KU-526-260

CHRISTIANITY:

THE COMPLETE GUIDE

Edited by John Bowden

With Anders Bergquist, Hugh Bowden and Norman A. Hjelm

Managing Editor: Margaret Lydamore

continuum

Continuum
The Tower Building, 11 York Road, London SE1 7NX

Copyright © Continuum 2005

First published 2005

British Library Cataloguing in Publication Data
A catalogue record for this book is available
from the British Library

ISBN 0-8264-8012-8

All rights reserved. No part of this publication may be reproduced or transmitted in any form or by any means, electronic or mechanical, including photocopying, recording or any information storage or retrieval system, without prior permission in writing from the publishers.

Designed by Benn Linfield
Line drawings by Rachel Bowden
Typeset by Fakenham Photosetting Limited, Fakenham, Norfolk
Printed and bound in Great Britain by CPI Bath

CONTENTS

CHRISTIANITY: THE COMPLETE GUIDE

- *The Guide* consists of 335 major **articles** in alphabetical order. Inserted into these articles are 166 **boxes**, set in a different type and sometimes with charts and diagrams, which provide concise detailed information on specific subject-areas. For example, the article on Heresy has a box listing all the main heresies; the article on Creeds has a box with the text of the main Christian creeds. There is also a **Who's Who** giving short biographies of over 400 major figures from Christian history, a **time chart**, a series of **maps**, a **glossary**, and an **index**.
- For *those searching for specific information* the place to start is the **index**. This acts as a kind of search engine for the book as a whole. It has more than 50,000 entries and points straight to the place to find information about any specific topic. Once there, readers can set their first question in a wider context by following the cross-references.
- *Those seeking to expand their knowledge* will see that some articles are printed in double columns and some in larger type which spreads right across the page. The latter are called **Gateway articles**, because they are meant to provide an easy and informative way into major topics such as the Arts, the Bible, Christian life, Death, God, the History of Christianity, Jesus, Other faiths, Prayer, Women in Christianity, Worship and so on. At the beginning of each Gateway article, an icon introduces other articles which open out from it: for example, the Gateway on Death points to Destiny and purpose, Life after death, Pastoral care, Resurrection, Sacraments, Sacrifice, Sin and Suffering.
- In the margin of every article references are given to other relevant articles, boxes or entries in the Who's Who which provide further information. Thus the article on Miracle includes references to Jesus of history, Kingdom of God, Saint, Pentecostalism, Critics of Christianity, Evidence, Science and theology and Mary. Icons are used as easily-recognizable pointers to boxes and Who's Who entries.
- No term goes unexplained. The glossary provides a basic vocabulary for those unfamiliar with words such as ecumenical, liturgy, magisterium or schism; otherwise the system of cross-references fills out the picture more fully and deeply the further it is pursued.
- All articles have lists of books for further reading and in many cases there are also references to useful websites.

CHRISTIANITY:
THE COMPLETE GUIDE

CHRISTIANITY: AN INTRODUCTION

In the New Testament, an anonymous author writing 'to the Hebrews' describes the faith of Christians in famous words as 'the assurance of things hoped for, the conviction of things not seen'.

At its heart, Christianity is about seeing the invisible in faith. A great twentieth-century theologian, Karl Barth, described a common attitude among Christians through history. He pictured himself watching from a window people in the street. They suddenly stop and gaze up into the sky, shading their eyes with their hands. They are looking at something hidden from his sight by the roof. In the everyday world this is probably an aeroplane, but the posture is telling. The apostle Paul, for example, evidently sees and hears something that is quite beyond the range of our observation and the measure of our thought, and so do the mystics. Elsewhere Karl Barth quotes an early follower of Francis of Assisi in the thirteenth century, one Berthold of Regensberg, who remarked: 'A man who looks directly into the sun, into the burning radiance, will so injure his eyes that he will see it no more. It is like this also with faith; whoever looks too directly into the holy Christian faith will be astonished and deeply disturbed with his thoughts.'

The heart of Christianity, then, is invisible, and the chief pointers to it are the actions of men and women down the centuries and in the present. One has only to look at individuals kneeling or standing to pray or meditate in churches; at monks and nuns gathered together to mark the times of the day in sung and spoken prayer and contemplation; at congregations of men, women and children coming to break bread and drink wine together on a Sunday morning, to see that they are not just talking to themselves or among themselves; their attention is focused elsewhere, on a realm which they try, sometimes with difficulty, to glimpse.

Christianity is first and foremost about people, and above all about groups of people. It has never been a religion for individuals. There would be no Christianity at all were it not for the actions of one charismatic figure, Jesus of Nazareth, for whose nature no words have proved an adequate description. Jesus could speak of and to the invisible, unimaginable God as 'Father', and show what can only be called a childlike trust in God, even if this trust resulted in his death. And his chief action was to call and inspire a group of men and women. They followed him during his lifetime and were convinced that, far from having been killed by an agonizing crucifixion, he was alive with and as God, who had given them a Spirit that endowed them with a new life in which all was well between them and God, so that they had nothing to fear.

The first group of followers of Jesus came to spread all over the world, forming countless other groups, and as these groups tried to explain to themselves and others, against the background of increasingly varied cultures, what had happened to them and what it meant, they developed an impressive body of thought and writing. This literature centred on the Bible of the Jews, Jesus' Bible, which they too used, calling it the Old Testament; to it they added a collection of their own, which they called the New Testament. The literature went on to comprise a great body of letters and sermons, theological and philosophical treatises, works relating to prayer and worship, morality and so on.

Christians certainly have been and are over-fond of words; Mrs Moore in E. M. Forster's novel *A Passage to India* famously speaks of 'poor little talkative Christianity'. But from the start Christianity has been far more than looking towards the invisible, however devoutly, and talking about the incomprehensible. One of the main reasons for its impressively rapid spread through the ancient world was that Christians cared. They cared for one another and they cared for those around them. Jesus talked and taught (though his words are remarkably few, memorable and succinct) and his focus was firmly upon God, but above all he cared and acted to show his care by healing men and women who were sick in mind and body. His parable of the Good Samaritan, the representative of a disparaged group who came to the help of a badly mugged traveller when others had passed him by, has echoed around the world. He told it as an example of neighbourliness and put at the heart of his teaching, after the need to love God, the command to 'love your neighbour as yourself'. His first followers obeyed that command to a degree which amazed those around them who did not share their faith or join their groups. An African theologian, Tertullian, writing around the end of the second century, quotes the admiring remark, 'See how these Christians love one another' – and those who make it are not being sarcastic.

At some times and some places they could have been, for during their history Christians have not in fact got on very well together. There have been several reasons for this. First of all, the mere fact that Christianity spread so widely geographically meant that it was constantly having to be expressed in relation to a considerable range of cultures and customs, and inevitably underwent a degree of change in the process. This and the mere translation of key words and ideas from one language to another could lead to misunderstanding. Secondly, differing convictions and a passion for what they believed to be the truth, sometimes about very important issues and sometimes about incidentals, led to distinctly different groupings or denominations within Christianity. Thirdly, and disastrously, Christianity has been marked by a singular hostility and antagonism among its adherents. The shortest document in the New Testament, the Second Letter of John, which takes up barely half a printed page, remarks: 'If any one comes to you and does not bring this doctrine, do not receive him into the house or give him any greeting; for he who greets him shares his wicked work.' This attitude was to persist and can still be encountered widely today.

From the first century onwards, Christians suffered martyrdom: they were put to death for their beliefs and practices by the Roman authorities, and Tertullian could describe the blood of the martyrs as the seed of the church. However, the *Book of Martyrs*, compiled by John Foxe in 1563, was not about those suffering death under pagan rule but about the killing of representatives of one group of Christians, Protestants, by another group of Christians, Roman Catholics. Sadly, the events it describes are only one chapter in a long horror story of the persecution of Christians by Christians.

Nor does the black side of Christianity stop there. The treatment of Jews by Christians is a reprehensible one, with its roots once again in the New Testament, where in the Gospel of John Jesus is made to remark of 'the Jews', 'You are of your father the devil, and your will is to do your father's desires. He was a murderer from the beginning, and has nothing to do with the truth, because there is no truth in him.'

As it progressed to a prominent position in the world, Christianity had to make compromises which took it away from its original ideals, not least with political authorities from the time when the Roman emperor Constantine in the fourth century not only gave it a privileged place but also decided to take a personal hand in its affairs. In East and West this alliance between Christianity and the state continued in its heartlands, and it was extended further with the exploration and consequent colonization of the globe. Time and again, reform groups have sought to bring its teaching and practices nearer to the gospel of Jesus of Nazareth.

The people who have lived out the history of Christianity, shaping it with their thoughts and actions, have also left visible traces of many kinds all over the world. Distinctive church buildings, with their spires, towers and domes, mark the physical landscape, and Christian architects have created amazing buildings from, say, Durham Cathedral in England to Gaudí's Sagrada Familia in Spain; the Christian holy book, the Bible, has not only conveyed the story and teachings of Jesus of Nazareth and his first followers, but through translations has shaped some languages, such as German and English, and has been the occasion for setting down many other languages in written form for the first time. Music, paintings, sculptures and countless pieces of decorative art created by Christians are among the treasures of Western civilization.

Christianity lies behind the creation of schools, universities and hospitals. Its major festivals and distinctive seasons are landmarks in the calendar, which for much of the world is still centred on the supposed year of the birth of Jesus.

Even faiths such as Judaism and Islam, which do not accept Christian claims about Jesus, honour him as one of the world's great religious figures, as a prophet sent by God; and many of those with no religious faith at all see him as one of the greatest men of all time. Although little is authentically known about him, his person has been the subject of countless paintings, sculptures, novels, plays, films and even musicals.

Christianity may have left its mark on the world, but today its public role, at least in the societies of the Western world, is diminishing. The degree to which these societies have become secularized is discussed and argued over; what is clear, however, is that religious practices are increasingly being privatized and individualized. So a decline in church membership, church attendance and so on may not be the whole story. We may be moving back to a situation famously described in the anonymous Letter to Diognetus probably written in the third century. What the writer says is this.

Christians are no different from other people in either country or speech or customs. They do not live in cities of their own, nor do they use a different language or lead a peculiar life. Their teaching has not been discovered by the thought and effort of busy men; nor do they champion a human doctrine, as some do. Yet while living in the Greek or barbarian cities in which they happen to be, and following local customs in clothing, food and other matters of daily life, they show forth a wonderful and admittedly strange type of citizenship. They live in countries of their own, but as visitors; they share the life of citizens but experience it as foreigners; every foreign land is their fatherland, and every fatherland a foreign land. They spend their lives on earth, but their citizenship is in heaven. In short, what the soul is in the body, Christians are in the world. The soul dwells in the body but is not of the body; Christians dwell in the world, but they are not of the world. The soul is invisible and is confined in a visible body; so Christians are recognized in the world, but their religious life remains invisible.

However, given those many traces that Christianity has left behind over two millennia, it can still be thought of as a land of its own, with an enormous population. By the year 2000 there were two billion Christians in the world and their number is growing at an enormous rate, notably in the southern hemisphere. In some places these Christians do indeed blend in with the population and follow local customs in clothing, food and other matters of daily life; elsewhere they stand out by their dress, their diet and their practices – and the *World Christian Encyclopedia*, published in 2001, calculates that over 45 million Christians suffered martyrdom in the twentieth century, and that there are still 166,000 martyrs each year.

Christians are divided into major churches or groups of churches that are called Roman Catholic, Orthodox, Anglican, Protestant, Independent, Pentecostal and so on – each with its own customs and practices which have often changed and developed over the years. Churches can change as they become established on different continents and in different cultures: what happens today in a remote corner of Africa or Latin America may be influenced by decisions made in Germany in the sixteenth century or Rome in the thirteenth; elsewhere, buildings and worship may bear the stamp of nineteenth-century colonizers who were also missionaries.

So on the one hand Christianity is a kaleidoscopic panorama of living people, continuing to shape their surroundings and make some mark on the societies in which they live, even, as in Africa, to the point of influencing governments and national constitutions. On the other hand, particularly on the continent of Europe, the marks of its presence left by Christianity are, in the literal sense, museum pieces. Architecture, sculpture, painting, music and song, literature, poetry, philosophy, proverbs and popular wisdom, customs and traditions, extending as far as dress and food and even relating to ways of living and to social patterns may have been deeply influenced by Christianity, but awareness of this fact has disappeared. Cathedrals are thronged, not by worshippers but by tourists, and their atmosphere often feels little different from that of a castle or a stately home. The numbers of those attending church regularly in all denominations has dropped dramatically.

Ignorance of even the most basic features of Christian belief and history is almost universal, and it is notable that on radio and television quiz programme contestants with an otherwise extensive range of knowledge cannot answer the most basic question about the Bible or Christianity. Even those who are still practising Christians usually have a very limited awareness of the wealth and diversity of their heritage, and of the very different ways in which their brothers and sisters in the faith in other groupings and environments look back to Jesus of Nazareth and the God about whom he taught.

Hence this *Guide*. It is intended as a guidebook to Christianity seen as a land, perhaps an unexplored, even foreign land. How it works is explained in the next article. Using *The Guide* will make it possible to form a far fuller picture than this Introduction can convey, and to see in some depth the character of one of the world's great religions.

JOHN BOWDEN

HOW TO USE *THE GUIDE*

One way of looking at Christianity is to see it as a landscape, indeed as a land – for many people today in fact a foreign land. Some of the features of the land are indicated in the Introduction; *The Guide* as a whole is an invitation to explore them in some depth.

The Guide is what it claims to be, a guide; it is not a dictionary or an encyclopaedia, though it has some similarities with such works. It is intended above all to encourage journeys through Christianity, particularly as Christianity is to be found today; to help readers to become familiar with its geography and its history, its scenery, its peoples and their various beliefs and practices.

Some of these journeys can be made without stirring from an armchair, simply by following the pointers included within *The Guide* itself; others may involve slightly more effort, such as going to a library to read some of the many books which are suggested for further reading, or turning on a computer and logging on to some of the websites about every aspect of Christianity which are constantly being created.

The Guide will make it possible to understand better who Christians are, why they exist in so many kinds, and what role they play in today's societies. It will make it possible to get some idea of the nature of Christian spirituality, prayer and worship; of Christian beliefs in the presence of God in today's world; of Christian thinking on moral issues and the Christian responses to the bewildering developments brought about by science, technology and modern economic forces. It will make it possible to look at the different institutional churches, their strengths and weaknesses, in a new way; to discover the enormous contribution that Christianity has made to the shaping of Western culture; to see church buildings, paintings and sculptures with new eyes; to recognize the motive force which Christianity has provided for much music, poetry and literature; and to appreciate its distinctive perspectives on the world.

Some readers will pick up *The Guide* out of sheer curiosity, as a book on Christianity of a kind that they have never seen before. For them we have tried to make it enticing on every page, encouraging them by its layout to allow themselves to be led on from one topic to another, entertained as well as informed by the writing and the format in which it is presented. The contributors have been asked to write in such a way that their articles can be understood by someone who comes to a topic with no prior knowledge whatsoever; and the articles should be accessible to those of any faith or none. In this respect this guide to Christianity tries to be no different from a guide, say, to Yemen or China. There is information here about arriving, getting around, the different regions and their contrasting features, the buildings, the art, the literature, which bear witness to a colourful and dramatic past. There is information about what the people there are like, what language they speak, their traditions, lifestyle, ideals, beliefs, the stories they tell.

Other readers will pick up *The Guide* out of a specific desire to know more about Christianity as a religion. For them we have tried to make it as comprehensive as possible without being too antiquarian. Wherever possible, articles begin with Christian thought, practice, diversity, worship or whatever as it can be encountered today, looking back to the past above all to explain why things are as they are. In some cases, such as the history of Christianity, that is not always possible, but we are aware of the frustration of looking up a topic only to have it laboriously explained by an account that begins by going back to the mists of time.

Yet other readers will want to know about Christianity as a movement which has left a deep stamp on Western civilization and contributed to its art, its thought, its values, its politics, its welfare system. We hope that *The Guide* will enable them to see all these things in a new light and add an extra dimension to them. *The Guide* will give them plenty to reflect on.

Others again may themselves be practising Christians with some knowledge of Christianity but a desire to learn more; in *The Guide* they can deepen what they already know and believe and extend their knowledge into new areas, increasing their awareness of the kaleidoscopic variety of Christianity and, we hope, increasing their understanding of other Christians whose views are very different from theirs.

Finally, there may be readers who are still looking for a faith to believe in and who have urgent personal questions of their own. They may be troubled by the problems and perplexities of life. Why am I here? Why is there so much evil and suffering in the world? How can I cope with a deep sense of guilt and failure? How is it possible to pray? How do Christians relate to those of other faiths? Is death the end or is there any hope beyond it? *The Guide* will show what kind of resources Christians have found to tackle these questions. Answers are attempted by looking at Christianity not only from the outside as a religion which can be visited and explored, but also from the inside, to show what it means and has meant to be a Christian in different ways, in different times and places. *The Guide* sets out to describe how and why people are and have been Christians, and why Christianity can exercise such a strong hold on them that it becomes the focal point of their being; why Christians have given up careers, possessions, even lives, for what they believe.

Keeping a balance between these two approaches, looking at Christianity from the outside with the eyes of a visitor, and standing within it and trying to convey what it means to outsiders, has not been easy. But we believe that both approaches must be held together, since only in this way is it possible to present Christianity as something that is not just a museum piece, but a rich and living faith which has much to offer.

It should be emphasized that because Christianity is such a diverse faith, straightforward accounts of it can rarely be given. You will very rarely find here statements such as 'Christians believe …', 'Christians do not …', because such statements can almost always be immediately contradicted. The more than 200 authors, men and women, from the United States, the British Isles, continental Europe and elsewhere in the world who have written for *The Guide* would have many differences of opinion between them were they to meet for a discussion. However, they are experts on their subjects, and together they form a forum; they are, if you like, guides with opinions of their own – other guides might have offered a different perspective.

A word or two about the form of *The Guide*. After the Introduction and this explanation of how to use *The Guide*, the body of the book contains a series of articles in alphabetical order, the shortest of around 1000 words and the longest of around 17,000 words. We have deliberately avoided lots of small articles, believing that the information they would contain can be presented in a better way. Most articles are set in double columns, but some are set across the full width of the page in larger type, and we have called them Gateways. Immediately below the title of each of these is a distinctive gateway icon ╓╖, followed by a list of the main articles to which the Gateway is an opening. Gateway articles are intended above all for readers who want to begin by getting a general orientation, to familiarize themselves with various major aspects of Christianity or to discover Christian approaches to key topics. We have avoided any kind of technical terms for the titles of these Gateway articles; they are listed in the box below:

Arts	Evidence	Other faiths
Authority	Exploration	Prayer and spirituality
Beliefs	Geography	Ritual and worship
Bible	God	Salvation
Christian life	History	Society
Church	Initiation	Story
Communication	Jesus	Symbols
Death	Journeys	Time
Destiny and purpose	Mission	Tradition
Diversity	Monasticism and religious orders	Women in Christianity
Ethics	Origins and background	World

References to subjects covered in more detail elsewhere in *The Guide* are given by printing the titles of the relevant articles in the outside margin of a page. Wherever possible the articles have been provided with suggestions for further reading, marked by the icon, and details of relevant websites, marked by the icon. Topics which are not dealt with in a main article are either discussed in the wider context to which they relate, or are covered by being treated in a box such as the one above. There are 166 of these boxes: some are on individual topics such as Christian Socialism, the Inquisition or the documents of the Second Vatican Council; some contain statistical information, such as the number of Christians on the various continents; some present biblical material at first hand and show the issues it raises, such as the fact that there are two different versions of both the Lord's Prayer and the Ten Commandments, and three and sometimes four versions of events from the life of Jesus; some indulge in the popular passion for lists, and bring together a whole series of related terms, such as councils of the church, Roman emperors, popes, the seven deadly sins and other groups of seven, or the architectural features to be found in a church. They are unsigned, and have been produced by the editorial team. Cross-references to them are given by the icon, followed by the numbers of the pages on which they are to be found. In addition, following the main articles in the book, also by the editorial team, there is a Who's Who of more than 400 prominent figures in Christianity; only a very select handful of individuals are given articles of their own. The Who's Who provides dates and basic information about the men and women covered. Cross-references to it are given by the icon. An arrow ············➤ indicates that the point of reference is to the further column.

The key to discovering specific information on a topic in *The Guide* is the comprehensive Index at the back of the book with its thousands of entries. It performs the same function as a search engine for electronic documents. It will lead to detailed information on an enormous range of subjects, equivalent to what other reference books give in their countless short articles. So readers wanting information on, for instance, an aumbry, a chasuble, a *debtera*, the Lambeth Quadrilateral, a Millerite or a triforium should first look here. While we have tried to ensure that articles are as self-explanatory as possible, it is impractical to explain everything every time; words used by Christians that fall outside the regular everyday vocabulary are explained in a short Glossary.

Where relevant, articles also contain illustrations, maps, charts and diagrams; we have also provided a Time Chart.

We have tried to make *The Guide* comprehensive, but there will be gaps in it. There will also be over-simplifications over which experts will shake their heads, and interpretations with which some readers will strongly disagree. That is inevitable. Throughout, our priorities have been to put readers first and ensure that they can understand and above all enjoy what they read. If *The Guide* transports them to new scenery and new horizons, we shall have achieved our aim.

JOHN BOWDEN

LIST OF ARTICLES

Capitals denote GATEWAY articles

LIST OF BOXES

LIST OF ILLUSTRATIONS

Colour plates appearing between pages 660 and 661

LIST OF MAPS

LIST OF CONTRIBUTORS

T. H. M. Akerboom, Assistant Professor in Patrology and History of Theology, Faculty of Theology, University of Tilburg, The Netherlands
Christianity in Europe: The Netherlands

S. J. Allen, Associate Lecturer, The Open University, Milton Keynes
Hildegard of Bingen

Diane Apostolos-Cappadona, Research Professor, Center for Muslim-Christian Understanding, Georgetown University, Washington DC
Dance, Iconoclasm, Painting, Sculpture, Symbols

Edmund Arens, Professor of Fundamental Theology, University of Lucerne
Political theology

S. Wesley Ariarajah, Professor of Ecumenical Theology, Drew University School of Theology, Madison, New Jersey
Interfaith dialogue

Paul Avis, General Secretary, Council for Christian Unity of the Church of England and Director, Centre for the Study of the Christian Church
Church

Paul Ballard, formerly teaching in Practical Theology in the Department of Religious and Theological Studies, Cardiff University
Death, Discipline, Law, Pastoral care

James Barnett, formerly Archbishop of Canterbury's representative at the European institutions and currently representing the Intereuropean Commission on Church and School at the Council of Europe
Human rights

Andrew Barr, formerly Head of Education and Religious Broadcasting, BBC Scotland
Radio (with William F. Fore), Television (with William F. Fore)

John Barton, Oriel and Laing Professor of the Interpretation of Holy Scripture, University of Oxford
Canon

Paul M. Bassett, Professor of the History of Christianity Emeritus, Nazarene Theological Seminary, Kansas City, Missouri
Holiness movement

Michael Battle, Vice President, Associate Dean for Academic Affairs and Associate Professor Theology, Virginia Theological Seminary
African American Christianity: Experience and thought

Tina Beattie, Catholic theologian and writer, and Senior Lecturer in Christian Studies, Roehampton University
Mary

Trevor Beeson, Dean Emeritus of Winchester Cathedral
Church of England, Communication, Dress (with Jennifer L. Lord), Journalism (with Frank D. Langfitt), Money, Organization, Persecution (with Anders Bergquist)

Anders Bergquist, Vicar, St John's Church, St John's Wood, London
Bible, Language, Letters, Messiah, Persecution (with Trevor Beeson), Psalms

John Berthrong, Associate Dean and Associate Professor of Comparative Theology, Boston University School of Theology, Boston, Massachusetts
Chinese religions and Christianity

John Binns, Vicar, Great St Mary's, The University Church, Cambridge
Coptic Christianity, Ethiopian Christianity

Ian H. Birnie, Educationalist, Inspector of Schools and Local Government Adviser, Lytham St Annes, Lancashire
Education

Michael Bourdeaux, President, Keston Institute, Oxford
Christianity in Europe: Russia

Hugh Bowden, Lecturer in Ancient History, King's College London
Constantine's 'conversion', Music and Christianity (with John Bowden), Mystery cults, Origins and background, Paganism, Roman empire, University (with John Bowden)

John Bowden, formerly Editor and Managing Director, SCM Press Ltd, London
Archaeology, Biblical criticism, Body, Books, Christology, Community, Devotions, Diversity, Evidence, Exploration, Faith, Festivals and fasts, Food and drink, Fundamentalism, Geography, Hope, Jesus, Jesus of history, Kingdom of God, Liberal theology, Life after death, Ministry and ministers, Miracle, Music and Christianity (with Hugh Bowden), Publishing, Resurrection, Schools, Secularization, University (with Hugh Bowden)

Carl D. Bowman, Professor of Sociology, Bridgewater College, Virginia
Brethren (with Melanie May)

Bo Brander, Lecturer in Systematic Theology, Lund University, Sweden
Ecotheology

Marcus Braybrooke, President, World Congress of Faiths and Co-Founder of the Three Faiths Forum
Covenant, Interfaith worship

Ian Breward, Emeritus Professor of Church History, Ormond College, University of Melbourne
Christianity in Australasia, Australia, Pacific Islands

Pierre Bühler, Professor of Systematic Theology, Faculty of Theology, University of Zurich
Hermeneutical theology

William R. Burrows, Managing Editor, Orbis Books, Maryknoll, New York
Mission

David G. Buttrick, Buffington Professor of Homiletics and Liturgics, Emeritus, Vanderbilt University, Nashville, Tennessee
Preaching

James M. Byrne, Associate Professor of Religious Studies, St Michael's College, Colchester, Vermont
Karl Barth, Enlightenment, Humanism, Natural theology, Neo-orthodox theology, Friedrich Schleiermacher, Thomism

William J. Callahan, Professor Emeritus of History, University of Toronto
Christianity in Europe: Spain

Ted Campbell, President, Garrett-Evangelical Theological Seminary, Evanston, Illinois
Protestantism

Jeremy R. Carrette, Lecturer in Applied Theology in the School of European Culture and Languages at the University of Kent, Canterbury
Psychology and Christianity

Mark D. Chapman, Vice-Principal, Ripon College Cuddesdon, Oxford
Authority, Holy, Society, Tradition, World

Mary Charles-Murray, Faculty of Theology, University of Oxford
Iconography

John W. Coakley, Feakes Professor of Church History, New Brunswick Theological Seminary
Christendom, Investiture Controversy, Middle Ages, Renaissance

Thomas Cocke, Chief Executive, NADFAS
Furnishings, Stained glass

Cynthia B. Cohen, Senior Research Fellow, Kennedy Institute of Ethics, Georgetown University, Washington DC
Bioethics

Dan Cohn-Sherbok, Professor of Judaism at the University of Wales at Lampeter
Jewish Christianity

Hugh Connolly, Vice-President and Lecturer in Moral Theology, St Patrick's College, Maynooth, Ireland
Sin

John W. Cook, Professor Emeritus at Yale University and President Emeritus of the Henry Luce Foundation
Architecture (with Allan Doig), Patronage

David Cornick, General Secretary, the United Reformed Church and Fellow of Robinson College, Cambridge
Congregationalism, United Reformed Church

Graham Cray, Bishop of Maidstone, Kent
Contemporary Christian music

Lawrence S. Cunningham, John A. O'Brien Professor of Theology, University of Notre Dame, Indiana
Martyr, Saint

James S. Cutsinger, Professor of Theology and Religious Thought, University of South Carolina, Columbia
Perennial philosophy and Christianity

Allan K. Davidson, Lecturer in Church History and Director of Postgraduate Studies, School of Theology, University of Auckland, New Zealand
Christianity in Australasia: New Zealand

Brian Davies, OP, Professor of Philosophy, Fordham University, New York
Evil

Celia Deane-Drummond, Professor of Theology and the Biological Sciences and Director of the Centre for Religion and the Biosciences at University College Chester
Environmental ethics

C. Scott Dixon, Senior Lecturer, The Queen's University of Belfast
John Calvin, Martin Luther

Allan Doig, Fellow of Lady Margaret Hall, Oxford
Architecture (with John Cook), Buildings

Ian T. Douglas, Professor of Mission and World Christianity, Episcopal Divinity School, Cambridge, Massachusetts
Anglicanism

Willem B. Drees, Professor of Philosophy of Religion and Ethics, Department of Theology, Leiden University, The Netherlands
Creation, Science

Jeremy Duff, Director of Lifelong Learning, Liverpool Diocese
Pseudepigraphy

Donald F. Durnbaugh, Professor Emeritus of Church History, Bethany Theological Seminary, Richmond, Indiana and Archivist, Juniata College, Huntingdon, Pennsylvania
Anabaptists

James H. Evans, Jr, Robert K. Davies Professor of Systematic Theology, Colgate Rochester Crozer Divinity School, Rochester, New York
African American Christianity: Churches

John Fenwick, formerly Anglican Co-Secretary of the International Commission for Anglican-Orthodox Theological Dialogue
Eastern-rite Catholic churches, Christianity in the Middle East, Orthodox churches

Ron Ferguson, Writer and broadcaster and former Minister of St Magnus Cathedral, Kirkwall, Orkney
Church of Scotland

Richard Fischer, Executive Secretary of the Church and Society Commission, Conference of European Churches, Strasbourg
Christianity in Europe: Introduction, France, Germany

Columba Graham Flegg, formerly Orthodox Chaplain to the University of Cambridge and to universities in Scotland
Catholic Apostolic Church

William F. Fore, Former President, World Association for Christian Communication
Radio (with Andrew Barr), Television (with Andrew Barr)

J. Denis Fortin, Professor of Theology, Seventh-day Adventist Theological Seminary, Andrews University, Berrien Springs, Michigan
Adventist Church

Martin Forward, Helena Wackerlin Professor of Religious Studies, Aurora University, Illinois
Global ethic, New Age movement, New religious movements, Other faiths, Traditional religions and Christianity, Zoroastrianism and Christianity

Arthur J. Freeman, formerly Professor of New Testament, Moravian Theological Seminary, Bethlehem, Pennsylvania
Moravian Church

Robin Gill, Michael Ramsey Professor of Modern Theology, University of Kent, Canterbury
Christianity in Europe: Great Britain, Social ethics

Harvey Gillman, Former Outreach Secretary, Quaker Home Service
Quakers (Religious Society of Friends)

Terryl L. Givens, Professor of Religion and Literature, James A. Bostwick Chair of English, University of Richmond, Virginia
Mormons

Roberto S. Goizueta, Professor of Theology, Boston College, Massachusetts
Hispanic Christianity, Liberation theology

Bruce Gordon, Reader in Modern History, University of St Andrews
Heinrich Bullinger, Huldrych Zwingli

Christopher Gower, Rector, St Marylebone Parish Church, London
Sickness and healing

Basilius J. Groen, Professor of Liturgical Studies and Member of the Southeastern European Research Programme at the University of Graz, Austria
Christianity in Europe: Greece

Gunnar Grönblom, Diocesan Dean of the Diocesan Chapter, Borgå, Finland
Christianity in Europe: Scandinavia

Christine E. Gudorf, Professor and Chair, Department of Religious Studies, Florida International University
Sexual ethics

Richard M. Gula, SS, Professor of Moral Theology, Franciscan School of Theology, Graduate Theological Union, Berkeley, California
Conscience, Moral theology, Professional ethics

Caroline J.-B. Hammond, Rector of the Benefice of Gamlingay and Everton, Bedfordshire
Historiography

Stephen Happel, late Dean, School of Theology and Religious Studies, The Catholic University of America, Washington DC
Culture

Elizabeth J. Harris, Secretary for Interfaith Relations for the Methodist Church in Britain
Buddhism and Christianity

Max Harris, Executive Director Emeritus, Wisconsin Humanities Council, University of Wisconsin, Madison, Wisconsin
Drama

Anthony Harvey, formerly Canon of Westminster Abbey, London
Marriage, Work

Brian Haymes, Minister, Bloomsbury Central Baptist Church, London
Baptist churches

Douglas Hedley, Fellow of Clare College, Cambridge and University Senior Lecturer in Philosophy of Religion in the Faculty of Divinity
Philosophy of religion

S. Mark Heim, Samuel Abbot Professor of Christian Theology, Andover Newton Theological School, Newton, Massachusetts
Free churches

Alasdair Heron, Chair of Reformed Theology, Erlangen, Germany
Freedom, Grace, Justification, Predestination, Reformed churches

Judith Herrin, Professor of Late Antique and Byzantine Studies, King's College London
Byzantium

Bernd Jochen Hilberath, Director, Institute for Ecumenical Research, Tübingen
Holy Spirit

Norman A. Hjelm, formerly Director of the Commission on Faith and Order, National Council of the Churches of Christ in the USA
Ecumenical movement, Lutheranism

Linda Hogan, Lecturer, Irish School of Ecumenics, Trinity College, Dublin
Feminist theology

Nicholas Holtam, Vicar, St-Martin-in-the Fields, London
Homosexuality

Morna D. Hooker, Lady Margaret's Professor Emerita and Fellow of Robinson College, Cambridge
Paul

Mary E. Hunt, Co-Director, Women's Alliance for Theology, Ethics and Ritual (WATER), Silver Spring, Maryland
Gay and lesbian theology

Kenneth Hylson-Smith, Former Bursar and Fellow of St Cross College, Oxford
Evangelicals, Industrial revolution, Oxford Movement, Puritans

Dale T. Irvin, Academic Dean and Professor of World Christianity, New York Theological Seminary, New York
History

Antje Jackelén, Associate Professor of Systematic Theology and Religion and Science, Lutheran School of Theology, Chicago, Illinois
Science and theology

David Jasper, Professor of Literature and Theology, University of Glasgow
Literature

Werner G. Jeanrond, Professor of Systematic Theology, Lund University, Sweden
Theology

Cheryl Bridges Johns, Professor of Discipleship and Christian Formation, Church of God Theological Seminary, Cleveland, Tennessee
Pentecostalism

James Turner Johnson, Professor of Religion, Rutgers University, Brunswick, New Jersey
War and peace

Alan Jones, Dean of Grace Cathedral, San Francisco, California
Christian Life

Patricia Beattie Jung, Associate Professor of Theology, Loyola University Chicago, Illinois
Sexuality

Ogbu Kalu, Henry Winters Luce Professor of World Christianity, McCormick Theological Seminary, Chicago, Illinois
Christianity in Africa

John L. Kater, Jr, Professor of Ministry Development, Church Divinity School of the Pacific, Berkeley, California
Christianity in Latin America

Alistair Kee, Emeritus Professor of Religious Studies, University of Edinburgh
Critics of Christianity, Politics

Henry Ansgar Kelly, Professor Emeritus (Medieval and Renaissance Studies), University of California, Los Angeles
Satan

David J. Kennedy, Vice-Dean and Precentor of Durham Cathedral and Lecturer in Liturgy, University of Durham
Forgiveness

Pamela M. King, Head of the School of Culture, Media and Environment, St Martin's College, Lancaster
Mystery plays

Ursula King, Professor Emeritus of Theology and Religious Studies, University of Bristol
Interfaith dialogue and feminism, Interfaith dialogue and spirituality

Wolfram Kinzig, Professor of Church History, University of Bonn, Germany
Creed

Frank D. Langfitt, Labor/Workplace Correspondent, National Public Radio, USA
Journalism (with Trevor Beeson)

David R. Law, Lecturer in Christian Thought, School of Arts, Histories, and Cultures, University of Manchester
Inspiration

José Manuel Leite, Minister in the Evangelical Presbyterian Church of Portugal
Christianity in Europe: Portugal

Andrew Linzey, Senior Research Fellow, Blackfriars Hall, University of Oxford and Honorary Professor, University of Birmingham
Animals

Tony Lobl, District Manager for the UK and the Republic of Ireland, Christian Science Committees on Publication
Christian Science

Jennifer L. Lord, Assistant Professor of Worship and Preaching, Lancaster Theological Seminary, Pennsylvania
Dress (with Trevor Beeson)

Eric Lott, formerly Professor of Hindu Studies, Department of Religion and Culture, United Theological College, Bangalore, South India
Hinduism and Christianity

J. Rebecca Lyman, Samuel Garrett Professor of Church History, The Church Divinity School of the Pacific, Berkeley, California
Heresy

Christoph Markschies, Professor of Early Church History, Humboldt-University of Berlin
Gnosis

Peter Marshall, Reader in History, University of Warwick
Counter-Reformation

Joseph Martos, Former Director, Russell Institute of Religion and Ministry, Spalding University, Louisville, Kentucky
Sacraments

Martin E. Marty, Professor Emeritus, University of Chicago, Illinois
Christianity in North America

Mickey L. Mattox, Assistant Professor of Theology, Marquette University, Milwaukee
Reformation

Melanie May, Dean of Faculty and Professor of Theology, Colgate Rochester Crozer Divinity School, Rochester, New York
Brethren (with Carl Bowman)

Dennis P. McCann, Alston Professor of Bible and Religion, Agnes Scott College, Decatur, Georgia
Business ethics

John McCarthy, Associate Professor, Department of Theology, Loyola University Chicago, Illinois
Destiny and purpose, Future

Mark A. McIntosh, Associate Professor of Spirituality and Systematic Theology, Loyola University Chicago, Illinois
Beliefs

Kenneth Milne, formerly Principal, Church of Ireland College of Education, Dublin and Historiographer for the Church of Ireland
Christianity in Ireland

Robert Morgan, Priest-in-charge, Sandford-on-Thames and Fellow of Linacre College, Oxford
Biblical theology, Revelation

Catherine Mulgan, formerly Head of History, South Hampstead High School, London
Holy Roman empire, Wars of religion

Luca M. Negro, Secretary for Communications, Conference of European Churches, Geneva
Christianity in Europe: Italy (with Luigi Sandri)

Jon Nilson, Associate Professor of Theology, Loyola University Chicago, Illinois
Council, Papacy, Roman Catholic Church, Vatican

Gaye Williams Ortiz, Professor in Communication Studies, Augusta State University, Augusta, Georgia
Cinema

Rod Pattenden, Co-ordinator, Institute for Theology and the Arts, Sydney, Australia
Community arts

George Pattison, Lady Margaret Professor of Divinity, University of Oxford
God, Sören Kierkegaard, Modernism

Kristian Paver, JCL, Judicial Vicar of the Diocese of Plymouth
Canon law

Martyn Percy, Principal, Ripon College Cuddesdon, Oxford
Conversion

Charles Pickstone, Vicar, St Laurence, Catford, London
Art and Spirituality, Arts

Carl A. Raschke, Professor of Religious Studies, University of Denver, Colorado
Jehovah's Witnesses

Hugh Rayment-Pickard, Vicar, St Clement and St James and Area Dean of Kensington, London
Calendar, Eternity, Time

Elizabeth Rees, OCV, Writer and speaker on Celtic studies
Celtic Christianity

John Rempel, Assistant Professor of Historical Theology, Associated Mennonite Biblical Seminary, Elkhart, Indiana
Peace churches

Joerg Rieger, Professor of Systematic Theology, Perkins School of Theology, Southern Methodist University, Dallas, Texas
Methodism

Jonathan Riley-Smith, formerly Dixie Professor of Ecclesiastical History, University of Cambridge
Crusades

Darrin J. Rodgers, Librarian, Fuller Theological Seminary, Pasadena, California
Assemblies of God

Christopher Rowland, Dean Ireland's Professor of Exegesis of Holy Scripture, University of Oxford
Apocalyptic, Eschatology, Prophecy

Louis Roy, OP, Professor of Theology, Boston College, Massachusetts
Scholasticism, Thomas Aquinas

Rosemary Radford Ruether, Carpenter Professor of Feminist Theology, Graduate Theological Union, Berkeley, California
Women in Christianity

Luigi Sandri, Journalist, Rome
Christianity in Europe: Italy (with Luca M. Negro)

Simon Sarmiento, Computer consultant
Internet

Thaddaeus A. Schnitker, formerly Professor of Liturgy, Diocesan Seminary, Catholic Diocese of the Old Catholics in Germany
Old Catholic churches

Robert Schreiter, CPPS, Vatican Council II Professor of Theology, Catholic Theological Union at Chicago, Illinois and Professor of Theology and Culture, University of Nijmegen
Contextual theology

Jan Schumacher, Associate Professor of Church History, Norwegian Lutheran School of Theology, Oslo
Pietism

David Scott, Rector, St Lawrence with St Swithun, Winchester and Warden of the Diocesan School of Spirituality
Journeys, Mysticism, Poetry, Prayer and spirituality, Prayer, Romanticism, Spirituality

Timothy F. Sedgwick, Clinton S. Quin Professor of Christian Ethics, Virginia Theological Seminary, Alexandria, Virginia
Ethics

Richard D. Shiels, Associate Professor of History, Ohio State University, Newark, Ohio
Great Awakening

Joseph D. Small, Director, Office of Theology and Worship, Presbyterian Church (USA), Louisville, Kentucky
Presbyterian churches

Jane I. Smith, Professor of Islamic Studies, Hartford Seminary, Connecticut
Islam and Christianity

Matthew F. Smith, Committee Manager, Waltham Forest Strategic Partnership and formerly Information Officer, General Assembly of Unitarian and Free Christian Churches, London
Unitarians

J. Alberto Soggin, Professor Emeritus, University of Rome
Waldensian Church

Andrew Spira, Course Director, Christie's Education, London
Decorative arts

Eric O. Springsted, Member, The Center of Theological Inquiry, Princeton, New Jersey
Philosophy

Margaret Spufford, OBE, FBA, Professor Emeritua Roehampton Institute, London and Benedictine oblate, Malling Abbey, Kent
Suffering

Scott W. Sunquist, Professor of World Mission and Evangelism, Pittsburgh Theological Seminary, Pennsylvania
Christianity in Asia

Michael H. Taylor, Emeritus Professor of Social Theology, University of Birmingham
Globalization, Poverty, Third World

Gerd Theissen, Professor of New Testament, University of Heidelberg
Evolution

Notto R. Thelle, Professor of Theology, University of Oslo
Japanese religions and Christianity

Kenneth Thompson, Emeritus Professor of Sociology, The Open University, Milton Keynes
Sociology and Christianity

Suzanne R. Thurman, Independent Scholar, Florence, Alabama
Shakers

Mark G. Toulouse, Professor of American Religious History, Brite Divinity School, Texas
Christian Church (Disciples of Christ)

Jeffrey A. Truscott, Professor of Liturgics, Trinity Theological College, Singapore
Initiation

Keith Walker, formerly Residentiary Canon, Winchester Cathedral
Icon

Philip Walters, Head of Research, Keston Institute, Oxford
Christianity in Europe: Eastern Europe

Graham Ward, Professor of Contextual Theology and Ethics, University of Manchester
Postmodern theology

J. R. Watson, Emeritus Professor of English, University of Durham
Hymns

Diana Webb, Senior Lecturer in History, King's College London
Monasticism and religious orders, Monasticism, Pilgrimage, Religious orders

Louis Weil, James F. Hodges Professor of Liturgics, Church Divinity School of the Pacific, Berkeley, California
Eucharist

Samuel Wells, Priest-in-Charge, St Mark's Newnham, Cambridge
Incarnation, Trinity

Paul Westermeyer, Professor of Church Music, Luther Seminary, St Paul, Minnesota
Church Music

Susan J. White, Associate Dean and Lunger Professor of Spiritual Resouces and Disciplines, Brite Divinity School, Texas Christian University
Ritual and worship, Ritual, Worship

Maurice Wiles, Regius Professor of Divinity Emeritus, University of Oxford
Church fathers, Doctrinal criticism

Catherine Williams, Associate Priest in the Ecumenical Parish of Bishop's Cleeve, Gloucestershire
Friendship, Love

Trevor Williams, Chaplain Fellow and Tutor in Theology, Trinity College, Oxford
Atonement, Sacrifice, Salvation

Ellen van Wolde, Professor of Old Testament Exegesis and Hebrew, Faculty of Theology, University of Tilburg, The Netherlands
Story

Richard Woods, OP, Professor, Department of Theology, Dominican University, River Forest, Illinois
Angels

Melanie J. Wright, Academic Director, Centre for the Study of Jewish-Christian Relations and Member of the Centre for Advanced Religious and Theological Studies, University of Cambridge
Judaism and Christianity

Everett L. Zabriskie III, Director of Development, New Brunswick Theological Seminary, New Jersey
Dutch Reformed Church

THE GUIDE

Adventist Church

There are a number of Adventist churches worldwide, but most of them are numerically quite small. By contrast, with a membership of over 14 million believers and established in some 200 countries, the Seventh-day Adventist Church is one of the fastest growing Christian groups in the world, particularly in parts of Africa, Asia and Central and South America. Belief in the imminent return of Jesus Christ as prophesied in the Bible is the characteristic doctrine of Adventists, which gives them their name (Advent = coming). This motivates them to preach the gospel to all people on earth and to live a life of commitment to God. Hence Adventists spend time in reading the Bible and prayer, and witnessing for their faith. They view the Bible as the written word of God – inspired by the Holy Spirit – and accept its unique normative role to shape their beliefs and conduct. At the heart of Adventist teachings is the gospel, provided through the death of Jesus on the cross, and given to all those who accept it. Such a gift of grace cannot be earned but, in response to God's love and gift of salvation, Adventists desire to follow God's will as proclaimed in the Ten Commandments and the Bible. The fourth commandment regarding the day of rest, the seventh-day sabbath (Saturday), is understood as God's reminder of his acts of creation and salvation, and is the day on which God invites all to worship God. Since Jesus observed the seventh-day sabbath while on earth, Adventists also follow his example in keeping this commandment.

Adventists also encourage a holistic and healthful approach to life and embrace vegetarianism, strong family values and positive lifestyles. Those who choose to accept God's offer of eternal life demonstrate their belief through baptism by immersion. Adventists also believe in the conditional immortality of human beings and view the intermediate state between death and the resurrection as a sleep. At the second coming of Jesus, the gift of eternal life will be given only to those who have trusted God, while those who are lost will be destroyed (annihilated) for ever.

Although Seventh-day Adventists view themselves as a continuation of the Protestant Reformation of the sixteenth century and consider their doctrinal roots to go all the way back to the early Christian church, their movement as such began in the mid-nineteenth century in the eastern part of the United States. Between 1831 and 1844, William Miller, a Baptist preacher in New York State, preached that Jesus would return to earth around 1843 or 1844. He had reached this conclusion after his study of the prophecies of the books of Daniel and Revelation. Some of his associates within the movement calculated a more specific date of 22 October 1844 for the end of the world. When Jesus did not appear on this date, Millerites, as his followers came to be called, experienced the 'great disappointment'. In the weeks that followed, thousands of disillusioned Millerites throughout North America abandoned the movement, if not religious life, altogether. A few, however, studied their Bibles further to find why Jesus had not returned. From this study came a new conviction that the Bible prophecies predicted, not that Jesus would return to earth in 1844, but that at that time he would begin a special ministry in heaven for his followers. The Seventh-day Adventist Church arose from this small group of ex-Millerites; prominent among its early leaders were James and Ellen White and Joseph Bates.

With the help of a few publications, this small nucleus of Adventists began to grow. Ellen White became the trusted and influential spiritual leader of the church for more than 70 years until her death in 1915. Adventists believe that she received God's special guidance as she wrote her counsels to the church. In 1860, at Battle Creek, Michigan, these early believers chose the name Seventh-day Adventist and in 1863 formally organized a church body with a membership of 3500. Their activities were largely confined to North America until 1874, when the church's first missionary, J. N. Andrews, was sent to Europe in response to enquiries from Switzerland. Missions to many other countries soon followed.

pp. 384–5

The Seventh-day Adventist Church has a representative system of government. There are four levels of organization extending from the individual church member to the worldwide church. The first level is the local church formed of individual believers. Next comes the local conference, which is made up of local churches in a given geographical territory. The third level is the union conference, which brings together local conferences within a wider territory such as a group of states or provinces, or a whole country. The fourth level is the general conference, made up of all unions in all parts of the world and subdivided into twelve geographical divisions. In 2003 there were 94 unions, consisting of about 520 conferences with approximately 110,000 churches and groups. In all its institutions worldwide, the church employed over 190,000 persons. Each level of church organization receives its authority through a democratic process of formation and election.

Life after death
Initiation
Reformation

For Seventh-day Adventists, all Christians are stewards of God's creation entrusted to them. One's time, influence, service and material and financial resources ultimately belong to God and should be used for God's glory and the sharing of the gospel. In principle, Adventists give voluntarily to the church a tithe (10%) of their revenues, together with additional offerings. The tithe is used to pay the salaries of pastors, evangelists and church administrators, while other expenses are covered by offerings.

In practice, however, about half of church members give faithful tithes and offerings to the church. In spite of some financial stress caused by declining or changing regional economies in recent years, the church nonetheless has been able to carry on a worldwide network of church activities.

Within its four levels of organization the church operates numerous institutions and programmes of outreach to the community. Since Adventists have a holistic view of the human person, they have developed numerous institutions to meet the needs of church members and the wider population. Health-care institutions such as hospitals, clinics and dispensaries offer a variety of care and treatments. Furthermore, disease-prevention programmes such as the Five-day Plan to Stop Smoking have benefited a vast number of people. Adventists also operate one of the largest church-owned educational systems in the world. Seeking to better humanity, they provide primary, secondary and tertiary education for over a million students. The success of these educational institutions may well account for the upward social mobility of the Adventist membership over the last century. Through programmes such as the Adventist Development and Relief Agency (ADRA), the church provides practical assistance to the poor and disadvantaged in many countries of the world, without regard for race, religion or nationality. The church also operates publishing houses, radio stations, youth camps and community service projects. Adventists have also been strong supporters of religious liberty and tolerance. Each year the Public Affairs and Religious Liberty department of the General Conference publishes a Religious Freedom World Report that provides a unique Adventist perspective on the state of religious freedom around the world.

Since its origins, the Seventh-day Adventist church has been concerned with the lack of unity within Christianity and has advocated a unity based upon the teachings of the Bible. Seventh-day Adventists have endeavoured to foster good relationships with other denominations. For many years they have attended functions of various Faith and Order commissions of the World Council of Churches as observers or participants, and have encouraged dialogues with theologians of other denominations. Yet, for different reasons, the church has not become a member of the World Council of Churches or other regional ecumenical bodies. Seventh-day Adventists view unity at a level transcending mere visible church organization and understand their mission to be universal in character. Membership of ecumenical organizations would put at risk their missionary activities and ability to communicate their message to all people. Given their strong principle of separation of church and state, they have also been reluctant to be associated with the political involvements of some ecumenical activities and organizations.

Geography ➤
Ecumenical movement
Church fathers ➤

J. DENIS FORTIN

C. Mervyn Maxwell, *Tell It to the World: The Story of Seventh-day Adventists*, Mountain View, CA: Pacific Press ^{2}1982; Richard W. Schwarz and Floyd Greenleaf, *Light Bearers: A History of the Seventh-day Adventist Church*, Nampa, ID: Pacific Press 2000; *The Seventh-day Adventist Encyclopedia* (2 vols), Hagerstown, MD: Review and Herald ^{2}1996

http://www.adventist.org

Africa, Christianity in

The history of Christianity is all too often presented as the history of a Western religion. However, there are communities in Africa that can claim an involvement in the Jesus movement from its very beginning. The Gospel of Matthew (2.13–15) relates how Jesus' family took refuge in Egypt to avoid death, and the Acts of the Apostles (8. 26–39) reports an encounter between the treasurer of the Nubian kingdom of Meroe, returning from Rome, and the apostle Philip. When Christianity abandoned its Palestinian roots, its new home in the Graeco-Roman world included the Maghrib, the western part of north Africa comprising the Atlas mountains and the coastal areas of what are now Tunisia, Morocco and Algeria; this became the main source of grain supplies for Rome and shared extensive commercial and cultural relations with Palestine and the Levant. It was only later that Christianity shifted its centre of gravity into barbarian Europe, where every effort was made to domesticate it and repackage it in the Western image which is the only one with which many people are familiar.

Recently, commentators have observed a reverse shift in the number of Christians from the northern hemisphere to the south. Statistics show that by the year 2000 most Christians in the world lived in Latin America, Africa and Asia, in that order, and that out of around 2 billion Christians in the world, 1.11 billion are non-white. Africa looms large again. Out of 210.6 million evangelicals, Africa tops the list with 69.5 million; out of 423.7 million Pentecostal/charismatic Christians in the world, 126 million live in Africa. Given the rapid birth rate, these figures will increase dramatically. There are more Anglicans in Nigeria (with a Christian population of 49 million) than in England and Europe put together.

The significance of Africa's role in the formation of Christianity was remembered in 1971 when the All African Council of Churches convened an emergency session in Alexandria to reflect on an indigenous confession of faith. Beginning with a famous catechetical school founded at the end of the second century, and including the Greek-speaking church fathers Clement, Origen and Cyril, theologians in Alexandria had been prominent in the task of consolidating Christian theology and identity amidst the constraints of Roman imperial culture. When the doctrines, organization, forms of worship and ethics of Christianity were still in the process of being established, African voices were powerful. The Latin church fathers Tertullian and Augustine were also Africans. The spread of Islam in the seventh century gradually dismantled certain aspects of African Christianity as it retreated into Coptic villages as a symbol of nationalism and as it struggled in Nubia (until the fifteenth century) and in Ethiopia to witness amidst harassment by various Muslim dynasties.

In the fifteenth century, Europe abandoned its crusades and initiated a more creative response to Islamic economic, cultural and political challenges. Using sea routes to circumvent the Muslims, new efforts were made to evangelize Africa, but both the slave trade and colonization were a brake on evangelization. Christian presence in Africa retreated into the *feitoras*, trading forts, of various European nations until from the nineteenth century onwards the large-scale missionary enterprise led to a resurgence in the hinterlands of the communities that lived south of the Sahara desert. However, no African was present at the World Missionary Conference held in Edinburgh in 1910; Asia, including Japan, was the focus of interest for the delegates. Contemporary Africa is, though, highly significant for Christianity in the twenty-first century. Its story can be told in four sequences.

The first period: early Christianity in North Africa

It is uncertain when Christianity came to Egypt and much of the regions to the west such as Cyrenia, Numidia and Mauritania. The story of Pentecost told in the Acts of the Apostles (chapter 2) indicates clearly that people from this region, Jews and proselytes, newcomers to Judaism, were present at the crucial launching of the church. The Coptic Orthodox Church claims that both Thomas and Mark were in Egypt during a persecution of the Jesus movement; that Thomas moved from here to India; and that Mark was the first of the over 100 *abunas* (patriarchs) of the church. The pattern of the expansion of Christianity indicates that there was a Christian presence in Egypt around 239 and that from 274 the percentage of Christians in the population grew at a significant rate, greater than the percentage growth rate for the rest of the Graeco-Roman world.

A number of reasons for this growth have been given. First, there were the political and social forces that shaped the movement, especially a shift in the class structure of membership as upper-class women joined and provided facilities for the predominantly lower-class church members. Equally crucial was the conversion of some Jews; their social and commercial prominence protected the fledgling movement in its early days. The measures of suppression and repression of the new religion, the intermittent persecutions under the Roman emperors Decius, Severus and Valerian in the middle of the third century and especially the severe persecution under Diocletian at the beginning of the fourth century, strengthened rather than weakened the churches. From this perspective, the urgent debates about purity and the action against *traditores* (those who gave up the scriptures in their possession when threatened with death) indicate the degree of commitment among the ordinary believers who served as everyday evangelists. This commitment, extending as far as martyrdom, was the key to Christian survival.

Persecution

Martyr

The power of the message of Christianity was important, but the indigenous world-view was also a factor in its acceptance. Traditional Egyptian religion contained elements which resonated with the new faith, like the myth of Osiris, whose death and resurrection were celebrated annually; moreover, it was in Egypt, at Nag Hammadi, that the richest collection of Gnostic papyri was found, dating from the fourth century.

Crusades

p. 501

Gnosis

The Christian message was brought near to local populations by the translation of the Bible into Coptic languages such as Sahidic (Upper Nile), Bohairic (Nile Delta) and Fayumic or Bashmuric (Middle Nile) from the third century on. The use of the Coptic language in the liturgy and Bible domesticated the message and aided personal witnessing, which was the most powerful form of evangelism in this period. Evidence of deep religious consciousness is shown by the proliferation of Christian art, especially the distinctive genre of icons. Indeed, the indigenous culture was reshaped, as is evident in the funerary artefacts found in a tomb excavated at Antinoe in Upper Egypt; however, mummification persisted, since indigenous religion proved resilient.

p. 122

Icon

Another lasting contribution of this region was the monastic tradition. In the early fourth century Antony of Egypt was a pioneer of the solitary life of the hermit, while another Egyptian, Pachomius, founded the first monastery in 320; his regulations were adopted by many monasteries in due course. The retreats of hermits and monks in the deserts and mountains contributed towards nurturing Christian spirituality and a sense of mission, and served as havens for the persecuted or those who had grown tired of the virulent politics of those years. In later years, as the gilded Christianity in metropolitan Alexandria was emasculated, monasteries would prove to be the surviving centres of the Jesus movement. It should be stressed that Christianity in Egypt flourished amidst resilient ancient mystery cults that would later enjoy a renaissance.

Coptic Christianity

Monasticism

p. 1144

Spirituality

Mystery cults

At some point in time, the Christian movement flowed west and exhibited a character typical of those far from urban centres and the learning and scholarship that they flaunted. Consequently, a different type of Christianity

CHRISTIANS IN AFRICA AT THE MILLENNIUM

Country	Population	Roman Catholic	%	Independent	%	Protestant	%	Anglican	%	Orthodox	%	Non-Christians	%
1 Algeria	**31,471,000**	20,277	**0.1**	65,000	**0.2**	3,400	**0.0**	200	**0.0**	1,800	**0.0**	31,380,323	**99.7**
2 Angola	**12,878,000**	8,000,000	**62.1**	880,000	**6.8**	1,930,238	**15.0**	4,000	**0.0**	0	**0.0**	2,063,762	**16.0**
3 Botswana	**1,622,000**	60,000	**3.7**	498,253	**30.7**	178,000	**11.0**	10,500	**0.6**	120	**0.0**	875,127	**54.0**
4 Burkina Faso	**11,937,000**	1,129,078	**9.5**	54,000	**0.5**	799,000	**6.7**	0	**0.0**	0	**0.0**	9,954,922	**83.4**
5 Burundi	**6,695,000**	3,827,541	**57.2**	23,000	**0.3**	800,000	**11.9**	500,000	**7.5**	1,400	**0.0**	1,543,059	**23.0**
6 Cameroon	**15,085,000**	3,989,401	**26.4**	590,000	**3.9**	3,120,000	**20.7**	900	**0.0**	1,200	**0.0**	7,383,499	**48.9**
7 Central African Republic	**3,615,000**	664,639	**18.4**	418,000	**11.6**	520,800	**14.4**	0	**0.0**	0	**0.0**	2,011,561	**55.6**
8 Chad	**7,651,000**	502,158	**6.6**	152,000	**2.0**	782,756	**10.2**	0	**0.0**	0	**0.0**	6,214,086	**81.2**
9 Congo-Brazzaville	**2,943,000**	1,451,178	**49.3**	370,000	**12.6**	500,000	**17.0**	0	**0.0**	400	**0.0**	621,422	**21.1**
10 Congo-Zaire	**51,654,000**	26,300,000	**50.9**	12,050,000	**23.3**	10,485,000	**20.3**	440,000	**0.9**	8,100	**0.0**	2,370,900	**4.6**
11 Egypt	**68,470,000**	550,000	**0.8**	225,000	**0.3**	550,000	**0.8**	2,500	**0.0**	9,317,066	**13.6**	57,825,434	**84.5**
12 Ethiopia	**62,565,000**	450,000	**0.7**	860,000	**1.4**	8,510,000	**13.6**	800	**0.0**	22,837,859	**36.5**	29,906,341	**47.8**
13 Gabon	**1,226,000**	745,000	**60.8**	180,000	**14.7**	233,000	**19.0**	0	**0.0**	0	**0.0**	1,078,756	**12.0**
14 Ghana	**20,212,000**	1, 925,000	**9.5**	2,920,376	**14.4**	3,360,000	**16.6**	250,000	**1.2**	1,600	**0.0**	11,755,024	**58.2**
15 Guinea	**7,430,000**	117,000	**1.6**	43,000	**0.6**	69,182	**0.9**	1,400	**0.0**	0	**0.0**	7,199,418	**96.9**
16 Ivory Coast	**14,786,000**	2,182,882	**14.8**	1,373,000	**9.3**	760,000	**5.1**	0	**0.0**	20,000	**0.1**	10,450,118	**70.7**
17 Kenya	**30,080,000**	7,000,000	**23.3**	6,607,000	**22.0**	6,375,000	**21.2**	3.000,000	**10.0**	740,000	**2.5**	6,358,000	**21.1**
18 Lesotho	**2,153,000**	806,529	**37.5**	254,000	**11.8**	279,000	**13.0**	102,000	**4.7**	0	**0.0**	711, 471	**33.0**
19 Liberia	**3,154,000**	150,000	**4.8**	538,500	**17.1**	430,000	**13.6**	34,500	**1.1**	0	**0.0**	2,001,000	**63.4**
20 Libya	**5,605,000**	45,000	**0.8**	14,000	**0.2**	4,500	**0.1**	150	**0.0**	106,642	**1.9**	5,434,708	**97.0**
21 Madagascar	**15,942,000**	3,662,363	**23.0**	510,000	**3.2**	4,090,000	**25.7**	320,000	**2.0**	4,400	**0.0**	8,341,237	**52.3**
22 Malawi	**10,925,000**	2,697,860	**24.7**	1,830,000	**16.8**	2,140,000	**19.6**	230,000	**2.1**	4,400	**0.0**	4,022,740	**36.8**
23 Mali	**11,234,000**	125,565	**1.1**	16,300	**0.1**	82,000	**0.7**	0	**0.0**	0	**0.0**	11,010,135	**98.0**
24 Mauritania	**2,670,000**	4,216	**0.2**	1,700	**0.1**	600	**0.0**	0	**0.0**	0	**0.0**	2,663,474	**99.8**
25 Morocco	**28,221,000**	22,076	**0.1**	147,000	**0.5**	4,100	**0.0**	450	**0.0**	740	**0.0**	28,043,524	**99.4**
26 Mozambique	**19,680,000**	3,110,000	**15.8**	1,490,282	**7.6**	1,750,000	**8.9**	68,000	**0.3**	500	**0.0**	13,261,218	**67.4**
27 Namibia	**1,726,000**	306,211	**17.7**	187,000	**10.8**	820,000	**47.5**	31,000	**1.8**	0	**0.0**	381,789	**22.1**
28 Niger	**10,730,000**	19,670	**0.2**	25,000	**0.2**	13,000	**0.1**	0	**0.0**	0	**0.0**	10,672,330	**99.5**
29 Nigeria	**111,506,000**	13,400,000	**12.0**	23,975,000	**21.5**	14,050,000	**12.6**	20,070,000	**18.0**	3,100	**0.0**	40,007,900	**35.9**
30 Rwanda	**7,723,000**	3,942,000	**51.0**	236,293	**3.1**	1,689,970	**21.9**	805,000	**10.4**	1,500	**0.0**	1,048,237	**13.6**
31 Senegal	**9,481,000**	441,031	**4.7**	14,000	**0.1**	9,800	**0.1**	160	**0.0**	0	**0.0**	9,016, 009	**95.1**
32 Sierra Leone	**4,854,000**	169,140	**3.5**	165,000	**3.4**	171,000	**3.5**	25,000	**0.5**	610	**0.0**	4,323,250	**89.1**
33 Somalia	**7,265,500**	200	**0.0**	5,500	**0.1**	1,100	**0.0**	30	**0.0**	91,753	**1.3**	7,166,917	**98.6**
34 South Africa	**40,377,000**	3,350,000	**8.3**	18,500,000	**45.8**	12,410,000	**30.7**	2,660,000	**6.6**	150,000	**0.4**	3,307,000	**8.2**
35 Sudan	**25,490,000**	3,148,593	**12.4**	150,000	**0.6**	796,000	**3.1**	2,320,000	**9.1**	150,000	**0.6**	18,925,407	**74.2**
36 Swaziland	**1,008,000**	40,000	**4.0**	460,000	**45.6**	153,200	**15.2**	40,000	**4.0**	0	**0.0**	314,800	**31.2**
37 Tanzania	**33,517,000**	8,283,000	**24.7**	638,000	**1.9**	5,530,000	**16.5**	2,650,000	**7.9**	12,500	**0.0**	16,403,500	**48.9**
38 Togo	**4,629,000**	1,122,995	**24.3**	110,000	**2.4**	480,000	**10.4**	0	**0.0**	0	**0.0**	2,916,005	**63.0**
39 Tunisia	**9,586,000**	19,000	**0.2**	30,413	**0.3**	670	**0.0**	100	**0.0**	270	**0.0**	9,535,548	**99.5**
40 Uganda	**21,778,000**	9,130,000	**41.9**	815,000	**3.7**	596,000	**2.7**	8,580,000	**39.4**	32,000	**0.1**	2,625,000	**12.1**
41 Zambia	**9,169,000**	3,070,000	**33.5**	1,580,000	**17.2**	2,705,000	**29.5**	220,000	**2.4**	6,400	**0.1**	1,587,600	**17.3**
42 Zimbabwe	**11,669,000**	320,000	**2.7**	4,700,000	**40.3**	1,440,000	**12.3**	64,000	**0.5**	6,000	**0.1**	5,139,000	**44.0**

Independent is used here for Christians independent of historic, organized, institutional, denominational Christianity. In some countries, Christians are affiliated to more than one church.

Source: David B. Barrett, George T. Kurian and Todd M. Johnson (eds), *World Christian Encyclopedia*, New York: OUP ^{2}2002

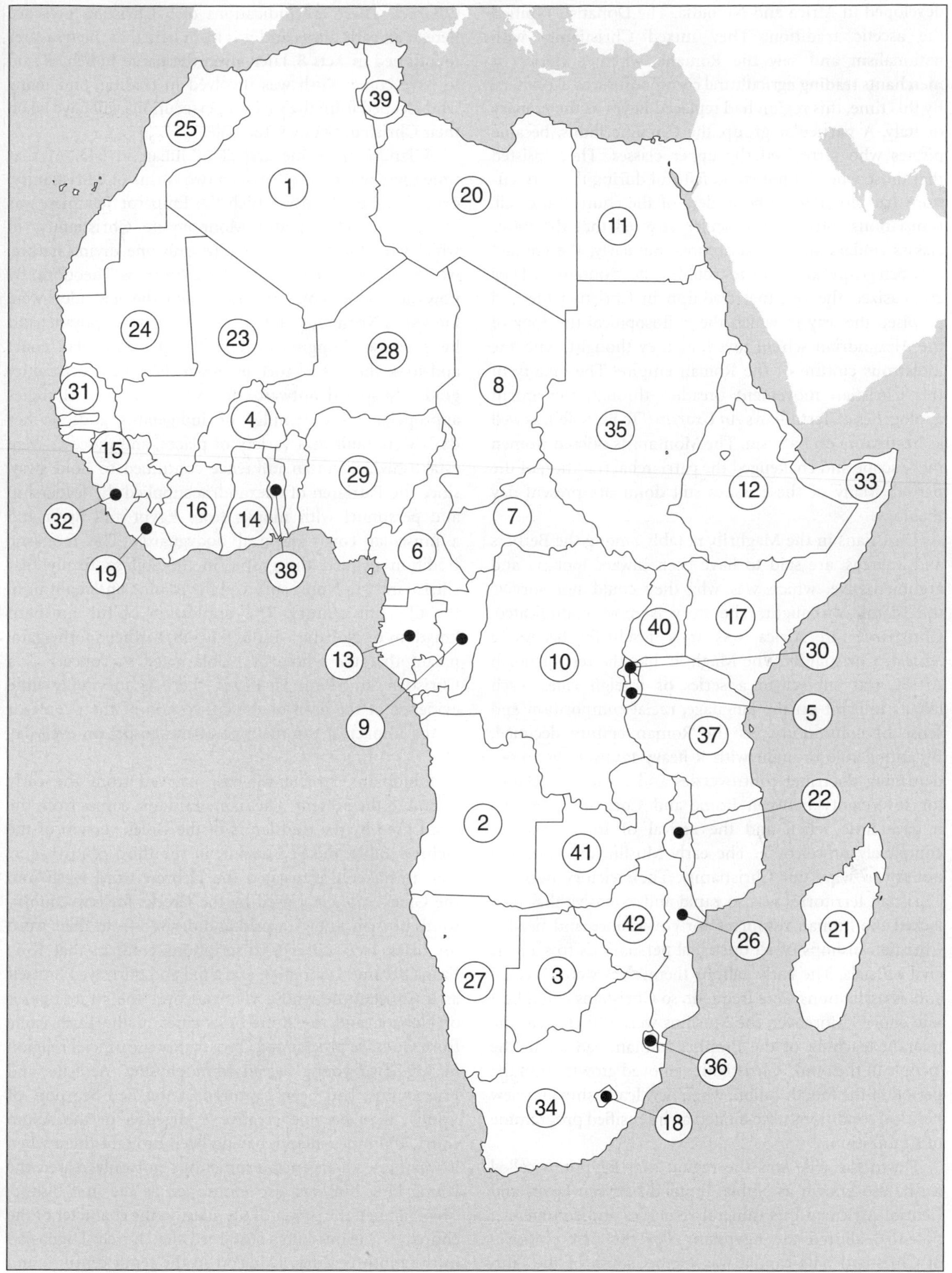
1
2
3
4
5
6
7
8
9
10
11
12
13
14
15
16
17
18
19
20
21
22
23
24
25
26
27
28
29
30
31
32
33
34
35
36
37
38
39
40
41
42

p. 520–1

developed in Africa and Numidia. The Donatists typified the ascetic tradition. They mixed Christianity with nationalism and saw the Romans, whether clerics or merchants trading agricultural commodities, as exploiters. By this time, this region had replaced Egypt as the granary of Italy. A particular group, the Circumcellions, became pirates who terrorized the upper classes. They insisted that those who did not stand faithful during the persecutions had no right to be leaders of the church; after all, translations into the vernacular ensured that the lower classes understood the scriptures. Similarly, the conflict between gospel and culture troubled the Montanists. They emphasized the spiritual tradition in Christian life and despised the way in which the philosophical theology of the Alexandrian school toyed, as they thought, with the idolatrous culture of the Roman empire. The vitality of this Christian movement breathes through the ardent apologetics of Tertullian's *Ad Uxorem* ('To his wife'), as well as his treatise on baptism. The Montanists offered women more scope and challenged the patriarchal tradition of the period. Many of these issues still dominate present-day theology.

Christology

Christians in the Maghrib, notably among the Berbers and Tuaregs, are said to have been inward-looking and argumentative, which was why they could not survive the Islamic onslaught. The story is more complicated. Christianity in Africa was only gradually becoming African Christianity. The Maghrib, like the rest of north Africa, was subject to a series of foreign rules; each left its imprint on the language, racial composition and sense of community. As the Roman empire declined, Byzantine rule brought with it heavy taxation, yet more damaging doctrinal controversies and competing claims for sovereignty between Rome and Constantinople. So it gave little relief, and the arrival of Islam was not completely unwelcome. The early Muslim dynasties did not try to wipe out Christianity. Their victory over the Christian territories was so rapid and extensive that they lacked the human resources for governance and needed Christian bishops of all doctrinal persuasions to serve as civil officials. The early caliphs themselves were insecure and assassinations were frequent, so Christians could be a safe choice. Moreover, the Muslims were still close to the tolerant teaching of the Prophet Muhammad about the 'people of the book'. Christianity enjoyed growth until the period of the fourth caliph, when new leadership and new political conditions necessitated an intensified programme of Arabization.

Down the Nile was the region that Egyptians called Kush, also known as Nubia. It stood between Egypt and Central Africa and its mineral resources and commercial potential allured the Egyptians. For the first centuries of Christianity its capital was Meroe, south of the Fifth Cataract. There are indications of a Christian presence here at an early stage, and it is from here that the treasurer mentioned in Acts 8, later given the name Judich, is said to have come; Kush was involved in trading, and many who escaped from the various persecutions will have taken their Christianity down the Nile.

A landmark is the arrival of Julian in 543. At that time there was rivalry between two forms of Christianity: orthodox Christianity, which the Emperor Justinian was trying to establish, and Monophysite Christianity, in which Christ was believed to have only one, divine, nature, which received the support of the Empress Theodora. By now the kingdom of Meroe had fallen; the new rulers were known as Nobatians. Julian, who was a Monophysite, and his successor Longinus, evangelized the Nobatian court and took the gospel further down the Nile. Christianity gradually spread outwards from the courts as churches appropriated the temples of indigenous gods, cathedrals were built in a variety of places, and dioceses were established. Egyptian influence continued to hold sway, since the Patriarch of Alexandria supplied the leadership and personnel with monks from Egypt and Syria and a muscular corps of local bodyguards. The monastic tradition planted the gospel in the soil so firmly that Christianity in Nubia survived the Islamic onslaught until the fifteenth century. The unification of the northern kingdom of Nobatia with Makurrah, further south again, meant that the whole of Nubia acted in concert as a Christian kingdom. However, there is inevitably little evidence of the level of the conversion of the people or of the impact of the message of the gospel on everyday life.

Ethiopian Christianity has survived from the early period to the present. The name Ethiopia comes from the word used by the translators of the Greek version of the Hebrew Bible, the Septuagint, in the third century BCE, who mistakenly translated the Hebrew word Kush into the Greek *Aithiopia*, used by the Greeks for any country south of their known world and derived from their word for black face, *aithiops*. Inscriptions confirm that King Ezana became a Christian as a child and portrayed himself as a Constantine whose victories over the straw houses of Nobatia and the stone-built cities of the Kush came from God. He proclaimed Christianity the official religion in 330. Two young Syrian Monophysites, Aedisius and Frumentius, had been captured at the Red Sea port of Adulis; they became creative evangelists in the Axum court, 100 miles inland, having been brought there when it was under a regency. Frumentius not only reared the young king but was also enthroned as the first bishop. This stamped the power of the state on the character of the church as various kings sustained the church: Digna-Jan in the ninth century; Dilna'od in the tenth century; and

A thirteenth-century rock-hewn church in Lalibela, in the centre of the Ethiopian highlands

Amda-Siyan, who restructured the church extensively in the fourteenth century.

The kings built many churches and monasteries, while Egypt supplied the patriarchs, the *abuna*. The Nine Saints or Sadaqan (Syrian Monophysite exiles) not only extended rural evangelization but established monasteries that became important in encapsulating the gospel. Soon rival abbots of monastic houses, insisting on the pre-eminence of their foundations, made church politics revolve around the three forces of king, *abunas* and abbots. When the power of Axum declined and the centre of Ethiopia shifted south from the area of the Tigre, the gospel continued to be incorporated into local culture. Jewish traditions of the early church were retained; there were innovations in worship that made use of traditional culture; and vigorous debates on observance of the sabbath and other finer points of theology.

Ethiopian contributions to Christian art, architecture, music, literacy and worship are enduring. The Ethiopian church, boasting a large number of extremely beautiful crosses, remained in splendid isolation until Europe rediscovered it in the fifteenth century in the quest for the mythical kingdom of Prester John, a legendary Christian priest-king of Asia. This contact saved it from the attacks of the Somali Muslim Ahmed Gran (the left-handed), who waged war on Ethiopia in the sixteenth century, but exposed it to disruptive foreign influences, especially the efforts to annex it to Rome. This created more internal debates, which by the nineteenth century had weakened the church.

Ethiopian Christianity

The story of Islam and Ethiopia is a long and complex one, because just as Jesus was sheltered in Egypt, so the prophet Muhammad was sheltered in Ethiopia: the king refused to repatriate him in spite of all the blandishments from his enemies in Mecca. He called for a tolerance that his followers reneged on.

In modern times the survival of Christianity was due to the powerful influence of two able monarchs, Yohannes IV (1872–89) and Menelik II (1889–1913). They dealt with the problem of foreign influence, held off the Mahdists from Sudan, defeated Italian attempts at colonization, and recovered the impetus from the Muslims, who had gained high political positions. Yohannes revitalized the church through four Coptic bishops, and evangelized the Galla, a people who had clung tenaciously through the years to traditional religion. Menelik established the structures of the modern Ethiopia that was inherited and developed by Emperor Haile Selassie (1892–1975).

The second chance: Iberian Catholicism

A new style of European response to the challenges of Islam was signalled by the Portuguese capture of Ceuta in North Africa from the Arabs in 1415. The immense consequences of this action, which was depicted as a crusade, included the recovery of the grain supply from Muslim control; it also provided valuable information about the extent of Arab trans-Saharan commerce in salt and gold that extended into Western and Central Sudan and the Senegalese Futa Jallon region. Psychologically, it prompted a series of striking maritime exploits. A nautical school established by Prince Henry at Sagres, the southernmost point of Portugal, experimented with sails, keels, compass and astrolabes. The Portuguese could venture into the Atlantic in the quest for a sea route to the source of spices, and encircle, block and cut into the Arab trans-Saharan gold trade from the south. Their aim was to reconnect with the empire of Prester John and convert the heathen. The combined motives of gold, glory and God fitted into the rhetoric of the period, the commercial motive being uppermost. Papal bulls offered the rights of patronage to the Portuguese monarch, authorizing him to appoint clerical orders for evangelization and to fend off competing European interests.

p. 700

The Iberian Catholic presence in Africa from the sixteenth to the eighteenth centuries had marked characteristics. Portugal was a small country and did not possess the manpower to control and evangelize the large territories 'discovered' between the years 1460–1520, stretching from Cape Blanco to Sumatra and Java. The settlers chose to stay on the islands and coastal regions of their shoestring empire. Iberian Catholicism was a social ornament, a religion of ceremonies and outward show, so in the islands and a few areas where they established a Christian presence on the mainland, there was formal adherence rather than strong spiritual commitment. Court alliances used religion as an instrument of diplomatic and commercial relationship. A missionary venture that insisted upon the transplantation of European models remained fleeting, superficial and ill-conceived. On the islands of Cape Verde and Sao Thome, the Portuguese built prototypes of Lisbon and established churches and cathedrals that also trained the pastors for ministry in the interior. In the Gold Coast of the Atlantic Ocean and at Kilwa in the Indian Ocean they built their first forts, but the only serious evangelization was among the *mestizo*, mixed-race children of the traders.

Evangelicals ➤
Great Awakening ➤

Incursions into the kingdoms of Benin and Warri (now part of Nigeria) soon failed as the Portuguese found pepper from India more profitable to trade in. The only enduring presence of Christianity was in the Kongo-Soyo kingdoms (in what is now Angola), lasting until the eighteenth century. Here some of the indigenous population were ordained to the priesthood, especially the children of Portuguese traders and gentlemen and some of the servants of white priests; however, the force of the ministry weakened with the changing pattern of trade and internal politics and the abolition of the Jesuit order. Celebrated cases such as the conversion of the Monomotapa, the chief of Mashonaland in what is now Zimbabwe, were soon overshadowed by disasters, and the Iberian presence on the East African coast had to compete against Indians and Arabs. The thirteen ethnic groups of Madagascar warred relentlessly against the Portuguese, while the Arabs of Oman reconquered the northern sector of the eastern coast. Finally, other European countries challenged Portugal for a share of the lucrative trade that had turned primarily into slave trading. Iberian domination collapsed; broken statues in certain parts of Africa remained to betray the missionary exploits of the past. By the end of the eighteenth century, 21 forts dotted the coast of West Africa; some had chaplains, but many did not. The chaplains were poorly paid with shoddy trade goods. The Dutch and Danish experiments that employed indigenous chaplains failed as well. The fleeting encounter with Christian presence in sub-Saharan Africa after the debacle on the Maghrib came to an end as the gospel bearers concentrated on making slaves of potential converts.

The resilient vision: abolitionism and evangelical revival

At the end of the eighteenth century, two forces combined to regenerate the evangelization of sub-Saharan Africa: abolitionism and evangelical revival. Spiritual awakenings occurred in many nations from the mid-eighteenth century into the nineteenth century. Their characteristics included an emphasis on the Bible, the cross, conversion experience, and a pro-active expression of faith. They were connected with abolitionism through the social activism of the evangelical movement, which proposed to put an end to the slave trade by gaining the co-operation of the chiefs who controlled the supply. An environment conducive to combating the slave traders was to be established through legitimate trade, a new administrative structure secured with agreements, and the use of Christianity as a civilizing agent.

The work of abolition was carried on by a network of philanthropists and religious groups across the Atlantic Ocean. Those involved were various groups of black Americans, including liberated slaves; Africans such as Ottabah Cuguano and Olaudah Equiano, former slaves living in Britain in the eighteenth century, who wrote vividly about their experiences; and entrepreneurs such as Paul Cuffee (1759–1817), a negro shipowner and businessman born in Massachusetts, who spent his resources building up a commercial enterprise between Africa, Britain and America. Motives again varied: religion, politics, commerce, rational humanism and local needs. In England, the Committee of the Black Poor complained about the increasing social and financial problems caused by the numbers of impoverished liberated slaves. In America, an African American élite became concerned about their welfare and planned to educate young people and equip them with skills for survival. Meanwhile, those slaves who took the dangerous option of deserting their masters and fighting on behalf of the British forces in the American War of Independence complained about the appalling conditions. They had perceived the war as an opportunity to be liberated; they absorbed the liberal constitutional ideology, and struggled against all odds in Nova Scotia and the West Indies to create a space in which to practise their ideals. Indeed, the next century would witness many rebellions in the West Indies. Liberated slaves also created a link between abolitionism and mission, between Enlightenment ideas and Christianity. They shared with the Republicans against whom they had fought the same ideals of individual enterprise, personal responsibility, equality before the law and freedom to practise religion.

In 1787 the British Government founded Sierra Leone as a haven for liberated slaves, but the colony nearly foundered because of attacks from local chiefs and the lack of adequate provisions for the new settlers. At this point, the Nova Scotians and West Indian Maroons were dispatched to Sierra Leone. They went out as missionaries to Sierra Leone in 1792 before any British missionary society was founded, and with a clear vision of building a new society under the mandate of the gospel. They took care to avoid the indigenous chiefs, who had been compromised through the slave trade. Indeed, they supported the separation of church and state in order to dissociate the missionary enterprise of redeeming Africa through religion from the patronage of the governors of trading companies. They set the cultural tone that nurtured thousands of freed slaves in Sierra Leone between 1807 and 1864. These freed slaves became agents of missionary enterprise throughout the west coast.

The liberated slaves who returned to Yorubaland, present-day south-west Nigeria, served variously as educators, interpreters, counsellors to indigenous communities, negotiators with the new agents of change, preachers, traders and leaders of public opinion in many West African communities. Adjai (Samuel) Crowther, who was made a bishop in 1864, personified their achievements. Furthermore, the Colonization Society recruited enough African Americans to found Liberia in 1822, and from this period until the 1920s African Americans were a significant factor in the missionary enterprise to Africa.

But other crucial factors determined the pattern of Christian presence in nineteenth-century Africa. The resurgence of the missionary enterprise led to an increase in the number of missionary bodies, individuals, theologies, motives, vocations and modes of funding and training. There was a widespread acceptance by the denominations, and the main feature of the enterprise was its popular appeal; it was voluntarily sustained by all classes of society in various countries. By mid-century, the faith movements encouraged individuals to venture into mission fields without institutional support. Many women seized their opportunity. The general optimism of the century set the tone, perhaps to the chagrin of Western Europeans who had started missions in the eighteenth century, before England and America became involved. Education, translation of the scriptures into indigenous languages and the founding of charitable institutions such as those for health care and artisan workshops domesticated the message and also changed the character of Christian presence.

Evangelism had a certain role to play in the resurgence: it reconciled the developed consciousness of individual responsibility with the Christian faith by fostering a close fellowship of believers; it served as an antidote to individualism; and its distinction between nominal, formal Christians and real Christianity resulted in a body of committed people who could be mobilized and deployed into mission. An organization emerged that could recruit, train, fund and provide a network with global centres. Logistics, access to indigenous people and organization changed the face of Christianity. The various evangelical groups reached beyond the individual to encourage the Christian way of life in families and society; radical discipleship and personal decision meant responding to a call to save the heathen. As America warmed to foreign missions, it brought enormous energy, optimism, vigour and human resources. The development of technology, the strength of the North Atlantic powers and the spread of civil and religious liberty created a viable environment for missions. Other racial theories such as being chosen, Covenant covenant, responsibility, civilization, destiny and other such ideas came later, and linked missions to imperial ideology. It is important to perceive the development of these ideas as well as their impact on the character of Christianity in Africa. The emphasis changed over time, and each phase compelled different rationalizations.

Roman Catholics revamped their organization and fund-raising strategies for missions in such a way that rivalry with Protestants influenced the pace and direction of the spread of the gospel. However, these changes coincided with new geo-political factors. By the middle of the nineteenth century, competing forms of European nationalism had changed the character of the contact with Africa from informal commercial relations into formal colonial hegemony. The Berlin Conference of 1884–5 partitioned Africa and insisted on formal occupation. It introduced a new spirit that overawed indigenous institutions and sought to transplant European institutions and cultures. The project of bringing civilization diminished the spiritual vigour of the missionary presence and turned it into cultural and power encounters. This explains the predominant strategy of the missionary movements in southern Africa of forming enclaves. Holy Ghost Fathers turned their plantation into a lucrative exploitation of young people at Bagamoyo, off the coast of Zanzibar. The white settler communities in East Africa established a tight control of ministry that spurned the cultural genius of the people. The Catholic missionary presence in the Congo colluded with the brutality of King Leopold until an international outcry in 1908 forced him to sell the colony to Belgium. The abusive Portuguese presence in Angola, Mozambique, Guinea Bissau and Cape Verde Islands would later provoke anti-clerical and Marxist response after the forced decolonization.

The story now becomes one of African Christian initiatives, hidden agendas and resistance to the system. In one place after another, indigenous prophetic figures inspired a charismatic response to the gospel and through their efforts Christianity grew. 'Native' agency became the instrument of growth. Some Africans gave voice to indigenous feeling against Western cultural iconoclasm and decision-making in the colonial churches. Using the promise in the Psalms that Ethiopia shall raise its hands to God, 'Ethiopianism' became a movement of cultural and religious protest. It delved back into its history to recover and re-contextualize its black traditions of emancipation which had been hidden from the consciousness of black peoples by colonial domination. In its religious guise, it breathed the hope that Africans would bear the burden of evangelization and build an autonomous church devoid of denominations and free of European control.

The Missionary News, 15 March 1936, showing an African town on the Congo River

A network of educated Africans spread across West Africa to evangelize, inculturate and create African Christianity. Their ideology was typified in *Ethiopia Unbound* by the Gold Coast lawyer, Casely Hayford, and *The Return of the Exiles* by Wilmot Blyden of Liberia. Mojola Agbebi and others changed their English names, wore African clothes and decided to leave the colonial religious establishment by founding African churches without the support of foreign aid. Missionary enclaves in southern and central Africa did the same. In Southern Africa, the American African Methodist Episcopal Church and its black ideology took on a strong charismatic religious tone. As racism divided whites and blacks in the Pentecostal impulse that came from Zion City, Indiana, the blacks claimed the names 'Zion' and 'Apostolic' and integrated symbols from indigenous religions to reshape the polity, liturgy and ethics of Western Christianity. Through mine workers, the movement percolated through the region. Between 1913 and 1990, the number of indigenous churches in South Africa grew from 30 to more than 6000. By the late 1920s, and in the middle of the influenza epidemic that came after the First World War, visions, dreams and prayer led some to tap the spiritual resources of the gospel, emphasize healing, incorporate African symbolism, use African musical instruments and African leadership. There was more scope for women, as there was with the Montanists of the early years. African indigenous churches (variously referred to as Zionists in Southern Africa, Aladura in West Africa and Arathi in East Africa) changed the face of Christianity in twentieth-century Africa.

However, a number of them separated and mutated into forms that had their roots in the original impulse; for instance, in Nigeria, the Zionist type, Cherubim and Seraphim, split into 51 groups between 1925 and 1975. Other genres emerged, that set up healing homes and, in the quest for miraculous power, use occult resources or clothe indigenous religion with a veneer of Christian symbolism. The fastest growing groups among them are the messianic forms in which the leader claims to be one or other person of the Trinity. These have moved away from the Bible as a focus. Sabbatarian forms have emerged that do not confess Jesus as Lord.

Some writers have incautiously romanticized the African indigenous churches as the African contribution to world Christianity; however, this characterization must be qualified, since the movement has widened beyond the pale of Christianity. Some revivalist groups are nationalist apologists; they repackage indigenous religion in statements of belief with a Christian format, a Christian structure and a resonance between the Bible stories and African religions. One group calls itself Godianism, another Orunmila and still another Afrikania.

The story of Christianity in Africa has always been linked with that of Islam. Islam benefited from colonialism and expanded south of the Sahara, not just because of *jihads* that led to the formation of states but also because Europe shifted from an idea that Islam was a form of superstition to the acceptance that since it acknowledged one God, it was superior to African religions. In his *Mohammed and Mohammedanism* (1874), the nineteenth-century historian Reginald Bosworth Smith provided an arsenal that combined evolutionary theory with arguments that Islam was a religion suited for primitive races; that a religion that prohibited the use of alcohol was best for the 'natives'. For other political reasons enshrined in the indirect rule strategy, official policy protected Islam, which used improved modes of communication to trade. The power of Islam has continued to hinder Christianity, even when the state adopts a secular ideology, because Islam perceives the state as an instrument for promoting religion.

A significant aspect of the nineteenth century was that as missionaries sowed the seed of the gospel, Africans appropriated it from a primal, charismatic world-view and read the translated scriptures in that light. Indigenous agencies recovered the spiritual resources of the gospel and challenged missionary Christianity to be fully biblical. This set the stage for the decolonization process that followed the world wars. New forces such as the implosion of the state challenged the heritage of African Christianity; and the collapse of the dictatorial states and attendant poverty probed the tensile strength of the church's stewardship. Inexplicably, charismatic and Pentecostal spirituality resurfaced to provide the energy for growth and sustainability in the midst of hostile circumstances.

New dimensions in African Christianity: power, poverty and prayer

Between the First World War and the emergence of political independence, several denominations sought to consolidate their enterprises, just as many religious entrepreneurs hatched various 'Christianities' out of a vibrant religious culture. The two world wars and economic depression created so much disquiet that the pace of revivalism and religious innovation increased. William Wadé Harris, for instance, trekked across Liberia and the Ivory Coast to the Gold Coast, preaching and healing. His ministry benefited the mainline churches and inspired charismatic movements. In the Congo, Simon Kimbangu prophesied that the global disorder indicated that God was passing on the baton from whites to blacks. His own imprisonment did not deter the growth of his movement. In the 1930s the Balokole movement spread from Rwanda through the Congo into Uganda, Kenya, Tanganyika and the Sudan. It urged repentance, holiness ethics and a closer relationship with Jesus. Examples could be multiplied to show that just as the wars increased African confidence and shifted the vision of cultural nationalists to the quest for political independence, so the efforts of missionaries to consolidate denominationalism were confronted by intensified, subversive, indigenous initiatives. Missionary response to nationalism was informed by individual predilections, the negative racial image of Africans and some liberal support; there were regional variations, as those in the settler communities responded with fright and the bulwark of apartheid laws.

Trinity

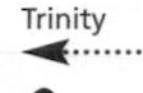

As the wind of change blew more brutally, it became clear that the missions had weak roots: few indigenous clergy, a dependency ideology, undeveloped theology, poor infrastructure and, above all, little confidence in their leaders. From the 1950s, Roman Catholics took the lead in a hurried attempt to train indigenous priests. Missions sought opportunities to ally with nationalists, because the educated élites were products of various missions and their control of power could aid their denominations in the rivalry for territory. This strategy entangled Christianity in the politics of independence.

Matters went awry when the élites mobilized the states into dictatorial one-party structures, castigated missionaries for under-developing Africa, promoted neo-Marxist Pentecostalism rejection of the dependency syndrome and seized the instruments of missionary propaganda such as schools, hospitals and social welfare agencies. The implosion of the state challenged the churches, but the failure of the states produced a rash of military coups, abuse of human rights and economic collapse. Poverty ravaged many African countries. The control of societies by military forces intensified inter-ethnic conflicts and civil wars. The religion of displaced people in refugee camps is a key aspect of contemporary African Christianity. Natural disasters such as drought in the Horn of Africa have made matters worse. Part of the problem can be traced to weak leadership, and Holy Spirit part to external forces that have used the continent as fodder in the Cold War by patronizing dictators, exploiting the mineral resources and manipulating huge debts that have burdened and permanently crippled many nations.

Feminist theology Meanwhile, the structure of the countries has changed dramatically as each has become more pluralistic. In many countries, Islamic rulers have dominated and Christianity has fought for space. A good example of the new dispensation is the Christian Association of Nigeria, which was formed in 1975 and brought many forms of embattled Christianity together to explore new models that could serve as calming factors in a difficult situation. As civil society was decimated, Christianity remained as the survivor. This explains why, at the end of the Cold War and the renaissance of Western interest in democratic structures, Christian leaders were chosen in one country after another to serve as the presidents of consultative assemblies that sought to renew hope and banish the pessimism that looked upon the problems of Africa as incurable.

A number of factors explain the survival of Christianity. The first is that the development of African Christian theologies from the mid-1970s enabled a critique of inherited traditions and theologies. In Southern Africa, the emphasis shifted from cultural theologizing to black consciousness; this sustained a black revolution against apartheid in South Africa, Namibia and Zimbabwe. The second is the rise of youthful charismatics. A commentator observed that in one country after another, young puritans emerged in urban settings from 1970 onwards. With a message of repentance and holiness ethics, secondary school and p. 836 university students transformed dowdy organizations like the Scripture Union and the Student Christian Movement into emotionally expressive charismatic movements. Mainline churches struck back with disciplinary rebuttals that forced them to form organizations that changed the face of Christianity. Those Pentecostal and Holiness groups that had emerged in the 1930–40 period benefited from the youthful revivals. Women featured prominently in these organizations and churches were compelled to create a space for charismatics or lose their members to new-fangled Pentecostalism.

This form of Christianity has changed shape in every decade, absorbing American prosperity preaching in the 1980s and reverting to traditions of holiness and petitionary prayer in the 1990s. Pentecostal/charismatic influence is growing rapidly in Africa, not least because of its cultural 'fit': it brings the resources of the gospel as answers to questions raised within the primal worldviews. Healing and deliverance feature prominently. As an instrumentalist response, charismatic Pentecostalism provides mechanisms for coping with economic collapse. The religious dimension is the inexplicable power of the Holy Spirit in Africa that has set the missionary message to work. The movement has flowed from urban centres into rural Africa.

A third feature of the times is the rise of Christian feminist theology, challenging the churches to become less patriarchal. Through many publications and programmes, churches are being compelled to ordain women and allow them to participate in decision-making processes.

There are two obvious challenges: whether the churches will mobilize their resources and use the new opportunities to combat poverty in pluralistic environments, and what the resurgence of Christianity in Africa could contribute to world Christianity. Two significant features are the explosion of African Christianity in the Western world and the emergence of charlatans. The churches in Africa are overflowing; many people boldly use biblical names for their businesses and political leaders declare themselves 'born again'. Charismatic and evangelical bodies are establishing crèches, Bible schools and universities and regaining a Christian hold of the family through education. Beyond quantitative growth there is much evidence of the deepening of the gospel in the lives of people who would have been lost to secularism. Contemporary Africa resembles a replay of early Christianity in the Maghrib.

OGBU KALU

John Baur, *2000 Years of Christianity in Africa*, Nairobi: Paulines 1994; Adrian Hastings, *The Church in Africa, 1450–1950*, Oxford: Clarendon Press 1994; Ogbu U. Kalu, *Power, Poverty and Prayer: The Challenges of Poverty and Pluralism in African Christianity, 1960–1996*, Frankfurt: Peter Lang 2000; Lamin Sanneh, *Abolitionists Abroad: African Blacks and the Making of West Africa*, Cambridge, MA: Harvard University Press 1999; Andrew F. Walls, *The Cross-Cultural Process in Christian History*, Maryknoll: Orbis and Edinburgh: T&T Clark 2002

African American Christianity

Churches

Almost every aspect of the life of the communities of worship and witness known as the African American or black church is shaped within the context of hidden and manifest meaning. Even their name has evolved, as along with people of African descent in general they have searched for language that is truly expressive of their identity: slave church, diaspora church, coloured church, Negro church, black church, African American church – each attempt to capture the genius and distinctiveness of these communities both succeeds and fails at the same time. Many of these churches proudly display and advertise their African heritage, often as part of their names, e.g. the African Methodist Episcopal Church, or the African Orthodox Church. Others attempt to embody a transcendence of race and culture by focusing on what they have in common with all other Christians, e.g. God's House of Prayer for All Nations, Inc.

These bodies range from regular and traditional worshipping communities to parachurch advocacy groups. Most of them are bodies that were founded and established by people of African descent, but many of them are part of larger European/Caucasian churches. They also span the spectrum from those bodies that are influenced by Jewish thought and practice, through those influenced by Islamic thought and practice, to those that are influenced by various forms of mysticism. In essence, the phenomenon referred to as the African American/black church is constantly evolving and changing. This attempt to describe it will be a snapshot; it will be a moment frozen in time that attempts to capture a moving image. Notwithstanding this reservation, certain salient features of this group of worshipping communities seem to be more or less permanent in their make-up.

All communities are compelled to deal with the issues of the self-esteem and self-worth of black people. They do this through their organizational structures, which provide opportunities for leadership often not available in the wider society for their members. They are all compelled to give an account of the social, political and economic injustices that frame the existence of their members. At times, some churches will confront the oppressive forces of the world directly. Other churches will focus on the importance of the spiritual realm as a way of refusing to cede ultimate power to the rulers of this age. They are all compelled to provide a space for the joyous praise of God. In some instances, this praise will be quiet and contemplative. On other occasions, it will be emotional and full-bodied.

Given the broad spectrum of groups that could conceivably comprise the black church, it is difficult to capture its scope and depth with any degree of specificity. The best attempt to date remains the classic work by C. Eric Lincoln and Lawrence Mamiya, *The Black Church in the African American Experience.* Based on exhaustive research on the major black church groups, this study provides crucial insight into the sociological dimensions of the African American church.

It is difficult to gauge the size of the total membership of African American churches for several reasons. The major denominational bodies range in size from the National Baptist Convention, Inc., with an estimated membership of 7 million, to a host of very small denominational bodies with memberships as small as a few hundred. In addition, the numbers of African American Christians in predominately white denominations is even more difficult to assess. It is safe to say that the influence of the black church, though lessened by the emerging power of a secular culture, remains significant in the black communities of the United States and beyond. The majority of black congregations (70%) tend to range in size from 100 to 600 members. While there are examples of larger congregations such as the Abyssinian Baptist Church in Harlem, New York, and the Concord Baptist Church of Christ in Brooklyn, New York, with more than 10,000 members each, the vast majority of African American churches have several hundred members.

This picture is changing with the advent of the mega-church phenomenon. These churches boast as many as 20,000 members or more. However, it remains to be seen what effect they will have on our understanding of the black church as a whole. What is becoming clear is that these mega-churches, whether black or white, often borrow significantly from the creativity of the historic black church. In terms of organization and activities, black churches are focused on several key constituencies. A recent survey showed that 51% of churches had a men's group; 67% had a women's group; 82% had a youth group; 92% had a Bible study group; and 92% had a midweek prayer meeting. 64% of the churches reported that lay people played a significant role in planning and conducting worship services. In contrast, only 38% of the churches had a senior citizens' programme, and only 29% had a programme for young single persons. These statistics suggests that the black church is well positioned to minister to the needs of persons until their latter years, and to the needs of married persons. Black churches may need to focus more resources on meeting the needs of the elderly and of single people in the community.

The notions of doctrine, worship and practices are useful categories when attempting to understand the evolution of predominantly white congregations in Europe and North America, but they must be seen in a different light when applied to the black church. The black church cannot be defined simply on that basis. It is the totality of worshipping communities throughout the African diaspora, Africans dispersed all over the world. The African American church, for example, is one expression of the black church. When we take into account the different dimensions of the black church throughout the world, a rich diversity is the result.

The common thread within the phenomenon of the black churches is, first, that in them doctrine, worship and church practice form a single fabric of faithful witness. Doctrine is not just about what is believed or confessed, but also about what funds and founds the life of the black Christian. Worship is not just about what is ritually celebrated or ceremonially observed on Sunday, but about allowing the power that funds and founds the life of the black Christian to emerge. Church practice is not about preserving a set of collective behaviours for the purpose of maintaining an institution, but about walking in that power. The essential features of the doctrine, worship and practice of the black church can be found in this affirmation: 'We believe in God who is the source of our existence. In him we live, move and have our being. We worship Jesus Christ who is present with us. Through him we are saved. We walk according to the power of the Holy Spirit who is our Guide. By him we are counselled and comforted.'

It is the ongoing work of the black theologian to assess this affirmation and to set out its implications. The doctrinal affirmations that ground the faith of the black church are tempered and forged in the struggle of daily living. It is life itself that compels the black Christian to seek doctrinal clarity. The self-understanding of the black church is rooted in an African religious sensibility. It is also, partly, a response to the experiences of enslavement, colonization and racial oppression. Yet what black Christians affirm is not primarily a reflection of the pathos of their existence, but in the final analysis a joyous affirmation of the possibilities of life in God.

The origins and the history of the black church lie in the convergence of several religious, social, cultural and political forces. The black church was the result of a quest for religious liberty, social cohesion, cultural integrity and political empowerment. During the eighteenth and nineteenth centuries within the United States the form and progress of the black church in the North differed in some respects from that in the South. Yet this multifaceted quest was evident in its emergence in both regions.

In the late eighteenth century, it was not uncommon for enslaved Africans to be found within European American congregations. This integrated worshipping community, however, was not a sign of any equality between the races. In fact, it was an act of prudence on the part of the slaveholders that they should keep strict surveillance on the slaves. In one or two instances, an all-black congregation would be allowed to gather, but only with the proviso that the preacher be white and the group had the permission of the slaveholder. Towards the latter part of the eighteenth century and into the early part of the nineteenth, independent black churches were established in South Carolina and in Georgia. These churches were the natural fruit of the clandestine praise meetings held by slaves. The difference was that these were churches, institutional counterparts to white churches, established in full view of whites, and often without their approval. In addition, the leadership of these churches was black. These early churches in the South endured much persecution. Their buildings were burned, their leaders were threatened, beaten and sometimes killed. Yet they persevered, their true prophetic witness not being fully appreciated until the end of the Civil War.

The beginnings of the black church in the northern United States can be traced to St George's Methodist Episcopal Church in Philadelphia. In 1787 Richard Allen and Absalom Jones, two African American members, left the church after they were pulled from their knees during prayers. They had stopped in a section of the sanctuary reserved for whites only. The roots of this dispute lay in the growing black membership of the church and the desire of the white membership to maintain separation between the races. Allen and Jones left to form black churches of their own. Jones established the first black Episcopal church in the United States, St Thomas' African Episcopal Church, and he was later recognized by the Protestant Episcopal Church in America as the first black Episcopal deacon. Allen founded the Free African Society, the civic and charitable service organization, and later the African Methodist Episcopal Church, the AME Church. Other church bodies followed, including the African Methodist Episcopal Zion Church and the African Methodist Episcopal Union Church.

In the South, black congregations would gather in small buildings with benches and a pulpit for the preacher; these basic structures provided them with a place of their own, free from the oppression of everyday life. Migrants to the North would first gather in homes for prayer meetings, but when the group became strong enough they would set up a church in the storefront of a building. These storefronts, again, had minimal facilities but performed the same function as the small southern country church in providing space for black congregations. They play a powerful role in countless African American communities, not least as welfare agencies.

The next significant period of black church establishment occurred nearly a century later with the founding of black conventions, i.e., the National Baptist Convention. In the early years of the twentieth century black Pentecostalism was born in a revival at the Azusa Street Mission in Los Angeles, under the influence of William J. Seymour, an African American holiness preacher from Texas. This renewal movement brought together black and white people in the unifying power of the Holy Spirit. The immediate significance of race was abrogated in this miraculous moment. One of the leaders of the movement was an African American Baptist minister, the Revd Charles Mason. In an extraordinary sequence of events, Mason ordained many white pastors, sending them out as apostles of the new dispensation. However, soon the demonic and divisive effects of racism entered the movement and it split along racial lines. The black Pentecostal movement resulted in the establishment of the Church of God in Christ, and the white Pentecostal movement, many of whose leaders had been ordained by Mason, resulted in the Assemblies of God church.

The relation of African American churches to other religious bodies has followed three distinct trajectories.

The first ecumenical efforts of black churches in the United States were directed towards bringing unity and solidarity among themselves. The Fraternal Council of Negro Churches (1934–64) was founded by the black social gospel proponent the Revd Reverdy C. Ransom, as an expression of the growing nationalism among black Americans and to combat the oppression and segregation that was predominant in the United States. The Southern Christian Leadership Conference was founded in 1957 and became closely identified with the Civil Rights Movement and its dynamic leader, Dr Martin Luther King, Jr. In 1963 the National Negro Evangelical Association was founded and later became the National Black Evangelical Association. This organization was established by black members of the predominantly white evangelical movement in the United States. White evangelicals were at best apathetic to black concerns about racial justice, and at worst explicitly hostile to these concerns. The National Committee of Negro Churchmen was established in 1967 in response to the challenges of the Black Power movement in the United States. It was later renamed the National Committee of Black Churchmen, then the National Conference of Black Churchmen, and finally, the National Conference of Black Christians. These are only a few of the efforts at internal unity which black churches have undertaken.

The second trajectory of the ecumenical efforts of the black church was evident in the participation of black theologians in the establishment of the Ecumenical Association of Third World Theologians (EATWOT). This consultation, begun in 1976, provided a global arena for discourse that included black theologians. In 1975, however, a serious ecumenical effort, the Theology in the Americas Project, sought to bring together theological voices from black American, Native American, Latino/a theologians and others for a historic conversation. Though these gatherings carried tremendous significance for the participants, unlike the efforts described above they were largely dominated by theologians and academics.

Pentecostalism

The third ecumenical trajectory involved conversations between black theological perspectives and other theological perspectives that went beyond the critique of social, political and economic forces that were often the main focus of the efforts described above. This third ecumenical moment has not yet been fully explored or developed. However, two examples have emerged with some prominence. The first is the relationship between black theological perspectives and Asian theological perspectives. These conversations centre on the significance of the Korean notion of *Han*, a word that means defeat, resignation and otherness, and its similarity to the pathos of much black religious expression. The second example is the relationship between black theological perspectives and Jewish theological perspectives. These conversations centre on the significance of a shared store of symbols (the exodus, Moses/Messiah, and the chosen people). This third moment moves from ecumenical conversations in the more traditional sense to an inter-religious dialogue.

Holy Spirit

Assemblies of God

The relationship between these ecumenical efforts and the broader ecumenical efforts of organizations such as the National Council of Churches and the World Council of Churches is a story of both hope and disappointment. While there have been moments when members of the broader ecumenical movement have put themselves on the line for the full inclusion of black churches, more often than not these organizations have been unable to pull themselves from the grip of racism and prejudice.

Ecumenical movement

JAMES H. EVANS, JR

James H. Cone, *Black Theology and Black Power*, Maryknoll, NY: Orbis 1997; James H. Evans, Jr, *We Have Been Believers: An African American Systematic Theology*, Minneapolis: Fortress Press 1992; C. Eric Lincoln and Lawrence H. Mamiya, *The Black Church in the African American Experience*, Durham, NC: Duke University Press 1995; J. Deotis Roberts, *Black Theology in Dialogue*, Philadelphia: Westminster Press 1987; Mary R. Sawyer, *Black Ecumenism: Implementing the Demands of Justice*, Valley Forge, PA: Trinity Press International 1994; Gayraud S. Wilmore, *Black Religion and Black Radicalism*, Maryknoll, NY: Orbis 1983

Experience and thought

African American Christianity is about the experience of being of African descent in North America and the subsequent understanding of how God identifies with African or black identity. The current ambiguity involved in being an African American or black American points to the complexity of describing such experience in relationship to Christianity. At the heart of what it means to be an African American Christian is the context of slavery of African people by Europeans. It is from such a context of slavery that such distinctive markers of African American Christianity as spirituals, preaching, shouting, 'testifying', civil rights and ultimately the black church experience come. In many ways, African American Christianity depends upon the narratives of how God identified with the Jews in their exodus out of Egypt and their delivery from slavery. It is important to be aware not only of these distinctive markers but of the overall sense of what African American Christianity has come to mean.

A revaluation of 'black identity' came about in the 1960s, when theologians and political leaders turned what was seen as a negative description, 'being black', into a spiritual vision of the reconstruction of a new humanity that was no longer defined by oppression, but by freedom. In American societies blackness simultaneously came to symbolize oppression and liberation. Blacks live in a society in which blackness means criminality, sub-humanity and anarchy. The goal of black theology is to attend much more closely to the nature of the fragile existence of blacks in North America and the Western world. The life of African Americans remains a very dangerous reality: a disproportionate number of black people are in prison, and die from homicide or HIV/AIDS. Today, blackness has also come to include all victims of oppression, who realize that the survival of their humanity is bound up with their liberation from whiteness. This current development of the good connotation of blackness applies just as much to Australian Aborigines as it does to African Americans. It is because of the perceived victory of the civil rights era that black identity has now become an international identity (e.g., blacks in South Africa, India, South America, etc.). In a world in which the oppressor defines authority in terms of whiteness, humanity means an unqualified identification with blackness. Black, therefore, is beautiful, despite the fact that oppressors have made it ugly. Currently, there is still some debate about whether the terms 'black Christianity' or 'African American Christianity' should be used. However, architects of African American Christianity begin their reflections on African American Christianity from the context of a different kind of church, born in American slavery.

The genesis of African American Christianity challenges the nature of the church and salvation often assumed by white or European Christianity. In a sense, African American Christianity understands the church as fundamentally a prophetic voice to the world. Thus the church, like the prophets of the Hebrew Bible, stands and declares the judgement of God upon other kingdoms. According to such prophets, reflection about God is not only rational discourse about ultimate reality, but practical justice meted out by the oppressed. More specifically, in order to be a Christian one must abide by the tenet that God always sides with the poor and oppressed. In this search for Christianity, we encounter the essential problem of African American Christianity: should there be any racial distinction in Christianity?

Prophecy

For some, racial distinction is a virtue, but to others it is a sin. The architects of African American Christianity became masters at articulating the sinfulness of racial distinction when they warned against the temptation of the dominant racial group to control the understanding of the nature of Christianity. In the United States, it is argued that race is the most pertinent criterion by which to judge one's human worth. The fallacy of this assumption is that the descriptive determination of 'race' simultaneously carries with it a fixed classification, i.e., race is not just a matter of skin colour but becomes a person's political character. And the one who claims to determine a person's race becomes that person's oppressor. Most people around the world did not have the opportunity to name themselves; they had to accept the identities that Europeans gave them. Asians had to accept being Asians, Africans had to accept being Negroes, Africans, etc., Indians had to accept being Indians. White domination was built on the assumption that whites might say who they were, independently of the needs and reality of other groups. From an oppressed understanding of human identity a society becomes possessed by racism and can determine racial difference only as a threat or as an encumbering chain.

The very need of the oppressor to define human beings racially once presupposed a natural science that explained physiognomical differences. And for economic and ideological reasons this racial taxonomy provided a hierarchical account of how so-called superior, racial identities related to lesser ones. Many white people declared that because people of different 'races' are 'different', they should develop separately. African American Christianity disagreed by proving to African Americans, to the world and to white people that race need not be a chain on human identity, but rather a blessing. However, this blessing is often reinterpreted through subtle attempts to re-establish white power dynamics.

There is a subtle force to racism that holds persons just as firmly as overt chains. This subtle thread of racism lies in the apparently 'normal' ways in which human beings define each other. Unfortunately, there is a tendency among dominant racial groups to single out those who are somehow seen as inferior, so that the dominant group does not feel so insecure. For example, when, say, a person of Greek descent becomes an American, he or she learns the slow process of losing that particular ethnic identity in favour of a dominant identity of being white. In other words, such a person is able to learn not to be black for the sake of dominant social prestige and to avoid being classified in an inferior group. Those of black African descent do not have such options. Instead of celebrating the particularity of being Nigerian, Ghanaian, etc., African Americans were stripped of such particularities in slavery and became black, thereby creating another human norm called white – something which Italians, Irish, Greeks, British, etc. could learn to be.

Suffering lies at the heart of African American Christianity. Christian faith is determined by what one does with suffering, especially as Jesus turned suffering ultimately into the redemption of humanity's sin. Because of the atoning work of Christ, faith in the Christian God who entered into suffering takes all human life seriously. The African American Church practises this redemption of suffering through all the distinctive features of black church experience so that the material universe may not be recalcitrant and alien to the work of Christ, and all of earthly reality will be transfigured to share in the glory of God, in which all things will be made new, including racial relationships, chief among which are the relationships between black and white people. This God, revealed in Jesus, helps persons to determine their identity apart from being strangers and oppressors and to understand God's reality in their very encounter with one another.

That Jesus naturally identifies with the African American experience of suffering lies at the heart of black church experience. In such experience, however, we encounter the problem of African American Christianity. How does such a particular experience avoid the exclusion of others? One answer is that the major voices of African American Christianity have provided a framework in which all people are invited to interpret their own particularity for the glory of God. In place of racist accounts which make persons valuable in the sight of God on the basis of the dominant group's political and biological attributes, African American Christians have encouraged accounts which tell the truth about the human situation. A key insight here is that one cannot simply proclaim a quintessential Christianity without first confessing from what perspective Christianity is being interpreted. So the question whether African American Christianity falls into its own trap of racism is answered by its contribution to interpreting Christianity always from particular perspectives. Only by particular criteria can the church universal ultimately describe God's faithful remnant.

It is from this conviction that it was protecting particular perspectives that African American Christianity became the driving force behind the Civil Rights movement. Here Martin Luther King, Jr (1929–68) enters the picture. If a person's createdness depends only on something described as racial difference, not everyone can be created equally. For major African spiritual leaders such as King, that is contrary – totally contrary – to the scriptures, which say that human value is determined by being made in the image of God, rather than in the image of white people.

King rapidly rose to prominence because he could combine the insights of both the European-American and the African-American understandings of Christianity. Although the published descriptions of his 'pilgrimage to non-violence' generally emphasized the impact of academic training, in more personal statements he acknowledged his black Baptist roots. In 1965 King recognized in the quiet recesses of his heart that he was fundamentally a clergyman, a Baptist preacher. This knowledge came from being the son of a Baptist preacher, the grandson of a Baptist preacher, and the great-grandson of a Baptist preacher. King's genius was his ability to relate mutually exclusive cultural traditions through the convergence of theological scholarship and the practice of the social gospel. Drawing upon a variety of intellectual and religious traditions (including Gandhi and Hinduism), he was able profoundly to affect the Civil Rights movement both by his experiences as a preacher's son at Ebenezer Baptist Church in Atlanta and as a diligent student of European theology at Crozer Seminary and Boston University.

At Boston, King ironically learned to criticize theological liberalism by adopting many of the ideas of Reinhold Niebuhr. This was ironical in that many people who knew King, knew him for his liberal world-view. However, King applauded Niebuhr for his rigorous analysis of liberalism in the twentieth century. What was perhaps most enlightening for King was Niebuhr's economic and moral analysis of capitalism, seeing that modern industrial civilization was responsible for 'appalling injustices', particularly the concentration of power in the hands of a small wealthy class. Agreeing with Niebuhr's analysis, King grew to believe along with Niebuhr that love and justice may not be achievable in an immoral society but nevertheless remain a leaven in society, permeating the whole and giving texture and consistency to life. King was particularly receptive to Niebuhr's criticism of love and justice as conceived in both white liberal and European theology. In European theology, individual perfection is too often made an end in itself, whereas white liberalism vainly seeks to overcome justice through what is rational to Europeans. King learned to see that liberalism confuses the ideal itself with the realistic means that must be employed to coerce society into an approximation of that ideal. Where King disagreed with Niebuhr, however, was in the extent to which Niebuhr's Christian realism failed to allow God's love truly to reign.

From all these American influences King learned to use America's public discourse and norms to articulate the best possible goal for African Americans. He used the United States constitution to show that its ideals remained unfilled, and that until they were fulfilled the United States would always be on the verge of war and chaos.

Community

King's theological education distinguished him from all but a few African-American preachers and temporarily separated him from his childhood environment, but theological studies ultimately led him to a deeper appreciation of traditional African American conceptions of Christianity, especially in times of public crisis. In his career as America's Civil Rights leader, King often reflected that when he was tempted to give up, he would always gain strength and determination from the African American church. He skilfully incorporated into his sermons those aspects of his theological training that affirmed his ties to the faith of his African American parents and grandparents. His father later affirmed that his son's roots in the African American preaching tradition remained strong even after years of graduate study. King's ability to blend these elements can be seen from his earliest known recorded sermon, 'Rediscovering Lost Values', to his most famous 'I have a dream' speech. King became a major architect of African American Christianity because he understood that his mission was to build a world not just for African Americans, but for all of God's people. Despite the many technological advances and material comforts of American society, King argued, humanity had lost the spiritual compass provided by a deep and abiding faith in God. King was trying to save America's soul. He insisted that all reality hinges on moral foundations espoused by Jesus.

A more controversial architect of African American Christianity is James Cone (born 1938). He best articulates the question: how does personhood survive in a world in which African humanity is deemed an illegitimate form of human existence? For Cone, the function of African American Christianity must be consistent with the struggle for political, social and economic justice. The black church is about ultimate reality, and must represent the prophetic word about God's righteousness spoken with impenetrable control. More specifically, for Cone, Christian theology must abide by the tenets of black theology. Theology is black, and this provides the best working symbol of the dimensions of divine activity in America. Therefore, black theology must become contextual language because there is no uninterrupted fact. Thus, theology cannot be written out of nothing, and it cannot be written for all times, places and peoples. For black theology, the task of theology is to qualify any universal language about God, and anyone who does advocate such a universal theology creates a doctrine in which God speaks only for the dominant society.

Contextual theology

For Cone, the role of black theology is essentially to focus the self-determination of a community by preparing to do anything the community believes necessary for its existence. Cone states that whites fail to recognize the fact that all decisions of value are made in the context of participating in a community. It is in the particular community that values are chosen, because the community provides the structure in which being persons is realized. Therefore it is not possible to transcend the community; it frames our being because being is always being in relation to others. Ultimately, the strength of Christianity for African Americans comes from the understanding that Christ is black. The sacrifice of Jesus' life constantly qualifies the setting and surroundings in which he is encountered: he would not dance for the devil in order to save the world's soul, nor would he buy Judas Iscariot's zealous plan to tackle the empire with force.

The strength of Cone's work is his avowal that focusing on Jesus means that we are not free to make Jesus what we wish him to be at certain moments of existence. For Jesus to be black symbolizes oppression and liberation in any society. This definition of being black entails the fall of dominant standards of intelligence, beauty and worth, all of which would have to be obtained outside of black identity, while at the same time being white assumes the proper control and manifestation of these standards in a protected normality. Being black assumes the human predicament of having to accept an imposed identity in which one has narrow choices: one can either redefine the alienation of being black into heroic identity or one can surrender to the demonic forces in the world which will use God-created differences to confuse and enchain persons. Jesus' blackness further defines the blackness of all victims of oppression, who realize that the survival of their humanity is bound up with their liberation from whiteness. Blacks live in a society in which blackness means criminality, sub-humanity and anarchy, so blacks must define their own community of behaving in this world in order to achieve a proper place, no matter what the cost. All that matters is dignity and liberation. Cone thinks that this understanding of blackness provides the best working symbol of the dimensions of divine activity in America. Therefore, African American Christianity becomes legitimate in its particularity, admitting that Christianity may not be understood for all times, places and peoples; instead, it is understood in its particularity – in this case, in the African American context. The task of systematic, black theology is to qualify any universal language about God, and anyone who does advocate such a universal God creates a theology in which God is not for the black community.

What is obviously difficult about African American Christianity is the way in which it reworks the Christian world-view to make racism the cardinal sin by which to judge all other categories. If one admits that Christianity can be understood only in its particularity, it seems suspect for other Christian thinkers to construct a method of blackness in which to address 'all' the categories of traditional theology. Further still, the problem for current African American Christians comes through the profound insight of the American-Ghanaian W. E. B. DuBois, author of *The Souls of Black Folk*, in which he identifies what as yet many do not wish to articulate, namely, the universal problem of racial discrimination in which anywhere in the world, regardless of race and nationality, the darker the shade of one's complexion, the more likely one is to fall into the category of the oppressed. This is where Cone's theology matures, seeking an understanding of Christianity not just for African Americans but for all those dominated by hegemonic forces and identities. Cone no longer confines God to the deliverance of African American people; now African American Christianity should illuminate the multiple human conditions so that those who are oppressed can see that their liberation is the manifestation of God's activity throughout the world.

One could say that African American Christianity has evolved to encourage the possibility of repentance for all those who oppress human freedom. Through the traditions of Negro spirituals, spontaneous worship, dynamic preaching, political involvement of churches and deep movements of God's Spirit among humanity, African American Christianity ultimately seeks to participate with all victims of oppression in situations of crisis. Perhaps it is here that we find the heart of what African American Christianity has come to mean, namely the human possibility to change communities through the radical movement of what Christians call conversion. African American Christianity invites the difficult conversion process in which it will be necessary for those of white identity to destroy their whiteness by identifying with members of an oppressed community. Being human in a condition of social oppression involves affirming what the oppressor regards as degrading.

Of course, African American Christianity contains many more perspectives and architects than those mentioned here, but the perspectives of King and Cone show how African American Christianity has become such a vital ingredient in understanding Christianity generally. No longer can those who claim to be Christians simply participate in 'God talk' without applying such speech to how they live their lives on behalf of the poor and oppressed.

What is beautiful about the black Jesus is that even when black people face the dominant culture of white Americans, who seem to have no intention of sharing goods and services equally, there is no capitulation to the temptation to fill hearts and minds with hatred or imaginations with revenge. This only breeds violence, in which death quickly follows. Instead, Jesus showed a different means, namely, how to live in such a way that creates a future: living in a way of non-violence. As history is being written, there is no doubt that African American Christianity will point to the kind of lifestyle that creates a future.

MICHAEL BATTLE

Michael Battle, *Reconciliation: The Ubuntu Theology of Desmond Tutu*, Cleveland, OH: Pilgrim Press 1997; George F. Bragg, 'The Story of the First Blacks, the Pathfinder Absalom Jones 1746–1818' in Carson Clayborne, *African-American Christianity* ed Paul E. Johnson, Berkeley, CA: University of California Press 1994; James Cone, *A Black Theology of Liberation*, Maryknoll, NY: Orbis 1990; W. E. B. DuBois, *The Souls of Black Folk* (1903), Greenwich, CT: Fawcett 1968

America, Christianity in Latin

Christianity in Latin America is not one tradition, but many. They continue to be lively, and therefore constantly changing, expressions of faith in the context of a region that itself displays enormous diversity, not only of geography but also of language, race, nationality and culture.

Since Christianity came to the region more than five centuries ago, it has not ceased to develop. The 'slices of life' described here by no means exhaust the panorama that is Latin American Christianity, but rather give a glimpse of some of the significant elements of that mosaic as they shape the lives of Christians at home in Latin America.

Folk Catholicism

It is 12 December in a hilly suburb of Mexico City. At the top of the hill, known both by its Spanish name, Guadalupe, and as Tepeyac, the name given it by Mexico's Aztec people, looms an enormous concrete building, the Basilica of Our Lady of Guadalupe. It can easily hold 10,000 worshippers, but on this day, the Lady's feast day, it is engulfed by more than 100,000 pilgrims.

The object of their devotion is a 500-year-old *serape* or shawl, hung behind bullet-proof glass high above the church's high altar. On the *serape* is an image identified as the Virgin Mary, but not as she appears in European art. She is brown-skinned and her features are more Aztec than Spanish; she is standing on the moon and is adorned with other symbols previously associated with Tonantzin, the Aztec mother of the gods, who had previously been worshipped at Tepeyac.

Mary

p. 733

According to legend, the image appeared miraculously on the *serape* of a young Aztec convert named Juan Diego,

11
9
8
10
12
6
13
17
5
7
15
3
2
14
4
1
16

CHRISTIANS IN LATIN AMERICA AT THE MILLENNIUM

Country	Population	Roman Catholic	%	Independent	%	Protestant	%	Anglican	%	Orthodox	%
① Argentina	**37,027,000**	33,750,000	91.1	2,050,000	5.5	2,295,000	6.2	19,000	0.1	158,000	0.4
② Bolivia	**8,329,000**	7,350,000	88.2	145,000	1.7	530,000	6.4	1,100	0.0	3,100	0.0
③ Brazil	**170,115,000**	153,300,000	90.2	25,500,000	15.0	30,200,000	17.8	125,000	0.1	170,000	0.1
④ Chile	**15,211,000**	11,800,000	77.6	3,820,000	25.1	382,000	2.5	12,000	0.1	23,750	0.2
⑤ Colombia	**42,321,000**	40,670,000	96.1	553,000	1.3	1,100,000	2.6	3,600	0.0	7,200	0.0
⑥ Costa Rica	**4,023,000**	3,660,000	91.0	108,000	2.7	330,000	8.2	1,600	0.0	0	0.0
⑦ Ecuador	**12,646,000**	11,900,000	94.1	225,000	1.8	240,000	1.0	1,600	0.0	1,800	0.0
⑧ El Salvador	**6,276,000**	5,723,000	91.2	710,000	11.3	530,000	8.4	400	0.0	0	0.0
⑨ Guatemala	**11,365,000**	9,600,000	84.5	1,030,000	9.1	1,450,000	12.8	1,800	0.0	0	0.0
⑩ Honduras	**6,485,000**	5,590,000	86.2	180,000	2.8	425,000	6.6	6,000	0.1	7,200	0.1
⑪ Mexico	**98,881,000**	92,770,000	93.8	2.900,000	2.9	3,800,000	3.8	187,800	0.2	100,000	0.1
⑫ Nicaragua	**5,074,000**	4,320,000	85.1	155,000	3.1	590,000	11.6	8,300	0.2	0	0.0
⑬ Panama	**2,856,000**	2,210,000	77.4	73,000	2.6	340,000	11.9	23,500	0.8	1,400	0.1
⑭ Paraguay	**5,496,000**	4,950,000	90.1	70,800	1.3	200,000	3.6	17,600	0.3	2,000	0.0
⑮ Peru	**25,662,000**	24,550,000	95.7	456,000	3.8	1,480,000	5.8	2,000	0.0	5,500	0.0
⑯ Uruguay	**3,337,000**	2,608,000	78.2	52,500	1.6	95,000	2.8	1,200	0.0	26,500	0.8
⑰ Venezuela	**24,170,000**	22,816,000	94.4	350,000	1.4	500,000	2.1	600	0.0	27,000	0.1

Independent is used here for Christians independent of historic, organized, institutional, denominational Christianity.
In some countries, Christians are affiliated to more than one church. In Latin America this dual affiliation is so high that it is impossible to calculate the number of non-Christians from the statistics.

Source: David B. Barrett, George T. Kurian and Todd M. Johnson (eds), *World Christian Encyclopedia*, New York: OUP [2]2002

who saw several apparitions of the Virgin Mary. She spoke to him in his own Nahuatl language, ordered him to have a shrine built for her on the hillside, and gave him the miraculous image as a sign to convince the sceptical church authorities.

The miracle of Guadalupe is reported to have happened on 12 December 1531, not quite 40 years after Christopher Columbus and his companions became the first Christians to set foot in what is now Latin America, and less than fifteen years after the Spanish conqueror Hernán Cortés overcame the mighty Aztec empire with its capital at what is now Mexico City.

The conquest of Latin America by Spain and Portugal resulted in the devastation of its native peoples, their culture and their religion. A shrine to Tonantzin once crowned the hill where the church of Guadalupe now stands, but like all the other holy places of the Aztec empire, it was ordered by Cortés to be destroyed in the bloody aftermath of invasion.

The conquest unleashed by the expeditions of Columbus was motivated in part by religion, but other more sinister purposes were also involved, purposes which ultimately influenced the nature of Latin American Christianity.

Throughout the sixteenth century, the kings of both Spain and Portugal enjoyed a special and highly favourable relationship with the Pope. Centuries of battle with the Muslim Moors, who held large parts of Spain prior to their defeat in 1492, had forged a Spanish culture closely identified with an aggressive Roman Catholicism; indeed, its monarchs were known as the 'Catholic kings'. The religious interests of the church were assumed to be identical with the economic, military and political interests of Spain (and Portugal as well). The kings of both countries enjoyed the benefits of an arrangement known as the *patronato*, which allowed them to nominate bishops, to oversee the internal working of the church in their territories, and to collect the tithes and offerings mandated by the church in return for providing for the clergy and religious institutions. The effect of this arrangement was to give the kings of Spain and Portugal nearly absolute control over the church within their territories.

Furthermore, the Pope awarded a number of recently discovered territories to the two countries. Portugal was given a sizeable portion of the eastern part of South America, which eventually became Brazil. With the exception of a few contested territories in and around the

Caribbean Sea, Spain exercised absolute authority over the rest of Latin America, from Mexico to the southern tip of South America.

The project of establishing firm control over the native peoples of Latin America and of overseeing the plunder of the natural resources of the region fell to the conquerors, their associates and successors. Franciscan, Dominican and Jesuit missionaries accompanied most of the expeditions by which control was established, and the official policy of both Spain and Portugal was to conquer and evangelize – that is, to impose military control but also to convert the native peoples to Christianity. In some parts of Latin America, the primary strategy was to resettle the native people in large plantations, called *reducciones*, where life was regimented by the conquering authorities and able-bodied workers were required to work under their command. In areas where large deposits of natural resources were found, the natives were forced to work in the mines. Working conditions, diseases imported to the Americas by the European conquerors and the stress of losing a treasured way of life took a terrible toll on the population; it is estimated that the native population, which stood at some 70 million when the Europeans arrived, had been reduced to 3.5 million within a century and a half.

Missionaries

The Inca people of Peru and Colombia and the Aztecs and Maya of Mexico had highly developed civilizations, with great cities, complex societies, sophisticated administrative and military skills, vibrant art, excellent systems of communication and rich literary traditions. Their cultures were, of course, different from anything previously known to the Europeans. Most of the other native peoples of Latin America were organized in tribes and were sustained by hunting, gathering, farming and trading.

The discovery of human sacrifice as an important element of the native religious life led the Europeans to determine that the cultures of the Americas were 'fatally flawed', and that the ultimate salvation of American souls required not only their conversion to Christianity but the elimination of native cultures. Indeed, early in the process of conquest and colonization Spanish Catholics debated whether conversion should be an integral part of their domination or whether, in fact, Americans belonged to a different species and therefore could be enslaved at will without regard to their spiritual well-being.

Some of the missionaries who had immediate contact with the native people in the course of their conquest saw no possibility of their redemption, and acquiesced in what soon became a brutal campaign of control and exploitation. Most, however, were appalled by the cruelty of the European occupation, and argued forcefully against the mistreatment of the American population.

Two of the missionaries who struggled valiantly on behalf of the American natives – and suffered persecution for their efforts – were Bartolomé de Las Casas and Antonio de Valdivieso, both now revered heroes of Latin American Christianity.

Las Casas was an early witness to the terrible abuse of the native peoples and preached forcefully against those responsible for the suffering, even accusing them of 'mortal sin'. He later became one of the first of many missionaries to argue the case for the native Americans before the Spanish court. Las Casas dreamed of a peaceful evangelization by example and teaching which would persuade the peoples of the Americas to embrace Christianity. But legal decrees establishing the rule of law and justice for the native people were ignored in the face of the obvious economic benefits from continued slavery, and Las Casas' efforts bore little fruit; he was driven from his duties as Bishop of Chiapas, Mexico, by the Spanish members of his own flock.

Antonio de Valdivieso was Bishop of Nicaragua in the mid-sixteenth century. Like Las Casas, he spoke in favour of the rights of the native people, preached forcefully against the cruelty of their masters, and requested intervention by the king of Spain. In 1550, he was assassinated by a small group of conquerors.

In spite of the efforts of such advocates, the native peoples of the Americas were conquered and converted as part of a single process. The Christian faith presented to them had the distinct flavour of Iberian Catholicism: passionate devotion, militant fervour and a dark sense of destiny. The American converts were taught that their domination was God's will, part of the plan by which their immortal souls would be saved from certain perdition.

In the colonies gradually established throughout the Americas, power remained in the hands of European military and government officials. The American-born descendants of the first settlers, known as *criollos*, enjoyed access to the wealth flowing into the colonial coffers but were denied a share in political power. In most areas of Latin America, the vast majority of the population were either native people or *mestizos*, of mixed ancestry, descendants of the offspring of the conquerors and native women. As the population of Latin America succumbed to the effects of conquest, large numbers of slaves from Africa were imported to take their place in the fields and mines of the conquerors. It was not until the nineteenth century that the *criollo* population, sometimes supported by other elements of society, succeeded in mounting successful revolutions against Spanish and Portuguese rule and achieving the political independence of the nations that today comprise Latin America.

The Christianity that evolved in this crucible demonstrated considerable diversity. In the urban centres there were wealthy monasteries, seminaries and cathedrals. The gold and silver pouring in from the mines was used for the lavish decoration of churches, and a European visitor would find the worship and devotional practices quite familiar. Latin American scholars, poets and musicians, many of them priests and nuns, produced a rich heritage of religious art that combined European and local elements.

Among the *mestizo* (mixed-race) and native populations, however, a very different form of Catholicism prevailed. There was little opportunity for serious teaching of Christian faith; conversions were often only nominal, and in many cases Christian terms and symbols were imposed on traditional deities and practices. The legend of Juan Diego and the Virgin of Guadalupe demonstrates how easily elements of Catholicism could be translated into native religious imagery. It is estimated that in the years immediately following, as many as 8 million Mexicans were converted to Christianity.

Because most of the rural and poor population had little regular access to the church's sacraments, the practices that evolved were sometimes quite different from official Roman Catholic teaching. The strict hierarchy and sense of dependence that were imposed by the colonial powers were reflected in a faith in which God, like the king of Spain, was almost impossibly distant and inaccessible. Day-to-day power was exercised by far lesser figures, whose rank in the hierarchy gave them influence in the heavenly court and who could be approached for favours in return for gifts, offerings or vows. There were saints who could be approached for almost any favour, in almost any crisis. In many cases, the veneration related to them was drawn not from Christian practice but from native traditions, and indeed, the saints are sometimes identified in the popular consciousness with traditional deities. Like devotion to Our Lady of Guadalupe, Latin American cults of the Virgin Mary often reflect the symbolism of the native peoples' Mother Goddess, while rituals attached to the image of the Crucified Christ are sometimes related to traditional gods of death. Given the experience of defeat and helplessness before the conquerors, it is not surprising that much of popular religion is devoted to rituals of survival under a system of patronage.

The traditional cycle of death and rebirth that marked the rhythm of much native religion, and the fatalism nourished by the experience of defeat, were used to reinterpret the story of the crucifixion and resurrection of Christ. The native peoples of the Americas found in the suffering and dying Christ a powerful symbol of their own ongoing crucifixion as a people; it is not surprising that Good Friday, the anniversary of Christ's death, came to be more widely observed than the Easter celebration of his resurrection. Easter itself is frequently related to the annual rebirth in spring; it is not uncommon to find a plate of sprouting grain placed on the altar of a rural Mexican church during the Lenten season which precedes Easter.

In this form of 'people's Catholicism', known as *piedad popular* or 'popular piety', the role of the clergy is often somewhat peripheral to the everyday practice of Christianity. There has always been a shortage of priests in relation to the many millions of Latin Americans who identify with the Roman Catholic faith; outside the cities, priests are often responsible for the oversight of enormous territories, where travel and communication are difficult even today. For many people in outlying areas, baptism might be the only moment in life when they actually have contact with a priest. Day-to-day rituals connected with marriage, coming of age, childbirth, illness and death are passed down from parents to children, often undergoing radical changes over time. The ideal of weekly attendance at mass is impossible to fulfil outside the cities, and has been replaced in popular piety by occasional festivals and commemorations throughout the year, often focused on the various saints who occupy a special place in people's devotion. Today, for millions of Latin American Christians who identify themselves as Catholics, the practice of their faith is determined not by the traditional disciplines of the church but by the customs of *piedad popular*.

Sacraments

In spite of the variations of faith and custom that have always marked Latin American Catholicism, the Roman Catholic Church continues to enjoy a unique place in the cultures of the region, the loyalty of millions of adherents, and a privileged position within its societies. In many countries, it remains the official religion of the state and vigorously defends the special rights that accompany its status. Nevertheless, in the modern era Latin American Christianity has developed in a number of ways that broaden its expressions and challenge the Catholic Church's traditional role.

Roman Catholic Church

Saints

Grassroots Catholicism

It is evening in a shantytown high above Caracas, Venezuela. As dusk falls, countless candles and lanterns twinkle across the hills. Though the skyscrapers of the city clearly visible in the valley are reminders that somewhere there is affluence and luxury, in this crowded community there is neither electricity nor running water. The houses are constructed of whatever materials are at hand: cast-off blocks and tin, odd scraps of wood, even cardboard. As night falls, a dozen people are making their way to one of the houses. Most are women, some clutching a small child by the hand; many are carrying Bibles like treasured possessions.

Calendar

Festivals and fasts

As they gather, they begin to sing. The words and images of their songs are drawn from the Bible. They tell the story of Moses, who led the people of Israel from slavery; of Joshua, who shepherded the people into the

Holy Week procession in Antigua, Guatemala

promised land; of Mary, who accepted the calling to give birth to Jesus in circumstances of poverty remarkably similar to their own. This gathering is a *comunidad de base*, a 'base community', its members drawn from the lowest rungs of the social ladder. Once people like these would have had almost no contact with organized Christianity; but in the 'base community' they sing, pray, and above all study the Bible. Those who cannot read rely on those who can; the conversation involves everyone. No one's opinion is ignored or overlooked.

Community

Base communities are associated with a particular style of Christianity known as liberation theology which emerged in Latin America during the 1970s, though its roots go back earlier. The Second Vatican Council, which was called by Pope John XXIII in 1962 to help the Roman Catholic Church to update itself in order to respond more adequately to the modern world, urged Catholics to rethink how their faith could have an impact on the world around them. When Latin American Christians began to consider their faith in the context of their own continent, they became aware that the situation of the poor majority was similar to that of the people of Israel described in the Hebrew scriptures and that of the Jewish nation during Jesus' lifetime. They began to analyse how the promise of liberation they found in the Bible could give hope to people whose lives seemed hopeless, and could inspire them to struggle to improve their situation.

Liberation theology

Council

Many priests and nuns were inspired by liberation theology to redirect their ministry, abandoning comfortable middle-class churches and the church's traditional alliance with those in power in favour of direct involvement with, and service to, the urban and rural poor. Their experience of the misery of the countryside and the shanty towns led many to seek for understanding of economic conditions through Marxist analysis. Eager for action that could improve the conditions of those they served, some supported the radical political and military movements that were emerging throughout Latin America. Not surprisingly, the armed forces turned on them and came to see radical Christians as the enemies of peace and stability. Many of the clergy and religious who worked with base communities, as well as the poor who made up their membership, were persecuted, suffering imprisonment, torture and death.

Persecution

At the heart of the movement were the base communities that sprang up in their thousands all over Latin America. People who had always been taught to accept their difficult fate as God's will responded in great numbers to the affirmation that God willed their well-being. They found hope in claiming the power to pray to God in their own name and participating in worship and reflection as equals before God. The stories of liberation found throughout the scriptures became the mainstay of their piety, and they became convinced that they could actually change their world. Jesus, who had always seemed a kindly but distant Lord best approached through his Mother, was now perceived as a militant and profoundly human advocate of the poor and dispossessed, a close companion who could inspire contemporary Christians to struggle against oppression. Demonstrations by large groups of newly-energized poor Christians became a common occurrence in many countries. In one country – Nicaragua – a revolution backed by many radical Christians actually succeeded in overthrowing a particularly brutal dictatorship and installing a socialist government in which three Roman Catholic priests served as cabinet ministers.

The social and political agenda of liberation theology foundered on the realities of globalization and the gradual realization that traditional approaches to social change had little power to resist the forces of world economy. A widespread revulsion against both the violence of radical guerrilla movements and the bloody military efforts to destroy them led to political compromises and the return to democratic governments in many places where military

Globalization

dictatorships had prevailed. But the experience of the base communities changed Latin American Christianity. It affirmed that ordinary people, including the poor, were an integral and valued part of the church, and brought their religious experience from the periphery to the centre of the church's life. It moved the institutional church to new efforts of education, and to reclaim its role as the advocate of those who suffer from the enormous inequalities of wealth that continue to plague the Americas. Most of all, it gave to people marginalized and ignored by society – the poor, women, children, members of racial and ethnic minorities – a sense of their own worth before God. It made the Bible and the deepest practice of Christian faith accessible to them. By taking their lives and perspectives seriously, it taught them to be actors in the human drama rather than spectators or passive victims. By valuing their experience and their opinions, it gave them a voice.

Macumba, Umbanda, Candomblé: Afro-Brazilian syncretism

It is Saturday night in a poor suburb of Rio de Janeiro, Brazil. In a plain concrete-block meeting hall divided at the centre by a low barrier, nearly a hundred people have gathered. One side of the hall is dominated by an altar; it is covered with plastic flowers, a crucifix, statues of the Virgin Mary and a number of saints, a rosary and other articles of devotion. The floor is covered with freshly-gathered leaves. The centre of attention is an elderly black woman dressed in white, who sits near the altar. This is the *chefe* (chief) or *mãe de santo* (mother of the saint), and this is her *terreiro*, or gathering place. Around the altar stand a number of figures, the women dressed in elaborate ceremonial skirts and blouses and white headscarves. These are the mediums, the initiates of the community. Nearby are several drummers.

On the other side of the barrier, several dozen suppli-cants are seated on makeshift benches. Many are of African descent, but others have distinctly European features. Most seem to be at home amid the poverty of the surroundings, but a few are obviously well dressed, and several expensive cars are parked nearby.

The drums begin the ceremony, and continue to mark the rhythm of the increasingly ecstatic proceedings. As the assistant of the *chefe* invokes the names of the spirits to be summoned, the mediums begin to dance. As their speed increases, they fall into a trance, exhibit marked changes of behaviour, and exchange their own clothing for elaborate costumes. Their speech, movements and even facial expressions seem to bear no relationship to their own personalities; it is as if they had become different people.

As the drumming and dancing subside and the mediums are calmed, one by one the spectators are led to meet with one of them. They exchange conversation, the medium offers advice and perhaps a ritual to be performed, and the spectators leave.

Macumba is the term used to describe a particular style of religion with African roots as it is practised in the city of Rio de Janeiro. As an organized phenomenon, it seems to date from the early twentieth century, but draws on rituals and beliefs brought from West Africa by the three to five million slaves who came to Brazil before the slave trade was abolished in 1851. A number of Christian saints are revered in Macumba, but in fact the figures are identified with Yoruba deities and spirits, and in Macumba the African identity of those invoked is an important part of its tradition.

Macumba preserves a complex pantheon of deities, including a distant (and largely irrelevant) creator god, as well as a number of other *orixás*, or gods, each with specific characteristics and identified with a Roman Catholic saint. Macumba also invokes a number of spirits of *pretos velhos*, or old black slaves, and *caboclos*, spirits of the dead of the Brazilian native peoples, both of whom are honoured for their wisdom. It is these deities and spirits who are believed to possess the mediums in Macumba ceremonies, and who are sought as the source of the advice given in the consultations that take place during the rites.

p. 342

The term Macumba is used for Afro-Brazilian religion in Rio which maintains strong ties to its African roots, including the use of drums as a vehicle for summoning the gods and spirits. Candomblé refers to a similar African-based faith in the north-eastern city of Bahia. Umbanda is the term used for all such Brazilian cults, but especially those that have evolved a more overtly Brazilian form of piety. Umbanda continues the worship of the African deities, but has reduced or even eliminated specific references to Africa and the use of drumming and animal sacrifice (considered indispensable in traditional Macumba). Umbanda is now an officially recognized religion, with many variants that include not only African elements but also components from nineteenth-century French spiritism and native Brazilian practices. It has been institutionalized in a variety of forms, some of which exercise considerable political power. (There is also another Afro-Brazilian cult, known as Quimbanda, which reveres the deity Exú, identified with the devil. Quimbanda also relies on traditional African religious practice but differs from the various forms of Umbanda in that it is undertaken primarily in order to do harm to others.)

All forms of Umbanda have a distinctly practical bent; the large number of deities and spirits available for consul-tation provide for a sense of immediate access to divine help in dealing with the human condition, whether diffi-culties with relationships, ill health or financial problems.

CHRISTIANS IN THE CARIBBEAN AT THE MILLENNIUM

The islands of the Caribbean were colonized from a remarkable mixture of countries: Britain, France, the Netherlands and Spain, and consequently the Christianity on them shows a particularly rich variety. Here are some details about the islands with the largest populations.

Country	Population	Roman Catholic	%	Independent	%	Protestant	%	Anglican	%	Orthodox	%	Non-Christians	%
(1) Barbados	270,000	11,000	**4.1**	17,500	**6.5**	85,158	**31.5**	77,300	**28.6**	300	0.1	78,742	**29.2**
(2) Cuba	11,201,000	4,367,909	**39.0**	135,000	**1.2**	190,000	**1.7**	3,600	**0.0**	1,400	**0.0**	6,503,091	**58.0**
(3) Dominican Republic	8,495,000	7,522,305	**88.6**	130,000	**1.5**	360,000	**4.2**	4,400	**0.1**	0	**0.0**	529,295	**6.2**
(4) Guadeloupe	456,000	433,000	**95.1**	1,120	**0.0**	22,500	**4.9**	0	**0.0**	0	**0.0**	42,752	**9.4**
(5) Haiti	8,222,000	6,520,000	**79.3**	430,000	**5.2**	1,440,000	**17.5**	105,000	**1.3**	0	**0.0**	632,576	**7.7**
(6) Jamaica	2,583,000	110,000	**4.3**	232,000	**9.0**	643,413	**24.9**	103,000	**4.0**	3,300	**0.1**	1,491,287	**56.7**
(7) Martinique	395,000	366,000	**92.7**	4,349	**1.1**	23,700	**6.0**	0	**0.0**	0	**0.0**	365,372	**6.6**
(8) Netherlands Antilles	217,000	150,862	**60.5**	2,100	**1.0**	23,000	**10.6**	2,550	**1.2**	0	**0.0**	178,512	**17.8**
(9) Puerto Rico	3,869,000	2,900,000	**75.0**	249,000	**6.4**	505,000	**13.1**	12,400	**0.3**	1,300	**0.0**	241,709	**6.3**
(10) Trinidad and Tobago	1,295,000	397,865	**30.7**	42,000	**3.2**	179,000	**13.8**	154,000	**11.9**	8,500	**0.7**	512,635	**39.6**

Independent is used here for Christians independent of historic, organized, institutional, denominational Christianity.
In some countries, Christians are affiliated to more than one church.

Source: David B. Barrett, George T. Kurian and Todd M. Johnson (eds), *World Christian Encyclopedia*, New York: OUP [2]2002

→

Barbados: The population is 80% black, and there are five indigenous black churches on the island, one Baptist, one Methodist, one Orthodox and two Pentecostal. Anglican clergy were among the first British settlers in 1626; the Protestant churches are a mixture of long-established bodies (Methodists and Moravians) and churches arising out of North American missions in the twentieth century. The largest church is Pentecostal, the New Testament Church of God. Catholicism is less influential than on other islands.

Cuba: Christianity came to Cuba through Spanish Dominican missionaries in 1512, soon after the arrival of Christopher Columbus. Christianity has not flourished under the Marxist regime of Fidel Castro established in 1959. The mass exodus in the early years after the revolution led to a catastrophic decline in the number of Roman Catholic priests and religious and of Anglicans generally. Statistics are not easy to obtain, but surveys indicate that only a tiny proportion of the Catholic population attend church regularly. The indigenous Iglesia Evangélica Pentecostal is the largest denomination in Cuba. The Anglican Church, which goes back to 1741, flourishes mostly in the towns and cities; all its priests are indigenous. The Methodists and Baptists also have significant presences.

Dominican Republic: Occupying two-thirds of the island of Hispaniola, discovered by Columbus in 1492, the Spanish-speaking Dominican Republic has been strongly influenced by Catholicism from its beginnings, but church attendance has steadily dropped over the last 50 years. Voodoo, which combines Catholic practices with traditional African rites, is also a major influence, as on Haiti. Protestantism entered the Republic relatively late, at the beginning of the twentieth century. There is an autonomous indigenous church, the Iglesia Evangélica Dominicana.

Guadeloupe: Guadeloupe is an overseas department of France and in the Roman Catholic Church the island is a diocese subordinate to Bordeaux. Magic and superstition flourish alongside Christianity. Seventh-day Adventists and Jehovah's Witnesses have the strongest presence after Roman Catholics.

Haiti: Haiti occupies a third of the Island of Hispaniola, but unlike the neighbouring Dominican Republic the language is French; it is the poorest country in the Western hemisphere. Voodoo is practised by a majority of Catholics. Protestant denominations are experiencing rapid growth, with many conversions of whole families from Voodoo. The Anglican church is largely made up of the élite, and has declined in numbers because of emigration.

Jamaica: Afro-Caribbean religions which combine Christianity with traditional African rites and spiritism flourish in Jamaica, arising not least from the effects of the Great Awakening in the mid-nineteenth century. One of the largest of these religions is Rastafarianism. The most prominent Protestant tradition is Pentecostalism; the Methodists and Moravians, who also have substantial communities, date from the eighteenth century, as does the Anglican Church. Roman Catholics are found largely among the poorer classes.

Martinique: Malevidan Spiritism has left its mark on the island, a mixture of Hinduism and Catholicism. The main deity is Maldevidan, who is depicted as riding a horse and is identified with Jesus Christ, and after him Mari-eman, a female divinity corresponding to the Virgin Mary. There are many temples on the island. The great majority of inhabitants are Roman Catholic; Protestantism arrived relatively recently and is still weak.

Netherlands Antilles: These two groups of islands are a self-governing part of the Netherlands. The main Protestant denomination is the United Protestant Church of Curaçao, which is a union of Lutheran and Reformed in origin and goes back to 1650.

Puerto Rico: Puerto Rico is a predominantly Roman Catholic country, but is also the scene of a clash between two traditions of Catholic culture, Hispanic and North American. In the Hispanic tradition the church is a supreme authority in matters spiritual and temporal; in the North American tradition the Catholic Church is experienced as a foreign element in a predominantly Protestant culture. Not least as a result of this, the church has remained conservative. Protestantism dates from the beginning of the twentieth century, Methodists and Adventists being strongly represented. The Pentecostal Church of God is the largest denomination after Roman Catholicism. Various forms of spiritism still exist.

Trinidad and Tobago: The islands have an unusual racial mix in population, with around 40% black and 35% East Indian. 22% of the population are Hindus. Roman Catholicism is strongest in urban areas and among blacks, whites and those of mixed race; the two most important Protestant denominations are the Presbyterian Church, with a membership of 95% East Indians, and the Pentecostal Assemblies of the West Indies. There is an unusually strong Orthodox presence, of the Greek and Ethiopian Orthodox churches.

The ritual acts imposed by the mediums may be a form of prayer, a gift of a favourite food or drink to be offered to the god, an act of charity or perhaps the sacrifice of a chicken. All are seen as gestures to gain the attention and favour of the god invoked. If the favour requested is not forthcoming, it is always possible to consult another deity or spirit.

While Umbanda maintains many of its ties to the religion of African slaves, it is now practised by Brazilians of all races and economic strata. Indeed, it is estimated that at least 10 per cent of the population of Brazil regularly practises some form of Umbanda, and that many others occasionally resort to it in times of personal crisis or conflict.

The Roman Catholic Church, with which more than 90 per cent of the population of Brazil is nominally identified, has officially opposed all forms of Umbanda as inconsistent with Christian faith. Nevertheless, many of those who practise it do so while continuing to identify themselves as Catholics participating fully in church rituals. The adoption of Christian names and titles for deities whose character is essentially African represents a form of syncretism in which two different perspectives and practices are combined to produce a new form with characteristics of both.

Hymns ➤
Great Awakening ➤
Evangelicals ➤

Syncretism is a common element in much of Latin American Christianity. Cults that preserve elements of African religion similar to Macumba or Umbanda can be found in a number of countries besides Brazil. They play a significant role in the religious life of Haiti, the Dominican Republic and Cuba. They can also be found in other places where African slaves were concentrated, such as Panama, Puerto Rico and Peru.

The religious beliefs of native peoples found in Latin American Catholicism demonstrate an element of syncretism in the *piedad popular* of the region. Like Umbanda, it has produced significantly new forms of religious faith and practice. But in *piedad popular* Catholic symbolism tends to incorporate and dominate the native traditions, while in Umbanda, the traditional African deities dominate the Christian imagery through which they are expressed. For that reason, the institutional church has been much more willing to incorporate the practices of *piedad popular* into its rites and permit its practices, while it has continued to be hostile to the growth of Umbanda and other cults of African origin.

Latin American Protestantism

It is Sunday morning in Colón, the principal city on Panama's Caribbean coast. In the large market in the centre of the city, business is being carried on as usual. Fish fresh from the early-morning catch are resting on ice, melting rapidly in the steamy heat; heaps of pineapples, guavas, mangos and bananas piled high in the scant shade provided by the vendors' stalls add bright colour and a sweet aroma to the scene. Most of the people moving slowly in the early morning heat are of Afro-Caribbean descent. The cries of the vendors and the conversations of the shoppers are a unique mixture of Spanish and English, often changing language in mid-sentence.

Meanwhile, services at Christ Church by-the-Sea, the oldest Episcopal church in Panama, are about to begin. The large window facing the altar depicts the figure of Christ with African features. The congregation that has gathered is entirely of Afro-Caribbean background. The elderly members of the congregation, who make up many of those present, have made no concessions to the oppressive heat: the women wear hats, while the men are dressed in coats and neckties. The bell rings to announce the beginning of the service; the organist plays the opening hymn, and the congregation joins in singing 'Blessed Assurance, Jesus Is Mine'. The words and melody were written in the United States by a prolific hymn writer associated with the evangelical revival moment in the nineteenth century, which was taken by Protestant missionaries to the islands of the West Indies and then accompanied Caribbean immigrants in their thousands when they came to Central America in search of work. The service continues according to the Episcopal Church's English-language Book of Common Prayer. The ritual reflects the training of the Anglican missionaries from England and the United States who oversaw the congregation for many years, and the memories of people whose families had been members of the Church of England on the islands of Jamaica or Trinidad for generations. At the same time, distinctively West Indian rhythms syncopate the music, and the cadence of the sermon is clearly related to the preaching style of black preachers in both the United States and the Caribbean.

Because West Indians spoke English, they were favoured as workers by the Americans who built the Panama Railroad in the mid-nineteenth century and the Panama Canal at the beginning of the twentieth. They were also brought to most of the Central American republics to work in the banana plantations that stretched along the entire Caribbean coast.

The conditions under which Afro-Caribbean West Indians lived and worked in Central America were rigorous and often dangerous. The companies that built the railroads and established the plantations were also given responsibility for housing, education and medical care. Because they considered that religion could be a useful tool for maintaining discipline and morale among their workers, companies often supported churches as well; indeed, the red sandstone from which Christ Church is built arrived in Panama from the United States as ballast in a ship, and the salary of the first Anglican priest was paid by the Panama Railroad Company.

Black immigrants from the Caribbean were subjected to discrimination throughout Central America. Under the duress of racial oppression, extreme poverty, and both formal and informal attempts by local governments to force them to adapt to the dominant Latin American cultures, most West Indians held tenaciously to their own identity, which they continued to define by their place of origin, their use of English, and their loyalty to the churches of the Caribbean islands.

While most Latin Americans of Caribbean descent today speak Spanish and have overcome most of the most blatant discrimination they faced throughout much of the twentieth century, many continue to affirm their distinctive identity by using English at home and in their worship. Elements of Latin American Christianity, especially its music, have now been incorporated into Afro-Caribbean Protestantism; mainstream churches that came to Central America with the West Indian immigrants have now been joined by other, locally-founded congregations that still preserve aspects of traditional Caribbean culture.

It is Thursday evening in a middle-class neighbourhood of Buenos Aires, Argentina. Large blocks of flats reminiscent of central Europe rise on both sides of the tree-lined street. As night falls, people begin to gather, singly and in couples, in the living room of one of the apartments. The name on the door reads 'Schroeder'.

Inside, as an animated discussion gets under way, conversation slips easily between Spanish and German. The governing board of the neighbourhood's Lutheran church is meeting to decide whether to incorporate more Spanish into the Sunday services. The older members of the group, most of whom immigrated from Europe as teenagers after the Second World War, argue the importance of maintaining the German language as a way of assuring fidelity to their Lutheran heritage. Younger members, born in Argentina, worry that by continuing to hold on to their ancestral language they are seriously limiting the appeal of their congregation and risk losing their own children, whose grasp of German is weakening.

The debate shaking the congregation is repeated all over Latin America, wherever European Protestant immigrants have settled. Like English-speaking West Indians, they rely on the churches that accompanied them to maintain treasured elements of their traditional culture, and struggle to maintain ties with the churches of their motherlands. With time, however, those bonds are weakened, and the Latin American members of mainline European Protestant traditions – German Lutherans, Dutch and Swiss Reformed, members of the Church of England – are faced with a difficult decision. Should they continue to hold on to their European customs, and thereby eliminate the possibility of broader involvement in the life of their community, or should they adopt the language and customs of the new country, risking the erosion and even disappearance of much that was distinctive about their religion? In most countries their number is very small, and as their congregations age and the younger generations are more thoroughly assimilated into the culture around them, issues of survival and adaptation become ever more pressing.

Church of England

It is Sunday morning in a suburb of Guatemala City, capital of the Central American republic of Guatemala. Rows of small, one-storey stucco houses stretch as far as the eye can see. Though many sprout television antennae, there are few cars in front of the houses. Most of the people in this neighbourhood work hard to feed and clothe their families and to scrape together the fees needed to keep their children in school.

Nearby, the bell of the local Roman Catholic church is ringing, warning people that mass is about to begin. But many of the residents do not hear it; long before, they have set out on foot or by bus to an open-sided shed located at the end of its street, where the pot-holed concrete gives way to mud. A hand-painted sign in front of the shed reads *Iglesia del Cordero de Dios* – Church of the Lamb of God.

Inside the church, with its rows of metal folding chairs, the congregation has gathered; most carry Bibles, all are dressed in the best clothes they own. Some are elderly; many arrive in large groups that include numbers of children. As the service begins, the sounds of tambourines and drums are heard over the enthusiastic singing of the worshippers. As the music dies away, a middle-aged man, dressed in black suit, white shirt and necktie, stands at the podium and greets the congregation. After a brief prayer, he invites the congregation to follow in their Bibles as he begins to read a passage from the prophet Jeremiah.

Lutheranism

Once the scripture reading has been completed, the figure on the stage begins to address his hearers. He repeats key words from the passage they have just heard, and explains their meaning. Soon his voice rises. In response, the audience becomes more animated; occasional exclamations from its members punctuate the sermon. Within minutes, the preacher is sweating, moving rapidly from one end of the stage to another; he is reminding his audience of the words of hope they have heard from the Bible, how God would 'bear them up on eagles' wings', and how the Spirit of God is even now among them, lifting them to the divine Presence. Soon the sermon has passed over into a prayer, as the preacher, his voice trembling with emotion, begins to ask God to bless those present. The congregation is on its feet, arms extended in the air

Dutch Reformed Church

Assemblies of God

Liberation theology

in an attitude of fervent devotion, eyes closed, swaying in rhythm with the preacher's words. Suddenly the preacher begins speaking in syllables unrecognizable to his hearers; a number of the congregation begin to pray in the same way. All recognize this phenomenon as glossolalia, or 'the gift of tongues', ecstatic speech which they believe to manifest the immediate presence of God's Spirit. As the fervour grows, several members of the congregation suddenly go rigid and begin to fall; only the attention of those around them prevents them from hitting the ground. Gradually, the energy begins to wane; the people who have been 'slain in the Spirit' awaken to consciousness, and the service draws to an end.

Pentecostalism

p. 216

Pentecostal Christianity arrived late in Latin America, mostly through the efforts of evangelists from the United States, where the movement began early in the twentieth century. It is marked by ecstatic worship and a strong belief that the 'gifts of the Spirit' mentioned in the New Testament, including not only 'speaking in tongues' but also miraculous healing and other dramatic signs of God's power, are available to Christians in the present as they were in the days of the early church. While there is still some contact with Pentecostal bodies in the United States, leadership is now almost entirely Latin American. Its leaders are charismatic, self-selected and validated by successful preaching and inducing the 'gifts of the Spirit' rather than by formal training; indeed, many have little or no formal theological education. Some have a reputation as healers, and their services are attended by large numbers of people seeking to be cured of disease or disability. Pentecostal Christians take the Bible very seriously, using it to search for guidance for personal problems but also as the focus of the exuberant and joyous worship that is the heart of this style of belief. While they identify themselves as Protestants, they have little contact with traditional Protestant churches. Pentecostal Christianity stresses a strict ethic of responsibility for one's own actions, and has little patience with vices such as promiscuity or the abuse of alcohol or drugs. It is often seen as an important social force encouraging family stability, personal honesty and hard work.

Radio
Television

Like the movement in the United States and elsewhere, Pentecostal Christianity in Latin America is found in small, neighbourhood meetings such as the *Iglesia del Cordero de Dios*, but also in enormous gatherings of many thousands, where worship relies on up-to-the-minute media such as elaborate sound systems, video, pop-style music and choirs of hundreds of voices to create an exciting setting for worship. Some Pentecostal churches also rely on mass media, including both radio and television, to propagate their message; many countries in Latin America have television stations with unbroken programming including worship, Bible teaching, news broadcasts from a Pentecostal perspective, on-the-air counselling, and even Christian dramas. While some congregations participate in loosely-organized denominations such as the Assemblies of God, most are independent, founded by their pastor and relying on contributions from the members for survival.

The Roman Catholic Church has opposed the growth of Protestant Pentecostalism, considering it to undermine the Catholic base of all Latin American cultures. It was particularly criticized by liberation theologians, both Catholic and Protestant, since it seemed to reduce Christian faith to an immediate experience of holiness that rarely issued in engagement with the misery of the continent. Yet some Roman Catholic congregations have themselves been captivated by the exuberance of the Pentecostal experience of faith, and many Catholic churches have now incorporated 'charismatic' elements – music, ecstatic prayer, 'speaking in tongues', an emphasis on healing – into their own worship. Meanwhile, some Pentecostal congregations have begun to take a more active role in addressing the social issues that afflict their congregations and communities. Furthermore, as base communities focus more on the spirituality of their members and less on a political agenda, there are obvious similarities between the two movements: an intense experience of community that provides a sense of identity and personal worth; respect for the individual, including those often excluded; a focus on the Bible as an important source for guidance in personal living; and reliance on the presence of God in times of crisis with no easy solutions.

During the last decades of the twentieth century, the growth of Pentecostalism has attracted millions of people whose previous allegiance, however tenuous, was to the Roman Catholic Church. It has radically changed the experience of Christianity throughout the continent. While reliable statistics are difficult to obtain, by the beginning of the new millennium Guatemala may well have become the first country of Latin America with a Protestant majority, almost entirely Pentecostal. Similar growth can be found in many other countries, including especially Brazil and Chile.

The brief glimpses of Latin American Christianity offered here can only begin to convey the depth and breadth of Christian traditions in Latin America. Each has a much richer history than that described here. Each is far more complex than these vignettes would indicate, and each continues to grow and change in dialogue with its context. The richness and variety of Latin American cultures is reflected in the multiple forms in which Christian faith is practised. Those expressions of Christian faith themselves continue to enrich and multiply that diversity in countless and valuable ways.

JOHN L. KATER, JR

📖 Clayton Berg, Paul Pretiz and Paul E. Pretiz, *Spontaneous Combustion: Grass-Roots Christianity, Latin American Style*, Pasadena, CA: William Carey Library Publishers 1996; Serge Bramley, *Macumba*, San Francisco: City Lights Books 1994; Diana DeG. Brown, *Umbanda: Religion and Politics in Urban Brazil*, New York: Columbia University Press ²1994; Gustavo Gutiérrez, *A Theology of Liberation*, Maryknoll, NY: Orbis and London: SCM Press ²1988; Margaret Hebblethwaite, *Base Communities: An Introduction*, Mahwah, NJ: Paulist Press 1993; José Miguez Bonino, *Faces of Latin American Protestantism*, Grand Rapids, MI: Eerdmans 1997; Robert A. Voeks, *Sacred Leaves of Candomblé: African Magic, Medicine, and Religion in Brazil*, Austin, TX: University of Texas Press 1997

America, Christianity in North

Main features

Newcomers who wish to understand North America, be they visitors or immigrants or inquiring scholars, will find themselves coping with the massive presence of Christianity there. More than 80 per cent of the people in Canada and the United States identify with the many versions of this faith.

These new observers are likely to be surprised as they encounter the different features of Christianity in North America. What surprises them will depend upon their own origins and experiences, and these tend to connect with the continents from which they come or from which they do their observing.

Asians other than Koreans who have not done much advance study will be surprised to see how dominant Christianity is in two nations which are both conventionally described as 'secular' and 'pluralist'. People from Korea are exceptional, because Christianity is strong in their nation as it is almost nowhere else in Asia. The new Asian arrivals or scholars may sight some Buddhist and Hindu structures and communities in some cities, but steeples of Christian churches dominate both the urban and rural landscapes.

Similarly, those who come from the Middle East, North Africa, or South East Asia to live in North America or who engage in studies there are likely to be Muslim or to have been surrounded by Islamic cultures. They, too, will find mosques in various places, since Islam is growing rapidly. Islam, however, had little role in shaping North America and most mosques exist in the shadow of Christian churches, which played a key role in forming its ethos.

Europeans, coming from the continent that is historically the main source for immigrants and tourists, will be likely to feel at home as they come across both Roman Catholic and Protestant churches and cultures. Given what we know about degrees of participation and involvement in most of both Eastern and Western Europe and the British Isles, it is safe to assume that most of these observers from across the Atlantic will be stunned to see how many churches are full, and how active their members are in their identification with and expression of Christianity. They may find Canada to be a bit more 'like home', since participation is not so great there as in most of the United States, but there is no mistaking the power of Christianity in Canada, too.

Africans from south of the Sahara will share Christian faith with North Americans and will feel partly at home, since their churches are often transformed expressions in later generations of missionary work originating in North America. They will find that African Americans make up a very strong segment of Christian life, but white Christianity has dominated. Africans are likely to find most of these white Christians to be somewhat more settled-in, quieter, more passive, if in many ways more entrepreneurial, than their African counterparts.

Latin Americans from 'Central America', though they share the North American continent with the United States and Canada, are not thought of as North American in religious censuses. People from there, conditioned by their awareness of the dominance of Roman Catholicism, are immediately aware that in the United States and Canada Catholicism, with which about 25 per cent of the people identify, is a minority in cultures largely and long influenced by Protestantism.

The fictional tourists or immigrants fresh off the plane or first-time students of the subject, before they explore further, will already have discerned six key elements. These characterized North American Christianity as *massive, dominant, shaping, active, settled-in* and largely *Protestant*. The continental regions from which the visitors come or in which the scholars study, however, will not themselves be the only expression of regionalism in their survey and discernments. North American religion itself is highly regionalized. It is not all one thing, defined by the amalgam of Christian creeds with which Americans interact in various ways. Even those who participate in groups defined by creed observe and practise their faith differently depending in part on where they are. Being a Baptist in Quebec is not at all like being one in Dallas, Texas. Being a Roman Catholic in Salt Lake City is quite a different experience from being a Catholic in Montreal or Boston.

The regions

In 1981 a *Washington Post* writer, Joel Garreau, wrote a book, *The Nine Nations of North America*, in which he

CHRISTIANS IN NORTH AMERICA AT THE MILLENNIUM

Country	Population	Roman Catholic	%	Independent	%	Protestant	%	Anglican	%	Orthodox	%	Non-Christians	%
Canada	31,147,000	13,017,945	41.8	1,680,000	5.4	5,350,000	17.2	820,000	2.6	580,000	1.9	9,699,055	31.1
United States	278,357,000	58,000,000	20.8	78,550,000	28.2	64,570,000	23.2	2,400,000	0.9	5,762,000	2.1	69,075,000	24.8

Independent is used here for Christians independent of historic, organized, institutional, denominational Christianity. In some countries, Christians are affiliated to more than one church.

Source: David B. Barrett, George T. Kurian and Todd M. Johnson (eds), *World Christian Encyclopedia*, New York: OUP [2]2002

Church of England

Congregationalism

creatively mapped regions that in most cases have no definite borders other than possibly the sea coasts. It is illuminating to note religious predominances in these regions. In religious terms two of them, which Garreau calls 'MexAmerica' and 'The Islands', belong to Latin and Roman Catholic America. One very distinct region, Quebec, is Canadian only and has no overlap southwards into the United States. The Christianity one encounters in the metropolis of Montreal, a quaint Quebec city, or in the Quebec countryside, the form of faith that shaped the province, is Catholic. A few mainstream Protestants and evangelical outposts may be there, but on a broad scale only Catholicism counts.

Council

From colonial times until at least the Second Vatican Council which ended in 1965, the Catholicism of the Quebecois was considered to be traditionalist and often repressive. The terms of Catholic life were clearly spelled out for a province of parishioners who regularly attended mass. French-speaking Catholics in recent decades have been a major element in Quebec separatism, a movement of people who feel slighted by English-speaking and largely Protestant Canada. A number of factors have cut into the power of Catholicism in recent decades. When mass attendance became a matter of conscience and not church law after the Second Vatican Council, statistics showing participation plunged drastically. Other factors in the decline there have been secularization processes shared with non-Catholic Canada and, many note, reaction by the offended faithful to widely-publicized sexual scandals involving Catholic priests.

Secularization

The second region mapped by Garreau is again quite distinctive. It includes the lightly populated 'Maritime Provinces' in Canada, but for the most part it is what Garreau also named it, the New England of the United States. If the visitors have any knowledge at all of the stories and histories of colonial America, they will know that this is the area sung about as 'Land of the Pilgrims' Pride' and, in part, 'Land Where Our Fathers Died'. Those pilgrims and fathers were almost all Protestants who arrived often as dissenters from the Church of England. They were Congregationalists, and many of their historic white wooden churches, three centuries later, still exist. They form the background to depictions of New England village greens. They carry on ministries in cities and town and country alike. They have lost place, however, to Roman Catholicism. Today not a single county in Massachusetts, Connecticut, New Hampshire, Vermont or Rhode Island – the latter having been settled by Baptists who insisted on religious freedom when Congregationalists were still 'established' by law – has more members of any church than do the Catholics. Church participation over all in New England, however, is much lower than it is in the North American South.

The heritage of New England in American Christianity is largely twofold. From colonial times, even though the churches were supported by law, they spread doctrines that emphasized individual liberty and the power of local congregations to determine their destinies. Some of these doctrines, stressed by dissenters against the establishment, many of whom then turned Baptist, moved with New England migrants to the American South, where the congregational style remains strong. The other heritage, that of urban Catholicism, manifests the power of the church in civil affairs in cities like Boston and Providence, where 'City Hall' was historically made highly aware of the wishes of Catholic bishops and congregants who were also voters. This was at a time when Catholics had less say in national politics. No Catholic ran for the presidency until 1928 and none won until John F. Kennedy of Boston did in 1960.

Third, the area that Garreau called 'The Foundry' is usually described as the 'rust belt'. This area includes the heavily populated East Coast south of New England and what someone has called the 'Industrial Riviera' around the Great Lakes, the home of giant manufacturing and transportation cities such as Detroit and Chicago, where the smokestacks of industry and of steam railroads in the nineteenth century were so manifest. Not a single

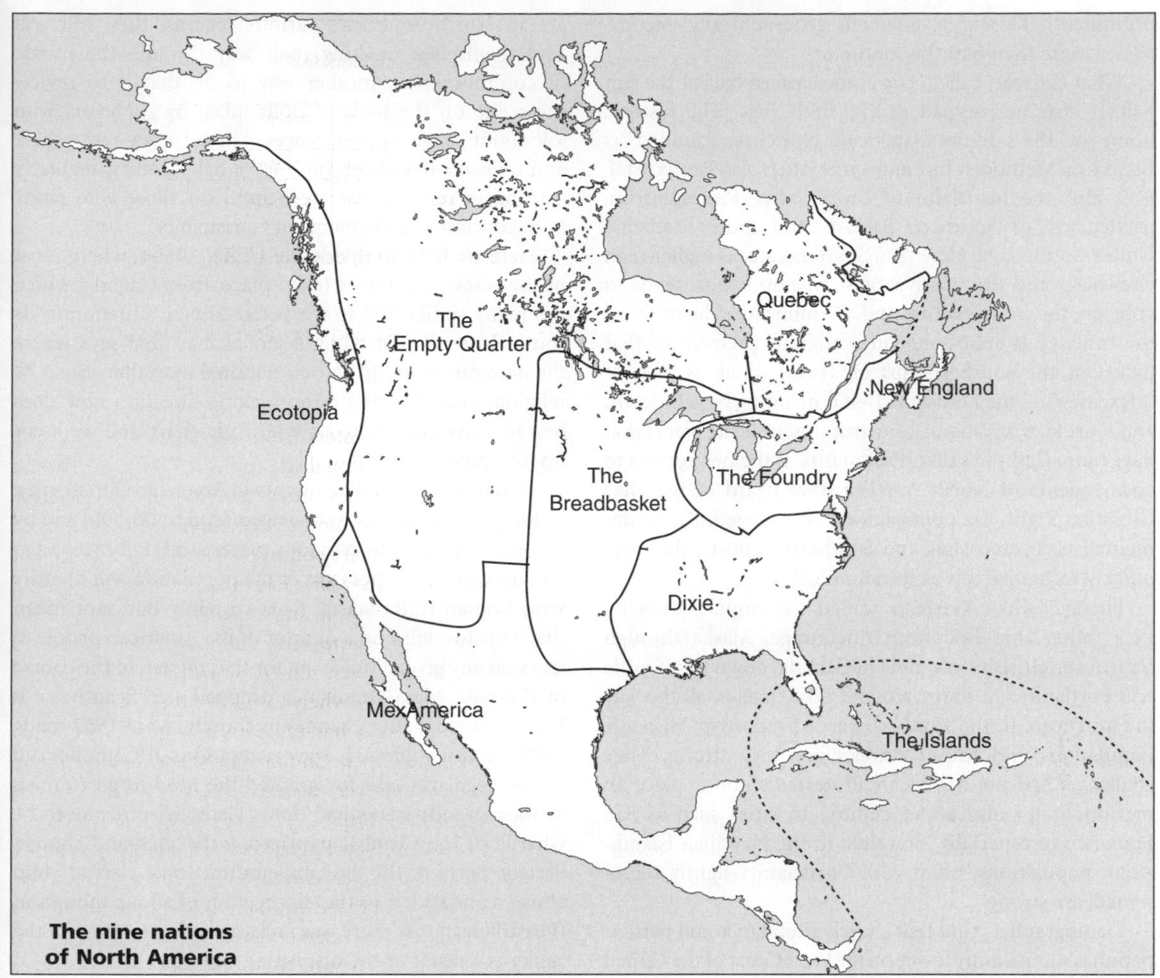

The nine nations of North America

county on the United States side of these Great Lakes houses any religious body larger than the Roman Catholic Church. Yet the populations in all these cities, for example Toronto on the Canadian side, include diverse elements, as do the huge metropolises at the east end of the rust belt, including New York, Philadelphia, Baltimore and Washington. Mainline Protestantism played a significant role in this whole 'belt', and its church buildings remain visible and its memberships active, but in many places it is being outpaced by African American and, increasingly, evangelical Protestants. Overall, Christians in the rust belt were among the pioneers and pace-setters in having to learn how to co-exist with other religious groups. For example, in this region there are more Jews than anywhere else in the United States, and Jewish-Christian relations are most visible and vivid there.

What Garreau called 'The Breadbasket' and 'The Empty Quarter' can be viewed as a single region in respect to religion. This is the Midwest, the farm belt; here are the prairies, the Great Plains, the Rocky Mountains and the Great Basin. To many Easterners some of this historically got listed as the 'Bible belt'. It is true that much of the pioneering and homesteading occurred there under the aegis of hardy Protestants who came directly from Europe or from the eastern United States. In the picture they present to other Americans, many of these citizens are relatively conservative religiously, and the term 'Bible belt' can be seen as an indication of the efforts made to give these conservative values a creative place in folk cultures and civic life.

Roman Catholic Church ◄

African American Christianity ◄

However, this vast area is anything but homogeneous. How can one generalize about an area that includes Salt Lake City, the capital of the Latter-day Saints, the Mormon world, perceived as being an off-shoot of Christianity; Winnipeg, with its large Ukrainian population; Lutheran and Catholic Minneapolis, St Paul and Milwaukee; and all the way south to Fort Worth, where Baptists are most

Mormons

prominent? This area, after all, geographically encompasses more than half the continent.

What Garreau called 'Dixie', the eastern half of the sun belt, is also stereotyped as the 'Bible belt'. The historic home of the African American churches, founded as Baptist or Methodist but now quite often also Pentecostal, it is also the heartland of conservative Protestantism, particularly of Southern Baptists and more moderate United Methodists. Here church attendance is higher than elsewhere, and the white Protestant population tends to vote on the conservative and Republican side most of the time. Only maps showing religious preferences that focus on the southern tips of Texas, which is part of 'MexAmerica', the Louisiana Delta including New Orleans, and Florida, with Miami as metropolis, indicate places that have more Catholics than Protestants. If the newcomers to and students of North America have heard of the New Christian Right, the political force of evangelicals, fundamentalists, Pentecostals and Southern Baptists, they will quickly recognize this as its domain.

Finally, what Garreau called 'Ecotopia' stretches in a rather thin line from Anchorage, Alaska through Vancouver, British Columbia in Canada, down past Seattle and Portland, San Francisco and Los Angeles, all the way to San Diego. In the southern part of this strip, Hispanic populations and thus Catholics are very strong. They challenge African American Protestants for a place in metropolitan politics and culture. In cities such as San Francisco or especially Honolulu in the Hawaiian Islands, Asian populations, often with Christianity lightly represented, are strong.

Demographers find that church attendance and participation is significantly lower on the West Coast of the United States than elsewhere in the nation. Scholars attribute this to many factors: some think that the beckoning of nature in the form of ocean and mountain distracts many from church participation or is an almost religious substitute for it. Others point out that this coastal strip was settled later than most of the rest of the nation, after frontier revivals had passed. The populations which came as part of the Gold Rush in the mid-nineteenth century and the California boom in the twentieth were so diverse and so preoccupied with other things that they devoted less attention to church. Still, anyone who consults the phonebook listings of congregations, looks at the steeples on the skyline, or perceives how cities and town and country work, will find great involvement among the churches.

Polls about religion

After the newcomers have checked in and generalized about American Christianity by comparing it to their own continents back home, and after they have noted how different Christian dominances and expressions are in North America's various regions, they still will find themselves working their way through the puzzle of commitments. Another way to do that is to review the scene on the basis of polls taken by surveyors who ask about religious preferences. These survey-researchers and pollsters have been busy for a half-century, regularly turning in reports that are helpful for those who study both continuity and change in Christianity.

Presbyterian churches ➤

Here we have to divide the United States, where most of the assessments have taken place, from Canada, which has many similarities to the better-known situation to its south. Instead of needing a global map that says where the newcomers are from or a national map that shows its religious reasons, the person seeking direction now does best to draw a diagram, a circle, a 'pie-chart' and see it cut up into pieces.

Here there is a certain stability in American Christianity, so long as one asks, as interviewers tend to do, 'Oh, and by the way, what is your religious preference?' Fifty years ago and now, about 25 per cent of the population will identify with Roman Catholicism. That certainly does not mean that a visitor will find a quarter of the American people at mass on any given Sunday or, for that matter, in the course of the year. Mass attendance dropped significantly, as it had in Canada, after changes in church law in 1967 made participation voluntary. New generations of Catholics did not so regularly take for granted the need to go to mass as their grandparents had done; Catholicism came to be what Pope John Paul II criticized as the 'pick-and-choose' variety. Early in the new millennium some clerical child abuse scandals led to the disaffection of some, though in the early response there was no large-scale desertion of the ranks as a result of the dispiriting exposés.

Through intermarriage with non-Catholics and some falling away, one might have expected to see the Catholic population decline. However, very large influxes of Hispanic populations, historically Catholic, from Mexico, Central America, Puerto Rico and Cuba, made up for such losses. Catholicism kept its quarter of the 'pie'.

The second near quarter belongs to people who identify themselves as 'moderate' or 'liberal' or 'mainline' Protestant. Or they may indicate to the pollster a preference for one of the church bodies ranked as 'mainline', the chosen term for what a century earlier might have been thought of as 'standard-brand' Protestant Christian. These included, first, three in the heritage of colonial America: the Congregationalist from New England, who, thanks to a merger in 1957 with the historically German 'Evangelical Reformed' body, became the United Church of Christ; the Episcopal Church in the USA, whose ancestors were established in southern colonies such as Virginia and the Carolinas; and the Presbyterian Church in the USA and related smaller Presbyterian bodies, which descended from settlers of the Middle Colonies such as Pennsylvania, New York and New Jersey. Those three denominations are thinly spread across the national map, with Episcopalians and Presbyterians being more at home in the South than are those of Congregationalist descent.

The second mainline cluster we might think of as the 'frontier denominations'. These included the northern Baptists, New Englanders who moved west early in the nineteenth century, while in the South their more conservative counterparts turned against mainline identification: the United Methodists, who had divided before the Civil War (1861–5) but reunited in 1939; and the Disciples of Christ, a body born in the United States, one that appealed to people whose other preferences would have led them to Baptist or Presbyterian churches.

Another set of denominations had mainly European continental roots, and were not originally English speaking. Largest among these are the Evangelical Lutheran Church in America, the result of many mergers of more moderate Lutherans (while the more conservative congregations came to make up the Lutheran Church – Missouri Synod, not to be thought of in the mainline camp); the Reformed Church in America, often of Dutch stock from New York and New Jersey but later at home in Michigan and elsewhere in the Midwest, which also has a more conservative counterpart at the edges of the mainline in the Christian Reformed Church; and the cluster of groups often typed as 'peace churches', Mennonites, Church of the Brethren and the like. They used to be seen as 'sects', bodies less exposed to other church bodies and worldlier ways, and they still adhere to many distinctive teachings from their particular heritage, but most observers classify them as sharing destiny with the mainline.

Third comes another quarter of the pie which sociologists call 'evangelical'. It includes the three already mentioned conservative counterparts to the mainline, the Southern Baptist Convention, by far the largest Protestant body; the Lutheran Church – Missouri Synod; and the Christian Reformed. For the most part, however, evangelicals are not typed by their denominations, be they, for instance, Evangelical Free Church or Assemblies of God, so much as by styles.

The hard-line element in this segment is made up of fundamentalists, the more moderate of whom are named evangelicals; on a slightly different track are Pentecostals. These three and the three denominations just mentioned today make up the most visible and vibrant cluster in largely-white Protestantism, and the visitor or newcomer welcomes some accounting for them.

Fundamentalists used that name for themselves and their party from the 1920s. They perceived growing divisions in major denominations over issues such as Darwinian evolution, higher criticism of the Bible, and progressive views of history and social action. Sensing a drift into liberalism or modernism, which they despised, and indifference or atheism, they formed party lines and engaged in struggles, most of which they lost, over who controlled and taught in the theological schools and who dominated the sending of missionaries and the mission fields. Having lost power struggles in the northern Baptist and northern Presbyterian bodies, they went off to found denominations of their own, and saw many of these then split as fundamentalists disagreed with one another. No denomination has 'fundamentalist' in its title; churches on this front may be Baptist or Presbyterian or Church of Christ (a conservative parallel to the Christian Church, Disciples of Christ). For the most part, fundamentalism is the word for a Protestant emphasis and way of organizing, often through 'para-churches', non-denominational organizations of a voluntary character.

Liberal theology
Modernism

The more moderate fundamentalists were put off by what they regarded as excesses or they were descended from more moderate strands that had never been fundamentalist. They dissociated themselves from the militants in the early 1940s. At first calling themselves neo-evangelical, they later dropped the 'neo-'. The foreign visitor who cannot easily make sense of all the subtleties could best fix them in mind by thinking of the evangelist Billy Graham, as representative as any individual could be of post-fundamentalist evangelicalism. Fundamentalists tended to be separatist, while evangelicals, who could agree with harder-line Protestants on most doctrines, plunged more freely into the mix of American life. They were more ready than their fundamentalist kin to pray with Catholics or sometimes to form coalitions with non-evangelicals for particular causes. Long seen as 'other-worldly' and 'non-political', in the 1970s they began to group as political conservatives and became a major player in local and national politics. Their old 'other-worldly' image also waned as they ranged into other aspects of public life, including entertainment, athletics, publishing, television and the market.

Peace churches

Evangelicals

At the side of these are Pentecostals. Their movement was born out of the holiness wing of Methodism and other revival churches almost precisely at the turn to the twentieth century. Attractive to whites and African Americans alike and now to Hispanics, this cluster of denominations has cognate groups in Pentecostalisms in sub-Saharan Africa, Central America, and other places where they tend to challenge mainline Protestant and Catholic heritages alike. There are, of course, Roman Catholic Pentecostals, but they are always numbered as having Catholic, not evangelical preferences. And Pentecostalism is a burgeoning movement in African American Protestantism.

Pentecostalism

Fundamentalism

Hispanic
Christianity

Newcomers from most continents other than Europe do

Evolution
Biblical criticism
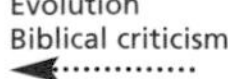

not need much defining when it comes to Pentecostalism. It grows so fast elsewhere that most visitors and immigrants might be more familiar with it than with Anglicanism (Episcopalianism in the United States), Presbyterianism or Lutheranism. The Pentecostalists came on the scene as revivalists, ready to show emotion, engaging in 'speaking in tongues', advocating spiritual healing and the like. They were long suspect among fundamentalists because, while they shared belief in an inerrant word of God, they read and heard it differently. They were open to more ready conversation with the Holy Spirit than fundamentalists would acknowledge. Pentecostalism used to be associated in the public eye with tent-revivals among the poor in the southern Bible belt. Now it prospers in 'mega-churches' in suburban malls and increasingly throughout the North. Many Pentecostals are in political coalition with other evangelicals, leaving behind their own older image of being not very 'this-worldly'.

With three-quarters of the American pie-chart accounted for, the newcomer or student of Christianity in North America will still find reason to learn about the final slightly larger than one-quarter segment. In that sector would be non-Christians such as those in the 2 or 3 per cent that 'prefer' Judaism; the growing comparable counterpart that prefers Islam; the fast-developing Latter-day Saints, seen more as 'a new religious tradition' than part of orthodox Christianity, 'New religious movements', and representatives of historically Asian religions such as Buddhism and Hinduism. Also in this sector are those with no preference or who are decisively non-Christian and non-religious. Depending upon who is counting, only about 8 or 10 per cent are in that group.

Mormons

New religious movements

What is left, then, is the sector of African American Protestants, a very visible 8 per cent of the population. They grew up first under the reluctant tutelage of slave masters and then, often subversively, in their own right under the slaveholders' noses. Then freemen, people who bought or were given freedom from slavery for various reasons, became free to organize the churches for the first time. The more independent and congregational among these were and remained Baptist. The more 'connected' across lines of individual congregations replicated the Methodism they knew in the South and in the urban North, and formed two major denominations and several movements of Methodism. In the twentieth century the fastest-growing element has been Pentecostal, as in the Church of God in Christ. Once at home chiefly in the South of the United States, these Christians moved into the urban North following job opportunities, especially during the two world wars.

The visitor or scholar from elsewhere may be puzzled as to why there are white and African American versions of Baptist, Methodist and Pentecostal movements, or why there are congregations largely segregated as to race in Catholicism and mainline Protestantism. Originally these divisions came about because whites excluded blacks or assigned them inferior status. After the Civil War many African Americans engaged in a kind of positive self-exclusion. There they could have more opportunities to govern themselves, to shape their mission and worship, and gain political coherence, especially in the cities. This resulting pattern of segregation on racial lines has been reinforced by the fact of residential realities. Even though the law generally protects the right of people to buy and live anywhere, in practice there is a kind of racial and class segregation. Since congregations are made up chiefly of people who live in adjacent neighbourhoods, this works against integration.

Of course, there is plenty of overt white racism keeping Christians of similar denominations apart; there are movements of black identity whose leaders fear amalgamation, suppression or second-class status. But whatever the reason, while many people of goodwill publicly rue the situation, profess repentance, and try to make amends, most Christians are still 'with their own people' in respect to race and class on Sunday or whenever they congregate.

Shifting of boundaries

The immigrant may ask whether there is much shifting of boundaries across these fluid and viscous lines of 'preference'. American Christians have come to be known as 'switchers', the pick-and-choose types mentioned in respect to Roman Catholicism above. In economic terms, this is both a 'buyers' market' and a 'supply-side venture'. That is, people make their demands and state their preferences. Then, if they make a commitment, it will be one that they, not their parents or forefathers, determined for them. On the supply side, there are always plenty of enterprising believers, often devout and sincere, who put together some new offering, some package. They advertise it, and it is alluring to some, who switch commitments.

In the case of Catholicism, some loss is compensated for by the arrival and commitment of Hispanic people of Catholic heritage. Mainline Protestantism has had no such infusion and no doubt has lost some people not only from the ranks of those holding membership and participating but also from the very idea of stating any preference. These are believed to have leaked to evangelicalism or into the 'no-preference' zone. Evangelicalism's piece of the pie is likely to have grown somewhat. The drama comes not through people crossing preference boundaries so much as because of the development of disparities within the sectors. In simplest terms, the evangelicals have 'worked their potential constituency' more efficiently and successfully than have Roman Catholics and mainline Protestants. They are more aggressive missionaries and evangelizers, more concerned about drawing people within clarified boundaries of faith, and more energetic about providing alternatives to the offerings of secular culture, as in the case of television, books, rock music and the like.

Physical environment

Any visitor or newcomer to or scholar studying a scene is likely to be attentive to the physical environment. North America, which includes spaces as vast as those in the Yukon in Canada and as cramped as an urban ghetto in Philadelphia, and which offers for view chasms such as the Grand Canyon and peaks like Mount McKinley, sharecroppers' crumbling cabins and the mansions of the wealthy at Palm Beach, is not a setting that can easily be reduced or homogenized. Similarly, the religious landscape and cityscape defy simple characterization. Mention Christianity and one thinks of church buildings. These vary from African American storefronts to Russian Orthodox cathedrals, from simple white clapboard Iowa Methodist churches to St Patrick's Cathedral in New York. One way to introduce American Christianity in respect to appearances, then, is to say that it is not likely that any two nations in history can offer such varied fare for producers of books on church art and architecture. Can nothing be said, then, to guide a visitor?

One line of division runs down between the tradition-minded celebrators of art on one hand and the advocates of simplicity on the other. Orthodox, Roman Catholic, Episcopalian, and 'high church' Protestants tend to stress the sacramental life. The pulpit for preaching has its place, but it shares this with a prominent altar for the mass or communion and, quite likely, pictorial adornments in stained glass and sculpture. At the opposite extreme, in Quakerism or New England Congregationalism, the stress is on simplicity. Here the pulpit or reading desk does dominate; the Bible on it says 'this is a house of the Word', the word preached and read. Here the stress will not be on the formal side of worship; make yourself at home, it invites, and be ready to listen.

More than the users and builders may know, visitors and expert analysts do quickly find homogeneities within the various strands of Christianity. The presence of a large tank in a sanctuary shouts, 'This is Baptist; when you come of age, we will immerse you.' When there are folding chairs in a storefront or a chapel, the visitor can anticipate a reshuffling of furniture depending upon what is to go on. Anchored pews suggest a congregation that is the object of the preaching and praying ministers. Movable seating is an invitation for people to get up, perhaps to dance, engage in processions, and testify. Enter a huge auditorium of a Christian 'mega-church' and you will note the absence of a cross or other Christian symbols. Such a place is made to look as much like an auditorium in a high school or convention centre as possible. It says, 'We have taken an analysis of the surrounding public's taste and interest, and have assessed that formal symbols of the church are forbidding; they imply so much familiarity with the stories that we celebrate that you will turn your back before we even get started.'

American Christians are likely to make arrangements for the collection of offerings. Not just the alms box that one would find in nations where the church has been established, but stacks of offering plates remind one that American Christianity is an unsubsidized 'pay as you go' venture. One may enter a European cathedral and find only a narthex and a nave. Where, the American tourist asks, are the rest rooms; where the rooms for religious education; for coffee hour; for socializing; for organizing voluntary activity? Almost all American churches have all of them. The sanctuary may suggest quiet, but we are active and we want to signal activity. Buildings

It is quite possible that these few paragraphs of reference call to mind scenes and settings that visitors will notice at once and find familiar. Still, they are only ideal types, stereotypes, efforts to describe significant representations. In the end, the physical setting is hard to find interesting because of its mere place, described as 'North American'. So one turns to the pattern of ideas one is likely to find characteristic of American Christians.

Distinguishing features

One could well start by running through a catalogue of creeds. On such terms, a person would invite the guest on terms like these: 'Many Americans are members of credal churches. Read the Westminster Confession, the Augsburg Confession, the Baltimore Catechism and the Thirty-Nine Articles and you will have entrées to Presbyterian, Lutheran, Catholic and Episcopalian life.' Yet few observers have ever found much clarified devotion to such confessional documents; most church members have never read them, and many of their clerical leaders consult them only in seminary or when some faction in a denomination engages in disputation. Rather than examine this credal scene, then, we will look at some relatively distinguishing features of American Christianity.

Creed

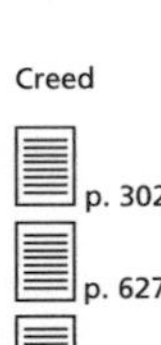

p. 302
p. 627
p. 303

First, and this sounds on the one hand obvious or, on the other, unsettling: American churches, across boundaries of regions and denominations are *American*. They are so in different ways in Canada, where there was no War of Independence, no sudden invention of ways to distinguish between religious and civil realms, and where many see almost no signs of 'civil religion'. Canadians tend to sanctify their particular environments, be these the Maritimes or the prairie provinces.

In the United States, matters are different. American Christians are heirs, or think they are heirs, of people who,

while they learned to distinguish religion from the civil authorities – some call this 'the separation of church and state' – have always tended to meld their church theologies with the moral and spiritual aspirations of the state. This phenomenon, as indicated above, can be unsettling. Christianity is supposed to be a global faith, and singing 'God Bless America' is usually done in terms of privilege,
p. 960
which means God has blessed, is blessing, and will bless America, no matter what God does to others. Similarly, it is very hard to picture that a secular and pluralist society could come up with moral and theological norms that are sufficiently congruent with what the churches profess that they can so congenially blend into each other.

In the eyes of many Americans, however, they do. Societies, including the most complex ones, tend to converge towards certain basics. Following the Spanish philosopher José Ortega y Gasset, I have chosen to call these *creencias*, which Gasset defines as beliefs so deep you do not know you hold them; they are not the beliefs that you have, but the beliefs that you are. In the United States many of these derived from, and were modified from, Christian themes.

For a sample, American Christianity was the main contributor to the notion that America has a mission. It is to be steward of its resources and of God's call and assignment. God has favoured this nation above others and given it a vocation. Now mission and stewardship
Ethics
and vocation do come from the Christian vocabulary, and not the Buddhist or Muslim, though these may have analogues influential in nations where they are dominant. The idea that the nation is morally accountable, in ways that transcend boundaries of believing groups or of believers versus non-believers, is not something one finds just anywhere. Nor is the notion that in a pluralist society one can and should hold to the integrity of creeds and hopes and practices that make one distinctive as, say, a Catholic and a Mennonite. This notion can be extended to a legitimation of the idea that American Christians are free to convert and even should make efforts at converting others.

Just as suddenly, firmly and briskly comes a parallel, some would say a conflicting, set of mandates: co-operate with the other; be tolerant; respect faiths alien to and even competitive with your own; use your faith resources to criticize society, but only up to a point. At that point you rally for the common good. Those are not Christian ideas heard everywhere and at all times; they developed on a particular soil. While there are egregious exceptions and occasions, times of violence and frequent violations of these civil convictions, most American Christians hold to them, however late, rare and exceptional they have been on the soil of most nations.

American Christianity, however, is not a mush, a mere amalgam of elements from the separate faiths designed to produce a civil faith for the common good. American Christians argue, as they always have, about what the common good is and how to achieve it. Sometimes they do this without reference to the political forum. Seldom in Christian history has there been such a set of initiatives as those that Canadian and United States Christians developed and put to work to produce voluntary associations early in the nineteenth century and ever after. These are agencies for education, delivery of health care and moral reform. The impulses behind them may lead eventually to political determinations, or some may find governmental support. But many do remain in the hands of the religious, and support of them is considered by Christians to be a good Christian thing.

At the same time, many of these do progress (or regress) into the political domain, where many Christians divide in their address to argument. The great flaws on American Christian soil 150 years ago were slavery, the banishing of Native Americans to reservations, and the development of corporate structures that could be destructive of human health and initiative. Christian churches sometimes were implicated in what many members saw to be evil in such situations, but many American Christians appealed both to distinctively Christian norms and to some more philosophically grounded contentions for the common good.

At the turn to the new millennium these arguments revolve about everything from war and peace or racial and economic justice to the troubling close-to-home issues that deal with abortion, euthanasia, homosexual practices and the like. Sometimes the non-Christian and non-believing spokespersons in the population utter plagues on 'both your houses', on the two sides or more in these arguments. What use is it, they ask, to argue on Christian grounds if Christians do not have their own act together, if each cancels the other out? What, conversely, do Christians bring distinctively to the debates? The questions are frequent, valid, and well stated. What they have not done is to convince most Christians to silence themselves and depart from the political scene.

The political scene is anomalous and difficult to address. Efforts to form what one nineteenth-century leader called 'a Christian party in politics' have usually been frustrated or rejected. Having denominational leadership speak for church bodies, on the other hand, often means that they are heard as unrepresentative citizens, criticized for stepping out of their spiritual roles, or not competent to make judgements. For such reasons, through the years American Christians, be they Catholic, mainline Protestant, evangelical, or whatever, have tended to organize in voluntary associations to witness, propagandize, raise funds, and, when necessary or possible, support specific candidates or oppose uncongenial legislation. They know that just as they gained moral credibility among those who agreed with them, they also took and take risks of the loss of favour among those who on political grounds oppose them.

Mention of leaders calls to mind the fact that no single polity, no single form of government, begins to characterize American Christianity. Some churches are hierarchical, among them the Roman Catholic and the Orthodox; some are connexional, such as the United Methodist; some, like the Episcopal and the larger Lutheran body, are episcopal but do not usually bow low to hierarchy; others are presbyterian, governed by 'elders', or synodical, making policy through conventions, or finally, congregational. For all the diversity, however, in a society where churches are not established by law and where citizens are free not to practise a particular faith or follow faith commitments at all, leaders have to be very responsive to lay members. They call on them for financial support of Christian causes; they try to persuade them to pursue certain moral ends; they have to do their best through rhetoric and example to make their version of the Christian message comprehensible and attractive.

Over half of American Christians are women. From the first they have been influential as congregants: for example, as those who nurtured the young in the faith, or in carrying out the works of love. Recognition of their leadership role in the rites of the church, however, was slow to come. Curiously, it came first not from the liberal churches but from groups like the Pentecostals, where women were licensed or ordained in preaching roles by the middle of the nineteenth century. Similarly, from the ranks of holiness groups, women were in the front ranks of leadership in the Salvation Army.

Finally, during the most recent half-century, almost all bodies except the Catholic and the Orthodox, the Southern Baptists and Missouri Lutherans, began to see a move from confining women in posts of auxiliary leadership, to their being ordained as clergy. This move was not, of course, the first time women served. The Roman Catholic religious orders of women, in a church that forbids their ordination, assigned significant roles and status to women. Today, in the churches that ordain women much of the leadership is passing into their hands. While ordination affects only a small minority of members, it preaches a message of equality that mere verbal assent to themes of equality had not effectively done.

To deal with American Christianity and use few names of persons may seem to be misleading to tourists and immigrants. While present-day Christians may honour some of their forebears, they have a reputation for not being very historically minded. Not many United Church of Christ members could discourse on the greatest theologian and evangelist in their heritage, Jonathan Edwards in the eighteenth century, or the more recent theological titan Reinhold Niebuhr. Christian Scientists, not regarded as Christian by so many others, will know of their founder Mary Baker Eddy and, similarly, Latter-day Saints will know the prophet Joseph Smith, but the nearer church bodies are to the 'standard brand', the less such figures stand out. Catholics have been served and ruled by major hierarchs such as John Carroll in eighteenth-century America, but the names mean little to most.

Organization

At the same time, within each generation and its aftermath, come leaders to embody movements that incarnate peoples' hopes. While Martin Luther King, Jr, was wildly unpopular among white Christians who resisted desegregation in the 1960s, he might well be thought of as the representative American Protestant of the last 50 years. Dorothy Day had a passionate following and set of admirers in and beyond Catholicism. For the most part, however, American Christianity does not live by its 'saints' and heroines so much as in response to contemporary persuaders and exemplars.

The future

In respect to the future, the question of the relative size of those bodies with Christian preference is often raised within the context of pluralism. Since Hinduism, Buddhism and especially Islam are growing more rapidly than Christianity, some wonder if that will fade in relative importance. Still, it has such a head start and large lead in statistics and cultural position that it will be hard for others to begin to overtake it. One set of projections suggested that about 85 per cent of the American people identify with the Jewish-Christian tandem of inheritances (and only about 2 or 3 per cent of that is 'Jewish') and that this dominance will decline in twenty years to about 83 per cent. Such projections may be rather fanciful, but they are suggestive of the public posture, the general favour and the at least residual and sometimes cultural and ecumenical prominence of American Christianity as it faces the future. Christians have been in North America for over half a millennium, which means that they are ageing. Yet their impulses of response to the Holy Spirit, as they interpret this, and their innovative spirit, also keeps them young and full of promise as they keep reassessing their place in world Christianity.

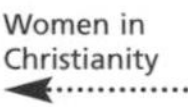

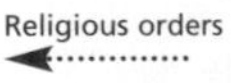

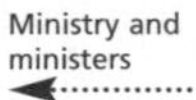

MARTIN E. MARTY

Sydney E. Ahlstrom, *A Religious History of the American People*, New Haven, CT: Yale University Press 1972; Joel Garreau, *The Nine Nations of North America*, Boston: Houghton Mifflin 1981; Martin E. Marty, *Pilgrims in Their Own Land: 500 Years of Religion in America*, New York: Penguin Books 1984; Mark A. Noll, *A History of Christianity in the United States and Canada*, Grand

Rapids, MI: Eerdmans 1992 and *The Old Religion in a New World*, Grand Rapids, MI: Eerdmans 2002

Peace churches

Anabaptists

Reformation

The term 'Anabaptists' denotes those who rebaptize. It is now used of a number of Christian groups, including the Amish, the Brethren and the Mennonites; it goes back to the time of the Reformation in the sixteenth century, when it was applied to a group of Protestant radicals.

Initiation
Counter-Reformation

As they studied the New Testament – which they took as their sole guide for belief and practice – these radicals concluded that the baptism of infants was not scriptural. Baptism was to be given only to those who confessed Christ and pledged to follow his commandments. So they ignored their earlier baptism as infants and were baptized again with adult or believers' baptism, hence their name.

Covenant

They shared the criticisms of the Roman Catholic Church made by other Reformers, notably Huldrych Zwingli, Martin Luther and John Calvin, but were convinced that these had halted half-way in their break with Rome. They urged the complete separation of church and state, rejected all force in religious affairs, and formed disciplined congregations based on the covenants of mature believers.

Although Anabaptists criticized the close links of the chief Reformers with government, they accepted the basic Reformation tenets of scriptural authority, salvation by grace through faith, and the priesthood of all believers. One widely-accepted description of Anabaptist belief had three components: 1. a conception of the essence of faith as obedience to the teachings of Jesus Christ (discipleship); 2. a view of the church as a voluntary body of believers, accountable to each other and separate from worldly society (non-conformity); and 3. a thoroughgoing ethic of love, which rejects all forms of violence (non-resistance).

The movement first appeared in the Swiss provinces in 1525, but spread rapidly all over Europe. However, both the Roman Catholic and the Protestant authorities suppressed and persecuted Anabaptists, and thousands were killed or banished. The brave manner in which they faced the sword, stake or noose convinced onlookers of the truth of their beliefs. Non-resistance, along with other tenets, was codified in a 1527 agreement, the 'Brotherly Union'.

In 1533 militant Anabaptists took over the Westphalian city of Münster, which they believed would be the 'New Jerusalem', the site of the Christ's Second Coming. When besieged (1534–5), they defended themselves by force and leaders instituted a reign of terror in the city. This uncharacteristic episode tarnished the reputation of all Anabaptists for centuries. More typically, they have long been recognized, with the Quakers (Religious Society of Friends) and the Church of the Brethren as historic peace churches.

Some Anabaptists survived by fleeing to the regions of Bohemia and Moravia in central Europe, where they found refuge in the realms of tolerant nobles. In 1528 one faction of the refugees, following the biblical mandates of passages from the Acts of the Apostles (chapters 2 and 4–5), adopted complete communalism of goods and production. They formed around 100 communities (*Bruderhofs*) that flourished in the second half of the sixteenth century, with a membership approaching 30,000. This communal movement took the name of an early leader, Jakob Hutter, and came to be known as the Hutterian Brethren or Hutterites. Driven from their homelands by the Catholic Counter-Reformation, they trekked eastwards, finally finding a new homeland in Southern Russia. From there, they migrated to North America in the 1870s, where by 2000 they were thriving in 425 colonies in the western provinces of Canada and the Northwestern states of the USA – the oldest communal group in history. In the 1920s a group in Germany led by Eberhard Arnold emerged, which joined forces with the Hutterian Brethren in 1931, though not now affiliated. This Society of Brothers or Bruderhof had ten communities in the USA, UK and Australia in 2002, with some 2000 members.

A few Anabaptists managed to survive in isolated valleys in the Swiss Alps and in Southern Germany, but many were forced to emigrate, often resettling in the colonies of British America, especially in Pennsylvania, where religious liberty was granted early. Others won limited toleration in the Netherlands, where they became known as Mennonites, after a second-generation leader named Menno Simons, noted for his doctrinal writings and pastoral concern. By the late seventeenth century, Mennonites in the relatively tolerant Dutch provinces had achieved considerable prosperity; they used their means to aid their co-religionists in Switzerland and the German lands, often by helping them to emigrate to the New World.

The Amish, named after their dominant leader Jakob Amman, also moved to North America. This movement arose out of a division among Mennonites in Switzerland, Alsace and Southern Germany after 1693. The last Amish congregation in Alsace disbanded in 1937. Despite considerable schism, Amish continue to flourish in the present day, with perhaps 80,000 adult members in several hundred districts, almost entirely in the United States. The Old Order Amish, who forbid the use of power-line electricity, automobiles and trucks, domestic telephones and almost all electronic devices, have captured the imagination of the wider society.

By the eighteenth century, small numbers of Mennonites were able to establish themselves in north Germany, especially in Krefeld on the Lower Rhine. Members introduced the textile industry there, which as it burgeoned brought wealth and esteem to the Mennonite entrepreneurs. A comparable development took place in Altona, a suburb of the port city of Hamburg. Here Mennonites flourished in the shipping and trading industries. A considerable number of Mennonites migrated eastwards, first into Prussia and later into South Russia. In the latter region, they were given permission to run their own affairs and prospered in agricultural communities. When, however, Czarist Russia began to place restrictions on their freedoms late in the nineteenth century, many of these Russian Mennonites emigrated to North America. This trend was heightened again following the two world wars, as they suffered under Communist domination. A number of Russian Mennonites found asylum in South America, especially in Paraguay.

European Mennonites were influenced by the renewal movement among European Protestants after 1675 known as Pietism, which sought to bring spiritual life and warmth to what had become rigidly dogmatic and formalized church structures. Some Pietists were expelled from the state churches; among these separatists, known as Radical Pietism, arose in 1708 the religious body known since the early twentieth century as the Church of the Brethren. The Brethren accepted many of the beliefs and practices of Mennonites except for the manner of baptism of adult believers; Mennonites poured water on the heads of those baptized, whereas Brethren insisted on total threefold immersion – which earned for them the nickname 'Dunkers'. By the year 2000, their world adult membership was approximately 300,000.

By the middle of the nineteenth century, the centre of Anabaptist life was in North America, although Mennonites persisted in small numbers on the European continent, in Germany, the Netherlands and France. This orientation changed with the challenge of the missionary movement in the late nineteenth and early twentieth centuries. The result is that in the twenty-first century more Anabaptists live outside North America and Europe than live within them. In 2000 total adult membership numbered around 2.1 million in 10,000 congregations in 64 nations. 55 per cent live in Congo, Indonesia, India and Ethiopia. A Mennonite World Conference, with a small headquarters office in Strasbourg, co-ordinates the interaction of hundreds of separate Anabaptist/ Mennonite conferences or bodies. About every five years, an international assembly brings together representatives from many nations for fellowship, inspiration and co-ordination, but not for binding actions.

A highly respected social agency, the Mennonite Central Committee (MCC), originally organized in 1920 to aid sufferers in Russia, conducts relief and rehabilitation projects around the world with a staff (largely volunteer) of more than 1500 and a budget of $63 million in 2000. Over the years its efforts have largely shifted from emergency relief to economic and educational advancement of the disinherited. A quarterly periodical, *A Common Place*, documents the far-flung MCC activity.

For many years suspicious of higher education, Mennonites and Brethren in North America selected their ministers from among their own membership by discerning qualities of piety, biblical knowledge and leadership. (Dutch and German Mennonites were the exception, from an early period favouring formally educated ministers.) They were self-supporting and, until recent times, male. The most conservative branches select their leaders by lot from those nominated, believing that the Holy Spirit will honour and bless those chosen. After 1875 Mennonites and Brethren began to sponsor numerous colleges, universities and seminaries (theological schools). Today theological education is the norm for pastors, although ministers may be selected who have had alternative forms of education. Worship services are non-liturgical, featuring fervent hymn singing and biblically-based sermons.

Pietism ◄

Since 1900 there has been an upsurge of scholarship on Anabaptist subjects. Originating in but not restricted to their own membership, research and publication has increased to a remarkable degree. One of the reasons is that scholars appreciate that in the course of time many of the beliefs of the early Anabaptists – such as religious freedom and separation of church and state – have become the favoured stances of most religious movements. Much of this scholarship appeared first in journals, the most respected of which is the *Mennonite Quarterly Review*.

Brethren ◄

Ecumenical relationships differ from region to region. Dutch and German Mennonites have co-operated ecumenically for many decades, but Mennonites in North America have been slow to join inter-confessional bodies. In 2001–2, the two largest American Mennonite groups, the Mennonite Church and the General Conference Mennonites, merged to form the Mennonite Church USA, with perhaps 120,000 members. There are innumerable smaller Anabaptist churches – more often the result of division over church practice rather than of doctrine – of which the largest are the Mennonite Brethren and Brethren in Christ, with membership principally in the USA and Canada. The Church of the Brethren is a member of both the National Council of Churches of Christ (USA) and the World Council of Churches (WCC) of Geneva. In the area of social outreach, Mennonites co-operate freely around the world with other religious agencies.

Mission ◄

Considered after their origin in 1525 as dangerous heretics – fit only for persecution – the Anabaptists of several family groupings today are still a religious minority. They are, however, widely respected for their sturdy witness for peace and justice and for their persistent readiness to aid sufferers around the world, regardless of race, creed or political adherence.

DONALD F. DURNBAUGH

The Mennonite Encyclopedia, Volumes 1–5, Scottdale, PA: Herald Press 1955–90; *The Brethren Encyclopedia, Volumes 1–3*, Ambler, PA: Brethren Encyclopedia Inc. 1983–4 (Vol. 4 forthcoming); Donald F. Durnbaugh, *Fruit of the Vine: A History of the Brethren, 1708–1995*, Elgin, IL: Brethren Press 1997; Cornelius J. Dyck, *An Introduction to Mennonite History*, Scottdale, PA: Herald Press [3]1993; John A. Hostetler, *Amish Society*, Baltimore, MD: Johns Hopkins University Press [4]1993; Donald B. Kraybill and C. Nelson Hostetter, *Anabaptist World USA*, Scottdale, PA: Herald Press 2001; C. Arnold Snyder, *Anabaptist History and Theology*, Kitchener, ON: Pandora Press 1995

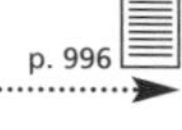
p. 996

Angels

In the biblical tradition of Jews, Christians and Muslims angels are believed to be immaterial spirits created by God to regulate the order of the world and serve as messengers in regard to human salvation. Similar spirits appear in the belief systems of many world religions. The English word 'angel' comes from the Greek *angelos*, which means something like 'announcer'. It was used to translate a number of Hebrew words for messengers and representatives of God.

The tendency of liberal theologians over the last two centuries has been to deny outright the existence of angels. In recent times, however, angels have again captured the attention of many ordinary believers and several major theologians. Reported experiences of angels have played a significant part in this recovery. But before we look at angels today, we must trace their history, beginning with the Old Testament.

In the earliest Hebrew scriptures, *mal'ak*, the Hebrew term for messenger of God, denoted a divine envoy, barely distinct from God, who appeared to inform, guide, protect or warn men and women individually, or the chosen people as a whole. Only rarely was the term used in the plural. So when the angel of the Lord appears to Abraham or to Moses in the burning bush, or goes before the Hebrews as a pillar of fire and a cloud, it signifies and effects God's actual presence.

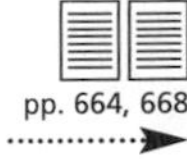
pp. 664, 668

Later identified as angels, the 'sons of God' appear as the divine retinue or 'heavenly court' or host of heaven. Other 'angels' include the 'Holy Ones', guardians of persons and places and worshippers of God; these were also known as 'servants', 'mighty ones', 'ministers' and 'watchers'. Mainly protective and benevolent, such beings were important as mediators between God and the patriarchs, judges and prophets. But 'destroying' angels sometimes also executed the wrath, judgement or vengeance of God. However, the Hebrew Bible says nothing about the creation of the angels or their fall.

Religiously, as a personification or sensible manifestation of the divine word or action, the use of the term 'angel' maintained the absolute sovereignty of God while affirming God's direct intervention in human affairs. The Hebrews did not think of angels as 'pure spirits', though, but portrayed them as ordinary if unusually powerful human beings or merely a heavenly voice.

Interest in angels reached its greatest peak during the two centuries between the last works in the Hebrew Bible and the first Christian writings, the so-called intertestamental period. By that time, the Jewish people were dispersed throughout the Mediterranean world, from Persia in the far east to Carthage, Gaul and Spain in the west. They were thus exposed to the literature and art of a great variety of cultures. Many left their mark on the Jewish conception of angels. The most significant development was an emphasis on the fall of the angels and the emergence of demonology in the books of Enoch, the books of Adam and Eve, the Martyrdom of Isaiah, the Sibylline Oracles, etc. But in the midst of some of the most imaginative descriptions, there also seem to be accounts of actual encounters with angels, including several from the books of Maccabees (e.g. 2 Maccabees 5.1–4).

Although the New Testament is clearly influenced by late Jewish beliefs and writings, the pattern of angelic description generally follows the ancient Hebrew tradition. But it also includes actual encounters, some of which are unexplained and mysterious. Angels bear important messages about births and deaths; they witness to divine manifestations, especially the resurrection and ascension of Jesus; they reveal to key figures information that changes the direction of their lives and ministry; they provide encouragement, protection and even direct assistance. The early church took angels in its stride as part and parcel of its religious world. Jesus himself seems to have shared the ordinary view of angels prevalent among the common people and particularly the school of Pharisaic Judaism to which he largely adhered.

Angels figure in the Gospels as messengers, as in the infancy accounts of Matthew and Luke and the resurrection accounts of Matthew and John. Angels also minister to Jesus following his temptation in the wilderness according to Matthew and Mark, but not Luke; and according to a disputed verse in Luke's Gospel (22.43) an angel strengthened Jesus on the Mount of Olives. Virtually all other references to angels are allusions to beliefs of the Jews or figure in stories and predictions of Jesus. This seems especially true of passages in which angels appear in numbers rather than singly.

In the letters of Peter and Paul, as well as other New Testament writings, angels are also portrayed as mighty forces orchestrating history and the cosmos itself, sometimes discordantly. The theme has most likely been developed from late Jewish teaching about the angels of the nations, as in Daniel 7.

As portrayed in the New Testament, angels look like human persons and communicate in the ordinary language of the people. Sometimes these manifestations are accompanied by unusual features, such as bright light or the dazzling appearance of clothes or faces. However, there are no wings, no haloes, no armour nor weapons.

The Bible names only two angels, Michael and Gabriel (three if Raphael, who appears in the book of Tobit, the biblical status of which is disputed by some Christians, is included). In 745 a synod in Rome prohibited theologians and liturgists from incorporating the names of any angels except these three. But another angel is named in Christian scripture, although little attention is paid to him or his highly unusual character. He resembles the destroying angel of Jewish tradition, and in the book of Revelation is called Abaddon in Hebrew and Apollyon in Greek (9.11). Both words simply mean 'destroyer' (20.1). He is referred to again later as the angel of the Abyss. In the Old Testament Abaddon is sometimes used as a synonym for *she'ol*, the place of the dead, and a number of commentators have assumed that Apollyon is another name for Satan. But he is clearly called an angel, and while his name might have been a title at one time, it has now become a true name. Originally, the other angels' names were also designations or titles: Gabriel means 'Strength of God', Michael means 'Who is Like God?', and Raphael means 'God Heals'. Similarly, Ariel (who is considered an angel in Milton's *Paradise Lost*) means 'Lion of God', and Uriel, who appears in the apocryphal book of Enoch, means 'Fire of God'.

In Christian tradition, because Gabriel makes announcements, he is assigned the task of blowing the final trumpet, an otherwise anonymous task described in the book of Revelation (11.15), but in 1 Thessalonians Paul probably had Michael in mind (4.16); Michael is also referred to in the letter of Jude (9).

Angels are first to announce the coming of Christ and the new covenant (Luke 2.9–13); at times they accompany Jesus in his ministry. According to Jesus' own testimony, they are our representatives and advocates, presenting our prayers to God (Matthew 18.10). However, despite this saying, which speaks of the angels of 'little ones', Jesus does not appear particularly to endorse the notion of guardian angels. But according to the Acts of the Apostles, as the early community of disciples grew, angels fostered and protected it (8.26; 10.3, 22). Jesus affirmed that on the day of judgement angels will accompany the Son of man at his return (Mark 8.38), gathering both the elect and those who have resisted God's rule (Luke 12.8–9). Finally, the letter to the Hebrews says that those who remained faithful to God throughout life and death will be accompanied by countless numbers of angels as they enter the heavenly Jerusalem (12.22).

Generally, in the New Testament angels are not only subject to the lordship of Christ but are to some extent even subservient to human beings, in so far as women and men are united with Christ in his death to sin and resurrection to the justice of God.

The heavenly host began to be organized in classes in the inter-testamental period and clearly achieved recognizable rank in early Christian writings. All the titles given the 'choirs' are found in the Bible, but the eventual pattern and even the inclusion of some of the names is not itself biblical. The same is true of the names of the angels. Apart from Michael, Gabriel, Raphael and the mysterious Abaddon, all are taken from extra-biblical Jewish, Christian and Muslim lore, whether folk-tales or more sophisticated extrapolations of scripture. Literally thousands of names were eventually given to angelic figures. Hence the official discouragement and eventual condemnation of the mania by the church, which was still issuing decrees on the matter as late as the fifteenth century and afterwards.

In general terms, the system of angelic orders was created by amalgamating several casual enumerations of the apostle Paul, who speaks of principalities, powers, virtues (or 'energies'), dominions or dominations, and thrones. Probably beginning with Irenaeus in the second century, to these were added 'angels' and 'archangels', as if they were different kinds of spirits, and finally the 'seraphim' and 'cherubim' from the Hebrew Bible.

In the Eastern church, arrangements of these divisions were made by Cyril of Jerusalem and John Chrysostom. In the West, Ambrose and Augustine produced similar lists. But the principal architect of the angelic hierarchy was an anonymous monk writing in Syria at the very end of the fifth century who called himself Dionysius after Paul's Athenian convert (Acts 17.34). Dionysius created a systematic interpretation of reality that reflected the developing orders in the church as well as the cosmic arrangement of angels and even civil society. But it was his doctrine of angelic choirs that caught the imagination of both Eastern and Western Christians, not least of all Pope Gregory the Great, through whom the Dionysian system entered the West with official approval.

Church fathers

Covenant

The angelic hierarchy received widespread attention in

Western Christianity chiefly after John Scotus Eriugena translated the writings of Dionysius into Latin in the ninth century. Commentaries on the angelic hierarchy developed by Dionysius became part and parcel of the standard theological works of the Middle Ages. Over a century before, it had been the subject of one of the remarkable visions (and subsequent paintings) of Hildegard of Bingen.

Hildegard of Bingen

After the Middle Ages, teaching about angels did not develop notably, and with the coming of the modern age, the industrial revolution and the Enlightenment, belief in them tended to migrate to the periphery of theological and even popular interest, except for the notion of guardian angels, chiefly taught to children, and their role in art. In both instances, the mighty beings of scripture and tradition became little more than decorations.

Industrial revolution Enlightenment

The return of interest in angels in the last decades of the twentieth century was sufficiently impressive for *Time* magazine to devote its Christmas 1993 cover story to the subject. It reported in rather startled terms that 69 per cent of the American public believed in angels. 46 per cent believed they had a personal guardian angel. Additional polls conducted by George Gallup and the National Opinion Research Institute reported similar findings. In November 1994 *Newsweek* magazine announced that 20 per cent of those they interviewed had had a revelation from God during the year and 13 per cent had seen or sensed the presence of an angel. More reports came in from Europe.

Books on angels became bestsellers, and films and television programmes continued to feature angels. They indicate that contrary to what is commonly thought, modern men and women still believe in angels (as well as in miracles) and claim to have experiences of them.

The Old Testament has many accounts of angelic experiences that seem to be more than later editorial embellishments, and in the New Testament, too, many references indicate some kind of actual experience with angels. In the Middle Ages, visions of angels may not have been a common experience, but the reports by Hildegard of Bingen in the twelfth century indicate more than a literary and artistic interest. According to even primitive accounts, Francis of Assisi received the marks of Jesus' wounds, the stigmata, during a vision of a seraph. In the fifteenth century, Joan of Arc was guided by the voices of angels and saints in her mission to liberate France. Teresa of Avila recorded several experiences with angels, including one of the most important in her life.

Some experiences remain wholly within the consciousness of a person with no identifying characteristics other than a voice. But many involve physical events. One of the most dramatic recent incidents occurred in the ranching hamlet of Cokeville, Wyoming, where a school

God creating an angel to overcome the devil, from the eleventh/twelfth-century Latin codex, *Visions of St Hildegard of Bingen, Book of the Works of God*

full of children was saved from disaster by the intervention of what were described as angels. Similar accounts were collected in the wake of the Oklahoma City bombing on 19 April 1996.

Such accounts, like the experiences themselves, will not convince sceptics that anything other than an over-excited imagination was at work. But for those who have had such experiences, no amount of cold water thrown on their interpretation will dampen their conviction that they have been helped in an extraordinary way by emissaries of God.

However, not all experiences of angels involve crisis appearances or even visions. Many seem related to the ancient connection of angels to divine worship. According to some theologians, especially in the Eastern Orthodox tradition, this is their primary activity and the liturgy is therefore where they are normally, if invisibly, encountered. But not exclusively.

The English writer Rosalind Heywood described a number of angelic experiences. Among them was what she called 'The Singing', a kind of humming that she interpreted as an indication of angel presences. Such audible encounters were known to the ancient world and accepted as a major aspect of religious experience in India in the form of Nada Yoga.

Christian writers had taken up the theme of *musica celestis*, the music of heaven, much earlier. In the fourteenth century, the English mystic Richard Rolle claimed to have heard the sweet music many times and called it the Song of Angels. In a short essay of that name written a few years later, the Augustinian mystic Walter Hilton corrected some of Rolle's enthusiasm, but affirmed that hearing celestial harmonies associated with angelic communication was one of the mystical gifts and gave instruction on differentiating between the authentic experience and various illusions. In the late twentieth century, the South African mathematical physicist Michael Whiteman described his own experience of angelic music.

The awareness of music emanating from outside the ordinary human world of instruments, radios and stereo sets remains one of the most interesting aspects of religious experience, even apart from association with angels. But its ancient and modern connection with the host of heaven, who have often been portrayed by artists such as Fra Angelico with a variety of musical instruments, adds a touch of mystery and beauty that fits in well with the great chants ascribed to angels in the writings of Isaiah, Daniel and the book of Revelation.

RICHARD WOODS, OP

Joan Wester Anderson, *An Angel to Watch over Me: Children's Encounters with Angels*, New York: Ballantine 1994; Gustav Davidson, *A Dictionary of Angels*, New York: Simon & Schuster 1994; Malcolm Godwin, *Angels: An Endangered Species*, New York: Simon & Schuster 1990; Megan McKenna, *Angels Unawares*, New York: Orbis 1995; H. C. Moolenburgh, *A Handbook of Angels*, Saffron Walden: C.W. Daniels 1984; John Ronner, *The Angels of Cokeville*, Murfreesboro, TN: Mamre Press 1995

Anglicanism

Anglicanism is the tradition and experiences of a body of Christians around the world, known as the Anglican Communion, who trace their roots to the ancient apostolic church through the Church of England and the See of Canterbury. In 1985, Robert Runcie, the then Archbishop of Canterbury, described Anglicanism like this:

> We have developed into a worldwide family of churches. Today there are 70 million members of what is arguably the second most widely distributed body of Christians. No longer are we identified by having some kind of English heritage. English today is now the second language of the Communion. There are more black members than white. Our local diversities span the spectrum of the world's races, needs, and aspirations. We have only to think of Bishop Tutu's courageous witness in South Africa to be reminded that we are no longer a church of the white middle classes allied only to the prosperous Western world.

At the beginning of the twenty-first century, Anglicans numbered approximately 73 million and were found in 167 countries as members of 38 national or regional churches. Numerically speaking, the largest of the churches in Anglicanism remains the Church of England, with over 20 million members. This number, however, needs to be qualified. Given that the Church of England remains the established church in the country, the national church, individuals are counted as members even if their participation in the life of the church is marginal or non-existent. In reality, the active membership in the Church of England is closer to 1 million, with average Sunday attendance approximately 800,000. The number of active Anglicans in England can be contrasted with active membership in other churches within the Anglican Communion. The Anglican Church in Nigeria, depending on the statistics quoted, has anywhere from 11 to 17 million active members. The phenomenal growth of Anglicanism in Nigeria in the twentieth century has been replicated across the Anglican churches in Africa. As a result, today more Anglicans (approximately 37 million or close to 50 per cent of the global Anglican community) live in Africa south of the Sahara than in any other part of the world.

Church of England

SEE

The word 'see' comes from the Latin *sedes*, 'seat', the chair or throne in his cathedral in which the bishop sits, and which was the first mark of his office. By transference, the city in which the bishop's seat is located is also called see.

Anglicans regularly talk of the See of Canterbury as the focal point of the Anglican Communion; Roman Catholics call the State of the Vatican City, the supreme authority in the Catholic Church in which the Pope has his seat, the Holy See.

The use of the word 'Anglican' in the titles of the churches in the Anglican Communion is a curious reflection of the history and current realities of global Anglicanism today. The Anglican Communion, as a family of churches, is a relatively recent phenomenon. It can be said that the Communion came into being in 1789, when the Episcopal Church in the United States threw off its colonial association with the Church of England and became the first self-governing Anglican church outside the British Isles. The same process of independence and growth was replicated a century and a half later when Anglican mission fields in Africa, Asia, Latin America and the Pacific became free from their colonial ties to England and the United States. Today, a map of the 38 churches in the Anglican Communion reflects the history of expansion of the British empire, with most Anglican churches located in what were previously colonies of England and/or the United States.

Many of the 38 churches in Anglicanism do use the word 'Anglican' as part of their official name, e.g. the Anglican Church of Canada, the Anglican Church of Kenya or the Province of the Anglican Church of South East Asia. Some Anglican churches, on the other hand, use the nomenclature 'episcopal', which describes the key role of bishops in Anglican life and witness, such as the Episcopal Church of Sudan, the Episcopal Church in the USA, or the Episcopal Church in Jerusalem and the Middle East. Still other Anglican churches do not use the words Anglican and Episcopal at all in their titles. This occurs for a variety of reasons, from 'Anglican' being an assumed name (the Church of England, the Church of the Province of the West Indies), to its lack of meaning in translation (Nippon Sei Ko Kai – the Holy Catholic Church in Japan), or because the 'Anglican' church in a particular nation or region has been joined with a wider ecumenical or p. 83 'united' church (the Church of South India, the Church of Pakistan). Whether using the word Anglican or not, the 38 churches of the Anglican Communion represent the living out of the Anglican tradition, or Anglicanism, in the contemporary global context of Christianity.

Given that most churches in the Anglican Communion somehow trace their roots to the Church of England, either directly or through another Anglican church, there is a direct lineage with the established church in England. Most Anglican churches around the world thus share many of the beliefs and practices of the Church of England. Although historically related to the universal church catholic through the Church of England, Anglican churches around the world are intimately connected to the celebration and embrace of the local cultures in which the church is embedded, and their life and witness grow out of it. Ordered public worship in the local vernacular languages has been a hallmark of Anglicanism since the English Reformation, with the translation of the Bible and the creation of a Book of Common Prayer in the language of the people, namely English, as paramount. Most Anglicans in the world today, following this vernacular principle, thus come together to worship God in their own tongue and cultural idiom using the Book of Common Prayer as translated and adapted to their local context. At the same time, English remains the *lingua franca* of Anglicanism. This reflects the close connection between the spread of Anglicanism in the nineteenth and twentieth centuries and the expansion of political and cultural power of the British empire in the same time period.

Anglicanism, consistent with the history and tradition of the established Church of England, has neither a proscribed confession outlining beliefs and doctrines nor a strong central authority structure that dictates norms and practices across the Anglican Communion. Being neither 'confessional' nor 'curial', Anglicanism embraces an elasticity and latitude of theological perspectives and practices that to some seem curiously inconsistent. Indeed, the determination of norms for identity and authority across the global Anglican Communion is hotly contested in Anglicanism today. Although there is a breadth of belief and practice across its 38 churches, there are a few points of reference to which most Anglicans in the world today would subscribe.

In 1886 in Chicago, Illinois, the bishops of the Episcopal Church in the United States, seeking to articulate points of agreement to which all non-Roman Catholic Christians in America could subscribe, articulated four fundamentals for a united Christian ecumenical witness. This 'quadrilateral' was affirmed, with slight revision, at the 1888 gathering of the bishops of the Anglican Communion known as the Lambeth Conference. The 1888 'Chicago-Lambeth Quadrilateral', as the four fundamentals have come to be known, affirms: '(a) The Holy Scriptures of the Old and New Testament, as "containing all things necessary to salvation", and as being the rule and ultimate standard of faith; (b) The Apostles' Creed, as the Baptismal Symbol; and the Nicene Creed, as the sufficient statement of the Christian faith; (c) The two Sacraments ordained by Christ Himself – Baptism and the Supper of the Lord – ministered with unfailing use of Christ's words of Institution, and of the elements ordained by Him; (d) The Historic Episcopate, locally adapted in the methods of its administration to the varying needs of the nations and peoples called of God into the Unity of His Church.' Over time these four tenets, although originally offered as an ecumenical vision of Christian unity, have become four fundamentals to which all Anglicans around the world subscribe.

Not possessing a confession as a point of unity or as a sufficient statement of belief and doctrine, Anglicanism

MEMBER CHURCHES OF THE ANGLICAN COMMUNION

The member churches of the Anglican Communion are as follows:

The Anglican Church in Aotearoa, New Zealand and Polynesia
The Anglican Church of Australia
The Church of Bangladesh
Igreja Episcopal Anglicana do Brasil
The Episcopal Church of Burundi
The Anglican Church of Canada
The Church of the Province of Central Africa
Iglesia Anglicana de la Region Central de America
Province de L'Eglise Anglicane Du Congo
The Church of England
Hong Kong Sheng Kung Hui
The Church of the Province of the Indian Ocean
The Church of Ireland
The Nippon Sei Ko Kai (The Anglican Communion in Japan)
The Episcopal Church in Jerusalem and The Middle East
The Anglican Church of Kenya
The Anglican Church of Korea
The Church of the Province of Melanesia
La Iglesia Anglicana de Mexico
The Church of the Province of Myanmar (Burma)
The Church of Nigeria (Anglican Communion)
The Church of North India (United)
The Church of Pakistan (United)
The Anglican Church of Papua New Guinea
The Episcopal Church in the Philippines
L'Eglise Episcopal au Rwanda
The Scottish Episcopal Church
The Church of the Province of South East Asia
The Church of South India (United)
The Church of the Province of Southern Africa
Iglesia Anglicana del Cono Sur de America
The Episcopal Church of the Sudan
The Anglican Church of Tanzania
The Church of the Province of Uganda
The Episcopal Church in the USA
The Church in Wales
The Church of the Province of West Africa
The Church in the Province of the West Indies
The Church of Ceylon
Iglesia Episcopal de Cuba
Bermuda (Extra-Provincial to Canterbury)
The Lusitanian Church (Extra-Provincial to Canterbury)
The Reformed Episcopal Church of Spain (Extra-Provincial to Canterbury)
Falkland Islands (Province of Canterbury)

'Extra-Provincial to Canterbury' means that the church falls within the Province of Canterbury, though it is not geographically situated there.

www.anglicancommunion.org

tends to a theological method with a certain amount of latitude and messiness. This can be confusing to those who would prefer a more systematic and well-defined approach to theology within Anglicanism. Anglicans do hold the Book of Common Prayer as a central point of unity and common life. While the Book of Common Prayer has been, and continues to be, translated many times in many different contexts around the Anglican Communion 'according to the various exigency of times and occasions', Anglicans the world over share ordered worship as laid down in the Prayer Book. In Anglicanism, then, the Book of Common Prayer stands as a common defining gift that sustains a theological method of *lex orandi lex credendi* (the law of prayer determines the law of belief). Following in the footsteps of the Anglican divine Richard Hooker and informed by his *Treatise on the Laws of Ecclesiastical Polity* (1594–7 with posthumous additions), Anglican beliefs and practices are tested by the three principles of scripture, reason and tradition in determining how the gathered community lives and worships. The local worshipping community, meeting in the parish church, is where the baptized gather to hear the Word of God proclaimed and the sacraments celebrated. Parishes, served by ordained priests and deacons, come together in defined ecclesiastical jurisdictions known as dioceses under the authority and care of a bishop. The manner of gathering dioceses into synods, provinces, and conventions constituting national or regional churches (e.g. the Church of the Province of West Africa, the Church of the Province of the West Indies, or the Anglican Church of South East Asia) varies within Anglicanism depending on the particular church's history or organizational structures.

Anglicanism does not have a single juridical structure that arbitrates relationships across the Anglican Communion. In other words, each church within Anglicanism is technically free to determine its own beliefs and practices. There are, however, expressions of relationship or 'bonds of affection' that tie the churches in Anglicanism into a mutually responsible and interdependent global communion. These 'bonds of affection' have developed over time in such a way that the common life of Anglicanism is expressed in a great variety of both historic and contemporary expressions. Perhaps the oldest

expression of unity in Anglicanism is the Archbishop of Canterbury. The recognition of bishops by the Archbishop of Canterbury is fundamental for Anglican identity. The Archbishop of Canterbury is the titular head of the Anglican Communion, the 'first among equals' of all the bishops within Anglicanism. He does not, however, have direct authority over other bishops in the Anglican Communion outside the Church of England. The Archbishop of Canterbury's capacity to recognize bishops as being in communion with the See of Canterbury, combined with his presidential authority to extend invitations to various inter-Anglican gatherings and make appointments to Communion-wide commissions, give him significant power within global Anglicanism.

One of the oldest and most significant gatherings within Anglicanism, over which the Archbishop of Canterbury presides, is the meeting of the bishops of the Anglican Communion known as the Lambeth Conference. Approximately every ten years, since 1867, the Archbishop of Canterbury has invited Anglican bishops to come together from the four corners of the globe to pray, to worship, and to take counsel together. Originally the bishops met at the abode of the Archbishop of Canterbury in London known as Lambeth Palace (from which the name of the conference is taken). Now, however, the number of bishops in the Anglican Communion has far exceeded the resources of Lambeth Palace. The most recent Lambeth Conference brought together over 750 bishops from around the Anglican Communion and met at the University of Kent in Canterbury for more than two weeks in July and August 1998. Lambeth 1998 issued various reports and agreed to over 100 resolutions, none of which is technically binding on any church in the Anglican Communion unless a particular national or regional church chooses to endorse it through its own legislative processes. Although not able to make binding pronouncements for the Anglican Communion as a whole, the gathering of Anglican bishops from around the world does have significant symbolic power to articulate norms and expectations for beliefs and practice in Anglicanism.

Conferences of bishops are just one form of international gathering within Anglicanism. In the twentieth century there were three significant Pan-Anglican Congresses that brought together lay people, priests and bishops from around the Anglican Communion. The first occurred in London in 1908, and the later two were held outside Great Britain, reflecting the increasing global reach and shift of power in the Anglican Communion. The Anglican Congresses of 1954 in Minneapolis and 1963 in Toronto signalled the beginning of a new contemporary Anglican Communion. Like the Lambeth Conference, Anglican Congresses do not have legislative juridical authority over the Anglican Communion. They do, however, have similar symbolic power, and as such the 1963 Congress was particularly influential. Its declaration entitled *Mutual Responsibility and Interdependence in the Body of Christ* presented a vision for Anglican common life beyond the old one-way giving and receiving norms of nineteenth- and early-twentieth-century missionary practices. In recent years a desire in Anglicanism for another Anglican Congress has emerged and a proposal to bring together lay people, priests and bishops from every diocese in the Anglican Communion in an 'Anglican Gathering', tentatively planned for 2008 in South Africa, has been developed.

Both the Anglican Congress of 1963 and the Lambeth Conference of 1968 recognized the need for increased communication and consultation in the expanding family of churches of the Anglican Communion. In 1971 a new body came into being in Anglicanism known as the Anglican Consultative Council (ACC). The ACC is a representative assembly of lay people, priests and bishops from every church in the Anglican Communion that meets approximately every three years to pray, worship and take counsel together for the common good of the Communion. It is the only legally incorporated entity representing the entire Anglican Communion. Although much smaller numerically than either the Lambeth Conference or an Anglican Congress, with no national or regional church in the Communion having more than three representatives, the ACC functions similarly to the other bodies with respect to reporting and resolutions. Once again, the ACC cannot make a pronouncement binding on any church in the Anglican Communion unless a particular Anglican church chooses to endorse it through its own legislative processes. To date, the ACC has met twelve times in various parts of the Anglican Communion from its first gathering in Limuru, Kenya, to its most recent in Hong Kong in 2002.

In addition to Lambeth Conferences, Anglican Congresses and the meetings of the ACC, another regular meeting, called by and presided over by the Archbishop of Canterbury, has come into being over the last two decades. Beginning in 1979 the 'heads' of the national and regional churches in the Anglican Communion, variously known as archbishops or presiding bishops and commonly referred to as Primates, have also come together regularly for prayer, worship and counsel. The Primates' Meeting originally took place every few years, but recently it has become an annual meeting. Like other inter-Anglican gatherings, the power of the Primates' Meeting resides not in legislative authority over the Communion but in relationships engendered and solidarities developed between the heads of the churches. There are some in the Anglican Communion who would like to see the Primates' Meeting exercise increased control and authority by articulating 'limits of Anglican diversity', but so far such a temptation to increased centralization of power in Anglicanism has been avoided.

Finally, there are a wide variety of both official and unofficial commissions, committees and networks across the Anglican Communion that also embody different forms of common life and witness in Anglicanism. At the official level, there are four 'standing commissions' in the Anglican Communion variously called into being by one or more of regular gatherings of Lambeth, the ACC or the Primates' Meeting. Current commissions are: the Inter Anglican Theological and Doctrinal Commission, the Inter Anglican Standing Commission on Ecumenical Relations, the Inter Anglican Standing Commission on Mission and Evangelism, and the newly-created Inter Anglican Standing Commission on Telecommunications. These commissions meet approximately once a year, report to the regular meetings and gatherings of the Communion such as ACC and the Primates, and their commissioners are broadly drawn from churches throughout the Anglican Communion. In addition to these standing commissions there are various other 'official' consultations, working groups and networks across the Anglican Communion such as, but not limited to: the International Anglican Liturgical Consultations, the Theological Education in the Anglican Communion Task Group, the International Anglican Family Network, the International Anglican Women's Network, the Network for Interfaith Concerns, and the Anglican Indigenous Network. The work of all of these inter-Anglican gatherings, consultations, working groups and networks is facilitated through a modestly staffed and financially strapped Anglican Communion Office located in London. A General Secretary and various programme directors staff the Anglican Communion Office. In addition to this London-based staff there is an Anglican observer at the United Nations in New York who represents the concerns of the Anglican Communion at the United Nations. These official bodies and staff are complemented by various 'unofficial' or independently organized initiatives around the Anglican Communion bringing together a wide variety of individuals and organizations such as missionary agencies and organizations, theologians and theological educators, Mothers' Unions, and those involved in urban ministry.

Questions of authority in the Anglican Communion and the limits of Anglican diversity have been exacerbated of late because of disagreements over issues of human sexuality across the Anglican Communion. On 2 November 2003 Gene Robinson was consecrated bishop of the Episcopal Diocese of New Hampshire in the Episcopal Church in the United States. This was a controversial act because Bishop Robinson is a homosexual man living in a life-long committed relationship with another man. Bishop Robinson's consecration, combined with an increasing openness to the blessing of same-sex relationships in some dioceses/churches of the Anglican Communion, notably the Diocese of New Westminster in the Anglican Church of Canada, has exacerbated differences over biblical interpretation across the Communion, while raising the question whether present organizational structures are adequate for responding in a time of crisis. Thus a primary question before Anglicanism today, addressed by an inter-Anglican 'Lambeth Commission' reporting to the Archbishop of Canterbury in October 2004, was: what are the acceptable limits of Anglican diversity and how will the Anglican Communion continue to live together as a family of interdependent yet self-governing churches that span the diversity of the world's cultural and social contexts? The conclusions were published as the *Windsor Report*.

Taken together, contemporary Anglicanism is a messy lot of Christians who are historically related through the See of Canterbury but who seek to love and serve God in their various locales and contexts as mutually responsible and interdependent sisters and brothers in Christ. In any family, tensions among siblings are bound to arise, and the Anglican family of churches is no different. Recent disagreements over the ordination of women and human sexuality have indeed created new tensions within global Anglicanism that threaten to splinter the Anglican Communion. At the same time, Anglicans around the world have increasingly discovered a new level of common witness, activism and solidarity, specifically in efforts in evangelism and in addressing the crushing concerns of international debt and the HIV/AIDS pandemic. The future of Anglicanism thus lies not in the many meetings and gatherings that occur across the Anglican Communion, nor in a shared heritage and relationship with the See of Canterbury, as important as these realities are. Rather, the future of Anglicanism rests in the Anglican Communion's common service and faithfulness to God's mission of reconciliation and restoration in a hurting and broken world.

IAN T. DOUGLAS

p. 836

Ian T. Douglas and Kwok Pui Lan (eds), *Beyond Colonial Anglicanism: The Anglican Communion in the Twenty-First Century*, New York: Church Publishing, Inc. 2001; Stephen C. Neill, *Anglicanism*, Oxford: OUP [4]1978; Frederick Quinn, *To Be a Pilgrim: The Anglican Ethos in History*, New York: Crossroad 2001; Stephen Sykes, John Booty and Jonathan Knight (eds), *The Study of Anglicanism*, London: SPCK 1998; Andrew Wingate, Kevin Ward, Carrie Pemberton and Wilson Sitshebo (eds), *Anglicanism: A Global Communion*, London: Mowbray 1998

Animals

Enlightenment p. 627

The way in which human beings treat animals has become a topical issue in moral philosophy. Since the 1970s, a wide range of books and articles have appeared challenging the traditional view that animals have no moral status, and most have been sharply critical of practices such as intensive farming and animal experimentation. This interest, largely generated by philosophy, has helped to spur on new generations of animal advocates who have taken animal rights into the political arena and been vocal for fundamental change.

One of the major philosophers associated with this movement, Peter Singer, attributes the moral neglect of animals to the indifference of the Christian tradition, and he is not alone in his judgement. Many philosophers and activists lament the historical record of Christianity. They point to the high, indeed exalted, position of humanity in creation embedded in biblical texts, and to the notion of 'dominion' specifically in Genesis as examples of how Christian thinking is irredeemably 'speciesist' in its attitude to other creatures. ('Speciesism' is defined as the arbitrary favouring of one species over another.)

There is force in the complaint that the right treatment of animals has been only a marginal issue in Christian ethics – at least, possibly, until recently. But in order to understand this apparent dismissal of animals, we need to understand how the shape of historical theology evolved in such a way that animals were precluded from impartial consideration.

The historic view

In his widely-read textbook, *Moral Philosophy*, published in 1889, the Jesuit Joseph Rickaby wrote: 'Brute beasts, not having understanding and therefore not being persons, cannot have any rights. We have no duties of charity or duties of any kind to the lower animals, as neither to stocks and stones ... Brutes are things in our regard.' Doubtless Rickaby's views were extreme even for his age. But they do highlight the major historical influences. Animals are deemed non-rational, hence they are not 'persons' with immortal souls. They are thus excluded from the sphere of direct obligation, which extends only to other humans. Even whether they suffer is debatable.

All these notions are found, to a greater or lesser extent, in the earliest Christian thinkers. Both Augustine and Thomas Aquinas regarded animals as non-rational. Thomas specifically denied that we have any duty to love animals or any moral obligation towards them apart from the prevention of direct cruelty, and only then if it brutalized the human perpetrator. All the classical Christian thinkers, including Augustine, Thomas Aquinas, Martin Luther and John Calvin, denied that animals have immortal souls. And René Descartes took that view even further by his scepticism about animal sentience. Animals, he held, were intricate machines devoid of self-consciousness. Without self-consciousness, indeed any consciousness at all, suffering was deemed illusory.

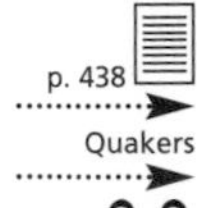

p. 438 Quakers

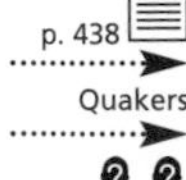

In case it is thought that these influences have melted away under the weight of post-Enlightenment thinking, it is worth noting that the *Catholic Catechism*, published in 1994, still retains echoes of earlier thought. Humans owe animals 'kindness' – which is certainly a departure from standard Thomism – but otherwise it is morally right to use animals for food, clothing, work and leisure, and also to experiment on animals 'if it remains within [unspecified] reasonable limits'. It is wrong to cause animals to suffer or die needlessly, but only because it is 'contrary to human dignity'. Most revealingly: 'It is likewise unworthy to spend money on them [animals] that should as a priority go to the relief of human misery. One can love animals; one should not direct to them the affection due only to persons' (24.16–18). In short: while 'kindness' is virtuous, animals still retain a largely, or wholly, instrumental value for human beings. Indeed, the *Catechism* declares that 'God willed creation as a gift addressed to man ...' (299). We have no direct obligation to animals. Our 'stewardship' means that we can use them, with very little restraint, for human purposes even when suffering is involved. Moreover, the needs of human beings are paramount. It is difficult to see how any situation of animal suffering, no matter how dire, could trump the stated prior obligation to relieve 'human misery'.

Given these influences, both historical and contemporary, it is hardly surprising that animals have failed to emerge as a strong topic of moral concern among contemporary churches. But it would be wrong to leave the matter there – as if the Christian tradition was incapable of change or of reforming itself. There have been, and still are, movements both of thought and practice which promise a more positive estimate of animal life.

Christ-like suffering

Although some voices within the tradition have denied that animals suffer, or, if they do, that their pain is not analogous to what humans endure, there has been a vocal sub-tradition which has opposed – on explicitly Christian grounds – the infliction of suffering. One major focus of what might be loosely termed the 'humanitarian movement' of the nineteenth century was the alleviation of specifically animal suffering. A wide range of Christian voices supported the anti-cruelty cause: for example, the evangelical Clapham Sect denounced sports such as bull-baiting and cock-fighting, as did the Quakers, who resolved as early as 1795 'against the practices of hunting and shooting for diversion ... let our leisure be employed in serving our neighbour, and not in distressing, for our amusement, the creatures of God'.

In a similar way, the founder of Methodism, John Wesley, opposed hunting and coursing, and also urged his congregations to care for their domestic animals. Exceptionally, he also preached in defence of animal immortality. An Anglican priest, Arthur Broome, founded the first national animal welfare society in the world, the English Society for the Protection of Cruelty to Animals (as it then was) in 1824. The Unitarian Frances Power Cobbe, together with the leading evangelical Lord Shaftesbury and Dr George Hogan, founded the British Union for the Abolition of Vivisection in 1886 to campaign for the end of animal experiments.

The theological rationale for this upsurge in sensitivity was best stated, perhaps unwittingly, by John Henry Newman in a sermon on the crucifixion preached on Good Friday at Oxford in 1842. Contemplating reports of cruelty to animals, Newman argues that what should 'move our very hearts and sicken us' is the realization that animals are morally innocent, 'that they have done no harm. Next that they have no power whatever of resisting; it is the cowardice and tyranny of which they are the victims that makes their suffering so especially touching ... there is something so very dreadful, so satanic in tormenting those who have never harmed us and who cannot defend themselves, who are utterly in our power, who have weapons neither of offence nor defence ...' And he concludes: 'Think then, my brethren, of your feelings at cruelty practised on brute animals, and you will gain one sort of feeling which the history of Christ's Cross and Passion ought to excite within you.' In other words, there is a Christ-likeness about the innocent suffering of animals (and also, Newman argues, about the suffering of children as well). Indeed, a moral equivalence is suggested: 'For what was this [cruelty inflicted on innocents] but the very suffering inflicted on our Lord?,' asks Newman.

Although there has been a paucity of theological reflection on the meaning of animal suffering, there are some developments that could harbinger a new orientation. Chief among them is the renewed emphasis upon the suffering of God in modern theology, most obviously associated with Jürgen Moltmann's landmark work, *The Crucified God*. In this theology, we are invited to see Christ's cross as the embodiment of God's co-suffering presence, which extends, at least in principle, to all creatures. If, as Moltmann suggests, 'God has made the suffering of the world his own in the Cross of his Son,' then it follows that *all* creaturely suffering – including that of animals – has been redeemed – at least in principle – through the Cross of Christ. Not only is the alleviation of suffering a Christ-like work; the specifically human task is to become co-redeemers of the burden of suffering which afflicts the animal world. Human beings are the servant species called to reflect and actualize God's redeeming purposes for all creation.

Liberating life

The second development that promises some theological reinforcement for a new perspective is provided by liberation theology. Although it must be said that its main exponents, namely Gustavo Gutiérrez, Leonardo Boff and Jon Sobrino, have been overwhelmingly concerned with human liberation, its core concern for the vulnerable and the oppressed resonates with those struggling for the liberation of animals from unjust treatment. If belief in God requires an urgent commitment to the establishment of justice, indeed is inseparable from it, then it is difficult to see how the wrongs inflicted on millions of fellow creatures can be left out of account. Gutiérrez acknowledges that liberation has primarily a christological sense: '*all* things have been created in Christ, *all* things have been saved in him (Col. 1.5–20)', but he fails to develop Paul's insight that the whole suffering creation – both human and non-human – is to be saved from bondage to decay (Romans 8.18–24). If only liberation theology had placed the liberation of humans within the wider, biblical context of the liberation of all life, then it could have provided a new impetus to regard animal suffering as a theological issue. This neglect is also evident in Boff's discussion of one of the most animal-friendly saints, Francis of Assisi. He understands even the example of Francis in a way that is centred wholly on human beings.

Liberation theology

Liberation theology is sometimes dismissed as 'advocacy theology', namely an attempt to utilize theology in order to advocate political or social change. But in fact almost all theology has – or should have – such a role. Correctly understood, all theology is moral theology in the sense that it is rooted in, and orientated towards, the fulfilment of this life in another. 'On earth as it is in heaven,' is the prayer of Jesus. What theology therefore expresses is some imagination, or lack of it, of what divine justice means for all God's creatures. In the light of God's generous work as Creator, exclusive moral preoccupation with the human species should seem parochial.

The earth as God's body

That insight has been championed in various ways by the third important development, ecological theology. One of the strengths of ecological theology is the way in which it overcomes the false dichotomy between 'flesh' and 'spirit' which has characterized historical theology. Ecotheologians seek to rediscover the sacredness of 'earthly things', including flesh and soil. Instead of being seen as wholly other and transcendent, God is to be located immanently in the glories of creation. Traditional

Ecotheology

theology, which speaks of incarnation, is offered a wider paradigm: the world as God's body. Sallie McFague is perhaps the most influential exponent of this view. Her work *The Body of God: An Ecological Theology* (1993) has been justifiably praised for helping Christians to reconnect with the earth, and for putting respect for nature on the church's moral agenda.

But McFague's approach – and that of other eco-theologians – is not unambiguously animal-friendly. In rediscovering the goodness of the earth, ecotheologians seem over-eager to embrace the notion of nature as 'red in tooth and claw' as God-given. McFague writes of how, 'If the earth is our home, then we need to attend to some of its most basic house rules'; but to discover certain natural processes is one thing, to regard them as normative is another. In the more extreme form provided by Matthew Fox, 'eat and be eaten' is the 'law of the Universe'. One is tempted to suggest that human beings might think differently if they were the subjects of predation.

Covenant ➤

The issue of predation in the natural world presents Christian theology with the obvious difficulty of how it can be reconciled with the loving God revealed in Jesus Christ. But however we may explain the contradiction, the issue is not adequately resolved by simply accepting it, or pretending that it presents no moral or theological difficulty. A similar problem can be discerned in the attempt by ecotheologians to deify the whole created world. Anne Primavesi expresses it this way: 'If nature is seen as "not God", then this licenses human control over it.' But if God is literally to be identified with everything in the world, then the possibility of redemption – including the redemption of animals from suffering and parasitism – is eclipsed. God cannot, logically, redeem him or herself!

Gay and lesbian theology ➤
Feminist theology ➤

The challenge of animal theology

While being some improvement on traditional understandings, these developments still do not offer an adequate account of animal life. Most centrally, they fail to provide a sufficiently theological, i.e. God-ward, view of animals as distinct from a purely humanistic one. To understand the force of this point, one needs to remember that Christianity – for almost all of its history – has regarded animals as being there simply for human use: as commodities, resources, tools, things. This 'instrumentalist' view still abounds, and manifests itself in acts of wanton cruelty in countries where conservative religious traditions are most prevalent: for example, bull-fighting and fiestas in Spain, hare coursing in Ireland, and 'sport hunting' (even 'Christian' bow hunting) in many states in the USA. If there is to be a better world for animals, then Christians need to break out of the traditional view that animals are here just for us and embrace the wider, more theological, view that they have value in themselves because they matter to the Creator.

A great deal of Christian thinking is still absurdly humano-centric: it assumes that the earth is made for human beings and humans are the only species that God really cares about. Critical reflection on biblical perspectives can – and should – provide some correctives. Although the Bible is not unambiguously friendly to either human or animal rights, there is a range of positive insights that need to be rediscovered and appropriated, for example: animals are fellow creatures; they have a value to God independently of their value to us; God's covenant extends to all living beings; human beings are accountable to God for their treatment of animals, and, most significantly, God's creating and redeeming love extends to all creatures. Indeed, if humans are made in the 'image of God' – and this same God is holy, loving and just – it follows that human dominion must similarly be loving and just.

These, and other, insights have been developed by an emerging group of 'animal theologians', such as Andrew Linzey, Stephen H. Webb, Stephen R. L. Clark, Jay B. McDaniel, John B. Cobb, Jr, Charles Birch, Lukas Vischer and John Berkman. They offer creative ways in which theology can address its own human-centred limitations, and facilitate a wider vision of peaceableness than the tradition has so far espoused. The challenge is whether Christian thinking can now offer an account of other creatures that begins to do justice to their Creator. If that sounds a tall order, it is worth remembering that Christianity has always – to some extent – been reinventing itself. Whether it can do so in the case of animals, as it once did in the case of slaves, has yet to do in the case of gays and lesbians, and is still trying to do in the case of women – is, as yet, unclear.

ANDREW LINZEY

📖 Charles Birch and Lukas Vischer, *Living with the Animals: The Community of God's Creatures*, Geneva: WCC Publications 1997; Stephen R. L. Clark, *The Moral Status of Animals*, Oxford: Clarendon Press 1977; Andrew Linzey, *Animal Theology*, London: SCM Press and Chicago: University of Illinois Press 1994 and *Animal Gospel*, London: Hodder & Stoughton, and Louisville, KY: Westminster John Knox Press 1999; Andrew Linzey and Dorothy Yamamoto (eds), *Animals on the Agenda: Questions about Animals for Theology and Ethics*, London: SCM Press and Chicago: University of Illinois Press 1998; Norm Phelps, *The Dominion of Love: Animal Rights According to the Bible*, New York: Lantern Books 2002; Stephen H. Webb, *On God and Dogs: A Christian Theology of Compassion for Animals*, New York: OUP 1998

Apocalyptic

Today, the word 'apocalypse' is likely first of all to conjure up the image of a threatening swarm of helicopters flying up the Mekong River over napalm-devastated Vietnam to the music of Wagner's 'Ride of the Valkyries' in Francis Ford Coppola's famous film *Apocalypse Now*. Or the doom-ridden scenarios of Hal Lindsey's *Late Great Planet Earth*, with its interpretation of current events in the Middle East as the prelude to an Armageddon, a devastating war which will all but destroy the planet and bring in the end time. Or, for those who know them, the enormous canvases of the early Victorian painter John Martin with their unique vision of cataclysmic devastation by fire, flood or earthquake, made all the more terrifying by the single figure often depicted as a spectator (see colour plate 1).

The word 'apocalypse', however, derived from the Greek *apokalypsis*, does not in fact originally denote the cataclysmic end of the world, but an 'unveiling', or 'revelation', a means whereby one gains insight into divine mysteries relating to the present, or to a particular historical situation. It offers the alternative perspective of God's own view. In Judaism and Christianity the term apocalypse denotes a particular literary type found in the literature of ancient Judaism, characterized by claims to offer visions or other disclosures of divine mysteries concerning a variety of subjects. Cataclysmic events described in these texts are also labelled 'apocalyptic'. We may best understand the enormous variety of material in the apocalypses, however, if we consider them not as eschatological tracts satisfying the curiosity of those who wanted to know what would happen in the future but as revelations of divine secrets whose unveiling will enable readers to view their present situation from a completely different perspective. Thus an apocalypse is to be read as not just being about disaster or the last days; it is applicable to every age, offering a way of discerning significant theological moments in history.

There are two apocalypses in the Bible, the book of Daniel in the Old Testament and the Revelation to John in the New Testament (often called the Apocalypse). However, they are only part of a far wider apocalyptic literature extending from the second century BCE to well into the Christian era, most of which has not survived. Some of it was translated into languages like Slavonic and Ethiopic, and has come down to us in that form; fragments of apocalyptic books have been found at Qumran among the Dead Sea Scrolls. The most important non-biblical apocalypse is the Apocalypse of Enoch, but there are also apocalypses of Baruch (Jeremiah's scribe), Abraham, Adam and Elijah, among others.

The titles of these apocalypses already indicate one distinctive feature of the literature: the revelations in them are received by figures from the past, often the very distant past. Even Daniel is presented as a Jewish exile at the Babylonian court of the sixth century BCE (the Revelation to John is an exception here). This device makes it possible for the key characters to present accounts of the future apparently from their own day, forecasting future events the occurrence of which can be verified. (The approximate date at which the apocalypses were composed can usually be determined from the point at which specific references to historical events give way to vague predictions.) The revelations are conveyed by dreams and visions, and make use of a great variety of symbols, notably animal and numerical symbols (in Daniel 7 four great beasts come out of the sea: a lion with eagle's wings, a bear, a leopard with four wings and four heads, and a terrible beast with ten horns, followed by a figure in human form who is presented to God, the Ancient of Days; all these inspire the picture of the blasphemous beast in Revelation 13, which is given the mysterious number 666). In the predictions, oppression and suffering is followed by the victory of God and the establishment of God's rule.

Symbols

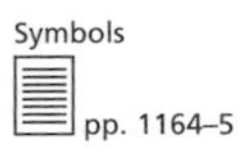

pp. 1164–5

Revelation

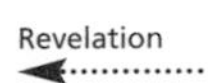

Apocalyptic has obvious links with the successors to the prophetic texts of the Hebrew Bible, and particularly with the future hope of the prophets. The concern with human history and the vindication of Israel's hopes echo prophetic themes, drawn particularly from the books of Ezekiel, Daniel and Zechariah. It has been suggested that a subtle change takes place in the form of that hope in the apocalyptic literature as compared with most of the prophetic texts in the Bible. It is placed on another plane, the supernatural and other-worldly (e.g. Isaiah 65–6, compare Revelation 21 and 4 Ezra 7.50). But evidence for such a change from the earthly to the supra-mundane is not in fact as widespread as is often alleged. More important is the subtle change of prophetic genre in the later chapters of Ezekiel, with its visions of a new Jerusalem, and the emergence of highly symbolic visions in the early chapters of Zechariah and the cataclysmic upheavals of its last chapters and the probably late eschatological chapters of Isaiah 24–7 and 55–6.

Prophecy

Eschatology

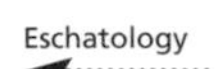

Bible

Antecedents of apocalyptic have also been found in the wisdom tradition of the Hebrew Bible, with its interest in understanding the cosmos and the ways of the world. Apocalyptic is concerned with divine wisdom, not only of the age to come but also of things in heaven (e.g. 1 Enoch 72ff.) and the mysteries of human existence, akin to features of the wisdom literature. The ability to practise astrology and to interpret dreams, oracles and divine mysteries relating to future events was attributed to certain wise men in antiquity. There is some trace of the role of such figures in the Hebrew Bible, e.g., in the Joseph stories in Genesis, and in the early chapters of Daniel. But the most obvious 'apocalyptic' or revelatory moment in the Wisdom corpus is the opening and dramatic climax

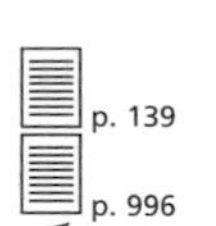

p. 139
p. 996

p. 845

of the book of Job. This climax enables Job's entirely reasonable stance to be transcended, and for Job to move from understanding on the basis of hearsay to understanding based on apocalyptic insight (Job 42.5).

The Book of Revelation has probably had more effect on Christian doctrine, art and literature than almost any other. No other biblical book has been treated at such breadth at every period of Christian history and the Fundamentalism main contours of the interpretation of it were already set within the earliest period of Christianity. It only occasionally prompts a quest for the meaning of the mysteries it describes (e.g. 17.9, compare 1.20 and 10.4). In this respect it is remarkably different from its counterpart in the Hebrew Bible, the book of Daniel, which is replete with the detailed elucidation of its apocalyptic allusions. Nevertheless, it has prompted scores of ingenious attempts to unlock its mysteries. Revelation, along with other prophetic books, has been used to interpret history. Here it hardly ever functions on its own but as part of a sophisticated pastiche of scriptural passages, to offer an eschatological scenario of a cataclysmic kind that despairs of human or political transformation in this age. So it has been treated as a complex prediction of the end of the world, having no connection with present ecclesiastical and political realities.

It can also be read against its original first-century context and attempts can be made to decipher its complex symbolism and its relationship to the particular circumstances in which Christians in late first-century CE Asia Minor found themselves. It can be seen as an allegory of the struggles facing the individual soul in its quest for p. 852 God. Or it can be applied to present realities, whether human or divine, as an interpretative lens with which to view contemporary history. Here it is not a matter of trying to apply the text to current events but rather seeing it as a gateway to a greater understanding of reality, divine and human, spiritual and political, which includes, but transcends, that offered by the human senses. In this way Revelation becomes a means of interpreting every age of human existence.

As a prophetic book, Revelation has offered space for women and men to enable their spiritual vocations to flourish, whether or not they are regarded as theologically qualified according to the canons of this age. The prophets and the mystics have found in it an inspiration to explore the inner life and to exercise a ministry denied by much else in scripture and tradition. Men and women radicals who have turned to it have found in its allusive text a licence to resist received religion and practice precisely because here a book of the Bible opens up a door for an experience of God which enables them to transcend the boundaries imposed by what was conventionally possible. The visionary appropriation of scripture offers the opportunity to 'see again' what had appeared to prophets and seers in the past or become a means of prompting new visions leading to discernment of higher spiritual realities.

The imagery functions in a way very similar to a modern political cartoon, challenging the presumptions of power and its oppressive consequences. The ubiquity of such an approach in Christian history is itself a reminder that the modern fundamentalist interpretation which sees the book as a road map to the end of the world is not the only way of reading it, and that for centuries it has served a very different, and more fruitful, purpose.

CHRISTOPHER ROWLAND

R. Bauckham, *The Theology of the Book of Revelation*, Cambridge: CUP 1993; I. Boxall, *Revelation: Vision and Insight*, London: SPCK 2002; J. H. Charlesworth, *The Old Testament Pseudepigrapha 1: Apocalyptic Literature and Testaments*, New York: Doubleday and London: Darton, Longman & Todd 1983; J. J. Collins, B. McGinn and S. Stein (eds), *Encyclopedia of Apocalypticism* (3 vols), New York: Continuum 2000; C. Rowland and J. Kovacs, *The Apocalypse, The Book of Revelation*, Blackwell Bible Commentaries, Oxford: Blackwell 2003

Archaeology

In 2002 an ossuary, a stone box used to contain the bones of the dead, dated to around 62 CE, was found with the inscription 'James, son of Joseph, brother of Jesus'. It was immediately hailed as the first ever contemporary artefact specifically to mention Jesus and thus as the most important discovery in New Testament archaeology, and was widely publicized in magazines and learned journals. However, even when the excitement was at its height, more sober scholars were pointing out that 'James, Joseph and Jesus' were as common names as 'Tom, Dick and Harry' in first-century Jerusalem, and that the association with James the brother of the Lord and Jesus of Nazareth was far from certain. A year later the antique dealer who owned the box was arrested for forgery, and all the hypotheses that had been built on the ossuary crumbled away.

Great expectations are attached to archaeological exploration. Indeed the discovery of evidence that would substantiate the Bible, along with the desire to collect valuable works of art from a past civilization, was the motive power behind its origin. The quest goes back a long way. For example Helena, mother of the Roman emperor Constantine, travelled in 326–8 CE to the Holy Land, where legend has it that she discovered the true cross; consequently she has even been called 'the first Christian archaeologist'. The search for relics and the wish to locate and visit places mentioned in the Bible, particularly in connection with the life of Jesus, have marked the history of Christianity.

However, modern archaeology is above all a systematic discipline that attempts to paint a much wider picture. It sets out to reconstruct life in past societies and settlements, the changes that took place in them, and the events which affected them, by making deductions from buildings, artefacts and other remains. Whatever interesting individual items may emerge in the process, it is the overall picture that is important.

The archaeology of Christianity can be said to have begun in the sixteenth century, when one Antonio Bosio (1575–1629) spent his life investigating the ancient Roman cemeteries, the catacombs. The results of his researches were published in 1632 in a book entitled *Roma sotterranea.* However, his work was widely ignored, and it would be more than two centuries until its concerns would be taken up again. Meanwhile, Christian antiquities were often being destroyed rather than investigated and preserved. It was Giovanni Battista di Rossi (1822–94) who produced a second *Roma sotterranea* in three volumes, and at the same time founded a journal of Christian archaeology and left a school of pupils to carry on his work. All this laid the foundation for reconstructing the life of the early Christians in Rome and interpreting early Christian art.

By contrast, archaeological investigation of the lands of the Bible began much later. It was preceded by journeys of discovery by intrepid explorers, like Edward Daniel Clarke, who travelled around the Holy Land at the very beginning of the nineteenth century in search of genuine biblical sites (he was very sceptical about the authenticity of the traditional sites that he was shown), and Edward Robinson and Eli Smith, who in the 1830s began the long process of constructing a map of ancient Palestine to superimpose on the present map, thus making it possible to identify and later excavate key towns and cities. Soon afterwards, archaeological societies were formed, and since then with major European and American universities and other foundations they have carried on a vast number of investigations, making it possible to build up a picture of life in the Near East which is steadily becoming more detailed.

Archaeology is a complex business. It begins with mapping and fieldwork, i.e. the examination of sites without actually excavating them; here aerial photography is invaluable. Then comes excavation, in which stratigraphy is crucial: in other words the different layers of remains in a site are carefully identified and dated, so that its history can be determined. This dating is established above all by the identification of different types of pottery which belong to different periods. More sophisticated

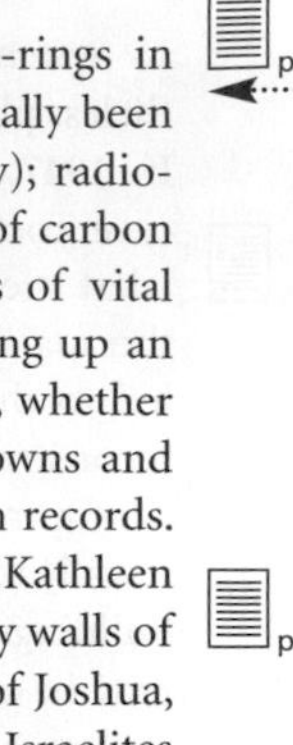
p. 1075

dating can be achieved by measuring the tree-rings in wooden objects against a scale which has gradually been established (this is known as dendrochronology); radiocarbon dating works by measuring the decline of carbon 14, present in all living things. Chronology is of vital importance for archaeology, not only for building up an overall framework, but also for establishing, say, whether evidence of the habitation or destruction of towns and cities matches up with what is related in written records. For example, the famous English archaeologist Kathleen Kenyon established that the demolition of the city walls of Jericho, thought to have taken place in the time of Joshua, in fact happened 1000 years before he led the Israelites into the promised land (Joshua 6), and Ai, which he is also said to have destroyed (Joshua 8), was uninhabited at the time.

p. 135

p. 325

In the middle of the twentieth century, archaeology in the Near East was dominated by the American scholar William Foxwell Albright, who created what came to be known as biblical archaeology by combining archaeology with biblical studies and historical geography, in an area extending from Syria-Palestine to Egypt and Mesopotamia. However, strictly speaking there is no such thing as biblical archaeology, or Christian archaeology: archaeology is a discipline in its own right, and in any case most of the light it sheds on the Bible, Jesus and Christian origins is indirect.

Exploration

Positively, archaeology enables us to picture, for example, life in Palestine at the time of Jesus or in the thriving cities at the eastern end of the Mediterranean in which Paul carried out his mission. Sometimes quite dramatic discoveries are made, like that in 1986 at Kinneret on the Sea of Galilee of a boat of the type used by fishermen at the time of Jesus. In 1968 the bones of a crucified man were found in a burial cave north-east of Jerusalem, bearing the marks of nails. But this evidence is only illustrative: there are no direct links with Jesus. A closer connection with the New Testament was provided by an inscription discovered in Delphi at the end of the nineteenth century that mentions one Gallio as proconsul of Achaea in 51 or 52 CE. In the Acts of the Apostles (18.12–17) Jews are said unsuccessfully to have brought Paul before Gallio's tribunal. The dating provided by the inscription gives us a firm chronological point of reference for Paul's activities, which the New Testament account lacks.

Paul

Negatively, as in the case of Jericho and Ai, archaeology can rule out traditional locations and datings. For example, what is pointed out as the tomb of Lazarus in Bethany does not seem to be a tomb, nor can it be dated to the first century. Question marks similarly hang over the holy places pointed out in connection with Jesus in Nazareth, the site of Golgotha and the tomb known as the Holy Sepulchre.

Systematic though archaeology may be, chance nevertheless plays a very great part in archaeological discoveries. In 1947, Bedouin looking for a lost goat came upon a cave containing jars of manuscripts that proved to be what are now known as the Dead Sea Scrolls, perhaps the major find of the twentieth century. This discovery led to the excavation of the neighbouring area and the reconstruction of the life of a distinctive Jewish religious community. Similarly, in urban sites where archaeology is usually impossible, excavations for the foundations of new buildings sometimes uncover ancient remains, and there may be a pause in the work to enable them to be studied and recorded. So further striking archaeological discoveries may be made, particularly since only a tiny fraction of Near Eastern sites, in an area so often torn by conflict, have yet been investigated.

p. 845

JOHN BOWDEN

W. F. Albright, *The Archaeology of Palestine*, Harmondsworth: Penguin Books 1960; John J. Rousseau and Rami Arav, *Jesus and his World. An Archaeological and Cultural Dictionary*, Minneapolis: Fortress Press and London: SCM Press 1996; William H. Stiebing, *Uncovering the Past*, New York: OUP 1994; George Ernest Wright, *Biblical Archaeology*, Philadelphia: Westminster Press 1960

Architecture

From late antiquity until the beginning of the twentieth century, the history of Western architecture has been seen as the history of Christian architecture. During that period, at least, ecclesiastical style has consistently been representative of the age.

Little is left of pre-Constantinian edifices either used or built by early Christians. This is partly a result of persecution, but also because active, successful and growing communities adapted their buildings continually and so thoroughly that only archaeological remains, scanty and difficult to interpret, are to be found in the lower levels of churches still in use. This is the case with some of the title-churches in Rome. These churches were first of all private houses in which Christians met, which had the name of the owner inscribed on a slab, Latin *titulus*, at the door, hence the name. One church in which remains can be found is San Clemente. The sole exception to this rule is the building converted for Christian use at Dura Europos in Syria.

Initiation

If architecture is to be distinguished from buildings, then Christian architecture, at least as it comes down to us, begins with Constantine and the 'Peace of the Church'. With the gift to the Pope of his Lateran Palace and the building of a basilica (the type of large public hall common in the Roman world) to serve as the cathedral of Rome, the status of Christianity (and its adherents) changed from the religion of a small minority to the object of imperial favour. The marks of Christian identity were extended, if not totally transformed. From a 'family' gathering, the eucharist developed in line with court ceremonial in the new architectural context of the basilica. Neither architectural nor artistic style were independent and distinctively Christian, but rather borrowed from the surrounding culture, with narrative in art only gradually gaining very particularly Christian interpretation. An early example of this is Sta Costanza which, reputedly being the burial chapel for Constantine's daughter, is in the usual circular form of a martyrium. The mosaics of the vaulting can be read either as straightforwardly classical designs, or the putti pressing grapes can be invested with Christian meaning. The late fourth-century mosaics in the chapels off the ambulatory have a more explicitly Christian narrative, showing Christ giving the keys to Peter and the law to Paul.

In its Christian version the basilica is a three- or five-aisled nave (a long hall) with a transept (a large place for clergy across the front of the nave) and apse (the half-domed area terminating the space that housed the altar). The quintessential Roman basilica was St Peter's, built over the tomb of the martyr between 320 and 340 at the base of the Vatican hill. The long nave and double aisles on either side were separated by four rows of 22 columns each. The roof was stepped so that the nave dominated the exterior elevations as well. At the east end of the nave was a transept and apse, and the whole was encompassed by a single decorative treatment. Just as the empire had Romanized the world, so the church adopted the current style and over several generations Christianized the empire.

The altar was not the only focal point for worship. It became necessary to incorporate baptisteries (fonts for the baptism of believers) into the architectural plans. Early baptisteries were built separate from basilica spaces because the ceremonies were considered private and mystically important in the lives of believers. Therefore the architecture for baptism took the shape of baths and memorial shrines, and baptisteries were usually built next to the basilicas. Normally, they had sunken pools at the centre and types of decoration that emphasized that baptism was an initiation into the Christian life.

In 330 Constantine transferred his capital to Byzantium on the Bosphorus and named it Constantinople. It became the centre of the Byzantine empire until it fell to the Turks in 1453. The city was to be the new Rome, but it was half destroyed in the Nika Riots of 532, directed against the emperor, and with it the churches of the Holy Wisdom,

ARCHITECTURAL FEATURES OF CHURCHES

Church buildings differ widely in their architectural features, depending on the period in which they were built and the tradition to which they belong. Here are the names for some of these features.

Aisle: Part of a church parallel to the nave of the church and separated from it by pillars.

Ambulatory: A semicircular aisle enclosing an apse, used in processions.

Apse: A vaulted end to a church, semi-circular or polygonal, at the east end.

Baptistery: A building containing the font and usually separate from the church.

Belfry: The upper level in a tower in which bells are hung. It comes from the Old French *berfrei* (tower) and has no connection with 'bell'.

Campanile: Italian word for bell tower, usually standing separate from the church.

Chancel: Part of the east end of the church containing the main altar and the places where the choir and clergy sit.

Chantry: A chapel in or adjoining a church, for the celebration of masses for the soul of whoever gave money for it to be built.

Chapel: An area within a church with a separate altar, in honour of a particular saint or the Virgin Mary (Lady Chapel). Chapel can also be used of a whole building: for example part of a school, college or hospital, a church in private hands, or, most commonly in the United Kingdom, of the buildings used by Non-conformists, as opposed to parish churches.

Chapter house: A building, attached to a cathedral by cloisters, usually octagonal, where the chapter, the administrative body of the cathedral, meets.

Choir: The part of the church where the choir sits, usually in the chancel.

Clerestory: The upper part of the main walls of a church, above the roofs of the aisles and containing a row of windows.

Cloister: An enclosed rectangular space surrounded by pavements to walk on, with a colonnade or arcade usually looking out on a garden on the inside and a plain wall on the outside.

Crossing: The place where the nave, chancel and transepts of a church meet.

Crypt: An area below a church, usually containing graves or relics.

Iconostasis: A screen in Byzantine churches separating the sanctuary from the nave, with three doors in it. It is usually a wooden or stone wall covered with icons, from which it takes its name.

Lych gate: A covered wooden gateway at the entrance to a churchyard, where the coffin could be rested (*lych* is Saxon for a corpse).

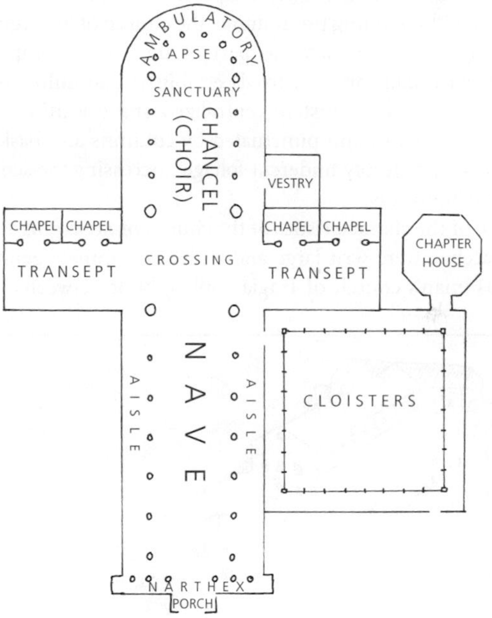

Narthex: A vestibule running across the nave, separated from it by columns or a wall.

Nave: The main area of the church, often with aisles either side of it.

Porch: The covered entry to a doorway; it is also called a portico if it has columns, like a temple.

Sacristy: A room in a church where vessels and vestments used at the eucharist are kept.

Sanctuary: The area around the main altar of a church.

Spire: A tall structure rising from the tower of a church and ending in a point.

Transept: The arms of a church with a cross-shaped ground plan, usually extending between the nave and the chancel.

Triforium: A passage in the wall with arcades, facing into the nave below the clerestory.

Undercroft: A vaulted room below a church. Another name for crypt.

Vestry: A room where the clergy robe for worship. Representatives of a parish used to meet in the vestry to transact the business of the parish, so the term also came to be applied to them as a body.

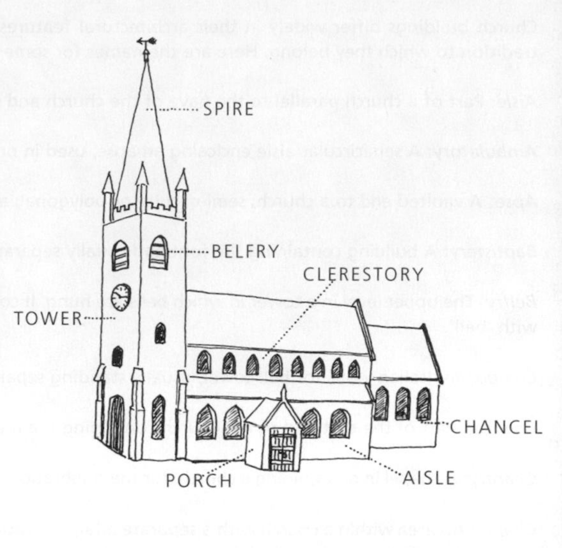

Holy Peace, and the Twelve Apostles. In the Emperor Justinian's rebuilding programme, the church of St Sergius and St Bacchus (which was part of the palace complex where Justinian formerly lived) established an influential pattern. It was an austere centralized space wafting up through galleries and punctuated by columns and basket capitals with deeply undercut foliage, increasing the sense of weightlessness.

All of the characteristics of the church of St Sergius and St Bacchus were writ large and with consummate genius in Justinian's church of Hagia Sophia, built between 532 and 537. From the outside the domes and half-domes billow upwards, enclosing a vast space lined with glinting marble and mosaics. The central space was reserved for the clergy and the imperial party. The empress and ladies of the court occupied the western gallery, and all others were in the lower side aisles. The hierarchical use of the sacred space gave the same message as Byzantine artistic depictions of Christ crowning the emperor, or giving the keys to Peter or the law to Peter or Paul – divine authority was vested in the papacy and the emperor, where earth and heaven met.

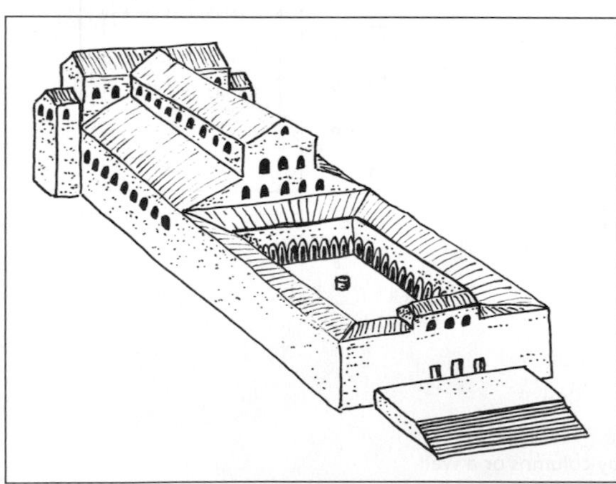

St Peter's, Rome (S. Pietro in Vaticano, begun 319)

In 800 Charlemagne was crowned by Leo III. This link with Rome was celebrated in a number of large churches modelled on St Peter's Basilica in his domains, such as the abbey of St Riquier near Abbeville in northern France. St Peter's had the added distinction of a double-storey transept at the west end of the nave. It also had a proliferation of towers: two at the crossing, two for staircases in the westwork, and two at the entrances, totalling nine in all. The westwork in its turn was the model for many others of the period, notably at Hildesheim.

Pilgrimages had a major effect on Christian architecture. To cope with the pressure of numbers the relics were removed from below the altar to an eastern chapel, the choir was raised above the nave, and the side aisles were wrapped round the east end to allow the progress of pilgrims round the relics without disrupting the daily offices of the church. As early as the beginning of the ninth century, the 'echelon apse system' emerged at St-Philibert de Grandlieu in the form of a rectangular ambulatory around the crypt with chapels radiating off it on the eastern side. With many people walking great distances to sacred sites, the architectural styles became better known and therefore somewhat homogenized. The basilica was still dominant, but was becoming greatly elaborated. Enlarged monastic communities like Cluny established a style of architecture that was widely imitated. Its tradition made a significant contribution to what is called the Romanesque style. In the second half of the tenth century the abbey church of Cluny II made a significant contribution to the echelon apse scheme, and its architectural forms spread via its many daughter churches such as Autun between about 1120 and 1132. In northern Europe Romanesque is characterized by round arches for windows and doors, barrel vaulting for roofs (again rounded structures), few windows and massive walls and piers to bear the pressure of the vaulting.

The splendour of the Cluniac elaboration of these elements is in sharp contrast to the austerity of Cistercian architecture. The rigorous asceticism of the Cistercian monastic rule and life was directly reflected in their architecture. It appears that the Cistercians delayed the building of great structures to house the order for fear of repeating the Cluniac example by succumbing to the temptation of architectural opulence. Bernard of Clairvaux set about establishing a strict and severe programme for a style of architecture to suit the asceticism of their lives. Clairvaux II was the first set of buildings to follow Bernard's programme, but little remains. The abbey of Fontenay is almost contemporary, however, and it has a barrel-vaulted nave, no clerestory, transverse barrel-vaulted side aisles with windows to add light to the nave – a formula repeated throughout Europe by the Cistercians.

In the wake of the Norman Conquest, the vast building programmes brought the Romanesque to England at St Albans, Canterbury, Rochester, Gloucester, Bury, Norwich, Ely and Durham. Durham was consecrated in 1133 and already by 1093 the rib-vault begins to appear, eventually being used throughout, and some of the arches are also pointed – all prefiguring the Gothic vault.

Out of the Romanesque environment and the waning popularity of pilgrimages came the form of Christian architecture called 'Gothic'. A convergence of theological teachings, religious practices and technological advances led to its predominance. With its combination of pointed arch and ribbed vaulting, Gothic made possible the creation of great spaces illuminated by vast areas of windows, made of stained glass. Ribbed vaulting with lighter infill allowed the structural load to be transferred outwards through buttresses so that the walls themselves, relieved of these forces, could be reduced to thin planes or vast windows. The weight of the buttresses, and thus their ability to withstand lateral forces from the vaulting, could be increased by adding pinnacles which contribute in turn to the vigour of the aesthetic effect.

The classic example of early Gothic is St Denis in the Île de France, but almost contemporary was the cathedral of Sens of about 1130 to 1164. Both show an innovative use of Romanesque characteristics heralding the new Gothic (then called 'modern') style. Sens reproduces the Romanesque layout of nave with ambulatory, but without a transept, and its double bays have a three-storey elevation deriving from Norman and English examples. Of the earliest group of Gothic buildings, the most astonishing is Notre Dame de Paris, begun in 1163. At 110 feet high it is a triumph of technology.

p. 792

Gothic was a truly international style that dominated Europe from Spain to Germany, Britain to Bohemia, from its origins in the middle of the twelfth century to the completion of the chapel of King's College, Cambridge, in 1515, with a vast array of national and local schools and traditions.

Though Gothic came to be superseded by adaptations of architectural styles from classical antiquity, it continued to be the architecture of many churches and underwent a major revival at the end of the nineteenth century. It continues to be popular for church buildings even into the twenty-first century, and shows up in cathedrals, parish churches, chapels and many other forms of building as well as in secular structures such as universities, offices and domestic buildings.

The Renaissance revived classical learning and architecture. The elements of architecture were taken from Roman classical precedent combined under strict laws of proportion and geometry. Filippo Brunelleschi's Pazzi Chapel was built in Florence in about 1430, long before the demise of northern Gothic. The whole design, from the façade through the interior space, was rigorously governed by a proportional system. On plan his Santo Spirito in Florence, begun in 1436, appears very traditional, but the aisles are treated as an ambulatory encompassing the nave, transepts and choir. Already it was seeking to create an encircling harmony.

Leon Battista Alberti travelled to Rome in 1432 and studied the remains of antiquity first-hand alongside the sole-surviving classical treatise on architecture written by Vitruvius. In about 1452 Alberti published *De Re Aedificatoria* in which he described the Vitruvian system of proportion. In the 1460s he designed S. Sebastiano in Mantua, closely modelled on ancient tombs and martyria.

The greatest building of the Renaissance, however, must be the new St Peter's in Rome. Pope Julius II was determined to establish Rome's (and the papacy's)

St Denis, Paris, founded 1137 by Abbot Suger

pre-eminence and focus of pilgrimage, and he engaged Bramante in 1506 to rebuild the Constantinian basilica of St Peter, now in a very poor state. It was to be a gigantic centralized martyrium. Bramante was not to complete the task, and was followed by Raphael, Peruzzi, Antonio da Sangallo, Michaelangelo and Maderno. Michelangelo's work introduces a new inventiveness to classicism. There is even a degree of visual instability troubling the calm rationalism of the Renaissance – a Mannerist device heralding the exuberance of the Baroque. Building the new St Peter's took huge financial resources, and Pope Leo X, Julius II's successor, resorted to selling indulgences in Germany to fund the project.

Martin Luther

It was in opposition to the sale of these indulgences that Martin Luther nailed his Ninety-Five Theses to the door of the castle church in Wittenberg in 1517 in an act which marked the beginning of the Reformation. The theological changes which this brought displaced the centrality of the eucharist by an emphasis on preaching, leading to a shift in the place of the pulpit and reducing the significance of the altar and sanctuary.

This meant that many earlier buildings had to adapt to the new ways. While large auditory churches for the new emphasis on the preaching of the Word were being constructed along classical norms and often on centralized plans, some previous buildings were altered to meet the demands of the new culture and to accommodate the shift of emphasis from the celebration of the sacraments. For instance the St Jakob church at Rothenburg-ob-der-Tauber, Germany, discarded its older altarpiece in favour of a newer, more acceptable one, and the stained-glass windows had to be changed to show the portraits of the Reformers. In the Netherlands between the seventeenth and nineteenth centuries a wide variety of centralized churches was built, from the Nieuwe Ronde Lutherse Kerk (of 1668–71) in Amsterdam, the Oostkerk in Middelberg (1647–67), the Nieuwe Kerk in 's-Gravenhage with a neatly pinched 'waist' (1649–56) and the Noorderkerk in Groningen (1665), to the Hervormde Kerk in Permerend (1853). Existing medieval churches were either partly (as at the fourteenth-century Maartenskerk in Zaltbommel) or wholly filled with pews to produce a close approximation to a transverse preaching-box. Few churches were destroyed, and then as often as not because of neglect, as at Gorinchem. Both in Europe and in Britain many were stripped of their art to combat idolatry, and of their treasures in the name of sobriety – and no doubt for other more worldly reasons as well.

Counter-Reformation ············➤

The ensuing Counter-Reformation produced some of the most spectacular architecture of the Christian tradition. The Baroque took the opportunity to emphasize instability, rupture and even conflict and made them the object of opulent display and celebration in a highly aesthetic treatment of the space for worship. Rich ornament was introduced, altar pieces were enlarged and made more ornate. An example of this treatment of architecture is seen clearly in the alterations that were made in the late-Gothic church of St Martin in Salzburg, Austria. In St Peter's itself, Bernini elevated the Chair of Peter above the High Altar in an extravaganza including the Holy Spirit in the form of a dove in a sunburst, clouds and angels levitating the chair and the triple crown of the papacy half-way between heaven and earth. The ecstatic message could hardly be clearer. Every element was charged with energy and set in movement; every surface was decorated and gleamed with the light of heaven; ceilings opened to reveal the glory of heaven as in the Jesuit church of S. Ignazio in Rome painted by Andrea Pozzo. There he shows the Jesuits evangelizing the peoples of the world. Jesuit missionaries transported the glory of the Baroque via Spain triumphantly to the New World. Eventually the rich décor of the Baroque evolved into the fantastic Rococo style. One of the great achievements of that period is the monastic church of the Vierzehnheiligen in Germany by the architect Balthazar Neumann.

After the Great Fire of 1666, Sir Christopher Wren took the opportunity to rethink the planning of Anglican churches in the 52 buildings needed for the capital. By no means all were from his hand, but St Mary-le-Bow and St Stephen Walbrook show important developments of the auditory design. His masterpiece was St Paul's Cathedral, which very significantly both borrows from and contrasts with St Peter's, Rome. It was a very English, and Anglican, Baroque building.

At the same time as the effervescence of the Rococo across Europe and in the New World, a movement in the New World created a Christian architecture of austerity and simplicity. The New England meeting house and some of the Protestant American churches were plain and unprepossessing by contrast with the excesses of the Rococo style. As the Christian tradition, in its many forms, spread into the New World, the Gothic, Renaissance, Baroque and Rococo all appeared in various forms, vigorously confronted with the austerity of American Protestant church architecture.

New American Christian architecture was built with an eye to the churches such as James Gibbs' St Martin-in-the-Fields, but interpreted in the idiom of the New England post-and-beam house. Later a spire was added and a neo-classical porch. Inside these buildings were auditory halls where the sermon was the supreme focal point of all worship. Originally the pulpit was raised half-way up between the first and second floors. A gallery was introduced on three walls at the second-floor level and on the ground floor there were, early on, booths for families to sit together, and eventually benches lined up in a row. The white, clapboard-sided building with a tall central spire on one end and an attached neo-classical entrance became the fixed image in the Christian tradition and continues to be repeated. Another favourite style to this day in America is that of the English parish church. This form was exported throughout the British empire, especially through the influence of the Ecclesiological Society, successor to the Cambridge Camden Society.

During the nineteenth century there was a huge surge in church building in England. In 1818 there was the stark realization that the Church of England was in a poor position to provide pastorally for the burgeoning city population, and an Act of Parliament established a commission for building new churches. Budgets were very constrained, and consequently the results were somewhat flimsy. In 1833 John Keble preached his Assize Sermon, which provided a catalyst for the high-church Oxford Movement; this revived the study of the liturgy and ceremonial of the medieval church. The Oxford Architectural Society and the Cambridge Camden Society focused interest on medieval Gothic architecture, with a preference for the 'Middle Pointed' or Decorated Style. The darling of the Cambridge Camden Society was the architect Augustus Welby Northmore Pugin, who worked with Sir Charles Barry on the Houses of Parliament. In 1836 he published *Contrasts, or a Parallel between the Noble Edifices of the Fourteenth and Fifteenth Centuries, and Similar Buildings of the Present Day, and Showing the Present Decay of Taste.* Between 1840 and 1846 he designed St Giles, Cheadle, for the Earl of Shrewsbury. Through the munificence of the patron he was, exceptionally, able to apply all the colour and ornament he thought necessary. The result was magnificent, but beyond the capabilities of most clients.

The archaeological revival of medieval style was superseded by more original use of Gothic forms by architects such as William Butterfield (as at All Saints, Margaret Street, London), George Edmund Street (St Philip and St James, Oxford), William Burges (Cork Cathedral), and George Frederick Bodley (All Saints, Cambridge and the Episcopal Cathedral, Washington DC). The international reputation of English Gothic architects was such that the commission for the Nikolaikirche in Hamburg was awarded to Sir George Gilbert Scott. A competition to build the Anglican Cathedral at Liverpool was held in 1901. The winner was the 21-year-old Giles Gilbert Scott with a modern, but still recognizably Gothic, design on a stupendous scale.

New styles have emerged from the new techniques and materials used in architecture in the late nineteenth and early twentieth centuries. For instance, concrete as a medium of construction has led to new ideas. At Oak Park in Illinois Frank Lloyd Wright designed Unity Temple in 1906, constructed of concrete slabs. He exercised enormous influence in Europe. Between 1923 and 1924 Auguste Perret built a church at Le Raincy in the *banlieu* of Paris. It was an aisled basilica in a concrete cage with the walls (made of precast concrete segments) dissolved in coloured glass by Maurice Denis. The style was no longer Gothic, nor any other recognizable historical style (though the description is reminiscent of the Cistercian); rather, the forms arose from the characteristics of the materials. The tall, thin columns support a concrete barrel vault with transverse barrel vaults in the side aisles. In the middle of the century Le Corbusier continued the exploration of the capabilities of concrete in his chapel at Ronchamp, as did Oscar Niemeyer in his cathedral for Brazilia in the form of a crown of thorns filled in with glass (see colour plate 19). Church buildings in the United States designed by Marcel Breuer use concrete in exciting ways, as at St John's Abbey, Collegeville, Minnesota (1961). In Japan, the Church on the Water (1988) and Church of the Light (1989) by the Japanese architect Tadao Ando are remarkable achievements, with a smooth, reflective polished concrete used within a strict geometry. Other material advances, such as the use of glass, have led to interesting innovations, for instance, in the Crystal Cathedral at Garden City, California, designed by Philip Johnson (see colour plate

Oxford Movement

20), or the new work by the British architect, Norman Foster. Many new forms of church architecture are taking shape as new materials and new technologies become available.

More recently, a new scale of architecture for Christian worship has been introduced called the 'mega-church movement'. So far, the architecture of these relatively new buildings borrows from secular models in order to hold large numbers of people. From the outside, these new Christian church buildings look more like shopping malls than churches. The arrangements of the interiors remind one more of arenas or amphitheatres than of sacred spaces. In the United States one of the earliest of these types is the Willow Creek Church in Illinois. One of the striking features of this building and others like it is the introduction of modern communication technology that presents images and amplifies the actions and sounds of the events immeasurably. So far the mega-church movement has not produced a unique Christian architecture that would be comparable to those styles of the past, but it is changing the definition of worship and eventually will possibly have a characteristic form that is authentic to this age.

It is fair to say, after all this evidence is considered, that many different styles at present characterize Christian architecture. Some of the movements have come and gone and what they have left behind now gives an impression which it was not originally intended to convey. Some of the movements have lingered on and continue to shape the way in which Christian communities call themselves together. At the same time a set of new styles introduced by the new possibilities that new materials and new technologies have made possible is emerging. So too is a postmodern phenomenon in Christian worship that may appear secular to this age, but intends to put 'old wine in new wine skins'. Or to put it another way, the multiple competing factors of our modern global society have led some Christian communities to abandon old forms of church architecture in search of something more relevant and hopefully enduring.

JOHN W. COOK AND ALLAN DOIG

📖 Xavier Barral i Altet, *The Early Middle Ages: from Late Antiquity to AD 1000*, Cologne, London and New York: Taschen 2002; Roger Dixon and Stephan Muthesius, *Victorian Architecture*, London and New York: Thames & Hudson [2]1985; Edwin Heathcote and Iona Spens, *Church Builders*, London and New York: Wiley 1997; Edward Norman, *The House of God: Church Architecture, Style and History*, London and New York: Thames & Hudson 1990; Rolf Toman (ed), *Romanesque: Architecture, Sculpture, Painting*, Cologne: Könemann 1997; Christopher Wilson, *The Gothic Cathedral: The Architecture of the Great Church 1130–1530*, London and New York: Thames & Hudson 1990

Art and spirituality

In 1951 the French writer and philosopher André Malraux suggested that the art gallery was the cathedral of the twentieth century. Art, it appeared, had become more religious than religion. This view of art was the culmination of a 200-year history which saw men and women coming to feel increasingly at home in the everyday world, and now looking to art rather than the churches to supply a sense of 'otherworldliness' – even if, in the bleak aftermath of World War II, there was an undeniably existentialist flavour to Malraux's dictum.

Since Malraux's time the already complex relationship between art and religion has become ever more convoluted. Today, art has virtually become chaplain to the secular society, spawning a generation of artists who deliver secular sermons and art critics more akin to theologians, while during a brief moment of magnificence in the 1960s and 1970s, art colleges became seminaries of revolt. In every major city and town across the Western world vast exhibition spaces continue to spring up like the cathedrals of old (even if, as often, their architecture is more striking than the works of art on display inside). For example, London's Tate Modern lies just across the river from the city's largest Christian cathedral, St Paul's, in a conscious rivalry that dated originally to the days when, as a power station, it was designed as a cathedral to electricity. Despite the great cost of its conversion, at the time of its opening in 2000 admission to the cathedral of art was free, while a large sum was levied for admission from visitors to its ecclesiastical neighbour.

The sacral nature of these spaces has instinctively been acknowledged by contemporary artists, who take every opportunity to exploit their resonance, whether positively, by creating works that are inward or delicate and respond to their charged environs, or negatively, by committing sacrilege and filling the galleries with inappropriate material designed to disconcert the ordinary viewers, most of whom are still rather orthodox in what they expect of a sacred place. Indeed, the result of this artistic guerrilla warfare has been partly to effect the gradual demythologization of art, which is now nearly as complete as that of religion a century ago.

Romanticism ➤

The process of looking for 'otherworldliness' in art began in the late eighteenth century, when German painters such as Caspar David Friedrich (1774–1840), in the thick of the romantic revolution, endowed apparently secular paintings of forests, oceans and mountains with what they saw as religious force, notably a sense of

Caspar David Friedrich, *Mountain Landscape*, 1835

boundlessness, of the sublime (that which lies 'beyond the threshold' of ordinary experience). This 'mystical' view of art in the Teutonic world was paralleled all over the West. In England, for example, the range stretches from Turner's sublime late paintings of light of the 1830s and 1840s to the awkwardly moralistic paintings of the mid-nineteenth-century Pre-Raphaelite Brotherhood, while in Victorian art as a whole there was a rather morbid emphasis upon a spiritualized eroticism that, largely suppressed in the public arena, was the closest that many Victorians came to a non-material world. In the US, vast landscape paintings exploited the mythology of the unspoilt American frontier region for an increasingly affluent and sedentary audience: this 'American sublime' appealed to the deeply religious instincts of a nation of religious refugees.

Things had been very different during the millennium that saw the Christian church as the principal patron of all the arts in the Western world. In this period (*c.*550–1550), almost all art was explicitly sacral, using standard Christian themes and iconography as determined by the church, which was responsible for almost all commissions. The arts served to embellish liturgy and places of worship, to instruct the faithful, to image the deepest fears and yearnings of the Christian and to woo the fickle hearts of the peasantry away from paganism by at least acknowledging the human body, denied, as it was, by most spiritual writing and preaching.

Paganism

Body

Even when the church's influence faded in the sixteenth century, the material capital of Florentine bankers proving a more potent influence on artists than any spiritual gold which the church could endow, the quality and sheer quantity of artworks that had been commissioned over previous centuries guaranteed a substantial afterlife for Christian themes in art, even if, in the ensuing secular world, the churches' ability to commission art of the highest quality was eclipsed by wealthier rivals. Certainly, much overtly Christian art continued (and continues) to be produced in the secular world of the Renaissance, Enlightenment and modern periods. For example, since the time of the sixteenth-century Protestant Reformation, art and its suppression have been used to characterize particular currents within Christianity, seen both in the emotionally charged altar-pieces of a Counter-Reformation church in Spain, and in the uncluttered, clean lines of a Calvinist building in Holland. Again, with the coming of the age of mass reproduction in the late

Renaissance

Enlightenment

Patronage

◄┈┈ Reformation

Counter-Reformation

nineteenth century, certain Christian images have become globally inevitable, such as Leonardo's *Last Supper* in Roman Catholic circles, or, in Protestant ones, Dürer's *Praying Hands* or Warner Sallman's *Head of Christ*, which was distributed free to all American troops in World War II. An estimated one billion reproductions of Sallman's art have been made since 1941. But, increasingly, these were exceptions. Ordinary people's religious instincts failed to be satisfied by the tightly-controlled Christian imagery popularly available, and instead secular artworks began to be invested with religious expectations.

In the second half of the twentieth century, this process of investment – to which art was especially suited thanks to its ability to evoke some 'other' world on the far side of Spirituality the frame – was termed 'spirituality'. Originally, in medieval times, 'spirituality' was opposed to 'temporality' to indicate the demarcation line between ecclesiastical and secular, especially with regard to church property. In seventeenth-century France, *spiritualité* became a technical term, indicating the personal relationship of human to God. But it was only in the second half of the twentieth century that the word came to indicate religious sensibility in secular guise, a convenient and identifiable definition of what is distinctive about religion (as opposed to other fields of human experience). Spirituality is thus a usefully vague word, able to point to a religious component in almost any aspect of human experience, from the writings of the mystics Mysticism to the mystique of music, dance or cookery: and it is in this sense that the spirituality of art is generally discussed.

The spirituality of art has become very important in countries where intellectual life is mistrustful of religion. For example, the work of the Abstract Expressionists in 1950s New York has generated an entire industry devoted to analysing their secular spirituality. These pioneering artists, mainly uprooted from communities with long traditions of religious practice, many of them Jewish or Christian refugees from Eastern Europe, are best known for their large, numinous abstract paintings which devour the viewer. For their audience, a generation with limited exposure to conventional religion and bored by the little they knew but who valued LSD and Zen, these works beautifully expressed the ineffable and were described as 'numinous' and 'sublime'.

Another example, this time from France, might be Germaine Richier's *Crucifix*, commissioned by the great Dominican theologian Père Couturier for his Alpine church at Assy in France in 1947. The corpus is an organic shape, more akin to a withered tree than a human figure. It sparked huge controversy, being thought to be too distorted, too painful and too 'existential'. The Assy project had initially received Rome's benediction but was then officially condemned and the Bishop of Annecy had Richier's *Crucifix* removed. It was only put back in its place by the altar in 1971.

Although rejected by the church authorities at the time (and still viewed with suspicion by some Roman Catholics), Richier (1902–59) is today acknowledged to be one of the major French sculptors of her day. Her work, which often combines human with animal or vegetable parts, is now seen as prescient of the ecological crisis that went on to dominate the latter half of the twentieth century. As she put it, 'no form, it seems to me, can be separated from the universe, the elements. It is therefore something more than an image.' Here is a church work that is actually of more importance to secular thinkers.

If these are extreme examples, there will, on the other hand, always be artists able to produce works of notable interiority or of stunning beauty, works of profound humanity or of social criticism that take their stand from a position well beyond the pale, works that break out new paradigms, perhaps using a new framework to make sense of the world, or which create a new sense of space that will inevitably be labelled 'spiritual' and will be particularly open to theological readings. The relationship between art and religion, at its best, can always be mutually enriching.

Increasingly, however, the contemporary art world is less interested simply in creating two- or three-dimensional images, and seeks rather to explore the fullness of life using any available means: video, performance or unrecordable 'actions'. There is also a blurring of boundaries between the different art forms. This 'postmodern' or 'whole-life' approach to art is removing the barriers between art and life and, inevitably, putting the whole question of the spirituality of art into doubt, just as theologically the traditional distinctions between immanent and transcendent, spirituality and temporality, are being radically challenged by postmodern theologians. Whether all art will disappear into craft (and whether religion will disappear into an extended humanism), developments that some, at least, are predicting, or whether art goes on to carve out a new territory for itself (perhaps fuelled by some global crisis that once more makes the world a difficult place to inhabit), the relationship between art and religion is always likely to be both problematic and creative.

CHARLES PICKSTONE

📖 Frank Burch Brown, *Good Taste, Bad Taste and Christian Taste: Aesthetics in Religious Life*, Oxford: OUP 2000; George Pattison, *Art, Modernity and Faith: Restoring the Image*, London: Macmillan and New York: St Martin's Press 1991; George Steiner, *Real Presences*, London: Faber and Chicago: University of Chicago Press 1989; Mark C. Taylor, *Disfiguring*, Chicago: University of Chicago Press 1992; Maurice Tuchman (ed), *The Spiritual in Art: Abstract Painting 1890–1985*, Los Angeles: County Museum of Art 1986

ARTS

Architecture, Art and spirituality, Books, Cinema, Community arts, Dance, Decorative arts, Drama, Icons, Iconoclasm, Literature, Music, Mystery plays, Painting, Patronage, Poetry, Sculpture, Stained glass, Symbols

From the Sistine Chapel in Rome to Canterbury Cathedral, from fifth-century mosaics in Ravenna to medieval books of hours, from early plainchant to Bach's *St Matthew Passion* and Verdi's *Requiem*, the importance of Christianity to all the arts is incontrovertible. Christianity is the single most important factor in the development of 2000 years of art, architecture and music in the Western world, whether as inspirer or patron, from the earliest Roman ivories, coins and catacomb art to recent commissions such as Coventry Cathedral or Los Angeles' Crystal Cathedral. Christianity is inconceivable without artistic expression, just as the study of the history of the arts is inconceivable without some knowledge of and feeling for Christianity. The churches have almost without exception used some or all of the arts to communicate – or even develop – the essence of the Christian faith in its many different historical expressions, just as Christianity in its turn has provided much of the most important subject-matter and modes of expression for the arts. A good knowledge of their relationship is therefore crucial to the understanding of Christianity.

The arts are arguably the richest expression of our humanity, condensing the whole gamut of human experience into image, symbol or sound. They are the most enduring expression of human freedom, working against the tides of necessity and constraint, a sign of the infinite scope of the human imagination, of the importance and given quality of inspiration and of the ultimate value of the non-utilitarian. The arts have also always been among the surest sources of consolation for the oppressed, the weary and those in pain; they fill the empty spaces in our dwellings, our time, our routine, our lives. They create utopias that allow escape from the particular historical age in which they are embedded but also present an outside platform from which to criticize or seek to reform. The arts celebrate the human body and human desire. In addition, the work of art is often Body
seen as giving access to some other world, as opening up a transcendent sense of otherness.

All these fields of human experience (except, until recently, the body) are fundamental, too, to Christianity. Therefore there has always been a natural kinship between Christianity and the arts, which has led equally to suspicion – or even to blatant rivalry – but also to a complete fusion.

The contents of any large art gallery mainly show the bond between the arts and Christianity (for example, 70 per cent of the pictures in the National Gallery in London are on Christian themes); on any one evening, well over half of London's concerts will include music written by Christian composers or for Christian purposes; a high proportion of extant architectural sites over 300 years old will be either churches or the ruins of religious sites. Even rock and pop music, it is claimed, can trace their descent back to Afro-Caribbean spirituals. p. 808

The relationship between the arts and Christianity is complicated by two additional factors. 1. The notion of 'the arts' is a relatively recent one, so that to speak of 'the arts' is to apply what is actually an anachronistic term to material and non-material artefacts that stretch back 2000 years. 2. For 1000 years of European and colonial history, the Christian churches were the major patrons (at times, the only patrons) of the arts, defining their subject-matter and style to such an extent that during this period the two might have appeared coterminous. It is only relatively recently that the arts have regained their autonomy and separate identity. Today by contrast the churches are minor players in the field of arts patronage, and have little influence. Christians are more likely to seek underlying or implicit religious themes or 'spirituality' in nominally secular works of art than to commission significant works themselves. Secular art works are thus as important as sacred ones to the contemporary Christian. In addition, a number of the newer arts (cinema, photography) have never been part of Christianity: their themes, however, may still be explicitly Christian, or at least show underlying Christian influence, and they, too, are treated here.

Spirituality

There are three possible (overlapping) directions in which Christianity's relationship with the arts may be explored.

The *thematic path* considers the wide range of arts that have been practised within or influenced by Christianity, as they appear today, and looks at some of their most common Christian themes.

The *historical path* seeks to understand Christian art works in terms of the circumstances of their origin.

The *theoretical path* takes the reader through what leading Christian writers and thinkers have said about the various arts and their relationship to Christianity.

The thematic path

Here a few brief signposts in the form of a table are followed by a more detailed description of the route. (Simply for ease of reference, the arts have been divided up into the traditional categories.)

	Creation	**Incarnation**	**Crucifixion**	**Resurrection**	**Church and Holy Spirit**	**Judgement**
Visual arts	Michelangelo, Sistine Chapel	Nativity scenes	*Isenheim Altarpiece*	Ravenna mosaic	Giotto, Scrovegni Chapel	Giotto, Scrovegni Chapel
Music	Haydn, *Creation*	Monteverdi, *Vespers*	Bach, *Passions*	Easter hymns	Mass settings	Requiem mass
Architecture	Domed churches	Baptisteries	Cruciform churches		Iconostases	Funerary chapels
Decorative arts		Christmas cribs		Easter garden	Vestments, reliquaries	Black vestments
Poetry and prose	John Milton, *Paradise Lost*	Wesley, hymns	*Dream of the Rood*	George Herbert; Gerard Manley Hopkins	Mystical poetry	Dante, *Divine Comedy*

The enduring value of the greatest Christian art across the centuries comes from its roots in humanity. Even someone who knows little or nothing about the Christian story may well be moved by Giotto's depiction of the grief of Mary at Jesus' death in the Scrovegni Chapel in Padua (1303–5), or by Monteverdi's glorification of Mary in his setting of the Magnificat in his *Vespers* of 1610. The greatest Christian themes have a universality about them that makes them accessible to anyone who can respond to art or music or architectural space.

However, much is inevitably lost without a more detailed understanding of the particular task the author or artist intended his or her work to perform. In Italy, for example, which contains an estimated 40 per cent of the world's artistic heritage, almost every site worth visiting demands explicit and detailed knowledge of some often obscure point of the Christian tradition. In the Scrovegni Chapel just mentioned, a large number of its most beautiful pictures illustrate the fictional life of Jesus' grandparents – even for Christians a little-known cycle of stories; the wonderful painting by Veronese on the theme of the supper of Gregory the Great in the sanctuary of Monte Berico above nearby Vicenza is similarly taken from a miracle story now virtually forgotten. That the richness of these works is still fresh today is a sign that these themes, although obscure, are fundamentally related to the human condition. It is also possible that their use of artistic media makes what they have to say more timeless than, say, contemporary sermons or manuals of devotion. But full appreciation of these works requires an understanding of their subject matter and of their world.

Among the key themes of the Christian arts are the following:

Creation. The great Christian themes, being loosely based on the life of Jesus, tend to follow the human life cycle. The exception is that of the creation, which has produced some of the greatest Christian works of art. The ceiling of the Sistine Chapel, Haydn's great oratorio of that name, Milton's *Paradise Lost* and a thousand medieval cycles of bronze or wood or fresco (e.g. the carved cycle outside the doors of S. Zeno Maggiore in Verona) which begin with the creation are all testimony to the enduring fascination of the question of our origin, purpose and sense of wrongness. It perhaps represents the greatest challenge for any artist or composer. Architecturally, the domed churches characteristic of Byzantium and later of the West are said to represent the dome of the sky as seen from below, and in a sense represent the divine depths and origin of the universe.

Annunciation, Visitation, Incarnation, Nativity. The human life cycle begins with conception and birth; in every age Christian artists have borrowed from the circumstances of their time to illustrate these domestic events. The images of the Annunciation by the angel Gabriel to Mary (Luke 1.26–38), always suggesting a gentle conception, while never implying that the angel Gabriel was anything other than a messenger, have conveyed a respectful and chivalrous notion of intercourse, divine and human; the image of Jesus in the crib or enthroned on his mother's lap is perhaps the most important single image of the Christian faith, persevering through all cultures and backgrounds, and suggesting the mysterious depths of the ordinary and domestic circumstances surrounding the birth of a child. The presence of animals widens the scope of this image not just to embrace the pets or farmyard animals with which the viewer might share their accommodation but to add resonance to Jesus' identity. The Visitation (of Mary mother of Jesus to Elizabeth mother of John the Baptist, Luke 1.39–45) again gives artists the chance to show the potential resonance of the perfectly ordinary scene of two women embracing, while the Massacre of the Innocents (the killing of the children by King Herod, Matthew 2.16–18), very popular in certain centuries, perhaps reflects contemporary feelings about the appallingly high levels of infant mortality endured across most of human history.

Musically, Christmas carols sung in homes and streets take up the vernacular and domestic themes implicit in the Nativity. The Christmas crib, first attributed to Francis of Assisi, is important in different cultures across the world, with Christmas markets selling crib figures throughout southern Europe to this day, while the legend of the three kings is illustrated early on in the fifth-century mosaics of Ravenna on the hem of the robe of Empress Theodora – a common motif later throughout Europe, where many kings and emperors saw themselves descended from one of the three.

ARTS

Jesus

Jesus' baptism, adult life and ministry. The adult years of Jesus' life apart from his baptism were of little interest to the early church; however, since then every aspect of this period of his life has been illustrated in art and become the subject of interminable numbers of hymns and sermons (some of them works of art in themselves).

Jesus' baptism (Mark 1.9–11) is crucial in architecture. For much of Christian history, baptisteries were separate buildings from churches, and generally octagonal (representing the eighth day of creation, the day of resurrection, the day without sunset which Christian believers enter in baptism). Many representations of the baptism of Jesus, from Ravenna mosaics to Piero della Francesca in the London National Gallery, show someone taking the plunge, as it were, entering a moment of commitment, with overtones of conversion or rebirth. The temptations which followed on from the baptism are often more discreet in the case of Jesus than for Antony, the pioneer monk, whose temptations in the desert reveal the peculiar and age-old mistrust of Christianity towards sexuality.

Jesus the teacher and Jesus the healer are particularly popular images during more settled times; all of Jesus' actual teachings are illustrated somewhere, especially the image of Jesus the Good Shepherd, which in ancient times was seen as a parable about the afterlife. Jesus as teacher affected architecture particularly in the design of pulpits and, after the Protestant Reformation, of churches that are little more than preaching boxes or, more contemporarily, places where the technology of mass communication can be installed.

Jesus' encounters, especially with women (the woman at the well, John 4.7–30; Mary Magdalene, John 20.11–18), are well illustrated, while pictures of Jesus at table, prefiguring the last supper, were painted by Veronese and many others.

p. 759

The miracles provide a certain scope for the arts, as artists and musicians try to show how the extraordinary can be juxtaposed to the everyday. In particular, the Transfiguration (e.g. Mark 9.2–8) is popular in Byzantine art, and at Ravenna in the basilica of Sant' Apollinare in Classe there is a magnificent example (see colour plate 3). Also popular are the wedding at Cana in Galilee (Jesus' first miracle, John 2.1–11); and Masaccio's depiction of the rather obscure miracle of the tribute money (the coin in the mouth of a fish, Matthew 17.24–7) in the Brancacci Chapel in Florence is unforgettable for the gentle seriousness of its characters.

Palm Sunday, Last Supper, Passion and Crucifixion. If birth and death are the two key moments of life, death is inevitably the easier to explore. Probably the bulk of all Christian art and music is concerned with it, as are the greater part of the Gospel narratives. The theme of Jesus' death, variously treated over the years as the death of a hero, of a righteous man, of a suffering servant, of the Son of God, of a political prisoner, of a lamb of sacrifice, according to historical period and current concerns, dominates all Christian artistic production. It can be seen everywhere, from Gothic churches designed in the shape of a cross to hundreds of thousands of artistic representations of every aspect of Jesus' passion (including the series of stations of the cross on the walls of two-thirds of the churches in Christendom), in every style from the extreme sentimentality of the late Baroque period to the depictions of Jesus' dignified kingship, which even at the moment of greatest suffering still dominates his captors, as, for example, in the mosaics of Ravenna.

p. 341
Christendom

Hymns, spirituals and popular works such as Stainer's *Crucifixion* rival difficult works such as the choral settings of the passion by a host of composers, most famously J. S. Bach, and Handel's *Messiah*, not to mention hundreds of settings of *Tenebrae*, the Reproaches and Lamentations for Holy Week by a wide range of composers.

Artistically, particular episodes capture the imagination: the kiss of Judas, the depiction of the *arma Christi* (the instruments of the passion), the *pietà* (Jesus' dead body cradled in his mother's lap reminding the viewer of the baby he had been only a few weeks beforehand in the liturgical year at Christmas.) Especially, the body of the dead Jesus hanging on the cross (except in some Protestant churches which historically have always objected to its misuse as a devotional object, to be kissed and venerated, in the fifteenth century) has dominated the Christian imagination since the early Middle Ages, often reflecting the social conditions of its time. The well-known *Isenheim Altarpiece* in Alsace, for example, reflects in Jesus' wounds the appalling skin diseases suffered by the patients in the hospital for which it was commissioned; similarly, Nicholas Serrano's *Piss-Christ* (1987), which shows a crucifix immersed in urine, dates from the height of AIDS epidemic in New York, when all body fluids were suspect. Accounts of the passion of Jesus were also responsible for the development of the passion play, moving performances of the passion of Christ that toured the medieval world. In the twentieth century these have been translated into celluloid, of which Mel Gibson's *The Passion of the Christ* is notable for its realistic brutality.

Resurrection and Ascension. The rather abstract concept of the empty tomb and the fact that Jesus' resurrection was unobserved have, strangely, meant that artistically the resurrection has had much less significance than the crucifixion. It is difficult to portray a joyful absence convincingly, and easier to depict pain than joy. The Byzantine tradition has always been better at depicting resurrection than that of the West. An important sub-theme is that of the harrowing of hell, where Jesus is shown leading Adam and Eve (followed by a whole crowd of souls) out of hell, stepping on little demons on the way. Music and literature have produced poems and mystical songs (including those by George Herbert famously set to music by the English composer, Ralph Vaughan Williams). The ascension is even more difficult to picture, as the flat-earth cosmology taken for granted by the Acts of the Apostles is so foreign to that of most art since medieval times. Sometimes it is signified simply by a pair of feet stuck on to the ceiling of a church.

Resurrection
Byzantium

Holy Spirit, Church. The descent of the Holy Spirit on the disciples and the founding of the church (Acts 2) is generally the last episode in cycles of the life of Christ such as Giotto's in the Scrovegni Chapel in Padua, a particularly fine example of the apostles gathered together in a room, receiving the Holy Spirit who will make them into the church. Church architecture has always attempted to reflect the supernatural origin of the Christian church with the concepts and tools of its day, and even today Christian architects struggle to create a sense of sacred space within their buildings. Musically the liturgy, what goes on in churches, has provided composers with vast opportunities; in particular, settings of the mass span 1000 years and reveal a vast richness of resources and texture, from the simplest chant to the vast choral and orchestral resources required for the requiem and other masses by such composers as Verdi, Brahms, Bernstein and Britten (never intended to be sung as part of a church service), who feel able to develop Christian texts in secular directions.

Holy Spirit
Music

Saints. From the Middle Ages, the lives of the saints became increasingly significant, with the growth of importance of relics and pilgrimage shrines. Many commissions in Christian art were for pictures or sculptures of particular saints (often the patron saint of the church, chapel or donor). Elaborate furnishings could be afforded by wealthy pilgrim sites, and beautiful reliquaries commissioned to hold their bones. Devotion to saints might also respond to particular needs: images of the penitent Mary Magdalene were common in the post-Reformation era, when the Roman Catholic

Saint p. 1075
Pilgrimage p. 850

Church sought to encourage the sacrament of penance; cities subject to plague might commission images of St Roch. The historical popularity of doctrines such as the Immaculate Conception and Assumption were accompanied by many paintings on these themes from painters such as Murillo.

Last Judgement. Springing from a desire for a final and definitive triumph of the righteous and what would today be called social justice, images of the Last Judgement were particularly important at times of social change. Painters were permitted an anarchic depiction of the forces of chaos, with ghoulish monsters devouring or punishing in kind (often remarkably explicitly by today's standards) those guilty of various sins; the denizens of hell might well include popes and kings. These images often have a vitality which today sometimes seems to compare favourably with the serried ranks of angels and righteous souls always depicted in parallel with the sinners, although this would probably not have been the case in the medieval world, when fear of death and judgement reigned supreme, affecting even such men as Samuel Johnson. Musically, this theme gave rise to the requiem mass, and, in literature, to arguably the greatest poem ever written, Dante's *Divine Comedy*.

The historical path

To understand art works and their relationship to Christianity, it is important to distinguish between the major phases of Christian cultural history. These might be characterized as follows:

Roman empire

First to fifth centuries: the outsider church. Up to the fall of the Roman empire, the early Christian church, with its eyes on an imminent end to the world, was, officially at least, hostile to the 'this-worldly' world of the arts, before finally making its peace with the arts shortly before the barbarian invasions. Naturally, little survives from this period except for some architecture, a few artefacts, the tomb-painting hidden deep in catacombs and some of the more durable church art, such as sarcophagi and notably the magnificent series of mosaics to be found particularly in Ravenna, Istanbul and Rome (notably, Sta Maria Maggiore).

Sixth to fifteenth centuries: the Christian empires. In both Eastern and Western Europe, the churches established a cultural monopoly in their respective spheres of influence, pursuing campaigns of cultural expansion and employing all of the arts to remarkable effect. No aspect of life was left ignored, from the popular to the most solemn, from the cradle to the grave.

Renaissance

Protestantism

Sixteenth to nineteenth centuries: the church and the world. From the Renaissance (*c.* 1500) and the destruction of Byzantium onwards, the wealth and influence of the churches decreased. The arts became increasingly autonomous, initially in Northern Europe, where the Protestant denominations discouraged the use of any of the arts (except music) within churches, while outside churches they were used principally for moral edification; and then in Catholic Europe, when a great revival of the Christian arts, the Counter-Reformation, finally burnt itself out in the nineteenth century.

Twentieth and twenty-first centuries: the contemporary world of spirituality. In the largely secular sphere of the contemporary creative arts, Christianity is able to use the autonomous world of the arts as independent evidence of religious or spiritual themes. This period sees the rise of new art forms (photography, cinema) that have never been under Christian influence.

	Outsider church: first to fifth centuries	Christian empires: sixth to fifteenth centuries	Church and world: sixteenth to nineteenth centuries	Contemporary world: twentieth and twenty-first centuries
Visual arts	Iconoclastic period: the church used mainly pagan prototypes. Early Byzantine period: few crucifixions or images of the suffering Jesus	Gothic art and sculpture: wall friezes, dooms, crucifixions, last judgement, icons	In the north: opposed to iconography or too poor. Romantic revolution in the south: Counter-Reformation, Baroque	'Spirituality' explores the boundaries of human existence: less emphasis on orthodox iconography
Music	Byzantine chant: unaccompanied singing mainly of psalms	Plainchant, polyphony, hymnody: Hildegard of Bingen (1098–1179) first named composer. Requiem masses	Congregational and choral church music	Contemporary composers (e.g. Tavener, Britten); development of popular music in church
Architecture	Basilica the distinctive Christian building. Hagia Sophia: round churches	Romanesque, Gothic, International Gothic	In the north: Gothic revival In the south: Baroque	Avid experimentation with new styles in the search for sacred space, e.g. the Crystal Cathedral
Decorative arts	Sarcophagi; mosaics	Stained glass, illuminated manuscripts, silverware, Books of Hours		
Poetry and prose	Early Christian hymns	Miracle plays, mass texts, pilgrimage texts	Invention of printing; pietistic hymns and poetry. Dante's and Milton's epics	Contemporary poets (e.g. Rowan Williams, R. S. Thomas) and hymn writers
Historical background	Eschatological enthusiasm; conversion of Constantine; barbarian invasions	Split between East and West; church has cultural monopoly and major patronage of the arts; crusades; slow cultural expansion and final development of nation states	Fall of Constantinople; Reformation and Counter-Reformation; industrial development	Two world wars, Auschwitz, Hiroshima, Cold War

We can now look at these broad historical outlines in more detail.

The outsider church. The early church emerged into a secularizing world where the state worship of Roman gods was devolving into a mass of small local, national and international spiritualities. As early as the beginning of our era, attendance at temple worship was declining, and oriental-inspired mystery religions were flourishing. With the development of Greek tragedy and comedy the dramatic arts, at first associated with religious festivals, had long become fully autonomous.

Mystery cults

Unsurprisingly, given the mishmash of hybrid spiritualities that characterized the time of the birth of Christianity and the general prohibition on images by their Jewish antecedents, the first Christians were fervently iconoclastic. Once Christianity became established, religious imagery rapidly began to emerge, initially largely based on pagan prototypes: first in the catacombs, used for

Origins and background

funerary decoration and (probably) in house churches; then in churches and for popular devotion at home. A great deal has not survived, but such as there is gives a good picture of the magnificent effects achieved by Christian art at the time of the barbarian invasions.

Of contemporary architecture, many magnificent examples of the basilica survive all across the Roman world.

Of the other arts, little trace of early Christian music has survived; the New Testament contains much evidence of Christian poetry and hymnody.

Middle Ages

The Christian empires. In the Middle Ages, at the high point of its secular power, the church was able to use the arts to create sacred spaces for worship, to proclaim its message to the unlettered, to decorate its buildings and to fill them with beautiful artefacts, to create a sense of the sacred apposite to worship, and to take its message out into the community.

During this period, the great Christian images and themes were developed by the international church: for example, mother and child, *pietàs*, stations of the cross, doom and last judgement, Adam and Eve, images of the various saints, and latterly the Christmas crib; these images became common currency across the Christian world. Similarly, a common liturgy encouraged the widespread development of certain musical settings and the production of beautifully illuminated manuscripts and private books of the devotion for the wealthy. A relatively uniform style of architecture also emerged to provide a common cultural identity against the non-Christian nations surrounding or occupying parts of Europe: this 'international Gothic' style is one of the few assured masterpieces of world culture, its light, airy and soaring spaces decorated with elegant tracery and richly-coloured glass invoking a conception of the soaring yet harmonious potential dignity of human beings in the service of divinity.

p. 1037

Reformation

The church and the world. From the Reformation onwards, Europe split into three, while Christianity itself became increasingly a global phenomenon. Northern Europe evolved into a series of secular states. The myriad small churches that ensued were either anti-iconic or did not have the resources to commission great works of art; such works as exist are largely for private patrons, generally outside church, or pietistic works of devotion printed for private use. The exception was congregational and choral church music, which flourished in all congregations except the very strictest. Eastern Europe, largely under Islamic occupation, remained in a relatively pristine state; southern Europe, still largely under the control of the Roman Catholic hierarchy, mounted a vast propaganda campaign for the hearts of its own people and against developments in the north; using every available means, emotional and intellectual, the Counter-Reformation commissioned grand works of music, architecture and painting which pushed the emotional impact of the Christian faith to (and in some cases beyond) its limits. Eventually, even in Protestant Europe, emotional life made a return, notably at the time of the eighteenth-century romantic revolution, which dealt with previously religious themes in an avowedly secular guise.

Counter-Reformation

Romanticism

As the Christian nations developed empires abroad, so they exported their national Christian denominations across the world. Although initially they simply reproduced their own artistic genres and commonplaces, such as 'English'-style village churches built across India, eventually they opened themselves to indigenous influence. The Christian art and especially music of Latin America is notable; in addition, African and Asian Christians have developed Christian themes in new and unexpected directions.

The contemporary world. At the height of the secularizing period of the arts there had always been a tendency for works of art to be treated as substitutes for religion, and this trend has continued. The contemporary world has seen a renewal of interest in the arts. Whereas through most of the twentieth century this largely took the form of using the arts as secular protest against the various establishments (political, religious, hierarchical, etc.), in the late twentieth and early twenty-first century the arts are seen as a way of exploring the boundaries of human existence. As such, labelled 'spirituality', developments in the arts are not incompatible with recent developments in religion, which have also become more personal, less other-worldly, more interested in the human body. Although in terms of resources available for patronage, the church is no longer a major player, there have been significant commissions, especially in terms of architecture (new cathedrals are among the few public commissions in any walk of life that are still regularly able to be financed). Church music has also experienced a particular period of vitality. Christian poetry and hymnody are also important (both Pope John Paul II and the Archbishop of Canterbury, Rowan Williams, are respected poets). Christian artists are rarely in the front line of critical attention, but many apparently secular artists are turning to the great Christian themes for inspiration, with often surprising results. Even if congregations are not now so large as during the early years of the twentieth century, the majority of church buildings are at the beginning of the twenty-first century probably better maintained than they have been for many years.

The theoretical path

The field of religion and the arts is only now in the process of becoming a formal academic discipline. Over the last decade, academic chairs have been created in various American and European universities and research projects established. Academically, therefore, the subject might be said to be in its infancy. Over the whole course of Christian history, however, it has been a topic of constant and often fierce debate.

For many readers the development of Christian aesthetics, in its rather cerebral abstraction, may not initially appear the most scintillating part of the Christian experience. Unlike, say, the great medieval cathedrals, which even today can be relatively easily admired and appreciated, the complex writings of their contemporary scholastic theologians can seem quite inaccessible. It is much easier to visit a cathedral or listen to the music of the Middle Ages than it is try to grapple with its theology, written from within the perspective of a very foreign world-view – one, for example, where the world was flat and human psychology in its infancy.

It is important to make the effort, because while casual viewers may believe that they understand cathedrals or music, it is only by reading contemporary sources that they can have any idea what these things meant to the men and women who built them or composed it, and also because the intellectual products of, say, the Middle Ages easily rival their surviving material artefacts. In the classical age, too, Augustine of Hippo, for example, who was dismissive of human creativity, was himself a master craftsman, a fully-trained classical rhetorician who, even when denigrating the arts, did so in a very skilful and attractive manner.

The principal difference in world-view between most of the Christian past and of today – which presents the key difficulty that contemporary men and women have in reading the historical Christian texts on theology and the arts – is that of the ubiquitous presence of another, superior, world above, beyond, before or after the present one in all previous periods of intellectual history. In fact, the modern period might almost be seen as a historical aberration in not having much faith (and certainly less practice) in another world. This makes it difficult to understand the majority of Christian writing about art. Most of the classical formulations of the subject begin by positing another world such as the world of heaven, and then either claim artworks as a vital link between the two worlds – pictures, for example, as icons of glory or polyphonic singing as an echo of the music of heaven, partially revealing the heavenly world to human beings – or else suggest that the other world is *so* other that no human artefact could possibly bridge the gap, and that it is blasphemous even to try.

Here, then, are the two major theories of Christian art. The one affirms the importance of the arts as a source of revelation of the divine supplementary to that in the Bible and church teaching; the other, the 'iconoclastic' view, denies the place of art altogether. These two contrary attitudes to art, one offering the possibility of religious art that brings heaven to earth, the other denying it, are found at different times throughout the whole of Christian history.

For example, in the eighth century the Eastern church was bitterly divided between the two views during what was called the Iconoclastic Controversy, a major spiritual and cultural crisis which affected every aspect of Roman civilization: church and court, academy and monastery. The church was under considerable pressure to ban all sacred art partly because of the increasing popularity of Islam, a fiercely anti-iconic faith with which the Christian church was engaged in a prolonged competition for the hearts and minds of people already suspicious of the theological justification for depictions of the holy; and partly because of the increasing influence of emperors and bishops from Asia Minor, especially Syria, parts of the world more likely to be Monophysite, i.e. to believe that Jesus had only one, divine nature, and who therefore disliked depictions of Jesus in material form. It was also a time of retraction for the Byzantine (eastern Roman) empire, and it is possible that this purging of icons was a comforting gesture, designed, perhaps, to allay God's clearly felt displeasure. The pro-icon Eastern church fathers were compelled over about 100 years, from the deposition of the Patriarch Germanus of Constantinople in 730 to the regency of Theodora in 843, to develop a sophisticated christology that would permit the use of icons in church in a world where icons were under suspicion and in many places had been destroyed, and those who supported them persecuted or exiled.

Christology

After some considerable theological exploration over this period, Nicephorus (758–829) and Theodore of Studios (759–826), two very different champions of the icon, produced a classical justification for Christian art: since Jesus was God embodied, his unique human body was an essential part of his divinity, even after the resurrection, not just an add-on to be quickly disposed of. Therefore, artistic depictions of the particularity of Jesus' body do not 'circumscribe' or limit his divinity (as the iconoclasts had complained). The divine had chosen to present itself through the material, the contingent and the particular, and since it is with particularities that the artist most happily deals, icons can be a valid channel of communication between the human world and the divine.

This complex and nuanced view of the incarnation did not find favour everywhere. Although, as we have seen above, ordinary Christian people did use art from the earliest times, the official absence of art was a useful early point of distinction between Christians and pagans as it had been for Jews, justified by the second commandment (Exodus 20.4), whose breach could be highly inflammatory, as Antiochus Epiphanes discovered when, as reported in 1 Maccabees 1.41ff., he erected a cultic statue in the Jewish temple, and triggered a huge Jewish rebellion led by the Maccabee brothers. In the Bible, therefore, as one would expect, there is little discussion of the subject except Paul's references to Christ as 'the icon of (the invisible) God' (2 Corinthians 4.4; Colossians 1.15), and perhaps the reference in John 12.3 to the odour of the ointment used to anoint Jesus filling the house, an uncharacteristically sensuous note.

Perhaps because of the abundance of popular representations of divinities of every shape, size and potency, the Western intellectual world into which Christianity was born was also suspicious of images. Socrates, as recorded by Plato, had regarded an artist's picture of something as a shadow of a shadow of its reality (the reality being, of course, not of this world), and this view was popular among philosophers and the educated. It was by this tradition that Augustine of Hippo in the fourth/fifth centuries was influenced in his writings about the arts: human reason was guided by a residual memory of absolute Truth – a sort of divine implant in human beings. This Truth was also Beauty, and so, although human beings might initially find external signs of beauty such as art works helpful, they should really mistrust them for fear that they might all too be seduced by the second best, for the real beauty of which people had a divinely planted intuition was of a different world altogether. With the Goths gathering on the flanks of Europe and the whole 1000-year-old western Roman empire about to go under, Augustine's pessimism about the this worldly beauty is entirely understandable. Gregory the Great, the last of the Latin doctors of the church, on the other hand, declared in 599 that 'we do no harm in wishing to show the invisible by means of the visible'.

The world of the Middle Ages, similarly, was really two worlds. As well as the divide between the popular practice of the arts and the high theory of the theologians, there was also a great chasm between the vale of tears of this life – the realm of kings little better than warlords, of frequent outbreaks of the plague, and of international religious communities much like the transnational corporations of today wielding vast economic power – and the other world, the next life, the place of universal justice. Art was commonly used to bridge the gap, and depictions of the final judgement (and its concomitant rewards and punishments) would have graced most churches and cathedrals.

For an example of medieval theology, in Thomas Aquinas' *Summa Theologiae* there is little explicitly about the relation between art and religion, although Thomas does state neatly what has by this stage become the standard threefold justification of religious art works, at least in the West: 'First for the instruction of the unlettered, who might learn from them as if from books; second, so that the mystery of the incarnation and the examples of the saints might remain more firmly in our memory by being daily represented to our eyes; and third, to excite the emotions which are more effectively aroused by things seen than by things heard', but it is difficult to look at the theological and cultural world of the Middle Ages – and certainly at Thomas' rather intellectual notion of beauty – without seeing it through the romantic and nostalgic spectacles of the Victorian period or more recent disciples of Thomas such as Jacques Maritain (1882–1973), or the artist and sculptor Eric Gill (1892–1940). Nonetheless, it is often argued that the real visual theology of this age is worked through in its architecture; Gothic cathedrals are regularly compared to the soaring achievements of scholastic theology. Scholasticism

If, however, medieval theologians were reticent about the arts, the popular religious culture of the Middle Ages, in its almost unbridled vitality, threatened to get quite out of control. A corrective was soon to be applied. 'Let not God's majesty be debased by untimely representation' ordered John Calvin (1509–64) in sixteenth-century Protestant Geneva. And a few miles to the south, the Roman 
Catholic Council of Trent (1545–63) was busy issuing draconian legislation as to what might or Council
might not be fittingly represented in religious art. Even the inclusion of a small dog in a *Last Supper* by the Italian painter Veronese was considered unseemly, and after the artist's appearance before the Inquisition in 1573 the painting was renamed *Feast at the House of Levi.* Thus both Protestant and Roman Catholic reforming theologians sought to control the arts as part of their attempt to

tighten up Christian discipline. On the one side, in the newly-Protestant world, they forced all the arts except music outside the church to create an other-worldly, intellectual purity as the ambience for worship in contrast to the robustly mercantile economy outside; on the other, all across the Roman Catholic world a sugary Baroque style rapidly became the uniform expression of religious art, a sad degeneration from the work of its founder, Caravaggio (1571–1610), the Roman low-life painter who used newly-available intuitions about human sexuality to give a sense of other-worldliness to his religious works.

It was in the romantic era of the eighteenth and nineteenth centuries, however, that the arts really took off on their trajectory to theological glory. Even secular writings about art and aesthetics became larded with religious terms and expectations. The process was particularly important in Germany where writers such as Friedrich von Schlegel, Friedrich von Schiller and Friedrich von Schelling found in the arts once more a satisfactory way to point to another world: aesthetic intuition, they suggested, provides humanity with access to the divine.

At this period, art and religion tended to be conflated, and the resultant blend became known as the 'sublime', a particular feature of eighteenth-century thought. 'Two things fill my soul with awe and wonder,' said Immanuel Kant, 'the starry heavens above and the moral law within.' The sublime, Kant suggested, 'forces us to abandon our merely empirical sensibility and draws us to a higher realm'. It is a conduit of the 'supersensible', and even if Kant himself did not believe that human beings had privileged access to what might lie beyond the world of appearances, others were quick to suggest that through the arts they might; Friedrich Schleiermacher, for example, suggested that the arts had a special role to play in evoking what he termed 'God-consciousness': 'If it is true that there are sudden conversions in men, thinking of nothing less than of lifting themselves above the finite, in a moment, as by an immediate, inward illumination ... I believe that more than anything else the sight of a great and sublime work of art can accomplish this miracle.' As culture became increasingly secularized, so art and artist became sacralized. The symbolist movement, for example, and later the surrealist and futurist movements, made loftier claims for themselves than even any religious fanatic could have dreamt of. For some, such as John Ruskin (1819–1900) in England, who began his writing career by suggesting that the ultimate task of the artist was to reflect in his work the beauty given by God to created things as a perpetual witness to his eternal glory (a variant on the usual 'other-world' theory), the strain of trying to keep art and Christianity together proved too much, and Ruskin was not the only one to abandon conventional Christianity.

The twentieth century saw a plethora of theories about art and religion, the majority trying to establish art as a link to some other world, whether explicitly religious or not. One example will suffice. The English writer and member of the Bloomsbury Group Clive Bell (1881–1964) claimed that 'art and religion are ... two roads by which men escape from circumstances to ecstasy. Between aesthetic and religious rapture there is a family alliance.'

Along with accounts of aesthetics in phenomenology (Gerardus van der Leeuw and Maurice Merleau-Ponty) and existentialism (Paul Tillich), anthropology (Mircea Eliade) and process theology (Alfred North Whitehead), one of the more interesting twentieth-century treatments is that of Jacques Derrida: a number of theologians have attempted to use his notion of *différence* – 'the absence that makes presence possible', the invisible dark hole, the unsayable 'radical alterity' that underlies the intelligible world – as a signal of transcendence, a theory that can be used to deconstruct texts and pictures alike and thereby glimpse divinity.

More recently, however, some writers on the arts see them as completely central to contemporary attempts to construct a theology appropriate to the more unified world that we currently inhabit, a world which is decreasingly dependent upon some other world to make sense of itself. If human beings invest increasingly in the here and now, then the arts, which at best are rooted in the material, the bodily and the everyday and yet which still seem to resonate profoundly, may be the best guides to exploring the infinite range of this present. As Rowan Williams puts it, 'any artist is going to be in the business of showing the world differently' – and the best artists are those who do this by enlarging the world, ideally 'without tearing the fabric of history and matter'. For Christians, he claims, the event of Jesus is 'the unsurpassable enlargement of the world' – the extreme case of what all art is about. Thus it may well be that our present world turns out to be particularly hospitable to these two old adversaries, and that art and religion may end up renewing each other, both occupying key roles in the new dispensation. Time will tell.

CHARLES PICKSTONE

Tom Devonshire Jones (ed), *Presence: Images of Christ for the Third Millennium*, London: Biblelands 2004; Richard Francis (ed), *Negotiating Rapture: The Power of Art to Transform Lives*, Chicago: Museum of Contemporary Art 1996; David Freedberg, *The Power of Images: Studies in the History and Theory of Response*, Chicago: University of Chicago Press 1989; Ena Giurescu Heller (ed), *Reluctant Partners: Art and Religion in Dialogue*, New York: The Gallery at the American Bible Society 2004; James Alfred Martin, *Beauty and Holiness: The Dialogue between Aesthetics and Religion*, Princeton: Princeton University Press 1990; Aidan Nichols, OP, *The Art of God Incarnate: Theology and Image in Christian Tradition*, London: Darton, Longman & Todd 1980

Asia, Christianity in

Asia is both the birthplace of Christianity and the continent where the followers of Jesus are most persecuted. With only about 8 or 9 per cent of the continent Christian, it is the least Christianized region of the world. And yet because Asia has such a huge population, this percentage amounts to over 315 million Christians and the numbers are growing. It is important to remember that, unlike Europe, the Americas, the Pacific and many countries of Africa, there is only one nation in Asia which can be considered a Christian nation: the Philippines. The diversity of Christianity in Asia is a product of the size of the continent (over 17 million square miles compared to 11.5 million for Africa), the diversity of languages (31 per cent of the world's languages), varied geography and ancient religions and kingdoms. All of the major 'world religions' originated in Asia, and most of the world's ancient empires have been found there too. Christianity is at home in Asia, but it has always been at home as a nomadic or refugee existence rather than as in a palace or among royalty. A sign of this nomadic Christian existence in Asia can be seen in the shifting centres of Christianity: from Jerusalem to Antioch to Edessa to Selucia-Ctesiphon to Malabar and today to places like Seoul, Singapore, Sabah and Xiamen. Christianity is a guest in Asia, and often an unwelcome or misunderstood one. History reveals for us something of why Christianity is still such a minority faith, but also why it is more 'Asian' today than it has ever been.

Persecution

Earliest history

Before the massive persecutions under the great empires of the Romans, Persians and Arabs, Christianity was spreading at a very rapid rate in West and Central Asia. Although early evangelization in Asia outside the Roman empire is shrouded in myth and mystery, it is clear that the smaller kingdoms of Armenia, Adiabene and Osrhoene were evangelized in the first century and all became Christian by the beginning of the third century. These were smaller kingdoms, however, which were dominated by the larger empires of Persia, Rome and later by the Arabs and Ottoman Turks. Until about 225 CE, Persia was controlled by the Parthians, a tolerant people who were mostly Zoroastrian. Thus there was a greater acceptance of Christianity in Persia under this 'Parthian peace' than

Roman empire

Zoroastrianism and Christianity

CHRISTIANS IN ASIA AT THE MILLENNIUM

Country	Population	Roman Catholic	%	Independent	%	Protestant	%	Anglican	%	Orthodox	%
① Bangladesh	**129,155,000**	235,000	**0.2**	536,000	**0.4**	160,490	**0.1**	0	0.0	160	0.0
② Cambodia	**11,168,000**	22.000	**0.0**	74,708	**0.7**	21,500	**0.2**	40	0.0	0	0.0
③ China	**1,262,557,000**	7,500,000	**0.6**	80,708,347	**6.4**	640,000	**0.1**	23,000	0.0	55,000	0.0
④ India	**1,013,662,000**	15,500,000	**1.5**	34,200,000	**3.4**	16,826,000	**1.7**	0	0.0	3,100,000	0.3
⑤ Indonesia	**212,107,000**	5,752,358	**2.7**	8,436,000	**4.0**	12,125,000	**5.7**	3,400	0.0	100	0.0
⑥ Japan	**126,714,000**	460,000	**0.4**	1,800,000	**1.4**	570,881	**0.5**	60,000	0.0	26,000	0.0
⑦ Laos	**5,433,000**	32,000	**0.6**	45,613	**0.8**	34,400	**0.6**	200	0.0	0	0.0
⑧ Malaysia	**22,244,000**	721,889	**3.2**	178,000	**0.8**	660,000	**3.0**	205,000	0.9	3,000	0.0
⑨ Myanmar	**45,611,000**	590,000	**1.3**	575,000	**1.3**	2,511,664	**5.5**	58,000	0.1	0	0.0
⑩ Nepal	**23,930,000**	7,000	**0.0**	551,000	**2.3**	14,561	**0.1**	0	0.0	2,500	0.0
⑪ North Korea	**24,039,000**	55,000	**0.2**	432,413	**1.8**	10,000	**0.0**	0	0.0	0	0.0
⑫ Pakistan	**156,483,000**	1,165,000	**0.7**	850,000	**0.5**	1,796,000	**1.1**	0	0.0	0	0.0
⑬ Philippines	**75,967,000**	62,570,000	**82.4**	14,330,000	**18.9**	3,775,000	**5.0**	120,000	0.2	0	0.0
⑭ Singapore	**3,567,000**	143,000	**4.0**	94,000	**2.6**	126,536	**3.5**	34,000	1.0	1,400	0.0
⑮ South Korea	**46,844,000**	3,700,000	**7.9**	7,700,000	**16.4**	8,870,000	**18.9**	110,000	0.2	5,000	0.0
⑯ Sri Lanka	**18,827,000**	1,260,000	**6.7**	331,120	**1.8**	102,000	**0.5**	55,000	0.3	0	0.0
⑰ Taiwan	**22,401,000**	300,000	**1.3**	451,093	**2.0**	400,000	**1.8**	1,650	0.0	0	0.0
⑱ Thailand	**61,399,000**	255,000	**0.4**	778,717	**1.3**	303,000	**0.5**	450	0.0	0	0.0
⑲ Vietnam	**79,832,000**	5,320,822	**6.7**	640,000	**0.8**	580,000	**0.7**	3,100	0.0	0	0.0

Independent is used here for Christians independent of historic, organized, institutional, denominational Christianity.
In some countries, Christians are affiliated to more than one church. Because in so many countries the percentage of the population who are Christians is so small, it is not meaningful to indicate the number of non-Christians, as in other tables.

Source: David B. Barrett, George T. Kurian and Todd M. Johnson (eds), *World Christian Encyclopedia*, New York: OUP [2]2002

in the Roman empire under the *Pax Romana*. Parthians Mission were, however, powerful people who prevented the spread of Roman rule to the East and who ruled from Syria to India and as far north as present-day Afghanistan. Both land and sea trade routes were open to the east, and so Christians spread the new faith as they travelled.

Like the Parthians, the Sasanians who next ruled Persia after 225 were also Zoroastrians. Christian monks and priests, often converts from Zoroastrianism, were trained first in Edessa and Nisibis, and later in many monastic schools throughout Mesopotamia. Education was in Syriac Calendar and followed the liturgical calendar. Unlike the Hellenistic and Latin forms of theology that developed in the Roman empire, early Asian theology and preaching was more 'Semitic' and poetic. Relationships with the Western churches were often more relationships of contrast or conflict than of co-operation. The Asian church, for example, inherited many of the divisions of the Western Orthodox churches church and so two main streams – an East Syrian or 'Nestorian' stream, and a West Syrian or 'Jacobite' church – flourished in the Parthian and early Sasanian periods. In spite of the terrible persecutions of the fourth century, the Persian church sent out missionaries, or wandering monks, who travelled across the rooftop of Asia to the Middle Kingdom: China. The first of these East Syrian monks arrived in the Chinese T'ang capital of Xian (Sian-fu) in the year 635, and it is likely that soon after Christians from Persia reached the Pacific Ocean. Thus Christian missionaries were officially received in China nearly 350 years before they would be received in Scandinavia.

The early spread of Christianity to India is generally related to the legend of St Thomas. This legend comes down to us in at least three traditions, but all record the doubting disciple of Jesus as having gone, or been sent, to the East. Whether Thomas actually planted the St Thomas Church in south-east India (south of Madras) and was martyred by angry Hindus in the late first century is debatable. What is not debatable is that Christianity has been present in South India from at least the second century CE, because third-century records describe this story. These records would not have been preserved if Christian communities had not been present in India as

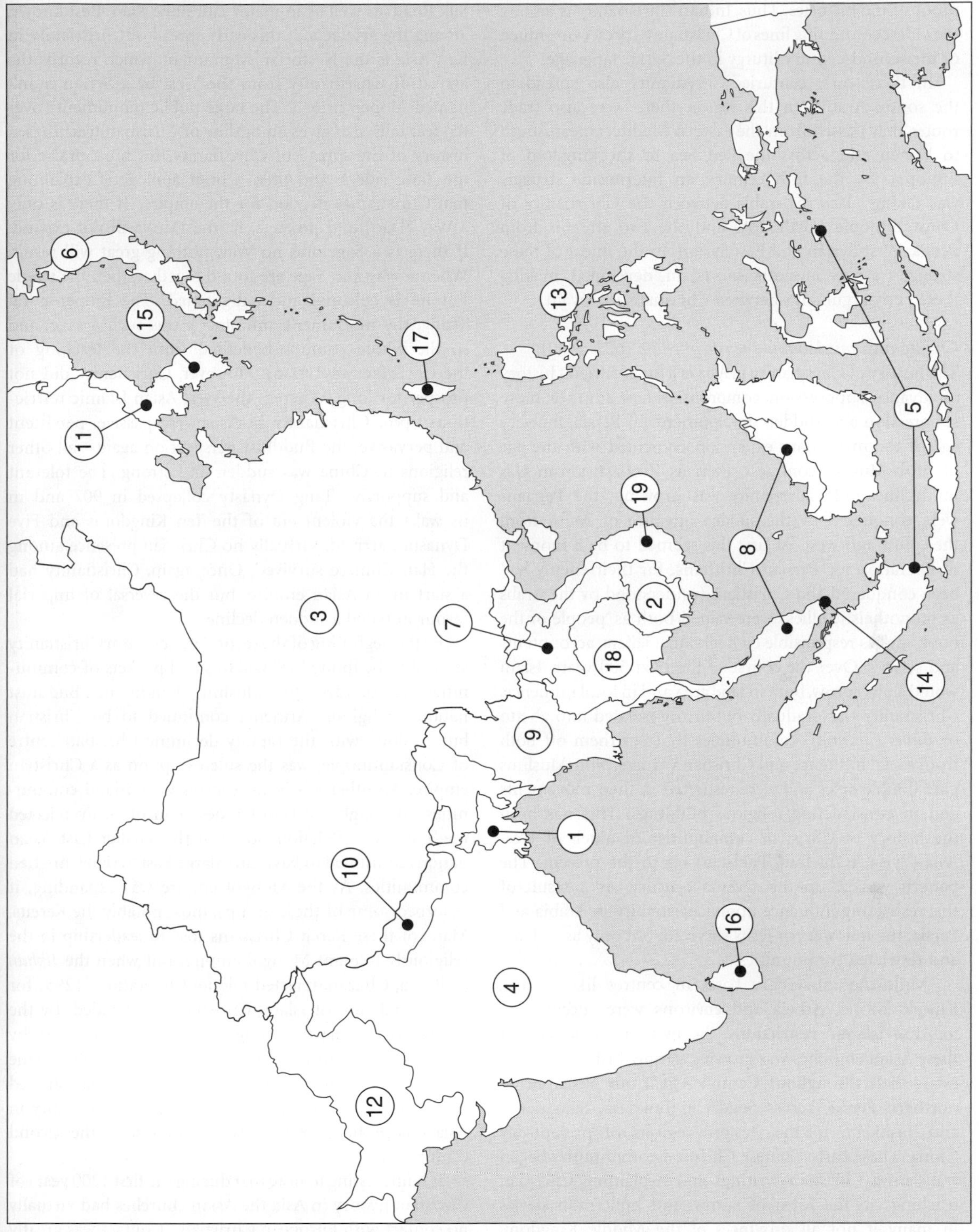
1
2
3
4
5
6
7
8
9
10
11
12
13
14
15
16
17
18
19

proof of the histories. Thus, Indian Christianity is among the oldest continuing lines of Christianity, preserving much of the second-century liturgy in the Syriac language.

In these early centuries Christianity also spread to the south: Arabia. In this region there were also trade routes that passed from the eastern Mediterranean south to Yemen and across the Red Sea to the kingdom of Ethiopia. By the fifth century an internecine struggle was taking place in Arabia between the Christianity of Constantinople (Orthodox) and the two streams from Persia: West Syrian and East Syrian. In the midst of these struggles a new monotheism, Islam, developed, making these petty arguments between Christians irrelevant.

Christianity, mission and the rise of Islam (627–1400)

The history of Christianity in Asia is a long, difficult history of advance, suppression, compromise, new advance, more suppression and sudden development. In Persia, the very age of the missionary expansion coincided with the age of Arab-Muslim conquest. Even as Zoroastrianism was in decline and Christianity was growing, the Persians were conquered by the sudden advance of Arabs from the south and west. At first this seemed to be a moment of liberation for Persian Christians, for their enemy had been conquered and Christians (understood by the Arabs as monotheistic allies) were valued both as 'people of the book' and as responsible civil servants: jailers, accountants and scribes. Over the course of the next 500 years, Islam would slowly grow, both in land area and in local influence. Christianity was gradually but firmly isolated into ghetto or *millet* (*dhimmi*) communities that cut them off both from social influence and Christian witness. Non-Muslims paid double taxes and were restricted in their movements and in constructing religious buildings. This has been the history of Christian communities in much of West Asia (Syria, Iran, Iraq, Pakistan) up to the present. The pattern was set in the seventh century. As a result of this restricting influence upon Christianity in Arabia and Persia, the followers of Jesus survived, but only as isolated and restricted communities.

While the missionary bases in centres like Nisibis, Kirkuk, Mosel, Arbela and environs were succumbing to Arab Islamic restrictions, the missionary activity of these Asian churches was growing strong. Bishoprics were established throughout Central Asia from Nishapur in northern Persia, across Sogdia in Bokhara, Samarkand and Tashkent, to the western regions of present-day China. These early Chinese Christian communities began translating Christian writings and explaining Christian teachings in the form of sutras, and built monasteries in many if not all provinces of the Middle Kingdom. Evidence of Christianity in China between the seventh and the tenth centuries is still being discovered along the 'Old Silk Road' as well as in major cities like Xian. Best known among the artefacts of this early spread of Christianity in East Asia is the Nestorian Monument, which records the arrival of Christianity from the West by a Syrian monk named Alopen in 635. The large public monument (over ten feet tall) also gives an outline of Christian teachings, a history of the spread of Christianity in China, praise for the Tang rulers, and then a brief apologetic explaining that Christianity is good for the empire. 'If there is only a Way (Dao) and no Sage, it (the Dao) will not expand. If there is a Sage and no Way, nothing great will result. When a Way and Sage are found together, then the whole Empire is cultured and enlightened.' The Emperor Tai Tsung, the monument announces, was such a sage, and so the whole country benefited from the teaching of the Christian way (Dao). However, Christianity did not prosper for long. Whereas the West Asian Islamic restrictions upon Christianity in Asia were passive, persistent and pervasive, the Buddhist persecution against all other religions in China was sudden and strong. The tolerant and supportive Tang Dynasty collapsed in 907 and in its wake the violent era of the Ten Kingdoms and Five Dynasties arrived. Virtually no Christian presence among the Han Chinese survived. Once again, Christianity had a start in an Asian empire, but the reversal of imperial favour initiated a sudden decline.

Exploration ➤

Chinese religions and Christianity

By the beginning of the second millennium Christianity seemed to be limited in Asia to small pockets of communities surrounded by Muslim, Hindu or Buddhist national religions. Armenia continued to be Christian but it, along with the rapidly declining Christian centre of Constantinople, was the sole exception as a Christian empire. All other Christian centres were island communities. Although the Han Chinese had officially rejected the 'Luminous Religion', some of the smaller East Asian nations continued to have fairly large East Syrian Christian communities. As the Mongol empire was expanding, it absorbed some of these groups, most notably the Kereits. Many of these Kereit Christians rose to leadership in the religiously tolerant Mongol empire. But when the *Ilkhan* of Persia, Ghazan, rejected religious toleration (1295) for the one religion of Islam, Christian hopes faded. By the fourteenth century the Mongol toleration was replaced by the Turkic-Muslim fanaticism and violence of Tamerlane (Timur: 1363–1405). Thus on the eve of Spanish and Portuguese exploration and colonization, Christianity in Asia was probably at its weakest point since the second century.

It is interesting to note that during the first 1200 years of Christian history in Asia the Asian churches had virtually no contact with European Christians. Contact was greatly restricted by the imperial divisions (Roman versus Persian empires) and later by both politics and theology (most of the Asian churches followed minority christological formulas rejected in the West). One exception to this generalization was the restrained attempt of the papacy to contact, encourage and build the Christian communities in Central Asia from 1245 until 1346. Ten separate missions of mostly Franciscan friars were sent out during this time to the court of the Yuan (Mongol) emperors (khans). These embassies are something of a historian's curiosity; their impact was very small, being limited to the minority people (mostly Mongols) who were overthrown in 1368.

Christology

European and Asian colonialisms

Contact with the global Christian community marks a whole new chapter on Christianity in Asia. This new contact was a mixed blessing. On the one hand, the arrival of the Portuguese was an encouragement to the struggling Christian communities in South India. On the other hand the Portuguese and later the Spanish in East Asia brought a militant and domineering form of Christianity that was new to Asia. Asian Christians had always been minority communities, dominated by militant Zoroastrian, Hindu, Buddhist or Muslim cultures. The Portuguese came as militant Christian sailors. Their goals, however, were not always the same as those of the local Christians. Indian Christians found the Portuguese helpful in defending the Christian communities against Muslim rulers, but rather a nuisance in their desire to make them European Christians, subservient to the Pope. Elsewhere, in Ceylon (Sri Lanka), Malacca, Siam (Thailand), Japan and over to Macao, the Portuguese established their 'shoestring empire' for trade and profit. Missionary work was of little interest to the captains and sailors. Religious orders, however, were quick to see the opportunities for missionary outreach. At first religious orders such as the Augustinians, Franciscans and Dominicans found their way on the Portuguese schooners, but the most innovative and newest order, the Society of Jesus (Jesuits, founded 1540), was the fastest-growing and had the greatest impact upon the way missionary work would be done in Asia.

A pattern of contextualization pioneered by the early Jesuit father Francis Xavier (1506–52) meant that missionary work would look different in different contexts. What this meant for Japan – bringing expensive gifts and wearing silk rather than cotton robes – was quite different from what it meant in India as carried out by Robert de Nobili (1577–1656). Jesuits, like the later Protestants in Asia, pressed beyond the safe regions of the European colonies. Matteo Ricci (1552–1610) studied the Confucian classics and earned the respect of royalty and literati alike, carrying out Christian witness in the shadow of the emperor. His literary works were published in Peking, and in time Korean Confucianists, making their pilgrimages to

Matteo Ricci and a Chinese official, from a seventeenth-century engraving

the Chinese capital, discovered some of these Confucian-Christian writings and brought them back to Seoul. Thus the earliest known Christian movement in Korea was spread from Peking, through Chinese works written by an Italian who studied missionary theory in India.

Religious orders

Another Jesuit, Alexandre de Rhodes (1591–1660), presented the Christian faith in Vietnam, devising a script and a new catechism that spoke to the Vietnamese situation. Vietnam saw the most rapid growth of Christianity in all of Asia up to the modern period. In many countries of Asia the Jesuit approach of accommodation came in conflict with the classic approach, especially of the Dominicans and Franciscans. By the early decades of the seventeenth century, Christianity was having the greatest impact ever on east and south-east Asia.

The sudden decline in Christianity in areas like Japan and China was not only the result of foreign governments or religious persecution; it was also the result of inter-church conflict. The papacy ruled that the Jesuit contextual approach allowed for too much accommodation and so it was no longer approved. Christianity went into rapid decline in China, as the only form of Christianity that was

acceptable to the empire was not approved by the papacy and the only form approved by the papacy (Dominican) was not approved by the Chinese emperor. In Japan the new Tokugawa Shogunate unified the empire and persecuted Christianity (beginning in 1614). All foreign priests were deported, the Christians went 'underground' ('Hidden Christians') and Christianity has never fully recovered in Japan.

Japanese religions and Christianity

Elsewhere in Asia small communities of Christians sprang up in south-east Asia, generally in close proximity to Portuguese trading ports and later Dutch centres (Java, Moluccas). In the Moluccas, Christianity struggled against the violence of the Portuguese and the militancy of the Muslim sultans. Christianity came to the Philippines from the east rather than from the west. Ferdinand Magellan first arrived in 1521, but major conversions did not begin to take place until the arrival of Miguel Lopez de Legaspi (1565), who was sent from Mexico both to develop the spice trade and to evangelize the people of the Philippines. Thus the development of Christianity, spread by *conquistadores* and monks, followed more the pattern of South and Central America than that of the rest of Asia. Once again, resistance to Christianity was felt from the Muslim sultans who at the same time were moving north from the 'Dutch Indies'. The Philippines became a Christian country by means of Spanish arms and preaching friars. West Asia during this same period came under the domination of the Ottoman Turks, and thus the churches of the region, including the Christian centre of Constantinople, were marginalized. In western Asia, Christianity continued in a survival mode as a *dhimmi* community. Thus by the beginning of the eighteenth century Christianity was growing as never before in South and East Asia, but in West Asia Christians laboured under Turkish Muslim rule.

p. 776

Protestant work in Asia came very late, most of the early work being done by chaplains attached to British, Danish or Dutch communities. The work of the chaplains was mostly for the 'expat' communities of Europeans, but many outstanding chaplains understood their calling to include local indigenous communities. Henry Martyn's (1781–1812) work, through the British East India Company in South and West Asia, resulted in the translation of the New Testament into Urdu and Persian. This marks a new approach to mission based not only on the acquisition of local languages, but also on the translation of scriptures into those languages; this became a Protestant priority. During the nineteenth century alone, Protestant missionaries and national church leaders translated the New Testament (or the whole Bible) into 59 Asian languages. During the first eighteen centuries of Christianity in Asia the Bible had only been translated into Syriac, Armenian, Georgian, Arabic, Malay (1733) and Tamil (1727).

The first Protestants to work in Asia, not as chaplains but as missionaries, were not English speaking. Often William Carey (1761–1834) is considered the 'Father of Protestant Missions', but in fact the earliest Protestant missionaries were German Pietists working in Danish territories, and supported by the Danish king and British evangelicals. Bartholomew Ziegenbalg (1683–1717) pioneered this work, arriving with his friend Henry Plutschau (1677–1752) in 1706. As Roman Catholic work was hampered by the struggles between the Jesuits and the papacy, Protestants were just beginning their greatest advance ever. From the last decade of the eighteenth century, Protestant missionary societies grew rapidly, both denominational and ecumenical (non-denominational), looking to the vast continent of Asia. Many of the trading companies and their colonial governments were not receptive of missionary work in their overseas lands. Missionaries learned the local languages, taught literacy and baptized the local people. These were the very people the trading companies needed to exploit in order to increase their profit margins. In time, uneasy alliances were built as missionaries helped with translations and in educating a civil-service sector, and European colonialists provided transportation and social order. The alliance was never simple or static.

Although all regions of Asia were of concern for Protestant missionaries, there was a certain mystique and concern for reaching the Chinese. The London Missionary Society developed a strategy to reach 'closed' China by establishing churches around China that would train overseas Chinese to reach their 'homeland'. This 'ring of light' approach was abandoned when Europeans forced China to open for trade through the 'unequal treaties' of the 1840s. Missionaries who had been working with overseas Chinese pulled up stakes from Malaya, Singapore and the East Indies and moved to one of the treaty ports of China. This early work was confused by the twin European concerns of selling opium and preaching Jesus. In addition, the often violent reactions against foreigners and foreign religion made the work especially difficult. And yet, the Protestant work in China exploded unlike any other field: medical work, educational work, agricultural work, publishing work. As with the Roman Catholic mission work in China, the Protestants also had many theories about how to reach this largest and most needy of nations. Should an approach of social uplift through the best of Western science and education be used, or should missionaries identify with the local farmers and people in the villages, preaching a Jesus of the poor and needy? Both approaches were used, and the results were mixed.

By the beginning of the twentieth century churches were established in most regions of Asia, if not among all language groups. One of the last nations to be open to missionary work was Korea, but as with the first Roman Catholics, Protestantism also first came to Korea through Koreans leaving (this time for Manchuria) for China and coming back with Christian literature. This time the literature was the Gospels translated into Korean. Thus Protestant Christian communities began in Korea before there was a resident missionary. At the very time Protestant missionaries were arriving (1884), Japanese influence was spreading, displacing the Chinese in the imperial court. The Protestant approach in Korea was adopted from the strategy of John L. Nevius, Presbyterian missionary to China. This method strongly emphasized training local leaders to lead self-supporting, self-governing and self-propagating churches. As a result, Christian leaders and Christian churches were closely identified with the local people and culture. The foreign oppressors, Japanese, insisted upon a foreign religion, Shintoism, and a foreign language, Japanese. Christians were among the most culturally Korean, the best-educated and also the most nationalistic. Protestants working in British India (from present-day Pakistan to Myanmar) had similar debates about the approach to take in a highly stratified country. Even those who tried to reach the upper castes in India ended up having a much greater impact upon the lower castes and the Dalits (outcastes). In many regions of India, beginning in the early nineteenth century, mass movements of people came to faith, creating problems of leadership training. As in other areas of Asia, medical work took off with the discovery of bacteria, the use of sterilization and vaccines. Thus by the end of the century Christianity became identified with schools and hospitals.

In the early twentieth century three new trends were observable in Asia. First was the growth of newer faith missions such as the China Inland Mission (1865, now the Overseas Missionary Fellowship). Secondly, at the turn of the century the first Pentecostal groups began work in Asia. By the 1920s, Asian Pentecostal evangelists (especially Chinese, Indian and Ceylonese) began to have a continent-wide impact. Finally, movements multiplied which worked to nationalize and unite churches and missions. The formation of the Church of Christ in Thailand, for example (1934), came from both Baptist and Presbyterian types of church government, and the Church of South India (1947) came from Anglican, Methodist and Reformed confessions. The Philippine Independent Church was founded in 1902 in part as an expression of Philippine independence and control over the church. This uniting and nationalizing of churches initiated a rapid growth of indigenous church leaders. National leaders such as Bishop Azariah of Dornakal were pioneers both  in new church and mission structures (India Missions Association, 1903) and in developing Asian theologies. Social transformations in Asia – both the resistance to foreign (European and Japanese) domination and the influence of Communist and democratic ideals – had a tremendous impact upon the development of Christianity in Asia. In these shadows one of the greatest evangelists of the twentieth century, John Sung, developed an extensive  ministry not only in China, but also among Chinese throughout East Asia. It was not until after the end of the Second World War, however, that the impact of these early national Christian leaders and other indigenizing trends had their full impact.

CHURCH OF SOUTH INDIA

The Church of South India is a landmark in the history of Christianity in that it is the first-ever union between episcopal and non-episcopal churches, i.e. churches which recognize the office of bishops in an ordered succession, and those which do not. It was formed in 1947 by a merger of part of the Anglican Church of India, Burma and Ceylon with the South India Methodist province and the South India United Church, itself formed in 1908 from a merger of Presbyterians, Dutch Reformed and Congregationalists. The union was based on the Bible, the Nicene Creed, the sacraments of baptism and holy communion, and the historical episcopate. A 30-year period for growing together was planned, and on the day of the union nine new bishops, drawn from all the traditions, were consecrated, to join the five existing Anglican bishops.

Membership of the Church of South India now numbers 3.8 million, comprising 14,000 congregations in 21 dioceses (including, for historic reasons, one in northern Sri Lanka). It runs 2000 schools, 130 colleges and 104 hospitals and has organized many rural development projects.

From the start there was hostility to the church from the Anglo-Catholic wing of the Anglican Communion, and one Anglican society cut off all official grants to South India. It was not until 1968 that the Lambeth Conference recommended that Anglican churches should re-examine their relationship with the Church of South India. The church developed a form of service for the eucharist which proved influential all over the world, but the way in which it came into being has not been followed elsewhere. Particularly closely associated with the church is Lesslie Newbigin (1909–98), a Church of Scotland missionary who was one of its founders, one of the original bishops to be consecrated to it, and its tireless champion.

 www.csichurch.com

After the fall of Japanese and European imperialism
With the collapse of the Japanese empire came also the collapse of the various European empires. Great Britain, France, the Netherlands and Portugal quickly scaled back or abandoned their Asian empires after the Pacific War. Suddenly, empires that had been neutral or partially supportive of Christian ministry were replaced by Buddhist-orientated governments (Sri Lanka, Burma, Laos, Cambodia), Hindu-dominated governments (Nepal, India), or Muslim governments (most of the Middle East, Indonesia, Bangladesh, Pakistan). Other countries, in Central Asia, came under the sway of Soviet Russia; the spread of Marxist materialism in China, Vietnam and other states of East Asia led to the rejection of Christianity as well as all religions. It appeared that only liberated Japan would be a fertile mission field. In fact, only in Japan (an imperial power) and Thailand (a non-colonized country) has Christian growth been nearly imperceptible. With the exodus of foreign powers came severe restrictions on, or even expulsions of, foreign missionaries. The result was that the national churches in places like India, Pakistan, Burma, Vietnam, Iran, Indonesia and China had to stand on their own. Within a generation or less (from 1945 to 1968) Christian churches had to accept and express Christian faith in their own contexts. In many countries this meant that the schools and hospitals were 'lost', being closed or nationalized. In Myanmar, for example, the newly-formed independent government in 1960 declared Buddhism the state religion; in 1962 all schools and hospitals were nationalized and all missionaries were removed. Consequently, leadership in health care, education and the church was lost overnight and the churches were pushed back upon their own resources.

In south-east Asia the spread of Communism was a major concern after the Pacific War. With North Korea, China and Vietnam becoming Communist, and Communist agents, often Chinese, spreading their teachings overseas, the governments of Malaysia and Indonesia responded. These responses often aided in the growth of Christianity. In Indonesia the government insisted that all citizens declare a religion as a way of excluding Communist sympathizers. Many declared themselves Christian and then later learned about what they had decided. The spread of Communism in Vietnam, first in the north and then in the south, meant great restrictions on and persecution of Christians. As East Asian nations moved into the global economy, greater openness to ecumenical contacts was a side benefit. As a rule of thumb, the years of restriction and persecution (in China from 1948 until about 1980) shattered the institutional structures of the churches, but have fanned the flames of Christian identity and courage. When global Christian contacts have returned, they have come as 'light support' but weighty encouragement to Christians in places like Vietnam, Cambodia, Myanmar and China. Christians in China have chosen different paths of faithfulness to the gospel. Some have chosen to work in harmony with the government. Leaders like Y. T. Wu in the China Christian Council and the Three-Self Patriotic Movement exemplify this approach. Others, like Wang Mingdao, opposed the government and chose to accept long-term imprisonment as punishment. The church in China continues with these two approaches, one working officially, legally and publicly; the other (not trusting the government) chooses to meet in unregistered house-churches. Both streams are growing at one of the fastest rates ever in the history of Christianity.

In South Asia, Christianity has also grown significantly under local leadership, although mostly among the lower castes and classes. Mass movements of Dalits in India have occurred, partly in defiance of the oppressive nature of Hinduism for those not in a scheduled caste. Dalits who become Christian are able to break out of the cycle of poverty, attend school and become teachers, pastors or doctors. In Pakistan, Christians also tend to be from lower-class families and a conversion is seen as a step down socially. Nepal was a closed Hindu kingdom from 1769 until it slowly began to open to the outside world in the 1950s. With most of the missionary work being done by Indians, the church today is growing rapidly. In fact, thousands of full-time Asian cross-cultural missionaries are working in all of South Asia, mostly within their own political borders.

Some of the largest churches in the world today are in South Korea. Before the partition of Korea, the strongest churches were in the northern regions. With the Korean War came terrible persecutions of church leaders and a massive exodus to the south. Today Korea is one of the largest mission-sending nations in the world. As with all nations in Asia today, Christianity in Korea has been shaped by the local culture. One of the characteristics of Korean Christianity is the daybreak prayer meeting. Most churches have well-attended prayer meetings each day of the week at daybreak. The influence of Christianity upon modern Korea can be seen symbolically by the number of crosses on the skyline of Seoul at night.

Minority status of Christian communities
Despite all the growth and indigenization of Christianity in Asia, it continues to be a minority religion with little support or protection from the national governments, except for the Philippines. This has been the case since the first century. What is different today is that these Christian communities are now more widely spread; they are in contact with each other; and church leaders often have a place at the table in social intercourse. As a minority faith, Christians are in daily contact with people of other faiths.

Thus inter-religious relationships are very important for Christians in every country of Asia. In general we can speak of four patterns of Christian relationships with people of other faiths in Asia.

1. There are countries that are more secular, or more concerned with international trade, which foster a pluralistic acceptance of religions. We might call this the new Parthian peace: a toleration of beliefs as the best way to encourage stability and trade. Often, because there is no real threat from other religions, these Christian communities have very little contact with people of other religions. The Republic of Singapore, Taiwan, Thailand and South Korea belong to this category.

2. There are countries where tolerance is a government requirement, but in fact Christianity is perceived as a threat at the local level. Even though Christianity has few if any restrictions in these countries, there will be intermittent persecution, which at times becomes fairly severe. In this category would be Turkey, Indonesia, India and Pakistan. In these countries there are often places of inter-religious dialogue and co-operation that make possible the healing of wounds and the reconciliation of estranged parties.

3. There are those countries where Christian activity is curtailed by the government. The restrictions placed by the government may be for religious reasons (as in Malaysia or Bangladesh) or secular reasons (as in China or Vietnam). The result is that Christian communities live a type of *millet* existence once again. Examples of restrictions that governments place on these communities vary greatly. In Malaysia, the name Allah cannot be used by Christians for God, making all Indonesian published Bibles officially illegal. In many countries each church must register and have approval for new buildings, and these legal requirements may be difficult or impossible to meet. When the governments are so restrictive, the persecution comes less from lay people in other religions. In fact this type of governmental persecution often drives people of other faiths closer together.

4. In Islamic republics like Yemen, Saudi Arabia and Iran, only limited Christian practice, if any, is allowed for others than foreigners. Non-Islamic practice in these Muslim lands is seen as an affront to the Muslim kingdom. Until 1990 Nepal was the only Hindu kingdom in the world, and although Christian foreign workers were allowed in the country to help with social, agricultural and technical programmes, no Christian witness was permitted. Now, however, the extreme forms of restriction placed upon Christians exist only in Muslim states, in Laos and in Bhutan (a Buddhist country). In these countries inter-religious relationships are almost impossible.

Another way of looking at the Christian existence as a minority community in Asian countries is to see how individuals and communities creatively adapt to their contexts. In China, Communist Party members are not allowed to be Christian, yet there are Party members and eager young intellectuals who are interested in the life of Jesus. Many attempt to follow Jesus, but refuse to be baptized. These 'culture Christians' often meet together to study the Bible and even pray, but they generally do not participate in normal church activities. In India, the dominance of Hindu culture and the close-knit ties in families around the Hindu faith and practices cause many Christians to refuse baptism. Baptism will cut them off not only from their families, but also from the possibility of Christian witness. These 'unbaptized believers', as they are called, try to be faithful to their religion without baptism. In some Muslim villages in South Asia where a *mullah* may be converted, leading those at his *masjid* or mosque to follow Christ, all of the external practices of the Muslim culture are retained. Only the beliefs change. Thus in these villages worship is held on Friday and prayers are said with men and women separated, in the name of Jesus the Messiah. Even with relaxed restrictions in most Communist countries of Asia, there are millions of Christians who meet in house churches, whether in villages or in large urban areas. In all of these communities mentioned above, the two threads which link them with the large 50,000-member church in Seoul or the Christian ashram, the place of spiritual retreat in India, is the study of the Bible and the present reality of Jesus alive and active today.

Asian Christianity today

By the beginning of the twenty-first century, Christianity in Asia has become a more vital religious force than in Europe. In all of Asia only 8 or 9 per cent of the population is Christian, but in contrast to Europe, nearly all of these Christians are active; they attend weekly worship and are concerned with Christian witness to non-Christians. The comparison with Europe is helpful in assessing both Christian presence and vitality in Asia today. In most countries of Europe today, less than 5 per cent of the population attends church on a given Sunday. In many Buddhist, Muslim, Hindu and Communist countries in Asia, more than 5 per cent of the population attends church, and the percentage is increasing. The vitality of a religion can be measured in several ways. In terms of numbers of adherents, in most countries of Asia the numbers and percentage of Christians are increasing. Two of the most rapidly growing Christian populations in the world are in Asia: Nepal and China. In terms of actual numerical growth, the Christian population in the People's Republic of China has grown faster than any church or empire ever in a single generation. Similar growth patterns are evident in other Communist East Asian countries (e.g.,

Cambodia, Vietnam), but the absolute numbers are far greater in China. With over 35 million Bibles published and distributed in China in less than fifteen years, we get some clue as to the growth of Christianity. In addition, the Christian population in some countries is growing more than 1.5 per cent faster than the population. This is the case in Bangladesh, Cambodia, China, Indonesia, North Korea, Laos, Mongolia, Myanmar (Burma), Nepal, Pakistan, Thailand and Turkey. In virtually every country in Europe, the Christian population is declining.

Another measure of Christian vitality is the number of new institutions and organizations that are started. It is very difficult to keep up with the new churches, denominations, Bible schools and mission societies which are developing in Asia. Independent churches-cum-denominations such as the Church of Bangkok, Jesus is the Lord Fellowship (Philippines), True Jesus Church (Chinese), as well as the over 100 Presbyterian denominations in South Korea, are signs of Christian vitality. Christian Bible Schools and training centres continue to proliferate, not only in countries that are becoming more open to Christian witness, but in almost all Asian countries. Even in countries that have a declining Christian population – mostly Muslim countries (Azerbaijan, Iraq, Kazakhstan, Kyrgyzstan, Tajikistan, Turkmenistan and Uzbekistan) – the decline is merely hiding another form of vitality. In most of these countries the decline is related to the Russian Orthodox exodus, but at the same time a smaller, but very diverse, growth of Protestant groups has begun. Other institutions such as missionary organizations are also growing rapidly in Asia. India, for example, now has over 130 indigenous missionary societies affiliated with just one Protestant umbrella organization: the India Missions Association. The number of societies and their members continues to grow.

Pentecostalism

Another measure of Christian vitality is the number of indigenous or local patterns that develop in each region. This is a sign that Christianity is not merely a foreign expression in Asian soil. Not only are there many newer Asian Roman Catholic orders, but also we see the Korean daybreak prayer meetings and the Chinese businessmen who become church planters as Asian patterns of Christian vitality.

Salvation

Atonement
Community

Asian Christian art and music continues to develop at a very rapid pace. Chinese Christian hymns and songs are being composed and published in China as well as Taiwan and among Chinese Christian communities throughout East Asia. In India and Sri Lanka Christian ashrams have developed as a uniquely South Asian structure for spiritual retreat and pilgrimage. Other pilgrimage sites, in the Roman Catholic tradition, have developed in Asia including Maryamabad in Pakistan, various sites of the Apostle Thomas in Madras (Mylapore region) and other ancient Christian sites in South India. With all of these signs of Christian vitality, Christianity still lives a fragile and tentative existence in Asia, the continent of its birth.

Holy Spirit
Miracle
Conversion

SCOTT W. SUNQUIST

Daniel H. Bays (ed), *Christianity in China, From the Eighteenth Century to the Present*, Stanford, CA: Stanford University Press 1996; Ian Gillman and Hans-Joachim Klimkeit, *Christians in Asia Before 1500*, Ann Arbor, MI: University of Michigan Press 1999; Robert Hunt, Lee Kam Hing and John Roxborogh (eds), *Christianity in Malaysia. A Denominational History*, Selangor, Malaysia: Pelanduk Publications 1992; Phan Phát Huôn, CSsR, *History of the Catholic Church in Viêt Nam*, Long Beach, CA: Cúu Thê Túng Thú 2001; Samuel Hugh Moffett, *A History of Christianity in Asia* (2 vols), Maryknoll, NY: Orbis 2000, 2003 and *History of Christianity in India* (5 vols), Bangalore: Church History Association of India 1984–92; Scott W. Sunquist, David Wu Chu Sing and John Chew Hiang Chea (eds), *A Dictionary of Asian Christianity*, Grand Rapids, MI: Eerdmans 2001

Assemblies of God

The Assemblies of God, the largest and most prominent Pentecostal denomination in the world, was organized in Hot Springs, Arkansas, in 1914 by a broad coalition of ministers who desired to work together to fulfil common objectives, such as sending missionaries and providing fellowship and accountability. Formed in the midst of the emerging worldwide Pentecostal revival of the early twentieth century, the Assemblies of God quickly took root in other countries and formed indigenous national organizations.

Pentecostals believe that the central message of Christianity is salvation – that individuals can be adopted into God's family by having faith that God will forgive their sins through the sacrificial death of Jesus Christ. Since salvation is faith lived out in community, a person must develop relationships with God and with fellow-believers. Pentecostal spirituality – an integration of this belief into daily life – draws heavily from Christian scripture. Believing that scripture offers a pattern for how all Christians should live, across time and cultures, Pentecostals attempt to restore what they view as the faith-filled life of the New Testament church. Pentecostals emphasize the power of God to transform lives, noting that New Testament believers, through the Holy Spirit, were given spiritual gifts and witnessed miracles and significant numbers of conversions. Pentecostal spirituality attempts to combine historic Christian beliefs with an acceptance of the contemporary practice of biblical spiritual gifts (notably healing and speaking in tongues).

The Assemblies of God affirms the historic doctrines of the Christian faith. The US Assemblies of God adopted its Statement of Fundamental Truths in 1916. The statement's sixteen doctrines remain materially unchanged and provide a basis for fellowship. Four of these beliefs, deemed cardinal doctrines, identify Christ as saviour, baptizer in the Holy Spirit, healer and soon-coming king. The statement also affirms the trinitarian view of the Godhead, justification by faith, biblical inspiration and infallibility, substitutionary atonement (the view that Jesus took on himself the punishment for sin that human beings rightly deserve), progressive sanctification and premillennial eschatology (the view that the second coming of Jesus will be followed by a period of 1000 years during which the saints will rule with him on earth). Two ordinances, baptism in water and holy communion, are practised. Assemblies of God organizations in other nations generally have adopted similar statements. It should be noted that a history or theology of the Assemblies of God from a global perspective has not yet been written. While most Assemblies of God adherents reside in Third-World nations, scholars lack enough up-to-date information to begin to form a comprehensive picture. Most scholarship, including this brief introduction, relies almost exclusively on Western (North American) sources.

While worship styles vary greatly in Assemblies of God congregations around the world, the common focus is on the activity of the Holy Spirit within the worshipping community. Worshippers seek to interact with rather than simply learn about God. Pentecostals often view highly-structured liturgies as impediments to the Spirit's guidance, instead preferring more informal services that allow for the spontaneity that characterized the worship of the first-century church. Still, many congregations have developed increasingly predictable services.

Sunday morning services generally include the following elements, although the sequence may vary: invocation, congregational singing, pastoral prayer (with the congregation praying vocally in concert), announcements, greeting of visitors, collection of tithes and offerings, special music, sermon (preceded by reading of the scriptural text and prayer), time of reflection or altar call response, and benediction. Appropriating Old Testament themes, services often include clapping of hands, use of orchestras, and lifting of hands in prayer and praise. Assemblies of God churches have long been noted for their contemporary church music.

The Assemblies of God is one of several denominations that emerged out of the Pentecostal revival at the beginning of the twentieth century, which had roots in the trans-Atlantic Holiness movement. Early Pentecostals drew from a complex tapestry of sometimes-competing beliefs, including the Wesleyan doctrine of entire sanctification, the Reformed emphasis on a baptism for empowerment for Christian service, the Plymouth Brethren notion of dispensational premillennialism (the view that God's dealings with humankind are divided into a series of periods or 'dispensations' beginning with an initial period of innocence and ending in the thousand-year reign of Christ), and the faith healing movement. Pentecostals, despite their historical and doctrinal differences, formed an identifiable movement because of their common commitment to the doctrine and experience of baptism in the Holy Spirit.

p. 171

Justification
Inspiration

While many sought spirit-baptism, it was not clear how to determine whether one had received it. Answering this question, the Kansas holiness evangelist Charles F. Parham identified a scriptural pattern – that the initial evidence of spirit-baptism was speaking in tongues. After students at his Bible school in Topeka, Kansas, began speaking in tongues at a prayer meeting on 1 January 1901, Parham, through his Apostolic Faith movement located in the south central states, had some success in promoting the restoration of the gift of tongues. Parham's identification of tongues as the evidence of spirit-baptism became a defining issue within the emerging Pentecostal movement.

Eschatology

However, it was not until the 1906 revival at the Azusa Street Mission in Los Angeles that this restoration became widely known. William Seymour, a black man and former student of Parham, led the Azusa Street Mission. The revival lasted for at least three years, reported to have non-stop services, day and night. This revival transcended all boundaries and brought together men and women from diverse religious, ethnic and national backgrounds. As news of the outpouring spread, ministers and lay persons from around the world made pilgrimages to Azusa to experience the remarkable revival and to seek to be baptized in the Holy Spirit. Participants became known as Pentecostals, named after the Jewish feast of Pentecost when the Holy Spirit was first given to the church and believers first spoke in tongues (Acts 2).

Most established churches did not welcome the revival, and participants were forced to form new congregations. By 1910, Pentecostals from Wesleyan and Reformed backgrounds had divided over the issue of sanctification. Many southern Pentecostals, including Parham, held to the Wesleyan teaching that the Christian experience contained three successive instantaneous experiences: justification (salvation), sanctification and spirit-baptism. Others held a Reformed view, teaching that sanctification was progressive, not instantaneous. According to this view, there were only two experiences: justification and spirit-baptism. While several entire Wesleyan denominations

Holiness movement

became Pentecostal, most Pentecostals who taught a Reformed view of sanctification existed in networks of independent congregations.

As the revival rapidly spread, many Pentecostals recognized the need for greater organization to promote doctrinal unity, co-ordinate foreign missions efforts, provide a legal charter for churches, and establish a ministerial training school. In 1914 about 300 ministers and laymen from twenty states and several foreign countries gathered in Hot Springs, Arkansas, and formed a co-operative fellowship, the General Council of the Assemblies of God. While most other US Pentecostal denominations were regionally defined or taught a Wesleyan view of sanctification, the Assemblies of God claimed a broad nationwide constituency and taught a Reformed view of sanctification.

Almost immediately, leaders were faced with a doctrinal dispute – whether to abandon traditional trinitarian formulations in favour of a view of God as one person, whose name, Jesus Christ, is redemptive. Responding to this dispute – known as the 'New Issue' – the Assemblies of God affirmed the doctrine of the Trinity and adopted its Statement of Fundamental Truths in 1916. Within a few years, the Assemblies of God established headquarters in Springfield, Missouri, formed Gospel Publishing House, and endorsed ministerial training schools. National organizations were quickly established in other countries. While many of these national organizations resulted from efforts of Assemblies of God missionaries, other bodies that affiliated with the Assemblies of God, as in Brazil, existed before the Assemblies of God was formed. The international fellowship, which adopted the name World Assemblies of God Fellowship in 1993, has witnessed significant growth.

Trinity

Fundamentalism ➤

In 2003, the Assemblies of God reported over 50 million constituents in over 250,000 churches and preaching points worldwide. National fellowships reporting at least 500,000 constituents included: Angola (1,607,538); Argentina (762,835); Brazil (19,005,026); Burkina Faso (800,000); Ghana (1,165,710); India (592,920); Ivory Coast (651,800); Kenya (1,035,750); Malawi (586,320); Mozambique (1,351,200); Nigeria (2,036,410); Romania (690,820); South Korea (2,250,000); United States (2,729,562). Notably, Yoido Full Gospel Church, an Assemblies of God congregation in Seoul, South Korea, is the world's largest local church, with over 700,000 members.

The Assemblies of God established schools to train its growing body of ministers. In the US a network of small Bible institutes, begun by local congregations and districts, were endorsed by the General Council of the Assemblies of God and evolved into accredited colleges and universities. In 2002, the nineteen endorsed US institutes, colleges, universities and a seminary enrolled over 15,000 students. In other nations, the Assemblies of God reported 1891 Bible schools and extension programmes – more than any other US-based denomination – that served over 90,000 students.

The US Assemblies of God has ordained women as evangelists and missionaries since 1914 and as pastors since 1935. While it was common to find women spreading the gospel during the denomination's first few decades, the percentage of women among US Assemblies of God ordained clergy declined from 11 per cent in 1977 to 9 per cent in 2002. In recent years the denomination has made an effort to include women and ethnic minorities in leadership roles. The role of women in ministry varies in Assemblies of God churches in other nations. Some national organizations restrict women in ministry; others, such as East Timor, are served by a female national leader.

Paradoxically, the Assemblies of God's restorationist vision has been both ecumenical and sectarian. Great diversity exists within the Assemblies of God, and leaders maintain it is more of a movement than a denomination. The local church enjoys the autonomy to determine its own destiny, and members come from a broad spectrum of religious backgrounds. Still, the Assemblies of God identified with the emerging fundamentalist movement after World War I and with the more conservative strain of the evangelical movement after World War II. The US Assemblies of God was a founding member of the National Association of Evangelicals (1942) and the Pentecostal World Conference (1947), but declined to join organizations led by more liberal denominations, such as the World Council of Churches. The charismatic renewal, beginning in the 1950s, led to significant grass-roots ecumenism, as Assemblies of God and mainline congregations began to come together to worship and to minister in their communities.

DARRIN J. RODGERS

📖 Edith L. Blumhofer, *Restoring the Faith: The Assemblies of God, Pentecostalism, and American Culture*, Urbana, IL: University of Illinois Press 1993; Stanley M. Burgess (ed), *New International Dictionary of Pentecostal and Charismatic Movements*, Grand Rapids, MI: Zondervan 2002; William K. Kay, *Inside Story: A History of British Assemblies of God*, Mattersey, England: Mattersey Hall Publishing 1990; Gary B. McGee, *People of the Spirit: The Assemblies of God*, Springfield, MO: Gospel Publishing House 2004 and *This Gospel Shall be Preached: A History and Theology of Assemblies of God Foreign Missions* (2 vols), Springfield, MO: Gospel Publishing House 1986, 1989

Atonement

A sense that the way things are does not match how they ought to be seems to permeate human life and to be the driving force behind individual, social and political efforts to reshape the world. Deep and often destructive differences then emerge over what is the right goal, where and how and why things have gone wrong, and how they can be put right. These issues can be and are raised in secular contexts without appeal to any god, yet often with religious passion. However, where God is excluded from the picture, the burden and challenge of putting things right and meeting the infinite yearnings of human beings must fall exclusively on finite human beings within the limited framework of finite physical existence.

By contrast, religions posit a goal or a state in which the true potential and meaning of human life may be achieved through conformity or union with some reality that transcends physical existence. Enormous differences emerge again over the nature of this reality, the part it plays in fulfilling human yearning, the extent to which it is personal or impersonal, involved in human life and history, or at odds with it.

Christianity is a religion which acknowledges a transcendent, personal, loving, creator God, who wills the good of the whole of his creation, above all of his human creation, but whose loving purposes have somehow been frustrated. The problem is traditionally understood as sin, a disruption of the intended relationship between humanity and God. Somehow human beings are both responsible for and victims of their predicament and unable to put things right.

The doctrine of the atonement is concerned with how the reconciliation between humanity and God has been effected through the life, death and resurrection of Jesus Christ. The noun literally means 'at-one-ment' or 'reconciliation', while the verb 'to atone' means to act in the way necessary to achieve reconciliation. As such, atonement is closely bound up with the themes of redemption (Latin *redimere*, 'to buy back' or 'ransom') and 'salvation' (Latin *salvare*, 'to save' or 'heal'), which focus respectively on what humanity is saved from and saved for – the new life opened up through Christ.

The fact that the barriers between humanity and God have been experienced and understood differently at different times and places is one reason for the diversity of interpretations of the atonement; another is the fact that the church never formally defined the doctrine and so left the way open from New Testament times to the present for Christians to express their beliefs through a variety of images and metaphors. Examination of these may help to illuminate a doctrine that cannot be expressed in a single formulation.

Historically, differences have emerged over the extent to which Christ is believed to have put things right by effecting a change in God's attitude to humanity and/or a change in human nature. This distinction is closely tied to the question whether it is the guilt of past sin that has to be addressed, or rather the transformation of the sinner. Interpretations of the atonement that are deficient in either respect must seem inadequate on their own, even if not devoid of insight. However, for many today who do not have a deep sense of sin or guilt, the atonement will seem remote and irrelevant unless it can be related to the sense of disorder and the search for meaning that is still very prevalent in the world.

God ◄

Sacrifice

Though the ritual slaughter of animals is not a familiar sight to most people in the West, this ancient and widespread symbol of reconciliation is still evocative. Sacrifice embraces a multitude of meanings. In the Old Testament numerous kinds of sacrifice are mentioned, with the main emphasis on animal sacrifice as the means God has provided to expiate or wipe out sin, understood mainly as ritual impurity.

Sacrifice

However, the meaning of sacrifice was profoundly enriched by the shift of emphasis from the physically unblemished animal to spiritually unblemished holy lives (cf. Psalm 51.16), and even more by the association of sacrifice with the death of martyrs. The problem posed by the belief that suffering was God's punishment for sin was met by the conviction that the righteous martyrs suffered for the sins of others, not for their own. They thus satisfied God's righteous judgement on sin and so opened the way to the reconciliation of sinners. The fact of death with atoning value connected readily with and enriched the concept of sacrifice.

Creation ◄
Sin
Martyr

To see Christ's death in this light as a sacrifice acceptable to God is to see it not in isolation, but as the culmination of a life acceptable to God: a life, according to the New Testament, marked by constant resistance to worldly power, privilege and judgement, and by the constant affirmation of the disaffirmed, outcasts and sinners. To see God in the light of Christ – indeed in Christ – was, in the first place, to see a divine love that embraced all, offering forgiveness and reconciliation as a gift, not as anything human beings could earn or deserve. In the second place, such a response demanded commitment to the same way of life, and perhaps even the same sacrificial offering in death.

Salvation ◄

The value of sacrificial imagery lies in its diversity not only as a rich resource for illuminating the reconciling work of Jesus, but as drawing his followers into sharing in his life and work. The danger lies in overlooking the development of sacrificial imagery and tying it too closely to the blood rituals of animal sacrifice in the Old Testament, or viewing it as a quasi-magical means of escape from the consequences of sin.

Ransom

In contrast to sacrifice, 'ransom' suggests some sort of deal with an enemy. Jesus' words in Mark 10.45, 'The Son of Man came … to give his life a ransom for many', may simply point to the costliness of his vocation, but sooner or later the question would be raised, 'to whom was the ransom paid?' The pioneering theologian Origen argued that it must have been paid to the devil, since we were not God's prisoners, but how could God do a deal Satan with the devil? A solution was to suppose that the devil was given what he asked for, and even had the right to demand, Christ's sinless soul, in exchange for the release of humanity (which had sold itself to the devil). However, the devil, not recognizing Christ's divinity, could not hold his soul and so was outwitted and defeated. Such ideas recur in the vivid image of Christ as the cheese on the mousetrap (Augustine), or the bait on the fishhook (Gregory of Nyssa). The image of ransom thus hinted at later transactional theories and at the same time served as a bizarre symbol of victory.

Complete denial of the devil's rights could suggest that humanity was the innocent victim of evil powers, a conception foreign to Christianity but widespread in the Gnosis early history of the church, as among Gnostics, and by no means absent from present-day interpretations of the human situation. However, the very idea was intolerable when viewed from the perspective of God's righteousness and omnipotence.

The problems posed by talk of the devil (dualism, i.e. two rival powers; the threat to God's omnipotence, etc.) could be met in three different ways: by a bold defence of the traditional imagery, by de-literalizing it in the search for its underlying significance, or by abandoning the battlefield metaphor in favour of alternatives.

The classic idea

The deception and defeat of the devil remained a popular theme for 1000 years, until displaced by more systematic  theories. In the 1930s, the Swedish theologian Gustaf Aulén labelled it the 'classic idea', and urged its revival as the best way of interpreting the atonement, not as a theory but as a drama celebrating Christ's victory. Against what he considered an excess of theorizing, Aulén appealed to the great paradoxes of God as Reconciler and Reconciled, and the devil as God's enemy and yet at the same time the agent of God's wrath. However, that would seem to place Christ's conflict with the devil in the heart of God himself – a paradox too far for theologians past and present, even Hymns though the imagery still resonates in Easter hymns. As it stands, the classic idea can too easily suggest a cosmic battle over humanity's head independent of human response, and dangerously close to the 'innocent victim' error. An alternative is to acknowledge the symbolic character of the theological language.

A solution offered by the theologian Paul Tillich is to treat the devil not as a separately existing being, but as a symbol of the demonic, understood as the destructive power unleashed by human beings when they worship what is less than God as God, turning to the finite or creaturely, in short, idolatry. Jesus stands out in the Gospel stories as resisting the claims of anything less than ultimate to have ultimate authority over him, whether political or religious authorities, public opinion, tradition, the Law of Moses, his mother and family, or even his own disciples. In so doing, he broke the power of the demonic, not by totally rejecting worldly powers and authorities, but by denying their ultimacy. He thus made actual the true potential of humanity to be united (reconciled) with God. As such Jesus was the Christ or, in Paul Tillich's words, the bearer of the New Being (cf. Tillich's *Systematic Theology*, vol. 2).

Those committed to Jesus as their ultimate concern are bound to resist all other claims to ultimacy; thus they share in his victory over all demonic powers and false idols. At the same time, the danger of Jesus himself becoming the object of demonic or idolatrous commitment is prevented by Jesus' acceptance of his own self-negation in death on the cross. To the anguished questions, Why does God allow the devil to exist? Why doesn't God destroy him utterly?, Tillich replies that the demonic springs from human freedom to turn from God, without which it would be impossible to turn to God in love. For God to destroy the devil would mean destroying humanity and defeating God's own loving purposes. God's wrath, on the other hand, may be understood as God's allowing the destructive consequences of alienation to run their course. Yet if human beings committed to false absolutes believe they can eliminate the truth of God, they deceive themselves.

A similar approach is found in the work of liberation theologians such as Gustavo Gutiérrez and Leonardo Boff. They draw attention to the threat of social or structural sin, not just individual sin. For them, the traditional view of God's absolute justice or law sets an example of authoritarianism that must be resisted.

Critics fear that Tillich's interpretation is too subjective and obscures the role of a personal God reaching out in love and forgiveness. Yet many find that his analysis sheds light not only on the story of Jesus but on terrible events and manifestations of evil in Christian and world history. Through Christ, world- or self-centred human beings are centred again on the ground of their being, in other words, they are reunited – reconciled – with God, and hence with each other. Different theories of the atonement are thus symbolic expressions of the variously experienced transition from estranged, disordered existence to human life as it is meant to be (though apart from Jesus not perfectly realized in this world).

Transactional theories

Satisfaction. In the absence of existentialist resources for reinterpreting the classic idea, Anselm of Canterbury, in his great treatise 'Why God-Man?', turned away from the metaphor of the battlefield to the metaphor of the law court in a feudal setting. He saw Jesus as not defeating God's wrath, but satisfying God's justice. While not denying the devil's existence, Anselm denied him any significant role. Sin stood between humanity and God, and sin was not to render to God God's due, i.e. perfect obedience. Disobedience took away God's honour. In the absence of the devil to blame, the full weight of sin falls on humanity. For Anselm, God's justice required punishment for sin, unless satisfaction could be made. But punishment would frustrate God's purposes in creation; yet finite humanity could not provide the infinite satisfaction merited by its infinite offence against God (the suggestion that it could earned Anselm's famous rejoinder, 'You have not considered the weight of sin!'). The solution lay in the God-Man, who as man was obliged to offer satisfaction, and as God could give infinite value to the satisfaction offered, namely his willing acceptance of death which, being sinless, he did not deserve. The gift of his life to the Father earned the infinite reward that the God-Man could then bestow on his fellow human beings to make satisfaction for their sins, and so reconcile them to God.

Anselm has been criticized for imposing necessity on God in the work of atonement, for quantifying sin, reducing forgiveness simply to the avoidance of penalties, and also for focusing Christ's atoning work on his death in isolation from his life, and even from his suffering. Anselm concentrates on how the fact of past sin and guilt has been dealt with by Christ. So though he takes sin seriously, he gives scarce attention to the transformation of sinners so that they will no longer sin.

Penal substitution. With the relegation of the devil, not only did responsibility for sin fall heavily on humanity, but responsibility for punishing it was vested directly in God. Long before the Reformation, Anselm's careful distinction between satisfaction and punishment gave way to familiar imagery of ransom or price; only now the price for our redemption had to be paid not to the devil but to God after all, whose sentence of death for sin rested on humanity. Thus the scholastic theologian Peter Lombard could write of Christ's death, 'This is the price of our reconciliation which Christ offered to the Father so that he may be appeased'; and though emphasizing the love of God, Thomas Aquinas could still write, 'No price had to be paid to the devil but to God.'

With a seemingly unconscious metaphorical shift from the civil to the criminal courts, the alternative of satisfaction or punishment gave way to the alternative of punishment or punishment, to be endured by sinful humanity or Christ as our substitute. That the price was offered to God, not the devil, allowed such ideas to be more readily assimilated with the language of sacrifice.

Reformation

Reformation theologians did not deliberately challenge the doctrine of the atonement they inherited, yet it was hardened in their hands. The feudalism of Anselm's day had vested supreme authority in the person of the king, but social and political changes gave rise to concepts of absolute law to which even kings and princes were subject. The demands of God's justice above all had to be met. Only Christ could bear the penalty of sin without suffering destruction. Thus Philipp Melanchthon wrote: 'Christ's benefits are these: to bear guilt and eternal death, that is to placate the great wrath of God', while the Augsburg Confession (1530) prepared by him proclaims that Christ suffered and died 'that he might reconcile the Father to us'. The same themes recur in John Calvin (though with greater emphasis on the love of God), and less so with Martin Luther (where the classic idea dominates). In Luther's view it was only by the imputation of Christ's righteousness to sinners that reconciliation with God could be assured. Thus justification, acquittal before God, was by faith alone, the acceptance of what was done.

p. 302

Criticism of penal substitutionary ideas has arisen on various counts: the absence of the idea of sinners transformed by the love of God; the rigid views of divine justice and retributive punishment; and the emphasis on change in God himself. Though arguably all theories of atonement are grounded in the antecedent love of God in sending Christ, it was against the apparent discontinuity between the loving Christ and vengeful Father that Aulén justifiably protested.

Subjective or moral theories

In contrast to Anselm, an emphasis on the transformation of the sinner is to be found in Anselm's near contemporary, the brilliant but unsystematic thinker, Peter Abelard. Though Abelard did not ignore Christ's dealing with the fact of past sin (of which he was unfairly accused), he emphasized the transforming power of Christ's love revealed in his willingness to die for the sake of sinners (see John 15.13). At the same time, fear of punishment was removed, since for Abelard, unlike Anselm, punishment was corrective, not retributive, and so no longer necessary for those 'corrected' by God's love. His emphasis on the

transforming power of Christ's love fed into the work of later theologians, such as Thomas Aquinas.

Abelard has been accused of 'exemplarism', the view that Christ reconciles us to God merely by setting a good example. Though this could be said of later theologians who appealed to Abelard's authority, he himself emphasized the necessity for grace to effect the personal response to the love of Christ: a love addressed to each individual, as he wrote to Heloise, not just a general example. The so-called 'moral theory' gained its profoundest systematic exposition with Friedrich Schleiermacher (1768–1834), though he could be accused of one-sidedness and of failing to recognize the power of evil. The tendency by Albrecht Ritschl (1822–89) and others in the nineteenth century to view Jesus as little more than a good example or teacher of righteousness is more open to the charge of 'exemplarism'. Its fault is to ignore the conditions necessary to recognize a good example. For many in his day, Jesus was a bad example. For Paul, a total reorientation of his life, virtually a change of identity (dying and rising with Christ), was necessary for him to recognize that Jesus was indeed a good example.

Paul

Further attempts to address the divine and human aspects of the atonement were made by the Scottish theologian John MacLeod Campbell (1800–72) and the Anglican Robert Campbell Moberly (1845–1903), who, emphasizing God's love, found his justice satisfied through Christ's perfect penitence for sin achieved through his identification with humanity.

Anglicanism ➤

The radical change in the twentieth century is seen in the virtual disappearance not only of the devil but also of God from many people's lives, and certainly of any sense of sin or guilt before God. Many factors such as psychology, sociology, evolutionary theory and advances in genetics have contributed to the spread of secularism. Yet the sense that what is does not match what ought to be continues to impress itself on human life, and the belief that reconciliation with God is the way to salvation and that it is to be found through Christ is still the conviction of many.

In conclusion, however weird or remote some theories of Jesus' atoning work may sound today, they rest on the same assumption and arrive at the same conclusion, that through his life, death and resurrection, whatever stood between humanity and God has been overcome, and the way opened for human beings to be healed and reconciled to God and each other. It is not theories of the atonement but the action of the Holy Spirit that makes this real for believers.

TREVOR WILLIAMS

📖 G. Aulén, *Christus Victor*, London: SPCK and New York: Macmillan 1951; P. S. Fiddes, *Past Event and Present Salvation*, Louisville, KY: Westminster John Knox Press 1989; L. W. Grensted, *A Short History of the Doctrine of the Atonement*, London: Longmans, Green 1920; C. E. Gunton, *The Actuality of Atonement* (1988), London and New York: Continuum 2003

Australasia, Christianity in

The term Australasia is a useful construct to cover the region south of the equator, including Australia, New Zealand and the Pacific Islands. Though there are large political and cultural differences, not to mention huge distances, there are also a number of commonalities based on trade, shared colonial history and patterns of migration. Missionary activity has been another important link, involving both European and Polynesian strands. At first sight, Christianity in this vast region appears to be a conventional replica of its parent churches, all of which have heavy cultural imprints. Missionary and migrant churches are often more slow to change than their founding bodies. Some Tongan Methodists still cherish missionary ministerial dress. Australian Lutherans suspect ecumenism, and have no pulpit and altar fellowship with any other Australian churches because of persecution experienced by their Prussian forebears.

A deeper look shows that there has been considerable adaptation. Anglicans modified episcopal authority with lay representation in synods over a century before the Church of England. That was partly theological conviction and partly pragmatism. Despite English opposition, American and Antipodean Anglicans helped to establish the influential Lambeth Conferences. The Synod of Oceania held in Rome in 1998 saw fit to attack the democratic tendencies of regional Roman Catholics. In New Caledonia, Kanak Christians have enculturated the gospel within Melanesian culture in ways that have alarmed both French settlers and successive French governments. Tonga has developed a theocratic monarchy, while in the Highlands of Papua New Guinea sin-sniffing is an important part of the life of some revivalist churches.

All the regional churches have had a strong missionary tradition both within the region and beyond it, in Africa, Asia and Latin America. Australian and New Zealand Christians saw divine providence in the planting of their colonies, as missionary bases for the evangelization of the north, as well as the Pacific. Though the original churches were British and European in origin, migration to Australia and New Zealand has significantly widened the denominational and religious spectrum since 1945. Most of the Orthodox churches now have dioceses, so that all the great traditions are now regionally present. Buddhists, Confucians, Hindus and Muslims are now significant minorities. Many Australians and New Zealanders have left their religious allegiance for various forms of humanism and New Age groups, while many others list themselves of 'no religion' in the census. Roman Catholics and Anglicans are the largest group, but various forms of Protestantism have been religiously and culturally influential. The churches played an indispensable role in community building in the colonies of settlement, providing not only places of worship, but also schools. They built a formidable network of charitable institutions and societies, including hospitals. Many newspapers were an alternative Christian pulpit.

The Church of England was briefly established as the state church in Australia, but the Church Acts of 1836/7 widened state aid to all the major churches, including Roman Catholics. Such assistance was valuable in expanding education, but by the 1860s and 1870s most colonies had established a free, compulsory and secular primary system. Roman Catholics set up a separate system, staffed by religious orders. Protestants relied on Sunday schools and youth movements to sharpen religious awareness, though until recently almost all schools in the Pacific Islands were provided by the churches. That system lasted until the 1960s–1970s, when state aid resumed throughout the English-speaking region and government schools became more common.

The formation of the Commonwealth of Australia in 1901 led to a formal separation of church and state, but in practice close co-operation has developed, especially in the provision of social services in both Australia and New Zealand. The recent appointment of Anglican archbishops as Governor General in both countries was a recognition of the place which that church occupies in the community, rather than a new establishment. Many of the constitutions of the newly-independent Pacific states, established from the 1960s onwards, give an honoured place to the Christian faith as one of the bases of national identity, though these states lack the financial resources to subsidize education and welfare. Independence has forced churches to reconsider their civic role, especially in Melanesia, where they are one of the major unitive institutions against the still-powerful tribal loyalties. Seventh-day Adventists have become one of the largest churches in parts of Papua New Guinea and find modification of their separatist heritage a great challenge.

Sectarianism was a potent force until the Second Vatican Council changed Roman Catholic attitudes and subverted Protestant stereotypes of Rome. Ecumenism was already a significant force among many Protestants in both conciliar and evangelical forms. Roman Catholic membership of Councils of Churches, together with some Orthodox participation, has opened up a wide range of co-operation in theological education and in contributions to public debate. Conservative Evangelicals and Pentecostals are suspicious of ecumenism. Regional reunions have occurred in the United Church of Papua New Guinea between Methodists and Congregationalists and in the formation of the Uniting Church in Australia from Congregationalists, Methodists and Presbyterians. A wider scheme in New Zealand failed.

Popular religion is incredibly varied, ranging from the Christian villages of the Pacific Islands to those who reject any religion, living in major cities. Others see religion as a private choice that ought not to impinge on any aspect of public or community life. Yet others have dropped out of church life, disillusioned but still strongly influenced by the Christian values of compassion, justice and integrity. European, Asian and Pacific migrants have brought aspects of their folk religion with them to Australia and New Zealand, but find it hard to keep their children faithful, for the churches' constituency is rapidly ageing.

All the churches show signs of cultural captivity, whether to racism and sexism, or to tribalism and intellectual fashion. There are also signs of vigorous new initiatives, the redrawing of boundaries between culture and gospel and theological explorations into areas like significance of land, which are regionally important. Regional Christian leaders have contributed to the world church in a variety of ways. Experience of an incredible variety of languages and cultures underlines diversity, as well as highlighting the need for a unity that reconciles and holds diversity together.

IAN BREWARD

I. Breward, *A History of the Churches in Australasia*, Oxford: OUP 2004

Australia

Encountering Australian Christianity is much more complicated than it was before 1950, when national leaders spoke of Australia as a Christian country and patterns of church allegiance remained much as they had developed during the nineteenth century. The major churches were Anglican, Roman Catholic, Methodist and Presbyterian, with Catholics comprising roughly a quarter of the population. Protestants were proudly British, loyal to the crown and empire and often dismissive of the Catholic sub-culture, with its stubborn Irishness and memories of English oppression. However, Catholics could not be ignored, because of their influence in the Labour Party, their philanthropic activities and their sporting prowess. Aborigines, by contrast, were religiously and politically invisible, and until the 1970s severely disadvantaged by racist laws and regulations that assumed that their future lay in assimilation to a white Australia. While missions to the Aborigines were very paternalistic, they helped

Council

Ecumenical movement
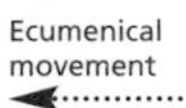

CHRISTIANS IN AUSTRALASIA AT THE MILLENNIUM

Country	Population	Roman Catholic	%	Independent	%	Protestant	%	Anglican	%	Orthodox	%	Non-Christians	%
(1) Australia	18,880,000	5,400,000	28.6	840,000	4.4	2,630,000	13.9	4,060,000	21.5	700,000	3.7	5,250,000	27.8
(2) New Zealand	3,862,000	495,000	12.8	190,000	4.9	931,219	32.4	825,000	21.4	6,000	0.2	1,414,781	36.5
(3) Papua New Guinea	4,608,000	1,380,000	29.9	270,000	5.9	2,610,000	6.7	308,000	6.7	400	0.0	39,600	0.9
(4) Antarctica	5,000	1,400	28.0	700	14.0	970	6.0	300	6.0	30	0.6	1,600	32.0

Independent is used here for Christians independent of historic, organized, institutional, denominational Christianity. In some countries, Christians are affiliated to more than one church.

Source: David B. Barrett, George T. Kurian and Todd M. Johnson (eds), *World Christian Encyclopedia*, New York: OUP [2]2002

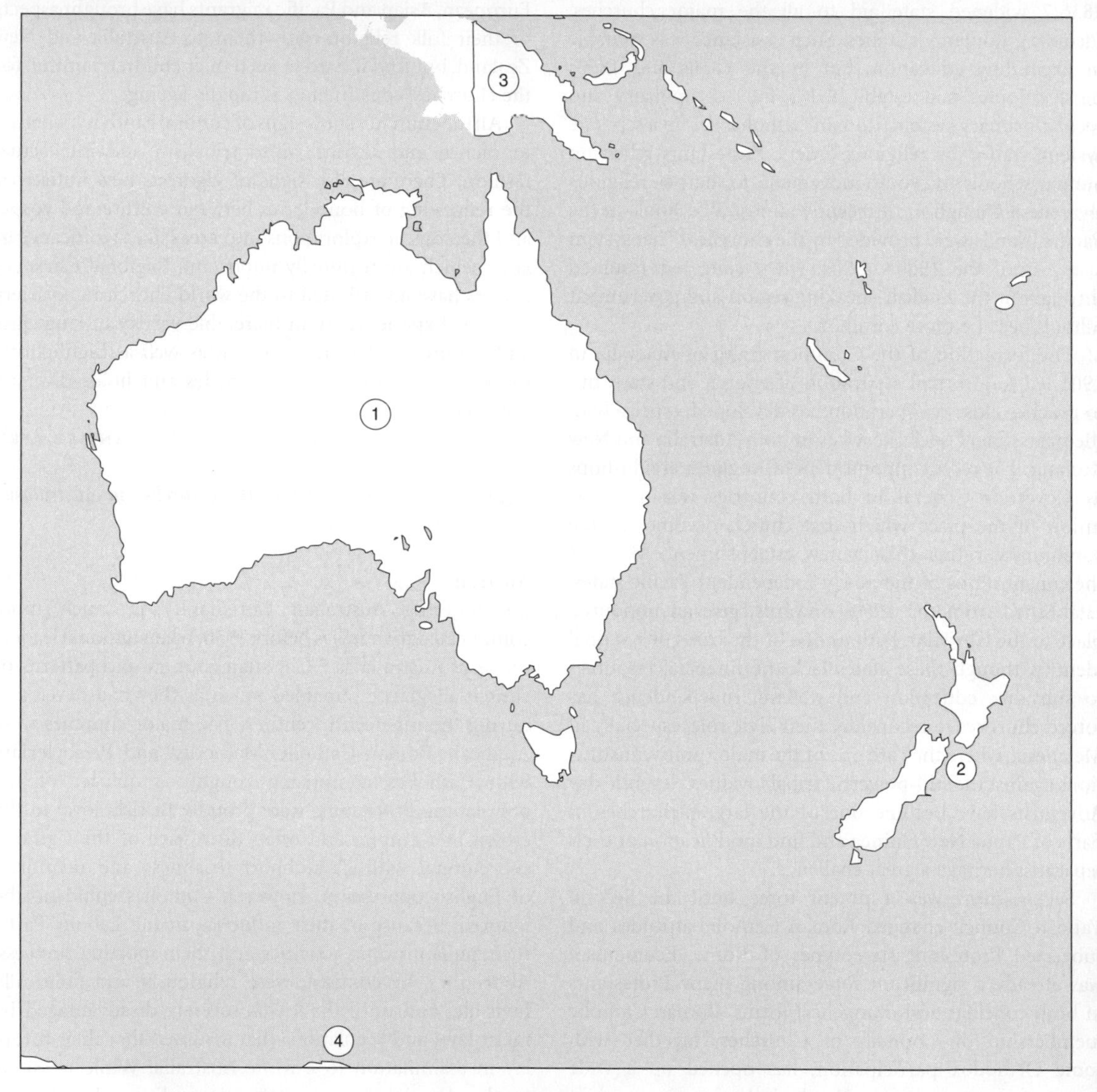

to preserve many communities from exploitation and destruction. Torres Strait Islanders, by contrast, had strong churches and their own clergy from the 1920s.

By the end of the twentieth century, there had been big changes in religious demography. Allegiance to the major Protestant churches had seriously diminished, with about one quarter of all the population claiming to be of no religion, or refusing state affiliation. Roman Catholics had become the largest denomination and Pentecostals the second largest in church attendance. Migration from Asia and Europe modified the Irishness of Catholicism. Orthodox in communion with Constantinople and Oriental Orthodox are almost 3 per cent of the population. Ethnic Protestants from Asia and the Pacific have also established strong churches. Aboriginal and Islander Christians now have significant numbers of clergy, and recognized constitutional status in the major churches and ecumenical bodies. Buddhism, Confucianism, Hinduism, Islam and Judaism all have a significant presence and prefer to speak of Australia's near 20 million people as a multi-faith country. In the cities and substantial towns, the church buildings and activities look rather similar to the patterns of Britain, Ireland and North America.

Outside this context, distance and geography make settlement very sparse. There are over 1300 remote Aboriginal settlements, often separated by thousands of miles over forbidding terrain and ill-defined tracks, scarcely negotiable even by four-wheel-drive vehicles. Many pastoralists are similarly isolated, as are mining towns. They are ministered to by patrol padres and sisters who sometimes can reach their scattered flock only by plane. Being Christian in such isolation is very different from urban discipleship, but nonetheless authentic. Ministry to the outback was pioneered in 1912 by the Presbyterian John Flynn, who not only provided occasional pastoral care, but also worked with early aviators to provide flying medical services to complement the Australian Inland Mission's simple hospitals, staffed by dedicated nurses, which saved hundreds of lives. Simple pedal radios were developed, through which even a child could call for medical help in an emergency. Anglicans and Methodists also developed similar distance ministries. The Anglicans' Bush Brotherhoods, staffed by energetic young English clergy who served for a term before returning home, were influential.

Aboriginal Christians were divided by scores of different languages and tribal rivalries, as well as huge distances. They were not deemed ready for ministry, except in a few faith missions, until the 1960s, when some of the major church missions changed their policy and began to prepare leaders for ordination. Worship was often outdoors under shady trees or an iron roof, but rarely in the Aboriginal languages, for most missionaries believed that learning English was essential to sharing in mainstream Australian society. The missions, like governments, frequently removed children from their families to cut ties with traditional culture and to hasten assimiliation. For many Aborigines the personal and social costs were heavy and life-long. Some of the stories are poignantly recorded in an official report *Bringing Them Home* (1997) and in the film *Rabbit-Proof Fence* (2002). Aborigines now number some 300,000.

Many of the missionaries regarded Aboriginal cultures as valueless and even satanic. With a few exceptions, such as the Roman Catholic Father Worms and the Lutheran Carl Strehlow, most did not learn the local languages and so had no access to the richness of the associated culture. Little attempt was made to link biblical themes with traditional cultures, so that there were some gross misunderstandings among those for whom poor English was a fourth or fifth language. For all the limitations of their teachers, many Aboriginal Christians valued hymns and Bible stories and made their own connections with their heritage. Twentieth-century leaders like the Lutheran Blind Moses, the Anglican deacon James Noble and the Churches of Christ pastor Douglas Nicholls showed what potential was imprisoned in white Christian certainties about white cultural and religious superiority.

These certainties did not change until the 1960s and 1970s. English, German, Irish and Scottish leaders saw no need to modify their heritage for Australian conditions, with a few exceptions. Shortage of clergy meant that standards of ministerial and priestly education were often lower than in the mother churches. Lutherans dropped German as their church language in the face of British hyper-patriotism in the First World War. Anglicans introduced synodical government and lay participation in the mid-nineteenth century because of the democratic temper of the Australian colonies and clear signals that the laity demanded a constitutional share in the use of their financial gifts. Similar requests from Roman Catholic laity at the same time were rejected by the bishops. A century later, the Second Vatican Council ensured that the laity had a limited part in diocesan governance and a more generous one in parishes.

Council

The other major change in the forms of Christianity in the latter part of the twentieth century has been the growing influence of North American Christianity. It has been especially strong in evangelical churches and congregations, seen in music and songs, education materials, types of fund-raising, pastoral care and counselling, evangelism, renewal programmes and religious literature. One of the most dramatic indications of that influence has been in Pentecostal churches and charismatic fellowships within the major churches. Their membership has grown dramatically, affecting Catholic-Protestant relations, introducing flexibility into liturgies and restoring the cultural legitimacy of vital Christian experience of the Risen Lord and the Holy Spirit. An important source of American influence has been the numbers of ministers who have studied and worked in the United States and Canada. Another form of Christianity that is hard to define is outside the churches. Composed of the disillusioned and unsatisfied, its numbers are hard to quantify, but they remain committed to belief in God, the primacy of love, the importance of social justice and compassion for the needy in Christ's spirit, even though they often reject classical explanations of his significance.

Relationships between Christian churches have varied greatly since the foundation of the colonies. Small sects such as Adventists and Plymouth Brethren were convinced that they alone had the truth. Anglicans could be both co-operative and insufferably superior towards mere Protestants, as well as being deeply divided between Anglo-Catholics and Sydney's Evangelicals. Ethnic divisions among Orthodox churches have been exacerbated by political divisions and the activities of bishops whose recognition is limited. The Congregational, Methodist and Presbyterian Churches united in 1977, forming the Uniting Church, but a substantial group of Presbyterians stayed out of the union. Lutherans had united in 1966. The National Council of Churches, with state councils of churches, is an important forum, which now includes Lutherans as well as Roman Catholics and many Orthodox communities, but many conservative Protestants remain outside ecumenical activities.

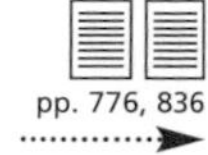
pp. 776, 836

Australian Christians have reflected the dominant convictions of their social context for over 200 years, as well as shaping an ethos that is strongly compassionate, committed to fairness, scornful of religious and moral pretence, and irreverent about authority. Aborigines did not see the process of colonization as anything so benign. They saw Europeans as utterly unscrupulous in their greed for land, treacherous, brutal and murderous when tribes tried to protect their land. Their experience of the legal system was equally negative. Only a minority of Christians actively protested on behalf of Aborigines and Islanders, though advocacy has increased significantly since the 1970s.

In other situations, the churches were remarkably creative. Given that tens of thousands of convicts were shipped from England after the foundation of New South Wales in 1788, the colonies (Tasmania 1802, Western Australia 1829, Victoria 1834, South Australia 1836, Queensland 1859) provided new opportunities to become useful and even prosperous citizens once their sentences were completed. Historians are divided about the effectiveness of the work of the chaplains to the convicts and the impact of the churches on the emancipists and their children, but the churches' education and pastoral care helped to raise moral horizons. The work of notable Christians like the Catholic lobbyist Mrs Caroline Chisholm prevented new arrivals from slipping into misconduct and criminality. Many churchmen such as the Congregationalist John West were influential in bringing to an end the transportation of convicts to the eastern colonies, though it continued in Western Australia till late in the nineteenth century.

The gold rushes of the 1850s coincided with the grant of responsible government, and the resulting immigration of tens of thousands of energetic young men transformed New South Wales, South Australia and Victoria. The churches were hard put to meet the need for ministers and priests. Many of the early places of worship were crude, for population movement was rapid and unpredictable, but by the 1870s many flourishing congregations had emerged, with fine churches and huge Sunday schools. Many of the miners who settled became successful businessmen and farmers, whose leadership in churches and communities was responsible for a dramatic expansion of educational and philanthropic activities, as well as helping to create remarkably religious communities with a high percentage of the population regularly attending worship. British visitors were struck by the energy and vision of the colonial churches, which had become self-governing, with leaders of great ability in major pulpits. Recruitment and financial support from Britain's Society for the Propagation of the Gospel and Society for the Promotion of Christian Knowledge remained important, with Anglican and Roman Catholic bishops retaining strong ties with England and Ireland until the 1960s. Christians saw colonization as a God-given opportunity for the British peoples, since Aborigines were not using the resources of the continent. Capitalists were honoured, and many repaid their community with astonishingly generous gifts, which still aid education, hospitals, social welfare and medical research, as well as the churches.

Churches were divided in their attitude to socialism and the emergence of the Labour Party in the late nineteenth century, though the excessive greed of many capitalists led to a terrible collapse in the 1890s and the slow emergence of some basic welfare provisions. Patriotism in the South African War and First World War was intense and often uncritical. Few voiced doubts about the justice of the Allied cause, just as few queried the White Australia policy embodied in legislation by the Commonwealth formed in 1901. Catholic Archbishop Mannix of Melbourne led a campaign against conscription which caused some Protestants to press for treason charges against him, though two anti-conscription majorities showed that support extended far beyond the Roman Catholic community.

Lutherans in South Australia were treated disgracefully by Protestant hyper-patriots in the war years, even when their sons were serving in the Australian forces.

Chaplains in the armed forces discovered that understanding of Christianity was very thin, though none of the churches really dealt effectively with that for the remainder of the twentieth century. Commemoration of the courage of the Anzacs at Gallipoli in 1915 in Anzac services on 25 April 1916 became a deeply religious annual ceremony for the nation and has remained so. Every congregation had an honours board listing those who had served and died. Communities had impressive stone memorials that were the focus for the annual services, though they were often classical rather than Christian. Clergy did not have a central role in the services, for Roman Catholics were forbidden to share in Anglican and Protestant prayers and hymns until the 1970s. Carefully crafted words and poems were read by returned servicemen, usually high ranking, so that none would feel religiously excluded.

Migration from Britain resumed strongly in the inter-war years, for commitment to a British Australia was still strong, though a sense of Australian identity was growing beneath the élites of church and nation. The increasing strength of the Labour Party led some in the churches to reconsider the significance of socialism, and what Christian contributions to a more just society might mean. Urgency was lent to that with the cruel economic depression of the 1930s and the intellectual bankruptcy of apologists for capitalism. The generality of church leaders were as puzzled as the rest of the nation about what to do, except to try to meet the needs of the unemployed. City Missions, Methodist Central Missions and Anglicans of various theological views embodied a gospel of compassion very effectively; this period saw the founding of the Brotherhood of St Laurence, now one of the nation's leading welfare agencies; Salvationists and Roman Catholics also did remarkable charitable work far beyond their denominational boundaries. Such welfare was continued in the latter part of the twentieth century. With government subsidies, the churches still are major providers in this area. Since the 1960s Christian networks and churches' committees have become much more radical critics of the existing social order, as well as pioneering initiatives on social problems about which there is sharp division, such as alcohol and drug abuse, treatment of refugees and prisoners, and careless exploitation of the natural environment.

Church–state relations in the nineteenth century were characterized by rejection of an established church as a way to a Christian nation. Church leaders contributed actively to debates on federation. Agreement on the separation of church and state was accompanied by a cautious acknowledgement of God in the preamble to the constitution. Many politicians have seen politics as a Christian vocation, but attempts to found confessional parties have not succeeded.

The churches have been an important source of inspiration in good times and bad, fostering an ethic of community service and generosity to the needy, presenting moral alternatives to received wisdom, as well as sometimes showing dismaying conformity to public opinion on issues such as gender roles, until late in the twentieth century. It has been a long struggle for women to share equally in the leadership and governance of the churches, let alone have equal employment opportunities. Conservative Evangelical and Pentecostal churches, Presbyterians, Lutherans, Roman Catholics, Sydney Anglicans and a minority of Anglo-Catholic dioceses have stood with the Orthodox churches and some migrant churches in rejecting ordination of women to ministry/priesthood. That has been very disillusioning to many women. Some have dropped out in the last two decades, although Anglicans finally ordained women in 1992, somewhat later than other Protestant churches. Catholics have begun to explore this new world cautiously.

Worship remained little changed until the 1960s, when new hymns and liturgical experiments began to gather momentum. Changes accelerated with the dramatic about-face of the Roman Catholic Church in permitting replacement of the Latin mass by an English version. Anglicans produced a new prayer book in 1978, followed by a more thorough revision in 1995. The Uniting Church's *Uniting in Worship* (1988) was a large resource book, but with the exception of the Orthodox churches and some small Protestant groups, there was a move away from set-piece worship towards more informal and participative patterns, with many clergy discarding distinctive dress.

Some Australian hymns had been included in denominational hymnals in the early twentieth century, but by the 1970s and 1980s large numbers of fine new hymns were being written, some set to traditional tunes, others with contemporary settings. In addition, gospel songs and choruses from North America spread rapidly. Australian churches had a strong choral tradition, but this diminished in the 1980s. Anglicans and Roman Catholics had local composers who produced settings for the eucharist and other services. Cathedral choirs continued to sing at the highest standard, as did choirs that specialized in period church music, but many worshippers were uncomfortable with modern tunes that were difficult to sing. The *Australian Hymnbook* (1977) and *Together in Song* (1999) are fine selections of traditional and contemporary hymns edited by an ecumenical committee. *Hillsong*, from a large Pentecostal church in Sydney, has been influential in Australia and beyond.

While no distinctive Australian architectural style for

churches has emerged, nineteenth-century Gothic is no longer the normative architecture. The expansionary years after 1945 saw a variety of experiments with new materials, interiors that emphasized the people of God meeting round word and sacrament, rather than rows of hearers or watchers. Stained glass became more contemporary, even abstract. Pentecostal churches were often converted commercial buildings, in which the performance of worship created the sacred, whereas other traditions still expected the building's sacred space to create an atmosphere of reverence. Where Orthodox Christians purchased redundant churches from other denominations, interiors were dramatically transformed to reflect Orthodox convictions about gathering in the presence of the saints. Their liturgies remain unchanged in content, except for some translations into English.

Theological learning in Australia has been dominated by the heritage of the great European theologians. Roman Catholics saw no need for any change. Protestant denominations reproduced their own traditions in their theological colleges, since for fear of sectarian rivalries universities deliberately excluded degrees in theology until Sydney introduced a post-graduate BD in the 1930s, with honorary teachers. Protestant theologians were divided

Biblical criticism

by their acceptance or rejection of modern biblical scholarship and liberal revisions of classical theology. The heresy trials of the Sydney Presbyterians Samuel Angus and Peter Cameron in the 1930s and the 1990s showed that the old tensions were far from dead. They were substantially modified by the development of ecumenical faculties in the major capital cities, usually linked with universities, the flowering of Roman Catholic scholarship after Vatican II, and increasing interest in the Australian context. Two Catholic universities were founded, one in Western Australia, the other uniting campuses in the eastern states. Australian scholars with international reputations contributed to dialogues between confessions, ecumenical scholarship and to lively debate within Australia, though these dialogues cannot yet be said to have interacted fully with major debates in the Australian community on environmental issues and refugee policy.

Popular religion is varied, but lacks the folk quality that characterizes much European Christianity, with its exuberant loyalty to local saints. Some of these festivals have come to Australia with migrants, but Australia as yet has no Orthodox or Roman Catholic saints whose sites are visited by pilgrims. Recent beatifications may change that. Strong currents of conservatism continue to flow in all Christian traditions, sweeping aside liberal optimists and their views in unexpected ways. The Uniting Church discovered that in the 1990s, when a group of liberals pressed for the ordination of practising homosexuals. No agreement could be reached, and so the status quo remained until limited permission was granted in 2003. Many have been deeply disillusioned by the failure of some Anglican and Roman Catholic bishops to deal adequately with sexual exploitation of minors by some clergy and religious. That led to the resignation in 2003 as Governor General of Dr Peter Hollingworth, the former Anglican Archbishop of Brisbane.

Many Aborigines still keep a connection with their primal religion beneath a Christian overlay, as do Torres Strait Islanders. Australian churches have experienced the same collapse of numbers at worship and decline of vocations to ministry, priesthood and religious life as many European and North American churches. Roman Catholics, Orthodox and some Evangelicals have been less affected, but many former Protestants appear to have opted for a mix of tradition and New Age eclecticism, which provide a framework of spiritual meaning focused on individual needs rather than the creation of permanent new religious communities.

For many Australians under 40, the churches no longer play a significant personal or community role. These people were never shaped by Sunday schools or youth groups, let alone family attendance at worship. Modest religious observances at state schools have virtually disappeared, though numbers of chaplains are increasing. Church parades of community groups are in decline as religious belief and observance becomes more pluralist, privatized and publicly marginal. Radio and television no longer broadcast Sunday services each week in prime time. Religious programmes and newspaper columns remain, but no longer have such a Christian focus. Yet beneath the surface of an increasingly secular Australia, religious questions continue to be asked outside the churches.

IAN BREWARD

📖 I. Breward, *A History of the Australian Churches*, Sydney: Allen & Unwin 1993 (privately reprinted 2004); W. W. and S. Emilsen (eds), *The Uniting Church in Australia: The First Twenty-Five Years*, Melbourne: Melbourne Publishing Group 2003; J. Harris, *One Blood: 200 Years of Aboriginal Encounter with Christianity*, Sydney: Albatross Books 1994; B. Kaye (ed), *Anglicanism in Australia*, Melbourne: Melbourne University Press 2002; P. O'Farrell, *The Catholic Church and Community in Australia: A History*, Sydney: New South Wales University Press 1992; R. Thompson, *Religion in Australia*, Melbourne: OUP 1995

New Zealand

Church buildings are iconic features in the New Zealand landscape. The simple, white, wooden, red-roofed country churches and the mixture of brick, stone and wooden urban structures often reflect a nineteenth-century transplanted piety. There are interesting examples of architectural adaptations to the southern context, with views looking out on natural scenery, or Maori carvings and decorations giving interiors a unique dimension. The worship within these buildings still draws on a northern hemisphere heritage but also incorporates varying southern influences. The Book of Common Prayer underlies much of Anglican worship, but *The New Zealand Prayer Book – He Karakia Mihinare o Aotearoa* (1989) includes services in the Maori language and imagery drawn from Aotearoa (the Maori name for New Zealand). At Christmas, traditional carols about shepherds and holly are now complemented with New Zealand hymns that refer to such things as musterers and the Pohutukawa (the New Zealand Christmas tree). Easter worship in autumn draws on language about death in nature and the expectation of new life.

Pentecostal churches and the influence of charismatic renewal from the 1970s stimulated the writing of a large number of scripture-based songs without distinctive antipodean imagery. The Pentecostal beginnings in community buildings have given place to the construction of large auditoriums that reflect North American patterns of gathering. Migration from the Pacific Islands is reflected in the Islanders' large church buildings. For them, the singing of the Lord's song in a strange land takes place in their own languages, reproducing the strong influence of the Christianity of their homelands. As their New Zealand-born children have become adults, the tension between the ways of their parents and the influence of the dominant culture have created new challenges.

The settler churches, transplanted in the nineteenth-century, struggle for congregations in the new millennium amidst New Zealand's secularity. In the nineteenth century over 73 per cent of the population identified themselves nominally as Anglicans, Presbyterians and Methodists. In 2001 that figure was just over 30 per cent, while those who identified themselves as having 'no religion' was 27 per cent. Only Roman Catholics, at 13 per cent, have managed to retain numbers in 2001 close to their nineteenth-century average of 14 per cent.

Church attendance figures in New Zealand for the larger churches, Roman Catholics apart, were always much lower than their nominal census figures. While New Zealand adopted a clause in 1877 declaring its universal primary education to be secular, Christianity has played a much more significant role in the country's life than has often been recognized. In the nineteenth century, an imported Protestant/Catholic sectarianism was reinforced and reshaped by Anglo/Celtic and French/Irish influences. The emerging denominational and ethnic mix resulted in a pluralistic society with its own distinctive religious character. Roman Catholicism, for example, was dominated by its Irish constituency and maintained its uniqueness by establishing, at considerable cost, its own separate system of church schools. For many committed Protestants the 'secular clause' was opposed because it excluded religious teaching in state schools. Catholics saw a refusal to give their schools state aid inequitable.

In the post-Vatican II world, with the decline of sectarianism and the promotion of ecumenism, political pragmatism overcame both sectarian and secular objections in the 1974 Conditional Integration Act. Private schools became eligible for government support. The secular opposition to teaching theology in the universities was overcome with the help of ecumenical co-operation in Dunedin in 1946 and in Auckland in 1990.

The influence of Maori, the indigenous population, on many aspects of New Zealand life, gained fresh prominence from the 1970s. That was seen in the renaissance of Maori language and culture, their continuing population growth, and assertion of their political rights. Anglican, Methodist and Roman Catholic churches that began as missions among Maori in particular responded to these changes. Anglicans adopted a new constitution in 1992 that gave autonomy to Maori, Pakeha (the Maori word for Europeans) and Polynesian *tikanga* or streams, with their own bishops united through a general synod. Methodists restructured their organization with Maori and *Tauiwi* (all others) representing separate voices in the governance of the church. Catholics appointed a Maori assistant bishop in 1988. The return from France to New Zealand in 2002 of the remains of the Catholics' founding bishop, Jean Baptiste Pompallier, was the cause of great celebration, particularly among northern Catholic Maori.

Missionary work began in 1814 when the Church Missionary Society (CMS), an Anglican evangelical group, commenced in the Bay of Islands. Wesleyan Methodist missionaries started their mission in 1822. Initial disinterest in the missionaries' message changed in the 1830s as Maori were increasingly attracted to Christianity by literacy, peace-making and European goods. Maori agents played an important role in promoting Christian teaching. The arrival of Catholic missionaries in 1838 exacerbated both sectarian and nationalistic divisions that were sometimes used by Maori to assert tribal identity. Churches, and worshipping and reading the Bible in Maori, were becoming more widespread as the threat of European colonization became more pressing. The English missionaries, notably Henry Williams, played a significant role in working with the British representative, William Hobson, in gaining Maori support for the Treaty of Waitangi in 1840 that established New Zealand as a British colony.

Mission

In identifying with the British crown, Protestant missionaries acted as guarantors that Maori would receive the rights and privileges of British subjects. The influx from 1840 of migrants, largely from Great Britain and Ireland, had the effect of swamping the Maori population. Under the adverse impact of musket warfare in the 1820s, European diseases and cultural dislocation, the Maori population declined markedly until its nadir was reached in 1896. The Pakeha pressure on Maori land gave rise to skirmishes, and conflict in the 1860s resulted in land confiscation. Over the following decades much of Maori land was alienated. While a small group of Anglican leaders protested publicly against the government's anti-Maori actions, from the 1860s the voice of church protest was virtually silenced. Pakeha churches were involved in providing ministry to settlers who were the beneficiaries of alienated Maori land. Some Maori leaders rejected missionary Christianity and developed movements with their own distinctive rituals which were an amalgam of traditional, cultural Christian and European influences and a response to colonial government and migration.

Te Ua Haumene's Pai Marire movement intended to be peaceful, but under the leadership of Keropa Te Rau and others was seen as fanatical. Te Kooti Rikirangi was unjustly arrested and deported to the Chatham Islands, where he developed his Ringatu faith. Escaping with other Maori to the North Island he reacted violently to the unwillingness of the government to make peace and became feared as a leader of guerrilla fighters. In 1883 he received a crown pardon. His church continues as an indigenous expression of Maori Christian spirituality focused on monthly gatherings in Maori traditional meeting houses. Te Whiti and Tohu at Parihaka in the 1870s and 1880s adopted non-violent protest in response to land alienation. They and their followers were arrested, but they helped to shape a significant pacifist protest tradition. Rua Kenana in the Urewera developed a distinctive community at Maungapohatu, drawing on biblical inspiration. The most successful of the Maori religious movements grew out of the healing movement led by Tahupotiki Wiremu Ratana during the influenza epidemic in 1919. By 1925 25 per cent of Maori belonged to the Ratana church. The church's religious message was complemented by its political activity. Ratana called for the Treaty of Waitangi to be honoured. Four of his followers successfully won the Maori parliamentary seats, and Ratana entered into a working arrangement with the Labour Party which was elected as the government in 1935.

George Augustus Selwyn, who arrived as the first Anglican bishop in 1842, attempted to hold together the roles of missionary and settler bishop to both Maori and Pakeha, but increasingly found himself stretched between mutually antagonistic communities. The College of St John the Evangelist, which Selwyn founded in 1843, was a far-sighted, multi-level, educational institution for Maori, Pakeha, and for a time Melanesian students, but it was difficult to sustain. It went through a number of changes, eventually emerging as a theological college. Selwyn's greatest achievement was in organizing the Anglican Church in 1857 on the basis of a voluntary compact with annual diocesan and triennial national synods in which bishops, clergy and laity shared governance in three houses. For its time it was an innovative response to the colonial situation, anticipating both synodical government and lay participation in the mother church. However, the assimilation of Maori within the Pakeha church structures limited the effectiveness of their own leaders. A Maori was appointed Bishop of Aotearoa in 1928 but was not put in charge of a diocese.

While Presbyterian migrants reflected the variety of denominational fissures that rent their church in Scotland, they largely avoided institutionalizing these divisions in New Zealand. There was, however, a geographical partition. The southern church reflected the Free Church ethos of its founding fathers, who established a Presbyterian settlement in Dunedin in 1848. The northern church, which in 1862 brought together churches north of the Waitaki River, reflected a more eclectic Presbyterianism. The two churches were united in 1901. Methodists achieved independence and unity in 1913, when the Primitives joined with the New Zealand Methodist Church as it separated from the Australasian Conference.

Smaller groups such as Baptists, Congregationalists and Quakers struggled in the nineteenth century to establish a national presence. The Salvation Army, while remaining small in size, developed a significant public profile through its community service. A strong revivalist element was fostered by the visit of overseas evangelists. While vigorous churches were in place before 1914, with active Sunday schools and youth movements, apathy rather than hostility was seen in the high rates of nominality.

Protestant churches were loosely aligned in campaigns to shape society according to their own evangelical or puritan outlook. That was seen in their concerns about Sunday observance and opposition to gambling and dancing, and particularly in their prohibition crusade. Prohibitionists nearly achieved victory in 1919. The failure of the churches to bring most working-class men into active church life was in part due to the churches 'wowser' (spoil-sport) image. In contributing to the restrictive dimensions of New Zealand society, the churches were ill-prepared for the loosening of these restrictions from the mid-1960s. Church membership went into steady decline as the baby boomers discarded their parents' religious commitments.

The Women's Christian Temperance Union was very effective in advancing a whole range of women's issues alongside prohibition, including universal suffrage. New Zealand was the first country in the world to give women the vote. It was another 40 years, in 1933, before the first woman was elected to parliament, and in 1993 only a small number of women had been MPs. In 2002 women were in office as Governor General, Prime Minister and Chief Justice. The first Anglican diocesan woman bishop in the world was ordained in 1990, and women have served as heads of all the major churches except the Roman Catholic. These firsts were starting points on a journey towards gender equality. Women's voices have ranged across the spectrum from those who accept male leadership and exclusive language to radical feminists who challenge the gendered patriarchal nature of the church and who offer inclusive models of being church.

New Zealand churches have made significant contributions to social service work. Despite opposition from the hierarchy, the Daughters of our Lady of Compassion, a Roman Catholic order, under its remarkable founder Mary Aubert, was sympathetic to all in need, irrespective of creed. Churches eschewed political involvement outside their own narrow moral agenda. Exceptional individuals broke out of this mould, such as the Presbyterian minister Rutherford Waddell, who protested against the exploitation of seamstresses in the 1880s and developed a range of innovative approaches to ministry. Church leaders were often most comfortable supporting the status quo. The First World War provides a significant example of that, with the churches sanctifying sacrifice and failing either to criticize the war or provide a satisfactory theological response to its suffering. New Zealand had one of the highest national rates of casualties, even although the conflict was on the other side of the world.

Following the First World War, Methodists adopted an American 'Social Creed'. Along with other churches they struggled, however, to find an effective response to the Depression of the 1930s beyond their noteworthy involvement in social work. The novel approach of the charismatic Methodist, Colin Scrimgeour, led to the founding of the Radio Church of the Friendly Road, but this was on the edges of the institutional church and was not sustained. The election of the first Labour Government in 1935 and its introduction of the social welfare state drew on church support and the contribution of individuals such as Arnold Nordmeyer, a Presbyterian minister and later leader of the Labour Party. The great interest in pacifism in the 1930s gained inspiration from Ormond Burton, a First World War veteran and Methodist minister. Methodists were over-represented among the conscientious objectors interned during the Second World War as the New Zealand government adopted a repressive approach to the rights of conscience.

The two decades after the Second World War were a boom time for the churches. Energetic ecumenism found expression in the National Council of Churches (NCC) founded in 1941, which during the war had attempted through the Campaign for Christian Order to set out a Christian foundation for society. Protestant churches shaped by a northern Christendom world and a comprehensive ecclesiology were involved in church union negotiations which culminated in *The Plan for Union* in 1971. This proposed the union of Anglicans, Congregationalists, Methodists, Presbyterians and the Churches of Christ. The slight window of opportunity was lost when Anglicans failed to gain the requisite majorities. The membership of these churches had peaked, and the opportunity to develop a Christendom-style church had already passed. Churches found themselves increasingly marginalized and became more preoccupied with their own denominational identity and structures, particularly Anglicans and Methodists as bi-cultural issues came to the fore.

The general consensus that had prevailed in 1959 when Billy Graham had been invited by the NCC to conduct crusades had also passed. Theological conflict was present in earlier decades, but divisions were sharpened in the 1960s as Lloyd Geering, the principal of the Presbyterian theological college, advanced views similar to those articulated in England by John A. T. Robinson. Geering was tried for heresy in 1967 and exonerated. The rift between liberals and conservatives became more pronounced. Over succeeding decades the liberal voice has declined and evangelicals have become more assertive. Through the Bible College of New Zealand evangelicals have developed an extensive theological educational enterprise. In the 1990s the Methodist and Presbyterian debates over homosexuality and ministry were tinged with acrimony and contributed to a Methodist group breaking away.

The rapid increase from the 1960s of Pentecostal churches such as the Assemblies of God, and New Life churches, and the impact of the charismatic movement on traditional churches promoted personal and church growth, often centred upon strong leaders. New alliances resulted in new forms of co-operation. The decline in the ecumenical movement has paralleled the decline of the mainstream churches. The considerable impact of the Second Vatican Council on Catholic church worship, religious orders and ecumenical endeavours resulted in a new spirit of openness between denominations. That has been difficult to sustain at the national level. Ecumenism finds expression in theological education and a wide variety of ventures. The decline in religious and priestly vocations has presented new challenges to Catholics. For Protestants, decline in membership has resulted in increased training and recognition of voluntary ministry.

The churches struggle to find their place in the new millennium. Wedding and funeral celebrants have rapidly pushed out clergy from their traditional roles.

The relative Anglo/Celtic homogeneity of the nineteenth century has been replaced by diverse ethnic membership reflecting increased migration from Asia, the Pacific and southern Africa. Cultural and theological diversity and the increasing marginality of Christianity in New Zealand society mean that the churches speak largely from the edge and not from the centre. The prophetic voice of the church has been sharpened. Opposition to apartheid, focused on rugby contacts with South Africa, culminated in a divisive protest in 1981, when churches and the country found themselves torn apart. The recognition of domestic racism and support for the work of the Waitangi Tribunal that investigates historical Maori grievances have brought a new realism to both churches and society. The Hikoi (walk) of Hope in 1998, organized by the Anglican Church and joined by others, was an expression of concern about how far New Zealand could act justly in the areas such as housing, poverty and education. While there is no consensus on either the role of churches or the nature of its voice, the Hikoi represented a reaction to monetarist policies that had reduced public and welfare services and exacerbated the division between rich and poor.

The future of Christianity in New Zealand will be expressed through different voices. Some will promote an individualistic and separatist piety, while others will seek to bring the biblical tradition and heritage into a dynamic interaction with the context in which people live. The Christian voices will increasingly be heard alongside those of other faiths and no faith. While the future of many of the small and even large church buildings as places of worship remains in question, the future of the church, without some unpredictable revival, will largely be around the edges of society.

Mission

ALLAN K. DAVIDSON

p. 776

A. K. Davidson, *Christianity in Aotearoa: A History of Church and Society in New Zealand*, Wellington: New Zealand Education for Ministry 2004; A. K. Davidson and P. J. Lineham (eds), *Transplanted Christianity: Documents Illustrating Aspects of New Zealand Church History*, Palmerston North: Dunmore 1995

Pacific Islands

Though there are cities on the Pacific Islands, village Christianity offers the best window on its distinctive features. Every aspect of life is touched by a sense of the sacred. Most of the community will be at worship on Sunday in their best clothes, which include eye-catching women's hats. Men and women often sit separately. Careful attention will be paid to family precedence. Each village will have its cherished church, ranging from Gothic style to simple small structures open to the breezes. The singing will be splendid and the sabbath will be kept with a strictness all but forgotten in European and North American Christianity.

Many parts of the region are isolated by huge distances of ocean. In Papua New Guinea, another kind of isolation is imposed by very rugged terrain, which can mean that a journey of a few miles on a map is a huge effort. Ships and aeroplanes have modified such distances, but not abolished them. Despite the beauty of the region, subsistence is very demanding, with diseases like malaria taking a heavy toll of life and energy, and cyclones suddenly wiping out years of work. Rising ocean levels threaten many atoll dwellers.

Europeans have divided the region into Melanesia and Polynesia, reflecting linguistic and physical differences. The former has hundreds of distinctive languages, while the latter is part of a large regional language group including Madagascar, Indonesia, Malaysia and the Philippines. Colonialism brought English, French and German as languages of government, with some Indian languages among the descendants of indentured labourers in Fiji. Combinations of English and local languages in Melanesia have become increasingly important for inter-tribal communication and some education. They are known as Pidgin or Kriol. Translating into so many languages has been a huge task, aided considerably by the Wycliffe Bible Translators' use of modern linguistics and technology.

Regional forms of Christianity reflect the impact of the colonial and missionary era, and important local adaptations, as well as comity agreements among some Protestant missions. Roman Catholic missions did not recognize such arrangements and saw Protestant converts as being as much in danger of damnation as pagans. Chiefs and villages were also often adept at advantageous choices of missions. The Spanish explorer De Mendana held a mass with Solomon Islanders as early as 1568, but there were no lasting missionary contacts until workers from the London Missionary Society landed in Tahiti in 1797. Tribal wars and culture shock led most to seek refuge in Sydney, but the victory of Pomare and the persistence of those who stayed led to significant Christian growth. John Williams built on this by placing Tahitian evangelists on other islands through the 1820s and 1830s, creating an indigenous Polynesian missionary movement whose religious and cultural impetus lasted well into the twentieth century, as far away as Papua New Guinea and the Solomon Islands, and Micronesia.

The London Missionary Society, Wesleyans and Anglicans complemented this movement, with informal comity agreements that were not always recognized by the Polynesians. When Wesleyans withdrew from Samoa to concentrate on Tongan and Fijian work, Tongan Methodists refused to leave. Anglicans began work in New Zealand in 1814, followed by Wesleyans. Bishops Selwyn and Patteson worked in the New Hebrides and Solomon

Islands with indigenous assistants. Canadian and Scottish Presbyterians worked in other parts of the New Hebrides, battling fevers and local hostility before strong local churches were established. By the 1850s, strong indigenous churches had emerged, with varying degrees of mission control. Rome had divided the South Pacific into Eastern and Western vicariates, both evangelized by French orders. The Picpus fathers worked from 1834 in what is now French Polynesia, while the Marist fathers worked in the west, including New Zealand, New Caledonia and the Solomons, from 1838.

The colonization of Papua New Guinea in the latter part of the nineteenth century by Australia and Germany brought further Roman Catholic religious orders to the region from France and Germany, as well as Lutherans from Germany and Australia. The colonial authorities' attempts to prevent sectarian rivalry by allotting territory were only partly successful. French Protestants from the Paris Mission replaced London Missionary Society workers in French Polynesia and New Caledonia and the Loyalty Islands.

Most features of primal religion were seen by the missions as incompatible with Christianity. Traditional cults, warfare, cannibalism and sorcery were replaced by Christian worship and morality, technology, literacy and simple health care in carefully organized villages. Outwardly, European influences may have seemed strong, but substantial indigenous features remained in views of the holy, family life, ideas about healing and initiation ceremonies that went underground in Melanesia. Some missions felt that Christianity had been too assimilated to local culture. Adjustment cults that were local adaptations of Christianity indicated that Christians in the Pacific Islands retained considerable capacity for dealing with religious and cultural change on their own terms. In Fiji, the introduction of indentured labour to work the sugar plantations brought Indian religions to the region, but there was little interaction, for missionaries ignored the Indians until Hannah Dudley worked among them from 1897.

Relations between Protestants and Roman Catholics were interwoven with tribal and village rivalries, with occasional conflicts in Tonga and the Loyalty Islands and aggressive behaviour by some missionaries over territory in Papua New Guinea when the Highlands were opened up from the 1930s. Grudging respect also grew, since church leaders on either side of the confessional divide with understanding of local cultures recognized that others had made important contributions to the challenge of inculturating Christianity. That was underlined in Japanese prison camps and occupation and in the challenge of rebuilding church life after the disruption of the Second World War. The convergence of Protestant and Roman Catholic ecumenism in the 1960s, co-operation in Bible translation, and regional councils of churches enabled Pacific Islander Christians to voice common concerns about French nuclear testing, outside exploitation of their natural resources and the impact of tourism.

Tribal loyalties and structures remained politically, socially and religiously important and are still a challenge to the unity of the nations that have emerged since the 1960s in the wake of colonial regimes where the language of government was English. French Polynesia and New Caledonia are legally part of France, though there was a strong independence movement among the Kanaks in the latter part of the twentieth century. Many of the new nations have constitutions that are strongly shaped by their Christian ethos. Some clergy have been influential political leaders since independence. In Bougainville, Fiji and the Solomon Islands there have been bitter civil conflicts that have underlined the continuing power of ethnic loyalties. Tribal fighting in the Papua New Guinea Highlands has re-emerged in the 1990s, with Christians torn between unity and tribal loyalty, not to mention the problems of financial corruption, in many parts of the region.

Worship in the region is still heavily stamped by the influence of the missionary era, though cautious adaptations have been taking place, aimed at incorporating local custom. Polynesian singing has wonderful exuberance, with village and church choirs an important part of the prestige system. The Uapou of the Cook Islands, the adaptation of traditional Fijian chants to Christian use and the prophet songs of Papua show how missionary and local culture have become blended. Traditional dancing has been more difficult to incorporate into worship, though the Papua New Guinean churches influenced by the revival movement of the 1970s and Pentecostalism have begun this. Distinctive regional features such as White Sunday have emerged in churches of London Missionary Society origin. For this one day of the year the subordinate status of children is reversed and they are waited on by adults, as well as wearing new white clothes. Special services at new year and in May, inheritances from the missionary period, have been indigenized. Though many popular hymns are translations by missionaries from their own tradition, they have acquired a distinctive rhythm and lilt. Since the 1960s some local Christians have been writing hymns, though they have been less influential than the widely-used choruses and songs of North American origin. Preaching styles have sometimes been shaped by local patterns of oratory. Some experimentation with local styles of architecture incorporated into church building has occurred, especially in Papua New Guinea, as has use of traditional religious motifs in interior decoration and furniture.

The variety of languages and cultures and the comparatively recent development of secondary and tertiary education have limited the emergence of indigenous theology accessible both throughout the region and beyond it. Church magazines and oral tradition suggest that there have been powerful and original minds at work interpreting the Christian faith from early in the nineteenth century. Ta'unga from the Cook Islands and Penisimani in Samoa are two examples. In New Caledonia Erijisi and Pwagatch gave the great missionary anthropologist, Maurice Leenhardt, indispensable insights as he expounded the richness of Kanak culture as a partner in the proclamation of the gospel. Theological colleges were begun in 1838 and 1844 in the Cook Islands and Samoa, giving pastors a solid grounding in both secular and sacred knowledge. Textbooks were translated into local languages, but in predominantly oral cultures the book-based theology of Europe was basically inaccessible and only a few had opportunities for study in the seminaries and colleges of the sending churches.

That has changed since the 1970s, with the founding of regional seminaries with highly-qualified staff, adequate libraries and scholarships for study in Europe, North America, Australia and New Zealand. Even more important has been the emphasis on enculturating the gospel in local cultures, instead of simply following the priorities of Europe and North America. The Melanesian Institute in Goroka, Papua New Guinea was founded by Roman Catholic religious orders, but speedily became ecumenical and published stimulating journals such as *Point* and *Catalyst*, as well as running superb orientation courses for the workers who came in significant numbers to meet the expanding needs of the churches in Melanesia after 1945. Christians on the Pacific Islands have in turn begun to make a widely recognized contribution to the world church, with a number of local seminaries such as Malua in Samoa upgrading their faculty and facilities in ways which will be important for the twenty-first century.

Popular religion still has close connections with primal religion, especially in Melanesia. Custom shapes the way the Bible is heard and embodied in daily life. Adjustment cults have been significant throughout the twentieth century. Apolosi Nai led such a movement in Fiji in the 1930s with political as well as religious emphases. The Hahalis Welfare Society in the 1950s was another attempt to capture the secrets of European wealth, repudiating aspects of Christianity, but adapting others, for religion, well-being, deliverance and prosperity are potently linked. Yet other dimensions of Christianity have also been lived profoundly. Many hundreds of Islanders died for their faith during the Japanese occupation. Peter To Rot Burua of New Guinea, who was martyred in 1945, was beatified in 1995. Similar heroism and integrity was shown in the civil war in Bougainville, where thousands died. In the Solomon Islands, the Melanesian Brothers (Anglican) have kept the respect of both Malaitans and the people of Guadalcanar despite the initial failure of peacekeeping on the part of Australia and New Zealand. The restoration of the rule of law by Australian military and police had been largely successful by late 2004.

Missions in the traditional sense have completed their work, with well over 90 per cent of the population professing Christianity. Meeting the challenges of the twenty-first century will test the regional churches. Many patterns established in the missionary era need to be re-examined in the light of mere positive attitudes to traditional culture, so that Christianity connects better with its strengths and insights. The boundaries between the sacred and the everyday need to be redefined, for the connections of religion and the political realities of independence are inadequate, whether one looks at the Christian kingdom of Tonga and the refusal of the chiefly élite to permit democratic constitutional change, or the unscrupulous exploitation by many Fijian chiefs of ethnic tensions between Fijians and Indians. Few clergy are able to comment helpfully on the temptations and possibilities of politics and business, or the drastic depletion of resources often associated with corruption, though there are some very discerning lay voices. There are serious problems of social breakdown, unemployment and major health issues which few communities have the capacity to address. Yet the social strength of the churches is a huge advantage.

IAN BREWARD

J. Garrett, *To Live among the Stars. Christian Origins in Oceania*, Suva: Star Printery 1985, *Footsteps in the Sea: Christianity in Oceania to World War 2*, Suva: Institute of Pacific Studies 1992 and *Where Nets Were Cast. Christianity in Oceania since World War 2*, Suva: Institute of Pacific Studies 1997; B. MacDonald Milne, *The Way of Service*, Leicester: Christians Aware 2003; D. Munro and A.Thornley (eds), *The Covenant Makers. Islander Missionaries in the Pacific*, Suva: Institute of Pacific Studies 1996; G. Trompf, *Melanesian Religion*, Cambridge: CUP 1991

AUTHORITY

Bible, Church, Creed, Councils, God, Ministry, Papacy, Tradition, Vatican

The problem of authority is undoubtedly one of the most contested of all areas of Christianity, since it relates directly to the various aspects involved in decision-making in the church. In particular it relates to the use of scripture and tradition, the role of the ministry and the relationships between church and state. Indeed, the problem of authority crystallizes many of the disputes which led to the division of Western Christendom in the sixteenth century and it still forms the most fundamental stumbling-block in attempts to resolve the remaining differences between the denominations. Christendom

The central question of authority is how it is possible to speak and act in the name of God. How can the institutions and leaders of the church claim to have supernatural origins and to be founded upon the divine commission of Christ? What is the divine and human legitimacy of the coercive power which is used in church and state? How does the authority that comes from another place relate to the institutions of this world, both ecclesiastical and civil?

Definitions

The history of the word 'authority' is illuminating: it derives from the Latin *auctoritas,* for which there is no direct equivalent in Greek. The New Testament word often translated as authority (*exousia*) is closer to the English 'power' (Latin *potestas*). The concept of *auctoritas* originated in the Roman law of inheritance: the person disposing of property (the *auctor*) guaranteed the help of the law to the inheritor against the claims of any third parties. The guarantee itself came to be known as the *auctoritas.* On this basis, the word came to be associated with particular people whose opinions carried special weight, sometimes on account of their social position, and sometimes because of their learning or the strength of their personality. Such a notion of authority came to be of supreme importance in Roman politics: the concept of *auctoritas* was quite different from that of *potestas,* which was associated with the magistrate and carried with it the possibility of coercion. In distinction, *auctoritas* was associated with the advice given by the senate. It functioned as a control on the unfettered power of the magistrates: authority thus functioned as a kind of indirect power guaranteed by social standing or learning. This sense of authority is reflected in the 'authorities' of the English legal tradition: judges, whose decisions carry legal and coercive power, are nevertheless wise to base their opinion on the 'authorities' of the legal tradition, even though there is no absolute requirement to do so. This might be referred to as 'enabling' authority rather than coercive power. To be effective, coercive power should be based on accepted authority.

Later, *auctoritas* was used by the Roman emperor Augustus, who as leading citizen or *princeps* saw his own status as the source of the power of the magistrates: all authority was personalized in the emperor. This led to confusion, since *auctoritas* came to be associated with the legal powers of the magistrate and depended on office rather than status. Following the centralization of power in the person of the emperor, all authority was invested in his will, becoming the basis for all other forms of authority: power and authority became difficult to distinguish. This double use of authority and the easy confusion between authority and power quickly found its way into Christian understandings of the term. Roman empire

Authority in the early church

There is no equivalent to the Latin word *auctoritas* in the New Testament, although there are obviously similarities between Jesus' role as an 'authoritative' interpreter of his own religious tradition and the claims made to speak with 'power' (*exousia*), a word which is used 95 times in the New Testament. The most important usage in the Synoptic Gospels connects Jesus' power with the power of God: it is the Son of man who is given the authority on earth to forgive sins (Mark 2.10). This is at the centre of many of the conflicts with his opponents: for instance, Jesus is asked by his detractors: 'By what authority (*exousia*) are you doing these things?' (Mark 11.28). The answer is implied in his actions, which are seen as displaying the power of God at work in Christ. In turn this is contrasted with the power of Beelzebul (Mark 3.22). This notion of *exousia* is akin to what the sociologist Max Weber called 'charismatic authority': it is a form of authority and legitimacy that depends on the spiritual endowments of the leader and is not open to rational explanation. Importantly, the word *exousia* is used of the power granted by Jesus to the twelve apostles to cast out demons (Mark 3.15). Charisma thus extended from one generation to the next. Similarly, Paul also speaks of having received power from Christ for the sake of 'building you up and not destroying you' (2 Corinthians 10.8; 13.10). The power of God resides in the apostle in order to fulfil a specific function. However, as later history testifies, to equate the power of God with the authority of God could lead to a magnification of the claims of the church.

Paul p. 750

It was not until the time of the jurist, Tertullian, at the turn of the third century, that the word *auctoritas* was used in Latin theology. Reflecting the changed use in imperial Rome, he saw it as referring to the absolute authority of God, equating it with the plenitude of power exercised by the emperor. In turn, such divine authority was soon identified with the authority of Christ, together with the authority of the tradition (in the sense of scripture and creed), and most importantly with the authority of the institution which Christ set up on earth. To some extent this can be seen as making charisma a matter of routine. At the same time, however, authority was also associated closely with the handing on of tradition as a kind of inheritance, guaranteed by the authority of the apostles as *auctores*. The bishop, as successor to the apostles, became associated with the handing on of tradition. By the time of Cyprian, Bishop of Carthage (died 258), the church was understood as the bishop's church. As Cyprian wrote in one of his letters, the church 'is the people united to its pontiff, and the flock abiding with its shepherd'. Cyprian equates episcopal authority with magisterial power which makes a claim beyond that of simply guaranteeing an inheritance: authority and power become indistinguishable. This meant that the (moral, spiritual and intellectual) authority of the bishop as guardian of the tradition could easily be identified with the power (and judgement) of God: for Cyprian, this was confirmed by spiritual experience. Here he is continuing the earlier tradition of Ignatius at the beginning of the second century: being subject to their bishop, the Magnesians and the Trallians are subject to God himself.

Augustine (354–430) later used the word *auctoritas* frequently, albeit unsystematically. He saw all human life as based on *auctoritas*, on inherited traditions of living, which formed the basis of human reason and language. However, because of the inherited weaknesses of human nature the only guarantee for truth was divine authority, embodied in Christ and handed down through scripture and the church. In a famous quotation he could write: 'I would not believe the gospel unless the authority of the church moved me to do so.' The resurrected Christ thus survived in the power of the Spirit in scripture and church. However, Augustine was reluctant to identify any particular offices, such as the apostolic sees, with the utter certainty of divine power. Instead, all people were to return to the scriptures as the ultimate guarantee and test of their authority, and the bishop was always to exercise his authority in relation to his flock.

Constantine's 'conversion'

Not unnaturally, the concept of authority underwent significant change following the establishment of Christianity as the official religion of the Roman empire, since two forms of authority and power, ecclesiastical and civil, both of which frequently resorted to theories of divine origin, had to be reconciled. This was complicated by the fact that bishops were soon officially included in the system of administration and were frequently involved in the functions of law and government. As a result the personal authority (as well as the coercive power) of the office-holder increased. The balance between the church and state was frequently questioned, as, for instance, in the formulation of Pope Gelasius I, who wrote to the emperor in 494, stressing the church's rule over the world: 'There are two principal authorities by means of which the world is ruled: the sacred authority of the bishops and the power of the royal office.' At least rhetorically, such a theory meant that the authority of the bishop, equated with the authority of God, could hold the power of the emperor to account.

The growth of papal primacy

Although Augustine's understanding of the church was not fundamentally hierarchical, others moved in different directions. Conflict, exemplified earlier by that between Cyprian and Pope Stephen over the validity of baptism by heretics, often focused on the relative degree of weight which attached to the authority of the different episcopal sees. There was often competition between important sees, for instance, those of Alexandria and Antioch in the East and Rome in the West. The pressing problem of how to resolve conflicts and the realm of appellate jurisdiction can be formulated in a simple question: to what extent did one bishop, even the Bishop of Rome, have the right to interfere in the jurisdiction of another? For Cyprian, all bishops shared in the one episcopate, which forbade, at least in theory, the intrusion of one bishop in another's business. At times 'ecumenical councils' of all bishops were called to settle certain doctrinal and moral disputes, although their authority and disciplinary powers were not universally recognized, nor was there agreement about whether they were to be convened by the ecclesiastical or civil powers, an issue that remained problematic until the modern period.

pp. 552–3

The question of the supremacy of Rome was central. Because of its association with the centre of imperial rule, Rome had always been accorded an important status as a patriarchate, although there is little evidence of primacy before the fourth century. By 343, however, Latin representatives at the Synod of Sardica claimed that deposed bishops could appeal to the Bishop of Rome, and by the time of Pope Damasus (366–84) there were complaints about his heavy-handed use of coercive authority. As time went on, however, the Pope gradually acquired his own legal authority to adjudicate and make decisions in conflicts, based on the commission of Peter ('on this rock I will build my church', Matthew 16.18), and exercised in terms of imperial power. In the Middle Ages, particularly after the pontificate of Gregory VII (1073–85), authority and power were gradually identified: the authority of the see of Peter was equated with the regal power of the papacy. This often led to conflict with the power of the state. The Pope, whose power stemmed from Christ, was sovereign not merely over matters spiritual, but also over matters temporal (plenipotentiary power). These two aspects of authority were later differentiated into the *ius administrationis* (those aspects of episcopal authority which could be exercised before ordination) and the *ius auctoritatis*, which required sacramental ordination. In a period when many popes came from notorious banking families, there were few remnants of the older theory of the *moral* authority of the Pope. Even during the conflicts between popes and councils in the fourteenth and fifteenth centuries the concept of authority was still equated with power: the papacy was simply displaced by the councils.

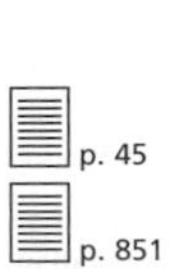

p. 45
p. 851
Investiture Controversy

The legalism of the late medieval church had ensured a massive bureaucratization of authority and power in the Curia. This concentration of ecclesiastical power was accompanied by an increasingly p. 1045 centralized teaching office (magisterium) associated with the authority of Rome, particularly in matters of faith. The Pope, as vicar of Christ, became the ultimate authority in doctrinal matters. This gradually developed into a doctrine of papal infallibility as maintained, for instance, by the philosopher William of Ockham (1285–1347), who later broke with Rome over the question of poverty. William claimed that the Pope had the authority to declare an authentic doctrine of the church which was binding on everybody. The papacy was thus charged with the *authorization* of doctrine. Such an understanding was to be developed still further at the Council of Trent, and at the First Vatican Council it received doctrinal formulation. Papal authority was exerted against the claims of national churches, even extending to the choice of bishops.

Authority in the Reformation

The concentration of power and authority in the papacy led to much opposition in the Middle Ages and early modern period, particularly after the great development in textual scholarship associated with figures like Desiderius Erasmus, which seemed to give Christ new life. The original text of scripture (and to some extent the tradition of the church) which had been rediscovered in new sources and critical texts was set against the personalized legal authority of the papacy, which had been reiterated at the Fifth Lateran Council of 1512–17. A new understanding of authority was developed on the basis of the direct communication of the 'Word of God'; against the word of the priest as the representative of the judgement of God, God alone was sovereign, acting directly through his Son, his Word, to whom scripture bore witness. It was not surprising that notions of authority were frequently subsumed under theories of sovereignty, which had been undergoing rapid development in the late medieval period.

This challenge to the office of the priesthood and the church sparked off Martin Luther in his great controversies of 1517–20. With Luther, the traditional sense of authority had returned with a vengeance, but reduced to the singular, incontrovertible and irreducible authority of the Word of God. The gospel functioned as the law of God and Christ alone was head of the church. The spiritual authority of the church was thereby transformed into a mere function of a higher authority (the Word of God) which existed externally to the church: the church itself stood under judgement. Reason, too, which had become increasingly important in the Middle Ages in justifying the authority of human law, was also challenged in the light of the Word of God. For John Calvin, too, the church was not infallible, but was subject to the word of the Lord. As he wrote in his *Institutes*: 'the only authorized way of teaching in the church is by the prescription and standard of God's Word'. Such a view has continued to shape Protestant understandings of authority until the present day: all institutions and authorities, both ecclesiastical and political, are open to question Anglicanism in the light of the Word of God; it has also found expression in Anglican theology.

Counter-Reformation The elevation of the principle of the authority of scripture was paralleled in the Catholic Reformation with the re-assertion of the authority of the Pope, enshrined in the elevation of an oral tradition which stood under the protection of the church and which was expounded by the teaching office. Here tradition was given a status equivalent to that of scripture. The authority of the original apostles was extended to the present by a theory of succession which gave to the bishops, as guardians of the tradition, something approaching the authority of Christ himself. On the Reformation side, Protestantism with the rise of Protestant orthodoxy, the authority of scripture itself was amplified to the extent that God himself was seen as its *auctor*: this conferred on scripture a quasi-juridical role in the questions of faith.

Authority in church and state

The relationship between the authority of the church and that of the civil ruler was also transformed in the Reformation: for Luther, there was a duty to obey the magistrate in worldly matters primarily on account of the need to restrain the wicked. Within the general priesthood of all believers, the Christian prince thus had a particular authority. Luther's Reformation had not fundamentally challenged medieval Christendom, but had merely boosted the claims of the civil authorities and their coercive powers.

For Huldrych Zwingli, although the Bible, which stood open for all to read and hear, similarly functioned as the authoritative criterion of faith, church order was to be regulated in its externals by the Christian magistrate, who had the power to excommunicate. Authority in church and state was based on the authority of God himself. The relative authority of the spiritual and temporal insitutions, together with the coercive power to be exercised by the civil authorities in the control of religion, remained a crucial point of distinction between the different strands of the Reformation. In England, for instance, the theory of the absolute sovereignty of the king meant that he was elevated to the position of head of the church, a situation that has survived into the modern period, although tempered by parliamentary control.

The clamour for authority

The development of the understanding of authority since the eighteenth century has been closely connected with changes in the exercise of power and authority in the state, together with a questioning of all authority in the time of the Enlightenment. The power exercised by the divinely appointed rulers in church and state (understood as external command) was frequently transformed into a form of authority that depended on the consent of the ruled: the Enlightenment principle of criticism meant that no authority in church or state could rest secure on its divine foundation, but had to be opened up to criticism and had to earn its legitimacy. Such an individualization and democratization of the concept of authority had profound effects on the theological and ecclesiastical understanding of authority and exercise of power. All authority was challenged, whether established in the scriptural principle of the Reformers, the rule of the Christian magistrate, or the Roman Catholic magisterium.

Enlightenment

In England, for instance, the opening up of the institutions of power to members of denominations other than the Church of England seemed to some an abuse of the divine right on the part of the king. This led in turn to a clamour for an alternative source of divine authority. The very first of the Tracts for the Times issued by the Oxford Movement in 1833 served to some extent as a manifesto for a rediscovered sense of the authority of the visible church and particularly of its ministry. The clamour for authority here seems to be coupled with a loss of ecclesiastical power; this is also reflected in the elevation of the papal claims to 'divine right' in the nineteenth century at precisely the time when the Pope's international prestige and temporal power were most under threat. Elsewhere, as with the rise of biblical literalism in the United States at the end of the nineteenth century and the rise of 'fundamentalism' in the twentieth, the thirst for an absolute certainty to compensate for the loss of ecclesiastical power in the wider society seems self-evident.

Oxford Movement

Fundamentalism

Some have seen the clamour for religious authority as a mask for the unbridled and often abusive exercise of power on the part of religious institutions and religious rhetoric. They ask whether all religious authority is not by nature oppressive, and whether the Christian gospel does not promise freedom but enforce obedience. Luther may have made the contrast between the authority of the church and the 'liberty' of the Christian a fundamental theme of his charges against Rome, but he conceived of freedom as a gift from God in which there could be no 'free will'. Such a conception of liberty, expressed as 'bondage', 'submission' and 'obedience', invites careful theological and psychological critique.

The future of authority

Such critiques indicate how important it is to legitimate the exercise of authority in the face of the absolutist claims of the past which confuse moral authority with coercive power. In the contemporary pluralist situation, coercive power has virtually disappeared from the church. Similarly the power which derives from the authority of office has frequently been questioned in all spheres of life including the religious. Because choice is possible and denominations compete with one another, obedience has to be a matter of consent and authority proved to be legitimate. Authority thus depends on the free choice of individuals in favour of something they have weighed and submitted to scrutiny, in the process continually transforming it. The final authority rests ultimately in the future. In the Roman Catholic Church some writers have developed understandings of authority which pay full attention to the notions of consent and legitimacy, as well as the contribution of the
p. 627
laity in the decision-making processes of the church. The *Catechism of the Catholic Church* states that the teaching office serves the laity (§ 2235–6). In other churches there has been a resort to 'experience' of the spirit as a source of authority and power, which some have seen as a rejuvenation of charismatic forms of authority, but which many have criticized on psychological grounds.

Authority is the current issue in the dialogue carried on within the Anglican Roman Catholic International Commission (ARCIC), the latest views of which are expressed in the 1999 document *The Gift of Authority*. It remains a key issue for all the churches today.

MARK D. CHAPMAN

ARCIC, *The Gift of Authority*, London: Catholic Truth Society and Toronto: Anglican Book Centre 1999; P. Avis, *Authority, Leadership and Conflict in the Church*, London: Mowbray and Philadelphia: Trinity Press International 1992; M. D. Chapman, *By What Authority?*, London: Darton, Longman & Todd 1997; G. Evans, *Problems of Authority in the Reformation Debates*, Cambridge: CUP 1992; B. Hoose (ed), *Authority in the Roman Catholic Church*, Aldershot: Ashgate 2002; J. M. Todd (ed), *Problems of Authority*, London: Darton, Longman & Todd and Baltimore: Helicon Press 1962

Baptist churches

The roots of the Baptists lie in the sixteenth-century
Reformation
Reformation. Although some have tried to claim that such communities of faith have always existed as the true church, a view known as landmarkism, Baptists have normally dated their origins from the early years of the seventeenth
p. 988
century in England. They have been Dissenters, Nonconformists, and today are one of the largest Protestant groupings in the world.

Baptists insist that nothing must compromise the sovereign rule of Jesus Christ, the one to whom all authority in heaven and on earth has been given (Matthew 28.18). Believing that they are taking the New Testament as their model, they emphasize a way of being the church that stresses the local congregation called together under the lordship of the living Christ. The local company of Christians can read the scriptures together, reflect on their meaning and, under the guidance of the Holy Spirit, act in ways they believe are the will of Christ. Having Christ, the Bible, the promised leading of the Holy Spirit and fellow Christians with the gift of faith, they need no imposed human authority to be the church. Such an approach, with no external ecclesiastical authority, was liable to lead to different forms of expression, and that has indeed been the case. What impelled Baptists to separate originally from other churches was the desire to be the true church, and they looked to the New Testament for guidance.

Internationally, Baptists are widespread, because of the strong missionary imperative that has been a creative feature of their life. At present there are 206 Baptist unions or conventions in membership with the Baptist World Alliance (BWA). A union or convention is made up of local churches on the basis of some brief statement of purpose or confession of faith. Often such unions are national, as in Scotland or Belgium, but there may be more than one union in the same country, as is the case in America. There are 44 million baptized believers associated through their unions with the BWA, the core of a community of 110 million in more than 200 countries. The goals of the BWA are to unite Baptists world-wide, to lead in world evangelization, to respond to people in need and to defend human rights.

The social and economic background of Baptists is very varied and always has been so. In the southern states of America, for example, some congregations may be very large and rich with considerable economic and political influence. In other parts of the world, Baptists can be found among the very poor, as missionaries have worked among them and established churches. Politically, Baptists can be found anywhere on the spectrum from radical left to moral majority right. Theologically, the spread may be as wide, from liberalism to fundamentalism.

Baptists stand in the Evangelical as distinct from the Catholic or Orthodox tradition of the faith. However, within this broad description there have been differences. The earliest Baptists comprised Arminians (those who believed salvation was offered to all) and Calvinists (who thought only God's elect were to be saved). When the BWA was formed in London in 1905, the first act the President asked the delegates to perform was to recite the Apostles' Creed. It was a way of declaring that Baptists saw themselves as standing in the apostolic faith and were not a sub-Christian sect.

Reciting a creed was an unusual thing for Baptists to do. It is not that creeds are not believed; rather, since creeds are human constructions, Baptists did not think they could have the authority some Christians attach to them. Early Baptists drew up confessions of faith as a means of explaining themselves to one another and to other Christians. Such confessions would be developed, and so they never had the authoritative status of creeds. No local congregation could impose its confession on another congregation.

For Baptists, the most important document is the Bible, by which all beliefs and practices must be tested, because the Bible has unique authority. Many Baptists call it the Word of God. However, there are significant differences among Baptists on the issue of biblical authority. Some congregations take a literalistic approach, affirming what the Bible says because it says it. So, for example, the numerically large Southern Baptist Convention in the United States has declared that no woman should be in pastoral authority over a man, that women should not preach or be ordained, because that is judged not to be biblical. By contrast, the Baptist Union of Great Britain has had recognized women ministers for many years. The British interpret the Bible differently and also base their union on a Declaration of Principle which does not affirm the supreme authority of the Bible with its story of Jesus, but the given authority of the risen Christ to whom the scriptures bear witness. Such distinctions can be found among Baptists, but generally speaking Baptists adopt a Calvinistic interpretation of the evangelical faith and so look to the Bible as the authority for faith and practice. Baptists have had a long tradition of biblical scholars, some of whom remain radical and critical in their approach to the text.

John Calvin

What distinguishes Baptists? Initially views connected with the doctrine of the church. For Baptists there are two fundamental and related understandings of the word 'church'. One is that great company of the redeemed that no one can number, the church known only to God, the one great universal church spanning all time and space, of which all Christians are members. Early Baptists called this the invisible church.

Liberal theology
Fundamentalism

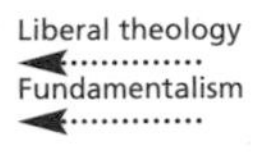

The second expression of the 'church' is the local gathered congregation of those who profess the faith of the gospel and live obediently by Christ. Two or three gathered in his name, listening to and obeying his word, are the church. It is the presence and recognition of Christ's authority that is essential for the true church (Matthew 18.20). The fellowship of believers, having the risen Christ among them, needs nothing more in order to be the church. Bishops, ministers, buildings, councils may be helpful, but they are not of the essence, which is Christ with his faithful people. So the local church meets regularly to order its life after the mind of Christ. Members have the responsibility and privilege of shaping the life of the church as they believe is right under Christ.

p. 1016

Creed

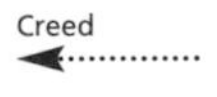

Who are members of the church? For Baptists, those who have heard God's call and come to trust Christ as saviour and follow him as Lord. Baptists stand in the believers' church tradition. The church is composed of those who have repented of their sin and turned to Christ. They are not necessarily born of Christian parents, but they are 'born again'; that is, they have responded in faith to the living call of God. This does not mean that every Baptist has been through a sudden 'Damascus Road' conversion experience. For many, the journey to Christian

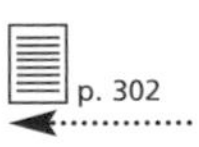

p. 302

Forgiveness

Conversion

commitment has been over several years. But the point is that every Baptist acknowledges that the initiative has been with God, evoking the free response of personal trust and faith. Both the work of God and the answering faith of the individual are crucial. Faith and trust cannot be forced or received by proxy. We are called by name and must answer for ourselves. This reflects the evangelical gospel of grace through faith.

Initiation

So it follows that if the church is made up of believers, and if baptism is the biblical mode of entrance into the church, then baptism is for believers only. That is the route Baptists eventually took. Baptism does not of itself make a person a Christian. It is those who trust in Christ who are baptized and become members of the church. Baptists have never set an age for baptism, insisting only on the candidate's confession of faith. Believers' baptism is not adult baptism. At their baptism candidates will be invited to give their testimony to faith in Christ. They will be questioned about their belief in the triune God, their commitment to Christ and their willingness to share the fellowship of the church. Upon such confession of faith they are baptized. Baptism usually takes the form of total immersion, being buried and raised with Christ. Some Baptist churches will welcome into membership those who have faith in Christ but are not baptized. Baptists welcome children, with services of thanksgiving, dedication and blessing.

Sacraments

Some but by no means all Baptists think of baptism as a sacrament, along with the Lord's Supper. These are occasions where God is graciously active. Thus baptism is not simply an act of personal testimony. It is one of the two God-ordained meeting places where God blesses his people. There is a similar division between Baptists over the meaning of holy communion. For some the emphasis is strictly one of symbol and memorial, recalling the death of Jesus. For others, Christ is present feeding his people in a meal that is more than a symbol. Many early Baptists took a sacramental view of the Lord's Supper and baptism, as did significant twentieth-century Baptist theologians in England. However, in the nineteenth century, perhaps in reaction against Anglo-Catholic emphases in the Church of England, a non-sacramental theology was developed.

Ministry and ministers ➤

Local Baptist churches hold regular church members' meetings. Everything that relates to the life of the congregation and Christian discipleship is potentially on the agenda. The outward appearance of the meeting may be that of a democracy, for all members may speak and each individual has only one vote. But at its best the church meeting is not an exercise in democratic power so much as a shared search for the mind of Christ. The church, after all, is that company gathered in his name to do his will and be his people. It must be admitted that local congregations can fall below this high standard, and prejudices and partisanship can become evident. But the vision of all whom God has called into the fellowship of the local church being members together under the rule of Christ, all potentially those through whom God may speak his word to the church, is an important one for Baptists.

It would be misleading to suggest that the unqualified independence of congregations is all there is to be said. Again, the practice among Baptists has varied, but most Baptist congregations have belonged to associations from which they have sought fellowship and help and in which they have recognized some measure of accountability. They have rarely used the word 'church' for these organizations and meetings, and precisely how they relate to the church remains a matter of dispute. However, the associations have produced their own confessions of faith, taken responsibility for ministerial preparation and support, encouraged the planting of new congregations and appointed their own association ministers.

Many Baptist churches are also members of national unions, such as the Baptist Union of Great Britain. These unions often came into being to support the mission of the churches both at home and abroad. Inevitably the organizations developed, taking responsibility among other things for ministerial recognition, national policies of mission, ecumenism and questions of relations with the government. However, it would be wrong to speak of the Baptist Church in Great Britain. For Baptists, the church is local, but churches gather in associations and unions. It is this that has made participation in ecumenical discussions difficult for Baptists. When it came to the question of whether the Baptist Union of Great Britain should join new ecumenical instruments a special debate was called at the Annual National Assembly of the Union and every single church had the right to vote.

Nonetheless, local Baptists have sought fellowship with one another in associations, national unions and internationally through the BWA. All of these have arisen as expressions of that fellowship that Christians have with one another in Christ and in order to further the missionary spread of the gospel.

By their baptism, church members share in the ministry of the church under Christ. Baptists have insisted on the priesthood of all believers. They have not developed a separated clerical group distinct from the laity. However, from their reading of the New Testament, they recognize that Christ gives pastors, teachers, leaders, to his church (Ephesians 4.11–13). Some early Baptists insisted that a local church was complete only when it had recognized and appointed spiritual leaders. Questions of preparation and recognition of ministers were an early matter of concern, since in England the universities were closed to Baptists. Hence the emergence of academies, such as the one in Bristol, founded by local churches in 1679.

Ordination is another contentious issue. Some Baptists ordain their ministers, seeing them not only as ministers of a local congregation but also as ministers in and to all the churches. Other Baptists, rejecting all talk of ordination, simply recognize their ministers. Some Baptists ordain deacons, who are local congregational leaders assisting the pastors in the spiritual care of the congregation.

Three other Baptist distinctives are the emphases on mission, religious liberty and human rights. Early Baptists did not have a strong sense of mission. But in the late eighteenth century new theological explorations into scripture, allied with the impact of a wider knowledge of the world through trade, led to a more evangelical form of Calvinism. William Carey, who went to India, was one of those who inspired the formation of what became the Baptist Missionary Society (1792). Thus Baptists were in the forefront of what has been called the modern missionary movement. Engagement in world mission and evangelism has been a feature of Baptists' life ever since. American Baptists in particular have developed many pioneer mission initiatives. Among such early missionaries Adoniram and Ann Judson went to Burma in 1812 and Charlotte (Lottie) Diggs Moon to China in 1873. The annual Lottie Moon Christmas Offering among Baptists has received more than $1 billion for missions. Mission has taken the forms of proclamation and evangelism, education, medical, agricultural and development work. The contribution of American Baptists to mission remains particularly noticeable, although Brazilian and Korean Baptists also supply large numbers of missionaries. The German Baptist Johann Gerhard Oncken (1800–84) interpreted the movement correctly when he declared every Baptist a missionary.

The issue of religious liberty has been with Baptists from the first. It was because there was not the freedom to practise the faith in England as some believed it should be practised that they went to Holland. Among them was John Smyth, who through study of the New Testament came to the conclusion that infant baptism was wrong. Smyth was influenced by the Mennonites. A group returned to England in 1612 to set up the first Baptist Church at Spitalfields, then just outside London. Their leader was Thomas Helwys. He wrote *A Short Declaration of The Mystery of Iniquity*, which was a defence of religious liberty for all. He specifically stated that the monarch had no authority when it came to that relationship between any individual and God. Helwys meant that all – Roman Catholics, Jews, Muslims, pagans – should enjoy religious freedom. The sovereignty of God over all, including the monarch, was the ground of human freedom.

This has remained an important issue for Baptists, who have championed the cause of religious freedom wherever it has been challenged. The first Baptist churches in America were in the New England colonies to which many Puritans emigrated, seeking religious freedom. Roger Williams founded the colony of Providence (now Rhode Island) in 1636, asserting complete freedom in matters of religion. A Baptist church was formed in Boston in 1665, but its members were persecuted for several years. The struggle for religious freedom in America was long, and Baptists suffered. But by persistent argument from leaders such as John Leland in Virginia the Constitution brought firm guarantees, expressed in the First Amendment which begins, 'Congress shall make no law respecting an establishment of religion, or prohibiting the free exercise thereof.' This led to a time of unparalleled growth of churches in the United States. The European experience was different, and even today the 'official' churches of the state can hinder Baptist work.

Mission

p. 776

Baptists believe in the separation of church and state. They have not denied that Christians should be good citizens, paying respect to those in authority, praying for them, and taking up the responsibilities of citizenship. But the state may not dictate to the church on issues of worship, ministry and evangelism. The church's fundamental loyalty is to Jesus Christ, and this has sometimes led to controversy and persecution by the state.

Human rights

Human rights have been an important concern for Baptists. Theologically, this has its roots in the assertion of the authority of Jesus Christ. The BWA maintains a Human Rights Commission, calls on churches to observe an annual Human Rights Sunday and makes an annual Human Rights award, the first recipient being President Jimmy Carter. Martin Luther King, Jr, was a Baptist.

Forms of worship among Baptist churches vary. Traditional patterns focus on the proclamation of the gospel with a simple outline of hymns, prayers and preaching. But the liturgical movement and the charismatic movement have also influenced Baptists. Congregational and choral singing are important features. The service of holy communion may be weekly, but is more likely to be monthly or even quarterly. Usually the local minister presides at the table, but lay presidency is not unusual. There are no official Baptist worship service books.

Anabaptists

Ecumenical movement

Again there is diversity among Baptists with regard to the ecumenical movement. British Baptists, for example, were foundation members of national ecumenical groups and of the World Council of Churches (WCC). The Southern Baptist Convention, the largest single Baptist group in the world, has consistently stood outside the WCC on the grounds that it is a council of churches, and a Baptist convention is not a church. There has been general caution about ecumenical engagements among Baptists on the world scale. However, this has not prevented local congregations from being active in local projects. Their form of governance makes it difficult but not impossible

for Baptists to engage in ecumenical conversations towards unity with another denomination.

BRIAN HAYMES

W. H. Brackney, *Baptist Life and Thought*, revd edn, Valley Forge, PA: Judson Press 1998; A. R. Cross, *Baptism and the Baptists*, Carlisle: Paternoster Press 2000; P. S. Fiddes, *Tracks and Traces. Baptist Identity in Church and Theology*, Carlisle: Paternoster Press 2003; C. W. Freeman, J. W. McClendon Jr and C. R.Velloso da Silva (eds), *Baptist Roots*, Valley Forge, PA: Judson Press 1999; J. L. Garrett Jr, *We Baptists*, Franklin, TN: Providence House 1999; A. W. Wardin (ed), *Baptists around the World*, Nashville, TN: Broadman and Holman 1995; J. E. Wood Jr, *Baptists and Human Rights*, McLean, VA: Baptist World Alliance 1997

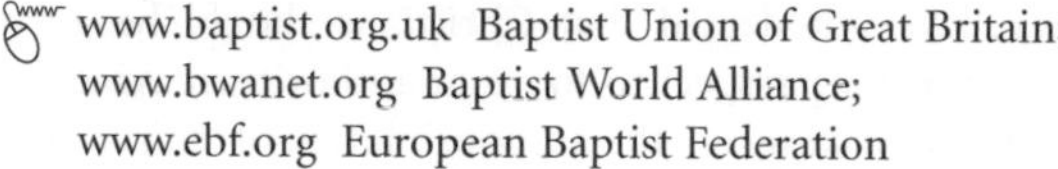

www.baptist.org.uk Baptist Union of Great Britain;
www.bwanet.org Baptist World Alliance;
www.ebf.org European Baptist Federation

Barth, Karl

Liberal theology

Karl Barth (1886–1968) was the most influential Protestant theologian of the twentieth century. Of the Swiss Reformed tradition, he studied theology in Germany at the high point of nineteenth-century Protestant liberalism, and his theological career can be regarded as essentially a reaction against that influence. Among his teachers were some of the greatest of the nineteenth-century liberal Protestant theologians, including Wilhelm Herrmann (1846–1922) and Adolf von Harnack (1851–1930).

As a young pastor in the Swiss village of Safenwil in the years before World War I, Barth struggled with the problem inherited from his liberal teachers, namely how to make the Christian gospel meaningful to people in the modern world. When war was declared in August 1914 Barth was astonished to find that his former teachers were signatories to a manifesto supporting the war aims of Kaiser Wilhelm II. He regarded this as a capitulation of Christianity to the world and it finished for ever his allegiance to theological liberalism.

Paul

Philosophy

In the early years of World War I Barth turned to intensive study of the Bible, and especially the writings of Paul. He later spoke of this period as one in which he discovered what he called the Bible's 'strange new world'. The result of this study was his book *Der Römerbrief* (*The Epistle to the Romans*, 1918), which tried to read Paul as Barth thought Paul himself would want to be read, and not through the lens of modern historical or cultural concerns. In this period Barth also gained valuable insights from several nineteenth-century writers, most especially Sören Kierkegaard, from whom he took the view that there can be no overcoming the 'infinite qualitative difference between God and man', a principle which was to be an abiding theme of his theology. The second edition of Barth's *Romans* (1922) emphasized the autonomy of revelation and rejected the emphasis in liberalism on the continuity between God and humanity. Only in paradox, argued Barth, can we begin to understand the relationship between humanity and the divine. As there is no way from humanity to God, we encounter God only through God's own revelation. The true revelation of God is Christ, but even this revelation is veiled, and the God that we know through Christ is always the hidden God. The paradox of revelation teaches us to read the Bible with fresh eyes. In it we do not find useful moral lessons or insights into history; rather, we find there the strangeness of God's revelation. It is in and through the Bible's contradictions, its clearly human and fallible nature, that the hidden God is revealed. Our understanding of revelation always involves both a 'Yes' to God and a 'No' to any assumption that we have grasped God through human understanding. Therefore theology for the early Barth is a thoroughly dialectical activity.

Revelation

In 1922 Barth moved to the University of Göttingen and subsequently to those of Münster and Bonn. In 1927 his *Prolegomena zur Christliche Dogmatik* (*Prolegomena to a Christian Dogmatics*) was published. From this point onwards it was clear that Barth was steering his own independent theological course which set him apart from many of those, including the great biblical scholar Rudolf Bultmann (1884–1976), who had shared his earlier theological concerns. The key point of disagreement was his view of human nature. Barth saw no possibility for a human basis for Christian faith and so eschewed any theological or philosophical anthropology which would imply such a starting point; his critics argued that some such 'point of contact' between God and humanity was inescapable and that to understand God's revelation one first had to understand humanity. Such fundamental theological differences led inevitably to a split and Barth eventually dissociated his theological project from those of Bultmann, Friedrich Gogarten, Emil Brunner and others with whom he had been in earlier agreement.

Barth was himself critical of his approach in *Romans* and the *Prolegomena*, considering it to be too influenced by existentialist concerns, and from the late 1920s onwards he sought to develop a theology which could be independent of what he saw as the corrosive influence of philosophy and anthropology. The long-term result was the enormous *Kirchliche Dogmatik* (English translation *Church Dogmatics*, 1936–81). For the Barth of the *Church Dogmatics* the proper subject of theology is the Word of God given to us in three ways: in Jesus Christ, in the scriptures, and in the proclamation of the church. While the primordial form of the Word is the person and being of Jesus Christ, and while scripture and the church's proclamation are themselves human activities and should not be identified with the Word as such, Barth nevertheless argues that the Word of God is truly encountered there also. God, through the power of the Holy Spirit, graciously allows scripture and the church's preaching of the Word to *become* the Word of God. This means that we are subject to the Word of God as revealed in the scriptures and that comprehending that revelation requires our engagement with the text of scripture. Yet Barth recognized that we bring to that engagement our own ideas, concerns, theologies, presuppositions, etc. But how are these human concerns related to the divine autonomy of scripture? Barth's theory of exegesis, in which he tried to balance the pre-eminence and autonomy of scripture with a recognition of the human presuppositions inherent in every act of interpretation, has been the subject of much criticism, and he never successfully explained how scripture could be autonomous and 'self-interpreting' without destroying a necessary and legitimate human interpretation of the text.

The *Church Dogmatics* discusses the central themes of Christianity (scripture, Trinity, doctrine of God, incarnation, human nature, reconciliation, and so on) with one over-riding and central focus: Jesus Christ. Barth's *Dogmatics* is essentially a christology. Given that God has chosen to incarnate himself in the person and life of Jesus Christ, we can understand humanity only through Christ, the alpha and the omega not only of humanity but of all of creation. For Barth, we cannot understand God without understanding the very humanity of God as revealed in Christ. It is the incarnation which gives us hope, for the last word is always God's 'Yes' to humanity in the person of Christ. Even sin then loses its power over us, for though we are sinners we cannot, in the end, escape God's forgiving grace. In the person of Christ we see both the God who saves and the humanity which is saved. In Christ God both takes on himself the rejection of humanity and offers to human beings grace and eternal life. Thus Barth radically subverts the classical Reformation doctrine of double predestination, in which some are saved and some are damned from all eternity, in favour of a doctrine of salvation centred on Christ which comes very close to asserting the view that all humankind is saved. Barth did not go so far as to avow this viewpoint openly, because God's freedom cannot be constrained, but it is implicit in his christological interpretation of the doctrine of election.

Barth's political thought was closely linked to his theology. In 1933 Hitler's National Socialist government formed the Evangelical Church of the German Nation (the so-called *Deutsche Christen*, 'German Christians') as a mechanism of control over German Protestants. Barth, then a professor at the University of Bonn, was among the first to oppose this subjection of the church to a political programme. In 1934 the Confessing Synod of the German Evangelical Church met at Barmen and produced the famous Barmen Declaration, a theological statement condemning the 'German Christians' for their capitulation to Hitler and affirming that there is only one Lord, Jesus Christ. The Barmen Declaration bears all the marks of the theology of its principal author, Barth, especially in its rejection of any form of natural theology which might provide the foundation for a Christian ethics. For Barth, there is only one source for ethics and for the political action that might follow, namely the command of the Word of God as found in the scriptures. God's absolute sovereignty calls into question all human activities and projects, over and against which God stands in judgement; there can be no compromise between Christianity and any political party, least of all one which would place its own leadership and ideology in a position of power over the Christian church. Barth's intellectual and personal courage cost him his university professorship, but it did not change his stance towards politics. While he continued to be actively engaged in social issues, Barth refused to advocate a distinctively Christian viewpoint on many contentious matters, a position which set him apart from many of his contemporaries but which was nevertheless consistent with his rejection of any natural theology.

p. 302

Ethics
Christology
Natural theology

Barth's theology continues to be the subject of debate. He has been attacked for his understanding of revelation, which seems to leave no room for human reason or judgement; for his rejection of even a tempered form of natural theology; for his christocentrism; and for his separation of revealed history from secular history. Even the atheistic 'death of God' movement of the 1960s has been attributed to Barth's influence, in so far as he destroyed for many the possibility of knowledge of God in and through the world. Nevertheless others, such as contemporary post-liberals and even some Roman Catholic theologians, find in Barth a necessary corrective to the influence on theology of secular philosophies.

Incarnation
Sin
Predestination

JAMES M. BYRNE

Karl Barth, *The Epistle to the Romans*, London: OUP [2]1933; *Church Dogmatics*, I/1–IV/4, Edinbugh: T&T Clark 1936–81; *How I Changed My Mind, 1886–1968*, Richmond, Va: John Knox Press and Edinburgh: T&T Clark 1969; H. U. von Balthasar, *The Theology of Karl Barth* (1971), Fort Collins, CO: Ignatius Press 1997; G. Hunsinger, *How to Read Karl Barth: The Shape of his Theology*, New York: OUP 1991

BELIEFS

Atonement, Bible, Church, Creation, Creed, Council, Evil, God, Holy Spirit, Incarnation, Jesus, Life after death, Resurrection, Salvation, Sin, Trinity

Asked to give a succinct summary of traditional Christian beliefs, someone standing at the centre of mainstream Christianity might give the following account.

Jesus of Nazareth induced in his followers a transition in their ways of life and thought. Accounts in the Gospels of Jesus' healings, parables and presence among outcast persons often suggest experiences of startling abundance and the reversal of expectations. This transformation of perception seems to have deepened intensely as a result of Jesus' crucifixion and what his disciples reported as a persisting experience of his resurrection (life beyond the power of death) and an outpouring of what they called the Holy Spirit within their life together. Christianity itself grows out of these transforming experiences, and Christian beliefs unfold in various ways at various times as an attempt on the part of Christian communities (or churches) to state in shareable form what they experience as the truths about reality disclosed through their ongoing encounter with God in Christ through the Holy Spirit.

Community

Sometimes, for the sake of clarity of teaching or in the case of divisive disagreements, these beliefs have been given expression in the form of precise statements of belief (or creeds), and sometimes in more extended authoritative teachings issued by large gatherings of the church meeting together in council. Leading Christian teachers such as Augustine of Hippo and Anselm of Canterbury also pointed to an inherently questing dynamism within belief, always leading the mind of the community on a deeper search for understanding, and thus in the direction of a contemplative enjoyment of the full truth to which statements of belief or teaching (doctrine) can only point.

A system of Christian beliefs is generally considered necessary on two counts. First, it sets a boundary to what Christians should believe (e.g., that the entire universe is a good creation of God) and therefore also identifies what Christians should refuse to believe (e.g., that matter is inherently evil). Secondly, beliefs are also valued as holding the mind open to what another important theologian, Thomas Aquinas, calls sacred teaching (*sacra doctrina*, i.e., the teaching that comes from God); this means that, in analogy to any other process of teaching, believers begin with certain basic principles (beliefs) whose full truth and significance they do not yet fully grasp, but by means of these principles they are enabled to grow in the habits needed to move towards understanding (these habits are called the theological virtues of faith, hope and love). If there were no beliefs to begin with, however, no growth could occur.

Thomas Aquinas

Faith

Hope

Love

For example, an apprentice auto mechanic is taught certain basic principles which she doesn't yet fully understand, but by believing these teachings she is able to begin to work on combustion engines; by practising her art she develops certain crucial skills and work habits, and thereby the reality of what she could at first only believe 'on faith' becomes more and more intelligible to her directly. Christians believe that the full intelligibility of God, unlike, say, the full truth of combustion engines, will become fully available only in what they sometimes refer to as the beatific vision, the vision of God which beatifies or blesses all who behold it in the life of the world to come. Then beliefs will be at an end, for they will have been transformed into knowledge and vision.

In the meantime, Christians hold a great variety of beliefs which they count as enabling them to practise and develop the skills they need to serve God and their neighbours in faith, to hope for God's gift of new life (usually called salvation), and to practise now the love of God which they believe will be the endless life of heaven. Clearly, then, beliefs are intricately related to these virtues that dispose one towards actual encounter with God. While one could presumably hold many Christian beliefs in a purely notional manner, without practising any Christian habits of life, such a form of believing would inevitably prove deficient as leaving one without any actual experience or taste of the divine reality to which the beliefs are intended to direct those who believe them. So what are the most basic beliefs of Christians? Of course there have been many different formulations, different emphases, and very often considerable disagreement over the centuries and across cultures, but here are at least some fairly central beliefs in barest form.

For Christians, belief in God is not primarily a matter of faith in the existence of God (a matter which many have held to be knowable by natural reason), but of belief in the particular identity of God as revealed in the community's experience of Jesus, the one he called Father, and the Holy Spirit. God is, Christians believe, the Trinity of this Father, Son and Holy Spirit. The development of this belief over time is richly complex (reaching a landmark formulation in the Nicene Creed), but it springs from the early community's experience of a divine activity in Jesus, making possible for believers a new relationship with God as loving Father and filling them with the Spirit. In time, this experience led to the belief that, while God is one perfect and complete reality, this divine life unfolds itself in the loving eternal expression by the Father of all the truth of God's life as the Word or Son of God, and that the loving power of this eternal self-sharing is God the Holy Spirit. The historical relationship between Jesus and the Father in their Spirit is believed to be the visible expression in time and space of this eternal relationality of trinitarian self-giving love. This gives rise to the belief that the Son and Spirit are of the same being with the Father, all one God, and therefore neither subordinate deities nor maximally significant creatures.

Reflecting on the experience of being invited into this divine relational life through Jesus Christ and by the power of the Spirit, Christians have also developed a number of beliefs about revelation itself, that is, about God's manner of disclosing divine life in the midst of time. Revelation is believed to be entirely a gift of God in which God as revealer (the Father) brings believers by the power of revelation (the Holy Spirit) into a life-changing encounter with the truth or Word of God's life (the Son). This understanding of revelation arose from a belief in Jesus as the incarnation of this Word or Son, eternally spoken by the Father, and born into time from Mary of Nazareth as Jesus. Beliefs about the relationship between the full humanity of Jesus and his full divinity came to a landmark expression in the Chalcedonian Definition. Belief in the incarnation holds that the life, death, and resurrection of Jesus is the unique expression in time of the eternal speaking (Word or Son) of the Father. But the same trinitarian activity of revelation is also believed to be unfolding throughout the creation, throughout history, and especially in the history of the people of Israel. The holy scriptures (Bible) of the Old and New Testaments are believed to be the authoritative or canonical (from the Greek word, *kanon*, for measure) witness to God's revelation.

Revelation

Mary

pp. 300–1

p. 1152

Canon

Belief in the incarnation of the Word as Jesus has important implications for Christian beliefs about humanity, for it leads to an understanding that human being and divine being are not somehow mutually exclusive. Not only are human beings believed to be created by God in the divine image, but in the light of Christian beliefs about Jesus humanity is also believed to be created for intimate and everlasting friendship with God. What do Christians mean by believing that humanity is the divine image? First, the idea draws a contrast between human authorities, who set up statues as their images among subject peoples, and the creator God, whose chosen images on

Church dogma, folio from *De universo* by Rabanus Maurus, 780–856

earth are free and living human beings. Sometimes humanity's imaging of God has been believed to lie within a feature of individual human existence (e.g., freedom or rational intelligence) and sometimes it has been believed to spring from the mutual sharing and relationship so fulfilling of human life (and reflective of the mutuality and loving relationality of the Trinity).

Jesus' humanity is believed to be fulfilled and perfected through his obedience to the Father, that is, through his enacting completely his identity as the Word or Son of the Father. In analogous fashion, humankind in general is believed to be called to its consummate state of human existence by living ever more fully into the new affiliation with the Father which is made possible by sharing in Jesus' own relationship with the Father. While Christian beliefs about how Jesus reconciles the world to God have taken a variety of forms, salvation is understood to have been accomplished by Jesus once for all in his death on the cross, and brought to life within believers through the power of the Holy Spirit. Some teachings on salvation have been conceived using metaphors from a legal domain; thus Jesus is described as suffering the punishment for human sin so that humanity may be forgiven and pardoned. Other conceptions have emphasized more the defeat of evil, sin and death through Jesus' complete fidelity to the Father and thus a winning of restored trust and friendship between humanity and God. Sin is likewise interpreted variously within Christian thought, but is always believed to involve a breach in relationship between humanity and God, only fully restored through the work of God in Christ.

Christians also believe that the whole universe is likewise created to reflect the divine glory and to share, according to the nature of each creature, in the eternal communion with God of a new creation. Belief in creation is belief that the universe exists not as the result of a cosmic battle or an overflowing emanation of divine life or random pre-atomic occurrences; Christians believe, rather, that the universe is the freely chosen creation of God's artistry and delight. Each creature is, by virtue of its sheer existence, a continuous event of divine giving and good pleasure. Because each creature is freely called into existence by God, its own reality is wholly gratuitous and free – not necessary, but reflective of divine grace and love. And this is believed to be the true source of all creaturely liberty and capacity to love freely beyond the claims of biology or culture.

Because God as creator is not one of the creatures but the reason why there is anything at all, God is not believed to be another 'being' in addition to the creatures. This belief in the creator's transcendence of all creatures also permits a belief in God's intimate involvement with all creatures (in ways that another being, no matter how powerful, could not offer). God's presence in the creation is, for example, not like a mutually exclusive presence of a human in the same physical space as a horse. God is the giver of both the human's and the horse's existence moment by moment. This also means that, according to Christian understandings of creation, every creaturely activity is in some sense also and simultaneously an act of God – as giving the creatures their existence and calling them to fulfilment. The relationship of Christian beliefs about creation to modern science is a matter of debate among Christians, but in general belief in God as creator need not necessarily be a substitute for scientific theories about the origin of the universe; belief in God as creator would simply presuppose that God causes the existence of whatever pre-cosmic events scientists believe may have led to the origins of space and time. And in an analogous way, Christian beliefs about the destiny of the universe go beyond any scientific speculations on the subject. While considerable detail and variety has grown up in Christian thought about the 'end', central to such beliefs is the conviction that the same Jesus who gave his life for all and was raised as the beginning of a new creation will be present to bring to light the truth of all creaturely existence and history, and to inaugurate the fullness of God's justice and loving communion through all and in all and for all beings. It remains a disputed question in Christian belief whether any creatures will ultimately and for ever refuse to share in this communion; but such a refusal would generally be believed to constitute the state of hell or damnation, while acceptance and joy in communion with God would be understood as the life of heaven or the consummation of the kingdom of God.

Science
Science and theology
Eschatology
Kingdom of God

MARK A. MCINTOSH

Jaroslav Pelikan, *Credo: Historical and Theological Guide to Creeds and Confessions of Faith in the Christian Tradition*, New Haven and London: Yale University Press 2003; Kathryn Tanner, *Jesus, Humanity and the Trinity: A Brief Systematic Theology*, Edinburgh: T&T Clark 2001; Thomas Aquinas, *Compendium of Theology*, St Louis: Herder 1948

BIBLE

Apocalyptic, Authority, Biblical criticism, Biblical theology, Canon, Eschatology, Fundamentalism, Inspiration, Jesus, Messiah, Origins and background, Paul, Prophecy, Psalms, Pseudepigraphy, Revelation

Title

Authority The Bible is the collection of Christian scriptures, that is, of texts that have religious authority for Christian belief and practice, and are regarded as in some sense 'the word of God' to God's people. The name derives from the Greek *biblia* ('books'), where the plural already indicates that it is not a single book, but a collection with a complex history. The Christian Bible is divided into two parts of unequal length, traditionally called the 'Old Testament' and the 'New Testament'. The origin of these titles is uncertain. The idea of the contrast between an 'old covenant' (or 'testament', the Greek word for both these is the same) given to Moses on Mount Sinai and a new covenant ratified in Christ is already in Paul (2 Corinthians 3.12–18), but the use of Old and New Testament as titles for the writings which bear witness to these covenants is later. It has been suggested that the titles were coined by Marcion (died 160), a ship-owner expelled from the Christian community in Rome in the second century for heretical views. He systematically contrasted the gracious and redeeming God taught by Jesus with a lesser creator God of the Old Testament; the association of the terms with a notable heretic would explain the reluctance of early Christian writers to adopt them.

Covenant

More recently, an anxiety not to seem to imply that God's first covenant, with Israel, has been superseded by his second covenant, in Christ, or that it is obsolete and inferior, has led many Christians to prefer the title 'First Covenant' or 'Other Covenant' to Old Testament, or to refer to the first part of the Christian Bible as the Hebrew Bible. This move can be misleading, in that while the Old Testament overlaps very considerably with the Jewish scriptures, Christians read them in a somewhat different order, and within a different framework of interpretation.

Origins

Jesus himself was rooted in the Jewish scriptures: Luke has him read from the scroll of Isaiah; asked to state which is the greatest commandment he responds with a quotation of Deuteronomy 6.4 and Leviticus 19.18; in a sense of abandonment on the cross he quotes Psalm 22.1. The first Christians were Jewish, and their scriptures were the Jewish scriptures, though they read these in Greek rather than Hebrew. In this sense there was never a church without the Bible, and that Bible, which was the Jewish scriptures understood in the light of Jesus' resurrection and the gift of the Holy Spirit, shaped the church from the beginning.

Resurrection

Holy Spirit

But it is equally true that the church has shaped the Bible in that the selection and ordering of the books of the Christian Bible were the results of decisions and processes within the church that can be investigated historically. When Paul wrote his letters to the churches in Corinth or Rome, he would not have supposed that he was writing 'scripture' in the same sense that Exodus or Isaiah were for him 'scripture'; it was a later action of the church that gave his writings scriptural authority, and indeed ranked them above Exodus or Isaiah as authoritative disclosures of Christian truth. An important motive for this development was the need to find ways of transmitting the apostolic faith to new and unforeseen Christian generations. Paul might no longer be alive, and the

CHAPTER AND VERSE

The books of the Bible are divided into chapters and verses. These divisions were not made by the original authors but much later. The original texts contained no divisions and did not even have much punctuation. However, as time went on the need arose to indicate sections about as long as paragraphs for reference and for liturgical use. Jews marked these out in the Hebrew Bible and Christians in the New Testament.

Stephen Langton, a professor in Paris who became Archbishop of Canterbury, devised the present system of chapters on the basis of Jewish practice and in 1205 used it in a copy of the Latin Bible (the Vulgate). From there it was incorporated into the Hebrew Bible and the Greek New Testament. However, the chapters often do not correspond to the literary structure of the book and can therefore give a misleading impression.

The system of verse numbering was created by Robert Stephanus (Étienne), a Paris printer who produced the first complete printed Bible in 1560. He too based the system on Hebrew practice for the Old Testament. He is said to have divided the New Testament into verses while riding on horseback from Lyons to Paris. Be this as it may, again the results are less than satisfactory. Sometimes a verse contains several sentences, and sometimes a sentence is divided between two verses; sometimes the words introducing a quotation are in the previous verse, and sometimes in the verse containing the quotation.

Although the Christian divisions in the Old Testament are closely based on the ones in the Hebrew Bible, they do not always correspond exactly. A modern English translation will usually note these differences in the margin. They can cause confusion if one is using a scholarly commentary that follows the Hebrew numbering. Thus in the Hebrew Bible Exodus 8.1–4 is numbered 7.26–9 and 8.5–32 is numbered 8.1–28; 1 Kings 4.21–34 is numbered 5.1–14 and 5.1–18 is numbered 5.15–32.

There are two special sources of confusion in the numbering of the Psalms: 1. Many Psalms are prefaced by musical directions and descriptive terms. In a Hebrew Bible these are counted as verse 1, with the psalm itself starting at verse 2. The Hebrew Bible verse numbers, which commentators often use, therefore run one ahead of the numbers printed in an ordinary English Bible. 2. There are slight differences in the way in which the 150 Psalms are counted in the Septuagint (LXX) and in the Hebrew text tradition. The LXX numbers generally run one behind the Hebrew numbers. The Orthodox and Roman Catholic Churches have historically followed the LXX numbering, which was used in the Vulgate (though recent Roman Catholic translations like the New Jerusalem Bible have moved to follow the Hebrew Bible). Non-Roman Catholic translations (AV, RSV, NRSV) use the Hebrew numbering.

The system of chapters and verses is so universally established that it is impossible to change it. However, useful as it is for finding passages in the Bible, its shortcomings need to be noted.

Chapters and verses are indicated by the book of the Bible followed by the chapter, then the verse, separated by a full stop or colon, e.g. Isaiah 7.14.

Lord might not yet have come in glory, but a Christian generation that did not know the apostle Paul directly could still allow its life to be shaped by his apostolic teaching.

Paul

The process of preparing a closed and authoritative list, usually referred to as the 'canon', is an important part of early Christian history. Its relation to the development of the Jewish canon continues to be investigated.

From a very early stage, the Bible was translated into other languages, notably Syriac and Latin: the Latin translation by Jerome, known as the Vulgate, was the Bible of the Western church down to the sixteenth-century Reformation, which saw the rapid spread of vernacular translations.

Reformation

Encountering the Bible

The way in which Christians have encountered the Bible and its contents has varied considerably over time and space. We have become so used to the idea that the Bible is readily available as a single volume, to be bought in almost any airport bookshop or found in a hotel bedroom, and that a group of Christians might meet to study it, each bringing their own copy, that it takes an effort of historical imagination to realize that the Bible has been readily available in this way only in the last quarter of Christian history. For the first three-quarters, most ordinary Christians would have encountered the Bible primarily through public worship and public teaching. Whole Bibles survive from the fourth century: Codex Sinaiticus and Codex Vaticanus, for example, possibly two

ANCIENT VERSIONS OF THE BIBLE

The first followers of Jesus were familiar with the Law and the Prophets, which they encountered in Aramaic translations called *Targums* as well as in Hebrew. As the early Christian movement spread into the eastern Mediterranean world, it quickly adopted as its Bible the authorized Greek translation of the Jewish scriptures called the *Septuagint* (LXX), which was very widely used among Jews dispersed through the world in the Diaspora. The LXX was so effectively adopted by Christians that it came to be regarded by Jews almost as a Christian book, and new Greek translations were prepared which were less amenable to Christian interpretation (Isaiah 7.14 is a famous case – the LXX's '*a virgin* shall conceive' was readily quoted by Christians in support of their messianic claims for Jesus). Early Christianity added to the Septuagint a collection of specifically Christian writings, which came to form the New Testament: what had originally been simply 'scripture' now became the 'Old Testament'.

Both Testaments of the Christian Bible were rapidly translated into a variety of languages, so that Christians inside and outside the Roman empire could read scripture in their own language. These early versions are important not only for the history and reconstruction of the biblical text, but also for the shaping of literature, culture, and even sense of national identity in different parts of the Christian world down to the present day. Each of the ancient versions has its own history, which can be complex. Sometimes a single translator accomplished heroic solo efforts, as Jerome did; more often, a body of translations was built up over a longer period. The Gospels and Epistles of the New Testament were often translated first, but not always. The Armenian translators of the fifth century began with Proverbs, because its pithy wisdom seemed to them the most practically useful part of the Bible.

It was obvious that Christian scripture would need to be translated into *Latin*, the language of Rome. The first Latin versions, made in various times and places from the Greek Old and New Testaments, are collectively known as the Old Latin. No complete Old Latin Bible survives, and there perhaps never was one. In 382, Pope Damasus I commissioned Jerome to revise the Old Latin of the Gospels and Epistles. This project gradually turned into a complete re-translation of the Bible, with reference to the Hebrew text: the famous Vulgate, which remained the official text of the Bible in the Roman Catholic Church until the mid-twentieth century.

Syriac was a language closely related to Aramaic, and widely used in the eastern Roman empire. Jews had already begun to translate parts of their scriptures into Syriac, and Christians developed this work from an early date. In the early second century, the church father Tatian harmonized the four Gospels into a single narrative, the *Diatessaron* ('[one] through four'); this, rather than the four Gospels, was for a while the official Gospel text of the Syriac churches. It was suppressed in the fifth century, when the Peshitta ('simple' or 'current') version was adopted as the authorized Syriac translation of the whole Bible.

Coptic Christianity

Coptic is the language of Egyptian Christianity. The New Testament was translated from Greek into both its dialects, Sahidic (used in Upper Egypt) and Bohairic (used in Lower Egypt), from the third century onwards. No translations of the Old Testament have survived.

Ethiopian Christianity

Translation of the Bible from Greek into *Ethiopic* probably began in the fourth and fifth centuries, although the surviving manuscripts are much later. The Ethiopic Bible is notable for the very wide selection of books included in its canon: as many as 81. This makes it a particularly rich source for the study of apocryphal and pseudepigraphical biblical traditions.

Although the Armenians embraced Christianity very early in the fourth century, the first biblical translations had to wait for the invention of an Armenian alphabet by Mesrop Mashtots 100 years later. He co-ordinated a large team of royally-sponsored translators, who worked on theological as well as biblical texts. Mesrop Mashtots also developed the Georgian alphabet. The *Armenian* and *Georgian* versions are closely related, and there continues to be much debate over whether the translators worked from Greek or Syriac originals.

Bruce M. Metzger, *The Bible in Translation: Ancient and English Versions*, Grand Rapids, MI: Baker Academic 2001

survivors of a set of Bibles commissioned by the Emperor Constantine as part of a programme of support for the church; their very size and costliness emphasize their character as valuable public property.

As well as encountering Bibles and Gospel books in church, where they were read aloud during p. 1037 the liturgy by clergy and readers who had the necessary and rare skills in literacy needed to read a text which (in the earliest centuries at least) lacked even punctuation and word division, Christians would become familiar with its contents through drama (passion plays, cycles of mystery plays), visual arts (stained-glass windows, mosaics) and songs.

Mystery plays

Stained glass

Books

The invention of printing in the late fifteenth century, coinciding with and making possible the

Reformers' programme of breaking an ecclesiastical monopoly of biblical interpretation, marked a decisive change in the way in which modern Christians encountered their Bible. Now they could read it themselves in their own languages. Ever since, there has been a continuous effort to give people access to Christian Bibles (or at least New Testaments) in their own languages; and this programme sustains the work of numerous Bible societies. It remains to be seen in what ways the internet and other new technologies of communication will affect the appropriation by Christians of their Bible.

Internet
Communication

Authority and interpretation

It is common to end a reading from the Bible in church worship with a statement such as 'This is the word of the Lord', and the claim that the Bible is 'the word of God' would command general assent among Christians. However, the sense in which that expression is to be understood, or the way in which the Bible is to be read and interpreted, have varied greatly in Christian history, and are now contested among many Christians. Early Christian writers understood the Bible to be, in a very direct way, divine speech: Pope Gregory the Great (reigned 590–604) will typically introduce a quotation from Exodus with the formula 'as the Lord says through Moses'. But the same writers were sensitive to the difficulty of taking all of the biblical text at surface value: sometimes it seemed to contradict itself, and sometimes it represented God as acting or speaking in reprehensible ways. These were taken not as indications that the Bible was not a divinely inspired text, but as intentional clues to alert the reader to the need to search for the true meaning of the text at a deeper level than the surface meaning. Just as the human person is flesh and spirit, so scripture might conceal a deeper spiritual meaning within the literal or fleshly meaning. This allegorical mode of reading, although scarcely practised now, was enormously widespread in the church until the sixteenth century. Practised by Origen, Augustine, the Cappadocians or Gregory the Great, and associated especially with the biblical scholars of Alexandria, it became formalized by the scholastic theologians of the medieval West, for whom the text might have four levels of meaning: literal (what happened), allegorical (doctrine), moral (ethical) and anagogical (where they pointed).

Church fathers
Scholasticism

Although it can appear to a modern observer that the allegorists were reading meanings into a text, they would themselves have insisted that they were drawing out meanings that the divine author had intentionally placed into the text for them to find. This immediately raised the question of how one might test whether a discovered meaning was true or not. Part of the answer was quickly found in the need for a reading to commend itself to the community of faith. Allegorical reading of the Bible was done in and for the church, so it would be up to the church to determine the legitimacy of any interpretation that the allegorist might humbly offer. By the late Middle Ages in the West, this had developed in practice into a system where the representatives of the institutional church could claim to determine the meaning of the Bible, sometimes in ways that were surprisingly far from what the text might obviously appear to say, and which tended to legitimate particular patterns of power within the church.

This is the indispensable background to the emergence of the doctrine of *sola scriptura* (scripture alone) in the Western Reformation. There was a deliberate attempt to wrest control of the interpretation of the Bible from church authorities, and to insist that any Christian could arrive at its meaning by direct and unaided study of the plain sense of scripture; there was equally an insistence that the life of the church should be shaped by nothing other than scripture taken in that plain sense. It is important to note that there was already reaction against allegory in earlier Christian centuries: John Chrysostom (347–407), for example, suspected that it allowed Christians

Reformation

ENGLISH TRANSLATIONS OF THE BIBLE

Unlike Jews and Muslims, members of the other two 'religions of the book', most Christians do not use their scriptures in worship and study in the languages in which they were originally written, but in translation. The Bible has been translated into well over 2000 languages.

The earliest known written English translation of any part of the Bible was produced by the Venerable Bede (*c.* 673–735), who at the end of his life translated some of the Gospel of John into Anglo-Saxon. This was about the same time as the Lindisfarne Gospels. However, translation of the Bible into English really began in the fourteenth century, around the time of Chaucer, and the first complete translation is associated with John Wyclif (*c.* 1384). It was revised by Wyclif's secretary, John Purvey, in 1397 and was widely used over the next century or so. It was followed by the translation of William Tyndale (1490–1536), from the Hebrew and the Greek; the New Testament was completed and printed in 1525, but Tyndale was burnt as a martyr before he could complete the Old Testament. Miles Coverdale (1488–1569)'s translation was from a strange mixture of sources: Martin Luther's German translation and the Latin Vulgate; it also incorporated some of Tyndale's translation. It was the first complete printed English Bible. Coverdale's translation of the Psalms was incorporated into the Book of Common Prayer, and is thus influential even today. A comparison with modern translations shows just how far it could differ from the original texts.

Four other major English Bible translations appeared before the classic King James/Authorized Version: Matthew's Bible (1537), a revision of Tyndale's work licensed for general reading by Henry VIII, to whom it was dedicated; the Great Bible (1539–41), based on Tyndale and Coverdale, which was the first official English church Bible, put in every church in England; the Geneva Bible (1560), a revision of Tyndale and the Great Bible, which though not officially authorized, became the most popular translation, used by Shakespeare and John Bunyan; and the Bishops' Bible (1568), a revision of the Great Bible on the basis of the Geneva Bible.

Roman Catholic exiles working on the European continent produced the Douai-Reims Version: the New Testament appeared in Reims in 1582, the Old Testament in Douai in 1609.

The King James Version (1611), also known as the Authorized Version, is so called because it was produced by a commission appointed by James I and was authorized to be read in churches. A revision of the Bishops' Bible, it also drew on the Reims version of the New Testament. Strangely enough, although it is regarded as a classic of English literature, of enormous influence, it took time to become established; for a couple of generations the Geneva Bible was more popular. The King James/Authorized Version was revised at the end of the nineteenth century (1881–5), but this Revised Version and its American equivalent, the American Standard Version (1901), never came to be used widely.

Since the Second World War a plethora of translations of the Bible into English have appeared, more than 500 of them. Some, like the influential translations of the whole Bible by the Roman Catholic Ronald Knox (1944–50) and the Protestant James Moffatt (1936), and of the New Testament by the Protestants J. B. Phillips (1958) and William Barclay (1969), were the works of individuals; most have been the works of committees. The best known of these are:

Revised Standard Version (RSV, NT 1946, OT 1952), revised as the *New Revised Standard Version* (NRSV, 1989)

Amplified Bible (AMB, NT 1958, OT 1965)

New English Bible (NEB, 1961), revised as the *Revised English Bible* (REB, 1992)

Jerusalem Bible (JB, 1966), made from the French *Bible de Jérusalem* and now replaced by the *New Jerusalem Bible* (NJB, 1985), a heavy revision based on the original languages

Today's English Version (TEV), also known as *The Good News Bible* (GNB, 1966), revised as the *Contemporary English Version/ Good News Translation* (CEV/GNT, 1996)

New International Version (NIV, NT 1973, OT 1978)

New King James Version (NKJ, 1979–82) A revision of the King James/Authorized Version

New American Bible (NAB,1987)

New American Standard Bible (NASB, 1971). It claims to be 'the most literally accurate translation'.

There are a number of reasons for the many different modern translations of the Bible, quite apart from the commercial advantages of publishing a new version. New manuscript discoveries and the work of biblical scholars constantly produce new readings of the text and insights into it; since living languages change over time, what seemed a good translation in one decade can seem dated or inappropriate in another; cultural sensitivity has led to importance being attached in some translations, say, to inclusive language; and above all, there are different philosophies of translation, which is inevitably always interpretation.

Some modern translations are almost paraphrases in their attempts to make the Bible speak to the modern world, departing a long way from the original texts; the Amplified Bible adds a great many words and phrases. These aside, there are two schools of thought on methods of translation. One, commonly known as the 'formal correspondence' school, tries to keep as close as possible to the wording and word order of the original Hebrew and Greek texts. The other, the 'dynamic equivalence' school, tries to put the sense of the text into the best modern English without following the original wording or word order. Of the versions mentioned above, the Douai-Reims, KJV/NKJ, RSV/NRSV, NAB and NIV could be classed as 'formal correspondence' translations; NEB/REB, TEV/CEV (GNB) and JB/NJB as 'dynamic equivalence' translations.

→

Denominational allegiances also play a role in Bible translations: the Douai-Reims, JB/NJB and NAB are 'Catholic'; KJV/NKJ, TEV/CEV and NIV are 'Protestant' and NEB/REB, RSV/NRSV 'ecumenical'.

The *Translator's New Testament* (TNT, 1991), by W. J. Bradnock and H. K. Moulton, is an interesting work, prepared by the British and Foreign Bible society for those with no knowledge of Greek who need to translate the New Testament into other languages. It seeks to be a bridge between the original language of the New Testament and the languages and cultures of the modern world.

The *New Century Version* (NCV, 1987) is a translation of the Bible primarily for children, using the most limited vocabulary possible; the *Living Bible* (LVB, 1971) has the same aims, but it takes liberties with the text and is dominated by a strongly evangelical theology.

Convenient parallel texts of the different versions can be found in: *The Complete Parallel Bible*, New York: OUP 1993 (contains NRSV, REB, NAB, NJB); *The Precise Parallel New Testament*, New York: OUP 1995 (contains the Greek NT, KJV, Douai-Reims, AMB, NIV, NRSV, NAB).

The relationships between all these translations can be expressed in a family tree.

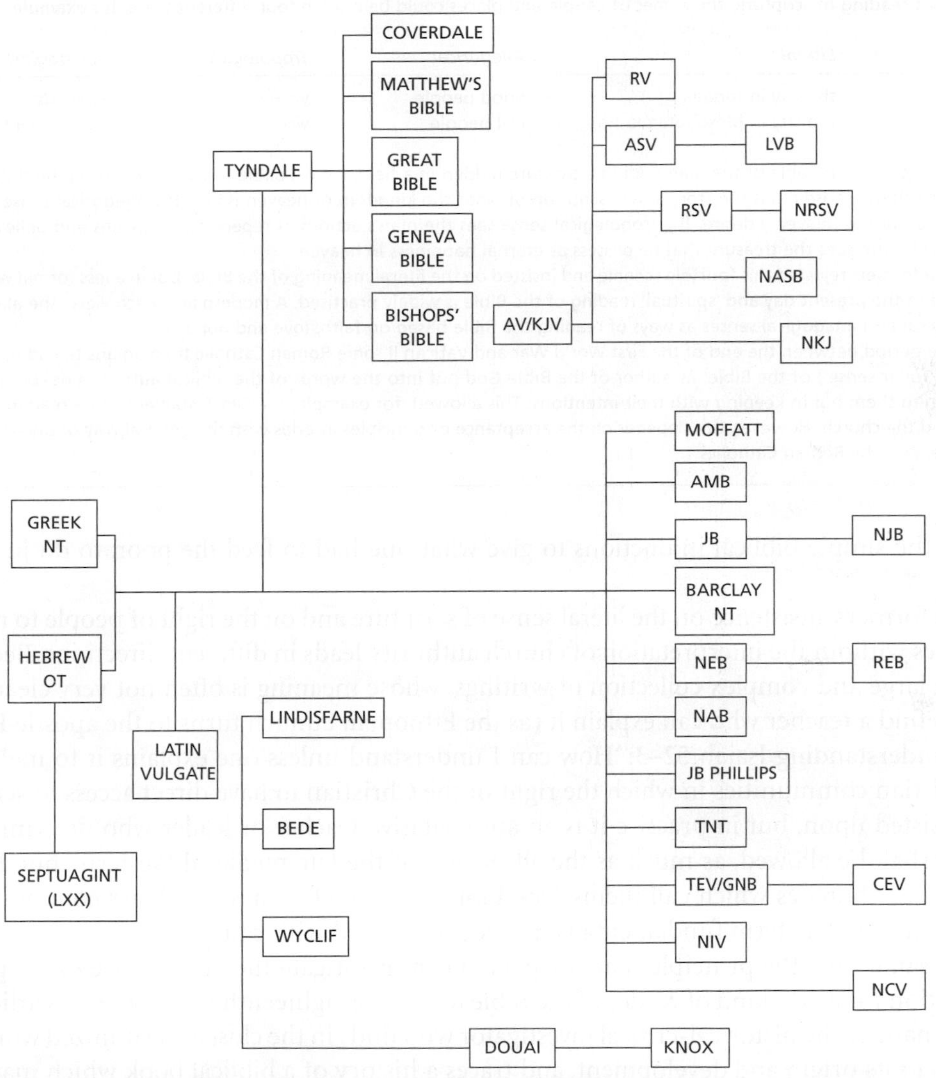

David Daniell, *The Bible in English. Its History and Influence*, New Haven and London: Yale University Press 2003; Bruce M. Metzger, *The Bible in Translation. Ancient and English Translations*, Grand Rapids, MI: Baker Academic 2001

Many of the Protestant English translations of the Bible can be found at www.biblegateway.com

SENSES OF SCRIPTURE

From theologians like Origen in the early church through the Middle Ages and beyond, the Bible was seen as having several different meanings or 'senses'. Scholastic theology described in a terse Latin couplet the four different senses which became established:

Littera gesta docet, quid credas allegoria
Moralia quid agas, quo tendas anagogia.

(The literal sense describes what happened, the allegorical what you may believe;
the moral sense what you may do and the anagogical sense where you may go.)

The moral sense was also known as the tropological sense.

On this reading of scripture, the names of people and places could be read in four different ways, for example:

	Literal	*Allegorical*	*Tropological*	*Anagogical*
Jerusalem	the city in Judaea	good people	virtues	rewards
Babylon	the city in Mesopotamia	evil people	vices	punishment

Similarly, in the parable of the man finding a treasure hidden in a field, selling all he has and buying the field (Matthew 13.44), the literal sense reads the story as a description of what the kingdom of heaven is like; the allegorical sense sees the hidden treasure as heavenly desire; the tropological sense sees the man's actions as repenting of his sins and believing; the anagogical sense sees the treasure that he possess as eternal happiness in heaven.

The Reformers rejected this fourfold scheme and insisted on the literal meaning of the Bible, but in a less formal way it has persisted to the present day and 'spiritual' reading of the Bible is widely practised. A modern approach views the allegorical, tropological and anagogical senses as ways of reading the Bible based on faith, love and hope.

In the period between the end of the First World War and Vatican II some Roman Catholic theologians talked of a *sensus plenior* ('fuller sense') of the Bible: as author of the Bible God put into the words of the biblical authors a deeper meaning unknown to them but in keeping with their intentions. This allowed, for example, the Old Testament to be read in terms of Christ and the church. However, this depends on the acceptance of principles at odds with the general way of understanding the Bible, even by Roman Catholics.

to evade the simple biblical injunctions to give what one had to feed the poor, to do justice, and so on.

The Reformers' insistence on the literal sense of scripture and on the right of people to read their own Bibles without the interpretation of church authority leads in different directions. Because the Bible is a large and complex collection of writings, whose meaning is often not very clear, there is a need to find a teacher who can explain it (as the Ethiopian eunuch turns to the apostle Philip for help in understanding Isaiah 52–3: 'How can I understand unless one explains it to me?'). So we find Christian communities in which the right of the Christian to have direct access to scripture is much insisted upon, but in practice it is an authoritative teacher or leader who determines what meaning shall be allowed, as much as the allegorists of the late medieval Western church. This is often true of churches which call themselves 'biblical', or of churches which are commonly called 'fundamentalist'. The term fundamentalism needs to be used with caution.

At the same time the principle that any person can investigate the literal sense of scripture is a precondition for a new kind of reader of the Bible in the late eighteenth century (with earlier anticipations), namely the historical-critical investigator who finds in the closely-scrutinized words of the text clues to its origin and development, and traces a history of a biblical book which may be very different from the traditional and inherited understanding – for example, using the tensions and inconsistencies of 1 and 2 Corinthians to reassemble a more complex dossier of at least three letters from Paul to the Corinthians, or suggesting that Isaiah as we have it is the work of more than one prophet, from widely different periods. Although historical-critical scholarship and fundamentalism are opposed to each other, they share in part a common root. It is perhaps still possible to articulate a doctrine of scriptural inspiration which does justice to what historical-critical scholarship has revealed of the complex genesis and development of the books of the Bible. Such a doctrine would start from the idea of the incarnation as the fundamental act of God's self-disclosure and would suggest that a God who acts through incarnation would similarly allow any scriptural self-disclosure to be mediated through human processes of transmission and development.

Incarnation

Here we shall be looking at the contents of the Bible against the background of the discoveries of scholars who have been studying it over the past two centuries. To look at the Bible in the light of its origins and against a historical background is not of course the only way of reading it; there are other very different approaches among present-day biblical critics, among whom there are those who insist that the text as we have it now is all that matters. However, when a collection of books has come into being over such a long period of time and in many cases the books themselves have undergone an organic development in their creation, their history cannot simply be ignored.

The Old Testament

It is impossible for a brief outline to do justice to the variety and complexity of the Old Testament, which is a collection of writings that has grown and been shaped over 1000 years and more; it constitutes a great classical literature in poetry and prose and includes many different genres and forms of writing. We shall be examining some of the main concepts that are usually encountered in study of the Old Testament and mapping out some of the issues most commonly investigated.

The Old Testament now exists in two main forms. The Hebrew text tradition, which is transmitted and commented on to this day within Judaism, is known as the Masoretic text, named after the Masoretic families (from *masoreh* = 'that which is handed on') who gave it decisive shape in the early Middle Ages. Until the Dead Sea Scrolls were discovered, the earliest Hebrew manuscripts

p. 845

BIBLICAL FIGURES AND WHERE TO FIND THEIR STORIES

Knowing the names of the main figures in the Bible is one thing; knowing where to find the stories about them is another. Most of the classic stories appear in the Old Testament. Here is a basic guide to whose stories appear where; it does not take account of just passing references. The famous figures from the New Testament mostly appear either in the four Gospels or in the Acts of the Apostles.

Aaron	Exodus 4–Numbers 20
Abraham	Genesis 12–25
Adam and Eve	Genesis 2–3
Cain and Abel	Genesis 4
Daniel	Daniel, especially 1–10
David	1 Samuel 16–1 Kings 2
Deborah	Judges 4–5
Elijah	1 Kings 17–2 Kings 2
Elisha	2 Kings 2–13
Enoch	Genesis 5
Esau	Genesis 25–8, 32–5
Esther	Esther 1–10
Goliath	1 Samuel 17
Isaac	Genesis 17, 21–8, 35
Isaiah	Isaiah, especially 6–8
Jacob	Genesis 25–35, 42, 45–7
Jeremiah	Jeremiah, especially 1–43
Job	Job, especially 1–2, 42
Joseph	Genesis 37, 39–50
Joshua	Deuteronomy 34; Joshua 1–13; Judges 1
Miriam	Exodus 16; Numbers 12, 20
Moses	Exodus 2–Deuteronomy 34
Naomi	Ruth 1–4
Noah	Genesis 6–9
Rachel	Genesis 29–33, 35
Rebecca	Genesis 24–7, 49
Ruth	Ruth 1–4
Samson	Judges 13–16
Samuel	1 Samuel 1–16, 25
Sarah	Genesis 17–21, 23
Saul	1 Samuel 9–31
Solomon	1 Kings 1–11

THE BOOKS OF THE BIBLE

The Old Testament

Remarkably, not all editions of the Christian Bible contain the same books in the Old Testament. The reasons for these differences lie right at the beginning of Christianity.

The Jewish canon, i.e. the authoritative collection of books of the Hebrew Bible, was finally completed at the end of the first century CE after a long process. The books were divided into three sections, Law, Prophets and Writings. But the Hebrew Bible had also been translated into Greek by Jewish scholars, and this version, known as the Septuagint, was used in the Greek-speaking Jewish world beyond Palestine, particularly in Egypt. It was the Septuagint that the Christians took over as their Old Testament, and it contained a number of books which were not in the Hebrew canon. (The Jews thereupon dropped it, because of the way in which the Christians used it as prophecy of Jesus as the Christ.) The Septuagint was divided into four sections, with books in a different order from the Hebrew Bible: Law, History, Poetry and Prophets. At this time the canon of the Septuagint was not firmly fixed, so differences arose between churches over which books were regarded as part of it. The table below gives both the books generally regarded as comprising the Septuagint and the books of the Orthodox Old Testament, which does not recognize the Odes (apart from the Prayer of Manasseh) and the Psalms of Solomon and has 4 Maccabees as an appendix. 1 Esdras is a variant collection of material from 2 Chronicles, Ezra and Nehemiah; 2 Esdras is Ezra/Nehemiah. The Septuagint book of Psalms has 151 psalms rather than 150.

Hebrew Bible	*Septuagint (Greek translation)*	*Roman Catholic Old Testament*	*Orthodox Church Old Testament*	*Protestant and Anglican Old Testament*
Torah				
Genesis	Genesis	Genesis	Genesis	Genesis
Exodus	Exodus	Exodus	Exodus	Exodus
Leviticus	Leviticus	Leviticus	Leviticus	Leviticus
Numbers	Numbers	Numbers	Numbers	Numbers
Deuteronomy	Deuteronomy	Deuteronomy	Deuteronomy	Deuteronomy
Former Prophets				
Joshua	Joshua	Joshua	Joshua	Joshua
Judges	Judges	Judges	Judges	Judges
	Ruth	Ruth	Ruth	Ruth
1 Samuel	1 Kingdoms	1 Samuel	1 Kingdoms	1 Samuel
2 Samuel	2 Kingdoms	2 Samuel	2 Kingdoms	2 Samuel
1 Kings	3 Kingdoms	1 Kings	3 Kingdoms	1 Kings
2 Kings	4 Kingdoms	2 Kings	4 Kingdoms	2 Kings
Latter Prophets	1 Chronicles	1 Chronicles	1 Chronicles	1 Chronicles
Isaiah	2 Chronicles	2 Chronicles	2 Chronicles	2 Chronicles
Jeremiah	1 Esdras	Ezra	1 Esdras	Ezra
Ezekiel	2 Esdras	Nehemiah	2 Esdras	Nehemiah
	Esther	Tobit	Esther	
Hosea	Judith	Judith	Judith	
Joel	Tobit	Esther	Tobit	
Amos	1 Maccabees	1 Maccabees	1 Maccabees	
Obadiah	2 Maccabees	2 Maccabees	2 Maccabees	
Jonah	3 Maccabees		3 Maccabees	
Micah	4 Maccabees	Job		Job
Nahum	Psalms	Psalms	Psalms	Psalms
Habakkuk	Odes	Proverbs	Proverbs	Proverbs
Zephaniah	Proverbs	Ecclesiastes	Ecclesiastes	Ecclesiastes
Haggai	Ecclesiastes	Song of Songs	Song of Songs	Song of Solomon
Zechariah	Song of Songs	Wisdom	Job	
Malachi	Job	Ecclesiasticus	Wisdom	
	Wisdom		Ecclesiasticus	
Writings	Ecclesiasticus			
Psalms	Psalms of Solomon			
Job	Hosea	Isaiah	Hosea	Isaiah
Proverbs	Amos	Jeremiah	Amos	Jeremiah
Ruth	Micah	Lamentations	Micah	Lamentations

→

BIBLE

Hebrew Bible	*Septuagint (Greek translation)*	*Roman Catholic Old Testament*	*Orthodox Church Old Testament*	*Protestant and Anglican Old Testament*
Song of Songs	Joel	Baruch	Joel	Ezekiel
Ecclesiastes	Obadiah	Ezekiel	Obadiah	Daniel
Lamentations	Jonah	Daniel	Jonah	Hosea
Esther	Nahum	Hosea	Nahum	Joel
Daniel	Habakkuk	Joel	Habakkuk	Amos
Ezra	Zephaniah	Amos	Zephaniah	Obadiah
Nehemiah	Haggai	Obadiah	Haggai	Jonah
1 Chronicles	Zechariah	Jonah	Zechariah	Micah
2 Chronicles	Malachi	Micah	Malachi	Nahum
	Isaiah	Nahum	Isaiah	Habakkuk
	Jeremiah	Habakkuk	Jeremiah	Zephaniah
	Baruch	Zephaniah	Baruch	Haggai
	Lamentations	Haggai	Lamentations	Zechariah
	Letter of Jeremiah	Zechariah	Letter of Jeremiah	Malachi
	Ezekiel	Malachi	Ezekiel	
	Susanna		Susanna	
	Daniel		Daniel	
	Bel and the Dragon		Bel and the Dragon	

The Apocrypha

Martin Luther's famous translation of the Bible into German (1534) followed the Hebrew canon for the Old Testament and put those books not in the Hebrew Bible between the Old Testament and the New Testament as 'Apocrypha, that is, books which are not held equal to the sacred scriptures, but nevertheless are useful and good to read'. Other Protestants took a far more negative view of them and they were dropped from Bibles completely. Another term used for them is 'deuterocanonical books'. The books concerned are:

1 Esdras	The Letter of Jeremiah
2 Esdras	The Prayer of Azariah and the Song of the Three Young Men
Tobit	Susanna
Judith	Bel and the Dragon
Additions to Esther	The Prayer of Manasseh
The Wisdom of Solomon	1 Maccabees
Ecclesiasticus or the Wisdom of Jesus ben Sira	2 Maccabees
Baruch	

The New Testament

The books of the New Testament comprise four Gospels; a history of the earliest church; a series of letters attributed to Paul, some addressed to communities and some to individuals; a series of letters (also called epistles) by other authors (Hebrews bears no indication of authorship in the text), and a visionary apocalypse. 1 and 2 Timothy and Titus are known as the Pastoral Epistles because of their subject-matter; James, 1 and 2 Peter, 1–3 John and Jude are known as the Catholic Epistles, because they are not addressed to a specific church (strictly speaking, this is not true of 2 and 3 John).

Gospel according to Matthew	1 Timothy	*Pastoral Epistles*
Gospel according to Mark	2 Timothy	
Gospel according to Luke	Titus	
Gospel according to John	Philemon	
Acts of the Apostles	Hebrews	
Romans	James	*Catholic Epistles*
1 Corinthians	1 Peter	
2 Corinthians	2 Peter	
Galatians	1 John	
Ephesians	2 John	
Philippians	3 John	
Colossians	Jude	
1 Thessalonians		
2 Thessalonians	Revelation of St John the Divine (Apocalypse)	

came from the ninth or tenth centuries CE. There is another older version of the Old Testament, transmitted in Greek rather than Hebrew. This is the collection of authorized Greek translations, begun in Egypt under Ptolemy II Philadelphus (308–246 BCE) for Greek-speaking Jews in Egypt, and completed perhaps in the first century BCE. It is known as the Septuagint (LXX), after the tradition that the Five Books of Moses with which the Old Testament begins were miraculously translated by 72 translators, who worked without being allowed to communicate with one another and whose identical results proved that their translation was divinely inspired. The story of this miraculous origin of the Old Testament is related in the Letter of Aristeas (probably written in the middle of the second century BCE), and is evidence of the very high prestige which the LXX enjoyed within the Jewish world.

The Masoretic texts and the LXX differ in the number of books they contain, in the order of the books, and in the form of text which they transmit of any particular book: thus LXX Daniel contains material which is not in MT Daniel, and MT Jeremiah contains material which is not in LXX Jeremiah. The Dead Sea Scrolls are of intense interest for the study of the Old Testament, because in preserving Hebrew biblical manuscripts of the late second century BCE to first century BCE they give us access to Hebrew texts that are much older than what previously were the earliest surviving texts of either MT or LXX. Unfortunately they do not allow any simple answer to the question which of the two text traditions is older or more 'original'. Cave 4 has yielded Hebrew text fragments of both the longer (later found in MT) and the shorter (later found in LXX) traditions of the book of Jeremiah.

The early Christian church adopted the LXX as its first scriptures, and the LXX continues to form the Old Testament of the Greek and Russian Orthodox churches. Jerome's Vulgate Latin Old Testament was largely prepared from Hebrew, but follows the line of LXX in coverage and order. The Reformers sponsored new vernacular translations directly from MT, which they regarded as more directly authentic than LXX, but retained features of the LXX order. The reader of an ordinary modern English version of the Old Testament will be dealing with what is basically a translation of MT, with corrections drawn from the LXX and other sources on the (frequent) occasions when the MT tradition appears to have mistaken the original sense of a passage. The books in an English Bible will follow the general order of the LXX. A major source of perplexity in translating the Old Testament in any period is that very little classical Hebrew writing has been preserved outside the Old Testament itself, and there is therefore little wider linguistic context to help to elucidate obscure or unusual words and expressions. Comparative philology and the study of earlier solutions of these difficulties as they are embedded in ancient versions or in traditions of rabbinic interpretation are important resources for solving these linguistic problems.

The Pentateuch

The first five books of the Old Testament are commonly known in Old Testament study as the Pentateuch (from the Greek *pentatoichos* = fivefold [book]); in Judaism they are known as the Torah (= law, instruction). Genesis, Exodus, Levitus and Numbers are sometimes thought to have circulated together before the addition of Deuteronomy, and the word Tetrateuch has been coined for this unity. Joshua follows directly from Deuteronomy, and so the word Hexateuch has been coined for the first six books of the Old Testament. The Pentateuch is represented as written by Moses: 'The Five Books of Moses'. Historical criticism, especially since the nineteenth century, has attempted to unravel a more complex history of composition and editing, without coming to any definite consensus.

WHAT'S IN THE PENTATEUCH

The Pentateuch, the first five books of the Bible, is also known as the Torah = 'law', 'instruction'.

Genesis
Two accounts of the creation of the world (1.1–2.4; 2.4–24); Adam and Eve (3); Cain and Abel (4); Noah and his ark (6–9); the tower of Babel (11); stories of Abraham and Sarah (12–25); stories of Isaac and Rebecca (24–7); stories of Jacob and Rachel (27–35); the story of Joseph (37–50).

Exodus
The Israelites are slaves in Egypt; Moses is born (1–2); God calls Moses in the burning bush (3–4); Moses and Aaron lead the Israelites out of Egypt with plagues, celebration of the Passover, crossing of the sea (5–14); Moses and his sister Miriam lead celebrations for the exodus (15); the Israelites journey through the wilderness to Sinai (16–18); the Law is given to Moses by God on Mount Sinai (19–24: Ten Commandments 20.1–17); instructions for making the tabernacle, a portable shrine, and for worship in it (25–31); the people worship the golden calf and are struck by a plague; Moses breaks the tablets of the Law God has given him (32); Moses pleads for the people and receives the Law again (33–4); the making of the tabernacle (35–40).

Leviticus
A collection of laws, still set at Sinai; chapters 17–26 are known as the Holiness Code, laws motivated by the principle 'You shall be holy; for I the Lord your God am holy' (19.2).

Numbers
The end of the time at Sinai. The book begins with a census, hence its name, and yet further laws (1–10). The Israelites journey on through the wilderness (10–20), sustained miraculously by manna and quails (11); spies are sent into Canaan, the land they are to be given, but bring back discouraging news (13); there are constant complaints (14; 16–17); more laws are given (18–19). Moses miraculously gets water from a rock; Miriam and Aaron die (20). Moses heals those bitten by snakes by holding up a bronze serpent; the Israelites win a battle and occupy territory (21). Balak king of Moab summons a prophet, Balaam, to curse them, but Balaam can only utter blessings (22–4). There are more disputes among the Israelites, but after another census has been taken they settle in the land east of the Jordan (25–36).

Deuteronomy
A speech given by Moses delivered in Moab just before his death. Chapters 12–26 are a distinct collection of laws, among other things centralizing Israelite worship in one particular place. The book also contains another version of the Ten Commandments (5.6–21); it ends with an account of the death of Moses, who is not allowed to enter the promised land, and the appointment of his successor, Joshua (34). Deuteronomy 34 is really Numbers 37; it continues the account in Numbers, the rest of Deuteronomy having been inserted at some stage.

The German biblical critic Julius Wellhausen (1844–1918), building on the work of predecessors such as Johannes Vatke (1806–82) and Karl Heinrich Graf (1815–69), is especially associated with the view that the Pentateuch is woven together from strands generally referred to as J, E, D and P. The strand J (short for Yahwist, so named because it uses YHWH as the name for God: JHWH in German, which is why the source is not called Y) is a body of narrative, the work of a writer who has been placed at various times from the tenth to the seventh century BCE, and is thought to have been active in either Jerusalem or Judah. E material is sometimes connected with the northern kingdom (Ephraim) and characteristically substitutes Elohim (= God) for the divine name YHWH. D material is concentrated in the book of Deuteronomy. P reflects the concerns of the Priestly establishment; as well as in Leviticus and Numbers, P material is found in Genesis and Exodus. Thus the first of the two accounts of creation (Genesis 1) in the more recent P version and the emphasis on division (*havdalah*) as the primary way in which God brought creation from chaos (dividing waters above the firmament from waters below, dividing light from dark, etc.) is matched by the emphasis in Leviticus on making proper division and distinction between things and qualities, especially holy from common and clean from unclean.

This kind of analysis can be applied to the account of the crossing of the sea in Exodus 14, and the reader may like to ask what the nature of the story is if one supposes that the verses attributed to J constitute an earlier version, and how and why the story is changed by the addition of the P material. The terms J and P especially continue to be widely used, even if it has proved difficult to disentangle the history of the formation of the Pentateuch as neatly as an earlier generation of scholars had supposed. It is important to remember that for Wellhausen and his successors the analysis of the Pentateuch was not an end in itself but part of an attempt to use the Old Testament to write a narrative of Israelite religion and institutions different from the story as the Old Testament presents it. Wellhausen's own reconstruction postulated a decline from the moral peak of the great ethical prophets of the ninth and eighth centuries to what he presented as the oppressive and formal legalism of Judaism as it developed after the return from exile. This view has been severely (and rightly) criticized for its failure to understand the true nature of observant Judaism, and for the contribution it may have made to the growth of German antisemitism, but such criticism should not be allowed to detract from the originality of Wellhausen's primary enterprise.

The Deuteronomists

p. 1152

The sack of Jerusalem by the Babylonians in 587 BCE with the destruction of the temple, the extinction of the monarchy as a political institution, and the taking into exile of the leading figures of the political, cultural and religious life of the nation, had profound consequences for the content and shaping of the Old Testament. An explanation was needed: how can YHWH have allowed this to happen to his chosen people? One ready answer saw the disaster as a just punishment for the sins of YHWH's people, understood both as religious apostasy and as the creation of an unjust society repugnant to him. Martin Noth (1902–68) suggested that the historical books from Joshua to 2 Kings inclusive could be read as a single historical work, a review of the history of Israel and Judah from the entry into the land to the beginning of the exile, intended to document the ways in which the nation had sinned, and the leaders responsible for that sin. He named it the Deuteronomistic History. The present book divisions into Joshua, Judges, 1 and 2 Samuel, 1 and 2 Kings are arbitrary functions of the length of a scroll. Noth suggested that the Deuteronomistic History was originally organized into five books. Deuteronomy formed a historical preface to the whole work, and the authorship (both of Deuteronomy and of the Deuteronomistic History) was associated with the scribal and administrative élite of Jerusalem in the seventh and early sixth centuries BCE. King Josiah (ruled *c.*640–609 BCE) is something of a hero of the Deuteronomistic tradition, and the account in 2 Kings 22 of the discovery in the temple of a book of the law and of the reforms which Josiah introduced on the basis of this discovery are evidence of the power of the Deuteronomic circles in the 620s; it is tempting to connect the 'book of the law' with some form of the book Deuteronomy.

The prophets

The Deuteronomists were also interested in collecting and editing the texts of some of the great pre-exilic prophets. Several prophetic books (e.g. Amos, Hosea) are prefaced with opening verses that date the prophecy in terms of the Deuteronomistic dating system, and a close study of the text shows traces of Deuteronomistic editorial activity. In the case of Jeremiah, the Deuteronomistic contribution to the book is very considerable, and there is a vigorous debate in current scholarship between those who (at one extreme) argue that the figure of Jeremiah is entirely a construction of

THE CROSSING OF THE SEA: TWO ACCOUNTS

The account of the crossing of the sea (scholars prefer to call it the 'Reed Sea' rather than the traditional 'Red Sea', to be more accurate) in Exodus 14.1–31 can be divided into two rather different narratives without much trouble. In the earlier one, JE, YHWH, the God of the Israelites, seems to have driven back the sea with an east wind; in the later version, P, the story is developed and amplified with the introduction of motifs like the hardening of Pharaoh's heart and the dividing of the sea into walls of water on either side.

JE	P
	14[1] Then YHWH said to Moses, [2]'Tell the people of Israel to turn back and encamp in front of Pi-ha-hiroth, between Migdol and the sea, in front of Ba'al-zephon; you shall encamp over against it, by the sea. [3]For Pharaoh will say of the people of Israel, 'They are entangled in the land; the wilderness has shut them in.' [4] And I will harden Pharaoh's heart, and he will pursue them and I will get glory over Pharaoh and all his host; and the Egyptians shall know that I am YHWH.' And they did so.
[5] When the king of Egypt was told that the people had fled, the mind of Pharaoh and his servants was changed toward the people, and they said, 'What is this we have done, that we have let Israel go from serving us?' [6]So he made ready his chariot and took his army with him, [7]and took six hundred picked chariots and all the other chariots of Egypt with officers over all of them.	
	[8]And YHWH hardened the heart of Pharaoh king of Egypt and he pursued the people of Israel as they went forth defiantly
[9]The Egyptians pursued them,	all Pharaoh's horses and chariots and his horsemen and his army, and overtook them encamped at the sea, by Pi-ha-hiroth, in front of Ba'al-zephon. [10]When Pharaoh drew near,
the people of Israel lifted up their eyes, and behold, the Egyptians were marching after them; and they were in great fear.	And the people of Israel cried out to YHWH;
[11]and they said to Moses, 'Is it because there are no graves in Egypt that you have taken us away to die in the wilderness? What have you done to us, in bringing us out of Egypt? [12]Is not this what we said to you in Egypt, "Let us alone and let us serve the Egyptians"? For it would have been better for us to serve the Egyptians than to die in the wilderness.' [13]And Moses said to the people, 'Fear not, stand firm, and see the salvation of YHWH, which he will work for you today; for the Egyptians whom you see today, you shall never see again. [14]YHWH will fight for you, and you have only to be still.'	
	[15]YHWH said to Moses, 'Why do you cry to me? Tell the people of Israel to go forward. [16]Lift up your rod, and stretch out your hand over the sea and divide it, that the people of Israel may go on dry ground through the sea. [17]And I will harden the hearts of the Egyptians so that they shall go in after them, and I will get glory over Pharaoh and all his host, his chariots, and his horsemen. [18]And the Egyptians shall know that I am YHWH, when I have gotten glory over Pharaoh, his chariots, and his horsemen.

BIBLE

JE	P
19 Then the angel of God who went before the host of Israel moved and went behind them; and the pillar of cloud moved from before them and stood behind them, 20 coming between the host of Egypt and the host of Israel. And there was the cloud and the darkness; and the night passed without one coming near the other all night.	
	21 Then Moses stretched out his hand over the sea;
And YHWH drove the sea back by a strong east wind all night, and made the sea dry land,	and the waters were divided. 22 And the people of Israel went into the midst of the sea on dry ground, the waters being a wall to them on their right hand and on their left. 23 The Egyptians pursued, and went in after them into the midst of the sea, all Pharaoh's horses, his chariots, and his horsemen.
24 And in the morning watch YHWH in the pillar of fire and of cloud looked down upon the host of the Egyptians, and discomfited the host of the Egyptians, 25 clogging their chariot wheels so that they drove heavily; and the Egyptians said, 'Let us flee from before Israel; for YHWH fights for them against the Egyptians.'	
	26 Then YHWH said to Moses, 'Stretch out your hand over the sea, that the water may come back upon the Egyptians, upon their chariots, and upon their horsemen.' 27 So Moses stretched forth his hand over the sea,
and the sea returned to its wonted flow when the morning appeared; and the Egyptians fled into it, and YHWH routed the Egyptians in the midst of the sea.	
	28 The waters returned and covered the chariots and the horsemen and all the host of Pharaoh that had followed them into the sea; not so much as one of them remained. 29 But the people of Israel walked on dry ground through the sea, the waters being a wall to them on their right hand and on their left.
30 Thus YHWH saved Israel that day from the hand of the Egyptians; and Israel saw the Egyptians dead upon the seashore. 31 And Israel saw the great work which YHWH did against the Egyptians, and the people feared YHWH; and they believed in YHWH and in his servant Moses.	

the editors of the book, and cannot be connected in any secure way with a historical figure, and those who (at the other extreme) argue that the book gives us a direct insight into the internal struggles of Jeremiah the son of Hilkiah; there are a number of intervening positions. That the Deuteronomists should have been interested in the pre-exilic prophets is natural; here were voices foretelling the very catastrophe that the Deuteronomists were attempting to understand. Ezekiel presents, however, a criticism of the Deuteronomistic theology: the catastrophe of 587 BCE is not a punishment for the sins of earlier generations but a punishment for the sins of the present generation; each generation suffers the consequence of its own sin (Ezekiel 18). And the book of Isaiah seems to reflect another enterprise, from the time of the exile, that of editing and commenting on a body of prophecy. It has long been recognized that the book contains material relating to the late eighth century BCE (the time of King Hezekiah), the later sixth century BCE (the imminent

WHAT'S IN THE DEUTERONOMISTIC HISTORY

In the Hebrew Bible, the historical books from Joshua to 2 Kings are known as the 'Former Prophets', as opposed to the 'Latter Prophets', the prophetic books. Modern scholars usually call them the 'Deuteronomistic History', after the widely held view that they form a single historical work shaped by the theology of the Deuteronomists. It is plausibly suggested that this history is divided into five parts, separated by significant speeches:

1. The wanderings in the wilderness and the conquest of the lands east of the Jordan: *Moses' speech: Deuteronomy 33*
2. The conquest of the lands west of the Jordan: *The last words of Joshua: Joshua 24*
3. The period of the Judges: *Samuel's speech: 1 Samuel 12*
4. Monarchy and empire: *Solomon's prayer at the dedication of the Temple: 1 Kings 8*
5. The divided monarchy in decline *(the work perhaps originally ended at 2 Kings 25.26)*

Joshua
Joshua sends spies across the Jordan (2). The Israelites cross the Jordan with dry feet (3–4) and conquer the land, destroying Jericho and Ai along with many other places; they massacre the inhabitants (5–12). The land is divided among the twelve tribes of Israel (13–22). Before Joshua dies he makes the people put away the gods they had served previously (23–4).

Judges
It proves that the conquest has not been as thorough as suggested by the book of Joshua; some of the tribes do not drive out those occupying their allotted land (1). The Israelites enter into a cycle of doing evil and serving the gods whom they are supposed to have put away; their God YHWH delivers them into the hands of their enemies; they repent and YHWH raises up saviours, 'judges'. This cycle persists throughout the book. The judges include figures like Deborah the prophetess (4–5), Gideon (6–8), Jephthah, who because of a rash vow has to sacrifice his daughter (11–12), and Samson, a man of enormous strength who is lured into the hands of the Philistines by Delilah. He finally kills all their leaders by pulling a temple down on them (13–16). The book ends with three episodes illustrating the prevalence of a high degree of lawlessness (17–21); its last words are 'In those days there was no king in Israel; every man did what was right in his own eyes.'

1 Samuel
The book begins with Hannah, who serves as a model for Luke's portrayal of Mary of Nazareth. She is a childless woman who gives birth to a son, Samuel, after praying to God. Like Mary, she sings a hymn of praise. Samuel is very special (1–3). There is still corruption and lawlessness in Israel and the Philistines even capture the sacred ark of the covenant; however, it returns of its own accord (4–6). Samuel too is a judge, but his sons are corrupt and the people want a king (8). Samuel chooses and anoints Saul (9–12). Saul is not a success; he falls out with Samuel and constantly has to fight the Philistines (13–15). YHWH chooses another king, who first appears in the unlikely guise of David the shepherd boy. David kills the Philistine giant Goliath and becomes a close friend of Saul's son Jonathan (16–18). Saul grows jealous of David, who becomes a fugitive, gathering his own supporters and even allying himself with the Philistines; finally the Philistines defeat the Israelites in a battle in which Saul and Jonathan die (19–31).

2 Samuel
David becomes king, first of Judah, a tribe of Israel, and then of all Israel (1–5). He establishes his capital in Jerusalem and builds a palace (he is not allowed to build a temple); he wins more victories and establishes the foundations of an empire (6–8). A very detailed account of the vicissitudes of his reign and the machinations over who will be his successor runs from chapter 9 until the end of the book and into the first two chapters of 1 Kings; it is known as 'the succession narrative' and is thought by many scholars to have been written relatively close to the events it describes.

1 Kings
The book begins with the death of David and the accession of his son Solomon (1–2). Solomon is a man of great wisdom; his judgement on the two women who claim the same child is legendary (3). He builds the temple in Jerusalem and establishes a great empire (4–10), but marries foreign wives and has temples built for their gods, so that YHWH threatens the end of his kingdom (11). Under Solomon's successor Rehoboam the kingdom which David had united splits into two, Judah in the south and Israel in the north (11–13). From here on kings of the two kingdoms are chronicled and evaluated in terms of the purity of their worship of YHWH; the north is almost always judged harshly. The account is interspersed with stories of prophets: an anonymous prophet (13), Elijah (17–19) and Micaiah (22).

2 Kings
The book begins with further stories of Elijah (1–2) and his successor Elisha (2–9); the chronicle continues and reports the end of the northern kingdom, which is overwhelmed by the Assyrians (18); the southern kingdom survives under Hezekiah, one of the 'better' kings, who is advised by the prophet Isaiah (19–20). The best of the kings is Josiah, who reforms worship on the basis of a book (which some scholars see as a first form of Deuteronomy) found in the temple (22–3). However, this does not turn the tide and the book ends with the capture of Jerusalem by the Babylonians; the leaders are led into exile (24–5).

ascendancy of King Cyrus of Persia and the fall of the Babylonian empire) and the beginning of the fifth century (the Persian period and the time of the restoration). The material is more tightly integrated than the conventional division into a First Isaiah (1–39), Second Isaiah (40–55) and Third Isaiah (56–66) allows, and it has recently been suggested that the poet responsible for the bulk of 40–55, with its message of hope for return and rebuilding, was himself the editor who attached his prophecy to Isaiah 1–39.

If the period after 587 BCE was decisive for the collecting and shaping of the prophetic books as we have them in the Old Testament, the phenomenon of prophecy was a good deal older, and persisted at least into the fifth century. Prophecy was by no means unique to Israel and Judah: prophets, organized even into official groups and employed by the state, are documented by texts from the early second millennium BCE discovered in Mari and Nuzu (or Nuzi) in north-western Mesopotamia. There are numerous references in the Old Testament to 'official prophets' similar to the Nuzu prophets, and the Old Testament itself seems to draw a distinction between these and the outstanding figures of biblical prophecy: Elijah, Amos, Hosea, Isaiah and the like. Amos disdained any official role (7.14, where 'I am no prophet nor a prophet's son' probably means 'not one of the sons of the prophets', i.e. not a member of any prophetic guild or group), and 1 Kings 22 presents us with a contrast between the freelance Micaiah and an impressive assembly of about 400 prophets evidently attached to the interests of King Ahab. The unconstrained prophetic voice announcing the will of YHWH for his people and rebuking their despondence continues in the time of the restoration and the rebuilding of the temple, in Haggai and Zechariah.

The Priestly Document and Old Testament law

It was the policy of the Persians, who defeated the Babylonians in 539 BCE, to allow subject people to worship their indigenous gods after their own traditions. For the exiles, this meant a return to the land and a degree of autonomous self-government (but not the restoration of the monarchy). It also meant the rebuilding of Jerusalem, and the construction of a second temple to replace the building constructed by Solomon and destroyed by the Babylonians. The restoration may also have been significant for the codification of law, especially of the legal material in Leviticus and Numbers associated with the P strand of the Pentateuch.

The sequence and chronology of the restoration is notoriously difficult to unravel from the account in the books of Ezra and Nehemiah, but an important episode is recounted in Nehemiah 8: Ezra the scribe reads 'the book of the law of Moses' to the people 'from early morning to mid-day', and they pledge themselves to the keeping of this law. This episode has been used to suggest that P was edited into its present form at the beginning of the restoration, or better when the restoration became an imminent prospect, as a manifesto for the return of the people to the land in a cultically pure state. This is not to suggest that the individual elements of P are compositions of the end of the sixth century: Leviticus and Numbers clearly contain material of great antiquity (e.g. the scapegoat ritual of Leviticus 16), and the institution of the priesthood is ancient. Much confusion has been caused, in discussion of the date of P and of similar subjects, by a failure to make the basic distinction between the date of the final edition of a body of material (the date at which it assumed exactly the form in which we find it in the pages of the Old Testament), the date of the earlier cycle of material incorporated into the final version and the date of individual stories and traditions which were incorporated into those earlier cycles.

In the period of the restoration, then, when there is a general consensus that the Pentateuch had become a closed body of material in something like its present form, at least two cycles of legal

THE CHRONICLER

The first and second books of Chronicles (in Hebrew the book is called 'Events of the days'; the familiar English title comes ultimately from Jerome) cover much the same historical ground as the first and second books of Kings, but with variations of emphasis and content. The work is probably from the fourth century BCE. The Chronicler shares the view of the Deuteronomists that blessings and misfortunes are rewards and punishments from God for the behaviour of king and people, but when the Chronicler's text is compared to the parallel passage in the Deuteronomistic history, some special concerns emerge: celebration of the achievement of David and Solomon in establishing the monarchy and the temple; an interest in the liturgy, practices and personnel of the temple; and the role of the Levites. Compare, for example, these accounts of the placing of the ark of the covenant in the temple newly completed by King Solomon:

1 Kings 8.1–6,10–11	*2 Chronicles 5.2–7, 11–14*
Then Solomon assembled the elders of Israel and all the heads of the tribes, the leaders of the fathers' houses of the people of Israel, before King Solomon in Jerusalem, to bring up the ark of the covenant of the LORD out of the city of David, which is Zion. And all the men of Israel assembled to King Solomon at the feast in the month Ethanim, which is the seventh month.	Then Solomon assembled the elders of Israel and all the heads of the tribes, the leaders of the fathers' houses of the people of Israel, to Jerusalem, to bring up the ark of the covenant of the LORD out of the city of David, which is Zion. And all the men of the Israel assembled before the king at the feast which is in the seventh month.
And all the elders of Israel came, and the priests took up the ark. And they brought up the ark of the LORD, the tent of meeting, and all the holy vessels that were in the tent; the priests and the Levites brought them up. And King Solomon and all the congregation of Israel, who had assembled before him, were with him before the ark, sacrificing so many sheep and oxen that they could not be counted or numbered.	And all the elders of Israel came, and the Levites took up the ark. And they brought up the ark, the tent of meeting, and all the holy vessels that were in the tent; the priests and the Levites brought them up. And King Solomon and all the congregation of Israel, who had assembled before him, were before the ark, sacrificing so many sheep and oxen that they could not be counted or numbered.
Then the priests brought the ark of the covenant of the LORD to its place, in the inner sanctuary of the house, in the most holy place, underneath the wings of the cherubim.	So the priests brought the ark of the covenant of the LORD to its place, in the inner sanctuary of the house, in the most holy place, underneath the wings of the cherubim.
And when the priests came out of the holy place,	Now when the priests came out of the holy place (for all the priests who were present had sanctified themselves, without regard to their divisions; and all the Levitical singers, Asaph, Heman and Jeduthun, their sons and kinsmen, arrayed in fine linen, with cymbals, harps and lyres, stood east of the altar with a hundred and twenty priests who were trumpeters; and it was the duty of the trumpeters and singers to make themselves heard in unison in praise and thanksgiving to the LORD), and when the song was raised, with trumpets and cymbals and other musical instruments, in praise to the LORD, 'for he is good, for his steadfast love endures for ever',
a cloud filled the house of the LORD, so that the priests could not stand to minister because of the cloud; for the glory of the LORD filled the house of the LORD.	the house, the house of the LORD, was filled with a cloud, so that the priests could not stand to minister because of the cloud, for the glory of the LORD filled the house of God.

There is much debate about the relationship between Chronicles and Ezra-Nehemiah – itself originally a single book, which was only divided in Christian Bibles from the third century CE, and not divided in Hebrew Bibles until the fifteenth century. Are these two works by different authors? Are they two works by the same author, conventionally called 'the Chronicler'? Were they originally a single work, which has been broken up in transmission?

Ezra-Nehemiah tells the story of the restoration of the people in the land after the time of exile, in the period of Persian control (late fifth to late fourth century BCE). The walls of Jerusalem are rebuilt, the community is gathered together as a people pure before God (mixed marriages are ended, those who cannot prove their descent are excluded), the law is proclaimed, the temple is rebuilt, and the rhythms of worship are re-established as the law directs. Although the outline is clear, the precise sequence of events is hard to reconstruct, and there continues to be much discussion about the date of the book, the dates of the historical persons Ezra and Nehemiah, and the relationship between them and the various phases of the restoration.

material had been woven into the law of Israel. The D tradition of reflection tends to emphasize the contractual character of the law: it is something to be kept as an act of obedience, and a condition of continuance in the land that God gives his people. The P tradition presents law as a consequence of living in a universe that God has made in the way in which he has made it. The law is rooted in creation, and to live according to the law is to live in tune with the order of things as they are made by God. Thus it is that we find in the Pentateuch both an emphasis on the revealed character of the law as given to Moses by YHWH on Mount Sinai and an emphasis on the natural character of the law as given in creation.

Wisdom

Wisdom is an important term in Old Testament study. In its most general sense it refers to a theological style that attempts to understand the world, and a human being's place in the world, p. 444 by reflection upon experience. The starting point for theodicy or practical morality is not a special utterance of YHWH ('the voice of the Lord came to me saying …') but careful attention to experience of life. One characteristic way of expressing this accumulated experience is in the distilled form of the proverb. Wisdom in this broad sense is found not only in the 'wisdom books' of the Old Testament (e.g. Proverbs, Ecclesiastes) but also in the use of proverbs or ideas of poetic justice in the pre-exilic prophets. The transmission of an accumulated body of experience in proverbs came to be characteristic of the training of an administrative élite. It has been suggested that this scribal wisdom had an institutional base in some kind of academy, possibly attached to the temple of Solomon, in which well-born young men were prepared to take a role in government; whether the institution existed or not, the 'young man' addressed in Proverbs or Psalm 119 is this kind of pupil.

For scribal wisdom, the keeping of the law is an important route to wisdom, alongside the careful study of lessons from observation. God will give wisdom to those who are faithful to the law, and they will enjoy high office and reputation: exactly the career path of two young heroes of the wisdom tradition, Joseph and Daniel (the story of Joseph in Genesis 40–8 also has the stamp of wisdom literature and it is not accidental that in the MT Daniel is found among the wisdom books rather than among the prophets).

Scribal wisdom tends to find itself in difficulty in the face of apparently innocent suffering (in Psalm 37.25 the psalmist simply denies that the difficulty ever arises). In books like Job and Ecclesiastes the method of doing theology by reflection on experience tends in a quite different, sceptical direction: the author questions the received wisdom about providence and divine justice, on the basis of direct (real or imagined) experiences of life. Such countervailing wisdom was a persistent phenomenon in Old Testament thought and this makes the sceptical wisdom books difficult to date. Ecclesiastes is generally assigned to *c.* 300 BCE and Ecclesiasticus is more precisely datable to the second century; however, Job, Proverbs and the Song of Songs are not really datable. Psalms, which is located among the wisdom books in both MT and LXX, is a special case.

Daniel and the beginning of apocalyptic

In the 160s BCE, there was a determined attempt to suppress the traditional observance of the Torah. The conflict that followed is probably better understood as a struggle between conflicting interpretations within Judaism of what Jewish identity and practice should be rather than as an attempt by foreign overlords to impose a Hellenizing programme, even if those who attempted to enforce new customs (Greek style gymnasia, attribution to YHWH of the Greek title Zeus Hypsistos, Zeus the

THE WISDOM BOOKS

The following biblical books, grouped together in a Hebrew Bible at the beginning of the 'Writings', are commonly called the wisdom books. They embody the theological concerns and strategies of Old Testament wisdom.

Job: The book is impossible to date; its dramatic setting seems to be in the time of the patriarchs. The ostensible question in the book is whether piety is correlated with prosperity. The Satan challenges God: if God inflicts suffering on Job he will curse God. But the scope of the book is soon enlarged to discuss the possibility and meaning of innocent suffering. Job's comforters, initially three, and then four with the addition of Elihu, articulate the traditional theodicy: there is no unmerited suffering; Job must have done something wrong. Job confounds them, but is himself left speechless when God speaks to him from the whirlwind: how can a creature grasp or question the ways of the Creator? The book has been read in many ways. Is God's great speech from the whirlwind the last word, or is the reader meant to take even this as irony?

p. 444

Psalms: The book of Psalms appears between the books of Job and Proverbs and thus is classed as a wisdom book. Certainly an important strand within the collection reflects the wisdom tradition; however, Psalms has come to mean far more than this in Christianity, and it therefore needs to be considered separately.

Psalms

Proverbs: A collection of proverbs, attributed mostly to Solomon, the great hero of the wisdom tradition, but also to Agur, Lemuel and 'the wise'. This is a body of accumulated wisdom and the reader – specifically the young man who is being trained for high administrative office in the service of the state – is incited to regulate his life accordingly. Much of the material goes back to the time of the Israelite monarchy and earlier, and is well paralleled in proverb collections from other countries in the ancient Near East, but in its present form the book is probably post-exilic. In Proverbs 8 a personification of Lady Wisdom speaks. This chapter has played an important part in debates about the Christian doctrine of Christ, with whom Wisdom (Greek *Sophia*) was early identified (1 Corinthians 1.24). Sophia plays a prominent role in some feminist theologies.

Ecclesiastes: With Job, this is a masterpiece of 'sceptical 'wisdom. Scholars date it to around 300 BCE, but as usual the words are attributed to Solomon. Observation of life, and especially the universality and inevitability of death, seem to undercut the possibility of ultimate sense or meaning. But the world is not so much void of meaning as full of contradictory meanings. The key word *hebel*, usually translated 'vanity' or 'futility', may rather mean 'absurdity'. Ecclesiastes is the Greek translation of the Hebrew Qoheleth, by which name the book is also known. It means 'speaker' – either in the sense of one who addresses an assembly or in the sense of one who presides over it.

The Song of Solomon: A collection of love poems which cannot be clearly dated, though the tradition again attributes them to Solomon. Their frank eroticism has led both Jewish and Christian traditions to read them allegorically, e.g. as expressing the mystical union between God and the soul, or between Christ and the church. It is interesting that the Reformers of the sixteenth century, who were generally hostile to allegorical interrelation of the Bible, remained reluctant to read this book 'literally'. More recently, the love poetry has come to be appreciated in its own terms.

In addition to these five works in the Hebrew canon, there are important additional wisdom books in the Greek canon (i.e. in the Apocrypha). These include:

pp. 128–9

The Wisdom of Solomon: The book was composed in Greek, quite possibly by an Alexandrian Jew and in the later first century BCE. The author explores the contrast between the 'righteous' and the 'wicked' and their relation to immortality. Some of Wisdom's speculations on life after death were used as scriptural support for the late medieval Roman Catholic doctrine of purgatory (and for the related system of indulgences), and hostility to this book was an important reason for the Reformers' rejection of the Apocrypha as having no authority for the determination of Christian doctrine.

Life after death

Ecclesiasticus: Latin 'church book', presumably from its use in early Christian centuries. It is also known as the Wisdom of Jesus ben Sira, or simply as Sirach. Ben Sira was a teacher of wisdom, perhaps operating in Jerusalem in the decades before the Maccabean revolt. His collection of proverbial material was translated from Hebrew to Greek by his grandson at some point after 132 BCE (see the prologue). About two- thirds of the original Hebrew text, which was thought to have been completely lost, was recovered in various manuscript discoveries during the twentieth century.

Katharine Dell, *Get Wisdom, Get Insight: An Introduction to Israel's Wisdom Literature*, London: Darton, Longman & Todd 2000; Leo G. Perdue (ed), *In Search of Wisdom*, Louisville, KY: Westminster John Knox Press 1993

TWO REMARKABLE WOMEN

Two books of the Bible bear the name of women:

Ruth tells the story of a young widow from the land of Moab, who returns to Bethlehem with her mother-in-law Naomi, who is also a widow. There Ruth comes to marry Boaz, with whom she has a son who is to be David's grandfather. If the book is dated before the exile, its purpose may have been to elaborate the genealogy of the Davidic kings. If it is dated after the exile, it may have been to emphasize the possibility of intermarriage (against the tradition of Ezra and Nehemiah). Whatever the date and purpose of the book, the central characters are drawn with notable sympathy and compassion, from Ruth's act of commitment to Naomi, 'Where you go, I will go ...' (1.16–18), to Naomi's consideration for Ruth and Boaz's generosity in different ways to both of them. The narrative conveys vividly the constraints on a woman's life-choices in the period, and the humanity which can transcend these constraints. In an English Bible, following the Septuagint, the book of Ruth is inserted after Judges because the story is set in the time of the Judges. This interrupts the flow of the Deuteronomistic History, and the Hebrew Bible puts Ruth towards the end of the Writings.

pp. 128–9

Esther is the story of a Jewish woman who becomes the favoured wife of the Persian king. Having come to political influence through the harem, Queen Esther uses her power to rescue the Jews from a pogrom planned by the king's wicked minister Haman. The anti-Jewish tensions of the plot suggest that the book might have been written in the time leading up to the Maccabean revolt (compare the stories of deliverance in Daniel). It is explicitly an explanation of the Jewish feast of Purim, and the story is retold at Purim every year to this day. In the Christian church, the book has been of more marginal importance, not least because God is never mentioned in it by name. The community at Qumran also seems not to have had a high opinion of it: it is the only biblical book not represented in the Dead Sea Scrolls.

Origins and background

p. 845

Most High God, etc.) and to proscribe old ones (circumcision, observance of the Torah) enjoyed the support of the Antiochene overlords of the Near East. The violent persecution of Jews faithful to the law and the counter-reaction of 167–164 BCE which came to be known as the Maccabean revolt are the likely context for some Psalms (especially 44, with its insistence on persecutions being for the Lord's sake and not for any sin the people have committed) and of Daniel.

The nightmare of 167 BCE posed the problem of theodicy more acutely even than the catastrophe of 578 BCE. The persecution of the faithful ones was a direct consequence of their fidelity to the law, and could scarcely be read as a just punishment for apostasy. Daniel offers comfort to the persecuted, in two forms. The familiar stories of Daniel and his companions, in the time of the exile, are retold to emphasize that those who remain faithful to the law will in the end be vindicated, and God will avenge himself on their accusers. The visions in Daniel 2 and 7–12 predict the imminent vindication of God's saints, as the judgement that has already been given in their favour in the heavenly court (Daniel 7) is worked out in the processes of human history. Daniel marks the emergence of a new genre of apocalyptic writing (from Greek *apokalypsis* = revelation, i.e. of the true nature of things in a heavenly perspective, and therefore of the future course of earthly history). The case of Daniel suggests that apocalyptic grew as much from wisdom traditions as from prophecy. It was a dominant genre of the literature produced between the Old and New Testaments, which in turn is an important part of the background to the writings of the New Testament. Daniel 12.2 is one of the few clear Old Testament references to the resurrection of the body, significantly in connection with a final judgement in which God's justice will be vindicated. Otherwise the Old Testament locates existence after death in Sheol, like the Greek Hades a shadowy place in which no meaningful relationship with God continues. The Maccabean revolt was also important for the development of the idea of martyrdom: the account of the death of a mother and her seven sons in 2 Maccabees 7 not only underscores the emergence of a doctrine of bodily resurrection but was so thoroughly appropriated by Christians that the Maccabean martyrs came to be regarded as Christian figures.

Life after death

Martyr

Christian theologies of the Old Testament

A number of attempts have been made to organize the rich and varied material of the Old Testament within a theological scheme conducive to Christianity. Among the best known are those of Gerhard von Rad (1901–71), who read the Old Testament as an account of God's salvation history which finds its fulfilment in Jesus Christ, and Walther Eichrodt (1890–1978), whose central organizing principle is covenant. As part of his larger theological exploration of glory, the Swiss systematic theologian Hans Urs von Balthasar (1905–87) produced what is in effect a one-volume theology of the Old Testament, but this has been little noted by Old Testament scholars. More recently, there has been considerable debate about the possibility or legitimacy of these overarching schemes, and about the relationship between the appropriation of the Old Testament by Christians and the use of the Hebrew Bible within Judaism. The traditional title 'Old Testament', whatever its origin, already suggests a recontextualization of the whole collection within a theology of successive covenants.

Covenant

It will be noticed that the theme of future messianic expectation is not a dominant, or even a strong, theme in the Old Testament. There are abundant references to the Lord's Messiah = Anointed; these are in the first instance references to the anointed king and would originally (as in Psalm 2 or Psalm 89) have related to a living person within the institutional structure of Israel. With the disappearance of the monarchy as an institution, thought not as an idea, the texts became free to attach themselves to new points of reference. The selection of a number of texts (especially prophetic) into a body of messianic prophecy which is then regarded as the essential 'message of the Old Testament' is an ancient Christian enterprise: the process can be seen already in the Gospels, and is presupposed in Justin Martyr's *Dialogue with Trypho the Jew*, interesting not least for preserving Trypho's protest that his scriptures are being misrepresented. The development of dialogue between Jews and Christians in the second half of the twentieth century has created a new context for the exploration of these issues.

Messiah

Judaism and Christianity

The New Testament

The Gospels

The Gospels (from the Old English 'godspell' = Greek *evangelion* = 'good news') are a fourfold presentation under the names of four different evangelists or Gospel writers of the life and teaching of Jesus, and of his suffering, death and resurrection. It is understood in Christian tradition that there is only a single gospel or 'good news'; hence the proper title 'The Gospel according to Matthew, according to Luke', etc. It is significant that the church retained a fourfold gospel with important differences between the versions rather than a single harmonized version. (From the middle of the second century such a harmonized version, the *Diatessaron* = 'weaving together', i.e. of the four Gospels, by Tatian, enjoyed a wide circulation in the early Christian East, but never became canonical.) There are also remains of Gospels over and above the other four (e.g. the Gospel of Philip, Gospel of Thomas), but these never enjoyed the same canonical status. It is, however, possible that they preserve authentic sayings of Jesus – such sayings, together with the sayings attributed to Jesus in the Qur'an, are known as the *agrapha* ('unwritten' [sayings]).

Matthew, Mark and Luke share a large body of material, sometimes in exactly the same words. Although some scholars believe that these similarities can be accounted for by oral tradition, it is generally believed that the first three Gospels stand in a written relationship to one another. They are commonly called the 'synoptic' Gospels, and the question of the relationship between them is called the synoptic problem; it is studied by comparing their texts as set out in the parallel columns in a synopsis. A synopsis also allows the reader to see how they differ in their treatment of a shared

p. 151
p. 152

text or story, and so to build up a picture of the characteristic concern and theological interests of each of the synoptic evangelists, and of the communities within which and for which they were writing (this enterprise is called redaction criticism).

p. 851

Early Christian tradition identified Mark as preserving especially the memoirs of Peter, and there is a general tendency to regard it as the oldest of the Gospels. Luke's Gospel is to be read together with the Acts of the Apostles; they are by the same author, and constitute a single work in two parts, with shared themes.

All four Gospels have been characterized as 'passion narratives with extended introductions'. Shared traditions about the suffering, death and resurrection of Jesus constitute the foundation of each Gospel, to which material about the earlier life of Jesus is added in ways that are characteristic of each writer, and are studied through redaction criticism.

It has been thought that Mark's lean narrative was written in and for a community for which suffering was a present reality. He begins his narrative directly with the baptism of the adult Jesus, and he alone ends with the flight of the frightened women from the tomb, perhaps leaving it to the liturgy to proclaim the risen Christ (the resurrection appearances in Mark 16.9ff. are generally believed to be a later addition). The perfection of Jesus' messiahship through his suffering and death casts a long shadow forward in Mark's book.

Matthew shapes Jesus' teaching into five discourses (perhaps in a reference to the five books of the Old Testament law), and is concerned with scribal traditions. Some have seen a self-description in his reference to 'every scribe trained for the kingdom of heaven' (13.52). Themes of judgement and separation are sharpened in his work. His use of the Old Testament can be usefully contrasted with Luke's by comparing their infancy narratives. Both wish to present Jesus as foretold by the Old Testament. Luke skilfully evokes the atmosphere of 1 Samuel. Matthew attaches particular episodes of Jesus' conception and infancy to particular texts in a more mechanical way.

Luke presents Jesus as reaching out in a particular way to foreigners and outcasts. Jesus sits more often at table with 'tax-collectors and sinners', and it is Luke alone who records the parables of the Good Samaritan and the Prodigal Son. Where Matthew emphasizes the note of judgement and demand in the teaching of Jesus, Luke draws out a note of inclusiveness and compassion.

Whether or not he knew the synoptic traditions, John is distinctive in the depth of his reflection on the meaning of Jesus' life and death. He selects miracles and other incidents with care, and makes them pegs for long passages of teaching. 'Johannine irony' is a particular feature of the construction of the Fourth Gospel. Someone makes a remark in one sense that the reader takes in another (e.g. Caiaphas' observation that 'it is expedient for one man to die for the sake of the people', 11.49). A seemingly innocent question (1.38: 'Rabbi, where are you staying/where do you abide?') proves to have an unexpectedly profound answer (15.10: 'Keep my commandments and you will abide in my love, as I abide in my Father's love'). This structured effect helps to create the sense of many-layered depth that pervades the Fourth Gospel. John attaches to his narrative a prologue, summarizing his story as that of the Word made flesh and dwelling among us. His sense of Jesus as the incarnation of the heavenly Word is so strong that it sometimes seems to lead him to depreciate Jesus' earthly experience of want or uncertainty (see 6.6).

As a genre the Gospels have no equivalent in the literature of the ancient world. Philostratus' *Life*  of the sage Apollonius of Tyana (died *c.* 98 CE), written in the middle of the third century, is a much longer biographical account, and the points of contact that it has with the Gospels (accounts of the master's teaching, miracles of healing) are explained by the fact that Philostratus is also writing about an important religious teacher.

FROM JERUSALEM TO ROME

Of the four evangelists, Luke alone writes a sequel to his Gospel, a history of the first days of the church under the title the Acts of the Apostles. Free from close dependence on the Gospel of Mark and other early material about Jesus, he shows himself to be a master story-teller. His grip on the forward momentum of his narrative is firm; its lines are clear; the events it describes are powerful; the characterization both of his main characters and the world in which they move is vivid. Chiefly through the fortunes of two figures, first Peter and then Paul, he shows how the Christian gospel moves, by divine providence and always under the guidance of the Holy Spirit, from Jerusalem, where Jesus had been crucified, to Rome.

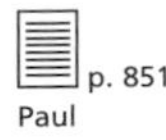
p. 851
Paul

Acts opens by repeating the end of Luke's Gospel, an account of the ascension of Jesus to heaven (1.1–12), but whereas in the Gospel Jesus seems to ascend soon after his resurrection, in Acts it is after 40 days. The disciples' next move is to make good their number, so that they are again twelve (1.15–26); however, the Twelve play little part in the story thereafter. Then, gathered together in a house, on the feast of Pentecost they receive the Holy Spirit in the form of a mighty wind and tongues of fire (2.1–13). Peter explains to puzzled outsiders what has happened in a long speech; such speeches recur throughout the book at key moments. Chapters 3–5 describe the life of the first Christians in Jerusalem, combining generalized accounts with specific episodes, most notably the death of Ananias and Sapphira in mysterious circumstances (5.1–11). We then discover that there is a split in the community between 'Hellenists', Greek-speaking Jews, and Hebrews; Stephen becomes the leader of the Hellenists (6.1–6). He is said to be hostile to law and temple, and in a long speech attacks the Jews, whereupon he is lynched (7.2–8.1). One Saul, later known as Paul, witnesses his death.

Saul becomes a persecutor of the church, and as a result of the persecution the Hellenists have to disperse, eventually finding a new centre in Antioch (11.19–27). Acting independently, after a strange incident with Simon the magician (8.9–24) the disciple Philip opens up a new road for the gospel in an encounter with an Ethiopian minister (8.26–40). Meanwhile, on his way to Damascus, Paul encounters the risen Jesus and becomes a Christian (9.1–22). Peter reappears on the scene and performs miracles in Joppa and Lydda (9.32–43); from there he is summoned by the Roman centurion Cornelius to Caesarea, where he has a vision which persuades him that no food is unclean (10.1–11.18), opening up the way to a church of both Jews and Gentiles. Peter returns to Jerusalem, where he is imprisoned by Herod, who has already killed James the brother of John; however, an angel frees him and he departs 'to another place' (12.1–17). That is the last we hear of him.

p. 902

The story is now dominated by Saul/Paul, based in Antioch, who embarks on the first of his famous missionary journeys (13.2–14.28). In Pisidian Antioch he too makes the first of a number of speeches. However, there is disquiet in Jerusalem at what he is preaching and what is known as the 'apostolic council' is called, at which the terms of Paul's future activities are agreed. By now James the brother of Jesus, who presides over it, is clearly the leading figure in Jerusalem (15.1–35). Paul's second (15.36–18.22) and third (19.21–21.17), journeys follow, taking him to the European mainland, notably to Philippi, Thessalonica and Corinth; he has no success in Athens (17.16–34). Between the two journeys there are encounters with what might be called 'imperfect Christians' (18.24–19.20). Towards the end of the third journey Paul makes a speech at Miletus which sounds a bit like a last testament (20.18–38), and in a way it is: despite protests from his friends he next feels constrained to go to Jerusalem (in fact to take money collected by his churches to the church there – a peace-offering the importance of which is evident in Paul's letters, but which is passed over by Luke). Fears are justified, Paul is involved in a riot and is arrested by the Romans (21.27–36).

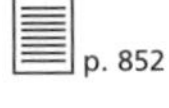
p. 852

From now on Paul is in Roman hands; he declares himself to be a Roman citizen, and this leads to a long process before he can be sent to Rome; various circumstances enable him to make long speeches, including two further accounts of his conversion (22.1–21; 26.2–29), one of them to King Agrippa. His dramatic voyage to Rome involves a shipwreck (27.1–28.14); once there he is put under house arrest, but preaches 'openly and unhindered to the end' (28.17–31).

Luke's story is a clear and simple one, but the thoughtful reader anxious to discover more about earliest Christianity may be left with a series of questions. Was it all as straightforward and uncomplicated as that? Close comparison with the letters of Paul where they cover the same ground show tensions and discrepancies (e.g. the money collected by the churches); in other respects much seems to be going on in the background, not covered by Luke, which represents quite major developments. What really happened in Jerusalem to lead to the emergence of James the brother of Jesus? By what ways were the 'brethren' who greeted Paul in Rome converted? Above all, who was 'Luke'? Here opinions are divided. Some, convinced by a series of passages in the first person plural ('we', 16.10–17; 20.5–15; 21.1–8; 27.1–28.16) believe that Acts was written by the 'beloved physician' mentioned in Colossians 4.14 as a companion of Paul; others feel that Acts (and 'Luke's' Gospel) are looking back from a rather later date.

p. 898

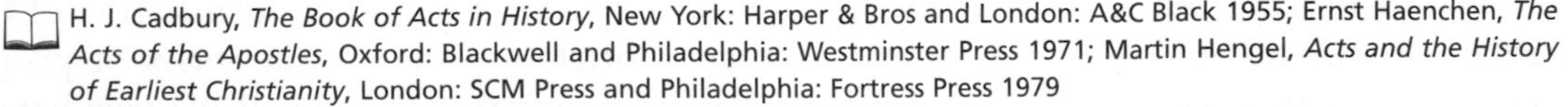

H. J. Cadbury, *The Book of Acts in History*, New York: Harper & Bros and London: A&C Black 1955; Ernst Haenchen, *The Acts of the Apostles*, Oxford: Blackwell and Philadelphia: Westminster Press 1971; Martin Hengel, *Acts and the History of Earliest Christianity*, London: SCM Press and Philadelphia: Fortress Press 1979

A wide range of dates has been canvassed for the Gospels within the range 60–90 CE. There is a particular significance in the possibility that the passion narratives came into their final shape in the period shortly after the sack of Jerusalem in 70 CE. This catastrophe led to a reshaping of Judaism, deeply influenced by the traditions of the Pharisees; at the same time Christian claims for the lordship and divinity of the risen Christ were proving impossible to contain within the framework of Jewish monotheism. The separation of Christianity as a religion distinct from the Judaism within which it was originally a movement was attended with great bitterness; this seems to be reflected in e.g. Matthew's violent hostility towards 'scribes and Pharisees', and such antagonism may well have been projected back into the Gospels' presentation of the Pharisees of Jesus' day. It has been an important task of recent New Testament scholarship to try to recover a picture of the Judaism of Jesus' time which is less coloured by the conflicts of the late first century CE.

Letters by or attributed to Paul

Because the Gospels stand at the beginning of the New Testament and because they seem to set before us directly the life and teaching of Jesus, it is easy to regard them as the primary documents of Christian faith and to forget that the letters (often called epistles) of Paul are older. Paul's account of the last supper in 1 Corinthians 11 or of Jesus' teaching on marriage in 1 Corinthians 7 are an earlier witness to the tradition than the related passages in the Gospels.

p. 665
Marriage

The collection of Paul's letters in the New Testament is arranged in order of length, with the longest (Romans) first and the shortest (Philemon) last. It has long been believed that Christians were responsible for the replacement of the roll (scroll) by the codex (a book with numbered leaves) as the dominant way of organizing a book; it has more recently been suggested that it was precisely the desire to organize the relatively short text of the Pauline letters for easy cross-reference that led Christians to prefer the codex format. The date and genuineness of the letters in the collection has been much debated. Four shorter letters (Galatians, Ephesians, Philippians, Colossians) represent themselves as having been written from prison, and are collectively known as 'the captivity letters'. Of these, Ephesians is widely believed to be by an author who is not Paul and who does not write in exactly his usual style, but who knows his mind and teaching intimately. The extent to which Colossians is wholly by Paul is also much debated, as is the location of his imprisonment (possibly Rome, at the end of his life, or, as is now more widely believed, Ephesus). The letter to the slave-owning Philemon belongs to this group, and strengthens the case for Ephesus.

Paul apparently dictated his letters. They show the occasional dislocations of thought and grammar characteristic of dictated text; the secretary who took them down sometimes adds his own greeting (Tertius in Romans 16.22) and Paul draws attention to a postscript that he adds in his own hand (Galatians 6.11). The dictated character of the letters is not always sufficiently remembered by those who scrutinize their minutest details for the nuances of Paul's thought.

The two letters to Timothy and the letter to Titus, collectively known as the Pastoral Epistles, are placed at the end of the main collection and, on the hypothesis that Paul's letters are arranged in descending order of length, outside it. They are concerned with the inner organization of the Christian community and the kind of behaviour appropriate to different categories of people within it. They suggest a degree of structure which is not otherwise evidenced in Paul's own letters, and a concern with the practical discharge of closely defined roles (such as those of the *episkopos* and the *diakonos*, of which 'bishop' and 'deacon' are misleading translations in this early context), which lead to a general belief that they are at least a generation older than Paul himself. The most widely canvassed dates are in the range 80–110 CE.

Ministry and ministers

THE APOCRYPHAL NEW TESTAMENT

The term 'Apocrypha' was originally applied to books contained in the Old Testament and used by the churches up to the Reformation which are not in the Hebrew Bible. 'Apocryphal New Testament' or 'New Testament Apocrypha' are modern terms, coined by scholars to denote books not in the New Testament which are similar in form or content to books which are in it. There is no definitive list of New Testament Apocrypha, not least because fragments of new works are still being discovered. The types of text include:

Gospels
The Coptic Gospel of Thomas
The Gospel of the Nazareans
The Gospel of the Ebionites
The Gospel of the Hebrews
The Gospel of Philip
The Gospel of the Egyptians
The Gospel of Peter
The Book of Thomas
The Apocryphon of James
The Dialogue of the Saviour
The First Apocalypse of James
The Second Apocalypse of James
The Letter of Peter to Philip

The Gospel of the Four Heavenly Regions
The Gospel of Perfection
The Gospel of Truth

The Sophia Jesu Christi
The Pistis Sophia
The Two Books of Jeu

The Gospel of Mary
The Protoevangelium of James
The Infancy Story of Thomas

The Gospel of Nicodemus
The Gospel of Bartholomew

Writings relating to the apostles
The Kerygma Petri
Paul's Letter to the Laodiceans
The Correspondence between Seneca and Paul
Pseudo-Titus

The Acts of Andrew
The Acts of John
The Acts of Paul
The Acts of Peter
The Acts of Thomas
The Acts of Peter and the Twelve Apostles

The Pseudo-Clementines

Apocalypses
The Ascension of Isaiah
Apocalypse of Peter
5 and 6 Ezra
Christian Sibyllines
The Book of Elchasai
The Coptic Gnostic Apocalypse of Paul
The Coptic Gnostic Apocalypse of Peter
Apocalypse of Paul
Apocalypse of Thomas

The standard edition is R. McL. Wilson and W. Schneemelcher, *New Testament Apocrypha* (2 vols), Cambridge: James Clarke and Louisville: Westminster John Knox Press 1971, 1973

Hebrews

In Christian antiquity the letter to the Hebrews was not generally thought to be by Paul, but came to be attached to the end of the collection of Paul's letters. It is written as a 'word of encouragement' (13.22), to urge Christians who are suffering persecution to stand firm in their faith. They have not yet suffered to the point of shedding their blood, but the writer fears that they will abandon their faith. Despite the traditional title, there is nothing in the letter to suggest that it is written to a group of Jewish Christians other than the way in which it draws on traditions about Old Testament priesthood. The author insists that, just as Jesus died once for all, so Christians have one unique opportunity to benefit from his sacrifice of himself; if squandered, the chance does not recur. As the writer reflects on the character of Jesus' once-for-all sacrifice, he presents him as a new high priest 'after the order of Melchizedek', who has made obsolete the Old Testament system of priesthood and sacrifice. The absence of any reference to the actual destruction of the temple suggests a date before 70 CE, although dates at the end of the first century continue to be canvassed. Sacrifice

Letters attributed to other apostles

The New Testament includes letters attributed to leading figures in the early Christian movement other than Paul. Even if not from the same hand as the Fourth Gospel, the three letters of John belong to the same milieu, and the simplicity of their reflection on love as the necessary heart of a Christian community recalls John 14.15 or 17.1ff. It is more difficult to connect the letters attributed to Peter, James and Jude with particular early Christian churches. With 1 John, they are known collectively as the Catholic Epistles (or letters) because they are addressed to all Christians in general rather than to any Christian individual or community in particular.

Revelation

The inclusion of this powerful example of Christian apocalyptic in the New Testament aroused complaints well into the fourth century. Its vivid imagery of the end of the world, of the final judgement, and of the heavenly Jerusalem, have been especially important for apocalyptic and millenarian movements in subsequent Christian history. Much scholarly ingenuity has been expended on its allegories and images, some of which appear to encode precise esoteric meaning. These would be a clue to the date and occasion of the book if they could be determined. Revelation has recently attracted much attention from scholars interested in the religious dynamics of an intense Christian group, possibly experiencing persecution, and its reaction to the oppressive power and symbolism of Rome.

ANDERS BERGQUIST

The Cambridge History of the Bible, 1. From the Beginnings to Jerome ed P. R. Ackroyd and C. F. Evans; *2. The West from the Fathers to the Reformation* ed G. W. H. Lampe; *3. The West from the Reformation to the Present Day* ed S. L. Greenslade, Cambridge: CUP 1975; Bruce M. Metzger and Michael D. Coogan, *The Oxford Companion to the Bible*, New York: OUP 1994; J. R. Porter, *The Illustrated Guide to the Bible*, Oxford: OUP 1995

Old Testament: John Barton, *Reading the Old Testament. Method in Biblical Study*, London: Darton, Longman & Todd 1984; Étienne Charpentier, *How to Read the Old Testament*, London: SCM Press and New York: Crossroad 1982; Richard Coggins, *Introducing the Old Testament*, Oxford: OUP 2001; J. Alberto Soggin, *Introduction to the Old Testament*, London: SCM Press [3]1989

New Testament: Paul Q. Beeching, *Awkward Reverence. Reading the New Testament Today*, New York: Continuum and London: SCM Press 1997; Étienne Charpentier, *How to Read the New Testament*, London: SCM Press and New York: Crossroad 1982; Luke Timothy Johnson, *The Writings of the New Testament*, Minneapolis: Fortress Press and London: SCM Press 1999; Edwin D. Freed, *The New Testament: A Critical Introduction*, Belmont, CA: Wadsworth and London: SCM Press 1994

Biblical criticism

Bible The Bible, Old and New Testaments, is the foundation document and ultimate authority of Christianity, and as such has a unique status. But at the same time it is a book that stands on bookshop shelves like any other book, is promoted commercially like any other book, and can be read like any other book. This is a relatively recent development: only 150 years ago, in mid-Victorian Britain, in a book, *Essays and Reviews*, produced by a group of Oxford scholars, the philosopher and classicist Benjamin Jowett caused deep offence by writing that the Bible could be interpreted 'like any other book': 11,000 clergy signed a petition against the volume and it was condemned by the church. But Jowett's view became commonplace, and having for so long been under the control of the churches in one way or another, from then on the Bible became open to scrutiny from the most varied perspectives.

Biblical criticism is the term used to describe this scrutiny by experts. It comprises sub-divisions such as textual criticism, philological criticism, source criticism, tradition criticism, form criticism, redaction criticism, rhetorical criticism, narrative criticism and, most recently, reader-response criticism. The terms may sound forbidding, but in fact all these disciplines are simply attempts to answer basic questions about the contents of the Bible. How do we know that the text we have is faithful to what the author(s) wrote? Are we sure that we know the meaning of the words used in the Hebrew Old Testament or the Greek New Testament? From where did the authors get their information? How was this information handed down? Does the fact that some of the contents of the Bible have been handed down in a particular form tell us anything about its origin? Can we detect anything of the purpose and intentions of the authors of individual books of the Bible? Criticism is a word with negative connotations, but in this context those connotations are absent: 'criticism' denotes no more than a questioning approach.

Yet the findings of biblical critics have frequently been felt to be predominantly negative. Biblical criticism began with the questioning of traditional views about the Bible, particularly that Moses wrote the first five books of the Bible, as had hitherto been believed, and went on to question whether the Gospels were written by those whose names they bear or whether Paul wrote all the letters attributed to him. But overall, the work of biblical criticism is positive, contributing to increasing understanding of the Bible and how it can be read.

Unfortunately, though, the activities and findings of biblical critics are not at all easy for most people to follow at first hand. In marked contrast to Judaism and Islam, where it is thought important to learn Hebrew and Arabic respectively in order to understand scripture in the language in which it was written, few Christians know any Greek and fewer still know Hebrew, relying instead on translations, not all of them without agendas of their own, which can sometimes be no more than paraphrases. Consequently those who do know Greek and Hebrew become élites who can discuss among themselves but have difficulties in communicating what they can see clearly to those without the necessary linguistic equipment.

Nevertheless, the basic outlines of biblical criticism can be easily understood even through looking at English translations of the Bible. To keep the subject within reasonable bounds, here we shall be looking only at the New Testament: the same kinds of questions arise in connection with the Old Testament, but on a much larger scale, because the Old Testament is so much bigger and contains such a wide variety of material.

Textual criticism

The first question that arises is: can we trust the text that we have? Has anything happened to it between the time it was written and the present? Here a simple exercise is illuminating.

Open one of the best-known modern translations of the Bible, the Revised Standard Version, and look at the Gospel of John, and you will find that a familiar passage is missing. The story of the woman taken in adultery, who is forgiven by Jesus, which normally stands at the end of chapter 7, is not there. Instead, it is printed as a footnote in italics. The New English Bible goes even further and prints the passage as an appendix to the Gospel on a separate page, under the heading, 'An incident in the temple'. Other translations do not go so far, but put it in square brackets or add a note of explanation. The explanation given is that the passage does not appear in the some of the most authoritative ancient manuscripts, and in others is put in the Gospel of Luke.

Something similar happens with the ending of the Gospel of Mark. In the Revised Standard Version the Gospel ends abruptly with the women going from the empty tomb saying nothing because they are afraid; the traditional ending to the Gospel, which describes appearances of Jesus to Mary Magdalene and the disciples, a missionary command from Jesus and mention of his ascension, is again printed as a footnote in italics. Again, it is pointed out that some authoritative witnesses do not contain the longer ending.

Exploration

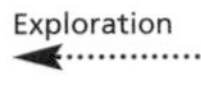

Finally, those brought up on the Authorized/King James Version will look in vain in modern translations for the words in italics in this version of 1 John 5.7–8: 'For there are three that bear record *in heaven, the Father, the Word and the Holy Ghost, and these three are one. And there are three that bear witness in earth,* the Spirit, the water, and the blood, and these three agree in one.' They aren't there at all, having been recognized as a late insertion into the text, so late that there is no serious manuscript support for it. The full passage is in the Authorized/King James Version, but no modern translations contain it.

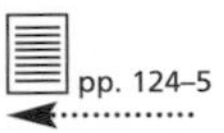

pp. 124–5

The New Testament has come down to us in manuscripts, laboriously copied from other manuscripts: the earliest texts we have are papyrus fragments from second-century CE Egypt and two great fourth-century manuscripts discovered in the nineteenth century. More than 5000 manuscripts exist today. In addition, ancient translations of the New Testament and quotations in the church fathers indicate the readings of Greek texts that we no longer have. Of course this vast array of manuscripts, all copied or taken down from dictation by hand, displays a very large number of variant readings – it is thought that there may be as many as 250,000 of these, but the number drops considerably when minor variations like misspellings, omissions, misreadings (or mishearings) and changes to grammar and spelling are left out of account.

In the second half of the nineteenth century there were high hopes that it would be possible to arrive at the original text of the New Testament by sorting manuscripts into 'families' and determining which manuscript was copied from which; in this process the 'best' manuscripts were identified and used as the basis for establishing the text. In 1881 two great British scholars, B. F. Westcott and F. J. A. Hort, were confident enough to produce a book entitled *The New Testament in the Original Greek*. Their views became highly influential.

p. 967

However, as time went on this approach became increasingly open to question: the evidence was complicated and the judgements of even the greatest scholars could be subjective. Despite the large number of extant manuscripts of the New Testament, a far larger number have been lost, and it is just not possible to establish genealogies; besides, during transmission one family has often been 'contaminated' by another.

Instead of attempting to establish families, New Testament textual criticism nowadays adopts a two-pronged approach. On the one hand scholars attempt to determine the historical background against which manuscripts were produced and the circumstances that influence them. On the other hand, where manuscripts offer different readings, they attempt to determine the original by rational arguments; here their work is exactly like that of classical textual scholars, and it was the poet and classicist A. E. Housman who laid down a key principle: 'the original reading is that which explains the origin of the other readings'.

We have no reason to doubt that we have substantially the Greek text of the New Testament as it was written: the work of scholars guarantees that there are no gross errors in it. But the form in which it is published indicates at a glance the many variations that cannot definitively be resolved. The text is prefaced by a list of the manuscripts and other sources on which the text is based; the text itself is printed, and below it, sometimes taking up half the page, are the variant readings found in other manuscripts that are significant for scholars and translators. In the standard edition, published by a group of international Bible societies and known as Nestle-Aland after its editors, variants are evaluated by letter: A indicates that the text is virtually certain, B indicates that there is some degree of doubt, C indicates that there is considerable doubt as to whether the text or the apparatus has the better reading, and D indicates that there is a very high degree of doubt about the selected reading.

Philological criticism

The Greek text, once established, has to be translated accurately, and for that to be done the meaning of all the words in the original text has to be determined. This is a particular problem with the Old Testament, because many words in the Hebrew appear only once and their meaning is by no means clear; informed guesses have to be made using comparisons with related Semitic languages. But the problem also occurs in the New Testament. Strikingly, the meaning even of one of the words of the Lord's Prayer is uncertain. The Greek for 'daily' bread is *epiousios*, which occurs only here, and it has been subject to much discussion: suggestions have been 'continual', 'for our need', 'for today', 'for tomorrow', 'for the future', 'belonging to the day'.

Granted, this is an extreme case; for the most part the New Testament does not present the same problems as the Old. However, an exploration of the way in which words in the New Testament are also used in contemporary literature and less formal documents written in *koine* Greek, the form in common use at the time, gives greater depth to them. They can be read against the background of the time without having inappropriate or extraneous connotations being attached to them. Here, as in textual criticism, study has run in parallel with classical studies and each has benefited from the other.

In a classic book, *The Glory of God and the Transfiguration of Christ*, Archbishop Michael Ramsey engaged in a notable exploration of the Greek word *doxa*, used in the New Testament to denote God's glory: how did a word which in classical Greek commonly meant simply opinion or notion come to denote such a supreme divine attribute? Investigation of 'New Testament words' can be very illuminating. Where words appear and in what context in the New Testament can be discovered through a concordance, an alphabetical list giving the reference and context for every word.

Source criticism

Where did the author of a New Testament book get his material from? Many of the books of the New Testament contain passages in which the author seems to be quoting from, or drawing on, someone else. Even Paul in his letters does this. In 1 Corinthians he quite specifically refers to earlier traditions about the eucharist and the resurrection which have been given to him, and some other passages which read like hymns, e.g. in Philippians 2 and Colossians 1, are thought to be quotations. Then Colossians and Ephesians, and 2 Peter and Jude, are so similar that it looks as if one has quoted the other. And most strikingly of all, the Gospels of Matthew, Mark and Luke are so closely related that it is possible to put the three of them in parallel columns. It is now almost

MANUSCRIPTS OF THE BIBLE

Hebrew Bible

Two small silver plaques from Jerusalem, dated to the seventh/sixth centuries BCE, are incised with the Aaronic blessing (Numbers 6.22–9), but these are not necessarily evidence of a *biblical* text. The earliest substantial manuscripts of the Hebrew Bible that we possess are those among the Dead Sea Scrolls, most notably a complete scroll of the book of Isaiah; there are also fragments of many other books. These date from the second/first century BCE. Before the discovery of the Scrolls, the earliest text containing biblical material was the Nash Papyrus, discovered in 1903, with the Ten Commandments and the Shema' ('Hear O Israel, The Lord our God is one Lord', Deuteronomy 6.1ff.). The Dead Sea Scrolls discoveries were particularly important because previously the earliest manuscripts of the Hebrew Bible dated from the end of the ninth and the tenth century CE. The finds confirmed the accuracy of the Jewish manuscript transmission as well as showing many interesting variants.

Another striking find was the discovery of the Cairo Geniza in 1896. A 'geniza' is a room in which sacred Hebrew books which are no longer usable are stored. Among many treasures, the Cairo Geniza contained a Hebrew manuscript of parts of the book of Ecclesiasticus, the Wisdom of ben Sirach, the very existence of which had been doubted (the book was thought originally to have been written in Greek).

Special importance attaches to a manuscript of the complete Bible dated 1008/9 CE, in the Firkovich collection in St Petersburg, still generally known as L (i.e. 'Leningradensis'), although it may come to be known by another sign now that Leningrad has reverted to its older name. The great textual scholar Paul Kahle identified L as the best witness to the Masoretic text of the Bible as transmitted in the ben Assher family. A modern edition of the Hebrew Bible as generally used by scholars and translators is essentially a direct transcript of L, mistakes and idiosyncrasies included. The editors then add a critical apparatus of variant readings from other Hebrew manuscripts or early versions, leaving readers to construct their preferred working text.

New Testament

The earliest text of the New Testament is a papyrus fragment found in Egypt in 1935, containing four verses of John 18 and dated to around 135 CE (Rylands papyrus, after the John Rylands Library in Manchester). More than 75 other papyri fragments of the New Testament have been found, mostly dating from the third century: the collections in which they appear are known as the Oxyrhynchus, Chester Beatty and Bodmer papyri.

Christian Bible

From the start, Christians used codexes rather than rolls (scrolls), as Jews did, for their holy scriptures. The codex consisted of parchment cut into rectangular pieces and stitched to form something like a modern book. The most important early codexes, all of the Greek Bible, are: Books

1. *Codex Sinaiticus* (fourth century). First discovered by the German scholar Constantin Tischendorf in the monastery of St Catherine on Mount Sinai in 1844, presented to the Tsar of Russia and bought by the British Library from the Soviet government in 1933. Referred to by the Hebrew character aleph = א.
2. *Codex Vaticanus* (fourth century). In the Vatican Library. Referred to as B. א and B may be the survivors of a set of 50 magnificent Bibles commissioned by Constantine for the leading churches of his empire. Indeed, it has been suggested that א was a trial product of this enterprise, which was then scaled down because it could not be continued at such a level of magnificence.
3. *Codex Alexandrinus* (early fifth century). Given by the Patriarch of Constantinople to James I in the seventeenth century, and now in the British Library. Referred to as A.
4. *Codex Bezae* (fourth to sixth century). Owned by a sixteenth-century Calvinist scholar, Theodore Bèze, who donated it to the University of Cambridge. Referred to as D.

The contribution that all these manuscripts make to establishing the original text of the Bible is studied by textual criticism.

Ernst Würthwein, *The Text of the Old Testament*, Grand Rapids, MI: Eerdmans and London: SCM Press 1980; Kurt and Barbara Aland, *The Text of the New Testament*, Grand Rapids, MI: Eerdmans 1990

universally accepted that Matthew and Luke used Mark as a source.

Luke wrote a second book, the Acts of the Apostles, and it is likely that he used other sources, but he is so skilful at disguising his material that these are very difficult to identify. At several points his narrative slips into the first-person-plural 'we', and it is thought that these may be a special source, even his own eye-witness account, but the 'we' could just be a stylistic device to add vividness. The same problem arises with the Gospel of John: did the author know and use the actual texts of Matthew, Mark and Luke, or did he use traditions that were also used by

THE GREEK NEW TESTAMENT

311 ΚΑΤΑ ΛΟΥΚΑΝ 23. 34–38

μενον Κρανίον, ἐκεῖ ἐσταύρωσαν αὐτὸν καὶ τοὺς κα-
κούργους, ὃν μὲν ἐκ δεξιῶν ὃν δὲ ἐξ ἀριστερῶν. 34 [ὁ
δὲ Ἰησοῦς ἔλεγεν, Πάτερ, ἄφες αὐτοῖς, οὐ γὰρ οἴδασιν
τί ποιοῦσιν.][5] **διαμεριζόμενοι δὲ τὰ ἱμάτια αὐτοῦ ἔβαλον
κλῆρον.** 35 καὶ εἱστήκει ὁ λαὸς **θεωρῶν. ἐξεμυκτήριζον**
δὲ καὶ οἱ ἄρχοντες λέγοντες, Ἄλλους ἔσωσεν, σωσάτω
ἑαυτόν, εἰ οὗτός ἐστιν ὁ Χριστὸς[b] τοῦ θεοῦ[b] ὁ ἐκλεκτός.
36 ἐνέπαιξαν δὲ αὐτῷ καὶ οἱ στρατιῶται προσερχόμενοι,
ὄξος προσφέροντες αὐτῷ 37 καὶ λέγοντες, Εἰ σὺ εἶ ὁ
βασιλεὺς τῶν Ἰουδαίων, σῶσον σεαυτόν. 38 ἦν δὲ καὶ
ἐπιγραφὴ ἐπ' αὐτῷ[6], Ὁ βασιλεὺς τῶν Ἰουδαίων οὗτος.

[5] **34** {C} *ὁ δὲ Ἰησοῦς ἔλεγεν, Πατήρ, ἄφες αὐτοῖς, οὐ γὰρ οἴδασιν τί ποιοῦσιν.* ℵ^{*,c} A C D^{b} (K *εἶπεν for ἔλεγεν*) L X Δ Π Ψ 0117 0250 *f*^{1} (*f*^{13} *omit δέ*) 28 33 565 700 892 (1009 *ποιῶσιν*) 1010 1071 1079 (1195 *ἅ for τί*) 1216 (1230 1253 *Ἰησοῦς ἐσταυρωμένος ἔλεγεν*) 1242 1344 1365 1546 1646 2148 2174 *Byz Lect* it^{aur,b,c,e,f,ff2,l,r1} vg syr$^{(c),p,(h,hmg),pal}$ cop^{bomss} arm eth geo Hegesippus Marcion Diatessaron^{a,earm,i,n} Justin Irenaeus^{lat} Clement Origen^{lat} Ps-Clement Eusebius Eusebian Canons Ambrosiaster Hilary Basil Apostolic Constitutions Ambrose Chrysostom Jerome Augustine Theodoret John-Damascus // *include ὁ δὲ...ποιοῦσιν. with asterisks* E // *omit* 𝔭^{75} ℵ$^{a\,vid}$ B D* W Θ 0124 1241 it^{a,d} syr^{s} cop^{sa,bomss} Cyril

[6] **38** {B} *ἐπ' αὐτῷ* 𝔭^{75} ℵ^{a} B L 0124 1241 cop^{sa,bo} // *ἐπ' αὐτῷ γεγραμμένη* C* // *γεγραμμένη ἐπ' αὐτῷ* it^{a} (syr^{c,s}) // *γεγραμμένη ἐπ' αὐτῷ γράμμασιν ἑλληνικοῖς καὶ ῥωμαϊκοῖς καὶ ἑβραϊκοῖς* (*see* Jn 19.20) C^{3} K W Δ Θ Π 0117 0250 *f*^{1} 28 565 700 892 1009 1010 1071 1079 1195 1216 (1242* *omit ἐπ' αὐτῷ*) 1242^{c} (1253 *omit γράμμασιν and first καί*) 1344 1365 1546 1646 2148 2174 *Byz Lect* (*l*^{60} *ἐπ' αὐτῶν γράμμασιν ἑβραϊκοῖς, ἑλλινηκοῖς, καὶ ῥωμαϊκοῖς*) (*l*^{70} *omit καὶ ἑβραϊκοῖς*) it$^{aur,(c),e,f,ff2,l,r1}$ vg^{cl} syr^{p,h} arm eth geo Acts of Pilate Cyril // *ἐπιγεγραμμένη ἐπ' αὐτῷ γράμμασιν ἑλληνικοῖς καὶ ῥωμαϊκοῖς καὶ ἑβραϊκοῖς* (*see* Jn 19.20) A (D *omit καί and καί*) (*l*^{950} *omit καὶ ἑβραϊκοῖς*) it^{b,d,q} vg^{ww} // *ἐπ' αὐτῷ γεγραμμένη γράμμασιν ἑλληνικοῖς καὶ ῥωμαϊκοῖς καὶ ἑβραϊκοῖς* (*see* Jn 19.20) X Ψ *f*^{13} 33 1230 // *ἐπ' αὐτῷ γράμμασιν ἑλληνικοῖς ῥωμαϊκοῖς ἑβραϊκοῖς* (*see* Jn 19.20) ℵ^{*,b} cop^{bomss}

[b b] **35** *b* none, *b* none: Bov Nes BF^{2} TT Zür Seg // *b* none, *b* minor: WH RV ASV RSV NEB Jer // *b* minor, *b* none: Luth // different text: TR AV

---

33 *ἐσταύρωσαν...ἀριστερῶν* Is 53.12 **34** *Πάτερ...ποιοῦσιν* Is 53.12; Mt 5.44; Ac 7.60 *διαμεριζόμενοι...κλῆρον* Ps 22.18 **35–36** *εἱστήκει...στρατιῶται* Ps 22.7–8 **36** *ὄξος... αὐτῷ* Ps 69.21

A page from a modern critical edition of the Greek New Testament. It shows part of Luke's account of the crucifixion of Jesus. Two important questions arise here: 1. Was verse 34 (And Jesus said, 'Father, forgive them, for they know not what they do') part of the original text? 2. Were the words 'in letters of Latin and Greek and Hebrew' part of the original text? The notes give the weight of manuscript evidence for and against each; the various letters and numbers (sigla) denote manuscripts of varying importance; quotations from the church fathers and other documents are also taken into account.

THE SYNOPTIC PROBLEM

When the first three Gospels, Matthew, Mark and Luke, are set side by side in three columns (the name for the book in which this is done is a synopsis = 'see together'), it is evident that they agree to a large extent in the order of the events that they describe and that there is considerable conformity in the wording of the stories they contain. So there must be some sort of literary relationship between them. The question is precisely what this relationship is.

p. 152

It is widely believed that Matthew and Luke used Mark as a source. Matthew and Luke also share approximately 200 verses of material not found in Mark. In the commonest solution of the synoptic problem, the Four Source Hypothesis, these 200 verses are thought to be derived from a shared source commonly known as Q (from the German *Quelle*, source). Mark is then the first of the Gospels; Matthew had Mark and Q and a further source (M), peculiar to himself; Luke had Mark, Q and a further source (L), peculiar to himself. But if Matthew had sight of Luke, or Luke had sight of Matthew, there is no need to postulate a Q. Another hypothesis, named after the New Testament scholar Johann Jakob Griesbach (1745–1812), regards Matthew as the earliest Gospel and Mark as making an abbreviated use of it. Scholars continue to debate variations of these two principal hypotheses and other solutions to the synoptic problem.

Whether the writer of the Fourth Gospel had knowledge of the synoptic tradition is much debated. There are points of detail which suggest that he did (the phrase 'pure nard' at John 12.3 which picks up Mark 14.3 and the details of the Feeding of the Five Thousand in John 6.1–14), but the selection and arrangement of the material, and the portrait of Jesus, are significantly different, as is the chronological placement of some events (the 'cleansing of the temple'; the placing of the crucifixion on 14 Nisan in the Jewish calendar, so that Jesus is crucified as the Passover lambs are slain; the synoptic Gospels place the crucifixion on 15 Nisan, which makes the Last Supper an actual Passover meal).

A look at any page in a synopsis where all three Gospels are in parallel will indicate many minor variations in wording: for example while Mark 9.1 has 'Truly, I say to you, there are some standing here who will not taste death before they see that the kingdom of God *has come with power*,' Matthew 16.28 has 'Truly, I say to you, there are some standing here who will not taste death before they see *the Son of man coming in his kingdom*.' Luke 9.27 differs yet again: 'But I say to you truly, there are some standing here who will not taste death before they see the kingdom of God.' There are similar variations in the wording of Q passages: for example, Matthew 12.28 has 'If it is by the *Spirit of God* that I cast out demons, then the kingdom of God has come upon you,' while Luke 11.20 has 'If it is by the *finger of God* that I cast out demons, then the kingdom of God has come upon you.' In many cases it may be impossible to determine what the original wording was: at best, the theological interests of the evangelist can be determined by a careful study of the Gospel as a whole, and they can be taken into account in an assessment of individual sayings.

Synopses not only indicate the variations in wording between the first three Gospels; they also indicate the variations in structure and the order in which they present the material. Matthew and Luke go their own ways where they do not have Mark to follow, i.e. in the birth stories and the accounts of the resurrection appearances. From the appearance of John the Baptist to the discovery of the empty tomb Matthew closely follows Mark's order, but adds compilations of sayings in five 'sermons', beginning with the Sermon on the Mount. He also adds further miracles, parables and other embellishments. Luke treats Mark differently: in 9.51 to 18.14 he presents what is known as 'the Lukan travel narrative', in which he presents much of the Q material which in Matthew is more dispersed within the framework provided by Mark, and material of his own.

p. 664
p. 668

Synopses are not widely available, nor are they used much by other than New Testament scholars. However, the information that they give so clearly is vital to a proper understanding of the Gospels. The synoptic problem is not just an academic exercise: understanding it is the way towards seeing the first three evangelists as creative figures each using traditional material in his own way to present three different theological pictures of the life, death and resurrection of Jesus. To ignore this and to take actions and sayings of Jesus at random from the Gospels and conflate them (as in the 'seven last words of Jesus from the cross') is to distort what little we actually do know.

p. 341

The synoptic problem can be studied further in E. P. Sanders and Margaret Davies, *Studying the Synoptic Gospels*, London: SCM Press and Philadelphia: Trinity Press International 1989

these three evangelists? Does his numbering of the first two miracles indicate that he was using a 'signs' source?

The Gospel of Mark opens up a yet wider horizon. It has been called a 'passion narrative with an extended introduction' and up to Jesus' entry into Jerusalem consists of a whole series of brief, self-contained episodes, hung together like pearls on a string, with no integral connection to one another. There are few details of time or place, and the way in which the episodes are linked is not necessarily chronological. It looks as if on the whole he has left this material intact and made his points by his arrangement of it. But where does it come from?

Source criticism tries to answer all these questions and in the process goes behind the New Testament writings as we have them to an earlier stage.

Form criticism

The approach that recognized the small units of which the first three Gospels are composed developed in the early twentieth century; it is known as form criticism. The

SYNOPSIS

Matthew 16.24–8	Mark 8.34–9.1	Luke 9.23–7
24 Then Jesus said to his disciples, 'If any one *would come* after me, let him deny himself and take up his cross and follow me.	34 And he called to him the multitude with his disciples, and said to them, **'If any one** would follow **after me, let him deny himself and take up his cross and follow me.**	23 And he **said** to all, **'If any one** *would come* **after me, let him deny himself and take up his cross** daily **and follow me.**
25 For whoever would save his life will lose it, and whoever loses his life for my sake will find it. 26 For what will it profit a man, if he gains the whole world and forfeits his life? Or what shall a man give in return for his life?	35 **For whoever would save his life will lose it; and whoever loses his life for my sake** and the gospel's **will save it. 36 For what does it profit a man,** to **gain the whole world** and **forfeit** his life? 37 For what can a man give in return for his life?	24 **For whoever would save his life will lose it; and whoever loses his life for my sake,** he **will save it.** 25 **For what does it profit a man** if he **gains the whole world** and loses or **forfeits** himself?
27 For the Son of man is to come with his angels in the glory of his Father, and then he will repay every man for what he has done.	38 **For whoever is ashamed of me and of my words** in this adulterous and sinful generation, **of him will the Son of man** also **be ashamed, when he comes in the glory of his Father** with **the holy angels**.'	26 **For whoever is ashamed of me and of my words, of him will the Son of man be ashamed when he comes** in his glory and **the glory** of the Father and of **the holy angels.**
28 Truly, I say to you, there are some standing here who will not taste death before they see the Son of man coming in his kingdom.'	9[1] And he said to them, **'Truly, I say to you, there are some standing** here who **will not taste death before they see** that **the kingdom of God** has come with power.'	27 But **I say to you** truly, **there are some standing here** who **will not taste death before they see** **the kingdom of God.**'

A synopsis (Greek = see together) is a volume which prints the texts of either the first three or all four Gospels side by side. New Testament scholars study the text in the original Greek, but synopses with English texts are also available. As this extract clearly indicates, there is a very close relationship between Matthew, Mark and Luke, along with a great many minor differences: sayings of Jesus appear in different Gospels in slightly differing forms. Because of the close relationship between them, Matthew, Mark and Luke are commonly known as the synoptic Gospels, and the question of the nature of this relationship is known as the synoptic problem.

To see the relationship fully, it is of course necessary to refer to the original Greek; an English translation cannot give all the nuances, for example when there are two different Greek words for 'who' and 'truly'. Agreements between all three Gospels are indicated in the text of Mark by both **bold and underlining**. Agreements only between Matthew and Mark are underlined; agreements only between Mark and Luke are in **bold**; agreements only between Matthew and Luke are in *italic*.

Burton H. Throckmorton, *New Revised Standard Version Gospel Parallels*, Nashville, TN: Nelson Reference and Carlisle: STL1992; for a discussion of the whole passage see E. P. Sanders and Margaret Davies, *Studying the Synoptic Gospels*, London: SCM Press and Philadelphia: Trinity Press International 1989, pp. 56–7

German K. L. Schmidt concluded from his study of the first three Gospels that up to the passion narrative these Gospels were composed of units of oral tradition that had originally circulated independently (the technical term for these units is pericope). As they were handed on, they assumed characteristic forms which made them easier to memorize and reproduce, forms which varied depending on their setting (German *Sitz im Leben*). For example, the structure of a miracle story, which will emphasize at the beginning just how serious the illness is that a miracle cures, will differ from a pericope which culminates in an unanswerable pronouncement by Jesus: 'Render to Caesar the things that are Caesar's', or, 'Let the dead bury their dead.'

Schmidt's pioneering work was continued by Rudolf Bultmann and Martin Dibelius, who investigated the whole of the Gospel material, each from a different perspective: Bultmann began from an analysis of the pericopes in the Gospels and compared them with similar forms in ancient literature; Dibelius sought to recreate the earliest Christian communities and identify the function the pericopes had in the life of the church. Both scholars arrived at remarkably similar conclusions.

What emerges from their work is that the material that goes to make up the first three Gospels was not just handed down, say, out of a desire to preserve the historical memory of Jesus. It had a function, and was handed down with a purpose, for use in preaching, teaching, worship, arriving at ethical principles and rules for behaviour within the community. So form criticism sheds much light on the life of the earliest church and the problems with which it had to deal; at the same time it makes the quest for the historical Jesus more difficult, because it shows how the church did not necessarily hand down the words of Jesus verbatim, but used them creatively for its own purposes.

Redaction criticism

The concentration in form criticism on the basic units of the tradition tended to minimize the role of the evangelists, who were seen as little more than compilers, and by the second half of the twentieth century this was felt to be a serious weakness. So attention shifted towards the contribution of the evangelists themselves, and the ideas that guided them as they made their own arrangements of the material. This approach was given the name redaction criticism.

Redaction criticism was not, in fact, a novelty. The name might be new, but what it denoted had been going on ever since the New Testament began to be read critically. In an extreme form, it is illustrated by the work of the great radical German theologian F. C. Baur in the first half of the nineteenth century, who looked for the 'tendency' of each of the New Testament authors and concluded that the New Testament reflects a clash between two parties in earliest Christianity, Gentile-Christian and Jewish-Christian. But it was now carried on in much greater detail and increased sophistication.

To keep to the first three Gospels: it is hardest to identify the concerns of Mark, because we do not know the state of the material he was using and whether some of it had been previously arranged. But it is clear that he has put the small units in a framework of his own, marked out by three predictions by Jesus of his passion and resurrection in 8.31; 9.31 and 10.32–4. Many scholars also want to attribute to Mark the way in which in this Gospel Jesus is concerned to conceal his true identity (the 'messianic secret') by commanding demons and disciples to be silent, and by giving cryptic teaching in parables in private to disciples who often fail to understand.

p. 759

The concerns of Matthew and Luke are easier to identify because we can see how they use the material in Mark, on which they base their Gospels. Both add stories about the birth and the resurrection of Jesus which extend his story at the beginning and end and which are also characterized by their basic interests. Here it is possible only to single out just a few motifs. For Matthew, Jesus is the great teacher, the second Moses, and his Gospel is structured with five great discourses, beginning with the Sermon on the Mount, a pointer to the five books of the Jewish Law. Matthew also regularly uses the formula, 'this was to fulfil what was spoken', to show how Jesus fulfils the Jewish scriptures.

Jesus of history

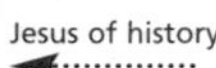

Luke's Gospel is markedly different; this is not least because it is the first volume of a two-volume work, to be concluded with the Acts of the Apostles, an account of the history of the earliest church. Because Luke is to tell this story of the church, which continues after the death and resurrection of Jesus, he tones down the emphasis in Mark on the expectation of an imminent end to the world. For him, Jesus is not so much the end of time as the centre of time. He arranges the material at the centre of his Gospel (9.51–19.27) to form a kind of travel narrative, which brings Jesus, an itinerant teacher, from Galilee to Jerusalem.

Redaction criticism reminds us that in their own way, working within the limits imposed on them, namely preserving the traditions which had come down to them, the evangelists were not just ciphers, but creative authors with personalities and interests of their own.

Literary criticism

So far the various types of criticism described have been predominantly historical; they seek to discover the historical truth about the Bible and the way in which it came into being, the processes by which it arose out of a

particular historical situation. And beyond doubt this is an important activity. Christianity makes great claims about Jesus, about what happened in and to him, and presents these as the truth; it also presents ethical teaching for the individual and society – and for all this the Bible is the evidence and the authority. Even though they indicate that the relationship between the Bible and history is a complex one, the findings of historical criticism play an important role in showing that while the Bible can be read like any other book, it is not a work of fiction.

However, during the final 30 years of the last century it became increasingly clear that the work of the biblical critics had obscured an important fact: the Bible is also literature. It contains great and complex stories that stand on the same footing as the greatest of world literature, and can also be studied by methods that have been developed in the secular study of that literature. Here the focus is not on what has gone on under the surface of the written text, as happened, say, in the search for sources or the elucidation of historical background, but on the text itself.

Literary criticism analyses the structure of narratives, their themes and the techniques employed in creating them, the forms of poetry to be found in the Bible, and so on. Thus in the New Testament, on a literary-critical approach the Acts of the Apostles is not seen primarily as historical evidence about earliest Christianity, to be checked out against other contemporary documentation and investigated for its accuracy and its sources, but as a story. Attention focuses on the way in which Luke relates this story and the points that he is trying to put over: above all that although the founder of Christianity had been crucified by the Romans, Christianity is still a faith that even governors and kings could believe in. In many respects Luke's book is a political book, and as in politics, speeches are important. So, too, on this approach, the many speeches in Acts are seen, not as recording what, say, Peter or Paul said at the time, but as spelling out the author's concern in a different way – a role which speeches play in other contemporary writings.

Story

Literary criticism is a very general term, and because it is so general, other narrower terms have come to be used alongside it. Here, in contrast to textual criticism and source criticism or form criticism, the boundaries are more fluid.

Rhetorical criticism

By the very nature of their activities, Christian leaders and missionaries were and are public speakers, and to speak effectively (and also in writings that serve the purpose of a speech when the author cannot be present, like Paul's letters, which were intended to be read out in churches) it was natural for them to make use of the rhetorical devices current in their time. Rhetorical criticism studies speech, language and communication in the world of earliest Christianity. It looks at the occasion for the speech or letter, the problems to be overcome in discussing the subject-matter effectively, the way in which the sympathy of the audience is gained, and the balance between emotion and argument. It analyses the different types of argument that can be used and the stylistic devices used in presenting them, from sarcasm and irony to passionate defence.

Rhetorical criticism makes it possible to read the speeches in Acts and particularly the letters of Paul in a new light and provides a vocabulary for talking about them. When is Paul on the defensive, when is he being manipulative, how effective are his words?

Narrative criticism

Narrative criticism studies the narrative parts of the Bible strictly as narratives. Its questions are not like those that are common in the traditional forms of biblical criticism, but focus directly on the narrative. How does the narrator compose the scenes? What is the function of dialogue in narrative? What is the purpose of repetitions in story? What knowledge is communicated to the reader and what is concealed? How does the narrator introduce the characters and how does he make them develop? Thus a narrative-critical approach to the Gospel of Mark, having noted that in it Jesus twice feeds a crowd, once of 4000 and once of 5000, would not go on to say that here the author used two sources and extrapolate from that; it would ask why the story had been told twice, and what the significance of the repetition was. Likewise, gaps in the narrative are not seen as points at which the author has no information; the narrative critic sees them positively and asks just as much about what the author does not tell us as about what he does.

It is natural to speak here about 'the author', but in fact narrative criticism prefers to speak of 'the text'. We cannot get at the person of the historical author or discover his intentions in writing the narrative. All we have is the narrative itself, and all our questions must be answered by it. Similarly, we cannot get at the original audience to which the narrative was addressed; we can only infer it from the narrative, by the way in which it is written. Thus, for example, the author of the Fourth Gospel assumes that the reader is not a Jew, is knowledgeable about the scriptures and familiar with the tradition about Jesus, but is ignorant of the geography of Palestine and Jewish rites (this reader is referred to as the 'implied reader'). But we are not the implied reader, and our knowledge and background is likely to be very different. So a key element in narrative criticism is a move from the 'implied reader' to the actual or real reader. Actual readers bring a whole kaleidoscope of presuppositions to a narrative, depending on their social background, previous reading, world-view, psychological make-up, and so on.

So narrative criticism is set against a sophisticated understanding of the relationship between reader and text, sometimes referred to as the 'reading pact'. But by its very nature, it will be most detailed in the treatment of the narrative, examining how it begins and how it ends, its plot, its setting, its characters and the interaction between them, the way in which the story is told and the time-span over which it elapses.

Since the Bible is a text which from the start has shaped people's thinking and stamped their ideas, whether it has been seen as a collection of authoritative statements of divine inspiration or of historically accurate accounts of past events, narrative criticism plays an important role in demonstrating that its nature is not exhausted by these two alternatives, and that the relationship between Bible and reader is much more complex. In this respect it serves as an important counter-balance.

Reader-response criticism

Yet another form of criticism takes to extremes the availability of the Bible like any other book. It focuses on the reader and the process of reading rather than the author and the text. The text, it is claimed, has no fixed or final meaning, no one 'correct' meaning. Its meaning is established by the interaction between the reader and the text: the meaning of the text is what happens when the reader reads it.

Reader-response criticism sets out to make readers aware of what they are doing when they are reading and offers words and concepts that enable them to talk about their experience and identify it more precisely. The reader has priority, not the text. It makes a difference whether the text is read by a man or a woman, a black person or a white person, someone living in a prosperous middle-class English suburb or someone living in a shanty town in South America or Africa. Readers' approaches are influenced by their backgrounds and their interest, whether these are mere curiosity, seeking the liberation of the oppressed, improving the status of women or preserving the status quo.

Feminist criticism

Reader-response criticism tends to be practised by professional biblical scholars in often highly technical works, but the way in which it focuses on the reader as well as the text is also a feature of one of the most important recent developments in studying the Bible. Feminist biblical scholars have introduced an entirely new perspective. They point out that the biblical texts were written by males, in a patriarchal culture, and consequently make all kinds of assumptions that modern readers cannot, or should not, share. For example, whereas traditional interpretation has seen Mary the mother of Jesus as a passive figure, whose main characteristic is her obedience, some feminist interpreters see her as a woman in charge of her own destiny, with faith and courage to go into the unknown comparable to that of the great Old Testament figure of Abraham. They single out the Magnificat, Mary's song of praise in Luke 1.46–55, with its emphasis on social justice, as an expression of a feminist theology and a liberation theology. Other feminist scholars set out to trace the 'hidden' story of women in earliest Christianity, for example by bringing out the role of women who followed Jesus in his ministry, like Joanna and Susanna (Luke 8.1–3), or exercised roles of leadership in the church, like Phoebe, Prisca, Mary, Tryphaena and Tryphosa and Julia (all mentioned in Romans 16). They point out that the male-centred nature of the sources has led to the exclusion of information about the role of women in the early church and that what there is tends to be overlooked, again because of male prejudices. Because of the nature of the sources, the possibility of major new findings through feminist approaches is limited, but the new perspective that they offer is perhaps the most important development in recent biblical criticism.

Mary

Feminist theology
Liberation theology

Commentaries and Introductions

How all these different approaches illuminate reading the Bible can be seen by studying individual books, or indeed the Bible as a whole, by means of commentaries. Commentaries on the Bible were written by the church fathers and the Reformers, and since the rise of modern biblical criticism they have proliferated. Sometimes they are published in series that cover the whole Bible or the whole of the New Testament; sometimes individual commentators choose just one book which speaks particularly to them. Sometimes the commentator is more prominent than the original author, as is the case with Karl Barth's famous commentary on Paul's Letter to the Romans; sometimes the commentators put themselves at the service of the elucidation of the text, as for example in C. K. Barrett's commentary on the Gospel of John. There are commentaries which focus more on textual criticism, and those, not least by feminist scholars, which focus more on the reader. The easiest way of finding what commentaries are available is to consult another genre of literature: the Introduction. The name Introduction is somewhat misleading here. Such a book is by no means a simple way in but discusses all the questions that need to be considered by a student before embarking on reading a book of the Bible; some Introductions are very technical.

Conclusion

In addition to all the approaches mentioned here, postmodern thought has also made its contribution to the interpretation of the Bible, though at present this contribution is too complex to be summarized briefly.

These various types of criticism do not diminish the stature of the Bible, as is often thought or feared, but on the contrary bring out the complex wealth of its content and the role readers play in reading it. One might perhaps compare an understanding of the Bible in the light of biblical criticism with an understanding of the world in the light of modern science. At one time the world was thought to have been created directly, as it is, by God, and God was thought to act directly in it through the forces of nature. The theory of evolution and many other scientific discoveries were seen as great threats to this belief. But it is possible to have a rich understanding of creation, even accepting the findings of science, especially when the role of the observer is taken into account. Similarly, at one time the Bible was thought to have been directly inspired by God, divinely dictated to authors who were merely the pens with which God wrote. Biblical criticism shows that the Bible did not come into being in this way, but it can still be seen as an inspired and authoritative work.

Science
Creation
Evolution
Inspiration

JOHN BOWDEN

Textual criticism: P. R. Ackroyd and C. F. Evans (eds), *The Cambridge History of the Bible, Vol.1*, Cambridge: CUP 1970; B. M. Metzger, *The Text of the New Testament*, Oxford: OUP [2]1968

Philological criticism: William Barclay, *New Testament Words*, London: SCM Press and Philadelphia: Westminster Press 1964

Source criticism: Raymond F. Collins, *Introduction to the New Testament*, London: SCM Press and New York: Doubleday 1983

Form criticism: Rudolf Bultmann, *The History of the Synoptic Tradition*, Oxford: Blackwell and Philadelphia: Westminster Press [2]1968; Martin Dibelius, *From Tradition to Gospel*, New York: Scribner 1967 and Cambridge: James Clarke 1971

Redaction criticism: Norman Perrin, *What is Redaction Criticism?*, Philadelphia: Fortress Press 1970; J. Rohde, *Rediscovering the Teaching of the Evangelists*, London: SCM Press 1968

Literary criticism: Robert Alter and Frank Kermode (eds), *The Literary Guide to the Bible*, Cambridge, MA: Harvard University Press 1987

Rhetorical criticism: A. N. Wilder, *Early Christian Rhetoric. The Language of the Gospel*, London: SCM Press 1964 and Cambridge, MA: Harvard University Press 1971; G. A. Kennedy, *New Testament Interpretation through Rhetorical Criticism*, Chapel Hill, NC: University of North Carolina Press 1984

Narrative criticism: Robert Alter, *The Art of Biblical Narrative*, New York: Basic Books 1981; Daniel Marguerat and Yvan Bourquin, *How to Read Bible Stories*, London: SCM Press and New York: Continuum 1999

Reader-response criticism: J. P. Tompkins (ed), *Reader-response Criticism: From Formalism to Post-Structuralism*, Baltimore: Johns Hopkins University Press 1990; Stephen Moore, *Literary Criticism and the Gospels: The Theoretical Challenge*, New Haven: Yale University Press 1989

Feminist criticism: Elisabeth Schüssler Fiorenza, *In Memory of Her. A Feminist Reconstruction of Christian Origins*, New York: Crossroad and London: SCM Press [2]1995

Commentaries and Introductions: Luke Timothy Johnson, *The Writings of the New Testament*, Minneapolis: Fortress Press and London: SCM Press 1999

Postmodern criticism: A. K. M. Adam, *What is Postmodern Biblical Criticism?*, Minneapolis: Fortress Press 1995

Protestantism
Pietism
Bible

Biblical theology

Most Christian theology has claimed to be 'biblical', i.e. to be in accord with the biblical witness as a whole, but the phrase 'biblical theology' originated in two strands of seventeenth- and eighteenth-century Protestantism, which aimed to secure the Reformers' emphasis on 'scripture alone'. It was applied first to collections of proof-texts supporting the statements of orthodox dogmatics, and secondly to Pietist critiques of those dogmatic systems which appealed to their scriptural and experiential base. The phrase has thus always had both a constructive and a critical intent. It can refer (a) to the activity of doing Christian theology by interpreting the Bible, or (b) to the resulting summaries of the doctrinal content of the Bible. Those textbook summaries were and sometimes still are typically organized in terms of dogmatics, mirroring the contemporary statements of Christianity that they aim to support or correct. 'Biblical theology' (of the Old and of the New Testament) was placed alongside 'critical introduction' to Old and New Testament in nineteenth-century German Protestant faculties. It is now used ambiguously to refer (a) to historical and linguistic studies of doctrinal topics or (b) to explicitly theological interpretations of a part or the whole of the Christian Bible.

The modern development of this theological sub-discipline is usually dated from a lecture given in 1787 by the German theologian J. P. Gabler, 'On the Proper Distinction Between Biblical and Dogmatic Theology', characterizing biblical theology as a historical discipline, descriptive but with normative implications. Gabler's concern was to preserve the authority of the Bible for modern Christianity by setting aside its time-conditioned elements. He later distinguished between a 'true' and a 'pure' biblical theology: the former, true to the texts, describes and systematizes the biblical teachings; the 'pure' was to be a distillation of what in the Bible remains timelessly valid.

That rationalist solution to the problem of untrue or morally unacceptable elements in the biblical witness, namely the identification of 'the true' and 'the pure' in the Bible, could hardly survive the subsequent recognition that as a collection of human writings (even if in some sense 'inspired') the whole Bible is conditioned by the times and places of each part's origins. However, Gabler's distinction helped to free biblical scholarship from its subservience to dogmatics and (contrary to his intentions) allowed it to pursue its historical agenda without reference to theological or church interests. This possibility was not much explored until recently, because as late as the 1960s the social location of the discipline and the interests of its practitioners were still overwhelmingly theological.

Biblical theology remained Christian and theological in the nineteenth century, when the new historical approach led G. L. Bauer to write separate theologies of the Old Testament (1796) and the New Testament (1800–2), and to distinguish between the different voices heard in each testament. Disciplinary specialization in the mid-nineteenth century permitted theologians to enquire about the unity of each testament, but the unity of the whole Bible was neglected by most critical scholars.

G. W. F. Hegel's belief that the divine Spirit moves through history made it possible for the Tübingen scholar F. C. Baur's pioneering historical research on Christian origins and the development of dogma in the 1830s and 1840s to be understood as the human intellect (finite spirit) attaining knowledge of God (infinite Spirit). In 1835 the first (and only) volume of the Berlin Hegelian philosopher W. Vatke's *Biblical Theology* implied a similar modern theology by tracing a dialectical development in the religion of the Old Testament. The breakdown of Hegel's synthesis brought about by pressure from more accurate historical study, and the eclipse of Hegel's metaphysics, left critical biblical studies without the strong Idealist framework that had initially made them overtly theological. Most scholars describing biblical religion were still themselves religious, and knew which parts of the Bible they as Protestants found most congenial (the prophets, Jesus, Paul), but the growing sense of historical distance and of the otherness of antiquity opened up a gap (or gulf) between biblical studies and dogmatics. This was not conducive to biblical theology of either Old or New Testaments, much less a unitary biblical theology.

In 1897 William Wrede, professor at Breslau, could even propose that the label 'New Testament theology' be replaced by 'the history of early Christian religion and theology', corresponding to best practice at the time. He was right that purely historical presentations of biblical ideas are history, but one might say that they could still be called theology, even after abandoning the dogmatics model, because they corresponded to the (liberal, non-dogmatic) theological interests and beliefs of their authors.

Authority

Wrede's proposal accepted the historical 'task and method' of biblical study, but underestimated its authors' aims and the social context of biblical study in Christian theological faculties which existed to train clergy for mostly conservative congregations. Liberal Protestant religious practice might dovetail with an approach to the Bible in terms of the history of religions, but not even in late nineteenth-century Germany was everyone a liberal Protestant. When 'culture Protestantism' was eclipsed following the First World War, continental Protestantism returned to more orthodox Reformation theologies, supported by more directly theological interpretations of scripture. These new variants of biblical theology, associated especially with Rudolf Bultmann and his pupils in the New Testament, and Walther Eichrodt and Gerhard von Rad in the the Old, made biblical interpretation powerfully theological until new paradigms emerged in the 1970s, reducing biblical theology to one interest among many.

Liberal theology

p. 702

The twentieth-century theological era dawned with Karl Barth's interpretation of *The Epistle to the Romans* (1919, second edition 1922). This powerful work challenged a biblical scholarship whose relationship to Christian theology depended more on the piety and institutional context of the professors than on the integrity of a theology that could communicate the Christian message in a post-liberal world. Biblical scholarship had investigated the human phenomenon of religion (which most of the scholars still practised), but did not (as historical and linguistic research) speak directly of God. That task was left to dogmatics. Biblical studies, Barth claimed, had become at best part of the history of theology, mere prolegomena to Christian theology properly so-called.

Karl Barth

Barth's animus against a biblical scholarship with roots in Enlightenment rationalism obscured for him its theological potential. His *Church Dogmatics* and theological commentaries contain much very fine theological interpretation of scripture, but it was Old and New Testament specialists, rooted in the liberal tradition yet dissatisfied with its theology and influenced by Barth, who developed new syntheses in biblical theology. Their Old and New Testament theologies respectively maintained the disciplinary separation of the testaments, and the phrase 'biblical theology' became less common than its reality. Most Christian Old and New Testament scholarship was

Enlightenment

Prophecy

Jesus

Paul

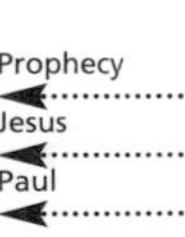

still religiously motivated, and much of this motivation was explicit, but while some German scholars explored again the theological and hermeneutical issues involved in making their historical research serve theological ends, personally religious English and American critics preferred patient textual analysis to novel theological syntheses. This scholarly distance from the religious interests motivating most biblical study led to the reaction of the 1940s and 1950s known as the 'biblical theology' movement. The unity of the Bible and its distinctive languages and revelatory character were put in the foreground. For some the movement offered simplistic substitutes for modern systematic or philosophical theology. This sometimes naïve biblicism was useful for teaching and preaching, but did not divert critical scholarship, and by the 1960s was largely discredited. Its legitimate aims to serve the church were pursued in more critical Old and New Testament theologies, which by the 1960s were spreading from German and Swiss Protestantism to English-speaking students, and Council Roman Catholics after the Second Vatican Council.

Dissatisfaction with Bultmann's negative theological evaluation of the Old Testament was a factor in the renewed quest for a unified biblical theology, but it was mainly Christian Old Testament scholars who explored the relationship of their own specialism to the New Testament and Christian theology. Gerhard von Rad's typological solution did not gain wide acceptance, but a generation later the massive labours of B. S. Childs, of Yale Divinity School, have influenced even some who reject his 'canonical criticism', the view that criticism of biblical books must relate to their final form and Canon place in the biblical canon. Old and New Testament and biblical theology have always been concerned to develop Christian readings of scripture, and as Western culture has become less Christian their constructive role has become more prominent than the critical, and biblical theological proposals which once were radical and critical (Martin Luther, Rudolf Bultmann and Ernst Käsemann) have come to seem relatively conservative.

The new diversity in contemporary biblical scholarship, with many authors decidedly untheological in understanding or interest, has stimulated revivals of biblical theology among those who now need to make their religious aims more explicit. The wide range of methods and approaches currently in vogue, and especially the challenge to the hegemony of historical studies, has led to new patterns of biblical theology. Some interpret only Bible the final form of the text, because that is what is read in Tradition the religious community. This theological interpretation of scripture can work with the new literary approaches whose variety has opened up a plethora of possibilities. Ethics Theologians who are politically engaged have usually preferred to seek new alliances with the social historical studies of Christian origins, Hellenism, and above all Judaism, which have also made further advances over the past 50 years. Their work has been sharpened by sociological questions and insights.

So long as Christian believers read their scripture as a source and (in some sense) a norm of their faith, they will always need theological interpretations of these texts, i.e. interpretations that clarify their Christian meanings and stimulate theological reflection. The many possible meanings of texts and plurality of methods make simple biblical answers to questions of Christian identity today impossible. Christian reading of scripture requires discernment, and presupposes the ever new and unpredictable activity of the Spirit. The on-going task of biblical theology is part of the church's on-going engagement with the scripture that bears witness to the revelation it claims to acknowledge. Biblical theology usually interprets small sections of the biblical material, corresponding to units in which scripture is usually heard, but there remains a place for larger overviews which suggest how the whole New Testament and the whole Old Testament and even the whole Christian scripture, may be seen to cohere.

ROBERT MORGAN

James Barr, *The Concept of Biblical Theology*, London: SCM Press and Minneapolis: Fortress Press 1999; B. S. Childs, *Biblical Theology in Crisis*, Philadelphia: Fortress Press 1970 and *Biblical Theology of the Old and New Testaments*, London: SCM Press 1992 and Minneapolis: Fortress Press 1993; S. E. Fowl (ed), *The Theological Interpretation of Scripture*, Oxford: Blackwell 1997; W. Moberly, *The Bible, Theology, and Faith*, Cambridge: CUP 2000; Robert Morgan with John Barton, *Biblical Interpretation*, Oxford: OUP 1988; H. Räisänen, *Beyond New Testament Theology*, London: SCM Press [2]2000; C. S. Scobie, *The Ways of our God*, Grand Rapids, MI: Eerdmans 2003

Bioethics

New breakthroughs in medicine and health care, such as the use of ventilators to support breathing and *in vitro* fertilization to overcome infertility, have heightened the ethical and social questions inevitably raised over the course of human history about whether and how to use novel biomedical measures. Christian bioethics addresses such questions, relying on the Bible and other writings, as well as tradition, reason and human experience. In this field, Christian thinkers and churches have responded to specific issues that have been thrust to the fore for those who must make pressing health-care decisions at the beginning of life, during life, and at life's end.

Issues at the beginning of life

Contraception. The Christian tradition today generally accepts the use of contraceptives to avoid pregnancy, although the Roman Catholic and Orthodox churches consider it morally wrong to do so. Until the twentieth century, Christian theologians had generally frowned upon the intentional prevention of pregnancy. Augustine, an influential church father, adopted a natural-law approach to human sexuality that led him to teach that it is wrong to engage in sex without intending its biological outcome, the conception of children. Thomas Aquinas repeated this view in the thirteenth century, maintaining that since procreation is the primary end of sexual relations, the use of contraception is a sin against nature. Protestants continued this ban on the use of contraceptive techniques in the sixteenth century, but not on the basis of natural law. Instead, they were concerned that these techniques might harm the woman and the foetus.

Anglican bishops startled the Christian world at the Lambeth Conference of 1930 when they introduced a new openness to the use of contraception into Christian ethical thought. They indicated that it is morally acceptable to employ contraceptive techniques if this is done responsibly by couples to affect the number and spacing of their children. Many Protestant churches were led by this Anglican initiative to accept contraception, often citing the need for family planning to enable parents to fulfil their obligations to existing children, overcome poverty, improve women's health, and further global ecology. The Roman Catholic and Greek Orthodox churches still condemn artificial contraception, holding that every act of sexual intercourse within marriage must be open to the transmission of life.

Abortion. Whether to engage in abortion is one of the most difficult decisions that women and their spouses can face. Significantly different views about the morality of proceeding with an abortion have emerged within the various Christian churches. To understand why this is so, we need to take a look at how Christian views of this practice developed.

Many among the church fathers held that it was wrong to end the life of the 'formed' foetus, which was the foetus that had grown to the point where it had developed a rational, as opposed to a vegetative or animal, soul. Borrowing from the Greek philosopher Aristotle, they took this 'formed' foetus to come into existence at 40 days after conception for the male and 90 days for the female. However, they viewed ending the life of the 'unformed' foetus (early embryo before the 40- or 90-day point) as a lesser sin that was akin to the use of contraception. They reasoned that to do so was not to destroy an ensouled being, but instead was to frustrate what they considered the proper end of sexual relations, procreation.

This view predominated within the Christian tradition until the discovery of the female egg or oocyte in the nineteenth century. Many scientists and theologians thereupon abandoned the view, widely held earlier, that a little man (*homunculus*) was carried in the male seed and nurtured to grow by the female womb. Instead, they acknowledged that the female egg plays an important role in bringing forth children and came to believe that conception, when sperm and oocyte merge, is the crucial event that marks the beginning of a human being. This scientific discovery was among the factors that led Pope Pius IX in the nineteenth century to condemn abortion from conception onwards within the Roman Catholic Church.

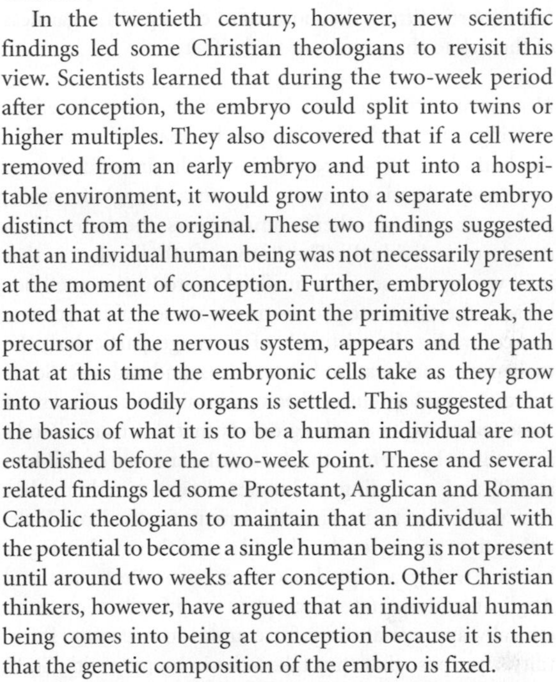

In the twentieth century, however, new scientific findings led some Christian theologians to revisit this view. Scientists learned that during the two-week period after conception, the embryo could split into twins or higher multiples. They also discovered that if a cell were removed from an early embryo and put into a hospitable environment, it would grow into a separate embryo distinct from the original. These two findings suggested that an individual human being was not necessarily present at the moment of conception. Further, embryology texts noted that at the two-week point the primitive streak, the precursor of the nervous system, appears and the path that at this time the embryonic cells take as they grow into various bodily organs is settled. This suggested that the basics of what it is to be a human individual are not established before the two-week point. These and several related findings led some Protestant, Anglican and Roman Catholic theologians to maintain that an individual with the potential to become a single human being is not present until around two weeks after conception. Other Christian thinkers, however, have argued that an individual human being comes into being at conception because it is then that the genetic composition of the embryo is fixed.

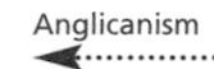

Not only scientific findings, but also Christian ethical and social understandings related to abortion were revisited in the twentieth century. The moral acceptability of abortion was taken to turn on weighing in the balance the importance of procreation as an outcome of sexual activity, the kind of protection owed to the foetus, the well-being of the woman, and the responsibility of the pregnant woman to make this choice. The Roman Catholic tradition, in assessing these values, retained the view that abortion is morally unacceptable in any circumstances. However, the doctrine of double effect within that tradition allows the life of the foetus to be ended when this is a foreseen but unintended consequence of a procedure designed to save the life of a pregnant woman. Many Orthodox commentators also maintain that abortion is wrong but would allow it when pregnancy puts a woman's

life at risk. Protestant and Anglican churches tend to give more weight to the unique circumstances of those considering abortion, giving significant weight to the health and well-being of the woman and placing the responsibility for the decision with the woman whose body is involved. Thus, in some Protestant and Anglican churches, abortion is considered a tragic but morally acceptable act when pregnancy has resulted from rape or incest, when it gravely threatens the woman's health, or when the foetus is found to have a serious abnormality. These churches take it to be morally questionable to have an abortion for less serious reasons. In more conservative Protestant and Anglican churches, however, the view prevails that the embryo and foetus should be protected from abortion from the moment of conception, regardless of the risk to the woman or to the foetus.

New reproductive technologies. Questions about the ethics of using novel medical techniques to create babies outside the body have arisen recently with the introduction of *in vitro* fertilization, gamete (sperm and egg) donation, and surrogacy (another woman bears the baby for a couple or individual). The Roman Catholic view is that it is wrong to use such artificial reproductive methods because they separate procreation from sexual intercourse and contradict the mutuality of marriage, particularly the exclusive sexual relation between husband and wife. Some Protestant and Anglican theologians also reject the use of these technologies on the grounds that this usurps God's sovereignty by opening the door to the creation of children at will and according to human design. Children, they fear, will come to be viewed as manufactured products, rather than precious gifts, should use of these technologies become widely accepted. However, most Protestant and Anglican commentators accept *in vitro* fertilization as an ethically appropriate way for couples to overcome infertility, a purpose that they take to be in keeping with God's plans. Yet they have not endorsed the use of the new reproductive technologies without reservation. Many maintain that more needs to be done to protect couples from the physical and psychological risks of these techniques and to develop ethical and social limitations on their use that make the well-being of the child a paramount consideration.

Some Christian commentators accept the use of *in vitro* fertilization but reject the use of the gametes or wombs of others to assist infertile couples to have children because they believe that this smacks of adultery. Others maintain, by contrast, that it is ethically acceptable to have the help of third parties to overcome infertility, for there is no offence against the informed and willing marriage partner. The principal question raised, they believe, is whether the rearing parents will provide a stable environment in which the child will thrive. There is concern across all Christian denominations that it may be difficult for the infertile partner to accept having a third party enter into the processes of procreation. Moreover, if secrecy is maintained to protect that partner from social discrimination, this may cause confusion for the future child about his or her parents and family lineage. The practices of egg donation and surrogacy also raise questions about the degree of physical risk that female donors and surrogates should suffer on behalf of others and about their economic exploitation.

The possibility of using cloning (in which the nucleus of a donated egg is removed and replaced by a cell from the person to be cloned; after this the egg is stimulated to develop into an embryo that is then transferred to a woman's uterus to be brought to birth) to bring children into the world has come under intense fire recently within the Christian tradition. Most Christian commentators oppose reproductive cloning out of concern that it would stand on its head the very meaning of procreation as a relational partnership between two people. Moreover, they view human beings as unique creatures who ought not be duplicated asexually. Reproductive cloning, they argue further, would introduce confusion into our understanding of parenthood, for who would be the parent of the cloned child – the cell donor? the egg donor? the cloned child's grandparents? Those Christian thinkers who would welcome reproductive cloning hold that it is an ethically acceptable way to enable otherwise infertile parents or those who might pass genetic disease to their children to have healthy children. However, sufficient questions have been raised about the risks of reproductive cloning to the health of the resulting children that all responsible Christian thinkers maintain that its use should be prohibited for the foreseeable future.

Stem cell research, embryos and chimeras. Research scientists have recently discovered the existence of stem cells in humans. These are the original, undifferentiated cells from which all specialized cells of the human body, such as the brain, blood and kidney cells, grow. Stem cells are found in human embryos, human sperm and eggs and living human beings. Their discovery is important, for if investigators can learn how these cells grow, differentiate and proliferate throughout the body, they can, hopefully, learn how to replace them when they are damaged, thus treating those with such serious conditions as Parkinson's disease, Alzheimer's disease or heart disease. However, two major ethical questions have arisen about stem cell research: 1. Should such research be pursued using early human embryos, since, as things currently stand, this would necessarily involve their destruction? 2. Should human stem cells be inserted into animals prenatally in order to study how they grow and develop, thereby running the risk of creating human-animal chimeras?

The attention of Christian thinkers thus far has largely focused on the first question. Many who view the human embryo as a human being from the moment of conception would prohibit all stem cell research that would lead to the destruction of early human embryos. They see this as a form of killing a human being. A second group of Christian thinkers maintains that the early human embryo is owed a degree of respect, since it might eventually develop into a human being, but until it passes the second week of development, it does not have the potential to develop into a human being. Therefore, they assert, the early embryo can appropriately be used in stem cell research. Some in this second group would only allow frozen embryos remaining at *in vitro* fertilization centres that are no longer needed for reproductive purposes to be used for stem cell research. Rather than discard these embryos, they maintain, it would reflect better stewardship to use them in research to help those who are seriously ill. Still others in this second group would, in addition, allow human embryos to be created specifically for stem cell research. A third group of Christian commentators maintains that the early human embryo is merely a clump of cells like any other human tissue and that it is ethically acceptable, even required, to use them for research that might benefit humankind. The various Christian denominations remain divided about the question of whether to use early human embryos in stem cell research, although they are in agreement that it is ethically appropriate to use adult stem cells for this purpose.

A second, troubling question that has just begun to be raised is whether it is ethically acceptable to study the development of certain neural human stem cells, such as those of the brain and retina, by inserting them into animal embryos and foetuses and observing how they grow and proliferate. To do so, many fear, could result in the creation of a human-nonhuman chimera and this, they maintain, would be contrary to both human and animal dignity. God created human beings as stewards of all other living creatures, giving them a special dignity and worth that would be denigrated were humans to be merged with animals at an early developmental stage. Moreover, God treasured all kinds of living creatures, as the story of Noah's ark relates, and it would be wrong to violate the integrity of animals by endowing them with human features.

Concern about the creation of human-animal chimeras has especially focused on the transfer of human neural or brain stem cells into animal embryos. Researchers maintain that since brain and other neural stem cells grow and differentiate rapidly at the prenatal stage and exhibit little renewal after birth, the only way to learn how they develop is to study them as they develop in embryos and foetuses. It would be ethically unacceptable, however, to use human embryos for this purpose, and so they have begun to insert human neural stem cells into animal embryos instead. This, some moral theologians fear, runs the risk of creating animals whose bodies house human brains and, ultimately of creating a combination human-nonhuman being. To date, however, stem cell investigators have found that when human brain cells are transferred to mice, they take up only a small percentage of the mouse brain and that the mouse brain governs the way that these human cells develop. Moreover, the human brain is much larger and has a more complex organization than the mouse brain. Consequently, even if human cells should completely occupy the mouse brain, that brain would still remain a small mouse brain with the relatively simple organization of the mouse brain. The same would be true, these researchers maintain, if chimpanzees, which are biologically closer to human beings than mice, were used in such research. Therefore, these investigators argue, the fear of creating human-animal chimeras through the transfer of human cells to animal embryos is misplaced and neither human nor animal dignity is violated by such research. This is a question that has just begun to be discussed and that promises to lead to the development of regulations limiting the ways in which cells and other materials from humans and animals can be mixed prenatally.

Questions during life

Genetic testing. The rapid pace at which we are discovering genes and their functions has provided an impetus to test individuals whose family history or bodily symptoms suggest that they are at risk of a serious disease or condition. Such tests enable medical professionals to learn whether these individuals have genes associated with such conditions.

Genes are tiny pieces of material found on chromosomes, which are minute threads of chemicals located in the nucleus of every cell. The threads in our chromosomes look like two long, paired strands that are tightly coiled together. These strands are composed of DNA (deoxyribonucleic acid). A gene is any given segment along this DNA that carries instructions telling a cell to perform a specific action. Some find it useful to picture chromosomes as a book that contains pages (genes) that are its units of organization. Thus the specific genes of each individual help to organize and characterize him or her, for they affect such features as hair colour and blood type. Genes can sometimes be changed or mutated in ways that may lead people to develop certain genetic diseases.

Genetic testing can be carried out to learn whether an individual has genes that may or will lead that person to develop a gene-based disease. Such testing can involve a laboratory procedure in which a small sample of blood is studied to learn whether a certain chromosome or gene is present. It can also be done by means of biochemical tests, such as those for the presence or absence of key proteins that are associated with certain genes or gene mutations.

Some Christians think that it is wrong to undergo such testing, for they believe that God gave us whatever genes we have and that we should not be involved in testing and possibly tinkering with them. To do so, they believe, is akin to eating the forbidden fruit in the Garden of Eden and to usurp what is rightfully God's domain. Other Christians respond that God not only created the world but also continues to act within it, calling upon us to assist in mending and renewing it in ways that accord with God's purposes. We are to use genetic information to alter the progression of disease and to care for those who are suffering. In these respects, genetic testing is no different from other forms of medical testing.

Genetic testing can reduce uncertainty for those with a family history that suggests that they are at risk of developing a serious genetic condition. It can also spur those who test positive to look into whether there is or soon will be treatment for the condition. Furthermore, the knowledge gained through testing can help individuals to make realistic decisions about their future and about having children. However, although knowledge can be a blessing, it can also be a curse. Genetic testing can raise difficult personal and ethical questions for those tested, for it may reveal information about which the person tested can do nothing, since there may be no treatment available for the disease at issue. In addition, an individual may learn not only about his or her own predilection to a genetic disease but also about family members who are affected by the disease. Moreover, test results may expose an individual to discrimination in employment and insurance. In view of such benefits and disadvantages, most Christian denominations recommend that those considering genetic testing should consult with genetic and pastoral counsellors before they decide whether to be tested.

Body
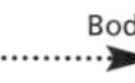
Resurrection
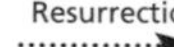

Gene therapy and germline interventions. The conviction that humans, as stewards of creation, have a responsibility to restore and renew the natural order in view of God's aims is a prominent feature of Christian moral thinking. Therefore, the various Christian traditions generally agree that we are to proceed cautiously in our efforts to understand and repair human genes that have gone awry.

Genetic interventions, in theory, could be carried out in the somatic or body cells of living persons and also in gametes (sperm and eggs) or embryos. The former interventions have become known as 'gene therapy' and the latter as 'germline interventions'. Germline interventions affect not only the children who are born of the treated gametes or embryos but also their line of descendants. Genetic interventions, whether into the genes of living persons or embryos, can be carried out for the purpose of therapy, that is, to cure or correct disease, or for the goal of enhancement, that is, to improve and heighten certain human characteristics.

Most Christian thinkers accept as ethical those genetic interventions aimed at curing disease in living persons. To date, however, gene therapy research has not been successful and, regrettably, has resulted in some deaths. It is considered extremely unsafe currently to attempt to treat genes in embryos, as we have no way of predicting the outcome for the resulting child and for his or her descendants. Christian commentators tend to maintain that neither somatic cell interventions into living persons nor germline interventions into embryos should be used in order to enhance and improve human beings. A major problem that they believe genetic enhancements would create is that individuals would engage in a series of them, each designed to give them or their children a leg up over others in a never-ending upward competitive spiral. Such individual decisions, taken together, could reintroduce a eugenic ethos into society grounded in arbitrary and un-Christian standards of human perfection. Many commentators argue that rather than try to enhance themselves and their children, Christians should embrace diversity within the human family and proclaim the equal value of all of God's children. Furthermore, they should work to overcome social stereotyping that puts those who are 'different' at a disadvantage.

Organ transplantation. The Christian view of the human body as real and good, rather than as ephemeral and evil, underlies the attitude of acceptance that Christian churches have taken to organ transplantation. Some Christians are hesitant to have their bodies cut open after death for fear that they will be blemished at the resurrection. However, Christian theologians have maintained that the doctrine of bodily resurrection, understood as an affirmation of God's power, does not present a barrier to organ donation. They point out that those whose bodies have been mangled at death, such as persons who have died in car accidents and war, will be raised up whole by God. They hold that the call to love one's neighbour provides a moral warrant for donating body parts from cadavers or living persons to those in need, but only when donors have made a voluntary decision during their lives to allow this. Indeed, it is love of neighbour that has provided the foundation of the various legal systems of organ donation which have been developed in many countries that have refused to allow organ conscription or commercial sale. The option of buying and selling human organs has generally been rejected by Christian and other thinkers because it would open the door to the exploitation and commodification of the human body, thereby violating the profound respect that is owed to the human person. Organ transplantation, however, still raises difficult questions about the allocation of scarce resources in a just manner in most countries. Many have attempted to adhere to canons of justice by providing available organs to those most in need and by encouraging more people to arrange to donate their organs after death.

Justice in distributing health care. The Christian tradition has, from its very beginnings, encouraged the provision of health care to those who are sick as a way to emulate Christ. Jesus healed those who were ill and disabled and, in Jesus' parable of the Good Samaritan in particular, taught that Christians should reach out to all in need of help. Today, in the face of complex systems of health-care delivery, we face difficult questions about how to provide health-care resources in a just manner to those in need. We have begun to realize that we do not have the resources to do all that it is possible for medicine to do and at the same time carry out other socially important activities. Consequently, we must make difficult decisions about who should receive health care, what sorts of health care to provide, and what quantities of health care to deliver.

Several standards of justice have been suggested by Christian theologians, including a first-come-first-served rule, an individual-need rule, and a utilitarian rule that would allocate health resources in ways that maximize the health of those in society in general. This diversity of standards has led to major differences of opinion among these thinkers about the moral relevance of such factors as age and lifestyle in decisions about the allocation of health care. Even so, most Christian theologians agree that a basic, decent level of health care should be available to all people, regardless of their ability to pay, as a matter of justice and love of neighbour. Just what would constitute such care, however, is often disputed. Moreover, some theologians, referring to the parable of the Good Samaritan, argue that those who can afford to pay for health care have a responsibility to contribute to the care of those who cannot. They maintain that those who have been gifted with the wherewithal to purchase their own health care can repay God and the community to whom they are indebted by contributing to the common good in proportion to the wealth they have received. To do so is at the core of what it means to be a Christian member of the human community.

Questions at the end of life

Withholding and withdrawing life-sustaining treatment. Medical advances are enabling health-care professionals to extend the lives of patients far beyond what was possible in earlier generations. These new capabilities raise difficult questions for Christians about how long to attempt to utilize life-sustaining treatment and whether it is ever right to refuse or to withdraw it. Many Christian theologians maintain that to extend the dying process through modern technology is to deny our mortality and our finitude, make an idol of life itself, and usurp God's prerogatives. Others believe that we must do everything possible to retain life for as long as possible until God takes it from us. The latter is a minority view in most Christian denominations.

A rough consensus exists among Christian theologians that we are not ethically required to use treatments that provide no reasonable chance of benefit to patients or that present burdens to patients and families that outweigh their benefits. This view has been adopted from the Roman Catholic tradition, which distinguishes between 'ordinary' or proportionately beneficial treatment and 'extraordinary' or disproportionately burdensome treatment. The former is treatment that offers a degree of good to the patient that outweighs its drawbacks, and the latter is treatment that offers no reasonable chance of providing such good or that creates harm that outweighs its good. 'Ordinary' or proportionately beneficial treatment should always be provided, whereas 'extraordinary' or disproportionately burdensome treatment need not be.

Jesus
p. 658

However, what is 'ordinary' treatment for one patient, such as the use of a ventilator to tide him or her over a temporary difficulty in breathing, can be 'extraordinary' treatment for another, such as one near death for whom the use of a ventilator would only prolong dying. Therefore the 'ordinary-extraordinary' distinction provides a general rule that must be individualized to the specific circumstances of each patient. There is some dispute among Christian thinkers about whether the use of artificial nutrition and hydration – the provision of nutrients and liquids through tubes – is the sort of treatment that can become 'extraordinary' in some instances or whether its use is always morally required. Christian theologians also differ about whether it is morally justifiable to withdraw antibiotics and artificial nutrition and hydration from patients who are in a permanent vegetative state. Those who object to doing so do not view these patients as being in the process of dying but instead maintain that they are living human beings who ought to be treated with all available measures.

Death

When patients are near death and in great pain and suffering, the doctrine of double effect developed within the Roman Catholic tradition would allow health-care professionals to relieve their pain and suffering by the use of analgesic drugs, even though doing so might indirectly hasten their death. This view has been adopted, albeit in somewhat different language, within the Orthodox, Protestant and Anglican traditions. The need to provide dying persons with palliative care and pain relief has been emphasized by the hospice movement, which was initially developed within the Anglican tradition. The hospice approach calls for providing those near death with supportive care, relief of pain and suffering, the company of others, and spiritual care, and yet not to prolong the process of dying through medical means.

Euthanasia and assisted suicide. Although the term 'euthanasia' broadly refers to a good death, it has come to mean bringing about death directly and compassionately in order to alleviate pain and suffering in a dying person. Hence, it is sometimes referred to as 'mercy killing'. Assisted suicide also means bringing about someone's death for compassionate reasons, but it is distinguished from euthanasia in that the final act that leads to death is performed by the individual involved, rather than another. The Christian tradition has long maintained that both euthanasia and assisted suicide are wrong. To commit these acts, many Christian thinkers argue, contradicts the creative and loving purposes of God who gave humans life; it reveals a failure of trust and faith in God, as well as a lack of gratitude. Moreover, some among these thinkers are concerned that such practices will diminish the communal bonds that God has established between humans and cut out of human fellowship those most in need of it. Indeed, if euthanasia and assisted suicide were to become accepted social practices, they declare, those near death might well feel pressure either to end their lives quickly or else to justify remaining alive. These thinkers fear that the question 'Why aren't you dead yet?' would not be far from the lips of those around them.

Some Christian theologians hold, to the contrary, that, as creatures made in the image of God, we are called to take responsibility for our lives as partners with God and that this can entail ending our lives when we are near death and in great pain and suffering. These thinkers believe that to force dying persons to remain alive in anguish is to assault their dignity in a way that serves no discernible spiritual or other purpose. Dean Inge, an Anglican theologian, once wrote of those near death, 'I do not think we can assume that God willed the prolongation of torture for the benefit of the soul of the sufferer.' Instead, theologians who support the use of assisted suicide and euthanasia maintain that God's will is to alleviate the suffering of those near death.

Finally, some Christian thinkers would allow euthanasia or assisted suicide only in rare, extreme, and exceptional circumstances akin to those of the person trapped in a burning car wreck with no way to escape. It would be morally acceptable, they believe, to kill the trapped person and it would also be morally acceptable to participate in assisted suicide and euthanasia for those near death who are experiencing intolerable pain and suffering who have no other way of being saved from a horrible death.

CYNTHIA B. COHEN

📖 *General*: Hessel Bouma III et al. (eds), *Christian Faith, Health, and Medical Practice,* Grand Rapids, MI: Eerdmans 1996; Stephen E. Lammers and Allen Verhey (eds), *On Moral Medicine: Theological Perspectives in Medical Ethics,* Grand Rapids, MI: Eerdmans 1998; Gilbert Meilaender, *Bioethics: A Primer for Christians,* Grand Rapids, MI: Eerdmans 1996; Sondra Ely Wheeler, *Stewards of Life: Bioethics and Pastoral Care,* Nashville, TN: Abingdon Press 1996

Questions at the beginning of life: Lisa Sowle Cahill, *Between the Sexes: Foundation for a Christian Ethics of Sexuality,* Philadelphia, PA: Fortress Press 1985; Church of England, Board of Social Responsibility, *Personal Origins,* London: Church House Publishing [2]1996; Ronald Cole-Turner, *Beyond Cloning: Religion and the Remaking of Humanity,* Harrisburg, PA: Trinity Press International 2001; John Connery, *Abortion: The Development of the Roman Catholic Perspective,* Chicago, IL: Loyola University Press 1977; Oliver O'Donovan, *Begotten or Made?,* Oxford and New York: OUP 1984

Questions during life: Ronald Cole-Turner, *The New Genesis: Theology and the Genetic Revolution,* Louisville, KY: Westminster John Knox Press 1997; Committee on Medical Ethics, Episcopal Diocese of Washington, DC, *Wrestling with the Future: Our Genes and Our Choices,* Harrisburg, PA: Morehouse 1998; Norman M. Ford, *The Prenatal Person: Ethics from Conception to Birth,* Oxford: Blackwell 2002; Ted Peters, *For the Love of Children: Genetic Technology and the Future of the Family,* Louisville, KY: Westminster John Knox Press 1996; David H. Smith and Cynthia B. Cohen (eds), *A Christian Response to the New Genetics: Religious, Ethical and Social Issues,* Lanham, MD: Rowman & Littlefield 2003

Questions at the end of life: Cynthia B. Cohen et al., *Faithful Living, Faithful Dying: Anglican Reflections on End of Life Care,* Harrisburg, PA: Morehouse 2000; Church of England, Board of Social Responsibility, *On Dying Well: A Contribution to the Euthanasia Debate,* London: Church House Publishing [2]1996; Committee on Medical Ethics, Episcopal Diocese of Washington, DC, *Assisted Suicide and Euthanasia: Christian Moral Perspectives,* Harrisburg, PA: Morehouse 1997

Body

From the beginning Christianity has shown signs of an ambivalent attitude towards the body. On the one hand, the body with its demands is seen as a burden, something that can drag Christians down and divert them from the way to salvation; on the other hand, the central Christian belief is that God assumed a body to save humankind and though that body, the body of Jesus, was disfigured and nailed to a cross, it was raised to new, immortal life in the resurrection.

The letters of Paul, the earliest Christian writings that we have, clearly demonstrate this ambivalence and already give some indication of how Christian thought would develop. In a famous passage in his letter to the Romans he laments his divided state: 'For I delight in the law of God, in my inmost self, but I see in my members another law at work with the law of my mind and making me captive to the law of sin which dwells in my members. Wretched man that I am! Who will deliver me from this body of death?' (Romans 7.23–4). He has to struggle to keep his body under control, to train like an athlete, 'I pommel my body and subdue it' (1 Corinthians 9.27), and he looks forward to the time when Jesus Christ 'will change our lowly body to be like his glorious body' (Philippians 3.21). Yet at the same time he has the highest possible view of the body. 'Do you know', he says to the Christians in Corinth, 'that your body is a temple of the Holy Spirit?' (1 Corinthians 6.19); indeed 'your bodies are members of Christ'; 'the body is for the Lord and the Lord for the body' (6.13, 15). This image was taken up in the third century by Origen when he remarked that Christians have learned 'that the body of a rational being devoted to the God of the universe is a temple of the God they worship'. Moreover, the image that Paul chooses to describe the church is the body: 'We, though many, are one body in Christ' (Romans 12.5); 'You are the body of Christ and individually members of it' (1 Corinthians 12.27). The bread broken at the eucharist is the body of Christ: 'Anyone who eats and drinks without discerning the body eats and drinks judgement upon himself' (1 Corinthians 11.30).

This love-hate relationship with the body is different from the dualistic approach to be found in Gnosticism, a movement contemporaneous with early Christianity, whose adherents saw matter as evil and the world created by a demiurge, an inferior being. For them, human nature was a spark trapped in a material body and deliverance came by being freed from that body through knowledge. This was a view that the church rejected, because it inherited from Judaism the view that God had made the world good and that matter, including the body, however problematical, was good also. Nor, over the formative years of Christian attitudes to the body, do we find a split between mind or spirit and body, of the kind that later led thinkers to conceive of a disembodied spirit or immortal soul. The church fathers were aware of the interrelationship of what they called heart (rather than mind, spirit or soul) and body: the heart was the centre of a person; it strove to control the body, and in turn the body shaped the workings of the heart.

The story of how attitudes to the body developed in Christianity after Paul is a complicated one, and made all the more difficult to follow because our sources for it are partial: we hear views about the body above all from men, often men of mature years who have chosen an especially disciplined life, almost always as leaders of the church; and on the rare occasions when women have a say, these too are high-born women who have chosen a life of austerity and virginity. But these are the views that have shaped Christian attitudes to the body over the centuries, and are still influential today.

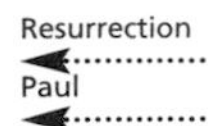

Being in the body means being subject to its drives, of which the two main ones are the appetites for food and sex, so it is not surprising that Christians were particularly concerned about coping with these. They were closely associated: 'Look to the body,' said the second-century church father Tertullian. 'Had there been any possibility of disjoining lust and greed, the private parts would not have been fixed to the belly itself. The region of these members is one and the same.'

Food and drink

From the beginning, fasting or abstinence from food for periods was seen as a means of controlling the body, and this practice became a fixed part of Christian life; with the rise of monasticism it was taken to extremes in a desert existence in which dedicated hermits lived constantly on the verge of starvation. Such privation, however, was the choice of only a few.

There are some parallels to this development over fasting in attitudes to sex, which were never positive: there was a male fear (we do not hear from women) of sexual urges and orgasms as being uncontrollable and messy in their outcome, so the mess was tolerable only if it led to something, i.e. it was a necessary part of the process of producing children. Initially, virginity was chosen by the Gnostics and the most radical groups like the Encratites, who combined it with dietary restraints. Paul had remarked, 'Concerning virgins I have no command from the Lord' (1 Corinthians 7.25) and thought it 'better to marry than to burn' (7.9). Clement of Alexandria was representative of a widespread attitude in seeking to control the body by freeing it from every kind of passion so that it could serve God; sexual intercourse was for conceiving children and should be engaged in as such a service, without an excess of pleasure.

Sexuality

Virginity became the ideal for controlling the sexual drives of the body in the fourth century. Among men it was the way of life chosen by the ascetic monks of the desert, but with them it was associated with the harshness of their existence away from civilization; among women it arose among well-to-do ladies in the cities whose circumstances allowed them to become embodiments of a profound Christian piety and who were to make a deep impact on the church. From these roots it spread to become the higher way of life. As Eusebius of Caesarea put it: 'Two ways of life were thus given by the Lord to his church. The one is above nature, and beyond common human living ... The more humble, more human way prompts men to join in pure nuptials and to produce children.' Although the formal regulations enjoining clerical celibacy were still a long way off, at this point what was to be the church's attitude to this aspect of the body was already well established.

Martyr

The most positive statements about the body are made in speaking not of what the body is but what it will one day be. They were prompted above all by the fate of the martyrs, which forced Christians to clarify the role and meaning of the body in salvation, in Christian life, and especially in death. Thus discussion of the resurrection of the body provides the richest material for Christian thought about the body in the first millennium. Augustine of Hippo was a theologian who tried to envisage what the risen body would be like: men, he argued, will have beards in heaven, because they must rise as handsome as possible. A hymn attributed to Thomas à Kempis is a classic example of this longing for the better, perfect body: 'O how glorious and resplendent, fragile body, shalt thou be, when endued with so much beauty, full of health, and strong and free, full of vigour, full of pleasure that shall last eternally!'

Origins and background

Canon

The problem for Christianity today, given the views of the body which have characterized it from the early centuries onwards, is to find a legitimate way of seeing the body here on earth in terms of the positive features in this picture, of celebrating the joys of food and sex, indeed the joys of the created and embodied world. This has resulted in the rise of what has been called body theology, or theologies of embodiment, which paradoxically have come into being because of the harm being done to human beings and the environment. Body theology is an offshoot from the concerns of feminist theology, liberation theology and ecotheology; in this last the world has been seen as God's body. Such a theological approach claims to be far more in keeping with the doctrine of the incarnation than traditional Christian theology. As Elisabeth Moltmann-Wendel remarks, a theology of embodiment 'seeks to give people once again the courage to use their senses, which atrophy in a rational culture, to stand by themselves and their experiences and accept themselves with their bodies, to love them, to trust them and their understanding, and to see themselves as children of this earth, indissolubly bound up with it'.

Paul

Feminist theology
Liberation theology
Ecotheology

p. 325 

However, whether such theology can establish itself within the churches as they now are, given their history of antipathy to the body and suspicion of it, is another matter.

JOHN BOWDEN

Peter Brown, *The Body and Society*, Berkeley, CA: University of California Press and London: Faber 1988; Caroline Walker Bynum, *The Resurrection of the Body in Western Christianity, 200–1336*, New York: Columbia University Press 1995; Elisabeth Moltmann-Wendel, *I Am My Body: A Theology of Embodiment*, London: SCM Press and New York: Continuum 1995; James Nelson, *Body Theology*, Louisville, KY: Westminster John Knox Press 1992

Books

Books have been vital to Christianity from a very early stage. However, it needs to be remembered that although like Jews before them and Muslims after them Christians have been called a 'people of the book', the beginnings and foundation of Christianity lie in a person, Jesus, and a group of followers whom he gathered around him. Though these followers took over the Greek translation of the Hebrew Bible as their book, their own scriptures, the New Testament, took some time to be brought together and recognized. The formation of these scriptures took place along with the formation of the book as we now know it; indeed it could be said that Christianity was instrumental in the creation of the book.

While Jews used parchment rolls (scrolls) for their scriptures, on the whole Christians used codexes. The codex consisted of leaves of wood, papyrus or especially parchment bound together in the form of a modern book. It evolved out of notebooks that travellers took around with them – a Roman invention. 2 Timothy 4.13 speaks of 'parchments' that Paul has left behind: some scholars think that these may have been such notebooks, but what they contained is a matter of conjecture. There were several reasons for this choice: the codex was more easily portable than the unwieldy and sensitive roll and could be kept in a 'bookcase'; it was easier to find a passage of scripture in a codex than in a roll; above all the codex, like the use of the Greek Bible (Old Testament) rather than the Hebrew Bible, distinguished Christians clearly from Jews and pagans. No New Testament manuscript known to us is written on a roll: all are papyri. When Christians later needed and could afford to produce longer works, further advantages of the codex were that both sides of the page could be used and more pages could be added to a volume.

There is a painting in the catacomb of St Peter and St

Marcellinus in Rome of a young man holding an open codex, and Constantine ordered 50 copies of the scriptures to be made in codexes for the churches in Constantinople. The earliest and most important extant texts of the Bible are codexes: Codex Alexandrinus, Codex Sinaiticus, Codex Vaticanus, the Latin names denoting where they were discovered. One authority has remarked that without the codex one may wonder whether Christianity would have survived.

The first Christian book may well have been a book of testimonies, an anthology of Old Testament passages that could be interpreted as witnesses to Jesus. Leaves from such a codex have been discovered in Egypt, though they come from a later date, and a collection of proof texts about the Messiah has been discovered among the Dead Sea Scrolls. The Old Testament was far too large a book to have been widely available in earliest Christianity; the codexes mentioned above all come from the fourth century. The length of the Gospels suggests that they were first produced each in a simple codex, consisting of just one stitched signature, or group of pages. From papyrus evidence, in the second century none of the earliest codexes seem to have contained more than two books of the Old Testament; in the third century the Chester Beatty papyri show that the four Gospels and Acts were in a single codex.

However, some Christian books were written on rolls. *The Harmony of the Four Gospels* (*Diatessaron*) produced by Tatian, found at Dura Europos in Syria and thus written before the destruction of the city in 256 CE, is on a roll; in the third century there was still a dispute in pagan circles in the cultured East as to whether a codex was a proper book. It is interesting that at this time there is no Greek equivalent to the Latin term codex.

Remains of a writing room (scriptorium) have been found at Qumran, where members of the community produced the Dead Sea Scrolls. The variety of hands in the earliest Christian papyri suggests that they were not produced in scriptoria. However, the church historian Eusebius reports that when Origen (*c.* 185–*c.* 254) dictated his works, 'there were ready at hand more than seven shorthand-writers, who relieved each other at fixed times, and as many copyists, as well as girls skilled in penmanship', all financed by Bishop Ambrose of Milan, and this cannot have been the first Christian scriptorium. Origen's scriptorium foreshadowed the scriptoria of the medieval monasteries and cathedrals, in which monks, together with lay scribes and illuminators from outside the monastery, copied and illustrated manuscripts.

Script

One distinctive characteristic of biblical manuscripts is the use of abbreviated forms of words of religious signifi-

p. 149

ΠΑΡΑΤΗΝΟΔΟΝΚΑΙ
ΗΛΘΕΝΤΑΠΕΤΙΝΑ
ΚΑΙΚΑΤΕΦΑΓΕΝ

est ager sanguinis u
diem. Tunc impletum
est per hieremiam pr

Propter quam causam non con
eosuocare dicens nuntiabo no
mens in medio ecclesiae laudab

Top: Greek uncials (Codex Sinaiticus, *c.* 350 CE)
Middle: Half uncials (Lichfield Gospels, *c.* 710–20 CE)
Bottom: Carolingian minuscule (Grandval Bible, 825–50 CE)

Messiah

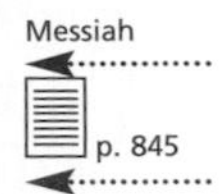

p. 845

cance, known as *nomina sacra* ('sacred names'). Certain words are contracted by omitting some vowels and even consonants and indicating the contraction by a line over the word. The main instances are the Greek words *theos* (God), *kyrios* (Lord), *Iesous* (Jesus) and *Christos* (Christ), but other words were given the same treatment. The system is widely and consistently used in manuscripts and is peculiar to Christianity. It is thought to have arisen out of the practice in Greek versions of the Old Testament of writing the name for God, YHWH, in Hebrew letters in the text.

Manuscripts were written in capital letters, known as uncials, in multiple columns with wide margins and spacing; the classic fourth-century codexes all take this form, as do the Book of Kells and the Lindisfarne Gospels. However, from around the seventh century onwards, uncial manuscripts were rapidly replaced by minuscule (small letters with ascenders and descenders) ones. The advantage of minuscule was that it was quicker to write and easier to read, important as the demand for books grew. Minuscule differed from region to region: there were

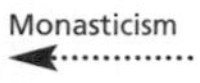

Monasticism

variants in Spain, southern Italy and Ireland, in addition to a Merovingian version in Charlemagne's own realm. This could cause difficulties. Moreover, the copying of texts led to many forms of corruption in them, from crude errors when scribes either had a deficient knowledge of Latin or Greek to learned alterations when they thought they knew better and altered the text deliberately. Beautiful though the Book of Kells may be, it has many errors in the actual text.

In his revival of the arts (known as the Carolingian renaissance), the Emperor Charlemagne set up a school at the abbey of St Martin in Tours. As its abbot he appointed Alcuin (*c.*740–804), who came from Northumberland and had been educated at the cathedral school of York. As well as obtaining texts from the most authentic sources, the libraries of Rome and Monte Cassino, and revising the text of the Latin Bible, the Vulgate, and the liturgical books of the church (it is to his work that we owe much of our knowledge of the classics), Alcuin presided over what he called a 'crowd of scribes' who developed the style known as Carolingian minuscule. This standardized writing practices: there were rules for the writing of each letter and how the pen was to be held. Uncials were incorporated at the head of texts and for chapter headings.

Faced with the competition from minuscules, uncial manuscripts gradually disappeared. An elegant form was used for special presentation volumes to high dignitaries; uncials were also retained for liturgical books, especially lectionaries, which had to be read in badly-lit churches. However, the style did not last beyond the twelfth century.

Illuminated books

The codex was admirably suited for illustration, since the space available was much increased and at the same time concentrated. In rolls illustrations were added haphazardly; the codex offered the opportunity for a full-page illustration. No illustrated rolls have survived and very few early illustrated codexes – none of Christian works; extant examples of these begin in the sixth century CE. Illustration itself, however, goes back at least to ancient Egypt, particularly the Egyptian Book of the Dead, extant examples of which date from the second millennium BCE.

Byzantium

An impressive Byzantine form of book was the 'purple codex' written in letters of gold and silver on purple vellum leaves. Three instances of this are the Rossano Gospels, with the illustrations gathered together at the front; the Rabbula Codex, a Syriac Gospel book containing probably the earliest manuscript depiction of the crucifixion; and the Vienna Genesis. In the West, notably Celtic Ireland and Northumbria, illustration drew on a range of pagan ornamentation, including interlacing designs and spiral patterns; there are also birds, beasts and fishes, but few

St Mark with his symbol, the lion, from the Lindisfarne Gospels

animals. These appear in the Lindisfarne Gospels, dating from the end of the seventh century, and the Book of Kells, dating from the end of the eighth. This tradition introduced the decorated initial, unknown in classical antiquity, but capable of being put to creative use on the book page.

Here again the age of Charlemagne is a landmark, and from then on the illumination (the wider term denotes decoration as well as illustration) of manuscripts developed steadily. Carolingian illumination fused the Eastern and Western styles in a brilliant way. The Godescalc Evangeliary (*c.*781), with the fountain of life in the form of a baptistery surrounded by birds and a stag, is a very early example, which actually antedates Charlemagne. Another fine example is the Utrecht Psalter of 830, in which the psalms are illustrated by expressive line drawings. The Stuttgart Psalter from the same period takes symbolic images from each psalm and by typology relates them to the New Testament. One book that particularly lent itself to illustration in the Middle Ages was the Revelation of John, the Apocalypse, an early example of which is the Bamberg Apocalypse (*c.*1010) made for Emperor Otto II.

Carolingian and Ottonian illumination evolved into

Romanesque, and in this France and England were particularly influential. Winchester became a centre of art, and it was here that the Benedictional of St Ethelwold was produced towards the end of the tenth century. But the Winchester Bible, produced between 1150 and 1180 and never completed, is the masterpiece of the school, standing alongside the St Albans Psalter as the best of English illuminated work.

In the Gothic period illumination followed contemporary style in architecture and culture, as is evident from the Psalter of St Louis, produced soon after the building of the Sainte-Chapelle in Paris in the middle of the thirteenth century. A contemporary English example of Gothic illumination is the Evesham Psalter, the first in a long series.

This period also saw the origin of the Book of Hours. This was a medieval book of devotion which contained prayers in honour of the Virgin Mary to be said at the canonical hours. Small, and lavishly illustrated and decorated, these books were prized by the wealthy, who commissioned them to their taste. The most magnificent is the *Tres Riches Heures* of the Duc de Berry; it contains illustrations not only of biblical scenes and lives of the saints but also of the duke's palatial residences.

If the Book of Hours was the prerogative of the rich, the poor were not forgotten. *Biblia pauperum* ('the Bible of the Poor') is the term used to describe illustrated books used for basic instruction in Christianity. Each page contained groups of biblical figures from the Old Testament and the New Testament, interpreted by means of typology as type and antitype, along with short Bible texts and verses to help in memorizing them. They appeared particularly in Austria and Germany in the fourteenth and fifteenth centuries and took the form of 'block books', i.e. each page consisted of a wooden block on which the illustration and lettering had been cut by hand.

Liturgical books

In addition to the Bible the main books of the Middle Ages, many of which were illuminated, were liturgical books. They existed in a complicated variety.

The missal. The missal (from the Latin *missa*, 'mass') developed between the tenth and thirteenth centuries. It was formed by the combination of a series of originally independent books used by the various people involved in celebrating the mass. These were:

The *sacramentary*: This was a book for the celebrant at the eucharist, who is presumed to be a bishop. It contained all and only the prayers that he said, namely the collects, the prefaces and the canons of the mass, and also the prayers he used at ordinations, consecrations, blessings and exorcisms. There are three famous sacramentaries. The early seventh-century Leonine Sacramentary is the earliest surviving book of prayers according to the Roman rite. It is not strictly a sacramentary, as it does not contain the canon of the mass but only the variable parts of the liturgy and is made up of a series of independent booklets. The eighth-century Gelasian Sacramentary contains texts for the whole year beginning with the vigil of Christmas and the canon of the Roman mass in almost its traditional form. A copy of the Gregorian Sacramentary was sent by Pope Hadrian I to Charlemagne as a basis for liturgical reform (it is known as the Hadrianum).

The *lectionary*: This contained only the epistles and gospels to be read at each feast. When the gospel readings were extracted and put in a separate book it is known as an *evangeliary*; the collection of epistles is known as the *epistolary*.

The *antiphonal*: This contained antiphons for both the mass and the daily offices. Over time, those used in the mass were put separately in a book called the *gradual*. Mary

The *ordo*: This gave the directions for the performance of the liturgy.

The *liber pontificalis* contained rites performed only by the bishop, like ordination and the consecration of churches.

There are also many copies of medieval *processionals*, following the usages for processions in various places. *Benedictionals* contained blessings.

The breviary. The breviary likewise arose out of the books used in the recitation of the daily office of the church. p. 1197 'Breviary' is short for the Latin *Breviarium sive ordo officiorum per totam anno decursionem* ('Short compendium or order for the offices of the whole year'). It developed in the eleventh century to bring together what were originally independent volumes, e.g. the psaltery containing the psalms and the lectionary containing the readings.

Penitential books contained directions for confessors, Forgiveness listing sins and the penances for them. They originated in the Celtic church in the sixth century.

Printed books

With the invention of printing in the fifteenth century the possibilities of disseminating Christianity through books became endless. At the same time the role of *the* book, the Bible, began to change significantly, with the sixteenth-century Reformation and its aftermath. Indeed Reformation it can be argued that the Reformation spread as widely and as strongly as it did above all because of the invention of printing, and that such a movement would have been impossible previously.

With the Reformation, in Protestant churches the Furnishings lectern with the Bible on it and the pulpit took over the prominent place formerly occupied by the altar. But as Bibles came to be more and more widely available the Bible became independent of any building or community and indeed in due course could be bought at a bookseller like any other book. Moreover, the mere distribution of Bibles was seen as a way of evangelization. The Gideon Bible found in virtually every hotel bedroom in the Western world is one indication of this. The Bible as a book became an object of symbolic importance: the form almost became more important than the content. The wry Mission comment of those experiencing Christian mission in the colonies is telling: 'At first we had the land and the white man has the Bible. Now we have the Bible and the white man has the land.'

Biblical criticism How the Bible came to be interpreted, and subjected to criticism, in these new conditions, is another story; here it is worth noting how the development led to yet more books. The Bible needed to be explained, and so a flood of commentaries, concordances listing the words of the Bible, dictionaries, biblical homilies and the like began and has never stopped growing.

Printing also saw the spread of other Christian books that had an influence far beyond Christianity. The 1662 Book of Common Prayer has made an enormous contribution to the English language and culture as a whole, Hymns and *Hymns Ancient and Modern*, which first appeared in 1860, spread the length and breadth of the British empire.  John Foxe's *Book of Martyrs* (1563) and John Bunyan's Literature *Pilgrim's Progress* (1682) were also prominent, and books of sermons were for long among the best-sellers of the book trade. But here the history of books becomes the Publishing history of publishing and the history of literature.

Of course the production of beautiful books did not Reformed churches end with the beginning of printing. On the contrary, new masterpieces were created. One of the earliest was Albrecht Dürer's *Apocalypse* published in 1498, with 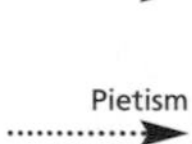 Pietism Anabaptists fifteen full-page woodcuts; he also illustrated two accounts of the passion of Christ and a life of the Virgin Mary. The invention of colour printing in the 1830s opened up vast new possibilities, taken advantage of at a very early stage  by William Blake. Against his visionary images can be set the first colour gift books of the 1840s, containing biblical Organization  texts in a Gothic font and richly decorated with motifs from illuminated medieval manuscripts. The twentieth century saw a wide variety of beautiful books, from Georges Rouault's colour aquatints for a *Passion* by André Church  Suarès to the striking black and white prints of Eric Gill.

More generally, over the past two centuries the sheer volume of inexpensive books has become all but impossible to cope with. If a book is what is defined by UNESCO as 'a non-periodical printed publication of at least 49 pages excluding covers', the pamphlets and tracts which also appeared in vast numbers in the nineteenth century do not count as books; however, the twentieth-century newcomers, the mass-market paperbacks, certainly do, and Christianity is extremely well represented in this format. Indeed, in an age of radio, television, CDs, DVDs and the internet, books of every kind are still vital to Christian thought and life.

JOHN BOWDEN

📖 P. R. Ackroyd and C. F. Evans (eds), *The Cambridge History of the Bible, Vol. 1, From the Beginnings to Jerome*, Cambridge: CUP 1970; G. W. H. Lampe (ed), *The Cambridge History of the Bible, Vol. 2, The West from the Fathers to the Reformation*, Cambridge: CUP 1976; Nicolete Gray, *A History of Lettering*, London: Phaidon Press 1986; John Harthan, *The History of the Illustrated Book: The Western Tradition*, London: Thames & Hudson 1981; Otto Pächt, *Book Illumination in the Middle Ages*, London: Harvey Miller Publishers 1986

Brethren

The Brethren movement began in August 1708 near Schwarzenau, Germany. Five men and three women, all religious refugees, most under 30 years of age, made a covenant of 'good conscience with God, to take up all the commandments of Jesus Christ as an easy yoke, and thus to follow the Lord Jesus ... even unto a blessed end'. They then descended into the river Eder to be baptized by immersion. One of them, chosen by lot, baptized Alexander Mack, who became their leader and first minister. Mack then baptized the rest.

These eight were mostly of Reformed Church background, although very much influenced by the radical separatist wing of seventeenth-century German Pietism and by the descendants of the sixteenth-century Anabaptists. Pivotal to their formation as a separate religious community was their decision to embrace what they considered the 'outward yet sacred' ordinances of the apostolic church as recorded in the New Testament. With this decision, they parted company from their radical Pietist associates who rejected church organization altogether in favour of a more spiritualized understanding of baptism, communion and church.

From the beginning, the Brethren embodied a high doctrine of the church as an intimate fellowship of believers whose life together is a means of grace. Collective study of the Bible to determine its meaning for their lives was paramount. No church hierarchy or called-out ministry was vested with the power to interpret scripture for the faith community; rather, the body as a whole – with each voice contributing – was seen as the recipient of the Holy Spirit's illumination. The body also had authority to discipline errant members, call members to the ministry, settle disputes within the fellowship, and conduct church business. Creeds, liturgies, hierarchies and buildings were considered inessential to the church. Instead, the church was realized in worship, fellowship and work, as members collectively sought the mind of Christ, strove for obedience, and dedicated themselves to 'the glory of God and their neighbour's good'.

In their efforts to be obedient, the Brethren emphasized adherence to the teachings of Jesus and the life of the early Christian communities. Their study of scripture led them to adopt immersion baptism of adult believers by a forward motion; a threefold love feast patterned after Christ's last supper (consisting of footwashing, a common meal, and the bread and cup); greeting members with a holy kiss; anointing for healing; non-resistance in general, including non-participation in war; non-conformity to worldly norms deemed incompatible with the life of the awakened Christian; and the judicious exercise of church discipline (the ban) against members who strayed from church teachings.

By 1735, nearly the entire European membership of the Brethren had transplanted itself to eastern Pennsylvania, following the migration path blazed by other German sectarians. Eighteenth-century growth was slow, but steady: at the end of the century there was a total fellowship of about 5000, including members and their families.

Though they laboured to preserve the unity of their small fellowship, Brethren struggled early on over theological and practical differences and questions of church discipline and authority. A notable early exodus of members was led by Johann Conrad Beissel, who believed that the Brethren placed too great an emphasis upon scripture as opposed to divine revelation. Shortly after his break from the Brethren in 1728, Beissel established a monastic community of celibate Pietists called Ephrata, which observed the seventh-day sabbath, certain dietary restrictions (including the avoidance of pork), and an austere asceticism coupled with a Christ-mysticism focusing upon divine love and spiritual marriage with Christ. Several Brethren ministers, and even two sons of Alexander Mack, joined Beissel's community for a time, yet by mid-century the threat to the survival of the Brethren had largely subsided. Today, the restored buildings of the Ephrata community have been transformed into a state historical monument by the Commonwealth of Pennsylvania.

Holy Spirit

A controversial Pietist teaching embraced by the Ephrata community as well as many of the early Brethren (including Alexander Mack) was the doctrine of universal restoration – that all souls would eventually be restored to God after a period of severe punishment. Brethren were careful to distinguish their belief from Universalism, which rejected punishment during the afterlife. Some Brethren ministers continued to embrace universal restoration up to the end of the nineteenth century, but were encouraged to keep the teaching private, lest it be misunderstood as Universalism by outsiders. Despite this attempt at a doctrinal distinction, some Brethren ministers and congregations joined the Universalist movement in the United States, and former Brethren became pioneers of Universalism throughout the southern United States.

Jesus

Eucharist
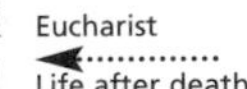
Life after death

Unitarians

Discipline
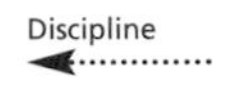

The nineteenth century was a time of rapid numeric growth and geographic expansion for the Brethren. By 1880 the church had grown to nearly 60,000 members. This rate of growth was sustained with little church organization, and led by an unsalaried ministry lacking in higher education and formal theological training. Beyond the local congregation, which was closely connected to, and overseen in part by, neighbouring congregations, the Brethren had only their Annual Meeting that had emerged during the previous century as a mechanism for preserving unity and resolving differences. Its decisions were rendered

PLYMOUTH BRETHREN

The Plymouth Brethren arose out of a Christian community formed in Britain in 1830, whose members sought to return to the simplicity of the earliest days of Christianity and to break down divisions among Christians. Numbers grew, and an influential teacher emerged in the form of a Church of Ireland minister, John Darby. Darby also founded groups elsewhere in the British Isles and on the continent of Europe. Plymouth Brethren had no organized ministry, but met every Sunday to break bread in a communion service. Their outlook was conservative and firmly biblical, and early members had a keen sense that the second coming of Jesus was near.

Despite their concern for unity, from the start the Plymouth Brethren showed a tendency towards division, and in 1849 'Exclusive Brethren', those who followed the strict views of Darby, split off from the mainstream movement, who came to be known as 'Open Brethren'; there were then further divisions among both groups over matters of principle. The movement went into decline in the second half of the twentieth century, though its members are still widespread in the British Isles, Europe and the United States. They are also involved in missionary work. Members have exercised an influence out of proportion to their numbers.

by the unanimous consent of all church members in attendance. By the mid-nineteenth century, however, when members were many and scattered, preserving unity proved difficult. As questions about appropriate practice and procedure multiplied, Annual Meeting responded by formalizing practices that had once been more flexible. Baptismal requirements, dress and discipline were all laid down specifically in an 'order of the Brethren'; that drew a clear boundary between Brethren, who were viewed as spiritual brothers and sisters, and outsiders, who were often considered 'nominal Christians', meaning Christian in name only.

Dress

Controversy over an increasingly exacting 'order' resulted in a three-way division during the early 1880s. One group of self-consciously 'progressive' Brethren interested in more aggressive evangelism (powered by innovations such as Sunday schools and revival meetings), and in less Annual Meeting control over the activities of individuals, formed the Brethren Church. This group itself experienced a split over fundamentalism/modernism during the 1930s, resulting in the formation of the Fellowship of Grace Brethren Churches. A second group retained the name German Baptist Brethren and hoped to steer a middle course that relied upon Annual Meeting to preserve distinctive Brethren practices while permitting innovation, particularly in the area of missionary outreach and evangelism. A third group, taking the name Old German Baptist Brethren and understanding itself to be preserving the 'ancient and primitive order' of the church, took a strong stand against religious innovations imported from outside groups and in favour of preserving distinctive practices such as plain dress, avoidance of musical instruments, plain meeting-houses for worship, and avoidance of various outside organizations.

Peace churches

Fundamentalism

After considerable debate, much of it focusing upon the desirability of the name 'Dunker', which had been loosely applied to the Brethren for generations, the middle group of German Baptist Brethren voted to adopt the name 'Church of the Brethren' in 1908. The name-change, however, was only the tip of the iceberg for a church whose identity was rapidly moving from an emphasis upon religious peculiarity to a self-conception of the Brethren as part of the Protestant mainstream of American society. By the 1930s, the Church of the Brethren had endorsed seminary level education, the salaried ministry, Sunday schools, participation in national elections, the construction of church buildings that were indistinguishable from other Protestant groups, musical instruments, a foreign missionary structure and countless other innovations. The practice of church discipline for violating church rulings was rapidly fading, as was 'plainness' as a symbol of religious distinction. Since the late nineteenth century, Brethren had established several post-secondary schools, the largest of which were thriving. These and other Brethren initiatives were overseen by a handful of permanent boards that were evolving into a permanent national organization. By 1930, Annual Meeting decisions were made by a delegate assembly that voted on and monitored ongoing programmes, most of them devoted to evangelism, missionary outreach, relief efforts and Christian education.

As Brethren moved into the American cultural and religious mainstream, even the old insistence upon avoiding military participation became ambiguous. Church guidance to young, male members during World War I was vague and conflicting, resulting in a variety of positions on military service. And even though Brethren clearly understood theirs as a 'peace church', Annual Meeting embraced a nuanced position during World War II that, while declaring all war to be sin, granted to individual members the freedom of conscience to make their own decisions about levels of involvement. As a result, the majority of Brethren during World War II opted for full military service. Even so, the Church of the Brethren in the twenty-first century continues to take strong stands in Annual Conference (Meeting) against military actions, military participation by its members, and violence in human relations generally.

The proliferation of home missions through local congregational outreach had by the early twentieth century developed into a full-scale foreign missionary movement that established Brethren missions in India, China, Nigeria and Ecuador, among other locations. From 1890 until World War II, such missions clearly constituted the focal point of Brethren programmes and activities. In 1955, a new foreign mission policy refocused mission from 'parenting' to 'indigenization' and thereby initiated a new era in mission, one of transferring control and pulling back from large-scale involvement. In 1978 a Latin American mission strategy, *mision mutua en las Americas*, emphasized the ecumenical stress on solidarity with the poor and on mutuality in mission. By the year 2000, the *Ekklesiyar 'Yan'uwa a Nigeria* (EYN, or Church of the Brethren in Nigeria) had more in attendance at weekly worship than the American Church of the Brethren, even though it is organizationally autonomous.

After World War II, at the time that funding and energy for foreign missions was waning, Brethren Service work of many varieties galvanized the outreach energies of the Brethren. In the wake of the Spanish Civil War, the Brethren Service Committee launched Heifer Project, which became an important, independent non-profit organization. Brethren were instrumental in the creation of CROP (Christian Rural Overseas Program), which was officially sponsored by Church World Service in 1947, opening its first office at the Brethren's Bethany Biblical

Seminary in Chicago. Brethren Volunteer Service became intensely involved in European reconstruction efforts after World War II, later establishing volunteer service projects around the world.

The Brethren, in the form of the Church of the Brethren, have been involved ecumenically, joining the World Council of Churches in 1948 and the US Federal Council of Churches (now the National Council of the Churches of Christ in the USA).

Membership of the Church of the Brethren has declined significantly over the last 40 years, to 136,000 in 2000. The membership is also aging, the median age being in the mid-fifties. Of the groups tracing their lineage to the Schwarzenau Brethren of 1708, the Fellowship of Grace Brethren churches, experienced the greatest growth during the last quarter of the twentieth century. The Old Order Brethren – Old German Baptist Brethren – maintain a thriving but small fellowship of less than 10,000 members who continue to dress in plain clothes, practise church discipline and hold Annual Meetings under a large tent, in much the same form as the Annual Meetings of the mid-nineteenth century. A number of smaller Old Order groups exist that have broken away from the Old German Baptist Brethren for a variety of reasons.

CARL D. BOWMAN AND MELANIE MAY

Carl F. Bowman, *Brethren Society: The Cultural Transformation of a 'Peculiar People'*, Baltimore: Johns Hopkins University Press 1995; Donald F. Durnbaugh, *Fruit of the Vine: A History of the Brethren, 1708–1995*, Elgin, IL: Brethren Press 1997; Donald B. Kraybill and Carl F. Bowman, *On the Backroad to Heaven: Old Order Hutterites, Mennonites, Amish, and Brethren*, Baltimore: Johns Hopkins University Press 2001; Dale R. Stoffer, *Background and Development of Brethren Doctrines, 1650–1987*, Philadelphia: Brethren Encyclopedia, Inc 1989

Buddhism and Christianity

In May 1969, Tissa Balasuriya, OMI, a Sri Lankan Roman Catholic priest, through the press publicly called on Christians to recognize that the Christian treatment of Buddhism in Sri Lanka had been wrong. He urged appreciation of Buddhism, and presented the Buddha as a man of deep spirituality. A barrage of correspondence followed, not all of which was positive. Many Buddhists, for instance, distrusted the call for brotherhood between Buddhists and Christians, fearing that it was a proselytizing strategy. One wrote, 'The kiss of the Vatican is the kiss of death. Let us Buddhists guard against these subtle moves by the Catholic Church.'

This correspondence was rooted in the legacy of Europe's global, imperial domination, when Christian missionaries, with a few honourable exceptions, condemned Buddhism as nihilistic and ethically impotent, a hell-risking dead end. The immediate consequence of this in Sri Lanka was a vigorous Buddhist revival motivated by antagonism towards Christianity. The reaction to Balasuriya revealed how easily mistrust could come to the surface, decades after the colonial era, mistrust even of those seeking better interfaith relationships.

Mission

Ecumenical movement

Christianity's relationship with Buddhism is long and it is marked by both conflict and rapprochement. And each context of encounter – Japan, China, Thailand, Tibet, Burma, Sri Lanka, the West – has been and continues to be different. There has been no one form of Buddhism for Christians to encounter, and there has been no unified Christian response. The nihilistic missionary construction of Buddhism in the eighteenth and nineteenth centuries, even in its own time, lay side by side with more positive Christian approaches. For instance Robert Childers (1838–76), a committed Christian, compiled with great empathy the first authoritative Pali-English dictionary to be published in the West. Today, a combination of postmodernist spiritual quests, interfaith dialogue and in-depth encounter has brought greater understanding, but the negative continues, taking its very fuel from the fact that rapprochement exists.

One of the earliest Christian recognitions of Buddhism comes with Clement of Alexandria (*c.*150–*c.*215), who wrote: 'Among the Indians some follow the instructions of the Buddha, whom they have honoured as a god because of his unusual holiness.' It is not impossible that there were Buddhists in Alexandria at this time. In north-west India, in the first centuries CE, Christian and Buddhist communities may also have been in contact. It is possible in fact that some aspects of Christian monasticism originally came from Buddhism. It is difficult now, however, to trace just how much encounter there was in these early centuries. Some authors have argued that some Gospel narratives have Buddhist origins, in a strand of speculation that began in the nineteenth century and still continues. What we can be certain of is that there was Christian-Buddhist encounter both in north-west India and along the Silk Route in the early centuries of Christianity. And in China, in the seventh and eighth centuries CE, significant encounter took place between Persians and Christians of the Syriac Church, often called Nestorians. By the medieval period a corrupted version of the Buddha biography had actually entered the Christian calendar in the form of St Josaphat (or Joasaph), a figure characterized by asceticism and awareness of suffering. But there is all too little concrete evidence of this interaction. Certainly, there was little 'memory', even in China,

Monasticism

to inform the era of European expansionism when the two religions again met.

China can again be taken as an example of encounter in this later context. Jesuit missionaries arrived there in 1583. For the first twelve years of their activities, they wore the cloaks of Buddhist monks and lived inside or alongside Buddhist monasteries. They found that the statue of Mary, Mother of God, was honoured by lay Chinese Buddhists as an image of the *bodhisattva*, Kwan Yin. It would be true to say that Buddhists in China at first saw the newcomers as living a form of Buddhism. But this absorptionist co-existence did not last. For the Jesuits began to point out the differences between Christianity and Chinese Buddhism. Controversy, leading at times to persecution, then gradually gained the upper hand.

Mary

Spirituality

Persecution

In South Asia also, Jesuits encountered Buddhism at this time. How to deal with both similarity and difference was again the issue. The solution of De Queyroz, chronicler of the Jesuits in Sri Lanka, was to attribute similarity either to ancient Jewish or Christian influence, or to the devil. 'The fact is,' he wrote, 'the devil has forestalled everything ... if we preach to those of further India and of Ceylon (for this sect has disappeared from many parts of India wherein it began) they reply that their Buddum or their Fo or their Xaka also took the shape of a man, though he was an eternal being ...'

Jesus

The Portuguese were followed into Asia by other imperial powers: the Dutch, the French and the British. The nineteenth century was key to the relationship between Christianity and Buddhism. Textual material was gathered by Europeans in Asia such as Rasmus Rask (Denmark), Alexander Csomo de Koros (Hungary) and Brian Houghton Hodgson (Britain) and fed into the curriculum of European universities. Eugene Burnouf was one of the first in Europe to collate this research, but missionaries and civil servants on the ground in Burma and Sri Lanka – Francis Buchanan, Benjamin Clough, Daniel Gogerly – preceded him. From the world of the academic, Buddhism then entered the popular. Edwin Arnold's 1879 poem, 'The Light of Asia', which presented the Buddha as compassionate hero, warm, sensitive, wise, was pivotal. It drew a generation of people towards the East, and laid the ground for the first converts to Buddhism. Novels that played with themes such as rebirth followed.

By the end of the nineteenth century the picture was complex. Most Christian missionaries in Asia, while insisting that respect and courtesy should govern Buddhist-Christian relationships, maintained a negative view of Buddhist doctrine and practice. The non-theism of Buddhism was presented as nihilistic and belief in rebirth as absurd. *Nibbana* (or *Nirvana*), the blissful goal of the Buddhist life, was wrongly interpreted as annihilation, and the exorcist ceremonies in popular Buddhism were condemned as devil worship. Others, however, were stressing what Christians could learn from Buddhism. Yet others again were turning away from Christianity to embrace Buddhism.

The twentieth century not only brought dialogue on to the Christian-Buddhist agenda, but also the practice of 'passing over' to come back and what can only be called hyphenated religious identity. By the 1960s, Christians in several Asian countries were reaching out towards Buddhism for genuine dialogue on the level of spirituality. In Japan, H. M. Enomiya Lassalle and J. Kachiri Kadowaki, Jesuits, were discovering that Zen meditation could contribute positively to Christian spirituality. In Sri Lanka, a pioneering group of young priests, Anglican, Protestant and Roman Catholic, were attempting to redress the distrust that the colonial era had generated: Lynn de Silva (Methodist), Yohan Devananda (Anglican), Aloysius Pieris (Catholic) and Michael Rodrigo (Catholic). De Silva called for an informed debate between Buddhists and Christians. Devananda established a Christian ashram, a place of retreat, which drew on Buddhist forms of spirituality; it eventually became an interfaith community with a strong emphasis on action for social justice. Pieris called on Christians to be 'baptized' in the waters of Asian spirituality as Jesus was baptized in the Jordan by John, and set up a centre for inter-religious encounter. Rodrigo, towards the end of his life, went to live in an entirely Buddhist village to engage in a dialogue of life. At the same time some Buddhists were actively engaging with Christians, for example the founders of the Network of Socially Engaged Buddhists, Thich Nhat Hanh from Vietnam and Sulak Sivaraksa from Thailand.

Within the field of inter-monastic dialogue, Thomas Merton, Trappist monk (1915–68), was a pioneer in his call for an international, inter-religious monastic, spiritual encounter. He died tragically on the second day of a meeting in Bangkok of L'Aide à l'implantation monastique (AIM – Inter-Monastic Aid). But AIM took forward his vision. In 1973, a meeting that it convened of Christian and non-Christian monks resulted in a series of East-West spiritual exchanges, mainly between Zen and Christian monastics. In 1978, the first two committees for monastic interfaith dialogue were formed in North America and Paris. Both still continue, with a wide range of activities and regular news bulletins. There is no doubt that both Christians and Buddhists have benefited and continue to benefit from this dialogue of silences, disciplines and devotion.

One important form of Christian-Buddhist encounter emerged through the Kyoto School of Japanese Buddhism. Founded by Nishida Kitaro, it sought to relate the concept of 'emptiness' in Zen Buddhism with Western philosophical ideas concerning self-awareness. Deliverance and elf-awareness, Kitaro argued, in the early years of the wentieth century, could be found at the point of absolute othingness where non-duality ceased. Christianity's early lialogue with Buddhism in the United States was much nfluenced by this. In 1980, the University of Hawaii tarted an East-West Project, and this gave rise to international Buddhist-Christian conferences. At the second, n 1984, what was known as the Cobb-Abe Group was ormed. John Cobb was a Protestant theologian and Maseo Abe a Buddhist of the Kyoto School. The 1987 conference, n turn, gave birth to the Society of Buddhist-Christian studies. And in 1997 a parallel organization, the European Network of Buddhist-Christian Studies, came into being. Both these bodies have moved much wider than the Kyoto School in their dialogue. Both attempt to combine the academic with practice. Meditation sessions, for instance, are held each day at the conferences of the European Network.

In the present, few Christians, once they have encountered Buddhism, remain untouched by it. In many ways, Buddhism is radically different from Christianity. Buddhists, for instance, do not look towards a creator God. Buddhas, enlightened beings who have seen into the truth of existence, are teachers of gods and humans. But the touching points between the two religions are numerous. Buddhism, as Christianity, is aware that something is wrong with our world. Whereas Christians might speak of alienation from God, Buddhists locate the cause in the patterns of selfish craving within the human mind and heart. The way out, Buddhists would say, is through destroying our greeds, hatreds and illusions through meditation, and the development of loving kindness and compassion. It is through emptying ourselves of the 'I' concept and the belief that we are separate from everything else in the universe. 'Just as a mother would protect her only child at the risk of her own life, even so cultivate a boundless heart of loving kindness towards all beings,' reads one ancient Buddhist verse. 'Hatred is never appeased by hatred in this world; by non-hatred alone is hatred appeased. This is an eternal law,' reads another. For at the heart of Buddhism lie the twin concepts of wisdom and compassion: a wisdom that can see into Truth; a compassion that can reach out to all beings in the cosmos.

Some Christians have found that their encounter with Buddhism has turned them towards Christian contemplative and mystical traditions. It is not unknown for a Christian monastic vocation to be found through contact with the deep spirituality of Buddhist monastic life. Others have found such help in Buddhist meditation practices that they have brought them into their own spiritual life, some preferring to be called Christian-Buddhist. And in countries such as Sri Lanka, Thailand and Cambodia Christians and Buddhists have found greater strength to work for social change through co-operation. Globally, Christian-Buddhist encounter is still in its infancy. It is an exciting encounter, one that has much to give to the wider inter-religious movement, and to human spiritual development.

ELIZABETH J. HARRIS

Kenneth Fleming, *Asian Christian Theologians in Dialogue with Buddhism*, Frankfurt am Main, etc.: Peter Lang 2002; Rita M. Gross and Terry C. Muck (eds), *Buddhists Talk about Jesus, Christians Talk about the Buddha*, New York and London: Continuum 2000; Thich Nhat Hanh and Daniel Berrigan, *The Raft is Not the Shore: Conversations Toward a Buddhist-Christian Awareness* (1975), Maryknoll, NY: Orbis 2001; Elizabeth J. Harris, *What Buddhists Believe*, Oxford: Oneworld 1998; Whalen Lai and Michael von Bruck, *Christianity and Buddhism: A Multi-Cultural History of Their Dialogue*, Maryknoll, NY: Orbis 2001; Aloysius Pieris, SJ, *Love meets Wisdom: A Christian Experience of Buddhism*, Maryknoll, NY: Orbis 1988

God

Buildings

From earliest times Christians needed shelter in various forms for the different aspects of their community life, most especially for celebrating the sacraments. The breaking of bread together, from its institution at the Last Supper onwards, took place indoors, first in the 'upper room' and soon thereafter in one another's houses. Though the sacrament of baptism at first did not require a built environment, the early growth of Christianity was urban rather than rural, and in the crowded towns and cities this sacrament, too, moved indoors. In the early years, especially during times of persecution, it would have been desirable for the setting of worship, the sacraments and teaching to be inconspicuous. As was the case with other religions, spaces were probably rented in tenements or public buildings. According to the literary tradition, the houses of wealthier members of the Christian community were partially or wholly put at the disposal of the community, though this is impossible to identify archaeologically with any certainty.

Sacraments
Eucharist
Persecution

Buildings were thus 'borrowed' for the growing family of the church, the *ecclesia* (at this early period the word, which is Latin for 'assembly' – the Greek word is almost the same – always referred to the worshipping community, never the building). There could be no more appropriate building to borrow for this large spiritual family than a pre-existing large family house. Worship at this time also went on in the synagogue, and the apostles continued for a while to teach in the synagogues and the temple itself.

Church
Origins and background

Establishing the Western prototypes

Growing opposition from the Jewish authorities increased the importance of the house-churches. The buildings do not appear to have been given any special sanctity by the performance of religious rites in them, and there is no evidence of the existence of Christian religious art until the end of the second century. The oldest remains that are traditionally identified as house-churches are to be found in Rome under the so-called 'title churches' (*tituli*). These churches were first of all private houses in which Christians met, which had the name of the owner inscribed on a slab, Latin *titulus*, at the door, hence the name. However, subsequent changes and wholesale destruction have removed what would constitute archaeological proof. It has been speculated that Roman society was extremely conservative and that the public rooms of first- and second-century houses of the Roman nobility preserved the general layout of the ancient houses of the original Latin settlements of at least a millennium earlier.

Of course examples vary greatly, but schematically there was an entrance from the street into the vestibule and then into the *atrium*, which was a large pillared hall with a tank of water (*impluvium*) in the middle. The *atrium* was either open to the sky or lit by skylights. Continuing along the main axis there was a room called the *tablinum* which was generally up a step or two but entirely open to the *atrium*. The *tablinum* was a figure of the original family homestead, the *atrium* being a vestige of the open yard with 'farm outbuildings' in the rooms either side. The *tablinum* had lean-to structures either side separated by columns or low walls. At the entrance to the *tablinum* always stood a stone table. The *tablinum* housed the sacred fire and the household gods, and its side-rooms held the family trophies and memorials. Teachers of oratory saw the house as a 'storehouse of memories'.

This building type could hardly have suited the growing Christian family better, and in the arrangement we can readily see features of later church buildings: the nascent porch/narthex (for catechumens, those seeking baptism), the pillared nave with font for baptism (*atrium* with tank or *impluvium*), the *tablinum* as a raised chancel with altar (stone table or *cartibulum*), and the choir aisles (side-rooms or *alae*). Just as the whole patrician family would meet in these inter-related spaces presided over by the *paterfamilias*, head of the family, who sat in a large chair in the *tablinum*, so the bishop would preside over his growing Christian family at the liturgy (whether eucharist or agape). It was a large urban family in a large urban house.

Initiation ➤

The building with its particular arrangement of rooms was charged with meaning when the Roman patrician family gathered, and with an easy shift of religious context this meaning changed when it was used by the Christian family. In Rome alone there are some eighteen churches that by tradition originated as such house-churches handed over in whole or in part for the use of Christian communities. These include S. Clemente, said to have been the palace of Titus Flavius Clemens, who was executed in 96 for 'superstition', and his wife Domitilla, who was exiled. Doubts remain whether the 'superstition' for which the consul died was that he was a Christian, especially given that it is barely conceivable that such a high-ranking patrician should be a convert to this new religion from the East. The claim persists, however, and the remains of the building are still much in evidence under the present church. Other *tituli* include S. Cecilia in Trastevere, S. Martino in Monti, SS Giovanni e Paulo and S. Prisca Pudenziana. These were brought together as the parish churches of Rome. It had been the ideal that the whole community should gather in one place as the *ecclesia* to celebrate the eucharist under the bishop of the city, but in a great city like Rome this had become impossible and presbyters who were given charge of the title church would perform the eucharistic liturgy. For centuries in Rome, and as late as 1870, it was the practice to have representatives of all the clergy and laity of the 'titles' represented at the Pope's 'stational mass', from which a fragment of the consecrated bread would be sent to the title churches to be placed in the chalice at the local celebration. It was clearly difficult to maintain the direct link between a bishop and the whole of his *ecclesia* even before Christianity became a permitted religion.

What appear to have been house-churches are still to be seen in Rome, but they are not complete enough to indicate with any certainty how different rooms were used. If these are indeed the remains of house-churches, then confiscation of Christian property or the great success and expansion of the church led to wholesale modification and destruction of early arrangements. The most complete existing house-church was a chance discovery in the provincial garrison town of Dura Europos by the Euphrates in eastern Syria. The house is by the city wall and was probably converted for use as a church in the 230s or 240s. In 256 the city was destroyed by the Sassanids (Persians) and never inhabited again. The town contained numerous other cult buildings, including a temple to the god Mithras and a synagogue. The house-church had a large room about 65 feet by 60 feet, with a small dais. There was a baptistery with Old and New Testament scenes showing David and Goliath, Christ healing the paralytic, and Christ walking on water. The font itself had depictions of the Good Shepherd and Adam and Eve, so the use of the room is beyond doubt. A third room could have been used for the instruction of catechumens.

There are literary references to other pre-Constantinian churches, and some archaeological fragments have been

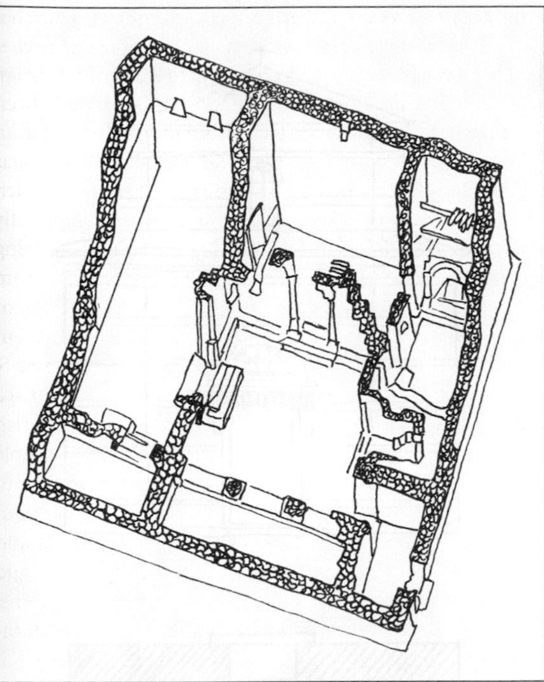

Dura Europos, house-church (the room for assembly is on the left, the baptistery back right)

roposed as possible candidates, but otherwise evidence s lacking for Christian buildings, except in the area of nemorial 'building', primarily in the form of catacombs. These have survived so well because the Romans recognized the sanctity of the body after death, even the bodies of executed criminals. The catacombs were constructed in ields made up of tufa, a soft volcanic stone that hardened after carving. 'Building' was a reductive, hollowing process where shelves were created in the walls of the labyrinthine unnels and galleries; bodies were laid on them and sealed n behind pottery slabs.

The buildings used and developed by the pre-Constantinian church reveal the self-understanding of the church as the family of God. The gathered *ecclesia* was the body of Christ, the bishop was the *paterfamilias*, and his chair was the symbol of his teaching, as the continuing embodiment of Christ in the world. The tremendous growth of the church was putting a strain both on this self-conception and on the buildings. Though the essential parts of a church and their disposition would in the main change little throughout the historical development of the built form, changes in context (historical, theological, political and geographical) would produce changes in self-understanding and consequently in the built form of the structures that housed and served the Christian community and its developing forms of worship. Other variations would be the result of the availability of building materials and technical and constructional expertise. A building was a common metaphor for the people of God; not surprisingly the buildings used by or developed for the *ecclesia* reveal much about what they thought this meant.

The prime example of the development of a new building type for the church in response to a radical shift in circumstances took place at the beginning of the fourth century. From the year 303 there was a particularly intense persecution under the Emperor Diocletian. It lasted until 306 in the West, and in 311 his successor Galerius issued a decree that allowed a degree of freedom of worship. Imperial power had been divided, and Constantius Chlorus was emperor in Gaul and Britain, where no one was martyred in his reign. On his death in July 306 his son Constantine was elected emperor by the army at York. He became locked in a struggle with Maxentius, who had meanwhile proclaimed himself emperor in Rome, for supreme power in the West. On his drive towards Rome before the decisive victory at the Milvian Bridge in 312 Constantine is said to have seen a vision of a symbol made up of the Greek letters *chi* and *rho*, called the labarum, and heard the words *In hoc signo vinces* ('In this sign you are victorious'). He was, and thereafter there was toleration; soon real privileges were accorded to Christians. Christianity was to become the state religion and the emperor supreme in all things temporal and spiritual, presiding at the Council of Nicaea in 325, and judging doctrinal disputes. In 330 he founded a new capital, Constantinople.

Constantine's 'conversion'

p. 1166

Council

p. 325

Full Christianization of the empire took some generations, but the forces were already at work. With persecution in the past and new imperial favour, congregations swelled. The old buildings became hopelessly inadequate and were radically rebuilt.

Perhaps as early as 313 Constantine may have given his old imperial palace of the Lateran to the Pope, whose role as *paterfamilias* of the Christian family in Rome was correspondingly edified (a not inappropriate word in this context). The rites and ceremonies of the church were becoming fixed and would now be considerably elaborated in line with the court ceremonial. A very grand church was built beside the palace, originally dedicated to Christ the Saviour (only much later rededicated to the two Johns). The great building was basilican, a secular form, previously used for commercial purposes or by the imperial administration as a law court. This new church was the cathedral of Rome, which the present building continues to be. Its capacity was greatly increased by the inclusion of double side aisles. The rounded apse for the bishop's throne was at the west end; the orientation of churches was not yet fixed but would be soon. The form of the basilica admitted a great deal of variation to suit

Papacy

local needs, and to some extent its ecclesiastical use would introduce elements from the Roman house-church, as at St Peter's in the Vatican, begun probably in 319. It was a five-aisled basilica, as at the Lateran, but it included a large colonnaded *atrium* or forecourt. The bishop's throne (which it might now appropriately be called) was in the apse, surrounded by his clergy behind the altar at the front edge (or 'chord') of the apse – all clearly reflecting the arrangement in the *tablinum* of the older house-churches. At St Peter's (and thereafter a fairly common

Martyr

arrangement) the tomb of the martyr (Greek *martys* = witness) was immediately beneath the altar; this is called a *confessio*, i.e. the tomb of one who has confessed the faith. The arrangement reflects the passage in the New Testament book of Revelation (6.9) which describes how 'when [the Lamb] opened the fifth seal, I saw under the altar the souls of those who had been slain because of the word of God and the testimony they had maintained'.

At this period shrines for martyrs and funerary basilicas were built in the cemeteries outside Rome. There are the basilicas connected to the round imperial mausolea, S. Constanza next to S. Agnese and the Tor Pignattara at SS Marcellino e Pietro; there are also the ambulatory basilicas of S. Lorenzo, S. Sebastiano and an unnamed building on the Via Prenestia, all built between about 320 and 380. When Christian martyrs were buried outside the walls of Rome, a martyrium or *cella memoriae* was often built to mark the spot, and a large hall would soon follow for agape ('love feast', associated with the eucharist) and funeral feasts on the anniversary of the martyrdom. The faithful would be buried nearby as at S. Sebastiano on the Via Appia. The martyrium as a form looks back to the Greek *heroön*, which was normally a small temple commemorating a hero and often sited over his tomb. Martyrs were the heroes of the faith, and their graves or places of martyrdom were likewise marked. Early martyria were located in Old St Peter's, St Paul's on the Ostian Way (marking his place of execution), and S. Agnese and S. Costanza (the tomb of Constantine's daughter). Constantine had martyria built in Palestine at the Church of the Nativity in Bethlehem (in 333) and the Holy Sepulchre (in 336). Both original churches had a martyrium, nave and atrium.

The form of baptisteries was closely related to that of martyria. In the baptismal act of witness the old Adam dies (a kind of martyrdom) and rises again in Christ. In the early church those who had not been baptized were not admitted to the eucharist, and baptism itself was administered in a separate space as at Dura Europos, so many of the earliest examples were completely separate from the church, as at S. Giovanni in Fonte beside the Lateran, reputed to be Constantinian, of 324, but perhaps a century later. Other baptisteries were octagonal (as in Ravenna at

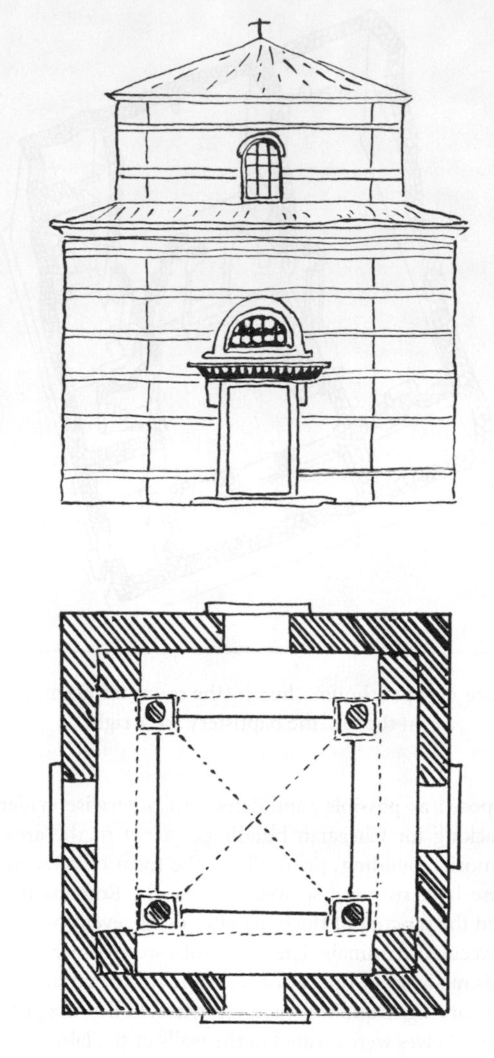

Building over the tomb of St John at Ephesus, elevation and ground plan

the baptisteries of the Orthodox and the Arians) or even cross-in-square; however, they were usually a centralized space because of the form of the rite. Subsidiary spaces were needed so that modesty could be preserved when candidates had to shed their old clothes and don a white robe. Baptism in this early period was of adults, and only much later when Christianity was at least nominally the religion of the whole populace did infant baptism become the norm, bringing the development of the font and its inclusion within the body of the church itself.

The interiors of the imperial foundations were

CATHEDRALS, CHAPELS AND CHURCHES

Abbey: An abbey was originally a complex of buildings in which monks lived, including a church; however, in many cases the only building left is the church, which is then itself called an abbey, as in Westminster Abbey.

Basilica: Strictly speaking, this is a technical term from architecture, denoting the earliest type of church building, modelled on Roman public halls. The basilica is rectangular with a long nave and usually side aisles; it has an apse at the east end. However, basilica is also used as the title of a church, as in the Basilica of St Francis in Assisi or the Basilica of St Thérèse in Lisieux.

Cathedral: The bishop's church, so-called because his *cathedra* (throne, or seat) is there. However, the cathedral is administered by its dean (or provost) and canons, who together form the chapter (so-called because at its meetings this body listened to a chapter from their rule). Cathedrals are the focal points of dioceses, which are named after the place where the cathedral is situated. A parish church used as a cathedral is called a pro-cathedral.

Chapel: The term chapel derives from the Latin *capella* (cloak), and was first used of the French *chapelles*, buildings which housed the pieces of the cloak which St Martin of Tours gave to a beggar, and by derivation other relics (the term chaplain comes from the name of the priest, *capellanus*, who looked after the chapel). Some of these chapels were masterpieces of architecture, like the Sainte Chapelle in Paris, built in 1248 by Louis IX. In England there are 'chapels royal', e.g. in the Tower of London, St James's Palace and Hampton Court. The church building within a school, college or hospital is also usually called a chapel. Chapel is also used in England of the buildings used for worship by Non-conformists, a practice widespread when chapels were differentiated from and contrasted with the Anglican parish churches. A chapel can also be an area within a church with a separate altar, in honour of a particular saint or the Virgin Mary (Lady Chapel).

Church: Church is the most widespread term used to describe the buildings in which Christians in a particular area worship. The term originally comes from the Greek adjective *kyriakon*, 'belonging to the Lord'. In countries where the church as an institution is established, the church is the focal point of a local area, the parish.

Minster: The term originally meant a monastic establishment, but as with the abbey, the monastery has disappeared and the term is applied to some cathedrals (York Minster) and large churches (Beverley Minster).

Oratory: Designated in Roman Catholic canon law a place for worship for the benefit of some community or assembly of the faithful; others may attend with permission. In this sense it differs from a church, which is for all. Oratories were founded by Philip Neri (1515–95), who also founded an order of Oratorians. Cardinal Newman founded the Birmingham Oratory in 1848 and the London Oratory (now the Brompton Oratory) in 1849.

Tabernacle: Some Baptist churches, non-denominational and other churches call the building in which they worship a tabernacle, after the portable sanctuary which the Israelites are said to have taken along with them in the wilderness.

breathtaking. Though pre-Constantinian Christianity is thought of as a religion of the poor, even the early house-churches were magnificently endowed with altar plate, as we know from records of confiscations. The interior of St Peter's itself, as described in the *Liber Pontificalis*, an early collection of the lives of popes, was lit by 32 silver hanging candelabra, a corona of lights before the apostle's tomb and four great silver candlesticks covered in scenes from the Acts of the Apostles. The shrine was of gold, the altar silver-gilt with hundreds of precious stones and surmounted by a solid gold cross. This became the norm for high-status churches. The embellishment of the building reinforced the already clear statements made by the imperial form and source of the structures: Providence had brought church and state together and 'the kingdom of this world will become the kingdom of our Lord and of his Christ' (Revelation 11.15). Christendom would become co-extensive with the empire. Christendom

The Eastern prototypes

Constantine gained complete control of both West and East by 324. In 330 he moved his capital to Constantinople, a new city founded in 325 on the site of the Greek city-state of Byzantium. There he built new churches, combining and adapting the remarkably flexible prototypes established in Rome. The destruction and fires of the riots of 532 directed against the Emperor Justinian destroyed most of the city, and today nothing but a few foundations from Constantine's time remain. Byzantium

The Church of Hagia Irene or Holy Peace was a Constantinian church, and nearby Constantius, Constantine's son, built the Hagia Sophia or Holy Wisdom

in 360. Hagia Sophia burned down in 404. Restored in 415, it was again badly damaged by the fires of the 532 riots. The domed basilica which arose on the site between 532 and 537 was to transform the desire for space and light into one of the most astonishing interiors the world had ever seen. The clear span of the vault was vastly bigger than anything in Rome. Unlike the Pantheon, it is not a dome resting on a cylindrical drum, but a shallow dome born aloft on billowing arched pendentives and semi-domes. It appears to be suspended like the vault of heaven. The impact on the contemporary worshipper would have been stunning. Not only had such an immense, seemingly unsupported structure never before been seen, but according to the contemporary chronicler Procopius the whole ceiling was overlaid with gold and the walls with polished marble. The interior glowed with richly coloured reflected and refracted light. It was an unforgettable sight and ever afterwards was the image to which church builders in the East returned. When Prince Vladimir of Kiev sent envoys, they reported that: 'We knew not whether we were in heaven or on earth ... we only know that God dwells there among men.' With that, the building type spread to vast new territories.

When built, Hagia Sophia was approached through an *atrium* into a porch, continuing on the axis into the nave. As with previous imperial churches, the liturgical furnishings were of the costliest materials – a golden altar inlaid with precious stones, a silver-plated screen in the front of the chancel, many lamps of gold, and an ivory pulpit inlaid with silver.

Many other large churches were rebuilt after the riots, including Hagia Irene nearby. This was another, though smaller-scale, domed basilica. Justinian completely rebuilt the capital, and his passion for building extended throughout the empire; sometimes the major furnishings and architectural elements were shipped complete from imperial workshops in the capital. Imperial churches arose as far away as the monastery of St Catherine on Sinai. This dates from between 548 and 565 and, since it served a stable and isolated monastic community, it is now the best preserved of all Justinian church interiors with its polished marble panels, semi-dome and mosaics (probably Justinian).

Icon
Monasticism
Heresy

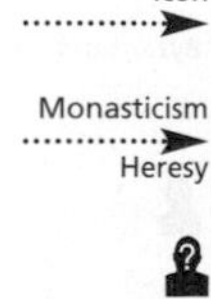

Under Justinian both the treatment of the interiors and the structure of the building emphasize order and unity, which were of primary importance to church and state: the one beset by doctrinal dispute and heresy, and the other by enemies within and without. In contrast to this the Roman basilica was essentially a sequential building, one spatial element opening into another with their hierarchical relationships parallel to the liturgical structure and the hierarchical structure of the Christian family. The domed basilica of the Eastern empire, especially as in the example

Interior of Hagia Sophia, Istanbul

of Hagia Sophia, remained suitable for processions, but the dome was a strong, not to say irresistible, centralizing force. Though Byzantine churches vary enormously according to local circumstances, centralized spaces are most common, especially versions of the Greek cross-in-square. From about the sixth century the main axis of the church was de-emphasized in worship when the Bible was carried in at the 'Little Entrance' and the eucharistic elements at the 'Great Entrance', in a procession which did not go along the central axis from the west but from side-chapels near the domed space. Around the same time it became common for the laity not to receive communion but simply to observe the liturgical action, so they no longer moved from east to west along the axis either. It was not until the fourteenth century in Russia that the iconostasis, the screen bearing icons, developed.

Other models of the Christian life gave rise to different building types, including the monastery. At the beginning of the fourth century the desert fathers lived solitary contemplative existences in isolated areas, but in 305 fame and followers prompted Antony of Egypt to organize his community of hermits in a series of small separate cells. Pachomius, who died in 346, founded the first community of men occupying communal buildings at Tabennisi, near Thebes in Egypt. More communities for men and for women followed under a rule, or way of life that he devised. Just over a century later, in 525, Benedict left his solitary cave at Subiaco and founded the great monastery at Monte Cassino in Italy under the rule that would become the norm for Western monasticism. The rule, the purpose of the order and the size of the community determined the arrangement of the buildings, but usually they were grouped about a cloister on the north side of the church, including a chapter house, refectory, infirmary and cells or a dormitory. As centres of education, learning and healing, and often in possession of large tracts of agricultural land, they flourished to the point that some became quite opulent, as at the magnificent and powerful abbey of Cluny. The Cistercians sought to reform monasticism, taking it back to its more austere roots, with a corresponding simplicity in its buildings. Though the Cistercian houses were all constitutionally separate, they were all built to a remarkably uniform plan, still to be seen at Fontenay near Montbard in France. The churches were barrel-vaulted and unornamented.

Mechanisms for change

Changes in the shape of a community, its sense of purpose, the balance of its activities, and its size, all play important parts both in the creation of prototypes and in the transformation of built form. These transformations lead to the development of new building types and the modification of the old. Building types are metaphors; they stand for the activities and communities they contain. When the activities and the communities change, the buildings must be made to respond to those changes – time is introduced into the 'matrix of meaning' that is the building. It truly becomes a 'house of memories' after the Roman pattern. It is because Christianity is a historical religion that memory and tradition are crucial to the maintenance of the faith. Churches of all kinds are built to house the central sacrament of the eucharist, which is a response to Jesus' command to 'do this in remembrance of me'.

Similarly, martyria and memorial chapels of all kinds keep the lives of the 'heroes of the faith' fresh for each generation. The built heritage of the church is a veritable matrix of memory. From the fifth century the cult of the saints became very strong; churches became reliquaries and relics became the object of pilgrimage. Buildings during the Romanesque period, i.e. around the eleventh century, had to cope with two new factors, display and crowd control. As at Old St Peter's, where the altar was above the grave of the martyr, relics were housed in or near altars, encouraging growing numbers of subsidiary altars in bigger churches. Large numbers of pilgrims had to be able to circulate round these subsidiary spaces so the basilica became greatly elaborated. The aisles of the basilica were wrapped round the apse as an ambulatory, often with radiating chapels as at St Sernin in Toulouse and Ste Foy at Conques, both pilgrimage churches on the route to Compostela. At Compostela itself the ambulatory wraps itself around three sides of the transepts, making a complete circuit of the church. There were also galleries at triforium level, and crypts as at Compostela and Canterbury, another major centre of pilgrimage.

These complex inter-related spaces required new complex inter-related vaulting. The complexity grew from the crossed barrel to the groined and, eventually during the Gothic period, the ribbed vault. The Gothic style emerged in Abbé Suger's rebuilding of the Abbey of St Denis near Paris between 1130 and 1144. His purpose in transforming the building was theological and historical. In his account of the rebuilding Suger expresses great admiration for the venerable fabric that he was pulling down to make way for his astonishing new work that was to integrate past and present. This heady mix would create a built form that would conquer the medieval world.

p. 792

The result astonished Suger's contemporaries. The structural system made greater height and light possible, allowing the mind of the observer to pass from the glories of the building to the splendour of the kingdom of God. The composite power of royal and religious history, transcendent theology and structural technology that made immense height and enormous windows possible overwhelmed the contemporary imagination and attracted powerful patronage. The style, with its immense potential for elaboration, spread far and quickly. Strictly speaking, all these considerations are architectural rather than of a building's functional form – their function is emblematic. They are concerned, however, with the use of the buildings and the nature and ends of the community that inhabits them. The arrangement, function and contents of a 'storehouse of memories' will always have to deal with the emblematic as well.

Patronage

As the historical tale unfolds, it becomes increasingly difficult to confine considerations to 'building' as opposed to 'architecture'. The Renaissance conception of man as the measure of all things meant that human scale and proportional systems played a very particular role in design during the period. The stylistic references shifted to the classical, and unity and coherence were of paramount importance, partly no doubt in response to schisms in the church as a result of the Reformation. The cool rationality of classicism gave way to the Counter-Reformation's exhibition of power and display. Movement, dynamism, exuberance, the Baroque, capture the drive of the moment.

Architecture
Renaissance

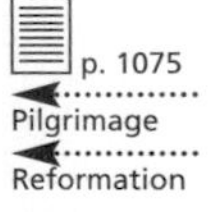
p. 1075
Pilgrimage
Reformation
Counter-Reformation

Ironically, while struggling together, both the Counter-Reformation and the Protestant churches developed a similar form, the auditory church. The Word was of paramount importance in Reformed theology and

Preaching

preaching an essential part of worship. In the first instance, during the sixteenth century in the Netherlands former Catholic churches were brought into Protestant use by radical re-orderings which usually re-orientated the interior from facing east, where the altar formerly stood, to facing south where a new pulpit with tester was installed. The interior was stripped of decoration and refurnished around the central pulpit. From the early seventeenth century, a variety of centralized plan forms were developed: square, octagonal and Greek cross, sometimes provided with galleries to increase the seating capacity within earshot. Church services were very static with little or no movement either by clergy or people. The Bible was not carried in procession, indeed no processions took place, and when the Lord's Supper was celebrated, it was set in order before the service and usually took place apart from the preaching space. The spaces spoke of unity and simplicity, and looked back to the early Christian community as an ideal.

In seventeenth-century England the problem differed somewhat from the Dutch context in that the altar maintained an importance as great as the pulpit in the Anglican Church. The Great Fire of London gave Sir Christopher Wren magnificent scope for the development of a new type of building. A total of 87 churches were destroyed and 51 were rebuilt, all of them under the direction of Wren; they became essays for his more sustained work on the design of St Paul's Cathedral. He was much exercised by the development of a plan appropriate for a modern church. For this he looked to ancient precedent in Vitruvius, the only classical architect whose treatise on architecture has survived, and also to Serlio, a Renaissance commentator. St Mary-le-Bow, for example, is based on his engraving of the Basilica of Constantine in Rome. Wren was also doubtless aware of Dutch auditory churches too, but his London churches show his astonishing ingenuity and originality. At St Stephen Walbrook and later at St Paul's, his main problem was to integrate a dome on eight equal arches with an aisled nave. At Christ Church Newgate Street he produced a two-storied basilica, a form perfected at St James, Piccadilly, with its beautifully integrated galleries and its vaulted nave and aisles. For St Paul's itself he produced many experimental designs, some cruciform with a domed crossing, others centralized, including the Great Model, which is a Greek cross with western vestibule. It had a great central dome supported by eight piers whose arches open on to eight smaller domed spaces functioning as an ambulatory. However, Anglican liturgical practice still demanded greater eastward movement. In the final design the cathedral has been stretched along its east-west axis, resulting in a long nave with a domed crossing and subsidiary domes vaulting the aisles. Wren's St Paul's was a fitting rival for St Peter's in Rome.

At this period scholars were engaged in serious study of early Christianity, including forms of worship and church buildings. The recovery of 'apostolic' forms would carry immense authority. They looked to early Christian and Byzantine churches, and to the temple of Jerusalem itself as prototypes. Some evidence exists to suggest that Wren used Hagia Sophia as a model in his studies for St Paul's. Wren's younger colleague Nicholas Hawksmoor, responsible for the next wave of London churches, also produced drawings for 'The Basilica after the Primitive Christians ... as it was in the fourth century in the purest times of Christianity'. Much of this research was speculative, and the built forms contained symbolic references rather than accurate reconstructions.

During the next century huge changes were taking place in European society. Remaining with the English example, there was increasing urbanization and the allegiance of the population at large, particularly 'the lower orders', shifted from the Anglican to the Non-conformist churches. Between 1801 and 1831 the number of communicants in Anglican churches on Easter Sunday had dropped from about 10 to 7 per cent of the population, while membership of Non-conformist churches had doubled from 2.75 to 5.5 per cent. The Anglican church just did not have the necessary buildings in urban centres. In 1818 the Church Building Commission was established by parliament with an initial grant of £1,000,000, and another £500,000 was to follow in 1824. The government was keen to guard against Non-conformism, atheism and potential revolution that, after all, was very real on the other side of the channel.

The face of reform was the Commissioners' Churches such St Peter's, Brighton, built by Sir Charles Barry between 1824 and 1828. They cost an average of £3000, cheap even by the standards of the day. It was against their thin and rather brittle use of the Gothic style that A.W. N. Pugin published his book *Contrasts*, in which he compared towns of the 1840s and 1440s, that is to say contemporary urban industrialism and pre-Reformation Catholic England. Built forms were charged with religious, moral and social significance. Ironically, his ideas struck a chord more with the Anglican Tractarians than with his own co-religionists. Beginning with John Keble's 'Assize Sermon' in 1833, the Oxford Movement emphasized continuity with the Catholic past, the sacraments, and spirituality expressed in ritual. The Cambridge Movement concerned itself with the reform of liturgy and church building. Its publications, including *The Ecclesiologist* (from 1841), gave clear prescriptions for the building and arrangement of churches, based for the most part on Pugin. Hand-in-hand with the British empire, Pugin's model of the neo-medieval English parish church spread around the world and was planted in the most unlikely contexts. In England by 1873 a full third of existing parish churches were 'restored', that is, made to conform to the model.

The twentieth century brought a new questioning of ecclesiastical forms from first principles. The new liturgical movement, the revival of biblical studies, the new ecumenism and a re-thinking of the whole mission of the church produced a new 'brief', and the Modern Movement in design produced new forms. Activity was particularly intense in France (with designers like Auguste Perret, Le Corbusier, Rainer Senn and Matisse, and churchmen like Père Couturier), Germany (Otto Bartning, Gottfried and Domenikus Böhm and Rudolf Swartz), England (Robert Maguire and Keith Murray), and America (Ludwig Mies van der Rohe, Marcel Breuer and Frank Lloyd Wright). Contemporary design of churches responds to changes in the liturgy and mission of the church, as was always the case, but now theological approach is so much more diverse and often addresses a greater range of community activities.

Existing churches, too, need to adapt to changing needs and circumstances, and there are pressures for every generation to make the building its own. That temporal dimension is extremely sensitive, because the forms of buildings become metaphors not only for the identity and history of the people who create and use them, but also for the society within which they live. The structure of buildings becomes a powerful symbol for social and religious structures, and the shaping and control of those symbols has been a contentious issue from the earliest days of the church: from the confiscations of church property during the persecutions to the imperial model under Constantine, to the appeal to various historical periods and precedents, to Modernist appeals to first principles for a new church for the new age.

ALLAN DOIG

📖 John Beckwith, *Early Christian and Byzantine Art*, New Haven and London: Yale University Press 1970; Paul Bradshaw, *Early Christian Worship*, London: SPCK 1996; J. G. Davies, *Temples, Churches and Mosques*, Oxford: Blackwell 1982; Gregory Dix, *The Shape of the Liturgy*, London: Dacre Press 1945; John Lowden, *Early Christian and Byzantine Art*, London: Phaidon Press 1997; Rowland Mainstone, *Hagia Sophia: Architecture, Structure and Liturgy of Justinian's Great Church*, London: Thames & Hudson 1997; Andrew Wallace-Hadrill, *Houses and Society in Pompeii and Herculaneum*, Princeton: Princeton University Press 1994

Bullinger, Heinrich

Heinrich Bullinger (1504–75), reformer and theologian, was born in Bremgarten, near Zurich, the son of a priest and his common-law wife. Such relationships were common in German and Swiss lands in the late Middle Ages and clerical marriage was therefore central to Huldrych Zwingli's reforms of the early 1520s.

Huldrych Zwingli

p. 1145

Bullinger was educated by men who were adherents of the *Devotio moderna*, that mystical movement of which Thomas à Kempis' *Imitation of Christ* is the classic product; this, in turn, influenced Bullinger throughout his life. After his school studies he matriculated at the University of Cologne in 1519, where he followed the traditional arts curriculum. While in Cologne he was first exposed to humanism and the church fathers. He returned to the Swiss Confederation in 1523 to serve as a teacher in the monastery school of the Cistercian house at Kappel, south of Zurich. During this period Bullinger came to know Huldrych Zwingli and was influenced by the latter's thought.

Humanism
Church fathers

At Kappel Bullinger implemented many of his humanist educational principles and eventually broke with the Catholic Church. After the introduction of the Reformation in Zurich in 1525 he wrote his first theological and historical works. Following Zwingli's death in October 1531, Bullinger was appointed chief minister in Zurich. He was still a young man and he faced a daunting task: the backlash against the Reformation was ferocious and the magistrates of the city were determined to control the clergy. Bullinger argued that the preaching of the gospel was central to the office of the Christian ministry, which could not be limited by any political authority. Nevertheless, he had to balance his concern that the gospel be freely preached with the political realities of the day. The consequence was an arrangement with the magistrates by which Bullinger strictly controlled the clergy of Zurich (approximately 120 rural and urban parishes) and co-operated with the civic rulers in all church affairs. His influence on every aspect of the Zurich church was enormous.

Reformation

As Zwingli's successor, Heinrich Bullinger led the first and most significant of the Swiss Reformed churches. He played a crucial role in the formation of Reformed theology during his almost 45 years of leadership. He was co-author of the First Helvetic Confession (1536), the *Consensus Tigurinus* (with John Calvin, 1549) and, most significantly, the Second Helvetic Confession (1566), the fullest statement of Reformed thought in the sixteenth century. Throughout his life Bullinger was loyal to the memory of Huldrych Zwingli and sought to defend his theology, yet his thought also had a distinctive tone. The covenant between God and humanity was central. Bullinger came from the southern German tradition of humanist reformers (i.e. Martin Bucer, Johannes Oecolampadius and Konrad Pellikan) that venerated the Hebrew Bible and the Hebrew language. The Old Testament was read as a book pointing to Christ, with an emphasis on the continuity between the

Reformed churches

p. 302

Covenant

two testaments. For Bullinger, the fulfilment of the ancient covenants between God and the Israelites was in Christ.

Bullinger's sacramental theology also had a strong covenantal character, as baptism was likened to circumcision and the Lord's Supper was treated as a memorial. Eucharist This is not to say that the eucharist was an empty ritual, for Bullinger argued forcefully that in eating the bread and drinking the wine a person was spiritually consuming the body of Christ. Faith in Christ was, for Bullinger, the absolute foundation of the Christian life, and all of his writings are strikingly centred on Christ. One aspect that distinguishes Bullinger from Zwingli is the almost mystical language in which he describes the unity of the believer with Christ in faith.

During the period from 1535 to his death Bullinger became the leading voice of the Reformed church in Europe. His works were widely printed and translated. The most well known was his *Decades*, a series of 50 sermons on all aspects of the Christian religion. The work was quickly translated into all the major languages of the day. An English translation appeared in 1587 and the book had such a high reputation that John Whitgift, Archbishop of Canterbury, instructed all his parish clergy to have a copy. At home Bullinger faced two major threats: Lutheranism Anabaptists the German Lutherans and the Anabaptists. Relations between Zurich and Wittenberg were poisoned by the split between Zwingli and Luther over the eucharist.

Martin Luther After Zwingli's death, Martin Luther made it clear that he would have nothing to do with Zwinglians, whom he condemned as heretics. Bullinger sought to build bridges to German Protestantism and he developed a good relationship with Philipp Melanchthon, but found himself continually forced to defend the Swiss churches against the charge of heresy. This shaped his theology profoundly as he sought to demonstrate the harmony of Reformed thought with the teaching of early church fathers. On the other side, the rise of Anabaptism in Zurich posed a major threat to Bullinger's church and he wrote against the radicals most vehemently. He saw the Anabaptists, not the Catholics or Lutherans, as the greatest danger to the Reformation.

Bullinger's influence as a European Reformer was based partially on his published writings, but perhaps even more on his correspondence and role as protector of religious refugees. His surviving letters (approximately 12,000) form the largest collection from the Reformation period and they demonstrate the breadth and depth of his influence across Europe. From England to Transylvania he was consulted as a patriarch of the Reformation, and his network of contacts and informants was unrivalled. He was an early supporter and patron of John Calvin and the two men worked closely together, though they were never close friends. They did not agree on many things but they did not allow their differences to appear in public. Their partnership did much to bring about the flowering of the Reformed faith in the second half of the sixteenth century. Calvin's theology would eventually eclipse Bullinger's writings, but in their day there was no doubt as to who was the senior partner.

BRUCE GORDON

Wayne Baker, *Heinrich Bullinger and the Covenant*, Athens, OH: Ohio University Press 1980; Bruce Gordon, *The Swiss Reformation*, Manchester: Manchester University Press 2002; Bruce Gordon and Emidio Campi (eds), *Heinrich Bullinger and Formation of the Reformed Faith*, Grand Rapids, MI: Baker Academic 2004

Business ethics

'Business ethics? An oxymoron if there ever was one!' Though this may be the common view, it is less likely to be held by persons who have had significant experience managing a business. Despite Enron and other trade names that have become a byword for corporate greed and predatory business practices, most business people know that if they stray too far from the law, not to mention prevailing moral wisdom, they risk getting themselves into serious difficulty. This unstated, but usually effective, minimal morality is reflected in perhaps the most basic rule of thumb known to business people, the so-called 'newspaper test'. In trying to decide whether to go forward with some new venture, policy or specific action in a given situation, ask yourself if you would go forward knowing that your response and its motives were to be reported tomorrow on the front page of the *New York Times*, *The Times*, or whatever else is the paper of record in your area. Ethics in business often may seem disturbingly thin and superficial, but it is not as such a contradiction in terms.

That this is so is just one more indication of the moral and spiritual impact of Christianity within Western civilization. To be sure, that impact has not been pervasive, nor can it be assumed to be permanent. Nevertheless, most of the major ethical benchmarks that now characterize Western civilization, such as the rule of law, human rights, freedom, equality, justice and compassion for others, have all emerged in one way or another in Western civilization's sometimes unacknowledged struggle with the legacy of Christian faith and practice. Though each of these, considered in the abstract, is neither logically dependent on Christianity nor genealogically traceable to exclusively Christian sources, their relationship to the basic moral and spiritual agenda of Western civilization is unmistakable, especially when viewed from outside that civilization.

This is no less true of ethics in the business world than it is of any other area of public moral concern. As in these other areas, business ethics in a Christian perspective distinguishes itself by entering into an ongoing conversation that includes not only reason and experience but also scripture and tradition. Christian business ethics may appear to be little more than common sense sprinkled with holy water, but with more careful observation one discovers that it is focused primarily on the question, 'What is God enabling me (us) to be and to do?' The fact that this question must be asked by Christians in business, no less than in any other walk of life, is clearly the legacy of scripture and tradition. There is no special ethic for business, if by 'special' one means that because 'business is business' it is exempt from the ethical expectations that commonly apply to all other areas of human interaction. No less than in politics or any other allegedly secular pursuits and professions, Christians in business seek to bring the resources of scripture and tradition to bear on what they understand to be reality and how they are to respond to it. To be sure, understanding what is going on involves reason and experience, but those who confess themselves to be Christian are constantly involved in shaping and reshaping both reason and experience, just as both scripture and tradition are constantly open to critical reassessment. Doing business ethics in this way may yield a rather uncommon common sense, with or without the holy water.

Substantively considered, business ethics in a Christian perspective is an extension of three fundamental themes, grounded in scripture and honoured in the traditions of historic Christianity: covenant, stewardship and vocation.

As the most characteristic expression of God's relationship with Israel, *covenant* is the principle through which most, if not all, Christian ethical concern is organized. The Ten Commandments are central to Christian faith and practice. Within that framework, as elaborated in the biblical stories of Israel's covenantal relationships, care for the ethical nuances of buying and selling in the market-place is a hallmark of faithfulness. The Holiness Code in Leviticus, for example, specifically upholds fair dealing and condemns various forms of fraud (19.9–17, 33–7); the significance of this is emphasized by the prophetic denunciations of the oppression of the poor and the use of unethical means to gain riches (as in Amos 5.12–15; 8.4–6).

God's chosen people are expected to distinguish themselves from neighbouring tribes and nations by refraining from predatory business practices not only among themselves but also in their dealings with strangers, widows and orphans, i.e., persons lacking the power to bargain effectively as equals. The reasons given for this higher standard of market-place morality are typically couched in terms of remembering the threats and promises given in God's covenant and Israel's own desperate experience of liberation from slavery in Egypt. The covenant thus provides not just an overarching framework for understanding the deeper theological significance of good business practices, but also detailed prescriptions regarding proper conduct in the market-place.

Stewardship, a concept familiar to many Christians in reference to their common obligation to make fair provision for the economic well-being of the church and its ministries, has come to be identified with the broader purpose of wealth, its acquisition, and disposition within the Christian moral life as a whole. Stewardship, in short, is the practical expression of a Christian's confession of faith in God the Creator. Creation, accepted in faith as a gift from God, like most gifts comes with strings attached. For all its seeming limitlessness, creation is characterized by a paradox of scarcity that provokes a deep anxiety in humanity, one that can either tempt people towards greed or challenge them to live faithfully as God's stewards. More like lease-holders than property owners, stewards are entrusted with the earth, to cultivate it and improve it, in faithful response to their master's directives. Thus in the perspective of stewardship those who would claim absolute ownership of this world's resources, implying that they are free to do with them as they please, are guilty of 'playing God', the ultimate form of idolatry. Here the meaning of private property and the rights conferred by ownership are both affirmed and yet qualified by a biblical vision of the challenge of living faithfully in this world. Within that vision, all things are to be regarded as resources for completing the work of creation by optimizing their value consistent with God's love for all creatures. Economic scarcity is thus more apparent than real; provisional, perhaps, but not definitive. This is the point of departure for Christian reflection, not just on the meaning and purpose of scarcity and its relationship to economic and social justice, but also on the imperative of environmental responsibility, the proper regard for the so-called silent stakeholders, the myriad forms of wonderful life, whose needs and desires must be given due consideration even as we pursue our own.

Creation

Covenant

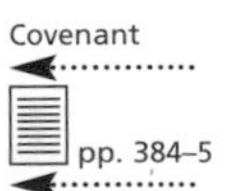

pp. 384–5

Rooted in scriptural memories of God's uncanny habit of calling specific persons to share in specific aspects of the work of liberating creation from sin and death, *vocation* captures a sense of the process in which Christians agree to participate in the adventure of stewardship and to order their own actions according to the provisions of the covenant. Those who are aware of their vocation are transformed, or at least are seeking to be transformed. For them, covenant and stewardship are no longer conundrums to be admired or criticized in abstraction from

Prophecy

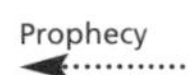

their own destiny, but are embraced as sacramental signs illuminating the path of moral and spiritual development. Business people who construe their lives as responding to a calling from God can no longer regard work as merely a job or even a career. When they are called specifically to business, this business activity must be regarded as a mission empowered by God. As in all forms of empowerment, responding to a vocation is risky, not only for them but also for others whose lives are affected by one's responses. Acknowledging one's vocation means engaging in a moral and spiritual struggle, first with one's own self – one's own fears, desires and aspirations – in order to overcome whatever obstacles may stand in the way of carrying out one's God-given mission.

At first sight, reconciling the scriptural witness with doing business in a capitalist environment may seem impossible. Many theologians have concluded that capitalism cannot be redeemed. Tradition, however, holds out other possibilities. Though it does record the legacy of Catholic monasticism and its equation of Christian discipleship with the vowed life of poverty, chastity and obedience, it also preserves the intellectual labours of Clement of Alexandria, Cyprian of Carthage, Thomas Aquinas, John Calvin and John Wesley, among others, who struggled to release the scriptural vision of business and economic life from its sometime captivity to utopian visionaries and their theologically motivated contempt for this world. In their work Christian ethics, to be true as well as effective, had to be based on a critical respect for the achievements of a civilization at least open to Christian influence, and a willingness to explore new truths precisely for the sake of the Christian mission.

In this process of moral and spiritual discernment, Thomas Aquinas and Calvin were probably decisive in the development of business ethics in Christian perspective. For Thomas, despite his reverence for Aristotle in so many ways, parts company with the philosopher precisely on the point whether a Christian can, in good conscience, engage in trade professionally. In Thomas' view one can, since there is nothing inherently sinful in seeking to make a living from buying and selling, provided that one's intentions are good. Aristotle, by contrast, taught that a gentleman should not engage in trade professionally, because the vices of merchants were inherent in the art of acquisition or money-making as such. The central theoretical issue for contemporary business ethics, however, is the moral logic of capitalism itself. Here Calvin's reinterpretation of the biblical arguments against usury, especially those based on Deuteronomy 23.19–20, which in effect overturned them, enabled Christians to participate fully in the development of the institutions of the modern Western financial system. The business of lending money at interest had been condemned by most patristic and medieval theologians, though the trend, particularly apparent in Thomas, had been to narrow the scope of the condemnation. Calvin's contribution was to release Christians from their lingering scruples about finance, and make it possible, as Max Weber famously argued, for a substantively Christian business ethics eventually to emerge.

Christians seeking moral guidance about business today are not likely to trouble themselves about the basic questions that Thomas Aquinas and Calvin struggled to answer. They tend to presuppose their answers as common sense, and focus on more pressing concerns such as where to draw the line between aggressive and predatory business practices. Some of the questions engaging the hundreds of millions of Christians employed in business are perennial, such as the relationship between law and morality, and what is distinctive of Christian business ethics beyond doing no harm, obeying the law and striving to emulate what is commonly regarded as best business practice. What is distinctive about Christian business ethics today is not that Christians operate with a substantively different code of ethics from that acknowledged by non-Christians. It is rather that Christians are seeking to grasp the deeper significance of their business activities. Finding a proper and harmonious balance between work, family, church and one's other social activities today seems more indicative of Christian commitment than worries over the morality of engaging in business as such. Christians seeking moral and spiritual integrity on such a basis may often be found in Bible study groups and other forms of fellowship, where, as one might expect, the discussion of the meaning of covenant, stewardship and vocation is intense and ongoing.

DENNIS P. MCCANN

Max DePree, *Leadership is an Art*, Garden City, NY: Doubleday 1989; James M. Gustafson, *Can Ethics be Christian?*, Chicago: University of Chicago Press 1975; Laura L. Nash, *Believers in Business*, Nashville, TN: Thomas Nelson 1994; Max L. Stackhouse, Dennis P. McCann and Shirley Roels with Preston Williams (eds), *On Moral Business: Classical and Contemporary Resources for Ethics and Economic Life*, Grand Rapids, MI: Eerdmans 1995; Ernst Troeltsch, *Protestantism and Progress: A Historical Study of the Relation of Protestantism to the Modern World* (1912), Boston: Beacon Press 1966; Max Weber, *The Protestant Ethic and the Spirit of Capitalism*, New York: Harper & Row 1958; Oliver F. Williams (ed), *Business, Religion and Spirituality: A New Synthesis*, Notre Dame, IN: University of Notre Dame Press 2003

Byzantium

Byzantium and its adjective Byzantine appear often in accounts of Eastern Christianity. However, it is far from easy to describe the multiple realities to which they refer.

The name Byzantion was given to a colony founded by Greeks from Megara, a city on the Gulf of Corinth, supposedly in the seventh century BCE. They chose a site marked by its potentially secure location on a bluff at the confluence of the Golden Horn estuary with the Bosphoros. With deep water forming its borders to the north, east and south, the only fortification required to enclose the colony was a wall to the west. From its elevation Byzantion could control shipping up and down the dangerous waters that link the Black Sea with the Sea of Marmora, which in turn flows into the Aegean at the Dardanelles. Later inhabitants explained Byzantion as a combination of the names of Byzas, the Greek leader, and Antes, his opponent in the battle to establish the colony, and minted coins in his name. The etymology of Byzantion remains unknown.

The survival of the colony may well have been due to its favourable trading position, tapping the lucrative transport of goods from the far north (amber, furs and wood) and from the Mediterranean (oil, grain, papyrus, flax and imported spices). Little is known of its history until Septimius Severus laid siege to the city at the end of the second century CE. Its unsuccessful resistance was punished by the demolition of the land wall, but the emperor later undertook the reconstruction of the colony's monuments, including a new hippodrome, colonnaded streets and possibly a theatre. New land walls were built strengthening the site and confirming its importance. On the acropolis, the highest point of the bluff overlooking the Bosphoros, two temples, dedicated to Rhea the mother of the gods and Fortuna, were constructed.

Apart from the legend that St Andrew founded the see of Byzantion and ordained its first bishop, Stachys, there is no record of the first Christian community. The city sent no bishop to the first ecumenical council held at Nicaea (325), though later sources record the existence of Bishops Metrophanes and Alexander at the time. It must have witnessed the growth of Christian communities, with Christians from the eastern Mediterraean travelling to the West and back: for instance, Irenaeus, Bishop of Lyons. Believers later celebrated two local Christian martyrs, Mokios and Akakios, whose shrines continued in existence for centuries, but Byzantion had no famous patron saints.

The history of Byzantion was dramatically changed when Constantine I decided to establish a new capital in the east of the empire. In choosing the colony for this role, Constantine took account of its strategic position, commanding the routes between Europe and the Near East and between north and south. In traditional ceremonies performed in 324, its new circumference was designated by ploughing a line, with gates in the western line and along the Marmara and Golden Horn. The city of Constantine, Constantinople, also called New Rome, was inaugurated on 11 May 330. It was considerably larger than the colony of Byzantion and as befits a capital had numerous new public monuments: the Forum of Constantine, hippodrome, palace, mint, and many fountains to distribute water for the expanding population. Ancient statues were brought from all parts of the empire to decorate the city. On top of the porphyry column in the Forum of Constantine, a statue said originally to be of Apollo was adapted to represent the emperor, while four antique bronze horses were later set up at the entrance to the hippodrome. With major colonnaded thoroughfares linking the fourteen regions and seven hills, imitating those of Rome, the new capital was constructed to impress.

In founding New Rome in the East, Constantine I clearly brought many of the features of Rome on the Tiber to the Bosphoros. He granted land and privileges to senatorial families who agreed to move east and established a grain supply from Egypt to feed the growing population. Few religious buildings can be attributed to Constantine. He may have planned the church of the Holy Apostles, to which the imperial mausoleum was attached; the cathedral church of Hagia Irene and churches of the local martyrs, Mokios and Akakios. In 337 he was buried with Christian ceremonies in the mausoleum, which was designed to house relics of all the apostles. His son Constantius II completed this church and translated the bones of the saints Timothy, Luke and Andrew to the site in 356–7.

What the capital lacked in local martyrs it made up for in its collection of relics. Nearly all Constantine's successors and their wives contributed to an impressive range of relics and objects associated with holy people. The true cross, discovered by Helena in Jerusalem, and relics of the passion (the nails, crown of thorns, sponge and lance) were sent to the capital for safe-keeping, while the veil, girdle and shroud of the Virgin were brought to her shrine at the church of Blachernai. By 454 the head of John the Baptist found a home at the monastery of Stoudios, and the remains of Stephen the first martyr were translated to the capital with great ceremony. Interestingly, the ancient temples of Constantinople were not demolished; in the sixth century they were adapted for secular use.

p. 1075
Council
p. 848
Martyr

In addition to these important relics, early Christian paintings (icons) of holy people, Christ, the Virgin, saints, bishops, holy men and women were avidly collected. In the use of the ancient technique of encaustic, painting in heated coloured wax, Constantinople encouraged

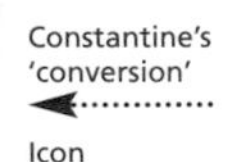
Constantine's 'conversion'
Icon

the development of a very specific Christian art form. While *eikon* means any image, religious icons are correctly associated with Constantinople. Some of the earliest surviving works are now in monastic collections such as that at the monastery of St Catherine at Mount Sinai, for example the famous sixth-century icons of Christ and of the Virgin and Child with military saints and angels.

Constantinople also played a major role in the expansion of ecclesiastical administration. Under Theodosius I the second ecumenical council was summoned to the capital in 381 and Constantinople was accorded second place in the hierarchy of Christian sees, behind Rome and ahead of Antioch, Alexandria and Jerusalem. These five centres were thus established as the leading sees of the Christian universe (*oikoumene*), each ruled by a bishop called patriarch or pope, and collectively identified as the pentarchy. This 'rule of five' took responsibility for maintaining correct belief and ecclesiastical discipline through the canons issued by ecumenical councils. The earliest collections of church law include all these canons and additional ones issued by provincial councils, for example at Antioch, Laodicea or Sardis.

The promotion of Constantinople was related to the fact that it was now the seat of imperial government; emperors of the fourth century and later rarely went to Rome. The see of Constantinople had to have an appropriately high rank, which was strengthened in the mid-fifth century by the claim that it had the same status and deserved the same honour as Old Rome. This raised the new capital to an equal position with the foremost centre of Christianity in the West.

Between Old Rome and New Rome, rivalry was inevitable. The Western capital was no longer the residence of Western emperors, who preferred Milan or Ravenna. It

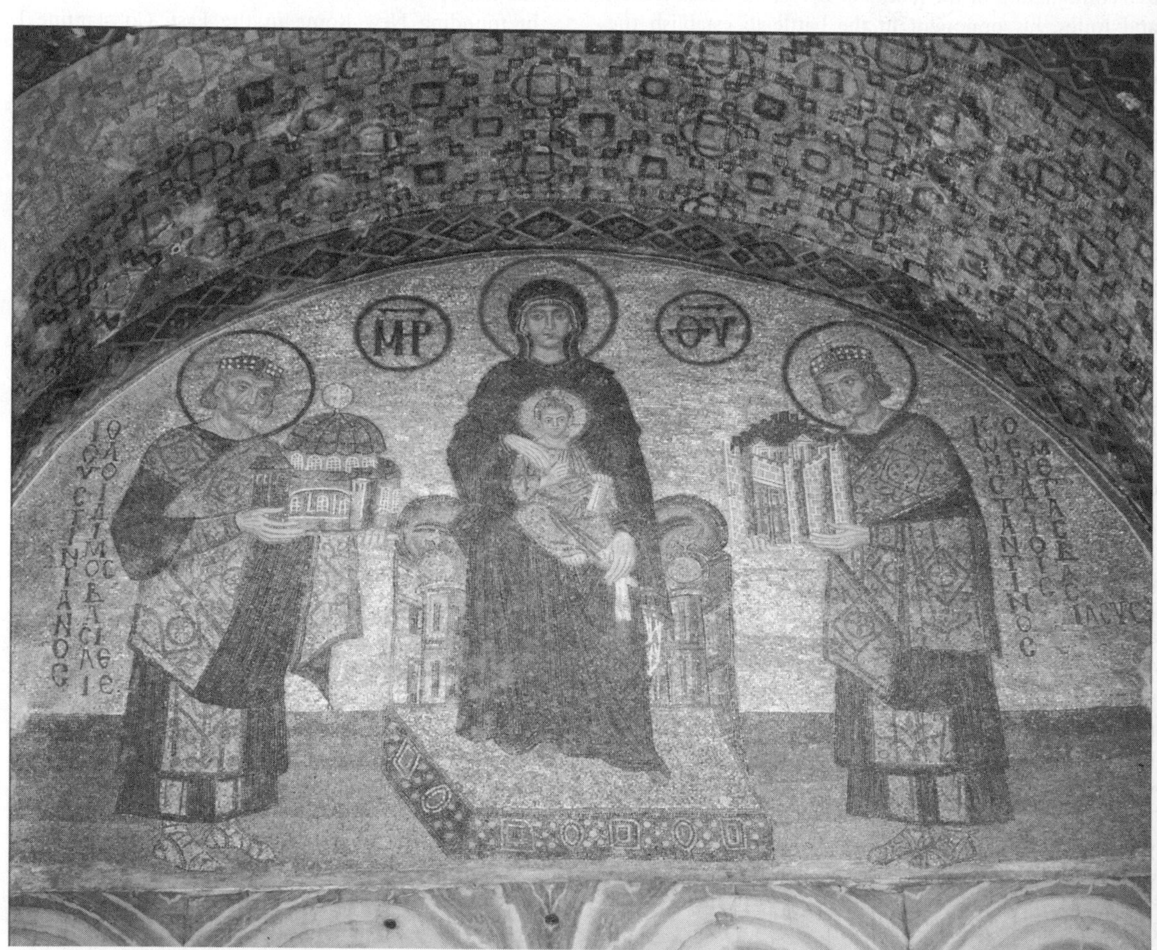

The Emperor Justinian offers Hagia Sophia and the Emperor Constantine offers the city of Constantinople to the Virgin and Child, mosaic in Hagia Sophia

fell to the Gothic forces of Alaric in 410 and was sacked by the Vandals in 455. With severely reduced resources, its bishop was obliged to assume a leading role, as Pope Leo I did in embassies to Attila (452) and in negotiations with Gaiseric (455). He accepted the Council of Chalcedon, over which his legates presided, but also emphasized the primacy of Rome, based on the Gospel text of Matthew 16.18. Christ's words to Peter, 'On this rock I will build my church,' became the major cause of friction between the two sees.

Meanwhile in the East, successive patriarchs of Constantinople enhanced their authority in direct association with imperial power. New Rome acquired not only relics, icons, holy men who founded monasteries, libraries of Christian writings and the most impressive churches, such as Hagia Sophia dedicated by Justinian in 537; it also developed its own system of canon law in Greek, based on the decrees of church councils. Patriarchs formed a court of appeal for differences between clerics in all parts of the empire. They headed the lists of ecclesiastical dioceses (*Notitia episcopatuum*), which were ranked according to historical importance, starting with Caesarea in Cappadocia (the see of Basil), Ephesus and Heracleia, and progressing down to the most recently-created bishoprics.

The honour due to Old Rome nonetheless secured its first place in this hierarchy of Christian sees. Pope Leo's successors insisted on this primacy and contrasted it with the insignificant early history of Byzantion. During the Middle Ages Rome expanded its control over the entire West, insisting that bishops journey to the city to receive the pallium of office. It also claimed a superior authority for its judgements (decretals) in Latin, which drew on Peter's foundation of the church of Rome. The combination of different sources of power and different methods of resolving legal problems set the two Romes on opposing trajectories, which were bound to clash.

By the ninth century Old and New Rome were further divided by linguistic differences compounded by local variations in service books, ecclesiastical ritual, the wording of the creed (with the addition of the *filioque* in parts of the West), and matters such as clerical celibacy. The central issue, however, concerned authority within the Christian world, which had been greatly altered by the Arab conquests of the East and Christian expansion in the West. While Constantinople supported the supreme power of the pentarchy, Rome stressed its own particular authority derived from Peter. These matters came to a head in the debates between Patriarch Photius and Pope Nicholas I in the 860s, with mutual denunciation and excommunication. Although relations were re-established and the two centres remained in close contact, the issue of Petrine supremacy continued to divide West from East.

In 1054 the Pope's legate, Humbert, Cardinal of Silva Candida, laid a bull of excommunication of Patriarch Michael Keroularios on the altar of Hagia Sophia, thus initiating mutual anathemas. Recent research on this event has reduced its significance and removed its previous name, the 'Great Schism'. Neither party held to the excommunication, which was considered a personal matter, and considerable intercommunion between Greeks and Latins continued to take place. In the course of the twelfth century, however, as Western crusaders brought their own practices into the Orthodox world of the East Mediterranean, the divergences became more and more apparent. The siege and conquest of Constantinople by the forces of the Fourth Crusade in 1204 forced the emperor and patriarch into exile in Nicaea, while the crusaders elected a Latin emperor. The appointment of a Latin patriarch of Constantinople (the Venetian Morosini) led to a complete schism. Pope Innocent III had demanded the submission of the Greek Orthodox East to Rome's authority as the condition of his support for the crusade, but the exiled Greek church remained fiercely independent. And in 1261, when the Byzantines regained the capital, patriarchs of Constantinople reasserted their control of the Orthodox churches in the East and ignored the Catholic Church of the West. Subsequent efforts to reunite the churches all failed.

Crusades

Canon law

While the city of Constantinople, New Rome, effectively replaced Byzantion, its inhabitants always continued to call themselves Byzantines (*Byzantioi*). The subjects of the Roman emperor were identified as Romans (*Romaioi*), but the 'people of Byzantion' clung to this name right through the empire's existence to its fall to the Ottoman Turks in 1453. And in their characterization of others as provincial, often with unsophisticated habits, they revealed their inherent superiority, based on the fact that they believed they lived in the most glorious, rich and important city in the world.

The term Byzantine was also connected with 'Byzant' or 'Bezant', the name given by Westerners to the gold coins issued by emperors of Constantinople from Constantine I to his namesake Constantine IX in the eleventh century. The fineness and stability of the gold *nomisma* made it a reliable and highly appreciated coin, especially among the silver currencies of the early medieval West. It also reflected the strength of imperial administration, which for over 700 years minted a 24-carat gold coin usually with a portrait of the ruling emperor or empress and relatives, and Christian symbols, images and inscriptions.

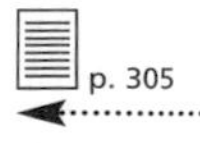
p. 305

Authority

The term 'Byzantium' was coined and adopted by sixteenth-century humanists to designate the medieval Roman empire. The epithet 'Byzantine', however, eventually passed into European vocabulary as a synonym for all its most reprehensible and morally disreputable

Humanism

features. From being a term used with pride by those born in the city of Constantine, it came to envelop a devious and cunning diplomacy, political instability generated by assassination and usurpation, or court intrigue by eunuchs, considered typical of the medieval empire of Byzantium – in short, all the worst aspects of a state that lasted over a millennium.

Fortunately, this is no longer so. 'Byzantium' now characterizes the tradition of imperial government, based on Roman law in Greek translation, and directed by an autocratic ruler in a highly ceremonial and colourful court. In artistic terms 'Byzantine' stands for a brilliant

Art
Architecture
Renaissance
Festivals and fasts
Middle Ages
Renaissance

development in medieval Christian art and architecture that influenced the artists of the Italian Renaissance. Its silks, ivories, liturgical silver, icons and even ceramics are displayed in all great museums. Scholars of Byzantium were also responsible for the transmission of classical culture, for instance of Homer and almost all of ancient Greek drama, which is known only from Byzantine manuscript copies with commentaries. It is also intimately connected

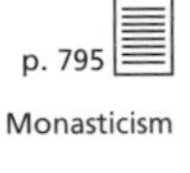

p. 795
Monasticism

with the development of specific Christian traditions symbolized by Mount Athos. Byzantine monasticism links the earliest Christian ascetics of the Egyptian and Syrian deserts with contemporary Orthodox monks.

In the field of religion, Byzantium is particularly important for the preservation and annotation of all early Christian writings, the Greek fathers of the church (Basil, Gregory of Nazianzos, Gregory of Nyssa and John Chrysostom) and the desert fathers, whose sayings and

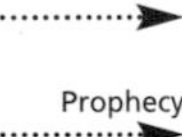

Jesus
Prophecy
Messiah

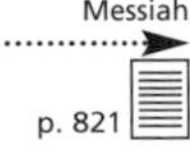

p. 821

rules for ascetics influenced all later monastic movements. Byzantium promoted the government of the early church through ecumenical councils and the rule of five great patriarchates (the pentarchy). With the support of the state, the church of Constantinople converted the medieval inhabitants of Bulgaria and Russia to Christianity. It carried the spiritual movement of Heyschasm, based on the Jesus Prayer, from Mount Sinai to all parts of the orthodox world. This remains an essential foundation of Orthodoxy.

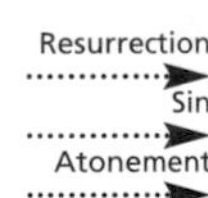

Resurrection
Sin
Atonement

Byzantium also remained the bastion of Christian belief in the East as the Ottoman Turks expanded their state and imposed the faith of Islam over vast areas of the Near East. As it was gradually encircled by hostile forces, Constantinople appealed to the West for military help. In 1453 only a few Italians responded and the emperor prepared to defend his city with inadequate forces. Even so, New Rome might have survived but for the invention of gunpowder. For it was a new military weapon, cannon, which could bring down sections of the fifth century walls and so destroy Byzantium. On 29 May 1453 the last emperor, Constantine XI, named after all his distinguished predecessors, died fighting on the walls, and the great Christian metropolis of the eastern Mediterranean became the capital of the Ottoman Sultan, Mehmed the Conqueror. It is now known as Istanbul.

JUDITH HERRIN

Cyril Mango (ed), *The Oxford History of Byzantium*, Oxford: OUP 2002; Cyril Mango and Gilbert Dagron (eds), *Constantinople and its Hinterland*, Aldershot: Variorum 1995

Calendar

Over the centuries the Christian church has developed an extremely detailed calendar – of seasons, fasts, festivals, holy days and saints days – which gives a sacred structure to the entire year. In pre-modern Europe (the Middle Ages and the Renaissance) the Christian calendar would have dominated people's day-to-day living. Even ordinary men and women would have been much more aware of festivals and saints days than of numerical dates and months. However, since the eighteenth century – with the development of a new scientific understanding of time – the Christian calendar has increasingly declined in public importance and awareness. Our modern public understanding of time is now largely non-religious, although the remnants of a Christian calendar still endure in the structure of public holidays, particularly at Christmas and Easter.

The Christian calendar is organized around the story of Jesus, beginning with the festival of Advent on the Sunday nearest to 30 November. On the Sundays of Advent, Christians reflect upon those prophets, such as Isaiah and John the Baptist, whom they traditionally believe to have foretold the coming of Christ, the Messiah. Advent ends with the festival of Christmas, on 25 December, when the birth of Jesus is celebrated. A few weeks after Christmas – the exact date depends upon the phases of the moon – the 40-day season of Lent begins with a holy day called Ash Wednesday. Lent is a period of preparation for the festival of Easter, when Christians remember Jesus' death and celebrate his resurrection. During the Sundays of Lent believers are reminded of human sin (wrong-doing) and the need for Jesus to sacrifice his own life. Lent ends with Holy Week when Christians follow day-by-day the events that built up to Jesus' resurrection on Easter Day. The most important day in Holy Week is Good Friday, when the church commemorates Jesus' crucifixion. Exactly 40 days after Easter, Jesus' withdrawal into heaven is remembered on Ascension Day. After a further ten days the church celebrates its own inauguration at the festival of Pentecost (or Whitsunday). The last major festival of the year is Trinity Sunday, which falls a week after Pentecost, in early summer. This narrative calendar of festivals and seasons is ɜppered with numerous saints' days: anniversaries of the ıurch's heroes and heroines. The foremost of the saints Mary, the so-called 'Blessed Virgin' and mother of Jesus, ıd she has not one but a number of days dedicated to ɜr memory.

The annual cycle is divided into 'seasons' that build ɔ to or follow the major festivals: Advent, Christmas, piphany, Lent, Easter and Pentecost. Each season has its wn mood: in Advent, longing and expectation for the rth of Christ; in Lent, preparation and penance before ıster; in Pentecost, reflection upon the life and role of ıe church. The succession of liturgical seasons turns ıe year into an annual drama, which gives a religious ructure not only to worship, but also to the whole of life. lthough the church seasons are distinct from the four asons of spring, summer, autumn and winter, the litur-cal seasons do tie in at important points with the natural cle. Easter falls in spring when new organic life in the ıtural world echoes the theme of Jesus' resurrection in e liturgical calendar. Christmas falls at the winter solstice he shortest day of the year, when the sun is over the uator at noon). This coincided conveniently with both e Roman celebration of Saturnalia (the festival of their ɔd Saturn) and the pagan festival of the Unconquered ın. The church was able shrewdly to offer Christmas as a stival that would replace existing religious practice.

The traditional Christian calendar is distinct from ose of some other cultures in making no official ovision for celebrating the safe arrival of the annual ırvest. The Jewish thanksgiving festival of Tabernacles, r example, has no equivalent in the Christian year. But e harvest was such a crucial event that the celebration harvest eventually worked its way into the formal lendar. In medieval times Lammas Day (literally 'loaf-ass' day) may well have served as a harvest thanksgiving the beginning of August, with ceremonies for blessing ecially-baked loaves of bread. Celebrations of Lammas ll survive in Scotland, but have died out elsewhere. The odern harvest festival is a creation of the nineteenth-ntury Anglican church and was officially recognized ıly in 1862.

Although there are links between the four seasons and e church year, the liturgical calendar marks a spiritual ther than a natural physical process. Augustine argued rongly that Christian time was not merely cyclical like e natural seasons, but was always moving forwards wards the second coming of Christ. Whereas the seasons e stuck in a pattern of endless repetition, the liturgical ar describes an arrow pointing towards salvation, the d of time and the kingdom of heaven.

As with all matters of religion, the structure of the urgical year has been the subject of many contro-rsies and differences in practice. What is called 'the church calendar' is in truth a family of calendars sharing a common underlying structure. Easter, Christmas and Pentecost are universally celebrated, but for the more Protestant churches the calendar itself is not very important. Quakers, for example, argue that 'all true and acceptable worship to God' is not 'limited to places, times, or persons' (15 Quaker 'propositions'). For Quakers it is the inward spiritual life that matters and not 'all the foolish and superstitious formalities'.

Saint

Mary

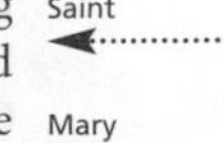

Quakers

The Eastern (or Orthodox) churches share the broad pattern of the Western (Roman) Church, but with many differences in emphasis and detail. The Eastern year begins before Advent on 1 September and is organized around Easter, 'the Feast of Feasts'. Next in importance are the 'Twelve Great Feasts', which include Christmas, Pentecost and four feasts of the Virgin Mary. The Eastern year is divided into three main sections: the triodion (the ten weeks before Easter), the pentecostarian (the weeks after Easter) and the octoechos (the remaining weeks of the year). The Eastern churches also have some unique festivals such as 'The Feast of the Protecting Veil of the Mother of God' (celebrated on 1 October) and 'The Feast of the Three Great Hierarchs' (celebrated at the end of January). There is a much greater emphasis upon fasting in the East and an altogether more rigorous calendar.

Orthodox churches

In the sixteenth century, the newly-established Protestant churches reformed the liturgical calendar by including only those festivals and ceremonies which had their origins in scripture. For example, the Augsburg Confession (1530) warned against 'traditions devised by man' and recommended celebration only of those festivals which 'are of service for tranquillity and good order in the church'. The Protestant churches regarded many aspects of the calendar as superstitious and anti-Christian. The keeping of saints' days was particularly objectionable to the Reformers, who argued that there was no basis in scripture for celebrating the lives of saints. The Protestant liturgical year was much more austere, with just a few key festivals like Easter, Pentecost and Christmas. Indeed, the Protestant churches put much more emphasis upon the celebration of Sunday as a weekly festival of the resurrection (which was the practice of the early church) than upon annual dates and seasons.

Protestantism

p. 302

The most controversial and complicated issue in the Christian calendar has been the dating of Easter. If these controversies seem pointless and bizarre to us today, we must remember that for Christians the day of Jesus' resurrection is the most important day in the history of the cosmos. Keeping Easter on the precise anniversary of the resurrection was a matter of the highest importance. We must also bear in mind the primitive state of pre-modern astronomical time calculation, which gave immense scope for differences of opinion about the true date of Easter.

Finally, we need to be aware that there is no record in the Bible about how the early church kept Easter, so that later Christians were left to argue about the practices of the first Christians. All in all, the question of the date of Easter was both highly charged and wide open to dispute.

Constantine's 'conversion'

The first of the so-called 'paschal controversies' arose in the second century and revolved around the importance of keeping Easter on a Sunday. The churches of Asia Minor followed the 'quartodecimanian' (Latin for fourteenth) practice of observing Easter according to the date of the Jewish Passover (i.e. the fourteenth day of the Jewish month Nisan), even if that day was not a Sunday. The Quartodecimanians (literally, 'the people of the fourteenth') argued that this was the practice of the apostle John. Their opponents argued that Easter should be celebrated on the Sunday following the Passover. The dispute raged through the second half of the second century, with the majority of churches sticking with the practice of keeping Easter on a Sunday. Though they formed their own sect, the Quartodecimanians had died out by the fifth century.

Religious orders

p. 966

Controversy did not end there, because there were further differences of opinion about the calculation of the date of the Passover. The traditional practice was to follow the Jewish method of dating Passover in relation to the vernal (or spring) equinox. The equinox occurs twice each year – in spring and autumn – when the sun crosses the equator, and day and night are of equal length. However, the Jewish calculation took no account of the position of the observer, which can make a significant difference to the calculations. Attempts to produce a better calculation were frustrated by astronomical incompetence on the part of the churches. As a result, Easter was often celebrated on quite different Sundays in different places. The Council of Nicaea in 325 CE tried to impose a standard calendar, but the Roman and Alexandrian churches continued to use different methods of calculation: Hippolytic and Metatonic respectively. The Metatonic method was the better of the two and enabled the production of a 100-year table of dates for Easter. In the subsequent two centuries there were various improvements to the calculations, culminating in a cycle devised by Bishop Victorius, which set the date for Easter for 532 years. The Victorian cycle was improved by 'Dennis the Little' (see also below) and later by the Venerable Bede. However, Victorius' method was not initially accepted by the church in Gaul (the Celtic churches), including the Northumbrian and Scottish churches. The matter was resolved at the Synod of Whitby in 664 after an acrimonious debate in which, according to Bede, the Celtic churches came grudgingly to see the error of their ways.

Origins and background

Council

These slow and haphazard attempts to standardize Christian time and worship were hugely significant for the development of Christianity. The liturgical year provide a global structure to time that would serve the church well in their international mission. The geographic reach of the calendar was given a vast boost by th Roman emperor Constantine in the fourth century. I 321 Constantine declared Sunday to be a legal holida throughout the empire and forbade commerce and nor essential work on the sabbath. The church was not slow t learn the lesson that it could expand quickly by convertin national or tribal rulers who were in a position to impos Christianity from above. The universal calendar mear that the celebration of festivals would be synchronized a over the planet. New Christians in all corners of the worl could feel part of the universal church by marking festiva in co-ordination with others around the globe.

In addition to the annual cycle, the Christian wee evolved its own calendrical structure. Sunday was a joyf celebration (or eucharist) of the resurrection and the were special days for fasting (Wednesday and Friday Those in religious orders, such as Benedictine monl and nuns, have every single hour of the day set asic for worship, work, eating or study. The day is structure around the 'liturgy of the hours' (otherwise known the Divine Office), consisting of seven periods of pray distributed through the day and night. Monks and nu literally give all their hours to God.

The rich and complex Christian calendar evolve over many centuries. Almost nothing is known about th festivals celebrated by the earliest Christians. It is assume that the first followers of Jesus (who still saw themselves Jews) would have observed the Jewish religious calenda It is clear that these early Christians kept Sunday as weekly celebration of the resurrection, with the sharing bread. It is probably the case that the early churches d not set much store by anniversaries, because they believe that the end of the world was imminent. Anniversari and other annual commemorations would have becon more important after the church re-framed its theolo to take account of the fact that Jesus had not con again. The celebration of Easter and Pentecost are th first documented festivals. Christmas and Ascension we celebrated by the fourth century, when the structure Holy Week started to take shape. The Christian calend is still developing with the addition of new saints ar commemorations.

Every calendar needs to decide two start points: a originating year and a date for the beginning of each ne year. The ancient Roman calendar counted years forwa from the founding of the city of Rome by Romulus ar Remus in what is now called 753 BCE. The Jewish calend counted forward from the *molod tohu* or 'nothingne immediately before the creation (Monday 7 Octob 3761 BCE). The practice of counting years from Chris

BIRTHDAYS AND NAME DAYS

When the dates of many figures in early Christianity are given, while the date of death may be firm, the date of birth usually has a c. (= Latin *circa*, 'around') against it. In fact for the first few centuries birthdays do not seem to have been marked particularly. We have virtually no clear information, but they may have posed problems for Christians because they were associated with other gods – in Greece the 'good daemon' and in Rome the Genius or Juno – who became guardian deities through life. Moreover the birthdays of Roman emperors were celebrated in a religious way. The church father Tertullian at the beginning of the third century remarks that he would prefer to see the dead commemorated on the day of their death rather than on their birthdays; Origen, slightly later, firmly remarked that he had carefully studied scripture and that nowhere in it was there mention of the celebration of the birthday of a just man. And the days of martyrs' deaths came to be described as their birthdays.

However, as Christianity became more integrated into society, pressure from outside to observe birthdays grew, and theological reasons were looked for to justify this practice. The key turning point came in the fourth century, when the birthday of Jesus began to be celebrated. The earliest evidence from this is a report by the church father Ambrose of Milan about a sermon on the birthday of the Redeemer preached on 25 December 353. The festival took on many of the features of the celebrations of the birthdays of Roman emperors.

Church fathers

Traditionally Christians named their children after saints and martyrs and the Roman Catholic 1917 Code of Canon Law even stipulated this, adding: 'If the parish priest cannot induce the parents to do so, he should add the name of some saint to that suggested by the parents and enter both in the baptismal register' (this has been replaced by the 1983 Code, which simply says that care should be taken not to give a name which is foreign to Christian sentiment). This practice led to the celebration in many countries of 'name days', the feast day of the saint whose name a person bore. Name days are still celebrated, and in some families are more important than birthdays. Symbols, colours and other elements associated with the saints' lives suggest various forms of appropriate celebration.

Canon law

p. 1076

birth did not start until the middle of the sixth century when a monk called 'Dennis the Little' coined the term Anno Domini (AD) or 'in the year of the Lord'. Dennis' idea took a while to catch on. By the eleventh century, however, the term Anno Domini was in standard use. In the eighth century the Venerable Bede added the term BC (Before Christ), although this was not a common term until much later. In the late twentieth century some academic historians started using the terms 'Common Era' (CE) and 'Before the Common Era' (BCE) in preference, respectively, to AD and BC, and in a multi-faith world this seems more appropriate. So it is the practice adopted in this *Guide*.

Although the Western Christian liturgical year starts at the beginning of December and the Eastern calendar at the beginning of September, the pre-Christian practice of starting the new year on 1 January has been standard in Christendom. Although this new year is not generally celebrated in the liturgical calendar, Methodist churches hold a Watchnight service on New Year's Eve to pray for the coming year.

The Julian Calendar (established by Julius Caesar on 1 January 45 BCE) was based upon the assumption that the average year is 365.25 days long (the so-called 'quarter-remainder' year). In fact the average year is 365.24219 days long. This may not seem a very significant error – after all, the Julian calendar was only 0.00781 days (about 11.15 minutes) out every year. The problem is that this error mounts up, so that after 128 years the calendar year was a full day out of synch. Pope Gregory XIII reformed the calendar in the late sixteenth century by making a correction of eleven days in October 1582 and adjusting the arrangements for leap years. The new Gregorian calendar was now only at 26.8 seconds' variance from the solar year, an error equal to one day every 3200 years. The Gregorian calendar has its drawbacks, primarily its lack of symmetry and regularity: the lengths of the months are irregular; days of the month fall on different days of the week; and the year cannot be divided into equal halves and quarters. However, although many subsequent reforms have been proposed, it is hard to imagine the Gregorian calendar being unseated in the foreseeable future.

The adoption by the various churches of the Gregorian calendar was a slow, painful and controversial process. The Protestant churches took much longer to accept the new system and it was not adopted in England until 1752. The Eastern churches also waited until 1924 to adopt the Gregorian calendar. Even today the churches of Jerusalem, Russia, Serbia and the monastic communities on Mount Athos persist with the Julian system. This explains why it is possible to visit some Orthodox churches and find them celebrating Easter and Christmas on a different Sunday from the Western Catholic and Protestant churches. The quest for a true world calendar continues, and has been pursued by some through ecumenical discussions and even in the United Nations.

Christendom

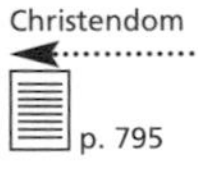
p. 795

The calendar is important to the church as a way of recalling and commemorating its sacred history. Festivals and anniversaries provide an effective mnemonic method

for Christian communities to keep in mind the life, death and resurrection of Jesus Christ. The calendar also provides a comprehensive curriculum for new church members seeking to learn the faith. As believers go through the year they are given a complete version of salvation history, the life of Christ, the major theological topics and the lives of the saints. With each passing year this knowledge is consolidated and developed. In a pre-literate society Christians would have been helped by cartoon-strip books, called 'paupers' almanacs', which gave pictographic information about the ecclesiastical festivals.

Scholasticism

Time

Fundamentally, the calendar affirms the belief that all time is sacred time. Christians believe that God created time and that time has a divine purpose. The calendar gives each day a special sacred significance and reassures the faithful that God is control of time and that life has a higher spiritual significance. Ironically, the message of the calendar is that time is only of secondary importance and that the true believer should be looking to the next life and not to this one. The ultimate purpose of the calendar is to direct the believer out of time altogether and into the eternal, time-less presence of God.

Humanism

HUGH RAYMENT-PICKARD

Thomas J. Talley, *The Origins of the Liturgical Year*, New York: Pueblo Press 1986; A. A. McArthur, *The Evolution of the Christian Year*, London: SCM Press 1953; E. G. Richards, *Mapping Time: The Calendar and its History*, Oxford: OUP 1999

Huldrych Zwingli

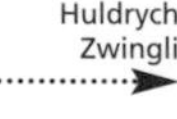

Calvin, John

Protestantism

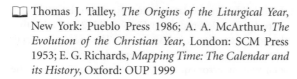

John Calvin (1509–64) was the premier Reformer of the second generation of Protestants and the author of the *Institutes of the Christian Religion* (1536), a work which, in its final edition, represented the most influential synthesis of the Reformed (or Calvinist) faith written in the sixteenth century.

Martin Luther

Calvin has always been a difficult figure for historians to grasp, for unlike those of Martin Luther (1483–1546), his theological works reveal very little about his character. Moreover, as Calvin actively discouraged any sort of cult of personality, few detailed portraits of the French Reformer remain. What little we know about Calvin's life was gathered after his death from the recollections of colleagues and biographers.

Born on 10 July 1509 in Noyon, a town in the region of Picardy in France, Calvin was sent by his father to the University of Paris. While in Paris, Calvin began to work on a degree of arts in the Collège de Montaigu and was immediately exposed to the cross-currents of intellectual life in the city. All colleges of the university placed a heavy emphasis on the philosophy of Aristotle (his works of logic in particular) and all students were fed a steady diet of grammar and rhetoric; but at Calvin's Collège de Montaigu there were other philosophical traditions in circulation as well, including the thought of the nominalists, which was proving so influential in the assault on medieval scholasticism, as well as the various schools of Augustinianism so central to the rise of evangelical theology. From around 1528 to 1531 Calvin was in Bourges and Orléans (again following his father's wishes), pursuing a higher degree in civil law. Historians have often emphasized the impact of his legal studies on the workings of his mind (as reflected, for instance, in his lifelong need for order and stability) but the most profound effect of his time in Orléans was his exposure to the methods and the teachings of the humanists. While in Orléans Calvin honed his talents as an interpreter of texts; he learned the most modern critical methods needed in order to understand a source in its context and he built on his philological skills, adding Greek to his knowledge of Latin and (once back in Paris) beginning the study of Hebrew. Calvin's first published book was not a work on religion but rather an edited commentary of the Roman philosopher Seneca's *On Clemency* (1532), a calculated attempt to make his name as a humanist author. It would have little impact on the world of learning, and it was only when Calvin turned his thoughts to religion that his fame began to grow.

Like the other main Protestant Reformers of the sixteenth century, Calvin has always been closely associated with one place: Martin Luther was in Wittenberg, Huldrych Zwingli was in Zurich, and John Calvin was in Geneva. From our perspective any other association seems hard to imagine, yet Calvin's connection to the imperial city was largely the result of fortunate timing. Once back in Paris, Calvin came under the influence of the local evangelical movement. At this stage he was still a fairly moderate Christian humanist, but he was becoming more and more critical of the Catholic Church. Thus when his friend Nicolas Cop, who had recently been appointed rector of the University of Paris, used the occasion of his inaugural address to give a Lutheran sermon and thereby bring down the wrath of the Catholic authorities on the evangelical community, Calvin was forced to join the other exiles and leave France. At first he resided in Basle, where he wrote the first edition of the *Institutes*, but it was on his way to Strasbourg, where he was headed in order to pursue a life of scholarship, that he made the most fateful decision of his life. While passing through Geneva, Calvin was recognized by the local Reformer Guillaume Farel, who convinced him to stay in the city and help him see through the Reformation. As Calvin later recalled it, 'he proceeded to utter an imprecation that God would curse my retirement and the tranquillity of the studies which I sought, if I should withdraw and refuse to give assistance when the necessity was so urgent'.

Apart from one short interlude while in exile in Strasbourg (1538–41), Calvin spent the rest of his life in Geneva. It is this association – the French Reformer and the imperial city on the borders of Switzerland – that history has best preserved. Calvin's influence on the Reformation in Geneva, and indeed on the history of the city during the sixteenth century, was immense; yet it was never easy for the Reformer to work in what was essentially a foreign country riddled by political intrigue. When he arrived, Geneva itself was the object of a political tug-of-war between the overlords of the city, the dukes of Savoy, and the neighbouring Swiss city-state of Berne, which had recently introduced the evangelical faith and was thus in full support of the Reformation in Geneva. Inside the city tensions were just as rife, as the supporters of Savoy (the Mamelukes) and the supporters of the confederation with Berne (the Eigenots) divided the populace. The arrival of Calvin and his uncompromising vision of a civic church just added to the tensions, and he would spend much of his life working to overcome the urban opposition. Calvin struggled against a faction within the city, led at first by Ami Perrin, a member of a prominent bourgeois family, who not only opposed the new ministry and the influx of foreign (mainly French) refugees seeking shelter in the city, but also resisted Calvin's attempts to see through comprehensive religious reform. Calvin referred to Perrin and his followers as 'Libertines', because of their lack of respect for his idea of godly order. On his death-bed Calvin spoke of the scale of resistance: they had abused him, taken shots at him, set their dogs on him. Ultimately, however, after a failed attempt at insurrection in 1555, the Libertines were finally quelled. Some were imprisoned, others were executed, and Calvin was left in relative peace to pursue his vision of the Christian community.

Calvin detailed his understanding of the faith in a huge flood of works – theological treatises, biblical commentaries, pamphlets, catechisms, church orders – most of which were published by the two great Genevan printers Henri Estienne and Jean Crespin. Like Luther, Calvin wrote in both Latin and the vernacular (in his case, French), and while his style was generally much more structured and formal than Luther's, he too showed great invention in the use of his mother tongue, sometimes creating new words in order to capture the meaning of complex Latin (such as the French verb *édifier* to relate the notion of building up, *aedificatio*). A large part of Calvin's literary legacy was not actually written by the Reformer at all, but recorded by stenographers as he lectured on the Bible or presented his many weekly sermons. However, he did write his most influential publication, the *Institutes of the Christian Religion* (1536), a work that went through numerous editions during his own lifetime (including a French translation). In the first edition, the *Institutes* was a fairly manageable compendium, just six chapters long, in the manner of a catechism. By 1559, the Latin edition numbered 82 chapters in four books, the most comprehensive synthesis of Protestant theology in existence, and the best guide to Calvin's thought on the nature of the Christian religion.

The *Institutes* (1559) is divided into sections according to the following themes: the doctrine of divine creation and providence; the doctrine of redemption and sin; the application of this redemption to the faithful (faith, regeneration, justification, predestination); and the nature of the godly community – by which is meant the church, the ministry and the sacraments. No single theological principle ties the work together (as, for instance, the theme of justification by faith unites the work of Luther), but it is clearly structured around the figure of Jesus Christ, in both his divine and human aspects. Book One examines how the individual may come to a knowledge of God. Calvin sees God in all creation, reflected in part in the natural order and partly intuited through a native sense of divinity. Because of man's fall from grace, however, human understanding of God is necessarily imperfect. Only through revelation can mankind come to know the creator, and that is the role of scripture and the Holy Spirit, for both will lead the believer to a deeper understanding of Jesus Christ. Book Two examines the centrality of Christ to the faith. In his analysis Calvin follows the sacred narrative from the Old Testament to the New, emphasizing how the coming of Christ represents a point of division: Christ is the mediator between the earthly and the divine; without Christ there is no redemption, for this act of sacrifice satisfies the debt of sin. Book Three turns to examine how the individual Christian can obtain grace and thus the benefits of Christ's sacrifice. Like all the Reformers, Calvin teaches that faith is the medium of sanctification. Through faith in the will and the Word of God believers share in the benefits of Christ's sacrifice, resulting in justification and sanctification. This later notion of sanctification was a theme prominent in south German and Swiss Protestantism, and it helps to explain why Calvin and his followers placed such stress on morality (for in this model good works follow justification). But perhaps the best-known principle of the faith in the *Institutes* was the article on predestination, an idea described as 'the eternal decree of God, by which he determined what he wished to make of every man. For he does not create everyone in the same condition, but ordains eternal life for some and eternal damnation for others.' Calvin referred to predestination as a mystery and did not expound it at great length. Its significance was left to later generations of Protestants to explore.

Reformation ← Justification
Revelation
Bible
Holy Spirit
Sacrifice
Predestination

John Calvin, John Wyclif, John Hus, Martin Bucer and other Reformers

Church · Tradition · Covenant · Ministry and ministers

In the final book of the *Institutes*, Calvin takes up the theme of the church and the issue of Christian order on earth. This is perhaps his most famous legacy, his idea of the godly commonwealth. In essence, Calvin's notion of the true church was the same as that of the other Protestant Reformers: the church is where the Word is preached and the sacraments are properly administered. Calvin rejected the Catholic idea that tradition was one of the foundations of the church. The only certain guide was the Word of God. With this as his premise, Calvin drew on scripture to develop a church for Geneva, all of which he detailed in the *Ecclesiastical Ordinances* (1541). Four offices comprised the body of ecclesiastical officials: pastors, teachers, elders and deacons. Paramount was the office of pastor, for the pastors were the men charged with the preaching of the Word and the administering of the sacraments. Calvin never wavered in his belief that the office of pastor was the linchpin of the Christian commonwealth. 'Neither the light and heat of the sun,' he wrote, 'nor food and drink, are so necessary to nourish and sustain the present life as the apostolic and pastoral office is necessary to preserve the church on earth.'

To help the pastors preserve the faith, teachers and deacons were appointed to watch over the church. The elders, however, were different in kind, for they were chosen from among the laity to oversee how the parishioners actually conducted their lives. Together with the pastors, the elders comprised the consistory, an institution first established in Geneva to regulate the morals and well-being of the community. Calvin's need for order was rooted in his theology. His understanding of the Law differed from that of Luther: the Law did more than just reveal the sinfulness of humanity; it served as an order for the covenant of God, so it followed that whoever observed the Law was in essence performing an act of faith. As a result of this conviction, Calvin sought order in every sphere of life, in both the civil and the spiritual world. As he remarked, 'it is only when we live in accordance with the rule of God that our life is set in order; apart from this ordering there is nothing in human life but confusion'. His desire to create the godly commonwealth in Geneva, an objective which met with so much success that it prompted the Scottish Reformer John Knox to claim that Geneva was 'the most perfect school of Christ that ever was ... since the days of the apostles', was derived from this article of belief.

Calvin's legacy was profound. The religion based on his work and his writings spread throughout the world. By the start of the seventeenth century Calvinism had taken root in France, Germany, Scotland, the Netherlands, many parts of eastern and southern Europe, and the American colonies. For many years Geneva served as a centre for the spread of Protestantism, establishing close ties with cities as far away as Heidelberg, Edinburgh and La Rochelle. Moreover, as later commentators would propound, many of Calvin's theological insights served as the basis for the intellectual and social revolutions that followed the confessional age. Scholars have claimed that many of the roots of the modern world can be found in Calvin's theology, from the principles of thought and behaviour associated with economic activism (and thus capitalism) and the scientific revolution to the phenomena of individualism, Puritanism, and the culture of doubt and anxiety. For Calvin himself, however, the ultimate consequences of his thought were always overshadowed by his efforts to grasp the meaning of scripture for the believer in the *present* – a search for understanding, he once wrote, which represented 'a continuous striving to the end of our lives'. John Calvin died in Geneva on 27 May 1564 and was buried, according to his wishes, in an unmarked grave.

C. SCOTT DIXON

William Bouwsma, *John Calvin: A Sixteenth-Century Portrait*, New York: OUP 1987; Alexandre Ganoczy, *The Young Calvin*, Philadelphia: Westminster Press 1987; Harro Höpfl, *The Christian Polity of John Calvin*, Cambridge: CUP 1982; Alister E. McGrath, *A Life of John Calvin: A Study in the Shaping of Western Culture*, Oxford: Blackwell 1990; François Wendel, *Calvin: Origins and Developments of his Religious Thought* (1987), Grand Rapids, MI: Baker Book House 1997

Canon

'Canon' when used of the Bible means the officially accepted, authoritative list of the books that comprise it. In the case of the development of the New Testament as we now have it, three stages were involved: writing, acceptance as scripture, and limitation to just 27 books.

The New Testament is not a flat, two-dimensional work, but one with a history. The earliest stage in that history was not the Gospels – even though they are of course concerned with the earliest relevant events, the life and work of Jesus – but the letters of Paul. Among those letters the first is not the one you first meet when you leaf through a New Testament (i.e. Romans), but the first letter to the Thessalonians. Most Christians take little interest in it, but it is the earliest piece of Christian writing that we possess, probably written within not much more than a decade of Jesus' crucifixion. In our New Testaments the Gospels come first because they are the story of Jesus, not because they were written first; and the letters of Paul begin with Romans, not because Romans was the first letter he wrote, but because it is the longest – the letters are simply arranged in descending order of length. But by tracing Paul's career from the book of Acts and correlating it with the various churches he wrote to, it is possible to work out the order in which they were written; and if you do that, you will find that 1 Thessalonians is the earliest letter.

p. 898

Jesus

We could say broadly that the New Testament came into being in three stages.

First, in the 40s and 50s CE, we have the letters of Paul. Paul knew a good deal about Jesus, his older contemporary, which he had learned from the disciples, although he never gives us a detailed account of Jesus' life; but he knew of course about the crucifixion and resurrection, and he recalls other traditions about Jesus, such as his institution of the Lord's Supper or eucharist (see 1 Corinthians 11.23–60).

Puritans

Secondly, from the late 60s onwards writers decided no longer to rely on oral memory for the stories about Jesus, but began to write them down, to make what we call the Gospels. Mark was almost certainly the earliest, followed by Matthew, Luke and John, later ones relying on earlier ones or perhaps on other collections, now lost, but adding material of their own. (Luke wrote a second volume, the Acts of the Apostles, but not necessarily immediately after compiling the Gospel: Acts may belong to the third stage.)

Thirdly, overlapping with the writing of the Gospels, the other letters in the New Testament (attributed to Peter and John and James) and the book of Revelation took shape. At the same time, probably in about the 90s CE, other letters were written and said to be by Paul, though most New Testament scholars think they are not really by him: examples are Ephesians and the so-called Pastoral Epistles, the letters to Timothy and Titus. From this period comes also the letter to the Hebrews, which some people in ancient times thought was by Paul, but which never says it is anywhere in the text.

Bible

There are thus three generations of writings in the New Testament: Paul; Gospels; pseudo-Paul, other letters and Acts. The present order of the books of the New Testament conceals this historical development from us.

But an account of how the books were written cannot be the whole story about how we come to have a collection called the New Testament. In addition, there had to be a recognition of these works as holy or inspired or authoritative: as scripture, in fact, rather than as merely miscellaneous Christian writings. Now the earliest

Paul
Authority

Christians did not call the Christian writings 'scripture', a title that was reserved for the Jewish scriptures, what we call the Old Testament. But they did come astonishingly soon to treat the first Christian writings with enormous respect and reverence. From the beginning of the second century Christian writers quote from Paul and the Gospels and treat them as absolute authorities. It is probably true to say that the New Testament writers did not think of themselves as writing 'scripture': 1 Thessalonians was not meant as a piece of the Bible, but as a real letter to a specific church. But on the other hand Paul did not think of his letters as merely casual documents, nor did the people who received them; they treasured them and applied them to new situations in the church's life, much as Christians do today.

The Gospels, similarly, were from the very early days read in the church's worship, and were treated with great reverence. It took only a few years for the New Testament writings to establish themselves as an authority alongside the Jewish scriptures. In fact, by the time the letter called 2 Peter was written, Paul's own writings are already being treated as scripture, because the writer says this: 'Our beloved brother Paul wrote to you according to the wisdom given to him, speaking of this as he does in all his letters. There are some things in them hard to understand, which the ignorant and unstable twist to their own destruction, *as they do the other scriptures*' (2 Peter 3.15–16). Paul is here being treated already as a piece of scripture, on a par with the 'other scriptures', that is, with what we call the Old Testament.

Holy

There is also a third element without which we would not have a New Testament. That is the growth of the idea not only that these particular books are holy, but also that no other books are of equal holiness. If you are to be able to include all the New Testament books within the covers of a single volume, there must be a limit to them – there must be what technically is called the 'canon', an authoritative list telling you which books qualify for membership. Now this development is surprisingly quite late.

Pseudepigraphy

Even in early times – indeed, even within Paul's letters themselves – there are warnings about not accepting spurious letters (see 2 Thessalonians 2.2); apparently other people wrote in Paul's name, and he distinguishes his own letters by telling us that he signs them in his own handwriting (Galatians 6.11; Colossians 4.18; he generally used a secretary for the main text, see Romans 16.22). But the rejection of specific writings as not part of the New Testament developed slowly, and it is not till the fourth century that we get definitive lists that exactly correspond to what is in our Bibles, and even then the books are not in quite the same order they are in ours. The great biblical manuscripts like the Codex Sinaiticus in the British Library contain extra books that we do not now regard as part of the New Testament. There was a plethora of alternative Gospels going the rounds in the second and third centuries, many of which we still have, but which the church eventually rejected, though elements from them passed into popular belief. Such elements are the names of the three wise men, or the tradition that the Blessed Virgin Mary's parents were called Joachim and Anna, which are not in 'our' Gospels. It is Athanasius, writing in 367, who first lists exactly the books we now have in the New Testament, and even he reports that there remain differences of opinion about a few marginal ones.

p. 149
pp. 128–9

So the canon even then remained slightly fuzzy at the edges, and it is only in medieval times that we start to get manuscripts containing only and exactly the books we now recognize, arranged in precisely the order we now have them. But it is important to get this matter into proportion. People quite late on in Christian history were a little doubtful about the authority of the third letter of John or the second letter of Peter; at the same time, on the other hand, they were quite disposed to read a work like the so-called Epistle of Barnabas as though it were more or less scripture. But no one was in any doubt about the status of the Gospels of Matthew or John, or the main letters of Paul. They had become authorities from astonishingly soon after they were written. The main heartland of the New Testament writings formed a Christian Bible from at the latest the mid-second century; it was only at the edges that doubts persisted, and that precisely because the books in question were not very central to Christian faith anyway.

The distinct stages of writing, acceptance as scripture and limitation to a particular list of books are also important when investigating the development of the Old Testament canon. The question of the Old Testament canon is much complicated by the fact that it crystallized in two different forms: a Greek form found in the Septuagint (LXX), i.e. the authorized Greek translation of the Jewish scriptures prepared in Egypt from the third century BCE onwards, and a Hebrew form, the Masoretic text (MT), attested in Bibles produced by the Masoretic tribal families of the ninth and tenth centuries CE onwards. It would be tempting to suppose that the Greek canon represented an Alexandrian version of the Jewish canon, and the Hebrew canon a Palestinian one, but the story may not be as simple. Both the Greek canon and the Hebrew precursor of what became the MT canon may have had an element of 'openness' to them at the time Christianity emerged; it is possible that biblical debate between Jews and Christians was a factor in the closure of the Jewish canon, and that there is a strong Christian contribution to the shaping of the LXX in particular. These are questions currently under debate.

In a Hebrew Bible the scriptures are divided into the

Law, the Prophets and the Writings. The Law, or Five Books of Moses, was probably a closed collection by the time of Ezra and Nehemiah, in the late fifth and early fourth centuries BCE: the earliest Old Testament canon. It used to be argued that the canon of the Prophets must have been closed by the 160s BCE, because Daniel (which was written in its present form at that time) is found among the Writings and not with the Prophets, where he would seem to belong. But is Daniel really among the prophets? His location with the wisdom books in a Hebrew Bible could be seen as an apter classification of a book that has strong ties to the Old Testament wisdom tradition. And Jesus himself is represented in the Gospels as speaking of 'the law and the prophets' (e.g. Matthew 7.12; 22.40), which might imply that in his time the Jewish scriptures were divided into two rather than three parts.

As in Christianity, so in Judaism there were arguments about the fringes of the canon. Jewish sources suggest some continuing discussion about whether Esther should be regarded as canonical or not. In Christian circles, a writer as late as the fourth or fifth century might raise more than an eyebrow at the fact that a book like Ecclesiastes was included in the canon of the Christian Bible. These complaints are not evidence that the canon was still undecided – rather the opposite – but they do attest the remarkable freedom which Christian writers sometimes allowed themselves in speaking of their scriptures.

JOHN BARTON

📖 John Barton, *Making the Christian Bible*, London: Darton, Longman & Todd 1997 and *What is the Bible?*, London: SPCK [2]1997; Étienne Charpentier, *How to Read the New Testament*, London: SCM Press and New York: Crossroad 1982; John W. Drane, *Introducing the New Testament*, Tring: Lion 1987

Canon law

Since the church is a complex reality of both the human and the divine, norms of behaviour are an inevitable and essential part of its life. From its very beginnings, the writings of the New Testament show how the early church community found it necessary to establish rules for the effective and fruitful living of the gospel message, particularly with reference to the structures of authority and ministry, the sacramental life of the community and the resolution of disputes and punishment of offences. As the church grew and spread throughout the Roman empire, local gatherings of bishops started to make regulations for their territories to meet the new challenges this presented. These canons were gathered into collections, sometimes ordered systematically, sometimes chronologically. The growing development and importance of the office of the Bishop of Rome also added to the production of laws, especially in the form of rescripts or replies to individual bishops who presented questions to the pope for resolution or guidance. By the twelfth century the often contradictory mass of these regulations, known as canons, had grown considerably, and the first attempt in Western Christendom to harmonize them into a single work was undertaken by a scholar at the University of Bologna.

In 1140, a figure about whom we know little, one Gratian, produced a collection of nearly 4000 texts which he sought to reconcile; he called it the *Concordantia Discordantium Canonum* ('Concordance of Discordant Canons'), and it is known as the Decree of Gratian. In the centuries that followed, a number of other collections were made, usually on the instruction of the Pope. These were published together with the Decree as the *Corpus Iuris Canonici* (Body of Canon Law) in 1582 by Pope Gregory XIII. This collection remained the standard text of canon law until the twentieth century. However, with the passage of time, there had been many additions and amendments, and the canon law had become confusing and inaccessible to the vast majority of the church. To remedy this, and following the modern continental tradition of codification, the first Code of Canon Law in the history of the Roman Catholic Church was produced in 1917 with the authority of Pope Benedict XV. This remained in force for over 60 years.

Nearly twenty years after the start of the renewal of the Roman Catholic Church initiated by the Second Vatican Council, on 25 January 1983, Pope John Paul II formally presented a revised Code of Canon Law to the Catholic world. The Council had dedicated much of its time to renewing the theological understanding of the church, centred upon the biblical image of the people of God. Greater emphasis was given to the reality of the particular church or diocese and the role of the bishop, and the importance accorded to the sacrament of baptism led to a renewed vision of the laity as sharers in the priestly, prophetic and kingly office of Christ. The influence of the ecumenical movement was also apparent. The 1983 Code was the culmination of a long process of translating this theology into canonical terms.

Council

Ecumenical movement

The Code consists of 1752 laws or canons applicable to the whole Latin Catholic Church, divided into seven books, covering nearly all areas of church life. Though all are ecclesiastical laws, they include a mixture of theological statements, recommendations, exhortations and concrete norms of action.

Discipline

Book One is largely theoretical and describes the basic legal concepts underlying the rest of the Code, such as law, custom and the subjects of the church's laws.

Book Two, the longest and perhaps most significant

book, is entitled 'The People of God', and deals with the diversity of canonical states within the church – lay, clerical or the various forms of religious life – and their respective obligations and rights. It also outlines the universal and local structures of leadership and consultation, the ministry of the Pope and the bishops and the key pastoral unit of the parish.

Mission

Book Three addresses those areas of ministry connected with the church's teaching office, including preaching, catechetics, missionary activity, schools and the means of social communication.

Book Four covers the fundamental canonical requirements for the valid and proper celebration of the seven sacraments – baptism, confirmation, the blessed eucharist, penance, anointing of the sick, holy orders and matrimony – and other liturgical matters.

Reformation
Sacraments
Justification

The slim Book Five contains norms concerning the acquisition, administration and alienation of the church's material goods.

Book Six deals with the delicate area of penalties for those who contravene the church's canons. This book is divided into two parts, the first covering the basic principles of penal law in the church, especially the understanding of culpability, and the second giving a list of specific offences and penalties.

Lastly, Book Seven sets out the structures and procedures of the church's tribunals or courts.

The Code provides a general framework of laws that govern the whole of the Latin Catholic Church. However, considerable freedom is left to the diocesan bishop to make local laws adapted to the pastoral needs, circumstances and culture of the people of his area. For greater pastoral effectiveness, such laws can on occasion also be made at the national level by the regular gathering of bishops of a country, known as the bishops' conference. Thus, whilst the Code lays great stress on the importance of maintaining communion between the bishops and the Pope, the appropriate levels of pastoral responsibility are recognized. Importantly, a separate Code was issued in 1990 for the 21 Eastern Catholic churches to respect and promote the unique traditions of eastern Christianity.

Church of England

Faith, love, grace and spiritual gifts always have first place in the life of the church and church law must always be of service to these. Canon law does not supersede them, but aims to provide an ordered environment in which they can be promoted and protected. The nature of the relationship between theology and canon law has always been a disputed matter throughout the history of the church, but although modern scholars belonging to different 'schools' of thought give more emphasis to one or the other, they all agree that there must always be an intrinsic connection between the two sciences. Theological reflection provides the values to which canon law gives concrete expression. Thus, as theology continues to expand human understanding of divine mysteries, canon law is called to reflect this.

Anglicanism
Theology

Canon law does share some similarities with other legal systems. However, its nature is unique since it is at the service of the mission of the church, the spreading of the gospel of salvation. It employs concepts such as equity and dispensation to ensure that the rigorous observance of the law does not harm the spiritual well-being of individuals. As the last canon of the Code succinctly puts it, the supreme law of the church must always be the salvation of souls.

At the time of the Reformation the role of canon law in the church was one of the issues challenged by the Protestant Reformers. The understanding of the time saw canon law as offensive to the principle of salvation by faith alone and as the expression of the unacceptable power of the Bishop of Rome. The new churches were often closely related to the civil authorities of the area and so left much of the law-making to them. However, seeing the need to provide some regulation of the internal life of the Christian community, particularly regarding membership and the administration of the word and sacrament, the Lutheran and Calvinist churches adopted the concept of 'church orders'.

In the modern era, most Christian churches have felt the need to adapt their internal laws to the new circumstances and challenges. The revision of canon law intended by the reformers of the Church of England in the sixteenth century was eventually completed in the second half of the twentieth century. The Canons of the Church of England were issued in the 1970s and have been frequently updated since that time. Besides reflecting the particular relationship with the state in matters of law resulting from establishment, the canons have sections on divine service and the administration of the sacraments, ordained ministers and their functions, the order of deaconesses, the lay officers of the church, church fittings, the ecclesiastical courts and the synods of the church. The canons are made by the General Synod, but must receive the royal assent before they have any force. Most of the other autonomous provinces of the Anglican Communion have similar collections of church law. Indeed, over the last decade, there has been a considerable revival in the study of canon law within the Anglican Communion.

Since the canon law or church order of every Christian church gives concrete expression to its doctrine of the church and its mission, it is inevitable that the study and revision of canon law should be an integral part of the ecumenical movement. As churches grow closer together as a result of theological dialogue, this will need to be reflected in their canonical structures. But although this was recognized by the World Council of Churches in 1974 in a document of the Faith and Order Commission, the contribution of canon law to the unity of the churches remains largely undeveloped.

KRISTIAN PAVER, JCL

Canon Law Society of Great Britain and Ireland, *The Canon Law, Letter and Spirit: A Practical Guide to the Code of Canon Law*, London: Canon Law Society 1995; J. A. Coriden, *Canon Law as Ministry: Freedom and Good Order for the Church*, New York and Mahwah, NJ: Paulist Press 2000; N. Doe, *Canon Law in the Anglican Communion*, Oxford: OUP 1998; L. Örsy, *Theology and Canon Law: New Horizons for Legislation and Interpretation*, Collegeville, MN: Michael Glazier 1992; M. Reuver, *Faith and Law: Juridical Perspectives for the Ecumenical Movement*, Geneva: WCC Publications 2000

Catholic Apostolic Church

The body which became known as the Catholic Apostolic Church, and sometimes though inaccurately as the Irvingites after one of its prominent early members, the Presbyterian Edward Irving, was formally constituted on 10 July 1835. On this day twelve 'apostles' who believed themselves to have been called by the Holy Spirit were designated for work as rulers of the church by seven independent London congregations which formed 'the Council of Zion'. This apostolic rule ceased on 3 February 1901 with the death of the last surviving apostle. Thereafter no ordinations to the major orders of its ministry were carried out; by its own choice the body fell into decline as, one by one, these orders ceased to exist. The last member of its episcopate died (in Germany) on 3 November 1960, its last priest (in England) on 16 February 1971, and its last deacon (in Australia) on 25 July 1972. Subsequently most of its remaining lay members have worshipped with other churches, though a few have restricted themselves to prayer-meetings led, where still possible, by members in the minor order of underdeacon. The title Catholic Apostolic Church was an accident of the 1851 church census in England, its members preferring to be known as 'congregations gathered under apostles' or simply as 'the Lord's work'.

There are still many Catholic Apostolic church buildings in existence, most notably two fine churches in London, one in Gordon Square and the other in Little Venice, Paddington. Those buildings which survive are now used by other Christians: for example, several have become cathedrals or parish churches of the Orthodox Church. Trustees are still appointed to deal with administrative and financial affairs. However, to all intents and purposes the Catholic Apostolic Church has now ceased to exist as an ecclesiastical body. It is a body that successfully completed considerable development in ministry and worship, demonstrating a remarkable fusion of Eastern and Western theology and worship.

One root of the Catholic Apostolic Church lies back in the events of the French Revolution. This gave rise in England to various societies and study-groups devoted to searching the scriptures for an eschatological interpretation of current events, seeking to determine which prophecies were as yet unfulfilled. The most significant of these groups gathered annually from 1826 to 1830 at Albury House (near Guildford), the home of the Anglican landowner and Member of Parliament Henry Drummond. One of their main conclusions was that current events were indicating the nearness of the 'last days', when the bowls of the wrath of God spoken of in the biblical Revelation of St John (chapter 16) were to be poured out, to be followed by the Second Coming of Christ and the ushering in of the 'millennium' of blessedness. Many of those who met at Albury were subsequently to play prominent roles in the Catholic Apostolic body, most notably Henry Drummond and Edward Irving. The meetings also gave rise to a prophetic journal *The Morning Watch*, edited by John Tudor.

Eschatology

A further development arose from the wide distribution of a pamphlet by an Anglican priest, James Haldane Stewart, calling for prayers for a new outpouring of the Holy Spirit upon the church. Miraculous instances of healing were recorded in south-west Scotland, together with prophetic utterances and speaking in tongues. These events were validated by a group from London led by John Bate Cardale, a lawyer. Similar events then took place amongst Roman Catholics in Bavaria in 1827, among Anglicans in London in 1831 and (the best known) at Irving's 'Scotch Church' in Regent Square. Eventually the disorders at this church received such notoriety that Irving, having been deposed by his local presbytery, was summoned to Scotland to be tried for heresy on the grounds that he had declared Christ's human nature sinful. He was found guilty on 13 March 1833 at a church court in Annan and deposed from the Presbyterian ministry. Irving was soon to be ordained to the Catholic Apostolic episcopate by Cardale, but then died on 8 December 1834 during a preaching visit to Glasgow.

Holy Spirit

As a number of charismatic congregations were expelled from their various churches, there was clearly a need for some sort of central government of these as yet independent yet like-minded groups. Many prophetic utterances had been calling for the restoration of apostles, the episcopate without apostolic rule being seen as having become a source of disunity rather than unity in the wider church. In November 1832 Drummond, in an ecstatic state of prophetic utterance, called Cardale to the apostolate during a prayer-meeting at Irving's house, and in December Cardale ordained Drummond to the episcopate as 'angel' of the newly-formed Albury congregation. This term was preferred to 'bishop' because it was considered to carry with it additional implications of spiritual rule in the last days. Drummond was prophetically called to the apostolate in September 1833, and further calls over the next two years completed a college of twelve apostles.

The body had two ecumenical aspects. During the period leading to its formation, members from most of the Western churches had been drawn into its ranks. Its membership was thus ecumenical, though it did not include members of the Eastern churches. More important, however, was the claim of the apostolic college to have been called to restore the broken unity of the wider church by acceptance of its spiritual rule. Hence 'testimonies' were delivered to all the principal rulers of church and state in Europe. Christendom, as the new Israel, was divided into twelve tribes, named after the tribes of the old Israel, each to be under the spiritual rule of an apostle. The body's ecumenical outlook was emphasized by its eucharistic hospitality offered to all baptized members of other churches.

Ministry and ministers

The college also set up appropriate orders of ministry to care for the needs of the various congregations. Acting on prophetic utterances, the apostles determined on a double fourfold structure. There were the traditional ministries of angel (bishop), priest and deacon, over which was set the apostolate, thus making a fourfold ministry of *order*. To the traditional ministries was then assigned a fourfold ministry of *character* corresponding to the four elements of the human psyche: the will, the imagination, the understanding and the affections. Thus, according to prophetic revelation at their ordinations, Catholic Apostolic clergy were designated respectively as elders (priests only), prophets, evangelists or pastors. Vestments of corresponding colours were worn: gold, blue, red or white. Purple, symbolizing rule, was worn by angels in charge of congregations and by apostles when visiting their tribes. Each apostle had a coadjutor (who might be designated an archangel) and all the principal clergy had designated helps in the same orders as themselves. A number of minor orders were also established, most notably deaconesses and underdeacons (subdeacons). Only certain of the clergy were 'separated', that is, in a paid full-time ministry, the majority continued to earn their living in secular occupations. Financing the full-time ministry was achieved through the payment of tithes in addition to the usual offerings given at church services.

pp. 354–5

In the initial days of the body each congregation continued to use its own inherited forms of worship. Such diversity was unacceptable to the apostles, who charged Cardale with the task of supervising the preparation of distinct liturgical forms that would reflect the particular witness of the body. After extensive research, involving experience of the worship of the various principal Christian communions, and a long period of development beginning with a first form for the eucharist in 1838, the final version of *The Liturgy and Other Divine Offices of the Church* was published in 1880. The beautiful office for the eucharist has aptly been described as Roman in form, Anglican in language and Eastern Orthodox in ethos.

The Catholic Apostolic body experienced three serious crises. The first related to the authority of the apostolic college in relation to that of the council of the congregations. In fact this reflected the apparently conflicting authorities of the apostolic and prophetic offices. It was settled by the college disbanding the council and declaring that the specific office of the apostolate was that of rule. The second was a gradual spiritual relaxation, described as a 'creeping apathy', evident as ministers passed away without any sign of the Second Coming of Christ for which the whole body was waiting. The apostles' response was the institution in 1847 of a rite of 'scaling', the laying on of an apostle's hands with chrism, to be administered to all adult members. Its effect was remarkable in that the apathy disappeared and members experienced a renewed sense of their calling and witness. The third arose as the death of apostles raised the question of the possible call of replacements. Prophetic utterances declared that apostles could not be replaced. However, in 1860 the angel of the Berlin congregation ecstatically called two angels, and in the next year a priest-elder, to the apostolate. The response of what was left of the original college was excommunication of all involved in such independent action. This excommunication led to a permanent schism and the setting up of what is now known as the New Apostolic Church.

The last surviving apostle died in 1901. As years passed, services had to be conducted by an ever-ageing and rapidly diminishing priesthood. As the clergy became too old and infirm to travel, members had to travel ever-increasing distances for as long as they were themselves able to do so. Following the passing of the last of the clergy, surviving members continued to gather for the reading of old homilies and the singing of the Litany and hymns, most but not all seeking the sacraments in other episcopal bodies. By the end of the twentieth century, the number of members still meeting together was reduced to a few hundreds, except in Germany, where the last surviving angel had ordained a number of young underdeacons who continued to maintain prayer-services.

COLUMBA GRAHAM FLEGG

📖 *The Liturgy and Other Divine Offices of the Church*, London 1880; R. A. Davenport, *Albury Apostles*, London: Neillgo Publications 1970, revised 1973; C. G. Flegg, '*Gathered Under Apostles*'. *A Study of the Catholic Apostolic Church*, Oxford: OUP 1992; P. E. Shaw, *The Catholic Apostolic Church*, New York: King's Crown Press 1946

Celtic Christianity

The huge growth of interest in Celtic Christianity over the last twenty years seems to have arisen in part from the answers it provides to some important questions. How can we live with looser and less centralized structures? What is the relationship between the beauty of the created world and Christianity? How can women find a voice in the church? Why are people so drawn to and spiritually moved by holy places? Whether, historically, the Christianity that existed among the Celtic peoples of the first millennium is the authentic provider of answers to these questions is immaterial to many. Today's pilgrimage places of the Celtic church – Lindisfarne, Iona, Bardsey, Monasterboice, St David's and many others – evoke a vision of what the church might have been like, and what the church could be like now.

In the last 50 years there have been enormous developments in the field of Celtic studies. In the early twentieth century a Cornish clergyman, Gilbert Doble, studied and translated the *Lives* of the Celtic saints and began to chart their travels. The picture has been broadened more recently by studies in historical geography, the examination of inscriptions and the excavation of significant sites, such as Whithorn in southern Scotland.

Alongside the historical and academic work there is a movement within present-day Christianity that finds the idea of the Celtic church attractive, alternative, spiritual and artistic. People pick from the wealth of culture that has come down to us from those days, such as legends of the saints, poems, sculpture, buildings and illuminated manuscripts which are often reinterpreted in contemporary modes of expression. Authors such as David Adam have made collections of prayers and the Iona Community has compiled worship books and composed hymns inspired by this tradition.

But who were the Celts and what gave rise to Celtic Christianity?

The ancient civilization of the Celts flourished for over 1000 years. In the fifth century BCE, Greek writers describe Celts living in the upper Danube region. It is a striking fact that when Paul wrote to the Galatians in western Turkey, they spoke a Celtic language. The Celts conquered Rome in 386 BCE and Delphi in 279 BCE. They were found in Gaul and Spain, and they moved westwards from France and the Low Countries into Britain, as the Germanic tribes and the Romans expanded their territories on the European mainland.

Celtic society was tribal, with elected chiefs who presided over tribal assemblies. Chiefs were also judges and commanded the army in time of war. Druids were professional teachers and priests, trained in tribal law and administration. Monks later took over much of their work. Bards were story-tellers, poets and minstrels. Druids and bards appear to have become Christian priests and monks. The Celts easily absorbed Christianity: they already believed in immortality and in the sacredness of creation. It has become a cliché to say that the Celts worshipped a triune God, but this fact is still acknowledged, although the Christian concept of a Trinity consisting of Father, Son and Spirit was new to these people.

Trinity

Christianity entered Britain through traders and travellers, through the Roman occupation, and through Christians emigrating from Gaul. There were periodic persecutions: we hear of Alban being martyred in the third century, and of two Christian soldiers named Julius and Aaron being executed at Caerleon in south-east Wales. In 313 the converted emperor Constantine gave Christians freedom to worship. A scattering of church foundations, lead cisterns for baptism and collections of communion vessels found across Britain suggest that Christianity spread easily in later Roman times. By then there were bishops in the provincial capitals of York, London, Cirencester and Lincoln; they are recorded attending church councils in Gaul, Italy and Bulgaria.

Persecution

Constantine's 'conversion'

In the English countryside, a number of villas became house-churches, as we can tell from their wall paintings and mosaics, which depict Christian themes. When the Romans withdrew in the first decade of the fifth century, life continued in these rural communities, and a villa was sometimes the nucleus of a later village, as the name implies. Romano-British Christian families appear to have kept their faith alive.

Many of the early British Christians known as the Celtic saints were monks and nuns. Monks lived in caves or huts, often grouped around a more experienced leader. Bishop Martin of Tours (*c.*316–97) was the best known of the early Western figures who pursued the monastic life. His friend and biographer, Sulpicius Severus, portrayed him as a Western Antony. Martin preached widely throughout the countryside, and is likely to have provided an important model for others in the Western church. Sulpicius Severus describes how the bishop lived in a wooden cell, surrounded by about 80 disciples, who dug out caves or lived in wooden huts, and shared all they possessed. The monasteries of Gaul developed a strong intellectual tradition, and from 400 CE their influence spread to Ireland and Wales.

Community

Paul

The remote monastic settlement of Skellig Michael, off the south-west coast of Ireland, dating from the seventh century

Monasticism

Saint

Pilgrimage

Journeys

In Celtic kingdoms, pastoral care was tribal: parishes had not yet evolved. Many Celtic saints were high-born members of their tribe. They might be sent to a nearby monastery for a good education; later they commanded their people's respect as they spoke about their faith. Priests and bishops were married. They often lived in monasteries, alongside monks and nuns who chose to remain celibate in order to be freer to pray and preach. Monastic communities came together to share food, work and worship. Craftsmen and their families also lived around a monastic compound.

Celtic monks and nuns, priests and bishops were often called 'saint' after their death. At this time, the title 'saint' simply meant someone wise and holy, or any good Christian who had died. Many Celtic monks, particularly in Ireland, became 'pilgrims for Christ', and left home in search of a solitary place which God would show them: somewhere unknown, where they could be alone with God. Many set sail in light, hide-covered boats, drifting with the wind and currents until they reached their new location. These men and women were not primarily missionaries, but when they settled in a new place, they had a profound impact on local people. Monks and nuns spread and flourished in the Celtic kingdoms of Ireland, Scotland and Northumbria, Wales, Cornwall and Brittany.

Throughout Celtic times, Ireland was a centre of monastic life and learning. St Patrick was a Briton who worked in Ireland in the fifth century. His remarkable autobiography, the *Confession*, is the only surviving account by a Celtic Christian of his conversion to God and his feelings about his life and work. He appears to have spread the gospel in the north of Ireland, around Armagh. Meanwhile, other missionaries, such as Déclán of Ardmore, lived and worked in the south. St Brigid is believed to have lived a couple of generations after Patrick; she perhaps died around 525. She founded a famous monastery of nuns at Kildare, 30 miles west of present-day Dublin.

A man of great promise who died young was the sixth-century monk Ciarán, who founded a community at Clonmacnoise beside the broad River Shannon, in the west of Ireland. Many of its buildings survive, including elaborately carved high crosses and a round tower. A contemporary of his was St Kevin, who established a monastery at the beautiful site of Glendalough, beside a pass through the Wicklow Mountains, 25 miles south of Dublin. Glendalough means 'Glen of the two lakes', and Kevin retired to live as a hermit beside one of them. St Brendan (died *c.*575) was a monk who chose the ocean as a focus for his monastic exile. *The Voyage of St Brendan*, written in about 780, was one of the most popular stories in medieval times.

Ninian was an early monk who worked in Galloway in south-west Scotland in the fifth century. The Venerable Bede briefly mentions him, and later the Northumbrians popularized his cult. Another early saint was Kentigern, a Briton who became Bishop of Glasgow in the sixth century. We know considerably more about St Columba (*c.* 521–97), who was born in Donegal into the royal family of the northern Uí Néill. He was an outstanding scholar, priest, poet and warrior. Columba established a community on the island of Iona, off the Scottish west coast, which became a centre of monastic life and learning throughout Celtic times. In response to an invitation from Oswald, King of Northumbria, a monk from Iona named Aidan founded a monastery on the island of Lindisfarne, which became a famous centre for manuscript art. The Book of Kells was created here, and so were the Lindisfarne Gospels. Its most famous abbot was an Anglo-Saxon, St Cuthbert.

St David (died *c.*589) worked in south-west Wales in what is now Pembrokeshire. He founded a monastery at St David's that was renowned for its austerity. His monks ploughed the fields themselves instead of using oxen, and spent the rest of the day reading, writing and praying. Further east, St Illtud's monastery at Llantwit Major in the Gower peninsula and that of St Cadoc at nearby Llancarfan became famous for their scholarship and learning. A collection of fine carved monuments survives at Llantwit Major. St Beuno was a missionary monk in north Wales in the sixth century. His niece, St Winifred, was the focus of an ancient and widespread cult; her healing well near the coast at Holywell has been a centre of pilgrimage from early times.

Many monks travelled across Cornwall to Brittany, and similarly, Breton monks evangelized Cornwall and Wales. One of these was St Cadfan, who is said to have made a foundation on Bardsey Island, off the tip of the Lleyn peninsula. Samson was a monk who trained at Llantwit Major, crossed Cornwall and later established monasteries in Brittany, including that of Dol on the north coast. He took an active part in Breton politics, and signed decrees of church councils in Paris in 553 and 557. There were some nine monasteries in Cornwall in Celtic times, and there are also early Christian remains in Cumbria and on the Isle of Man, where Vikings intermarried with Christian Celts. Their carved crosses display a unique style of Christian art.

Celtic Christianity and culture were extinguished in lowland Britain by the Saxons and the Normans, but in some of the more remote regions, such as the Scottish highlands, Celtic monks (Culdees) survived throughout medieval times until the Reformation. In the nineteenth century, Alexander Carmichael collected poems and prayers chanted by farming and fishing communities in the Scottish highlands and islands which preserve elements of Celtic theology and thought. Beautiful prayers to accompany everyday activities such as lighting the peat fire and herding the cattle are found in Carmichael's *Carmina Gadelica*.

Reformation

It is not easy to come close to the Celtic saints, since most of their biographies were written in medieval times, centuries after their lifetime. However, the sites where Celtic monks, nuns and missionary couples lived and worked can still be seen in the more remote parts of Britain, Ireland and Brittany. Their huts, holy wells and chapels are often set in beautiful landscapes: sheltered valleys, dramatic headlines and rocky islands. Archaeology, the study of sites, of place names, inscribed stone and early texts can provide us with further clues about how these men and women lived and the unique ideals they held. However, most of their writings and their magnificent works of art have perished as a result of attacks by Vikings, Saxons, Normans, the Reformation and the ravages of time. What survive today are only pieces of a very large jigsaw puzzle; they provide us with no more than a few clues about Celtic peoples, their thought, their beliefs and their way of life.

Archaeology

Books

ELIZABETH REES, OCV

📖 E. G. Bowen, *Saints, Seaways and Settlements in the Celtic Lands*, Cardiff: University of Wales Press 1969; Ian Bradley, *Celtic Christianity: Making Myths and Chasing Dreams*, Edinburgh: Edinburgh University Press 1999; Alexander Carmichael (ed), *Carmina Gadelica: Hymns and Incantations*, Edinburgh: Floris 1994; Thomas O'Loughlin, *Saint Patrick: The Man and His Works*, London: SPCK 1999; Elizabeth Rees, *Celtic Saints, Passionate Wanderers*, London: Thames & Hudson 2000; Charles Thomas, *And Shall These Mute Stones Speak? Post-Roman Inscriptions in Western Britain*, Cardiff: University of Wales Press 1994; Esther de Waal, *World Made Whole: Rediscovering the Celtic Tradition*, London: HarperCollins 1991

Chinese religions and Christianity

The Christian movement has grown rapidly in the countries of East Asia. Korea has a very large and vibrant set of churches. Japan, though with a much smaller percentage

Christianity in Asia

of Christians, also has a strong Christian presence. In China, Taiwan and Hong Kong, the Christian churches have not only revived but are growing rapidly. Many of these East Asian Christians are deeply committed to a dialogue with their traditional cultures. They no longer believe that to be Christian is to become a convert to all aspects of Western culture. Many Asian Christians have taken the lead in dialogue with the religions of China.

Chinese religions

When Christians first arrived in China, they would have encountered basically three major forms of indigenous Chinese religion and one import from South and Central Asia, Buddhism, which played a vital role in Chinese religious life. Islam would also arrive in China from the West to become part of the Chinese religious mosaic, but much later than either Buddhism or Christianity.

The first of the indigenous traditions was Daoism. Although not as well known in the West as Confucianism or Buddhism, Daoism is the great native Chinese religious complex, and Daoists played a vital role in the first great dialogue between the Christian movement and the Chinese religious world. Religious Daoism traces its roots back to the writings of some of the greatest philosophers of the classical age in China (roughly from 551 BCE to 221 BCE). The two most famous texts are the *Daodejing* of the legendary Laozi and the works of Master Zhuang, a collection of writing now known as the *Zhuangzi*. As with so many of the great texts of this era, all later Chinese intellectuals, regardless of their specific religious affiliations, honoured and enjoyed works such as the *Daodejing* and the *Zhuangzi*. Nonetheless, organized religious Daoists from the second century of the Common Era believed that they shared a special affinity with these early texts.

Mission
Orthodox churches

At the end of the second century CE a number of great teachers arose and began the organization of the various Daoist sects, some of which still exist today in the Chinese cultural world. The period from the second century to the ninth century was the era of the great flourishing of the Daoist religious movements. Texts were revealed, temples were built, organized priesthoods were ordained, emperors were converted, and great debates were held with Confucians and Buddhists about the true nature of the Dao, or the Way.

Confucianism always likes to think of itself as the oldest of the Chinese religious traditions. Although it is identified with the teachings of Master Kong or Confucius, as he is known in the West (551–479 BCE), Confucians hold that they are really the disciples and students of the great sage kings and ministers of China's mythic past. Confucianism was ultimately proclaimed the official state ideology in the second century BCE. However, by the time of the decline and fall of the great Han empire at the end of the second century CE, Confucians were tired, and confused by the fall of their dynasty. Rather like the fall of Rome at the other end of the Eurasian landmass, the demise of the Han marked the end of the first phase of Confucian intellectual and religious dominance in the Chinese cultural world.

The third indigenous religion of China is the popular or folk religion of the common people. It takes a bewildering variety of forms, and all the élite traditions, such as Confucianism, Daoism and later Buddhism, made use of its common sensibilities. It is a religion of nature and spiritual forces, celebrating the ties of family, of the world of spirits of mountain and sea, of geomancy, chants, divination by diverse methods, talismans, feng shui, spirit writing and the propitiation of the ghosts of the dead. Many scholars believe that ancient Chinese folk or popular religion is closely related to shamanism as found throughout northern Asia. Along with Confucianism, popular religion is always intimately linked to the life of the family.

The fourth religion of China was imported, like Christianity, from the West. Buddhism, which entered China via the Silk Road through Central Asia, was already recognized as an emerging religious alternative to Daoism and Confucianism by the second century CE, though the great Buddhist period in China was slightly later. Actually, Buddhism and Christianity must have arrived in China at about the same time, though Christianity only made its impact felt after Buddhism had secured a successful and often dominant place in the intellectual and religious life of medieval China.

The Nestorian mission

In the sixth and seventh centuries CE the great Christian missionary church was the Church of the East, or the Nestorian Church. The Nestorian Church's activities stretched from Persia in the West to the grandly revived Tang dynasty (618–907) in China. A stone monument records the arrival of Alopen, a Nestorian missionary, in 635 at the Tang capital, beginning the first great dialogue between the Christian movement and Chinese religions. After a series of ups and downs, it was also recorded on another imperial stone monument that in 781 the Christian movement achieved recognition as a legitimate religion in China. The story of this early and highly successful mission was forgotten until these stone monuments were rediscovered during the even larger Catholic mission to China in the sixteenth and seventeenth centuries. These stele were extremely important for the later Christian missions because they demonstrated that the Tang emperors had decided to accept the Christian church into the Chinese empire.

What is even more exciting about the Nestorian mission is that the Nestorian priests and scholars were active ırtners in the inter-religious dialogues of the Tang period. is clear from reading the various Chinese translations of hristian material that the Nestorian missionary-scholars ere skilled at presenting the Christian faith in terms ıat would make sense to the Chinese audience while maining faithful to the fundamentals of the Christian ith.

Two stories of this kind of dialogue are illustrative the interaction between Christians and Daoists and uddhists in the Tang dynasty. One of the most famous all Daoist temples is the grand Lou Guan Tai temple mpound south of the modern city of Xian in north-west hina. Although the story, like the great stone monuments, as been lost in the haze of history, it goes something like is. The Daoists of Lou Guan Tai befriended the Chinese holar-monks and priests of the new Nestorian Church. lthough Buddhists were not allowed to build within Lou uan Tai, the Daoists not only allowed the Nestorians to ork in their temple compound, they even encouraged the estorians to build their own Da Qin pagoda on Daoist nds. The Da Qin pagoda still exists today and is being udied and restored as an important archeological site.

It is also recorded that when some famous Japanese lgrim monks came to the Tang capital Chang'an in the ırly ninth century, they were supported and encouraged their translation work by a Nestorian priest. The estorian priest was skilled in the various languages of dia, Central Asia and China and was hence able to assist e Japanese monks, probably including such luminaries Kukai of the Shingon School and Saicho of the Tendai hool, in preparing texts to take back to Japan. It is fascinating to contemplate the role of these learned Christian issionaries as colleagues in dialogue with equally learned aoist and Buddhist friends from across East Asia.

Although we do not understand the reasons why, the estorian mission to China was not successful and the ıristian movement disappeared as part of the Chinese ligious mosaic. There were some sporadic attempts by e medieval papacy to send missionaries to China during e heyday of the Mongol empire, but these were minor comparison to the earlier Nestorian mission and the uch larger and sustained mission begun in the sixteenth ntury.

ıe Jesuit mission

ıe second great dialogue between the Christian ovement and the religions of China began in earnest the sixteenth century with the justly famous Jesuit ission to China. The Catholic mission included priests om many different Roman Catholic orders, but it was e Jesuits who were able to establish a foothold in China ıring the last days of the Ming dynasty (*c.* 1590–1644) d the founding of the Qing dynasty (1644–1911). The Jesuits were acutely aware that China was a huge, proud and powerful empire with a profound and rich cultural history. Led by the able Matteo Ricci, they realized that the only way they would have access to the hearts and minds of the Chinese people was to become scholars of the Chinese tradition, and they set out to learn about Chinese philosophy and religion with a passionate intensity.

The Jesuits had an ambivalent attitude to the Chinese philosophical and religious tradition, but fundamentally rejected it. First, while they were favourably disposed to many aspects of Chinese culture, they believed that this ancient culture still needed the infusion of the saving message of the Christian gospel. Moreover, they came to respect parts of the Chinese religious heritage but rejected other aspects rigorously. For instance, they decided that they could accept the Confucian Way as a form of pagan philosophy and ethical culture much like the best of late Graeco-Roman philosophy. Secondly, they saw nothing wrong with the five cardinal virtues of the Confucian tradition as long as these virtues were completed or perfected by the revealed truths of the Gospels and traditions of the Catholic Church. Many Chinese literati agreed with the Jesuits and accepted the new wisdom from the West and converted to Christianity without forsaking the core of the ethical teachings of the Confucian Way. The Jesuits offered dialogue and wisdom and not negative confrontations.

If the Jesuits developed a profound respect for the Confucian Way, the learned scholar-missionaries completely rejected any such positive interpretation of Chinese Daoism, Buddhism and folk religious practices and beliefs. If Confucianism could be accepted as a profound form of social ethics, all the other religions had to be spurned as negative forms of superstition and error. This view was congruent with the way many Confucian scholars also viewed the other religions of China. But in the end the Jesuit mission was crippled by negative theological rulings from Europe about its positive view of Confucian philosophy and ritual. The Jesuits argued that Confucian ritual was lawful because it was not ultimately a form of idolatrous worship, but the Pope ruled against them and forbade Chinese converts to take part in traditional Chinese family, community and state Confucian ritual.

The Protestant missions

When the Catholic mission was floundering on the shoals of the controversy over Confucian ritual practice, in the middle of the nineteenth century Protestant missionaries arrived in China. This was also a period of great decline in the power of the Chinese state, leading to the fall of the Qing dynasty and what the Chinese call a semi-colonial period for the Chinese people. The Protestant missionaries were

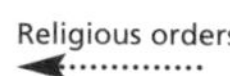

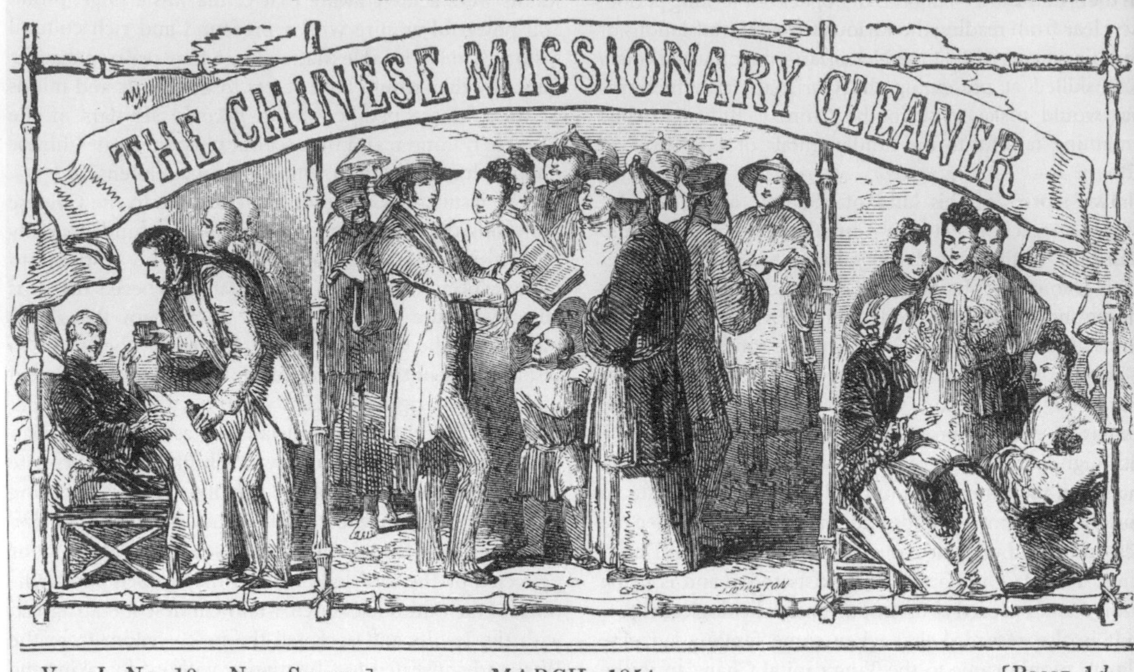

THE CHINESE MISSIONARY CLEANER

VOL. I. No. 10. NEW SERIES.] MARCH, 1854. [PRICE 1*d*.

*** This publication is the organ of the Chinese Evangelization Society; and the friends of China are earnestly requested to promote its circulation.

CHINESE EVANGELIZATION SOCIETY,

17, RED LION SQUARE.

Front page of *The Chinese Missionary Cleaner*, March 1854, published by the Chinese Evangelization Society

much less inclined to take a positive approach to dialogue with Chinese religions. While some great missionary-scholars such as James Legge – the greatest translator of the Chinese classics into English – had a high regard for the Confucian Way, many other Protestant missionaries affirmed that all traditional Chinese philosophy and religion would need to be replaced by the teachings and rituals of the Christian faith. But even in spite of the negative theological judgements on the Chinese religious scene by the Protestant missionaries, many individual missionaries engaged in positive exchanges with individual Chinese scholars and Daoist and Buddhist monks.

Although this period was not very positive in terms of the intentions of the Christian missions, it was very important because the Chinese were learning a great deal about Western culture. The initial Chinese reaction was extreme caution in accepting foreign influences. With the arrival of the imperial West during the Opium Wars in 1839, the Chinese were justly worried that Western Christianity was being imposed on them at the end of tl barrel of a gun. After suffering defeat after defeat at tl hands of the aggressive Western powers from the midd of the nineteenth century to the middle of the twentie century, it was amazing that many Chinese continued have a positive understanding of anything about Weste culture. During this period there was a steady grow of the Christian movement, and many of the Chine converts retained a more positive regard for their trad tional culture, a feeling not always matched by the Weste missionary community.

With the victory of the Communist movement the civil war in China in 1949 and the foundation of tl People's Republic of China, it appeared that Christiani was in dire shape. The Chinese Communists we uniformly hostile not only to the Christian movement b to all forms of religion, Chinese or foreign. The peri from 1949 to the reforms of Deng Xiaoping after the dea of Mao in the late 1970s was a terrible time for all religio n China. Daoists, Confucians, Buddhists, folk religionists, Muslims and Christians were all persecuted. The only good outcome is that with the end of the Cultural Revolution, Chinese Christians were no longer viewed as the dupes of Western missionaries.

A sea change was also taking place in the Western Christian world as China was going through the throes of the last stages of Mao's rule. In the early 1960s, the Second Vatican Council called for positive dialogue between the Roman Catholic Church and the religions of the world. The change in Roman Catholic thinking about relations with the other religions was closely followed by similar changes in the attitudes of the members of the World Council of Churches. The Christian churches now affirmed that they might appreciate the other religions; in time Christians even agreed that there might be many positive things to be learned from dialogue with the other religions. This new regard for positive dialogue and mutual enrichment began a fourth phase of the Christian encounter with the Chinese religions.

A wider vision

In many ways there has been a return to the insights of the Jesuit missionaries, but with an even more inclusive vision. Along with the dialogues with Confucianism, Christians have begun conversations with Daoists, Buddhists, Muslims and followers of the folk religions. One can only imagine that some of the Buddhist monks who sought dialogue with Christians in the 1920s would have been delighted with the new dialogues emerging all over the Chinese cultural world.

With the long Chinese experience with religious pluralism, many Chinese intellectuals believe that they have valuable insights to offer to the emerging inter-religious dialogues now encouraged by the Christian movement around the world.

JOHN BERTHRONG

John H. Berthrong and Evelyn Nagai Berthrong, *Confucianism: A Short Introduction*, Oxford: Oneworld 2000; Julia Ching, *Chinese Religions*, Maryknoll, NY: Orbis 1993; Bob Whyte, *Unfinished Encounter: China and Christianity*, London: Collins Fount Paperbacks 1988

Christendom

Nowadays, the word Christendom is most often used to describe a society that considers itself Christian and undertakes sanctions and other measures to maintain itself as such. In its purest sense, Christendom had its heyday long ago in the Middle Ages, and is no more. But the Christian faith continues to carry the seeds of the idea of Christendom.

The German theologian and sociologist Ernst Troeltsch (1865–1923) grasped the essence of the phenomenon when he described the prevailing concept of 'church' in Western Christianity from late antiquity up to the time of the Reformation and contrasted it with the concept of 'sect', a type of religious organization which also made its appearance in the Middle Ages, though it is more characteristic of the modern age. Whereas 'sect', for Troeltsch, denotes an entity which one joins by choice, its members distinguishing themselves clearly from those who do not belong to it, 'church' denotes an entity into which one is born and which suffuses the society to which it pertains. Whereas the sect receives its members by their own decision to be baptized as believers, the church baptizes its members as infants – an event over which they evidently have no control, but through which everyone in the society is, as Troeltsch put it, 'welcome to partake of the goods of salvation'. Such was the spirit of Christendom.

Church

Council

The fourth and fifth centuries CE were the crucial formative period of Christendom. It was in 313 that the Roman emperor Constantine (died 337) declared toleration for Christianity and brought the long period of official persecution to an abrupt end, in the wake of the military victory that he owed, as he thought, to the intervention of the Christians' God. Constantine did not actually seek to be baptized until the end of his life, but he favoured the Christian church throughout his reign: he supported clergy financially, exempted church lands from taxation, ordered the allocation of construction materials for church buildings and food for Christian widows and virgins, and intervened in the controversies over the heresies of Arianism and Donatism. He thus set Christianity on the path to becoming the official religion of the empire, though it was not until the end of the fourth century that subsequent emperors began to enact the body of legislation – enshrined eventually in Book 16 of the Theodosian Code of 438 – that in effect declared the empire Christian, prohibiting both paganism and heresy and establishing the bases for state support of the church.

Constantine's 'conversion'

Persecution

pp. 520–1

Law

Paganism

Heresy

Alongside these legal underpinnings of Christendom, its theological underpinnings found classic expression at about the same time in the writings of Augustine (354–430) who, out of a profound distrust of the powers of the unaided will of fallen human beings to choose what is right, argued for the forcible closure of the churches of the schismatic Donatists, as well as (most famously in his influential work *The City of God*) for the suppression of polytheism. The institutions and beliefs of Christianity were becoming a feature of society itself, a given rather than a matter of choice.

Society

Middle Ages

Church of England ➤ Lutheranism ➤ Christianity in the Middle East Papacy Roman empire pp. 552–3 Christianity in North America ➤ Christianity in Africa Ethiopian Christianity

The period of about 1200 years that followed Augustine's time was the great age of Christendom – or rather of Christendoms, for many distinct Christian societies appeared in this period. Not all Christians, to be sure, inhabited Christian societies; it is important to remember the churches that have survived from the seventh century until the present under Islamic rule, for example in Syria, Egypt and Persia. But in other places Christian societies flourished. Western Europe, where the Roman papacy constituted a unifying principle within, though in constant tension with, the shifting principalities and other temporal authorities of that large region, was just one of these Christendoms. Another was the Byzantine commonwealth centred on Constantinople, which until its fall to the Ottoman Turks in 1453 directly continued the institutions of the old Roman empire in the Greek-speaking areas of the north-west Mediterranean. To the north, the conversion of Slavic princes in the ninth and tenth centuries created another area of Christendom; the Slavic churches were always closely related to Constantinople but, from the fifteenth century onwards, Moscow became a pre-eminent centre in its own right, calling itself the 'third Rome' in succession to Constantinople. Armenia, though often subjugated by other powers, maintained an identity as a Christian nation from the time of the conversion of King Trdat III at the beginning of the fourth century. And far to the south in Africa, Christian kingdoms survived in Nubia (in present-day southern Egypt and Sudan) from the sixth to the twelfth century, and in Ethiopia from the fourth century until the mid-twentieth.

Wars of religion Reformation Anabaptists Secularization ➤ Geography ➤

The demise of Christendom has been a major feature of the modern era. The wars of religion triggered by the Protestant Reformation in sixteenth- and seventeenth-century Europe played a crucial role in that demise. One could say that the idea of Christendom – to which the major Protestant groups (excepting the Anabaptists) as well as the Catholics continued to subscribe – even caused those wars, in the sense of allowing no room for a choice of belief, and therefore no remedy but violence for irreconcilable differences of belief; and it was in the aftermath of those wars of religion, in the late seventeenth  century, that such Enlightenment thinkers as John Locke (1632–1704) began to argue for the necessarily voluntary character of religious belief and consequently the necessity of tolerating the beliefs of others. In the two centuries since the American and French Revolutions, such toleration has become a basic tenet of most states outside the Islamic world.

Christendom, in its classic form of a society in which citizens are perforce Christians, is thus largely a thing of the past. But the idea of Christendom has not entirely disappeared, in two senses.

In the first place, churches with roots in the era of Christendom retain important vestiges of it even as they adapt to, or even positively embrace, the changed conditions of modern society. Perhaps the most obvious examples are the historic national churches that retain some small degree of support or special recognition from the state, as for instance in England or Germany. But more profoundly, there is in every church that practises infant baptism, whether Protestant, Anglican, Orthodox or Roman Catholic, a certain echo or resonance with the old idea of Christendom – an affirmation of Christian faith as something that we do not simply choose as individuals but that also, itself, shapes and suffuses the social structures into which we are born. Such churches, historically rooted as they are in pre-Enlightenment ideas, can never embrace modern individualism without some lingering, even if only semi-conscious, reservation, some vestigial memory of Christendom.

The idea of Christendom has also, in the second place, survived in a more explicit albeit changed form, namely in the idea of a voluntarily Christian society. This idea has had an important history in the USA, a nation that almost immediately after its formation, in a constitutional amendment of 1790, decisively repudiated the old Christendom by forbidding the state to legislate in matters of religion. The amendment itself, however, received widespread support from many Christians, who thought of it as opening the way to a more rather than less Christian nation, in which, as the American pastor John Henry Livingston (1746–1825) wrote, 'truth is left to vindicate her own sovereign authority and influence'. The resulting free market of religious ideas in the USA quickly gave rise to a lively abundance of churches and sects and produced the paradox, often baffling to foreign visitors, of citizens who embrace the resolutely secular principles of the Constititution and at the same time aspire to a vision of a fully Christian nation. Even though prominent segments of American society have become as secularized as the societies in Europe where Christianity is in steep decline, still the percentage of Americans who belong to churches has risen steadily over the last two centuries and continues to rise; and the political influence of such Christians, secular republic or not, is not inconsiderable.

The USA is not the only society with such a critical mass of Christians. Today's strong numerical growth of Christians in nations south of the equator (who now outnumber those in the north) is well known, and it is among these nations that the historian Philip Jenkins has recently foreseen the rise of a 'new Christendom' within the next several decades, indigenized to its various cultures but also markedly traditionalist in comparison to the permissiveness of Western culture, and typically in competition with Islam. What specific form such a new Christendom might take, and what it may have in common with the old Christendom, is not clear, but apparently the idea of a Christian society is far from defunct.

JOHN W. COAKLEY

Peter Brown, *The Rise of Western Christendom. Triumph and Diversity AD 200–1000*, Oxford: Blackwell 1996; Roger Finke and Rodney Stark, *The Churching of America 1776–1990*, New Brunswick, NJ: Rutgers University Press 1992; Judith Herrin, *The Formation of Christendom*, Oxford: Blackwell 1987; Philip Jenkins, *The Next Christendom: The Coming of Global Christianity*, New York: OUP 2002; Alan Kreider (ed), *The Origins of Christendom in the West*, Edinburgh: T&T Clark and Harrisburg, PA: Trinity Press International 2001; Ernst Troeltsch, *The Social Teaching of the Christian Churches* (2 vols, 1931), London: Allen & Unwin 1956 and New York: Harper & Row 1960

Christian Church (Disciples of Christ)

The Christian Church (Disciples of Christ) traces its beginnings to the early national period in America. Disciples point to the work of four founders to describe their origins. All four men had ties to the Presbyterian Church. Barton Stone (1772–1844), the only one born in America, served as pastor of two Presbyterian congregations in Kentucky. In 1801, he served as the sponsoring pastor for the Cane Ridge revival, drawing an attendance of between 10,000 and 30,000 during the Second Great Awakening. The camp meeting revivals brought controversy. Stone withdrew from Presbyterianism and, with others, formed a loose association of congregations resolving 'to sink into union with the body of Christ at large'. These congregations took the name Christian and gained strength in North Carolina, Southern Virginia, Kentucky and Ohio.

Thomas Campbell (1763–1854) and his son Alexander (1788–1866) were Scottish-Irish Presbyterians who came to America in 1807 and 1809 respectively. In 1808, Thomas withdrew from the Presbyterian Church in Pennsylvania when he was rebuked for serving the Lord's Supper to Christians not associated with his brand of Presbyterianism. A year later, he formed the Christian Association of Washington, Pennsylvania. Shortly after this event, his family arrived. Alexander, 21 years old, quickly became a leading figure. Members of the Christian Association adopted the name 'Disciples'. By 1830, with the help of the evangelist Walter Scott (1796–1861), who had arrived from Scotland in 1818, the movement grew rapidly and formed congregations in Pennsylvania, Ohio and West Virginia.

In 1812, Alexander Campbell affirmed believers' baptism by immersion as the proper Christian baptism. This led to a brief (1815–30) affiliation with Baptists. Disciples disrupted Baptist life by seeking reform. They urged Baptists to eschew denominational names in order to unite around the simplicity of the apostolic faith, illustrated by the Disciples' commitment to 'no creed but Christ'.

Initiation
Baptist churches

During the 1820s, Campbell's Disciples ('Campbellites') and Stone's Christians discovered one another. By 1832, they had worked out a formal union that combined about 22,000 members. This union left a legacy of two names. Present-day congregations are known as 'Christian' churches, while their members are called 'Disciples'. In 1968, the denomination adopted its current name, the Christian Church (Disciples of Christ).

In the United States and Canada, Disciples membership stands at around 790,000, divided into some 3700 congregations. Nearly 8 per cent are African Americans, with much smaller percentages of Hispanics (just under 1 per cent) and various Pacific Asian Disciples (just over 0.5 per cent). The states of Texas, Indiana, Kentucky, Missouri and Ohio contain about one third of all North American Disciples. In addition, the church's Common Global Ministries Board co-ordinates work among some 2.7 million indigenous Christians across the world who call themselves Disciples.

Presbyterian churches

Disciples divide their church's work into three manifestations, working within a voluntary and covenantal arrangement: local, regional and general. Congregations control their own affairs and support various ministries of their own choosing. Most contribute financially to the regional and general work. Disciples have 33 regions across the United States and Canada. Regional offices support congregations and provide for co-operation in wider ministries.

Great Awakening

Church work among Disciples is managed by a General Assembly that meets every other year. A General Board plans for the church in between assemblies. Eleven administrative units specialize in ministries related to such things as higher education, home missions, overseas ministries and benevolence work. The Church Finance Council manages the Disciples Mission Fund, an annual fund that combines interest on investments with congregational giving, to support general and regional ministries. Disciples give approximately 30 million dollars annually, on top of operating costs, for local, regional and general church outreach ministries.

Early Disciples hoped to unify the church by restoring the faith and practices of the earliest congregations described in the Bible. For this reason, their worship included the weekly celebration of the Lord's Supper, open to all who professed Christ. Contemporary Disciples continue this practice. Their early commitment to believers' baptism also continues. Though contemporary congregations welcome infant-baptized persons into church membership without rebaptism, most continue to practise only believers' baptism by immersion.

During the late nineteenth century, leaders among Disciples embraced the scientific spirit that swept American Protestantism after 1870. They fashioned a critical approach to the Bible open to the newest developments in scientific understanding and human knowledge. As Disciples shared this budding 'liberal' vision, they began to doubt that any group of Christians, even the ancient Christians, could truly capture the divine message in its entirety. This realization strengthened their historic commitment to ecumenism.

Biblical criticism

Disciples are perhaps best known for their deep yearning for Christian unity. They are founding members of both the National Council of Churches of Christ in the USA and the World Council of Churches. Disciples have served both organizations in key leadership roles. In the late 1980s, Disciples and the United Church of Christ formed an ecumenical partnership. Together, they have helped to shape Churches Uniting in Christ (CUIC), the partnership of nine denominations that grew out of the Consultation of Church Union (COCU), a group seeking, since the 1960s, to support Christian unity.

United Reformed Church
Ecumenical movement

Today, because of their commitment to an educated faith, Disciples sponsor seventeen colleges and universities and four theological seminaries. Each of these schools is diverse, with the vast numbers of students coming from religious affiliations other than Disciples. They also maintain support for three 'foundation' houses located at the University of Chicago, Vanderbilt University and in Claremont, California. These houses support Disciples masters and doctoral students in non-Disciples institutions.

Shifts among Disciples towards more liberal views ironically led this movement devoted to church unity to experience two schisms. The first had been building since the Civil War period, when sectional loyalties contributed to theological differences. In 1906, the Churches of Christ (160,000 members who opposed the use of instrumental music during worship) claimed a separate identity. Disagreements about baptism, biblical interpretation and the structure of missionary societies continued among Disciples in the first half of the twentieth century. In the late 1960s, as Disciples restructured their church life, approximately 750,000 conservative members withdrew to form the Christian Churches and Churches of Christ.

MARK G. TOULOUSE

Winfred E. Garrison and Alfred T. DeGroot, *The Disciples of Christ: A History*, St Louis: Bethany Press 1948; Lester G. McAllister and William E. Tucker, *Journey in Faith: A History of the Christian Church (Disciples of Christ)*, St Louis: Bethany Press 1975; Mark G. Toulouse, *Joined In Discipleship: The Shaping of Contemporary Disciples Identity*, revised and expanded St Louis: Chalice Press 1997; D. Newell Williams (ed), *A Case Study of Mainstream Protestantism: The Disciples' Relation to American Culture, 1880–1989* Grand Rapids, MI: Eerdmans and St Louis: Chalice Press 1991

CHRISTIAN LIFE

Body, Community, Conscience, Discipline, Dress, Education, Evil, Faith, Festivals and fasts, Food and drink, Freedom, Friendship, Grace, Holy, Hope, Initiation, Justification, Law, Love, Marriage, Martyr, Prayer and spirituality, Ritual and worship, Sacraments, Saint, Sexuality, Sickness and healing, Sin, Suffering, Work

What does it mean to follow Jesus? What was he like? What do his followers do and what are their distinguishing characteristics? It seems as if there are as many answers as there are Christians. There is a tendency to identify Christianity with a single set of authorized beliefs. Not only is there no such single set of beliefs, there is no absolute path to being Christ-like, either. This is partly because the subject of 'Christian life' is the place where many of the historical, theological and psychological challenges of being a Christian come home to roost. Christian life has been played out in different ways throughout history and, over the centuries, Christians have argued about, for example, issues of grace and free will, sexuality and social justice. There are also distinctive 'pieties' in the various traditions and sometimes the differences are radical, particularly around issues about who is included and who is excluded from the community of faith. Jesus

There are at least three challenges in examining Christian life. The first is the discrepancy between faith and practice. Mahatma Gandhi's statement, 'I love your Christ, but I hate your Christians; they are so unlike him,' expresses the disconnection between what Christians believe and what some of them do. The tension between 'Christian' and 'Christ-like' is constant. The second challenge has to do with the varieties of Christian belief and practice throughout history. Christ has been made both Marxist and Fascist, both a liberator and a defender of the status quo, and his followers have modelled themselves on their particular and often distorted image. The third is focused on the way the Christian faith and life is framed. Does the practice of Christianity answer questions, or does it deepen them? Is it a matter of aspiration or prescription? For some, Christianity is all answers. For others it is a journey into deeper questions.

1. *Faith and practice.* The first challenge (the discrepancy between faith and practice) is not, of course, confined to Christianity. People of all faiths fail to live up to their stated beliefs. Religious practice is the way people live into what they believe. It takes time, and the person trying to follow the way of Jesus has always a long way to go. Hypocrisy is an ever-present possibility for any one who aspires to live a committed life. Human beings grow into the roles they eventually play in the world by acting as if they were already familiar with and proficient in them. The authentic life begins with acting 'as if' something were the case. Act 'as if' justice mattered even in the most corrupt situations and justice will then have a chance. Often what trips up both people of faith and those who criticize them is a crippling idealism. Because of the high idealism involved, all forms of piety and practice are easily caricatured and a sense of humour and irony is essential for the life of faith.

2. *Varieties of belief.* The second challenge is not as daunting as the first, since there are discernible common traits on which most Christians agree with regard to spiritual life and practice. Just because 'Christian life' means different things to different people, that doesn't mean that there

aren't common threads to which most Christians cling. But we shouldn't assume a consensus. Imagine a conversation between Christians from different periods of history. Would Augustine, Florence Nightingale and the evangelist Jerry Falwell have very much in common? How far would they have a shared vision? In fact, how far can we assert that there are any Christians at all? W. H. Auden suggested that there are not even Christians in church, 'for Christianity is a way, not a state, and a Christian is never something one is, one something one can pray to become'. In one sense Christianity has not happened yet.

3. *Answers and questions.* The third challenge has to do with emphasis on religion being a matter of either answers or questions. Each emphasis has its drawbacks – one tends to embrace rigidity and the other to exult in ambiguity. The metaphor of the theatre can be helpful in bringing the two together. The director Peter Brook writes that theatre is 'the meeting place between the great questions of humanity – life, death – and the craft-like dimension, which is very practical, as in pottery. In the great traditional societies, the potter is someone who tries to live with great eternal questions at the same time he is making his pot.' It means becoming part of a tradition. Thus 'Christian life' is a matter of both grace and practice, both gift and craft.

In spite of differences, common patterns emerge. Christians, on the whole, are for peacemaking rather than war and for reconciliation rather than retaliation. The practical morality of giving a cup of cold water to someone in need is central. 'And whoever in the name of a disciple gives to one of these little ones even a cup of cold water to drink, truly I say to you, he shall not lose his reward' (Matthew 10.42). And, because self-righteousness and moralism are the traps into which believers fall, penitence is also essential: 'The sacrifice of God is a troubled spirit; a broken and contrite heart, O God, you will not despise' (Psalm 51.17).

We can also understand this third challenge by looking at the way in which the various traditions approach the mystical life (which is the way we express our longing for God). Protestantism has always been suspicious of mysticism because it suggests that we can live a godly life through the practice of certain disciplines. It implies that one can work at being a Christian. The classic Protestant would want to emphasize grace in contrast to works, what one is given rather than what one does. Of course these distinctions don't play out well in real life. Life is something one has to 'work' at, and at the same time it is a gift. The mark of Christian life is freedom, and yet the tendency is to hedge it around with laws. Those who claim that the Christian life is all a matter of faith often get themselves in a psychological bind because 'faith' then becomes an impossible and exacting 'work'.

Protestantism

Mysticism

Imitation and participation

Not all Christians agree as to what the rewards and responsibilities are in following Jesus. Nevertheless, there are distinguishing marks, even if the tradition is fuzzy in some places and contradictory in others. There are two ways of understanding the way the Christian character is formed. Do we try to be like Jesus, or do we somehow actually share in his life? The first way is by imitation. We read the stories in the New Testament and try to do what Jesus did. He is the pattern and the model for the Christian life. This finds a modern manifestation in the evangelical question one is to ask when one is in a moral dilemma. 'What would Jesus do?' The second way of understanding how people grow into being Christians is to think of their actually participating in the divine life. Christians are not only to 'imitate' Christ; they also share in his life by being members of his body. Those who favour the idea of participation would see their character begin to form by being committed to certain acts like prayer and sharing in the eucharist, which is also 'the body of Christ'. Being a Christian is not only acting in a certain way but also being part of a community.

Eucharist

The Bible is the central source for discerning how a Christian is called to be in the world. It is, however, a poor handbook of morals. Much of it is more a collection of cautionary tales about how not to behave. In cultures where the Bible has been read over and over again Christians still behave badly, but they cannot do so with a good conscience. These texts follow the imitation/participation pattern. That is why the dominant metaphor for Christian life is that of a journey or pilgrimage. We are always on the move. Images from the Old Testament of the Exodus and the Exile become metaphors of the spiritual life used by such writers as John Bunyan, Dante and Augustine.

Bible

Journey

Pilgrimage

Obvious basic texts are the Ten Commandments in the Old Testament (Exodus 34) and the so-called Sermon on the Mount (the Beatitudes) in the New (Matthew 5). Certain other key texts from the New Testament exhort the Christians to foster certain habits of behaviour and practice. The strand of the tradition which emphasizes imitation (giving a cup of water) celebrates human solidarity. It represents a call to Christians in the modern world to practise selfless giving, and to work for an alleviation of conditions in which others are sick, oppressed or imprisoned in the unjust conditions of an unbalanced global economy.

pp. 384–5

p. 385

The strand which favours participation celebrates the mystery of human identity. 'We are God's children now; what we will be has not yet been revealed. What we do know is this: when he is revealed, we will be like him' (1 John 3.2). And, 'Let us love one another. Whoever does not love does not know God' (1 John 4.7–21). Another important text which brings together the two ideas of imitation and participation is Philippians 2.6: 'Who, although he existed in the form of God, did not regard equality with God a thing to be grasped.' Yet another is 2 Corinthians 5.17: 'So if anyone is in Christ, there is a new creation: everything old has passed away; see, everything has become new!' There are also the well-known 'Taking up the cross' texts in the Gospels, of which Matthew 10.38, 'and whoever does not take up the cross and follow me is not worthy of me', is an example.

From these texts, the tradition developed the view of a life patterned on the seven virtues – made up of the four cardinal virtues of prudence, temperance, courage, justice (taken from classical Greek philosophy and considered to be necessary to follow the good life for all people) and the three theological virtues of faith, hope and love. There are also the seven 'corporal' works of mercy: feed the hungry, give drink to the thirsty, give shelter to strangers, clothe the naked, visit the sick, minister to prisoners, and bury the dead. The old word 'charity' emphasizes the practical dimension of Christian love.

In sum, Christian life is centred on the mystery of death and resurrection (the Easter mystery), so to be a Christian is to take on a whole new kind of life and to 'die' to an old pattern of living. The Christian is 'buried with Christ' and raised with him in faith. 'For you have died and your life is hidden with Christ in God' (Colossians 3.3). That is why the tradition speaks of Christian life as a process of mortification, not in order to be morbid but in order to discern where true life comes from.

Resurrection

What, then, is a human being from the point of view of Christian life? What kind of people are Christians? The mystical tradition defined a human being as made in the image of God (and, therefore, free). A human being is a *capax Dei* and *Deo congruens* – has a capacity for God and leads a 'God-shaped' Christian life, and therefore shares in the divine life – actually participating in it – as a way of transformation. In the Eastern church the process is called *theosis*, deification: 'God became one of us that we might share in the divine life.' In fact one early writer could talk of the 'humanity of God'. Christian life is nothing less than sharing in God's life, primarily through contact with the community and by sharing in the sacraments.

MARKS OF THE CHRISTIAN LIFE

From the beginning, the characteristics of the Christian life have been summed up in lists. The earliest is by the apostle Paul in his letter to the Galatians (5.22–3):

The fruit of the Spirit: love, joy, peace, long-suffering, gentleness, goodness, faith, meekness, temperance. The Vulgate, the Latin translation of the Bible, adds modesty, continence, chastity, to bring the number to twelve.

The seven gifts of the Holy Spirit: Christians took over seven qualities from a list in the book of Isaiah (11.2) as gifts of the Holy Spirit: wisdom, understanding, counsel, fortitude, knowledge, piety, fear of the Lord. In fact the Hebrew text, followed by the English translations, has only six 'gifts'; piety has again been added by the Vulgate.

The seven corporal acts of mercy: Jesus' words in Matthew 25.35f. about the actions which distinguish the blessed from the cursed at the judgement of the Son of man have become seven corporal acts of mercy: Feeding the hungry, giving drink to the thirsty, clothing the naked, harbouring the stranger, visiting the sick, ministering to prisoners, burying the dead.

The seven spiritual acts of mercy: These came to be paralleled with the seven corporal acts of mercy: Converting the sinner, instructing the ignorant, counselling the doubtful, comforting the sorrowful, bearing wrongs patiently, forgiving injuries, praying for the living and the dead.

The seven virtues: Leading Christian theologians like Augustine and Thomas Aquinas took over the four cardinal virtues from Plato and Aristotle: prudence, temperance, fortitude and justice. To these were added three 'theological' virtues to produce another set of seven: faith, hope and charity.

Negatively, Christians were warned to avoid the

Seven deadly sins: Pride, covetousness, lust, envy, gluttony, anger, sloth.

Two characteristics of Christian life are therefore freedom and joy. Freedom requires that the question of being human remains open. Joy naturally flows from the experience of being truly free. The ancient formula to describe human purpose was 'The glory of God is a human being fully alive.' This suggests an open vision of human nature which finds its fulfilment in being orientated towards God. We are what we do with our attention. We are to 'attend' to God and to each other and this loving attention gives rise to the fully human community. The poet Dante's vision of heaven is a place of radical mutuality – complete unity in unimaginable diversity. How then are Christians to behave? Lady Julian of Norwich, the fourteenth-century mystic, wrote: 'God is kind in his being.' And Christians are to be 'kind' too – not simply in acts of benevolence but by being the sort of people who are loving and compassionate. Kindness also suggests family relationship as in 'kindred'. Christians are to be 'kind' in all three senses: benevolent; the sort of people who treat all people as their kin; in allegiance to the God who has made them into the sort of people who are kind to one another.

The way, then, that Christians participate in and/or imitate the life of God-in-Christ is through prayer, both private and corporate, and through participation in the sacraments (baptism and the eucharist). The three great images of Christianity – the Woman with her Baby, the Broken and Ruined Man, and the Communion of Persons (known by the theological terms incarnation, redemption and Trinity) – offer an understanding of prayer as pregnancy, suffering and communion. Christian life is much more than behaving in a certain way. It is becoming a certain kind of person through a process of allowing these images to work on one in a long process of transformation. In fact one image is that of our being pregnant with ourselves. We are midwives to each other in a process of formation. There is suffering, too. Above all there is communion. The

Trinity

LAUGHTER

Christianity is not generally associated with laughter. The New Testament never says that Jesus laughed; the Rule of St Benedict often warns against laughter: 'The tenth degree of humility is, when a monk is not easily moved and quick for laughter, for it is written: "The fool exalteth his voice in laughter."'

In the Hebrew Bible the aged Sarah laughs ironically at the thought that she might conceive a child; God laughs at the rulers of the earth conspiring against him (Psalm 2) and at the wicked (Psalm 37.13; 59.8). In later books, such as the Wisdom of Ben Sirach (Ecclesiasticus) which the Rule of St Benedict quotes, laughter has become a sin.

The phrase 'laugh to scorn' is a very common one: being laughed to scorn is the fate of the upright man (Job 12.4), and it is the reaction that Jesus gets when he tells the crowd that the daughter of the ruler of the synagogue is not dead but sleeping (Mark 5.40). In one Gnostic work, the Apocalypse of Peter, Jesus is not really crucified: another man dies in his place, while the living Christ stands by and laughs. Only in the Beatitudes does laughter appear in a more positive sense: those who weep now will one day laugh.

p. 659

It is perhaps because of the negative character of such laughter that Christian views about it are so negative. Only against this background is it possible to understand the strange late medieval custom of 'Easter laughter', the *risus Paschalis*, in Bavaria. At the Easter mass the priest would include funny stories and comical songs, even with *double entendres*, in his sermon to make the congregation laugh as a challenge to death.

A more secular tradition describes occasions for heavenly laughter. A famous anthology of German folk songs, *Des Knaben Wunderhorn* ('The Boy's Magic Horn'), dating from the beginning of the nineteenth century but allegedly containing medieval material, contains a vivid description of heavenly joys, set to music by Gustav Mahler as the last movement of his Fourth Symphony. When a feast day comes, not only is there an abundance of meat, fruit and vegetables, but even the fishes swim up gladly to be caught. 'Eleven thousand virgins are bold enough to dance, and even St Ursula (a traditionally gloomy saint) laughs.'

p. 1076

Karl-Josef Kuschel, *Laughter. A Theological Reflection*, London: SCM Press 1994

dominant image is that of a banquet to which everyone is invited. We don't live in isolation. The impulse towards society is in our nature. The principle is 'being is communion'. Participation in society is necessary for becoming fully human. Thomas Aquinas wrote 'God is not solitary'; nor are we. In fact, Christian life is a kind of love affair in which we seek to love and be loved in one communion. The mystics believed that Eros is natural to human beings. We long for God. That's the way we are built, and Christian life which tries to by-pass the passions is no life at all. We were made by love for love.

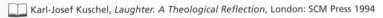

Life has a narrative structure

Story

Christians live their lives as a story – a cycle of dying and rising. The central metaphor is that of Easter – the Paschal mystery – of death and resurrection. To be fully alive is to share in that baptismal cycle of dying to an old self and living into the new. This mystery is expressed in the two great sacraments of baptism (the dying and the rising) and the eucharist (the anticipation of the full communion of all things).

Human life has a narrative structure and stories link us with issues of choice and the life of the will and of the imagination. Our distinctive spirituality, or take on life, is a matter of which story we choose to tell ourselves about ourselves. How do we arrange the bits and pieces of our experience and how do we glue them together to form a picture we can understand? Every narrative has a beginning, a middle and an end. It is a journey.

The late Joseph Campbell, expert on world mythology, wrote that a myth or story has a fourfold function to relate us to God, the world, others and our deepest selves. A fourfold structure of Christian life can be discerned through paying attention to these four relationships. Prayer, living fully and responsibly in the world, being just and loving, and being committed to self-knowledge, are the building blocks of spiritual rule of life.

The mystics saw Christian life in terms of rebirth/transformation (Gregory of Nyssa's *Life of Moses*) or as the consummation of a love affair (John of the Cross). Others spoke of life as 'the school of love' and the models were Jesus, the disciples, Mary. The principle was that everything that happened to Jesus, by analogy happens to us. This is how Christians can interpret their experience in the cycle of his life, death and resurrection. In another way, they can interpret our lives as recapitulating the experience of the apostles. Just as the apostles were enthusiastic, cowardly and bewildered, so are the Christians who come after them. Yet another way is to see oneself like Mary – obedient to the overshadowing of the Holy Spirit – and become pregnant with new possibilities. Like Mary, every human being is 'the container of the uncontainable'.

Mary

Christian life is expressed in certain disciplines that reinforce the narrative structure of that life. Most Christians would agree that reading the Bible (in private prayer and study as well as in communal worship) is central, as is sharing in holy communion. Both practices build the Christian character by giving it shape and direction. The Bible provides the architecture of the way Christians think about themselves and the world.

The embodied life

In spite of the centrality of the body in the Christian understanding of the work of Christ, the church has a poor history with regard to its understanding of and teaching about sexuality and the body. The body, however, is of central importance for Christian life. It is a sacrament of God's presence among us. As obvious as it sounds, it is the way we relate to each other. As the tradition has it, the body is the place where God chooses to dwell. The basic goodness of sexuality and its enjoyment is affirmed, as is the use of food and drink and the disposition of wealth. The traditional monastic vows of poverty, chastity and obedience express one way of living the embodied life, as does marriage and other committed relationships.

Body

There is risk and hope in human connectedness and the Christian life is a connected life; it has been defined as 'the art of making connections'. These connections are manifested physically by water (baptism), bread and wine (eucharist), oil (healing), and sexual intercourse (marriage). There is a connection between receiving the bread and wine in the eucharist and action in the world (social justice).

The fully embodied life is a connected and integrated life of body, mind and spirit that requires attention to the narrative structure of human lives. They are going somewhere and will come to an end. That is why preparing for death is important and why practices of self-simplification are central. The three traditional disciplines of prayer, almsgiving and fasting (rather like Campbell's fourfold structure of myth) express three basic relationships: prayer in respect to God, almsgiving in respect to others, and fasting in respect to ourselves.

Death

The goal of the converted life is to find God in all things and is based on the conviction of the unity of reality. Everything is connected. Ignatius Loyola tells us that those advanced in the spiritual life constantly contemplate God in every creature. This life is based on trust, the immediate relationship we have with God, since a human being is, by definition, the place where God chooses to dwell. Human beings aren't meant to be solitary, and we find out who we are and what we are about in the company of others, through a constant process of conversion. The traditional Benedictine greeting is, 'Please pray for my conversion, as I pray for yours.'

Gregory of Nyssa saw life as an unending progress of discovering how God is at work among humanity, and sin as refusal to keep on growing in this discovery. 'This is true perfection: not to avoid a wicked life because we fear punishment, like slaves; not to do good because we expect repayment, as cashing in on the virtuous life by enforcing some business deal. On the contrary, disregarding all those good things which we hope for and which God has promised us, we regard falling from God's friendship as the only thing dreadful, and we consider becoming God's friend the only thing truly worthwhile.' And, finally, John of the Cross says it all: 'In the end we shall be examined in love.'

ALAN JONES

Bernard McGinn, *The Foundations of Mysticism: Origins to the Fifth Century*, New York: Crossroad 1991; Elaine Pagels, *Beyond Belief*, New York: Random House 2003; Timothy Radcliffe, OP, *I Call You Friends*, London and New York: Continuum 2001; Esther de Waal, *The Celtic Way of Prayer*, New York: Doubleday, Image Books 1996

Christian Science

The Church of Christ, Scientist, consists of the mother church in Boston, Massachusetts (The First Church of Christ, Scientist) and nearly 2000 branch churches worldwide. Its membership spans 139 countries. It was founded by Mary Baker Eddy in 1879 and its core mission is to bring spiritual healing to humanity.

The church provides an array of resources for those seeking spiritual answers, including worship services on Sundays and Wednesday evenings, Sunday school for children and teenagers, and a global speakers' bureau. It publishes the newspaper *The Christian Science Monitor* and a variety of books and magazines. It also offers websites, radio programmes and Christian Science campus organizations at many colleges and universities, all for public audiences. Accounts of healing are given in public meetings each Wednesday evening and in the various Christian Science magazines. People tell how the power of prayer has healed disease, emotional and mental problems and broken relationships, and dealt with financial challenges and many other concerns in their lives.

There are no ordained clergy. The Bible and Mary Baker Eddy's main work *Science and Health with Key to the Scriptures* are considered pastor of the mother church and its worldwide branches. Men and women committed to a full-time public healing ministry are listed in *The Christian Science Journal*. Equality between women and men, spiritually and in practice, is valued. Both men and women conduct services in churches and the five-person body entrusted with transacting the business of the church, the Christian Science Board of Directors, consists of both men and women.

The term Christian Science refers not to the church organization but to a universal, practical system of prayer-based healing available and accessible to all. Many readers of all backgrounds regard *Science and Health* as an entry point to their own practice of systematic spiritual healing. While it is used as a textbook by members of the Church of Christ, Scientist, it is also read and appreciated as a non-denominational practical guide by adherents of other faith traditions (or none). Since September 2000 the full text of *Science and Health* as well as the Bible has been available to read on the spirituality.com website.

The basic teachings of Christian Science set forth in *Science and Health* include these concepts: God is divine Love, Father-Mother, supreme. The true nature of each individual as a child of God is spiritual. God's infinite goodness, realized in prayer, heals. Each individual's connection with God is unique and unbreakable. Some important synonyms for God are: Mind, Spirit, Soul, Principle, Life, Truth, Love.

Mary Baker Eddy, as the author of *Science and Health* and founder of the Church of Christ, Scientist, broke through barriers of illness, poverty and social conservatism to establish a system of spiritual healing and made it available to all. She wrote a book that has been read by millions, founded a church, a college – the Massachusetts Metaphysical College – and a successful business, the Christian Science Publishing Society. In addition to launching several magazines, in 1908 at the age of 87 she founded *The Christian Science Monitor* whose mission is 'to injure no man, but to bless all mankind'. It is published both in print and on the web.

As interest in women's history, spirituality and healing grows, Mary Baker Eddy is increasingly recognized as a vibrant and perceptive thinker, reformer, philanthropist, entrepreneur and business woman, as an outstanding inspirational writer and speaker, a remarkable healer and teacher, and one of the few women to found a successful religious movement. In 2002 the Mary Baker Eddy Library for the Betterment of Humanity was opened in Boston,

Massachusetts. It is a resource centre where scholars, researchers, journalists and the general public can 'explore the power of ideas' and find answers to their questions about Mary Baker Eddy and topics related to her life, ideas and achievements.

TONY LOBL

Mary Baker Eddy, *Science and Health with Key to the Scriptures*, Boston, MA: Christian Scientist Publishing Co. 1875; Mary Baker Eddy, *Mary Baker Eddy: Speaking for Herself*, Boston, MA: Writings of Mary Baker Eddy 2002; Gillian Gill, *Mary Baker Eddy*, Cambridge, MA: Perseus Books 1998; Richard Nenneman, *Persistent Pilgrim*, Etna, NH: Nebadoon Press 1997; Yvonne von Fettweis and Robert Warneck, *Mary Baker Eddy: Christian Healer*, Boston, MA: Christian Science Publishing Society 1997

www.churchofchristscientist.org;
www.csmonitor.com;
www.spirituality.com;
www.marybakereddylibrary.org

Christology

Jesus

What was Jesus? Even during his lifetime people were asking the question, and after his crucifixion they asked it even more urgently, since although he had been executed he was experienced as alive; he was seen and heard. The question was not asked out of interest or curiosity, but was literally one of life and death, for those who asked it felt that Jesus had transformed their whole existence, had brought them from death to life, had 'saved them'.

Salvation
Council

Because our major evidence about Jesus' life, contained in the New Testament Gospels, is shaped by the experience of his resurrection, it is not always easy to determine what explanations of his person were given during his lifetime and what later. But we can safely say that at a very early period Jesus was said to be a prophet, was spoken of as messiah, was associated with a mysterious figure called the Son of man, and was even called son of God (though against a Jewish background that term did not have the depth of meaning it came to assume later; it meant perhaps something like 'godlike'). And he was Lord and Saviour.

Messiah
p. 661

What Jesus believed himself to be or claimed to be is again difficult to determine because of the nature of the evidence. But in the letters of Paul, the earliest Christian writings that we possess, we can read what may even be a hymn which Paul is quoting, describing him as being in the form of God, taking the form of a servant, being born in human likeness, crucified, and then exalted even higher than he had been by God (Philippians 2). The Gospel of John begins by claiming that in the beginning the Word (another title used of Jesus) was with God and was God (John 1), and in it Jesus later says, 'I and the Father are one' (John 10.30). So from the beginning Jesus was seen as related to God in a special way.

Paul

But in exactly what way? If Jesus was God, and God the Father in heaven was God, weren't there two Gods? And didn't that break apart the whole tradition of Judaism with its strict belief in one God and the emphasis on the oneness of God that was an important element of Hellenistic philosophy in the time of Jesus? These questions were discussed for many centuries after the death of Jesus as they still are, and the technical term for the discussions is christology, in Greek 'talk about Christ' ('Christ' from the Greek *Christos*, is the same word as the Hebrew 'Messiah', and means 'anointed one'), just as theology is 'talk about God'. Because questions about what Christ was were so closely related to questions about how he brought salvation to those who believed in him, christology has always been indissolubly connected with soteriology (talk about salvation).

Much of the discussion about christology was carried on initially in Greek and later in Latin by learned churchmen, especially bishops, but we should not underestimate the keen interest among ordinary people, especially in the east of the Roman empire, where much of it took place. We are told that the nature of Jesus was hotly argued about in barbers' shops. In the controversy sparked off in the fourth century by Arius, who argued that Christ had not existed for all time, songs were written and slogans coined, such as 'There never was a was when he wasn't.' In official circles the debate was not always carried on peacefully: at one crucial council, in Ephesus in 431, monks used strong-arm tactics in support of the side that they favoured. And over it all stood the figure of the emperor. In 325 the Emperor Constantine called and presided over the first 'ecumenical' (= worldwide) council which, among other things, defined the nature of Christ. It was vital for the Roman empire to be united, and arguments about Christ among Christians were posing a threat to this unity.

From the start, reflection on the nature of Christ has always had wider dimensions than theological argument. Here we shall be following intellectual developments, but it should not be forgotten that the discussion was always carried on within the ongoing life of Christians. Christians prayed and worshipped, and their experiences here profoundly shaped what they believed about Christ. Over the course of time Christ was depicted in the graphic arts, and representations of him influenced the piety of churchgoers, not least the illiterate. Singing and speaking words in a church of a particular architectural style with stained-glass windows, statues and paintings, can have a powerful effect. Countless hymns were written, making it possible and indeed popular to *sing* even the most technical doctrinal definitions. A Victorian hymn still popular today, 'Come, ye faithful, raise the anthem', is a perfect expression of what became the officially sanctioned christology. It begins with 'God eternal, Word incarnate' who, 'ere he raised the lofty mountains, formed the sea, or built the sky' was moved by love eternal to die, and ends with the words 'consubstantial, co-eternal, while unending ages run'.

But the words of this hymn, orthodox though they may be, seem to have brought us a long way from the Jew Jesus of Nazareth. What happened to make them possible?

The first titles to be associated with Jesus, like prophet, messiah, high priest, saviour, all depicted so to speak earthly roles that were attributed to him. Moreover, two other titles gave him what might be called a heavenly role: he was said to be the Word of God and the Wisdom of God. All these terms appeared in the Hebrew scriptures, and in the authoritative Greek translation of them (the Septuagint), which the earliest Christians used as their Bible, and were current in the Judaism of Jesus' time. To say that Jesus was the Wisdom of God and the Word of God was particularly significant, since in Judaism these two terms had become personified, and God's Wisdom or Word was seen as assisting God at the creation of the world and delighting in his handiwork (e.g. Proverbs 8.22–31). 'Word' proved to be a particularly important link term with the Greek world.

In a Jewish context the key questions were: *who* was Jesus, what had he come to do and by what authority? But as Christianity moved out into the intellectual world of Greek philosophy the question changed. *What* was Jesus? What was his nature, and how did that nature relate to the divine nature of the one God? Outside their original background, the earliest titles of Jesus came to be thought inadequate and either disappeared (like Son of man) or were given a heightened meaning (like Christ, Son of God). This development might not have taken place as soon as it did, or to the degree that it did, had it not been that Jewish Christianity, the Christianity of Jesus' first followers, disappeared after the Roman capture of Jerusalem in 70 CE and further punitive actions against Jews. Jewish Christians, too, were inevitably caught up in the disaster. Jewish Christianity all but disappeared except for small pockets, some of which were still in existence at the time of the rise of Islam in the seventh century.

We have scattered evidence of some Jewish-Christian groups and their views about Jesus; their names later came to be included in the lists of 'heretics'. For example, the Ebionites (in Hebrew, 'poor men') are said to have believed that Jesus was the human son of Mary and Joseph and that the Holy Spirit alighted on him at his baptism. Often mentioned alongside the Ebionites, though their background is rather different, are the Docetists (from the Greek 'semblance'), Christians with Gnostic views. They believed that Jesus was not really crucified but only 'seemed' to suffer. Simon of Cyrene, reported in the Gospels as having carried Jesus' cross, was crucified, and Jesus laughed from on high at the ignorance of the bystanders. This solution to the problem of how the saviour of the world could have been crucified by the Romans, to which we find many kinds of response in early Christianity, found its way into Islam.

Hymns
Gnosis

But the mainstream discussion centred on the question what Jesus was, what his nature, his make-up was. It was believed to be by virtue of this nature that he brought salvation. In a world strongly influenced by the Greek philosophical tradition, there were two key words, *logos* and *ousia*, 'word' and 'essence' or 'substance', in the discussion. As the discussion became more complex, these words were joined by a number of others.

Logos (Latin *verbum*) proved an extremely useful term for interpreting Jesus. It was the Greek translation of the Hebrew *dabar*, used in the Old Testament to denote the mode of God's communication with human beings, a 'word' which sometimes seemed almost to take on an existence of its own. At the same time, in Greek philosophy, notably among the Stoics, *logos* denoted something like reason, the rational principle behind the universe. Moreover, *logos* was actually used of Jesus, as we have seen, at the beginning of the Gospel of John. What better term for explaining what Jesus was? The earliest Christian theologians to offer a defence of Christianity, known as the Apologists, in the second century, and notably Justin Martyr, used *logos*, not least in arguing that Christ played a role in creation. As we shall see, *logos* later also was a key term in discussions about the make-up of Christ's person.

Bible

Ousia (Latin *substantia*), 'substance', denoted being, essence, that which makes something what it is. Thus God has divine *ousia*. As John Henry Newman put it in a famous hymn, the divine *ousia* is 'God's presence and his very self, and essence all-divine'. Human beings have human *ousia*. So the question 'What is Jesus?' became 'What is the *ousia* of Jesus?' What is the relationship of his *ousia* to God's *ousia*?

The definitive answer to this question was given at the Council of Nicaea, convened by the Emperor Constantine in 325. Among rulings on many different matters it produced the first version of a creed, known as the Nicene Creed (the 'Nicene' Creed recited in churches today is a later expanded version of this creed, produced at the Council of Constantinople in 381). This stated that Jesus was 'of the *ousia* of the Father, God from God, light from light, true God from true God' and *homoousios* with the

Jewish Christianity
Constantine's 'conversion'
Creed
Heresy

p. 1211

Father. This term *homoousios* (Latin *consubstantialis*), 'of the same substance', was highly controversial, because it did not appear in the Bible, and there were protests at its inclusion, but it was felt to be the only term that fully expressed Jesus' divine status. The Word that was made flesh in Jesus was God, in exactly the same sense as God the Father is God.

The creed made many other statements about Jesus, indeed it was largely about him: of the 24 lines of the original just three are about God the Father and one about

Holy Spirit

the Holy Spirit (interestingly, the creed, which begins 'We believe', ends simply 'and in the Holy Spirit': how the Holy Spirit related to Jesus was the subject of a complicated discussion at a later stage, which we shall not be investigating here). The creed says that Jesus was 'begotten' of the Father, not made, and that all things in heaven and on earth were made through him. He came down from heaven and was 'made flesh' and 'became man'; he 'suffered', rose again and will come to judge the living and the dead. Significantly, nothing is said about what Jesus said and did during his earthly life. This was to have major consequences for christology.

pp. 552–3

What had made the creed so necessary had been the arguments put forward by the presbyter Arius, mentioned above. From what we know of him, he seems to have taught that Christ, or God the Word, was a creature and not God by *ousia*; he was not eternal but had been created by God before all time to be an agent in creating the world; and he was made son of God as a reward for his righteous life. In other words, God the Word was not 'God' in the same sense as God the Father was. This was Arius' way of facing the problem of how to relate the God who does not change and does not suffer, God as God is in himself, to the Word who becomes incarnate, suffers and dies for the salvation of the world. And here in fact in many ways he did more justice to the Gospel record than his opponents. However, they could not accept the inferior status that Arius gave to the Word (such a Word could not bring salvation), and he was branded a heretic. Nevertheless, at the time Arius had a strong following. In fact Nicaea did not put an end to Arianism: this proved to be a potent force in subsequent decades and then flourished particularly among the Goths as a result of their evangelization by Ulfilas.

Once Arius' attempt at a solution had been ruled out, attention inevitably turned to the question of the relationship between the divine nature and the human nature in Christ. Here again the nature of the salvation brought by Christ was a key question. To bring salvation Christ had to be God, God as the Father was God; but for humankind to be saved, in Christ God had to assume human nature completely. 'That which is not assumed is not saved' was a fundamental principle.

In the debate that followed we meet with a number of technical terms that are central to it. The Greek term used for 'nature' now tended to be not *ousia*, but its near equivalent, *physis.* The divine nature was denoted by the term *logos*, which we have already met; the human nature was denoted either by the Greek *sarx* (flesh) or *anthropos* (man in the sense of human being). Though in some contexts, as in the Nicene Creed, *sarx* and *anthropos* could be used as equivalents, *anthropos* indicates far more clearly that the *logos* was united with (and therefore also saved) the human soul (Greek = *psyche*). Here a difficult balancing act was needed: put too much emphasis on the role of the divine *logos* and insufficient justice is done to the humanity of Christ; put too much emphasis on the humanity and either the *logos* is again brought dangerously near to suffering and change, or the unity of the person of Christ is endangered.

Broadly speaking, we find two schemes within which the relationship between the divine and the human nature of Christ was discussed: for short, *logos-sarx* and *logos-anthropos.* Not only were these advanced by different groups; they were also focused on different centres: Alexandria in Egypt and Antioch in Asia Minor. It is no coincidence that in Antiochene theology, represented among others by the theologians Diodore of Tarsus, John Chrysostom, Theodore of Mopsuestia and Nestorius, there was a much stronger tradition of biblical exegesis. Alexandrian theology, the dominant figures in which were Athanasius and Cyril, was characterized far more by philosophical reflection in the Platonic tradition.

In the christology of Alexandria with its *logos-sarx* scheme, Jesus' soul seems to be almost completely ignored. The *logos* takes over in Jesus and is responsible for his spiritual and moral actions: it is the subject of virtually all that is said of Christ. The body, the *sarx*, is the instrument of the *logos*, the organ through which it acts. This Alexandrian scheme succeeds in presenting Jesus as a unity of thought and action, but emphasizes the divinity to such a degree that the humanity seems on the verge of disappearing. And in the most extreme representative of the Alexandrian school, Apollinarius, it does disappear altogether.

As with Arius and others who were later declared heretics, the lack of reliable sources makes it impossible to portray Apollinarius' teaching precisely, but he seems to have argued that only the unchangeable divine Logos could save humankind and that Christ did not have a human mind or soul. He had only one nature. Apollinarius was an important influence on what later came to be called Monophysitism.

With its greater emphasis on the humanity of Jesus, the christology of Antioch and its *logos-anthropos* scheme had the opposite problem, that of holding together the person of Jesus. Antiochene theologians took seriously the New Testament statements that Jesus was hungry, thirsty and suffered; therefore he had to have a human soul and a real inner human life. But if that was the case, if Jesus was a man, *anthropos*, with a soul, how did his inner human life relate to the inner divine life? Did Jesus experience and do some things as human but others as divine? Wasn't he near to becoming two persons in one?

Here discussion was complicated by the ambiguity of another term that came into play around this time (in passing, it should be pointed out that many of the terms mentioned here took time to become technical terms with a clear and fixed meaning and that translations from Greek to Latin and vice versa also led to misunderstandings). *Hypostasis* was a Greek word which in some contexts was equivalent to *ousia* (*substantia*), but in others came near to denoting a separate being (the Latin *persona* seemed to move even further in this direction). So when Antiochene theologians used *hypostasis* to describe the natures of Jesus it could be thought that they were saying that there were two persons in Jesus. This particular usage was a crucial factor in a complex and often acrimonious debate that also involved a good deal of ecclesiastical skulduggery. It came to a head over Nestorius, Patriarch of Constantinople. Rightly or wrongly (and again we have a problem with the sources), he was accused of teaching that there were two separate persons in the incarnate Christ; he was deposed at the Council of Ephesus in 431 and later banished. His refusal to accept a new title for the Virgin Mary, *Theotokos* ('mother of God'), which had arisen in the atmosphere of monasticism and Alexandrian christology, contributed to his downfall.

Again an emperor, Marcian, intervened to resolve the situation by calling a council, which was held at Chalcedon, just outside Constantinople, in 451. It aimed to correct the excesses of both Alexandrian and Antiochene christology and to produce an orthodox definition of the Christian faith. This 'Chalcedonian Definition' affirmed previous creeds, notably that of Nicaea and its revised Constantinopolitan version, condemned a series of errors, and stated the doctrine of the Christian church. The divine and human natures were united in the one person (Greek *hypostasis*) of Jesus Christ (the technical term for this is 'hypostatic union'). The definition said that Jesus was one and the same Son, perfect in Godhead and manhood, truly God and truly man, with a rational soul and body, consubstantial with the Father according to his Godhead and consubstantial with us according to his manhood, acknowledged in two natures without confusion, change, division and separation ... And it continues in this vein. We have reached the terms of 'Come ye faithful, raise the anthem' and countless other hymns of praise.

The Chalcedonian Definition has since been very widely regarded as the church's authoritative statement of the relation of the human to the divine in the person of Christ, and it continues to be the starting-point for much reflection on christology today. But it was vigorously contested at the time, and has defined disagreement as well as agreement in subsequent Christian history. The Alexandrian church felt that the Definition conceded too much to Nestorius and his followers; it insisted on Cyril's preferred formula that there was 'one nature of God the word made flesh'. This position was commonly termed 'Monophysite', although both modern scholarship and official church dialogues have preferred to move away from the traditional and over-simplifying labels. The Armenian church followed the Alexandrian, and so did those Syrian-rite Christians who were later called 'Jacobites'. There is evidence that Nestorius himself was content with the Chalcedonian Definition, but some at least of his followers felt that it conceded too much to the Alexandrian position. This 'Nestorian' point of view is represented today in the Syrian-rite Church of the East, also called the 'Assyrian Church'. Disagreement with Chalcedon has been a defining characteristic of the Oriental Orthodox churches. Controversies over christology became entangled with political allegiances in the Byzantine period, and this is one reason why the later history of Eastern christology is too complex to summarize here. Attention turned in particular to the will of Christ, and a group of Monophysites argued that there was only one will in Christ (Monothelitism).

Orthodox churches

Nevertheless, what came to be known as 'Chalcedonian orthodoxy' became the basis of Christian teaching about the person of Jesus, which was to be accepted without question throughout most of the church.

The 'solution' laid down by Chalcedon was framed against a particular philosophical background and in the course of theological discussions which started from particular presuppositions. What if this background and these presuppositions changed? Despite the tendency so often evident in Christian doctrine to appeal to a 'faith once delivered', which does not change, we now know that no ideas are timeless. Moreover the very way in which the debate over Christ was carried on in the first five centuries had one fundamental weakness: to all intents and purposes it passed over the life of Jesus of Nazareth between cradle and grave. The debate had become all too schematic, dominated by abstract terms like *logos* and *sarx*, *physis* and *ousia*, *hypostasis* and *prosopon* (Greek 'countenance' or outward appearance, yet another term brought in to solve the christological puzzle).

Reformation

The first major change came at the Reformation, but in some ways it had been heralded in the eleventh century by Anselm of Canterbury in his work *Cur Deus Homo* ('Why the God Man', 1098). In this work Anselm linked the person of Christ closely with his saving work; and by stressing his role as mediator introduced a distance between God and

Jesus that had to be bridged by the atoning self-sacrifice of Jesus. It should also be noted that over this period in visual terms Western depictions of Christ came to focus quite markedly on his suffering, in stark contrast to the traditional emphasis in the East on his reigning in glory.

The Reformers maintained the classical christological definitions, but with them the emphasis shifted markedly from the nature of Christ to his role in redemption. Here the discussion was complicated by being entangled in the controversy with the Roman Catholic Church over the nature of the presence of Christ in the eucharist. Christ, as the second person of the Trinity, was seen above all as the sole mediator (*Christus solus*) between God and humankind, and his work consisted in giving himself for the salvation of humankind. He was seen as having a 'threefold' office, of prophet, priest and king, and his works of salvation were systematized under these headings. So strong was this focus on Christ's work that Philipp Melanchthon could summarize christology in a famous phrase: 'To know Christ is to know his benefits.'

There were differences between Lutherans and Calvinists. John Calvin took more of an 'Antiochene' line. For him it was the human nature united with Christ that died on the cross. He put a particularly strong emphasis on the unity of the divine and human natures in Christ as the foundation of communion between God and human beings. He saw Christ at work outside the spatial and temporal limitations of his humanity through the Spirit (the Lutherans labelled this view the *extra Calvinisticum*). Martin Luther was more 'Alexandrian', insisting that on the cross God himself, the incarnate God, took the place of sinful human beings and died for them. The two natures were firmly united in and from the incarnation.

Incarnation

Enlightenment

It was in the Enlightenment that a major crisis arose for christology. New ways of thinking raised problems here for which the traditional categories seemed to provide no answer: the philosophical background had become an alien one; a rational empirical approach challenged the authority of Christian doctrinal claims and questioned the elements on which they were based, particularly the idea of the miraculous which seemed to be so much a part of the story of Christ; and a revealed morality did not fit in with the ethical demands presented in that story. This marked the beginning of a new story, that of the quest of the historical Jesus. Starting with the fragment of a major work by H. S. Reimarus entitled 'On the Aims of Jesus and his Disciples' published by G. E. Lessing after Reimarus' death, scholars began to investigate the Gospel material critically in the hope of rediscovering the real Jesus under the guises in which the church had portrayed him. This story will be told elsewhere, but by the nature of things it runs parallel to, and often becomes entangled in, the ongoing development of christology.

Jesus of history

Discussion of christology in modern times has been wide-ranging and varied. For the past two centuries, many of the great theologians have written on it. It has ranged from making a particular philosophy so dominant that the distinctive features of Jesus almost disappear to a fundamentalist emphasis on Jesus that leaves no room for interpretation in terms of any kind of philosophy, with many variants in between.

At the risk of oversimplification, perhaps the easiest way of marking a way through the complex discussions is to distinguish between christologies which in one way or another essentially presuppose the classic Chalcedonian Definition as a given (let us call them christologies 'from above'), and those which do not (christologies 'from below'). The former basically begin with at least some of the classic doctrinal statements about Christ and attempt to reinterpret them in terms of new situations – philosophical, cultural, social and so on. The latter begin from Jesus of Nazareth, as far as he can be known in the conditions of modern study, and develop a contemporary understanding of his significance in the light of that study without necessarily referring to or accepting the traditional categories of Christian doctrine and all its claims.

Of the great modern theologians, both Karl Barth and Karl Rahner can be seen as basically offering christologies 'from above' within the European Christian tradition, and they have been followed by many other theologians. Further afield, particularly with the expansion of Christianity through missionary work and engagement with different cultures, attempts have been made to restate the meaning of the person of Christ for Asians, Africans, black Americans. The christologies here, too, are just as much 'from above', even if they may not immediately seem to be so.

Many of them, particularly those arising from oppressed peoples, are closely related to a type of christology which developed in the nineteenth century in Lutheranism and was taken up in Anglicanism, known as kenotic christology. The term derives from the Greek *kenoo*, 'empty' and arises from a passage in Paul's letter to the Philippians which speaks of Christ 'emptying' himself. This was understood to mean that at the incarnation the son of God gave up all his divine attributes to share human suffering. Versions of kenotic theology can be found in a variety of contexts. In black theology Jesus is spoken of as the black Christ who provides the necessary soul for liberation in black suffering. Korean Minjung theologians find the suffering Christ in the persons of the suffering Minjung, the socially and economically oppressed. Indian Dalits see Jesus involved in the struggles of the outcaste Dalits. Japanese Burakumin see him among them wearing a crown of thorns. As ever, new representations of Jesus in art have accompanied these interpretations.

South African Christ

But Christ can be depicted in more active roles: in African christology, for example, he is seen as the chief, the master of initiation, the ancestor, the healer. This approach can refer back to a long tradition of Christ as victor over the powers of evil. And following the writings of Pierre Teilhard de Chardin, some Asian christologies take up the idea of the Cosmic Christ, in whom not only human and divine but also cosmic dimensions are centred, in a process of coming to be.

What all these christologies have in common is that in one way or another they assume the special, unique, divine status of Christ and do not question it (that is why, even if they do not always seem it, they may be said to be 'from above'). They presuppose the results of the centuries of development up to Chalcedon and do not feel the need to justify this basic presupposition again. What they argue for may not be fully 'orthodox' in the traditional sense, but it is bound up with elements of orthodox christology in the same way as other variant christologies were bound up with mainline christology in the past. They are concerned to present a positive view of Christ in a new situation.

By contrast, on the same presuppositions feminist theologians, with their growing realization that women and their thought have been woefully under-represented in Christianity, have been among the more radical critics of traditional christology. For many of them the view that Christ was a male and so only the male can be the image of Christ, and that women are the passive objects of his redeeming work, is a major defect of Christianity. It is also the basis of the denial to women in many traditions of the role of representing Christ and his work for the community in the ordained ministry. The maleness of Jesus even seems to imply the maleness of God. Thus, for example, Rosemary Radford Ruether could even write an article entitled 'Can a Male Saviour Save Women?'

On the positive side, though, feminist christologies have contributed to a recovery of the identification of Christ with the Wisdom of God which was made by the church fathers. In both Hebrew (*hokhmah*) and Greek (*sophia*) wisdom is feminine, and 'Lady Wisdom' has become the focal point of much research and discussion (Elisabeth Schüssler Fiorenza has written of *Jesus: Miriam's Child, Sophia's Prophet*).

Problems are equally caused for christology by the question of the relationship between Christianity and other religions. Because of its claims about Jesus,

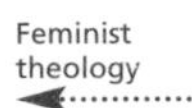

Judaism and Christianity

Islam and Christianity

Christianity quickly came into conflict with Judaism and, after the appearance of Muhammad and his new teaching, with Islam. Yet the three faiths have common roots: Jesus was a Jew, and in many respects there is continuity as well as conflict between Judaism, Christianity and Islam. Any consideration of the relationship between Christianity and other faiths finds christology at the heart of the problems that arise there.

It is this that makes the other approach to christology, 'from below', so important. What picture of Jesus, his nature and his role, do we get if we begin from what we can discover about his person, his life, his claims, his actions and the response to all this in our earliest sources? The failure of any form of the quest of the historical Jesus shows that it is impossible to get back to 'Jesus as he was'. But might not a re-examination of the original testimony to Jesus lead to a new interpretation that could be the basis of a better understanding of his role, a more positive vision of how he is to be represented within the church that developed from him and a more fruitful encounter with other faiths? Karl Barth's contemporary, Rudolf Bultmann, was already a striking example of this approach, disregarding classical christology and even demoting Jesus to a presupposition of Christianity. Two less radical, but promising, re-examinations of christology starting from Jesus were made in the 1970s by the Roman Catholic theologians Edward Schillebeeckx and Hans Küng.

At precisely the same time as the books by Schillebeeckx and Küng, the appearance of Geza Vermes' *Jesus the Jew* signalled a renewal of interest in Jesus on the part of Jewish scholars and further books by Vermes and by John P. Meier (*A Marginal Jew*) have explored the place of Jesus in the Judaism of his time. While many of the issues discussed here belong more properly in the context of the discussion of the historical Jesus, they are of course deeply relevant to christology.

Books like these indicate not least the kind of rethinking that needs to be done in christology. Yet again in the 1970s, a start was made on this in a collection of essays edited by John Hick, entitled *The Myth of God Incarnate*. While its specific focus was the doctrine of the incarnation, it nevertheless raised major questions for the whole structure of christology. It caused a public stir and provoked a number of responses, and perhaps this public outcry against it prevented its questions from being taken further. But they are still there on the table and represent an agenda to be taken up in future discussion.

JOHN BOWDEN

John Bowden, *Jesus: The Unanswered Questions*, London: SCM Press 1988 and Nashville, TN: Abingdon Press 1989; James D. G. Dunn, *Christology in the Making*, London: SCM Press and Philadelphia: Westminster Press 1980; Aloys Grillmeier, *Christ in Christian Tradition* (3 vols), Oxford: Mowbray and Louisville, KY: Westminster John Knox Press 1975–96; John Hick (ed), *The Myth of God Incarnate*, London: SCM Press and Philadelphia: Westminster Press 1977; Hans Küng, *On Being a Christian*, London: Collins and New York: Doubleday 1978; Volker Küster, *The Many Faces of Jesus Christ*, London: SCM Press and Maryknoll, NY: Orbis 2001; John P. Meier, *A Marginal Jew* (2 vols), New York: Doubleday 1966; Rosemary Radford Ruether, *To Change the World. Christology and Cultural Criticism*, London: SCM Press and New York: Crossroad 1981; Edward Schillebeeckx, *Jesus. An Experiment in Christology*, London: Collins and New York: Doubleday 1979; Elisabeth Schüssler Fiorenza, *Jesus: Miriam's Child, Sophia's Prophet*, New York: Continuum and London: SCM Press 1995; Geza Vermes, *Jesus the Jew*, London: Collins and Philadelphia: Fortress Press 1973; Anton Wessels, *Images of Jesus*, London: SCM Press and Grand Rapids, MI: Eerdmans 1990; Frances Young, *From Nicaea to Chalcedon*, London: SCM Press and Philadelphia: Westminster Press 1983

CHURCH

Buildings, Community, Diversity, Ecumenical movement, Geography, History, Initiation, Ministry and ministers, Mission, Organization, Sacraments, Pastoral care, Sociology of religion

From the beginning Christianity has been a religion of communities: with Jesus a group of itinerant disciples, then in the cities of the first-century world small groups meeting in the house of a more well-to-do member, and finally substantial communities with buildings of their own, all linked together in an organization (later organizations) which spanned and still spans the world. The English word 'church' (and its German and Dutch equivalents) comes from the Greek *kuriake*, 'belonging to the Lord'. The French have quite a different word, *église*, also from the Greek, in this case *ekklesia*, meaning assembly. *ekklesia* is the word regularly used for both a local Christian community and the Christian community as a whole, made up from individual communities.

Many dimensions

The Christian church has many dimensions. First of all it is an *institution*. It is much more than an amorphous movement. And 'the church' is not simply a catch-all sociological category in which to place the discrete churches. In spite of differences and divisions, the church can be seen as an identifiable visible community in time and space, though the Christian claim is that there is more to the church than that – it is the mystical body of Christ. The Christian church as such has a recognizable history; it has pervasive (though not common) structures; and it certainly has a set of overall beliefs, goals and values that sustain its identity. As an institution, the church lends itself to empirical description and analysis.

Secondly, the church has an *intellectual* dimension. From the beginning the church has had an ongoing intellectual life; it has generated a theological industry. Today anyone, Christian or not, church member or not, may choose to study Christian theology, but over history theologians have normally had a sense of working in the community of the church and out of a particular church tradition. They may be said to work on the ideology of the institution. Theology

Thirdly, the church has a *mystical* dimension. This includes the private prayer and contemplation of ordinary Christians and of religious, as well as the ordered public worship of the church. It concerns the heart and the feelings and the sense of the presence of God. It includes the formation of Christian character and the way that suffering is borne with patience. The mystical dimension is that side of the church's existence that is most mysterious, yet it is also arguably the most important of all. It is, in the words of the letter to the Colossians, the life that is 'hidden with Christ in God' (3.3). Mysticism Prayer Worship Christian life

Singular and plural

Christians often talk about 'the church' as though there were only one. In hymns, prayers and confessions of faith 'the church' invariably occurs in the singular. The most widely used and authoritative of creeds, the Niceno-Constantinopolitan Creed (finalized in 381 CE), refers to 'the one, holy, catholic and apostolic church'. Occurring as it does in the creed, this statement is a confession of faith. In spite of the visible disunity of the church and the sinfulness of its members, its limitations Creed and lack of faithfulness to its apostolic mission, to the eyes of faith it is ultimately one. It is vital to Christians to believe that the church is one and that there is only one church. Just as there is one God and one Jesus Christ, so there is necessarily only one church. A New Testament statement of this axiomatic unity of the whole Christian economy invokes 'one body and one Spirit ... one hope ... one Lord, one faith, one baptism, one God and Father of all' (Ephesians 4.4–6).

Yet the most obvious feature of the church to strike an impartial observer is that it is not one but many, not singular but plural. The church takes many forms and bears many names. Its members tend to style themselves, not simply Christians, but Roman Catholics, Orthodox, Anglicans, Lutherans, Presbyterians (or Reformed), Methodists, Baptists, Evangelicals, Pentecostals and a host of others. These brand names represent to some extent different ways of worshipping, believing and living as professed disciples of Jesus Christ. In the course of 2000 years of church history distinct traditions, streams of Christian practice and reflection, with organizational structures and theologies to match, have emerged, flourished, declined and sometimes disappeared. The impressive church of North Africa, of Tertullian, Cyprian and Augustine of Hippo, was swept away by waves of invasion in the early centuries of our era.

The most obvious sign of the plurality of churches is probably the extraordinary variety of church buildings. In some towns and cities every street corner sports a church of a different denomination. Where a church of the dominant denomination stands, rival denominations have felt the urge to build a church right opposite. In London, Westminster Abbey partly predates, in its existing form, the Norman Conquest (eleventh century). For less than a century (since 1912) the massive Methodist Central Hall (not 'cathedral' or even 'church') has stood across the road, a challenge to Anglican hegemony as the church by law established. For a little longer has stood Westminster Cathedral (completed 1903, consecrated 1910), the seat of the Roman Catholic cardinal archbishop. In small towns and villages, Non-conformists built their chapels as close as they could to the parish church, even in the churchyard itself, if possible, in a bid to claim sacred turf.

Reformation

In countries touched by the sixteenth-century Reformation, church buildings have passed through various ownerships. In Europe parish churches and cathedrals more than 500 years old were of course from the beginning under the jurisdiction of Rome and were served by clergy who looked to the Pope as Christ's earthly representative. At the Reformation, when the papal jurisdiction was repudiated, they often came under the authority of the state and of a bishop who looked to the crown for his legal authority. Today in England ecumenical goodwill sometimes makes it possible for the same ancient church to be used by Roman Catholics again. Such churches or chapels may well display a record of priests that makes no distinction as it passes from Roman Catholic to Anglican and back again. As far as Anglicans at least are concerned, the one church and the one ministry of word, sacrament and pastoral care have continued down the ages, essentially unaffected by political upheaval and changes of political allegiance.

Martin Luther
Justification

Lutheranism, on the other hand, is an example of a Christian tradition that has a sharper sense of historical discontinuity. Lutherans believe that Martin Luther (1483–1546) was raised up by God to bear witness to the lost truth of justification by faith and to reform the church. Lutherans continue to have a strong sense of confessional identity which they are loath to compromise (as they see it) by uniting in any organic way with other churches. Some Lutherans, particularly in Germany, have a strong sense of a new beginning, of a new expression of church springing up in the sixteenth century. Yet they happily worship in medieval churches and cathedrals where their unreformed ancestors heard mass for the living and the departed, offered prayers and gifts at the shrines of saints and made their confession to a priest. The continuity is at least as strong as the discontinuity.

When Christianity with its churches is looked at as a global phenomenon, what holds it together is probably as apparent as what breaks it into fragments. It may even look quite cohesive, though far from monolithic. Many churches there may be, but they all worship God through Jesus Christ in the power of the Holy Spirit. With the notable exceptions of the Religious Society of Friends (Quakers) and the Salvation Army, they practise similar forms of Christian initiation (baptism and confirmation of some sort) and celebrate the eucharist (holy communion, mass or Lord's Supper) as their central rite. They ground their faith in God's revelation found in the Bible (which they read and teach assiduously) and most use the historic creeds (the Apostles' Creed and the Niceno-Constantinopolitan Creed) in worship or at least as theological reference points. Almost all have a form or forms of ordained ministry, distinguished from the unordained laity. The overwhelming majority of Christians are in churches that have the threefold ministry of bishops, priests (presbyters) and deacons, but some ordain only presbyters (ministers or pastors) or only presbyters and deacons, while their senior ministers simply have wider responsibilities. Considered phenomenologically, as a community of believers, the Christian church is a comparatively unified entity.

Revelation
Bible

It is, however, at the institutional level that the multiplicity and diversity of churches is most apparent. The one church of Christ confessed in the creed as an article of faith may indeed be universal (catholic), but the individual churches are also now found throughout the world. During the twentieth century, in fact, Christianity has become the most extensive and universal religion in history. At the beginning of the twenty-first century there are Christians and Christian churches in every country.

Church, denomination and sect

Three quarters of the totality of two billion Christians in the world today belong to traditional denominations and churches. Of the almost 34,000 distinct Christian denominations in the world today, most are small and local, while about one third of the total are the larger, traditional denominations. Churches do not normally refer to themselves by the levelling sociological term 'denomination', but by the theological term 'church'. In the past, larger well-established churches would dismiss their more recent smaller rivals as 'sects'. The New Testament church has sometimes been described as a sect of first-century Judaism. That designation is neither correct nor helpful, since the followers of the Way (as the first Christians were called) saw themselves as the true or renewed Israel, the church of the (old) covenant.

Covenant

'Church' has a range of meanings today, just as it did in the apostolic church, when the apostle Paul could speak of the church in a certain town or city, the generic church in which apostles, prophets and others ministered, and the church as the mystical body of Christ. The particular meaning depends on the context in which the word is used, from the local congregation or parish to the national church and beyond to the universal church. To take an English Anglican example, the statement 'I belong to the church' may refer to the parish (symbolized by the parish church building), to the Church of England as a national church, or to the universal church of Christ. The diocese (the sphere of the bishop's oversight and other ministry) is also 'church' because it is a community in which word, sacrament and pastoral care are ministered by those who have pastoral responsibility (the bishop and other clergy). While this sense of church is seldom articulated explicitly by Anglicans, it remains important to Roman Catholic self-understanding.

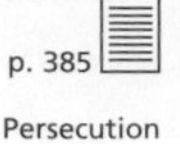

While churches are now too polite to condemn each other as 'sects', the term is still used descriptively in the sociology of religion. Max Weber (1864–1920) and Ernst Troeltsch (1865–1923) rehabilitated this time-worn term of disparagement, the latter developing a suggestive polarity of church-type and sect-type Christian communities in his *The Social Teaching of the Christian Churches*, 1912 (English 1931). Sects, typified by the medieval movements of protest and reform over against the all-powerful hierarchies of the Roman Catholic Church, were characterized (according to Troeltsch) by lower social origins, alienation from the state, individualism, lay initiative, intensity of conviction, conversion and exclusive membership. However, Troeltsch pointed out that the sects preserved aspects of the authentic message of Jesus (the radical discipleship of the Sermon on the Mount) and of primitive Christianity. They followed Christ through rejection persecution and death.

p. 385 Persecution

'Sectarian' is still used – even by the responsible media – as a term of abuse and as equivalent to 'extremist' and 'fundamentalist' (particularly of feuding groups in Northern Ireland). The sectarian mentality is bigoted, unreasonable and anti-ecumenical. But 'sect' as a term of opprobrium has been giving way in popular imagination to 'cult', an anthropological term that has been absorbed into everyday speech. A cult is a sect with mystique, and the word often has sinister overtones. Cults are supposed to have fiendish initiation rites and to brainwash their devotees. Their power-hungry charismatic leaders are evil and/or insane and often sexually abuse their deluded followers. If the thought-control processes prove insufficient, they retain their reluctant members by threats. Cults are even more alienated from modernity than sects and have bizarre eschatological expectations – 'doomsday scenarios'.

In reality the difference between church, sect and cult is a matter of degree. One person's sect is another's church. Among the thousands of denominations there must be many that fit the sociological description of a sect and not a few that deserve to be called cults. The ugly features of sect and cult have too often found a place in the mainstream churches. In the ecclesiastical glasshouse these labels are invidious and have a habit of boomeranging on their users.

Joining the church

The subject of membership of the church involves subtleties and paradoxes. All Christian communities have ceremonies of initiation and understandings of belonging. Almost all have a defined pattern of initation, of which baptism and confirmation (or chrism in the case of the Orthodox) are the focal sacramental moments. But there is uncertainty (at least among Anglicans) about whether baptism constitutes complete Christian initiation, about the meaning and purpose of confirmation, and about whether baptized children should be admitted to holy communion before confirmation. One huge achievement of the ecumenical movement is agreement on a common (i.e. mutually recognized, interchangeable) baptism. But this is not universal, as not all Greek Orthodox would accept non-Orthodox baptisms and most Baptists – believing that baptism administered to infants is not real baptism – will re-baptize, on profession of faith, those who come to them from churches which practise infant baptism.

Furthermore, a distinction should be made between membership of the one, holy, catholic and apostolic church, given in baptism, and membership of a particular Christian denomination or local church. Local membership is important to traditions of independency or congregationalism (such as Baptist churches) where Christians enter into a covenantal commitment to one another in a gathered church of professed believers. This emphasis leaves Baptists with the problem of the place and status of children within the Christian community. They are considered not to be old

GATHERED CHURCHES AND TERRITORIAL CHURCHES

Many churches, particularly in the Protestant tradition, are gathered churches, i.e. their members come together to meet and worship at a particular church from a variety of places surrounding it. However, in countries where there are established churches, recognized by the state as the church of that country, as in England, and historically in the Roman Catholic and Orthodox Church, the churches are territorial, i.e. they have defined administrative areas, each with differing degrees of seniority. Some of these are:

Parish: In England, the area under the pastoral care of a Church of England priest. Nowadays, however, in many cases, particularly in country areas, parishes have been combined and are looked after by groups of clergy, known as team ministries.

Rural (or area) deanery: A group of parishes in a given area.

Archdeaconry: An area delegated to an archdeacon by the bishop in a diocese.

Diocese: The area governed by a bishop. (American Lutherans use the term *synod* instead.) In the Eastern church the diocese is called an *eparchy*.

Archdiocese: A diocese of which the bishop is an archbishop.

Province: A group of dioceses adjacent to one another, governed by an archbishop.

Thus the parish churches of St Andrews, Stewton and St Martin, Welton le Wold are looked after by the Louth team ministry; they are in the deanery of Louthesk, in the archdeaconry of Louthesk, in the diocese of Lincoln, in the Church of England province of York.

enough to understand and therefore to profess the faith responsibly in baptism. Do they belong to the church or not?

At the other end of the spectrum Anglicanism places almost all its emphasis on membership of the Body of Christ through baptism and is relaxed about denominational loyalty. In the Church of England all baptized parishioners are deemed to belong. Ministry is offered to all who will receive it, and parishioners, whether baptized or not, have a right to the ministrations of the clergy, particularly in rites of passage. Members of other Christian churches who worship in the parish church may designate themselves also members of the Church of England and so have their names put on the church electoral roll for the purpose of taking part in church government at every level. The problem that a weak notion of membership brings is that of nominal adherence.

Around half the population of England is a member through baptism of the Church of England, but those who can realistically be described as churchgoers are only several millions (though there is a larger constituency that has some form of pastoral contact with the Church of England). Does the scale of nominal membership discredit the Anglican approach to ministry and mission? Before leaping to this conclusion or assuming that the Church of England is a 'worst case scenario', we should reflect that nominal membership is an issue for all churches. Of the one billion Roman Catholics in the world only a fraction attend weekly mass or make their confession to a priest. But backsliding is even more difficult to cope with in gathered church traditions, where individuals have been baptized and welcomed into membership on profession of faith and testify to having been 'born again'.

Mutual acceptance

Much of the energy of the ecumenical movement continues to go into attempts to bring about 'mutual recognition' or acceptance between separated churches. This endeavour builds on the fact of a common baptism and the common basic faith that this implies. Agreement in the fundamental faith of the creeds is not particularly difficult to achieve, but issues of ministerial validity and of sources of authority or oversight in the church are more intractable. Growth in mutal acceptance is attained step by step with corresponding gains in practical co-operation. The Anglican-Methodist Covenant in England of 2003 is an example of mutual recognition and commitment that tries to heal the wounds and divisions of the past but falls short of complete communion.

Churches that are 'in communion' have largely interchangeable ministers and members (e.g. the British and Irish Anglican churches and most of the Nordic and Baltic Lutheran churches through the Porvoo Agreement; the churches of the Anglican Communion and the Old Catholic churches through the Bonn Agreement; Anglicans/Episcopalians and Lutherans in North America). But eucharistic hospitality (welcoming each other's members to receive holy communion) is practised more widely. The Church of England invites baptized communicants who are in good standing in other trinitarian churches to receive the sacrament at the eucharist in Anglican churches. However, eucharistic hospitality is still the exception. The Roman Catholic Church does not extend it to Protestants or Anglicans, except in exceptional or unique circumstances, including grave pastoral need. No Roman Catholic is permitted to receive the sacrament from an Anglican or Protestant minister in any circumstances. Orthodox churches are equally strict. This lack of reciprocity remains a cause of hurt.

Great and small

Some churches are numerically huge: the Roman Catholic Church is a single global church with approximately one billion (a thousand million) members. It thus comprises one half of all the Christians in the world and one sixth of the world's population. Its doctrine of the church has two main foci: the 'local church' or diocese and the universal church. In Roman Catholic teaching the universal church of Christ is closely but not exclusively identified with the institutional Roman Papacy Catholic Church centred in Rome and ruled by the Pope. The parish is not as important for Roman Catholics as it is for Anglicans (particularly Anglicans of the highly territorial Church of England), and the idea of the national church is foreign to Roman Catholicism.

The Orthodox churches, though much smaller than the Roman Catholic Church, come second with something in excess of 200 million members, including the family of Oriental Orthodox churches. For the Orthodox, the church is primarily the community gathered by the bishop at the eucharist. Orthodox churches are 'autocephalous': they are self-governing, with their own patriarchs and metropolitans, not ruled by a quasi-papal authority. They do not accept the jurisdiction of the Pope or his personal infallibility, and the senior bishop of the Orthodox family of churches, the Ecumenical Patriarch of Constantinople, enjoys nothing approaching papal status. Like the Roman Catholic Church, the Orthodox churches hold that they comprise the church: the one church is coterminous with Orthodoxy. Although they are deeply involved in the ecumenical movement and were among the founders of the World Council of Churches in 1948, this does not imply any formal recognition of other Christian churches. The Orthodox hold that the faith and practice of Orthodoxy – and therefore of Christianity itself – is essentially unchanging and unchanged and therein lies its authenticity.

The Anglican, Lutheran, Reformed and Methodist families of churches muster between 70 and 80 million members each, while 52 million of the various shades of Baptists are affiliated to the Baptist World Alliance. The Moravians, on the other hand, while they form a global church like the Roman Catholics, total less than a million members worldwide. There are tens of millions of

Christians in local or regional independent Pentecostal and Evangelical churches, mainly in the southern hemisphere. While the traditional, mainstream churches are declining relative to the world population (though not absolutely because of substantial accessions to these traditions in the developing world), the Pentecostal and independent Evangelical churches are growing rapidly, in both relative and absolute terms.

Pentecostalism
Evangelicals

The diversity and multiplicity of the church may, of course, be seen as one of its strengths. Like a great tree it has grown huge branches, laden with luxuriant foliage. The energy that it generates is so intense that it has forced its way into many different historical forms and is still multiplying. As fast as the centripetal impulse of Christianity, seen today in the ecumenical movement, can help churches to discover their common ground, to work together and in some instances to enter into close relationships through binding agreements, the centrifugal impulse throws other parts of the church apart, continually spawning fresh currents of Christianity and therefore new churches.

The church of Jesus?

We should pause at this point to wonder at the apparent incongruity between the church as it has become – a great society spanning the centuries and the globe, sometimes an empire in its own right – and its unpromising beginnings in the group of confused and unreliable disciples whom Jesus called to work with him. Scholars are virtually unanimous that Jesus did not consciously intend the church as we know it and did not foresee it. Jesus believed that his mission was the harbinger of the end-time *(eschaton)*. Divine judgement would supervene and through cataclysmic events God would make a new beginning. He therefore did not expect his cause to be carried forward through history in institutional form.

Jesus

But before we jump to the conclusion that the church and Jesus have nothing to do with each other we should remember that ancient Israel also was the church of God, called to be God's instrument for the blessing of all humankind. Jesus called Israel to repentance, signifying the renewal of Israel by appointing twelve leaders who would have seats of judgement in the kingdom. Jesus linked his approaching suffering, death and vindication with the coming of God's kingdom. The inter-testamental period had seen the development of ideas of a godly remnant, a faithful, persecuted community that would carry forward God's cause. The New Testament identifies the apostolic community with this divine purpose and sees Jesus' death and resurrection as the cataclysmic events that had been foretold, bringing a new beginning to birth. The mission of the apostles was to carry the good news (gospel) into all the world and to all nations before the ultimate fulfilment of God's purpose in history.

p. 1152
Kingdom of God
Resurrection

So there are threads of continuity as well as the obvious discontinuity. However, the eschatological framework of Jesus' ministry is a standing challenge to the over-institutionalization of the church. There is a need for continual conversion back to Jesus and the kingdom. Sometimes it is good to ask, 'What would Jesus think of us now?'

Monopoly and pluralism

During the past century or so there has been a conceptual revolution in the way in which diversity and unity are understood. For by far the greater part of church history, unity has been understood in an exclusive and monolithic sense, i.e. as uniformity. Uniformitarianism was a dominant ideological world-view in all disciplines. In theology Vincent of Lérins (early fifth century) famously proposed the test of orthodoxy, *quod ubique, quod semper, quod ab omnibus creditum est* (what has been believed everywhere, always and by everyone), known as the Vincentian canon.

CHURCH

It was assumed, for basically socio-political reasons, that there could be only one valid way of worshipping, believing and practising the Christian life. Only one church could be accommodated in a state and that one was the authentic one. The security of the state was thought to be incompatible with religious pluralism. Notwithstanding the relativizing principle of *cuius regio eius religio* (the religion of the state followed that of the ruling house) after 1555, theologians saw the various Christian traditions as competing expressions of Christianity and of church. One church was the 'true church'; all others were 'false churches'. It was then necessary to tell which was which.

Both the sixteenth-century Reformers and their Roman Catholic opponents developed sophisticated tests of the true church. For the Reformers the true church was identified by the true preaching of the gospel and the right administration of the sacraments. Second-generation Reformers added the test or mark of pastoral oversight or effective discipline which was arguably implied in the ministry of word and sacrament. Champions of the Roman Catholic Church in the Counter-Reformation such as Cardinal Bellarmine (1541–1621) countered with claims of universality, antiquity and numerical superiority, among others. Thus the Protestants tended to apply a qualitative test and the Roman Catholics a quantitative one.

Counter Reformation

Constantine's 'conversion'

From the conversion of Constantine (312 CE) until the nineteenth or even early twentieth centuries uniformity of belief and of worship was enforced in Europe. Religious and political requirements were seldom distinguished. In the medieval period, dissident movements such as the Bogomils, Cathars, Waldensians, Hussites and Lollards were ruthlessly persecuted. The 'magisterial' Reformers (those identified with the ruler and the state) urged the suppression of the Anabaptists and Separatists (who rejected the idea of a state or folk church). In England 1559 and 1662 marked major religious settlements enforced by Acts of Uniformity. Not until 1828–9 were disabilities suffered by Protestant Non-conformists and Roman Catholics lifted in England. The Roman Catholic Church affirmed liberty of conscience and of religion only at the Second Vatican Council in the early 1960s.

Heresy

p. 988

Meanwhile, the exclusive claims of the churches and the traditions they represented were being eroded by changes in the intellectual climate. The *philosophes* of the French Enlightenment brought a critical rationalism to bear on various forms of unquestioned, traditional authority, including that of the Roman Catholic Church. The historical movement that succeeded the Enlightenment adopted a comparative method that had a relativizing effect. Later, political philosophers and social scientists (notably Karl Marx, 1818–83, and Émile Durkheim, 1858–1917, respectively) showed how belief and morals were influenced by social and economic factors, while depth psychologists (pre-eminently Sigmund Freud, 1856–1939) uncovered comparable determinative factors hidden in the unconscious.

Enlightenment

Critics of Christianity
Psychology and Christianity

Economic changes were decisive in prompting the churches to make a virtue of necessity and for the first time to embrace diversity on ideological grounds. One generally recognized aspect of the process of secularization that has removed the churches from the centre to near the margins of public life in Europe has been the diversification and specialization of institutions. This process, no doubt driven by economic factors, was accompanied by the break-up of state-sponsored religious monopolies and the recognition of a diversity of religious institutions within one state or nation.

Secularization

Difference and development

A prior condition for the churches to be able to acknowledge the sinfulness of wilful division and to begin to seek to heal the wounds of the body of Christ is acceptance of the validity of difference within Christianity. When they accept that a diversity of expressions of Christianity and of church are here to stay, they can begin to accommodate themselves to it. That means recognizing that each one may have something to teach the others and that the form preferred by one particular church may lack something that others can offer. That recognition leads to trying to understand each other better and therefore talking and even worshipping together. For the past century, since the International Missionary Conference in Edinburgh in 1910, the ecumenical movement has stood for the recognition of difference and the imperative of reconciliation and mutual affirmation, notwithstanding differences. Through theological dialogue and shared mission, it has achieved a substantial mapping of common ground and the exposure of negative stereotypes and caricatures, and has narrowed down the real, apparently intractable differences between the churches.

Ecumenical movement

Difference takes both historical (diachronic) and contemporary (synchronic) forms. The theory of the proper development of belief and practice, famously proposed by John Henry Newman in *An Essay on the Development of Christian Doctrine* (1845), challenges all claims (by the Roman Catholic Church and the Orthodox churches) to have preserved the primitive pattern of Christianity unchanged or (in the case of 'restorationist' Evangelical and Baptist churches) to be replicating it directly today from the pages of the New Testament. The subversive potential of development theories is incalculable and poses a threat to the authorities in the historic churches and to the dogmas and structures that they seek to uphold. What it gives with one hand, it takes away with the other.

p. 851

Thus the papacy may be said by some to be a salutary later development (which seems to validate the papacy); but it follows from the theory of development that Peter could not have been the first pope, awarded his authority over his brethren by Jesus according to Matthew's Gospel (which undermines official Roman Catholic claims). It may be argued that the ordination of women is a necessary and helpful recent development (a development, not a sheer innovation). But this argument inadvertently highlights the fact that Jesus appointed only males as his apostles (which undermines the argument from divine intention). It is therefore not surprising that Newman and other proponents of development attempt both to have their cake and eat it by insisting that Christianity develops while remaining essentially the same. Authentic developments preserve the genuine identity of Christianity and of the church, while inauthentic developments destroy this. Thus a viable theory of development demands a set of tests (such as Newman proposed) and an authority that decides whether the tests have been met (for Newman this had to be the Pope, whose formal judgement was infallible – Newman's assumption being that a probable answer was not enough and that one had to know with certitude). If there was development, there was change and therefore difference. 'You cannot have Christianity and not have differences.' Differences were to be argued about and therefore the church was a polemical institution.

Diversity and mission

The synchronic diversity of Christianity and its institutional expression in the churches plays a crucial part in the success of its contemporary mission. Its diversity reflects the multiplicity of cultural environments with which the churches engage, and to which they respond, in their local contexts. The infinitely diverse forms of human need and aspiration can probably find a purchase somewhere in the many-faceted expression of Christian belief and worship. Thus the more successful the church's mission is, the more diverse church life becomes. Diversity can thus be seen as a function of mission.

However, success in mission – the numerical growth of the church – can bring adverse consequences for the churches as institutions. The greater the diversity, the more difficult it becomes for constituted authority to exercise control. To be geared up for mission means to be adaptable and flexible and open to new movements of the Spirit. This cannot be achieved without some loosening of institutional ties. When the grip of the institution is weakened, accountability is weakened and there is less constraint on the exercise of power by charismatic leaders over their followers. So mission and institution are in tension.

As historic institutions, churches guard their identity. They preserve and propagate narratives that tell of their journey in history, of the saints and heroes, especially the martyrs, who by their life and death have defined Christianity and church in that tradition. For Anglicans, the story includes Augustine of Canterbury (but also increasingly the Celtic saints), Alfred the Great, Thomas à Becket, Julian of Norwich, Henry VIII and Thomas Cranmer, Elizabeth I and Richard Hooker, Charles I and William Laud – and that only goes as far as the English Civil War in the mid-seventeenth century. The Methodist identity story seems circular rather than linear: everything circles around the work of John and Charles Wesley 250 years ago, and Methodists are held by their gravitational field. Lutherans adhere to Martin Luther, and the answer to every question facing the Lutheran churches includes a discussion of what Luther said and did about it. The identity narrative of all churches is embedded with numinous symbols. Though the emphasis varies, such symbols as the cross, the Bible, the eucharist and the priesthood/pastorate are the common possession of all churches. Other symbols distinguish and divide the churches from each other: the Pope for Roman Catholics, the anointed sovereign for the Church of England, parity of ministers for Presbyterians. The narratives of the churches increasingly intertwine, in a way that brings both mutual support in an increasingly indifferent world and mutual critique leading to changes in attitude and practice. The history of the church as a society or institution has been full of surprises: no doubt there are many more to come.

Symbols

PAUL AVIS

Paul Avis, *The Anglican Understanding of the Church*, London: SPCK 2000 and *Anglicanism and the Christian Church*, revd edn, London: T&T Clark 2002; Daniel Hardy, *Finding the Church*, London: SCM Press 2001; Adrian Hastings (ed), *A World History of Christianity*, London: Cassell and Grand Rapids, MI: Eerdmans 1999; Hans Küng, *The Church*, New York: Sheed & Ward and London: Burns & Oates 1971; Richard McBrien, *Catholicism*, revd edn, New York: Harper Collins 1994

Church of England

Most English people live near to a church, and the overwhelming majority of these buildings house congregations of the Church of England. There are over 16,000 of them, more than 7000 of which were built between about 1080 and 1600. A few are even older, and a number were built during the twentieth century, but most of the rest belong to the nineteenth century, though their architecture is similar to that of the medieval period.

Buildings

The buildings vary considerably in size, but outside they are often surmounted by a tall, pointed spire or a sturdy, crenellated tower, which helps to make them the most prominent structures in their locality and in rural areas visible for several miles. The size of the older churches was often determined not so much by local need as by the amount of money available from landowners and a desire to give glory to God through splendid architecture. Community rivalry was not unknown. Some small towns and villages boast enormous churches, for example Thirsk in Yorkshire, Northleach in Gloucestershire and Lavenham in Suffolk. These are known as 'wool churches' because they were built and endowed by local merchants in the late medieval period who thrived on the flourishing English wool trade. Far fewer churches were built between the sixteenth century and the Gothic revival in the nineteenth century.

Besides local churches, the Church of England has 42 much larger buildings known as cathedrals. This name is derived from the Latin *cathedra* (chair) and indicates that it is the church where a bishop has a special chair, often described as a throne, from which he presides over the 250 or more local churches constituting a diocese. Most of the cathedrals were built during the period 1000–1600; some are of great size and splendour and are numbered among the finest buildings in the world. As a result of population growth and movement to urban areas in the nineteenth century, more cathedrals were required, and these were usually created by adapting large local churches. The twentieth century saw the building of new cathedrals in Liverpool, Guildford and Coventry – the last of these replacing a medieval building destroyed by wartime bombing.

The local churches belong to parishes, of which there are just over 13,000. These are territories of varying size which cover every square mile of English soil. This parochial system, as it is called, dates from the twelfth century, and the boundaries of some rural parishes have hardly been altered since then. Where there has been urban growth, however, they have changed considerably and often do not coincide with any definable community.

The parishes enjoy a high degree of autonomy, though an increasing number of administrative matters, such as clergy stipends and housing, are now handled by the diocese, as well as provision for educational and youth work. Since the 1960s groups of parishes in rural, and sometimes in inner-city areas, have been united to form team or group ministries. These are served by teams of clergy, some of whom may be specialists in educational or social work, and when the team is successful a more dynamic church life develops. The focus of unity in the diocese is the bishop, who is acknowledged as having pastoral oversight over the whole territory.

The name Church *of* England, not the Church *in* England, indicates that it was once literally the church of the whole nation. It is impossible to understand the Church of England without some knowledge of its place in English history. Tracing its origins to the conversion of the English people to Christianity during the seventh century, the church has for most of its existence been closely integrated with the life of society. During the Middle Ages it was impossible to draw a clear line of demarcation between church and state, and the great upheaval of the sixteenth-century Reformation sprang as much from a desire for political independence from continental Europe as it did from disagreement with the religious doctrines of the Church of Rome.

The ostensible cause of the formation of the Church of England, as a separate church from the Church of Rome, was Henry VIII's (1491–1547) desire to divorce his wife Catherine of Aragon, who had been unable to bear him a male heir, in favour of Anne Boleyn. To achieve this he flouted the Pope's authority and embarked on a course which led to his being recognized as supreme head on earth of the Church of England and broke the bonds between England and Rome. The break was received with mixed feelings, as is evident from what happened next. Under Henry's boy successor Edward VI (1537–53) the church moved further towards Protestantism, but when Mary (1516–58) succeeded him on his death, papal supremacy was again recognized and much of what had been achieved in the previous two reigns was undone. However, with a firm hand Elizabeth I (1533–1603) finally repudiated papal supremacy and was given the title 'supreme governor' of the church.

Architecture
Protestantism

As a result of the complex toing and froing in the sixteenth century, unlike the other churches of the Reformation, in which militant Protestantism was the dominant force for change, the Church of England retained some crucial elements of the Catholic tradition, and these remain an integral part of its life today – expressed in an episcopal ministry, an emphasis on the sacraments, use of the historic creeds, and the observance of the Christian year. It therefore sees its history in terms of continuity, and the lists of clergy often displayed in parish churches frequently go back to the thirteenth or fourteenth centuries, when the parish was founded.

Organization
Ministry and ministers
Sacraments
Creed
Calendar

Some other traces of the past also remain. The Church of England is an established church, in other words a state-related church. The sovereign is the temporal head of the church and the church carries out his or her coronation. Bishops and some cathedral and parish clergy are appointed by the Crown, though the church now has a large say in their choosing. Twenty-six of the diocesan bishops have seats in the House of Lords. At the national and local levels the Church of England normally presides over community celebrations and commemorations. During the last 100 years the formal links between church and state have been considerably modified in the direction of greater freedom for the church, but a sense of partnership between the two is still widely recognized, and the church regards whatever privileges it may retain as providing opportunities of service to the community.

History

Everyone living in England resides in a parish and has the legal right to attend its church (sometimes there is more than one) and, subject to certain conditions, to have the use of it for baptisms, weddings and funerals. Until the second half of the twentieth century most people who did not belong to another branch of the church or another religious faith described themselves as 'C of E', even if they

Middle Ages
Reformation

rarely attended an act of worship. Their number is now smaller, though not insignificant, and in communities with a long history, a large proportion of the population still regards the parish church as 'our church' and often raises considerable sums of money for its repair. The Church of England sees itself as being available to and at the service of all, and in market towns and villages the parish priest is usually a leading member of the community.

The amorphous nature of the relationship between the Church of England and those who reside in its parishes makes it difficult to calculate its numerical strength. And while the life of the local church depends on the vigour of those who are deeply committed to its beliefs and witness, there is never any desire to disown those whose attachment is more tenuous. Statistics gathered for the year 2000 provide a broad-brush picture. The usual Sunday attendance is 878,000 adults and 180,000 children and young people. Total weekly attendance, incorporating those who attend church services on weekdays rather than Sundays, is 1,031,000 adults and 243,000 children and young people. Easter Day attendance is 1,626,300 and Christmas Eve/Christmas Day attendance 2,851,600. There are 168,020 baptisms and 232,550 funerals, just over half of which were held in crematorium chapels.

Schools ➤

Pastoral care ➤

The chief public activity of the Church of England is the offering of worship to God. Virtually every local church, except in some thinly populated rural areas, has at least one service every Sunday; many have two, some have three. Most of these are celebrations of holy communion, but there are also non-sacramental services – Morning and Evening Prayer or family services – where the emphasis is on the Bible. Besides Sunday services, weekday acts of worship are common and, again, these may be either holy communion (most common) or a biblical service.

Worship

The content of these services is to be found in either the Book of Common Prayer or *Common Worship*. The former, which took shape during the Reformation, was authorized in 1662 and was the only service book in general use for more than 300 years. The latter, authorized in 2000, contains some of the material of its predecessor and also much new material compiled during a 40-year period of experiment and innovation. This is now widely, though not universally, used and offers a considerable variety of choice to those responsible for the ordering of worship. Hence the common use of booklets and leaflets to aid congregations. Several different hymn books are also in use, and the ceremonial accompanying services are very varied, as are the robes worn by those who lead the worship. Robed choirs are less common than they were 50 years ago.

Hymns

For many years it has been customary for community commemorations and celebrations to include a service in the parish church. Remembrance Sunday, royal weddings, jubilees and deaths attract large numbers to these services. In rural areas the harvest festival remains popular and community organizations everywhere often mark milestones in their life with an act of worship. Westminster Abbey, St Paul's Cathedral and other cathedrals provide venues for these at national and regional levels and their number overall is increasing.

The church was a pioneer in the field of education in England and at the end of 2000 was still responsible for 9700 primary and secondary schools, educating 925, 891 pupils. During that year 37,489 candidates aged above ten were prepared for confirmation. Many parishes have youth organizations, offering a choice of levels of Christian education, and even more have at various times of the year study groups and lectures for adults.

The pastoral care of parishioners, whether or not they attend church, has always been a high priority for the Church of England. Visiting the sick, comforting the bereaved, counselling the perplexed and generally being available for spiritual and other forms of advice is one of the primary duties of the clergy. In country parishes where populations are small, the priest may well know every one of his or her parishioners and call regularly at their homes, but this is much less easy in towns where community life is weaker. In these circumstances the ministry of the parish priest may be confined to those who attend church or who are contacted through baptisms, weddings and funerals. In well-developed parishes lay people now share in the pastoral work and sometimes there is co-operation with doctors and social workers over particular problems.

Although the laity are now more active in the life of the Church of England than at any other time in its history, the leadership provided by the clergy remains the key to the well-being of the church's work in its parishes. In 2000 there were 8872 full-time parochial clergy, of whom 1068 were women. In addition there were 2083 priests, about half of them women, who received no stipend and provided part-time services in the parishes, as well as a distinctive witness in their places of work. Women were admitted to the priesthood in 1994, but the use of male clergy whose ministry is exercised mainly in their secular occupations goes back to the 1960s.

Training for the priesthood takes a variety of forms. The ideal training for a full-time priest is a university degree followed by one or two years of vocational preparation at a theological college. Candidates without a degree spend three years in a theological college. Several regional courses have, however, been recently established to provide theological and pastoral training on a part-time basis at evenings and weekends. These are designed chiefly for those who will minister without a stipend, i.e. unpaid.

Besides the clergy who exercise pastoral ministries

in parishes there are over 1200 engaged in specialist work in the armed forces, schools, hospitals, prisons and industry. Others are involved in social work and some in broadcasting and publishing. The cathedrals are staffed by a dean and three or four canons who are responsible for the family worship and a great variety of educational and pastoral work associated with these much visited buildings. They may also have other responsibilities in the diocese. Archdeacons – two or more in every diocese – share with the bishop in the oversight of the parishes, and particularly in the administration.

The Church of England, in common with the other provinces of the Anglican Communion and the Roman Catholic and Orthodox Churches, has episcopal leadership. That is to say, the mission of the church in every diocese is centred on the ministry of a person – a bishop – rather than on the work of a committee or council. In England each of the 43 dioceses has a bishop who provides the overall leadership, is responsible for the ordaining of priests, the institution of clergy to the care of parishes and the administration of confirmation to those (36,387 in 2000) who enter into the full communicant life. Since the demands on the bishop of a diocese for these and many other pastoral and administrative matters are heavy, each has the assistance of one or more suffragan bishops. These have the authority to undertake all the functions of a bishop, though in practice their duties are defined by the diocesan bishop. Every parish church has a special chair for the bishop to occupy when he is present and to indicate always that pastoral responsibility for the parish is ultimately his. Bishops play some part in the lives of their local communities as well as in the life of the church.

There are two Archbishops in England, of Canterbury and York. Each is responsible for a diocese and their authority is not essentially greater than that of any other diocesan bishop. But the Archbishop of York has some leadership responsibilities among the dioceses in the north of England and the Archbishop of Canterbury likewise in the south, though he is also recognized as the Church of England's national leader and as the focus of unity for the world-wide Anglican Communion. He exercises his leadership largely through influence, rather than by authority, and inevitably this depends greatly on his personality and gifts.

Anglicanism

From the second half of the twentieth century onwards, there has been a very considerable increase in

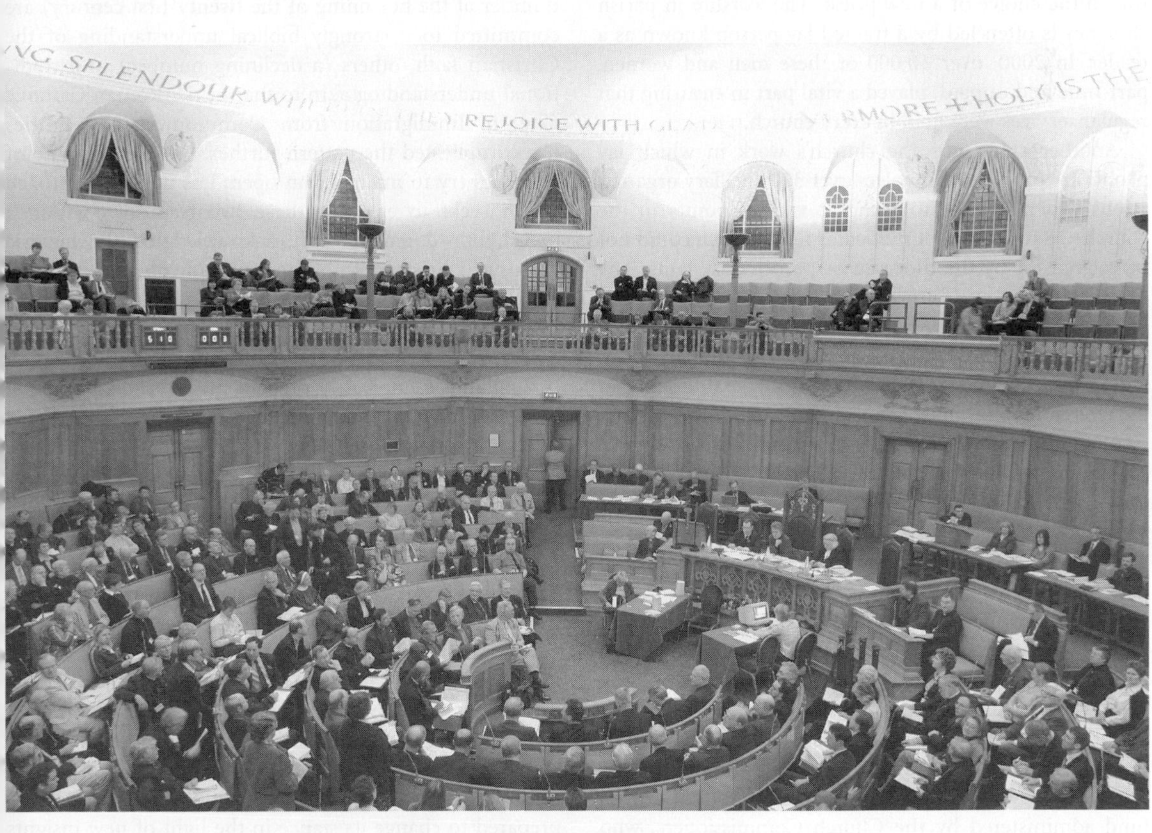

General Synod of the Church of England

the participation of the laity in almost every aspect of the Church of England's life. This is the result, partly of a renewed understanding (shared with most other Christians) of the corporate nature of the church, partly of a decline in the number of clergy, and partly of financial problems requiring lay involvement in the raising and spending of money. Local churches are, at their best, a partnership between clergy and laity, and at diocesan and national levels the laity are an integral part of the decision-making. This takes place in a synodical system incorporating the bishops and elected representatives of the other clergy and the laity. One of the consequences of this system, inaugurated in 1970, is the need for many meetings. The power of bishops has also been reduced, though their authority in matters relating to doctrine remains. Every parish has a church council, consisting usually of the clergy and about twenty lay members, who are elected annually and are involved in virtually every aspect of church life. Two of the lay members, named churchwardens, are the bishop's representatives in the Evangelicals parish and, among other duties, are legally responsible for maintaining worship in a vacancy, i.e., when a parish is temporarily without a priest; they also play an important role in the choice of a new priest. The worship in parish churches is often led by a trained lay person known as a reader. In 2000, over 10,000 of these men and women, part-time and unpaid, played a vital part in ensuring that regular services were held in every church.

p. 836

Another sphere of the church's work in which lay people are prominent involves over 300 ancillary organizations which came into being at various points in the church's history to meet particular needs which could not be catered for by the diocesan or parochial systems. The Mothers' Union was founded in l876 to uphold the virtues of family life and now has 750,000 members in English parishes and also overseas. The Modern Churchpeople's Union was founded in 1896 to advance liberal thought in the church and has only a small membership. The Central Council of Church Bell Ringers was founded in 1891 and still flourishes, but experience suggests that it is easier to found an organization than it is to close it down when its usefulness has ended.

Money

The finances of the Church of England are complex and at the turn of the century were causing anxiety. Until the 1830s, bishops, parish priests and clergy were paid from Ethics historic endowments attached to their particular offices. Church buildings were maintained, or neglected, by local landowners. This system could not survive the demand for new parishes and churches created by the growth of the industrial towns during the nineteenth century. So the endowments were gradually pooled to form a central fund administered by the Church Commissioners, who eventually became responsible for the stipends and housing of all the clergy. The maintenance of church buildings became the responsibility of the parishioners. Although the income of the Church Commissioners was for some years adequate for the discharging of their responsibilities, the changed economic circumstances of the nation in the late twentieth century led to an ever-increasing shortfall in the amount of money required to keep the clergy adequately paid. In 2000 the Commissioners contributed about £30 million to clergy stipends and over £100 million to clergy pensions. This left the parishes to find over £600 million for the payment of their clergy, the upkeep of their churches and vicarages, and for diocesan and national ministries, including clergy training. Financial constraints have required many small parishes to be united with their neighbours and this has coincided with a decline in the number of clergy available to serve them.

The Church of England's beliefs are those of Anglicanism as a whole, but a greater variety of emphasis is exhibited than in other parts of the world because of the nature of its origins. There is still a marked contrast between Evangelicals who emphasize the beliefs and practices of the Protestant Reformation and Catholics who are 'high church'. Some parishes (an increasing number at the beginning of the twenty-first century) are committed to a strongly biblical understanding of the Christian faith, others (a declining number) to a traditional understanding akin to that of the Roman Catholic Church. Immigration from Commonwealth countries has complicated the pattern further. But the majority of churches try to maintain an open, less defined approach which seeks to embrace these two traditions within a broad, non-dogmatic faith, acknowledging the historic creeds of Christendom but leaving individuals (including the clergy) free to make their own interpretations based on intellect and experience.

All of this can give the impression that the Church of England is hopelessly divided in its beliefs or that it believes next to nothing. But most of its members regard freedom from imposed dogmas as a strength, rather than as a weakness, and value the variety as an enrichment of corporate faith. The same is true of the variety of forms of worship that tend to express the different faith traditions, though the lack of a single prayer book to serve as a unifying element can cause some confusion among mobile worshippers and some lowering of liturgical standards.

On ethical matters the Church of England tends to take a pastoral, rather than a legalistic, approach. While promoting the broad principles of Christian morality, it can be tolerant of deviations provided these are clearly the best, or the least worst, courses of action in situations of particular difficulty. Furthermore it is prepared to change its stance in the light of new insights or constructive developments in society. Thus artificial methods of contraception, remarriage after divorce and, in some circumstances, abortion are now acceptable. Homosexual activity is no longer regarded as a barrier to church membership, though opinion is divided about its permissibility for the clergy, among whom there is a significant number of men and women of homosexual orientation. This issue has become particularly acute in recent years. On matters of social ethics, bishops and General Synod committees often express opinions in public about the plight of racial minorities, the poor and the homeless, as well as on war and peace. This sometimes leads to conflict between the church and various organs of government.

At the beginning of the twenty-first century the Church of England, like most other Western European churches, particularly those that were once closely integrated into their national culture, was faced with a number of serious problems. The alienation of the working class from the church can be traced back to the time of the Industrial revolution and by the mid-nineteenth century was virtually complete. The twentieth century saw the gradual but accelerating weakening of the attachment of the middle class, and by the end of that century the effects of this were clearly visible in much smaller congregations in most churches, shortage of clergy and acute financial problems. These factors, combined with the growth of secularization, resulted in the church being consigned to the margins of society.

Attempts to deal realistically and dynamically with an unprecedented situation have so far been hampered by a marked reluctance to face unpleasant facts and an equal reluctance to question the value of traditional forms of church life based on the parochial system. Resources are now too thinly spread for this system to provide the basis for renewal. The office of bishop, now confined largely to the crisis-management of a declining institution and the pastoral care of a dispirited clergy, allows little scope for visionary leadership and has become unattractive to those who might offer such leadership. High hopes were pinned on the new Archbishop of Canterbury, Rowan Williams, when he was appointed in 2003, but whether he is in a position to bring about much-needed changes is another matter.

TREVOR BEESON

📖 Owen Chadwick, *The Victorian Church* (2 vols, 1966, 1970), London: SCM Press 1987; Eamon Duffy, *The Stripping of the Altars. Traditional Religion in England 1400–1580*, New Haven: Yale University Press 1992; Adrian Hastings, *A History of English Christianity, 1920–2000*, London: SCM Press 2001; Kenneth Hylson-Smith, *English Christianity from Elizabeth I to Elizabeth II* (3 vols), London: SCM Press 1996–8

Church of Scotland

The Church of Scotland is a part of the world-wide family of Presbyterian churches. It is Scotland's national church, although it is free from state interference in its life, worship and doctrine.

Presbyterian churches

Any visitor to Scotland will easily find the Kirk (as the Church of Scotland is often called). As part of its responsibility as the national church, the Kirk has divided Scotland up into territorial regions called parishes, and it has church buildings in every parish. Its adult church membership is just over 600,000 out of a population of 5 million; in the early 1950s the Church of Scotland boasted a signed-up adult membership of 1.2 million.

The Kirk's places of worship vary from cathedrals to fine Victorian buildings to modest hall churches. Visitors will usually find a simplicity of style in both architectural design and furnishings. This emphasis on simplicity is not accidental; it reflects the worship and theology of the Kirk. As part of the Reformed tradition, the Church of Scotland believes that the individual soul has access to a gracious God, through Jesus Christ, unmediated by priesthood or church regulation. While beauty is honoured, it must serve, rather than distract from, the core simplicity of the gospel message.

Industrial revolution
◄ Reformed churches

The Church of Scotland understands itself as both Catholic and Protestant. It is Catholic in that it sees itself as being part of the universal church, with its roots in the earliest Christian communities; and also in that its primary statements of faith are the historic Apostles' and Nicene Creeds, approved by the great councils of the Catholic Church.

Secularization ◄
Creed
Council

The Kirk is also Protestant in that it stands within the Reformed tradition of Christian faith. At the heart of this tradition is the doctrine known as 'justification by grace through faith': this means that the individual finds salvation not through the accumulation of good works or the fulfilment of certain ecclesiastical conditions, but through the free, unmerited love of God as expressed in the life, death and resurrection of Jesus Christ.

Justification
Salvation
Christianity in Great Britain ◄

The worship of the Church of Scotland expresses both simplicity and diversity. The Kirk's main service book, the Book of Common Order – unlike the Roman Catholic Missal or the Church of England Book of Common Prayer – was provided as an example rather than a worship book to be followed rigorously. Some congregations follow the Book of Common Order very closely, while most others adapt the orders of worship provided. A good number follow a lectionary of scripture readings, while others do not. The Kirk celebrates two sacraments: baptism and holy communion.

Worship
Sacraments

A normal Sunday morning service, usually lasting for about an hour, will consist of hymns, prayers, scripture

Bible

readings and sermon. The Bible is regarded as the 'supreme rule of faith and life', though there is diversity in interpretation within the Kirk. In some congregations, the Bible will be interpreted in a literalistic way; in most others there will be a variety of emphases. In other words, within the parameters of the Reformed tradition, the Kirk is a 'broad' church.

Celtic Christianity

A distinctive part of Scottish Presbyterian worship is the singing of metrical psalms, many of them set to old Scottish traditional and folk tunes. These verse psalms have been exported to Africa, North America and other parts of the world where Presbyterian Scots missionaries or émigrés have been influential.

Organization
Reformation
Ministry and ministers

In its government, the Church of Scotland is presbyterian. The New Testament Greek word *presbuteros,* means 'elder', and the presbyterian system involves government by ministers and elders. At the local level, each congregation is governed by a kirk session, whose chairman, normally the congregation's ordained minister, is referred to as the 'moderator'.

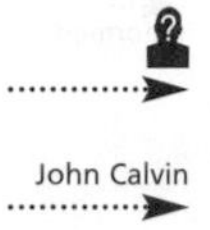

John Calvin
Predestination

Elders – who, despite the name, can be of any age over 21 – are drawn from the congregation. They are either invited by the kirk session or voted in by the congregation, normally because of their Christian character and commitment. Most elders have pastoral responsibility for a district within the parish. The Kirk has had women elders since 1966, and women ministers since 1968.

At the heart of Presbyterianism is the doctrine of 'the priesthood of all believers'. The ordained minister is seen as the congregation's spiritual leader and teacher, rather than as a priest who mediates the mysteries of faith. The Presbyterian priesthood is understood as a corporate function exercised by all the believers.

Presbyterianism is therefore a comparatively egalitarian and democratic form of government. It has no bishops. Above the kirk session is the presbytery, a regional assembly made up of equal numbers of ministers and elders. It has both missionary and supervisory functions.

The supreme court of the Kirk is the general assembly of the Church of Scotland. Made up of equal numbers of ministers and elders from all over Scotland, this annual week-long gathering hears reports from its boards and committees whose remits cover matters such as doctrine, ministry, national mission, world mission, education, stewardship, social responsibility and finance.

The best part of one day is given over to a report of the Assembly's church and nation committee. This report seeks to make Christian comment on many aspects of national, and even international, life. Up until the establishment of Scotland's own parliament in 1999 – a cause supported by the Kirk for more than 50 years – the general assembly of the Church of Scotland was often portrayed in the media as the nearest thing to Scotland's parliament.

This honoured place in Scottish life reflects the role of the Kirk in the shaping of the modern Scottish nation. It is not known for sure when Christianity first came to Scotland, but the first recorded missionary movement is associated with St Ninian, who settled in Whithorn in Galloway towards the end of the fourth century. The next great missionary movement began in 563, when St Columba established his community on the island of Iona. Both Ninian and Columba were part of what is known as the Celtic Church, which differed from the Roman Church on matters of organization, emphasis and style rather than doctrine. The Celtic Church gradually became subsumed under the Roman order, and Catholic Christianity, under the leadership of the Pope, continued in Scotland until the time of the Reformation.

Protestant ideas came to Scotland from mainland Europe. Scotland proved to be fertile soil for the seeds of the Reformed faith. The Protestant Christians in Scotland understood themselves as being the inheritors of the legacy of Ninian and Columba; indeed, they saw their roots as being in the early church.

Under the courageous, vigorous leadership of John Knox (*c.* 1513–72), the Calvinistic version of Protestantism prevailed in Scotland. John Calvin's brilliant, rigorous mind put the sovereignty of God at the heart of his theology, and his emphasis on predestination (the foreknowledge of an all-powerful God working its way out in human history) shaped much Scottish theological thinking.

Scotland was declared to be a Protestant country in 1560, but it was nearly a century before the Presbyterian revolution was secured and the Church of Scotland became officially Scotland's national church. John Knox's dream of a church and a school in every parish gradually began to be realized, and the Kirk was the unchallengeable founder of the modern Scottish educational system. Its egalitarian ideas also had considerable influence on the political and cultural life of the nation.

Over the centuries there were several presbyterian secessions from what became known as the Auld Kirk ('Old Church'), the most serious of which was the Disruption of 1843, in which about a third of the ministers and members of the established church left to form the Free Church of Scotland. In 1900, the Free Church and the United Presbyterian Church united to form the United Free Church, and in 1929 the Church of Scotland and the United Free Church joined together. The Free Church and the Free Presbyterians are referred to as the 'Wee Frees' and are proverbial for their strict observance of Sunday.

Some members of these denominations refused to join the united bodies, and there have been further secessions from the continuing Presbyterian churches. Most of the disagreements over the centuries have been about links with the state, or perceived laxity in confessional statements.

How to understand it all? Think Presbyterianism, think coffee. The Church of Scotland is the decaffeinated version of Presbyterianism. As you move to the right, starting with the Free Kirk and moving through to the Reformed and Associated Presbyterian churches, the theological caffeine gets stronger and stronger. When you reach the outer fringes, you're nearing 100 per cent proof.

Although Scottish Presbyterianism has specialized in splits, the twentieth century has been a time of unification. The Church of Scotland has been much involved in ecumenical discussions, though plans for a united church involving the Church of Scotland, the Scottish Episcopal Church, the Methodist Church and the United Reformed Church were thrown out at the Kirk's general assembly in 2003. Traditional Presbyterian suspicion of bishops and hierarchies played an important part in this decision.

Like all British mainstream churches, the Church of Scotland is concerned about diminishing influence. As a national church with a declining membership, the Kirk is currently facing painful questions about identity and strategy in the postmodern era.

RON FERGUSON

📖 J. H. S. Burleigh, *A Church History of Scotland*, London: OUP 1960; G. Donaldson, *Scotland: Church and Nation through Sixteen Centuries*, Edinburgh: Scottish Academic Press ²1972

Church fathers

The leaders and writers of the early church whose work played a major role in determining the life and thought of the church in its first, formative centuries, are known as the church fathers. The use of the term (or of its near equivalents such as 'the fathers' or 'the holy fathers') goes back to the very start of the church's development. The word 'father' was in regular use as a way of speaking of either a bishop or a teacher. At that time those two roles were much more often combined in a single person than they are today. So the use of the word in the phrase 'the fathers' related naturally to these two closely integrated functions.

Today scholars tend to speak of the period during which the church fathers were active as the 'patristic' period (from the Latin for father, *pater*), and the study of them is known as patristics. Books summarizing the work of the church fathers and listing the literature about them are called patrologies.

There was and is no official or authorized list of 'the fathers', though there is general consensus about the main names that would unquestionably figure in any account of those in mind when the term is used. There is nothing surprising in that. The same is true in the case of the other principal authority for determining Christian thought and life, the Bible. Although the main outline of the canon was established by about the end of the second century, the precise contents of the various lists of canonical books that have come down to us continued to vary in detail for a long time after that.

Bible Canon

Four distinguishing marks may be said to characterize those regarded as meriting the title of church father: orthodoxy of doctrine, acceptance by the church, holiness of life, and belonging to a sufficiently ancient stage of the church's existence.

In the case of *orthodoxy of doctrine* there is an inevitable degree of circularity. The importance of the appeal to the writings of the fathers, especially from the fourth century on, when that appeal became particularly important, was to help determine the orthodox interpretation of the scriptures where that interpretation was in dispute. So if orthodoxy was a distinguishing mark of someone's right to the designation 'father', his writings were also a contributory factor in determining what that orthodoxy was. But the requirement of orthodoxy was never regarded as implying infallibility. Individual fathers were not treated as an absolutely reliable guide to truth on their own. Even admirers of so outstanding a father as Augustine could admit that he was occasionally guilty of error. It was the corporate witness of the fathers taken together, rather than the teaching of any single father in isolation, on which the church relied for a true understanding of the gospel.

Acceptance by the church is a further corollary of the emphasis on the corporate rather than individual status of being a church father. Not only is the significance of the fathers for the church a corporate rather than an individual matter; the process of coming to be regarded as a church father depended on the positive appraisal of the church. Even though there was no official list of church fathers formally agreed by church authority, wide acceptance within the church as a whole was seen as a necessary criterion. Successful appeal to someone's teaching in an ecumenical council, for example, was a clear sign that that person was rightly to be seen as one of the fathers, through whom the faith was being authentically handed down to future generations of Christians.

Authority

Council

As for *holiness of life*, most, but not all, of the generally acknowledged fathers were canonized. Augustine, for example, is commonly referred to today as St Augustine. A church father was valued not just for his intellectual acuity in discerning the shape of Christian truth, but also as one who exemplified that truth in his devotion and leadership of the church's broader life of worship and service. Sadly, a number of the most influential of those universally acclaimed as 'church fathers' would seem to have rated rather poorly on this score. Cyril of Alexandria, for example, a key father particularly in the view of the Orthodox churches, was highly criticized in his lifetime, and not only by his enemies, for the strong-arm tactics of his political leadership.

Heresy
Doctrinal criticism

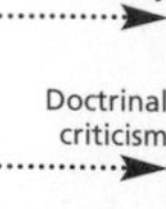

When it comes to *belonging to the ancient church* the limits of what can appropriately be described as the 'ancient church' have obviously kept changing. Those who did most to establish the practice of appealing to 'the fathers', like Basil of Caesarea and Gregory of Nazianzus in the fourth century, did so in order to emphasize that their teaching was not their own invention but something that had been handed down to them by the faithful leaders of the church in the past. But in the course of time Basil and Gregory themselves came to be seen as key figures in this process of the faithful handing on of Christian truth, outstanding church fathers in their own right. In principle there is no logical end-point to 'the age of the fathers'. But in practice in the course of the second millennium there has grown up a generally agreed definition of when it should be regarded as reaching its close. Like all such periodizations of history, it is a useful convention, though inevitably in some measure an arbitrary one. The end is marked not by any particular date but by the lives of John of Damascus (*c.* 655-*c.* 750) in the East and Isidore of Seville (*c.* 560–636) in the West. Both were prolific authors, much of whose work involved intensive summarizing of earlier patristic authors and played an important role in passing it on to the medieval world.

Feminist theology
Women in Christianity
Orthodox churches
Roman Catholic church
Scholasticism
Protestantism
Trinity
Christology
Reformation
Anglicanism

The attitude of the different mainstream churches to this 'age of the fathers' as a clearly defined entity is far from uniform. The Orthodox churches have paid least attention to the dividing line. The fathers, for them, are simply the first, admittedly highly important phase of a continuous living process of transmitted life that has gone on in fundamentally the same way from the very beginning and continues essentially unchanged in the life of the church today. Roman Catholics tend to see the time of the fathers as a first period in the clarification and handing on of Christian truth, which was followed by the age of scholasticism; and that, with its different characteristic style, tends to be seen as an advance on the earlier age of the fathers. Protestants have been inclined to value the work of the fathers more selectively, giving great weight to developments in the doctrines of the Trinity and the person of Jesus down to the time of the Council of Chalcedon (451 CE), but regarding other aspects of the patristic age and even more the centuries that lie between it and the Reformation with serious suspicion. Among Anglicans, study of the fathers was for a long time seen to be of crucial importance as providing a court of appeal in support of their interpretation of scripture over against the interpretations followed by other Protestant churches.

The twentieth century has seen the growth of a more critical-historical approach to the fathers. This has led us to see them more closely in relation to the historical and philosophical context of the Hellenistic world in which they lived. It has also had the effect of reducing the sharp line of distinction that has always existed between the 'fathers', who were recognized by the church as orthodox, and the 'heretics', who were also often church leaders and gifted Christian writers but who were judged by the ancient church to be guilty of serious error. Both groups tend now to be seen as men who in their attempts to express and live their Christian faith in a changing cultural setting all contributed, by way of action and reaction, to the gradual emergence of traditional Christian doctrine. But the line, though blunted, is not erased. Some now regarded as 'church fathers' like Tertullian and Origen were in the patristic age itself regarded with too much suspicion to be treated as 'church fathers', though they were nonetheless recognized as having made an important positive contribution to the developing doctrines of the church. Others who were condemned as out-and-out heretics, like Arius and Apollinarius, are still put in that category.

The long-established term 'church *father*' and the related term 'patristics' have not unnaturally come under critical scrutiny from feminist scholars. But even those who have expressed a desire to see the development of 'matristics' have acknowledged that such a study could not start until after the end of the patristic age. Though some women did make a significant contribution to the life of the early church, none of those who held the kind of position or influence characteristic of the fathers were women. But feminist scrutiny has also brought more fully to light the male orientation of so much of the underlying anthropology that they inherited both from their biblical and Hellenistic sources, and its deep-seated influence on much of the teaching and practice built up in the patristic age.

We shall be looking at the life and thought of some of the major church fathers in chronological order.

Major series of English translations: *The Ante-Nicene Christian Library* ed A. Roberts and J. Donaldson (1866ff.), reprinted as *Ante-Nicene Fathers* (1884ff.), Peabody, MA: Hendrickson 1994; *A Select Library of Nicene and Post-Nicene Fathers* ed P. Schaff and H. Wace (1886ff.), reprinted as *Nicene and Post-Nicene Fathers*, Peabody, MA: Hendrickson 1994 (*these texts are available online at http:/www. ccel.org.fathers*); *Ancient Christian Writers* ed J. Quasten and J. C. Plumpe, Westminster, MD: Christian Classics 1946ff.; *The Fathers of the Church* ed L. Schopp, Washington, DC: Catholic University Press of America 1947ff. (in articles on individual fathers, references to these editions are given in abbreviated form)

THE APOSTOLIC FATHERS

'Apostolic fathers' is the name given to the authors of the earliest Christian writings outside the New Testament. These comprise:

The *Didache* (or *Teaching of the Twelve Apostles*): A document, unknown before its discovery in 1883, giving directions about catechesis, liturgy and ministry. Its contents are striking and not easily integrated into our other knowledge on these topics. Its provenance and date are still much debated, with Syria and c.100 CE as likely possibilities. It is a useful reminder of how diverse early Christian belief and practice were in different localities.

Clement of Rome, *Letter to the Corinthians*: A letter of counsel, written c.96 CE, arising out of a challenge to the authority of the leaders in Corinth.

Second Letter of Clement: A pseudonymous homily of unknown authorship, dealing particularly with the issue of penance.

Ignatius of Antioch, *Letters*: Seven letters, one to Rome and six to churches in Asia Minor, which Ignatius had visited briefly while being taken to Rome where he was to die as a martyr. Written c.110 CE.

Polycarp of Smyrna, *Letter to the Philippians*: A short letter, valued chiefly because Polycarp was reputed to have sat at the feet of the evangelist John and lived to a great age as Bishop of Smyrna before dying as a martyr in 156 CE. A moving account of his martyrdom is also sometimes included among the writings of the apostolic fathers.

Papias of Hierapolis, *Fragments*: Only fragments of the writings of this Asian bishop survive. He was not regarded with the same veneration that was accorded to Polycarp, but the surviving fragments of his work were valued for the information they give about how the canonical Gospels came to be written.

The Letter of Barnabas: An anonymous tract, probably of Alexandrian provenance, using a highly allegorical interpretation of scripture to support a Christian over against a Jewish understanding of the Old Testament scriptures.

Hermas, *The Shepherd*: A long work, involving a series of visions, by a layman in Rome calling for repentance and reform in the life of the church. It had wide circulation and respect in the second and third centuries.

The Letter to Diognetus: An attractive writing of unknown origin, defending the church from attacks current in the Roman world. Although historically included among the writings of the apostolic fathers, it is more akin in content, and probably in date also, to other late second-century writings, generally grouped together under the title 'the apologists'.

Selected texts in English: *The Early Christian Fathers* ed H. Bettenson, Oxford: OUP 1956; *The Later Christian Fathers* ed H. Bettenson, Oxford: OUP 1970; *Documents in Early Christian Thought* ed M. Wiles and M. Santer, Cambridge: CUP 1975
Comprehensive work of reference: J. Quasten (ed), *Patrology* (4 vols, 1960–86: vol. 4 ed A. Di Berardino), reissued Notre Dame, IN: Ave Maria Press 1994
Biographical studies: H. F. von Campenhausen, *The Fathers of the Greek Church*, London: A&C Black 1963; *The Fathers of the Latin Church*, London: A&C Black 1964; Frances M. Young, *From Nicaea to Chalcedon*, London: SCM Press and Philadelphia: Fortress Press 1983

Apostolic fathers (first and early second centuries)
This is the name, first given in the seventeenth century, to the authors of a miscellaneous group of the earliest surviving writings immediately after the New Testament period.

In some cases nothing at all, not even the name, is known of the authors themselves. The period in which the works were written covers roughly the years 70–135 CE. The earliest of the works is therefore likely to be of an earlier date than the latest writings of the New Testament. They are not the only surviving writings of a Christian provenance to come from that period. But others of similar date, some of which have only been recovered recently, are for the most part further removed in ethos from the emerging Christian orthodoxy, having a more Gnostic flavour than these writings of the apostolic fathers. Some of the latter (Clement's *Letter*, the *Shepherd of Hermas* and the *Letter of Barnabas*) were so highly regarded by their contemporaries and immediate successors in the church that they occasionally appear in early lists of canonical books. But they largely disappeared from view between the fifth and sixteenth centuries. After their rediscovery they came to be highly valued as rare links between the scriptural writings and the much fuller body of patristic

Gnosis

writings from the late second century on – precious glimpses into what used to be called 'the tunnel period' of the immediate post-New Testament age. The more straightforwardly historical approach of much modern scholarship tends to study them in closer conjunction with the later writings of the New Testament, which overlap with them in date of composition, than was customary in the past.

Martyr

Clement and Ignatius are the two figures who have elicited the most interest and exercised the greatest influence in the course of the church's history. Clement's name appears as second or third bishop of Rome after Peter in later succession lists. That he was a leader in the church of Rome at the end of the first century is not in doubt. Whether there was at that time a 'bishop' of Rome, as the office was later understood, is open to question, and Clement is probably better seen as simply the senior presbyter. His letter is a sustained argument for an ordered ministry, whose authority needs to be accepted, and draws heavily on Old Testament and Stoic ideas. In the course of his argument he describes the established ministry as standing in a tradition of apostolic appointment. His remarks have been used at times to support a much more precise notion of the unbroken succession of bishops from the apostles than their context will easily allow.

Ignatius of Antioch was bishop of the important Eastern diocese of Antioch. His voice conveys a more charismatic and personal faith, as he looks forward to martyrdom as a fulfilment of union with Christ from which he has no wish to be rescued. But he too speaks of the need for obedience to the one bishop, with the accompanying ministry of presbyters and deacons, as the antidote to division in the face of external threat. His words too have been used on occasion as conveying a more universal advocacy of episcopal ministry than their immediate context need imply.

Sacrifice

📖 M. Staniforth, *Early Christian Writings: the Apostolic Fathers*, revd edn, Harmondsworth: Penguin Books 1987 (contains English translations of most of the texts); Simon Tugwell, *The Apostolic Fathers*, London and New York: Continuum 2002

Justin Martyr (*c.* 100–*c.* 165)

Justin Martyr is the outstanding figure among a number of second-century Christian writers usually grouped together under the generic title, 'the apologists' (others, not described here, include Aristides and Athenagoras of Athens, Theophilus of Antioch and Minucius Felix, probably from Africa). Our knowledge of Justin's life comes mainly from his own writings, and the details given there may sometimes owe more to literary fiction than to accurate reporting. Born of Greek parents in the region of Samaria, he was drawn to the teaching of Stoic, Peripatetic, Pythagorean and finally Platonist philosophers in Ephesus, before being converted to Christianity around 130 CE. He himself became a teacher of Christianity as the true philosophy in Rome, a conception of his role that he symbolized by adopting the traditional philosopher's cloak. And it was in Rome around 165 CE that he finally died a martyr's death for his refusal to offer sacrifice.

An 'apologist' is one who offers an 'apology' for (or, in modern terms, a defence or vindication of) Christianity in response to contemporary criticisms of it. Justin's overall purpose was to show that the apparently far less sophisticated Christian faith was in fact the true wisdom only partially reflected in the best philosophies of the ancient world. The first of his three surviving works, *Dialogue with Trypho*, is directed against Jewish attacks on Christianity and belongs to his Ephesus period; the other two, his first and second *Apologies*, were written during his time in Rome and deal with Roman attacks on the faith.

The *Dialogue with Trypho* purports to be the account of a public debate between himself and a Jewish scholar, Trypho. It is probably based on a real occasion of public debate, but in the form in which we have it, it has clearly been written up in a manner that expands Justin's role and emphasizes its success, while turning Trypho into a man of straw. The central theme is Justin's demonstration of how completely Christianity fulfils the prophetic aspects of the Jewish scriptures. The primary weapon in Justin's armoury is an appeal to the figurative meaning of the prophetic scriptures wherever a more literal or straightforward interpretation of them would seem to go against the Christian case.

The *First Apology* takes the form of an official petition to the emperor, Antoninus Pius, but it is unlikely that it was formally presented in this way. Nevertheless it was certainly intended to rebut understandings of Christianity that underlay action against Christians by state officials. Although Christians did not offer sacrifices, which were regarded as the basic form of divine worship, they were not atheists; they had a more transcendent, immaterial understanding of God. So too their refusal to participate in official sacrifices was not evidence of sedition; in every other respect they were loyal subjects of the emperor, committed to the highest standards of morality. There was nothing in their behaviour to justify the punishments meted out by some magistrates to Christians simply on the basis of their confessing to the name of being Christian.

All these are themes that recur in the writings of other apologists as well. Justin is distinctive for the special emphasis that he lays on his primary theme, namely that Christianity is the fulfilment of the best, particularly the Platonic, aspects of traditional thought. Despite the many errors and shortcomings of the ancient philosophers which

Justin was not afraid to criticize sharply, much of Stoic ethics and Platonic ideas of divine transcendence were valid insights that derived ultimately from the best philosophers' participation in the divine Logos (or Reason). And since that divine Logos was also Christ, Justin could even speak of Socrates as a 'Christian before Christ'. He also took up a notion already suggested in the Hellenistic world to the effect that many of the positive ideas in the Greek world had been derived historically from Moses, who was prior to Plato in time and said to have been an influence on his thought.

So Justin taught that Christ was the divine Logos or Son of God, who had appeared to the patriarchs in the theophanies (appearances of God) recorded in the Old Testament and had finally lived on earth as Jesus of Nazareth. He was god, but distinct from the fully transcendent Father, who could not properly be thought of as appearing in visible form to the patriarchs or living in a physical form as Jesus. By these means Justin sought to integrate the Christian faith as he knew it with the best insights of the Graeco-Roman world in which it was beginning to put down its roots. It was not a sell-out to the philosophy of the day, but it was not a way of integrating the two which was to satisfy the church in the long run. For in the centuries that followed the church went on to pursue the task of affirming Jesus Christ not simply as the divine Logos and Son of God, but also as one who was fully co-equal with the Father. However, Justin deserves to be assessed not by criteria that still lay in the future but by his positive and creative response to the challenges facing the church in his own day.

St Justin Martyr: The First and Second Apologies translated L. W. Barnard, New York and Mahwah, NJ: Paulist Press 1997; L. W. Barnard, *Justin Martyr: His Life and Thought*, Cambridge: CUP 1967; E. F. Osborn, *Justin Martyr*, Tübingen: J. C. B. Mohr (Paul Siebeck) 1973

Irenaeus of Lyons (*c.* 130–*c.* 200)

Irenaeus was Bishop of Lyons towards the end of the second century. He probably came originally from Asia Minor, as he speaks of having heard Polycarp of Smyrna in his youth. Like other leading figures in the Western church in the second century, Greek was his native tongue. Two of his writings are available to us: a five-volume work entitled *Against the Heresies*, which is a detailed refutation of Gnosticism surviving in a Latin translation, and *The Demonstration of the Apostolic Preaching*, a short outline of the faith rediscovered only at the beginning of the twentieth century in an Armenian translation.

The conflict with Gnosticism, which is the theme of his major work, has also served to shape the distinctive contours of his own thought. It has three main focal points.

The first of these is *the sources of the faith*. Gnostics appealed to a variety of sources in support of their beliefs: a wide range of scriptures, some of which, like the Gospels of Philip and of Thomas, were Gnostic in their general orientation; highly figurative (in Irenaeus' view, absurd) interpretations of the scriptures they had in common with the main church; and a chain of oral transmission of esoteric teaching, claimed to go back through a succession of teachers to secret teaching given by Jesus himself. Irenaeus responded by limiting the scriptures to which appeal could rightly be made. Although any formal fixing of the scriptural canon belongs to a later date, the writings to which Irenaeus appeals coincide very closely with the subsequent list of books accepted into the biblical canon. He is the first to claim that there can be only four Gospels, just as there are four principal winds. And those scriptures are to be interpreted in the light of tradition (or 'rule of faith', to use Irenaeus' favoured term), handed down openly in the public life of the church. Moreover the church itself is under the authority of its presbyters and bishops, who can trace their episcopal succession in the public domain back to its apostolic origin – in Rome's case to Peter himself.

p. 145

Canon

Tradition

Authority

p. 851

The second is *the one God*. Gnostics, influenced by the intractable problem of evil, attributed the creation of the physical world to a demiurge, a creator god distinct from the supreme God or the Father of Jesus Christ. Irenaeus would have none of it. Christian faith was emphatically monotheistic. There could be only one God, properly so called. The Christian God was the creator of the physical as well as of the spiritual world. It was true that the production and ordering of that world was done through the Logos and the Spirit but they are 'the two hands of God', so that together Father, Son and Spirit are one God.

Evil

The third is *the plan of salvation*. For Gnostics the essence of salvation was the rescue of spiritual beings from the world of matter in which they were tragically enmeshed. For Irenaeus it was the redemption of the whole order that God had created, including the material. Evil is the work of demons, and human involvement in it was a result of Adam's disobedience. Unlike Augustine, who sees Adam's fall as that of a fully endowed, mature human being, Irenaeus attributes it to the immaturity of the newly created Adam before he had had time to grow up into the maturity that was God's purpose for him. So throughout history God has been at work with a divine plan (or 'economy', to use Irenaeus' word) of salvation. The Old Testament, with its stories of theophanies and prophecies, is the account of the presence and activity of the divine Logos in the execution of the early stages of that plan. The coming of Christ, the divine Logos (or

Gnosis

Salvation

Philosophy
Satan

Reason) fully present in a human life, is the climax of that preparatory stage. In his life and death Christ as man retraces the steps of the first Adam and emerges triumphantly obedient, and as God wins a cosmic victory over the forces of Satan. But the completion of this plan lies still in the future. Just as Christ retraced the path trodden by Adam in his human life, so he will ultimately 'recapitulate all things in himself', a key phrase Irenaeus takes from Ephesians 1.10. And this includes the physical creation. Irenaeus argues strongly for the resurrection of the body and also a renewed earth as foretold in prophecies like that of a new Jerusalem in the book of Revelation.

Resurrection
Revelation

Although *Against the Heresies* is a somewhat rambling work with a dismissive attitude to those against whom he writes, Irenaeus is the first writer of post-New Testament times whose surviving writings provides so broadly based and balanced an account of Christian theology as a whole. He is often praised as 'the first catholic theologian', with a strong and healthy hold on the importance of tradition. But we need to recall that for Irenaeus tradition was a static concept. He thought that he was doing no more than repeat the teaching of the apostles. Nor could he have imagined the changes in catholic theology that still lay ahead.

Heresy
p. 750

Irenaeus: The Proof of the Apostolic Preaching translated J. Smith, New York and Mahwah, NJ: Paulist Press 1992; D. Minns, *Irenaeus*, London: Geoffrey Chapman 1994; G. Wingren, *Man and the Incarnation*, Edinburgh: Oliver & Boyd 1959

Paul

Tertullian of Carthage (*c.* 160–225)

Tradition has it that Tertullian's father was a centurion in the Roman army, that Tertullian studied law in Rome and may also have practised there as a lawyer for a time. But the reliability of that tradition is open to question. We know nothing for certain about his life before he emerges as a prominent member of the church in Carthage, who wrote his many treatises in the last few years of the second century and the first decade of the third.

The most striking feature of Tertullian's writings is his use of language. He is the first major theologian to write in Latin (Irenaeus, the one significant Western theologian before him, wrote in Greek). Tertullian wrote in a concise, pungent, aphoristic style, a style well geared to the art of polemic, in which he excelled with much use of wit and sarcasm, and one also well suited to giving sharp and memorable expression to the tenets of Christian faith.

Trinity

Two of the most quoted of his aphoristic sayings may serve both to illustrate his linguistic style and at the same time to indicate a dominant characteristic of his own thought. 'What has Athens to do with Jerusalem?'; 'I believe because it is absurd' (the forcefulness of the sayings is even more striking in Tertullian's Latin: *Quid Athenis et Hierosolymis?* and *Credibile est quia ineptum est*). Tertullian is not in fact as hostile to philosophy as the first saying might suggest. While he was not influenced by Platonism, the philosophy that played so dominant a role in the thought of many of the fathers, especially in the East, Stoicism was a powerful influence on him, not only in relation to ethical teaching, as it was with many early Christian writers, but also in his understanding of God and of the soul. The word 'spirit', for example, did not indicate for him an immaterial reality but, as for the Stoics, a highly refined form of matter. Nor was the second saying as extreme or as anti-rational as it might appear. All early Christian thinkers accepted the givenness of revelation and of scripture in a strong sense, and Tertullian's sense of it was stronger than most. But he was not averse to giving reasons for accepting revelation in that way; his argumentative skills were acute and powerful.

Three groups may be picked out as recipients of Tertullian's polemic: the Roman state, Christian heretics and lax believers. An example of the first group of writings is Tertullian's *Apology*, a powerful plea against the unreasonable and unlawful character of the official persecution of Christians. Other apologetic writings go on the offensive, presenting reasoned criticism of such features of civic life as idolatry or the public games.

The prime example of the second group is Tertullian's massive five-volume work, *Against Marcion*. Marcion, impressed by Paul's sharp contrast between law and gospel, had argued that the Old Testament, with its account of the creator God and his punitive justice, was incompatible with the gospel and should not be regarded as a Christian book. Tertullian is in his element demolishing Marcion's attempt to produce a version of the New Testament scriptures, shorn of all positive reference to the Old Testament. But Tertullian's rightful insistence that the justice of God was not a concept to be set aside contributed in his own case not only to the implacable rigour of much of his ethical teaching but also on occasion to vivid and exultant accounts of the eternal torments of hell awaiting those now responsible for the sufferings and martyrdom of Christians.

Another work, *Against Praxeas*, was to have a particular influence on later doctrine. Praxeas (probably a pseudonym) had emphasized the oneness of God in a way that seemed to undermine the distinct identities of Father, Son and Holy Spirit. In his response Tertullian argues for the compatibility of insisting on both the unity of the Godhead and its threefold character. Although, like all trinitarian thinkers of his time, he gives a more secondary status to the divinity of the Son than the church was ultimately to affirm, nonetheless the language of 'substance' and 'persons' as the way to refer to the unity and threefold being of God respectively, the language that orthodoxy was eventually to adopt, derives from Tertullian's use of it in his *Against Praxeas*. The clarity of Tertullian's mind and his feel for language, which this and others of his anti-heretical writings display, made an important contribution to the emerging pattern of Christian doctrine.

However, Tertullian was concerned not just with the beliefs of Christians but every bit as much with their practice. He wrote many treatises on matters of Christian conduct and church discipline. In the course of time his dissatisfaction with what he saw as lax standards on the part of ordinary Christians and lax disciplinary procedures on the part of many clergy led to an increasingly rigorous tone in his writings. This was partly influenced by the attraction he felt towards the Montanist movement, which taught a special coming of the Holy Spirit calling Christians to more demanding forms of discipleship. Whether this led to his formally leaving the main church and joining a schismatic sect is not clear. It certainly led him to modify his understanding of the church, so that in his view it was the spiritual quality rather than the authorized office of the clergy that had the primary call on Christian obedience.

Despite the large contribution that Tertullian made to the development of Christian doctrine, he was never classified as one of the church fathers in the ancient world. This was partly because he was not, to the best of our knowledge, ordained, and even more to the fact that in his final years he was so closely linked to the Montanist schism. In any event it is easier to admire Tertullian than to like him. Alongside the clarity of his mind and the forcefulness of his reasoning there is a harshness of attitude and an unscrupulousness in argument that does not seem altogether appropriate in a father of the church.

📖 *Tertullian's Treatise against Praxeas* translated E. Evans, London: SPCK 1948; *Tertullian: On Penitence and On Purity* translated W. P. le Saint, Ancient Christian Writers 28, Westminster, MD: Newman Press and London: Longmans Green 1959; *Tertullian: Apology* translated T. R. Glover, Loeb Christian Library, London: Heinemann and Cambridge, MA: Harvard University Press 1931/1968; T. D. Barnes, *Tertullian, A Historical and Literary Study*, Oxford: Clarendon Press [2]1985; E. F. Osborn, *Tertullian, First Theologian of the West*, Cambridge: CUP 1997

Origen of Alexandria (*c.* 185–*c.* 254)

Origen is pre-eminent among early Christian authors before Augustine. He stands out not only for the volume and range of his writings, but also for their intellectual power and spiritual depth. He was a major influence on many of the fathers who followed him in the next two centuries. He was never in fact accorded the title 'church father'; even in his lifetime his orthodoxy was being called into question, and as that orthodoxy became more precisely defined in the fourth century, the questioning became sharper, until at the Second Council of Constantinople in 553 his writings were formally condemned. Nevertheless he cannot be left out of the ranks of the fathers today.

Council

Origen was born of Christian parents in Egypt, probably in the 180s. Two stories from his early years, whether historically reliable or not, illustrate well the intensity of his Christian commitment. When his father was martyred in 202, he is said to have been prevented from rushing out to join him in martyrdom only by his mother's expedient of hiding his clothes; he is also said to have castrated himself in literal obedience to the injunction of Matthew 19.12. He was well versed in philosophy (he is said to have sat at the feet of a Platonic philosopher, Ammonius Saccas), as well as being a devoted student of scripture. The overriding character of his life's work was to interpret the scriptures in a way which taught a vision of God and a way of life consonant with a broadly Middle Platonist understanding of the world.

Discipline ◀·········
Philosophy

For many years Origen taught Christian faith both at an elementary level to new converts and at a more advanced level to other Christians in Alexandria. Whether his school was a formal catechetical school of the Alexandrian church or had a looser relationship with the diocese is not clear. In any event conflict with the Bishop of Alexandria led to his moving to Caesarea in 231, where he was ordained priest; he stayed there, continuing to write and preaching regularly, until he died in 251 as a result of torture received in the first empire-wide persecution, launched by the Roman emperor Decius. He also travelled in pursuit of his researches, and was sometimes invited by other churches to arbitrate on matters of doctrinal uncertainty or dispute (*The Dialogue with Heraclides*, only discovered in 1941, is a fascinating account of such an occasion).

Schools
Persecution

Origen's productivity as a writer was prodigious. Much has been lost, and much of the still considerable volume of work that has survived has done so only in (not always wholly reliable) Latin translations. The greater part of his writing was directly concerned with scripture. The *Hexapla* was a massive work of textual scholarship, compiled over many years. It set out the text of the Old Testament in six columns – the Hebrew text, the Hebrew text transliterated into Greek characters, and four Greek translations, those of Aquila, Symmachus, the Septuagint and Theodotion (with three further Greek translations added at some points). It was highly esteemed in the ancient world, but only fragments have survived.

Biblical criticism

In his work on scripture Origen deals more extensively

with the Old Testament than with the New (though he did write lengthy commentaries on Matthew, John and Romans, substantial parts of which survive). Most of his writings on scripture take the form either of commentaries or of homilies. In both cases the work was normally taken down by stenographers and exhibits both the liveliness and the prolixity of the spoken word. At one point Origen speaks of scripture as requiring a threefold interpretation: literal, moral and spiritual. But he does not adhere to that particular formula in his own practice. More often he uses the simpler distinction between literal and allegorical interpretations. In the course of his commentaries he frequently puts forward a variety of possible interpretations, not always feeling the need to commit himself to one as in his judgement the true one. In his homilies on books such as Leviticus, Numbers and the Song of Songs he finds the allegorical approach indispensable, and draws out of the text a profound account of the journey of the soul into ever deeper knowledge and love of God. His use of allegory is a Midas touch that can turn the most unpromising material into gold. But it also enhances the risk, never far away in the work of interpretation, that the interpreter is liable to find in the text the meanings that he or she wishes to find there.

p. 126

In addition to Origen's extensive writings on scripture, three other surviving works deserve mention in illustration of the range of his scholarly output. His *Contra Celsum* (Against Celsus) is the longest and most wide-ranging example of early Christian apologetic, written in response to a much earlier attack on Christianity by a pagan philosopher of that name. *On Prayer* deals with philosophical difficulties, biblical teaching and practical issues related to prayer. *De Principiis* (On First Principles) is not a systematic account of Christian doctrine, but does deal with a number of central problems about God, Christ and human freedom, sin and salvation. It offers the best overall account of his Christian beliefs.

Persecution
Martyr

At the outset of *De Principiis* Origen expresses his firm commitment to the basic tenets of Christian belief but also thinks it appropriate to undertake bold speculation in an attempt to give as full and coherent an account of those beliefs as possible. The picture that he offers stresses the transcendent unity of God the Father, the distinct and eternal existence of the Son within the Godhead as the perfect image of the Father's goodness, the eternal nature also of created souls whose fall into sin gave rise to the physical world, the crucial redemptive role of Christ (the eternal Son conjoined to the one unfallen soul) and the hope of a final restoration of all fallen souls in fulfilment of the loving purposes of God. It was the speculative elements in this audacious vision that led later generations in particular to accuse Origen of unorthodoxy. Unfortunately the surviving text of the *De Principiis* is a Latin translation from the time when his orthodoxy was much in dispute, and that fact has affected its reliability. Determining the precise nature of Origen's theological beliefs, and the degree of tentativeness with which some of his bolder speculations were intended to be regarded, is a complex and difficult matter. But for most readers of Origen today, the primary reaction to his work is one of intense admiration for the intellectual creativity and spiritual quality of his writings.

Origen: The Song of Songs, Commentary and Homilies translated R. P. Lane, Ancient Christian Writers 26, New York and Mahwah, NJ: Paulist Press and London: Longmans, Green 1957; *Origen: Contra Celsum* translated H. Chadwick, Cambridge: CUP 1953; *Origen: De Principiis* translated G. W. Butterworth (1936), New York: Harper & Row 1966; H. Crouzel, *Origen*, Edinburgh: T&T Clark 1989; J. W. Trigg, *Origen*, Atlanta: John Knox Press and London: SCM Press 1985

Cyprian of Carthage (died 258)

Cyprian, a man of wealth and a rhetorician by training, had only been a Christian for two years when in 248, with the strong support of the laity, he was elected Bishop of Carthage, the most important see apart from Rome in the Latin West. Within a few months of his election, under the Emperor Decius Christians were for the first time persecuted throughout the Roman empire; other severe persecutions were to follow, and provided the context for his whole episcopate until he was himself put to death as a martyr on 14 September 258.

Cyprian saw the persecutions as God's judgement on the sinfulness of the church. He himself withdrew from the city to avoid arrest, so that he could provide the church with much-needed leadership throughout that testing time. The persecution and its aftermath gave rise to a series of contentious issues. The extensive collection of Cyprian's letters and a few short but important treatises show how he dealt with them; these writings exercised an important influence on subsequent generations.

Many of those who, unlike Cyprian, stayed in Carthage had to choose between offering incense to the Roman gods or being thrown into prison and possibly put to death. Those who followed the latter course were accorded great veneration. Some of these 'confessors', including those who were later to die a martyr's death, claimed that their costly Christian witness gave them the right to grant forgiveness and readmission to the church to those who had 'lapsed' by participating in the required pagan worship. Cyprian insisted that so serious a sin as apostasy could be forgiven, if at all, only by the bishop, acting in conjunction with the whole church, after a prolonged period of penance. Any premature readmissions would both discourage the true penitence required of the lapsed if they were to receive God's forgiveness and also contaminate those into whose fellowship they were being prematurely restored. Meanwhile a schismatic group in Rome, under the leadership of Novatian, moved in the opposite direction and argued that any readmission of apostates would fatally contaminate the church. Over against Novatian, Cyprian viewed the church as a school for sinners rather than a home for saints, but a school with very strict disciplinary rules. In the course of time he did modify slightly the very strict rules for readmission, as pastoral needs in the face of renewed persecution seemed to demand. His central conviction was that the matter of the readmission of penitents must be kept firmly in the hands of the church as a whole, under the guidance of the bishop.

This view of the church as the one ark of salvation, with firm boundaries separating it from the outside world, was severely tested by the schisms, which, like that led by Novatian, arose out of conflicting responses to the readmission of those who had lapsed under persecution. What was to be done about those who had received baptism within a schismatic body, and then wanted to join the catholic church? Cyprian argued that the saving rite of baptism could take place only within the one true church, which schismatics had by definition repudiated. So those who wanted to join the catholic church needed to be 'rebaptized', or more accurately to be baptized, since their initial 'baptism', even if following the church's form of rite exactly, was not a true baptism at all, having taken place outside the one ark of salvation. But the Church of Rome followed the different policy of requiring only a laying on of hands; this marked the reconciliation of penitents, admitting them into membership of the true church and thereby enabling the baptism they had already received to have its true saving efficacy.

This disagreement between Carthage and Rome raised another problem for Cyprian. If the unity of the local church is grounded on the figure of the bishop, what happens to the unity of the universal church when the bishops of different churches come into conflict? Cyprian believed that episcopal authority was something in which every bishop shared equally. In his dispute with Rome he was prepared to accept different practices in the different churches, but Rome claimed to have the greater authority and expected Carthage to give way. Cyprian argued that although the promise of power to forgive was first given to Peter alone (Matthew 16.18–19), it was subsequently given to all the apostles together (John 20.19–23). The single gift to Peter was thus not a gift signifying the primacy of the Bishop of Rome, but the single nature of the episcopal gift shared by all the apostles.

Some of Cyprian's letters and treatises relate to topics outside this particular complex of issues, such as the eucharist, the Lord's Prayer and almsgiving, and these were highly regarded by the later church. But it was his leadership of the church through the traumatic years of persecution and his subsequent martyrdom that was his primary legacy to his successors. In North Africa in the fourth century he was universally regarded as the founder figure to whom all sections of the church looked back for inspiration and support for their own beliefs. And it was his writings and views about baptism and the church in particular to which they turned. But they did so selectively. In the bitter divisions between Donatist and catholic at the time of Augustine, the Donatists with their puritan outlook appealed to Cyprian's fear of the contamination of the church by association with apostasy and his refusal to recognize the validity of sacraments outside the one true church, while the more cosmopolitan Augustine built on his recognition of the church as made up of sinners as well as saints. The less emotionally involved assessment of a modern admirer is perhaps more likely to give credit to the combination of firmness of principle and flexibility of practice with which he faced the particular conditions of unremitting disruption and successive crises that marked his ten-year episcopate.

Forgiveness ◄
Heresy
Sacraments
Initiation ◄

De Lapsis and *De Unitate Ecclesiae* ed and translated M. Bévenot, Oxford Early Christian Texts, Oxford: Clarendon Press 1971; Peter Hinchliff, *Cyprian of Carthage*, London: Geoffrey Chapman 1974; J. Patout Burns Jr, *Cyprian the Bishop*, London: Routledge 2002

Eusebius of Caesarea (*c.* 260–*c.* 340)

Eusebius was first and foremost a learned and painstaking scholar. In his early years he played a part in building up the great library at Caesarea, originally based on the library of Origen, who was a great hero in his eyes and a dominant influence on him. Some of his writings reveal the characteristic style and interests of a reference librarian – his *Onomasticon* (or *On the Place-Names of Holy Scripture*) is a biblical gazeteer, incorporating information on the etymology of the Hebrew names, and his *Chronicle* (surviving only in an Armenian translation) provides a chronology of world history in columnar form, showing the relationships in date between biblical and non-biblical histories.

But Eusebius was also the bishop of an important diocese, Caesarea, to which he was appointed about 313, the time of the ending of the great persecution, and one which he held until his death around 339. In that capacity he was to play a substantial role in the ecclesiastical and political events of those momentous years.

The combination of research scholar and ecclesiastical

politician offers a clue to the understanding of much of Eusebius' career, not least his most important writing, his *Ecclesiastical History*. This account of the rise of the church from its first beginnings to Eusebius' own day is a vital source for our knowledge of that early period of church history; limited though that knowledge is, it would be much more limited without Eusebius' account. He has justly been dubbed 'the father of church history'. The work is not polished and literary, in the manner of the great Greek historians of the ancient world. Its distinctive feature is the large number of direct citations from the writings of earlier Christian authors, many of which, though available to Eusebius in the library at Caesarea, have not survived. This structure gives the work a somewhat rambling appearance, but it is more than a mere collector's chronicle. Eusebius is concerned to tell the story of the growth and transformation of the church from its small beginnings to its very different status in his own day. But there appear to have been several editions, Eusebius bringing the work up to date a number of times as persecution spread, abated and then gave way gradually to the favourable settlement under Constantine. The climax of the story is thus blurred, and the interpretation of his history as a whole a subject of continuing dispute. But the work remains an indispensable window on to the church between the apostolic age and the Constantinian settlement.

Historiography

Constantine's 'conversion'

Many of Eusebius' other writings belong in spirit to the pre-Constantinian world in which he grew up. Two major works of apologetics, the *Preparation for the Gospel* and the *Proof of the Gospel*, develop the apologetic arguments of earlier writers on a grander scale, characteristically involving far more direct quotation from pagan writers, drawn once again from the resources of Caesarea's library. His own understanding of Christ and Christ's relation to the Father continues to ascribe a secondary status to the Godhead of the Son of a kind that had characterized the theology of most writers in earlier times. But that approach was coming under increasing challenge, and Eusebius found himself running into ecclesiastical difficulties. His (qualified) support for Arius led to his temporary excommunication at a synod at Antioch in 324 in the run up to the Council of Nicaea. Eusebius was reluctant to accept the findings of the council, with its description of the Son as 'of one substance *(homoousios)* with the Father', though in the end he felt able to give it an interpretation he was prepared to accept. But the general pattern of his understanding of the Trinity remained resistant to the new direction that Athanasius and others were trying to give it. And he even showed himself a powerful controversialist in his two writings against Marcellus, an extreme exponent of the unity of the Godhead, entitled *Against Marcellus* and *On Ecclesiastical Theology*. Here too his tendency to quote directly from those he was seeking to confute has been an invaluable source in the task of reconstructing Marcellus' own beliefs.

Heresy

Christology

Persecution

Trinity

The new Constantinian age did lead to one striking and significant development in Eusebius' writings towards the end of his life. In 336 he delivered a *Panegyric* to celebrate the thirtieth anniversary of Constantine's accession. It is (as was the nature of panegyrics) wholly uncritical of Constantine. For such an occasion that was, perhaps, inevitable. But seeing in Constantine the one who, under God, had brought the church out of its fearsome persecution into its new favoured status in the Roman world, Eusebius treats the empire as an earthly image of the heavenly kingdom, and compares the role of Constantine as emperor with that of Christ. And at the time of his death he was engaged in writing a *Life of Constantine* in similar vein.

Eusebius: The History of the Church translated G. A. Williamson, revd edn, Harmondsworth: Penguin Books 1989; *Eusebius: The Life of Constantine* translated A. Cameron and S. G. Hall, Oxford: OUP 1999; T. D. Barnes, *Constantine and Eusebius*, Cambridge, MA: Harvard University Press 1981; D. S. Wallace-Hadrill, *Eusebius of Caesarea*, London: Mowbray 1960

Athanasius of Alexandria (*c.* 296–373)

Athanasius contra mundum ('Athanasius against the world'): this Latin tag neatly encapsulates the traditional picture of Athanasius as standing over against the rest of the world, and, when everyone else had been led astray by Arian heresy, single-handedly defending the cause of orthodoxy and thereby ensuring the preservation and triumph of the true faith. Although there have always been a few dissenting voices, that has been the dominant account of Athanasius accepted within the church until recent times. Modern scholarly work has substantially altered it, but not wholly destroyed it.

Athanasius was elected Bishop of Alexandria in 328, though he was apparently below the canonical age for such a position. He inherited a diocese divided on two issues. The first was on the terms on which those who had lapsed in the final burst of persecution before the coming of Constantine should be allowed to return to the church. (This was the Melitian schism, named after Melitius, Bishop of Lycopolis in Egypt, who took a hard line and ended up founding a separate church of his own.) The second was on the teaching of Arius (who had recently been condemned at the Council of Nicaea in 325).

Athanasius proved to be a forceful leader, but one not averse to using strong-arm tactics to assert his authority. His determination to see the condemnation of Arius rigorously enforced, a condemnation extended also to anyone who gave Arius support or who taught in ways at all similar to his, brought him into conflict with other church leaders and with imperial policy. He was exiled from his see on three occasions, once having to spend some years in the West and at another time hiding in the Egyptian desert, where he had the strong support of the monks. Some of the opposition that led to his exile was prompted by his high-handed and violent treatment of opponents, but his unwavering rejection of any form of teaching that he could associate with that of Arius was also a significant factor.

The fundamental issue which divided Athanasius from Arius, and also from many other bishops who did not necessarily side fully with Arius either, concerned the divine nature of the Son. The mainstream Christian writers of the second and third centuries had all regarded the Son as divine, but had also seen him as in some loosely defined sense secondary to the Father. The Son on this view certainly belonged to the threefold Godhead, but in a manner that made his incarnation as Jesus of Nazareth an intelligible notion, where that of the Father would not have been. Arius pushed this emphasis so far as to speak of the divine Son as 'created' by the Father – though in a way quite distinct from all other creatures, since they were all created by or through the Son. Athanasius would have none of it. For him such an account undermined the saving significance of Christ. He thought of human salvation as divinization, our becoming 'partakers of the divine nature'; and that, he insisted, was something that could only be imparted by one who was fully divine in himself. The Son was the Father's true Son; there was no difference between the divinity of the one and the divinity of the other. Athanasius' position had its own difficulties, which his opponents could and did bring against him: how then were Father and Son the 'one God' that Christian faith also affirmed them to be? And did such an understanding of the Son allow for the fully human nature of Christ? These were questions with which the church was to wrestle throughout the next century. Athanasius did not ignore such questions, but he did not do a lot to meet them. He saw his essential role as outlawing any form of teaching that disparaged the unqualified divinity of the Son in any way. And in that task he was successful – at no small cost to himself.

It is not surprising, therefore, that his most substantial surviving work should be entitled *Against the Arians* in three books (though some scholars are doubtful about the authenticity of the third). It is a sustained and highly rhetorical polemic against the general position outlined above and that he dubs 'Arian', the form of its appeal to scripture being the primary object of his attack. The details of Athanasius' exegetical arguments are not always very convincing; their most striking positive characteristic is his determination to give precedence to the overall intention of the scriptural writings in assessing the implication of the biblical witness for the church's faith.

This emphasis is reflected in his best known work, *On the Incarnation*. In it he presents with force and clarity an account of what has become the classic form of the Christian story: the creation of humanity in God's image, the fall with its penalty of death, the taking of a human body by the divine Word, Christ's death and resurrection, and thereby his opening of the way to the completion of God's purpose that created human beings might be made partakers of the divine nature. That was the vision that Athanasius was determined to safeguard at all costs.

As a result, much of his life was involved in controversy and political intrigue. A number of his writings are carefully devised defences of his own role in the ecclesiastical conflicts of his day. In the past these have largely been allowed to determine the church's understanding of the period, but are now rightly subject to much more critical scrutiny.

Christology ◄

Incarnation ◄

However, Athanasius was an equally determined pastor of his diocese and promoter of the ascetic life. Several of his *Festal Letters*, sent out each year to announce the beginning of Lent and the date of Easter, have survived. Sometimes written in conditions of great difficulty, as when he was in exile from his diocese, they show him at work as the provider of strong spiritual encouragement and guidance. His *Life of Antony*, the famous pioneer monk (though there are doubts as to how directly in its present form it comes from his pen), was an important influence in spreading the ideals of ascetic practice and the monastic life. The period that Athanasius spent in exile in the West played a significant role in the establishment of monasticism in the Western empire.

Letters

Monasticism

Athanasius, On the Incarnation in E. R. Hardy (ed), *Christology of the Later Fathers*, London: SCM Press and Philadelphia: Westminster Press 1954, pp. 41–110; *Athanasius. The Life of Antony* translated R. C. Gregg, New York and Mahwah, NJ: Paulist Press 1980; T. D. Barnes, *Athanasius and Constantius*, Cambridge, MA: Harvard University Press 1993

Ephrem the Syrian (*c.* 306–73)

The church fathers are often sub-divided into the 'Greek' and 'Latin' fathers, as if that was a comprehensive distinction which embraced the fathers in their totality. But Christianity spread eastwards as well as westwards from its point of origin in Palestine. In the East, in the general area of Mesopotamia, there grew up a body of Christians whose native tongue was Syriac, a dialect of Aramaic, the main language of Palestine at the time of Jesus. That Christian body has continued in existence as the 'Church

Language

of the East' to this day. As that church looks back to its founding fathers of the early centuries, an unchallenged pride of place is given to Ephrem the Syrian.

Ephrem was born of Christian parents in the early years of the fourth century, in Nisibis, a frontier town of the Roman empire close to its border with the Persian empire. (In modern terms it is in south-eastern Turkey near the border with Syria.) We know little of Ephrem's life there. He was ordained deacon, taught in the catachetical school and preached there for many years. In 363 Nisibis was ceded to Persia as part of the settlement following the death of the pagan Roman emperor Julian the Apostate in a disastrous Persian campaign. Ephrem, with the Christian community more generally, moved to Edessa, 100 miles to the West, where he lived and continued his activities until his death ten years later.

Heresy

He was an extensive writer, and much has come down to us: mostly in the original Syriac, but some in Armenian translation. He was not merely a theologian, but also a musician and a poet. Notable among his prose writings are commentaries on books of the Bible. But it is his verse for which he is primarily renowned. His poetry takes two main forms: verse homilies and hymns. The latter, of which more than 400 survive, are the most distinctive and highly valued of all.

A theologian whose most characteristic form of expression is through hymnody is a surprising phenomenon to modern Western ears. But the theological tradition has often emphasized the role of imagery and of symbolism as an appropriate, even the essential, medium for our speech about the infinite and ineffable God. It is in their use of imagery and symbolism that Ephrem's hymns excel. Much of the symbolism he employs is derived from scripture, and is therefore familiar to the Western reader. But that scriptural imagery is further enriched by his use of other, less familiar Semitic sources. Both the church and scripture, for example, are likened to a harp on which God plays.

The central themes of Ephrem's hymns are similar to those of the Greek and Latin fathers. Topics such as virginity, the church and the way of faith all lend themselves naturally enough to poetic treatment. Most notable is his effective use of paradox. The paradoxical conjunction of opposing images is a powerful way of giving expression to the orthodox doctrine of the incarnation, with its insistence on the inseparable but unconfused union of the divine and the human in the one person of Christ. It is perhaps more surprising that many of his hymns should not merely expound the paradoxical character of incarnational faith, but should also be specifically directed against heresy. It was not only the earlier heretics of his own area, like Bardaisan and Mani, against whom he wrote, but also the contemporary Arianism that was being so fiercely contended in the Graeco-Roman world of his own day. Ephrem knew no Greek, so he can hardly have been conversant with the intricacies of that controversy. But he was unhappy with all attempts at formal definition of God. The way in which such attempts at definition made use of terms appropriate to the created order seemed to him to involve a limitation of God. That in his eyes was the great sin of heresy, Arianism in particular. The truths of orthodoxy, which found expression in his paradoxical conjunction of conflicting images, defied definition, but were the true ground of wonder and of worship.

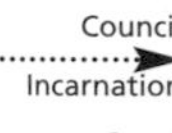

Council
Incarnation
Creed

The Christian community to which Ephrem belonged had developed from the same beginnings as the Christianity of the Western and the Eastern Orthodox traditions, but had done so in the context of a very different culture. Ephrem's writings constitute a fascinating and invaluable insight into this very different style of Christian belief and expression, in a form which owes little to the influence of the West.

Ephrem the Syrian: Hymns translated K. McVey, New York and Mahwah, NJ: Paulist Press 1989; Sebastian Brock, *The Luminous Eye: The Spiritual World of St Ephrem*, Rome: Cistercian Publications 1985

Ambrose of Milan (*c.* 339–97)

Ambrose came from a distinguished Christian family. His father had held the high office of prefect of Gaul; he himself was trained in law, and was appointed a provincial governor in Italy with his headquarters in Milan. In 374 he was involved in controlling riots that had broken out in the city over a contested election for a new bishop of Milan in place of Auxentius, who had recently died. The outcome was a popular call, with support from both parties, that Ambrose be appointed bishop. Although Ambrose was still only a catechumen, being instructed in the Christian faith, this was agreed; he was baptized, ordained and then made bishop. After a period of intensive study, he took up the reins of office.

The job was no easy one. A long-drawn-out controversy over the teaching of the presbyter Arius, who held that God the Son was inferior to God the Father, had caused much turmoil in the East, but had not impinged so fiercely on the Western church. A council held at Nicaea in 325 had produced a creed stating the orthodox faith and banning Arius, but this did not find support everywhere, and by Ambrose's time the division between the supporters and opponents of the Nicene Creed had become marked. Auxentius, and the larger part of the church in Milan, had been non-Nicenes. Ambrose was a firm supporter of the Nicene faith, as he demonstrated clearly from the start of his episcopate. Moreover, in the course of his time as bishop there the empress, Justina, whose sympathies were firmly with the non-Nicenes, was to establish her court at Milan. The bishop of the city had a difficult role to play, pastorally, ecclesiastically and politically.

Ambrose soon showed himself to have outstanding gifts in relation both to the general life of the church and to the special needs of the time. He was an outstanding preacher. His knowledge of Greek, unusual among Latin churchmen of his day, enabled him to draw on the rich resources of the Greek fathers, especially the allegorical interpretation of the Bible by Alexandrian theologians like Origen. His sermons were a significant influence on Augustine, assisting him on his journey to conversion and to catholic Christianity. Ambrose also did much to encourage the ascetic life and the cult of the martyrs. His composition of hymns, remarkable both for their literary form and their religious feeling, made an important contribution to the future of the church. Some of his most significant writings are of an ecclesiastical and liturgical character: his *De Officiis* (On Duties), modelled on a work of the Roman orator Cicero with the same title, was a manual of ethical teaching especially directed to the clergy; and his *De Sacramentis* (On the Sacraments), sermons taken down from his preaching (doubts about their authenticity have now generally been laid to rest), are a witness to his liturgical interests and provide us with valuable insight into the sacramental practice and understanding of the church of Milan at the time.

But much of Ambrose's energy was devoted to furthering the cause of Nicene orthodoxy against still powerful opposition. His writings of a more doctrinal nature are not outstanding, but his actions were forceful and effective. He marshalled popular support to thwart the empress' request to have a church allocated for use by Arian Goths, an important element within the army. The confrontation involved a long 'sit-in' in the church building by Ambrose and his supporters, which required conviction of purpose and a steady nerve. At the Council of Aquileia in 381 he dominated the proceedings with ruthless persistence to endure the condemnation of two leading anti-Nicene bishops. His resolute and at times overbearing zeal on behalf of catholic orthodoxy was a major force in ensuring the triumph of a Nicene faith in the West at the same time that it was finally establishing its supremacy in the East.

Most notable of all Ambrose's activities were his relations with a succession of emperors. As the state became increasingly committed to Christianity, new issues continued to arise about the appropriate relationship between church and state. Ambrose successfully dissuaded two successive emperors, Gratian and Valentinian II, from allowing a strongly backed appeal for the restoration of the Altar of Victory to the Senate House in Rome. Even the more powerful and more committedly orthodox Theodosius was subjected to the same pressure. When Theodosius had ordered the local bishop to restore out of church funds a synagogue at Callinicum which Christian zealots had burnt down, Ambrose browbeat him into rescinding the order by refusing to continue with the eucharist until he had agreed to do so. Two years later Ambrose rebuked Theodosius for ordering a massacre of some 7000 people in Thessalonica in reprisal for the murder of a Roman officer, and refused to admit him to communion until he had done public penance. Ambrose's masterful authority and his moral courage are not in question. But the two dramatic stories of his exercise of that authority over Theodosius well illustrate the potential for good and the grave danger of abuse in the church's exercise of power in relation to the state that is evident from later history.

Hymns

Select Works and Letters in *Nicene and Post-Nicene Fathers* vol. 10 (includes *On the Duties of the Clergy*); Theological and Dogmatic Works in *The Fathers of the Church* vol. 44 (includes *On the Sacraments*); F. Homes Dudden, *The Life and Times of St Ambrose*, Oxford: Clarendon Press 1935; N. B. McLynn, *Ambrose of Milan: Church and Court in a Christian Capital*, Berkeley, CA and London: University of California Press 1994; D. H. Williams, *Ambrose and the End of the Arian-Nicene Conflicts*, Oxford: OUP 1995

Cappadocian fathers (fourth century)

The Cappadocian fathers is a name given to a trio of church leaders and theologians, all coming from Cappadocia in Asia Minor, who played a decisive role in the period leading up to the Council of Constantinople in 381. The three were Basil of Caesarea (or Basil the Great), his friend Gregory of Nazianzus, and Basil's younger brother Gregory of Nyssa. They were very different from one another in temperament, which led at times to strained relations between them, but they also had many things in common.

They all came from a well-to-do and cultured background, and all had a thorough, primarily rhetorical training, which for Basil and Gregory of Nazianzus included six shared years in Athens. All three followed their years of study with some time spent in an ascetic community before going on to ordination, public ministry, and in due course episcopal office. Origen was an important influence on each of them (Basil and Gregory of Nazianzus in their early years jointly produced an anthology of selections from Origen's writings, entitled the *Philokalia*, 'Love of the Beautiful', and Gregory of Nyssa followed not only Origen's style of biblical interpretation but also his unusual hope for a final universal salvation); Origen's influence fuelled their difficult goal of achieving an integration of classical learning and ascetic piety. Finally, in the public sphere they were all unreservedly committed to the doctrine of a co-equal Trinity, following the teaching of the Council of Nicaea, over against a hierarchical view, especially as propounded at the time by Eunomius of Cyzicus.

Trinity

Basil (*c.*330–79) was the natural leader of the three and a born administrator. In 370 he was appointed Bishop of Caesarea in Cappadocia, where he continued until his death in 379. These were nine years of vigorous and effective ministry. He had already written a major work, *Against Eunomius*, and during his episcopate he wrote a treatise, *On the Holy Spirit*, which argued the case for the full personal divinity of the third member of the Trinity as well as of the Son. But the time had come not just for argument but for action. For Basil this involved a courageous confrontation with the emperor, Valens, who was a supporter of the 'Arian' or 'Homoian' party in the church rather than their opponents, the 'Nicenes'. It also involved securing the appointment of bishops with Nicene sympathies to vacant sees, even if this meant the appointment of his two closest allies, the two Gregories, against their wishes to minor sees in his area. His energetic leadership made a major contribution to the turning of the tide in a Nicene direction, which was to culminate in the wholehearted adoption of the Nicene way of faith at the Council of Constantinople just two years after his death.

Holy Spirit

Journey

But Basil's activities were not restricted to doctrinal matters. He was a vigorous supporter of the monastic ideal. His understanding of that ideal was a strongly social one, emphasizing both social relations within the monastic community itself and the relation of the community to the wider society, involving regular welfare activities on behalf of those outside the monastery walls. To this end he drew up rules for monastic communities (which are still operative in the Eastern church) and furthered an extensive building programme.

Monasticism

Letters

Gregory of Nazianzus (329/30–389/90) fully shared Basil's enthusiasm for classical culture, ascetic piety and the Nicene faith, but he did not share his taste for public life. It was with reluctance that he succumbed to his father's pressure and was ordained priest; and though unable to avoid Basil's appointment of him as bishop of the out-of-the-way town of Sasima, he never actually took up the duties of that office. It was to the ascetic life that he felt most strongly drawn. But he was an outstandingly gifted preacher. Between 379 and 381 he ministered to the small Nicene congregation in Constantinople, a city of predominantly Arian sympathies. His preaching had a remarkable impact, particularly a group of five sermons, known as his *Theological Orations*, in which the essential tenets of a Nicene faith were set forth with dazzling rhetorical force. It is these compositions in particular that led to his being widely known in the Eastern church as Gregory the Theologian. A more immediate result of their enthusiastic reception was that, when the Bishop of Constantinople died in 380, he was appointed to the see and, when the president of the Council of Constantinople died in the next year, he was given that role also. He was not a success, and before the year was out he had resigned his offices and retired to a monastic life in his home town of Nazianzus.

Gregory is also notable for his poetic writings. Adopting the traditional forms and style of classical poetry, he used them as a medium of expression both for Christian beliefs and for an autobiographical record. It was one more way of integrating classical culture and Christian faith.

Gregory of Nyssa (*c.*330–*c.*395) followed more closely in his elder brother's steps. Soon after Basil's death, for example, he took up the cudgels in defence of his brother in another lengthy work, also called *Against Eunomius*, and played a full part as a bishop at and after the Council of Constantinople in ensuring the triumph of the Nicene faith. But it was not work for which he had either the gifts or the inclination that his brother had. It is as a writer on the spiritual life that he excels. His *Life of Moses* and *Homilies on the Song of Songs*, drawing on the allegorical interpretation of the Bible that he had learnt from Origen, are profound treatments of the spiritual life; by adapting the biblical imagery, they describe the way of virtue as an unending journey into the mystical darkness that envelops the mystery of God. Though not a profound philosophical thinker, Gregory brings together Platonic and biblical understandings of God's transcendence in a way that has played a fundamental part in the subsequent doctrines and piety of the church.

All three of the fathers were frequent writers of letters, many of which have survived. These help to provide us with a better understanding of them as human beings, with their hopes, their frustrations and their failings, than is possible with most of the earlier fathers, whom we know only through their more formal writings.

📖 *St Basil. The Letters* (4 vols) translated R. Deferrari, Loeb Classical Library, London: Heinemann and Cambridge, MA: Harvard University Press 1950; *Gregory of Nazianzus: The Theological Orations* in E. R. Hardy (ed), *Christology of the Later Fathers*, London: SCM Press and Philadelphia: Westminster Press 1954, pp. 111–214; *Gregory of Nyssa: Life of Moses* translated E. Ferguson and A. J. Malherbe, New York and Mahwah, NJ: Paulist Press 1978; Anthony Meredith, *The Cappadocians*, New York: Continuum 1995

John Chrysostom (*c.*347–407)

John Chrysostom was born in Antioch of well-to-do Christian parents around the middle of the fourth century. Although he is now often referred to simply as 'Chrysostom', that second half of the designation was never in fact a part of his name. It was a descriptive appellation, not given to him, it would seem, until well after his death. It means 'Golden Mouth', and reflects what was perhaps his outstanding characteristic: the rhetorical power of his preaching.

In his early years John received a rhetorical training at the feet of Libanius, the leading pagan rhetorician of his day. His initial plans were to embark on a career as a lawyer. But all that changed with his baptism, at, his biographer Palladius tells us, the age of 18. To delay baptism to such an age was nothing unusual at that time in Christian families as socially distinguished as the one into which John had been born. It is not enough to say that John took his Christian commitment seriously; he took it in the extreme and unqualified manner that characterized everything he did. For him commitment to Christianity involved commitment to a rigorously ascetic way of life. For the first two years, while his mother was still alive, he pursued his ascetic regime from within his mother's house. But after her death he withdrew to the hills, where the extreme nature of his ascetic practices did permanent injury to his health. The breakdown in his health brought him back to Antioch, where he was (reluctantly) ordained deacon in 381 and subsequently priest in 386.

It was there that he made his name as a preacher. For twelve years, from 386 to 397, he exercised a remarkable preaching ministry. A large number of his sermons from that period have come down to us. Many of them form long series of primarily exegetical sermons, as he worked his way steadily through one of the Gospels or one of the letters of Paul. The sermons tend to fall into two halves: the first half straightforward exegesis of the passage for the day; the second half, apparently unrelated, treatment of some moral or social problem of the moment. His manner of interpreting scripture follows lines generally characteristic of Antiochene Christianity. It shows little inclination for allegory and generally follows the straightforward meaning of the text. However, the 'straightforward' meaning of the text for John was not the historical sense, as it might be understood by a modern scholar, but its spiritual and moral application to the lives of the members of his congregation. He took up that same concern directly in the second part of his sermons. If John had had to abandon the life of a solitary ascetic in the hills, he had not abandoned the ideals that had first driven him to undertake such a life, either for himself or for those to whom he preached. The moral and social shortcomings of his congregation were denounced with relentless oratorical power. The ostentatious affluence of the rich and their neglect of the needs of the poor are frequent targets of his scathing denunciation. So too are the attractions of the theatre and the racecourse. But one needs also to acknowledge that it was not only those who succumbed to such social temptations who received the lashing of his tongue; Jews and heretics were the recipients of equally violent condemnation.

In 397 John was taken from Antioch, without any prior consultation or consent on his part, and made Bishop of Constantinople, the imperial capital. The vigour of his preaching was as powerful as ever, and won him a following among the crowds who came to hear him that he was never to lose. But it did not find so warm a welcome everywhere. Thinly veiled attacks on the powerful empress, Eudoxia, made him an enemy who could do him much harm. Nor did his rigorous treatment of some of his clergy or his less than diplomatic attitude towards other leading Eastern bishops win him many ecclesiastical friends. Almost from the start he came under attack from the emperor's household and from ecclesiastical courts. He was deposed at a synod at The Oak, a suburb of Chalcedon, and sent into exile in 403; but very soon he was recalled because of popular disapproval and unrest. The next year he was exiled again to Armenia. Even from there his influence continued to be felt. Finally, while being transported to an even more remote place of exile in 407, he died. It was a death which his admirers came to see as a form of martyrdom. In 438 his remains were brought back to Constantinople and reinterred in the cathedral.

The great reverence that has been accorded to John Chrysostom ever since is rooted in his relentless pursuit of personal piety, the balance of his biblical exegesis, the power of his preaching, his fearlessness and forthrightness in face of the powerful and his compassion and concern for the poor.

📖 *St John Chrysostom. Baptismal Instructions* translated P. W. Harkins, Ancient Christian Writers 31, Westminster, MD: Newman Press and London: Longmans, Green 1963; *St John Chrysostom. Homilies on St John* in The Fathers of the Church, vols 33 and 41, Washington, DC: Catholic University Press of America 1957 and 1959; J. N. D. Kelly, *Golden Mouth*, Ithaca, NY: Cornell University Press 1995

Jerome of Bethlehem (*c.* 345–420)

Jerome's rightful claim to a place among the most distinguished figures in the history of the early church depends primarily on his outstanding achievement as a biblical scholar. The two other most distinguishing marks of his life are his firm commitment to and propagation of the ascetic life and the bitterness of his polemic against the many with whom he crossed swords.

He was already in his thirties when he first adopted the ascetic way, but it remained a dominant motif throughout

Niccolo Colantino, *Jerome healing a lion*, S. Giorgio Schiavoni, Naples

the remaining years of his long life. A happy initial period, lived with a group of like-minded friends in Aquileia in North Italy, ended abruptly with Jerome's departure for the East because, for reasons that are not clear, life in Aquileia had become too uncomfortable for him to remain. The ten years from 372 to 382 that he spent in the East included a period of three years as a hermit, and were followed by three years in Rome, where he acted as secretary to Pope Damasus. That was a task that he enjoyed and one that gave scope for the exercise of his skills at the heart of the

Biblical criticism 

church's life. He was a successful promoter of the ascetic cause, and was particularly influential in encouraging the adoption of the ascetic life by a number of wealthy and talented widows. But these activities, and particularly the sharpness of his criticisms of his opponents, made him many enemies. When Damasus died in 385, it proved impossible for Jerome to stay on in Rome. Once again he left under a cloud and travelled east. This time he established a monastery for men near Bethlehem (with a nearby convent for women under the direction of Paula, his closest friend among the Roman matrons whom he had encouraged and supported in the ascetic life). He was to remain there for the remaining 34 years of his life.

Throughout that long life, and particularly during his final years in Bethlehem, he was engaged in literary activity, as biblical scholar, translator and prolific correspondent. The outstanding feature of his scholarship was ability with language. His proficiency in Greek, the fruit of serious study during his first period of residence in the East, led him to embark on a series of translations that would make the writings of the Greek fathers more accessible to the Western church. Eusebius and Origen particularly attracted him for the breadth of their learning and the calibre of their exegesis. He not only adopted Origen's use of allegory in general, but also drew extensively on Origen's commentaries in the composition of his own. It was an attraction and a dependence that he came to regret in later life. In the closing years of the fourth century Origen came under a cloud as being too unorthodox a writer. And in his anxious attempts to preserve his reputation for firm orthodoxy by disassociating himself from any taint of Origenism, Jerome became embroiled in a bitter dispute with his erstwhile close friend, Rufinus of Aquileia, a fellow translator of Origen.

But Jerome's greatest work was his translation of the Old Testament from Hebrew into Latin. After his arrival in Bethlehem he set about improving his rudimentary knowledge of Hebrew with this goal in view. It was not only the size of the task and the linguistic difficulties involved that made this so courageous an undertaking. The church had always looked on the Septuagint, the Greek Old Testament, as the God-given scriptures of the church. The switch to another version was bound to meet with opposition in the church, among ecclesiastics and laity alike. It was not only a matter of minor variations in the text; it also involved the exclusion of the books we know as the Apocrypha, which were not part of the Hebrew canon as they were of the Septuagintal one. Jerome's primary defence of his decision was that it would be impossible to get Jews to take a Christian interpretation of the Old Testament seriously unless Christians used the same version of those scriptures as the Jews themselves. But Jerome's undertaking was not only a courageous one; it was also a superbly successful one. His translation, known to us as the Vulgate, was to serve the church splendidly for many centuries to come.

To the end of his life Jerome continued to write – letters, commentaries and fiercely polemical treatises. But he was never a man at ease with either himself or the world. At the heart of his achievement lies an unresolved tension, with which he wrestled unsuccessfully all his life. He wrote superbly, in a Latin style rooted in the great tradition of Greek and Latin culture. Yet he also saw that culture as the enemy of his biblical faith, something to be renounced in the name of the ascetic piety to which he was committed. In his dreams he was tormented by the notion that he was at heart more influenced by the Roman orator Cicero than by Christ, however much he might claim to be using the fruits of his Ciceronian culture in the service of Christ's church. It was a tension that he never resolved, a torment from which he never found release.

📖 *Jerome: Select Letters* translated F. A. Wright, Loeb Classical Library, London: Heinemann and Cambridge, MA: Harvard University Press 1933, 1991; J. N. D. Kelly, *Jerome*, London: Duckworth and New York: Harper & Row 1975

Augustine of Hippo (354–430)

Augustine stands head and shoulders above his contemporaries and other fathers of the early church for the quality of his mind, the depth of his spiritual insight and the extent of his influence on the subsequent history of Christianity in the West – albeit that that influence may not always have been for the good.

Augustine's *Confessions*, a title that implies praise of God as well as acknowledgement of sin, is not an autobiography in the sense that we understand that term today. Its underlying motif is a meditation on the restlessness of the human heart until it finds its rest in God. Nevertheless it does provide a reflective outline of Augustine's early life. Born of Christian parents in North Africa in 354, he was first drawn to value the pleasures of the mind above those of the body by a philosophical writing of the Roman orator Cicero. Religiously he was drawn to the dualistic teaching of the Manichees, best seen as an extreme form of Christian heresy which denied any responsibility of God for evil, regarding it as inherent in the material world. Pursuit of a career as a teacher of rhetoric took Augustine to Milan, where the mystical writings of neo-Platonism, the thoughtful preaching of Ambrose and the persistence of his mother Monica all contributed to his conversion to catholic Christianity in 386. He had already parted from his uneducated but long-time sexual partner and mother of his son with a view to a marriage appropriate for his burgeoning career. But after his baptism both the career and the prospect of marriage were abandoned. He spent the next five years with a small community of friends, first in Cassiciacum near Milan and then at his home town of Thagaste in North Africa, living a life of study, writing and contemplation, with the primary emphasis moving gradually from philosophy to the study of scripture. In 391 he reluctantly accepted ordination as a priest in Hippo, and four years later was consecrated bishop, an office he was to hold until his death 35 years later.

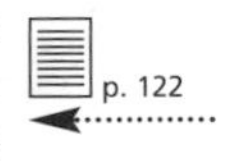
p. 122

Heresy

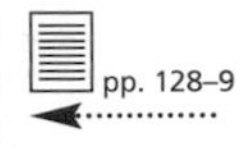
pp. 128–9

The heavy demands of his pastoral office, which Augustine fulfilled with the utmost assiduity, did not curb the flow of writing on which he had already embarked. In him philosophical and scriptural concerns were blended together at a greater depth than in any other early Christian writer. But the particular directions that those writings were to take were greatly influenced by the ecclesiastical and political circumstances with which he was faced throughout his years as priest and bishop.

The catholic church in Hippo when Augustine began his ministry there was considerably outnumbered by the Donatist church in the town. The Donatists were a puritan group in North Africa, who believed that the catholic church had lost its holiness by its failure to stand absolutely firm in the great persecution of 100 years before. They claimed that they themselves therefore, having broken away in protest at the time, were the only true church and that only their sacraments had any validity. In responding to their claims Augustine was led to reflect deeply on the nature of the church. Its primary characteristic was not holiness, but love; and it was not the way of love to separate oneself from those who had failed in their Christian living. Holiness was the church's goal; separation, when the pure and true church, now known only to God, would be made known, belonged not to the present but to the final judgement at the end of time. The church as we know it is the field where wheat and tares grow together until the harvest. Moreover the validity of baptisms and ordinations could not be dependent on the holiness of their officiant, or how could anyone know if he or she was truly baptized or not? Augustine, always anxious for reconciliation with the Donatists, did allow the validity of their baptisms and their ordinations, but insisted firmly that these could become efficacious only when those who had received them were reunited with the universal, catholic church. It was a view of the church which, like much else in Augustine's teaching, was to have great influence on the later church, Catholic and Protestant alike.

The sack of Rome in 410 was a traumatic experience, of great symbolic significance throughout the Roman world. Might it not, reflective pagans asked, be due to Rome's abandonment of her ancestral gods in favour of Christian worship? This drew out from Augustine a lengthy, wide-ranging book, *The City of God,* which was to prove, along with *The Confessions,* his greatest legacy to subsequent European culture. The two cities, the earthly city and the city of God, are two fundamental principles operative in human history – the principles of self-love and of the love of God. The two cities are not to be identified with church and state (we have already seen that for Augustine the church was emphatically a mixture of saints and sinners); nor are they to be identified with good and evil (the secular realm has its own proper function within the purposes of God). Augustine's perceptive reflections on pagan worship and philosophy, on the need for public order and justice, and on their relation to the peace and justice of the heavenly realm, were a fruitful source of inspiration for the ideals and practices of Western society for centuries to come.

One problem was dominant for Augustine throughout his life – the problem of evil. It was the Manichees' apparent solution to the problem that had drawn him to them for the whole decade of his twenties. Having rejected their linking of evil to matter, how was he to account for it? The philosophical approach of his early writings, drawing on the Platonic identification of good and being, suggested that evil was not a part of the creation for which God was responsible. It was a disorder of the will. But how then was it so deeply seated in human life? The biblical account of the fall, and especially Paul's use of the idea of Adam's sin as the point of entry for sin into the world with consequences for all his descendants, was itself his point of entry for dealing with the problem. Adam's sin (or the angelic fall that lay behind even that) was not just a case of a sinful choice that subsequent men and women might or might not choose to follow. Rather, it had introduced a disorder into the basic structure of human life which we as individuals are powerless to overcome. What was needed was a transformation of our deepest desires. Only then could we begin to choose and do the good. But that initial transformation was outside the range of our powers.

The need to grapple with this problem, never far away from him, was reinforced by another contemporary issue of dispute in the church, primarily associated with the name of Pelagius. Pelagius, a reformer from Britain, was horrified by the laxity of practice in religiously conformist Christian Rome. For him God's grace was always at hand. What was lacking was our will to call upon it and that was within our power. Augustine's teaching seemed to him to be a dangerous dissuasive from what was needed. Augustine in his turn was determined at all costs to maintain the priority of divine grace in all human beings do, even in their response to God's call to salvation. At first he insisted on a mysterious and unfathomable conjunction of human willing and God's gift of grace. But under pressure in controversy he was led to give a clear priority to the gift of grace. Nor towards the end of his life did he flinch from the logical implications of that insistence on the priority of God's grace, namely that one seems led to assert the predestination of a fixed number of the elect for whom alone that gift is destined to be given. It was a conclusion that did not win general consent then, and certainly has not done so since.

Augustine's other work of outstanding importance was his *De Trinitate* (On the Trinity), a substantial work in fifteen books written over a period of twenty years. This was not a work driven by immediate controversy, as so much of the writing of the fourth-century Greek fathers on the subject of the Trinity had inevitably been. Rather scripture, philosophy and contemplation are once again profoundly interwoven. He seeks to illuminate the mystery of the traditional threefold nature of God by the analogy of mind, knowledge and love in the one human soul. But it is only by the way of devotion, in which our souls are themselves being recreated in God's image, that true, but still incomplete, progress can be made in the apprehension of God's being.

These brief accounts of a few of Augustine's most significant works do little justice either to the range of

Sin ➤
Grace ➤
Trinity ➤
Evil

his writings as a whole or to the quality of those primary writings themselves. Deep reflection on the nature of signs and on how knowledge is possible for human beings underlies all his reflections on our knowledge of God. It is this dimension in his work that has made it so fruitful an inspiration for such a diversity of Christians since his own time. But his legacy has been a mixed chalice. Sometimes in controversy he was led to affirm extreme views that have had a fateful influence on later history. His recognition of the inescapable contamination of the social context of human lives led him to speak of an inheritance not only of Adam's sin but also of his guilt; and his way of affirming the priority of God's grace led him to speak of the predestination of a limited number of the elect, leaving all others with no way of escaping their sinful condition or the punishments that would ensue from them. These aspects of the great Augustinian heritage of the Western church render him a good exemplar of one of his own strong convictions, namely that human life in this age, even at its best, always falls short of perfection.

Augustine, City of God ed Gillian Evans, Harmondsworth: Penguin Books 2004; *Augustine, The Confessions* translated Henry Chadwick, Oxford: OUP 1992; *Augustine. Later Works,* translated J. Burnaby, London: SCM Press and Philadelphia: Westminster Press 1955 (this includes substantial parts of *De Trinitate* and two other works, one relating to the Pelagian and one to the Donatist controversy); Peter Brown, *Augustine of Hippo: A Biography*, Berkeley, CA: University of California Press and London: Faber & Faber 1967; Henry Chadwick, *Augustine*, Oxford: OUP 1986; Serge Lancel, *St Augustine*, Notre Dame, IN: University of Notre Dame Press and London: SCM Press 2002; John Rist, *Augustine: Ancient Thought Baptized*, Cambridge: CUP 1994

Cyril of Alexandria (died 444)

In the year 412 Cyril was elected to succeed his uncle, Theophilus, as Bishop of Alexandria. It was a bitterly disputed election, not completed without bloodshed, an omen of things to come. In the course of the 32 years that Cyril held the office of bishop he earned a reputation, even among some of his supporters, for his ruthless exercise of political and ecclesiastical power. It was said that he was a true nephew to Theophilus, who had been a major influence in securing the downfall and exile of John Chrysostom, Bishop of Constantinople, earlier in the century at a synod held at The Oak, a suburb of Chalcedon, which Cyril also attended as a junior member of Theophilus' entourage.

Alexandria was a particularly volatile city at the time. Cyril undoubtedly contributed to its unstable condition by his repressive measures against heretics and his confrontational attitude towards paganism. It was during his episcopate that the pagan philosopher, Hypatia, was stoned to death by a mob in a Christian church. A more acceptable face of Cyril's crusade against paganism is to be seen in his polemical writings, particularly that against Julian the Apostate.

Paganism

The year of Cyril's election was also the fortieth anniversary of the death of Athanasius, the most illustrious of Cyril's predecessors as Bishop of Alexandria. By the time that Cyril was appointed, Athanasius' insistence on the full co-equality of the Son's divine nature with that of the Father had effectively won its long-drawn-out battle against those who sought, in one way or another, to give a secondary status to the divinity of the Son. But difficulties were still being felt about whether the Athanasian emphasis was compatible with the true humanity of Jesus, and if so how. No one did more than Cyril to overcome those misgivings. His doing so was the fruit of his very considerable theological, and equally considerable, if less attractive, political skills.

Cyril produced a substantial body of biblical interpretation, particularly commentaries on the Old Testament and a massive commentary on the Gospel of John. His primary concern in all his exegetical work is with the overall doctrinal or theological thrust of the scriptural writings. Allegory plays a considerable part, as it had always done in the Alexandrian milieu, but it is allegory kept under control by its subservience to what Cyril sees as the broad theological message of the text. These general characteristics of his exegesis are particularly marked features of his Commentary on John. If John's Gospel can be said to represent a theological interpretation of the earlier Gospel tradition, Cyril's commentary can be described as providing in its turn the same style of interpretation of the Johannine Gospel. His exegetical skills were the basic resource underlying his powerful contribution to the doctrinal conflicts of his day.

Among those who had fully accepted the reaffirmation of the Council of Nicaea at the Council of Constantinople in 381, there were two conflicting schools of interpretation. The one, drawing primarily on the traditional emphases of Antiochene Christianity, spoke of two realities (*hypostases*), one human the other divine, conjoined in Jesus to form a looser, more external, personal unity (*prosopon*). Only if one could speak of the two different *hypostases* as the distinct subjects of differing sayings and actions of Jesus (ascribing, for example, the sufferings to the human *hypostasis* and the miracles to the divine) was it possible to do justice to the real humanity of Christ without in the process denying the impassibility and omniscience of the transcendent God. The other, allied to more characteristically Alexandrian ideas, insisted that such an interpretation did not do justice

pp. 1210–11

Christology

to the one who, for the salvation of humankind, in the incarnation 'humbled himself and took upon him the form of a servant'. The divine Son must, Cyril argued, be seen as the subject of all the words and saving deeds of the incarnate Jesus. Only so could they be 'saving' deeds. The divine Son could speak or act sometimes in his human and sometimes in his divine capacity, but always it was the divine Son who was the true subject of the words and deeds of Jesus. Words spoken and acts done in his human capacity did not impair in any way the impassibility or omniscience of his fully divine nature. Jesus was indeed made up of two natures (*physeis*), but they had come together to form a single *hypostasis*. Both accounts had serious difficulties to contend with that exponents of the other were not slow to point out.

Spirituality

Various reasons ensured that it was Cyril's approach that was to win the day. For all the questions that may be (and were) asked about how successfully it does justice to a real humanity in Jesus, it was the more fully worked out and the better able to give expression to a gospel of divine concern for the human race. But other factors played an equally important role, when the issue came to a head. In 428 Nestorius, an outspoken champion of the more characteristically Antiochene approach, was appointed Bishop of Constantinople. The time for serious theological evaluation was past. Terminological confusion and ecclesiastical rivalry took control. In such a context Cyril was a far stronger player than Nestorius, and Nestorius was forced out of office and into exile. Seven years after Cyril's death, at the Council of Chalcedon in 451, a definition of the faith was agreed which hailed Cyril as an outstanding champion of the true faith. But it was a more moderate statement than that for which Cyril had campaigned in the heat of the controversy. Nestorius in exile could argue that it did not exclude what he had stood for. But he was left in exile, while the name of Cyril was venerated.

Cyril of Alexandria: Select Letters translated L. R. Wickham, Oxford Early Christian Texts, Oxford: Clarendon Press 1983; John A. McGuckin, *St Cyril of Alexandria: The Christological Controversy*, Leiden: E. J. Brill 1994

(Pseudo-) Dionysius the Areopagite (*c.* 500)

Acts 17.34 recounts that one of those converted by Paul's address to the Council of Areopagus in Athens was a member of that council, named Dionysius. Early in the sixth century a group of writings, in which Christian thought and Neoplatonic philosophy are closely integrated, was put into circulation under the name of Dionysius the Areopagite. Neoplatonism had already been a substantial influence on Christian theology, but the integration of the two in these writings is far closer than is to be found in any earlier Christian writer. If a pseudonym suggesting that they belonged to the early days of the church was needed to allow them a serious chance of being given a favourable reception, Dionysius, being the name of the first Christian associated with Athens, the home of Greek philosophy, was a natural choice. It was also a very effective one. Until well into the sixteenth century the writings were almost universally accepted as coming from the apostolic age, and their influence on the development of spirituality was thus greatly enhanced. That the attribution of the writings to Dionysius is a false one is beyond question. Moreover, by inference from the dates of works on which they draw and the time at which other writers first refer to them, it is possible to date them with some confidence to the early years of the sixth century in Syria.

Philosophy

The corpus of writings attributed to Dionysius is not large: four relatively short treatises and ten letters. The character of the theology that they were so successfully designed to inculcate can be seen by looking at them in turn.

The Divine Names is a reflection on the many names used of God in scripture. But its final emphasis is that, rich though these names are, they still belong to the conceptual realm, whereas the inscrutable, transcendent One lies beyond the conceptual realm and so beyond all names.

The Mystical Theology describes the way of the soul to union with God or divinization. The treatise speaks of the affirmative (or 'cataphatic') way and contrasts it with the way of denial (or 'apophatic' way). It is the first occurrence of that particular formulation, which was destined to figure so largely in subsequent theological reflection. The apophatic way is seen as more appropriate to the nature of a God who utterly transcends the conceptual realm. But even straightforward negation is not enough; union with God involves the negation not only of affirmations but of negations also, as the believer passes outside the realm of knowledge altogether.

The Celestial Hierarchy uses the Neoplatonic framework of a changeless One, from which derives a process of emanation and return, to give a Christian account of revelation from God and union with God. To this end Dionysius draws on the scriptural references to angels and develops a hierarchy of nine orders of angels, arranged in three triads. The biblical imagery is given a spiritual interpretation, showing how enlightenment derives ultimately from God, and how a path of purification, illumination and perfection is made possible for us.

The Ecclesiastical Hierarchy (or 'our' hierarchy, as the author regularly calls it) goes on to show how this way from and to God is embodied in the worship of the church. Once again there are nine orders in all, made up of three triads: the sacraments, the clergy and the laity. The nature of the sacraments, the hierarchical structure of church order and the manner in which the liturgy is conducted are all given a spiritual interpretation as embodying the way of purification and contemplation.

Two features of the writings stand out. Most notable is the extreme to which the apophatic way is taken, so that even the negation of images is seen to fall short of what is needed to do justice to the utter transcendence of God. Mysticism of so radical a kind does not always combine easily with more formal worship and the ordering of the church's life. However, for Dionysius the mystical way remains rooted in the hierarchical and liturgical life of the church and in the imagery of scripture, however firmly and frequently its literal sense may need to be negated. It is not only the spurious claim to the authority of the apostolic age that has contributed to the continuing interest in and influence of these writings. It is also the calibre of the writings themselves with their dual emphasis on the radical transcendence of God and on the role of the imagination as a means towards apprehending a way of spiritual illumination in and through the traditional scriptures and liturgies of the church.

Pseudo-Dionysius: The Complete Works translated C. Luitheid, Classics of Western Spirituality, New York and Mahwah, NJ: Paulist Press 1987; Andrew Louth, *Denys the Areopagite* (1989), London and New York: Continuum 2002

Gregory the Great (*c.*540–604)

Gregory was born into a wealthy and aristocratic Christian family, and rose to hold the office of prefect of Rome in 573. The next year he abandoned that life, sold his property, devoting the proceeds to charity and to the establishment of monastic foundations, and himself became a monk. But five years later he was called to ordination and the service of the papacy, first in Constantinople for five years and then back in Rome. In 590 he was himself elected pope, serving in that office until his death in 604.

Like many other leading figures in the early Christian world, he was torn between the contemplative life of the monastery and the active life of public affairs. But more successfully than most, he struggled to integrate the two into a holistic vision. He did much to encourage the monastic life, for which he always maintained a deep longing. Its primary purpose was a training in the contemplative life. But the fundamental quality of life developed by monastic piety was not suited only for the monastery. The inner stability of purpose to which it aspired was highly pertinent to both private and public life as well. In his running of the papacy, he entrusted many of the most important positions to monks. Gregory himself was a skilled and conscientious administrator, a quality much needed in as unsettled an era as that through which he lived. The breakdown of imperial power in the West had left an important role for the papacy to play in maintaining social and political stability. His early experience as prefect of Rome stood him in good stead, particularly in dealing with invasions by Lombards from the north. There was also more scope than ever for the charitable activities of the papacy, which Gregory oversaw with dedication and skill. He was the first to adopt the title 'servant of the servants of God' as a designation of the Pope's office, and he came closer to living up to that ideal than many of his successors. Moreover, with the changing political scene in the West, the church was less inclined to restrict its attention to the heartlands of the empire. That was the context which helped to give rise to Gregory's most famous missionary initiative: the sending of Augustine (of Canterbury) with a team of monks to undertake the difficult task of the conversion of Britain.

Mysticism

Gregory's strong dual commitment to the contemplative and the active life is the more impressive in one who was acutely subjected to the sufferings of ordinary life. To the disturbed social and political conditions of his time may be added his own constant sufferings from ill-health. It is not surprising that the misfortunes of the world, which he strongly affirmed to be God's world, should have led him at times to speak of the period through which he was living in apocalyptic terms as the end of the age, and to do so with a sense of immediacy not seen since apostolic times.

Gregory was not an original writer, but one well versed in the traditional teaching of the church, especially the work of Augustine, which he saw it as his duty to apply to the changing conditions and needs of his own time. His writings also reflect clearly the teaching and pastoral duties of his office, and his deep respect for both the contemplative and the active life.

His many writings on scripture (the *Moralia* on Job from his days in Constantinople and the many homilies on scripture given during his years as pope) follow the traditional pattern of distinguishing the literal or historical sense from the spiritual; the spiritual itself is often divided into the allegorical and the moral, so that he works sometimes with a twofold, sometimes a threefold distinction. It is the spiritual, and particularly the moral sense on which the stress is laid, because that is the point at which the application of scripture to the lives of his readers or hearers is effected. His *Pastoral Rule,* written just after his accession to the papacy as he himself was coming to terms with his new office, is a succinct and practical guide to priestly office. The authenticity of his *Dialogues* has been questioned, but the great majority of scholars accept them as genuine. With their many stories of the miracles of the saints, they are intended for a more

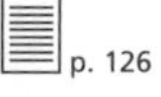
p. 126

Gregory the Great, eighth-century ivory diptych, Monza Cathedral

general readership than his other writings. The miracles are not meant to be treated just as wonder stories. Like the records of scripture they need to be interpreted; it is their moral message that is all-important.

Gregory embodies perhaps better than anyone else the spiritual and pastoral intention of so much of the scholarship and writings of the church fathers. It is this rather than any outstanding intellectual contribution that led to his being included (along with Ambrose, Jerome and Augustine) as one of the four 'Doctors of the Church' recognized by the Western church of the Middle Ages. His overriding pastoral concern is evident in his writings and in his practice, particularly in his emphasis on the need for flexibility in giving guidance to the very varied lives and needs of different men and women, and on the appropriateness of different customs in culturally different parts of the world. The ordering of the church, the exposition of scripture and the ministrations of the clergy were, like the Pope himself, intended to serve the servants of God.

📖 *St Gregory the Great: Pastoral Care* translated Henry Davis, Ancient Christian Writers 11, Westminster, MD: Newman Press and London: Longmans, Green 1950; *St Gregory the Great. Dialogues*, The Fathers of the Church vol. 39, Washington, DC: Catholic University of America Press 1959; Robert Markus, *Gregory the Great and his World*, Cambridge: CUP 1997; Carole Straw, *Gregory the Great. Perfection in Imperfection*, Berkeley, CA: University of California Press 1988

Maximus the Confessor (*c.* 580–662)

Maximus was born into a well-to-do family in 580. Having enjoyed a good education, he achieved the position of first secretary to the Emperor Heraclius in Constantinople when still in his early thirties. But in about 614 he abandoned his career and became a monk. Unlike many other leading fathers of the church whose ecclesiastical career began in the same way, this was not for him the first step to ordination and the episcopate; though he was to play a prominent role in the ecclesiastical affairs of his day, he remained an unordained monk to the end of his long life. The first period of his monastic life was spent in two monasteries in the neighbourhood of Constantinople. But the invasion of the Persian armies led to the dispersal of his monastery and his eventual settlement in the West, first at Carthage and subsequently in Rome. It was to be nearly 30 years before he would return to Constantinople, in even more distressing circumstances than those that had led him to leave it.

Maximus had already begun on a career of scholarly writing before leaving the East, but his time at Carthage was his most prolific period as a writer. Two distinctive but not untraditional forms provide the structure for many of his most important works. His *Quaestiones* (Questions), *Ambigua* (Difficulties) and *The Ascetic Life* are all cast in a question and answer form; his *Centuries* (or *Chapters*) *on Charity* and on *Theology and the Incarnation* are both made up of sets of a hundred aphorisms – four and two hundreds respectively.

His *Quaestiones* deal with problems arising from the scriptural text, the *Ambigua* with problems in the writings of Gregory Nazianzus, for Maximus an almost equally sacrosanct source of tradition, and also of Dionysius the Areopagite, another major influence on his thought. His creative interpretation of the problems that he finds in these, for him, authoritative texts is an instructive illustration of how it was possible for the Christian tradition to develop and to change without any explicit repudiation of its sources. *The Ascetic Life* and *The Centuries on Charity* are a reminder that the intended goal of all Maximus' writings was the inculcation of the way of self-denial and of love as the path to union with God, not only for monks but for every Christian.

His theological vision was on the broadest, cosmic scale. He envisaged a unity of God, humanity and the rest of creation, in which nothing is lost of the distinctive character of each. The foundation stone of this whole vision was a transformation of our disordered world brought about by the incarnation. It was not just the presence of God as the divine Word but the presence there of the incarnate Word, fully God and fully human, on which that transformation depended. The Council of Chalcedon had attempted to settle long-standing disputes about the basic understanding of the incarnation in a way that was well suited to Maximus' vision of the whole by its insistence on the existence of two natures, one fully divine and the other fully human, in the one Christ. But it had not succeeded in uniting the whole Christian world. Some, who came to be known as Monophysites, objected that the way in which the Chalcedonian formula spoke of the two natures of Christ did not do adequate justice to their union in the incarnation. In Maximus' time an attempt to find a path that might reconcile the division between Chalcedonians and Monophysites had given rise to the suggestion that the sense of a divided Christ might be overcome if it were agreed that, though having two natures, Christ had only one will (a view known as monothelitism). To this Maximus was implacably opposed. Even though in action will was a function of the one person, it was still at root an inalienable aspect of human nature. A true human nature must therefore have its own will. In his eyes, therefore, monothelitism was incompatible with a view of the incarnation as involving a union of the fully divine and the fully human, and so was totally unacceptable. During his time in Carthage and in Rome, Maximus was active in securing the rejection of the belief in the Western church.

To the emperor, who had secured the support of the patriarchate of Constantinople to the monothelite compromise, this forthright rejection of the monothelite view was totally unacceptable. It spelt the frustration of all his attempts at a reconciliation that would overcome the serious divisions within the empire. So in 653 Maximus, along with the Pope, was arrested in Rome; he was then taken to Constantinople, condemned and sent into exile. In 662 he was recalled to Constantinople, and when further attempts to get him to modify his position met with total rejection, he was tortured (his tongue and right hand, the organs through which his defiance had been expressed, were both amputated) and sent back to an even more remote place of exile. He died shortly after arrival there. Less than twenty years later, at the second ecumenical Council of Constantinople in 680, the dyothelite (two wills) position for which he had stood so resolutely and suffered so severely was formally agreed to be the true teaching of the church.

Maximus was well versed in both the Western and Eastern traditions. He contributed to their development with a remarkable degree of intellectual and spiritual sensitivity. Subtle and precise in his understanding of the detail of those traditions, he was also, in line with the apophatic tradition, well aware of the inadequacy of human language for the theological task, something that he had imbibed from the writings of Dionysius. All this adds to the tragic nature of his courageous 'confession' of his faith in the face of exile, torture and death. One may well want to ask: was he right to see the precise account of incarnation for which he stood as something essential to the religious vision which was at the heart of his faith? Patristic theology is notable both for the grandeur of its spiritual vision and for the precision of some of the definitions of its faith. But the types of understanding involved in those two notable aspects of the tradition are not easy or natural bedfellows.

Incarnation ◄
Council ◄
Christology ◄

📖 *Maximus the Confessor: The Ascetic Life* and *The Four Centuries on Charity* translated Polycarp Sherwood, Ancient Christian Writers 21, Westminster, MD: Newman Press and London: Longmans, Green 1955; *Maximus the Confessor: Selected Writings* ed and translated G. C. Berthold, New York and Mahwah, NJ: Paulist Press 1985; Andrew Louth, *Maximus the Confessor*, London and New York: Routledge 1996; Lars Thunberg, *Man and the Cosmos: The Vision of Maximus the Confessor*, New York: St Vladimir's University Press 1985

MAURICE WILES

Cinema

In 1911 the yet-to-be-pioneer film-maker William DeMille (brother of Cecil B.) described the movies as 'galloping tintypes (which) no one can expect … to develop into anything which could, by the wildest stretch of the imagination, be called art'. DeMille would no doubt be amazed by the popularity of film into the next century; despite initial misgivings about its potential, film has developed into a universal medium of entertainment and education. It has also become a meaningful art, in that through it are expressed the basic themes of human knowledge and existence; it has its own kind of 'religious imagination' from which can be discerned an experience of transcendence. Indeed it can be said that the cinema, along with the theatre and the novel, is a place where the central questions about life are being asked today.

Religious language and symbols continue to come alive in contemporary media culture: Christianity has as its living heritage a storehouse of symbolic, narrative and sacramental resources. The early film-makers saw religious themes as the most popular to put on the silver screen. The first biblical spectacular was *King of Kings* (1927) by Cecil B. DeMille, and it became meaningful to many, including a German Lutheran pastor named H. E. Wallness. He was so moved by the film that he decided to devote his life to the Christian ministry. He had a parish in Prague when Hitler invaded Czechoslovakia, and saved 350 Jewish children from the Gestapo. He wrote to DeMille after the war to let him know how much the film had affected him, through making Jesus come alive in his imagination.

Film, with its moving images, has a potent capacity to wash over us; it has been said that movies are felt by the audience long before they are understood. Just as in the theatre the audience unconsciously blocks out the physical limits of the proscenium arch in order to engage fully with the play, so those in the cinema are completely absorbed mentally into the on-screen action, experiencing little if any sense of emotional or geographical distance. Not only emotions, but attitudes and values come out of film, because film, like religion, can affect feelings towards oneself and one's neighbour, as well as reflect hopes and fears of our world. The cinematic technique of using light and darkness in denoting good and evil is one example of how film can influence our understanding and interpretation of what we see on the screen.

The term 'grace on the screen' which has been used of the cinema suggests that the perennial themes of popular film – those of freedom, authenticity, love and justice – have to do with the basic stuff of existence, which is permeated with divine grace. The recognition that films can provide a useful point of contact between faith and culture was indicated in a 1971 document from the Pontifical Council for Social Communications entitled *Communio et progressio*: 'Many films have compellingly treated subjects that concern human progress or spiritual values. Such works deserve praise and support' (no. 144). To mark the centenary of cinema in 1996 the Vatican released its list of films that it declared offer 'artistic or religious merit'. Many of the films on the list could be termed 'religious films', such as *A Man for All Seasons* and *The Gospel According to St Matthew*, but a surprising number are films that have no overt religious or theological purpose but can certainly be 'read' from spiritual or theological perspectives: *2001: A Space Odyssey*, *It's a Wonderful Life*, *The Wizard of Oz* and *Schindler's List*.

The story of Jesus has constantly been the subject of theological and cultural reinterpretation. It is a story that film-makers cannot leave alone, whether it is offered in the shape of controversial films such as *The Last Temptation of Christ* (Martin Scorsese, 1988) and *The Passion of the Christ* (Mel Gibson, 2004), a modern-day critique of the media (*Jesus of Montreal*, Denys Arcand, 1989), or even a parody of the institutional church (*Life of Brian*, 1979). The Gospel narratives offer everything that a good film could want: a suspenseful plot, all-too-human characters, an exotic location, an ultimately uplifting and inspirational ending.

Pier Paolo Pasolini, *The Gospel According to St Matthew*, 1964

In mainstream film, many modern heroes are in fact Christ figures, who experience the kinds of things Jesus did or who personify the righteous, loving, self-sacrificing Christ. Christ figures in film can identify with Jesus' suffering, liberate people who are persecuted or enslaved, or rescue people from an evil force: films such as *Superman*, *ET the Extra-Terrestrial*, *Pale Rider* and *Cool Hand Luke* are only a few that have flagged up parallels to the gospel. Clint Eastwood once explained that he has always been interested in the supernatural mythical hero who brings spirit to discouraged people, or encourages them to fight for their own rights. George Lucas realized the power of the mythological archetypes of good battling against evil in his *Star Wars* series of films, and this battle is also central to two recent box office successes, the Harry Potter films and *The Lord of the Rings* trilogy.

Saints and sinners have been the subjects of many classic films: Charles Laughton starred in *The Hunchback of Notre Dame* (1939) with a stunning performance that set the hunchback's suffering within the context of the Passion. Priests and nuns are popular stereotypical characters in films ranging from *The Bells of St Mary's* to *Dead Man Walking*. The millennium saw an increased number of films with apocalyptic themes (*End of Days*, *Armageddon*).

Mel Gibson, *The Passion of the Christ*, 2003

Some of the most affecting cinematic performances have been portrayals of religious conversion and sacrificial love (*Tender Mercies, The Mission*).

Although film-makers may consciously endow their works with spiritual overtones (Ingmar Bergman said that film goes far beyond ordinary consciousness 'deep into the twilight room of the soul'), ownership of the cinematic experience is the key to the meaning of art. We learn to understand ourselves when we encounter art, and the imparting of meaning is a role of both the film maker and the audience. Entering into a second century of cinema as sophisticated consumers of moving images, we can recognize that the genius of film is to transport us beyond the projected image to a place where we can examine our values, explore ideals that are personally freeing and affirming, and reflect upon our own responses to what we have seen and heard on screen.

GAYE WILLIAMS ORTIZ

📖 C. Deacy, *Screen Christologies*, Cardiff: University of Wales Press 2001; R. Johnston, *Reel Spirituality*, Grand Rapids, MI: Baker Academic 2000; C. Marsh and G. Ortiz, *Explorations in Theology and Film*, Oxford: Blackwell 1997

COMMUNICATION

Books, Cinema, Drama, Internet, Journalism, Letters, Music, Painting, Poetry, Preaching, Publishing, Radio, Sculpture, Television, Worship

Jesus At the centre of the Christian religion stands a communicator. Christians believe that Jesus had unique insights into the nature of God and his dealings with the human race. He also had insights into the character of human life and the ways in which men and women find fulfilment. If true, these insights must be of supreme importance for the well-being of individuals and communities, and it was in the unbending conviction that they are true that Jesus devoted a brief period of his short life to sharing them with those of the Jewish community into which he was born who were ready to listen to his words and observe his way of life.

The number of those who responded positively by accepting his insights and allowing them to provide a new basis for their own understanding and way of life was very small, and it was not long before Jesus was publicly executed as a threat to the established religious and political orders. But inasmuch as the message he taught and exemplified was seen by his followers as an expression of divine truth, there was no possibility of their keeping it to themselves. Of its very nature, it must be Church shared with others. Thus the church, which developed from what is now regarded by Christians as an act of divine communication, has always had the imperative to communicate at the heart of its life.

Today there are estimated to be about two billion people who profess to be Christians, located in almost every part of the world, and although there is now a marked decline in religious Geography observance in many Western countries, Christianity is still expanding quite rapidly in Africa, Asia and Latin America. At the beginning of the twentieth century there was a widely-held belief among Christians that within a generation the entire human race would have heard and probably accepted the message of Jesus. This proved to be an over-optimistic assessment, and since then there has been a resurgence of some other major religious faiths, notably Islam, but even so the growth of the Christian community from a handful of followers of a crucified teacher to a massive worldwide presence, accomplished in less than twenty centuries, is a matter for wonder. It is the result of highly effective communication, though some of the methods employed and the insights shared are open to question.

As at the beginning, the spoken word has always been the primary form of Christian communication, though not all its forms have been equally effective. Such knowledge as we have about the life and teaching of Jesus originated in an oral tradition. Jesus did not write any books, and it was not until several decades after his death that attempts were made to commit this tradition to writing. Today sermons, lectures, seminars, discussions and personal conversations are all ways in which Christian insights are shared, though public utterances, such as sermons in which audiences only listen, are not considered to be a very helpful form.

From the very beginning, letters between churches and individuals have played an important role in communication; many of them have been preserved, and it is notable that a substantial part of the New Testament consists of letters.

Bible The Bible itself has a unique place among the channels of Christian communication, since it contains virtually all that is known about Jesus, provides the religious and social background of his life and teaching, and gives important evidence of the impact this made on his immediate circle and some who came afterwards, notably Paul of Tarsus. Wide circulation of the Bible had, however, to await the invention of printing in the mid-fifteenth century, and even then its personal use was confined to the limited number of those who could read. Now it is readily available in a variety of English translations, none of which makes it an easy volume to comprehend. It contains several different forms of literature and, like all collections of ancient documents, it is couched in the thought-forms of cultures very different from our own. Its study requires patience and skill for the fullest understanding of its message. The same is true of the writings that date from the post-biblical era, but the Christian religion has inspired some of the finest literature in history and today writers of every kind seek to share their faith with others by means of articles and books, poems and plays.

Paul

pp. 124–5

In the pre-literate world visual images were essential to Christian communication. Early Christians decorated the walls of the catacombs in which they worshipped with paintings of biblical scenes and symbols that had significance for faith. Medieval churches were treasure houses of religious art expressed in painting, mosaic, sculpture and stained glass. The architecture of the buildings themselves was, and remains, a powerful expression of the faith that inspired their creation. A leading twentieth-century philosopher said that he had been converted to Christianity by gazing on Lincoln cathedral. At certain times in history, for fear of idolatry, there has been a reaction against this use of religious art and, not least in Britain, much of great value has been destroyed. Today, however, there is a new recognition of the importance of the eye as a vital gateway to communication, and the second half of the twentieth century saw the beginning of a new partnership between the church and the artist. This still has a long way to go before its potential is fully realized.

p. 325
Symbol
Stained glass

Again, music has played a major part in the communication of the Christian faith. Some of it was composed for use in worship, some simply for performance, but among these compositions are examples of the highest human achievement. Happily, there has been no serious dislocation of the church/musician partnership, and the concert hall as well as the church building has become a place of deeply religious experience and aspiration. From the mystery plays of the Middle Ages onwards, drama, too, has been an important form of communication, and in the twentieth century musicals like *Godspell* and *Jesus Christ Superstar* have played a part. Nor should the role of the cinema be forgotten.

Mystery plays

The advent of radio, television and other electronic forms of mass communication has brought new opportunities that Christians have sought to exploit, with varying degrees of success. But religious insights are not easily shared through these channels, and after a period of creativity in the 1970s and 1980s, the opportunities for serious religious broadcasting have been greatly reduced.

More significant than any of these means of communication, however (though it has embraced all of them), has been the life of the church. Jesus, the communicator, formed a small community that would not only continue to share his insights with others but also demonstrate how these insights might be expressed in human life. 'See how these Christians love one another,' remarked one of the church's earliest opponents, and he was not being cynical. In spite of many serious shortcomings and not a little sordid corruption, across the centuries the church has managed to attract to its community individuals who are searching for life's meaning and through their involvement have embraced the Christian faith.

Worship – the church's chief activity – is, if rightly ordered, the most powerful means of communication for many people. By means of words, movement, colour and music, and the bonding which their corporate use creates, Christians express something of what they have learned

COMMUNICATION

from Jesus about loving God and loving one another. For participants and observers this can be compelling.

Love
Sickness and healing
Education
Pastoral care

But Christians are required not only to love God and one another, but also to extend their love to others who are outside the church's life, especially those who are in need of any kind. The Good Samaritan is a central Christian icon, and although Christians have all too frequently failed to follow the injunction of Jesus, 'Go and do likewise,' some of them have, both individually and corporately, made major contributions to human welfare in the realms of health, education and social reform. Less visible, except to their recipient, but not the less influential, have been the countless acts of care and compassion extended to neighbours in time of need. Christian action communicates, and without this non-verbal form of communication all other efforts to share the Christian message are likely to fail.

Destiny and purpose
Faith

In considering these efforts at communication it is important to recognize that while Christians are always under an obligation to share their insights with others, they are never in a position to impose them on others as if these insights belonged to the same category as some scientific truths. Because the insights involve ultimate questions concerning origins, meaning, purpose and destiny, they require an act of faith, that is to say, a personal conviction that the insights communicated by Jesus point to how things are in the divine/human encounter, and a readiness to base one's life, in trust, on this disclosure.

That said, it must immediately be acknowledged that there is no single pattern of movement to faith. Because the human personality is so varied that every human being can be described as unique, response to religious revelation is bound to differ greatly. What is more, the response is never complete, but involves a lifelong quest for greater depth of insight, with the distinct possibility that feelings and faith may wax and wane according to changing experiences, perceived and unperceived.

This being so, it follows that Christian communication is not as simple and straightforward as many of the most fervent propagators of the faith seem to believe. Here a line must be drawn between valid communication and propaganda. Propaganda involves the distortion of information and the exploitation of emotion in ways that mislead and reduce the freedom of the recipient to make a considered choice. Examples of this in the history of the church are not difficult to find and remain common. Preachers, convinced of the truth of their message, sometimes use a mixture of promise and fear to evoke a positive response from their listeners. The linking of missionary work with food aid in underdeveloped countries runs the risk of producing what are sometimes called 'rice Christians'.

Constantine's 'conversion'
Reformation

Historically, the expansion of Christianity has owed much to mass conversions, when from personal conviction or political expediency rulers have imposed Christianity on their subjects. In 313 the Emperor Constantine, though not himself a Christian, made Christianity a favoured religion in the Roman empire, and this led to a rapid increase in the size of the church. When Augustine led a mission from Rome to England in 597 he was pleased to discover that the queen of Kent was already a Christian, and on Christmas day of that year, shortly after the conversion of the pagan king, 10,000 people were baptized. During the colonization of Latin America by the Spanish and Portuguese conquistadores in the sixteenth century innumerable Indians were baptized under duress, and at this time it was recognized throughout Europe that the religion of the ruler would also be the religion of the people. Protestant and Catholic allegiance was enforced by penal sanctions, including execution, during the English Reformation. It was not until the nineteenth century that Non-conformists and Roman Catholics in England were freed from serious disabilities.

Whenever religious or political systems are enforced, control of information and censorship are never far away. William Tyndale, who translated the New Testament and part of the Old Testament into English in the early sixteenth century, encountered fierce opposition from the leaders of both church and state in England who believed that the reading of the Bible by individuals would lead to differences of opinion about its meanings and thus undermine the stability of society. He fled to the continent, where he was eventually strangled and burnt at the stake. Since 1557 the Roman Catholic Church has had an Index of books that its members are officially forbidden to read or possess. This ceased to have juridical force in 1966, though it was retained as having moral authority. Roman Catholic writers on religious subjects are supposed to obtain permission from their bishop before publication, known as the Imprimatur (Latin: 'let it be printed'), though this is widely ignored. Nonetheless it is by no means uncommon for theologians who depart from the official Roman line on matters of doctrine to be called to account by the Vatican and, in some instances, to lose their licence to teach or even face excommunication. In less authoritarian churches that lack these sanctions, controversial books are sometimes publicly denounced by bishops and other church leaders, often on the grounds that they are likely to disturb the faith of the laity. The freedom of Salvation Army officers to write for publication is severely constrained.

Vatican

More significant in the modern world than any of these direct pressures, however, is the fact that a very large number of people are still born and nurtured in Christian surroundings and within a broadly Christian culture. The influence of this continues to be great, and accounts for most of those involved in the life of the churches. The validity of the faith of such people is not to be discounted. The communication of Christianity, as of other belief systems, takes place in many different ways and can only be evaluated, should this be called for, by the effect it has on the lives of individuals and communities.

Besides the communication to others of the Christian faith, the church, in common with all other organizations, requires strong lines of internal communication to enable information to be exchanged and decision-making to be shared. Many of the methods used for the sharing of faith with unbelievers are used for this purpose, but other methods can be found within the churches. Most local churches have a monthly magazine or newsletter, the quality of these publications ranging from the highly professional to the embarrassingly amateur. Some Church of England dioceses publish tabloid-style newspapers paid for by advertisers, but these are now threatened with closure whenever diocesan budgets are stretched, since they are not without cost. Bishops occasionally write pastoral letters on particular subjects that are read from church pulpits in their diocese. All of them employ press and information officers. Most of the other mainstream churches have similar systems for keeping in touch with their members; national weekly newspapers, although generally under private ownership, play an important part in the conveying of information to the clergy and lay leaders.

In some parts of the world, mainly the USA, Christian organizations have their own broadcasting stations or purchase air time on other, commercial, networks. They are used mainly as a means of communication for hell-fire preachers and during the 1980s had massive audiences and incomes, but scandals involving money and the sexual morality of the preachers took them off the main channels and they are now confined to small, local stations. The Vatican has a radio station that disseminates the official views of the Roman Catholic Church on ecclesiastical, social, political and sometimes doctrinal matters. Its audiences are small, but its information and opinion are frequently reported on by the international news media.

Although the potential of the internet is only just beginning to be explored by Christians, it is playing an important role in communicating every aspect of Christianity and maintaining contact between Christians. Instantaneous communication all over the world is possible through email, and there are websites of every conceivable kind, making available libraries of books, a plethora of information and a point of contact for churches and organizations.

Except in those parts of the world where Christianity is spreading rapidly, it may be said that the churches generally give much lower priority to communication than might be expected in bodies that exist primarily to communicate something they believe to be of the utmost importance. The reasons for this are many and varied, but all are related to the fact that with the passage of time the once vibrant Christian communities have become preoccupied with maintaining their present institutional life in a world where a high proportion of those who have acknowledged religious needs and aspirations do not feel drawn to express these in churches. This is a dangerous situation, for churches that do not grow tend to wither away.

On the other hand, it must be recognized that highly effective communication by the church does not necessarily guarantee success, as success is commonly understood: massive support, increased influence. The insights communicated by Jesus are, Christians believe, true, life-enhancing, and the secret of human happiness and fulfilment. But they are not offered at bargain price. Their cost is the heavy one of life motivated by sacrificial love, and the fact that Jesus died a lonely death on a cross is the clearest possible indication of their demands. It is not to be expected, therefore, that the best lines of communication of the Christian faith will necessarily lead to crowded churches or prosperous Christian organizations. Indeed, where such exist there may be good reason for enquiring what insights are being communicated. New truths, or different understandings of truths already revealed, are still needed, and the communication process will continue for as long as religious insights are required.

TREVOR BEESON

Community

Communities have been of vital importance to Christianity throughout its existence. One of the first things that Jesus did was to create an itinerant community of twelve disciples who were to follow him, and there are indications of other groups in his lifetime, not least the women who also went with him. The first communities became a church, and from then on the church became the dominant form of community in which, according to Paul, 'there is neither Jew nor Greek, there is neither slave nor free, there is neither male nor female; for you are all one in Christ Jesus' (Galatians 3.28).

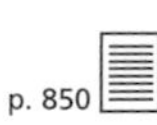
p. 850

Church

However, this vision faded, and as Christianity grew and expanded the churches became vast international organizations, institutions in which the personal dimension came to be lost. And in our time, as many of these institutions are going into decline in the Western world, religion, including Christianity, is increasingly being privatized and individualized; beliefs and allegiances are chosen in accordance with personal preference, and the dimension of community often disappears. A further problem is that the word community is now so widely used and of so many groupings that it has become virtually meaningless. Ethnic communities, the local community, community services, the wider community, the international community, religious communities, just 'the community' – all these terms are applied to people, often large numbers of people, who are largely unknown to one another and whose cohesion is by no means obvious.

So it is important to see how substance can be given to the word 'community' by looking at the different forms that it has taken in Christianity, alongside and with that of the church.

In one of the earliest summary descriptions of the first Christians, the Acts of the Apostles remarks that 'the company of those who believed were of one heart and soul, and no one said that any of the things which he possessed was his own, but they had everything in common' (4.32). This picture may be somewhat idealized, but there is plenty of evidence elsewhere for the community spirit which it conveys. The Greek word for 'in common' is *koinos*, and the noun from it, *koinonia*, is fundamental to the nature of earliest Christianity. The translation of *koinonia* is fellowship, and Paul ends one of his letters, 'The grace of the Lord Jesus Christ and the love of God and the fellowship of the Holy Spirit be with you all' (2 Corinthians 13.14). These words found their way into the Anglican Book of Common Prayer at many places, as an alternative ending to a service in place of a blessing; they are still widely used, and are known simply as 'the grace'.

For Paul the word *koinonia* denotes more than belonging together in a close-knit community; it means sharing in something: here a bond that is brought about by the Holy Spirit. He also can talk of the *koinonia* of the blood of Christ, the sharing in Jesus' death and resurrection that is celebrated in the eucharist, the holy *communion*. And *koinonia* has a practical dimension. A major concern of Paul's was to collect money from the churches that he founded in Macedonia to bring relief to the hard-pressed Jerusalem community: this he calls a *koinonia* of service (2 Corinthians 8.4). This sharing can be so close that the community can be called the body of Christ, with each of its members dependent on the other (1 Corinthians 12.27).

A related word, central to the Orthodox churches, is the Russian *sobornost*, almost impossible to translate. Its core meaning is unity, a unity that, as in Paul's 'grace', flows from Father, Son and Holy Spirit. This unity transcends emotions, ideas and identities and has immense horizons. It is a mystery to be understood more with the heart than with the mind, but it is centred on baptism, the eucharist, service to others in love, and contemplation. It overcomes loneliness, alienation and fragmentation and binds Christians closely together.

With the growth of the churches the sense of community became more difficult to maintain. From being small groups meeting in houses, Christians became large groups worshipping in large buildings, and although the ideal of community, fellowship and unity remained, there were those who felt that the realization of this in the churches was not enough. So 'alternative' communities came into being and have existed in and with the church ever since. The first such communities were groups leading the monastic life in the Egyptian desert, who under the guidance of Pachomius (*c.*290–346) were organized into small groups living together. Here lie the roots of later monasticism, with houses providing the setting in which groups of men and women could live in close community, sharing prayer and worship and bound by vows.

The Middle Ages also saw the foundation of religious orders, some static communities of men or women, living together under a common rule and sharing in work and worship; others were itinerant groups, again under vows, but travelling around the world to preach the gospel rather than staying in one place. 'Society' is another term that came to be used of their community, as in the case of the Society of Jesus, founded by Ignatius Loyola in 1540. The Brothers and Sisters of the Common Life, like the Beguines and Beghards in northern Europe, also lived in communities but without being bound by vows. Fraternities were founded to meet the religious and social needs of both clergy and laity, gathering regularly for meals and seeking to provide ways of reconciling disputes among their members.

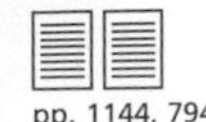

pp. 1144, 794

The Reformation in the sixteenth century, after which the Protestant churches developed in many directions, saw the formation of a whole variety of communities, brought together and held together by persecution and consequent migration, needing to stay together to survive in a foreign land. Among them were such varied groups as the Amish, who originated in Germany in the seventeenth century and then migrated to the United States; the Shakers, who originated in Lancashire in 1747 and under their leader Ann Lee emigrated to New York state; and the Herrnhutter, a group of Moravians formed in 1722 in the Saxon village of Herrnhut, who ever since have provided annual sets of Bible readings (in German, the *Losungen*).

Paul
Reformation
Holy Spirit
Eucharist
Shakers

Moravian Church
Orthodox churches

The nineteenth century saw a 'Catholic' revival outside the Roman Catholic Church and a resurgence of the communal life, in which attempts were made to adapt monasticism to the modern world. Among many new foundations were the Anglican Society of St John the Evangelist, founded in Oxford in 1865 by R. M. Benson, and the Community of the Resurrection (now at Mirfield, Yorkshire), founded in 1892 by Charles Gore.

In modern times it is sometimes difficult to distinguish between communities, fellowships and movements, which can themselves form communities in different places. The Fellowship of Reconciliation was founded on the outbreak of the First World War in 1914 as a Christian pacifist movement. The Iona Community was founded by George Macleod in 1938 with the aim of both rebuilding the ruined Benedictine abbey on the island and working in Scottish industrial areas; it originally consisted of clergy and laymen from the Church of Scotland, who spent three months a year on Iona in preparation for their missionary work; now it is composed of both men and women drawn from all the churches and its rules are more flexible. Other notable Christian examples are the Taizé Community in France, founded in 1940 by Roger Schutz, for work with young people; Focolare in Italy, founded in 1943 by Maria Lubich, a predominantly Catholic lay movement; and L'Arche, which forms communities for those with learning disabilities, founded by Jean Vanier in France in 1964.

Church of Scotland

Monasticism
Middle Ages
Religious orders

Perhaps most notable of all in the modern world, though, are the so-called 'base ecclesial communities' in the Roman Catholic Church of Latin America, the

Christianity in Latin America

TAIZÉ

The Taizé community was founded by Roger Schutz, a Swiss layman, in 1940. He and his sister Geneviève bought a house in Taizé, a small village in Burgundy, close to the line which divided Vichy France from occupied France and well placed for welcoming refugees, including Jews. They had to leave in 1942 but Brother Roger, as he came to be called, returned in 1944 with a group of others: after the war, with Geneviève, they first looked after war orphans, and later welcomed German prisoners of war. The first community was formed in 1949, making a commitment to sharing and simplicity of life.

The Taizé community now consists of over 100 brothers, Protestants and Catholics, from many countries. They earn their living and accept no donations. Some work among the poor in America, Asia and South America, sharing their wretched conditions. In Taizé, thousands of young people from all over the world are welcomed every summer by the brothers for Bible study, prayer, and exploration of the problems of world society, in activities which enable them to deepen their understanding and faith. Two communities of Roman Catholic sisters in the next village are also involved in the work. Every year after Christmas, tens of thousands of young people meet in a European city as part of a 'pilgrimage of trust on earth' that the community has been engaged in for 25 years.

 www.taize.fr

Liberation theology

grassroots communities. These active small groups, which came into being in connection with the rise of liberation theology, see themselves as a new way of being the church. They read the Bible together and relate its message to the community, and they share in projects to meet local needs. They came into being in the late 1960s and flourished for a decade or more. However, as the Roman Catholic hierarchy expressed its disapproval of liberation theology they went into decline and the focus of their activities shifted from the social to the devotional. Nevertheless, the idea spread to Africa, Asia and beyond, and base communities can still be found round the world.

Mystery plays

In today's world, in which even the oldest and most intimate community, the family, has in many places broken down, the need for community is greater than it has ever been and countless communities of various kinds have come into being, lasting over shorter or longer periods of time. Some are Christian; others acknowledge their debt to Christian models but have other dominant ideals, like self-sufficiency; yet others are secular in spirit.

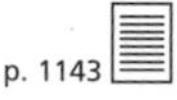
p. 1143

Spirituality

Many communities, especially those with available accommodation, offer themselves as bases for retreats, spaces of time during which individuals can come to stay and deepen their spirituality with periods of silence and the possibility of various forms of teaching and guidance.

JOHN BOWDEN

Catherine D. Doherty, *Sobornost. Eastern Unity of Mind and Heart for Modern Man*, Notre Dame, IN: Ave Maria Press 1977; Faith and Order Commission, *Partakers of the Promise. Biblical Visions of Koinonia*, Geneva: WCC 1993; Fellowship for Intentional Communities, *Communities Directory: A Guide to Intentional Communities and Cooperative Living*, Rutledge, MO: FIC [3]2000; Margaret Hebblethwaite, *Base Communities. An Introduction*, London: Geoffrey Chapman and Mahwah, NJ: Paulist Press 1993

http://www.ic.org, the website of Intentional Communities, provides a directory of communities

Community arts

Down the ages, Christians have been involved in events which have involved whole communities, such as pageants, processions, carnivals and mystery plays, and many of these forms of community art still survive to the present day, perhaps most notably in the passion play held every ten years in the German village of Oberammergau, which involves just about the whole population.

However, community arts are not just limited to keeping past traditions and forms alive. The umbrella term covers a wide range of creative and innovative practices which are deliberately set within the particular conditions of a local community and call for the participation of community members, activating the imagination and creating choices in a given situation. This intention is based on the clear assumption that such artistic activity will generate change. Activities can include street theatre, mural art, installations, performances as well as more open forms such as festivals and events, types of playback theatre, pavement art, poetry groups, local history, literary narratives, and so on. The list can seem endless when the arts are explored for their community-building capacities in creating an audience, in sharing stories and in focusing creative energy.

Such creative activity has become of increasing importance to local communities in terms of their history, identity and their negotiation of change in an increasingly multicultural and socially diverse context. This importance has grown as a result of increased leisure activity as well as a general valuing of cultural life and a greater perception of the role of the arts. In the face of increased globalization and a trend towards a monochrome urban environment, there has been a re-valuing of individual creativity and the diversity of local cultures.

The arts are a valuable means through which the church can express its identity and contribute to the life of a local community. The life of the imagination, which funds the creative arts, is a crucial component of theological reflection. This is seen in a local community where the elements of the Christian faith find their expression in the forms of a particular culture. An awareness of a local culture provides resources for exploring relevance and vitality through the imagination of faith.

By their very nature the arts explore, interpret, expose and celebrate the complexity of life and its many choices. Since the 1960s, through movements for social change and action, they have been used to offer alternative views, to parody prevailing ideals, and to re-imagine new possibilities. In terms of community development, the arts communicate new possibilities as well as assist in the process of a community's negotiation of change and in mediating internal points of tension.

Many churches, particularly in areas of rapid social change, have sponsored or played host to arts workers by giving space to community theatres or providing studio and work spaces. A number of churches have formalized these relationships into programmes where artists are considered to be in residence in the life of the local community.

Artists-in-residence may be individual writers, performers or visual artists who seek to develop their ideas through being exposed to a specific community. They may also be called upon to facilitate the production of artistic projects in collaboration with community members. They may oversee and produce, for example, a wall mural, a theatre production or an exhibition of children's artwork, or develop a choir. Churches endowed with property are able to create these possibilities for development, led by a skilled and creative innovator.

This model of relationship has, in some places, been extended to hosting larger groups such as theatre or dance companies, providing space for artists' studios, or dedicating space for community arts initiatives in partnership with local government. A number of churches now run art galleries or performance spaces as part of their overall mission. A range of recent projects has seen artists of international stature install works or lead programmes in these community-based settings. The range of funding support received, from local government through to national arts councils, has underscored the importance of this community focus.

A further extension of these dynamics is the operation of a more formalized arts programme in which, rather than playing host, the church has taken the initiative in organizing and promoting its own programme in collaboration with local artists and performers. Some churches have developed or contributed to larger festivals and regional events, thereby recovering a role for the church as a major patron of the arts. Major commissions of artworks have also resulted from the goodwill that has been built up through these creative partnerships.

Globalization

Patronage

Given that these initiatives are connected to the specific conditions of a local community, a number of projects have been aimed specifically towards the welfare concerns of the local population. This may be, for example, an art or writing class for homeless people in the inner city, or a photographic project for youth at risk. In turn, some churches have become key providers of community development projects. Here, using the resources of the arts, local communities have sought to re-imagine their future and in response have developed projects that, for example, reclaim waterways, re-vegetate parklands, or find creative ways of dealing with visual graffiti.

Many of these projects respond to ideas about the quality of life in a local community. They affirm the role of the imagination in human development and the need for people to play and re-create the culture in which they find their life. It is an appropriate role for the church to be part of this re-creative activity as it still remains a key provider of hope in the life of any local community.

The benefit of artistic interaction with the wider community is that it helps to shape the mission of the church and in turn questions and enlivens its worship. This shaping of the tradition occurs in the midst of new urban realities and the complex conditions of postmodern society. A valuing of the imagination and human creativity is an essential part of the expression of faith in any community and re-affirms the ability of a tradition to change and embrace new challenges.

Mission

ROD PATTENDEN

Fiona Bond, *The Arts in Your Church: A Practical Guide*, Carlisle: Piquant 2001

Congregationalism

Congregational churches may be found in many parts of the world. American Congregationalism resulted from European migration in the seventeenth century. In other parts of the world Congregational churches were children of the modern missionary movement. Congregationalists were also known as Independents; it is by no means clear when the term 'Congregationalist' was first used, but it seems to have arisen about the middle of the seventeenth century in England, around the time of the Commonwealth.

Baptist churches
Reformation

The roots of Congregationalism are to be found in the left wing of the sixteenth-century Reformation. There was a feeling that reform was not going fast enough, nor was it radical enough. In Europe this feeling motivated the work of men such as Conrad Grebel and Menno Simons; however, it was not articulated in England until the 1580s, when a handful of radicals began to develop a coherent ideology of 'separatism'. Robert Harrison (died *c.*1585), John Penry (1559–1603), Henry Barrow and Robert Browne (*c.*1550–1633) all emerged from the radical tradition fostered around the urban centres of East Anglia: Cambridge, Norwich, Thetford and Bury St Edmunds.

They urged 'reformation without tarrying for any' (in Browne's famous phrase), and called on the faithful to 'separate' from the apostate and godless multitudes of the parish churches of England to live lives of true holiness. Following Christ demanded a distinctive lifestyle, as Barrow put it, '... reducing all things and actions to the true and primitive pattern of God's Word'. The truly faithful should shun the national church, for its ministers were ordained by bishops and maintained by tithes, rather than presbyters chosen, appointed and paid by the people. Further, its worship was unscriptural, based on a Prayer Book all too Romish in tendency, and its government an unhappy mingling of courts sacred and secular. All that had to be rejected for the narrow way, the faithful walk.

Ministry and ministers

Such sentiments were seen as politically seditious as well as theologically erroneous by the Elizabethan establishment. Persecution, exile and martyrdom were to be the lot of the separatists. Barrow and Penry were executed in 1593. Browne and Harrison, along with some other members of their congregation, endured the difficulties of exile in the Netherlands. They settled first at Middelberg in Zeeland. During 1582 Browne set out his views in a series of books, *A Brief Treatise of the Reformation without Tarrying for Anie*, *A Treatise upon the 23 of Matthew* and *A Book which Sheweth the Life and Manner of all True Christians.* There he set out his understanding of the church as a gathered company of Christians, in covenant together under God, with minister, officers and people held together in mutual contract (an idea later translated into political philosophy with much profit by John Locke).

Covenant

The separatists were not Congregationalists, although it can be reasonably argued that they were the precursors of Congregationalism. In 1606 a separatist congregation was formed in Scrooby in Lincolnshire under the leadership of John Smyth (*c.*1554–1612) and John Robinson (*c.*1575–1625). Within two years it had split, but both congregations under the respective leaderships of Smyth and Robinson sailed for the Netherlands. Smyth, a true smouldering radical, rebaptized himself, and his congregation became the precursor of the Baptists. Robinson's flock eventually settled at Leyden. He was a sensitive, gracious pastor and his congregation grew. However, the Netherlands was not England. Language remained a barrier and there were subtle theological disagreements between the exiles and their hosts. It was not surprising, therefore, that in 1620 a large section of the congregation decided to set sail, first for Southampton and then New England. William Brewster (*c.*1560–1644), the Scrooby postmaster who had been a member of the original congregation of 1606, was one of them. The group is better known as the Pilgrim Fathers. Brewster died the first Governor of Plymouth Colony.

The development of Congregationalism in New England and the full expression of Independent ideas during the Commonwealth and Protectorate were closely related. Thomas Goodwin (1600–80) and John Owen were both influenced by John Cotton's *The Keyes of the Kingdom* (1644) in their exploration of the nature of Congregationalism. Cotton had been the vicar of Boston in Lincolnshire for 21 years before emigrating in 1633 to become the Congregational minister at Boston in New England. Goodwin, later the President of Magdalene College, Oxford, was one of the five members of the Westminster Assembly who put his signature to the Independent dissenting coda, *An apologeticall narration.* Owen, Dean of Christ Church, Oxford, from 1651 to 1660, was the finest of Congregationalism's seventeenth-century apologists, particularly in his elucidation of the relationship between the particular local church and the church catholic. It is his orderly and catholic understanding of Congregationalism that lies behind the most important Congregationalist declaration of faith, the Savoy Declaration of 1658.

The restoration of the monarchy in 1660, the passing by the English parliament of the Act of Uniformity in 1662, which required ministers to use only the Book of Common Prayer, and consequent legislation, meant a dramatic change of fortune for Congregationalists. A period of persecution of varying intensity between 1662 and the passing of the Toleration Act of 1689 proved Congregationalism to be an ideology ideally adapted for such stressful times. It passed through the fire into the calmer days of the eighteenth century, developing its own culture and emphases.

Religious freedom had been granted to dissenters in 1689 at the cost of civil liberty. Their sphere of activity was defined by that legislatively enforced social apartheid. Banned from grammar schools and excluded from higher education, they developed the dissenting academy, a blend of school and theological college that nurtured progressive experiment in education and played a quietly supporting role in the emergence of modern science. They forged a spirituality born of engagement with the Word and the elegant simplicity of worship in meeting houses which emphasized both light and learning. The shared responsibility of Church Meeting developed skills of debate and the handling of business that was later to translate effortlessly into the council chamber and the trade union meeting.

It was during these years that Isaac Watts (1674–1748) turned psalmody into hymnody, gifting the Christian world with a new art form, along with Philip Doddridge (1702–51), whose ecumenical generosity and passion for the love of God flowed into a practical Christianity the effects of which were writ large in the institutions of his home town of Northampton and in one of the treasures of English devotional writing, *The Rise and Progress of Religion in the Soul.*

Congregationalism in Britain grew exponentially between 1715, when its estimated membership was just under 60,000, and 1851, when the religious census recorded 655,935 Congregationalists. Part of the reason for that growth was the impact of the evangelical revival of the 1740s that brought Methodism to birth, part the shifts in population caused by the industrial revolution. During those years non-conformity was immensely adaptable, and because it did not need legislative permission to build new churches (as did the Church of England), it moved with the people. In doing so it was instrumental in bringing a new commercial, entrepreneurial class to political influence. In the persons of men such as Titus Salt, the Bradford alpaca prince, the carpeting Crossleys of Halifax and the Colman mustard dynasty of Norwich, Congregationalists rose to economic power, and it was clear that the political status of dissent had to change. The history of Congregationalism in the nineteenth century therefore combined the fight for civil rights with the rise to respectability until, symbolically, in 1889, the Congregationalists opened their own college, Mansfield, in that bastion of Anglican establishment, Oxford.

In common with most Protestant denominations, Congregationalism experienced a liberalizing and redefinition of its inherited Calvinism in the nineteenth century, but in the early years of the twentieth century its greatest theologian since Owen was P. T. Forsyth (1848–1921), whose work has frequently been described as a precursor to that of Karl Barth.

Twentieth-century Congregationalism was marked by a growing ecumenical commitment, which was to result in 1972 in the union of the Congregational Church in England and Wales with the Presbyterian Church of England to create the United Reformed Church. Just over 25% of Congregational churches opted not to join the union. The majority formed the Congregational Federation, others the Evangelical Federation of Congregational Churches, while a few remained as independent congregations. In 2003 the Congregational Federation had a membership of 10,234 gathered in 297 congregations. The Evangelical Fellowship of Congregational Churches has 128 affiliated churches across the United Kingdom.

DAVID CORNICK

Daniel Jenkins, *Congregationalism: A Re-statement,* London: Faber 1954; R. Tudur Jones, *Congregationalism in England 1662–1962,* London: Independent Press 1962; Geoffrey Nuttall, *Visible Saints: The Congregational Way 1640–1660,* Oxford 1957; Alan Sell, *Saints Visible, Orderly and Catholic: The Congregational Idea of the Church,* Geneva: WCC and Pittsburgh, PA: Pickwick Publications 1986

Hymns

Conscience

Conscience is something that we all know we have, even if it is difficult to explain what it means or how it works. We know that we have a conscience because we stand for certain convictions that we compromise only at risk of losing our integrity. We know our conscience is operating when we struggle over deciding what to do. Achieving clarity about conscience has been complicated by the ways in which the theological tradition has spoken about it and by our tendency to confuse the moral conscience with the Freudian psychological notion of the superego.

Evangelicals
Methodism
Industrial revolution

Conscience is rooted in the biblical notion of the 'heart'. In the biblical view of the make-up of human beings the heart is the ultimate source of physical, emotional, intellectual and volitional life. It is the 'mission control centre' of the moral life. In the heart dwell the insights, intentions, desires, memories, fears and hopes that express one's moral character and influence one's moral actions. In the Old Testament, when young King Solomon was about to assume the throne of his father, David, he is said to have asked not for a long life or even for power over his enemies but for 'an understanding heart' (1 Kings 3.1–9). Solomon asked for wisdom, a conscience that would enable him to make prudent judgements. The rightly-ordered heart has an instinct and inclination for what is good, whereas the misdirected heart produces sin (Mark 7.21; Luke 6.45). To live out of the heart in the biblical sense includes everything that we would ascribe today to the 'head and heart' working together to reach a considered judgement about what ought or ought not to be done.

John Calvin

The medieval debates spoke of conscience as a function of the intellect or of the will. The era of the Roman

Presbyterian churches
United Reformed Church

Moral theology
Community

Catholic moral manuals made conscience a rationalistic operation that applied principles to cases in a deductive way. Today we speak of conscience holistically as the integration of thinking, believing, feeling, intuiting and imagining. Conscience is not a distinct faculty but the whole person integrating a range of operations in coming to know moral values and to judge in the light of them.

Bible
Psychology and Christianity

We can distil the wisdom of the tradition on conscience for our contemporary understanding of it by distinguishing three dimensions of the one operation. Conscience is a *capacity*, a *process*, and a *judgement*. As a capacity, conscience is our innate ability to discern what is good and right from what is evil and wrong. This is the sense in which we 'have' a conscience. But conscience is also something we 'do', a process of being informed. This is the practised ability of doing our moral homework – acquiring insights into moral questions, informing ourselves of values and obligations, and learning what it means to be persons of faith, virtue, integrity and goodwill. Conscience as judgement is the 'work' of conscience. For Christians, the judgement 'I must do this' comes after they have made a sincere effort to discern wisely and well through prayer and serious study. It takes place in the deepest sanctuary of the heart, where one is alone with God.

Martin Luther
Education

Once we have decided that it is morally right to do something, then the dignity of the primacy of conscience requires that we adhere to our decision. This is the force of Martin Luther's famous statement, 'Here I stand, I can do no other.' Officials of the Roman Catholic Church were convinced that he was wrong in some of his opinions, but his own prayer and study led him to conclude otherwise. To act according to conscience means to be true to our inner convictions, informed by a sincere effort to discover what is right. To be true to his conscience, Luther had to take a stand on what he believed to be right.

A core belief of the Christian tradition about the primacy of conscience is that God judges the interior state of one's soul, that is, the sincerity of the heart in striving to choose what is right more than in doing it. Even if we inadvertently misread the situation and get some of our information wrong, we must still do what we believe to be right. God accepts our sincerity and forgives our mistaken knowledge. But if we do not even try to find out what is right or are careless in the process of being informed, then we are guilty, at least for our negligence, even if not for the full weight of the wrong that we do. The goal of acting in conscience is to bring together our sincere desire to discern well with the best course of action to take.

Freedom
Authority

This understanding of conscience is sometimes mistaken as a stand for individual freedom and against authority. But to claim the primacy of conscience as the ultimate court of appeal does not mean that conscience stands independent of authority. Conscience and authority are dialectically related. They are neither identical nor totally separable. While the judgement of conscience is always made *for* oneself (what I must do), it is never formed *by* oneself. Conscience is a community achievement. After all, the root meaning of the word 'conscience' is 'knowing together with'. This meaning makes it clear that moral knowledge is social. We form our moral convictions and learn of moral obligations from some dependence on our social groups and their authorities. These include not only the human sources of family, friends, colleagues, laws and customs of civil society, and the knowledge of experts in the field which pertains to the decision we have to make, but also specifically religious sources, such as the Bible and the teaching of the church. In the process of becoming morally responsible, the conscientious person would want to attend to the wisdom of such authorities, not to take the place of conscience but to inform it. Obedience to authority is no excuse for going against a sincerely-informed conscience.

One way of clearing up the confusion about the relation of conscience to authority is to distinguish the moral conscience from the Freudian notion of the superego. Psychologists of the Freudian school tell us that we have three structures to our personality: the id, that unconscious reservoir of instinctual drives largely dominated by the pleasure principle; the ego, the conscious structure which operates on the reality principle to mediate the forces of the id, the demands of society and the reality of the physical world; and the superego, the ego of another superimposed on our own to serve as an internal censor to regulate our conduct by using guilt as its powerful weapon.

As we develop through childhood, the need to be loved and approved is our basic need and drive. We regulate our behaviour so as not to lose love and approval. As a matter of self-protection, we absorb the standards and regulations of our parents, or anyone who has authority over us. The authority figure takes up a place within us to become a kind of psychic parent or police officer keeping an eye on our behaviour and giving us commands and setting out prohibitions. Since we carry this authority with us in the unconscious structure of our mind, the voice of this authority is always and everywhere present to us. It tells us that we are good when we do what we have been told to do, and it tells us that we are bad and makes us feel guilty when we do not do what we should. In short, the external authority now internalized as the superego takes over the function of the moral conscience and we act out of the obligation to be obedient lest we lose love and approval.

The moral conscience, by contrast, exercises responsible freedom: the freedom of wanting to do what we ought to do as virtuous persons because we own the values that we are expressing. External authorities are sources of wisdom by which we come to know what is valuable and what life looks like when we are faithful to values, but the external authorities do not take over the function of conscience. On the basis of personally appropriated convictions, we decide whether or not to follow the guidance of authority in this instance.

Conscience, then, is our innate capacity for moral discernment, the process of discerning, and the judgement we make in the light of the truth that we discover. Throughout our lives, we learn from various authorities how to become sensitive to value, to learn virtue, and to discover what is right and what is wrong. This puts conscience in constant dialogue with the various sources of moral wisdom. But ultimately we have to make up our minds for ourselves. We do not act in conscience by pinning our souls on another and abdicating responsibility. If we spend our life doing what we are told to do by someone in authority simply because the authority says so, or because that is the kind of behaviour expected by the group, then we never really make our own moral decisions. For moral maturity we must be our own person. It is not enough just to do what we are told. To act with a mature conscience, we must be able to perceive, choose and identify with what we do. In short, we create our character and give our lives meaning by committing our freedom, not by submitting it to someone in authority. We cannot claim to be virtuous, to have strong moral character, or to give direction to our lives if we act simply on the basis that we have been told to act that way. As long as we do not direct our own activity, we are not yet free, morally mature persons responding to what God is calling us to do in the deepest resources of our hearts, our conscience.

RICHARD M. GULA, SS

Sidney Callahan, *In Good Conscience*, New York: HarperCollins 1991; Linda Hogan, *Confronting the Truth*, New York and Mahwah, NJ: Paulist Press 2000; Charles M. Shelton, *Achieving Moral Health*, New York: Crossroad 2000

Constantine's 'conversion'

The conversion of the Roman emperor Constantine on the eve of the Battle of the Milvian Bridge in 312 CE has been seen as a key turning point in the history of Christianity, to be compared with the similarly dramatic conversion of Paul on the road to Damascus. Before Constantine's reign Christians had been a persecuted minority; after his reign every Roman emperor but one was a Christian, and the Christians were to be found in positions of influence throughout the Roman empire. Was this transformation the consequence of one moment of revelation, or was it more complex?

The first decades of the fourth century were years of dynastic struggle in the Roman empire. Two emperors abdicated, and one more, Constantine's father Constantius I, died within a year of taking office. There were disputes between adoptive sons and biological sons over who should succeed, with the result that by 310 at least six men were claiming the title Augustus, meaning senior emperor, when five years earlier there had been only two. One of the six was Constantine, who had been encouraged by his troops to claim the imperial purple, and was in effect a usurper. A combination of deaths and civil wars allowed Constantine to fight his way to power and by 324 he was sole emperor. According to the stories that grew up later in his reign, it was during the course of these wars that something happened that was to change history.

The tradition that Constantine had a 'moment of conversion' to Christianity always associates that moment with his campaign in 312 CE against one of his rivals, Maxentius, who had proclaimed himself emperor and was occupying the city of Rome. Two different stories are told in the sources. According to Eusebius in his *Life of Constantine*, Constantine, before setting out to march into Italy, prayed to the god his father had honoured, and was rewarded by a vision in the sky of a cross-shaped trophy accompanied by the words 'by this conquer'. Lactantius, in his work *On the Deaths of the Persecutors*, says that Constantine had a dream the night before his battle with Maxentius in which he saw the *chi-rho* symbol, a monogram made from the first two Greek letters in the name of Christ.

Both accounts were written some time after the events, and Eusebius makes no mention of a vision or a dream in his earlier *History of the Church* – nor is it referred to in the surviving speeches made in honour of Constantine. To make things more complicated, a speech made two years before this does refer to a vision Constantine had, given to him by the sun god Apollo. From that point on, he minted coins with the symbol of the sun on them – a practice that continued after the defeat of Maxentius.

It is difficult to know how to interpret the evidence, but one possibility is that there was no dream or vision in 312, and that Christian writers had adapted the story of the pagan vision of 310. The worship of the Unconquered Sun had been associated with emperors, including Constantine's father Constantius I, for the preceding 50 years. Whether Constantine himself thought that the Unconquered Sun, or Apollo, was the same as the God of the Christians is unclear. There are signs that he continued to think in 'pagan' terms after 312. The seven days of the week were named after the seven planets (Sun, Moon, Mars, Mercury, Jupiter, Venus, Saturn), and it had

Paul

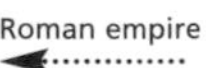
Roman empire

Baptism of Constantine, thirteenth-century fresco

become established that legal activities did not take place on Sundays. When Constantine modified this practice to allow the freeing of slaves on Sundays he did so explicitly because it was the day of the Sun, not because it was the day that marked the resurrection of Jesus. Constantine did undergo baptism, but only on his death-bed. Some writers of the time claimed that he actively legislated against non-Christian practices, such as animal sacrifice, but the evidence for this is slight, while it is known that he permitted the building of temples to his family.

Resurrection

Sacrifice

Whatever Constantine may have believed, it remains true that Christianity benefited from his reign. He gave Christian clergy exemption from the duty of holding public office (a privilege that 'pagan' priests usually enjoyed), he allowed churches to inherit property, and he became involved in the internal disputes of the church. He called a number of councils of bishops to try to settle doctrinal differences between them, of which the most important was the Council of Nicaea in 325. How much Constantine was interested in the disputes, or indeed understood their subtleties, is not clear, but it is certain that he saw a harmonious and prosperous Christian priesthood as vital for the well-being of his empire. The result of his interventions was the emergence of a single Christian church within the empire, with the emperor overseeing it. For some modern observers this was the moment when the simple Christianity of the apostles and of the early church was overwhelmed by secular power, while for others it was the point of the final triumph of the faith. For Constantine it was probably a matter of pragmatism: the better the God of the Christians was served by his clergy, the more likely he would be to aid the emperor.

Council

At the time of Constantine's death Christianity was probably still the religion of a minority of the inhabitants of the empire, and although there were powerful Christians, it had made little progress among the rich and powerful in the major cities. However, by the end of the fourth century it was the dominant religion of the empire, and non-Christians could be dismissed as mere country bumpkins (in Latin *pagani*, from which the word 'pagan' comes).

Not all of this was Constantine's own work: persecution of Christians in the eastern parts of the Roman empire was ended by the Emperor Galerius shortly before his death in 311, and the 'edict of Milan' of 313 commonly attributed to Constantine, which supported toleration of all religious practices including Christianity, was actually the work of his co-Emperor Licinius, although it was issued in the name of both men. In any case, large-scale persecution had never been a frequent or long-lasting phenomenon, and Christianity had been able to grow gradually over the preceding three centuries with only occasional episodes of repression.

Nonetheless, the reign of Constantine was important, above all in making Christianity visible. Archaeology has revealed remarkably little about Christianity in its first three centuries: very few Christian buildings have been identified from before the fourth century, and Christian images and inscriptions are rare. By involving themselves in Christian affairs Constantine and his successors made it respectable to be a Christian even in the highest social circles, and by allowing churches to inherit property they made them wealthy. The long-established practice of rich patrons supporting public building works now included Christian patrons erecting Christian basilicas. Christian symbols, above all the cross and the *chi-rho*, became part of the iconography of the emperors, and as a result spread through the empire they ruled. In these ways and others Christianity became part of the general culture of the Roman empire. It was not through a single event, or through the advocacy of a single ruler that the Roman empire became a Christian empire. It was a gradual process, in which Constantine played an important, but perhaps not entirely intentional, part.

HUGH BOWDEN

Averil Cameron, *The Later Roman Empire*, London: HarperCollins 1993; Alistair Kee, *Constantine versus Christ*, London: SCM Press 1982

Contextual theology

Theology has the study of God as its object. Since Christians believe God is ultimate perfection, the language of theology has often tended to match that absolute character. It tries to express realities in universal ways that do not admit of exception, speaking of God as all-powerful, all-knowing and the like. In the same manner, the Christian revelation was presented as being universally intelligible to all human beings. Because Western theology arose in a socially powerful and culturally uniform area, this universal character of theology was further emphasized.

Paganism
Persecution

However, the spread of Christianity outside the Western cultural sphere in the nineteenth and twentieth centuries raised questions about the capacity of theology to speak about 'that which is believed everywhere, at all times, by all people' (to quote Vincent of Lérins, a theologian from the ninth century). As Western Christianity moved into very different cultural settings in Asia and Africa, it became increasingly apparent that all theology is articulated by concrete human beings, who live in particular circumstances, and who bring specific concerns to their reflection on God. Up until the middle of the twentieth century those who did not fit into the established (Western) pattern were considered immature or not sufficiently developed to speak according to the norm (that is, the European West). But with the coming of independence to former European colonies in Africa and Asia, Christians in those settings began asserting the right to speak in their own fashion.

Archaeology
Christianity in Africa
Buildings
Christianity in Asia
Christianity in Latin America

This process began among young African theologians in the 1950s. By the 1970s, it had spread to Asia and Latin America, as well as among ethnic minorities in the United States. It was at this time that 'contextual' theology began to be produced more consciously. Contextual theology asserted that theological expression does not stand on a platform outside specific contexts. Those contexts influence what questions are asked, what constitutes an appropriate answer to those questions, and which questions are more important than others. For example, in the 1960s and 1970s, European and North American theologies were preoccupied with how to make sense of faith in God in the face of the increasing secularization of society. This question did not have the same urgency in Africa, where nearly everyone presumed the existence of God and of an unseen world. Europeans responded that Africa was not yet 'developed' enough to face this question. Once Africa had caught up with Europe, it too would be asking it. But African theologians could assert that their point of departure was different, and should be accepted as such.

Patronage

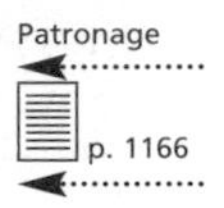

p. 1166
Secularization

From the mid-1970s onwards, there was an increasing interest in how specific contexts shaped questions in theology, and how those same contexts made some answers more suitable than others. Different terms are used to describe this phenomenon. 'Contextual' theology was the preferred term in Protestant circles in the World Council of Churches. Roman Catholics, on the other hand, tended to speak of this phenomenon as the 'inculturation' of the faith, that is, how the message of Christianity entered a particular culture. There was also sometimes talk of 'local' theologies, to be differentiated from theologies that tried to be 'universal' in scope. While there are nuances of meaning between these terms, for general purposes they all try to say the same thing.

Ecumenical movement
Theology
Revelation

In the 1970s and 1980s, these theologies developed in cultural areas outside the West (but also among cultural minorities in North America). They found their focus around one of two poles. Some focused especially on issues of identity, and how their (non-Western) identity made them distinctive. Culture was a prime defining category, and emphasis was placed on differences between cultures. Others were concerned with the social problems that needed to be faced, such as poverty, political oppression and racism. These theologies attended especially to the social structures that constrained human flourishing, and asked questions about how a theological answer might promote change. Many of these theologies were known as liberation theologies, because they aimed at human liberation.

The identity theologies looked for specific African, Asian or native identities to inform thinking about God. They flourished in the first instance in former European colonies seeking independence. As time went on, groups oppressed by majorities even within these settings also looked for distinctive identity. Thus Dalit theologies arose among low-caste and no-caste groups in India. Burakumin theologies among leather workers in Japan would be another example. Hispanic or Latino theologies arose in the United States among people who were pushed to the social margins because they were of Latin American descent. The same was true in that country for people of African descent, who created black theologies. Social groups that were not ethnic minorities, yet nonetheless were striving against the powerful classes within their societies, found similar distinctive identity. This was the case for the Minjung groups in South Korea.

Specific cultural identities could also become rallying points for social change. This was most evident in the development of black theologies in South Africa, which mobilized sentiment against apartheid.

As time went on, people who were part of the majority cultures in Europe and North America sought to create theologies distinctive to their needs and aspirations. Among the first were women creating feminist theologies in the 1970s. By the beginning of the twenty-first century, feminist theologies were in almost their third generation. In their most recent manifestations, they admit of a highly differentiated understanding of the plight of women in different class and social settings. Ethnic differences among women have been the basis for developing womanist (African American) and *mujerista* (US Latina) feminist theologies as well. In Africa, the Circle of Concerned African Women Theologians has been working towards similar differentiation from white feminist thought. By the 1990s, gay and lesbian theologies also started to emerge. In yet other instances, people in majority cultures felt that the academic theology developed in the West did not meet them where they were, and efforts were made to create local theologies within majority culture contexts. One finds such theologies in Europe, North America and Australia.

Culture
Poverty
Globalization ·········➤
Liberation theology
Postmodern theology ·········➤
Hispanic Christianity
African American Christianity
Feminist theology
Gay and lesbian theology

As a result of all of these efforts, by the beginning of the twenty-first century there was a much wider acceptance of the idea that all theology is contextual, i.e., all theology arises out of a specific context. Universalizing theologies continue to exist, but even these generally show an awareness of their own particular setting. With the advent of globalization in the late 1980s, the intermingling of global and local factors made simple designations of 'universal' and 'local' even more problematic. The homogenizing tendencies of globalization in many instances heightened further the sense of the local and the contextual. Likewise, postmodern thinking has meant that 'culture' is no longer seen as a clearly-bounded union of territory, language and custom. Particularly in urban settings, where migrants from many distinct cultures came together in a single place, specific cultural boundaries for a theology are more difficult to draw. But even in the midst of these difficulties, the social location of the theologian (i.e., the theologian's class, gender, race and the like), the relative social power of those engaging in theology, and the intended goals have come to influence how theologies are read today. Even as highly diverse societies seek means of greater cohesion, it is unlikely that theology, as an expression of the faith of Christian believers, can ever pretend to be utterly universal in a non-reflective way. Contextual theologies are likely to continue to be part of the Christian intellectual landscape for a long time to come.

ROBERT SCHREITER, CPPS

📖 Sigurd Bergmann, *God in Context: A Survey of Contextual Theology*, Aldershot: Ashgate 2003; Stephen Bevans, *Models of Contextual Theology*, revised edition, Maryknoll, NY, Orbis 2002; Robert Schreiter, *Constructing Local Theologies*, Maryknoll, NY: Orbis and London: SCM Press 1983 and *The New Catholicity. Theology between the Global and the Local*, Maryknoll, NY: Orbis 1997; Clemens Sedmak, *Doing Local Theology*, Maryknoll, NY: Orbis 2002

Conversion

The word 'conversion' has its own history outside religion. As a noun, it can mean to change or to switch something. Adaptation, transformation, renovation, alteration or transfer can all be implied in the use of the term. Money can be converted from one currency to another; a small family saloon adapted and converted, to be transformed into a rally or racing car; a barn renovated and converted into a spacious home. But in religious usage, the term tends to denote something else: a radical change, either from one religion to another, or from no religion to the dramatic discovery of faith, and a new relationship with God. When religious people speak of conversion, they normally refer to the idea that – irrespective of their faith tradition – a major and drastic revolution has occurred in people's lives. They are now 'saved'; they have been 'born again'; they are now part of the 'true faith'.

There are good reasons for religious people to understand conversion in this revolutionary way, rather than in the more adaptive and mellow way that the term is normally used in secular language. Consider, for example, Paul the apostle, one of the first and most dramatic converts to Christianity. The book of Acts records that Saul (his pre-Christian name) was a zealous persecutor of Christians. But while on the road to Damascus, he has a dramatic encounter – bright light is seen, and the voice of Jesus heard – which makes Saul temporarily blind. He emerges from his blindness a convert to a new faith. Paul's 'Damascus road experience' (a phrase drawn from the Bible that has since become part of ordinary everyday language) is a typical figure of speech for what many regard as religious conversion: 'I once was blind, but now I see', is how the hymn writer John Newton put it.

But Paul's dramatic conversion is not a prototypical experience, a template that should frame and judge all other conversions. Paul came to Christianity some years after Jesus is said to have risen and ascended, which begs a question about the other apostles, who had known Jesus in his earthly life. At what point, one might ask, were the disciples converted from Judaism to Christianity? The Bible is somewhat silent on the matter. The resurrection stories suggest that the disciples were fearful and joyful in equal measure, but whatever they made of the resurrection appearances that they were seeing and experiencing, they still attended 'the temple'. At the end of the Gospels, the followers of Jesus are still Jewish, even if, like their master, they are out of sorts with the Pharisees and Sadducees. Traditionally, the Christian church dates its birth from the feast of Pentecost, another dramatic 'conversion' story, in which the disciples receive the Holy Spirit. This may be so, but even in this narrative – also recorded in the book of Acts – there is no obvious Christian identity to appeal to. Indeed, it is interesting to note that the New Testament at no point gives a definition of what a Christian actually is. Of course, there are hints and clues in stories – 'repent and believe', 'follow Jesus', 'receive the Holy Spirit', 'eat and drink in remembrance of me' – but no formal creed or description by which one can make decisive judgements that include or exclude believers.

That said, the first Christian communities that emerged were marked by difference. When Christians began to understand that their beliefs and practices no longer 'fitted' with the worship of the temple and synagogue, they began to meet in their own homes, and perhaps in meeting rooms too, just as Jesus and the disciples had once eaten together in an upper room. They chose a modest title to describe these gatherings – the Greek word *ekklesia* – which simply means assembly. In the Hellenic world of the first century CE, every major town had its own *ekklesia*, the assembly that dealt with civic matters, law, commerce and the general policing and welfare of the population. Such assemblies would have been run by men, and normally it was only men who could attend.

Church

But Christian assemblies were different from the beginning. Women would be present – and they might speak too. Children might be there also. Apart from Jews, there might be Greeks and other ethnic or national groups. And, most revolutionary of all, slaves were also admitted. In other words, from the very beginning of Christianity, its assemblies were radically inclusive. Or, put another way, Christians converted the way that we understand assemblage: their *ekklesia* was for everyone. Belonging to this community of faith no longer depended on where or to whom you were born; it rested solely on the willingness of the individual, family or other group to be converted, and then to belong. It is also important to remember that for these first 'converts' to Christianity, there was no New Testament, there were no creeds, and there was very little in the way of church structures. But it still meant leaving one religion for another. So converting to Christianity, for the first generation of believers, was often a costly business; it meant believing that Jesus was the Son of God, and then being filled with the Holy Spirit – but it could also mean persecution and martyrdom. Nonetheless, it was a simple faith, with a radical message – and it spread like wildfire.

Paul
Women in Christianity

Bible
Creed
Jesus

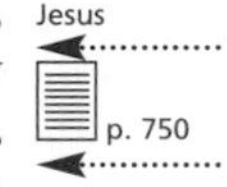

p. 750
Resurrection
Persecution
Martyr

Yet Christianity was a pragmatic and accommodating religion, almost from the very beginning. Conversion took many forms. Christian missionaries, as they began to spread throughout Europe, and also eastwards towards India, discovered that where the more familiar elements of a culture were retained, there was likely to be more success in introducing a 'new' religion. It has been pointed out, for example that by thinly overlaying pagan festivals and sacred places with Christian interpretations, missionaries made it easier for people to become Christian – so easy that actual conversion seldom occurred. If this cultural appraisal, which relates to the seventh century, is correct, then it is probably also true that people cannot easily give up what they have yet to fully embrace. Although he was baptized a Christian, the Emperor Clovis (466–511) would not forsake his ancestral gods for political reasons: 'The people that follow me will not allow me to forsake their gods.' And although Christianity gradually 'trickled down'

Origins and background
Festivals and feasts
Holy Spirit
Paganism

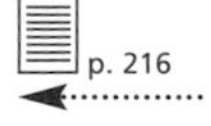

p. 216

Community

from the élite converts (the early European monastically-based missionaries normally worked on the wives of kings, princes and rulers, converting them to Christianity first) to the masses, the process taking hundreds of years, elements of paganism continued to survive.

It was no different for the European missionaries who set forth in the nineteenth and twentieth centuries. Faced with practices that appeared not to correspond with ordinary inculturated Westernized Christian values, missionaries often had to adapt their message and practice to secure conversions. In a moving account of his missionary work among the Masai of Africa, the Roman Catholic missionary Vincent Donovan finds his accounts of the Christian faith profoundly challenged. There is not only the language barrier to overcome. There are also cultural and conceptual difficulties for the would-be missionary as he attempts to communicate the Christian faith. For example, the Masai insist that the whole tribe is baptized; the idea that individuals can be included or excluded from the rite offends them. Moreover, and more profoundly, tribal baptism turns out to be a radical fulfilment of the gospel. As the tribal elder, Ndnagoya explains, the catechesis has become part of the culture: the lazy have been helped by those with energy, the stupid supported by the intelligent, and those with faith have aided those who have little. The tribe can truly say 'we believe'; this is just one of many ways in which Donovan has his eyes opened.

Pentecostalism

The rituals that surround conversion can vary considerably. Baptism is the standard point of initiation into Christian faith, but there are differences of opinion on the right circumstances and age for baptism. The Roman Catholic Church, the Orthodox, Anglicans and most mainline Protestant denominations practise infant baptism. Their sacramental view of baptism recognizes that the child is brought into a saving relationship with Christ even before the child can reason or articulate anything that might imply consent to conversion. Normally, the rite of confirmation (and its equivalents) allows those same children a public opportunity to own the baptismal faith for themselves as they reach the beginning or end of childhood (i.e., between the ages of seven and fourteen).

Initiation

Education

Some Protestant denominations, while not denying the importance of baptism, emphasize the need for the personal conversion of an individual first. Often, such a conversion has been marked by baptism by full immersion, and for some Pentecostal churches it is also marked by speaking in tongues as a sign of conversion. Classically, the great revivalist and evangelistic rallies and crusades of the last 300 years have placed a stress on individuals 'knowing Christ personally' and making a personal response to a call for repentance and faith. From John Wesley's 'strangely warmed' heart to Billy Graham's appeal to millions packed into stadiums to 'get up out [their seats]', and 'be born again', conversion has continued to be part of the vocabulary of Christian churches.

In the latter part of the twentieth century, the rise of new Christian movements has witnessed new developments in ritual that mark conversion. Some new churches practice a form of Christianized Bar Mitzvah, the Jewish rite which marks the passage of a youth from childhood to adulthood. The ritual can include walking over a specially constructed (and symbolic) bridge, and being blessed by the pastor and by parents. New types of catechetical material have also been developed, some of which are designed to act as a catalyst for conversion. The global success of the Alpha course has allegedly been responsible for hundreds of thousands of conversions worldwide. Equally, many missionary agencies and their materials can make similar claims, with some justice. In the Roman Catholic Church, the effectiveness of the new rites of initiation and catechesis have also led many to renew their

ALPHA

Alpha is an extremely successful course extending over ten weeks which promotes an evangelical type of Christianity to people looking for answers to questions about their lives. It has been followed by more than 2,000,000 people, and more than 25,000 courses are currently being run all over the world, on every continent. The participants meet for a meal, listen to a talk and then divide into small groups to discuss the week's topic, which usually takes the form of a question, many of them beginning 'How can I . . .?' (be sure of my faith, be filled with the Holy Spirit, make the most of the rest of my life), or 'Who is . . .?' (Jesus, the Holy Spirit). In the middle of the course the group has a day or a weekend away together.

Alpha originated in the Anglican church of Holy Trinity, Brompton, in London, and began its meteoric rise through the work of the Revd Nicky Gumbel, a former barrister who was ordained and joined the church, taking responsibility for the course in 1990 and being appointed Alpha chaplain. His book *Questions of Life* provides the syllabus.

 Nicky Gumbel, *Questions of Life*, Eastbourne: Kingsway and Colorado Springs, CO: David C. Cook 1993

 http://alphacourse.org

faith and religious commitment, moving from nominalism to activism in their belief and practice.

Conversion is a term that is usually associated with the transformation of an individual or community. Some scholars consider that there are three distinct elements to conversion: tradition, transformation and transcendence. Tradition refers to the religious context in which change takes place; transformation covers the specific changes (e.g. thoughts, beliefs, practices etc.); transcendence refers to the divine encounter that may be the catalyst for change. This leads scholars to conclude that five types of conversion can be identified: tradition transition – moving from one faith to another; institutional transition – changing allegiance within a faith, such as moving from one denomination to another; affiliation – an individual or group with no previous religious commitment joining a religious group or faith; intensification – renewal of faith within a tradition; and apostasy – rejection and defection of faith, but embracing a religion that is based on the previous religious convictions.

Some scholars also theorize that conversion in the contemporary Western world is partly the product of particular social, cultural or psychological contexts. One of these contexts may be a sense of crisis, in which religion offers a new coherent pattern of organization and meaning for the convert, and makes better sense of the world than any social, therapeutic or psychological alternatives. For some, embracing religion may be a deliberate rejection of secularity, and an attempt to rebel against materialism. Other scholars point out that the secular, capitalist and postmodern Western world leads many to a quest for meaning. In this scenario, conversion is understood as a motif within a journey – from nothingness to meaning. The rise in the popularity of new religious movements may support this hypothesis.

Conversion remains a term that is primarily used by the world's major faiths and by many new religious movements. It has no precise meaning, except to signify that the person or group now belongs to a faith in a new way, and that this belonging is marked by rituals, which in turn recognizes that some profound transformation has taken place. The origins of most of the world's major religions also lie in there being some sense in which their founders have been converted: from passivity to activity, and from one understanding of their faith to a new one, which is normally the cue for others to convert to this new understanding. Jesus himself came to 'fulfil' the law and the prophets, but in his ministry so radicalized the reading and understanding of the Jewish faith that his followers converted, albeit through a series of encounters and progressive evolution in their belief and practice.

At the beginning of the third millennium, conversion remains an important issue for churches, and for also non-Christian faiths. In the case of Christian faith, many mainstream denominations now focus as never before on evangelization, re-evangelization and on Christian education. With society increasingly moulded by more secular values, and with generations now being raised that have 'gospel amnesia', the task of conversion has become more demanding, and more imagination is required. Christian knowledge can no longer be assumed to be widespread and embedded within society. Correspondingly, many patterns of evangelism that were once avidly practised by churches are now being set aside in favour of longer-term programmes that seek to impart religious knowledge and Christian education within the public sphere. Often this is done through schools and other public institutions, and it also occurs in those contexts where the church is responsible for marking birth, marriage and death. However, such activity does not normally facilitate conversion; but it does begin to recreate the context in which churches might once again be able to talk about tradition, transformation and transcendence with some confidence.

Schools

At present, the churches normally have to settle for less than this, acknowledging that while many continue to affirm a belief in God, and may also value spirituality, they nonetheless choose not belong to churches or to other religious organizations. Persuading individuals and communities to convert ultimately requires the creation and nourishment of appropriate contexts. Ultimately, without conversion there is only organic growth, which quickly slows. This is often followed by a process of atrophy that many churches have experienced during the twentieth century.

Spirituality

Arguably, churches, in their response to this milieu of modernity, need to rediscover both their courage and confidence in the hope that they offer the world. It is that hope that has converted millions down the ages, and continues to do so in a new millennium in many parts of the world. For Christians, conversion is never a matter of turning to a programme, formula or organization for transformation and salvation. True conversion is to a person, namely Jesus; and it is a new or unique encounter with Jesus, as Paul on the road to Damascus would testify, that continues to be the central motif in any normative conversion narrative.

Journeys

New religious movements

MARTYN PERCY

E. S. Jones, *Conversion*, London: Hodder & Stoughton 1960; A. D. Nock, *Conversion*, London: OUP 1933; Martyn Percy (ed), *Previous Convictions: Conversion in the Present Day*, London: SPCK 2000; L. Rambo, *Understanding Religious Conversion*, New Haven CT: Yale University Press 1993

Coptic Christianity

The church in Egypt is a vibrant, growing, hospitable church. Accurate numbers are not available, but it is estimated that between 10 and 15 per cent of the population of Egypt is Christian, with the vast majority members of the Coptic Orthodox Church. It is the largest Christian community in the Middle East and has been growing in numbers and vitality during the last 50 years.

Christianity in the Middle East

The word Coptic means Egyptian, from the Greek *aiguptios*, which became in Arabic *qibt*, which in turn was pronounced Copt. It testifies to the proud claim of the Christian community that they trace their origins back to the ancient Egyptians, in contrast to Greeks or Arabs who arrived in later centuries – for the Copts, comparative newcomers.

Orthodox churches

Not only are Copts conscious of the antiquity of their civilization but they are also constantly reminded of the age of the church, which looks back to the earliest days of the Christian story. The young Jesus, Matthew's Gospel tells us, was taken by Mary and Joseph to Egypt to escape the wrath of King Herod, and while some might dispute the historicity of this episode, there is no reason why it should not have happened, since travel between Bethlehem and Egypt was not difficult. Certainly the Copts are in no doubt that the story is true, and many churches and other sites commemorate incidents in this journey.

p. 664

The foundation of the church took place, again according to an old tradition, within a decade or so of the resurrection, when Mark the Evangelist preached in Egypt. The huge new cathedral in the Abbasiya area of Cairo is dedicated to Mark, and contains his remains. It is also a centre for Coptic learning and culture of all kinds.

Resurrection
Monasticism

In the early Christian centuries the church thrived in the urban areas, especially Alexandria, and was mainly Greek speaking. A tradition of learning and teaching was already present, and by the end of the second century the catechetical school of Alexandria, a school at which distinguished teachers taught advanced theology, had been founded. Origen was one of its principals. Alexandria produced a distinctive type of theological thought which shaped the theology of the church. Among the theologians of Alexandria were Athanasius, who struggled to uphold what is now the traditional doctrine of the Trinity, and Cyril, who insisted on the unity of the person of Christ against those who distinguished the human and the divine natures too clearly. The thinking of these figures dominated the ecumenical councils of Nicaea (325) and Chalcedon (451), both summoned by the Byzantine emperor in Constantinople and held in the neighbourhood of the capital.

Church fathers

Trinity
Christology
Council

In the years following the Council of Chalcedon the church in Egypt became divided. There were many reasons for this. The doctrinal disagreement concerned the person of Christ, with the Egyptian church following the teaching of Cyril with its firm insistence on the single nature of Christ, sometimes called Monophysitism, and fearing that the Council of Chalcedon with its language of two natures and one person in two natures was compromising this vital principle. Then there was local opposition to the domination of Constantinople as well as a developing Coptic culture and language that encouraged a distinct Egyptian identity. Attempts to bridge the gap failed, and the conflicts were resolved from an unexpected quarter when the new military force in the region, the Arabs, invaded in 639 and conquered Alexandria in 642. At least some of the Egyptian church seems to have greeted the Arabs as liberators. The invasion completed the separation from the church of Constantinople. As a result the Coptic Orthodox Church is one of five churches – the others being the Armenian, Syrian, Ethiopian and South Indian churches – which are Orthodox churches but separated from the other national Orthodox churches of Russia, Greece and elsewhere. These are sometimes called Monophysite, but this title is to be avoided since it has come to refer to a heretical teaching that the Copts do not hold. The name 'non-Chalcedonian' is to be preferred. The vast majority of Egyptian Christians are Coptic Orthodox, with a much smaller number still loyal to the Greek Orthodox Church, which retains its relationship with Constantinople. Only now, after 1500 years of separation, are discussions under way to achieve reunion between these two families of Orthodox churches.

Perhaps the greatest gift of the Egyptians to the worldwide church is monasticism. The growth of the monasteries is closely allied to the emergence of a truly Coptic as opposed to Greek Christianity. Around 250 preaching in the Coptic language began, and in 251 Antony set out to live the ascetic life in the desert. It was a simple life of solitude, fasting, prayer and a struggle against the devils, and was described by Athanasius of Alexandria in his *Life of Antony*, which, it has been argued, is the most influential book in the history of the church after the Bible. Antony's example was followed by that of Pachomius, who founded several communities, which, unlike Antony's informal groups of hermits, lived in regulated communities, called coenobia. Around the same time Shenute of Atripe became abbot of the White Monastery near modern Akhmim, which in spite of the harsh regime that the founder maintained attracted huge numbers of local peasants, estimated at one point as 2200 monks and 1800 nuns. From Shenute's communities a Coptic literature emerged. Monastic life was developing more or less simultaneously in Syria and Palestine, but the monasteries of Egypt were pre-eminent.

Since the Arab invasions of 639–42, Egypt has been ruled by Muslims and the church has been a minority, sometimes persecuted and always discriminated against. The Copts are conscious of the long tradition of martyrdom. The Coptic calendar starts to count the years, not with the birth of Christ, but with the accession of the Emperor Diocletian (284–303), which initiated a period of fierce persecution, and is called the 'first year of the martyrs'. Persecution has been intermittent, but remains part of the experience of the church. Today reports of the killing of Copts by Islamic fundamentalist groups are distressingly frequent occurrences. It is remarkable that the church has survived these pressures and sufferings and still constitutes over 10 per cent of the total population. It is even more remarkable that in the second half of the twentieth century there has been a dramatic revival.

The features of the modern Coptic Church are continuous with the characteristics of its early greatness. There have been two outstanding leaders, or popes, as they are known. Cyril VI (1959–71) was a monk venerated for his holy life, who developed the role of the church in the ecumenical movement, and who had good relationships with the leadership of the day. By contrast, under Shenouda III (1971–) relationships with the government deteriorated and were reflected in the church. These resulted in his confinement under house arrest from 1981–5. He is a popular preacher whose weekly addresses draw several thousands of listeners.

As in Greek Alexandria, education is valued, with strong Sunday schools, a vibrant youth movement and a tradition of teaching in the parishes which has enabled a growing sense of community and Coptic identity. This has developed in part in response to growing Muslim radicalism. Also the monasteries have grown. The monastic revival is especially associated with the figure of Matta el Meskin, or Matthew the Poor, a pharmacist who became a monk in 1948, then a hermit, then the spiritual father of the monastery of St Macarius, north of Cairo. Monasteries combine, as they always have done, a strict ascetic life with many monks living in nearby hermitages. These form thriving communities, developing desert agriculture among other activities. Numbers are constantly changing, but the larger monasteries have well over 200 members.

Large Coptic communities have grown up in many parts of Western Europe and in the USA. In spite of an uncertain and volatile political situation in Egypt, the church demonstrates considerable vitality both in Egypt and in the West, with the riches of its tradition and culture becoming better known and valued.

JOHN BINNS

Bat Ye'or, *The Decline of Eastern Christianity under Islam, from Jihad to Dhimmitude*, Rutherford, NJ: Fairleigh Dickinson University Press 1996; D. Chitty, *The Desert a City. An Introduction to the Study of Egyptian and Palestinian Monasticism under the Christian Empire*, Oxford: Blackwell 1966; W. Dalrymple, *From the Holy Mountain*, London: Flamingo Books 1997; Matthew the Poor, *The Communion of Love*, New York: St Vladimir's University Press 1984; J. Watson, *Among the Copts*, Brighton: Sussex Academic Press 2001; B. Watterson, *Coptic Egypt*, Edinburgh: Scottish Academic Press 1988

Council

The Second Vatican Council, announced quite unexpectedly by Pope John XXIII barely three months after he had become Pope, and held between 1962 and 1965, is a great landmark of the twentieth century, not only for the Roman Catholic Church, but also for Christianity at a whole. 2860 Catholic bishops, accompanied by theological experts, and joined by non-Catholic observers, produced a collection of documents which brought far-ranging changes to the way in which Roman Catholics thought, acted and worshipped, and how they related to those of other faiths and the secular world.

Ecumenical movement

Councils and other assemblies have shaped and characterized Christianity since its very first days. Councils and council-like structures are common in most Christian churches. They go by different names: synod, assembly, conference, convention, etc. They operate at the congregational, local, regional and national levels. In them the church, embodied in certain representative members, gathers to deal with issues of major importance. Alone among the Christian churches, the Roman Catholic Church is organized and unified on a worldwide basis, so that a council can make decisions binding upon the whole church (such a council is called 'ecumenical' = worldwide). However, difficulties of communication and travel have made ecumenical councils rare in the church's history, and Catholic scholars list only 21 such councils in the 2000 years of the church's existence. Because what was to become the Roman Catholic Church divided from what was to become the Orthodox Church in the eleventh century, only the seven of these held before that time are universally recognized as truly ecumenical.

What is known as the 'apostolic council' is reported in the New Testament (Acts 15); this was clearly a special event and not comparable to subsequent councils. In the next two centuries synods and councils were held on a number of occasions, bringing together bishops of different areas to resolve controversial issues which threatened the unity of the church: these could be theological, disciplinary or practical, like the date of Easter.

Calendar

Gregory the Great likened the first four ecumenical councils to the four Gospels in their importance. In fact

COUNCILS OF THE CHURCH

Traditionally, 7 councils are held to be ecumenical, i.e. councils of the universal church, by both Eastern and Western churches; the Roman Catholic Church recognizes another 14 councils as having ecumenical authority. These 21 councils are:

1. Nicaea (325): Convened by the Emperor Constantine and traditionally attended by 318 bishops. Its prime aim was to bring unity to the church by dealing with the controversy surrounding Arius, who argued that God the Son was subordinate to God the Father. It produced a creed (though this is not what is commonly referred to as the 'Nicene' Creed).

2. Constantinople (381): Convened by the Emperor Theodosius I to effect a final resolution of the Arian controversy, which Nicaea had not settled. It endorsed the teaching of the Council of Nicaea and issued a creed (the classic creed of Christianity known as the 'Nicene' Creed).

3. Ephesus (431): Convened by the Emperor Theodosius II in the hope of settling the controversy surrounding Nestorius, who was thought to teach that there were two separate persons in the incarnate Christ. The council had a troubled course. It was convened by Cyril, Bishop of Alexandria, and excommunicated Nestorius before Nestorius' supporters or the papal legates appeared. It gave formal approval to the title *Theotokos*, 'Mother of God', for Mary. When the Syrian bishops who supported Nestorius arrived they had a rival meeting and excommunicated Cyril. They and Cyril were reconciled two years later.

4. Chalcedon (451): Convened by the Emperor Marcian to deal with the controversy surrounding Eutyches, who at the opposite extreme to Nestorius was accused of confusing the two natures in Christ. It produced the Chalcedonian Definition, a classic statement of belief in the person of Christ.

5. Constantinople II (553): Convened by the Emperor Justinian I to resolve the controversy over the so-called 'Three Chapters', three works sympathetic to Nestorius which had been condemned by the emperor in an edict ten years previously, in the face of opposition from the West. The Three Chapters were condemned and the authors, Theodore of Mopsuestia, Theodoret of Cyrrhus and Ibas of Edessa, anathematized, i.e., expelled from the church.

6. Constantinople III (680–1): Convened by the Emperor Constantine IV to deal with monothelitism, the view that there was only one will in Christ. It affirmed that there were two wills in Christ and reaffirmed the Chalcedonian Definition.

Iconoclasm

7. Nicaea II (786–7): Convened by the Empress Irene to end the iconoclastic controversy. It decreed that the veneration of images is a matter of respect and honour, but absolute adoration is reserved for God. It was the last universally recognized ecumenical council.

8. Constantinople IV (869): The first council to be recognized as ecumenical only by the Western church. It was convened by the Emperor Basil I to condemn Photius, Patriarch of Constantinople. Photius had clashed with the Pope, who had refused to recognize him; in return he had issued an encyclical against some Roman practices and later instigated a council which excommunicated the Pope (these events are referred to as the Photian Schism). The condemnation of Photius brought only temporary peace between East and West.

9. Lateran I (1123): The first council to be held at Rome, in the Lateran Palace, convened by Pope Callistus II. It abolished the right claimed by lay rulers to confer on bishops and abbots the ring and crosier which were the symbols of their office (the so-called Investiture Controversy).

Investiture Controversy

10. Lateran II (1139): Convened by Innocent II to condemn the teachings of Arnold of Brescia, a reformer who attacked the worldliness of the church and sought to revive the ideal of apostolic poverty.

11. Lateran III (1179): Convened by Alexander III. It restricted the right to elect the Pope to a college of cardinals, among whom there had to be a two-thirds majority.

12. Lateran IV (1215): Convened by Innocent III. The most important of the Lateran Councils, which marks the culmination of papal power. Its decrees were extremely pragmatic; all Christians were required to go to confession and receive communion once a year; strict measures were taken against heretics; Jews had to wear special clothing. The foundation of new religious orders was banned. The council also legislated for crusades.

Crusades

13. Lyons I (1245): Convened by Innocent IV to deal with what he called 'the five wounds of the church': the degeneration of the church, the failure to recapture the Holy Land, the invasion of Hungary by the Tatars, the schism with the Eastern church, and the conflict between the church and the emperor. The council excommunicated the emperor and ordered the preaching of a new crusade, but this came to nothing.

14. Lyons II (1274): Convened by Gregory X to win back the Holy Land, bring about reunion with the Eastern church, and reform the church. Many famous theologians attended; Thomas Aquinas died on the way there. In fact the Eastern church was required to capitulate over its differences with the Western church, including the acceptance of the insertion of the Latin word *filioque* into the creed: the Holy Spirit proceeds from the Father 'and the Son'.

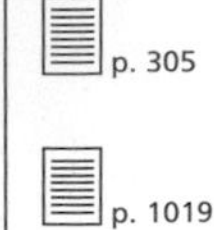

p. 305

15. Vienne (1311–12): Convened by Clement V, the first of the Avignon popes, to deal with the Templars, who were accused of heresy and immorality, and to promote a new crusade. The Templars were suppressed and King Philip IV of France promised to go on a crusade within six years. The council also issued decrees against the Beguines and Beghards, who were (wrongly) accused of immorality. More positively it made provision for the teaching of oriental languages in five universities to further missionary work.

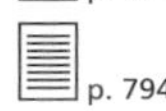

p. 1019

p. 794

16. Constance (1414–18): Convened by John XXIII, one of three popes in office at the same time (the others were Gregory XII and Benedict XII) to end what is known as the 'Great Schism', when there were rival centres of authority for Western Christianity in Avignon and Rome. It famously issued the decree *Haec Sancta* ('This holy synod of Constance'), which is the culmination of conciliarism. The decree states that the council is above the Pope, and on this basis the council resolved the schism by deposing John XXIII and Benedict XIII (Gregory XII resigned). (Because John XXIII was never officially recognized as pope, the most famous twentieth-century pope felt free to use his name.) The council called for general councils to be held regularly (at intervals of at most ten years), but this never came about. It also acted against John Wyclif, ordering his body to be removed from its burial place in consecrated ground, and infamously condemning to be burnt at the stake Jan Hus, the Bohemian reformer, to whom it had given safe conduct.

17. Basle (1431–49): Convened in Basle by Martin V to carry forward the work of the Council of Constance. Another troubled council. Martin V died before it met and Eugenius IV dissolved it. The council refused to accept this, and reaffirmed the position of Constance that the general council is superior to a pope. In 1433 the Pope reversed his former decision, but the council continued to be hostile to him and issued decrees relating to papal elections and the role of cardinals. It also settled the Hussite question by making concessions to the Bohemians, against the papal position. In 1437, a dispute with the Pope over the location of a proposed council with the Orthodox Church led to a major split: the council wanted Basle, but the Pope and the Orthodox wanted somewhere in Italy. Eugenius transferred the council to Ferrara, and subsequently to Florence, but many members remained in Basle and excommunicated the Pope; they were driven out in 1448 and ended the council in Lausanne in 1449.

18. Lateran V (1512–17): Convened by Julius II. A relatively insignificant council, concerned mainly with disciplinary decrees. For this reason it was condemned by Luther as having nothing to say about the Christian faith.

19. Trent (1545–63): Plans for a council to reform the Roman Catholic Church in the face of the challenge of the Protestant Reformation began as early as 1537, but it was not until 1545 that the council finally met in Trent, convened by Paul III. All in all it met for 50 months under three popes: Paul III (1545–7), Julius III (1551–2) and Pius IV (1562–3). The suspensions of the council were caused by political tensions, notably between the Pope and the Emperor. It did great work in reforming both dogma and discipline. In dogma it worked on those doctrines which were attacked by the Protestants: the authority of the Bible and the misuse of scripture; the role of tradition; original sin and the doctrine of justification; the doctrine of the sacraments; and the doctrine of purgatory. Its disciplinary measures were aimed at orientating the church on pastoral care, the clergy being there to preach the gospel and dispense the sacraments. Here it emphasized the role of bishops, as representatives of the Pope. Immensely influential, though perhaps not going as far as had been hoped, the council shaped Roman Catholic life until Vatican II.

20. Vatican I (1869–70): Convened by Pius IX, it was intended to deal with a large range of subjects relating to both faith and morals. However, the outbreak of the Franco-Prussian war on 18 July 1870 led to its adjournment, and the moral issues were not discussed. The council began by preparing a document on modern errors and discussing church discipline and canon law. Before its closure it went on to decree the infallibility of the Pope when speaking ex cathedra, i.e. with the full formal authority of his office.

p. 291

21. Vatican II (1962–5): Convened by John XXIII, who died in 1963, and continued by Paul VI. The documents it produced brought far-reaching changes to the life and thought of Roman Catholics. They led, for example, to the replacement of Latin by the vernacular in worship and communion in both kinds for the laity, a doctrine of the church as the people of God, and a changed attitude to other Christians, those of other faiths and the secular world.

The First Vatican Council, 1870, by an unknown artist

there is a slight difference between them: Nicaea and Constantinople settled fundamental theological questions once and for all; the positions laid down at Ephesus and Chalcedon did not resolve all the controversy in every region of the church.

The councils from Nicaea in 325 to Constantinople IV in 869 were all held in the East and were convened by the emperor. Beginning with Lateran I in 1123 they were convened by the Pope. The Fourth Lateran Council in 1215 was totally dominated by Pope Innocent III.

However, in the fifteenth century, when the Roman Catholic Church had rival centres of power in Rome and Avignon and at one point there were three claimants to the papal throne, 'conciliarism' became appealing. This theory maintained that the authority of a council was superior to that of the Pope. Therefore, a council could send any false claimants packing. It could also depose a corrupt or incompetent pope and elect a new one. 'Conciliarism' was short-lived, although the Second Vatican Council affirmed the corporate authority of bishops exercised in union with the Pope. Thus, the Roman Catholic Church holds that an ecumenical council is the supreme authority in the church only so long as it is convened by and presided over by the Pope (or his representative), and its decrees and regulations are approved by him.

Papacy

Roman Catholic Church

JON NILSON

N. P. Tanner, *The Councils of the Church. A Short History*, New York: Crossroad 2001; *Decrees of the Ecumenical Councils* (2 vols), Washington DC and London: Georgetown University Press 1990

Counter-Reformation

It is difficult to comprehend the Roman Catholic Church today without some understanding of the process of

THE DOCUMENTS OF VATICAN II

The Second Vatican Council (1962–5) was a turning point and defining mark in twentieth-century Roman Catholicism. It approved and issued a series of documents on a variety of questions. Each bears a Latin name which, as is customary with official Roman Catholic documents, consists of the opening words of the document.

The Constitution on the Sacred Liturgy *Sacrosanctum concilium*
Decree on the Means of Social Communication *Inter mirifica*
Dogmatic Constitution on the Church *Lumen gentium*
Decree on the Catholic Eastern Churches *Orientalium ecclesiarum*
Decree on Ecumenism *Unitatis redintegratio*
Decree on the Pastoral Office of Bishops in the Church *Christus dominus*
Decree on the Up-to-date Renewal of Religious Life *Perfectae caritatis*
Decree on the Training of Priests *Optatam totius*
Decree on Christian Education *Gravissimum educationis*
Declaration on the Relation of the Church to Non-Christian Religions *Nostra aetate*
Dogmatic Constitution on Divine Revelation *Dei verbum*
Decree on the Apostolate of Lay People *Apostolicam actuositatem*
Declaration on Religious Liberty *Dignitatis humanae*
Declaration on the Church's Missionary Activity *Ad gentes divinitus*
Decree on the Ministry and Life of Priests *Presbyterorum ordinis*
Pastoral Constitution on the Church in the Modern World *Gaudium et spes*

Austin Flannery (ed), *The Basic Sixteen Documents of Vatican II*, Dublin: Dominican Publications 2003; Walter M. Abbott (ed), *Documents of Vatican II: In a New and Definitive Translation with Commentaries and Notes by Catholic, Protestant and Orthodox Authorities*, New York: Crossroad 1990

transformation Catholicism underwent during the later sixteenth and seventeenth centuries. By convention, this process is known as the Counter-Reformation, though some scholars prefer Catholic Reformation, in order to make the point that it was more than just a negative reaction to the threat of Protestantism, and that early shoots of renewal could be detected before anyone had heard of Martin Luther.

It is hard to exaggerate the sense of crisis among Catholic leaders in the middle years of the sixteenth century. The spread of 'heresy' seemed unstoppable. England and the Scandinavian kingdoms had broken with Rome, Protestantism was making strong inroads in France and the Netherlands, and also (especially among the nobility) in Poland, Austria and Hungary. Even the Catholic heartlands of Italy and Spain seemed under threat. Worst of all was the situation in Germany, where by the mid-1550s Bavaria was the solitary significant Catholic state, and barely a quarter of Germans were still Catholic. There was widespread agreement that what was needed was a General Council, to reform the abuses which had fuelled Protestantism, and to co-ordinate the Catholic response. Papal anxieties about this caused long delays; in the fifteenth century, a series of councils had promoted the doctrine of 'conciliarism', asserting that their own authority trumped that of the Pope. But Paul III finally convened a council in the north Italian town of Trent in 1545. It sat in three sessions, 1545–9, 1551–2 and 1562–3, through five pontificates, and its achievements were momentous.

Some, including the Holy Roman Emperor Charles V, had hoped that the council would make concessions to the Lutherans to restore religious unity in Germany. But the early sessions of Trent were largely concerned with countering Protestant doctrines and providing definitive statements of Catholic belief on such matters as justification (condemning Luther's notion of justification by faith alone), the importance of good works, the number of the sacraments (seven, to the Protestants' two), the equal authority of church tradition with scripture. This greater doctrinal clarity set the boundaries of Catholic orthodoxy for centuries to come, and made it easier to launch a counter-attack against Protestant positions.

Holy Roman empire
Protestantism
Martin Luther
Justification
Sacraments
Tradition

Later sessions of Trent were more concerned with reform: seminaries were to be set up in each diocese to train new priests, and bishops were ordered to reside in their dioceses. There was a fierce row about whether such residence was required 'by the law of God', raising the question whether bishops held their office directly from God, or only as delegates of the Pope. In fact, Trent fudged this crucial issue. Only in the twentieth century did the Second Vatican Council affirm the principle of episcopal 'collegiality'. There is no doubt, however, that papal

Council

authority emerged much enhanced from the Council of Trent. Pius IV (1559–65) confirmed its decrees, reserving to himself their interpretation, and his successor Pius V (1566–72) undertook some important tasks the council had left undone, such as standardizing the text of the mass – the 'Tridentine rite' beloved of modern Catholic traditionalists ('Tridentine' is the adjective meaning 'of Trent').

Wars of religion
p. 345
Vatican

The implementation of Trent's decrees went hand-in-hand with an overhaul of the Roman Curia (central administration), which organized cardinals in so-called congregations to oversee such matters as liturgy, the Inquisition, the Index of prohibited books, and the 'propagation of the faith' (origin of the word propaganda). The Vatican began to take on characteristics of a modern state, and the cardinals seemed less like squabbling medieval nobles and more like papal administrators. The growing authority of the papacy was not just institutional, but moral. In contrast to lax and corrupt Renaissance popes, a series of austere figures occupied the papal throne in the later sixteenth century: Pius V (canonized 1712), Gregory XIII (diplomat turned reformer) and Sixtus V (an ascetic Franciscan friar).

Saint
Religious orders

The greater vitality exhibited by the papacy was mirrored at lower levels in the church. There were many examples of a new type of pastorally-minded reforming bishop. The model was Charles Borromeo, Archbishop of Milan 1564–84 and canonized in 1610. Equally significant was the appearance of new religious orders, reacting against the perceived laxness of late medieval monks, friars and nuns. The Capuchins, for example, were a break-away branch of the Franciscans, aiming to recapture the original ideals of Francis of Assisi.

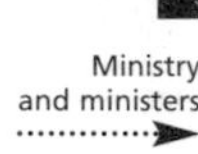

Ministry and ministers

Without doubt, the most important of the new orders was the Society of Jesus, founded by the Spanish former-soldier Ignatius Loyola in 1534, and ratified by the Pope in 1540. The Jesuits have been called the 'shock troops' of the Counter-Reformation, and they were its biggest success story: by the early seventeenth century there were 13,000 Jesuits in thirteen provinces across Europe. Combining the discipline of the traditional religious orders with activism and flexibility, the Jesuits became educators and preachers against heresy. Local bishops often distrusted them, but they enjoyed the support of the papacy. (Jesuits took a special fourth vow of loyalty to the Pope.)

Pilgrimage

It was not just men who felt the call to new forms of religious life. Orders of nuns such as the Ursulines and Visitandines were founded with the aim of nursing the poor and the sick. But the authorities were uneasy with the concept of public female ministry, and in the seventeenth century strict 'enclosure' was forced on these orders. When the Englishwoman Mary Ward tried to set up an order of activist nuns on the model of the Jesuits she ended up imprisoned by the Inquisition. Catholic women made important contributions to the Counter-Reformation, but from behind convent walls and through the interior life of the spirit. The mystical writings of the Spanish Carmelite nun Teresa of Avila (died 1582, canonized 1622) stand, with the *Spiritual Exercises* of Ignatius Loyola, as the greatest devotional works of the era.

By the middle of the seventeenth century, much of the territory lost to Protestantism in Central Europe had been regained, though this owed as much to Catholic military successes in the Thirty Years War as to missionary effort. In some ways, however, this can be seen as the starting point rather than the conclusion of Catholic reform. Leaders of the Counter-Reformation did not merely wish for formal allegiance. They wanted a new type of Catholic lay person, better educated in the faith, more likely to attend mass and go to confession regularly, less prone to superstition and participation in riotous local festivals. Some scholars see the Counter-Reformation as a campaign of mass indoctrination on an unprecedented scale, a reform of popular religion that paralleled the Protestant Reformation as much as it opposed it. Yet how successful it was in these aims is open to question.

Folk beliefs about fairies and witches persisted alongside orthodox Catholicism in parts of rural Spain, Italy and Ireland into modern times. There is also considerable evidence that though Catholic reformers presented the saints as examples of heroic virtue, models to be emulated, many ordinary lay people continued to regard them as they had in the Middle Ages – as powerful supernatural beings whose job was to effect healing. The success of the Counter-Reformation on the ground depended very much on the abilities of the local clergy, but the establishment of seminaries was an extremely slow process, not achieved in many places until the eighteenth century. Even then, seminary-educated priests often found it difficult to relate to the concerns of rustic parishioners.

It seems, in fact, that the Counter-Reformation was most successful where it made accommodations with the culture of the people, rather than merely rejecting it. The Jesuits (and other orders, like Vincent de Paul's Lazarists) were in the forefront here, in missions undertaken in rural France and Italy. Villages would be evangelized by groups of missioners, employing a full range of theatrical techniques such as plays, processions, melodramatic preaching – appeals to the senses and the emotions characteristic of medieval religious culture. There was success, too, especially in Germany, in building on the tradition of a 'sacred landscape', encouraging the revival of popular pilgrimage to holy sites, where, for example, consecrated hosts were said to have bled.

The question of the degree to which Tridentine Catholicism could accommodate itself to local and traditional cultures was at its most pertinent outside

Europe. For it was during the Counter-Reformation that Catholicism became for the first time a truly global religion. Franciscan and Dominican friars followed in the footsteps of the Spanish *conquistadores* in the New World, and the Jesuits too were soon on the scene, in Africa and Asia as well as the Americas. It seemed that God was providing a plentiful harvest of new souls, to compensate for those lost in the winter of the Reformation in Europe. There were astonishing successes – thousands of indigenous people were baptized in the Philippines, and in Mexico and Peru. But there were disappointments, too. As the missionaries became aware, many 'converts' practised a 'syncretistic' religion, blending the most appealing elements of the new religion with their ancestral practices. Periodic crack-downs on 'idolatry' in the Latin American colonies provoked resistance and rebellion. In Japan, missionaries created a thriving local church without the assistance of European arms, but Japanese Catholicism was virtually extinguished by a ruthless persecution in the early seventeenth century. Catholicism made less impact in the ancient civilizations of India and China, though some Jesuits made progress with Chinese élites by adopting Mandarin dress and teaching that Christianity was compatible with Confucian practices like ancestor veneration. Rival missionaries feared the baby was being thrown out with the bathwater, and 'Chinese Rites' were condemned by the papacy in the early eighteenth century.

A movement for reform and modernization, yet deeply rooted in tradition, the Counter-Reformation wore an often repressive face. But this was balanced by an extraordinary creativity, in devotional expression and in the artistic achievements of the Baroque, as well as by many examples of individual sanctity. An impulse towards standardization and centralization was tested by the ever greater complexity and diversity of the Catholic world, within and beyond Europe. For good or ill, the Counter-Reformation made the modern Catholic Church, in all its contradictions.

PETER MARSHALL

📖 J. Delumeau, *Catholicism between Luther and Voltaire*, London: Burns & Oates and Philadelphia: Westminster Press 1977; M. A. Mullett, *The Catholic Reformation*, London and New York: Routledge 1999; J. W. O'Malley, *The First Jesuits*, Cambridge, MA 1993; R. Po-Chia Hsia, *The World of Catholic Renewal 1540–1770*, Cambridge: CUP 1998

Covenant

Many people today will come across the word covenant only if they are signing a legal agreement or making a donation to a charity. This technical use of the word obscures its importance in the Bible, where it emphasizes God's personal relationship with human beings. The word is used in various senses in the Bible and in Christian thought. In recent years, an important issue in Jewish-Christian relations has been the relationship of the 'old' and 'new' covenants.

Mission
Bible
Judaism and Christianity

In the Hebrew Bible the word usually translated 'covenant' is *berit*; in fact *berit* has a much wider range of meanings, depending on the context; it can mean 'promise', 'agreement' or just 'relationship'. Although the Hebrew Bible speaks of many different covenants, the word *berit* is never used in the plural. Covenants may be between God and individuals, such as Noah or Abraham (Genesis 9.8–11; 15.18–19 and 17.1–14); between God and Israel (Exodus 19–24; 34 and Deuteronomy 28–31); and between two human individuals, such as David and Jonathan (1 Samuel 18.3; 20.8; 23.18) – here the agreement may be given added solemnity by being made 'before the Lord' (1 Samuel 20.8; 23.18). Breaking a marriage covenant was therefore seen as an offence against God as well as against one's partner (Proverbs 2.17; Malachi 2.14). Above all *berit*, drawing on the ancient Near Eastern language of diplomacy and contract, compares the relationship of God with his people to human relationships as they are expressed in oaths, gifts and obligations.

Covenants to which God is party are of three types. In the first type, God freely makes a commitment. For example, God promises Noah that there will never again be 'a flood to destroy the earth' (Genesis 9.11). Secondly, God may impose an obligation on others, perhaps in return for a promise. For example, God gives Abraham the land of Canaan and demands that he and his descendants should 'be circumcised' (Genesis 17.1–14). Thirdly, the parties to the covenant may mutually agree certain commitments. At Sinai, the Israelites, to whom God promised the land of Canaan, freely affirmed that 'everything the Lord has said we will do' (Exodus 24.3).

Architecture

For Jews, the ideas of covenant and being a chosen people are closely related. Circumcision affirms a boy's entry 'into the covenant of Abraham our father'. Some rabbis stressed that God's special relationship with Israel in no way limited God's concern for all people. They referred to God's covenant at creation with Adam and all people (Ecclesiasticus 17) and God's covenant with Noah (Genesis 9. 9). In this covenant God allowed human beings to kill animals for food, but warned that they should not consume the blood and that God would demand satisfaction for the killing of another human being. The rabbis developed this to suggest that Gentiles (the children of Noah) were required to observe seven commandments that included the setting up of law courts and the prohibition of idolatry. The requirements imposed on Gentiles by the early church may reflect the laws of Noah (Acts 15.29).

Sacrifice

In the Hebrew Bible sacrifices are offered in connection with the making of a covenant; at the lawgiving on Mount Sinai Moses pours blood from sacrificial animals on the altar and on the people before reading to them the book of the covenant. He refers to this as the 'blood of the covenant' and this image also comes to be used in the New Testament, except that there the victim whose blood is shed is Jesus (Hebrews 10). The synoptic Gospels and Paul Paul also relate the covenant to the blood or death of Jesus (Mark 14.24; Matthew 26.28; 1 Corinthians 11.25). Eucharist Thinking of the Last Supper as a Passover meal, they link God's rescue of the Israelites to Jesus' rescue of his Atonement followers from sin and compare his death to the slaughter of the Passover lamb (1 Corinthians 5.7). The Greek word used in the Septuagint translation of the Hebrew Bible to render *berit* is *diatheke*, which usually means last will or testament (Galatians 3.15ff.), another reason why writers in the New Testament (a term which, literally translated, is in fact New Covenant) could relate the new covenant of which they speak so closely to the Last Supper and death of Jesus.

New Testament material about the relationship of the covenant with Israel and the covenant in Jesus Christ is Jesus ambiguous. Jesus said that he had come to fulfil and not to abolish the Law and Prophets (Matthew 5.17). New Testament writers refer positively to the covenant with Abraham (Acts 3.25), but sometimes the old covenant of the letter is compared unfavourably to the new covenant of the Spirit (2 Corinthians 3.6; Galatians 4.24ff.). The letter to the Hebrews speaks of Jesus Christ as the 'mediator of a new covenant' (9.15), which 'is superior to the old one' (Hebrew 8.6).

p. 1152

This sense of the superiority of the new covenant has been common in Christian thinking. It has led many Jews and some Christians today to avoid the term Old Testament (i.e. Old Covenant). For many centuries, the church – in a doctrine known as supersessionism – claimed to be the 'new Israel' and to have taken over the promises made in the first, old covenant. In the twentieth century, however, other Christians, recognizing that centuries of Christian anti-Judaism caused much Jewish suffering and was a fatal preparation for the Holocaust, have affirmed that the covenant with the Jewish people is unbroken. In 1980, Pope John Paul II spoke of the people of God of the Old Covenant 'which has never been revoked'. A Church of Scotland report says: 'Paul affirms that our Christian calling in no way abrogates the divine election of the Jewish people.'

The traditional view that the first covenant has been replaced by the new covenant calls in question God's faithfulness to God's promises and ignores the continuing spiritual richness of Jewish life. It also presumes that Jesus was a critic of Judaism, whereas many scholars today speak of him as 'a faithful Jew'. It may also reflect a misunderstanding of Paul's teaching, although there is continuing debate on what Paul meant in Romans 9–11, where he dismisses the view that God had rejected his people (Romans 11.1).

p. 302

Some Christians maintain the traditional view that the covenant in Christ has replaced the covenant with the Jewish people and that Christians should therefore engage in missionary activity to convert Jews. Others hold that through Christ Gentiles are admitted into the one covenant, but this view is criticized because it fails to recognize the distinctiveness of Christianity and does not make room for Jews who convert to Christianity. The so-called double covenant theory seeks to address this, claiming that there are two distinct, although related, covenants. This implies that there are at least two 'peoples of God'. Some Christians are worried that this calls in question the uniqueness of their faith; others, such as the Korean theologian Choan Seng Song and the American theologian Rosemary Radford Ruether, see no reason why Jews and Christians should claim a privileged position. They suggest that the idea of covenant should be extended to other faith communities. Such an extension of the term may, however, drain it of meaning and not make sense to members of other religions. Some Christians see the return of many Jews to Israel as a sign that God is faithful to his covenant, but many Christians do not attach a theological meaning to the creation of the state of Israel and would base their attitude on international law.

Some traditional Jews see the state of Israel in religious terms, but many citizens of Israel are secular. Some recent Jewish thinkers, such as Richard Rubenstein, have also questioned the concept of covenant, arguing that the Holocaust showed that God was unable or unwilling to meet his side of the agreement by protecting his people. Irving Greenberg suggests that after the Holocaust there is now a new 'voluntary covenant' initiated by the Jewish people in response to a divine invitation to share in the work of redeeming the world.

In Christian thought, several Reformation writers gave particular attention to the idea of covenant. John Calvin affirmed the continuity of the old and new covenants, which were so alike that 'in reality the two are actually one and the same'. The notion of the covenant helped Calvinists to reconcile the sovereignty of God with the human desire for assurance. Covenant theology (also known as 'federal theology', from the Latin for covenant, *foedus*) linked a first covenant with Adam, that Adam broke; however, a second covenant (from eternity) gave the elect forgiveness and eternal life on the basis of Christ's sacrifice. Covenant theology underlies the Westminster Confession of 1647.

The term covenant was also used in the religious and political sphere, especially in Scotland, where the National Covenant of 1638 united opposition to Charles I's attempt to impose a Scottish prayer book. The alliance of Scottish Presbyterians and English Parliamentarians, established in 1643, was called a Solemn League and Covenant. Concepts of covenant were also applied by Puritans in establishing settlements in the New World.

The idea of covenant has been revived in ecumenical circles. In 1964 the Nottingham Faith and Order Conference of the British Council of Churches adopted *Proposals for a Covenant*. More recently, the Church of England and the Methodist Church have entered into a covenant.

The term covenant has also been used of the individual Christian's relationship to God. In some churches baptism is regarded as a covenant between God and the believer (cf. 1 Peter 3.21). John Wesley introduced a New Year Covenant service, in which the believer rededicated his or her life to Christ, 'accepting with joy the yoke of obedience'. Marriage has also been seen as a covenant between two people made in the presence of God (cf. Malachi 2.14). The marriage service in the Book of Common Prayer includes a prayer that the couple will 'perform and keep the vow and covenant betwixt them made'.

This use of the word covenant in describing the individual believer's relationship with God, at a time when the word is most common in a legal context, is an important reminder that the Bible uses covenant to speak of God's personal relationship with individual and a people. The God of the Bible is to be thought of in personal terms and is a God who can treat a human being as a friend (2 Chronicles 20.7).

MARCUS BRAYBROOKE

Tony Bayfield (ed), *He Kissed Him and They Wept*, London: SCM Press 2001; Marcus Braybrooke, *Christian-Jewish Dialogue: The Next Steps*, London: SCM Press 2000; John Bright, *Covenant and Promise*, Philadelphia: Westminster Press 1976 and London: SCM Press 1977; E. W. Nicholson, *God and His People: Covenant Theology in the Old Testament*, Oxford: Clarendon Press 1986; David Novak, *Jewish-Christian Dialogue: A Jewish Justification*, Oxford: OUP 1989; H. Watt, *Recalling the Scottish Covenants*, London: Thomas Nelson 1946

Creation

The word creation is used both of the world as such (here it is synonymous with reality, or nature) and of the moment of creation (origination), if such a moment can be defined. It expresses fundamental ideas about both God and the world.

God

God

Talk of creation is a way of articulating the difference between God and the world – the one is creator, the other creation. These are not only different, but stand in an asymmetrical relationship: God transcends (surpasses) the world; furthermore, as the world's creator, God is prior to the world.

Puritans ←

Ecumenical movement ←

In Christianity, talk of creation asserts that God is the sole source of reality. It thus stands in contrast to polytheistic views and other creation myths. It opposes especially the idea that the world is due to both a good and an evil divine principle (dualism). If God is sole creator, there is no need for any raw material, in contrast to the Platonic tradition, where a demiurge is supposed to form the world out of raw material (as in Plato's *Timaeus*). This understanding of God's full freedom is articulated especially in the doctrine of *creatio ex nihilo*, creation out of nothing.

←

Marriage ←

The world

World

In respect of the world, the doctrine of creation implies that the world is not autonomous and does not explain itself. However, this need not exclude the idea that phenomena within the world may be explicable on the basis of earlier conditions and general regularities. Seeing the world as creation does not imply that the world is totally unintelligible, except for a theological understanding; however, it does indicate that the world is not ultimately intelligible without reference to God.

That the world is God's creation, with God understood as loving, implies that the world is valued positively. The world is not an illusion, but real. Nor is it a prison, with spiritually significant aspects of existence (say a 'soul') destined for some other reality. Rather, the material, created world is the place where human beings and God are in relation. By describing the world as 'creation' the Christian tradition connects facts and values, an 'is' and an 'ought', even though modern philosophy has challenged, with good arguments, the argumentative adequacy of such connections.

The beauty and intricacy displayed in nature has impressed people. Quite a few have been puzzled by the existence of the world and its regularities. Such experiences have been articulated in some of the 'arguments for the existence of God', especially cosmological arguments (from a beginning) and arguments from design or purpose. Arguments based upon beauty, order and design can be challenged by pointing to contrasting experiences with imperfection, inefficiency or cruelty, and to alternative ways of understanding the existence and qualities

p. 507

of natural order (e.g. that of David Hume, 1711–76). The most significant set of alternative explanations has come from science. Though such experiences and the possibility of such alternative explanations block any direct argument from features of the world to God, they do not rule out seeing the world as God's creation.

Science

It might even be said that the rise of science was possible because the world was seen as God's creation. The free God could have created a different world. Since God is believed to be trustworthy, we may also expect the world to be reliable and orderly, rather than unruly. Hence, as creation, the world is seen as a 'contingent order'. Empirical explorations are needed in studying such a contingent order, as one cannot find out how the world is by thinking alone. Mathematics is also needed to articulate the regularities that reflect God's reliability. Along such lines, references have been made to the Christian understanding of the world in order to explain why modern science developed in Western Europe rather than in China or in Arab civilizations. However, technological and socio-economic developments have played a role alongside religious ideas in creating conditions that made the rise of science possible. And even if the idea of creation has been essential to the rise of science, this does not imply anything about the truth of the idea itself (though it might counterbalance the equally naïve criticism that Christianity has always obstructed the development of science).

Science and theology

Natural theology

Is the creation of a world to be understood scientifically?

Medieval treatises referred to natural phenomena as the 'six days' work' (since the creation story in the first book of the Bible, Genesis, is structured in six days of creation, followed by a seventh day of divine rest). By contrast, some theologians in modern times have held that theological and scientific understanding are distinct. They may co-exist without interference. The theologian Karl Barth (1886–1968) wrote in the introduction to the volumes on creation in his *Church Dogmatics* that the doctrine of creation has nothing at all to do with the natural sciences. Rather, creation is to be understood in terms of the covenant between God and Israel. Science cannot add or detract from faith, nor can faith add to or detract from science. The bypassing of the natural sciences by theology also has roots in the ideas of Friedrich Schleiermacher (1768–1834). He saw the sense of absolute dependence as central to religious life. Such dependence was not to be understood in historical terms (e.g., my dependence upon my parents). Rather, this dependence is ontological in kind; it is part of our being. At every moment my existence is dependent upon God. If God were to withdraw his continuous support for the world, the world would not be. This is expressed in terms of *creatio ex nihilo*, but it could also be articulated as *creatio continua*, continuing dependence upon God's preserving and sustaining action. Such ways of conceptualizing 'creation' avoid making any connections with the results of the natural sciences. They also serve piety by dissociating the notion 'creation' from 'origination', as if creation referred merely to some event in the far past. However, the risk here is that the religious symbol of creation is disconnected from the world known by other means; as a result the concept is emptied and its usefulness is undermined, for instance in discussions of ecological responsibility.

Bible

Karl Barth

Covenant

Friedrich Schleiermacher

At the other end of the spectrum there are those who understand the world known through the sciences as God's creation (e.g., Ian Barbour, Ralph Burhoe, Paul Davies, Arthur Peacocke, John Polkinghorne and Robert J. Russell). Quite a few such religious thinkers come from the UK or the USA, perhaps because of the respected tradition of natural theology in the UK, in contrast to the greater influence of theologians such as Barth and Schleiermacher on the European continent, and because of the greater need for apologetics for science in the USA.

A 'science and theology' movement has developed worldwide in the last few decades. Discussions have dealt with origins and with the nature of reality. The understanding of divine action in these contexts is of major importance for theology. Is God supposed to act in opposition to natural processes, intervening in the natural process? Many contributors to modern theology and reflections on science seek to avoid such a crude interventionist view of divine action, out of appreciation of the integrity of natural processes and for theological reasons. For if God needs to intervene in processes God has created, would that not diminish our esteem for the Creator? Thus, other ways of thinking about divine action have been explored.

Some have explored the idea that God might act within the framework uncovered by the sciences, given that there seems to be looseness in this framework. Quantum physics may be interpreted as indicating that reality is not determinate from moment to moment. And models of chaotic and complex systems have suggested that determinate systems may be unpredictable and sensitive to minute differences. Others have suggested that there might be metaphysical ways of understanding that would be consistent with science and allow for a sensible notion of divine action. Process philosophy, a view of reality articulated by Alfred N. Whitehead, Charles Hartshorne and others, is one such proposal. This model has given up on *creatio ex nihilo*; God is involved in the creative process rather than its origin. Furthermore, this model uses mental categories for elementary events. Again, others are more sceptical about such models of divine action, for both scientific and philosophical reasons and for theological ones, as it makes God a God of the gaps, even if these are not gaps in current knowledge but in reality. Conceiving divine action in such a way exacerbates the problem of evil, since God could have interfered (without being noticed) to prevent horrendous evil. Thus, rather than conceiving of divine action in natural processes, some prefer to think of natural processes as the way God acts. This approach goes back to some of the medieval theologians, who articulated a distinction between primary and secondary causality – the latter being what we now call natural processes. God's primary causal role would be to create and sustain the laws of nature.

The discussion about whether or not the theological and scientific understandings of reality are significant for each other has taken various forms. This discussion is not merely about origins, since science affects the understanding of reality (including time and space, matter, life and consciousness) at all moments, and thus in principle all theological ideas. Many such ideas, e.g. about Jesus Christ and about salvation, were articulated in terms of a flat earth with the heavens above. Hence, new understandings of reality challenge more than the doctrine of creation in the narrow sense. Just as it is a mistake to limit the debate on the relationship between theology and science to the understanding of creation, so it is also a mistake to reduce the debate about creation to one about the impact of modern science. Creation is an issue about which Christianity has seen conflicts, both among Christians and with adherents of alternative views, from its early days up to modern fundamentalism and the New Age.

Creation and creationism

Opinion polls in the USA in and after 1991 invited respondents to choose from three possibilities: 1. God created human beings more or less in their current form at some moment less than 10,000 years ago; 2. human beings came into being in a long evolutionary process which was guided by God; 3. human beings originated in a long evolutionary process in which God played no role. Less than 10 per cent opted for the last, naturalistic alternative; almost 50 per cent chose the first, creationist, one. In European countries 'creationism' has been less of an issue, but there too it is of some influence, whether as an indigenous standpoint or as an export from American fundamentalism and evangelicalism. 'Young earth creationism' emphasizes the sudden creation of life on earth less than 10,000 years ago. Human beings and apes have no common ancestors. Geological strata and fossils mostly arose in a single worldwide flood.

It is sometimes assumed that creationism is a last remnant of old convictions. This is mistaken; present-day creationism is the late product of a historical development.

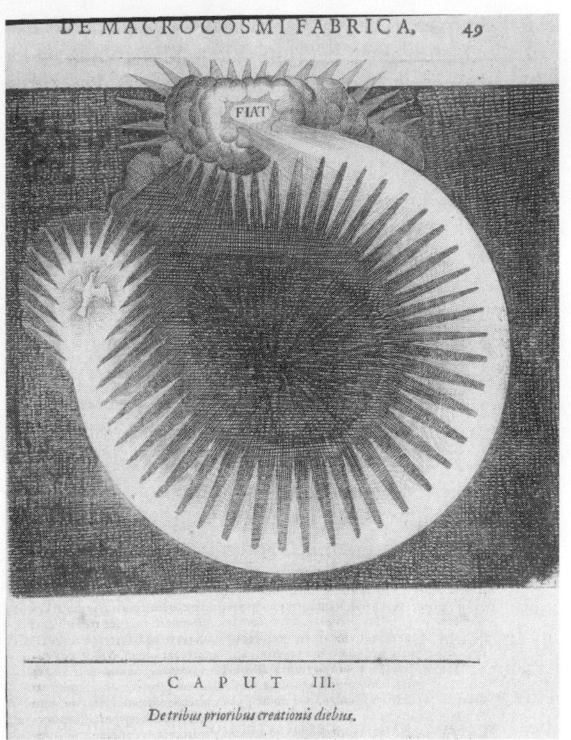

The will of God creates the macrocosm or occult version of the creation with God, Father, Son and Holy Spirit from Robert Fludd, *Utriusque Cosmi Historia* 1617–24

Evil

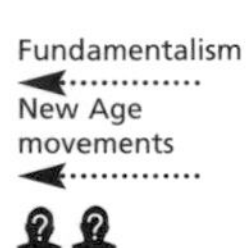

Major theologians of the past such as Augustine and Thomas Aquinas reconciled theological ideas and other knowledge of their time. When evolutionary biology became prominent in the latter half of the nineteenth and in the early twentieth century, most orthodox Christian thinkers accepted an old earth. Sometimes the days of Genesis were interpreted as periods; after all, the Psalms say that for God 1000 years are like a day. Others argued that the first lines of the Bible could be read as referring to very different moments in natural history. 'In the beginning, God created …' could be taken to refer to *creatio ex nihilo* in a distant past. The next line, 'The earth was without form and void …', could refer to a much later moment, when God re-created an orderly world out of chaos. Fossils and geological layers could thus date from a distant past, while the biblical narrative would still have its human time-scale, which counts in generations rather than in millions of years.

Not only did orthodox believers reconcile their faith with evolution; the botanist Asa Gray and the minister and amateur geologist George F. Wright were even active defenders of Charles Darwin's ideas. Evolution became

a major target in the 1920s when three American states forbade the teaching of evolution in public schools, and a biology teacher in Tennessee, John Scopes, was prosecuted for such teaching. Since then, publishers and authors have avoided conflicts by leaving the theory of evolution out of the textbooks. The main concern of the anti-evolution moment was moral: science had produced the poison gases used in World War I, and was replacing the law of Christ by the law of the primeval forest. An anti-élitist sentiment also played a role: why should a few scientists determine the views of millions of Christians?

Society

But even then, major advocates such as William Bryan Jennings understood the days of Genesis as longer periods. They would be taken literally as periods of 24 hours just to make the creationist view ridiculous. However, such literalism became the dominant position in the early 1960s, i.e. just after the centennial commemorations of Darwin's *The Origin of Species* (1859), the apparent Russian dominance in space with the unmanned Sputnik (1957), and the first manned space flight (Yuri Gagarin, 1961). In the USA these had prompted a state-subsidized modernization of curricula in the sciences, including biology, which was presented with evolution as the organizing principle. This evoked resistance from some parents, and thus set the stage for 'young earth creationism', resulting in a continuing series of court cases and public controversies over teaching and textbooks.

p. 131

There are various dimensions to these controversies. Some question science directly, e.g. the adequacy of evolutionary explanations, indicating missing links in natural history and presenting apparent counter-examples. Some shift the discussion to the philosophy of science, and question whether evolution is a scientific theory. Is it falsifiable? But is falsifiability the criterion? And there are issues of policy. If evolution is nothing but 'a theory', why not give equal consideration and teaching time to alternatives? This abuses the range of meanings of the word 'theory', as the term may refer to any suggestion in a conversation ('I also have a theory as to how this murder happened') as well as to consolidated pieces of knowledge, confirmed in experiments and practice. It is hard to imagine that in geography people would want to give the same time to teaching that the earth is flat as to teaching that it is spherical, with the argument that both are theories.

Origins and background

What seems to drive the controversies is concern about social and religious values. In a debate on 16 June 1999 in the US House of Representatives over a shooting in a school two months previously, the Republican leader read out with approval a letter stating that it had not been the weapons that led to this killing. The shooting was a consequence of divorces, of child care where children lived according to the laws of the jungle, of computer games, of contraception and sterilization which keep families small, of moral relativism, and 'because our school systems teach the children that they are nothing but glorified apes who have evolutionized out of some primordial soup of mud'. The debate about creation is not just about origins, but is part of a much larger theological and social concern about modern society. In its motives and in treating biblical ideas as alternatives for (and of a kind with) scientific theories, creationism is a modern phenomenon.

In the Bible, creation is not a theory. The Bible has no philosophical or cosmological treatises, and the origin of the world is not treated in general terms. Even the book of Genesis is mostly about the patriarchs of Israel, though it begins with a saga about the origins of the world, of humankind (Adam and Eve), and of the various peoples of the world (the sons of Noah). Modern people who open the Bible may thus think that we first learn about God in general as the creator of the world before hearing about God as the God of Israel. However, most scholars hold that religious understanding began with the particular experiences of Israel, the experiences of exile and exodus. In due course the relationship between these people and their God has been modified, resulting in the remarkable claim that their God is not one of the tribal gods, but the Only One, the Maker of heaven and earth.

Two episodes in this process were important.

When the leadership of Judah was in exile in Babylon, in the sixth century BCE, they were far from the temple, the place where God was to be worshipped. However, even there they could praise the Lord, for their Lord was not limited to his own country, but present everywhere. The dominance of the Babylonians was not to be understood as the victory of their god over the God and protector of Israel; rather, the predicament of those in exile was understood as a punishment from God for failing to live up to God's intentions.

In the second century BCE, in the period of Roman and Greek influence, we find the sole explicit reference in the Bible to *creatio ex nihilo*, in 2 Maccabees 7.28. (This is one of the deutero-canonical books – books not part of the Hebrew canon but present in early Greek translations and accepted by the Roman Catholic Church as part of scripture.) However, *creatio ex nihilo* is not a philosophical reflection, but is offered in a highly threatening situation. An oppressive king seeks to suppress Jewish identity by forcing Jews to eat pork. Seven brothers refuse. They are tortured and killed. When the seventh son is about to be killed, his mother encourages him by saying that God has created heaven and earth from nothing, and will also be able to restore him and his brothers on the day God chooses. This is not said to explain the cosmos but to stress God's power as infinitely surpassing the power of the oppressive king.

The account in Genesis 1 is also about Jewish identity. The seventh day, the day on which God rests, is a reference to the sabbath of the people. The book of Genesis as a whole is structured by lists of generations, of descendants. The story of the seven days ends with the same formula (Genesis 2.4), the only place where this is not said of human beings but of the world. Thus the narrative about the seven days of creation is a phase in the genealogy of Israel.

There are other biblical texts that offer or imply views of creation, giving voice to values prevalent in different settings. In the second chapter of Genesis the narrative concentrates on human beings in their relationship to God and each other, while treating the rest as background. Whereas in Genesis 1 God creates by giving orders, the next chapter has a more physical image of making (dust, breath, a rib). In the Psalms, references to God's creative works and acts are an encouragement to praise and find comfort in the Lord, without opting for a single tradition as to how God 'did it'. Images of making like a potter and commanding like a king occur side by side (Psalms 8; 19; 33; 148). In the later parts of the book of Isaiah, references to God as creator stress the universality of God's authority, in order to make clear that the Persian king, Cyrus, has a function in God's plans here and now. In the book of Job, God's majesty, far beyond human understanding, is expressed partly by references to creation. In Proverbs a reference to God as creator expresses a moral consideration: 'Who oppresses the poor, insults his Maker' (14. 31). And in an earlier passage about wisdom being present at creation (Proverbs 8.22–31), the point is not to present a theory about processes in the beginning but rather to stress the importance of wisdom for living the life God intended. The Bible does speak of God as creator, but it is not limited to a single model or theory as to how God has been creator. And God is spoken of as creator for a variety of reasons, almost none of which resembles the aims of scientific description and the explication of processes of evolution and origination. Thus, to put science and the biblical understanding of creation in direct competition, as in creationism, is to neglect their different natures and functions.

Creation and polemics

Creation is not only an area for discussion among Christians, who sometimes have opposing views. There are also major differences of opinion with those outside the main Christian tradition. The New Age movement does not have a well-defined body of ideas, but its views in some respects resemble those of the Gnostics of earlier times. In New Age books such as the *Course in Miracles*, the material and messy world is not understood as having been created by God, nor is it valued positively. Rather, the world is a painful illusion that will lose its significance when one awakens and comes to spiritual insight. The tendency to understand good and evil in terms of knowledge and ignorance, symbolized as light and darkness, is also Gnostic. Thus, suffering is our own failure and salvation our own responsibility (an attitude which increases our guilt when we fail in reaching the blessed state).

Suffering
Salvation

The Christian understanding of creation acquired its present form through controversies with Gnostic ideas in the first two centuries of Christianity, for instance in Irenaeus of Lyons' books *Against the Heresies*. The other major heresy in the second century CE was articulated by Marcion, who was expelled from the Christian community in Rome in 144. He sought to cleanse Christianity from Jewish elements. He argued that the Old and the New Testaments presented two radically different ideas about God: the creator of this ambivalent world, who sees justice as 'an eye for an eye', could not be the same as the loving Father of Jesus Christ, who speaks of grace and forgiveness.

Psalms

In spite of Marcion, the Christian tradition in its major confessional statements has retained both the Old and New Testaments, and combined belief in God as creator of this world and as the Father of Jesus Christ. The notion of creation affirms God's relation with us and our world and the world's reality and value.

pp. 984–5

p. 139

WILLEM B. DREES

Ian G. Barbour, *Religion and Science*, San Francisco: Harper 1997; Willem B. Drees, *Creation: From Nothing until Now*, London and New York: Routledge 2002; Ronald L. Numbers, *The Creationists*, Berkeley, CA: University of California Press 1993; Arthur Peacocke, *Theology for a Scientific Age*, revised edition, London: SCM Press 1993; M. Ruse (ed), *But Is It Science?*, Buffalo, NY: Prometheus Books 1988; Gerd Theissen, *Biblical Faith*, London: SCM Press and Philadelphia: Fortress Press 1985

Creed

Creeds are short summaries of central tenets of the Christian religion. The English term creed itself goes back to the Old English *créda*, which again is derived from Latin *credo*, 'I believe'. Creeds usually have a threefold structure in accordance with the three persons of the Trinity, Father, Son and Holy Spirit, and are recited in worship. The ancient name for creed is Greek *symbolon*, Latin *symbolum*. Why this term, which originally means a token serving as proof of identity, was used to designate creeds is controversial. Initially, it may have referred to the baptismal act within

Trinity
Worship
Gnosis

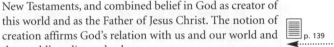

EARLY CREEDS OF THE CHURCH

The Apostles' Creed

Tradition has it that when the apostles set out to preach the gospel throughout the world, each contributed a clause to the creed. However, its origin seems more mundane. Elements can be traced back to a creed which developed in Rome around the end of the second century, but the final form dates from around 700. Both Latin and Greek texts circulated.

I believe in God the Father almighty, creator of heaven and earth;

And in Jesus Christ, his only Son, our Lord, who was conceived by the Holy Spirit, born of the Virgin Mary, suffered under Pontius Pilate, was crucified, dead and buried. He descended to hell, on the third day rose again from the dead, ascended to heaven, sits at the right hand of God the Father almighty, thence he will come to judge the living and the dead.

I believe in the Holy Spirit, the holy catholic church, the communion of saints, the forgiveness of sins, the resurrection of the body, and the life everlasting.

The Old Roman Creed (before 341)

I believe in God the Father almighty.

And in Jesus Christ, his only Son, our Lord, who was born of the Holy Spirit and the Virgin Mary, crucified under Pontius Pilate and buried, on the third day he rose from the dead, ascended to heaven, sits at the right hand of the Father, thence he will come to judge the living and the dead.

And in the Holy Spirit, the holy church, the forgiveness of sins, the resurrection of the body.

The Creed of Nicaea (325)

This creed differs from what is commonly known as the Nicene Creed; it contains a bare assertion of belief in the Holy Spirit and ends with a condemnation (anathema). The original is in Greek.

We believe in one God, the Father all-governing, creator of all things visible and invisible;

And in one Lord Jesus Christ, the Son of God, begotten of the Father as only begotten, that is, from the essence of the Father, God from God, Light from Light, true God from true God, begotten not created, of the same essence as the Father, through whom all things came into being, both in heaven and in earth; who for us men and for our salvation came down and was incarnate, becoming human. He suffered and the third day he rose, and ascended into the heavens. And he will come to judge both the living and the dead.

And in the Holy Spirit.

But those who say, Once he was not, or he was not before his generation, or he came to be out of nothing, or who assert that he, the Son of God, is of a different *hypostasis* or *ousia*, or that he is a creature, or changeable, or mutable, the Catholic and Apostolic Church anathematizes them.

The Creed of Constantinople (381)

What is commonly known as the Nicene Creed was in fact promulgated by the Council of Constantinople. The original is in Greek.

We believe in one God, the Father all-governing, creator of heaven and earth, of all things visible and invisible;

And in one Lord Jesus Christ, the only-begotten Son of God, begotten of the Father before all time, Light from Light, true God from true God, begotten not created, of the same essence as the Father, through whom all things came into being, who for us men and because of our salvation came down from heaven, and was incarnate by the Holy Spirit and the Virgin Mary and became human. He was crucified for us under Pontius Pilate, and suffered and was buried, and rose on the third day, according to the Scriptures, and ascended to heaven, and sits on the right hand of the Father, and will come again with glory to judge the living and the dead. His kingdom shall have no end.

And in the Holy Spirit, the Lord and life-giver, who proceeds from the Father, who is worshipped and glorified together with the Father and the Son, who spoke through the prophets; and in one, holy, catholic and apostolic Church. We look forward to the resurrection of the dead and the life of the world to come. Amen.

The Chalcedonian Definition

The Chalcedonian Definition is widely regarded as the classic statement of belief in the person of Christ. However, its promulgation was followed by two centuries of controversy and it is even now not universally accepted by Christians. The original is in Greek.

Following, then, the holy fathers, we unite in teaching all men to confess the one and only Son, our Lord Jesus Christ. This selfsame one is perfect both in deity and also in human-ness; this selfsame one is also actually God and actually man, with a rational soul and a body. He is of the same reality as God as far as his deity is concerned and of the same reality as we are ourselves as far as his human-ness is concerned; thus like us in all respects, sin only excepted. Before time began he was begotten of the Father, in respect of his deity, and now in these 'last days', for us and on behalf of our salvation, this selfsame one was born of Mary the virgin, who is God-bearer in respect of his human-ness.

[We also teach] that we apprehend this one and only Christ – Son, Lord, only-begotten – in two natures; without confusing the two natures, without transmuting one nature into the other, without dividing them into two separate categories, without contrasting them according to area or function. The distinctiveness of each nature is not nullified by the union. Instead, the 'properties' of each nature are conserved and both natures concur in one 'person' and in one hypostasis. They are not divided or cut into two *prosopa*, but are together the one and only and only-begotten Logos of God, the Lord Jesus Christ. Thus have the prophets of old testified; thus the Lord Jesus Christ himself taught us; thus the Symbol of the Fathers has handed down to us.

The Athanasian Creed

The so-called Athanasian Creed was widely used in the Western church and was included in the Anglican Book of Common Prayer. It is much longer than the creeds quoted above and consists of two main sections, one stating the doctrine of the Trinity and the other the doctrine of the incarnation. It begins and ends with threats of everlasting damnation. It has long been known that the creed is not by Athanasius; the original is in Greek and is thought to date from the fifth century. The opening Latin words are *Quicunque vult* ('Whosoever will [be saved]'), and the creed is also known under this name.

which the creed was recited, indicating its ritual and legal character. Not until the second half of the fourth century did it become exclusively the name for the creed, emphasizing its function as the 'rule' and 'criterion' of orthodoxy, as a sign of recognition and distinction.

The three most important early Christian creeds, the Apostles' Creed, the Creed of Constantinople (often erroneously called the 'Nicene' Creed) and the Athanasian Creed, are recognized by a large majority within Christianity. As such they also serve to mark the differences *vis-à-vis* other religions or dissenting Christian views. Thus they contribute to defining Christian identity.

Even now, scholars have been unable to arrive at a consensus on the origins of the creeds. It used to be suggested that the earliest creed dates back to the beginning of the third century and was probably composed in Rome, but this theory has recently come under serious criticism. It is undisputed, however, that no unequivocal testimonies are found prior to the middle of the fourth century. From the second half of the second century onwards there is firm evidence for the existence of so-called 'rules of faith', doctrinal summaries which were formulated *ad hoc* in theological controversy, especially against Gnostics. They resemble creeds quite closely, except that their overall structure is not fixed and their wording is fluent. Various forms of the rule of faith may be found in one and the same author.

From the end of the second century onwards there is also evidence for the existence of baptismal interrogations. In North Africa, immediately before baptism, catechumens – those who had been undergoing training to become Christians – had to answer certain questions about their faith, mentioning not only the Father, the Son and the Holy Spirit, but also the church. In Rome, too, around the middle of the third century it was customary to interrogate the catechumens about their faith prior to baptism. The Roman interrogatory creed, too, probably had a trinitarian structure. At the same time, the use of interrogatory creeds is also attested in Palestine, Cappadocia and Alexandria. Apparently, the baptismal questions were closely linked to baptism in the name of the Father, the Son and the Holy Spirit. The oldest questions are therefore probably the result of a revision of the formula which occurs in Matthew 28.19 and the early Christian document the Didache (Teaching of the Twelve Apostles) 7.1, 3, 'baptize in the name of the Father and of the Son and of the Holy Spirit'. This revision was carried out in order to emphasize the binding character of the baptismal act and its theological significance.

p. 245

Fixed formulae summing up basic tenets of the Christian faith in declaratory form are first found in the West in the context of the Arian controversy. The most important creed, which was at the centre of the trinitarian debate of the fourth century, is the creed passed by the first ecumenical Council of Nicaea in 325. Some of its contents were later incorporated into another creed associated with the second ecumenical council, held in Constantinople in 381. This creed is the most widespread of all creeds today and is accepted by virtually all churches throughout the world.

Christology

Council

Gnosis

In the West, the first conclusive evidence for the existence of creeds is not found until the middle of the fourth century, when the Roman Church apparently promulgated a formula which must be considered as the immediate ancestor of the Apostles' Creed. In its present form it is not attested until the eighth century. In the Orthodox churches this creed never became very widespread. It is therefore often considered a typically 'Western' creed.

Initiation

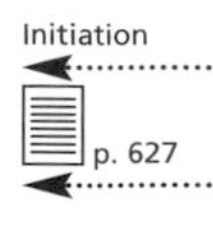
p. 627

Church

CONFESSIONS OF FAITH

Whereas creeds are recited in public worship, confessions of faith are definitions of the beliefs of particular denominations. Some have had wider political significance. They have been mainly composed for the churches of the Reformation. Here are some of the most important.

Augsburg Confession (1530): Composed by Philipp Melanchthon. A fundamental definition of Lutheranism.

First Helvetic Confession (1536): Drafted by Heinrich Bullinger and others as a confession of faith for the whole of German-speaking Switzerland: basically Zwinglian but with Lutheran elements.

John Calvin

French or Gallican Confession (1559): Basically the work of John Calvin. It was adopted by the first national synod of Protestants in Paris.

Belgic Confession (1561): Drawn up on the basis of the Gallican Confession, it established Calvinist principles in the Low Countries.

Second Helvetic Confession (1566): Drafted by Bullinger, and soon accepted in all Swiss Protestant churches. Basically Calvinist, it is important for the Reformed churches of Switzerland, France, Scotland.

Formula of Concord (1577): The last of the classic Lutheran statements of faith.

Canons of Dort (1619): A series of articles asserting Calvinist principles.

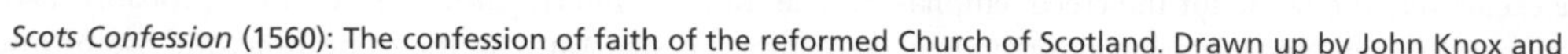

Scots Confession (1560): The confession of faith of the reformed Church of Scotland. Drawn up by John Knox and others.

Westminster Confession (1646): The basic statement of faith for Presbyterians.

Theological Declaration of Barmen (1934): Defines the belief of the church in the face of threats from Nazi Germany.

Confession of Belhar (1982–6): Against apartheid. One of the doctrinal standards for the Uniting Reformed Church in Southern Africa.

This is even more true of a Latin confession of faith which was erroneously attributed to the church father Athanasius (died 373) and was therefore called the Athanasian Creed or *Quicunque vult* (after its first two Latin words, 'Whoever wishes [to be saved]'). It was composed in southern Gaul in the second half of the fifth century. It is made up of a series of doctrinal statements originally in Latin that are not introduced by 'I/We believe'. Nor is there a threefold structure. In addition, in most churches its liturgical use is very limited, if it has not been completely dropped. One could therefore argue that it is no creed at all, but rather a doctrinal statement. It deals with the doctrine of the Trinity and of Jesus Christ. In the Middle Ages it was handed down together with the Apostles' Creed and the Nicene Creed in the West and was subsequently also accepted by the churches of the Reformation, whereas it is largely unknown in Eastern Orthodoxy.

Holy Roman empire

Lutheranism

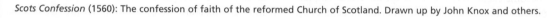

In addition to these early Christian creeds there are a number of confessions of faith from later periods. It is arguable whether they ought to be called creeds at all, since they neither display the threefold structure of the early Christian texts nor are they usually recited in worship. They are, therefore, often called 'confessional writings' and have usually contributed to defining a particular 'confession' in a denominational sense by being incorporated in church orders. Among the most important Protestant confessions is the Augsburg Confession, which was composed by Philipp Melanchthon (1497–1560), the famous Reformer and friend of Martin Luther, for the Diet (the assembly of the princes of the Holy Roman empire) held in Augsburg in 1530. It is fundamental for the definition of Lutheranism. In its first part (Articles 1–21) it explains Christian doctrine from a Protestant perspective. In its second part (Articles 22–8) certain abuses in the life of the church are censured. The Augsburg Confession is also contained in the Book of Concord published in 1580. The aim of this work was to unite the German Lutherans by assembling basic Lutheran doctrinal texts and introducing them with the Formula of Concord of 1577, an objective which was only partly achieved.

Whereas the Augsburg Confession has become the common denominator of virtually all Lutheran churches, within the Reformed tradition there is a much greater variety

ARTICLES OF FAITH

Articles of faith are sets of statements which define important doctrines for particular groups. As such they stand alongside creeds and confessions. Here are some of the most important ones:

Twelve Articles (1525): The main demands put forward by the peasants in the Peasants' War, seeking the right to elect their own pastors and to have fair living and working conditions. Luther approved of the articles, but was against the use of force to implement them.

Ten Articles (1536): The first articles of faith issued by the Church of England on the urging of Henry VIII.

Smalcald Articles (1537): A doctrinal statement drafted by Martin Luther and approved by Lutheran theologians and rulers at Smalcald in Thuringia.

Six Articles (1539): Articles imposed on the Church of England by Henry VIII to stop the spread of Reformation doctrines and practices.

Forty-Two Articles (1553): A collection of doctrinal statements issued with royal mandate to which all clergymen, schoolmasters and graduates were to subscribe. Probably never formally approved and never enforced. They formed the basis for the Thirty-Nine Articles.

Thirty-Nine Articles (1563): Doctrinal statements approved by the Church of England to define its position. In one form or another Anglican clergy have been required either to subscribe to them or recognize them as a historic statement of faith.

Lambeth Articles (1595): Nine doctrinal statements issued by the Church of England on the predestination to salvation of a definite number of people from eternity. Never authorized.

Irish Articles (1615): 104 articles of faith adopted by the Irish Episcopal Church, replaced in 1635 by the Thirty-Nine Articles.

Gallican Articles (1682): The rights and privileges demanded by the clergy of France arising out of a dispute between King Louis XIV and Pope Innocent XI.

Organic Articles (1802): Napoleon's provisions to regulate public worship and define the relations between church and state in France.

Twenty-Five articles (1808): John Wesley's adaptation for Methodists of the Anglican Thirty-Nine Articles.

of credal documents. There is no collection of confessional writings comparable to the Book of Concord. The Second Helvetic Confession (*Confessio Helvetica posterior*) of 1566 is important for the Reformed churches of Switzerland, France, Scotland, etc.; the Belgic Confession (*Confessio Belgica*, 1561) for the Dutch and affiliated churches; and the Westminster Confession (1646) for Scottish and American Presbyterianism. Churches which hold a strict predestinarian doctrine often fall back on the Canons of the Synod of Dort (1618/19). In addition, Reformed churches often appeal to the Heidelberg Catechism (1563) which, being a catechism by genre, shows very clearly why it is premature to identify creeds and confessional writings.

An important confession from the twentieth century is the Theological Declaration of Barmen, passed by a synod of the German Confessing Church in May 1934. By means of this Declaration (which was originally not meant to be a confession), the synod rejected the rule of the (Nazi) state over the church and all attempts at ideological infiltration. It emphasized that the sole source of its proclamation was God's Word in Jesus Christ as attested in holy scripture.

The Barmen Declaration has influenced a number of modern confessions, such as the Confession of Belhar (1982–6), which takes a strong stand against apartheid and has found widespread support in Reformed churches. Thus it is one of the standards of unity (along with the Belgic Confession, the Canons of Dort and the Heidelberg Catechism) for the new Uniting Reformed Church in Southern Africa.

Whereas in the Protestant churches confessional writings abound from the Reformation onwards, neither the Roman Catholic Church nor the Western churches possess texts of equivalent status. In Roman Catholicism canon law, conciliar texts and papal decrees largely fulfil the function of defining the legal and doctrinal identity of the church, whereas Eastern Orthodoxy sees Christian

Reformation

Canon law

doctrine enshrined in the writings of the church fathers and the canons of the seven ecumenical councils. The foremost credal formula here is the Nicene-Constantinopolitan Creed.

Initiation

In the Anglican tradition the Book of Common Prayer of 1549/1662, incorporating, among other texts, the Thirty-Nine Articles of Faith of 1553/63, plays a major role, though it is more liturgical than doctrinal.

Congregationalism
Methodism
Baptist churches

Finally, Congregationalist, Methodist and Baptist churches all have their own confessions.

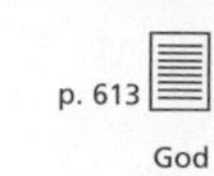

p. 613
God

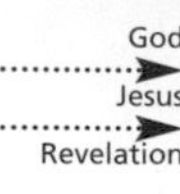

Jesus
Revelation

Many modern Christians find it difficult to confess their faith with the old creeds. They find the idea of a virgin birth or of a last judgement as expressed in the Apostles' and Nicene Creeds offensive to their beliefs. It is therefore important to realize that creeds have been set out by human beings and are not divine revelation. They are meant to aid Christians in expressing their faith in a responsible and coherent manner. They are therefore by no means immutable, and have in the past often been adapted to changing needs and historical situations. Today they may be changed, too. Any attempt to change the creeds should, however, be done in the awareness that the Apostles' and the Nicene Creeds have been adopted by most Christian churches and are important to believers from various cultures. Therefore, new creeds should be used side by side with the old ones rather than replace them altogether.

Holy Spirit

Apostles' Creed

p. 750
p. 850

From the beginning of the fifth century it was thought that the Apostles' Creed had actually been composed by the apostles themselves. Legend had it that each clause was written by one of the Twelve, although the precise attribution of the clauses varied. In the Middle Ages the legend was also repeatedly represented in book illuminations and in church art. First doubts as to its authenticity were uttered at the Council of Florence (1438–45); in the middle of the century it came under attack by the famous Italian humanist Lorenzo Valla (died 1457) and by the Bishop of St Asaph and later of Chichester, Reginald Pe(a)cock (died 1460/1). Since the beginning of modern research into the creeds in the middle of the seventeenth century the Apostles' Creed is no longer believed to be a product of the Twelve.

In its present form the creed (usually abbreviated T for *textus receptus* = received text) is first attested in the eighth century. There was, however, a precursor called the (Old) Roman Creed (R), which is first attested around the middle of the fourth century. Whereas until very recently it was assumed that R in turn ultimately dates back to the beginning of the third century, there is now reason to believe that R had its origin in a creed submitted by Marcellus of Ancyra (died 374) to a synod at Rome in 340/1 and adopted by this synod. However, this hypothesis has not yet found unanimous support.

From the fourth century onwards the Apostles' Creed formed part of a liturgical ritual before baptism, called the *traditio* and *redditio symboli*, i.e. the 'handing over' and 'repetition' of the creed. The bishop made the creed officially known to the catechumens and exhorted them about its contents. At a later point during the preparations for baptism, the catechumens, in turn, had formally to repeat the confession.

It is perhaps because of this essentially didactic purpose that the structure of T is very simple. It is divided into three articles. First it expresses belief in God the Father who has created heaven and earth. Then Jesus Christ, the Son of God, is mentioned. Important details of his incarnation are recapitulated (virgin birth, crucifixion, descent into the underworld, resurrection, ascension). The fact that the historical figure of Pontius Pilate is mentioned here has always struck scholars. It was probably included in order to indicate the particular point in history where the Jesus story is located.

It is also said that at the end of days Christ will return to judge humankind, both dead and alive. Belief in the Holy Spirit is the subject of the third article. It is connected with a series of statements relating to the church, the forgiveness of sins and the end of the world. This has led to some confusion, since it is not clear whether we are actually supposed to believe in the church and what follows or whether these clauses are meant to be explanations of the work of the Holy Spirit. There is a slight change in wording here in Protestant versions of the creed: Martin Luther advocated the translation of *sanctam ecclesiam catholicam* by 'the holy Christian Church', since in the context of the Reformation 'catholic' came to be understood as referring to the Roman Church, whereas originally it had simply meant 'general, universal' (which, of course, also implied orthodoxy).

The Apostles' Creed has often been at the centre of doctrinal controversies. There are literally hundreds of expositions of its content. Its beauty lies in its simplicity.

In the Western churches the Apostles' Creed is probably the most popular of all ancient creeds. In Eastern Orthodoxy, however, it is regarded as a 'Western' creed and plays no major role.

Nicene Creed (Nicene-Constantinopolitan Creed)

The so-called Nicene Creed is often seen as the most solemn of early Christian creeds. In some denominations it is recited at high feasts only. Its origins go back to the first ecumenical council. In 325 numerous bishops and theologians were summoned by the Emperor Constantine (emperor 306–37, sole ruler from 324) to hold a synod at Nicaea in Asia Minor (modern Iznik/Turkey). Constantine

FILIOQUE

The word *filioque* is Latin for 'and from the Son'. It has for centuries been a bone of contention between Roman Catholic and Orthodox theologians and was one of the factors leading to the split between the Western and Eastern Churches in the eleventh century. Why this was so is a complex story.

The creed formulated at the Council of Constantinople in 381 stated that the Holy Spirit 'proceeds from the Father', 'procession' being the technical term used to describe the distinguishing feature of the Holy Spirit, which is not begotten or created. The doctrine had been developed in particular by the Cappadocian fathers. However, there were theologians who argued that the Holy Spirit proceeds not only from the Father but also from the Son, a doctrine known as 'double procession'. Double procession was maintained by some Eastern theologians, such as Cyril of Alexandria, though without using the actual word procession, but it was predominantly a Western doctrine, though there too by no means unanimously accepted. Fatefully, the doctrine came to be stated in the Western, Latin version of the 381 creed with the insertion of the word *filioque* at the Council of Toledo in 589, and in Western churches *filioque* is still in this creed, inaccurately called the Nicene Creed, today.

Church fathers

The insertion was not accepted overnight, and Pope Leo III (795–816) had the text of the original form of the creed inscribed on two silver tablets and deposited at the tomb of St Peter in Rome. But popular practice was against him, and through the Franks in particular the *filioque* version spread widely, reaching Rome by the end of the millennium. Eastern monks in Jerusalem were offended at hearing it sung in Jerusalem at the beginning of the ninth century, but it was Photius, Patriarch of Constantinople (*c.*810–95), who was the first to denounce it vigorously. From then on it soured relations between East and West; when the *filioque* was finally given official sanction by Pope Benedict VIII in 1017, it proved the last straw, and in 1054 the great schism followed. All attempts since to reach some agreement have proved fruitless, though it has to be said that there are many theologians today who would be in favour of removing the *filioque* from the Western creed. In 1990 the Lutheran World Federation authorized omitting the *filioque* when the creed is said at ecumenical events which include the Orthodox.

asked the council to decide on various controversial matters, primarily relating to the question as to how best to understand the relation between God the Father and his Son Jesus Christ. Some time before the council, the controversy had been sparked by the Alexandrian presbyter Arius, who claimed that the Son was not co-eternal with the Father and did not originate from the Father, but was made out of nothing. The council condemned Arius' views and signed a creed (often called N), the origins of which are unclear. There is reason to believe that it goes back to a local creed used somewhere in Syria or Palestine, but this is no more than a plausible hypothesis. In its form as revised at Nicaea, however, it is not identical to what ecclesiastical tradition calls the 'Nicene Creed'. This becomes immediately obvious from the third article, which simply says 'And (we believe) in the Holy Spirit', with no further qualifications.

N's emphasis was on the first two articles instead, affirming the divine status of the Son by calling him 'of one substance with the Father' (*homoousios*). Apparently this Greek term was suggested by the emperor himself. Since, however, it is not biblical, opposition to its inclusion in the text of the creed was considerable. This is why N was by no means immediately adopted in the church. Instead, throughout most of the fourth century there were bitter struggles between the leading theologians of the time over the precise nature of the doctrine of the Trinity.

The controversy was finally settled at the second ecumenical council in Constantinople in 381 by issuing another creed. It is this text which tradition refers to as the Nicene Creed but which modern scholars usually call the Niceno-Constantinopolitan Creed (abbreviated to NC or C). The dissimilarities between C and N suggest that C cannot be simply regarded as an extended revision of N, but is, rather, a different text. Later generations, however, called it the Nicene Creed because it was considered fully to express the faith of Nicaea. By comparison with the Apostles' Creed, C is much more clearly marked by the theological debates of the time. The relationship between God the Father and his Son Jesus Christ is more fully described ('of one substance with the Father', Greek *homoousios*). It is said that before his incarnation Christ co-operated in the creation of the world.

In comparison with the creed of 325, C contains a much extended third article on the Holy Spirit. The reason for this is that from *c.*360 it was argued by theologians such as Athanasius of Alexandria and Basil of Caesarea that the Spirit, too, was of divine origin and status and had to be regarded as being, as it were, on the same level with the Father and the Son. At the council this led to considerable controversy with a group known as Pneumatomachians ('Spirit-fighters'), who denied that the Spirit was fully divine. Ultimately, this group found no majority for their views. Yet, interestingly, the final text of the creed does not say that the Spirit is of the same substance as the Father and the Son. The reason for this

is unknown, but it is sometimes said that the *homoousios* was not included in this passage in order to find a compromise with the Pneumatomachians. However, a dogmatic decree of the council stated this doctrine in no uncertain terms.

In addition, the Holy Spirit is seen as the giver of life who proceeds from the Father and the Son. In the Old Testament he spoke through the prophets. In the Middle Ages the idea that the Spirit proceeds from the Father 'and the Son' (Latin *filioque*), which is only expressed in the Latin versions of C, provoked a long-lasting and tortuous controversy between Western and Eastern theologians and partly contributed to the ultimate split between the Latin and the Orthodox churches. Today ecumenical dialogue has led to much progress on that score. For many Western churches it is no longer a problem to omit the *filioque*.

p. 507

As in the Apostles' Creed, this is followed by the mention of the church and the forgiveness of sins, in this instance coupled with baptism and the resurrection of the dead and life everlasting. In contrast to the Apostles' Creed, C specifically expresses belief in the church, so that one may ask whether there are not actually four articles rather than three. Then again, baptism for the remission of sins is 'only' confessed or acknowledged and the final resurrection is said to be 'expected'. The third article therefore has a somewhat uneven structure.

The Nicene-Constantinopolitan Creed of 381 is today the most widespread creed in Christendom. It unites Christians throughout the world.

Jesus of history

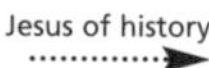

WOLFRAM KINZIG

Creeds and confessions of faith: B. A. Gerrish, *The Faith of Christendom: A Sourcebook of Creeds and Confessions*, Cleveland, OH: Meridian Books 1963; J. N. D. Kelly, *Early Christian Creeds*, London: Longman [3]1972; E. Routley, *Creeds and Confessions: From the Reformation to the Modern Church*, London: Duckworth 1963; J. Pelikan and V. Hotchkiss (eds), *Credo: Historical and Theological Guide to Creeds and Confessions of Faith in the Christian Tradition* (5 vols), New Haven: Yale University Press 2003; F. M. Young, *The Making of the Creeds*, London: SCM Press and Philadelphia: Westminster Press 1991; *Ecumenical Creeds and Reformed Confessions*, Grand Rapids, MI: CRC Publications 1987

The Apostles' Creed: C. E. B. Cranfield, *The Apostles' Creed: A Faith to Live By*, Edinburgh: T&T Clark and Grand Rapids, MI: Eerdmans 1993; Hans Küng, *Credo: The Apostles' Creed Explained for Today*, London: SCM Press and New York: Continuum 1993; L. H. Westra, *The Apostles' Creed: Origin, History, and Some Early Commentaries*, Turnhout: Brepols 2002

Critics of Christianity

The detractors

There have been critics of Christianity since the day the Sadducees arrested the apostles in Solomon's Portico (Acts 4.1–2), but they have not all been critical of the same thing. First of all there is a criticism that Christians do not believe. The followers of the high priest (as described in Acts 5.17ff.) complain that the Christians are not orthodox Jews. Towards the end of the second century Celsus (as represented by Origen in *Contra Celsum*) complained that Christianity was not Platonist (enough). Secondly there is a criticism that is not necessarily a rejection of Christianity but rather a criticism of the grounds on which it has been defended. At the end of the eleventh century the Christian Gaunilo, a monk of Marmoutiers (as represented by Anselm in *Cur Deus Homo?*), rejected Anselm's ontological argument for the existence of God put forward in the *Proslogion*. At the end of the eighteenth century David Hume, in his *Dialogues Concerning Natural Religion*, criticized the argument from design. However, Hume's friends in the Scottish Enlightenment, Adam Ferguson, Adam Smith and Dugald Stewart, never thought of him as an atheist. There is a third type of criticism, which actively seeks to destroy Christianity by undermining its historical basis. The first exponent of this approach was H. S. Reimarus in *The Aims of Jesus and his Disciples* (published posthumously in 1778), in which he argued that the meagre historical evidence which we have about the life of Jesus does not support the claims that are made for the Christ of the church.

The functionalists

These criticisms have been concerned with the truth of Christianity, but there is a much more damaging criticism, namely that Christianity should be characterized not with respect to truth or falsity but with regard to its social functions. In the period 1840–1940 the great masters of suspicion each in turn identified a different function. Earlier critics concluded that on rational grounds Christianity as presented *could* not be believed; modern critics concluded that on moral grounds it *should* not be believed.

Ludwig Feuerbach (1804–72). Today Feuerbach is remembered merely as the precursor of Karl Marx, one of the fiercest critics of Christianity, but in the 1840s he was the leading critical philosopher in Germany, perhaps in Europe. His reputation stems from his criticism of religion (for him, as for most nineteenth-century critics, as a matter of course this was Christianity), but his influence on the creation of the social sciences is seldom recognized. Feuerbach laid the foundations for the study of the social construction of our view of reality. He identified a dialectical movement within human consciousness that has been described rather dauntingly as a process of externalization, objectification and internalization. It is this process which is traced at the beginning of his most famous work *The Essence of Christianity* (1841). 'Man – this is the mystery of religion – projects his being into objectivity, and then again makes himself an object of this projected image of himself, thus converted into a subject.' If this statement were true it would dismantle religion at a stroke. While theists and atheists debate the rational basis of religion, Feuerbach claims to expose the process by which it is socially constructed. While philosophers evaluate arguments about the existence of God, Feuerbach demonstrates that God is a human creation.

For Feuerbach there is something mysterious about religion, but the mystery lies not in another world but in this world. The mystery concerns the attributes not of God but of man. What distinguishes man (and he knew nothing of inclusive language) from other animals is human consciousness, consciousness of the species. Through I-Thou relations, individuals are able to develop not only self-consciousness but self-criticism. Or rather this is the end-point of the process, when philosophical analysis has developed.

Feuerbach believed that religion precedes philosophy, in the life of individuals as well as whole societies. Thus at an early stage, before abstract philosophical distinctions can be made, religion is the medium in which the process develops. Through their understanding of their own limitations people are able to conceive of a being who would be unlimited. Understanding their own faults, they can conceive of a being who would exhibit perfection. Instead of conceiving of unlimited power, they conceive of a being of unlimited power. Instead of conceiving of moral or aesthetic perfection, they conceive of a being who encompasses perfect goodness and beauty. This, then, according to Feuerbach, is the function of religion. It enables societies to develop self-consciousness and self-criticism: it leads to the formation of ideals and aspirations. However, the process is carried on at an unconscious level, and because of this there are important consequences.

This is Feuerbach's projection theory of religion. Human beings unconsciously project aspects of their being away from themselves. These become objective in the form of God or gods. And finally, the idea of God, the belief in the existence of God, acts back and controls human thought and behaviour. Thus moral ideals that could have no force in society are conceived of as divine commandments. As the laws of God these ideals now have authority and come to control individual behaviour and to inform the legal system of society itself. And this, according to Feuerbach, is the 'mystery of religion'. It explains the main division of his book *The Essence of Christianity* into Part I, 'The True or Anthropological Essence of Religion', and Part II, 'The False or Theological Essence of Religion'. The previous debate between belief and unbelief saw the winner take all. If God exists, then religion is true in its entirety; if God does not exist, then religion is entirely false and without value. Not so, according to Feuerbach. Religion has truth and value as long as its true subject is identified. Its mystery lies in what it discloses, not about God but about man. He calls it a mystery because it embodies knowledge that was not in the consciousness of those developing religion. Thus religion should be studied and certainly not dismissed. The division of the book implies not only that there is truth and value in religion, but also that it embodies truths not otherwise recognized. But the implication is that these truths cannot be recognized so long as God is taken to be the subject of religion. He claims that his analysis will be positive as far as the human elements in religion are concerned, but that it will be experienced as negative as far as the non-human (i.e. the divine) is concerned.

Feuerbach displays none of the hostility towards religion so characteristic of atheistic attacks. That is because for him religion is the process by which, primitively and unconsciously, societies identify and formulate their truths about the world, together with their moral and aesthetic values. He deplores and dissociates himself from atheism when it entirely rejects religion. The division over religion is not whether to reverence and affirm the divine attributes, but whether to see these attributes as belonging to God or to mankind. Real atheism is not the denial of the existence of God, but the lack of faith and commitment to what might be called the divine attributes.

In Feuerbach's time increasing numbers of Europeans found that religious belief lacked credibility. The projection theory of religion provided them with a way of continuing to value religious traditions, traditions that were important to them personally and to European civilization more generally. There was, however, a further element that made Feuerbach's position attractive, namely devotion. The attitude of devotion, rather than belief or ritual practice, lies at the heart of religion. Feuerbach recommended that people be devoted not to God, but to those attributes which had previously been identified as divine. Meaningful lives and indeed European civilization could continue if people were devoted to attributes such as sacrificial love and forgiveness, attributes which, incidentally, Feuerbach the philosopher claimed were disclosed in religion but not incorporated into philosophy. This was the continuing mystery and fascination with religion. Feuerbach's criticism of Christianity is not only original but also disarming. He comes not to bury it, but to praise it; yet the terms in which he praises it reject its traditional metaphysical foundations.

It is not difficult to criticize the projection theory. It does not provide an account of the origins of religion at all. The phenomenology of religion is a more productive method for dealing with that question. Projection requires a screen, and the projection theory actually requires a previous belief in God in order to function. However, the projection theory does raise serious questions for Christianity. For example, Paul taught that 'the head of every man is Christ, the head of a woman is her husband, and the head of Christ is God' (1 Corinthians 11.3). Is this revelation or projection? Is Paul here revealing the ontological order of the universe, as it is by nature: God, Christ, man, woman? Or is he projecting into the heavens an existing, oppressive social order from which he benefits? The projection theory raises the question whether much of Christian thought, organization and practice is the religious legitimation of the life of a fallen world. In the long term this is a much more embarrassing and damaging criticism.

Paul

Karl Marx (1818–83). Marx is remembered as a materialist philosopher, a moral crusader and an economist. He is also remembered as a critic of religion. In fact he formulated three criticisms of religion, corresponding to each of these fields.

First, religion is the reversal of reality. Here Marx simply takes over Feuerbach's projection theory. 'The basis of irreligious criticism is this: man makes religion; religion does not make man.' Religion reverses reality. Religion creates the illusion that there is another world which is more real and lasting than this world, that there is a Creator who creates mankind in his own image. For Marx this is to get things exactly the wrong way round. The religious world is simply a 'reflection' of the human world. It is man who creates the social world and the picture of what is real. The criticism of religion is the demystification of its illusory account of reality. The importance of this process is not simply that it corrects a false picture, but that it ends human alienation. When all creativity and value are assigned to a divine being, human beings are alienated from their own responsibilities and possibilities. That way lies fatalism and dependence. As with Feuerbach, the criticism of religion is undertaken on behalf of mankind. Marx therefore begins by taking over Feuerbach's criticism of religion, but thereafter their paths diverge.

Industrial revolution

Feuerbach could see a 'mystery' in religion and continued to unpack it during the rest of his career. Marx accepted this criticism and having stated it moved on. He did not make a career out of criticizing religion, and indeed criticized those who did.

In this context the importance of the criticism of religion for Marx is that it becomes the premise of all other forms of criticism. It shows the way and provides a model for his own philosophy. For example, the German philosopher G. W. F. Hegel had formulated a high doctrine of the state. Marx saw in it the same reversal of reality in which the state became more real than human beings, bestowed citizenship on individuals and had the power of life and death. But is this not the same reversal as in religion: the idea of community gains objective status over against society, acts back and controls human life. Or again, Marx saw the same reversal in money. Money is not a natural phenomenon. It is a social product, which gains objective reality over against society. It acts back to control individual lives and to bestow worth and value. This criticism of religion becomes the key to Marx's criticism of the other institutions of society. In each case they represent a reversal of reality that produces human alienation.

If the first criticism of religion is philosophical, the second is moral and includes one of the most famous phrases from the corpus of Marx's writings. 'Religious suffering is at the same time an expression of real suffering and a protest against real suffering. Religion is the sigh of the oppressed creature, the heart of a heartless world, and the soul of soulless conditions. It is the opium of the people' (*Critique of Hegel's Philosophy of Right: Introduction*). In the first part of this famous passage Marx appears to praise Christianity. In the midst of the worst period of the industrial revolution there was a protest against the suffering of the proletariat. The protest came not from the monarchy or the state, not from the aristocracy or the new bourgeois class. The protest, the only protest, came from the Christian religion, which gave voice to the cry of the poor in face of heartless and soulless conditions. And yet his praise of religion is qualified. If Christian voices were raised in prophetic denunciation, more often they were raised in the justification of the status quo. 'It is the opium of the people.' The metaphor of opium was common in 1844, coming within two years of the end of the opium wars with China. In the nineteenth century opium had a particular place in society. Medicine could diagnose many illnesses but had no cure for them. In conditions of suffering, hopelessness and despair there was opium. It made the intolerable tolerable: it reconciled people to their lot. And for Marx this was the function of Christianity. By legitimizing the political, social and economic order of things it enticed the suffering poor into the acceptance of their poverty. The rich man in his castle, the poor man at his gate: this was not just the order of things, it was the divine order of things against which there should be neither protest nor rebellion. Religion as the opium of the people stole from their minds the imagination to see that things might be different and stole from their hearts the courage to change history. This is the same reversal of reality, the same projection into the heavens of the current arrangements here on earth.

To the philosophical criticism is added the moral protest. In a real sense it is biblical criticism come home to expose Christian indifference. It sounds like the word of God spoken by a man who in his most famous photograph looks every inch an Old Testament prophet, a man whose Jewish family on both sides included many famous rabbis from Poland, Hungary, Italy and Holland.

There is, however, a third criticism of religion to be found in Marx's works, and it is the one which has gained him a place as one of the three great masters of suspicion. It derives from the last stage of his development, as he formulated his historical materialism. It begins with another famous sentence: 'The philosophers have only interpreted the world, in various ways; the point, however, is to change it' (*Eleventh Thesis on Feuerbach*). The philosophers have interpreted the world. Hegel had justified the course of history, culminating in the form of the Prussian state. Marx might just as well have said that the theologians have interpreted the world in various ways, justifying the suffering of this life with the bribe of the reward of the life to come. Always the same justification, the same reversal of reality, the same mistake. A mistake, yes, but not a simple mistake. It was an incorrigible mistake, one that refused to be corrected in the face of increasing and incontestable evidence. Feuerbach had described the formation of consciousness; Marx now called it 'false consciousness'. Why was the false picture of reality perpetuated and defended by philosophy and theology in the face of the facts? Here suspicion arises. The present arrangement of things, legitimated by religion, suits the interests of the ruling class against the interests of the ruled. Since the Roman emperor Constantine in the fourth century, the Christian church has thrown in its lot with the rich and powerful, thinking that the interests of religion were best served when it legitimized the interests of Caesar. This is Marx's theory of ideology. An ideology is a (false) picture of reality that suits the interests of the powerful against the weak, the rich against the poor. His third criticism of religion is that Christianity is itself such an ideology or at least more often than not legitimizes the ideology of the ruling class.

Friedrich Nietzsche (1844–1900). If Marx criticized Christianity because of its oppressive functions, Nietzsche criticized it because of its debilitating effects. Neither took time to debate the existence of God. Nietzsche's philosophy begins with the declaration of the 'death of God', a phrase which is much more significant than an assertion of atheism. As a boy Nietzsche was deeply religious and indeed it was thought by his family that he would follow his father as a Lutheran pastor. As so often happens, it was when he was a student at Bonn that he lost his religious faith. This was a personal tragedy for him, but he came to reflect on it as an instance of a deeper movement in European culture. His life had been based on his religious faith, but then the whole of European culture was likewise based on religious premises, for example the rather naïve belief in science that there are such things as facts. But if increasingly people no longer subscribe to these premises, then the foundations of European civilization are dismantled: the possibility of truth, the justification of morality and the sense of aesthetic judgements. The death of God is therefore a metaphor for the loss of the foundations of European culture. In *The Gay Science* the Madman comes at noontime with his lantern to announce the impending doom, but he comes too early. Nietzsche's analysis proved to be prophetic, and it was a century later before the full effects of secularization were experienced in Europe.

Secularization

In the face of this rising tide, project Canute attempts to roll back the waves and re-establish the religious foundations. However, for Nietzsche, if the loss is at first experienced negatively, it opens up the possibility of establishing new foundations. And this is the beginning of his criticism of Christianity. He does not seek to return to the past because the effects of Christianity have been so destructive on the development of European civilization. He offers two criticisms.

Nietzsche's basic criticism of Christianity is that it is against nature. When the early church emerged from Palestine into the Roman empire proper it came under the intellectual influence of the sophisticated Idealist philosophy of Plato. The two were structurally similar: there is another world that is eternal, perfect and spiritual in contrast to this world which is transitory, flawed and material. Christianity was influenced by Platonism's evaluation that the spiritual was good and the material evil. In European history there is evidence to support Nietzsche's contention that Christianity has condemned the natural life, seeing it as inimical to the spiritual life. But if the Idealist, religious premises have been set aside, this judgement can be reviewed.

Take the example of aggression. In the development of animals and human beings aggression has been absolutely fundamental to the individual and society. Neither could have survived or prospered without it. It is therefore good and its absence is bad. Christianity, however, has condemned it. Nietzsche claims that it should be sublimated and used to achieve ends appropriate to contemporary society. Christianity has been suspicious of the passions. Nietzsche claims that by being sublimated, the new virtues become the old passions in an enhanced state. (This is not so very different from Adam Smith's view a century before

God

that there are some social goods that can only result from the exercise of self-interest.) Christianity has excommunicated the instincts; Nietzsche wishes to harness them (to baptize them). This is the motivation behind his 'revaluation of all values'. Nihilism represents the loss of faith in all values, but Nietzsche wishes to overcome nihilism not by a return to Christian values but by a return to what he considers original, natural values. These values are natural and they arose not from idealism but from materialism, from physiology – even chemistry.

Not surprisingly, therefore, Nietzsche draws the conclusion that Christianity has led to degeneration and to decadence. He can point to remnants of the older order of things even within contemporary society, representing it in rather élitist, even classicist, terms. At an earlier stage society depended on certain dominant individuals. Nietzsche describes them as noble, aristocratic. The majority, described by Nietzsche with the disparaging term 'herd', rely on these leaders. Society develops through this natural arrangement as long as the noble values are acknowledged. But then comes Christianity to condemn the noble values and to substitute the virtues of weakness, piety and submission. This revaluation feeds the *ressentiment* of the herd against the rulers. And now in Christian democratic Europe the lunatics have taken over the asylum, the herd has displaced the exemplars of the noble values.

This is, of course, a very selective reading of European social history, and Nietzsche was well aware that members of the aristocracy have failed to exhibit the noble values, while individuals born into the herd have emerged to display these same values. The situation is ambiguous, but Nietzsche takes it into account with a move that at first sight seems equally ambiguous.

Nietzsche's second criticism is that Christianity is the religion of the herd. (According to Paul it was certainly drawn from the lower classes of Roman society.) For Nietzsche it is not a religion of striving but of acceptance. It fosters the attitude of dependence. 'God was in Christ reconciling the world to himself' (2 Corinthians 5.19). It is a faith that someone else has done something for you, something that you could not do for yourself. For Nietzsche, that is the attitude of decadence that leads to regression. However, it is at this point that Nietzsche makes a distinction between the Christ of faith and Jesus as a 'free spirit'. Jesus exhibits the noble values and calls on people to follow him. It is a demanding life, a narrow way and a straight gate through which few will enter. This is Nietzsche's final criticism of Christianity. Christianity is a religion of decadence in which faith in what has been done substitutes for belief in what is required. Here is a contrast between the religion *about* Jesus and the religion *of* Jesus. The terminology might be ambiguous, but the meaning is clear: Christianity is un-Christian.

Sigmund Freud (1856–1939). With Freud we come to another critic who has moved beyond proofs for the existence of God. As a psychiatrist he presents us not with an argument but with a diagnosis. Religion is not a mistake; it is a form of mental illness. As the founder of psychoanalysis, Freud offers a psychoanalytic account of the origins, function and fate of religion in the life of the individual and of society life. His early career was in neuro-anatomy, but he turned from the brain to the mind when he became convinced of the importance of the unconscious. There are repressed forces, desires and fears, based in the unconscious, which come to influence behaviour. In his account of the Oedipus complex, Freud famously claimed that infants go through a period in which they have sexual desires for their other-sex parent and a desire to be rid of the rival parent. Everyone goes through these unconscious processes. Most people achieve a healthy adult outcome, but some develop neuroses that can be uncovered only by a psychiatrist. Freud places religion in the neurotic sphere of human life: his criticism of religion emerges as he uncovers its 'real' origins and functions. 'Real' can be placed in quotation marks because Freud claims that the psychoanalyst can uncover the real sources of behaviour which remain unconscious and even alien to the subject.

A good example of this is to be seen in Freud's earliest attempt to apply psychoanalysis to religion, 'Obsessive Actions and Religious Practices' (1907). The article contains an interesting, suggestive thesis. Obsessive neurotic actions are typically performed repeatedly but also precisely – cleaning a room, washing the hands, walking by a prescribed route. When questioned, the subject will give reasons for these actions, reasons that seem entirely inadequate to the observer. The subject is unaware of the real reasons that, for Freud, are frequently associated with feelings of anxiety and guilt concerning early sexual traumas. The actions have a meaning and a function for the subject, but the analyst may be able to discover their real meaning and function and hence cure the neurosis so that the actions can be dispensed with. The parallel with religion is clear, although it must be said that Freud fails to develop his argument properly; the parallel could have been illustrated with better examples. It is said, metaphorically, that obsessive actions are performed 'religiously'. If the process is interrupted the subject will return to the beginning, otherwise it will not 'take'. In religion a ritual must be completed using precise words gestures and actions, performed in a particular place by a prescribed person. Otherwise it will not take, will not be efficacious. Reasons will be given, stated in detail and with conviction, but these will not seem adequate to the observer. The ritual actions will have a meaning and function for believers: Freud as psychoanalyst will offer to uncover the 'real' reasons, the 'real' meaning and function. And this is his criticism of religion. It does not disclose reality to us, but obscures it. It does not reveal a higher world outside us but rather the traumas of a lower world within us. Freud offers not simply an account of religion but a cure from it.

As one of the main contributors to modernity Freud is an essentialist. He was still publishing the results of his biological research into his forties. He clearly expected to be able to give an account that would be true of all members of a species. Turning to religion, he expected to uncover the same origins and function of religion that are true for all members of the human species. He was not content with an account that was sociological or culture-specific. Everyone is neurotic, to some degree: one's participation in religion must be an expression of neurosis. Religion, Freud tells us, is 'a universal obsessional neurosis'. In contemporary religious studies there is a movement away from essentialism. The origins and development of religions are related to geography, climate, social structure and individual identity formation. Individuals who are neurotic will participate in religion – neurotically – but that does not mean that religion is nothing but the expression of neuroses.

In his early essay Freud applied psychoanalysis to individual behaviour, but he was intrigued by anthropological research being undertaken at that time into the communal rituals of aboriginal peoples. In *Totem and Taboo* (1913) he identified two features of totemic religion: the ambivalence towards the father (symbolized by the totem animal) and exogamy forbidding marriage within the tribal group (avoiding incest). Thus while aboriginals (and anthropologists) might give reasons for totemic practices, Freud saw in totemic religion the two elements of the Oedipus complex. Freud assumed totemism, as animism, to be the earliest form of religion. As an essentialist he assumed it to be a universal form common to all human societies. As an evolutionist he identified it as the first of three stages of the development of societies. As a psychoanalyst he simply asserted a parallel between the three stages of social development and the three stages of individual development. (None of these assumptions would be accepted today.) If the first stage of individual development is concern for the self (animism), the second stage sees the individual child coming to terms with the parents, specifically the father. This is the subject of Freud's last work, *Moses and Monotheism,* in which he deals with Judaism as the religion of the Father. There is more than enough sex and guilt in the Bible for Freud to interpret Judaism as the vain attempt by a people to deal with their inherited corporate guilt. (In this Freud accepted the already dated views of Jean-Baptiste Lamarck, 1744–1829, on inherited acquired characteristics.) Once again he fails to use the best material. The Last Supper, the eating of the body and blood of the Son, links very well with the original totemic meal from which he claims religion arose.

In *The Future of an Illusion* (1927) Freud deals with the third and final stage in development. For the individual it is adulthood and the adjustment to the social world at large. For society it is the emergence of science (a progression reminiscent of Auguste Comte). Religion is the means by which individuals and societies deal with their neuroses. Science (represented by psychoanalysis) comes to cure them of their neuroses. On this account religion functions like Marx's opium: it enables people to live with their neuroses instead of tackling them. Perhaps one of the great illusions of the twentieth century was psychoanalysis itself.

Culture criticism

There have been critics of religion in the twentieth century, but none to compare with the great masters of suspicion. One reason for this has been the change in the place of religion in Western culture.

Nietzsche anticipated a time when the religious foundations of Western culture would be removed. This movement we now call secularization, the process by which education, health, welfare, indeed all aspects of day-to-day life have their meaning and justification with respect to this world as opposed to another world. Where previously religion bestowed meaning on all aspects of life, secular culture bestows its meaning and value on religion, which has now itself become an aspect of secular life. In these circumstances those who wish to contest the possibilities of life or the structures of society need not first take on religion. The Danish theologian Søren Kierkegaard said that only two kinds of people understand religion: those who are passionately for it and those who are passionately against it. In the modern world of the twentieth century fewer people have been passionately against religion. There was an assumption that it would decline and eventually disappear. This eurocentric view ignored the fact that religion continued to thrive in the USA and indeed was flourishing throughout the rest of the world. However, in the last quarter of the twentieth century it became evident that the assumption of decline was not entirely confirmed even in Europe. Ironically, it was the modern world itself that came under sustained criticism rather than religion.

Culture

Søren Kierkegaard

It was Nietzsche's fear that Western culture would never be rid of God: that is, that religious assumptions would underlie even secular thought. We have already seen examples of this in Freud's essentialism and Nietzsche's warning that ideas of truth or facts depend on religious assumptions. Jacques Derrida has led the deconstruction of many of the assumptions that the Enlightenment

Enlightenment

project took for granted. The attack has not taken the form of a criticism of religion, though institutional religion has sometimes been included in a cultural class-action suit. So, for example, Jean-François Lyotard in *The Post-modern Condition* (1979) claims that grand narratives are no longer credible. Examples of grand narratives include Hegel's absolute idealism and Marx's historical materialism, systems that bestow meaning on individuals and events. But Eschatology the Christian doctrine of providence or eschatology would also fall within this class. In so far as Christianity continues to provide the metaphysical underpinning of modernity, it is indirectly criticized by postmodern writers. However, as we have seen, modernity was fiercely critical of religion. On the basis of the-enemy-of-my-enemy, we should not be surprised to find that there is actually a renewed interest in religion among some postmodern thinkers. As the philosopher Luce Irigaray observes, 'Sociology quickly bores me when I'm expecting the divine.'

ALISTAIR KEE

Giles Fraser, *Redeeming Nietzsche: On the Piety of Unbelief*, London and New York: Routledge 2002; Graham Ward (ed), *The Post-modern God: A Theological Reader*, Oxford: Blackwell 1997

Crusades

Crusades were not the only 'holy wars' fought by Christians, but they were the most radical in their ideology and the Forgiveness most attractive to ordinary men and women. The church, which has been reluctant to give unequivocal approval to other forms of warfare, endorsed them wholeheartedly. p. 476 Pilgrimage From the twelfth century to the seventeenth the consensus of the teaching of the bishops was that qualified men had a moral obligation to volunteer. This was reinforced by the support of men and women universally regarded as 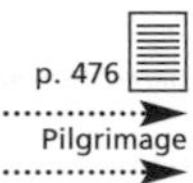 saints: Bernard of Clairvaux, Thomas Aquinas, Bridget of Sweden, Catherine of Siena, even probably Francis of Assisi. From Urban II in 1095 to Innocent XI in 1684, pope after pope wrote or authorized the despatch of letters, including many general ones, in which the faithful were summoned to crusade, offered spiritual privileges if they responded and threatened with divine judgement if they did not. These letters comprise an impressive, coherent and consistent body of teaching. The popes also recognized a new type of religious institute in approving  p. 1019 of and privileging the military orders. At least five general councils legislated for crusades. Two of them, the Fourth Council Lateran Council (1215) and the Second Council of Lyons (1274), published the constitutions *Ad liberandam* and *Pro zelo fidei*, which were among the movement's defining documents.

And yet it is astonishing that none of the authors of the best-known multi-volume histories of the twentieth century, René Grousset, Steven Runciman and the American team led by Kenneth Setton, were prepared to state clearly what a crusade was and that when definition became a subject for discussion it proved to be controversial. Four 'schools' of historians were identified in the debate that followed. *Generalists* believed that any attempt at definition was more limiting than helpful and held that any Christian religious war fought for God, or in the belief that its prosecution was furthering God's intentions for humankind, was a crusade. *Popularists* proposed that the essence of crusading lay in a prophetic, eschatological exaltation arising collectively in the peasantry and the urban proletariat. *Traditionalists* treated as authentic only those expeditions launched for the recovery of Jerusalem or in its defence. *Pluralists*, on the other hand, maintained that many campaigns in other theatres of war, preached as crusades and fought by men and women who had taken crusade vows and enjoyed crusade privileges, were as authentic as those to or in aid of Jerusalem.

Most historians are now pluralist. They describe crusades as penitential war-pilgrimages, which were legitimized by the popes as representatives of Christ. Their cause – the recovery of property or defence against injury – was 'just' in the traditional Christian sense, but was related to the needs of all Christendom or the church, rather than to those of a particular nation or region. Crusaders were volunteers who took a public vow, enforceable by the church and signified by the wearing of a cloth cross. They were also penitents, who performed their military service as a penance to expiate their sins, of which the church granted them a full remission. From 1198 this remission was reformulated as a plenary indulgence. Pilgrimage terminology was often used of crusaders, and some of the privileges they enjoyed, particularly the protection of themselves, their families and properties, were associated with those of pilgrims.

Many crusades were preached long after Jerusalem had faded from the scene, and from almost the first they manifested themselves in different theatres: the eastern Mediterranean region, of course, but also North Africa, Spain, the Baltic shores, Poland, Hungary, the Balkans and even the interior of Western Europe. It follows that the Muslims, who provided the opposition in North Africa and Spain as well as in Palestine, Syria, the Aegean and later the Balkans, were not uniquely significant, since crusaders were also engaged against Pagan Wends, Balts and Lithuanians, Shamanist Mongols, Orthodox Russians and Greeks, Cathar and Hussite heretics and Catholic political opponents of the papacy.

From the fourth century to the sixteenth most Christian thinkers believed that God or Christ could and would authorize the use of force, either personally or through an intermediary. Scriptural support was not hard to find in the Old Testament, but most theologians followed Augustine of Hippo, the greatest theoretician of Christian violence, in maintaining that it was also provided in the New Testament. They regularly referred to Luke 3.14 (the advice of John the Baptist to soldiers), Luke 22.36–8 and 49–51 (the swords at the Last Supper and in the Garden of Gethsemane), John 18.10–11 (Peter and the sword in the Garden of Gethsemane) and Romans 13.4 (Paul on the coercive authority of the state). Although force could only be employed within certain parameters, which came to be expressed in the criteria of just cause, legitimate authority and right intention, the idea that in certain situations its use was positively pleasing to God became embedded in Christian thought. Until the nineteenth century, moreover, the majority opinion was that acts of violence were not in themselves evil, but were morally neutral and took ethical colouring – bad or good – from the perpetrators' intentions. In the eleventh century this belief had been reinforced by a growing conviction that death while engaged in righteous violence could be martyrdom, although it co-existed rather uncomfortably with concerns about the disposition of fighters and their ability, even when engaged in a just war on the church's behalf, to avoid occasions of sin.

The theology of war developed rapidly in the second half of the eleventh century because the radical reformers who had seized control of the papacy felt threatened in a civil war that had broken out in Italy and Germany. Three scholars who had sought refuge with the most zealous of Pope Gregory VII's supporters, Countess Mathilda of Tuscany, set out to justify the use of force on behalf of a reforming church. Anselm of Lucca anthologized the writings of Augustine, scattered throughout 40 years of authorship, and made them coherent and usable. Bonizo of Sutri took up the idea of martyrdom in battle, which had been expounded by popes from the ninth century, and John of Mantua justified the authority of the papacy to summon knights to fight in its defence, basing his argument on the incident in the Garden of Gethsemane when Peter had drawn a sword on Jesus' behalf. Although as a priest Peter had not been permitted to wield the sword himself, he and his successors the popes had authority over it, since Jesus had told him to put it back into its scabbard rather than throw it away.

It was another idea – that the perpetration of violence could itself be a penitential activity – which was truly revolutionary. Although it is possible that this is to be found embryonically in the so-called Barbastro indulgence issued by Pope Alexander II in 1063–4, so many doubts have been expressed about that isolated and enigmatic fragment that it is safer to date its introduction to the early 1080s, when Pope Gregory VII 'ordered … Mathilda (of Tuscany) to fight the Emperor Henry for the remission of her sins'. It was pointed out at the time that this mandate was unprecedented – as indeed it was – and that Gregory was 'inciting to bloodshed … secular men seeking release from their sins'. His justification for it was explained by one of Anselm of Lucca's priests when he transmitted a blessing to Mathilda's army in 1085. 'We were (he wrote) to impose on the soldiers the danger of the coming battle for the remission of all their sins.'

This presented the faithful with an entirely new form of warfare. But while it put certain expressions of violence on much the same meritorious level as fasting, prayer and works of mercy, it would never have been easy to justify the inflicting of pain and loss of life, with the consequential distortion of the penitent's internal disposition, as a penance simply because he was exposing himself to danger, however unpleasant the experience might have been for him. The achievement of Pope Urban II, the preacher of the First Crusade, was to give the idea a context in which it could be presented more convincingly, because he associated warfare for the physical liberation of the Holy Sepulchre with the most charismatic of all traditional penances, pilgrimage to Jerusalem. This had a theoretical advantage over Gregory's formulation, because violence was now associated with an act which was indubitably penitential. The danger and physical hardships of the coming expedition still had significance, of course, but they no longer provided the main justification for treating the war as a penance; instead they gave added value to a penance that was primarily justified through its association with pilgrimage. Over time, the penitential nature of crusading was to some extent to be diluted by ideas of chivalric duty, but the movement never entirely lost the notion that a crusader's service was, or should be, grounded on sorrow for sin.

Crusading came into being with Urban's formal summons to the First Crusade at Clermont on 27 November 1095. After an epic campaign the city of Jerusalem fell to the crusaders on 15 July 1099. If it had not done so, it is likely that the movement would have been still born, since there are signs that senior churchmen were worried by the new theology of penitential war, but any potential criticism now faltered. The achievement of the first crusaders, who without horses and pack-animals – they had nearly all died within a year – and without any overall commander or system of provisioning, and encumbered by non-combatants, had marched into Asia and after two terrible years had taken Jerusalem, 2000 miles from home, was an inspiration for centuries. Once the conviction that God had intervened on their behalf was fixed in the minds of Western men and women, nothing, not even catastrophe, could expunge it, because

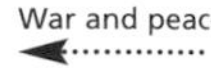

CRUSADES TO THE HOLY LAND

First Crusade: Preached by Pope Urban II at the Council of Clermont in 1095. Four major contingents set out, led by noblemen. They captured Antioch in 1098 and Jerusalem in 1099. Four crusader states were established.

'People's Crusade': Disorganized attempts, the most famous led by Peter the Hermit and Walter the Penniless. They only got as far as Byzantium and were annihilated (1096).

Second Crusade: Crusader bull issued by Eugenius III in 1145, protecting crusaders' property and families. The crusade was proclaimed by Bernard of Clairvaux. French and German contingents were led by King Louis VII and Emperor Conrad III. The crusade collapsed in 1148 after a failed attempt to capture Damascus. Subsequently Saladin reoccupied much of crusader territory including Jerusalem in 1187.

Third Crusade: Crusader bull issued by Gregory VIII in response to the failure of the Second Crusade and the fall of Jerusalem (1189). The crusade was led by Richard the Lionheart of England and Philipp II Augustus of France. Philipp returned after the capturing of Acre; Richard conquered Cyprus, but the crusade did not get to Jerusalem (1192).

Fourth Crusade: Promoted by Innocent III and launched in 1202. Led by several French noblemen with the involvement of Venice, which provided the transport. Under the influence of the Venetians, and their trade rivalry with Constantinople, the Crusade was diverted to Constantinople, which it captured and looted in 1203.

Children's Crusade: 1212. Thousands of children set out to free the Holy Land, only to be lost, shipwrecked or sold into slavery.

Fifth Crusade: The last crusade in which the papacy played an active part. It was launched in 1218 after an elaborate plan had been made for a crusade at the Fourth Lateran Council (1215), and consisted largely of French crusaders. Its goal was Egypt as a base for an attack on Jerusalem but little was achieved. Francis of Assisi went out and met the Muslim sultan.

Sixth Crusade: Led by Emperor Frederick II, not least for his own political motives, and launched in 1227. He was excommunicated by the Pope. This robbed him of support and what achievements he had were through diplomacy.

Crusade of Louis IX of France: Launched by Louis IX in 1248 with papal support. It again focused on Egypt but had little success: Louis IX was captured and had to be ransomed.

failure in the future could always be explained not as a demonstration that crusading was against God's wishes, but by the fact that his present instruments were too unworthy to carry it out. Although crusading took some time to establish itself as a regular activity, the shocked reaction of the West to the loss of Jerusalem to Saladin in 1187 led rapidly to its institutionalization and to the establishment of a system of clerical taxation to subsidize future expeditions and ensure recruitment. The thirteenth century was the high point of the movement, but even after the loss of Palestine in 1291 crusaders continued for centuries to defend Christian possessions in the eastern Mediterranean region against the advance of Islam.

Crusading was too useful an instrument for it to be confined to expeditions in the East. It was associated with an assault on the Balearic Islands in 1114 and thereafter it became a feature of the reconquest of the Iberian peninsula. Granada, the last Muslim stronghold in Spain, fell in 1492, after which crusading spread along the North African coast, where a string of beachheads was established as far east as Tripoli. The movement reached the Baltic region in 1147, where it came to be particularly associated with the Teutonic Knights. The states of Finland, Estonia and Latvia were its creations. Crusading was first proposed against political opponents of the papacy in 1135; and for the second half of the thirteenth century and most of the fourteenth there was almost continual campaigning in defence of papal interests in Italy. It was preached against heretics in Western Europe in the early thirteenth century. The most famous crusades of that kind were the Albigensian Crusades (1209–29) and the Hussite Crusades (1420–31). From 1188 to 1500 there was hardly a year when a crusade was not being fought somewhere.

The last crusades of the classic type were probably the expedition of Sebastian of Portugal into Morocco in 1578 and the Armada against England ten years later. By then, however, the Muslims were deep into Europe and resistance to them had mutated into another form. Crusade leagues, which had originated in the fourteenth century, were alliances of front-line powers, representing their interests rather than those of Christendom as a whole, although the participants were granted crusade

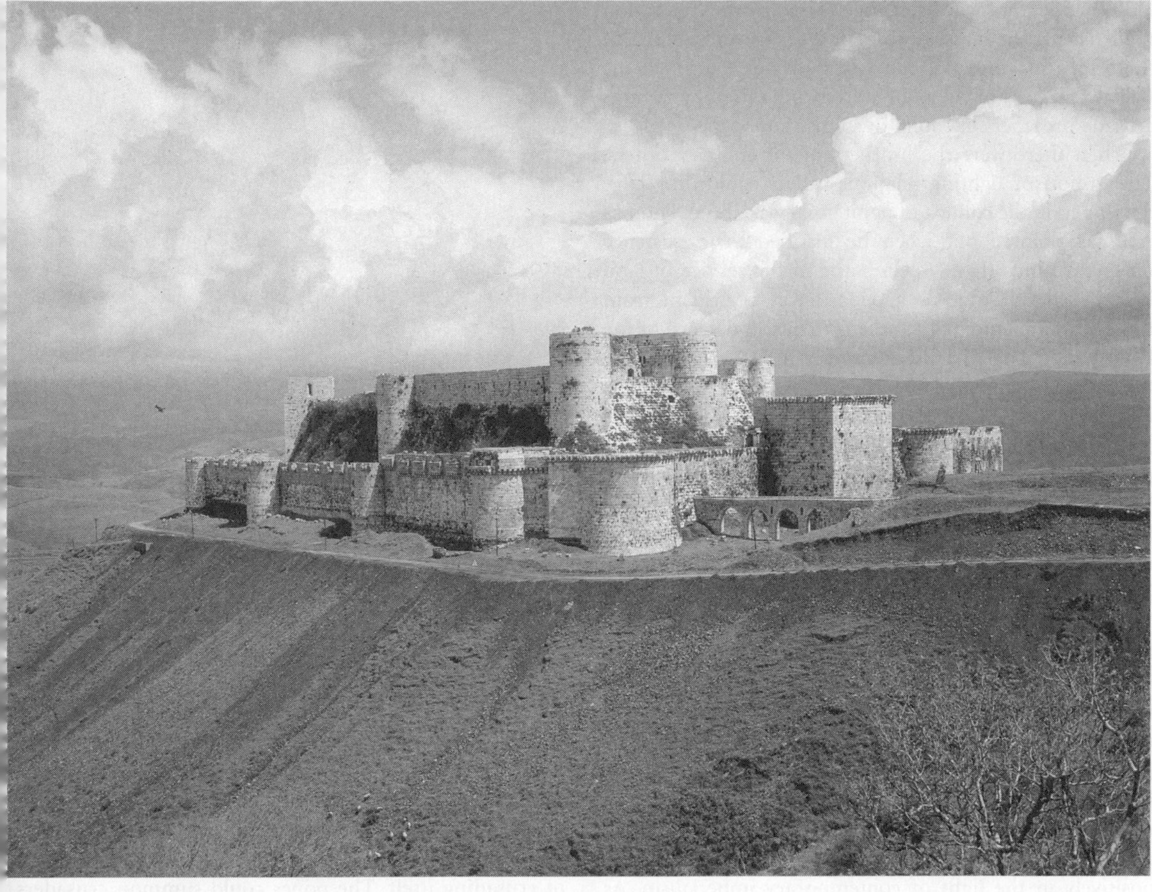

Crusader fortress of Krak des Chevaliers, Syria, 1142–1271

privileges. Leagues of this type won the battle of Lepanto in 1571, defended Crete between 1645 and 1669 and began the recovery of the Balkans in 1684. But by then crusading, unfashionable and despised by intellectuals, was in rapid decline, although the island of Malta, ruled by the Knights Hospitallers of St John, remained a centre of activity until its loss to Napoleon in 1798.

Although it was common for the armies to contain mercenaries who had not taken the cross, the nucleus of every crusade had to consist of crusaders. Men and women with a wide range of perceptions, cerebral as well as emotional, were inspired to join or to provide intellectual or material support, but taking part appealed particularly to a certain type of European armsbearer: pious and guilt-ridden; usually a member of a kin-group predisposed to respond positively through attachment to family traditions of pilgrimage, the veneration of certain saints, the benefaction of particular religious houses and later chivalry and crusading itself; and often associated with other enthusiasts in a network centred on a committed feudal lord. Merchants, artisans and city burgesses also took part. And there were large numbers of poor non-combatants attached to the early expeditions. These contributed little and were a source of concern for the leaders, who felt responsible for them, but they could not be prevented from joining because as pilgrimages crusades had to be open to all. In the early thirteenth century the papacy tried to solve the problem of non-combatants by encouraging everyone to take the cross while allowing those who were 'unsuitable' to redeem their vows for small sums of cash. This was to lead to the notorious 'sale of indulgences' and it is hard to tell how effective it was. On the other hand, the growing practice of transporting the armies by sea imposed on the poor the need to pay passage fees which few of them could afford, and the popular crusades of the thirteenth and early fourteenth centuries, the Children's Crusade (1212), the Crusades of the Shepherds (1251, 1320) and the Popular Crusade

(1309) appear to have been engendered by the frustration that ensued. The masses never left the stage entirely and in the fifteenth century, as the Turks advanced through the Balkans, armies of the poor were being raised by famous crusade preachers like John of Capistrano.

Then there were the brothers of the military orders. The notion of fighting religious orders could only have developed in the context of penitential warfare, as Thomas Aquinas pointed out when he justified their existence on the grounds that: 'To do battle in the service of God is imposed on some as a penance, as is evident from those who are enjoined to take up arms in defence of the Holy Land.' The first brothers of a military order were the Knights Templar. They were followed by the Knights Hospitallers of St John and then by many others, including the Teutonic Knights and the Knights of Santiago, Calatrava and Christ. Although the Templars were suppressed in 1312, the Knights Hospitallers of St John and the Teutonic Knights created highly original theocratic polities, the order-states of Rhodes, Malta and Prussia. Their orders still survive today.

From 1098 onwards settlements were established in the Levant in the wake of crusades. Most migrants to them had never been crusaders, the vast majority of whom returned home once their campaigning was over, but many historians – and the public at large – have come to believe that a prime motivation for crusading was materialistic. This conviction seems to have originated in the nineteenth century, when French and British politicians, artists and historians viewed the crusades very positively in the light of contemporary imperialism. As imperialism itself came to be discredited in the 1920s and 1930s, the crusades, stripped of their ideology, began to be interpreted in social and economic terms by economic historians, who had, of course, inherited from the imperialists the idea that crusading was an early example of colonialism, in spite of the fact that no economic history of it has ever been written. Common to all theories of materialistic motivation is the absence of evidential proof and a refusal to acknowledge that the evidence that has come to light points in a different direction, at least with respect to crusaders to the East. These men seem to have been ideologically motivated, although many must have regretted the vows they had made on the spur of the moment in fevered public gatherings, fired by preachers who were employing all the razzmatazz needed to create religious hysteria and gain recruits.

The emotions whipped up by the preachers help to explain the atrocities that were often associated with groups of men preparing to depart. The most notorious of these, the persecutions of European Jews, were characterized by attempts to force baptism on them and by calls for vengeance, expressed in the language of the vendetta.

Crusaders, from a thirteenth-century floor tile in S. Giovanni Evangelista, Ravenna

Virulent anti-Judaism, which featured in the preparations for almost every crusade to the East in the central Middle Ages, demonstrated how weak the church was. This impotence stemmed paradoxically from the nature of crusading itself. The popes could summon crusaders, tax the church to provide funds, arrange for shipping, work to establish peace in Western Europe while a crusade was in the field and discuss strategy with the leaders, but they were helpless thereafter, because as priests they, and their representatives in the armies, were prevented in law from bearing arms or physically directing them. For the conduct of a campaign they were totally dependent on the lay volunteers who had taken the cross. Many crusades were characterized by indiscipline and by a kaleidoscopic shifting of allegiances as minor lords moved from one contingent to another, or armies and individuals came and went.

Although the introduction of taxation meant that subsidies to individual crusaders could be employed as a measure of control, indiscipline remained a feature. The rhetoric which persuaded audiences to commit themselves to a strenuous, expensive and dangerous activity so heightened emotions that turbulent forces were unleashed. Two levels co-existed in the crusading movement, one institutional and the other charismatic; and the institution needed charisma if a crusade was to be launched at all.

JONATHAN RILEY-SMITH

C. Hillenbrand, *The Crusades. Islamic Perspectives*, Edinburgh: Edinburgh University Press 1999; N. J. Housley, *Religious Warfare in Europe, 1400–1536*, Oxford: OUP 2002; J. S. C. Riley-Smith (ed), *The Oxford Illustrated History of the Crusades*, Oxford: OUP 1995 (reprinted as *The Oxford History of the Crusades*, Oxford: OUP 1999) and *What were the Crusades?*, Basingstoke: Palgrave Macmillan [3]2002; F. H. Russell, *The Just War in the Middle Ages*, Cambridge: CUP 1975

Culture

Christianity has an ambiguous relationship to cultures. Its claim is that God became a particular human being in Jesus of Nazareth, who saved the entire world, indeed the universe. One singular divine intervention in Jewish culture had universal saving effects. This profound belief established Christianity's missionary impulse. In the Gospel of Matthew (28.19), Jesus is said to have commanded his followers to preach and baptize throughout the world. At the same moment, however, this belief that God had acted decisively in Jesus enshrined a tension within Christianity itself. Missionaries soon began to cross cultural and religious boundaries. When they preached faith in the person of Jesus, should this also include the particularity of Jewish cultural customs and religious laws? One of the first controversies within the Christian community, discussed by the apostle Paul, focused on whether Christians could eat the 'meat sacrificed to idols' (1 Corinthians 8.7–13; Acts 15.19–20). What was Paul's solution? One could legitimately eat such meat, but it was better not to do so, so as not to scandalize one's neighbour. However, clearly Christ was not bound to a single cultural and religious expression.

Converts to Christ rapidly assumed cultural religious habits marked by local indigenous patterns of behaviour, language, worship and understanding. The images and concepts used in preaching in Antioch differed from those used in Damascus, Alexandria, Corinth, Thessalonica, Armenia or Rome. Christians prayed in Aramaic, Syriac, Armenian, Greek, Coptic and Latin. Once these local differences took root, where was the norm for determining communion across great distances and historical continuity with the first preacher, Jesus?

Quickly, differing forms of Christian expression vied for authenticity. Some believed that 'knowing' was enough: Gnostics drew the veil from the confusion of the cosmos. Others thought that maintaining their Jewish legal and dietary laws would maintain unity. The tradition represented by the church fathers Ignatius of Antioch and Irenaeus of Lyons argued that the norms for continuity and communion were to be found in the Christ proclaimed by the apostles and the scriptures. This norm also required close adherence to the local bishop. Rapidly, worship was codified around major Christian episcopates and language groups: Antioch, Alexandria, Armenia, Damascus, Jerusalem, Rome. The collection of books called the Bible was established by 200 CE. The Apostles' Creed was circulated early in oral form as a norm for doctrine emerging from the trinitarian baptismal liturgy. All of these – liturgy, creed, government of the church by bishops, the number of books in the Bible itself – emerged from the commitment to the person of Jesus of Nazareth as universal saviour. The book, the bishop, the apostles and the creed were the marks of communion and continuity.

Canon
Bible
Creed

The internal tensions of this claim became evident in the controversy over icons from 725 to 842 in the Eastern churches. Icons or images of Christ and his mother were condemned by patriarchs and emperors because they attempted to present the invisible God in cultural clothing. Cultural images were idols; icons were to be destroyed. Icon worshippers, however, claimed that iconoclasts no longer believed in the incarnation of God. After much conflict, the Second Council of Nicaea in 787 approved the appropriate veneration of images, but made it clear that these were not to be identified with the Godhead. However, the controversy continued unabated for cultural and theological reasons until the death of the Emperor Theophilus in 842. It re-emerged in the Western Church especially during the Reformation. Huldrych Zwingli, the Swiss Reformer, could state that no vehicle was necessary for the Spirit. Christianity transcended cultures; indeed, it had no need of them.

Icon
Jesus
Iconoclasm
Council
Mission

Paul

Christian commitment to Jewish cultural origins, then to the tradition of the apostles and the scriptures, established norms by which local cultures were to be formed and judged. One might wear the same clothes as nonbelievers or speak their language in liturgy, but one could not behave as they did. If culture is a set of meanings and values that inform a way of life, then Christianity not only had many different cultural expressions; it also claimed that there was a normative dimension within those cultures. How was it possible to think through, let alone live, this dual claim to pluralism and normativity? Did it mean a single determinative Christian culture or something more complex? On the one hand Christianity was to evangelize the world by becoming part of its diversity; on the other, it had to maintain its unique normative status. These questions are still urgent today.

Food and drink

Gnosis

Classicist and historical culture

Contemporary men and women inhabit a historical culture in which they could not imagine anything other than being immersed in diverse cultures. Each of these

cultures has a history, and since the eighteenth-century Enlightenment, human beings believe themselves to be intrinsically affected by historical events. Human beings change in the course of history. They are shaped by history and they shape it, thereby shaping one another. Western post-industrial cultures would find it impossible to imagine themselves otherwise since the Enlightenment and the political revolutions of the nineteenth century.

Enlightenment

An older view of culture, the one that informed most of Christian history, is classicist. Not only was Christ normative, but Culture itself (with a Capital C) had a normative dimension; barbarians did not have culture. They should be colonized and educated according to the proper cultural models. They should accept the ideal paradigms of beauty, philosophy and religion offered to them by the civilized. To the classicist mind, the pluralism of historical cultures is an incidental fact, something that does not affect the inner kernel of things.

The classicist notion of culture naturally married up with the normative nature of Christianity. Christ was the universal saviour who divided his adherents from the non-believers and the damned, just as classicist culture divided the Greeks and Romans from the tents and hovels of the barbarian nomads. Christian theologians found positive norms in the culture that reinforced the gospel: Athens could speak to Jerusalem. They borrowed philosophy, art, music, garments for worship, and so forth. Although they condemned Hellenistic morals, they assumed responsibility for the rest of the Hellenistic cultural empire. The classics of Christian culture that emerged were permanent acquisitions that determined how people should speak, live, work and love. To educate oneself in such a classic Christian culture meant imitating the ideal models, living by the eternal truths, and promulgating permanent laws. Change of any sort was a cultural decline from the ideal norm.

History

Hence, wherever there was Christian worship, doctrine and moral behaviour, a single cultural norm for Christians appeared. Especially after the schism of 1054 the Eastern churches looked to Constantinople for their norms; the Western churches looked to Rome. To live by the 'proper' liturgical books, Charlemagne had turned to Rome for his model (*c.*790). The Jesuits in China, after trying to evangelize from within Chinese culture, were informed by Pope Clement XI (died 1721) that they must cease their adaptations. The classicist does not believe that there can be plural religious expression. The normative nature of faith in Christ is identified with a particular cultural expression of that faith. Circumstances of time and place are merely accidental, and can be ignored in the light of the essential nature of truth and values. Cultures are the husk around the kernel of doctrine, the clothing that can be discarded in favour of the naked truth. And the Truth was Christ conveyed (to their mind) with the true Culture.

Chinese religions and Christianity

The contemporary notion of culture is empirical and historical. There are as many cultures as there are systems of meaning and values. Pluralism reflects the intrinsic nature of human cultural expressions. Pluralism is not simply accidental to the human condition. Being affected by history means being located in a particular place and time, with the recognition that others may view the world differently. For Christians to be able to preach to the diverse cultures of the world presupposes that teachers have deepened and enlarged their own horizons to understand those cultures. To be able to study such cultures creatively means determining not only their failings in meaning and value, but also their positive qualities. The authentic preacher in contemporary cultures mines the resources of a culture to discover where the 'signals of transcendence' might be.

High and low culture

The differences between classicist and historical cultures have often been enshrined in Western thought and action by calibrating the distinctions between high and low culture. High culture and fine art are normative; they model what is enshrined in museums. A 'high priesthood' of art critics decides what is or is not a 'classic' to be included. Low culture is historically mobile, local, craft-laden, and sometimes sentimental kitsch. The presumption that the intensities of high art in music, painting or sculpture are the only proper religious expression is a 'classicist' view of Christianity. It assumes that there is something magically transformative about high culture – that mere acquaintance with it will change the participant. When one absorbs high culture, one will no longer be a barbarian. Not to be able to appreciate such high religious art shows at least ignorance, if not moral laxity.

On the other hand, low culture, the expression of the under-educated and often poorer classes, has its own religious dimensions. Low Christian culture is historical; it is an expression in common sense of an individual's, a community's, or a tribe's understanding of how to live in the world as Christians. Such common-sense religious expressions can be particular to a culture; they may or may not be translatable into another. Low culture is concrete; it shows a willingness to apply itself to every particular situation. Low culture is always incomplete, ready to be amended and/or reworked, depending upon the circumstances. Low culture is expressed in sayings, proverbs, stories, songs, lore and ready-made symbols.

High culture sees those 'low' expressions as limited often doctrinally unclear or ethically ambivalent. It tries to reform them, remove them or erase them from the emerging culture. Such was the attitude of sixteenth-to nineteenth-century European missionaries to Mexico, South America, India, Africa and Indonesia. High religious culture, classicist culture, understands itself as the archetype of all religious expression. Low religious culture with its sentiment, its poor craftwork, its dogmatic insecurities deserves to be uplifted, remade in the likeness of the true Christian Culture.

To include low culture in legitimate religious expressions, not to judge it 'lesser', is to operate from the point of view of 'historical' and empirical culture. Historical culture sees both classicist norms in high culture and the historical plurality of human expressions in low religious cultures and attempts to relate them coherently. The inclusion of historical religious cultures 'de-classicizes' religion. High culture then enters a dialogue with low cultural expressions, competing with them in the public rhetoric of religious convictions.

Christianity has been expressed in high and low cultures since its beginnings. Pilgrim badges for journeys and holy water for houses and churches compete with Michelangelo (1475–1564) and Raphael (1483–1520). Caravaggio's (1573–1610) deliberate transgression of the boundaries between high and low culture made his paintings much desired by some connoisseurs and equally reviled by those church leaders who commissioned them. But if Christians include both high and low culture, the norms of the classicist and the history of ordinary, common-sense expressions in their understanding of their religion, how do they maintain their commitments to the normative Christ and the pluralism of culture?

Christ and culture

In a classic book of 1951, H. Richard Niebuhr described five models for the relationship of Christianity to cultures. Despite the historical inaccuracies of all typologies, his analysis is useful in the way it can locate the ambiguities of the dialogue between Christianity and cultures. In a sense, the first two models are the opposite ends of the spectrum. The final three are in the middle.

First, Christianity is located in opposition to culture. Sin and evil exist in the world, as in the Gospel of John; holiness is the mark of the Christianity community. The role of believers is to judge the culture, condemning its evils. Christianity opposes culture; it has its own 'cultureless' absolute norms. This parallels a 'classicist' understanding of culture.

Secondly, Christianity collapses into culture. Christianity no longer offers any norms to the culture; it absorbs all its moral principles from the cultural situations in which it finds itself. Typologically, this is often attributed to 'liberal Christianity' of the nineteenth century prior to World War I. Christianity simply agrees with the prevailing cultural norms for knowledge and action.

Thirdly, Christianity is above culture, lifting it towards God, but never able to achieve its goal, since God always exceeds cultural expressions. Christians accept that they must live in a material world, but they always hope to rise above it. Matter itself has some ambiguity in this model. Revelation nonetheless provides a superior, i.e. 'supernatural', wisdom and love that far surpasses culture. Christianity must therefore reign over cultures. Niebuhr attributes this position to Thomas Aquinas, Roman Catholicism and certain forms of Anglicanism.

Fourthly, Christianity and culture remain eternally in a paradoxical relationship. The tension will never be resolved. Essentially, this type permits room for dualists who believe that matter and spirit are incompatible, however necessary. Here church and state, the sacred and the profane, spirit and matter, are constantly vying for the allegiance of the believer. Neither wins until the eschatological victory of God over the world.

Finally, Niebuhr argues that Christianity should be the transformer of culture. Culture is sinful, but God's creative power can heal the fallibility and malice because creation was once good in itself. Implicitly, this model believes that culture is a good medium in which it would be possible to embody Christian values in the culture. A Christian culture, at least one that honoured its values, could be developed with the grace of God.

The mutual dialogue of Christianity and culture

The final model that Niebuhr proposed remains the one that most Christians see matching their history. In 'ordinary' times, Christians enter a dialogue with particular cultures in such a way that both are marked by the interchange. To be able to preach the gospel to all nations requires the ability to preach to every class in high and low culture in a way that permits them to absorb the message. This position believes that the introduction of Christian ritual, customs and doctrine into another culture will prompt the development of that culture, further enhancing its resources.

This position recognizes that the 2000-year-old dialogue between Christianity and culture is an already established conversation between two cultures. It studies the past with this intercultural dialogue in mind. One of the cultural partners in conversation has explicitly Christian values, themes, worship and books, and the other may have only fleeting acquaintance with these. The relationship between these two cultures may have all the attitudes Niebuhr describes: opposition, collapse, superiority, paradox and transformation. Each model has an attitude towards the other culture, its people and its moral practices: disdain, capitulation, arrogance, tension and optimism. How a particular Christian culture treats the other culture is the strategy that matters in the current context.

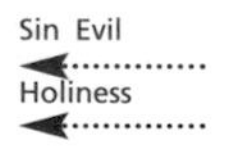

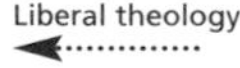

A genuinely dialogical understanding and practice

of Christianity and cultures would entail that in each instance the Christian culture facing a new situation would learn as well as teach. It would provide resources and discover new ones in the art, literature, music, dance and moral behaviour of the other culture. Where there is good in the culture, the Christian culture would reverence it. Where there is malice, it would exhort to conversion.

Body

The mutuality of intercultural, inter-religious dialogue in the encounter between Christianity and cultures acknowledges the diversity of peoples, cultures and social arrangements, but it does not leave aside the norms, the Sexuality principles and the belief in permanent teachings that have been markers of Christian belief. But the dialogue Marriage trusts to the operation of the Spirit in the interchange. This mutuality believes that the truth to be explored will be enriched by some of the knowledge, attitudes and behaviour received in the discussion. What is permanently true in church teaching is the meaning in a context in which the truth was discovered and defined. To enter into cultural dialogue about even the most profound truths of Christian faith may change the language, but the meaning will be enriched and remain in continuity with the previous cultural interpretation.

STEPHEN HAPPEL

Hans Belting, *Likeness and Presence: A History of the Image before the Era of Art*, Chicago: University of Chicago Press 1994; Peter Berger, *A Rumour of Angels: Modern Society and the Rediscovery of the Supernatural*, New York: Anchor Books and Harmondsworth: Allen Lane 1970; Jacques Dupuis, *Toward a Christian Theology of Religious Pluralism*, Maryknoll, NY: Orbis 1997; H. Richard Niebuhr, *Christ and Culture*, New York: Harper & Row 1951; David Tracy, *Dialogue with the Other: The Inter-Religious Dialogue*. Louvain: Eerdmans/Peeters Press 1990

Dance

One of the most curious aspects of Western cultural history is that while Christianity patronized and legitimated Architecture architecture, music and the visual arts, even sculpture, Music it never affirmed or commissioned dance. Rather, the Sculpture majority of Christian texts referring to dance provide either proscriptions or condemnations but not definitions or explanations. The difficulties with the presentation and

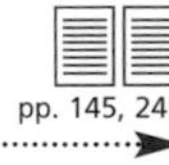

pp. 145, 245

reception of liturgical dance encountered by both dancers and Christian congregations alike, especially following the Council reforms of the Second Vatican Council, were heightened by the prejudices against Christian dance. However, there Church fathers had been a tradition of and a role for dance within the history of Christianity, and significant historical events either allied or separated Christianity and dance before the formation of the liturgical dance movement in the early twentieth century and the mid-twentieth-century conciliar decrees that regenerated the Roman liturgy.

Without doubt, the variations in Christian attitudes towards dance have affected the history of dance. Behind them lies the conflicting and often ambiguous Christian attitude to the human body. This often militated against the acceptance of dancing, as a sacred or a secular activity, at distinctive moments in Christian history and within the differing divisions of Christianity. Thus, the relationship between dance and sexuality – whether interpreted as an expression of chastity, physical union, an act of lust, or the ideal of cosmic harmony in Christian marriage – was dependent upon the attitude towards the human body characteristic of the time.

The fundamental Christian attitude towards dance, as towards the other arts, was ambivalent. There were two sets of interpretative lenses: the Hebraic, which proscribed the visual, and the Hellenistic, which understood the beauty of form, whether in the arts or the human body, as a metaphor of the divine. The Hebrew and Christian scriptures relate narratives that are similarly ambivalent: Miriam's dancing to praise God (Exodus 15.20) was contradicted by her participation in the lascivious dance in tribute to the golden calf (Exodus 32.19). A near-naked David danced joyfully around the ark of the covenant and was censured for it (2 Samuel 6.14), but music and dancing greet the return of the Prodigal Son (Luke 16.25). Celebrating the divine intervention that saved her city and her people, the Jewish heroine, Judith, performed a dance of thanksgiving (Judith 15.12–13), while a dancing Salome became the primary symbol, and perhaps victim, of sexual lust (Mark 6.21–8).

Over the early centuries, however, the question for Christian theologians and believers alike became whether these scriptural references expressed an appropriate course of earthly action or simply a heavenly ideal. From classical Greek culture, the early Christians inherited both the word *choros* and the activity of choral dancing. Dance, according to the aesthetic theories of the classical Greeks, affected the soul and furnished an expressive mode for the overflowing spiritual awareness that was otherwise inexpressible. Documentation in several early Christian texts including the Didache, the apocryphal Gospels and a variety of patristic treatises provided an argument for choral, or circle, dancing as an appropriate and praiseworthy mode of Christian spirituality.

Affirmations of circle and processional dances incorporating both religious leaders and the members of the congregation, i.e. a form of 'folk dance', are found in the writings of several early church fathers including Clement of Alexandria, Origen, Gregory Thaumaturgus, Gregory of

Nyssa, Gregory Nazianzus and John Chrysostom. Christian believers – male and female – took part in the *choroi* either as liturgical events in themselves or as the all-night sacred dance festival described by the fourth-century church father and historian, Eusebius, in his *Life of Constantine*. These forms of 'sacred dance' were deemed to be a natural expression of 'joy', a mode of 'adoration', part of the path to 'salvation' and earthly mirrors of the blessed heavenly dancing of the angels, martyrs and saints.

At the same time Basil the Great, Ambrose and Augustine condemned all forms of liturgical dance, and any and all of the women who danced. These influential fourth/fifth-century fathers advocated the meaningful but symbolic nature of the 'Dance of the Blessed' as they decried the dangers of its earthly performance. Once again, the crucial fourth-century transformations of Christianity into the imperial religion brought changes in attitude towards women, the human body and dance. As the status of women in the church was modified from active and public participation to passive and discrete concurrence, ecclesiastical pronouncements condemning their participation in 'frivolous dances and indecent movements' were issued and enforced. The truth of the matter was simply that any participation by women in sacred dancing was perpetually suspect, given the temptations it was believed to present to men.

The fundamental, if not primary, function of the early church councils was to instruct the faithful in matters of doctrine and practice. From the sixth century onwards, we find multiple condemnations of 'shameless dancing' in churches, churchyards and sacred festivals. These castigations were accompanied, more often than not, with denunciations of 'unseemly art' and 'excessively embellished music'. Without doubt, the primary issue was not aesthetic or even theological, but rather one of control. The Christian liturgy was essentially a communal activity that both unified and identified members of the community. In it the ecclesiastical hierarchy strove to establish a 'set' order of worship and a regularized series of ritual actions that could be easily recognized by 'the average Christian'. The identification of some forms of dancing as 'shameless' and some dancers, i.e. women, as inappropriate would become a codified position against sacred dance. Although artistic and archaeological evidence provides documentation that 'sacred dance' flourished into the fifteenth century, the ecclesiastical testimony represented by the confirmations and clarifications of these early proscriptions reads otherwise.

During the early Middle Ages, from 500 to 1100, the church solidified its position as an authoritarian power over both secular and sacred matters. The continuing regulations of all forms of liturgical activities culminated in the decrees issued from Charlemagne's imperial court at Aachen which codified the order, language and music of the liturgy as well as the liturgical calendar, the liturgical language and liturgical vesture. Opposition to religious dance throughout conciliar and papal documents in the form of disciplinary measures against those, especially women, who participated in sacred dance is indicative of the common opinion that dancing was a degenerate activity.

Calendar

Dress

However, this otherwise 'official' position must be balanced by the artistic and archaeological evidence, which includes the music and sacred choreography credited to Isidore of Seville. This Spanish bishop supported the principle of a Christian liturgy rich with dance and music as stated at the seventh-century Council of Toledo. He was credited with the design of the Mozarabic mass, which incorporated *los mozos de coro*, or dances by choristers, the most famed of which were *los seises* ('the sixes'). These dances take their name from groups of six altar boys who danced in Seville Cathedral before the reserved sacrament on the feasts of Corpus Christi and the Immaculate Conception. Sacred dancing appears to have flourished in the eighth and ninth centuries, especially as the customary processions that accompanied the circumambulations of the relics of saints or martyrs in celebration of their holy days. Additionally, references in hymns and sermons indicated the continuing presence of dance in Christian rites and liturgies, including the eleventh-century emergence of the flagellants in Germany, France and most especially Spain.

Women in Christianity

Festivals and feasts

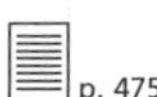

p. 475

The fundamental ambivalence that characterized the Christian attitude towards dance witnessed new heights in the High Middle Ages, from 1100 to 1400, as ecclesiastical pronouncements vacillated between bans or controls on liturgical dance. The existence of patterns of a labyrinth on the floors of French cathedrals suggests dancing in complex patterns, especially at Easter; there were carefully choreographed processions, and theatrical dance segments in mystery and morality plays. An age of dramatic and emotional expressions, the twelfth and thirteenth centuries were the time of the *plancthus*, that is, religious plays on the theme of the sorrows of the Three Maries and the era of those monastic orders, particularly the Franciscans and Cistercians, who identified dancing as a religious value. Fourteenth-century hymn writers created themes for ring and processional dances, as well as songs for the healing dances that grew in popularity between the fourteenth and seventeenth centuries. A Dance of Death was practised in churchyards and this became a didactic motif in sermons and works of art. Hans Holbein painted a famous example. It became the most widely identified sacred dance during the Black Plague (1347–73).

Mystery plays

Religious orders

Dance carols were composed; and a new spirituality of dancing emerged in the *chorizantes*, or ecstatic dance

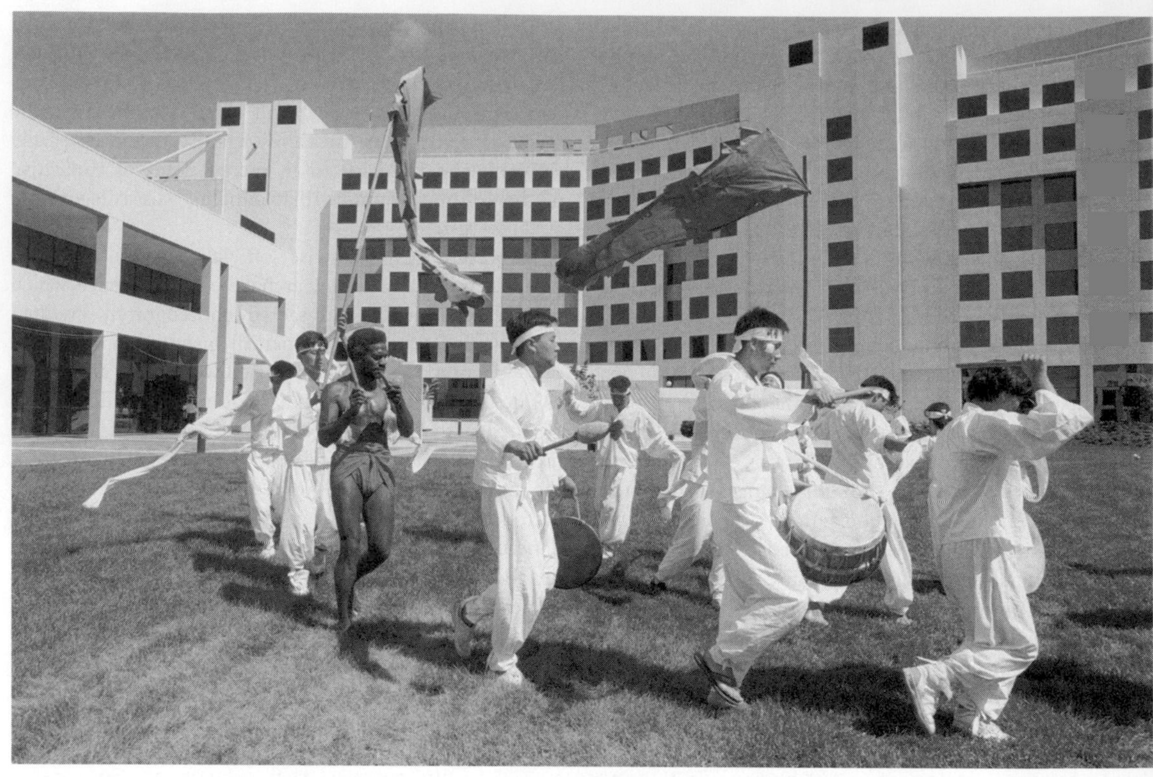

Korean dance rehearsal for the World Council of Churches Assembly, Canberra 1971

sects. St Vitus' Dance in Germany, St Anthony's Fire and the Tarantella in France and Italy were all forms of manic dancing which seized large groups of people. Concurrently, between the Council of Auxerre in 573 and the Council of Paris in 1212 conciliar decrees condemned or at the very least curtailed dance. However, it was the decrees of the Lateran Councils (1123–1215) that presaged the language of denunciation and condemnation that would be codified at the Council of Trent in 1563. The fundamental fear of the body, sexuality and sex conjoined with the suspicion of women and the desire for reform, so that the denial of sacred dancing corresponded with the definitions of clerical celibacy.

The Protestant traditions permitted no dancing during liturgical services because of the Reformed view that the arts were a distraction from worship, the suspicion if not outright fear of women and sexuality, and the desire for a 'cleansing' and remodelling of the liturgy. So for both Roman Catholics and Protestants alike, dancing was no longer a part or element in services and rites of worship or sacraments. Sacred dancing was ostracized from Christian worship with only the occasional exception of a specific sect such as the Shakers or events like the performance of *los seises* (see above), which still takes place today. This enforced removal of dance encouraged the development of social dancing and secular dance, including theatrical dance, performance and entertainment.

Shakers

However, early in the twentieth century, the principle and practice of sacred dance was resurrected in American modern dance. The pioneering dancers/choreographers, Ruth St Denis and Ted Shawn, not only created a style, a troupe and a school for this new performance technique; they also understood that dance was essentially spiritual. They explored the formal relationships between dance and religion in their choreography and classes, and eventually led dance back into the church. St Denis aspired to fulfil her dream to choreograph religious theatrical dance and simultaneously created modern liturgical dance, even performing at the age of 80 as the Virgin Mary and as Mary Magdalene in the premiere of her *Blue Madonna* in 1959. Her husband, Ted Shawn, had studied to be a Methodist minister but found himself drawn to dance and choreography as his form of religious expression. The Scottish Rite Temple in San Francisco became the site of one of his earliest liturgical choreographies for a complete church service in 1917. This new movement of liturgical, or sacred, dance flourished in early twentieth-century America, especially in the Episcopal and Protestant traditions. William Norman Guthrie, then rector of St Mark's-in-the-Bowerie church, choreographed a controversial *Annunciation* in which six women garbed in loose, flowing, white garments danced barefoot *à la* Isadora Duncan. This avant-garde presentation was deemed so scandalous that St Mark's was suspended from communion with the Episcopal Church of America. The liturgical dance movement gathered momentum; this ultimately led to the formation of the Sacred Dance Guild in the late 1950s with rapid expansion throughout the 1960s, 1970s and 1980s.

Nor has the movement been confined to North America, although that is where it has flourished most. In Europe, too, liturgical dance is practised by varied groups of people and in different situations. Its importance in Christian education is recognized, and those working with disabled people in particular know of its therapeutic value.

Deemed both a retrieval of the early Christian practice of congregational and processional dancing and a modern creation, liturgical dance has sought to re-incorporate sacred movement into the liturgy and sacramental rites. The creation of rhythmic, or dance, choirs similar to singing choirs; dance performances for the community; danced congregational prayers; and inclusive congregational dancing are among the possibilities for inclusion of sacred movement in the liturgy. The central questions whether these liturgical dances should be choreographed and/or performed by professionals or amateurs; whether the spiritual or aesthetic dimensions should be emphasized; and whether the congregation should participate or merely serve as an audience, became the controversies of the 1970s and 1980s. At the beginning of the twenty-first century, dancing has re-emerged as once again voices are raised in the debate whether 'sacred dance' is a heavenly ideal or an earthly action.

DIANE APOSTOLOS-CAPPADONA

Doug Adams and Diane Apostolos-Cappadona (eds), *Dance as Religious Studies* (1990), Portland: Wipf & Stock 2001; Eugene L. Backman, *Religious Dances in the Christian Church and in Popular Medicine*, London: Allen & Unwin 1952; Marilyn Daniels, *Dance in Christianity: The History of Religious Dance through the Ages*, New York: Paulist Press 1983; J. G. Davies, *Liturgical Dance: An Historical, Theological and Practical Handbook*, London: SCM Press 1984; Carlynn Reed, *And We Have Danced: A History of the Sacred Dance Guild 1958–1978*, Austin, TX: The Sharing Company 1978; Margaret Taylor, *A Time to Dance: Symbolic Movement in Worship* (1967), Austin, TX: The Sharing Company 1981

www.psalm121.ca/dance for a list of Christian dance resources

DEATH

Destiny and purpose, Life after death, Pastoral care, Resurrection, Sacraments, Sacrifice, Sin, Suffering

Death is strikingly prominent in Christianity. In churches in the Roman Catholic tradition the figure of a dead or dying man hanging on a cross is omnipresent, in the form of crucifixes, paintings and other depictions. And in Protestantism, which rejected such visual representations, there is constant talk of death: death as the result of sin, which has infected the whole human race, and in particular the death of Jesus, who through the blood he has shed has saved men and women from the punishment that they deserve. Because death is the end of all human beings, and was marked in particular cultures by special rites long before Christianity, Christian views about death and the practices surrounding it differ widely, and are almost impossible to chronicle.

Jesus

Atonement

One way of seeing the varying attitudes to death among individual Christians living in different ages would be to go into an ancient village parish church, say in Britain. Round it is the churchyard, in which countless people have been buried down the centuries, their graves marked with tombstones bearing inscriptions which can testify to anything from 'sure and certain hope in the resurrection to eternal life', the words from the Book of Common Prayer with which their bodies were committed to the ground, to a blunt acknowledgement of the loss which the death has caused or some sentiment expressed to cope with the situation: 'Don't grieve for me now, don't grieve for me never. I'm going to do nothing for ever and ever.' Inside the church there are more tombs, perhaps in the floor, or as elaborate decorated monuments, from depictions of the family to stark skulls and crossbones, again attesting the different ways in which death has been faced.

It is possible to become so familiar to the proximity of church to churchyard, and the burial of bodies even inside the church that it is easy to forget how strange this might seem, say, to visiting Jews or Muslims, who make a firm separation between their places of worship and the last resting places of their dead. Here Christianity is unique.

The origin of this practice lies in the veneration of those who voluntarily gave their lives for their faith: the martyrs, who date back almost to the beginning of Christianity. Their earthly remains were reverently preserved, and by around the fourth century the places where they were put, not least the famous catacombs in Rome, had become focal points of worship. The elaborate stone coffins, sarcophagi, bear rich figurative decoration, and as well as being important Christian works of art are also valuable sources for our knowledge of Christianity, as are the wall paintings which can be found in the catacombs. The remains of the saints were thought to be especially holy and capable of performing miracles themselves; bodies came to be divided up and distributed between different centres. These 'relics' played an important part in the piety of the Middle Ages.

Martyr

Sculpture

The meaning of death

Bible

The writings in the Hebrew Bible that the Christians took over as part of their holy scriptures, the Old Testament, in turn vary in their attitudes to death.

There is a radical acceptance of death as the limit of human life. Throughout most of the Old Testament death is thought of as the end (Psalm 6.5). At best the dead person's shade moves on into the shadows of Sheol, the Hebrew name for the underworld (Isaiah 38.18), where the spirit is cut

CATACOMBS

The term probably comes from the Greek *kata kumbas*, 'in the hollows', and denotes extensive systems of passageways with niches off them, used for underground burial. Such passages can be found in various places round the Mediterranean, but the most famous are in Rome, where there are 41 catacombs dating from the second half of the second century CE. It used to be a popular belief that the early Christians worshipped in the catacombs, but this is highly unlikely; however, by the fourth century the eucharist was being celebrated at tombs of martyrs, and Pope Sixtus II is said to have been executed in the catacomb of Praetextatus during the persecution of Christians by Valerian (258). Christians also took refuge in the catacombs during the barbarian invasions.

Work on building the catacombs continued until the fourth century: they consisted of systems of underground galleries often on several levels, connected by stairs. Bodies were buried in the floors of these galleries or in niches carved out in their sides, larger or smaller, simpler or more elaborate, depending on the importance of those buried in them. The wall paintings and sarcophagi in the catacombs provide valuable evidence of the life of Christians in the period in which they were used. The most important catacombs are:

Via Appia: St Callistus, St Praetextatus and St Sebastian;
Via Ostiensis: St Domitilla Aurelia Vetus, St Commodilla;
Via Labicana: St Marcellinus, St Peter.

With the rapidly growing cult of martyrs, the catacombs became too cramped for the pilgrims who came to visit them, and an increasing number of buildings were constructed above them; there were also cemeteries at ground level. Gradually relics were brought up, and later transferred to churches all over Rome; as a result the catacombs came to be largely forgotten. It was only with the beginnings of Christian archaeology in the sixteenth century that they were rediscovered and their importance appreciated.

Martyr p. 1075 Archaeology

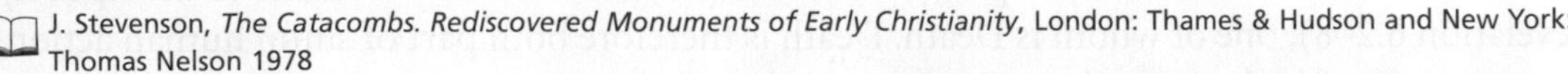
J. Stevenson, *The Catacombs. Rediscovered Monuments of Early Christianity*, London: Thames & Hudson and New York: Thomas Nelson 1978

off from God. At best a man can be 'gathered to his people' (Genesis 35.29). The normal allotted span is the proverbial three score years and ten (Psalm 90.10). Death may come as the fitting end of a life of blessing and prosperity (cf. David, 1 Chronicles 29.25). More often, however, death is a fearful prospect. Not only can it strike at any time, in war or famine or accident, but there is also pain and separation, both from one's people and from God (Psalms 55; 102). It is, however, possible to die bravely and honourably (2 Samuel 1.23).

Such a bleak scenario comes to be modified, but is indicative of key crucial beliefs about God as creator. The first is that, apart from God, all things are contingent and are dependent on God for their existence. God has made human beings in his love and mercy, setting the limits of life, including death. In the biblical Hebrew tradition there is no inevitable, natural immortality, 'The Lord gave and the Lord has taken away; blessed be the name of the Lord' (Job 1.21). Indeed, the temptation for Adam and Eve is to be like God: immortal and omniscient (Genesis 3). Whether, as has sometimes been held, unfallen humanity was destined to live for ever, the point remains that only God is the source of life and the creature is confined to time and space.

God

This has a number of implications. First, as in modern existentialist philosophy, the inevitability of death shapes the meaning of life. Goodness is to be found in the land of the living (Psalm 27.13). Life is a gift to be treasured and lived out in trust and obedience. That is why the Christian tradition has always condemned suicide as well as murder. To take life, especially one's own, is to act as God, though on occasion suicide might be justified (Saul, 1 Samuel 31.4). But the bottom line, which cannot be ceded, is that only God is the author and finisher of life.

In our own day this discussion has become especially significant. On the one hand, anxiety about 'weapons of mass destruction' represents the need to try to control our powers of destruction and to preserve some vestige of a sense of the sanctity of human life. On the other hand, advances in medical science have given us the ability to sustain life. Not only do people live longer, but also the processes of dying can be increasingly arrested through medical procedures such as transplants and mechanical aids. Clinical death is normally understood as loss of the 'brain stem' functions, without which there is no possibility of an independently sustained existence. But what do we mean by life when there is no quality of life at any level? The issues are complex and detailed and are one of the main concerns of bioethics. Much Christian response has been to condemn anything that can be understood as the taking of life. The fear is that the universal sanctity of life will be eroded. Others, however, will argue from the need for life to have certain basic qualities that there are circumstances when what appears to be a living death can legitimately be terminated by euthanasia or assisted suicide. More frequently, however, those anxious about the over-prolongation of life will support the medical argument that in some circumstances the management of a disease may conflict with the need to sustain life. In this case it is possible, for example, to administer a painkiller knowing it will possibly be fatal, or to withdraw care. But in such cases, it is argued, death is understood to be strictly a secondary effect.

Bioethics

In the biblical tradition, death is linked with sin and punishment. In the Genesis myth death is bound up with the consequences of the fall (Genesis 3.14–19). Physical death is understood in this wider context. It becomes a metaphor of the brokenness and degradation of the human condition, but no less real for that. Life can be turned into a living hell, and death is part of the process of destruction. This is most vividly depicted in the imagery of the 'four horsemen of the Apocalypse' (Revelation 6.2–8), one of whom is Death. Death is therefore both part of sinful human action and a consequence of it (Lamentations; Romans 6.23).

However, death is also associated with the remedy for sin, an essential element in redemption and salvation. Sacrifice is not an easy concept for the modern mind. It has often been associated with a price that is paid. But the main thrust of the biblical material is on the release of life to enable communion. Sacrifices in the law of Moses were primarily about building a bridge between God and the people. They were shared, often literally, as at Passover, by being part of a communal meal.

Against this background, in Christianity the death of Jesus can be seen as a culmination of his total obedience to his Father's will and the outpouring of his life for the world. In death, as in life, he identified himself with the broken, the poor and the outcast. Somehow through death the alienation of death has been overcome. A new relationship between God and humanity has been inaugurated, guaranteed by God in the faithfulness of his Son.

This focus on the death of Jesus in Christianity radically alters the understanding of death. Death is already past. The death of Christ is a gateway into new life. This is symbolized in baptism. The Christian has already died and has been born anew (Romans 6.5–11). Physical death, therefore, is not an end to life but an entry into a new phase of life. But here and now the new life begins; though there is still a continuing struggle to overcome sin, the crucial battle has been won. The disciple is now enjoined to live the life of obedience, service and love that Christ himself lived, and it was this that from the start led to martyrs.

Initiation

After death

Whereas ancient Israel did not have a meaningful belief in an afterlife, this belief was to change in the period prior to the birth of Jesus. Evil was the problem. What is the explanation of the apparent success of the wicked and the frequent sufferings of the righteous? The early assumption was that in the end the evil ones would get their deserts (Psalms 37; 73). Even the exile of the Hebrew people in Babylon was coped with in this way (Isaiah 40.12–31). However, a crisis came under the

Evil

Origins and background

policies of Antiochus Epiphanes (died 163 BCE), who sought to change the very nature of Judaism. The fragile Jewish community suffered what today would be called ethnic cleansing: an attempt forcibly to acculturate its members to Greek cultural patterns. Those who resisted were ruthlessly persecuted, while those who collaborated prospered (1 Maccabees 1–2).

Out of this came the concept of resurrection. How can the victory of evil and death be reversed? The answer was through a fresh act of creation by God. The old, violent world would be assigned to a final death; but a new world would emerge, a kingdom of peace and justice in which the righteous would rule. It would, however, include those faithful who had died. They would be brought back to life, made to stand again, be raised (Daniel 12.2). The imagery used to depict this vision was very varied and could be quite lurid, as in apocalyptic literature, of which the books of Daniel and Revelation are the clearest biblical examples.

Apocalyptic

It is this doctrine that permeates most of the New Testament, but with another new twist. The fulfilment of God's promises of the new heaven and the new earth (Revelation 21) has been given substance by the resurrection of Jesus Christ. Jesus did not survive death but was brought back from the dead by God (Acts 2.32). In that event the new age has begun. It is Paul who sets this out most fully (1 Corinthians 15.20–8). The church exists between the decisive event of Christ's death and resurrection and the final completion and outworking of that process. Death, in a very real sense, has been conquered (1 Corinthians 15.54).

The early church was not primarily interested in life after death but in getting ready for the coming of the kingdom in which the faithful would participate. About what happened in the meantime there was no unanimity. Those who had died might now be asleep (Revelation 6.11), or with Jesus (Philippians 1.23) or, in an image that was popular later, in Abraham's bosom (Luke 16.19–31); but they remained dependent on the creative activity of God (2 Corinthians 4.14). Whether those Christians expected an early completion of the kingdom, as is often assumed, or, more probably, accepted that the timetable was unknown, their faith was in the promise of God who had given assurance in the resurrection of Jesus.

Kingdom of God

However, as the church moved out into the Graeco-Roman world, Christians encountered other models of how life after death was understood. The dominant concept can be briefly characterized as the immortality of the soul. The human person was thought to comprise the body, the will, the mind and the soul. It is the latter that belongs to and partakes in the ultimate levels of existence. The soul tends towards perfection, unity, God, our true home. The body is only temporary, often thought of as evil or as a tomb for the soul. It was inevitable that Christian apologists had to take account of this very different framework. Indeed it can be argued that the emergent understanding of life after death was an amalgam of the Judaistic, biblical belief in creation and resurrection and the Hellenistic belief in the soul.

Body

As this process crystallized out in the Middle Ages, it was effectively a two-stage eschatology or doctrine of the end, but one that was inherently unstable. Briefly, here death is followed by a period of waiting before the final judgement and the eternal state of heaven and hell. This is classically summarized in the doctrine of 'the four last things'.

Eschatology

Death, the first, brings to an end the earthly life of the individual. The soul leaves the body and enters the outer portals of heaven. However, the church always avoided any notion of the soul somehow being divine. The soul is a creature, made by God, and placed in the body. This avoids, on one hand, the idea of the eternal existence of the soul, as propounded by Origen (*c.* 185–*c.* 254) on the basis of Platonism, or, on the other, of Traducianism, a view held by Tertullian and even considered by Augustine, that the soul, like the body, is passed on from generation to generation.

Dance of Death, engraving by Jacob Ridinger, eighteenth century

Each person is a unique individual, created and willed by God; but the soul is so made as not to die, children inheriting their souls from their parents.

Interest, however, was increasingly paid to the interim period. From being a time of rest in Abraham's bosom it came to be seen as a time of preparation before judgement and so a time of possible repentance and redemption. Thus the notion of purgatory emerges. As the church in heaven (triumphant) and on earth (militant) is one, so all souls, living or departed, are together before God in praise and intercession. It is possible, therefore, to pray for the dead. There were traces of this cult right back into the time of the catacombs, though it was not clearly formulated. Praying for the dead became a major activity in monastic houses, and the laity secured prayers on behalf of themselves and their family. Later the practice spilled out into parish churches, and rich and powerful patrons would endow chantry chapels, either free standing or within a larger church, employing priests to say masses for the dead. The notion of penances, especially in the form of indulgences, as developed in the medieval church, tended to quantify and make mechanical the process of the remission of sins which led to the abuses against which Luther rebelled in the sixteenth century. The practice of prayers for the dead and indulgences, reinterpreted by the Council of Trent (1545–63) and subsequently, is still practised; so is praying for the dead in Orthodoxy and High Anglicanism, both as general intercessions and for particular people. Interestingly, a sense of the common fellowship of the whole church, while not usually expressed in terms of intercession, has permeated parts of the Protestantism in recent times.

Patronage
Forgiveness
 p. 476

Three groups were excepted. First, a few special persons were deemed to have been taken straight into heaven. These were Enoch (Genesis 5.24), Moses (Jude 9), Elijah (2 Kings 1.11), Jesus as the resurrected one, and Mary. As the type of the true Christian Mary is the mother of the faithful whose intercession is most direct and effective. Secondly, the saints also have access to God in heaven and may be venerated and called on for intercession. Thirdly, there are those in limbo, outside the full blessedness of the beatific vision. Here are the saints of the Old Covenant and the unbaptized, like the still-born or birth-deaths, who are innocent of personal guilt.

Mary
Saint
Covenant

The Reformers inherited this medieval model but rejected the notion of purgatory as unscriptural and a threat to the simple reliance on God's mercy. The result was to make the moment of death crucial, as it is at that point that the fate of the soul is decided and there is no possibility of subsequent repentance.

Living with death – the pastoral dimension

The pastoral practices of the church embody the beliefs held about death. Many variations can be found in the history of the Western tradition.

In the early church it was the hope of resurrection that shaped practice. Such a belief made the Graeco-Roman custom of cremation repugnant; it was felt to be an obstacle to a future resurrection. The bodies of the faithful were buried, often in catacombs. The funeral was a time for rejoicing (the funeral colour was white), especially over those who had borne steadfast witness in the face of persecution, and in the Celtic church funeral celebrations included feasting.

Celtic Christianity

It was with the emergence of medieval Christendom that the classic patterns of Catholic practice were laid down. The constant threat of death was real. The reminder was in the mass and depicted in paintings and carvings, notably in the Dance of Death, in which actors, dressed as skeletons, representing various members of the community, reinforced the message of death as the great leveller. This was also a motif on the memorials of the great and good, where a skull and sometimes a skeleton were carved into the tomb. Death is the great common experience, 'Ask not for whom

Christendom
Dance

 the bell tolls. It tolls for thee,' John Donne reminded his Elizabethan congregation. 'In the midst of life we are in death,' affirmed the 1662 Anglican Book of Common Prayer. Indeed such would have been the common experience until the end of the nineteenth century. All manner of devotional exercises and literature offered spiritual wisdom and understanding. The wise Christian lives in a state of preparedness.

With the onset of death every endeavour is made to ensure that the dying person is prepared. In Roman Catholicism confession is made and absolution given, and, possibly, communion is administered (this is traditionally known as the *viaticum*, Latin for 'provision for a journey'). Extreme unction, which consists of symbolic anointing and commendatory prayers, is given. (It often appears that this rite carries with it a sense of finality and so it is sometimes resisted; but that is a misunderstanding, since it derives from rites of healing and can be received on other occasions and more than once.) At the point of death prayers are said for the departing. The family and close intimates have also gathered to make their farewells and to see that worldly concerns are in order as well as to share in the last rites. The model death in the tradition can be seen in John Henry Newman's poem *The Dream of Gerontius*, so dramatically set to music by Edward Elgar.

A considerable literature, *ars moriendi*, or the art of dying, emerged as literacy grew and printing gave access. These, typically, are devotional instructions for priest, family and the dying.

The funeral is a key rite of passage for all concerned: for the deceased, who is sent out into the unknown of the next world; and for those left behind who have to accept loss, learn how to say p. 1256 farewell and to adjust to the new situation. This is a solemn time. The colour is black or purple. It is also, in Orthodoxy as well as in Roman Catholicism, recognized as a process. Even in modern Catholicism there is a recommendation for a vigil before the Requiem Mass. That mass includes prayers for the departed and, classically, the *Dies Irae,* reminding all of the day of judgement. Commemorative masses can be said regularly over the next year, including the anniversary of death. There is clear pastoral value in this, as it helps to articulate publicly the grieving process, which can take up to two years or more. In earlier times mourning rites would have been more elaborate, marking off the time of transition and the restoration of normality.

Since the latter part of the nineteenth century, prompted by the lack of space for burial grounds in large cities and not least for hygienic reasons in the circumstances of the time, the practice of cremation has spread, and it may well become the chief form of Christian funeral practice. The Roman Catholic Church has announced that it is not prohibited, and many Protestant churches have actively supported it.

In Protestantism there are local mourning customs, reflecting the social relationships in the community. There is also a strong emphasis on being personally ready for death. Preaching has often stressed the fate of the reprobate and the bliss of heaven. There is also a supply of pious reading, including spiritual classics such as Jeremy Taylor's *The Rule and Exercise of Holy Dying.*

Protestantism Above all the desire is for a 'good death'. In classical Protestantism there was little formal ritual. The concept of the priesthood of all believers meant less reliance on clergy and put the family at the centre. Memorials of the sixteenth and seventeenth centuries often show the family at prayer. The dying person was expected to leave affairs in order. Above all, as death was approaching, what was looked for was an expression of the assurance of faith. The moment of death was crucial for the fate of the soul, since there was no possibility of subsequent repentance. To know that one's loved one died trusting in Christ was to be assured that he or she was safe in God's hands. Last words, therefore, were deemed important and often piously recorded, and death scenes used as hortatory material.

The consequence of such a perspective was that the funeral itself was of less importance; it was simply a means of reverently disposing of the body. If anything, it would be an occasion, through a sermon, to exhort the living to take heed of the closeness of judgement.

The modern world has seen great changes. While the old beliefs and practices are still widely preserved, today there is an uncertainty about death. It is only on state occasions that something of the solemnity of earlier, more formal, society can still be seen. It may be that contemporary society has lost the benefit of recognized and public stages of mourning.

First, there is an ambiguity about death. Any Victorian family would have been familiar with death, not least of the young. That did not make grieving any the less, but perhaps enabled people to cope better. Today, however, through higher standards of living and medical technology, people are expected to live longer. Death can thus be a forgotten threat, something that should not happen or should be delayed. It is hard to accept the death of children or even of the middle-aged. It also makes it hard to acknowledge terminal disease. We can always hope for a new cure.

At the same time, the twentieth century has been the most violent in human history. It is difficult now to understand the social trauma caused by the First World War, evidenced by ubiquitous war memorials and national remembrance. The dead became simultaneously victims and heroes. Yet through the horrors of war and mass destruction, shown ever more vividly on the media, it is possible to become inured to death.

Secondly, death has been sanitized. It has been taken off the streets and out of the home, and into the hospital or old people's home. The funeral director manages all the details. We are silent about death. Bereavement is played out in private and not in the community. There is a major pastoral discussion about how much and when and to whom the prognosis of death ought to be given.

Thirdly, and most significantly, the hospice movement has been established. Its roots, in the United Kingdom, are explicitly Christian. The aim is to provide, through palliative care and a supportive, caring environment, the possibility of a 'good death' for those with terminal disease. It has made a widespread and a major contribution to the way in which death as a social and personal reality is perceived. There are, across the country, specialized units in hospitals, nursing homes and domiciliary services, both religious and secular in ethos.

Fourthly, the funeral is the last Christian occasional rite to be almost universally observed, though there is a move to humanistic and other forms of ceremony. But here, too, there have been considerable pastoral changes. Countering the fragmentation and anonymity of contemporary society, there is an emphasis on personalizing the rite. This often takes the form of a eulogy, perhaps given by a member of the family or a friend. The stress is on thanksgiving for a life lived. There is seldom reference to judgement, but to God's mercy and care, and the rest into which the deceased has entered.

Fifthly, these developments have been broadly informed by the growing understanding of the dying and grieving processes on which pastoral care of the dying and the bereaved, in common with counselling or social work, can draw. The emphasis, therefore, is on the needs and development of the persons involved.

PAUL BALLARD

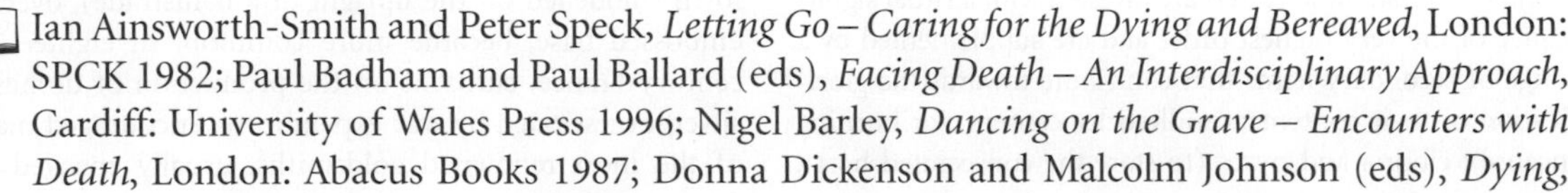

Ian Ainsworth-Smith and Peter Speck, *Letting Go – Caring for the Dying and Bereaved*, London: SPCK 1982; Paul Badham and Paul Ballard (eds), *Facing Death – An Interdisciplinary Approach*, Cardiff: University of Wales Press 1996; Nigel Barley, *Dancing on the Grave – Encounters with Death*, London: Abacus Books 1987; Donna Dickenson and Malcolm Johnson (eds), *Dying,*

Death and Bereavement, London: Sage 1987; Peter Jupp and Clare Gittings (eds), *Death in England – An Illustrated History*, Manchester: Manchester University Press 1999; Peter Jupp and Tony Rogers (eds), *Interpreting Death – Christian Theology and Pastoral Practice*, London: Cassell 1997; Bill Kirkpatrick, *Going Forth – A Practical and Spiritual Approach to Dying and Death*, London: Darton, Longman & Todd 1997

Decorative arts

The distinction between 'decorative' or 'applied' art, in which artistry is applied to functional objects, and 'fine' art, in which the aesthetic, emotive and theatrical impact of images is valued for its own sake, developed during the Renaissance. Prior to this time, most artistry or craftsmanship was applied to objects that served some form of practical purpose. In a Christian context, such purposes could be utilitarian, as in the case of a pyx, used to store the consecrated host; or they could be symbolic, as in the case of a crosier, carried by a bishop as a symbol of his pastoral office. Story-telling was also one of the purposes of images, as the Bible was not translated into vernacular languages in the West until the fourteenth century, making it impossible for most Catholic Christians to understand the scriptures. It was not until the sixteenth century, when artists raised themselves above artisans, on account of their intellectual and literary scope, that the distinct notion of 'applied' art – considered by some to be a poor relation to 'fine' art, because it was sullied by its association with the banality of functional life – evolved.

Renaissance
p. 485
Story
Middle Ages

The functional aspects of the Christian religion, however, are by no means secondary to its intellectual ones. On the contrary, they are integral to its vision, and the material culture that has developed around them is crucial to its expression. Of all the functions performed by the various Christian churches, the celebration of the eucharist is the most universal. The objects that have developed to serve this sacrament – including chalices, patens and ecclesiastical vestments among many others – are a direct expression of its significance. They are usually made of metals, fabrics and other materials, and are therefore classed today among the 'applied' arts of the church.

Eucharist
pp. 354–5
p. 1257

The most important of these objects are the paten and chalice: the vessels used to contain the body and blood of Christ in the form of consecrated bread and wine. In the Roman Catholic Church, in which the bread and wine are believed to be actual transubstantiations of the body and blood of Christ, these vessels are invested with a ritual significance of the very highest order and are supplemented by a range of secondary items that contribute towards the glorification of their contents: candlesticks; censers (for burning incense); ciboria and pyxes (to store the consecrated host); monstrances (to display the host on the altar). Such objects are usually made of silver or base metal, sometimes gilded and encrusted with precious stones or other rich materials. Throughout the Middle Ages, discussions were held about the appropriate material for the sacramental vessels. Should they glorify Christ with splendour or imitate him with simplicity? Horn was outlawed as a sacramental material because it came from a creature that contained blood; glass was only very occasionally used because of its fragility; gilt copper was common (though the bowls of chalices were often made of silver to avoid contamination from *verdigris*, copper oxide). Pewter (an alloy of tin and lead) was also common, partly because it was considered to stand between silver and lead, thereby combining the divinity and humanity of Christ in an appropriately symbolic way, and partly because it was cheaper; pewter objects were also made, throughout the Middle Ages, to be buried, unconsecrated, with clergymen.

Roman Catholic Church
p. 1068

The form of the Catholic chalice developed over the ages. Archaeological research suggests that some of the earliest chalices were made of glass. The earliest known chalices are made of copper and silver and date from the eighth century; they have large bowls, evidently made to serve a large congregation. In the twelfth century, sanctity came to be invested almost exclusively in the clergy, on account of the sacrament of their ordination, and frequent communion with Christ through consumption of the consecrated bread and wine was withdrawn from the laity (except at Easter). Priests were empowered to receive communion on behalf of the congregation – 'vicariously' – and chalices were reduced in size accordingly. The traditional form of Catholic chalice consists of a cup, supported on a stem, emphasized at its centre by a prominent knop, over a spreading foot. Until the sixteenth century, the most common form of foot was splayed out like the end of a trumpet. It was often engraved or decorated with enamels; a hexagonally-shaped base was introduced to stop the chalice from rolling when it was laid on its side to drain, after use. In the sixteenth century, the classical baluster form (modelled on the upright of a balustrade), over an embossed base, became more common. In eighteenth-century France, cutbacks on the production of domestic silver, necessitated by war expenditure, encouraged many of the most renowned goldsmiths, usually engaged on lavish dinner services, to produce ecclesiastical wares. Some of these makers, such as Juste-Aurèle Meissonier and François Germain, had trained in Italy, where they picked up elements of the Baroque style, which they transformed into the Rococo style. The end of the eighteenth century saw a return to classicism in the form of the lighter neo-classical style, as reflected in the works of the Valadier workshop in Rome (1738–1817).

From the thirteenth century, when the eucharistic elements were withheld from the laity, the occasion at which the congregation communed most directly with the sacraments was the elevation of the host. At this moment, the celebrating priest, standing with his back to the congregation, raised the consecrated bread and wine above his head for all to see. Such practices generated new forms of culture and belief. The legend of the Holy Grail, for instance, gave rise to the notion that merely to gaze upon the grail – the lost cup used by Christ at the Last Supper, the ancestor of all chalices – would be to commune spiritually with its contents. The evolution of 'optical communion' – communion by gazing – led to a number of further developments. The feast of Corpus Christi, instituted by Pope Urban IV in 1264, was celebrated with a procession of the sacrament around the church or town, in a monstrance: a new purpose-designed type of mounted vessel in which the consecrated bread (in the form of a wafer) is raised up and exposed between two discs of glass or cut crystal, to be contemplated visually by the faithful.

Similar developments took place in relation to relics, the bodily remains or possessions of saints, venerated for their auspicious powers and preserved in reliquaries (from the Latin *relinquere*, to leave behind or relinquish). Relics have been venerated by Christians since the earliest times, and reliquaries made of wood, bronze, silver and clay survive from the fourth century onwards. In the ninth century the fraudulent trade in bogus relics led some authorities to decree that relics should not be displayed without reliquaries. When the cult of pilgrimages got under way in the tenth century, lavish reliquaries – a major attraction in the new pilgrimage churches (such as Santiago de Compostela in Spain and Conques in France – see colour plate 4) – became especially common.

Reliquaries can take many forms. The earliest examples are simple boxes, sometimes painted or decorated with images in relief, or phials (bottles for sanctified oil from shrines). Until the thirteenth century, reliquaries were usually closed structures, concealing the relic from view. Many such pieces were made in the form of miniature buildings, covered with gilt bronze or ivory figurines and enamelled plaques, imitating the large-scale sculpture and stained glass of real churches. Ivory, which was frequently made into plaques in the Middle Ages, for use as diptychs, triptychs and book covers, was mostly imported from Africa or recycled from classical objects; in the north, where ivory was more scarce, whalebone and walrus tusk were used. Enamelled objects were produced in specialist areas such as Limoges and the Rhine and Meuse valleys. The techniques used in the manufacture of such objects were set out in detail by the twelfth-century monk, Theophilus (possibly a pseudonym for the metalworker Roger of Helmarshausen), whose manual of painting, glassmaking and metalworking, *De Diversis Artibus*, was used throughout the Middle Ages.

In the thirteenth century, the new practice of communing with Christ by gazing at the host (during its elevation at the altar and during Corpus Christi processions) was reflected in the design of reliquaries, in many of which the relic was exposed behind crystal to be viewed by the faithful. Reliquaries were also produced in the form of the limbs from which the bones to be venerated originally came; heads, arms, fingers and feet are the most common.

The different attitudes of the various Christian churches are reflected in differences between the sacramental vessels they use. The Orthodox Church, for instance, shares with Roman Catholicism a belief in the transubstantiation of

Orthodox churches
Festivals and fasts

The Tassilo Chalice, 788

Saint
p. 1075
Pilgrimage

Church of England
Reformation
Ritual
Architecture
Furnishings
Council
p. 1256

the eucharistic elements into the body and blood of Christ, but unlike the Catholic Church, which has almost always offered the bread alone, it offers communion to the communicant 'in both kinds' (bread and wine). Particles of the consecrated bread are placed in the chalice with the wine (and a little hot water), and are served to the communicant on a spoon, called a labis. In keeping with this idiosyncratic tradition, Orthodox chalices tend to have broad stable bases with relatively small cups, resembling mounted bowls as much as vessels to drink from. The attitude of Protestants towards communion as a commemorative act, in which the bread and wine symbolize rather than become the body of Christ, is also reflected in their sacramental vessels. Following the Reformation in the sixteenth century, the Anglican church restored physical consumption of the bread and wine to the congregation, thereby necessitating the return of larger vessels. The cultic associations of the traditional shape and the Catholic name 'chalice' were replaced by the simply named 'communion cup', modelled on the domestic wine glass. Plain flagons, resembling large tankards, were introduced to replenish the cups; ornamentation and iconography were kept to a minimum. Ritual objects such as reliquaries, pyxes, monstrances, ciboria, paxes (small flat tablets which worshippers kissed when offered the kiss of peace) and almost all images – which were considered to be idolatrous – were abolished. On the other hand, alms dishes to receive money for distribution to the poor were introduced at this time. In the Dutch and Scottish churches the simple form of a beaker, without a foot, was sometimes used for communion.

The furniture of churches was similarly affected. The highly-dressed altars, placed against the east end of medieval churches (90 degrees to the axis of the church) to elevate the eucharist above the faithful, were replaced by simple tables placed 'table-wise' in the centre of the church. Antipathy towards signs of unnatural ritual veneration at communion was so strong among some Protestants that even the low altar-rails that replaced the elaborately painted and carved rood screens (used to veil medieval choirs) were outlawed.

The Roman Catholic Church also recognized the need for reform at this time and, prompted by the threat of Protestantism, instituted its own reforms at the Council of Trent (1545–63). In contrast to the Protestant approach to reform through rationalization, the Catholic approach attempted to intensify the emotional appeal of the church through dramatization of its cultural forms. With regard to church interiors, for instance, the consecrated host was ritually displayed on the altar in exuberant, monumental tabernacles. Examples were designed in the most theatrical Baroque style by Gian Lorenzo Bernini and others from the sixteenth century onwards.

Despite the radical simplification of the Protestant aesthetic, elements of the decorative styles of the Middle Ages did eventually return to the Protestant Church after the Reformation. During the 1630s, William Laud, Archbishop of Canterbury, advocated a revival of certain aspects of medieval style in order to revitalize the Church of England, which he considered to have been impoverished by the dispiriting restrictions of the Puritans. Laudian communion cups, for instance, incorporate a prominent knop and Gothic ornament, in a distinctively medieval manner, while retaining the size of a communion cup. Despite Laud's committed Anglicanism, such changes were controversial, as they appeared to be tainted with Catholic 'popery'. As a result, signs of medievalism did not appear again until the end of the eighteenth century when the style – chiefly in its Gothic rather than Romanesque form – was revived as part of the romantic nationalism that swept across Europe. The style was initially used, along with Rococo and chinoiserie, as a wayward alternative to the rationalism of the Enlightenment, reflected in classicism. At this stage it was used as a domestic style, bringing a sense of fervour and nostalgia to an otherwise detached and genteel world. It was not until the beginning of the following century that it became associated, almost exclusively, with religious values.

In Britain, this shift was marked by the intensive promotion of the Gothic by Augustus Welby Pugin, who invested it with moral values – a fervent religiosity and a spontaneous and innocent understanding of the 'true principles' of craftsmanship – which he believed to have prevailed in the Middle Ages. His interest in Gothic architecture was partly responsible for his conversion in 1835 to Roman Catholicism, which followed the granting of political and civil liberties to Roman Catholics in Britain in 1829.

Pugin designed all manner of church fittings including metalwork, furniture and vestments. Besides reviving medieval styles, he prided himself on the revival of medieval techniques such as the application of enamel plaques to silver objects. It was an irony of his time that although he rejected the technical short-cuts of the industrial revolution as demeaning to the integrity of craftsmen, much of the metalwork that he designed was electroplated by the company that made it, the Birmingham firm of John Hardman.

Pugin was equally influential with regard to church vestments. Vestments are the ritual garments, originally deriving from the everyday dress of early Christians (i.e. the formal dress of Roman citizens), by which the clergy are invested with their power of office. For many centuries, the vestments have been ascribed symbolic meanings – such as the 'burden of suffering', the 'mantle of hope' – and in some traditions the clergy recite appropriate prayers in relation to these symbolic meanings as they put the garments on. Codes of liturgical colours, determining the colours to be worn for the various feasts and seasons in the church calendar, were also developed. Since the Middle Ages, the principal colours have been white (used for the feasts of Christ and the Virgin), red (for the Passion of Christ and the martyrs), black (for Good Friday and mourning) and green (for Sundays between Trinity and Advent and between Epiphany and Lent). These changed through the ages, and until the nineteenth century, were subject to considerable variation across Europe.

In the European tradition, the chief vestments are the chasuble (a poncho-like gown, worn by the celebrant of the eucharist, and open at the sides to allow free movement of the arms), the cope (a processional cloak, open at the front, fastened by a clasp called a morse, but covering the arms), the cope hood (a symbolic remnant of a hood, often lavishly decorated with embroidered ornament), the orphrey (a broad band of imagery or ornament attached vertically to the front and back of a chasuble or cope) and the mitre (headdress of a bishop).

Until the sixteenth century, the most prestigious examples of these vestments were made of silk, richly embroidered with figurative panels. During the seventeenth and eighteenth centuries, embroidered iconography was largely replaced by lighter materials with woven floral patterns. In Protestant Europe, all forms of vestments were outlawed and clergy were required to wear dark gowns. In Britain the surplice, a plain white linen overgarment, originally used by all levels of the clergy, was allowed, despite intense resistance from Puritans, who wanted to see all traces of traditional practice removed. The nineteenth-century Gothic revival saw a revival of medieval-style embroidery in Britain, largely championed by Pugin. As the technique of richly raised embroidery was all but forgotten in Britain, the earliest realizations of Pugin's designs for embroidered vestments had to be executed by a firm of military and ceremonial embroiderers. Many pieces that were later designed for Anglican churches were made by amateur embroideresses working in newly-founded sisterhoods. Such communities were encouraged by the medieval revivalists with a view to restoring a degree of monastic fervour to the Anglican Church.

The Gothic revival was accompanied by a revival of ritualism, and by the final decades of the nineteenth century most ecclesiastical art reflected Gothic influence. Some freedom to experiment in this area was created by the fact that many of the ecclesiastical wares produced at this time were designed by the architects of the churches they were made for: William Butterfield, William Burges, George Edmund Street and G. F. Bodley. In order to preserve national pride, and to proclaim their anti-Catholicism, some English supporters of the style – members of the Ecclesiological Society (founded as the Cambridge Camden Society in 1839) – insisted that British designers should use English sources for their designs, rather than Italian or French ones that had Roman Catholic associations. Manifestly devotional images such as the Sacred Heart and the Immaculate Conception were avoided.

Calendar ◄

Church plate, ecclesiastical vestments and altar design are of particular importance among the arts of the church because, of all the applied arts, it is these that are the most specifically shaped and determined by Christian theology. But other crafts have also been abundantly patronized by the church. Many spectacular designs in ironwork and tiles survive. Stained-glass windows are the glory of many churches throughout northern Europe; they were scarcely developed in Spain and Italy and not at all in the Orthodox Church. The medium arguably reached its peak during the twelfth and thirteenth centuries, when the technique of production and the type of image produced were at their most fully inter-dependent. At this period, images were made up of pieces of stained (as opposed to surface-painted) glass called 'pot metal'. The outlines of the figures were directly linked to the way in which the glass panels were assembled: both were achieved by means of the lead strips that linked the glass fragments. In subsequent periods, more complex images with a wider range of colours were made, using enamel paints that could be applied to larger sheets of clear glass, independent of their construction, and then fired. At the Reformation, the usefulness of glass in keeping birds and rain out of churches ensured that it survived in more abundance than other forms of imagery (e.g. at Canterbury Cathedral). However, the combination of Protestant iconoclasm, technological advances in the production of clear glass and a growing taste for views of landscape eventually ensured the demise of coloured glass until the nineteenth century, when the medieval techniques of staining glass were revived.

Stained glass

Iconography ◄

Iconoclasm

The legacy of the nineteenth century was the association of Christian religiosity with the Gothic style. While this association was fundamental to the revival of interest in Christianity in the nineteenth century, it is arguable that it became a burden in the twentieth, when its claims to historical authenticity became confused with conservatism and resistance to change. The challenge of the twentieth century has been to reconcile ecclesiastical design with the aesthetics of modernism and, above all, with abstraction.

ANDREW SPIRA

E. Duffy, *The Stripping of the Altars: Traditional Religion in England 1400–1580*, London and New Haven: Yale University Press 1992; James Gilchrist, *Anglican Church Plate*, London: Michael Joseph 1967; Pauline Johnstone, *High Fashion in the Church: the Place of Vestments in the History of Art from the Ninth to the Nineteenth Century*, Leeds: Maney 2002; M. Rubin, *Corpus Christi: the Eucharist in Late Medieval Culture*, Cambridge: CUP 1994

DESTINY AND PURPOSE

Covenant, Creation, Death, Eschatology, Evil, Evolution, God, Hope, Kingdom of God, Life after death, Predestination, Resurrection, Salvation, Sin, Suffering

For most of us, life is largely made up of day-to-day tasks: making sure the laundry is done, or the children are at school, or the car has been repaired, or the last customer has been attended to at the close of a business day. The rhythm of the day-to-day becomes all consuming; there seems to be little else to life than the often thankless completion of these tasks. At times this rhythm can also provide the sort of comfort that regularity allows: when this task is done I can finally rest, or after this month's work the family can take a short break. Thoughts of 'destiny' or the question of the 'purpose of it all' seem quite remote in this kind of living. 'Destiny' and 'purpose' are terms that are more likely to occur in the speech of a political leader or the writings of a philosopher than in the conversation with a customer or the interchange between a wife and husband.

Yet most of us have had the experience of this day-to-day rhythm being broken. Maybe it comes with a news story about the grinding starvation and death faced each day by millions throughout the world; maybe it comes with the birth of a new child; maybe it comes with the burial of a parent; or maybe in a moment of study when we realize just how complex the brain is, or how fragile the environment may be, or how random the paths of development over billions of years might be that somehow let us be who we are now. It is at times like these that the remoteness of talk about 'destiny' and 'purpose' is overcome and questions arise: 'What is the point of it all?' or 'What should I be doing with my life?' or 'What responsibility do I have for the faceless hungry that I hear about, or the well-being of the grandchildren of my child's grandchildren?' The more momentary joy, fatigue, boredom or anxiety of the day-to-day is put against the background of a different horizon, one which reveals the always present but never quite satisfied desire to make sense of it all and to act in harmony with that sense.

More often than not this combination of sense and action is lived out rather than thought about. In this respect 'destiny' and 'purpose' are very practical issues, even if the terms seldom come up in our day-to-day exchanges. The way we live our lives announces what we understand the purpose of life to be, or what we understand the purpose of the world to be, or what we think our destiny is. As the Christian theologian Paul Tillich notes, all of us have 'ultimate concerns', even if our ultimate concern is not to be concerned about anything. More likely, however, this ultimate concern might be about our own security, or care for our children, or wealth, or the betterment of others.

What we understand to be 'the purpose of things' and how we live our 'destiny' is immediately related to our ultimate concerns. While the issues surrounding 'destiny' and 'purpose' can by no means be reduced to each person's deepest involvements, the idea of 'ultimate concern' suggests one way in which the remote notions of purpose and destiny, ideas that have a religious dimension, function in our everyday lives.

In modern discussions, 'purpose' and 'destiny' are seen as concepts that refer to the identity of a person, or object, or structure, by disclosing how it relates to the world around it (what is its purpose?) and to the actions that are appropriate to or for it in that world (what is its destiny?). It is important to make a distinction between purpose and design. Something may be designed or structured to produce a particular result: a hammer is much better than a hand for driving in nails.

However, purpose may override design: I may use the hammer to keep a window open. The same holds true for 'destiny'. 'Destiny' is not the same thing as fate. While it seems certain, for instance, that the fate of all living beings is death, our destiny, as individuals or as a whole, refers more properly to what we do with life knowing that death is our fate.

The discussions within the study of the various sciences – historical, life, social and natural sciences – over the last 200 years have made all enquiries about purpose and destiny much more nuanced. This is because they have identified laws, probabilities and statistical regularities which lead to understandings of existence as radically determined for some, and as radically random for others. Nevertheless, for a variety of reasons – drawn sometimes from arguments about quantum theory, sometimes from chaos and complexity theory, sometimes from evolutionary biology or from neurology – it still seems warranted, even necessary, to recognize that the cosmos and its history are more than a series of complex, necessary causal structures, more than design or fate. The need for a distinction between purpose and design, between destiny and fate in the existence of the cosmos and history suggests that any contemporary discussion of purpose and destiny should ask at least three types of questions: 1. questions that clarify where we have been, from the origin of the universe to the present; 2. questions about what are the realistic possibilities for the future given all that we know about the past; and 3. questions about who, not just what, we are. We need to approach the issues of purpose and destiny from the best-informed perspectives in all areas of enquiry about our deep and recent history, about the possibilities for our action, and about our identity.

Science

History

The Christian tradition has had a long history of discussion about the purpose and destiny of all of creation, of the human person, and of social groups and nations. In this history it has developed a rich vocabulary to speak about the right order of existence in relation to God, to others and to the world; a rich vocabulary to describe the recurring trends in human history; a rich vocabulary to describe what the end of that history might involve. It has struggled with several debates over the destiny of all to salvation, various forms of predestination, and the place of grace and free choice. It has struggled with various formulations about the power of sin and the human history of sin to distort even our best intentions to pursue good ends. Calling attention to the seemingly goal-directed structure of so much of existence, it has even offered a 'proof' for the existence of God based on purpose and destiny.

Grace

Freedom

p. 507

In short, considerations of purpose and destiny have been woven into almost every facet of a Christian perspective. The briefest of summaries of this perspective might run: live and die with the believable hope that all creation has a purpose, the fullness of existence in relation to God, and that this purpose has become a destiny in the death and resurrection of Jesus. Thus this Christian perspective is a thoroughly practical one: live in a particular way. Speculation about design and future events, states or conditions, serves to reinforce the assurance that even when designs and plans seem to falter – when bad things happen to good people, when the promise of God seems to be forgotten, when death seems most the moment of being forsaken – God abides.

Jesus

Christian life

The sense that the purpose of existence must be supplied by human intention and action seems to be corrected at almost every turn in this Christian perspective. The Christian tradition asserts that salvation, living fully in relation to God, is the purpose of existence, and at the same time that this salvation is a gift of a gracious, often enigmatic God. Various genres display this fundamental conviction of the Christian tradition: it appears in the story of Israel; it appears in the prophetic visions of a restored land and rebuilt temple after the exile; it appears in the vision in the Jewish wisdom literature that whatever may be thought and said about the right road to salvation, things

p. 1152

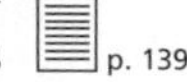
p. 139

are not what they seem and the future is God's; it appears in the philosophical and theological disputations about whether human action merits salvation or displays its presence, about whether the human will is so distorted by sin that nothing but God's creative love can bring its desires to good. The typical Christian conviction is that the destiny of all creation is basically a freely-offered gift of God and not the work of the will.

Revelation

The imagery and conceptual apparatus used to discuss both purpose and destiny in the Christian tradition have certainly at points obscured the more practical side of the issues. This is probably for the most part the case in the sometimes vivid portrayals of after-life and judgement along with the sometimes detailed calendrical speculation about when the end-time would come. This way of presenting the destiny of all of existence – in the imagery of a revelation about a future event or a future location – has, at its best, encouraged consolation in times of seeming hopelessness, or caution about a naively optimistic perspective of the future. At those times when the presentations have been taken as a report of future events, the practical concerns associated with Christian destiny have been lost in conjectures about future worlds, unneeded anxieties about engagement with a created world, or undue confidence in the certainty of election.

Philosophy

p. 504

The same is true when the Christian discussion has relied heavily on philosophical systems. In the early encounter with the classical Greek world and various forms of middle and neo-Platonism, sometimes very fine distinctions were drawn between providence, destiny, purpose, fortune, fate and chance. Throughout these discussions the Christian position on monotheism, its belief in one God, remained steadfast: fortune and fate were not rival powers to God in the consideration of the future and of destiny. Providence was the way God ordered matter, but providence included fortune, fate and chance, each with their own spheres of control, and none ever competitive with God or determinative for human action. Yet at points even these clarifying discussions seemed to take on a life of their own, more concerned with mapping speculative hierarchies of being than informing the Christian call to live and die in an assured hope.

Paul

This same potential to clarify and obscure the Christian position on purpose and destiny occurred with the discussions of predestination. Rooted in several phrases from the letters of Paul and passages of the Hebrew scriptures, as well as in the fundamental conviction that salvation is the fullness of life with God and not a creation of the human will, speculation at times ran rampant regarding the precise limits of human freedom, the extent of the distortion of human willing by sin, the role of human action in receiving the gracious gift of salvation, the relation of God to human freedom, the relation of knowledge to necessity, and the relation of eternity to temporality. A wide variety of positions on predestination were expressed in these debates, from a reliance on the role of human action in bringing salvation, to various forms of double predestination, a determination of God for the salvation or damnation of the individual soul seemingly irrespective of the life of the individual.

Ethics

Psychology and Christianity

For many today, such considerations about predestination are of little value. So much has changed in our views of cosmology, of the structure of human desires and consciousness, of our ability to appreciate the role of imagination in the formulation of religious perspectives. Thus the current discussions of purpose and destiny are less in debt to these past speculations and more in conversation with the scientific and ethical issues that shape the world today. Evolutionary biology has generated a fundamental discussion about the place of random variation, chance, natural selection and a fundamentally non-anthropocentric view of life. Neurophysiology and psychology have vastly expanded the discussion of the factors that seem to shape how we conceive our individual and social destinies. The discussion of the first seconds of existence in the 'Big Bang' and the conditions which that initial singularity established for the range of existence in the universe affect the discussion of destiny on a grand scale. The discussion of political theorists and economic historians about the intractable issues of poverty and their effect on what people perceive to be the purpose of life or the future for their children has moved the discussion of Christian purpose and destiny into the realm of political action and liberation.

Poverty

Liberation theology

At few points in the discussion of Christian thought does there seem to be as wide a gap in the way the discussion of a topic was carried out in the past and the way it is now structured. The discussion of purpose and destiny had for so long in the Christian tradition been shaped by philosophy, particularly various forms of Platonism, that the transfer of these terms into the context of the natural, life, social and historical sciences of today has been one of the major incentives for important and often unresolved discussions about the relation of Christianity to science as a whole.

Sociology

Because of the recognition that 'purpose' and 'destiny' in the Christian context are practical concepts, concepts which shape human identity and action rather than compete with science for the most adequate description available of the cosmos or the development of various life forms, contemporary Christian thought about purpose and destiny is shaped more by an appreciation of the role of imagination in the structuring of possibilities for human action and social transformation than by previous discussions of predestination and the hierarchy of providence, fortune and fate. The foundational biblical narratives for the Christian tradition – the narratives of the proto-history of creation, the election of the Hebrews and the exodus, the exile in Babylon and the re-establishment of the temple, and the accounts of the life, death and resurrection of Jesus – continue to disclose realistic possibilities for the practical configuration of identity and action which are at the heart of the consideration of destiny and purpose.

Each of these narratives suggests different aspects for the consideration of purpose and destiny. The Genesis narratives of the proto-history do not compete with accounts of geology, paleontology or evolutionary biology over the unique origins of the human species; rather, they offer to the imagination a world where order is always surrounded by chaos, where the human seems inclined simultaneously to the most amazing feats and at the same time to its own self-destruction. The exodus and election stories offer the imagination a world in which slavery and oppression are not the destiny of God's chosen, and yet the freedom of redemption offered by God is also a struggle. It is a picture where the purpose of life is displayed less in order than in action, action which, at least in the short run, is the occasion of more suffering and confusion than consolation. The destiny of the kingdom guaranteed by a covenant with God crashes with the exile in Babylon and the destruction of the temple in Jerusalem. Again for the imagination, any sense that the destiny of God's chosen or the accomplishment of human purpose is measured by security, power or wealth seems to be corrected. And if the purpose of human existence is somehow modelled as a discipleship, as it is in the Christian Gospels, then the imagination is given a very confrontational perspective: the purpose of our lives may indeed challenge us to chasten our desires for domination or pleasure or wealth, and to live with a purpose that is not our own, or not measured by the best descriptions of our natural states.

Covenant

It is an imaginative picture that dares to suggest that authentic human purpose involves feeding the hungry and clothing the naked and that authentic human destiny leads to crucifixion. In this enigmatic challenge, there is a constant affirmation that existence is purposeful and that the destiny of existence as 'salvation' is already at hand; at the same time there is the disquieting suggestion that the gracious gift of this destiny is a demanding one that can take us to places where the discussions of chance and randomness are less than adequate for getting at the practical dimension of authentic Christian purpose and destiny.

JOHN MCCARTHY

James K. Beilby and Paul R. Eddy (eds), *Divine Foreknowledge: Four Views*, Downers Grove, IL: InterVarsity Press 2001; Peter C. Hodgson, *God In History: Shapes of Freedom*, Nashville, TN: Abingdon Press 1989; David Tracy, *Plurality and Ambiguity: Hermeneutics, Religion, Hope*, San Francisco: Harper & Row and London: SCM Press 1987

Devotions

Periods of quiet prayer and meditation, often observed daily by Christians, are known as devotions. They may take many forms, but often include meditations on a passage from the Bible or a Christian spiritual writer, silence, and prayer. In the Protestant tradition, written material to aid devotions is available in many forms, from small booklets to large books; for example the Bible Societies provide notes for daily Bible readings, and an enormous amount of material appears on the internet.

In the Roman Catholic tradition, devotions tend to be more formal and make more use of visual aids: rather than focusing on Bible passages they tend to centre on images of Jesus and the Holy Spirit, Mary, the saints and the eucharist. The forms and themes of these devotions often seem strange to those who are not Catholics, but they become more understandable when we look at the context in which they arose. They come from a time and culture in which the majority of people were illiterate and therefore could not read books, so they are focused on things that could be seen and touched.

In the Orthodox tradition, too, the focal point of devotion is visual, in the form of icons. A major role is also played by the continual repetition of the Jesus prayer, 'Lord Jesus Christ, Son of God, have mercy on me.'

Thomas Aquinas

Icon

p. 821

Hymns

Devotion to Jesus

In a church which venerated martyrs from a very early date and prized and honoured their material remains, their relics, it was natural for devotions to be fixed not only on, say, Jesus, but on a particular part of him. The thirteenth century saw the beginnings of devotions to the Sacred Heart of Jesus, which seem to have arisen out of contemplation of the wound inflicted on Jesus at his crucifixion, from which blood and water flowed; these were seen as the source of the church's sacraments of eucharist and baptism. Mystics, notably Mechthild of Hackeborn (died 1299) and Gertrude (died 1302), had visions of this heart, and it is mentioned by Julian of Norwich (*c.*1342–1416) in her 'Shewings': 'And therewith He had me recall His dearworthy blood and precious Water which He let pour out for love and He shewed me His blissful heart.' Originally practised by comparatively few devout Christians, this devotion was promoted in the seventeenth century first by the Jesuits and Francis de Sales (1567–1622), later by the French missioner John Eudes (1601–80), and above all by Margaret Mary Alacoque (1647–90), a nun of the Visitandine order founded by Francis de Sales; in 1765 it became a feast of the church. Early in the nineteenth century devotions to the Sacred Heart of Mary also came to be observed.

p. 1075

Mary

In the Middle Ages various churches, in places as far apart as Beirut and Bruges, claimed to have relics of the blood shed by Jesus, and although Thomas Aquinas argued that all Jesus' blood returned to him after his resurrection, popular devotion begged to differ, and feasts of the Precious Blood were celebrated during the nineteenth century. A Feast of the Precious Blood was established in 1849, but was abolished in 1969, after the Second Vatican Council. Westminster Cathedral in London is dedicated to the Precious Blood.

The Name of Jesus became an official focus of devotion in the Middle Ages, marked by Latin hymns, the most famous of which is still sung in English as 'Jesus, the very thought of Thee' with the verse 'Nor voice can sing, nor heart can frame, nor can the memory find a sweeter sound than Thy blest Name, O Saviour of mankind.'

Many Christians other than the Orthodox focus on Jesus through the Jesus prayer and by making the sign of the cross. A procession along the Stations of the Cross is held in many churches in the Catholic tradition in the period before Easter; on Good Friday Anglicans hold a service from noon to 3pm, known as the Three Hours' Devotion, a period of prayer and meditation based on the 'seven last words of Jesus'.

Devotion to Mary and the saints

The chief form of devotion to Mary is the rosary, a string of beads for counting prayers. The rosary developed out of

THE STATIONS OF THE CROSS

1 Christ is condemned to death
2 Christ receives the cross
3 His first fall
4 He meets his mother
5 Simon of Cyrene is made to bear the cross
6 Christ's face is wiped by Veronica
7 His second fall
8 He meets the women of Jerusalem
9 His third fall
10 He is stripped of his garments
11 He is nailed to the cross
12 Christ dies on the cross
13 His body is taken down from the cross
14 His body is laid in the tomb.

The Stations of the Cross commemorate fourteen selected incidents in the journey of Christ to his crucifixion: they are depicted by plaques either in churches or in the open air. In the Catholic tradition processions along them are made on Good Friday; at each station there is a pause for prayer and meditation. This practice was probably inspired by the pilgrimages made in Jerusalem from Pilate's house to Calvary, which pilgrims wanted to repeat on their return home. The number of stations initially varied from five to thirty: the number fourteen was fixed by Pope Clement XII in 1731, comprising nine scenes from the Gospels and five from popular tradition (3, 4, 6, 7, 9).

THE SEVEN LAST WORDS OF JESUS ON THE CROSS

Matthew	*Mark*	*Luke*	*John*
4. 'Eli, eli, lama sabacthani: My God, my God, why have you forsaken me?'	4. 'Eloi, eloi, lama sabacthani: My God, my God, why have you forsaken me?'	1. 'Father, forgive them, for they know not what they do.' 2. 'Today you will be with me in paradise.' 7. 'Father, into your hands I commend my spirit.'	3. 'Woman, behold your son ... behold your mother.' 5. 'I thirst.' 6. 'It is finished.'

In many churches, Good Friday is marked by a devotional service based on the 'seven last words of Jesus', with hymns, prayers and short sermons. Although this is now predominantly a Protestant and Anglican form of devotion, it in fact originated with Peruvian Jesuits in the seventeenth century; it is an instance in which modern Protestants have picked up Roman Catholic devotional practices. The seven last words have also inspired a number of pieces of music, notably a string quartet with this title by Joseph Haydn; the nineteenth-century French composer Theodore Dubois wrote an oratorio in eight movements, *The Seven Last Words of Christ*, based on them.

However, an examination of the 'seven last words' as set out above, and a closer consideration of the Gospel passages in which they appear, shows that to bring together seven 'last words' is to conflate three different presentations of the dying Jesus, each with different theological emphases. In Matthew and Mark Jesus' only words are an apparent cry of despair (though this is a quotation from a psalm which ends in hope, 22.1). In Luke Jesus dies an exemplary death, to be closely imitated by Stephen, the first Christian martyr, in the Acts of the Apostles (Acts 7.59–60). In John, Jesus is sovereign as he hangs on the cross, commending the Beloved Disciple and his mother to each other and dying with the statement of a task fully performed: the words 'It is finished,' in Latin *consummatum est*, are better translated 'It is accomplished.'

THE ROSARY

The rosary consists of five (sometimes fifteen) sets of ten beads (called decades), each separated from the next set by a larger bead; a pendant of two large beads separated by three small ones and a crucifix is attached to the string with a medallion at the joining point. One way of using the rosary is to say the creed while holding the crucifix and then use the five beads above it for the Lord's Prayer, three Hail Marys and the Gloria. The Lord's Prayer is said on the medallion and then Hail Marys are said on the small beads and the Gloria and Lord's Prayer on the large beads until the cycle is completed.

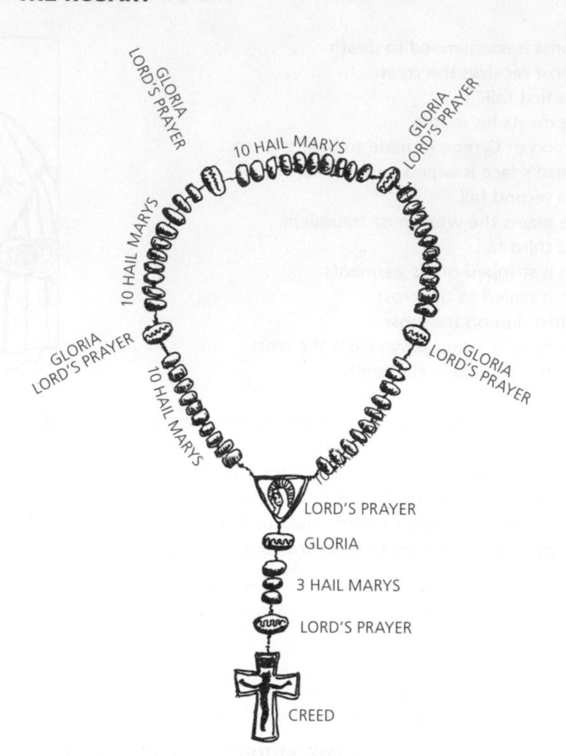

the monastic repetition of a particular prayer a set number of times; in the Eastern churches this practice developed instead into the Jesus prayer.

Saint

Another form of devotion to Mary is the litany, a long series of praises of Mary like 'Mistress of the Angels', 'Star of Heaven', interspersed with the address 'Holy Mary'; this seems to have originated in private devotions, but from around the sixteenth century came to be used publicly, in a simpler form, especially at times of war and epidemics. One particularly famous example is the Litany of Loreto, which originated at the shrine there of the 'Holy House', the house in Nazareth where Joseph and Mary lived, which was supposed to have been transported to Italy by angels. There are countless other hymns and prayers to Mary, some of them very ancient.

p. 1068

Devotion to Mary also takes the form of making pilgrimages to shrines at places like Walsingham, Guadalupe, Lourdes and Fatima, where the Virgin is believed to have appeared. And shrines of the Virgin adorned with flowers and surrounded by lighted candles in virtually every Catholic church bear witness to everyday veneration of her. From the seventeenth century, the month of May has been consecrated to Mary for special observances.

Pilgrimage
p. 733
Sacraments
pp. 484–5

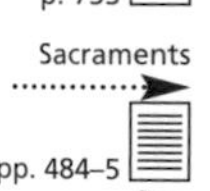

Alongside devotion to Mary goes devotion to the saints, particularly patron saints associated with particular groups or places, who are believed to provide help in times of danger and distress. Testimony to such devotion can be found in the many petitions for favour or thanks for blessings received in Catholic churches all over the world expressed in forms which range from illustrated tablets fixed to the wall to scraps of paper pinned on a board.

Eucharistic devotion

With the establishment in the thirteenth century of the doctrine of transubstantiation, i.e. the view that the bread and wine consecrated at the eucharist change their substance (but not their appearance) and become the body and blood of Christ, the way was opened up for the elements, and particularly the eucharistic bread in the form of a wafer, the host, to be themselves the object of devotion, outside the eucharist itself. From the fourteenth century on the host was exposed for adoration, enclosed in a monstrance, a glass container set in an elaborate frame

AVE MARIA

p. 967

This prayer, which for Roman Catholics comes second only to the Lord's Prayer, is based on a combination of the words spoken to the mother of Jesus by the angel Gabriel and by her kinswoman Elizabeth in the Gospel of Luke (1.28, 42). The first part of the prayer, 'Hail Mary ... Jesus', first appears in the eleventh century; the second part does not appear until the sixteenth century.

Ave Maria	Hail Mary
Ave Maria, gratia plena, Dominus tecum, benedicta tu in mulieribus, et benedictus fructus ventris tui, Jesus. Sancta Maria, Mater Dei, ora pro nobis peccatoribus, nunc et in hora mortis nostrae. Amen.	Hail Mary, full of grace, the Lord is with thee. Blessed art thou amongst women and blessed is the fruit of thy womb Jesus. Holy Mary, Mother of God, pray for us sinners, now and at the hour of our death. Amen.

usually with gold or gilded rays extending from it, on a stand by which it could also be held up or carried.

The service of Benediction of the Blessed Sacrament developed, often following evening prayer, during which the sacrament is exposed, eucharistic hymns are sung and Christ is praised in his sacramental presence. Thomas Aquinas wrote a great hymn *Tantum ergo*, which belongs in this context; in English it runs, 'Therefore we, before him bending, this great sacrament revere; types and shadows have their ending, for the newer rite is here; faith, our outward sense befriending, makes the inward vision clear.' At its most public, eucharistic devotion is expressed in colourful public processions with the eucharistic host at the feast of Corpus Christi; at its most private in figures quietly kneeling in a chapel in which the eucharistic elements are reserved, primarily for taking to the sick and infirm.

JOHN BOWDEN

J. V. Bainvel, *Devotion to the Sacred Heart of Jesus: The Doctrine and its History*, London: Burns Oates & Washbourne 1924; John Macquarrie, *Paths in Spirituality*, London: SCM Press and New York: Harper & Row 1972

Discipline

In every human grouping or institution, discipline in some form, whether formally constituted or informally exercised by custom or consensus, is inevitable. Such discipline performs three interlocking functions. 1. It provides a framework that enables the individual to enter into and participate in the organization. 2. It gives shape and order to the community so that it can perform its agreed functions. 3. It sets boundaries and sanctions whereby the group can deal with disruption and dissidence in an orderly and acceptable manner. The way discipline is understood and exercised is affected by many factors. It is bound to reflect the cultural assumptions that are around at the time, such as notions of authority and acceptable personal behaviour. This is as true of the church as of other social institutions such as the state or the family.

Authority

Discipline for individuals

Not surprisingly, discipline in the church is there to serve its primary aims and beliefs. The Christian community is the company of those who believe in God as found in and through Jesus Christ and have undertaken to walk in his way of witness and service in the world. This means that for Christians discipline is there, in the first instance, to enable the community and the individual to grow into that way of life. Indeed the first followers of Jesus were called 'disciples', which means 'learners', from the Latin *discernere*. They were also called 'the people of the way', those who follow Jesus' path. The Gospels tell of Jesus calling together a group of people, not always easy to define but clearly with a core of men and women, to 'be with him' (Mark 3.13–14). This was not unusual; John the Baptist (John 1.35) and other rabbis (Mark 2.15) had disciples, as do teachers in other religions. The aim is to learn from the master wisdom and understanding for life.

Festivals and fasts

p. 848

This image has persisted, and the heart of Christian discipline is designed to facilitate the process. A 'practising Christian', using today's parlance, is expected to adhere to a minimal discipline, usually defined in terms of joining regularly, normally on 'the Lord's Day' (Sunday), with the church in its place for worship, instruction (Bible reading and exposition) and, in many traditions, the eucharist. For the sacramental traditions this is centred on weekly attendance at the eucharist and confession. Protestants lay the stress on preaching. The modern liturgical movement, however, has drawn these two traditions closer together. The monitoring of such discipline has been at the heart of

Christian life
Eucharist
Forgiveness
Preaching

Pastoral care

pastoral care exercised by priest, minister, elder or church meeting, according to the tradition.

Devotions

p. 342

p. 1143

Some Christians will enter into stricter levels of discipline or practice. All traditions encourage models of devotion and education as means of advancing in the Christian life. These will include the use of devotional aids and literature, such as books of prayers or the use of the rosary; personal counselling through the confessional or spiritual directors; services and meetings, such as Benediction or Bible study; going to retreats, courses or conferences; and regular habits of private prayer.

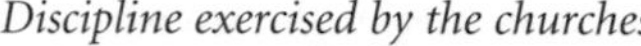

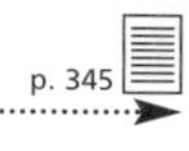

p. 345

For others there is a calling to enter into an order or similar community. All clergy are, in some sense, under a form of discipline, which differs from tradition to tradition. But the monastic and other orders offer a stricter way of life, whether in a community or working in wider society. There are also, attached to some of the older orders, 'tertiary' orders for those who take vows without withdrawing from everyday life.

Discipline exercised by the churches

Organization

All the churches have their own constitutions reflecting their understanding of the nature and purpose of the church, which are their authority structures. There are, broadly speaking, four models of church authority.

Canon law

Church of England

Council

Counter-Reformation

p. 1045

1. Within Western Catholicism there is a highly sophisticated body of canon law expressing the church's faith, morals, discipline and other formal activities. It has accumulated and been revised over the centuries. Its roots are in the New Testament and the first decisions of the church (Acts 15). Subsequent councils and authoritative statements have added to it. In the Middle Ages, with Gratian, and reinforced by the Counter-Reformation, canon law entered its modern centralized phase. This was brought to a climax at the First Vatican Council (1870) with the promulgation of the doctrine of papal infallibility, when the pope speaks *ex cathedra*, i.e. with the full weight of his office. The magisterium, or teaching authority of the Roman Catholic Church, resides in the Pope with the bishops.

Persecution

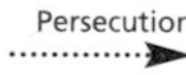

2. The Orthodox and Anglican traditions, in their own particular ways, represent forms of 'hierarchical federalism'. The local churches, whether thought of as dioceses, provinces or patriarchates, are under the bishops, who are themselves bound together in the common faith and tradition. Here there is more variation and a consensual notion of authority.

3. Synodical government, as found, e.g., in Methodism and Presbyterianism, vests ultimate authority in a general assembly, usually of a national church. Decision-making and discipline are exercised through a series of councils from the local to the national.

4. In the congregational form of government, as found, e.g., among Baptists, Congregationalists and some Pentecostals, authority is vested in the church meeting of members, with its own constitution.

Church discipline and state discipline

Christian discipline is not, however, unaffected by the wider context. Christianity has always recognized two powers: the sacred or ecclesial (of the church) and the secular or earthly. The relationship between these two down through history has shaped the practice of that authority.

In the Catholic West, in the Middle Ages, the Pope claimed that as Christ's representative he was over the emperor. It had been the teaching of Augustine that the powers of the secular arm could be called in to give force to papal jurisdiction. Hence, e.g., the practice of the Inquisition to turn heretics over to the state or to call for a crusade against heretics. With the rise of the nation state and secularism the relationships have been increasingly regulated through concordats or treaties negotiated between sovereign powers, giving the Roman Catholic Church recognized rights and freedoms.

In Eastern Orthodoxy the emperor was seen as the image of God's ruling power and thus the protector of church and state, though not himself a priest or bishop. In Anglicanism, Henry VIII, by taking on himself the title 'supreme head' of the church, set himself in a very similar position, subordinating the church's authority and canon law to the sovereign in parliament. Over the last century or so the Church of England has been given power to control its own internal affairs, though still as established by parliament. To some extent Protestantism in Germany and elsewhere is similarly established.

The Free Church model, which pertains wherever a church has no formal state relationship, separates church from state. The churches exercise their discipline by their own authority, under the sovereignty of Christ. But of course they are also within the jurisdiction of the state and are given only such freedoms as the state allows. This can often lead to tensions and the need sometimes to assert the freedom of the gospel, perhaps under persecution. In the West, such churches are understood as voluntary associations.

Discipline as correction

It is within this context that discipline in its meaning of correction is exercised. From the beginning there has been a need to rebuke and control those who have brought dissension or shame upon the church. The purpose of such discipline is, however, clear: it is to bring back restoration and harmony. Indeed the biblical words can be translated both as 'chastisement' and as 'instruction'. This does not mean that such authority has always been exercised justly

THE INQUISITION

The Inquisition was a Roman Catholic institution which actively fought against heresy and sought out alleged witches, sorcerers and alchemists. Its foundation is generally attributed to Pope Gregory IX in 1231, but it was in the making before then, when movements like the Cathars and the Waldensians were thought to be posing grave threats to the church and had to be combated. The first inquisitors were drawn mainly from the Dominican and Franciscan orders and appointed in areas where heresy was thought to be rife. They relied for their effectiveness on co-operation with the secular authorities, and where that was not forthcoming, as in Great Britain and most of northern Europe, there was no Inquisition.

The inquisitors were responsible only to the Pope, and had jurisdiction over all Christians. Those suspected of heresy, witchcraft or whatever were given time to confess and seek absolution, but if they did not they were interrogated in secret in the presence of witnesses. They were not told what they were accused of or allowed witnesses in their defence, and lawyers were hard to come by because they did not want to incur the suspicion of heresy themselves. In 1252 Pope Innocent IV authorized the use of torture to obtain confessions. On conviction, or admission of guilt, the accused could be sentenced to a wide range of penalties, from regular penance, fasting or pilgrimage to confiscation of property and imprisonment, in serious cases for life. Those who refused to recant were handed over to the secular arm, which alone could impose the death penalty, and were burnt at the stake. The accused could appeal to the Pope before sentencing and the Pope was the supreme authority for the inquisitors.

The Inquisition declined in the fifteenth century with the lessening of the threat from the Cathars, but in 1478 a new Inquisition, the Spanish Inquisition, was set up – this time not by the Pope, but by Ferdinand and Isabella with the Pope's permission. It was directed primarily against apostate former Jews and Muslims in an attempt to enforce religious unity. The first inquisitors, based in Seville, were so severe that Sixtus IV had to intervene, but he was quite ineffective in curbing the Inquisition. Indeed in 1483 he was persuaded to appoint a Grand Inquisitor for Castile. The first to hold this office, the Dominican Tomás de Torquemada, has become the symbol of the inquisitor who mercilessly uses torture and has his victims burnt at the stake. The public ceremony at which sentences were pronounced and carried out, the *auto-da-fé* ('act of faith'), became spectacular, often held in the presence of royalty, and involving a procession, solemn mass, oath of obedience to the Inquisition, a sermon and the reading of the sentences. However, those found guilty were not handed over to the secular powers or burnt during this ceremony. The Spanish Inquisition was finally suppressed only in 1834; the last *auto-da-fé* was in Mexico in 1858.

In 1542 Pope Paul III established the Roman Inquisition to combat Protestantism. It was headed by a commission of six cardinals, the Congregation of the Inquisition. Except under one or two popes it was far more moderate than the Spanish Inquisition, and although theoretically it had general authority, its activities were limited to Italy. Once Protestantism had ceased to be a threat to unity there, the Roman Inquisition increasingly became one of the instruments of papal government, responsible for maintaining pure faith and morals in the Catholic Church. When Pope Pius X reorganized the Curia in 1908 the Inquisition came to be known officially as the Holy Office, and in 1965 Pope Paul VI reorganized it and renamed it the Congregation for the Doctrine of the Faith.

or well. There are too many instances of power struggles and cruelty to be complacent. Yet the ostensible motive has always been to seek the reconciliation of those who apparently have broken faith by word or deed.

Following the New Testament (cf. Matthew 18.15–17), there have been traditionally three levels of action. The first is at the semi-informal, personal and private level. For most this will be experienced as pastoral care, as an appeal to recognize that something has gone wrong and needs to be righted. This will be done in ways appropriate to the tradition: confession, pastoral conversation, counselling. In Roman Catholicism the admission of sin is accompanied by an act of penance. This should be regarded as an act of reparation and reflection. Sometimes, indeed, the penitent has 'to make it up' with another. But at the same time the failure has also torn the fabric of the community and the relationship with God. It is appropriate therefore that this be recollected and given some kind of expression – not to exact retribution but to formalize the act of restoration. The grace of God is always seeking to reconcile the sinner which is sealed in the act of repentance.

Grace

The second move is to formalize the situation if personal appeal fails. It is at this stage that recourse is made to the constitutional provisions for dealing with disputes, whether through the canonical courts or other structures. This can range from processes of law backed by the civil authority to proceedings that are closer to a tribunal trying to come to an acceptable solution within a Christian community.

Thirdly, if there seems no hope of resolution, the most extreme act of discipline is excommunication or expulsion by refusing the key sacrament of communion. Where the cultural ties are closely intertwined this could be tantamount to total social exclusion. But even today, where the churches are marginal to the culture, it is a step that is not taken lightly. In any case, there is always the possibility of restoration.

Sacraments

Forgiveness

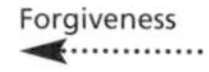

Individuals, groups or whole communities can be

DISCIPLINE IN THE CHURCH

'If your brother sins against you, go and tell him his fault, between you and him alone. If he listens to you, you have gained your brother.

But if he does not listen, take one or two others along with you, that every word may be confirmed by the evidence of two or three witnesses.

If he refuses to listen to them, tell it to the church; and if he refuses to listen even to the church, let him be to you as a Gentile and a tax collector.

Truly, I say to you, whatever you bind on earth shall be bound in heaven, and whatever you loose on earth shall be loosed in heaven.'

(Matthew 18.15–18)

This passage in the Gospel of Matthew indicates the first beginnings of a judicial procedure in the church and the first indication of a process of excommunication. Given that Jesus gave no instructions for the formation of an organized church, it seems likely that these words do not come from him, but from the early church itself.

excommunicated. Ecclesiastical schism has often been expressed in these terms. One of the marks of twentieth-century ecumenism has been the gradual breaking down of such barriers between communions. There is still some way to go. Most Protestants now accept one another. There have been major steps between Orthodox and Roman Catholics. But other divisions are still present, even if considerable progress has been made towards healing them.

Ecumenical movement

PAUL BALLARD

Paul Avis (ed), *The Christian Church – An Introduction to the Major Traditions*, London: SPCK and Ohio: Pilgrim Press 2002; J. A. Coriden, *An Introduction to Canon Law*, London: Geoffrey Chapman and New York and Mahwah, NJ: Paulist Press 1991; N. Doe, *Canon Law in the Anglican Communion – A Worldwide Perspective*, Oxford: OUP 1998; R. Newton Flew (ed), *The Nature of the Church*, London: SCM Press and New York: Harper & Brothers 1952; Stewart Lamont, *Church and Society – Uneasy Alliances*, London: The Bodley Head 1989

DIVERSITY

Adventist Church, African American Christianity, Anabaptists, Anglicanism, Baptist churches, Catholic Apostolic Church, Christian Church (Disciples of Christ), Christian Science, Church of England, Church of Scotland, Congregationalism, Coptic Christianity, Dutch Reformed Church, Eastern-rite Catholic churches, Ethiopian Christianity, Free churches, Jehovah's Witnesses, Lutheranism, Methodism, Moravian Church, Mormons, Old Catholic churches, Orthodox churches, Peace churches, Pentecostalism, Protestantism, Quakers (Religious Society of Friends), Reformed churches, Roman Catholic Church, Shakers, United Reformed Church, Waldensian Church

A tour of the Christian world would leave a breathtaking series of colourful scenes in the memory. In Moscow, the Orthodox Church's Easter eucharist is celebrated with timeless splendour: processions pass through the screen of icons separating off the altar in an act of worship performed by a community which never kneels. Christ is depicted as reigning in majesty, even from the cross, and the celebration seems to bring heaven to earth. In the villages of Italy, France and Spain, by contrast, the Roman Catholic churches with their crucifixes and representations of the dying Jesus are focused on suffering, and frescoes often depict a terrifying last judgement; light and hope come from the shrines to the Virgin Mary and the many candles lit in her honour by individuals who go there through the day to kneel and pray.

Icon

p. 1253

Mary

Further south, in Ethiopia, Christianity has still retained its Semitic form: male Christians are circumcised as in Judaism, and the devout observe the sabbath regulations on Saturday as well as worshipping on Sunday. Replicas of the Israelite ark can be found, and there is sacred dancing with a decidedly Old Testament flavour. In utter contrast, in Protestant Switzerland the interiors of the churches are whitewashed and bare: there are no paintings or statues; there is no stained glass, since images are prohibited; nor are there organs. Instead, there is the pulpit, the lectern and the Bible, the word of God.

Iconoclasm

Across the Atlantic, in Pennsylvania, an equally radical attitude is adopted by the Amish, conservative in their renunciation of modern technology, which leads them to reject the use of electricity and travel in horse-drawn buggies, immigrants coming from a fierce pacifist tradition. And in the comfortable suburbs of the United States, and to a far lesser degree Europe, attendance at churches with a kaleidoscopic variety forms part of the fabric of an everyday life in which in most respects church members do not seem to differ much from their non-churchgoing neighbours. Not only does the regular cycle of worship mark the year, but churches are still the places where Christians and non-Christians alike come together to mark events ranging from national thanksgivings to memorial services for murder victims.

Christianity in North America
Christianity in Europe

Festivals and fasts

These scenes hardly begin to touch on the diversity of Christianity. This diversity could be heightened by portraits of the varieties of Roman Catholic and Pentecostal worship in Latin America; by a contrast between the staid worship of the Dutch Reformed Church in South Africa and the colourful exorcisms and faith healings in the Independent African churches; by the exuberant singing and clapping of black congregations in the Caribbean; and in Asia by the gigantic congregations in the churches of Korea or the struggling and long-persecuted churches of China.

Christianity in Latin America

Christianity in Asia

DIVERSITY

Food and drink · Sexual ethics · Women in Christianity · Jesus

The range of Christianity is mind-boggling, with denominations (groupings of churches) running into the tens of thousands at the end of the second millennium, so much so that it is tempting to speak of Christianities in the plural. Certainly, phrases like 'Christians believe', 'Christians think', 'Christians do not ...', which are used commonly enough, prove on closer inspection to be far too simplistic. Some Christians are pacifist and some are not; some Christians drink alcohol and some do not; some believe it sinful to practise artificial contraception and some do not; some believe that men and women should have the same status within the churches and some do not.

Holy Spirit

Yet all this diversity derives from a single source, Jesus of Nazareth, and all Christians trace their origins back to him and see the work and worship of their churches as the doing of his will on earth. In whatever form, the great diversity of Christians pray through Jesus, whom they acknowledge as Lord, to God, in the Holy Spirit, and hold as an ideal the hope of 'one church, one faith, one Lord'. But attempts by one particular tradition to define itself as 'the true church', the only authentic form of Christianity, come to grief on the sheer weight of evidence for Christian diversity: empirically Christianity has constantly been in a state of flux, of growth, of diversification, and will continue to be so.

Why has this happened?

History · Mission · Roman empire

First of all, the legacy which Jesus left behind was open-ended. He left no written instructions, and his teaching is not focused on any institution which would arise after his death. Strangely, the disciples whom he chose do not seem to have played a major role in shaping the earliest church. How the church spread and took form was governed not least by local circumstances: for example, in Syria and Palestine during the first century there were many wandering prophetic Christian preachers with no fixed abode, spending a short time in a village before moving on; by contrast, in the urban world of the Greek cities where Christianity arrived at a very early stage, settled communities formed around the houses in which Christian converts met. Language, culture and philosophy gradually changed Christian thought, worship and practice as Christianity expanded both eastwards and westwards, through Persia to India, and from France to northern Europe. And whereas during the period of the Roman empire communications between the churches were relatively easy, at other times churches became isolated and developed customs of their own.

Because of all these factors, as time went on, one form of Christianity was on occasion to give rise to another form which differed quite substantially in its pattern of worship, the priority given to specific tenets of faith, and its attitude to society. The complex of factors which make up these forms has been conveniently referred to as a 'paradigm', a term taken from the history of science which denotes a constellation of beliefs, values, techniques and so on shared by the members of a given community, and the change in paradigm as a paradigm shift. Six major forms of Christianity can be identified, regardless of whether or not the term paradigm is used to describe them.

Jewish Christianity · Language · Persecution

The first form of Christianity was a Jewish Christianity, which had spread over Palestine and Mesopotamia and was centred on Jerusalem. The languages which it used were Semitic, above all Hebrew (for the scriptures) and Aramaic. Because of the disruption and persecution in connection with the destruction of Jerusalem by the Romans in their wars against the Jews (above all in 70 CE), Jewish Christianity went into decline.

Jewish Christianity was succeeded by a Christianity which had grown up in the Hellenistic-Greek world, with the formation of a Greek-speaking imperial church and the development of a body of dogma. Out of this grew the Orthodox churches.

Papacy

In the West, Christianity took a different course, which resulted in medieval Roman Catholicism, with the rise of the papacy and its claim to rule over the church, a system of Roman law, the

DIVERSITY
Forgiveness
Reformation
Bible
Enlightenment
Science
Exploration
Philosophy
Postmodern theology
Ecumenical movement

dominance of Latin as the church language, a celibate clergy and a complex system of reparations for sins committed.

A change took place in the West when abuses in the Roman Catholic Church and an attempt to return to the original sources of Christianity led to the Reformation and the formation of 'Protestant' churches. Especially as a result of the work of Martin Luther and John Calvin in the sixteenth century, these reformed churches protested against the neglect of the 'Word of God', and reshaped themselves in a manner they believed to be more in keeping with the Bible. The Church of England, which occupies a distinctive position between Roman Catholicism and Protestantism, also came into being at this time.

The seventeenth- and eighteenth-century Enlightenment brought a change of a different kind which this time did not produce a new church or group of churches, but rather created so to speak a split across all the churches. The successes of modern science in transforming people's lives and their challenge to traditional beliefs, the new discoveries arising from exploration of the universe, past and present, radical new developments in philosophy with the rule of reason, and the social revolutions, notably in France and America, motivated by the idea of human rights, led not only to hostility to religion but also to revisions of Christianity which would make it compatible with the modern world. There was criticism of every aspect of Christian belief and practice, eagerly pursued and accepted in some of the churches but fought against tooth and nail in others.

A final change is taking place now, at the end of the twentieth and the beginning of the twenty-first century, as disillusionment with some of the legacies of the Enlightenment has set in among many Christians, and there are even calls to go back to the form of Christianity current before the rise of historical criticism. The term postmodernity is regularly used in the northern hemisphere to denote the new situation; the forms of Christianity which are flourishing to an amazing degree in the southern hemisphere by-pass modern developments in Christian thinking and have direct recourse to the Bible and experience of the spirit as self-evident realities.

These various forms did not follow one another in history, but perhaps with the exception of Jewish Christianity have continued to exist side by side. The Orthodox churches, the Roman Catholic Church with its papal claims to primacy, the Reformation churches and the Anglican church still flourish today, in a world where there are also many Christians who find it difficult to give full allegiance to the church to which they belong because they feel that its way of thinking is too fixated on the past and has not grappled with the problems of life in the modern world, and many Christians for whom belief in the gospel and experience of the spirit transcends any institutional form. At the end of the second millennium there were 1057 million Roman Catholics, 342 million Protestants, 215 million Orthodox and 79 million Anglicans. In addition to these there are more than 400 million Christians belonging to the myriad of other denominations, independent, charismatic and Pentecostal, which have formed in more recent times and which are constantly increasing.

Given the circumstances in which Christianity has grown and spread, it is not at all surprising that there should be such diversity, and is evident that diversity will always be a characteristic of Christian communities. How far that diversity is tolerable is a question which is answered in different ways by different churches: for example, the limits of diversity are set more narrowly in the Roman Catholic Church or Orthodox churches than they are in the Protestant and Anglican churches. This issue of the 'limits to diversity' has proved an especially thorny problem in the ecumenical movement and is still far from being resolved. One thing, though is clear. However vigorous the quest for unity, and the concern not to allow Christianity to be overly diluted by alien elements, there can never be anything like uniformity of beliefs and practices. What is regrettable is that there often seems to be little recognition of the inevitability of diversity and the tolerant acceptance of it, and little attempt to understand the nature of the historical legacy of Christianity and the complex theological questions to which this gives rise. Sadly, Christianity has always been characterized by hostility and reciprocal exclusion of its members and communities. It is here that lessons need to be learned.

JOHN BOWDEN

Hans Küng, *Christianity. Its Essence and History*, London: SCM Press and New York: Crossroad 1995; Ninian Smart, *The Phenomenon of Christianity*, London: Collins 1979; *The World Christian Encyclopedia* ed David B. Barrett, George T. Kurian and Todd M. Johnson, New York: OUP [2]2001

Doctrinal criticism

Fundamentalism
Biblical criticism
God

The term 'doctrinal criticism' is modelled on the more familiar and far more widely established concept of 'biblical criticism'. The word 'doctrine' indicates agreed teachings of the church. It is not a precise term, but one that stands midway between 'dogma' (a particular doctrine regarded as fixed and inalienable) and 'theology' (less formal accounts of Christian beliefs where a measure of speculation and change are to be expected). The boundaries between the three are not always clearly defined. It is not surprising, therefore, that proposals that doctrine should be subject to critical assessment and to change have neither been readily accepted nor wholly ruled out in the past.

Trinity
Incarnation

Heresy

Historiography

The use of the distinctive term 'doctrinal criticism', particularly in Britain in recent decades, derives from an article by George Woods (1966). He defines it as 'the critical study of the truth and adequacy of doctrinal statements', and argues that it is as urgently needed in academic theology as biblical criticism has shown itself to be in biblical studies. That the need for it was particularly acute at that time was in large measure due to the success of the practice of biblical criticism. This had shown conclusively that traditional Christian beliefs could not be derived directly from the Bible with the degree of certainty claimed for them in the past and believed by many to be essential for a viable religious faith. In response to this dilemma it was tempting to turn to the central agreed doctrines of the church as having the requisite degree of certainty in themselves, however ambiguous their relation to the biblical text might turn out to be. But such a proposal had two grave drawbacks. The doctrinal statements of the church have a history, just as the biblical text has. If the biblical text is rightly subjected to critical study, must not the same be true for doctrinal texts? Nothing would be gained by replacing a discredited biblical fundamentalism with a form of doctrinal fundamentalism. Moreover, Christian doctrine takes for granted a transcendent reference to God. In a cultural context where such reference is widely regarded as meaningless (particularly the case at the time and place where Woods was writing), that aspect of doctrinal statements also seems to call for some justification.

In the light of that analysis of the problem, doctrinal criticism clearly needs to include both a historical and a philosophical dimension. It has not been formally subdivided into a list of different named styles of criticism, as biblical criticism has been. But historical and philosophical questioning can each take a variety of different forms, and what is involved in doctrinal criticism can best be seen from the range of different questions that need to be raised to test the truth and adequacy of doctrinal statements, beginning with the historical end of the spectrum.

Many basic doctrines, such as the doctrines of the Trinity and incarnation, were established in the early centuries of the church's life by way of fierce controversy with what came to be seen as heretical beliefs. Only limited sources have survived from that period, and questions need to be asked about their reliability. The writings of those judged heretics have largely been destroyed. Most of what we know about them comes from the highly polemical writings of their orthodox opponents. This means that the sources of our knowledge about the establishment of these crucial doctrines are both incomplete and extremely one-sided. Their history has been written almost exclusively by the victors in the controversies.

One of the ways in which victors characteristically write the history of doctrinal debates in which they have proved victorious is to present the doctrinal outcome as the only possible valid interpretation of the founding events of Christian history. Since we have grown up with that outcome as the established orthodoxy of many centuries' standing, we are strongly predisposed to believe them. That predisposition applies not only to the believer, but to the cultural historian also. It needs the self-conscious adoption of a critical stance to be able to read the story of the development of doctrine as the story of genuinely open possibilities, which is certainly what it was for those who lived through it. When we learn to do that we begin to see that these sociological and church-political motives helped to fashion the particular doctrinal outcome that prevailed. Political reasons were often an important factor in determining what credal text came to be adopted by the church.

Christian doctrines have always been claimed to be based on the teaching of scripture, and to constitute a coherent Christian understanding of the world as a whole. But both the understanding of the scriptures and the philosophical assumptions about the world which were common assumptions to both sides of those early doctrinal debates were very different from those characteristic of the modern world. It is not easy, but neither is it entirely impossible, to enter into the mind-set of those who laid down the pattern of early Christian doctrines. It is a process that is necessary for a properly historical understanding of those doctrines. However, doctrine is concerned not only with what was believed then but with what we should believe now. So the doctrinal critic cannot be content only with the task of trying to clarify what those ancient doctrines meant to those who professed them then. He or she needs to ask also whether our changed understanding of the nature of scripture and our different philosophical and other assumptions about the nature of the world in general affect the reasonableness of our believing those same doctrines today – and, if they do make a difference, in what way those doctrines need to be modified.

So historical questions of this kind lead, not only to a different understanding of the history of doctrine, but also to a different evaluation of the role those doctrines may rightly play in contemporary Christian belief. At this point historical questioning points to and merges with a more philosophical range of questions. In the nineteenth century the Anglican bishop Charles Gore spoke of Hellenism providing 'a language fitted, as none other has ever been, to furnish an exact and permanent terminology for doctrinal purposes'. Such an understanding of language is no longer tenable. And that carries the further implication that our own linguistic terminology and philosophical views are no more exact or permanent than those of early Christian times. Moreover, the difference between the prevalent Platonist outlook of the age of the church fathers and the modern historical consciousness of our own time is such that the thoughts of the one age cannot be straightforwardly translated into the context of the other. So the doctrinal critic must be critically aware of both the ancient and the modern, but in subservience to neither. Contemporary Christian doctrine arises out of an always shifting interplay between ancient and modern horizons. In consequence, it is not only ancient doctrine that is seen by the doctrinal critic as in need of change; contemporary doctrine, too, can only be seen as provisional in character.

Christology ◄

Woods' original article stressed the problematical character of reference to the transcendent in the modern era. Recent reflection on this problem tends to emphasize how our speech about the transcendent (and therefore about God) has as much kinship with that of the poet or the artist as with that of the logician or the research scientist: it owes as much to the creative imagination as to formal reasoning. The truth and adequacy of its language is a matter of the appropriateness of its imagery as much as of the logical cogency of its arguments. And that imagery is a part of the Christian tradition that we inherit, not something we devise for ourselves. This way of understanding the fundamental language of Christian doctrine is sometimes regarded as militating against the approach of doctrinal criticism. But that is a mistake. As poetry and art are rightly evaluated and assessed by the disciplines of literary and artistic criticism, so doctrine too needs to be subjected to an appropriate style of criticism. What this understanding of language shows is not that doctrinal criticism is inapplicable, but that it is a more variegated and elusive process than is sometimes realized. Feminist critiques of the language of fatherhood with reference to God and its often hidden influence on the structure of traditional doctrine are one specific example of such doctrinal criticism at work.

Poetry

Feminist theology

Nevertheless, there is strong resistance to the approach of doctrinal criticism today. It is argued that doctrinal criticism is exclusively concerned with the work of historians and philosophers to the neglect of anthropologists, musicians and poets, that it is too detached or neutral. However, doctrinal criticism does not depend on the critic's adopting a wholly detached or neutral standpoint. No such standpoint exists. But only the most extreme and implausible form of postmodernism would claim that that ruled out the possibility of reasoned, critical questioning. And it is the exercise of that kind of critical reflection that is at the heart of doctrinal criticism. Doctrinal criticism is diametrically opposed to any type of theology that takes over the inherited doctrines of the past without first submitting them to appropriate critical scrutiny in the light of the best contemporary knowledge of the world. There are plenty of forms of conservative and confessional

Postmodern theology

◄

Language ◄

theologies currently in vogue which need to be challenged in that way.

MAURICE WILES

📖 Maurice Wiles, 'The Consequences of Modern Understanding of Reality for the Relevance and Authority of the Tradition of the Early Church in our Time' and 'Looking into the Sun' in *Working Papers in Doctrine*, London: SCM Press 1976, pp. 89–107 and 148–63; *The Making of Christian Doctrine*, Cambridge: CUP 1967; *The Remaking of Christian Doctrine*, London: SCM Press 1974; G. F. Woods, 'Doctrinal Criticism' in F. G. Healey (ed), *Prospects for Theology*, London: James Nisbet 1966

Drama

For many early Christians, the idea of Christian drama would have been a contradiction in terms. This was largely due to the inevitable association of 'theatre' with popular Roman spectacles that relied on live violence and obscenity for their mass appeal. When medieval church authorities or later Puritan clergy denounced the theatre, they tended to do so in language borrowed from earlier condemnations of the Roman games.

But Christianity is a religion grounded in the story of a God who repeatedly acts in human history in strikingly dramatic and even theatrical ways. Many of the biblical miracles are reported as spectacular acts before a watching audience. Old Testament ceremonial was a fully sensory medium. At the heart of the Christian story is the narrative of the Word become flesh (John 1.14), the transformation of the disembodied divine word into the embodied speech, gesture and action of the fully human Jesus of Nazareth. The transformation of dramatic text into theatrical performance bears striking parallels to this central episode in the Christian story. It is not surprising, therefore, that, despite its frequent condemnation of the stage, Christianity has given birth to a wide variety of dramatic texts and theatrical performances, many of them remarkably popular in nature.

Mystery plays ➤

The Christian drama of medieval Europe included a wide range of forms, from small enacted dialogues added to the liturgy at Easter and Christmas to spectacular outdoor dramatizations of all or part of the Christian narrative. The sequence of plays known as the English Cycle Plays, which flourished from the early fifteenth until the late sixteenth century, told the Christian story of the world from the creation to the last judgement. Staging methods varied. The York Cycle plays, for example, were wheeled through the city streets on pageant wagons during the annual festival of Corpus Christi, stopping to perform

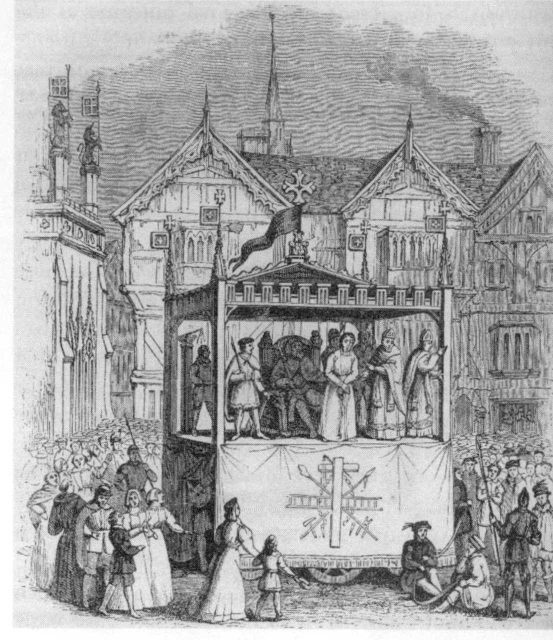

Mystery play performed in Coventry in the sixteenth century

before waiting audiences at various points along the route. The entire sequence of plays lasted from dawn to sundown on an English summer day. The York Cycle (or mystery) plays were revived in 1951. Selections are now performed in the city every four years.

Other Christian dramatic traditions with their roots in the Middle Ages focused on the life, death, and resurrection of Christ rather than on the whole sweep of Christian history. Passion plays were especially popular on the continent of Europe. Most were staged outdoors over a period of several days and involved spectacular scenic effects, notably an elaborate hell-mouth that opened and closed mechanically to admit the demons and the damned and frequently shot fireworks into the air. The best-known modern Passion play, presented every ten years in the Bavarian village of Oberammergau, was first staged in 1633.

Other surviving late medieval dramatic traditions include the annual *Misteri d'Elx*, in the Spanish town of Elche, which dramatizes the Assumption of the Virgin Mary, and the widespread Hispanic tradition of mock battles between folk actors dressed as Moors and Christians. Elche's mystery play has maintained a continuous tradition of performance for over 500 years. Equally old are the Festivals of Moors and Christians, which can now be found in villages and towns from the Andes to the Philippines. In many cases, they are performed in honour of the local patron saint. The most spectacular examples, involving thousands of actors and the explosion of several tons of gunpowder, can be seen each year in Alcoy (Spain) and Zacatecas (Mexico).

Not all Christian drama, however, is communal and festive. Some of Europe's best professional playwrights wrote passages which engage with Christian themes. This is the case even with William Shakespeare: in his *Measure for Measure* (1604), Isabella pleads for her condemned brother's life in explicitly Christian terms. When Angelo tells her sternly, 'Your brother is a forfeit of the law,' Isabella replies:

> Why, all the souls that were were forfeit once;
> And He that might the vantage best have took
> Found out the remedy. How would you be,
> If He, which is the top of judgement, should
> But judge you as you are? O, think on that,
> And mercy then will breathe within your lips,
> Like man new made (II, ii).

Whether or not they were themselves practising Christians, most of Shakespeare's contemporaries wrote plays that deal with Christian themes. A professed atheist like Christopher Marlowe wrote *Doctor Faustus* (*c.* 1590), which dramatizes the danger to the soul's salvation of traffic with the devil, while Cyril Tourneur wrote *The Atheist's Tragedy* (1611), which argues that vengeance should be left to God.

The same was true on the continent. Spain's most celebrated playwright, Pedro Calderón de la Barca, wrote nearly 200 plays dealing with the conflicting demands of love, honour and religion. Some have proved remarkably durable. A version of *The Constant Prince* (1629), which dramatizes the heroic martyrdom of a Portuguese Christian prince, was staged to international acclaim by the experimental Polish director Jerzy Grotowski in 1965. France's most famous dramatist, Jean Racine, was less prolific but no less concerned with Christian themes. *Phèdre* (1677), whose plot is borrowed from classical mythology, is arguably about the tensions between predestination and free will within the Christian scheme of things. Racine's last two plays, *Esther* (1689) and *Athalie* (1691), draw directly on biblical material for their plots.

In the first half of the twentieth century, there was something of a self-conscious revival of Christian drama in Europe, spearheaded by Paul Claudel in France and T. S. Eliot and Christopher Fry in England. Eliot's plays in particular met with critical acclaim and popular success. Both *Murder in the Cathedral* (1935) and *The Cocktail Party* (1949) deal, directly or indirectly, with the theme of Christian martyrdom. Both have enjoyed a number of revivals. But Eliot's plays are somewhat fastidious. They lack the vigour of the earlier Christian drama of the medieval and Elizabethan periods, which happily mixed soaring poetry and bawdy humour, theological reflection and sexual escapades.

In his book *Mimesis*, the literary critic Erich Auerbach argued that this mixed style was a natural outgrowth of the Christian narrative, according to which God did not ask human beings to become disembodied spirits, but instead became human himself, eating, drinking, and talking with publicans, prostitutes, fishermen and tax collectors. Christian drama at its best remembers the good news of God's acceptance of humanity and, as befits so irreducibly bodily a medium, enters into an unflinching engagement with the full range of embodied human experience.

MAX HARRIS

📖 Max Harris, *Theatre and Incarnation* (1990), Grand Rapids, MI: Eerdmans 2005 and *Carnival and Other Christian Festivals: Folk Theology and Folk Performance*, Austin, TX: University of Texas Press 2003; William Tydeman (ed), *The Medieval European Stage, 500–1500*, Cambridge: CUP 2001; Greg Walker (ed), *Medieval Drama: An Anthology*, Oxford: Blackwell 2000

Dress

What do Christians wear? Do they distinguish themselves from others through dress? The answers to these questions will depend on the century or the nationality of the Christian group in question. There are also distinctions between the dress of Christian lay persons and the dress of those Christians ordained to leadership in the church.

Some Christians have dressed in order to distinguish themselves from those around them; others have dressed to blend in with the society in which they live. Members of religious orders have historically worn distinctive dress, with nuns in full habit, monks in flowing robes, and symbols of hierarchy within these orders symbolized through other stylistic changes in dress. In many parts of the world a group of Christians is called 'plain people', named after the style of their garments.

Religious orders

Amish and Old Order Mennonites are representative of Christians wearing distinctive dress: they have one outfit for cold months and another for warm months. The dress of these sects is influenced by the notion that change is worldly and their dress should be as it was in the sixteenth century: men wear broad-fall (drop-front) trousers, women wear cape-dresses; zip-fasteners are not permitted, and clothes are sewn with buttons or, better still, hooks and eyes. Some branches of these groups even distinguish themselves by their choice of the number of braces/suspenders for men (one or two). Less strict

Peace churches
Anabaptists

VESTMENTS

Eucharist

Vestments is an old word which once simply denoted garments; now, however, it is used almost exclusively for what the clergy of some churches wear when they celebrate the eucharist. Vestments derive from the formal dress of the Roman nobility and seem to have been introduced in the fourth century. In the Western church they traditionally consisted of:

Alb: a long white garment reaching to the feet, sometimes brought together by a girdle at the waist.

Amice: a rectangular piece of white linen tied with tapes, which originally served as a neckerchief, to protect other vestments from sweat. Amices are sometimes 'appareled', i.e. they have a long stiff narrow piece of material of the same kind as that of the outer vestments, and in the same colour.

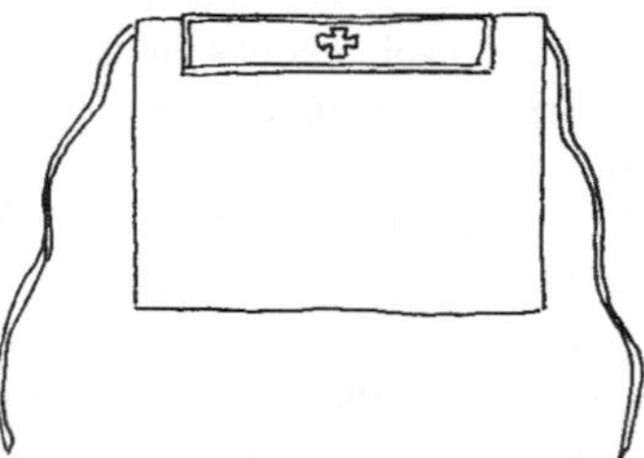

Stole (top right): A strip of material about four inches wide made of plain or embroidered textiles, often in the liturgical colour of the season. It is worn round the neck and its ends, which are often decorated and tasselled, reach below the knees. It probably derives from the scarf worn by Roman officials as a sign of rank.

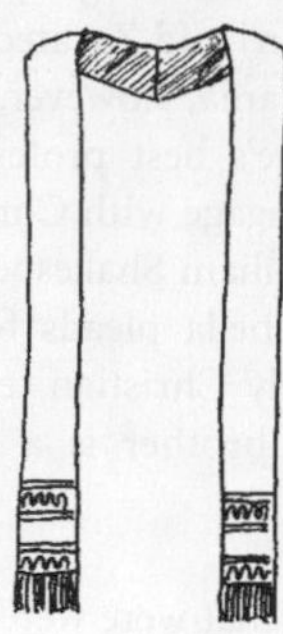

Maniple: A strip of material slightly narrower than the stole and of the same colour, looped over the left wrist and fastened underneath. This too was originally a sign of rank.

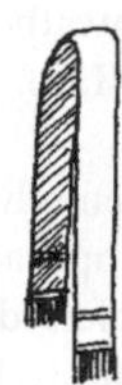

Chasuble: A 'cloak' originally made from a semi-circular piece of material with the ends sewn together to form a tent-shaped garment (there was a hole in the centre for the head). It is usually made of heavy material, often in the liturgical colour of the season, and decorated: the chasubles of the Middle Ages were particularly splendid.

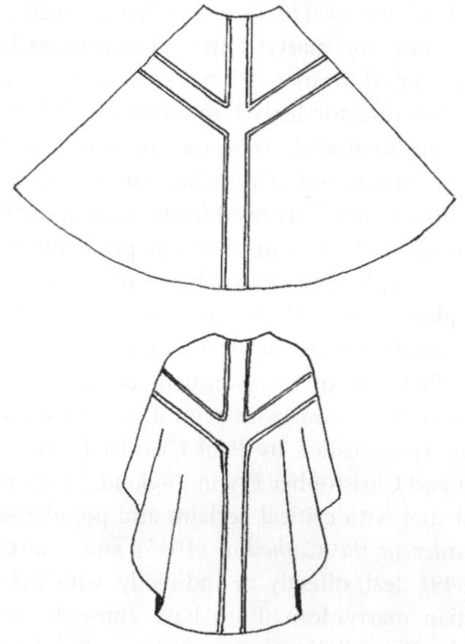

At a high mass, where there were three ministers, the priest (who celebrated), the deacon and the sub-deacon, the priest would wear the chasuble over his alb; the deacon would wear a *dalmatic*, a wide-sleeved over-garment reaching down to the knees, often decorated. The sub-deacon would wear a *tunicle*, a similar garment but less elaborate in its decoration.

Most vestments in the Orthodox churches are parallel to those customary in the West:
Sticharion = alb
Zone = girdle
Orarion (worn by deacons) or *Epitrachelion* (worn by priests and bishops) = stole
Phelonion = chasuble
Sakkos (but in the Orthodox churches this is a sign of dignity, worn by the patriarch and bishops) = dalmatic

Vestments which have no parallels in the West are:
Epigonation: a stiff square of material hung from the zone; originally probably a form of handkerchief
Epimanikia: cuffs to the *sticharion*.

In the West, after the Second Vatican Council there were changes to the use of vestments; the maniple has disappeared, except in the most traditionalist churches, and the amice has been incorporated into the alb as a hood.

Mennonites often still favour simplicity of dress, although their clothing could be described as generally American/Western in style. Women of these groups may still opt for some small head-covering, observing admonitions in the New Testament. Yet even these two groups can be seen as somewhat outside the mainstream of Christian life and practice. One only needs to look at other nations to find more examples. Some African Christians upon baptism will adopt a uniform that identifies them with Christianity and a particular congregation/denomination.

We can find just as many examples of the ways in which Christians assume a non-distinctive dress. The reforms of the Second Vatican Council freed nuns in full habit to adopt clothing of their cultural context. Here is an example of a Christian choice to fit in with a culture rather than exercise immediate visual identification to distinguish oneself from one's culture. And this description applies to many Christians around the world: they wear clothing appropriate to their cultural context.

In addition to dress distinctive because of its differences from or consonance with culture, Christians may wear distinctive dress on the basis of its formality or informality. In the context of the African American church Christians will gather for the Sunday service in their best, formal, dress (including magnificent hats worn by the women). This is an example of what, in many places, has been a long-standing practice of putting on one's best clothes to come before God in the Sunday assembly. On the other hand, there are Christians who intentionally dress less formally. Again this choice is associated with an understanding of liturgical services; these Christians attend services that are known as 'informal worship' or 'contemporary worship' as opposed to 'traditional worship', and dress accordingly.

There is a category of Christians who practise another type of distinctive dress: simplicity. These Christians are not Amish or Mennonites who wear identical prescribed outfits, but rather those who wear clothing of their cultural context, yet strive to be moderate in style, expense, and the number of garments they own. Concerns about economic justice and priority of values help some Christians to determine their style of dress: choice of garments are not dictated by the latest styles in fashion magazines but by a utilitarian understanding of clothing as protective garments that are not made (for instance) by sweatshop labourers. These considerations reflect the various ways that Christians understand themselves to be in but not of the world.

Some Christians strive to make choices about clothing that are not dictated by vanity. Many late medieval sermons (among sermons of other centuries!) spoke strongly to women in the congregation, on the basis of remarks in the letters of Paul exhorting them to simplicity for the sake of their soul's salvation, and the morality of the community. There is an interesting tension between Christians who practise simplicity of dress for economic and/or moral reasons and those Christians for whom expensive clothing is a sign of God's blessing. One thinks of some Evangelical and Free Church bodies in this regard, especially those broadcasting on television.

Council
Women in Christianity
Paul

In some countries Christians may adopt a distinctive style of dress upon baptism or reception into church membership that carries political danger: Christians in India and certain parts of the Middle East have suffered oppression because their dress identifies them as people who do not align themselves with the current political powers and dominant belief systems.

African American Christianity

Other Christians have worn a form of cultural dress which changed when they emigrated from their home country and chose non-distinctive dress to fit into a new cultural context. Asian Christians and African Christians may live in countries where Western-style dress is the norm, yet may dress distinctively in clothing from native lands in order to connect their heritage with current context.

Christianity in Asia

The Emperor Justinian and his court, with Archbishop Maximian, wearing formal Roman dress, still recognizable in present-day vestments, S. Vitale, Ravenna

Eucharist

Most, but by no means all, of the clergy wear a distinctive dress while leading worship in church, and some – a dwindling number – wear a means of identity when out and about in the community. No one pretends that any of this is an essential element of the Christian faith, but at various times robes have been the cause of acute controversy, and even today they can cause division in local churches. They were the best clothes of an ordinary Roman citizen from the second to the sixth centuries and were therefore worn by all those attending worship on Sunday. It was not until the sixth century, when this form of vesture went out of fashion in the Mediterranean world but was retained by the conservative clergy, that it acquired any religious meaning. Today robes are worn partly to emphasize the importance of what is taking place in worship, partly to highlight the distinctive role of those leading worship, and partly to express the historic origins and continuity of the occasion. It is also suggested sometimes that the vestments worn at the eucharist clothe the priest in a certain anonymity, desirable in worship which is not focused on any minister but on the sacrificial offering of Christ.

Orthodox churches

When not leading worship in church, clergy in Britain still may wear a black cassock, an ankle-length coatlike garment; however, in the United States even Episcopalians and Roman Catholics wear suits and shirts with a clerical collar. Until fairly recently all Anglican bishops and archbishops wore purple cassocks, but some now wear black to identify themselves with the rest of the clergy. Roman Catholic bishops wear black cassocks, with a purple waistband; if they are cardinals the waistband is scarlet.

The outdoor dress of the Orthodox clergy is black cassock, gown and hat. The shape of the hat varies from country to country, and bishops and priest-monks wear over their hat a long veil that extends down the back. In some countries the parish clergy wear tall 'stove-pipe' hats and always in Russia a pair of strong boots.

At the sixteenth-century Reformation the new Protestant churches reacted strongly against the use of special robes. This was partly because of the belief that all forms of elaboration and colour in churches distracted congregations from centring their worship on the God who revealed himself in Jesus Christ and who may be approached without the need for mediating persons or objects. Apart from Scandinavia, where the Lutheran Church continued to use vestments to demonstrate continuity with the past, the Protestant churches settled on forms of a black academic gown, sometimes with a white ruff or collar. This simply distinguished the minister from the rest of his congregation and invested the worship with appropriate austerity and dignity. In some of these churches, however, the minister wore no distinctive dress. Today the ministers of the Church of Scotland and other Presbyterian churches wear gowns, as do many of the ministers of the Methodist, United Reformed and Baptist churches, but in churches of an evangelical tendency everyday clothes are normal.

Quite distinct from any other Christian tradition, however, is the Salvation Army which, since its foundation in the nineteenth century, has combined evangelical fervour with a deep commitment to social work among the poorest. True to its name and highly-disciplined organization, members of the Salvation Army wear a uniform when on duty – offering worship in their meeting places or out of doors, normally accompanied by bands and banners, or engaged in social work. The uniform worn by men is of a semi-military style, with a peaked cap, while that worn by women is chiefly characterized by a Victorian-style bonnet. In both instances the black material is decorated with deep red, signifying the blood of Christ.

The reversed white clerical collar is less commonly seen in the streets of Britain and the rest of Northern Europe, including France, than it was for most of the twentieth century. This is because in an increasingly secularized society the clergy prefer to be of less distinctive appearance when outside their churches, believing that this eases their relations with non-churchgoers. What can be a useful badge of identity is therefore in danger of being lost, though until the latter part of the nineteenth century the clerical collar was not worn outside continental Europe.

TREVOR BEESON AND JENNIFER L. LORD

Dutch Reformed Church

The Dutch Reformed Church today can be recognized as such only in the Netherlands, the Republic of South Africa and the United States. Its worship, sacraments, and Christian ethics would not distinguish the Dutch Reformed from other similar churches such as the Scottish Presbyterian, the German Reformed, the Korean Presbyterian, or a number of others.

Reformation

The rise and fall of the Dutch trading empire is the historical context in which the Dutch Reformed Church arrived in many nations. The church continues only in the nations where Dutch heritage and current trade continue to have a large impact. Churches in countries with the Reformed faith expanded out of Europe and into the wider world by the process of trade.The Reformed went to new worlds not for religious freedom or for imperial conquest, but to trade. They had religious freedom at home. Being traders at home, they were accustomed to competition and organized themselves to compete in local situations the world over. And the Dutch began Reformed churches over all the world but none of them exactly alike. They were infused with 'Dutchness', accommodating to individual difference and encouraging effective economic interaction.

p. 1145

Gerhard Groot (1340–84), who in 1382 founded the Brotherhood of the Common Life, is the source of the Dutch Reformed Church. The daily life of the Brotherhood formed a value set that we might call 'Dutchness'. The now generally accepted Western values of toleration, individual value and a regard for human dignity characterized the people who lived in the Low Countries. The consistent interaction with the sea, in fishing, in trade and in the constant battle to wrest agricultural land from the sea developed a cultural milieu which valued truth, productivity and acceptance of individual difference. Groot and the Brotherhood implemented the practical life in the living of Christian faith. Their community was marked by study of the Bible and practical piety. They were not monks. They did not beg. Where the structure of the Western church had held authority over all of life, and had now begun seriously to abuse that authority for personal gain, the Brotherhood earned their living as teachers. From them came vernacular translations of the Bible, in Dutch as early as 1477, and schools. Their schools produced some of the best teachers in Europe, as well as Thomas à Kempis, Wessel Gansevoort and Rudolph Agricola, all of whom preached and taught well before Martin Luther.

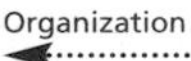
Organization

Monasticism

Secularization

One of the Brotherhood's students, Geert Geerts (1467–1536), the illegitimate son of a Roman Catholic priest, marks the second source of the Dutch Reformed Church. The Bible was the particular province of this most noted of the Dutch humanists, known more commonly by the translation of his name into Latin – Desiderius – and Greek – Erasmus. Desiderius Erasmus' translations of the Bible from the original Hebrew and Greek texts began the study of the Bible as a human document, as well as God's

Bible

Word. It is an approach to scripture that continues to this day. In his treatment of the Bible, he ploughed the ground Reformation in which the seeds of Reformation grew. His work gave public voice to the idea that new knowledge was possible, that knowledge was more than simply dependence on proper interpretation of the ancient authorities. As he lived and wrote, and was criticized and condemned by church authority, he did so with a soul formed by Dutchness. The p. 1016 Dutch temperament defined free thinking in that time. And the culture of the Low Countries was the soil in which they grew.

In all the cultures surrounding the North Sea and the Baltic, distinct differences had developed between those who farmed, those who fished, and those who herded animals. Often in northern Europe, these differences produced different languages, as in the dialects of Scandinavia and the distinct languages of Dutch and Frisian. However, in the Low Countries, for many reasons which are unclear, the stresses of difference were overcome by a perception of those who lived there that they were one people. In the overcoming, the values of acceptance of individual difference and widespread economic interaction became the forming values of the Dutch culture. And the culture – the 'Dutchness' – formed the particular expression of Christian faith among this people.

This 'Dutchness' became the ethos of the Dutch Reformed expression of Christianity in the conflicts of Wars of religion sixteenth-century Europe. As Philip II of Spain tried to turn back reform and re-establish Roman Catholicism in the Low Countries, the blood of martyrs became the seed of the church. Guy de Bres and his compatriots wrote the p. 302 Belgic Confession in 1561 as a witness that their faith was indeed the Christian faith and not a corruption, as was being claimed. Ursinus and Olivianus were assigned by Frederick the Elector to the task of writing a catechism to reconcile the Lutheran, Zwinglian and Calvinistic wings of the German Reformation, producing the Heidelberg p. 627 Catechism in 1563.

Respect for human dignity and difference was expressed in 1565 by a group of nobles who signed a solemn league known as the Compromise, committing themselves to defend the Netherlands against the despotism of Philip II of Spain, seeking protection from persecution and religious toleration. When they reached the court of the Regent, Margaret of Parma, they were described as a troop of beggars. The metaphor caught on. The League of Beggars was formed, and common people began to wear the 'Beggars' medal'. Field preaching and the 'cleansing' of churches in which the religious artifacts of Catholicism were removed became causes for yet more persecution. The emerging church became known as 'The Church under the Cross' and its emblem was the Lily Among the Thorns, taken from Song of Songs 2.2, 'As a lily among the thorns'. Deliverance came finally through William, Prince of Orange, who raised an army and led the Low Countries through war to the Union of Utrecht in 1579, the foundation of the Dutch Republic and the Dutch Reformed Church. With the Synods of Wesel, Embden, Dort and Middleburgh, the creation of church order and organization was begun; the Classis (the name for the local authority) of Amsterdam began functioning in 1582. Doctrinal controversy, notably the Arminian controversy, continued and was finally settled at the Synod of Dort in 1618–19. Since 1620, the Canons of Dort, the Belgic Confession, and the Heidelberg Catechism have remained as the distinctive doctrinal standards of the Dutch Reformed Church and its daughter churches.

While the Dutch took their church with them wherever they traded, the major daughter churches are those in the United States and in South Africa. In both cases, the qualities and values of 'Dutchness' have been formative for the whole life of the nation, but in very different ways.

The Dutch Reformed Church was the first and formative expression of Christianity in the *United States*. An employee of the Dutch East India Company, Henry Hudson, began the Dutch trading outposts in North America in 1609. His success led to the forming of the Dutch West India Company, which began the colony of New Netherland. As the established church of the colony, the political, economic and social leaders were all numbered among its adherents. The native population were treated in typical Dutch fashion – as trading prospects. But as the primary commercial product in the beginning was beaver pelt and as the fashion for beaver pelt in Europe did not last, the colony was less of an economic success than the other projects of the Dutch West India Company in the Caribbean, and was therefore not well supplied with personnel or capital. In the larger picture, war was imminent between the two main European maritime powers, the Dutch and the English. It broke out in 1664, and four English frigates were sent to New Netherland. The English captain, Richard Nicolls, informed the governor of the colony, Peter Stuyvesant, 'In his Majestie's name I do demand the towne, situate upon the island commonly known by the name of Manhatoes with all the forts thereunto belonging.' As Stuyvesant had no resources with which to fight, the colony passed to the English without a shot being fired and New Netherland became New York. The 'Dutchness' continued, however. Despite the change in political sovereignty, the values of acceptance of difference and the need for economic interaction continued to undergird the life of the colony. Under English rule, the Dutch Reformed Church continued to increase and the social and economic leaders continued to come from its ranks, with only the political leadership adhering to the now established Anglican Church. When the American Revolution took place, the Dutch Reformed Church supplied numerous generals, statesmen, and eventually Presidents, and as the new country began, the values of 'Dutchness' continued to shape all of American life.

The story went somewhat differently in *South Africa*. There, too, the Dutch Reformed Church is the formative expression of Christianity. In 1652, the Dutch East India Company sent Jan van Riebeeck to establish an outpost, which soon grew into a colony at Capetown on the Cape of Good Hope. As in New Netherland, and in all the Dutch settlements, the Company insisted that the language of commerce and politics be Dutch and that the established religion be the Dutch Reformed Church. So, in South Africa the political, social and economic leaders were all adherents of and formed by the Dutch Reformed Church. In Africa, however, there was a native population which sold its own into slavery, unlike the native population encountered in North America, and in 1658 the first of many shiploads of slaves arrived in the colony. The agriculture was hard in the arid regions. Soon, the European population moved towards the interior and, finding very arable land, built an agricultural life that required large numbers of slaves. There, further and further removed from the governmental authority, the Dutch abandoned a life of trade and became landed farmers, economically dependent on the institution of slavery. In this milieu, where the slaves most often outnumbered the colonists, the 'Dutchness' of accommodating individual difference and the high regard for human dignity were overwhelmed in the press of an economic necessity which required slavery.

Over the years, the Dutch Reformed Church began to shift its doctrinal and theological views to accommodate the slave holdings of the majority of its members, ending finally in claiming the support of God for apartheid, the government-imposed classification of human beings by race. In 1982, the Belhar Confession of the Dutch Reformed Mission Church, an offshoot of the established church and other Reformed churches, through the World Alliance of Reformed Churches, declared apartheid to be heresy, thereby helping to set in motion the process that led to its end. The Belhar Confession may one day join the Belgic Confession, the Heidelberg Catechism and the Canons of Dort as a confessional standard of many Reformed churches.

EVERETT L. ZABRISKIE III

📖 Donald Bruggink (ed), *Guilt, Grace, and Gratitude – A Commentary on the Heidelberg Catechism Commemorating its 400th Anniversary*, Grand Rapids, MI: Eerdmans 1963; G. D. Cloete and D. J. Smit (eds), *A Moment of Truth: The Confession of the Dutch Reformed Mission Church, 1982*, Grand Rapids, MI: Eerdmans 1984; Daniel J. Meeter, *Meeting Each Other in Doctrine, Liturgy, and Government*, Grand Rapids, MI: Eerdmans 1993; Marcel Pradervand, *A Century of Service – A History of the World Alliance of Reformed Churches, 1875–1975*, Edinburgh: St Andrew Press 1975

Eastern-rite Catholic churches

Pope John Paul II once spoke of the need for the church to breathe with both lungs – Eastern as well as Western. For the best part of a millennium there have been repeated attempts (for various motives) to re-unite the two halves of the church, one in the West and the other in the East, which have been separated as the 'Roman Catholic Church' (also conveniently in this context described as the 'Latin Church') and the 'Orthodox churches' since the eleventh century. The Eastern-rite Catholic churches are one of the visible fruits to date of such attempts. (These have also been called 'Uniate' churches, though the term today has pejorative overtones and is employed less than formerly. It was first used by opponents, Russian Orthodox and Latin Poles, of the 1595 Union of Brest, which brought together the Ukrainian and Roman Catholic churches.)

Roman Catholic Church

Orthodox churches

The very existence of the Eastern-rite Catholics, and the various circumstances in which they came into being, are highly contentious matters down to the present day. It was to be expected that the Roman Church, with its particular self-understanding, should have attempted to win over separated Orthodox churches in order to contribute towards restoring unity to the Christian church as a whole, but the methods used were often unworthy of the high ideals. Deception, bribery and violence all too often accompanied Rome's attempts to bring Eastern Christians into her fold.

One, which still leaves a bitter taste in the mouth of the Orthodox, was the so-called Union of Florence in 1439. This took place as the city of Constantinople was being encircled by Turkish forces. The Orthodox delegates were promised Western aid as long as they accepted a number of Roman demands, one of them the inclusion of the controversial term *filioque* ('and from the Son') in the creed. Desperate, they capitulated. Back home they found that the Orthodox faithful generally rejected the union: 'Better the sultan's turban than the Latin mitre' sums up the attitude. In any case the promised Western aid was not forthcoming, and Constantinople fell to the Turks, betrayed, as it saw it, by the Western church.

History

p. 305

The Union of Florence produced no lasting results. The same was not true of the Union of Brest. After some years of Jesuit preparation, at a Council at Brest-Litovsk in

1595 the majority of Orthodox bishops agreed to a union. Those who wished to remain Orthodox were savagely persecuted by the authorities. Their property was seized and given to the 'Uniates'. Violence was used against them. The tragedy has continued down to the present day.

After the Soviet invasion of Eastern Europe in 1945, Eastern-rite Catholic jurisdictions were suppressed and their members forcibly joined to the Orthodox Church. Many resisted, and there was inevitably violence and injustice. The situation was particularly bad in the Ukraine. It is to the shame of Orthodoxy that the Patriarchate of Moscow supported the Soviet policy in this regard. Following the collapse of Communism there have been renewed disturbances as former 'Uniates' have sought to return to their former obedience. The situation remains a running sore between the Roman Catholic Church and the Orthodox Church.

Christianity in Europe

p. 289

Away from Europe, there are parallel stories, with the result that alongside most Orthodox and Oriental Orthodox churches there are Eastern-rite Catholic communities. Some of these are very small, others are now larger than the original Orthodox community. Often these secessions – which now have their own hierarchies and institutions – have weakened the mother church and contributed to its decline. The witness of Christianity to Islam in particular has been severely damaged.

In Eastern Europe political realignment and boundary changes were often a significant factor in the formation of Eastern Catholic communities. Orthodox in the territory of Roman Catholic rulers might find themselves 'absorbed' in this way. Elsewhere there was often a specific policy of 'targeting' individuals and communities by Roman 'missionaries', often Jesuits. Such a policy exploited tensions and rivalries in the Orthodox community, resulting in rival Orthodox and Catholic patriarchs.

India furnishes a particularly sad example of the effects of Roman-backed interference. On discovering the ancient Syrian community in South India, the Portuguese sought to bring it under papal obedience. At the Synod of Diamper in 1599 the Portuguese Archbishop Menezes required the local clergy to abandon many of their traditional Eastern practices and place themselves under Roman obedience. Thus, for example, clerical marriage was forbidden. Countless precious manuscripts were destroyed by the Roman Catholic authorities on the grounds that they contained 'heresy'. The Syro-Malabar Church which descends from this incident is still one of the largest in India to this day, and is currently debating to what extent it should purge itself of Western accretions to its liturgy and practices.

Ecumenical movement

There is one group of Eastern-rite Catholics for whom no Orthodox counterpart exists. These are the Maronites, based in Lebanon. The Maronites claim always to have been in communion with Rome, and certainly have been so since the twelfth century. They therefore tend to be particularly vigorous in their rejection of the adjective 'Uniate'.

The story of the Eastern-rite Catholics is a tragic one. Despite some good intentions, it nevertheless shows some of the worst sides of both Orthodoxy and Roman Catholicism. In Eastern Europe many of the issues remain unresolved to the present day. Particularly sad, perhaps, is the way in which Eastern-rite Catholics are often looked on with suspicion by Western-rite Catholics. Used to a relatively monolithic uniformity, many Western Roman Catholics do not consider the Easterns, with their range of very different rites and practices, to be true Catholics.

The existence of the Eastern-rite Catholics has, however, had some important positive consequences for the Roman Catholic Church. As the pressures for change in the Latin Church built up prior to the Second Vatican Council, the Eastern-rite jurisdictions provided some important precedents. Their very existence, with their ancient practices, showed that it was possible to be in communion with Rome and, for example, worship in the vernacular or have married priests. This meant that it was difficult to argue that such matters were absolutes in the life of the church, and that therefore change might be possible. Thus, to use the two examples just given, vernacular worship is now the norm in the Latin Church, and although the marriage of priests has not yet been universally permitted, there are now a number, including some married Anglican priests who have been received into the Roman Catholic Church. The Eastern-rite Catholics have opened up the way for change in the Roman Catholic Church. They also serve as a permanent reminder of the richness and diversity that can exist in the church.

JOHN FENWICK

John Binns, *An Introduction to the Christian Orthodox Churches*, Cambridge: CUP 2002; Norman A. Horner, *A Guide to Christian Churches in the Middle East*, Elkhart, IN: Mission Focus 1989

Ecotheology

The word ecotheology first appeared towards the end of the 1980s within the framework of the work of the World Council of Churches' programme on Justice, Peace and the Integrity of Creation. From the 1990s onwards it became the key term for denoting theological reflection on ecological issues and the global crisis of the environment.

Ernst Haeckel coined the term ecology in 1866 in the wake of the publication of Charles Darwin's *The Origin of Species* in 1859. Besides turning the generally accepted theory about the stability of the species on its head,

Darwin's book also contributed to the emerging view that the organic life of the biosphere is interacting and intimately linked – a point to which the churches paid hardly any attention at that time.

The prevailing view of nature hitherto had been highly reductionist. It was assumed that dissecting organisms and material objects into their smallest constituencies would lead to an ever greater understanding of the structure and function of the natural world.

The discipline of ecology gradually developed along five mutually interdependent main lines: the scientific line, where the collaboration and interaction of biotopes (regions uniform in environmental conditions and their animal and plant populations) and organisms are the primary focus of interest; the history-of-the-environment line, which studies different kinds of environments, the occurrence of the species, their origin and extinction; the socio-political line, where the interaction between human beings and the environment comes into focus; the religious-philosophical line, for which the very being of biotopes, organisms and matter is the starting-point; and the ethics-focused line, where issues of justice and of guilt are the objects of study.

In 1927 the zoologist Charles Elton wrote *Animal Ecology*, the first major work on ecology. It was a description of the sociology and the economy of animals, i.e. the way in which they gather and consume food. Elton describes how the nourishment moves between the various species. It is through his book that the term 'food chain' has become established.

Yet another step in ecological research was taken in the mid-1930s, when the Oxford botanist A. G. Tansley began to speak of ecosystems. An ecosystem is a biotopical unit, larger or smaller, in which all the organisms interact, consume one another and together constitute the precondition for the survival of the system. The major breakthrough for ecological reflection was, however, achieved through the works of the Odum brothers during the 1950s and 1960s. Eugene Odum's *Fundamentals of Ecology*, in particular, became a classic. Odum considers smaller ecosystems as well as the entire biosphere as units in which the well-being of every individual unit is dependent on the ecological balance within the system as a whole. With Odum, the foundation for ecology had in fact been laid. The complexity and the wonder – as well as the fragility – in the world of nature is studied on the basic assumption that the ecosystem under investigation will remain in balance unless subjected to destructive interference, primarily caused by human beings.

However, the 1990s saw a marked rise in interest in ecology. The turbulent and chaotic events in the universe and in the history of the environment of our planet came increasingly into view. Not least a book by Donald Worster, *Nature's Economy. A History of Ecological Ideas*, began to see the assumed balance of ecological systems and of the environment as problematic.

Ecological systems are understood today as working models rather than as exactly definable realities. The efforts to achieve a balanced environment assume some vision of what such an environment would be like. From the perspective of the history of the environment there is no lasting state of balance. The cosmos is a chaotic and turbulent but fascinating and fragile home for living beings, who in the perspective of the history of the environment appear to be in balance only exceptionally, at least when considered by a subjective human being.

Science ◄

The first directly ecological lecture to attract international attention was 'Called to Unity', given by Joseph A. Sittler in 1961 during the World Council of Churches General Assembly in New Delhi. Sittler saw not only humanity but creation as a whole as being called by God to unity. However, his lecture remained an isolated event throughout the 1960s. Theological interest in creation was at that time exclusively in the social dimension and did not attribute any intrinsic value to nature itself. In several theological contexts, the natural world was merely considered as the stage on which human life and work took its shape and on which social issues were pressed.

Creation

Environment ethics ◄

1974 saw the publication of *The Limits to Growth: A Report for the Club of Rome*, which marked the beginning of urgent attention of the threats to the environment. The World Council of Churches met in Bucharest in the autumn of 1974 and for the first time the issues of the environment were on the agenda. That meeting introduced the term 'sustainability'. The following year, 1975, the General Assembly in Nairobi formulated a programme entitled 'A Just, Participatory and Sustainable Society', which expressed a vision for a just and sustainable society, in which everyone could participate.

From the very beginning, however, tensions within global Christianity have been great. Since the 1970s the ecological concerns of the rich world have challenged the primary requirements for reasonable living conditions in the Third World. Environmental issues and a just sharing of earth's resources are unavoidably linked and in a global context must be considered together.

Third World

In the 1980s the concept of sustainability was replaced by the phrase 'the integrity of creation' in the churches' work on the environment. At the same time the term 'sustainability' became established in secular society, not least through the work of Lester Brown and his survey entitled *The State of the World. Worldwatch Institute Report on Progress toward a Sustainable Society* (published annually since 1984). In 1987 the so-called Brundtland Commission published its report, in which the phrase 'sustainable development' links sustainability to development.

The churches took up the term again in the 1990s, pointing out the risk of misinterpreting sustainable development as sustainable financial development. In reaction, they then launched the concept of 'sustainable communities'. This concept is intended to take account of the situation of the poor as well as the sufferings that the ecological web endures.

However, during the 1980s, the focus was on 'the integrity of creation'. This term denotes the intrinsic integrity of creation, which must be protected and honoured on the grounds that it is permeated by God's creative presence, even though human beings are not, from their position, able to communicate with God through creatures. As a result of the work of the Protestant theologian Jürgen Moltmann and others, the perspective in the theology of creation shifted from the presentation of the human being as the crown of creation to the view that the crown of creation is the sabbath rest of all creatures with God. The text in Paul's letter to the Romans (8.23ff.) in which Paul describes how all creation groans for freedom from the shackles of mortality came to be linked to that perspective.

Ecotheology generally gives much scope for reflection on how human beings relate to creation. Through the writings of Douglas John Hall, particularly *The Steward. A Biblical Symbol Come of Age,* in Western theology the term 'steward', which in the past had had exclusively pastoral connotations, became the primary anthropological term for expressing the relationship of human beings to creation. In ecotheology, 'steward' has been described as being a co-relation in relation to the rest of creation, using the character of Jesus as Immanuel, i.e. God with us, as its model.

Jesus

Eastern theology has also contributed to the reflection on the place of human beings within the ecological weave. Here the concept of the microcosm has been brought into focus. Taking Genesis 2.7 as the starting-point, Orthodox ecotheology presents human beings as, in a physical sense, a miniature universe (made from the dust of the earth), in which matter has been arranged for the purpose of reflecting its origin and adoring its creator. By allowing these two anthropological concepts mutually to challenge one another, the microcosmic motif in humanity binds human beings to the ecological weave and makes the human being the liturgical minister of all creation, singing the praise of the creator and offering intercession on behalf of all creation. The motif of stewardship denotes the active responsibility of human beings for this fragile web.

Orthodox churches

Ecotheology has always included a strand of apologetics. This tendency began with a much-debated article by Lynn White, Jr, in *Science* in the spring of 1967, entitled 'The Historical Roots of Our Ecological Crisis', in which White claimed that Christianity, particularly in its Western form, is the cause of the environmental crisis.

Young people concerned about the future of the planet, World Social Forum, Porto Alegre, Brazil 2003

The Western form of Christianity has separated creation from the creator, and the same type of Christianity has turned human beings into external exploiters, by giving them the role of rulers of creation, put there to govern it. A major part of ecotheology has been devoted to responding to White's accusations. Creation has been given its own integrity, and human beings have been dethroned from their government and turned into affectionate stewards. However, not even White claims that theological reflection is without value for ecological work. On the contrary, he emphasizes that the ecological awareness and attitude of human beings is dependent on their religious view of nature and of creation as well as of their own future.

Other writers have pointed out that every society that has economized with natural resources for a considerable period and has lived in ecological harmony has done so out of a religious attitude and considerable reverence for the God-given creation. So ecotheology is a call for further reflection on the sacredness of creation and its relation to the creator as well as on the place of human beings within the ecological web and as exercising stewardship in a microcosm.

BO BRANDER

Douglas John Hall, The *Steward. A Biblical Symbol Come of Age*, Grand Rapids, MI: Eerdmans 1990; David G. Hallman (ed), *Ecotheology, Voices from South and North*, Geneva: WCC Publications and Maryknoll, NY: Orbis Books 1994; Dieter T. Hessell and Rosemary Radford Ruether (eds), *Christianity and Ecology. Seeking the Well-Being of Earth and Humans*, Cambridge, MA: Harvard University Press 2000; Paulos Gregorios, *The Human Presence. An Orthodox View of Nature*, Geneva: WCC Publications 1978; Donald Worster, *Nature's Economy. A History of Ecological Ideas*, Cambridge: CUP [2]1994

Ecumenical movement

Ecumenism – expressed as the ecumenical movement – is broadly identified as commitment towards the unity of the church. While it is to be seen as one movement, its wide variety of emphases, models, and goals have made its life complex and for some even problematic. In his sermon at his enthronement as Archbishop of Canterbury (1942), William Temple famously described the ecumenical movement as 'the great new fact of our era'. Whether that judgement still stands is perhaps an open question.

The word 'ecumenical' is derived from the Greek *oikoumene*, which was used as long ago as the fifth century BCE to designate 'the inhabited world'. In the New Testament the word is rarely used, and when it does occur it usually, though not always, refers to the whole world (Matthew 24.14) or the Roman empire (Luke 2.1). Gradually, the word came to be used for the whole church, specifying its universality. It is also widely used to describe the seven 'ecumenical councils' of the early church convened from the fourth to the eighth centuries and held by most Christians to be authoritative. It should further be noted that in Eastern Orthodoxy the Patriarch of Constantinople is designated the 'Ecumenical Patriarch', to reflect his standing as the first among equal patriarchs. Since the fall of the Byzantine empire in the fifteenth century, usage has been confined to ecclesiastical concerns, albeit with varying emphases and connotations.

In the early twentieth century the term 'ecumenical' came to denote the whole church, quickly becoming firmly attached to the movement for church unity, not least in respect to that movement's concern for global mission. In 1951 the Central Committee of the World Council of Churches (WCC) defined ecumenical as pertaining to everything that relates to 'the whole task of the whole church to bring the Gospel to the whole world. It therefore covers equally the missionary movement and the movement toward unity.' Most frequently, now, the word is defined as 'the whole inhabited world'.

The fundamental reality behind the ecumenical movement is the reality of church division. Even though schism in an institutional sense did not occur widely in the earliest church, the phrase 'undivided church' is perhaps fictional. Historians have shown us that the tensions in the early church were as great as those of our own day, yet the New Testament consistently describes unity as the will of God for God's people. This conflict – between unity and division – has marked Christianity throughout its history.

History

As a result of the formulations concerning the nature of Christ at the Council of Chalcedon in 451, a persisting fracture took place between what we now know as Oriental Orthodox churches ('non-Chalcedonian') on the one hand and the Eastern Orthodox and Western churches ('Chalcedonian') on the other. In 1054 the Eastern church centred on Constantinople and the Western church centred on Rome divided. The split was over political issues, but also over a Latin term, *filioque*, in the Nicene Creed which affirms that the Holy Spirit 'proceeds from the Father *and the Son*'. The idea of the Spirit proceeding from the Son was intolerable to the Orthodox East. And, of course the sixteenth-century Reformation, led by Martin Luther, John Calvin, Huldrych Zwingli, Thomas Müntzer and hosts of others, divided the churches in the West between Roman Catholics and Protestants. For somewhat different reasons, although the theology of the Reformation played its role, what is now the Church of England, led by Henry VIII, also broke from Rome in that century. Major divisions all – but these historical ruptures are not the whole story of division in Christianity.

Christology
p. 305
Church of England

Protestants, it would seem, have particularly been prone to fragmentation. The rise of Protestant sects took place in the shadow of national churches, e.g., in the United Kingdom and the Nordic countries, where groups – Reformed, Free Church, Pentecostals – left the established Anglican and Lutheran churches for theological, political and social reasons. In North America the forces of immigration and race abetted those of theology, politics and economics to create a kaleidoscopic map of denominations, sects and Christian movements. During the twentieth century, churches in the Third World have been formed for a variety of reasons, not least to counter the power of dominant churches and traditions from the North; this is seen most strikingly in the myriad of newly-formed African Independent churches. An important consequence of the reality of division has been the loss of credibility suffered by the Christian missionary movement: why should the Christian message be believed if its churches and adherents are unable to demonstrate unity among themselves?

Council
Orthodox churches
Christianity in North America
Third World
Christianity in Africa
Mission

Movements in the nineteenth century were expressions of Christian unity. These, however, were movements of individual Christians, often laity, dedicated to particular

p. 836

causes: the YMCA and YWCA, the Sunday School movement, student Christian movements, and various mission and Bible societies. What has come to be regarded as the ecumenical movement of churches is commonly dated from the World Missionary Conference held in Edinburgh, Scotland, in 1910. This was a meeting of Protestant and Anglican mission societies and agencies; neither Roman Catholics nor Orthodox were present. Its purpose was largely to assess the state of missionary efforts throughout the world and to foster new initiatives in mission. The two persons most closely identified with this event were an American, John R. Mott (1865–1955), and an Englishman, J. H. Oldham (1874–1969).

From the Edinburgh conference three streams of ecumenical concern developed among the churches, although World War I slowed down their activities. The International Missionary Council (IMC) was officially established in 1921 at Lake Mohonk, New York, by seventeen Protestant national missionary bodies, thirteen from the West and the remaining four from Asia, Africa and Latin America. Immediate tasks taken up by the IMC included securing the rights of German missions after the war, special mission efforts towards Jewish and Muslim peoples, mission work by Protestant churches in Latin America and Africa, and the production of Christian literature. Much of the work of the IMC centred upon major global mission conferences which brought together church missiologists and mission officials. In 1961 the IMC was integrated into the WCC as its Commission on World Mission and Evangelism.

A second stream of ecumenical concern flowing from Edinburgh was what came to be known as the Life and Work Movement. Initially led by Nathan Söderblom (1866–1931), Archbishop of Uppsala and Primate of the Church of Sweden, this was seen as a church movement for Christian service, not least in respect to questions of war and peace. One of its watchwords was 'service unites while doctrine divides', a slogan which has subsequently – in the light of political and ideological clashes – proven questionable. Significant conferences of Life and Work were held in Stockholm (1925) and Oxford (1937). This movement joined with a third stream from Edinburgh to form the World Council of Churches in 1948.

War and peace

This third stream was Faith and Order. Whereas at Edinburgh there was a relatively conscious effort to steer away from divisive theological and doctrinal debates, the American episcopal bishop Charles H. Brent (1862–1929) felt that matters of theology, doctrine and ecclesiology could not be avoided. After the Edinburgh conference he spoke to his own church body about the need for unity, expressing his own conviction that a 'world conference on Faith and Order should be convened'.

Again World War I intervened, but in 1927 over 400 persons, representing Orthodox, Anglican, Reformation and free churches gathered in Lausanne, Switzerland, under the leadership of Bishop Brent, 'to register the apparent level of fundamental agreements within the conference and the grave points of disagreement remaining'. Subsequent world conferences on Faith and Order have been held in Edinburgh (1937), Lund, Sweden (1952), Montreal (1963) and Santiago de Compostela, Spain (1993). The Standing Rules of Faith and Order state that the purpose of the movement is 'to affirm the oneness of the Church of Jesus Christ and to keep before the churches the gospel call to visible unity in one faith and one eucharistic communion, expressed in worship and in common life in Christ, in order that the world may believe'.

Faith and Order, along with Life and Work, came into the World Council of Churches at its formation. It has remained as a commission of the WCC, and after Vatican II the Roman Catholic Church joined Faith and Order as a full member. Perhaps the most celebrated accomplishment of Faith and Order is the 'convergence document' on *Baptism, Eucharist, and Ministry*, adopted by churches meeting in Lima, Peru, in 1982. The most widely translated and distributed document in modern ecumenical history, this statement demonstrates a remarkable level of agreement in three areas of considerable controversy among the churches. By 1990 official responses from 190 churches, including the Roman Catholic Church, had been received by Faith and Order, published in six volumes by the WCC as *Churches Respond to BEM*.

In 1920 the Holy Synod of the Church of Constantinople, largely through the work of Germanos, Archbishop of Thyateira (1872–1951), issued an encyclical, *Unto the Churches of Christ Everywhere*. The Dutch theologian who became the first general secretary of the WCC, W. A. Visser 't Hooft (1900–85), described this encyclical as 'an initiative which was without precedent in church history'. The Holy Synod in this encyclical reminded churches everywhere of the devastating effects of World War I, the rivalries and tensions between churches, and the gospel's clear demand for mutual love and unity. Here was a call for a league or fellowship (*koinonia*) of churches, modelled much after the League of Nations, which was at that time coming into existence.

In many ways this encyclical from Constantinople marked the beginning of the movement towards the formation of the World Council of Churches. In July 1937 it was proposed that Life and Work and Faith and Order each appoint seven members to a provisional committee responsible for the WCC 'in process of formation'. World War II prevented a first assembly planned for 1941, and it was not until later, in August 1948, that the WCC was officially formed at its first assembly in Amsterdam. Some 147 church bodies from 44 countries were represented

– virtually all Christian communions except the Roman Catholic Church.

The Amsterdam assembly declared that 'The World Council of Churches is a fellowship of churches which accept our Lord Jesus Christ as God and Saviour'. In 1961, at the third WCC assembly, in New Delhi, this official basis was amplified, the WCC being seen as 'a fellowship of churches which confess the Lord Jesus Christ as God and Saviour according to the scriptures, and therefore seek to fulfil together their common calling to the glory of the one God, Father, Son and Holy Spirit'.

The WCC has developed into an organization made up in 2003 of 342 churches in more than 100 countries; its headquarters are in Geneva. The Roman Catholic Church is not an official member of the WCC, but it works closely with the Council at many points. Through its programmes of mission, relief, racial and economic justice, and theological reflection, the WCC has had a great influence on the lives of churches throughout the world and has brought about a considerable amount of unity of purpose, effort and fellowship.

The WCC has not been without its tensions. An international controversy was stirred up by the Council's Programme to Combat Racism which, particularly from the late 1960s to the early 1980s, led many critics to conclude that its work to end apartheid in southern Africa was more political – even violently so – than it was ecclesial. Such criticism has by now been substantially silenced. Points of tension have also marked the WCC's life as it sought to hold churches from East and West together during the Cold War, as it has sought to establish meaningful dialogue with non-Christian faiths and ideologies, and as it has supported churches and countries of the Third World in their struggles to overcome economic and political domination from northern powers.

The WCC is now debating its *raison d'être* and its future. Is there compatibility between the Council's concern for visible church unity and its programmes of social justice? Do the churches still have the will – spiritual and financial – for a global Christian movement such as is represented by the WCC? Is the Council marked by a dominant 'Protestant' mentality to the disadvantage of its Orthodox participants? Might there not be a broader ecumenical table which could include the churches of the WCC as well as the Roman Catholic Church, and a far wider representation of evangelical and Pentecostal bodies than at present? Questions such as these mark present debates about the global ecumenical future.

Of course there are a number of expressions of the ecumenical movement other than the WCC. Chief among these is the Roman Catholic participation in endeavours for visible church unity.

This was clearly not the case for more than half of the twentieth century, although Rome frequently expressed its desire for reunion with the Orthodox churches of the East. In that connection the historic meeting in 1964 on the Mount of Olives in Jerusalem between Pope Paul VI and Ecumenical Patriarch Athenagoras as 'two pilgrims with eyes fixed on Christ' and their subsequent agreement (1965) to 'remove from the memory and from the midst of the church the excommunication of 1054' was momentous.

Rome was invited to participate in early Faith and Order activities, but the reply of Cardinal Gasparri, Secretary of State to Pope Benedict XV, was ambivalent at best, and World War I discouraged further invitations. Shortly after the first world conference on Faith and Order at Lausanne in 1927, Pius XI in his 1928 encyclical *Mortalium animos* negatively assessed the nascent ecumenical movement and asserted: 'There is only one way in which the unity of Christians may be fostered, and that is by promoting the return to the one true church of Christ of those who are separated from it; for from that one true church they have in the past unhappily fallen away.' Ecumenism in this view was a one-way street: return to the one true church of Rome.

However, in 1949, in the decree of its Holy Office *Ecclesia sancta*, the Roman Catholic Church began positively to assess the ecumenical movement 'among those who are dissident from the Catholic church' yet 'believe in Christ the Lord' as 'an inspiring grace of the Holy Spirit'. The Second Vatican Council (1962–5), called by John XXIII, saw a decisive shift in the Roman Catholic attitude towards the ecumenical movement and, indeed, brought that body into vital contact with other Christian traditions. The Council's Dogmatic Constitution on the Church, *Lumen gentium*, and especially its Decree on Ecumenism, *Unitatis redintegratio*, firmly placed the Roman Catholic Church in the wider movement towards visible unity between the churches.

p. 291

Immediate consequences were the admission of the Roman Catholic Church to the WCC Commission on Faith and Order, extensive co-operation with other church bodies on issues of social justice, and the establishment of bilateral theological dialogues with other churches. The 1995 encyclical of Pope John Paul II, *Ut unum sint* ('That They May Be One') reaffirms, following Vatican II, the 'irrevocable commitment' of the Roman Catholic Church to ecumenism as 'an organic part of her life and work'.

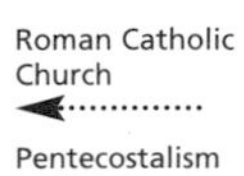

For more than 30 years there have been a number of theological dialogues on national and international levels between churches. The purpose of these dialogues has been to assess theological, doctrinal and ecclesiological differences and to work for greater convergence and common understanding. A number of traditions have seen the goal of these dialogues as the reconciliation of diversity and

Justification

Pope John Paul II visits the World Council of Churches, 1984

the attainment of visible unity, often described as 'full communion'. In the 1970s the Faith and Order movement stated that such communion between churches would involve four elements: common confession of the historic Christian faith, reciprocal acknowledgement of and access to the two sacraments of baptism and eucharist, mutual recognition of ordained ministries, and common decision-making.

Sacraments

Ministry and ministers

An agreement of what amounts to full communion was reached in 1920 between the Church of Sweden and the Church of England after negotiations which began in the first decade of the century. Other early twentieth-century conversations have taken place between Anglicans and Roman Catholics (1921–6), Anglicans and Orthodox (1930–), Anglicans and Old Catholics (1931), and Lutherans and Reformed (1947–).

Perhaps the earliest product of such dialogue in recent years is the Leuenberg Church Fellowship of 1973 which now comprises over 100 churches – Lutheran, Reformed, and most recently Methodist – principally in continental Europe, although some church bodies in Latin America and Scandinavia are also members. The Porvoo Common Statement, presented in 1992 and now ratified by more than ten churches, has established full communion between the Anglican churches of the United Kingdom and Ireland and the Lutheran churches of the Nordic and Baltic countries. In the United States such dialogues have brought the Evangelical Lutheran Church in America into full communion with the American member churches of the World Alliance of Reformed Churches (the Presbyterian Church [USA], the Reformed Church in America, and the United Church of Christ) (1997), the Episcopal Church (1999), and the Moravian Church (1999). There are many other instances of dialogue bringing about full communion between churches on every continent.

Perhaps the most striking result of dialogue, even if it has not brought about full communion, is the *Joint Declaration on the Doctrine of Justification* signed by the Vatican and the member churches of the Lutheran World Federation in Augsburg in 1999. This declaration affirms that while some theological differences remain between the two traditions concerning the doctrine of justification, they are not to be seen as 'church-dividing'. Moreover, the sixteenth-century condemnations of this doctrine levelled by each tradition against the other have been lifted as no longer applicable. This *Joint Declaration* represents, to say the least, a significant ecumenical advance.

Clearly there are many shapes to ecumenical endeavours. As early as 1905 a council of churches was formed in France. In subsequent years such councils have been formed – at local, national, and regional levels – in every part of the world. The twentieth century has seen the organic union of churches, notably in India and Pakistan, but also in the United Kingdom and the United States. Multilateral dialogues between nine churches in the US over the past 30 years or more have finally resulted in the inauguration in 2002 of 'Churches Uniting in Christ', although this relation is lacking in the structural commitment that goes with organic union.

Quite apart from church union, the ecumenical movement is in many places expressed by co-operative efforts in matters of social justice, relief and refugee services, commitment to peace at points of international warfare or tension, etc.

The issues facing the ecumenical movement are literally too many to number. Chief among them, doubtless, is the matter of 'ecumenical reception'. How are major ecumenical agreements – e.g., agreements of full communion – which are reached by theologians and ecclesiastical bureaucrats made meaningful on other levels of church life? How is full communion expressed between parishes of agreeing traditions? Is the goal 'that all may be one' anything more than lip service to biblical and historical ideals?

Other burning issues have yet to be faced, such as the relation between co-operation and communion; the relation between the unity of the church and commitment to social, racial, economic, and ecological justice; the formal inclusion within the total ecumenical fellowship of previously – for whatever reason – excluded partners (evangelicals, Pentecostals, Roman Catholics); the limits to diversities – e.g., theological, political, sexual variations – within united and uniting churches; and the relation of ecumenism between churches and dialogue with other religious faiths and ideologies.

The Groupe des Dombes stems from the work of Abbé Paul Couturier in France, a Roman Catholic pioneer for Christian unity who in 1935 championed the cause of a Week of Prayer for Christian Unity, now a well-established tradition throughout the world (18–25 January of each year, to coincide with the Feast of the Conversion of St Paul). In 1937 Abbé Paul started the Groupe des Dombes at the Cistercian abbey of Les Dombes near Lyons, France, consisting mainly of Roman Catholics and Protestants from France and Switzerland. Their purpose was common discussion and prayer in an atmosphere of love and friendship. In 1991 this group published *Pour la conversion des Eglises* which appeared in 1993 in English as *For the Conversion of the Churches.* The concluding sentences of that small publication are noteworthy:

> Many words have been said and many documents written; but too often actions are slow to follow, and this situation becomes worse as the years go on. May our congregations and communities have the courage to confront their practice with the convictions that have already been approved by the ecumenical movement. May they progress as their conversions progress and at the appropriate time celebrate acts of reconciliation which will be symbols of the thresholds that have been crossed. In this way confessional conversion will serve ecclesial conversion and enable the church to give a credible witness to its conversion to Christ.

NORMAN A. HJELM

📖 John Briggs, Mercy Oduyoye and Georges Tsetsis (eds), *A History of the Ecumenical Movement: 1968–2000*, Geneva: WCC Publications and Grand Rapids, MI: Eerdmans 2004; Jeffrey Gros, Eamon McManus and Ann Riggs, *Introduction to Ecumenism*, New York and Mahwah, NJ: Paulist Press 1998; Groupe des Dombes, *For the Conversion of the Churches*, Geneva: WCC Publications 1993; Michael Kinnamon, *The Vision of the Ecumenical Movement and How it Has Been Impoverished by its Friends*, St Louis: Chalice Press 2003; Nicholas Lossky et al. (eds) *Dictionary of the Ecumenical Movement*, Geneva: WCC Publications [2]2002; Harding Meyer, *That All May Be One: Perceptions and Models of Ecumenicity*, Grand Rapids, MI: Eerdmans 1999; Jon Nilson, *Nothing Beyond the Necessary: Roman Catholicism and the Ecumenical Future*, New York and Mahwah, NJ: Paulist Press 1995; Konrad Raiser, *Ecumenism in Transition: A Paradigm Shift in the Ecumenical Movement?*, Geneva: WCC Publications 1991; Ruth Rouse and Stephen Neill (eds), *A History of the Ecumenical Movement: 1517–1968* and Harold E. Fey (ed), *A History of the Ecumenical Movement: 1948–1968* (one volume edition), Geneva: WCC Publications 1993

Education

Education is a key process in our world. We live at a time when more and more education is being provided for more and more people and costing more and more money. Those of us who live in the developed world have a significant experience of education; we have been to school, college and university and know what benefits education can bring. Those who have not had this experience are at a disadvantage, for as the World Bank points out, when people have just a little education, their families are smaller, their children healthier, their economic prospects better. Education is perceived as being decisive to the process of human development and to that of communities and societies. But what is education?

Mark Twain, the American author and humorist, remarked, 'I never let my schooling interfere with my education,' echoing the comment of the seventeenth-century statesman George Savile Halifax, 'Education is what remains when we have forgotten all that we have been taught.' Such statements remind us that we would not describe a person who had simply mastered a skill, for example the wiring of an electrical connection, as educated. For a person to be educated, that person should possess more than skills, more than know-how. Mr Gradgrind, the headmaster introduced by Charles Dickens in his novel *Hard Times*, advises a member of staff to restrict teaching to facts, 'Facts being sufficient for life'. But it is not sufficient for a person to be well informed for us to describe him or her as educated. To describe people as educated requires that they have some understanding of principles, some ability in reasoning, some notion of what is valuable. In describing such a person as educated we refer to his or her state of mind. As R. S. Peters put it, 'In this respect, also, "education" is like "reform"; for it would be as much of a contradiction to say "my son has been educated but has learnt nothing of value" as it would be to say "my son has been reformed but has changed in no way for the better".'

The word 'education' derives from the Latin verb *educare*, which relates to the process of 'leading out', that is to say, developing the full purpose of someone or something. So we might say that an army does not fulfil its purpose if it stays in the barracks or a ship if it never puts to sea. To speak of the education of a person is therefore to speak of the development of his or her full potential, the fulfilment of the purpose of personhood. Education and questions about the meaning of being fully human are therefore inseparable, and the process of education is value-laden. If our view of human fulfilment is humanistic, we will have a humanist view of the purpose of education; if Christian, a Christian view of that purpose. So it is that philosophers and political theorists from the classical world to the present day have given the highest priority to education which provides persons with the opportunity not only to gain in knowledge but also to acquire a range of attitudes and values. Education is important because it is about changing people.

Schools

The term 'Christian education' has been used in two distinct ways: first to describe a 'frontier' activity of Christians, namely an engagement with general education, the form of education provided by national or local government, and second to describe an 'internal' activity of the community concerned with Christian nurture.

Christians and education

Christians cannot be disinterested in education, for it is self-evident that the concept of education includes assumptions about the nature of persons. Education presupposes an individual whose development will be influenced by personal decision, personal relationships and society. This

Humanism

Renaissance

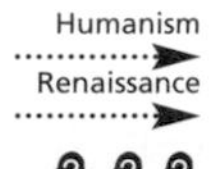

position constitutes a historic view of the development of persons: the future of persons is not biologically predetermined but open. It is an enabling function of education to provide opportunities for persons to become more aware of their nature and of their potential for development in relationship with others and the world. Education provides persons with opportunities to think through

Reformation

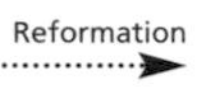

questions of personal function, 'What can I do?'; questions of obligation, 'What ought I to do?'; and questions of

Destiny and purpose

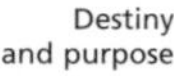

destiny, 'What might I become?'. Discourse encouraged by education in relation to such issues faces persons with questions about human distinctiveness, the nature of reality, whether life has meaning or purpose and what may be hoped for.

From the time of the early church Christianity has been involved in 'general education'. The provision by Christians

University

of schools, colleges, universities and teacher-training establishments has frequently been in advance of governments

Industrial revolution

taking responsibility for education. In many countries churches have negotiated with government schemes of shared responsibility for the provision of education. While Christian values and beliefs inform education in church schools, Christian commitment to general education as a force for humanization is shown when schools are maintained in countries, for example India, which forbid

Bible

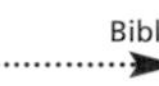

attempts to Christianize through schooling.

Accordingly, Christians engage in the ongoing debate about the objectives of education in rapidly changing societies, emphasizing the importance of approaches to learning that feature openness, rational enquiry and the development of personal autonomy. From this it follows that we should expect Christians to be critical of any approach to education, curriculum planning or teaching style that seeks to reduce persons in respect of the economic or citizenship needs of society. Similarly an education incorporating values and beliefs that are not open to scrutiny and realistic consideration will be rejected as indoctrinatory.

A key issue in the first centuries of Christian history was how the church should respond to the classical education experienced by the young in schools. The curriculum, comprising philosophy and elements of Greek and Roman literature, conveyed values and beliefs that the leaders of the church did not want their members to encounter. Schools with a Christian foundation were not the norm for some time; consequently, the church could seek only to influence general education by broadening the range of beliefs and values encountered in education. As the political position of Christianity in medieval Europe strengthened, the church became the major provider of education. At this time, the classical tradition in the curriculum was accepted, but in institutions with a strong Christian ethos. The position of general education in society was strengthened by the rise of Christian humanism during the Renaissance period. Leading reformers of the time, Desiderius Erasmus, Martin Luther and John Calvin among them, argued that general education, the preserve of an élite, should be expanded and made available to all. We see in this proposal the recognition of the benefits of an educated population for society as a whole. The rise of denominations following from the Reformation had a very particular impact on general education. The potential of education as a powerful influence for the unity of society was disrupted, as denominational provision of general education became a source of division and on occasion extremism in society. There were exceptions to this trend as Christians responded to fundamental changes occurring in society. Robert Raikes in England (1735–1811) and the reforming mill-owner Robert Owen in Scotland (1771–1858) launched movements to offer education to the rapidly growing populations of countries experiencing the industrial revolution.

In the case of Raikes, the movement he initiated, which came to be known as the Sunday School movement, is misunderstood if it is thought to be a sabbath exercise in religious instruction. Raikes had broad educational aims, seeking first to develop skills of literacy and numeracy and to foster positive citizenship, and secondly to present Christian values through the study of the Bible.

The nineteenth century saw major changes in the provision of primary, secondary and higher education throughout the world as it experienced industrialization. The idea of education for all, first argued by the Reformers, Erasmus, Luther and Calvin, was taken up by organizations representing the working classes and became a need of developing economies. Economic pressure gave rise to arguments about the nature of the curriculum, seen as education for skills acquisition and thus challenging the humanistic ideals of education for personal development. The churches, the chief providers of education until this time, had to give way to state provision on a massive scale, and this has led to their marginalization in the field of education in the twenty-first century.

The final decades of the twentieth century were marked by the increasing impact on society of developments in science and technology, of rapid social change resulting from the process of secularization, and the increasing mobility of people both within countries and across continents. The need for a highly-skilled workforce has become more urgent in nation states intent on maintaining economic growth, and this in turn has increased pressure on the curriculum of schools. Nations have moved to replace the traditional freedom of schools to devise a curriculum with a 'national curriculum' that guarantees the learning experience of all pupils in all schools. Christian schools dependent on governmental funding have had to accept the requirement that the national curriculum be taught, a circumstance reducing further a Christian presence in 'general education'.

Education and the Christian community

Christian education as an internal activity of the church is concerned to prepare and sustain the community in the life of faith. Such Christian education is not only an education 'about' Christian faith, but also education 'in' the Christian faith.

Through the ages Christian education in the church may be said to have had three characteristic features.

First, the acceptance that a direct experience of the Christian life is a necessary precursor to any education aiming to support persons in living that life themselves. The primacy of an experience of Christian living is enunciated by Augustine of Hippo, who together with Hippolytus of Rome was responsible for establishing the patterns of education that shaped centuries of Christian catechetics. Augustine said, 'Do not seek to understand in order that you may believe, but believe in order that you may understand.' Secondly, the focused and continuous nature of the provision of education. Education is focused on key moments in the developing life of faith: baptism, confirmation, first communion, personal profession of faith and the celebration of these 'stages' in the journey of faith, in special services and festivals. This approach adopts an attitude to education which is continuous, lifelong, never finished, and is in conflict with any approach that aims simply to make new members of the church.

From the second century the church formally identified the catechumenate, those preparing for membership of the church. The curriculum and the methods of teaching came under the control of a catechism which carried the authority of the church. Prominent features of catechesis were: formal instruction, normally given after baptism; the requirement of participation in the worship of the church; and support for family life in the home and positive personal relationships. From time to time revisions to the process have been introduced in the face of changes in society and in an attempt to combat the ignorance of the people more effectively. For instance, at the time of the Reformation, Luther introduced his *Smaller Catechism* to combat that ignorance. More recently, on Easter Day 1971, the Sacred Congregation for the Doctrine of Faith of the Roman Catholic Church issued a new *Catechetical Directory*. 'The purpose of this Directory is to present the fundamental theological-pastoral principles, taken from the magisterium of the Church and especially the Second Vatican Council, for the guidance and better co-ordination of the ministry of the word.' The aim reflects the concerns of catechetics down the centuries, to combat ignorance of the faith among congregations.

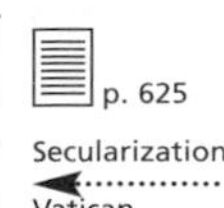
p. 625
Secularization
Vatican

A difference in approach from that of the Protestant, Anglican and Roman Catholic churches is to be found in the Orthodox Church. In the Orthodox Church the child of Christian parents receives baptism, confirmation and first communion as an infant and through that process becomes a fully-ordained member of the community of faith. Practice in the Protestant and Anglican churches from the Reformation and in the Roman Catholic Church has been ambivalent about the place of the child in the church. The importance of personal experience, a moment of conversion, or a conviction of faith has been stressed, particularly in Protestant churches, with worship and preaching made subservient to that experience. These stances on membership have led to markedly different approaches to Christian education. Education in the Orthodox Church addresses the person as a member of the church and is concerned with the requirements of living the life of faith, whereas in the Protestant, Anglican and Roman Catholic traditions education is directed towards a moment of decision for membership at a point in the future.

Orthodox churches

Thirdly, both teacher and taught are held together in a relationship that is personal and reflects their common position as members of the community of faith. The teacher passes to the learners the living heritage of the community, and the learners appropriate that tradition in their own experience. The personal nature of the relationship between teacher and taught marks a difference between education which is personal and instruction which is functional, requiring no such relationship. Augustine of Hippo remarked with no little insight, 'Where there is no love, there is no education.'

Baptism

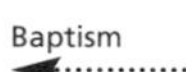

Christians and the theory of education

The twentieth century is notable for the significant growth in the study of the process of education and in our

Kingdom of God

Psychology and Christianity

Liberation theology

knowledge and understanding of how people learn. At the heart of this development was the work of Sigmund Freud, the founder of psychoanalysis, and the group that gathered round him in Vienna, which included Alfred Adler and Carl Jung. Adler and Jung through their studies in psychology enriched our understanding of the nature of childhood, which in turn fuelled the growth of studies in the application of psychological knowledge to the practice of educational psychology. The research programmes of two scholars, Jean Piaget and Erik Erikson, are examples of the development in the study of education, developments which have challenged many of the approaches traditionally employed by educators within the Christian community. The work of three Christian scholars, Paulo Freire, John Westerhoff and James Fowler, is an indication of how the church is attempting to learn from general education research.

Jean Piaget was concerned to explore the cognitive development of children. How do children acquire knowledge, by what processes do they perceive and understand? How do they form beliefs, develop concepts and move to structure their lived experience into coherent patterns? What can be known about the process that leads from the dependency of infancy, through childhood and adolescence, to that position of rational autonomy which is the mark of an educated person?

Piaget researched these questions through the medium of conversations with children. These conversations led him to propose a developmental model of personal progress, based on a series of inter-linked phases of growth. Each phase represented a period of stability in the gradual maturation of a person. Each phase was susceptible to breakdown as children's perceptions were challenged by their lived experience. Piaget believed cognitive development to be a natural process, which could be delayed or even arrested, yet was ultimately inevitable: a consequence of the process of biological, intellectual and social maturation. He proposed a model for education that encouraged movement through the phases, arguing that the child's ability to know, think and understand was to some extent determined by the stage in the developmental process reached. Since the objective of education was to support and enable the development of the child, the aim of teaching should be the provision of opportunities for learning that would progress the maturation of the child. Piaget's methodology for achieving developmental growth was to adopt an approach to teaching and learning which produced 'cognitive conflict' in the child's mind, requiring children to re-think what they knew, or had understood or believed.

Through his teaching based at the University of Recife, *Paulo Freire* brought education and theology into a dynamic relationship. He set out to explore the consequences for society of taking seriously a theology of the kingdom of God that promoted justice and peace. Through a programme of literacy education that has echoes of Christian education with the industrial poor of Europe 200 years earlier, Freire demonstrated that it was possible to 'conscientize' destitute communities to the oppressive social realities that marked their daily lives. His philosophy and theology of education were influential in the development of Latin American liberation theology. By deliberately focusing the power of education to humanize the urban poor, Freire placed the full contemporary understanding of education at the heart of Christian education strategy. The influence of Piaget's studies on the cognitive development of persons has been especially marked.

Freire was open to the criticism that in striving to influence the nature of that personal development directly he was engaging in indoctrination and ignoring a necessary objectivity in the process of education. He made no apology for his stance; on the contrary, he argued that neutrality was no more possible in education than in science. His belief was that education is about changing people, freeing the downtrodden, liberating the poor, and providing opportunities for personal maturation by strongly challenging what people believed and understood. Education was to provide opportunities for people to reflect on their experience, to think through their relationship with society, and to consider how they might act in the world and on the world, with a resultant deepening of 'cognition' to be compared with archaeology, in this case an 'archaeology of consciousness'.

Erik Erikson, a social psychologist, sought to understand better the process of developing selfhood. How is personal development affected by family life? How does living in the wider community and one's encounter with its institutions affect personal development?

Erikson proposed a model of the life-cycle that represented the journey of a person through a series of stages. Each stage was a crucial step in the process of maturation, a journey that could be halted or even reversed by the manner in which the person faced up to the inevitable challenges and crises encountered. Erikson identified eight stages in the process of maturation, five relating to the period of childhood and youth, and three to adulthood and old age. Hence human development is a process reflecting the building of personal character. The character of a person is formed by and consequent upon a period of trial and testing at each stage in the cycle. It follows that progress may falter and development cease; indeed, there may be regression to a previous stage. Where development continues towards adulthood, the inherent strengths of persons, forged on the journey, and their weaknesses are carried forward to the next stage. We may point to the period of adolescence which characteristically presents a person with a crisis of personal identity, or the 'mid-life crisis' commonly regarded as a feature of adulthood.

Erikson identified 'trust' and 'mistrust' in human relations as a key factor in determining how a person deals with the crises of a particular stage. Where individuals move on to a further stage they observe that a balance of trust has been achieved and will be observable. Erikson calls the resulting virtue 'faith'. In 'faith' the inner world of the person, for instance children's need for food and love, and the outer world of their experience, their experience of mother, achieve a balance.

James Fowler's theory of 'faith development' reflects the work of Erik Erikson. In using the word faith, Fowler, like Erikson, has in mind something broader than mere religious faith. He argues for the universality of faith and is concerned to explore the nature of faith, rather than the content of faith.

Fowler argues that the word faith should be understood as a verb and regrets the limitation of usage imposed by the English language when compared to Greek or Latin. The Greek verb *pisteuo* and the Latin *credo* allow the broader use of faith as in, 'I trust', 'I commit myself', 'I pledge allegiance to'. Such an understanding makes clear that faith is about engagement with the world, shaping it to our expectations of life. Fowler's research base comprises interviews with considerable numbers of adults exploring the answers to the questions: Does life have meaning or purpose for you? What gives your life meaning? Where and when do you experience wonder, awe, ecstasy? What events, persons, relationships or experiences have most decisively shaped your way of seeing and moving into life? The suggestion that faith should be understood as a propensity in all persons is controversial within the church and there is further challenge in Fowler's identification of six 'stages of faith'. His suggestion that faith development is sequential, individuals moving from one stage to the next as their faith development progresses, requires acceptance of the proposition that faith is not once-and-for-all but is subject to change. Faith may progress, that is, move towards a position of maturity, or regress.

The acceptance of Fowler's theory for internal programmes of church education would be far-reaching. Traditional approaches to internal education have focused on the achievement of positions of security, baptism, confirmation and the like. The application of Fowler's theory would direct the focus to the moving of individuals on from such positions to an increasingly mature understanding of their faith and of the necessity of lifelong learning.

John Westerhoff is prominent among those who have explored the incorporation of stage-development theory into the practice of Christian education. He reflects Fowler in using the word faith as a verb. His understanding is that faith is to do with ways of behaving that involve knowing, being and willing. The content of persons' faith is reflected in their world-views and value systems, but faith itself is something they do. Faith can be understood as an action. It results from our actions with others, it changes and expands through our actions with others, and it expresses itself daily in our actions with others.

In his proposals for an approach to Christian education incorporating the theory of 'stage development', Westerhoff emphasizes the crucial importance of a direct experience of Christian living. He also places participation in the 'liturgy' at the heart of the process of faith formation. His understanding of liturgy is broad, encompassing the whole work of the church, both in worship as the community of faith and as a community of people acting in society as the body of Christ. Westerhoff's Christian education materials and the approaches they adopt require a radical reconsideration of traditional catechetics, the process by which persons are initiated into the Christian community's faith, revelation and vocation. The challenge inherent in Piaget's work is that of relating what the church wishes to teach to the stage of cognitive development achieved by the learner. The notion of 'readiness for knowledge', 'readiness for understanding', has hardly entered the realm of internal education. If Piaget is right, much that the church has traditionally sought to teach has been inaccessible to the learners, given the stage of their cognitive development. Westerhoff begins to explore the consequences of the acceptance of general education theory for internal programmes. His proposal that the church provide opportunities for the experience of committed Christian action in society as part of the programme of education is a proposal for an approach to understanding belief by encountering 'the way, the truth and the life' in general human experience.

Faith ◄

Education in the modern world

Education in the modern world has a demonstrable objective, the transformation of the individual. This objective presents a challenge to the received tradition of Christian education in home, school and church. As we have seen, through the centuries education has been directed at familiarizing the faithful with the tradition. Children have been the targets of taught programmes which sought to inculcate biblical knowledge and knowledge of the doctrines and the liturgy of the church. The 'faithful' learner was one who 'knew', not one who questioned! Education, encouraging the development of the autonomous person, a person of independent mind and spirit, is viewed as a process challenging the authority and tradition of the church. In the Western churches,

Tradition

Protestant, Anglican and Roman Catholic, it is thought to be at least partly responsible for the widespread loss of young people from the church.

The development of the theory of education through the last century offers new opportunities for education within the Christian community to enrich the knowledge and understanding of the faith. These very advances do, however, pose a dilemma for the church. The tradition of Christian education has been to focus on the nurture of faith in a context of shared values, attitudes and beliefs. The importance of an experience of Christian living has been held to be crucial to this process. This insight from the past is supported by what we now know about how people learn and it therefore remains critical to the process of understanding Christian belief that the church be seen to be creatively engaging with society. However, the nature of contemporary life makes urgent the task of equipping Christian people with the knowledge, skills and understanding to enable them to think critically about faith in a world seemingly apathetic or antagonistic to that faith. Education can be a resource in the development of the mature Christian adult. Alternatively, some will judge the risks to be too great and choose to retreat from a process that inculcates questioning rather than acceptance in the learner.

Biblical criticism ➤

Fundamentalism ➤

IAN H. BIRNIE

Postmodern theology ➤

Environmental ethics ➤

📖 John I. Elias, *A History of Christian Education*, Melbourne, FL: Krieger Publishing 2002; James W. Fowler, *Stages of Faith: The Psychology of Human Development and the Quest for Meaning*, New York: Harper & Row 1981; Paulo Freire, *Pedagogy of the Oppressed*, Harmondsworth: Penguin Books 1972 and New York: Continuum 2000 and *Cultural Action for Freedom*, Harmondsworth: Penguin Books 1972; R. S. Peters (ed), *The Concept of Education*, London: Routledge & Kegan Paul 1967; John Sutcliffe (ed), *A Reader for Christian Educators*, Birmingham: Christian Education Publications 2001; John H. Westerhoff, *Will Our Children Have Faith?*, New York: Harper & Row 1976 and *Bringing Up Children in the Christian Faith*, New York: Harper & Row 1980

Enlightenment

At the beginning of the third millennium, the Enlightenment of the seventeenth and eighteenth centuries in the West can be seen in retrospect as one of the great turning points in human history. The era gave us the agricultural and scientific revolutions, the emergence of democratic states and a market economy, the beginnings of modern medicine, the weakening of the powers of traditional religion and principles which resulted in the extension of basic rights to women and minorities.

Yet despite these achievements there are many today who see in the Enlightenment a fundamental turn for the worse in human history. They point to the environmental destruction wrought by industry; to the damage done to indigenous cultures by Western colonial expansion; to the increased bureaucratic controls exerted by the modern nation state; and, in religious matters, to the profound challenge to traditional modes and structures of belief engendered by the application to religious belief of the tools of scientific reason such as critical methods of modern biblical scholarship and the comparative method in the study of religions. To many people the achievements of the Enlightenment have left a legacy which appears destructive of traditional wisdom, promotes hostility to religious authority, and empties the world of the sense of the sacred which is intrinsic to a religious world-view. This is a significant contributing factor in the emergence of various fundamentalisms which mark all the great religious traditions at the beginning of the twenty-first century. Yet it is not only those who advocate a return to traditional modes of religious practice who think in this way. Critics of global capitalism, including many in the environmentalist movement worldwide, express a hostility to the Enlightenment as the origin of much that they reject in modern life. So, too, many proponents of postmodernism in philosophy and cultural criticism see the Enlightenment as symptomatic of a false and unfounded idea of the power of reason to analyse and comprehend an unavailable 'true' world.

Today the Enlightenment is perceived as both the time in history when humankind came of age and began to overcome the darkness imposed by ignorance and religion and, alternatively, as a time when human beings began to develop an arrogance which has been damaging to our great religious traditions, has destroyed much of our natural habitat, and has given us a false pride in our technological and scientific advances. The Enlightenment has become a symbol for competing and conflicting understandings of our contemporary religious, political, environmental and economic situation. Our concern here is with the impact of the Enlightenment on religion, and in particular Christianity; yet, understanding how the Enlightenment viewed religious belief can help us to comprehend not only the significance of the Enlightenment as a whole but also many of the ideological divisions which mark global society today.

What, then, was the Enlightenment? The term refers to a long period between around 1650 and 1800 when groups of free-thinkers emerged, particularly in France, who were intent on grounding knowledge in the exercise of critical reason. This emphasis on rationality, freedom of thought new concepts of human nature, the scientific investigation of the natural world and ideals of progress frequently brought its proponents into dispute with established Christian teachings. Many intellectuals, disgusted with the conflict which religion had brought to Europe since the Reformation, relished the opportunity for criticism which the times allowed. Yet Enlightenment ideas were also employed to defend particular Christian doctrines and to modify Christian belief along lines more amenable to the spirit of the age. Modern Christian apologetics is very much the product of Christian responses to the Enlightenment critique, but equally, many anti-religious concepts and movements such as materialism, secularism and atheistic humanism have their roots in the period.

It could be claimed with some justification that the concept of original sin was the single Christian doctrine most opposed by the Enlightenment *philosophes*, a group of French thinkers who pursued a variety of intellectual interests: scientific, mechanical, literary, philosophical and sociological. They believed that humanity was characterized by the dignity bestowed by reason and the pessimistic anthropology of the doctrine of original sin was an affront to this dignity. Jean-Jacques Rousseau (1712–78) claimed that there is no original depravity in the human heart and that 'all the morality of our actions is in the judgements that we ourselves make of them'. For Rousseau, human beings are essentially good, and while they are responsible for the evil they do, this responsibility is purely natural and has no theological overtones of disobedience to the divine commandments. In rejecting original sin Rousseau repudiated the need for a saviour and thus denied the whole Christian dispensation. However, the Enlightenment did not offer a unified vision of humanity to counter the Christian view, but rather a series of critiques which undermined the integral relations of the Christian belief system and cast the hitherto dominant Christian anthropology as simply one alternative among others.

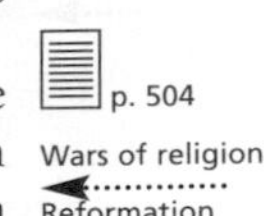
p. 504

Wars of religion

Reformation

In deism, the view that there is a God who is the ultimate source of reality but who does not intervene in the natural course of events, the Enlightenment found a focus for many of its ideas without abandoning religion completely. The search for a simplified religion was quite early on epitomized by the 'Five Common Notions' of Lord Edward Herbert of Cherbury (1583–1648), the first clear statement of the principles of deism which he set out in his *De Veritate* (*On Truth*, 1624). In the middle of the seventeenth century the Cambridge Platonists advocated a rational religion which spurned enthusiasm and what they saw as the irrationality of contemporary Calvinism. Later, John Locke (1632–1704) argued that religious ideas should be clear, simple and within the bounds of reason; this premise led many to attack the doctrine of the Trinity and gave support to the deists in their battles with the orthodox.

Trinity

The title of John Toland's (1670–1722) *Christianity Not Mysterious* (1696) alerted its readers to his claim that God only required belief in what was rationally acceptable. Samuel Clarke (1675–1729) challenged the doctrine of the Trinity and Anthony Collins (1676–1729) averred that the messianic prophecies of the Old Testament were not fulfilled in Jesus. In the so-called 'Deists' Bible', *Christianity as Old as the Creation* (1730), Matthew Tindal (1655–1733) presented the Christian gospel as an instance of what could be known through reason or nature and claimed we should judge revelation not by its claims to authority but only by means of our rational estimation of its moral and religious value.

Against the deists, Bishop Joseph Butler (1692–1752), in his *Analogy of Religion* (1736), argued that both nature

THE CAMBRIDGE PLATONISTS

The Cambridge Platonists were a group of seventeenth-century Cambridge theologians standing between the Puritans and the High Church Anglicans, Calvinism and materialism. They sought to reconcile Christianity with the rising sciences and faith with reason. Their main members were Benjamin Whichcote (1609–83), Ralph Cudworth (1617–88), Henry More (1614–87), John Smith (1618–52) and Nathanael Culverwell (died *c.* 1651).

Puritans

Though coming from a Puritan background they reacted against Calvinistic ideas of the total depravity of human beings and the sheer sovereignty of God: against William Laud, Archbishop of Canterbury, they denied that ritual, dogma and church government are essential to Christianity; and against the political philosopher Thomas Hobbes, they argued that morality was more than obedience to a will. For them reason, seen as an inner light lit by God, was all-important, and they believed that it could judge both natural and revealed religion. In their views they were influenced by Plato and Neoplatonism, hence the name given to them. Their background gave them a broad view of reason and a conviction that right and wrong are part of the order of things. This emphasis on morality led them to be called atheists by some and to be seen by others as forerunners of eighteenth-century deism.

R. L. Colie, *Light and Enlightenment. A Study of Cambridge Platonists and Dutch Arminians*, Cambridge: CUP 1957

and the scriptures were problematic. By means of an analogy between nature and revelation Butler aimed to 'show … that the system of religion, both natural and revealed, considered only as a system and prior to the proof of it, is not a subject of ridicule, unless that of nature be so too'. This argument was effective against deists but less so against atheists, who could simply object that neither the evidence from scripture nor from nature is convincing.

Disputes over atheism had begun early in the Enlightenment period. In the first decades of the seventeenth century there was a strong attack on atheism from Christian theologians, ostensibly aimed at authors from the ancient world such as Lucretius. The real targets were, however, somewhat closer to home, for the divine had already become problematic in the thought of some philosophers. René Descartes (1596–1650) used God as a convenient plank in his philosophical system, much to the chagrin of his contemporary Blaise Pascal (1623–62), who ridiculed the pretensions of reason to grasp Miracle the transcendent. Pascal, a prescient early critic of the Enlightenment, was a brilliant exception in his time, for in the early Enlightenment natural theology seemed so evidently true to most Christian theologians that the atheist, real or hypothetical, was often thought to be lacking the full faculty of reason. Many Christian thinkers believed that the evidence for divine providence in nature was so powerful that it was sufficient both to counter the arguments of atheists and also to temper the enthusiasm of overly naïve and superstitious Christians.

Arguments from design were ubiquitous in the late seventeenth and early eighteenth centuries, and the discoveries of Isaac Newton (1642–1727) only seemed to lend weight to the idea that the world and everything in it was designed by the hand of the provident Creator. But the orthodox were well aware that the world was Evil permeated with evil as well as good. In order to explain how bad things happened in a world of providence some had recourse to speculating that those who suffered the misfortunes of flood, famine, lightning or shipwreck had received just punishment for their sins. But Voltaire's poem *The Lisbon Earthquake*, written in the aftermath of the disaster of 1755 and subtitled *An Enquiry into the Maxim 'Whatever is, is Right'*, vehemently attacked the idea of natural or divine benevolence and marked a turning point in the confident theologies of providence.

In the high Enlightenment in France in the second half of the eighteenth century there were a number of prominent thinkers who were not afraid to express their disbelief, especially among those close to the Baron Paul Henri Thiry d'Holbach (1723–89). D'Holbach's *The* p. 1082 *System of Nature* (1770) was a sustained materialist attack on Christian revelation, the immortality of the soul, divine providence and even the God of deism. In his *Letter on the Blind* (1749), Denis Diderot (1713–84), editor of the great *Encyclopédie* (1751–72), expressed his materialism through the character of the blind British mathematician Nicholas Saunderson, who claimed on his deathbed, 'If you want me to believe in God you must let me touch him.' Other leading materialists included Claude-Adrien Helvétius (1715–71), whose *De l'esprit* (*On the Spirit* 1758) argued that humans are completely determined by their environment, and Julien Offray de La Mettrie (1709–51), whose works *Histoire naturelle de l'âme* (*A Natural History of the Soul*, 1745) and *L'Homme machine* (*Man a Machine*, 1747) were both widely condemned. While such explicit atheism was rare, even among the leading *philosophes*, those who did affirm a materialist position were significant forerunners of modern naturalism.

Although David Hume (1711–76) is more accurately described as a sceptic than as an atheist, his critique of the power of reason dealt a severe blow to the rational natural theology of deists and orthodox alike. In his essay 'On Miracles', in *An Enquiry Concerning Human Understanding* (1748), Hume attacked an important plank of eighteenth-century Christian apologetics, namely the claim that miracles are guarantees of divine revelation. He argued that 'the ultimate standard, by which we determine all disputes, that may arise concerning them, is always derived from experience and observation'. We know the laws of nature through constantly repeated experience and a miracle is by definition a violation of this experience and of these laws. Hume concludes that 'as a uniform experience amounts to a proof, there is here a direct and full *proof*, from the nature of the fact, against the existence of any miracle'.

New scientific discoveries sometimes seemed to lend weight to the atheists' cause. While the emerging sciences as such were not inherently inimical to Christian beliefs, many new discoveries did appear to contradict existing doctrines. The French scientist Georges-Louis Leclerc Comte de Buffon (1707–88), raised several contentious questions regarding the development of species, including the human species itself, and his calculation of the age of the earth challenged existing estimates based on biblical genealogy. The Swiss naturalist Abraham Tremblay (1710–84) became famous among materialists, who took the results of his experiments on the fresh water polyp as an opportunity to argue that there was no soul or guiding immaterial principle of life, only matter itself.

The new possibilities for knowledge offered by the scientific method contributed to what later scholars were to call the 'demystifying' of life and the weakening of the grasp of religion on the popular imagination. This is exemplified in the decline in belief in witchcraft which was an important indication of the weakening of traditional Christian beliefs, and the emergence of more secular forms of thought; although the last judicial execution of a 'witch' was as late as 1782 (in Switzerland), belief in witches had already been discredited among large segments of the population. Also, advances in medical knowledge led to a change in popular attitudes towards suicide and mental illness, which came to be perceived within psychological and not theological parameters.

Disputes over belief and doctrine found parallels in attempts to weaken the political power of the churches. This often took the form of pleas for religious toleration. The most significant defender of religious toleration in the early Enlightenment was the enormously influential French Protestant Pierre Bayle (1647–1706). For Bayle, the truth of religious belief lies within the conscience of the individual, so there is little point in blaming those who hold heretical beliefs, as they can believe in no truth other than that which they hold in conscience. When the inviolability of conscience is recognized, Bayle argued, toleration is the only adequate response, and as conscience is placed in us by God, to go against our conscience is to go against God: 'The law that forbids a man to blind himself to the light of his conscience is one from which God can never dispense us since, if He were to do so, He would be permitting us to scorn or to hate Him.'

While Bayle remained a Christian, later advocates of toleration were more critical of the churches. Most prominent was Voltaire (1694–1778), one of the most stinging Enlightenment critics of Christianity. The celebrated French polemicist attacked Christianity to the point of committing himself to its destruction. His anti-Christian polemic is exemplified in the *Dictionnaire philosophique* (*Philosophical Dictionary*, 1764). In a highly inventive manner he combined fable, invention, history, observations on the natural world and philosophical acumen to ridicule Christian beliefs, while simultaneously informing, delighting, and at times scandalizing his readers. Voltaire's caustic wit brought religion down from the exalted heights of metaphysical truth to the lowlands of custom and culture. This form of cultural criticism was a powerful weapon in the *philosophes*' battle to bring religion under equal scrutiny and criticism with all other forms of human culture and behaviour. A favourite literary device became the visit of outsiders to Europe, where they commented on the peculiar habits and customs of the natives, a genre exemplified by the *Lettres persanes* (*Persian Letters*, 1721) of Baron Montesquieu (1689–1755).

This increased awareness of the customs and beliefs of other cultures raised crucial issues for Christian theology and the dominant role of the Christian church (e.g. is Christ the only revealer or saviour?) and made it possible for Christians to begin to contemplate the possibility of

NTENELLE MÉDITANT SUR LA PLURALITÉ DES MONI

Conscience

Bernard le Bovier de Fontenelle, 1657–1757, French scientist and man of letters, reflecting on the plurality of worlds

their own religion as one among many and not as the single true religion. This signals a seismic change in the history of Christianity, for it effectively marks the end of the possibility of maintaining 'Christendom' as a totalizing concept embracing and unifying all humanity.

Christendom

Voltaire's increasingly vehement anti-Christian campaign, during which he coined his famous phrase *Écrasez l'infâme* ('crush the infamous one', i.e. Christianity), came to a head in the 1760s with the Calas affair, which gave rise to his *Traité sur la_tolerance* (*Letter On Tolerance*, 1763). The son of a Huguenot family in the south of France was found dead, and local rumour had it that he was killed because he wished to convert to Roman Catholicism. The young man's father, Jean Calas, was arrested and executed on the basis of flimsy evidence motivated more by religious hatred than the due process of law. To Voltaire the event was further proof of the evils generated by religion: whether the son wished to convert or not and whether the father was guilty or not, one of the two had been killed unjustly for a religious motivation.

Other faiths

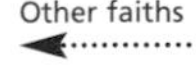

It was events like the Calas affair and the abiding memory of the 1572 St Bartholemew's Day massacre of Huguenots which helped make France the battleground

Secularization

between the established power of the church and the secular spirit which was emerging among the intelligentsia. In other European countries such as England and Holland, where the influence of the church had been tempered by the power of the state, there was less bitter antagonism.

p. 1043

In Austria under the reforming emperor Joseph II (1741–90) the government embarked upon the appraisal and appropriation of church property; almost one third of the monasteries in the empire were closed and their property confiscated by the state. Joseph's reforms were in no manner designed to extirpate Christianity, but rather to simplify it and make it a useful and productive part of the lives of his subjects. The new Catholicism of the Austrian empire was to be rational, functional and moral, based on firm Enlightenment principles of utility and practicality. Yet these reforms failed, most notably because of their overbearing nature (e.g. the banning of coffins).

Romanticism

Still, Joseph II saw himself as a reformer of Christianity, not its destroyer, and in many countries Enlightenment ideas were utilized in defence of religion. In Germany, Holland, Scotland, Switzerland and the new United States of America there were thinkers who were not hostile to Christianity but who wished to transform it in line with the temper of the times. For example, in the United States, while Thomas Paine (1737–1809) was hostile to Christianity, Thomas Jefferson (1743–1826) was more representative of the time; he produced his *Jefferson Bible* (1820) with the aim of purging the message of Jesus of what he saw as its extraneous and non-rational elements.

Biblical criticism

In Germany the complex relationship between Christianity and Enlightenment can be seen in the careers of Christian Wolff (1689–1754) and Johann Salomo Semler (1725–91), the two greatest Protestant theologians of the eighteenth century. Both sought to bring Enlightenment ideas to bear on Christian theology, Wolff through his rationalist dogmatics and Semler primarily through his historical treatment of Christian origins. In the eighteenth century this rational theology struggled for dominance in many German Protestant universities with Pietism, which stressed individual salvation and moral seriousness. The key figures in the Pietist movement were Philipp Jakob Spener (1635–1705) and Count Nicholas Ludwig von Zinzendorf (1700–60). In his *Pia desideria* (*Pious Desires*, 1675), Spener advocated a renewal of Lutheran worship, more practical and devotional sermons, reading of the Bible by the laity, and a more interior and experiential form of belief. Pietism stood in contrast to the Enlightenment tendency to reduce religion to the minimum of rational beliefs and opposed the propensity of Lutheran orthodoxy to defend belief through recourse to rational theology. Yet it shared certain characteristics with its age, such as the emphasis on the moral commitment demanded of the individual and a mistrust of ecclesiastical power.

Pietism

Friedrich Schleiermacher

Through the emigration of Moravians and others, Pietism helped shape the development of Protestantism in America. John Wesley (1703–91) and Charles Wesley (1707–88) were greatly influenced by the movement, thus tempering the development of rational theology in eighteenth-century England. The philosophy of Immanuel Kant (1724–1804) shows distinct marks of his Pietist upbringing (e.g. his mistrust of organized religion and emphasis on moral duty, faith and individual responsibility), and the Pietist stress on emotion and personal conviction also served as a background influence on the development of German Romanticism.

In a more critical vein, Gotthold Ephraim Lessing (1729–81) published the biblical criticism of Reimarus as the famous *Fragments* (1774–78) and promoted religious toleration in his *Nathan der Weise* (*Nathan the Wise*, 1779), which also expressed his hostility to all positive, revealed religion. The biblical scholarship of Semler, Reimarus and others served to weaken the status of the Bible as divine revelation and paved the way for modern biblical criticism. In the later German Enlightenment Johann Gottfried von Herder (1744–1803) and the celebrated Johann Wolfgang von Goethe (1749–1832) initiated the shift away from the Bible and the traditional questions of theology towards a new emphasis on nature, human sentiment, and folk traditions, thus giving impetus to the emerging Romantic movement. Thinkers such as Friedrich Heinrich Jacobi (1743–1819) and Johann Georg Hamann (1730–88) opposed rationalism in religion, and the critical philosophy of Kant spelled the death of systems of dogma based on reason (at least among Protestants), inverting the traditional relationship between religion and morals. 'Religion,' said Kant, 'is the recognition of all duties as divine commands.'

Although many of the most significant Enlightenment figures were hostile to Christianity, the era's contribution to the Christian religion was not its destruction but rather a modification and renewal of its theology, polity and practice. Close study of the Enlightenment reveals not the cold rationalism that is all too often presented as its *leitmotif*, but rather a complexity of shifting trends and influences. Modern Christian thought began when Friedrich Schleiermacher (1768–1834) reformulated dogmatics in response to the thought of Kant and, just as the modern world is inescapably a product of the Enlightenment, so also is modern Christianity.

The Enlightenment is perceived today as the origin of much that is good and much that is destructive in modern life. Yet it is possible, looking back on the period, to form a judgement about its real significance, in terms of both its achievements and its limitations. Critics of the Enlightenment come from many perspectives: environmentalists, radical postmodernists and religious fundamentalists make strange yet frequent bedfellows in their attacks on the rationalism unleashed by the *philosophes* and others 300 years ago. In some respects their criticism is accurate; it is true that we have wreaked destruction on our environment, that we have undermined not only traditional religious belief but many of the institutions – such as the nuclear family – which it sustained, and what postmodernists aver may well be true, that in our cultural hubris we overestimate our powers of reason at our peril.

Yet is it not the case that such protests appear as misguided attempts to blame history for our present lack of wisdom? Few in the West would wish to return to a world where morality was truly governed by religious authority, where the technological advances of modernity were absent, or where the Enlightenment principle of the common rationality of human beings had not given us greater equality for women. In their hostility to the Enlightenment, do not its critics often betray a nostalgia for a time of consensus, purity, or sacredness – of nature or of religion – which never really existed? And do not many educated, Western, critics of the Enlightenment, in making common cause with those who are often hostile to the values of freedom of expression and of enquiry which are among its greatest achievements, contribute to a future even more uncertain than the present which they too easily lament? It is not so much the Enlightenment as such that is to blame for the perceived ills of the present, but rather our inability to deal wisely with its achievements. Despite its controversial legacy, the fundamental principles of the Enlightenment, such as freedom of thought, the dignity and rights of the individual, rational methods of problem solving, and a shared human nature, continue to be the principles best suited to undergird our hope for the future.

JAMES M. BYRNE

James M. Byrne, *Glory, Jest and Riddle*, London: SCM Press 1996 (US title *Religion and the Enlightenment: From Descartes to Kant*, Louisville, KY: Westminster John Knox Press 1997); Isaac Kramnick (ed), *The Portable Enlightenment Reader*, New York: Penguin 1995; Roy Porter, *The Creation of the Modern World: The Untold Story of the British Enlightenment*, New York and London: Norton & Co. 2000; W. R. Ward, *Christianity Under the Ancien Régime: 1648–1789*, Cambridge: CUP 1999; John W. Yolton et al. (eds), *The Blackwell Companion to the Enlightenment*, Oxford: Blackwell 1991

Environmental ethics

Christianity has traditionally thought of itself as being concerned with the salvation of souls, so why should it turn its attention to environmental questions? While some authors still believe that the Christian gospel has little to say on such matters, others are more convinced that environmental concern is at least implicit in the Christian message, even if not explicit. In addition, Christianity needs to face the charge that it is in some way responsible for environmental destruction by fostering attitudes that led to a detachment from the natural world, through its emphasis on human supremacy.

Few can now doubt the scientific findings that point to environmental strain. For example, the rate of loss of biodiversity due to human interventions has been estimated at over a hundred times that caused by base extinction rates during the course of evolution. Human intervention can be direct, e.g. through hunting, or indirect, through destruction of habitat and climate change.

Women in Christianity ◄

Climate change was at one time the subject of some dispute, but the weight of evidence for it is accumulating. Senior respected scientists have demonstrated convincingly that it is taking place, often at an alarming rate. The increase in global temperature recorded in the twentieth century represents a greater change than that recorded over the past 10,000 years. The rising sea levels and the increase in climate extremes has led to the prediction that there will be 150 million environmental refugees by 2050 if the rate of change continues. It is becoming increasingly obvious that the poorer nations of the world are likely to suffer the worst of the impacts of climate change, since nations such as Bangladesh are low-lying, and are ill-equipped to deal with rising sea levels. Much of the climate change is caused by burning of fossil fuels, leading to the release of carbon dioxide, and associated global warming through the 'greenhouse effect'. Deforestation leads to a similar effect on climate, as well as having a direct impact on biodiversity. A combination of factors, including over-consumption by the world's richer nations, alongside an ever-growing population and rising pollution levels, together with diminishing natural resources, all contribute to environmental damage. So questions to do with the environment can no longer be separated from wider issues of social justice.

Third World

While it is reasonable to suggest that environmental concern is not built into a traditional reading of the Bible, it is possible to read the text in the light of these concerns and find insights that have been missed in the past. Such a reading is similar to feminist readings of the biblical text, though this time it is from the perspective of the earth. More conservative theologians may not wish to undertake such a radical interpretation, but are still willing to refute

Feminist theology

the charge that the early chapters of Genesis led to a domineering attitude to the natural world. They insist, rather, that the dominion spoken about in Genesis 1.26 refers to *dominion over* rather than *domination of* the earth. Such dominion leads to an ethic of careful and Creation responsible stewardship. This ethic puts creation care at the heart of the way Christians should behave towards a created world that is declared good by God.

Not all Christian ethicists agree that the theme of stewardship is sufficient to focus attention to the earth and treat it with the care it deserves, and arguably needs. Bible Writers in this vein are convinced that we need a much more radical sense of seeing ourselves as connected intimately with the earth and all its processes. In particular, they believe that stewardship is still too centred on human beings, implying that we can act like 'managers' of the planet. The question now becomes: how can we move away from human-centred attitudes in order to develop a greater sensitivity to and kinship with species other than our own? One way this might be done is through moving towards a greater focus on the earth and its creatures as sacred in and of itself. Another way is to stress the individual worth of each and every creature, giving Animals non-human species *intrinsic* worth, that is, value in and of themselves. This is in contrast to what they perceive Orthodox churches as the *instrumental* worth of non-human species that has dominated ethical approaches in the past, namely, using other species for human benefit alone. It is not surprising that Christian scholars drawn to the idea of intrinsic worth of all creatures are also attracted to other religious traditions, such as Buddhism or even animism.

The Gaia hypothesis is also instructive for many, for this theory suggests that the earth acts as a whole in a feedback process so that environmental conditions remain fit for life to exist. This implies, for some, that we need to remind ourselves of the interconnectedness of all parts of the earth, not just in terms of origin, if we adopt evolutionary theory, but also in terms of present function. Christian ecofeminist writers, while they vary considerably in their style of feminism, commonly believe that domination of the earth is linked to the domination of women. According to this view, the interlinked oppressions need to be dealt with at a number of levels, including the social and economic levels. Of course, more conservative positions would argue that such shifts are moving too far away from distinctive Christian approaches to the issue.

In addition to such reflections on the worth of the earth in and of itself, other scholars are particularly concerned to highlight the social issues connected with environmental concern. In particular, such scholars argue that the move towards settled urbanized culture has reinforced detachment from the land, at least in the so-called 'developed' economies. In some poorer nations of the world questions about environmental issues are not a luxury, but questions about survival. The Johannesburg Summit on Sustainable Development that took place in 2002 made this quite clear, for questions to do with environmental practice could not be separated from the needs of the poorer communities. This discussion was of great concern to many Roman Catholic theologians and scholars, who have traditionally given a great deal of attention to issues of social justice. It is one reason, perhaps, why Pope John Paul II has called for the need for 'ecological conversion'. Scholars writing in this vein have turned to biblical accounts to reinforce their ethical approach, arguing that the biblical record, especially the Old Testament, points to a deep relationship between people and land. In the book of Jeremiah, the disobedience of the people has effects on both the fate of the people and that of the land. While this devastation was obviously on a much smaller scale than that of today, the point is clear enough: in the tradition shared by Jews and Christians there is a close connection between God, humankind and the land. Of course, secular writers have stressed the need to develop a land ethic, but Christian authors writing in this vein want to go further in emphasizing the need for a rediscovery of Christian community understood in ecological terms.

Alongside these traditions, Eastern Orthodox theologians have played a prominent role in the conversation about environmental concern, believing that humanity needs to turn away from its own attachment to material things. Such attachment leads to forms of consumerism that are at least indirectly responsible for the environmental crisis. In this context, environmental ethics is about a rediscovery of both the ascetic tradition and the worth of creation as celebrated in Orthodox worship. In particular, once the earth is viewed as God's gift, it becomes imperative to treat it with love and respect. Moreover, the Orthodox view puts great emphasis on the goodness of creation, including humanity as in some sense representing the whole of the created order. In this case a strong sense of the difference between humanity and other non-human creatures is combined with an equally strong sense of the way in which all of life must necessarily participate in the life of God if its existence is to continue. In addition, the Orthodox view is that through participation in the Divine Liturgy, the church can serve to remind humanity of its dependence on God and God's gift of life to all creaturely existence.

Of course, there are difficult decisions to make when it comes to what course of action to take first, given the enormity and scale of the problems faced. Ethical decision-making is notoriously difficult in this area, and secular approaches have tended to adopt the precautionary principle. This states that we need to act cautiously vhen it comes to making environmental decisions, which re often expressed in terms of costs and benefits. The lifficulty is that in many cases one simply does not know f harm will follow or not: those who are more radical nvironmentalists will interpret a lack of knowledge as eing sufficient reason to avoid change, while those who re more committed to new technologies will go ahead *nless* there is positive evidence of harm. The language f sustainability is also common currency, most often neaning that action is justified only if it can be shown hat it will not have a detrimental effect on future generaions. Such predictions of effects are complex, and are tied p with political and economic issues. Some authors have rgued that in order to deal with such questions we need to raw on the theological tradition of wisdom, including the bility to express such wisdom in practical ways through rudential decision-making. This classical tradition of rudence is not the same as the precautionary principle, ince while it includes the notion of caution, it also ncludes ideas such as circumspection, or paying attention o circumstances in the present; foresight, or knowledge bout the future; taking counsel; and the ability to make xceptions to any rules in place.

Some Christian ethicists are critical of paying attention o either local communities or virtues, as they believe hat this fails to take adequate account of the global ature of environmental problems. They call for a greater osmopolitan sense of environmental concern, one that vill facilitate international agreements and common overnment policy. Of course, environmental ethics in this ontext is necessarily political, though it is fair to suggest hat such virtues as prudence are not necessarily restricted o individual decision-making, but include domestic and olitical dimensions as well. A discussion in this context lso needs to include questions about justice, and how and o what extent non-human species can be included in the anguage of rights and justice. Christians are divided on vhether such rights language or the language of justice is ppropriate for the non-human sphere. It is also reasonable o suggest that those who have adhered to animal rights rom a Christian perspective have tended simply to extend uman-centred rights to animals, rather than shifting the ocus of value from humans to non-humans.

Overall, environmental ethics as demonstrated by Christians shows considerable diversity, but all are agreed hat humanity needs to become more aware of its impact n the global commons. For some this is best done by dentifying religious issues as those that underlie damaging ttitudes to the environment. They argue that we need to ay far more attention to the way humanity has become ttached to consumer modes of living and culture, calling or a deeper repentance and change in human behaviour o simpler styles of living. Others point to the social justice issues implicit in environmental concerns, arguing that we no longer have the luxury of treating environmental concern as if it were an optional extra for Christian believers. Others again point to the biblical record as a source for inspiration for models such as stewardship or prudence. More radical forms of ethics arise out of more radical forms of ecotheology, where a new image of God Ecotheology is being developed in order to give greater attention to the love of God for the non-human world, and the inclusion of all creation in the story of salvation.

Christianity sits somewhat uneasily between modernity and the rise of modern science, which it accepted, even Science if it did not directly facilitate, and other more critical religious movements which put far more emphasis on the sacredness of all of life. While Christians disagree in the way environmental concern needs to be expressed, most will agree that fostering love and respect for the environment is an integral part of what it means to live a Christian life ethically and responsibly.

CELIA DEANE-DRUMMOND

Robin Attfield, *The Ethics of the Global Environment*, Edinburgh: Edinburgh University Press 1999; R. J. Berry, *God's Book of Works*, London: Continuum 2003; Steven Bouma-Prediger, *For the Beauty of the Earth: A Christian Vision of Creation Care*, Grand Rapids, MI: Baker Academic 2001; Celia Deane-Drummond, *The Ethics of Nature*, Oxford: Blackwell 2004; Paulos Gregorios, *The Human Presence: An Orthodox View of Nature*, Geneva: WCC 1978; IPCC, *Climate Change 2001: Synthesis Report of the Third Assessment of the Intergovernmental Panel on Climate Change*, Cambridge: CUP 2001

Globalization

Eschatology

Eschatology is not an easy word to define. Strictly speaking, it is to do with the study of the 'last things', events concerned with endings, usually events which will bring history and this world to its close. Yet the word is used in a variety of different senses. Thus we can find it used to describe the fate of the individual believer's soul after Life after death death, the termination of this world order and a setting up of another, events like the last judgement and the resur- Resurrection rection of the dead, and as a convenient way of referring to future hopes about the coming of God's kingdom Kingdom of God on earth, irrespective of whether in fact they involve an ending of the historical process. Typically, many biblical passages are about a future hope and its fulfilment in this world.

The bulk of the Jewish literature which has come down to us views salvation in the context of history. Thus the Salvation dominion of God over all flesh is intimately linked with the belief in God as creator and liberator. Whether the urgency for deliverance was strong or not, the formative p. 1152 experiences of the Jewish nation, the exodus, spoke of the deliverance and triumph of the people of God, the manifestation of the mighty hand of God in human affairs. Thus it is impossible to imagine that salvation could be considered as in any way complete without reference to the fulfilment of that hope for God's kingdom on earth.

For Jews, the promise of a final vindication of the Jewish people and the establishment of a new order in which God's ways would prevail was a belief which had its roots in the covenant relationship itself (2 Samuel 7.8–14). So the prophetic hopes for a righteous leader who would act as God's agent in delivering his people (Isaiah 11), many of which were themselves derived from Covenant promises based on the covenant with David (Psalms 89; 132; Psalms of Solomon 17; Qumran texts 1Qsa 2; 1QS 9.11), exercised their own influence on the imagination of the Jewish writers. Two features of the eschatological expectation during the centuries preceding the birth of Jesus are the conviction that before this age came about, a p. 661 period of severe distress, of political and cosmic disorder and upheaval, would have to be endured; and the belief that a new age of peace and justice would come on earth. Belief in the coming of a new age of peace and justice is firmly rooted in the Old Testament (e.g. Isaiah 11; Ezekiel 40ff.; Zechariah 8.20ff.; 9–14). Some Jewish writers looked forward to a time when the nations would join Israel in worshipping the one God (Zechariah 8.20; Psalm 72.10f.; Revelation 21.26).

The heart of the early Christian message is eschatological: Messiah the coming of the promised Messiah and the pouring out of the prophetic Spirit. For most New Testament writers there is still an unfulfilled element in the process of salvation. Believers may have tasted of the heavenly gift and partici- Holy Spirit pated in the Holy Spirit (Hebrews 6.4), but they look forward to a future of bliss, and while they wait they endure the privations, merely tasting the glory to come. We need to appreciate how pervasive this tension is between what Paul believers have already experienced in Christ *now* and what they still have to wait for (the *not yet*).

The resurrection of Jesus is important within the New Testament. For Jews and early Christians it was an essential Hope component of the future hope. To speak of the resurrection of the dead was to speak of the life of the age to come. From time to time in the New Testament we have hints of the very close link between resurrection and the eschatological events (e.g. 1 Corinthians 15.20; Philippians 3.21). The resurrection of Jesus of Nazareth is the first-fruits, an anticipation in which a key feature of the 'last days' (Acts 2.17) becomes a reality in the old age. Thus in so far as the first Christians spoke of the resurrection of Jesus and made it a cornerstone of their existence, they were affirming that for them the future hope was already in the process of fulfilment and was not merely an item of faith still to be realized at some point in the future. By stressing the centrality of resurrection, the early Christian writers were making eschatology the key to the understanding of their lives. The early Christian proclamation that Jesus was raised from the dead may be regarded as an alternative way of expressing the conviction which confronts us in the teaching of Jesus: God's kingdom is at hand (Mark 1.15): in Jesus' resurrection the life of the age to come has drawn near.

The New Testament writers looked forward to an imminent manifestation of the righteousness of God, when Jesus returned as Lord to complete the process which had started in the events of his ministry, culminating with the cross and resurrection. The word *parousia*, which denotes the belief in the coming of Christ from heaven to fulfil the eschatological purposes inaugurated in his life, death and resurrection, is often used to refer to this complex of ideas in Christian eschatology (e.g. Matthew 24.27–31 compare Mark 13. 26; 1 Corinthians 15.23–6; 15.23–6; 1 Thessalonians 4.17). The departure of the 'Son of man' to God was only a temporary phenomenon, for he would be revealed (1 Corinthians 1.7; 1 Peter 1.7) and would bring about the times of restoration of all things foretold by the prophets (Acts 3.21). That would happen soon (Romans 13.11; Revelation 22.20), though the New Testament writers are uniformly unwilling to be too specific about the exact date (Mark 9.1; 13.32; 1 Thessalonians 5.1; cf. 2 Thessalonians 2.2f.). The return of Jesus on the clouds of heaven was linked with the convictions about the resurrection, in that it was the consummation of a promise of which the resurrection of Jesus was the guarantee. However, the early Christians believed that the eschatological salvation was not wholly future, particularly since the new age had broken into the old in the resurrection of Jesus: the experience of the Spirit, such a dominant feature of early Christian religion, cannot be understood apart from the eschatological perspective.

Paul hints that experience of the Spirit is closely linked with the eschatological hope. Thus, in outlining the present period of travail in Romans 8.18ff., he speaks of Christians being the ones who have the first-fruits of the Spirit (v. 23). The implication is that despite having already tasted of that glory (cf. Hebrews 6.5), even Christians long for a greater liberation still to be made manifest; Christians, too, therefore join in the travail of the messianic woes which precede the coming of God's kingdom. Similarly, in Acts 2.17 the pouring out of the Spirit on the day of Pentecost is a fulfilment of an eschatological promise from the book of Joel. The experience of the Spirit was seen as the present expression in the life of the individual and the community of that eschatological reality, which had been manifested in the resurrection of Jesus of Nazareth from the dead.

The Spirit Paraclete promised in the Gospel of John, the comforter or advocate, is a successor to Jesus, a compensation by his presence for Jesus' absence with the Father, and enables the disciples to maintain their connection with the basic revelation of God (14.18–19, 25–6; 15.26). The emphasis on present experience of future hope is a feature of the Gospel of John. 2 Peter 3 and the parables at the end of Matthew 24 are often suggested as indirect evidence of writers wrestling with the non-fulfilment of hopes for the future. There are just a few systematic presentations of eschatological belief which tend to be fragmentary in character and linked with the management of specific pastoral problems. A comprehensive scheme may be found in the seventh book of the church father Lactantius' *Institutes* (v. 18), written in the early fourth century; it is also linked with pagan and Jewish prophecy. In the history of Christian doctrine hope for the establishment of God's kingdom on earth faded, and the emphasis came to lie on the transcendent realm as the goal of the Christian soul. This differs from the core beliefs of the first Christians, who prayed for God's kingdom to come on earth and the divine will to be done on earth as in heaven.

CHRISTOPHER ROWLAND

Jürgen Moltmann, *The Coming of God: Christian Eschatology*, London: SCM Press 1996; Christopher Rowland, *Christian Origins: An Account of the Setting and Character of the Most Important Messianic Sect of Judaism*, London: revd edn, SPCK 2002

Eternity

Throughout their history, Christians have looked for ways to express the ultimate and superlative character of God. So it has been said that God is all-loving, all-knowing, all-powerful and so on. It is in this spirit of attributing to God the highest imaginable qualities that Christians have also said that God is 'eternal'. We humans live finite lives of just a few years. But as the highest imaginable being and lord of time, God was taken to be unrestricted by time, in other words an eternal deity without beginning or end.

The descriptions of God in the Bible illustrate this very well. Psalm 90 declares that God exists 'from everlasting to everlasting'. The author of the letter to the Hebrews argues that God is not like earthly objects that perish with time. God's years have 'no end' (Hebrews 1.12). Revelation speaks of a God 'who was, and is and is to come' (Revelation 4.8). Although there are many biblical references to God's eternal nature, the Bible contains no theory of eternity and its relationship to time. When the biblical writers called God 'everlasting', their principal motive was to pay God a compliment, rather than to develop a theory about God. For subsequent theologians, however, the question of God's 'eternity' has been extremely complicated and has raised fundamental issues about the core doctrines of the incarnation, the Trinity and the simplicity of God.

Incarnation
Trinity

To understand the difficulty, we need to distinguish between two very different understandings of eternity: 'eternity as infinite time' and 'eternity as timelessness'. In everyday speech we generally use concepts of eternity in the first sense, to mean an infinite expanse of time. So if I say that a tedious meeting 'went on for ever' I am thinking of eternity as an unrestricted duration. This is the way in which the biblical writers speak of eternity – as endless days or unrestricted time. Christian theologians, by contrast, have tended to see God as outside time, eternal in the timeless sense. This distinction is not just a game with words: one concept equates eternity with time, the other sees eternity as the very opposite of time.

The concept of a timeless eternity has its roots in the philosophy of the ancient Greek philosopher Plato, who came to have a very significant influence on Christian theology, particularly through the writings of Augustine. Plato had argued that it is not possible to have true knowledge of things that change in time. We can only really know something that never changes, something timeless. So the highest and most valuable knowledge, for Plato, was knowledge of the eternal. Platonic philosophy provided a way for early Christian theologians to understand God's eternity as timeless and unchanging. The theory of God's timelessness persists to this day through the enduring influence, particularly in the Roman Catholic Church, of the theologian Thomas Aquinas.

Thomas Aquinas

If we start to think of God as a timeless eternity, we soon run up against some major problems. If God is timeless and unchanging, how is it possible for God to act in time? How could God bring about a time-bound creation? How could God become time-bound in the person of Jesus? How could a timeless God have any meaningful connection whatsoever with our world of events? If God were to act, or even to think a thought, God would have to do so at a particular moment, which would make God subject to time and change. In order to remain timeless, God would have to persist in a static state. As Thomas Aquinas put it, 'the form of eternity lies in ... uniformity'.

God
Jesus

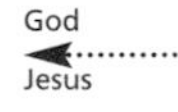

The Bible, however, had always depicted God in a dynamic relationship with our world of time. God is described as a 'living God', unlike the static, lifeless idols made of wood and stone. He created the world, acted

Time

THE ETERNAL GOD

Lord, you have been our dwelling place in all generations.
Before the mountains were brought forth,
or ever you had formed the earth and the world,
from everlasting to everlasting you are God.

You turn men back to the dust,
and say, 'Turn back, O children of men!'
For a thousand years in your sight
are but as yesterday when it is past,
or as a watch in the night.

You sweep men away; they are like a dream,
like grass which is renewed in the morning:
in the morning it flourishes and is renewed;
in the evening it fades and withers.

(Psalm 90.1–6)

Of old you laid the foundations of the earth,
and the heavens are the works of your hands.
They will perish, but you endure;
they will all wear out like a garment.
You change them like raiment and they pass away;
but you are the same, and your years have no end.

(Psalm 102.25–7)

in miraculous ways, became part of the world through Jesus Christ and promised to transform the world into his 'kingdom'. So if God is eternal, it must be a kind of eternity that allows God to be involved with time. Perhaps, then, it is better to think of God's eternity as the totality of time so that God is understood to be present at every moment of time but not restricted to any moment of time. So we experience time as a succession of events, but God experiences all time as a single cosmic event. The Scottish theologian John Duns Scotus (*c.* 1265–1308) arrived at this kind of conclusion, arguing that God 'has the power to produce an infinite number [of events] simultaneously'.

The theological problem of eternity is most complex when we consider the doctrine of the incarnation, which says that God became a time-bound person in Jesus Christ. If Jesus was truly human, he must have experienced time as a succession of events, as we do. But how is the time-experience of Jesus compatible with an eternal divine nature? Most Christians agree that this paradox cannot be properly explained: this is where faith takes over from theological understanding.

A central article of Christian faith is the belief that Christians will not die, but will be released from the restrictions of time and will join God in his eternal life. Since the days of Paul, Christians have also believed that it is possible at special times for people to have experiences of the eternal – perhaps in prayer, contemplation or moments of revelation. These experiences are a 'foretaste' of the eternal life to come. Paul believed that he had been transported for a period into heaven (2 Corinthians 12.2). Augustine shared a similar moment in prayer with his mother. Many Christian people will speak about mystical experiences when 'time stood still'. Such episodes are difficult to explain, but they do show that 'eternity' is a key part of Christian religious experience and not just a theological concept.

HUGH RAYMENT-PICKARD

Paul Helm, *Eternal God*, Oxford: Clarendon Press 1988; Brian Leftow, *Time and Eternity*, Cornell Studies in the Philosophy of Religion, Ithaca, NU: Cornell University Press 1991; William Lane Craig, *Time and Eternity: Exploring God's Relationship with Time*, Wheaton, IL: Crossway Books 2001; Alan G. Padgett, *God, Eternity and the Nature of Time*, New York: St Martin's Press 1992

ETHICS

Bioethics, Business ethics, Conscience, Global ethic, Homosexuality, Human rights, Professional ethics, Sexual ethics, Social ethics, War and peace

Ethics lies at the heart of Christianity. In describing their lives in relation to God, Christians cannot avoid using categories like good and evil, right and wrong. And as they have reflected on ethical questions over the centuries they have built up a whole body of teaching that can be called Christian ethics. Whether or not Christian ethics is distinct from other kinds of ethics is an extremely complex question, because Christians have always been part of a wider society and have not only adopted ethical standards from the world around them but also found others criticizing their ethical standards as deficient (as for example, in the toleration of slavery or the inferior status of women in Christianity until a relatively late date). What can be done, though, is to look at the nature of Christian ethics and establish its main characteristics.

Society
Women in Christianity

Christian ethics at the least involves the study of what Christians ought to do and ought not to do; it has often led to views which are thought to be binding on those who are not Christians as well. It is descriptive and prescriptive. Christian ethicists describe and compare what other Christians have said and done, assess those accounts and actions, and develop their own normative account of Christian ethics.

The material for studying Christian ethics is made up of a great variety of Christian writings. Sermons and letters have an occasional character that comes from addressing the concerns of particular communities. Devotional writings seek to deepen a sense of the presence of God, often in the context of the moral decisions of daily life. These writings range from morality stories to meditations on death and dying. Broader moral teachings are given in commentaries on scripture, in catechisms that summarize the basics of Christian life, and in teaching documents that include the texts of lectures, tracts, essays, and the official teachings of a church. Other writings address specific cases in order to offer moral judgement and guidance. In the Roman Catholic tradition these judgements were organized in a systematic manner to form a moral theology and casuistry in order to offer guidance to priests who heard the confession of sins. Largely developed in the context of the university as that first began in the twelfth and thirteenth centuries, systematic treatises in Christian ethics develop more comprehensive accounts of Christian faith and the moral life.

Preaching
Letters
Death

p. 625
Moral theology
University

It has been argued that five inter-related questions run through writings on the Christian moral life, reflecting the history of ethics from Aristotle (384–322 BCE) to Friedrich Schleiermacher (1768–1834) and beyond. How is God understood and what is God doing and calling Christians to do? What is the nature of the good, of what is claimed to be moral? How do human persons come to know what is moral and how are they enabled or empowered to act morally? What are the moral demands or principles that indicate what should be done? How should the world and particular situations in it be morally analysed and understood? In short, the questions of Christian ethics are questions about God, the moral good, moral responsibility, and moral judgement.

The answers given to these questions of Christian ethics draw variously on the Christian story as told in the Old and New Testaments and understood within the Christian tradition; understandings of the world, for example, views about the natural world, history, and the human person; fundamental, philosophical assumptions about the nature of things such as the nature of truth or

Bible

THE TEN COMMANDMENTS

Exodus 20.1–17	*Deuteronomy 5.6–21*
God spoke all these words, saying, 'I am the Lord your God, who brought you out of the land of Egypt, out of the house of bondage.	God said, 'I am the Lord your God, who brought you out of the land of Egypt, out of the house of bondage.
1. You shall have no other gods before me.	1. You shall have no other gods before me.
2. You shall not make for yourself a graven image, or any likeness of anything that is in heaven above, or that is in the earth beneath, or that is in the water under the earth; you shall not bow down to them or serve them; for I the Lord your God am a jealous God, visiting the iniquity of the fathers upon the children to the third and the fourth generation of those who hate me, but showing steadfast love to thousands of those who love me and keep my commandments.	2. You shall not make for yourself a graven image, or any likeness of anything that is in heaven above, or that is on the earth beneath, or that is in the water under the earth; you shall not bow down to them or serve them; for I the Lord your God am a jealous God, visiting the iniquity of the fathers upon the children to the third and the fourth generation of those who hate me, but showing steadfast love to thousands of those who love me and keep my commandments.
3. You shall not take the name of the Lord your God in vain; for the Lord will not hold him guiltless who takes his name in vain.	3. You shall not take the name of the Lord your God in vain; for the Lord will not hold him guiltless who takes his name in vain.
4. Remember the sabbath day, to keep it holy. Six days you shall labour and do all your work; but the seventh day is a sabbath to the Lord our God; in it you shall not do any work, you or your son, or your daughter, your manservant, or your maidservant, or your cattle, or the sojourner who is within your gates; for in six days the Lord made heaven and earth, the sea, and all that is in them, and rested the seventh day; therefore the Lord blessed the sabbath day and hallowed it.	4. Observe the sabbath day, to keep it holy, as the Lord your God commanded you. Six days you shall labour and do all your work; but the seventh day is a sabbath to the Lord our God; in it you shall not do any work, you or your son, or your daughter, your manservant, or your maidservant, or your ox, or your ass, or your cattle, or the sojourner who is within your gates, that your manservant and your maidservant may rest as well as you. You shall remember that you were a servant in the land of Egypt, and the Lord your God brought you out thence with a mighty hand an outstretched arm; therefore the Lord your God commanded you to keep the sabbath day.
5. Honour your father and your mother, that your days may be long in the land which the Lord your God gives you.	5. Honour your father and your mother, as the Lord God commanded you; that your days may be prolonged, and that it may go well with you, in the land which the Lord your God gives you.
6. You shall not kill.	6. You shall not kill.
7. You shall not commit adultery.	7. Neither shall you commit adultery.
8. You shall not steal.	8. Neither shall you steal.
9. You shall not bear false witness against your neighbour.	9. Neither shall you bear false witness against your neighbour.
10. You shall not covet your neighbour's house; you shall not covet your neighbour's wife, or his manservant, or his maidservant, or his ox or his ass, or anything that is your neighbour's.	10. Neither shall you covet your neighbour's wife; and you shall not desire your neighbour's house, his field, or his manservant, or his maidservant, his ox, or his ass, or anything that is your neighbour's.

The Ten Commandments (also known as the Decalogue, Greek for 'ten words') appear twice in the Old Testament. In the book of Exodus they are given directly by God to Moses on Mount Sinai; in Deuteronomy they appear in Moses' report to the people Israel of God's speech 'to all your assembly at the mountain out of the midst of the fire'. Deuteronomy 5.22 states that the commandments were written upon two tables of stone.

There are slight variations in the two versions, most notably in the motivation for observing the sabbath: in the Exodus version this is God's rest after creation; in Deuteronomy it is the exodus from Egypt. In the last commandment, in Exodus the neighbour's wife is simply included in the list of the neighbour's possessions; in Deuteronomy she heads the list.

Church fathers

Augustine regarded the commandments against coveting one's neighbour's wife and his other possessions as two separate commandments and to keep the number ten combined the prohibitions against making other gods and against making false images. He was followed by Roman Catholics and Lutherans, so that there are two different Christian versions of the Ten Commandments

The date and original setting of the Ten Commandments have been much discussed. There is a general consensus that the collection is ancient, and came to be incorporated into the wider body of legal material in Exodus and Deuteronomy. The commandments are not comprehensive in their coverage: they are addressed to the male Israelite head of a household, one of a peer group of men who each had oxen and maidservants which the others might covet. Adultery is forbidden, presumably as an offence against the wronged husband, and because it would call into question the legitimacy of the children of his line; nothing is said of other sorts of extra-marital sex. These limitations are a clue to the origins of the collection, and it has been suggested that the Ten Commandments should be read as a codification of Israel's criminal (as opposed to civil) law.

There are surprisingly few references to the Ten Commandments in the Old Testament (Hosea 4.2 and Jeremiah 7.9 are possible allusions). Later Jewish tradition identifies 613 commandments in the Torah, all of which are regarded as equally significant, but the presentation of the ten in Exodus and Deuteronomy seems to preserve a memory of their special standing. The lawyer's question to Jesus, 'Which commandment is the first of all?' (Mark 12.28), may be an echo of a contemporary debate about whether it is right to give any commandment priority over others. If it was intended to categorize Jesus as an adherent of 'the ten' or 'the 613', he typically sidesteps the issue by naming neither, but rather Deuteronomy 6.4 and Leviticus 19.18. The continued Christian emphasis on the ten may then be an instance of the church's continuation of an Old Testament tradition that fell out of use in Judaism, or a specifically Christian recreation.

The Ten Commandments were compact enough to use in Christian worship, or to be set up in churches, and were much favoured by the Reformers. They were a familiar sight at the east end of English parish churches until the reorderings of the late nineteenth and twentieth century and were very well known to generations of Anglican worshippers through their mandatory use at the beginning of the Holy Communion service in the Book of Common Prayer. The Fourth Commandment especially has needed reinterpretation to make it workable in a contemporary Christian setting; this transfer of the sabbath commandment from Saturday to Sunday has sometimes been contested within Christianity. The Ten Commandments are little used in present-day Christian worship, although they maintain a hold on the Christian imagination, especially among Protestant Christians.

THE SERMON ON THE MOUNT

Through Christian history the Sermon on the Mount has been regarded as the quintessence of Jesus' teaching. It can be found in the Gospel of Matthew, chapters 5 to 7. Jesus goes up a mountain, sits down, and teaches his disciples; when he stops speaking the crowds are astonished at his teaching. The Sermon begins with the Beatitudes, 'Blessed are', and also contains the Lord's Prayer. Many of Jesus' most famous sayings are in it, including what are known as the 'antitheses', because of their form: e.g. 'You have heard that it was said ... but I say to you', along with the instruction not to be anxious about the morrow, but to look at the birds of the air and the lilies of the field, which God cares for. It ends with a series of warnings.

p. 659
p. 967

Scholars today do not think that the 'sermon' as given in Matthew's text was delivered by Jesus on one particular occasion: it was composed from sayings of Jesus by the evangelist Matthew, who in fact structures his Gospel with five sermons in all. Material contained in it appears in a different context in the Gospel of Luke.

Exalted teaching though the Sermon on the Mount is, it raises a number of difficult questions. To whom is it addressed? To the followers of Jesus or to a wider audience (it is said at the beginning to be for the disciples, but the crowds are also mentioned at the beginning and the end)? Is it meant to strengthen the teaching of the law or to do away with the teaching of Moses (both emphases can be found)? Is it meant to be taken literally throughout, or are some of the sayings exaggerations, of the kind to be found elsewhere in the teaching of Jesus? Is it dominated by the expectation of an imminent end of the world, so that its ethic is thought to apply only for a limited period?

All these questions are the subject of constant discussion. As so often with biblical texts, it is easier to talk about the Sermon on the Mount in general terms than to come to grips with precisely what it says.

W. D. Davies, *The Sermon on the Mount*, Cambridge: CUP and Nashville, TN: Abingdon Press 1966

the relationship between the eternal and temporal; the particular history and experience that form communities and individuals. Just as the questions of Christian ethics mutually inform each other, so too do the sources of Christian ethics.

Specific accounts of the Christian moral life differ in their use of sources and in the answers they give to the questions of Christian ethics. What matters is what sources they use and how comprehensive and consistent are the answers they give. Despite differences, historical and contemporary

Christian ethics share some common convictions about God, the moral good, moral responsibility and moral judgements.

Love of God and neighbour

Just how distinctive Christian faith and ethics are is a question that is central to Christian understandings of God in relationship to what is morally good. Does Christianity claim distinctive religious and moral 'truths' in contrast to others? In a sense it does, since Christianity is a particular, historical religion. For example, the truths of Christian faith and life conveyed in the various writings of scripture are not simply examples of some universal truths about God or some universal moral principles that have parallels in other religious and moral traditions. Instead, Christians claim that the story of scripture culminates in Jesus, who reveals and effects a new relationship with God that results in a new way of life.

Jesus

Christian life

How Jesus reveals and effects the moral life is variously understood, but it is always understood in the light of the New Testament Gospels which tell the story of Jesus' life, ministry and teachings as fulfilled in his death and resurrection, in his being raised into God. The character of this life is itself understood in terms of love, the love of God and the love of neighbour. As Jesus says in what is called the Great Commandment, 'You shall love the Lord your God with all your heart, and with all your soul, and with all your mind. This is the greatest and first commandment. And a second is like it: You shall love your neighbour as yourself. On these two commandments hang all the law and the prophets' (Matthew 22.37–40; Mark 12.30–1; Luke 10.27).

Resurrection

The integral relationship between the love of God and the love of neighbour may be understood by the central place of worship in the Ten Commandments. The Ten Commandments are the basic commandments that God gives to the Hebrew people. Christians accept these basic commands for their own lives as well. The first four commandments ground life in God. You shall have no other gods but me. You are not to make any graven images and worship them. You are not to take the name of God in vain. And you are to keep holy the sabbath. The last six commandments are moral commands. You are to honour your father and mother, murder no one, be faithful in marriage, and neither steal nor lie. These moral commandments indicate what is to be done in order to live in community in such a way that individual persons are honoured and respected. This requires an attitude that is not self-centred. This is stated in the last of the Ten Commandments: You shall not covet. At the centre the sabbath commandment emphasizes the need to set aside time to rest in God, to give thanks and praise, apart from any human attempt to achieve goodness or happiness.

The Ten Commandments thus express the basic Jewish and Christian conviction that the moral life is grounded in God. In the love of God the moral goods of life are rightly ordered. Misplaced or distorted love is the nature of sin and idolatry. The human problem is not simply or narrowly a matter of wrong actions (sins) but is a state of being (sin) in which relationship to God is lost or broken. Only in the knowledge of God's love is relationship with God restored and the works of love are enabled or empowered. Christians love because they are loved by God.

Sin

Love

In terms of action, for Christians the works or acts of love are closely tied to the care of the stranger, of those in need, and of the enemy, those who wish us harm. This is clear from the Sermon on the Mount. It is a reflection of the Exodus tradition of the Hebrew people, who had been strangers in need. The disparity between such teaching and the actual life of Christians is reflected in the earliest Christian writings in the New Testament, for example, Paul's first letter to the Christian community in Corinth. Nonetheless, Christian teachings express a larger vision in which all people are acknowledged, forgiven for the harm they have done, and cared for. This is reflected in the movement from the early church's development of a fund for the poor within the church, through the development of hospitals to care for the sick and dying both within and outside the church in the fourth century, to the contemporary articulation of claims of justice and basic human rights for all persons.

The universal thrust of Christian understandings of love begins in a community of faith that understands itself to be a new people, the people of God. That means that ethics always addresses not only the relationship of the Christian community to the world around it but also the relationships that form the Christian community as a distinct people.

Moral responsibility and Christian practices

In addition to questions about God in relationship to what is morally good, Christian ethics has addressed the question of moral responsibility, of how persons come to know and do what is good. For example, Roman Catholic thought as developed by Thomas Aquinas (1225–74) has understood the human person in terms of powers and capacities, specifically in terms of mind, will and body. These powers develop over time, depending on the choices we make. A person develops habits, either good or bad. The good person is a person of temperance, fortitude, prudence, and justice – what are called the cardinal virtues. However, the full development or perfection of the human person depends upon relationship with God. Given relationship with God through Jesus Christ, human powers are perfected in what are called the theological virtues of faith, hope and love.

Thomas Aquinas

p. 216

In contrast, beginning with Martin Luther (1483–1546) and John Calvin (1509–64), traditional Protestants have been suspicious of the Roman Catholic language of virtue because it seemed to them to over-emphasize human action in changing oneself and one's relationship with God. In contrast to what they called works of righteousness, they understood the human self to be caught between human strivings and the power of God's grace or what is called justification by grace. Humans are radically turned in upon themselves. They seek their own reward. In their failures they come to see the impossibility of fulfilment within the law of striving. Only in their emptiness do they experience the grace of God that turns them in love towards God and neighbour. The Christian moral life is, therefore, best understood in terms of law and gospel, judgement and grace, mortification and vivification, cross and resurrection. Faith, hope and love are not the perfection of human powers but simply divine gifts.

Justification

Grace

Roman Catholics, Protestants and other Christians have developed other accounts of moral agency. Contemporary accounts, for example, may draw upon evolutionary biology, sociology, and developmental psychology in understanding moral and faith development, including the differences between women and men. What is central to all accounts is to make sense of human responsibility in the light of understandings of how Christians are formed in relationship to God. This leads back to the practices that form Christians or at least leave them open to God's grace.

Education

The question of what practices are central to Christian faith and life is the question of 'ascetics', which is addressed in Christian thought in ascetical theology. While the word 'ascetic' means discipline, the word also has the connotation of self-denial. This is natural, as the word 'ascetic' initially referred to the discipline of preparing to compete in an athletic event. Through practice certain interests and capabilities are strengthened while others are weakened. This requires time, effort and the denial of some things for the sake of others.

Discipline

As reflected in the Ten Commandments, prayer and worship are practices of Christian faith integral to the Christian life. Prayerful reading of scripture is vital to Christian worship. In the light of the reading of scripture and its proclamation in the sermon, persons see the world and

Prayer

Worship

themselves differently. Together the reading of scripture, prayer and worship draw persons more fully into the love of God and neighbour.

Poverty

Besides engaging in what are called mental or religious exercises, Christians have physically disciplined their lives. Whether as solitary ascetics, members of monastic communities, or in the simplified life of the Christian in the world, they have seen that riches can ensnare the soul in the love of particular goods. This has lead to broad moral discussion and advice about poverty and wealth. Analogous to pacifism and the renunciation of lethal force, some have claimed that voluntary poverty is at least an ideal. To renounce worldly possessions and stand naked before God is to know that the blessing of life is beyond possessions, a matter of grace lived in love that embraces friend and stranger alike. Others have rejected voluntary poverty as irresponsible and called for using wealth to care for others and, more radically, to change society so that all may share in the basic goods of society.

Food and drink

Beyond such questions of what sabbath rest requires and what poverty entails, Christians have considered questions such as what occupations are consistent with Christian faith, what is the place of fasting and feasting, what is the need for daily prayer and devotions, how one's money is spent, how much of one's income should be given to church and charity, who needs to visit the sick and care for the poor and those in need, and how much time should be given to play and more generally to care for the self. These are questions of lifestyle or what some have called holiness of life. They highlight the basic fact that Christian ethics struggles to prescribe a way of life that is always, to varying degrees, counter-cultural.

Moral issues and judgements

Particular moral judgements are often debated and developed in different directions, but Christian ethics has nonetheless focused on a specific set of moral concerns. Given the central concern for what is required to be the people of God living a holy life and the particular claims to care for the stranger and those in need, Christian ethics has paid particular attention to questions about family and household, the sanctity of life, and justice in church and society.

Marriage
Paul

Jesus' own teaching called persons out of the household and yet also spoke of the holiness of marriage. As reflected in the churches founded by the apostle Paul, Christian faith and life begin in the household, and yet the household and the church as the household of God were not to be identified with the patriarchal order that dominated late antiquity. Instead there developed an understanding of the holiness of marriage given in the love between husband and wife and in the gift of children. Alternatively, celibacy and monastic communities offered alternative households as ways of forming a holy life. In contemporary Christian ethics many have sought to liberate sexual relations from what are viewed as the negative attitudes of the tradition towards sex and from the continuing patriarchal exercise of power and authority. For all, the family and households matter because they are the basic community in which persons live their lives.

Moral questions about the sanctity of human life are equally central to Christian ethics. Life is understood as a gift from God. The prohibition against murder extends to all persons. Abortion, infanticide and suicide are in general morally wrong. Ethical reflections have then focused on exceptions to this general stance and on such questions as when human life begins and what should be done and what need not be done to sustain and extend it. Such matters continue to be central to contemporary bioethics.

Perhaps the greatest divide among Christians has been whether the sanctity of life morally requires or prohibits that life itself should be taken in order to protect the innocent lives of others.

Jesus' renunciation of the use of force in his own life, culminating in his crucifixion, led some to believe that Christians should be pacifists and renounce the use of lethal force. However, others observe that early Christians also granted authority to the state and, by implication, to its use of lethal force in certain situations. The conflict between these views was heightened after Christianity became the established religion of the state. There are equally differences among Christians as to whether the death penalty should be imposed for grave crimes such as first-degree murder.

From the perspective of pacifism, to make Christian faith a requirement of citizenship is to create an unholy alliance that corrupts Christianity by making it a servant of the state. To accept the authority of the state is to rationalize and sanctify the taking of human life in defence of the state. Other Christians have believed that Christians have a duty to serve or support those who serve the state, such as police, magistrates, servants of the court and soldiers. In a fallen world it is necessary to protect the innocent and that includes, when all else fails, killing those who attack the innocent either by directly attacking individual persons or by attacking the government itself.

In *The City of God* Augustine of Hippo (354–430) offered the first full defence of the state and the Christian duty to support the state. For this perspective human beings live in two related but distinct cities: the human city and the city of God. The human city is not to be confused with the heavenly city, in which there is perfect freedom and the peace that is redemption. In a world torn by private interests, however, the human city is necessary in order to establish the basic order needed for society to survive, to protect innocent lives, and to enable true religion. Further, the establishment of Christianity as the religion of the state was understood to serve the mission of the church and to serve the state by instructing citizens and rulers about their obligations, including the limits of the power of the state. Central to such social teachings have been issues of justice, especially economic justice and the just use of force as developed in what is called just war theory.

Each age addresses its own distinctive moral challenges. The social injustice of slavery, industrialization and the unrestrained power in politics were primary concerns of the nineteenth and twentieth centuries expressed in such movements as the Social Gospel and Christian Socialism. Contemporary concerns for social justice have focused on the liberation, equality and self-determination of those who have been oppressed and marginalized by the dominant society – peoples of different races and cultures, women, the poor, gay and lesbian persons and disabled persons. This has led to the critique of traditional Christian ethics and the development of Christian ethics from the perspective of particular peoples. Broader concerns for social and political justice address the globalization of the world economy and with that the divide between the rich and the poor, the loss of indigenous cultures, the weakening of traditional ties of households and communities, the world arms trade and the increasing violence and genocide by governments and peoples, and the destruction of the natural environment.

pp. 1132, 1131

Differences and traditions in Christian ethics

Differences in answers given to the questions of Christian ethics – which is to say understandings of God in relationship to what is morally good, how one comes to know and is empowered to do the good, and what Christians should do – cannot be narrowly identified with different Christian traditions or churches. Differences are part of the ongoing conversation about the answers to the questions of Christian ethics in the light of particular situations and understandings of the sources that inform those answers. For example, monastics have a different set of moral concerns from those whose focus is on people who live and work in society. The monastic Rule of St Benedict has different concerns from Augustine's treatise *On Christian Marriage*. Other differences in moral

Monasticism

judgement arise over time because of new understandings and new challenges. Different answers to the question of when a human person's life begins depend in part on different understandings of human development. The answer to the question whether or not interest on loans to those in need is justified depends in part upon the kind of economy a society has, for example a barter economy where there is no capital investment versus a mercantile economy where money is invested at some risk in order to buy and sell goods at a profit.

Still, broad differences in the general conception of Christian faith and the moral life are reflected in the different ways in which the historical division of Christian churches into, e.g., Orthodox, Roman Catholic, Anabaptist, Protestant and Anglican have spoken about the purpose of the Christian life. The Orthodox, for example, speak of *theosis*, divinization, or more broadly of participation in the divine life. Anglicans share with the Orthodox the language of participation and with Roman Catholics the language of beatitude, of happiness and fulfilment in God, given in contemplation and the vision of God. In the Roman Catholic tradition Thomas Aquinas develops such understandings in more particular ways. Contemplation is to be understood as a kind of love and friendship with God. Protestant Reformers are more likely to speak of the sovereignty of God, the will of God, and the glory of God. Standing outside the state because they reject its use of lethal force, Anabaptists more narrowly focus on discipleship and following in the bloody trail of martyrs.

Anabaptists

Martyr

Contemporary Christian ethics is distinguished from its historical roots by being formed in the context of religious freedom. When Christianity was the established religion of the state – or in the case of the Anabaptists was formed in opposition to established religion – Christian faith was understood as necessarily social, as tied to what it means to be a people. In contrast, as Ernst Troeltsch described in *The Social Teaching of the Christian Churches* (1911), with religious freedom came the growth of a more individualistic type of Christianity. He called this type of Christianity mystical. The focus was on the indwelling spirit of God with little need for church organization or social teachings. The development of the 'mystical type' happened in all traditions. Whether the emphasis is on the more Protestant evangelical experience of conversion and new life or more traditional Catholic spiritual direction and mysticism, the focus of Christian faith is on matters of the spirit. At its extreme Christian ethics is narrowed to the spirituality of the individual.

Spirituality

In contrast to the 'mystical type', other contemporary Christian ethicists have claimed an integral relationship between Christian faith and the moral life. These responses have varied greatly, even while reflecting the different historical Christian traditions of Orthodoxy, Catholicism, Anabaptism, Protestantism and Anglicanism. Some have identified the work of God closely with social and political movements and so have spoken of the end of the Christian life in terms of such images as liberation and the kingdom of God. Others have emphasized the distinctiveness of Christian faith and the moral life while refusing close identification with any particular social and political movement.

Kingdom of God

Theories, casuistry and comparative ethics

Theories of ethics have sought to make sense of the differences within and between different kinds of ethics, past and present, in terms of claims about the essential nature of ethics. Theories of ethics have often focused on one of the central questions of ethics, particularly the nature of the good or the purpose of actions, virtues like the qualities and character of the moral person, or obligations, norms and principles. So, for example, ethics may be distinguished in terms of ethics of the good, virtue ethics, and ethics of obligation.

More broadly, a distinction is often made between teleological ethics and deontological ethics. This is sometimes expressed by contrasting 'the good' with 'the right'. Teleological ethics sees the moral life in terms of an end (Greek *telos*), which is good. Drawing on Aristotle, Roman Catholic ethics is in this sense generally teleological. In contrast to teleological ethics, deontological ethics (an ethics of duty, Greek *deon*, what is binding) sees the moral life in terms of obligations, of what is right. It focuses on what binds or calls us to act morally. Especially as developed in Protestant thought, morality rests upon the absolute binding character of the will of God or, as expressed by Immanuel Kant (1724–1804), in the universal moral law.

As an alternative to strict teleological and deontological theories, some contemporary theorists have sought to incorporate the claims of both in more comprehensive theories of responsibility. Developed by H. Richard Niebuhr in *The Responsible Self* (1963), theories of responsibility focus on the historical character of the human person. Stories tell of the relationship over time, in history, between the goods of life and some larger purpose or end. In this way stories provide a sense of the end of our lives as tied to goods and values that themselves carry their own obligation. The moral life is a matter of telling the story of our life in a way that makes sense of the obligations and the larger purpose and end of life as they mutually inform each other.

Story

Other theories of ethics have focused on the knowledge of the good or the right, what traditionally is spoken of as conscience. Some have claimed that moral knowledge is a kind of natural knowledge, a reading of moral duties or ends in the world about us. Christians have expressed this understanding in terms of belief in a natural law or a law of reason that all persons can grasp. Others have instead claimed that moral knowledge is a matter of intuition, whether by way of reason or emotions. At the extreme, some Christians have claimed that Christians know what to do only in their individual encounter with the living God.

Suspicious of the possibility of defending a common reading of nature or a moral intuition, yet others have sought the essential conditions of moral claims themselves. The moral is what is prescriptive and universal, applicable to all, in order to have human life. Murder and lying are, for example, universal moral principles. Finally, others have rejected any foundational claims for ethics. They claim that moral knowledge is always particular, known only in adopting a particular moral life. Such radically historical understandings of moral knowledge have most recently been the basis for claiming the distinctiveness of Christian ethics.

In the midst of the twentieth-century explosion of theories of ethics, there has also been a renewal of casuistry, especially in the area of bioethics but also in other areas such as just war theory and business ethics. Moral issues in a pluralistic society have led to this increased attention to specific moral cases. Differences in the foundations of ethics, including religious foundations, are initially put aside even while such foundations are acknowledged as central to people's particular moral judgements. Instead, cases are addressed in order to identify where there is consensus about what should be done or where there are simply outstanding differences. This has led Christians to identify the common moral convictions and judgements they share with others.

The renewal of casuistry has also contributed to comparative religious ethics. Through a systematic study of the ethics of different peoples, comparative religious ethics seeks to describe and compare the ethics of different peoples in order to further respect for the integrity of distinct peoples and to identify ways in which outstanding moral issues in a pluralistic, multicultural world might best be addressed. Through such studies Christians also may gain understanding of what may be distinctive about Christian ethics.

TIMOTHY F. SEDGWICK

James F. Childress and John Macquarrie (eds), *A New Dictionary of Christian Ethics*, London: SCM Press 1986 (US title: *The Westminster Dictionary of Christian Ethics*, Philadelphia: Westminster Press 1986); Robin Gill (ed), *The Cambridge Companion to Christian Ethics*, Cambridge: CUP 2001; James M. Gustafson, *Protestant and Roman Catholic Ethics*, Chicago: University of Chicago Press 1978; Stanley Hauerwas and Samuel Wells (eds), *The Blackwell Companion to Christian Ethics*, Oxford: Blackwell 2004; Albert R. Jonsen and Stephen Toulmin, *The Abuse of Casuistry: A History of Moral Reasoning*, Berkeley: University of California Press 1988; Robin W. Lovin, *Christian Ethics: An Essential Guide*, Nashville: Abingdon Press 2000; Wayne Meeks, *The Origins of Christian Morality*, New Haven: Yale University Press, 1993; H. Richard Niebuhr, *Christ and Culture*, San Francisco: Harper SanFrancisco 2001

Ethiopian Christianity

Monasticism

Most churches look to the life of Jesus as forming the historical period in time that brought their church into existence. While not disagreeing, Ethiopians date their origins a further millennium or so earlier, to the time of King Solomon. The Queen of Sheba, in the course of her visit to Solomon, entered into a relationship with the king and gave birth to his son, who was named Menelik. Menelik was brought up in the court of Solomon until in adult life he returned to Ethiopia, taking with him the Ark of the Covenant from the temple at Jerusalem. It found its way to Axum, and there it remains to this day, in the treasure house attached to the cathedral, guarded by a monk who never leaves it and ensuring that nobody else approaches it. On his death the monk appoints his successor. The coming of the Ark to Ethiopia is narrated in the *Kebra Negast*, or the Glory of the Kings, a book that in its present form is an Arabic writing from the thirteenth century.

This story brings out some of the themes that give the Ethiopian Orthodox Church a unique place in Christian history.

The Menelik story suggests a close relationship with Judaism. There have been strong trading links with Israel since the time of Solomon, when the existence of the port of Eilat, or Aila, is recorded in 2 Kings. We can assume continual traffic along the Red Sea, and a natural extension of first Jews and then Christians along the coasts into Arabia and Ethiopia. While the rest of the church decided not to follow the Old Testament law (Acts 15.4–11), Ethiopia has retained many Jewish customs and practices. The dietary laws of the Old Testament are observed; boys are circumcised, usually after eight days; Saturday, the sabbath, is kept holy as well as Sunday; and the ministry of the church includes the order of *debtera*, as well as bishop, priest and deacon. The order is modelled on the Levites of the Old Testament and leads the dancing in church. During the famine of 1984 the tribal group called the Falasha were identified as Jews and airlifted to Israel. These Jews followed some Christian practices, such as monasticism, and demonstrate a further dimension of cultural interaction between the two faiths. The languages of Christian Ethiopia, Ge'ez, the classical ecclesiastical language, and the modern Amharic and Tigrean, are Semitic.

Ministry and ministers

Positive relations have also generally been maintained with Muslims. The prophet Muhammad is said to have taken refuge in Ethiopia during war in Arabia. As the Arabs expanded, the Christian kingdom found itself surrounded by Muslim sultanates, but apart from a devastating invasion by Ahmed ibn Ibrahim al Ghazi, known as Gran or 'the left-handed', between 1518 and 1543, peaceful relations have generally prevailed. Today Muslims comprise around 40 per cent of the total population and are growing both in numbers and economic influence, which leads to anxiety on the part of many Christians.

Taken as a whole, the Ethiopian experience shows the common roots of the three great monotheistic faiths and the possibility of co-existence and even mutual influence.

Worship shows both Jewish and African influences. Churches are reputed to be modelled on the temple at Jerusalem, with a threefold design. Usually they are circular, following traditional architectural style, although some are of a rectangular basilica shape. At the heart of the church is the *tabot*, a plate that is laid on the altar and represents the Ark of the Covenant, and is used to impart holiness to the Temple. If the church is round, there is a central circular sanctuary, to which clergy only have access. Around this is a further circular space called the *qiddist*, where those who are going to receive communion stand; around that again is the *qene mahlet*, where the *debtera* sing and perform the slow stately liturgical dance called *aquaquam*. Most of the congregation, however,

Easter celebrations in Ethiopia

remains outside, hesitant to enter into a place of such awesome holiness. The design of the building shows the Jewish roots of the church, and the deep sense of holiness suggests an African sensitivity to the sacredness of place.

The church is deeply rooted in the life of the community. It is staffed by large numbers of priests, deacons and *debtera*, with over 100 clergy attached to a large church. The liturgy, or *qidasse*, is celebrated daily in many churches, with large numbers of people attending. The rhythm of the life of the community is set by the church's year. 250 days a year are appointed as fast days when no animal products can be eaten, and food can be taken only after midday. These are followed by the festivals, when there are processions, dancing and singing as well as worship: examples of these are the feast of the Exaltation of the Cross, or Mesqal, and, most impressive of all, Epiphany or Timqat, when the *tabots* of the churches are carried in procession to a stretch of water where water is blessed after a night of prayer.

Monasticism is strong, tracing its history to the Nine Syrian Saints who arrived in the late fifth century, founding monasteries in different parts of the country. The most famous of these monasteries are Debre Damo in Tigray, which can only be reached through being pulled to the top of a mountain by a rope, and Debre Libanos, north of Addis Ababa. There are over 800 of them, with many thousands of monks and nuns.

The centres of Ethiopian culture are reminders of the long history of the church. Axum in the north is the ancient capital. Here two young Syrian Christians from Tyre, Frumentius and Aedesius, were brought after their boat was shipwrecked. They grew up in the court of the king, Ezana, and some time after 340 Frumentius was consecrated as first bishop for the Ethiopians by Athanasius of Alexandria. The relationship with the Coptic (Egyptian) Church has continued, so that the Ethiopians are often but misleadingly referred to as Coptic. The church is therefore included as one of the five non-Chalcedonian Orthodox churches. Along with those of Egypt, Armenia, Syria and South India it has rejected the understanding of Christ's

Coptic Christianity
Orthodox churches

nature set out at the Council of Chalcedon (451) and has instead affirmed the single nature of Christ. The tradition that the Coptic Patriarch sends a single archbishop to Ethiopia continued until 1929 when four Ethiopians were consecrated to assist the Coptic archbishop, and then in 1959 Patriarch Basilios became the first Ethiopian to lead the church. Thus through most of its history this large church had a single foreign archbishop. Today relations have been strained after the Coptic Pope established a separate hierarchy of bishops for the newly-independent Eritrea, leading to the establishment of a separate church.

From Axum the capital moved to Roha, which was renamed Lalibela after the great king of the early twelfth century. Lalibela constructed his capital as a new Jerusalem and built twelve carved monolithic churches, which remain the most celebrated architectural site of the country. These churches are carved from rock and so are all below ground level, surrounded by courtyards and connected by tunnels. Rock churches are also found in other parts of the country (see page 7), especially in Tigray in the north.

During the seventeenth century Gondar became the capital. In this period a rich tradition of learning and scholarship developed, and has been passed to succeeding generations using mainly oral teaching methods. Boys are taught to read and can continue to learn, travelling from teacher to teacher begging for their livelihood, and absorbing language, liturgy, theological tradition, poetry (called *qene*), music and dancing. A respected teacher will probably have studied for over 30 years. This enduring tradition has preserved a rich and vibrant Ethiopic culture of which the Orthodox Church has been the custodian.

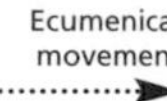

Today the church administration is found in Addis Ababa, which became the capital in 1887. The church has survived the fall of the empire in 1974 and the murder of Haile Selassie in 1975, and a period of brutal communist rule which confiscated the huge landed wealth of the church, but which failed to eradicate its roots in the loyalty and commitment of local people. If anything, it affirmed them.

While the distance of the Ethiopian Orthodox Tawehedo Church, to give it its full title, from the centres of Christianity has caused it to be isolated, it is important in world Christianity for several reasons. It is large, with a membership of over 30 million, and, since church-going is still strong, it is probable that it is the largest of the national Orthodox churches in terms of regular Sunday church attendance. It is an indigenous African church and so exercises an appeal in the Caribbean and among black Christians, and Rastafarians also look towards Ethiopia. While modern Western missionaries and an economically powerful Islam are making some inroads into its traditional influence, it remains the church of about half of Ethiopia, and is active in the ecumenical movement, gaining the respect of many throughout the world.

Various other churches have been growing over the last

RASTAFARIANISM

Rastafarianism is a religious movement which officially began in Jamaica in 1930. It started in the slums, but spread to the middle class and from Jamaica all over the world. Rastas, as its members are called, are now estimated to number around 700,000. The movement takes its name from Ras (Prince) Tafari, the name of a former emperor of Ethiopia, Haile Selassie I (1892–1975), before his coronation, and considered divine, and the Messiah. Rastas believe that black people are a reincarnation of the ancient people of Israel, who once lived in Ethiopia. They were expelled from there to Jamaica because of sins against their God, but they will be redeemed and return to Africa, where they will exercise lordship over white people. They see Ethiopia as a heaven on earth.

A key figure in the formation of Rastafarianism is Marcus Garvey (1887–1940), a black Jamaican who encouraged black people to unite and establish a nation of their own in Africa, leading a 'Back to Africa' movement. His place is second only to that of Haile Selassie. However, neither Haile Selassie himself, who was a devout Christian, nor Marcus Garvey, were actually involved with the Rastafarians. This did not, though, prevent scenes of mass hysteria when Haile Selassie came to Jamaica in 1966. April 21, the date of his visit, has become a Rastafarian holy day.

Because the beliefs and practices of Rastas have not been systematized, it is difficult to give a clear account of them. However, hostility towards white people and a sense of the superiority of black people were prominent from the start. Rastas claim that white missionaries and preachers disguised the fact that Adam and Jesus were black; this mistrust also extends to the Bible, which they interpret selectively: they see Jesus as having predicted the coming of Haile Selassie. They see Jamaica as Babylon, a place of oppression to which they have been exiled. A distinctive belief is 'I and I', a way of describing the oneness of two persons: God in human beings.

Rastas observe a biblical injunction not to cut the hair, hence their distinctive hairstyle (dreadlocks). Women have at best a subordinate role. Vegetarianism is widely practised. Their rituals include the use of *ganja* (marijuana) as a holy herb mentioned in the Bible, the singing of revivalist hymns and reggae music. The most famous Rasta is the reggae singer Bob Marley (1945–81).

Leonard E. Barrett, Sr, *The Rastafarians*, Boston: Beacon Press 1997 century, with some estimates suggesting that up to 10 per cent of Christians, perhaps more than 5 million, belong to one of the various Protestant churches. These include both the relatively well-established Mekane Yesus (Abode of Jesus) Evangelical Church and newer Pentecostalist groups. The Mekane Yesus Church is in fact probably the fastest-growing Lutheran church in the world.

JOHN BINNS

A. Atiya, *A History of Eastern Christianity*, Notre Dame, IN: University of Notre Dame Press 1968; C. Chaillot, *The Ethiopian Orthodox Tawehedo Church Tradition*, Paris: Inter-Orthodox Dialogue 2002; W. Ullendorff, *Ethiopia and the Bible*, London: OUP 1968

Eucharist

Christian faith is primarily embodied in a common meal, called the eucharist, which means simply 'giving thanks'. It can be claimed that the eucharist is the action which most fully embodies the many dimensions of Christian faith. It is a sacred meal because it is an encounter with the Holy One; it is nevertheless food, a human meal. It is important to begin here because, as we shall see later, the meal aspect of the eucharist eventually came to be minimized under the impact of a very different concept of the holy: material things were, because of their physical nature, seen to be too ordinary to embody a spiritual reality. In a religion whose central claim is that God has come into the world in the life of a fully human person, Jesus Christ, it is strange that such a denigration of the ordinary should have occurred.

A human meal is far more than merely the ingestion of food. Animals ingest food for the nourishment of their bodies, and it is certainly possible for a human being to ingest food merely as a response to physical hunger. But a meal in human experience embodies more than physical nourishment, important as that is. A meal is a social event. A meal is where we share a basic human activity (the nourishment of our bodies) in a context of conversation, of friendship and of love. In this context, the nourishment symbolizes the nourishment of our full humanity on the foundation of our fundamental human need to sustain our physical bodies in life. The meaning of the eucharist must not be separated from this claim about the significance of a meal for human beings. A meal eaten alone is void of this larger signification of the interrelatedness and the interdependence of our lives. A meal shared in the context of friendship and love teaches us, through our appetites and senses, that none of us live only for ourselves. A meal embodies our participation in the human family. In the eucharist we find a fundamental expression of the Christian understanding of sacrament: an outward sign of the invisible working of God's grace. Thus the eucharist is the spiritual food that Jesus gave to his disciples at a final supper as at their many meals together, but it is also a meal in which Christians receive and experience that spiritual food through the ordinary physical realities of bread and wine.

Sacraments

Today, if you were to tour various Christian churches, the liturgical rituals themselves, as now commonly celebrated, would largely seem to contradict this basic assertion. Although you would find many celebrations of the eucharist in a variety of styles that reflect the wide range of Christian traditions, the meal aspect of the service would probably be minimal. Eating and drinking and interaction would more often be experienced in the social event of a coffee hour or other gathering after the service; that separation itself is the consequence of the distinction between the sacred eating and drinking which take place during the liturgical rite and the ordinary eating and drinking and social exchange which take place at the coffee hour.

As for the eucharistic rituals themselves, you would see a great deal of variation from one congregation to another. In some places the rite would be austere, with little ritual action, little or no music, and a heavy emphasis upon the verbal aspect of the service, especially the sermon. But you might also visit a community in which the ritual is extremely elaborate, one which might be associated with historical films where kings and bishops are robed in splendid garments and live in a world that seems very different from our own.

Holy

There could also be countless variations between these two styles. Such variations might include a strong ethnic element that would be reflected in the musical and cultural elements of a liturgy; ethnic differences might also include the use of various languages, some currently spoken and others that are ancient ritual languages preserved only in public worship. There would also be differences in terms of leadership. In some rites, one minister might fulfil a clearly dominant role as the person who has the authority to perform the sacred action, while other participants are understood to take secondary or seemingly inferior roles. But you might also find assemblies in which there is a sharing of roles, suggesting that there are different and complementary gifts of leadership, and in which the full participation of the entire assembly in the liturgical action is the presumed norm, in fact, essential.

Food and drink

It would be impossible to summarize the extraordinary diversity that now exists among the different Christian traditions with regard to the ways in which the eucharist is celebrated. Yet this rich mosaic of ritual practices takes its origin from a meal (in reality, many meals) which Jesus shared with his followers. How is it that such diversity was

EUCHARIST

'Was ever another command so obeyed? For century after century, spreading slowly to every continent and country and among every race on earth, this action has been done, in every conceivable human circumstance, for every conceivable human need from infancy and before it to extreme old age and after it, from the pinnacles of earthly greatness to the refuge of fugitives in the caves and dens of the earth. Men have found no better thing than this to do for kings at their crowning and for criminals going to the scaffold; for armies in triumph or for a bride and bridegroom in a little country church; for the proclamation of a dogma or for a good crop of wheat; for the wisdom of the Parliament of a mighty nation or for a sick old woman afraid to die; for a schoolboy sitting an examination or for Columbus setting out to discover America; for the famine of whole provinces or for the soul of a dead lover; in thankfulness because my father did not die of pneumonia; for a village headman much tempted to return to fetish because the yams had failed; because the Turk was at the gates of Vienna; for the repentance of Margaret; for the settlement of a strike; for a son for a barren woman; for Captain so-and-so, wounded and prisoner of war; while the lions roared in the nearby amphitheatre; on the beach at Dunkirk; while the hiss of scythes in the thick June grass came faintly through the windows of the church; tremulously, by an old monk on the fiftieth anniversary of his vows; furtively, by an exiled bishop who had hewn timber all day in a prison camp near Murmansk; gorgeously, for the canonization of St Joan of Arc – one could fill many pages with the reasons why men have done this, and not tell a hundredth part of them. And best of all, week by week and month by month, on a hundred thousand successive Sundays, faithfully, unfailingly, across all the parishes of Christendom, the pastors have done this just to make the *plebs sancta Dei* – the holy common people of God.'

Dom Gregory Dix, *The Shape of the Liturgy*, London: Dacre Press 1945, p. 744

generated from within what was simply the pattern of Jewish table fellowship 2000 years ago?

To begin to understand this, we must consider what can be known of the table fellowship of Jesus and his disciples. The image that comes most frequently to mind, even for people who have never actually attended a celebration of the eucharist, would probably be a depiction of what is usually called the Last Supper (as seen, say, in the famous painting of that name by Leonardo da Vinci). There are, of course, countless paintings of this subject by many artists from many nations. These depictions vary, often extensively, in detail, and are more likely to reflect the culture in which the artist lived and worked than to be a historical depiction of the society in which Jesus lived.

Jesus

Painting

p. 1152

In such paintings, even the food on the table may vary in ways that reflect the local culture at the time the painting was made. There is, for example, a painting of the Last Supper from the sixteenth century by a German artist in which there is a roasted pig on the table, certainly a reflection of German eating habits rather than of any Jewish supper in the first century. In other words, such paintings over the centuries take the biblical event of the last supper of Jesus with his disciples and use it as a point of departure for situating the event in their own time and culture. This offers us, in fact, an important insight into the understanding of the eucharist itself as grounded in that final supper of Jesus with his disciples, yet continuing to be a living and present reality which believers of every generation are invited to share in the context of their own real world.

If artistic depictions of the last supper inevitably employ the cultural realities of the artist, the descriptions of the supper which we find in the New Testament put us more closely in touch with table fellowship at the time of Jesus. Nevertheless, New Testament accounts do not tell us all that we want to know. For example, scholars have long debated whether that final meal was or was not the Passover meal. It is generally accepted that even if it was not itself the Passover meal with its specific ritual pattern, it was nevertheless a meal shared on the eve of the Passover and thus imbued with much of its meaning – a celebration of God's mighty work in delivering the Jewish people from slavery in Egypt.

What is evident in the last supper narratives is that the unusual words of Jesus at his blessing of the bread and wine took place in the context of a meal, albeit a religious meal. Perhaps it was the kind of fellowship meal that Jesus had shared many times with his followers. In addition to the New Testament references to these intimate meals, there are also the narratives about the feeding of very large gatherings of people who had come to hear Jesus preach or to see him heal. In these texts the vocabulary is quite similar to that of the last supper narratives, when Jesus 'took the bread and broke it'.

In other words, there is not simply one meal that is the source for the Christian eucharist, but rather many meals, many occasions on which Jesus shared food and drink either with his disciples, or with larger groups of followers, or with a multitude of people. All of these events contribute to the church's understanding of the eucharist. And we must also note, as a hinge point between such meals that took place prior to the death of Jesus and meals at which he was seen after his resurrection, the extraordinary event that is described in the immediate wake of the crucifixion. The Gospel of Luke (24.13–35) tells how the disciples presumed that Jesus was dead and buried and that all their hope in him as the saviour of his people had come to nothing. Yet on the road to the town of Emmaus, a stranger joined two of the disciples who were fleeing Jerusalem in despair. When the stranger remained with them for supper, they recognized that it was Jesus himself, risen from the dead, who was known to them now in the breaking of the bread.

It is this last event that leads directly to the Christian eucharist. It is at Emmaus, and in later reflection upon that experience in the lives of the disciples, that we see the beginning of a memorial meal in which the disciples would continue to encounter the risen Lord from that time onward. Sharing of the bread and wine at the eucharist became a kind of cumulative experience in which the whole reality of table fellowship with the Lord and his abiding presence came into focus in the holy meal.

If the basic meaning of the eucharist is so clearly that of a sacred meal, how did it come about that its original context, an ordinary gathering of devout Jews around a table to eat and drink together as an expression of their common life, gradually disappeared? As we saw earlier, the separation of the eucharistic blessings of the bread and wine were eventually seen to pertain so clearly to the realm of the sacred (as distinguished from the ordinary) that all associations with a common meal were excluded from the eucharistic rite. But this was not the original reason for the separation of the blessings from the context of a meal.

It is important to remember that during the first three centuries after the life of Jesus, his followers were subjected to persecution, often, ironically, because they were considered to be atheists who would not offer homage to the gods officially recognized by the Roman state. During such periods of persecution, it would have been difficult for Christians to gather without arousing suspicion, especially when their gathering would involve the social event of a common meal. From the beginning of the second century CE there is documentary evidence that Christian assemblies were taking place and were being noticed by Roman government officials. To avoid such easy recognition, the blessings of the bread and wine were separated from the context of a meal and were attached to the reading of scripture that the Christian community had adapted from the Jewish synagogue service. If we remember that the earliest Christian community was made up of Jews, then this use of a Jewish model of liturgical prayer seems a perfectly normal development, since the Jewish followers of Jesus understood their faith as the fulfilment of their messianic expectation. In other words, they continued to worship as Jews, but their forms of prayer were transformed by the impact of their faith in Jesus. It is quite appropriate to think of the early Christian community as a sect of Judaism that was defined by its proclamation of Jesus as the awaited Messiah, as distinct from other Jewish groups who could not accept that claim. Thus its forms of worship were developed from within the Jewish liturgical context and not as those of a separate religious community.

Resurrection ◄

Messiah

This simple form of worship was the blessing of bread and wine that were then shared in communion even in times of persecution, often under cover of darkness in the early hours of the morning. In this way, during difficult times, Christians could more easily avoid detection. This basic pattern, with various elaborations as the ritual developed in new contexts, has continued as the fundamental pattern of the eucharist up until the present day. In spite of wide diversity in ethos and style, this basic shape of the eucharistic rite has been the primary form of the church's prayer throughout two millennia.

The separation of the eucharistic blessings from the context of a meal, however necessary it may have seemed in times of persecution, shifted the understanding of the eucharist in the life of the church. This development gradually transformed the meaning of the eucharist in dramatic ways. The inevitability of such a shift is perhaps not immediately obvious. If we reflect on the ordinary character of a meal as a mode of human social interaction, the reason becomes more evident. In the context of a meal, no matter how formal, there is always the give-and-take of conversation and exchange among persons gathered at the table. For the early Christians, this context shaped the social interaction among members of the community. Once the meal was removed, the blessings of the bread and wine attracted an intensity of focus, since they now stood in bold relief within the eucharistic prayer. Although no more sacred or solemn in themselves than they were in the meal context, when standing alone the two blessings gained a dramatic emphasis which became embodied within a ritual texture.

Persecution ◄

This was to be emphasized all the more in the fourth century, when the celebration of the ritual shifted from an intimate space to the grandeur of a public basilica. This process was, of course, gradual. Christians could not have anticipated the effects that would result from the liberation of the church by the Emperor Constantine early in the fourth century. With recent memories of persecution and martyrdom, Christians could not be certain that the emperor's favour would continue. In that regard, we may say that the full realization of their liberation unfolded in a century-long process, by the end of which we see the emergence of Christendom as an alliance of church and state which has continued, with various mutations, into our own time.

Constantine's 'conversion'

Martyr

In alliance with the Roman state, the church began to grow dramatically in numbers. This came about not only because of the end of the persecutions, but also because of increasing favour shown to the church by the emperors. Gradually, models of authority and leadership in the church were based upon those of the secular government. With regard to the office of a bishop, for example, what had been seen essentially as a ministry of pastoral oversight and care of God's people as the primary teacher and preacher of the community, became an office understood more in terms of authority and power. This shift was visually embodied in the replacement of the bishop's chair by a throne and other ritual trappings associated with imperial authority. The impact of this new situation upon the eucharist was enormous.

Ministry and ministers

Creed

During times of persecution, Christians had often been obliged to meet for their secret gatherings in the homes of the wealthiest members. With the liberation of the church and the influx of new members, it was imperative to find yet larger spaces for worship. Through the patronage of the Emperor Constantine, large basilicas (more or less the equivalent of a modern town hall) were adapted from secular to liturgical use by the church. Eventually the church's need for large spaces for assembly led to the construction of basilicas intended only for the use of the Christian community in its worship. Again, the construction of such buildings was possible only through the patronage of the royal family or people of great wealth.

Buildings

These large buildings greatly influenced the general understanding of the liturgical action and the way the roles of liturgical leadership were embodied. The new situation contrasted radically with the earlier gatherings in private homes. The placing of traditional rituals in this new context also required ritual changes; for these, the church simply adopted the models already associated with, for example, the entrance of public officials into these buildings. This was, in fact, a common-sense decision dictated by the demands of the much larger space in which Christian worship was to take place.

Another consequence of this new situation was the beginning of a separation between liturgical leaders and the general assembly of the people at the eucharist. This, too, was dictated by the shift to a larger building. If a person was to be seen as the liturgical leader, then a more defined and elevated space was required for the chair from which the person would preside and for the altar from which the sacred blessings would be proclaimed. Again, this model was already present in the assemblies that had taken place in the secular basilicas where matters of public business had been presented to the people. The basilica architecture virtually obliged the church to come to understand liturgical leadership in this way, and initiated a transformation in the way the actions of the president were understood.

The most notable impact of this new situation upon the role of the president at the eucharist is in the extraordinary elaboration of the prayer proclaimed by the president for consecrating bread and wine. Early texts indicate that such prayers had originally been comparatively brief and to some degree spontaneous. They might include a thanksgiving to God, a reference to the institution of the eucharist by Jesus at the last supper, and a plea for the Holy Spirit to act by consecrating the gifts and the people as they shared them in communion. In fact, a eucharistic prayer from the early third century is similar in structure to the statement of faith (creed) which candidates professed at their baptism. This suggests that the proclamation of the eucharistic prayer by the president serves as a kind of credal frame for the consecration of the bread and wine.

From the fourth century onwards, however, the eucharistic prayer (sometimes called the anaphora, after the Greek for 'offering') became greatly lengthened and was adapted to the rhetorical style of secular public declamation. It was specifically when the community began to worship in large public buildings and as the clergy became separated from the assembly into the sacred area around the altar that the president assumed verbal dominance that eclipsed the other liturgical ministers.

During this same period, the participation of the laity became less significant within the eucharistic rite itself. The sense of the eucharist being a shared action under the leadership of the chief pastor gave way to something more like a performance in which the ordained fulfilled all the significant roles. This diminution of the role of the laity also affected the norm that the participation of the laity involved not merely attendance but also communion, i.e. receiving the consecrated bread and wine. During the first three centuries of Christianity, this was the culmination of the eucharist: communion fulfilled the purpose of the eucharistic blessings not merely for the clergy but for the entire assembly. The bread and wine were consecrated for the communion of the whole assembly as a sign of their unity in Christ.

By the late fourth century, however, we find sermons in which the preacher laments that even the newly baptized are not coming to communion. The explanation given is that it is the awareness of sin that keeps people from communion, but that they should repent and come to receive the sacred gifts. It is clear that communion is still understood as normative at that time, even as we learn that laity are in practice beginning to refrain from regular communion.

As the church expanded into northern Europe, and as the acceptance of Christian faith was often linked to the adherence of the local king or ruler, the old adage that 'the faith of the king is the faith of the people' led to the baptism of large numbers of people. These newly baptized were initiated into the church without the benefit of the training that had been the norm during the early centuries. Poor preparation for baptism thus led to the further separation between clergy and laity. It must be admitted, however, that at this time, the education of the clergy was only slightly better than that of the laity.

In this context, clergy did not encourage communion, but rather fostered a piety in which looking at the consecrated bread became a substitute for communion. This so-called 'piety of vision' refers to the common emphasis that the laity, who were accustomed to receiving the eucharistic bread and wine very infrequently, could receive God's grace simply by looking upon the sacred elements. Christians of the early centuries would have found this unimaginable. This attitude, however, held sway for several centuries during which laity participated in the eucharistic liturgy through attendance and eventually through the formalized piety of vision. This was embodied in a liturgical novelty where the bread and wine were lifted up for the people to adore at the time of the recitation of the words of Jesus, 'this is my body; this is my blood' (referred to as the 'elevation'). The communion of the laity had declined so dramatically that at a council in 1215 (Lateran IV), the bishops decreed that the laity must communicate once a year, at Easter.

Another effect of these developments was a significant change in attitude regarding the church's understanding of itself. In the first centuries of Christianity, the primary image of the church was that of 'the body of Christ'. In other words, this phrase was essentially a reference to the whole community of God's people. 'The body of Christ' referred to all the baptized members of the church. The consecrated bread and wine that were received in communion served as a kind of mirror to the community of its identity, and were thus referred to as 'the body and blood of Christ' derivatively.

The presence of Christ was essentially identified with the community of faith. This view is supported by the practice of referring to a newly-baptized Christian as 'another Christ', so profound was the identification of Christ with the members of his body. The eucharistic elements were understood to be instruments of the presence of Christ because he had declared them to be his body and his blood. They were the food which nourished that presence in the eucharistic community itself. This teaching was powerfully expressed by Augustine in a sermon (no. 227) that he preached to his people in North Africa. He said: 'You are the bread on the altar. Be what you see. Receive who you are.'

By the end of the first millennium, however, the distinction of the consecrated bread and wine from any hint of connection to ordinary food and drink was complete. The presence of Christ was no longer identified with the church as his body but rather with the sacred elements.

What had once been a sacramental mirror to the community had now become the entire focus of Christ's presence. The phrase 'the body of Christ' had come to refer uniquely to the sacred elements. A theory was developed to explain this understanding of eucharistic presence that was known as transubstantiation. This theory asserted that, once consecrated through the repetition of the words of Christ, which were viewed as the consecratory part of the eucharistic prayer, the bread and wine no longer existed; they were, in effect, annihilated. The total otherness of the consecrated bread and wine was now complete; the separation of the blessings from the context of an ordinary meal had come to its logical extreme, but at the cost of the early church's understanding of a sacrament.

p. 1068

Devotions

What had developed was a kind of sacramental literalism that viewed the consecrated bread and wine with such awe that consuming them – the purpose for which Jesus had instituted them at that final supper – had ceased to be the custom for the vast majority of Christians. The consecrated bread and wine were accorded such awesome reverence that they came to be treated as a sacred talisman, as objects which imparted blessing outside the common sense of their nature as spiritual food and drink. In effect, their symbolic meaning, what they signify as the living memorial of Christ's death and resurrection, had moved into a by-path that eroded the basic sacramental sense. The true holiness of the consecrated gifts of bread and wine is found in the very fact that these were the ordinary food and drink of the table, and that Jesus had embraced common food as the means by which his followers would be sustained in faith for generations to come.

Council

Church

Although it would be unrealistic today to suggest that every celebration of the eucharist should take place in the context of a meal, it should be evident at this point that an awareness of the grounding of those blessings in eating and drinking offers a fundamental insight into the meaning of the eucharist: it is the spiritual food of Christian faith because it is, first of all, food, something which human beings require if they are to live.

Community
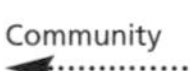

The relation of the eucharist to ordinary food also reveals what we might call 'the prophetic dimension' of the eucharist. When the meaning of the sacred elements, even out of reverence, is limited, history reveals that it is possible to ignore the implications of the eucharist with regard to the hunger of the world. The very fact that the sacred elements are the food and drink necessary to life implies that for Christians there is an inescapable link between their eucharistic significance and the appalling reality of starvation around our world. Here the signifi-

Communion, Holy Trinity Cathedral, Accra, Ghana

cance of the eucharist obliges a person of faith to look beyond ritual and into the world where that ritual is celebrated.

The Passover meal, from which the last supper of Jesus with his disciples drew much of its meaning, was a meal of liberation. For Jews, the Passover was the celebration of God's mighty work in bringing their people from slavery into freedom. The eucharist sends Christians out into the world, each to be 'another Christ' in service to the world that Christ redeemed. One of the most radical claims of the gospel is that Jesus identified himself with the most needy, the sick, those in prison, those without food, and taught that whoever reaches out to meet those needs is in fact serving him. A eucharistic piety which is grounded in the reality of the world always sends believers into that world as instruments of Christ's presence.

The twentieth century saw the beginning of a significant renewal in the church's understanding of the eucharist. This was fostered by the recovery of an understanding of the church grounded in the baptismal identity that all Christians share, which affirms a unity of the church that transcends denominational barriers based upon hierarchical differences. Although the ecumenical movement has not brought about the visible unity of Christians as quickly as many once hoped, it has led to dialogue and also to sacramental sharing. Increasingly, Christians of one tradition are receiving the eucharistic gifts at liturgies of another tradition; this has become a sign of deepening reconciliation among communities. Such sharing would indicate that a more common theology of the sacraments, particularly the eucharist, is emerging. In addition, the church is reclaiming the baptismal imperative that the eucharist be a sign of the unity of Christ's body.

Ecumenical movement

LOUIS WEIL

Gerard Austin, OP (et al.), *Eucharist. Toward the Third Millennium*, Chicago: Liturgy Training Publications 1997; William R. Crockett, *Eucharist: Symbol of Transformation*, New York: Pueblo Publishing Co. 1989; Nathan Mitchell, *Cult and Controversy: The Worship of the Eucharist Outside Mass*, New York: Pueblo Publishing Co. 1982 and *Eucharist as Sacrament of Initiation*, Chicago: Liturgy Training Publications 1994; R. Kevin Seasoltz, *Living Bread, Saving Cup*, Collegeville, MN: The Liturgical Press 1982

Europe, Christianity in

Introduction

The European continent is not a region of the world in which Christianity today seems to be at its most alive and dynamic. But it is certainly the most original and atypical region. Whereas everywhere else religious practice is developing, Europe seems to be a strange enclave: its religious heritage is extraordinarily rich, but religious practice is in continual decline.

And yet here, as elsewhere, Christianity continues to be a strong influence on culture, mentalities and customs, at the same time nourishing the faith of numerous people, parishes and communities.

A 1990 survey on the values of (Western) Europeans indicated a quite widespread situation: those who share Christian faith are far more numerous than those who go to church. Sociologists call this 'believing without belonging'.

Whereas 70% of Europeans believe in God, only 29% go to church at least once a week. 40% never go to church; 5% go once a year; 8% go at Christmas, Easter, etc., and 10% go once a month. But 61% believe in the existence of the soul, 43% in a life after death, 53% in sin and 33% in the resurrection of the dead. More recent surveys seem to indicate a slight increase in belief among the youngest age groups.

However, differences are hidden underneath the similarities. The Roman Catholic countries of the south are more religious than the Protestant countries of the north. In the Republic of Ireland, which has a large Catholic majority, church-going is very high, as it is in Poland. In France, a country the vast majority of whose population is Roman Catholic, church-going is very low, a fact explained no doubt by its history.

We can distinguish three major spheres of Christian influence in Europe: a Roman Catholic zone in the west, the south and the centre; a Protestant (and Anglican) zone in the north; and an Orthodox zone in the east. Throughout the continent the Christian population is made up of close to 50% Catholics, 25% Orthodox and 25% Protestant. All in all, Christians form more than 75% of the whole population. Refining this further, we can distinguish five major types of Christian affiliation: the Roman Catholic countries (Poland, Italy, Spain and the Republic of Ireland); the Anglican and Protestant countries (Great Britain and the Scandinavian countries); the mixed zones (Germany and Switzerland); an Orthodox area (from Russia to Greece, through the Ukraine, Romania and Serbia); and a secular region (France, Belgium, the Netherlands, perhaps England and the Czech Republic) in which those who do not claim to belong to any religion form between 50% and 60% of the population.

The traditional or 'historic' churches are tending to see their membership diminish in favour of the younger evangelical, Pentecostal or charismatic churches. A large number of people find a living faith in a warm and deeply emotional community atmosphere. Traditional Roman Catholicism and Protestantism, which centre more on formal worship or reflection – are trying to combine these with and appeal to feeling. Orthodoxy, now for more than ten years freed from the yoke of Communism, is centred on the beauty of its worship, which has always been able to touch the whole of the human being.

Pentecostalism
Roman Catholic Church
Protestantism
Orthodox churches

Choose almost any city or region on the continent, between Lisbon and Moscow. Take time to go for a walk and you will be at the beginning of a extraordinary journey across the centuries. You will discover the wonders that religion has contributed to a prodigious cultural wealth, at a great depth: architecture, sculpture, painting, music and song, literature, poetry, philosophy, proverbs and popular wisdom, customs and traditions, extending as far as dress and food and even relating to ways of living and relating and to social patterns.

There are good reasons for speaking of a 'European social model', a subtle mixture of individualism and collective solidarity, in interaction with other currents of thought and conviction. Here mention should be made of the predominant role of the Renaissance, the Enlightenment and non-religious humanism, often in conflict with religion in its efforts to establish the freedom of the sciences and the arts, democracy, human rights and the pre-eminence of law.

Renaissance
Enlightenment
Humanism

That has led to the autonomy of the political and religious domains and to a more or less forced 'privatization' of religion. This private character of religion is probably not to be found anywhere else in the world. Nevertheless, the cultural role of the religions has not diminished even now.

Among the religions, Christianity – Roman Catholic, Orthodox, Protestant, Anglican – has by far the strongest presence. But despite its history of 2000 years, it is not the earliest, since it was preceded by Judaism, not to mention religions – Greek and Roman, Celtic and Germanic – which have disappeared. Islam came later, but for centuries put its stamp on European civilization, above all in Spain and south-east Europe. It is also the religion of 98% of the population of Turkey, a member country of the Council of Europe (whose headquarters are in Strasbourg, France) and a candidate for entry into the European Union.

Anglicanism

Of course the cities or regions of Europe by no means bear the same kind of witness to the influence of religion on this civilization. Sometimes it is above all the wealth of a particular tradition that proves impressive. That is the case in the regions where such a tradition predominates strongly: Orthodoxy in many of the countries of Central and Eastern Europe and in Greece; Roman Catholicism in the 'Latin' countries of the south-west and centre of Europe; Lutheran Protestantism in the Nordic countries. Elsewhere, it is the way in which the traditions exist side by side and even become interwoven: that is the case where the sociological weight of several traditions stands side by side, for example in Germany, Switzerland or the Netherlands. The case of Great Britain is more complex: Anglicanism dominates in England, but Roman Catholicism is certainly present, while the Reformed Protestant tradition has the greatest influence in Scotland.

Wars of religion

Far from the persecutions of religious minorities and bloody conflicts with a strong religious component which have torn Europe apart, peaceful relations and, increasingly, mutual respect and even co-operation between Christian confessions and religions are being translated into everyday life over a large part of the continent. Elsewhere, relations are tense or mistrustful, in particular between minority and majority churches. Yet elsewhere, more or less cruel conflicts have only just stopped, or are still continuing, for example in Northern Ireland and in the Balkans. In all these cases, true reconciliation will require learning once again to listen to one another and to talk with one another, with patience, honesty, courage and goodwill. And first of all justice will have to be done to the victims and a process of social reconstruction will have to be set in motion.

Paul

Music

p. 274

In countries which belonged to the Warsaw Pact up to the demolition in 1989 of the Berlin Wall and the Soviet system and which formed part of the Eastern bloc, the Christian cultural and religious heritage has suffered much from partial or total destruction. Buildings have been re-used for non-religious purposes (the storage of military, agricultural or other material). However, many buildings, some of them very old, are still there to bear witness to the fervour of many generations of believers. And everywhere, restoration projects are now on the increase and new buildings are being constructed. Among them are not only places of prayer but also medical and social centres, schools, information bureaux and hostels. Tourists are welcome here for cultural and spiritual pilgrimages. That is the case in Romania, where on the initiative of the very dynamic Orthodox Metropolitan of Isai, they are invited to discover the magnificent monasteries, the interiors and exteriors of which are covered with frescoes, symbolically retracing the whole history of the Bible and the Christian people down to the present day.

Poetry

Painting

Icons

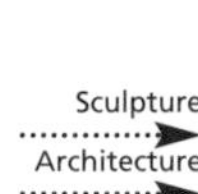

Sculpture

Architecture

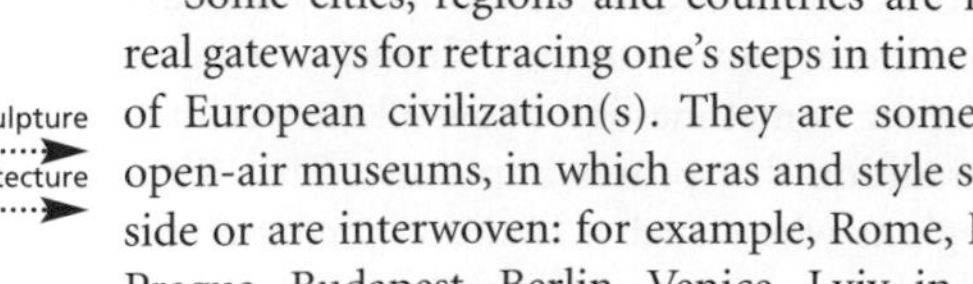

Some cities, regions and countries are in themselves real gateways for retracing one's steps in time to the origins of European civilization(s). They are sometimes virtual open-air museums, in which eras and style stand side-by-side or are interwoven: for example, Rome, Paris, Vienna, Prague, Budapest, Berlin, Venice, Lviv in the Ukraine, Moscow, St Petersburg, London, Amsterdam, Bruges and Ghent, Augsburg, Granada, Lisbon or Strasbourg.

It all depends on what interests you: Graeco-Roman antiquity; the Byzantine or Ottoman empire; the Middle Ages or the Renaissance; the golden age of tolerance between Judaism, Christianity and Islam in Andalusia; the Anglican and Protestant Reformations and the Roman Catholic Counter-Reformation; Baroque, Romanesque, Gothic or neo-Gothic art, classical or neo-classical art, or contemporary art? Are you fascinated with the majestic universe of cathedrals or monasteries? Or by the idea of a pilgrimage along the routes to Compostela, or in the footsteps of Martin Luther, John Knox or John Hus? Are you interested in fortified churches? Or perhaps in the churches and monasteries of the Orthodox tradition – sometimes built entirely of wood? What about the often-disturbing testimonies of the life and faith of Jewish communities, long victims of discriminations and exclusions, and regularly persecuted? How about perhaps following Paul on the European stages of journeys when he was founding, strengthening and building up the first Christian communities?

Or perhaps you're more attracted by music. There are plenty of festivals and concert halls, churches and open-air venues. There will be countless works to stir you, to make you dream, to move and uplift you: Mozart, Bach, Handel, Monteverdi, Schütz, Messaien, Elgar and so many others. And whether or not combined with music, we should not forget sacred song, from Gregorian chant to classical church choral music and the singing of Taizé. Sometimes the words are backed by rock and blues or other contemporary music, and are often living professions of faith, the medium of a real evangelization. Or do you prefer poets, novelists, philosophers, some profoundly concerned with or interested in religious reflection, such as theologians, others inspired by the occasion? There is a wealth of choice.

Are you more interested in painting? The cultural influence of religion here is remarkable, from Cranach, Grünewald, Giotto, Caravaggio and Fra Angelico to Chagall and Stanley Spencer, through Brueghel, Rembrandt, Dürer, Michelangelo, Leonardo da Vinci, Titian, Raphael, Georges de La Tour, El Greco and Doré, to mention only a few.

Nor should the marvels of Byzantine art be forgotten. The icons are more than masterpieces: they are real objects of worship, windows on to the beyond and a universal catechism. The art of painting them ('writing' them) goes back to a very ancient mystical tradition. Andrei Rublev's icon of the Trinity is famous the world over.

What about sculpture and architecture? The museums, public squares, special sites in ruins, historic centres and some streets in towns and cities have magnificent witnesses to the past. Architecture is brilliantly expressed in the extraordinary daring of the cathedral builders, in the myriad churches, basilicas, synagogues, mosques, convents, abbeys, monasteries, chapels, bishops' palaces, fountains, gates, arches, cemeteries, tombs and houses of different style, down to the catacombs outside Rome. In the south east of Europe Romanesque and Gothic art mix, with a predominance of the former. In the north east Gothic art prevails over Romanesque art. Baroque art is concentrated in central Europe, around the Alps. In the east there is Byzantine art, with some admixtures, in a zone extending from the Baltic as far as former Yugoslavia, the dividing line between the Christianity of the East and the West.

Europe influenced by Christianity also displays the art of tapestry, the decoration of manuscript books, of painting on wood, on glass and on fabric; stained-glass windows, marquetry and mosaic.

The audiovisual media also show signs of Christian inspiration in numerous films for cinema and television. European cinema can boast famous directors such as Zeffirelli, Bunuel, Rosellini, Bergman, Scorsese, Pasolini and others. A large number of films touch indirectly on questions of a religious and spiritual nature, often by way of moral, social and humanitarian questioning, in scenarios dealing with relations between individuals or social and political questions. Sometimes this happens within the framework of detective or historical films or films which speak of war and resistance, colonialism and the struggle for freedom, and sometimes even within comic films made for a mass audience.

The influence of Christianity also appears or flourishes in an increasingly successful art-form, the comic strip. Subjects are treated here with the same variety as cinema, and the same creativity: there is humour, a concern to educate, a serious effort to relate history, the aim of provoking or compelling reflection, of denouncing or arousing admiration. Comic strips set out to describe doubt, the quest for meaning, anxiety, sickness, despair, utopia or tenacious hope; they touch on the question of suffering and death, evil or a sense of the absurd, injustice and the struggle for dignity and human rights. All these themes lie at the heart of religion.

You can choose a route round a city, a region, a country or several countries to pursue a particular theme. Thousands of tourist offices are at your disposal throughout Europe to help you to discover particular aspects of cultural history at a deeper level.

The churches are increasingly emphasizing their heritage and the way in which they have contributed to shaping cultures generally. For at least two reasons this is the case, whether they are very old or more recent, in a majority or in a minority. First, out of respect for the building and the works which form part of the treasure of their region and country, and beyond that to all humanity. Then because when it comes to beliefs and convictions, we are in an age of pluralism. Belonging to a church has become a matter of personal choice, on the part of the population in general and among young people in particular. It has become quite legitimate and normal for Europeans to abandon all religious allegiance and practice, to change beliefs or to cobble together the content of what they want to believe. In these circumstances, to emphasize the cultural dimension of religion is an excellent way for the churches to establish or renew contact with people who do not have the strongest or most regular links with them.

Buildings

There are now countless initiatives at every level on the theme of 'faith and culture'. They include thematic exhibitions in churches or other places; concerts; museums; or routes following in the steps of a particular 'saint' or witness of faith whose action and influence deserve to be saved from oblivion. One might mention Mother Teresa, Albert Schweitzer, Dietrich Bonhoeffer, John Comenius, Francis of Assisi, Pope John XXIII and the Ecumenical Patriarch Athenagoras as examples. There may be commemorations of significant or symbolic dates, the anniversary of the birth or death of an eminent person, or of an extraordinary event, which sometimes is thought to have been miraculous. The events commemorated can also be tragic, like those related to the disastrous consequences of antisemitism, reinforced by a certain Christian anti-Judaism: the Holocaust and the death camps of the twentieth century.

Books
Stained glass
Cinema

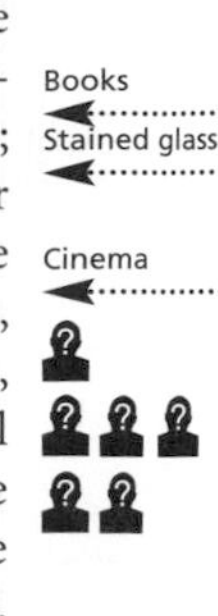

p. 685

Objects aimed at emphasizing the religious heritage come up against unexpected obstacles. Here is an example from Strasbourg in France. A parish decided to transform the interior of its church to make it also a reception centre. The aim was to provide a service and to proclaim the gospel in an original way. Located at the heart of a UNESCO world heritage centre, every day it sees the toing and froing of thousands of people who come shopping or to take a walk. There are large numbers of children, but some of them end up exasperating their parents with their behaviour. Why not offer somewhere where children can be left, to play or engage in educational activities? That could be a way of making contact with some of their parents, and the activities offered might include discovering famous figures of the Bible so that the children could acquire the basis of a biblical education while playing among themselves. Sometimes conversations with the parents turn to more personal, spiritual and religious questions, or to questions about life generally. This is a way of showing perhaps an unexpected or original face of the church in the city.

But the archaeological work that is legally required has revealed frescoes of great value that the church is

CHRISTIANS IN EUROPE AT THE MILLENNIUM

Country	Population	Roman Catholic	%	Independent	%	Protestant	%	Anglican	%	Orthodox	%	Non-Christians	%
① Austria	8,211,000	6,200,000	75.5	73,000	0.9	413,570	5.0	3,100	0.0	155,000	1.9	1,366,330	16.1
② Belgium	10,161,000	8,222,396	80.9	40,000	0.4	125,000	1.2	10,800	0.1	48,500	0.5	1,714,304	16.9
③ Bosnia-Herzegovina	3,972,000	681,135	17.1	750	0.0	2,700	0.1	0	0.0	700,000	17.6	2,587,415	65.1
④ Bulgaria	8,225,000	90,000	1.1	580,000	7.1	95,000	1.2	0	0.0	5,886,450	71.6	1,573,550	19.1
⑤ Croatia	4,473,000	3,960,000	88.5	11,386	0.3	26,000	0.6	0	0.0	250,000	5.6	225,614	5.0
⑥ Czech Republic	10,244,000	4,135,936	40.4	350,000	3.4	400,000	3.9	1,200	0.0	60,000	0.6	5,296,864	51.7
⑦ Denmark	5,293,000	33,200	0.6	36,000	0.7	4,639,710	87.7	4,800	0.1	1,400	0.0	577,890	10.9
⑧ Finland	5,176,000	6,400	0.1	77,700	1.5	4,635,000	89.5	170	0.0	55,900	1.1	400,830	7.7
⑨ France	59,080,000	48,600,000	82.3	1,325,000	2.2	910,000	1.5	13,200	0.0	660,000	1.1	7,571,800	12.8
⑩ Germany	82,220,000	28,700,000	34.9	728,000	0.9	30,420,000	37.0	27,000	0.0	680,000	0.8	21,665,000	26.4
⑪ Greece	10,645,000	62,000	0.6	228,000	2.1	21,400	0.2	3,600	0.0	9,900,000	93.0	430,000	4.0
⑫ Hungary	10,036,000	6.330,000	63.1	165,000	1.6	2,560,000	25.5	0	0.0	90,000	0.9	891,000	8.9
⑬ Ireland	3,730,000	3,159,896	84.7	19,000	0.5	31,500	0.8	134,000	3.6	1,550	0.0	384,054	10.3
⑭ Italy	57,298,000	55,680,000	97.2	415,000	0.7	446,000	0.8	10,600	0.0	91,000	0.2	655,400	1.1
⑮ Netherlands	15,786,000	5,450,000	90.8	490,000	3.1	4,238,853	26.9	8,600	0.1	7,400	0.0	5,591,147	35.4
⑯ Norway	4,461,000	45,000	1.0	136,000	3.0	4,200,000	94.1	2,000	0.0	1,600	0.0	76,400	1.7
⑰ Poland	38,765,000	35,743,000	92.2	330,000	0.9	195,000	0.5	0	0.0	1,030,000	2.7	1,267,000	3.8
⑱ Portugal	9,875,000	8,970,000	90.8	277,000	2.8	135,000	1.4	3,050	0.0	1,200	0.0	488,750	4.9
⑲ Romania	22,327,000	3,237,000	14.5	290,000	1.3	2,380,000	10.7	450	0.0	19,000,000	85.1	*********	0.0
⑳ Russia	146,934,000	1,500,000	1.0	7,800,000	5.3	1,630,000	1.1	3,300	0.0	75,950,000	51.7	60,050,700	40.9
㉑ Slovakia	5,387,000	3,660,186	67.9	23,000	0.4	600,000	11.1	0	0.0	21,000	0.4	1,082,814	20.1
㉒ Slovenia	1,896,000	1,659,006	87.5	31,000	1.6	32,000	1.7	0	0.0	12,000	0.6	161,944	8.5
㉓ Spain	39,630,000	38,080,000	96.1	320,000	0.8	120,000	0.3	12,000	0.0	2,250	0.0	1,095,750	2.8
㉔ Sweden	8,910,000	175,000	2.0	60,000	0.7	8,420,000	94.5	2,880	0.0	120,000	1.3	132,120	1.5
㉕ Switzerland	7,386,000	3,260,000	44.1	160,000	2.2	3,040,000	41.2	13,300	0.2	26,000	0.4	886,700	12.0
㉖ Turkey	66,591,000	30,500	0.0	78,000	0.1	32,500	0.0	2,100	0.0	227,655	0.3	66,220,245	99.4
㉗ Ukraine	50,456,000	5,578,901	11.1	8,500,000	16.8	1,340,000	2.7	0	0.0	27,400,000	54.3	7,637,099	15.1
㉘ United Kingdom	58,830,000	5,620,000	9.6	2,140,000	3.6	5,050,000	8.6	26,000,000	44.2	370,000	0.6	19,650,000	33.4
㉙ Yugoslavia	10,640,000	546,557	5.1	185,000	1.7	95,000	0.9	400	0.0	6,046,000	56.8	3,767,043	35.4

Independent is used here for Christians independent of historic, organized, institutional, denominational Christianity.
In Europe in particular there is often a marked difference between nominal members of churches and those who are active within them. In some countries, Christians are affiliated to more than one church; in the case of Romania this produces a number of Christians greater than the population of the country.

Source: David B. Barrett, George T. Kurian and Todd M. Johnson (eds), *World Christian Encyclopedia*, New York: OUP [2]2002

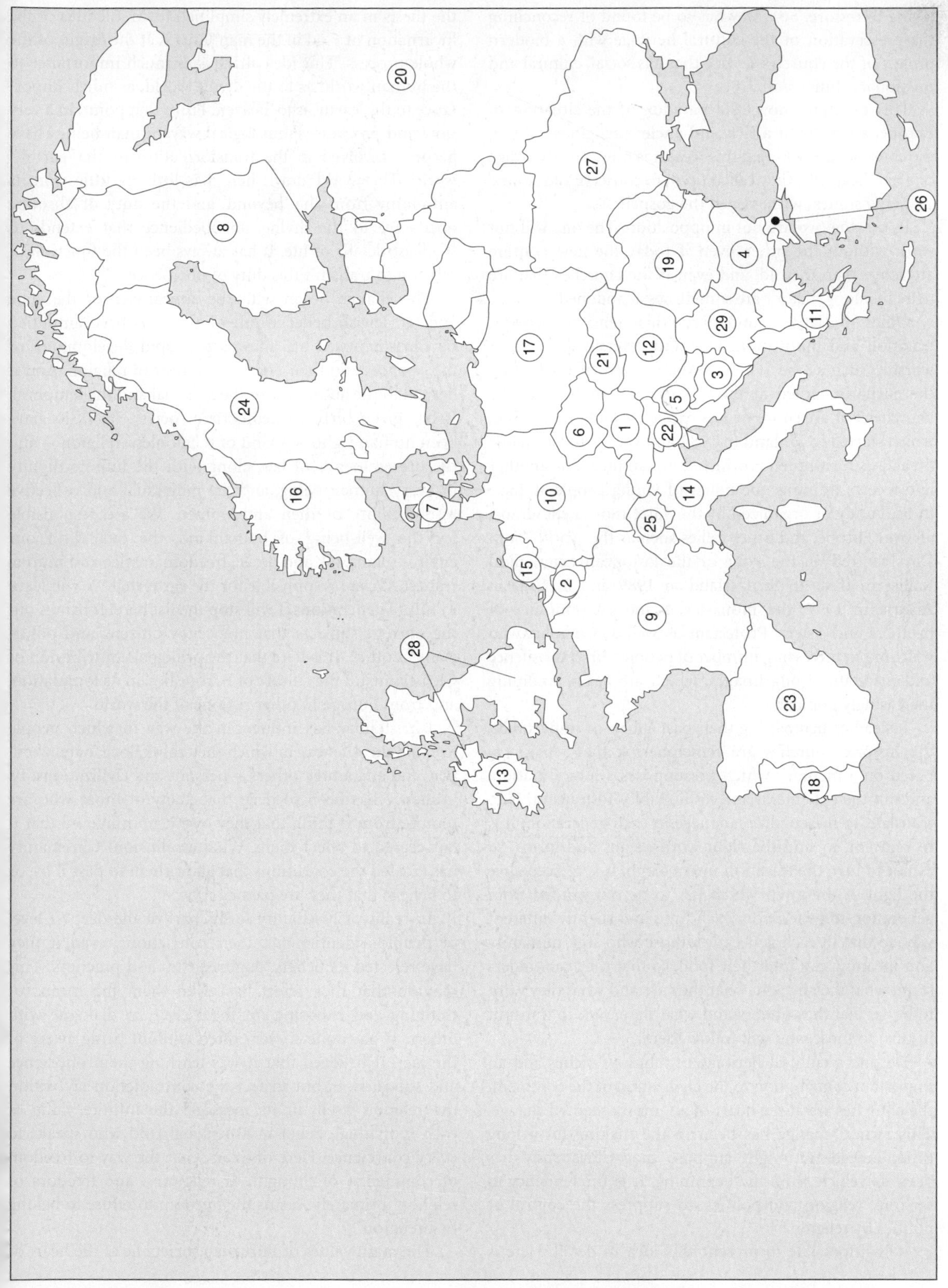
20
8
24
16
7
28
13
27
17
21
12
29
19
4
26
11
3
5
22
1
6
10
14
25
15
2
9
23
18

Incarnation
Jesus

trying to restore. So a way has to be found of reconciling the preservation of the cultural heritage with a modern project of the church's service that has social, cultural and missionary dimensions.

This example shows the paradox of the situation in Europe, a land with a rich and ancient religious culture: the churches are asking if this wealth is more an advantage or a handicap. Are they called upon to conserve 'old stones' or 'living stones', witnesses to the gospel?

In fact the two are not in opposition. The one will not work without the other, even if today the new is more attractive than the old, and even if the churches that are heirs to a long history are sometimes abandoned.

Science
Human rights
Environmental ethics

Other initiatives underline this tension between tradition and innovation: new and diversified forms of worship such as the 'Thomas Mass', a way of celebrating the eucharist aimed at those who are remote from the churches but are more or less explicitly looking for God, which started in Finland in 1989 and spread to Germany; breakfasts for women at which they can meet one another and receive training; the rallies of young people at Taizé in Burgundy or organized by the Taizé movement almost all over Europe, and other rallies such as the World Youth Days centred on the Pope or the European Ecumenical Rallies in Basle in Switzerland in 1989 and in Graz in Austria in 1997; the monasteries and communities of brothers and sisters, Protestant as well as Catholic, who welcome an increasing number of people thirsty for silence and meditation; pilgrimages, which are again becoming increasingly popular.

Instead of bemoaning their past 'glory' or importance, the historic churches are remembering that religion is based on a memory which presupposes a long duration, and not the ephemeral and fashionable. To transmit is to translate, to re-actualize language in each generation; it is to reinvent, to find the right words, signs and forms, so as not to turn the tradition into a tomb. It is to keep alive the light of the torch which has to be transmitted from generation to generation, each time in a slightly different way, so that in each generation those who seek humanity and meaning can find their food, so that they can understand what they live on, what they are and what they want to be, so that they understand what they want to transmit in turn to those who will follow them.

Despite a cultural heritage of fabulous riches and an important contribution to the civilization of the continent, the churches are at the heart of an unprecedented change. This radical change has been in the making for a long time; indeed we might suppose that Christianity has been its vehicle from the beginning. It is the tendency to separate religion and politics, to suppress the control of politics by religion.

Politics

It is impossible to present this idea in detail. Here is the thesis in an extremely simplified form: the idea of the incarnation of God in the man Jesus is at the origin of the whole process. This idea attaches as much importance to the human world as to the divine world, as much importance to the 'earth' as to 'heaven'. From that point, in a very slow and progressive but logical way, human beings have become involved in the transformation of the 'earthly' world. The world 'down here' has little by little won its autonomy from the 'beyond' and the duty of absolute obedience to the divine, an obedience that extends to the least details of life. It has always been the function of religion to transmit this duty of obedience.

The change began with the appearance of the state and the Jewish belief in one God. It has been amplified by Christianity. It has allowed the rapid development of the sciences and their emancipation from religion. And it has led to the autonomy of the spiritual and the temporal. It has given birth to democratic society. Its fruits have been human rights – a kind of religionless 'religion' – and the pre-eminence of law, along with the infinite dignity of every human being, and the individual and collective responsibility of men and women. We are responsible for the well-being of humankind, the quality of our environment, war and peace, freedom, justice and mutual respect. We are responsible for the earth that we will leave to future generations. I will stop the list here. It brings out the current subjects that preoccupy citizens and politicians in office. It is here that the principal contribution of Christianity to the culture of Europe lies, in its foundation, and from Europe in other regions of the world.

Christianity has influenced the way in which people live and die, the way in which they think, love, hate, work, play and encounter 'others' – persons and civilizations. Its influence has been so deep that many of those who are remote from it think that they owe it nothing and that it has ceased to affect them. What an illusion! Christianity has created the conditions that allow them to pass it by, or to believe that they are passing it by.

In reality, Christianity forms part of the deepest level of people's identity and their convictions, even it they have rejected its beliefs, dogmas, rites and practices. This religion that they reject has given them the means of thinking and choosing for themselves, in dialogue with others. It has done so very often without being aware of the fact. It believed that it was teaching them obedience and submission, but in fact the contradiction lay within the religion itself, in its message: the infinite value of each individual, belief in a personal God who speaks to every conscience. Here one can sense the way to freedom of conscience, of thought, or religion – and freedom of religion ultimately means the freedom to refuse to belong to a religion.

The main values of European society lie at the heart of

Christianity, and at least in nucleus in its message. They include the fight against intolerance and the rejection of the death penalty, the work on memory and on the exchange of memories, and dialogue with other religions and currents of thought. This is even more important than ever after 11 September 2001. The churches are becoming involved here in an increasingly more concrete way, at local, regional or national levels, but also together on the European level. The aim is to 'deepen communion with Judaism', to 'cultivate relations with Islam' and to move to the 'encounter with other religions and ideologies'. These are extracts from the *Charta Oecumenica* signed in Strasbourg in 2001 by the Conference of European Churches (CEC) and the Council of European Episcopal Conferences (CCEE). They invite all the churches on the continent to develop a culture of dialogue and co-operation, among themselves and with other religions and convictions.

The CEC brings together the Anglicans, Protestants and Orthodox, the CCEE the Roman Catholics. They are aware of their 'common responsibility in Europe' to help to 'reconcile the peoples and cultures', to 'safeguard creation' and to 'take part in the construction of Europe'.

In concrete terms the CEC is developing a critical and constructive dialogue with the institutions of the European Union, the Council of Europe, the Organization for Security and Cooperation in Europe and the United Nations, in close relations with the Roman Catholic Church. It is helping the churches to develop common positions which it passes on to political organizations, relating to questions of bioethics and biotechnology; sustainable development; global solidarity, peace and security; human rights and religious freedom, etc.; and also to the significance and the aim of the building up of Europe and the role of the churches.

This dialogue does not aim to re-establish religious control over politics. It is precisely because that is prevented from returning by the back door that dialogue and co-operation are possible, desirable and desired, even by atheistic political authorities. Religion does not make people afraid, since no one any longer believes that it will dominate the political and social order. Its voice has become one voice among others in the democratic debate. That is why it is listened to seriously and with interest. That is the great novelty.

Granted, the autonomy of the temporal and the spiritual has not been explicitly realized everywhere, for example in certain countries with a recent democratic tradition or with Orthodox Christianity. In Russia, one of the aims of the church is to 're-clericalize' society.

In the majority of the other countries believers and religious institutions are simply trying to bear witness to their faith. They invite listening, dialogue, support. They do not seek to impose it, knowing that is a vain hope. Their society is no longer religious, i.e. controlled by religion. But the spiritual quest and thirst are there, omnipresent. They exist among many people in an open or confused way, all the more so since this approach is now made in the form of questioning, in freedom. The churches have lost their power. Paradoxically, that is a great opportunity for them, since they can devote themselves fully to a crucial task, that of offering help to numerous people engaged in a spiritual quest and of offering the authorities and the public at large reports and ethical reflections on social questions.

Although religion may no longer be a political power in Europe, its vocabulary and some of its traditions form part of everyday life. Sports journalists constantly use terms such as 'crucifixion', 'resurrection', 'way of the cross', 'descent into hell' or 'miracle' to describe the exploits, efforts or sufferings of the champions. Reporters write of 'going into the wilderness' after the electoral failure of a political official. Biblical and religious themes are massively used in advertising, and a number of current proverbs and phrases draw their origin from the Bible or religious traditions: 'lose one's soul', 'a Judas kiss', 'an eye for an eye, a tooth for a tooth', a 'scapegoat', a 'lost sheep', 'rendering to Caesar what is Caesar's', 'Damascus road experience', 'judging a tree by its fruits', 'throwing the first stone', 'the salt of the earth', 'a good Samaritan', 'no one can serve two masters', 'don't put new wine in old bottles', 'kill the fatted calf', 'be transported to the seventh heaven', the 'wheat and the chaff', 'daily bread'.

Finally, don't be surprised by the impressive number of holidays. Some are national festivals. Many are a Christian heritage, a reminder of the time when Christianity had transformed Europe into a territory of 'Christendom'. Without forgetting what it owes to Christianity, this region of the world has become one of political pluralism. It is on the way to becoming more a region of cultural and religious pluralism. This protects diversity, being based on a foundation of principles and values inscribed in the message and internal dynamic of Judaism and Christianity.

Festivals and fasts

Christendom

RICHARD FISCHER

Grace Davie, *Religion in Modern Europe: A Memory Mutates*, Oxford: OUP 2000

Eastern Europe

Practically all the major Christian denominations are to be found in Eastern Europe. Together with Russia, it is the heart of the Orthodox world. It contains the traditional 'fault-line' between Western and Eastern Christianity, which partially coincided for centuries with the frontier between the Habsburg and Ottoman empires, and along with the Iberian peninsula, it is that part of Europe which saw a confrontation of Christianity with Islam: the Turks reached the gates of Vienna in 1529 and 1683. This confrontation had a lasting effect, right down to the conflict in the Balkans in the 1990s.

Secularization ➤

The countries that border or straddle this frontier are religiously mixed. In the Transylvanian part of Romania there is a strong Calvinist and Lutheran presence. Hungary is Roman Catholic, Reformed and Lutheran. Belarus is both Orthodox and Roman Catholic. Ukraine has several rival Orthodox jurisdictions and a strong presence of Roman Catholics and Eastern-rite Catholics, as well as growing numbers of Baptists and Pentecostals.

Eastern-rite Catholic churches

Eastern-rite Catholicism is a phenomenon of the borderlands in Central and Eastern Europe. From the late-sixteenth to the mid-eighteenth century in areas of Catholic political power Orthodox communities in Ukraine, Poland, Lithuania, Transylvania and elsewhere were brought into communion with Rome and papal jurisdiction while being allowed to retain all their traditional Orthodox rites and customs. These churches were all declared illegal in Communist times; their resurgence over the last decade presents challenges for inter-church relations and ecumenism in the region and more widely.

Orthodox churches

Orthodox churches tend to be named after their host nation-states, and there is a tendency for the churches to think of themselves as the natural faith of a particular people. There is close identification between the Orthodox Church and the nation in Bulgaria, Serbia and Romania (and in the Caucasus, Georgia, and also Armenia, where the Armenian Apostolic Church has this in common with the Orthodox churches). In some of the predominantly Roman Catholic countries in the area there is also a clear identification between a people, its culture and its faith. The best-known such country is Poland; others are Lithuania, Slovenia and Croatia. The rival traditions of religious self-identification in the almost identical countries of Croatia and Serbia, on either side of the 'fault-line', were tellingly invoked while Yugoslavia collapsed in the 1990s.

Council ➤
Ecumenical movement ➤
Liberation theology ➤
Feminist theology ➤

In several of the countries the identification of one leading church with the nation was bolstered under Communism, either because the Communist regime favoured one church to the exclusion of others (Romania) or, conversely, because the church became a symbolic alternative to the official ideological system (Poland, Lithuania).

In the fourteen years since the end of Communism the new environment for the churches has meant that they now increasingly resemble their counterparts in Western Europe. They are now already, or are tending to become, minority bodies in a pluralist and increasingly secular world.

The idea of a 'spiritual East' and a 'materialist West' has been shown to be a false stereotype. In Eastern Europe, the Poles and Slovaks are very religious; not so the very secularized Czechs and eastern Germans. In the late 1990s professed atheists ranged from 0% in Romania to 40% in former East Germany, compared to a European average of 5%. The general context, however, was increasing secularization. By 1999 surveys throughout the region were showing an average 15% decline in religious practices since 1991 (Poland remained an exception). There was a difference between town and country (in Slovakia attendance at mass ranged from 80% in villages to 3% in the towns) and there was a discrepancy between nominal and practising Christians (in late 1999 40% of the citizens of the Czech Republic said that they were Roman Catholics, but only 5% said that they attended mass).

A basic question facing the churches in the post-Communist countries is one that is also facing the churches in the West: what should be the role of a church in a pluralist society? Some argue that Christians must accept the situation of ideological pluralism and contribute vigorously to the debate. Others take the view that Christians should make a resolute stand in the face of pluralism and secularization.

There is a general tendency throughout Eastern Europe for church members (laity, clergy and hierarchs alike) to be more traditionalist and conservative than their Western European counterparts, though of course liberal individuals and groups are certainly to be found in the Eastern European churches. East-West disagreement arises over such issues as the ordination of women, homosexuality and abortion. Part of the reason is that during the Communist period the churches in Eastern Europe had no exposure to developments that had taken place in world Christianity since the Second World War, such as the Second Vatican Council, the ecumenical movement, the growth of black churches, and new theologies (liberation, feminist). There is now widespread concern at the influx of liberal and secularized ideas, to an extent that has caused, for example, Archbishop Jan Sokol in Slovakia to say: 'We must bar our doors to the West.'

Perspectives of this kind have coloured debate in the Eastern European churches on the question of accession to the European Union. In Poland a nationalist Roman Catholic newspaper which reflects the views of perhaps 12% of the population has warned against a 'wave of garbage, a postmodernist, liberal slush of pseudo-values – this is what Europe is offering us today … this is all too high a price for being together with the West'. However, the opponents of joining the EU are generally in a minority in the churches.

In some countries clergy have been vocal in urging their flock to support particular political parties, and have often been politically involved themselves. In 1999 a synod of the Roman Catholic Church in Poland warned priests to avoid politics as part of its effort to bring church practices into line with the Second Vatican Council. It said that the church did not 'identify with any party' and that no party had 'a right to represent it'. However, it called on lay Catholics to be generally active politically, and defended the right of priests and bishops to set out 'Catholic criteria' for public life.

Most of the churches in the countries concerned were structurally crippled and restricted by Communist governments. They were at best tolerated (East Germany), at worst forbidden any visible existence (Albania). They are still dealing with this legacy. They have had a lot of ground to make up in outreach to the population. In the early 1990s there was very little public understanding of religion. The Hungarian churches co-operated in producing a handbook for the media, but at a very elementary level 'just so that they don't confuse Baptists and Buddhists'. Under Communism there was also a restriction on the training of clergy. According to the statutes of the Bulgarian Orthodox Church a parish should consist of between 300 and 400 families. Today a severe shortage of priests means that every country priest has several parishes to serve; in the towns, a priest may be responsible for as many as 10,000 families. 'The "parish" as a meaningful entity doesn't exist in Bulgaria,' said a young Christian from that country in 1995. In that same year 40% of Hungary's Catholic parishes were still without priests; in the Czech Republic the ratio of one Roman Catholic priest to 5600 church members compared to the European average of one to 1295.

A general lack of resources and infrastructure explains the extreme dismay with which the indigenous churches throughout Central and Eastern Europe have been reacting to the sudden influx of all kinds of foreign missions and sects. Many of these evangelistic organizations have huge financial and technical resources that cannot be matched by the indigenous churches, and are quite happy to use the promise of material prosperity to attract converts. 'People will come running when they hear the dinner bell,' commented a representative of one American mission. The impression is easily created that such 'sects' are simply the aggressive tools of Western secular materialist interests operating under the guise of religion. There has been a natural desire to curb the activities of these new bodies, and new legislation has been introduced in many post-Communist countries to place restrictions on them. Now that mission work is possible again in Eastern Europe, rivalry and recrimination often arise between denominations which consider themselves 'traditional' and those which are perceived as 'new', with the former accusing the latter of 'sheep-stealing'.

The only Eastern European country where there is state-sponsored suppression of minority religions is Belarus: in summer 2002 three Baptists were fined 200,000 roubles each for 'singing religious songs' in the open air and police broke up a Hindu meditation ceremony in a public park. In Georgia chronic and violent aggression against religious minorities has been organized by individual Orthodox clergy, with the secular authorities either unable or unwilling to curb it.

Another cause of tension between denominations is the restoration of church property. In Communist times the state authorities often favoured one church over another and handed over to it buildings belonging to another denomination, so there is now the issue of rival claims to the same property. In Romania, for example, the 'favoured' Orthodox Church received over 2500 churches belonging to the Eastern-rite Catholic Church when the latter was de-legalized in 1948. Since 1989 the two churches have been wrangling over their return. By 1998 the Eastern-rite Catholics had received fewer than 100 churches.

p. 685

In some parts of Eastern Europe antisemitism is a problem. In 1999 Polish police and army units had to intervene to remove over 300 crosses from the former Auschwitz concentration camp, installed by Roman Catholic nationalists in protest against exclusive Jewish claims to the site. There is also widespread scapegoating of Roma (gypsies), and nationalist and right-wing groups frequently justify their programmes in religious language.

Nevertheless, despite rivalries and recriminations, there are genuine and successful ecumenical initiatives at all levels. Orthodox and Protestant Christians were conspicuous among 70,000 who attended a December 1999 youth meeting of the ecumenical Taizé community in Warsaw. In 2000 the Roman Catholic Council of European Bishops' Conferences under the presidency of the Czech Cardinal Miloslav Vlk pledged itself in Prague to stepping up 'practical and thematic co-operation' with non-Roman Catholics. In the same year the Roman Catholic Church in Poland agreed to a joint recognition of baptisms with the country's seven largest minority churches. Again in 2000 in the Czech Republic Roman Catholic representatives attended the consecration of the Hussite church's first woman bishop, while the Pope voiced 'great regret' over the martyrdom of the fifteenth-century Czech reformer John Hus.

p. 274

There is great tension between the Moscow Patriarchate and the Vatican, but Roman Catholic-Orthodox relations in Eastern Europe are more cordial. In 1999 the Pope visited Romania, the first visit by a reigning pontiff to a predominantly Orthodox country, and was greeted enthusiastically. The visit followed an agreement by Romania's long-feuding Orthodox and Eastern-rite Catholic churches to resolve their disputes through a series of diocesan commissions. The wars in former Yugoslavia were waged for years under the banners of rival faiths, but in April 2000, in a sign of interfaith reconciliation, a religious council was set up in Kosovo, bringing together Catholic, Orthodox and Muslim leaders and modelled on a similar body functioning in Bosnia-Herzegovina.

One major topic of debate throughout Eastern Europe is the prospect of joining the European Union. In the late 1990s delegations of bishops from Poland, the Czech Republic and Hungary visited Brussels and returned fully convinced that the EU was the way for the future. Generally speaking, Roman Catholic and Protestant leaders and clergy are in favour of accession, as is the leadership of the Romanian Orthodox Church. Church approval has given a significant boost to the campaign to mobilize public support in these countries.

The attitude of the churches to the EU reflects the fact that new church leaders in Eastern Europe are increasingly orientated towards the West. Eastern European churches are now better represented in European consultative bodies: more have joined the World Council of Churches, and Eastern Europeans comprise half of the 34 Roman Catholic bishops' conferences. There has been expansion of local contacts and assistance: hundreds of Polish priests, for example, are working in Western Europe. Eastern European Christians were very involved in producing the *Charta Oecumenica* in March 2001.

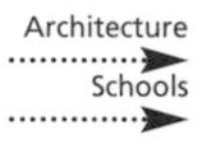

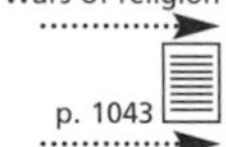

The churches in Eastern Europe are facing a range of challenges. Some of these are specific to the legacy of Communism, and some are shared with the churches in Western Europe. In 2000 Cardinal Glemp, the head of the Roman Catholic Church in Poland, apologized for the 'sins and failures' of church members, accusing citizens of moving too easily from 'the sins of Communism to the sins of capitalism', while singling out antisemitism and Communist-era collaboration among his country's Roman Catholic clergy; and the Roman Catholic bishops of Lithuania expressed regret for their church's 'involvement in nationalist conflicts'. 'Filling the great space of freedom has created problems in all post-Communist countries,' says Fr Daniel Herman, spokesman for the Czech Catholic Bishops' Conference. 'The church expected more people to identify with it, but its priorities were sometimes mistaken. Today, we're still busy evaluating the role of religion in our national life.'

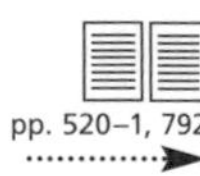

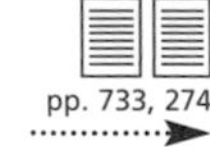

PHILIP WALTERS

Irena Borowik (ed), *The Future of Religion: East and West*, Krakow: Nomos 1995; *Church-State Relations in Central and Eastern Europe*, Krakow: Nomos 1999; Irena Borowik and Miklos Tomka (eds), *Religion and Social Change in Post-Communist Europe*, Krakow: Nomos 2001; Ina Merdjanova, *Religion, Nationalism, and Civil Society in Eastern Europe: the Postcommunist Palimpsest*, Lewiston, Queenston and Lampeter: The Edwin Mellen Press 2002; Patrick Michel, *Politics and Religion in Eastern Europe*, Cambridge: Polity Press 1991; William H. Swatos, Jr (ed) *Politics and Religion in Central and Eastern Europe: Traditions and Transitions*, Westport, CT: Praeger Publishers 1994
The one English-language journal devoted to Christianity in Eastern Europe is *Religion. State and Society: the Keston Journal* (quarterly from 1992; formerly called *Religion in Communist Lands*, 1973–91)

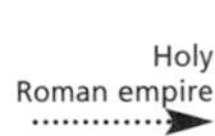

France

From the perspective of the Roman Catholic Church, France is sometimes called 'the oldest daughter of the church'. This title can perhaps be justified by its history. France played a prominent role in the evolution and development of Western Christianity from the Middle Ages onwards both in evangelization and in artistic and spiritual creativity (it has a wealth of amazing cathedrals and saw the birth of Gothic architecture) and made an important contribution in education (the schools of Charlemagne), society and politics (the place of the papacy and the clergy in the building and affirmation of the state, the wars of religion between Protestants and Roman Catholics). It has also been a rebellious daughter: from the thirteenth century on, 'Gallicanism' was a nationalist form of Catholicism that challenged many of the claims to power of popes.

The territory of what is now France has been the home of many key figures and events of Christianity: as well as Charlemagne (*c.*742–814), there is his predecessor, the Merovingian king Clovis (*c.*466–511), whose baptism was a key event; the foundation of the great monasteries of Cluny and Cîteaux; the rise of the Albigensian or Cathar movement in the south and its violent persecution by the church in the twelfth century; the formation of distinctive types of spirituality in the seventeenth century; the Enlightenment and the French Revolution, which posed such a challenge to Christianity – the list is endless. In the twenty-first century it is the land of Taizé, the community in Burgundy with a worldwide influence, and of Lourdes, the world-famous pilgrimage centre.

In the sixteenth century a phenomenon developed which contained the embryo of what would later become 'laicity', the regime, quite specific to France, of an advanced separation between the state and the churches and religions. To protect themselves from the 'encirclement' represented by the Germanic Holy Roman empire (which supported the Roman Catholics), the French kings (who were Roman Catholics) became accustomed to ally themselves with the Protestant kings and princes of Germany, Denmark, Sweden and so on. Political power became autonomous from the church. This element alone does not explain why for almost a century (since 1905), the legal order in France has enforced the separation of the churches from the state. That should mean the end of a long conflict between the Roman Catholic Church and the state; but this conflict, although much diminished today, continues to stamp French mentalities and realities. In fact, laicity is also the result of compromise and does not exclude a degree of pragmatism.

According to a 2001 survey, France, with around 59 million inhabitants, is composed of 69% Roman Catholics and 2% Protestants. 7% of those asked said that they belonged to other religions, among them 6% to Islam and 0.8% to Judaism. There are also Orthodox and Anglican Christians, and 22% of the population said that they were non-believers or atheists.

A survey made some years ago revealed an amazing fact: of 1.8 million people who claimed to be 'near to Protestantism', almost 27% were in fact Roman Catholics. Spread very widely in most regions, Protestants are less rare in Alsace, in the department of the Gard and in the region of Montbéliard. In the sixteenth century one third of France was Calvinist. An intense religious persecution during a century (1685–1787) in which Protestantism was outlawed led many members of the RPR or 'Religion Claiming to be Reformed' to flee. They found refuge in Switzerland, Holland, Germany, Russia and the British Isles. Today French Protestantism remains in the Reformed tradition, except in the East, where it is predominantly Lutheran.

The main churches and unions of churches are the Roman Catholic Church, the Reformed Church of France, the Church of the Augsburg Confession of Alsace and Lorraine, the Lutheran Evangelical Church of France, the Reformed Church of Alsace and Lorraine, the Protestant Gipsy Movement of France, the National Union of Reformed Evangelical Independent Churches, the Federation of Evangelical Baptist Churches, the Apostolic Church and the Union of Free Evangelical Churches. Christians attached to the smaller churches are Pentecostals, evangelicals of various denominations, Mennonites, Methodists, Adventists, Orthodox, Anglicans or members of the Salvation Army.

Generally speaking, even when they are limited to a few matters, relations between the churches are quite good, and at all events acceptable. Sometimes they are excellent between religious leaders, as in Marseilles, where they are contributing towards making specific improvements in relations between Jewish, Christian or Muslim individuals and groups. These good relations can be attributed to the churches and religious groups themselves, but also to the lay regime which establishes the neutrality of the state *vis à vis* all religious groups. The way in which the French distance themselves from religion also plays a role here, as does the churches' habit of expressing their perspectives on social questions in a modest way, in other words in the form of propositions and not affirmations or absolute condemnations. Even the most reticent of them end up by admitting that they do not have a monopoly of morality or even of spirituality. They accept the contradictory and public debate with the representatives of other religious or philosophical traditions, including humanists and atheists. But they can also be clear and firm when fundamental values seem to them to be at stake. Not all the churches and their members adopt this attitude, but the vast majority do.

After the wave of intra-Christian ecumenism that followed the Second Vatican Council, there has now been more of a return towards allegiance to a particular church, in France as elsewhere. Despite that, understanding and co-operation between churches and Christians continues to develop at the official level and among the faithful. The most committed are often impatient for new progress in relations. Christians who do not practise regularly find it difficult to understand the significance of the distinction between the different Christian traditions. Two of the main reasons here are the lesser importance of religion as an identity factor and a profound lack of religious culture. The Protestants cited above, together with some others, form part of the Protestant Federation of France (FPF). The aim of the FPF, created in 1905, is to 'bring its members closer, to co-ordinate their actions and to help them to assume their responsibilities'. The mission of the FPF is also to represent Protestantism to the public authorities and media and to express itself publicly in spheres where Protestants think that they have to bear a particular witness which they want to be heard in public debate. It also has the task of watching over the defence of religious freedom in France and in the world, of encouraging dialogue with the churches and associations that are not members of the FPF, and promoting shared relations and initiatives with non-Protestant Christian churches. Thus for example after the shock of 11 September 2001, the President of the FPF took the initiative in proposing an inter-religious celebration: this took place two days later in the Episcopalian cathedral in Paris, where the president of the Republic, the prime minister, the government and officials responded to the call from representatives of the major churches.

On the Roman Catholic side, what is broadly the majority position is pressing towards an attitude of openness to other Christians. Co-operation or alliance with them is often sought, even if it is often the case that in practice 'ecumenical activity' can signify 'Roman Catholic activity with which Protestants or Orthodox are associated, sometimes at the last moment'. Is it their minority position that drives other Christians to associate with their Roman Catholic partners from the start when they want to launch an ecumenical initiative? But in general the other Christians are largely over-represented and favoured in relation to their numerical importance in the media, chaplaincies, meetings and various consultations. This is one of the effects of Roman Catholic good will and laicity, which encourages the expression of pluralism and diversity. On the national level there is a Christian council presided over by three figures: one Orthodox, one Protestant and one Roman Catholic. Such councils are beginning to see the light of day at the local level. The delegates of other churches are often invited as observers or participants to official meetings of Roman Catholic conferences and vice versa. Tensions or problems sporadically appear over practices that are thought to be negative, like proselytism on the part of groups which have more or less derived from Protestantism. This is the case when these groups indiscriminately criticize the other churches and imagine that they hold the sole 'truth'. This then recalls the not so distant time when a number of Roman Catholics saw other Christians as members of 'sects'.

Today the Roman Catholic Church is carrying on theological dialogues with so-called 'evangelical' Christians, having long engaged in conversations with the Reformed and the Lutheran, and certainly the Orthodox. These last, who are very much in a minority, are concentrated in the big cities and for the most part derive from immigration from Eastern Europe. Some arrived after the Russian Revolution of 1917 and others after the fall of communism. Despite their small number and feeble resources, they seek to play an active part in ecumenical life. They radiate the strength and beauty of their liturgy and the depth of their theological thought. They are living lines of communication between the Christianity of the East and the Christianity of the West. So they are more valuable than ever, since they forcibly affirm the cultural and religious particularisms in Europe, including those at the heart of Christianity.

Churches of a certain size have developed organized or occasional relations with other religions. The authorities and the faithful have come to know each other better; sometimes theological or spiritual questions are examined, or there is greater familiarization with the history and practices of others. Islam in particular is being helped to find its place. From time to time it is the current situation, peaceful or tragic, that dictates the common dialogue and initiatives: social, cultural, educational or ethical questions, or religious freedom and human rights; humanitarian conflicts or dramas in the world; the building of Europe and international relations; ecumenical events, sometimes extending beyond frontiers.

The churches and their associations are very active in society. Often in an innovative way they perform significant services at the level of education, culture, charitable works, health and social and humanitarian projects. They are clearly present in the population in relation to community life generally. They can be critical of the public powers or show their approval or support. In an *ad hoc* way they can be consulted or associated with projects by the public authorities, in the same way as non-governmental associations.

In fact the regime of separation is not absolute. In some parts of France there are local rights where religions benefit from state recognition.

There is great diversity, despite the main emphases to be found among Roman Catholics and Protestants. To put it simply, it could be said that religious practice is weak among people who declare an allegiance to Christianity, around 10%, except in the 'evangelical' churches, whose members are more active. But Christians continue to be attached to the celebrations which mark the stages of life: baptisms, marriages, funerals, and to a lesser degree the great festivals of Christmas and Easter. Many children do not receive religious training from the church, and only in exceptional cases is there religious teaching in state schools.

The major churches are divided roughly between supporters of innovations and supporters of traditions, with a whole range of nuances and degrees. But other splits are just as important: an emphasis on reason or on experience, looking inwards or social commitment, the local or the universal, the particular church or the ecumenical movement. Thus some churches, parishes or communities with a Protestant, evangelical or charismatic character organize campaigns of evangelization in which they put the emphasis on personal conversion to Jesus Christ. In these rallies the emphasis is on a warm and welcoming atmosphere, on music and song, and on the use of simple and vivid language. That appeals more to the imagination and the emotions than to any great effort at reflection. Others concentrate their activity on groups targeted by age and socio-cultural and professional background. The concern is to help small groups to revisit their everyday lives in the light of the gospel. This is done, for example, by the various movements of Catholic Action. Yet others express their spirituality by involvement in forms of practical and social Christianity: social and political involvement in protest against situations of injustice and social exclusion, and proposals to improve the victims of such situations, groups for mutual aid and support, charitable and humanitarian action, work with strikers, refugees and asylum seekers, those without documents, prisoners or prostitutes, and welfare, medical and social work among the sick, old and handicapped.

Often different forms of spirituality can be combined.

One conviction is common to most Christians: they are convinced of the importance of periodical meetings to remind them of their numbers and make them feel stronger together, to encourage one another and to reflect on new forms of presence and witness, to learn to get to know one another better and to co-operate, but also in order to exist a little longer in the public arena and the media in a society which is accustomed to seeing religion as a private matter. Two examples of these gatherings are the Catholic World Days of Youth and the Contacts with Protestants (CAP), held every four years in the East of France.

Another feature common to many Christians and the church is the organization of public debates on topical subjects in which the ethical and social dimension are important. Theology remains healthy and is varied, among Protestants and minority Orthodox too. However, its creativity is declining, along with its capacity for originality in the face of new challenges – globalization, the building up of Europe, anthropology and technical progress. Its involvement in the great intellectual discussions is quite limited. Popular religion is expressed in the form of traditional piety in the framework of the churches, as in pilgrimages or processions. Other forms are situated mid-way between the church, psychology, esotericism and the paranormal: exorcisms, appearances, healings. Yet others perhaps do not merit the term religious: divination, practices of 'personal flourishing' which mix elements of diverse origins, often from the East. The 'free market' of the religious, allied to the development of individualism and the loss of influence of the religious institutions on the content of beliefs, is encouraging the blossoming of a popular *à la carte* religion.

RICHARD FISCHER

A. Dansette, *A Religious History of Modern France* (2 vols), Freiburg: Herder 1961; H. Foreman, *A New Look at Protestant Churches in France*, Bromley: Marc Europe 1987

Germany

Germany is one of the countries of Europe – along with England, Switzerland and France – whose role in the history of Christianity has been particularly significant. If France gave John Calvin to the movement of the Protestant Reformation, Germany produced Martin Luther, whose thought and action had a considerable impact on the history of Europe – not just its religious history – and beyond. By his translation of the Bible into German, Luther certainly brought these basic texts close to the people, but at the same time he also gave the modern German language its form. Protestantism has also put a profound stamp on German culture at the level of philosophy and theology. German Protestantism has made an essential contribution to Protestant biblical and theological research throughout the world. German history was formed around the event of the Reformation in the sixteenth century, a real religious revolution. This clearly identified two camps, Roman Catholic and Protestant, leading to conflicts in which religion and politics were intertwined. When peace returned, these two camps were recognized on the principle *cuius regio, eius religio*: the religion of the ruler determined the religion of the subjects in a given territory. Here it must be remembered that it was not until the nineteenth century that Germany became a united state; until that time what we call Germany was made up of a series of states, each with its own ruler.

Theology
Biblical criticism
Reformation
Wars of religion

During the Nazi period the Roman Catholic Church was in effect rendered powerless to oppose Hitler; its political party, the Centre Party, had been abolished and a concordat between Rome and Germany regulated relations between church and state. Moreover the majority of the Protestant church was dominated by the 'German Christians', partisans of Hitler. A 'Confessing Church' was created in reaction to this; under the influence of the Swiss Reformed theologian Karl Barth and the German Lutheran pastor Hans Asmussen in 1934 it published the Barmen Declaration, a text of spiritual resistance to Nazism. Two Lutheran theologians, Martin Niemöller and Dietrich Bonhoeffer, engaged in active resistance. The former was put in a concentration camp, the latter was hanged by the Nazis.

Karl Barth

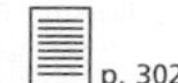
p. 302

After the Second World War and the collapse of the Hitler regime, the two great Christian churches contributed in a decisive way to the rebuilding of democratic structures. They were given a certain moral authority and their role in society was institutionalized in the Basic Law of 1949. The Protestant church in particular also played a key role in the peaceful revolution in the German Democratic Republic that led to the reunification of Germany officially proclaimed on 3 October 1990.

In Germany, with a population of more than 82 million, more than 55 million belong to one of the two Christian confessions. 27.4 million are Protestants and 27.4 million are part of the Roman Catholic Church; a minority adheres to other Christian communities. These include above all the Orthodox churches of Germany, the Old Catholic Church and the free Protestant churches. The Jewish community numbers around 130,000 members, and it is thought that there are around 3 million Muslims from 41 nations, the majority from Turkey. Protestants are more numerous in the north, Roman Catholics in the south.

John Calvin
Martin Luther

The main churches and unions of churches are the Evangelical Church in Germany (EKD: this is not in fact the name of the church but that of a functional structure which

Protestantism
Philosophy

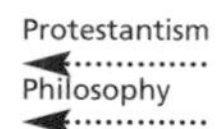

brings together 24 regional churches – Lutheran, Reformed and United; all the Lutheran regional churches but one, Württemberg, also form the United Evangelical Lutheran Church of Germany, VELKD); the Roman Catholic Church; the Orthodox churches in Germany; the Federation of Parishes of Free Protestant Churches (Baptists); the Old Catholic Church and the Evangelical Methodist Church. Other Christians are Anglicans, Mennonites, Adventists or Pentecostalists, or belong to the Federation of Free Protestant Parishes of Germany, the Salvation Army, the Church of the Nazarene, the Mülheim/Ruhr Christian community and the Protestant Fraternal Union.

At the end of the nineteenth century, after the failure of Bismarck's battle against Roman Catholicism – which he accused of threatening German unity and identity – the Roman Catholic Church was able to organize itself and find its place in society. Today it works closely with the EKD both on the religious level and on ethical and social questions. For the first time, in 2003 a big ecumenical meeting (Kirchentag) was organized in Berlin on a national scale by both Protestants and Catholics. Hitherto they had done this alternately and separately every two years, each time attracting around 100,000 people, many of them young. Numerous other Christian churches also play an active part in this major event, as do individuals and groups from all over the world. The questions discussed and messages adopted by these meetings – prepared above all by responsible lay people – are disseminated widely throughout society.

University

Since the 1961 Protestant Kirchentag the question of dialogue with Jews has played a major role. Because of the elimination of the Jews organized by the Germans during the National Socialist dictatorship, the Protestant churches in Germany consider that they owe a special debt to Israel. The consensus texts adopted in this connection speak of the 'rejection of antisemitism' and the 'recognition of the share of responsibility and blame borne by Christians for the Holocaust'. The emphasis is put on the 'indissociable bond between the Christian faith and Judaism', and on 'the eternal election of Israel', and attention is drawn to 'the significance of the state of Israel'.

Judaism and Christianity

p. 685

The EKD plays an important role in the organization called the Leuenberg Church Fellowship, which brings together almost all the Protestant churches in Europe. In 2001 it published a theological document entitled 'The Church and Israel: A Contribution by the Churches deriving from the Reformation in Europe on Relations between Christians and Jews'. No text produced by the churches has ventured so far in the quest for dialogue with Judaism. The document recognizes Judaism as a way of salvation and puts in question the classical affirmation of Reformation theology that Christianity has replaced Judaism.

The Roman Catholic Church in Germany is also carrying on a dialogue with the Jews and strongly approves of the initiatives and gestures by the Vatican in this direction, as for example the declaration of repentance made by Pope John Paul II, which recognizes the responsibility of Christians for persecutions and sufferings inflicted on the Jews throughout history.

The two major churches are also seeking to intensify contacts and relations with representatives and members of other religions present in their country.

The Roman Catholic and Protestant churches are recognized as corporations under public law. They benefit from a church tax levied by the state administration and are present in state schools through confessional religious teaching. They carry on important medical, social and educational work under the umbrella of the Roman Catholic *Caritas* and the Protestant *Diakonisches Werk*. They are in fact big employers (with around 500,000 staff). Churches and Christian organizations continue to play an important role in society despite the increase in 'departures from the church' motivated by a refusal to pay the church tax.

Apart from religious teaching in state schools, the intellectual influence of the churches is also exercised through faculties of theology integrated into the university state system, though here Catholics and Protestants still work separately. It is likewise evident in the academies, a type of training centre for adults that is available to the public as a whole. Finally, the churches are very much present in the various media and address public opinion in various ways, notably by publishing memoranda and works of every kind. The joint letter of the churches in 1997 on 'the Economic and Social Situation in Germany' provoked a big public debate. The churches are listened to by political authorities, even if they are not always followed, as in certain discussions connected with bioethics and biotechnologies. They have ecclesiastical delegates whose task is to maintain relations with the authorities at different levels, including the federal level. The EKD also has a very active office in Brussels for relations with the institutions of the European Union. This office co-operates closely with that of the Conference of European Churches (CEC).

The EKD is very much involved at the ecumenical and international level with the World Council of Churches and the Lutheran World Federation. At the European level it works actively within the CEC and the Leuenberg Fellowship. It has an important service and network of aid, humanitarian action and development on a global level, as does the Roman Catholic Church. The major charitable works of the churches are financed by the voluntary gifts of the faithful. Since 1993–4 the churches have had a bias in favour of Central and Eastern Europe in their actions of solidarity and partnership, with the aim of encouraging self-help.

Among Protestants, those taking part regularly in worship are very few: around 4%. This percentage must be higher in those churches that in principle meet only as committed members. Thanks to the religious teaching at school and other aspects of the presence of the churches in society, the religious socialization of young people is largely assured.

Even if indifference towards the churches is a reality among some of the population, the perspectives and the themes that they develop are certainly present in public discussion. For the moment, the churches do not feel that they have been relegated to the private sphere. Present in many ways in the organizations and institutions of society, Christians perhaps do not feel much need to invent new forms of witness to the gospel and expressions of their faith.

Because of the visible presence of the churches in Germany, questions and debates, including the airing of theological and religious views, are far more present in the media and in public opinion than in France. Many theological tendencies are present, from existentialist theologies and a theology of the cross, through evangelical theology to political theology, feminist theology and liberation theology.

RICHARD FISCHER

📖 John Ardagh, *Germany and the Germans*, Harmondsworth: Penguin Books [3]1995; Klaus Scholder, *The Churches and the Third Reich* (2 vols), London SCM Press 1987, 1988

Great Britain

Christianity in Great Britain has a number of distinctive features. It has two established churches, i.e. state churches, the Presbyterian Church of Scotland and the Anglican Church of England. Only the Church of Scotland is unambiguously Protestant or Reformed. Yet, despite having these established churches, for the last three centuries all parts of Great Britain have also had Dissenting or Non-conformist churches to rival them. In addition, unlike much of Roman Catholic Europe, anti-clericalism is still comparatively uncommon, at least within mainland Britain.

However, there are a number of other features that also characterize Christianity in the Great Britain, as in many Western countries today. During the twentieth century churches experienced very considerable institutional decline. This decline shows no signs as yet of halting. An increasing number (especially the young) now identify with no religion, never attend church, and express scepticism about traditional Christian beliefs. Even though most people still identify themselves loosely as 'Christian', both New Age beliefs and outright scepticism now attract a sizeable minority.

Establishment continues to puzzle many North Americans (as well, perhaps, as the British themselves). More familiar with a separation between church and state in a context of relatively high church-going, they frequently express surprise that bishops sit in the House of Lords, that their appointment can still be vetoed by the Prime Minister, and that the Archbishop of Canterbury receives widespread media attention. And this is despite the fact that less than a tenth of the British attend church regularly. In Ireland establishment was abolished in 1871 and in Wales in 1920. Yet in England and Scotland, so far, it remains intact. Not surprisingly, there is considerable disagreement within society at large about its significance and within the churches themselves about its desirability. Some British view it, together with the monarchy, as an element of moral stability in an otherwise pluralist society, whereas others see it as an anachronism or even as a hindrance to the churches themselves.

Although both are established and national churches, the Church of Scotland and the Church of England are distinct. The monarch is technically 'head' of the Church of England but only a member of the Church of Scotland. The Church of Scotland also lacks direct political power, having no formal representation in the House of Lords or even in the Scottish Assembly. Moderators within the Church of Scotland (it has no bishops) are elected solely within the church, and the Prime Minister is without any power of veto over their appointment. The Church of Scotland also (in theory at least) follows the teaching of John Calvin, is a branch of worldwide Presbyterianism and identifies itself clearly with the Reformation.

Political theology ◄
Feminist theology ◄
Liberation theology ◄

Presbyterianism
Church of Scotland ◄
Church of England ◄
Evangelicals

The Church of England, along with the comparatively small Scottish Episcopal Church and the Anglican Churches in Wales and Ireland, is internally divided about identifying closely with the Reformation. Evangelical Anglicans, a growing presence in all of these churches, tend to see themselves as Reformed and Protestant. Anglo-Catholics, on the other hand, generally do not. That Anglican clergy are allowed to marry, have an emphasis upon biblical study and preaching, and are not required to be obedient to papal teaching and authority, all tend to point to a Reformed identity. That Anglicans have bishops and primates, celebrate the eucharist regularly, and often wear vestments, point rather to a Catholic identity. It has been argued that this ambiguity was a deliberate product of the Elizabethan Settlement, the reshaping of the Church of England under Queen Elizabeth I (1533–1603). Tired of the religious wars of the sixteenth century, the English constructed a church that was 'comprehensive', embracing both its Catholic and its Protestant wings; closely related to the state; but also relatively powerless. As a consequence, outright hostility to mainstream churches is comparatively rare in Britain. Some interpret this as British indifference

New Age movement ◄

to all things religious, but others as a mark of British tolerance.

Congregationalism
Baptist churches
Methodism
Pentecostalism

If Britain has generally escaped anti-clericalism, establishment, both in England and Scotland, has long generated religious dissent. Independent (later Congregationalist) and Baptist churches competed strongly with Anglicans in England (and Wales) in the seventeenth and eighteenth centuries, as did Methodists in the nineteenth century and Pentecostals in the second half of the twentieth. In Scotland, Presbyterians finally gained ascendancy over Anglicans only in the late seventeenth century, but themselves experienced radical divisions in the eighteenth and nineteenth centuries. As a result, Free Presbyterians built churches to rival Church of Scotland churches in almost every parish during the second half of the nineteenth century. Alongside this Non-conformist dissent, Irish immigration from the mid-nineteenth century onwards helped Roman Catholic churches to flourish in Britain by the mid-twentieth century. As most other church congregations in England, Scotland and Wales declined in the first half of the twentieth century, Roman Catholic congregations, in contrast, tended to grow. It was only in the second half of the twentieth century that they too began to decline.

Sociology of religion ➤

One of the most visible products of this inter-church rivalry has been an abundance of church buildings throughout Great Britain. The British population doubled in the first half of the nineteenth century and again in the second half. This century also saw a rapid process of industrialization and urbanization. The unique government census of church-going in 1851 captured the very moment when the population turned from being predominantly rural to predominantly urban. It was also a high point of church-going, with approximately four in ten people in England and Wales attending church or chapel on the census day. Today, in contrast, less than one in ten would be found in church or chapel on a similar Sunday. The census also showed that a very active campaign of church and chapel building was already under way. Despite rapid rural depopulation, this campaign continued strongly in the second half of the nineteenth century in rural as well as urban areas. In many parts of Britain, especially in Wales, church and chapel provision considerably exceeded rural populations by the beginning of the twentieth century. Rapid suburbanization ensured that many city centres also had a serious over-provision of church buildings by this time. Most mainline denominations in Britain (apart from Roman Catholics, who built more prudently) have been struggling with this problem ever since.

If most of these features of Christianity are distinctively British, the rapid decline of visible aspects of church life in the second half of the twentieth century is not. With the major exception of the United States, most Western countries (including Australia and New Zealand) have experienced a very similar decline. Church-going rates across denominations (now including Roman Catholics) have declined rapidly, especially among the young, as have baptisms, confirmations, Easter and Christmas communicants, Sunday school attendances, church membership rolls, church marriages, ordinations and vocations to religious orders. In addition, opinion polls also suggest a gradual decline in traditional Christian beliefs, especially, again, among the young. There are indications of church-going rises in some former Soviet Union countries, of continuing resilience in staunchly Roman Catholic countries such as Poland and Malta, and of growth in a number of conservative, evangelical churches. Yet these do not nearly offset the very considerable and ongoing overall declines in organized Christianity apparent in most Western countries.

Alongside this decline in organized religion, there has also been a considerable increase (this time including the United States) of those identifying themselves with no religion. Opinion polls are the major source of evidence in this area, but they do need to be approached with some caution. If people in Britain today are asked bluntly, 'What is your religion?', eight in ten will still identify themselves as 'Christian' (as they did in the 2001 population census). However, if they are asked more gently, 'Do you regard yourself as belonging to any particular religion?' only six in ten offer any religion at all. If this group is then asked to name the specific church or congregation that they belong to, the proportion drops again. Whichever method is used, those who respond positively tend to be older and more middle class and female than those who do not.

There is much debate among sociologists of religion about whether this is an ongoing change or a passing generational difference. Some believe that as people grow older, so they tend to turn back to organized religion. Others argue that this is a new and damaging trend for the churches, with young people today, unlike previous generations, receiving little or no socialization in organized Christianity. If the latter, then it may be less likely that the young today will become active as they grow older in churches that are largely unfamiliar to them.

Cumulative evidence from opinion polls collected since the 1940s in Britain does seem to point to ongoing changes in religious belief. Again caution is needed, since many opinion poll questions in this area tend to lack sophistication. None the less, compared decade by decade they do suggest three broad conclusions. The first is that traditional Christian beliefs have tended to decline; the second that stated disbelief has increased; and the third that New Age beliefs have held steady or even increased. So, overall there has been a decline in belief in a 'personal' God, in the divinity of Christ, and in the possibility of life after death. There has also been a corresponding increase in scepticism, or at least a switch from 'don't know' to disbelief. At the same time, a quarter of the population now state that they believe in reincarnation, more people believe in ghosts today than in the past, and a sizeable minority apparently trusts horoscopes.

Again there is much debate among sociologists of religion about how to interpret this confusing picture. Steve Bruce, for example, argues that it is clear evidence of Western secularization. As the population at large becomes increasingly pluralistic, affluent and educated, so religious organizations in the West tend to become less prominent. Christian beliefs and practices that were once widely shared by predominantly rural local communities become less convincing and significant for people in modern Britain and elsewhere. Bruce is also sceptical about the depth of New Age beliefs, regarding them as weak substitutes for the Christian beliefs that once genuinely shaped the lives of the British. He expects mainstream churches in Britain to wither away, some within the next generation. And he sees most people in Britain leading increasingly secular lives uninfluenced by any church teaching.

However, sociologists such as Grace Davie tend to interpret the evidence rather differently. She concedes that churches both in Britain and in most of Europe have lost members and churchgoers over the last few years. Yet she relates this loss more to a general decline within voluntary associations than to any process of secularization. People have become more individualistic and less inclined than in the past to join voluntary organizations, but this does not necessarily mean that they have thereby become less religious. She argues that in Europe at large there is still a religious memory and resilient religious belief that survives and mutates despite institutional decline. In the future this is likely to take different forms, but, while humans still search for meaning and purpose in life, it is unlikely to disappear altogether.

An important part of the debate between Steve Bruce and Grace Davie and their counterparts revolves around how to interpret the religious scene in the United States. Church-going rates there are at least double those in the British mainland. Grace Davie argues that it has been a long-standing mistake of European sociologists of religion to assume that American resilient churches are the exception and European declining churches the real trend of modernity. She argues that there are forces peculiar to Europe that have tended to generate this decline. Steve Bruce, on the other hand, maintains that American churches are actually much weaker and less significant than at first they might appear. For him they are either an exception to Western secularization or, more likely, themselves a variant of secularization.

This debate has important implications for predictions about the future of Christianity in Great Britain and beyond. If Steve Bruce is right, then liberal denominations are unlikely to survive the erosions of increasing secularization. Small-scale sects may survive, but only by severing their ties with society at large. Most people in the future will pay little or no attention to religion in any shape or form. If they do, it will have little effect upon their daily lives. If Grace Davie is right, then churches will adapt to changing social patterns. Church-going may change in the future and, say, the religious media or the internet might become more important, but religious beliefs and practices are unlikely to disappear, since they serve a human need. Indeed, evidence about the political significance of religious fundamentalism in the modern world, such as 11 September 2001, might support this position. For Steve Bruce it is a temporary throwback to pre-modernity, whereas for Grace Davie it is reminder of the resilience and potency of religion even in the modern world.

Secularization ◄

Fundamentalism

Secularization was a key concept for both Durkheim and Weber in the early phases of the sociology of religion and remains contentious among sociologists today. It is quite possible that the multi-faceted nature of ancient religious traditions, Christianity included, renders them hard to locate as social phenomena. On the one hand, Christianity in Great Britain can be depicted as weak and insignificant, subservient to the state through its established churches, and contributing to individual lives only as a leisure activity. On the other, it can be seen as a key factor in shaping moral lives, in challenging secular powers and in providing a resource for meaning and purpose even for those using its rituals but occasionally.

The moral implications of Christianity have long been of concern in Britain. Many evangelical Victorians were convinced that the eternal punishment for the wicked in hell was an essential doctrine for the maintenance of morality in society. The Anglican theologian F. D. Maurice challenged this doctrine and was deprived of his chair at King's College London for doing so. Interestingly, he made this challenge on moral grounds, believing that eternal punishment was itself immoral, as was the attempt to enforce morality through it.

Life after death

While many Christians in Britain today might regard this particular debate as antique, there is none the less empirical evidence that active church-going does encourage moral belief and action. For example, active church-goers are three times more likely than nonchurch-goers to be involved in voluntary work in the community. Many child-care groups, youth clubs, charity shops, and care-of-the-elderly services depend heavily upon church-goers. Using evidence from opinion polls, it appears that on balance church-goers are more altruistic and honest than nonchurch-goers. Significantly, those adult nonchurch-goers who were church-goers as children tend to retain these values more than do nonchurch-goers who were also nonchurch-goers as children. The evidence here can be exaggerated (clearly not all church-goers are altruistic or honest) but it is now well established. p. 795

British churches still face many unresolved issues. There are divisions within most denominations between traditionalists and non-traditionalist congregations, between charismatic and non-charismatic congregations, between growing and declining congregations, and between financially self-supporting and financially subsidized congregations. Issues to do with sexuality (especially Homosexuality homosexuality) and gender (especially women priests and bishops) also tend to divide denominations sharply. Yet the New Testament provides ample evidence that such divisions are not new. More widespread theological Calendar education and shared ecumenical experience may yet set these divisions in a wider perspective.

ROBIN GILL

Steve Bruce, *God is Dead: Secularization in the West*, Oxford: Blackwell 2002; Grace Davie, *Religion in Britain since 1945. Believing without Belonging*, Oxford: Blackwell 1994; *Religion in Modern Europe: A Memory Mutates*, Oxford: OUP 2000; Robin Gill, *The 'Empty' Church Revisited*, Hampshire: Ashgate 2003; Adrian Hastings, *A History of English Christianity, 1920–2000*, London: SCM Press 2001; Doreen Rosman, *The Evolution of the English Churches 1500–2000*, Cambridge: CUP 2003

Greece

Greece is proud of being the first European region to have been reached by Christianity. According to the Acts Paul of the Apostles (especially chs 16–18), the apostle Paul Eastern-rite Catholic churches preached the gospel in Philippi, Thessalonica, Beroea (Verria), Athens and Corinth. His letters to the young Christian communities of Thessalonica and Corinth are also important New Testament documents.

At present, almost all Greeks are, at least nominally, Christians. About 97% of the population of over 10 million belong to the Orthodox Church, more or less the state church. The centre of ecclesiastical administration is Athens. The archbishop is president of the 'Holy Synod of the Hierarchy', the ruling body. The synod consists of all bishops. They number about 80; many dioceses are only small. For practical reasons, there is a 'Permanent Holy Synod' with a much smaller membership. It often meets and its membership changes every year (except for the Archbishop of Athens).

The proclamation of the Greek war of independence against the Turks in 1821 has left its mark on the church. It resulted in the breaking off of relations between the Orthodox churches Church of Greece and the Ecumenical Patriarchate of Constantinople. The self-governing Church of Greece was eventually recognized by Constantinople in 1850. However, the church in several parts of the country, notably Crete, the Dodecanese and Mount Athos developed independently and fall directly under the jurisdiction of the Patriarchate of Constantinople, with its centre in Istanbul. The northern Greek provinces of Macedonia, Thrace and Epirus also belong to the Patriarchate but, for the time being, they are part of the Church of Greece.

About 7 million Greeks have emigrated and now live in North and South America, Western Europe and Australia. They, too, are taken care of by the Patriarchate of Constantinople.

Several hundreds of thousands of Orthodox still follow the old Julian calendar, created by Julius Caesar, which now lags thirteen days behind the Gregorian calendar, a reformed and more accurate calendar introduced in 1582 by Pope Gregory XIII and from then on used in the Western world. In 1924, the Orthodox Church adopted the Gregorian calendar by order of the Greek state, but some of the faithful rejected this renewal and later formed independent ecclesiastical organizations, such as the True Orthodox Church; these are the ones who use the Julian calendar.

Other denominations and religions in Greece are only small minority groups. The largest group is that of the Muslims in Western Thrace, who probably number about 110,000. Moreover, among the nearly 1 million foreign immigrants there are several hundred thousand Muslims, mainly from Albania and the Middle East. The phenomenon of numerous Muslim and other immigrants clearly shows that Greece, for many decades a country of emigration, has now become a country of immigration.

About 50,000 Greeks are Roman Catholics, including 2000 who adhere to the Eastern rite. Among the foreign immigrants there are also many Catholics, numbering at least 200,000. Most of them are Poles, Filipinos, Chaldeans from Iraq, Ukrainians, Western Europeans and Africans.

Jehovah's Witnesses number about 45,000. They are not foreigners, as their opponents often assert, but ethnic Greeks. Approximately 25,000 Greeks are Protestants. There are also at least 10,000 Western European and Northern American Protestants. Smaller groups are the Armenians, the Jews and the Scientologists, who number about 5000 each. There are also even smaller groups, such as Anglicans, Baptists, Pentecostals, Mormons, Seventh-day Adventists, Buddhists and Baha'i. Up to the Second World War, over 50,000 Jews lived in Thessalonica, but they were killed in the Holocaust. Many other Jewish communities were also destroyed in the Holocaust.

There are several thousand Greeks who have been baptized in the Orthodox Church but have now embraced classical Greek religion and worship the twelve gods of

Olympus. They aim at a 'pure Hellenism' without any Christian or Jewish influences. Many of them believe that the Greek race and blood are superior to all other nations.

Freemasonry is a special case; it is regarded as a heretical religion by the Orthodox clergy. Freemasonry and Orthodoxy are considered incompatible.

Religious and national elements are closely connected. The current Greek constitution, revised in 2001, has been drafted, like its predecessors, 'in the name of the holy, consubstantial and indivisible Trinity'. It lays down that the 'prevailing religion in Greece is that of the Eastern Orthodox Church of Christ' and that, regarding dogma, 'the Orthodox Church of Greece, whose head is our Lord Jesus Christ, is indissolubly united with the Great Church of Christ in Constantinople and with any other Church of Christ which has the same creed ...' (Article 3).

The close constitutional bonds between Orthodoxy and the Greek state are revealed in many ways. Religious and national festivals often coincide. Processions and parades may be combined. On the Feast of the Annunciation on 25 March, the uprising of 1821 against Ottoman domination is also commemorated. On 28 October, the day of the Greek 'no' to the Italian ultimatum in 1940, which brought Greece into the Second World War, the festival of Mary's Protecting Veil is also celebrated. Traditionally, Orthodox churches celebrate this festival on 1 October, but in Greece the date was changed (1952) so that it could coincide with the 'day of no'. On 15 August, both the Dormition of the Mother of God and Mary's patronage of the Greek military forces are celebrated. The Greek president and members of parliament are sworn in 'in the name of the Holy Trinity' on the assumption of their duties. However, non-Orthodox may take a different oath. An Orthodox bishop can accede to office only after being presented to the Greek president. The Ministry of National Education and Religious Affairs has close links with the Orthodox hierarchy. According to the constitution, it is not allowed officially to translate the Bible into modern Greek without permission of the Orthodox Church (Article 3). Further, the training and salaries of Orthodox clergy and theologians as well as the construction and maintenance of Orthodox places of worship are paid for by civil authorities. In exchange, the church turns over one third of its income to the state. The Jewish community and several Muslim institutions also enjoy financial support from the state. This regulation does not apply either to the other non-Orthodox groups or to the True Orthodox Church.

Both clergy and politicians often define the relationship between Orthodoxy, the Greek state and the Greek people as an 'indissoluble bond'. It often looks as if the true Greek is Orthodox and, conversely, the true Orthodox is Greek.

Nevertheless, there has often also been tension between the ecclesiastical hierarchy and those in parliamentary and government circles. In particular, the government decision in May 2000 that on new ID cards religion should no longer be mentioned gave rise to a sharp conflict between the church leadership and the socialist government. Church leaders argue that the Orthodox religion is an indispensable element of 'Greekness' and that the government decision promotes 'atheism', 'globalization' and 'spiritual bankruptcy'. The government claims that the European Union demands such a decision and, furthermore, that religion is a private matter and that the compulsory mention of religion promotes discrimination against the non-Orthodox. The fact that about 3 million Greeks support a petition against the government decision also means that two-thirds of the Orthodox Greeks did not sign it and that in this matter the church leadership cannot count on the support of the majority of the people.

Globalization

Anyone who visits Greece can observe that the Orthodox Church is an essential part of Greek society. In daily life, the church plays an important role by way of the rites of passage. Although a separate civil marriage is possible, the vast majority of couples prefer to be married in church. Almost all funerals take place with Orthodox ceremonies. Since the Orthodox Church is convinced that cremation is not only bodily but also spiritually destructive, cremation is currently impossible; however, legislation to introduce cremation is in preparation.

Festivals and fasts ◄

Good Friday and Easter form the climax of the Orthodox Holy Week, known as Great Week, indeed of the whole liturgical year. Then, nearly all Greeks attend church services. The passion, death and resurrection of Christ are extensively re-enacted and visually dramatized. For many foreigners, too, these rituals, e.g. the procession and lamentations on Good Friday and the stately reading of the resurrection gospel on a podium outside the church during the Easter vigil, are moving events. The annual festival of the local community's patron saint, which includes music and dance as well as pilgrimages to noted shrines, such as those of Mary on the island of Tinos and of St Nektarios on Aegina, are other highlights.

However, except for the great religious festivals and despite the devoutness and frequent church attendance of a part of the population, many baptized Greeks are religiously indifferent. Or they feel bitter about the clergy, complaining of scandals and traditional right-wing attitudes within the church.

At most types of school, Orthodox religious education is compulsory. However, the number of curriculum hours has been reduced in recent years. Outside school, there are special catechism hours in church institutions. Many dioceses also provide courses in Byzantine music and iconography, foreign languages and even information theory. For candidates for the priesthood there are seminaries. Those who want to study Orthodox theology can do so at the state universities of Athens and Thessalonica.

Retreating from the busy world and living within a monastic community is a feature of Greek Orthodoxy. There are at least twice as many nuns as monks. The women's convent in Ormylia (Chalcidice) and the twenty monasteries and other monastic houses on Mount Athos are famous for their liturgy and asceticism. At least in liberal circles, the Athos monks are also notorious for their warnings against 'modernism', 'ecumenism' and 'inter-religious dialogue'. Mount Athos enjoys a semi-autonomous political status in Greece and can be visited only by men.

Nearly all churches and religions carry out an extensive diakonia, i.e. social care for the needy. In most Orthodox dioceses the weak and poor are supported by the so-called 'Desks for the Poor' and 'Parish Centres of Charity'. There are church homes for the elderly, blood donor centres and scholarship programmes for students. In many parishes a free meal is offered daily to between 50 and 100 poor, homeless or sick people, and the elderly and prisoners are visited. However, the extent and character of this charity work differs: in some dioceses a lot happens for those who need help – usually without advertisement – whereas in others there is little to be proud of in this respect.

According to the Greek constitution, freedom of religious conscience is inviolable and every 'known religion' is free (Articles 5 and 13). Non-Orthodox pupils do not have to attend the compulsory Orthodox religion classes at school if they declare that they do not wish to do so.

Nevertheless, in practice all non-Orthodox religious groups complain about discrimination. They feel that the position of the Orthodox Church as the dominant religion and the frequent identification of Greek with Orthodox leave hardly any room for the non-Orthodox.

However, several factors are bringing about changes in the thinking of many Greeks about religious majority and minority groups, about their 'own' identity and 'otherness': better education, the positive experiences of Greek foreign workers with other churches in Western Europe, Greek membership of the European Union, European legislation and the judgements by the European Court of Human Rights on Greek violations of religious freedom.

In spite of this, for most Orthodox hierarchs and also for many politicians and other Greeks, religious multiformity and multiculturalism remain undesirable. In their view, Orthodoxy is the only moral guarantor for the Greek nation.

BASILIUS J. GROEN

Kallistos Ware, *The Orthodox Church*, Harmondsworth: Penguin Books [4]1997

Celtic Christianity →
Books →
Reformation →
Church of England →

Ireland

Patrick, born in Britain in the fifth century to a Romano-British official who was a Christian deacon, is acknowledged as 'the apostle of Ireland'. He first saw the country when he was captured near his home in Britain by Irish pirates and sold into slavery in Ireland. Having escaped after several years, he became convinced of his vocation to bring Christianity to the Irish and in later life returned, as a bishop, to the land of his captivity. The church that he and his successors established soon developed along predominantly monastic lines, and many Irish monasteries such as Glendalough, Clonmacnoise and Bangor became famous centres of scholarship and produced such important examples of Christianity as the sculptured high crosses, the Book of Kells and the Ardagh chalice. Indeed, at a time when the Roman empire was crumbling and the church suffering from considerable disruption, many Irish missionaries travelled to Britain and the continent and earned for Ireland the title 'island of saints'.

Ireland, whether north or south, is still widely regarded as one of Europe's most religious countries, where the level of church-going and other forms of religious observance is much higher than is generally the case on other parts of the continent. In Northern Ireland in particular, religious and political traditions are so closely aligned that there can be little doubt that the great majority of Catholics are 'nationalists', treasuring their cultural Irishness, while the great majority of Protestants are 'unionists', for whom Britishness matters at least as much as Irishness, and often counts far more. They view with deep suspicion any overtures from the 'Catholic' Republic that might lead to political unity, despite the great changes that have taken place in the Republic, in the last century in particular, towards making it a pluralist society. Church leaders have constantly made the point to the outside world that the troubles in Northern Ireland are not a religious war, yet undoubtedly the nationalist/unionist strife has strong religious overtones.

This link between religion and politics in Ireland has its roots as far back as the Protestant Reformation in the sixteenth century, and aspects of it have their origins several centuries before that, when the slow but sure conquest of Ireland by England began in the late twelfth century. The English conquest of Ireland was not a sudden event, like the Norman victory over the English in 1066. It was piecemeal, with many setbacks. However, little by little the country came under English rule, centuries before the Reformation, and at the same time the church was also made to conform to English forms of worship and organization. As early as 1217 the English monarch ordered that only Englishmen were to be appointed to any office as bishop or to any cathedral positions in Ireland. Therefore, when Henry VIII renounced allegiance to the

Pope, the church in Ireland was required to follow the English pattern, and in those parts of the country under English authority the changes made in England by the Reformation, including the requirement to use the Book of Common Prayer, were imposed on Ireland. Henceforth, only the Anglican 'Church of Ireland' was recognized, and remained the state or 'established' church until 1871.

The conquest of Ireland by the British crown was only completed following the victory by the Protestant William of Orange over the Catholic James II at the Battle of the Boyne in 1690 (from whom the name 'Orangemen' for Irish Protestants derives). Irish resistance was largely broken, and a policy of large-scale confiscation of the estates of Irish chiefs, who were Roman Catholics, and transferring ownership of them to landowners from Britain (or to Irish landowners who conformed to the Church of Ireland) led to a situation in which in the early eighteenth century 86% of Irish land was in Protestant hands. This policy of 'plantation' had particularly lasting effects in the province of Ulster, where a great majority of the new landowners and their tenants were Scottish Presbyterians. Contemporary antagonisms in Northern Ireland are a fusion of the political, religious and cultural differences rooted in the plantation of Ulster in the early seventeenth century.

The British crown, being Protestant, could, according to the norms of post-Reformation Europe, require its subjects to conform to the faith espoused by the state, and the Ulster Presbyterians were regarded by both the government and the Church of Ireland as dissenters, excluded from political power, as in time would be Quakers, Methodists and other Non-conformists. But a series of 'penal laws' enacted in the decades after the Battle of the Boyne were directed at the Roman Catholic population in particular. Roman Catholics were subjected to many restrictions where public worship, education and admission to the professions were concerned, and while these disabilities were gradually eased, and in some cases were rarely implemented, the overall result of the penal laws was to give control of government and society to a Protestant (Anglican) ascendancy class which dominated Ireland for the greater part of the eighteenth century and the early decades of the nineteenth.

By the late eighteenth century Irish resistance to British rule had revived and found expression in the Society of United Irishmen, which drew much of its inspiration from Ulster Presbyterians who were fired with French revolutionary fervour for religious equality and political change. This Irish republican movement was led by Theobald Wolfe Tone, an Anglican, and a small number of Roman Catholics and Protestants who espoused the related causes of religious freedom and political independence. The United Irishmen's insurrection of 1786 failed, as did several later attempts to achieve freedom from British rule by violent means, though each in turn was regarded as keeping the flame of resistance burning. The Irish parliament, which had been a buttress of Protestant Ascendancy power in Ireland, was abolished, and in 1801 Ireland was ruled directly from Westminster as part of the United Kingdom of Great Britain and Ireland. As most barriers to Roman Catholic participation in parliamentary life were removed, inevitably, by degrees, most Irish Members of Parliament were Roman Catholics and were committed to at least some degree of Irish independence. The Roman Catholic Church had retained the allegiance of the great majority of the population and embarked on a vast programme of church building. A major programme of educational and medical provision under church auspices got under way, largely through the work of religious orders of men and women, several of which, now worldwide, were founded in Ireland. Nineteenth-century philanthropy was more often than not provided by churches, particularly at times of famine, and if relief work was sometimes tinged with proselytism this was by no means universally so. Great numbers of Irish people emigrated through economic necessity, especially in the wake of the Great Famine of 1847–8, but there were also those, of all religious traditions, predominantly though by no means exclusively Roman Catholic, who were imbued with a missionary spirit to serve abroad.

English politicians, in particular the Liberal Party led by W. E. Gladstone, sought to bind Ireland to Britain by redressing Irish grievances and, as an earnest of this, removed the Church of Ireland's privileged position as the 'established church'.

The movement for Irish independence culminated in 1922 in an Anglo-Irish Treaty whereby 26 of the 32 counties of Ireland (92.6% Catholic) achieved virtual independence, the 6 north-eastern counties of Ulster (66.5% Protestant) remaining within the United Kingdom with a degree of local autonomy.

The religious minorities in both jurisdictions faced uncomfortable times. In the formative years of the Irish Free State social legislation (especially where matters of contraception, divorce and censorship were concerned) was strongly imbued with Roman Catholic social teaching, and state policy to revive the Irish language and hopefully replace English as the vernacular alienated many Protestants. A new constitution for the Free State came into operation in 1937. It acknowledged the 'special position' of the Holy, Catholic, Apostolic and Roman Church as 'the guardian of the Faith professed by the great majority of the citizens'. This article fell far short of what influential voices in Dublin and Rome would have wished, and was subsequently decreed by the courts to confer no privileged position before the law on any members of that church. Furthermore, the same article 'recognized' the Church of Ireland, the Presbyterian Church in Ireland, the Methodist Church in Ireland and the Religious Society of Friends (Quakers), as well as the Jewish congregations and other religious denominations existing in Ireland at the time. In any event, the clause was removed from the constitution of Ireland by referendum in 1972 by a majority of 5:1. The fact that leading figures in the Irish language revival movement (particularly Douglas Hyde) and in the Anglo-Irish literary and dramatic renaissance at the turn of the century (not least W. B. Yeats, J. M. Synge and Sean O'Casey) were Protestant illustrated the Protestant contribution to both political and cultural nationalism. Roman Catholics in Northern Ireland could make no such claim to a part in achieving unionist ambitions and were subjected to varying degrees of discrimination, especially at local government level, well documented by official enquiries.

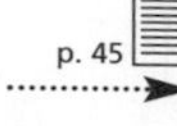
p. 45

Waldensian Church

By the late twentieth century, the larger Irish churches, all of which had retained their unity despite the partitioning of the island, were being impelled towards greater reconciliation, not least by the constant rebuke to their ministry posed by communal bitterness and violence. This was particularly evident in Northern Ireland, but was symptomatic of inter-church relationships that were far from perfect throughout the country. The Second Vatican Council (1962–5) provided the occasion and the inspiration for a considerable outpouring of ecumenical feeling from the 1960s onwards, and in 1973 regular ground-breaking meetings began between the leaders of the Roman Catholic Church and the member churches of the Irish Council of Churches (Orthodox, Anglican and Protestant). These talks have by degrees been placed on a more structured basis, the churches concerned being mindful of their contribution to division in past years and of the urgent need for ecumenical effort.

Paul

Council

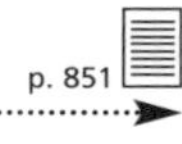
p. 851

Ministry and ministers

It needs also to be recognized that the Irish churches have not been preoccupied with internal problems to the exclusion of a wider ministry. Over the years they have made great contributions both at home and overseas to the welfare of countless numbers of people. Whether in the form of the traditional missionary efforts to Africa, India and elsewhere or, more recently, by providing personnel and other resources to bring aid to developing countries, Irish men and women have attempted to show the world a more attractive face of Irish Christianity than that which more usually hits the headlines.

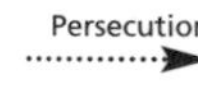
Persecution

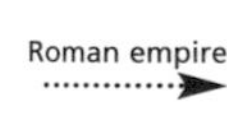
Roman empire

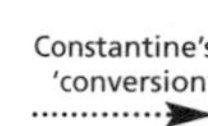
Constantine's 'conversion'

KENNETH MILNE

Brendan Bradshaw and Daire Keogh (eds), *Christianity in Ireland: Revisiting the Story*, Dublin: Columba Press 2001; D. L. Cooney, *The Methodists in Ireland: A Short History*, Dublin: Columba Press 2001; P. J. Corish, *The Irish Catholic Experience: A Historical Survey*, Dublin: Gill & Macmillan 1985; Finlay Holmes, *The Presbyterian Church in Ireland: A Popular History*, Dublin: Columba Press 2000; Kenneth Milne, *A Short History of the Church of Ireland*, Dublin: Columba Press [4]2003

Papacy

Italy

For most people, 'Italian' means 'Roman Catholic', since Italy is home to the Holy See, the centre of Roman Catholicism. However, while this Christian church has been dominant in Italy and still is, it should not be forgotten that the Italian religious panorama is enriched by some significant and ancient minorities, such as the Jews (who lived in Rome long before the Christian era) and the Waldensians (Italy's Reformed church, whose roots go back to the twelfth century).

Christianity was brought to Italy at the dawning of the church. The Acts of the Apostles informs us that the apostle Paul and his companions sailed from Malta towards Italy. When they arrived in Puteoli (Naples), the writer tells: 'there we found fellow-Christians, and were invited to stay with them for seven days; and thus we came to Rome. And the Christians, when they heard about us, came from there as far as the Market of Appius and Three Inns [on the outskirts of Rome] to meet us' (28.14–15).

So Paul was not the first to evangelize Rome, even if his influence was crucial for the establishment of Christianity. If the arrival of Paul in Rome is witnessed by the New Testament, Peter's presence in the capital of the empire is recorded only by an ancient tradition, speaking of the martyrdom of Peter and Paul in Rome towards the 60s CE. Roman Catholics consider Peter to be the first 'pope', and subsequent bishops of Rome as his successors, even if many historians think that the early Christian community of Rome did not have a single bishop but rather a collegial form of episcopacy, exercised by a group of presbyters.

During the first three centuries, not least because of persecutions, the power of the Bishop of Rome was in practice – with a few exceptions – limited to Latium, the region around Rome. But in the fourth century, when the emperors declared Christianity at first a 'lawful' religion (Constantine) and then the official religion of the whole empire (Theodosius), papal influence began to extend to all Italy and beyond.

By the end of the fourth century the whole of 'pagan' Italy had become Christian. And it remained so in the following centuries, because the 'barbarian' people who invaded the peninsula also converted to Christianity, if they were not Christians already. From the eighth to the tenth centuries, papal power declined as a result of particularly difficult social conditions and the fact that some great Roman families had managed to get control over papal elections. But the role of the papacy rose again at the dawning of the second millennium, and was gradually strengthened in all regions, even if Italy was politically divided into various principalities and independent republics.

Italy was politically united again only in the nineteenth century, with the Risorgimento led by the kings of Piedmont (the Savoy dynasty). On 20 September 1870 the Piedmontese army entered Rome, putting an end to the temporal power of the Pope, which had lasted since the eighth century.

Pope Pius IX excommunicated the Savoy family and retired to the Vatican as a 'voluntary prisoner'. The 'Roman question' would not be solved until February 1929, when the Italian dictator Benito Mussolini and Pope Pius XI signed the Lateran Pacts: the Holy See recognized Rome as the capital of the Kingdom of Italy, and Italy assured the independence of the State of Vatican City (44 hectares), which was born that very day, with the Pope as supreme sovereign. The Lateran Pacts included a treaty, a concordat (giving several privileges to the Catholic Church in Italy) and a financial agreement. The treaty clearly affirmed that 'the Catholic, Apostolic and Roman religion is the sole religion' of the Italian state (Article 1).

At the end of the Second World War, with the fall of Fascism and the abolition of monarchy, the constitution of the new Italian Republic (1947) stated in Article 7 that the relations between the state and the Catholic Church were ruled by the Lateran Pacts, while relations with confessions other than the Catholic Church should be ruled by special 'agreements' (Article 8).

In 1984 the 1929 Concordat was revised, *de facto* abolishing Article 1 of the Lateran Treaty. Only then were the first agreements with other religious confessions signed (with the Waldensian/Methodist Church and the Jewish Union). With the new concordat the Catholic Church received a new system of financing, which would later also be adopted by the state in the agreements with other religious bodies. This is the so-called '8 per 1000' system, whereby taxpayers can decide to assign 0.08% of their taxes to a denomination of their choice.

According to Roman Catholic doctrine, the Pope is the Bishop of Rome, and all his powers in the church derive from this office. In practice, however, he does not govern the diocese of Rome directly, leaving this task to a 'vicariate' led by a cardinal whom he nominates. The Pope is also the primate of Italy, but after the Second Vatican Council (1962–5) an Italian Bishops' Conference (CEI) was set up, as in other countries. However, while bishops' conferences in the rest of the world elect their president and secretary, in Italy these are directly chosen by the Pope.

The Roman Catholic Church in Italy has a formidable organization: 225 dioceses with approximately 300 bishops; 25,000 parish churches with 37,000 priests, both religious and secular; 80,000 nuns; and a large number of different institutions (schools, hospitals, cultural centres, publications). Some of these institutions are directly linked to CEI or to individual dioceses, while others answer to religious orders or lay movements. The Bishops' Conference also controls *Avvenire*, the Catholic national daily newspaper; the *Osservatore Romano* is the Vatican daily newspaper, representing semi-officially the thought of the Holy See.

Organization

More than 90% of Italians are baptized into the Roman Catholic Church. From this point of view the country is still strongly Roman Catholic, but in the last decades growing secularization has deeply affected the country's religious landscape. Apart from baptism and other 'rites of passage' (confirmation, marriages and funerals), religious practice is shrinking, so that even the CEI speaks of Roman Catholics as a 'minority' in Italian society. According to recent surveys, regular attendance at Sunday mass is steadily decreasing, dropping from 35% in 1985 to 29% in 2002. Only 15.7% of young people between the ages of 18 and 24 regularly attend mass.

Vatican
Secularization

Furthermore, Italians seem to be less and less inclined to conform to the guidelines of the Roman Catholic hierarchy on moral and social issues. Only in 1970 was divorce made legal in Italy. In May 1974 there was a referendum on the law, and the Roman Catholic hierarchy strongly urged the faithful to vote to abolish it. However, 60% of the electorate voted to keep the law. The same thing happened in May 1981, when in a referendum 70% of the electorate voted to keep the law on abortion, once more against the advice of CEI.

From the end of the Second World War to the early 1990s the Christian Democrats ruled the country, representing more or less the 'long arm' of the Roman Catholic hierarchy in the political field. The political unity of Roman Catholics came to an end after the breakdown of the Berlin wall in 1989, and the party collapsed, in parallel to the crisis of the Italian Communist party, at that time the strongest Communist party in Western Europe. Today there are still political parties that have the adjective 'Christian' in their name, but the CEI does not want to be directly linked with them, as it was with the Christian Democrats. Rather, the bishops call on all 'Catholic' politicians – whether right-wing, centre or left-wing – to defend 'Catholic values'.

Italian Catholicism boasts some of the most famous saints of the worldwide church, including Benedict (sixth century), Francis of Assisi (thirteenth century), Catherine of Siena (fourteenth century), Luigi Gonzaga (sixteenth century), John Bosco (nineteenth century) and Pope John XXIII (twentieth century), who was declared 'blessed' in

2000. The Italian church has sent a host of missionaries all around the world. Most popes have been Italians: in 1978 the election of the Polish Pope John Paul II interrupted a continuous chain of Italian popes lasting for 455 years.

In the last decades, there has been a significant growth of lay movements in Italy, engaged in both social work and spiritual renewal. Even if now reduced in numbers, the movement of grassroots communities or Catholic dissent has played an important role in the renewal of the church in the wake of Vatican II, and in challenging the identification of Roman Catholicism with the Christian Democrats. However, these groups have always been marginalized by the hierarchy. Other lay movements, on the contrary, have good relations with the bishops, such as the Focolare movement and the Sant'Egidio Community, both engaged in ecumenical activities and peace efforts, and now also active in other countries. After Vatican II the importance of Catholic Action, a lay movement that was very strong in the decades from 1930 to 1960, has diminished, but the Associations of Catholic Workers (ACLI) have kept their social influence.

The Waldensian Church was granted civil rights in 1848 by King Charles Albert of Savoy, and with the Italian Risorgimento, the movement for Italian unity in the second half of the nineteenth century, started opening churches, schools and cultural and social institutions all over the peninsula. Baptists, Methodists and the Salvation Army also started their work in Italy during the Risorgimento. Together with the Waldensians and the Lutherans they now form now the Federation of Protestant Churches in Italy (FCEI), established in 1967. The Waldensians and Methodists united in 1975; there has been close co-operation between the Waldensians/Methodists and the Baptists since 1990.

Fundamentalism

Pentecostalism

The Pentecostal movement began in Italy in the 1920s, and suffered harsh persecution from the Fascist regime. Pentecostals in Italy at present number over 250,000 believers, while the FCEI member churches have a membership of about 70,000. Together with other denominations (Plymouth Brethren, Adventists, independent churches etc.), evangelical and Protestant Christians number between 400,000 and 450,000, i.e. slightly less than 1% of the Italian population. There are also a growing number of 'immigrant' churches, mainly of African and Asian background.

Because of Fascist persecution there are now only 30,000 Italian Jews, half of them living in Rome. Muslims were almost non-existent in Italy until the last two decades of the twentieth century. Since then, the continuous flow of immigrants from Muslim countries has made them the second religion of Italy, with about 1 million believers. Other religious groups include Buddhists (mainly coming from Buddhist countries, but with a growing number of Italian converts), Hindus, Sikhs and Jehovah's Witnesses (who claim a membership of about 400,000).

LUCA M. NEGRO AND LUIGI SANDRI

R. E. Hedlund, *The Protestant Movement in Italy: Its Progress, Problems and Prospects*, South Pasadena, CA: William Carey Library 1970; M. F. Ingoldsby, *Up and Down Catholic Italy*, New York: Vantage Press 1985

The Netherlands

At the beginning of the twentieth-first century the churches in the Netherlands are clearly less flourishing than they were a century ago. At the same time, the need for new insights and new forms of spiritual experience is being expressed everywhere. Religion keeps cropping up in unexpected places. In his speech on New Year's Day 2002, to the surprise of many people the Mayor of Amsterdam pointed out the importance of religion for the city. While he felt that the separation of church and state was justified, he went on to say that the authorities were trivializing the role of religion in our times. He concluded that society needed more cohesion, and looked to religion as a moral standard and to the churches as social communities to provide this. Others have taken precisely the opposite view. In the wake of the attacks of 11 September 2001 and in the discussion of the integration of immigrants, a great aversion to fundamentalist aspects of religion has developed. This criticism of religion has been focused above all on Islam, but also on the more orthodox Protestant organizations in the Netherlands. In short, there is not only an increasing recognition of the role of religion in society but also a discussion of what kind of religion is acceptable.

Markedly individualistic expressions of spirituality are also becoming increasingly evident. The spontaneous lighting of candles and the laying of flowers and cuddly toys on the scene of a road accident, or a murder, or a fight which ended with a fatality and so on are rituals which show sorrow and indignation above all on the part of individuals, but also are a sign of shared grief.

Of all the religious tendencies in the Netherlands, the church and Christianity still have the largest following. It is unthinkable that the church should withdraw from discussions about society. The church has its place at the centre of social upheaval and should be an oasis for the many people who are in search of insight into themselves, redemption and happiness.

The involvement of the average church member has decreased markedly in recent decades. In the Netherlands Christianity, at least in its organized form, has become more and more the religion of a minority. The pillars of faith are crumbling rapidly and the churches have become 'ordinary' social organizations. At the same time their membership has declined. Whereas in 1980 still 75% of the population of the Netherlands were church members, by 1990 this number had dropped to 62%; according to figures from the Central Bureau of Statistics (CBS) in 1999 it was 60%. According to the Social and Cultural Planning Bureau (SCP), in 1980 50% of Dutch people regarded themselves as members of a church; in 1999 this had dropped to 37%. The discrepancy between these figures arises from a difference in the specific questions asked; however, the tendency is clear.

Not only has the number of church members dropped; so too has their involvement in the churches. In the Roman Catholic Church, for example, church attendance has dropped from 1.2 million in 1980 to around 400,000 today. The number of church marriages in this period has more than halved. And this development will presumably continue for some time because the younger generations are increasingly beginning to dominate the picture, and they are less involved than the older generations. The SCP forecasts that in 2010 only 13% of the Dutch population will be Catholic, 9% Protestant and 6% Muslim; 67% will not belong to a church.

However, in 2004 there are still churches and communities that are growing: Pentecostal communities, Evangelical communities, Jehovah's Witnesses and conservative Reformed churches. The great growth in the first two groups is largely because of 'new' Dutch people. They organize and promote themselves in a distinctive way. They combine a clear religious message that does not tolerate doubt with firm social control. They have a sense of exclusiveness, of being different from other churches and the rest of the world. This puts pressure on them to convince others, their own children or outsiders that they have the truth. Those who leave such churches have to pay a heavy emotional and social price. Conversely, the other churches are beginning to drop their exclusive attitudes and become more ecumenical. As a result, the need for individuals to remain members of the churches is declining. The pressure to engage in mission is disappearing: implicitly or explicitly, at home children get the impression that they can choose what they want to believe in. Churches that take this course lose members.

While there is a separation between church and state in the Netherlands, that does not mean that the authorities are no longer concerned about religious life. To give some important examples: the government subsidizes the restoration and maintenance of historic church buildings and contributes to the cost of confessional teaching and church and confessional public broadcasting; moreover, gifts to the church are allowable against tax and the government is involved in paying for the training of ministers. However, this support is not for the church *qua* church but rather for the church as the owner of national monuments (along with other owners) or in the framework of the collective financing of private initiatives (teaching, broadcasting). There is no question of subsidizing the structure of churches; however, there is financial support for specific tasks and areas like the spiritual welfare of prisoners and members of the armed forces.

Many people no longer organize their lives round their beliefs or profess them publicly. That does not mean that religion has become unimportant, but rather that the need to confess and experience oneself in a tangible group has declined. In recent years the Christian churches have lost their monopoly. This is above all the consequence of social developments such as individualization, the tendency of people to detach themselves from traditional associations and to direct their lives in their own way, and pluralization, the rise of a variety of religions and world-views to choose from. The religious market offers a choice of appropriate rituals or insights for every situation, and individuals are increasingly selecting their own religious positions.

Secularization

It is sometimes argued that the Netherlands is becoming more and more secularized, and the decline in church attendance and the marginalization of the churches are cited as evidence of this. However, a more nuanced picture of religious developments in the last five decades seems called for. Not only have social changes taken place, but the churches have also undergone a transformation. As early as 1955 the Synod of the Dutch Reformed Church called on its members to show a new solidarity, 'a new and powerful expression of togetherness in the world'. A year earlier, the bishops of the Roman Catholic Church already recognized this new social commitment: 'It is appropriate to our time to live in more openness and to make more open links between ourselves and others.'

Dutch Reformed Church

That, and not primarily the break with the church or the shift from the secular to the profane, was the most important event that took place in the religious sphere in the course of the 1960s. Christians no longer isolated themselves and kept out of world events, but were actively present in the public arena, often at the service of a deliberately broader ideal than a confessional one. Emphasis was placed on the public significance of religion, of ethics and of the churches themselves. Religious organizations – churches, schools and the wider social arena – became the instruments by which society was served. Although many of these organizations began to play down their religious character, they continued to exercise a powerful influence on society. Nor did religious influence on society come only from church organizations. The social movements that characterized the Netherlands from the 1960s to the middle of the 1980s were often inspired by religion. Moral energy was primarily fuelled by the convictions of people who had grown up in a religious milieu, whether or not they kept their links with the church. However, not all the religious activism of the 1980s was progressive; that is clear from the extensive anti-abortion movement, supported by many Roman Catholics and orthodox Protestants.

Somewhere towards the end of the 1980s this social activism inspired by religion suddenly stopped. The social movements lost influence, just as the old church organizations had done. The public hostility to traditional forms of religion also stopped. It was replaced by a greater openness to spiritual experiences, above all among young people. Religion became more individualistic and more diffuse, less moralistic and more spiritual. The renewed academic interest in religion, noticeable since the end of the 1980s, fits into this, coinciding precisely with the new interest in spirituality.

Now that the traditional churches have lost their monopoly, the religious market is wide open to a whole variety of suppliers. Immigrants from other parts of the world are bringing their own forms and experience of religion: exotic variants of Christianity, of course Islam, but also Hinduism, Buddhism and Winti, an Afro-Suriname religion. New Age seems to be a label that covers an extremely varied set of courses, lectures, therapies and rituals. These activities are focused on the individual seeker and do not necessarily lead to the formation of a community which meets at set times.

New Age movement

There is a growing discrepancy between the number of church members and the number of people with an interest in religion. In 1996, the latest survey in a long-term sociological investigation, 'God in the Netherlands', the first results of which were published 30 years previously, noted that clearly not all religious practice assumes the form of involvement with a church. A substantial number of people who call themselves believers or religious and for whom religion has a special significance in life do not feel the need to be associated with a church. In other words, there is a gulf between religious questions, needs and interests on the one hand and what is offered by the institutional church on the other.

For Dutch people, interest in religion lies primarily in the private sphere, especially in finding appropriate rites of passage for important moments in life and in bringing up children: 70% to 75% of the population recognizes that here religion is of some importance. This moral and ritual function of religion is recognized at the social level by a large majority. In other words, many people feel that religion is to some degree important for preserving values and norms (72%); for contributing towards a better society; and also for providing rituals for commemorations (70%), and for coping with disasters (63%). Granted, the social role of religion is thought of as being of less importance than its moral and ritual functions, but on average around 50% of the population accept it to some degree.

Although the view of public opinion is that the Netherlands is a secularized country, one can say that it is a land of believers. Despite the ongoing move away from the church, two out of three Dutch people believe in the existence of God or a higher power. A majority regard themselves as believers and sometimes pray. Various surveys show that these circumstances have remained relatively stable over the years. Atheism is not growing. On average, Dutch people find themselves somewhere in the no man's land between unbelief and Christian orthodoxy. Half of those outside the churches have some interest in religious beliefs. The survey by the SCP has produced the even more striking finding that belief in life after death, heaven and religious miracles even increased during the 1990s. And it is above all those in the youngest generations, born after 1970, who are showing a renewed interest in religious matters.

T. H. M. AKERBOOM

📖 A. J. A. Felling, J. W. M. Peters and O. Schreuder, *Dutch Religion: The Religious Consciousness of the Netherlands after the Cultural Revolution*, Nijmegen: ITS 1991; R. N. Eisinga and H. A. G. M. Jacobs, *Social and Cultural Trends in the Netherlands 1979–1990: Documentation of National Surveys on Religious and Secular Attitudes in 1979, 1985 and 1990*, Amsterdam: Steinmetz Archive Publications 1992

Portugal

From its earliest origins, Portugal has been a country with very close connections to the Roman Catholic Church. In 1179 its first king, Afonso Henriques, declared himself a vassal of the Pope in order to gain independence from the kingdom of Castile-León. From then to the present day there has been a series of alliances and concordats with the church, and even after the 1974 revolution, which led to a new constitution that provided for a secular state and separation between church and state, a concordat between the Vatican and the state signed in 1940 giving the Roman Catholic Church a special position continued to remain in force, though it is currently being revised.

'To be Portuguese is to be Roman Catholic' is a statement that, explicitly or implicitly, continues to be used to describe the church situation in Portugal. Statistics continue to prove that this is the case, indicating that 90% of Portuguese are Roman Catholics, but sociological studies show that the number of practising Catholics does not exceed 15% (and in the south it is as low as 3% or 4%). While it cannot now be said that Catholicism is the legal religion of the country, most Portuguese families want their members to be baptized, married or buried by the Catholic church. To be Protestant is to be 'alien' in a Portuguese context.

It is difficult, if not impossible, to say when the first non-Roman Catholic Christians appeared in Portugal. Historians point to a series of intellectuals, writers and traders who proved sympathetic to the new ideas arising out of the Lutheran reform, but the first Reformed Christians did not appear until much later. The first Portuguese known publicly to have embraced Protestantism was João Ferreira de Almeida (1628–91), who was the also the first to translate the Bible into Portuguese.

Almost all the Protestant churches in Portugal are the result of missionary work by foreign churches from the middle of the nineteenth century on, and mainly at the beginning of the twentieth century. The oldest Protestant church (which is Presbyterian) was founded on the island of Madeira in 1838 by a missionary couple from Scotland. Methodists and Anglicans began their activities in the north of Portugal, around Porto, with chaplains from abroad; the Baptists are connected with the missionary work of the American Southern Baptist Church.

For decades, Portuguese Protestantism was limited to groups of foreigners living in the cities, mainly Porto and Lisbon. A constitutional law of 1826 allowed foreigners to be Protestants and even to build churches, but this was illegal for native Portuguese. Nevertheless, the first native Portuguese Protestant communities began to appear, as a result of close contact with foreigners, marriages and (illegal) missionary work. The context in which Portuguese Protestantism arose has given it two negative characteristics that are very marked in some areas: a 'ghetto' mentality, and hostility to Roman Catholicism. And in a country with such a marked Catholic stamp, the Protestant presence has been viewed with mistrust and wrongly identified with political ideologies, especially left-wing ideologies.

Protestant churches are not recognized as such; in 1971 they were legally classed as 'religious associations' and put on the same level as associations in sport and recreation. But they were barred from many activities such as teaching in schools, broadcasting on radio and television or having chaplains in hospitals, prisons and the armed forces. For many years it was not possible to construct church buildings, so many churches were housed in rented garages or similar spaces, adapted for the purpose. This often led to a ban from the local authorities on the grounds of illegitimate use. Pastors are not allowed to have their occupation on their passports because it is not legally recognized.

Being used to one church, most Portuguese were puzzled when a variety of Protestant churches arose at the beginning of the twentieth century, especially Baptists, Pentecostalists and Brethren; to make the situation worse, there was rivalry and non-co-operation between them. The names of these churches were also foreign. So they all tended to be lumped together as 'Protestants', which was a derogatory term. They were seen as 'children of the devil', as being under foreign influence, Communist, and so on. In this context the need arose to create a Portuguese Evangelical Alliance, and this was formed in 1925 in an attempt to overcome the divisions and promote understanding. For a long time the Alliance was an organization which only individuals joined, but later churches, communities and Christian groups have affiliated to it. Prior to the Second Vatican Council (1962–5) contacts between the 'historical' churches and the Roman Catholic Church were only just beginning, and were non-existent in the Evangelical Alliance, which was dominated by anti-Roman sentiment.

Ecumenism in Portugal can be said to date from the second half of the 1960s. At this time the Lusitanian Church (now integrated into the Anglican Communion) and the Presbyterian Church became affiliated to the World Council of Churches, and since then have sent representatives to the Conference of European Churches. A new political and social situation arose in Portugal with the 1974 revolution, which led to a certain cooling of ecumenical relations between the various churches, and especially among the hierarchy of the Roman Catholic Church, at every level. In the same year the Portuguese Council of Churches was created; at present this is the most representative body in ecumenical dialogue for non-Roman Catholics.

Anglicanism
Presbyterian churches
Ecumenical movement

In 2000 parliament approved a new law of religious freedom. This new law is discriminatory in that it does not apply to the Roman Catholic Church, but it does recognize the existence of other churches in Portugal and grants them some of the rights that the Roman Catholic Church has. However, most people do not think that it will put an end to religious discrimination and the unequal treatment of churches. The concordat exists to maintain the privileges of the majority church.

The establishment of the democratic regime in Portugal saw the rise of a number of neo-Pentecostal charismatic churches, coming above all from Brazil. These churches are flourishing. They are generally anti-Roman Catholic, anti-ecumenical and engage in a proselytism without frontiers. In addition some Orthodox churches have appeared, but these are not recognized by the Ecumenical Patriarch of Constantinople.

Pentecostalism

JOSÉ MANUEL LEITE

📖 C. de Azevedo, *The Churches of Portugal*, New York: Scala Books 1985

Russia

Russia, of course, extends far beyond Europe, but it is part of Europe as well. If you fly from Shanghai to London, after the first hour you are over Russia – Siberia – and so you are for the next eight hours. Beneath you, if it is daylight and in the winter, you see an unbroken expanse of forest and snow clearings, marked only by an occasional river and settlement on its banks. This utter monotony, however, conceals a network of peoples and languages astonishing in its diversity.

Persecution ➤

Even many people who have visited Moscow and St Petersburg as tourists think of Russia as a land of onion-domed churches, gilded and glinting in the sun. The reality is different. At the end of 1991 fourteen Soviet republics became independent states, each containing its own particular mix of people and languages. Yet this did not mean that the 'Russia' that remained was now a land of uniformity. Far from it. It used to be said that the old Soviet Union resounded to over 100 languages, despite Stalin's insistence that all should learn Russian through the education system. Russian citizens everywhere are rediscovering their old traditions, underpinned by their keenness to preserve their diverse languages, which never died out.

Orthodox churches

The Russian Orthodox Church exists everywhere, but often only as the religion of the colonizers who spread out from Muscovy from the sixteenth century onwards. The 'Encyclopaedia of Religion in Russia Today' (projected English title: the text is so far only in Russian) being prepared by Keston Institute, Oxford, and its Russian team of researchers states that once you have crossed the Urals into Siberia, Russian Orthodoxy is no longer the dominant religion. You find, instead, a bewildering diversity: Catholicism, Protestantism, Buddhism, revivals of pagan or ethnic religions, sects ancient and modern in all their variety.

So, go to Ulan Ude, the capital of the Buryatia, close to Lake Baikal in the far east of Siberia, and you will find one of the world's most lively Buddhist cultures, glorying in its revival after decades of repression. Visit Khanty-Mansiisk in Western Siberia, a massive region of tundra and marsh, and you will find pagan rites openly and vigorously performed.

Paganism

But Russia's European heartland, too, is not uniformly committed to Russian Orthodoxy. The republic of Tatarstan (capital Kazan) on the Volga is half Muslim: it is where Ivan the Terrible defeated the Tatars in the sixteenth century, but the vanquished retained their religion even during the Communist period. Go down to the far south. Today it is impossible to travel freely in some of the six regions of the North Caucasus, such is the instability and – in Chechnya – the ferocity of anti-Russian revolt. Each region is a separate melting-pot of Islam, Russian Orthodoxy and other diverse local religions and cultures.

Also in the south, Kalmykia, bordering on the Caspian Sea, is Europe's only Buddhist enclave. Its religion was exterminated by the Soviets, but is now vibrant again. Halfway between Moscow and the Urals ancient paganism has come alive again in the regions of Chuvashia and the Marii El.

There is one feature of Christianity – indeed of the whole of religion – in Russia today which defines its special quality: the first attempt in the history of the human race, under the Communists, to eradicate religion. *Gosateizm* ('state atheism') sounds a neutral enough expression, but this word conceals a policy which was not only systematically brutal, but brought catastrophe into the lives of hundreds of millions of people. Tactics may have changed over the years, but Lenin's ultimate aim of converting Russia into a religion-free society was never renounced for 70 years.

The Russian Orthodox Church had a privileged and protected position under the tsars, even though its independence was subjugated to imperial control. Lenin nationalized all church property and initiated the imprisonment and murder of clerics who resisted the new policy. Under Stalin all believers – not only those who stood out for their opposition to atheism – were treated as criminals and millions perished, men and women who even today have no memorial, not even their names recorded in the book of history.

Human beings suffered the worst tragedy, but the devastation of church buildings followed close behind. There was some alleviation during the period of World War II, when many priests and pastors were liberated from the camps and several thousand churches re-opened, but Nikita Khrushchev launched yet another campaign of imprisonment and church closure (1959–64). Khrushchev's fall saw no improvement, merely freezing the status quo. Leonid Brezhnev forced church leaders to toe the party line and proclaim that believers enjoyed all the freedom they needed. Anyone who made public the true facts – Western observers, as well as Soviet citizens – suffered calumny. Gradually a human-rights movement emerged, especially after the Soviet Union signed the Helsinki Accords in 1975, which theoretically rendered Soviet practice open for public inspection. 'Helsinki monitors' in many of the Soviet republics suffered systematic harassment and imprisonment. Behind the outstanding figures of Andrei Sakharov, the nuclear physicist, and Alexander Solzhenitsyn, Nobel-Prize-winning novelist, there were now tens of thousands of religious activists who risked their freedom and sometimes their lives to make the truth known. These men and women, including such groups as the women's Council of Baptist Prisoners' Relatives, were often denounced by the leaders of the official Baptist Union; and the ruling body of the Russian Orthodox Church, the Moscow Patriarchate, forced into conformism by the fist of the Soviet anti-religious establishment, denounced any independent voice. The scars which this betrayal inflicted have not completely healed even today and go some way to explain why 'reform' in the Orthodox Church is treated virtually as heresy by the Patriarchate, whose basic personnel never changed. Modern translations of the Bible and the use of Russian (as opposed to the tradition Old Church Slavonic) in the liturgy are excluded, with the repression of any reformist-minded priests.

Enter Mikhail Gorbachev in 1985, elected in the aftermath of the short and disastrous rule of Andropov and Chernenko. After he had been a year in office, the Chernobyl disaster (April 1986) apparently had the effect of persuading Gorbachev to add respect for human rights and religious liberty to his manifesto of *glasnost* (openness) and *perestroika* (refashioning the system). Believers experienced religious liberty for the first time in Soviet history. Without any grasp of how to use this, it was not always an easy ride. So many of those who fought for their ideals did not find the space to exploit them in the new Russia.

For example, the Moscow Patriarchate has never forgiven Fr Gleb Yakunin, a former prisoner of conscience, for having uncovered evidence in the Soviet archives of the collaboration that took place between so many bishops and the KGB. Disciplined by his own hierarchy, he was forced to leave the official church and exercise his priesthood in a 'dissident' branch of the Russian Orthodox Church.

1988 inaugurated the Orthodox Millennium, marking 1000 years since the baptism of Prince Vladimir of Kiev. Most believers looked on this as a miracle: the event fell in the first year since the Revolution of 1917 when it could be celebrated on the streets and in the media. The Russian Orthodox Church regained its freedom overnight and the triumphalism accompanying these scenes of joy was to be the mark of the official church, which explains much of what one sees and experiences in visiting it today.

Gorbachev promised a new law on religious liberty and delivered this in 1990, thus striking out the legal justification of Stalin's persecution, his Law on Religious Associations, which had been on the statute book since 1929.

The scars of persecution have not healed. Today, however, they are more mental than physical, so many visitors to Russia are unaware of them.

In terms of rebuilding, an astonishing amount has been achieved in a decade and a half. You could visit not only Moscow and St Petersburg, but also dozens of provincial cities, and be bowled over by the beauty of the restored churches, the gleaming colours of which give so much character to the central districts.

Rivalling the Kremlin, on the banks of the Moscow River, is the golden dome of the Cathedral of Christ the Saviour, one of the world's most massive and ornate churches. It replaces a predecessor of the same name, pulled down on Stalin's orders in 1937 (the event is preserved on cine-film). The architects planned to construct a tower block on the site, surmounted by a statue of Stalin big enough to rival the Christ in Rio de Janeiro. It never happened. The ground was marshy, cracks appeared, old women said the ground was cursed – so they dug out the foundations and constructed a swimming pool instead. But not all Muscovites are happy with the reversal of history enshrined in the new building. The untold billions of roubles were exacted by Moscow's Mayor Luzhkov from the *nouveau-riche* business community as a kind of hush money, they say. The decoration is ugly. Nor is the location a good one. Why not spend the money, they ask, on new and more modest buildings in the endless square kilometres of the featureless outer suburbs?

By contrast, the transformation of the Kazan Cathedral in St Petersburg, formerly the premier atheist museum in the Soviet Union, into a beautiful church again, is a wonder to behold. To talk to the dedicated priests, icon painters, masons and carpenters at work inside is a spiritual experience in itself.

Theological education, which was reduced to just two seminaries on Russian soil, is now re-established, at least half of 80 or so dioceses having their own schools for training the clergy. But here one becomes aware of the scars. It is one thing to restore a building, quite another to equip it with books and trained teachers. Too many have been drafted into these establishments without the necessary training (where indeed could this have been found?). The broad base of what is considered essential theological instruction in the West is simply absent. The result is narrowness, exclusiveness, even a mentality which wishes to turn the clock back to pre-1917 and see the church regain the position of privilege which it once enjoyed.

This is not and cannot be healthy. One obvious result is that the church – at least at official level – has turned in on itself. It presents a magnificent 'show': the liturgy, superbly sung, often by a professional choir, and dramatically enacted by ranks of richly robed priests and deacons, has power, depth, sincerity, theological meaning to attract the young and make converts, but it often also conceals the deficiencies which lie below the surface.

Fr Martyri, a priest in a central Moscow church, did model social work, tending the poorest of the poor and the physically handicapped. His superiors felt that this created the wrong image for tourists who visited his church. He lost his parish and eventually emigrated to Germany.

At its highest level, the Russian Orthodox Church has become anti-ecumenical, but this does not prevent East-West contacts, direct from parish to parish, which can often be spiritually rewarding.

The Moscow Patriarchate often proclaims that Orthodoxy is the religion of the land and the people. This may have been true in the Middle Ages, but it ceased to be so soon after. The Old Believers split from the mother church at the end of the sixteenth century over the issue of liturgical reforms that they would not accept. The schism was violent and has never been healed. The scattered Old Believers are rebuilding their communities in the many places distant from Moscow to which they were dispersed.

The Catholic and Lutheran Churches penetrated the hinterland almost imperceptibly with the opening-up of Russia to commerce and the import of foreign workers from the eighteenth century onwards, especially as a result of the reforms of Peter the Great. Nor were they always treated as renegades or a threat to the theological unity of the country. You can see a potent symbol of this in the historic heart of St Petersburg. On the Nevsky Prospect (opposite the Kazan Cathedral) stands the Catholic Church of St Catherine. Close by are a Lutheran and an Armenian Apostolic Church. The Nevsky was once nicknamed the 'street of tolerance'.

In Communist times Roman Catholicism was virtually wiped out on Russian soil although it retained its presence in Lithuania, incorporated into the Soviet Union at the end of World War II. Yet every major city had its Roman Catholic church, estimated to number some 300 in total. The anti-Catholic stance of the Moscow Patriarchate has ensured that there have been many and continuing battles over the return of these properties. However, whether or not they have regained their original buildings, an influx of foreign priests has ensured that the majority of Roman Catholics today can receive baptism, confirmation and communion somewhere in the major cities at least.

Lutherans predate other Protestants. Like the Roman Catholics, they came in with the influx of foreign – mainly German – workers, and commercial personnel and congregations sprang up in many cities. Soviet repression was almost complete, the more so since they were viewed as having ties with Germany. In recent years the renaissance of Lutheranism has been one of the most notable features in the religious life of Russia. However, there are five separate groups, not unified under a single administration.

The Russian 'Baptists', as the evangelicals are commonly called, originated in the second half of the nineteenth century and have long since ceased to bear the marks of an imported religion. Nothing is more truly Russian than the fervent singing of hymns (to Western tunes) by a full congregation in one of the many large churches.

However, the achievement of religious liberty in recent years has not come without the experience of deep pain on the way. After a relatively trouble-free first ten years, Stalin sought to eliminate the Baptists in the 1930s. The war years saw the creation of an All-Union Council of Evangelical Christians and Baptists, which the system forced into conformity. When new restrictive legislation regarding ministry to young people was forced on the church in the early 1960s, a strong and well-organized group, inspired by Pastor Georgi Vins and others, objected. A schism resulted, the ensuing bitterness pervading the life of Russian Baptists even today. So in many places one finds the 'reform' Baptists now enjoying freedom of worship, but in different churches from the 'official' Baptists.

There is also a revival of Methodism and no less than seventeen different branches of Pentecostal or charismatic churches can be identified. All of these were completely repressed in the Soviet period, as were the Quakers. They, like the Seventh-day Adventists, are now enjoying a period of greater freedom than they have ever experienced before in their history.

Anti-sectarianism is almost a disease in today's Russia. The media, backed by spokesmen from the Russian Orthodox Church, have whipped up a near-frenzy against the incursion of foreign missionaries. Yet many of these represent respected Christian traditions and among Baptist missionaries, for example, there are Russians and Ukrainians, as well as Americans and Koreans. Russia has been besieged, too, by Jehovah's Witnesses, Mormons, Moonies, Scientologists and representatives of various oriental religions.

Some of this activity pre-dates the collapse of Communism, but Gorbachev's new law of 1990 facilitated it. So great was the concern that a debate erupted about the legitimacy of these activities. Old-time Communists, who had been deprived of a voice in the new society, saw this as an opportunity to begin to exercise their muscle again. Governors in the various regions began, in an uncoordinated way, to pass their own local laws aimed at restricting sectarian activity. They established committees in which the strident voices of former atheist activists could be heard, though now backing the Russian Orthodox Church against Protestants and Roman Catholics indiscriminately, as well as the new sects. In fact, the main wave of foreign missionary activity soon passed over Russian territory, which was not left inundated. For the vast majority of Russians, what the missionaries offered held only temporary appeal. 'Anti-sectarian' indignation lost its focus, being replaced by systematic attack on Protestants and especially Roman Catholics.

During the 1990s the debate escalated, resulting in the promulgation of a completely new law in 1997, which swept away some of Gorbachev's reforms. The Russian Orthodox Church is recognized, in the preamble, as making the 'special contribution of Orthodoxy to the history of Russia and to the establishment and development of Russia's spirituality and culture'. Islam, Judaism and Buddhism are recognized as also being 'traditional' religions. When it comes down to the detail, the inadequacy and self-contradiction of this law becomes evident. Apparently, any religion may be considered traditional if it existed fifteen years previously (i.e. in 1982). But this year was Brezhnev's heyday and many mainstream denominations – not least the Roman Catholics and the Lutherans – were virtually deprived of official recognition at that time. The penalty for not being traditional is that every excluded group must re-register every year for the next fifteen, in order to prove its credentials and 'become' traditional. In the meanwhile, the right to publish, to own property and much else, is restricted.

Probably the main thrust of this law was intended to control sectarianism. Predictably, it has introduced confusion instead of clarity. Lawyers represent minority groups and fight for their rights against the Orthodox 'establishment', pointing out that the law does not conform to international conventions to which Russia is a signatory. Groups hindered, albeit temporarily, by the new law include the Salvation Army and the Moscow Anglicans.

Meanwhile, a vast amount of religious activity of the most varied kind continues, either unmolested or suffering hindrances from time to time. The one certainty that emerges is that the strength of the Russian Orthodox Church is less imposing than it seems on the surface, though its re-emergence as a power in the land is one of the major factors of post–1991 society. It has to learn to use its own strengths to compete in the 'market place' or – better – to rediscover ecumenical principles which it theoretically espoused when it participated so influentially in the activities of the World Council of Churches from the 1960s to the 1980s.

MICHAEL BOURDEAUX

📖 Michael Bourdeaux (ed), *The Politics of Religion in Russia and the New States of Eurasia*, Armonk, NY: M. E. Sharpe 1995; Nathaniel Davis, *A Long Walk to Church: A Contemporary History of Russian Orthodoxy*, Boulder, CO: Westview Press [2]2003; David C. Lewis, *After Atheism: Religion and Ethnicity in Russia and Central Asia*, Surrey, England: Curzon Press and New York: St Martin's Press 2000; Michael Rowe, *Russian Resurrection: Strength in Suffering – A History of Russia's Evangelical Church*, London: Marshall Pickering 1994; John Witte and Michael Bourdeaux (eds), *Proselytism and Orthodoxy in Russia: The New War for Souls*, Maryknoll, NY: Orbis 1999

Scandinavia

Scandinavia comprises the area between Greenland in the west, Finland in the east, Norway in the north and Denmark in the south. It is often said that the countries within this area are very similar in terms of politics and religion, and from an outsider's perspective that is true. But from within, as from within a family, it is possible to see differences between individual sisters and brothers.

The Scandinavian countries are usually thought to be predominantly Protestant. However, it has not always been the case. They gradually became Christian through missionaries from the south and west. The first known missionary to Denmark and Sweden was Ansgar, who came to Sweden in 829 and was received by the king himself. He came from north Germany and his mission was so appreciated by the church in Rome that he was made Bishop of Hamburg, a diocese which at that time included all Scandinavia. But the mission from the south was only partially successful. Later on, missionaries also arrived from the British Isles, firmly establishing Christianity here. Mission

Their strategy was to convert the kings, earls and nobility. This top-down approach to mission also decided when a nation was to be considered Christian, which was when the king and all his men had been baptized. Denmark came first, followed by Norway around 950. The Swedish king was baptized around 1000, the year that Iceland's 'Allthing' decided that it was a Christian nation. Christianity arrived in Finland around 1150 from both the east and the west: the Orthodox Church from Russia, and Swedish crusades towards the east.

Though church provinces in the far north were led from Rome, they gradually developed into national churches well before the Reformation. The church and politics were already closely intermingled. The signs of a national church were already present during the Middle Ages: the church buildings, the parish with all its inhabitants baptized, the bishop as head of the diocese, and Christian kings and a council that defended the Christian faith. One nation, one law, and one faith became true for the Scandinavian countries. All inhabitants were required to belong to the church. In some cases bishops were as much politicians as spiritual leaders. Reformation
Ecumenical movement ◄

The ideas of Martin Luther reached the far north very quickly. As early as 1523, one of Luther's students brought his ideas to the newly-elected king in Stockholm. This marked the beginning of the Swedish and Finnish Reformation; the Reformation arrived in Denmark, Norway and Iceland a little later. Of course, to begin with there were conflicts between the old and new faiths, and the whole area was not totally Lutheran until around 1600. New ideas of liberalism, tolerance, socialism, rationalism and positivism arrived in the nineteenth century, mostly from England. High rates of literacy led people not only to read the Bible, but also to interpret it and draw their own conclusions. Lay preachers became popular and common- Lutheranism place. New associations were founded and free churches established. In Denmark, Norway, Iceland and Finland most of the new movements remained within the national church, but in Sweden many free churches were established.

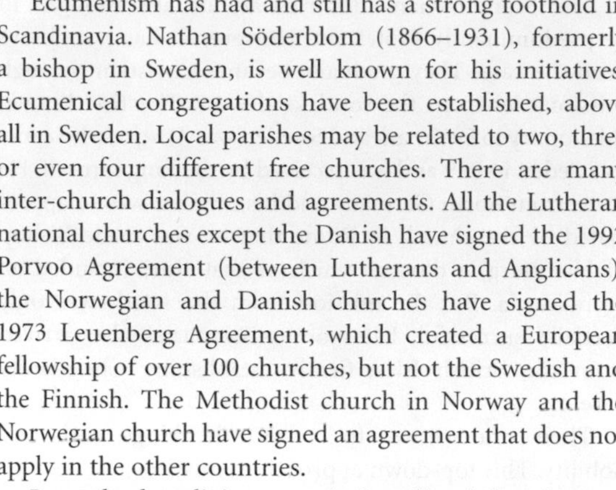

Ecumenical movement

Ecumenism has had and still has a strong foothold in Scandinavia. Nathan Söderblom (1866–1931), formerly a bishop in Sweden, is well known for his initiatives. Ecumenical congregations have been established, above all in Sweden. Local parishes may be related to two, three or even four different free churches. There are many inter-church dialogues and agreements. All the Lutheran national churches except the Danish have signed the 1992 Porvoo Agreement (between Lutherans and Anglicans); the Norwegian and Danish churches have signed the 1973 Leuenberg Agreement, which created a European fellowship of over 100 churches, but not the Swedish and the Finnish. The Methodist church in Norway and the Norwegian church have signed an agreement that does not apply in the other countries.

Recently, the religious map in Scandinavia has changed a lot. During the second half of the twentieth century large numbers of immigrants arrived in Norway, Sweden and Denmark, while Finland and Iceland have far fewer. In the first three countries there is a significant Muslim population. Many other religions not represented in Scandinavia before are now active and visible. So it is no longer true, as it was 20 or 30 years ago, that Scandinavia is mono-religious and mono-cultural.

A large majority of the population of Scandinavia belongs to the Lutheran national churches. The numbers are: Denmark 87%, Finland 85%, Iceland 90%, Norway 86%, Sweden 85%. Moreover, most people want to be baptized, married and buried by the church, though many of them are no longer even members. For example, in Finland in 2002, 87% of all newborn babies were baptized into the Lutheran folk church, though only 85% of the population were members of it. The difference is even higher in the case of burial.

Confirmation has long played a prominent role in the Scandinavian countries. Most fifteen-year-olds are confirmed; the lowest proportion is in Sweden, slightly less than 60%; in Finland, 90.5% were confirmed in 2002.

When it comes to church attendance the picture is completely different: an average of 10% in all Scandinavian countries attend church at least once a month. However, this is not because of hostility to the church; it is just not typical for Scandinavians to go to church every Sunday. They attend church only for special occasions.

Denmark
The Reformation church reached Denmark at the beginning of the sixteenth century, and the present constitution of the Lutheran church dates from 1849. Since the beginning of the last century, the Lutheran church in Denmark has had parishes and parish councils that govern local life in the churches, including the election of pastors. The parishes are organized into 111 deaneries and 10 dioceses, plus the Faroe Islands and Greenland. As early as 1947, women were allowed to become pastors and bishops, and currently two bishops are women.

In the nineteenth century some Christian movements had a great influence on church life in Denmark. One was inspired by the Danish pastor, writer and politician N. F. S. Grundtvig. Another important movement, 'Tidehverv' ('the Epoch'), argued that the church should focus on preaching the gospel and avoid engaging in other activities.

About 85% of the 5 million inhabitants belong to the Lutheran Church; 1% belong to other Protestant churches and about the same percentage to the Roman Catholic Church.

The Evangelical Lutheran Church is the Danish national church and as such is supported economically, legally and politically by the state. Constitutionally the ruling king or queen must belong to this church and the national church was supposed to have its own ecclesiastical law and be separated from the state from 1849 onwards. However, this is not yet the case: the church has no governing body and one of the state departments runs the church. Each diocese has a bishop who has very little power. At the local level, the parishes and the parish councils are largely independent. While the Lutheran church can be considered a state church, religious freedom is not restricted. All citizens have the right to belong to whatever church or religious community they choose. Nevertheless, only the Lutheran church enjoys state subsidies.

Religious education is included in the school curriculum except for children between the ages of twelve and fourteen; this is to allow for confirmation preparation. Those who do not want to be confirmed need not follow the religious education course at this time. Children over fifteen can be exempted from religious education provided that they and their parents so wish.

The role and status of the church in society are most prominent at the local level; the church has no national structure. Moreover, in keeping with the 'Tidehverv' movement, the Lutheran church is not expected to take stands on social and political issues.

Finland
As Finland was part of Sweden in the sixteenth century, the Reformation reached the country at the same time as in Sweden. In 1809, Finland became a Grand Duchy of the Russian empire. The Lutheran Church, however, remained the state church of Finland. The Ecclesiastical Act of 1869

loosened the bonds between church and state and made the church almost totally independent of the state.

Nearly 85% of the population belong to the Lutheran Church, which still has a special legal position in society. The same applies to the Orthodox Church in Finland, which is even more dependent on the state than the Lutheran Church and receives a substantial financial contribution from the state. It comprises 1.1% of the population. Other main religious communities are Roman Catholics (0.1%), Jehovah's Witnesses (0.4%), Pentecostals (1.1%) and Free Churches (0.4%). Almost 12% belong to no religious community at all.

The Lutheran Church has close to 582 parishes and 9 dioceses, administered by 10 bishops. The parish council is the supreme decision-making body within a parish. All members of the parish over the age of 18 have the right to vote in parish council elections. The supreme decision-making body for the entire church is the synod, which determines the doctrines, policies, and finances of the church. It meets twice a year.

The dioceses are headed by a bishop and a diocesan chapter. Until very recently, the bishops were appointed by the President of the country, and the diocesan chapters were part of the state administration.

The Lutheran Church is governed by the Ecclesiastical Act, which can be changed only by the synod but has to be approved by the Finnish parliament. Parliament has, however, no right to change the amendments proposed by the synod. The Orthodox Church does not have the same right as the Lutheran Church. Its affairs are also governed by a law, but that law can be changed by the state regardless of the opinion of the church. However, this happens very rarely. Both churches have the right to tax their members. This right of taxation does not apply to other religious communities. There has been religious freedom since 1923; a new act of religious freedom came into force on 1 August 2003.

All pupils of comprehensive schools have the right to religious education according to their own religion, and this is financed by the school. Those pupils who belong to no religious community and do not want to take part in religious education are required to attend classes in ethics and philosophy instead.

The status of the Lutheran Church in Finnish society, both at the local and national levels, is relatively strong. Since most of the Finnish population belongs to this church, there are rarely conflicts between church and society. If and when the church takes a stand on a specific issue, attention is paid to it.

Iceland

Christianity was established as the national religion in Iceland in 1000. Since Iceland was part of Denmark in the sixteenth century, the Reformation was implemented in 1541. As a result of this, the church came increasingly under the power of the crown. In 1874, a new constitution was established, which allowed for freedom of religion. During the nineteenth century, the effects of rationalism and other religious currents were widely felt.

Lutheranism is now the official religion of the republic. Relations between church and state are facilitated by a ministry of church affairs. There is only one diocese, the bishop of which is elected by the pastors and the theological professors in the university.

The highest legislative authority of the church is the Church Assembly. It has 21 elected representatives, 9 clergy and 12 laymen, and a lay person as the moderator. The highest executive authority is the Church Council, which is comprised of two clergy and two laymen, and is presided over by the bishop.

About 90% of the population belong to the Lutheran Church, while another 7% belong to other religious groups. All persons over 15 years of age have to pay a due to the religious community to which they belong or to the University of Iceland, if they choose to be outside all such communities. The state collects these dues along with taxes and distributes them to the respective community or the university.

Religious education is one of the subjects in the schools and is primarily considered mandatory. Even though those who are not interested in taking this course of study can be exempted from this subject, very few exercise this right.

Norway

Christianity came to Norway before the end of the first millennium. Since Norway was part of Denmark in the sixteenth century, the Evangelical Lutheran faith became established as the official religion of Norway in 1539. In 1660, the Lutheran Church was placed entirely under state control.

The Church of Norway is still a state church, with the king continuing as its official head. The government makes decisions on church matters like the appointment of bishops and pastors, liturgy, and even clerical robes. Parliament is responsible for the budget of the church.

There has been tension between the church and state for many years. The appointment of bishops has, in some instances, created friction. The media shows a great interest in church matters. There are also a number of church newspapers, which keep readers well informed.

There are about 1600 churches and chapels. The whole country is geographically divided into 1310 parishes, 103 deaneries and 11 dioceses. Parish work is led by a pastor and an elected parish council.

The General Synod of the church meets annually. 80 of the 85 delegates are members of the diocesan councils.

The National Council of the Church, led by a lay person, is the executive body of the synod. As part of the state administration, the Ministry of Education, Research and Church Affairs plays an important role in the governing of the church.

Although the Lutheran Church is a state church, freedom of religion is guaranteed by the constitution. By law, any religious community may apply for an annual contribution from the state. The sum of all contributions is to be approximately equivalent to the official budget for the Lutheran Church and allocated proportionally. When a community is granted a state contribution, it may also apply for a contribution from the local municipality, based on the sum of local expenditures to the Lutheran Church, also allocated proportionally.

The Lutheran Church accepts women pastors. At present, 14% of the clergy, and two of the 11 bishops are women. Strong lay movements in the last two centuries have shaped the Lutheran Church by establishing congregations under lay preachers in prayer-houses.

Although the independence of the Lutheran Church from the state and local municipalities has increased significantly of late, the relationship between church and state has been the subject of debate in recent decades, and commissions have been appointed to discuss alternatives.

All pupils in the schools have to take part in religious education, since the subject Christianity, Religion and Ethics is part of the school curriculum. This has been disputed by some parents, but so far they have not been able to effect change in the national courts.

Sweden

Christianity in Sweden traces its beginnings back to the ninth century, but was not firmly established until around 1000. The influence of Christianity grew gradually. At the end of the fourteenth century, the Nordic countries were united in a confederation. In 1520, the king contrived to have two bishops executed in Stockholm, which became the signal for a movement of national liberation, both from the confederation and from the Pope. The leader of this movement, Gustav Vasa, was crowned king of Sweden in 1523. He introduced the Reformation in 1527.

Gustav confiscated all property belonging to the bishops, but promised instead to finance the administration of the church. This meant that the Lutheran Church became a state church. It remained so until 2000, when it became an independent body with regard to the state, almost on equal footing with other religious communities. Parliament enacted a short and general church law; all other regulations are contained in the church order adopted by the synod.

The Lutheran Church has 13 dioceses and more than 2000 parishes. Each diocese is led by a bishop, a chapter and a diocesan council. On the national level, the decision-making body is the synod with 251 members, elected directly by all church members and meeting twice annually. In addition, there are the Synod of Bishops and the Central Board chaired by the Archbishop of Uppsala.

As a consequence of the new relationship between the Lutheran Church and the state, the implementation of religious freedom can be said to be almost total. Over 85% of the population belong to the Lutheran Church. There are a large number of free churches, but the Roman Catholic and the Orthodox Church also have a large number of members, 1.7% and 1.2%. Muslims make up somewhat less than 1% of the population.

All pupils have to take part in religious education whether or not they belong to a religious community, because the education is considered to be non-confessional.

The percentage of the population taking part in different church rites is considerably lower in Sweden than in the other Scandinavian countries. Only slightly more than 70% of all infants are baptized and a little less than 60% are confirmed. About 60% of all marriages take place within the Lutheran Church and more than 30% are civil ceremonies. Only with regard to burials is the percentage at the same level as in the other Scandinavian countries. About 90% are buried within the Lutheran Church, 5% within other denominations and 2% according to civil rites.

There are both differences and similarities between the Scandinavian countries with regard to the religious situation. In certain parts of each country, religion plays a much more dominant role than in others. The practice of religion seems to diminish with urbanization and increase with the age of the population. At the same time, younger people seem to be very open towards new religious ideas, while most of them continue to take part in the church rites.

GUNNAR GRÖNBLOM

Spain

'All Spaniards are Catholics, either good ones or bad ones,' remarked a clerical observer about the state of religion in mid-twentieth century Spain. This sweeping assertion disguised the reality of religious alienation already prevalent among sectors of the population, especially the working class, but in a nominal sense it had some validity. By 1950, religious minorities, Protestants, Jews and Muslims, numbered less than 100,000. By the early twenty-first century, this pattern had changed to a degree as immigrants arrived in considerable numbers from Morocco and Eastern Europe, especially Romania. The number of Muslims and Orthodox Christians in the country has increased, as has membership of certain Protestant churches, notably Jehovah's Witnesses. There is also a small Jewish population of about 10,000. Accurate figures on the size of religious minorities are difficult to come by, but it is likely that they number about 1 million in a population of 42 million. The vast majority of the population continues to identify with Roman Catholicism, although for many religious practice takes the form of observing the traditional rites of passage, baptism, marriage and burial in the church. But when asked to state their confessional identity by pollsters, from 75% to 85% of Spaniards (depending on the survey) still declare that they are Roman Catholic.

In spite of the qualifications that must be made about the quality and extent of religious practice among Catholic Spaniards, the persistence of this pattern of identification with Roman Catholicism still reflects the force of centuries of the country's religious history. Christianity had arrived early in Roman Spain. Indeed, according to tradition and legend still commemorated at the pilgrimage shrine to St James in Santiago de Compostela, the apostle began the conversion of the population. By the second and third centuries, Christianity had taken firm root in Roman Spain. Christians were subject to periodic waves of persecution, especially during the rule of the emperor Diocletian. The conversion of the emperor Constantine and the later adoption of Christianity as the official religion of the empire during the fourth century solidified the foundations of Roman Christianity. But the tribal invasions of the later fifth century ended Roman rule in the Iberian peninsula and introduced a period of conflict among the invading peoples that ended with the triumph of the Visigoths. The conversion of the Visigoths to Latin Christianity in 589 began a cultural and religious renaissance that produced outstanding figures, such as St Isidore. Over time, the Visigothic monarchy began to suffer from serious internal weaknesses and collapsed before the Muslim invasion of the early eighth century which left one small Christian kingdom surviving in the northern mountains of Asturias.

Christianity and the church by no means disappeared in Islamic Spain, although there were occasional outbursts of persecution. There were also periods of accommodation, particularly during the cultural and intellectual flowering of the caliphate of Cordova during the tenth and early eleventh centuries. It opened to Christian thinkers a wealth of knowledge from classical antiquity that had been preserved by Islamic scholarship over the centuries. But the fundamental fact in the history of the Spanish medieval kingdoms was the *Reconquista*, a centuries-long effort to reconquer the lands lost to the Muslim invaders. The so-called Reconquest was a long, episodic and, at times, chaotic process, but the defeat of the Muslim army at the battle of Navas de Tolosa in 1212 sealed the fate of Islamic Spain, although the small Moorish kingdom of Granada survived until conquered by Ferdinand and Isabella in 1492.

As the Spanish kingdoms of Castile and Aragon conquered more and more territory, they acquired a significant population of Jews and Muslims. The question of how to deal with them lay at the centre of official policy for centuries. For a time, there was a certain 'live and let live' policy, what some historians have called *convivencia*, among Roman Catholics, Jews and Muslims. But by the end of the fourteenth century, this world of practical accommodation gave way to what would become relentless pressure from the Crown and the Roman Catholic population to impose religious uniformity. During the fifteenth century, civil disabilities were imposed on Jews, while pogroms and other pressures caused many of them to convert to Christianity. Matters came to a head during the reign of Ferdinand and Isabella when in 1478 they established the Inquisition, primarily to deal with converted Jews (*conversos*) who were accused of observing their old faith in secret. Unconverted Jews were dealt with summarily through expulsion in 1492. Muslims suffered the same fate, although they managed to survive longer. They, too, were forced to convert to Christianity and were finally expelled, beginning in 1609. By the time this long process was over, the Spanish kingdoms had achieved their goal of religious uniformity, enforced by a vigilant Inquisition, which from the 1540s onwards also turned its attention to eliminating individuals accused of Lutheranism.

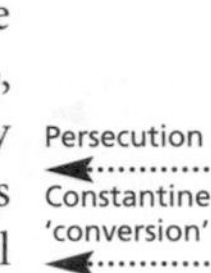
p. 345

Pilgrimage

Persecution

Constantine's 'conversion'

The emergence of liberalism in nineteenth-century Spain undermined the close relationship between throne and altar forged over the centuries. Successive liberal governments maintained Roman Catholicism as the official religion of the state, but they introduced reforms that undermined the wealth and privileges enjoyed by the church through the eighteenth century. The Inquisition was abolished, while the vast landed properties of ecclesiastical institutions were sold at public auction for the benefit of the public treasury. In 1835–6, the male religious orders were suppressed, although they would reappear during the last quarter of the century. The liberal state supported the diocesan clergy financially, although the resources provided could not compare with the wealth enjoyed by the church in earlier times. The progressive constitution of 1869 introduced religious liberty for the first time in the nation's history, while in 1873, the First Republic proposed the outright separation of church and state. But the installation of a conservative constitutional monarchy in 1874 ended these experiments. The church recovered its official monopoly, although the constitution of 1876 allowed religious dissenters, perhaps 10,000 in number, the private practice of their religion. Economic development and the

Religious orders

emergence of a more secular culture moved the church, however, to the centre of public controversy as a virulent anti-clericalism emerged which sometimes took violent form as during a wave of church burnings in Barcelona during the summer of 1909.

Jesus
Conversion
Bible

With the Second Republic (1931–9), church and state were separated and the religious orders subject to strict government controls, especially in education. The rising of the generals in 1936 against the Republic provoked a bitter civil war, in which about 7000 priests and religious perished as a wave of reprisals swept through the republican zone. With the triumph of General Francisco Franco and the Nationalists, the church recovered the privileges it had enjoyed prior to 1931 and acquired more in the process. This comfortable relationship began to erode during the 1960s as a result of the influence of the Second Vatican Council and the increasing pace of economic development. The death of Franco in 1975 opened the way to democratization. The constitution of 1978 ended the long history of Roman Catholicism as the state's official religion and recognized the right of all Spaniards to full and complete religious liberty. The separation of church and state was, however, far from complete. The government continues to subsidize clerical salaries, although at a reduced level, while it provides a generous subsidy to Roman Catholic schools, which have an enrolment of more than 2 million students. Religious minorities, Protestants, Jews and Muslims, have benefited from the new constitutional arrangements, although it is interesting that the government did not sign formal agreements with them until the early 1990s.

Wars of religion
Protestantism

Roman Catholicism remains the dominant confession in contemporary Spain in spite of the growth of religious minorities. It possesses an elaborate organizational structure based on the national episcopal conference (established in 1966), dioceses, parishes and a multitude of devotional and charitable associations, approximately 10,000 in number. But studies by sociologists of religion have shown a progressive decline in levels of religious commitment and practice since the 1960s, especially among young people and urban populations. The secularizing trends of recent decades are likely to continue.

Great Awakening

WILLIAM J. CALLAHAN

William J. Callahan, *Church, Politics and Society in Spain, 1750–1874*, Cambridge, MA: Harvard University Press 1984 and *The Catholic Church in Spain, 1875–1998*, Washington, DC: Catholic University of America Press 2000; Frances Lannon, *Privilege, Persecution and Prophecy: the Catholic Church in Spain, 1875–1975*, Oxford: OUP 1987; Stanley G. Payne, *Spanish Catholicism*, Madison: University of Wisconsin Press 1984

Evangelicals

The word evangelical comes from the Greek *euaggelion* and the Latin *evangelium*, words which mean 'good news', the old term for which is 'gospel'. Nowadays, it is used most frequently of churches or movements which regard as the hallmarks of Christianity the preaching of the gospel of Jesus, personal conversion experiences, the Bible as the sole basis of faith and an active programme of evangelism winning people over to Christ. However, evangelicalism has a long and complex history.

Martin Luther and his disciples were known as 'evangelical', as opposed to the followers of John Calvin who called themselves Reformed, and the Lutheran Church in Germany is called the Evangelical Church. However, evangelicalism in its modern phase originated in the first half of the eighteenth century. At that time individuals, churches, groups and movements emerged in North America and Britain with the same prime concerns as those of present-day evangelicals, concerns that have remained as core, distinctive elements in the evangelical tradition.

In the last 50 years of the seventeenth century, and as a consequence of religious persecution, there was a mass exodus of Protestants: Huguenots from France, Silesians, Saltzburgers from Austria and Moravians from their European homelands. They were passionately concerned to promote a type of vital Christianity in which the Bible, intensity of fellowship through small group gatherings and evangelistic missions were much in evidence. They emigrated to North America, Britain and elsewhere and exercised their powerful evangelical influence wherever they went.

It was in New England that modern evangelicalism first manifested itself in the New World. Typically, this took the form of church renewal and revival. During such times there were sudden, spontaneous, noteworthy and sometimes sustained increases in the extent and intensity of the commitment of church members in a particular area to their Christian faith and practice, with remarkable signs of rejuvenation. This was accompanied by a wave of conversions among both 'outsiders' and 'nominal' believers. Solomon Stoddart, the minister at Northampton in the state of Massachusetts, witnessed five such periods of exceptional spiritual activity in over 50 years of service to that small community up to his death in 1729. Under his grandson and successor, the learned and highly influential Jonathan Edwards, there was a spectacular surge forward for the church in the town in 1733–4, with many lives transformed, and a massive impact on the whole spiritual and moral life of the community. What was accomplished was reinforced and given a more secure and lasting foundation by the visits of the first international

Protestant evangelist, the Englishman George Whitefield. Whitefield was a key figure in the Great Awakening of the 1730s and 1740s that fundamentally changed the whole character of the church in North America and introduced social and cultural characteristics that have endured to the present day.

Other revivals occurred in various parts of North America throughout the next 70 years, and towards the end of the century camp meetings helped to perpetuate the revivalist tradition. These were outdoor, often very emotive, gatherings in which preaching was interspersed with prayer. It was also in that era, but more especially in the following century, that American evangelists carried on the work of proclaiming the gospel both in their native land and abroad.

American revivalism continued to play its part in the evangelical culture of the United States, the revival of 1857–60 being of particular note. During the closing decades of the nineteenth century various holiness movements were inaugurated in which the possibility of a 'second blessing', producing instantaneous sanctification, was proclaimed. In the early years of the twentieth century, and especially in Los Angeles in 1906, experiences of 'Spirit baptism' were reported that resulted in the establishment of Pentecostalism as a separate denomination. In the latter half of the twentieth century all churches and denominations, including the Roman Catholic Church, were powerfully and permanently coloured, and in many cases transformed, by the charismatic movement, and this added a new dimension to evangelicalism in North America and throughout the world.

The combined effect of all this evangelical activity, bolstered and maintained by the ministries and efforts of innumerable pastors, clergy and lay people, was to give the North American church both in the United States and in Canada a distinctly evangelical ethos.

The history of the evangelicals in Great Britain has had parallels with that outlined for North America, but with important differences.

Revival first appeared in Wales. Its origins and progress there were connected with the concurrent but almost separate labours of Howell Harris, the Revd Daniel Rowland and the Revd Howell Davies in the 1730s, a few years prior to the English revival. A revival in Cambuslang and Kilsyth in Scotland was likewise almost completely independent of what happened in England, although it began in 1742, at which time the English revival had been in full flood for about three years.

The revival in England was spearheaded by George Whitefield, and the brothers John and Charles Wesley. Its main components were, or became, open-air preaching, various types of small group meetings for 'seekers' and believers, and the use of lay preachers.

Unfortunately, in the course of about 80 years the new revival fellowship of believers experienced painful and at times bitter differences of opinion, and this soon resulted in long-term fragmentation. There was first of all the split between the Arminians, who stressed free will and were led by the Wesley brothers, and the Calvinists, who emphasised predestination and who looked to Whitefield as their leader. The ebullient Selina, Countess of Huntingdon, in her Calvinistic enthusiasm, built her own chapels and formed a Connexion which later, and much to her regret, became a separate denomination. The Wesleys remained faithful members of the Church of England, but in the 1790s, after their deaths, a new denomination, Methodism, was established, which in the following few decades itself divided into Wesleyan Methodism, the Methodist New Connexion, the Primitive Methodists and the Bible Christians.

At first the Presbyterians, Baptists and Congregationalists, the so-called Old Dissent, were not greatly touched by the revival. Nonetheless, during the nineteenth century they flourished, and they exercised a massive influence, exemplified in the ministries of Robert William Dale in Birmingham and Charles Haddon Spurgeon in London, and by the development of a highly important 'Nonconformist conscience'.

Then there were evangelicals who remained stalwart members of the Church of England. During the nineteenth century there was an impressive increase in the number of them, and in the prominent part they played in the life of the country. In the previous century they had been a small and much maligned and even persecuted minority. By 1830 they represented between one eighth and one quarter of the Church of England clergy. As the century progressed the proportion grew, and a number of these priests were remarkably dominant in local life. Some evangelicals became diocesan bishops.

As the evangelicals became more established, they widened their concerns. This was most powerfully demonstrated with the activities in the late eighteenth century and the early nineteenth century of the evangelical pressure group, the Clapham Sect. Under the leadership of William Wilberforce, it achieved much in the way of reform. Most notably it played a large part in bringing about the abolition of slavery. Subsequent to this, there was the outstanding work of Lord Shaftesbury, who was instrumental in introducing some of the foremost Victorian social reforms, including the hugely important amelioration of working conditions resulting from the Factory Acts. Added to this were the countless evangelical societies for the relief of poverty and social need and for the promotion of overseas missions, and such evangelical organizations as the Church Army and the Salvation Army. The growing strength of evangelicals and awareness

Methodism

Holiness movement

Pentecostalism

Church of England

p. 836

THE CLAPHAM SECT

This name was given at the time to a group of Anglican Evangelicals, active between around 1790 and 1830, who lived in the south London suburb of Clapham. They campaigned for the abolition of slavery and promoted missionary work in England and abroad. Their most famous figure was William Wilberforce (1758–1833); the group also included Henry Thornton (1760–1815), a banker whose home served as a centre; John Venn (1759–1813), rector of Clapham; Charles Grant (1746–1832), a director of the East India Company; Lord Teignmouth (1751–1834), a governor general of India; James Stephen (1758–1832), a leading barrister; Zachary Macaulay (1768–1838), father of the famous historian and at one time governor of Sierra Leone, all of whom lived in Clapham, and Charles Simeon (1759–1836), vicar of Holy Trinity Cambridge and founder of the Church Missionary Society, and Hannah More (1745–1833), who did not.

Wealthy and politically conservative, members of the group appealed to the rich and were able to mobilize public opinion and influence parliament. As well as abolishing the slave trade in 1807 and slavery in the British colonies in 1833, they established and supported a colony for ex-slaves in Sierra Leone. They were instrumental in founding the Church Missionary Society and legalizing the sending of missionaries to India, worked for prison reform and against cruel sports, and financed schools founded and tracts written by Hannah More. They nevertheless believed in the preservation of the status quo in society.

E. M. House, *Saints in Politics: The 'Clapham Sect' and the Growth of Freedom,* London: George Allen & Unwin 1971

of their shared interests led representatives from a number of denominations and countries to form the Evangelical Alliance in London in 1846.

Most of the nineteenth century was therefore a golden age for the evangelicals, but during the last two decades there were ominous signs of decline, division and dissention. By the early years of the twentieth century not only were their numbers shrinking, but they were a beleaguered minority. They were rent by internal strife and preoccupied with aggression against liberal theology and, in the case of the Church of England evangelicals, against high church ritualism. This unsatisfactory state of affairs persisted with only short-lived interludes until the 1950s.

Soon after the Second World War there was a pronounced and sustained evangelical renaissance that has persisted until now. The evangelical movement grew so substantially that it is currently a major force in all Protestant churches, and evangelicals worldwide have a great sense of their common heritage and their shared beliefs and practices. The World Evangelical Fellowship was formed in 1951, three years after the World Council of Churches was formed, and more than 100 million people are now affiliated to it. Gatherings such as the international conferences on world evangelization encapsulate an awareness of universal identity, unity of purpose and mission. The Inter-Varsity Christian Fellowship (subsequently named the Universities and Colleges Christian Fellowship) and Campus Crusade for Christ are often the dominant Christian organizations among university students. In particular, individual evangelists have presented evangelical beliefs to vast audiences, most notable among them the American Baptist Billy Graham. It is also noticeable that many of the most thriving churches in the world are evangelical. The evangelicals have certainly moved a long way since the pioneer days of the eighteenth century.

KENNETH HYLSON-SMITH

D. W. Bebbington, *Evangelicalism. A History from the 1730s to the 1980s*, London: Unwin Hyman 1989; Kenneth Hylson-Smith, *Evangelicals in the Church of England 1734–1984*, Edinburgh: T&T Clark 1988; M. A. Noll, D. W. Bebbington and G. A. Rawlyk (eds), *Evangelicalism. Comparative Studies of Popular Protestantism in North America, the British Isles, and Beyond, 1700–1990*, New York and Oxford: OUP 1994; G. A. Rawlyk and M. A. Noll (eds), *Amazing Grace. Evangelicalism in Australia, Britain, Canada and the United States*, Grand Rapids: Baker Book House 1993; W. R. Ward, *The Protestant Evangelical Awakening*, Cambridge: CUP 1992

EVIDENCE

Bible, Holy Spirit, Jesus, Miracle, Paul, Prophecy, Science, Tradition

Some strands of Christianity have claimed and continue to claim that all the necessary evidence for the 'truth' of Christianity can be found in the Bible. In the modern world this view is generally labelled 'fundamentalism' and considered extreme, but until perhaps 150 years ago it would have been widely accepted. The idea of 'truth' included both claims for Christianity as the only correct religion, and claims that the narrative accounts in the Bible were historically accurate. Other conservative groups would claim that the continuing inspiration of the Holy Spirit in the lives of Christians – either as directly experienced, or as revealed in the history of the church – provided a separate strand of evidence for the truth of the Christian message, the validity of which is usually tested against the standard of the Bible. Various developments, particularly in natural science, but also in philosophy and criticism, have challenged the reliability of the evidence of the Bible in various ways, and while the history of Christianity has involved more or less violent attempts to suppress evidence which was seen to conflict with the evidence of the Bible, the challenge of external evidence has also led to more fruitful developments in Christian thought.

Fundamentalism

Appeals to evidence in support of the claims made by and for Jesus go back to the earliest days of Christianity. Jesus himself is said to have appealed to evidence when messengers came from John the Baptist to ask whether he was 'the one who is to come' or whether they should look for another (Matthew 11.2–6/Luke 7.19–23). He replied, 'Go and tell John what you hear and see; the blind receive their sight and the lame walk, lepers are cleansed and the deaf hear, and the dead are raised up, and the poor have good news preached to them.' This appeal is first to the miracles that he does and secondly, since his words are a loose quotation from the book of Isaiah, to prophecy.

When Paul writes to the church in Corinth about the importance of the resurrection he refers to his own experience of the risen Christ, but in addition he passes on what he had been told: that Christ appeared to Cephas (Peter), then to the Twelve, then to more than 500 brethren at one time, most of whom are still alive, then to James and then to all the apostles (1 Corinthians 15.3–8). He also uses the same kind of argument when in an earlier chapter of the same letter he writes about the institution of the eucharist, on the night when Jesus was betrayed (1 Corinthians 11.23–6). What he says is based on a firm tradition.

Paul

Resurrection

Just before Paul writes about the resurrection, in speaking of the death of Jesus he, too, refers to prophecy. Jesus died 'according to the scriptures'. What happened to Jesus was not some random act of violence or dreadful tragedy; it was part of God's plan, which could be read in the writings of the Jewish Bible. This appeal to scripture runs right through the New Testament from beginning to end. The Gospel of Luke constantly takes pains to show Jesus explaining to the disciples how everything had to happen as it did; the Gospel of Matthew has a series of passages saying that 'all this took place to fulfil what the Lord had spoken by the prophet': in connection with the virgin birth (1.22f.), Herod's massacre of the children (2.18), the withdrawal of Jesus to Galilee (4.15) and so on. For the Gospel writers, the evidence for Jesus is in the scriptures, and so strong is this evidence that it shapes the whole way in which his story is told.

Early Christians also claimed that the evidence for Christianity lay in the present, in the experience of the Spirit in the life and actions of believers. In the account of the giving of the Holy

Spirit at Pentecost in the Acts of the Apostles, bystanders mock the Christians and say that they are drunk. However, Peter explains what has really happened, and ends by saying, 'God has poured out this Holy Spirit which you see and hear' (Acts 2.33). The truth of Christianity was shown by experience, and this experience led to tangible expressions of love and exemplary ethical behaviour. Christians showed the authenticity of their beliefs by bringing forth the fruit of the Spirit.

Messiah Salvation

The appeal to miracles, the appeal to tradition, the appeal to scripture, and the appeal to experience can be found at the beginning of Christianity, and these appeals are still made today as evidence for the truth of Christian faith. For many Christians there is complete continuity in this respect from the first days of Christianity on. Jesus was the Messiah whose death and resurrection were foretold in the Old Testament, who has brought salvation, and whose followers have been given the Holy Spirit, which has opened their eyes to see the action of God through history to the present day and into the future.

Beliefs Bible

Over the first thousand years of Christianity the beliefs about God, Jesus and the world which had been established by the earliest claims were developed into a comprehensive system, with its focal point in the Bible. In the Middle Ages the Bible was a school book and the source of teaching for liberal arts, the devotional book of the religious, the authority for professional theologians. It was the source of all knowledge, the answer to everything. It reigned supreme. There may have been different ways of interpreting it, but its truth was not doubted. And even if some might have had doubts, there was no way of substantiating them because there was no other evidence to which to appeal. The Bible was the basic evidence for Christianity. Indeed, it was seen to be the basic evidence for all human history, as indicated by the publication in 1660 of James Ussher's *Sacred Chronology*, which used the evidence of the Bible, interpreted somewhat questionably in places, to fix the year of the creation of the world as 4004 BCE.

Authority

However, such claims were open to challenge, and the figure who marks the first beginnings of that challenge is none other than the great astronomer Galileo Galilei (1564–1642). Galileo was utterly convinced of the truth of the new astronomical view of the world put forward by Nicolas Copernicus, who suggested in a work published in 1543 that the earth revolved around the sun rather than the sun around the earth. However, at the same time he was aware that this view went against the teachings of the Bible and the church. So he tried to find a way of reconciling two apparently conflicting truths. In 1615 he wrote an open letter arguing that both scripture and nature proceed from the word of God, but nature is inexorable and immutable, whereas the Bible often speaks figuratively to accommodate itself to human understanding. Once evidence emerges in the scientific sphere as to a particular state of affairs, that must be accepted; the authority of the Bible may not be made binding on scientific questions. There is a difference between knowledge which has a demonstrable basis and does not depend on interpretation, and knowledge over which argument is legitimately possible, where interpretation is involved. There is no way of suppressing the former truth; even the Pope is powerless here.

What is so important about Galileo's letter is its recognition that there was now a second source of knowledge, outside the Bible, which can also claim to be sound evidence. Galileo himself hoped that the two truths, the truth of the Bible and the truth of astronomy, could be reconciled, but he was condemned by the church, and the problem that he had discovered was thus made infinitely more serious in the long term.

Twenty years later a Frenchman living in Bordeaux, Isaac de la Peyrère (1596–1676), encountered a different problem. 'Ancient Chaldaean calculations, the earliest documents from Egypt, Ethiopia and Scythia, newly discovered areas of the earth including unknown lands to which Dutchmen have sailed' pointed to the existence of peoples who probably did not descend from Adam. Like Galileo, de la Peyrère could not doubt the truth of what had been discovered, but he too wanted to preserve the authority of the Bible so that there were not two sources of truth but one. His solution is indicated in the title of the book he wrote, *The Pre-Adamites.* In it he pointed out that the Bible itself suggests that there were human beings before Adam, and that Adam was the father only of the Jewish race (here he appealed to the apostle Paul). Nowadays de la Peyrère's argument is no more than a historical curiosity, but it enabled him to look the evidence straight in the face and take it more seriously than it had been taken before. He suffered very much the same fate as Galileo: he fell into the hands of the Inquisition and was forced to recant; his book was publicly burnt. Attacked by both Catholics and Protestants as 'the most pestilential theory ever held in the church', his solution quickly disappeared, but the problems it set out to deal with remained.

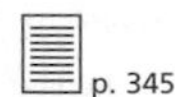
p. 345

Exploration

Centuries of exploration, not only of the globe, but of new areas of science, such as geology and evolutionary biology, and of human history and prehistory, produced more evidence that appeared to offer an alternative truth to that of the Bible and 'revealed' religion. The period of the Enlightenment, which began more or less at the time of Galileo's death, saw new developments in philosophy, including new ways of interpreting the Bible. The symbolic figure here is Benedict de Spinoza (1632–77), a Dutch Jewish philosopher who was an early pioneer in biblical criticism.

Enlightenment

From now on, all the evidence to which Christians had previously appealed was open to checking. Miracles were no longer universally convincing evidence of the divinity of Jesus. The philosopher David Hume (1711–76) made a devastating attack on them, arguing that no testimony for any kind of miracle has ever amounted to a probability, much less to a proof; he went on to say that what could be said about miracles also applied to prophecies. The tradition to which appeal had been made was examined in detail by critical historians and was found to contain many dubious elements, if not downright forgeries; the appeal to experience was confronted with the question 'experience of what?'; and the Bible was subjected to the most detailed scrutiny of all. The rise of biblical criticism is a story in itself.

Biblical criticism

Much has happened in the more than three centuries since the question of the two sources of truth, the two sets of evidence, i.e. the Bible and the wider world now being increasingly explored, was first raised by pioneer thinkers.

From the start, reactions to this new evidence have been mixed. The first questioning of the traditional evidence for Christianity as a result of a developing new view of the world was met with implacable hostility by the churches (indeed it was not until 1992 that the Roman Catholic Church officially 'pardoned' Galileo), and this opposition continued, indeed still flourishes today, on both the Catholic and the Protestant side, not least in various forms of fundamentalism. But at the same time it has to be recognized that the period of the Enlightenment, which marked the beginning of the real accumulation of the new evidence, was marked by considerable hostility to the churches, and to Christianity itself. So the atmosphere in which the evidence was gathered and assessed was never a calm and neutral one; this evidence was all too often seen on the one hand as a threat and on the other as a weapon. And in many respects this is still so today.

Evolution

Ministry and ministers

It is certainly the case that many of the discoveries of the last three centuries seem seriously to question Christian claims: the theory of evolution seems to contradict the biblical account of creation; studies of the development of ministry in the earliest church seem to contradict the claim that Jesus himself appointed the first ministers; the Bible now seems a book all too evidently written by a whole variety of authors, often with different perspectives and convictions, and influenced by the conditions of their time, so that it can no longer be appealed to as an authority which

EVIDENCE

Diversity · p. 845 · Geography · Heresy

has so to speak come down from heaven. But appearances here can be misleading. What is striking in the accumulation of evidence is the richness of the picture of Christianity which has emerged, from its origins to the present, a Christianity thought out and lived out by men and women with immensely varied gifts and temperaments and convictions, acting as individuals or in positions of corporate responsibility. The Dead Sea Scrolls open up a completely new perspective on the world of the first Christians and thanks to archaeological investigations we can walk with eyes open in the footsteps of Jesus and Paul. We can now trace this Christianity in different circumstances and in different parts of the world as it grows and spreads, and often read opposing sides of the same story, as in the case of, say, the Gnostics in the second century and the persecuted Albigensians in the thirteenth century. Hitherto obscure figures, particularly women, emerge from the darkness and add to the kaleidoscope of the Christian tradition. Much of the new evidence is not directly relevant to specific points of dispute or controversies, but broadens our understanding.

Unfortunately, the range of the 'evidence about Christianity' in the widest sense is all too little known, and this knowledge still remains limited to a comparative few. In the modern world, with its tremendous potential for communicating information, all the signs are that for whatever reason, there is considerable ignorance about the Christian past and present. Whether this is because of an inability on the part of scholars and teachers to present the evidence adequately, a lack of concern in the churches to encourage learning and exploration, or insufficient realization on the part of Christians of how much there is to be discovered and enjoyed, is a matter for debate. That is a pity, because a greater appreciation of all the evidence about Christianity leads to much less antagonistic viewpoints.

On the evidence now available, many of the old conflicts can be seen in a new light: doctrinal disputes can be relativized; points of historical divergence can be revisited and reconciliation worked for; views once held simplistically and doggedly need not be abandoned completely, but can take a better form. The new evidence does not threaten to destroy the authority of either Bible or tradition completely; but it does call for the nature of this authority regularly to be reassessed in the light of constantly changing circumstances.

JOHN BOWDEN

Klaus Scholder, *The Birth of Modern Critical Theology*, SCM Press 1990

Evil

Suffering

We tend to use the word 'evil' to refer to or to describe what is truly and horrendously appalling. But 'evil', and its equivalent in other languages, was once just a general term of disapprobation. And we need to bear this fact in mind when it comes to the topic of Christianity and evil. In common with contemporary usage, Christians have sometimes employed the noun 'evil' as a synonym for words like 'catastrophe', 'depravity', 'malignity' and 'vileness'. And they have often taken 'evil' as an adjective to mean 'calamitous', 'depraved', 'malevolent', 'vile', and so on. But their understanding of 'evil' has also been much more inclusive. They have often employed it where we would settle for nouns like 'fault' and 'harm', or for adjectives such as 'bad', 'disagreeable', 'hurtful', 'inadequate', 'incorrect', 'undesirable', 'unfortunate', or 'unpleasant'. In Christian thinking, evil is exceedingly commonplace. It is exemplified by moral monsters and extreme suffering. But it is also there in minor misconduct and passing discomfort. It is anything but rare or unusual.

Christian approaches to evil

Some people have said that belief in the reality of evil is incompatible with belief in Christianity. But Christians have always positively included evil in their view of how things are. The Gospels frequently portray Jesus as assisting those in the grip of evil. They speak about him healing the sick. They also report him as both attacking and accepting those behaving badly. And they see him as himself the victim of evil. The evangelists are very conscious of the fact that Jesus suffered and died. 'He was crucified, suffered death, and was buried' is what Christians would actually call an 'article of faith'. The fact of there being evil is part of what Christians believe as Christians. In this sense, it is anything but incompatible with their teaching.

Nor is it incompatible with what they believe in so far as they value the writings of the Old Testament. For these also give due weight to evil. According to the book of Genesis, it was the desire to know the difference between good and evil that led Adam and Eve out of Paradise (Genesis 2). And sickness, pain, suffering and human wrongdoing are everywhere noted in other Old Testament texts. One of them, the book of Job, tackles the notion of evil head on. Bad things often happen to good people. But how come? In the book of Job we read about a righteous man who does no evil but is afflicted by misery. He asks, 'Why?' Friends offer answers and the victim comments on them. Readers of the book of Job are clearly being called upon to do likewise.

But what sort of comment can be made about the suffering of an innocent person? The ending of the book of Job only says that this can sometimes have its place in a world made by God. Job's question 'Why?' is eventually greeted by a response. God answers Job 'out of the whirlwind'. But he does not give Job reasons why Job has fallen on hard times. Instead, he insists on the enormous difference between himself, as Creator, and creatures, as his products. And Job backs off, confessing himself to be ignorant of the ways of God (cf. Job 38–42). In the New Testament, however, pain and suffering are put into a special context. The apostle Paul, for instance, says that the blameless Jesus shared in human pain. But he adds that his agony was a triumph of goodness over evil. In Paul's view, innocent suffering is puzzling. But Paul also thinks that the sufferings of Jesus (his passion and death) are, in a sense, intelligible in that they show us what human goodness and God are like. For him, as for other New Testament authors, the death of Jesus was a victory since it resulted from his unequivocal adherence to goodness and since it was followed by God's act of raising him from the dead.

In terms of this theology, at least one instance of innocent suffering teaches us how to be good as people. It also teaches us what good people can expect from God. And this is a theology which Christians other than Paul have tried to emphasize. In, for example, the thinking of Thomas Aquinas (1225–74), the death and resurrection of Jesus show him to be a model for us, because of what led him to it (his fidelity to his teachings and actions). Thomas also says that it shows us that God is in favour of those who share in what Christ was about. Indeed, he adds, those who share in what Christ was about are already starting to share in the very nature of God.

Thinking with reference to the Christian doctrine of the Trinity, Thomas (in common with all orthodox Roman Catholics) holds that God, from eternity, is an unchanging life of love. He also takes the death and resurrection of Jesus, together with his life as a whole, to be God's way of drawing people into what the Trinity is all about. On Thomas' account, the story of Jesus is, so to speak, a projection on to history of how God views human beings. And he sees the end of the story as one in which pain, suffering, and sin are wiped away as people come to enjoy God's own happiness. In this he echoes the Second Letter of Peter, according to which Christians are destined to 'become partakers of the divine nature' (a theme much emphasized in Greek Orthodox theology). Thomas also echoes the Gospel of John. According to this work, which strongly emphasizes the divinity of Christ, Jesus says that his disciples are his friends, not his servants (John 15.13). And he speaks of his death as comparable to what his disciples can expect. But he also describes it as a return to his heavenly Father, and he promises that his disciples will come to join him as objects of his and his Father's love. In terms of this theology, evil is something destined to pass away for those who are allies of Jesus.

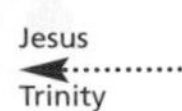

But what of the evil which we now encounter daily? Is there such a thing as a Christian view of this? To some extent there is. Hence, for example, Christians have consistently taught that moral evil is contrary to God's will and that human ethical thinking must always be complemented by an account of human behaviour which brings God into the picture. For Christians, conclusions as to what is morally good and bad are ultimately theological ones. Then again, Christians have always taught that evil is always somehow subject to God. Some people have taken evil to be a positive and active force almost equal to God. But this has never been a mainstream Christian view, though Augustine of Hippo toyed with it for a while. For Christians in general, evil always falls within God's providence and no evil takes him by surprise or represents a threat to him and his intentions. According to some Christians, it is actually a means by which God brings his plan for the created order to fruition. Hence, for example, one New Testament author writes: 'Count it all joy, my brethren, when you meet various trials, for you know that the testing of your faith produces steadfastness' (James 1.2–3). The suggestion here seems to be that adversity can improve character. And this is an idea that many Christians have emphasized.

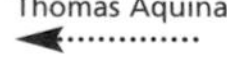

The problem of evil

But what about the fact that there is evil at all? With this question we approach a topic which has greatly engaged

THEODICY

Theodicy means 'the justification of God' (from the Greek). The term was first used by G. W. F. von Leibniz, who in 1710 wrote a book called *Essais de Theodicée sur la bonté de Dieu* (Essays of Theodicy on the Goodness of God). However, the problem denoted by theodicy, namely how the suffering and evil in the world can be reconciled with a good and just God, is an age-old one. The Greek philosopher Epicurus (347–270 BCE) already argued: 'If God wants to prevent evil, but cannot, then He is not all-powerful; if He can prevent evil, but will not, then He is not good. If He has both the power and the will to eliminate evil, then why is evil in the world?'

Many attempts have been made in the history of Christianity to answer this question. Evil has no existence and is a lack of good, so the creator is not responsible for it. Moral evil is the result of man's free choice, which is necessarily sinful. God allows evil but does not approve it and will overcome it in the end.

The French Enlightenment philosopher Pierre Bayle (1647–1706) argued powerfully that the existence of evil is incompatible with the existence of a good, just, omnipotent God, and it was against him that Leibniz wrote his book, arguing that this world was the best of all possible worlds. However, Voltaire in his *Candide* (1759) wittily and devastatingly destroyed this argument in the wake of the great Lisbon earthquake of 1755. Subsequent events, not least Auschwitz, have made any new argument impossible to construct. The question remains the most difficult of all for any religious believer.

both Christians and those unsympathetic to Christianity. Sometimes referred to as 'the problem of evil', it basically boils down to the question, 'How can there be evil if Christians are right to say that God exists and that he is as they take him to be?' Christians do not just claim that God exists. They also traditionally hold that God is omnipotent, omniscient, and perfectly good. But if all that is so, does it not seem to follow that there would be no evil? For would not an omnipotent, omniscient and good God prevent it? Evil seems to be no illusion. So does it not cast doubt on the reality of God?

Some have felt that it does, since they cannot see how God there could be any evil at all if God really existed. On their account, 'God exists' and 'Evil exists' are contradictory statements. Why? The argument often goes like this: 1. If God exists, he knows about evil and is able to prevent it occurring. 2. If God is good, then he would prevent evil in so far as he knows about it and is able to prevent it. 3. Since evil exists, it therefore follows that God cannot exist. According to this line of thinking, evil actually proves that there *could not* be a God. It is not just suggesting that, given evil, there being a God is unlikely or improbable. It amounts to the claim that 'God exists' is not even possibly true.

But evil has also led people to be critics of Christianity with an eye on the notions of the likely and the probable. For, without asserting that evil shows that atheism is necessarily true, some have felt that it certainly renders God's existence pretty incredible. They ask whether there are not many instances of suffering which could have been prevented by God. Those pressing these questions commonly concede that a good God might countenance evil in so far as it leads to some good which could not come about without it. But, they think, there is evil which leads to no good and which therefore indicates, even if it does not prove, that there is indeed no good, omnipotent and omniscient God.

How have Christians responded to these lines of reasoning? There is no simple answer to this question, since Christians have taken a variety of stands. All of them naturally hold that evil does not disprove God's existence or render it unlikely. But just as they have disagreed about other matters, they have also been in dispute as to why this is so. People sometimes suppose that there is such a thing as 'the' Christian answer to the problem of evil. But that is not the case. There is no response to the problem of evil which commands the assent of all who call themselves Christians. Yet it is possible to indicate some of the major ways in which Christians have answered the charge that evil and God could not, or probably do not, co-exist.

Christians and the problem of evil

One of these takes us back to the fact that Christianity accepts the reality of evil as part of its creed. It is, of course, possible for people to have inconsistent beliefs. But that evil exists seems to be an essential element in the Christian view of things. So some Christians have argued that the existence of evil does not call their faith into question since it is part of that faith. On their account, what would be incompatible with Christianity and its belief in the existence of a good, omnipotent and omniscient God is the assertion 'There is no evil', not the observation that this assertion is false. And there is obviously something to be said in favour of this line of argument. Given, for example, what the Bible says of God, sin and suffering, it seems odd to suggest that God could not or might not exist, given the fact of evil. The biblical picture seems to incorporate evil into its picture of God and his activity. The biblical God is, for instance, a forgiver of sins. And God is a source of distress for the wicked. The biblical God seems almost by definition to be able to exist together with evil.

But in what sense can evil be said to exist? Some Christians have argued that it does not really exist at all.

Along with Mary Baker Eddy (1821–1910), these have held that evil is simply an illusion. More commonly, however, Christians have suggested that evil is essentially an absence or privation of goodness. You can find this view in, for example, the writings of Augustine. On his account, what makes suffering or wickedness bad is that it always amounts to a *lack* of some kind. For Augustine, 'evil' or 'badness' are not the names of independently existing individuals. Nor are they the names of positive qualities or attributes. Rather, they are words we use to signify a gap between what *is actually there* and what *could be* there (and *should be* there) but *is not*. There can be people, but there cannot, so Augustine thinks, be 'baddities' (things whose nature is captured simply by saying that they are bad). There can be wooden boxes, just as there can be wooden chairs. But, Augustine argues, while 'wooden' signifies a positive property, shareable by different things (like boxes and chairs), 'evil' or 'bad' do not. Just as to say 'There is nothing here' is not to say of *something* that *it* is here, so, in Augustine's view, to say that *there is* evil is not to say that there is any real individual or any positive quality. And Augustine regards this conclusion as significant with respect to the topic of God and evil, since he takes it to imply that evil cannot be thought of as something caused to exist by God. He thinks that it would be mad to say that nothing is bad or defective or sinful. But he also holds that evil is not something *created* or *createable*. For Augustine, its 'reality' is always a case of something missing, and it is totally parasitic on the existence of what is good.

So Augustine's position (one shared by many medieval thinkers) is that evil cannot be thought of as directly produced by God. According to Augustine, God can only directly produce (i.e. create) distinct individuals and positive characteristics. And Augustine sees all these things as good. In his view, therefore, God directly produces nothing but what is good. And many Christians have agreed with him on this. Yet might it not be thought that God brings about evil in an indirect way, by somehow permitting or allowing it? And, with an eye on the problem of evil, might it not therefore be argued that much evil is justifiably tolerated by God? Some Christians have said that the answer to these questions is 'Yes'. On their account, a great deal of evil, though not willed directly by God, is correctly accepted by him as the means to one or more goods which could not come about without it.

Some, for instance, have suggested that a world without problems and hardships would be morally static and that God is warranted in putting up with them for the sake of moral dynamism. Their argument goes like this: 1. We could not develop morally and spiritually if we were created with a clear vision of God. 2. God allows difficulties and perils so as to place us at a distance from God, to give us the opportunity to move towards God as free individuals and not as subjects automatically drawn to God because we clearly see God for what God is. On this account, our world, with its various evils, can be viewed as a 'vale of soul-making' in which some evil is a necessary element. A related view tries to supplement this account by arguing that there could be no serious moral options open to people in a world without at least some evil. The argument here goes like this: 1. It is good that people should have the ability to choose to do great good and great harm. 2. Their ability to do this depends on them knowing about the likely consequences of their choices. 3. They can only know about such consequences if they are already familiar with naturally occurring evil.

Christian Science

Are these good arguments? They clearly incorporate truths. The evil we encounter evidently does, at least sometimes, prompt people to improve at the moral level. It often has exactly the opposite effect, but there are times when it goads people to greater virtue. And it is manifestly true that we know how to do good and harm only because we have learned about good and harm in the first place. But the arguments just summarized are also open to question. The first presumes that people with a clear vision of God could not freely respond to God as they ought. And one might very well wonder why anyone should suppose that this is the case. One might also wonder whether it is compatible with at least one central Christian belief. For Christians typically teach that the blessed in heaven enjoy the vision of God. And they do not take this vision to destroy human freedom. The second argument also seems somewhat suspicious, since it is not obviously true that people could only know how to do good and harm because bad things have happened. That is how things work as the world goes now. But might there not have been people able to know about good and evil without evil having previously occurred? For that matter, might there not have been people without there being any evil at all?

In response to this last question, Christians generally agree that the answer is 'Yes', if that answer is understood as affirming that one can be human without doing wrong. Early in the book of Genesis, Adam and Eve are described as living in a blissful state marred by no blameable actions on their part. And Christians have tended to find nothing amiss in the notion of there being people who never commit any sin. Indeed, so they claim, Christ was such a person (cf. Hebrews 4.15). But can God *ensure* that people never commit sin? If God cannot, then maybe the occurrence of some evil can be ascribed to people and not to God (thereby supporting belief in God's goodness). And many Christians have held that this is where the truth about God and evil lies, which brings us to something commonly called 'the free will defence'. According to this: 1. Much evil consists in, or is the result of, what people freely choose to do. 2. It is good that there should be a world with agents able to act freely. 3. Even an omnipotent God cannot guarantee that free people act well. 4. Therefore, much evil is explicable in terms of God allowing for the possible consequences of God willing the good of human freedom.

The free will defence has been solidly endorsed by large numbers of Christians. And some of them have extended it with an eye to evil which cannot be ascribed to human beings and which cannot be thought of as springing from their choices. Let us agree that people who choose wrong are bad and that bad human choices can have harmful consequences. We might still wonder about the source of natural disasters, sickness, and the like. Some instances of these might be attributable to people because of their treatment of the environment or because of their lifestyles. But many of them seem to be outside human control. And, some Christians have suggested, these are also the result of free will, though not of human free will. Why? Because, so it has been said, they are the consequences of choices made by malicious non-human agents – demons, devils or fallen angels. In the first two chapters of the book of Job, a figure referred to as 'the Satan' has the power to inflict hardship. And, some Christians have urged, naturally occurring evil can be traced to free, malevolent, non-human agency.

Yet does it make sense to say that what a creature of God might freely do could be independent of God's activity? Or, to put the question another way, does the free will defence make Christian sense? Some Christians, at least, have thought that it does not. Why? Because they take God to account for the continued existence of all that is real apart from God. And they therefore conclude that nothing can come to be unless God makes it to be. In developing this conclusion some have simply denied that there is any creaturely freedom. On their account, God determines (or, as some have said, predestines) all that comes to pass. But other Christian thinkers have rejected the free will defence while also insisting that there are creatures who are genuinely free. Thomas Aquinas is a classic example. He offers philosophical arguments in defence of the claim that people have freedom of choice. But he also maintains that even human free choices must be caused by God since God is the reason why creatures exist at all. For Thomas, God, as Creator, accounts for there being something rather than nothing at any time. Since he takes people to belong to the realm of 'something', he concludes that their being and acting as they are is also God's doing.

Some would reply that Thomas must therefore be a determinist. But he and his allies would say that this would be the case only if God is thought to be part of the created order. If I push you down the stairs, then your tumbling down is involuntary. It is the effect of my acting on you so as to modify you. For Thomas, however, God the Creator cannot act on anything so as to modify it. Why? Because Thomas believes that God makes everything to be just what it is. And he thinks that God makes freely acting people to be just what they are. So he concludes that God makes people to be those who freely act as they do, and in this sense he rejects the free will defence. On his account the human free choice is one of the forms that God's action takes. In his view, God is the cause of everything's action since God gives everything the power to act, and preserves it in being, and applies it to action.

In that case, however, what is to be said about human wrongdoing? Is this brought about by God? Thomas denies that it is, since he takes it to consist in a failure to act and since he does not think that a failure to act can be something created. And this is a conclusion which many other Christians have adopted. Some of them, however, have also wanted to say (as Thomas does not) that God has absolutely no part to play in the coming to pass of human wrong action. On their account, he stands to it as an outside observer. Some have even suggested that he is also its victim. The idea here is that God's essential goodness must mean (a) that he shares in human pain as that is inflicted on people by others, and (b) that God, as God, is therefore capable of suffering and is himself affected by evil. And, so it has been urged, this is a thought which ought to give rise to hope on the part of Christians. People in distress can be driven to say that because of their suffering they cannot believe in God. For some Christians, however, God and suffering are not to be thought of as irreconcilable with each other because God in his innermost being also suffers. This conclusion, however, is something of an aberration when viewed against what Christians have tended to say since the early days of Christianity. Those who have believed that Jesus was truly divine have, of course, agreed that suffering can be ascribed to God because it can be attributed to Jesus as a human being. But they have not wanted to say, as the view just referred to does, that suffering affects the very divine nature. More typically, they have said that Jesus suffered as man, not as God. And they have taken the divine nature to be neither changeable nor able to be acted on or modified by anything creaturely.

Evil and the goodness of God

One might also note that what we might call 'traditional' or 'orthodox' Christianity has something to say which cuts across attempts to suggest that the problem of evil can be dealt with by trying to show that God is justified in allowing for the occurrence of evil. In discussions of God and evil, 'justified' often seems to mean 'morally justified'. Those who think that evil shows that the existence of God is impossible or unlikely frequently begin by supposing that God must be morally good. Then they offer reasons to suppose that a morally good God would not countenance the evils that exist. So they conclude that God certainly, or probably, does not exist. And the friends of God sometimes argue in a similar way. They often begin by supposing that if God exists then he is morally good. Unlike God's foes, however, they go on to suggest that God's moral integrity can be defended in spite of anything which might be taken to suggest otherwise. In other words, in much debate about God and evil the scenario looks rather like a conflict between lawyers in a courtroom. The accused stands in the dock. Is he or is he not guilty of the crimes with which he is charged? He is guilty if he can be convicted of behaving badly. On the other hand, he is innocent if he can be proved to have behaved well. But does it make sense to think of God behaving *either* well or badly? Or, to put the question another way, does it make sense to suppose that there is a problem when it comes to his moral goodness?

Most Christians from the fourth to the seventeenth centuries would have said that it does not. They would have observed that God's goodness does not lie in his conforming to a code of ethical conduct such as that binding on people. And in taking this line, they could have appealed to the Bible (as, indeed, they often did). The Old and New Testaments never suggest that God acts, or is obliged to act, according to standards over and against God. The picture presented is utterly different and is typified by the speech of God at the end of the book of Job. Here God asks 'Shall a fault-finder contend with the Almighty?' (Job 40.2). This question is typical of the position of the Bible when it comes to the behaviour of God. Authors of the biblical texts sometimes wonder why nasty things happen. But they never suggest that they do so because God, in spite of appearances, is being morally good and acting as a good moral agent. More commonly, they say that evil is a mystery which God understands and with which he can cope. In other words, they do not seek to explain it as we might seek to explain examples of evil in scientific or personal terms. Meteorologists can explain why there are droughts. And psychologists (perhaps) can explain why some people act as they do. But biblical authors tend not to see evil as explicable in these sorts of ways. This is partly because, like many Christians down the ages, they are conscious of the fact that God is just not part of the world and is, therefore, as deep a mystery as evil itself.

Evil and its origin

Yet the Bible and the writings of post-biblical Christians do contain some non-scientific accounts of where evil comes from. One, which has been especially influential, attributes it to the fall of Adam and Eve as recounted in the book of Genesis. Here we are told that Adam and Eve eat from a forbidden tree and were punished by God, who drove them from the garden of Eden and made them live in a world subject to pain and suffering. Reflecting on this account, some Christians have attributed evil to the disobedience of Adam and Eve. Paul speaks of Adam as the one through whom sin and death came into the world (Romans 5.12). And many Christians after Paul have referred to 'original sin', which they have taken to be the fault of Adam and Eve, and which they have also thought of as the source of at least some of the evils with which we are familiar. One needs to note, however, that Christians have also disagreed about how to understand the Genesis account of Adam and Eve. One should also note that they have, correspondingly, differed in their accounts of original sin.

Some of them have taken Adam and Eve to be historical individuals whose fall (the original sin) introduced evil into the world and left all of their ancestors sharing in their guilt (the stain of original sin). An obvious objection to this belief seems to lie in the fact that empirical research clearly favours the view that the human race did not derive from just two human beings. Another obvious objection lies in the fact that one can only be guilty of something that one has done oneself. So many contemporary Christians treat the story of Adam and Eve not in historical terms but as a way of telling us something about human nature in general. They have, for instance, said that the story should be read as a way of teaching that people are naturally prone to sin and are always in need of divine assistance. And it is evidently true that people do seem naturally prone to sin or wrongdoing. But why is this so? One cannot explain why it is so just by noting that it is, in fact, so. One needs to ask, 'What accounts for the tendency in people to go in for what is bad?'

The Bible offers no clear answer to this question. Even the book of Genesis does not do so. It attributes pain and suffering to what Adam and Eve chose to do. But it does not explain the mechanism. It does not tell us how pain and suffering sprang from their action. Nor does it give us any clear idea as to what might have prompted them to fall. And this, of course, means that, whether they read Genesis literally or not, Christians, on the basis of the Bible, lack a serious explanation for evil. But this is what many of them concede. Many of them would say that, in this life, evil can no more be explained than God can.

BRIAN DAVIES, OP

📖 Marilyn Adams, *Horrendous Evils and the Goodness of God*, Ithaca, NY: Cornell University Press 1999; M. B. Ahern, *The Problem of Evil*, London: Routledge and New York: Schocken Books 1971; P. T. Geach, *Providence and Evil*, Cambridge: CUP 1977; John Hick, *Evil and the God of Love*, London: Macmillan and New

York: Harper & Row [2]1975; Daniel Howard-Snyder (ed), *The Evidential Argument from Evil*, Bloomington and Indianapolis: Indiana University Press 1996; Kenneth Surin, *Theology and the Problem of Evil*, Oxford: Blackwell 1986; Peter Vardy, *The Puzzle of Evil*, London: HarperCollins 1992

Evolution

For many people, the notion of evolution is an argument against Christian faith, but for others it is a challenge to formulate that faith more credibly. It was developed by scientists who were familiar with theology. Charles Darwin (1809–82) had studied theology. He had been influenced by William Paley (1743–1805), who had seen a proof for the existence of God as the constructor of nature in the adaptation of creatures to their particular environments. Paley was convinced that species had remained constant since creation. This accorded with everyday experience. Creatures produce their like: a cat always produces only cats. J. B. Lamarck (1744–1829) was bold enough to claim, contrary to appearances, that species had developed in a long evolution. He thought that creatures bequeathed acquired characteristics to their descendants through assimilation. Nature transmitted their successes in learning to subsequent generations. Change in species would then be a directed process.

Darwin was the first to take the decisive step of explaining the evolution of life by variation and selection in his book *On the Origin of Species by Means of Natural Selection* (1859; A. R. Wallace also did so at the same time). Species developed as the result of creatures producing new forms of appearance through chance hereditary changes (mutations). These changes did not automatically further assimilation to the particular environment, but some changes had a higher value for adaptation than others. Darwin's ideas about these chance changes were unclear; the Augustinian monk G. Mendel (1822–84) was the first to provide part of the explanation by his laws of heredity; another part has been provided by modern molecular genetics. Today we know that the recombination of genes along with small mistakes in 'copying' genes is the cause of the variety of forms of life which is the first factor in evolution.

For Darwin the second factor was that by analogy with a human breeder, nature selects the most appropriate variants from those which have arisen fortuitously from nature. Their selection can be explained quite naturally without the assumption of a purposeful process. Here he transferred to nature the insights into population theory of T. R. Malthus (1766–1834), a former pastor. According to Malthus the population increases geometrically (2, 4, 8, 16), and thus very much more rapidly than the food supply, which increases arithmetically (2, 4, 6, 8). The consequence is a constant struggle over a sparse supply of food. Famines and other catastrophes adjust the population density to the food supply. In this struggle the strongest prevail. By analogy, Darwin assumed that in nature all creatures produce a surplus of offspring, who compete over food and living space. Consequently the worse-equipped variants have less chances of multiplying, are annihilated and die out, whereas the better-adapted variants win through in the struggle for life. Changes take place in species through natural (i.e. unplanned) selection, in the direction of forms with a more effective capacity to adapt. Human beings, too, have developed from higher primates on the basis of these natural laws of evolution.

Darwin's theory of evolution is a biological theory. However, time and again it has been extended beyond the sphere of biology in two directions. We know that life was preceded by a long phase of material (or chemical) evolution in which the presuppositions of biological evolution (e.g. combinations of carbons) were created. We can explain the origin of life from the self-organization of matter. But the history of humankind, too, has been interpreted as a new phase of evolution, as a cultural phase after its biological phase. In it the play of mutation and selection has been transformed into progress by trial and error. Many people are attracted by a comprehensive theory of evolution which comprises material, biological and cultural phases; it promises that we can draw all our knowledge into its framework. Like a myth, it can be shaped as a narrative, but it transcends science strictly speaking.

The theory of evolution, seen in purely biological terms, already poses four threats to theology: 1. It dethrones human beings. They lose their central position as the crown of creation. They do not derive directly from God but from higher primates. Possibly they are only a transition. Human beings in the image of God seem to be replaced by human beings in the image of apes. 2. It demystifies creation. The assimilation of species to the environment is not the result of any purposeful action; chance and necessity explain the increase in the organization and complexity of life. The theory of evolution interprets the world without teleology (i.e. without orientation on a purpose or a meaning). 3. It undermines ethics. In nature the fitter win through without any heed for weaker forms of life. Human solidarity seems to be an illusion in the struggle for life. 'Social Darwinism', which goes against Darwin's intentions, serves to justify racial policies and lives on in some neo-liberal ideas. 4. The theory of evolution explains the world without God. Certainly attempts are made time and again to reserve unexplained areas as places for the intervention of God for example the origin of the first life or of human beings. But these areas are disappearing. We always have a better explanation for what seemed inexplicable. Biology and the natural sciences compel us to rethink God's action in the world.

No wonder, then, that the fight against the theory of evolution became a central concern of fundamentalism (especially in the southern states of the USA). 'Creationism' insists on a literal understanding of the account of creation: all the species were created originally, the world is relatively young and the earth was formed by a global flood. Creationism attempts to present these biblical data as a scientific framework for research and to make teaching this view compulsory in school by law. Against this background, in 1925 the biology teacher J. T. Scopes, who had taught that human beings were descended from the animal kingdom, was condemned in the 'first monkey trial' in Tennessee. However, generally a secularism which sought to keep schools free from the influence of religious teaching became established. When in 1981 creationism was nevertheless again introduced into schools by law, this law was abolished in the 'second monkey trial' in 1982. A comparable draft law in Louisiana failed in 1987 before the US Supreme Court. Many theologians appeared before the court arguing in favour of the theory of evolution. As early as 1950 the Roman Catholic Church had affirmed the theory of evolution in the encyclical *Humani generis*, though with reservations (which were later dropped). In any case, in the main Protestant churches it was taken for granted that scientific results should be accepted.

The peace between religion and science is based on a certain consensus that science and religion raise different questions: science investigates the facts, theology investigates meaning and value. The sciences give their answers in a mathematical language, religion in metaphorical language. But there are points of contact: religion relates to the whole of reality, and perceives this whole as creation. In this creation it includes creation as known by the natural sciences. Science in turn has implicit presuppositions, for example that the world can be known with the help of mathematics, which can be the object of religious wonderment. Despite different questions and different systems of language, science and religion are in dialogue. There are four main points in this dialogue.

Human beings – no longer the centre and crown of creation?

In 1850, in a public discussion, Bishop Samuel Wilberforce asked Thomas Huxley, a zealous defender of the theory of evolution, whether he would prefer to be descended from apes on his grandfather's or his grandmother's side. Thereupon Huxley sensibly replied that he would rather be descended from apes than from such a bishop. This

'The Lion of the Season', *Punch* cartoon on Darwin's theory of evolution, 25 May 1861

Creation

p. 700

anecdote shows that for many, the doctrine of evolution was reduced to the view that human beings were descended from apes. But the evolutionary picture of human beings is more than a theory of descent; it also relativizes their special status generally and sees their existence as transitional. What does theology have to say about these three aspects of the evolutionary picture?

Science
Science and theology

At a very early stage theologians (for example John Henry Newman, 1801–90) accepted the theory of descent. The affinity of all creatures can be the basis for a deep religious experience. Something of us lives and suffers in all creatures. We have the same genes as they do. The biblical account of creation can be read metaphorically: it contains an intimation that the world and life came into being in stages. Why should not God have given the possibilities of life to a few forms or even just to one, for everything to develop from it? The problem is not that human beings are descended from apes, but that they are the products of chance and necessity. But even according to modern scientific knowledge human beings have reason to be amazed at their existence. In its soft version, the so-called 'anthropic principle' says that improbably the cosmos has been created in one particular

way and not otherwise, so that it could bring forth life and human beings. If a few basic data were slightly different, life would be impossible. The harder version of this principle even says that the cosmos had to bring forth life and human beings. Of course the anthropic principle is no proof that human beings were willed in the cosmos. But in the light of religious faith it can make the world transparent to something else. Moreover it is primarily focused on all life, and not specifically on human beings. So we must ask: do human beings have any special status in the living world?

Beyond question this special status of human beings has been relativized by biology and the theory of evolution. Experiments show that even the higher apes have self-awareness. They too can form the beginnings of traditions. We find the preliminary forms of language even in whales. There seem to be only differences of degree between human beings and animals. As we already saw, the way in which human beings are embedded in nature can also be the source of an experience of affinity with all creatures. But in addition this location in nature brings out even more clearly the characteristics which occur only in human beings. These include religion. While in their relationship to one another human beings differ from animals only by degree, their sense of transcendence makes them different from animals in principle. So is theology right to see the special status of human beings consisting in their having been made in the image of God – even if being in the image of God is only one of the images with which the human sense of transcendence is expressed? According to the Bible this means that human beings have responsibility for creation – today perhaps even by holding the threads of evolution in their hands.

The first creation story in the Bible (Genesis 1.1–2.4) sees human beings as the last work of creation. With them the world seems to have been completed. But human beings cannot be the last stage in evolution. Are they perhaps just a transition to something new? That certainly would not conflict with biblical faith. In its later strata the Bible itself says that human beings live at the interface between two worlds. They have already crossed the threshold to a new world, but as biological creatures are imprisoned in the old world. Thus inspired by the Bible and the theory of evolution, the Jesuit theologian and palaeontologist Pierre Teilhard de Chardin (1881–1955) could develop the vision of an overall cosmic development in which Christians are the advance guard of a new world. The evolutionary process leads from cosmogenesis through biogenesis to noogenesis, to the transformation of all things into the Spirit of God. His interpretation of Christian faith which thus affirmed the world exercised a strong fascination on many people. His limitation was that he interpreted this overall development in terms of purpose: it is working towards a goal. By contrast, the theory of evolution allows no final causes.

Has the demystified world no meaning or purpose?
The theory of evolution holds that life is the product of chance. Can chance explain the purposeful construction of organisms? Wouldn't that be paradoxical? But chance events form only one factor in evolution. A second factor, selection, is the reason why there are ever more complex adaptations of the organism to the environment. If we want to see the world as more than a senseless game, we must consider this second factor. All forms of life are based on efforts to assimilate to an external reality. That is external selection. But their blueprints do not allow just any further development. Even if it were an advantage for rhinoceroses to grow wings, they could not do so because of their internal structure. Here an internal selection is at work alongside external selection.

In human beings evolution has produced creatures with a cerebrum and reason. In so far as they have developed by external selection, they must correspond to external structures of reality. If they are capable of rationality, it is because the objective reality to which they have adapted is full of rationality. In fact the longer we investigate reality with our cerebrum, the more we are convinced of its rationality, of which our subjective reason, as Albert Einstein remarked, is a mere reflection. Now internal selection also plays a role in the development of the cerebrum (and thus of the human being). What we know is adapted to the principles by which our brain is constructed. We do not know the world in itself, but as it has been assimilated by our cerebrum. We cannot construct just any realities we like with our cerebrum.

Here we come upon an amazing state of affairs: if with our reason we develop a priori mathematical formulae without objective reality in view, we often note that these formulae are capable of describing nature a posteriori. We produce a mathematical language from ourselves, and surprisingly nature is composed in this language. It is as if we had laid down the rules of chess and discovered that nature, too, plays chess. This correspondence can no longer be explained by an adaptation governed by biology. The complications of higher mathematics have not contributed to the survival of the organism. Rather, with evolution we have entered a sphere transcending biological evolution. Alongside the improbable anthropic match between the universe and human beings, here we experience an 'epistemic' match: we can know the world. Even if we do not depict reality in knowledge but reconstruct it, our constructions have the status of knowledge. We discover in reality an order which is akin to us. The physicist Werner Heisenberg (1901–76) pointed out that in individual experiences this order can come as close to us as another human being. So did the supposedly meaningless play of chance simply allow the discovery of this overwhelming sense? But does that justify the cruel struggle for life? Doesn't it remain morally repulsive, particularly for creatures whose cerebrums allow them to empathize with others?

The struggle for opportunities in life – and the discovery of morality

For men and women with humane sensibilities the struggle between creatures over the distribution of resources is a serious challenge. Big fish eat little fish, and the little fish compete over who can best escape being eaten, the big fish over who can eat the little ones most effectively. All this contradicts what we regard as morally desirable among human beings. Social Darwinism wanted to make a norm of the discovery that in the biological struggle the fittest survives: this is also how it should be among human beings. That is clearly an illegitimate inference, from what actually happens to what should be, i.e. an example of the naturalistic fallacy. But many observations seem to confirm that in the world the right of the stronger does in fact prevail. So is the Christian and humanistic ethos of love of neighbour a delusion? Is it an attempt by the inferior to bind the superior with the chain of conscience? Is it a slave rebellion in morality, as Friedrich Nietzsche remarked?

Though the view is controversial, it can be argued that the biblical ethic is against selection. In biological evolution aggression against those who are not related genetically goes hand in hand with solidarity with those who are. This combination of modes of behaviour gives a good chance of survival. But the Bible develops an ethic in which enemies are to be loved and closest relations are to be hated. It tells of a people which was threatened with annihilation and nevertheless survived. It bears witness to Jesus of Nazareth who was crucified and who nevertheless became the basis of new life. Just as life once succeeded in partially escaping the law of entropy by producing an increasing complexity of forms of life contrary to this law, so too cultural evolution must have succeeded in escaping the principle of selection: in culture it has been replaced by the soft selection of ideas and modes of behaviour. Its basic maxim, coined by the philosopher Karl Popper, is that it is better for hypotheses to die than human beings. It is better to convert than to die. It is better to die a symbolic death than real death.

At an advanced stage of evolution the reality to which all creatures have to adapt by hard selection proves to be a reality which does not want the death of sinners, but that they should convert and live. Adaptation to it does not mean developing superiority to others in order to survive in the struggle for life, but love of the weak who have no chances of survival. Granted, as biological creatures we are still subject to the laws of biological evolution, but as human beings we have taken a step beyond the biological laws of evolution and are making the transition from biological to cultural evolution – as the conversion, rebirth, renewal and of each individual.

But if God is the ultimate reality, or stands behind reality as its creator, then isn't God acting in a contradictory way, first by selection in biological evolution and then by the overcoming of selection in cultural evolution? Here we should remember that already in biological evolution there is not only a struggle which involves suppressing and killing but also a rivalry through sexual attraction: flowers do not fight each other but compete for opportunities in life. Some attract more insects than others. Human beings, too, can develop such a capacity for attachments: by an evolution in love they can even develop attachments to things that are not attractive, precisely because scarce life needs their help. Here they are picking up what is already prefigured in nature, but can be developed into something new by identification with other life and sensitivity to its need.

The requirement to adapt is never suspended from an ultimate reality, not even the pressure of selection itself; rather, hard selection through death is replaced by a soft selection of ideas, attitudes and patterns of behaviour. Aggressive rivalry is toned down by help in solidarity, even if this happens only in that small sphere which is accessible to shaping by culture. But perhaps in this small sphere human beings are intended to go beyond biological evolution as the first free beings to transcend nature? However, if human beings are achieving their own evolution, is there any role for divine action? How are we to imagine it?

Critics of Christianity ←

The world of evolution – a world without God as creator?

There are two possibilities of linking scientific explanations of the world to theological interpretations of the world. First, scientific results can be interpreted in religious terms (which invites the charge that they are simply being repeated and given an illegitimate religious colouring). But science limits itself in an ascetic way to knowledge. It brackets out the emotional and motivational significance of what is known. The religious interpretation therefore has a distinctive feature: it works out the significance of what is known for human beings. But a cosmic religious amazement at the order in nature often gives intimations of something beyond what is accessible to science: it helps us to understand the traditional language of religion, praise and thanksgiving of the creator. Above all it lends the world a cognitive transparency of transcendence.

Hence the second task, of formulating traditional theological statements about transcendence in such a way that they are not in tension with the natural sciences, without exploiting the gaps in knowledge that still exist. We have to look for something that indubitably exists and is presupposed in all scientific knowledge and yet in principle escapes it. There is such transcendence in the midst of life. Creation out of nothing is experienced at the moment when the future which is not yet enters the present, immediately to sink into the nothingness of the past. 'Being' is a transition from not yet being to no longer being. Strictly speaking, everything that we know scientifically no longer exists. For any signal that goes from an event and reaches our observation and knowledge takes place at a finite speed, limited by the speed of light. Thus not only do we see the light of extinct stars in the sky, but in principle no observation, no sense datum ever reaches what is in fact the present but is its chronologically shifted effect in the past.

In science we experience being only in its traces in the past (however close these may be to the present). If God makes all being new every moment, in principle this event is not accessible to scientific observation and knowledge because its strict presence escapes the natural sciences. Such creation from nothing is not identical with the much-discussed big bang at the beginning of the (present?) universe; it is the action of God on all being at every moment which takes place crosswise to time. This

Faith

is where faith has its origin. In the light of faith it is then possible to thumb through the whole world at a secondary stage and have intimations of God in what others state as facts. That is also true of the miracle of evolution: that we are children of a universe which in an improbable way has been created with us in view and we in an improbable way for it.

A further connection between evolutionary thought and religion is becoming increasingly important: religion is a product of evolution. If we recognize its evolution so far and the direction it will take in the future we can make a responsible contribution to its further development. Nowadays the theory of evolution is especially applied to religion in socio-biology: here belief in God is either interpreted as a beneficent illusion, which brought its adherents an advantage in selection, so that it extended with them. Or religion gave groups an advantage in survival through basic factors on which every society is dependent: a basis for authority, an assurance of the truth in oaths, coping with fate and disaster and an obligation to reciprocal giving. In addition, attempts have been made to explain the religious ideas with which religion exercises this function through a cognitive psychology. In religion we become productive on the basis of cognitive schemes and categories which have come about by evolution. As we have seen, there are those who want to use such theories to demonstrate that religion is an illusion. But one cannot conclude that a notion is true or untrue from its genesis: that is the 'genetic fallacy'. An analogy can make that clear. In its biological 'utility' religion can be compared with being in love. The recognition that erotic desire contributes to the preservation of our species is plausible even without any theories from socio-biology. This is not to say anything about the truth and untruth of what the eyes of those in love perceive. Perhaps aspects of the world open up to them which otherwise we wrongly overlook. Religion is a love of being, in which something dawns on us of the depths of reality that we do not otherwise perceive. In religion the 'eyes of the heart' (Ephesians 1.18) see with categories which are deeply rooted in our brain and came into being through evolution. What is decisive is that they see *something*. They see it on the basis of an inner transformation of the person which we experience most intensively in love. When asked what God meant to him, a German scientist recently began by replying in terms of a benevolent socio-biological interpretation of religion. He said that for him God was 'a hypothesis which has more positive than negative effects on the living, even if it is wrong'. Then he added: 'Love is an intimation of what could be if the hypothesis is right.' The New Testament also says: 'God is love. And whoever abides in love abides in God and God in him' (1 John 4.16).

GERD THEISSEN

P. Boyer, *The Naturalness of Religious Ideas. A Cognitive Theory of Religion*, Berkeley and London: University of California Press 1994; Charles Darwin, *On the Origin of Species by Means of Natural Selection* (1859), Harmondsworth: Penguin Books 2004; *The Descent of Man, and Selection in Relation to Sex* (2 vols, 1871), New York: Gramercy Books 1998; Albert Einstein, *Ideas and Opinions* (1954), New York: Gramercy Books 1988; John Polkinghorne, *Science and Theology*, London: SPCK 1998 and Minneapolis: Fortress Press 1999; Gerd Theissen, *Biblical Faith. An Evolutionary Approach*, London: SCM Press and Philadelphia: Fortress Press 1984

EXPLORATION

Archaeology, Biblical criticism, Doctrinal criticism, Evolution, Journeys, Mission, Science, Theology

The urge to explore seems to be deeply rooted in human nature, and for better or worse to resist any attempts by either the church or society to prevent it from going too far. The range of exploration extends from the vast expanses of the universe to the make-up of the human genome, over all the areas in between. And perspectives on its results can be positive or negative. How these different attitudes have come about will emerge as the story unfolds.

When the first explorers sailed from Portugal and Spain on their voyages of discovery from towards the end of the fifteenth century onwards, they set in motion a chain of discoveries extending far beyond the routes and countries which they were initially seeking. These discoveries were to have a tremendous effect on Christianity and its understanding of the world, but their significance was only slowly realized, and it was not until around a century later that they made an impact.

Up to this time the Bible had been the unquestioned source of all truth. From Augustine onwards it had been accepted that the book of mysteries was also an encyclopaedia containing all useful knowledge, sacred and profane. There may have been many differences over how it should be interpreted, but no one doubted its essential truth, and even had they done so, there would have been no convincing way of substantiating such doubts. The Bible was thought to contain authoritative information, not least about history, geography and astronomy, and dominated study in these areas. But that was to change.

Bible 

The navigational instruments on which the explorers relied, and which had been developed by Muslim Arabs, took bearings from the stars, and were used in careful observation of the heavens. As a result of an age-old interest in astrology and because of the use of the stars in navigation, at the end of the Middle Ages astronomy was the science that had accumulated the most important collection of data derived from observations and accurate mathematical calculations. As these data accumulated they conflicted more and more with the accepted theory, compatible with the Bible, that the sun revolved around the earth, to the point that this theory became past rescuing and had to be replaced by another theory, incompatible with the Bible, that the earth revolved around the sun.

In the biblical view the earth was surrounded by the ocean on every side, beyond which was darkness. Palestine lay at the centre, with Jerusalem at its navel, and the earth was divided into three continents, Asia, Africa and Europe, inhabited by the descendants of the three sons of Noah, Shem, Ham and Japheth. The maps on which this geography was portrayed were circular. But the new areas now discovered had inhabitants of which the Bible was quite ignorant; they seemed to have no connection with the history recounted in the Bible and no religion that could be related to the God to whom the Bible bore witness. And as they were extended to include new lands, the circular maps had to give place, eventually, to globes that presented a very different picture.

The duration of the reigns of the rulers of some of these new lands caused yet more problems for biblical authority. They seemed to go back to before the traditional date of creation, 4004 BCE. The Egyptian dynasties had already posed this problem, but it was resolved by arguing that the

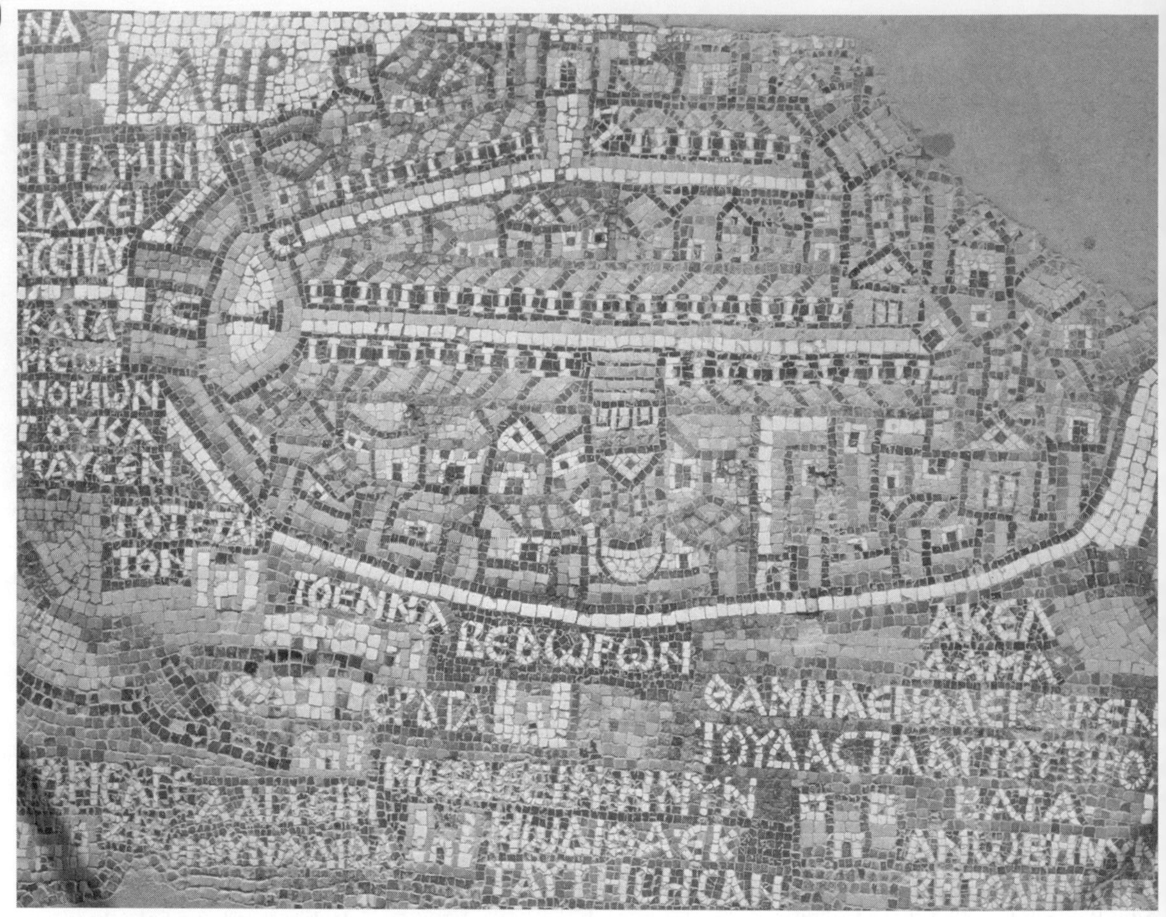

Jerusalem, from the oldest extant map of Palestine (sixth century), church of St George, Madaba, Jordan

Egyptians had invented the first eight dynasties to enhance their glory. However, this desperate expedient was shattered by the discovery that Chaldaean and Chinese chronology posed precisely the same problem, and these chronologies could not have been falsified.

By the middle of the seventeenth century a body of incontrovertible knowledge about astronomy, geography and history had been accumulated which presented a different 'truth' from that claimed for the Bible, and instead of being the norm of all truth, the Bible was increasingly put in question. Nor did the process of exploration stop there. At the beginning of the nineteenth century Charles Lyell in Scotland pioneered the discipline of geology and for the first time provided overwhelming evidence that the earth was immeasurably older than had been believed; in France Georges Cuvier led the way in the study of comparative anatomy which was the basis of vertebrate paleontology, two foundation stones for the theory of evolution for which Charles Darwin gathered the evidence in the 1830s in another voyage of exploration, in HMS Beagle, in the 1830s. The result was his *On the Origin of Species*. Explorations into every aspect of the universe continued, and are far from being completed.

This whole process of exploration was, and often still is, seen as an attack on Christianity. At Enlightenment every stage, particularly after the Enlightenment and its hostility to 'revealed' religion, attempts were made to use the new discoveries against Christianity, and on the Christian side equally vigorous attempts were made to disprove and discredit them. This antagonism is far from being a thing of the past.

However, antagonism has by no means been the only reaction to the explorations and discoveries that produced the modern picture of the world and the universe in which it is set. Some of the great pioneers such as Isaac Newton and Charles Darwin themselves had a deep interest in Christian theology and worked with the positive intention of reinterpreting it. And as well as the opponents, virtually from the start there were those who in a positive spirit accepted the new findings and embarked on their own voyages of exploration through the Bible and Christian tradition. Although the term often used for their activities is 'criticism', they were not hostile critics of Christianity; here criticism is a neutral term which means something like 'questioning exploration'.

Critics of Christianity

A landmark in this exploration of the Christian heritage is the work of a family of scholar-printers in Paris called Stephanus (or Estienne). They not only printed Bibles in the customary Latin but also the Old Testament in Hebrew and the New Testament in Greek. Here they were faced with the decision what text to print, for many manuscripts were in circulation, differing slightly depending on the 'family' of handwritten texts from which they came. Robert Estienne's 1550 Greek New Testament was the first to contain not only the text he chose as being the best, but also details of variations to be found in other manuscripts: the science of textual criticism had begun.

The next stage of exploration was carried on by scholars in studies and libraries, and consisted in reading the books of the Bible with a more critical eye than before. A French priest, Richard Simon (1638–1712), examined the first five books of the Bible attributed to Moses (the Pentateuch) and argued that they could not all have been written by him. Quite apart from the describing of Moses' death in them, the many instances of duplicate narratives and the variation in style ruled this out. Moses, Simon argued, wrote only the laws; the rest was written by annalists, chroniclers. A French Catholic physician, Jean Astruc (1684–1766) then conjectured from the different terms used for God in these books that Moses made use of two pre-existing documents. And from there the theories of the formation of the Pentateuch and the rest of the Old Testament developed and became increasingly complex.

Johann Gottfried Eichhorn (1752–1827), a professor at Göttingen, carried the exploration further by comparing the books of the Bible with other extant Semitic literature. He wrote 'Introductions' to both Old and New Testaments, systematically outlining the composition and sources of the books in them; he introduced a term 'higher criticism', now obsolete, by which he denoted the study of questions about the Bible above the level of textual criticism. In the New Testament, during the nineteenth century, the relationship of the New Testament Gospels, especially the first three, to each other, was a major preoccupation; this came to be known as the 'synoptic problem'.

p. 151

By now the exploration of the Bible and the Christian tradition was by no means confined to studying written words. It extended to the archaeological investigation of places associated with the Bible and the history of Christianity. A first start was made on this investigation in Rome when excavations were made in some of the basilicas there; later, Antonio Bosio (1575–1629), who has been called the father of Christian archaeology, discovered and investigated catacombs.

Buildings

However, it was not until the nineteenth century that the widespread archaeological investigation that was to illuminate the world of Christianity really began. Napoleon's invasion of Egypt in 1798 marks the beginning of a period when exploration of the Middle East became much more possible. And the invasion itself brought a first important discovery: French soldiers extending the foundations of a fort uncovered a stone, the famous Rosetta Stone, inscribed with parallel Greek and Egyptian texts, the latter in two scripts, one of which was hieroglyphic. Here, appearing quite by chance, as was subsequently to happen on so many occasions later, was the key to opening up Egyptian culture and history. An equally important discovery opened up the civilizations of Assyria, Babylonia and Persia. An English army officer, Henry Rawlinson, perilously venturing along a narrow ledge or hanging suspended in a cage, over a period of four years from 1835 on laboriously deciphered what is known as the Behistun inscription, a vast text carved into a cliff in the Zagros mountains in Persia, written in three parallel versions of cuneiform.

This marked the beginning of the creation of a detailed background against which to set the Bible, and the nineteenth century saw a great blossoming of archaeology. What had originally begun as treasure-seeking and antiquarianism became a science when the discoveries of geologists, especially their dating of the strata of the earth's surface, could be brought into play to date findings.

Stories of chance discoveries abound: Count Constantin Tischendorf spent twenty years visiting libraries in the Near East and in 1844 at St Catherine's Monastery on Mount Sinai discovered one of the most important manuscripts of the Greek Bible, the Codex Sinaiticus, about to be consigned to the flames for fuel. In 1887 Egyptian farmers discovered a series of tablets at El-Amarna containing letters illustrating the political situation in Canaan round about the time the Israelites were supposed to have arrived there. In 1945, a series of jars containing papyri codices of more than 40 previously unknown Gnostic works from the third to fifth centuries CE was found near the village of Nag Hammadi in Upper Egypt in a dramatic chain of events which included murder and the burning of some of the codices as accursed. In 1947 Bedouin goatherds searching for a lost animal on the cliffs beside the Dead Sea discovered jars with scrolls which provided the earliest texts of the Hebrew Bible and documents describing the life of a sect existing round about the time of Jesus.

p. 149

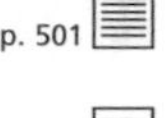

p. 501

p. 845

And alongside these chance discoveries, more systematic exploration of the lands of the Bible continued. Edward Robinson and Eli Smith began a survey of Palestine in 1838, and by 1845 a German exploration society had been formed. The Palestine Exploration Fund was founded in 1865 and the American Palestinian Exploration Society in 1870. The period after the Second World War saw Jewish scholars and archaeologists joining in the exploration of the land from which Christianity emerged and the sites associated with Jesus, shedding yet more light on them and producing artefacts such as ossuaries, stone containers for bones, sometimes closely connected with Jesus and his family. This story of exploration has been repeated, perhaps less dramatically, all over the world, illuminating all periods of Christian history.

Jesus
Evidence

Exploration of the earth and all that is in it continued unabated in the twentieth century and for the first time human beings travelled beyond the earth, setting foot on the moon. Satellites circle the earth and other planets, and the universe is beginning to yield up more of its secrets. Is there a different kind of life on other planets, and if so what significance might that have for the claims of Christianity? The story of exploration is far from over.

Here again are questions for Christians to face positively rather than negatively. Speculation on the consequences of extraterrestrial life began long before any kind of space vehicle had been devised. Such issues were raised, for example, by the Christian writer C. S. Lewis, who in 1938 in his *Out of the Silent Planet* described a visit to Mars and in 1943 in his *Perelandra* (also known as *Voyage to Venus*) a visit to Venus by his hero Elwin Ransome.

Exploration and the urge to explore both the Christian tradition and the world in which it is handed down are important because they show that Christianity is not just a set of beliefs and practices fixed once and for all, but a living faith which constantly adjusts itself to an ever-expanding and ever-changing world. Sometimes the consequences of discoveries about the world and about Christian tradition take a considerable time to emerge; these discoveries are by their very nature always fragmentary and their significance inconclusive and open to revision. The future is certain to produce further findings about the nature of human beings and the universe and the character of Christianity that prove both threatening and liberating. Nevertheless, if followed through and reflected on, exploration can lead to a richness of understanding and a greater openness.

JOHN BOWDEN

Henning Graf Reventlow, *The Authority of the Bible and the Rise of the Modern World*, London: SCM Press and Philadelphia: Fortress Press 1984; Klaus Scholder, *The Birth of Modern Critical Theology*, London: SCM Press 1990; William H. Stiebing, Jr, *Uncovering the Past*, New York: OUP 1994

Faith

Perhaps the most famous definition of faith in the whole of Christian literature appears in the New Testament letter to the Hebrews: 'Now faith is the assurance of things hoped for, the conviction of things not seen' (11.1). The passage then turns to the very beginning of things, 'By faith we understand that the world was created by the word of God, so that what is seen was made by things which do not appear', after which it becomes a long history of the acts of faith of characters in the Hebrew Bible from Abel and Noah, through Abraham and Moses, to David and Samuel and the prophets, ending with a list of the sufferings for their faith undergone by men and women of later times.

Here already are the two aspects of faith which were ultimately identified and distinguished far more formally: the fact that the world was created out of nothing by God came in Christianity to be called the faith which is believed (Latin *fides quae creditur*), an article of faith; the trust shown by the 'great cloud of witnesses' (Hebrews 12.1) came to be called the faith by which it is believed (Latin *fides qua creditur*), the act of faith.

Abraham, praised in Hebrews for 'going out, not knowing where he was to go' at God's command (11.8), is also a key figure of faith for the apostle Paul (Romans 4). 'In hope he believed against hope, that he should become the father of many nations … He grew strong in faith as he gave glory to God, fully convinced that God was able to do what he had promised' (4.18, 21). Abraham is a prime example of faith for Paul by virtue of his constant attitude of trust; he is in the right before God, justified, not by virtue of anything that he has done, but simply through his faith. Here faith is presented in contrast to 'works', any form of human achievement; it is a childlike attitude that accepts God's gifts and promises in sheer trust and obedience, without striving to gain God's favour by any actions. That this characteristic of faith can easily be misunderstood is evident from the Letter of James, which criticizes it sharply: 'Show me your faith apart from your works, and I by my works will show you my faith' (2.18). For the author, faith without works, seeing brothers or sisters starving or in rags and not feeding or clothing them, is dead, and Abraham is an example because of his works, in sacrificing Isaac (Genesis 22) rather than because of his faith (2.21).

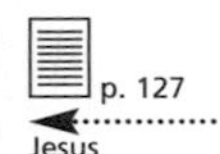
p. 127
Jesus

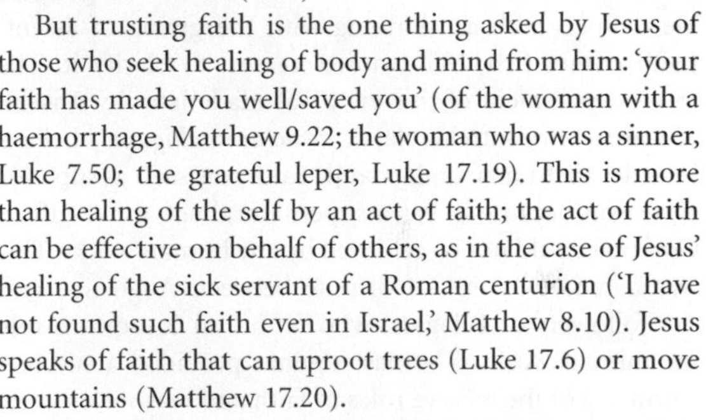

But trusting faith is the one thing asked by Jesus of those who seek healing of body and mind from him: 'your faith has made you well/saved you' (of the woman with a haemorrhage, Matthew 9.22; the woman who was a sinner, Luke 7.50; the grateful leper, Luke 17.19). This is more than healing of the self by an act of faith; the act of faith can be effective on behalf of others, as in the case of Jesus' healing of the sick servant of a Roman centurion ('I have not found such faith even in Israel,' Matthew 8.10). Jesus speaks of faith that can uproot trees (Luke 17.6) or move mountains (Matthew 17.20).

In the New Testament, those who have faith are said to believe and are called believers; English has different words here for noun and verb, but the Greek of the New Testament and also some modern languages, notably German, have one term for both (*pistis/pisteuein, Glaube/glauben*). This explains the apparently strange phenomenon that the Gospel of John never once uses the noun 'faith'; however, it uses the verb 'believe' around 80 times, more than any other New Testament book. Here too, having faith, i.e. trust in Jesus, is just as central a feature as in the other Gospels: 'You believe in God, believe also in me' (John 14.1). However, it is worth noting that in a modern context the two words 'faith' and 'belief' have drifted apart:

Paul

Justification

Exploration

belief now tends to mean having a belief about something which falls short of really knowing; faith is expressed in beliefs, but belief is not faith. To be 'faithful' is to show loyalty and trust, but there is no such word as 'belief-ful'.

Trust is generally the significance of the term faith in the biblical writings, but faith as believing something to be true also appears in the New Testament. The letter of Jude speaks famously of 'the faith which was once for all delivered to the saints', and which has to be fought for. This faith, which here clearly has some intellectual content, is delivered by God; in other words, it can be said to be revealed. A growing body of revealed truth comes into being, soon to be referred to quite simply as 'the Christian faith'. The earliest outline statements are referred to with the term 'rule of faith' (Latin *regula fidei*); these brief statements developed into summary creeds and confessions prefaced by the words 'We (or I) believe'.

Revelation

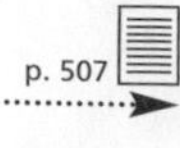

p. 507

Biblical criticism

Creed

Bible

In the course of ongoing theological reflection, which from early times was linked with philosophy, the question arose how revealed truths are related to knowledge achieved through reason. So in the early church the contrast between faith and works gave way to the contrast between faith and knowledge, and between faith and reason. In the long discussion that followed, faith and knowledge were generally seen as complementary; the differences were over the relative roles each of them played. In what became the mainstream, Augustine saw faith as enhancing knowledge, making it possible to understand things that otherwise could not be grasped. He defined faith as 'thinking with the giving of assent'. Faith comes first, but requires reason to clarify it. The clearest statement of this view was made later by Anselm of Canterbury with his classic *credo ut intelligam*: 'I believe in order that I may understand.' Faith was seen as superior to reason because it was a supernatural act, a free gift of God that could not be achieved by any human works. This was a famous point of dispute between Augustine and the followers of Pelagius, who found an important role for human works. Thomas Aquinas provided a succinct summary of the relative roles of faith and reason: 'As grace does not destroy but perfects nature, so it is right that natural reason should serve faith as the natural tendency of the will to love serves love.'

Jesus of history

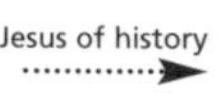

Evil

Authority

Reformation

At the Reformation, Martin Luther led the way in a return to the understanding of faith as trust and the central issue of justification by faith; the Roman Catholic Church for centuries differed here, arguing that faith justifies only when it is motivated by a supernatural love which leads to the doing of good works. Today an agreement between Roman Catholics and Protestants over justification by faith has been reached, but there can hardly be said to be any agreement in answering the problems which next arose, with the Enlightenment, over the understanding of faith when those beliefs which were held as a matter of faith clashed with the new knowledge which geographical and intellectual exploration was bringing everywhere. Time and again, 'the faith' was challenged by science, and rationalists came to argue that all the necessary truths of religion could be known without faith and without the divine revelation that preceded faith. This problem is still with us today. The philosopher Immanuel Kant sought to solve it by his *Critique of Pure Reason*, arguing that it was impossible to have knowledge of things in themselves, and therefore impossible to establish the existence of God by any proof: here he claimed to have denied knowledge in order to make room for faith. However, this means that faith becomes a mere attitude with no objective content.

Enlightenment

Yet another challenge to faith arose with the historical criticism of the Bible and the Christian tradition. What had long been thought to be a timeless and unchanging deposit of faith, 'the faith which was once for all delivered to the saints', even the Bible itself, was seen to have undergone historical development. Jesus was put in the context of his time and became part of an ongoing history, a very different figure from Christ as understood by the churches. Hence a further contrast arose between the 'Christ of faith' and the 'Jesus of history': here, faced with a shifting mass of historical evidence the reliability of which seemed constantly changing, the option of choosing the Christ of the faith of the church and personal experience has seemed to many the only way forward, even if this leaves the gap between faith and knowledge as wide as ever.

The most radical statement about faith is attributed to the second-century Latin theologian Tertullian, *credo quia impossibile est* ('I believe because it is impossible'; what he actually said was *certum est quia impossibile est*, 'it is certain because it is impossible'). In the light of the problems facing faith, to which, of course, could be added the moral problem of faith in a good God in the face of so much evil, this is one solution adopted today. Another is to accept an authority, that of the Bible or the church, and have faith in that, not seeking to understand the ultimate reasons why. But there will always be those who feel that an attempt must be made to reconcile faith and reason, faith and knowledge in some way. Here the fundamental elements to be taken into account are the personal attitude of the believer, the recognition that faith requires trust and commitment, and respect for the findings of modern knowledge, but coupled with an awareness that there are still more things in heaven and earth than are dreamt of.

JOHN BOWDEN

📖 Avery Dulles, *The Assurance of Things Hoped For: A Theology of Christian Faith*, New York: OUP 1996; K. W. Clements, *Faith*, London: SCM Press 1981; John

Hick, *Faith and Knowledge*, London: Macmillan 1967; Wilfred Cantwell Smith, *The Meaning and End of Religion* (1963), reissued Minneapolis: Fortress Press 1994 and *Faith and Belief* (1979), reissued Oxford: Oneworld 1998

Feminist theology

Feminist theology began by criticizing traditional theologies for their lack of attention to women's experience, though it moved quickly to the reconstruction of theological categories from a feminist perspective. Though diverse, at its core feminist theology calls into question the theological assumptions that justify patterns of male dominance in church and society. Religious beliefs that either implicitly or explicitly convey the idea of female subordination are littered throughout the Bible and theology. These initially became the focus of feminist criticism, particularly in early seminal works such as Rosemary Radford Ruether's *Religion and Sexism* (1973) and Kari Borresen's *Subordination and Equivalence: The Nature and Role of Women in Augustine and Aquinas* (1968). The beliefs that men more perfectly embody the image of God, that only men can represent Christ in the liturgy, or that women are created subordinate to men are among the beliefs commonly repeated in the tradition. And although these beliefs tend to reflect the cultural assumptions of particular historical periods, feminists regard them as unacceptable distortions of the gospel message.

Of course, the view that women are subordinate to men is not only conveyed through explicit teachings. Subtle forms of misogyny are also endemic. Moreover their influence often persists long after the more overt expressions of women's inferiority have disappeared. According to many feminists, the (virtual) absence of female images for God, despite the conviction that God is neither male nor female, exemplifies the misogyny of the tradition. So too does the passive role constructed for Mary in the life of the church. Thus at the heart of the feminist critique is this conviction that the theological tradition through the centuries has radically compromised the original (egalitarian) vision of Christianity.

While often regarded as a child of the 1960s, feminist theology has a long heritage in the church, though the term 'feminist' is itself a modern invention. Early examples of what one would today call feminist beliefs (and practice) were evident among medieval writers such as Julian of Norwich and Hildegard of Bingen. Not only was Hildegard influential as a mystic who enjoyed prophetic visions, she also had an active role in the life of the medieval church through her preaching and administrative work. Moreover, Christine de Pizan, writing in the early fifteenth century, engaged in what we would today call feminist biblical criticism. And in the nineteenth century Elizabeth Cady Stanton, Sarah Grimke and Lucretia Mott each challenged the prevailing patriarchal ethos of church and society on what could be regarded as feminist principles. Indeed in the late nineteenth century there was a flowering of Christian feminist writing and activism, much of it highly contentious at the time. The publication, in 1895–8, of Elizabeth Cady Stanton's *The Woman's Bible*, in which she criticized the biblical texts she regarded as detrimental to women's equality, was one such occasion of controversy. The central claim of *The Woman's Bible* is that the cause of women's subordination lies in their enslavement to patriarchal religion and that biblical texts are implicated in the construction of that subordination. The retrieval of these and other neglected precursors of contemporary feminism within Christianity has highlighted the significance of women's participation in the life of the church historically and, in the process, has created a more comprehensive account of the past.

Political theology

African American Christianity
Liberation theology

These early developments notwithstanding, contemporary feminist theology emerged in the late 1960s alongside the critical perspectives of political, black and liberation theologies. It is therefore appropriately situated within the broader theological context of the late twentieth century. The Second Vatican Council, which encouraged theologians to respond to the 'signs of the times'; the turn to politics in the writings of Jürgen Moltmann, Johann Baptist Metz and James Cone; and the efforts of liberation theologians to 'do theology from the underside of history' all provided important resources for feminist theologians. Moreover, particularly in the USA and Europe, the women's movement, with its all-encompassing critique of patriarchy, provided both practical and theoretical resources for this fledgling discipline. However, the early advocates of feminist theology in no way anticipated the diversity of women's experience. Viewed with the benefit of hindsight, these initial attempts to theologize from women's experience now seem extraordinarily naïve. Yet once women began to engage in theological reflection, the differences among women came to the fore. Whereas initially the racial, ethnic, economic and geographical differences between women were neglected, in the last two decades this precise issue has become a dominant theme in feminist theological discourse. While this in part reflects the postmodern preoccupation with the politics of difference, the main impetus has come from women of colour and Third-World women.

God

Mary

Women in Christianity
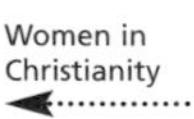

Hildegard of Bingen

Particularly since the mid-1980s the differences among women have been to the foreground in theological reflection. Thus womanist theology pioneered by Delores Williams and Katie Canon emerged from the

African American community. It attempted to tackle the sexism within that particular theological and cultural context, while simultaneously challenging the sexism and racism of the dominant society. Hispanic women in the United States, too, have named their distinctive theological perspective as generating *mujerista* theology, a neologism coined by Ada Maria Isasi-Diaz. Among Third-World women post-colonial themes predominate. Mercy Amba Oduyoye from Ghana, Virginia Fabella from the Philippines and Ivone Gebara and Elsa Tamez from Latin America each attend to the symbiotic relationship between Christianity and indigenous traditions in the maintenance of sexist beliefs and practices. Feminist theologians from Asia have also draw attention to a similar dynamic, while developing theological themes that reflect the cultural uniqueness of Asian Christianity. As a result feminist theology is now a pluralistic and intercultural theology, one that best reflects the catholicity of the Christian tradition.

Hispanic Christianity
Ministry and ministers ➤

In addition to contesting the shape of traditional theological reflection, feminist theologians have also engaged in discussions of biblical, doctrinal and ethical themes. Though initially regarded as a separate theological discourse, feminist perspectives now take their place alongside others in the domain of contemporary theological debate. Thus the biblical scholar Elisabeth Schüssler Fiorenza has pioneered a form of biblical hermeneutics that, though intended as a tool to identify the neglected biblical history of women, has now been appropriated by other biblicists. Her 'hermeneutic of suspicion' draws attention to the manner in which biblical (and theological) texts are the products of literary and cultural élites and argues that they must therefore be read as such. This feminist textual criticism combined with archaeological and historical investigation has contributed greatly to our knowledge of the social and religious lives of biblical women and in the process has created a more inclusive and accurate picture of the Christian biblical heritage.

Sexuality ➤
Bioethics ➤
Human rights ➤
War and peace ➤
Biblical criticism

In the field of systematic theology much of the focus has been on the theology of God, and in particular on the manner in which the patriarchal models and exclusive language function to exclude women from full participation in the church. Yet the consistent conviction among Christian feminists is that these patriarchal models can be interpreted in the light of the long-held Christian belief that all discourse about God is culturally generated. It is metaphorical, provisional and ultimately capable of renewal. Sallie McFague, Elizabeth Johnson and Delores Williams have each written theologies of God which are inclusive while simultaneously being traditional. Thus God is imaged as Friend, as Mother and as She Who Is. Moreover, reinterpretations of trinitarian theology speak of God as 'Creator, Redeemer, Sustainer', rather than as the all-male 'Father, Son and Holy Spirit'. Feminists have also debated the theological significance of the maleness of Jesus. Traditional theologies of Mary, too, have been criticized on the grounds that in these Mary usually functions as the passive handmaid of the patriarchal church, embodying and reinforcing conservative views about women's identities. Moreover, the church's institutional structures as well as its models of ministry have been the subject of feminist theological reconstruction. Debates about the ordination of women also continue, though feminists now regard the ordination of women as part of the struggle for a more inclusive, collaborative and prophetic form of Christian ministry.

Feminist theologians have also been prolific writers on ethical themes. Some follow the liberal paradigm, arguing for equal rights and privileging autonomy and freedom. Others strive to revalorize women's traditional association with caring through the development of an ethic of care. Themes of identity and power also predominate, particularly in feminist discussions of sexuality and of bioethics. Moreover in the context of social ethics, feminist ethicists have intervened in debates about human rights, citizenship and war and peace. Indeed feminist ethical thought illustrates well the broader trend that has seen feminism progress from the margins into the mainframe of theological reflection. Thus although it began as a form of criticism, feminist theology is today more appropriately regarded as a novel, perhaps even radical, development of the tradition. Its goal is to bring feminist perspectives to bear on inherited theological categories and in so doing to transform the discipline in its entirety.

LINDA HOGAN

Hyun Kyung Chung, *Struggle to Be the Sun Again: Introducing Asian Women's Theology*, Maryknoll: Orbis and London: SCM Press 1990; Elisabeth Schüssler Fiorenza, *In Memory of Her: A Feminist Theological Reconstruction of Early Christian Origins*, New York: Crossroad and London: SCM Press 1983; Ada Maria Isasi-Díaz, *En la Lucha: Elaborating a Mujerista Theology*, Maryknoll: Orbis 1996; Elizabeth Johnson, *She Who Is. The Mystery of God in Feminist Theological Discourse*, New York: Crossroad 1992; Susan Frank Parsons, *The Cambridge Companion to Feminist Theology*, Cambridge: CUP 2002; Rosemary Radford Ruether, *Sexism and God-Talk*, Boston: Beacon Press and London: SCM Press 1983; Delores Williams, *Sisters in the Wilderness: The Challenge of Womanist God-talk*, Maryknoll: Orbis 1993

Festivals and fasts

The Christian calendar is marked by a whole series of festivals and periods of fasting or abstinence from certain kinds of food and drink. In most traditions the year starts with Advent, which begins on the fourth Sunday before Christmas. Then come Christmas, Epiphany, Lent, Easter, Ascension Day and Pentecost. This cycle is interspersed by festivals of Jesus, Mary and the saints. Easter and the festivals related to it, such as Lent, Ascension Day and Pentecost, have movable dates; the other festivals have fixed dates. In church calendars important feasts came to be printed in red ink, so they were known as 'red-letter days'.

From around the time of the Emperor Constantine onwards feasts came to be celebrated over eight days (known as an 'octave'): Easter, Pentecost and Epiphany were the first feasts to have octaves; saints days followed until there was such a proliferation that steps had to be taken to reduce it. In the Western church today the only octaves still celebrated are those of Christmas, Easter and Pentecost.

Advent

The season of Advent, peculiar to the Western churches, takes its name from the Latin *adventus*, 'coming'. It dates from the fifth or sixth century and was the last season of the church's year to develop. It extends over the four Sundays before Christmas Day.

It was originally a period of fasting, but the element of fasting gradually disappeared, and the season came to be seen more as a time of preparation. On the Sundays sermons were originally preached on the coming of Christ. In due course a second theme was added, the Second Coming of Christ at the end of time, and this led to sermons on the 'four last things': death, judgement, heaven and hell. Both themes are marked in the hymns traditionally sung during Advent: 'Hark the glad sound, the Saviour comes, the Saviour promised long' and 'On Jordan's bank the Baptist's cry announces that the Lord is nigh' contrast with 'Lo, he comes with clouds descending, once for ransomed sinners slain' and 'Come, thou long-expected Jesus, born to set thy people free'. Occasionally the themes of Advent are celebrated in Advent carol services, but in modern times Christmas themes have come to appear earlier and earlier.

The days of Advent are marked by an Advent calendar, supposedly devised by a Munich housewife tired of being asked by her children when Christmas would come. Religious Advent calendars, culminating on December 24 with a depiction of the baby in the manger, are now inevitably being swamped by calendars on commercial themes. Many churches have an Advent evergreen wreath, into which four candles are inserted and lighted, one more each week, to symbolize the light of the world. In Moravian homes and churches three-dimensional paper stars with a light in them are hung from the beginning of Advent to Epiphany. This custom has not spread widely, but another custom, that of the Christingle, has. At a Christingle service during Advent, or on Christmas Eve, a 'Christingle' is given to the children. This consists of an orange, representing the world, with a lighted candle stuck in it to symbolize Christ. Nuts, raisins and sweets on pointed sticks symbolize God's good gifts.

Moravian Church
Calendar
Food and drink

Christmas

The word Christmas means simply 'Christ's Mass'. Names in other languages are more evocative: *navidad* (Spanish) and *natale* (Italian) mean 'nativity', and *Weihnachten* (German) 'holy night'. Christmas Day, celebrating the birth of Jesus, is usually celebrated on 25 December, but the Russian Orthodox Church and the Armenian Church celebrate Christmas on 6 January and the Ethiopian Orthodox Church on 7 January.

The actual date of Jesus' birth is unknown. There are two theories about the choice of 25 December: 1. That was the date of a Roman festival of the invincible sun, and Christians took it over to celebrate Christ, the sun of righteousness; 2. It was calculated in the third century as nine months after the spring equinox, believed to be the date of the creation of the world and therefore an appropriate date for its new creation in Christ.

Christmas seems first to have been observed in the early fourth century, but its origins are obscure. It has come to be the most popular of all Christian festivals, observed in one way or another by Christians and non-Christians alike.

The mixture of religious festival and secular celebration characteristic of modern Christmases has been there from early times. In the seventeenth century, Puritans in England and North America actually banned the observance of Christmas for this reason. The ancient Roman festival of Saturnalia was held in December, and was an occasion for feasting and drinking, and the Yule log and decorations with holly and mistletoe come from old Germanic winter customs. The Christmas tree originated in German mystery plays as a symbol of the tree of paradise and was popularized through its introduction into Victorian England by Prince Albert. The Christmas crib, a representation of the manger in which Mary put the baby Jesus, was first introduced by Francis of Assisi (1182–1226).

Puritans

Santa Claus, who comes at Christmas, is a corruption of the Dutch Sinterklaas, St Nicholas. Nicholas of Myra (in present-day Turkey) was a shadowy fourth-century saint who among other things brought pickled boys back to life, an exploit commemorated in icons and in

Benjamin Britten's cantata *Saint Nicholas.* On his feast day (6 December) he was believed to visit children with warnings and gifts.

Christmas is preceded by carol services which take a variety of forms. A popular one is a sequence of readings from the fall of Adam and Eve to the coming of Christ, interspersed with carols, which is particularly associated with King's College, Cambridge. Roman Catholics have long celebrated the first Christmas mass at midnight, and 'midnight mass' has also become popular in the Anglican tradition. Other churches hold late-night candlelight services on Christmas Eve.

Some customs originating in a winter northern hemisphere have been transplanted directly to a summer southern hemisphere, but they have also been changed. Christmas is a summer festival in Brazil with picnics and Forgiveness fireworks, culminating in a procession of priests to church to celebrate midnight mass. In Mexico on the days before Christmas, children re-enact Mary and Joseph's search for a place to stay.

Epiphany

The first evidence of a feast of Epiphany comes from Gnosis Gnosticism in the second century. The Greek *epiphania* means 'manifestation', and was a term used at that time among other things for the ceremonial visit of a king or emperor or the appearance of a deity to a worshipper. The festival was celebrated on 6 January, for reasons that are not entirely clear. It appears in the Eastern churches in the third century, as a festival second only to Easter, where it was and still is associated with the baptism of Jesus. There are special blessings of water and administration of baptism at this time. When the festival spread to the West it celebrated the manifestation of Jesus to the Gentiles, in the persons of the magi or wise men who came to visit his cradle. By contrast, in the East the magi came to be associated with Christmas and Epiphany with the wedding in Cana at which Jesus turned water into wine.

Towards the end of the fourth century the Western and most of the Eastern churches in fact each adopted the other's festival in honour of the birth of Jesus; this led to the 'twelve days of Christmas', a celebration extending from 25 December to 6 January.

Lent

Lent comes from the Middle English *lenten*, 'spring'. It Council started in the fourth century, after the Council of Nicaea, as a 40-day period during which candidates were instructed Initiation in preparation for baptism at Easter. The last week of Lent was particularly important, and from the same period it came to be called a 'holy week'.

In the Eastern churches, four special Sundays prepare for what is known as the great fast: the Sunday of the Pharisee and Publican; the Sunday of the Prodigal Son; Meat-Fast Sunday, after which meat is not to be eaten; and Cheese-Fast Sunday, after which the fast is extended to include cheese, eggs, butter and milk. In the Roman Catholic Church, three Sundays before Lent marked a pre-Lenten season; named Septuagesima, Sexagesima and Quinquagesima (roughly 70, 60 and 50 days before Lent), they originated as a special time of prayer for protection against war, famine and plague. They appear in the Anglican Book of Common Prayer but have been dropped in modern liturgical revisions.

The observance of Lent today begins on a Wednesday, called Ash Wednesday, on which in the Roman Catholic Church and some forms of Anglicanism those who are present at the eucharist have their foreheads marked with ash in the sign of the cross. This symbolizes their sinfulness and need to repent; during the first millennium Lent was also a time of public penance in which those who had committed grave sins were sprinkled with ashes.

It was customary also to go to confession on the day before Lent to receive absolution, or in the ancient term to be 'shriven'. This practice has given its name to the day before Ash Wednesday, Shrove Tuesday. Nowadays on the European continent and elsewhere, Shrove Tuesday is a virtually secular carnival day (and in many places the culmination of several days of carnival); Mardi Gras ('Fat Tuesday', from the custom of using up the fats in the home before Lent) in New Orleans is a famous example.

The fourth Sunday in Lent, just over half-way through Lent and therefore sometimes called 'Mid-Lent Sunday', has many other names. In Anglican churches it is best known as 'Mothering Sunday', and on it children who attend worship are provided with bunches of spring flowers to give their mothers, thus making the day one of the more widely-attended festivals. In Victorian times domestics were given time off to visit their mothers and take presents of flower and cakes. The Sunday is also called 'Refreshment Sunday', because a relaxation of fasting on that day became customary; in England simnel cakes, specially rich fruit cakes, used to be baked. Yet another name is *Laetare* (Latin 'rejoice') Sunday, after the first word of the opening antiphon set for the eucharist on that day.

The next Sunday used to be known as Passion Sunday, and from then on all crucifixes and other images in church were veiled in purple. However, reforms in the Roman Catholic Church abolished the title in 1969 and restricted the practice to Holy Week; other churches that observed it have followed suit. Nevertheless the title Passiontide for the period from then until Easter has been retained.

Holy Week

Holy Week is the week leading up to Easter; in the Eastern churches it is known as 'Great Week'. In Jerusalem as early as the fourth century the events of Jesus' final week there, from the welcome by crowds waving palms on his entry to his crucifixion, burial and resurrection, were re-enacted dramatically, and from there Palm Sunday processions and veneration of the cross spread to other churches.

Palm Sunday. In the Catholic tradition Palm Sunday opens Holy Week, usually with a procession that can start from outside the church building and with the blessing of palms. The long account of the last events of the life of Jesus (the 'passion', or suffering) from Matthew's Gospel is read at the eucharist.

Maundy Thursday. The next major observances are on the Thursday, known as Maundy Thursday. A ceremony of foot-washing, which originated in the Middle Ages, has been revived in modern times; an anthem from this ceremony in fact gave its name to the day. The anthem was set to words from the Gospel of John, 'I give you a new commandment' – Latin *mandatum*, of which Maundy is a corruption. This day also marked the end of the period of penance undergone by sinners. In the Eastern Orthodox churches there is an evening service with readings from the various accounts of the passion of Jesus in the New Testament. In the Catholic tradition it is customary to celebrate the eucharist in the evening, to commemorate the Last Supper. After this the altar is stripped of its linen and the candles are removed; it is then washed with water and wine.

Good Friday. The Friday before Easter is known in the Western churches as 'Good' Friday and in the Eastern churches as 'Great' Friday, and marks the day on which Jesus of Nazareth was crucified. Just as the celebration of the resurrection of Jesus at Easter has left its mark on Sunday, the first day of the week, as a day of worship and rejoicing, so from the second century Good Friday left its mark on other Fridays as a day of fasting and penance. Resurrection

In the Roman Catholic Church the day is commemorated in churches by prayers and readings, especially of the

The Pope's Easter blessing, St Peter's, Rome

account of the passion in the Gospel of John; the veneration of the cross, in which the worshippers come forward to kiss a crucifix; and the distribution of communion from the sacrament reserved from the Maundy Thursday eucharist. Anglican and other churches hold a three-hour service between noon and 3 pm consisting of sermons, p. 341 hymns and prayers often centred on Christ's 'seven last words from the cross'. There is no celebration of the eucharist in the Eastern Orthodox Church, and at Vespers, the evening service, there is a solemn re-enactment of the burial procession of Jesus, represented by the epitaphion, a piece of material bearing an image of his dead body.

p. 341

The devotion of the Stations of the Cross is also practised in Catholic churches on Good Friday; the stations are usually represented by plaques on the walls of churches, but in many Catholic countries there are long 'ways of the cross', often up to a hilltop, with the stations as shrines along the way.

p. 685

In the Middle Ages Good Friday took on increasingly antisemitic overtones and it was unsafe for Jews to venture out on the day. In the Anglican Book of Common Prayer Holy Spirit one of the prayers for the day asks for mercy upon all 'Jews, Turks, Infidels, and Hereticks' and asks for their salvation among 'the remnant of the true Israelites'. These antisemitic overtones have been removed in recent liturgical revisions and there is now great sensitivity on the issue.

Easter

The word Easter comes from the Old English *eastre*, the name for a spring festival. In Greek and Latin the festival is called *pascha*, from the Greek equivalent to the Hebrew *pesach*, 'Passover'. Pascha produces the adjective 'paschal', which is regularly used for things associated with Easter such as the paschal lamb and the paschal candle. Easter is the earliest Christian festival and celebrates the resurrection of Jesus of Nazareth from the dead. Its date is flexible, and is chosen as the first Sunday after the full moon that occurs on or next after the spring equinox (21 March). This means that it can fall on any Sunday between 22 March and 25 April.

The most important of all Christian festivals, in the early church Easter was preceded by a vigil in which the scriptures and psalms were read. In the Roman Catholic tradition, followed also by many Anglicans and Lutherans, during this vigil there is a blessing of new fire, the lighting of the paschal candle, the blessing of the font and the baptism of new Christians, and a service of scriptural readings. This culminates in the celebration of the Easter Eucharist eucharist. In the Eastern churches the Easter eucharist is

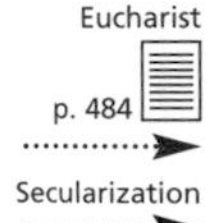

p. 484

preceded by a procession representing a vain search for the body of Jesus, followed by the announcement 'Christ Secularization is risen'. The procession leaves the church in darkness, but when it returns lights are lit everywhere. In the United States the interdenominational dawn Easter service is so popular that it is covered on radio and television.

The candle lit at the vigil from the new fire which is kindled is usually a large one; it has the date of the year inscribed on it, together with the sign of the cross and the Greek letters alpha and omega, and five grains of incense are inserted into it, symbolizing the five wounds inflicted on Jesus. It is lit for worship through the season form Easter until Pentecost, and at all baptisms.

Post-Easter festivals

Ascension Day. The festival celebrating the Ascension of Jesus is traditionally dated as the fortieth day after Easter; however, some churches observe it on the Sunday nearest to that day. The Ascension was initially celebrated at Pentecost, but a separate festival arose during the fourth century.

Pentecost. The name comes from the Greek *pentecoste*, fiftieth day, and is given to the Sunday that falls on the fiftieth day after Easter. It commemorates the descent of the Holy Spirit on the apostles related in the Acts of the Apostles (chapter 2), which occurred on that day. The feast is first mentioned in the second century. The whole period of 50 days after Easter was also called Pentecost in the early church, and there were baptisms at the beginning and end of the season. In Northern Europe Pentecost in fact became more popular than Easter for baptisms and in England came to be called Whitsunday after the white garments worn by candidates.

Trinity Sunday. A feast of the Holy Trinity was first inaugurated in the early tenth century and proved so popular that it spread through northern Europe, being established in Rome in the fourteenth century. Some religious orders, such as the Dominicans and Carthusians, and the Anglican and Lutheran churches, named the Sundays for the rest of the church's year Sundays 'after Trinity' instead of 'after Pentecost' as in the Roman Catholic tradition, but with the revision of their books of worship the Lutherans and Anglicans have adopted the Roman Catholic naming.

Corpus Christi. In the Roman Catholic Church and other churches in the Catholic tradition this festival is held on the Thursday after Trinity Sunday and celebrates the sacramental body and blood of Christ. It has been traditionally marked by a procession through the streets in which the host, the bread consecrated at the eucharist, is carried in an elaborate monstrance. However, the procession has become less common in recent times, partly because of the secularization of society and also because the focus of the significance of the eucharist has

A TABLE FOR FINDING EASTER

Golden number	Day of the month	Sunday letter
XIV	March 21	C
III	22	D
	23	E
XI	24	F
	25	G
XIX	26	A
VIII	27	B
	28	C
XVI	29	D
V	30	E
	31	F
XIII	April 1	G
II	2	A
	3	B
X	4	C
	5	D
XVIII	6	E
VII	7	F
	8	G
XV	9	A
IV	10	B
	11	C
XII	12	D
I	13	E
	14	F
IX	15	G
XVII	16	A
VI	17	B
	18	C
	19	D
	20	E
	21	F
	22	G
	23	A
	24	B
	25	C

0	A
1	G
2	F
3	E
4	D
5	C
6	B

THIS Table contains so much of the Calendar as is necessary for the determining of *Easter;* to find which, look for the Golden Number of the year in the first Column of the Table, against which stands the day of the Paschal Full Moon; then look in the third column for the Sunday Letter, next after the day of the Full Moon, and the day of the Month standing against that Sunday Letter is *Easter Day.* If the Full Moon happens upon a Sunday, then (according to the first Rule) the next Sunday after is *Easter Day.*

To find the Golden Number, or Prime, add one to the Year of our Lord, and then divide by 19; the remainder, if any, is the Golden Number; but if nothing remaineth, then 19 is the Golden Number.

To find the Dominical or Sunday Letter, according to the Calendar, until the year 2099 inclusive, add to the Year of our Lord its fourth part, omitting fractions, and also the number 6: Divide the sum by 7; and if there is no remainder, then A is the Sunday Letter: But if any number remaineth, then the Letter standing against that number in the small annexed Table is the Sunday Letter.

For the next following Century, that is, from the year 2100 till the year 2199 inclusive, add to the current year its fourth part, and also the number 5, and then divide by 7, and proceed as in the last Rule. Note, that in all Bissextile or Leap-years, the Letter found as above will be the Sunday Letter, from the intercalated day exclusive to the end of the year.

The Christian festival of Easter is celebrated on the first Sunday after the spring full moon and therefore varies from year to year between 21 March and 25 April. This table for calculating the day on which Easter will fall is printed in the Anglican Book of Common Prayer.

shifted from the elements of bread and wine to the whole action of the service.

The Transfiguration. This festival, commemorating the occasion when Jesus took three disciples up a mountain, where Moses and Elijah appeared and he was transfigured (Mark 9.2–13), has always been a major festival in the East since its origins in the seventh century. It is celebrated on 6 August, but the Syrian and Armenian churches keep it on the seventh Sunday after Pentecost. It did not become established in the West until 1457, when Pope Callistus III ordered its universal celebration to commemorate a victory over the Turks at Belgrade. It is observed there on the same day except in some Lutheran churches, which observe it on the last Sunday after Epiphany.

Festivals of Mary

The first festivals of Mary were celebrated in the Eastern church after the Council of Ephesus in 431 which named her 'Mother of God', and in the Orthodox churches the Mary four festivals commemorating her are: The Nativity (8 September); The Presentation in the Temple (21 November); The Annunciation (25 March); The Dormition, or Falling Asleep (15 August). The festival of Hypapante ('Meeting'), celebrating the meeting of Simeon and Anna with the infant Jesus and his parents in the temple described in the second chapter of the Gospel of Luke is the equivalent of the Western Feast of the Purification, but is not a festival of Mary.

Four major festivals were introduced in Rome in the seventh century and are celebrated today in the Roman Catholic Church: The Nativity of the Blessed Virgin Mary (8 Paganism September, now the Feast of the Immaculate Conception); The Purification of the Blessed Virgin Mary (2 February), known as Candlemas because a procession with candles was held; The Annunciation (25 March); The Assumption (15 August). There are many other local festivals of Mary, such as the feasts of Our Lady of Lourdes (11 February) and Our Lady of Guadalupe (12 December).

Festivals of the saints

Martyr

Commemorations of martyrs were among the very first of the church's festivals; they took place on the anniversaries of their deaths. The first such commemoration, of St Polycarp of Smyrna, is recorded as early as 155 CE. This is a century earlier than the feast of St Peter and St Paul (29 June), which was established in 258.

Saint

Originally each church had its calendar of saints' days, and it was some time before it began to be standardized; even then it took around 500 years, from the fourth to the ninth centuries. After that, new local additions to the calendar were made until at last in 1634 Rome gained full p. 1077 control over the veneration and canonization of saints. The proliferation of saints meant that in both the Eastern and the Western churches there were several, often many, saints for each day of the year. This was one of the excesses Reformation which the Reformation opposed, and in the Church of England, the Book of Common Prayer prescribed the observance of a very slim, essentially biblical, list: St Andrew (30 November), St Thomas (21 December), The Conversion of St Paul (25 January), St Barnabas (11 June), St John Baptist (24 June), St Peter (29 June), St James (25 July), St Matthew (21 September), St Michael and All Angels (Michaelmas, 29 September), St Luke (18 October), St Simon and St Jude (28 October) and All Saints Day (1 November). After the Second Vatican Council the saints' days were revised and many legendary saints, such as St George, were abolished, but new saints are being added all the time. In the Anglican Church the Lectionary that lists the observances of the year is now full of commemorations, not just of saints, but of a whole variety of figures who have served the churches in various ways.

All Saints Day and All Souls Day occupy a singular place in the church year. A reference to a feast celebrating all Christian saints, known and unknown, occurs as early as the fourth century, when it was assigned to the first Sunday after Pentecost, a date still observed in the East. In the West, in 610 Pope Boniface IV established a feast of All Saints on May 13; in the next century Gregory III transferred it to 1 November. This move was to have major consequences in Britain and Ireland, where 1 November marked the end of the summer, when animals were brought in for the winter. The souls of the dead were also thought to visit their former homes at this time. As a result, the eve of All Saints Day, a holy eve or 'Halloween', came to be associated with a variety of pagan beliefs and customs. Although many attempts to stamp it out were made in the Protestant tradition, it persisted, and was transported to North America by Irish immigrants, who helped to make it a major children's festival. The following day, 2 November, came to be observed as a day for the commemoration of the dead from the beginning of the second millennium onwards; at this time in southern Europe people pay ceremonial visits to the graves of members of their family.

Harvest festivals and fasts

Harvest thanksgiving. In the early church, there were festivals for offering the first fruits of the harvest; the dates of these differed, depending on the location and the crops. In medieval England 1 August was called Lammas ('loaf-mass') Day and bread was baked from the new wheat and blessed at the mass. However, it became more usual to commemorate the completion of the harvest and the customary date was 11 November, St Martin's Day, or Martinmas. After the Reformation the Christian harvest thanksgiving disappeared in England, and all that was left was secular merrymaking. However, it continued in the Netherlands from which the Pilgrim Fathers sailed, and probably led to the observance of Thanksgiving in North America. In England in 1843 a Cornish Anglican vicar revived the Lammas custom, but on the first Sunday in October; harvest festivals then became extremely popular and now they probably come second after Christmas in their appeal to the public at large.

Rogation days. The three days before Ascension Day are known as Rogation Days (from the Latin *rogare*, ask). In rural societies they were observed by processions round the fields in which litanies were recited, praying for good weather for the crops and deliverance from plague and famine. With the increasing urbanization of society these observances have largely died out and been replaced by special masses.

Ember days. Ember days are four sets of three days of prayer, fasting and penitence, on Wednesday, Friday and

Saturday, around the beginning of each of the seasons of the year. Their dates are: after the third Sunday of Advent, the first Sunday in Lent, in the week of Pentecost, and in the week after Holy Cross Day (14 September), a feast commemorating the recovery of the supposed True Cross from the Persians by the Emperor Heraclius in 614. They are probably agricultural festivals introduced into the Christian year. Until recently they were also times of ordination to the priesthood in the Roman Catholic and Anglican churches.

JOHN BOWDEN

Adolf Adam, *The Liturgical Year: Its History and Its Meaning After the Reform of the Liturgy*, New York: Pueblo Press 1981; Alan McArthur, *The Evolution of the Christian Year*, London: SCM Press 1953; Thomas J. Talley, *The Origins of the Liturgical Year*, New York: Pueblo Press 1986; Francis X. Weiser, *Handbook of Christian Feasts and Customs: The Year of the Lord in Liturgy and Folklore*, New York: Harcourt, Brace & World 1958

Food and drink

Food and drink lie at the heart of Christianity: its central act of worship is a communal meal at which, now symbolically, bread is eaten and wine is drunk. This meal arose out of the last supper that Jesus had with his disciples before his death, which in turn had been preceded by many shared meals, often in the company of the most disreputable members of society. One of the images with which Jesus described the kingdom of God was a feast, to which the outcast and oppressed came first. The heavenly banquet subsequently came to be seen as one of the great joys of heaven. A particularly earthy vision of it is given by a tenth-century Irish saint, Brigid, revived for the twentieth century by the American composer Samuel Barber as one of his 'Hermit Songs'. Brigid writes how she would like to have the men of heaven in her house with vats of good cheer laid out, the three Marys and people from every corner of heaven, and Jesus with them. She would like a great lake of beer for the King of Kings, and she would like to be watching everyone drinking it through all eternity.

The openness of the way in which everyone is welcome at the feast is paralleled by an equal openness over what food is eaten. Jesus himself is reported as saying that nothing which enters people defiles them, but what comes out of them (Mark 7.15), and in the Acts of the Apostles (chapter 10) Peter has a vision in which a great sheet descends to earth, let down by four corners, containing all kinds of animals, reptiles and birds. Peter is invited to 'kill and eat' but refuses three times: each time he is told that nothing here is unclean, since God has cleansed everything.

Origins and background

The background to this dream is the controversy that split Christianity at the very beginning and was one of the main factors that eventually led to its emergence as a separate religion. Judaism had dietary regulations that forbade the eating of certain kinds of living creatures and in particular the consumption of their blood, and Jews who became Christians continued to observe these regulations; did pagans who became Christians also have to observe them? Paul, the great missionary to the pagans ('the Gentiles') said no, but the authorities of the mother church in Jerusalem said yes. In the end the matter was settled at an 'apostolic council', which ruled that pagans who became Christians had to 'abstain from the pollutions of idols and from unchastity and from what is strangled and from blood' (Acts 15.20). Paul's own view was that the most important thing was not to affect those who were not strong-minded. 'Food will not commend us to God. We are no worse off if we do not eat [meat offered to idols], and no better off if we do ... But if anyone sees you, a man of knowledge, at table in an idol's temple, might he not be encouraged to eat food offered to idols? And so by your knowledge this weak man is destroyed' (1 Corinthians 8.8–11).

Paul

The prohibition against eating meat in which there was blood, from animals that had not been ritually slaughtered according to Jewish practice, continued to be extremely influential. Converts to Christianity in second-century Rome had to abstain from black puddings, which were particularly popular. The church father Tertullian complains to the pagan authorities: 'You tempt Christians with sausages of blood, just because you are perfectly aware that the thing by which you thus try to get them to transgress they hold unlawful.' Clement of Alexandria and John Chrysostom spoke out against consuming blood, and in fourth-century Persia drinking blood was offered to Christians as a way of escaping martyrdom.

Eucharist

Kingdom of God

Martyr

Feasting and sacrifice

The mention of meat sacrificed to idols is a reminder that in the ancient world feasting, and particularly eating meat, was bound up with the practice of sacrifice. The religious practices of the world in which Christianity emerged had sacrifice at their centre, and with sacrifice, especially among the Greeks and Romans, went the idea of the shared meal. In the Greek world the killing of domesticated animals always and only took place in ritual circumstances. Jesus' last supper was not only one in a series of many meals he shared with his disciples; it was held at the time of the Jewish Passover, the feast which commemorated the exodus of the Israelites from Egypt, at which lambs were killed and eaten by those taking part.

Sacrifice

Jesus

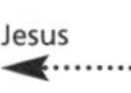

p. 851

For the Jews, too, until the destruction of the Jerusalem temple in 70 CE, sacrifice was an essential part of their religious practice.

By a complex process, Jesus came to be identified with the Passover lamb, and the eucharist came to be understood as a sacrificial meal. It thus came to perform the function of traditional sacrifices, the rejection of which was one of the most striking features of emergent Christianity.

At Passover, Jews eat unleavened bread, i.e. bread made without the use of yeast. The exodus from Egypt was sudden, and there was no time to wait for bread to rise. Unleavened bread, in the form of wafers, became the type of bread customarily used in the eucharist in the Western church, but the custom in almost all the Eastern churches seems to have been to use leavened bread: at the time of the split between the churches in 1054 this was a major factor. Nowadays, though, leavened bread is often used in Western churches for its greater symbolism (see, e.g., Matthew 13.33).

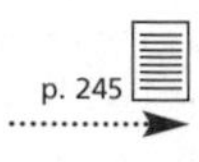
p. 245

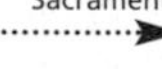
Sacraments

Although the eucharist itself became a symbolic meal, more substantial eating was and is associated with it. A religious meal called the agape (love feast) was held in the early church in close association with the eucharist, but because it was open to abuse it disappeared by the third century; however, the agape has been revived in modern times in communities with no minister to celebrate the eucharist as an appropriate way of celebrating fellowship. Until recently blessed bread (*pain bénit*) was distributed after mass in French and Canadian churches, and in Orthodox churches the remainder of the loaves used at the eucharist are distributed to people afterwards (this is known as the *antidoron*, Greek for 'instead of the gift').

The Gospel of John presents in the person and actions of Jesus almost a complete compendium of food and drink. He is the 'bread which came down from heaven' (6.41) and provides food to feed a multitude (6.1–14), the instigator of a miraculous catch of fish (21.1–14), the source of living water of which whoever drinks will never thirst again (4.14), the true vine (15.1), and at a wedding feast turns water into wine (2.1–11). Most importantly, in his very person he provides food for those who believe in him: 'For my flesh is food indeed and my blood is drink indeed. He who eats my flesh and drinks my blood abides in me and I in him' (6.55–6).

Christian influences on eating

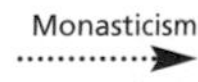
Monasticism

As time went on, developing Christianity introduced feasts and foods of its own, often Christianizing existing pagan customs and giving them new associations. Through Christianity these feasts and foods have survived the decline of religious observance in Western Europe and are still enjoyed by those who would not call themselves practising Christians.

Christmas replaced the midwinter celebration of Saturnalia; though many of its most familiar features, like Christmas dinner, derive from the Victorians, there are Christmas meals at Camelot in the Arthurian legends. On the eve of Ash Wednesday, the first day of Lent, the season of fasting, people first went to confession, to be 'shriven', hence Shrove Tuesday, and then ate pancakes, to use up ingredients forbidden during Lent. This turned into a longer period of pre-Lenten celebration, known as Carnival or Mardi Gras ('Fat Tuesday'). Hot cross buns are said to derive from cakes offered to the goddess Astarte in ancient times, originally decorated with horn marks which were later changed to a cross. Easter eggs, a symbol of the renewal of life in springtime, came from celebrations associated with the goddess Eostre.

Fasting and abstinence

Jesus and his disciples were criticized for not fasting, and Jesus was called a 'glutton and a drunkard' (Matthew 11.19), but he did not condemn the practice, and fasting became one of the many ascetic features of Christianity. Like Jews, Christians fasted twice a week, but on different days: as the Didache, a first-century document, puts it: 'Let not your fast days be with the hypocrites: they fast on Mondays and Thursdays, but you should fast on Wednesdays and Fridays.' Over the centuries numerous regulations about fasting developed, in preparation for baptisms, ordinations, consecrations and receiving communion at the eucharist, and for purposes of penance and intercession. Lent, the period of fasting before Easter, originally lasted only two days, but by the fourth century had been extended to 40, at which it remained. Further fasts were added in the Eastern church, notably in Advent.

Fasting originally meant abstaining from food for the whole of a day, or over long periods limiting oneself to one simple meatless meal a day, but came to be relaxed. Over time, in the Western church, the regulations about when fasting was necessary were also relaxed, and since the Second Vatican Council it has been required in the Roman Catholic Church only on Ash Wednesday and Good Friday.

Another, but related, practice grew up alongside fasting, namely abstinence, i.e. not eating certain kinds of food. One form of abstinence was practised by early Christian groups referred to by the church fathers as Encratites; they rejected wine and meat and were so extreme that they were considered heretical. The early monks in the desert lived only on bread, salt and water, and equally strict abstinence has been practised in a number of the religious orders.

The best-known form of abstinence is the Roman Catholic practice of not eating meat on Fridays, substituting fish on that day; however, this has ceased to be a meaningful practice in a world where fish are being caught

Walter Dendy Sadler, *Friday*

to the point of extinction and are often more of a luxury than meat.

In the Orthodox churches there are five levels of abstinence: 1. abstaining from meat; 2. abstaining from meat, eggs, milk, butter and cheese; 3. abstaining from meat, eggs, milk, butter, cheese and fish; 4. abstaining from meat, eggs, milk, butter, cheese, fish, oil and wine; 5. abstaining from all foods and beverages except bread, water, juices, honey and nuts.

Christianity has never been strong on the treatment of animals, and despite numerous contemporary efforts to make a case for vegetarianism, there is little outside the general history of fasting and abstinence to support this in the tradition. However, particularly in the face of our modern intensive farming and fishing practices, an increasing number of Christians are becoming vegetarians out of respect for the world and what they see as the God-given life of its non-human inhabitants.

Animals

Alcohol and temperance

Along with corn and oil, wine is regarded in the Old Testament as one of the staple products of fertile land and one of the joys of life. In the ancient world the custom was to drink wine with water. Only exceptional individuals, Nazirites such as Samson (Judges 13.4), totally abstained from wine and spirits. Given the scarcity of pure drinking water, for much of Christian history it was in fact safer to drink wine or beer. The monastic orders preserved brewing as a craft during the Middle Ages, and there are around a dozen abbeys in Europe which still produce beer and sell it commercially, the six best-known of them Trappist and in Belgium, with names like Chimay, Orval and Westmalle. Liqueurs, too, are associated with monastic orders: the Benedictines produced the liqueur named after them in 1510 and the Carthusians of La Grande Chartreuse first produced liqueurs made of green and yellow herbs in 1607.

Temperance, abstaining from alcoholic drinks, dates from the very beginning of the nineteenth century. Churches in North America were the first to introduce pledges of abstinence, and under their influence temperance societies rapidly developed, spreading first via Ireland to Great Britain and then on to the European continent. Methodists and Baptists, Quakers, Mormons, Christian Scientists, Seventh-day Adventists and Jehovah's Witnesses have all made abstinence a condition of membership, but this was relaxed in the Methodist Church in the middle of the twentieth century. At celebrations of the eucharist these churches substitute unfermented grape juice for wine.

Though asceticism, abstinence, fasting and temperance run through the history of Christianity, delight in the good things of creation is also a constant feature of the tradition. However, the ecological crisis has moved Christians, too, to think about the consequences of their eating and drinking, for the environment and for the economy of poor nations. They have not always been in the forefront of movements for change, but they have been learning the need for it.

JOHN BOWDEN

Shannon Jung, *Food for Life: The Spirituality and Ethics of Eating*, Minneapolis: Fortress Press 2004; Christoph Markschies, *Between Two Worlds*, London: SCM Press 1999

Forgiveness

Jesus

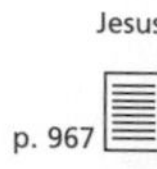

p. 967

Forgiveness lies at the very heart of Christianity. The one prayer that Jesus taught his disciples, the Lord's Prayer, asks God for forgiveness, while at the same time indicating that forgiveness is something that men and women should show to one another. Forgiveness was a key aspect of Jesus' activity. He claimed the power to forgive sins, and when challenged about this with the question, 'Who can forgive sins but God alone?', tells a paralysed man brought to him on a stretcher to take up the stretcher and walk – which the man thereupon does (Mark 2.5–12). When Peter asks Jesus how many times he is to forgive his brother, as much as seven times, Jesus replies, 'Not seventy times, but seventy times seven' (Matthew 18.21–2) – in fact limitlessly, like the creditor who releases a debtor from a debt of ten thousand talents, an almost unimaginable sum (Matthew 18.23–7). The Gospel of Luke records an encounter between Jesus and a 'woman of the city who was a sinner', probably a euphemism for a prostitute. He tells those who object to the forgiveness of which he assures her that 'her sins which are many are forgiven for she loved much; but those who are forgiven little, love little' (7.47–8).

Conversion

p. 848

Resurrection Sin Death

It was a basic conviction of the followers of Jesus after his death and resurrection that he had overcome the destructive forces of sin and death and restored human beings to a right relationship with God, an extension of the liberating power that those who met Jesus experienced during his lifetime in the form of forgiveness. In the early church forgiveness is most closely associated with water baptism, and the Nicene Creed affirms, 'We believe in one baptism for the forgiveness of sins.' This baptism is spoken of in the twofold imagery of cleansing and drowning. Baptism 'washes away' or deals with sin but is also understood as representing the 'death' of an old way of life, which is 'buried' in the baptismal waters so that the Christian may then be 'raised up' to walk in newness of life. But before baptism Christians were required to go through a process of learning and personal discipline, the catechumenate, which involved repentance, confession and absolution (this became the term used for the authoritative forgiveness of sins). In this way they became members of the church and free from sin – at least in theory.

Creed

Initiation

But as time went on it became clear that Christians continue to sin after baptism. Indeed, the New Testament can both speak of the Christian being set free from sin and also say that 'if we say that we have no sin, we deceive ourselves' (1 John 1.8). Paul speaks of refusing to be mastered by sin and yet experiencing an on-going struggle with sin (Romans 7). This presence of sin after baptism continued to be a live question in early church debates. Repentance, confession and absolution were necessary time and again, and associated with them penance was, the action required to show that the repentance was genuine. All these form a complex connected with the forgiveness of sins in the church, and each needs to be considered separately to understand how forgiveness has been understood over the centuries.

Repentance

In the New Testament, the word usually translated as repentance (Greek *metanoia*) means literally 'turning' in the sense of 'turning right round', a complete reversal of attitudes and motives. In particular, the word is used of a turning or conversion towards God or Christ in faith and a turning away from sin, usually understood as the failure to keep God's commandments. In Mark's Gospel, John the Baptist proclaims a baptism of repentance for the forgiveness of sins (Mark 1.4) and Jesus begins his ministry with the call to 'repent, and believe the good news' (Mark 1.15). Matthew and Luke's accounts of the preaching of John the Baptist broaden the reference; those called to baptism must bring forth fruit worthy of repentance (Matthew 3.8; Luke 3.3); in other words, the call is to a change of behaviour and attitude. Luke illustrates this as John the Baptist exhorts tax collectors to collect only what is due, and soldiers to resist extorting money from anyone by threats or false accusations (Luke 3. 13–14).

In the synoptic Gospels (the Gospels of Matthew, Mark and Luke) Jesus combines with his offer of forgiveness a call to repentance. This is illustrated by his concern for 'tax collectors and sinners', those who failed outwardly to keep the Jewish law and so placed themselves outside the community of salvation as commonly understood by the rabbinic Judaism of his day. Jesus' daring table-fellowship with such outcasts, which so scandalized his opponents, was a means of showing to them that they could be accepted into God's kingdom through repentance and faith: 'Those who are well have no need of a physician, but those who are sick; I have come to call not the righteous but sinners to repentance' (Luke 5.31–2). Luke in particular emphasizes this theme in the great parables of Luke 15: the lost sheep, the lost coin, and the lost son; the emphasis is that those who are 'lost', who are outside God's kingdom are 'found' and restored through repentance.

Luke's Gospel concludes with the statement that 'repentance and forgiveness of sins is to be proclaimed in his (Jesus') name to all nations, beginning in Jerusalem

(Luke 24.47), a theme which is illustrated by the sequel to the Gospel, the Acts of the Apostles.

Despite the prevalence of references to repentance in the synoptic Gospels and Acts, there are no references in the Gospel of John and very few in Paul. This is principally because both authors, in their reflection upon human sinfulness and the possibility of salvation, employ other theological categories.

While repentance is essentially an inward disposition of the heart and will, in Christian practice it is given clear expression in liturgical rites. The archetype is the liturgy of baptism, which celebrates salvation, the passing from death to life, from darkness to light. For example, in the Roman Catholic rite for the Christian Initiation of Adults, where the norm is initiation at Easter, the preparatory period of Lent, called the period of purification and enlightenment, includes rites for self-searching and repentance. This is an important aspect of the conversion that is demanded by accepting the rites of initiation. The initiation services of the Church of England include the specific question to the candidates or to the parents and godparents in the case of the baptism of infants: 'Do you repent of the sins which separate us from God and neighbour?' The answer to be given is: 'I repent of them.'

Similarly, the post-baptismal form of commissioning those able to answer for themselves as Christian disciples includes the question: 'Will you persevere in resisting evil, and, whenever you fall into sin, repent and return to the Lord?' The answer is: 'With the help of God, I will.'

The eucharist, as the church's regular renewal of the baptismal covenant, also usually includes the invitation to repentance through confession and absolution. This was a particular concern of rites emanating from the Reformation, which looked to Paul's warnings in 1 Corinthians 11 about the dangers of partaking in the sacrament unworthily, and so incorporated weighty forms of examination and penitence. The Book of Common Prayer (1662) of the Church of England, for example, includes a rehearsal of the Ten Commandments, with the congregational response, 'Lord, have mercy upon us and incline our hearts to keep this law,' and a demanding congregational exhortation inviting the examining of conscience in the light of God's commandments, of restitution and satisfaction for offences against a neighbour, and the willingness to forgive others. Those invited to communion are those who 'do truly and earnestly repent' of sins, while the form of general confession includes the words, 'We do earnestly repent, and are heartily sorry for these our misdoings.' It should also be stated that the rite stresses God's mercy upon those who are truly penitent.

While repentance is regarded as essentially an inward disposition in Protestant theology, although it must be matched by the intention to lead a new life, in Roman Catholic and Orthodox practice, inward contrition and outward participation in the sacramental rite of penance, with confession to and absolution from a priest (under the seal of utter confidentiality), are necessary to show true repentance. This brings us to the question of confession.

Confession

Biblically, the word confession (Greek *homologia*) is used in two senses: confession of faith or confession of sins. Prayers of confession of sins are found in the Hebrew scriptures in passages such as Nehemiah 1.4–11; Daniel 9 and in the so-called penitential Psalms (6; 32; 38; 51; 102; 130; 143). In the Gospels, the response to the preaching of John the Baptist was confession of sins (Matthew 3.6), and there are various examples of individuals acknowledging their sinfulness (Matthew 6.12; Luke 5.8; 15.21; 18.13). The letter of James includes the exhortation, 'Confess your sins to one another, and pray for one another, that you may be healed' (James 5.16), while the First Letter of John assures the believer of forgiveness upon confession: 'If we confess our sins, he who is faithful and just will forgive us our sins and cleanse us from all unrighteousness' (1 John 1.9). In the church's liturgical tradition, there are two traditions of confession, corporate or general confession and individual confession.

Psalms

Within corporate worship, certain texts have a penitential character or reference. The petition *Kyrie eleison* ('Lord, have mercy') is found in many historic liturgies as the characteristic congregational response within litanies; this tradition has continued in the Orthodox churches, while in the West by the eighth century, the petitions tended to be omitted, leaving a ninefold pattern of *Kyrie eleison* (three times), *Christe eleison* (three times) and *Kyrie eleison* (three times). The *Trisagion* ('thrice-holy'), 'Holy God, holy and strong, holy and immortal, have mercy upon us', is characteristic of Orthodox worship, and the communion anthem *Agnus Dei* ('O Lamb of God, who takes away the sins of the world, have mercy upon us') established itself in the Western mass from the seventh century. Corporate confession of sins did not become a feature of the Roman Catholic mass (except as a preliminary devotion for eucharistic ministers called the *confiteor*, 'I confess'), but became almost universal in Protestant worship from the Reformation onwards. For example, in the Anglican tradition forms of general confession and general absolution are provided for Holy Communion and Morning and Evening Prayer. A penitential rite was introduced into the Roman Catholic missal of Paul VI (1969): while this makes provision for general confession and a form of absolution, it is simply a prayer for forgiveness; the actual forgiveness of sins is mediated only through the rite of penance, which we shall be looking at shortly.

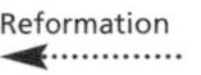

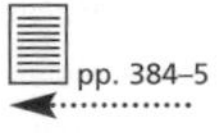

Forms of general confession usually include an acknowledgement of sin, a statement of contrition and a petition for forgiveness. Sometimes explicit reference is made to the death of Jesus as the means by which sins are forgiven. Some forms of general confession, reflecting the instruction in the letter of James, 'Confess your sins to one another …', include an acknowledgement that confession is made both to God and also to fellow members of the church, e.g., 'I confess to almighty God and to you, my brothers and sisters, that I have sinned …'. At various points in Christian history attempts have been made to give this instruction real expression. John Wesley (1703–91), the founder of the Methodist movement, established 'band' meetings for those who were intent on pressing on towards scriptural holiness; these meetings included the opportunity for members to interrogate one another on their manner of life and motives, thus establishing a kind of corporate confessional.

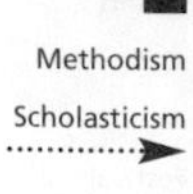

Methodism
Scholasticism

There are two strands in the tradition of individual confession. The first is personal private confession as a daily or regular expression of Christian discipleship and the life of prayer. In the patristic church this was deemed sufficient for the forgiveness of minor sins, and was sometimes accompanied by voluntary abstinence from the eucharist for a period. More serious sins were liable to public penance, which included formal exclusion from the eucharist, and such sins tended to be defined by church synods and councils. Such private individual confession has continued throughout Christian history with varying degrees of emphasis across the differing Christian traditions. Since the beginning of printing, popular books on daily devotion stress private confession as one of the parts of prayer, alongside adoration, intercession and thanksgiving, while there is also a long tradition of personal preparation, including penitential prayer, before receiving communion at the eucharist.

Council

Books

Prayer

The second strand is individual confession to another person. This approach emerged from between the fifth and eighth centuries in monastic communities, especially those of the Irish Celtic tradition. Here the emphasis was on spiritual direction, a form of spiritual counsel that evolved and flourished with the rise of monasticism. The penitent would come to a spiritual director (increasingly over time, though not invariably, a priest), make confession (referred to as auricular confession), and receive spiritual counsel. In contrast to public penitential discipline, which, as we shall see, was usually administered only once after baptism, this form of private confession could be undertaken many times. As it gradually spread and became recognized across the Western church, it was usually permitted only for minor sins. However, by the beginning of the second millennium it came to eclipse the public form of penance. This was partly because of the unpopularity of public penance, but also because of developments in the nature of the priesthood and the increasing importance of absolution.

Justification
Monasticism
Celtic Christianity

The status and 'separateness' of the priesthood increased from the time of Pope Gregory VII (1073–85), while in Europe generally there was re-emergence of individual consciousness during the eleventh and twelfth centuries. Whereas previously forgiveness had to be preceded by doing penance, now increasingly priestly absolution was granted immediately after confession, to be followed by the fulfilment of penances, which themselves were now understood as making satisfaction. While scholastic theologians debated the nature of the rite of penance, some placing the emphasis on contrition, some on making confession, and some on absolution, the last of these grew in importance. Absolution was understood as the priestly exercise of the office of the keys, the power to forgive or retain sins (Matthew 16.19), and as the 'form' of the sacrament, while contrition, confession and satisfaction constituted the 'matter'; in other words, upon true confession (contrition, confession, satisfaction), forgiveness and restoration was mediated through the absolution. In the Western church this was confirmed by the Fourth Lateran Council of 1215, which made individual confession to a priest obligatory at least once a year and in particular in preparation to receiving the sacrament at Easter. The newly-established pattern retained the tradition of giving spiritual counsel: this in turn led to the publication of numerous manuals for priest confessors setting out advice for the performance of the sacrament.

At the Reformation, Martin Luther retained forms of individual confession and absolution, but he did not regard them as mandatory. Rather, he regarded the ministry as pastorally important for those who could not quieten their own conscience. He rejected, however, any form of satisfaction. Luther placed particular stress on absolution as a word of grace from God mediated through the pastor. The doctrine of justification by faith required that nothing be added to the authoritative word of absolution; faith embraced the scriptural promise. In England, Thomas Cranmer, the author of the Book of Common Prayer, also retained individual confession and absolution for certain pastoral circumstances. An exhortation at Holy Communion recommended private confession if a person could not quieten his own conscience, while also asserting the sufficiency of general confession. A form of absolution, including the phrase 'I absolve you from all your sins', was retained in the order for the visitation of the sick, to follow confession if the sick person should 'feel his conscience troubled with any weighty manner'. John Calvin and other continental Reformers tended to reject auricular confession, preferring to make provision for the public corporate penance, and rejecting confession and absolution as a sacrament because it lacked any outward and visible sign instituted by Christ. They also rejected any sense of the priest as a mediator between God and humanity; the Protestant stress on direct access to God through Christ meant that in most traditions confession and the reception of forgiveness were essentially inward and spiritual in both corporate worship and private prayer.

In the Roman Catholic Church, the Council of Trent required individual auricular confession for all mortal sins. The order for confession was published in the Roman Ritual of 1614, superseding a whole series of local rites. In the Orthodox tradition, the act of confession is preceded by the reciting of Psalm 51 and two prayers for forgiveness. Following an exhortation from the priest, absolution is given. There are a variety of absolution prayers; the ancient forms ask God to forgive the penitent; to these were added in the seventeenth century an indicative form, 'I ... do forgive and absolve thee from all thy sins', approximating more closely to the Roman rite. With the decline in regular reception of the bread and wine at the eucharist, auricular confession came to be used as a prescriptive form of preparation to receive the sacrament.

Absolution

Absolution is the authoritative declaration of the forgiveness of sins in response to confession. In the New Testament, the power to 'bind' or 'loose' sins was conferred on Peter in Matthew 16.19: 'I will give you the keys of the kingdom of heaven, and whatever you bind on earth will be bound in heaven, and whatever you loose on earth will be loosed in heaven,' on the church in Matthew 18.18, and on the apostles in John 20.23: 'Receive the Holy Spirit. If you forgive the sins of any they are forgiven; if you retain the sins of any, they are retained.' In the Roman Catholic and Anglican traditions, the authoritative declaration of God's forgiveness is reserved to the priesthood.

As with confession, absolution is administered either corporately or individually. In the Roman Catholic tradition, sacramental absolution is pronounced only through the Rite of Penance. While a rite for reconciliation of several penitents with general confession and absolution makes provision for general absolution, this rite is seldom used and is not authorized by all bishops' conferences. The norm remains individual absolution following individual confession. The form of absolution runs: 'God, the Father of mercies, through the death and resurrection of his Son has reconciled the world to himself and sent his Holy Spirit among us for the forgiveness of sins; through the ministry of the Church, may God give you pardon and peace, and I absolve you from your sins in the name of the Father, and of the Son, and of the Holy Spirit.'

Forms of individual confession and absolution are given in many Lutheran, Anglican and some other Protestant service books. They are understood as an appropriate pastoral provision for some, but are not requirements of church membership. The well-known adage 'All may, some should, none must' is often quoted. The historic phrase 'I absolve you' (Latin *ego absolvo te*) has proved to be controversial in non-Roman traditions. Despite the fact that it was retained in the service for the visitation of the sick in the Book of Common Prayer, some Anglicans are concerned lest it undermines the divine prerogative to forgive; in such cases phrases such as 'you are absolved from your sins' replace the indicative form.

Churches in the Protestant tradition usually provide some forms that are prayers and others which are declarations. For example, the form provided in the British 1999 Methodist Worship Book is a declaration: 'God, the Father of all mercies, through Jesus Christ his Son, forgives all who truly repent and believe in him. By the ministry of reconciliation given by Christ to his Church, I declare that your sins are forgiven, in the name of the Father, and of the Son, and of the Holy Spirit. Amen.' General absolution, following general confession, is a well-established form of prayer in most liturgical churches. While the current Roman missal includes an 'absolution' as part of the penitential rite, the prayer is couched in the subjunctive: 'May almighty God have mercy on us, forgive us our sins, and bring us to eternal life.' This does not constitute sacramental absolution. In the Anglican tradition, the general absolution is regarded as fully efficacious for the forgiveness of sins; the most common form is: 'Almighty God, who forgives all who truly repent, have mercy upon you, pardon and deliver you from all your sins, confirm and strengthen you in all goodness, and keep you in life eternal; through Jesus Christ our Lord. Amen.' A deacon or lay person using the above prayer must substitute 'us' for 'you'.

In Protestant churches, the word absolution is seldom used; rather, the prayer following confession is understood as a declaration or assurance of pardon and often quotes scripture. An example would be: 'Christ Jesus came into the world to save sinners. Hear then the word of grace and assurance of pardon: Your (or Our) sins are forgiven for his sake.' This form of absolution could be said by any Christian; it is not reserved to ordained ministers of the word and sacraments.

Ministry and ministers

Penance

The word 'penance' is from the Latin *poenitentia*, used in the Vulgate to translate the Greek word *metanoia*, usually translated 'repentance' or 'conversion'. In current liturgical use it is most often used to designate forms of service for confession and absolution of sins. So, in the Roman Catholic Church, the Rite of Penance was authorized

Penitents processing through Seville during Holy Week

in 1973 as part of the liturgical reforms initiated by the Second Vatican Council. Previously, the word penance was most commonly used of those undertaking penitential discipline and, more narrowly, of 'doing' or performing a penance, a form of spiritual exercise or activity to show contrition for sins committed.

Discipline

In the early centuries of the church, patterns of penitential discipline were developed for those who fell into sin after baptism. The issue of post-baptismal sin is apparent in the New Testament documents (1 Corinthians 5.11, 13; 2 Corinthians 2.5–11; Hebrews 6.4–6; Matthew 18.15–18; 1 John 5.16, 17; 1 Timothy 5.19–22). These passages illustrate how different Christian communities engaged with the realities of serious sin. The possibility of exclusion from the community or excommunication is clearly envisaged, while some passages also suggest restoration. 1 John includes reference to 'mortal sin', the letter to the Hebrews states that it is impossible to restore again to repentance those who have fallen away, reflecting the seriousness of apostasy.

In the post-apostolic period, the fullest descriptions of emerging patterns of penitential discipline are given by the church father Tertullian in *De poenitentia*, reflecting North African usage at the beginning of the third century and in the contemporary Syrian church order the *Didascalia Apostolorum*. In the latter, the bishop, who stands in the place of God, must be stern: he must judge offenders, excluding them from the church, but nevertheless show mercy upon repentance. If an offender is repentant, the bishop then assigns certain weeks of fasting and prayer according to the offence, with exclusion from the church and so from the eucharist. After the period of exclusion is completed, the penitent is then received back into the church through the laying on of hands. This public reconciliation to the church was the outward sign of reconciliation to God. In some communities penitents were required to wear sackcloth and ashes as an outward sign of contrition. This restoration was comparable to baptism, and like that sacrament, it could only be administered once, although there were debates about the restoration of those who lapsed more than once because of repeated persecution. Indeed, the process of restoration was in many ways parallel to that required of candidates for baptism.

At Rome, this parallelism with baptism was further strengthened by making the fast of Lent the time both for

FLAGELLANTS

Flagellants were men who beat themselves with whips in public processions; there were also women flagellants, but they whipped themselves in private. The practice arose in the thirteenth century in Perugia, spreading from there throughout Italy and then to Germany and the Low Countries. It seems to have been prompted by a plague, anarchy in the Italian states, and prophecies of the end of the world by Joachim of Fiore.

Flagellation already had a long history: from the fourth century onwards clergy and laity practised it as a means of penance. The difference was that in the Middle Ages the flagellants organized themselves into brotherhoods. Their characteristics were devotion to the Virgin Mary and also a concern for social reform. The movement was given added impetus in the fourteenth century by fear of the Black Death. Though condemned by Pope Clement V in 1549, the flagellants survived in Germany into the fifteenth century; they became a sect, wearing a white habit with a red cross and processing to the centre of the city twice a day; they were persecuted by the Inquisition. In Italy, public processions were still being held in the nineteenth century.

the final preparation of candidates for baptism and the period of penitential discipline. The rite of excommunication took place before the eucharist on what became known as Ash Wednesday because the penitents received the imposition of ashes. The penitents were publicly readmitted to the church's fellowship on the Thursday before Easter by the laying on of hands and initiation was celebrated at the Easter vigil. This in time led to the adoption of Lent as a penitential season for the whole church, beginning on Ash Wednesday and extending to Easter, approximating to the time (40 days and 40 nights) that Jesus spent in the wilderness being tempted by the devil (Mark 1.12–13).

A number of factors led to the gradual demise of public penance. One was that many aspects of it were voluntary; rather than being imposed, it often had to be sought, and this proved to be a disincentive. Moreover, just as many delayed receiving baptism because of fears about post-baptismal sin, so many were reluctant to enter penitential discipline because it could only be administered once, thus raising concerns about subsequent sin. The process was public and could hold people open to disgrace; some penitential processes were overly harsh and severe. During the sixth and seventh centuries many sought reconciliation only *in extremis*.

As public penance fell into decline, so it was replaced by private confession. Here, the word penance became associated with the imposition of tariff penances, or practical responses to sins confessed. Penitential manuals and tables set out suggested penances for particular sins. These ranged from set periods of fasting or prayer to requirements for a change in lifestyle as a remedy to habitual sins. For example, the sexually immoral had to revert to chastity, the thief had to repay what had been stolen, the lazy had to give themselves to work. On satisfactory completion of the penance, the offender could be restored to eucharistic fellowship. In time, where the penances were particularly long and demanding, and so unlikely to be fulfilled, alternative penances were granted which were deemed to be equivalent. Often this meant undergoing shorter, more severe, spiritual exercises, or if a person was wealthy, payment of money could replace the traditional tariffs.

This development appears to have made the gift of money the penance itself rather than a thank-offering for restoration on fulfilment of the traditional penances. It laid the foundation for the eventual sale of indulgences, which in the sixteenth century became a major catalyst for the Reformation. The dispute arose in the context of the development of the doctrine of purgatory, that the faithful departed must undergo a period of purgation after death to make them fit to behold the beatific vision of Christ in glory. As a means of raising revenue for the papacy, indulgences guaranteeing the forgiveness of sins could be purchased to reduce or even eliminate the period of purgation. Luther's insistence that justification is by faith reasserted forgiveness as a divine gift mediated by God alone and in this sense not through the power of the church or the priesthood.

Life after death

In contemporary rites of reconciliation, the Roman rite retains the imposition of an act of penance or expiation to make satisfaction for sin. The rite understands this as both an atonement for past sins and also as an aid to new life and antidote to weakness. The rite states: 'The penance should correspond to the seriousness and nature of the sins. The act of penance may suitably take the form of prayer, self-denial, and especially service to neighbour and works of mercy.' While non-Roman rites tend not to make an act of penance mandatory, the pastoral helpfulness of positive acts in response to forgiveness is recognized.

Atonement

The twentieth century has seen the re-evaluation of rites of penance. A number of factors have contributed to this. First, the renewal of baptismal theology has led to a fuller appreciation of penance as a restoration of baptismal dignity, rather than as an aspect of church discipline. Second, insights from the human sciences, notably

INDULGENCES

In the Roman Catholic Church an indulgence (from the Latin *indulgentia*, kindness, tenderness), is the remission of punishment for sins after they have been confessed and forgiven. Absolution forgave sins and wiped them clean, but sinners still had to accept punishment. That punishment might consist of doing penance in one form or another; penance in this life might not be enough, so they were to expect further punishment in purgatory.

By tradition there are various kinds of indulgence: universal indulgences which may be obtained anywhere, and local indulgences; perpetual indulgences which are available at any time, and temporary indulgences; and especially partial indulgences, which remit only part of the punishment, and plenary indulgences, which remit it all. The first plenary indulgence was granted by Pope Urban II on the occasion of the First Crusade in 1095: 'Whosoever out of pure devotion and not for the sake of gaining honour or money, shall go to Jerusalem to liberate the Church of God, may count that journey in lieu of all penance.' An example of a partial indulgence is the indulgence of 40 days granted by Pope Innocent II in 1132 to those who visited the church of Cluny and contributed towards it.

Crusades

The association of financial contributions with indulgences proved fateful: indulgences financed many of the cathedrals and other buildings in Europe and the system was abused by the senior clergy, the more unscrupulous of whom profited from it personally. Indulgences granted to finance the rebuilding of St Peter's in Rome helped to spark off Luther's Reformation; Thesis 21 of the 95 Theses which he pinned to the door of the Castle Church in Wittenberg in 1517 states: 'Therefore those preachers of indulgences are in error, who say that by the Pope's indulgences a man is freed from every penalty, and saved.' The Council of Trent put an end to the abuse of indulgences, and subsequently Pope Pius XV revoked all indulgences associated with financial payments.

In present Roman Catholic teaching indulgences may apply to both the living and the dead (they are discussed in the *Catechism of the Catholic Church*, 1471–9). Those who wish to gain them must be in a state of grace and perform whatever good work is prescribed.

Psychology and Christianity

psychology, have led to reflection on the place of guilt, memory and experience of life in human consciousness. Third, there has been a recovery of the church's ministry of healing. This has stressed the desire for wholeness at all its levels, rather than simply cure, and so the relational, spiritual and environmental aspects of healing have become important. Fourth, while spiritual counsel has always formed part of this ministry, the late twentieth century has seen a very significant development in the use of spiritual direction and the adoption of a structured rule of life that often includes auricular confession. While the Roman Catholic Church has entitled its revised services the Rite of Penance, equivalent rites in other churches are often described as 'rites of reconciliation'. This reflects an understanding that the ministry encompasses reconciliation with God, with the church, with other Christians and other human beings, as well as seeking personal and inward reconciliation in the disintegrated aspects of an individual's personality. The outcome is that rites of reconciliation are now understood essentially as an expression of pastoral care rather than church discipline, and as part of the Christian's desire for wholeness and a fuller experience of the reconciliation Christ came to bring.

Sickness and healing

Sacraments

The Roman Catholic Rite of Penance was promulgated in 1973. The rite uses the language of conversion (*metanoia*), and sets penance in the context of baptism, citing Ambrose of Milan: 'The Church "possesses both water and tears: the water of baptism and the tears of penance"'. The rite of penance achieves both forgiveness from God and reconciliation with the church. Penance has four constituent parts: contrition, confession, an act of penance and absolution. Three forms are provided: the first the rite for reconciliation of individual penitents; the second the rite for the reconciliation of several penitents with individual confession and absolution; and the third the rite for reconciliation of several penitents with general confession and absolution.

The form for individual penitents comprises the reception of the penitents, including welcome and invitation to trust in God; an optional reading of the word of God; confession of sins with appropriate counsel and the acceptance of an act of penance or satisfaction, an act of contrition and the absolution (accompanied by the priest extending his hands over the penitent's head, or at least extending a hand towards the penitent); a proclamation of the praise of God; and a dismissal. This remains the norm for Roman Catholics. The other two rites are seldom used.

Forms for the reconciliation of a penitent may also be found in contemporary prayer books of Anglican, Lutheran, Methodist and Reformed Churches. They follow a similar pattern to the Roman form, the main differences being a fuller provision for the ministry of the word, avoidance of the language of satisfaction, and different approaches to the absolution.

DAVID KENNEDY

James Dallen, *The Reconciling Community: The Rite of Penance*, Collegeville, MN: Liturgical Press 1986; Martin Dudley and Geoffrey Rowell (eds), *Confession and Absolution*, London: SPCK 1990; Joseph Favazza, *The Order of Penitents: Historical Roots and Pastoral Future*, Collegeville, MN: Liturgical Press 1988

Free churches

In its least precise usage, this term encompasses those Protestant churches that do not belong to one of the major confessional families of the Reformation: Lutheran, Reformed, Anglican. What is described in this way is a large portion of the world Christian community, but one so varied that it is difficult to unify historically or theologically. It ranges from Baptists, Mennonites and Quakers to holiness churches, Adventists and Pentecostals. The term itself appears to date from 1843, when a group of ministers led by Thomas Chalmers left the Church of Scotland to found a communion separate from state control and support, which they called the Free Church.

According to varied meanings of the word 'free', the term can designate three overlapping but non-identical groups of Christian communions.

1. It can refer to those who reject in principle the existence of any state religion because the true church can be formed only by voluntary personal conversion and covenant. These 'believers' churches' originate with the Anabaptist movements of the Reformation era (of whom Mennonites are a direct descendant), with precursors in the work of John Wyclif, the Hussite movement and the Waldensians. The Anabaptists invented the role of churches as voluntary societies within the political state. The believers' church movement re-emerged independently in England among separatist congregations inspired by Puritan reform. Baptists developed in this setting, eventually to become the largest denominational family among believers' churches. For such communions, the church must be composed only of confessing, regenerate believers. Thus baptism is limited to professing believers and membership comes only through voluntary, adult decision. A church composed of such members is governed as directly as possible by the inspiration of the Holy Spirit in the interpretation of scripture, without bondage to the prior authority of historical creeds or state rulers. Because these groups stress the autonomy of individual congregations and the equal voice within the congregation of each covenanted member, they practise a democratic polity in church governance. Believers' churches are free churches in that they are free from government direction, free of traditional credal norms and free in each member's liberty of voice and vote on all matters of faith and practice.

All Protestants affirm the authority of scripture, but all have likewise recognized that interpretations of the Bible will differ. To maintain apostolic continuity and identity, some means of authoritative determination of scriptural teaching is required. Reformers rejected the magisterium of the bishops, the unique teaching authority of the Pope, and much of the received theological tradition of the Roman Catholic Church. In turn, they placed great weight on other, remaining standards, such as historic creeds (and new confessions), fixed liturgies and a learned ministry. Believers' churches took the dramatic further step of dropping even these elements, affirming no creed but scripture, sharing no fixed liturgy and ordaining the theologically uneducated as well as (or even in preference to) the scholarly. The simple and variable form of worship is one of the most characteristic features of these communities. The local congregation, in the collective discernment and decision-making of its members, becomes the authoritative interpreter of scripture for its own life. These groups were well aware that this programme could work only with a very unusual and disciplined community. Hence the care with which the personal testimony and religious experience of each prospective new member was judged by the congregation as a whole, and the care with which discipline was administered to those within the church. Hence also the emphasis on individual and small-group study of the Bible and on intensive common prayer, as the context for congregational decision-making.

Church membership is an active decision, on the part both of the applicant and the congregation. This strengthens the members' sense of responsibility and fosters lay co-operation and leadership in all areas of the church's life. Historically, free church congregations attracted adherents because of their intimate piety, egalitarian order and undiluted biblical focus. They were and for the most part remain small, family-like communities, with highly participatory structures. More recently the polity of congregational autonomy has proved consistent with the emergence of mega-churches. These huge individual congregations function as denominations unto themselves and find precedent in the congregational principles of the free churches, even while they may differ from them in many ways.

2. 'Free churches' can refer to those who sought the liberty to practise their own form of the church alongside an established or territorial church. This includes the original believers' churches in their historical contexts, but others in addition. In particular it refers to those who held this position historically in England. There, Presbyterians, Congregationalists, Baptists and Methodists were all 'dissenters' or 'non-conformists'. They did not conform to the teaching and discipline of the Church of England, and they sought relief from legal sanctions against their

Authority
Bible
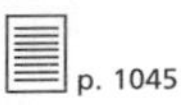
p. 1045
Creed
Protestantism
Reformation
Lutheranism
Reformed churches
Anglicanism
Baptist churches
Peace churches
Holiness churches
Adventist Church
Pentecostalism
Community
Discipline
Covenant
Anabaptists

Waldensian Church

Puritans
Holy Spirit
Presbyterian churches
Congregationalism
Methodism
Church of England

own forms of church life. Together, these groups formed the National Free Church Council in 1892, united not by a shared doctrine of the church but by their status within an Anglican establishment. By conviction, some of these groups were willing to accept or seek status as a state church if circumstances allowed, and in fact enjoyed or had enjoyed that status in some location outside England.

3. 'Free churches' (in the broadest meaning) can refer to a large composite set of churches, composed by combining categories 1 and 2, but eliminating any in 2 that may belong to the magisterial Reformation confessions (such as Presbyterians), while adding yet additional bodies. These additional bodies are groups whose origins postdate the free church revolution in church and state and which do not explicitly belong to the Lutheran, Reformed or Anglican communion (for instance, Pentecostals). Most of these churches emphasize individual conversion. Many share the congregational polity of the believers' churches, while differing from them on other issues such as baptism. The only sense of 'free' that is shared among them is a freedom from subscription to a specific, received confessional tradition.

Christian Church ➤
Assemblies of God ➤
Conversion

Historically, the development of free churches was centred in the English-speaking world and in a predominantly Reformed theological context. 'Free church' remains a common designation in countries such as Germany and England, where an established church persists, while in the US free churches are not distinguished by this contrast and so are often spoken of as non-credal or believers' churches. Such groups are planted in virtually all parts of the Christian world, and many churches with no genetic links to earlier free churches have independently developed similar forms (as with some African independent churches).

The establishment of religious liberty is an essential contribution of the free churches to modern pluralistic society. The United States of America became the preeminent home of the free church movement, in two senses. First, free churches (in all of the senses above) grew there through the emigration of those religiously oppressed in their home countries. Second, religious freedom in civil society was advocated as a fervent religious principle by major figures such as Roger Williams of Rhode Island (a Baptist, 1603–83) and William Penn of Pennsylvania (a Quaker, 1644–1718), and above all by the Baptists as a group. Some of the more deistic of the nation's founders opposed religious establishment in the federal government in a desire to protect the state from religious conflict. These rather different but converging motives – the desire for freedom to be the true church and the desire to keep disagreement about the true church from swamping government – resulted in the first amendment to the US constitution. That amendment led to a new chapter in church history, since the national government was forbidden any state church and the existing established churches in individual states were disestablished (though this process took a number of decades). As a result, all churches in the US became free churches in social fact, though not necessarily by theological conviction or in internal polity. Revivalism was a strong force in the growth of free churches and they have exhibited a strong commitment to mission. Much of the evangelical style of US Protestant church life is rooted in a free church background. By division and innovation, many new American born denominations arose, ranging from holiness groups such as the Church of the Nazarene to the Christian Church (Disciples of Christ) and Pentecostal churches such as the Assemblies of God.

Philosophy ➤

S. MARK HEIM

D. F. Durnbaugh, *The Believers' Church: The History and Character of Radical Protestantism*, Scottdale, PA: Herald Press 1968; J. L. Garrett (ed), *The Concept of the Believers' Church*, Scottdale, PA: Herald Press 1969; F. H. Littell, *The Free Church*, Boston: Starr King Press 1957; *From State Church to Pluralism: A Protestant Interpretation of Religion in America*, New York: Macmillan 1971; E. A. Paine, *The Free Church Tradition in the Life of England*, London: Hodder 1965

Freedom

The term 'freedom' is employed, defined and interpreted in many different contexts and horizons – theological, metaphysical, philosophical, scientific, political, social or individual. It can be understood primarily negatively, as freedom from, or positively, as freedom for. Few concepts are so widely appealed to in today's world, or understood in so many different ways or with so many different undercurrents or agendas. Its application in Christian thought and theology has links across to all these other fields.

Explicit philosophical and anthropological reflection on *eleutheria*, 'freedom', is originally a fruit of ancient Greek and Hellenistic philosophy, from Plato and Aristotle to the later Stoics. Free citizens were defined in the first place by contrast to the slave, who belongs to and must obey someone else; they were also profiled as the free citizens of a Greek city-state by contrast with barbarians living under despotic rule. Yet this freedom was not absolute or arbitrary: they were subject to the law and their freedom included responsibility before it. This dialectic is expressed in classical Greek philosophy in political terms, but then in later Hellenistic thought also in theological or metaphysical dimensions corresponding to the Stoic ideal of human life in harmony with the Logos, the cosmic reason or law.

This dialectic also raises the classical philosophical puzzle of freedom versus determinism: are people really free, or do they only appear to be so? This puzzle can be felt in various ways: classically as a metaphysical conundrum, in recent centuries as a scientific question in a universe apparently ruled by mechanical laws, as an issue of the foundations of ethics in the tension between autonomy and universal values, as a psychological dilemma in the light of explorations of the human unconscious, or as a sociological problem in view of manifest or concealed social pressures and forces shaping apparently 'free' human behaviour.

Hebrew and Jewish society also included both free people and slaves, but this generally did not lead to the same kind of philosophical reflection on the political quality and human value of freedom as in the Greek world. In the Old Testament the central theme in this connexion is not so much 'freedom' (as opposed to slavery) as 'liberation of God's people from slavery' – originally in the exodus from Egypt, later in the return from the Babylonian exile. God's mighty acts of redemption in history are both a memory out of the past and grounds of hope for the future, graphically expressed and dramatically experienced, for example, in the feast of the Passover. Freedom here is theologically grounded and orientated on the future rather than geared to the exercise of freedom in the here and now, though it can be anticipated along the way. This is also largely true of Judaism through the centuries – a reflection both of its biblical roots and its history.

In the New Testament Jesus took up this prophetic tradition of promise in his preaching of the imminent reign of God and of the coming Son of man – an apocalyptic figure symbolizing both hope of liberation and promise of judgement. In witnessing to his cross and resurrection, Jesus' followers came to proclaim him as this future Son of man whom they were to expect as Saviour and Judge. In his controversies with Judaizing Christians (vividly reflected in the letter to the Galatians), Paul then pointed up the theme of the freedom given by Christ in a new way: as freedom from the Law in the sense of cultic observances relating to meals, circumcision and the like. Paul insisted, 'For freedom Christ has set us free.' This admittedly was chiefly a cultic and religious freedom: the New Testament church does not, for example, appear to have questioned the institution of slavery even among Christians. (Nor indeed did the church, by and large, for another 1700 years.)

In the history of Christian thought up to the early modern period the issue of freedom tended to arise particularly in the area of the hope of salvation. That human beings do have some capacity or ability that can be called 'freedom of the will' in relation to the affairs of normal life was not generally seriously doubted (however difficult it might be actually to define either of the concepts 'freedom' or 'will'). The mainline Augustinian tradition of Western theology, however, held that this freedom did not extend to a capacity to 'earn' or 'merit' blessedness, which depended primarily or solely on the grace and election of God. This position was if anything radicalized by Martin Luther with his insistence on the 'bondage of the will' to the devil because of original sin – a position shared in broad outline by the generality of the Reformers. (Where Roman Catholic theology held that original sin was wiped out by baptism, the Reformers were more radical, insisting that this sin remains in the baptized, and even if it does so only as a mere non-activated inclination to sin, is still in itself sinful.) An important consequence was that in this perspective such a fettered human freedom could not be regarded as the highest or most characteristic feature of human existence or human identity – though Luther's early writing on *The Freedom of a Christian Man* did offer significant impulses for new reflection on the nature and value of human freedom in a theological perspective. Similarly, the struggles for religious freedom unleashed by the Reformation did contribute in their own way to a new sense of the right to resist tyrants; and this came in turn to strengthen the appeal of a broader call for liberty.

Sin
Reformation

Such calls, only occasional and sporadic in the Middle Ages or the era of the Reformation, were to become a defining feature of the modern era and very often to burst the matrix of Christian thought that had at least partly nurtured them. Examples are the Puritan Revolution in England; the philosophical contributions of Thomas Hobbes, John Locke and Benedict de Spinoza; the philosophy of the Enlightenment; the thought of Jean-Jacques Rousseau and Voltaire in the background to the French Revolution with its cry for 'liberty, equality, fraternity'; the revolution of the North American colonies and the American Constitution; the thought of John Stuart Mill in the nineteenth century and the (admittedly politically less effective) contributions of German Idealism, to say nothing of later twentieth-century thinkers or the numerous examples of 'freedom struggles' and 'liberation theologies' seen in the last century. An interesting product of this development is that whereas Roman Catholic (and some Protestant) theologies were long very suspicious and sometimes hostile to these secular developments, recent generations have seen a new theological engagement with social and political ethics, with human rights and with the theme of divine and human freedom.

Jesus
Paul

ALASDAIR HERON

 Leonard Hodgson, *For Faith and Freedom*, Oxford: Blackwell 1956, reissued London: SCM Press 1968

Salvation

Friendship

Few of us would doubt the importance of friendship; of having close and fulfilling relationships with others who are like-minded and with whom we can relax and be truly ourselves. Many have said that having friends and being a friend to others is an essential part of what it means to be human. Often we take this for granted, without considering what is involved in the process of relating at a deep level to others.

In the Graeco-Roman world friendship was considered to be an essential component of civilized society and was highly valued. The Greek philosopher Aristotle (384–322 BCE) remarked that none of us would choose to live without friends even if we had everything money could buy. Friendship was for him the very fabric of a happy and healthy society. Aristotle influenced the Roman orator and philosopher Cicero (106–43 BCE), whose treatise *On Friendship* (*De Amicitia*) became the seminal work exploring the value of friendship throughout the Western world, and has influenced many writers and thinkers down the centuries.

For Christians, relating to others is always to be set within the context of the believer's relationship with God, who is three in one, traditionally described as Father, Son and Holy Spirit. At the very core of God is a deep expression of relatedness. God is in essence a community of love and friendship as the three persons of the Trinity – Father, Son and Holy Spirit – exist and work together. The Old Testament says that all people are made in God's image (Genesis 1.27) and therefore contain within their being something of God. This is why people long to be in community, in relationship with God, with themselves, and with each another. For Christians this also explains why friendship can be a source of wholeness and joy, since it mirrors the divine way of working and existing.

Trinity

Community

In the Old Testament Abraham is called God's friend (2 Chronicles 20.7) and God is said to speak with Moses as a friend (Exodus 33.11). Various deep human friendships are witnessed to also, in particular the friendships between David and Jonathan (1 Samuel) and Ruth and Naomi (Ruth). These relationships speak of faithfulness and loyalty, and have been seen as an allegory of God's love and commitment to the chosen people of Israel. Within the New Testament the concept of friendship is broadened and deepened as Jesus illustrates commitment to people from all walks of life, irrespective of creed, race or gender. He is known to be the friend of 'tax-collectors and sinners' (Matthew 11.19), and calls his disciples 'friends' because they share with him the knowledge of God (John 15.15). For Jesus the calling to be a friend is of the highest significance and may lead to the laying down of one's life for another (John 15.13). For Christians, Jesus' death on the cross fulfils these words and demonstrates God's love for the entire world.

Jesus

Homosexuality

During the eleventh and twelfth centuries the Christian church in the West saw a great flowering in the practice of Christian friendship, particularly within monastic communities. Thoughts on the importance and nature of friendship were explored by people such as Anselm of Canterbury (*c.* 1033–1109), Bernard of Clairvaux (1090–1153), William of St Thierry (*c.* 1085–*c.* 1148), and most importantly Aelred of Rievaulx (*c.* 1110–67), an English Cistercian monk living in North Yorkshire. Aelred's major work *Spiritual Friendship* (1150–63) was widely read throughout Europe in the twelfth century and became very popular.

Aelred believed that deep relationships were essential for spiritual health and growth. As novice master at Rievaulx Abbey he introduced a system of mentoring built on deep and lasting friendships. These relationships enabled monks living celibate lives in community to experience and enjoy love and loyalty to another person and so grow in faithfulness and commitment to God. Aelred went as far as to translate 'God is love' (1 John 4.8) as 'God is friendship', demonstrating the high importance to be placed on friends. Among the monastic houses in medieval Europe there were a number of deep friendships, the most famous being the relationship between Francis of Assisi and Clare.

In comparison with these medieval relationships many of our own modern-day friendships seem shallow. The medieval writers bear witness to friendships that are deep, intense, strong, stable, creative and long lasting. Having a close friend enables one to grow more fully into one's own identity as one is loved and accepted and then encouraged to explore and develop within a context of unconditional love. Anselm speaks of having his friend imprinted on his heart, like a waxen seal, and carrying his friend deep within himself. Thoughts such as these help people to continue to be friends at great distances and through many years, continuing profound communion with one another even when apart.

The medieval writers on friendship describe relationships that contain sweetness, joy and sometimes great passion. There is fierce commitment, both to one another and to God. This commitment transcends death and is eternal, because it comes from God. Thus friends are to help one another to walk through life, meeting Christ within each other on the way, and finally to ascend towards God. The culmination of a true friendship will come in heaven when all are united to one another and to God.

Possibly because of such intensity within relationships, through envy of exclusivity and from the fear of homosexuality, particular friendships came to be looked upon by the church with deep suspicion and have been firmly discouraged from the fourteenth century almost to the present day.

In recent years there has been a rediscovery of the works of these medieval friends, and of the value of 'celibate passion'. This has happened alongside a new flowering of the value of friendship within the Celtic tradition. From the Gaelic church we learn of the *anam cara*, or 'soul-friend'. In this tradition friends recognize within each other relatedness at a deep level, and they strive to explore and meet Christ within each other. The Celtic tradition says that friends have always been joined in an ancient and eternal way, and the recognition of this allows a level of intimacy, which releases new possibilities within oneself. The *anam cara* relationship is one that desires the best for another and makes time for growth and spiritual development at a deep level.

Friendship, then, is an expression of love and faithfulness between people. It transcends shared interests and common pursuits and at its deepest and most committed can be a source of great security and joy. Friendship is a place where people can be free to explore who they truly are and grow into who God calls them to be. For Christians, friendship with others can help believers to explore and grow in friendship with God, and walk in the way of Christ. True friendship is a source of great joy and fulfilment and requires commitment, loyalty and love.

CATHERINE WILLIAMS

C. S. Lewis, *The Four Loves,* London: Fount 1960; John O'Donohue, *Anam Cara,* New York: Bantam Books 1999; Michael Pakaluk (ed), *Other Selves. Philosophers on Friendship,* Indianapolis, IN: Hackett 1991; Aelred of Rievaulx, *Spiritual Friendship,* Kalamazoo, MI: Cistercian Publications 1977; Elaine Storkey, *The Search for Intimacy,* London: Hodder 1995

Fundamentalism

Nowadays, the word fundamentalist is just as likely to conjure up the image of a Muslim suicide bomber or a member of an ultra-Orthodox Jewish group in Jerusalem as a conservative Christian from the American mid-West who insists on the literal truth of the Bible. Use of the term has spread widely over the past decade, and there is also talk of Hindu or Buddhist fundamentalists. Unfortunately, as the application of the term has been extended, fundamentalist has become a more and more diffuse designation, so that it has become increasingly difficult to establish precisely what is meant by it.

The origin of fundamentalism is clear enough. The term is a comparatively recent one. It is derived from a series of twelve booklets published in the US between 1910 and 1915 entitled *The Fundamentals: A Testimony to the Truth.* Three million of these booklets, written by leading evangelical churchmen, were circulated free of charge among clergymen and seminarians. They were on five main topics: 1. The literal inerrancy of the originals of each book of the Bible; 2. The virgin birth and deity of Christ; 3. The substitutionary view of the atonement; 4. The bodily resurrection of Christ; 5. The imminent return of Christ. 'Fundamentalist' as the name for those who take their stand on these fundamentals was first used in print in 1920. Of these five 'fundamentals', insistence on the literal inerrancy of the Bible is the best known and most widely emphasized; fundamentalists tend to use the Bible as a collection of 'proof texts' that infallibly support their views.

Bible p. 613 Atonement Resurrection

By and large, fundamentalism was a response to the declining impact of traditional revivalist Christianity in America during the early years of the twentieth century caused by the social change brought about by immigration and industrialization, and the threat posed by the findings of biblical criticism and evolutionary views about the origin of the universe. Fundamentalist views spread around the world above all in evangelical circles, though not necessarily labelled 'fundamentalist'; these circles saw themselves as evangelicals, preaching the gospel; 'fundamentalist' tended to be used by opponents as a derogatory term.

Great Awakening Biblical criticism Evolution Evangelicals

It took time for fundamentalists to become an effective force in public life, and only in the 1970s did they gain a high public profile in the United States, following a decade of radical change which saw the rise of the civil rights movement, the women's movement, gay rights and the legalization of abortion. Not least the increasing prosperity of their supporters, highly-organized fund-raising and the generosity of wealthy businessmen contributed to their success. From then on fundamentalists established a variety of organizations, the best known of which is Jerry Falwell's Moral Majority (founded in 1979), and came to dominate, if not virtually monopolize, Christian radio, television and publishing, to the degree that today the adjective 'Christian' has been commandeered to denote programmes and books of a fundamentalist kind. American Christian fundamentalism has been generally associated with right-wing conservative views, but there are also left-wing radical fundamentalist organizations, such as Sojourners, founded by Jim Wallis and active among the poor of Washington, DC.

Radio Television Publishing

The political views of Christian fundamentalists also have a strongly apocalyptic colouring, and most major recent international events, from the foundation of the state of Israel to the 2003 Iraq War, have been associated with a coming end of the world which is expected to follow the course outlined in the book of Revelation, with a

Apocalyptic

great conflict at the Armageddon mentioned in Revelation 16.15. These millenarian expectations are expounded not only in books that claim to be serious interpretations of the Bible, but also in a new and rapidly growing genre of end-time novels.

If the American version is the most powerful form of Christian fundamentalism, 'fundamentalism' has also been identified in Eastern Orthodoxy, with its exaltation of traditionalism, its antagonism to the West, its often-expressed opposition to the ecumenical movement and its mistrust of dialogue. Even more, there is said to be a fundamentalism in the Roman Catholic Church, in which at the beginning of the twentieth century there was marked opposition to modernism under Pope Pius X. Movements such as Opus Dei and that headed by Archbishop Lefebvre have been called 'fundamentalist', and so too have many of the standpoints taken by Pope John Paul II.

Ecumenical movement

Modernism

p. 836

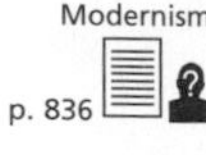

What is the justification for lumping all these together, along with the examples of fundamentalism that are to be found in other religions? Studies of fundamentalism in the various religious traditions have identified a number of features that fundamentalists have in common.

Fundamentalists in any religion are essentially an opposition movement, and their characteristic beliefs can be defined just as clearly by stating what they are against as what they are for. They are above all opposed to the ongoing process of secularizing social change which is often referred to as globalization, and which brings with it the erosion of religious traditions and values, to relativism and pluralism, and to sophisticated patterns of interpretation which would seem to qualify what is said in authoritative texts.

Globalization

By contrast, fundamentalists believe in a unified and revealed truth, the sources of which are inerrant and absolutely authoritative, and allow of no misunderstanding. However, they are selective in the parts of the tradition that they emphasize, the passages of scripture that they focus on, and the features of modernity that they reject (for example, they are happy to make use of modern means of mass communication).

Eucharist

What fundamentalists accept or reject is largely determined by charismatic leaders who govern and guide communities and organizations, and often introduce their own highly personal emphases. Groups have firm boundaries, and there are strict rules for the behaviour of their members.

p. 1068

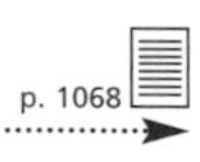

Fundamentalists are essentially confrontational. They are convinced that they and only they are right and, for example in a Christian context, that those who do not agree with them are not true Christians. This makes them unwilling and indeed incapable of engaging in forms of dialogue that might lead them to revise their positions.

Protestantism

Fundamentalism remains a strong, if not a growing, force which still attracts millions. And in a world where values have been so eroded, there is great good in much of what it stands for. But serious questions remain about its essential characteristics, and when it turns in the direction of fanaticism it can only fan the flames of conflict.

JOHN BOWDEN

James Barr, *Fundamentalism*, London: SCM Press and Philadelphia: Westminster Press 1977; Kathleen C. Boone, *The Bible Tells them So*, Albany, NY: SUNY Press and London: SCM Press 1989; Martin E. Marty and R. Scott Appleby (eds), *Fundamentalisms Observed*, Chicago: Chicago University Press 1991

Furnishings

Church furnishings are as varied as the Christian communities that use them. Climate, economics, politics are as important as theology in determining their character. This has been true from the period when the faith was spreading within the Roman empire, and suitable furnishings had to be provided from the cold forests of Northern Europe to the deserts of the Near East. Moreover, while the needs of a particular time and place may prompt the introduction of furnishings such as combs, fans and fly whisks, they may remain part of the apparatus of worship long after those needs have become irrelevant.

One crucial distinction has to be made among furnishings, however, and that is between those used directly in worship, especially the eucharist, and those associated with the convenience and/or comfort of the officiants and of the congregation.

The altar might be expected to be the most significant piece of furniture in a church, since it is on the altar that the eucharist is celebrated. Yet it is rarely the finest, oldest or most valuable object in the building. Different denominations stress different aspects of the eucharist, and this affects their treatment of the altar, or, as some prefer to call it, the holy table. At one extreme, the Catholic belief is that the sacrifice of Christ is repeated at each celebration of the eucharist. The consecrated elements of bread and wine become the body and blood of Christ, not figuratively but literally. Thus the altar should express its function as a place of sacrifice, and what is more appropriate than stone to recall the altars of both ancient Israel and pagan antiquity? At the other extreme is the Protestant conception of the eucharist as a commemorative meal re-enacting the last supper of Jesus and his disciples. For such a purpose, a wooden table around which people can gather is a more appropriate and convenient model.

In fact throughout history, the demands of practicality or aesthetic preference have blurred these stark contrasts. A large block of stone, however rich in symbolism, is difficult

Church centred on altar

Church centred on pulpit

FURNISHINGS

Different Christian traditions have widely different views about how churches should be furnished. In churches in the Roman Catholic, Orthodox and Anglican traditions the altar occupies a central place; in many Protestant churches (the Lutherans are an exception here) the term altar is not used, but table, and the focal point of the building is the pulpit. Again Roman Catholic, Orthodox and Anglican churches may be rich in ornamentation, whereas churches arising out of the Reformation may insist on the strictest simplicity. Here are some furnishings which can be found in churches:

Altar: A table, originally of stone, on which the eucharist is celebrated. After the Reformation it was replaced by a communion table made of wood. The high altar is at the top of a series of steps at the east end of the church. Reforms of worship brought about at the Second Vatican Council, and also implemented in other churches, required the celebrant to face the congregation. Since this is impossible with the altar in this position, the high altar is often left unused and a new altar is placed at the other end of the chancel, close to the nave.

Ambo: A raised platform from which the Bible can be read, and from which sermons are sometimes given.

Aumbry: A recess within the wall of a church in which liturgical vessels and books were kept. In Anglican churches bread and wine consecrated at the eucharist for distribution to the sick (reserved sacrament) are kept there.

Candle: Candles on the altar are lit during the celebration of the eucharist. At Eastertide a large Paschal candle decorated with a cross, the Greek letters alpha and omega (the first and last letters of the alphabet, the beginning and the end), the date of the year and five grains of incense is placed on a large free-standing candlestick. In the Catholic tradition candles are lit and placed as devotional offerings in stands in front of representations of the Virgin Mary and the saints.

p. 1166

Cross and crucifix: A cross or crucifix (a cross bearing the figure of the crucified Jesus) may be found in many parts of the church; crosses are sometimes carried in processions at services. An important medieval form of crucifix was known as the rood, the Saxon word for cross, and was placed on a screen in front of the chancel.

Font: A container for water used in baptisms, usually made of stone and covered with a lid. The font usually stands symbolically near the church door; in some churches it is in a separate building, the baptistery.

Frontal: A frontal (also referred to as an antependium) is a detachable decorative covering which is hung in front of an altar: it can be made of embroidered textiles, precious metals or wood. The colour of the frontal can change with the seasons of the church's year.

pp. 1164–5

Lectern: A stand used to support books used in worship, especially the Bible. It often takes the form of an eagle with the book placed between its outstretched wings, an eagle being the symbol of St John the Evangelist.

Misericord: A protruberance on the underside of the seat of a hinged choir stall. In the Middle Ages, when the person in the stall had to stand for long periods during monastic services, he could turn the seat up and rest on it (the Latin term means 'mercy'). Misericords are often decorated with carvings.

Monstrance: A container for the eucharistic bread (host), usually consisting of a circular glass window with gold or silver rays emanating from it. This is used at the devotion of Benediction or the Exposition of the Blessed Sacrament.

Organ: Organs in churches go back to the tenth century. Especially in cathedrals and large churches, these are 'great' organs, with impressive arrays of pipes and elaborate carved and decorated casings, set high on the wall and with an organ 'loft' for the organist. They may be supplemented by 'positive' organs, comparatively small instruments which can be moved around where they are needed.

Pew: A fixed wooden seat in a church, long enough for several people to use. A box pew has a high wooden enclosure all round and is entered by a small door.

Piscina: A stone basin in a niche near the altar for washing the vessels used at the eucharist.

Pulpit: A raised stand of stone or wood from which sermons are preached, often with a flight of steps leading up to it. Some Anglican churches still have a three-decker pulpit, with a reading desk, a stall and the preacher's stand one on top of the other. Many pulpits have a *tester*, a sounding board, above them.

Pyx: From the Greek meaning 'wooden container'. A receptacle used for carrying the bread consecrated at the eucharist to the sick, usually put in a bag to be suspended from the neck by a cord. However, pyxes are in fact made from precious metals like silver. With devotions to the Blessed Sacrament, the pyx came to be part of the furnishings of a church, being kept within the tabernacle; it could also be suspended from the ceiling of a chapel.

Reliquary: A container for a relic. These may be caskets or boxes, richly decorated, and sometimes with a glass panel so that the contents may be seen. They are sometimes contained in stone structures, which are called shrines, dedicated to the relevant saint or martyr.

Reredos: A wall or screen made of wood or stone, usually decorated, and placed behind an altar.

Rood Screen: From the Anglo-Saxon *rōd*, cross. A screen between the nave and the chancel, on the top of which was placed a cross or crucifix, sometimes with the Virgin Mary and St John beside it.

Stall: A carved seat of wood or stone, often constructed as a series, for the choir and clergy, placed in the chancel.

Stoup: A container for holy water, usually near the entrance to a church.

Tabernacle: An ornamental receptacle to contain the bread consecrated at the eucharist, usually in the shape of a miniature building. It is placed at the back of the high altar in Catholic churches.

Table: The term preferred to altar in the Reformation tradition.

to adapt or even move. One ingenious compromise was to make a travelling altar of a small stone slab that could be set into or on top of any convenient surface.

The size of an altar has varied in a similar ways, balancing the need to have sufficient space to consecrate the elements with the overall look of the sanctuary. The slender evidence that survives from the early times of Christianity indicates that altars were relatively small, rarely more than a yard in any dimension. Once the custom developed of celebrating mass immediately over the holy relics of a saint or martyr, the altar grew longer to cover the implied coffin below. By the end of the Middle Ages, the altar could be up to three or four yards in length and would be surrounded with tall curtains, powerfully emphasizing the physical reality of the dramatic mystery by which the bread and wine became the body and blood of Christ.

After the Reformation, both the Catholic and Protestant traditions rejected this type of structure. At the Council of Trent the Roman Catholic Church established detailed regulations for the way in which the eucharist should be celebrated by the priest and received by the people, and architects responded by creating elaborate settings, rather than enlarging the altar table itself. At times the actual surface on which the mass was celebrated was almost obscured by the painting or sculpture above, itself perhaps enclosed within a monumental architectural setting, and by the ornamental frontal below and in front of the altar, whether this was of rich textiles or of inlaid stone or marble.

In the Church of England, the stone altar slabs of the Middle Ages were deliberately broken up or economically turned upside down and reused as paving, to be replaced by long wooden tables around which the communicants could gather. To ease this procedure the table was set, as they put it, 'table-wise', i.e. along the east/west axis of the church in deliberate contrast to 'altar-wise', i.e. on a north/south axis, where the medieval altars stood.

A powerful section of the church remained determined to keep the altar as the devotional focus of the east end of the church building and ensure reverence for it as more than a convenient surface. After a century of strife, this view prevailed. The classic Anglican altar, though set at the east end and protected by rails, was modest in size, usually of wood but occasionally of stone or marble, like a side table in a great house. However, once controversy revived in the 1840s as to the nature of the eucharist and Protestants within the church felt threatened by claims of the real presence of Christ at the eucharist, the facts of history were forgotten and stone altars were declared illegal in the Church of England. The revival of Catholic sympathies thereafter not surprisingly led to a revival of medieval Catholic models for altars, and by the period between the two world wars the so-called English altar, with its riddel posts supporting hangings and refined decorations, had returned to the dimensions popular 400 years earlier.

p. 1075
Saint
Martyr

Reformation
Council

The liturgical reforms of the second half of the twentieth century across all parts of the Christian church have led to a return to favour of early Christian models, free-standing and often not just of stone but of unworked rock. It remains to be seen how the wheel will turn again.

The other crucial item of furnishing in a church building is the font. From the earliest times, admission to full membership of the Christian community has been a solemn occasion, involving careful preparation and culminating in passing through water, whether literally by full immersion in a river, pool or tank, or symbolically by aspersion, with water sprinkled from a bowl. As with altars, the competing demands of liturgy, historical and regional traditions and aesthetics led to a wide range of alternatives in giving physical expression to the font.

Initiation

The original pattern of baptism in a river, a symbolic Jordan, or pool remained current for centuries, particularly where a crowd of adults was baptized, as in the mass conversions of so-called barbarian tribes. However, once Christianity became established as the faith of a whole community, it was vital to create rites to include everyone, Sin especially children, who, as the doctrine of original sin was developed, faced eternal banishment from heaven if they died before baptism. In England this led first to the fashioning of barrel-shaped fonts, large enough to immerse infants, and then to shallower vessels holding enough water simply to sprinkle them. The practice of full immersion for adults never disappeared, however, and in recent years has returned to popularity.

The third most important item of furnishing in a Preaching church is a place for proclaiming the word. Here practical considerations have always been paramount, with theology generally having to bow to common sense. The crucial questions are: who is to be addressed, and where – is it within a closed community or is it directed to a wider world, is it in a tiny rural chapel or a vast cathedral? Whether reading the scriptures or preaching a sermon, until very recent times speakers had to struggle first and foremost to be audible. They had to be elevated so that Icon their voices could carry, yet such elevation inevitably conveys superior dignity over those below.

The classic arrangement evolved by the early church was for a pair of pulpits (called ambones, the plural of ambo), balancing each other on the chancel screen, which separates the sanctuary or chancel from the nave, the body of the church. Such symbolism was powerfully evoked by the Anglican George Herbert (1593–1633) as demonstrating the balance that should exist between the key elements of prayer and preaching.

Ambones were essentially for liturgical use within church Religious orders buildings. When the preaching orders, the Dominicans and Franciscans, began to address great crowds, whether in halls or in the open air, they needed temporary boxes that could be moved and adjusted in height as required. By around 1500, the idea of regular preaching had reached down to the parish church and fixed wooden pulpits became standard features. The Reformation, with its strong emphasis on preaching, naturally reinforced the focus on pulpits and they became ever more dominant in church interiors, sometimes almost obscuring the altar from view. This dominance was yet further increased by the heightening of pulpits to two or three layers, known as two-deckers or three-deckers, with separate levels for the minister to preach and to pray and for the clerk to lead the congregation's responses.

While the Victorians literally cut these towering structures down to size, they thought highly of preaching and their pulpits were substantial affairs, often of stone and adorned with carving. It is not until recent decades that the concept of a raised pulpit has itself fallen from favour. Preachers now prefer to speak from light moveable desks so as to be on the same level as their listeners, in every sense, rather than being raised several feet above them.

Screens, though not used directly for worship, have been the next most important church furnishing over the centuries. Their prime purpose has been to define space and direct the use of it. They can be temporary or fixed, of simple boards or in rich marbles, transparent or closed. They can be regarded as anything from a security fence to a mark of honour and respect. As far as one can tell, it was in the latter role that screens first became common in churches. In the first St Peter's in Rome, the sanctuary was delimited by spiral columns, allegedly from the Temple of Solomon, to give dignity and symbolic protection. The pierced marble screens (transennae) also found in churches of the period had the more practical purpose of distinguishing the different rooms that had now developed within churches, without blocking sound and light between them.

In the Eastern churches, the screen between the sanctuary, reserved for the clergy, and the congregational space of the nave became ever more substantial until the iconostasis, the screen bearing icons, formed a continuous barrier from wall to wall and floor to ceiling. In the West, while screens in great churches could be massive affairs, capable of carrying singers and instruments, they tended to be sufficiently open in their upper parts for sound and image to travel through. In the West it also became ever more acceptable for lay people of sufficient status to penetrate into the 'sacred' zone.

It was, moreover, acceptable to use a substantial screen to divide a church building into spaces for devotion and for the other activities which to twenty-first-century people seem more everyday. Most Christian institutions, whether designed for the care of the old, the young, the sick or for education, would have a chapel at their centre, and the screen would distinguish an ante-chapel for assembly from the chapel for worship. In a great church, over time the nave had frequently become a public forum.

Ivory throne of Maximian, Archbishop's Palace, Ravenna

After all, the church was the largest covered public space, at least in Northern Europe. In Old St Paul's Cathedral in London, the nave was notoriously where appointments were made, servants engaged, transactions sealed. The solid screen to the east preserved the worship area of the choir undisturbed.

Screens can also be used to define private areas within a church, perhaps a chapel belonging to a family or guild or a vestry for storing textiles and metalwork, or to divide different social classes or genders. When crowds gathered in Renaissance Italy in town squares to hear the great preaching friars like Bernardino, temporary screening and curtains were erected to divide the men from the women and so prevent lustful glances and matchmaking.

Though the picture most people have today of a church interior is dominated by seating, concern for the comfort of the congregation is a late development in Christian worship. Traditionally seats were reserved for the privileged – hence the significance of the *cathedra*, the bishop's chair in his principal church, where he sat to speak with authority. Such a seat would originally be moveable, however splendid, for example the sixth-century ivory-panelled throne of Archbishop Maximian of Ravenna.

The earliest seating built into the structure was the bench around the semicircular apse behind the altar. Here the most important priest would preside over the eucharist, flanked by the other ministers. More extensive seating became desirable with the establishment of the monastic Rule of Benedict, with its regular cycle of communal worship. Fixed wooden seating was installed in the choir not only to give some relief for weary limbs but also to place the community in due order. With the growth of endowments for particular positions in monasteries and cathedrals, the seat or stall belonging to that office became its emblem, so to this day a cathedral canon 'owns' a particular stall in the choir.

Monasticism

Throughout these centuries, the laity were expected to stand, as they still do in the Orthodox tradition. The only provision for the elderly or infirm was stone plinths or benches which in some buildings ran along inside the walls (though moveable wooden seating could also be introduced on special occasions). However, the congregation would not be expected to remain static but would move around, again as in Orthodox churches to this day.

This was changed in the late Middle Ages as the sermon became a regular part of worship even at parish level. The very highest in the land were already accustomed to having their private 'pew', where they could sit or kneel at their devotions, protected by screens and curtains from draughts and idle gazes. This practice, in England at least, spread down to include all substantial property owners, and for centuries most parish churches would contain one or more of such private pews, reserved exclusively for the owners, their families and dependents. Seating for the less grand, though still propertied, consisted of substantial benches, sometimes adorned with carving.

Church of England

By the time that the Church of England was re-established after the dislocations of the Civil War, the standard pattern was to seat all the congregation in uniform pews, sometimes known as box pews, i.e. closed seats with benches set under breast-high screening, to give not just some privacy but some relief from the cold and damp of the as yet unheated building. Simple benches were reserved for the poorest or youngest, for instance charity school children. In the mid-nineteenth century this comfortable system came under severe attack from reformers, who saw the property rights embodied in the carefully allocated pews no longer as symbols of a divinely-ordained hierarchy but as affronts to the equality of believers. The reformers' ideal was for everyone to share a uniform system of seating. They also regarded open seating as conforming more to contemporary advances in comfort and hygiene. (Popular usage confusingly defied the reformers' correctness and continued to call the new open seats by the traditional word pew.) So influential was this trend that by 1900 hardly a church or chapel of

Renaissance

any religious denomination had escaped total re-seating of this kind.

Reaction a century later has been equally strong. The nineteenth-century ranks of pews are now in turn regarded as too formal and rigid, expressive of past and oppressive social structures. The current preference is for chairs, allegedly more flexible (but who will move them?) and more domestic, in keeping with current trends in worship.

THOMAS COCKE

Thomas Cocke et al. (eds), *Recording a Church: An Illustrated Glossary*, Council for British Archaeology [3]2002; Christopher Howkins, *Discovering Church Furniture*, Princes Risborough: Shire Publications 1980; Gerald Randall, *Church Furnishing and Decoration in England and Wales*, London: Batsford 1980

Future

Any statement about future events is a risky affair. Fortune-telling, astrology and oracles may be a pleasant entertainment for many or a diversion from the demands of the everyday, but few of us are likely to think that the future is really accessible through such practices. At the same time the future does not seem to be completely unavailable to us. We take out insurance for a motor or for health care or for retirement because we know that a collision or an illness or old age are all distinct, even likely, possibilities. We make appointments for a meeting, or buy travel tickets well in advance, assuming that our actions now have a very definite bearing on the future. We make promises to return a book, or repay a loan, or to love someone, all of which assume that the future will be sufficiently like the present that our actions now and in the past will be continuous with what is yet to come in our lives.

We worry about the possibility of global warming, or nuclear destruction, or genetic engineering because we are sure that the measures that we take now at national and international levels will create a better future for yet unseen generations. Yet we know that unforeseen events can rapidly change all our best-thought-out projections. Even within as short a time-span as the last century, who could have predicted penicillin, or the internet, or the destruction of Hiroshima? Indeed, any statement about future events is a risky affair, but that fact neither stops us from making such statements nor stills our need to plan and promise, to worry and project. In everyday ways we live part of our lives now, part of our lives in the past, and part of our lives within the future.

Christianity has a long history of entertaining the risky business of making statements about the future. Words and concepts like prophecy, final judgement, predestination, heaven, apocalypse, hope or despair, the millennium, the rapture and the resurrection are all essentially dealing in some way with statements about the future. As one major Christian theologian, Karl Rahner, observes, Christianity is largely a religion of the future. Simply put, it is impossible to understand Christianity without understanding the ways that it approaches the future. So what does it say? A professor of New Testament studies, Craig C. Hill, suggests that what Christianity says about the future can be summed up in two words: 'God wins.' While alarmingly simple, this observation is neither inaccurate nor a bad place to begin.

Maybe the first thing to note is that Christianity 'says' something about the future; it deals with the future by the way in which it *speaks* about the future. Like most aspects of a Christian perspective, the understanding of the future has its sources in the Bible with its long and varied traditions and in the experiences of those who call themselves Christians. So the language of prophecy, or apocalyptic, the images of resurrection or a final judgement, are all rooted in more specific narratives and songs, prayers and political reflections that are part of the long literary heritage we know today as Christianity.

It should not be surprising, then, that the understandings of many of the words and concepts used to speak of the future have changed over time, with cultural, historical and linguistic shifts. Likewise it should not be surprising that Christianity has not used a single vocabulary or set of ideas to understand the future. Sometimes it speaks of victory, sometimes of rest, sometimes of comfort, sometimes of fire. Sometimes the way it speaks is consoling, sometimes anxious, sometimes predictive, sometimes filled with threat. Christianity exhibits a wide diversity of images, concepts and genres when dealing with the future. It is crucial to recognize this kind of diversity in what it says about the future for at least two reasons. First, the Christian tradition seems to relish a diversity of ways of speaking about the future without being bothered by logical contradiction. Secondly, and directly related to this, Christianity does not speak about the future in the same way a newspaper reports events. Rather, Christian speech about the future is embedded in genres quite distinct from that of an accurate report. Christianity testifies about the future, prays about the future, issues warnings about the future based on the present; it hopes and imagines possibilities for the future and encourages actions and attitudes, given this present and given these hopes. Christian language about the future is not worried about contradictions, nor for that matter about exact calendars of the future, precisely because it does not report the future as a set of already determined events just waiting for the curtain to be lifted. So someone asking about what Christianity has to say about the future and expecting a prediction of events from a reading of the book of Revelation like that seen when the tabloid newspapers predict the end of the world will undoubtedly be disappointed to realize that Christianity actively discourages this way of speaking about the future.

But that is not to suggest that the way Christianity speaks about the future is simply a jumble of words and images assembled without any sort of integrity. Rather, there is a rough coherence to the way that Christianity understands the future, a coherence which is evident not in a unified set of descriptions or concepts, but in the conviction that the language about the future is inescapably *theo*-logical. All Christian language about the future is in some way about what God (*theos* in Greek) is and what God does. It is about how Christianity understands the relation of God to all that exists, specifically as God's creation.

In fact Christian talk about the future is not radically different from Christian talk about creation. Just as the Christian view of creation is not a report of events but a description of a kind of relationship between God and all that exists, a relationship described as making and sustaining, so too the Christian view of the future relates to how the relationship between God and existence will continue and what existence might look like in this perspective. Christian talk of and thought about the future does not arise out of a desire to know about the future but out of the conviction that God is a God of the future, a God of promise.

One way of speaking about this dimension of God in Christianity is to speak of the 'final things', in Greek *eschata.* These 'last things' – typically death, life after death, judgement, the consummation of existence and the kinds of faith, hope and love which characterize a life lived with the conviction that these issues and images are an important part of a relationship with God – are considered in a part of Christian thought called 'eschatology' (Greek for 'words about the end'). Again, it is important to emphasize that Christian talk about these last things is not a report about the events that will happen with an individual's death, or with the end of the universe; almost all but the most fundamentalist contemporary Christian theology maintains that eschatology is about an aspect of the relationship of existence to God, not about particular future events.

Given this odd kind of reference for Christian talk of the future, what more can be said about the 'rough coherence' among the various images and concepts used by Christians to say something about the future? This 'rough coherence' is basically a combination of several elements within the Christian faith that together establish a perspective on the future.

It may be obvious, but it is quite basic to the Christian understanding of the future to assert that there is a genuine future. Basically, this means that a Christian perspective takes the idea of the 'new' very seriously. Rather than viewing history as an endlessly repetitive cycle of the same eternal ideas or patterns, the Christian perspective views the future as the arrival of something in the relationship with God that can be unexpected, transformative and genuinely new. Without this perspective the singular event of Jesus could never be understood as a 'new covenant'. Jesus Covenant

At the same time the future is understood to be continuous with the past and present. The ways in which this continuity is maintained may be astonishing at points even to the Christian, but 'newness' is never completely severed from what has gone before. Even the 'new covenant' does not destroy the old; even the destruction of the world by a flood in the legend of Noah does not lead to a wholly new world. Understanding the future is informed by understanding the past. Each new generation, each new age does not need a new saviour, or a new creation. Even in the new, the startling, the disruptive, even in the seemingly obliterating events that can affect the life of persons or whole groups, there is the conviction that the new future that is ahead can be trusted as both what arrives from a God of the future and what is continuous from this same God as the God of the past. Creation

The foundation of this trust for the future is the basic sense that in any age God is a God of salvation, a God who heals, renews, recreates, redeems and sustains. Thus the future is a future for salvation that has already occurred in the person and event of Jesus. This fundamental testimony of the Christian perspective calls for a constant reconsideration of the life, death and resurrection of Jesus. The resurrection is the central symbol of the Christian faith that any future is never a truly radical rupture from the past. The resurrection is understood to be the 'first fruits', the fulfilment of the true promise fulfilled, of what the future will be. Because the future is not simply what is yet to come, because the future is already present in the resurrection of Jesus, the life of the Christian is a fundamentally hopeful one, even in the recognition that death is also the future of all of existence. Eschatology

While this future is a future for salvation it is simultaneously a future that is ambiguous. It is a future in which the hope grounded in the resurrection does not displace responsibility, struggle, disappointment, deception or destruction. Seldom does such hope offer either lives of security or theological positions of victory and comfort. The resurrection is never discontinuous with rejection and crucifixion; the prophet's announcement of the word of God is rarely comforting. Thus the sense of hope associated with the Christian future is only partially squared with our commonsense version of hope. Christian hope is less the Fundamentalism promise of victory on the other side of adversity than it is the foundation for responsibility, for the expectation of the ambiguous twist in even the seemingly best achievements of our existence.

Salvation
Kingdom of God

So while it is true that the Christian understanding of the future might be summed up in the two words, 'God wins,' it must be equally balanced by the aphorism, 'winning isn't everything'. The future remains in an essential way God's future for existence. Every programme of 'salvation', whether proposed by a church or a culture or a political platform, remains fundamentally 'under suspicion'. In more classical Christian imagery, the kingdom of God may be at hand, but it is never in an institution. Thus even in the most radical Christian claims for a theocracy, the rule of God, or for a single, holy church, there is always the reminder from the Christian perspective that because the future is still to come, even with the presence of the resurrection, the present remains ambiguous.

Because of the essential role of the person of Jesus for the understanding of the Christian future, it may seem as if this future is a future of 'persons'. While in the Christian perspective it is certainly true that the future is personal – a future for salvation of all persons of all times – it is likewise a future for all creation. Like the creation image, the Christian understanding of the future puts God in relation to all that exists. It does not lift the person out of creation but rather renews this creation. Sometimes the language of the Christian tradition even speaks of 'divinization'. Because of the inclusion of all creation in the future, the relationship of responsibility to all others, to the forgotten of the past, to future generations, to the earth and its environment, is part of a Christian perspective.

In a culture where accurate descriptions of facts and events are the most significant measure of truth, any talk of the future – other than to note that nothing is really certain – seems to make little sense. But Christian talk about the future is not 'risky' in this sense, since it is not really about predictable, datable facts and events. When Christian language about the future becomes this kind of fortune-telling, it inevitably fails, sometimes generating scepticism about Christianity as a whole, sometimes encouraging various allegorical or mystical readings. Such language is 'risky' because it testifies to a relationship with a God of the future, and in doing so establishes a way of life rather than a calendar. It is a way of life based on the foundational image and narrative of the death and resurrection of Jesus, a perspective in which the future is in a certain, but yet unknown, way already here.

In fact for the most part we carry out our lives with an implicit hope that our actions now have a bearing on the future; every action we undertake confirms this anticipatory understanding about the future, suspended between an ongoing faith in life based on a past that has brought us to the ambivalent situations in which we now live, and a hope about what we are yet to do, to further or correct, to delight in or suffer through in a time yet to come. Christian talk of the future is at home in the evocative language of prayer, in the directive language of ethics, and in the symbolic representations of our human and cosmic situations. If there is a fundamental appropriation of a Christian way of life, it is marked by this kind of realistic hopefulness in a relationship with the future, a risky responsibility which lies somewhere between the sense that our actions now will determine with certainty the shape of future existence and the sense that the future is out of our hands, so unhinged from the present and past that all we can do is await what it brings. Rather than philosophical or imaginative speculations about future realms, heavens or hells, or the precise description of the 'moment of death' or the 'meaning of judgement', or the 'experience of eternal life', or the date of the 'millennium', contemporary Christian talk of the future deals more with current human responsibilities for future generations, for the structures of threat, oppression and degradation that we continue to create for personal, social and cosmic life. It is for this reason that it commonly deals with ecology, or the threat of nuclear war, or liberation from the institutions of economic, political and social oppression, or the importance of contemporary astrophysics or evolutionary biology for the shape of future existence.

If Christianity confirms a modern perspective that any talk about the future is a risky business, it does not locate this risk in error. The risk is that of worshipping inappropriate gods of the past, of not doing our best to be responsible for the future. It is the risk of losing hope amidst the ambiguities of the present.

JOHN MCCARTHY

James Buckley and L. Gregory Jones (eds), *Theology and Eschatology at the Turn of the Century*, Oxford: Blackwell 2001; Craig C. Hill, *In God's Time: The Bible and the Future*, Grand Rapids, MI: Eerdmans 2002; Gerhard Sauter, *What Dare We Hope? Reconsidering Eschatology*, Harrisburg, PA: Trinity Press International 1999

Homosexuality ➤

Gay and lesbian theology

Gay and lesbian theology is theoretical reflection on biblical sources, human experience, ethical questions, and their implications for religions that have developed in response to the challenge of homosexuality as a healthy, respectable, even holy lifestyle. The concerns of bisexual and transgender people are increasingly coming to theological expression as well. Sometimes 'queer theology' is used as an umbrella term for reflection based on a range of sexual expressions that go beyond the heterosexist norm. These theological approaches also have Jewish, Buddhist and other religious starting points, though here we shall focus on the Christian sources. They are engaged in against a background of hostility from the churches, whose standpoint is that homosexuality is sinful.

Same-sex love is a major point of contention in most Christian churches. This is at once odd and explicable. It is odd because 'love' is so basic to Christian religious teaching. It is hard to explain why same-sex love is condemned while heterosexuality, even if it results in violence or divorce, is always seen as good in itself. This is explicable by the heterosexual bias that has held sway in Christian churches for millennia. Anti-homosexual behaviour has resulted from that bias, including discrimination against gay and lesbian people in most aspects of Christian life. Gay and lesbian theology addresses this bias and seeks to correct it.

Gay and lesbian theology arose in conjunction with feminist, black, liberation and other theological approaches that begin with the experiences of those who are marginalized and who attempt to bring their concerns into the mainstream. Gay men and lesbian women began to articulate their experiences of oppression and to claim their place as respected members of the Christian faith community in the 1960s. In fact the Council on Religion and the Homosexual, an early advocacy group, was founded in San Francisco in 1964. This was even before the Stonewall Riots in New York City when gay and lesbian people fought back against police interference, an event commonly cited as the beginning of the contemporary gay rights movement. So religious efforts were among the first forms of gay/lesbian activism in the United States.

Theological work in this arena has always been intimately connected with social change, given the central role of religion in that process. Gay and lesbian theology unapologetically puts a case. Examples of early work in the field include the writings of John McNeill, a Jesuit priest, who was dismissed from his order because of his support for gay and lesbian people. His book *The Church and the Homosexual* (1976), a supportive treatment of gay/lesbian inclusion in Christianity, is one of the first examples of gay theology. Another early example is the creative ministry of the Reverend Troy Perry, a Protestant minister who left his home denomination to found what became the Universal Fellowship of Metropolitan Community Churches in 1968. The MCC is a predominantly queer Christian denomination with more than 300 churches around the world.

Among the earliest work by lesbian women is a memorable article by Sally Miller Gearhart, 'A Lesbian Looks at God the Father' (1972), in which she explores from a feminist perspective how patriarchal Christianity disregards the experiences of all women, especially of lesbian women. She co-wrote *Loving Women/Loving Men* (1974) with William R. Johnson, the first 'out' gay man ordained in 1972 by a Christian denomination, the United Church of Christ. Carter Heyward, an Episcopal priest, later brought her lesbian feminist perspective to a range of systematic theological issues, including Jesus, the church and salvation. These early works set in motion a cascade of books, articles, journals, academic gatherings and websites that make up the field of gay and lesbian theology.

Jesus
Church
Salvation

Membership, ordination, sexual ethics and marriage are among the major issues treated by gay and lesbian theology. Some Christian churches, both at the congregational and denominational levels, have raised the question whether gay and lesbian people, especially those who are sexually active and honest about it (that is, not celibate as some church teachings require), can be members in good standing. This has caused an exodus by LGBTQ people (LGBTQ is the abbreviation for lesbian/gay/bisexual/transgender/queer, which is used frequently in the literature) from many conservative Christian communities, for example, the Mormons and Southern Baptists. It has occasioned an influx of LGBTQ people into such welcoming groups as the Unitarian Universalists, the United Church of Christ and, of course, the Metropolitan Community Churches. Most mainline Christian denominations have an LGBTQ advocacy group, such as Affirmations (Methodist), Integrity (Episcopalians), and More Light Presbyterians. Two gatherings of all of these groups have been held under the aegis of Witness Our Welcome, conferences of hundreds of LGBTQ people and their supportive allies. There is a new kind of Christian ecumenism in this coming together of people from myriad denominations for worship, education and strategizing.

Sexual ethics

The Roman Catholic Church has published a series of official teachings which make clear that homosexual orientation is 'intrinsically morally disordered', while homosexual acts are 'objectively evil'. This does not mean, however, that homosexuals cannot be Roman Catholics. It means that they are considered sinful by the institutional church in so far as they express their love sexually. The many lesbian nuns and gay priests and religious brothers are evidence of the fact that Roman Catholic membership is not restricted on the basis of sexuality.

An increasing number of Roman Catholics reject the official teaching, emboldened by Roman Catholic theologians who use traditional Roman Catholic social justice claims to ground Roman Catholic gay and lesbian theologies. Robert Goss's work on Jesus as 'queer' and Mary E. Hunt's attempts to construct a Roman Catholic feminist lesbian theology are among these efforts. Activist groups like New Ways Ministry provide counselling, retreats and

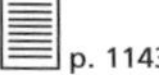
p. 1143

other theological resources for LGBTQ Roman Catholics and their families.

Ministry and ministers

Ordination of homosexuals is another vexed issue. While most churches admit that they have ordained many gay and lesbian people who are closeted, i.e. silent about their sexuality, the ordination of honest homosexuals is a matter of great debate. It is hard to imagine why a church that values honesty would reward lying. But it proves how virulent the opposition to homosexuality can be when even honesty is trumped by sexuality in the eyes of those who reject the goodness of same-sex love. Much of the theological work on ordination has been done in denominational papers, seminary seminars and the like. The theological issue rises and falls on the matter of the morality of homosexuality, not on some special matters regarding ordination.

The most celebrated case is the ordination in 2003 of the Episcopal Bishop Gene Robinson of New Hampshire, the first openly gay Anglican bishop. Conservatives in that denomination threaten to split off from the main body over their disagreement on the matter. But Bishop Robinson and his supporters insist that the process of his election was just like that of any other bishop and, therefore, a valid and licit – if extremely controversial – election. In the ordination ceremony of Bishop Robinson, the strongest opposition expressed had to do with gay male sexual activity, not with Bishop Robinson himself. It was quickly dismissed by the presiding bishop as already having been discussed, signalling that a major task for Christian churches is to live with disagreement on these matters. When women were ordained in the Anglican communion, similar threats of reprisal were expressed but not carried out on any large scale. This time may prove to be different, with large numbers of Anglican bishops in developing countries voicing opposition, another indication of how strongly people feel about sexuality.

Anglicanism

Methodists, Presbyterians, Disciples of Christ, Lutherans and others discuss ordination endlessly with no consensus. Baptists, Missouri Synod Lutherans and other evangelical groups do not even debate what is considered a closed matter. Church trials and other disciplinary moves have been made against those who, in ecclesial disobedience, transgress the rules and ordain homosexuals. Likewise, those who have been ordained and later make public their sexuality come in for equal censure. The theological grounds cited in opposition refer to heterosexuality as the norm according to scripture and tradition. Opponents reject claims to the moral neutrality of homosexuality and claims to the goodness of fidelity in same-sex relationships. Proponents cite these as reasons in favour of the right to testing one's call to ministry regardless of sexuality.

As homosexuality is increasingly accepted in contemporary culture, and as theological arguments are mounted to demonstrate that sexual diversity, as we now understand it, can be squared with Christian teachings on love and justice, the arguments begin to fall away, as in the case of Bishop Robinson. Moreover, as it becomes clear that many LGBTQ people serve with distinction in the ministry, including many 'out' pastors in denominations such as the United Church of Christ, the likelihood of these rules changing increases. The theological struggles played out in annual meetings, general conferences and the like have devastating consequences for the faith of many LGBTQ people who experience themselves as the object of generalizations and condemnations.

Roman Catholics handle the matter of ordination of homosexuals by mandating celibacy for their all-male clergy. They require their priests to refrain from marriage, as well as from genital sexual activity. Thus the matter of sexual orientation, in theory, has no bearing on one's suitability for ordination, since no Roman Catholic priest can licitly engage in sexual activity of any sort. The paedophilia scandal and cover-up in the United States has revealed that many priests are sexually active, that many of them are gay, and that a few are active in criminal ways, namely with under-age persons, mostly males. All of this has led Roman Catholic officials to suggest that in the future same-sex orientation may well be a bar to ordination. The ban is not yet in place, but even the threat of it has caused great consternation among seminarians, many of whom are in fact gay.

Sexual ethics is another contested matter for Christian theology. For some denominations, like institutional Roman Catholicism, the mere fact of homosexuality is considered sinful. For others, homophobia or heterosexism is sinful. The range of ethical views is enormous. Much of the discussion focuses on sexual acts, and whether it is morally acceptable to engage in same-sex genital activity. There is a predictable split between those who say yes and those who say no. Much of the opposition is grounded in natural law approaches; much of the support is grounded in the social sciences and anecdotal material from healthy, happy people who live in same-sex relationships.

Some of the more controversial ethical work simply assumes that same-sex relations are morally neutral and probes just what kinds of activities are morally permissible. For example, with the HIV/AIDS pandemic, the theologian Robert Goss has questioned whether the use of condoms for gay male sex is a moral imperative, or whether gay men can choose to run the risk of infection for the pleasure they experience without condoms. Some feminists have raised the question of just what constitutes 'good sex' from women's perspectives. They conclude that it is not so much the so-called bedroom, or micro-ethical, issues that are at stake. They suggest it is the more political and economic matters of women's consent and safety, of sexual trafficking and prostitution, which require ethical attention.

Same-sex marriage is another major issue in gay and lesbian theology. Predictably, there is strong division even among groups who favour it and those who do not. Some opponents suggest that it will cheapen or destroy heterosexual marriage. Others argue that it is a contradiction in terms to call even the most committed same-sex relationship a marriage. Those in favour argue that a covenant is a covenant regardless of the gender constellation of those making the commitment, and that marriage confers a certain social and spiritual legitimacy on relationships to which they ought to have access. Still others who favour the right to same-sex marriage question the wisdom of it, arguing that it will compromise gay and lesbian liberation by privileging couples, albeit same-sex ones. The Christian ethicist Marvin Ellison explores the range of opinions on the question in his book on the topic.

Much of the foundational theological work on lesbian and gay issues is completed. Scriptural studies on relevant biblical passages, the so-called 'clobber texts' which are used to argue that homosexuality is against the will of God, include both positive and negative interpretations. John Boswell's landmark book on Christianity and homosexuality offered a solid foundation for later studies of just how same-sex love was understood throughout the history of the Christian tradition. He argued that some male saints were probably lovers, and that the early Christian communities showed evidence of a certain acceptance of homosexuality. Continued historical work bolsters his position, though some argue that homosexuality as such cannot be claimed until the early twentieth century.

Bernadette Brooten looked at women's homoeroticism in the Christian scriptures. She concluded that in the case of two women lovers the transgression was not so much at the level of gender, that is, two women instead of a man and a woman. Rather, it was the fact that they treated one another as equals, transgressing the normative hierarchical model of one lover in power (on top) and the other submissive (on the bottom) that was the real cause of scandal and censure.

Studies of medieval monastics found examples of same-sex lovers in convents. Their gender boundaries were porous – women acting as men, claiming their lovers were really angels – with all manner of fanciful activity found in some fascinating texts. Gay and lesbian theology relies on such material to demonstrate the wide variety of sexual expressions visible throughout Christian history.

Today thousands of lesbian and gay Christians write, lobby, preach and pray, claiming that their sexuality is conducive of and not a barrier to holiness. Bisexual Christians are increasingly vocal about their situations. They correct the mistaken impression that they have more than one lover at a time. They make it clear that they experience their love for both women and men, and consider it consistent with Christian ethical norms. Some even suggest that a God who loves all humanity is a model of bisexuality, a claim their opponents find abhorrent. Transgender persons bring another theological lens. Texts such as Galatians 3.28, 'neither male nor female', for example, take on new meaning when read through their filter.

The fluidity of sexuality, both in the human community and in individuals over a lifetime, demands theological and ethical dynamism. This is what gay and lesbian theology attempts to provide. For those who query what remains stable, one Christian response is the values of love and justice with which all persons expect to be treated. Living out those values is proving to be a major challenge in contemporary Christianity and promises to become even more complex with increasingly diverse sexualities.

MARY E. HUNT

📖 John Boswell, *Christianity, Social Tolerance, and Homosexuality*, Chicago: University of Chicago Press 1980; Bernadette J. Brooten, *Love Between Women*, Chicago: University of Chicago Press 1996; Marvin E. Ellison, *Same-Sex Marriage?*, Cleveland: Pilgrim Press 2003; Robert Goss, *Jesus Acted Up: A Gay and Lesbian Manifesto*, San Francisco: HarperSanFrancisco 1993; Carter Heyward, *Touching Our Strength: The Erotic as Power and the Love of God*, San Francisco: Harper & Row 1989; Mark D. Jordan, *The Silence of Sodom: Homosexuality in Modern Catholicism*, Chicago: University of Chicago Press 2000; John McNeill, *The Church and the Homosexual*, Boston: Beacon Press 1976

GEOGRAPHY

African American Christianity, Christianity in: Africa, Latin America, North America, Asia, Australasia, Europe, Middle East, Mission

As well as having a history stretching back over 2000 years, Christianity also has a geography. It spans the world. Of the 6 billion inhabitants of the globe at the beginning of the third millennium, around one-third were Christian. Of these there are 560 million Christians in Europe, 480 million in Latin America, 360 million in Africa, 313 million in Asia and 260 million in North America.

History

Modern accounts show that it is misleading to think of Christianity as a Western religion, soon leaving its origins in Galilee and Judaea for the Greek world of the Mediterranean, then spreading northwards for more than a millennium through Europe, from the fifteenth century crossing the Atlantic to the Americas and finally establishing itself in Africa in the nineteenth century.

From the start Christianity also spread eastwards, with the trade routes as far as India and then beyond, and southwards down into Africa. For more than 1000 years most Christians lived in Asia and North Africa. Earliest Christianity was predominantly eastern (in terms of the then inhabited world) and the major developments and events in the first centuries took place around the eastern end of the Mediterranean with its many lines of communication and densely populated cities. With the rise of Rome after the toleration of the Christian religion by the Emperor Constantine in 312, the makings of a split between East and West developed, but at first Jerusalem, Antioch, Alexandria and Constantinople were the main focal points. This split between a Latin-speaking West and a Greek-speaking East, still evident, say, in the ongoing existence of the Roman Catholic Church and the Orthodox churches, continued to characterize Christian thought and practice even after the rise of Islam. Surprisingly, despite the subsequent westward spread of Christianity, for more than a millennium Christians remained much more numerous in the East (there were 3 million Christians in Egypt around 1200); it was not until around the thirteenth century that the balance shifted as a result of the great decline in the number of Eastern Christians because of persecution and plague, after which Western Christianity became dominant and remained so.

Constantine's 'conversion'

pp. 552–3

Roman Catholic Church

Orthodox churches

Outside Europe, great empires which no longer exist stamped the pattern of Christianity on the globe. For example, the 424 million baptized Roman Catholics in Latin America have their roots in colonization from Portugal and Spain: Brazil now with 153 million Roman Catholics was part of the Portuguese empire; Mexico now with 93 million Roman Catholics was Spanish, as across the Pacific were the Philippines with 62 million. The British empire furthered the spread of Anglicanism, which now has a communion of over 70 million members, 20 million of whom live in Nigeria alone. Christianity and colonization went hand in hand.

Anglicanism

Diversity

The diverse forms of Christianity which exist all over the world owe their varied characteristics in part to the local cultures and customs which had existed previously, to the characteristics of the particular European churches or missionary societies which became established there, and also, last but by no means least, to the political and economic consequences of the arrival of the European empire-builders. Christianity in Latin America was inevitably affected from the start by the fact that it was the source of boundless supplies of silver which was plundered for Europe. To safeguard these both church and society were given hierarchical and feudal structures which put those on the receiving end of the gospel at the lowest level of society, lorded over and exploited by the colonizers.

Here is the source of the 'top-down Catholicism' which in the latter part of the twentieth century was challenged by the advocates of liberation theology. The story was repeated in a similar way in Africa.

Liberation theology

What is surprising is that, given its close alliance with colonial empires that eventually collapsed, Christianity has flourished to an amazing degree in their territories. Indeed, in Africa after the Second World War Christian leaders played a prominent part in helping some states to achieve viable independence. And what is even more surprising is that Christianity is growing in the territories of former empires at a phenomenal rate. This growth is occurring within the Christian churches which were founded at the time of the first colonizers and those arising from the work of nineteenth-century missionaries, but alongside them, especially in Africa, a whole series of new independent churches and sects have come into being, which are deeply influenced by local cultures and local patterns of worship and belief. Many of these groups are charismatic and Pentecostal, and alongside faith healing and speaking in tongues believe in demon possession and practise exorcisms.

Pentecostalism
p. 1081

As a result, a great shift in the geographical distribution of Christians is taking place. Whereas once Christianity was split between West and East, now the split is between North and South, and by the middle of the twenty-first century the Christians living in the South will be in the majority. Even now the largest Christian communities are in Africa and Latin America, and the higher birth-rate in the South, despite the ravages of poverty and AIDS, will itself bring about this change. The Christian countries in the North have static or declining populations, whereas many of the countries of the South with Christian inhabitants are experiencing population explosions. Furthermore, while Christianity is stagnant or in decline in much of Europe and North America, in the South conversions are adding to the large numbers of new Christians born into the faith.

In Brazil the Protestant Pentecostalist Universal Church of the Kingdom of God gained millions of followers in the space of less than twenty years; in the Philippines the Catholic charismatic El Shaddai movement gained as many adherents over the same period, and both have the potential for global expansion. Korea has the world's largest single Christian congregation of more than half a million members, the Full Gospel Central Church in Seoul, and in Nigeria the Redeemed Christian Church of God in Lagos is another mega-church.

The growing Christianity of the South differs markedly from that in the North, and here too, political and economic factors are playing their part, most notably the poverty and exploitation that are the legacy of colonialism and the urbanization brought about by the spread of the global economy. However, paradoxically, although circumstances in the Roman Catholic Church in Latin America led there to the rise of a liberation theology with a political dimension under the influence of Marxism, elsewhere, the focus of southern Christianity is on personal salvation rather than on political problems.

In many respects this Christianity is closer to the Christianity of the earliest days. In the face of poverty and the constant threat of death there is a greater sense of the supernatural and a desire for prosperity and health. There is no doubt about the possibility of miracles, and about the malevolent activity of hostile powers which have to be combated. Against this background the Bible can be read almost as if it had been written yesterday. This makes religion in the South on the whole more conservative in its beliefs and moral teachings.

Miracle
Bible

Of course there are marked differences within the Christianity to be found in the southern hemisphere, associated not least with the origin of the churches. Many churches in Africa are members of the World Council of Churches, in which they have a common focal point, but because

Ecumenical movement

the Roman Catholic Church is not a member of the WCC, this is not the case with the churches in Latin America. Again, in Latin America the rising new churches have to define themselves over against a society which is predominantly Roman Catholic; in Africa traditional religion and Islam are also key factors.

However, common to both continents is the ongoing spread of the charismatic, Pentecostal movement, which is changing the old patterns of allegiance. For the last generation the number of Protestants in Latin America has been increasing by an average of 6 per cent per year, so that they now form a tenth of the predominantly Roman Catholic population. Over the same period there has been a similar increase among Roman Catholics in Africa, where the growth rate is comparable.

Statistics from the year 2000 show that the largest Christian populations after the United States are in Brazil, Mexico, the Philippines, Nigeria, Ethiopia and Congo/Zaire. Although the United States is in the northern hemisphere, a major reason for the continuing strength of Christianity there is immigration from the south. For example, the Hispanic population, from Mexico, the Philippines and elsewhere, already forms a majority of the inhabitants of the state of California and will soon do so in Texas; this group, made up to a large extent of young Roman Catholics, will contribute to growth and change in American Roman Catholicism.

Hispanic Christianity

In addition to the way in which it can speak directly to the situation of people in the southern hemisphere with its promises of health and salvation, Christianity also has a great appeal in the gigantic cities which are forming there, like Lagos in Africa, and Mexico City and São Paolo in Latin America. As in the earliest days, in these vast urban conglomerations Christianity provides a place to belong, tangible communities which can offer a sense of belonging and provide mutual help.

The current geographical shift associated with the rapid population increase in the South is likely to change the very face of Christianity and make many generalizations and assumptions about it obsolete. By 2025 it is forecast that the figure of 2 billion Christians currently alive will have grown to 2.6 billion. Of these, the number of those living in Europe will actually have declined to 500 million (by contrast, thanks to immigration from the South, Christians in North America will have increased to 290 million). Elsewhere, though, the Christian population will have increased by between one third and one half, with 640 million Christians in Latin America, 633 million in Africa and 460 million in Asia. Africa and Latin America will contain half the Christian population of the world. Of course, statistical projections can be misleading, and changes in the distribution of the world's resources, so urgently needed, together with the greater use of birth controls, the spread of literacy and education, and so on may alter the picture; however, the move of the focal point of Christianity southwards seems unstoppable.

The Christians of the North to some degree can still exert influence over those in the South through the financial resources that they can make available; but given a shift in this balance of power, southern Christianity is likely itself to influence global Christianity, and even make its mark in the heartlands of Europe.

JOHN BOWDEN

Philip Berryman, *Religion in the Megacity*, Maryknoll: Orbis Books 1996; Philip Jenkins, *The Next Christendom*, New York: OUP 2002; E. R. Norman, *Christianity in the Southern Hemisphere*, London: OUP 1981; *World Christian Encyclopedia* ed David B. Barrett, George T. Kurian and Todd M. Johnson, New York: OUP [2]2002

Global ethic

On what basis can Christians enter into meaningful and life-giving dialogue with those of other faiths? It is difficult to earth dialogue in theology, which is usually divisive. For example, the different interpretations that Christians and Muslims have of Jesus often make him a conflict-ridden figure. Partly for this reason, and to some extent because inter-religious relations have often been violent and sometimes continue to be so, there has been an increasing tendency in recent years for interfaith dialogue to focus on ethics rather than theology. There has also been a growing recognition that, in our inter-related world, such ethics must command widespread assent. So there has been a high-profile attempt to identify a global ethic upon which members of different religions, and even secular people of goodwill, can agree.

The recent search for such a global ethic began with a strong Christian input. In the 1980s the distinguished theologian Hans Küng coined the phrase 'No peace among the nations without peace among the religions'. For Küng, this means there must be dialogue between the religions and an investigation of their foundations. From his enthusiasm blossomed a number of conferences, and these prompted the Parliament of the World's Religions, meeting in Chicago in 1993, to issue a 'Declaration toward a Global Ethic' which received widespread support. Since 1993, a number of conferences have commented upon the document, and organizations promoting a global ethic are mushrooming in the USA and Europe; probably too many, since some seem to be in competition with others, which seems richly ironic to critics, even friendly critics, of the enterprise.

There were of course significant stepping-stones on the way to this global ethic. The General Assembly of the United Nations adopted the Universal Declaration of Human Rights on 10 December 1948. Since then, interfaith organizations like the World Conference on Religion and Peace and the International Association for Religious Freedom, as well as conferences organized by the Unification Church and the Brahma Kumaris, have made significant statements about the role of religions in establishing and sustaining peace. From 1997, UNESCO has again become interested in clarifying and publicizing the aims and ideals of a global ethic.

The 'Declaration toward a Global Ethic' promoted what it calls four irrevocable directives. They are: commitment to non-violence and respect for life; commitment to a culture of solidarity and a just economic order; commitment to a culture of tolerance and a life of truthfulness; and commitment to a culture of equal rights and partnership between men and women. These are worthy aims, but the formulation tends to suggest that religions promote these admirable aspirations, whereas very often they tolerate and even encourage repressive and intolerant practices. For example, the role of women has often been exploited and undervalued by religions.

Other faiths

Indeed, although the Parliament of the World's Religions represents a spectrum of the world's religions, its title is a misnomer: those who attend are not democratically appointed representatives. Moreover, although people from many religions signed up to the declaration, it was primarily the work of a small group of Christians.

Interfaith dialogue

Moreover, some distinguished advocates of the global ethic have tended, surprisingly, to oversimplify the issues at stake. For example, some of its proponents assume too easily that religions ought to accept the authority of, or at least work with, secular, international organizations. The former President of Iran, Ali Khamenei, stated: 'When we want to find out what is right and wrong, we do not go to the United Nations; we go to the Holy Qur'an.' He went on to say, more colourfully: 'For us the Universal Declaration of Human Rights is nothing but a collection of mumbo-jumbo by disciples of Satan.' His is by no means the only view in contemporary Islam on ethics, peace and human rights. Proponents of a global ethic need to understand and deal with the impulses that lead many religious people to say and believe such things; otherwise they will condemn their important project to sentimental, platitudinous irrelevance.

It is important not be sentimental and simplistic about core values, or locate agreement and even difference between religions in the wrong places. What is needed is not only an ethic of agreement but also an ethic for coping with disagreement, where religions have wronged others. For example, many Christians in India are Dalits, the 'oppressed' or 'burdened' ones, marginalized and even dehumanized by many other Indians, who have little reason to value or trust the teachings of the Sanskrit traditions of Hinduism, which imposed and justified the caste system and condemned them as out-caste people. Any attempt to formulate a global ethic has to recognize the need for justice and the integrity of creation, and avoid any spurious harmonization that papers over profound inequities.

The global ethic is a brave and admirable attempt to harness the resources of the world's religions to positive and universal ends. Yet religions cannot just be applied like balm for the soul in order to produce desirable ends like peace and justice. They must not simply admire their theoretical resources. They have to reform themselves in the contemporary world, if they are truly to be homes for the human spirit. Attempts are being made to consider what the implications of a global ethic are for business, the armaments industry, the care of the environment and other centrally important matters for the future of humankind

Poverty

and, indeed, the planet itself. The next few years will see what results arise from this questioning, and whether sufficient members from all religions can be persuaded to work together to achieve justice, peace and good practice for wider groups than their own community.

MARTIN FORWARD

Hans Küng, *Global Responsibility. In Search of a New World Ethic*, London: SCM Press and New York: Crossroad 1990; and *Yes to a Global Ethic*, London: SCM Press 1996; S. B. Twiss and B. Grelle (eds), *Explorations in Global Ethics: Comparative Religious Ethics and Interreligious Dialogue*, Colorado and Oxford: Westview Press 1998

Globalization

Globalization is a relatively new word for a process that has been going on for hundreds of years. The different parts of the world have been moving closer together for a very long time as people have travelled and traded with each other and nations have built their empires and established and ruled their colonies. One familiar sign of this movement today is the increasing range of goods and services bought from other countries. Since about the 1970s this process has intensified and accelerated, mainly due to advances in information technology, television and telecommunications, and cheaper air travel. It becomes easier and easier to do business with people over enormous distances. The world shrinks to a 'global village'.

Communication

A great deal of discussion has focused on the economic aspects of globalization. Indeed for many the global economy is all that globalization is about. Gradually and then rapidly the economic system known as capitalism, characterized by the so-called 'free-market'and unfettered opportunities to buy and sell in open competition, has swept other systems to one side. A dramatic example of this was the collapse of the state-centred socialist economies of Eastern Europe in the early 1990s. It led many to believe that capitalism was the only economic system that worked and the only one left. Its driving forces include international financial institutions like the World Bank, the International Monetary Fund and the World Trade Organization; the world's seven or eight most powerful economies (G8), above all the United States; financial markets like Wall Street in New York and the City of London; and the vast transnational companies whose turnover and influence is greater than that of many smaller nations put together.

Culture

Many regard this global economy as benign. It has its problems, but has vastly improved the living standards of millions of people and, by creating more wealth, can raise many millions more out of poverty. Its adoption by poorer nations through structural adjustment policies which open them up to the advantages of international trade can only do them good.

Economic globalization also has many critics, and their numbers are growing. Some want radical reform and some want an end to the system altogether. Many see it as a threat to the environment. Capitalism with its commitment to growth and consumption uses up too many of the earth's resources. It is greedy for gain. Its manufacturing processes pollute the air and water and endanger the fragile interdependencies of nature (and the atmosphere). It is responsible for global warming and its perils.

An even more serious criticism is perhaps that the global economy, while making some people much better off, is bringing few benefits to vast numbers. On the contrary it is making and keeping millions of them poor. Vast areas of the world, such as most of Africa, have been left out or rather have been exploited for cheap raw materials and cheap labour while receiving little in return. As a result the world can be seen to move in the opposite direction, away from integration, as the gap between rich and poor gets wider and a growing sense of injustice drives people apart. One oft-quoted example of this injustice is the contrast between the freedom of those with money and capital to move it across national borders and around the globe in order to invest or speculate and make more money, and the lack of freedom of people without money to move from one country to another as 'economic migrants' to try to make a living. Capital does not require a visa. Poor people do.

Central to reform is the recognition that a largely unregulated global economy, where private companies and their share holders can overrule elected governments, must be controlled by stronger nation states and improved systems of global governance. The United Nations, the World Trade Organization and international courts would be examples. These must be democratic, so that everyone has a say and the economy is made to work for the good of all and to pay for services like universal education and health care, which are not usually best dealt with on a purely commercial basis.

A second, much debated way in which globalization produces both integration and division has to do with culture. Superficially McDonalds and Coca-Cola seem to be everywhere. More profound is the way in which Western urban ways of living and Western values like individualism and consumerism are becoming universal and threaten to erode the many and varied cultures of the rest of the world. No culture is entirely good or bad in itself, and all cultures can benefit from criticism and interactions. The problem arises when people feel that their own cultural identity or sense of who they are and their pride in themselves are under threat. So once again, alongside the attractions of an affluent way of life, there is resistance to globalization. It can be fairly gentle and amount to respect and tolerance for, even appreciation and enjoyment of, cultural diversity. It can, however, be far more aggressive and amount to what has been called a 'clash of civilizations' or 'Jihad versus McDonalds'.

What has Christianity to do with globalization? First, it has been part and parcel of it from the beginning and has contributed to it in several ways. At the heart of Christianity, and not only Christianity, is a universal claim and drive to bring the whole world within its fold. This claim is that the God made known in Christ loves and redeems all humankind and all humankind is called to love and serve the God made known in Christ. This was the conviction which energized the missionary expansion of the early church and in more recent centuries the missionary movements from the West to Africa, Asia and South America. It was not always easy for missionaries to distinguish between the quality of the divine love they proclaimed and the superiority of the Western cultures with which their faith had become entangled. As globalization made progress, this same Western Christianity generally lent its support to capitalism (some see a kinship between capitalism and the Protestant work ethic) and intensified the opposition to communism and the state-centred socialist economies, though the fact that there are now more Christians outside the Western world than within it has contributed to a questioning of both these attitudes.

Protestantism

Secondly, those who understand Christianity as offering not only salvation from sin but good news to the poor will take seriously the challenges posed by globalization, as it appears to aggravate the sorrows and deprivations of millions of women, children and men. Christianity will find it difficult not to regard 'making globalization work for the poor' as an essential part of its mission, and tackling issues like fairer trade rules, global governance and a more holistic approach to the good life than mere economic growth will provide, as central to its life and work. True to Jesus' solidarity with the poor, it will look for ways to maximize the potential of its own presence in almost every place to become a global network of solidarity.

Salvation

Thirdly, Christianity will have to deal with the issue of unity and diversity on a much larger scale than simply within its own ecumenical movement. Its relation to culture, indeed its own inability to be expressed in anything but cultural and relative forms, is one aspect of it. Its attitude to other religions is another. Religion, since the events of 11 September 2001 if not before, is recognized as a critical factor in globalization. It can all too easily become the ally of divisive forces like injustice, fear and the loss of self-respect. It can all too easily turn to fundamentalism, uncritical of itself, intolerant of others, corrupting its universal vision into an unthinking and oppressive superiority, in the attempt to assert its people's identity.

Diversity
Ecumenical movement
Fundamentalism

Alternatively, many religions speak the language of coherence, reconciling one humanity to a common life under God. They, Christianity among them, could complement the tough realism which the power struggles of the world require with an inspiring ideal of a global city even more hospitable than the new Jerusalem envisaged in the book of Revelation. It would be a holy place for Christians, Jews, Muslims and all peoples of faith; it would be a home with open gates for all the nations from North, South, East and West; it would be a community built on what is sometimes referred to as a 'global ethic' of mutual respect, tolerance, basic human rights, co-operation and kindness.

Global ethic

MICHAEL H. TAYLOR

📖 CAFOD, *The Rough Guide to Globalisation*, London: CAFOD 2000; H. E. Daly and J. B. Cobb, *For the Common Good: Redirecting the Economy Toward Community, the Environment, and a Sustainable Future*, Boston: Beacon Press 1989; Hans Küng, *A Global Ethic for Global Politics and Economics*, London: SCM Press 1997 and New York: OUP 1998; Samuel P. Huntington, *The Clash of Civilisations and the Remaking of World Order*, New York: Simon & Schuster 1997; Rob van Drimmelen, *Faith in a Global Economy*, Geneva: WCC Publications 1998

Gnosis

The Greek term *gnosis* is used with two different meanings which need to be distinguished carefully. First, the term means knowledge; secondly, it is used to denote a current or a number of religious philosophical systems in antiquity. It is found in the first sense in the Bible and the writings of the period between the Old and New Testaments; it is used in the second sense in the history of Christianity.

The Greek term gnosis ('knowledge')
Knowledge was a central value for the ancient world, as we can see, for example, from Plato, who probably coined the term 'gnostic'. The term *gnosis* also appears relatively frequently in the Greek translation of the Old Testament, the Septuagint. There it is used in the sense of recognition, experience or insight, very often as an equivalent to the term 'revelation'. *Gnosis* is given by God. Since in the Septuagint the Greek word is translating a Hebrew term,

the meaning here differs from that in classical Greek texts: in the Jewish world *gnosis* denotes a unity of thought and action, of rational knowledge and sensory perception, whereas Greek thought makes a strict distinction between these. The use of *gnosis* in the New Testament is shaped by the meaning of the term in the Hebrew Bible; it also extends to right action.

Paul

However, a new understanding of the term appears in the correspondence between the apostle Paul and the community in the port of Corinth, where Christians are proud of their knowledge (1 Corinthians 8.1; 13.2, 8). Paul criticizes this and reminds his readers of the 'weak' who are coming to grief as a result of the conceit and lovelessness of those who claim to have superior knowledge. Scholars do not agree on the spiritual tradition from which this high esteem for knowledge in Corinth comes, but most probably it originates in Hellenistic Judaism.

In a late New Testament work, the First Letter to Timothy, the unknown author writing under the pseudonym of Paul warns his readers against the 'godless chatter and contradictions of what is falsely called knowledge (Greek = *gnosis*)' (6.20). Here for the first time we can see a group of Christians who attribute their consciousness of a distinctive theological competence to particular doctrines which are not shared by the majority in the church and who claim a special knowledge. In the second century such groups spread widely and were called 'gnostics' by their opponents; using the formulation from 1 Timothy their doctrine was designated 'knowledge' (*gnosis*, falsely so called). A few representatives of this trend also seem to have called themselves Gnostics (a first example is attested by the middle Platonist philosopher Celsus, *c.* 178, the target of Origen's *Against Celsus*, 5.61).

Creation ➤

The first great scholarly conference on gnosis, held in Messina, Sicily, in 1966, agreed to make a clearer distinction between the general interest in knowledge and antiquity and the particular groups. It used gnosis to describe a 'knowledge of divine mysteries reserved to an élite' and 'Gnosticism' to designate 'a particular group of systems in the second century CE'. However, this proposal has not become fully established, partly because it goes against the ancient terminology.

Church fathers ➤

Gnosis as a designation for a number of philosophical religious systems in antiquity

A whole series of sources attests that within Christianity from the second century onwards, and increasingly also outside its boundaries, as in Judaism and the grey zone between the ancient religions, systems became established in which 'knowledge' (*gnosis*) became a central factor in human redemption. It is difficult to demarcate such systems and groups exactly, and any such demarcation presupposes a modern definition, because the phenomenon was seldom seen as a unity in antiquity. Most of the systems now assigned to gnosis the following features in common, though of course these features also shape many other religious and philosophical movements in antiquity: 1. The experience of an utterly transcendent supreme God; 2. The introduction of further divine figures to mediate between this supreme God and human beings; 3. The characterization of the world and matter as evil or at any rate defective creation (in contrast, say, to the views of Platonism); 4. The establishment of an independent creator God, who is referred to by the Platonic term 'craftsman' (demiurge) and who relieves the supreme God of responsibility for the defective world. He is partly described as ignorant, and partly also as evil; 5. The explanation of all this by the narration of a mythological drama about a divine element which falls from its sphere into the evil world, slumbers as a divine spark in human beings of a particular class and can be liberated; 6. A redeeming knowledge about this state which is given only by a redeemer figure who descends from a higher sphere and ascends again; 7. Redemption through the knowledge that God (or a divine spark) is in the knower; 8. The predestination of a particular class of people for this knowledge; 9. A marked tendency towards dualism which can express itself in the differentiation between the supreme God and the 'craftsman' in the concept of God, in the opposition of spirit to matter, or in the differentiation of classes in the doctrine of human nature. It makes sense to call these systems gnosis, because *gnosis* is of central importance: failed knowledge leads to a divine fall and the creation of the world; successful knowledge leads to redemption. Through their knowledge, those who know partly become their own redeemers.

Systems which can be called Gnostic are cited, paraphrased or commented on critically by their opponents in the mainstream church. Traces of original Gnostic texts can be found above all in the works of five theologians from the time of the Roman empire: Irenaeus of Lyons, Clement of Alexandria, Origen (in his Commentary on the Gospel of John), Hippolytus of Rome and Epiphanius of Salamis (on Cyprus). Moreover in 1945 a whole library of original Gnostic texts in leather-bound codexes was discovered at present-day Nag Hammadi in Upper Egypt. These contain Gospels (e.g. the Gospel of Thomas), letters of apostles (e.g. James to Cerinthus), apocalypses (two apocalypses of James) and acts of apostles (e.g. The Acts of Peter and the Twelve Apostles); there are also texts which are clearly not Gnostic and are critical of gnosis. It is particularly difficult to demarcate a further group of sources: non-Gnostic texts which contain individual motifs or groups of motifs (e.g. the so-called Hermetic books, a collection of religious and philosophical writings attributed to Hermes Trismegistos, the thrice-greatest Hermes, a later name for the Egyptian

THE NAG HAMMADI LIBRARY

In 1945, peasants near the town of Nag Hammadi in Upper Egypt discovered a large jar containing twelve papyrus codices (i.e. manuscripts in book form rather than rolls), and part of a thirteenth, probably dating from the fourth century CE. The works they contain are entitled gospels, letters from apostles, revelations (apocalypses) and theological treatises. They are written in a form of Coptic and most of them are Christian, but of the kind of Christianity known as Gnostic. They are particularly important because otherwise we know of Gnostic views predominantly from reports by their opponents. Here the Gnostics speak for themselves.

The texts are referred to by NHL (Nag Hammadi Library) followed by a Roman numeral to denote the number of the codex and an Arabic number to denote the tractates in each codex, e.g. NHL VIII, 3. Some works exist in multiple copies.

I, 1	The Prayer of the Apostle Paul
I, 2	The Apocryphon of James
I, 3 and XII, 2	The Gospel of Truth
I, 4	The Treatise on the Resurrection
I, 5	The Tripartite Tractate
II, 1; III, 1; IV, 1	The Apocryphon of John
II, 2	The Gospel of Thomas
II, 3	The Gospel of Philip
II, 4	The Hypostasis of the Archons
II, 5 and XIII, 2	On the Origin of the World
II, 6	The Exegesis on the Soul
II, 7	The Book of Thomas the Contender
III, 2 and IV, 2	The Gospel of the Egyptians
III, 3 and V, 1	Eugnostos the Blessed
III, 4	The Sophia of Jesus Christ
III, 5	The Dialogue of the Saviour
V, 2	The Apocalypse of Paul
V, 3	The (First) Apocalypse of James
V, 4	The (Second) Apocalypse of James
V, 5	The Apocalypse of Adam
VI, 1	The Acts of Peter and the Twelve Apostles
VI, 2	The Thunder, Perfect Mind
VI, 3	Authoritative Teaching
V1, 4	The Concept of our Great Power
VI, 5	Plato, Republic 588A–589B
VI, 6	The Discourse on the Eighth and Ninth
VI, 7	The Prayer of Thanksgiving
V1, 7a	Scribal Note
VI, 8	Asclepius 21–29
VII, 1	The Paraphrase of Shem
VII, 2	The Second Treatise of the Great Seth
VII, 3	Apocalypse of Peter
VII, 4	The Teachings of Silvanus
VII, 5	The Three Steles of Seth
VIII, 1	Zostrianos
VIII, 2	The Letter of Peter to Philip
IX, 1	Melchizedek
IX, 2	The Thought of Norea
IX, 3	The Testimony of Truth
X, 1	Marsanes
XI, 1	The Interpretation of Knowledge
XI, 2	A Valentinian Exposition
XI, 3	Allogenes
XI, 4	Hypsiphrone
XII, 1	The Sentences of Sextus
XII, 3	Fragments
XIII, 1	Trimorphic Protennoia

The English texts are published in James M. Robinson (ed), *The Nag Hammadi Library in English*, Leiden: Brill ^{3}1988

god Thoth, seen as the father of all knowledge). Dating all these sources is a particular problem; they can come from any time between the second and fourth centuries. Whether there was a gnosis before Christianity depends, among other things, on this dating.

The source material shows that gnosis in fact consisted of groups which resembled pagan philosophical schools in gathering round particular charismatic teachers who were isolated from the religious majority groups by their élitist consciousness. However, there were sometimes considerable doctrinal differences between the heads or founders of schools and their pupils. The Marcionites and Valentinians are examples of such great schools.

The ship-owner Marcion, who lived in the middle of the second century and was active in the Christian community in Rome, from which he was expelled, is said to have taught two gods, an unknown good God proclaimed by Jesus and Paul and a further inferior creator god. He made the first attempt at an edition of the New Testament which was scholarly by the standards of antiquity, though it was rejected by the mainstream church because it treated the text very freely. An Egyptian teacher  by the name of Valentinus, who lived in Rome at the same time, developed out of elements of the biblical creation story and features of contemporary Platonic philosophy a mythological system as a preface to the biblical account.

A GNOSTIC HYMN TO CHRIST

This hymn comes from the Acts of John, a Gnostic work dating from the second or third century CE.

'Glory be to you, Word:
Glory be to you, Grace.' – 'Amen.'
'Glory be to you, Spirit:
Glory be to you, Holy One.
Glory be to you in glory.' – 'Amen.'
'We praise you, Father:
We thank you, Light:
In whom darkness does not dwell.' – 'Amen'

'Follow my dance,
see yourself in me, I am speaking,
and when you have seen what I do,
keep silence about my mysteries.
You who dance, understand
what I do, for yours is
this human suffering,
which I am to suffer.
For you could by no means have
known what you suffer, unless to you as Word
I had been sent by the Father.'

It was set to music by Gustav Holst (*Hymn of Jesus*, op.37); its ideas are also reflected in Sydney Carter's famous 'Lord of the Dance'.

Like Platonists, the Valentinians understood elements of God as eternal ideas (though they did not call them 'ideas' but 'eternities'); they constructed a fall in the cosmos of ideas by which they explained the origin and also the redemption of the world. In the end the original unity of all the elements with the divine is restored.

We can understand the development of such systems, which represent a synthesis of elements of biblical texts and philosophical theories, as an attempt at mission with which theologians who saw themselves as Christians sought to address the educated. Like the Platonists, they tried to elucidate Christian answers to the universal questions of the origin of evil and of human beings and their responsibility through stories and thus make them more understandable and credible. There had long been models for this missionary strategy in Hellenistic Judaism; as the example of the neo-Platonist Plotinus (205–70) shows, genuine Platonists were no more convinced than prominent Christian theologians in succeeding centuries. However, the Persian Mani (216–76) developed a gnostic system made up of traditional Zoroastrian motifs and borrowings from a variety of ancient religions into a world religion.

CHRISTOPH MARKSCHIES

📖 B. Layton (ed), *The Gnostic Scriptures*, New York: Doubleday and London: SCM Press 1987; James M. Robinson (ed), *The Nag Hammadi Library in English*, Leiden: Brill ³1988; Christoph Markschies, *Gnosis: An Introduction*, London and New York: T&T Clark 2003

GOD

Atonement, Beliefs, Christology, Covenant, Creation, Evil, Holy Spirit, Incarnation, Jesus, Kingdom of God, Mysticism, Natural theology, Philosophy of religion, Prayer and spirituality, Ritual and worship, Theology, Trinity

'God' is a word we learn in our earliest childhood, and even very young children can use it with a certain level of competence. Seven-year-olds can discuss whether God is a being who lives in heaven, a kind of presence spread throughout the universe, or an idea 'inside you'. In these simple ideas they show an ability to deal with the concepts of theism (God as a being separate from and superior to the universe), pantheism (God as identical with the totality of the universe) and a spiritual, interiorized religion. Some will also explicitly connect God with Jesus, setting the stage for the specifically Christian idea of God. Naturally, children cannot have the same level of understanding as adults, but it is clear that even as adults, we come to the idea of God with deep-rooted presuppositions as to what the term itself means or ought to mean.

However, these presuppositions not only relate back to our childhood conceptions of God, but also to the immense cultural, intellectual and historical discourse that has grown up around the word. The singular psychological and cultural power of the word and its associations is so great that even the most rational thinker can have difficulty in being entirely objective about it. When the Scottish poet Edwin Muir described the Protestant God as 'three angry letters in a book', he spoke for many who experience God only as an alien, threatening, power, associated with the most negative aspects of patriarchy. Such associations have to be acknowledged and dealt with if the word is to regain anything of the positive meanings it has in Christian usage.

What, then, have Christians meant by 'God'? For much of Christian history the dominant idea of God has, broadly speaking, been what is called 'classical theism', theism being derived from the Greek word for God, *theos*. This is an idea that reflects both philosophical thinking about God and important elements in the Bible. It is both essentially simple but also capable of complex philosophical analysis and extension. The God of classical theism is beyond space and time, infinite and eternal. God is the all-powerful creator, who created all things out of nothing simply by a command. God cannot be influenced by any external factor and therefore cannot suffer, being, in the terminology of medieval theology, 'pure activity'. But God is not simply all-powerful. God is also supremely good, and God's purpose in creating the world was to bring about the maximum possible distribution of goodness and happiness. In creating, God did not simply act upon impulse, but wisely and with complete foresight of all the consequences. That is to say, God is all-knowing or omniscient. God therefore foresaw that there would be much pain and suffering in the world, but judged that this was, so to speak, a price worth paying for giving freedom to all creatures and for the supreme goodness of the final glory to which creation would providentially be steered. In the exercise of this providential care, God does not overrule the freedom of creatures, but does intervene in history to ensure that the divine purposes are fulfilled.

Bible

Suffering

Freedom

In Christian versions of theism such intervention is supremely exemplified in the incarnation, when God took human flesh in the life of Jesus. Such specific interventions are not to be confused with God's omnipresence – that is, God's presence, simultaneously, to every aspect of creation without, however, being identified with it. At the end of time, God will bring history to a close, and

FORMS OF BELIEF IN GOD

Over the ages, belief in God and in the way in which God is related to the world has taken many forms, which are described by technical terms. These are the main ones:

Agnosticism: Denotes uncertainty whether or not there is a God to whom human beings can be related. However, the term tends to have negative connotations. It was first used in the nineteenth century by T. H. Huxley, who argued that God is unknown and unknowable.

Animism: The view that natural phenomena are endowed with personal life. The term was first used by the anthropologist E. B. Tylor in the nineteenth century as a 'minimum definition of religion'.

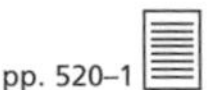

Atheism: The belief that there is no God. There are many variations of atheism with different motivations. God may be denied as being incompatible with the evil and suffering in the world, as God is denied by Ivan in Dostoievsky's novel *The Brothers Karamazov*; talk of God may be dismissed as meaningless, as in some forms of linguistic philosophy; or God may be said to be a human projection or wish-fulfilment, as happens in Feuerbach and Freud. Most common of all is the atheism of indifference.

Enlightenment

Deism: The view, originating in the Enlightenment, that there is a God who is the ultimate source of reality but does not intervene in natural and historical processes. God is like the clockmaker who makes a clock and then leaves it to run.

pp. 520–1

Ditheism: Belief in two gods. In some forms of ditheism one god may be good and the other evil, but the term can also be used of 'heretical' forms of Christian belief which recognize, say, the divinity only of God and Jesus and not the Holy Spirit.

Zoroastrianism

Dualism: The belief that the world is governed not by one God but by two eternal divine principles, one good and one evil. This is characteristic of Manichaeism and Zoroastrianism.

Monolatry: Worship of one God without claiming that he is the only god. This seems to have been practised in periods of the religion of Israel. It is sometimes also called henotheism.

Monotheism: The view that there is only one God, the creator and ground of everything that exists. Judaism, Christianity and Islam are all monotheistic religions.

Panentheism: The view that everything is in God. It differs from pantheism by holding that God is more than the universe and from theism in holding that the world is not external to God. Its main proponent has been the philosopher Charles Hartshorne,

Pantheism: The view that the universe is the mode of appearance of a single reality and that therefore nature and God are identical. The term did not appear until the Enlightenment, but the idea itself is ancient. It can have two different emphases: 1. God is real and the world is mere semblance and in the end unreal; 2. God is immanent within the reality of the world.

Polytheism: The belief that there are many gods.

Theism: The view that there is a personal God, creator and sustainer of the universe, whom human beings should worship and obey. Judaism, Christianity and Islam are all theistic religions, though the characteristics that each attribute to God vary.

Tritheism: The belief that there are three Gods, not, as in the Christian doctrine of the Trinity, one God in three persons.

creation to its ultimate perfection. Generally, this is seen as involving rewarding the righteous with an eternal life in which they share the joy of heaven, beholding God face to face and 'fully enjoying him forever' (in the words of a Scottish catechism), whilst also punishing wrong-doers with eternal damnation and all the pains of hell. Particularly in modern times, however, some versions of theism have inclined towards 'universalism', that is, the view that God will bring all creatures and not only the chosen few to final blessedness. Although we can conceive right ideas about God, God is intrinsically beyond all representation, invisible and ineffable, infinite and immortal.

Life after death

If this, very roughly speaking, has been the dominant Western Christian idea of God, it should at once be added that this idea has been interpreted and presented in many different ways and with many different nuances.

More philosophical forms of theism, for example, often highlight the connection between the idea of God and the category of 'Being'. They might insist that the most important aspect of God is that God is pure Being, Being-Itself or the Being whose essence is 'to be'. This sounds extremely abstract, but it rests upon some fairly basic ways of thinking about things. To understand this, let's begin by reflecting on what it is we are really saying when we ask, 'What's that over there?' The reply could vary according to what the questioner thought we were interested in. The Greek philosopher Aristotle, for example, listed ten basic categories we use in describing any particular entity. Using these categories we can say *what* a thing is (its essence), *where* it is, *what state* it is in, *where* it is going, etc. But unless we can say that what we are talking about *exists*, that it 'has' being, or that it 'is', none of the other categories will have any real reference. To say that God 'is' is therefore the most basic and the most necessary thing to be said about God, the peg on which everything else hangs.

For philosophers in the Platonic tradition it was also true by definition that being is intrinsically good. It is good to be and bad not to be. Everything, in so far as it has some share in being, therefore also has some share in goodness, no matter how limited. Conversely, the supreme being of God manifests itself in supreme generosity, such that God cannot and will not withhold being from anything that could possibly exist.

Philosophy

It should be said that not all versions of classical theism are Christian. Judaism, Islam and some forms of Hinduism would share many elements of God as described thus far, but without the specific appeal to the incarnation. The same would be true of philosophical forms of theism that limited our knowledge of God to what we could know from nature without recourse to special revelation (and especially emphasizing their independence from Bible and church). Such philosophical theism was especially important amongst thinkers of the early Enlightenment, such as Jean-Jacques Rousseau.

Enlightenment

Classical theism is, then, a complex mix of elements, and in modern times it has come under increasing pressure, both from the side of philosophy and from that of faith. In terms of Christian belief, for example, it is hard to see how the divine attribute of impassibility (not being affected by anything external) can square with the biblical picture of a God who is moved and grieved by both the faithlessness and the sufferings of God's people. Theologians have become generally uncomfortable with such philosophical aspects of classical theism and feel that it prejudices God's sovereignty and freedom of action, as well as God's personality. At the beginning of the modern period the French philosopher Blaise Pascal declared that the God of his Christian faith was 'the God of Abraham, of Isaac and of Jacob, not the God of the philosophers', and this cry has been taken up many times since. Yet although (for example) the definition of God as pure Being seems to belong to another thought-world from that of the Bible and the God of Abraham, Christian thinkers from early times claimed that God's reply to Moses from the burning bush – I AM THAT I AM – proved the legitimacy of making a connection to philosophical ideas of Being. Thomas Aquinas, whose theology has had a normative role in the Roman Catholic Church, insisted in the light of this that 'HE WHO IS' is the best possible name for God.

Thomas Aquinas

Although Christian theists have always claimed that the chief basis for holding to the picture of the theistic God is that this is indeed the God of the Bible, an important supporting element in theistic belief has been a group of arguments that have attempted to prove or, at least, to give added assurance to, belief in God's existence (although, again, many modern Christians balk at the idea

THE NAME OF GOD

As well as being spoken of as God (Hebrew *'elohim*), the God of the Old Testament is also referred to by the name YHWH (which in some English translations is rendered 'the LORD', using capital letters throughout). By the time of Jesus, Jews no longer pronounced the name and used substitutes like 'My Lord' or 'the Name'. It is often referred to as the Tetragrammaton (Greek for 'four letters'). Because the divine name was not spoken there is no indication from Jewish sources of how it was pronounced; however, transcriptions in the writings of the early church fathers suggest that the pronunciation was Yahweh and this rendering is used in, for example, the Jerusalem and New Jerusalem Bibles, and in scholarly discussion.

The Jewish scribes provided the consonantal Hebrew text of their Bible with indications of vowels above and below the letters; the text bearing these signs is known as a 'pointed' text. When they came to YHWH they gave it the vowels of the word for 'My Lord', *ªdonay* (the superior letter being pronounced as a very short vowel which could also sound like a short 'e'), to remind the reader to use the substitute. In the late Middle Ages, however, Christian readers attached the vowels of *ªdonay* to the consonants of YHWH, producing the name Jehovah, a form which never existed. This form can be found in the King James Version at Exodus 6.3, where God says to Moses of his appearances to Abraham, Isaac and Jacob, 'but by my name JEHOVAH I was not known to them'.

This form of the name also appears in Protestant hymns, for example the well-known 'The God of Abraham praise who reigns enthroned above'. This contains the line 'JEHOVAH, Great I AM, by earth and heaven confest': here 'I am' reflects what has been thought to be the meaning of the name. When God appears earlier in the Moses story at the burning bush, Moses asks for God's name so that he can tell the Israelites; God's reply is 'I AM WHO I AM ... Say this to the people of Israel, "I AM has sent me to you"' (Exodus 3.14). The Hebrew verb 'to be' is made up of the three letters *hyh*, so there is thought to be a play on words here with YHWH. The Greek translation of the Old Testament, the Septuagint, translates 'I AM' as 'He who is', using the participle form (literally = the [one] being); this was very useful for Jewish philosophers of the time of Jesus, such as Philo, who sought to demonstrate that Jewish thought was on a par with that of the Greek philosophers. However, the Hebrew text does not have the connotations of 'being' in the philosophical sense.

Jesus is said to have addressed God with the intimate Aramaic word 'Abba', a term used, say, by a son to a loving father; it appears untranslated in Mark's account of Jesus' prayer in the Garden of Gethsemane, and also twice in Paul's letters (Romans 8.15; Galatians 4.6).

of any sort of 'proof' of God's existence: surely God is not an object to be proved or disproved but a being to whom we can only relate in love, worship and faith – or else reject?).

These arguments or proofs are often divided into two broad categories, arguments a priori (that is, arguments that are based purely on logical considerations without appeal to experience) and arguments a posteriori (that is, arguments that proceed from experience).

The most influential of the a priori arguments for the existence of God is what became known as the ontological argument for the existence of God ('ontological' coming from the Greek word for 'being' and, as we shall see, the argument hinges on the question of Being). It is best known in the version given by Anselm, the eleventh-century Archbishop of Canterbury, and it is worth looking at this in some detail, because of its pivotal role in the history of thinking about God, and because it points to important elements in both philosophical and religious approaches to the question of God. Indeed, it has been argued that all other arguments for the existence of God can be boiled down to the ontological argument. We shall return to that claim later, but first let us look at the argument itself.

Modern readers coming to the argument for the first time are likely to see it as a supreme example of verbal trickery – just the kind of logic-chopping that we intuitively feel to be inappropriate in relation to God. If we read Anselm's argument in context, however, we will see that it is part of an intense and passionate meditation in the form of an extended prayer. Anselm does not begin with logic, but he turns to logic and reason to secure the idea of God that he already holds in faith. Without faith, he insists, we could not begin to understand God. His starting-point, then, is not logic but, in his phrase, 'faith seeking understanding'. On the other hand, if he cannot be sure that God really exists, then all the hopes and longings he has invested in his faith will be in vain.

Faith

Thomas Aquinas

ARGUMENTS FOR THE EXISTENCE OF GOD

The most famous arguments for the existence of God were put forward by two medieval theologians, Anselm of Canterbury (1033–1109) and Thomas Aquinas (1224–74).

Anselm's argument is known as the *Ontological Argument*. It runs like this: God is 'that than which no greater can be conceived'. Now we can conceive of such an unsurpassably great being. If this being exists only in our minds, it is not that than which no greater can be conceived, for we could conceive of something greater, namely this being existing in reality. So this being, God, must exist in reality.

Thomas Aquinas put forward five arguments, which are known as the *Five Ways*.

First Way: The argument from motion
1. Nothing can move itself.
2. If every object in motion has a mover, then the first object in motion needed a mover.
3. This first mover is the Unmoved Mover, called God.

Second Way: Causation of existence
1. Things exist that are caused by other things.
2. Nothing can be the cause of itself.
3. There cannot be an endless chain of objects causing other objects to exist.
4. Therefore there must be an Uncaused First Cause, called God.

Third Way: Contingent and necessary objects
1. Contingent beings are caused.
2. Not every being can be contingent.
3. A being must exist which is necessary to cause contingent beings.
4. This necessary being is God.

Fourth Way: The argument from degrees of perfection
1. One may say of two objects that one is more beautiful than another.
2. There are therefore degrees of a quality.
3. Perfection of that quality must exist as a standard by which qualities are measured.
4. That perfection is God.

Fifth Way: The argument from intelligent design
Common sense tells us that the universe works in such a way that we can conclude that it was designed by an intelligent designer, God. In other words, all physical laws and the order of nature and life were designed and ordered by God.

The first way is a version of what is known as the *cosmological argument*, moving from creation to Creator; the fifth way is known as the *teleological argument* or the *argument from design*. A famous version of it was put forward at the end of the eighteenth century by William Paley, in his *A View of the Evidences of Christianity*. Among other things he argued that anyone finding a watch on the seashore would infer that it was the creation of an intelligent mind and that the universe displayed similar features. The argument had been criticized at the time by the philosopher David Hume and was dealt a deadly blow by Charles Darwin.

The *moral argument* for the existence of God starts from the absolute claim that ethical demands seem to have upon us. The 'ought' involved in them is so unconditional that it has to derive from an absolute source of values, God. This too is challenged by the recognition that there are many different moralities, constructed by human beings.

The various arguments for the existence of God carry little weight today. W. H. Auden seems to have the last word in his 'Friday's Child':

> All proofs or disproofs that we tender
> Of His existence are returned
> Unopened to the sender.

John Hick, *Arguments for the Existence of God*, London: Palgrave Macmillan and New York: Seabury Press 1971; H. P. Owen, *The Moral Argument for Christian Theism*, London: George Allen & Unwin 1965

So, he asks, what do we think of when we think of God? He answers this question with a striking definition of God as that-than-which-nothing-greater-can-be-thought. But now imagine that that-than-which-nothing-greater-can-be-thought does not exist! What follows? Why, the paradox that we would then be able to think of something greater than that-than-which-nothing-greater-can-be-thought – namely, something that is not only that-than-which-nothing-greater-can-be-thought but that also exists (since, Anselm says, it is 'greater' for something to be than for it merely to be thought or, as he puts it, only 'in the mind' and not 'in reality'). Therefore that-than-which-nothing-greater-can-be-thought necessarily exists. In other words, we can't think of God without thinking of God as existing. Indeed, we can be surer of God's existence than of anything else of which we can think. In this way, Anselm believes his faith has been secured against doubt.

Even in its own time the argument provoked heated discussion. One contemporary critic claimed that by the same logic we could prove the existence of an imaginary earthly paradise. Anselm replied that this was missing the point, since his argument was not about the 'greatest' instance of any particular earthly phenomenon, and that there could be only one Being to whom the argument applied.

Most (but not all) of those who have subsequently attempted to prove the existence of God have preferred to start with aspects of our experience, rather than with what is seen as a mere definition.

One popular argument has been to look at the structures of our world and to claim that they are not self-sufficient but must depend on another, higher Being (these are called cosmological arguments, from the Greek *cosmos* = world). So, for example, when we look around us we see all sorts of instances of cause and effect. Indeed, it would seem impossible for the world to exist at all if there were not some universal principle of causality operative within it. But if the chain of causes ran backwards indefinitely we would have to ask how it ever got going in the first place. Surely there has to be some first cause to ground it all and stop everything from sliding into endless relativity? Thomas Aquinas offered 'five ways' of proving God's existence along these lines, using ideas from the then dominant Aristotelian cosmology, namely, the arguments from motion, causality, contingency and necessity, degree and design.

Science

The Aristotelian view of the world collapsed with the rise of modern science, but the argument from design lived on to become especially popular in the natural theology that flourished in England from the seventeenth century onwards and that reflected the outlook of the early scientific revolution. Nature, it is said, shows us innumerable instances of incredibly intricate and finely-tuned relationships within organisms or environments. Now, if we look at a mechanism like a watch we realize at once that someone must have designed it. Such complexity cannot have occurred by chance. Given that what we see in nature surpasses even the finest products of human contrivance, then, there must exist a great Designer who has designed it all!

Evolution

The exploration of nature which led Charles Darwin to the theory of evolution started out under the influence of this kind of thinking. Darwin, like many others, approached nature with the conviction that greater knowledge of the workings of its mechanisms would throw more light on the wisdom and skill of the Designer. Evolution, however, was to prove the biggest counter-argument to this theory, since it seems to offer an account of the origins of things that does not depend on anything other than natural causes ('natural selection'). Turning the design argument on its head, the modern Darwinian biologist Richard Dawkins has famously spoken of the blind watchmaker: if any non-random process plays the role of watchmaker in the universe, it is blind.

The claim that all such arguments can be reduced to the ontological argument may seem at first odd, since they seem to start from opposite ends, the one from a mere definition without reference to experience, the other from experience. In an argument that has shaped the whole of modern thinking about God, however, the German philosopher Immanuel Kant claimed just this. How so? As Kant saw it, those who argued from causality and design were right to say that we cannot but think of the world as held together in a coherent and unified system of causes and purposes. Science itself demands that we do so and that in the face of any novel or inexplicable event we don't just shrug our shoulders and say 'So what?' but ask 'Why? What caused this? What are its effects likely to be? What is it for?' This is a necessity of thought, as Kant put it. But, he added, a necessity of thought is not the same as a necessity of being, though this is just what the ontological argument tries to prove. The structures of our minds do not necessarily reflect the way things really are. So maybe we cannot but think of God as existing (if we think of God at all), but it doesn't follow that God really exists. The arguments for the existence of God therefore tell us more about the workings of our own minds than they do about God.

Since Kant, then, those who would argue for the existence of God have tended to look more at what it is in human beings that drives them to the thought of God and to examine what that thought means to them. This shift is sometimes termed 'the turn to the subject', i.e. to the human subject of religious belief, rather than attempting to demonstrate the objective basis of belief. Kant himself led the way by suggesting that a more important argument was to be found in our moral needs – that the idea of God underwrites our striving for moral perfection, since (together with the idea of immortal life) the idea of God holds out the promise of a final coincidence of virtue and happiness, something we certainly don't see in the world as it is. Others have looked instead at the phenomena of religious experience, at the sense of dependence that we typically feel in relation to the universe, or at claims of some direct mystical vision of God. In great modern traditions such as existentialism and some forms of psychoanalysis the question of God has become inseparable from the question of the self, such that finding our true self or becoming who we are is seen as inseparable from coming to know God. In the light of this kind of approach older attempts to construct theoretical arguments for the existence of God seem much too abstract and speculative. Human needs and human aspirations now stand at the centre – as in one redefinition of God as our Ultimate Concern (rather than, say, the First Cause or the Great Designer).

Critics of Christianity

Although such 'subjective' arguments are appealing in so far as they bring us closer to the sphere of the religious life itself, they also expose the idea of God to what is called 'reductionism', i.e. an approach that reduces God to 'nothing but' the projection on to an infinite canvas of what is, at bottom, a human need or aspiration. Reductionism became widespread in the nineteenth century, largely following the German philosopher Ludwig Feuerbach, who claimed to show how all ideas about God could be reduced to material needs. When, for instance, we call God 'love', all we are really doing is declaring that love is for us the highest value. Karl Marx and Sigmund Freud are two especially influential proponents of this approach, seeing religious ideas as reflecting social and psychological realities, respectively, and, what is worse, therefore obstructing human flourishing. They argued that all progress depends on humanity turning away from God and refocusing its attention on itself.

Whereas earlier criticisms of the idea of God had tended to call merely for a more rational idea of God, conceived of less in human terms (so that God became little more than the initial agent who set the world in motion, a position known as deism), the nineteenth century saw a positive rise in atheism, a rejection of all belief in God and the view that such belief could only be injurious to humanity. The most dramatic version of this militant atheism was Friedrich Nietzsche's declaration

that 'God is dead!' Without God, Nietzsche claimed, humanity could at last become free to create its own values, to reinvent itself in whatever way it chose.

Some very recent theological approaches have tried to incorporate the insights of reductionism and even atheism. In the 1960s there was even a paradoxically-named (and short-lived) movement called the 'theology of the death of God'. More recently, so-called 'non-realists' (a term chiefly associated with the British philosopher of religion Don Cupitt) follow Kant and reject 'realism', the view that there really is a being out there corresponding to our idea of God. Nevertheless, against Marx, Nietzsche and Freud they see the idea of 'God' as a valuable unifying symbol for our highest and most important ideas and principles. Such contemporary non-realism offers itself as a new form of faith, a purer kind of religion that has learned to detach itself from anything that smacks of scientific or metaphysical speculation as well as outgrowing any childish dependence on a supernatural comforter.

Secularization

Of course the problem of evil has been an especial challenge to the whole theistic picture. Already in biblical times people were asking, 'Why did God create a world such as this when God could foresee that there would be so much suffering in it?' In a famous formulation the early modern philosopher Gottfried Leibniz declared that, despite all the suffering in it, God created this world because God could see that it was the best of all possible worlds. Beginning with the Lisbon earthquake of 1755, however, a whole series of catastrophic events has seemed to mock this optimistic claim. The twentieth-century experience of battles such as the Somme and Verdun, in which millions perished in horrendous conditions, of the Holocaust and the atom bomb, seemed to call for a fundamental revision in our idea of God. Could a God who allowed such things (let alone a God who actively willed them) be worthy of worship, even if this God existed? In the words of Fyodor Dostoievsky's fictional atheist, Ivan Karamazov, if God allows such things, then I'm handing him back the ticket; I don't want to be part of his great plan if it's bought at such a price.

Christians no less than others have been affected by such experiences. Both Jewish and Christian traditions have rediscovered the biblical figure of Job. For centuries Job had been presented as a model of patience, submitting himself to the inscrutable will of a God who had inflicted such terrible torments upon him. Now (and much more faithful to the biblical text!) Job was presented as the angry voice of protest, refusing to take the advice of his friends and to trust unquestioningly in God's superior wisdom and, instead, challenging God to defend himself. This, it has been argued, is a much more truthful way of relating to God than the traditional emphasis on submission and obedience.

If the cumulative force of theological and philosophical criticisms of theistic ideas and the impact of the mass horrors of the twentieth century led some to non-realism, it led others to important reformulations of the idea of God.

One idea to gain in popularity has been panentheism, literally all-in-God-ism, i.e., a kind of combination of pantheism, the belief that God is in all things, and theism. Although the supremacy of a personal God is still acknowledged, the world is no longer seen as external to God but as being itself an expression of or participating in God's own dynamic self-development. This has been especially associated with what is called 'process theology'. Part of the appeal of this is that it incorporates an evolutionary view of the world. It also offers a new approach to the problem of evil, since God is no longer thought of as looking down on human suffering from afar, but as feeling the pain, making God 'a fellow sufferer who understands' (A. N. Whitehead). The idea of eternal life is similarly revised, so that instead of being a kind of endless existence after death it becomes the eternal value of our lives within the life and memory of God – 'a pulse in the eternal mind'

GOD

(the ultimate hope in Rupert Brooke's poem 'The Soldier'). Some panentheists, however, have seen the divine process of the universe as culminating in a final splendour, with something closer to the traditional eschatology and stressing Christ as the Omega-Point (final goal or conclusion) of history. The speculative Jesuit scientist-theologian Pierre Teilhard de Chardin is an especially striking example of such an approach. Possibly some of the more Westernized forms of Hinduism that were widely propagated in the late nineteenth and early twentieth centuries also influenced panentheism. In any case, like such Neo-Hinduism, panentheism also seems to offer a solution to the problem of why there are many faiths. Each is now seen as a different, historically- and humanly-conditioned expression of one underlying mystical vision.

Hinduism and Christianity

Panentheism has had some influence among Christian thinkers, but many theologians have preferred to move away from philosophical strategies and to refocus thinking about God on the figure of Jesus. This is often traced back to the dramatic reformulation of the theological agenda at the hands of the Swiss Calvinist theologian Karl Barth, although Barth himself acknowledged his kinship with precursors such as Rudolph Otto and Sören Kierkegaard, not to mention John Calvin, Martin Luther and Paul! If Barth began by insisting on the 'infinite qualitative difference' between God and human beings, asserting that God is the 'Wholly Other', such insistence was only half of the picture. Early Barthian theology was often known as 'dialectical theology', and if the denial of humanity's capacity for knowing God was one pole of the dialectic, God's gracious self-revelation in scripture and, above all, in Jesus was the other and ultimately more important pole. Only in God's self-revelation in Jesus, Barth claimed, do we have a basis for knowing him.

Paul

Whereas Barth's focus on Jesus is very much concerned with Jesus as revealing the transcendence of God, others have seen Jesus more in terms of God surrendering all those attributes of omnipotence and omniscience that made his non-intervention in a world given over to evil so scandalous. This tendency is often referred to as 'kenotic christology' (Greek *kenosis* = emptying), where Jesus is an image of a God who has emptied himself of all his attributes of power and authority and 'humbled himself in the form of a servant, even to death on a cross' (Philippians 2.6–8). Geoffrey Studdert-Kennedy (an army padre in the First World War) gave forceful expression to such ideas in a series of popular books, whilst Dostoievsky's novels *The Idiot* and *The Brothers Karamazov* heralded a line of literary and cultural explorations of what a 'powerless' God might mean. In the complex map of modern thinking about God some forms of kenotic christology have been incorporated into a panentheistic and process vision which sees this self-emptying as part of a larger process which also has its moment of future glory, while other forms have moved closer to the theology of the death of God, emphasizing the illegitimacy of any 'triumphalist' talk of God.

Christology

An important feature of the last 25 years has been the re-emergence of a vigorously trinitarian emphasis in theology. Like process thought, this seems to allow for a more dynamic, living image of God than that provided by classical theism. As with the renewal of christological thinking, this too owes much to Karl Barth. It has been pointed out that while the church has professed its faith in God as Trinity from the Council of Nicaea (325) onwards (when the doctrine was formally agreed upon), most of the time it has spoken of God as more or less solely identical with the Father and, in the Western Church at least, has hardly spoken of the Spirit at all. Although the new trinitarianism has received impulses from various sources, it has often been marked by the specific influence of the theology of the Orthodox churches of the East. For many the beauty of this vision of God is best expressed not in verbal theology but in the famous Old Testament Trinity icon by the Russian fifteenth-century icon painter Andrei Rublev, showing the angelic figures who visited Abraham in Genesis 18 and who have often been identified in Christian thought as a revelation of the Trinity.

Council

Orthodox churches

Icon

Another area in which older elements of the Christian tradition have re-emerged has been in the debate about religious language. For much of the twentieth century this debate was dominated by attempts to respond to the strong claims of logical positivism that the only meaningful sort of language was language that could be verified or falsified by experiment and experience. Philosophers in this tradition pointed out that Christians and other believers consistently refuse to allow the way they use 'God-talk' to be pinned down. Christians say God is a loving Father – but surely no loving human father would stand by and watch his child dying of cancer without doing all he could to help. Yet, although God is all-powerful, God does nothing about the sufferings of his children. 'Ah!' the Christians say in reply, 'but God is not like a human father, God's love is a different kind of love.' This did not satisfy the exasperated critics, who insisted that a love that is compatible with every conceivable state of affairs is meaningless. There has to be some point at which you can say, 'If God is loving, then this follows or that is excluded,' but believers just go on shifting their ground and, as a result, God is dying the death of a thousand qualifications. The fact is, the critics claimed, that religious language is emotionally expressive and doesn't really make any truth-claims about how things are in the world and is therefore meaningless. In response, sympathetic philosophers and many theologians expended great efforts in pointing out that there are in fact many diverse ways of using language meaningfully apart from that of science, and we should not try to impose such arbitrary stipulations on the actual complexity of living language. Instead, we should try to understand and to respect the different 'language-games' being played. The religious 'language-game', especially, was said to be something *sui generis*, playing by its own rules and not at all in competition with the language of science.

Language Philosophy

More recently there has been a rediscovery of earlier traditions of negative (or apophatic) theology. The central idea of this kind of theology is that none of our human categories of thought could adequately name the supreme identity of the Godhead, and they must all be negated or retracted when used of God. This theology was often associated with mystical elements in Christianity. Its most famous source was a fifth- or sixth-century writing put into circulation under the name of Dionysius the Areopagite, an Athenian philosopher who according to Acts 17.34 debated with Paul and was believed subsequently to have been converted. In his short book *The Mystical Theology* (Pseudo-)Dionysius writes of God that 'It [note: not 'He'] is not sonship or fatherhood and it is nothing known to us or to any other being. It falls neither within the predicate of non-being nor of being. Existing beings do not know it as it actually is and it does not know them as they are. There is no speaking of it, nor name nor knowledge of it.' We seem to find a similar teaching in the more pithy and less technical medieval English text known as *The Cloud of Unknowing*, where we read 'that of God Himself can no man think'. In texts such as *The Cloud*, it should be added, this denial of any intellectual, knowledge-orientated access to God is complemented by an insistence that we can, nevertheless, come to 'know' God in the mode of love, through the heart but not the head.

Mysticism

These kinds of texts certainly resonate with modern uncertainties as to how to think and speak of God. They have been especially fruitful in helping religious thinkers to respond to the forceful assault on the whole idea of 'onto-theology' (the equation of God with Being or the conception of God as the highest Being, discussed above), carried out by the German philosopher Martin Heidegger and taken forward in the philosophy of deconstruction. Quite apart from the kinds of objections to theistic belief stemming from reductionism and from reflections on the problem of evil, Heidegger argued that the Christian idea of God and the way of talking about God-as-Being found in Christian philosophy were actually guilty of compounding modern humanity's alienation from Being. Heidegger suggested that although we are constantly seeking a perfect

Evil

perspicacity, when our intuitions and thoughts become, as it were, transparent to Being, Being-Itself constantly eludes our grasp. The instant in which we name it or conceptualize it, it escapes us – and, he asserted, Christian theology has been one of the most persistent offenders in confusing the ability to conduct an abstract theoretical discourse about Being with the actuality of Being's own presence. We have to unlearn our theology, he suggested, before we can re-learn our sense for Being – and only then might we once more come to be in a position really to think about God. As the deconstructionists would put it, the meaning of what it is for God to be (and, therefore, all the other beings that are dependent on him) is infinitely deferred, always promised, but never arriving. But, the apophatic theologians can retort, genuine theology never did believe that it had perfect intuitions or perspicuous concepts of God. Mystical theology has always known and taught that God is indeed God by virtue of his infinite interior mysteriousness, always beyond anything we can say. Reflection on the problematic nature of talking about God is not to show weakness in the face of secular criticism but to be faithful to the tradition itself, which has always been more linguistically sophisticated than its detractors (and some of its defenders) have realized.

It would be hard, perhaps impossible, to sum up the current trends in Christian thinking about God. The task is made even more complex if we take into account the insights of other faiths – and even if we wish to preserve certain distinctly Christian emphases, it is today impossible to think seriously about God without at least addressing the question as to how the Christian idea of God relates to the ideas of God or of divine or ultimate truths found in other religions. To make predictions about future developments would be still more hazardous. Nevertheless, some general observations seem relatively safe.

Other faiths

First, it seems that unreconstructed classical theism is continuing a steady decline in philosophical and popular status despite a number of vigorous attempts at reanimation. Secondly, however, it has become clear that Christian faith itself is not tied quite so exclusively to classical theism as was at one time assumed. Trinitarian and apophatic emphases offer a subtly richer, deeper and more dynamic way of thinking about God. But, thirdly, although the crisis to which they were responding was real enough, the proposal of death-of-God and secular theologians that 'God' was no longer a necessary part of Christian experience or thought can be seen as an over-reaction. 'God' remains a continuing element in the human attempt to understand the world and our place in it. How God is to be understood, pictured, experienced or worshipped, however, is as open a question as it has ever been. Our time, therefore, is one in which thinking about God calls for a more than usual sensitivity to historical tradition, an awareness of the best available scientific world-picture, and a readiness to attend to and to learn from the voice and imagination of religious belief itself.

GEORGE PATTISON

Karen Armstrong, *A History of God*, London: Heinemann 1993; John D. Caputo (ed), *The Religious*, Oxford: Blackwell 2002; John D. Caputo, Mark Dooley and Michael J. Scanlon (eds), *Questioning God*, Bloomington, IN: Indiana University Press 2001; Philip Clayton, *The Problem of God in Modern Thought*, Grand Rapids, MI: Eerdmans 2000; Don Cupitt, *Taking Leave of God*, London: SCM Press 1980; John Hick (ed), *The Existence of God*, London: Macmillan 1964; George Pattison, *A Short Course in the Philosophy of Religion*, London: SCM Press 1997; Graham Ward (ed), *The Postmodern God*, Oxford: Blackwell 1997; Merold Westphal, *Overcoming Onto-Theology*, New York: Fordham University Press 2001

Grace

'Grace' is a word which has fallen into disuse in contemporary English (in spite of the new popularity of the hymn 'Amazing grace' in the last 30 years). Something of its meaning is retained in such expressions as 'grace before meals' (meaning a prayer of thanks), 'grace and favour' (relating to gifts by a ruler), 'gracious' in the sense of 'generous' or 'benevolent', 'gratitude', 'congratulation' or 'graceful'. In the negative sense 'graceless' is still sometimes employed to describe awkward, clumsy and thankless behaviour. This range of meanings reflects the associations of the Latin term *gratia* as it came to be developed and applied in the history of Western Christian theology.

p. 476
Martin Luther
Reformation

Gratia was related to *gratus*, which passively meant 'beloved, dear, acceptable, pleasing, agreeable', and actively 'thankful, grateful'. It probably derived, like the Greek *chairo* (rejoice) and *charis* (gift, endowment, thanks), from the Sanskrit root *har-jami*, meaning love or desire and consequently also appreciation, enjoyment or thankfulness. *Charis* is the New Testament word usually translated as 'grace'.

Charis was chiefly used in the Greek translation of the Hebrew Bible, the Septuagint, to translate the Hebrew term *ḥen*, 'favour' or 'mercy'. A word of similar meaning, *ḥesed*, was rendered in Greek by *eleos*, 'pity' or 'mercy'. In their theological application these terms express the goodwill and patience of God, particularly in dealing with Israel or with individuals. Contrary to widespread opinion, the Hebrew scriptures do not chiefly present a wrathful or vengeful God, but a God of mercy and forgiveness, longsuffering and compassionate, patient and healing – and see these norms at the same time as the highest standard for human behaviour.

Sacraments
Paul

In the New Testament it is Paul who speaks most frequently of the divine *charis*. The theme is particularly developed, for example, in his letter to the Romans. God's *charis* and God's gifts – *charismata* (though Paul more commonly uses the singular) – are the foundation of Christian life, and these are realized and given in the crucified and risen Jesus Christ. This involves on the one hand a break with the Jewish tradition – for salvation is now presented as given by grace through faith in Jesus Christ, not achieved by obedience to the Law – but on the other its continuation on a deeper level: God has not rejected his ancient people, but in Christ has opened the covenant for the Gentiles along with them (Romans 9–11).

Salvation
Law
Covenant

In spite of Paul, the church in the early centuries showed a marked tendency to interpret the Christian message as a 'new law', based on obedience rather than on grace. This view was especially vigorously maintained around 400 by Pelagius. He criticized Augustine's view that human beings are incapable of saving themselves by works of obedience from the consequences of the fall, and depend totally on divine grace for salvation. The church followed the lead of Augustine and Jerome, and condemned Pelagianism. The following centuries, however, saw a widespread inclination to semi-Pelagianism. This did not deny the importance of grace but also stressed the significance of human co-operation with it. In Western medieval theology some trends were more Augustinian in this respect, others veered to semi-Pelagianism. In practical terms, however, prominent aspects of medieval practice and piety were blatantly Pelagian, particularly the emphasis on 'merit(s)' and the traffic in indulgences. In 1517 this provoked a protest from Martin Luther and set the Reformation in motion. *Sola gratia*, 'by grace alone', was to become one of its main watchwords, along with *sola fide* ('by faith alone'), *sola scriptura* ('by scripture alone') and *solus Christus* ('by Christ alone').

At the same time, the understanding of grace in the theology of the Reformation differed sharply from that of the preceding centuries. From the eleventh century, Western medieval theology had undertaken a far-reaching intellectual and philosophical project to develop a synthesis of 'nature' and 'grace', and in the process to articulate and systematize the theological concept of grace. This was done in more than one direction and with varying theological emphases: there were differences of emphasis, for instance, between the Dominican and the Franciscan approaches. In general, however, the forms of divine grace were related on the one hand to anthropology and ethics (including the Christianized version of Aristotle's teaching on the 'virtues') and the workings of grace in the human soul, and on the other to the development of the system of the seven sacraments (baptism, confirmation, confession, the eucharist, marriage, ordination and extreme unction). These were understood as 'forms and causes of grace', i.e. as mirroring the specific grace they conveyed, and as being intimately bound up with the institution of the church as the sacramental ark of salvation.

In this context, justifying grace came to be subdivided into such categories as 'prevenient', 'operating', 'co-operating', 'assisting', 'subsequent', 'accompanying' and the like. These stages were related to a form of individual 'order of salvation' which in a typical and widely-used version began in a person's merely not resisting grace, then advanced through increasing co-operation between grace and free will until finally it reached a stage of justification understood as perfect righteousness achieved by the increasingly harmonious interplay of grace with merit. Further distinctions came to be drawn – for example between 'uncreated grace' and 'created grace', 'common grace' and 'special graces'.

Apart from the tendency to semi-Pelagianism (highly

impressive though this entire edifice was), such systematizing went far beyond either the Bible or the earlier church. It could also have the effect of objectifying grace as a supernatural force and of detaching it from God. (This tendency was reflected, for example, in a well-known hymn of Cardinal Newman which speaks of 'a higher gift than grace ... God's presence and his very self'.) Consequently the Reformation generally departed from this understanding of grace and returned, following Paul in particular, to a more dynamic and personal emphasis on grace as the graciousness of God. Much more recent Roman Catholic theology has also adopted this insight. This does not mean that the questions medieval theology sought to address are not valid or significant, but its specific use of the category of grace must now be regarded as problematic.

ALASDAIR HERON

Great Awakening

The Great Awakening was a popular religious movement in the British colonies in the mid-eighteenth century that might be considered the American counterpart to Britain's Evangelical Revival.

Historians disagree over how or even whether to use the term and over its causes and consequences. Joseph Tracey, *The Great Awakening*, published in 1842, was the first book to use the term and spell it with initial capital letters. Today most scholars use it to describe a wave of religious revivals that swept across the northern and middle colonies in the years 1739–41. Many also use it more broadly, as it will be used here, to describe a popular movement associated with revivals of religion over three decades beginning in the 1720s. Historians often say that it was followed by a Second Great Awakening (*c.* 1798–1832), and sometimes add a Third (*c.* 1890–1920) and a Fourth (beginning about 1950).

The term 'Great Awakening' denotes a vast inter-colonial movement marked by a wave or waves of revivals of religion. The term 'revivals' denotes local phenomena in which significant numbers of people experienced religious conversion. Conversion, by definition, happens to individuals. Here 'conversion' does not mean a change from one religion to another but rather an experience that is taken to be the beginning of the Christian life.

These are all Protestant concepts. Some seventeenth-century English Puritans rejected the concept of a universal or catholic church, which includes all baptized believers in Christendom, and strove to create 'pure' churches which included only the 'saints'. Those Puritans who settled Massachusetts Bay believed that the saints could be identified at least provisionally because they would have evidence of experiencing conversion. Herein lies a concept key to revivals and awakenings alike: becoming a Christian requires a 'new birth' that is an identifiable, often highly emotional, experience. Pockets of American clergy from religious traditions other than Puritanism in places outside New England held a similar concept. Among these clergy were Theodore Frelinghuysen, a pastor among the Dutch Reformed in Raritan, New Jersey, and William Tennent, a Scots-Irish Presybyterian who trained men for the pastorate in a 'Log College' in Neshaminy, Pennsylvania, and his son Gilbert, pastor in New Brunswick, New Jersey.

Bible

Dutch Reformed Church

American Puritans expected conversion to be a prolonged process that followed a predictable pattern. Occasionally numbers of people acknowledged conversion at the same time, as part of the process of joining the church. These 'seasons' were sometimes called 'harvests' or 'seasons of grace' but were not often called 'revivals of religion'. Puritanism had passed by the beginning of the eighteenth century, conversion experiences became rare and religion was widely perceived to be in decline. Across England, Scotland and the American colonies networks of clergy prayed for a 'revival of religion'. Here the term seems to have meant a reversal of the decline without referring specifically to what would come to be called 'revivals'.

Evangelicals

Solomon Stoddard, pastor in Northampton, Massachusetts, had witnessed five periods in which significant numbers had been converted and joined his church in the course of a 57-year ministry which ended in 1729. He called these 'harvests'. Frelinghuysen, Tennent and others preached for conversions and witnessed numbers of their flock respond emotionally, beginning in 1726. Jonathan Edwards, Stoddard's grandson and successor at Northampton, met with similar success and wrote the first revival narrative, *The Faithful Narrative of the Surprising Work of God in Northampton, Massachusetts, in 1734–5 ...* (1737). It came to the attention of the Englishman Isaac Watts, who arranged for its publication in London. John Wesley was among the Englishmen who read it and the narrative helped to inspire Wesley to preach for such revivals in England and Wales. Henceforth Protestants began using the term 'revivals' to mean local phenomena such as Edwards had described, in which significant numbers of residents experience religious conversion and join the church.

Conversion

Hence the Great Awakening was an American manifestation of an Anglo-American movement. English Puritans brought the key suppositions to New England. Edwards' narrative was published in England before it was published in America. Through Wesley and Watts it had an impact upon England and Wales. And George Whitefield, the Awakening's greatest preacher, came from England to America in 1739.

Protestantism
Puritans
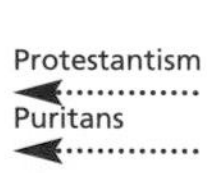

John Wesley preaching from his father's tomb

Whitefield was an Anglican cleric, a college friend and evangelical collaborator with John Wesley. Still in his early twenties, Whitefield was controversial for his emotional preaching. Many Anglican bishops had closed their churches to him, but he had drawn large crowds by preaching outdoors, beginning in Bristol in February 1739. He arrived in Delaware the next October and remained in the colonies until January 1741. A polished orator, he was said to be capable of making a grown man cry simply by saying the word 'Mesopotamia'. A pioneer in the use of the media and the art of publicity, he was a phenomenon by himself. He caught the fancy of Benjamin Franklin, a rational sceptic, who printed Whitefield's journals and recorded carefully his own observations of the man. It was Franklin who determined that Whitefield's voice could be heard by 30,000.

Whitefield spent approximately a third of these fifteen months in Savannah, Georgia, where he held a clerical appointment, and two-thirds travelling and preaching revivals. Gilbert Tennent accompanied him on much of his tour. At one point in the spring of 1740 approximately 40 other clergy, most of them former students from William Tennent's Log College, travelled with them. His tour was most effective in the middle and northern colonies where there were cities. He was triumphant in Philadelphia, New York and Boston and preached in many smaller communities as well. Masses came to hear him and often he preached outdoors. They came expecting to be converted, and hundreds were. Itinerant evangelical preaching continued after Whitefield left. Gilbert Tennent actually surpassed Whitefield's success in New England in the summer and fall of 1741, and a corps of other like-minded clergy undertook preaching tours of their own. Edwards did some travelling in the Connecticut River Valley and subsequently published the sermon he preached in Enfield, Connecticut, *Sinners in the Hands of an Angry God* (1741), a classic hell-fire sermon that has become the most famous publication in our day of the Great Awakening.

Even before the Awakening had begun in the southern colonies it was dividing the Congregational and Presbyterian churches farther north. The Age of Reason was dawning and some found the emotionalism excessive. Others wished to emphasize doctrine. Many objected when revivalists assumed that no one was a Christian who had not experienced an emotional conversion. Gilbert Tennent preached *The Danger of the Unconverted Ministry* (1740) in Pennsylvania and warned his audience against heeding the words of any clergyman who could not personally claim a conversion experience. Whitefield himself wrote similar words in his published *Journals*. Pro-revival Presbyterians, called 'New Side Presbyterians', were driven from the 'Old Side' Synod of Philadelphia by June 1741, and formed their own Synod of New York in 1745.

In New England it was local churches, which would come to be called 'Congregational', that divided. Many of these were in towns that previously had only one church. Here the two camps were called 'New Light' and 'Old Light'; here, too, supporters of revival were thought to hold something new. In many towns the two groups managed to co-exist within one church. Schisms often occurred, however, where New Light laity worshipped in churches with Old Light pastors. Approximately 150 new 'Separatist-Congregational' churches were created across Massachusetts and Connecticut. Eventually most of these churches became Baptist.

Two events brought concerted action against the Awakening by New England authorities. James Davenport, one of the lesser itinerants, came to New London, Connecticut, worked his audience into a frenzy, led them out onto the wharf and burned books of theology along with jewellery, trinkets and other books. Already uncomfortable with the New Light challenge, the Connecticut legislature outlawed itinerant preaching in 1743. Whitefield returned to America in 1744 to resume his tour. Religious authorities in Boston, both local pastors and the Harvard faculty, issued a written denunciation of Whitefield and his kind. The result was that the most pro-revival Christians in New England worshipped in local Separatist churches while revivals led by highly visible itinerants became quite rare.

South of Maryland, however, the Great Awakening had only just begun. The South had very few large communities or large churches. In this region the Awakening never included anything like the mass meetings Whitefield had led up north in 1739–41. But Whitefield had preached in smaller communities such as Williamsburg, New Bern, Beaufort, and Savannah in those years and left a scattering of converts across the area. William Robinson, a Log College graduate, found some of these and organized the first New Side Presbyterian congregation in Virginia in 1742. He had been commissioned to evangelize in the South by Gilbert Tennent's group, the New Side Presbyterians in New Jersey. New Side Presbyterians from Delaware sent Samuel Davies to evangelize Virginia five years later. Davies created a preaching circuit for himself that covered five counties in the centre of the colony. Authorities in Virginia sought to outlaw itinerant preaching, as the Connecticut legislature had done a few years earlier, but Davies was able to secure legal recognition for a newly-formed Hanover Presbytery in 1755. About the same time two Separate-Baptists, Elder Shubael Stearns and his son-in-law Elder Daniel Marshall, had migrated from Connecticut to Sandy Creek in North Carolina. Stearns and Marshall brought the Awakening with them from Connecticut as Robinson and Davies had brought it from New Jersey and Delaware. The church they formed at Sandy Creek in 1754 grew to 600 members within a year. The two men then struck out across areas of Virginia, South Carolina and Georgia, preaching and forming Baptist churches. Marshall and Stearns organized the Sandy Creek Baptist Association, consisting largely of churches they had formed, in 1758.

Congregationalism
Presbyterian churches
Enlightenment

When did the Great Awakening end? Whitefield continued to commute between England and America and to tour the colonies preaching for conversion until he died in 1770, but he never again enjoyed the success he had known in 1739–41. There were sporadic revivals, even localized waves of revivals, over the second half of the eighteenth century. Christians whose faith had been forged in revival fires kept the embers alive in Separatist and Baptist churches. However two wars, the French and Indian War (1755–63) and the American Revolution (1776–83), consumed the passions and resources of the next generation. Church membership fell to its lowest level in American history by the end of the American Revolution, but this time of decline proved to be an interlude. A Great Revival began in the South in 1785 and waves of new revivals began in Connecticut in 1798, in Kentucky in 1800. Hence historians conceive of the Great Awakening ending with the French and Indian War and a Second Great Awakening following a generation later.

Baptist churches
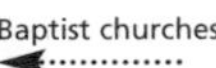

Jonathan Edwards emerged as the leading apologist for the Awakening, Charles Chauncy as the most outspoken opponent. Chauncy, pastor of a large church in Boston, dismissed the work as the product of fallible human emotions in a sermon entitled *Enthusiasm Described and Cautioned Against* (1742). By then Edwards had already defended it in *The Distinguishing Marks of a Work of the Spirit of God* (1741). Acknowledging that the work included extraordinary emotional outbursts and a variety of excesses, Edwards argued that these neither prove nor disprove the divine origin of the work but might be understood as natural reactions to the experience of the supernatural. The argument continued when Edwards published *Some Thoughts Concerning the Present Revival*

of Religion in New England (1742) and Chauncy retorted with *Seasonable Thoughts on the State of Religion in New England* (1742). In this debate the Old Light Chauncy laid the groundwork for a rational expression of Christianity which evolved over the next two generations, culminating in American Unitarianism. Edwards in turn laid out ideas which proved to be important for New Light Congregationalists, New Side Presbyterians, Separatists, Baptists and other evangelicals for the next century.

Unitarians

The legacies that have been claimed for the Great Awakening are legion. Clearly the Awakening produced a proliferation of churches and divided many churches into two general camps, evangelical and rational. The Awakening produced a proliferation of colleges as well, including Princeton in the middle colonies, Dartmouth and Brown in New England. America's first religious magazine, Thomas Prince's *Christian History* (1743), was published to record this work and to sustain it. It is more difficult to document claims that the Great Awakening prepared the colonies to declare their independence from England, overthrow traditional hierarchies and create the world's most democratic society. Clearly, however, the Awakening changed American religion, and one aspect of this change can be called 'democratization': clergy lost some of their traditional power over church life; laity took it upon themselves to form new churches and to dismiss and call preachers of their own liking.

University

Revelation

Tradition

Church

American evangelicalism is also a legacy of the Great Awakening. Evangelicals believe the Christian life begins with an identifiable, often emotional, conversion experience. Many Evangelicals work to organize revivals of religion. Whitefield was but the first of a long line of professional revivalists that included Charles Grandison Finney, Dwight L. Moody and Billy Graham. He was also the first of a long tradition of Christians called 'Methodists' who set out to revitalize Christianity in America, as Wesley did in England. Edwards was not the first local pastor to preach for conversion, but Edwards established key foundational concepts for generations of evangelicals. Puritanism passed with the seventeenth century; evangelicalism emerged in the Great Awakening of the eighteenth. These two have been the most influential religious traditions in American history. In the end it was Anglo-American Protestantism that was reborn.

Salvation

Methodism

RICHARD D. SHIELS

Michael Crawford, *Seasons of Grace. Colonial New England's Revival Tradition in its British Context*, New York: OUP 1991; Alan Heimert, *Religion and the American Mind: From the Great Awakening to the American Revolution*, Cambridge, MA: Harvard University Press 1966; William G. McLoughlin, *Revivals, Awakenings and Reform*, Chicago: University of Chicago Press 1978; Harry S. Stout, *The Divine Dramatist. George Whitefield and the Rise of Modern Evangelicalism*, Grand Rapids, MI: Eerdmans 1991; W. R. Ward, *The Protestant Evangelical Awakening*, Cambridge: CUP 1992

Heresy

The Christian affirmation of saving belief in Jesus has been shadowed by the denial of ideas that are suspected of compromising this central confession. 'Heresy' is the theological term that describes the denial by certain Christians of what the main body hold to be 'orthodox' beliefs. 'Orthodox' derives from the Greek word for 'right opinion', and in Christianity this word defines the truth as received by revelation, preserved by tradition, and embraced by the community of believers or church. 'Heresy' is therefore distinct from 'blasphemy' in Judaism and Islam because it is not strictly a sin against God, but rather a deliberate corruption of the correct teaching of the community. 'Schism' is defined as the separation of Christians over a disagreement involving matters of discipline or organization, but not necessarily over wrong beliefs. 'Apostasy' is another term that refers to the deliberate abandonment of Christianity entirely.

Historically and theologically, definitions of 'heresy' are therefore tied to the definitions of 'orthodoxy' within Christian communities. Verbal arguments as well as physical force have been employed to curtail individuals and beliefs considered to be harmful to the content of salvation or to the community. Different periods of Christian history as well as diverse forms of Christian communities have used the label 'heretic' in distinctive ways. In the present ecumenical age, when the varied Christian communities are seeking to find common theological ground, these categories have been used less frequently. However, charges of heresy and administrative procedures for trial and discipline are used in various branches of Christianity today.

The invention of heresy

The original Greek word 'heresy' literally meant 'choice' or 'sect'. It referred to one's selected philosophical or religious community. Josephus, the first-century CE Jewish historian, therefore referred to different sects within Judaism as 'heresies'. As the Christian movement spread through the urban centres of the Roman empire, converts to this new religion set themselves apart from both the ancient traditions of Judaism, by no longer practising dietary laws or circumcision, and of Graeco-Roman polytheism, by refusing to offer sacrifice to the many gods. This rejection of the dominant polytheistic religion of the Romans could lead to persecution and death. Thus, teachings about the significance of Jesus or the nature of God or of human beings were critical to defining and defending the emerging religious identity of ancient Christians. Christianity offered a saving theology, but it was also a separating theology. Not surprisingly, some who disagreed deeply with other interpretations of scripture or the significance of salvation felt that by their degree of doctrinal differences their opponents were 'un-Christian' in their beliefs. Their wrong beliefs compromised their spiritual identity. In the New Testament and other early writings factions were called 'heresies' (Acts 5.17 or 1 Corinthians 11.19). Though they were natural within a growing movement, these divisions were potentially harmful to the unity and faith of the small missionary communities.

In second-century Christian literature the word 'heresy' was detached from the original meaning of 'sect', and defined as the wilful rejection of correct and saving teaching. 'Heresy' was not mere intellectual disagreement, but a demonic corruption of divine truth. The points of theological disagreement were laid out in written treatises with reference to what were considered to be the true sources of Christianity as received from Jesus and preserved in apostolic tradition and scripture. This period therefore saw a number of significant controversies, while Christianity grew as a movement. The rejection of certain ideas helped to define and establish what became the 'orthodox' tradition. Unfortunately, because the 'heretical' works were often destroyed by their opponents, since they were thought to be dangerous, we know mainly about these ideas only through their enemies. It is difficult to recover what was actually taught or meant. The ideas of the 'heretics' were presented polemically and in a hostile light and seen as contrasting with the truth of orthodoxy. Heretics were labelled by their founder's name or their theological error to show that they were not followers of Christ, but preferred a human authority. This naming itself therefore creates a distance from the Christian tradition. Thus, we have 'Gnosticism' from false knowledge (*gnosis*) or 'Arianism' as the teaching of a man, Arius. Heretics were characterized by speculation rather than revelation, arrogance rather than humility, philosophy rather than scripture, and secrecy and disorder rather than public and moral communities. Heresy was therefore a spiritual and theological corruption that threatened the true community. Before Christianity received imperial patronage from the Roman emperor Constantine in 313, those who were labelled 'heretics' could simply leave a community and begin a new one. There was no central authority to enforce definitions, though teachers and bishops in various places wrote to one another to inform friends and allies about local conflicts and dangerous ideas.

Persecution ◄

The legal and broader geographical enforcement of heresy emerged as the church in the fourth century formulated a central affirmation of belief through councils and creeds. As the statements of belief were defined and ratified by a majority of bishops representing the church, the emperor enforced these decisions. This political policy followed the Roman tradition of encouraging a united piety to bring peace to the empire. Those who disagreed were often exiled or banned from communication with the community. For a time dissenting communities continued within the Roman empire, but by the end of the fourth century the emperors passed laws, including the confiscation of property, and enforced them to maintain the unity of one orthodox church. To the horror of many, the first execution of a heretic happened in the late fourth century: Priscillian was accused of sorcery, a charge that had always been a capital offence in Roman law. To be a 'heretic' when Christianity was an established religion was therefore to be a social as well as spiritual outcast. 'Heresy' was not viewed as mere dissent, but rather as destructive to public spiritual and political well-being.

Roman empire

Theological snapshots: a catalogue of errors

Because the ancient period saw the emergence and self-definition of Christianity as a new religion, many of the 'heresies' named at this time became as it were classic types of theological error against which the positive teaching of 'orthodoxy' continues to be defined. Chronologically later groups or individuals would be accused of holding the theological positions that were condemned centuries earlier. Thus, thinkers who questioned the doctrine of the Trinity in the seventeenth century were called 'Arians'. The timelessness of 'error' mirrored the eternity of revealed truth. Yet, these controversies also show continued reflection on difficult questions concerning God and human existence.

Trinity

God

What is the relation between God and evil? One of the first major answers to this question was Gnosticism, which seemed to focus on a dualism or opposition between God and the material world. Creation was a mistake, and the material world was evil. Jesus as incarnate God therefore only appeared to be human, but in fact remained a wholly divine spirit and uncontaminated by matter or evil. Salvation was deliverance from the material world. In rejecting this reading of scripture and human existence the orthodox were led to affirm God as a powerful creator, the material world as good, and the true suffering and humanity of Jesus as God who became flesh. Salvation through resurrection was the defeat of death and evil. In later history Christians who denied the humanity of Jesus or the goodness of creation, such as the Cathars in twelfth-century France, would be labelled Gnostics.

Evil

Gnosis

Creation

Constantine's 'conversion' ◄

HERESIES

A 'heresy' is a belief or set of beliefs which conflict with the 'orthodox' Christian faith. Heretics were condemned, expelled from the church, persecuted and sometimes killed. However, it should be remembered that many 'heretics' did not deliberately reject 'true' teaching but formed part of the process of establishing that teaching. They offered alternative views which in due course the church felt went too far.

Most heresies are named after either the instigator of the views in question or the view that came to be condemned.

Heresies named after the view condemned

Adoptionism (or Adoptianism): The view that Jesus is not the true, but the adopted Son of God. Adoptianism is used for the version of this view which arose in Spain in the eighth century, put forward by Elipandus, Bishop of Toledo, and Felix, Bishop of Urgel; Adoptionism is a blanket term used to describe a variety of views in the early church from Ebionitism onwards, which saw Jesus as merely a man gifted with divine powers.

Docetism: The view attributed to some in the early church that the humanity and sufferings of Jesus were only apparent (*dokein* = Greek 'to seem') rather than real.

Modalism: A form of teaching about the Trinity which held that the distinction between the persons in the Godhead was not permanent.

Monarchianism: A third-century view which by emphasizing the unity (= monarchy) of God failed to recognize the independent existence of the Son. One form of it was:

Patripassianism: The view that God the Father suffered as God the Son.

Subordinationism: Views in which the Son was seen as subordinate to the Father or the Holy Spirit was seen as subordinate to both Father and Son. Such views were held by early church fathers (Justin, Irenaeus) who were not seen as heretics, but were condemned in the form held by Arius.

Heretics who gave names to heresies

Apollinarius → Apollinarianism (fourth century): He seems to have denied that Christ had a human mind or soul.

Arius → Arianism (fourth century on): He seems to have held that the Son of God was not eternal but created by God the Father before the world.

Bardaisan → Bardaisanism (154–222): A speculative thinker who lived in Edessa; his teaching about Christ was docetic and he denied the resurrection of the body. He had a dualistic view of the world and probably influenced Mani.

Bogomil → Bogomilism (tenth century on): Founder of a movement in the Balkans which believed that the world had been created by the devil and that matter was evil. Adherents logically held a docetic view of Christ. The movement spread into Europe and influenced the Cathars.

Donatus → Donatism (early fourth century): A rival Bishop of Carthage whose followers argued that the validity of the sacraments depended on the worthiness of those administering them; they refused to accept as ministers those who had shown weakness in persecution.

Eutyches → Eutychianism (fifth century): He held a form of Monophysitism, the view that Christ has only one, divine, nature, claiming that Christ's manhood was not 'consubstantial' with ours.

Mani → Manichaeism (third century on): Founder of a strictly ascetic group which held a dualistic view of the world, believing that there was a perpetual fight between light and darkness. These views seem to have grown out of Gnosticism.

Marcion → Marcionitism (second century): Marcion rejected the Old Testament as revealing a cruel creator god who was not the God of Jesus Christ and who represented law. Of the New Testament he accepted only ten letters of Paul and an edited version of the Gospel of Luke: these presented the gospel of grace.

→

Montanus → Montanism (second century): Founder of an ascetic and apocalyptic group which believed that it was experiencing the spiritual gifts of the end-time.

Pelagius → Pelagianism (fourth/fifth centuries): The British theologian is thought to have held the view that human beings can gain salvation through their own efforts, quite apart from divine grace.

Priscillian → Priscillianism (fourth century): Bishop of Avila in Spain, he became the leader of a highly ascetic group, fell foul of the church and was executed.

Sabellius → Sabellianism (third century): Little is known of him; he gave his name to a form of Monarchianism.

Other heretical groups

Cathars (known as Albigensians in France and Patarenes in Italy) (twelfth/thirteenth century): A reform movement which posed a major challenge to the church with its claim to be practising a purer form of the gospel. Its views were dualistic, holding that matter was evil; this led to an ascetic life with a rejection of the sacraments and many teachings of the church.

Ebionites (first/second centuries): The name means 'the poor ones'. A group of Jewish Christians who believed that Jesus was the son of Joseph and Mary on whom the Spirit descended at his baptism. They were ascetic and observed the Jewish law.

Gnostics (second century on): Literally 'the knowers'. This movement, which attached supreme importance to 'knowledge' (of God and human destiny), held a dualistic view, distinguishing between the god who created the world and the supreme God. Sparks of divinity are contained in human beings and these can be rescued from matter and restored to where they belong. Gnosticism took many forms.

Lollards (end of fourteenth century): The name comes from the Middle Dutch *lullen* ('sing softly', from which 'lullaby' also comes) and was first used in a derogatory sense ('mumblers' or babblers of nonsense'). It was originally used of the followers of John Wyclif but also came to denote others who wanted to reduce the power and wealth of the church in England at the end of the fourteenth century. Lollardy has been described as Britain's only native medieval heresy. As well as having political aims the Lollards also emphasized the authority of the Bible, personal faith and divine election.

Mandaeans: A still-surviving group in Iraq/Iran with dualistic views, like the Manichaeans believing in an eternal conflict of light and darkness and seeing the soul as imprisoned in the body and awaiting redemption.

How could Jesus be divine if God is One? Some early Christians believed that Jesus was a very good man who had been inspired by God and filled with the Holy Spirit like a prophet. This position was labelled 'adoptionist', since Jesus was only adopted by God at birth or at his baptism rather than eternally sharing God's divine nature as God's Son. Other Christians described Jesus as divine by describing him as the 'Word of God' who came into the world, took human nature, and truly suffered. However, objections were made to this theology by those who believed that this division between God and his Word compromised biblical monotheism. These people were called 'monarchians' or 'modalists' because they affirmed the one power or rule of God. The one God was called by different names ('Father', 'Son' and 'Holy Spirit'), depending on the saving activity. This position was rejected in orthodox trinitarian theology because it denied the eternal existence of the three persons of the Trinity as revealed in scripture.

In the fourth century many of these questions were resolved through a series of ecclesiastical councils called by the Roman emperor. The Council of Nicaea in 325 put forward a creed to combat teachings by Arius, a priest from Alexandria, about the nature of Christ. After several decades of controversy and further councils, the Council of Constantinople in 381 affirmed a doctrine of the Trinity as eternal and sharing the same being. 'Arianism' seems to have been characterized by a separation between the Father and the Son based on nature; God as eternal by definition could not generate a Son with the same nature. This teaching appeared to compromise the divinity of the Son. In later centuries the term Arianism has often been applied to any position that seemed to deny the full divinity of the Son.

Christology ← Council Holy Spirit ← Creed Incarnation

This credal affirmation of incarnation and Trinity did not solve theological controversies entirely. A position called Apollinarianism defended the divinity of the Son by arguing that the divine Word replaced the human soul in the incarnation. This was opposed by the orthodox teaching that in order to save humans, Jesus must be fully

Grace
Sin
Predestination

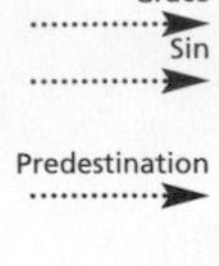

p. 1016

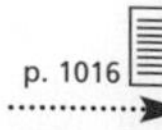

human and fully divine, i.e. at once possessing both a human body and soul as well as being the Incarnate Word. Struggles to understand and teach this theology led to bitter arguments in the Eastern Mediterranean that were nourished by ecclesiastical rivalry between the bishops of the major Eastern cities, Alexandria and Constantinople. Cyril of Alexandria wished to emphasize the unity of the person of Christ in the incarnation, and accused Nestorius of Constantinople of Arianism. Nestorius wished to affirm the reality of both natures through their distinction, and in response he found Cyril to be Apollinarian. A compromise was reached after the Council of Ephesus in 431; Nestorius was exiled and Cyril accepted 'two natures'. Yet, in some of his writing Cyril referred to 'one nature of the Word incarnate'. Later theologians affirmed this description, and were labelled Monophysites (one nature). The Council of Chalcedon in 451 affirmed a two-nature christology. However, the Eastern Orthodox Church has been split until very recently between those who accept Chalcedon and those who reject the two-nature christology (the Oriental Orthodox churches).

Orthodox churches
Papacy

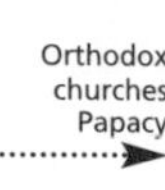

Holy

How may the church be holy? In the Western Mediterranean the Donatist movement began in North Africa after an intense imperial persecution in 303. Some members of the clergy were accused of surrendering the scriptures in their possession to the Roman authorities; it was believed that as a result of this their ordinations and the sacraments that they administered were invalid. The church was thus tainted by the sin of the clergy. After the Peace of the Church in 313 under Constantine, divisions existed in the church between those who were willing to accept these clergy and those who rejected this position. The church of North Africa was divided over this issue for a century. Called after an early leader, Donatus, the Donatists were at one point the majority movement in North Africa, representing the local and ancient traditions of purity. The 'catholic' party argued that God was the author of the sacraments, so the impurity of the clergy could not compromise the church. In 411 a council at Carthage found the catholics to represent the valid form of Christianity, and the Donatists were ordered to disband. Physical coercion was eventually necessary to suppress the movement. In the Middle Ages a similar argument over the pollution of the church by clergy buying and selling offices would be raised again.

Waldensian Church

Sacraments

Salvation

How is one saved? Another defining theological controversy of antiquity was the Pelagian controversy, named after a British teacher, Pelagius. He was a spiritual teacher in Rome who taught that Christians were individually responsible for fulfilling the commandments of God. Grace co-operated with free will in order to complete virtuous actions. Augustine of Hippo rejected this interpretation which he saw as compromising the initiative of grace that comes from God and heals the will crippled by original sin. Humans are unable to save themselves, but are dependent on God alone. Although the church did not accept all Augustine's ideas on predestination, they affirmed the initiative of grace. This argument concerning nature and grace or the relation between human will and divine power has been renewed numerous times, as when Protestant Calvinists have been in conflict with Arminians and Roman Catholic Jesuits in conflict with Jansenists.

The use of force in religious conflict

If heresy was a spiritual danger to the health of a Christian society, political states united with the church in the East and West developed various means for disciplining theological disunity. After the fall of Rome, Christianity in the West was a missionary religion, often in conflict with indigenous religions. Heresy was less a threat; survival itself was at stake. As Christianity formed a central structure of authority through the renewal of the papacy in the West in the eleventh century, charges of heresy became more common. Medieval heresy was different from the ancient forms, for many 'heresies' were in fact movements reflecting social changes such as urbanization or contact with the Eastern Mediterranean, and did not arise from individual theologians. However, challenging the authority of the church was increasingly seen as spiritually disobedient, and therefore heretical.

Several groups ironically embraced common reform goals of the time, but in a more radical form. Responding to the rise of a money economy, the Waldensians (followers of Peter Waldo) formed a lay movement whose members wished to embrace a life of poverty and preaching; they translated scripture without authorization. The Spiritual Franciscans, after the death of Francis of Assisi, criticized the wealth of the church and predicted the end of the Age. John Wyclif's teachings on the wealth of the church, the authority of scripture, and the authority of the laity gave rise to the Lollards (mumblers) in England. These movements were suppressed by law, and some members were executed.

Theological conflicts also occurred. In Southern France the dualistic movement called Cathars (the pure ones) or Albigensians (those from Albi), which saw good and evil as being in perpetual conflict, denied the goodness of matter and the reality of the incarnation. When debates with the Cistercians and Dominicans failed to persuade them, the Pope called a military crusade against Southern France. Peter Abelard, an early scholastic theologian, was condemned by a council for his teachings on the Trinity. Study of the Greek philosopher Aristotle was initially prohibited in university theology for fear of a 'double truth' theory that gave equal credence to both reason and revelation. Mystical movements such

Pedro Berruguete, *St Dominic and the Albigensians*, fifteenth century

as the Beguines, women who lived in community without permanent religious vows, were also condemned.

During this period church and society developed different tactics to oppose heresy. Certain controversial definitions were legislated, such as transubstantiation for the eucharist. An official body of theological experts to help local bishops was established – the Inquisition. This was not a constant presence in European Christianity; rather, it existed for specific needs in various geographical areas. The emphasis was theoretically upon converting the heretic, calling him or her to repent, and also to inform on others in order to stop the theological danger from spreading. Execution was in fact failure, since it meant that the person would not recant, and was delivered to the state to be burned. However, the increasing use of physical torture, sophisticated manuals of interrogation and secret proceedings whipped up criticism and fear. Many uneducated persons confessed simply to be freed. The king of France cynically accused a religious order, the Knights Templar, of heresy in order to seize their income. Ironically, Joan of Arc was burned as a heretic in 1481 and canonized as a saint in 1909.

If the Inquisition of the thirteenth century created theological unity for a time, the breaking apart of the church in the sixteenth century during the Reformation brought more violence. These divisions, because of a number of religious, social and political factors, produced a number of Christian churches that viewed certain others as 'heretics'. Persecution was regularly used by established churches against dissenters within their region, ranging from excommunication to physical punishment to death. The range of views on the sacraments was the key to persecution within most Christian groups, though the emerging Unitarians were executed for their denial of the Trinity. Anabaptists were executed for their rejection of state authority and denial of infant baptism. The execution of Roman Catholics under Elizabeth was linked to treason, for fear of war with Spain. These Reformation 'heretics', however, became revered martyrs to the groups they represented.

Reformation
Discipline
Unitarianism
Anabaptists
Martyr

Heresy in modern Christian pluralism

After a century of conflicts and wars, a pragmatic religious tolerance was established in Europe. The co-existence of different forms of Christianity was accepted, though members of dissenting groups within certain regions often had limited civil rights or barriers to full citizenship. In North America freedom of religion was eventually legalized nationally after the American Revolution. Christians had defended the right of the conscience in religious matters, but secular states began to legislate protection of individual religious freedom. The emergence of science created new tensions, as in the trial of Galileo by the Inquisition or later reactions to Darwin.

Wars of religion
Conscience
p. 794

In the modern era, therefore, heresy remains only as a religious charge within the beliefs and disciplines of particular ecclesiastical bodies. Often the issue has been framed as a challenge to religious authority by secular cultural developments such as democracy or critical historical scholarship. The historical criticism of biblical authorship or interpretation has provoked more than a century of controversy. For example, in the nineteenth century John William Colenso, the Anglican Bishop of South Africa, was tried and condemned for heresy over his denial that Moses was the author of the Pentateuch, the first five books of the Bible traditionally attributed to him, and of universal salvation. At the beginning of the twentieth century Albert Schweitzer wrote a controversial book on the historical evidence for Jesus, and was allowed to go to Africa as a medical missionary only if he agreed not to teach. Among some conservative Protestant groups these arguments concerning literal biblical interpretation have continued to the present day.

p. 345
Biblical criticism
Jesus of history

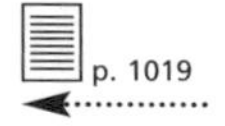

p. 1019

Secularization
Modernism

The growth of secular states, a diversity of cultures contained by Christianity, and an increasing individual freedom within Christianity has also led to controversy. In the nineteenth century the Roman Catholic Church condemned the rise of secular learning and political freedoms in the 1864 Syllabus of Errors and the 1907 condemnation of Modernism. The Second Vatican Council brought certain new definitions of authority, yet individual theologians may be disciplined for teaching in conflict with the Roman Catholic tradition. The claims of indigenous cultures in various parts of the world to interpret Christian teachings in the light of their traditions has also challenged certain doctrinal ideas. Some African Christians have wished to defend traditional ancestor rites. Finally, for other Christians, heresy – in an age of increasing individualism – ironically has become a self-chosen title to represent spiritual integrity and independent thinking over against any traditional institution.

J. REBECCA LYMAN

Harold Brown, *Heresies. Heresy and Orthodoxy in the History of the Church*, Grand Rapids, MI: Hendrickson Publishers 1998; Virginia Burrus, *The Making of a Heretic*, Berkeley: University of California Press 1995; David Christie-Murray, *A History of Heresy*, Oxford: OUP 1989; Malcolm Lambert, *Medieval Heresy. Popular Movements from the Gregorian Reform to the Reformation*, Oxford: Blackwell 1992; Pietro Redondi, *Galileo Heretic*, Princeton: Princeton University Press 1987; Maurice Wiles, *Archetypal Heresy. Arianism Through the Centuries*, Oxford: OUP 2001

Theology

Hermeneutical theology

Biblical criticism

'Hermeneutical' comes from the Greek verb *hermeneuein*, which means 'interpret, understand, translate, explain'. When theology, as responsible talk of God, is called hermeneutical, the adjective means that it essentially has to do with interpretation and understanding and is best understood from this perspective.

Friedrich Schleiermacher

We can see this most simply, first, from the fact that from earliest days theology in the Christian sense has been devoted to the interpretation of the Bible. Down the centuries theologians have laboured to interpret the biblical texts, and make them speak to new times in a new way. They have developed different methods of doing this. The first beginnings of interpretation and understanding – which are themselves the subject of reflections and narratives – are to be found in the Bible itself. Thus for example in Luke 24, on the way to Emmaus, the risen Jesus himself becomes the interpreter of scripture, and in Acts 8.30 Philip raises *the* hermeneutical question when he asks the Ethiopian court official, 'Do you understand what you are reading?'

But because the basic issue is to see how the word of God in scripture addresses people and makes demands on them, hermeneutical theology is also concerned with those to whom this word is expressed. In this sense, hermeneutical theology is bound up with all too human procedures. In fact, even in daily life we are confronted with questions about interpretation and understanding: 'How am I to interpret that?', 'What did you mean by that?', 'Did you understand what I said?' These are everyday hermeneutical questions. In asking them we are already engaged in hermeneutics, perhaps without knowing it.

We are most intensively engaged in hermeneutics when we ask ourselves how we understand our lives. And this question is posed time and again as we deal with biblical texts. These texts become mirrors in which we can understand ourselves. The French philosopher Paul Ricoeur once remarked, 'To understand a text is to understand oneself in the face of this text.' In this sense the category of self-understanding is fundamental to hermeneutical theology.

Understanding always moves to and fro between two poles: on the one hand the text in its historical context and on the other the reader in his or her concrete historical situation. Thus hermeneutical questions are raised for theology in all its disciplines, from exegesis through church history and systematic theology to practical theology: these questions aim to make the ancient text once again living proclamation.

Over the course of the centuries, the idea became established that a specific hermeneutic must be used for scripture. Early Protestant orthodoxy spoke of a sacred, as opposed to a profane, hermeneutic. Modern historical criticism posed a radical challenge to this: it claimed the freedom to read the biblical texts like any other documents of human civilization. This principle has gone down in the history of hermeneutics as the Semler principle, so-called after an eighteenth-century German exegete. It did away with the difference between a sacred and a profane hermeneutic and opened the way for a universal hermeneutic. At the beginning of the nineteenth century the German theologian Friedrich Schleiermacher deliberately adopted this approach, thus opening up the possibility of making hermeneutics too a key topic of philosophy and the humanities. Interestingly, in this context as well as talk of a 'hermeneutical theology' as opposed to other theologies, there is also talk of a 'theological hermeneutic'. What is the specific character of such a hermeneutic by comparison with other hermeneutics?

Modern historical criticism requires that the text should be read in accordance with critical rules and a strictly defined method. Its meaning is to be ascertained in its historical context, independently of any faith that can be evoked in us by it today: any such faith must remain in the background. Here the historical distance which separates us from the text is deliberately emphasized. The text is made an alien entity, so that it is not appropriated or commandeered too hastily.

In the twentieth century the aspect of appropriation came to the fore once again as a result of the encounter between theological hermeneutics and existential philosophy. The programme for this was laid down by the theologian Rudolf Bultmann (in conversation with the philosopher Martin Heidegger), along with a variety of Bultmann's pupils like Ernst Fuchs and Gerhard Ebeling. Bultmann combined the use of modern historical criticism of the biblical texts with an existentialist interpretation of them. In other words, he argued that interpretation of the text is really achieved only when readers finally understand their own existences in the light of the text. Thus interest is concentrated on what is at stake in the text. Following Sören Kierkegaard, Bultmann calls this the existential message of the text, or its kerygma (from the Greek verb *kerussein*, 'proclaim').

On the basis of an intensive study of Martin Luther's theology and hermeneutics, Gerhard Ebeling made it his task to think through the whole of theology as hermeneutical theology. His basic category is the word-event: in the word a presence of God comes about which creates faith in men and women as a completely new trust which has an effect on the whole of their lives.

What are the present challenges for hermeneutical theology?

Certainly today there is a far greater plurality of methods. For a long time historical criticism had a strong monopoly; today, however, there are many more approaches, and that has also led to new ways of dealing with the biblical texts. Thus today historical criticism is being supplemented in a fruitful way by insights from structuralist linguistics, rhetoric, narrative theory or reader theories from literary criticism. Sometimes, however, the new approaches also deliberately compete with historical criticism and enter into critical discussion with it. That is the case, for example, with the psychoanalytical interpretation of biblical texts, which detect in them traces of psychological developments and the beginnings of ways of assimilating them better. Socio-political interpretation is a comparable approach: this interprets the texts in terms of balances of power and structures of oppression and at the same time looks in them for models for social and political action (as for example in the various liberation theologies).

On the basis of these different methods, critical questions are now being asked about the modern presuppositions of theological hermeneutics, for example by theologians grappling with the hermeneutical implications of 'postmodern' thought. These relate to the claim to universality, which is challenged in order to put more emphasis on the fundamental, concrete context, both of the text and its interpreter. A one-sided orientation on the intention of the text or its author is also thought to be difficult. Rather, attention needs to be paid to what the text expresses in a hidden or distorted way (Paul Ricoeur calls this the 'hermeneutics of suspicion').

Postmodern theology

That makes it necessary to think through once again insights which were thought to be well-established, for example the relationship between text and reader. In classical hermeneutics it is assumed that the text has a single, original meaning, which is hidden in it and can be extracted from it through exegesis as so to speak a finished product. Today, an often ambivalent diversity of possible meanings can be detected in the text which depend upon readers as well. Readers play an active part in the construction of meaning by their reception of the text. The meaning of a text does not simply lie in a text as a finished product, but comes into being in the constant interaction between the effect of the text on the reader and the creative reception of the text by the reader.

The ecumenical dialogue also has to be taken up afresh in a hermeneutical perspective, in two directions. First, the question arises how far hermeneutics can become a method of ecumenical dialogue: here work is now being done on an 'ecumenical hermeneutics'. On the other hand, there is also a need to engage in inter-confessional dialogue in connection with hermeneutics. Roman Catholic and Orthodox hermeneutics shape their interpretation of scripture more strongly by the principle of tradition, associated with the councils or the teaching authority of the Pope, the magisterium. By contrast, Reformation hermeneutics claims scripture itself as a principle for criticizing the tradition on the basis of its 'scripture alone', *sola scriptura*. Work needs to be done on these differences in the light of the new hermeneutical approaches.

Ecumenical movement

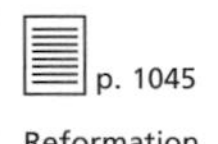

p. 1045

Reformation

The abiding concern of hermeneutical theology is always with men and women as they are addressed and challenged by God to discover themselves and be themselves, through all these questions and considerations, and all the problems that they raise. 'You are the man,' says the prophet Nathan to King David in 2 Samuel 12.7, after telling him a parable as a mirror for understanding himself before God.

PIERRE BÜHLER

Werner G. Jeanrond, *Theological Hermeneutics. Development and Significance*, New York: Crossroad Publishing Company 1991 and London: SCM Press 1994; Anthony C. Thiselton, *New Horizons in Hermeneutics. The Theory and Practice of Transforming*

Liberation theology

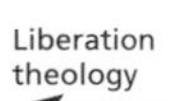

Biblical Reading, Grand Rapids, MI: Zondervan 1992; David Tracy, *Plurality and Ambiguity. Hermeneutics, Religion, Hope*, San Francisco: Harper & Row and London: SCM Press 1987

Mysticism

Hildegard of Bingen

Women in Christianity

Hildegard of Bingen (1098–1179) is one of the most significant women in Christian history. An influential abbess, mystic, prophet, preacher, scholar, composer, poet, dramatist, scientist and adviser to churchmen, kings and emperors, she would have stood out in any age. As a woman who took a public role in the male-dominated church of the medieval period, her achievements are nothing short of remarkable.

Some might argue that Hildegard's life represents a brief anomaly in the history of Christianity. Hildegard was born on the eve of the twelfth century – a time which witnessed a renaissance in the European economy and European society and a development of church organizations and religious thought. Her life epitomizes this renaissance in the diversity of her writings and activities. She was born in Bermersheim, a German settlement not far from Mainz, the tenth child of parents of noble birth, and just before her eighth birthday she was dedicated to the Benedictine monastery of Disibodenberg.

p. 788

Hildegard suffered ill heath all through her life and scholars have speculated that this, along with her prophetic gifts, led to her being placed, not in a typical convent setting, but with the anchoress Jutta, who occupied a cell attached to the monastery. This might seem a cruel decision, given that the life of an anchoress was to be spent in solitary confinement. Yet the fame of Jutta's piety was such that by the time Hildegard took her vows (*c.*1113), the anchoress' cell had grown into a thriving convent. Under Jutta's care Hildegard received religious instruction. Scholars may disagree on exactly what Hildegard learned from Jutta, but during this time she became familiar with the works of Aristotle, Augustine, Boethius and Isidore of Seville, as well as contemporary scientific writers.

p. 301

Jutta died in 1136 and Hildegard was unanimously elected to succeed her. By all accounts she was an authoritative and capable leader. In 1150, despite opposition from the abbot of Disibodenberg, Hildegard founded her own independent convent, Rupertsberg, on the banks of the Rhine near Bingen. Such was its success that Hildegard later founded a daughter house near Eibingen, which she visited twice a week until her death.

While Hildegard excelled in her demanding role as abbess, she is best known as a mystic and prophet. In 1141, she stated that she was commanded by God to reveal her visionary and prophetic gifts to the world. Although the medieval church was able to point to female prophets in both the Old and New Testaments, the emergence of mysticism and the role played by women in this movement was a new phenomenon. Christian mysticism was seen as a divine gift – a direct communion between an individual and the divine. Although this experience could be augmented through prayer, fasting, study and meditation, it could not take place unless one had been chosen by God to receive it.

p. 804

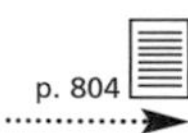

It may seem surprising, given women's limited public role in the church, that we find a fair number of women mystics from this later medieval period. Perhaps it was the very nature of mysticism that made it seem less threatening to male church leaders, but credit should also be given to the women themselves who, despite the misogyny of the times, were able to convince churchmen of the genuineness of their experiences. Hildegard's public revelations came to be accepted by all, including Bernard of Clairvaux and Pope Eugene III (the latter confirmed Hildegard's visions at the Synod of Trier, 1147–8). Known as the 'Sibyl of the Rhine', Hildegard drew followers from all corners of Germany and France who wanted to hear her words and advice.

But Hildegard was no mere cult figure. Her recognition by the church and, in particular, her religious writings demonstrate the depth of her experience and the scholarly foundation of her work. These writings embraced a wide range of subjects and have been compared to the works of Dante and William Blake. Her two major books, *Scivias* (Know the Ways) and *Liber divinorum operum* (Book of Divine Works), serve as a record of her visions and of her own critical interpretation of these experiences. Some manuscripts included illustrations of the visions, and it is thought that at least one might have been prepared under Hildegard's direct supervision (although only a facsimile of this manuscript survives). She also wrote a discourse on human vices and virtues, *Liber vitae meritorum* (The Book of Life's Rewards), commentaries on the Gospels, the Athanasian Creed, and the Benedictine rule as well as the first known liturgical morality drama *Ordo Virtutum* (Play of the Virtues) and two saint's lives, those of St Disibod and St Rupert.

While these works might cast Hildegard as a subject fit only for theologians and 'serious' scholars, she has recently gained popular interest through her other works, most notably her music. Her *Symphonia harmoniae caelestium revelationum* (The Symphony of the Harmony of Heavenly Revelations) is a collection of 77 songs including hymns, responsories, sequences and antiphons. Hildegard's compositions were first popularized in 1982 with an LP entitled 'A Feather on the Breath of God'. Her lyrical words and inspiring melodies go well beyond conventional Gregorian chant and twelfth-century poetry.

Moreover, her talents were just as appreciated in her own time as today, and several of her works were commissioned by fellow monastic institutions.

Hildegard is also recognized as Germany's first woman doctor and scientist. This honour relates to her two scientific treatises, *Physica* (Natural History or Book of Simple Medicine) and *Causae et curae* (Causes and Cures or Book of Compound Medicine). The first is an encyclopaedic study of the natural world and its medical applications, and the second a work on the human body and the causes and treatments of disease. This second treatise is particularly interesting as it not only deals frankly with issues of gynaecology and sexuality, but also counters some of the church's long-held views on these issues. Hildegard's scientific inclinations also led her, for some unknown reason, to create a language, a mixture of Latin and German, which consisted of an alphabet of 23 characters and a list of 900 words. Her secular writings may not have made a great impact upon her own age, but they do show us the workings of a logical and enquiring mind at a time when experimentation and scientific methodology were seldom employed and rarely encouraged.

Even with this long list of written accomplishments, Hildegard might still be overlooked in terms of her public influence had it not been for the fact that she did not live in isolation. Her correspondence includes letters to and from no fewer than four successive popes, Bernard of Clairvaux, Thomas Becket, nine other archbishops, nine bishops, 49 abbots, 23 abbesses and numerous priests, monks, nuns and religious communities. Hildegard also wrote and received letters from two emperors and many kings and queens of Europe. These letters display a knowledge and understanding of the religious and political issues of her day. She chided Emperor Frederick Barbarossa for his dispute with Pope Alexander III; she advised Queen Eleanor of Aquitaine on her recent divorce from Louis VII; and she warned Henry II of England of the consequences of failing to rule his kingdom justly. Hildegard was often asked to give theological pronouncements on difficult issues and in her advice to churchmen she was heeded as an equal and, at times, a superior authority. Even Bernard, a man who had little time for women, wrote that he could not presume to instruct or advise Hildegard since by her mystical experiences she had been elevated above himself and indeed, the whole of humankind. For any churchman to gain such recognition would have been extraordinary; for a woman it was astounding.

Nor was Hildegard content to carry on her public work from the cloister. Regardless of church injunctions against nuns leaving their convents, she travelled widely to Cologne, Trier, Würzburg, Bamberg, Frankfurt, Rothenburg, Metz and several other towns and monasteries of Northern Europe. Many of these visits were in fact

God's people on earth building churches, from the eleventh/twelfth-century Latin codex, *Visions of St Hildegard of Bingen, Book of the Works of God*

preaching tours – an extraordinary venture for a woman of this period, as the church had long condemned women preaching in church or speaking in public on church matters. Nevertheless, she is said to have addressed church men and women within monasteries and chapter houses and occasionally to have preached in public, all with the full support of the church.

This was achieved despite Hildegard's frequent bouts of ill health and in addition to the duties and responsibilities entailed in the running of a successful and active convent. Her management of her convent was not only time-consuming but, sometimes, controversial. On one occasion she was criticized for allowing only the daughters of the nobility to join, and her nuns were accused of dressing up in a degree of finery not in keeping with the Benedictine rule. Hildegard vigorously defended both her nuns' attire and her admittance policies, but her arguments may perhaps have been more reflective of her notions of class than of theology. In the last year of her life she was again involved in a dispute, this time with the churchmen of Mainz. The controversy concerned the burial at Rupertsberg of a noble whom the Mainz clergy claimed was excommunicate at the time of his death. Hildegard was requested to exhume the body from the consecrated ground, but she claimed that the man had been reconciled to the church before death, and refused to comply. Rupertsberg was placed under interdict. Hildegard, however, stood her ground and after months of correspondence the interdict was finally lifted in March of 1179. Six months later, Hildegard died at the age of 81.

Ecotheology
Postmodern theology
p. 1077

Hildegard never received formal canonization. The process was begun in the 1220s, but foundered in 1243 for reasons unknown. A local cult flourished, however, and Hildegard's name was added to the Roman martyrology in the sixteenth century. Her convent, Rupertsberg, was destroyed in 1632 during the Thirty Years War. Its daughter house at Eibingen carried on in a much-depleted state until 1803. Yet the memory of their founder was not forgotten and the cult of Hildegard survived. Today she is recognized as the patron saint of Eibingen, and in 1904 a new convent was dedicated to Hildegard near this site.

Wars of religion
Pilgrimage

S. J. ALLEN

Mark Atherton (ed), *Selected Writings of Hildegard of Bingen*, Harmondsworth: Penguin Books 2001; Sabina Flanagan, *Hildegard of Bingen. A Visionary Life*, London and New York: Routledge 1989; Fiona Maddocks, *Hildegard of Bingen. The Woman of Her Age*, New York: Image Books 2003; Barbara Newman, *Sister of Wisdom – St Hildegard's Theology of the Feminine*, Berkeley: University of California Press 1997; Hildegard of Bingen, 'A Feather on the Breath of God', Hyperion CDA66039, 1984

Hinduism and Christianity

Christians encountering Hindu religious life for the first time are often bewildered by the sheer profusion of imagery. So many divine names and sacred stories, complex rituals and esoteric metaphysics – and much more – to be made sense of. In the West and among modern Hindus in India religious practice has been greatly simplified, with more exotic traditions curtailed. Yet, it is precisely the mystique of its otherness, its difference from Western Christian thought and culture, that has attracted such large numbers of Westerners to Hindu religion in the second half of the twentieth century. The one million globally who have become Hare Krishna devotees, or the estimated ten million attracted by the acclaimed spiritual powers of the South Indian 'God-man' Satya Sai Baba, are only part of the many who have aimed to move to a higher level of spiritual awareness and energy by accepting the authority of a modern Hindu guru. Western New Age thinking and values may be well adrift from authentic Hindu spiritual tradition, but the practice of yoga and the cultivation of inner powers, belief in karma, avatars, reincarnation, mantras and suchlike are clearly indebted in part to Hindu influence. Even eco-sensitive spiritualities and the more relativist and pluralist world-view of postmodernism have close affinity with important strands of Hindu thinking. Emigration from India during colonial and more recent times, resulting in the spread of some six million Hindus across the globe, is just one reason for these trends in today's cultural mix.

New Age movements

In Hindu tradition there are many strikingly different ways in which sacred power manifests itself. In India countless holy places – by rivers and their points of confluence, on hills and even Himalayan glaciers, in cities and in forests – invite pilgrimage with the story of divine epiphany there. Gaining 'vision' (*darshan*) of God in that place, 'seeing' the central image, is the climax of every pilgrim journey, more important than acquiring merit from it. The whole year, too, has its many sacred moments, some days and seasons being dangerously inauspicious, others times of festive celebration, such as Divali ('row of lights') with its central theme that light overcomes darkness. Each great moment of transition in life's journey is also marked by sacred ritual. And all these acts become potent through the reciting of sacred verses (*mantras*), usually from the huge corpus of Sanskrit scriptures of which the Vedas are primary. In these ways the life of Hindus is nurtured by all-pervasive structures of the sacred.

The many names of gods and heroes may mystify the outsider, but devout Hindus increasingly emphasize that in reality there is one God of all. Two great gods in particular have captured Hindu devotion. Around Vishnu ('Pervader') and Siva ('Auspicious') strong communities of faith have gathered, and at least from about the time of Jesus, great waves of passionate devotion have swept India. Vishnu followers usually worship him in one or other of his ten most important avatars ('descents'), especially as Rama and Krishna. Rama's reign on earth, after many heroic struggles, is celebrated as a perfect expression of the *dharma*, or 'right ordering', looked for in all cosmic life. But many devotees also feel overwhelming warmth of love for Rama, as they do for Krishna, the passionate divine lover who enchants by his flute-playing and dancing. 'Have faith in nothing but me alone; I will set you free from all your sins,' is his message to those who love and trust him. Siva, too, though celebrated in stories depicting striking paradoxes such as his ascetic and erotic character, is especially loved as the 'Lord of Dance' and as the one who drinks and holds in his throat the poison meant for his followers.

It is not only ecstatic poetry and dance, pilgrim journeys, festivals and sacred ritual that express the Hindu spirit. There are also the astonishingly sophisticated efforts to express the transcendent dimensions of Hindu faith in systematic forms of discursive reasoning. Christian scholars have reflected on two more than any others. *Vedanta* means the 'end (or intention) of the scriptures'. The non-dualist (*advaita*) interpretation by the philosopher Sankara (*c.*700-*c.* 750) and the 'non-dualism (defined by) distinctions' of Ramanuja (*c.*1017–1137) have dominated this Hindu theological discipline. Put simply, for both these teachers all life in essence shares unbroken continuity of being. For Sankara, though, anything less than unconditioned oneness of inner selfhood and consciousness is tinged with unreality and illusory *maya*. For the theistic vision of Ramanuja, the relationships intrinsic to creation and our social existence are ultimately real. Yes, perceptions unenlightened by divine love are imperfect, but they are not unreal. The basis for this relational vision, then, is both the wonderful greatness of God and God's 'inseparable bond', first with his 'love-drowned' devotees and then with all creation. Of the interlinked triad – God, souls, material creation – none must ever be seen as less than completely real. Naturally, the embodying of a divine avatar (i.e. a deity in human form), too, is completely real. A self-body image is dominant here: this whole universe is the 'inseparably related body' of God, its inmost Self.

Clearly these are not only very distinct ways of interpreting Hindu scriptures and of envisioning life. They have, in differing ways, provided crucial insights for Christians in India seeking more contextual expressions of faith.

It is often argued, though, that Hinduism is not a set of beliefs, nor any particular spiritual path, but the living out of a very broad range of cultural values. Again *dharma* is the word encapsulating this 'right ordering' of life. Everything has its rightful place. For example, society is ordered hierarchically into castes – far more complex than the traditional four: Brahmins (empowered with sacred knowledge), Kshatriyas (with warrior and princely power), Vaishyas (for commerce and economic power), Sudras (the toiling and artisan 'feet' in this social body). Each soul's *karma* – the inescapable effect of actions in past lives – determines which status a person is born into. However, the role of caste and belief in *karma* is changing rapidly. The militant World Council of Hindus (VHP) declares that caste must have no determining place in Hindu life. Yet, the humiliating social status of many of the 20 million once known as 'out-caste' (now Dalits) is still a reality, especially in some rural areas.

Hindu *dharma* has at least three more important aspects. Giving to the poor and needy is called *dharma*. Then, the protection of the cow, Hinduism's most sacred animal, has always been at the centre of 'non-injury/compassion to all life'. Recently militant Hindus have again made this a rallying cry in opposition to Muslims. 'Non-injury/compassion to all life', a maxim so beloved of 'great-souls' (*mahatmas*) of the past, has tended to be forgotten of late. And there are the four life-stages: celibate study of scripture and sources of dharmic knowledge, family life and worldly duties, a period of 'refuge' in the forest, and at last wandering free from all dharmic duties in search of the final goal, *moksha* (liberation).

Christian attitudes towards Hindu thought and practice have been far from uniform. In Britain's parliament in 1813 the evangelical social crusader William Wilberforce described Hindu gods as 'absolute monsters of lust' – not atypical of one prominent Christian perception, as is seen in the derogatory language used from the sixteenth century onwards by numerous missionaries, Catholic and Protestant. Others, though, especially after the early twentieth century, have not only been deeply appreciative of aspects of Hindu spirituality; in some cases their scholarship has even enhanced Hindu self-understanding. Many more have formed binding friendships with Hindus, that between C. F. Andrews and M. K. Gandhi being an outstanding example.

With the globalizing of Hindu communities, in educational, medical, technological, commercial, literary and media life, throughout the Western world today a Hindu presence is now commonplace. By far the most significant Hindu-Christian encounter, however, is that between the nearly 30 million Indians who are Christian and their fellow-Indian Hindus. Three interlinked factors have made for strained relationships in recent years. Some 60 per cent of Indian Christians originate from what most now call the Dalit ('crushed', 'broken') communities. Indeed, leaders – Christian theologians among them – from the many distinct Dalit groups seek to create a common Dalit identity as the only way to build up their people's self-confidence and liberate them from past oppression. The anti-Hindu ideology of B. R. Ambedkar (1891–1956), a key figure in shaping the Indian constitution and a champion of the outcastes, is their main inspiration, but biblical liberation motifs are also prominent. Secondly, militant Hindu nationalists, recently having become politically powerful, argue that all Indians are 'Hindus'. To be born in the sacred motherland that is Bharat means that culturally one is bound to Hindu norms, values and world-view. This, thirdly, means that those religions not indigenous to India – Christianity and Islam in particular – are suspect as anti-national, and their adherents are told by some exponents of Hindutva, the intolerant nationalist Hindu ideology, either to identify themselves as Hindus or leave India. In particular, attempts to convert Hindus, including Dalits and tribal peoples, to these 'non-Indian' religions are opposed with increasing vigour.

Politically, then, the situation is explosive, though some

social analysts urge a clear distinction between militant Hindutva and genuine Hindus. In any case, at a social level friendships are frequent, many cultural values and events are shared, and interfaith reflection still takes place, especially among those Christian theologians committed to more authentic contextualization of their faith. But the tensions are increasingly felt.

Even Christian attempts at inculturation in worship or spiritual lifestyle are suspect in the eyes of today's militant Hindus. Becoming more 'Hindu-like' is seen merely as a strategy to make more converts from among Hindus. Radical Christian Dalits, too, resent any reversion to classical cultural forms, theologically or liturgically, as the 'Brahmanizing' of the church, in other words as a return to the symbols of their former oppression. The history of the struggle to be more 'Indian' began with the remarkable Italian Jesuit, Robert de Nobili (in India 1605–50), accused by Portuguese ecclesiastics in Goa – intent on replicating the religious life of their homeland – of duplicity and fatal compromise with Hinduism when he aimed for the conversion of high-caste Hindus by adopting many of their ways of worship, dress and lifestyle. Theologically far more sophisticated continuities were worked out by the self-styled 'Hindu-Catholic' Brahmabandhav Upadhyay (1861–1907). An example is his interpretation of the dynamic mystery of the Trinity in terms of Vedanta's *sat-chit-ananda* (the supreme One as 'being-consciousness-bliss'). Many others have similarly sought to integrate Catholic and Hindu contemplative ideas and practices, setting up Hindu-style ashrams, i.e. places of spiritual retreat, and being seen as guru-like teachers. To Western Christians seeking a higher plane of spiritual being, Shantivanam ashram in South India, led for many years by Bede Griffiths, has been an important centre.

Trinity

Christianity in North America

At the liturgical level an 'Indian mass' has integrated elements of Hindu worship: removing footwear, sitting cross-legged, burning camphor, scattering flower petals, singing indigenous *bhajans* (devotional songs), praising divine names. More contextually fitting iconography and wider forms of creative expression by artists such as Jyoti Sahi is another important source for looking at the interpenetration of Christian faith and Indian cultures (see colour plate 21). The Dancing Lord, for example, is a frequent image in Sahi's work. And primal imagery is more often found than classical forms.

Iconography

Christianity in Latin America

Christian-Hindu dialogue takes place at many levels in India, from everyday neighbourly points of meeting to the more specialist forms mentioned above. Globally, too, there is dialogue – as at the World Council of Churches, in the journal *Hindu-Christian Studies*, in centres such as that for Vaishnava and Christian studies at Oxford or for Dharmic studies at Cambridge, or in numerous more local and grassroots meeting points. At times effective dialogue is hampered by an uncritical complacency: 'But in essence there are no differences; each is but a path to the same goal; in Hinduism all these paths are found, though most perfectly in Vedanta.' Equally obstructive, as Hindus perceive it, is a Christian absolutism insisting that only in Christ is there fullness of truth and salvation. Even so, fruitful meeting-points have been found and are surely crucial for the future of both faiths.

ERIC LOTT

Wesley Ariarajah, *Hindus and Christians: A Century of Protestant Ecumenical Thought*, Grand Rapids, MI: Eerdmans 1991; H. Coward (ed), *Hindu-Christian Dialogue: Perspectives and Encounters*, Maryknoll, NY: Orbis Books 1989; Diana Eck, *Encountering God: A Spiritual Journey from Bozeman to Banares*, Boston: Beacon Press 1993; Klaus Klostermaier, *A Survey of Hinduism*, Albany, NY: Suny Press [2]1994; Julius Lipner, *Hindus: Their Religious Beliefs and Practices*, London: Routledge 1994

Hispanic Christianity

In his Apostolic Exhortation *Ecclesia in America*, Pope John Paul II challenges all Americans to think of themselves as one entity, one 'America'. John Paul II's challenge is today more appropriate than ever, given the recently-released US Census Bureau projections which indicate that by the end of this century Hispanics will constitute one third of the US population.

The ongoing Latin American 'reconquest' of the United States has particular significance for the Roman Catholic Church in the United States. Between two-thirds and three-quarters of all US Hispanics are Roman Catholic. In ten years, a majority of all Catholics in the United States will be Spanish-speaking.

At the same time, one should remember that the 'US Latino' or 'US Hispanic' community is, in reality, numerous different communities with different histories. The largest numerically, the Mexican-American community, actually predates the contemporary United States. Mexicans first became Mexican *Americans* not when they emigrated to the United States but when, in 1848, the United States annexed half of what was then Mexico. Thus Mexicans did not cross the border; the border crossed them.

The second largest group, Puerto Ricans, have their own unique history, one that also involves conquest. As a result of the Treaty of Paris, which ended the Spanish American War in 1898, Spain ceded the island to the United States, and Puerto Rico eventually became a commonwealth of the US. Puerto Ricans are thus United States citizens, but without representation in the US Congress. The same treaty gave the United States increased influence over the government and economy of Cuba, though Cuba remained technically independent. While Cubans emigrated to the United States throughout the twentieth century, the largest influx occurred after Fidel Castro took power in 1959. Cuban Americans are the third largest Latino group. While all three groups can be found throughout the United States, Mexican Americans are primarily concentrated in the Southwest and Midwest, Puerto Ricans in the Northeast, and Cuban Americans in Florida.

Another important difference – one becoming increasingly important – is that of religion. Though historically a small minority in Latin America, the mainline Protestant churches which gained influence in the nineteenth century throughout the continent are today joined by the burgeoning evangelical and Pentecostal communities which form an increasingly visible and influential part of both Latin American and US Hispanic Christianity. Between 20 and 40 per cent of Hispanics belong to Evangelical or Pentecostal churches. At the same time, such figures can be misleading, since many Latinos are what religious scholars call 'pluriconfessional', that is, they participate in different churches simultaneously (e.g., attending Roman Catholic mass on Sunday and Baptist Bible study on Wednesday evening). Moreover, Latino Protestantism usually has a certain Latino 'flavour' that reflects its Roman Catholic cultural ambience and heritage.

Despite the differences, however, common threads run throughout the histories of the various US Latino communities. All Latinos share, for instance, the historical heritage and experience of '*mestizaje*' (racial-cultural mixture). The Latin American culture and people are the products of five centuries of racial and cultural intermixing. In North America, the British colonists exterminated the indigenous people; to the South, the Spanish killed millions of Amerindians, either through the illnesses brought from Europe or through outright violence, but the Spanish also intermingled with the native peoples.

In the Caribbean region, the mixture was less between Spanish and Indians than between the Spanish colonists and the Africans brought to the islands as slaves. The result of this history has been a culture that still reflects the influence not only of Spanish culture but also of African and/or Amerindian cultures. And, of course, as Latinos settle in the United States, a 'second *mestizaje*' takes place: immigrants assimilate influences from the larger US culture. Thus, living as part of a *mestizo* people means always living on the border, culturally and psychologically; one never feels completely at home on either side.

This same *mestizo* heritage is reflected in the religious faith of Latinos. The world of Latino religiosity is a world of 'both/and' rather than a world of 'either/or'. This 'both/and' world is manifested, above all, in the *mestizo* character of Latino popular religion. At the very heart of the Mexican experience of *mestizaje*, for example, stands the figure of Our Lady of Guadalupe. The historical experience of *mestizaje* originated in the violence of the conquest, in the violation of indigenous women by Spanish conquistadores. As the child of violence, the child of the violent European conqueror and the violated indigenous woman, the *mestizo/a* has historically suffered scorn and humiliation, which he or she has internalized in the form of self-deprecation and self-hatred. In his classic work *The Labyrinth of Solitude*, the great Mexican poet and writer Octavio Paz poignantly described this process whereby the dehumanization suffered at the hands of European conquerors becomes, over generations, a deep-seated self-hatred. The child of the conquistador father and the violated mother is ultimately ashamed of both parents who gave him or her birth through this primordial act of violence.

Protestantism

Evangelicals
Pentecostalism

p. 733

However, the appearance of Our Lady of Guadalupe in December 1531 signals a turning-point, or axial point, in the history of Latin American *mestizaje*. In the Guadalupe event, '*la Virgen morena*' ('the dark-skinned virgin') appears to an indigenous man, Juan Diego, on a hill outside what is now Mexico City. The narrative recounts several encounters between '*la Morenita*' and Juan Diego, in the course of which she repeatedly assures him that, despite his own sense of worthlessness *vis-à-vis* the Spaniards, he is her most beloved, favoured child. As she continues to reassure him, Juan Diego gradually develops a sense of his own dignity as a child of God. In their first encounter, she commanded Juan Diego to ask the Spanish bishop in Mexico City to build a church on the hill where she had appeared. Juan Diego resisted, arguing that he was not worthy to be charged with such a mission. The Lady insisted, so Juan Diego eventually went to the bishop's palace to make the request. At first, the bishop would not even receive the poor indigenous man. Later, the bishop received him, but did not believe him. Finally, the Lady gave Juan Diego a 'sign' to take with him, a bouquet of flowers she had ordered him to pick from a nearby hilltop. Since all knew that such flowers could not grow at that time of the year, they would recognize the miraculous nature of the sign. So Juan Diego put the flowers in his *tilma*, or cloak. When the indigenous man arrived at the bishop's palace and opened the cloak to reveal the flowers, another miraculous sign appeared, an image of the Virgin imprinted on the cloak. Stirred and convinced by these signs, the bishop relented and ordered that the Lady's wish be granted.

Here the traditional roles are reversed: the dark-

Mission
Reformation
Counter-Reformation

skinned Lady and the indigenous man themselves become the messengers of God, evangelizers to the Spanish Roman Catholic bishop, who is portrayed as the one in need of conversion. In addition, the narrative and accompanying images also exemplify a fascinating religious, symbolic *mestizaje*. Tepeyac, the hill on which the Virgin appeared, was well known to the Nahuas (the indigenous people to whom Juan Diego belonged) as the place where they worshipped the mother goddess Tonantzín. Likewise, the Virgin's clothing was adorned with a mixture of Christian and Nahua symbols.

Council
Devotions
Pilgrimage

According to the Mexican-American theologian Virgilio Elizondo, the Mexican nation as we now know it could not have emerged had it not been for the Guadalupe event. In 1531, the indigenous peoples of Mexico had been destroyed by the conquering Spaniards; those who had survived the onslaught were demoralized and in despair. It was at this very moment of deepest anguish that Our Lady of Guadalupe appeared, to accompany them in their suffering, confirm them in their dignity as children of God, and herald the dawn of a new era of hope. Indeed, the image that Juan Diego saw and that, to this day, remains emblazoned on the cloak as it appears in the Basilica of Our Lady of Guadalupe in Mexico City, is that of a pregnant woman (unique in the history of appearances of Mary). *La Morenita* gives birth to a new people, a *mestizo* people. Moreover, dark-skinned Guadalupe's ability to relate the Christian faith to the indigenous world-view, adopting and adapting indigenous symbols to the Christian world-view, made possible the evangelization of Mexico.

p. 533

Though paradigmatic, Our Lady of Guadalupe is hardly the only example of the *mestizaje* that has taken place not only in race and culture but also in religion. And it is precisely in its religious faith that the US Latino/a community most fundamentally affirms its distinct history and identity as a people of God – and, therefore, a people of dignity – in the face of marginalization and oppression.

Enlightenment

The term 'popular religion' denotes much more than a series of religious practices, symbols, narratives, devotions, etc. Rather, the terms refer to a particular world-view, an epistemological framework that infuses and defines *every* aspect of the community's life. Popular religion is not only a particular way of being 'religious'; it is also a particular way of living life. Indeed, the very distinction between 'religion' and life is itself called into question by a faith that is at the heart of every aspect of the community's life. Arguably, then, even that minority of Latinos and Latinas who do not consider themselves explicitly religious reflect – even if only implicitly or obscurely – the world-view, values, epistemological perspectives underlying Latino popular religion. For popular religion lies at the very origins, the very heart of the *mestizo* Latino/a culture itself.

The Christianity that was first brought to the Americas from Europe was a pre-Reformation Iberian, medieval Christianity. In this form of Christianity, religious faith was expressed and lived out primarily through images, symbols, rituals, and religious practices; these were what defined Christian identity. Though the Protestant and Catholic Reformations took place in Europe in the sixteenth century, these did not begin to make an impact on the life of Latin American Christianity until generations later. As European Christians became increasingly concerned with drawing clear lines between what was Roman Catholic (or 'orthodox') and what was Protestant (or 'heretical'), post-Reformation Christianity attached increased importance to doctrines and confessional beliefs as criteria of 'orthodox' Christian faith. In Roman Catholicism, this emphasis on correct doctrine reached an apex in the Council of Trent. Yet Latin America did not experience the full impact of this evolution of Christianity from a faith primarily identified with religious practices, devotions, pilgrimages, symbols, narratives, etc., to a Tridentine faith primarily identified with dogma.

Moreover, the ritual-based Christianity that had taken hold in Latin America had found reinforcement, first, through the analogously ritual- and symbol-based religions of the Amerindians (these similarities thus facilitated the process of religious *mestizaje*) and, secondly, through the Baroque Catholicism that would be brought to the 'New World' by the Iberian colonizers of the seventeenth century. This latter exhibited a profoundly dramatic sense of life and the cosmos, as reflected in the many *autos sacramentales* of the period. Such a sense of life-as-theatre and the cosmos-as-stage reinforced the essentially *performative* character of Latin American Christianity, which had been inherited from both the original Iberian missionaries and the indigenous religions.

These popular religious practices reflect and express a particular world-view, one in which the human person sees himself or herself as part of a relational network and a temporal continuum embracing all of reality, material and spiritual. This organic, holistic world-view underlying US Latino culture is at odds with post-Enlightenment notions of time and space, the material and the spiritual, and the person's place within time and space, within the material and the spiritual dimensions of reality.

First, the world-view underlying these popular religious celebrations reflects a particular notion of the human person, a particular 'theological anthropology'. Indeed, this aspect is often what Euro-Americans find most striking about US Latino popular religion, namely, its decidedly communal character. Whether *vis-à-vis* his or her family, *barrio* (district), ancestors or God, the Latino/a

AUTOS SACRAMENTALES

This Spanish term can be translated literally as 'sacramental acts'. The *autos sacramentales* began in Spain around the fifteenth century as dramas, presented at the feast of Corpus Christi, rather similar to the old English mystery plays. They were usually allegorical; sometimes not a single human character appeared. The characters were personifications of the virtues, the vices and the elements, like Faith, Sin, Air. In the sixteenth century they developed into dramatic presentations with the mystery of the eucharist as the theme. The most famous author of *autos sacramentales* was Pedro Calderón de la Barca (1600–81), who wrote around 70 of them, the most famous being *The Divine Orpheus*, *The Devotion to the Mass* and *The Captivity of the Ark*. The *auto sacramental* was preceded by a procession through the streets in which priests carried the eucharistic host under a decorated canopy. The performance was as splendid and elaborate as the locality could afford and with its music and splendour took a strong hold on people's imagination. The dramas were banned in Spain in 1765 by Charles III but continued to be presented in smaller towns there for some time and in Latin America.

A. A. Parker, *The Allegorical Dramas of Calderon: An Introduction to the 'Autos Sacramentales'*, Llandysul, Ceredigion: Dolphin Book Company (Tredwr) 1943

always exists in relationship. This is evident in the familial character of the *Dia de los Muertos* (Day of the Dead) celebrations, where so much care is taken to affirm and reinforce family ties, with both the living and the dead. It is also evident in the public, communal processions of Good Friday, where the people accompany Jesus Christ in his passion and accompany each other on the way of the cross, thereby identifying their own personal struggles with those of Jesus and their companions.

Even Jesus is not an autonomous, self-sufficient individual; even he is defined by his relationships, especially his relationship to his mother, Mary. The special place of Mary in Latino popular religion should thus come as no surprise; if everyone's identity is constituted by the relationships and communities which have birthed and nurtured them, then it is impossible truly to know Jesus without also knowing his family, especially his mother.

Another important way in which Latino popular religion reflects an organic world-view is by affirming the interconnectedness of the material and spiritual dimensions of reality. One of the most widely-recognized cultural manifestations of this particular characteristic of Latino culture is the so-called 'magical realism' of so much Latino and Latin American literature, where the historical and spiritual worlds often intermingle almost willy-nilly. Events and characters that to an outsider may appear as 'magical' or 'fantastic' are to the Latino merely one more aspect of everyday existence, one more dimension of reality, a reality rich and diverse enough to encompass the 'magical' as well as the mundane, the ethereal as well as the material. Thus, for example, the ritual of placing a deceased relative's favourite foods or photographs on his or her grave, or on a home altar, during the *Dia de los Muertos* celebrations in order to give pleasure to the deceased person presupposes a world-view in which there is no clear separation between the spiritual and material realms. Here, the deceased person is really present and participating in every aspect of our everyday lives. Indeed, what is called into question by such rituals is precisely any definition of the 'Real' which clearly circumscribes the Real, excluding from the definition any non-empirical reality. The non-empirical world is as 'real' as, if not more real than, the empirical world – without, however, denying the importance of the latter.

The popular religious traditions of Hispanic Christians thus embody pre-modern, pre-Enlightenment aspects of the Christian tradition that today are often dismissed in the face of modern individualistic and rationalist notions of faith. Where individualism can lead to loneliness or isolation, and rationalism to emotional aridity, the *manera de ser* of Hispanic Christians, the way they are, remains an important resource for modern Christians. What is called for, however, is a genuine openness to the presence of Hispanic Christians at the very heart of twenty-first-century Christianity. In the Americas particularly, that means a commitment to become a truly *American* Christianity that witnesses to a Christ who transforms human borders from barriers that exclude into privileged places of human and divine encounter.

Jesus

Mary

ROBERTO S. GOIZUETA

Ana María Díaz-Stevens and Anthony M. Stevens-Arroyo, *Recognizing the Latino Resurgence in US Religion*, Boulder, CO: Westview Press 1998; Timothy Matovina and Gary Riebe-Estrella (eds), *Horizons of the Sacred: Mexican Traditions in US Catholicism*, Ithaca, NY: Cornell University Press 2002; Peter Casarella and Raúl Gómez (eds), *El Cuerpo de Cristo: The Hispanic Presence in the US Catholic Church*, New York: Crossroad 1998; Justo González, *Mañana: Christian Theology from a Hispanic Perspective*, Nashville: Abingdon Press 1990

Historiography

God Jesus Story

Is God active in history, and, if so, why do the righteous suffer? Or is God a passive, suffering God, 'alongside' God's people in their troubles, and if so, what use is God? This is the dilemma of Christian historiography in its simplest form. After all, Christianity is a story (and 'story' is short for 'history'), the story of God's relationship with the world and with humankind. Jesus as God's 'Word' encapsulates both story and reason, and all Christian historical writing is composed of both the recounting of facts and evidence, and analysis and judgement about them. Historiography is the study of how people have recorded and analysed evidence about the past, usually to some extent in narrative (i.e. story) form.

Reformation

Who did the storytelling? And why did they attempt it? We can also ask, who is writing the story of Christianity today? What will our generation pass on to the future? Academic textbooks? Popular fiction? Newspapers? Internet sites? Christian historiography is usually a response to, a reflection on, the circumstances of a writer's own time; perhaps also a challenge to readers to rethink their Christian priorities and allegiances. In the present day, historiography can challenge the threat of fundamentalism, which is a deliberately unhistorical way of practising Christianity.

Bible

pp. 128–9

Karl Barth

Christianity is a historical faith. One of its great strengths is that it is often seen to be firmly rooted in reality which is open to proof. So however much difficulty scholars and scientists may have with God creating 'out of nothing', or with the historical basis for the history books of the Old Testament, few would deny that a man called Jesus lived and then was crucified, 'under Pontius Pilate'. What is more, the Christian Bible is arranged in such a way as to conform to the standard of a historical book. It has a beginning in Genesis (the Creation), and an end foretold in the Revelation to John (the Last Judgement). The individual scriptures of Christianity are arranged so as to emphasize this – they begin at the start of the human story, work their way through God choosing a people, keeping faith with them, chastening, rescuing and restoring them, and then (in the New Testament) fulfilling God's promises to them by sending God's Son Jesus the Messiah.

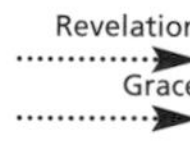

Revelation Grace

This is not the only way the story could have been told. The Jewish Bible arranges the books of the Old Testament in a different order, thus telling a different collective story. But in the Christian arrangement, the story moves in an ordered sequence from past to present to future, which helps its readers to see it principally as a divine drama of faith history, with plot and character development, and eventually a resolution.

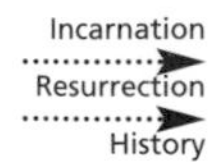

Incarnation Resurrection History

Is there a difference between the story of faith and the history of Christianity, such as some have claimed to exist between the Christ of faith and the Jesus of history? The spectre of objectivity looms over the historian of Christianity. The German historian Leopold von Ranke (1795–1886) argued for scientific objectivity in historiography, but in practice all historians know this to be impossible. Can one who stands outside the community of believers understand properly their motivations, or record accurately their convictions? Can those within that community break free of presuppositions which colour their attitude and distort their use of evidence (and even, should they)?

One outline of the historian's task suggests that any writer of Christian history needs to do research, evaluate and analyse evidence, to offer insights into the value of the findings, and to express them accurately and memorably. Modern professional historians almost without exception write from a detached viewpoint, offering no clue to their own faith perspective, and no reflection on the interconnection of divine and human in historical writings. This is partly a reaction against the partiality and partisanship of previous generations. Then Christian historiography was almost always written from a national or sectarian viewpoint, so as to make detached study of, say, the Reformation, impossible – one had to be on one side or another. Now one has to be on nobody's side instead. In the second half of the twentieth century, progress has been made in freeing Christian historiography from this narrow focus, through the influence of writers like Kenneth Latourette (1884–1968), Stephen Neill (1900–84) and Jaroslav Pelikan (1923-) in restoring the balance by considering the ecumenical perspectives in historiography, and by attempting to reach beyond the restricted sphere of the Western church. Latourette in particular was motivated by a concern to promote a global perspective on church history, and, himself a Protestant, was careful to give full weight to Roman Catholicism and Orthodoxy in his writings.

Until relatively recently, Christian historiography as an academic discipline has played second fiddle to theology. Among modern writers, Karl Barth (1886–1968) made the case most forcefully for the rejection of historical-critical study of the Bible or the past as a means to truth, insisting instead on the supremacy of revelation and grace. His view may commend itself within the Christian community, but it has nothing to say to those outside. In the end historiography, by perceiving patterns, coherence and identity in human affairs over time, is more likely to elicit dialogue between faith and unbelief than is theology.

Belief that human nature is constant, that humankind is governed by a sinful propensity towards wrongdoing and self-destruction, and above all that the events of the incarnation, cross and resurrection, being unrepeatable, disprove the possibility of a cyclical view of history; all these are to some extent common ground for Roman Catholics and Protestants, though alien to more optimistic and liberal thinkers. All these ideas have played their part in denying importance to historiography as a vehicle for divine truth. In simple terms, classical 'pagan' historiography viewed time as cyclical, while Christianity operates with a linear concept of time, of progression towards a determined goal. The cyclical view lets in the argument that the same sort of events produce the same sorts of results, and hence that study of the past helps decision-making and strategy in the present. It is reinforced by those who believe that 'human nature' (usually left undefined) is a constant, and that with enough data, historiography can predict future outcomes. If this is a gross over-simplification, it is still true to say that human beings have an inclination towards perceiving, even constructing, patterns and coherence in events and over time, which both inclines them towards the practice of historiography and encourages them to see the past as a source of guidance and moral insight. This, after all, is how many Christians principally use their main history book, the Bible.

The Christian historian with whom Christians are most familiar is a Bible writer, Luke (first century CE). He tells his story, in his Gospel and the book of Acts, from the conception of Jesus to the missionary journeys of Paul, ending in Rome. His narrative is written from a clear faith perspective, with a coherent progression and sequenced unfolding of plot and character. The Spirit which Luke finds moving in events corresponds in his writings to the sense of God's providence which was to be important to later Christian historians. This was a belief that God's people were not at the mercy of blind chance, or inexorable fate, but under loving and merciful guidance. Educated 'pagans' would have recognized Luke-Acts as historiography of a sort, for their own historians in this period were also recording the deeds of significant men, not without reports of miraculous events (albeit from a sceptical standpoint).

Historians of Christian faith have mostly been men (whether scholars or men of affairs), often sectarian in outlook, arguing for a partisan view of God or the church. This goes back to the beginning of Christian historiography proper in the fourth century CE with Eusebius of Caesarea (*c.*260–*c.*340). His work reveals sympathy with the Alexandrian school of theology in general and with Origen in particular, and also support for the Emperor Constantine, whom Eusebius portrays as the human embodiment of God's divine rule, with no pretence to impartial judgement of events. By harmonizing the different chronologies prevailing in the various polities of his own day, Eusebius took a significant step forward in making Christianity intelligible to a non-Christian readership. Eusebius was a man of affairs, a bishop in the Eastern Church, but his most immediate successors were not. In the fifth century CE Socrates Scholasticus (*c.*380–*c.*450) gave a much more detached account of the first Christian emperor, as well as preserving valuable evidence about the doctrinal disputes of the church. He, like Sozomen, another early fifth-century historian from Palestine of whom we know little, and others after Eusebius also wrote history as 'pagans' would have understood it – records of, and reflections on, the great deeds of the powerful, starting from where their avowed historical predecessors had left off.

This era of early Christian historiography seemed to give way to a dark age after the fall of the Roman empire, when historical writing dwindled into chronicle and hagiography, abandoning the key historical hallmarks of research, evidence, analysis, progression, causation. But historiography never really stood still. The first English Christian historiographer, Bede (*c.* 673–735), not only had a vital impact on the controversy over the dating of Easter, but also shaped the historical thinking of a millennium and more by devising a chronology based on events happening *anno Domini* (AD). It is so pervasive that although this terminology has changed out of courtesy to other faiths to Before Common Era/Common Era (BCE/CE), use of the incarnation as *the* pivotal point in all human history has not. Bede's account of the coming of Christianity to Britain is also important for the way in which events in history are conformed to, and interpreted by, events and characters from the Bible. This is a trend first apparent in the earliest records of Christian martyrdoms; it was followed by later historians too, notably John Foxe (1516–87), whose *Actes and monuments* (known as Foxe's *Book of Martyrs*) broke new ground in using contemporary oral sources from (among others) the poor.

Calendar

Paul

Martyr

With the Renaissance came a fresh impetus to the writing of history. Medieval scholasticism began to be challenged by the new humanism, and scholars began looking at original texts and sources, and started to question the validity of given truths. The classic example is Lorenzo Valla (1407–57), using historical analysis to expose a document known as the Donation of Constantine as a forgery. By the time the Reformation began to make its impact, a new kind of historiography was being pioneered by Niccolo Machiavelli (1469–1527; especially in his *Discourses on Livy*). It was practical, political, concerned with the past for the sake of the present, and not interested in divine providence. The challenges to Christian historiography did not stop there. The intellectual revolution of the Enlightenment encouraged writing of history without reference to or concern for God, which could be hostile to Christianity. So for Edward Gibbon (1737–94), Christianity was responsible for sapping the vitality of 'pagan' Rome.

Renaissance

Scholasticism

Humanism

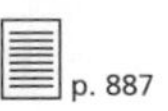

p. 887

Enlightenment

In the nineteenth century, intellectual upheaval caused by the new historical-critical study of the Bible, and the challenges posed by Darwinian theory (*The Origin of Species* was published in 1859), left Christianity struggling to find its way back to a sense of the presence and providence of God in human affairs. Karl Marx (1818–83) was developing an alternative way of writing history which jettisoned the Christian conception of the unique value Kingdom of God of individual persons, and God's guiding care for them, in favour of impersonal economic and social processes, and the destiny of masses, not individuals.

Still more did Christianity face a crisis of historical understanding in the twentieth century, in which the horrors of two world wars, Holocaust and multiple genocide made the doctrine of divine providence governing history even more of a historiographical challenge (if not a lost cause).

Historiography is far from being an intellectually sterile discipline. Well-written Christian histories have borne Feminist theology fruit, shaping and directing the church and the thinking of individual Christians by the way they describe patterns and periods in history. Historiography helped Christians to see how doctrine had developed, especially in the controversial historicist writings of Ferdinand Christian Baur (1792–1860). Baur broke new ground not only by

investigating the development of Christian doctrine over time (instead of treating it systematically, and using texts and sources without reference to date and context), but Predestination also by investigating the motives and perspectives of each individual text. His insistence on historical-critical method as the only way to establish the truth of evidence Miracles led him to cast doubt upon miracles and for that matter Christology christology itself, so it was hardly surprising that his work was never accepted in the mainstream of Christian thought.

His work was built upon by his fellow liberal historian Adolf von Harnack (1851–1930), to overturn the conception found in Eusebius, Thomas Aquinas and beyond of doctrine as an unchanging deposit of faith. The views of Baur and Harnack were too extreme for many, but their influence has been profound, in affirming the possibility, as Joseph Barber Lightfoot (1828–89) also did, Exploration of engaging fully with the challenges of new scientific and textual discoveries, rather than denying or avoiding them.

New theories of the church's role in history were developed to supersede those which were no longer tenable – Philip Schaff (1819–93) argued for the church as not a timeless given, but a living, developing organism with its roots firm and secure, yet always growing. He, like others including John Henry Newman (1801–90), found their faith enlivened and challenged by new study of the church fathers, whose writings cast light on the historical challenges of their own day. Chief among these Church fathers was Augustine of Hippo (354–430). Augustine himself was no historian, which makes it ironic that his *City of God* provided the most acute insight into the overarching dilemma and challenge of Christian historiography – how to square God's providence with the suffering of his faithful people. Where the writers of the Bible's historical books mostly equated suffering with sin and success with righteousness (as many Christians do today), Augustine argued that no earthly ruler or kingdom could be identified with the kingdom of God. Earthly dominions might possess larger or smaller proportions of virtue and strength, but all earthly kingdoms were separate from the city of God, which was to be realized only on the other side of eternity. This argument, sprawling and unwieldy though its expression is, still makes the best response yet to those challenges to belief in divine providential goodness which have rocked the past century.

Where does Christian historiography go from here? In the past 50 years it has become more ecumenical, less sectarian, more interdisciplinary. It has begun to be shaped by the insights of feminism and the experiences and stories of the worldwide, not just the Western, church. But some of the problems it attempts to explore are unlikely to change. There will always be debate over what Martin Luther (1483–1546) called the 'hiddenness of God' in human affairs; there will always be argument about whether history is a random sequence of events in a meaningless but ineluctable process, or an intricate providential divine plan, or, as John Calvin (1509–64) saw it, a dynamic working out of the predestination of the elect and the damned. Finally, if we accept that no scholar, or school of history, ever has the complete picture, the whole truth, and that complete objectivity in historiography is impossible, it remains a vital principle that writers of Christian historiography should understand their own presuppositions and context, and also make them plain for their readers. In the end, perhaps Luther best sums up the challenge: while we are in this world, and so see only God's back, not his face, Christians will always find history to consist of both meaning and mystery.

CAROLYN J.-B. HAMMOND

M. Bauman and M. I. Klauber (eds), *Historians of the Christian Tradition: Their Methodology and Influence on Western Thought*, Nashville: Broadman and Holman 1995; E. E. Cairns, *God and Man in Time: A Christian Approach to Historiography*, Grand Rapids, MI: Baker Books 1979; R. G. Hall, *Revealed Histories: Techniques for Ancient Jewish and Christian Historiography*, Sheffield: Sheffield Academic Press 1981; C. T. McIntire (ed), *God, History and Historians: An Anthology of Modern Christian Views of History*, New York: OUP 1977; W. Pauck, *Harnack and Troeltsch: Two Historical Theologians*, London: OUP 1968

HISTORY

Byzantium, Christendom, Constantine's 'conversion', Counter-Reformation, Crusades, Enlightenment, Great Awakening, Historiography, Holy Roman empire, Industrial revolution, Investiture Controversy, Middle Ages, Mission, Reformation, Renaissance, Roman empire, Wars of religion

To understand Christianity as it is today, with its great diversity of beliefs, styles of worship, social practices and cultural customs, it is important to know of its historical past. That history is long and complex, and marked by a number of significant turning points. Taken together, that history portrays a religion that is marked by constant transformations and renewal, even as it maintains continuity across the ages. In the brief account that follows the story of Christianity is recounted through a single overarching narrative, leaving numerous points of detail to be filled in elsewhere in the *Guide.*

Emergence of the Christian movement

Christianity was born on the western edge of Asia, at the crossroads of several civilizations, in a land under Roman imperial rule and at a time of historical upheaval. At the centre of its historical drama of salvation is Jesus of Nazareth. Born to a young Jewish mother, he was raised in the ways of Israel and around the age of 30 began an itinerant ministry. His message that the kingly reign of God was at hand, and the accompanying works of wonder that he performed, inspired a small band of followers, many of them at the margins of society. Confrontation with the religious authorities in Jerusalem brought him a gruelling death on a cross at the hands of the Roman military. Yet that was not the end of the story, for shortly after his death some among his followers, most notably women, claimed that his tomb was empty. Others claimed that he had appeared to them in his resurrected body. God had raised him from the dead by the power of the Spirit, they said. The crucified Jesus was now the Risen Lord whom God had appointed to reign over all the earth. Emboldened by that same Spirit, these followers soon found their way from Galilee and Jerusalem to other cities of the ancient Mediterranean world and beyond, spreading the message of the Risen Christ and organizing new bands of followers in his name.

Jesus
Kingdom of God
Miracle
Resurrection

Like the opening bars of a great symphony, the message and practice of these early followers or apostles has continued to be played out across the ages and in diverse cultural locations wherever Christianity has spread. During the first years the movement was a party or sect within the boundaries of Judaism. Known simply as the Nazarenes, their message that Jesus was the long-expected Messiah was distinctively Jewish in content. Within a decade or so of the death and resurrection of Jesus, however, dispersion of these followers to other cities in the region, most notably the city of Antioch, brought them into direct contact with non-Jewish (or Gentile) peoples. Some of these Gentiles began to embrace the new message of Jesus. It appears from the New Testament that in Antioch these Gentile followers first began to share table fellowship with Jewish followers of Jesus without undergoing conversion to Judaism (which included male circumcision), thereby breaking the dietary codes of Judaism. The Acts of the Apostles says that the followers of Jesus were first called 'Christians' in Antioch. Indeed, in a sense it is in Antioch that Christianity as a new religion was truly born. It took more than a century for the separation between Judaism and Christianity

Messiah
Origins and background

CHRISTIAN

The first followers of Jesus were Jews and to begin with had no special name with which to identify themselves: they were 'believers', 'brethren', 'disciples', 'saints' and claimed to follow the 'way'. The term 'Christian' (Greek *christianos*) is said first to have been applied to them in Antioch by outsiders (Acts 11.26). The form ending in *–ianos* (Latin *–ianus*) also appears in connection with political figures: the Gospels speak of Herodians and elsewhere there is talk of Caesarians; the term has also been said to have been derogatory. Be this as it may, it was used only rarely by early Christian writers, and then usually in reporting an outsider's view; this is the case with the two other instances in the New Testament (Acts 26.28 and 1 Peter 4.16). The appearance of the word marks a stage when the followers of Jesus began to stand out against the Jewish background from which they came and to become a separate movement.

to be finally realized. Nevertheless, these two streams of a faith that traces itself back to Abraham remain intrinsically connected, and Christianity can never shed its Jewish roots.

Judaism and Christianity

At the same time Christianity quickly began to grow beyond these Jewish roots and to take on a greater array of cultural expressions as it spread to new regions of the world. The melody took on new complexities as the message of Jesus was translated into new contexts. Paul, a zealous Jewish Pharisee who became a tireless Christian missionary, was a key figure in this regard. Among the new communities he founded were those in Asia Minor and then on the European mainland. In a body of letters that became part of the New Testament he translated the Christian message into new categories, drawn from the urban life of the Hellenistic world through which he moved.

Paul

The first Christian communities in the cities of Greece and Asia Minor began to reflect aspects of their surrounding intellectual and religious world. In Rome the Christian community was forced to deal with new political challenges, while from Alexandria Christians began to express their faith in the distinctive Hellenistic idioms of that great Egyptian city. By the early second century the spread of Christianity eastward into Syria reached beyond the Roman empire to the city of Edessa, where distinctive Semitic tones of a Syriac tradition began to be heard.

Driving this process beyond the borders of Israel was a universal vision of Christ's rule that was often parallel to the vision of other ancient political kings and emperors who sought to conquer the world. The difference was that these early followers of Jesus had expansionist tendencies without worldly imperial power. How far these apostles went is unknown for the most part, but ancient tradition locates Thomas as far away as India. Their message was carried not by armies of warring kings but by merchant ships and caravans, along the well-travelled trade routes that crossed the ancient world. Its appeal was to the middle classes and the poor at first, although later to members of the upper classes, at least in the Mediterranean world.

p. 750

One factor at work was the social inversion Christianity proclaimed. The world into which the apostles first travelled was one where only the élite had honour, privilege and power. The story of a powerless Jesus who was dishonoured in his own land but was raised up by God resonated with people facing similar situations in their own lives. The ethical considerations that derived from this message figured prominently in the early Christian movement as it spread from city to city. Many early communities showed an egalitarianism among women and men that was remarkable for its day. Slaves found a message of hope for emancipation. Those who were considered aliens or strangers in the cities where they resided found a message that made them family to one another. The egalitarian and liberationist character of the message became a permanent prophetic critique embedded deeply in Christian teaching and practice through the ages. Often it was directed against the institutional centres of Christian power itself that eventually emerged.

Women in Christianity

The cross-cultural and liberationist impulse of the first generations of Christian faith was accompanied by a third, an ascetic impulse, that led many to break their ties with the world of family, wealth and marriage in order to be joined to the new household of God. In the desert regions of Syria this asceticism often took the extreme form of individuals living in the wild, eating grasses and going without clothing. More often the ascetic impulse was lived out in community where individuals exercised discipline, practised sobriety, and lived as if the end were near. The Christian rite of initiation, baptism, symbolized both the washing away of sin and death to the old order of the world. As opposition within the Roman imperial order emerged, this ascetic impulse became linked to the practice of self-sacrifice through suffering and death in martyrdom. Christianity was an illicit religion within the Roman empire during its first three centuries. From time to time fierce storms of persecution broke out leading to a number of highly visible public executions. The courage that these martyrs showed was the most effective inducement to early Christian faith.

Food and drink
Initiation
Martyr
Persecution

As the message of the apostles took root and new communities were formed in various urban locations, the task of maintaining continuity with the original message and faith fell to a new generation of leaders. Individuals were ordained to these offices through a consecrating rite of the laying on of hands, in which the Holy Spirit was believed to be conferred upon the person being ordained. At first, types of church leadership seem to have varied: we hear of overseers (Greek *episkopos*, from which our words episcopal and bishop come), presbyters ('elders') or priests, and deacons ('servants') or ministers. The teachings of the apostles, in the form of several collections regarding Jesus (the Gospels) as well as letters from Paul and others (the Epistles), were preserved and passed on by an anonymous generation of scribes. By the end of the second century, Christian worship regularly included the reading of one or more passages from these books along with an interpretation of their meaning and application, and the sharing of the sacramental meal or eucharist (thanksgiving).

Holy Spirit
Ministry and ministers
Worship
Eucharist

Christians looked to their leaders for what other religions provided for their devotees. Bishops and priests were asked to bless marriages as priests of other religions did. The bread and wine that were part of the eucharist were understood in sacrificial terms that were familiar from the various local temples and shrines around them, and soon only the bishop or priest could handle them. The leadership of women appears to have been an early casualty to this development in Christian life. Although women are listed among the early ranks of Christian leaders, after the second century there is a deafening historical silence regarding women as bishops or presbyters.

By the end of the second century there was a general consensus among most of those who called themselves Christian that churches were led by bishops who were the successors to the apostles and who consecrated elders, deacons and others in leadership. Early in the second century one early Christian bishop, Ignatius of Antioch, used the word 'catholic', meaning 'of the whole', to describe the church that gathered with its bishop around the table of the eucharist.

Ignatius knew of various beliefs that he considered to be outside the acceptable boundaries of Christian teaching. For instance, there were some who were called Docetists, who believed that Jesus did not have a real body, but only appeared (Greek *dokein*) to have come 'in the flesh'. By the middle of the second century, varieties of this teaching were flourishing in the Christian world. Others affirmed that Jesus was truly a human being in the flesh, but they disputed whether he was more than that. These Ebionites (as they were later called) appear to have remained closer to the Jewish roots of Christianity. By the third century their camp had all but died out. Christianity was well along the way to being an overwhelmingly Gentile religion.

pp. 520–1
Jewish Christianity

Defining and defending the Christian faith

Language

By the end of the second century Christian communities could be found from Spain to Afghanistan and most likely even India. The most common Christian language was *koine* Greek, the everyday language spoken by ordinary people, the language of the New Testament itself. In the city of Edessa a vibrant Syriac literary tradition had taken root, while up the River Nile Egyptian was being used to express the meaning of Christian faith. Around the city of Carthage in North Africa Latin was becoming the dominant language of Christians, while Punic and possibly other indigenous tongues might have been used there as well. Bishop Irenaeus of Lyons tells us around 180 CE that he had preached to the Celts in his city in northern France, although whether it was in their own language or not we do not know, while from Alexandria a decade later or so Pantaenus set off to preach in India.

Letters
Community
p. 1037

The consciousness of being part of a widely-flung movement was strong. Christians celebrated the fact that they came from diverse homelands. Holding them together were the networks of fellowship woven back and forth by travellers. Letters continued to be exchanged. The treatises of bishops or other teachers in one place were copied and read in another. There was no central authority, although the heads of churches in the great cities of the Mediterranean (Rome, Alexandria and Antioch) commanded considerable prestige. Collegial relations of fellowship and communion (*koinonia*) found expression through various gatherings of church leaders in councils, and in the sense of sharing a common life of worship, or liturgy.

p. 1152

Yet differences did arise. The second and third centuries produced a burst of new intellectual activity. One teacher in Rome early in the second century in particular began to challenge the connection with Israel. Marcion taught that the God of the New Testament was a God of love, who was different from the God depicted in the Old Testament. His teachings caught on and he organized a new body of churches that reached almost as far across the world as the catholic communion did.

Gnosis

Another group of intellectual leaders who appeared first in Alexandria and Rome around the same period taught that Jesus was the purveyor of a secret body of knowledge that he passed on to his disciples in the form of mystery teachings. Drawing upon Hellenistic philosophy as well as various strands of both Jewish and Egyptian mystical teachings, these Gnostics, as they were known (from *gnosis*, the Greek word for knowledge), forged a substantive Christian alternative to the catholic party's position regarding salvation. Gnosticism appears never to have become more than the faith of an intellectual élite among the Christians. A number of its adherents appear to have been absorbed after the third century by the Manichaean religion, which was founded by the Persian prophet Mani.

The intellectual challenge of Gnostics from within the ranks of Christianity, as well as that from opponents outside the church, occasioned a number of responses from catholic intellectual leaders in the second century. As a group these catholic writers are often referred to as the apologists. Among the earliest of their number was Justin Martyr in Rome, who wrote both a longer and a shorter 'apology' to the Roman emperor, seeking to defend the legitimacy of the Christian religion in the empire. Irenaeus of Lyons was another influential apologist, as was Tertullian in North Africa and Clement of Alexandria. A lesser-known catholic figure from this period, Bardaisan in Edessa, and perhaps the greatest Christian theologian of all time, Origen of Alexandria, were both declared heretical by later catholic authorities, but both deserve to be remembered among the apologists who helped defined catholic tradition in the second century.

A number of other controversies in the second and third centuries helped to define early catholic identity and practice. One of them was the New Prophecy movement, also known as Montanism, which challenged the catholic leadership on issues such as women's leadership. Another was occasioned by Sabellius, whose strict monotheism taught that the one God had appeared in three modes as Father, Son and Spirit. Writing against a similar position Tertullian argued in Latin that God was one substance but three distinct persons, thus setting forth the basic contours of the doctrine of the Trinity. It is important to note that for these early Christian teachers, doctrine and piety were closely related. Like many others in the ancient world, Christians believed that true philosophy resulted in a virtuous life. True doctrine was therefore just as evident in the witness of martyrs such as Perpetua and Felicitas as it was in the teachings of Tertullian or Origen.

Trinity

The making of an imperial church … and beyond

The fourth century witnessed a radical change in the political status of Christianity in the Roman empire, the effects of which were felt far beyond the Roman borders. Christian numbers within the Roman world had been steadily growing. Large portions of the urban population identified themselves with the illegal religion, and in places members of the clergy had even become respected community figures. Christians had begun to meet for public worship in separate buildings known to Roman political authorities and the general public alike. Yet after more than two centuries of official hostility and occasional persecution, churches were not necessarily ready for political establishment.

Buildings

The first kingdom we definitely know to have embraced Christianity as the religion of the state was Armenia. The story is richly cloaked in theological tradition surrounding Gregory the Illuminator and the conversion of King Tiridates II around the year 300. Within a relatively short time after this the Armenian script was created and Christian scriptures were translated into the language. Christianity was soon intertwined with Armenian national identity.

The conversion of the Roman imperial order in the fourth century had a far greater impact upon the history of world Christianity. The key figure in this turn of events was the Roman emperor Constantine. In 313, while battling for control of the western region, Constantine issued an edict that legalized Christianity under his rule there. Several years later, after securing control over the entire empire, he moved first to lift all restrictions on the churches, then extended imperial support to them. By 330 the building of a new imperial city called Constantinople was well under way. The only religion to be practised in this new imperial capital was Christianity. On his death-bed in 337 Constantine himself finally underwent Christian baptism. In the few short years of his lifetime, Christianity went from being an illegal religion to the official creed of the Roman emperor.

Constantine's 'conversion' was the first step towards a great synthesis of religion, state and culture in the Roman world. This synthesis took another 60 years to secure, and was interrupted by a brief period of imperial reversion to the ancient gods of Rome under the Emperor Julian. At the same time, it also set in motion forces that led to further splits and diversity in the churches. A decade or so after Constantine's death the first great wave of Christian persecution occurred in the Persian empire, as Rome's ancient enemy came to perceive Christianity to be the religion of the Roman state. Zoroastrianism was the official religion of the Persian state, and Christians found themselves increasingly under persecution for their faith.

Zoroastrianism and Christianity

Within the Roman world, competing political and theological visions fractured Christianity into several diverging church traditions, despite the best efforts of bishops and emperors alike to maintain the unity of church within the imperial state. The two most important theological controversies that emerged early in the fourth century to divide the churches began almost immediately after Constantine legalized the faith. In Roman North Africa (the provinces of

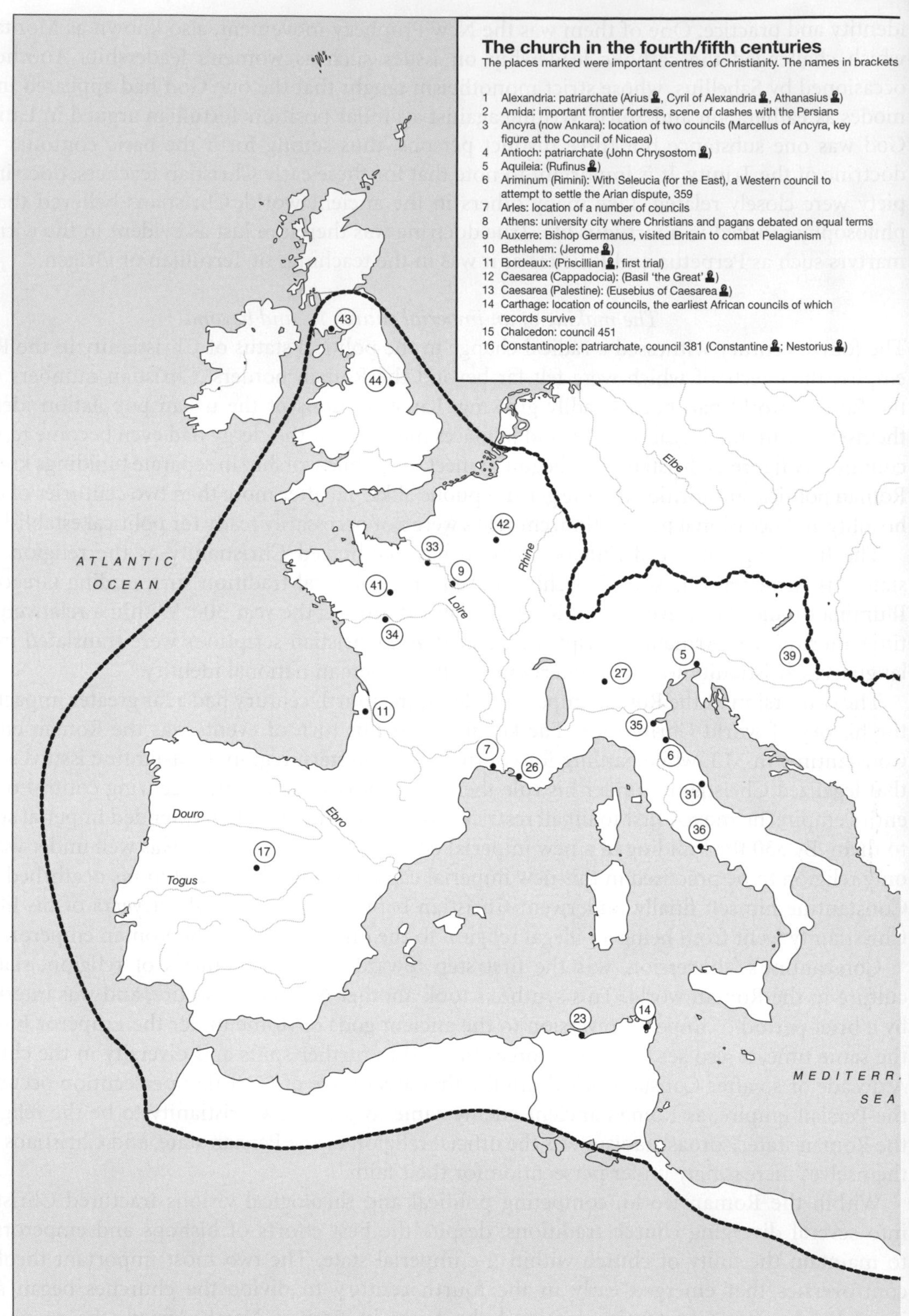
The church in the fourth/fifth centuries
The places marked were important centres of Christianity. The names in brackets
1 Alexandria: patriarchate (Arius, Cyril of Alexandria, Athanasius)
2 Amida: important frontier fortress, scene of clashes with the Persians
3 Ancyra (now Ankara): location of two councils (Marcellus of Ancyra, key figure at the Council of Nicaea)
4 Antioch: patriarchate (John Chrysostom)
5 Aquileia: (Rufinus)
6 Ariminum (Rimini): With Seleucia (for the East), a Western council to attempt to settle the Arian dispute, 359
7 Arles: location of a number of councils
8 Athens: university city where Christians and pagans debated on equal terms
9 Auxerre: Bishop Germanus, visited Britain to combat Pelagianism
10 Bethlehem: (Jerome)
11 Bordeaux: (Priscillian, first trial)
12 Caesarea (Cappadocia): (Basil 'the Great')
13 Caesarea (Palestine): (Eusebius of Caesarea)
14 Carthage: location of councils, the earliest African councils of which records survive
15 Chalcedon: council 451
16 Constantinople: patriarchate, council 381 (Constantine; Nestorius)
ATLANTIC
OCEAN
MEDITERR.
SEA
Elbe
Rhine
Loire
Ebro
Douro
Togus
43
44
42
33
9
41
34
11
7
26
27
5
39
35
6
31
36
17
23
14

are of significant figures associated with these places. The black line indicates the frontier of the Roman empire.

17 Cordoba: (Hosius of Cordoba, adviser to Constantine at the Council of Nicaea)
18 Der Mar Antonios (present-day name): (Antony of Egypt ♟)
19 Edessa: (Ephrem the Syrian ♟)
20 Ephesus: council 431
21 Gangra: council held against excessive asceticism
22 Hadrianopolis: scene of death in battle of the emperor Valens, 378, attempting to crush revolt by Goths
23 Hippo: (Augustine of Hippo ♟)
24 Jerusalem: patriarchate (Cyril of Jerusalem ♟)
25 Laodicea: (Apollinarius ♟)
26 Marseilles: (John Cassian ♟)
27 Milan: (Ambrose of Milan ♟)
28 Nazianzus: (Gregory of Nazianzus)
29 Neocaesarea: location of council
30 Nicaea: council 325
31 Nursia: (Benedict of Nursia ♟)
32 Nyssa: (Gregory of Nyssa ♟)
33 Paris: episcopal buildings on the Île de la Cité
34 Poitiers: (Hilary of Poitiers ♟)
35 Ravenna: location of the Roman imperial court in the fifth century
36 Rome: patriarchate (Leo the Great ♟)
37 Sardica: council 343 to determine the orthodoxy of Athanasius ♟
38 Seleucia: With Ariminum (for the West), an Eastern council to attempt to settle the Arian dispute, 359
39 Sirmium: important pro-Arian council, 357
40 Tabennisi: (Pachomius ♟)
41 Tours: (Martin of Tours ♟)
42 Trier: (Priscillian, second trial ♟)
43 Whithorn: reputedly the earliest church in Scotland (Ninian)
44 York: scene of death of the emperor Constantius, 306

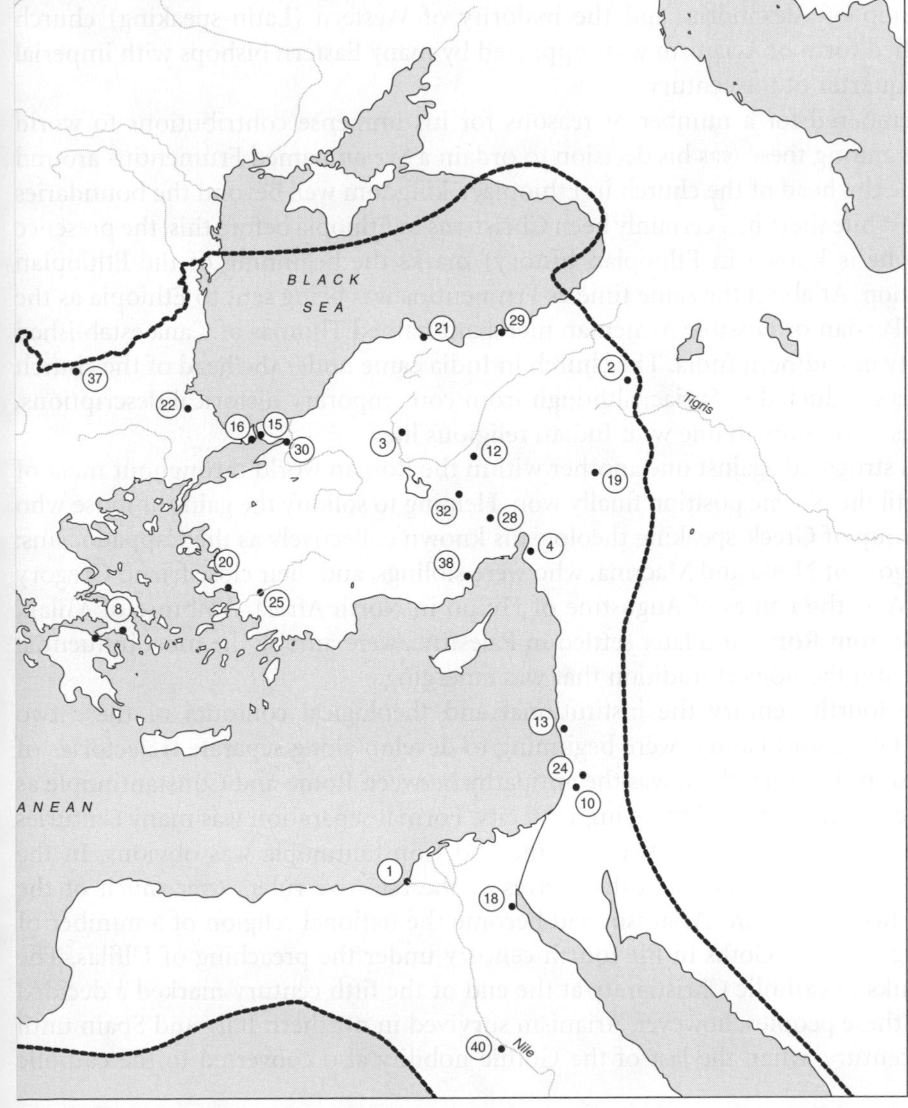

Islam and Christianity

Byzacena, Africa Proconsularis, Numidia and the three Mauretanias), a dispute that started over the status of clergy who were suspected of having collaborated with imperial authorities during the persecution erupted into a full-fledged schism after 315. Two parties, known as Donatists and Catholics, emerged in separate communions. Their churches lived side by side for several centuries in North Africa until Islam effectively put an end to organized Christianity in the region.

Council
Creed

The other major dispute that erupted in the first quarter of the century is known as the Arian controversy. Primarily theological in nature, it concerned the proper Christian understanding of the nature of Jesus in relation to God. This debate was the main occasion for Constantine to convene the Council of Nicaea (325), whose theological decision that Jesus Christ was of the same substance as the Father eventually became the standard of orthodox faith for the majority of churches in the world. One of the decisions of Nicaea was to promote a short creed that summarized its position. Eventually this creed was extended to become what is known today as the Nicene Creed, a universal symbol of orthodox Christian faith. Among the fourth-century proponents of the Nicene position were Athanasius, Bishop of Alexandria, and the majority of Western (Latin-speaking) church leaders, while a modified form of Arianism was supported by many Eastern bishops with imperial backing until the last quarter of the century.

Euthiopian Christianity
Christianity in Africa

Athanasius is remembered for a number of reasons for his immense contributions to world Christianity. Not least among these was his decision to ordain a Syrian named Frumentius around the year 350 to become the head of the church in Ethiopia, a kingdom well beyond the boundaries of the Roman empire. While there had certainly been Christians in Ethiopia before this, the presence of Abuna Salama (as he is known in Ethiopian history) marks the beginning of the Ethiopian national church tradition. At about the same time as Frumentius was being sent to Ethiopia as the head of the church, a Persian or possible Armenian merchant named Thomas of Cana established a Christian community in southern India. The church in India came under the head of the church in Persia. Worship was conducted in Syriac, although from contemporary historical descriptions, some of their practices were more in line with Indian religious life.

Arians and Nicenes struggled against one another within the Roman world throughout most of the fourth century until the Nicene position finally won. Helping to solidify the gains of those who supported it were a group of Greek-speaking theologians known collectively as the Cappadocians: Basil of Caesarea, Gregory of Nyssa and Macrina, who were siblings, and their close friend Gregory of Nazianzus. In the West the names of Augustine of Hippo in North Africa, Ambrose of Milan, and Jerome who came from Rome and later settled in Palestine, were among the most influential in shaping a distinct Latin theological tradition that was emerging.

By the end of the fourth century the institutional and theological contours of these two theological streams – Greek and Latin – were beginning to develop along separate trajectories of faith. Fuelling the tensions between them was the antipathy between Rome and Constantinople as the latter displaced the former as the reigning imperial city. Formal separation was many centuries away, but by the year 600 the distance between Rome and Constantinople was obvious. In the meantime, Germanic tribes had established themselves as the effective rulers over much of the western region of the Roman empire. Arianism had become the national religion of a number of these tribes, beginning with the Goths in the fourth century under the preaching of Ulfilas. The conversion of the Franks to catholic Christianity at the end of the fifth century marked a decided turn in the history of these peoples; however, Arianism survived in northern Italy and Spain until the end of the sixth century, when the last of the Gothic nobility also converted to the catholic faith.

One of the spiritual practices that continued to cut across the frontiers of the various churches was asceticism. A book by Athanasius on the life of an Egyptian hermit named Antony helped to popularize the message on a mass scale in the fourth century. Towards the latter part of the century a new organized form emerged from the deserts of Egypt to become a major vehicle of mission and renewal for churches throughout the world. The key element in the success of this new institutional form of asceticism (or monasticism, as it was now called) was a community rule written by an Egyptian named Pachomius. A steady stream of visitors from across the Christian world visited the monasteries of Egypt and adapted the community rule in new versions of their own.

Monasticism

Monasticism carried on the spiritual heritage of self-sacrifice that martyrs had previously exemplified. It took up the tasks of education and community care as well. Monasteries became schools, health-care facilities, places for Christian travellers to stay, and centres for spiritual life. Through monastic practices women in particular found a degree of social freedom that allowed them to exercise gifts of ministry and spirituality that might otherwise have gone unexpressed. Most of the women whose names are known to us from the Christian movement of the fourth to sixth centuries, including Melania the Younger, Eustochium and Olympias, were ascetics. They were rural dwellers from Syria and Egypt as well as members of the upper classes of Rome and Constantinople. Their number included young girls on the verge of marriage at the age of twelve as well as widows and grandmothers who had already raised families. Practitioners of monasticism, men and women alike, became the most effective evangelists of the Christian world after the fourth century. Included among their numbers in the fifth century were luminaries such as the Nine Saints in Ethiopia, Benedict in Italy, and a Briton named Patrick who was the first effective missionary of Christianity to Ireland, a land that lay beyond the ancient boundaries of the Roman empire.

Schools

The fifth century brought a new round of theological debate to the churches of the Roman world. The controversy that gave rise to them focused on the relationship between the divine and human natures in the person of Jesus Christ. On the one side were a number of teachers and bishops most often identified with the school of theology that had emerged in Alexandria. The Alexandrians, as they are often called, held that the mystery of salvation was best represented by speaking of the one incarnate person, Jesus Christ, in whom the divine nature took on human flesh. The most capable exponent of this position in the fifth century was Cyril of Alexandria.

On the other side of the increasingly hostile debate were those who found in the language of one nature an impious mixing of human and divine characteristics. They believed that the transcendence of God required a more careful articulation of the two natures, divine and human, which were conjoined in Jesus Christ. Those who shared this perspective gathered around a group of teachers who identified themselves historically with the theological school at Antioch, most notably Theodore of Mopsuestia. They were not afraid to use the terminology of two natures and even two persons to describe Jesus Christ. The position that brought them into direct conflict with their Alexandrian opponents, however, was their refusal to call Mary *Theotokos* (Mother of God). A sermon to this effect delivered by one of their number, Nestorius, who was Bishop of Constantinople early in the fifth century, set in motion the controversy that culminated in the Council of Chalcedon in 451, which is considered the fourth ecumenical council of the ancient church.

Mary

Chalcedon sought to resolve the debate by defining Jesus Christ as being two natures joined in one personal union. This was the position of the Latin churches, expressed in a *Tome* that Pope Leo had sent to an earlier council and was accepted as orthodox at Chalcedon. It also became the position, after several more decades of controversy, of the Greek-speaking churches in communion with the Bishop of Constantinople. A number of churches in Egypt, however, refused to accept the Chalcedonian position. By the sixth century the support for their position (called Monophysite by their detractors) included churches both inside and beyond the boundaries of the Roman empire, among them the Egyptian (Coptic), Ethiopian, Nubian, Armenian and Syrian (Jacobite) communions.

During the last half of the fifth century those who adhered to the two-nature teaching were suppressed by a combination of political and theological efforts that deprived them of their foothold in the eastern Roman world. Forced into exile by the emperor, they found a hearing for their doctrine further east among the Persian churches. After the fifth century, the two-nature doctrine became the confessional position of the dominant churches of Persia, India, Central Asia and China, whose liturgy was in Syriac. The patriarch (or catholicos) of these churches resided in the Persian capital of Seleucia-Ctesiphone. In the Mediterranean world they were usually called Nestorians, after the Bishop Nestorius whose teachings were ruled heretical at the Council of Chalcedon in 451, but they are known today as East Syrian (or Assyrian).

The end of antiquity and the beginning of Christendom

The early decades of the seventh century found world Christianity centred upon patriarchs or popes in Seleucia-Ctesiphone, Alexandria, Constantinople and Rome. A separate national church in Armenia looked to its own patriarch for leadership, while the Ethiopian church continued to look to the Coptic pope in Alexandria as its head. The divide between the eastern Mediterranean world (or East Roman empire) that looked to Constantinople as its centre, and the western Roman world, now fragmented into various Germanic kingdoms but still nominally a part of the Roman empire, was intensified.

Among the most important Christian East Roman rulers of this period were Justinian and Theodora, in whose reign the fifth ecumenical council (Constantinople II, 553) was convened. Also during this period an official mission from Constantinople to Nubia was launched, which succeeded in converting the royal household of that African kingdom to Christianity. Justinian did much to codify the ancient Roman tradition of law and advanced the power of emperors over the church in Constantinople beyond any of his predecessors. During this period for the first time the title 'Ecumenical Patriarch' came into use for the head of the church in Constantinople. In the western Mediterranean world Pope Gregory the Great (*c.*540–604) overshadowed all others of the era and did much to enhance the theological significance of the Roman office of pope in the absence of effective imperial rule in the region.

Perhaps the most important person to affect world Christianity in the seventh century, however, was neither Latin nor Greek but an Arab prophet named Muhammad (570–632) from the cities of Mecca and then Medina. Guided by a series of new revelations that Muhammad claimed to have received from God and that were recorded in the Holy Qur'an, the movement called Islam burst upon the ancient world with a combination of unparalleled religious fervour and military strength. Within a few short decades, Arab forces inspired by the Islamic faith toppled the Persian empire and assumed control of Syria, Palestine, Egypt, Roman North Africa and Spain, shaking the East Roman empire to its core. Within a century approximately half of the Christians of the world lived under Muslim rulers as religious 'minorities' who were taxed, restricted in their public expression, and often persecuted for their faith.

Chinese religions and Christianity
Buddhism and Christianity

The Arab advances in the seventh century took place at a time when the T'ang dynasty in China was turning its attention toward the West. The Chinese had already shown an interest in Buddhism, which had entered their land from across the Persian frontier. In the seventh century, they began to show an interest in other Persian and Syrian religions as well. The flow of Persian merchants into the Chinese capital city by way of the Silk Road brought Christians, along with Buddhists, Manichaeans and Zoroastrians, into the Middle Kingdom (as China was known), to open up the first sustained encounter between Christian faith and Chinese culture. The number of Christians in China during the T'ang dynasty was never very large. Changes in the Chinese imperial attitude towards the West and the spread of Islam into Central Asia combined to bring about an end to this first Christian mission to China by the tenth century. Nevertheless, their effort left an important legacy that was only rediscovered many years later.

About the same time that Christian monks from the east were making their first appearance before the Chinese emperor T'ai-tsung in 635, to the west their counterparts were appearing in the court of Edward I in England. Sent by Gregory the Great from Rome, these Latin missionaries to the Anglo-Saxons succeeded in bringing all of England eventually within the realm of Christian belief. Meanwhile, monastics from further west in Ireland began itinerant missionary work among the Germanic peoples in Gaul and in Northern Italy. A century later Anglo-Saxon monks such as Boniface and nuns such as Lioba were influential in spreading Christianity throughout central Germany and in regions along the frontier of the Franks.

The Franks were the dominant political power in what is now Western Europe, and by the eighth century their kings had developed an alliance with the Pope in Rome. This alliance reached a new dimension under Charlemagne, whom Pope Leo III crowned as emperor on Christmas Day in 800. During the following century the power of the Roman popes continued to grow both administratively and theologically in the West.

Charlemagne's coronation was not well received in Constantinople, where Roman emperors and empresses continued to occupy the imperial throne. Within a single generation in the seventh century, the East Roman (or Byzantine) empire had lost more than half its territories to the Arabs, including many of its most important food-producing regions. Yet despite such losses, it continued to sustain a vibrant Christian religious and cultural life, far surpassing in both economic and intellectual terms the civilization that was emerging under the Franks to the west. Drawing upon the spiritual inheritance of the first six centuries, the churches of the Greek-speaking world addressed the new challenges of their day by building upon the doctrinal foundations laid by the ancient teachers and the great ecumenical councils of Christian tradition that began with Nicaea.

Several significant theological controversies took place during these years in the East Roman world. One happened on the eve of the Arab conquest and concerned the question of whether Jesus Christ had one will or two. What came to be considered the sixth ecumenical council (Constantinople III, 680–1) rejected the 'monothelite' or one-will doctrine and extended the Chalcedonian pattern of two natures to encompass the two wills united in one person in Jesus Christ.

Several decades later an even more divisive controversy broke out in and around Constantinople over icons, or holy images, including those of Jesus, Mary and the saints. Such icons had long been a part of the devotional practices of the Greek churches. During the first quarter of the eighth century some, including the emperor, came to see their use as violating the biblical prohibition against images. They were soon known as 'iconoclasts'. The fact that devotion to icons was especially strong among monastic communities beyond imperial control, and that the emperors did not reject the use of their own images for political purposes, suggests that the struggle was political as well as theological.

Icon

Iconoclasm

The issue was the occasion for what eventually became known as the seventh ecumenical council (Nicaea II, 786–7), which determined that devotion paid to icons was not the same as worship that alone belonged to the Trinity. Important support for the orthodox position came from John of Damascus (*c.* 655–*c.* 750), a theologian who had once served in the employment of the Muslim government in Syria and who had extended the doctrine of the incarnation to encompass the liturgy, icons and other such material means by which humanity encountered the divine nature.

The rich legacy of spiritual life which the churches of the Greek-speaking world bequeathed p. 821 to world Christianity during this period includes the practice of *hesychia* (holy silence) and the devotional use of the 'Jesus prayer'. Among important centres for Christian spirituality the p. 795 monastic community on Mount Athos still ranks as one of the foremost in history, while the work of Simeon the New Theologian (949–1022) continues to influence Christians worldwide.

Constantinople opened up a new mission in the ninth century to the Bulgars and the Slavs who had established kingdoms to its north. This was followed in the tenth century by the conversion of the ruling house of the Russian people. Meanwhile in the West, the ninth and tenth centuries witnessed the advance of Christianity among the inhabitants of Scandinavia, who were brought into the family of churches that looked towards Rome for the bearer of tradition. This new wave of expansion reached as far as Iceland in the year 1000. Thus at the end of the first millennium, the movement that began in Galilee and Jerusalem reached from China and India in the east to Ethiopia in the south, to Russia and Sweden in the north and to Iceland in the west.

Christian history from 1000 to 1453

Western Europe was a bewildering political patchwork of landed estates and kingdoms at the beginning of the second millennium. Its people spoke an array of languages. Most lived in villages or towns on the estates and worshipped in churches whose bishops and priests were fully ensconced within the feudal political system. Catholic Christianity alone provided the cohesive force for a common civilization. Latin was no longer spoken as the day-to-day language in Europe, but it was still the language of liturgy and scholarship and the means by which the élite could communicate with one another. Latin was not only the language of the church but also the carrier of a classical Roman past, linking these lands tenuously with the glories of the imperial heritage. The situation thus favoured the emergence of a strong institutional papacy.

Against this background a series of reformers succeeded in the eleventh century in asserting for a time the authority of the papacy over against that of secular rulers in the churches in what became known as the Investiture Controversy. Among the changes they institutionalized were the appointment of cardinals from throughout the Latin church, election of the Pope by the college of cardinals, universal celibacy of the priesthood, and an end to the practice of purchasing ecclesiastical appointments (called 'simony', after Simon Magus, who attempted to buy the power of bestowing the Holy Spirit for money, Acts 8.18–19).

Conflict continued to mark the relationship between Constantinople and Rome, which had already been strained during the last half of the ninth century when the Romans insisted on adding p. 305 a word, *filioque* ('the Holy Spirit proceeds from the Father *and the Son*'), to the time-honoured creed of Nicaea and Constantinople. There had also been differences over the form of bread to be used in the eucharist and the proper ways of fasting. The crisis reached boiling point in 1054, when a papal delegation in Constantinople excommunicated the Ecumenical Patriarch, who responded in kind. The result was a split between the Eastern and Western churches which still has not healed.

A decade later a new Muslim dynasty known as the Seljuk Turks took Armenia, forcing many there into exile in Cilicia in the south-east corner of Asia Minor. In 1071, at the battle of Manzikert in Armenia, the Seljuk Turks handed the Byzantine empire one of the most devastating defeats in its history, leaving all of Asia Minor open to Turkish occupation and only the western end under Constantinople's rule. The Turks then turned their attention to Palestine. Facing hostile armies on several fronts at once, in 1081 a Greek emperor turned to Rome in search of military assistance.

Several decades earlier in Spain, the army of a Christian king had captured the city of Toledo from Muslim forces, opening up a new era of Christian reconquest in that region. The response to these events led Pope Urban II in 1095 to call upon the rulers of the West to take up a war under the cross, or 'crusade', against the Muslims in the Holy Land and Spain, thereby opening up a new era in the history of world Christianity.

The first waves of crusaders never made it to the Holy Land, turning instead on Jews in Germany. Still others were lost trying to cross Asia Minor. Eventually the armies of the crusaders succeeded in establishing Latin rule in Palestine and Syria, but the effort was soon reversed by Muslim forces from Egypt under the rule of Salah ad-Din (Saladin). The reconquest of Spain was more successful, but left in its wake a militarized history of violence and a legacy of royal control over the appointment of new bishops in conquered territories that would continue for centuries to come. Throughout Europe new cities were rapidly emerging during this period, fuelled in part by expanding trade and a revived monetary economy. Crusading was soon linked to commerce among notable ports such as those of Venice and Genoa. Several more attempts by Western forces to take Palestine failed, while a fourth crusade in 1204 sacked Constantinople and established a Latin ruler on the throne of that ancient Christian city. Constantinople never completely recovered from this ignominious chapter of intra-Christian relations.

The religious fervour of the crusades that was unleashed within Western Europe came to be directed not only against Jews but also against others who were deemed 'heretical' by the growing institutional apparatus of the papacy. The new urban economy brought with it new political associations, as artisans and traders played a more significant role in Western life. New religious views were taking hold. Some, such as the Cathars in southern France whose roots can be traced to eastern Europe, were the object of violent suppression and extermination called forth by Rome. Others, such as the lay Christian movement that came to be known as the Waldensians, succeeded in gaining a foothold and surviving. Still others, including the new order of Franciscans and Dominicans, eventually gained acceptance from church authorities and were able through their practices of apostolic poverty and mendicancy (begging for their living) to spread their message throughout the West and beyond.

Waldensian Church
Religious orders

New intellectual currents were also emerging in Europe during these years, encouraged both by Western intellectual contact with Islam through Spain and by the growth of new urban centres. Among the most important results of this development were the rise of scholasticism, the development of new universities, and the work of thinkers such as Hildegard of Bingen, Anselm of Canterbury, Thomas Aquinas and William of Ockham. The next century gave rise to what historians have often called the Renaissance, a movement that sought to recover more of the classical intellectual wealth of Graeco-Roman antiquity and led to lasting contributions in the arts, sciences and humanities in the West.

Scholasticism
University

Six decades of Latin rule in Constantinople in the thirteenth century after the crusaders conquered it during the Fourth Crusade, in 1204, had the opposite effect. The Greek empire and the Ecumenical Patriarchate survived in exile in the kingdom of Nicaea until Greek forces retook Constantinople in 1261. One of the outcomes of this period of exile was the development

Siege of Constantinople by the Turks in 1453, unknown artist

of independent national churches within the Byzantine communion, such as that of the Serbian people. In Palestine, Syria, Armenia and Egypt indigenous churches all suffered serious disruptions at the hands of the Western Latin crusaders, while to the north the Russian kingdom found itself facing the combined hostile forces of Swedes and Teutonic knights. p. 1019

Further to the east, a new political force arose in the thirteenth century that eventually changed the equation of power from China to Rome. A new empire took shape under a Mongol ruler named Temujin, or Genghis Khan ('Great Ruler'), whose mission was to unite all nations and religions under one universal law. At the height of the empire he founded, Mongol rule extended from the Pacific Ocean to Europe. During its first century Mongol rulers allowed for a relatively high degree of religious pluralism. A number of influential women among the nobility, including the wives of several great khans, were Christians, while the men mostly practised shamanism, a form of religion centred on the shaman, a religious figure believed capable of communicating with the spiritual world when in ecstasy and of healing the sick. One of the first Mongol rulers to break with this pattern was Kublai Khan, the grandson of Genghis Khan, who converted to Buddhism. After conquering Baghdad in 1258 Mongol rulers in Persia flirted briefly with Christianity before converting to Islam at the beginning of the fourteenth century. New waves of persecution opened up shortly after that against Christians in the Persian world and intensified under the reign of terror unleashed against them by the armies of Timur the Great (also known as Timurlane or Tamburlane) in the last decades of the fourteenth century.

A new Muslim dynasty in Egypt known as the Mamelukes came to power in the thirteenth century, seizing Palestine and Syria before turning to the south to bring about the end of the Christian kingdom of Nubia. Ethiopia remained the lone Christian kingdom in Africa by the fourteenth century, and its churches found themselves facing new pressures from Islam on several sides. A new emphasis upon Ethiopian continuity with Judaism, made concrete in the revival of the ancient story of the Queen of Sheba's relationship with King Solomon, helped revitalize Ethiopian Christian identity during this period.

Political developments at the beginning of the fourteenth century in the West led to the papacy being moved from Rome to Avignon near the border of southern France, where it remained for nearly seven decades. Shortly after the office was returned to Rome in 1378, two competing claimants were canonically elected pope within several months of each other and by the same body of cardinals, resulting in mutual excommunications and further institutional turmoil. The Great Schism in the papacy lasted four decades, during which every bishop and priest in Western Europe was excommunicated by one or other of the popes. The end of the schism came in 1417 and coincided with an age of renewed conciliar activity in the West as well as increased powers of national kings over the institutions of the church. Two decades later one of the last attempts to bring Latin and Greek communions together took place at the Council of Ferrara-Florence in 1438–9. The council was conducted on theological terms dictated by the Latin West, and failed to achieve any lasting success among the churches of the Byzantine East.

A new Turkish dynasty known as the Ottomans had come to power in 1300 in Asia Minor, and soon after had begun their assault upon the dwindling domains of the empire of Constantinople. Meanwhile to the north the city of Moscow was growing in importance as a major ecclesiastical centre. The churches of Russia elected a new metropolitan of Moscow in 1448 for the first time without the blessings of the Ecumenical Patriarch of Constantinople. Five years later in 1453 the Ottoman Turks mounted their final assault on the city of Constantinople, ending a 1000-year experiment in Christian empire.

The birth of the modern world

The fourth century had witnessed the conversion of the Roman imperial order and the subsequent synthesis of Christian and Graeco-Roman culture in the Mediterranean world. The fifth to tenth centuries witnessed the progressive conversion of various peoples to the north, original inhabitants and newer immigrants alike. The result was a shift northwards in the political centre of the Western Roman world and the thorough synthesis of Christian Latin and Germanic cultures. The unified religious-cultural construct called Christendom that emerged by the tenth century remained more

HISTORIC CENTRES OF CHRISTIANITY

Jerusalem: Jerusalem is not just a historic centre of Christianity; it is a holy city for Jews, Christians and Muslims. Historically, it was the scene of the last days of Jesus and the rise of Christianity, and already at that time was a powerful symbol for Jews as the city of David. As Psalm 137 puts it: 'If I forget you, O Jerusalem, let my right hand wither! Let my tongue cleave to the roof of my mouth ... if I do not set Jerusalem above my highest joy.'

The first, mother, church was in Jerusalem and exercised considerable influence: Paul, who came from Asia Minor and worked in the Greek-speaking world, felt it important to maintain good relations with Jerusalem, and a dangerous visit there led to his imprisonment and subsequent death. But Jerusalem was captured by the Romans in 70 CE during the Jewish War and the Christians fled. This marked the end of its supremacy, though it remained one of the major patriarchates of the Christian church.

For Christians, too, Jerusalem became a powerful symbol, the subject of countless hymns and visionary writings, from the Holy City, the new Jerusalem, descending from heaven to earth in the Revelation of John (21.2) to William Blake's Jerusalem 'builded here, among those dark satanic mills'. If these are social visions of a new earth, there is also 'Jerusalem my happy home, when shall I come to thee?' and 'Jerusalem the golden with milk and honey blessed', the heavenly resting place awaiting the faithful.

The Old Testament book of Ezekiel speaks of Jerusalem as being at the middle of the earth, and until the age of the explorers this was accepted as a revelation about the form of the earth. That Jerusalem was the earth's centre was asserted by Christians from Jerome to Pope Urban, who preached the First Crusade; this view also appears in Dante. A popular medieval account, *The Travels of Sir John Mandeville*, even claims that a spear standing erect at the Holy Sepulchre casts no shadow at the equinox.

This view was reflected in early maps: The *Mappa Mundi* ('map of the world'), now in Hereford Cathedral, drawn in 1290 and the only complete wall map of the earth to have survived from the Middle Ages, has Jerusalem as the centre of the world and east, not north, as the map's top. Countries and oceans are squeezed and stretched to fit into the map's centre.

Crusades

But Jerusalem is above all an earthly city, always entangled in the politics of its time, and here its image as the 'holy city' plays a major role. Attempts were made in the Crusades to win it back for Christianity and from 1099 to 1291 there was a Latin Kingdom of Jerusalem. However, Christianity, with its somewhat different attitude to holy places from that of Judaism and Christianity, has refined its views since then.

Antioch: It was to Antioch that Greek-speaking members of the Jerusalem church fled after persecution and in Antioch that they were first called Christians. Antioch was the base for Paul's first activities and was a very important centre for earliest Christianity. In size and importance it was the third city of the Roman empire. By the fourth century it also ranked third as a patriarchal see after Rome and Alexandria, but after that it declined, being eclipsed by the power of Constantinople.

Antiochene theology was distinctive. It contrasted with Alexandrian theology, and came into conflict with that in a number of disputes. In interpreting the Bible it put more emphasis on the literal and historical sense and in teaching about Christ put more emphasis on his human characteristics and moral choices. Since supporters of Alexandrian theology often had the upper hand in these disputes, Antiochene theologians like John Chrysostom, Theodore of Mopsuestia and above all Nestorius were mistrusted and worse.

Rome: Christianity reached Rome at a very early stage. Tradition has it that Peter arrived there in 42 CE; certainly Paul found Christians there before him when he arrived in Rome as a prisoner twenty years later. Both Peter and Paul are said to have been buried there and St Peter's is said to be built on the site of the former's crucifixion. The growing importance of Rome for Christianity is bound up with the growing importance of its bishop, in due course *the* Pope (the title was also given to other bishops, notably the Bishop of Alexandria). Over the centuries the focal point for Christians moved westwards, and although in 330 the Emperor Constantine inaugurated his new capital Constantinople, whose church soon came to dominate the Eastern Mediterranean, by the end of the first millennium Rome had achieved undisputed supremacy in the West.

Pilgrimage

Rome has long been a place of pilgrimage for Christians. Bishops are summoned by the Pope to make the journey *ad limina apostolorum* ('to the tombs of the apostles', the phrase now used to denote the visits which they are required to make to report on their dioceses) and others go voluntarily, with special favours granted those who make the pilgrimage in a Holy Year. It has a wealth of associations with the history of Christianity, from the catacombs and its many basilicas to the Vatican itself. But if it stands for one thing in Christianity, it is for authority: '*Roma locuta est, causa finita est*' ('Rome has spoken, the case is closed') is a famous saying, which some say goes back even as far as Augustine.

Alexandria: Alexandria had the largest community of Jews in any city in the ancient world and also a legendary library, burned down in mysterious circumstances at a date which cannot be fixed. It was also the second city of the Roman empire. The Jews there were Greek-speaking, and it was for them that the Septuagint translation of the Bible was made. Traditionally the foundation of the church there is attributed to the evangelist Mark, but this too may well be legend. A Catechetical School with a succession of heads, modelled on Plato's Academy in Athens, is also said to have existed from the second to fourth centuries, but this may be yet another legendary construction.

→

What is not legend is that in the third century CE Alexandria became famous as a centre of Christian thought through the work of Clement of Alexandria and Origen. It also had two famous bishops, Athanasius and Cyril. At the council of Nicaea in 325 it was ranked second after Rome, but it too came to be eclipsed by the rise of Constantinople.

Alexandrian theology was heavily influenced by Platonism. Its interpretation of the Bible tended to be allegorical and spiritual, and in teaching about Christ it emphasized the role of his divine nature and the unity of his person. Monophysitism was a logical outcome of this theology; it was officially rejected, but proved extremely influential in the church.

Constantinople: Byzantium, which became Constantinople when Constantine made it his capital and residence in 330, had a Christian population from an early date: legend has it that the church was founded by the apostle Andrew. In 381 the first Council of Constantinople recognized that Constantinople was 'now the new Rome' and ranked its bishop second only to Rome. At the Council of Chalcedon it was given a large area of jurisdiction in the Balkans and Asia Minor. Paradoxically its importance grew with the Muslim conquests: many bishops whose dioceses had been over-run took refuge in Constantinople. It was also the base for the expansion of Christianity, in a Byzantine form, into most of Eastern Europe including Russia, and this, together with its increasing power and prominence, led to tensions, hostilities and an eventual split with Rome in 1054. Hostility to Constantinople in the West is embodied in the disastrous Fourth Crusade, during which the Crusaders captured the city (1204). When the city was captured by the Turks in 1453 the patriarch was granted authority over the Eastern churches, but in the course of time these became independent and the patriarch now has authority essentially only over Constantinople, Mount Athos, and some dioceses in Greece and the islands.

Byzantium

p. 795

Kiev: In 957 Princess Olga of Kiev paid a state visit to Constantinople, where she was baptized by the patriarch and took the Christian name Helena, that of the mother of Constantine. She built a church in Kiev in honour of Holy Wisdom (St Sophia; it was rebuilt on a grand scale in the next century) . After her displacement as regent and a period of renewed paganism, in 988 her grandson Vladimir was also baptized and another famous church, the 'Tithe Church', was built and monasteries established, including the Monastery of the Caves. The Nestorian Chronicle, the earliest account of the history of the state of Rus, was compiled here around 1113. By the twelfth century Kiev had more than 400 churches and was famed for its art, frescoes and mosaics. The architecture and worship of Kievan Russia was Byzantine and showed Greek influence. Kiev was also the residence of Ilarion, a learned monk who was the first Russian head of the church of Rus, from 1051–4, just before the split between the Eastern and Western churches. Kievan Russia was subsequently invaded by the Mongols in 1240 and this and other factors led to the decline of Kiev. Nevertheless, until 1448 the Metropolitan of Kiev was head of the Russian Church, but subject to Constantinople.

Moscow: Although the Metropolitan of Kiev was head of the Russian Church, from 1328 he resided in Moscow. From 1448 the Russian bishops elected their own patriarch, and with the fall of Constantinople in 1453 Moscow achieved supremacy in Russia. In 1589 Metropolitan Job of Moscow was ranked fifth as patriarch after the patriarchs of Constantinople, Alexandria, Antioch and Jerusalem. However, Moscow had an even more exalted view of itself: after Rome and Constantinople it was 'the third Rome'. It felt itself equal to the Western Roman imperial empire, even if Western emperors and kings would not recognize this. The doctrine was worked out by a monk, Filofei of Pskov, who in a letter to the Grand Prince of Moscow, Vasilij III in 1510, wrote: 'Two Romes have fallen, but the third stands, and there will never be a fourth.' This doctrine was given up with Peter the Great and the rise of St Petersburg in the seventeenth century, but has surfaced again in post-Communist Russia in anti-Western circles.

Canterbury: Augustine established his first church in Canterbury, rather than in London, when he arrived from Rome in 597. He organized England into two church provinces, the other being York, and for a long time there was a struggle for precedence between them, but in the fourteenth century Canterbury proved victorious. The archbishop became Primate of All England, and as the Church of England spread round the world, the leading figure of the Anglican Communion. Canterbury is the focal point of the Anglican Communion, and most recently has been the place where the conference of Anglican bishops from all over the world meet every ten years. However, the residence of the Archbishop of Canterbury is at Lambeth in London, and the conference is known as the Lambeth Conference.

p. 47

Geneva: In the Protestant world, Geneva is perhaps the nearest equivalent to Rome, Constantinople or Canterbury, in that it is the home of the World Council of Churches, the World Alliance of Reformed Churches and the Lutheran World Federation. In Geneva the Reformation took a particularly radical form and in fact the first 'heretic' to be killed by Christians, Servetus, was burnt at the stake there in 1553.

1536 saw the acceptance of the Reformation in Geneva, which became a separate city state, and the arrival of John Calvin, who introduced a Presbyterian form of church government; a consistory, to co-operate with the civil authorities in matters of law and order; and an academy, to train clergy from all over the world. The political neutrality of Switzerland favoured the choice of Geneva as the base for the organizations which it hosts.

Reformers
John Calvin

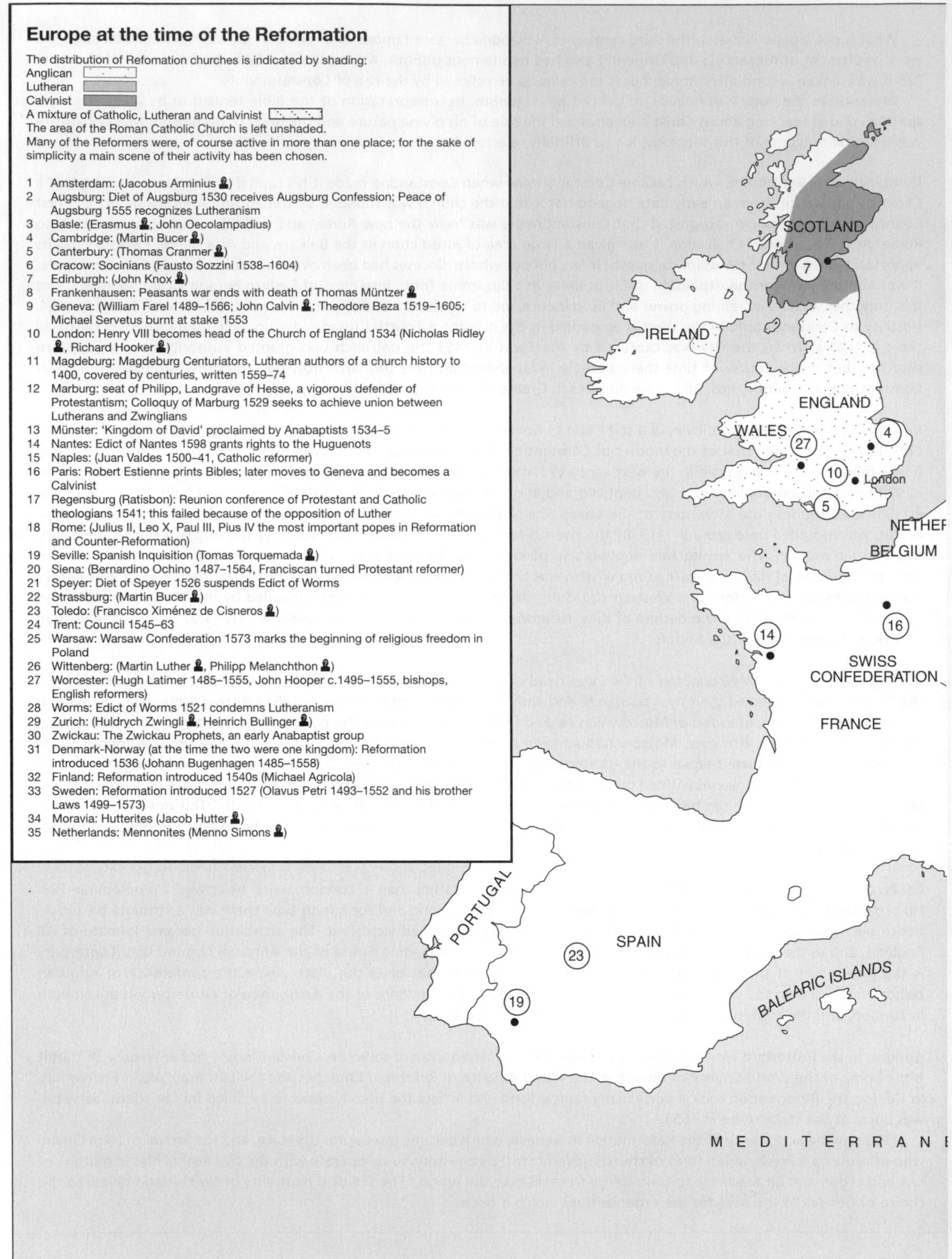
Europe at the time of the Reformation
The distribution of Refomation churches is indicated by shading:
Anglican
Lutheran
Calvinist
A mixture of Catholic, Lutheran and Calvinist
The area of the Roman Catholic Church is left unshaded.
Many of the Reformers were, of course active in more than one place; for the sake of simplicity a main scene of their activity has been chosen.
1 Amsterdam: (Jacobus Arminius)
2 Augsburg: Diet of Augsburg 1530 receives Augsburg Confession; Peace of Augsburg 1555 recognizes Lutheranism
3 Basle: (Erasmus; John Oecolampadius)
4 Cambridge: (Martin Bucer)
5 Canterbury: (Thomas Cranmer)
6 Cracow: Socinians (Fausto Sozzini 1538–1604)
7 Edinburgh: (John Knox)
8 Frankenhausen: Peasants war ends with death of Thomas Müntzer
9 Geneva: (William Farel 1489–1566; John Calvin; Theodore Beza 1519–1605; Michael Servetus burnt at stake 1553
10 London: Henry VIII becomes head of the Church of England 1534 (Nicholas Ridley, Richard Hooker)
11 Magdeburg: Magdeburg Centuriators, Lutheran authors of a church history to 1400, covered by centuries, written 1559–74
12 Marburg: seat of Philipp, Landgrave of Hesse, a vigorous defender of Protestantism; Colloquy of Marburg 1529 seeks to achieve union between Lutherans and Zwinglians
13 Münster: 'Kingdom of David' proclaimed by Anabaptists 1534–5
14 Nantes: Edict of Nantes 1598 grants rights to the Huguenots
15 Naples: (Juan Valdes 1500–41, Catholic reformer)
16 Paris: Robert Estienne prints Bibles; later moves to Geneva and becomes a Calvinist
17 Regensburg (Ratisbon): Reunion conference of Protestant and Catholic theologians 1541; this failed because of the opposition of Luther
18 Rome: (Julius II, Leo X, Paul III, Pius IV the most important popes in Reformation and Counter-Reformation)
19 Seville: Spanish Inquisition (Tomas Torquemada)
20 Siena: (Bernardino Ochino 1487–1564, Franciscan turned Protestant reformer)
21 Speyer: Diet of Speyer 1526 suspends Edict of Worms
22 Strassburg: (Martin Bucer)
23 Toledo: (Francisco Ximénez de Cisneros)
24 Trent: Council 1545–63
25 Warsaw: Warsaw Confederation 1573 marks the beginning of religious freedom in Poland
26 Wittenberg: (Martin Luther, Philipp Melanchthon)
27 Worcester: (Hugh Latimer 1485–1555, John Hooper c.1495–1555, bishops, English reformers)
28 Worms: Edict of Worms 1521 condemns Lutheranism
29 Zurich: (Huldrych Zwingli, Heinrich Bullinger)
30 Zwickau: The Zwickau Prophets, an early Anabaptist group
31 Denmark-Norway (at the time the two were one kingdom): Reformation introduced 1536 (Johann Bugenhagen 1485–1558)
32 Finland: Reformation introduced 1540s (Michael Agricola)
33 Sweden: Reformation introduced 1527 (Olavus Petri 1493–1552 and his brother Laws 1499–1573)
34 Moravia: Hutterites (Jacob Hutter)
35 Netherlands: Mennonites (Menno Simons)
SCOTLAND
7
IRELAND
ENGLAND
WALES
27
4
10
London
5
NETHEF
BELGIUM
16
14
SWISS
CONFEDERATION
FRANCE
PORTUGAL
SPAIN
23
19
BALEARIC ISLANDS
MEDITERRANE

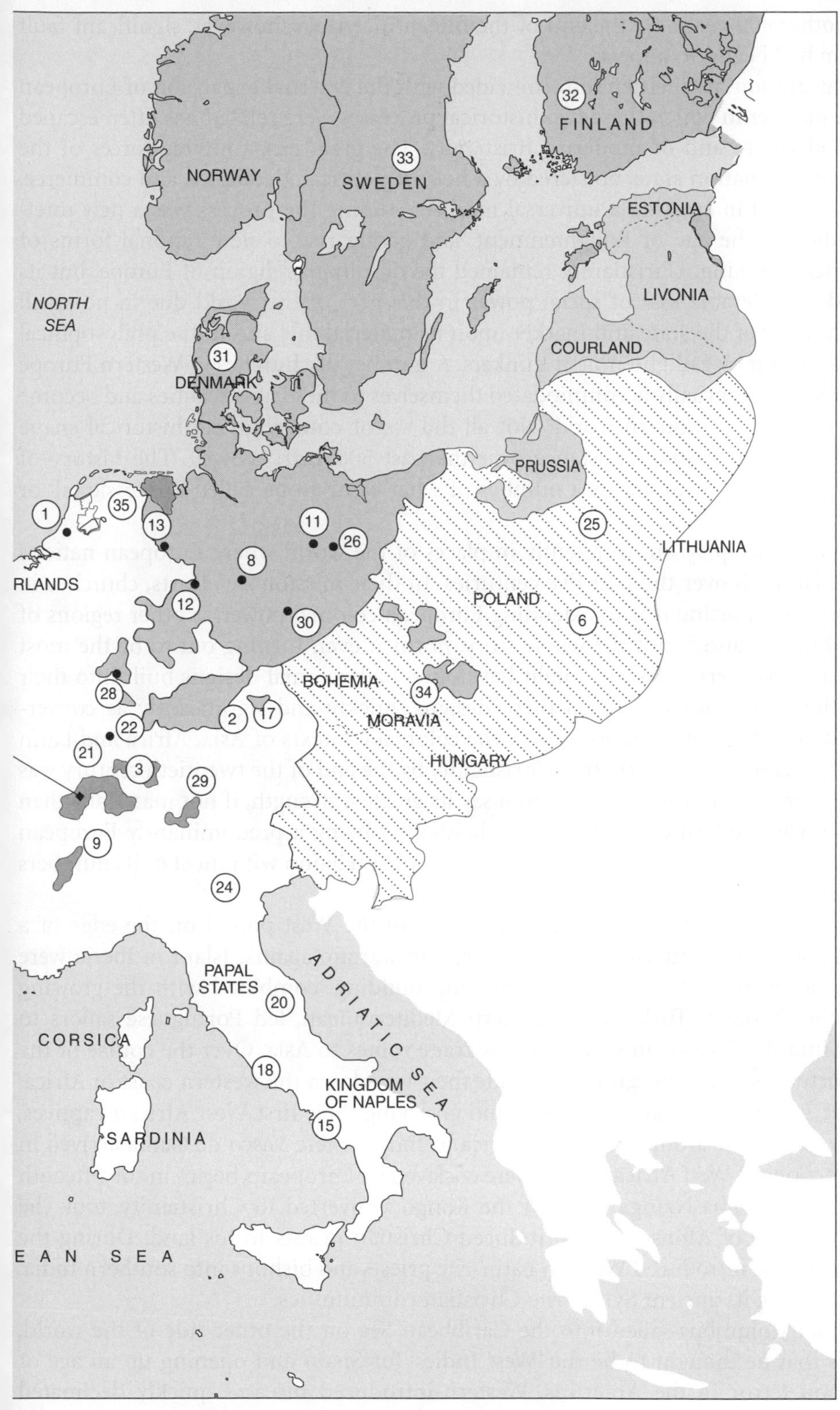
NORWAY
SWEDEN
FINLAND
ESTONIA
LIVONIA
COURLAND
NORTH SEA
DENMARK
PRUSSIA
LITHUANIA
POLAND
RLANDS
BOHEMIA
MORAVIA
HUNGARY
PAPAL STATES
CORSICA
SARDINIA
KINGDOM OF NAPLES
ADRIATIC SEA
EAN SEA
1
2
3
6
8
9
11
12
13
15
17
18
20
21
22
24
25
26
28
29
30
31
32
33
34
35

or less intact for another 400 years. By the end of the fifteenth century, however, significant fault lines in Christendom had begun to appear.

The internal disintegration of Christendom coincided with the external expansion of European colonial power. The manner in which these two historical processes were related has often escaped historians of the modern era and of modern Christianity. The great new unifying forces of the modern world became the nation state, bolstered by a host of political ideologies, and commerce, which eventually succeeded in creating a universal market. Guiding the process was a new intellectual spirit embodied in the age of Enlightenment, and giving rise to new rational forms of scientific and historical thinking. Christianity remained the dominant religion of Europe, but its institutions suffered considerable loss of social power in this part of the world due in no small part to the encroachments of the state and market upon its material life, and to the philosophical criticism launched against it by Enlightenment thinkers. A number of churches in Western Europe and its settlement colonies eventually accommodated themselves to these new realities and become comfortable partners with the modern world. Not all did so, of course, giving historical shape to a persistent tradition of Christian resistance over the past 500 years as well. The history of dominance and resistance plays out across a number of what came to be called 'confessional' or 'denominational' traditions.

Dominance and resistance play out differently in places of the world where European nations extended their colonial reach over the past five centuries. In their missionary efforts, churches in the West often played a supporting role in extending European colonial power to other regions of the modern world. But this also is not the whole story, nor is it even turning out to be the most critical part of the story. Western missions might have often had colonial designs built into their initial efforts, but the results often changed these designs quickly and significantly as conversions took place and new churches were formed in the colonial contexts of Asia, Africa and Latin America. It is in these regions of the world that Christianity by the end of the twentieth century was registering its greatest growth, and some might even say its greatest strength, if not materially then at least intellectually. The modern era began with Christianity being a predominantly European religion in the world. It is ending with Christianity being a global religion with most of its numbers in Africa, Latin America and Asia.

Geography

The opening stage of this modern era found Christians in the West poised on the edge of a new crusade against Islam. Four hundred years of Christian warfare against Islam in Iberia were coming to a close. Meanwhile, advances in Western ship-building, combined with the growing political power of the Ottoman Turks in the eastern Mediterranean, led Portuguese sailors to venture out further into the Atlantic in search of new trade routes to Asia. Over the course of the fifteenth century, Portuguese ships progressively made their way down the western coast of Africa, establishing strategic military posts along the way and enslaving their first West African captives. Eventually they charted a route around southern Africa to India, where Vasco de Gama arrived in 1498. The first conversions of West Africans who were enslaved by Europeans began in the fifteenth century, while in 1506 Mvemba Nzinga, ruler of the Kongo, converted to Christianity, took the Portuguese Christian name of Afonso, and introduced Christian priests to his land. During the same period the Portuguese introduced Western Latin-rite priests and bishops into southern India, causing disruptions among its ancient Syriac-rite Christian communities.

In 1492 Christopher Columbus sailed into the Caribbean Sea on the other side of the world, claiming the islands that he thought to be the 'West Indies' for Spain and opening up an age of colonial conquest and terror in the Americas. Western-introduced diseases quickly decimated the indigenous populations, and many were forced to live under severe conditions of oppressive labour. African slaves also began to be imported to work in the Americas, their numbers growing exponentially as the demand for plantation labour increased. By the end of the century the Atlantic Ocean had been virtually turned into an African lake, so great was the number of Africans who had been shipped across it. Resistance to the abuse of the native population (although rarely to the enslavement of Africans) came from the ranks of religious orders who sent members to work in the Americas, the most notable among them being Bartolomé de Las Casas. Despite the hardships to which they were subjected, Native American conversions began soon after the Spanish arrived. A new form of indigenous Catholicism emerged, symbolized by the legend of the appearance of the Virgin of Guadalupe, or the brown-skinned Virgin Mary, to a Native American farmer named Juan Diego in 1531.

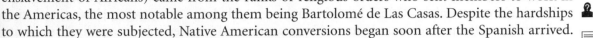

p. 733

Hispanic Christianity

De Las Casas was in Spain in 1520 to present his case for the defence of the indigenous peoples before the newly-enthroned king of Spain, Charles I, who had just been elected by the German princes as Emperor Charles V. The following year, in 1521, another European churchman, a German by the name of Martin Luther, appeared before Charles V at the Diet, the assembly of the princes of his empire, held at Worms, to present his case for reforms. Along with other humanist scholars of his day, Luther had turned his attention towards the scriptures as the primary source for Christian teaching. Unlike many others, however, Luther had openly rejected the authority of the Pope and the role of the church in dispensing grace through the sacraments. Human beings are justified by faith in Jesus Christ directly, he argued, and not by any work that either the individual or the church might perform. Preaching was to play a more prominent place in worship, which was to be conducted in the language of the people to facilitate their reception of the Word of God for themselves. On these and other points Luther was regarded by Rome as heretical, and had he not gained the support of his prince in defiance of the emperor, the life of the reformer would have no doubt been cut short.

Martin Luther

Papacy Grace

Sacraments

Justification

Preaching

Luther's ideas spread rapidly in the 1520s throughout Europe, aided in large part by the recently-invented printing press, to set in motion what came to be called the Reformation. In Switzerland the Reformation was led by Huldrych Zwingli and John Calvin. Calvin's influence in particular was great, and his ideas soon spread to followers in France (where the Protestants were called Huguenots), Holland and England. In Scotland John Knox played a leading role in introducing Calvin's programme for church reform to set in motion the formation of a Presbyterian church.

Books

Huldrych Zwingli

John Calvin

Presbyterian churches

A more radical branch of the Reformation known as Anabaptism emerged in Switzerland, Austria and Southern Germany and quickly spread to northern and eastern Europe as well. The Anabaptists rejected infant baptism, and formed congregations of believers without priests. Most rejected the authority of civil rulers in matters of Christian life and faith, and refused to participate in war. A number of their communities found refuge for a time in regions of eastern Europe, but for the most part the Anabaptists were violently persecuted by Protestant and Roman Catholic rulers alike.

Anabaptists

In England King Henry VIII separated the church from papal authority in the 1530s and nationalized the monasteries, but did not embrace the rest of the Reformers' platform. Following Henry and several decades of religious conflict in which a number of church leaders lost their lives for heresy, a distinctive Church of England tradition emerged with its Book of Common Prayer, under the authority of the crown and the Archbishop of Canterbury. A number of dissenting voices who soon became known as Puritans could be heard to argue for more Reformed measures along Calvinist theological lines.

Church of England

Puritans

Lutheranism
Brethren

By the middle of the sixteenth century Europe was bursting with reformers and new religious ideas. Some were mystical, others apocalyptic. Some argued against the sacramental power of the church, others rejected the historic Christian doctrine of the Trinity. In many cities the projects of reformers coincided with those of the city councils, which were dominated by the rising class of urban artisans and merchants called the 'burghers' or 'bourgeoisie'. In eastern Europe Roman Catholic and Orthodox communions were now joined by Hussite, Lutheran, Calvinist, Brethren and Socinian communions. Often there was violence. And always there were printers producing books, many of them anonymously to avoid persecution, which they sold to rapidly disseminate the new ideas.

Humanism

Reform had been in the works for some time among humanists and church leaders within the Roman church communion. The Council of Trent, which met between 1545 and 1563, institutionalized many of these efforts, especially those pertaining to clerical abuses, and set the direction for the Roman Catholic Church within Europe for the next 300 years. There were also important new currents of spiritual renewal in the Roman Catholic Church in the sixteenth century. The *Spiritual Exercises* of Ignatius of Loyola is one of the lasting contributions from this period. The Society of Jesus, or Jesuits, founded by Ignatius, quickly became a highly effective missionary order on behalf of the Roman Catholic cause both within and beyond Christendom. Another sixteenth-century spiritual figure was Teresa of Avila, whose works came to be read by Roman Catholics and Protestants alike.

Reformed churches
Anglicanism
Peace churches

By the end of the sixteenth century, Christianity in Western Europe was solidifying into a number of confessional church formations. Alongside the Roman Catholic Church were now, among others, Lutheran, Reformed, Anglican and Mennonite churches. In a number of places Protestant churches became aligned with emerging national state formations, but following a period of religious wars in central Europe, by the middle of the seventeenth century a new spirit of tolerance was emerging. Religious differences played a significant role in England's Civil War in the middle of the seventeenth century, but by the end of the century England had legalized most dissenting groups.

The colonial venture in the Americas

The church in Latin America in the sixteenth and seventeenth centuries was torn by the contradictions of the colonial setting. Although laws were issued protecting the rights of indigenous peoples, abuses continued relatively unabated. Institutionally the church was dominated by royal colonial interests. No bishop from the Americas was allowed to attend the Council of Trent, as Charles V believed the issues discussed there did not concern them. Pastoral ministry among the poor was mostly carried out by members of various orders. Some Jesuits went so far as to organize native Americans into separate villages and armed them for self-protection against the colonialists, but in the long run their effort proved futile. Franciscans followed Spanish soldiers into the area that is now the US South West and began working among the native peoples in the sixteenth century, founding mission churches that are still part of the south-western landscape today.

Quakers

England's colonial venture in North America was launched in the first decades of the seventeenth century primarily on mercantile grounds. To these were soon joined the cause of religious dissent, as Puritans and Quakers undertook new settlements in order to escape persecution in England. Convinced that the divine hand of providence was guiding their cause and bolstered by a doctrine of divine election that set them apart, Puritans in New England went to war against any Native American inhabitants who resisted the seizure of their land. In Pennsylvania the Quakers negotiated payment for land for their colony, but even here European immigrants soon forced native Americans off their land. Both Virginia and Massachusetts began importing kidnapped Africans for slave labour, and by the middle of the seventeenth century had passed laws maintaining the descendants of these Africans as well in slavery for life, belying any uncritical claims that these colonial episodes were unqualified ventures in Christian freedom.

Christianity in the East in the sixteenth and seventeenth centuries

Charles V could not give his full attention to extinguishing the flames of reform in his territories in the sixteenth century in part because he was engaged in continuous warfare with the Ottoman Turks to his east. Following the capture of Constantinople in 1453 (which the Ottomans renamed Istanbul), the Ecumenical Patriarch became an *ethnarch*, or ruler of a subjugated people within the Ottoman empire. The Patriarch was now appointed by the Muslim ruler and held office at the ruler's pleasure. Educational opportunities for Christians were curtailed, and the ability of bishops to exercise spiritual leadership hampered. The influence of European powers at the Ottoman court further added to the difficulties of the Ecumenical Patriarchate as both Roman Catholics and Protestants sought to advance their theological agenda within the Orthodox world. Western theological influences in general increased through this period. Further to the east the Syrian-rite churches (Syrian Orthodox and Assyrian) continued to suffer decline in their numbers due not only to the harsh conditions of Islam governance under which they lived, but now also to proselytism by Roman Catholic orders.

To the north the demise of Constantinople and the overthrow of Mongol rule in Russia by Ivan the Great in 1488 left Moscow, which by then had became known as the 'Third Rome', as the most powerful centre for Orthodox church life. A form of extreme nationalism began to emerge for the first time in the Russian church during this period, especially visible during the reign of Ivan IV (also known as Ivan the Terrible), who in 1547 assumed the title of 'Tsar' (or 'Caesar'). Fifty years later the Union of Brest brought many Polish Orthodox churches into communion with Rome while allowing them to maintain their Orthodox liturgy. The following century the introduction of liturgical revisions intended to bring the Russian church into greater conformity with Greek Orthodox practices led to a schism of the 'Old Believers' in the Russian Church.

Eastern-rite Catholic churches

Portuguese excursions further east into Asia brought to these regions Roman Catholic missionaries such as Francis Xavier, colleague of Ignatius of Loyola and missionary to India and Japan. In China, Matteo Ricci and other Jesuits began to translate Catholic faith into a Confucian philosophical idiom. Ricci and his colleagues were granted permission by the emperor early in the seventeenth century to take up residence in the imperial Chinese city of Beijing. Among their first converts were a small number of Chinese scholars, including Xu Guangqi, Li Zhizao and Yang Tingyun, who are sometimes called the 'Three Pillars' of Chinese Christianity. The Jesuits initially argued that Chinese converts should be allowed to continue practising ancestral rites, but after a period of controversy the Vatican finally forbade such practices in the eighteenth century, marking the end of an important early effort toward inculturation in Asia.

Intellectual currents in Europe and North America

The seventeenth century's confessional formations gave rise in Western Europe in the eighteenth to a new age of scholastic orthodoxy. Meanwhile the growing intellectual movement in philosophy known as the Enlightenment had begun to mount a significant challenge to a number of the tenets of traditional orthodox Christianity. The philosopher René Descartes provided a concise

formulation of some of the founding principles of the Enlightenment when he wrote, 'I think, therefore I am.' No longer was God to be the centre of the intellectual universe, but rather the thinking individual whose gaze is turned upon the objective world of nature. The authority of the past, communicated in the form of tradition, was soon challenged in the name of intellectual progress. The intellectual gains of rationalism and scientific experimentation could soon document claims to truth in a way that Christian dogmas resting on faith, tradition or divine revelation alone could not. By the end of the eighteenth century a thinker such as Immanuel Kant could argue that his was a world 'come of age', free from the tutelage of church and tradition.

Revelation

A number of Enlightenment thinkers sought to bridge the divide between reason and revelation by turning towards more reasonable interpretations of Christian teaching, or by applying methods of common sense reasoning to the interpretation of the Bible. Others responded to both traditional dogmatic orthodoxy and the newer Enlightenment rationality by turning to various expressions of mysticism or pietism, which favoured spiritual experience of the heart over dogmatic forms and intellectual knowledge of the head.

Mysticism

Roman Catholics continued to experience spiritual vitality in its various religious orders and communities. One that flourished in France in the early seventeenth century but was eventually suppressed by Rome on suspicions of heresy was Jansenism, with its centre in the abbey of Port-Royal in Paris. Towards the end of the century in Germany Pietists began to organize *collegia* or small groups for prayer and spiritual renewal that represented a Protestant form of monastic renewal within the state-sanctioned churches. Among the many Pietist groups in the eighteenth century in Germany the Moravians stand out for their contributions in theology and worship. Pietists were also the first Protestants to join Roman Catholics in sending missionaries beyond Western Christendom to spread the Christian faith.

p. 1016

Pietism

Moravian Church

In England the counterpart to Pietism was a movement brought about by a series of popular revivalists, most notably John and Charles Wesley. The Wesleyans or Methodists (as they were derogatorily called) were organized into highly-disciplined bands and societies for the purpose of promoting 'scriptural holiness' among the masses. Combining heart-felt religion with rigorous moral discipline, Methodists succeeded in becoming an effective mass movement among the emerging industrial poor.

What came to be called the Great Awakening spread from England to North America in the middle of the eighteenth century, where outbreaks were recorded up and down the eastern seaboard. Previous to this period Anglican missionaries had sought to evangelize among the Africans held in slavery, with little success. It is in the Awakening of the eighteenth century that we find the first significant conversion of Africans to Christianity in North America. By the end of the century the 'invisible institution' of Christian slave religion had formed on plantations of the south, while independent African American Christian churches were emerging in the north.

African American Christianity

The age of revolution and the ambiguities of freedom

The end of the eighteenth century in both North America and Europe was a time of great political change. Two revolutions in particular are important for the emergence of the modern state. In 1776, thirteen English colonies in North America launched a collective War of Independence that came to fruition in the formation of the United States of America in 1789. That same year the French Revolution began, marking the death of the Ancient Regime and the ascendancy of the modern nation-state in Europe. One of the first amendments added to the new US Constitution was a statement preventing the government from establishing a particular religion or hindering the freedom to practise religion. The principle of disestablishment eventually became the norm of modern European nations, further eroding the synthesis of Christendom.

The principles of freedom that drove the revolutionary agenda forwards in Europe and North America were ambiguous at best. By the middle of the eighteenth century in England an equally momentous industrial revolution was under way, giving rise to the modern industrial city and the economic life it sustains. Conditions for workers in these urban industrial regions were far from conducive to a life of freedom. In many cases poor districts in the modern city became indistinguishable from the prisons that these cities boasted, and innumerable lives were lost to the workings of the modern industrial machine.

Quakers were among the first Christians in eighteenth-century England to oppose the transatlantic slave trade, and by the end of the century a significant abolitionist movement was under way. But abolitionism remained mostly a minority opinion in the West. Numerous arguments were advanced on multiple fronts – social, economic and even religious – supporting the institution of chattel slavery. Freedom remained confined to those of European descent.

On the other side of the world from the Americas, England's colonial hold over India was deepening by the end of the eighteenth century. A group of English merchants in 1600 had first organized the East India Company, and the first English trade ships reached India in 1608. Ships of the company reached China in 1637, and by 1700 a trading house was established at Guangzhou. In India the Company's influence increased until they seized virtual military control of the country in 1757. The English government proceeded to assume control over India in 1773, turning the subcontinent into a colony of the Christian nation of England.

Early ecumenical trends

At the end of the eighteenth century, several new Protestant missionary societies were organized in England to support the effort to expand Christianity in various places outside Europe. One of these, the London Missionary Society, was organized across confessional boundaries. Similar efforts were undertaken in the US, Germany and elsewhere early in the nineteenth century, expanding Protestant missionary efforts significantly while opening up opportunities for inter-confessional co-operation. Roman Catholic efforts in foreign missions continued throughout the century to be the work primarily of its orders, co-ordinated through the Office for the Propagation of the Faith in Rome. Rarely, if ever, did Catholics and Protestants work together in mission during this period.

p. 776

The global expansion of Western churches and Western culture colours much of the history of eighteenth-century Orthodox Christianity in the East as well. Peter the Great of Russia cast his lot with the processes of Westernization early in the century. Under Peter, the 'Spiritual Regulation' of the churches was introduced in 1721, putting the Russian church under the authority of a lay official appointed by the government and greatly reducing the power of the patriarch. Over the course of the rest of the century spiritual leadership of the Russian church increasingly passed into the hands of monks and nuns, and a revival of monasticism took place despite government efforts to curtail it.

Roman Catholic missionaries had long been at work among the Orthodox churches of Syria, Armenia and Persia, as well as India, seeking to gain proselytes from these Eastern church traditions to Rome. The decision by a group of Orthodox churches in Antioch to unite with Rome in 1724 took this process to a higher level. Rome permitted those churches that recognized its authority to retain their own Orthodox rites, including married clergy. The churches gained the advantage of Western support while maintaining their identity, at least in part. The Melkite schism, as it came to be known among the Orthodox, was deemed to be a far greater threat to Orthodox life than individual proselytism of believers had been. Thirty years later in 1755 the Synod of Constantinople, which continued to function more or less throughout the Ottoman period as an effective council, issued a Decree on Rebaptism, denying the validity of the Western rite. Catholics and Protestants who might seek to join the Orthodox church thereafter had to undergo rebaptism in the Orthodox rite. A new low in East-West Christian ecumenical relations had been reached.

Within the Greek Orthodox communion, the latter part of the eighteenth century saw a movement for liturgical renewal that had its roots in a controversy begun on Mount Athos. A group of traditionalists known as Kollyvades (named after a dish of boiled wheat, kollyva, used in memorial services as a symbol of the resurrection) had objected to changes in traditional liturgical practices. Within a few decades the movement had spread to other parts of the Greek Orthodox communion, whose churches continued to look to the Ecumenical Patriarch and the Holy Synod in Istanbul for leadership. The Kollyvades sought to renew the liturgical life of Orthodoxy through restoration of ancient traditions, stemming the tide of Westernizing influences and strengthening Orthodox identity in the process.

The nineteenth century in Europe

In the aftermath of the French Revolution a general named Napoleon Bonaparte was appointed First Consul and launched a series of military operations to dominate Europe. Riding on the currents of these military excursions, French political (anti-monarchical) and cultural influences spread as far as Sweden and Russia to the north, and into Greece in the south. A series of new democratic revolutions broke out across Europe, culminating in 1848 in a partial victory for democratic forces in the revolution in Germany. In France the monarchy was restored for a period, but the pressure for more liberal democratic reforms continued until 1852 when popular vote established a new liberal government.

From Germany the concepts of philosophical idealism forged by Gottfried Leibniz, Immanuel Kant, Friedrich von Schiller and above all G. W. F. Hegel opened up even more expansive intellectual visas in the early nineteenth century. Hegel conceptualized history as the realm in which Absolute Spirit had divided from itself and was dialectically moving towards achieving its own self-realization, which was the *telos* or goal of history. Art and religion were but lesser-developed stages of this self-realization which achieved its highest expression as philosophy. History for Hegel was a process of assimilation in which forms and ideas of one period were overcome or taken up into those of the next. He mapped this movement dialectically through the concrete course of the history of world civilization from Asia to Europe, conveniently situating Germany as the end of history.

Critics of Christianity

Among Hegel's philosophical disciples in the mid-nineteenth century one in particular emerged as a critic of Christianity who sought to turn Hegel's system against itself. Karl Marx heard in the French Revolution the opening salvo of a wider revolutionary movement that he believed was destined to sweep free-market capitalism and the bourgeois class from the stage of history. His detailed analysis of the manner in which capitalism turned human beings into objects to be exploited, coupled with his grand theory that material economic forces determine intellectual ideas, took philosophical criticism in a radically new materialist direction. Marx believed that the working class, whose exploited labour was the source of capitalism's wealth, was destined to overthrow its oppressors and create a new classless society. Religion (especially the Christian form that belonged to the German bourgeois class) was both the opiate of the masses and their sigh for liberation. Like the state, it was destined soon to disappear. Marx laid the philosophical foundation for international Socialism and Communism in the nineteenth and twentieth centuries. His criticisms of religion, economy and society were major influences in twentieth-century theologies.

Friedrich Schleiermacher was a contemporary of Hegel who swam in the same philosophical waters of German idealism, but charted a different course in terms of theological legacy. Schleiermacher took up the task of answering the Enlightenment critics of Christianity, or those whom he called 'the cultured despisers of religion'. Often called the father of modern theology, Schleiermacher argued that religion was not a function of science or of dogma, but rather a feeling of absolute dependence, allowing him then to interpret historical dogmas for their subjective or intuitive meaning. Schleiermacher is sometimes also called the father of modern hermeneutics, for his work in exploring the philosophy and practice of interpretation.

Hermeneutical theology

The effect of German idealism and criticism upon biblical studies resulted in the creation of a new form of biblical studies that eventually became known as historical (or higher) criticism. By the end of the eighteenth century some scholars were ready to argue that much of what we have in the Bible is little more than 'pious frauds' and ancient legends invented to illustrate or support religious beliefs. Over the course of the nineteenth century scholars laboured to determine what might be considered history and what might be myth. Evidence both inside and outside the biblical texts was used to identify the various historical and literary strands upon which biblical writers had drawn. Higher criticism challenged many of the assumptions of common-sense readings of biblical texts, and to many seemed to pose a direct challenge to the source of Protestant religious authority.

Biblical criticism

Equally as challenging to many Christians in the West in the nineteenth century was the publication in 1859 of Charles Darwin's *The Origin of Species*, in which he set out his theory of evolution. Human beings were not created by a special act of God. Rather, they evolved from lower forms of primates, who in turn had evolved from other less-developed forms of life. The entire process was a long and arduous journey guided by the laws of natural selection and survival of the fittest. Darwin's thesis challenged the notion of a direct or special creation, and even allowed for an atheistic interpretation of the origins of life.

Evolution

The modern state, philosophical criticism, modern theology and science combined to pose a challenge to all the churches in Europe in the nineteenth century. Added to these for Rome was the political challenge of Italian national politics. Catholic life was dominated by the 32-year reign of Pius IX, which began in 1846. In 1864 he published an encyclical entitled *Syllabus errorum* (Syllabus of Errors) that condemned a wide range of modern doctrines including rationalism, socialism, liberalism and the separation of church and state. Failing to stem the changing tide of modern life on a number of fronts, including such matters as marriage and divorce, the Pope called for a general council to meet in Vatican City in Rome in 1869. Vatican I, as the council was known, was cut short in 1871 by civil war. But by then its work was mostly done. One of its most important acts was the promulgation of the doctrine stating that the Pope, in the exercise of his office as teacher of all Christians, is infallible in matters concerning faith or morals. Faced with the challenge of modern life rapidly changing the world around it, the Roman Catholic Church found refuge in the notion of the Pope's infallible office.

p. 1045

The nineteenth century in the Americas

The first decades of the nineteenth century brought a new revolutionary spirit to Latin America and the Caribbean. The name of Simón Bolívar (1783–1830) stands out in the struggle for independence of several South American nations. In Mexico the struggle for liberation from Spain took more than a decade. Independence brought the abolition of slavery, fostering the development of a more integrated society in Latin America than had previously been the case. The Catholic Church, which had been so closely connected with both the Spanish and the Portuguese colonial regimes, initially suffered a considerable loss of influence after independence, although it soon was able to reforge its alliances with the new Latin American leadership. Protestant missionaries from north of the border were not invited into Latin America until the last decades of the nineteenth century, and then it was more out of a desire for building schools than planting churches.

New waves of religious revival were sweeping the US during the first half of the nineteenth century. Transcendentalism, utopianism and a host of other religious ideals were in the air. Unitarians, Universalists and a variety of Restorationists contributed to the increasingly crowded denominational field of churches. Protestant cultural dominance lent a strong anti-Catholic ethos to US cultural life in the nineteenth century that at times broke out in anti-Catholic violence. There were also episodes of violence directed against what appeared to many to be quasi-Christian movements, such as the Mormons. The US as a nation was on the move westwards, and immigration continued to push native Americans from their lands. Inspired by the secularized millennial vision of a 'Manifest Destiny', the US declared war on Mexico, brought Texas into the Union and annexed the region from New Mexico to California.

Unitarians

Mormons

From the days of the Puritans a particular strand of Christian perfectionism could be found in American religious life. In the nineteenth century individual perfectionism took a decidedly Wesleyan turn in its holiness emphasis, while continuing to be the engine of social reform that was being pursued through a variety of new voluntary associations. The abolitionist movement gained strength in the north among the churches, and along the way helped birth a new movement for women's rights. Women were also becoming more prominent in the leadership of various churches, and in 1853 Antoinette Brown became the first woman ordained to the ministry in the Congregational Church (she later became Unitarian).

Holiness movement

The issue of slavery was becoming more divisive in churches and the nation at large. Finally in 1860 Civil War broke out when the southern states declared their secession from the Union. The end of the war brought the emancipation from slavery, but only a brief period of Reconstruction ensued, followed by the onset of a new era of discrimination and racial terror. Throughout this period black churches in America became the centre of community life and the most important institutions of social development.

During the last decades of the century, growth in European immigrants brought significant increases in the US urban population. Efforts towards urban reform, including temperance and the first expressions of what came to be called the Social Gospel, took on new urgency. Cities were becoming more culturally diverse as Jews from eastern Europe, Italians from southern Europe, Chinese from eastern Asia and African Americans from the US south crowded in together. By the opening of the twentieth century a new multicultural city was emerging in places like New York, Chicago and Los Angeles.

p. 1132

Global Christian movements in the nineteenth century

Christianity as a whole was becoming more diverse in the nineteenth century as Western missionary efforts began to increase rapidly the numbers of converts in Asia and Africa. Following the American Revolution of 1776 former slaves from Canada, the US and England, inspired by the ideals of freedom with assistance from British abolitionists, succeeded in planting a colony in West Africa in Sierra Leone. From here mission efforts further inland were launched, the most famous

Slave auction in the USA in the nineteenth century

being that along the Niger River under the leadership of Samuel Ajayi Crowther (*c.*1806–91), the first African ordained to the Anglican church episcopacy. Various new mission efforts were launched in southern and eastern Africa as well. By the end of the nineteenth century, European commercial interests were fuelling the drive to colonize all of Africa, and at the Berlin conference of 1884–5 the European powers divided the continent among themselves.

European colonialism dominated the history of Christianity in nineteenth-century Asia as well. The Ching dynasty in China had extended its control over territories as extensive as any previous Chinese dynasty. The superior technology of the English military forced the Chinese government to open more ports and accept unequal treaties. The Treaty of Nanjing in 1842 provided Protestant missionaries with protections and access to the country. Within a few decades a steady stream of missionaries had begun, reaching its peak in the twentieth century.

Protestants and Catholics were not the only ones to send missions across Asia in the nineteenth century. Russian interests had reached across Siberia into Alaska, where traders began operating in the middle of the eighteenth century. The first Russian mission to Alaska was founded in 1794, and even after the US assumed control of the region in the 1860s the Russian Orthodox Church continued to grow.

Nineteenth-century Russia was the land of Fyodor Dostoievsky and Leo Tolstoy, of great tsars and impoverished peasants, of monasteries and cities. The emancipation of the serfs in 1861 marks an event as important in Russian history as was the Emancipation Proclamation two years later in the US. In 1881 Konstantin Pobedonostsev, a fierce opponent of Western democratic political ideas and of religious pluralism, became head of the Holy Synod in Moscow. Roman Catholics, Protestants, Jews, Buddhists and others suffered persecution under his rule.

To the south, the last decades of the nineteenth century saw the demise of the Ottoman empire and the rise of autocephalous (self-governing) churches in the Balkans. Increased Western mission efforts directed towards Islamic countries posed the greatest challenge to the ancient Orthodox churches of the East (Armenian, Coptic, Syrian and Assyrian), since most of those who became either Protestant or Roman Catholic were proselytes from other Christian traditions. A series of reforms begun under Patriarch Cyril IV in Egypt in the middle of the century, which included the founding of the Coptic Orthodox College and expansion of educational programmes for women, helped to strengthen the Coptic communion internally while preparing it for greater participation with other churches of the world in the ecumenical movement of the twentieth century.

Coptic Christianity

The twentieth century

Thus the twentieth century began with Western churches everywhere exerting their influence on world Christianity. Riding on the back of Western colonialism and imperialism, Western missionaries had won converts and planted churches in virtually every region of every continent. Control of the mission churches remained mostly within the 'sending' church in Europe or North America, reproducing the colonial relations that characterized global political dynamics. Western missions had reproduced the confessional and denominational divisions that were characteristic of Western Christianity in the modern period as well. Such divisions often reflected social and cultural differences found in the European or North American contexts, leading some to begin to question their relevance to new contexts as they sought to work together in mission. Several Protestant confessional bodies had begun to work together on an international level, and from the Anglican Communion had come an invitation to the other separated churches of the world to work together for unity in matters of faith and order. The first steps towards the development of more indigenous forms of theology as well as towards ecumenical co-operation were being taken at the beginning of the twentieth century.

These efforts were given a major boost forward by the World Missionary Conference held in Edinburgh, Scotland, in 1910. Delegates from almost all major branches of Protestant Christianity gathered there to consider the situation and seek the best ways to advance the cause of world missions. The Conference helped to give impetus to the search for Christian unity in matters of faith and order, and to the search for a more relevant witness in matters of life and work in the world. It took more than a decade for these other conferences (Faith and Order, and Life and Work) to be organized, but eventually they were, giving definitive institutional form to a distinct ecumenical movement in the twentieth century.

Ecumenical movement
Christianity in Asia

Anti-colonial sentiments were growing throughout Asia during the first decades of the twentieth century. In India, where Christians represented a small minority and Western missions were often associated with British imperialism, a new generation of Indian Christian leaders, many of whom were more open to dialogue with other religions, was in the making. Meanwhile in China, where the Ching dynasty was coming to an end, many were grappling with the ambiguities of harbouring strong anti-foreign sentiments while seeing the need to adopt aspects of Western science and education that characterized the modern world. The 1911 nationalist revolution under Sun Yatsen brought an end to thousands of years of traditional imperial rule and the traditional educational system of Confucian learning that supported it. A new generation of national Chinese Christian leaders emerged both within churches historically related to Western mission bodies and in new independent Chinese churches.

In Africa an even more radical form of Christianity was emerging as a number of indigenous prophetic or charismatic church leaders began to organize new independent African churches. Often these leaders came out of the Western mission churches, which did not permit Africans to assume positions of leadership. Such African initiated churches adapted more readily traditional African cultural and religious practices, paid more attention to local concerns such as healing and witchcraft, and gave more attention to the work of the Spirit in their midst.

Churches in Western Europe were equally grappling with the challenges of modern life, including rapid advances in science, the growing industrial order, and new radical political theories during these years. During the first decades of the century many were optimistic about the so-called 'progress' of human (or better, Western) civilization. The horrors of the world war fought in the trenches of Europe, in various colonial lands, and out on the seas, between 1914 and 1917 put an end to such dreams. In the aftermath of that war the realization grew among many that Western Christendom was finished, and that churches in Europe no longer influenced the culture the way they once thought they could.

Science

Biblical criticism, liberal theology, the new social sciences and the study of world religions all made their impact upon the traditional Christian intellectual world in North America as well during the first decades of the twentieth century. Here, especially in the US (less so in Canada which continued to have more in common with Europe), the clash between these newer Protestant theological currents and more traditional forms of evangelical faith led to a protracted struggle between those who were eventually known as 'fundamentalists' and the so-called 'modernists'. The Social Gospel movement was at its peak during these first decades of the twentieth century in North America as well, while a host of urban mission efforts sprang up from the evangelical and holiness branches of Protestant Christianity in both England and the US.

Liberal theology
Sociology
Other faiths
Fundamentalism

From these same streams of holiness and revivalist Christianity in the US, a new Pentecostal movement emerged in the first decade of the twentieth century, announced to the world by a revival that took place in Azusa Street, Los Angeles, led by an African American preacher named William J. Seymour. The signature event of this new Pentecostal movement was speaking in unknown tongues, a practice that would became the single most important identifying mark of Pentecostalism worldwide in the twentieth century. Although it quickly adjusted in North America to the reigning paradigms of Protestant denominationalism, elsewhere in the world Pentecostalism continued to thrive as a movement more than an institution, gaining adherents often without being noticed by those at the institutional centres of theological power.

Pentecostalism

Roman Catholics in Western Europe and North America faced the challenges of modern society in the first decades of the twentieth century from the perspective of Vatican I. Papal encyclicals condemned modern materialism, theological liberalism, *laissez-faire* capitalism and atheistic socialism. To many in the Roman Catholic Church, Latin America seemed to represent a 'new Christendom', for it seemed to be most free from the anti-Catholic pressures of modernity that were affecting the church in the North. The problems of social inequality and ruling oligarchies in Latin America posed a different set of challenges to the church, however, and by the third decade of the century organizations such as Catholic Action among the university students and laity had begun to address problems of social reform.

Countries represented at the Second Vatican Council, 1962–5

The numbers in brackets after each country indicate the number of delegates present:

1 Albania (3)
2 Algeria (6)
3 Angola (7)
4 Arabia (23)
5 Argentina (68)
6 Australia (38)
7 Austria (16)
8 Bahamas (1)
9 Belgium (27)
10 Bermuda (1)
11 Bolivia (22)
12 Botswana (1)
13 Brazil (217)
14 British Honduras (8)
15 Bulgaria (2)
16 Burma (8)
17 Burundi (5)
18 Cambodia (2)
19 Cameroon (11)
20 Canada (100)
21 Cape Verde (1)
22 Central African Republic (5)
23 Ceylon (9)
24 Chad (5)
25 Chile (35)
26 China (67)
27 Colombia (58)
28 Congo (Brazzaville) (4)
29 Congo (Kinshasa) (47)
30 Costa Rica (7)
31 Crete (1)
32 Cuba (6)
33 Czechoslovakia (5)
34 Cyprus (1)
35 Dahomey (5)
36 Dominican Republic (5)
37 Ecuador (25)
38 Egypt (14)
39 El Salvador (8)
40 Ethiopia (7)
41 Falkland Islands (1)
42 Finland (2)
43 France (144)
44 Gabon (3)
45 Gambia (1)
46 Germany (61)
47 Ghana (7)
48 Great Britain (48)
49 Greece (6)
50 Guatemala (11)
51 Guinea (3)
52 Guyanas (3)
53 Haiti (7)
54 Honduras (7)
55 Hungary (12)
56 Iceland (1)
57 India (93)
58 Indonesia (32)
59 Iraq (14)
60 Iran (4)
61 Ireland (31)
62 Israel (3)
63 Italy (451)
64 Ivory Coast (6)
65 Jamaica (1)
66 Japan (16)
67 Jordan (5)
68 Kenya (11)
69 Korea (12)
70 Laos (3)
71 Lebanon (2)
72 Lesotho (3)
73 Liberia (2)
74 Libya (4)
75 Malagasay Republic (19)
76 Malaysia (5)
77 Mali (8)
78 Malta (3)
79 Mauritius (1)
80 Melanesia (6)
81 Mexico (68)
82 Micronesia (3)
83 Morocco (2)
84 Mozambique (8)
85 Netherlands (15)
86 New Guinea (13)
87 New Zealand (6)
88 Nicaragua (8)
89 Niger (1)
90 Nigeria (26)
91 Norway (3)
92 Pakistan (13)
93 Palestine (3)
94 Panama (9)
95 Paraguay (14)
96 Peru (44)
97 Philippines (46)
98 Poland (59)
99 Polynesia (8)
100 Port Guinea (1)
101 Portugal (29)
102 Puerto Rico (6)
103 Reunion (2)
104 Rhodesia (6)
105 Romania (2)
106 Rwanda (4)
107 Senegal (5)
108 Seychelles (1)
109 Sierra Leone (2)
110 Singapore (1)
111 Somalia (1)
112 South Africa (26)
113 South West Africa (2)
114 Spain (87)
115 Spanish Sahara (1)
116 Sudan (5)
117 Swaziland (1)
118 Sweden (1)
119 Switzerland (11)
120 Tanzania (27)
121 Thailand (8)
122 Togo (3)
123 Trinidad and Tobago (6)
124 Tunis (1)
125 Turkey (3)
126 Uganda (11)
127 Ukraine (1)
128 Upper Volta (6)
129 Uruguay (15)
130 USA (247)
131 Venezuela (29)
132 Vietnam (17)
133 West Indies (2)
134 Yugoslavia (28)
135 Zambia (10)

Note: this map is not exhaustive.

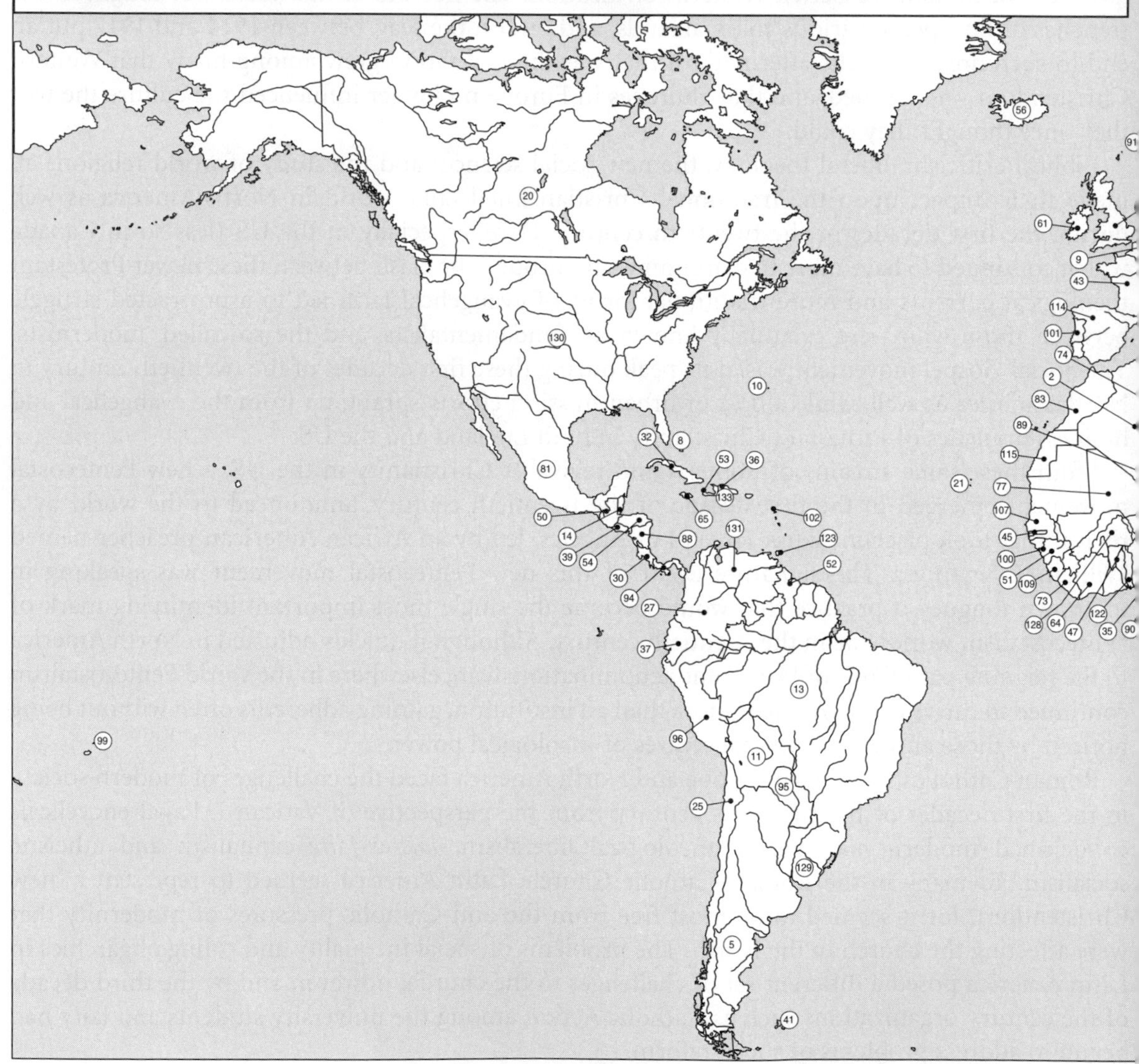

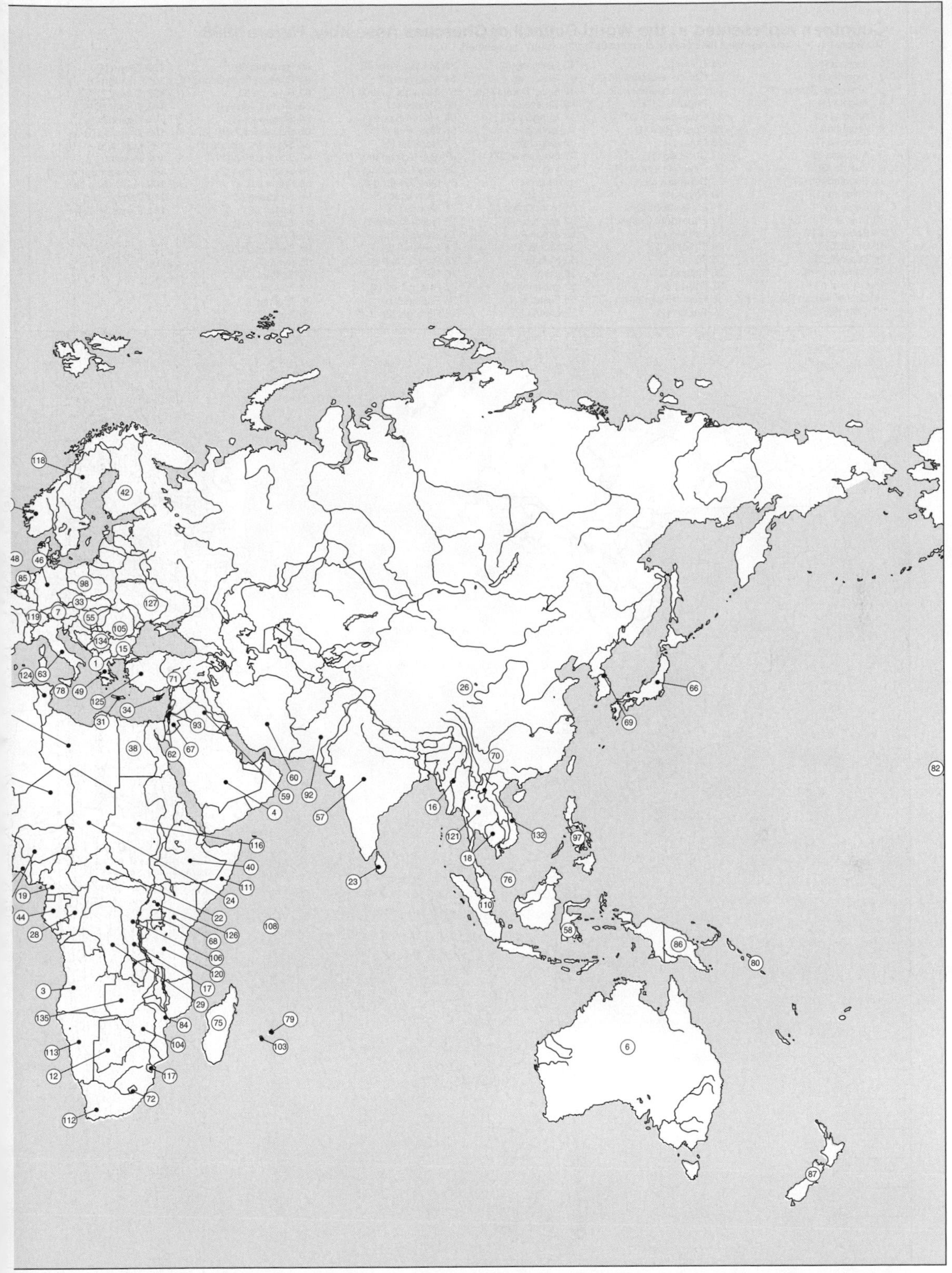
118
42
48
46
85
98
33
127
7
119
55
105
134
15
1
124
63
78
49
125
71
34
31
93
38
62
67
60
92
59
4
57
26
66
69
70
82
16
121
18
132
97
116
40
111
24
22
126
68
106
120
17
29
19
44
28
108
23
76
110
58
86
80
3
135
113
12
112
72
117
104
84
75
79
103
6
87

Countries represented at the World Council of Churches Assembly, Harare 1998
The figures in brackets represent the number of churches in the country represented.
1 Albania (1)
2 Algeria (1)
3 American Samoa (1)
4 Angola (4)
5 Antigua (3)
6 Argentina (7)
7 Armenia (1)
8 Australia (3)
9 Austria (3)
10 Bangladesh (2)
11 Belgium (1)
12 Benin (1)
13 Bolivia (2)
14 Botswana (1)
15 Brazil (5)
16 Burundi (2)
17 Cameroon (6)
18 Canada (7)
19 Central African Republic (1)
20 Chile (5)
21 China (2)
22 Congo (Brazzaville) (2)
23 Congo (Democratic Republic) (7)
24 Cook Islands (1)
25 Costa Rica (1)
26 Cuba (1)
27 Curaçao (1)
28 Czech Republic (4)
29 Denmark (2)
30 Egypt (4)
31 El Salvador (2)
32 Equatorial Guinea (1)
33 Estonia (1)
34 Ethiopia (2)
35 Fiji (1)
36 Finland (2)
37 France (4)
38 French Polynesia (1)
39 Gabon (1)
40 Germany (4)
41 Ghana (4)
42 Great Britain (13)
43 Greece (2)
44 Hungary (2)
45 Iceland
46 India (8)
47 Indonesia (27)
48 Iran (1)
49 Ireland (1)
50 Italy (3)
51 Ivory Coast (2)
52 Jamaica (3)
53 Japan (4)
54 Kenya (8)
55 Kiribati (1)
56 Latvia (1)
57 Lebanon (3)
58 Lesotho (1)
59 Liberia (2)
60 Madagascar (3)
61 Malaysia (2)
62 Marshall Islands (1)
63 Mexico (1)
64 Mozambique (1)
65 Myanmar (3)
66 Namibia (1)
67 The Netherlands (7)
68 New Caledonia (1)
69 New Zealand (5)
70 Nicaragua (2)
71 Nigeria (7)
72 North Korea (1)
73 Norway (1)
74 Pakistan (2)
75 Papua New Guinea (2)
76 Peru
77 Philippines (4)
78 Poland (4)
79 Portugal (2)
80 Romania (4)
81 Russian Federation (1)
82 Rwanda (2)
83 Sierra Leone (1)
84 Singapore (1)
85 Slovak Republic (3)
86 Solomon Islands (2)
87 South Africa (11)
88 South Korea (2)
89 Spain (2)
90 Sri Lanka (2)
91 Sudan (2)
92 Suriname (1)
93 Sweden (2)
94 Switzerland (2)
95 Syria (2)
96 Tanzania (3)
97 Taiwan (1)
98 Thailand (1)
99 Togo (2)
100 Tonga (1)
101 Trinidad (1)
102 Turkey (1)
103 Tuvalu (1)
104 Uganda (1)
105 Uruguay (1)
106 USA (25)
107 Vanuatu (1)
108 Western Samoa (2)
109 Yugoslavia (3)
110 Zambia (4)
111 Zimbabwe (4)
Davis Strait
Denmark Strait
Norwegian Sea
Hudson Bay
North Sea
Baltic Sea
NORTH ATLANTIC OCEAN
Mediterranean Sea
Gulf of Mexico
Caribbean Sea
Gulf of Guinea
SOUTH ATLANTIC OCEAN

ARCTIC OCEAN
ARCTIC OCEAN
Laptev Sea
East Siberian Sea
Kara Sea
Barents Sea
Chukchi Sea
Bering Strait
Bering Sea
Sea of Okhotsk
Aral Sea
Caspian Sea
Black Sea
Sea of Japan
Yellow Sea
East China Sea
PACIFIC OCEAN
Philippine Sea
Bay of Bengal
South China Sea
Gulf of Aden
Red Sea
Celebes Sea
INDIAN OCEAN
Coral Sea
Mozambique Channel
Tasman Sea
81
62
53
57
7
21
72
88
95
97
48
74
46
10
65
98
77
91
34
90
61
84
19
104
54
82
96
16
47
75
86
107
64
60
111
8
68
58
69

HISTORY

The landscape of Orthodox Christianity was greatly affected by events related to the world war. Shortly after its outbreak in 1914, the ruling Turkish authorities of the Ottoman empire launched a systematic genocide against Armenian and Assyrian Christians. Over the next several years both communions suffered deaths estimated to amount to millions and further dislocation from their traditional national homelands. The war brought the Russian government of the Tsar to the point of collapse. In the ensuing period of civil war the Bolsheviks, a Communist party headed by Vladimir Lenin, came to power. They executed the Tsar and his family, deposed the Patriarch of Moscow, disestablished the Orthodox Church, and set in motion seven decades of religious oppression. Within a few years the borders of Russia were expanded to encompass several other former nations in what was then called the Soviet Union.

Persecution

The war brought about the end of the Ottoman empire and a degree of greater freedom for the Orthodox churches in territories formerly under its rule. Greater contact with Western churches, both negative and positive, had been going on for some time. Looking at the situation across the world, the office of the Ecumenical Patriarch in Istanbul in 1920 issued a pastoral letter inviting the churches of the world to form a league of churches similar to the League of Nations then in process. Already planning for a World Conference on Faith and Order was under way. That conference took place in 1927, drawing together representatives from most Protestant and several Orthodox communions. A decade later, delegates to a Second World Conference on Faith and Order voted to join their movement to that of the parallel movement for Life and Work to create the World Council of Churches, which finally held its inaugural assembly in 1948 in Amsterdam.

The decade of the 1930s was a time of totalitarianism. In the Soviet Union Joseph Stalin solidified his grip on the nation, while fascist governments were in power in Italy, Spain and then Germany. The world economy was in the grip of a great depression when Italy invaded Ethiopia in 1935. Two years later Japan, which had already annexed Korea in 1910, went to war against China. Meanwhile republican forces battled fascists in Spain from 1936 through 1939 in civil war. Then in 1939 German armies under Adolf Hitler annexed Czechoslovakia and invaded Poland, igniting what was soon known as World War II. Within Europe, Hitler and the Nazis began the systematic extermination of Jews, a holocaust that by the end of the war in 1945 cost over 6 million Jews their lives. In the decades following 1945 the role that Christians worldwide had played in either passively or actively supporting the Jewish Holocaust during these years became the occasion for fundamental rethinking on the part of every major branch of world Christianity the matter of its teaching regarding Judaism. In the Pacific the war was brought to an end when the US dropped two atom bombs on major cities in Japan, almost instantaneously wiping them off the face of the earth. While a far lesser degree of Christian soul-searching took place around this event, a strong international movement against nuclear weapons did emerge, and by the 1960s had become part of a wider global peace movement in which numerous individual Christians and churches participated.

The close of World War II brought about a new era in East-West relations with the rise of the Cold War. Two superpowers – the US and the Soviet Union – were soon lining up client states across the globe to support them in their confrontation. The nations of Eastern Europe were drawn into the Soviet political orbit as Communist states, while nations from Western Europe, the US and Canada formed the North Atlantic Treaty Organization (NATO) pledged to stop Soviet aggression in Europe. In 1949 the nationalist government in China fell to Communist forces under Mao Tse-tung, but within a decade China was forging an independent Communist path. A movement of non-aligned nations was organized with India, which gained independence from England in 1947, and figured prominently. The formation of the United Nations provided one of the few effective forums for discussion across these ideological divides in the post-1945 world.

Christians on both sides were affected by the Cold War. In Western nations churches with few exceptions lined up with various degrees of enthusiasm to support their governments. Under Communism Christians in the East faced severe restrictions, infiltration of their hierarchy, and often open persecution, as hostile governments, guided by the supposed logic of Marxist theory, sought to suppress religion as a counter-revolutionary force. In China the Communists expelled all foreign missionaries in 1949, but while the government attempted to bring churches under state oversight, outright persecution of those that did so was minimal until the period of the Cultural Revolution in the 1960s. A number of churches in China resisted government registration on the other hand, giving rise to an underground Chinese movement of persecuted Protestant house-churches and a separate Catholic Church that continues today.

In the southern hemisphere de-colonization was well under way by 1945, and a new era of ecumenical theology arose in its wake. By the 1960s the Civil Rights movement in the US was under way. Churches in the US played a critical role in organizing and carrying out this struggle for the liberation of African Americans. A similar movement in South Africa against the system of apartheid likewise took shape in the 1960s, and continued until the South African apartheid regime finally came to an end in the 1990s. Across the globe a movement for women's liberation also gained strength over this period.

The 1960s were without a doubt a momentous decade in world Christian affairs. Not least among the events that made it such was the general council of the Roman Catholic Church known as Vatican II that met from 1962 to 1965. Citing the need for an 'updating' (*aggiornamento*) in the church, Pope John XXIII called for the council in 1959 shortly after assuming office. After a period of preparation, bishops and theologians from across the world, joined by observers from other Christian communions and even other religions, worked together to produce a body of documents that taken together charted a new course for the church's faith and ministry. Vatican II defined the Roman Catholic Church as the definitive sacrament of salvation given by God to humanity, but recognized valid signs of salvation in other Christian communions, which were now called 'separated' siblings. Among the liturgical reforms it called for worship in the vernacular languages of the people. A new sense of the role of the church in the modern world was articulated, one that called for more active engagement with thought forms as well as problems faced by the present age.

Vatican II helped propel a number of theological movements forward, at points converging with the more general anti-colonial sentiments that were at large across the world. Among Catholics and Protestants alike the theological movement for indigenization in Africa and Asia accelerated. By the 1970s the terms contextualization or inculturation were being used to describe efforts to appropriate for theological reflection the dynamic resources of diverse world cultures. From Latin America, Southern Africa, India and the African American community in North America, to be joined by women from all across the globe, new forms of discourse and reflection emerged in what were generally known as liberation theologies. Rather than seeking to answer questions posed by modern forms of disbelief, as Western theology since the Enlightenment had tended to perceive its task, liberation theologies sought to answer theological questions posed by poverty, injustice and oppression. The results were often controversial, and by the 1990s Christian communities either formed around or explicitly committed to pursuing an agenda set by liberation theology remained few. Liberation theology fared best in the academic centres of Christian life – somewhat of an irony given its commitments to being an effective agent on behalf of the poor.

Liberation theology

During the last quarter of the twentieth century the theological movement that grew fastest among the poor was not liberation theology but Pentecostalism. Explosive growth began to be noted in Latin America by researchers in the 1970s. By the end of the century, the phenomenon was recognized as worldwide in scope. In Africa, Latin America, parts of Asia, and parts of Europe Pentecostals and neo-Pentecostals (or charismatics, as the latter are also known) have helped Christianity to grow at rates greater than ever before in its history.

Christianity in Europe

At the same time Western Europe, which at the beginning of the modern era was the most Christianized continent and throughout most of the modern era continued to be the major source of missionary efforts for expanding Christianity, passed through a sustained phase of 'de-Christianization' under the forces of secularization. While many Europeans continue to consider themselves Christian in a general cultural sense, few attend worship on a regular basis, have their children baptized, or participate in a meaningful way in the faith of the community. Europe has become in some ways the least Christianized continent on earth at the beginning of the third millennium.

Secularization

Christianity in North America

North America has witnessed a similar decline over the past quarter century in what are often called the 'mainline' Protestant churches. American evangelicalism, on the other hand, has shown itself to be a growing force both at home and around the world. Since the 1970s evangelicals worldwide have developed a global network of relations through organizations such as the Lausanne Conference on World Evangelism, or through 'para-church' ministries and the work of charismatic individuals. The figure of Billy Graham stands out as an emblem of the global reach of the US evangelical message. No person in the history of world Christianity, save perhaps for his contemporary, Pope John Paul II, has brought the message of the gospel to more people on earth over the past two millennia.

Globalization

Thus we stand at the beginning of a third millennium. The end of the Cold War and the economic processes of globalization have abolished borders east and west while at the same time a worldwide resurgence of Islam has increased tensions with Christianity in virtually every corner of the globe. Within Christianity the changes have been enormous. Churches that for thousands of years considered themselves bound to particular territories have through global migrations and the gains of conversions found themselves rapidly de-territorializing their identities. Russian and Greek Orthodox traditions no longer belong only to people who are of Russian or Greek descent. At the same time there are growing Baptist, Pentecostal, Seventh-day Adventist and Salvation Army communities in Russia. The typical Christian is no longer from London or Geneva, but from Buenos Aires or Lagos.

The vast majority of the nearly two billion people on earth who have been baptized belong to the Roman Catholic communion, and their numbers are increasing. The fastest growing segment of world Christianity, however, may well be those who worship in Pentecostal or charismatic communities. Christians now belong to well over 30,000 different denominations or separate churches on earth. They speak nearly every language now in use, and use several languages in worship that have not been regularly spoken for 1000 years or more. Christian scriptures have been translated into hundreds of languages, many of them in only the last half century. In many parts of the world, however, the use of video and audio tapes is supplementing the use of written words in day-to-day Christian life. World Christianity is a highly diverse, and still diversifying, movement at the beginning of the twenty-first century.

DALE T. IRVIN

Peter Brown, *The Rise of Western Christendom. Triumph and Diversity 200–1000 AD*, Oxford: Blackwell 2002; Adrian Hastings (ed), *A World History of Christianity*, London: Cassell and Grand Rapids, MI: Eerdmans 1999; Dale T. Irvin and Scott W. Sunquist, *History of the World Christian Movement, Vol.1: Earliest Christianity to 1453*, Maryknoll, NY: Orbis and Edinburgh: T&T Clark 2001 (Vol. 2 in preparation); John McManners (ed), *The Oxford History of Christianity*, Oxford: OUP 2002; Samuel Moffett, *A History of Christianity in Asia* (2 vols), Maryknoll, NY: Orbis 2001, 2003; *The Penguin History of the Church:* 1. Henry Chadwick, *The Early Church*; 2. R. W. Southern, *Western Society and the Church in the Middle Ages*; 3. Owen Chadwick, *The Reformation*; 4. Gerald R. Cragg, *The Church and the Age of Reason 1648–1789*; 5. Alec R. Vidler, *The Church in an Age of Revolution;* 6. Owen Chadwick, *The Christian Church in the Cold War*, Harmondsworth: Penguin Books 1990–3

Holiness movement

It seems an irony that one branch of the Christian church should bear the name 'holiness movement', for Christianity as a whole has essentially always been a 'holiness movement'.

The 'membership' of the holiness movement is quite amorphous, but in so far as perhaps half of it has organized itself into denominations and ecumenical enterprises, it is represented by two North American alliances: the Christian Holiness Partnership (CHP) and the Interdenominational Holiness Convention (IHC). The CHP, by far the larger, was born in 1867, in Vineland, New Jersey, as the National Camp Meeting Association for the Promotion of Holiness (NCAPH); the IHC in 1947, in Salem, Ohio.

Conservatively estimated, the world 'membership' of the holiness movement is about 8.5 million, with a constituency somewhere between 14 and 15 million. Just under half of its membership and constituency is divided among its five largest representative bodies: the Church of the Nazarene (1.4 million members), the Salvation Army (1 million), the Church of God (Anderson, Indiana, 0.6 million), the Wesleyan Church(es) (0.4 million) and the Free Methodist Church(es) (0.4 million). These numbers are all approximations and may mislead, in part because of widely-variant organizational patterns: the Church of the Nazarene and the Salvation Army are organized as international bodies; the Wesleyan and Free Methodist churches are both federations of independent national churches; and the Church of God (Anderson, Indiana) is a worldwide communion of independent congregations.

There are several other reasons for noting the numbers only as approximations. Perhaps the most important is the fact that many Christians are in every way but denominational membership Wesleyan/holiness people. This would include persons in various Methodist bodies (e.g. the historic African American Methodist churches in the US, the United Methodist Church and the Wesleyan Methodist Church in the UK) which still serve at least as many as 4 million holiness people. Important, too, is the fact that a large number of constituents, though quite faithful Christians through their respective holiness congregations, refuse to join because they choose not to accept one or more of the rather strict mandatory behavioural 'rules' for members characteristic of holiness groups. Hence the reason for looking at both 'membership' and 'constituency'.

There are two key figures in the establishment of the holiness movement. The first is John Wesley (1703–91), Oxford scholar and Anglican priest, and founder of Methodism. He held that the doctrine and experience of 'scriptural holiness' are central and essential to Christian faith, including its social action and its evangelizing. For Wesley, God graciously grants assurance of both justification and entire sanctification, holiness, to the believer. However, assurance of entire sanctification may not come immediately or instantaneously; it is a divine gift that may require time and experience to recognize. The internal witness of the Holy Spirit is the sole evidence that God has granted it. One retains this gift only by continuing dependence in faith upon the atoning work of Christ. The relationship of unconditional love to God and neighbour should mature with experience, but it may be lost (as is also the case with justification). Should it be lost, the Lord may graciously renew it through confession and repentance, enabled by grace.

Justification

Holy Spirit

The second key figure is Charles Grandison Finney (1792–1875), an American evangelist who established himself at Oberlin, Ohio, where he eventually became president of the college which had been founded there as a joint Presbyterian and Congregational effort, and which was the first co-educational and first racially integrated

Methodism

institution of higher education in the nation. Finney transformed revivalism in America. Like Wesley, Finney insisted that entire sanctification is a work of grace, but unlike him, Finney emphasized the role of the human will in accepting and retaining it. Wesley emphasized spiritual cleansing and freedom; Finney emphasized spiritual power over sin. His emphases came to prevail in the holiness movement by about 1900. They became critically important in sustaining the idea that the movement is essentially a revival movement, an idea that some holiness people are now questioning as the study of Wesley himself has revived. In important ways, the differences between Wesleyan and Finneyite emphases were factors in the formation of the two different alliances in the holiness movement.

Revivalism and the frontier spirit are of a piece and they dominated the original North American context for both Wesley's and Finney's understandings of the doctrine and experience of entire sanctification until World War II; they still carry great influence. Impatience with temporizing and with intellectual reflection has fed revivalism's urgent call for immediate decision. Many, perhaps most, North American holiness people expected an instantaneous divine response to an abrupt, usually emotion-laden, decision to 'be saved', or to 'be sanctified'. In addition, their missionaries outside North America passed this understanding on to those to whom they ministered. The seeker decides 'now' and God responds to the decision 'now'. The focus was upon entrance into these religious experiences; many, certainly not all, holiness people tended to treat further growth in grace as of secondary importance or with clichés. So, while some revivalists and pastors, a minority, followed Wesley and seriously encouraged both immediate commitment and growth in grace, the far greater proportion of the energy of the movement went into evangelizing, at home and abroad.

The name Christian Holiness Partnership dates only from 1997. Its roots lie in the National Camp Meeting Association for the Promotion of Holiness (NCAPH). This association was formed by prominent Methodist Episcopal preachers who had held a remarkably successful camp meeting in Vineland, New Jersey. The meeting had intentionally emphasized John Wesley's doctrine of entire sanctification in an atmosphere of intense prayer, Bible study and preaching. Its pastor-organizers felt that more such meetings should be planned, and the NCAPH was the means for doing so.

The reputation of the NCAPH as a sponsor of intense, effective, well-focused and well-ordered holiness camps brought invitations to hold campaigns in every section of the US, including the South and Canada. Encampments of more than 1000 tents and congregations of more than 10,000 were common. Usually reliable eyewitnesses reported that 20,000 attended the 1868 camp meeting in Manheim, Pennsylvania.

By the time that the NCAPH officially changed its name, in 1893, to the National Association for the Promotion of Holiness (commonly, the National Holiness Association [NHA]), it had held about 60 campaigns. The NHA spawned and encouraged the development of regional, state, county and local holiness associations. It exercised no control over these, but usually had cordial relationships with them and its advice was often sought, and sometimes given without being sought. The independence of the satellite associations allowed for more ecumenical co-operation than was desired by the Methodist-run NHA; these satellite groups often became the nuclei for new denominations. By the beginning of World War II, episcopal Methodism, increasingly committed to social action, had grown indifferent to the proclamation and teaching of Wesley's doctrine of entire sanctification, but now there were dozens of holiness bodies taking up the cause. The NHA, very much aware of changing circumstances, opened its doors more widely to non-episcopal Methodist membership and leadership. In 1942, it elected its first non-Methodist president, and its membership list grew ever more ecumenical. In 1971, the NHA again changed its name to reflect a Canadian and Caribbean presence in its membership, and to recognize that several of its member denominations were planning to become international organizations. 'National' no longer described the organization. Other concerns too, especially those related to higher education and a recommitment to ministry to the poor, helpless, and outcast, changed the character of the NHA from a holiness rally and a meeting place for holiness people to share concerns informally to a forum for discussion of mutual denominational problems. So it became the Christian Holiness Association (CHA). In 1997 Christian Holiness Partnership (CHP) was chosen as yet another new name, so as better to describe the structure and purpose of the organization as it now is.

The Interdenominational Holiness Convention (IHC) was born in 1947 as the Inter-Church Holiness Association, but it quickly adopted its current name. It arose largely, but not entirely, as a critique of what was perceived as 'worldliness' within the holiness movement, especially with respect to the behavioural 'rules' and practices. It is composed of some 30 small denominations. None of them has more than 15,000 members. Most are much smaller and most are post-World War II objectors to mergers or schisms from larger holiness denominations.

The long-time leader of the IHC was Harold E. Schmul, pastor of the Salem, Ohio, congregation in what had originally been the Allegheny Conference of the Wesleyan Methodist Church. When the Wesleyan Methodist Church

Holiness camp meeting, Wichita, Kansas, 1909

and the Pilgrim Holiness Church merged in 1968, Schmul, who had already become the principal leader in the IHC, led the Allegheny Conference out of the merger and into independence as the Allegheny Wesleyan Methodist Connection. Schmul's *Convention Herald*, his long-time management of an active publishing enterprise, and his establishment and direction of an annual indoor camp meeting and convention in Dayton, Ohio, have been the principal instruments in maintaining his strong sense of character as a peacemaker and have gone a long way in maintaining reasonably cordial relationships between the IHC and the NHA/CHA.

'Spreading scriptural holiness' has spurred the holiness people since their earliest days as a movement, and then as an aggregation of denominations, to engage in vigorous programmes for missionary work, including clinics, hospitals and schools at all levels. In the US, Canada and the UK, higher, liberal arts, education, including the establishment of universities, is both a cause and an effect in maintaining denominational and traditional identity and mission.

Almost every holiness denomination has a missionary corps and takes great interest in its work. Since the late 1970s, most missionaries have been preparing indigenous representatives to carry on all aspects of the work of the given denomination in the given area. This has produced wholly indigenous districts in the international denominations, and fully-organized sister denominations in the federating denominations. Some of the missionized countries now send and receive missionaries, e.g., Argentine Nazarenes have missionaries in Africa, and Korean Nazarenes have sent missionaries to the US and Canada. The Nazarenes (considered as an international church), with 1.4 million members, have about 600 missionaries in 60 countries. The Wesleyan Church (considered as a worldwide federation), with 400,000 members, has active missionary work in about 20 countries.

Education has also played a strong role in the missionary work of the holiness people and early on the movement expended great energy in social action. This tended to die out during the Great Depression and then on through the 1970s, when the great push was for acceptance in society at large. But in the 1970s the movement's social conscience revived, especially with respect to the needs of the urban poor and minorities. It is now very strong, even though the majority of the movement's adherents are politically conservative.

Until the 1990s, the Sunday morning worship services

of the holiness people were almost universally indistinguishable in form from the informal but orderly practice of American evangelicals in general. This still holds true for at least half of the holiness congregations. The greatest difference lies in the greater openness of the holiness people to spontaneous testimonies, exclamations of agreement or praise and calls to immediate spiritual decision. However, this is only a matter of degree. The holiness movement has never rejected form but it has eschewed formality or formalism. The bare bones of Book of Common Prayer rituals are clear in celebrations of baptism and the Lord's Supper, and in the services for marriage and burial. Vigour and explicit emotional expression mark worship. People still value the sincere, spontaneous 'Amen', 'Praise the Lord', etc. Applause, absent for about 80 years, has returned, but it is not universally encouraged, for it seems to many to draw attention to human performance rather than to divine worship.

Bible
Papacy
Church

Talk of uniting ebbs and flows among holiness bodies. The Wesleyans and Free Methodists have come close to merging on several occasions, and the Nazarenes and Wesleyans have entered exploratory conversations. Almost every holiness denomination is the result of, or has experienced, at least one merger – far more mergers than schisms. A varying number participate together in the planning and writing of materials for Christian education in local congregations, such as quarterly Sunday School lessons. The Church of God (Anderson), the Wesleyans and the Nazarenes have had representatives on the Faith and Order Commission of the National Council of Churches of Christ in the US (NCC), but the denominations of the holiness movement have generally stayed aloof from the World Council of Churches and the NCC. All of the larger holiness groups and some of the smaller ones have maintained at least co-operative relationships with the National Association of Evangelicals (NAE), and a number of their scholars participate in the NAE-related Evangelical Theological Society. Hesitation over interdenominational co-operation has usually vanished at the local level as pastors and congregations have usually been quite active in local ministries. The Nazarenes belong to the World Methodist Council; the Wesleyans have belonged to it on occasion, as have the Free Methodists.

Eucharist
Holy Spirit

p. 1037

Ecumenical movement

PAUL M. BASSETT

Paul M. Bassett (ed), *Holiness Teaching – New Testament Times to Wesley*, Boston: Beacon Hill Press 1997; Melvin E. Dieter, *The Nineteenth Century Holiness Movement*, Boston: Beacon Hill Press 1998; Albert F. Harper, *Holiness Teaching Today*, Boston: Beacon Hill Press 1998

Holy

In the Christian tradition the word 'holy' is most commonly used as an adjective in terms such as 'Holy Name', 'Holy Word', 'Holy Bible' or 'Holy Spirit'. Most often this use serves to associate the object with what is divine in the sense of giving to it an association with a power that derives from beyond this world. For instance, the Bible is holy because it relates the teachings and stories about God and the world; similarly, the Pope is called the 'Holy Father' because his authority over the 'holy catholic church' is ultimately not his own but is of divine origin, like the church itself.

Alongside the institutions and documents of Christianity which are understood as holy there are also the rites and practices of the Christian churches which have been concerned with 'sanctification', with making things holy through ritual acts of blessing or special forms of worship. These ritual acts have usually been connected with the distinctive actions of Christian priesthood. For instance, the elements of bread and wine are understood as being made holy through the actions of the ordained priest who celebrates the eucharist and who summons down the Holy Spirit to make holy the ordinary things of human life. Similarly, many other things are set apart for religious use and thereby become holy – cups and plates can become sacred or holy vessels through their use in Christian liturgy; or they are set apart for particular purposes – 'holy water' is used to make other things holy through sprinkling, or 'holy oils' are used for rites of anointing in baptism or before death. Sometimes such holy objects gain a special name because of their sacred use, as with the chalice and paten of the eucharist.

More often than not, it is the adjectival sense of 'holy' that has been the main emphasis of the Christian understanding of holiness. Although things that are holy might appear to the casual observer to be exactly the same as things which are profane, what makes them holy is the fact that they are set apart and reverenced or respected as holy or special. This understanding can be traced back to the Old Testament and the Hebrew root *qds*, which means separation – that which is holy is holy or sacred simply because it is separate from that which is not holy or profane. In turn its holiness depends solely on its association with God rather than any quality inherent in the object.

A good illustration of this use is the 'holy ground' which surrounded the burning bush when God's glory was manifested to Moses in the book of Exodus (Exodus 3.5); the ground may have looked identical, but it was holy because of what had been manifested there. Throughout the Old Testament holiness is frequently connected with God's revelation and evokes something of the atmosphere of awe and fear before the divine: Moses is forced to hide his face for fear of looking at God. Holiness is thus linked with God's otherness and transcendence, or what has been called God's 'awesome sacrality'. Even here, however, holiness remains a relative term. What is holy or sacred makes sense only in relation to that which is profane or not holy.

Although it is God's holiness which separates God from the world, it is also that holiness which vindicates Moses' message as a revelation that comes from God. The holiness of the awesome presence of God in the experience of the burning bush is what guarantees the validity of what Moses has to say. Similarly, the experiences of the prophets – for example the extraordinary vision of holiness in Isaiah, chapter 6 – are used by the Old Testament writers to justify the truth of what they have to say or their calling as prophets. The experience of holiness is connected with supernatural authority; even today in ordination services the vision of Isaiah is read out to emphasize the sacredness or holiness of the calling to Christian ministry. Similarly, one of the ancient prayers of the eucharist, the Sanctus, or 'Holy, Holy, Holy', derives from Isaiah's vision and comes at the climax of the eucharistic prayer where God's transforming power is invoked to consecrate the elements.

At the same time, throughout the Jewish and Christian tradition, what is holy has often been associated with specifically religious practices or rites and those who maintain them. A supernatural or 'holy' authority is conferred on those who control access to sacred places and who lead sacred rites. In the Old Testament the noun *qodes* was linked with the priestly cult associated with the Jerusalem temple and in particular with the 'holy priesthood' which protected the sacred centre of the faith, the 'holy of holies'. Many thinkers in the Christian tradition, from as early as the time of Cyprian of Carthage in the third century, consciously applied these Old Testament models of a holy priesthood controlling access to holy things to the Christian priesthood, which in turn became increasingly associated with the power to make things holy. Much medieval theology depended on such a conception of a priesthood whose principal role was to offer the holy sacrifice of the mass on behalf of the living and the dead. In popular practice the eucharistic bread was treated as holy in itself and became the object of religious rites independent of the communion service. At the Reformation many of the Protestant churches rejected the institution of a holy priesthood in favour of a more functional model of ministry. Repeated conflict over the holiness and authority of ministry has characterized debates between, and sometimes within, the different denominations.

Alongside the emphasis on the holy priesthood there also developed in the Old Testament a long list of legal regulations, the so-called 'holiness codes' of the book of Leviticus, where proscriptions were placed on certain practices to ensure the attainment of holiness, primarily through avoiding contamination with what was ritually unclean. This can be seen, for instance, in the injunctions for what was allowed on the sabbath, which became the 'taboo day'. By the time of the New Testament, as Marcus Borg writes, 'to be holy meant to be separate from everything that would defile holiness. The Jewish social world and its conventional wisdom became increasingly structured around the polarities of holiness as separation.' Holiness was thus associated not merely with particular cultic religious activities but with the whole approach to life.

Prophecy

Jesus

Jesus undoubtedly questioned many of the distinctions between sacred and profane and pure and impure. He sought to overcome some of the tendencies towards separation by deliberately siding with outcasts and sharing fellowship with outsiders including Samaritans and tax collectors, or even with those in a state of constant impurity (as with the haemorrhaging woman, Mark 5. 24–34). Indeed, for Jesus, the 'politics of holiness' can be understood as part of a healing power that cleanses people from their defilement rather than a permanent state of opposition between sacred and profane. For Jesus, holiness was as much a disposition of the heart as obedience to a set of religious and ethical instructions.

Authority

Sacraments

Understanding holiness: the sacred and the profane

Christianity shares its emphasis on the holy with other religions: indeed 'the holy' is often understood as one of the universal categories characterizing all religions. Although the holy is often difficult to define, there are two main understandings of it that have been influential in the modern study of religion. Both are helpful in trying to understand the role of the holy in Christianity: the first focuses on the understanding of the holy as that which is separate from the profane, and the second on the holy as experience of the irrational.

Many scholars have sought to clarify the understanding of 'the holy' in terms of separation and apartness. In an influential article published early in the twentieth century the Swedish scholar Nathan Söderblom distinguished between the poles of clean and unclean and sacred and profane, building on concepts that had been pioneered by the early anthropologists. These included *mana* (a sort of contagious religious force) and *taboo* (that which had to be avoided). In essence, holiness was a supernatural and irrational power associated with particular people or places or times. As was common at the time, Söderblom felt that religions developed from a primitive to a more modern form, a movement characterized by the growth and codification of specific rites and ceremonies aimed at

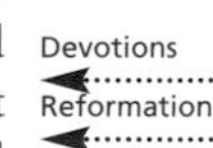

Devotions

Reformation

Ministry and ministers

HOLY PEOPLE, HOLY PLACES AND HOLY THINGS

In Christianity a variety of people, places and things are called holy: here are some of them.

Holy City: Jerusalem.

Holy Club: The name given to the group of Methodists formed at Oxford by John Wesley.

Holy Coat: The seamless garment worn by Jesus, claimed as a relic by Trier cathedral in Germany and the parish church of Argenteuil in France.

Holy Communion: Another name for the eucharist or mass.

Holy Cross Day: 14 September: the feast of the exaltation of the cross.

Holy Door: A door in the façade of St Peter's Rome, bricked up and opened only during a Holy Year by the Pope.

Holy Family: Jesus, Mary and Joseph.

Holy Father: A title of the Pope.

Holy Ghost: Archaic term for the Holy Spirit.

Holy Grail: In legend the cup used by Jesus at the Last Supper and later by Joseph of Arimathea to catch the blood flowing from Jesus' wounds when he was on the cross. However, in some accounts, e.g. Wolfram von Eschenbach's *Parzifal*, the grail is a precious stone fallen from heaven.

Holy Innocents: The children of Bethlehem massacred by Herod the Great.

Holy Island: This usually refers to Lindisfarne, off the coast of Northumberland, England.

Holy Lance: A relic kept in St Peter's Rome, believed to be the lance which pierced the side of Jesus at the crucifixion.

Holy Land: Palestine/Israel.

p. 795

Holy Mountain: Mount Athos in Greece.

Holy Name: The name of Jesus. In the Middle Ages Franciscans engaged in special devotions to the Holy Name; they instituted a Feast of the Holy Name and a Litany of the Holy Name; churches are also dedicated to the Holy Name.

Holy Office: A body instituted to deal internationally with heresy, known as the Inquisition. Since the Second Vatican Council it has been called the Congregation for the Doctrine of Faith.

Holy Oil: Oil used for anointing at baptisms, confirmations, consecrations and coronations.

Holy Orders: The offices of bishop, priest and deacon.

Holy Places, The: The main sites in Palestine to which pilgrimage is made.

Holy Roman empire: The territories ruled by the emperor, from the time of Charlemagne onwards.

Holy Saturday: The day before Easter Day.

Holy See: The see ('seat, throne') of the Bishop of Rome, i.e. the place from which he exercises authority.

Holy Sepulchre: The cave in Jerusalem where according to tradition Christ was buried and from which he rose.

Holy Shroud: A relic kept in Turin with the imprint of the front and back of a human body marked with the traditional stigmata, wounds in hands, feet and side.

Holy Spirit: The third person of the Trinity.

Holy Synod: The supreme organ of government in the Russian Orthodox Church.

Holy War: The title of a book by John Bunyan written during his time in Bedford Gaol; the full title, which indicates is contents, is *The Holy War made by Shaddai upon Diabolus, for the Regaining of the Metropolis of the World, or, The Losing and Taking again of the Town of Man-soul.*

Holy Water: Water blessed for special purposes.

Holy Week: The week preceding Easter Day, beginning on Palm Sunday.

Holy Writ: Another name for the Bible.

p. 476 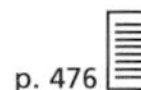

Holy Year: A year proclaimed by the Pope in which a special indulgence is granted to pilgrims to Rome.

cultivating a sense of holiness. This often meant ensuring that boundaries were established from what was not holy, and differences from the profane or ordinary world were emphasized: for instance, taboos on certain practices or activities prevented contamination of the holy.

A similar relational understanding of holiness was developed at much the same time by the French sociologist Emile Durkheim in *The Elementary Forms of Religious Life*. Religions, he claimed, 'presuppose a classification of all things known to men, real and ideal, into two distinct kinds', the sacred and the profane. The sacred is surrounded by a variety of rituals and taboos that constitute 'religion'. This is defined by Durkheim as 'a unified system of beliefs and practices relative to sacred things (things set apart)'. Most crucially, religion is a social phenomenon and is fundamentally a set of 'beliefs and practices which unite into a single moral community, called a church, all those who adhere to them'. Indeed, for Durkheim, religion is primarily concerned with the task of social integration. The corporate worship of that which is holy (the most primitive form of which he believed to be the tribal totem) creates what he calls a 'collective effervescence' where men and women 'believe themselves transported into an entirely different world from the one they have before their eyes'. In this way clan or group identity is constantly re-invigorated through the impact of the holy on the life of the community.

For Durkheim, while the holy was a product of human beings (in that it did not exist apart from human activity), it could nevertheless exert a very real influence on the lives of men and women and in this sense could be said to be 'real'. Consequently he was able to see all religions as ultimately based on corporate identity affirmed through worshipping that which was considered to be holy. It is hard to overestimate the importance for Durkheim of the building up of a corporate identity through the worship of the holy. Christianity offers a good example. From its very beginnings it has stressed the importance of the community built up through sharing in the mystical identity of the 'body of Christ' which is first conferred through the rite of baptism, and which is reaffirmed through liturgical actions which re-inforce a corporate memory.

However, since Durkheim sees nothing in religion beyond the worship of the social, he cannot distinguish between the different religions, all of which fulfil much the same function. Indeed, he asks: 'What essential difference is there between an assembly of Christians commemorating the principal moments in the life of Christ, or Jews celebrating either the exodus from Egypt or the giving of the Ten Commandments, and a meeting of citizens commemorating the institution of a new moral charter or some great event in national life?' While he is tied to a developmental view of religion which fails to see the many different layers at work in religions as practised, Durkheim's classification of the sacred and the profane and his elevation of the importance of social integration through worship of the holy has been deeply influential on sociological and anthropological interpretations of religion.

More recently, Mircea Eliade developed the relational understanding of holiness in his book *The Sacred and the Profane*. Retaining Durkheim's distinction between the sacred and the profane as different ways of classifying the world, he also interpreted the categorization in terms of the 'power' and impact of the holy and the profane on the lives of men and women: the different categories defined the way in which human beings existed in the world. Most importantly, the two categories could make contact, which meant that the sacred could make an impact on the profane world through 'hierophany', the manifestation of the other world in this world: it is this understanding that allows him to develop a theory of sacred places and times. In similar vein, in her thoroughgoing engagement with both Christian and non-Christian sources, the anthropologist Mary Douglas has also sought to show how different conceptions of the holy can serve to maintain social distinctions.

What is central to these relational understandings of 'the holy' which run through from Söderblom to Douglas is the notion of holiness as the means whereby human identity is maintained by a process that moves beyond the ordinary realms of experience (the profane) towards something interpreted as transcendent and usually taken as divine and thus as beyond question. Social and corporate identity is bestowed through an identity conferred by the holy, which, simply because it is holy, cannot be questioned. This leads to what Roy Rappaport called a 'closed loop of authority and legitimacy'. In Christianity the various things described as holy (which vary between the different denominations) confer a sense of identity on those who venerate them as holy: the repetition of the holy eucharist, for instance, acts as a means for fostering identity in Christian communities. The fact that access is controlled through a 'holy priesthood' who interpret a 'holy scripture' has led to many vigorous criticisms of Christianity, not least from socialists influenced by the thought of Karl Marx.

For Nathan Söderblom there was far more to holiness than the simple affirmation of communal identity through religious activity. Holiness also implied a set of moral injunctions whereby it became possible for human beings to separate themselves off from the world through obedience to a set of moral codes and thus to attain holiness themselves. In this way the holy thing itself would retain its separateness and, furthermore, part of its holiness could rub off on the human being involved in the careful protection of its separateness. This understanding can be seen in the Old Testament: the people of Israel, as that nation set apart from the rest of the nations by God, was considered God's holy people, and its holiness was rooted in that of God: 'You shall be holy, for I the Lord your God am holy' (Leviticus 19.2).

Holiness was a quality that could be transferred, and often the process of transfer involved a deliberate attempt to remove oneself from the unclean or the commonplace through obedience to a set of rules or through particular acts of discipline or self-control. Human holiness was thus an achievement of obedience to the moral law. It also came to be associated with those holy people who Holiness movement subjected themselves to the rigours of asceticism and bodily purgation as the Qumran community did. By New Testament times the Old Testament word for holiness was translated by the Greek word *hagios*, which was applied to God himself (as in John 17.11) but was also later used for specific saints. It implied a pure conduct of life in obedience to a set of moral injunctions.

Similar ideas quickly developed in the early church, partly because of the importance of holiness codes in establishing a sense of identity among the first generations of Christians who marked themselves off from pagan society. In 1 Peter, for instance, the ideas of holiness that once applied to the people of Israel were transferred to the 'holy nation' of the church (2.9). It was a mark of holiness or sanctification that Christians would behave in ways marked out from their neighbours. It did not take long for Christianity to adopt very strict codes of purity, placing taboos on the defilement of holy places and things: for instance, after childbirth women had first to be cleansed ('churched') before they could regain admission to the community.

Much Christian spirituality has focused on the attainment of holiness through gradual ascent towards union with God himself. The idea of 'becoming holy' or Celtic Christianity Spirituality becoming divine was one of the leading characteristics of Christian spirituality from the beginning, especially in the Eastern churches. Through a disciplined life of prayer and contemplation the Christian was thought to ascend Reformation from the material world towards the spiritual world and was eventually united with the being of God himself. Such spirituality is most clearly expressed in the work of  so-called Dionysius the Areopagite or Pseudo-Dionysius, who wrote in about the year 500. His writings have continued to be influential. The attainment of holiness was often accompanied by a rigorous asceticism. Indeed, the discipline required for true holiness could lead to extraordinary acts of self-abuse and a negative view of the body, as is perhaps most clearly exemplified in the impact  of Jerome's teachings on his followers, some of whom allegedly starved themselves to death. In the Western tradition much monastic spirituality has stressed the attainment of holiness through an austere life of prayer and contemplation, as in the writings of the great Spanish mystics Teresa of Avila and John of the Cross in the sixteenth century.

Other forms of Christian spirituality, however, have sought to see holiness as something that can be attained by all Christians in their ordinary everyday lives, as with the injunctions of Jeremy Taylor, an Anglican bishop of the seventeenth century, who in his *Holy Living* and *Holy Dying* sensed God's presence in everybody and everything: 'God is wholly in every place ... God is in every creature: be cruel towards none.' Such an emphasis on the practical attainment of holiness has also been an important aspect of evangelicalism, particularly those branches stemming from John Wesley. With this tradition it is clear that holiness is not regarded as something for either the professionally religious or for the religious expert, such as the monk or nun, but is something open for all to attain. It is what has been described as 'inner-worldly asceticism'.

This activist approach to Christian living and the emphasis on seeing the holy in everyday life has been much challenged in recent years. The rise of various forms of other-worldly spirituality and the clamour for holiness and mystical experience as something set apart from the world make it increasingly difficult to stress the mundane character of holiness. The quest for spirituality is often seen as a dimension of life separated from other areas. Some other Christians, however, have sought to understand God's creation itself as worthy of reverence, or holy, and have developed ecological theologies or creation-centred spiritualities. The most influential figure in this movement has been the American priest, Matthew Fox.

Similarly, and perhaps as a counter-cultural reaction to the increasing complexity of modern life, many Christians have sought to revive pre-modern forms of spirituality. These include the romantic re-creation of Celtic spirituality as well as a revival of pilgrimage to holy places which are set apart from the everyday world. These movements serve as a challenge to the rational and word-based inner-worldly religion of the Reformation by stressing the otherness and the difference of the Christian message from the secular world.

Understanding holiness: experience and irrationality

This understanding of holiness as an expression of otherness and irrationality has been stressed by some modern writers on the holy. Alongside the important accounts of the holy given by Söderblom and Durkheim and their successors there is another influential theory of the holy which was pioneered by Rudolf Otto in his classic book *Das Heilige*, first published in 1917 and translated as *The Idea of the Holy*. His particular emphasis is conveyed by the subtitle: *An Inquiry into the Non-Rational Factor in the Idea of the Divine and its Relation to the Rational.* Otto understood 'the holy' as another category for interpreting the world alongside the rational explanations of the scientific method. Whereas for Söderblom holiness was a quality applied to the object, Otto was more concerned with the human experience of the holy: he focused on that feeling of awe when encountering the sacred.

Such an experience was quite distinct from the experience of anything else; it could not be exhausted by the rational understanding of God or by 'the essence of deity'. For Otto, there was a non-rational factor which was not merely 'accidental' to religion but which marked a third and more important factor beyond the moral and the rational: this he classified as the 'numinous'. This *sensus numinis*, Otto felt, was 'rediscovered in a vague and general way' by Friedrich Schleiermacher, who, in his influential *Speeches on Religion* of 1799 characterized religion as the sense and taste for the infinite. Religion was thereby grounded in that feeling of unity or holiness that underpinned everything else in the world. It was this mysterious sense of oneness that allowed the observer to penetrate the innermost heart of things, to gain access to the elusive thing-in-itself. Otto's idea of the holy as a religious faculty of cognition thus becomes the means by which human beings are able to glean something of the mysterious depth of reality and to confer meaning on the world. This form of cognition, which has been called 'intuition', is never available through reason, since reason merely leads to a form of knowledge always mediated through the limitations of the human understanding. The experience of holiness, however, expresses a certainty which can never be attained through scientific thought.

Most importantly for Otto, 'the holy' was a common human experience felt in holy places and through holy rites, which nevertheless pointed beyond the commonplaces of human understanding towards the mystery of the universe itself. Because such an experience was shared by all people, Otto did not confine his understanding of holiness purely to the practices of Christianity, but was able to glimpse something of the deeper nature of reality during his extensive travels. Writing home to Germany during one of his journeys, for instance, he spoke of his experience of synagogue worship in Mogador in Morocco. After hearing the words 'Holy, Holy, Holy, Lord God of hosts, heaven and earth are full of your glory' from the book of Isaiah sung in unison, he wrote: 'I have heard the *Sanctus, sanctus, sanctus* of the cardinals in St Peter's, the *Swiat, swiat, swiat* in the cathedral in the Kremlin, and the *hagios, hagios, hagios* of the patriarch of Jerusalem. In whatever language these words are spoken, the most sublime words that human lips have ever uttered, they always seize one in the deepest ground of the soul, arousing and stirring with a mighty shudder the mystery of the other-worldly that sleeps therein.'

While Otto shared much of the cultural arrogance of his generation, his understanding of the holy paved the way for much future work in religious studies and theology. In particular his identification of the holy as a 'mystery', as something 'wholly other', quite different in kind from anything else, proved influential on the great Swiss Protestant theologian, Karl Barth, who shortly after reading Otto's book established a new form of theology based on a conception of God as 'wholly other'. Barth was later to dismiss *The Idea of the Holy*, since he felt it failed to establish holiness on the righteousness of God and instead derived it from the human feeling of the numinous. Other theologians and students of religion also adapted Otto's thought, often reshaping it in accordance with their own purposes.

Karl Barth

Friedrich Schleiermacher ◄

The stress on the irrational and the transcendent was challenged by those who sought to stress the immanence of God and who felt that modern science left little space for the irrational and transcendent. The hugely influential liturgical reforms of the Second Vatican Council in the 1960s, for instance, served to redirect worship away from the God associated with the mystery of the mass performed by a sacred priesthood set apart from the people. Instead of a mysterious liturgy celebrated in the sacred language of Latin, the Roman Catholic Church adopted a very simple and accessible form of worship which was open to all and which used the vernacular. Other churches quickly followed suit. Churches were architecturally re-ordered and the focus was frequently placed on the act of communion, with an altar sited in the midst of the community. This served to stress God's immanence in the worshipping congregation (which had always been maintained in Protestant churches), rather than his separation and transcendence. Many sacred buildings took on increasingly secular roles and it was often difficult to distinguish the sacred from the profane.

Council

Buildings

At the same time many theologians from different churches questioned the possibility of the category of holiness altogether and sought to 'secularize' religion by removing from it many of its supernatural and mythical qualities. Particularly influential were the German theologian Dietrich Bonhoeffer and the English bishop John A. T. Robinson, whose *Honest to God* provoked a vigorous debate in the English-speaking world in the 1960s. However, many saw the loss of the supernatural, irrational and mythical or the 'holy' elements of Christianity as tantamount to the destruction of its historical heart. Many others felt that by holding to irrational beliefs the churches had become hopelessly outdated: from the 1960s there has

Christianity in Europe

been a massive decline in church attendance in Western Europe.

In recent years, however, some Christians have consciously sought to distance themselves from the world by stressing the otherness and transcendence of Christianity – this can be seen in the revival of teachings on sexual purity and the resistance to the 'secular' agenda of human equality and rights as well as to secular scientific understandings of the world. This reaction to such a perceived loss of holiness in the 1960s has often been focused on the role of women in the church and particularly in ministry, as well as more recently on the acceptability of homosexual relationships. It is claimed that since the church is holy it is set apart from the current fads of modern society. This clearly demonstrates the complexity of the category of the holy, with its various emphases on otherness, sacredness and irrationality.

Women in Christianity
Homosexuality
Byzantium

Conclusion

Christendom

Although the understanding of the holy in the Christian tradition is much contested, the two main trajectories outlined above point to an objective and a subjective dimension of holiness. That which is holy is marked off from that which is profane and confers a sense of identity on those who worship it, or regard it as holy. Indeed almost anything can be categorized as holy or profane: wooden images, various vessels, parts of buildings, which in themselves are neither special nor valuable, can take on the character of holiness, and natural phenomena, like wells, can easily be treated as holy. Similarly a rag or a bone can take on a special meaning by being associated with a particular holy person or event. Throughout the Middle Ages the holiness that the saints displayed in their lives was considered to have survived in some form in their dead bodies and in their personal possessions that were venerated as holy objects in their own right. Holiness is an irrational and therefore often seemingly arbitrary category and seems to have little to do with the inherent qualities of the object. At the same time those who venerate things as holy and who gain their identity through separation can also expect to sense a feeling of holiness. This experience can act as a guarantee for the authenticity of revelation, and has been understood as conferring a sense of certainty on the believer. However, whether the feeling of holiness is ultimately grounded in anything beyond human experience is always open to question. The future of holiness is bound up with the survival of transcendence itself.

Revelation

MARK D. CHAPMAN

📖 Stephen Barton (ed), *Holiness Past and Present*, London and New York: T&T Clark 2003; Mary Douglas, *Purity and Danger* (1966), London and New York: Routledge 2002; Emile Durkheim, *The Elementary Forms of Religious Life*, New York: Free Press of Glencoe 1995; Mircea Eliade, *The Sacred and the Profane*, New York: Harcourt Brace Jovanovich 1959; Rudolf Otto, *The Idea of the Holy* (1923), Oxford: OUP 1971; Roy Rappaport, *Ritual and Religion in the Making of Humanity*, Cambridge: CUP 1999

Holy Roman empire

Long after the Roman empire had collapsed in the West in the fifth century, it remained a symbol of order and unity. (The Eastern Roman empire, with its capital at Constantinople, had little relevance and was slowly diminishing in power.) When Charlemagne, king of the Franks, had conquered a vast area from the Elbe to beyond the Pyrenees, he considered himself ready to revive the old concept. But this was to be a specifically Christian empire, almost co-extensive with Western Christendom. In 800 Pope Leo crowned Charlemagne as Emperor of the Romans, seeing him as a strong and high-minded ruler capable of bringing order and civilization after many years in which anarchy and barbarism had seemed to be winning. In this way an institution was created which was destined to last 1000 years in one way or another, under its better-known later title of Holy Roman empire. Allied with the popes, the emperors claimed religious as well as secular authority. They believed that the unity of Christendom depended on the alliance of these two powers ruling the world, one priestly and one royal.

In reality, it was Charlemagne who was master of both the church and the empire, although the Pope had conferred the crown on him. This shared authority was to lead to endless controversy in the future as pope and emperor each claimed supremacy. Even sooner, the territorial extent of the new empire was threatened. Charlemagne's successor was so weak that his own sons deposed him, and then quarrelled with one another. The Partition of Verdun in 843 divided the empire into three roughly equal kingdoms; eventually France and Germany were to develop from the western and eastern portions. The third brother, Lothar, ruling the centre, retained the title of emperor: but in reality Charlemagne's empire co-extensive with Western Christendom had been broken up, never to be fully restored.

The kingdom of Germany was first to recover from the years of anarchy that followed. Otto the Great (936–73) aimed to restore Charlemagne's inheritance, including the secular headship of Christendom. He managed to gain temporary control over much of Italy, and force the election of his own candidates as popes, but his real success was in Germany. This set a precedent, with several

Charlemagne enthroned between Pope Leo III and Bishop Turpin, from Charlemagne's tomb, cathedral treasury, Aachen

emperors powerful as rulers of Germany, but running into failure and revolt when they tried to gain control of Italy. These southern campaigns gave popes the chance to pose as guardians of Italian autonomy, and were an ingredient in the long-running feud between emperors and popes known as the Investiture Controversy. It was during these years, in 1157, that the adjective 'Holy' was added to the title of the institution. This was also the time when several emperors, notably Frederick Barbarossa, fulfilled their obligations to the church in a new way, by going on crusade.

Pope Innocent III, who became Pope in 1198, was able to exploit the empire's weakness when there were rival candidates after Henry VI's death in 1197 (the two groups of supporters became known as Guelphs, the Pope's supporters, and Ghibellines, supporters of the emperor). Under him the Pope's pretensions reached their greatest extent.

This long-running quarrel ended when Charles IV was crowned emperor in 1355, and realized that his real power base should be Germany. He abandoned to the Pope the territorial rights over Rome and Italy for which many of his predecessors had fought, and no later emperor tried to recover them. He gave the empire a constitution, the Golden Bull of 1356; this laid down which princes should have the right to elect the emperor (election, rather than hereditary succession, was a Germanic practice) and how the emperor's heir could be pre-elected as king of the Romans. The seven listed at this time (the rulers of Brandenburg, the Palatinate, Bohemia, Saxony, and the Archbishops of Cologne, Mainz and Trier) were to remain until the seventeenth century, when an eighth, the ruler of Bavaria, was added. It also settled the role and membership of the Imperial Diet, the assembly of the princes of the empire. Yet Charles had little interest in the concept of the empire as a united Christian state, and aimed primarily at the advancement of his own family.

During the later fourteenth and fifteenth centuries the individual states of Western Europe grew in importance, while the papacy lost moral authority in exile in Avignon. From 1379 there were two popes (this period is known as the Great Schism) with the rulers of Europe supporting rival candidates, bringing the papacy into enormous disrepute. Many believed that only a general council of the church could remedy the situation. But with two competing popes, which of them had the authority to summon one? After rival councils were called, it fell to the Emperor Sigismund, in his role as the secular chief of Christendom, to push the antipope John XXIII to call a council to Constance in 1414. With one pope deposed and the other forced to abdicate, the council proceeded to lay down how future popes should be elected, and that general councils should meet periodically. It had healed the Great Schism, but the Pope and the various national groups of clergy could not agree on measures for the reform of the papacy as a whole.

Papacy

Council

They were also highly suspicious of any future attempts by the emperors to take a controlling interest in church affairs.

Investiture Controversy ◄

In the opinion of Lord Bryce, its most famous historian, the Holy Roman empire reached its lowest point in the reign of Frederick III (1440–93). He gave away huge privileges to the individual German princes, hastening Germany's decline in relation to her neighbours France and Spain, where national unity was growing. Frederick was the second Habsburg to be emperor, and this family was to provide all the emperors until the eighteenth century. From now on the empire becomes at base an Austrian monarchy, with its jurisdiction over the rest of the empire merely titular, but used as a means of extending the power and prestige of the House of Habsburg.

Crusades ◄

By the time Maximilian I (1493–1519) succeeded to the throne, it was generally recognized that the empire was long overdue for reform. The new emperor established an Imperial Court of Justice, but his attempts to create an effective representative assembly for the empire in place of the Diet failed. The Holy Roman empire never succeeded in adapting to the forces of change sweeping Europe in the sixteenth century. The emperor remained politically weak and always short of money, while the individual German princes grew in power, and several of the independent cities became very rich.

However, Maximilian managed to consolidate the Hapsburg claim to Hungary by betrothing his granddaughter and his grandson to the king of Hungary and his sister respectively. No one then could have foreseen that in 1526 the young king of Hungary would drown after the battle of Mohacs against the Turks, leaving only his sister and brother-in-law Ferdinand as heirs, and thus adding Hungary to the Hapsburg lands.

When Maximilian died in 1519 his grandson, Charles V, had to raise enormous sums to bribe the electors in order to become emperor. The kings of both England and France entered the lists; because Charles had inherited Spain and the Netherlands from his mother and grandmother, the other European rulers regarded him as a potential menace. The election took the attention of all Europe at a crucial time for the future of the empire.  Martin Luther had made public his attacks on the papacy only two years earlier, but the uncertainty over the election and troubles in Spain kept the new young emperor from calling the Diet of Worms to tackle this problem until 1520. By then the new ideas had swept across Germany, never to be eliminated.

Counter-Reformation ➤

As a devout Roman Catholic, Charles took his duties as God's vice-gerent extremely seriously. He was deeply hurt by the unwillingness of the popes to co-operate with him in reforms of the church that he believed would bring the Protestants back into the Roman Catholic fold. There had been calls for a general council of the church to initiate reforms since the Diet of Nuremberg in 1523, but the popes feared that such a meeting would curtail their power, as had happened at the Council of Constance in 1414, and increase that of the emperors. Corrupt popes were also unwilling to end practices in which they had a vested interest.

Protestantism

Wars of religion ➤

Unlike his predecessors, Pope Paul III, elected in 1534, was willing to summon a council, but its meeting was delayed by the war between Charles V and the king of France. It finally met at Trent in 1545, the location chosen because it lay within imperial territory but was easily accessible from northern Italy. Paul III's relations with the emperor became increasingly strained as it became apparent that the two men had vastly different expectations of what the council might achieve. Charles saw it as an instrument for removing the abuses which had been a major factor in driving Protestants to leave the church; the Pope wanted to concentrate on precise definitions of doctrine, which would make it easier to denounce heretics but make the reconciliation sought by Charles even harder to achieve. When plague broke out in Trent, the Pope used it as an excuse to move the council to Bologna, where he had greater control since it lay within the Papal States. Here he was able to ensure that no compromises were made of the kind for which Charles had hoped.

By 1555 Charles was utterly worn out. He had had to fight against France and the Turks, and against rebels within his territories including the Protestant princes of Germany. The effort of fighting on so many fronts and at the same time confronting the Lutherans proved to be beyond one man's capacity, all the more so as Charles was fundamentally a man of peace with a profound belief that religious and political unity should go hand in hand. He abdicated in that year and divided his inheritance between his brother Ferdinand, who became Holy Roman emperor, and his son Philip, who was to rule Spain and the Netherlands. By now the old ideal of one faith, one government was truly shattered. Within Germany, the Protestant subjects of the emperor would not give him the old allegiance.

Ferdinand II (1619–37), succeeding after two weak rulers, was determined to recover the lost authority and the lost lands of the empire. He had been educated at the new Jesuit university of Ingoldstadt, one of the institutions by which much of southern Germany had been won back in the Counter-Reformation surge of the later sixteenth century. He took his religious responsibilities as Holy Roman emperor very seriously, perhaps the last emperor to do so. Early in his reign he crushed the Protestant rebels in Bohemia and recovered the whole of that kingdom for the Roman Catholic Church. His Edict of Restitution, issued in 1629, ordered that all church property seized by the state since 1555 should be restored to the Catholics. He also planned to recover both Denmark and Holland in alliance with his fellow Hapsburg ruler in Spain. But his high-handed methods alienated even his Catholic subjects, and Sweden's intervention in the Thirty Years War brought him defeat.

The Peace of Westphalia in 1648 marks the start of the last stage in the decline of the Holy Roman empire. The individual rulers of Germany were granted full sovereignty within their territories, the Edict of Restitution was repealed, the division between Catholic and Protestant areas was accepted as permanent, and the empire suffered significant losses of territory. The independence of Holland and Switzerland was formally recognized, and lands were ceded to France and Sweden.

The Holy Roman empire had become a loose confederation of German-speaking states; when Vienna was attacked by the Turks in 1683, it was saved by the intervention of the king of Poland, not the German princes. It was the last time the empire fulfilled one of its old responsibilities as the protector of Europe against Muslim invaders from the East. A century later Frederick the Great, king of Prussia (one of the individual German states which had become more powerful than Austria), compared meetings of the Imperial Diet with dogs in a yard baying at the moon. The Hapsburgs continued to use the empire purely to further the interests of their own house, and put their effort into winning new lands to the east of Austria, their true homeland. By now they were usually known as emperors of Austria.

It was left to Napoleon to bring the empire to a close. Having defeated the emperors of Austria and Russia, and made himself emperor of France, he decided the time had come to finish off the old relic. In 1806 several German princes started proceedings by repudiating the authority of the last emperor, Francis II, who decided to abdicate. Thus ended just over 1000 years of the Holy Roman empire. In the words of Voltaire a generation earlier, it 'was neither holy, nor Roman, nor an empire'.

CATHERINE MULGAN

📖 James, Viscount Bryce, *The Holy Roman Empire*, London: Macmillan 1866; Donald A. Bullough, *The Age of Charlemagne*, London: Elek Books [2]1973; M. Fernandez Alvarez, *Charles V*, London: Thames & Hudson 1975; Andrew Wheatcroft, *The Habsburgs*, London: Viking Books 1995

Holy Spirit

Throughout the history of the Christian church the Holy Spirit (once referred to by the more archaic term Holy Ghost) has been an experience rather than a topic for thought, discussion or speculation. The Acts of the Apostles reports how after the resurrection of Jesus, on the feast of Pentecost, his followers were gathered together in one place when suddenly 'a sound came from heaven like the rush of a mighty wind, and it filled all the house where they were sitting. And there appeared to them tongues as of fire, distributed and resting on each one of them. And they were all filled with the Holy Spirit' (2.1–4). From time to time groups have appeared claiming direct experience of the Holy Spirit, and in the twentieth century one such group, Pentecostalism, is the most rapidly growing part of Christianity. The Gospel of John reports how after the resurrection Jesus appears to his disciples behind closed doors and breathes on them, saying, 'Receive the Holy Spirit. If you forgive the sins of any, they are forgiven; if you retain the sins of any, they are retained' (20.22–3).

Following from this, in the historic tradition of the church the Holy Spirit has been seen as given through a succession of sacramentally ordained ministers, i.e. as at work in and through the structure of the church. At the same time, the Holy Spirit has also been seen as active far more widely, permeating the creation and raising up witnesses to God beyond the limits of the church. The language of poetry and praise has proved the best way, perhaps even the only way, to talk of the Holy Spirit. *Veni, Creator spiritus* ('Come, Holy Ghost, our souls inspire'), composed in the ninth century, is one of the greatest of Christian hymns, sung in versions ranging from plainchant to the tumultuous setting in the first movement of Gustav Mahler's Ninth Symphony; 'Come, thou Holy Paraclete', written in the thirteenth century, is a love song to the Holy Spirit; and Bianco da Siena in the fifteenth century expressed deep longing for the Holy Spirit in 'Come down, O Love divine'.

Hymns

It may be almost impossible to talk of the Holy Spirit, but pneumatology, the doctrine of the Holy Spirit, particularly in the Bible, is part of Christian theology, so we can look at some aspects of belief in the Holy Spirit, and how the Spirit came to be seen as being equal with the Father and the Son in the doctrine of the Trinity.

Trinity

The Holy Spirit in the Bible

Bible

A look at the Old Testament shows us the wealth of biblical experiences of the Spirit. The Hebrew word *ruach*, which is translated by Spirit, usually refers to a dynamic, creative and inspiring force of life. Though in individual cases figures may achieve their ends by extraordinary human capabilities – as in the story of Samson and his hair – in the end it is the divine Spirit that gives leaders their charisma. The Spirit descends on a man, as upon Gideon (Judges 6.34), Jephthah (Judges 11.29) and Saul (1 Samuel 11.5–12), and as a result they do great deeds of deliverance.

With King David, Israel's experience of the Spirit reaches a new stage: the *ruach* no longer intervenes almost in a flash in situations of extreme need; rather, it becomes a permanent gift bestowed on the anointed one, the one chosen by God. As the faith of Israel becomes increasingly orientated on the future, the notion of the king being endowed with the Spirit of God becomes that of the Messiah as the longed-for king of salvation (cf. Isaiah 11.2; 42.1; 61.1). Interestingly, there is almost no appeal to God's Spirit in any of the prophets from Amos to Jeremiah. Even in Ezekiel, prophetic proclamation is not described as a gift of the Spirit of God or a task imposed by the Spirit. However, this changes in the latter parts of the book of Isaiah known as Second and Third Isaiah (chapters 40–66). God puts his Spirit upon his servant (42.1); God's Spirit rests on his anointed (61.1); the 'Holy Spirit' (63.10) bestows the prophetic gift – in connection with an anointing. In retrospect, in this perspective Moses is then seen as a prophet endowed with the Spirit (cf. 63.11,14),

Festivals and fasts ◄
Messiah
Prophecy
Pentecostalism ◄
Ministry and ministers ◄

indeed in Isaiah 59.21 the outpouring of the Spirit on all the people (house of Israel) promised in Ezekiel 39.29 is understood as a prophetic gift. Thinking about the nature of the Spirit did not continue like this, but from now on prophecy and the gift of the Spirit (inspiration) belonged together.

In the exile Israel came to experience that God creates new and abiding life by his Spirit. Like the prophetic Word and the inspiring Spirit, now the creative Word and creative Spirit of God are combined. Finally, in the p. 139  wisdom literature Word, Spirit and Wisdom can appear interchangeably with a creative function (cf. Sirach 24; Wisdom 7.22; 9.1). Here we should note that Spirit does not denote a dimension within the Godhead but the power to live that God gives human beings through his grace. God's Spirit can bestow new life even on dead bones. The Resurrection vision of this in Ezekiel 37 is not yet about a resurrection at the end of time. The aim of the gift of the new Spirit is a Tradition  new community of men and women. They are given a new heart (Ezekiel 36), a new capacity for relationship. It is noteworthy that the Spirit itself becomes a gift to be given at the end of time. The phrase 'Holy Spirit' appears in only three passages in the Old Testament (Isaiah 63.10,11; Psalm 51.11). Here 'holiness' means above all sovereignty.

Jesus Jesus' disciples were inspired by the experience that the two great hopes which had been expressed since the exile in the scriptures and which were being kept alive in various currents of early Judaism were being fulfilled:  Jesus was the Messiah anointed by the Spirit; they were those who had been given his Holy Spirit. The 'sin against the Holy Spirit' mentioned in Mark 3.28f. is to reject Jesus Paul and to dispute his spiritual authority. For Paul, those who have died and risen with Christ in baptism (Romans 6) have attained the freedom of the children of God through the Spirit (Galatians 5). It is important for them not to Creed surrender this freedom and once more become enslaved to Council 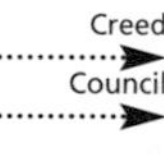 spirits and powers that destroy it. Anyone who has become a new person in Christ and through his spirit is a member of the body of Christ. This body is given life by the Spirit, who bestows his gifts (charisms, 1 Corinthians 12–14;  Romans 12). These gifts of the Spirit are not primarily extraordinary gifts but basic Christian forms of behaviour; they are not given for private use but for the building up of Community the community; they are not to be boasted about but must be seen against the background of the crucified Christ.

According to the synoptic Gospels, before Easter Jesus is the only bearer of the Spirit (the only charismatic). The outpouring of the Spirit at Pentecost to which Luke then bears witness in Acts 2 is the outpouring of the Spirit on all flesh which was promised in the book of Joel (2.28–9) for the end time. In the power of this Spirit Christians proclaim to all nations the gospel of Jesus the Christ (the one who has been anointed by the Spirit).

In the Gospel of John the Spirit is presented above all as the Spirit of truth. As the Paraclete (Greek for advocate) he stands by the disciples when they bear witness to Christ. Whoever believes has the experience of being reborn through the life-giving Spirit (cf. John 3), the Spirit of the Father and the Son. Through this Spirit believers are given power to lead a new life in keeping with the God who is spirit and life, light and truth, the God who is love. More clearly than in Paul the Holy Spirit not only appears as the one in whom the Father acts on believers in the Son and binds the fellowship of believers to the fellowship of God (1 John 1.1–4); he also joins Father and Son together in a fellowship of life and action, and thus is the Spirit of the Father and the Son.

The Holy Spirit in the history of the church

In Christian teaching, the experience of the Spirit communicates true knowledge of God and the self and ensures the truth of the gospel and the apostolic tradition. This experience is often held in a tension between the immediacy of the activity of God and the need for it to be mediated through human beings and human institutions. The charismatic renewal movements that have come into being throughout church history appeal to experiences of the Spirit and its gifts. This can lead them to oppose the existing order and put themselves outside the church or be forced out of it. An appeal to the Spirit and rigorism in ethics often go together; theologians of the early church such as Tertullian and Origen criticized those in office who, as they thought, did not have the Spirit.

How did the Holy Spirit come to be confessed as God, as the Father and Son are God? This happened in a struggle towards a proper understanding of the Holy Spirit that was above all carried on in monastic circles. Belief in the divinity of the Holy Spirit was formulated in the creed of the Council of Constantinople in 381: 'We believe in the Spirit [Greek *pneuma*], the Lord and Giver of Life, who proceeds from the Father, who with the Father and the Son is worshipped and glorified, who spoke by the prophets.'

For Athanasius, the champion of orthodoxy, the divinity of the Spirit arose from the distinction between Creator and creature that had been established at the Council of Nicaea in 325. Jesus Christ, the Lord, the Logos, the Son, is not a creature but the eternal word of God. He is of one and the same being with the Father. Behind this creed of Nicaea stands the conviction that we are saved only when God himself has acted in us in Jesus Christ. Athanasius uses the same argument in the controversy with a group known as the Pneumatomachoi (spirit fighters) who rejected belief in the divinity of the Holy Spirit. 'Now if the Holy Spirit were a creature, through him we would have no fellowship with God; rather, we would be conjoined with a creature and alienated from the Godhead, because we would not share in it. But since it is said of us that we share in Christ and God, it has been demonstrated that the anointing and seal in us do not belong to the nature of created things but to that of the Spirit, who conjoins us with the Father through the Spirit who is in him.' Athanasius is referring to what is said of Christians, i.e. to the tradition and the creed of his time, to experience and testimony. The Cappadocian father Basil, who played a key role in shaping the theology of the Council of Constantinople in 381, which defined the divinity of the Holy Spirit, even if he was unable to take part in it, does not engage in any speculation about the Spirit either. He refers, rather, to the baptismal creed and prayer (of the eucharist). Here we can recognize an axiom that played an important role in the early church, *lex orandi, lex credendi*: the law of faith corresponds to the law of prayer. As Basil puts it in one of his letters, 'We believe as we are baptized, and praise as we believe.'

So the Spirit belongs on the side of the Creator; that is why he is called Holy and 'Lord'. That is why it is confessed that he proceeds from the Father, the source of the Godhead. The doxology, 'Glory be to the Father and to the Son and to the Holy Spirit', attests that the Holy Spirit is on a level with the Father and the Son. The insertion of the Holy Spirit into the third article of the creed thus attests the divinity of the Holy Spirit, without explicitly calling him 'God' or saying that he is 'of the same substance'. What the council puts in technical theological language in a separate doctrinal letter substantiates the creed, which can content itself with the language of the Bible and of worship. This is an extremely interesting insight to apply to ecumenical relations.

Further development took different courses in East and West. At the end of the first millennium alienation between East and West was so far advanced that unity between the two churches was shattered, and in 1054 each side excommunicated the other. Among other things, there was a dispute as to whether the Spirit proceeded from the Father (alone) or from the Father and the Son (Latin *filioque*). However, this was not the cause of the split; it simply served to justify it after the event, as it still does.

Augustine left Western theology a mixed legacy: the Spirit is the bond of love and the communion between Father and Son; it is the gift of the Father and the Son. This is expressed in the verse of the well-known hymn, 'O Holy Spirit, Lord of grace': 'As thou in bond of love dost join the Father and the Son, so fill us all with mutual love and knit our hearts in one.' Augustine expresses the unity of God above all with the help of psychological analogies (the Spirit who expresses himself in knowledge and love lives as a parable for God, the Father, who expresses himself in the

Pentecost by the Master of Santo Domingo de Silos, twelfth-century Romanesque stone relief

Logos and the Spirit). Here too, however, the speculations are not remote from life but concern human salvation. The Holy Spirit dwells in human beings and gives them the fullness of his sevenfold gifts.

p. 216

Religious experience and worship provide the context for the theology of the Holy Spirit even more clearly in the Eastern churches. That the Spirit gives life is expressed in the Armenian and Syrian churches by the way in which they speak of the Spirit as mother, or describe the Spirit in feminine imagery. Just as Eve, the mother of life, was formed from Adam's rib, so the Holy Spirit, as the mother of the new life, is thought to be the 'rib of the Logos'.

p. 305

The mystery of God, the incomprehensibility of God's nature, is so important to theologians like Simeon the New Theologian (949–1022) and Gregory Palamas (*c.* 1296–1359) that they distinguish between the being of God and God's 'uncreated energies'. Human beings can share in these.

Augustine spoke of the procession of the Spirit 'from both' (Latin *ab utroque*). This can be taken as a variant on the formula 'from the Father through the Son' which was also current in the East. But the way in which the Western church used 'procession' as the main term to describe the way in which both the Son and the Spirit originated in the Father proved problematical. The Eastern church wanted  to distinguish the way in which Son and Spirit originated because this was the one thing that distinguished the persons: the Father is without origin, the Son is 'begotten',  the Spirit 'proceeds'. It is certainly possible to say 'and from the Son' in the sense of 'from the Father through the Son' when speaking of the Trinity as it manifests itself in history, but this statement must not be transferred to the 'immanent Trinity', to the life of God in himself. The East was concerned to understand the Father as the source of the Godhead. No more can be said about the mystery of God.

Despite the different conceptions of the Holy Spirit in the doctrine of the Trinity in the Eastern and Western churches, it has to be noted that the stumbling block for the Greeks was not primarily the *filioque* in itself but the fact that the addition of 'and from the Son' was an alteration to the original canonical text of the creed of 381. That was an offence against canon law, and showed p. 291 contempt for the tradition, but not until the attacks by the Latins in subsequent centuries, and especially the atrocities at the sack of Constantinople in 1203 during the Crusades Fourth Crusade, was an atmosphere created in which the *filioque* too was said to be the expression of the Latin papal quest for supremacy. Now the theological problem was entangled in ideological issues. So it was political interest on the one hand and different structures of thought and speech on the other, together with different views of the binding nature of church doctrine or the authorities Symbols behind it, that led to the failure of efforts at reunion at the councils of Lyons II in 1274 and Ferrara/Florence in 1438.

The doctrine of the Holy Spirit in the Latin Middle Scholasticism Ages had two focal points: on the one hand scholastic thinking within the framework of the doctrine of the Trinity and the doctrine of grace and the virtues; on the other the spiritualist movements within the church which showed subversive or even schismatic tendencies within the church. Here the abiding problems of a theology of the Holy Spirit proved to be the relationship between the Trinity as it is eternally and as it manifests itself in history, Christology between christology (the doctrine of the person of Christ) and pneumatology (the doctrine of the Holy Spirit), between charisma and office, grace and freedom, the direct experience of the Spirit and the Spirit as communicated through the sacraments, freedom and firm discipline.

Reformation At the time of the Reformation an attempt was made to resolve the problem of how salvation is communicated, which by then had become an oppressive one, with recourse to the doctrine of the Holy Spirit on the basis of the creed  of the early church. Martin Luther did not understand the Holy Spirit as a supernatural power in human beings but strictly as something that is encountered personally; the Holy Spirit creates faith and can only be accepted in faith. Philipp Melanchthon reacted to the increasing interest in the connection between faith, experience and ethical action by giving a psychological description of the activity of the Spirit. John Calvin's theology seems to be the one that is most strongly stamped by the Holy Spirit. The Holy Spirit appears not only as a co-operator but as creator; as a bond it communicates fellowship with Christ.

The institutional church and those holding office in it generally have reservations about charismatic, spiritualistic movements, indeed may reject them altogether, as is evident from a whole series of controversies. Moreover, the doctrine of the church (ecclesiology) in the West has a very marked christological stamp. So Orthodox theologians in the East accuse the West of concentrating solely on Christ and forgetting the Spirit. In the Roman Catholic Church the situation has changed since the Second Vatican Council. Charismatic movements have also found a place in it, particularly if they are not critical of the church and its ministry. In the Second Vatican Council's Constitution on the Church, *Lumen gentium*, the concentration on Christ in ecclesiology is corrected by reference to the Spirit. The Spirit is the principle of life in the church; it is the motivation behind service in the church and marks the difference between Christ as the sole mediator of creation, and the church that is the sign and saving instrument of the saving activity of God.

The reality and activity of the Spirit today

A great variety of images can be found in the Bible, worship and spirituality for the activity and effect of the Spirit: wind, breath, living water, fire, dove, finger of God, oil, seal, key, kiss, and also peace, joy, love, fellowship, gift. These images all point to a greater reality. It is common today to think, 'that's only a metaphor', as if it were inferior to a fully thought-out concept. But in reality what is expressed by a metaphor cannot be better expressed through a concept; it can be expressed adequately only in an image, in a metaphor. The metaphor invites further thought. That is very much the case with the doctrine of the Holy Spirit; it does not consist of logical concepts but of metaphorical pointers.

From the history of the experience and theology of the Holy Spirit it seems better not to concentrate on one metaphor, but to bring several together and reflect on them. Some complexes of images have crystallized out of the history of charismatic experiences and reflections on the Spirit: the Spirit is like/the Spirit appears as and brings about life, truth, freedom, love as gifts. These metaphors can all be derived from the quite biblical statements of the creed of 381.

Throughout history the Spirit has been experienced as holy and sanctifying; not only is it a divine gift, but it is also the divine Giver (along with the Father and the Son). That is why the church confesses in its creed that the Holy Spirit is the 'Lord' who 'proceeds from the Father and the Son' and 'with the Father and the Son is worshipped and glorified'.

The activity of the divine Spirit shows itself in its power to create life and bring to life. In the 'one baptism for the forgiveness of sins' it gives new life; this is realized in the 'one holy, catholic and apostolic church'; through the resurrection of the dead the spirit is consummated in the 'life of the world to come'.

This Spirit of life is the Spirit of truth, 'who has spoken through the prophets'. Some creeds of the early church extend this statement by mentioning the apostles and the evangelists, or follow the Gospel of John in calling the spirit Paraclete, the eschatological witness to the truth. As the life-giving spirit that testifies to the truth and is the basis for freedom the Holy Spirit is the gift of divine love. Since Augustine, the characteristics of the Spirit have been summed up in this description. Both the Spirit and love express themselves in the same way: by emerging from themselves to be with and in others. There is a good expression in Paul's letter to the Romans which has been used as a key statement about the nature of the Spirit and of grace: 'The love of God has been poured out in our hearts by the Holy Spirit which has been given to us' (5.5).

To talk about the Holy Spirit it is necessary to begin from the workings of the Spirit. This means beginning from the experiences of the Spirit in history and attempting to approach what can be called the reality and especially the personhood of the Holy Spirit. It means beginning from specific experiences as experiences given by God's Spirit, and it must always be remembered that while the nature or the person of the Holy Spirit cannot be understood, it can nevertheless be traced in the experience of the Spirit who gives himself.

The Holy Spirit is the event of loving encounter, the sphere which Father and Son themselves enter, which binds them into a unity in love. To this degree spirit and love as characteristics of the divine life are at the same time the specific characteristic of the Holy Spirit.

In speaking of the Holy Spirit as person, if personhood is understood in terms of an autonomous subject, the person of the Holy Spirit appears to withdraw completely into the inner life of the Trinity. But if personality is understood in the light of that movement by which the spiritual loving subject goes beyond itself in order to be itself with others, the Holy Spirit appears as the primal image of personhood, which consists in being for others. The Holy Spirit is himself by allowing the Father and Son to be themselves in the other.

Living in the Spirit

Life in the Holy Spirit of God means accepting life as a gift, giving space to other life, living in relationships, allowing oneself to be freed and to free others, expecting all that one does to be completed by God. It could be summed up in the prayer: 'That we might no longer live for ourselves but for him who died for us and rose again, he sent from you, Father, as the first gift for all who believe, the Holy Spirit, who continues the work of your Son on earth and makes all things holy.'

Creation, nature, life, the human spirit exist by the life-giving Spirit of God and are permanently dependent on him. To talk of the creator Spirit must not disguise the fact that the Spirit is beyond human control. Moreover, the creation is always to be seen from the perspective of the new creation: it is also ravaged, fallen, oppressed creation, in need of liberation and longing for fulfilment. Talk of the Spirit also involves speaking out about the suppression of God's creative spirit and giving expression to the hope of a new creation. To live in accord with the Holy Spirit thus works for the preservation of creation and the advancement of freedom and justice.

Church ← Creation

The Holy Spirit gives the new life that has been made manifest in Jesus from the Father. It enables men and women to overcome the selfish behaviour they have inherited or acquired and to build up a community of true life and true freedom. The church which serves the Spirit as an instrument of the Spirit's power to sanctify and to heal is permanently characterized by a tension between the binding force of the Spirit and a free power which is beyond human control. The church does not live by itself but by the life-giving Spirit of God; and it does not live for itself but realizes itself in being there for others. As the sacrament of the Spirit for the world it exists as a way towards the final fulfilment, the fellowship of all men and women in the fellowship of the God who is Trinity, a fellowship that is brought about by the Spirit.

BERND JOCHEN HILBERATH

📖 Stanley M. Burgess, *The Holy Spirit: Ancient Christian Traditions*, Peabody, MA: Hendrickson ³1997, *The Holy Spirit: Eastern Christian Traditions*, Peabody, MA: Hendrickson ²1993 and *The Holy Spirit: Medieval Roman Catholic and Reformation Traditions*, Peabody, MA: Hendrickson 1997; Sinclair B. Ferguson, *The Holy Spirit. Contours of Christian Theology*, Downers Grove, IL: InterVarsity Press 1997; Veli-Matti Kärkkäinen, *Pneumatology. The Holy Spirit in Ecumenical, International, and Contextual Perspective*, Grand Rapids, MI: Baker Academic 2002; Jürgen Moltmann, *The Spirit of Life: A Universal Affirmation*, London: SCM Press and Minneapolis: Fortress Press 1992; John V. Taylor, *The Go-Between God. The Holy Spirit and the Christian Mission*, London: SCM Press and Philadelphia: Fortress Press 1972

Homosexuality

'Homosexuality' is a word first coined in 1869 by the Swiss Dr K. M. Benkert to describe the experience of people attracted to the same sex. It is used to describe both a person's identity and his or her behaviour. In the 1960s homosexuals themselves introduced the word 'gay' as a way of naming their identity positively. The use of the word 'queer' to describe homosexuals was originally a term of abuse, emphasizing deviancy, but in the late twentieth century it became for some a way of describing themselves as different from the heterosexual majority.

Official church teaching, while mostly being hostile to homosexual behaviour, accepts that some people have a homosexual identity. The presence of homosexuals within the church has been tolerated as long as they are invisible and silent. Officially, they have also been required to be celibate. In the second half of the twentieth century there was a growing social and cultural acceptance of homosexuals particularly but not only in Northern Europe and North America. Now the open presence of gay Christians in all denominations is challenging the church's traditional understanding not just of homosexuality but also of sexuality and human identity, as well as of authority and conformity in patterns of Christian discipleship.

Gay and lesbian theology
Sexuality
Authority

The discussion of homosexuality is one of the most contentious of current moral debates within the church. Consequently it is also one of the most creative and interesting, including an important revision of homosexuality in history and theology. This has still to find its place in the institutional church, which has experienced discussion of this issue as divisive and therefore as threatening. The question is whether the positive and full acceptance of homosexuals within the church is an expression of God's justice, truth and love or an accommodation with the world's self-serving values that corrupt the God-given 'traditional' Christian teaching.

Paganism

Bible

Six biblical passages are cited as specific and clear evidence that the scriptures are against homosexual acts: Genesis 19, in which the destruction of Sodom and Gomorrah is attributed to divine punishment for male homosexual acts; Leviticus 18.22 and Leviticus 20.13, which prescribe that a man who lies with a man as with a woman has committed an abomination and both parties to the act should be put to death; Romans 1.26–7, which includes female and male homosexuality as examples of degrading passions and an expression of idolatry; 1 Corinthians 6.9–10, which lists those who will not enter the kingdom of heaven and includes *malakos* and *arsenokoites*, translated in the New Revised Standard Version as male prostitutes and sodomites; and 1 Timothy 1.10, which includes *arsenokoites* in a list of those for whom the law is intended to bring the disobedient to conform to the glorious gospel of the blessed God.

However, interpretations of these passages fall into three types, with different implications.

First, there are those who see the 'plain meaning' of these texts as the denunciation of homosexual practices which are contrary to the will of God. This view of scripture can be criticized for not recognizing the contradiction between taking the plain meaning of these texts and ignoring the equally plain statement in Leviticus that the death penalty is to be imposed for homosexual practices. Nor does it explain why these particular texts are selected as having absolute and universal application today, while others are set aside. For example, scant attention is paid nowadays in Christianity to the prohibition in Leviticus against eating shellfish (11.12). However, those who use scripture in this first way would cite the teaching of Jesus and other New Testament texts to counter the imposition of the death penalty, and the significance of Jewish food laws was modified in the teaching of Jesus (e.g. Matthew 15.10–20) and the early church (e.g. Acts 11.1–18). Some of those who read scripture in this way further strengthen their understanding of homosexuality by stating that it is helpful to move beyond specific texts. For example, the specific scriptural teaching against homosexual acts gains positive expression in what is said about human sexuality and heterosexual marriage in Genesis 1 and 2.

Second, there are those who challenge this first interpretation of scripture by careful analysis of the texts. Identifying the context of each particular passage and examining the meaning and translation of individual words allows for much less certainty about the condemnation of homosexual practices than might at first sight seem obvious. The story of Sodom is really about a breach of hospitality. The condemnation in Paul's letter to the Romans is of homosexuality associated with idolatry and paganism. The meaning and translation of specific Greek words is a great deal more complex than is apparent from the plain meaning of the English Bible. This approach requires of the church a revision of the significance of these particular texts.

However, both of these approaches to scripture are undermined by the third, which recognizes that these texts do not address the contemporary reality of homosexual Christians. The serious part of our modern concern is for people who are homosexual not by deviance from their heterosexual nature, nor by preference or choice, but because of their given identity. They seek to form stable, faithful, adult, loving sexual relationships, and as Christians they want to do so within the context of the church of which they are baptized members.

Moral arguments

The key theological division is between those who believe that homosexuality is inherently sinful and those who accept that some people are homosexual because that is how they have been made. For the former, no discussion is wanted because it gives the illusion that there may be circumstances in which homosexual behaviour might be acceptable. Their difficulty is in maintaining this position without appearing to be intolerant.

Christian ethics have never been simply biblical ethics. All Christians recognize that there is moral order within the structure of creation, though there is debate about its exact content. This is stated explicitly by Paul in Romans 1.20 and is reflected in the strands of universal wisdom within the Bible, including those in the teaching of Jesus. Moral arguments will therefore always seek support from what can be discerned in divinely-ordered nature as well as from the Bible. Moral arguments are always constructed by using God-given reason drawing on scripture, Christian tradition and reason. Where there is disparity between the various sources, Christians are obliged to follow their consciences, properly informed by the resources of the church as well as by their own individual experience.

The first of the approaches to scripture outlined above seeks support from the natural order through the spiritual, psychological, social and physical complementarity of male and female. It adds, from arguments again rooted both in scripture and the natural ordering of society, that sexual relationships should be confined to marriage. The theological rationale of this view of homosexuality is that we live in a world that is 'fallen' from the original pattern of God's creation. That some people are homosexual is a distortion of what it is to be truly human and an expression of our sinfulness that cannot be supported by the church. On this view, the church claims to 'condemn the sin but love the sinner', and offers either 'healing' or the acceptance of celibate homosexuals within its membership.

There is no single explanation of the causes of homosexuality, and there has been much discussion about the balance between genetic, psychological and social causes. Many people experience ambivalence about their sexual orientation at some stage in their life. A minority of people find themselves to be solely attracted to people of the same sex. For whatever reason, they are made that way. For Christian homosexuals to be offered only either behavioural conformity to heterosexual norms or celibacy might be considered a serious loss of dignity and injustice. It is worth noting that some South African Christians, including Archbishop Desmond Tutu, with their experience of apartheid, have identified the church's official teaching about homosexuality as discriminatory and unjust.

There have always been homosexuals within the church, and they now show a growing confidence and visibility. The recovery of their history has been an extremely interesting, if still incomplete, modern project. John Boswell, for example, collected liturgical evidence of rites for solemnizing the unions of 'brothers' in some European Roman Catholic and Orthodox churches between about 500 and 1500. Similarly, Alan Bray's documentation of funeral monuments for same-sex Christian partnerships is startling. The significance of this evidence cannot be read directly into a modern context. Nevertheless, the existence of these relationships provides encouragement for the view that we are not dealing with a novel, modern and culturally bound problem.

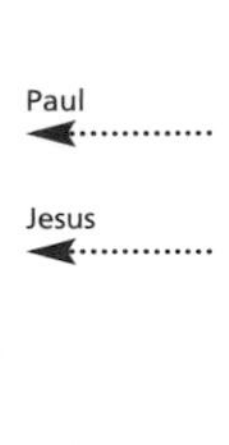

Contemporary issues

The questions raised in the Christian discussion of homosexuality focus crucial issues for the church in relation to sexuality in general. In contemporary culture, sexuality is associated with consumerism; that is, people themselves are treated as a commodity or sex is used to help advertise and sell products or ideas. This strikes many Christians as a serious distortion of humanity. Furthermore, the Western obsession with individual fulfilment can be seen as decadent, and this is particularly apparent to Christians from the less economically developed world. The religious critique of the culture of contemporary sexuality is not one that is confined to homosexuality.

In our highly sexualized society, relationships gain sexual expression more rapidly and more frequently than ever before. There is undoubtedly a problem for the church about how people now find themselves, including their sexual identity, for this requires personal experience and exploration. This is a major challenge to the Christian commitment to lifelong fidelity in sexual relationships. The cultural pressure on those who are ambivalent in their sexual orientation has been to conform to heterosexual norms. This has been a source of much anxiety and pain for those who are thereby denied their homosexuality by being drawn inappropriately into marriage. In a culture increasingly tolerant of homosexuality, it is possible that this sort of ambivalence will draw some people into homosexual relationships who don't really belong there. The ambivalence of the churches here will be apparent if this is a matter of regret, and homosexuality is seen as second-best. Equally, the zeal of campaigners may prevent the recognition that some people could get stuck in a pattern of behaviour in which they do not truly find their authentic selves.

Reformed churches Most of the Reformed churches have opened up the debate on homosexuality because of the recognition that there are a significant number of homosexual Christians, including clergy, in the church. Mere tolerance of these people as long as they remain invisibly homosexual is no longer acceptable. Secrecy about homosexual activity encouraged a culture of furtive promiscuity in which relationships lacked the public expression by which marriages receive social and legal support to help sustain them in times of difficulty. If homosexuals are to be openly accepted, the blessing of same sex unions will inevitably and properly follow. This would ease the church's decision about how to recognize the registration of civil partnerships.

The official Roman Catholic position on homosexuality is rigid and closed to the possibility of change, even though there is lively debate about sexuality among church members. The acceptance of homosexual relationships would challenge the systematic structure of the church's teaching in which the possibility of procreation is an essential purpose of sexual intercourse. The acceptance of homosexual relationships would deny this and have the additional consequence of allowing that a sexual relationship can be established outside marriage. This would be challenging for this church's teaching about both the use of artificial contraception and marriage.

It has been difficult for homosexual Christians to find a voice and get a hearing from their churches, even when those churches say that they want to listen to the experience of gay Christians in order to learn from them as, for example, with the Anglican Church following the 1998 Lambeth Conference. Yet there have been discernible changes. In November 2003 the consecration of a homosexual in a committed relationship as Bishop of New Hampshire in the Episcopal Church of the USA is seen by both sides of this debate as a watershed both within and between the various denominations. It is certain there will be very rapid developments in both Christian thinking and church order.

NICHOLAS HOLTAM

James Alison, *Faith beyond Resentment: Fragments Catholic and Gay*, London: Darton, Longman & Todd 2001; John Boswell, *Same Sex Unions in Pre-Modern Europe*, New York and London: Vintage Books 1995; Gareth Moore, OP, *A Question of Truth: Christianity and Homosexuality*, London and New York: Continuum 2003; Alan Bray, *The Friend*, Chicago: University of Chicago Press 2003; John Stott, *Same Sex Partnerships? A Christian's Perspective*, Grand Rapids, MI: Fleming H. Revell 1998; (Roman Catholic) Congregation for the Doctrine of the Faith, *Declaration on Certain Questions Concerning Sexual Ethics (Persona humana)*, 1975; *Letter ... on the Pastoral Care of Homosexual Persons (Homosexualitatis problema)*, 1986; Working Party of the (Church of England's) House of Bishops, *Some Issues in Human Sexuality: A Guide to the Debate*, London: Church House Publishing 2003

Hope

Jesus

Christianity all too often appears over-preoccupied with the past. Its beliefs, its practices, its forms of prayer and worship and the architectural settings in which these activities take place, together with discussions of the intellectual questions which arise from being a Christian, are all dominated by what has been said and done in the past, which is regarded as the norm for the present day. To some degree this is inevitable; Christianity owes its origin to a figure of the past, Jesus of Nazareth, and what he said and did, and forms of Christianity which disregard the past and its precedents all too easily run the risk of running wild and losing the essential features which make Christianity what it is. But the past can also become such a burden on Christianity that it becomes distracted from its original and essential focus, the future. In technical theological terms, Christianity is an eschatological religion, and hope for the future is a key element.

Future Eschatology

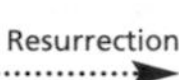

Hope is a central feature of earliest Christianity and is closely associated with the resurrection. The First Letter of Peter describes its readers as having been 'born anew to a living hope through the resurrection of Jesus Christ from the dead' (1.3) and describes testifying to the faith as 'making a defence to any one who calls you to account for the hope that is in you' (3.15). The Ephesians are said formerly, when separated from Christ, to have been 'having no hope and without God in the world' (2.12). For Paul, the armaments of the Christian are 'the breastplate of faith and love and for a helmet the hope of salvation'; the Abraham who is the prime example of faith because he trusted that God would give him descendants, though he and his wife were past the age for having children, 'in hope believed against hope' (Romans 4.18). Along with faith and love, hope is one of the three great virtues. By its very nature hope requires trust. 'Now hope that is seen is not hope. For who hopes for what he sees? But if we hope for what we do not see, we wait for it with patience' (Romans 8.24–5). That does not mean, though, that for Paul hope is an uncertain matter. His God is a God of hope: 'May the God of hope fill you with all joy and peace in believing, so that by the power of the Holy Spirit you may abound in hope' (Romans 15.13).

Resurrection Anglicanism Paul

The hope associated with the resurrection was that Jesus would come again, as judge of the living and the dead, to usher in the final consummation of the world, and it dominated the thoughts and shaped the attitudes of the first generation of Christians. When the first coming had not taken place, the focus of hope began to shift. Ignatius of Antioch (*c.*35–*c.*107), whose writings are contemporary with some books of the New Testament, while still connecting hope with the resurrection, most frequently uses the term hope to denote Christ himself, calling him 'our hope' or 'our common hope'. This shift represents a major change: here hope is no longer an attitude but the name of the source of blessings in the present, with whom Christians will be after they die. It is not a dynamic for living life in the world with eyes fixed on the future.

The shift marks the beginning of a long process in which hope was to play an increasingly subordinate role in Christian thought. Certainly there are discussions of hope in great theologians such as Augustine and Thomas Aquinas, but they lack the dynamic of the early days. There is none of the sense of being on a journey led by the God who once led Abraham out of Ur of the Chaldaeans and the Israelites out of Egypt, a sense which is expressed in a well-known Victorian hymn: 'One the object of our journey, one the faith which never tires, one the earnest looking forward, one the hope our God inspires'.

The centrality of hope for Christian faith has been recovered only relatively recently, above all through the writings of one German theologian, Jürgen Moltmann, whose *Theology of Hope* appeared in German in 1964 (English 1967). Interestingly enough, this rediscovery was prompted by the reading of a dense three-volume work, *The Principle of Hope*, by a German philosopher, Ernst Bloch, expelled from East Germany and forced into exile in Tübingen, to Moltmann's university. What was distinctive about Bloch's work was that, although an atheistic Marxist, he was strongly influenced by the Jewish and Christian belief in a messiah. As he pointed out, eschatological awareness, and therefore hope, came into the world through the Bible, and his book is a complex discussion of what an eschatological sense can mean today. Deeply influenced by it, Moltmann argued that Christianity had banished from its life the future hope which was its motivating force and had relegated the future to a beyond, whereas the biblical testimonies are full of a future hope for this world. The atheists, in the person of Bloch, he argued, had reclaimed the future hope, which was at best still cherished only by marginal sects, while in mainstream Christian thought it was a mere appendix.

Moltmann's own book, too, is by no means easy reading, and the issues with which it engages from the perspective of an eschatological approach to Christianity centred on hope are no longer those of the present day. But the book was a theological best-seller of its time and its concern, a restoration of hope to the centre of Christianity and what this means for the life and thought of the Christian churches, is still important. One of the roles expected of the Christian churches today is that they should offer hope, and should have a clearly thought-out basis for doing so. A Christianity characterized by a sense of being engaged in a journey embarked on in hope, of bringing real hope to those who at present have no hope, and inspired by a vision of the kingdom of God, would be in a stronger position than it is now.

Kingdom of God

JOHN BOWDEN

Ernst Bloch, *The Principle of Hope* (3 vols), Cambridge, MA: MIT Press 1995; Jürgen Moltmann, *Theology of Hope*, London: SCM Press and New York: Harper & Row 1967

Human rights

Journey

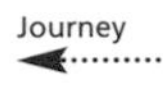

Human rights exist to affirm the dignity of every person. Although the term is relatively modern, protection of the rights of individuals has been necessary for as long as individuals or groups have been oppressed. In the Roman Republic, the tribunes of the people were charged to protect the lives and property of 'plebeians' from the middle of the fifth century BCE. In the Old Testament humankind is said to have been made in the image of God (Genesis 1.26) and the prophet Elijah rebuked King Ahab for his consent to the judicial murder of Naboth (1 Kings 21). Paul wrote that in Christ there is neither Jew nor Greek, slave nor free, male nor female (Galatians 3. 28ff). In Great Britain the Magna Carta of 1215 and the Bill of Rights of 1689 limited the power of the monarchy. Nevertheless, slavery was not abolished in the British Dominions until 1833, and women could not vote in France until 1945.

Messiah

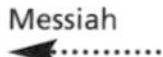

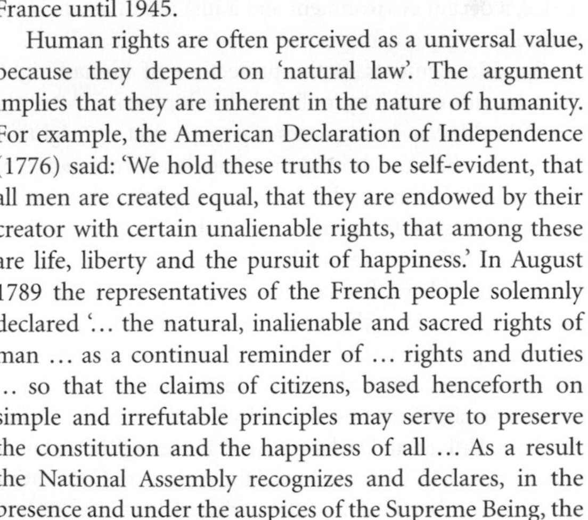

Human rights are often perceived as a universal value, because they depend on 'natural law'. The argument implies that they are inherent in the nature of humanity. For example, the American Declaration of Independence (1776) said: 'We hold these truths to be self-evident, that all men are created equal, that they are endowed by their creator with certain unalienable rights, that among these are life, liberty and the pursuit of happiness.' In August 1789 the representatives of the French people solemnly declared '... the natural, inalienable and sacred rights of man ... as a continual reminder of ... rights and duties ... so that the claims of citizens, based henceforth on simple and irrefutable principles may serve to preserve the constitution and the happiness of all ... As a result the National Assembly recognizes and declares, in the presence and under the auspices of the Supreme Being, the following rights of man and of the citizen.' The American Declaration, with its reference to the creator, implies a religious principle. The French declaration, with its reference to the Supreme Being, is more equivocal.

The theoretical expression of human rights must be worked out in practice. So rights are categorized in three 'generations'. The first concerns the equality of all and their entitlement to freedom from state interference. For example, in the French Declaration, men are born and live free and equal in their rights (Article 1). The aim of political association is the preservation of the natural and irrefutable rights of freedom, property, security and resistance to oppression (Article 2). Today the mainstream Christian traditions support the principle of inherent human rights. That principle is not negated by disagreement over issues such as the rights of an unborn child. On the other hand, extremist political movements may be unacceptable because they are perceived to infringe the rights of a proportion of the population. A policy leading to the intolerant treatment of immigrants would be an example.

Economic rights belong to the 'second generation'. They include secure employment, decent conditions, a fair wage and social and cultural security. In this area specific provisions are open to debate and depend on regulation. For example, according to some usually more left-wing political analyses, the individual freedom of first-generation rights can lead to capitalist exploitation of the labour of other people. Regulation of social issues by legislation or taxation is an aspect of political debate. In the late eighteenth century, however, Jeremy Bentham went further in his 'utilitarian argument'. He said that legislation should ensure the greatest good of the greatest number. He described human rights as 'nonsense on stilts'.

'Third-generation' emerging rights aim to guarantee peace, a decent environment and a just use of assets in the future.

Specific elements in the protection of human rights may be influenced by political developments. After the First World War it was necessary to protect the rights of minorities because boundaries had been redrawn. The League of Nations and a number of national constitutions made specific reference to that. Nevertheless, from 1933 to 1945 the Nazis not only ignored but attacked the rights of Jews, Roma and many dissidents. After the Second World War there was continued abuse of rights, for example in Central and Eastern Europe or in South Africa, though abuse was by no means confined to those regions. A significant post-war declaration was the United Nations Universal Declaration of Human Rights of 10 December 1948. There followed the American Convention of 22 November 1969 and the African Charter of 28 June 1981. These definitions were agreed between nations and recognized internationally.

Education ➤

Nevertheless, the effect of international agreements is limited. Because they apply to states, they depend on the preparedness of all parties to conform and become available to the citizen through the state and domestic law. On the other hand the European Convention of 4 November 1950 was the first human rights instrument to be internationally guaranteed. The member states of the Council of Europe (currently 45) are bound to observe its provisions and to accept the decisions of the European Court of Human Rights based in Strasbourg. A significant achievement has been the development of a substantial body of 'jurisprudence' based on the European Convention. It is related to Strasbourg's role as the court of last resort. Cases only become admissible in Strasbourg when all domestic remedies have been exhausted. So questions before the court can involve a process in which the citizen is effectively the plaintiff and the sovereign state is the defendant. This is tantamount to the indictment of a state on the part of a citizen. The judgements of the Strasbourg court are an essential element in the application and interpretation of universal values (although there is also an American court).

In so far as human rights are a 'universal value', they are the prerogative neither of a religion nor of a political standpoint. Article 9 on freedom of religion and conscience therefore makes no reference to a particular religion. A related issue is the Council of Europe's work in the field of education. It favours dialogue, of which an important aim is getting to know the other better and avoiding the imposition of one's own views. Religious proselytism is therefore discouraged, although Article 9 includes the right to manifest one's religion. The same principle is set out in the European *Charta Oecumenica* (see below). The signatories commit themselves to dialogue with all people of goodwill (II.12).

The principle is applied in different ways. In France, a long history of religious conflict led to the separation of church and state in 1905. The principle known as *laïcité* guarantees freedom of religion while denying any religious involvement to the state or the government. The law of 1905 was associated with the development of the *école laïque* at the end of the nineteenth century. Education is a right, but there are no religious symbols in French schools. Assumptions about the belief of pupils would be an infringement of their right to freedom of thought and conscience. Nevertheless, there are countries in Europe where religious organizations have a role in the school, while in Germany, for example, the curriculum still includes knowledge of a confessional tradition. In practice, therefore, the relationship of rights to natural law does not preclude cultural diversity or the influence of history, culture or the local context.

Perceptions evolve in other respects as well. As it applies or interprets the European Convention, the Strasbourg court sometimes has to make difficult decisions that may appear to be like ethical judgements. A terminally ill and seriously handicapped woman was not allowed to realize assisted suicide because Article 2 guarantees the right to life. A woman, the cost of whose gender reassignment operation had been borne by her country's health service, was judged to have the right to marry and found a family (Article 12) as well as to change her birth certificate and national insurance number.

Traditionally, Christians might have been expected to agree with the first judgement and to disagree with the second. In both instances medical developments have given rise to difficult questions that did not exist before. In the second instance, the fact that surgical techniques had become available to relieve personal suffering was a challenge to the prevailing law that marriage could only be to a person who was of the other sex at birth. It is impossible for the law to ignore scientific (and other) developments, as it may also be similarly difficult for theology. In the plurality of the twenty-first century there will be continuing dialogue.

It could be expected, especially with the collapse of the totalitarian regimes, that there would be greater consensus over social and economic rights and over security for the future, and there is a procedure for collective complaint under the European Social Charter. Nevertheless, issues such as immigration are not easily resolved. Globalization and free trade are perceived to result in unreasonable distribution of wealth and to lack of opportunity in the poorer countries of the world. On the other hand, the European Union is involved in a joint parliamentary assembly with the countries of Africa, the Caribbean and the Pacific (ACP). The resultant trading partnership offers some redress. The USA is party to an American trading agreement that embraces the whole continent. However, global injustice continues to threaten peace and security in the longer term.

More generally, perceptions about the church and human rights have developed, particularly in recent years. Blatant examples of bigotry and persecution in the sixteenth century apart, it was not until 1871 that Gladstone's government passed the Universities Tests Act that opened degrees and offices to men (*sic*) of any religion or of none, rather than giving privileges to members of the established church. Missionary organizations today engage in 'humanitarian' work, for example in providing access to education and medical care. Though the underpinning of this work by a confessional tradition makes it neither intrinsically better nor worse than that of other partners or contributors, it expresses the churches' commitment to all 'generations' of human rights. In this respect, the signing of the *Charta Oecumenica* in Strasbourg in 2001 was particularly significant.

Christianity in Europe

The signatories were the Conference of European Churches (CEC), to which almost all Orthodox, Protestant, Anglican, Old Catholic and independent churches in Europe belong, and the Council of European Bishops' Conferences (CCEE). All Roman Catholic Bishops' Conferences in Europe are represented in the CCEE. In addition to a commitment to work together, these bodies undertook to seek agreement with one another on the substance and goals of our social responsibility, and to represent in concert, as far as possible, the concerns and visions of the churches *vis-à-vis* the secular European institutions; to defend basic values against infringements of every kind; and to resist any attempt to misuse religion and the church for ethnic or nationalist purposes. They also undertook to respect other religions and to defend freedom of religion and conscience among people of other religions and world-views (III.7).

In the nature of the case there continue to be disagreements. Some, but by no means all, of them are perceived to relate to denominational points of view. In a talk at the University of Strasbourg in 1991, Metropolitan Daniel of Moldova said that every religion bases human dignity on man's relationship to God. He then referred to the lack of reference to the Almighty or to religion in the justification of human rights philosophy. He asked whether that does not make human rights a new religion or rather a substitute for religion. It follows that a different point of view about a particular issue need not imply a lack of commitment to human rights. Indeed, contributions by the churches should include raising difficult questions. In the early 1970s the ecumenical community at Taizé organized a Council of Youth. Its slogan was that participants could be signs of contradiction according to the gospel. The different reactions of people from either side of the Iron Curtain showed how it is possible to examine even what one supports and to do so critically.

Globalization

p. 274

That kind of contribution is particularly valuable when difficult questions relate the general principle of the relationship of individual freedom to the responsibility to take account of the rights and needs of others. For example, the Commissioner for Human Rights at the Council of Europe organized a colloquy at the end of 2002 about convergence and divergence in human rights, culture and religion. In the report on the colloquy participants agreed that, in conferring rights, the fundamental texts include an equal level of responsibility. They said that democracy and religion share a commitment to recognition and respect of other people. All analysis must be accessible if it is to contribute concordantly or discordantly to the evolution of human understanding.

JAMES BARNETT

Erich Weingärtner, *Protecting Human Rights, A Manual for Practitioners,* Geneva: Conference of European Churches 1994; Scott Davidson, *Human Rights,* London: Open University Press 1993; François Audigier and Guy Lagelée, *Human Rights,* Strasbourg: Council of Europe 2000; *Charta Oecumenica,* Geneva: Conference of European Churches 2001; *European Convention on Human Rights,* Strasbourg: Council of Europe 1950; *European Social Charter,* Strasbourg: Council of Europe 2001

For Council of Europe material see http://www.coe.int

Humanism

The modern English words 'humanist' and 'humanism' (and their equivalents in other European languages) have their roots in the Latin *humanitas* (humanity). The term 'humanist' (Latin *humanista*) was coined during the Italian Renaissance; it was first used colloquially to describe contemporary teachers of Greek and Latin literature, writing and rhetorical skills, and was later broadened to include anyone committed to classical learning. Modern use of the term 'humanism' (Latin *humanismus*) developed from attempts to distinguish the study of the classics from more scientific subjects, but has since come to carry a variety of meanings, not all of them clear.

Renaissance

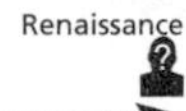

Scholars during the Renaissance derived their understanding of the idea of a distinct area of study from the Latin philosopher and orator Cicero's oration *De Oratore* (55 BCE) and his *Pro Archia* (62 BCE); here the great Roman orator defended what he called the *studia humanitatis ac litterarum* (study of the humanities and letters). In the Renaissance, the *studia humanitatis* meant the study of grammar, rhetoric, history, poetry and moral philosophy, a considerably more narrow focus than that advocated by Cicero (which would have included, for example, geometry and arithmetic). Yet the Renaissance humanists saw themselves rediscovering the learning of classical antiquity within a Christian context and placed themselves self-consciously in opposition to what they saw as the increasing sterility of the scholastic theology of the previous centuries.

p. 887
Education
Scholasticism
Body
Women in Christianity

The pre-eminent scholar of the early Renaissance was Francesco Petrarch (1304–74), known as the 'father of humanism'. An admirer and imitator of the eloquence and style of Cicero, Petrarch encouraged the study of ancient Rome, revived the classical Latin style and taught his contemporaries to think of the centuries between the ancient and contemporary worlds as an age of darkness, a label which is still with us. In his *On His Own Ignorance and the Ignorance of the Many* (1371), he attacked the scholars in the universities; in a Socratic mood he ridiculed their pretensions to knowledge and their admiration for Aristotle, arguing that Plato was more suited to Christian thought. His love poems, for which he was famous in his day, contributed significantly to the development of the romantic spirit in Western literature. Among other achievements he wrote works of morality and biographies of ancient heroes, composed orations, rediscovered ancient texts (including some of Cicero), and used textual analysis to identify medieval forgeries of ancient documents.

Philosophy
Theology

Petrarch's contemporaries and successors carried on the new ideas. Giovanni Boccaccio (1313–75) is best remembered for the stories in his *Decameron* and his *Genealogy of the Gods*, a collection of myths which was an early effort at the study of religion. Coluccio Salutati (1331–1406), an important figure in Florentine politics, was one of the first to use the term *studia humanitatis*; among his protégés was Poggio Bracciolini (1380–1459), who devised an innovative form of script for the new literary sensibility. Others in both the fourteenth and fifteenth centuries rediscovered some of the most important works of classical poets, philosophers and historians.

Both before and after the fall of Constantinople to the Muslims (1453), an influx of Greek scholars to the West increased knowledge of Greek literature and considerably broadened the resources available for study. The renewal of interest in classical sources stimulated Christian thinkers to return to early Christian thought. Among the most significant of the Renaissance theologians and philosophers were Nicholas of Cusa (1401–64), whose theology drew on neo-Platonic sources to develop a *via negativa* for speaking of God, i.e. saying what God was not, and Marsilio Ficino (1433–99), the most important neo-Platonist of the Renaissance. In this context critical analysis of texts became common practice and had some important results, most notably when Lorenzo Valla (1405–57) used historical-critical methods to demonstrate that the Donation of Constantine, a document purporting to be from Constantine and giving widespread political powers to the popes, was in fact an eighth-century forgery. The era also saw a vibrant interest in education, the development of the liberal arts, the promotion of personal development, the cultivation of the body as well as the mind and even a developing interest in the education of women (who were banned from the universities and most professions).

It is significant that the Renaissance humanists for the most part were not greatly concerned with philosophy and theology as they were understood and practised in the late-medieval university. Rather, they were primarily concerned with history, with literature and with rhetoric (the effective use of words and the art of composition).

Many of these scholars were not clerics and so were not educated in the scholastic tradition of commenting on venerable authors. Rather, many came from varied areas of life such as teaching, medicine, the law and government bureaucracy; thus their interests reflected the traits and aspirations of their professions. This goes some way to explaining their emphasis on the human qualities needed to succeed in the world. The very modern ideal of achieving one's human potential emerges in such tracts as the oration *On the Dignity of Man* of Ficino's student Giovanni Pico della Mirandola (1463–94), in which he daringly has God suggest to Adam that he is without limit and is free to determine his own nature, either to become more like God or more like the beasts. Yet such freethinking was not without its dangers, and the age was clearly not one of unqualified tolerance in religious matters; Giordano Bruno (1548–1600) went to the stake for a philosophical theology that was regarded as too pantheistic.

Where Renaissance humanism did influence religion it was significant. The renewal of interest in classical sources (including the Bible), the criticism of scholastic theology, increased attention to human experience in the world, an emphasis on individual freedom and autonomy over and against the constraints of the church, and the explosion of books and pamphlets which accompanied the invention of moveable type, all provided a background within which reforming movements could take shape. Although the connections between Renaissance humanism and the Reformation should not be exaggerated, there are nevertheless noteworthy links. In northern Europe many scholars learned from their Italian counterparts. In Germany humanism flourished at Heidelberg and elsewhere, and in England humanists such as Thomas Linacre (*c.*1450–1524) and William Latimer (*c.*1460–1543) encouraged the study of the classics. John Colet (1467–1519) promoted the study of scripture, yet also drew on the revival of neo-Platonism in Italy.

The foremost humanist of northern Europe was Desiderius Erasmus of Rotterdam (*c.*1469–1536), whose most important achievement was the publication of a Greek New Testament with a Latin translation and commentary (1516). In making the New Testament available to scholars in the original language Erasmus undermined the hold that church theologians had on the interpretation of the text, and it was his Greek edition which Martin Luther used to translate the New Testament into German. Further, Erasmus' ridicule of clerical pretensions and ignorance in his *In Praise of Folly,* and his attempt to encourage a more simple form of Christian piety in his *Enchiridion* (designed as a basic handbook for the ordinary Christian), encouraged a renewal of lay spirituality independent of church oversight.

Despite these influences, the Reformation's stress on sinfulness did not sit easily with the humanists' emphasis on human dignity and freedom, and Luther broke with Erasmus on the question of the freedom of the will. Nevertheless John Calvin (1509–64), Philipp Melanchthon (1497–1560) and other Reformers demonstrated the value of their classical learning through the weight that Protestantism gave to humanist education. On the Roman Catholic side the Jesuits, attempting to keep the aristocracy of Europe loyal to Rome, developed schools that emphasized many of the central elements of the *studia humanitatis.* Thus both Roman Catholic and Protestant education carried the ideals of the Christian humanists of the fourteenth and fifteenth centuries into the Enlightenment and, in an attenuated form, into the modern university.

Sin

Protestantism
Religious orders
Schools
Enlightenment
University

When we consider 'humanism' in the context of the Enlightenment of the seventeenth and eighteenth centuries its meaning takes on a non-Christian, indeed at times anti-Christian, flavour. Although not using the terms 'humanism' or 'humanist' to describe themselves, thinkers such as Voltaire, Jean-Jacques Rousseau, Denis Diderot, David Hume and others tried to move away from a Christian concept of human life as one lived in the context of the history of salvation under the guidance of a personal God to one in which human beings find their value and dignity through free exercise of reason in the world. Rousseau's insistence on the innocence of each human heart (a direct rejection of the Christian doctrine of original sin), Diderot's reflections on materialism, Hume's critique of miracles and Voltaire's cry of 'crush the infamous one' (i.e. the Christian church) all indicate an attempt to develop a 'humanism' free from theological foundations.

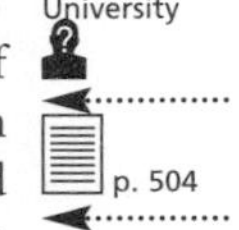

p. 504

Books

Reformation

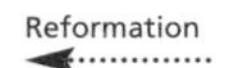

Thus the Enlightenment ushers in various forms of modern secular humanism that remain significant in Western societies today. In the modern period, however, there is little coherence in the meaning of 'humanism' and the term as such has lost much of its explanatory value. In our current pluralistic context there are Marxist humanists, scientific humanists, pragmatic humanists, existential humanists, Christian humanists and others. There are those who reject both the Renaissance and the Enlightenment notions of 'humanism'. Martin Heidegger (1889–1976) claimed that all humanisms must be rejected because they are grounded in metaphysics; his disciple Jean-Paul Sartre claimed that 'existentialism is a humanism', meaning that humanism is whatever you want it to be; some ecological advocates claim that the term 'humanism' reflects a new 'speciesism' which gives unjustified priority to *homo sapiens* over other species; postmodernists who follow the nihilistic philosopher Michel Foucault claim that the whole concept of 'man' (i.e. humanity) is an

invention of a recent date, one soon to be wiped away like a name written in sand by the seashore. Under such influ-ences, many Western schools and universities have given less and less attention to the *studia humanitatis*. However, there are also those who think that the corrosive educational, psychological, social and cultural effects of this trend away from the study of the humanities are already evident in Western society.

JAMES M. BYRNE

Myron P. Gilmore, *The World of Humanism, 1453–1517*, New York: Harper & Brothers 1952; Gerhard Hoffmeister, *The Renaissance and Reformation in Germany*, New York: Ungar 1977; J. Kraye (ed), *The Cambridge Companion to Renaissance Humanism*, Cambridge: CUP 1996; Paul O. Kristeller, *Renaissance Thought and Its Sources*, New York: Columbia University Press 1979; Charles E. Trinkhaus, *The Scope of Renaissance Humanism*, Ann Arbor: University of Michigan Press 1983

Monasticism

Hymns

Jesus Hymns have always been a part of Christian worship. Jesus and his disciples sang a hymn after the last supper (Mark Paul 14.26), and Paul twice exhorted the early Christians to join together, 'speaking to one another in psalms and hymns and spiritual songs, singing and making melody with your heart to the Lord' (Ephesians 5.19; Colossians 3. 16). The psalms would have come from the Jewish tradition, and the hymns and spiritual songs probably included refrains such as 'Alleluia' and 'Holy, holy, holy' (known as the Tersanctus or Trisagion), perhaps with passages of scripture added. There is evidence of hymn singing around the year 105 CE, when the younger Pliny, governor of Bithynia in Asia Minor, wrote to the Emperor Trajan and described Christians 'assembling together early in the morning and singing by turns a song to Christ as a god'. This is corroborated by a third-century writer, Caius, who described 'psalms and odes; such as were from the beginning written by the faithful, hymns to the Christ, the word of God, calling him God'.

Celtic Christianity

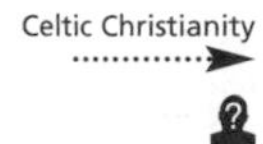

The words 'from the beginning' suggest that the practice of hymn writing and hymn singing began very early in the history of the church. One of the earliest Greek hymns, 'Hail, gladdening light', was described by Basil, who died in 379, as 'old'. It was sung at the lighting of the lamps:

> Now we are come to the sun's hour of rest;
> the lights of evening round us shine;
> we hymn the Father, Son, and Holy Spirit divine.

This beautifully simple hymn takes us back to the days of the first Christians in the Roman empire. It was translated by John Keble (1792–1866) and became one of the many ancient hymns made available in the nineteenth century through translation. The greatest of the translators was John Mason Neale (1818–66), who admired both the plainness of the Greek hymns and the grandeur of the Latin ones, and loved to feel that the church in the age of Queen Victoria was somehow in touch with the pure simplicity of the Christian poets of the early years.

The greatest of the early Latin poets were Prudentius (348–*c.* 410), who wrote 'Of the Father's love begotten', and Venantius Fortunatus (*c.* 530–609), who wrote 'The royal banners forward go' and 'Sing, my tongue, the glorious battle'.

Fortunatus' hymns were written for a convent in Poitiers, which is a reminder that the tradition of hymn singing was kept alive during the Middle Ages chiefly through the monasteries. The practice had been regularized and strengthened by Ambrose (340–97), Bishop of Milan, 'the father of church song'; it is doubtful whether he wrote the *Te Deum*, which has been attributed to him, but he certainly introduced some system into the singing of hymns in services. In monasteries and convents hymns came to be associated with times of day, such as 'Now that the daylight fills the sky', or 'Before the ending of the day'. Others were for particular seasons, such as Advent ('O come, O come, Immanuel'), or Pentecost ('Come, Holy Ghost, our souls inspire'). Yet others contrasted the brief life on earth with the joys of heaven, as in the splendour of Neale's translation from a twelfth-century hymn by Bernard of Cluny:

> Jerusalem the golden,
> With milk and honey blest,
> Beneath thy contemplation
> Sink heart and voice oppress.

Beside these hymns from the great monasteries of Western Europe there was another tradition of Celtic hymn writing, most famously demonstrated in 'St Patrick's Breastplate' and in the hymns of Columba. Together with the Greek and Latin hymns, they were revived in the nineteenth and twentieth centuries and given tunes, either from plainsong, or other ancient melody (such as the old Irish music used for Patrick's hymn), or modern tunes written specifically for those hymns. S. S. Wesley's AURELIA, for example, was written (as its golden name suggests) for 'Jerusalem the golden'. It is now used for 'The church's one foundation', but its impressive resonance is a reminder of how important music has always been to the hymn experience. This was one of the major reasons for the success of *Hymns Ancient and Modern* when it was printed in 1861 with music and words together.

The story of 'modern' hymnody begins with the Reformation, during which the Protestant exiles from persecution under Mary Tudor sang metrical psalms. Only one of these survives in common use:

> All people that on earth do dwell,
> Sing to the Lord with cheerful voice;
> Him serve with fear, his praise forth tell,
> Come ye before him, and rejoice.

The grand tune for these words, the OLD HUNDREDTH (because this was a metrical version of the hundredth psalm), was probably responsible for the survival of this psalm when so many others have been forgotten: but the metrical psalms formed the basis for much Protestant worship in England for 200 years, and in Scotland for even longer. They were greatly loved by John Calvin and his followers, who were distrustful of the latitude of hymns, whereas the Lutheran church was not. Martin Luther himself wrote some wonderful metrical versions of the psalms, notably the powerful 'Ein feste Burg' ('A safe stronghold our God is still', Psalm 46, translated by Thomas Carlyle), and 'Aus tiefer Noth' ('Out of the depths I cry to thee', Psalm 130, translated by the greatest of many translators from the German, Catherine Winkworth). In the nineteenth century, Winkworth and others did for German hymnody what Neale had done for ancient hymns. They produced singable versions of magnificent hymns by such poets as Paul Gerhardt, Joachim Neander and Martin Rinkart ('All my heart this night rejoices', 'Praise to the Lord! The Almighty, the King of Creation!', 'Now thank we all our God').

In the aftermath of the Reformation, psalm singing dominated worship, but a few hymns began to be written, and in the seventeenth century the first English hymn books were produced. The stage was set for the arrival of the first great hymn writer, Isaac Watts (1674–1748), whose hymns were clear, singable, and robust. 'When I survey the wondrous cross' and 'O God, our help in ages past' are probably the greatest hymns in the language. They are only two of many magnificent hymns and psalms written by Watts: his work dominated English hymnody of the dissenting tradition for over 100 years. His contemporary was Joseph Addison (1672–1719), whose hymn 'The spacious firmament on high' was, like the hymns of Watts, an expression of the splendour of the creation and its creator. Both writers, in their different ways, were responding to an age of Newtonian physics. Other hymn writers followed, notably Philip Doddridge (1702–51) and Anne Steele (1717–78), who was the first woman hymn writer to become celebrated.

It was natural that when the Methodists began their work in the 1730s they should have used hymns. As the preface to the 1933 *Methodist Hymn Book* memorably put it, 'Methodism was born in song.' John Wesley was a great translator of German hymns, but it was his brother Charles (1707–88) who really used the hymn form to express the full range of Christian spirituality. Charles's hymns were enthusiastic, energetic and dramatic: they were concerned with Christian experience, often with wonder and amazement. The hymn which he wrote to mark his conversion, 'Where shall my wondering soul begin?', poses a question that indicates his joy at the new birth. He went on to write a vast number of hymns in which one can often feel this excitement, though Wesley was also capable of being reflective and of writing on the great festivals of the church ('Hark, the herald angels sing'; 'Christ the Lord is risen today').

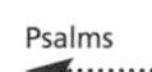

The evangelical revival, working at the same time as the Methodist movement though often in controversy with it, laid great emphasis on the sacrifice of Jesus Christ on the cross and on the salvation of souls by his blood. Perhaps the greatest of hymns from this source is 'Rock of Ages, cleft for me', by Augustus Montague Toplady (1740–78), with its description of the cleansing power of the sacred blood. It was this 'amazing grace' of God that was the central emphasis of the hymnody of John Newton (1725–1807) and William Cowper (1731–1800), who collaborated to produce *Olney Hymns* (1779), a classic volume of evangelical revival hymns, including not only Newton's 'Amazing grace' and 'Glorious things of thee are spoken' but also Cowper's 'God moves in a mysterious way', and 'Hark, my soul! It is the Lord'. Another of his hymns states the central evangelical position so powerfully that it has become unsingable:

> There is a fountain filled with blood
> Drawn from Emmanuel's veins;
> And sinners, plunged beneath that flood,
> Lose all their guilty stains.

In the nineteenth century, hymn writing became less strident, until the pendulum swung back again with the campaigns of Dwight L. Moody and Ira D. Sankey and the publication of Sankey's *Sacred Songs and Solos*, which went through many editions from the 1870s onwards. Before that, however, there had been some fine writing from the romantic period poets, such as Reginald Heber (1783–1826) and James Montgomery (1771–1854). Gradually hymns became accepted into Church of England services, culminating in the publication of *Hymns Ancient and Modern* in 1861. That book, containing classic hymns such as 'Abide with me' and 'Praise, my soul, the King of Heaven', both by Henry Francis Lyte (1793–1847), was the pre-eminent book in Britain and the empire until the coming of the *English Hymnal* in 1906. In successive

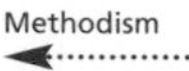

nineteenth-century editions it was able to add hymns soon after they were written, such as 'For all the saints, who from their labours rest', 'The church's one foundation' and 'The day thou gavest, Lord, is ended'. The inclusion of hymns that are both 'ancient' and 'modern' has continued in every succeeding edition up to its newest, *Common Praise* (2000).

The nineteenth century also saw a great increase in the number of hymns by women, including 'Just as I am, without one plea' by Charlotte Elliott (1789–1871) and 'Take my life, and let it be' by Frances Ridley Havergal (1836–79); Cecil Frances Alexander (1818–95) produced in 1848 the first really successful hymns for children, including 'All things bright and beautiful'; and there was also a marvellous outpouring of great American hymns, such as 'Dear Lord and Father of mankind' by John Greenleaf Whittier (1807–92). Interestingly, this was not originally written as a hymn but, like John Henry Newman's (1801–1900) 'Firmly I believe and truly' and 'Praise to the Holiest in the Height' formed part of a long narrative poem. The relationship between hymns and poems is an interesting one: such is the demand for hymns that many poems have been set to music as hymns, some, like these, more successfully than others.

At the beginning of the twentieth century there was a huge reservoir of hymns to draw upon, used with great skill by Percy Dearmer (1867–1936) in *Songs of Praise* (1925). The enlarged edition of this book (1931) contained hymns such as 'Morning has broken' by Eleanor Farjeon (1881–1965) and 'Lord of all hopefulness' by Jan Struther (1901–53).

After the Second World War there was a period of consolidation, followed by what has been called 'the hymn explosion', in which writers such as Albert Bayly (1901–84), Fred Pratt Green (1903–2000) and others, many still living, enriched worship with hymns that were serious and traditional, yet also fresh and modern. A hymn such as 'Tell out, my soul, the greatness of the Lord', by Timothy Dudley-Smith (1926–), demonstrates how an ancient text, the Magnificat, can be given new life. At the same time there have been less orthodox contributions such as 'Lord of the dance' from Sydney Carter (1915–2004), and socially-aware hymns from the writers associated with the Iona Community in Scotland. Never before, perhaps, has there been so much variety in hymn and tune writing, or so much activity all over the world. In almost every country where there is a Christian church, there has been a need to find or create texts, local or universal, that will address God in praise and prayer, that will teach the gospel, and that will reflect individual religious experience, drawing on the great heritage of the past and adding the testimony of the present.

Orthodox churches

Music

Byzantium

J. R. WATSON

Lionel Adey, *Hymns and the Christian 'Myth'*, Vancouver: University of British Columbia Press 1986; Louis F. Benson, *The English Hymn*, New York: George H. Doran 1915; Ian Bradley, *Abide with Me*, London: SCM Press and Toledo, OH: Gregorian Institute of America 1997; Donald Davie, *The Eighteenth-Century Hymn in England*, Cambridge: CUP 1993; J. R. Watson, *The English Hymn*, Oxford: OUP 1997 and *An Annotated Anthology of Hymns*, Oxford: OUP 2002

Icon

Sergei Fyodorov is a Russian icon painter (icon writer, as purists would try to insist). An icon is a flat picture, typically painted on wood, which usually represents Jesus, the Virgin Mary or a saint. Fyodorov is now in his forties, and his splendid work is to be found in significant Orthodox churches in Russia, but also in England in Canterbury, Rochester and Winchester Cathedrals, Westminster Abbey, and numerous other churches, including the tiny rural church of St Mary's, Twyford, in Hampshire. He was brought up in Russia as an atheist and the word 'God' had no place in his vocabulary. He chose to study art in Moscow and one day visited the famous Tretiakov Gallery, home to some of the most treasured icons in existence. Standing quietly before the work of Andrei Rublev, the famous fifteenth-century icon painter, Fyodorov was seized by a mysterious and transcending disclosure. He had no intellectual framework by means of which to interpret this critical experience, and only with time and the help of priests and friends did he realize that he had been visited through the agency of icons by the living God. His life was changed and he discovered his vocation as an icon painter in the service of the Russian Orthodox Church.

It can be no surprise that this story is rooted in Russia. Although icons today are to be found in many parts of the world, and certainly in European and American Roman Catholic, Anglican and Protestant communities, the tradition of icons and their appreciation in theology and the church is rooted in Christian Orthodoxy. Whether or not all church art was originally and in the early centuries of the type found now predominantly in Orthodox churches is a matter for debate. It was certainly widespread, but with time the symbolic and Platonic art of the Eastern churches developed one particular tradition and the more representative art of the Western churches developed another that was somewhat different. The achievement of the Orthodox churches of the East was clearly extraordinary. A visitor has only to look at the remaining decoration in the church of Hagia Sophia, Istanbul (formerly Constantinople); the mosaics in the monastery of Kariye Camii, also in Istanbul (created before 1335), which survived in all their magnificence because the invading Muslims painted them over and thus unwittingly preserved them; the Virgin of Vladimir, created in Constantinople around 1131 and an early gift to Russia, which accompanied Russian forces as they went into battle and is now housed in a church adjacent to the Tretiakov Gallery in Moscow; or the work of Andrei Rublev, to begin to gauge the cultural, artistic and religious achievement of the Eastern churches. The Virgin of Vladimir by itself must rank as one of the great artistic peaks in human endeavour: its aristocratic beauty, the profound intensity of the Virgin's suffering face and the helpless, clinging love of the Christ child quietens the viewer, exalts the human spirit and communicates the gospel through visual imagery.

Perhaps a dozen or so icons have been preserved that were painted before *c.*725. The period from around 725 to 842 witnessed the iconoclastic controversy, during which those in power, for puritanical and political reasons, ordered the removal and destruction of icons from all churches. The religious and artistic loss that resulted from this violence is incalculable.

Icons come in many forms. They may be painted on wood or metal; they may take the form of embroidery, mosaic or murals. Three-dimensional icons taking the form of statues faded quickly from the early tradition. The tendency in icon imagery is towards dematerialization, and statuary, however inspired, suggests earthiness. The method of making an icon doubtless varies in some measure depending on the artist and the medium of his work; perhaps the most common form is an icon painted on wood.

Icon painting is a canonical art; in other words it manifests the dogma and teaching of the Orthodox Church. Thus the icon painter is an obedient servant of the church and it is the church that authorizes his work. It is also insisted that the icon painter must be a believer leading a prayerful and Christian life. The truth of Christianity lies for the Orthodox partly in what the church teaches, but also in the illumination given to those open to the activity of the Holy Spirit. These two witnesses support each other and always agree. There is a tradition that the image of the subject to be rendered externally as an icon must appear first in the painter's heart. This appearance is understood as God's gift completing human endeavour. I remember commissioning Sergei Fyodorov, on behalf of the Chapter of Winchester Cathedral, to paint an icon of St Swithun, patron saint of the cathedral and perhaps never painted as an icon before. I supplied the little historical information we have of the saint's life. The icon did not appear. After conversation I supplied information about the holy legends of the saint. The imaginative and ecclesiastical perceptions of Fyodorov were released, met by the inspiration of God. The image appeared in his heart and the icon was completed in about a month (see colour plate 17). Conversely, a distinguished contemporary Russian icon painter was suspended from his prestigious post to spend time in Siberia. He was deemed to have grown proud and needed to learn the wisdom of humility.

Icons composed roughly after the sixteenth century and until recent times usually seem to express a diminished intensity of vision. The reason for this seems to be that Western artistic influences gained access into the painter's mentality and execution of his work; this was all part of the Westernizing of Russian culture and politics so encouraged and enforced by Peter the Great. Figures became more three-dimensional and the icon told more of a plain story, typical of Western artists painting in the service of the church such as Michelangelo or Rubens. One benefit of the collapse of Communist rule has been that in recovering the roots and tradition of Orthodoxy renewed attention has been given to the requirements of this canonical art.

Mary
Painting
Iconoclasm

Wax encaustic was originally used as the medium to hold mainly mineral sources providing the colour for icons, but after the iconoclastic controversy of the eighth and ninth centuries egg tempera (egg tempered by water) replaced the molten wax. Oils have never been used for painting icons. Gesso, chalk or even alabaster mixed with size to make a gluey substance that quickly hardens is first applied to the wooden support for the icon. A pummel is used to polish the surface. Wealthy institutions might add gold leaf at this stage, overlaying bole, made up of red or yellow earth, and linen strips might be fixed to places where cracks could appear in the wood. Then comes the paint, and finally the varnish.

The nature of this process is significant in two ways. First, the icon painter is involved in the spiritualization of matter. He is continuing the process of incarnation, perfectly realized in Jesus Christ. His work looks towards the spiritualization of all that can be spiritualized at the end of time. Secondly, reflecting this theological and spiritual point but at the practical level, the use of gesso and perhaps of gold leaf means that light striking the icon passes through the paint and is reflected back, thereby illuminating the paint.

Incarnation

Some scholars have called attention to some extraordinary portraits from Fayum, near Cairo, as the origin of the particular art of icons. They may well be a possible source, but hardly the origin. The desert dwellers from whom they come were contemporary with the birth and rise of Christianity. They were members of a mystical and Platonic sect, Gnostic in complexion, who expressed their art in funeral portraits. These portraits are extraordinarily beautiful, half length, with a three-quarter pose

Gnosis

and represent the subject, just dead, in the full bloom of his or her maturity. They are two-dimensional and employ bright colours, the eyes of the subject somehow defying death and gazing into eternity. Whatever encouragement the portraits gave to the art of icon painting, it is clear at the same time that the tradition was transformed. Pagan p. 848 art became Christian art. Content and form continued, but in a new manner.

If we enter an Orthodox church in the grand tradition we will find that such churches vary in shape and that the icons are put in different places. Nevertheless, a certain Buildings order is apparent. The church itself, with its decoration, is an icon, an image of the universe reconciled to God by the gospel. The narthex, the porch through which one enters, is often understood as the place where redemption begins, the nave where Christians, faithful but full of need, look about them at the representations of holy figures, knowing that the temporal world is subject to the spiritual world and open to its influence: hence a large icon of Christ Pantocrator (Ruler of All) appears in the centre of the dome. Above all, worshippers look before them, towards the sanctuary.

The church building is most itself and alive when worship is in progress, and we can see that worshippers Church will feel in the neighbourhood of heaven as they meditate on the icons around them, finding the most profound help coming from contemplation of the iconostasis (the icon stand) and what lies beyond it in the sanctuary. Over the centuries the iconostasis developed from images Prayer placed on a stone barrier before the sanctuary. It defines symbolically the division between heaven and earth. The voice of the priest during the eucharist, invisible behind the large iconostasis, represents the voice of God. When he and his acolytes appear through the royal (central) doors Eucharist of the iconostasis with the elements of the eucharist, it is heavenly food for earthly people. All this means that the iconostasis not only divides but also unites. Christ, the mediator, brings together heaven and earth, and this is symbolically represented by the iconostasis.

Symbols A fully developed iconostasis in a significant church might be ten or twelve feet high and as broad as the point where nave and sanctuary meet. It will be made of wood and capable of carrying a multitude of icons in several tiers. It is penetrated by three doors: the royal door in the centre, the door to the sacrifice to the north, and the deacon's door to the south. It is the face of heaven. The royal door is decorated with icons of the Annunciation and the four evangelists. Above the door is an icon of the Last Supper. Holy liturgists fill the jambs north and south. Saint Immediately to the south is an icon of Christ or the saint to whom the church is dedicated. Immediately to the north is an icon of the Mother of God, as the Orthodox call the Blessed Virgin Mary. Moving outwards, to the north and south are icons of archangels or sainted deacons. Other icons, perhaps of local saints, lie north and south again of these. Above the icon of the Last Supper and making a tier by itself is what is called a *deesis* or tchin. This is the place of prayer in particular. In the centre is Christ Pantocrator. On his right is the Mother of God. On his left is John the Forerunner, as the Orthodox call John the Baptist. Next on either side are the archangels Michael and Gabriel. Then on either side are the apostles Peter and Paul, with local saints on either side of them. Above this in a separate tier come the feasts of the church, as many as sixteen. Above these in a separate tier there are prophets, with Christ in the centre. At the very top of the iconostasis come the patriarchs, perhaps with an Old Testament Trinity at the centre. Worshippers may or may not identify each holy subject on the iconostasis. What they will apprehend, however, is the communion of saints, the neighbourhood of heaven and the redemptive process upon which they have entered.

What do icons mean? Icon painting is a unique form of art, for which prayer and right belief are more important qualifications than artistic skill, crucial though that is. It is church art, illustrating and conveying the truth of the Christian religion. It is a canonical art authorized and judged by the church. Tradition determines much, but not all, of the outline of the figure(s) painted, and particular colours for particular subjects are well known. It would be a mistake to conclude from this that icon painting is a repetitive exercise for those with dulled intellects and imagination. Rather, it is a form of prayer and theological realization, a penetrating and manifesting of what is. I recall visiting Sergei Fyodorov after he had completed painting a holy figure. Intelligent and imaginative as he is, used to painting icons as he is, I found him quite exhausted. The effort of the icon painter is primarily spiritual: all that he or she is, physical, mental and spiritual, strains in a one-pointed ascent to meet the subject being painted and to transmit this faithfully to the support. Further, icon painting is a symbolic art. A symbol points towards the thing symbolized and carries something of what it points to in itself. So it is written in the Life of St Stephen the Younger (died 765), 'An icon is a door.'

The icon is demanding for worshippers as well as for the painter. Quietness of heart and attentiveness are crucial. The worshipper needs a one-pointed ascent of heart, mind and body to receive what the icon can give. A friend of mine visited the cathedrals in the Kremlin, Moscow. He was part of a tourist party. As the party entered a cathedral he noticed an old lady, oblivious of the party, standing and gazing at an icon. Forty minutes or so later the party left the cathedral and the lady was still in the same position.

TYPES OF ICON

Icon painting is a very formal art, and this formalism also extends to its themes. Certain figures, and certain postures, appear time and again. Here are some of them.

Christ

Christ Pantocrator: Represents Christ as defined at the Council of Chalcedon, unifying divinity and humanity.

Mary

Virgin Kyriotissa: Mary sitting solemnly on a throne with the divine child on her lap.

Virgin Hodegetria: Literally 'She who shows the way'. The Virgin and child are both shown looking at the viewer.

Virgin Eleousa and *Virgin Oumilenie*: Mary the merciful, the Virgin of loving kindness: the faces of mother and child are touching affectionately. *Eleousa* refers to the feelings of the mother, namely mercy; *Oumilenie* refers to the feeling of the child, affectionate tenderness. One of the earliest and most famous instances of this form of icon is the twelfth-century *Mother of God of Vladimir*, taken from Constantinople to Kiev in 1131 and thence to Moscow; the child has its arm round its mother's neck. The *Mother of God Glykophilousa* ('The sweetly kissing one') icon from the seventeenth century shows the Virgin caressing her child.

Virgin Orans: A twelfth-century icon which depicts the Virgin with hands upraised in prayer, her child depicted in a medallion on her chest.

Other common themes for icons are the Nativity, the Presentation of Jesus in the Temple, the Four Scenes of the Holy Passion, the Four Scenes of the Resurrection, angels, saints and their lives, churches and monasteries, the Holy Trinity and further scenes from the life of Jesus.

Byzantine icons, organized by subject, together with icons of the Coptic and Ethiopian Church can be found at www.iconsexplained.com

The iconoclastic controversy clarifies the position. Iconodules (image lovers) favoured icons, claiming tradition, Christ's humanity and present experience in support. Iconoclasts rejected icons. As the church wrestled for right belief in the person of Christ, some emphasized especially his humanity, others his divinity. To some iconoclasts the humanity displayed in icons detracted from Christ's divinity. God is transcendent and ineffable. This aniconic stance was supported by the Jewish and Muslim belief that images are fraudulent and may even descend to animism and worship of the representation. The self-regard of iconoclastic emperors was also involved, for the images of Christ were construed as being in competition with images of the emperor in the devotion of the people. The controversy raged and included violence, but was decided eventually in favour of the iconodules, those who venerated icons. The fundamental argument, beyond that of appeal to tradition, was succinctly provided by John of Damascus. Indeed God is ineffable, but in Christ God has appeared in human form. The letters of the New Testament support the view that Christ is the image of the living God (Philippians 2.6; Colossians 1.15; Hebrews 1.3), and since God has appeared in human form, the image of the icon is valid. All those representations that honour and exalt Christ may be painted, and it is for this reason that every icon is named in visible lettering, determining the excellence of what has been painted but setting limits at the same time. The icon is venerated but not worshipped. Hence the Orthodox habit of bowing before icons and kissing them, reserving worship for God alone.

The best icons are superbly beautiful, expressing the Orthodox perception that beauty is an attribute of God and, in its sacred manifestation, to be cherished. Let's look at three of them.

Andrei Rublev's (*c.*1360–1430) *The Holy Trinity*, now in the Tretiakov Gallery, Moscow, is perhaps the most popular icon in existence, and reproductions can be found in many Western homes (see colour plate 16). It measures 44 × 55 inches and shows three figures at a table. In the background we can see a tree and a house. Rublev has taken a traditional subject and transformed it. Genesis 18, which describes the visit of three angels to Abraham in the guise of three travellers, is the biblical foundation of the composition. Each figure has angels' wings and a wand, sign of the sacred dignity of the angel, a messenger of God. The oak of Mamre and Abraham's house are in the background. But just as in Genesis the three visitors

God

are suddenly seen as angels and, indeed, as an epiphany of God, so these three figures are distinguishable as the three persons of the Trinity. The Orthodox have a profound sense of the ineffability of God and the Trinity is pictured only through this disguised image. God the Father is on the left as we look, God the Son in the middle, and God the Holy Spirit on the right. The heads of Son and Spirit incline to the Father deeply. He inclines to them less so. The middle figure of the Son is raised above the others since we enter the mystery of the Trinity through the revelation of the Son. Each figure closely resembles the others, but is subtly different. The table is also an altar, on which stands a cup that is also a chalice. There is a perfect harmony in the composition: the colours are gentle and pure, the figures lyrical. Icons of this subject painted after Rublev's follow his pattern. If we took a pair of compasses, pressing one point into the centre of the composition, and described a circle beginning with the crown of the Son's head, the circle would pass down the Spirit's back and up the back of the Father, touching the Spirit's and Father's feet on the way. This circular motion suggests the eternal movement of love between the persons of the Trinity as it slowly revolves in its eternal harmony. At the same time we notice the linear and static form of the three persons. The integration of circular motion and static linearity is part of the genius of the painter, wonderfully suggesting the reality of God.

Trinity

The subject *The Great Martyr George and the Dragon* is also popular as an icon and in reproduction. One example, dating from the fifteenth century and the Novgorod School, Russia, measuring 19 by 27 inches, is displayed in the Metropolitan Museum, New York. The name George derives from a Greek word meaning 'husbandman', farmer. According to tradition George, a Cappadocian, rose through the ranks of the army, and was martyred for his Christian faith. He is also the famous dragon-killer who rescued a princess. At the top of the icon, in the right-hand corner, we see the segment of a circle, representing the division between heaven and earth. A hand appears from this realm, fingers raised in blessing, with the name of Jesus Christ inscribed nearby to indicate the divine blessing on the action performed. St George's white horse tramples the dragon under foot. The icon shows the three levels of human existence, ranking evil at the base – the end of the dragon's tail is often depicted coming out of a dark hole – the human conflict in the middle, as good wrestles with evil, and the divine blessing and encouragement at the top of the icon. The white horse is a symbol of the ascent of humankind up the spiritual, moral and Christian path of life. The motionlessness and dematerialization of George reminds us that the battle relates to our lives of prayer and morality. A cross at the end of his lance and the name of Jesus Christ tell us from whom victory comes. The radiance of this icon, the colour white so apparent in its painting, reflects the radiance of heaven.

p. 1076

Thirdly, there is the icon of *St John the Forerunner*. This is a very popular subject, largely because it forms part of the *deesis* or place of prayer which can be found prominently positioned on every iconostasis. St John the Baptist also figures strongly in the liturgy of the Orthodox Church, so that he is an esteemed saint among the faithful. He is pictured sometimes with wings, as an angel, an indication of the celestial element within his human form and the Old Testament prophecy of a 'messenger' (Greek *angelos*, 'angel') who would prepare the way for Christ (Malachi 3.1). One example was painted by Sergei Fyodorov in 1994–6 and can be found in Winchester Cathedral. It is painted on an ash support and forms part of the *deesis.* St John is therefore positioned to the left of Christ. The background is gold leaf, the saint is half length, with a three-quarter profile and he is looking to his right, that is, to Christ Pantocrator. His garment is green, which assists the total colour harmony of the nine figures of the *deesis.* His face is long, thin and pained, suggestive of the urgency of his prophetic vocation and coming martyrdom. His hair is somewhat dishevelled and his garment is jagged in contour. John is a desert dweller, anticipating the desert saints, committed to a perilous task. He is the one figure among the eight (excluding Christ) with both hands extended towards the central figure. This is because John has no biography; he is a voice only, and crying out in the wilderness. It would be presumptuous to single out one icon as painted even better than the others but there is an authority and immediacy about this icon that impresses deeply. The painter told me that this was the saint with whom he identified most. Sergei Fyodorov had broken with his family in Russia, embraced the poverty and uncertainty of the human element of the Orthodox Church at that time, and eked out an impecunious existence in the east end of London when first I met him.

The beauty of icons is sacred and not profane, inspiring, not seductive. According to Feodor Dostoievsky, 'Beauty will redeem the world'. The Western church has been suspicious of beauty, but it is an attribute of God supremely honoured by the Eastern church.

KEITH WALKER

L. Ouspensky and V. Lossky, *The Meaning of Icons*, New York: St Vladimir's Seminary Press 1983; J. Baggley, *Doors of Perception*, London: Mowbray 1987; G. Limouris (ed), *Icons: Windows on Eternity*, Geneva: WCC Publications 1990; P. Sherrard, *The Sacred in Life and Art*, Louisville, KY: Golgonooza Press 1990

Iconoclasm

The demolition of the rock-cut Buddhas at Bamiyan in Afghanistan in March 2001 and the toppling of statues and paintings signifying the political power of Saddam Hussein and his government in 2003 have both been identified by the media and political commentators as 'acts of iconoclasm'. The misuse, or perhaps better said the overuse, of the word icon to denote anything from the identifying labels on a computer screen to representations of major athletes and film personalities has coloured the contemporary usage of its opposite, iconoclasm. Thus, the distortions of an athlete's image or the vandalizing of a work of sacred art are both categorized as 'acts of iconoclasm'. The historical roots of Christian attitudes towards iconoclasm, however, have a significant and distinct heritage.

More often than not, the term iconoclasm was defined as the act of destroying, especially as in the smashing, of images. Iconoclasm has had two specific historical references in Christianity: the eighth- to tenth-century Byzantine iconoclastic controversies and the sixteenth- to seventeenth-century Protestant Reformation. The term, etymologically rooted in the Greek words for 'the breaking of icons', was commonly believed to have entered into Christian parlance with the controversies over the meaning and use of icons in Eastern Christianity. However, the historical reality is another matter, since from its origins Christianity had a divided attitude towards icons, images and imagery. This arose from the prohibition against making images contained in the Ten Commandments of the Hebrew Bible on the one hand and the Hellenistic advocacy of the beauty of form on the other. And in fact iconoclasm is older than Christianity and has a variety of historical expressions, especially with relation to that category of visual imagery identified as 'idols' or 'idolatrous'. In point of fact, there are at least nine identifiable and theologically significant displays of iconoclasm throughout Christianity's 2000-year history.

The earliest form of Christian iconoclasm was the destruction of pagan images, or idols, in late antiquity. Called for by observance of the proscription of images in the Mosaic law, this 'cleansing' was interpreted as a defence of the singular integrity of the Christian God. This eradication of 'the pagan' was directed equally towards sacred, i.e., idolatrous, and secular images, and had its theological foundation in texts from both the Bible and the church fathers. Works of art – mosaics, wall frescoes, sculptures and ceramic objects – were either physically destroyed or buried, and thus removed from view and use.

The second identifiable phase of Christian iconoclasm was the well-documented Byzantine iconoclastic controversies of the eighth to tenth centuries. Here class and politics influenced religious values as the dialectic of Hebraic versus Hellenistic attitudes towards the image resurfaced, one might say 'with a vengeance'. For almost 200 years, imperial and ecclesiastical powers vacillated between iconoclasts (image-breakers) and iconodules (image-worshippers); consequently icons and other cultic objects were damaged, destroyed, renewed or replaced. The three central but interrelated theological issues – the meaning of the incarnation, the Christian attitude towards matter, and Christian redemption – were resolved by the Syrian monk John of Damascus, whose defence of the icons was predicated on John 1.14: 'And the Word became flesh, and dwelt among us.' He affirmed this statement by declaring that the incarnation defined the divine recognition of the human need to see in order to be on the path to salvation. As a result of these theological and political debates Eastern Christianity promulgated a series of clear pronouncements defining the meaning, creating and functioning of the icon, which was likened to 'a window to the event'.

Incarnation

The third and little-known expression of Christian iconoclasm was the Carolingian iconoclastic controversy, which occurred just before the reign of Charlemagne as Holy Roman emperor. Charlemagne played a central role in this reinterpretation of the relationship between the Hebraic and the Hellenistic as the word came to be favoured over the image, especially figural imagery found in carved and sculpted works. Again as much a political and social situation as the Byzantine had been, this 'Western' iconoclastic controversy was based on a series of moral and theological arguments against the unbridled ecclesiastical use of figural art which was interpreted as verging upon, if not actually, pagan in nature. The controversy was resolved in the *Libri Carolini (Caroline Books)* that were issued by the Synod of Frankfurt in 794. This lengthy document advocated the sixth-century position of Gregory the Great that images were the *biblia pauperum* ('Bible of the poor') and appropriate in so far as they instructed the unlettered in the narrative history and morality of Christianity.

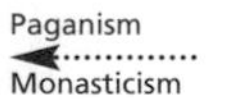

The fourth and often-overlooked statement of Christian iconoclasm was the Cistercian iconoclasm that flourished during the twelfth century. Once again, one of the fundamental 'fears' of the iconoclastic attitude seems to have come to the forefront: that the beauty of the visual arts would distract the worshipper's attention and thereby become a hindrance rather than an endorsement of prayer, contemplation and devotion. Bernard of Clairvaux not only pronounced the visual arts a deterrent to faith but also denounced the allocation of funds that might otherwise have alleviated the suffering of the poor. Cistercian monasteries and their adjoining cathedrals were 'cleansed' of offending and perhaps unnecessary works of art. At the same time Abbot Suger, the theological

Nach wenigh Predication
Die Caluinsche Religion
Das bildens furmen fiengen an
Das nicht ein bildt dauon bleib stan
Kap Monstrantz, kilch, auch die altar
Und west sonst dort vor handen war.
Zerbrochen all in kurtzer Stundt
Gleich gar vil leuten das ist kundt.
Anno Dnj. M. D. LXVI
XX Augusti

Destruction of relics and statues in church, April 1566

Architecture

mastermind of the first Gothic cathedral, advocated the necessity of the existence and the contemplation of the beautiful as both scripturally 'fitting to God' and spiritually affective for the believer.

Enlightenment

The fifth display of Christian iconoclasm was that made during the Protestant Reformation. The multiple perspectives of the Reformers were evident in the variety of their opinions on images. Martin Luther acknowledged the didactic value of art and recognized the real and potential 'abuses' of art, while opposing 'cleansing' in a violent or destructive manner. Huldrych Zwingli banned art as a distraction from worship and prayer as he supervised the process for the closing, 'cleansing' and reopening of medieval churches. Although John Calvin initially defended the didactic function of Christian art, he supported a 'cleansing' of churches while clearly opposing violence. The followers of these Reformers, however, practised extreme forms of iconoclasm – breaking, smashing, burning, looting and demolishing – which resulted in undecorated and severely plain churches, and constant criticism of the Roman Catholic and Eastern Orthodox Christian incorporation of 'the visual' within theological and cultural reference points.

The sixth mode of Christian iconoclasm began with the French Revolution and affirmed the Enlightenment quest for freedom from such traditional, oppressive institutions as 'the church'. The reality of this destruction was the recognition of the fundamental nature of the truly fine line between iconoclasm as a religiously-motivated impulse and iconoclasm as an act of vandalism. To ascertain, perhaps to assert, that form of individual liberation that resulted in human freedom, advocates of the Enlightenment and the French Revolution sought to dispel superstition and authority ungoverned by reason. Superstition became synonymous with idolatry; thereby, iconoclasm became an appropriate and justified political activity.

The seventh milestone of Christian iconoclasm, which has only recently been analysed, was the regular activity of colonial expansion, especially as practised in the Americas.

The missionary zeal for evangelization, fused with the emotive investigations of the Inquisition and the concern with 'the other' stemming from the Council of Trent, was situated within any primal, or polytheistic, religion. The fundamental defence of colonial-expansion iconoclasm was that it safeguarded the sovereign integrity of the Christian God and rooted out of the 'evils' of superstition related to idols, idolatry, and paganism. Similar in motivation and deed to the fourth- to sixth-century destruction of classical art in Mediterranean culture, this newer form of Christian iconoclasm wrought havoc on the indigenous traditions of the peoples of the 'New World'.

The eighth, and clearly controversial, demonstration of Christian iconoclasm was the process of the secularization of Christian art evident from the sixteenth-century Reformation. The transformations wrought by these Reformers extended into the world of Christian art, artists, patrons and clergy. The cultural shift towards the removal of art from the Reformed churches resulted in a transfer of art into the civic and domestic spheres, and commensurately, a shift in themes, motifs and styles away from scriptural narrative or devotional inspiration towards landscape, portraiture and genre scenes. The process of secularization was affected in Roman Catholicism from the mid-eighteenth century onwards as artists and patrons turned their attention from religious themes or spiritual inspiration towards historical or personal imagery.

The ninth, and little considered, presentation of Christian iconoclasm is the early twentieth-century artistic trend towards abstraction. Most clearly evidenced in the absence of the figure, the development of abstraction as a painted and sculptural style signified a transformation of artistic interest in the human, or for that matter any recognizable form. These artists – painters and sculptors alike – sought out new ways of valuing and seeing human experience confirmed in the destruction of the convention of the figural representation. Though not a form of iconoclasm practised through the destruction of work, this 'abstracted iconoclasm' was predicated upon the annihilation of the figural.

The cultural-political-social-religious-theological phenomenon we identify as iconoclasm is clearly a complex one. Iconoclasm is a concept overloaded with the baggage of diverse meanings, historical events and cultural expressions. It was founded upon a series of presuppositions, from the existence of idolatry and a fear of the visual to the ambiguity of religious attitudes towards the body and the power of images. Similarly, Christian iconoclasm has had a complex and meandering history affecting the exchange of power, authority and visual culture.

DIANE APOSTOLOS-CAPPADONA

p. 345
Council

Charles Barber, *Figure and Likeness: On the Limits of Representation in Byzantine Iconoclasm*, Princeton: Princeton University Press 2002; Alain Besançon, *The Forbidden Image*, Chicago: University of Chicago Press 2000; David Freedberg, *The Power of Images*, Chicago: University of Chicago Press 1991; Dario Gamboni, *The Destruction of Art. Iconoclasm and Vandalism since the French Revolution*, New Haven: Yale University Press 1997; John of Damascus, *On the Divine Images*, Crestwood, NY: St Vladimir's Theological Press 1997; John R. Phillips, *Reformation of Images: Destruction of Art In England, 1535–1669*, Berkeley: University of California Press 1973; Lee Palmer Wandel, *Voracious Idols and Violent Hands*, Cambridge: CUP 1999

Secularization

Iconography

Iconography is an academic discipline essentially concerned with the study of images. It is concerned to examine what is significant and interesting about imagery, rather than what may be regarded as art. Its chief interest is in the interpretation of images and it lies at a crossroads with other disciplines, intersecting with those other intellectual areas that have visual subject matter as the starting point of their investigations. It is therefore both a concept and also a method of study.

However, beyond this very generally agreed description there is a good deal of confusion as to the real nature of iconography. It is in the midst of an identity crisis, which is part of the wider contemporary crisis within art history itself. This crisis is due also to the growing significance of images in all areas of historical study. Thus in contemporary thinking iconography is becoming a matter of increasing scholarly interest and reassessment. The best way to gain some deeper understanding of the character of iconography and of the problems involved in its study is to consider its development historically.

Symbols

The interpretation of imagery in symbolic terms goes back to the sixteenth century, to Cesare Ripa, whose book *Iconologia* (1593) became the first of a continuing series intended to aid artists in the study of classical allegorical images. Although throughout the following centuries iconographers described, classified and interpreted images, Ripa remained really the first and only scholar to offer a plan for, and a description of, the conditions for a logic of images. The sixteenth century also saw a marked interest in one special form of iconography, that of portraits. However, preoccupation with portraiture did not become widespread until much later, in the nineteenth and early twentieth centuries. The model used for studying imagery was that of texts, i.e. pictures were something to be deciphered. It is this that explains the name of the discipline itself, 'iconography', which is derived from two Greek words, *ikon* (image) and *graphein* (to write), and also the alternative name for the study, 'iconology', deriving originally from Ripa; this refers to the Greek term *logos*, meaning thought or reason. The two terms are closely connected, and are sometimes used interchangeably and sometimes, rather, to point out the different emphases. Both names were revived in the twentieth century by the art-historical school connected with Aby Warburg. But since this double naming can cause confusion, in modern studies there is a general preference for the term iconography.

Because of its preoccupation with symbolism, iconography has proved to be a particular stimulus for the study of Christian art, the specific value of which derives almost entirely from its content. One of the earliest Christian iconographers was Johannes Molanus (Jan Vermeulen), whose book on sacred pictures and images, *De Picturis et Imaginibus Sacris* (1570), was intended to show artists how Council they might, in the spirit of the Council of Trent, represent biblical and religious subject matter. The rediscovery of p. 325 the catacombs in the sixteenth century also provided an important spur to the development of Christian iconography. In 1896 André Didron published his *Christian Iconography* in two volumes that were intended to lay out the principles of 'sacred archaeology'; they represent the culmination of the old approach to the discipline within this sphere.

It will be noted that these developments are in Renaissance Painting the Western tradition of Christianity. Discussion of iconography, whether in the form of subject matter or methodology, is a Western rather than an Eastern Christian preoccupation. In relation to visual representation Western Christianity has always shown greater freedom of expression, and so lends itself better to iconographical study. It has no one form of imagery that must Icon be deemed canonical, as is the case with the Eastern icon, where the content and style are traditional and a matter of ecclesiastical control.

In the eighteenth century the iconographical method of studying images was eclipsed by the work of J. J. Winckelmann, whose *History of the Art of Antiquity* (1764) is often regarded as the first true history of art. Winckelmann introduced into the discussion the idea that what is of importance in any work of art is its artistic elements and style, rather than its content. And after Winckelmann, style became to some extent the controlling feature of study, until iconography was revived and reconstituted in its modern form and as a serious academic discipline. Although fundamental work was done in France by scholars such as Émile Mâle, and in America by Charles Rufus Morey, iconography would henceforth always be associated primarily with the names of Aby Warburg (1866–1929) and Erwin Panofsky (1892–1968).

Warburg's work was by any criterion exceptional. His settled belief was that the image is inextricably associated with culture as a whole. He had an extraordinarily imaginative insight into the complex mutual relations of things, and so in contradistinction to Winckelmann and the later formalists his understanding of artistic style was that it is essentially interwoven with all other aspects of culture, rather than merely an indicator of it. Content, too, became of essential importance. Warburg's aim was to discover how other cultural forms interacted with the artistic image, and the image with them. So he developed an interdisciplinary approach to art, which ranged widely across various cultures, including the non-European, in order to assemble associated forms, memories and symbols. It was for this reason that he always arranged his images in groups in what he referred to as a 'picture atlas'. Although he wrote and lectured, and made a special study of the iconographical meaning of the cycle of the frescoes in the Palazzo Schifanoia at Ferrara, his work had its real expression and embodiment in the library which he established in Hamburg, and which was brought to England in 1933.

It was left for his follower, Panofsky, to give Warburg's beliefs a systematic formulation. With Panofsky iconography reached its peak, and in the mid-twentieth century was responsible for lasting achievements in the analysis of European figurative art, especially in the area of medieval and Renaissance painting, where the subject matter was concerned with the religious and political life of the state. Panofsky was interested above all in meaning, and therefore for him the subject matter of works of art was all-important. He regarded iconography as an interpretative search in which all other disciplines meet. In 1939 he published his famous essay 'Iconography and Iconology' as the introduction to his book *Studies in Iconology*. Because he thought that iconography is the extensive reality which underlies all cultural study, he held that any monument can be read not simply as a work of art, but as a cultural symbol of its age, and that this is true of any artefact and of any culture. His approach, therefore, has been said to be not so much a method as a general law, almost a form of philosophy, bordering on epistemology. He also drew a distinction between iconography as the study of subject matter and iconology as the study of the intrinsic meaning of works of art. By the latter he meant seeing through the work and into the mind of the culture that produced it. Basing himself on Ernst Cassirer's doctrine of symbolic forms, he offered a clearly-defined procedure for investigating the meaning encoded in art works, by setting up an elaborate tripartite system of signification. These various levels of significance were not to be regarded as actually distinct categories, but simply useful ways of speaking about the interrelated facets of an image as such. An illustration of his practice is to be found in the essay 'Et in Arcadia Ego: Poussin and the Elegiac Tradition' (1936).

Panofsky's work has been of immense influence, and the iconographical method still remains central to all cultural enquiry. One of his key phrases, 'ways of seeing', became the title of a book by the English art critic John Berger, who drew attention to the social and economic dimensions in works of art, while Kenneth Clark's celebrated TV series *Civilization* promoted the idea of art as expressive of the history of civilization. In terms of landscape, however, Panofsky had been anticipated iconographically by John Ruskin, who had treated Turner's landscapes as a text for expounding moral lessons, taking his model from biblical exegesis (*Modern Painters*, 1843).

Iconography nevertheless has not been without its difficulties or its critics. Panofsky had been primarily a student of the Renaissance, and his work was not suitable for application to all types of image. Over-enthusiastic pursuance of his ideas and methods by later scholars brought iconography into a measure of disrepute, particularly in the misuse of texts. A tendency developed which reduced art simply to the level of illustration of certain kinds of texts. The position of iconography was further undermined by postmodernism, under the influence of the philosopher Roland Barthes, which emphasizes the inherent instability of meaning in itself, and Panofsky's conception of iconology as a form of knowledge was criticized for being dependent upon a correspondence theory of truth. So currently not all scholars agree on the importance of iconography either for general or for specific studies.

However, within art, and in particular within the study of Christian art, iconography remains fundamental; so does its relationship to texts, without which it cannot function. But the connection of images and texts is now seen as more complicated, and it is recognized that sometimes the visual and the literary traditions can function quite independently of each other. Images must sometimes be approached simply on their own terms, and elements of style have been found to be meaningful in ways that iconographers have not always fully appreciated. Neurophysiology and psychoanalysis, semiotics and reception theory, gender studies, deconstruction and other methods, which go under the general term of 'critical theory', are now also regarded as important in helping iconography to reinterpret itself. It has been said that iconography will always be difficult because it relates two different things, a non-concrete idea called an image, and a material reality called an artwork. And it is perhaps the intellectual issue of meaning and form that will always remain problematic.

Yet despite all the criticism, it was the iconographical interest in subject matter which originally created two of the oldest instruments for analysing works of art, and which have become indispensable tools of permanent value to scholarship. These works are *The Index of Christian Art* at Princeton University, which catalogues images from the chronological and geographical standpoint, and the classificatory system of Henri van de Waal known as *Iconclass*, which deals primarily in themes. These resources and the data that they provide have become invaluable tools for research, not merely for art historians but for workers in other fields also. And since many works of art are information-based, iconography remains intimately connected with knowledge, even if interpretation is now considered to be a more difficult matter than was previously thought.

Iconography then, although it is undergoing a renewal and to some extent a redefinition, by offering now a more flexible, and indeed a more Warburgian, approach to the study of images, continues to be a productive area of scientific research. It touches now on almost every issue of visual representation. All these points were particularly well illustrated by the millennium exhibition that was held at the National Gallery in London entitled *Seeing Salvation: The Image of Christ*. The exhibition showed how images are able to create ways of seeing as well as being reflections of them. It showed the relationship of iconography to function, in demonstrating the uses to which images were put. It showed the power of images to communicate across centuries by their ability to explore the basic experiences of human life. And it showed too how Christianity, through its own theological concerns, has enriched the interpretative range of Western art. Finally, it showed how the iconographical approach is not simply auxiliary to historical and theological studies but is an intrinsic element of them. Iconography can be seen here for what it is: an essentially indirect method, rather than an authoritative point of view, but one for which a good deal of technical skill is required.

MARY CHARLES-MURRAY

B. Cassidy (ed), *Iconography at the Crossroads*, Princeton, NJ: Princeton University Press 1993; E. Cassirer, *The Philosophy of Symbolic Forms* (4 vols, 1923–9), New Haven: Yale University Press 1955–96; W. J. T. Mitchell, *Iconology. Image, Text, Ideology*, Chicago: University of Chicago Press 1986; E. Panofsky, *Studies in Iconology: Humanistic Themes in the Art of the Renaissance* (1939), Magnolia, MA: Peter Smith 1972; D. Preziosi (ed), *The Art of Art History: A Critical Anthology*, Oxford: OUP 1998

Princeton Index of Christian Art: ica.princeton.edu (subscription service); *Iconclass*: www.iconclass.nl

Incarnation

The doctrine

God Trinity Jesus

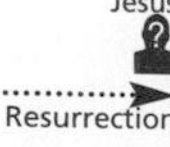

Resurrection

Stated formally, the Christian doctrine of the incarnation is that at a particular moment in history, God, the second person of the Trinity, the eternally beloved Son, known sometimes as the Logos or Word, took flesh in the person of Jesus of Nazareth and, growing from infancy to adulthood, walked on earth in human form. Yet throughout his birth, life, death, resurrection and final exaltation, this human being, Jesus, at no time ceased to be divine, the second person of the Trinity; nor did he at any time cease to be human; nor did he at any time cease to be one person, albeit a person with both a divine and human nature; nor did at any time the divine and the human, the Creator and the creature, cease to be distinct orders of being. In revealing himself in this way, God displayed God's character, demonstrated the depth and irrevocable extent of God's love for the world, showed the significance of humanity in God's eternal purpose, and focused the relationship between the Trinity and creation in a single life, defining the mediation of God to humanity and the representation of humanity to God. Incarnation is thus the foundational Christian doctrine from which all other doctrines flow. This doctrine needs to be explained, since what it says and the way in which it says it is not easy to grasp in today's world.

Origins

Bible Covenant p. 1152 Paul

For Christians, the Old Testament is the story of how God's people falteringly seek to imitate God's holiness and keep their covenant with God. The tension in the story is always whether God will overcome Israel's truculence and restore the companionship that is God's promise and God's purpose. In good times Israel fostered this relationship, focused through the offices of prophet, priest and king; through leaders such as Moses, Samuel, David and Elijah. And yet the northern kingdom's eighth-century obliteration and the southern kingdom's sixth-century exile exhibited estrangement from God. Sensing that Babylon, and the foreign rule that characterized life after the return, represented exile from God as well as from the land, the scriptures of the later period begin to articulate a longing for a figure who would not only restore Israel's fortunes but, more significantly, embody reunion with God. These sentiments reappear in the inter-testamental literature and the Dead Sea Scrolls.

p. 996 p. 845

Meanwhile, in the wisdom writings, together with the Apocrypha, God becomes a more remote being, and therefore the manner of God's communication with the world, including the Jews, becomes more problematic. Less personal intermediate agencies begin to emerge, such as Word or Wisdom. Centuries of Greek philosophy had explored the manner in which the one unchangeable God could, without affecting its nature, engage with the world. Word and Wisdom became modes in which this communication could be understood, and they started to take on almost a 'personality' in some portrayals. Philo of Alexandria, a Jewish near-contemporary of Jesus, saw God as a mystery, and the Logos as the intelligibility of God and the rationality of the world – what today we might call its logic. Philo began to use terms like 'second God' and 'Son of God' in relation to the Logos.

The Gospels portray the incarnation in narrative form. Each takes a similar shape. They begin with some form of declaration or revelation of the incarnation. The period of Jesus' ministry is one of symbolic and allusive gestures that presuppose divine power and authority within an undoubtedly human body. At some stage in the passion and resurrection narratives in each Gospel, Jesus' incarnate identity is definitively revealed or understood. For example, in Mark there is an announcement of Jesus as Son of God in the opening verse (1.1); the baptism (1.11) and transfiguration (9.7) are moments of disclosure; in his trial, Jesus says he is 'the Messiah, the Son of the Blessed One' (14.61–2); and at the moment of his death, the centurion realizes 'Truly, this man was God's Son!' (15.39). Meanwhile in Matthew and Luke, the opening proclamation comes in the form of an angelic announcement to Joseph (or Mary) that Mary, while remaining a virgin, will conceive through the power of the Holy Spirit. They also have the baptism, transfiguration and passion stories, but more than Mark they stress the significance of the resurrection narratives in confirming the identity of Jesus as the man-from-heaven. John takes the language of incarnation into a new dimension. His Gospel comes to a resounding climax in Thomas' words, 'My Lord and my God!' (20.28). But even more significantly, his prologue delves back into the existence of Jesus and his identity as the Logos before he became flesh, back as far as the beginning of all things: 'In the beginning was the Logos ... And the Logos became flesh and lived among us ... ' (1.1,14). This proclamation becomes the touchstone of all future understandings of the incarnation.

Paul's letters do not narrate, or even argue for, the incarnation; instead they presuppose it. 'When the fullness of time had come, God sent his Son, born of a woman,' Paul says in Galatians (4.4); God sent 'his own Son in the likeness of sinful flesh,' he says in Romans (8.3); and in Colossians he asserts that in Christ 'the whole fullness of deity dwells bodily' (2.9; cf. 1.19). Meanwhile, elsewhere in the New Testament similar assumptions are found: the letter to the Hebrews states that Christ 'is the reflection of God's glory and the exact imprint of his very being' (1.3), and in the book of Revelation Jesus says, 'I am the Alpha and the Omega ... the beginning and the end' (22.13). One

VIRGIN BIRTH

Virgin birth is in fact often used to denote the belief that Jesus was *conceived* by Mary as a virgin 'by the Holy Spirit' and without sexual intercourse with a man. That is all that is said in the New Testament. However, a second-century apocryphal Gospel, the Protevangelium of James, describes Mary as giving birth miraculously, with her sexual organs intact, so the belief developed that she remained a virgin even after giving birth. This gave rise to the title 'ever virgin', which was given to Mary at the Council of Constantinople in 553.

p. 145

pp. 288–9

p. 664

The virginal conception of Jesus is mentioned only in the Gospels of Matthew (1.18–25) and Luke (1.26–38). That Matthew and Luke agree over it is significant, since their narratives about the birth of Jesus are otherwise so different. However, this virginal conception plays no further part in these two Gospels, nor is it mentioned in any of the other books of the New Testament. It is far from having the significance of the other miraculous event associated with Jesus, namely the resurrection. Yet it is affirmed in both the Nicene Creed and the Apostles' Creed and has been a fixed part of the Christian tradition from the second century on.

pp. 300–1

p. 852

The Gospels indicate that Mary had other children after Jesus. In Mark 6.3, those who hear Jesus with astonishment ask: 'Is not this the carpenter, the son of Mary and brother of James and Joses and Judas and Simon, and are not his sisters here with us?' After the death and resurrection of Jesus it is James, known as 'the brother of the Lord', who surprisingly becomes the leader of the Christian community in Jerusalem, rather than one of Jesus' disciples. Those who nevertheless want to affirm the perpetual virginity of Mary have to explain these brothers and sisters of Jesus as sons of Joseph by an earlier marriage, or as cousins. Also striking in this passage is the fact that Jesus is unusually referred to as 'son of Mary', with no mention of a father. This has given rise to much speculation. Explanations range from the view that Mary was already coming to be venerated when this story circulated, to the view that here we have an insinuation of the illegitimacy of Jesus. The most extreme view is that Jesus was a child resulting from the rape of Mary; remarks by Celsus, a second-century critic of Christianity quoted by Origen, who speaks of Mary having had a child by a Roman soldier, Panthera, are also thought to point in this direction. That four women of doubtful morality are mentioned in the genealogy of Jesus in Matthew is noted as perhaps another hint of illegitimacy.

Church fathers

Since birth from a woman with no involvement of a male is so extraordinary, it is not surprising that explanations, however offensive to traditional believers, have been sought. But given the lack of evidence, no explanation can be substantiated. The inexplicable is therefore largely discussed in theological terms: the virgin birth is a miracle; it cannot be reduced to a historical fact or reduced to a historical event. It is symbolic of the creative power of the God who formed the universe from nothing.

Devotion to Mary has been strong from the second century onwards, and this has undoubtedly contributed to the affirmation of the virgin birth despite all difficulties and criticisms. The desire to avoid the chain of original sin (which later led to the claim that Mary, too, was immaculately conceived) and the emphasis on virginity in the early church were doubtless major factors, but they do not totally explain an enormously popular belief.

Sin

passage in Paul's writings has a similar pivotal significance to that which John's prologue has in the Gospels: that passage is in Philippians. Paul, apparently quoting an even more ancient hymn, says that Christ 'emptied himself, taking the form of a slave, being born in human likeness ... and became obedient to the point of death ... on a cross' (2.7–8). John's sense of pre-existence and Paul's sense of humility have been central to the Christian imagination throughout the history of the church.

There is no doubt that Jesus was recognized by the earliest Christians as both a man and God, and as much as they sought to imitate him as a human example, they continued to worship him as divine. The need to establish a clear stance in relation to Judaism, and to articulate an appropriate proclamation in relation to the world-view of the Mediterranean Gentile mind, pushed the theologians of the early centuries to express the conviction of the incarnation in the Latin and Greek philosophical vocabulary of their time. In the first place it was affirmed that there was still only one God. The fact that Jesus had been both God and human did not mean either that there were two gods (the God of the Jews and Jesus Christ) or that Christ was simply a temporary mode of God's existence and thus that heaven was empty while Jesus walked on earth until he ascended and returned (Modalism or Sabellianism). The doctrine of the Trinity emerged as theologians articulated that the inner life of the one God is a unity of three persons, Father, Son and Holy Spirit, and that while all that the incarnate Son revealed of God is true of the whole of God, that which Jesus experienced in the flesh, most significantly his death, did not change the character of the everlasting God. In other words, God fully lived in Jesus, but when Jesus died, God did not cease to be.

pp. 520–1

In the second place it was affirmed that Jesus, while undoubtedly God, was just as much a human being. This is the territory usually called christology. Between the fourth and seventh centuries, discussion raged among theologians of east and west over how Jesus could have a human nature and will, and also a divine nature and will, while still being one person, rather than two. The Chalcedonian

Christology

p. 301

Definition of 451 preserved this understanding of Christ, and has remained the touchstone of orthodox understandings of the incarnation. But its abstract terminology and heavy dependence on philosophical understandings of terms such as nature and person sometimes seem as distant from the Jesus of Galilee as they are from the Christ of contemporary faith and experience.

pp. 1210–11

What the doctrine affirms

Søren Kierkegaard

1. *Jesus is truly and fully human.* Søren Kierkegaard offers a parable to clarify the nature and purpose of the incarnation. A king fell in love with a humble maiden. He considered how he might woo her. If he were to court her with the trappings of majesty, she might love him for the wrong reasons. Yet if he were to dress up as a person of her own class, her love, if it came, would be founded on deceit. Thus he must become a person of her own class if he is genuine in his desire to win her heart. For Kierkegaard, as for the theologians who agreed the Chalcedonian formula, the idea that Jesus only seemed to be a human being but was really a veiled form of God all along, an idea known as Docetism, misses the point entirely.

Kierkegaard's story is helpful in that it stresses that the reason for the incarnation is God's unwavering and unearned love for the human race. This is not some biological or cosmological stunt, but an eternal and costly gesture of grace. The consequences of this are that Jesus was subject to the contingencies of human existence. He had physical limitations: he could not be in more than one place at one time, he needed food and drink, he needed rest. He was part of the intellectual and cultural fabric of his time: he started life as a child, he needed to be taught, he did not have an encyclopaedic knowledge, he was a Jew, he shared many of his people's assumptions about the world. He experienced profound human emotions: he was tempted, angered, grieved, abused and executed.

It is worth noting that Jesus' assumption of human nature must alter, or at least refine, an understanding of what it means to be human. If Jesus was fully human, while remaining God, it implies that those parts of human nature that withdraw from God are not intrinsic to being human. Sin is not essential to human identity, because Jesus was a human being but did not sin. If Jesus is a human being, he must be the definitive human being. Incidentally, this alleviates familiar difficulties with the debate between evolutionists and creationists over human origins. For the definitive human being is not Adam (or Eve) but Christ. Christian history is not linear but christocentric, centred on Christ.

Sin

Evolution

It has often been observed that many people's misgivings about the church can be traced back to prior scepticism about the genuine humanity of Jesus. Many of the church's shortcomings are due to its simple, clumsy, incorrigible humanity. But Jesus' humanity, if it was indeed genuine, must have had clumsy, incorrigible aspects just as much. Did he have a beautiful singing voice? Was his taste in food and art always the best? Did he have a good sense of humour? If these are questions contemporary Christians ask of one another, they must be questions that help to take the incarnation seriously.

Church

It is sometimes said that, in becoming human, God took humanity into the divine being. But the emphasis, especially in the prologue to John, on the pre-existence of the Logos, begs further questions. Was humanity always at the centre of God's purposes, long before human beings walked on earth? Was the 'shape' of God always such that God intended to take flesh at a certain point in history? Was the flaw in the created order, the frustration of God's design that is generally called the fall, inevitable, and did the incarnation take place primarily to reverse its consequences? Or would God have become incarnate even without the fall, to embody God's purpose to dwell with God's people for ever? Finally, which attributes of human life did Jesus retain after his resurrection and ascension to glory? Are they the same ones as he had prior to taking human form at a particular point in history, or did something change in God at the moment of the virginal conception? Theologians have never reached a consensus on these issues.

2. *Jesus is fully and truly God.* The weakness of Kierkegaard's parable is that it is so committed to avoiding Docetism, so concerned to stress the humanity of Jesus, that Jesus' abiding divinity may be obscured. This is often the case with accounts of the incarnation. Those accounts that are inspired most closely by Paul's description of Christ 'emptying himself' (Philippians 2. 5–11) are sometimes called kenotic (from the Greek word for emptying), and come close to saying that God ceases to be God in becoming human. The Chalcedonian understanding is that, while Jesus took on human nature, he was still God in personality. This was true from the very beginning of his life: there is no place for the heresy of adoptionism, that suggests that God bestowed Jesus with divinity, say, at his baptism, or rewarded him with divinity at his resurrection. Incarnation refers to the embodied presence of God in Jesus' whole life – conception, birth, ministry, death and resurrection.

But kenosis still presents the doctrine of the incarnation with a serious challenge, because it takes seriously that Jesus set aside omnipotence, omniscience, omnipresence and immutability. Those theologians who stress the setting aside of these traditional attributes of God are often the same theologians who doubt the value of such attributes in the first place. There seems an impasse between those who stress Jesus' divinity and those who emphasize the 'pouring out' of God in God's love for the world. Perhaps a neglected avenue of compromise is to attend further to the depth of the relationship between Jesus and the Father, a relationship frequently noted in the Fourth Gospel (John 5.19–23; 10. 14–30; 14. 1–6).

If, as we saw above, Jesus' full humanity must refine our notion of what it means to be human, then, just as much, Jesus' full divinity must refine our understanding of God. Whether or not God is to be understood as immutable or omnipotent, the God revealed in Jesus is undoubtedly passionately devoted to the poor, radically open to the outcast, extraordinarily hospitable to sinners, and prepared to shape his whole life for those he loves. Jesus' encounters with working people, marginalized groups and ruthless authorities are not just beautiful gestures: because he is God incarnate, they are definitive paradigms of the truth about existence.

But this can exacerbate a further problem, which is that the Chalcedonian Definition does not fully elaborate on how Jesus, being both God and human, remains one person. The danger lies in seeing divine and human personhood in absolute, exclusive terms – in perceiving a zero-sum equation in which if Jesus is one, he cannot be the other. The secret is to see the extent to which Jesus' being divine enlivens and illuminates his humanity, and to see how Jesus' being human focuses and intensifies the love of God. Again, the incarnation redefines the Christian understanding of both humanity and divinity.

The strongest imperative that ensured that the divinity of Jesus prevailed in the debates which formed the fourth- and fifth-century creeds was the requirement that Jesus be not just Lord but Saviour. In a sense, the doctrine of the incarnation works backwards: Jesus is worshipped because he (and he alone) saves; only God can save; therefore Jesus must be God, and if he was God in his passion and resurrection, he must have been God all along. If Jesus is not fully God, he cannot save – and if he is not fully human, that salvation cannot take root in human life.

It is this affirmation that the incarnation brings salvation which causes dissent in many quarters. Unitarianism and deism are two approaches that deny the incarnation, seeing no necessity for the significant figure of Jesus to be understood as God. The liberal Protestants of the nineteenth century strove to understand the personality of Jesus, but notoriously portrayed a character very much like their own. In contemporary studies the incarnation is most often questioned because of its apparently negative consequences for interfaith dialogue. In this case, dialogue becomes the normative principle in the way that salvation was for the early church. The danger in asserting the need of the incarnation to bring salvation is that the details of Jesus' life – in short, his humanity – become obscured, and incarnation becomes simply a device by which God saves the world. This almost mechanical portrayal of the incarnation is alien to the narrative of the Gospels.

The Incarnation, cartoon for a stained-glass window in sixteenth-century style designed by André Didron and drawn by Auguste Ledoux

Salvation

Critical challenges

The era of the Enlightenment not only turned the focus of reflection away from traditions handed down and towards the self; it also made the venerated traditions subject to unprecedented critical scrutiny. Of the criticisms of the Chalcedonian tradition made during and since the Enlightenment period, four stand out, and can be described as anthropological, historical, philosophical and moral.

Unitarians
Enlightenment
Liberal theology

1. *The anthropological critique* of the incarnation emerges from the study of Christianity alongside other religions. One influential study, describing three strands common to most religious experience, sees incarnation as a pervasive feature, like mysticism and a sense of the numinous. It is not hard to find the details of the incarnation – such as the virginal conception – replicated in other religious traditions. The most controversial word in this line of criticism is 'myth'. In the most general terms, myth is a

Interfaith dialogue
Mysticism

way of talking about an overarching reality of which the experience of, or belief in, God, or gods, is a part. The Christian doctrine of the incarnation thus emerges as a significant form in which one tradition understands the self-communication of the numinous – but by no means the only, or even the definitive, form.

Theologians committed to broadly Chalcedonian understandings have responded to the anthropological critique in two ways. On the one hand they have questioned whether a description of the Christian doctrine of the incarnation that compares it so closely with similar concepts in other religions truly does justice to the detail and complexity of the Christian understanding. For example, which other tradition speaks of the weakness of God, and of a power that overcomes through weakness, in the way that Paul does in 1 Corinthians 1? On the other hand, in common with the postmodern turn, they have questioned the assumptions of anthropology – that it is possible to stand in some supposedly neutral place and speak objectively of all traditions, while allegedly having no tradition (or religion) of one's own.

Feminist theology

2. *The historical critique* of the incarnation begins with discomfort at the dissonance between the apparently simple language of the Gospels and the labyrinthine complexity of the credal formulae. Out of this contrast comes a chorus of suspicious voices. There are conspiracy theorists, who suggest that Paul or some other early leader hijacked the historical figure of Jesus and loaded on him a back-breaking assortment of metaphysical longings. There are inter-testamental historians who see so much eschatological expectation in the contemporary literature that Jesus becomes little more than a container for the religious fantasies of his time. There are early church historians who find it hard to disentangle the historical Jesus from the practices and beliefs of the first Christians.

Jesus of history

Theologians committed to the tradition tend to argue that the debates of the fourth and fifth centuries were inevitable given the diversity of the accounts of Jesus in the New Testament. They tend to see that diversity as a strength rather than a weakness, since it attests to a much wider experience of the incarnation than any one conspiracy could bring about. And they see no reason to detach a historical figure of Jesus from the faith of the early church, since they recognize that it was the early church that wrote the New Testament, and that witness, rather than historical research, has been at the heart of Christianity all along.

3. *The philosophical critique* of the incarnation is most identified with the German eighteenth-century

Enlightenment figure G. E. Lessing. His claim that 'accidental truths of history can never prove the necessary truths of reason' epitomizes what came to be called the 'scandal of particularity', namely that salvation is achieved in a particular person in a particular place at a particular time, at the heart of incarnational faith. This philosophical position underlies the anthropological critique. The logic is that Jesus exhibited some more generally significant feature underlying the reality of the cosmos. This logic was picked up by the German philosopher G. W. F. Hegel. Hegel saw all knowledge as the synthesis that arises out of the transcendence of a contrasting thesis and antithesis. Thus God, as absolute Spirit (thesis), objectifies himself in world history (antithesis), and is reconciled in the incarnation (synthesis). Hegel's sweeping account illustrates a tendency in the doctrine of the incarnation after Lessing: either they part company with the historical realities of Jesus' life (like Hegel), or they part company with any significant sense of his divinity (like most liberal Protestantism of the nineteenth century).

4. *The moral critique* of the incarnation is voiced in contemporary theological discussion most from a feminist perspective. How important is it, that when God took human form, that form was male? If Jesus was fully human, and yet a man, does that mean that women are an insignificant or derivative aspect of 'full humanity'? If, as many early theologians asserted, 'the unassumed is the unhealed', i.e. unless God took on every attribute of human nature, humanity would not be saved, can a male saviour save women? This moral critique is in fact still part of the scandal of particularity. There is no doubt that for much of the church's history, the maleness of Christ was by many taken for granted as essential to the character of his divinity. This view is much less common today (although by no means a thing of the past), and the character of Jesus' full humanity is more often found in his complete trust in God and his identification with the most estranged and excluded groups in society.

Contemporary significance

The doctrine of the incarnation is the central doctrine in Christian theology, from which all other doctrines flow. The person whom the disciples recognized as God among them became the saviour who brought God's purposes to a climax, was identified with the creator who had shaped his life to be for humanity from the very beginning, and became the source of the Holy Spirit who empowered the life of the church. Of the many things that could be said of the importance of the incarnation in Christianity today, three stand out.

1. *The embodied character of God inspires the embodied character of Christian theology.* God's self-communication in Jesus involved passionate commitment, heartbreaking

frustration and excruciating suffering. Christian theology in the light of the incarnation can never be detached speculation on other-worldly traditions. Embodiment in this sense means taking seriously the lived realities of the practices of the church, that body of people who have explicitly committed themselves to find the truth about God and themselves by following Jesus. It means recognizing that just as Jesus became incarnate in a particular (Jewish) culture and (first-century) time and (fervidly rebellious) context, so theology must attend to its culture, time and context today. It means keeping a constant dialogue between the theoretical aspects of the credal tradition, and the practical outworkings of that tradition in discipleship and community life.

2. *The coming of Jesus in human form defines the character of God.* Christmas, the feast of the incarnation, expresses the mystery of God's limitless yet unfathomable love for humankind. The unknown God has made God known, and now nothing that can be known of God can contradict what has been revealed of God in Christ. If the incarnation lies at the centre of Christian devotion, it must also determine Christian understandings of the body. If Christ took on a human body, then the human body is, as Paul says, a 'temple of the Holy Spirit' (1 Corinthians 3.16). The body is hugely significant in contemporary reflection, from eating disorders to cloning, but no such reflection can ignore the significance of the incarnation. The human body is the place where God revealed everything humanity needed to know about God.

3. *The shape of God's life in Christ is normative for ethics and mission.* Mission inspired by the news of salvation in Jesus' cross and resurrection characteristically seeks to convince, convert and transform the stranger. By contrast, mission inspired by God's incarnation in Jesus is much more inclined to see faithfulness in simply going where Christ went, being with the people Christ was with, doing the things Christ did. Theologies of liberation, particularly in Latin America, stress that the first disciples discovered Jesus among the poor, with outcasts, women, notorious traitors, and the 'least', before they ever speculated on his pre-existence or virginal conception. Likewise, Jesus was not blind to the political dimension of the oppression of his times: an incarnational ethic must attend not just to the individual body, but to the corporate embodiment of sin under whose domination so many of the world's poor suffer today.

SAMUEL WELLS

Donald Baillie, *God Was In Christ*, London: Faber and New York: Scribner 1948; J. N. D. Kelly, *Early Christian Doctrines*, revised edition London: Continuum 1985 and San Francisco: Harper SanFrancisco 1978; Jaroslav Pelikan, *The Christian Tradition: A History of the Development of Doctrine*, Vol. 1: *The Emergence of the Catholic Tradition, 100–600*, Chicago: University of Chicago Press 1971; Rosemary Radford Ruether, *Sexism and God-Talk: Toward a Feminist Theology*, Boston: Beacon Press and London: SCM Press 1983; John V. Taylor, *The Christlike God*, London: SCM Press 1993

Industrial revolution

The industrial revolution that was to transform the face of the world began in Britain in the second half of the eighteenth century. As well as the dramatic changes in manufacture, transport and communication that it brought about, it resulted in a tremendous increase in the size of the population and a dramatic movement from the countryside to the towns and cities. The growth of the manufacturing industries and the workforces employed in them also led to inhuman working conditions and appalling living conditions. However, up to the last quarter of the nineteenth century the churches, and most obviously the Church of England, which was the church of the nation, were alarmingly unresponsive to all this. There were spasmodic attempts to confront the problems posed, but these were unco-ordinated, and only papered up the cracks. They smacked of first aid when major surgery was necessary. They were frequently the result of individual initiatives or the action of voluntary bodies, rather than moves by the churches or denominations themselves to adopt new and suitably radical policies or take effective action. There was little evidence of incisive collective thinking or concern to respond appropriately to what amounted to the most dramatic and comprehensive metamorphosis in the history of the country.

Festivals and fasts ◄

Body ◄

Church of England

Mission ◄

Part of the problem was complacency or a preoccupation with internal, domestic matters. The Church of England's phalanx of bishops, deans, other dignitaries and priests, impressive cathedrals and 10,500 mostly ancient parish churches created a false sense of security, permanence and invulnerability.

Liberation theology ◄

The Anglican ministry, and to an extent its membership, was to a great extent class-bound. Parish priests and the various high office holders in the established church hierarchy, including its bishops, continued to be dominated by the sons of noblemen and gentlemen. There were more aristocratic bishops in 1800 than in 1700, and the rectories and vicarages of the land were manned by members of the privileged classes throughout the Victorian era, despite the founding of theological colleges. The dominance of such a social élite, who had little if any

Ministry and ministers

first-hand prolonged contact with the labouring classes or understanding of them, made it difficult for the church to cope with the consequences of unprecedented industrial and agricultural revolutions. The national church never established an effective rapport with vast numbers of the new 'lower order' people, and they in turn were alienated from all forms of organized Christianity. This was most blatantly apparent in the ease and splendour of living enjoyed by many of the bishops, deans and canons in their secluded, elegant cathedral closes, so splendidly depicted in the Barchester novels of Anthony Trollope. The whole situation was a tragedy of massive proportions, with calamitous short, medium and long-term repercussions.

p. 836

The Church of England seemed unaware of the increasing irrelevance of its structure and organization. It seemed unconcerned to make the root and branch reforms that were required if effective ministry was to be provided for the growing mass of disfranchised, disadvantaged and disorientated manual workers spawned by the new industrial system. The parishes were situated in places where medieval communities had existed. They were concentrated in the rural South and Midlands. Many country parish churches were at best found to be excessively large for the populations they served, or at worse were stranded like beached whales in depopulated areas. In contrast, densely-populated and rapidly expanding industrial towns and cities were inadequately provided with either churches or clergy.

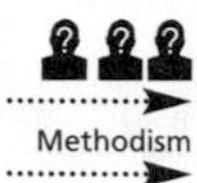

Methodism

Great Awakening

Furnishings

The church was resented and made even more unattractive than it might otherwise have been by pew rents, poor preaching, dull services and the requirement for worshippers to be suitably dressed. It is not surprising that exhausted, illiterate or semi-literate manual workers found counter-attractions more appealing than attendance at local church services. It seems that the labourer disregarded church and chapel not because of disbelief, but out of apathy, indifference and hostility. Working-class literature was often violently anti-clerical, anti-church and anti-chapel, but infrequently atheistic, agnostic or anti-Christian.

Evangelicals

Oxford Movement

p. 1131

The Victorian age was very religious, but this was not a classless religion. The evangelicals thrived in certain towns, and it was a triumphant age for their voluntary religious societies and associations. The high church revival, witnessed by the Oxford Movement, by the ministry of the 'slum priests' in the latter part of the century and by the various forms of Christian Socialism, also contributed to an appearance of healthy church and chapel life. Nonetheless, much of this vibrancy and fruitfulness of ministry was restricted to the middle and lower-middle classes.

Buildings

Immediately after the Napoleonic Wars, parliament accepted responsibility for the provision of new churches in populous areas, but this was a somewhat knee-jerk reaction dictated by fear of social discontent, and was not repeated. The evangelical Church Pastoral Aid Society, founded in 1836, and the high church Additional Curates Society, started in 1837, provided extra assistant clergy and other workers, but such valiant efforts merely scratched the surface of what were deep-seated problems. It was the same later in the century with the Salvation Army and the Church Army. All these magnificent endeavours were mere palliatives. They did not entail the essential restructuring and reorganization of the church. When the repeal of the Test and Corporation Act of 1828, the Catholic Emancipation Act of 1829, the Reform Act of 1832 and the proposals of the newly-created Ecclesiastical Commissioners of 1835 started to threaten or alter the status quo, there was vehement opposition from almost all sectors of the established church.

In the midst of such damaging conservatism and lack of response to change, it was a monumental disaster that the Church of England in effect drove out many of its most ardent and able evangelists and pastors – clergymen such as George Whitefield (1714–70) and John (1703–91) and Charles (1707–88) Wesley. The Methodists, and other denominations to some extent, stepped into the breach created by the inactivity of the national church. With their willingness to build cheap, functional chapels in strategic places; with their adaptability, their itinerant and lay preaching, concern for evangelism and call for conversion and sanctification; and with their greater ability to mobilize the laity in spreading the gospel and in serving others, they were a powerful force. Their numerical expansion was phenomenal, especially in the period from the late eighteenth century to the third quarter of the nineteenth century.

Nonetheless, although the Methodist achievement was impressive, its ability to attract members of the labouring classes was limited. Its outreach was largely confined to artisans and those who were more literate; and other mainline dissenting bodies were even less successful. Also, by the third quarter of the nineteenth century, Nonconformists were gradually losing much of their former cutting edge. Chapels became havens of the respectable, showing little concern for those beyond their warm fellowships. When any radical thinkers appeared, with a determination to engage with the manual workers, the poor and the dispossessed at first hand, as with William Booth (1829–1912), the founder of the Salvation Army, hackles were raised, barriers were erected, and not infrequently individuals were cold-shouldered or even expelled from the denomination concerned.

From the latter part of the nineteenth century to the present day both the Church of England and the Free Churches have undergone a major decline as measured by church membership or attendance at services. Perhaps the most worrying aspect of the slither downwards in numbers was the loss of many of the middle classes. They had been at the heart of the Victorian church and had provided most of its leadership. Their defection in ever increasing numbers from the late nineteenth century onwards was a massive blow. Allied to this was the inability of the churches to attract the managers, administrators and technocrats of the second industrial revolution in any great numbers, especially in the post-First World War era.

All this must not be interpreted as a total catastrophe. It is only one side of the picture. After all, despite the inability of all the denominations, and the Roman Catholics, to attract the labouring classes in great numbers, by 1851 about 70 per cent of the population attended a church or chapel. There were also many, largely unsung, achievements. It needs to be remembered that the churches were the trail-blazers in the provision of schools, societies for the relief of suffering in a multitude of forms, and service to communities. There is no way of measuring the benefits conferred on others, and the goodwill generated by the untold and immeasurable acts of kindness and charity to their neighbours shown by local churches and chapels and their members. In so many ways they and a host of societies acted as salt and light in society. Theirs is a record in this respect that is unparalleled by any other group, or by any other followers of alternative faiths and ideologies.

Nevertheless, despite all these provisos, the failure of the churches to attract and hold a large proportion of the industrial working population, and latterly of the middle classes, remains a mammoth disaster. It is a story that can be repeated for other societies throughout the world. Why this is so is a matter of much debate; the fact is almost indisputable.

p. 1245

KENNETH HYLSON-SMITH

Owen Chadwick, *The Victorian Church* (2 vols), London: A&C Black 1966 and 1970; S. Gilley and W. J. Sheils (eds), *A History of Religion in Britain. Practice and Belief from Pre-Roman Times to the Present*, Oxford: Blackwell 1994; K. S. Inglis, *Churches and the Working Classes in Victorian England*, London: Routledge 1963; H. McLeod, *Churches and Society in England 1850–1914*, London: Palgrave Macmillan 1984; M. Smith, *Religion in Industrial Society. Oldham and Saddleworth 1740–1865*, Oxford: Clarendon Press 1994

Schools
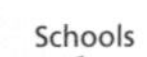

INITIATION

Conversion, Creed, Education, Forgiveness, Prayer, Ritual, Sacraments, Schools, Sin, Worship

Whatever claims religions may make about the truth of their doctrines, it remains true that most people in the world follow the religion of the family and community into which they were born. Even so, becoming a member of a religious group is an occasion normally marked by some kind of ritual, and this is what is meant by initiation. Baptism is usually the most important element in Christian initiation, but it can take many forms.

In a Philippine Lutheran Church on a Sunday morning, a three-month-old baby is being baptized. The church is a simple cement-block structure. The font is a small metal bowl on a wooden pedestal. Surrounding the font are the baby's family and several *commadres* and *compadres*, or 'godparents', who will share the responsibility of bringing the baby up in the Christian faith. The pastor baptizes the child by scooping water in his hand and then letting it fall over the baby's head. He lays his hand on the baby's head while praying an ancient prayer for the child's strengthening in grace to everlasting life.

In a large Roman Catholic congregation in the United States, five adults are being baptized at the Easter Vigil. Dressed in toga-like garments (with swimming apparel underneath), they, along with the entire congregation, are gathered around the baptismal pool – a cross-shaped structure containing twenty inches of water. Each candidate steps into the pool and kneels. With one hand on the candidate's forehead and another on the back of the candidate's neck, the priest pushes the candidate forward into the water three times while saying, 'I baptize you in the name of the Father, and of the Son, and of the Holy Spirit.' Afterwards, the newly baptized receive a white garment as a reminder of being 'clothed with Christ', and also a candle symbolizing enlightenment by Christ. After praying that the newly baptized receive the gift of the Holy Spirit, the priest goes to each and, after dipping his thumb in a special oil, marks the sign of the cross on the forehead of each while saying, 'Be sealed with the gift of the Holy Spirit.' The spice-like aroma of the oil fills the church.

Festivals and fasts

Holy Spirit

A congregation of Russian Baptists is gathered at a river for a baptismal service. The candidates speak briefly about their personal faith and why they desire baptism. Each is led into the shallow river. The minister recites a formula that refers to the Trinity. Wrapping his left arm around a candidate's upper back, and placing his right hand over the candidate's hands (which the candidate has placed over his face), the minister pushes the candidate backwards into the water and then quickly pulls him out again. The newly baptized emerges from the water to receive embraces from members of the congregation.

Trinity

Just as there are different ways of administering baptism, so there are different reasons why people come to baptism. Many were brought as infants by their parents. The parental decision may have been in response to quasi-superstitious fears or social expectations. Ideally, however, it reflects a conviction that baptism is a gift of grace that initiates one into a living relationship with Jesus Christ and the church, the fellowship of believers who will help nurture the baptized infant's faith in Jesus.

Grace

Jesus

By contract, others – adolescents or adults – come to baptism because of a conscious 'decision'. A person hears the Christian message (the 'gospel') and accepts its central claim that the crucified and

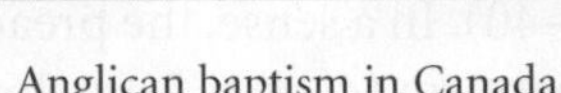

Anglican baptism in Canada

Pentecostal baptism in the Indian Ocean, Zanzibar

risen Jesus is humanity's Lord and Judge whose final word will be one of forgiveness and grace. The person commits him/herself to Jesus and rejects all other 'saviours'. In effect, the person experiences 'conversion': the radical re-orientation of values, morals, and allegiances. This is popularly known as a 'born-again' experience. Baptism is an outward demonstration of this spiritual renewal and initiation into the community of those who are likewise committed to Jesus Christ.

Community

Properly speaking, there is not a distinction between churches that baptize infants only and those that baptize only adults; rather, it is between churches that accept candidates of all ages and those that accept only confessing adults. Churches which have a long history of baptizing almost exclusively infants (e.g., Roman Catholic, Anglican, Lutheran) have recently developed programming and rituals for initiating adults. Hence, when it comes to initiatory practice, generalizations are out of place.

As we shall see, Christian initiation has a long and complex history and even in recent times has undergone significant changes.

Initiation in the classical world

Religious life in the Mediterranean world into which Christianity was born was completely bound to social and political life, so acceptance into the political community also meant acceptance into the religious community. Although this acceptance might have involved religious ritual, it is not usually considered to be initiation. However, there were certain mainly Greek cults – usually referred to as 'mystery cults' – where initiation was the central ritual act. Initiates would go through nocturnal ceremonies – apparently involving light and dark, and the revelation of secret objects or possibly the telling of secret stories – and might expect special favours from the gods as a result. Nevertheless, this kind of initiation would not necessarily make the initiate a member of a real community: it is likely, for example, that few of those initiated into the rites of the Great Gods on the island of Samothrace would ever visit the temple again after their initiation. In contrast,

Mystery cults

Christian understandings of initiation stress its relationship to membership of a community of worshippers.

Initiation in the New Testament

A distinctive feature of Jesus' ministry was his eating with 'sinners', 'outcasts' and other socially unacceptable people, something that earned him a reputation as a 'drunkard' and 'glutton' (Matthew 11.19). In fact, Jesus ate with anybody, and access to meal fellowship with him was completely free and open. There was no prerequisite initiatory rite, for the meal itself was the initiation. Spiritual conversion followed later as a consequence of the personal encounter with Jesus.

Even though meal fellowship was continued by the earliest Christians (cf. Acts 2.42), baptism became the means for initiating people into the church (Acts 2.38–9, 41). Indeed, Acts and the Paul writings of Paul contain numerous references to baptizing, which suggests that baptizing was Mission understood as central to the early church's mission in the world.

Although early converts were initiated into the church with a process that included water baptism, there is not complete certainty about what else was included in the early church's initiation. There probably was some sort of instruction of the convert, as is perhaps indicated by the encounter between Philip and the Ethiopian eunuch (Acts 8.26–40). In a sense, the preaching of the apostles itself served as instruction that led to conversion and baptism (cf. Acts 2.14–36; 10.34–48). Initiation is also likely to have involved a formal expression of faith in Jesus Christ by the initiate, although there are no explicit baptismal professions in the New Testament. Acts mentions the laying on of hands in connection with baptism in several places, but no consistent pattern emerges. References throughout the New Testament to 'sealing' or anointing (Acts 10.38; Ephesians 1.13; Revelation 7.3, 4) may indicate a literal anointing with oil, but there are no explicit references to anointing as an initiatory rite.

The early church

p. 245 A late-first-century or early-second-century Greek document known as the Didache gives the following shape of Christian initiation: 1. an instructional period (of unspecified length); 2. an immediate period of baptismal preparation consisting of a one- or two-day fast by the candidates, baptismal ministers and the entire church; 3. water baptism either by immersion (a complete dunking in water) or affusion (a pouring of water over the candidate), perhaps accompanied by a trinitarian formula ('I baptize you in the name of the Father, and of the Son, and of the Holy Spirit'), and 4. the beginning of participation in holy communion, although it is unclear whether this first communion was the culminating act of initiation. The Didache says nothing about a profession of faith by the candidate.

The *First Apology* of Justin Martyr (died *c.* 165), a Syro-Palestinian who lived in Rome, also indicates a time of pre-baptismal instruction (length unspecified) and fasting (ch. 61). Justin's use of credal language concerning the name of God (viz., 'the Father and Lord of all ... Jesus Christ who was crucified under Pontius Pilate, and ... the Holy Spirit who predicted through the prophets ...') may indicate the manner of confession spoken by the candidate within the baptismal rite or may refer to the formula used by the baptizing minister during the administration of water. Unlike the Didache, Justin indicates that baptism culminates in the newly baptized participating fully in the Eucharist church's worship, especially in holy communion.

An early-third-century Greek document commonly known as the *Didascalia Apostolorum* ('The Catholic Teaching of the Twelve Holy Apostles and Disciples of our Saviour') witnesses to a somewhat expanded initiatory pattern. The first step was a period of instruction supervised by the bishop. The initiation rite began with the bishop anointing the candidate's head with oil while laying on his hand. This laying on of the hand/anointing was accompanied by the reciting of Psalm 2.7 ('You are my son, this day I have begotten you'). Other ministers anointed the candidate's entire body, and the candidate was then washed while some formula (an 'invocation of the divine names') was recited. As indicated by Justin, baptism culminated in full participation in church life, including holy communion.

Two other Syrian documents from this same period show a similar ritual sequence. The Apocryphal Acts of the Apostles (second to third century) and the Acts of John both give descriptions of baptism that include pre-baptismal anointings, followed by water baptism, and then reception of holy communion.

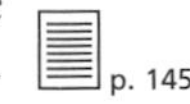
p. 145

An important witness to initiation in the Western church of the late-second and early-third centuries is the North African theologian Tertullian (*c.*160–225). His treatise *De baptismo* (198–200 CE) indicates that the initiates (catechumens) participate in a catechumenate, or period of instruction (length unspecified), and that immediately before baptism they fast, pray and confess their sins. Some time before the baptism, the initiates renounce the devil in the presence of the bishop and congregation. In the baptismal rite itself, the initiates re-affirm this renunciation and are asked if they believe in each person of the Trinity. Upon an affirmative answer, they are submerged or immersed – three times in all. The newly baptized then receive an anointing with oil known as 'chrism', a marking with the sign of the cross, and the laying on of hands, a gesture associated with the gift of the Holy Spirit. Finally, they partake of their first communion, which also includes a cup of milk and honey.

The *Apostolic Tradition*, attributed to Hippolytus of Rome (*c.*215), describes a rather lengthy process of initiation. To begin with, prostitutes, brothel keepers, actors, circus performers and other persons whose work was considered immoral or too closely associated with paganism were immediately refused admission to the initiatory process unless they renounced their professions. Because of their connection to the pagan state, government officials and soldiers likewise had to abandon their work. Those admitted as catechumens (the words means 'hearers') underwent a three-year period of ethical and biblical instruction and participation in Christian worship, but were not permitted to receive holy communion. Catechumens who appeared competent were officially admitted as candidates for baptism. During the final preparation period, their Christian conduct was examined, and they underwent daily exorcisms (rites for the expulsion of evil). On the Thursday before the rites of initiation, the candidates bathed and then fasted on the following Friday and Saturday. The bishop performed a final exorcism on Saturday, and that night was spent in a vigil ('watch') which included readings and instruction. Early on Sunday morning, the candidates removed their clothing and had their entire bodies rubbed with exorcised oil. The baptism took place in a manner similar to Tertullian's description: a threefold questioning about the candidates' faith accompanied by a threefold submersion or immersion. Afterwards, the newly baptized were again anointed, and after putting their clothing on they proceeded to the main assembly hall, where the bishop laid hands on each while praying for them to be made worthy of receiving the Holy Spirit. The bishop then anointed them and 'sealed' them (i.e., marked them with the sign of the cross). Finally, the bishop gave each the 'kiss of peace'. Following these rites the newly baptized joined in the congregation's celebration of holy communion, where they received a special cup of milk and honey as a symbol of their entry into the promised land. During the weeks after baptism, the candidates may have had additional instruction on the sacraments by the bishop.

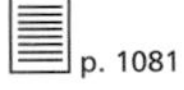
p. 1081

During the fourth and fifth centuries, all aspects of initiation from the catechumenal rites to the post-baptismal teaching (mystagogy) were reorganized. Easter emerged as a preferred time for the initiatory rites, while the season of Lent, which preceded Easter, became the time of final preparation. According to Cyril of Jerusalem (*c.*315–86), a bishop and theologian, those to be baptized at Easter, or the 'ones to be enlightened' (Greek *photizomenoi*), attended an introductory lecture during Lent, as well as a series of eighteen lectures on the creed. The rites of initiation began with the

Satan

candidates renouncing Satan and receiving an anointing on the head. Next they stripped off their clothing (imitating Christ's nakedness on the cross) and had their entire bodies anointed as a symbol of participation in Christ's 'richness'. The washing was administered with the threefold credal interrogation and was followed by another anointing that represented reception of the Holy Spirit. The initiatory process then culminated in the newly baptized receiving their first communion.

In Rome during the fourth and fifth centuries, the initiatory process was becoming rather complex. An official rite for enrolment into the catechumenate included the giving of blessed salt to the catechumen. The catechumenate itself involved instruction and numerous rites of exorcism. At the beginning of Lent, the catechumens were officially elected to baptism and thereby became known as *competentes*. During this time of final preparation, the *competentes* were 'given' the creed (i.e., the Apostles' Creed), in a rite known as the *traditio symboli.* Probably on the third, fourth and fifth weeks of Lent, the initiates experienced the 'scrutinies', or examinations of their Christian conduct. The baptismal service included a pre-baptismal anointing, a triple washing/triple confession of faith, clothing of the newly baptized in white garments, an anointing on the head, a prayer with the laying on of hands invoking the Holy Spirit and a second anointing on the head, both performed by the bishop, and finally first communion, which included a cup of milk and honey. These rites were conferred on both adults and infant candidates. Notably, a bishop's administration of post-baptismal rites associated with the Holy Spirit was a feature peculiar to Roman and North African initiation in the early church.

Outside Rome, other rites were incorporated into the initiatory process during the fourth and fifth centuries. In Milan, the newly baptized had their feet washed by the bishop. Some time after

p. 967

initiation, they were 'given' the Lord's Prayer ('Our Father'). In the Christian East (e.g., Jerusalem, Antioch, Egypt), rites for the renunciation of Satan (*apotaxis*) and adherence or dedication to Christ (*syntaxis*) began to appear. In addition to the solemn handing over of the creed to the candidates (*traditio symboli*), there was also a 'giving back' of the creed (*redditio symboli*) by the initiates before the bishop.

The Middle Ages

Middle Ages

During the early Middle Ages the period of the catechumenate was shortened. From about the seventh century, candidates for baptism were primarily infants, so a long process of learning and spiritual formation was out of the question. Consequently the catechumenate was reduced to the last three weeks of Lent and involved mostly exorcistic rites. In Rome baptism took place during the vigil of Easter. The rites today associated with confirmation, i.e. the laying on of hands and prayer for the Holy Spirit together with a signing of the forehead with holy oil known as 'chrism', both administered by the bishop, followed immediately. (Notably, early on in non-Roman Western churches, baptism did not include post-baptismal rites reserved for the bishop.) The newly baptized infants were then given holy communion.

It has been noted that as the Middle Ages progressed, Christian initiation was marked by four significant changes:

1. *The celebration of confirmation apart from the baptismal rites.* The performance by the bishop of post-baptismal rites linked with the conferral of the Holy Spirit eventually spread from Rome to other European churches. But because dioceses were large and travel difficult, this confirmation was often delayed until the bishop could be present. Many people were never confirmed, although they would have had their first communion some time shortly after baptism. The church eventually decreed that a person must be confirmed by the age of seven.

2. *The celebration of first communion apart from initiation.* While infants were given communion into the twelfth century (by means of the priest dipping his finger into the wine and then placing it in the child's mouth), concerns about spilling consecrated wine led to the withdrawal of the cup from the laity. This effectively ended the communion of infants, since they had never been given the bread. However, the communion of infants did not cease entirely until after the Council of Trent Council in the late sixteenth century.

3. *The dissociation of initiation and Easter.* The fear that children who died without receiving baptism thereby forfeited salvation led to *quamprimum* baptism (baptism as soon after birth as possible). Easter therefore ceased to be the dominant time for Christian initiation. In some places, however, baptism at Easter remained the norm until the thirteenth century.

4. *The development of three distinct rituals of initiation, all separated in time.* The most significant consequence of the fragmentation of initiation into separate rites is that confirmation became a sacramental rite which conferred the Holy Spirit for increased grace, strength to engage in spiritual warfare, and spiritual maturity. Severed from confirmation and first communion, infant initiation ultimately became infant baptism only. Usually baptism was celebrated in private, with only the priest, candidate, parents and sponsors present.

The Reformation

Reformation

Although they continued the practice of infant baptism, leaders of the early Lutheran, Reformed and Anglican churches reshaped Christian initiation in three significant ways. First, they all produced baptismal rites in the vernacular so that those present could participate intelligently. Secondly, they streamlined the rites of initiation. While retaining most of the traditional ceremonies in his first 'little baptismal book' or *Taufbüchlein* of 1523, Martin Luther (1483–1546) eliminated many of these in his second *Taufbüchlein* of 1526, namely, breathing on the child, the conferral of salt, the first exorcism, the *effeta* (opening of the ears), two anointings (before and after the washing) and the giving of a lighted candle. He argued that such rites tended to obscure the importance of the essentials, namely, the washing and the intercessory prayers for the child. The Zurich reformer Huldrych Zwingli (1484–1531) likewise produced two baptismal  rites (1523, 1525), the second of which was a more radical revision of the medieval rite. He rejected secondary ceremonies (exorcism, anointing, candle) because they had no biblical basis. John Calvin (1509–64) also abolished all secondary ceremonies, leaving only the washing accompanied by the traditional trinitarian formula. The first Anglican Book of Common Prayer of 1549 retained ceremonies like signing with the cross, exorcism, the procession to the font, and the conferral of a baptismal garment and anointing. But the second Prayer Book of 1552 abandoned all of these except for the signing with the cross and a threefold dipping of the child into the font.

Thirdly, with the exception of Luther, the Reformers stressed the public celebration of the rites of Christian initiation. For Zwingli and Calvin, the celebration of baptism before a Christian congregation was important because the act signified God's will to save. Both the 1549 and 1552 Book of

Common Prayer explicitly directed that baptism be celebrated within the public worship of Sunday or other holy days.

Peace churches

Baptist churches

Radical groups like the Mennonites and Baptists initiated only believing adults in order to ensure a church of committed Christians rather than a church of all members of society. For them, baptism was not God's saving action, but a means of giving public witness to a conscious decision of faith and conversion. Since infant baptism was considered illegitimate, those baptized in infancy would be 'rebaptized' upon their mature conversion – although this was not considered a rebaptism, but the person's only true baptism.

Luther, Zwingli and Calvin all rejected the medieval teaching that confirmation was a sacrament for the conferral of the Holy Spirit. For them, baptism bestowed the Holy Spirit and was therefore complete Christian initiation. No subsequent completion or augmentation of baptism was necessary. Accordingly, none of these Reformers produced a confirmation rite. Yet they did approve of a reformed 'confirmation' connected with catechetical instruction and examination of a child's faith. A particularly important figure in the history of Protestant confirmation was the Strasbourg Reformer Martin Bucer (1491–1551), who emphasized the examination of the candidates' knowledge of the basic tenets of the Christian faith. His influence is particularly evident in *A Simple and Religious Consultation* by a reforming Archbishop of Cologne, Hermann von Wied (1447–1552), which contained a confirmation rite with the following order: an examination of faith (based on the catechism), a vow of faithfulness and obedience to the church, intercessory prayers, the laying on of hands accompanied by a formula invoking the Holy Spirit, and a hymn. The Consultation was translated into English and was drawn on in the making of the Book of Common Prayer. Reformed churches in Calvin's Geneva used a similar type of confirmation.

The influence of Bucer is evident elsewhere. Common features in Lutheran confirmation rites included instruction which prepared candidates for receiving communion, a confession of faith and vow by the candidates, the laying on of hands, and congregational prayer for the newly confirmed. Bucer's influence is also apparent in the 1549 Book of Common Prayer. The confirmation rite was preceded by a question and answer-type catechism covering the Apostles' Creed, the Lord's Prayer, the Ten Commandments, and other material. The major elements of the rite itself, at which the bishop presided, included the traditional Western confirmation prayer for the sevenfold gifts of the Spirit, a marking with the sign of the cross on the candidates' foreheads, and the laying on of hands accompanied by a trinitarian formula. A greeting of peace (between the bishop and those being confirmed), a prayer and a blessing concluded the rite. Rubrics prescribed the necessity of regularly-scheduled catechetical instruction (once every six weeks on a Sunday or holy day), and proscribed the communion of anyone who had not been confirmed – the latter being a way of emphasizing catechetical instruction. The 1552 Prayer Book put even more emphasis on instruction, revised the language of the prayer for the sevenfold gifts, omitted the marking with the sign of the cross, and provided a new formula for the laying on of hands.

pp. 384–5

Modern initiation

Perhaps the most important development in Christian initiation in modern times has been the recovery of the adult catechumenate. Leading the way was the Roman Catholic Church with its *Rite of Christian Initiation of Adults* (RCIA), 1972. RCIA recognizes four periods in the initiatory process: 1. the period of evangelization and pre-catechumenate; 2. the catechumenate; 3. the period of purification and enlightenment; and 4. the period of post-baptismal catechesis or mystagogy. These four periods are punctuated by three rites or 'steps':

CATECHISMS

A catechism (from the Greek word *katecheo*, make to hear, instruct) is a document presenting Christian teachings. From earliest times teaching was passed on to new converts and children orally: the process was known as *catechesis* and those being taught were called *catechumens*. Catechesis often took the form of questions and answers.

Although forms of catechism were produced in the Middle Ages in the Catholic Church, it was in the churches of the Reformation that the catechism became prominent. Some famous ones are:

Protestant and Anglican

Luther's Catechisms (1519): Martin Luther produced two catechisms, the Small Catechism for the use of parents instructing their households, and the Large Catechism for the use of pastors and teachers. Both cover the Ten Commandments, the Apostles' Creed, the Lord's Prayer, baptism, confession and holy communion. They are basic documents in Lutheranism.

Geneva Catechism (1542): Produced by John Calvin and written in French. It is in question-and-answer form and has five sections: on faith, the law, prayer, the Word of God and the sacraments.

Catechism of the Book of Common Prayer (1549): Its inclusion in a prayer book was an innovation. It deals with baptism, the Apostles' Creed, the doctrine of the Trinity, the Ten Commandments, duty to God and neighbour and the Lord's Prayer.

Heidelberg Catechism (1562): Basically a Calvinist catechism, it became the standard of doctrine in the Palatinate, but translated into English and Dutch it had a wider influence.

Westminster Catechisms (1648): There are two catechisms, the Larger and the Shorter. The Larger is a restatement of the teaching of the Westminster Confession; the Shorter, in question-and-answer form, famously beginning 'What is the chief end of man?', was very influential in Presbyterianism.

Roman Catholic

Roman Catechism (1566): The flood of Protestant catechisms prompted this Roman Catholic response, the 'Roman Catechism' of 1566, which was written in Latin. It is not in question-and-answer form but is an exposition of the creeds, sacraments, Ten Commandments and prayer for parish priests.

A Catechism of Christian Doctrine ('Penny Catechism') (1859): The basic text used by English Roman Catholics since the middle of the nineteenth century. Its roots lie in English catechisms produced by Catholic exiles on the European continent from the beginning of the seventeenth century. Although it uses quite theological language, the catechism was intended for use by the Catholic laity, including schoolchildren. It has been revised many times and has been in constant use for almost 150 years. It remains in print, although no longer costing a mere penny.

Baltimore Catechism (1891): An English-language version of the Roman Catechism for Catholic schoolchildren, commissioned by American Roman Catholic bishops meeting in Baltimore. The first version contained 100 questions, the second 421, and the third 1274. Sections covered the relationship between God and humanity, the creed, the church and the sacraments, the commandments and Christian life, and the last things. It was much used until the Second Vatican Council, when it became less popular and was succeeded by the 1992 *Catechism of the Catholic Church*.

The Catechism of the Catholic Church (1992, English 1994): This catechism follows basically the same structure as the Roman Catechism but is a volume of more than 600 pages with almost 3000 paragraphs.

Education

1. *The rite for acceptance into the order of catechumens*, which involves questions about the prospective catechumens' reasons for coming to the church and their willingness to accept the gospel. This rite also includes signing with the cross (one or more). During the catechumenate, a time of training in the Christian life, the church prays that God will strengthen the faith of the catechumens and deliver them from the power of evil.

2. *Election or the enrolment of names*. This rite, usually celebrated at the beginning of Lent, marks the final preparation for baptism. The godparents are required to affirm the faith of the catechumens. Afterwards the catechumens are formally enrolled as candidates for baptism by the inscription of their names on a list or in a book. From this point the catechumens are referred to as the 'elect'. The last three Sundays of Lent are marked by the scrutinies (rites of self-searching

and repentance), exorcism and a solemn giving and reciting back of the Apostles' Creed and Lord's Prayer.

3. *The celebration of the sacraments of initiation at the Easter vigil.* Of central importance are the baptismal washing, followed by the 'explanatory rites' (clothing with a white garment and the presentation of a baptismal candle), and confirmation with its prayer for the conferral of the Holy Spirit and anointing. If the celebrant is a priest, he will also administer confirmation.

This entire RCIA process can last for months or even years. Anglicans and Lutherans in the United States have made similar adaptations of the ancient catechumenate, although the latter church has no tradition whereby a bishop presides at the rites of Christian initiation.

The Roman Catholic Church also baptizes infants, using a separate form of service. Normally, Roman Catholics will receive their first communion at the age of seven, after their first confession. Those baptized in infancy are later confirmed by the bishop.

The 1970s saw Lutherans and Anglicans in the US attempting to restore the early unitive shape of Christian initiation, in which confirmation was the completion of Christian initiation rather than a separate rite. The baptismal rites of these churches, adaptable for both infants and adults, include a post-baptismal prayer for the sevenfold gifts of the Holy Spirit and a sign of the cross/anointing, rites traditionally associated with confirmation. At the same time these churches attempted to play down confirmation by separating it from first communion and by making it one use of an affirmation (or re-affirmation) of baptism rite.

Lutheranism

In the Evangelical Lutheran Church in America, confirmation is understood as a process of spiritual formation and education, rather than as a rite. This process culminates in a solemn affirmation of baptism that uses the same rite for marking restoration to membership and reception into membership from a non-Lutheran Church. In the Episcopal Church, confirmation is likewise preceded by a period of catechetical instruction that culminates in an affirmation of baptism. The Episcopal confirmation rite, in which a bishop is presiding minister, is also used for reception into membership and other occasions for affirmation of baptism. For these churches, confirmation is in no sense a rite of initiation, especially since neither rite grants admission to holy communion. Both churches allow children under the traditional confirmation age to receive holy communion. But neither church has a rite for first communion, since they understand baptism itself to constitute admission to the sacramental meal.

Methodism
Presbyterian churches

Methodists and Presbyterians, likewise, baptize candidates of all ages. It is expected that those baptized in infancy will receive catechetical instruction and publicly affirm their faith in a rite of 'confirmation'. In these churches, policies on first communion vary widely.

Anabaptists

Churches with Anabaptist roots (e.g., Baptists, Mennonites) baptize only those mature enough to make their own confession of faith. A rite of confirmation is unnecessary, since the personal confession of faith takes place at baptism. The preferred mode is immersion. Infants are 'dedicated' with the hope that they will eventually make a profession of faith and be baptized. It is assumed that parents of dedicated infants will raise them in the church. Usually only the baptized receive holy communion in these churches.

Most Pentecostal churches likewise baptize only confessing adults by submersion, but emphasize the importance of a second baptism in the Holy Spirit that is manifested by such charismatic gifts as speaking in tongues and healing. In these churches baptism effectively admits one to the fellowship of holy communion.

JEFFREY A. TRUSCOTT

Maxwell E. Johnson, *The Rites of Christian Initiation: Their Evolution and Interpretation*, Collegeville, MN: Liturgical Press 1999; Aidan Kavanagh, *The Shape of Baptism: The Rite of Christian Initiation*, Collegeville, MN: Liturgical Press 1978; Hughes Oliphant Old, *The Shaping of the Reformed Baptismal Rite in the Sixteenth Century*, Grand Rapids, MI: Eerdmans 1992; *The Rites of the Catholic Church: Study Edition*, Collegeville, MN: Liturgical Press 1990; E. C. Whitaker, *Documents of the Baptismal Liturgy*, revised and expanded by Maxwell E. Johnson, Collegeville, MN: Liturgical Press 2003

Inspiration

To speak of the Bible as inspired is to claim that God speaks to human beings through this collection of ancient writings and that the Bible therefore possesses a higher status and greater authority than other, non-inspired works. The key texts cited to support the inspiration of the Bible are 2 Timothy 3.16 and 2 Peter 1.21, which are taken by some scholars as evidence that the Bible claims inspired status for itself. Elsewhere in the Bible information concerning inspiration is scanty and ambivalent. Sometimes it is implied that God himself has written the text (Exodus 24.12; Deuteronomy 5.22), or that the biblical writers are merely repeating words which God has dictated to them (Ezekiel 11.5; Isaiah 48.16; 61.1; Micah 3.8; Matthew 22.43; Acts 1.16; Hebrews 3.7; cf. 2 Samuel 23.2; Mark 12.36; 2 Peter 1.21). On the other hand, there are passages in the Bible which allow individuals a degree of freedom in how they carry out the task for which God has commissioned them (Exodus 31.1–11; Judges 6.34; 11.29; 13.24–5; 1 Samuel 10.6; 16.13; Number 24.2; Hosea 9.7; Micah 3.8; Ezekiel 2.2; 11.5; Isaiah 11.2; 42.1; 61.1). Here 'inspiration' seems to reside in the divine-human relationship. There is no suggestion of God dictating a message to the biblical writer.

The Bible's limited teaching on inspiration thus raises more questions than it answers. For much of Christian history this did not present a problem, nor did the church ever feel it necessary to fix as orthodox a particular theory of inspiration. Occasionally, individual church fathers mention inspiration during their discussion of other, more pressing issues, but offer no systematic theory. In the early church the dominant view was the 'instrumental' theory of inspiration. This is heavily influenced by the Platonic view of inspiration as an ecstatic state in which the god overrides the individual's personality and rational faculties in order to communicate his message. In the Middle Ages, the 'classic' theory fused this view with ideas drawn from Aristotelianism, arguing that God is the 'principal efficient cause' who makes use of the inspired writer as the 'instrumental efficient cause' in order to compose the biblical texts.

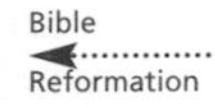
Bible Reformation

It was only with the Reformation that the doctrine of inspiration became a major theological issue. The Protestant rejection of Roman Catholic tradition, and Martin Luther's claim that scripture alone (*sola scriptura*) was the authoritative source and criterion of Christian life, thought and practice, necessitated making the status of the Bible as secure as possible. The challenge posed by the Enlightenment to the credibility of the Bible intensified this concern with the basis of biblical authority still further, for the natural sciences undermined the concept of supernatural intervention that underlies inspiration. Historical criticism of the Bible cast further doubts on God's authorship of the Bible by exposing the human character of the biblical writings.

Enlightenment

Three approaches have been developed to meet this challenge to the concept of inspiration. One approach is to abandon the concept altogether. This has been the *de facto* approach of much modern biblical criticism, and has been openly called for by some scholars on the grounds that 'inspiration' is a vague and loaded term. The other two approaches, which may be described as 'word-centred' and 'non-verbal' theories, attempt to find some way of retaining the concept of inspiration.

Biblical criticism

Word-centred theories – traditionally described as 'conservative' approaches – locate inspiration in the very words of the Bible. They received their first sustained exposition from the theologians of the era of Protestant orthodoxy (*c.*1600–1750). More recent theories of word-centred inspiration have been proposed by Louis Gaussen and, above all, by the nineteenth-century Reformed theologians of Princeton Seminary, Archibald Alexander, Charles Hodge, Archibald Alexander Hodge and Benjamin Breckinridge Warfield, at whose hands word-centred inspiration received its most sophisticated defence. Word-centred theories are characterized by their common commitment to verbal and plenary inspiration, and the view that the Bible cannot err. Verbal inspiration

Church fathers

means God does not inspire merely the biblical writers or their message but has inspired the choice of the very words they employ. Plenary inspiration means that all of scripture is inspired in the same way, a view held by both Roman Catholicism and Protestantism. The Council of Trent threatened with exclusion from the church all those who failed to acknowledge the inspiration of the biblical writings 'in their entirety and with all their parts', Council a view which was reaffirmed at the First Vatican Council. Plenary inspiration has also been vigorously defended by evangelical scholars such as Warfield and René Pache, who claim on the grounds of 2 Timothy 3.16, 1 Thessalonians 2.13, Revelation 22.18–19 and Matthew 5.18 that the doctrine is taught by the Bible. Its supporters also argue that to doubt the inspired status of a single word of the Bible is to set in motion a process that would ultimately lead to doubting the inspiration of all of scripture.

Word-centred theories are also characterized by their insistence on the inerrancy of scripture. The Roman Catholic argument is based on the divine authorship of scripture: if God is the ultimate author of scripture, then whatever is in scripture must be true. The Second Vatican Council, however, moved away from the strict inerrancy defended in earlier papal pronouncements and limited inerrancy to matters essential for faith. The Protestant concern with inerrancy is a consequence of the doctrine of *sola scriptura*. Since for Protestantism the only legitimate foundation for theology is the Bible, this foundation had to be made absolutely secure, an action which was felt to be possible only by affirming the Bible as the inerrant expression of the divine will. The inerrancy of scripture is, furthermore, guaranteed by the character of God. God cannot contradict himself, nor does God lie. Consequently, since God is ultimately the author of the Bible, it is inconceivable that the Bible could include errors. Supporters of biblical inerrancy also fear the corrosive effect of conceding the presence of a single error in the Bible. If the Bible contains one error, why should it not contain many more, including errors concerning the fundamental doctrines of the faith? The most important argument advanced by evangelical scholars in support of the inerrancy of the Bible, however, is that in such texts as 2 Timothy 3.16, 2 Peter 1.21 and John 14.26 the Bible itself claims to be inerrant.

Supporters of biblical inerrancy address the issue of Holy Spirit problematic material in the Bible by harmonizing apparently contradictory biblical passages. They also appeal to original autographs, arguing that it is not the present copies in which the inspiration of the biblical texts lies but the original documents composed by the biblical writers. Any 'errors' present in the Bible are caused by the failure of scribes to copy accurately the original texts composed by the biblical writers.

The strength of the word-based approach is its respect for the text and its consequent ability to apply inspiration to the whole of the Bible. Its weakness is that it commits the believer to accepting dubious material as divine revelation. It is also debatable whether word-centred approaches can do justice to the temperament and personality of the biblical writers, which is clearly discernible in many of the biblical texts.

Non-verbal theories situate inspiration not in the words themselves but in the message conveyed by those words or in the processes that led to the composition of the Bible. The inspiration of the biblical text is the result of this allegedly more fundamental, non-verbal inspiration, which is not tied to the precise wording of the biblical texts. There is great diversity among non-verbal theories of inspiration because of disagreement over the nature of the non-verbal dimension in which biblical inspiration is held to reside.

In the nineteenth century, William Sanday subsumed inspiration under the doctrine of providence, arguing that inspiration involves God's selection, first, of Israel as a whole and, secondly, of specific individuals as instruments to carry out his purpose. He explained the problematic material in the Bible by arguing that although the divine message shines through the biblical texts, these texts nevertheless bear the traces of the earlier, more primitive stage of the religious consciousness from which they have emerged. He also made a distinction between primary and secondary inspiration, arguing that the level of inspiration of the biblical material diminishes according to how far removed it is from primary inspiration in much the same way as light and heat grow weaker as they travel further from the sun.

At the same time, Charles Gore argued that all nations have a special vocation in God's purpose, and consequently every nation 'has its inspiration and its prophets'. Whereas other nations were inspired to develop the arts and sciences, however, Israel's inspiration was 'supernatural', and was for the purpose of achieving the 'fundamental restoration of man into that relation to God which sin had clouded or broken'. Because the biblical writers have been granted only a general insight into God's purpose, however, they are sometimes mistaken about the specific times when divine action is to take place. This lack of detailed knowledge, combined with the fact that the Spirit works through the flawed humanity of the biblical writers, accounts for the errors in the Bible.

In the twentieth century, for Austin Farrer inspiration consisted in God's bestowing an apprehension of divine mysteries on selected human beings by allowing them to participate in the divine perspective on reality. Such supernatural knowledge is recorded in the images of scripture, especially those used by Christ. We can appreciate the inspiration of the Bible only in so far as we allow ourselves to be moved by the biblical images.

William Abraham takes the human teacher as the starting point for his theory of inspiration. The teacher's inspiration of his students is a 'polymorphous concept' that takes place within all the other acts that a teacher performs, such as supervision, teaching and writing. Similarly, divine inspiration is not a single act alongside the other acts of God but is present within and expressed through God's various dealings with humankind such as leading Israel out of Egypt and raising Jesus from the dead. Just as pupils may misunderstand aspects of their teacher's lesson or may make errors in note-taking, so too it may be the case that the biblical writers have not always fully understood the divine message. However, just as a compilation of all the pupils' notes would give us a fairly accurate account of the teacher's lesson, so too the Bible – despite occasional problematic material – provides a reliable expression of the divine will.

Other non-verbal approaches situate inspiration in the community in which the biblical texts were produced. Modern biblical scholarship has made us aware that sacred writings reproduce not merely the words of an important religious figure but also the response of the community to these words. This has prompted scholars such as Friedrich Schleiermacher at the beginning of the nineteenth century and Karl Rahner and Paul Achtemeier in the twentieth to argue that inspiration is centred in the tradition of the community of faith and the application of that tradition to new situations confronting the community of faith in the present.

A recent view advanced by David Law holds that inspiration should be understood in terms of the ability of the biblical texts to mediate a sense of the presence of God to the reader here and now. It can be argued that the Bible can be understood as a collection of 'ciphers' or symbols which create a 'vision' of 'Transcendence' or God, but only when the individual enters their world by existentially appropriating them and lives his or her life in their light. The Bible's contradictions and inconsistencies constitute an essential aspect of its capacity to point to Transcendence, for they create existential ambiguity, which can be resolved only through the existential concern of the individual in his or her interaction with Transcendence.

The strength of non-verbal approaches is that they seem to account for the problematic material in the Bible more easily than word-centred conceptions of inspiration. Such material is due to the human fallibility of the biblical writers and to the historical and cultural conditions in which they were writing. However, it does not detract from the basic message underlying the biblical text. This means that non-verbal theories are committed to the gradation of scripture. Those passages which mediate a spiritual message are 'more inspired' than those which do not.

It is precisely the strength of the non-verbal approach to inspiration that constitutes its weakness, however, for the result of situating inspiration in an underlying message would seem to be that the text as such loses importance. The words are merely the vehicles for the biblical message, but the message as such is not dependent on these specific words and there may well be today more appropriate ways of expressing the contents of the biblical message. Consequently, because it is only the Bible's 'message-bearing' parts that are inspired, it becomes difficult to affirm the inspiration of the Bible as a whole.

DAVID R. LAW

William Abraham, *The Divine Inspiration of Holy Scripture*, Oxford: OUP 1981; Paul J. Achtermeier, *The Inspiration of Scripture*, Philadelphia, PA: Westminster Press 1980; Robert Gnuse, *The Authority of the Bible. Theories of Inspiration, Revelation, and the Canon of Scripture*, Mahwah, NJ: Paulist Press 1985; David R. Law, *Inspiration*, London: Continuum 2001; Bruce Vawter, *Biblical Inspiration*, Philadelphia, PA: Westminster Press and London: Hutchinson 1972

Interfaith dialogue

The relationship of Christians to peoples of other religious traditions has been an issue for the church from the very beginning. The first struggle for Christianity, as a faith born within the Jewish tradition, was to define its relationship to Judaism. Paul's letter to the Romans is a good example of an effort both to acknowledge this relationship and yet to claim freedom for the church as an emerging new faith community. But soon Christianity came into closer contact with the Graeco-Roman world and the church was itself transformed primarily into a 'Gentile' church. The writings of the first few centuries of the church provide a fascinating array of Christian approaches to other religious and philosophical traditions, marked both by accommodation and adoption and by hostility and conflict.

Other faiths

Judaism and Christianity
Paul

More important for the present situation, however, is the more recent history of the emergence of the concept and practice of 'dialogue' as a way of defining the relationship between Christians and those of other religious traditions. Dialogue also has implications for the life, ministry and theology of the churches.

Much of the church's interest in other religious traditions in the nineteenth and twentieth centuries was closely related to its missionary activities. Missionaries

Mission
Paganism

who went into Asia, Africa, the Americas and elsewhere came into contact with vibrant religious communities. These communities of faith had their own philosophies, scriptures and spiritual heritages that had been established over centuries. Missionaries responded to these heritages in many ways. Some rejected them as 'pagan' and worked towards the conversion of those who treasured them. Others attempted to study them in great depth. Few attempted to interpret the gospel in terms of the traditions that they encountered. Christianity in the mission fields developed all this in subsequent years.

p. 776
Ecumenical movement
Third World

The calling together of the world's mission agencies and missionary societies for an ecumenical World Missionary Conference in 1910 in Edinburgh marked the beginnings of a more systematic attempt to understand the Christian relationship to other religious traditions. This conference, which is also seen as the beginning of the modern ecumenical movement, was called primarily to develop a joint strategy for the evangelization of the world in that generation. At the conference, however, several missionaries, especially from Asia, challenged Christian assumptions about other religious traditions and called for a closer look at the religious life of others, if only to make the preaching of the gospel more relevant to their context.

Hinduism and Christianity

By the second World Missionary Conference (Jerusalem, 1928), scholarly interest both in comparative religion and in exploring the relationship of Christianity to other faiths had grown considerably. An influential book of the period was J. N. Farquhar's *The Crown of Hinduism* (1913), which argued that Christ fulfilled the longings and aspirations of Hinduism. In the United States the rise of liberal Protestantism was accompanied by the call to join the adherents of other religious traditions in the struggle against secularism. These developments influenced the Jerusalem conference to speak about the positive 'values' in other religious traditions and of the need to join hands with them in confronting the growing secular culture.

After the meeting, several groups felt uneasy about the 'message' that came out of the Jerusalem conference. They felt that the uniqueness of Christ and the challenge that the gospel brought to other religious traditions had been compromised. The controversy deepened with the publication in the USA of the *Report of the Commission of Appraisal of the Laymen's Foreign Mission Enquiry* (1933), edited by W. E. Hocking. This report was critical of the exclusive attitude of Christians towards other faiths and claimed that the challenge to Christian faith came not from other faiths but from anti-religious and secular movements.

This report, and the deep divisions that it caused, led the leaders of the missionary movement (which had by now been organized into the International Missionary Council) to call upon Hendrik Kraemer, a well-known Dutch missiologist, to write a preparatory volume on the biblical and theological basis for mission for the third Missionary Conference to be held in Tambaram, near Madras (1938). Kraemer's book, *The Christian Message in a Non-Christian World* (1938), following the theology of Karl Barth, argued that the gospel is in 'discontinuity' with all religious traditions, challenging them to respond to the unique and decisive act of God in Jesus Christ. Kraemer argued that all religions, including Christianity as a religious tradition, in all their heights and depths, are part of the sinful human rebellion against God. This made the proclamation of the gospel, with the challenge to obedience, the primary vocation of the church.

Kraemer's position, however, created a big controversy during and after the meeting, especially in Asia. The post-Tambaram debates, and especially the Rethinking Christianity movement in India, called for a radical review of the theology of religions that drove the missionary enterprise. This call was intensified with the post-war independence of many of the Third World nations. Now they were faced with the task of nation-building alongside neighbours of other religious traditions.

The post-Tambaram controversy eventually led the International Missionary Council and the World Council of Churches (which had come into existence in 1948) to call for a joint world-wide study on 'The World of God and the Living Faiths of Men' (*sic*). This study was undertaken with the help of study centres in many parts of the world. P. D. Devanandan, who led the study in India, argued that the Christian approach to other religious traditions needed to be considered along with people of other religious traditions. He organized meetings of people of different religious traditions at his study centre in Bangalore, India, and introduced the concept of 'dialogue' in his address to the third assembly of the World Council of Churches in New Delhi (1961). The International Missionary Council became part of the WCC at this assembly, making it possible to have a unified discussion of a subject that was becoming both deeply controversial and divisive.

The subsequent discussions and consultations within the WCC framework eventually led in 1971 to the creation of a sub-unit on Dialogue with People of Living Faiths and Ideologies within the programme structure of the WCC. Interfaith dialogue had now become an institutional reality, but the controversy would not go away. The Nairobi assembly of the WCC (1975) was a watershed in the institutionalized expression of the concern for dialogue. At this assembly the very concept and practice of dialogue was challenged fiercely as compromising the uniqueness and finality of Christ. Fears were expressed that dialogue would lead to syncretism and would compromise the missionary vocation and mandate of the church.

The issue was so divisive that after the assembly the Central Committee of the WCC called for a special consultation of all parties to the Nairobi debate at Chiang Mai, Thailand (1977). This meeting, on the theme 'Dialogue in Community', considered all dimensions of the issue and produced 'Guidelines on Dialogue with People of Living Faiths and Ideologies' that provided the basis for the continuation of dialogue within the programme structure of WCC and its promotion in the member churches. The Guidelines did not resolve all the issues. But they provided a basis for the continuation of dialogue and identified the areas in which more conversation was needed.

The Orthodox branch of the church has not developed its own positions in relation to dialogue, but Orthodox churches, as an essential part of the WCC, have been active in the discussions on dialogue within the WCC.

The differences in theological emphases between the Protestant and Roman Catholic traditions would also show in the way they related to other religious traditions, the Anglicans taking a middle way. The Protestants, placing christology at the centre of their theological approach, for instance, would argue that there was 'no salvation outside Christ'. Roman Catholic theology, with its emphasis on ecclesiology, had developed the position (in the Middle Ages) that there was 'no salvation outside the church' (*extra ecclesiam nulla salus*). But gradually this hard line was toned down in discussion about the state of those who had lived before Christ (like Abraham and Moses), and those who in our day, for no fault of their own, have had no access to the Christian message.

These concerns led to the development within the Roman Catholic Church of the concepts of 'implicit faith' or 'faith by intention', according to which one is not 'lost' simply because one was born at a particular time or place which made it impossible to become part of the historical expression of the church. This position held that the salvation offered in Christ is mysteriously available to all who seek to fulfil the will of God; it is possible to be incorporated into the church by intention.

These thoughts were developed in the 1960s by two prominent Roman Catholic thinkers, the French cardinal Jean Daniélou and the German theologian Karl Rahner. They provided the basis for the positive developments that were to take place at the Second Vatican Council (1962–5).

In 1963 Pope Paul VI created the Vatican Secretariat for Non-Christians, and on 6 August 1964 issued a significant encyclical, *Ecclesiam suam*, which emphasized the importance of positive encounter between Christians and peoples of other religious traditions. In addition, the Vatican II document 'Declaration on the Relationship of the Church to non-Christian Religions' (*Nostra aetate*), promulgated in October 1965, spelt out the pastoral dimension of this relationship. Other key documents, including 'The Dogmatic Constitution of the Church' (*Lumen gentium*) and 'The Decree on the Church's Missionary Activity' (*Ad gentes*), had important comments that pointed towards the need for dialogue with other religious traditions.

Vatican II itself, however, did not work out the meaning and implications of dialogue. This was left to the Secretariat for Non-Christians. The Secretariat (later to be named the Pontifical Council for Interfaith Dialogue) had struggles over dialogue not dissimilar to that of the WCC sub-unit on Dialogue with the Vatican Congregations for the Propagation of the Faith and the Doctrine of the Faith. Two documents, one on 'The Attitude of the Church towards the Followers of Other Religions: Reflections and Orientations on Dialogue and Mission', and the other on 'Dialogue and Proclamation', had to be worked out to allay the fears of compromise and to stabilize the official standing of the dialogue concern within the Roman Catholic Church.

Vatican

Official recognition of dialogue within both the WCC and the Vatican led to the promotion of the concern within the churches in all parts of the world. Many churches developed their own guidelines for their specific contexts. Bilateral and multilateral dialogue activities between Christians and other religious traditions at the local, national and international levels began to grow at a rapid pace. The world seemed to have become 'irreversibly interfaith'.

Salvation
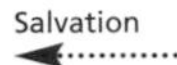

Etymologically the word dialogue, from the Greek *dia* and *logos*, means a full, thorough or exhaustive conversation. In the context of interfaith relations it might be defined as 'truth-seeking conversation'. Basically, dialogue depends on a new approach to religious plurality in which religious traditions respect one another and seek a relationship based on accepting the integrity and 'otherness' of the other. This means that each religious tradition defines itself, removing prejudices and misconceptions. Differences between dialogue partners are not treated in terms of 'right' and 'wrong' but as matters for fuller understanding and dialogue.

A number of the principles have been highlighted in the many documents and volumes that have come out on the issue. Dialogue happens not between religious traditions but between people of different faiths. The primary aim of dialogue is the building up of relationships or the creation of a 'community of communities'. Dialogue requires openness, and thrives on mutual trust. Therefore, informed understanding, critical appreciation and balanced judgements about each others' beliefs and convictions enhance the quality of dialogue. Dialogue provides the partners with the opportunity to speak openly and clearly about their own faith commitments. In this sense, it is an 'encounter of commitments' and a

Council

p. 290

Fundamentalism → Women in Christianity → Global ethic →

place for authentic witness. It should not, however, be used to manipulate one another or as a secret tool for mission. Dialogue is not intended for syncretism, for the creation of a universal religion, or for arriving at superficial consensus or false harmony. It is a truth-seeking conversation in which all partners are led to the discovery of new dimensions of truth. There is a legitimate place for mutual criticism in the exercise of dialogue. Self-criticism, mutual correction and mutual enrichment are the natural fruits of all honest and sincere dialogues.

Globalization →

While some see dialogue as an engagement primarily to build relationships, mutual understanding and harmony, others see in dialogue the potential for each of the religious traditions to grow and to be transformed as the result of its deep engagement with others. Still others see in dialogue the beginnings of the lowering of the boundary walls between religious traditions that would eventually lead to a new religious awareness and a spiritual revolution. But all agree that dialogue is not just an academic or intellectual activity; it is also a 'spirituality' and 'a way of life' that should inform all dimensions of life.

Interfaith worship

Dialogue became prominent with intentionally organized *dialogues of discourse* where persons of different religious traditions came together to converse on specific questions of doctrinal, social or of academic interest. But long before such encounters had been envisaged there had been the *dialogue of life* in places where peoples of different religious persuasions had lived together for centuries. This important dialogue is also going on in our day. S*piritual dialogues* happen where persons of different religious traditions or monastic communities meet for prayer, meditation and to practise one another's spiritual disciplines. There have also been increased instances of interfaith prayer and worship services and the emergence of interfaith liturgical material. Beyond these, there is also the *dialogue of action* in which persons come together to engage in concrete actions for justice, peace, preservation of the environment, defence of human rights and so on. Also on the increase are *institutional dialogues* in which religious traditions seek membership in interfaith organizations for the purpose of sustained dialogue and joint action.

Christology Holy Spirit Church Mission

The concept and practice of dialogue has made an impact on the Christian faith in many ways, the most important being its challenge to traditional Christian theology. Initially it called into question its theology of religions. Gradually it has also begun to make an impact on the contemporary formulations of doctrines of Jesus Christ, the Holy Spirit, the church and mission. At the pastoral level attempts are under way to give new guidance on such issues as interfaith prayer, multifaith worship, interfaith marriages and religious education in multifaith contexts.

At the same time, the enterprise of dialogue has also come under pressure over the rise of fundamentalism, militant expressions of religion, and the rise of violent conflicts in the name of religion. There are new pressures on religious traditions to engage in dialogue on such issues as the role of religion in public life, the place of women in religion and society, religion and economics, and religion and human rights. The attempts on the part of religious traditions to agree on a 'global ethic', to draw up a charter for 'united religions' (to parallel the United Nations), to co-operate in the development of an 'earth charter' and to draw up commonly agreed principles on 'human responsibilities', etc., point to the growing conviction that the future of religious traditions lies in their capacity to engage in dialogue and co-operate on common issues that affect all humankind.

More recently, there is also a growing concern about the future of religion itself in the context of rapid changes, vast population movements and the impact of a global secular culture that accompany the processes of globalization. Thus in some parts of the world the future of the religious life of humankind has itself become a subject of intense interfaith dialogue.

One striking feature of interfaith dialogue has yet to be touched on. So far women have played little part in it, nor has interfaith dialogue been of explicit concern to feminist theologians. Many dialogue practitioners are unaware that interfaith dialogue is strongly embedded in the patriarchal structures of existing religions and includes many exclusive sexist practices and deeply androcentric (male-centred) ways of thinking. Most writers on dialogue have paid scant attention to the difference that gender variables make to the practice and theology of dialogue. This issue needs to be looked at separately.

S. WESLEY ARIARAJAH

📖 *Dialogue with People of Living Faiths and Ideologies*, Geneva: WCC 1979; *Attitude of the Church towards Followers of Other Religions: Reflections and Orientations on Dialogue and Mission*, Vatican: Pontifical Council for Interreligious Dialogue 1984; S. Wesley Ariarajah, *Not Without My Neighbour: Issues in Interfaith Relations*, Geneva: WCC 1999; S. J. Samartha (ed), *Faith in the Midst of Faiths*, Geneva: WCC 1977 and *Living Faiths and the Ecumenical Movement*, Geneva: WCC 1971; R. B. Sheard, *Inter-religious Dialogue in the Catholic Church since Vatican II: An Historical and Theological Study*, Queens Town, Canada: Edwin Mellen Press 1987

Interfaith dialogue and feminism

The feminist movement exists worldwide in many different forms and shows a great deal of diversity. When defined

The World's Parliament of Religions, Chicago, 1893

inclusively, feminism can be understood as any form of opposition to the discrimination and oppression of women and the numerous efforts to overcome these and achieve the liberation, equality and full humanity of women. As such, it is a movement for women but not exclusively of women, which has widened out to more inclusive gender concerns relating to both women and men.

Feminist thought and critical gender ideas are now exercising considerable influence across religious boundaries with challenging, transformative implications for all religions. However, Christian feminist theologians do not widely engage in the study of other religions, nor are they generally closely involved in the practice of interfaith dialogue.

Nevertheless, the feminist critique of religion has been furthest advanced in Christianity and Judaism. At the same time, women from other religions – whether Hinduism, Buddhism, Islam, Sikhism, Chinese, Japanese or African religions, or native religious traditions – are now applying feminist analyses to their respective faiths. Thus a growing number of women from different faiths, together with women scholars of religion, are contributing towards a transformation of world religions by criticizing the male-centred assumptions of their scriptural and doctrinal heritage and by recovering muted female voices and experiences from the past or engaging directly in interfaith conversations. Women from different faith communities are now also increasingly in touch with each other at the grassroots level, sharing their different understandings of faith as well as their experiences of oppression and visions of liberation.

Women have participated in interfaith dialogue since the World's Parliament of Religions in 1893, but their presence and participation have been largely left unrecorded in standard historical accounts. At the time of the Chicago event, the parliament was hailed as a breakthrough for women in religion, and equal presentations by men and women were the stated aim, but this aim remained far from being realized. Closer examination of the proceedings shows that there were nineteen women plenary speakers (about 10 per cent), of whom seven were already ordained ministers, among them the Revd Antoinette Brown Blackwell, the first Christian woman to be ordained (in 1853); she could already speak about 40 years in the ministry. The women speakers came mostly from American liberal Protestant traditions, Universalists or Unitarians, but there were also important contributions from some Jewish women and an Indian woman. Alice Fletcher from Harvard University was the only speaker at the parliament who concerned herself with 'The Religion of the North American Indian', a topic of considerably more interest today than to our forebears. The historical and spiritual significance of the powerful dynamic of the then new women's movement was clearly expressed in the speeches of 1893, founded on a strong belief in the independence and power of women and the full share they must have in all areas of religion and spirituality. Yet even today we are still a long way away from their vision that 'one-half of the religious world' should enjoy equal participation and representation in religion.

Feminist theology

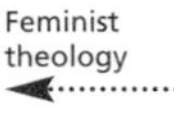

Unitarianism

To acknowledge the growing contribution of women and make it more visible, the World Council of Churches created the Ecumenical Decade of Churches in Solidarity with Women (1988–98). This led to a great deal of global dialogue among different Christian women, but interfaith dialogue was rather marginal to it. The same can be said about the dialogue among women members of the Ecumenical Association of Third World Theologians (EATWOT), although women theologians from Asia have shown greater sensitivity and interest in religious pluralism and interfaith dialogue than their sisters from other parts of the globe.

Although relatively small in numbers, women from different faiths are now coming into dialogue with each other, but an examination of contemporary interfaith dialogue from a critical gender perspective shows that feminism still remains by and large 'a missing dimension of dialogue'. The challenge of feminism for interfaith dialogue means that insights from feminist theory can be brought to bear on interfaith dialogue and the theology of religions. Women of faith around the world are frequently very active in dialogue groups at grassroots level without being visible as official spokespersons of interfaith dialogue. In fact, women from all faiths can be found in dialogue groups at local, regional, national and international levels, but their voices are not as frequently heard or fully reported in public as those of men. The official dialogue meetings convened by international interfaith organizations, large religious institutions or smaller religious and academic groups are usually still very male-dominated, with their work mostly reported by 'spokesmen'. This situation is directly connected with issues of religious leadership and representation, so far still mostly a male prerogative, and also with the historical and theological accounts given of interfaith dialogue. This raises issues of the respective authority of different voices engaged in dialogue, of representation, of styles of communication, and of major themes of dialogue pursued by women and men.

Third World ➤

Contemporary women's experience and the theoretical perspectives of women's research in religion, theology and philosophy raise fundamental questions about dialogue in an interfaith context. The challenge of gender may be the most difficult one for men in positions of religious leadership, for while it is hard enough to accept the 'other faith' in a dialogue situation, such faith is usually at least encountered through another man. As in other contexts, woman is doubly other in interfaith dialogue: she is of another faith and of a different gender, except where women of faith are in dialogue with each other, which now happens more and more among women around the world sharing their experience of faith and spirituality.

Global ethic ➤

Women's dialogue is not only of significance for the future shape of all interfaith dialogue but also raises questions for women themselves. Do feminist insights have universal application, or only a limited socio-cultural relevance? To what extent are religions a liberating force and to what extent are they an oppressive force in women's lives? The existence of this dilemma in all religions is further compounded by the fact that some women consider their own faith as mainly liberating, whereas they see other religious traditions as mostly oppressive. Much of the dialogue of women of faith with each other has occurred at the level of shared stories and experience, of experiments with worship, liturgies and spirituality, without necessarily being accompanied by critical theological reflection. At present interfaith dialogue, though continuously increasing among men and women around the globe, still remains very gender-specific and restricted. While men's dialogue has not yet appropriated the insights of women's own dialogue, the interfaith dialogue among women has not yet sufficiently called into question the male-centredness and exclusiveness of male dialogue. Thus the two different forms of dialogue provide a mutual challenge for each other in the light of greater gender awareness.

Out of the experience of interfaith encounter and dialogue a Christian theology of religions has been developed in which current discussions often revolve around the tripartite model of exclusivism, inclusivism and pluralism. Although these categories make no reference to gender, on closer examination they nevertheless turn out to be thoroughly male-centred and unsatisfactory, as they do not take women's faith experiences into account.

However, it is not only interfaith dialogue which is challenged by gender perspectives; the existence and continuing growth of such interfaith dialogue also provides a challenge for feminist reflections. The feminist theologies developed by Christian and Jewish women thinkers have not yet critically wrestled with the challenge which global religious pluralism poses for women's theology and spirituality, although some women from the so-called Third World, especially Asia, have begun to be involved in interfaith encounter and are reflecting on questions of interfaith dialogue and practice. This raises further questions of how women's interfaith dialogue challenges existing structures and institutions so that dialogue can become truly 'en-gendered'. At present there is a lack of religious diversity among participants in most feminist theological circles; there is also a lack of any theology of religious diversity and interfaith dialogue in most feminist theology; and lastly, there is a lack of feminist participants in most interfaith meetings.

Much still needs to be done to change the asymmetrical imbalance between women and men in interfaith dialogue. The 1993 global interfaith Declaration Toward a Global Ethic affirms among other things a 'commitment to a culture of equal rights and partnership between men and women' which requires the abolition of patriarchy, of the domination of one sex over another and of the exploitation of women. These goals do not exclusively apply to secular matters alone, but must be equally realized in the realm of religion. If religious institutions and religious life are to be transformed in this direction they must listen to the voices of women of faith. Religious authorities and institutions must give full space to an equal participation of women in all areas of religious life, and that includes the area of interfaith dialogue. The dynamic of feminism must transform interfaith dialogue so that it becomes truly inclusive of religious and gender diversities and fully affirms the experiences of women. It also must become ecumenical in a truly global sense by engaging seriously with religious experiences outside Western culture, especially those of the great Asian wisdom traditions.

URSULA KING

📖 Paula M. Cooey, William R. Eakin and Jay B. McDaniel (eds), *After Patriarchy. Feminist Transformations of the World Religions*, Maryknoll, NY: Orbis 1991; Rita M. Gross and Rosemary Radford Ruether, *Religious Feminism and the Future of the Planet. A Buddhist-Christian Conversation*, London and New York: Continuum 2001; Hans Küng and Karl-Josef Kuschel (eds), *A Global Ethic. The Declaration of the Parliament of the World's Religions*, London: SCM Press 1993; Maura O'Neill, *Women Speaking. Women Listening. Women in Interreligious Dialogue*, Maryknoll, NY: Orbis 1990

Interfaith dialogue and spirituality

Theological discussions about the interrelationship of the various religions tend to concern themselves with comparative understandings of God, revelation, salvation, the uniqueness and universality of Christ and Christianity or the nature of the church and universal truth claims, and not so much with spiritual growth and transformation.

Yet spiritual growth and renewal take place when people of different faiths encounter each other and reflect in dialogue together on the spiritual meaning of their beliefs and practices, and even more when they share in interfaith worship, prayer and meditation, meet in retreats, or share in depth some of the experiences and struggles of their lives.

A spirituality for interfaith dialogue is at present emerging with growing clarity and strength. We are only in the beginning phases of this movement towards such a spirituality, which is still in the process of being born, but it will grow and eventually assume greater fullness and maturity. That means that it is possible only to discern its direction and dynamic rather than present a definite description and complete picture.

Spirituality

Spirituality is difficult to define. Many different definitions have been proposed, some of which are explicitly religious and linked to a particular faith whereas others are much wider and include interfaith as well as secular meanings. For many centuries spirituality held a special place in Christian theology and practice; linked to the human search for holiness and perfection, it meant above all the search for God. Today, though, the concept of spirituality has been cut loose from its Christian theological roots and is now universally applied across different religious traditions, even though many non-Western languages possess no directly corresponding word for 'spirituality'. Instead of being related to particular theological doctrines, spirituality is now primarily understood anthropologically as a potential dimension latent within every human being, whether young or old, of whatever social and cultural background. This potential requires development, nurture and growth; it involves an in-depth exploration into what it truly means to become a fully human being. Thus spirituality is seen as intrinsic to the human subject, as an inner dimension relating to a general search for meaning, wholeness, self-transcendence, in relation and connectedness with others. The spiritual can be linked to all human experiences, but it has a particularly close connection with the imagination, with human creativity and resourcefulness, with relationships – with ourselves, with others, with God or with some other ultimate centre of all realities. Spirituality can be connected with a sense of celebration and joy, with adoration and surrender, but also with struggle and suffering.

Suffering

Though spirituality is a perennial human concern, its historical expressions, practices and teachings vary from culture to culture and are dependent on different times and places. Like all other human experiences, spirituality exists primarily in the plural – Christian spirituality is different from Jewish, Muslim, Hindu or Buddhist spirituality and that of other religions, and a Christian spirituality for interfaith dialogue will again be different from all of these.

God
Revelation
Salvation
Church

Spirituality can be understood in three different ways: as lived experience and a pattern of life (or discipline); as the spiritual teachings that grow out of this (for example, counsels on how to lead a good life; on finding liberation or salvation; or how to gain holiness and perfection); as the systematic, comparative and critical study of spiritual experiences and teachings of different religions. The development of a spirituality for interfaith dialogue is occurring in all of these three dimensions.

Interfaith worship

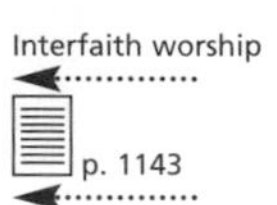
p. 1143

Spiritual experience and patterns of life emerging within and out of interfaith dialogue are still comparatively rare, since believers of different faiths engaged in the experimental and experiential process of dialogue are, numerically speaking, still very few. Immersed in

Judaism and Christianity
Hinduism and Christianity
Buddhism and Christianity
Islam and Christianity
Japanese religions and Christianity

a new venture, they are exploring a 'spirituality across borders' and discovering new paths through a deep personal engagement not only with their own faith but also with that of others, including encounters with people belonging to such different religious traditions as Judaism, Hinduism, Buddhism, Islam or Japanese spirituality, for example. Entering others' spiritual worlds and practices can lead to experiences of richness and fruitful convergence, but also to new questions and uncertainties. Wesley Ariarajah has identified 'dialogue and spirituality: can we pray together?' as one of the pressing issues of interfaith relations. The objections to interfaith prayer and worship are many, including the fear of eclecticism and syncretism, but as Ariarajah convincingly argues, this is not an academic question but is related to the urgent practical concern to find an authentic spirituality for our time, a holistic spirituality which can heal and transform individuals and communities by overcoming some of our differences.

A new spirituality nourished by interfaith dialogue has perhaps been furthest developed in the dialogue between Christians and Buddhists, and this is also true of the dialogue among women of different faiths. A wide variety of Buddhist teachings and practices, particularly the different forms of Buddhist meditation, have deeply influenced Christians from diverse denominational backgrounds across the world. The number of people who experience a 'double belonging' and can find a spiritual home in more than one faith is slowly but steadily growing.

Important individual Christians who have pioneered interfaith spirituality in their own lives have been among others Swami Abhishiktananda (a French Benedictine, Dom Henri le Saux, 1910–1873, who took on an Indian  identity), the British Benedictine Bede Griffiths (1906–93) and the American Trappist monk Thomas Merton (1915–68). Their lives and those of other interfaith pioneers have influenced many people to explore the spiritual depths of a faith other than their own.

Growing out of these experiences we now possess a growing number of teachings and counsels relating to spiritual advice drawn from more than one religious tradition. This is a rather fluid body of knowledge that is informally transmitted through reading or teaching in small groups. To give a few examples: Buddhist and Christian spiritual practices have been discussed for many years in the journal *Buddhist-Christian Studies*, reflecting insights and experiences gained through dialogue groups and encounters between Christians and Buddhists. The writings of the Sri Lankan Jesuit Aloysius Pieris have exercised a wide influence on seeking an appropriate spirituality for interfaith dialogue, as have those of the Spanish Indian Raymond Panikkar. The British Jesuit Michael Barnes has explored the sharing of the practices of prayer, meditation and yoga as well as the activity of compassion between people of different faiths in his book *God East and West*. Shared spiritual experiences and practices are described in several publications on Hindu-Christian, Jewish-Christian, Muslim-Christian and other interfaith dialogues. Such an interfaith spirituality arising from different forms of encounter and dialogue – whether that of a shared life, joint action, theological reflection or religious experience – possesses the characteristics of openness and humility, of willingness to listen, learn and change, an element of patience and attentiveness, of discovery and celebration, but at times it also includes experiences of frustrating incompleteness with only fragmentary glimpses of a greater wholeness which still needs to be searched for and achieved. Individuals and groups engaged in interfaith spirituality share the experience of relating to something greater than themselves, learn to create bridges across their distinct differences and to give to each other the gift of love and common purpose.

The Indian theologian Samuel Rayan understands spirituality as linked to openness and what he calls 'response-ability'. This term does not denote accountability, but the ability to respond to the many different dimensions of reality, to different things, events and people. This includes the ability to respond to the realities of other faiths and their spiritual horizons and insights. We have to cultivate a deep inner awareness to develop such openness. Only then can we discover the mysteries, meanings and revelatory moments of other faiths where the power of the Spirit breaks through again and again into the continuing stream of our historical brokenness and becoming. In Rayan's view, the more open we are, the more spiritual we are; the more realities to which we are open, the greater the spirituality; the greater the depths and the profounder the meanings of reality to which we are open, the more authentic the spirituality.

The last dimension concerns systematic study and reflection on interfaith spirituality. This occurs today in a global community with unprecedented means of communication that are helping us to evolve a new relational consciousness in the human community. On the one hand this means that we can begin to see the spiritual heritage of all faiths as common to all humanity; on the other hand the very fact of the differences of our faiths, our spiritual traditions and disciplines implies a 'dialogical imperative', the very necessity of communication and dialogue. The different faith communities are now making their spiritual resources globally available and accessible. An excellent example of this is the large series on World Spirituality under the general editorship of Ewert Cousins; others are the ongoing work of the Parliament of the World's Religions and of the United Religions Initiatives.

After the end of colonial rule and of Christian missions from a position of superiority, interfaith encounter can now occur in the context of an equal partnership in dialogue. The contemporary practice of dialogue is itself an event of religious significance, and that is why it is particularly important for the further development of spirituality. Encounter with people of other faiths and the serious engagement in interfaith dialogue can be experienced as an appeal, an invitation, a challenge, a magnificent opportunity to take the spiritual uniqueness of others seriously and appreciate their differences. Interfaith dialogue makes people first discover the pluralism of spiritualities themselves – and that can be a sobering, a difficult, but also a strengthening discovery. But it also makes them find new paths and lands of the mind and soul; it makes them experience different traces and touches of the Spirit which can spiritually uplift and strengthen us.

The great faith traditions of the world are not isolated fortresses to be conquered but homes of the Spirit where the whole human being can be nurtured and strengthened. If we do not look at religions exclusively from the outside, seeing nothing more than defective institutional settings and structures, but discover their deeper spiritual resources, we become aware that all the spiritual traditions together present us with immensely rich and diverse spiritual streams from which we can all drink. Our spiritual heritage is part of the human history on this globe, but it also is so much more – a revelation of an inexhaustible divine ocean of love, compassion and mercy, and a promise of the possibility of human dignity and wholeness. We can also see that the ethical codes of different faiths can help us construct what has been called a 'global ethic' for conflict resolution, for the overcoming of violence, poverty and inequality, and for learning the art of peacemaking. To develop an appropriate spirituality for interfaith dialogue may well be the great spiritual event of our time, full of the greatest significance for the future well-being of the human community.

URSULA KING

📖 S. Wesley Ariarajah, *Not Without My Neighbour. Issues in Interfaith Relations*, Geneva: WCC, Risk Book Series 1999; Michael Barnes, *God East and West*, London: SPCK 1991; Ewert Cousins (ed), *World Spirituality: An Encyclopedic History of the Religious Quest*, New York: Crossroad, 1985– and London: Routledge & Kegan Paul 1986– ; Rita M. Gross and Rosemary Radford Ruether, *Religious Feminism and the Future of the Planet. A Buddhist-Christian Conversation*, London and New York: Continuum 2001; Aloysius Pieris, *Love Meets Wisdom. A Christian Experience of Buddhism*, Maryknoll, NY: Orbis 1988

Interfaith worship

The growing interaction between members of the world religions at all levels of society has increasingly raised the question whether people of different faiths can or should pray together. Especially in Western society this is a new issue to which few churches have given much attention, although it is relevant both to a variety of civic and public occasions and to family life. In most cases, practice is well in advance of thinking about interfaith worship, so that there is now a need for more reflection to help Christians to decide whether, when or where it is appropriate.

It is usual to distinguish between public interfaith forms of worship and more personal occasions, for example, ceremonies to mark the marriage of two people who belong to different religions. There are also communities, like colleges or conferences, whose members belong to different faiths but wish to give a religious expression to their life together and their commitment to shared values. There are many public occasions when people of different religions want to join together, for example after a tragedy such as the attack on the World Trade Center on 11 September 2001; to pray for peace, as at the Days of Prayer at Assisi convened by Pope John Paul II; or to mark a special occasion such as the millennium. Occasions will vary from country to country depending on 'church-state' and interfaith relationships.

Besides the difference between public and private occasions, broad distinctions can be made between several types of interfaith worship. Members of one faith may invite guests of one or more other faiths to attend their usual act of worship. The guests' presence may be acknowledged just by a special greeting, or a visitor may be asked to read from his or her scriptures, say a prayer or perhaps speak. Christians might choose hymns centred on God rather than on Christ to make it easier for Jews and Muslims to participate. If the service is a eucharist, there are different views about inviting members of other faiths who may wish to receive communion. Christians invited to other places of worship will normally observe traditional practices such as removing shoes before entering a temple or mosque, or covering the head before going into a synagogue or gurdwara. One or more of the visitors may be invited to speak and perhaps to share in the ritual, especially at Shinto or Native American ceremonies. Visitors may be given food offerings which are customarily shared among devotees (*prasad*), although some Christians see this as partaking in food offered to idols, which Paul discouraged (1 Corinthians 8).

Global ethic ◀⋯⋯
Eucharist
Paul

The most common forms of interfaith worship are those in which members of each faith in turn offer prayers, readings or devotional songs – perhaps in alphabetical or historical order of the religions. Prayers specific to a particular tradition are offered in the presence of people of other faiths, but no prayers are said together. This clearly ensures the distinctiveness of each faith tradition, but besides making the occasion over-long, may emphasize difference rather than commonality, leaving those present observers rather than participants. At such 'serial interfaith observances' people are said to 'be together to pray' rather than 'praying together'. Such events evade theological questions about the relation of religions to each other.

Initiation ➤

Death ➤

Another form of interfaith worship is designed as a united service. The various readings, prayers and devotional songs are linked together round a central theme, such as peace, protection of the environment or celebration of a special event. Participants may be invited to join in an affirmation or act of commitment, to say prayers together and to sing well-known hymns. Symbolic actions to express unity may be introduced, such as giving everyone a flower or a lighted candle. Critics say these liturgies obscure the distinctiveness of religions. The venue may give a special character to the event, as for instance in the case of the Commonwealth Day Act of Witness held each year in Westminster Abbey. Many temples, however, are not designed for congregational worship. Some argue that interfaith worship should be in a neutral building, but this may deprive it of colour and character.

Unitarians ➤

Yet another form of worship could be described as 'universalist', a term which would apply to some services of the Bramo Samaj and the Unitarian Universalists, who regard all religions as human searchings for the divine rather than authoritative revelation. Such an approach has considerable appeal today for those who see themselves as 'spiritual' but do not identify with a particular faith community.

The most common personal occasion for interfaith services is marriage. It is no longer unusual for the couple being married to belong to different religions. Traditionally most faith communities have been unsympathetic to this, and some have rejected those who are said to have 'married out'. Others have encouraged the woman to convert or insisted that the children be brought up in the man's faith. Many faith communities have been reluctant to bless such marriages or to provide any religious ceremony. This, however, is changing slowly but inevitably, as religious diversity comes to be recognized as part of the contemporary landscape in many countries. Marriage law is different in each country. The situation is most complex in countries like Britain, where the religious and legal ceremonies may be combined. Where the legalities are a matter for civic authorities, there is greater freedom to devise an appropriate liturgy, which may be a beautiful and inspiring celebration. When one partner is a Christian, couples may hold this in church; others will think a neutral venue is more appropriate.

Marriage

The faith identity of children of a 'mixed marriage' may be a problem for the parents. A simple service of thanksgiving or naming, which includes material from two religions, may be devised, but rites of initiation presume membership of a particular faith community. Parents may therefore leave it to children to make a decision when they are older.

At death, it is normal for the funeral to be in accordance with the dead person's own religion, but surviving partners may want ministers of their religion to participate in the service.

Interfaith worship for voluntary groups will vary enormously. Those attending a dialogue conference may feel an important dimension of religious life is missing if there is no opportunity for worship or silence. It is common, therefore, for each of the faiths represented to lead a time of prayer or meditation.

Although interfaith worship is still new to many people, it dates back more than a century. The 1893 World's Parliament of Religions had times of silence, and the opening session included some hymns and an invitation to all present to join in the Lord's Prayer. Gandhi included hymns and readings from many traditions at his ashram's evening prayers. In Britain, the initiative was taken by Unitarians, and a collection of services was published in 1924. In 1953, the World Congress of Faiths held an all faiths' service to mark Queen Elizabeth II's coronation and has continued to hold such services.

Interfaith worship is not intended to replace a community's regular worship. It is for special occasions. Its different patterns reflect the varied theological views of Christians towards other religions. Some Christians may not take part in any such liturgies for fear that the uniqueness of Jesus Christ may be compromised. Others who recognize that God's Spirit is present in all religions may participate in some services but fear that services which are centred on a particular theme or are universalist obscure the centrality of Christ. Yet other believers who hold that the mystery of the divine transcends all creeds and language may find a form of worship that consists in a series of prayers, readings and songs rather sterile, and prefer a united service which emphasizes the common humanity of all God's children. They often claim that interfaith worship is a symbol of hope in a divided world and an effective way for people of different faiths to make a joint commitment to seeking peace and justice, to serving the needy and protecting the planet.

MARCUS BRAYBROOKE

Jean Potter and Marcus Braybrooke (eds), *All in Good Faith: A Resource Book for Multi-faith Prayer*, London: World Congress of Faiths 1997; Paul Puthanangady (ed), *Sharing Worship, Communication in Sacris,*

Bangalore: National Biblical Catechetical and Liturgical Centre 1988

Internet

The internet has revolutionized human communication like nothing else since the invention of printing. The modern telegraph, telephone, radio and computer have been integrated into a new medium unlike any other. It means much more than connections between computers. It also means connections between people, and the access those people have to stored information. The internet is as much a collection of communities as a collection of technologies, and its success largely depends on satisfying community needs.

Development of the underlying technologies began around 1978. Commercial connections to the internet started about 1992, and it is now dominated by commercial interests. The internet is so named because it is an interconnection of networks. It links many small groups or individuals to form a single large group. What is unique about the internet is the potential global reach, and global compatibility.

However, that reach is still limited in practice. In November 2003, less than 11% of the world's population had internet access. 62% of North Americans and 28% of Europeans (58% in the UK) were internet users, while in Africa only 1% of the population had access. In two major African countries with significant Christian populations, Nigeria and Uganda, the figures were only 0.1% and 0.2%. Within Latin America and the Caribbean the average was 7%, in Asia 6%, Oceania 2%, and in the Middle East 5%, although there were very wide variations between individual countries. The UK had the fifth highest number (34 million) of internet users in the world, after the USA – 185 million, China, Japan and Germany (see www.internetworldstats.com for current details).

The reduction of this global 'digital divide' is a major challenge which the United Nations and the International Telecommunications Union is trying to meet. Seven of the ten countries with the largest Christian populations, i.e. Brazil, Mexico, China, Russia, the Philippines, India and Nigeria have low figures for internet use. Growth rates in all continents are, however, extremely high, averaging 90% per year.

After two decades, the internet is becoming a commodity service, and its use has accelerated with the widespread adoption of browsers and World Wide Web technology. The internet will continue to evolve at the same high speed as the computer industry. It now provides new services such as audio and video streams, and supports portable devices which make possible internet access without wires. Underlying network technologies are also changing, e.g. broadband residential access and use of satellites. The most pressing question is not technological, but how the process of change will be managed, given the proliferation of global stakeholders and the need for large investments. If the internet stumbles, it will not be for lack of technology, vision or motivation.

Communication

Why is internet communication different?
'Online communication', sending and receiving electronic mail (email), making and reading web pages, is not like any medium that has ever existed before, and trying to understand it fully by analogy will not work. It is more instructive to look at the specific ways in which online communication differs from earlier media.

Language. Since the invention of the telephone, spoken communication has been mostly informal. Online communication returns us to the world of written informal language of previous centuries, when people wrote frequent letters to each other. Our customary informal speech characteristics are hard to translate to writing. There are no nonverbal cues. Inflections are difficult. You cannot change the meaning of a sentence by the way you pronounce words.

Speed. Online communication is immediate. You can write a message, send it, and get a reply back in a few minutes. Although there are occasionally delays, it is rare for an electronic message to take as long as the fastest postal letter. With electronic messaging, you can reach the other side of the earth as fast as the house next door.

Interactivity. Online text communication is not interactive. In face-to-face communication, if you are saying something unpleasant and you see a look of pain on someone's face, you may stop, or even change what you say. On the telephone you can hear changes in breathing or exclamations. These nonverbal cues are useful. When you write an email you cannot know how it will be received, and once you have sent it, you can't take it back.

Audience. Telephones are normally one-to-one. Radio, television and newspapers are one-to-many media, but unless it is your station or newspaper, you cannot control what is said. Online communication is a one-to-many medium in which anyone who participates at all can talk as well as listen. The property of one sender, many recipients combined with anyone can send is the most significant of the internet's differences. You can reach hundreds of thousands of people – if you can get their attention.

Nonlinearity. Ordinary speaking and printed documents are fundamentally linear. You start at the beginning and when you get to the end you stop. Online communication, especially the web, supports a style of writing called hypertext, in which you can write a short summary and provide links to more information without distracting the reader who does not want more detail. Writing well in hypertext is a distinctive skill.

Privacy. If you show a paper document to one unauthorized person, the extent of damage is relatively light. In online communication you cannot do this without giving away a copy of it, which in turn gives others the ability to give copies away. Any electronic leak of private information can rapidly become global. It is very difficult to keep something secret on the internet.

Permanence. Unlike telephone systems, online messaging stores everything; it requires a conscious act to erase a stored message, and not just your copy of the message, but the sender's copy, and possibly many others made at intermediate points. You should assume that every message you have ever sent is still somewhere.

Authenticity. A copy of electronic information is indistinguishable from the original. There is no intrinsic meaning to 'original'. When you get information, it is not always easy to be certain of the sender's identity or that the information is authentic. Modern techniques to detect forgeries, like digital signatures, exist but are not widely used.

Competing for attention. The person reading what you write is often alone and yet you probably do not have his or her complete attention. People have other options, and if you don't hold their attention they will go away. If you are not brief, most will ignore you, though by proper use of hypertext techniques it is possible to be both brief and detailed at the same time.

Respect for authority. The internet has a certain anti-authoritarian flavour to it. The design of the infrastructure neither requires nor welcomes central control. The concepts of national sovereignty, state and governmental power are startlingly vague in this context. National laws about what people can and cannot say vary widely and enforcement is problematic.

Social issues

When using the internet, people behave differently from when they are doing other things. The internet also offers new opportunities for misbehaving. It is crucial to be aware of some of these.

Stereotyping and masquerading. Many stereotypes are keyed to appearance. In online communication, you form your sense of 'who they are' based on purely intellectual and verbal cues. It is easy to use online communication to deceive people about who you are. No one need know your age, sex, race, nationality or any other aspect of you that doesn't come out in your writing. This is very liberating to people who know how to take advantage of it. Conversely, it can be very dangerous, for example with children. A widely-circulated cartoon from *The New Yorker* in July 1993 shows two dogs talking in front of a computer screen; one tells the other, 'On the internet, nobody knows you're a dog.'

Sense of safety. From the earliest days of computers, psychological studies showed that people were usually more willing to type secrets into a computer than they were to tell somebody in person. Many people feel safer using written online messages than using the telephone or talking in person.

Intimacy and inhibition. Again, from the earliest days researchers have discovered that most people are less inhibited online than in spoken language. The immediacy of the medium encourages people to respond without thinking, and nearly every user of online communication has experienced the desire to write regrettable things that they wouldn't want published in the newspaper.

Accountability. One by-product of all this is that cowardly acts are easier. Saying something offensive, and the online equivalent of running away, is too easy, and such remarks are quite often made on the internet. Experienced users of online communication tend either to develop the ability to ignore such offensive messages or else to drift away from visiting such internet venues.

Community. In years past, it was difficult to form strong communities unless people lived near one another. Telephony and broadcasting did not often do a very effective job of forming geographically-dispersed communities because they were either one-to-one, or else did not give very many people the opportunity to speak. Communities linked by online communication can be geographically diffuse and more specialized. Groups form regularly around mutual interests; all the participants need to share beyond the interest that defines their group is internet access and a common language. Online Christian groups of all kinds have formed (for example, Yahoo Groups, www.groups.yahoo.com, has over 5000 listed as Christian), and some of these have developed into real and lasting communities of value to the participants.

Spurious authority. Some people mistake what they read and learn about on the internet for the kind of knowledge that comes only from first-hand experience. The internet is not a fully adequate substitute for personal interaction, through face-to-face discussion with real people, preferably in *their* own habitat and cultural context.

Disruption. Every hour spent communicating online is an hour not spent doing something else.

Christians on the internet

Christian usage reflects the restricted geography of internet users. North American Christians currently dominate, with other English-speaking countries coming second, non-Anglophone Western Europeans third, and the Global South is scarcely represented as yet. This balance will not change much over the next decade unless the global 'digital divide' is significantly closed. It is not surprising therefore that so far the major Christian voices on the internet use the English language and reflect the theological balance of American Christianity, with strong representation of Protestant and often conservative viewpoints.

Thousands of local church congregations, regional church judicatories (dioceses, presbyteries, etc.) and national or international religious bodies (from the Vatican, www.vatican.va, to the Russian Orthodox Patriarchate, www.russian-orthodox-church.org.ru, and the Southern Baptist Convention, www.sbc.net) use email extensively in their daily operations and have 'official' websites describing their beliefs and reporting their official policies and activities. More often than not, these sites are aimed primarily at keeping their own existing members well informed; they are not really designed to attract outsiders to take part, or non-believers to become Christians.

Websites of official church institutions (like religious newspapers and magazines which are owned by official bodies) can of course be expected to promote the official policies of those bodies and to express the views of denominational church leaders. These positions may not always be shared by all, or even by a majority of, church members. Indeed, members of a particular Christian congregation do not necessarily share all the views of their local pastor.

Because it is so easy to do, many individuals or minority groups now have websites. The recent development of 'weblogs' (blogs), personal journals, usually offering the opportunity for personal comments by readers, published as web pages via 'blogging' applications requiring no technical skills of any user, has led to a huge growth in the expression of personal opinions. Many weblogs have a religious orientation, including thousands written by individual Christians, both clerical and lay. See for example *Blogs for God*, www.blogs4god.com. Some of these sites promote a single issue or an extreme viewpoint and thus are able to gain a much wider audience for such views than is possible by other means.

There are also privately owned multifaith sites such as the huge www.beliefnet.com and major academic websites devoted to Christian theology, such as www.ccel.org, www.divinity.library.vanderbilt.edu/lib or www.library.yale.edu/div/electext.htm.

Many influential Christian websites are outside the control of official church bodies, owned for example by church publications such as *Christianity Today*, www.christianitytoday.com, or the *Church Times*, www.churchtimes.co.uk, or by non-profit voluntary groups such as *Ekklesia*, www.ekklesia.co.uk, *Christians on the Internet*, www.coin.org.uk, *Ship of Fools*, www.ship-of-fools.com or *Anglicans Online*, www.anglicansonline.org. Many of these sites also sponsor open discussion groups using email or bulletin boards. These give excellent opportunities for the expression of a diversity of viewpoints.

There is a 'virtual church' out there with parish web pages, special interest groups, diocesan public relations machines, blogs, newsgroups, mailing lists and chatrooms. It can be easy, when we encounter this, to mistake it for the real thing and to reach misguided conclusions on the basis of these virtual encounters. While much can be learned from this, it all has limitations, because of its spurious authority.

This caution applies to secular press reports just as much as to information from 'official' church websites. For example, in America a far larger proportion of the population will be found worshipping in some church every Sunday than will be found in Australia. But it would be unusual for American newspapers to report routinely on bishops' Christmas and Easter sermons. In Australia many more people play sport on a Sunday morning than go to church. Australia (like most of Western Europe) is a much more secular society than the USA. But it is quite normal for Australian newspapers to report regularly on sermons of bishops and to ask them for comments on matters of social concern. This does not indicate that Australians are more religious, but only that the Australian secular media has a different outlook on religion from its American counterpart.

Religion is one of the largest areas of internet use: in January 2004 the search engine Google had indexed over 29 million pages containing the word 'Christian'.

The most detailed survey so far of religious internet use is a 2001 survey of North Americans (see www.pewinternet.org for details) which found that 3 million people a day (and in total 28 million Americans) had used the internet to get religious and spiritual information. This was a quarter of all American users – more people than had used internet dating services.

Some more detail from the survey shows that 91% of them were Christians, compared to 71% of the American population. They were more devout in practising their religion than most Americans. They rated internet use as less important than personal prayer, communal worship or community service. Their most popular uses of the internet were to discover more information about their own faith, or about social issues, to email prayer requests, to download religious music, or to buy books or other religious materials. Nearly a third subscribed to one or more electronic mailing lists of a religious kind. A majority had a favourite website affiliated with their own religious denominational group.

Religious internet users appear to differ from many secular communities in that they do not use the internet much to find a new religious organization to join, but rather to connect better with the one to which they already belong. Nearly two-thirds believed that the internet provides easier access to religious information than is readily available offline, and half had sought information on faiths other than their own. Of particular interest is the number (44%) who found that access to prayer and devotional materials was easier online. Those who were not active members of a congregation relied on the internet to find information that others would normally discover within their offline faith community. Purely social activity online (chat rooms, games, dating agencies) among people of like-minded religious views was of much less interest. Word-of-mouth offline was the major way that people learned of good internet sites to visit.

Middle Ages

Over one third believed that the internet has a 'mostly positive' effect on the religious life of other people, and nearly two-thirds that it encouraged religious tolerance. However, more than half thought that the internet made it 'too easy' for heretical or cult-inspired groups to promote themselves in harmful ways.

Although few at present use the internet as a substitute for a physical church, predictions have been made by another American survey organization (see www.barna.org) that within the next ten years 10% of Americans, largely the young, may rely solely on the internet for their religious experience. These millions of people will include some who have never belonged to any Christian body; but many who will have dropped out of traditional church activities may find that the internet acts for them as a refuge from a 'bricks and mortar' church. There is no reason to suppose that this behaviour will be confined to North America, although the percentages may be less in other areas.

Papacy

SIMON SARMIENTO

Investiture Controversy

In its most precise meaning, the term 'Investiture Controversy' refers to the conflict in the Western church in the late eleventh and early twelfth centuries over the question whether lay rulers had the authority to bestow upon a new bishop or abbot the ring and staff (crosier) that were the signs of his office. But its significance goes far beyond what that apparently technical question itself may seem to imply. The controversy stands both as a crucial episode in the history of religious authority and as a symbol of fundamental questions about the relation of the 'spiritual' and the 'temporal' that are still with us.

Authority

The complex background to the controversy cannot be described here in detail, but two elements should be mentioned: the so-called 'proprietary church' and the claims of the German kings to rule by divine right. The term 'proprietary church' refers to a practice that had developed after the demise of imperial Roman government in the early Middle Ages, especially in the German states, whereby a lay person could own a church or monastery and accordingly bequeath it to heirs, give it as dowry or otherwise dispose of it, just like any other property. The system of the proprietary church stood in some tension with the ancient principle of the jurisdiction of bishops, but it proved tenacious, especially within the chaotic social conditions that prevailed after the break-up of the Carolingian empire. As for German ideas of kingship, these had always asserted the king's chosenness of God and gave royalty itself a sacral character. It followed naturally that the king should have rights and responsibilities over the church. The kings of the Ottonian and Salian dynasties in the tenth and eleventh centuries therefore easily assumed the right to nominate bishops and abbots and to preside over episcopal elections. Such evident royal control, along with the fact of the 'proprietary church' itself, suggests that by the mid-eleventh century the church in German areas – and indeed this was true in the West generally – had come under the control of powerful laity.

The Investiture Controversy resulted from the challenge mounted by reform-minded clerics and especially by the papacy against such lay control of the church. The beginnings of the controversy came in the pontificate of Leo IX (1048–54), who moved against what he and the other reformers saw as the two major evils of simony – that is, the 'sale' of ecclesiastical office, even indirectly or in return for gifts rather than money – and clerical marriage (nicolaitism), which embroiled clerics in kinship ties. At this early stage in the reforms the Pope had the support of the German king, who in fact had helped ensure his election; and Leo's immediate successors continued these moderate reform policies. But within the papal curia more radical ideas were already emerging, which began to be translated into action later, after 1073, when the archdeacon Hildebrand (a figure of influence at Rome since the time of Leo) became Pope as Gregory VII.

In 1075 Gregory prohibited the investiture of clerics by lay persons altogether, in effect fundamentally challenging not only the system of the proprietary church but also the German kings' claims to rule by direct divine mandate. In the same year, in a document called *Dictatus papae*, he declared that only the Pope could depose or reinstate bishops, and furthermore that the Pope possessed the authority to depose emperors. For Gregory, therefore, the spiritual authority that resided in the church not only was the reserve of clerics, and was thus to be kept from the laity, but also, if necessary, was to be asserted over kings, whose authority was temporal and thus inferior. It was not long before Gregory came into open conflict with the German king Henry IV. He excommunicated and deposed Henry in 1076, for interference in the election of the Bishop of Milan, but granted absolution to him in 1077 after the king, having lost the support of the German bishops and of some of the nobility, came before the Pope himself and did penance, in a famous scene in which he stood barefoot in the snow at the gates of the fortress of Canossa at the base of the Apennines. But by the time Gregory excommunicated him again, in 1080, Henry had reconsolidated his power, and this time responded to Gregory by setting up an antipope and mounting a military attack on Rome, forcing Gregory into exile, where he died in 1085. In spite of this humiliation, however, the issues that Gregory raised continued to demand attention, such that in the ensuing decades legal compromises had to be made in the German empire as well as in France and England between the claims of temporal rulers to intervene in ecclesiastical affairs and the church hierarchy's now insistent assertion of its own prerogatives. And for more than 200 years after Gregory's death, indeed until the French monarchy began to contain the papacy in Avignon (1305), the popes continued to articulate his claims for papal authority over both church and world.

What is the long-term importance of the Investiture Controversy? In spite of the intentions of its protagonists – and perhaps to the horror of a pope like Gregory VII, had he been able to perceive the future – we can see that the controversy marked precisely, for better or worse, a crucial moment in the undermining of a unified, theocratic, world-view in Western Christianity. Whereas Islam, for instance, has preserved such a world-view, the Christian West has seen over many centuries a relentless process of bifurcation between the spiritual and the temporal, between the secular and the religious. We may think of the modern separation of church and state as the landmark event in this process, yet the Investiture Controversy played a crucial role in setting the process going. In spite of the fact that our society depends for its very existence on the bifurcation of secular and religious, on the cordoning-off of religious faith, that is, as something from which other aspects of public life are to be protected, nonetheless, as Gregory VII himself knew, such a notion is as foreign to the central insights of Christianity as to those of any of the other great religions.

JOHN W. COAKLEY

📖 Uta-Renate Blumenthal, *The Investiture Controversy: Church and Monarchy from the Ninth to the Twelfth Century*, Philadelphia: University of Pennsylvania Press 1988; Gerd Tellenbach, *Church, State and Christian Society at the Time of the Investiture Contest*, Brighton: Harvester Press 1970

Islam and Christianity

For more than fourteen centuries Christians and Muslims have faced the reality of living and interacting with each other. The responses of each community have been guided religiously by their own scriptures and theological positions, and practically by the reality of conquests and the shifting tides of political power. Often at the same time as religious spokespersons have been challenging the nature of the other faith and even its right to exist, cultural, commercial and personal relationships have been developed and maintained. Today as changing political, economic and social realities result in growing numbers of Muslims living in the West, new attempts are under way in both communities to understand one another and to find ways of living together.

When the religion of Islam arose in the seventh century CE, the Christian world was deeply divided. East and West were seriously at odds, and each contained within itself deep tensions and disagreements. It is little wonder that the new Islamic faith appeared to Christians as simply another Christian heresy. The fact that within a century Heresy of the death of the Prophet Muhammad in 632 Islam had spread across much of the known world was for many Christians both frightening and theologically incomprehensible. Muslims, for their part, saw Christians primarily as they were referred to and portrayed in their sacred scripture, the Qur'an, which they believe to be God's divine word. The Prophet Muhammad understood his role as the final prophet of a monotheistic faith to which Jews and Christians were the earliest adherents and the recipients of earlier revealed scriptures, namely the Torah, the Psalms and the Gospel. Muslims believe that these scriptures were corrupted by the communities to which they were sent, and thus were abrogated by the Qur'an. However, the special relationship accorded by the Muslim scripture to Jews and Christians as the people of the book provides the basis for the Islamic perspective on Christian–Muslim relations.

Muslims have always found it impossible to understand why Christians impugn the oneness of God by calling Jesus the son of God. The Qur'an specifically denies that possibility, although it holds the person of Jesus in high esteem. Referred to in 93 verses, Jesus is said to have been Jesus born of Mary the Virgin, been a righteous prophet, and Mary performed miracles. He also will be a sign of the coming of the day of judgement. Because the Qur'an attests that Jesus was not crucified, Christians have seen in it a denial of their essential doctrines of incarnation and the Trinity. Incarnation Nonetheless the Qur'an refers to Christians as people of Trinity compassion and mercy, able to enter paradise as long as they do not impugn God's oneness, and nearest in love to Muslim believers.

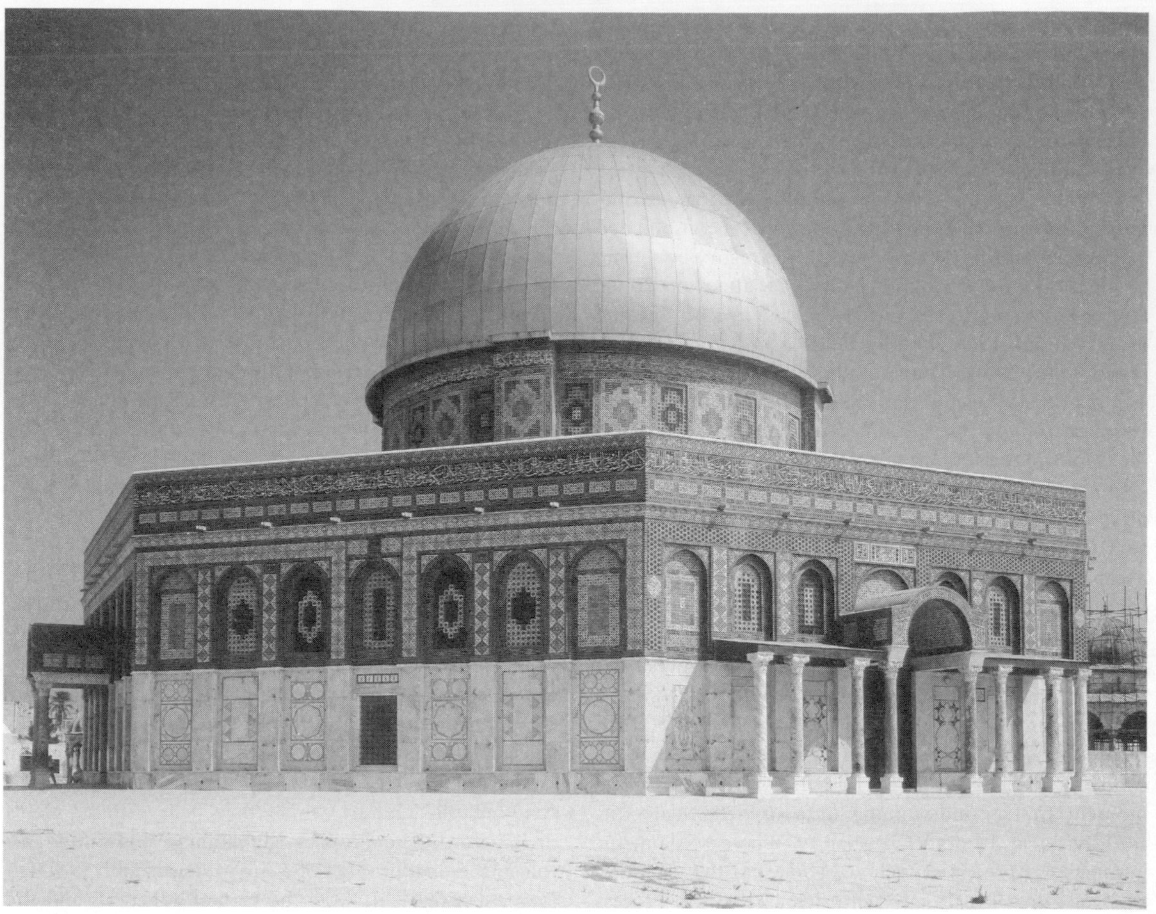

The Dome of the Rock, Jerusalem

As the Prophet Muhammad encountered the refusal of the Jews and Christians to accept his prophetic teachings, his community came to understand itself as the bearer of a faith that was related to, but different from, the existing religions of the Jews and Christians. This faith became known as Islam, submission to the one God. With the growth and spread of the Muslim religion, the people of the book were treated as minorities under the protection of Islam, believers in God despite their refusal to accept the Prophethood of Muhammad. Adult male Christians were thus not required to convert, although they had to pay a poll tax. A Christian woman was not allowed to marry a Muslim man, but the Qur'an does allow the marriage of a Muslim man to a Christian woman.

Christianity in Europe

In the early eighth century Islam moved across North Africa, occupied Spain, and tried unsuccessfully to advance into southern France. For some Christians the arrival of Islam as the new form of rule was seen as liberation from the tyranny of fellow Christians rather than as a menace or even a challenge to their faith. Christians remained the majority in much of what was nominally Muslim territory for a number of centuries. In the early years of the growth of Islam, the people of the book generally enjoyed friendly relations with Muslims and Christians and occupied high positions in the courts of the caliphs. As time went by, however, Muslim attitudes towards Christians tended to harden, with the result that free practice of the Christian faith often became more difficult.

One of the most successful ventures in interfaith relations seems to have been the early days of the five-century Muslim rule in Spain. Especially during the ninth and tenth centuries, Christians, Muslims and Jews lived in relative harmony, creating a culture rich in scientific and cultural achievements. Gradually this peaceful situation changed, and was supplanted by the intolerance, prejudices and mutual suspicion that more often have characterized relationships between the communities. In 1492 the monarchs Ferdinand and Isabella, having re-conquered Spain for Christianity, expelled Muslims or forced them to convert, bringing to a final end any hope of further Muslim-Christian harmony in the Iberian peninsula. The example set earlier, however, is often cited to show what is possible in terms of inter-communal existence.

Perhaps the most noteworthy example of unhappy engagement between Christians and Muslims over the centuries was the period of the Crusades, which lasted from the tenth to the thirteenth centuries. Always considered the Holy City by Christians, from the beginning of Islam Jerusalem has also been a place greatly venerated by Muslims. Its Dome of the Rock and al-Aqsa mosques are located on what is considered the third holiest site after Mecca and Medina. Muslims first occupied Jerusalem in 638, and for more than four centuries Christians for the most part were allowed to practise their religion freely there. That co-existence was shattered when, in 1095, Pope Urban II called for a crusade to recapture the city for Christianity.

Many of the crusading efforts were grossly misguided and ended in disaster. In the beginning, at least in the eyes of the West, there were crucial victories as well as the temporary attainment of the prize of Jerusalem. Initial crusader zeal gave way to territorial squabbling on the part of Christian rulers, however, and by 1187 the Christian hold on the Holy Land was effectively ended. The Muslim leader Saladin regained Jerusalem for Islam nearly a century after the first Christian invasion. Further crusading attempts over the next several centuries failed to regain the revered prize. The Crusades remain a serious blot on the history of interfaith relations, and are portrayed by many Muslims today as the beginning of a multi-faceted series of Western imperialist invasions of Muslim lands.

The Christian West in the Middle Ages found it very difficult to formulate a coherent vision of Islam, constrained by its own narrow horizons as well as by a lack of sufficient and accurate information. Both scholastic and popular writings tended to be contemptuous and even abusive of the Prophet, portraying him throughout his life as a prime example of sensuality, immorality and violence. This analysis was based both on critique of what they thought they knew about the life and teachings of the founder of Islam and on the actual experiences Christians had of Muslims invading their lands and profaning their churches. Christian thinkers such as Martin Luther and John Calvin at the time of the Reformation portrayed Muhammad as equal to the devil, and the Qur'an as foul and shameful. These images have remained strong in Christian consciousness, and continue to present a serious obstacle to the fostering of harmonious Christian-Muslim relations.

Throughout the Middle Ages and beyond, the vast majority of Muslims had little if any knowledge of the western regions of Christendom, as well as little interest in discovering anything about lands they considered bleak and remote, inhabited by peoples they thought to be little more than barbarians. A body of Islamic literature did develop dealing with Christian doctrine, however, for reasons of polemic and refutation. Relatively rare instances of Christian-Muslim interaction were usually characterized by debate grounded in each party's assurance that its own scripture was infallible. Missionary activity, especially on the part of Dominican and Franciscan friars, continued in the hope of converting Muslims to Christianity. This activity had the fortunate consequence of encouraging more serious study of Islam and Arabic on the part of Western scholars. It has long been recognized that one of the most significant and lasting contributions of the medieval Muslim world to Christendom was to provide access for Western scholars to the great classics of Greece and Rome by their translations from Arabic, from which they were rendered into European languages.

Christendom
Crusades ◄
Mission

Throughout the Middle Ages Christian and Muslim interactions were marked both by strife and warfare and by occasions of harmonious relations. Official tensions and hostilities at the political level were often balanced by local co-operation and even friendships between members of the two faiths. The seeds of mistrust and antipathy sown from the rise of Islam to the fall of Constantinople in the middle of the fifteenth century continued to grow in the following centuries. The rise of rationalism, a fascination on the part of the West with the cultural trappings of the East, and the necessities of international political and economic exchange soon moved the worlds of Islam and Christendom closer.

One of the key elements in current relationships between Muslims and Christians is the fact of Christian missions to Islamic lands, begun by the mendicant orders in the thirteenth century. Among the various Roman Catholic religious orders working for many years in the Muslim world has been the Jesuit order founded in 1534 and characterized both by scholarly work on Islam and close personal relationships with Muslims. Protestant missions did not appear with any serious intent until the Pietist movements of the eighteenth century, perhaps most notably with the founding of the Baptist Missionary Society. A major pioneer in Christian mission to Muslims was Henry Martyn (1781–1812), whose work in India is acknowledged in the continuing interfaith activity of the Henry Martyn Institute in Hyderabad.

Middle Ages ◄
Religious orders
Pietism

Protestant missions grew vigorously between the time of the French Revolution and the beginning of World War I. Their driving force was the hope of bringing Muslims to the faith of Christianity and the ultimate disappearance of Islam itself. While most Protestant missionaries developed warm personal relations with the Muslims they served, their attitudes towards the faith and its founder were rooted in the heritage of Christian denigration of Islam. This heritage is exemplified by such notables as Samuel Zwemer (1867–1952), the so-called 'apostle to Islam', a Dutch American from Michigan who was a pioneer in the Student Volunteer Movement. And it is still illustrated today, both subtly and blatantly, in the preaching of a number of prominent evangelicals and in the curricula of some theological schools training persons for ministry to, and conversion of, Muslims. Over the past century Christians in fact have realized relatively few conversions of Muslims to Christianity despite their efforts and their belief that Islam is on the wane. While Muslims acknowledge the important humanitarian service provided by many missionaries, the negative Christian attitudes towards Islam that they see illustrated both in missionary activity and in much academic scholarship has had a chilling effect on the promotion of harmonious relationships between members of the two faiths.

One of the harshest realities affecting Christian-Muslim relationships over the past century has been the movement of Western imperialism, with which missionary activity often has been associated. It is difficult to over-estimate the continuing repercussions across the Islamic world of Western colonialism. After World War I the Ottoman empire was dismembered, and the League of Nations established Western mandates over most of the Middle East. From the middle of the twentieth century on, Muslim countries have fought for liberation from what they see as the yoke of Western imperialistic rule, manifested in a variety of ways. Many of the current movements of political (sometimes extremist) Islam are directly rooted in a response to what they see as a long history of Western (Christian) incursion into Muslim territories and Western denigration of their faith and its founder, to the so-called 'orientalism' of much Western scholarship about Islam, and most lately to Western Christian political and moral support of the Zionist presence in the heart of the Muslim Middle East.

These factors have, in recent years, led to the growth of extremist Islamic or so-called 'Islamist' groups, whose leaders and members have not hesitated to turn to violent actions in response to what they see as unwanted Western intrusions into the heartlands of Islam, for no good purpose other than that of self-interest, especially to gain access to oil. Many Muslims live in poverty under undemocratic governments that are sustained by the patronage of the United States. Furthermore, most Muslims believe that the United States is not even-handed in its Middle Eastern strategy, especially in what they see as its uncritical support of the policies of Israel towards the Palestinian people. So, although the majority of Muslims condemned events such as the stunning attack upon mainland USA on 11 September 2001, many also hold that the USA reaped what it had sowed.

Although radicalized and politicized groups of disaffected Muslims use the products of Western technology (as diverse as state-of-the-art armaments and access to the internet) to further their cause, they also remember and draw upon the long history of Muslims' suspicion of Christians to gain widespread support for their actions. Indeed, in February 1998, al-Qaida ('the base') formed an alliance of revolutionary Islamic groups called the 'International Islamic Front for Jihad against the Jews and Crusaders'.

Jihad means 'struggle' and not 'holy war', as some mistakenly believe. Indeed, its majority interpretation tells of the struggle of every human to do what is right and just. Even its minority interpretation that permits warfare against others has mostly emphasized defensive struggle to protect Muslims and their religion, not aggressive action. However, like fundamentalist groups in every religion, al-Qaida and its allies find it impossible to accept the wide diversity of religious customs in Islam, believing that their interpretation is the only authentic one. For this reason, they are willing to kill other Muslims as well as outsiders. Moreover in protesting against the 'orientalism' of others, which they believe misrepresents them and their religion, many Muslims, especially but not only 'fundamentalists', have not recognized their own 'occidentalism'. This leads them to interpret Westerners, not as they themselves would, but from a very narrow viewpoint based upon Islam's self-identification, which outsiders do not share. They believe that it is that final, perfected religion for humanity. Indeed, many Muslims, poor and unrepresented by their countries' leaders, have taken comfort and pride in this claim for their religion. For the most part, they have not seen that others are not persuaded by it. Nor have they reckoned, as Christians have had to as part of their recent dialogue with Jews, that such supersessionary beliefs often dehumanize others, leading to violence against members of other religions and even against those who hold alternative viewpoints within the same faith.

In fact, just as, in and since the reforms of the Second Vatican Council, Roman Catholics have struggled to reinterpret their faith in ways that are appropriate for the contemporary world, so also many groups of Muslims have begun the process of renewing their faith, to take account of issues such as gender equality. In particular, a number of recent works by South African Muslims have outlined transformed and updated interpretations of Islam. Significantly, many such Muslims worked with members of other religions to protest against apartheid policies there, and learned much about and from them. It may well prove to be the case that current and future reformations of Islam will emerge, not from the traditional heartlands of Islam, but from Diaspora communities, whose members have had to learn to live as minorities and struggle to interpret the beliefs and customs of their host communities.

Indeed, new to the very recent history of the relationship between Christianity and Islam is the increasing presence of Muslims in Western Europe as well as in America. After the Turkish capture of Constantinople in the fifteenth century, Islam took hold among considerable numbers of East Europeans. Recent conflicts in such places as Bosnia reflect historical tensions. In the middle of the twentieth century a new kind of Islamic movement westward occurred as virtually all of the countries of Western Europe received Muslim 'guest workers', many of whom remained to claim citizenship. New forms of encounter are arising as the public practice of Islam comes up against national policies of the separation of state and religion.

Relations between Muslims and Christians today cannot be said to be improving in parts of the world where the two communities have co-existed for long generations. In many regions of Asia, Africa and the Middle East, political tensions, historical antagonisms and economic realities create conditions in which religio-political dominance seems to be a more preferable alternative than peaceful habitation. Some countries, particularly in Africa, are finding that after centuries of living together without conflict, they are experiencing pressures from both evangelical Christians and revivalist Muslims that serve to polarize the communities in new and unpleasant ways.

Many efforts are under way in different contexts and venues to bring Muslims and Christians together for conversation and to help them work together to resolve religious conflicts. Centres for dialogue and action have existed for many years in different parts of the world. For Roman Catholics, the Second Vatican Council from 1962 to 1965 signalled the start of new ways of thinking about and relating to other religions, and its statement that the church 'has a high regard' for Muslims clearly pointed towards understanding. The Secretariat for Non-Christians, later called the Pontifical Council for Interreligious Dialogue, has been the vehicle for promoting this new attitude and for formulating new initiatives at dialogue. In the 1960s Roman Catholic guidelines for dialogue between Christians and Muslims were published, and have since been revised several times.

The establishment of the World Council of Churches in Geneva, Switzerland, in 1948, whose members include Protestants and Orthodox but not Roman Catholics, provided the opportunity for other forms of Christian dialogue with Muslims. The first such organized dialogues took place in the late 1960s, and have continued regularly in various parts of the world, with various agendas and different constituencies. The name of the WCC unit concerned with interfaith dialogue has changed several times; most currently it is called 'Inter-Religious Relations and Dialogue'. In the United States the National Conference of Catholic Bishops and the National Council of Churches have fostered the work of interfaith relations and sponsored a number of ongoing dialogues. Many Christian theologians – Protestant, Roman Catholic, Orthodox and Anglican – have moved theologically to positions of greatly enhanced tolerance and even appreciation of the faith of Islam.

Muslim reflection on Christianity over the last several decades has taken place primarily through recent, and now growing, attempts to think seriously about the reality of religious pluralism. Many Muslims are struggling to balance what the Qur'an says about Christianity, as well as about religious diversity, with the long history of stormy relationships between the communities. They are also affected by what they see as contemporary Western Christian support of political policies and activities with which they deeply disagree, and by the anti-Western and anti-Christian rhetoric of revivalist Islam.

Muslims in America and Western Europe find themselves subject to many conflicting pressures. Some adhere to the view that they should take an isolationist stand and eschew involvement in Western public life, including interfaith activities. All Muslims living in the West are keenly aware of the persistent negative stereotyping of Islam on the part of the media, of the prejudice and fear that continues to linger and be manifested in the general public, and of the deep concerns they themselves have about elements of Western society and the dangers of becoming too deeply involved in its ethos. As recent world events have ratcheted up the level both of Western Christian fear of Islam and of interest in knowing more about Islam, many Muslims are responding by sharing information, holding mosque open-houses to which Christians are invited, and accepting invitations to meet and talk with Christians about their faith and practice.

Vatican

As they think about relating to Muslims, Christians now must deal with the heritage of what they have long seen as Muslim aggression and invasion, as well as their own history of prejudice and misunderstanding. Getting a perspective on this history is complicated by the reality of international instances of terrorist activity perpetrated in the name of Islam. Muslims who are trying to promote better interfaith relations are recognizing that they must come to terms with a past that they see riddled with Christian territorial intrusion and with deep-seated antipathy toward Islam and its Prophet. The immediate future seems to hold the promise both of continued alienation between the faiths regionally and globally, and the hope that the urgency of reaching mutual understanding, appreciation and co-operation will be

Ecumenical movement

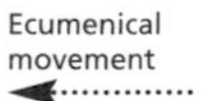

understood to be vital to the well-being of a large measure of humankind.

JANE I. SMITH

Hugh Goddard, *A History of Christian-Muslim Relations*, Chicago: New Amsterdam Books 2000; Yvonne W. Haddad and Wadi Z. Haddad (eds), *Christian–Muslim Encounters*, Gainesville: University Press of Florida 1995; Jane I. Smith, 'Islam and Christendom' in John L. Esposito (ed), *The Oxford History of Islam*, New York: OUP 1999; R. Marston Speight, *God Is One. The Way of Islam*, New York: Friendship Press [2]2001; Kate Zebiri, *Muslims and Christians Face to Face*, Oxford: Oneworld 1997

Japanese religions and Christianity

Most visitors to Japan are impressed by the apparent harmony between the various religions. People belong to more than one of them. Statistics show that most Japanese are Buddhists, but at the same time they are registered as Shintoists and participate in the traditional Shinto rituals. From time to time they may also be involved in religious practices and rituals which are not particularly Buddhist or Shinto, but may be characterized as folk religion or popular cults, sometimes closely related to Daoist practices. Even though few Japanese regard themselves as Confucians, the traditional social structure and relationships are still to a great extent moulded by Confucian ideals. In addition, aspects of Christianity have been integrated into Japanese society. Bach and Handel are among the composers featured in the music world; Christmas is celebrated with music and Christmas cakes; it is not uncommon for parents to want to send their children to Christian kindergartens and schools in order to give them a touch of Christianity; and wedding ceremonies in churches and Western-style wedding chapels are quite popular.

The impression of peaceful co-existence between religions is generally correct, and is often hailed as a model for multi-religious harmony. But it is necessary to add several modifications in order to avoid misunderstandings. Particularly when it comes to Christianity, there has been and still is potential for conflict with the other religions. One of the traditional images of religious co-existence in Japan may indicate some of the limitations of peaceful co-existence. According to traditional thinking, Japanese religious and spiritual life is described as a tree: Shinto is at the roots as the indigenous religious tradition, Confucianism is regarded as the stem and branches, and Buddhism as the flowers and fruits. The metaphor suggests that the three spiritual traditions are not separate

Japanese Christian convert, seventeenth century

units, but belong together as an organic whole, sharing the events of life and death: Shinto generally takes care of the rituals and events of this life, Buddhism takes care of death and dying and the next life, while Confucianism provides the traditional social framework. If Christianity is not included in the tree, that is not only because it is a relative newcomer (only since the sixteenth century), but also because there are features of Christianity which make such integration difficult.

The most obvious obstacles to integration are two aspects of foreignness associated with Christianity. First, Christianity is primarily thought of as foreign because it was introduced from Europe and America as a Western religion, and in contrast to other alien traditions such as Buddhism, Confucianism and Daoism; it seems to be more resistant to transformation by Japanese culture, and generally maintains a sense of foreignness. Secondly, and perhaps more importantly, mainstream Christianity generally claims a uniqueness that is alien to most Eastern traditions, appealing to a divine revelation which demands exclusive allegiance from its members. In a society where popular wisdom expects religious traditions to share the spiritual life of the citizens, such exclusive attitudes tend to create tension and conflict. There are similar reactions not only to Christianity but also to ideologies with exclusive claims like Marxism, and aggressive religious movements that ignore or reject others, like some movements within the Buddhist tradition and some new religions. At present, however, it seems as if traditional exclusivism and intolerance in Japanese Christianity are being replaced by a spirit of peaceful co-existence and openness.

The present trend, at least for mainstream Protestant churches and the Roman Catholic Church, seems to combine traditional claims for uniqueness with an inclusive openness that leads to peaceful co-existence, dialogue, and even co-operation where that seems useful.

This peaceful co-existence can be described at various levels. At the level of congregational life, Japanese Christianity has become much more tolerant in relation to non-Christian religious practices. Rituals related to funerals and ancestor worship were traditionally rejected as idol worship, and strict churches advised members not to attend Buddhist funerals, even for departed friends, neighbours and family members. Any gestures that might indicate worship or veneration in Buddhist temples or Shinto sanctuaries would be avoided. Now most mainstream Christians would have no problems participating in such occasions. At funerals they would take part in the traditional offering of incense or, more commonly, show their respect by offering flowers. Some Christian leaders would even express their respect in Buddhist temple halls by bowing or prostrating themselves in front of the Buddhist images. Christians seem to be more reluctant about Shinto rituals, particularly because Shinto is somehow associated with the emperor system and nationalistic attitudes. In general, however, Japanese Christians are more relaxed when it comes to local religious festivals, the expected support of local shrines, or even having the family's Buddhist shrine for the ancestors in their home (usually taken care of by the oldest son). Such tolerance is not necessarily shared by segments of conservative evangelicals and charismatic Christians, who maintain or even re-emphasize traditional negative attitudes.

At the level of academic reflection there seem to be various trends. Many Japanese theologians have been more interested in Western theology and philosophy than in engaging in dialogue with indigenous religious traditions. This is also partly because Japanese religions seem to be directed to the past and fail to deal with the pressing political and social concerns of the present world. On the other hand, a number of theologians have been seriously grappling with the challenge from Buddhist philosophy and religious experience. Particularly since the 1950s and 1960s a number of Christian study centres and dialogue institutions, Protestant and Roman Catholic, have actively promoted study and interfaith dialogue, and contributed to reflection about what it means to be a church in a culture moulded by non-Christian religions. The broader international dialogue, particularly between Buddhism and Christianity, has to a great extent been initiated in Japan.

At the level of social and political activity Christians have tended to be much more critically involved in society than the adherents of most other religions. This has strengthened the feeling that Christianity is an outsider alienating itself from others. On the other hand, this spirit of active involvement has also challenged other religions to reconsider their role in society, and prepared the ground for interesting constellations. A number of reform movements, particularly in the Buddhist community and among new religions, have been inspired by Christianity and have copied Christian activities in social work, teaching and missionary activity. In many cases interesting forms of co-operation have developed between Christians and reform-minded religious leaders. Important initiatives since the 1960s and 1970s have included common efforts to protest against nationalism, militarism, race and sex discrimination and co-operation for peace (The World Conference on Religion and Peace began in Japan) or organizing conferences and networks for dealing with common concerns of religions in a secular society.

At the level of spiritual search and sharing there have been a great variety of interfaith contacts, particularly between Buddhists and Christians. More than 100 years ago individual Japanese Christians began to investigate how to integrate Zen and other meditative practices into Christian spirituality. Some may be described as 'hyphenated Christians', that is, Christians who in various ways have integrated Buddhist, Confucian and even Shinto elements into their spiritual ways. Particularly since the 1960s, a number of organized efforts to investigate the possibility of integrating Buddhist practices into Christian spiritual life have emerged: missionaries, pastors and priests practising Zen under Buddhist masters; a series of conferences and retreats at which participants 'share' their spiritual ways; exchanges between Western and Eastern monastics; Christian retreat houses and monasteries adapting Buddhist meditation or Shinto forms of worship.

Even though there is an openness for dialogue and co-operation with other religions, with these interesting ventures the dialogue is mostly carried out by a limited number of interested groups and individuals. The majority of Christians are generally tolerant in their attitudes, but not particularly concerned about establishing such relationships.

The first documented encounters between Christianity and Japanese religions took place immediately after the  Mission arrival of Francis Xavier and the Jesuit mission in 1549. The Jesuits had extremely positive impressions of the Japanese, and reported favourably on their cultural and intellectual abilities. They also established friendly relations with the Buddhist leadership as they entered new places. Eager as they were to find indigenous terms in order to make their faith more easily understood, the Jesuits were led to adopt quite a lot of Buddhist terminology. From the Buddhist point of view, consequently, Christianity seemed to be just another denomination of Buddhism. As the missionaries gradually discovered that the terminology failed to distinguish their teaching from Buddhism, they changed policy and began to denounce Buddhism. The inevitable result was, of course, broken relationships and an increasingly negative stance on the part of Buddhism as well.

The general tone of later relationships seems to be consistently negative. Buddhism and other religions were denounced as diabolic inventions, morally degenerate, and opponents to be conquered; and the Buddhists responded with aggressive propaganda against the foreign intruder. What finally led to a complete break was the fact that Japanese authorities feared that the Christian mission was a tool for Portuguese colonial ambitions, and hence introduced a series of restrictions that led to the final proscription of Christianity in the early seventeenth century. Buddhism was eventually given a central position as a semi-national religion and main agent for the oppression of Christianity. Buddhist scholars were used as advisers in religious matters, and they consistently denounced Christianity as an evil religion. Buddhist priests were entrusted with the investigation and elimination of Christianity and other 'evil religions' and maintained that role for the more than two centuries of national isolation.

The initial contact between Christians and other religions after the forced re-opening of Japan in 1854 presented no basis for a meaningful relationship. From the Buddhist point of view, Christianity was still a fatal enemy, and there was no room for concessions. Consequently, Buddhist leaders made desperate attempts to combine patriotism and religious apologetics in order to stigmatize Christianity as a national threat. From the Christian point of view, Buddhism and other religions were regarded as so weak and dated that they could be ignored, a sentiment which was generally shared by Japanese intellectuals and political leaders.

In 1873 the Japanese government ordered the removal of the notice boards proscribing Christianity and introduced a policy of tacit recognition. As Christianity gradually expanded beyond the narrow boundaries of the treaty ports, the deep-rooted influence and power of Buddhism also became more obvious. The missionaries and Japanese Christians could no longer ignore Buddhism; at least it had to be regarded as a serious enemy. This reluctant recognition of the power of Buddhism led in the 1880s to a paradoxical change of relationship. On the one hand, Christians engaged in Buddhist studies in order to be prepared for the coming struggle. On the other hand, this apologetic concern initiated contacts that gradually led to a new respect for the other. Some leading Buddhists had similar experiences in the encounter with Christians, resulting in some cases in a courteous friendship between the antagonists.

These Buddhists mostly belonged to the progressive parties of their respective sects. They were painfully aware of the crisis of Buddhism, and saw the Christian expansion as a real threat. But as reformers they were also stimulated by the challenge from Christianity and believed that the situation would change as soon as their reforms were adopted. This combination of reform zeal and increasing confidence *vis-à-vis* Christianity contributed to more friendly attitudes, and in various ways prepared the ground for the coming dialogue.

While the waves of Westernization in the 1880s had created a favourable climate for Christian expansion, the 1890s were characterized by a nationalistic reaction, strongly anti-Western and anti-Christian. It is no exaggeration to say that Buddhism rode this nationalistic wave, making every effort to defame and stigmatize Christianity as superstitious, dangerous and incompatible with the national polity. Buddhists engaged in fervent anti-Christian propaganda, including even violent persecution and destruction of church buildings in the provinces. Given this background, it is significant to note that the 1890s, for all the nationalistic and anti-Christian sentiments, were also the period during which the peaceful dialogue reached a decisive breakthrough. There were several elements in this dynamic.

First, the Japanese Christians finally managed to convince their critics that it was possible to combine Christian faith and patriotism. Secondly, along with the new emphasis on patriotism, the churches developed a theology that advocated the need for the Japanization of church life and theology. Such a new emphasis on Japanese traditions – slightly anti-Western and anti-denominational, but also influenced by Western liberal theology – naturally led to a renewed interest in Japanese indigenous traditions, including Buddhism. Among the Buddhists, several reform movements advocated the need of a New Buddhism, and to a great extent it was Protestant Christianity that provided models for reform and modernization. In addition, chairs of comparative religion were established at various universities, with teachers promoting dialogue and tolerance. The World's Parliament of Religions in Chicago in 1893 provided the model for a similar Japanese small-scale parliament of religions in 1896, the so-called Buddhist-Christian Conference. The conference was actually the first official and public encounter by leading religious leaders in Japan, and may be regarded as the symbol of a new era of religious tolerance and co-operation.

As Japan entered the twentieth century, the mutual antagonism between religions in Japan gradually yielded to greater tolerance and co-operation. One trend that may be characterized as the establishment dialogue, that is, a government supported or favoured co-operation between the established religions, mobilized Buddhists, Shintoists and Christians to support and nurture national spirit and morality against so-called dangerous ideas represented by socialism, Marxism and anarchism. Another trend may be called the anti-establishment dialogue, that is, a co-operation between reformers and radicals within different religions who were critical of the mainstream conservative and nationalistic tendencies. A third trend may be characterized as a spiritual dialogue, that is, represented by numerous individual Christians who in various ways found it necessary to engage in an inner dialogue with other religious traditions in order to integrate these – positively or negatively – in their Christian spiritual life.

NOTTO R. THELLE

📖 George Elison, *Deus Destroyed: The Image of Christianity in Early Modern Japan*, Cambridge, MA: Harvard University Press 1973; Mark R. Mullins (ed), *Handbook on Christianity in Japan*, Leiden: E. J. Brill 2003; James M. Phillips, *From the Rising of the Sun: Christians and Society in Contemporary Japan*, Maryknoll, NY: Orbis 1981; David Reid, *New Wine: The Cultural Shaping of Japanese Christianity*, Berkeley, CA: Asian Humanities Press 1991; Notto R. Thelle, *Buddhism and Christianity in Japan: From Conflict to Dialogue, 1854–1899*, Honolulu: University of Hawaii Press 1987

Jehovah's Witnesses

Liberal theology ◄

Jehovah's Witnesses is a Christian millennialist movement, i.e. a movement that believes in a coming thousand-year kingdom of Christ on earth. It took root in America during the late nineteenth century and has gained notoriety during the last century for aggressive door-to-door proselytizing and for refusing to swear allegiance to the flag and to the United States government.

With worldwide headquarters in Brooklyn, New York, the 'Witnesses', as they are often called, publish *Awake!* and *The Watchtower* magazines, which serve as tools of evangelism and as authorized means of imparting doctrine to the faithful. The Witnesses are estimated to have about 800,000 members within the United States and between 3 and 4 million adherents around the globe.

Jehovah's Witnesses do not consider themselves a 'church', nor do they have anything resembling church structures. They meet in what are dubbed 'kingdom halls', which often resemble lodges, university classroom buildings or community centres.

The beginnings of the movement are associated with the ministry of Charles Taze Russell (1852–1916), a haberdasher from Pittsburgh, Pennsylvania, who in 1872 launched the International Bible Students' Association and in 1879 an organization called Zion's Watch Tower Tract Society. The movement adopted the name Jehovah's Witnesses in 1931 under the leadership of Joseph Franklin Rutherford (1869–1942), a Missouri lawyer who was Russell's successor. The new name was taken from Isaiah 43.10, where God declares to his servants: 'You are my witnesses.'

Rutherford considerably refined the scope and techniques of door-to-door missionary work. A proponent of the 'new' electronic media of his day, he equipped Witnesses with portable phonographs and 78rpm records of his talks. In 1925 he prophesied that the patriarchs and prophets of ancient Israel would soon be coming back to earth along with Jesus. Before he died, Rutherford purchased a shiny new automobile in which to chauffeur Abraham, Isaac and Jacob around Southern California, where he resided at the time.

After Russell's death the leadership of Jehovah's Witnesses passed to Nathan Homer Knorr (1905–77), who was also president of the Watchtower Society. Knorr is best known for having discontinued the use of phonographs and for employing detailed Bible study and the delivery of 'personal testimonies' to would-be converts. Knorr also oversaw the New World Translation of the Bible, which is utilized by the Witnesses to justify their distinctive doctrines. Subsequent heads of the Jehovah's Witnesses include Frederick Franz, the movement's eminent theologian, and Milton Henschel, who took over in 1993.

The teaching of Jehovah's Witnesses focuses largely on predictions concerning Jesus' imminent return to earth and the gathering together of God's 'elect' in accordance with biblical prophecy. Generations of Jehovah's Witnesses have anticipated and pegged Jesus' Second Coming in precise periods or years, which have included 1914, 1918, 1925, the early 1940s, 1975 and 1994.

Each time these predictions have not panned out: the Witnesses have either switched the date for Jesus' arrival or reinterpreted the meaning of scripture regarding the Second Coming. Since the early years Jehovah's Witnesses have maintained that Jesus already has returned, or will return, 'invisibly' to earth before making his rule and kingdom manifest.

p. 506

Jehovah's Witnesses are considered to be either aberrant or heretical by most mainline churches and denominations because their doctrinal positions, while derived to a certain extent from the Bible, are significantly at variance with traditional Christianity. By the same token, Taze himself considered much of traditional Christianity to be 'apostate', and like other sectarian figures maintained that the views of Jehovah's Witnesses were the only authentic rendering of God's revelation to humanity.

Jehovah's Witnesses today have adopted the stance that the Watchtower Society itself is the sole, trustworthy channel of God's communication to the human race. In the last twenty years Jehovah's Witnesses have on occasions been branded by their detractors as a 'cult' because of their tight-knit organization, authoritarian habits, fundamentalist ideology and custom of 'shunning' those who leave the fold. However, such a denotation is both reckless and misleading, in so far as the Jehovah's Witnesses follow much the same pattern of development as other millennialist forms of sectarian Christianity.

The chief disagreement of Jehovah's Witnesses with traditional Christianity centres on the doctrine of the Trinity. Jehovah's Witnesses insist that there is only one God who exists in one person and that Jesus is not identical in any way with God, even God in the flesh. Jesus was merely a perfected human being. Jehovah's Witnesses have also taught that Jesus was actually the archangel Michael who took on corporeal form, and that he did not 'rise' from the dead in a physical body. In contrast to traditional Christianity, they do not acknowledge that God is either all-powerful or all-present.

Trinity

Christology

Finally, Jehovah's Witnesses deny the reality of hell and the eternity of the human soul. They are adamant that no one outside their own organization can be saved, and that genuine sainthood is available to no more than 144,000 within their body. Jehovah's Witnesses believe that the 144,000 alone will be resurrected in the last days and that the remainder of humankind will be obliterated upon death.

They consider much of Christian practice, including the celebration of Christmas and the use of the symbol of the cross, to be 'pagan' in character. They contend that 'Jehovah' is the only true designation for God, even though most modern scholars agree that the origin of that word consists in a misreading of the biblical name Yahweh, resulting from the placement of alternative vowel markings in the medieval texts with the ancient Hebrew consonants. Hebrew itself has no letters for vowel sounds.

Membership of Jehovah's Witnesses revolves significantly around evangelism and regular sessions aimed at sharing effective stratagems for communication and persuasion. Sometimes these sessions resemble corporate sales meetings.

Witnesses are expected to devote a major portion of their life to spreading the word as far as possible, which involves logging their hours on the street. The well-recognized zeal of Witnesses for proselytizing reflects their strong expectation that the world itself will soon be coming to an end. Formal admission requires baptism by immersion.

CARL A. RASCHKE

James A. Beckford, *The Trumpet of Prophecy: A Sociological Study of Jehovah's Witnesses*, New York: Wiley 1975; Heather Botting, *The Orwellian World of Jehovah's Witnesses*, Toronto: Toronto University Press 1984; Marley Cole, *Jehovah's Witnesses: The New World Society*, New York: Vantage Books 1955 and London: Allen & Unwin 1956; M. James Penton, *Apocalypse Delayed: The Story of Jehovah's Witnesses*, Toronto: Toronto University Press [2]1998

JESUS

Beliefs, Bible, Biblical criticism, Christology, Eucharist, Evidence, Incarnation, Jesus of history, Kingdom of God, Messiah, Miracle, Origins and background, Resurrection, Women in Christianity

The movement which came to be known as Christianity derives from Jesus, who grew up in Nazareth, a small village in Galilee. Although the most common system of dating today is centred on the year of his birth, it was not devised until the sixth century and is generally thought to be inaccurate. Jesus was probably born at the end of the reign of Herod the Great (37–4 BCE). He is often referred to as Jesus Christ, or just Christ: here Christ is not a surname but a title (the Greek term for Messiah) which is used in worship and in reflection on the significance of his person in the light of his death and resurrection, reflection which is called christology. Since the means of investigating what Jesus said and did against the background of his own time became available as a result of what is known as the quest of the historical Jesus, the name Jesus of Nazareth has predominantly been used of the figure of Jesus in history, but the name Jesus is also used in devotion to address a divine person who has more than historical characteristics. Calendar Devotions

The evidence

From the eighteenth century on, attempts have regularly been made to prove that Jesus never existed and that his figure is in some way a personification of the ideas which led to the founding of the new religion of Christianity or the result of a combination of a series of existing myths. However, there is sufficient evidence about Jesus to rule out this view, which cannot stand up to detailed examination. What is far more problematical is that the nature and amount of the evidence about Jesus is such that it leaves plenty of scope for use of the imagination in filling up the many gaps. The result has been a great variety of pictures of Jesus, supposedly in his historical context; however, in many respects these prove to be self-portraits of the authors and their ideals.

What are these sources? Jesus is mentioned in several first-century non-Christian authors, most notably the Jewish historian Josephus (though the paragraph about Jesus in his *Jewish Antiquities* is thought by many to be a later Christian insertion); the Roman writers Tacitus, Pliny and Suetonius make brief allusions to him. However, these do not add anything to what we are told by our main sources, the New Testament Gospels. The earliest Christian documents we have, the letters of Paul, also of course give information about Jesus, but it is striking just how sparse this information is by comparison with the Gospels. Paul

As well as the New Testament Gospels there are a number of apocryphal Gospels. Some survive in fragmentary quotations which have been known for a considerable time, others have become known only recently, as the result of a find of papyri at Nag Hammadi in Egypt in 1945. In addition, in the New Testament outside the Gospels, e.g. in the letters of Paul, and in other early Christian writings there are a number of detached sayings of Jesus, called agrapha (literally 'unwritten'), which have been handed down out of any original context. p. 145 p. 501

How far the apocryphal Gospels add to our information about Jesus rather than tell us about the views of the people who wrote them is currently a controversial matter. The four New Testament Gospels, Matthew, Mark, Luke and John, though resembling biographies in appearance, are in fact theological and literary portraits. The material of which the authors made use was handed down by word of mouth in small units, usually with little or no indication of time or place. These units are not necessarily connected chronologically in a historical sequence, but have been strung together thematically, in a number of cases probably even before they came to the evangelists. What Jesus had said and done appeared to his followers in a new light after his death and their experience of his resurrection, and stories about him and reports of his teaching were handed down above all for a practical purpose, to inspire and guide the communities which were forming.

Just how complex and creative the process of writing the New Testament Gospels was can be seen from a comparison between them. In 1776 the New Testament scholar J. J. Griesbach published an edition of the Gospels in which the texts of Matthew, Mark, Luke and John were printed in columns p. 152 side by side (the book was entitled *Synopsis* = Greek 'see together'). This layout alone demonstrated that the first three Gospels are closely related and that the Fourth Gospel stands apart from them. p. 151 The precise nature of this relationship has been discussed ever since; it is known as the synoptic problem. It is a complicated matter and often ignored (synopses are very little used outside the world of New Testament scholarship and teaching), but is fundamental to understanding just how the Gospel portrait of Jesus is a mixture of what he thought and did and how this was interpreted, developed and even altered by the evangelists or the traditions they used.

Basically the same saying of Jesus can appear in different wordings in different Gospels (Matthew 16.28: 'There are some standing here who will not taste death before they see the Son of man coming in his kingdom'; Mark 9.1: 'There are some standing here who will not taste death before they see the kingdom of God come with power'; Luke 9.27: 'There are some standing here who will not taste death before they see the kingdom of God'). In Matthew 16.18 the famous saying 'You are Peter, and on this rock I will build my church' appears only in Matthew, but in a context common to the first three Gospels: either Matthew has added it, or Mark and Luke have omitted it. Some pp. 658, 759 sayings, parables, miracles appear in only one Gospel. And most clearly of all, as the Gospels come to an end the nature of the theological picture drawn of Jesus in each of them becomes particularly p. 341 clear: the 'last words' from the cross are quite different in Matthew/Mark, Luke and John, and so are the accounts of the resurrection: Mark originally ended abruptly with no account of any appear- p. 668 ances of Jesus; for Matthew these appearances occur only in Galilee, but for Luke they occur only in Jerusalem.

Moreover because Jesus was believed to be the Christ, the Messiah, the first Christians looked Prophecy for prophecies of his coming in their Bible, the Greek translation of the Hebrew Bible, which came to be called the Old Testament. In the light of his resurrection Jesus' life and death were seen in the context of the Hebrew Bible, which also made its contribution to colouring the accounts of what he said and did. The book of Zechariah in particular has left a strong mark on the account of the passion and resurrection.

It is important to be aware of the nature of the evidence about Jesus of Nazareth. By its very nature it makes certain things impossible. No biography of Jesus can be written, because there are so many gaps in the story, so many unknowns, and we have no reliable chronological framework. We do not even know how long his public activity lasted: was it three years, or only a year or so? Nor can we trace any way in which his thinking may have changed or developed; he may have become increasingly aware that his words and actions would result in his death, but the indications of this in the Gospels can be demonstrated to be the work of the evangelists.

Archaeology On the other hand, archaeological investigation of Syria/Palestine at the time of Jesus and study of the increasing number of documents from his time that have become available have contributed to a much fuller picture of the world in which Jesus lived, and Jewish scholars have joined Christian scholars in shedding light on the beliefs, practices and social conditions of his day, This picture makes much clearer the environment to which Jesus belonged and the origins and background of the rise of Christianity.

Life

Despite the many problems and uncertainties a consensus has now formed among scholars on a basic outline of the life of Jesus. It runs like this.

Jesus was a Jew. He was born and spent his early days in the Galilean village of Nazareth. He had several brothers and sisters and grew up in the home of Joseph, a building craftsman, who had married Mary, Jesus' mother. The situation has to be put this way because the Gospels make it clear that Joseph was not Jesus' physical father. At one point (Mark 6.3) Jesus is strikingly called 'son of Mary', apparently in contempt; the Gospels defend Mary against immoral behaviour and say that her son was conceived of the Holy Spirit.

Mary
p. 613
Holy Spirit

Jesus learned his father's trade and received a basic education at the local synagogue, coming to know parts of the Hebrew Bible and the religious traditions of his people. He may well have been unable to read or write, and he probably spoke Aramaic with a smattering of Greek.

During the 20s he joined the movement of John the Baptist, a prophet of doom who called for repentance in the face of the imminent judgement of God. John told his followers that they could escape condemnation in this judgement if they were baptized by him in the river Jordan. Jesus accepted this baptism and for a while joined the group of John's ascetic followers. John was later executed as a claimant to messiahship by the local ruler, Herod Antipas, but by then Jesus had parted company with him and gathered followers of his own. Throughout Jesus' lifetime there was rivalry between the followers of John and the followers of Jesus, and this rivalry continued for quite some time even after Jesus' death.

p. 848

The core of Jesus' followers was made up of twelve disciples whom he chose as symbolic representatives of the twelve tribes of Israel. Unusually for a Jewish teacher, he also had women around him, most notably Mary Magdalene, with whom he seems to have had a special relationship. There is no indication that any of his family were among his followers during his lifetime; indeed it is said that they thought him mad. However, Jesus' brother James abruptly appears as leader of the Jerusalem church at a very early stage and the Fourth Gospel pictures Jesus' mother Mary standing at the foot of the cross.

p. 850
p. 850
p. 852

Jesus' teaching was above all about God and the kingdom of God, or God's kingly rule. He addressed God in prayer with the intimate term 'Abba', 'dear Father'. God's love and generosity never failed, but his judgement on those who oppressed the outcast and the needy would be terrible. Jesus spoke of God's kingly rule in parables, stories which anyone could understand and which draw on images from the countryside: flowers and sheep and birds, and the activities of sowing and harvest, making bread and cleaning the house. He was always concerned to make people think for themselves, and among his parables are stories of dishonest people, like the steward faced with losing his job who fraudulently alters bills to make potential new employers favourably disposed towards him. Moreover, he indicated that those who entered the kingdom of God first would be a disreputable lot, the men and women who were at the very edge of society or outside it: prostitutes, tax collectors, the 'unclean' who did not observe the ritual regulations binding on all Jews. In that kingdom they would all recline together at a great banquet and there would be much rejoicing.

Prayer

Jesus anticipated the banquet of the kingdom of God in meals which he shared with his disciples

THE PARABLES OF JESUS

Parable	*Matthew*	*Mark*	*Luke*
Barren fig tree			13.69
Friend at midnight			11.5–13
Good Samaritan			10.25–37
Great supper			14.15–24
Hidden treasure	13.44		
Labourers in vineyard	20.1–16		
Leaven	13.33		13.20–21
Lost coin			15.8–10
Lost sheep			15.4–7
Marriage feast	22.1–14		
Mustard seed	13.31–2	4.30–2	13.18–19
Net of fish	13.47–50		
Pearl of great price	13.45–6		
Pharisee and tax collector			18.9–14
Pounds			19.11–27
Prodigal son			15.11–32
Rich fool			12.16–21
Rich man and Lazarus			16.19–31
Seed growing secretly		4.26–9	
Sower	13.3–9	4.3–20	8.4–15
Talents	25.14–30		
Tares in field	13.24–30		
Ten virgins	25.1–13		
Unjust judge			18.1–8
Unjust steward			16.1–13
Unmerciful servant	18.21–35		
Wicked husbandmen	21.33–46	12.1–12	20.9–18

Jesus taught in parables. Many of them are about the kingdom of God, the main theme of his preaching, and begin with the words 'the kingdom of God (in Matthew "of heaven") is like ...' a treasure hidden in a field, a net, a pearl of great price, seed growing secretly. Others have a striking main character (the good Samaritan, the prodigal son, the rich fool); sometimes these characters can be of doubtful morality (the unjust steward, the unjust judge).

The parables are drawn from everyday life and give us a vivid picture of social conditions in Jesus' day. Those featured in the parables are usually ordinary people going about their ordinary tasks: men waiting in the market place to be employed, women making bread at home, the sower working in the fields.

At one point, after the parable of the sower, an interpretation is given: the sower is a preacher, and the path or the rocky places on which the seed falls are types of hearers, who are lured astray by the devil or accept the word only superficially. It is suggested that the parables are understandable only to disciples; this form of teaching is to keep their message secret from outsiders (Mark 4.10–12). This view led to allegorical interpretations of other parables in the church: e.g. in the parable of the good Samaritan, the Samaritan was Jesus, the inn to which the wounded man was taken was the church, and the two pence given to the innkeeper were the two sacraments. At the end of the nineteenth century the parables were thought each to be focused on a single universal truth, e.g. in the parable of selling everything to buy a field with a hidden treasure in it, the principle of sacrificing a lesser good for a greater. However, it is now generally agreed that the parables use the imagery of Jesus' day to present his message as vividly as possible. Other Jewish teachers of the time used parables, though the most striking examples are later than Jesus. In modern times, both Franz Kafka and Oscar Wilde have composed parables of the same genre.

How the parables of Jesus are to be interpreted today is the subject of a large body of literature which explores them in the context of modern literary criticism.

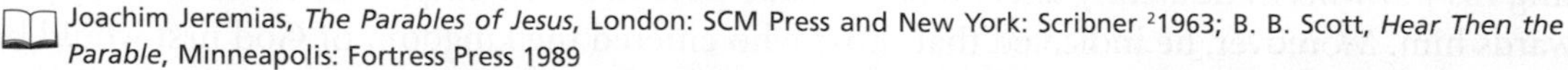
Joachim Jeremias, *The Parables of Jesus*, London: SCM Press and New York: Scribner [2]1963; B. B. Scott, *Hear Then the Parable*, Minneapolis: Fortress Press 1989

THE BEATITUDES

Matthew 5.1–12	*Luke 6.17, 20–6*
Seeing the crowds, he went up on the mountain, and when he sat down his disciples came to him. And he opened his mouth and taught them, saying:	And he came down with them and stood on a level place, with a great crowd of his disciples and a great multitude of people ... and he lifted up his eyes on his disciples, and said:
Blessed are the poor in spirit, for theirs is the kingdom of heaven. Blessed are those who mourn, for they shall be comforted. Blessed are the meek, for they shall inherit the earth. Blessed are those who hunger and thirst for righteousness, for they shall be satisfied.	Blessed are you poor, for yours is the kingdom of God. Blessed are you that hunger now, for you shall be satisfied. Blessed are you that weep now, for you shall laugh.
Blessed are the merciful, for they shall obtain mercy. Blessed are the pure in heart, for they shall see God. Blessed are the peacemakers, for they shall be called sons of God. Blessed are those who are persecuted for righteousness' sake, for theirs is the kingdom of heaven. Blessed are you when men revile you and persecute you and utter all kinds of evil against you falsely on my account.	Blessed are you when men hate you, and when they exclude you and revile you, and cast out your name as evil, on account of the Son of man.
Rejoice and be glad, for your reward is great in heaven, for so men persecuted the prophets who were before you.	Rejoice in that day, and leap for joy, for behold your reward is great in heaven; for so their fathers did to the prophets. But woe to you that are rich, for you have received your consolation. Woe to you that are full now, for you shall hunger. Woe to you that laugh now, for you shall mourn and weep. Woe to you, when all men speak well of you, for so their fathers did to the false prophets.

The Beatitudes appear in Matthew's Gospel at the beginning of his Sermon on the Mount and in Luke's Gospel at the beginning of his Sermon on the Plain. Luke's version ends with a series of woes. There are other obvious differences between the two versions. Matthew's version is in the third person, Luke's in the second. Matthew shows a tendency to 'spiritualize', e.g. in his 'poor in spirit', Luke – as elsewhere in his Gospel – is concerned about the relationship between riches, poverty and discipleship of Jesus. As in the case of the Lord's Prayer, it is impossible to determine which of the two versions is original.

p. 385

and with the outcast. That is one of the most prominent features of the traditions about him. And it was at a last supper on the night before he died that with blessings over bread and wine he initiated the symbolic meal which Christians have celebrated ever since.

Eucharist

Jesus had the power to heal people, and again his healing of the mentally ill by exorcisms are among the best-attested of his actions. Those with mental illnesses were thought to be possessed by demons, and the driving out of these demons was seen as a defeat of the devil, Satan, and a sign of the coming of the kingdom of God.

Sickness and healing

p. 1081

Satan

In his ethical teaching, concentrated above all in the Sermon on the Mount, Jesus both relaxed the Jewish tradition in which he had been brought up and made it more strict. He was prepared to take a relaxed attitude over the observance of the sabbath and over ritual cleanness and on numerous occasions put his views into practice publicly. But when it came to the fundamental

p. 385

Ethics

issues of loving God and one's neighbour his teaching was so radical as to seem impossible to fulfil. Not only is killing forbidden, but even anger; not only is adultery forbidden, but even lascivious thought; there must be no retaliation, but a turning of the other cheek.

It is difficult to know how Jesus spoke of himself, since it is here above all that later tradition and the evangelists have demonstrably rewritten what he said and attributed claims to him which he did not make. It is highly unlikely that he ever spoke of himself as Messiah or said that he was the son of God. If he gave any title to himself at all, it will have been the enigmatic Son of man, a term which scholars have been trying to explain satisfactorily for more than a century. But so strong was the force of his personality, so powerful were his actions and words, that he was in a position to point away from himself to the God who was the be-all and end-all of his existence.

Jesus seems to have expected the coming of God's kingdom in the very near future. In one saying (Mark 9.1) he prophesies that those standing around him will not taste death until they see the kingdom of God come with power. His twelve disciples will then sit on thrones judging the twelve tribes of Israel (Luke 22.30). It may be that like his gifted propagandist Paul, Jesus felt that he could hasten the coming of the kingdom of God by his own actions. Be this as it may, for reasons which are not completely clear, at some point he resolved to go from Galilee to Jerusalem, to confront the religious and political leaders of the people. He travelled with his followers, both men and women. There he attracted hostile attention to himself by a symbolic action in the temple in which he disrupted the activities of the money-changers and those who sold birds for sacrifices, traders essential to the worship of the temple. He also announced the destruction of the temple, which God would replace with a new one. The Jewish authorities turned on him, and one of his disciples, Judas, told them of a place where he could be arrested inconspicuously. After the last supper with his disciples, Jesus went to the garden of Gethsemane, from where he was taken away to trial and execution by crucifixion, probably in 30 CE.

Because the interests of the evangelists seem to dominate most strongly in the accounts of the trial of Jesus, it is difficult to identify the precise charges brought against him and by whom he was finally condemned to death. His criticism of the temple comes up in accounts of his trial, but is then said to be false witness; this would be an essentially religious crime. However, the placard which is said to have been fixed to the cross in three languages stated that Jesus was 'king of the Jews', in other words yet another claimant to the messiahship, and therefore guilty of a political crime. At all events, only the Romans could administer capital punishment, and the cruel method of crucifixion was distinctively theirs. On whatever charge, Jesus died on the cross. His disciples cannot have expected this, since they all fled in terror; only some women disciples are said to have stood at a distance, watching the scene. The site of his crucifixion is said to have been 'the place of the skull' (Mark 15.22), Greek = Golgotha, Latin = Calvary.

Joseph of Arimathea is said to have asked for Jesus' body (Mark 15.43). According to the narrative he bought a new linen shroud, which is thought by some to have been preserved as the Turin Shroud, which bears the image of a man on it. However, this shroud has been dated by several independent experts to the fourteenth century. He then laid the body in a tomb in the rock (the traditional location of which is marked by the Church of the Holy Sepulchre), which was later found by women followers to be empty. Whether at this point we are in the realm of legend and in fact Jesus was buried in a common criminal's grave is a matter argued over by scholars.

pp. 850, 851

After his death Jesus appeared to his followers, initially to Mary Magdalene and to Peter, then to various of his disciples. This is claimed by one of the earliest Christian documents we have, Paul's first letter to the Corinthians (15.3–8). Although he had never met Jesus in the flesh, Paul himself

1. John Martin, *The Great Day of His Wrath*, 1851–3

2. John Martin, *The Plains of Heaven*, 1851–3

3. S. Apollinaris in Classe, Ravenna, interior showing apse and mosaic of the Transfiguration with St Apollinaris and lambs below it, sixth century

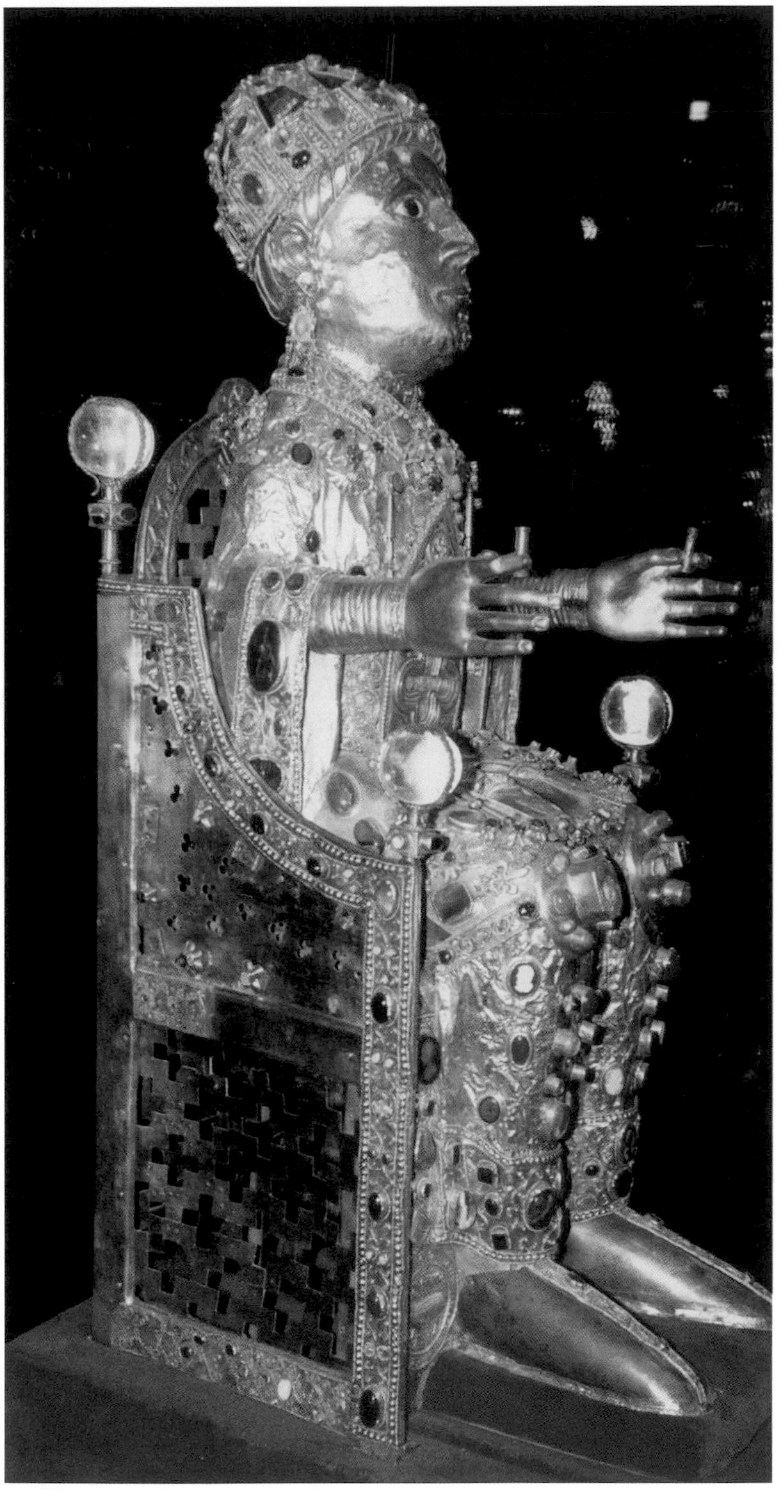

4. The Majesty of Ste Foy, *c.* tenth-century reliquary, Treasury of the Abbey Church of Conques

5. The Resurrection of Lazarus, mosaic cycle, S. Apollinare Nuovo, Ravenna, sixth century

6. Giotto, The Resurrection of Lazarus, Scrovegni Chapel

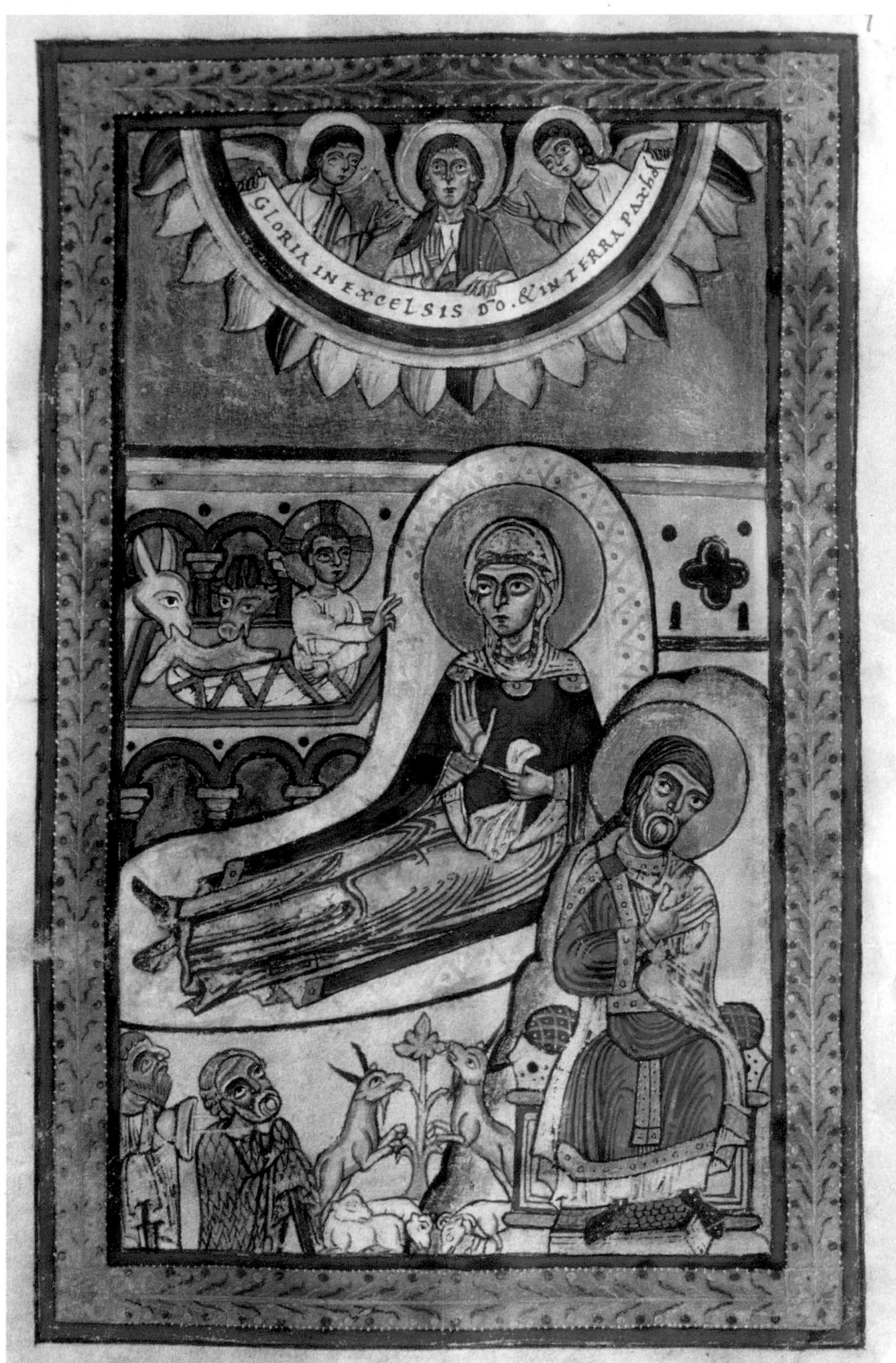

7. Nativity from twelfth-century illuminated manuscript Bible from Helmarshausen, near Kassel, Germany

8. Matthias Grünewald, The Virgin Mary, from The Nativity, *Isenheim Altarpiece*, *c.* 1515

9. Hieronymus Bosch, *Christ carrying the Cross*

10. Pieter Brueghel the Elder, *Dulle Griet* (Mad Meg)

11. Procession through Paris with monstrance, fifteenth century

12. John Lydgate and Pilgrims leaving Canterbury, from the end of the Prologue to *The Canterbury Tales* in an edition produced 1433–62

13. Nicolo Dorigati, The Concluding Session of the Council of Trent

14. Patricio Morlete Ruiz, *The Sacred Heart of Jesus*, Mexico, nineteenth century

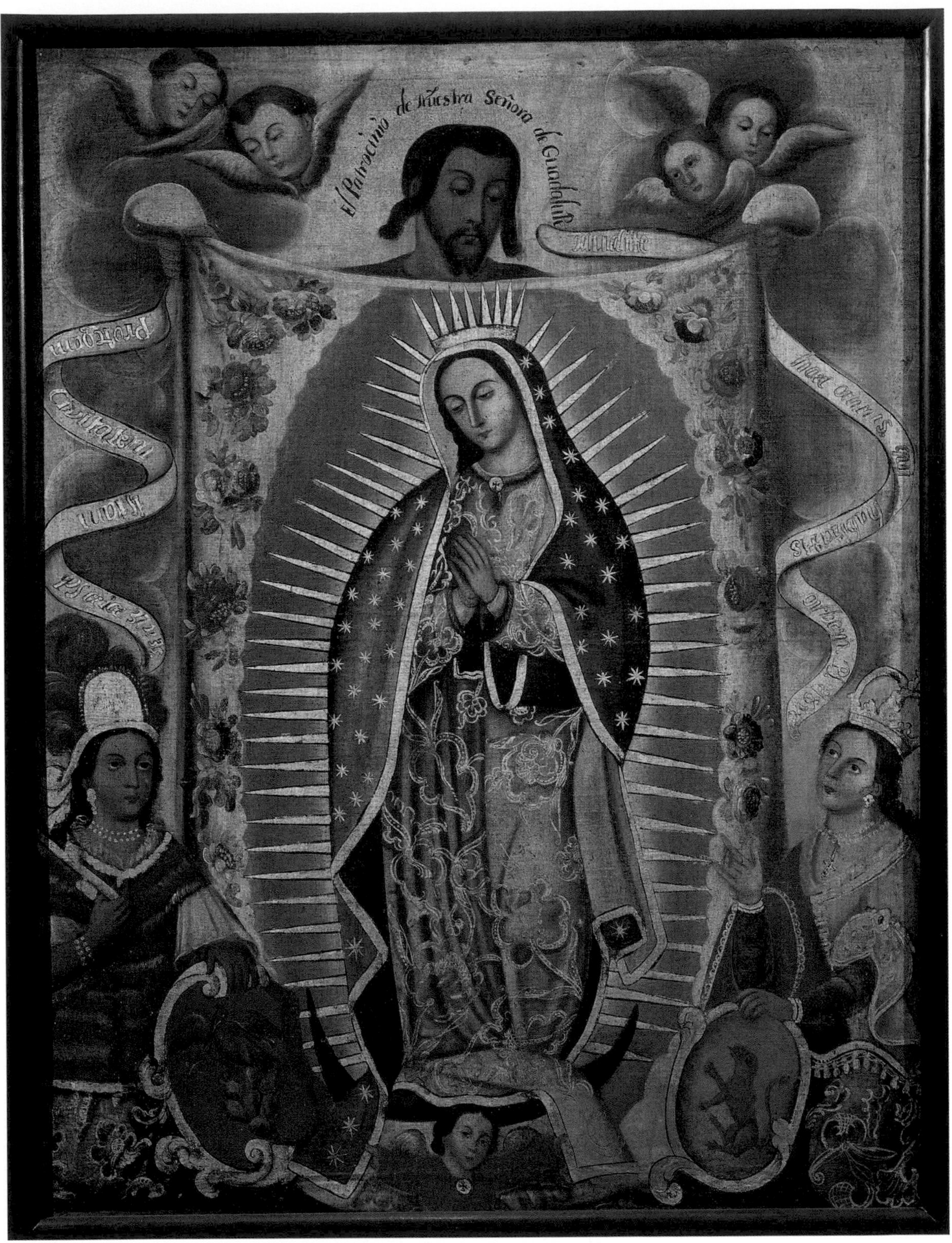

15. *Our Lady of Guadalupe*, by an unknown artist, 1745

16. Andrei Rublev, icon of *The Holy Trinity*, fifteenth century

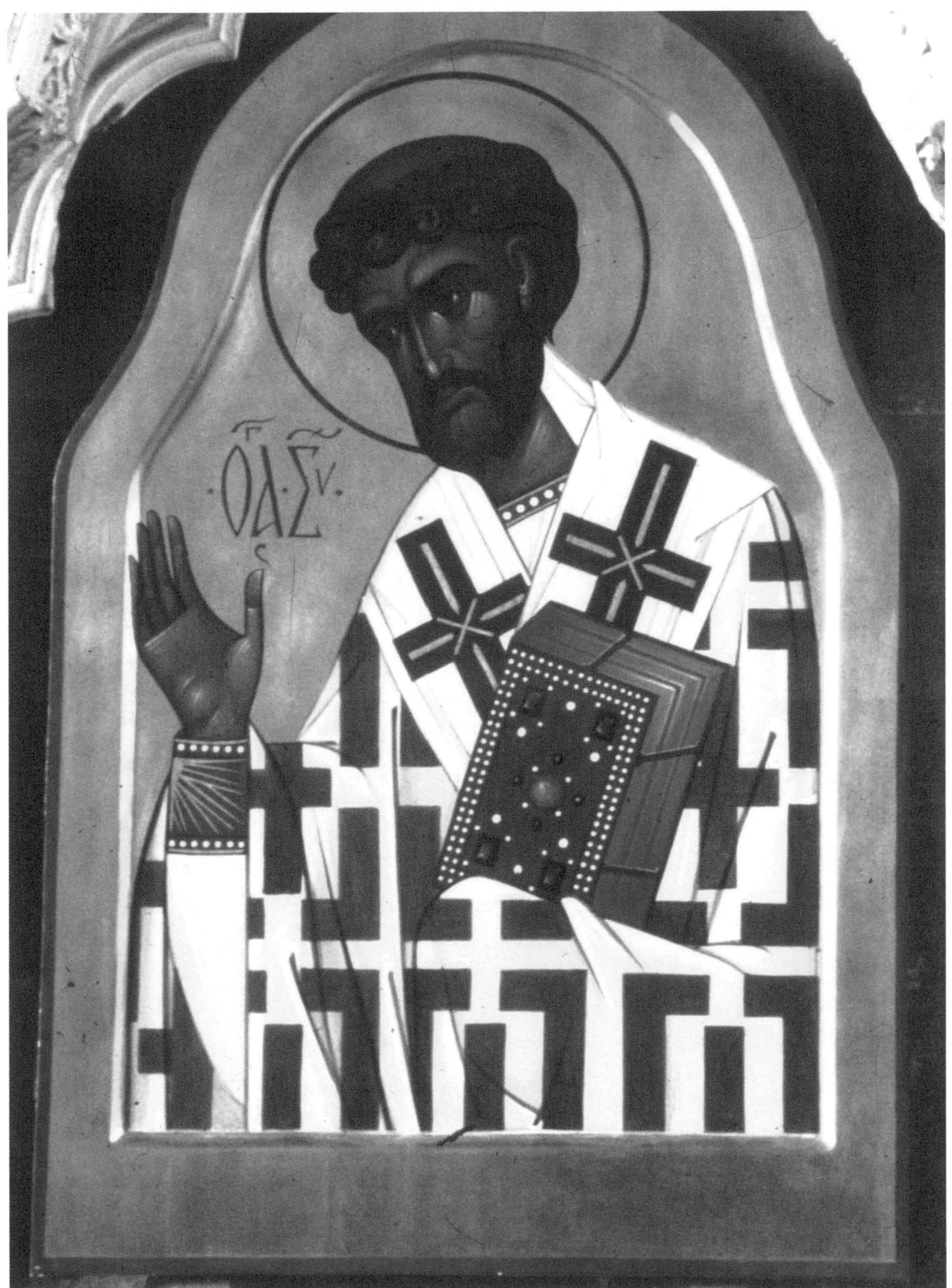

17. Sergei Fyodorov, icon of St Swithun, Winchester Cathedral

18. Interior, parish church of Vaujont, Longarone, Belluno, Italy, designed by Michelucci in 1968

19. Interior, Brasilia Cathedral

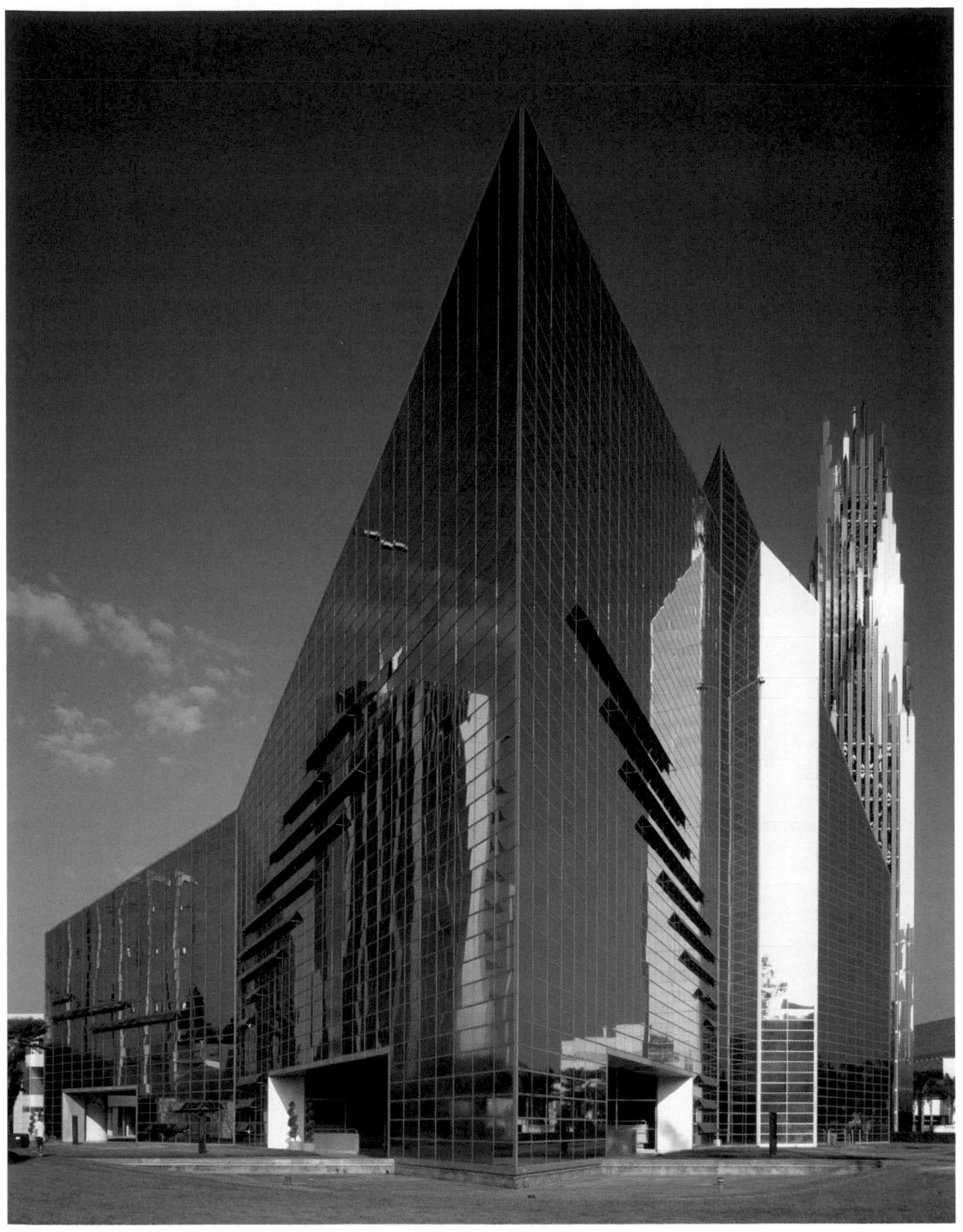

20. The Crystal Cathedral, Garden Grove, California, designed by Philip Johnson, 1980

21. Jyoti Sahi, *Washing Feet*

TITLES OF JESUS

Lists of 'titles of Christ' in reference books often extend to 100 entries and more, with such exotic ones from the Book of Revelation as 'Lion of the tribe of Judah' (5.5), 'Root of David' and 'Morning Star' (22.16). However, quite apart from the fact that many of these 'titles' are not strictly titles, but represent the rich imagery which came to be used of Jesus by the first Christians in prayer and praise, 'titles of *Christ*' is a problematical expression. For 'Christ' is itself a title, not a name: the name of the person to whom it was given was 'Jesus of Nazareth'. What titles, if any, Jesus gave himself, and what titles were given to him during his lifetime is a different matter. Answering this question is complicated by the fact that the Gospels which contain these titles are also written from an ardent faith in the resurrection and exaltation of Jesus, and the possibility cannot be ruled out that some titles in them are projections of this faith back on to the earthly Jesus.

The titles used in connection with Jesus during his lifetime are:

Christ (Greek *Christos*)/*Messiah* (Hebrew *meshiach*): In the Gospels Jesus hardly ever uses the title Christ (Messiah) of himself: the only exceptions are Mark 9.41, 'Whoever gives you a cup of water in the name of Christ'; Matthew 23.10, 'Neither be called masters, for you have one master, the Christ'; and Luke 24.26, 'Was it not necessary that the Christ should suffer these things and enter into his glory?' Twice, in indirect speech (Matthew 16.20 and Luke 4.41), Jesus is said to have told his disciples not to speak because they knew he was the Christ. However, the narrative knows that the title 'Christ' or messianic expectations were attached to Jesus: by his followers (e.g. Mark 8.29); his opponents (Mark 14.51); and the Romans (Mark 15.32).

Messiah

Son of God: This title is not used often in the Gospels, and when it is, it does not have the significance that it does in the creeds and later Christian belief. In the Hebrew- and Aramaic-speaking world, 'son of', when used in connection with God, denotes character more than physical descent: 'son of God' is one who reflects God in what he says and does. When it does appear in the Synoptic Gospels, it is on the lips of those possessed by demons (Mark 3.11; 5.7) or in a divine saying from heaven (Mark 1.11; 9.7), or by Jesus' disciples (Matthew 14.33; 16.16).

Son of man: Literally 'the son of the man'. This title appears often in the Gospels and hardly at all in the rest of the New Testament. It is the title that is most likely to have been used by Jesus himself. It is used only by Jesus, in three different contexts: 1. in sayings about the earthly life of the Son of man (he has nowhere to lay his head, Matthew 8.20; he comes eating and drinking and is called a glutton and a drunkard, Matthew 11.19); 2. in sayings about a future appearance of the Son of man in an apocalyptic scenario (Jesus tells his judges that they will see the Son of man seated at the right hand and coming with the clouds of heaven, Mark 14.62; the Son of man will come in glory with the angels and separate the sheep from the goats in judgement, Matthew 25.31); 3. in sayings about the future suffering of the Son of man (Mark 8.31; 9.31; 10.33). Which of these groups of sayings goes back to Jesus, and what is the background of the term Son of man, which Jesus sometimes uses as if it is referring to someone else ('Whoever is ashamed of me and my words … of him will the Son of Man be ashamed', Mark 8.38) is still hotly disputed by scholars.

Lord (Greek *Kyrios*): In the Gospels,'Lord' is used as a polite form of address, equivalent to our 'Sir'; in the rest of the New Testament, however, it becomes the most exalted of titles. *Kyrios* was the word used in the Greek translation of the Hebrew Bible, the Septuagint, as a substitute for the divine name, YHWH.

Prophet: The term prophet is often used in connection with Jesus. When people take offence at him, Jesus remarks that 'a prophet is not without honour except in his own country' (Mark 6.4); but like John the Baptist before him he was apparently regarded by people as 'a prophet like one of the prophets of old' (Mark 6.15). and as he enters Jerusalem to the acclamation of the crowds they say, 'This is the prophet Jesus from Nazareth in Galilee' (Matthew 21.11).

p. 858

Son of David: The crowds welcoming Jesus into Jerusalem also shout out 'Hosanna to the Son of David' (Matthew 21.15), a title which has already been used in requests to him for help from a Canaanite woman whose daughter is possessed by a demon (Matthew 15.22) and two blind men outside Jericho (Matthew 20.30). Matthew in fact begins his Gospel with a genealogy which in the very first verse claims that Jesus is David's son (1.1). In Jesus' time there was an expectation that the Messiah would come from the house of David.

also claimed to have seen Jesus, and this vision transformed him from a persecutor of Christians to one of the most influential figures in Christian history.

Legacy

Because his words and actions were focused on God and God's kingly rule, and he expected God to intervene in the course of the world in the imminent future, Jesus left behind him a minimal

WHO KILLED JESUS?

p. 685

In the Gospel of Matthew, Pontius Pilate, prefect of Judaea, washes his hands in public and states that he is innocent of the blood of Jesus. Thereupon the crowd responds, 'His blood be on us and on our children.' Over the centuries these words led to the most terrible treatment imaginable of Jews by Christians, who claimed that 'the Jews' were the murderers of God, and to a deep-seated Christian anti-Judaism.

But precisely who was behind the crucifixion of Jesus? Were the Jews to blame, and if so which Jews, since they cannot all be lumped together? And what about the role of the Romans? Although it is very difficult to discover the historical course of events, given the nature of the accounts in the four Gospels, written after Christians had come to believe that Jesus had been raised from the dead and deeply coloured by that faith, it is important to make an attempt to study the texts carefully, if only to correct pernicious views held for so long in the past.

There are references to the crucifixion of Jesus in non-Christian sources, notably the *Annals* of the Roman historian Tacitus (XV, 44) and the *Jewish Antiquities* of the Jewish historian Josephus (XVIII, 63–4), though the latter passage has been supposed to be a Christian insertion. However, the only detailed accounts are in the four Gospels.

When reading them, it is important to be aware of a major difficulty facing Christians preaching about Jesus. Their message was in fact that the son of God, the Messiah, who had appeared according to the scriptures and had been raised to the right hand of God, had been executed by the Roman authorities in a manner reserved for slaves and criminals. In other words, their Jesus was apparently a condemned felon. We might therefore expect to find attempts in the Gospels to exonerate the Romans and put the blame elsewhere, and indeed we do.

Of the four Gospel accounts, Matthew follows Mark closely. However, he adds to Mark an appearance of Pilate's wife, who has had a dream about Jesus and is convinced that he is righteous, and is the one evangelist who depicts Pilate washing his hands. In Luke (only) Jesus is sent to Herod Antipas, the local ruler: Herod sends him back to Pilate and both Herod and Pilate explicitly say that he is not guilty. Finally, instead of saying that Jesus was son of God, Luke has the centurion standing at the foot of the cross say that he was 'innocent'. The Gospel of John is more even-handed.

Messiah

So did the Romans merely confirm a death sentence pronounced by Jewish authorities? Here it is important to note differences in the accounts. In Matthew and Mark there is a nocturnal trial before Caiaphas and 'scribes and elders': two charges are levelled against Jesus, prophesying against the temple (this is dropped because of conflicting evidence) and claiming to be the Messiah, and he is condemned to death, though his claim to be the Messiah does not play a further role. He is mocked as a 'prophet'. In Luke Jesus is interrogated before the Jewish council in the morning, but this is not a formal trial; some think that it is a basis for a denunciation to Pilate. In John Jesus is interrogated by the high priest Annas and is sent on to Caiaphas, who is confusingly said to be the high priest that year. Readers already know that Caiaphas wants Jesus' death: some time before, he has remarked that 'it is expedient for you that one man should die for the people' (John 11.50).

The attitude of the people towards Jesus also varies. In Matthew and Mark they turn against Jesus, apparently influenced by the local aristocracy. In Luke the people call for the crucifixion, but a large crowd follows him to his execution lamenting. In John the people do not figure at all.

The evidence in the sources is complex and sometimes confusing. At all events, though, it is generally agreed that the Jews could not themselves inflict a death sentence, nor is it evident what charge against Jesus could have carried one. Jesus seems to have been condemned under Roman law: the notice pinned to the cross, 'Jesus of Nazareth King of the Jews', is formulated from a Roman perspective.

Kingdom of God

But why was Jesus crucified? It seems most likely that, coming from the country to Jerusalem, he fell foul of the local aristocracy, who were closely associated with the running of the temple, and the Roman authorities. He is said to have prophesied against the temple and performed a symbolic action to 'cleanse' it, and his talk about the kingdom may have been seen as a political challenge. There were other 'prophets' at the time of Jesus who gained a following and came to a violent end (Judas of Galilee in 6 CE, a Samaritan prophet in 36 CE and Theudas in 44–6 CE: Judas and Theudas are mentioned in Acts 5.36–7). Jesus seems to have met his end in a similar situation.

Simon Légasse, *The Trial of Jesus*, London: SCM Press 1997

legacy of teaching or other instructions. He produced no written documents, and what documents we have containing sayings of his give a Greek translation of them. Even the prayer which he is said to have taught his disciples, the Lord's Prayer, also regarded as a succinct summary of his teaching, has been preserved in two different versions, a common source of which is not easy to identify. Although a movement developed with amazing speed after his death, Jesus left no instructions for its organization or practices, say, in the form of a community rule of the kind discovered at Qumran. Inspired by what they believed to be the living Spirit sent by God, which was the Spirit

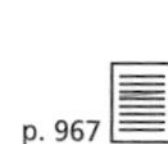
p. 967

p. 845

of Jesus who had died and been raised again, the first Christians treated the words of Jesus freely, as is evident from the Gospels, and combined event and interpretation in narratives, sometimes, as in the case of the miracle stories, in such a way that it is difficult to distinguish between event and interpretation at all.

Jesus of Nazareth becomes Jesus who is the Christ, and the heavenly figure begins to swallow up the earthly figure. Yet there is always a need to distinguish between the two, for if Jesus is the norm and the criterion for Christianity, this Jesus must be a real figure and not a projection. Even if it is impossible to write a biography of him or paint a portrait which depicts all his features, the attempt has constantly to be made.

Without Jesus there would be no Christianity. Yet Jesus lived and died a Jew and in his independence from Christianity as it developed over the centuries has always proved a challenge to it, the source of criticisms of forms of Christianity which have forgotten its origins and strayed too far from what Jesus thought, believed, did and lived for.

JOHN BOWDEN

Gerd Lüdemann, *Jesus after 2000 Years*, London: SCM Press and Amherst, NY: Prometheus Books 2000; John J. Rousseau and Rami Arav, *Jesus and His World*, Minneapolis: Fortress Press and London: SCM Press 1996; E. P. Sanders, *Jesus and Judaism*, London: SCM Press and Philadelphia: Fortress Press 1985; Gerd Theissen, *The Shadow of the Galilean*, London: SCM Press and Philadelphia: Fortress Press 1987; Gerd Theissen and Annette Merz, *The Historical Jesus*, London: SCM Press and Minneapolis: Fortress Press 1998

It is often said that the four New Testament Gospels, Matthew, Mark, Luke and John, are four different theological and literary portraits of Jesus, and that at the beginning and end of the Gospels, the nature of the picture of Jesus drawn in them becomes particularly clear: this is striking above all in the accounts of the death and resurrection of Jesus.

Such statements can be easily passed over and their significance underestimated. Their significance becomes much more evident if it is possible to see precisely how the Gospels differ from one another. This is not easy, since it is not practicable to compare them using the text of a conventional Bible. So to help matters, on the following pages you will find summaries of the New Testament passages relating to the birth stories, the last supper and institution of the eucharist, the passion narratives and the resurrection narratives, together with some explanatory comments in each case. You are invited to draw your own conclusions.

THE BIRTH STORIES

Matthew		Mark	Luke		John
1.1–17	Genealogy	None	1.5–25	In Jerusalem, an angel appears to Zechariah, an elderly priest, and tells him that his barren wife Elizabeth will conceive. She does so and keeps hidden for five months.	None
1.18–25	Mary is betrothed to Joseph but is found to be with child. Joseph resolves to divorce her quietly, but an angel appears to him in a dream and tells him not to fear to take Mary as his wife, as the child is conceived of the Holy Spirit.		1.26–38	In the sixth month, in Nazareth, an angel appears to Mary, a virgin, and tells her that she will bear a son whose name will be Jesus.	
2.1–12	Jesus is born in Bethlehem. Wise men come from the East to Jerusalem in search of him, to the disquiet of King Herod. Chief priests and scribes say that he is born in Bethlehem. The wise men follow a star and worship him, bringing him gifts. They return home without informing Herod, as they had been commanded.		1.39–56	Mary hastens to Elizabeth and sings a song of praise (*Magnificat*). She stays three months.	
			1.57–80	Elizabeth gives birth to a child, John (the Baptist), who grows up and is in the wilderness. Zechariah sings a song of praise (*Benedictus*).	
2.13–15	An angel tells Joseph to flee to Egypt to escape Herod and remain there until Herod's death.		2.1–7	The emperor orders a census and Joseph and Mary go from Nazareth to Bethlehem. Mary gives birth and lays her son in a manger.	
2.16–18	Herod has all the male children under two in Bethlehem killed.		2.8–20	Angels appear to shepherds in the field who go to Bethlehem to see the child.	
2.19–23	After Herod's death Joseph and family return; not, however, to Bethlehem but to Nazareth, for fear of Herod's successor Archelaus.		2.21	Jesus is circumcised on the eighth day.	
			2.22–38	Jesus is taken to Jerusalem for the purification of the family. The righteous Simeon holds him in his arms and blesses him (*Nunc Dimittis*). The prophetess Anna gives thanks to God.	
			2.39–40	The family returns to Nazareth and Jesus grows up.	
			2.41–52	The family goes annually to Jerusalem for Passover. When Jesus is twelve he is left behind in the temple where his parents find him among the teachers.	
			3.23–38	Genealogy.	

Neither Mark nor John relates the circumstances of the birth of Jesus. In Mark, Jesus appears as a grown man, who after being baptized by John the Baptist begins to preach in Galilee. The Gospel of John has a prologue describing how the Word (Greek *Logos*) becomes flesh, and then has John the Baptist witnessing to the beginning of Jesus' activity.

Both Matthew and Luke give genealogies of Jesus, Matthew at the beginning of his Gospel, Luke at the beginning of Jesus' ministry, after his baptism. These differ in the ancestors given: while in Luke Jesus' ancestry is traced back to Adam, 'the son of God', in Matthew Jesus is described as 'the son of David, the son of Abraham'. In Matthew the genealogy is the other way round, starting with Abraham; it strikingly mentions four women, all apparently of questionable morality, among Jesus' ancestors: Tamar, Ruth, Rahab and Bathsheba.

Both Gospels have an annunciation by an angel (but one is to Joseph and one is to Mary) and in both Jesus is born in Bethlehem. The wise men and the star appear only in Matthew, as do the massacre of the innocents and the flight of the holy family to Egypt. Luke has left the greatest stamp on the tradition with the census, the birth in a stable, the appearance of angels to shepherds and their visit to Bethlehem. He also adds two stories bridging the gap between Jesus' infancy and his maturity: his presentation in the temple and his being left behind in the temple, where he amazes the teachers.

THE LAST SUPPER AND THE INSTITUTION OF THE EUCHARIST

Matthew 26.26–9	*Mark 14.22–5*	*Luke 22.17–19*	*Paul (1 Corinthians 11.23–6)*
Now as they were eating, Jesus took bread, and blessed, and broke it, and gave it to the disciples and said, 'Take, eat, this is my body.'	And as they were eating, he took bread, and blessed, and broke it, and gave it to them, and said, 'Take, this is my body.'	And he took a cup, and when he had given thanks he said, 'Take this and divide it among yourselves; for I tell you that from now on I shall not drink of the fruit of the vine until the kingdom of God comes.'	For I received from the Lord what I also delivered to you, that the Lord Jesus on the night that he was betrayed took bread, and when he had given thanks, he broke it, and said, 'This is my body which is for you. Do this in remembrance of me.'
And he took a cup, and when he had given thanks he gave it to them, saying,	And he took a cup, and when he had given thanks he gave it to them, and they all drank of it.	And he took bread, and when he had given thanks he broke it and gave it to them, saying, 'This is my body.'	In the same way the cup, after supper, saying, 'This cup is the new covenant in my blood. Do this, as often as you drink it, in remembrance of me.'
'Drink of it, all of you, for this is my blood of the covenant, which is poured out for many for the forgiveness of sins. I tell you that I shall not drink again of this fruit of the vine until that day when I drink it new with you in my Father's kingdom.'	And he said to them, 'This is my blood of the covenant, which is poured out for many. Truly, I say to you, I shall not drink again of the fruit of the vine until that day when I drink it new in the kingdom of God.'		For as often as you eat this bread and drink the cup, you proclaim the Lord's death until he comes.

There are four accounts of Jesus' last supper in the New Testament, in the Gospels of Matthew, Mark and Luke (there is none in the Gospel of John), and one in Paul's First Letter to the Corinthians. When they are set side by there are significant differences between them. The main ones are:

1. In Mark and Matthew the sayings with which Jesus interprets his actions are parallel ('This is my body', 'This is my blood'); Paul has 'This is my body', 'This cup is the new covenant'.
2. In Mark and Matthew the blood is said to be 'of the covenant'; in Paul the cup is 'the new covenant'.
3. In Mark and Matthew there is no explanation of the body, the blood is explained as being be poured out 'for many'. In Paul the bread is Jesus' body 'for you'; there is no such explanation with the cup.
4. The command to repeat the actions appears only in Paul.
5. In Luke the action with the cup precedes the action with the bread.

These variations reflect how the tradition was not handed down word for word; interpretations of the significance of Jesus' last supper played a role from the start. Scholars argue that the texts of Paul and Mark are the earliest. The direct command to drink blood in Mark is striking, since Jews were forbidden to consume blood; this is thought to favour Paul as the earliest text, since he speaks rather of 'the new covenant in my blood'. In that case, the phrase 'drinking blood' would have been used in non-Jewish Christian communities, where such offence would not be felt.

THE PASSION NARRATIVES

Matthew		*Mark*		*Luke*		*John*	
26.30–46	Jesus and his disciples go to the Mount of Olives. Jesus prophesies that Peter will deny him. Jesus prays in Gethsemane while the disciples sleep.	14.26–42	Jesus and his disciples go to the Mount of Olives. Jesus prophesies that Peter will deny him. Jesus prays in Gethsemane while the disciples sleep.	22.39–46	Jesus goes to the Mount of Olives 'as was his custom', followed by his disciples. He prays in agony and an angel strengthens him while the disciples sleep.	18.1–11	Jesus goes to a garden across the Kidron valley, to which Judas leads soldiers to arrest him. Simon Peter cuts off the ear of the high priest's slave.
26.47–57	Judas betrays Jesus. One of Jesus' followers cuts off the ear of the high priest's slave. The disciples flee.	14.43–52	Judas betrays Jesus. One of Jesus' followers cuts off the ear of the high priest's slave. The disciples flee. A young man in a linen cloth is seized but escapes naked.	22.47–53	Judas betrays Jesus. One of Jesus' followers cuts off the ear of the high priest's slave. Jesus heals him. The disciples flee.		
						18.12–14	Jesus is led off to Annas, father-in-law of the high priest.
26.57–68	Nocturnal trial before Caiaphas (Sanhedrin).	14.43–65	Nocturnal trial before Caiaphas (Sanhedrin).				
26.69–75	Peter denies Jesus.	14.66–72	Peter denies Jesus.	22.54–62	Peter denies Jesus.	18.15–17	Peter denies Jesus.
				22.63–5	Jesus is mocked and blindfolded.	18.19–24	Annas questions Jesus.
				22.66–71	Hearing during the day before the Council.	18.25–7	Peter denies Jesus twice more.
27.1–2	Jesus is led off to Pilate.	15.1	Jesus is led off to Pilate	23.1–7	Jesus is led off to Pilate. Pilate finds no fault with him but the crowd claim he is a troublemaker from Galilee. This means he is under Herod's jurisdiction and Pilate sends him to Herod.	18.28	Jesus is taken to Pilate but the Jews cannot enter the praetorium for fear of being unclean for the Passover.
						18.29–40	Pilate goes in and out of the praetorium, questioning both the Jews and Jesus. Jesus talks of the nature of his kingship. Pilate asks what is truth. The crowd ask for Barabbas.
27.3–9	Judas commits suicide.						
				23.8–12	Herod questions Jesus who is silent. Soldiers mock and abuse him. Jesus is sent back to Pilate. Herod and Pilate become friends.		
27.11–26	Jesus appears before Pilate but is silent. Pilate's wife asks Pilate to have nothing to do with Jesus, who is righteous. The crowd chooses Barabbas rather than Jesus to be released. Pilate washes his hands.	15.2–15	Jesus appears before Pilate. The crowd chooses Barabbas rather than Jesus to be released.	25.25–25	Pilate wants to release Jesus but the crowd protests and asks for Barabbas to be released.	19.1–16	Pilate scourges Jesus and the soldiers dress him as a king. The crowd demand that Jesus should be crucified but Pilate wants to release him. Eventually Jesus is presented to the crowd as king and handed over for crucifixion.
27.27–31	Jesus is mocked and struck by the soldiers.	15.16–20	Jesus is mocked and struck by the soldiers.				
27.32–44	Jesus is taken to be crucified. Simon of Cyrene carries his cross. He is mocked by the crowd and two robbers crucified with him.	15.21–32	Jesus is taken to be crucified. Simon of Cyrene carries his cross. He is mocked by the crowd and two robbers crucified with him.	23.26–38	Jesus is taken to be crucified along with two criminals. Simon of Cyrene carries his cross. A crowd including many women laments Jesus who tells them not to weep for him but for themselves.	19.17–22	Jesus bears his own cross to Golgotha.
						19.23–4	The soldiers by the cross cast lots for Jesus' robe.
						19.25–7	Jesus commends his mother Mary, and the beloved disciple, standing below the cross, to each other.
				29.43–43	One of the thieves mocks Jesus, the		

→

Matthew		Mark		Luke		John	
					other asks to be remembered and is promised paradise.		
27.45–54	Darkness over the land for three hours. Jesus cries out and dies. The curtain of the temple is split, tombs are opened and saints come out. The centurion by the cross says that this was the son of God.	15.33–9	Darkness over the land for three hours. Jesus cries out and dies. The curtain of the temple is split. The centurion by the cross says that this was the son of God.	23.44–8	Darkness over the land for three hours. Jesus commends his spirit to God and dies. The curtain of the temple is split. The centurion by the cross says that Jesus was innocent.	19.28–30	Jesus says 'I thirst', is given a sponge of vinegar and dies with the words 'It is finished'.
						19.31–7	The soldiers break the legs of the criminals crucified with Jesus, but Jesus is already dead. His side is pierced and blood and water come out.
27.55–6	Women stand by the cross.	15.40–1	Women stand by the cross.	23.48–9	The multitude go home beating their breasts. Jesus' acquaintances and women followers stand far off.		
27.57–66	Joseph of Arimathea asks for the body of Jesus and puts it in a new tomb, which is guarded by the authorities.	15.42–6	Joseph of Arimathea asks for the body of Jesus and puts it in a new tomb.	23.50–4	Joseph of Arimathea asks for the body of Jesus and puts it in a new tomb.	19.38–42	Joseph of Arimathea asks for the body of Jesus and puts it in a new tomb.

The Gospel accounts of events between Jesus' arrival in the Garden of Gethsemane and subsequent arrest and his crucifixion and subsequent burial, traditionally known as the passion narratives, show significant similarities and also differences. As elsewhere, the relationship between the first three Gospels is particularly close; the Gospel of John goes its own way, with its own theological emphases. It is worth noting how Matthew, Mark and Luke relate to one another.

Mark, the earliest Gospel, mentions a young man in a linen garment who flees at Jesus' arrest; this is not taken up by any other evangelist.

Matthew basically follows Mark, but makes some insertions. He gives an account of the suicide of Judas Iscariot; he also adds an appearance of Pilate's wife, affirming Jesus' innocence, and has Pilate washing his hands. Tombs are opened and saints appear at the crucifixion of Jesus, and when he has been buried, a guard is set on his tomb.

Luke varies more noticeably from the account in Mark and has more additions. An angel strengthens Jesus as he prays in Gethsemane; Jesus heals the high priest's servant, who has his ear cut off. Instead of a nocturnal trial before Caiaphas (the Sanhedrin), Jesus is interrogated during the day; he is mocked and blindfolded before this, rather than just before the crucifixion, as in Mark and Matthew. Pilate initially finds no fault with him, and sends him off to Herod Antipas, the local ruler. Women accompany Jesus to the cross and remain watching to the end. Jesus has a conversation with the two thieves crucified with him, and after his death the centurion at the foot of the cross does not say that he is son of God, but that he is innocent.

In John, Jesus is first questioned by Annas, father-in-law of the high priest. Peter denies Jesus three times. There is a long scene involving Pilate, Jesus and the Jews. Pilate has to keep going in and out of the praetorium because if the Jews entered it they would become defiled. Jesus carries his own cross. He is in command of his life to the end. His legs are broken and his side pierced.

These variations are extremely important and more than just an academic exercise, because although the crucifixion of Jesus is mentioned in non-Christian sources, the Gospel accounts are the main evidence for it. One of the blackest aspects of Christian history is the way in which Jews have been persecuted and killed 'because they killed Jesus'. A careful examination of the evidence here shows that the question 'Who killed Jesus?' is a much more complex one.

p. 662

THE RESURRECTION NARRATIVES

Matthew		*Mark*		*Luke*		*John*	
28.1–7	Mary Magdalene and the other Mary go to the tomb, which has guards on it. An angel rolls away the stone with an earthquake and terrifies the guards. He tells the women to say to the disciples that Jesus is going before them to Galilee.	16.1–7	Mary Magdalene, the other Mary and Salome go to the tomb. They see that the stone has been rolled away and enter the tomb where they meet a young man in white. He tells them to tell the disciples and Peter that Jesus is not there but is going before them to Galilee.	24.1–10	Women, later said to include Mary Magdalene, Joanna and Mary the mother of James, go to the tomb and find the stone rolled away. Two men in dazzling clothes appear and remind them how Jesus told them when he was in Galilee that he had to rise on the third day.	20.1–10	Mary Magdalene comes to the tomb and sees that the stone has been taken away. She runs to Simon Peter and the beloved disciple, who run back. They go into the tomb and return home.
						20.11–18	Mary encounters Jesus, thinking he is the gardener. He tells her not to touch him because he has not yet ascended to the Father.
28.8–10	The women hasten to tell the disciples. Jesus meets them and tells them to tell the brethren to go to Galilee.	16.8	The women flee and say nothing to anyone because they are afraid.	24.11	The women think this an idle tale.		
				[*24.12*	*Most ancient authorities omit this verse*]		
			[*The Gospel ends abruptly and there are no accounts of any resurrection appearances. Some manuscripts have added what is clearly a secondary conclusion.*]	24.13–32	Jesus appears to two disciples on the road to Emmaus.	20.19–23	Jesus appears to the disciples in the evening, behind closed doors, gives them his peace and breathes the Holy Spirit on them.
28.11–15	The soldiers are bribed to say that the disciples stole the body while they were asleep.			24.33–5	The two return to Jerusalem where they are told by the eleven disciples that Jesus has appeared to Simon.		
28.16–20	The eleven disciples go to a mountain in Galilee where Jesus orders them to make disciples of all nations.			24.36–49	Jesus appears and asks for food to show that he is not a spirit. He explains the scriptures to them and tells them to remain in the city.	20.24–8	A week later Jesus appears again; this time Thomas, who was not there previously, sees and believes.
				24.50–3	Jesus leads the disciples out to Bethany, blesses them and parts from them. They return to Jerusalem.	21.1–23	Jesus appears to the disciples by the Sea of Tiberias in an extended scene which involves a miraculous catch of fish.
					[*The Acts of the Apostles describes how Jesus appears to the apostles in Jerusalem over 40 days and then ascends to heaven, after which the Holy Spirit is given.*]		

When the resurrection narratives from the four Gospels are set side by side, it can be seen that they run far less in parallel than the accounts of the passion and crucifixion of Jesus which precede them. Mark's account is the briefest. Matthew introduces an earthquake and the story that the guards at the tomb were bribed to say that the body of Jesus was stolen while they were asleep. The women are told by an angel that Jesus is going before them to Galilee. Jesus himself commands the disciples to go there, where he bids farewell to them on a high mountain. In Luke everything takes place in Jerusalem: the angel's command to go to Galilee becomes 'Remember how he told you when he was in Galilee that he had to rise on the third day.' Jesus appears on the Emmaus road and in a closed room, where he eats a portion of fish to show he is not a spirit. Then he leads the disciples out to Bethany where he parts from them. In the Gospel of John Mary is the main figure by the empty tomb; then the disciples meet, first without and then with Thomas; Jesus appears to them and breathes the Holy Spirit on them. An appendix to the Gospel (chapter 21) has Jesus appearing by the Sea of Tiberias and after a miraculous catch of fish giving commands to Peter.

Jesus of history

Hermann Samuel Reimarus (1694–1768), a professor of oriental languages in Hamburg and a committed advocate of a religion of reason, wrote a *Defence of the Rational Worshippers of God.* However, he only circulated it privately during his lifetime and it was not until after his death that the famous Enlightenment figure Gottfried Ephraim Lessing published a series of seven fragments from it without naming the author. In the last and longest of these fragments, entitled 'On the aims of Jesus and his disciples', Reimarus claimed to be distinguishing what Jesus really said and taught from the (false) account of the New Testament writings. Basically, he argued that Jesus was a traditional Jew who believed that he was the long-foretold Messiah. Jesus' disciples, Reimarus said, at first believed his claims, but after his death they revised the whole story of his career and made the earthly kingdom of Jesus a heavenly one.

Reimarus proved to be the first of a long series of figures who sought to recover this 'real' Jesus, convinced that beneath the portraits of Jesus in the New Testament Gospels there was another Jesus, whose features had been overlaid and distorted by the later church, to which the evangelist belonged,. There were sufficient of them for Albert Schweitzer to write an account of their efforts, which first appeared in 1906 and then in a much-expanded second edition in 1913; in English it was published as *The Quest of the Historical Jesus,* though not in its full form until 2000. It has been recognized as one of the most important books ever written about Jesus, and its basic insight, described below, has proved itself time and again since.

The 'quest' went through a number of stages. Following Reimarus, in the early decades of the nineteenth century a first group of scholars attempted to explain the miraculous features of the Gospel accounts of Jesus in rationalistic terms: they were particularly interested in explaining away the miracles. Thus they argued that the water which Jesus was thought to have turned into wine at Cana was a wedding gift of good wine which he had brought and stored in another room; his walking on the water involved a half-submerged log; the feeding of the five thousand was the infectious consequence of Jesus' setting an example by sharing his provisions; those supposedly raised from the dead had merely been in a coma, and so on. Jesus did not really die on the cross; the secret society of the Essene brethren sheltered a Jesus who had not really died, keeping him in hiding, from which he emerged to make his 'appearances'.

These attempts were mocked by David Friedrich Strauss (1808–74), who in a famous *Life of Jesus* translated by the novelist George Eliot used the notion of myth to explain the Gospel accounts. In them, he argued, motifs which appear in the Old Testament or are widespread in the history of religion are transferred to Jesus. For Strauss, everything before the baptism of Jesus was myth. Many of the stories about Jesus are modelled on the stories about Elijah and Elisha, like the calling of the disciples and the healings. The nature miracles are paralleled in other religions; Strauss even entitled a chapter containing a collection of them 'Sea Stories and Fish Stories'. There is no deliberate deception in the Gospels, but rather a vivid sense of mythical imagination. Strauss's view in this book (30 years later he wrote a second, much more conservative, Life) was predominantly negative.

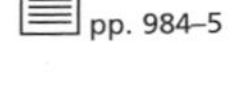

pp. 984–5

Enlightenment

Here, though, it differed from what were to prove by far the most popular writings about Jesus during the latter half of the nineteenth century. These attempted to present a coherent picture of Jesus by removing words and actions which were thought to be inauthentic and supplying material to fill the many gaps in the Gospel account. In keeping with nineteenth-century liberalism, Jesus was seen above all as a personality, and his teaching, his conduct and the impact he made on his contemporaries were all described with the aim of bringing out this personality. Such an approach was necessary because if Jesus was no longer regarded as the divine Son of God who performed miracles, he had to be given other qualities so that he had enough stature to be a sufficiently convincing replacement of the Christ of the church's tradition. Two bestsellers of the 1860s, Ernest Renan's *Vie de Jésus* and J. R. Seeley's *Ecce Homo,* tower above a host of inferior efforts in attempting to do this.

Messiah

Liberal theology

When Albert Schweitzer surveyed all these works, he could demonstrate that rather than discovering Jesus as he really was, they were projecting the authors' own views and ideals on to him: they were no more than mirror reflections. Moreover, this basic insight proved not only to apply to the books about which he wrote; it could be applied to a very large number of the books written about Jesus during the twentieth century, in which Jesus has been depicted as a divine propagandist, the founder of a secret society, the 'man for others', a clown, and a magician. As church structures and authority have grown weaker, as theology has become more specialized and the taste for sensation has increased, these new pictures have ranged over an increasingly wide spectrum, venturing into areas like the sexuality of Jesus which were previously taboo.

Miracle

The rise of the new discipline of biblical criticism in the second half of the nineteenth century had raised questions about how the biblical evidence for the life of Jesus should be interpreted, questions arising from the nature of the Gospel accounts. This development, particularly in Germany, coincided with a new emphasis on the role of the church, or the community, in Christian faith.

Biblical criticism

The new climate was heralded by a little book by Martin Kähler, published in 1892, with the cumbersome title *The So-Called Historical Jesus and the Historic, Biblical Christ.* In it he argued that the quest of the 'historical' Jesus was a dead end: it was impossible to write a life of Jesus or to psychologize him; the sources just did not allow it. What mattered was the 'historic' Christ, the living Christ who was encountered in the church, whom Christians worshipped as 'Lord'.

Rudolf Bultmann, a gifted New Testament scholar, went even beyond Kähler. Along with Karl Barth he represented a new strand in theological thinking which emerged after the collapse of liberal theology after the First World War. Known as kerygmatic or dialectical theology, this was a theology of proclamation which stressed that God and the Word of God had no points of contact with the events of history. Bultmann held that not only was it impossible to write a life of Jesus, it was not even necessary: Jesus was the presupposition for Christian theology, not part of that theology. It was important only to know that he had existed, not what he had said and done. Radical though this view was, in the circumstances of Germany between the wars and well beyond the Second World War, it proved highly influential.

Theology

However, Bultmann's view was never generally accepted, and even among his pupils it was eventually challenged. 1953 saw the beginning of a 'new quest' of the historical Jesus, a major representative of which was the German scholar Günther Bornkamm (1905–90). While accepting that it was impossible to write a 'life' of Jesus, this new group of scholars argued that it would be quite fatal if scepticism were to lead to a complete lack of interest in Jesus of Nazareth. They believed that while names, places, events and dates might be beyond our reach, it was nevertheless possible to reconstruct something of the 'selfhood' of Jesus.

Here the ground was laid for a return to a view that had been neglected since Schweitzer (and his contemporary Johannes Weiss) had put it forward at the beginning of the twentieth century. In dismissing all the liberal pictures of Jesus, Schweitzer had seen Jesus against the background of his time as a prophetic Jewish figure, using the thought patterns of his own time, dying in the hope of bringing in the kingdom of God. But he concluded that this Jesus could not be significant for the modern world, and opted instead for 'reverence for life'. In the 1970s the Jewish Jesus at last came into his own, and what had been largely a history of Protestant scholarship was widened by the work of both Jewish scholars, the pioneer among whom was Geza Vermes, and Roman Catholic scholars, whose findings were popularized by Edward Schillebeeckx and Hans Küng.

Kingdom of God

One of the most striking instances of the continued interest in the historical Jesus is the Jesus Seminar, first convened in 1985 by the American scholar Robert W. Funk. Its on-going project has been to evaluate the historical significance of every shred of evidence about Jesus from antiquity (about 30–200 CE). Over the past twenty years more than 200 scholars from North America and beyond have taken part in its semi-annual meetings. Having completed its evaluation and interpretation of the Jesus tradition, the Seminar is now turning its attention to analysis of the historical value of materials about and by the first generation of Jesus people, e.g. the Acts of the Apostles and the letters of Paul. The distinguishing features of its method are that discussions are carried on as a public forum and are concluded with a ballot among those taking part to test the consensus of the group about the relative value of an item as historical evidence.

Today, then, research into the person of Jesus is as lively as ever, and few would argue that a quest for the historical Jesus is either illegitimate or impossible. Although lip-service is often paid to Schweitzer's book, it is probably little read now. Nevertheless, his story of the quest of the historical Jesus remains an important cautionary tale, and there are still lessons to be learnt from it in assessing the most recent studies of Jesus.

Among the more controversial recent scholarly books on Jesus, John Dominic Crossan's *The Historical Jesus: The Life of a Mediterranean Jewish Peasant* and John P. Meier's *A Marginal Jew. Rethinking the Historical Jesus* fill out the historical Jesus with a wealth of detail from his time. E. P. Sanders, *Jesus and Judaism,* probably remains the best book about Jesus after Schweitzer.

JOHN BOWDEN

Günther Bornkamm, *Jesus of Nazareth*, London: Hodder & Stoughton and New York: Harper & Row 1960; John Bowden, *Jesus: The Unanswered Questions*, London: SCM Press and Nashville, TN: Abingdon Press 1988; Rudolf Bultmann, *Jesus and the Word* (1934), London: Collins Fontana and New York: Scribner 1958; John Dominic Crossan, *The Historical Jesus: The Life of a Mediterranean Jewish Peasant*, New York: Continuum and Edinburgh, T&T Clark 1993; Martin Kähler, *The So-Called Historical Jesus and the Historic, Biblical Christ* (1892), Philadelphia: Fortress Press 1964; John P. Meier, *A Marginal Jew. Rethinking the Historical Jesus*, New York: Doubleday 1994; H. S. Reimarus, *Fragments*, Philadelphia: Fortress Press and London: SCM Press 1971; E. P. Sanders, *Jesus and Judaism*, London: SCM Press and Philadelphia: Fortress Press 1985; Albert Schweitzer, *The Quest of the Historical Jesus. First Complete Edition*, London: SCM Press and Minneapolis: Fortress Press 2000; Geza Vermes, *Jesus the Jew* (1973), London: SCM Press and Minneapolis: Fortress Press 2003 http://religion.rutgers.edu/jseminar, which also lists a wide range of books associated with the Jesus Seminar

Jewish Christianity

Following his death, Jesus was proclaimed as Messiah by Jewish followers who continued to embrace a Jewish lifestyle. Together with fellow Jews they worshipped in the synagogue and kept the law. Prior to the destruction of the Jerusalem temple in 70 CE, a number of these individuals sought refuge in the neighbourhood of Pella. According to the church father Irenaeus, these Jewish Christians practised circumcision and persevered in the observance of the law. As followers of Christ, they believed that Jesus was the son of Joseph and Mary and was appointed to the office of Messiah because he was descended from David (see the genealogy in Matthew 1.1–16) and had led a holy life. Separating themselves from those pagans – the Gentiles – who had also joined the followers of Jesus, they viewed themselves as the true heirs of the kingdom of God.

During the latter half of the second century and continuing into the third century, relations were strained between Jewish and Gentile Christian communities. The early church had produced the canon of the New Testament, whereas the Jewish Christian community remained faithful to its own Hebrew gospel. Although little is known about the development of Jewish Christianity from the middle of the second century CE until the rise of Islam in the sixth century, the church father Epiphanius (*c.* 315–403) records that communities existed as far away as Mesopotamia. He writes further that these Jewish Christians had synagogues and elders like the Jews, and engaged in similar religious practices.

With the rise of Islam, little is known about the history of the Jewish Christian community, apart from various converts. Throughout the Middle Ages Jews were frequently compelled to convert to Christianity: these forced converts should be distinguished from those Jews who embraced Jesus as their Messiah and Saviour. Even though Jews were persecuted in the Middle Ages, a number of prominent Jewish officials were permitted to hold high office, particularly those who had converted to Christianity. Baptism served as the means whereby such individuals were able to attain acceptance into general society.

As in the Middle Ages, Jews in post-medieval society were regarded with contempt. Despite such sentiments, Jewish Christians during this period were actively engaged in disseminating Jewish learning. Among those who were active participants in this renaissance of Jewish literature were Paul Nunez Coronel, Alfonso de Zamora and Alfonso d'Alcala, who aided Cardinal Francisco Ximenes de Cisneros (1436–1517) in preparing the Complutensian Polyglot Bible, a Bible which had the Hebrew, Greek and Latin texts printed in parallel. A former rabbi of Safed, Dominico Irosolimitano, taught Hebrew at Rome after accepting the Christian faith. Another Jew from Safed, Giovanni Baptista Jonas, converted in Poland in 1625 and became professor at the University of Pisa and subsequently a Vatican librarian. In the first half of the sixteenth century the German Jew Paulo Riccio became professor of philosophy at the University of Pavia, and helped Christians to gain a greater knowledge of Jewish literature.

By the nineteenth century Christian missions to the Jews led to the recreation of Jewish Christianity. Such steps were initially taken by Joseph Samuel Frey and Ridley Herschell, who inspired the London Society and the British Society for Promoting Christianity among the Jews. By the end of the century, there were nearly 100 such bodies labouring among Jews in various parts of the world. As a consequence, nearly 250,000 Jews were converted. One of the most important missionary agencies was the Hebrew Christian Testimony to Israel, which was established in 1893 by David Baron and C. A. Schönberger in the east of London. Their aim was to draw Jews to Christ and demonstrate that Jews and Israel are inseparable.

Alongside the developments that were taking place in Great Britain, Christian missionaries were active in Europe. In 1882 the first Jewish Christian mission was established by Joseph Rabinowitz. Following his conversion in Jerusalem, he returned to Kishinev, where he gathered together numerous adherents of his doctrines. This new movement called itself 'Israelites of the New Covenant'; at their gatherings they used a liturgy composed of a mixture of Jewish and Christian elements. Rabinowitz's endorsement of a Jewish lifestyle, combined with an acceptance of Jesus' messiahship, was shared by another Jewish Christian, I. Lichtenstein, a Hungarian rabbi.

In the first few decades of the twentieth century, steps were taken to establish an international body of Jewish Christians. The creation of the Hebrew Christian Alliance provided a framework for Jewish believers to unite together. While the Hebrew Christian Alliance underwent considerable growth in the United States, the mission to the Jews continued apace. By 1927 there were many missionary bodies in those places in England, Scotland and Ireland which had sizeable Jewish populations. These British societies did not confine their efforts to the United Kingdom; on the continent there were missionary groups in France, Germany, Poland, Austria, Czechoslovakia and Hungary. Similar missions were also established in the Middle East and Asia.

Paralleling the growth of the youth movement within the Hebrew Christian Alliance of America, Jews for Jesus emerged in the early 1970s out of the Hebrew Christian movement. Initially its founder, Moishe Rosen, had worked as a Hebrew Christian missionary. By the late 1960s he

had become disenchanted with the Hebrew Christian movement. Resolved to reach Jewish youth, he founded Jews for Jesus. Rosen and his followers were determined to teach through drama, song and testimonials about what it means to be Jewish while accepting Jesus as the Messiah. The ideology of the movement was based largely on the beliefs Fundamentalism of American fundamentalist Christianity. Members were insistent that the Jewish component of the movement's ethnic identity should be a vital feature of the faith.

Simultaneously a major shift was taking place among Hebrew Christians. Increasingly, Jewish believers were anxious to form Messianic Jewish congregations where they worshipped Jesus (Yeshua) in a Jewish manner. Unlike many of the older members of the Hebrew Christian movement, the youth were determined to identify with their Jewish roots. In their view, the acceptance of Yeshua should be coupled with a commitment to the cultural and religious features of the Jewish faith. Among the leaders of the youth was Manny Brotman; through his influence the earliest Messianic literature was produced which stressed the Jewishness of faith in Yeshua. Another important figure was Joseph Finkelstein, who organized a singing group which wrote its own music and also introduced choreographed dance worship as well as testimonies from the singers.

At the 1975 Hebrew Christian Alliance of America Conference, the issue of changing the name of the movement was debated and carried. Previously the Alliance had been composed of Jewish believers from various Christian denominations. At this conference, charismatic forms of worship were introduced including raising of hands, clapping to the Lord, and singing in the spirit. Another issue which divided the movement was the question whether Jewish believers should live a Jewish lifestyle. Some members believed that it was desirable to follow Jewish traditions as long as they were in accord with scripture.

Over the ensuing decades Messianic Judaism has grown in numbers. Today there are over 150 Messianic synagogues worldwide. There are currently three major organizations which serve as the overarching structure for the Messianic community: the Union of Messianic Jewish Congregations (UMJC), the International Alliance of Messianic Congregations and Synagogues (IAMCS) and the Fellowship of Messianic Congregations (FMC), as well as two minor groups: the Association of Torah-Observant Messianics and the International Federation of Messianic Jews.

Messianic Jews insist that despite accepting Yeshua as Messiah and Saviour, they remain true to the tradition. Despite the variations in Messianic belief and practice, Council Jewish believers are adamant that they are fulfilled Jews. The Jewish community, however, has united against the Messianic movement, regarding it as deceptive, disloyal and dangerous. Critics of Messianic Judaism insist that the Messianic movement is a betrayal of the Jewish faith. In their view, it is impossible for Jews to accept Jesus as Messiah and Lord. In Israel, Messianic Jews are denied entry into the country under the Law of Return. Yet despite such universal rejection, Messianic Jews continue to proclaim their loyalty to the Jewish tradition and to other Jews who have denounced them as furthering the destruction of the Jewish nation.

DAN COHN-SHERBOK

📖 Dan Cohn-Sherbok, *Messianic Judaism*, London: Continuum 2000; *Voices of Messianic Judaism*, Baltimore: Lederer 2002; Shoshana Feher, *Passing Over Easter*, Ann Arbor: UMI 1985; Carol Harris-Shapiro, *Messianic Judaism*, Boston: Beacon Press 1999; David Rausch, *Messianic Judaism*, Lewiston, NY: Edwin Mellen Press 1982

Journalism

The United States

If you were a religion reporter for a US newspaper in the 1950s when President Dwight D. Eisenhower was in office, you would have spent most of your time covering Christian institutions (predominantly Protestant ones), writing about Sunday sermons, church announcements, ordinations and the national meetings of various denominations. You would have tailored many of your stories to a narrow religious audience, say those interested in the inner workings of the Protestant Episcopal Church (as it was then called). Some of your coverage, particularly the church announcements, would be designed to lure in advertising dollars from local parishes. By modern journalistic standards, many of your stories would have been considered dry and routine. Your job, religion writer, would have stood near the bottom of the newsroom pecking order. And if you left for a better position, most of your colleagues would have had little interest in what was widely viewed as a low-status beat.

If you covered religion today in the United States, your status, your approach and your subject-matter would in many ways be dramatically different from what it was a half-century ago. You would still spend the vast majority of your time covering Christianity – after all, most of the country identifies itself as Christian. But instead of focusing almost exclusively on Protestantism, you would also write a great deal about Roman Catholics, who have 65 million adherents in the US. Although the Second Vatican Council would have generated stories in the 1960s, the turning point for Catholic coverage came in the late 1970s when Pope John Paul II travelled to the United States on a tour that galvanized the nation.

You would still cover the occasional denominational meeting, such as the United States Conference of Catholic Bishops, that church's governing body in the US. But with reduced travel budgets and declining editor interest, you would write only about those meetings that guaranteed stories of broad interest, such as a battle over a hot issue. A prime example came in the summer of 2003 when the normally staid Episcopal Church, part of the worldwide Anglican Communion, saw a sharp rise in press attendance at its general convention because it was fighting over the election of its first actively gay bishop, the Revd V. Gene Robinson of New Hampshire. The Episcopal Church convention and the ensuing controversy over the election led the front pages of US newspapers for days.

Shifting away from institutional coverage, you would write more about broader trends and issues, such as the intersection of Christianity and politics. Subjects would include President George W. Bush's 'faith-based initiatives', designed to provide federal funding to faith-based social programmes, as well as the religious beliefs of individual candidates running for state and federal office. You might also explore the growing relationship between Christianity and American pop culture, a rich territory ranging from Christian rock and the phenomenally popular 'Left Behind' novel series which foretells the world's end to the battle over Mel Gibson's film, *The Passion of the Christ*, one of the most heavily publicized and financially successful movies in history.

More so than in the past, you would focus on stories about conflict and scandal, even investigating institutions such as the Archdiocese of Boston, the epicentre of the Roman Catholic Church's sex abuse crisis, in which leaders shuffled priests who abused youths from job to job. *The Boston Globe*'s coverage of the scandal won the Pulitzer Prize for Public Service, the highest award in newspaper journalism and a badge of honour in the industry.

While still spending as much as 85 per cent of your time covering Christianity, you might devote much of the rest of it to exploring the crazy quilt of faith that America has become in the past four decades. You would visit mosques and write about Muslims after the 9/11 attacks on the Pentagon and the World Trade Center in New York. You might cover a Hindu or Buddhist festival. If you were in a community with a significant Jewish population, say in the north-eastern part of the country, you would certainly write about them, in part because they have influence disproportionate to their numbers. There are approximately 5.2 million Jews among the US population of more than 280 million.

Religion reporters, then, and the landscape that they cover have changed in the past half-century. Much of the change has been driven by immigration; political changes have also played a role in expanding the parameters of the religion beat. The Revd Dr Martin Luther King, Jr, brought faith front-and-centre in the Civil Rights movement, one of the major domestic issues of the 1960s. The Supreme Court's decisions to legalize abortion and also to ban school prayer helped set the stage for the so-called 'culture wars' which echo today in the debates over gay marriage in which Christian conservatives are vocal and well-organized participants. Christian conservatives have also played an important role in US electoral politics. In the 2000 election, white evangelical Christians – loosely defined as people who believe in the inerrancy of scripture, the importance of spreading the gospel, and the necessity of maintaining a personal relationship with Jesus – were George Bush's core constituency, providing 35 to 40 per cent of his votes.

Anglicanism

Today, at least 400 US newspapers have a reporter spending at least some time covering religion, though only 100 to 150 of those reporters spend the majority of their time on the subject. There are, however, signs that religion coverage may be increasing. Certainly, the front pages of today's newspapers are filled with stories related to religion in ways they were not fifteen years ago. Some observers think that journalistic coverage of Christianity and religion has become more sophisticated and even-handed. Among the factors driving better religion reporting are sporadic efforts to educate religion writers on the nuances and complexities of the beat. Nevertheless, despite improving coverage, religion writers are sometimes caught flat-footed. When the 9/11 attacks occurred, few journalists had much grounding in political Islam and they most often lacked a network of sources in local Muslim communities.

Music

Cinema

In addition, theologians and some of the faithful also complain that the stories they find most relevant, articles on the healing and comforting power of faith or how faith drives volunteerism, remain undercovered. While the top dailies tend to dominate the major awards in religion journalism, some of the best work can nevertheless be found outside the nation's power centres, New York and Washington. The United States also has a variety of denominational publications, usually monthlies, which generally serve the interests only of members. However, certain independent publications such as *The National Catholic Reporter*, *Commonweal* and the Jesuit-run *America* magazine produce thoughtful and balanced reporting on sensitive issues, including the controversial reign of Pope John Paul II.

Christianity in North America

Islam and Christianity

The United Kingdom

During the second half of the twentieth century all the British mainstream churches suffered serious erosions of membership in the face of growing secularization.Yet the amount of space allocated to religious matters by many newspapers, particularly the serious broadsheets, increased greatly. There were two reasons for this, the first being that

Secularization

the churches became more newsworthy, the second that in fierce circulation wars newspapers dared not ignore the still substantial number of actual and potential readers who had religious interests. This remains true today.

The increased newsworthiness of the churches owes much to the fact that, in their different ways, they entered into a process of reform such as had not been experienced for several centuries. This was often interesting in itself but, more importantly, was nearly always controversial and thus provided those elements of conflict required for lively journalism.

In 1963 an Anglican bishop, John Robinson, published a modest paperback, *Honest to God,* which condensed into readable form the work of three important twentieth-century academic theologians. This was heralded by a Sunday newspaper article headlined 'Our Image of God must Go', and as a consequence of the subsequent uproar the original print-run of 6000 copies of the book went on the day of publication; in the end well over a million copies were sold in 17 different languages. Without the press this could not have happened. Later, controversies over changes in forms of worship, the ordination of women to the priesthood and, most recently, attitudes to homosexuals provided abundant material for news reporters and editorial writers.

The changes initiated in the Roman Catholic Church by the Second Vatican Council (1962–5) also attracted widespread news interest, though it was the decision of Pope Paul VI not to change his church's official position on birth control that aroused the greatest controversy and attention. The worldwide travels of Pope John Paul II broke new ground and received wide press coverage. The English free churches claimed less space, partly because their size is much smaller, but also because their style of leadership is different – less personal and more collaborative. Bishops and popes offer journalists more tempting targets for praise and blame than do moderators and committees.

Today the British broadsheets all have their religious affairs correspondents (the title was changed from 'churches correspondents' in the 1990s to accommodate other faiths) who, unlike many of their European counterparts, are not theologically equipped but use their professional reporting skill to cover, with varying degrees of accuracy and comprehension, pronouncements and events. Editorials on important religious issues are common and usually well informed. Church leaders are sometimes invited to contribute articles on contentious matters or at major festivals such as Christmas and Easter.

The tabloid newspapers are different. Their readers are judged to be much less interested in religious issues or what is happening in the churches, so these areas of news tend to be ignored unless they produce sensation or scandal. It is also the case that the degree of responsibility and integrity displayed by the tabloids is now very low and that the churches, particularly the Church of England, suffer unduly the lack of deference to Britain's historic institution shown by the press since the 1960s. Successive Archbishops of Canterbury have at times suffered rough treatment at their hands and in 2004, following an external review of its national information office, the Church of England recruited to its staff a specialist tabloid journalist.

Regional and local newspapers are different again. They carry a great deal of church news, often without regard to its significance, and many have weekly religious reflections contributed by local clergy. Their attitude to the churches, as to other local organizations, is always friendly, since they rely on them for news and, for circulation's sake, cannot risk offending many of their members. The chief problem at this level is blandness and boredom, which is not the fault of the journalists.

A similar problem affects the churches' own newspapers and journals. In England the Anglican and Roman Catholic churches each have two national weekly newspapers and the Roman Catholics a particularly good weekly news-review. The Methodist and Baptist churches each have a weekly paper, and the United Reformed Church and the Church of Scotland have monthly magazines. All are essentially house journals, inasmuch as their contents are confined mainly to news and ideas about the institutions they serve. Their readerships, which vary considerably in size but are never very large, tend to consist of clergy and the keenest laity. The Salvation Army uses its weekly newspaper as a tool of evangelism and to this end distributes it in pubs at weekends, but sales owe more to affection for the Army than to enthusiasm for its contents.

All the other church newspapers are owned by independent commercial organizations and trusts, which should in theory make for a robust independence and lively content. In practice, however, their precarious financial positions discourage risk-taking and severely restrict the number and type of journalists that can be employed. They are published on a shoe-string, and none of the churches regards them as important enough to be worth subsidizing, which says as much about the churches as it does about the papers.

FRANK LANGFITT AND TREVOR BEESON

National Catholic Reporter www.ncronline.org;
Commonweal www.commonweal.org;
America www.americamagazine.org;
Church Times www.churchtimes.co.uk;
Church of England Newspaper www.churchnewspaper.com;
Catholic Herald www.catholicherald.co.uk;
The Tablet www.thetablet.co.uk;
Methodist Recorder www.methodistrecorder.co.uk

JOURNEYS

Celtic Christianity, Christian life, Crusades, Exploration, Life after death, Mission, Paul, Pilgrimage

Journeys and the idea of the journey have played a significant part in the history of Christianity. The scriptures which Christians took over from the Jews begins with the story of Abraham, setting out for an unknown destination; Jesus goes on a journey to Jerusalem to meet his fate; Paul preaches the gospel on a series of missionary journeys. Later, Christians journey on pilgrimage and the idea of such a journey occurs regularly in Christian literature; and from Gnosticism to the present day there is the notion of the human soul as being on a journey to God.

p. 1152

Gnosis

A journey is a simple notion. Everybody knows what a journey is. Being alive as a human being is to move, however slightly. Movement is a sign of life. A journey usually involves a change of scene, some effort, occasional discomfort, and invariably juggles our thoughts and opinions into some sort of new configuration. Journeys change us. In our Western culture we are lucky to be able to go on so many and varied journeys, made possible by the availability of transport, and of an increasing number of places to stay in comfort and security. In fact, once you start looking at it, the whole world seems to be on the move, making the idea of 'journey' less and less out of the ordinary. It is possible to fly over the North Pole and be in Oxford on the same day.

We need an adjective to help us talk about journeys now, like 'significant' journeys, in order to distinguish a journey to the shops from a journey to the moon. Not only distance and effort turn a journey into a significant journey; there are many other aspects of it. A journey is about the people we meet, the type of destination, the planning, the people we go with, the terrain and landscape, the point in our lives at which it comes, the way the experience affects our behaviour, values and the future course of our lives, the route, the means of transport, the money we have to spend on it. Journeys and pilgrimages seem to be quite similar ideas, but one difference is that with a journey, the travelling itself seems to be of importance, more so than on a pilgrimage, where the end point is often of the greatest significance.

Take, for example, the journey Thomas Merton made to Asia in 1968, after twenty years as a Trappist monk in America. He had prepared for it through his growing interest in Eastern religions. He had fought for it by continued attempts to get permission to travel abroad. His expectations were high, his contacts numerous, and his personal investment in it was great. The *Asian Journal*, a diary Merton kept, records that journey. In the journal every step of the way has its significant moments. The journey ended in Merton's accidental death in the Red Cross Centre in Bangkok. The journey back to Kentucky was in the hold of a military aircraft along with the bodies of those killed in the Vietnam War. That journey, and in a sense the journey of Merton's life up to that point, took on a great significance for many searching for a spiritual way in the twentieth century. The journeys of the 'saints' become paradigms for many others who are searching for meaning. That just shows us how many aspects there might be to a journey entered on in the spirit of faith and adventure.

The Old Testament journeys

Bible The great Old Testament journeys were largely about discovery, conquest and exile. The narrowly defined religious element to the journeys went side by side with a search for land, although that search was in response to God's will for the people. The descriptions of the journeys are multi-layered, their significance for different generations having to be peeled back to sense different and authentic motives for moving from A to B. With journeys there is a real question about the way things are described and what motives lie behind the description. So with the Old Testament stories there is always an agenda to understand. The geography often takes second place to the theology, and we would be right to wonder if the theology sometimes creates the route. Having said that, we inevitably need a route, and a physical basis for the journey. The theological task is to understand the relationship between geography and theology. Three great journeys of the Old Testament stand out. They are the journey of Abraham (Genesis); the journey of the early Israelites in the desert searching for the promised land (Exodus); and the journey into exile in Babylon by the sixth-century Jews and their return (Jeremiah, Ezra and Nehemiah).

Abraham migrated from Haran southwards to Canaan (Shechem), where he built an altar to the Lord who had appeared to him. He moved on and pitched his tent on a mountain with Bethel on the west and Ai on the east, north of Jerusalem, where he built another altar. He journeyed southward into the Negeb (Genesis 12.6–9), and later returned to his earlier encampment between Bethel and Ai. To avoid strife between his own herdsmen and those of his brother-in-law Lot, Abraham went to Mamre near Hebron. His pursuit of Lot's enemies took him north up into Damascus (Genesis 14), and later he returned south to the Negeb and sojourned in Gerar. While they were in the Negeb his wife Sarah bore him a son, Isaac. God's testing of Abraham led him to take Isaac to the land of Moriah (near Jerusalem?) and offer him as a burnt offering (Genesis 22.2). Sarah and Abraham died and were buried in the cave of Machpelah, east of Mamre (Genesis 25.7–10). Abraham's grandson Jacob was also buried at Machpelah after a life of journeying. On one of his journeys he had a dramatic dream encounter with God at Bethel (Genesis 28.10–17). As a result of that experience he vowed, 'If God will be with me, if he will protect me on my journey and give me food to eat and clothes to wear, so that I come back safely to my father's house, then the Lord shall be my God (28.20).'

Later in the history of Israel came the greatest journey of them all, the *exodus*. It seems hardly possible to describe this journey simply in geographical terms. So much of importance on the journey was spiritual in nature. Yet the journey began in 'the land of Rameses', and Moses led the Israelites away from slavery in Egypt to freedom in the promised land. This sense of his leadership arose from his experience of God on Mount Horeb. The party of ill-equipped and frightened slaves went by the 'way of the wilderness', and there are at least three different theories of the route they took. The traditional route leads southwards after crossing the Red Sea to the southern end of the Sinai peninsula. Two or more direct northerly routes have been proposed. At least two p. 382 possible positions for Mount Sinai, where Moses received the Ten Commandments, have also been proposed: one in the north at Jebal Helal, and one in the south at the base of the Sinai peninsula. The journey included occasions of great recalcitrance and disobedience. Moses himself could only see the promised land, but not enter it; that was Joshua's privilege and responsibility. This journey, both the travelling and the settlement, is the core experience of Israelite faith, and has had an enormous influence both on the Hebrew and Christian mind. It is burnt into the Jewish psyche to this day.

It was on the journey that the law was given, and on the journey that the law was disobeyed, and the whole journey was guided by God, in a cloud by day and a pillar of fire by night. The journeying aspect of the exodus is most powerfully taken up in contemporary theology in the more general ideas of 'liberation'. The release from slavery and oppression has become the rallying cry of black and other minority groups. As powerful, and yet not so familiar, is the idea that on a journey God speaks, reveals himself, as both guide and direction, 'the way, the truth and the life'. It was on a journey that the persecuted Jesus stopped Paul in his tracks, on a journey that Balaam was directed by an angel (Numbers 24), and at the end of a long journey that the Wise Men discovered the infant King.

Liberation theology

The *exile*, or the Babylonian captivity, took place between 604 and 539 BCE, when a significant proportion of the population of Judah was deported in two groups (2 Kings 24.14–16; 25.11), under the orders of the Babylonian king Nebuchadnezzar. According to Ezekiel 1–2 they were permitted to return after the Persian ruler, Cyrus, had captured Babylon around 539 BCE. The literature of exile as we see it in some of the psalms is particularly poignant, reminding us of the significance of a journey that forcibly takes people away from home: 'By the waters of Babylon I sat down and wept, when we remembered Zion' (Psalm 137.1). Such poetry of exile speaks for many other tragic journeys which people have been forced to make on account of their faith. The postcard sent from Etty Hillesum to a friend and thrown from the train taking her to her death at Westerbork concentration camp in September 1943 is a reminder of another journey, another tragic exile. Etty wrote: 'Christine, opening the Bible at random I find this: "The Lord is my high tower." I am on my rucksack in the middle of a full freight car. Father, Mother, and Mischa are a few cars away. In the end, the departure came without warning. On special sudden orders from The Hague. We left the camp singing. Father and mother firmly and calmly, Mischa, too. We shall be travelling for three days.'

Psalms

Jesus and geography

The comparative geographical stability of Jesus within a fairly well-defined cultural context makes for an interesting dimension to the notion of journey in the Christian tradition. Luke is the evangelist who understands the importance of place in Jesus' ministry, and shows this in particular in the journey that he constructs in Luke 9.51–19.27. Luke sets the extended passage as a journey fixed on Jerusalem, but the mission in Samaria had great significance too. Luke uses geography and the journey to make strong theological points. In a sense the biblical critics have to put a microscope to the journeys of Jesus. There is none of the broad sweep of an Exodus or an Acts. In the Gospels we find a subtle concern for the place of Jerusalem in relation to Galilee in the mind and work of Jesus, and for those places where his ministry became impossible or was hampered. Paul journeyed from one distant place to another; he was conscious of the difference between Jew and Gentile and tried to bring unity among those who came to be followers of Christ. But Jesus journeyed with a strong sense of mission to the Jewish community, and to 'go up to Jerusalem' was a significant journey, because it was a journey to the heart of the Jewish establishment. There he had a mission to challenge, and eventually to transform.

Jesus

So journeys in the Gospels take on a metaphorical quality. It is not so much the travelling that is important, but the implications of the travelling. Within Jesus himself, we could say, there was a spiritual journey, the final stage of which was the journey to the cross. That journey was to become ritualized in time as a liturgical, or dramatic representation of the theology of the cross in the devotional journey known as the stations of the cross. The journey to Emmaus (Luke 24.13–35) was Luke's way of explaining the significance of Jesus' death to the early Christian communities,

p. 341

JOURNEYS

Resurrection

and how it was a miracle of his continued presence in both word (revealing the scriptures) and sacrament (breaking of the bread).

The journeys of Paul, and mission

The significant journeys of religious believers always have an element of God being present, and of the sense of God sending people out for God's purposes to be fulfilled. Journey and mission have often gone hand in hand: the Latin *mitto*, from which the word mission comes, means 'I send'. The journeys of Paul the apostle, in the middle of the first century CE, were vitally important journeys for building up the spirit, strength and wisdom of fragile communities of Christians. They were a personal commitment to Christ's work and teaching. Paul's letters and his journeys were two aspects of his missionary zeal. He made three significant journeys, travelling through Greek-speaking countries, predominantly Gentile but with Jewish colonies and synagogues in many cities. He set out on each of them from Antioch. On the first journey (Acts 13.2) he set out with Barnabas, and founded churches in southern Galatia, in Asia Minor, which are probably those addressed in his letter to the Galatians. On the second (Acts 15.36) he went with Silas, overland to Derbe, through 'Galatian Phrygia' (Acts 16.6), then northwards as far as 'opposite Mysia', and to the coast at Troas. From there, in response to a vision, he went to Macedonia, where the churches of Philippi and Thessalonica were founded. Paul went via Athens to Corinth where, joined by others, he stayed eighteen months, founding the local church. He sailed to Palestine, visited Jerusalem, and returned to Antioch (18.22).

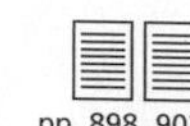
pp. 898, 902

On the third missionary journey Paul spent two-and-a-quarter years in Ephesus (1 Corinthians 16.8; Acts 19.8–10) and founded that important church. At Ephesus he kept in touch, by messengers (1 Corinthians 1.11; 2 Corinthians 7.6) and by at least one personal visit (2 Corinthians 1.23–2.1), with Corinth. He then travelled through Macedonia to Achaia where he spent three months, returned to Philippi, and sailed with the delegates of the churches for Jerusalem. At Miletus he called the elders of the Ephesian church to him, and took his farewell of them. At Jerusalem Jewish hostility resulted in Paul's arrest and removal to Rome.

We see with Paul the beginning of the idea of journey as a 'mission', and that ideological thrust to travel, that desire to influence the beliefs and customs of others with the gospel, entered into the bloodstream of the Christian church very early on. It begins as early as the mission statement at the end of Matthew's Gospel: 'Go therefore to all nations and make them my disciples; baptize them in the name of the Father and the Son and the Holy Spirit, and teach them to observe all that I have commanded you. I will be with you always, to the end of time' (Matthew 28.19f.). It is from this point that we see Christianity moving out into the entire world. For example, there was the mission of Augustine to Britain (597), and the Celtic mission to Ireland and from Ireland to northern Britain. The Celtic spirit is particularly interesting with regard to journeys because very often the journeys were not mission inspired but penitential. The voyages of Brendan in the sixth century seem often to be random, moving by the Spirit, or as a result of liturgical necessity: Easter here, Pentecost there. The motive for the journey was one of simply throwing oneself on the goodwill of God, and being led by the Spirit to do his will, finding places to settle and pray and lead an ascetic life.

Journeys like that of the Empress Helena, Constantine's mother, or of the abbess Egeria, both in the fourth century, mark the beginning of pilgrimages which become a prominent feature of Christianity, whether to local shrines which can be visited in a day, or involving long journeys to remoter places like Canterbury, Santiago da Compostela, Rome or the Holy Places in Palestine. But

Von sant Brandon ain hübsch lesen. was er wunders auff dem mör erfaren hat.

St Brendan the Navigator, from *The Marvellous Adventures of St Brendan and his Monks*, 1499

there was also a darker form of pilgrimage in the form of the Crusades to the Holy Land, which brought death and destruction rather than healing and fulfilment.

Different again in style and intention were the journeys of the Jesuit missions. Peculiar to the Jesuits is a special vow to travel for ministry anywhere in the world that the Pope may order, an indication of the missionary aim that motivated Ignatius Loyola (1491–1556) and his companions  from the beginning. The history of the missionary societies is largely a history of journeys, and what an interesting and dramatic history that has been. Volumes have been written about them.  p. 776 David Livingstone (1813–73) is one in whom the history of mission and of exploration became completely entwined. Annie Taylor (1855–1920), a member of the China Inland Mission, was the first woman traveller through Tibet. Her motto, among continual attacks from brigands and the vagaries of unknown territory, was, 'I left it all with Jesus and had perfect peace.'

Journey and story

The journey becomes an allegorical motif into which spiritual teaching is placed. There is nothing like the story of a journey to attract and keep the ear of a listener. This was not new at the time of Jesus; far from it. There is some element of it in the exodus itself. It becomes much plainer to see in the stories of Jonah, Tobit and Ruth, and in the continuing literary traditions of Christian literature. *The Pilgrim's Progress* (1678 and 1684), written by John Bunyan, is the best-known example. Christian, the pilgrim, sets off on a journey and has all sorts of experiences, meeting different people and situations that test his mettle. There is no pretence that this is a real journey, but it is a real experience of the Christian journey. We too can experience a slough of despond, and a valley of despair. To put these archetypal experiences into journey form gives the added dimension of time to the Christian experience, a lifetime's journey. From that emerges the idea that life is a journey from birth to death and beyond.

Story

The literary genre of journeys that have Christian themes is large and labyrinthine. It would include the material that gathers round 'The Quest of the Holy Grail'. This was the search for the cup used by Jesus at the Last Supper, which according to legend later belonged to Joseph of Arimathea, and its effects on those who saw it were made to correspond closely to the effect of holy communion upon those who received it. The story of Joseph of Arimathea travelling to England with the Holy Grail and building the first church in the country at Glastonbury was described in a book originally written by William of Malmesbury about 1129. Chaucer's *Canterbury Tales*, begun in 1387, gathers a multitude of moral tales round a journey from London to Canterbury. C. S. Lewis (1898–1963) wrote a series of seven 'Narnia' stories for children. They were begun in 1950 with *The Lion, the Witch and the Wardrobe* and weave an ostensibly Christian allegory on a journey that begins by going through a wardrobe, and ends with *The Last Battle* of good against evil.

Journey and metaphor

The genius of the gospel method in which the crucial journey was an inward one of faith is taken up in our day by the process of psychology. The journey inwards produces the story that our minds tell. It is sometimes referred to as the faith journey. We do not have to go anywhere physically to be going on a journey. We can travel in our dreams, in our attitudes, in our decision-making through the labyrinths of our minds. Connecting journey archetypes to contemporary experience has been the hugely influential task of Carl Gustav Jung (1875–1961), and of Mircea Eliade, particularly in his book *Le mythe de l'eternel retour: archetypes et repetition.* So the concept of extended time necessary for the journey as we understand it becomes a matter of the moment, the eternal now. The journey, said T. S. Eliot in *Four Quartets,* is 'now and always'. In John's Gospel the meaning is not in the ground covered or the places visited, but in the eternal presence of Christ. The journey for Nicodemus was back into the womb to be reborn.

Psychology

Eliot's poem 'Journey of the Magi' gains its powerful effect from the combination of an actual physical, geographical journey of the Magi to Bethlehem and the spiritual or psychological journey of Eliot's own experience of coming to baptism in 1927. The poem reaches out to the human experience of change and challenge, and is an example of the way archetypes express and communicate deep symbolic truths. Journeying is an endlessly fruitful metaphor for human life and beyond, and Eliot has put this as movingly as anyone in the twentieth century: 'the end of all our exploring will be to arrive where we started and know the place for the first time' (*Four Quartets*, 'Little Gidding').

The heavenly journey

Death is seen as an end of the journey, but also as the beginning of another. 'Go forth upon thy journey, Christian soul! Go from this world! Go in the name of God, the omnipotent Father ...' (Commendation of a Soul, Western Rite). The soul is understood to be in progress through a period of testing, or purgatory, before it can enter into the fullness of glory. Being an area shrouded in mystery, the stories about such journeys are many.

Within the Christian tradition, as most theologians believe, Jesus descended to the realm of existence which is neither heaven nor hell in the ultimate sense, but a place or state where the souls of pre-Christians waited for the message of the gospel, and to where the penitent thief passed after his death on the cross (Luke 23.43).

Later, as described in Acts 1.9, Jesus is seen ascending into heaven. The disciples looked up to witness the final earthly sight of their beloved Lord. The ascension of Elijah, or his translation into heaven, is dramatically described in 2 Kings 2.1–18. Elisha is witness to this: 'Suddenly there appeared a chariot of fire and horses of fire which separated them from one another, and Elijah was carried up to heaven in a whirlwind.' A Jewish tradition preserved in the Assumption of Moses describes Michael and the Devil contesting for the body of Moses. This is alluded to in the Letter of Jude (v. 9). The Ascension of Isaiah, an apocryphal work well known in the early church, describes Isaiah's ascent in ecstasy through the heavens and the revelations made to him there. Paul says that he knows a man (himself) who was caught up to the third heaven (2 Corinthians 12.2–4), and in Gnosticism the divine spark believed to be imprisoned in the flesh of human beings ascends to the world from which it came on a perilous journey.

Other authors have taken the opportunity to describe the journey beyond death in much greater detail. Dante's *Divine Comedy* is a classic journey narrative in which the poet travels for a week at  Easter 1300 from dark forest on this side of the world down through Hell. Eventually Virgil, who has been Dante's guide, takes the hand of Beatrice and leads her through the nine planetary and stellar spheres to the Empyrean. Bernard of Clairvaux takes the place of Virgil and presents Dante  to the Blessed Virgin Mary, at whose intercession the poet is granted a glimpse of the Beatific Vision.

On a more modest scale, the poem 'Peace' by Henry Vaughan (1622–95), which is also sung as  a hymn, encapsulates the interrelation of the human and divine journeys. The soul longs for the journey heavenwards. Christ comes down and draws the soul back with him to that 'country far beyond the stars ... above noise and danger [where] sweet peace sits crowned with smiles', and to the 'one, who never changes, Thy God, thy life, thy cure'.

A celebrated poem, *The Dream of Gerontius*, by John Henry Newman (1801–90), was first 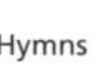 published in book form in 1866. It is a vision of a just soul leaving a body at death and of its subsequent meeting with the angels. It has been set to music by Edward Elgar, and two of the poems in it are well-known hymns: 'Firmly I believe and truly' and 'Praise to the Holiest in the height'. Another Hymns of Newman's hymns, 'Lead, kindly light', appealing to God to help him through the dark nights of his troubled thoughts, gives some simple and wise counsel for the journey: 'Keep thou my feet; I do not ask to see the distant scene; one step enough for me.' Eventually, he puts his faith in God to

Hieronymus Bosch, Tunnel of light, from *Paradise*

lead him 'o'er moor and fen, o'er crag and torrent, till the night is gone, and with the morn those angel faces smile, which I have loved long since, and lost awhile'.

DAVID SCOTT

Monica Furlong, *The End of our Exploring*, London: Hodder & Stoughton 1973 and New York: Coward, Mcann & Geoghehan 1974; Donald Coggan, *Meet Paul. An Encounter with the Apostle*, London: SPCK 1997; T. S. Eliot, *Four Quartets*, London: Faber and New York: Harcourt, Brace & World 1942; Herbert G. May (ed), *Oxford Bible Atlas*, London: OUP ³1985; Thomas Merton, *Asian Journal*, New York: New Directions Publishing 1988; Thomas O'Loughlin, *Journeys on the Edges: The Celtic Tradition*, Maryknoll, NY: Orbis 2000

Judaism and Christianity

Judaism is a religious tradition that developed in the Middle East from beginnings among the people of Israel around 4000 years ago. Judaism is strongly associated with Jewish identity, which is acquired by birth (traditionally, any child of a Jewish woman is regarded as Jewish) or, less frequently, by choice (by undergoing an appropriate form of conversion to Judaism). However, not all Jews are adherents of Judaism. Particularly in the USA and Israel (the countries with the largest Jewish populations) many Jews are non-religious and understand Jewishness in ethnic or cultural terms.

Just as relations between Judaism and Christianity stretch across 2000 years, so they take many forms. Judaism and Christianity encounter one another textually, in the writings of numerous authors. There is also a tradition of organized or institutional Jewish-Christian relations. In medieval Europe, for example, Jewish rabbis were forced to engage in public disputations with Christian scholars, who hoped to use such stage-managed events to refute Judaism and win converts. (The most protracted of these was the Disputation of Tortosa, which ran to nearly 70 sessions in 1413–14.) More recently, interfaith bodies, notably the various Councils of Christians and Jews and the World Council of Churches' Office on Inter-religious Relations and Dialogue, have brought groups of Jews and Christians together to consider points of commonality and difference in an atmosphere of mutual respect and enquiry. Running alongside these formal events and written explorations are many everyday interactions and encounters between Jews and Christians. Though they sometimes go almost unnoticed, such professional and social contacts are undoubtedly significant in shaping individuals' perceptions of each other's – and their own – faith traditions.

What motivates Jews and Christians to engage in dialogue with one another today? Some Christians wish to explore the Jewish roots of their faith. Others want to come to terms with the history of Jewish-Christian relations, especially Christian anti-Judaism and the churches' share of responsibility for the Holocaust. Still others are conversionists, regarding positive relations as preparation for missionary activity directed at Jews. For their part, Jews may be interested in relations with Christians because they are conscious of living as a religious and ethnic minority in societies shaped directly or indirectly by Christianity. Alternatively, they may view the development of relations in pragmatic-defensive terms, as a way of minimizing the potential for future violence born of misunderstanding. Finally, in recent years, some Jews have sought to work out a theology of Christianity and make sense within a Jewish religious framework of Christianity's successes as a world religion.

Origins and background

p. 1152

Christianity and Judaism have each changed immeasurably since the first century CE. Jesus did not teach the sophisticated doctrines developed over centuries by the Christian churches, and the founding texts of rabbinic Judaism were written several centuries *after* the Christian Gospels. However, the character of present relations is substantially influenced by ancient agendas. Jewish-Christian dialogue wrestles with the implications of the fact that Christianity grew out of early Judaism, and was for many years essentially one of several parties within it. Christianity regards Judaism as its point of departure, theologically and historically speaking, and claims to be its heir. Jesus and his disciples were Jews. Many of Jesus' teachings (his approach to religious law; his reference to God as 'Father') resemble those of the Pharisees, a reforming movement that emerged in the second century BCE. Light has been shed on Jesus' apocalypticism by comparing it with material in the Dead Sea Scrolls, and his miracle-working bears similarities to that of figures described in the Mishnah and Talmud, compilations of the

Jesus

Interfaith dialogue

Apocalyptic

p. 845

Miracle

teachings of leading Jewish scholars, dating from 200 and 500 CE respectively but containing earlier material. After Jesus' death, his followers were regarded, by themselves and others, as Jews: according to the Acts of the Apostles, Peter and others participated in Jerusalem temple worship (Acts 2).

Crusades Pilgrimage
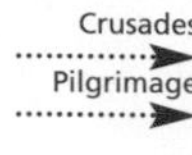
Council

Reformation Church fathers Martin Luther

Constantine's 'conversion'

Anabaptists
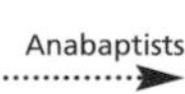

Disputes as to the means by which the Jesus movement should incorporate non-Jews (Gentiles) led to the gradual separation of Christianity from Judaism. (This divergence, often called the 'parting of the ways', should be understood as a process rather than a one-off event.) While some demanded that Gentiles should convert to Judaism and observe the commandments, advocates of a contrary position triumphed at a meeting in Jerusalem (the so-called 'apostolic council', Acts 15). Their victory triggered a chain of debates on Christian attitudes towards Jewish religious law: if it was not necessary for all, was its observance essential for any Christians? Today, many churches keep the commandments to a modest degree (typically, those in Exodus 20), but Christianity has generally interpreted passages like Galatians 3.10–14 and Romans 3.20 to mean that such practice is superfluous, and even detrimental to the salvation of the individual, Gentile or Jewish. The church fathers held that Judaism was superseded (fulfilled and abolished). Faith in the expiatory function of Jesus' death was alone capable of reconciling people to God; Christians had inherited the promises made to biblical Israel. After Constantine made Christianity a permitted religion (312 CE), such theology informed social and political policy. While Christians and Jews continued as religious rivals, the balance of temporal power between them was tipped decisively in Christianity's favour.

Covenant
p. 662
Enlightenment

Paganism
p. 1197
Biblical criticism

Much of the history of Jewish-Christian relations has been shaped by this theology of supersessionism. On the one hand Christianity regarded Judaism as redundant. The fact that Jesus died by a Roman method of execution (crucifixion) was played down, and the blame increasingly shifted on to his Jewish opponents (the charge first appears in the New Testament). Building on Matthew 27.25, 'His blood be on us and on our children', their guilt was conflated with that of later generations of Jews who rejected Jesus' messiahship. On the other hand, the church authorities afforded Jews a degree of protection; in this respect, they fared better than pagans and heretics. This was partly because Jews were seen as the first guardians of the scriptures that Christianity now called the Old Testament. Typological readings of biblical texts were also used to argue against exterminating Jews, since their survival in a subjected state enabled them to serve as a warning sign of the fate awaiting those who rejected the church. These inherently ambivalent attitudes, articulated by the church fathers, were largely unchallenged until the twentieth century. Christians viewed Jews through the lens of faith, rather than on their own terms, as an autonomous reality. Conversely, once Christianity had become a fundamentally Gentile entity, Judaism found it to be of little doctrinal interest. Jews produced some polemical texts that decried Christianity as absurd and heretical, but for the most part these were generated in reaction to Christian pressures, rather than out of a desire to propagate Judaism among Gentiles.

The Middle Ages were a particularly violent period in Jewish-Christian relations. In 1095, Pope Urban II preached the first Crusade, to wrest the 'Holy Land' from Muslim rule and facilitate Christian pilgrimage. Although European Jews were not Urban's target, they were easy prey for the Jerusalem-bound armies. Despite the efforts of some authorities, there were massacres and forced conversions, particularly in the Rhineland. And in the aftermath of these traumas, the Fourth Lateran Council (1215) required Jews to adopt distinctive clothing (ensuring their visible difference). Other legislation marginalized them economically (prohibiting them from land-ownership and the professions) and restricted the practice of Judaism (banning synagogue construction, for example).

The Reformation did not substantially change Jewish-Christian relations. Luther's *On the Jews and their Lies* (1543) blends Christian theology and negative images of Jews from European folklore. In addition to rehearsing older criticisms of Judaism, it describes Jews as parasites, bloodthirsty murderers and devil worshippers. The text (decisively rejected by Lutherans today) is distinguished by its ferocity, but with the exception of some Anabaptists, none of the Reformation leaders, or the churches that they founded, differed from Luther in regarding conversion to Christianity as the sole means by which a Jew might be saved. In England, Shylock in Shakespeare's *The Merchant of Venice* (1596) is the embodiment of the hated Jew. By the late eighteenth century, negative images of Jews were so firmly entrenched in the popular imagination that while critical of traditional Christianity, many European Enlightenment thinkers did not reject anti-Judaism, but infused it with contemporary scientific or pseudo-scientific thinking on race and nation. Emancipation (civil and political rights in their countries of residence) was offered to Jews with the expectation that they would reciprocate by assimilating to non-Jewish norms – that as Jews they would disappear.

While the advent of modern biblical criticism impacted significantly on the understanding of Christian origins, and to an extent on Christian-Jewish relations, it was really only in the aftermath of the Holocaust, when over 6 million Jews were murdered (two-thirds of European Jewry), that mainstream churches, shocked by continuities between Christian anti-Judaism and Nazi antisemitism, began to re-evaluate their teachings on Judaism. Nazism

ANTISEMITISM

Christianity is unfortunate in that its authoritative foundation document, the New Testament, undoubtedly contains passages which are hostile to the Jews. Their presence in the Christian Bible has contributed to a long history of discrimination, oppression, even demonization of Jews by the Christian church. This Christian attitude is often referred to as antisemitic, but the term antisemitism was coined as recently as 1879 in a modern context. It is inappropriate for two reasons. First, it implies discrimination against all Semites (the term is traditionally understood to denote the peoples descended from Shem according to Genesis 10, which would include Arabs). Secondly, when spelt anti-Semitism with a hyphen it suggests opposition to Semitism, and there is no such thing. It would be more correct to talk of anti-Judaism, but the use of anti-Semitism is now probably too widespread to be eradicated.

Two passages which highlight anti-Judaism in the New Testament (unfortunately they are not the only ones) are to be found in Matthew 27.25, where the people calling for the crucifixion of Jesus are made to say 'His blood be on us and on our children!', and John 8.44, where Jesus is made to say to 'the Jews', 'You are of your father the devil, and your will is to do your father's desires. He was a murderer from the beginning, and has nothing to do with the truth, because there is no truth in him.' In the light of these statements Jews came to be seen as the murderers of the Son of God, whose guilt was handed on from generation to generation.

There is no disputing the hostility to the Jews which runs through Christian history and is expressed even by theologians of the stature of Augustine and Luther. It is expressed even more shockingly in the history of Christian art, in the ways in which Jews are depicted, the portrayal of alleged crimes and blasphemies which they commit, and of the punishments inflicted on them in hell. And these hostile images encouraged acts of physical violence against Jews and the persecution of them. Precisely how all this fed into the Nazi extermination of the Jews in the 1930s and the 1940s and its relation to nineteenth-century racist theories is a complex matter; however, since the horrors of Auschwitz and other death camps, Christians from church leaders like the Pope, through those responsible for the words used in Christian worship, to theologians and beyond them to countless church members, have made it clear that any kind of Christian hostility to Judaism must be brought to an end and have taken steps to remedy the situation, even if they cannot rewrite history.

But the damning passages remain in the New Testament. To counteract them it is pointed out, first, that the New Testament Gospels which contain them were composed in the period after the Roman destruction of Jerusalem and the temple there in 70 CE, in a period when Christians, whose movement had originated as a sect within Judaism, were breaking away from Judaism and incurring much hostility in the process (in John 16.2 Jesus is made to prophesy that his followers will be expelled from synagogues). The Jews themselves were also attempting to cope with this blow and were engaged in a process of wholesale reform. The Jewish Bible, the Christian Old Testament, contains much about a previous destruction of Jerusalem and its temple, in 587 BCE by the Babylonian king Nebuchadnezzar; there it is seen as punishment for the past sins of the people. So both Christians and Jews would naturally see the destruction of the second temple in these terms: the crucial difference between them was that Jewish thinkers saw it as God's judgement on the Jewish people for their sins, to which they must respond with a purer form of Judaism; Christian thinkers saw it as God's rejection of the Jews for killing God's Son. Unfortunately words written in a particular historical situation came to be seen as God's Word and exercised the disastrous influence that they did.

Secondly, it is pointed out that the answer to the question 'Who killed Jesus?' cannot be read off the Gospels in a simplistic way. Attempts to do this, or to portray the crucifixion on the basis of a literal reading of the Gospels, as in the controversial 2004 Mel Gibson film *The Passion of the Christ*, are misleading. A careful reading of the texts in the light of the historical situation suggests that those responsible for the death of Jesus were the Roman authorities, since they alone could inflict the death penalty, and among the Jews at most members of the local Jerusalem aristocracy who saw him as a threat.

Church fathers ◄
Martin Luther ◄

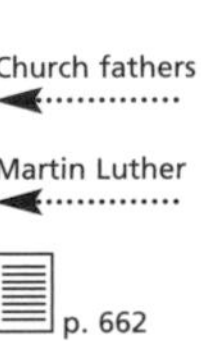
p. 662

The question of anti-Judaism, like so many issues in which Christians now seem called upon to disown attitudes going back to the very beginning, thus requires a new approach to the very basis of Christianity.

Richard L. Rubenstein and John K. Roth, *Approaches to Auschwitz*, Atlanta, GA: John Knox Press and London: SCM Press 1987; Heinz Schreckenberg, *The Jews in Christian Art. An Illustrated History*, London: SCM Press 1996

was dependent on race theory for its notion of 'the Jew' as biologically inferior, and exploited modern bureaucratic forms of organization in order to implement the Holocaust, but it borrowed much of the 'grammar' of persecution from Christianity. There are, for example, correspondences between the Nazis' Nuremberg Laws (1935) and medieval anti-Jewish legislation. Moreover, many leading Nazis were church members, and the churches in Europe and beyond were largely disinclined to protest against the assault on Jews. Centuries of anti-Judaism had created a culture in which few non-Jews included Jews within their sphere of care and concern. The years since 1945 have witnessed sustained efforts to reverse this trend. Increasing numbers of Jews and Christians participate in dialogue, for example, in which they hope to understand and learn from each other without denying their own religious traditions.

In contrast to the processes of differentiation at work in earlier periods, much post-war Christian-Jewish interaction has focused on the identification of a close relationship or correspondences between the religions. Some believe that Judaism and Christianity have so much in common that they are two sides of the same coin, and that one may speak of a 'Judaeo-Christian' or Jewish-Christian tradition. Christian advocates of such a position typically emphasize the insights of biblical scholarship on Jesus' Jewishness. Theologically, they question supersessionism, arguing that Jesus' death either admitted Gentiles into the God-Israel covenant or created a new parallel covenant for them, but did not signal the end of God's relationship with the Jews. A move from interest in mission to Jews towards witness (less coercive sharing of experience) or even joint Christian and Jewish mission to a secular world goes along with this theological change. Such ideas inform many institutional statements on Jewish-Christian relations, including the Vatican II document *Nostra aetate* (1965) and subsequent Catholic documents, and the recent cross-denominational Jewish document, *Dabru emet* (2000). These texts affirm Jesus' Jewishness and recognize a special bond linking Jews and Christians. *Nostra aetate* commends dialogue and joint biblical studies, and condemns prejudice, especially antisemitism. Among other things, *Dabru emet* suggests that Jews should welcome the fact that through Christianity, hundreds of millions of people have entered a relationship with the God of Israel. Touching on the topic of the state of Israel, which persists as a source of misunderstanding and tension between Jews and Christians, it notes that Jews can both welcome the support some Christians give to Israel and recognize that Jewish tradition mandates justice for non-Jews (including Christians) living in a Jewish state.

pp. 128–9

p. 291

Not all Jews and Christians would, however, see Judaism and Christianity as so closely intertwined. Some (typically, more conservative) Christian groups hold to supersessionism and continue to advocate mission to Jews. Orthodox Jews regard the religions as essentially different from each other. For them, Judaism is *sui generis*. It is the embodiment of divinely revealed teaching, mediated to the Jewish people through a unique covenant with God. Many Jews (and many Christians) are also sceptical about Christianity's long-term ability to exempt Judaism from its missionary endeavours. They point out that since the continuance of Judaism poses fundamental questions to Christianity in a way that other religious traditions (such as Islam or Buddhism) do not, the impetus for Christianity to generate anti-Judaic teaching and activity is ever-present.

Jewish Christianity

Those who believe Judaism and Christianity to be fundamentally different argue that, rather than trying to effect change within specific areas of Christian doctrine, attempts to overcome past tragedies must approach each religion's account of itself holistically and seriously if they are to succeed. For example, much organized dialogue concentrates on issues such as common ethical teachings, or locating Jesus within first-century Judaism. However, this approach is arguably of limited effect, since not only does it focus on a period and a character of little significance in the lives of contemporary Jews, but it also ignores the fact that the redemptive function of the crucifixion and resurrection is far more central to the religious experience of many Christians than the individual activities and teachings of the historical Jesus. In a similar vein, some commentators would query the assertion, voiced in *Nostra aetate* and *Dabru emet*, that Jews and Christians share common scriptures. While Jews and Christians share the Hebrew Bible (although they number and order its constituent books differently), Christians know it as the Old Testament, and read it in the light of the New Testament. Jews regard it as the written Torah (the Law, together with the Prophets and Writings), and supplement and interpret it in the light of the oral Torah (Mishnah and Talmud), which is traditionally also believed to have been delivered at Sinai to Moses.

Belief that Judaism and Christianity, while bearing some superficial similarities to one another, are essentially different in nature, does not necessarily rule out positive Jewish-Christian relations. However, in a sense it makes truly meaningful discourse between Judaism and Christianity as belief systems impossible, or at the very least extremely difficult. Non-theological dialogue has, therefore, been the preference of some Christians and Jews, and particularly of many Orthodox Jewish authorities.

As previously, future relations will be influenced by historical contingencies as much as theology. It seems likely that the trajectories sketched above will persist. The post-Holocaust reconstruction of Jewish-Christian relations is still in its infancy. Many of those who have devoted time to its study and practice would question the extent to which the average Jew or Christian 'owns' the various statements that have been released. A great deal remains to be done both in terms of disseminating the new thinking and in learning from the everyday experiences of ordinary synagogue and church members. There has also been little discussion to date of some particularly controversial issues, such as the place of Messianic Jews and Hebrew Christians (Jews who believe that their Jewishness is completed as a result of their acceptance of Jesus as Messiah, and that there should be now, as in the earliest period, a distinctive Jewish Christianity). Their claim to be both Jewish and

Christian challenges not just the traditional teachings of Judaism and Christianity but also the assumption underpinning Jewish-Christian relations, namely, the belief that Judaism and Christianity are to a greater (or lesser) extent separate entities. Additional factors will exert their influence on Jewish-Christian relations in the future, too. Many churches are increasingly non-European in membership and outlook. For African, Asian and Latin American Christians, responses to the Holocaust and relations with Judaism generally are of less immediate concern than those with, say, Islam. But at the same time, new perspectives on the dialogue may be opened up by their contribution. For its part, Judaism is affected by high rates of marriage between Jews and non-Jews (including Christians) and Orthodox Judaism's refusal to recognize Progressive Jewish procedure in matters of personal status (marriage; divorce; conversion). If dialogue is to stay relevant to the lived experience of Jews and Christians, it must take account of the shifting, disputed nature of Jewish identity today.

In short, the history of relations between Judaism and Christianity, and Jews and Christians as historical agents, does not make easy reading. But particularly since the Holocaust, dialogue and other activity has begun to chip away at the heritage of mistrust and opposition, and open up genuine avenues of reconciliation.

MELANIE J. WRIGHT

Edward Kessler and Neil Wenborn (eds), *A Dictionary of Jewish-Christian Relations*, Cambridge: CUP 2005; Jacob Neusner, *Jews and Christians: The Myth of a Common Tradition*, Philadelphia: Trinity Press International and London: SCM Press 1991; Marc Saperstein, *Moments of Crisis in Jewish-Christian Relations*, Philadelphia: Trinity Press International and London: SCM Press 1989; Michael Shermis and Arthur E. Zannoni (eds), *Introduction to Jewish–Christian Relations*, New York and Mahwah NJ: Paulist Press 1991; Hans Ucko, *The People and the People of God: Minjung and Dalit Theology in Interaction with Jewish–Christian Dialogue*, Münster: LIT Verlag 2002; Melanie J. Wright, *Understanding Judaism*, Cambridge: Orchard Academic 2003

Justification

'Justify' has the general meaning of straighten, put right or prove right. In Christian thought, however, it has a special connection with the justification of the ungodly, in other words with the justifying of those who because of sin are in themselves not 'right' with God. The main biblical sources of teaching on the subject are Paul's letters to the Galatians and the Romans, but it was with the Reformation that the issue erupted into the centre of theological debate. The theme of justification was radically sharpened and highlighted by the Reformers. Their teaching was in turn warded off by the Council of Trent on behalf of the Roman Catholic Church.

Reformation
Council

The general position common to the three major Reformation traditions in the sixteenth century (Lutheran, Reformed, Anglican) is stated by Philipp Melanchthon in the fourth article of the 1530 Augsburg Confession: 'They teach that men cannot be justified in the sight of God by their own strength, merits or works, but that they are justified freely on account of Christ through faith, when they believe that they are received into grace and that their sins are remitted on account of Christ who made satisfaction for sins on our behalf through his death. God imputes this faith for righteousness in his own sight (Romans 3 and 4).'

The main points in this condensed statement are: justification of the ungodly – and all humans belong to this category – is an act of free divine grace. It cannot be earned or deserved by merits or works. It is based on the satisfaction for sins offered by Christ in his death on the cross and is appropriated simply by faith, which God regards as righteousness.

Martin Luther had come to this conviction through his long struggles to find assurance that he was acceptable to God in spite of his own personal doubts, temptations and inadequacies. His rediscovery and reappropriation of Paul led to a shifting of the location of justification: no longer, as generally in medieval theology, the end of a process of purification and perfecting, but rather its basis and beginning. This reorientation brought with it a re-evaluation of the concept of faith as radical personal trust, not merely the simple acceptance of truth as delivered by ecclesiastical tradition or authority. In medieval theology and piety, by contrast, faith tended to be valued less highly than other virtues, especially love. A further important aspect was summed up in the phrase *simul justus et peccator*, 'simultaneously justified and a sinner', meaning that people can live with their own sinfulness instead of despairing over it because their righteousness in God's eyes lies elsewhere. Justification in this sense is described as forensic: it depends on a divine judgement that contradicts and so overrules empirical reality.

Martin Luther
Paul
Faith
Love

Although many other issues were involved in the Reformation, Luther was convinced that the doctrine of justification by grace through faith was the root of the whole matter, and came in later years to describe it as 'the article by which the church stands or falls'. This insistence on the centrality and supremacy of the doctrine of justification remains to the present day a feature of traditional Lutheran teaching. Other Reformation traditions maintain

Sin
Lutheranism

the doctrine in substantially similar form, but are less inclined to treat it as the pivot and horizon of the whole Christian faith.

Shortly after Luther's death the Council of Trent issued (in January 1547) a lengthy Decree on Justification which did in fact tacitly accept many of the points made by the Reformers (and in particular ruled out Pelagianism, the view that human beings can work towards their own salvation), but also anathematized a range of views in a series of 33 canons, many of which were clearly intended to target the Reformation. However, the council neither explicitly admitted that it had learned from the Reformation nor did its anathemas mention specific Reformers by name, instead using the formula 'If any one says ...' The decree and the canons are thus open to considerable interpretation and reinterpretation. This became a major enterprise in Roman Catholic theology in the twentieth century, running alongside a wide-ranging revival of Roman Catholic interest in the theology of the Reformation.

pp. 520–1

Ecumenical movement

These reconsiderations bore ecumenical fruit in 1999, when representatives of the Roman Catholic Church's Council for Christian Unity and the Lutheran World Federation met in Augsburg to sign a *Joint Declaration on the Doctrine of Justification.* This statement recognizes differences of emphasis and expression in the teaching of the two traditions, but stresses their compatibility within a 'differentiated consensus'. The Declaration did, however, come under criticism from Lutheran theologians in Germany who accused it (a) of confusing rather than clarifying the issues and (b) of failing to conclude that agreement on 'the article by which the church stands or falls' must logically lead to full mutual ecclesiastical recognition – a demand which the Roman Catholic Church resists. Another weakness in terms of ecumenical diplomacy is that it was only the Lutheran World Federation that was involved in reaching this agreement, and not the other Reformation traditions, although they too subscribe to the doctrine of justification solely by grace through faith.

A further issue considerably discussed in recent Protestant theology is whether or how the sixteenth-century language and teaching on justification is still vital and alive for people in the modern world. The *Joint Declaration*, for example, is barely readable, let alone comprehensible, for people without an extensive theological training and familiarity with the history of theological controversy on the subject in the early modern period. (The same applies to many of the utterances of its critics.) There are similar problems with most texts produced in ecumenical diplomacy, but they are perhaps especially acute in this area, where so many of the issues involve patterns of thinking deeply coloured by the controversial theological thought of the sixteenth and seventeenth centuries – for example, in the understanding of 'sin', the notion of 'grace' or such concepts as 'satisfaction'. The message of justification by grace through faith remains at the heart of Christian belief, but the way it is expressed, formulated and explained demands more than the repetition of past formulae that may no longer resonate.

ALASDAIR HERON

Hans Küng, *Justification. The Doctrine of Karl Barth and a Catholic Reflection*, New York: Thomas Nelson 1964 and London: Burns & Oates 1965; Lutheran World Federation and Roman Catholic Church, *Joint Declaration on Justification*, Grand Rapids, MI: Eerdmans 2000; William Rusch et al. (eds), *Justification and the Future of the Ecumenical Movement: The Joint Declaration on the Doctrine of Justification*, Collegeville, MI: Liturgical Press 2003

Kierkegaard, Søren

Søren Aabye Kierkegaard (1813–55) was a Christian writer whose reputation largely rests on a series of pseudonymous works he produced between 1843 and 1846, together with a couple of later works and, finally, a blistering attack on established Christianity that took the form of a series of polemical pamphlets published in the last year of his life. In a virtuoso blending of satire, fiction, literary criticism and philosophy, under various pseudonyms Kierkegaard explored many of the tensions between religion, ethics and a culture influenced both by Romanticism and by the newer rationalistic philosophy of Hegelianism. The works of a more literary tendency – *Either/Or, Repetition* and *Stages on Life's Way* (which include, among other things, three novellas) – and those of a semi-philosophical nature – *Philosophical Fragments, The Concept of Irony, Concluding Unscientific Postscript* – collectively constitute an indictment of the inadequacy, the complacency and even the despair of aesthetic, ethical and philosophical views of life that stop short of recognizing human beings' inability to redeem themselves and their consequent need of redemption by the incarnate God of Christian faith.

Romanticism
Philosophy

Kierkegaard's position is often described in terms of the three 'stages' of the aesthetic, the ethical and the religious that mark the progression of the self from a natural lifestyle orientated on pleasure, through the acceptance of society's moral demands, to the inwardness of religion. This pattern is found in Kierkegaard, but it is only one element in a larger, dynamic whole. It is, for example, importantly modified by a sharper, more dualistic pattern of either/or in which the self is at every stage challenged to an act of radical self-choice. Elsewhere the issue is seen in terms of 'repetition', a return to the self's original aims, only at a higher level, or of embracing the freedom revealed in anxiety. Kierkegaard also speaks of the 'religiousness A' that human beings can achieve by their own self-examination and of the 'religiousness B' that is entirely dependent on divine revelation. But in all these ways of thinking about the self and faith, the ultimate act of faith that alone can deliver us from despair is something that constantly eludes the grip of a theoretically-orientated view. Theory, Kierkegaard held, is necessarily orientated towards the universal, to what is always and everywhere the case. The particular has interest only as exemplifying a universal law or lesson. The same is true of ethical theory, where matters of right and wrong are debated in terms of universal principles and values. On Kierkegaard's view, however, existence is always particular and concrete. I cannot take a detached or disinterested view of my own existence. On the contrary, I experience it as something quite unique, posing moral and existential problems that cannot be resolved by appealing to general laws. Thus in *Fear and Trembling*, Kierkegaard emphasized how God's call to Abraham took the almost immoral form of the command to sacrifice Isaac, a command which Abraham obeyed (says Kierkegaard's pseudonym) 'by power of the absurd', believing against all appearances that God's original promise (that through Isaac Abraham would be blessed with many descendants) would nevertheless be fulfilled and that he would get Isaac back.

This tension between the universalizing approach of theory and the singularity of existence is perhaps even further heightened in *Philosophical Fragments*, where Kierkegaard insists on seeing the incarnation as the 'absolute paradox' and Christ as existing 'incognito', so utterly is he veiled from the eyes of a merely theoretical reason. Like all fundamental existential questions, the question of faith can only be addressed subjectively, passionately and, although Kierkegaard never used the expression 'leap of faith', in the light of a qualitative leap from theory to subjectivity. 'Subjectivity is truth,' he declared in the *Postscript*. But even our normal human subjectivity is not beyond suspicion, and in a later pseudonymous work, *The Sickness unto Death* (1849), Kierkegaard analysed the various forms of despair that afflicted a subjective self which failed to understand itself as owing its life to God and being offered the gift of forgiveness in Christ.

It is not possible to do justice to the range of Kierkegaard's intellectual and literary strategies in a short introduction, and one can only point out that these pseudonymous works not only contain some extraordinarily acute psychological analyses of modernity's divided self, alongside some of the most painstakingly precise criticisms of idealist logic, but they also contain many passages of glittering prose, literary criticism, and one of the most genial commentaries on Mozart's *Don Giovanni* ever written.

Yet, astonishingly, Kierkegaard also produced a constant stream of religious meditations, usually referred to as 'edifying' or 'upbuilding' or 'Christian' discourses, that almost equal the great pseudonymous works in bulk and that he himself declared to be the real key to his writing. Ironically, however, they were more or less overlooked by his contemporaries and have been similarly neglected in the secondary literature. As he put it in his self-explanatory work *The Point of View for My Work as an Author*: 'the world took with its right hand what I offered with my left, and with its left hand what I offered with my right'. These discourses do not so much contradict the message of the pseudonyms as deepen it, illustrate it and demonstrate its biblical and theological bases. Where the pseudonyms are dominated by such dramatic or bathetic figures as Johannes the Seducer, the complacently happily-married Judge William, the carousing and misogynistic symposiasts of *In Vino Veritas* and the grim patriarchal figure of Abraham, the discourses turn to such figures as 'the woman who was a sinner' of Luke 7, the lilies and the birds of the Sermon on the Mount, and the worshipper who, in becoming as still and quiet as the sea, receives anew the imprint of the divine likeness. Here the message is not so much 'fear and trembling' as inexhaustible gratitude for the 'good and perfect gifts' mentioned in James 1.17, a text which Kierkegaard described as his 'favourite'. *Works of Love* (also written in the form of discourses) has become a modern classic – albeit a controversial one – on the meaning of Christian love. Several of these religious discourses were specifically written as devotional addresses in preparation for receiving communion, revealing a deep and essentially orthodox sense of Christ's presence in the sacrament.

p. 385

Kierkegaard's work was not unnoticed by his contemporaries (as many commentators claim), though it is true that his influence was chiefly posthumous. His final attack on establishment Christianity's conflation of church and state sent ripples throughout Scandinavia and was soon noted also in Germany. By the early 1900s Kierkegaard was being read by theologians and avant-garde intellectuals across Europe. Not only were all the major theologians of the German-speaking world of the first half of the twentieth century significantly influenced by him – Karl Barth, Rudolf Bultmann, Paul Tillich and Dietrich Bonhoeffer, to name but a few – so too were writers and philosophers of the rank of Franz Kafka, Miguel de Unamuno, Martin Buber, György Lukacs and, not least, Martin Heidegger, who gave existentialism an unmistakable Kierkegaardian stamp. If Kierkegaardian themes of anxiety, guilt, despair, freedom and death were perhaps most to the fore in existentialism, the more recent waves of

postmodernism have brought to the fore the Kierkegaard of irony, pseudonyms, indirect communication, aesthetics and, in Anglo-Saxon philosophy, of a highly nuanced approach to ethical problems.

p. 967

It was perhaps inevitable that Kierkegaard's insistence on the subjective and existential nature of faith, together with his use of copious autobiographical references in his works, should have made his own life a part of his meaning for posterity. The story of the oppressive weight of his elderly father's sense of religious guilt, of his feeling compelled to break off his engagement to the lovely and intelligent Regine Olsen, his experience of public humiliation at the hands of the satirical journal *The Corsair,* his quarrels with leading theologians and churchmen and his sudden death at the height of his attack on the establishment have all invited comments which range from making him a saint to debunking him. A man who combined the urbane literary style of a nineteenth-century man-about-town with the intense devotion of an old-style Pietist, who wrote both philosophy and upbuilding discourses, who knew the extreme ranges of the comic and the tragic, and who, not least, saw himself as a new Socrates – such a man is, of course, very interesting. But whatever we are tempted to make of Kierkegaard the man, the works he produced in an extraordinarily intense fever of creativity remain among the landmarks of modern religion and theology.

Eschatology
Pietism
Evil

GEORGE PATTISON

Kierkegaard's Writings (26 vols) ed H. V. and E. H. Hong, Princeton: Princeton University Press 1987–2000; *Kierkegaard's Papers and Journals. A selection,* translated by A. Hannay, Harmondsworth: Penguin Books 1996; Alastair Hannay, *Kierkegaard. An Intellectual Biography,* Cambridge: CUP 2002; Bruce Kirmmse, *Kierkegaard and Golden Age Denmark,* Bloomington IN: Indiana University Press 1990; George Pattison, *Kierkegaard and the Crisis of Faith,* London: SPCK 1997

Salvation
Paul

Kingdom of God

Jesus
Papacy

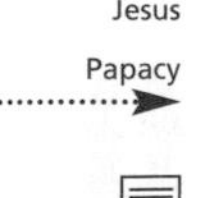

p. 658
Reformation

The central theme of Jesus' message was the coming of the kingdom of God (the Gospel of Matthew always speaks of the kingdom of heaven, to avoid mentioning the divine name). It is the subject of a great many of his parables, which compare the kingdom of God to a grain of mustard seed which becomes the greatest of all shrubs (Mark 4.30–2), or treasure hidden in a field or a pearl of great price which it is worth selling everything to buy (Matthew 13.44–5), and many individual sayings refer to it. Sometimes the kingdom is said to be here now ('If it is by the finger of God that I cast out demons [which Jesus does], then the kingdom of God has come upon you', Luke 11.20); at one point it is even said to be 'within you' (Luke 17.20); sometimes it is imminent ('There are some standing here who will not taste death before they see the kingdom of God come with power', Mark 9.1). The Lord's Prayer contains a request for the coming of the kingdom.

There has been much discussion about whether Jesus spoke of the kingdom as being present or future, whether he brought the kingdom (a view termed 'realized eschatology') or merely announced it (a view termed 'future eschatology'), but whatever the finer points to be considered, it is clear that the kingdom is inextricably bound up with the person and activity of Jesus. He marks a decisive turning point that means salvation for those who accept him and judgement for those who do not. The coming of the kingdom affects the whole future of the world. Here Jesus is taking up the Jewish hope, widely attested in the literature of the time between the Old and New Testaments, that God will establish his rule on earth and do away with evil, bringing peace and justice to all.

Notably, Jesus never speaks of God as king, nor is the kingdom of God in his sayings a realm: the term denotes God's kingly rule, through which evil is defeated. Nevertheless, the imagery of the kingdom does also have a spatial element: Jesus speaks of entering the kingdom, and depicts it as a great feast: many will come from east and west and sit at table with Abraham and Isaac in the kingdom (Matthew 8.11); tax collectors and prostitutes will enter it before self-righteous Jews (Matthew 21.31).

The term 'kingdom of God' does not occur very often outside the synoptic Gospels; when it does, it denotes in a general way the salvation that believers can expect. Paul speaks of 'inheriting the kingdom' (1 Corinthians 6.9). The striking absence of talk of the kingdom in the development of Christianity after Jesus led the Roman Catholic biblical scholar Alfred Loisy to remark, 'Jesus preached the kingdom of God; what came was the church.'

In fact the kingdom of God came to be identified with the church. Augustine in his *City of God* still identified only the invisible body of the elect within the church with the kingdom of God, but by the Middle Ages the identification of kingdom and church had become part of Roman Catholic theology. The Pope, in a line going back to the apostle Peter, holds the keys of the kingdom. By contrast, Reformers argued that the kingdom is not to be identified with any organization; they emphasized the contrast and conflict between the kingdom of God and the kingdoms of this world. By now there was talk equally of the kingdom of God and the kingdom of Christ: they came to be used interchangeably: in Reformation theology the kingdom was understood as the invisible rule of Christ exercised over believers through the Holy Spirit and the preaching of the Word.

One point of controversy now was whether it was possible for Christians to work towards bringing in the kingdom of God, say by evangelization and missionary work, or whether that lay solely in God's hands. During the nineteenth century, the kingdom of God was interpreted in terms of the establishment of an ideal Christian society. With leading liberal theologians such as Friedrich Schleiermacher and Albrecht Ritschl, the Christian colouring was still marked, but the ideal came to be secularized and the kingdom was seen as achievable through progress, increased prosperity and social development.

The kingdom was the focal point of the Social Gospel, a form of Protestantism which developed in the industrial cities of North America at the end of the nineteenth century and the beginning of the twentieth, and was associated with Walter Rauschenbusch. The Social Gospel was concerned with social as well as individual salvation and the transformation of society.

Reaction against this liberal view of bringing in the kingdom by practical action developed at the beginning of the twentieth century. It was led by biblical scholars. In his pioneering *Jesus' Proclamation of the Kingdom of God*, Johannes Weiss again emphasized that the background to Jesus' teaching was the Jewish expectation of the kingdom of God: this could not be built up by human effort but would break into history suddenly, transforming the world and judging it. Weiss's ideas were taken up by Albert Schweitzer, who saw Jesus' determination to be crucified as an attempt to force God to bring in the kingdom.

This eschatological, apocalyptic view might have seemed irrelevant to liberal Christians, but the outbreak of the First World War and the cataclysmic upheavals that followed created a climate in which such views were far more plausible than the liberal tradition. However, that climate was not to last, and the notion of the kingdom of God as an ideal society governed by truth and justice returned. It also appears in liberation theology and other contemporary theologies concerned for social change.

Perhaps the most powerful use of a term which has now been employed in so many ways and in so many contexts that its meaning has become vague and blurred is as an antithesis to the church, a reminder that Christianity must be concerned for more than its own institutional future as the church. At the same time, awareness of its origins is still a reminder that not every use of the term 'kingdom of God' can claim the support of Jesus of Nazareth.

JOHN BOWDEN

R. S. Barbour (ed), *The Kingdom of God and Human Society*, Edinburgh: T&T Clark 1993; C. H. Dodd, *The Parables of the Kingdom* (1935), London: Collins Fontana and New York: Scribner 1961; H. Richard Niebuhr, *The Kingdom of God in America* (1937), Middletown CT: Wesleyan University Press 1988; Norman Perrin, *The Kingdom of God in the Teaching of Jesus*, London: SCM Press and Philadelphia: Westminster Press 1963; W. Willis (ed), *The Kingdom of God in Twentieth-Century Interpretation*, Peabody, MA: Hendrickson 1987

Language

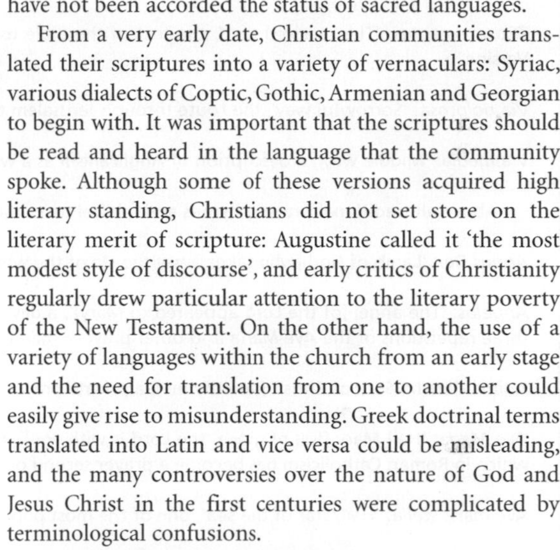

Christianity has no sacred language: no theological tradition, that is, of identifying a particular language as the language of God, or as a privileged medium of revelation, in the way that Arabic is a sacred language in Islam because it is the vehicle of God's revelation in the Holy Qur'an. The Christian scriptures were written in Hebrew, Aramaic and Greek, and the study of these languages has therefore always been important to Christians, but they have not been accorded the status of sacred languages.

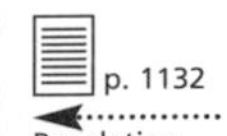
p. 1132
Revelation

Bible

From a very early date, Christian communities translated their scriptures into a variety of vernaculars: Syriac, various dialects of Coptic, Gothic, Armenian and Georgian to begin with. It was important that the scriptures should be read and heard in the language that the community spoke. Although some of these versions acquired high literary standing, Christians did not set store on the literary merit of scripture: Augustine called it 'the most modest style of discourse', and early critics of Christianity regularly drew particular attention to the literary poverty of the New Testament. On the other hand, the use of a variety of languages within the church from an early stage and the need for translation from one to another could easily give rise to misunderstanding. Greek doctrinal terms translated into Latin and vice versa could be misleading, and the many controversies over the nature of God and Jesus Christ in the first centuries were complicated by terminological confusions.

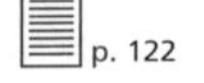
p. 122

Apocalyptic

pp. 1210–11
Trinity
Christology
Liberation theology

Though Christians were at least to begin with aesthetically indifferent to language, in practice particular Christian traditions tended to give pride of place, and in effect to sacralize, certain registers of language, particular the language of worship. An obvious example is the special status given to Latin in the Western Roman Catholic tradition, in which the eucharist was celebrated in Latin up to the middle of the twentieth century; to the English of the Book of Common Prayer, still prized by many in the Anglican tradition; or to the King James Version of the Bible in many parts of English-speaking Christianity. Special 'church languages' are often earlier forms of a vernacular, as is the case with Old Church Slavonic in Russian Christianity, or Ge'ez in Ethiopic. It is worth

Worship
Eucharist

A LITTLE LATIN ... AND SOME GREEK

It is almost impossible to explain many terms employed in Christianity without referring back to Greek or Latin. And this is not surprising. After all, Greek and Latin were the languages used in its earliest days. The New Testament was written in Greek, as was the version of the Jewish Bible which the Christians made their Old Testament. Greek continued to be the language of the Eastern churches, while in the West Latin was used for over a thousand years, until the Reformation; the Roman Catholic Church continued to worship in Latin until the1950s, and its priests were taught in Latin. To this day papal encyclicals are written in Latin and referred to by their first words, e.g. the 1967 *Populorum progressio* (The Development of Peoples).

Knowing the dominance of these languages helps us to understand why in English Christians are said to belong to churches (Greek *kyriake* = of the Lord); the corresponding adjective is ecclesiastical or ecclesial, from another Greek word for church (*ekklesia* = assembly, those called forth; the Latin is *ecclesia*). The body of the church building is called the nave (Latin *navis* = ship), because it can look like an upturned boat; in some traditions the main form of worship is called the mass (from the last words of the service, *Ite, missa est* = 'Go, you are dismissed'). There are countless other examples.

Latin terms are also still used untranslated, as if everyone will know what they mean; for example:

Ad limina apostolorum: 'To the threshold of the apostles'; bishops going to Rome to report to the Pope are said to make an *ad limina* visit.

Ex opere operato: 'By the act done', used of the sacraments. A sacrament is valid regardless of the moral standing of the one administering it or receiving it.

Simul justus et peccator: 'At the same time righteous and a sinner', the state of one who has been justified by faith.

Textus receptus: 'The received text', the text of the Bible used in the first printed versions and underlying the King James Version.

Via dolorosa: 'Sorrowful way', the route through Jerusalem taken by Jesus to his crucifixion.

Via media: 'Middle way', a description of Anglicanism as a way between Roman Catholicism and Protestantism.

Above all traditional prayers, hymns and biblical texts known as canticles have Latin names. Here are some of them:

Agnus Dei: 'Lamb of God [who takes away the sin of the world]', from John 1.29; said or sung in the mass.

Angelus: 'The angel [of the Lord appeared to Mary]', a devotion in the morning, at noon, and in the evening, consisting of three repetitions of the *Ave Maria* and other prayers, marked by the ringing of a bell.

Anima Christi: 'Soul of Christ' [sanctify me], a private prayer used at the eucharist.

Ave Maria: 'Hail Mary [full of grace, the Lord is with you]', the words addressed by the angel Gabriel to Mary in Luke 1.28, which in Roman Catholicism has become a prayer second only to the Lord's Prayer.

Ave maris stella: 'Hail, star of the sea', one of the most popular hymns to Mary.

Ave verum corpus: 'Hail true body', a medieval eucharistic hymn.

Benedicite: 'Bless [the Lord, all works of the Lord]', the song of the three children cast by King Nebuchadnezzar into a burning fiery furnace, contained in an addition to the biblical book of Daniel.

Benedictus: 'Blessed [be the Lord God of Israel]', from Luke 1.68–79; a morning canticle. The word is also used to denote the words 'Blessed [is he who comes in the name of the Lord]', said or sung in the eucharist after the *Sanctus*.

Credo: 'I believe', the 'Nicene Creed', said or sung in the eucharist.

Dies irae: 'Day of wrath', a medieval text known as a sequence, which forms part of the traditional requiem mass (mass for the dead).

Gloria: 'Glory [to God in the highest]', an ancient hymn of praise composed on the model of the Psalms

→

Jubilate: 'Rejoice [in the Lord, all you lands]', Psalm 100.

Magnificat: '[My soul] magnifies [the Lord]', Mary's song of praise from Luke 1.46–55.

Miserere: 'Have mercy [upon me O God]', Psalm 51.

Nunc dimittis: 'Now dismiss' , Simeon's song of praise from Luke 2.29–32.

Pater noster: 'Our Father', the Lord's Prayer.

Pie Jesu: 'Blessed Jesus [Lord, grant them rest]', sung in requiem masses between the *Sanctus* and the *Agnus Dei.*

Regina coeli: 'Queen of heaven', an Eastertide hymn to the Virgin Mary.

Requiem: 'Rest [eternal]', the first words of the mass for the dead.

Salve regina: 'Hail [holy] queen', one of the earliest antiphons (refrains) sung to the Virgin Mary.

Sanctus: 'Holy, [holy, holy, Lord God of hosts]', from Isaiah's vision of God in Isaiah 6.3; said or sung in the eucharist.

Stabat mater: 'The mother stood [by the cross]', a hymn describing the sorrows of Mary mother of Jesus at his crucifixion.

Te Deum: '[We praise] you God', a hymn of praise to God the Father and God the Son.

Veni creator: 'Come creator [Spirit]', medieval hymn, often used in ordination services.

Venite: 'O come [let us sing to the Lord]', Psalm 95.

Vexilla regis: 'The royal banners [forward go]', a hymn celebrating Christ's triumph on the cross.

Greek terms are less frequent outside the Orthodox churches, and unlike the Latin ones, some have been brought into use only by modern scholars. They include:

Agape: 'Love'; this is the term used in the New Testament to denote love between Christians, as distinct from *eros*, which is thought to have more sexual connotations. It also denotes a meal, or 'love-feast', held in the early church which was closely connected with the eucharist.

Kerygma: 'Proclamation', the original message preached by Christians is referred to as the kerygma.

Kyrie eleison: 'Lord, have mercy', the beginning of a ninefold prayer in the eucharist.

Parousia: 'Presence' or 'arrival', originally used of the ceremonial arrival of an emperor, in Christianity it came to denote the second coming of Jesus.

Pasch: 'Passover'; the word is used of both the Jewish Passover and the Christian Easter. The adjective 'paschal' is far more common.

Pentecost: 'Fiftieth day', the name for the festival commemorating the descent of the Holy Spirit on the apostles.

Trisagion: 'Thrice holy', another name for the *Sanctus*.

pointing out that the use of particular registers of language is also related to the question of power: the use of, say, English rather than Latin was driven by a desire not only to make the Bible more accessible but also to reject Roman authority. The power factor in connection with the use of language is still evident in modern battles over the use of inclusive language, which is of a special concern to feminist theology. Feminist theology

Whether the language of worship should be traditional and time-honoured, sometimes to the point of incomprehensibility, or immediately understandable, using the idioms and familiarity of everyday speech, is still a hotly debated question. At the moment the revisers are in the ascendant, but although they have often brought new life to the liturgy and made it more accessible, their work has inevitably been utilitarian and prosaic, and above all transient, as possible forms of service change and multiply, to the point that when large congregations from different church backgrounds meet it is not even certain that p. 967 without a text before them they will say the Lord's Prayer together in the same words.

An alternative to this flexibility and modernization of language is the language of poetry: John Donne and Shakespeare, Milton and Gerard Manley Hopkins, for example, cannot be rewritten in modern English although they use archaic forms of expression or words which need Poetry a dictionary to explain them. Poetry, like music, makes such a deep impression precisely because it remains the same, and remaining the same actually grows on people over the years, as they get to know it more deeply and it takes on profoundly personal associations. The repetition of time-honoured language makes it, as we say, 'part of us'. This is particularly the case with worship, and it is perhaps a deep insight into the very nature of the brain and its activity that traditional forms of words tend to be better recalled by a person who is dying.

As we shall see, philosophical discussions about meaning and truth in the twentieth century came to be focused on questions of language, and here perhaps the importance of the poets has been underestimated. Poets have tended simply not to address the problems that philosophers struggle with, using language to create rather than to describe in precise terms. Yet at times even poets have acknowledged the impossibility of expressing aspects of God in language.

Story Genesis 11.1–9 (the story of the Tower of Babel) is Holy Spirit the classic biblical explanation of the variety of human Pentecostalism languages, and the starting point for a rich current of reflection on the nature and history of human language in the early church and the Middle Ages. Some identified the language used before the building of the tower, spoken also by Adam and Eve in the Garden of Eden, with an Philosophy existing human language still in use after Babel. Hebrew was the commonest candidate. Others said that while this language had been lost on earth, it might perhaps be  experienced again in heaven. Dante Alighieri (1265–1321) held both views in succession. The Acts of the Apostles (2.1–13) deliberately presents the Day of Pentecost as the antithesis of Babel. After the Holy Spirit has descended on the gathering of apostles, Peter addresses crowds outside in a speech. In amazement they respond: 'How is it that we hear, each of us in his own native language? Parthians and Medes and Elamites and residents of Mesopotamia, Judaea and Cappadocia, Pontus and Asia, Phrygia and Pampylia... we hear them telling in our own tongues the mighty works of God.' In the new Christian society, perfect communication is once again possible. This spontaneous understanding of a single utterance by hearers of different languages, as described by Luke, is properly called *xenolalia*. This is different from the commoner *glossolalia*, or 'speaking in tongues', a spontaneous and uninhibited utterance, often highly tonal or musical, which is regarded in some (especially charismatic) Christian circles as a gift of the Holy Spirit. Glossolalia is seldom recognizable as human speech, and in a group of glossolalic Christians there is usually a person to 'give the interpretation' of the utterance.

Building the tower of Babel, from *Hymns to Saints and Martyrs*, eighteenth-century Coptic manuscript

Language became an important concern of twentieth-century Christians in two ways.

1. From the beginning of the century, questions of language became central to philosophical discussions of meaning and truth. What are Christians talking about when they use their language of faith to make claims about God and the world? Does talk of God refer to a reality apart from those who are doing the talking, or is it simply a way of describing some ideal that does not really exist? Analytic philosophers, often called logical positivists, notably A. J. Ayer, argued that religious and metaphysical statements were literally meaningless, because they could not be either verified or falsified. Other philosophers, such as R. B. Braithwaite, argued that religious language did not need to be subjected to the test of verification because it was essentially non-descriptive: its prime function was

to express commitments to certain ideals, often in the form of stories or parables. Yet others, notably Ludwig Wittgenstein in his later philosophy, argued that religious language can be understood only within the context in which it is generally used. If this approach is taken even further, it leads to the question whether meaning and truth are notions which can be applied generally at all, a position characteristic of postmodernism. The Cambridge theologian Don Cupitt, with his view that language is a way of imposing some order on reality, but that human beings simply skate on its surface like water-boatmen, represents an extreme position. At all points, Christian theologians came to be involved in the discussion, like the Oxford philosopher and later Bishop of Durham Ian T. Ramsey, who argued that the demand for verification could be met by an appeal to experience here or in a world to come which would conclusively confirm or refute beliefs; meanwhile, these could be meaningfully expressed by parables and metaphors. The philosopher John Hick produced a similar theory of eschatological verification, again arguing that the truth or falsehood of religious language would be proved at the end of the Christian's journey through life.

What God-talk refers to and in what forms it is legitimate are still central questions for Christian theology.

2. Important parts of English-speaking Christianity, particularly in the United States, have became concerned with the need to find 'inclusive language' renderings of the Bible and the liturgy; that is, to shape a language which does not presuppose the primacy or normalcy of maleness by, for example, using 'mankind' in the sense of 'all people'. This issue is part of a wider feminist concern, that the language which we use is fatally male-centred, carrying with it assumptions which are no longer valid. Yet changing the language is by no means easy, since at present the desired new forms generally do not exist and need to be created. Moreover, in many cases it is not just a question of language but of conceptuality; the world-view and the concepts behind much of the language of the Bible and the liturgy are no longer ours.

In a more arduous version of the inclusive language issue, the challenge is to frame a language for speaking about God that does justice to God's personhood without applying particular gender to God. This is particularly difficult, again not least because the need for a change in language is inextricably bound up with a change in conceptuality.

These issues arise in languages other than English, but have been discussed with particular intensity among English-speaking Christians, and have led, in the opening years of the twenty-first century, to special controversies within Roman Catholicism.

Language is a key issue for Christians, but it also needs to be remembered that it is not essential for, say, Christian prayer and worship. Christian negative (apophatic) theology emphasizes that God cannot be spoken of; and silence is a key element in a wide range of traditions from the Quakers to the Trappists. A psalm speaks of the heavens telling the glory of God: 'There is no speech, nor are there words; their voice is not heard; yet their voice goes out through all the earth, and their words to the end of the world' (19.3–4).

Mysticism

Postmodern theology

ANDERS BERGQUIST

Don Cupitt, *The Long-Legged Fly. A Theology of Language and Desire*, London: SCM Press 1987; Frederick Ferre, *Language, Logic and God*, London: Eyre & Spottiswoode 1962; John Macquarrie, *God-Talk*, London: SCM Press and New York: Harper & Row 1967; Brian Wren, *What Language Shall I Borrow? God-Talk in Worship*, New York: Continuum and London: SCM Press 1990

Law

Journey

All societies and groups need a framework of law to regulate their common life. This can be mediated through custom and tradition, but also more formally in a recognizable legal system. In the Western world, the law is based either on Roman civil law or Anglo-Saxon common-law systems. Jurisprudence, or the systematic study of law, traces the complex history of Western law and its application at all levels today. The church has a complex relationship to this legal system. It has clearly influenced its development, leading to its domination for over a millennium; but the church is also subject to the law as an institution within society, whether as a powerful presence or as a minority. This ambiguous relationship raises a number of issues.

Society

The source of law

There is always a sense that the law is above society and regulates it. Yet the law is always embedded in a changing reality to which it has to respond. In our time this is apparent in relation to rapid technological and scientific advances and new political alignments. The problem is to secure the basis of law in its positive practical expression. Broadly speaking, there have been two answers to this problem.

First, the concept of natural law in its Stoic form was introduced into Roman law as a philosophical basis for the traditional assumption that law came from the gods. Stoicism believed that there is a divine *logos* or ordered reason that informs all things both natural and moral. Humanity finds its fulfilment in conducting its affairs

Human rights

in accordance with this reason, which in ethical terms is shaped by the virtues. The law, therefore, seeks to conform society to it in the particular situation of the time.

The early church, drawing on the Prologue to John's Gospel (1.1–14), could interpret the Stoic ethic in terms of the common reason that is universally available and believed to be embodied in its fullness in Jesus. Similarly, Thomism the medieval Thomist tradition, which has been at the heart of Roman Catholicism, has understood the natural law as being available to human reason, confirmed and Secularization supplemented by revelation or divine law. The secularizing tendencies of the post-Renaissance world tended to detach natural law from its religious basis to make it part of the laws of nature. The notion of natural law remains a strong element in legal reasoning, as exemplified by the English law presumption of 'natural justice'.

Alongside natural law can be put the notion of revealed or 'divine law'. This is not in contradiction to natural law, for presumably both come from the same source in God's creative will. It is an additional source of law drawn directly from faith sources. In Christianity the sources Bible have universally been the scriptures as the word of God. In Roman Catholicism the Bible is interpreted through the magisterium, the teaching office centred on the Pope. Papacy At one point in the Middle Ages the popes were regarded as a primary source of law. However, the norm has been to recognize two sources of law: the sacred and the secular. Today the scope of sacred law is effectively limited to the church itself and has only advisory authority beyond. In the Byzantine East the emperor, and subsequently the tsar, was regarded as the divine protector of the society Reformation in God's name. The Reformers insisted on going back to the scriptures alone, thus effectively separating the secular from the sacred.

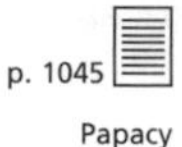
p. 1045

The second, essentially modern and secular, answer is to base the authority of the law on the democratic will of the people. Representative institutions, such as parliament or congress, act under the mandate of the democratic process. But as can be seen from the history of the past century, this can be fickle and dangerous, using the law to support regimes that are clearly repugnant. There is therefore an ever-present need to try to ensure the independence and authority of the law which can be appealed to, at least in theory.

Martin Luther

John Calvin

Structurally the separation of powers offers certain checks and balances between the legislature, the executive and the judiciary. Similarly, there are appeals to historical or moral reasoning. Marxism claims to provide a scientific analysis of human history that justifies the law. The Western democratic tradition usually finds its justification in some form of utilitarianism, arguing that 'the greatest happiness of the greatest number' both preserves liberty and takes care of the needs of the oppressed and wronged. More recently the notion of human rights, stemming from the French and American Revolutions of the eighteenth century, has been appealed to as safeguarding the needs of individuals and groups.

The churches, as institutions within society, can participate in the democratic processes. Thus they can influence the shape of the legal system. It is also true that most churches see democracy as a proper way of embodying aspects of a Christian understanding of freedom and responsibility.

The theological task of the law

Theologically the church has always regarded the law as part of God's providential dealing with humanity. On the basis of the theory of natural law this has been understood as being true of all legitimate authority, whether Christian or not, and even in persecution. Yet there has also been an ambiguity, since positive law as experienced in practice can be subjected to the critique of prophetic protest.

Thus in the New Testament there are two different approaches to the power of the Roman empire. Paul (Romans 13.1–7) and Peter (1 Peter 2.13–17) saw the Roman state as at least maintaining a framework of law and order which curbed the powers of chaos. However, in the book of Revelation (13.11–17) the emperor is seen as a destructive beast coming out of the abyss. Hope lies in the promises of God alone.

The classic expression of this ambiguity is the 'two kingdoms' theory that goes back to Augustine's *City of God*. Humanity lives simultaneously in the city of destruction and the city of God which will be revealed in the future consummation. Meanwhile the secular power has the task of shoring up the bulwarks against evil and chaos. This is true of pagan or Christian authorities. Within that city the church can live out its task as representative of the celestial city.

With the Reformation the medieval Roman Catholic interpretation of the two spheres was severely challenged in the name of restricting papal authority to the religious. A sharp distinction was made between the temporal and the spiritual. Each was to remain in its own sphere, though the magistrate or ruler had a duty to safeguard the freedom of the proclamation of the gospel, an issue that arose under Hitler. The fear of chaos made Martin Luther resist the Peasants' Revolt of 1525. In Calvinism, however, the church had the duty to monitor the state's conduct of its stewardship. This safeguarded the critical function of the church in ensuring that the law is in accordance with the word of God.

For the Reformers the law had a specific spiritual task. It was there primarily to curb the power of wickedness and to punish evildoers. But it also was there to remind all men and women of their fallen and sinful state and to point them to the grace of God. To this John Calvin added a third task. For Christians the law also made clear the path of righteousness, a spur to godly living. It is this that lay behind the Reformed tradition's emphasis on sanctification, as illustrated by John Wesley, and on developing the godly commonwealth, as was attempted in New England. The law, thus understood, can make a positive contribution to human welfare.

Law and morality

This last point indicates the close but complex relationship between law and morality. First, at any given time the legal system reflects more or less the social values and expectation of the day. At a time of rapid change it may represent earlier values. Indeed the law is usually 'behind the times' and may therefore be a useful brake on social movement. At other times it may be that the law permits behaviour not yet widely accepted. In other circumstances the law may be partisan and enforce the will of a powerful minority.

The law, however, is meant to stand for a sense of justice and of values that have intrinsic worth. It is possible, therefore, to see the law as having a didactic function, guiding the community's conscience. Thus, for instance, the law can protect the rights of minorities or promote acceptable attitudes in such areas as race relations.

However, there is a limit to its educational purpose. Of itself the law cannot change the inward disposition. It can only enforce outward conformity, though this may provide a framework for change. Nor can it deal with the subtleties of the particular personal situation, even where, as is normal in British courts, every effort is made to take all factors into account. Lines have to be drawn which are to some extent arbitrary and may appear to be heavy-handed.

The law, therefore, is never perfect or above criticism. It has constantly to be adjusted to take account of changing circumstances, social attitudes and technological developments that affect matters of life and death or the ordering of society. The law itself may be unjust. *In extremis* this may well result in social protest or even revolution in the name of a higher justice, processes that can be destructive as well as constructive.

The church has always claimed to be an advocate of justice and social well-being. That is an aspect of its prophetic voice. How this is done will vary very much, depending on the circumstances and what resources are available to be deployed. In Western democracies the churches are rightly part of the lobby system, putting out their critiques, perspectives and suggestions into the market place of political debate and policy. There is no guarantee, however, that the Christian voice will have unanimity or that the churches themselves are above criticism or reform.

The law and pastoral practice

Pastoral care

In its pastoral practice the church faces two issues in relation to the law. The first is the need to comply with the law of the land. Where the law is constrictive and even persecutory there may be some delicate decisions as to how to balance the perceived desire for legitimate freedoms and the threat of persecution that may well put members in danger. Such questions arise even in situations that would not be regarded as severe. Cultural assumptions embodied in the law can pose hard choices. In Western society, however, the need is usually to comply with regulations that may appear restrictive but are designed to ensure proper care for health and safety, professional standards or equal opportunities. It is in the interests of the churches to be seen to be attaining high levels of practice and contributing to the welfare of the wider society.

The other issue is an enduring dilemma. How is it possible both to maintain the moral standards that are often set out in law or regulations and yet at the same time to offer freely accessible non-judgemental acceptance to those who have fallen short or find themselves ostracized? This problem is well set out in the attitude of the elder brother in Jesus' parable who grudges the welcome given to the returning prodigal son (Luke 15.11–32). Pastoral questions often centre on morally divisive matters such as divorce, gender orientation or family quarrels. The tension becomes particularly acute when the issue cuts across divided public opinion. The church, through confession and pastoral counselling, has always accepted a duty to the troubled person. Only through such an accepting attitude, mirroring Jesus, can the real healing process take root. Yet there have to be standards and norms that represent key values. However, the judgements thus made necessary can easily turn into a condemnatory moralism that both demonizes the victim and debases the humanity of the perpetrator. Moreover, it is often the righteous whose attitudes are most in need of judgement. That is not to say that there are not proper ways of dealing with people who may be a danger to themselves or others, or whose condition requires specialist treatment or even restraint and remedies administered according to the law. It is often impossible to avoid hurt. All that can be done is to act with integrity and compassion and trust in God to overcome the deficiencies.

The law and grace

One of the concerns that run through the pages of the New Testament is the relation between the Jewish Law, the Torah, and the emergent church that has suddenly burst out into the pagan, Gentile, world. Does this mean the abolition of the law and thus the denial of the church's historical roots? The answer is symbolized in the insistence that the Hebrew scriptures be retained in the Christian Bible.

The classical expression of this problem is the Lutheran Justification doctrine of 'justification by faith'. Martin Luther, claiming Paul to derive it from Paul, drove a sharp division between the Torah which, while of divine origin, paradoxically has the effect of condemning humanity in its sin and which is powerless to help, and grace, which is God's unmerited gift of salvation in Christ. It is impossible, Luther argued, to claw a way out of the pit through greater obedience to the law. Only in Christ is it possible to enter into a new life of fellowship and freedom in God.

p. 906 Modern scholarship, however, has questioned this interpretation of Paul. Certainly the gospel is grace and Grace there is an ambiguity about the law in Paul. But the law itself is an act of grace given as part of the saving release from slavery. Nor is it simply a set of regulations, but Covenant rather an invitation to the people to enter into a covenant relationship that is also response. It provides a model of Israel's relation with God, including provision made for forgiveness and restoration. From it, the rabbis insisted, come wisdom and understanding and a deep relation with God (see Psalm 119). Paul's negative attack seems harsh and even perverse.

There is, however, more to be said. Paul honours the law that is God's gift and self-revelation. The law is not abrogated, but fulfilled in the law of love (Romans 13.10). The issue is not the Torah but whether the Gentiles have to become Jews in order to become Christians. To answer this Paul goes behind Moses to Abraham (and even Adam), to a primal act of faith that carries the universal promise before the law existed. He deduces that both Jew and Gentile, indeed all humanity, are included and that they can live side by side until they come together in the fullness of God's kingdom (Romans 9–11). Meanwhile the Torah can afford a resource for the daily pastoral task of helping Christians to cope with the pressures of life and to grow in love (see 1 Corinthians).

Jesus Paul, moreover, is echoing Jesus, whose attitude to the law is found in his response to the question about its essential nature (Mark 12.28–34). That is to be found in the commands to love God and neighbour. These are in line with Jesus' teaching elsewhere (Matthew 5–7) and Prophecy with prophetic practice. Indeed Jesus had a reputation of opening the law up and including the outcast, the sinner, the oppressed and even the Gentile. To live the law is to be shaped by love.

So for both Jesus and Paul the Torah keeps its place as the manifestation of God's covenant of grace. Yet that is not the final word, because it points to the inclusive

p. 898

nature of salvation. Is not Abraham found in the Torah? The danger, perhaps, is to miss the challenge and grace of love and to relapse into taking the Torah's commands with unwarranted literalism, forgetting that the first as well as the last words are grace, hope, faith and love, and that the greatest of these is love.

PAUL BALLARD

Jacques Ellul, *The Theological Foundation of Law*, London: SCM Press and New York: Seabury Press 1961; H. L. A Hart, *The Concept of Law*, Oxford: OUP 1978; Colin G. Kruse, *Paul, the Law and Justification*, Leicester: Apollos 1996; A. R. Vidler, *God's Strange Work*, London: SCM Press 1963; N. T. Wright, *The Climax of the Covenant – Christ and Law in Pauline Theology*, Edinburgh: T&T Clark 1991

Letters

From the beginning of the Christian movement, letters have been used in a variety of important ways by Christians. Some of these ways draw on, or develop, the use of letters in antiquity. Stylistically, the letter collections of the Roman politician and orator Cicero (106–43 BCE), never originally intended for publication, and of the orator and writer Seneca (*c.*4 BCE–65 CE), of which 124 published in 20 books survive, were important models for later Christian writers. The same careful craftsmanship can be seen in the letter collections of such diverse Christian figures as Sidonius Apollinaris (*c.*430–86), the statesman and Bishop of Clermont, and the great humanist Desiderius Erasmus (*c.*1469–1536), who consciously follow classical models.

Letters, of whatever kind, are important primary sources for historians of Christianity, in every period. They have the advantage of conveying a first-hand perspective, but one has to be sensitive to the purposes which may have shaped that perspective. An example of this skill would be the letters of the politician Pliny (61–112 CE), the Roman senator and governor of Bithynia and Pontus in Asia Minor, who gives us early evidence about activities of Christians in his province. These letters are shaped to make a deliberate statement about the personality and beliefs of the author, and about his view of the social and literary world of which he is a part.

The collections of letters from emperors are bodies of legal material which are important for the development of Roman law. Episcopal letters were to become similarly important for the development of church law.

Some of the commonest Christian uses of letters prove to be remarkably persistent in Christian history. Letters are a vital means of communication between churches. Together with personal visits by himself or trusted colleagues, Paul's letters are one of the chief ways in which he tried to encourage the churches he was in personal touch with to remain in right Christian belief and practice.

He developed the letter-writing conventions of his day in distinctively Christian ways, as in his theologically charged salutations. Letters by Paul, letters in the name of Paul which may not be by him, and some comparable letters attributed to other early Christian leaders such as Peter, John, James and Jude, came to be accorded scriptural status, and form what are also called the New Testament epistles.

It is interesting that a passage from a New Testament letter, along with a passage from a Gospel, has been a fixed element in the celebration of the eucharist from around the seventh century to the present day. The style of the letter, which seems less formal than a narrative or a sermon, makes a more immediate impact on the audience, though whether Paul ever intended the reading of his letters to be perpetuated in this way is another matter.

Letters continued to be an important way for churches to share news and to encourage one another after the apostolic period. Accounts of early Christian martyrdoms commonly take the form of a letter (e.g. the martyrdom of Polycarp, *c.*155, recounted in a letter from the church at Smyrna to the church at Philomelium). But letters were also a way in which a prominent Christian leader (Clement of Rome, Ignatius of Antioch) could communicate with a variety of churches.

Bishops in particular used letters to communicate with one another. They announced their appointment in circular or *systatic letters*, the sending and receiving of which were ways of signalling communion and excommunication. *Letters of orders* (letters from a bishop certifying a person to have been duly ordained) and *letters dimissory* (a request from one bishop to another to ordain a person on the first bishop's behalf) are still in current use as ways of guaranteeing the integrity of a person's ordination. Bishops consulted each other in letters (Cyprian of Carthage had a long correspondence with Firmilian of Caesarea in the mid-third century). They used letters to communicate with their own clergy (Cyprian again), or with their whole diocese, particularly through Festal Letters that announced the date of Easter, and took the opportunity to comment on the urgent matters of the day. The Festal Letters of Athanasius of Alexandria in the fourth century are an especially rich series. Letters expressing the administrative and legal decisions of bishops were fundamental for the formation and development of church law. The *episcopal registers* of the Bishop of Rome are centrally important for the development of Western canon law; the letters of Basil of Caesarea form the basis of canon law in the Christian East.

In the Roman Catholic Church, from the time when they became the established source of authority, popes have written to the bishops of the church on matters of doctrine and practice. From the eighteenth century these have been called encyclicals; in recent times encyclicals have also been addressed to 'all men of goodwill', as in the case of John XXIII's 1963 encyclical *Pacem in terris* ('Peace on earth').

Bible

Christians have always exchanged letters, especially for advice and spiritual direction; many classic writings on prayer and interior life originate as letter collections. Examples include Francis de Sales' letters to Jeanne de Chantal, a widow who founded a new religious order for women who could not take the austere life of the established orders, in the sixteenth century; or the letters of Baron Friedrich von Hügel, the great Modernist with a deep interest in mysticism, and of the Benedictine Abbot of Downside Abbey, Dom John Chapman, early in the twentieth. Some private letter collections were not originally intended for publication, and give poignant expression to affective relationships between Christians. John Chrysostom's letters to Olympias, a rich widow in Constantinople who devoted her life to the care of the sick and poor, date from the beginning of the fifth century; and Abelard's correspondence with Heloise (if it is authentic) from the twelfth. A very few purely private letters survive from Christian antiquity, written on papyrus which has been preserved by the dry atmosphere of the sands of Oxyrhynchus in Egypt, around 100 miles south of Cairo, where they were discovered from the end of the nineteenth century onwards. These give some insight into the ordinary concerns of Christians.

Eucharist

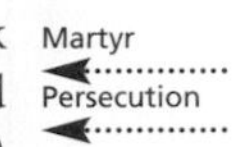
Martyr
Persecution

p. 245

A letter might provide a convenient form in which a Christian writer could cast a work intended for wider circulation. Gregory of Nazianzus and John Chrysostom in the fourth century each discussed the nature of Christian priesthood in letters to a friend excusing their own reluctance to be ordained; Blaise Pascal used the letter form to brilliant controversial effect in his satirical *Lettres Provinciales* (1656–7) against the Jesuits. In modern times, the format of the fictional letter has been used to communicate Christianity to the widest possible audience. The most famous series is C. S. Lewis' *Screwtape Letters* (1942), which allowed him to write an inverted apologetic for Christianity in the guise of letters from a senior to a junior devil; Lewis also wrote *Letters to Malcolm. Chiefly on Prayer* (1964). However, there have been other sets of letters that have proved equally popular. *Dear Mr Brown. Letters to a Person Perplexed about Religion* (1961), by the influential liberal preacher and theologian Harry Emerson Fosdick, presented a more questioning approach than that of C. S. Lewis.

Festivals and fasts

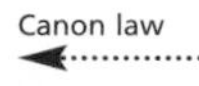
Canon law

Papacy

Writing manifestly fictional letters is one thing; claiming the authority of someone else is another. This phenomenon can also be found in Christian letter-writing. Because Christians have sometimes wanted to give authority to a point of view by connecting it with a significant figure,

ENCYCLICALS AND OTHER LETTERS

An encyclical is a pastoral letter written by the Pope for the whole Roman Catholic Church on matters of doctrine, morals, or discipline. From earliest times letters addressed to the church were issued by the Pope, but the first to be called an encyclical was *Ubi primum,* issued by Benedict XIV in 1740. It was about the duties of bishops. The title is taken from the first words of the document, which is usually in Latin. Encyclicals have been regularly used only from the time of Pius IX (1846–78): they are normally addressed to the bishops of the church, but some have been addressed to 'all men of good will' (particularly John XXIII's famous 1963 encyclical *Pacem in terris).*

Some notable encyclicals are:

Leo XIII

1891 *Rerum novarum* (Of new things) On capital and labour.
1893 *Providentissimus deus* (The God of all providence) On the study of holy scripture.

Pius X

1907 *Pascendi* (Feeding the Lord's flock) On the doctrines of the modernists.
1909 *Lamentabili sane* (With truly lamentable results) Condemning the errors of the modernists.

Pius XI

1928 *Mortalium animos* (The minds of men) This condemned the ecumenical movement, forbidding Roman Catholics to be involved.
1931 *Quadragesimo anno* (In the fortieth year = after *Rerum novarum*) On the reconstruction of the social order.
1937 *Mit brennender Sorge* (With the deepest anxiety) On the church and the German Reich.

Pius XII

1943 *Divino afflante spiritu* (Inspired by divine spirit) On the study of the Bible, commemorating the fiftieth anniversary of *Providentissimus deus.*
1943 *Mystici corporis* (Of the mystical body of Christ).
1950 *Humani generis* (Disagreement and error among men) Against some false doctrines threatening to undermine the foundations of Catholic doctrine.

John XXIII

1963 *Pacem in terris* (Peace on earth) On establishing universal peace in truth, justice, love and freedom.

Paul VI

1965 *Mysterium fidei* (The mystery of faith) On the doctrine and worship of the eucharist.
1967 *Populorum progressio* (The development of peoples).
1968 *Humanae vitae* (The transmission of human life) On birth control.

John Paul II

1981 *Laborem exercens* (Through work) To celebrate the ninetieth anniversary of *Rerum novarum.*
1990 *Redemptoris missio* (The mission of the Redeemer) On the permanent validity of the church's missionary mandate.
1993 *Veritatis splendor* (The splendour of truth) Certain fundamental questions of the church's moral teaching.
1995 *Evangelium vitae* (The gospel of life) On the value and inviolability of human life.
Ut unum sint (That they may be one) A commitment to ecumenism.
1998 *Fides et ratio* (Faith and reason) The relationship between them.
2003 *Ecclesia de eucharistia* (The church draws its life from the eucharist) An important restatement of eucharistic doctrine.

Papal communications are and have been also described with other terms:

Brief: A shorter, less weighty letter than a bull.

Bull: A general term for a papal letter, indicating that it is authenticated by a leaden seal (Latin *bulla*) and carrying great authority.

Constitution: Giving a decision on matters of faith or discipline addressed to the whole church.

Decree: A pronouncement on matters affecting the welfare of the church.

Decretal: A papal reply on a particular issue which serves as a precedent for other similar issues. The term *Rescript* is an equivalent.

Motu proprio: A letter written on the Pope's personal initiative (the meaning of the Latin term) with his personal signature.

they have not been immune to the temptation of forgery. Here, though, a distinction must be made between forgery in the sense of deliberately claiming the authority of a famous author for a text that has nothing to do with him or her, and may have been composed centuries later, and pseudepigraphy, the common ancient practice of circulating the writings of a disciple or follower under the name of a master, in the belief that one is expressing or developing the master's thought. There may be letters in Cyprian's corpus that are not by Cyprian, but which are close to him in date and are continuous in subject and approach with Cyprian's material. It is a different matter if (as some have claimed) the letters attributed to Ignatius of Antioch (*c.*35–*c.*107) are actually compositions of the third or fourth century.

The various Christian uses of the letter have as their context the changing technology of communication of successive Christian generations. Early and medieval letter-writing was dependent on having carriers travelling in the right direction; Paul's letters contain many references to the uncertainty of post. Later, some official and episcopal correspondence might use the imperial post service. The nineteenth-century invention of a universal and affordable postal service, in the West at least, was a precondition for the flourishing of 'spiritual' letter-writing in the early twentieth century. The publication of daily newspapers all over the world offering the possibility of writing 'letters to the editor' has made it possible for just about anyone to have a say in the public forum by means of the letter.

Letters from bishops and other clergy to the Christians in their care is by no means a thing of the past. Many bishops write a monthly letter which is published in the diocesan magazine, and parish magazines regularly begin with 'The Vicar's Letter', which offers clergy an opportunity to express themselves on a wider variety of topics and to a wider audience than would be possible from the pulpit.

Last and by no means least, Christians, like others, write letters to friends and loved ones from whom they are separated and with whom letters provide the only means of contact. Few of these are ever published, but there have been a number of books of moving last letters written by those executed under the Nazi regime, which often contain profound testimonies of faith. Most strikingly of all, this period and these circumstances gave rise to a classic of modern Christian theology, Dietrich Bonhoeffer's *Letters and Papers from Prison.* Bonhoeffer was arrested on suspicion of being involved in the plot against Hitler of 20 July 1944 and imprisoned in Berlin's Tegel prison. Through the good offices of friendly guards he was able to maintain a correspondence with his friend Eberhard Bethge, serving in the German army in Italy. In this correspondence, which included quite extensive essays as well as the letters, he not only gave a detailed account of how he continued to read and study and pray in prison, but also produced the outlines of a new theology for a 'world come of age' in which God had been forced to the periphery of life which in places is so radical that readers have been struggling with it ever since.

Pseudepigraphy

ANDERS BERGQUIST

Athanasius, *Select Works and Letters*, Nicene and Post-Nicene Fathers, Edinburgh: T&T Clark and Grand Rapids, MI: Eerdmans 1991; Dietrich Bonhoeffer, *Letters and Papers from Prison. The Enlarged Edition*, London: SCM Press and New York: Macmillan 1971; John Chapman, *Spiritual Letters* (1935), London and New York: Continuum 2003; Cyprian, *Letters*, Washington, DC: Catholic University Press of America 1964; Harry Emerson Fosdick, *Dear Mr Brown. Letters to a Person Perplexed about Religion*, New York: Harper & Row 1961; Hans-Josef Klauck, *Letters in Antiquity and in the New Testament*, London: T&T Clark 2003; Friedrich von Hügel, *Letters to a Niece* (1929), London and New York: HarperCollins 1995; C. S. Lewis, *The Screwtape Letters* (1942), London: HarperCollins 1998 and Grand Rapids, MI: Zondervan 2001.

Liberal theology

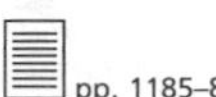
pp. 1185–8

Labels can be attached to a great variety of theologies, and these can be helpful in indicating their characteristics; however, 'liberal theology' is not really one of them. The term is vague and has many different shades of meaning. Sometimes it seems to be used simply to denote a theological approach of which another, more conservative, theologian disapproves.

The most specific and widely-accepted application of the term is to a trend in nineteenth and early twentieth-century Protestantism concerned to reinterpret traditional theology. In general, these liberal theologians argued for a different treatment of dogmas and creeds by adopting a historical approach to the sources of Christianity, taking into account the progress of science and other disciplines and the impact of philosophy on theology.

Protestantism

For them the Enlightenment was the great watershed, and in particular the implications of the developments arising from it. Immanuel Kant (1724–1804) had brought about a revolution in philosophy by restricting the scope of what can be considered certain knowledge of the world. Human beings, he argued, can have no certain knowledge of things-in-themselves, of natural phenomena and events; they do not discover order in nature but impose order on it. This conclusion cast doubt on the validity of traditional

Enlightenment

Philosophy

THE HISTORY-OF-RELIGIONS SCHOOL

The 'history-of-religions school' (German *Religionsgeschichtliche Schule)* is the rather cumbersome name given to a group of German Protestant scholars, most of whom completed their theological training in the University of Göttingen at the very end of the nineteenth century. The best known of them are Johannes Weiss (1863–1914), Wilhelm Bousset (1865–1920), Ernst Troeltsch (1865–1923), Rudolf Otto (1869–1937), Wilhelm Heitmüller (1869–1926) and Hugo Gressmann (1877–1927). Convinced that a radically historical approach to Christianity was needed, making use of philology and archaeology, they put the Bible and early Christian literature against the background of the cultures of the time and in so doing demonstrated Jewish, Babylonian, Persian and Hellenistic influences on Christianity.

At the same time the members of the school were concerned to make their findings known to as wide a public as possible in the conviction that a clear explanation of their findings would make Christianity acceptable to a far wider audience. They were successful in doing this by producing a series of interesting and highly readable books and reference works which sold in large numbers.

Karl Barth

The turn away from the historical approach to Christianity which took place after the First World War under the influence of theologians like Karl Barth led to the decline of the history-of-religions school, many of whose members in any case died young. However, their approach did not fade away completely, and methods that they developed like form criticism and tradition criticism continued to play a role in biblical studies. The questions they asked never became irrelevant, even if they were pushed on one side until well after the Second World War. There is certainly more interest now in the world in which Christianity came into being than in questions of Christian theology and doctrine, and while the findings of the school are long out of date and masses of new evidence have shown many of their wilder conjectures about the extent of alien influences on Christianity to be wrong, they represent an important step in the discovery of its origins and background.

Natural theology

p. 507

natural theology, including the classical arguments for the existence of God. But Kant found room for God: he saw human beings as thinking, moral beings who transcend nature and Christ as an ideal. God rounds off this moral approach, though he is not a God who can be worshipped and prayed to.

Friedrich Schleiermacher

Friedrich Schleiermacher (1768–1834), who may be called the father of liberal theology, took things one stage further. For him this view of religion, and Christianity, was not enough. While for Kant there was no way to God through science, for Schleiermacher there was no way to God through morality either. Right and wrong, he argued, are right and wrong whether or not God is brought in. So he turned to religious experience and described the essence of religion in terms like feeling, sense and taste; he eventually settled on the phrase 'the feeling of absolute dependence' (by which he meant something more than a mere emotional feeling).

Each in his own way, Kant and Schleiermacher thus restricted the possible scope of theological statements and marked out the area within which the liberal theologians wrote and thought. Albrecht Ritschl (1822–89) was the key figure here. He attempted to base Christianity on the New Testament, which he saw as purely factual and historical: Jesus is the man who exerts supremacy over nature. Ritschl thought and wrote in terms of worth and value, presenting theology as a series of 'value judgements'; in his approach he spoke about the worth and value of God, which was mediated through Jesus in the church. As a community, those who triumph over nature in this way form the kingdom of God, which will gradually redeem and transform society. In his *The Christian Doctrine of Justification and Reconciliation* (1870–84), Ritschl sought to bring together the major themes of the New Testament with the spiritual needs of his contemporaries.

Paul

Sin

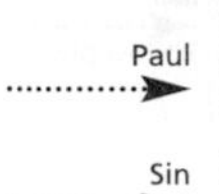

Kingdom of God

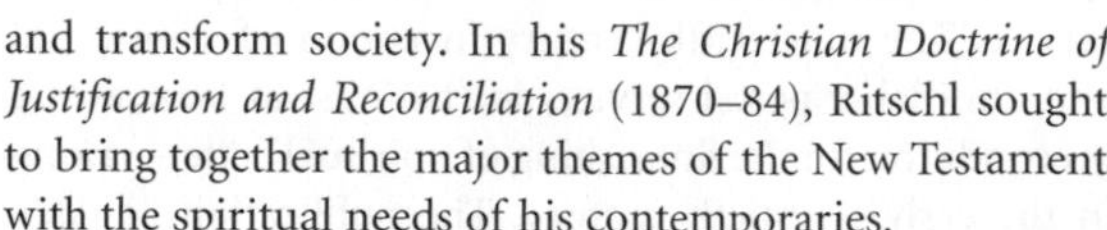

Other major figures in this liberal tradition were Wilhelm Herrmann (1846–1922), whose main work was *The Communion of the Christian with God* (1886); Ernst Troeltsch (1865–1923), whose 1898 essay 'On Historical and Dogmatic Method in Theology' was a classic demonstration of the consequences of accepting the historical method and the historical consciousness that goes with it; and Adolf von Harnack (1851–1930), one of the greatest church historians, who stated his beliefs in a famous book translated as *What is Christianity?* (the original German title was *Das Wesen des Christentums,* 'The Essence of Christianity', 1900). The original title is significant because one of the aims of the liberal theologians was to identify the timeless essence of Christianity, following earlier attempts such as that of the philosopher Ludwig Feuerbach (1804–72) in his *The Essence of Christianity* (1841) and *The Essence of Religion* (1845). In so doing they made a distinction that was influential over a long period, between the religion of Jesus and the religion about Jesus. The former, they held, was simple and practical, the latter was metaphysical and supernatural, and was more the creation of the apostle Paul and those who came after him.

In contrast to traditional Protestantism, liberal theology did not take sin very seriously; it was seen as a lack of spiritual awareness, an ignorance of God's true nature, and consequently notions of salvation and atonement did not play a major role.

Theologians with similar views can be found over the same period in Britain, France and the United States. In Britain mention could be made of the poet Samuel Taylor Coleridge (1772–1834), Matthew Arnold (1822–88) and F. D. Maurice (1805–72) along with the Catholic Modernist George Tyrrell (1861–1909); in France of Ernest Renan (1823–97); in the United States of Horace Bushnell (1802–76) and Walter Rauschenbusch (1861–1918). Simply to list these names confirms just how loose a label 'liberal theology' is.

In Germany the First World War and its consequences brought about the death of liberal theology; many of the liberal theologians of the time were fatally identified with jingoistic German nationalism. This point was hammered home by the Swiss theologian Karl Barth (1886–1968), who introduced a completely different kind of theology which rejected any continuity between God and humanity and saw the relationship between the human and the divine in terms of paradox and theology as dialectical, involving both a yes and a no. In a Germany dominated by the rise of a Nazism which attempted to exploit Christianity for its own ends and in which the remnants of a liberal theological approach were diverted into a nationalistic 'German Christianity', Barth's approach came to reign supreme, and elsewhere in the world, coupled with biblical theology which in many respects bracketed off the questions asked by the liberal theologians, it was widely influential.

However, because Barth offered no grounds for believing in God and totally dissociated God's action in the world from anything that can be ascertained by human investigation (for him there could be no such thing as natural theology), there was no alternative for disillusioned disciples like Paul van Buren (in his *The Secular Meaning of the Gospel*, 1963) but to follow another nineteenth-century theme running from J. P. F. Richter (known as Jean Paul, died 1825) through G. W. F. Hegel, Sören Kierkegaard and Friedrich Nietzsche and proclaim the 'death of God'.

Yet the questions asked by the nineteenth-century liberal theologians refused to go away, and in the 1960s and 1970s they returned with a vengeance in works like John A. T. Robinson's *Honest to God* (1963), *The Myth of God Incarnate* (1977), edited by John Hick, and Don Cupitt's *Taking Leave of God* (1980), all of which attracted immensely wider audiences than the theology which had preceded them. These three so different authors, too, cannot be lumped together as 'liberal theologians' – John Robinson explicitly called himself a 'radical' in the sense of one who goes back to the roots – but they shared the concerns of what had been called liberalism.

In recent times the Barthian position has gained new popularity, and forms of neo-orthodox theology, particularly the 'radical orthodoxy' group that started in Cambridge in the 1990s, are establishing positions against the background of postmodern thought. In a world of commercial and political exploitation, war and terrorism, 'liberal' is taken to be an outmoded and disreputable term. And there are elements of truth in this view. However, all the evidence is that the issues that preoccupied those to whom the unsatisfactory term 'liberal' has been applied, in praise or in censure, will never cease to occupy human minds.

Neo-orthodox theology

JOHN BOWDEN

Karl Barth, *Protestant Theology in the Nineteenth Century. Its Background and History* (1952), London: SCM Press and Richmond, VA: John Knox Press 1972; Mark D. Chapman, *Ernst Troeltsch and Liberal Theology: Religion and Cultural Synthesis in Wilhelmine Germany*, Oxford: OUP 2001; Garry Dorrien, *The Making of American Liberal Theology: Imagining Progressive Religion 1805–1900*, Louisville, KY: Westminster John Knox Press 2002 and *The Making of American Liberal Theology: Idealism, Liberalism and Modernity 1900–1950*, Louisville, KY: Westminster John Knox Press 2002; James Richmond, *Faith and Philosophy*, London: Hodder & Stoughton 1966

Karl Barth

Biblical theology

Liberation theology

Liberation theology is not a crystallized system of thought but a historical movement with roots within the history of the Christian churches in Latin America, particularly the Roman Catholic Church. Emerging as a distinct theological movement in the late 1950s and early 1960s, liberation theology can trace its origins to numerous dramatic shifts taking place at that time in the church and society. Three among these were particularly significant: 1. The interpretation of Third World poverty in terms of the 'dependency theory', namely that the low level of development in less economically developed countries is caused by their dependence on more economically developed countries; 2. The rapprochement between the church and the world effected at the Second Vatican Council and later at the second General Conference of the conference of Latin American Bishops, held at Medellín, Colombia in 1968; and 3. The rapid growth and increasing influence of 'base ecclesial communities' throughout Latin America.

Christianity in Latin America

From the sixteenth century to the present, Latin American countries have been defined by their status as colonies, first as political colonies of Spain and Portugal and later as economic colonies of the United States. Throughout the region, the process of colonization has been accompanied by a devastating, seemingly intractable poverty. Over the years, Latin American political economists have attempted to understand and interpret this history in order to address the social and economic problems of Latin America. In the 1950s and early 1960s, the classical liberal model of development located the roots of poverty in inadequate economic growth: therefore the problem of underdevelopment could be solved by encouraging and facilitating rapid economic growth through industrialization.

By the next decade, however, an alternative model had become increasingly prominent and influential, the 'dependency model'. Dependency theory held that Third World underdevelopment was the direct result of First World development. Serving as a storehouse for cheap labour and natural resources for the rich countries of the First World, the Third World (including Latin America) played a crucial role in the global economy and would thus never be permitted to develop economically; the insatiable desire to purchase more and more consumer goods at ever cheaper prices required the impoverishment of the Third World labourers who produced those goods for export to North America, Europe and Japan. Thus the possibility of 'development' within the extant global economic system would for ever remain an illusion; the system itself was fundamentally flawed and unjust. Only if the poor could 'liberate' themselves from their enslavement to this global system could they ever hope to live in dignity. What was called for was not development but liberation from a system whose success demands that the poor who comprise the vast majority of the world's population be excluded from participating in the economic decisions that affect their daily lives. Latin American development would take place only when the Latin American poor themselves became full participants in that decision-making process.

Liberation theologians took this key insight and applied it to theology. Latin American Christians had to stop depending on theologies imported from outside and instead begin to articulate a theological vision rooted in the experience of Latin American Christians themselves. The development of a theological reflection rooted in the everyday experience of Christians, particularly those who live in poverty and struggle for justice, was given 'official' p. 291 support in the Second Vatican Council's Constitution on the Church in the Modern World. In that document, Catholic bishops from around the world called for the church to identify itself with the sufferings, joys and hopes of its members, to discover there the face of the crucified and risen Christ. A few years later, at the Medellín conference, the bishops of Latin America explicitly took up the challenge of Vatican II. They examined the actual historical experience of the Latin American people, and in the light of that experience asked questions such as 'Where do we find Jesus Christ present in this historical reality?' and, 'How can we understand the church's identity and mission in the light of this historical reality?'. Reading the scriptures in the particular context of the Latin American church, they concluded that the poverty and oppression under which the great majority of Latin Americans live was contrary to the will of God and that therefore the church had to enter into solidarity with the poor and their struggles, becoming a church *of* the poor (not just a church *for* the poor or even a church *with* the poor).

By calling for a transformation, the Latin American bishops were generally perceived to be endorsing a grassroots movement already under way throughout the continent, namely, the base ecclesial community movement. This movement consisted of small communities of poor Christians who came together regularly to pray, read the scriptures, and support each other in their struggle to put the gospel into practice in their everyday lives. Often, such attempts to apply the gospel in their concrete circumstances would involve the communities in civic or political activity, whether seeking the installation of a sewerage system in a village, building a health clinic, or demonstrating on behalf of workers' rights. It was in the context of their participation in these communities that many liberation theologians developed and articulated their ideas. In so doing, they sought to ground their theological reflections in the experience of the struggling poor of Latin America.

Liberation theology emerged, then, at a time when the poor throughout the world were claiming their rightful place on the stage of world history. The first systematic attempt to articulate such a theology appeared in *A Theology of Liberation* (1973), the author of which was a Peruvian priest named Gustavo Gutiérrez. This book, considered the 'Magna Carta' of Latin American liberation theology, is now a theological classic.

Like most liberation theologians, Gutiérrez was educated in Europe. His theological work, however, has been rooted in his experience as a pastor among the poor. He has always identified himself primarily as a pastor and only secondarily as a theologian. While often holding academic positions, liberation theologians usually remain active in base ecclesial communities or other poor communities, for they understand their theological reflection as an attempt to explain how and where the God of Jesus Christ is revealed in the experience of the marginalized.

Fundamental to liberation theology is its claim that political neutrality or impartiality is impossible in the theological enterprise. Either theology is born out of the struggle of the oppressed for their liberation or else, whether explicitly or implicitly, directly or indirectly, it becomes a tool of oppression. To the extent that theologians remove themselves from the political arena in their quest for 'objectivity', such supposed objectivity functions as an implicit support for the unjust status quo. Silence in the face of oppression (for fear of not being 'objective') is not neutral but condones the oppression. Far from implying neutrality, silence implies consent.

Once the impossibility of an impartial, politically innocent theology is recognized, once it is admitted that theologians must take sides, the question arises which side they ought to take. For liberation theologians, as for the Latin American bishops at the Medellín conference, the answer to this question is clearly set out in the Bible, especially the Gospels: the Christian is called to take the side of the poor. Gustavo Gutiérrez speaks of two major overarching themes in the Bible: 1. the gratuity and universality of God's love; and 2. within that universality, God's 'preferential option for the poor'. Though the first theme may appear to contradict the second, in reality it implies it. The universality of God's love implies God's preferential option for the poor. To say that God's love is universal is not to say that it is neutral. In fact, the universality of God's love *precludes* an 'objective', 'neutral' God. If God's love is made manifest in human history, and if that history is characterized by a conflict and division between the powerful and the powerless, a neutral God would be one whose neutrality, like that of the supposedly neutral theologian, would serve to condone the unjust status quo. According to Gutiérrez, then, Christians are called to make a preferential option for the poor because God makes a preferential option for the poor. Yet such an option does not exclude the powerful and wealthy; it is, after all, a 'preferential', not an exclusive, option. Precisely because God loves the wealthy, God calls them to conversion, since their actions (or their inaction) are as dehumanizing to them as they are to the victims. Moreover the poor are themselves called to make an option for the poor. That is, the poor must enter into solidarity with their poor brothers and sisters, accompanying them in their struggle, rather than abandoning them in order to pursue wealth and power.

Yet the preferential option for the poor remains an abstract precept unless it can be concretely implemented. This requires the 'translation' of the biblical imperative into the contemporary context. Liberation theologians at this point draw upon the social sciences to help them understand their contemporary historical context; one cannot apply biblical precepts in the present context unless one has an accurate understanding of that context (e.g., the socio-economic causes of poverty and thus the types of social action that would be most effective in attacking those causes).

The very term 'liberation' requires interpretation and translation into the contemporary context. Gutiérrez distinguishes three dimensions of liberation, all of which are interrelated aspects of a single liberation process. The first aspect is liberation from all forms of social, political and economic oppression. At the second level of liberation, the poor no longer assume that their suffering is willed by God or by fate; rather, they come to see that suffering as an injustice that has social, historical, human causes. Consequently, they now accept the responsibility of struggling against the suffering of the poor and become active historical agents. The third level refers to the deepest, most fundamental aspect of the liberation process, Jesus Christ's own work of saving humankind from sin and death. While human beings can and must participate in helping to bring about the first two dimensions of liberation, this third form of liberation can be effected only by Jesus Christ; here, liberation is understood as pure gift. Human beings can do nothing themselves to bring about liberation in this, its deepest sense. At the same time, Gutiérrez always insists that none of the three levels of liberation – not even this third level – can be understood apart from the other two. Though men and women cannot themselves bring about their ultimate liberation (i.e. liberation from sin), they can and must work to eradicate the concrete, historical manifestations of sin in the world, those unjust social structures that are the result of human sin and that promote sin by fostering avarice, violence and other forms of sinful behaviour. That is, liberation is a single process with three dimensions, none of which can be separated from or understood apart from the others.

Atonement
Salvation
Sin
Bible

Attempts by Gutiérrez and others to explain 'liberation' in a holistic way, however, did not prevent liberation theologians from coming under severe criticism, especially from those who perceived in liberation theology a reduction of Christian faith to simple political activism and, more specifically, to Marxist revolution. Such criticisms appeared, for instance, in the 'Instruction on Certain Aspects of the Theology of Liberation' issued in 1984 by the Vatican's Congregation for the Doctrine of the Faith (the Vatican's official theological 'watchdog'). That document, however, did not single out any specific theologians for criticism. In 1986, the Vatican issued a second document, 'Instruction on Christian Freedom and Liberation', which was more positive in tone, emphasizing the importance and delineating the parameters of an 'authentic' theology of liberation. Concerned that 'some' liberation theologies were ignoring the spiritual dimension of Christian freedom, the Vatican nevertheless insisted that, properly understood as rooted in Christ's own saving work, the notion of liberation is indeed central to the Christian message.

Vatican

Along with most other liberation theologians, Gutiérrez saw an opportunity for dialogue in such criticism. Consequently, the development of liberation theology in the last two decades of the twentieth century was marked by increased dialogue with both critics and supporters outside Latin America itself. In a new introduction written in 1988 for a revised edition of *A Theology of Liberation*, Gutiérrez acknowledged how the dialogue with his critics had, for example, made him more sensitive to the unintentional connotations of some of the terminology that he used in his writings. In the revised edition, for instance, the term 'class struggle' was replaced in several instances by the term 'social conflict', presumably to avoid the Marxist connotations of the former. In the new introduction Gutiérrez also described the extended dialogues he had developed with theologians of marginalized groups around the world. These dialogues had served to deepen his appreciation of non-economic forms of oppression such as racism and sexism, which would now assume an important place in his own theological reflection.

In the last twenty years, a theme that has become increasingly explicit and central to the writings of liberation theologians has been that of spirituality, especially the spirituality of the poor. Though this theme had never been absent from Gutiérrez's writings, in the 1980s he wrote two books explicitly on spirituality, *On Job* (1987) and *We Drink from Our Own Wells* (1984). Both set forth a spirituality rooted in the suffering and faith of the poor. During this period, the Salvadoran Jesuit theologian Jon Sobrino also wrote his influential *Spirituality of Liberation* (1988).

Spirituality

The future of liberation theology remains a topic of debate. Numerous observers have suggested that liberation theology has passed into history, along with other social movements born in the 1960s, and there is no doubt that the events of the last twenty years, including continued pressure from the Vatican and the failure of socialist movements in Latin America and around the globe have made an impact on the movement. Yet the very methodology of liberation theology demands that theology change in response to changed circumstances and contexts. At its most basic, liberation theology is simply an attempt to read the Bible and Christian tradition from the perspective of the poor. Hence as long as there are poor persons there will be liberation theology. Indeed, when asked about 'the future of liberation theology' Gustavo Gutiérrez responds that he is not concerned about the future of liberation theology; he is concerned about the future of the poor in Latin America.

Resurrection

ROBERTO S. GOIZUETA

Ignacio Ellacuría and Jon Sobrino (eds), *Mysterium Liberationis: Fundamental Concepts of Liberation Theology*, Maryknoll, NY: Orbis 1993; Gustavo Gutiérrez, *A Theology of Liberation*, Maryknoll, NY: Orbis and London: SCM Press [2]1988; Paul Sigmund, *Liberation Theology at the Crossroads: Democracy or Revolution?*, New York: OUP 1990; Jon Sobrino, *Christ the Liberator: A View from the Victims*, Maryknoll, NY: Orbis 2001

Life after death

Cardinal Newman's famous poem *The Dream of Gerontius*, written in 1865 and given an added dimension when set to music by Edward Elgar in 1899, depicts the death of an old man and what happens after it. Gerontius dies, having made a last confession of faith, surrounded by the prayers of his friends and the church; his soul awakens refreshed and feeling an amazing lightness and, escorted by an angel, passes a host of demons 'hungry and wild to claim their property, and gather souls for hell'. The soul then hears a choir of 'angelicals' singing the praises of Christ in 'a grand mysterious harmony', and after that the echoes of his friends still praying for him round his deathbed, along with the voice of the angel of the agony, also supporting him. Gerontius goes before his judge: what then happens is not said in the poem and is expressed in the oratorio only by a series of cataclysmic chords. The angel announces that the soul is safe, 'consumed, yet quickened, by the glance of God', and finally, to the accompaniment of the voices of the souls in purgatory, lowers it into the 'penal lake' in which it will lie, supported by masses on earth and prayers in heaven, until after its night of trial it will be woken 'on the morrow'.

Newman's vision is poetic and personal, but it is inspired by the views of death and what comes after it that had grown up in the Roman Catholic tradition of his time and were expressed in the words of requiem masses. We are a long way here from early Christian ideas of the resurrection of the body: resurrection is barely hinted at, and there is certainly no suggestion of the soul rejoining the body. Moreover, the last judgement seems already to have taken place; the soul serves its sentence in purgatory after being in the overwhelming presence of God.

Christian views of life after death are in fact extremely complex, because they have developed out of a long history, taking in ideas from surrounding cultures and being affected by a variety of theological questions that arose over the course of time. The resurrection of the body may be the dominant Christian belief, but resurrection belief itself is far from simple, and in some contexts is supplemented with other views to such an extent that it seems almost to disappear.

The Hebrew Bible, which Christians took over as their Old Testament, sees the afterlife as a grey, shadowy existence: in Sheol, the underworld, people are not punished or rewarded, nor do they experience pleasure or pain. Their life is like sleep. In a last desperate attempt to discover how to avoid his doom, King Saul has a wise woman summon up the spirit of the prophet Samuel, who complains about being disturbed (1 Samuel 28). The Hebrew view closely resembles the view of the state of the dead in the classical world of Greece and Rome: they live a wraith-like existence in Hades, the realm of the dead. In Homer's *Odyssey*, the hero, like Saul, brings up a seer, Teiresias, to learn his future, and many other of the dead also appear to him.

In the classical world, a select few experience different fates: the really wicked are punished in Tartarus and the good and the great attain the Elysian fields or are like stars in the skies. In contrast to this, in the second century BCE in the Jewish world the notion of resurrection developed. This happened at a time when attempts were being made to Hellenize Judaism and abolish its most fundamental practices. A revolt developed among the Jews, led by the Maccabee brothers, in which many suffered martyrdom for their faith. It was felt intolerable that these should simply perish and have no reward. They had to be vindicated, and this ethical demand was met by the notion that their bodies would be raised by God. A similar demand for justice and vindication is at the heart of the Christian belief in the resurrection of Jesus and of those who followed him. However, for both Jews and Christians it was by no means clear when a general resurrection would take place, nor even who would be raised.

Jesus himself said little about the afterlife. His preaching was of the kingdom of God, the kingly rule that God would bring in, along with a new order of things. When asked a complicated question by the Sadducees, who did not believe in resurrection, about which of seven successive wives would be a man's wife in the resurrection, he retorted that in the resurrection people neither marry nor are given in marriage but are like the angels in heaven, and went on to turn the issue to the nature of God (Matthew 22.29–32). Little can be read into this debating point, nor is Jesus' promise in Luke's Gospel to the penitent thief crucified with him, 'Today you will be with me in paradise', a basis for further speculation.

Given that resurrection was something that in Christianity was expected to take place in what became an ever-receding future, it was natural for attention to turn to a notion that had been developed among the élite, in Greek philosophy, of the immortality of the soul. There it emerged in the context of reincarnation (Greek *metempsychosis*), but because of its incompatibility with the notion of resurrection, reincarnation was never a Christian belief. For the Greek philosopher Plato the soul existed before birth and survived death; the body was a prison from which the soul was released into a wider existence. In Gnosticism there was the belief that a spark of divine matter had fallen and become imprisoned in the body; this had to be freed so that it could begin the ascent to the heaven from whence it came. The Christian who came nearest to views like this was Origen, who believed that the soul existed before the body, but this view was not accepted by the church. Rather, the soul was seen as immortal but not pre-existent.

However, because of the dominant role played by the resurrection of the body, despite frequent mention of 'the immortal soul', the reflection on the immortality of the soul in the full sense has not played such a major role in the Christian tradition as might be imagined: soul and body are always closely linked. Yet it was believed that the soul lived on when the body died, and speculation turned to what happened to the soul from then on, until it finally rejoined the body in the resurrection. If resurrection had begun as an essentially ethical concept, as the action by which wrongs were definitively righted, with the emphasis on the soul, the danger came to be that of 'losing one's immortal soul' and suffering eternal damnation. In the early church baptism became the passport to salvation, but as the Letter to the Hebrews points out: 'If we sin deliberately after receiving the knowledge of the truth (i.e. after baptism), there no longer remains a sacrifice for sins but a fearful prospect of judgement, and a fury of fire which will consume the adversaries' (10.26–7). Sin after baptism brought damnation, and this led some to postpone it as long as possible, in order to minimize the risk of sinning. This rigorist position proved to be too harsh, but it did leave its mark on the development of the notion of penance, which extended beyond this world into the next.

Origins and background

Martyr

Forgiveness

Kingdom of God

Following on from the emphasis on the need of baptism for salvation and the idea of a place where sinners could do penance for their sin after death, the afterlife began to take on a structure that included stages other than the ultimate destinations of heaven and hell.

Limbo was the destination for those who had not been baptized. It was thought to contain the souls of those who lived before the coming of Jesus and therefore before they could hear the preaching of the gospel; between Jesus' death and resurrection, in what came to be called the harrowing of hell he was believed to have gone there to free its inhabitants, a conviction expressed in the phrase in the Apostles' Creed 'He descended into hell'. However, limbo was also thought to be the abode of unbaptized infants, who had not been personally guilty in any way, but because they had not been baptized were excluded for ever from heavenly bliss.

Creed

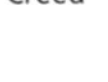

Purgatory was the place where Christians who had died in a state of grace underwent purification until they were fit to attain to the vision of God. This doctrine was in the making from the time of Augustine onwards, but was developed fully only in the twelfth and thirteenth

Gnosis

Francesco and Sperindio Cagnola, *The Last Judgement* (detail), Children in Limbo, Church of the Trinity, Piedmont

centuries. Thomas Aquinas formulated it in great detail and it was defined at the Councils of Lyons (1274) and Florence (1439). The classic description of purgatory is in the second book of Dante's *Divine Comedy*.

Council

The doctrine of purgatory had a major influence on the practices of the living. Those in purgatory could be helped by the prayers of the church and the celebration of masses on their behalf: this led to the endowment of chantries, chapels in cathedrals dedicated specifically for this purpose. Time in purgatory could also be reduced by indulgences: the remission of punishment for sins in return for penitential actions (such as going on pilgrimages or crusades). Purgatory was rejected by the sixteenth-century Reformers and led also in churches of the Reformation tradition to the rejection of prayers for the dead.

p. 476

Widespread and powerful though Roman Catholic imagery is, views about life after death differ in other Christian traditions. Because the doctrine of purgatory developed after the split between Eastern and Western churches, it is not found in a developed form in the Orthodox churches, though they do offer prayers for the dead; there are various private views about life after death in Orthodoxy, including the notion of a state similar to purgatory and the idea of custom houses or toll houses through which the soul passes on its way to paradise or to hell. The doctrine of purgatory was rejected by the churches of the Reformation, for whom the dead sleep until raised for the Last Judgement.

Orthodox churches

Reformation

The notion of the Last Judgement has a long history. The Hebrew prophets, especially Amos, spoke of a 'day of the Lord' which would bring judgement on the wicked, and the details of this judgement, on individuals and nations, were developed in apocalyptic literature. Jesus spoke of the coming of the Son of man for judgement, and in a parable described how the criterion for judgement would be whether those appearing at it had fed the hungry, given drink to the thirsty, welcomed the stranger and visited the sick and those in prison (Matthew 25.31–46). A division would be made between the 'sheep' and the 'goats': those who had not performed any of these acts would depart 'into the eternal fire prepared for the devil and his angels'. Another parable similarly speaks of the 'wheat' and the 'tares' (Matthew 13.24–30). This proved to be a powerful source of inspiration for medieval Christianity.

Prophecy

Apocalyptic

Jesus

Though shorn of the central figure of Christ reigning in glory by an insensitive later architect, the gigantic fresco of the Last Judgement in the cathedral of Albi, in southern France, gives a vivid depiction of the fortunes of the saved and the damned. Across the top of the fresco are angels; below them on the left (Christ's right hand) in three ranks are apostles, saints and the risen who are deemed worthy of the joys of heaven; on the right is a shadowy void separating sinners awaiting their punishment from those in heaven. Across the bottom of the fresco is a depiction of the torments of the damned, punishments devised as appropriate retribution for the seven deadly sins, with an imaginative flair reminiscent of the work of Hieronymus Bosch. Such paintings, and similar carvings on the west fronts of cathedrals, would have made a powerful impression on the people of the Middle Ages.

Another tradition about judgement grew up in Christianity, the one reflected in Cardinal Newman's poem. According to this, judgement does not take place only at the end, but after death; then the soul enters the presence of God and the verdict on it is given. A twentieth-century version of this view holds that at death individuals have one last, free and fully self-determining choice to accept God and the life-giving stream which flows from God, or reject or ignore God.

The medieval Roman Catholic Church knew precisely who would be going to hell. The Council of Florence (1438–45) decreed that 'no one remaining outside the Catholic Church, not just pagans, but also Jews or heretics and schismatics, can share in eternal life but will go into the everlasting fire'. Today conservative evangelical

The Last Judgement, twelfth-century tympanum of the Abbey Church, Conques

Christians are equally convinced that all those who do not call upon the name of Jesus Christ and are saved will likewise be damned.

To more sensitive modern minds the idea that part of the pleasure of the blessed in heaven is given by the knowledge that others are suffering perpetual torment in hell is abhorrent, but the notion of hell has proved very persistent.

From an early period the very idea did cause problems for some Christian thinkers. Origen was one of several early Christian theologians who believed in a 'restoration of all things' (Greek *apocatastasis*) in which even the devil would be turned to the good, and a similar view was put forward by radicals in the sixteenth-century Reformation. However, universalism, the view that in the end all would be saved, remained very much a minority view (Origen was condemned) and it was not until the nineteenth century that belief in hell came to be challenged. Unitarians rejected hell, and the Anglican theologian F. D. Maurice lost his professorial chair at King's College, London, for teaching that the Greek for 'eternal' in 'eternal punishment' need not have the meaning 'everlasting'. A Church of England report in 1995 rejected universalism but suggested that those who rejected God faced eternal death, not eternal punishment: in other words, hell was empty.

While vivid imaginations can make a lot of hell, heaven is far more difficult to envisage or depict, and the stereotyped images of angels eternally playing harps have taken their toll. Jesus gave glimpses of God's kingdom, called the 'kingdom of heaven' in the Gospel of Matthew, in which those who have been starving and suffering outcasts receive a joyous welcome at a great banquet. And Augustine memorably wrote: 'There we shall rest and see, we shall see and love, we shall love and praise. Behold what will be at the end without end. For what other end do we have, if not to reach the kingdom of God which has no end' (*City of God* 22, 305).

The Revelation of John speaks of the descent of the heavenly city in which there will be no more crying or pain (21.1–4). These two images are above all social images, taken up in the later Christian phrase 'the communion of saints', in which dead and living followers of Christ are united in him.

Unitarians

In fact, however, for many of the great writers of the Christian tradition the ultimate destiny for Christians

Suffering is not so much a place, heaven, but the presence of God and enjoyment of what is called the beatific vision. This is expressed in terms of the beloved and the lover, as it is in the hymn by F. W. Faber which ends: 'Father of Jesus, love's Faith Hope reward, what rapture will it be, prostrate before thy throne to lie, and gaze and gaze on thee.'

All this having been said, though, a very large number even of practising Christians seem to have abandoned belief in any life after death. In Christian thought and worship, 'eternal life' has regularly been interpreted as a quality of life here and now, rather than as something to look forward to and hope for. This reinterpretation has been given expression, e.g. in recent revised forms of worship, where the words with which the bread and the wine are distributed at the eucharist, 'The body/blood of Christ bring you to everlasting life', have been replaced by 'keep you in eternal life'.

Powerful secular arguments, accepted by some Christian theologians, militate against any belief in life after death.

First, all the evidence suggests that the life of the mind depends absolutely on the functioning of the brain and Body that this is determined by the state of our bodies. We are our bodies, and when those bodies degenerate and perish, so do we, and that is the end of us. Just as our lives and experiences are from the beginning governed by our bodily make-up, so too it is impossible to think of any life apart from the body. Moreover our thought-processes, our perceptions, our values, our capacity to understand and interpret are so governed by the historical and social environment in which we live and the others whom we encounter that it is impossible to visualize ourselves existing in a totally different context with none of the Bible characteristics which have made us what we are.

Secondly, it is said that the desire for personal survival is wishful thinking. To want to perpetuate our own existences is sheer selfishness, a desire for consolation in the face of evil and suffering and a refusal to come to terms honestly with our natural mortality. The idea of a better world to come, 'pie in the sky when we die', has all too often been used down history to counter attempts to improve the conditions of life as it is really lived by the suffering, the poor and the oppressed. To be focused on the need to improve living conditions and eliminate social injustices here and now is the mark of true humanity.

These arguments are indeed strong ones. Yet if they are accepted and taken account of, the form of Christianity which emerges seems to lack many of the fundamental aspects of traditional Christian faith. What becomes of pp. 124–5 the very idea of God, of the hope that runs throughout Christian belief and practice, if there is nothing beyond this life? Why engage in worship in which images of a future after death occur so frequently, and recite creeds that so firmly state belief in 'the life of the world to come'? What can be said in the face of all the suffering and hurt and injustice in the world that cry out for some recompense? By the very nature of things, here we are moving in the realm of the unknowable. Yet in spite of all the objections, there are still powerful factors, not least faith and hope, which move a great many Christians to say, 'Nevertheless ...'

JOHN BOWDEN

Ladislaus Boros, *The Moment of Truth: Mysterium Mortis*, London: Burns & Oates 1965; Oscar Cullmann, *Immortality of the Soul or Resurrection of the Dead?*, New York: Macmillan 1958; Kenneth E. Kirk, *The Vision of God*, London: Longmans Green 1931; Hans Küng, *Eternal Life?*, London: Collins and New York: Doubleday 1984; Robert Ombres, OP, *The Theology of Purgatory*, Dublin: Mercier Press 1978; Geoffrey Rowell, *Hell and the Victorians*, Oxford: OUP 1974; J. B. Russell, *A History of Heaven: The Singing Silence*, Princeton: Princeton University Press 1977; Church of England Doctrine Commission, *The Mystery of Salvation*, London: Church House Publishing 1995

Literature

T. S. Eliot wrote in 1935 that 'the Bible has had a *literary* influence upon English literature *not* because it has been considered as literature, but because it has been considered as the report of the Word of God. And the fact that men of letters now discuss it as "literature" probably indicates the *end* of its "literary" influence.' The difficulty of considering the Bible as literature is evident inasmuch as it has by many, in varying ways, been regarded as written under the direct inspiration of God. Furthermore, the unity imposed upon it in the establishment of its canonical status has tended to obscure the enormous variety and differences of purpose in the books of the Old and New Testaments. Nevertheless, the Bible indisputably contains some of the greatest literary works ever written and in various genres: the narratives of Genesis, many of the Psalms, the almost-tragedy of the book of Job, the love songs of the Song of Solomon, the intense passion narrative of Mark's Gospel and the hymn to love of Paul's First Letter to the Corinthians, chapter 13. In English, this literature has been well served by the genius of translators like William Tyndale (*c.*1494–1536) and Miles Coverdale (*c.*1487–1569), culminating in the great King James Version of 1611, one of the monuments of English literature. Study of the Gospels in the twentieth century by scholars like Karl Ludwig Schmidt (1891–1956) have placed them firmly in the traditions of oral literature, begging comparison with the fourth century *Apophthegmata Patrum* (Sayings of the Desert Fathers) and even the later collections of the legends of Faust in Germany.

In the literature of the early church, it was not uncommon to enfold Christian teaching within the 'lives' of saints and martyrs, somewhat after the manner of the Gospels. One of the most influential of such works is the *Life of Antony*, written in the middle of the fourth century CE, and usually attributed to Athanasius. Though like the Gospels this is hardly biography, it is often vivid and dramatic in its descriptions of the early ascetic life of the desert. Some 50 years later, Augustine's *Confessions* (397–8) are not only an extended meditation on God but also an intensely moving account of Augustine's conversion, establishing a literary genre in Christian writing that many others, as diverse as John Bunyan and John Henry Newman, have followed. The *Confessions* were first rendered into English in 1620 by Sir Tobie Matthew, and have frequently been translated since.

There are not many examples of early Christian poetry, but one of the finest is *The Pearl*, a cycle of seven poems written in Syriac by Ephrem the Syrian (*c.*306–73), referring back to the 'pearl of great price' in Matthew 13.45–6. These poems were written as hymns, and from the fourth century hymns in Greek became more common, followed later by Latin hymns. The great hymns of the Italian bishop Venantius Fortunatus (*c.*530–*c.*610), *Vexilla regis prodeunt* ('The royal banners forward go') and *Pange lingua gloriosa* ('Of the glorious body telling'), are still sung in English translation.

In the English Anglo-Saxon tradition, the Venerable Bede of Jarrow (*c.*673–735) also composed hymns and a treatise, *De Arte Metrica*, but is best remembered for his great *Ecclesiastical History of the English People* (731). However, the greatest work of Christian literature in Old English is undoubtedly *The Dream of the Rood*, fragments of which are found in Northumbrian runic inscriptions on an early eighth-century cross in Ruthwell, Dumfriesshire, as well as in a complete version in the tenth-century Vercelli book that found its way to Northern Italy. It is clear that the poem was widely known, and of interest not only as magnificent literature, but for its use of the pagan literary form of the riddle, through which the Christian themes of Passiontide shine. The later Middle Ages are rich in the literature of piety, from the hymns and prayers of Anselm of Canterbury (1033–1109) and the mystical sermons of Meister Eckhart (*c.*1260–*c.*1328) to the great canticles of Francis of Assisi (1182–1226). Francis' *Cantico del Sole* (Canticle of the Sun) was magnificently translated into English by Ezra Pound in 1910. In prose, the *Ancrene Wisse* (*c.*1230) is a handbook for anchoresses, notable for its use of metaphor and natural imagery, and anticipating the mystical writings of the author of *The Cloud of Unknowing* (*c.*1350) and Dame Julian of Norwich's (*c.*1342–*c.*1420) *Revelations of Divine Love*.

It is in the Passiontide liturgy in the tenth century that we find the beginnings of the flowering of modern European drama. The Easter trope (a trope is a sentence, set to music, introducing a chant in the mass) *Quem quaeritis* ('Whom do you seek?') dramatizes the exchange between the angel and the women at the empty tomb (Mark 16. 6–7), a dialogue that probably formed the basis for the great folk dramas of the fifteenth-century mystery cycles. Their portrayal of biblical history from Genesis to the resurrection moved from the church to the streets with elements of comic spectacle and satire mixed with Christian piety. From them and the later morality plays it was but a step to the Renaissance stage of William Shakespeare. The best-known English morality play is the early sixteenth-century *Everyman*, probably derived from a Dutch original and enacting the theology of the good death as Everyman realizes his dependence on good deeds in the last hour of his life.

Mystery plays

The literature of medieval chivalry fully enters the canon of spiritual literature, after the Arthurian romances of the twelfth-century French poet Chrétien de Troyes, with the *Queste del Saint Graal* (*c.*1225), which presents the quest for the Grail – the dish from which, according to the story, Jesus ate the paschal lamb at the Last Supper (in other traditions it is the cup which contained the wine that he blessed and gave) – through myth and legend, as a guide for the spiritual life in the court rather than the cloister. Underlying the Christian symbolism are layers of Celtic myth which, through a process of reworking, became the basis for the legends of King Arthur. These reached their peak in late medieval literature with Sir Thomas Malory's *Le Morte d'Arthur*, printed by William Caxton in 1485, which binds the Christian story with English history. In his Preface Caxton describes Arthur as the one 'which ought most to be remembered among us English men tofore all other Christian kings'.

The flowering of humanism in late medieval literature prepared much of the ground for the culture of the Reformation in Europe. Giovanni Boccaccio's (1313–75) great work *The Decameron* tells tales of scurrilous churchmen and monks and was probably an influence on Geoffrey Chaucer's *Canterbury Tales* (*c.*1387), although Chaucer's ribald clerics (akin to the lazy priest in William Langland's poem *Piers Plowman*, *c.*1370, who knew his Robin Hood better than his paternoster) are balanced by the figure of the poor parson, rich in 'holy thought and work' and 'that Christ's gospel truly would preach', and the *Tales* conclude with a serious example of medieval preaching on the seven deadly sins. But the outstanding medieval Christian poet is Dante (1265–1321), whose *Divine Comedy* is a vision of hell, purgatory and heaven,

Humanism

Reformation

deeply influenced by Thomas Aquinas and scholastic theology yet universal in its poetic claims. In an important essay of 1929, T. S. Eliot praised Dante's 'visual imagination' and his ability to make 'the spiritual visible'.

The Renaissance saw the flowering of Christian humanism in the writings of Erasmus of Rotterdam (*c.* 1469–1536), whose profound scholarship of the ancient Christian world was balanced by his biting *In Praise of Folly* (*c.* 1510), a witty satire against ecclesiastical institutions and an example of the literary ridicule of the church that finds its apex in the grotesque exaggerations of François Rabelais (*c.* 1494–1553) and his popular giants Gargantua and Pantagruel (in works which anticipate the modern novel) with their background in the medieval Feast of Fools, at which minor cathedral officials mimicked sacred ceremonies. (Writing in the Soviet Union in the 1930s, Mikhail Bakhtin used Rabelais' writings to condemn Stalinist oppression through the assertion of carnival and creativity in popular art forms.) Rabelais' mention of Utopians indicates the fame of the work of Sir Thomas More, whose political essay (written in Latin and translated in 1551) entitled *Utopia* (1516) was composed in close association with Erasmus and advocates the freest toleration of religion on an island of perfect government, endowed by More with language and poetry. The work of a Catholic martyr under Henry VIII, *Utopia* was later seen as the source of Anabaptism, Mormonism and even Communism.

Another Christian martyr, but a Protestant one, was John Foxe (1516–87), who was a playwright and a historian, chiefly remembered for his *Book of Martyrs* (Latin 1554, English 1563). This account of the victims of papist tyranny under Queen Mary gained wide readership through its homely style derived from Protestant oral tradition, indicative of the power of literature in religious dispute.

With the flowering of the English Renaissance there was a growing critical sense of the role of literature, exemplified in Sir Philip Sidney's *Apology for Poetry* (1595), an anti-scholastic defence of fiction. Sidney argues vigorously for the imaginative element necessary in true education, his poetic gift evident in his daring use of theologically coloured terms like 'erected wit' and 'infected will' in his defence of poetry, so that those 'with quiet judgements will look a little deeper into it, [and] shall find the end and working of it such, as, being rightly applied, deserveth not to be scourged out of the Church of God'. Sidney, like his fellow poet Edmund Spenser (1552–99), embeds theological themes in the fabric of his verse. For example, Spenser's *Hymn of Heavenly Beauty* (one of *Fowre Hymnes*, 1596) beautifully expounds the idea of *kenosis* or 'self-emptying', drawing on Philippians 2.6–11 ('For man's deare sake he did a man become').

Scholasticism Renaissance Drama Evil p. 444 Anabaptists Mormons Prayer Christology

The influence of the English Geneva Bible on Shakespeare and Elizabethan and Jacobean drama is incalculable, drawing ultimately on the fluid English of William Tyndale. Through the pen of Shakespeare the universal voice of tragedy speaks, modified by the language and perspectives of the Gospels, the Pauline epistles, Augustine and Thomas Aquinas. In recent times the Christian foundations of Shakespearean tragedy has been affirmed, described by George Steiner as construed of 'a close yet liberal conjunction of the antique and the Christian world-view', and by Ulrich Simon as we watch *Othello* drawn by an 'emotional compassion with Christian or more-than-Christian tears'.

Later in the seventeenth century, John Milton (1608–74) drew upon the traditions of epic literature in *Paradise Lost* (1667), mixing classical and biblical inspiration in the opening lines to re-describe the drama of the fall and examine the problem of evil, as poetry rather than theological argument seeks to 'justify the ways of God to men' (Book 1, line 26) in a major contribution to the question of theodicy. Milton's vast rehearsal of the story of Genesis 2–3 earned him the apprehension of his fellow poet Andrew Marvell (1621–78), who feared that he would 'ruin (for I saw him strong)/The sacred truths to fable and old song'.

In the eighteenth century this fear of literary invention in the face of biblical 'truth' was expressed again by Samuel Johnson in his 'Life of Milton' (in *Lives of the English Poets*, 1779–81), where he asserts that 'truth allows no choice, it is, like necessity, superior to rule', and Milton is only preserved 'by religious reverence from licentiousness of fiction'. Milton, it might be said, is the last of the great Renaissance Christian humanists.

It was Dr Johnson who coined the term 'metaphysical poets' for those poets of the seventeenth century, among whom are the Anglican clergy George Herbert and John Donne, whose witty and punning verse is saturated in their reading of the King James Bible and the Anglican Prayer Book. This had its origins in Archbishop Cranmer's books of 1549 and 1553 (and in particular Cranmer's prayers called the Collects) and its culmination in the Book of Common Prayer (1662), which remains a monument to English language and devotion to the present day. In the seventeenth century, too, the Puritan John Bunyan (1628–88) wrote the Christian allegory *The Pilgrim's Progress* (1678), which has a good claim to be the first great English novel. So great was its influence on both piety and literature that by the end of the eighteenth century it was often, with the King James Bible, the only book in many English households, while numerous works of literature drew directly upon it, above all, perhaps, Charlotte Bronte's *Jane Eyre* (1847). A rival claimant to be considered the first true novel is *Robinson Crusoe* (1719) by Daniel Defoe. Although interpreted by, among others, Karl Marx as an illustration of economic theory in action, *Robinson Crusoe* is also a profoundly religious work, a story of spiritual rebirth through the reading of the Bible.

Apart from classics of spiritual literature such as Bishop Jeremy Taylor's *Holy Living* and *Holy Dying* (1650–1) – the poet Samuel Taylor Coleridge called Taylor the Shakespeare of English prose – the seventeenth century is notable for the rise in Enlightenment defences of the reasonableness of Christianity, above all the *Pensées* of Blaise Pascal (1670, English 1688), which establish both the necessity and the limits of human reason. The greatest example of such argumentation in the eighteenth century is Bishop Joseph Butler's *Analogy of Religion* (1736), a defence of revealed religion in beautiful and measured prose.

At the end of the century, however, a new note is struck in the Romantic literature of Samuel Taylor Coleridge, Johann Gottfried Herder and others in England, Germany and France, where the theology of the Enlightenment and critical, historical readings of the Bible join with a fresh sense of the power of poetry in a new literature that is both passionate and prophetic. William Blake dines with the prophets Isaiah and Ezekiel in his 'Memorable Fancy' (1790), and the atheist Percy Bysshe Shelley in his *Defence of Poetry* (1821) reflects upon the effect of the 'poets' Moses, David and Isaiah on the mind of Jesus and transfers the claims of the Bible (as described by the translators of the King James Bible) to that of the 'great poem' as a 'fountain for ever flowing with the waters of wisdom and delight'.

During the course of the nineteenth century, the continued rise of historical criticism of the Bible and the new 'quest for the historical Jesus' (which produced its own literature in works like Ernest Renan's *Vie de Jésus* (1863) with its portrait of the Holy Family described by Albert Schweitzer as '"Christian" art in the worst sense of the term') was coterminous with the rise of the European novel. Following her extraordinary labours in translating David Friedrich Strauss's notorious *Life of Jesus Critically Examined* (1816), the young George Eliot (Marian Evans) (1819–80) turned to fiction as the vehicle for her post-Christian 'religion of humanity'. Her novels such as *Middlemarch* (1871–2), it has been recently argued, anticipate in many ways the 'postmodern' turn in the Christian theology of our own time.

The later nineteenth century saw the huge popularity of the novel of doubt, above all Mrs Humphry Ward's *Robert Elsmere* (1888), which portrays the tortured life of an Anglican clergyman who loses his faith, dismissing the resurrection as 'legend' and Christianity as mere mythology. At the same time, the European novel was becoming a major vehicle for theological reflection in the hands of writers like the Russian Fyodor Dostoievsky (1821–81) in works like *Crime and Punishment* (1866) and *The Brothers Karamazov* (1880), while in Denmark, Søren Kierkegaard (1813–55) used various literary devices and forms to explore an existentialist theology that ran counter to much of the conservative Christianity of his day.

The twentieth century saw the continued importance and development of the novel: James Joyce's extraordinarily difficult *Finnegans Wake* (1939) has been described as the culmination of the Christian epic tradition that began with Dante. At a more popular level, the fictional writings of C. S. Lewis (1898–1963) have sustained a tremendous popularity, but it is perhaps the Roman Catholic novelists who have been most creative, from the English Graham Greene (1904–91), to the French François Mauriac (1885–1970) and the American Flannery O'Connor (1925–64). In the liberation movements of the post-colonial world of the later twentieth century, the novel has continued to be a vehicle for religious expression both for and against Christianity. For example, the Kenyan author Ngugi Wa Thiong'o wrote his novel *Devil on the Cross* (1980, English 1982) as a political detainee. It is a searing indictment of neo-colonial Africa through a narrative that is fed by biblical forms and motifs from the Gospels.

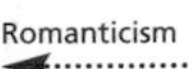

Romanticism

Christian drama experienced something of a revival in the earlier part of the twentieth century, though this has not been sustained except, perhaps, through the medium of the cinema. In Germany Hugo von Hofmannsthal (1874–1929) and in France Paul Claudel (1868–1955), both devout Roman Catholics, wrote major plays, while in England T. S. Eliot's *Murder in the Cathedral* (1935) was written for a Christian stage (Canterbury Cathedral) and a Christian audience, yet attracted broad popularity and is literature of the highest order. In 1951 the medieval mystery plays of the York cycle were revived in outdoor performance and have continued to be performed in the open air in York.

Cinema

Jesus of history

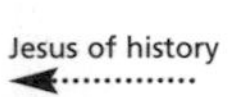

At the end of the twentieth century, the postmodern turn in literary criticism and later literature itself posed new challenges for the Christian writer and for the literary traditions that have been surveyed in this article. According to the critic J. Hillis Miller, 'deconstructive' readings of texts have set up a new opposition between sacred and secular literature. Parables in the Bible, Miller argues, are articles of faith, while parables in modern literature from Franz Kafka to the present day are articles of doubt in which 'it is impossible to know whether or not it is true or counterfeit'. In contemporary literature we have returned to the issue of truth, and for the Bible, perhaps, the question posed by T. S. Eliot at the beginning of this article. Is its primary claim to be considered as literature inextricably linked to the claim that it is the report of the Word of God – and therefore true?

DAVID JASPER

David Daiches, *God and the Poets*, Oxford: Clarendon Press 1984; David H. Hirsch and Nehama Aschkenasy (eds), *Biblical Patterns in Modern Literature*, Chico, CA: Scholars Press 1981; David Jasper (ed), *Images of Belief in Literature*, London: Macmillan 1984; David Lyle Jeffrey (ed), *A Dictionary of Biblical Tradition in English Literature*, Grand Rapids, MI: Eerdmans 1992; David Jobling, Tina Pippin and Ronald Schliefer (eds), *The Postmodern Bible Reader*, Oxford: Blackwell 2001; Alister E. McGrath (ed), *Christian Literature: An Anthology*, Oxford: Blackwell 2001; David Norton, *A History of the Bible as Literature* (2 vols), Cambridge: CUP 1993; Patrick Sherry, *Images of Salvation: Art, Literature and Salvation*, London and New York: T&T Clark 2003

Love

If one were to sum up the practice of the Christian religion in a single word, that word might be 'love'. One could go so far as to say that Christianity is at its very heart a journey of discovery to find out what 'love' means, and then to practise it.

There is much confusion about the word 'love' in contemporary society. This single word is used to describe a wide range of attitudes and feelings, from a fondness for a particular food or object, to a passion for a pursuit or hobby, to sexual desire, to a total and overwhelming selfless commitment to another person or to God.

Incarnation
Jesus

For a Christian also, the term 'love' can be approached in a variety of ways that speak of a commitment between God and humanity, and also between peoples striving to live alongside one another. This 'love' operates at various depths and at its best can raise human beings to a new and mature level of relating, beyond their normal capacity.

Trinity
Bible

'Love' is the defining personal characteristic of God, so much so that the New Testament writer John can say 'God is love' (1 John 4.8). In reaching this conclusion a long history of the development of God's revelation of himself as 'love' had already been experienced and recorded. According to Christian belief, God exists as one-in-three, the Trinity, residing in love as Father, Son and Holy Spirit. This love, existing before creation, calls everything into life; it is the animating principle in the universe. In the Old Testament God's first loving act is seen to be the creation of the world, including the first humans, traditionally known as Adam and Eve, who are the archetypal humans, made in God's image, and containing the capacity to love and create within their very being (Genesis 1).

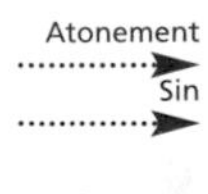

Atonement
Sin
Covenant

Throughout the history of the Jewish people God continually calls the Israelites into relationship with him. This loving commitment is given the name 'covenant'. In the book of Genesis God makes an eternal commitment to his people in the words: 'You shall be my people, and I will be your God.' This is reiterated many times throughout the Old Testament, and while the Israelites break the covenant from time to time because of their actions and 'turning away', God's love for them is so strong that God cannot let them go. Because love is part of God's personality God is not diverted by disobedience. God's fidelity and generosity are likened to a faithful husband's love for his often-erring wife, or that of a patient and loving parent for a recalcitrant child. This comes out particularly clearly in the books of Hosea, Ezekiel, Isaiah and Jeremiah, where God asks of Israel, 'How can I give you up?' (Hosea 11.8) and states, 'I have loved you with an everlasting love' (Jeremiah 31.3).

In response to this eternal loving commitment God calls upon God's people to love with their whole personality. In the book of Deuteronomy God's people are commanded to love God with all their heart, soul and might (Deuteronomy 6.5). The ability to love God at this level is a gift from God and is sustained by remaining in relationship with God.

The Hebrew word *ḥesed* is often used for this expression of covenant-love. This word has a range of meanings that we might translate as loving-kindness, mercy, goodness, piety, solidarity and steadfast love. It is an attitude of devotion and commitment that is without end.

In the New Testament the commonest Greek word for love employed by the first-century writers is *agape*. This word is used very infrequently in classical Greek, where it refers to the noblest and highest form of love. It is a dignified term referring to that which is beyond price.

According to the Christian doctrine of the incarnation, love, which is the very essence of God, took human form in first-century Palestine in the person of Jesus of Nazareth. At this point in history it became possible to witness love personified at first hand. Through the person of Jesus all are able to see God's love for humanity (John 3.16). This love was demonstrated in many acts of compassion: healing, forgiveness and acceptance. Jesus expanded the boundaries of what it means to love by accepting all people, including sinners, outcasts and the disadvantaged, and by desiring the best for them. In this way all are to be included and transformed by relationship with God. This belief is echoed in the words of a popular Christian hymn: 'love to the loveless shown, that they might lovely be'.

God's supreme loving act is demonstrated on the cross, where Jesus, God the Son, is sacrificed, taking upon himself the evil and wayward behaviour of the world. The doctrine of the atonement claims that this act released people for all time from their sin and brought them back into a full and permanent loving relationship with God, which nothing can sever. God's self-sacrifice was such an overwhelming and powerful expression of love that death itself was defeated and therefore Jesus Christ was raised from the dead. This is the pivotal act of Christianity and is celebrated by Christians on Easter Day, and borne witness to in all Christian acts of worship.

The dramatic events of Jesus' death on the cross and his resurrection from the dead can call forth a deep level of gratitude which may result in conversion to the way of Jesus Christ and a corresponding change in belief and lifestyle.

An acknowledgement that God loves them personally in such a total, unconditional, extravagant and eternal manner can open people up to new ways of being which invite God into their lives more deeply. Paul records this change in his letter to the Galatians: 'The life I now live in the flesh I live by faith in the Son of God, who loved me and gave himself for me' (Galatians 2.20). In this experience, as their hearts respond to God's love offered as a free gift, so God the Holy Spirit works within them, empowering them to love with the power of God's love.

In turn, the discipline of exercising such love makes the relationship with God deeper and more intimate, with the ultimate aim of being united in love with God, though this fulfilment will be fully realized only after death. The spiritual discipline of loving and seeking mystical union with God was particularly explored and developed by medieval mystics such as Meister Eckhart (*c.* 1260–*c.* 1328), Julian of Norwich (*c.* 1342–*c.* 1420), Teresa of Avila (1518–82) and John of the Cross (1542–91).

In Christianity, love always involves being in community with God's people, who are seen as brothers and sisters. Christians rarely practise their faith in isolation from others. To be in loving relationship with God and other people is a fundamental tenet of the Christian faith, to such a degree that the church is said to constitute the 'body of Christ' on earth. It has been said that 'love' is the life-blood of Christ's body – that which enables all to live.

Jesus' commandment to love God and one another (Matthew. 22.35–40) was expressed in the very early days of the faith in gatherings for fellowship in people's houses. These meetings almost always included participating in a communal meal called an 'agape', or 'love-feast'. All classes in society and both genders would eat together, which was an unusual occurrence in the ancient world. The agape meal gradually became incorporated into the eucharist or holy communion which most Christians celebrate today. In some Christian communities agape meals are also still enjoyed.

The love of God is to be shown in the day-to-day lives of Christians. This is the prime way in which God's loving acts demonstrated by Jesus during his earthly life are continued. Agape love may be worked out in acts of service, particularly ministering to people in need. Christianity has always been marked by works of charity, giving to the poor, care of the sick and dying, constant efforts for reconciliation, and seeking justice for the oppressed. Many charitable organizations have a Christian base, as do a considerable number of educational establishments and hospitals; indeed schools and hospitals emerged out of Christianity.

p. 836

Schools

Throughout history various Christians have shown an ability to love other people that seems to come directly from Jesus. Such a person in our own time could be said to be Mother Teresa of Calcutta, who reminded Christians of their responsibility in the words of Teresa of Avila: 'Christ has no body now but yours, no hands, no feet on earth but yours. Yours are the eyes through which He looks compassionately on this world. Christ has no body now on earth but yours.'

Conversion

Paul

Love is also expressed in seeking to bring the good news of God to all people so that all may have the chance to hear that God loves them unconditionally and will not let them go. Love includes allowing space for people to be themselves and empowering them to find and fulfil their God-given potential.

Holy Spirit

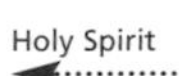

Agape love – the unconditional love of God – extends to all, and therefore the Christian commandment is to love not just those who are easy to love, but also those who might be considered 'unlovely', such as enemies, and those who persecute or do evil acts. This level of loving is impossible to attain in one's own strength, and is achievable only with the inner working of the power of God. The First Letter of John in the New Testament makes the pertinent point that if we cannot love those around us who we can see, we are incapable of loving God whom we cannot see (4.20)

Community

The apostle Paul, writing to the church in Corinth in the first century CE, spoke of love in some of the most beautiful words ever written (1 Corinthians 13). This passage, traditionally called the 'Hymn to Love', is often used at weddings and funerals and is one of the best-loved and most well-known passages in the Bible. For Paul, love alone matters, wins through and endures. He writes of love as an attitude that never treats others unfairly, that doesn't look for the bad but is always seeking the good. Love is not weak or sentimental, but is robust, venturesome and utterly open to the complexity of human relationships. No hardship or rebuff will bring love to an end, but love which is genuine will always persist. True agape love can never fail because it is of God's very essence and is therefore eternal. These words are deeply challenging and set a yardstick of relating which has the ability to deal with an unpredictable world and can transform individuals and communities.

Within Christian theology there has for some time been a debate about the difference between the Greek words

Pastoral care

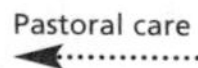

Time Eternity

agape and *eros*, both of which may be translated as 'love'. *Agape*, as we have seen, refers to love that is committed to another, whether or not that object or that person displays anything of worth. Agape love is capable of being shown equally to the beautiful and the repulsive, the good and the bad, the useful and the useless. Agape love desires what is best for the beloved without seeking any reward. This love is not swayed by the response of the loved one, and does not require mutuality in order to be exercised.

The term *eros* is also used of love, and from it we get the word 'erotic'. This is love that is called forth by the attractive qualities of the object or person who is loved. The commonest experience of eros is 'falling in love' with another. Human sexuality finds its fulfilment in this expression of love, as do many types of friendship and companionship. However, some Christians have felt uncomfortable with love expressed as eros, considering it to be dangerous and not always capable of being controlled. Along with the idea of eros love has gone the belief that it can lead to faults such as lust and greed, and can distract people from their devotion to God. Augustine of Hippo (354–430) believed there to be a polarization between sexual love and love for God (*amor dei*). This led to an emphasis on ascetic and monastic celibate love for God at the expense of love between the sexes.

Psychology

In the light of the discoveries of modern psychology Christians are beginning to reassess the importance of eros love in human relationships. Intimate relationships are part of what it may mean to be fully human. Sexual love is ordained by God for the continuation of creation, and finds its prime expression in stable, committed sexual relationships, traditionally lifelong marriage. The importance and joy of this way of relating is witnessed to in the Old Testament book Song of Solomon, which is a celebration of passion between male and female. Many human relationships may begin as eros love, but with time, commitment, and the help of God can mature into agape relationships that are sustainable even through the very worst of times. Probably the most important work on this is the Swedish theologian Anders Nygrén's *Agape and Eros* from the 1950s.

Reformation

Ethics

The principle of 'love' informs Christian ethical and moral thinking, holding to the belief that Christians are called to love others as Christ loves them (Ephesians 5.1–2) – that is, in an accepting and forgiving way. It is people who are to be loved rather than laws, and therefore morality is people-centred. Thus it is important to take time to think and pray through the most loving response in a given situation and not jump in with a set answer or moral code. This way of looking at things can be confusing for those who adhere to a set 'right or wrong' code of practice, and it has provoked the accusation that some Christians are 'woolly-minded'.

Religious orders

All this can be summed up in something like a short creed. Love is the very essence of God, and God lives in a relationship of love within himself through the three persons of the Trinity: Father, Son and Holy Spirit. Through love God calls everything into being and sustains it throughout time and eternity. This love is most clearly displayed in the person of Jesus Christ, who demonstrated God's love for all creation in both his living and dying. In response to this, men and women can open themselves up to be filled with this love, which they then practise towards others in acts of service, justice and hospitality, and as a way of following Jesus. All love comes from God, and is a gift freely given. People can experience the joy and empowerment of loving God and one another because God takes the initiative and loves them first (1 John 4.10).

CATHERINE WILLIAMS

Erich Fromm, *The Art of Loving* (1975), New York: Perennial 2000; C. S. Lewis, *The Four Loves* (1960), London: HarperCollins Fount 1998; Henri J. M. Nouwen, *The Inner Voice of Love*, London: Darton, Longman & Todd 1997; Anders Nygrén, *Agape and Eros* (1953), London: SPCK 1982; Mother Teresa of Calcutta, *No Greater Love*, New York: New World Library 2003; Robert Way, *The Garden of the Beloved*, London: Darley Anderson 1975

Luther, Martin

Martin Luther (1483–1546) was a German monk, professor and theologian whose personal quest for salvation ultimately led to the rise of the European Reformation and the division of Western Christianity.

Born in Eisleben, a small town in the German principality of Mansfeld, Luther attended Latin schools in Eisenach, Mansfeld and Magdeburg before entering the University of Erfurt in 1501 to begin a course of study in the liberal arts. Like many of his fellow students, Luther had been sent to university by his parents in order to take a degree in law. In 1505, however, just as he began the course of higher study, he experienced the first of many spiritual crises that would prove so pivotal in his life. Struck down by a bolt of lightning, Luther called on Saint Anne, promising to become a monk if she would protect him. True to his vow, he entered the monastery of the Observant Augustinian friars in Erfurt, where he quickly distinguished himself for his piety and his learning. In recognition of his talents, Johannes von Staupitz, vicar-general of the order, sent Luther on a diplomatic mission to Rome in 1510, and soon after his return transferred him to the University of Wittenberg, where Luther replaced

Staupitz as Professor of Bible Studies. Luther would spend his life in Wittenberg, which is why the Reformation movement originated in this small Saxon town.

While in Wittenberg, Luther was active in a number of different roles: he was a university professor, a preacher in the city church (1514), district vicar of the Observant Augustinians in Saxony (1515–18) and ultimately dean of the faculty of theology (1535). But most of his time was spent developing his theology, preaching before congregations, lecturing to students, debating with theologians, and above all publishing religious works in German and Latin.

Luther was one of the most prolific writers of the century, and his books brought him lasting fame. By the year 1519, at least 45 separate works were on the market written either by Luther or about him. On his death approximately 700 works in his name were circulating throughout the German lands in over 4000 editions. In the year 1520 alone he published three of his most important Reformation tracts (*To the Christian Nobility of the German Nation*, *The Babylonian Captivity*, and *The Freedom of a Christian*). At the same time, he had an extremely busy social life, and part of his lasting impact on history was due to his ability to gather men of similar religious views together in support of his reform theology. Luther was fortunate to have some of the best theological minds in Germany join him in Wittenberg, including important Protestant thinkers such as Johannes Bugenhagen, Justus Jonas and Philipp Melanchthon. Often they joined Luther and his wife Katherina (a former nun, the daughter of an impoverished Saxon nobleman, whom he married in 1525) at the large Augustinian monastery (a gift from his prince) which served as their home. There, surrounded by students, colleagues and his own children, Luther would sit for hours in conversation, while others would record his words for posterity in a series of works that became known to later generations as *Table Talk*.

In most histories of the Reformation, the point of origin is 31 October 1517, for that is the day on which Martin Luther is presumed to have posted his Ninety-Five Theses to the door of the castle church in Wittenberg. Reference to this act did not surface until after Luther's death, but even if there is more legend than fact behind it, there is no doubt that on this day he sent a copy of his theses to Archbishop Albrecht of Mainz. The theses were critical of the Roman Catholic practice of indulgences, and they soon found an eager audience, especially once they were translated from Latin into German. Albrecht forwarded his copy to Rome, with the result that Luther was invited to appear in Rome (8 August 1518) under suspicion of heresy. At that stage Luther's prince, Elector Friedrich the Wise of Saxony, intervened in an effort to protect his famous Wittenberg professor and managed to change the site of the hearing to the German city of Augsburg. Luther's meeting with the papal legate Cardinal Cajetan in Augsburg (12–20 October 1518) was his first appearance before the Catholic authorities to answer for his theology.

A debate in Leipzig with the Ingolstadt professor Johannes Eck took place the following year (4–14 July 1519), but on neither occasion did Luther recant, and indeed before the end of the debate with Eck he had gone so far as to question the authority of the Catholic Church, reject the claim to infallibility made by pope and councils, and associate himself with the condemned heretic John Hus. In response to his defiance, Pope Leo X issued *Exsurge domine* (15 June 1520), a bull threatening excommunication, declaring Luther a heretic and forbidding the faithful 'to read, assert, preach, praise, print, publish, or defend' his opinions. The following year the emperor Charles V endorsed the excommunication with the publication of the Edict of Worms (26 May 1521), thereby placing Luther under the imperial ban while repeating the demand to avoid his works, 'since they are foul, harmful, suspected, and published by a notorious and stiff-necked heretic'.

Papacy

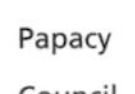

Council

p. 700

Luther and his followers were now fugitives in the eyes of both church and state, and we may the trace the rise of the Reformation as a broader historical movement to the publication of the Edict of Worms. From that point onwards, Luther emerged as the leader of the Reformation in the German lands. His most direct involvement was in his own principality of Saxony, where he supervised the various stages of reform, from the appointment of evangelical pastors, the reduction and eventual elimination of Catholic forms of worship, the introduction of a Lutheran service in the churches, the reform of the schooling and welfare systems, and the creation of the institutional church; from the offices of ecclesiastical rule to the organs of governance and the establishment of the Lutheran visitation (1528), including guidelines for the visitation of the churches and priests in Saxony to determine the 'faithfulness' of the pastors and churches and to set up a structure of correcting any errors. But Luther also played a central role in the general process of Reformation in the German lands, intervening personally in cities such as Erfurt, Bremen, Magdeburg and Nuremberg, as well as in territories such as Prussia, Hesse and Brandenburg, or serving in a broader sense as a figure of inspiration and authority for the emerging Protestant powers.

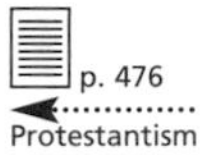

p. 476
Protestantism

Of course, the German Reformation was always more than just the vision or the will of a single man. Even in his own lifetime, indeed even in his own town of Wittenberg, Luther was often unable to control the course of Reformation. Evangelical theologians such as Andreas Carlstadt and Thomas Müntzer emerged with

Justification
Salvation
Bible

Martin Luther preaching to the faithful, and communion with the chalice

Sacraments

alternative visions of reform, and in the south German lands Lutheranism was always less significant than the theology of Huldrych Zwingli, or the later teachings of John Calvin. But his status as the founder of the German Reformation was never challenged, and he remained the single most important Protestant reformer in Germany until the end of his life.

Huldrych Zwingli
John Calvin
Forgiveness
Ministry and ministers

When Luther posted his Ninety-Five Theses in 1517, he did so in order to end the abuses associated with the sale of indulgences. He was writing with a view to historical events, and he would continue to write in this manner until the end of his life. Most of his theology, from his initial breakthrough to his later reflections, took shape as a dialogue with the world around him. In the beginning it was a personal dialogue, marked by deep and lasting spiritual doubts. While still a monk in the Augustinian order in Erfurt, Luther grew increasingly convinced of his inadequacy before God. Although he was true to his rule and observed what was expected of him, he felt that he could not meet the conditions set by God. Eventually he began to doubt that sinful man could ever meet the divine expectations, and it was his concern with this question – What if sinful man is unable to meet God's preconditions? – that led him to his most significant theological insight. He found it in Romans 1.17: 'For therein is the righteousness of God revealed from faith to faith: as it is written, The just shall live by faith.' To be justified, to stand in a right relationship with God, sinful man could do nothing except live by faith and rejoice in God's grace, his 'undeserved, unmerited divine favour to humanity'. This was the foundation principle of Luther's theology – *sola fide*, justification through faith alone – and it represented a fundamental challenge to the theology and the praxis of the medieval Roman Catholic Church, for it undermined the notion of good works, which meant that the religious culture associated with the practice (from the buying of indulgences and the giving of alms to the duties of penance and the struggles of confession) no longer had a role to play in the quest for salvation.

Lutheranism
Sin

Decades would pass before the full implications of the Lutheran concept of justification would be completely understood. Many of Luther's other theological insights, however, had a more immediate impact on the course of Christian history. His reliance on the Bible, for instance, which is often referred to as the principle of scripture alone (*sola scriptura*), provided him with a method of interpretation and a sense of legitimacy for his views, which enabled him to reject the claims of the Catholic authorities and cast doubt on the corpus of medieval theological thought.

Luther's reading of the Bible also led to new insights about the nature of the Christian religion, including his reduction of the seven sacraments of Roman Catholicism to (ultimately) the two Lutheran sacraments of baptism and the Lord's Supper. Only in these two, he concluded, do we find the divinely instituted sign and the promise of the forgiveness of sins.

A similar approach led Luther to reject the traditional distinction between the secular and the spiritual world. Instead, he spoke of the 'priesthood of all believers', by which he meant the communion of all true Christians equal before God and joined by baptism. The church was no longer the Church of Rome. On the contrary, Luther declared as early as 1520 that he believed the papacy to be the seat of the Antichrist. In his view, the true church was wherever people gathered to listen to the Word and worship in Christ's name, and this no longer meant the hierarchical institutions of Roman Catholicism but the 'godly communities' of the early Reformation movement. In time, however, the Lutheran church would evolve as a national or a territorial church, founded upon Luther's principle of the priesthood of all believers and articulated in his more general ideas about the relationship between the church and the state. In his work *On Secular Authority* (1523), Luther distinguished between two forms of rule, the rule of the church and the rule of the state, concluding that both were divinely ordained spheres of authority and that both, as long as each kept to its proper sphere, were necessary for a Christian state. This was the theoretical foundation for the evolution of the Protestant church.

Martin Luther has always played a role in Germany history beyond that of a great theologian. From the very beginning he was the symbolic centre of the Reformation movement. Artists and authors used his image in various forms in order to fashion a sense of Protestant community. Later generations would do the same thing, reworking his image to match the changing times and project a distinct sense of national identity. But his role was more than just symbolic. At the heart of Luther's legacy to his nation was his contribution to German culture. In the sheer number of his publications alone, Luther helped to bring about a media revolution, as the printed word, now available in the form of cheap pamphlets written in the vernacular, began to shape public culture.

He also made fundamental contributions to the evolution of the German language, investing it with an eloquence and an authority it did not possess before. In this field the most profound contribution was his translation of the Bible into German, with the New Testament appearing in 1522 and the complete Bible finished by 1534. Luther's Bible became the most influential text in German history, not only in its contributions to the making of the language but also in its shaping of the sense of national identity.

Indeed, Luther's whole life was a long dialogue with the German nation. He began as a theologian, writing works of pastoral guidance and spiritual comfort, and over the course of his career he would offer his opinions on a wide range of issues, from the foundations of a happy marriage to whether it was just to charge interest on goods and the role of the state in the reform of education. In 1546 he died in Eisleben, the town of his birth, while mediating in a controversy between the counts of Mansfeld. His body was taken to Wittenberg, where it was interred in the castle church.

C. SCOTT DIXON

Roland H. Bainton, *Here I Stand: A Life of Martin Luther* (1950), Harmondsworth: Penguin Books 2002; Martin Brecht, *Martin Luther. His Road to Reformation, 1483–1521*, Minneapolis: Fortress Press 1985; *Martin Luther. Shaping and Defining the Reformation, 1521–1532*, Minneapolis: Fortress Press 1990; *Martin Luther. The Preservation of the Church, 1532–1546*, Minneapolis: Fortress Press 1993; Richard Marius, *Martin Luther. The Christian between God and Death*, Cambridge, MA: Harvard University Press 1999; Heiko A. Oberman, *Luther: Man between God and the Devil*, New Haven, CT: Yale University Press 1986

Lutheranism

Martin Luther
Paul
Books
p. 476

Lutherans did not start out to be what they have largely become. Martin Luther (1483–1546) did not even want the name: 'I ask that no reference be made to my name; let them call themselves Christians, not Lutherans. After all, the teaching is not mine. Neither was I crucified for anyone. St Paul, in 1 Corinthians 3, would not allow the Christians to call themselves Pauline or Petrine, but Christian. How then could I – poor stinking, maggot-fodder that I am – come to have people call the children of Christ by my wretched name? Not so, my dear friends; let us abolish all party names and call ourselves Christians, after him whose teaching we hold.' Luther obviously did not prevail. The movement he unintentionally started in 1517 when in Wittenberg he called for a public disputation on the power and efficacy of indulgences by posting ninety-five points for debate, usually referred to as 'theses', has become what appears to be a very large, global denomination. One among many.

Holy Roman empire
Christianity in Europe
Roman Catholic Church
Reformation

What Luther and his original colleagues actually intended was to make certain important proposals about the meaning of the Christian message that when – and if – accepted would bring about reform in the church. In complicated ways that involved the Emperor Charles V (1500–58) of the Holy Roman empire, royalty and politicians in the German states and soon in Scandinavia, a number of popes, and countless theologians of various points of view, the Lutheran movement grew up alongside both the Roman Catholic Church and a number of other Reformation movements. In time it lost its provisional character, and a denomination was born.

Salvation
Justification

The original proposal of the Lutheran Reformation was that the Christian message, the gospel, should be seen in accordance with the Bible as God's gracious offer of unmerited salvation in Jesus Christ, the message of 'justification by grace through faith'. The famous hallmarks of Luther's cause were (in Latin phrases which Lutherans still love to use): *sola gratia* (by grace alone), *sola fide* (by faith alone), *sola scriptura* (by scripture alone). This basic understanding of the gospel was accompanied by other calls for reform: to give both the bread and wine to communicants at the mass, to conduct the mass and to provide the Bible in local languages, to allow priests to marry, and to provide for greater freedom in church government. As these proposals developed, theological refinements – subtle and not so subtle – widened the gap between Rome and the Lutherans.

p. 302

Luther's proposal was fleshed out in the Augsburg Confession, a document of 28 articles written by his colleague Philipp Melanchthon (1497–1560), signed by nine German territorial rulers, and presented in 1530 to the emperor, Charles V. Fatefully, it was not agreed to by the theologians of the 'other side', the Roman Catholic Church, and thus a complex historical process was started which resulted in the establishment of the Lutheran church as the official church of a number of the German states and of all the Scandinavian countries. The Augsburg Confession still stands in the twenty-first century as the authoritative statement for Lutherans around the world. From this point on, and for this reason, Lutheran churches would always be known as confessional churches.

Creed

The Lutherans themselves had a number of bitter theological controversies, especially after Luther's death in 1546. It was not until 1580, when The Book of Concord, a formidable collection of seven Lutheran documents following the three 'ecumenical creeds' (Apostles', Nicene and Athanasian), which covers over 700 pages in its English edition, was agreed to that Lutherans attained something like unity. Many Lutheran churches today continue to hold The Book of Concord as authoritative in its totality.

The spread of the movement

Pietism

Mission

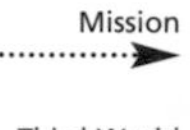

Third World

Even as post-Reformation Lutheranism was being consolidated – some would say ossified – in scholastic and orthodox terms, and even as the movement was being renewed by the 'religion of the heart' usually referred to as Pietism, there was expansion. Initially this expansion also involved political accommodations to states. Lutheran churches became established state churches in large portions of Germany and all of Scandinavia. These were territorial and national church bodies that claimed the name of Luther, even though they had no structural ties to one another. The legacy of this has been important for European history, not least in Germany in the time of both twentieth-century world wars. In Eastern and Southern Europe, Lutherans have been and remain distinct minorities.

Christianity in Africa

Christianity in Asia

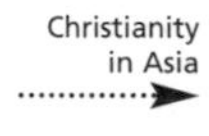

The state-church reality for European Lutherans began to break up only towards the end of the twentieth century. There are still complicated relations between church and state even in the most pluralistic and secular of these countries. In Germany the state since World War I has no longer controlled the church, but many would say that the *Landeskirchen*, territorial churches, still occupy positions of privilege. In the Nordic countries, only the Church of Sweden has taken the full step of disestablishment from the state, in 2000.

Christianity in North America

Christianity in Latin America

It was, of course, emigration which brought Lutheranism to the new world of North America. The name 'Lutheran' first appeared in 1564 in what is now Florida, but it is known that this was a name applied to French Huguenot settlers by Spanish Roman Catholics who regarded all Protestants as 'Lutheran'. It was in 1638 that the first Lutheran settlement, by Swedes in what is now Delaware, Pennsylvania and New Jersey, was established. Pastors from Germany and Sweden worked with these people, the first ordination of a Lutheran pastor in North America taking place in 1703. The first Lutheran church body, the Ministerium of Pennsylvania, was established in 1748 by the person generally regarded as the father of American Lutheranism, Henry Melchior Mühlenberg (1711–87), who had absorbed Lutheran Pietism when a student at Halle in Germany.

For generations Lutherans in North America faced 'the language problem'. Virtually all Lutherans were immigrants or their descendants who did not speak English. This isolated Lutherans both from large segments of American society and, in point of fact, even from each other. It is, moreover, a fact that must be seen together with the generally conservative character of Lutheranism in respect both to theology and social ethics if – especially in the nineteenth and early twentieth centuries – the distance between Lutherans and the predominant American culture is to be understood. Things have, to be sure, changed. There are now only two large Lutheran churches in the United States: the Evangelical Lutheran Church in America, a body of more than 5 million members which has become quite thoroughly American and ecumenical, and the Lutheran Church – Missouri Synod, a body half the size of the former, which remains theologically ultra-conservative and ecumenically uninvolved. While both of these bodies have grown, so that nationality is no longer a major factor, the racial and cultural diversity of North America is not at this time vividly reflected in these churches.

Both European and North American Lutheran churches sent missionaries in considerable numbers to what is now regarded as the Third (sometimes called the Two-Thirds) World. Lutheran Pietists from Germany went to Tranquebar, India, in 1706. The first significant Lutheran presence in Africa, in the first half of the nineteenth century, was in Ethiopia, followed by missions throughout the continent. After World War II these missions became fully indigenous church bodies. In 2001 there were over 11 million Lutherans in Africa, the largest church bodies being in Ethiopia, Madagascar, Tanzania, Namibia, South Africa and Nigeria.

In Asia in 2001 there were over 7 million Lutherans, the largest groups being in India and Indonesia. The nearly 4.5 million Lutherans in Indonesia are found largely among the Batak people of North Sumatra. In real terms, this is perhaps a genuine 'folk church', which in 1951 formed its own confession of faith (deemed by Lutherans throughout the world to be in harmony with the Augsburg Confession of 1530). The Bataks have taken a surprisingly prominent leadership role in the overwhelmingly Muslim Indonesian society.

There are slightly more than a million Lutherans in Latin

America, the largest group being in Brazil, descendants of German immigrants of the nineteenth and early twentieth centuries. Slowly but surely, Lutherans in Brazil have shed their European ways and have begun to take their place in the crucial Latin American struggles for economic and social justice.

Throughout the world, in 2001, Lutherans numbered over 65 million, with the European churches accounting for more than 36 million of these. It is clear, however, that Lutheranism is growing most rapidly in the southern hemisphere, most notably in Africa. In today's world, the territorial churches of the secularized north are just beginning to see the ways in which the countries in which the Lutheran movement began are now themselves lands ripe for mission.

The Lutheran World Federation

Efforts to establish a global identity for Lutheran churches began early in the twentieth century. The Second World War brought a halt to these efforts, but in 1947 representatives of 47 churches in 26 almost exclusively northern countries met in Lund, Sweden, to form the Lutheran World Federation (LWF). The process leading to this was a difficult one, since Lutherans were found on both sides of the global war. The action was necessary, however, in order to undertake joint rescue and relief for those who had suffered the ravages of war, common initiatives in mission, joint efforts in theology, and a shared response to the ecumenical challenge. The Federation was then seen as 'a free association of Lutheran churches'.

The LWF, with headquarters in Geneva, Switzerland, had grown by 2002 to number 136 member churches in 76 countries. These churches account for more than 62 million of the 65 million Lutherans in the world. Perhaps the most highly organized international denominational body apart from the Roman Catholic Church, the LWF carries on major activities in ecumenical relations, theology and study, humanitarian assistance, human rights and peace issues, mission and development, and communication services. Its staff in Geneva numbers about 90 persons from some 25 countries. Its international programme, Lutheran World Service, employs about 90 international staff from 31 nations who work alongside about 4000 national staff.

One highly significant action taken by the Federation was in 1984, when the membership of two small white churches in southern Africa was suspended because of their practice of apartheid at the eucharist. This took place after a lengthy debate in which the Federation determined that this practice was a *status confessionis*: in other words, on the basis of faith and in order to manifest the unity of the church, apartheid had to be rejected totally. After lengthy study, counsel and visitation the suspension of membership was lifted in 1991.

An ecumenical step of considerable importance was taken by the LWF together with the Roman Catholic Church in 1999. After a number of years of mutual study and dialogue, the two bodies signed – in Augsburg, Germany, the scene of the meeting with the emperor in 1530 – a *Joint Declaration on the Doctrine of Justification.* This statement affirmed that the Reformation controversy concerning justification by grace through faith is no longer a church-dividing issue between the two bodies. Sixteenth-century condemnations levelled at each other – in Lutheran confessional documents and at the Roman Catholic Council of Trent – were lifted. Lutherans and Roman Catholics still have major points of difference – ministry, papacy, the role of the Virgin Mary, etc. – but this Declaration represents perhaps one of the most significant ecumenical developments of the past five centuries.

Justification

Geography

Ministry and ministers
Papacy
Mary

The LWF no longer sees itself as a 'free association'. Its constitution now provides the organization with a self-understanding as 'a communion of churches which confess the triune God, agree in the proclamation of the Word of God and are united in pulpit and altar fellowship'. In a landmark step, the LWF's Council of 48 persons, at least 40 per cent of whom must be women, is now equally divided between representatives of southern and northern churches with no regard for the size or wealth of those churches. In 2003 the LWF expanded its official name to 'The Lutheran World Federation – A Communion of Churches'.

Lutherans: identity and issues

Lutherans are usually identified as generic Protestants, alongside many other denominations and sects. Nearly five centuries of history have made this identification virtually indelible. If, however, the definition of the Lutheran movement given here – as a proposal concerning the gospel to the church catholic – is correct, Lutheran churches throughout the world should be perpetually unsettled. Whether they are is a serious question.

From the beginning, the Lutheran movement has occupied a kind of middle ground, between Roman Catholics on the one hand and more radical Reformation movements on the other. Luther had no desire to do away with the form of the mass, for example. His critique of the mass was primarily theological, although he held on passionately to a doctrine of the 'real presence' of Christ 'in, with, and under' the bread and wine. This was in sharp contrast to the Swiss Reformation of Huldrych Zwingli (1484–1531) and to the Anabaptists. The position of John Calvin (1509–64) in Geneva was more nuanced, but still to the left of Luther. Most Lutherans structure their liturgy in the historic shape, the *ordo*, of the mass, and under the influence of the modern and ecumenical liturgical movements presiding ministers increasingly again use traditional eucharistic vestments.

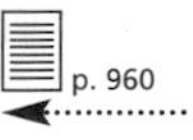
p. 960

Huldrych Zwingli

John Calvin

pp. 354–5

Nor did the Lutherans entirely do away with more 'catholic' forms of episcopal church government. Lutheranism is marked by considerable diversity (and controversy) at this point. Bishops in historic succession are found, among other places, in Sweden, Finland and Tanzania; bishops are 'coming into' historic succession in the United States and Canada as a result of ecumenical agreements with Anglican or Episcopal churches. Leadership in other countries is structured more along episcopal (without historic succession) or even secular corporate models. Increasingly, questions of traditional episcopal polity (church governance) are being faced in the light of new ecumenical arrangements.

Ecumenical movement

A strong case can be made that the Lutheran proposal concerning the gospel is taking the shape of what many call 'evangelical catholicity'. Jaroslav Pelikan (born 1923), an American theologian who has recently become a member of the Orthodox Church in America, in an important work of 1964, written when he was a Lutheran, built on the distinction made by the Lutheran Paul Tillich (1886–1965) between 'Protestant principle' and 'Catholic substance' in his understanding of the Lutheran Reformation. '"Catholic substance" … means the body of tradition, liturgy, dogma, and churchmanship developed chiefly by the ancient church … "Protestant principle" is a summary term for the criticism and reconstruction of this Catholic substance which Luther and his Reformation carried out in the name of the Christian gospel and with the authority of the Bible.'

A host of issues, then, face the Lutheran churches. Three can be singled out.

1. *The theological identity of Lutheranism.* Lutherans have consistently been described as 'confessional', a reference to their founding documents from the sixteenth century. But centuries have now intervened. What does this mean now? The sad fact is that many Lutherans remain unwilling to view these 'founding documents' within the contexts of their original histories. This is a strange phenomenon, especially for a movement that in many ways pioneered the modern 'historical-critical' study of the Bible. Failure to see the confessions as sixteenth-century documents has both made idols of those documents and hidden what may be their richness and relevance for the church of the twenty-first century.

Biblical criticism

Old practices, provincialisms and prohibitions, moreover, have largely disappeared: e.g., with a few exceptions Lutherans have for more than a generation ordained women, and increasingly women have become bishops. Theological training – especially at advanced levels – is now undertaken in ecumenical institutions. A number of theological disciplines, such as the large field of critical biblical studies, disregard denominational labels almost completely. Certain Lutheran theologians of the twentieth century – e.g., Dietrich Bonhoeffer (1906–45), Rudolf Bultmann (1884–1976), Anders Nygrén (1890–1978), Paul Tillich, Wolfhart Pannenberg (born 1928) – have influenced Christian theologians in all traditions.

Women in Christianity

In this situation, what is to be the identity of Lutheranism? Is there a doctrinal, liturgical, or experiential uniqueness to the Lutheran movement? What is the role today within global Christianity for 'Catholic substance' and 'Protestant principle'?

2. *The ecumenical challenge to Lutheranism.* The new situation of Lutheranism – after nearly five centuries – is nowhere more dramatic than ecumenically. Lutherans have been leaders in the formation of the modern ecumenical movement in the twentieth century, as witnessed by the pioneering contributions of the Archbishop of the Church of Sweden, Nathan Söderblom (1866–1931). Since the Second World War the cause of 'the quest for the visible unity of the church' has been significantly advanced by bi-lateral theological dialogues between traditions, and Lutheran churches – often through the Lutheran World Federation – have been thoroughly committed to that process. Before Lutherans and the Roman Catholic Church agreed to the *Joint Declaration on the Doctrine of Justification* of 1999, in the 1990s nearly all the Lutheran churches of the Nordic and Baltic lands and the Anglican churches of the British Isles reached an agreement of full communion with the signing of the Porvoo Common Statement. In the United States the Evangelical Lutheran Church in America has declared full communion with the Episcopal Church (Anglican), the three American member churches of the World Alliance of Reformed Churches, and the Moravian Church. Significant agreements have also been reached between the Church of England and the Evangelical Church in Germany in the Meissen Agreement, and between Anglicans and Lutherans in Tanzania and southern Africa. All of these agreements have been built on 30 or more years of bi-lateral theological dialogues. Moreover, other theological dialogues are moving ahead in various parts of the world.

What is to be the significance of these agreements? Many, to be sure, regard them as primarily theological exercises that have little effect on day-to-day church life; for many ecumenism is not an exciting enterprise. Others see them as the reconciliation of differences and diversities that have plagued Christian church bodies since even before the Reformation of the sixteenth century. No set of issues is more momentous for Lutherans – and others – than the twenty-first century advances. Is the provisional character of the original Lutheran movement – its 'proposal concerning the gospel' – to determine ecumenically the future of Lutheranism itself?

3. *Lutheran mission in a globalized context.* Questions of identity and ecumenical agreement are, it is tritely said,

for the sake of the overall Christian mission in the world. The issues are not simply academic or theoretical. The new realities faced by Lutherans and all Christians are determined by new economic, political, social and religious realities, often grouped together under headings such as 'globalization' or 'the new pluralisms'. And new realities are also seen in undiminishing global threats to life: war, the arrogant presumptions of the one global 'super power', the pandemic of AIDS, the persistence of poverty and injustice in all but a few areas of the world. The record of Lutheranism has not always been exemplary in the light of such challenges. One needs only to think of centuries of tense relations between Lutherans and the Jewish people, beginning with Luther himself; or of the tradition of 'Lutheran quietism' in respect to social issues, culminating in the failure of some German Lutherans boldly to respond to the Nazi movement before and during World War II.

Lutherans and, indeed, all churches face daunting futures that are marked by both opportunities and obstacles. Do the traditions – Lutheran and other – possess resources of truth, imagination, courage and generosity to meet the new tests of the present and of the future?

NORMAN A. HJELM

E. Theodore and Mercia B. Bachmann, *Lutheran Churches in the World: A Handbook*, Minneapolis: Augsburg Press 1992; Carl E. Braaten and Robert W. Jenson (eds), *The Catholicity of the Reformation*, Grand Rapids, MI: Eerdmans 1996; Günther Gassmann and Scott Hendrix, *Fortress Introduction to the Lutheran Confessions*, Minneapolis: Fortress Press 1999; Eric W. Gritsch, *A History of Lutheranism*, Minneapolis: Fortress Press 2002; Eric W. Gritsch and Robert W. Jenson, *Lutheranism: The Theological Movement and Its Confessional Writings*, Philadelphia: Fortress Press 1976; Robert Kolb and Timothy J. Wengert (eds), *The Book of Concord: The Confessions of the Evangelical Lutheran Church*, Minneapolis: Fortress Press 2000; Jaroslav Pelikan, *Obedient Rebels: Catholic Substance and Protestant Principle in Luther's Reformation*, New York: Harper & Row 1964; Jens Holger Schjørring, Prasanna Kumari and Norman A. Hjelm (eds), *From Federation to Communion: The History of the Lutheran World Federation*, Minneapolis: Fortress Press 1997

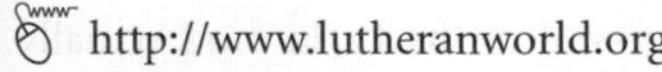
http://www.lutheranworld.org

Marriage

No religion can or should claim credit for marriage. Customarily defined as 'a voluntary union of a man and a woman for life', it has existed in all known ages and cultures, and has until recently been unchallenged as a necessary and desirable element of any stable family and social life. Christians, like Jews and members of other faiths, instinctively believe that it is ordained by God, and find confirmation of their belief in Genesis 2.24: 'Therefore a man leaves his father and his mother and clings to his wife, and they become one flesh.'

Globalization

Poverty

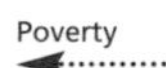

Judaism and Christianity

Not that marriage has always had the same form. In Europe and in countries colonized from Europe strict monogamy has been the rule – doubtless under the influence first of classical and then of Christian culture. In the ancient Middle East, as in the Hebrew scriptures, polygamy was countenanced (and practised by those who could afford it), and it is still allowed under Islamic law. In parts of Africa both polygyny and polyandry are practised; in other societies a strict matriarchy is the determinant factor of the family structure.

More important (at least for our purposes here) is the variety of reasons for which marriage has been undertaken. Marriage may be seen primarily as a partnership initiated by romantic love and sustained by mutual devotion, but it has also been entered upon to effect the transfer of property and to secure an inheritance; to cement a political or dynastic alliance; to give national rights to an alien; to give legitimacy to a child already conceived or born; to improve career prospects through social and political liaisons; to give livelihood and security to a vulnerable member of the opposite sex. It gives rights in law, it preserves the family name, it may lighten the burden of personal taxes; but, being more than a contract, it is assumed to be a lifelong relationship and requires a process of law to be dissolved. Its domestic structure has normally been patriarchal, with the wife expected to care for home and children while the husband earns a living. Today, new and more liberal patterns are being devised, which assign a more equal share both of duties and of work opportunities to each partner.

The interest of the state in this institution is mainly focused on arrangements for divorce. Since marriage is generally perceived as socially desirable, the procedures for terminating it are strictly controlled. In Britain until the nineteenth century, divorce was virtually unobtainable by ordinary citizens; under modern legislation it is still restricted by a number of conditions that have to be fulfilled. But that some marriages are likely to become unsustainable (particularly when the support of traditional social patterns breaks down) is a fact that legislators have to reckon with. It is the purpose of the law to ensure that the parties to a divorce are fairly treated and that adequate provision is made for the offspring of the marriage. Securing these objectives necessarily introduces delay and expense into the legal proceedings, and is the main disincentive offered by the state to those who contemplate divorce.

But the fact that there is virtually universal legal provision for divorce does not mean that it is universally acceptable morally. Fidelity in marriage is a disposition that is generally admired and warmly encouraged by moralists; and few people doubt that providing a permanent and stable family background for children should so far as possible take priority over the pursuit of conjugal and sexual happiness for its own sake. In the Hebrew scriptures there are aphorisms in praise of marital fidelity and stability (Proverbs 5.18 and elsewhere); the prophet Malachi deplored precipitate abandonment of a first wife (2.14–15); and Roman moralists extolled the virtues which led to a secure and lasting marriage. Yet almost all recognized that divorce may on occasion be the only practical and humane course for a spouse to take, and society as a whole did not think that a second or third marriage was in any way diminished or contaminated by the first.

Discipline

Jesus

Among moral and religious teachers, Jesus stands out as having been particularly severe on divorce. He went so far as to pronounce that remarriage after divorce is tantamount to adultery, which was a capital crime in the code of law attributed to Moses (Leviticus 20.10). How this teaching was to be proclaimed and expressed in the lives of his followers has been a problem for the church from earliest times. The formulation of Jesus' saying in Matthew's Gospel (5.32) apparently allows for an exception ('Anyone who divorces his wife except in the case of *porneia*' – a word of disputed meaning, which probably has the sense here of an adulterous relationship). Many believe that this represents an early attempt by the church to turn the general condemnation of divorce into a community rule. Similarly, when Paul refers to a 'command of the Lord' forbidding separation and divorce (1 Corinthians 7.10–11), he has to allow that if this is turned into a rule for church members there must be some flexibility in the case of marriages in which one partner is a pagan ('the Pauline exception'). Ever since, churches have had to wrestle with the tension between on the one hand giving faithful expression to Jesus' condemnation of divorce through the lives of their members, and on the other offering support, counsel and compassion to those who have failed (as many always will) to live up to this ideal.

Pastoral care

The Roman Catholic Church has historically taken up the most rigorous position, denying the possibility of divorce and remarriage to any of its members who were validly married in the first place and refusing access to the sacraments to those who have failed; and for a certain period (roughly the first half of the twentieth century) the Church of England espoused the same doctrine and followed the same policy. At the other end of the scale, the Orthodox churches have always been prepared, in certain conditions, to recognize second, or even third, marriages, and the Reformed churches have also found it possible to have divorcees among their members while seeking nevertheless to express something of Jesus' profound disapproval of divorce through their church life and discipline.

Sacraments

We need not pursue the history of these debates in detail; but the practical need for churches to regulate the divorce of their members has from time to time made it necessary to advance a distinctively Christian definition of what, as we have seen, is essentially a civil and secular institution. In the early centuries of its existence the church had little control over the marriage contracts and ceremonies arranged for its members. These were a matter for the civil authorities, and church discipline was confined to the question whether those who had divorced and remarried should be penalized or excluded. What form the actual marriage took was outside ecclesiastical control, and in fact varied quite widely in different parts of the world. But the extensive acceptance of the jurisdiction of the church in the West from the twelfth century onwards made it possible for church authorities to enforce a standard form of marriage and the fulfilment of a standard set of conditions if a marriage was to be recognized as valid. This allowed, in effect, a possible escape route for those whose marriages failed: if it could be shown that an essential condition had been absent, the marriage could be declared null and void, and the spouses would be free to re-marry without disciplinary consequences. Accordingly, ecclesiastical courts were put in place to determine individual cases.

But what were these essential conditions? One of these was that both the man and the woman should have given their consent to the union freely – a principle which is at the heart of all civil legislation and forms of marriage. A second was that the parties should have formally made a commitment of exclusive and lifelong attachment to one another. A third was that the marriage should have been publicly witnessed. All these were generally agreed. But in many cases these conditions had already been fulfilled at the moment of formal betrothal; and betrothal was not marriage. It could be broken off at will. What, then, was the essential feature of marriage – what Augustine called *quiddam conjugale,* 'the conjugal something' – which decisively united a Christian couple at the moment of their marriage according to the rites and ceremonies of the church? A clue was found in the Latin (and actually misleading) translation of the Greek word *mysterion,* which Paul used in Ephesians 5 to describe the nature of the marriage relationship as a reflection of that between Christ and his church: *sacramentum.* If the marriage of Christians was a 'sacrament', then, like baptism, it could never be undone. It was 'indissoluble'. And at what point did this take place? For Augustine, it was the moment of the solemn commitment of the spouses to one another. But later, a clue was found in a possible interpretation of Genesis 2.24: the phrase 'one flesh' (of man and wife) could be held to mean that it was the first act of sexual intercourse that constituted marriage. In which case, only a consummated marriage would be a sacrament. The other elements were sufficient to create a valid marriage, but only one that was consummated would be sacramental, and therefore indissoluble.

The effect of this legalistic search for the 'conjugal something' was to place immense emphasis on the rites of marriage and the first act of intercourse, so obscuring the fact that the one scriptural passage which gives content to the notion of 'Christian marriage' (Ephesians 5, the passage containing the word *mysterion*) concerns, not the rites and actions inaugurating a marriage, but the long-term marriage relationship itself. This passage is quoted or alluded to in almost every marriage service in churches of all denominations, and is the main basis for the claim that Christianity has a distinctive contribution to make to understanding the potential of the marriage relationship. 'Husbands should love their wives as they do their own bodies'; in doing so they reflect and are inspired by the love of Christ who 'loved the church and gave himself up for her' (Ephesians 5.25–8). And although the author (who may or may not be Paul – this is disputed by scholars) takes for granted the subordination of the wife to the husband and does not explicitly suggest that there should be a reciprocal and equal relationship of self-giving love between husband and wife, it is reasonable to suppose that had he lived in a more egalitarian age he would have followed the logic of his argument and encouraged the wife to love her husband in the same exalted terms.

But there is another contribution that the Christian tradition has been able to make. The Book of Common Prayer describes marriage as 'the vow and covenant betwixt them made'. This takes its cue from Malachi 2.14 ('your companion and your wife by covenant') and also from a passage in Hosea (2.16–20), where the prophet is inspired to see marriage as a symbol of the covenant relationship between God and his people. The distinctive feature of a covenant (as opposed to a simple contract) is that the parties may still be bound by it even when one of them has broken its terms: the belief that God had made a 'covenant' with Israel implied that God was not necessarily released from it, however faithless and disobedient his people became. In the same way (we may infer) a married couple are bound by their 'vow and covenant' in such a way that the faithlessness of one need not be a pretext for the other to renounce it: the relationship is to be one characterized (in Hosea's words) by 'righteousness, justice, steadfast love and mercy'.

In essentials, then, the Christian understanding of marriage runs along the same lines as that of the majority of human beings. Marriage is a lifelong union of a man and a woman based on free consent; it is solemnized by formal vows and is publicly witnessed; the physical union of the spouses, which should be exclusive, serves to deepen their commitment and their joy in one another and enables them to found a family; and their relationship is sustained by mutual love. But this immensely demanding and fulfilling relationship is immeasurably strengthened and deepened by resources which Christians believe are given by grace as well as nature: an infinite capacity to forgive, to amend and to seize on a new beginning after every failure. These are such as to raise 'the holy estate of matrimony' from being an ordinary social institution to being a parable of the love of God and a sacramental expression of his influence on the lives of his creatures. In short, marriage belongs (as the traditional formulation has it) to the realms of both creation and redemption.

Grace

It is when we consider the traditional way of seeing the *purpose* of marriage that recent changes become apparent. Traditionally, marriage was thought to have three purposes. These (as set out in the introduction to the marriage service in the Book of Common Prayer) are 'the procreation of children' and their nurture, 'a remedy against sin', and 'the mutual society, help and comfort' of the spouses. The first of these is based on Genesis 1.28, 'Be fruitful and multiply', and continues to hold pride of place in the Jewish understanding of marriage. The second reflects the medieval distrust of physical sexuality and is an echo of (one understanding of) Paul's warning, 'It is better to marry than to burn' (1 Corinthians 7.9). The third is an inference from Genesis 2.18, 'It is not good that the man should be alone; I will make him a helper as his partner.' These purposes have by no means been rendered obsolete; but they have been somewhat re-interpreted and have been drastically rearranged in order of importance.

p. 898

Covenant
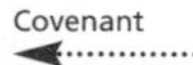

Procreation is now seldom regarded by Christians as the first purpose and is relegated to second place, partly to allow for necessarily childless marriages, but mainly because the sexual union of man and wife is now universally seen among the churches as 'unitive' as much as 'procreative': the Church of England's marriage service in *Common Worship* (2000) speaks of 'the delight and tenderness of sexual union and joyful commitment', and only then proceeds to refer to 'the foundation of family life'. (In the Orthodox tradition the primary purpose of marriage has always been understood to be the conjugal love and mutual service of the couple.) As for the 'remedy against sin', the ideal of chastity before marriage is one on which it is hardly realistic to insist in contemporary Western society, and this 'purpose' of marriage is now normally interpreted as a reiteration of the basic proposition that

p. 245

Love
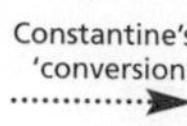
Constantine's 'conversion'
Persecution

the marriage bond is exclusive and lifelong in its sexual expression. In this form, these purposes are uncontroversial. The distinctive contribution of Christianity is to bring to bear on this understanding the experience and pursuit of the kind of love which is imaged in Paul's great analysis of it in 1 Corinthians 13, in the belief that such love is the primary human resource, enhanced and empowered by divine grace, that makes it possible to measure up to the lifelong commitment of the spouses to one another which constitutes the covenant between them and which is implied by Jesus' unequivocal condemnation of divorce. Such a union, Christians believe, receives God's blessing as a divinely ordained calling; it is strengthened by his grace, and may be seen and experienced as a sacramental embodiment of Christ's love for his church. In an age of increasing longevity and of general preoccupation with short-term satisfactions and provisional relationships, this vision of the true potential of marriage as a lifelong, exclusive and totally committed partnership continues to offer a challenge, as well as an opportunity for deep emotional and spiritual fulfilment, to an increasingly sceptical and materialist society.

ANTHONY HARVEY

Zygmunt Bauman, *Liquid Love: On the Frailty of Human Bonds*, Cambridge: Polity Press 2003; J. Dominian, *Passionate and Compassionate Love*, London: Darton, Longman & Todd 1991; A. E. Harvey, *Promise or Pretence? A Christian's Guide to Sexual Morals*, London: SCM Press 1994; Helen Oppenheimer, *Marriage*, London: Mowbray 1990; Edward Schillebeeckx, *Marriage: Secular Reality and Saving Mystery*, London: Sheed & Ward 1965; Report of the Commission set up by the Archbishop of Canterbury, *Marriage, Divorce and the Church*, London: SPCK 1971

Martyr

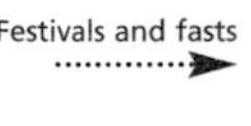
Saint
Architecture

Festivals and fasts
Relics

The Greek word *martys* and related terms mean 'witness'. In the New Testament the word appears quite frequently with the generic meaning of one who testifies to facts (e.g. in a legal sense) but in Luke-Acts it takes on the more specific meaning of those who bear witness to the deeds of Jesus in their experience: 'You will receive power when the Holy Spirit comes upon you; and you will be my witnesses in Jerusalem ...' (Acts 1.8; see Luke 24.48). The Book of Revelation calls Jesus 'the faithful witness' (1.5) and the 'faithful and true witness' (3.14).

By the second century the term 'martyr' slowly took on the technical meaning of one who died or suffered for the public confession of the Christian faith. It is in that precise sense that the word is used in *The Martyrdom of Polycarp*, a late second-century text describing the trial and execution of Bishop Polycarp of Smyrna who died *c.* 155. By the end of the century a distinction was made between those who died for the faith (martyrs) and those who suffered some penalty – exile, condemnation to the mines, loss of goods – for the faith (confessors). The church father Tertullian, writing in North Africa in the late second century, speaks of those in prison who will soon face the arena as *martyres designati* – those destined to be martyrs.

Christianity was a proscribed religious movement from the middle of the first century until Constantine's edict of toleration in the early fourth century. The Roman historican Tacitus in his *Annals* has Nero making scapegoats of Christians for the burning of Rome. Persecutions of the Christians tended to be sporadic and somewhat localized until the middle of the third century, when the Emperor Decius triggered an empire-wide persecution in the year 250 by demanding that everyone sacrifice to the Roman gods for the sake of the empire itself. This was a demand with which Christians could not comply, and those who did not suffered a range of penalties. Subsequent persecutions under the emperors Valerian and especially Diocletian at the very beginning of the fourth century were the most extensive and bloody.

Scholars still debate why the Christians were proscribed and on what legal basis. The most plausible reason may be that Romans saw the Christian belief that God alone could be worshipped and that therefore acts of devotion to the Roman gods were impossible as treachery undermining *pietas*, that religious sense which provided the harmony between the gods and the fortunes of government and thus generated the prosperity of the civil order. We have quite a large martyrdom literature that either repeats or elaborates the judicial process against Christians. These *Acta* indicate that Christians could have had their freedom had they been willing to make a liturgical gesture towards the gods of Rome or the 'genius' of the emperors. Their obdurate refusal to do so seemed, in the eyes of the Roman authorities, to be acts of treason.

The age of Roman persecution made an enormous impact on the subsequent shape of the Christian tradition. The depiction of the martyr as a figure to be emulated in the literature produced by the martyrdom period has many consequences. Now we see the origin of the cult of the saints; the rise of a certain kind of church architecture (for shrines or for churches exalting the martyred saints); a liturgical cycle of feasts which would go in tandem with the church year of major feasts recalling the birth, death and resurrection of Jesus Christ; the importance of relics and their place in the devotional life of the church; and the place of the martyrs as models of Christian fidelity. The literature about their lives and deeds increased, although some of the legends were extravagant elaborations of the more sober actions that had come down from antiquity.

The power of martyrs to inspire did not die out with the end of the Roman persecutions. Their memory was maintained both in worship and in popular devotions and in the proliferation of literature about them. They were held up as the ideal of the Christian life. In the thirteenth century, for example, Anthony of Padua was inspired to join the Franciscans after reading of the martyrdom of some friars who had attempted to evangelize the Muslims of Morocco. In the sixteenth century, as she tells us in her autobiography, Teresa of Avila thought about running away from home with her brother to enjoy martyrdom at the hands of Muslims in North Africa. John Foxe's *Book of Martyrs* (published in 1563) who suffered at the hands of Catholics during the Marian persecution went through four editions in his own lifetime and was a staple part of Protestant reading for generations after his death. A plethora of nineteenth-century novels (e.g. John Henry Newman's *Callista*) set out a romantic vision of early Christians being exposed to the wild animals in Roman circuses (true) while attempting to escape persecutions by hiding out in catacombs (most certainly not true).

What constituted martyrdom was easy enough to determine in the period of the Roman persecutions. The matter was succinctly stated by Augustine of Hippo: *non poena sed causa* – it was not the punishment but the reason for the punishment that determined who was a martyr. Medieval theologians like Bernard of Clairvaux and Thomas Aquinas considered the question as to whether the seven Maccabee brothers killed in the Jewish rebellion against Antiochus Epiphanes in the second century (1 and 2 Maccabees); the Holy Innocents, the children massacred by Herod the Great in an attempt to kill the infant Jesus; or John the Baptist could be considered martyrs, since they had suffered before Christ. Thomas' response was that they were true martyrs since they died unjustly in defence of truth connected to or an anticipation of the saving mysteries of Jesus Christ.

The question of the criteria for martyrdom was not a mere exercise in medieval scholastic intellectual discrimination. This question has arisen again in the contemporary period. Did Edith Stein die in a concentration camp *in odium fidei* (out of hatred of the faith, i.e. on the part of her killers) or did she die because she was a Jew? Did Oscar Romero, shot at the altar in El Salvador, die as a martyr or as a victim of political murder? Did the vast number of those who died at the hands of the Stalinist or Nazi regimes die because of their faith or because they were considered class or political enemies? Some theologians have argued that their deaths were motivated not so much by hatred of the faith as by hatred of the values that Christianity upheld but which were inimical to the

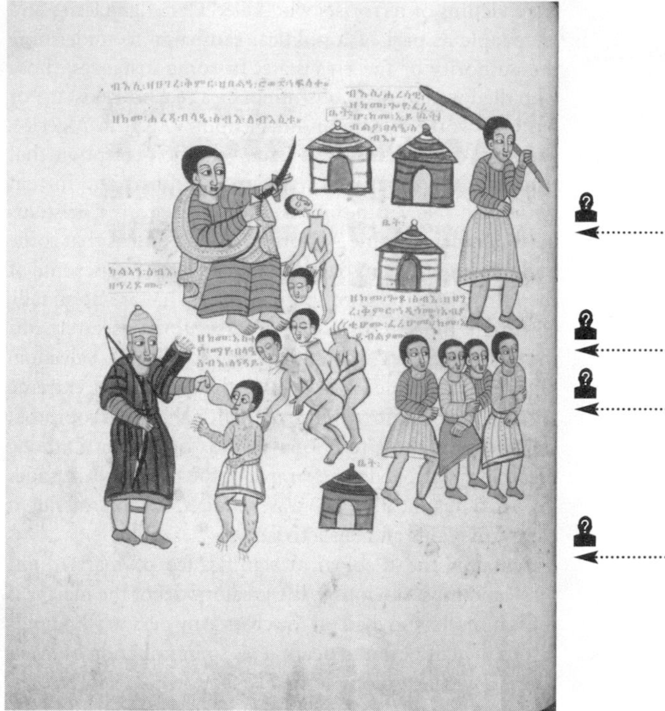

Martyrdom of St Sebastian and others, seventeenth-century Ethiopian manuscript

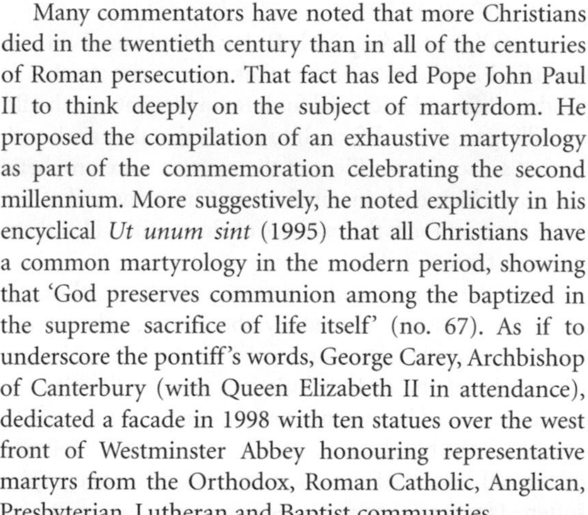

impulses of the totalitarian state. In the words of one thinker, they died *in odium caritatis* (out of hatred of the Christian doctrine of love).

Many commentators have noted that more Christians died in the twentieth century than in all of the centuries of Roman persecution. That fact has led Pope John Paul II to think deeply on the subject of martyrdom. He proposed the compilation of an exhaustive martyrology as part of the commemoration celebrating the second millennium. More suggestively, he noted explicitly in his encyclical *Ut unum sint* (1995) that all Christians have a common martyrology in the modern period, showing that 'God preserves communion among the baptized in the supreme sacrifice of life itself' (no. 67). As if to underscore the pontiff's words, George Carey, Archbishop of Canterbury (with Queen Elizabeth II in attendance), dedicated a facade in 1998 with ten statues over the west front of Westminster Abbey honouring representative martyrs from the Orthodox, Roman Catholic, Anglican, Presbyterian, Lutheran and Baptist communities.

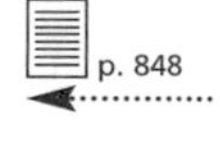
p. 848

p. 700

The more recent cases of those martyred in Central America, in Algeria, in Africa, Pakistan, and even in Sicily (killed by the Mafia) have raised the issue of martyrdom once again. In some of these cases it is clear that those killed were victims of terrorists who killed Christian clerics and lay people as part of a political campaign to undermine the authority of the civil state. In some instances, those who died were indigenous minorities (e.g. in Pakistan) or pastoral workers from another country (e.g. in Algeria). In either case what was at issue was the perception that somehow the Christians were an alien force, and in that sense their fate was not unlike that of the early Christians in the Roman empire. A more troubling note is that some exemplary Christians have been killed by persons, some of them in official positions, in countries that are nominally Christian. Indeed, some of the persecutors (as surely was the case in places in Central America like El Salvador) killed in the name of a politics that combined extreme anti-Marxism with a kind of nationalistic fervour that called on the most reactionary kinds of Roman Catholic piety. Some invoked the example of the medieval Crusades for such justification as was required to kill dissident clergy, religious and lay activists.

What is the theological significance of martyrdom? First, and most obviously, the great model of the martyr is Jesus himself who died on the cross. Any person who holds fast to the faith even to death does so in imitation of Jesus. The early martyrdom text, *The Martyrdom of Polycarp*, sees in the death of the aged bishop a re-enactment of the passion of Jesus, as the frequent allusions to the passion narratives of the Gospels makes clear. Indeed, the compiler of the acts of the martyrs of Lyons (late second century) says that those who died in the circus would not even have dared called themselves martyrs 'for it was their joy to yield the title of martyr to Christ alone, who was the true and faithful witness, the firstborn of the dead, and the prince of God's life'.

Jesus

Council

Orthodox churches

Secondly, as John Paul II has emphasized in his encyclical *Veritatis splendor*, there are some truths so fundamental and so crucial for human life that one should be willing to give up life itself to ensure that they are heard. In that sense, the sacrifices of the martyrs were prophetic gestures which both inspired other Christians and at the same time set forth the excesses of those who killed them for their faith.

Symbols

Over the course of the centuries the 'picture' of the martyr was largely shaped by the iconography of art. Christian piety had at its disposal a whole range of images that spoke of the early tribulations of the Christians in the Roman world: Lawrence with his grill; Catherine with her wheel; the blind Lucy with her detached eyes. It is one of the sad ironies of our own day that this iconography, softened by the passing of time into stereotype, must now be replaced with a new martyrdom iconography: barbed wire, the electrode, the noose and the firing squad. Such an iconography reminds us that martyrdom is as old in Christianity as the stoning of Stephen described in the Acts of the Apostles and as contemporary as the beheaded Trappist monks who were murdered for their faith in Algeria in the last decade of the twentieth century.

Iconography p. 1076

LAWRENCE S. CUNNINGHAM

Daniel Boyarin, *Dying for God: Martyrdom and the Making of Christianity and Judaism*, Stanford, CA: Stanford University Press 1999; Brad S. Gregory, *Christian Martyrdom in Early Modern Europe*, Cambridge, MA: Harvard University Press 1999; Herbert Musurillo (ed), *The Acts of the Christian Martyrs*, Oxford: Clarendon Press 1972; Robert Royal, *The Catholic Martyrs of the Twentieth Century*, New York: Crossroad 2000

Mary

The Virgin Mary is a ubiquitous but enigmatic presence in Christian history and culture. In the West from the fourth century until the Reformation she was a central figure in the Christian faith, and her legacy endures in European art, architecture, literature and music. Her traditional role as the mother of Jesus in Roman Catholic theology and devotion has continued to flourish alongside less orthodox representations in contemporary culture, from the parodies of the pop singer Madonna (Madonna is Italian for 'My Lady', a name used especially for statues and pictures of Mary) to a range of cinematic and artistic representations. In the East, from the Council of Ephesus in 431, when she was accorded the title 'Mother of God', she has also been venerated in the Orthodox churches. Yet the vast majority of people today know little about Mary's doctrinal and historical significance, beyond Christmas card images of the stable in Bethlehem and the visit of the three wise men.

How did this relatively minor biblical figure become one of the most familiar and contested symbols, capable of inspiring sublime artistic achievements and furious religious debates? Is there any relationship at all between the images and devotions that have proliferated around her and the poignancy of the young Jewish villager who, according to the Bible, conceived a child by the Holy Spirit, laid her newborn baby in a manger, became a refugee fleeing to protect her child from Herod's armies, and finally stood at the cross watching her son being tortured to death? The biblical story resonates with the hopes and sufferings of many ordinary people throughout history, but does not explain her elevation to the position of Queen of Heaven, Mother of God and now post-Christian cultural icon. The biblical Mary seems to stand in stark contradiction to the historical development of her cult.

In attempting to unravel the significance of Mary for

the Christian story, it is important to bear in mind the varied ways in which she is perceived and represented. For Orthodox and Coptic Christians she is an iconic presence of maternal compassion and wisdom, in forms of Christianity that remain modelled to a large extent on the practices and beliefs of the early church. In Roman Catholicism, her image reflects the developments and changes that have continuously taken place in Western theology and worship, from the earliest Marian doctrines and devotions to the flourishing of her cult in the High Middle Ages and later to the Counter-Reformation and the modern era. During the Reformation, the non-biblical basis of the cult of Mary led to its rejection by the Reformed churches, and even today Mary occupies a relatively insignificant position in Protestant Christianity. There is, however, a growing ecumenical movement that seeks to heal the divisions of the past, and this includes a re-examination of Mary's role in the incarnation. In addition to these various Christian representations, Mary features prominently in the Qur'an and is therefore an important figure in Islam, and the New Testament identifies her closely with the people of Israel and the Jewish tradition. It may be that in future years she will be seen as a potential point of unity for Christians, Jews and Muslims, as followers of the world's three great monotheistic faiths seek to discover shared symbols of belief.

Perhaps the most controversial question for Christians continues to be the extent to which there is biblical justification for the place of honour accorded to Mary by Roman Catholics. Non-Catholics often mistakenly believe that Roman Catholics worship Mary (the term used is mariolatry, excessive devotion to Mary), although there has always been a distinction in Roman Catholic doctrine between the veneration owed to Mary as the Mother of God (known by the Greek term *hyperdoulia*) and the adoration owed to God alone (*latria*). The Roman Catholic understanding of the church encompasses the saints in heaven as well as the earthly church, and Catholics believe that it is possible for all the saints, and especially for Mary, to pray with and for God's people on earth. In seeking to explore the origins of devotion to Mary in the Bible and the early church, it is important to bear in mind the ways in which the church fathers elaborated upon biblical stories and themes. The church fathers sought to explain the incarnation in terms of symbolic meanings and analogies, so that a rich world of ideas and beliefs developed through the complex interaction of scripture, philosophy and culture, in ways that were particularly significant for the early development of the Marian tradition.

Mary in the Bible

Mark's Gospel, believed to be the earliest, has the fewest references of all the Gospels to Mary. There is no infancy narrative, and when the author does describe an encounter between Jesus and his mother it seems that Jesus is distancing himself from his family or disclaiming any special relationship to them (Mark 3.31–5), although there are different interpretations of this scene, which also occurs in the two other synoptic Gospels (Matthew 12.46–50 and Luke 8.19–21). Matthew's Gospel tends to focus on Joseph rather than on Mary in telling the story of Jesus' conception and birth (Matthew 1.18–24). This is the only Gospel that refers to the visit of the wise men to the infant Jesus, the flight into Egypt and Herod's massacre of the children (Matthew 2.1–18). Luke's Gospel contains the fullest account of Mary's role and is the main source for the Marian tradition. As well as his description of the angel Gabriel visiting Mary with news that she is to become the mother of Jesus ('the annunciation'), Mary's visit to her cousin Elizabeth ('the visitation'), and the birth (Jesus' 'nativity'), the Gospel author includes the account of the shepherds visiting the manger, the circumcision of Jesus, the finding of Jesus in the temple when he was twelve, and his childhood in Nazareth (Luke 1 and 2).

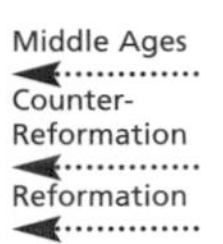
Middle Ages
Counter-Reformation
Reformation
Ecumenical movement

John's Gospel, believed to be the latest and most theologically developed of the Gospels, includes two references to Mary that Roman Catholic interpreters have always seen as highly significant. The description of the wedding at Cana refers to Mary's intervention when Jesus performed his first miracle (John 2.1–10), and there is also a reference to Mary at the foot of the cross (John 19.25–7). The Acts of the Apostles refers to Mary being present among the believers after the ascension of Jesus into heaven (Acts 1.14), but the letters of Paul and other New Testament writings make no mention of her, although there is a reference to Christ being 'born of woman' (Galatians 4.4–5). References to a woman crowned with stars in the Book of Revelation (Revelation 12. 1–17) have traditionally been associated with Mary and have inspired many paintings of the Immaculate Conception. They are still used as the liturgical readings for the Feast of the Assumption, although modern biblical scholars argue that they do not refer directly to Mary but to the church.

Saint

As well as New Testament references to Mary, the early church interpreted many Old Testament texts as prophecies or typologies of the coming of Christ – a method of interpretation that is seen as problematic today because of its Christian appropriation of the Hebrew scriptures. Nevertheless, this kind of typological reading is important for understanding the significance of Mary, particularly with regard to interpretations of the story of creation and the fall in Genesis 1–3. Some church fathers saw in Luke's story of the annunciation a symbolic resonance with the story of creation in Genesis, so that Mary's virginal maternal body was associated with the virgin earth from which the first Adam was created by

p. 1197
Church fathers
Incarnation

Bible
p. 664

Lorenzo di Credi, *The Annunciation*, sixteenth century

Christology

God. In the most significant and enduring interpretation, Mary was identified with the figure of Eve, first woman of the new creation, partner to the second Adam referred to in the New Testament (see Romans 5.12–19; 1 Corinthians 15.22, 45–9). The main basis for this association was what is known as the *Protoevangelium*, or 'first good news' of the coming of Christ, when God says to the serpent in Genesis, 'And I will put enmity between you and the woman, and between your offspring and hers; he will crush your head, and you will strike his heel' (Genesis 3.15). From the second century CE, Mary was seen as the woman in whom this promise to Eve was fulfilled, an interpretation that was given added impetus by a mistake in the official Latin translation of the Old Testament, the Vulgate, which used 'she' instead of 'he [or 'it' in some translations] will crush your head'. Another Old Testament text quoted in relation to Mary is the Isaiah prophecy, 'Therefore the Lord himself will give you a sign: The virgin will be with child and will give birth to a son, and will call him Immanuel' (Isaiah 7.14). Some attribute this Marian association to a mistranslation of the word 'virgin' that might more accurately be rendered 'maiden'. Mary's Magnificat (Luke 1.46–55) resonates with Old Testament themes, particularly with the words of Hannah, mother of Samuel (1 Samuel 2.1–10).

p. 145

Mary in the early and medieval church

Two related influences help to explain the rapid development of the cult of Mary in the early church. On the one hand, there was the theological need to formulate a defence of the incarnation against various religious and philosophical movements that denied either Christ's humanity or his divinity. Mary's virginal motherhood became a focal point for these early debates. Her virginity attests the divine origins and nature of Christ. It constitutes the vertical dimension of the incarnation, which is the belief that in Christ, God intervened miraculously to transform and redeem humankind by an act of supernatural creative power. Mary's motherhood affirms the full humanity of Christ, and constitutes the horizontal dimension of the incarnation. Christ shared the human condition from conception to death, and he was fully incorporated into the history of humankind from the beginning. It was as a result of the Nestorian controversy in the fifth century that Mary was proclaimed 'Mother of God' (*Theotokos*, or 'God-bearer'). John Henry Newman in the nineteenth century argued that all subsequent doctrinal and devotional developments in the Marian tradition are consistent with these early Christian beliefs about Mary as the New Eve and Virgin Mother of God.

But the fact that the Council of Ephesus prompted displays of popular jubilation in the streets points to the other factor that contributed towards Mary's significance in the early church. In a culture that still practised widespread devotion to the mother goddesses of the ancient Greek, Roman and Egyptian worlds, there was perhaps a need for a symbol of maternal power in Christianity. Mary is sometimes described by modern interpreters as the goddess of the Christian religion, and although this runs the risk of over-simplification (early Christians were at considerable pains to differentiate between their forms of worship and belief and those of the surrounding cults), she undoubtedly represents the maternal feminine dimension of the Christian tradition. In recent decades we have begun to understand more about the deep psychological desires and impulses associated with the maternal relationship, and this might go some way to explaining the enduring appeal of the cult of Mary.

One of the earliest documents associated with the Marian tradition is the second-century apocryphal gospel known as the *Gospel* or *Protoevangelium of James*, the popularity of which suggests an early desire to expand on the biblical narrative about Mary. This tells the story of Mary's conception by her elderly parents, Anne and Joachim, her birth and early life, and her marriage to Joseph and the birth of Jesus. The account of Mary's conception and birth closely echoes that of Jesus' conception and birth in Luke's Gospel. The figure of Anne is modelled on the Old Testament figure of Hannah, and there are also symbolic associations with the story of Abraham and Sarah in the Book of Genesis. The *Protoevangelium* formed the basis of much medieval literature such as the thirteenth-century *Golden Legend* (*Legenda Aurea*), and the story of Mary's life inspired many works of art such as the frescoes by Giotto in the Arena Chapel in Padua, the mosaics in the church of Santa Maria in Trastevere in Rome, and the stained-glass windows in Chartres Cathedral. Other influential early Marian texts, known as the *Transitus* stories, date from about the fourth century onwards and concern the dormition or falling asleep of Mary at the end of her earthly life.

Feasts of Mary

These accounts of Mary's dormition are significant because they provide evidence of early beliefs associated with the doctrine of the assumption. This is one of two Marian doctrines promulgated by modern popes. The doctrine of the immaculate conception was defined as dogma by Pope Pius IX in 1854, and the doctrine of the assumption was defined by Pope Pius XII in 1950. Immaculate conception denotes the sexual conception of Mary without sin by her parents, and is quite different from the doctrine of the virgin birth (the belief that Jesus was conceived without sexual intercourse), with which it is often confused. Both these doctrines trace their origins back at least to the fifth or sixth centuries, when there is evidence that belief in the sinless perfection of Mary and in her bodily assumption into heaven had become widespread if not universally accepted. Mary's nativity has been celebrated as a feast in the Eastern church since the latter part of the sixth century, and the feast of her conception since the late seventh century. In the Western church it was probably first celebrated in Ireland or England in the early eleventh century, from where it spread into northern Europe and Spain. As with many beliefs associated with Mary, the Feast of the Immaculate Conception arose more from popular devotion than from theological argument, and intense theological debate surrounded the subject until well into the seventeenth century. Although Orthodox Christians celebrate the feasts of Mary's conception and her assumption or dormition, they do not accept the dogmas promulgated by the Roman Catholic papacy. Protestants also reject the dogmas because they regarded them as unbiblical.

For Orthodox Christians, devotion to Mary is woven into the rich patterns of worship that shape the liturgical year, and of the twelve great Orthodox feasts, four are directly associated with the Mother of God: The Nativity of the Mother of God (8 September, also celebrated as the Birth of Mary in the Roman Catholic Church), the Presentation of the Mother of God in the Temple (21 November), the Annunciation of the Mother of God (25 March, celebrated as the Feast of the Annunciation by Roman Catholics), and the Dormition (Falling Asleep) of the Mother of God (15 August, known by Catholics as the Feast of the Assumption). Roman Catholics also celebrate the Feast of the Immaculate Conception on 8 December. The liturgies for Orthodox Marian feasts draw upon the language and symbolism of the early Greek Church, so that they offer a majestic and awe-inspiring vision of the cosmic significance of the incarnation. Icons are an integral part of Orthodox worship, with famous images of Mary such as the Hodegetria communicating a sense of timelessness achieved through the faithful perpetuation of an artistic tradition that has changed very little through the centuries. Combining power and tenderness, her image has a transcendent quality that speaks to the universality of the human condition, symbolizing the divinization of humanity in the incarnation through the delicate interplay of love and suffering, grief and hope.

Stained glass
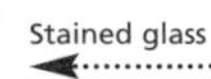
Icon

p. 605

Marian devotion

Devotions

Roman Catholic devotion to Mary tends to be more prolific and diverse in its practices and symbols, with a continuous tradition of prayers, litanies and works of art that constantly adapts and develops to reflect changing cultural and spiritual perceptions. This close relationship between cultural values and religious symbols in the Catholic tradition means that in every era representations of the Virgin Mary can be read as prismatic reflections of the ways in which Christians understand themselves in relation to God, to nature and to the community around them. From her emergence as a Byzantine empress after the Council of Ephesus until the Middle Ages, Mary is an imposing and majestic figure. Her status reflects her divine motherhood, in an era when Christ was understood primarily as the conquering king of the universe who liberated all of creation from its captivity to death and decay. But from the twelfth century onwards, Western Christianity became more focused on the humanity of Christ. Several explanations have been offered for this. It was an era that saw the beginnings of individualism, with a growing emphasis in Christian art and devotion on human spirituality, psychology and experience. Mary began to be associated with the feminine soul as the bride of Christ in imagery inspired by the Song of Songs, and she also became invested with the qualities of the Lady of the courtly love tradition, in highly eroticized expressions of spirituality that today might be interpreted as a form of sublimated sexuality among male celibates. It has also been argued that the suffering associated with the Black Death and with economic and social hardship in the fourteenth century led to a devotional focus on the suffering of Christ and his mother, who became known around that time as the *Mater Dolorosa*, or Mother of Sorrows. The

p. 613
Festivals and fasts
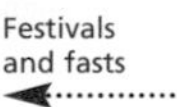

famous hymn of Mary at the foot of the cross attributed to Jacopone da Todi, the *Stabat Mater*, is believed to have been written in the early fourteenth century and still inspires many modern musical composers.

Music

But there have always been multiple strands to Marian devotion in the Roman Catholic Church, encompassing both the sublime creative achievements of the great Marian prayers, hymns and liturgies, and more popular forms of devotion that are often influenced by the indigenous religions and folklore of particular geographical regions. As well as the major Marian feasts that form part of the liturgical year, there are numerous other feasts and festivities associated with her, and prayers and litanies such as the *Angelus*, the rosary, the *Ave Maria*, the *Salve Regina*, the Litany of Loreto and the Magnificat form part of the regular patterns of Roman Catholic prayer.

Devotions

Late medieval art and devotion constitute a high point in the Marian tradition. The rejection of devotion to Mary and the saints and the iconoclasm that accompanied it during the Reformation brought to an end the vast maternal cult of the medieval church. While the Roman Catholic understanding of Mary has always attributed to her an active role in the incarnation because of her willing agreement to become the mother of Jesus, Reformers such as John Calvin and Martin Luther represented her as entirely passive and therefore as lacking any special honour or privilege in relation to Jesus. Protestants denied the intercessory power of Mary and the saints in the life of faith, and the doctrine of salvation came to be more exclusively focused not on the incarnation as a whole but on the cross alone. In the Anglican Church of the seventeenth century there were still pockets of devotion to Mary, particularly among high churchmen, the so-called Caroline divines, but only with the growth of ecumenism in the twentieth century has there been a real resurgence of interest in Mary in Anglo-Catholicism, although not at the more evangelical end of the Anglican spectrum.

Iconoclasm

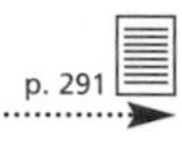
p. 291

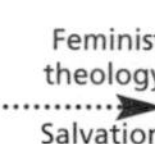
Feminist theology
Salvation
Liberation theology

Roman Catholic devotion to Mary in the Counter-Reformation and early modern era was often associated with a reaction against the growing rationalism of the age, with works such as the highly popular *Glories of Mary*, published by Alphonsus Liguori in 1786, suggesting a tendency towards sentimentality and extravagance. Today, the most widely known image of Mary in modern Roman Catholic churches is probably that of the Immaculate Conception as she appeared to Bernadette of Lourdes – a beautiful, pale-faced young girl in a blue robe, whose image is far removed from the majestic mother of early medieval art. The nineteenth and twentieth centuries also saw the continuing phenomenon of Marian apparitions (appearances) such as those at Lourdes (1858), Fatima (1917) and Medjugorje (since 1981), creating a revitalized cult of pilgrimages to Marian shrines that has grown steadily throughout the last century. There are now an estimated 100 million visitors per year to Christian shrines in Europe alone, many of which are associated with the Virgin Mary.

Mary and the Second Vatican Council

The most significant influence on modern Marian theology and devotion has of course been the Second Vatican Council. The issue of Mary was the most controversial of all the matters addressed by the Council, with intense debates between those who wanted to issue a separate document on Mary attesting to her unique significance and privilege in the Roman Catholic faith, and those who advocated a more integrated approach that would emphasize her role in relation to the church as well as in relation to Christ himself. In the end, the latter group won by a small majority, and the council's teaching on Mary was incorporated into the document on the church, *Lumen gentium*. There was a marked decline in devotion to Mary following the council, when many Roman Catholics enthusiastically rejected the more flamboyant or mystical aspects of the pre-conciliar church in the name of modernization and progress. However, since the 1970s there has been a revival of Marian devotion and theology both among conservatives and among liberal Catholics. While conservatives have upheld Mary as a model of obedient maternal femininity and contemplative spirituality, some Roman Catholic feminists have reinterpreted her significance as a potentially liberating symbol of women's call to equal participation in the life of the church, including the priesthood, criticizing the degree of passivity in the traditional portrayal with its emphasis on submission. Liberation theologians have seen in her a powerful affirmation of God's special love for the poor and solidarity with the oppressed. Her Magnificat includes the words 'He has brought down rulers from their thrones but has lifted up the humble. He has filled the hungry with good things but has sent the rich away empty' (Luke 1.52–3), and this has led the Magnificat to be read in social as well as spiritual terms by those who argue for a politically-engaged Christianity to challenge the economic and political injustices of the modern world. As the mother of the crucified Christ, Mary has also become a focus of inspiration and courage for the many mothers of Latin America whose children disappeared and were tortured and killed during the regimes of the 1970s and 1980s.

The tradition about Mary forms a vast and multi-layered aspect of Western history, culture and spirituality. Despite this, until recently there has been little scholarly or popular interest in her cult outside traditional Roman Catholic circles. However, with a growing number of people today looking anew at the spiritual and cultural heritage of the Christian tradition from many different

APPEARANCES OF THE VIRGIN MARY

Numerous appearances (often called apparitions) of the Virgin Mary to individuals have been recorded down the centuries and are still recorded today. Some of these reported appearances have given rise to famous pilgrimage centres. Here are some of them:

Walsingham 1061: Appeared to Lady Richeldis de Faverches, a widow who lived in Walsingham, Norfolk, and asked her to build a replica of her house in Nazareth. The house became one of the greatest pilgrimage sites in Europe but was destroyed under Henry VIII, apart from one chapel, the Slipper Chapel, which was rebuilt in the 1920s by an Anglican priest, Alfred Patten; it is again a pilgrimage centre.

Guadalupe 1531: Appeared in Guadalupe, Mexico, to a young Aztec, Juan Diego, ordering him to build her a shrine and imprinting a miraculous image on his shawl. The basilica now there is visited by 100,000 pilgrims each year on the anniversary of the appearance.

Paris 1830: Appeared in Paris to a nun, Catherine Labouré, instructing her to have a medal struck and showing her the model for it. Millions of copies of the medal were struck and circulated all over the world. As a result of the effect this medal had it was known as the miraculous medal.

Lourdes 1858: Appeared eighteen times in a cave in Lourdes in southern France to Bernadette Soubirous, revealing herself as 'The Immaculate Conception'. The place has since become a major pilgrimage centre to which many pilgrims go in the hope of being healed.

Knock 1879: Appeared along with Joseph and John the Evangelist in a church in Cnoc Mhuire (Knock), County Mayo, Ireland to Mary Beirne and fourteen other women, after which miraculous healings were associated with the church.

Fatima 1917: Appeared to three children in Fatima, Portugal, calling for prayer and repentance and predicting the conversion of Russia.

Medjugorje 1981: Appeared to six children in Medjugorje, Bosnia, and many times afterwards; she still appears to them. She calls for conversion, faith, prayer, fasting, peace and reconciliation. Pilgrims go there from all over the world, but the events have not yet been recognized by the Roman Catholic Church.

www.walsingham/org.uk; www.lourdes-france.com; www.knock-shrine.ie; www.fatima.org; www.medjugorje.org

perspectives, it seems likely that this rich and relatively untapped resource for theological, historical and cultural understanding might yet have new and surprising insights to offer.

TINA BEATTIE

Tina Beattie, *God's Mother, Eve's Advocate: A Marian Narrative of Women's Salvation*, London and New York: Continuum 2002; Raymond Brown, Karl P. Donfried, Joseph A. Fitzmyer and John Reumann (eds), *Mary in the New Testament*, Philadelphia: Fortress Press and New York: Paulist Press 1978; Hilda Graef, *Mary: A History of Doctrine and Devotion*, combined edition, London: Sheed & Ward 1994; Jaroslav Pelikan, *Mary Through the Centuries: Her Place in the History of Culture*, New Haven and London: Yale University Press 1996; Marina Warner, *Alone of All Her Sex – the Myth and the Cult of the Virgin Mary*, London: Vintage Books [2]2000

Messiah

The claim that Jesus of Nazareth is 'the Messiah' has been a central feature of Christianity from the beginning, but it masks some complex questions. What did the first Christians mean when they identified Jesus as 'the Messiah'? How large a part did messianic expectation play in the imagination of Jesus' Jewish contemporaries? How many of them were searching for a messiah, and what sort of a messiah were they searching for? The identification of a particular person as the Messiah is central to Christianity, but has not (with some important exceptions) been a preoccupation of Jews in medieval or modern times. Was this true also of the Jews of Jesus' day? How far did the early Christians reshape the concept of Messiah in the light of their experience of the death and resurrection of Jesus?

Jesus

Origins and background

'Messiah' is a rough transliteration of a Hebrew word *mashiach*, which simply means 'anointed' (person or

thing). Persons and things could be anointed with oil, as a sign that they were set apart for God's service. Priests and prophets might be messiahs, anointed ones, in this sense, and Isaiah 45.1 describes even the Persian king Cyrus as the anointed agent of God's purpose ('my messiah, whom I have chosen'), but the concept of messiah became Paul attached particularly to the kings of David's line. David himself was anointed by Samuel (1 Samuel 16.13), and according to the words of an anthem composed by Handel in 1727 and sung ever since during the anointing of every English king and queen at their coronation, 'Zadok the priest and Nathan the prophet anointed Solomon king'.

The majority of references to 'messiah' are specifically to the Davidic monarch: he is the one who is chosen and anointed to rule over God's people, and to guarantee their prosperity (cf. Psalm 89). However, with the end of the Davidic line with the exile in Babylon after the capture of Jerusalem in 587 BCE, and the failure of attempts to re-establish it after the return from captivity, the idea of the Messiah so to speak took on a life of its own. Without an earthly king to attach themselves to, the messianic texts of the Old Testament could be read in new ways: as relating to a future messianic age, for example, rather than to a present or future messianic person, or as relating to an earthly Jewish king who would rule over a people liberated from Roman rule.

It is not easy to trace the precise development of messianic ideas at the time of Jesus. Intense images of future hope took a variety of forms in Jewish literature Resurrection and politics in the period between the Old and New Testaments, in texts which are often hard to date, and  p. 661 whose relationships to one another are not easily determined. Rabbinic texts are later, but often embody older levels of tradition; they are a potentially important source, p. 845 to be handled with care. The Dead Sea Scrolls give a fascinating insight into the beliefs of the community that established itself in Qumran, and had adherents in various towns in Palestine, but the members of the Qumran sect were often (as in their attitudes to the temple in Jerusalem) at odds with most of their contemporaries. From our various sources, we know that there were those whose hope was for a political leader, a this-worldly figure who would re-establish the Jewish monarchy, and there were those who looked for a more cosmic redemption, at the hands of a figure not wholly contained within this-worldly categories. Texts associated with Qumran speak of a Teacher of Righteousness, and of a final confrontation between forces of light and forces of darkness, but it has not been possible to draw a definite connection between such beliefs and early Christian ideas. What was initially thought to be a reference to a 'pierced Messiah' in the Scrolls (4Q285) caused considerable interest, but closer inspection showed the phrase to be active rather than passive: it is the Messiah who is doing the piercing (in the context of the final battle?).

We are left with the impression, then, of a wide-ranging group of messianic ideas, which different Jewish groups could develop in different ways. Among those Jews who did make messianic ideas central to their hopes we must include the earliest Christians. Paul quite regularly refers to Jesus as Christ, the Greek equivalent of Messiah, indeed the use of the title becomes so routine that it rapidly takes on the character of a personal name. In the Gospels, Jesus' claim to messiahship is prominently sustained, though in an interesting way. In the synoptic Gospels, no sooner has his messianic identity been acknowledged than Jesus commands that it be kept secret.

This motif of the 'messianic secret' is clearly linked to another motif, the contrast between the speed with which expelled demons recognize who Jesus is, and the obtuseness with which the disciples fail to recognize who he is, until the turning-point of Peter's confession at Caesarea Philippi (Mark 8.27–33; Matthew 16.13–23; Luke 9.18–22). William Wrede, who analysed the motif of the 'messianic secret' in a famous book of 1901, held that it was a way of bridging the uncomfortable gap between what the earliest church claimed about Jesus (that he was the Messiah) and what Jesus had actually claimed about himself (no such thing). Wrede's analysis seems oversimplified now, but it does alert us to the difficulty of establishing how Jesus understood his own life and work, and of relating that to the understanding that the church came to have of him after his resurrection.

The titles used of Jesus in the Gospels, like 'Son of man' and 'son of God', have been exhaustively examined. To a reader of the Gospels who has absorbed, often unconsciously, the way that these titles function in Christian tradition as claims to messianic and divine identity, it can come as a surprise to discover how many questions surround them. What Aramaic phrase did Jesus use of himself that might lie behind the Greek phrase 'the son of the man' in the Gospels? Was it, on his lips, anything more than a characteristic way of referring to himself as an individual human being – 'me, this mother's son'? At what point and how did it come to be associated with the 'one like a son of man' in the heavenly judgement scene of Daniel 7, and what in any case does the complex imagery signify? In the process of Christian reflection on the death and resurrection of Jesus a phrase which he may well have used of himself in relation to his humanity has become an important statement of his divinity. So too with the acknowledgement by the centurion standing at the foot of the cross that Jesus was 'the Son of God' (Mark 15.39; Matthew 27.54). In origin, this idiom need not have meant more than 'a truly good or godly person', but the phrase acquired new levels of meaning in Christian reflection.

Given the originally close connection between the idea of the Messiah and the Davidic kingship, it would not be surprising to find that some of Jesus' Jewish contemporaries who had a specifically messianic hope were looking for a royal and political figure to redeem Israel in a political sense, a particular human being who would restore the autonomous kingdom of Israel. There are clues in the Gospels that some of Jesus' contemporaries thought that he might be that person: for example, genealogies trace his descent from David; a blind beggar asks for help, repeatedly calling Jesus 'son of David' (Mark 10.47), and the crowds who welcome Jesus into Jerusalem cry out, 'Hosanna! Blessed is the kingdom of our father David that is coming' (Mark 11.9) or 'Hosanna to the Son of David' (Matthew 21.9). It helps to explain the sequence of his trial if these political ideas are in the background of the narrative. In 132–5 CE, the second Jewish revolt against Rome was led by the insurrectionist Simon Bar-Kokhba, who presented himself as a messianic figure. His name ('son of the star') is an allusion to the star mentioned by Balaam in his prophecy in Numbers 24.17 ('a star shall come forth out of Jacob, and a sceptre shall rise out of Israel'), which also appears with a messianic connotation in the story of Jesus' birth (Matthew 2.1–12). However, it seems very unlikely that Jesus saw himself as a messiah in this sense. A few scholars have maintained that he did, but the zealot way of political violence is too much at odds with the general tenor of Jesus' teaching and person as presented in the Gospels to make this a convincing key to the way in which he understood himself. We should perhaps look instead to his words over the bread and the cup at the Last Supper, with their evocation of the new covenant of Jeremiah 31, or to his silence before Pontius Pilate, with its echoes of the suffering servant of Isaiah 52.13–53.12.

It is impossible to establish with certainty how many of these associations were in Jesus' own mind, and how many of them are connections that the earliest Christians made concerning him: there is no intrinsic reason why the second should not have grown organically out of the first. At any rate, it is in references like this, and in memories of his characteristic ways of speaking, that we may trace the roots of the Christian construction of Jesus as the Messiah, which developed in hindsight after the resurrection. He is of David's line, and the royal traditions of the dynasty of the anointed gather round him, but his kingdom is beyond as well as within this world. He is a divine as well as a human figure. He redeems his people by his suffering and death; he is the suffering servant of Isaiah, making atonement for the sins of the people. He will come again at the end, to be the instrument of God's final judgement. Every element of this composite has a background that can be traced with greater or lesser difficulty in the various Judaisms of Jesus' day, but the whole is a distinctively Christian construction. The dynamic that drives it is the Christian community's response to the overwhelming experience of the risen Christ, and it is this that continues to legitimate the construction for Christians.

Having identified Jesus as Messiah in this Christian sense, Christian preaching and apologetic began to single out those elements of Old Testament prophecy that supported the construction. This process of selection and arrangement can be seen clearly in Matthew's use of Old Testament proof texts, and is fully developed in Justin Martyr's *Dialogue with Trypho the Jew* (mid-second century CE). Indeed, the Old Testament came to be read by Christians as principally a prophetic account of the Messiah who was to come. The fact that this is a peculiarly Christian reading explains an unhappy near-constant in Christian attitudes to Jews. Successive generations of Christians have tended to blame Jews for failing to recognize a truth that ought to have been obvious, that Jesus is the Messiah they have been searching for, and is the fulfilment of the messianic prophecies of the Old Testament. Jews are therefore 'perverse' or 'obtuse', and should be treated accordingly. In reality, Jews have had quite different principal concerns – to order life according to the Torah, to shape the Jewish community as a people holy to God, to establish a secure Jewish homeland – and they have not typically brought to their Bible the messianic interests that Christians have brought to their Old Testament.

Judaism and Christianity

A minority of 'Messianic Jews' have in modern times absorbed the Christian messianic agenda entirely. Other Jewish groups, like the seventeenth-century followers of Shabbati Zvi or the twentieth-century Lubavicher Jews, have followed a Messiah, but not one who operates within anything like a Christian theology of redemption.

Jewish Christianity

p. 665

Christian messianism has always included the expectation that the Messiah will return to execute God's final judgement upon the world. This expectation has been particularly intense in the currents of Christian millenarianism which have flowed more or less strongly throughout Christian history, and there are various individuals who have claimed to be, or whose followers have claimed them to be, the returned Messiah. On the basis of Revelation 13, this returned Messiah is sometimes paired with Antichrist (i.e. anti-Messiah), the false Messiah, who is able to mislead people precisely because he looks so much like the true Messiah. Just as their followers have identified some as the true Messiah, their opponents have identified others as Antichrist. The identification of the Pope in particular as Antichrist is a recurrent feature of extreme Protestant polemic from the time of the Reformation onwards. Although Antichrist may appear to belong wholly to the realm of Christian imagery, there is in fact a background to this figure in both Jewish and pagan thought in late antiquity.

ANDERS BERGQUIST

William Horbury, *Jewish Messianism and the Cult of Christ*, London: SCM Press 1998 and 'Antichrist among Jews and Gentiles' in Martin Goodman (ed), *Jews in a Graeco-Roman World*, Oxford and New York: OUP 1998; Sigmund Mowinckel, *He That Cometh. The Messiah Concept in the Old Testament and Later Judaism*, Nashville, TN: Abingdon Press 1954 and Oxford: Blackwell 1956; William Wrede, *The Messianic Secret* (1901), Cambridge: James Clarke 1971

Methodism

Methodism has its origins in an eighteenth-century renewal movement within the Church of England. Unlike many other renewal movements, however, it does not primarily grow out of doctrinal differences. There are particular doctrinal concerns but no special teachings, and there is no new or different definition of the church. Methodism, even after it eventually became a church of its own (first in 1784 in the United States of America), agrees with the Church of England's definition that the church is the gathering of the faithful where the word of God is preached and the sacraments are administered. This definition matches the understanding of the classical Protestant traditions as well.

Church

p. 303

Preaching

Sacraments

Nevertheless, Methodism broadens the horizons of the church, and the concern for renewal that was characteristic of early Methodism and its founder, John Wesley (1703–91; Wesley remained an Anglican priest all his life), was far-reaching. Perhaps most characteristic is the fact that this renewal was worked out in the context of the lives of the common people who were often overlooked by the establishment church. In the social transformations of early industrializing England Wesley, and to an even larger degree certain groups among the later Methodists called 'Primitive Methodists', saw their mission in maintaining connections with those who had to endure much of the pressures of the new world. They did this not only by preaching to them but also by living in solidarity with them. The Methodist concern for renewal included 'holiness of heart and life', seeking to unite both 'knowledge and vital piety'. Methodists saw God's grace manifest in people's lives and in the world being transformed, and they sought to support this transformation further by developing communal structures through the formation of small groups and accountable communities. At the same time, they also encouraged fresh engagement with the Bible and the traditions of the church; in Wesley's own case this included a broad concern for the early traditions of the church. The name 'Methodist', originally a nickname designed to make fun of the disciplined lifestyle of John and Charles Wesley and some of their friends, captures these concerns.

Industrial revolution

Doctrine, practice and worship

The creative spirit of Methodism, which appreciates and appropriates a broad range of traditions and forms, can be seen in its doctrine, practice and worship. Wesley's initial response to the need for doctrinal guidance of the maturing Methodist movement was to publish a number of his sermons in an open-ended collection, the so-called Standard Sermons. Doctrine developed through sermons differs from credal statements and confessions in that it is more responsive to the pressures of real life and cannot easily be pressed into a rigid system. Doctrinal reflection in this approach is developed quite literally 'on the way'; the Standard Sermons were written over the course of several decades and reflect the varying concerns of the Methodist movement.

This approach displays a theological vigour that is characteristic of Methodism, even though it has at times been forgotten. John Wesley drafted 25 Articles of Religion (abridged from the 39 Anglican Articles of Religion and thus in basic agreement with the stream of traditions in the church which these Articles reflect) and a Sunday Service (abridged from the Anglican Book of Common Prayer) only on the occasion of the institution of an autonomous Methodist church in the United States. In this context, Methodism became a church largely for pragmatic reasons, because there was no established church structure like the Church of England through which the sacraments would be administered. The contemporary United Methodist Church still recognizes these Articles among its doctrinal standards, together with the Confession of Faith of the Evangelical United Brethren Church (another church body with Methodist roots which united with the Methodist Episcopal Church in 1968 to create the United Methodist Church), 53 of John Wesley's Standard Sermons, his *Notes Upon the New Testament*, and the so-called General Rules.

All these elements must be seen in relation, and Methodism has been at its best when it has held them in constructive tension in the midst of its ongoing involvement in the pressures of real life. This characteristic Methodist concern for doctrine as embedded in the challenges of real life is also reflected in the structure of the Book of Discipline of the United Methodist Church, which begins with a historical statement that tells the history of the church up to the present. Only within this context does it move on to its Constitution and Doctrinal Standards.

Since there is no hard-and-fast distinction between doctrine and life in the Methodist tradition, its doctrinal standards contain guidelines not only for faith but also for practice. Wesley's Standard Sermons have a practical bent, and the three parts of the General Rules sum up the spirit of the early Methodist movement when they encourage all who seek 'the power of godliness' to do no harm, to do good, and finally to 'attend upon all the ordinances of God'. This last part includes attendance in worship, at holy communion, prayer, and other activities that are commonly seen as more specifically related to the church. Nevertheless, the three parts belong together and broaden the perspective of what the church is. The General Rules reflect the nature of Methodism and describe a way of life in resistance to society's ills (including for instance 'drunkenness', not merely as a moral but as a social problem which ruined many working-class families, slave-holding, and 'the putting on of gold and costly apparel').

In the history of Methodism, there has been a constant struggle between such alternative lifestyles and the adherence of the mainline to the status quo, reflected in a number of splits within Methodism. In the USA the Methodist Episcopal Church split over slavery in 1844, and the Protestant Methodist Church split off because it rejected bishops in favour of a more democratic church government. In England, the Primitive Methodists split off because they wanted to maintain closer connections to the working classes.

Like its doctrinal emphases, Methodist worship has also been shaped by its history and its context. John Wesley's liturgy, the so-called Sunday Service, steeped in the Anglican tradition and the Book of Common Prayer, was quickly set aside in the United States, as the needs of the developing nation and of the frontier took over. Nineteenth-century revival style had little in common with Wesley's Sunday Service. Early Methodist worship in the United States focused strongly on preaching and was mostly led by laity, not clergy. Both men and women shared in leadership. An ordained minister would be present often not more than once a year since ministers (the so-called 'Circuit Riders') travelled great distances from church to church.

At the same time, however, such freedom to shape worship did not exist in many of the overseas missions. In the Methodist missions in Africa, for instance, strict supervision was the norm. The missionaries, both from Britain and the United States, controlled the patterns of worship, including dress and other cultural matters, and saw no harm in imposing their own respective traditions. In recent decades Methodism has once again developed worship styles that reflect its context, and the heavy hand of the missionaries has subsided. In the US, in a climate of renewed liturgical interest, Methodism has rediscovered the older patterns of worship informed by the Anglican Book of Common Prayer. In this context, holy communion has again assumed a more central place, partly reflecting Wesley's own emphasis on frequent communion. Nevertheless, in contrast to many other mainline denominations, no overarching pattern of worship exists in Methodism as a whole. Methodist forms of worship continue to be worked out in relation to the particular contexts and histories where Methodism finds itself.

Despite these differences, however, Methodism generally reflects Wesley's own concern for a broadening of the horizons of the church. This can be seen, perhaps most significantly, in a broad understanding of the means of grace. Wesley expands the traditional list of the means of grace (holy communion, prayer, scripture) to include works of mercy, a move that reflects the way in which he lived his life. Works of mercy are, therefore, not merely good deeds but also channels through which Christians receive God's grace. In this sense, Methodist concern for people at the margins is closely related to its worship. While it is understood by most denominations that worship is the place where members partake of the means of grace, the Methodist heritage allows Christians to understand more clearly that works of mercy offer a similar opportunity. Consequently, social involvement and works of mercy broadly conceived are integral parts of the Christian life whereby, as in worship, Christians maintain and refresh their relation with God. Wesley himself went so far as to claim that if there is a conflict between works of piety and works of mercy, the latter are to be preferred. A similar attitude is also reflected, of course, in the threefold structure of the General Rules, which pulls together life and worship in its own way.

Grace

Worship

Characteristic of Methodism as a whole, therefore, is a strong and broad doctrine of grace. God's grace is encountered not only in worship but also in Christian practice. Grace surrounds the whole of individuals' lives, starting long before they become Christians ('prevenient' = 'going before' grace), and does not rest even once they have become Christians (justifying grace is followed by sanctifying grace). This strong emphasis on God's grace also gives a particular twist to the Methodist understanding of holy communion. Participation in this sacrament is open not only to members of the church (as is the case in most other denominations) but also to those 'who earnestly repent of their sin and seek to live in peace with one another', as the liturgy of the United Methodist Church puts it. God's grace is at work in all of humanity, and all who seek to respond to it are welcome at the holy communion table.

Great Awakening

Eucharist

Mission

Organization and character

Organization

The authority to make decisions for the church as a whole lies not with individual leaders or churches but

Wesley's Chapel, City Road, London

with a collective body called 'Annual Conference' which meets once a year and includes all ordained clergy and usually an equal number of representatives of the laity in shared responsibility. Methodism in all of its various manifestations understands itself as a connexional church. From early times the term 'connexion' has been used to describe Methodism as a church linked through circuits and districts (the Methodist Church's rough equivalents to parishes and dioceses in the Anglican Church). Despite Wesley's own rather authoritarian leadership, this emphasis on connexion resembles the early organization of the Methodist movement in groups of bands and classes, which encouraged the responsible participation of each member. Even those churches in the Methodist tradition which have bishops understand themselves as connexional churches. The United Methodist Church, for example, understands itself as a connexion of annual conferences, where bishops function as general superintendents. United Methodist bishops are elected and consecrated to office, rather than ordained. They have no special sacramental role and their task is to represent the connexion. The ultimate authority in Methodism is to be found in the connexion itself. This emphasis on the connexion has also implications for the self-understanding of individual churches and congregations. Congregations are not autonomous but are accountable to the connexion, a fact that is reflected even in the property laws. The connexion rather than an individual congregation owns church property.

Having begun as a movement in England and as a church in the USA, Methodism is now global. While early Methodist mission in England was strongly related to those who experienced the pressures of early industrialization, and early Methodist mission in the United States was geared to the needs of the frontier, in the nineteenth century the interests of Methodist mission shifted overseas. Not surprisingly, the overseas missions of British Methodism followed in the footsteps of the British empire, particularly in Africa, and the overseas missions of United Methodism, strongly rooted in the United States, were often present where the interests of the US economy were at stake, particularly in Latin America. Both movements also had their own respective interests in different places in Asia. Today, there is increasing recognition of this history, and many of the Methodist churches in Asia and Latin America have chosen to become independent. These moves towards independence and autonomy have often been in resistance to various forms of dependency on the mother churches, but a certain dependency remains, particularly where there is continued monetary support.

Furthermore, conflicts still occur where vestiges of the two types of Methodism, one British and the other US-orientated, encounter each other abroad. Nevertheless, the balances are slowly shifting and Methodism is growing particularly in Africa and Asia, while its numbers in England and the US show some decline. Statistically, the United Methodist Church in the United States is still the numerically largest church in Methodism with 8.5 million members, down from 11 million in 1968. Outside the US, United Methodism claims 1.3 million more members. The next largest Methodist church outside the United States is the Korean Methodist church with 1.3 million members. In England, Methodists now number less than half a million members. In Australia and Canada Methodism underwent a different development when it entered into unions with Presbyterian and Congregationalist churches, forming the Uniting Church of Australia and the United Church of Canada. The diverse Methodist churches come together in the voluntary association of the World Methodist Council; this encourages multilateral dialogue and ecumenical relations with other church traditions.

The social background of Methodism is quite diverse. In its early beginnings, Methodism in England found strong resonance among those who were not served by mainline Anglicanism, particularly those pressured in various ways by early industrialization such as workers and artisans. In the United States, Methodism's success was likewise not with the establishment but with pioneers on the frontier and others who had to re-orientate themselves in a new world and who would not necessarily go back to the established churches from which they came. In its early days Methodism would even include African Americans and slaves (in the late eighteenth century 20 per cent of Methodists in the United States were black). As Methodism became more main stream, however, it lost many of its connections to the grassroots of society and moved into the middle class. In the United States of the nineteenth century, African Americans were pushed into forming separate Methodist churches, which still exist today, such as the African Methodist Episcopal Church (with 3.5 million members the largest African American Methodist church), the African Methodist Episcopal Zion Church and the Christian Methodist Episcopal Church. Other splits from the mainline Methodist church that resisted the move into the middle class include the Wesleyan Methodists, the Free Methodists, the Salvation Army, and other churches related to the Holiness movement such as the Church of the Nazarene. Offshoots of the missions of an upwardly mobile Methodist Church in the United States, many of the Methodist churches in Asia and Latin America reflect its middle-class orientation. In Africa, on the other hand, Methodism may be closer to remaining a church of the people, even though it often includes membership from the lower middle classes.

African American Christianity

Holiness movement

In the light of its history it is not surprising that Methodism has a natural inclination towards ecumenical relationships. The Constitution of the United Methodist Church, for instance, contains a clear commitment to ecumenical relationships and many Methodist churches are among the members of the World Council of Churches. In an ecumenical climate, however, which has at times been more geared to disembodied doctrinal discourse than to practical solidarity among the churches, Methodism may have a special contribution to make. While Wesley was indeed engaged in debates about doctrinal differences, for instance with a particular Calvinist form of the doctrine of predestination, his own approach to ecumenical relations was eminently practical. In his famous Letter to a Roman Catholic he concludes: 'If we cannot as yet think alike in all things, at least we may love alike. Herein we cannot possibly do amiss. For of one point none can doubt a moment: God is love; and he that dwelleth in love, dwelleth in God, and God in him (1 John 4.16).' There is a sense in the Methodist traditions, all the way back to Wesley's own ministry, that ecumenical relationships, including ecumenical conversations about doctrine, need to be built 'from the bottom up', from the perspective of shared Christian action. While all Christians can be expected to agree that God is a God of love and grace, each denomination might be seen as exploring particular ways to live with this insight. Perhaps it is as Christians join hands in the midst of the pressures of real life that ecumenical relations can be worked out in such a way that they do not eradicate what is distinctive of each tradition. In this case, Methodism may be seen as a step in the right direction.

Ecumenical movement

JOERG RIEGER

📖 *The Book of Discipline of the United Methodist Church*, Nashville, TN: The United Methodist Publishing

House 2000; Ted A. Campbell, *Methodist Doctrine: The Essentials*, Nashville, TN: Abingdon Press 1999; Theodore Jennings, *Good News to the Poor: John Wesley's Evangelical Economics*, Nashville, TN: Abingdon Press 1990; Albert C. Outler (ed), *John Wesley*, New York: OUP 1984; Joerg Rieger and John Vincent (eds), *Methodist and Radical: Rejuvenating a Tradition*, Nashville, TN: Kingswood Books 2003; John Wesley, *Explanatory Notes Upon the New Testament*, London: Epworth Press 1950; *John Wesley's Sermons: An Anthology* ed Richard P. Heitzenrater and Albert C. Outler, Nashville, TN: Abingdon Press 1991; Charles Yrigoyen, Jr, and Susan E. Warrick (eds), *Historical Dictionary of Methodism*, Lanham, MD and London: Scarecrow Press 1996

Middle Ages

What are we to think of the millennium from 500 CE to 1500 CE, give or take a century on either end, and more specifically about Christianity in the Middle Ages? Why have people found it meaningful to lump those ten or so centuries together and think of them as something distinctive? Typically, the concept of 'Middle Ages' has served, and continues to serve, as a particularly useful foil for people's understanding of the faith of their own day.

Reformation

Protestantism
Humanism
Renaissance
Scholasticism
Bible

The idea of Middle Ages is old, but it is of the essence of the idea to be more recent than the period itself. For the idea was invented specifically to designate something that was over and done with, that is by definition not ours any longer. It made its first appearance in the writings of the Italian humanists of the fourteenth and fifteenth centuries, who ushered in the Renaissance. These writers were enamoured of the culture of ancient Rome, the spirit of which they aspired to recover from what they saw as a long period of neglect and obscurity. It was as a kind of necessary corollary to this programme of revival or rebirth of antiquity that the humanists began therefore to speak of the centuries that intervened between the ancient decline of the Roman empire itself on the one hand and the present day on the other as an entity in their own right, a 'middle' period. The great early humanist Francesco Petrarch (1304–74), who was among the first to think in these terms, actually considered himself to be still inhabiting the wretched time 'in the middle' between what he called the 'happy age' of antiquity and what was for him still only a hypothetical future revival of that age. But slightly later humanist writers like the historians Leonardo Bruni (1369–1444) and Flavio Biondo (1388–1463) began to situate themselves confidently in the new age, lauding the renewal of the cultural virtues of antiquity that they saw under way, and regarding the period that separated their own society from that of antiquity, the middle or intervening period, as something finished. It was Biondo who began to speak of that middle period as roughly a millennium in length, thus giving it more or less precise limits and potentially a shape of its own. Although it was not until the seventeenth century that scholars such as the German historian Christoph Cellarius (1638–1707) would attempt to write the history of this *medium aevum* or 'Middle Age' (which is oddly pluralized in English but remains singular in German and French) in its own right with its position in the universal history of the world, nonetheless the idea of the Middle Ages was in place already the end of the fifteenth century – a product, as we see, of the self-awareness of the Renaissance.

That idea of the Middle Ages as something finished and done with – as the period bounded by antiquity on one side and our own modernity on the other – has lasted since the time of the humanists. Evidently people continue to believe that antiquity and modernity are themselves discrete realities. But perceptions of what sort of realities these are have often shifted.

The early humanists, though they were certainly Christian in religion, were not particularly thinking about religion when they called the Middle Ages to mind. It was not until the sixteenth century that the idea of Middle Ages acquired a specifically religious focus. This was largely the work of the Protestant Reformers. Humanism, indeed, had continued to be a strong force and had shaped the minds of many of these Protestants. In particular the reform-minded humanist Erasmus of Rotterdam (*c.* 1469–1536) prepared the way for the Protestants – though he himself never embraced their cause – by developing the idea that Christian faith in its pure form had belonged to the era of classical antiquity, and that it was not only classical culture that had become obscured in the intervening 'middle' period, but the true Christian faith as well, and thus the faith itself needed to be revived or recovered. For Erasmus, the major villain in this story was the scholastic thought of the later Middle Ages, which, in his view, smothered the simple faith of the New Testament with hair-splitting and dry speculation. So he produced an edition of the Greek New Testament in 1516 that used the tools of humanistic literary study to establish the text with pointed disregard of the scholastics and other medieval traditions of biblical interpretation, in a way that closely paralleled his own and other humanists' attempts to re-establish contact with ancient pagans like Cicero or Seneca by a direct and informed encounter with their works.

Taking their cue in part from Erasmus, whose Greek New Testament they made much use of, the Protestants raised the cry that the true biblical faith had to be recovered from the obscurity to which the medieval centuries had consigned it. For them the evil of the Middle Ages was in the church itself; the Reformers regarded the papacy, especially as it had behaved from about the late fifth century onwards, as the chief agent of corruption, and routinely identified the Pope with the biblical figure of the Antichrist. In the Protestants' view, of course, it was their own movement that marked the end of this papal tyranny. The millennium of the Middle Ages emerged then more or less clearly in learned Protestant literature – most famously in the *Centuries of Magdeburg* (1559–74), a multi-volume Protestant collection of documents aimed at exposing the church's infamy, century by century – as the long epoch when the true gospel languished in obscurity. What the Middle Ages had left behind, in this view, was the formative period of the church, its golden age; and conversely to leave the Middle Ages behind was to open the possibility of restoring that golden age.

But though the dream of recovering the early church's faith from medieval obscurity had power for the Protestants, there was actually something more fundamental at stake for them in their approach to the Middle Ages. This was the question of the proper relation between scripture and 'tradition'. For the Protestants, it was absolutely fundamental that only scripture could be God's true and dependable revelation; everything else in the history of the church was only 'tradition', and as such highly fallible. Thus for them even the admirable early church was not right all the time, and what it was right about was neither more nor less than its adherence to the scriptures; and by the time of the Middle Ages that adherence had been lost, in the Protestant view. Protestants gave various answers to the question of when the loss had occurred – that is, when 'tradition' had gone seriously wrong. The Lutherans and Calvinists were content to place the moment well after the Emperor Constantine's embrace of Christianity in the fourth century, while the Anabaptists, who faced persecution from the governments of their own time, placed it earlier. But for all of them, the history of the 'tradition', approached in the light of scripture, was something to be cautious of.

The negativity of the Reformation approach to the Middle Ages remained deep in the Protestant grain, and in a certain sense deepened over time. By the eighteenth century, Enlightenment thinkers had joined the Protestants in disparaging the medieval church, adding their own emphasis on the superstition and ignorance that supposedly dominated the medieval centuries so as to make them, in Voltaire's celebrated opinion, unworthy of any attention except as an object of scorn. Protestants, for their part, did not share the religious scepticism that informed such a view and regarded Voltaire and his ilk with suspicion. Yet even so the Enlightenment trends affected Protestant thinking profoundly. For in the resurgence of personal piety that marked that period in Protestant history, in part indeed as a reaction to Enlightenment scepticism, the individual person became the locus of authority in matters of religion, and the authority of the church in its own right declined, in a way that paralleled the Enlightenment philosophers' emphasis upon the individual's exercise of reason – and in that very vaunting of the individual, Protestants tended to lose track of the value of tradition, the collective experience of the Christian past. The result has been that from the eighteenth century on, much Protestantism, especially in the powerful pietistic strain usually called 'evangelical', has heeded Voltaire's advice and pointedly ignored the Middle Ages altogether (and often the earlier Christian centuries as well, excepting only what is recorded in the books of the New Testament).

So it has been of the essence of the idea of the Middle Ages to designate something – a culture, a world, a religious outlook – that is not our own any longer. But not everyone has viewed this as a good riddance. Roman Catholics, from the early days of the Reformation onwards, have always had a more positive attitude to medieval Christian tradition. Already soon after the appearance of the *Centuries of Magdeburg*, the Catholic scholar Caesar Baronius (1538–1607) wrote his massive *Ecclesiastical Annals* to refute its anti-papal claims and earned such stature within the church that he came close to being chosen pope himself; and from Baronius' time onwards a continuous train of Roman Catholic historians has taken up his legacy, embracing and defending the whole history of their church, including its medieval history, against Protestant attacks. Then in the nineteenth century, interest in rehabilitating the Middle Ages began to extend far beyond Roman Catholic circles, as an important thrust of the Romantic movement. The novelist Walter Scott (1771–1832), for example, and the art critic John Ruskin (1819–1900), among many others, expressed deep longing for the chivalric values of the feudal society of the Middle Ages, which they imagined as preserving social order and human dignity in pointed contrast to the impersonal and utilitarian industrial society of their own time. This was also the heyday of the revival of Gothic architecture, of which we see evidence all around us still. This Romantic medievalism (as it has come to be called) also had broad influence in religious circles, not only among Catholics but also among other Christians. Among Anglicans, for instance, the Oxford Movement emerged in the mid-nineteenth century, assertively to reclaim pre-Reformation Christian traditions that the Reformers had scorned, and at about the same time a similar impulse emerged in some Protestant circles, for example in the writings of the American theologian John Williamson Nevin (1803–86), against the individualistic evangelicalism that had become the dominant form of Christianity there.

Papacy

Authority
Evangelicals
Tradition

Lutheranism
John Calvin
Constantine's 'conversion'
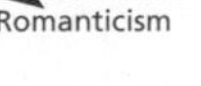
Anabaptists
Romanticism
Architecture
Enlightenment

Oxford Movement
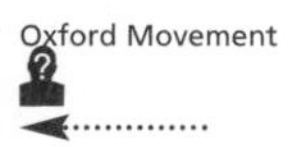

In the twentieth century and now in the twenty-first, attitudes to the Middle Ages have become more complex, amidst a great burgeoning of research into every aspect of the period. Nonetheless, one senses that the place of the European Middle Ages in people's imagination still depends upon its otherness, its being not ours – and that that otherness still elicits in people, variously, the impulses of both rejection, on the one hand, and longing, on the other, that we can discern in our forbears. In either event, it remains a natural course of action when we think about our own age to set up the Middle Ages, in their essential non-modernity, as a backdrop against which to see its contours.

Council

As we have seen, the idea of the Middle Ages is European in origin and application. Can it still be a useful interpretative concept when we try to break out of the Western-centredness that has characterized much writing about the history of Christianity and try instead to approach the Christian religion in more global terms? Did world Christianity also have its Middle Ages?

In the strict sense, perhaps no, for the Renaissance and Reformation that both developed the concept of the Middle Ages and themselves stood to mark its end-point were European events through and through. Although it is true that Christianity in its European forms has had no monopoly on reform or renewal, there were no Reformations or Renaissances in non-European Christianities in the sense of movements whose very self-awareness made necessary the idea of Middle Ages.

Culture

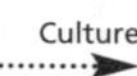

But if the reasons for placing the end-point of the European Middle Ages where we do made no analogously clear mark on the history of Christianity outside Europe, the same is not true of its start-point. For the end of antiquity, the crucial event for conceptualizing the beginning of the Middle Ages of Christian Europe, is arguably the decisive event in the history of Christianity as a world religion as well.

It is true that in many ways antiquity did not end at all. Roman emperors continued to reign from Constantinople until 1453; the classical inheritance continued strong even in the West; and the phrase 'late antiquity' has entered historians' vocabulary to refer to the vigorous culture of the era that straddled the border between antiquity and Middle Ages. Nonetheless, the Roman empire shrank drastically in size between the fifth and the eighth centuries. Not only did the Western portion of empire essentially disappear, but also much of the Eastern portion fell to the forces of Islam within a few decades of the death of Muhammad (632). For Christianity in its full geographical scope, there was an enormous significance in leaving the era of the old Roman empire behind. For it had been in almost every sense the child of that empire, having experienced most of its growth and development, within the *limes*, the imperial borders. Although some Christians had been present beyond those borders – in Persia, in the remoter areas of Britain – they formed very small subsets of the whole. When the emperors themselves embraced the faith, beginning in the fourth century, it seemed to Christian observers such as Eusebius of Caesarea to be God's own next major move in the history of salvation past the incarnation itself. It was in this Roman context that the Great or Catholic Church had emerged, with its authority firmly invested in bishops who claimed to be the heirs of Christ's apostles; it was the bishops who took the first decisive steps to define the faith, and established the content of the Bible; and when the emperors joined the faith, it was under their protection and support – the authority of the empire itself – that the Councils of Nicaea and Constantinople and Ephesus and Chalcedon were held to express the faith definitively. All of this happened within the matrix of the Roman empire.

Orthodox churches
Roman empire

But when that matrix receded – that is, at the moment when we traditionally say that the Middle Ages was under way – the Christian movement had to adapt to multiple other cultural contexts. The transition to a new situation was gradual, to be sure, and cannot be pinpointed in any given moment, yet Augustine's *City of God*, written between 413 and 427, gives the moment its purest expression, even if Augustine himself would not have been aware of all of the implications of what he was saying. In that book, Augustine countered pagan critiques by adducing evidence to show that Christianization of the empire had not made the world worse, but at the same time he also tacitly criticized the established Christian view that it had made the world better. The world will have its ups and downs and cultures will come and go, but though the 'heavenly city' of the saints has members currently residing in the 'earthly city' of human society, its welfare pointedly does not depend upon the welfare of that earthly city nor, conversely, does it assure the earthly city's welfare, even though its citizens are bound to love their earthly neighbours. Thus Augustine disengaged Christianity from the culture in which it had grown up, and in that sense wrote, in effect, a constitution for Christianity as a world religion, not intrinsically connected to any particular human society, though potentially present in all human societies.

Thus the Middle Ages made Christianity a world religion, which took root now in various very separate and distinctive cultural settings in distinct ways. In the East, we have the typical forms of Christianity that emerged in the aftermath of the Council of Chalcedon. These were the non-Chalcedonian ('Monophysite') churches of Syria, Egypt, Armenia, Ethiopia, who were already at odds with the Chalcedonian orthodoxy of the Roman emperor in the East in the wake of Chalcedon and then, with the advent of the rule of Islam under which, by and large, they found themselves from the mid-seventh century onwards, a decisively separate Christian tradition. Similarly, the East-Syrian Christian tradition, which had always existed in Persian territory and was never closely tied to the Roman empire, became all the more separate after Chalcedon when it retained the Antiochene ('Nestorian') view of christology, and then likewise was to live its life under the rule of the Islamic caliphs – and was to spread across Asia to India and China. The East Romans (Byzantines), for their part, became just one Christian expression among many, early on almost exclusively among Greeks and then, from the tenth century onwards, expanding their influence north to the Slavs.

What about an end-point, then, to the Middle Ages in this broader, even global, sense? Perhaps we can still locate the end-point at roughly the same time as for the Middle Ages of Europe, but for different reasons. For what marked the end – though perhaps it would be more accurate to speak of a partial eclipse – of the world Christianity of the medieval period was the emergence of a new kind of world Christianity in the sixteenth century, which quickly became a dominant force. This was the great modern world mission movement launched from the West, which would eventually establish churches everywhere of the Western types, Roman Catholic at first and later Protestant as well.

But now at the beginning of the twenty-first century, the old medieval form of world Christianity – the heirs of which have in fact maintained their traditions – seems remarkably contemporary. For reasons that have to do with both the successes and failures of modern missions from the West, world Christianity is now struggling to transcend the forms and legacies of those missions, as the old Christendom of the West becomes a smaller and smaller part of the whole. The inexorable motion of every part of that whole is now towards 'indigenized' or 'inculturated' Christianities. So it is that historians now escort those medieval non-Western Christianities out of the shadows into conspicuous places of their own on the stage of Christian history. Thus once more, though in a new mode, the idea of the Middle Ages helps us see both what we have lost and what we desire.

JOHN W. COAKLEY

Peter Brown, *The Rise of Western Christendom*, Oxford: Blackwell 1996; Norman Cantor, *Inventing the Middle Ages*, New York: William Morrow 1991; Alice Chandler, *A Dream of Order: The Medieval Ideal in Nineteenth-Century English Literature*, Lincoln, NE: University of Nebraska Press 1970; Wallace K. Ferguson, *The Renaissance in Historical Thought*, Boston: Houghton Mifflin Co. 1948

Middle East, Christianity in the

Christianity is a Middle Eastern religion. That fundamental fact is worth stating, as Christianity today is so strongly identified in popular perception with 'Western' society and culture that any involvement in the Middle East is seen as an intrusion – an illegitimate trespassing – into domains which 'belong' to others.

Christology

Situated at the meeting place of Europe, Asia and Africa, the region is of religious and political significance to hundreds of millions of Jews, Christians and Muslims worldwide. At several times in the last 2000 years (including the present time) it has been the focus of intense international interest. Inevitably there are many different perspectives on events there, making generalizations difficult. All of this has impacted heavily on the Christian presence in the region.

The regions listed in the Acts of the Apostles as being represented in Jerusalem on the Day of Pentecost include North Africa ('the parts of Libya near Cyrene'), modern-day Turkey ('Cappadocia, Pontus and Asia, Phrygia and Pamphylia') and substantial parts of the area now known as the Middle East ('Parthians, Medes and Elamites, residents of Mesopotamia, Judaea ... Egypt ... Arabs ...', 2.8–10). The list gives an immediate impression of an ethnic and linguistic diversity that has in many respects continued to the present day. The modern blanket term 'the Arab world' often misleadingly disguises the fact that different histories and traditions are found in the Middle East. A modern Iraqi, for example, is proud of his country's Mesopotamian heritage, as the modern Egyptian is of his country's Pharaonic civilization.

Mission

Although the New Testament concentrates on the westward spread of Christianity, principally through the ministry of the apostle Paul, there was a simultaneous expansion north, south and eastward, into regions that can broadly be described as Armenian, Coptic and Syriac-speaking. A substantial part of this expansion lay outside the Roman empire into Mesopotamia and Persia (now broadly Iraq and Iran). Despite periods of persecution, the church generally made steady headway. Varying proportions of the local populations became Christian, and the translation of the scriptures and liturgy into the diverse vernaculars began. By the early seventh century CE there was a substantial Christian presence throughout the Middle East, including the Arabian peninsula.

Christendom
Paul
Roman empire
Persecution

p. 122

The pre-existing ethnic and linguistic diversity interacted with two other factors. The first was political. The Middle Eastern provinces lay on the frontier of the Roman empire (and its continuation based at Constantinople from the fourth century onwards). In many of them there was a desire for independence from Roman/Byzantine rule. At times this took on a religious aspect expressed in

Council
Pilgrimage
Jesus

the second factor, which was theological. Following the cessation of the persecution of Christians in the Roman empire, a series of councils sought to address theological disputes by producing definitive theological formulae to which all were expected to subscribe. There were genuine theological emphases and differences. Often it was difficult to find precise Semitic equivalents for Greek terms. But frequently rejection of a formula favoured by the emperor was a way of expressing a desire for political as well as ecclesiastical independence. The result was a regrettable fragmentation of the Christian presence into a variety of communities with different linguistic, liturgical and theological allegiances. The healing of these divisions was prevented by what has been the defining experience of all Middle Eastern Christianity – the rise of Islam.

Initially the Arab invasions of the seventh century CE simply introduced a Muslim Arabic-speaking ruling class into the existing situation (rather like the Norman élite in Anglo-Saxon England following the Battle of Hastings). In most places Christians continued to form the majority of the population for many centuries and provided a large proportion of the educated and professional services. However, whereas in medieval England the Normans gradually adopted the language of the people they had conquered, the reverse happened in the Middle East. The existing vernaculars gradually gave way to Arabic as increasing numbers of the population became Muslim.

Reasons for the gradual absorption of the majority of the populations by Islam are complex. At times of armed conflict (*jihad*) there were undoubtedly some forced conversions through fear. More significant in the long run seems to have been the status afforded to Christians in a Muslim society. The technical term is *dhimmi.* Christians were recognized by the Qur'an as a 'people of the book' and given a certain degree of protection, but essentially they were second-class citizens, denied many of the legal and social privileges afforded to Muslims, and always vulnerable to attack at times of tension. The simple act of conversion to Islam would remove all these disabilities. Conversion of a Muslim to Christianity, on the other hand, would in most cases result in death for the convert and the person who had sought to win him for Christ. At times Christians could reach high positions of influence at the courts of the Caliphs, but the cumulative result of the general situation was that the Christian population diminished over the centuries. The process was hastened by certain events (see below). Eventually most Christians even abandoned their own language for Arabic, the ancient vernacular surviving only as the language of worship.

What is remarkable is that, after nearly one and half millennia of such a situation, there is any Christian presence in the Middle East at all.

The 'internal' dynamic of Christian-Muslim co-existence in the Middle East has been profoundly affected by 'external' factors. The Church in the Middle East has suffered from two contradictory approaches from the rest of the world church (and that of Western Europe in particular). These are neglect and interference.

External Christian interest has been in the Middle East as the lands of the Bible. The tradition of visiting the region on pilgrimage can be traced back at least as far as the fourth century CE. When conditions allow, hundreds of thousands of Christians from around the world visit the 'Holy Land' to see the places where Jesus walked. Such an approach is perfectly understandable, but it is often accompanied by an attitude that sees the intervening centuries as largely irrelevant. The modern pilgrim wants to get in touch with the time of Jesus. Everything else is potentially a distraction. This includes the existing indigenous Christian community, which is usually not understood by visitors, and seems alien and at best peripheral to their perfectly laudable intentions.

This is not simply a result of self-preoccupation on the part of Western Christians (though that strongly exists). Christianity as a faith is less dependent on a relationship with its homeland than is, for example, Islam. For the Muslim, pilgrimage to Mecca is one of the five pillars of Islam and something to be striven for. For most Christians around the world visiting the holy sites carries no such sense of strong obligation. Such a visit is seen as an 'extra', not an essential. Most of world Christianity would continue unaffected if the Christian presence were totally lost from Israel/Palestine. Worldwide Islam, by contrast, would find it impossible to conceive of the removal of a Muslim presence from the Arabian peninsula.

The practical effect of the current prevailing Christian attitude is indifference to the situation of their co-religionists in the Middle East. Sympathetic attitudes occasionally acquired on a pilgrimage to the area are seldom translated into a burning commitment to the indigenous Christian population. Where strong commitment does arise, it is usually directed elsewhere (see below). An example may be seen in the occupation of the Church of the Nativity in Bethlehem by Palestinian fighters in 2000. Though there were some international protests, the whole worldwide Christian population was not moved to action and protest. Had the Ka'aba in Mecca been occupied by armed Christians, the Muslim response around the world would almost certainly have been very different.

Middle Eastern Christians often see themselves as neglected by modern Western governments, which afford religious freedom to Muslims in their own countries, but seldom insist on similar rights for minority Christian groups in Muslim countries. Saudi Arabia, for example, is an ally of Britain and the United States, but will not tolerate any of its citizens becoming Christian, or the building of churches. Understandably, the Christian cause in the Middle East is seen as being sacrificed to the West's strategic and diplomatic needs.

This neglect of the Middle Eastern Christian presence and heritage by the wider Christian community can be illustrated in many other areas. There have, for examples, been accusations that Israeli archaeologists have deliberately removed Christian artefacts at certain sites, leaving only ancient Israelite ones, as part of a policy of obliterating anyone else's legitimate links with the Holy Land. If true, such action parallels the documented destruction by the Turkish authorities of Armenian Christian buildings in eastern Turkey, to destroy the evidence that there was ever a Christian presence there. Most Western Christians are unaware of such issues.

Paradoxically, the indigenous Christian communities of the Middle East have probably suffered more from interference than neglect. Often, such interference has been well intentioned; at other times less so.

From the surrender of Jerusalem to the armies of the Caliph Omar in 638 there has been a Christian desire to see the places where Jesus and the apostles lived and taught restored to Christian control. Attempts to achieve this have broadly fallen into two categories – the military and the missionary – with very often a considerable overlap between them.

In the centuries immediately following the Arab conquests of the Middle East there were numerous campaigns by the Christian emperors in Constantinople to recover the lost provinces. The emperors saw themselves as the protectors of the Christians under Muslim domination. It was their duty, therefore, to try either to liberate them, or at least to alleviate their situation by diplomacy. Much of the Christian population shared the same assumptions: one day they would be set free. Such a situation inevitably resulted in the Christian population falling under the suspicion of disloyalty to Muslim rule, and made the community an inevitable target for reprisals whenever the military or political situation deteriorated.

A far stronger abiding legacy, however, has been left by the crusades of the eleventh, twelfth and thirteenth centuries. Theoretically, these began as an attempt to assist the Byzantine emperor to regain Jerusalem and its environs in the aftermath of the anti-Christian campaigns of the Caliph Hakim. Very quickly, however, they degenerated into a 'land-grab' by Western European rulers and adventurers. The Western record of atrocities towards the Muslim population is well documented – as is the frequently more chivalrous attitude of the Arab leadership. Middle Eastern Christians were used to a degree of diversity (the different jurisdictions frequently co-existed) of which those coming from the monolithic Latin-rite West had no experience or sympathy. Frequently, Eastern Christians were treated no better by their Western co-religionists than their Muslim neighbours. This lack of understanding and sympathy towards Eastern Christianity was brought home horrifically when the Fourth Crusade in 1204 sacked Constantinople itself, committing terrible atrocities and hastening the final collapse of the Christian empire in the Eastern Mediterranean.

The Crusades were thus a double disaster for Middle Eastern Christians. They resulted in the final severance of contact and communion between Eastern and Western churches, while ironically at the same time increasing the suspicion and hostility with which they were viewed by their Muslim rulers and neighbours. From the Middle Ages onwards the decline of Christianity in the region quickened. The involvement of the Great Powers in the region in the early twentieth century following the collapse of the Ottoman empire and the resultant fact that it was the West that 'created' the modern map of the Middle East (by determining the boundaries of the new Arab states and by sanctioning the creation of a Jewish state) perpetuated a sense of external control, motivated by Western self-interest.

The legacy of this continues down to the present. Warnings of a 'crusade' against Islam form an important strand in the rhetoric and self-understanding of radical Muslim groups such as Al-Qaida. Any Western involvement in the region (such as the Gulf Wars of 1991 and 2003) has to be accompanied by strenuous efforts by Western politicians to avoid 'crusade' language and imagery. At the same time such involvement risks compromising the indigenous populations still further in the eyes of their neighbours. Opposition to the American occupying forces in Iraq in 2003 included the call to 'drive out the infidel'. Hatred of foreign Christians can easily be transferred to local Christians.

The situation has been further complicated over the years by the missionary motive. At times attempts to win Muslims to Christ have been independent of military and political activities, at others they have accompanied them. The Roman Catholic Church has been active in the Middle East for centuries. While there have been genuine attempts to convert Muslims, much Roman Catholic activity has, however, been directed at bringing indigenous Christian populations under papal obedience. This has resulted in schisms in most of the ancient churches of the Middle East. In the case of the Church of the East, the greater part of the community actually transferred its allegiance to Rome and now forms the Chaldaean Church (which is particularly strong in Iraq). Most of the other churches now have a Roman Catholic counterpart – Armenian Catholics, Coptic Catholics, Syrian Catholics, etc.

Mission

Crusades

Eastern-rite Catholic churches

Protestant missions in the Middle East, while motivated more strongly by the desire to evangelize, have usually had little success in winning Muslims. Instead, members of indigenous Christian communities have tended to transfer their allegiance to the missionaries' communities, sometimes despite the discouragement of the missionaries themselves. Thus from the nineteenth century there have been small groups of Protestants (often designated 'Evangelical') in all parts of the Middle East – the Coptic Evangelical Church, for example.

p. 1152 Evangelicals

A parallel example of transferred focus is provided by Anglican attempts in the first half of the nineteenth century to win Jews. While the first Anglican bishop in Jerusalem was a converted rabbi, very soon the church began to attract Arab Orthodox Christians, and recent Anglican bishops of Jerusalem have been Palestinian Arabs.

More recently again, proselytism by a range of small, often American-based, groups has added to the confusion. Such groups often see the emergence of the state of Israel as a fulfilment of biblical prophecy and have little understanding of or sympathy for the ancient Christian communities, whom they see as having failed in their evangelistic task.

Arguably, then, despite the frequently sacrificial and heroic lives of the missionaries, well-intentioned Christian evangelism from outside the region has also been a disaster for Middle Eastern Christianity. It has further divided the already fragmented Christian communities. Most recently, it has brought into existence groups with little sympathy for indigenous culture or for the possibility of expressing Christianity within it. It has tended to strengthen in Muslim minds the identification between Christianity and Western culture and political perspectives.

Is it possible for an Arab to be a Christian? For some Muslims the identification between Islam and Arab identity is so strong that Arab Christians are regarded as traitors to Arab identity. The late nineteenth and early twentieth centuries saw a great deal of discussion on this topic, as the collapse of the Ottoman (Turkish) empire raised the question of what form its successor states should take. Some Middle Eastern Christian writers argued for states with a broadly secular basis, in which Muslim and Christian would be equal before the law. This was part of the original intention of the now discredited Ba'ath party in Iraq. As an improvement on the *dhimmi* status forced on Christians by *sharia* law, it had obvious attractions. Later developments in the Middle East have tended to obscure this indigenous Christian commitment to Arab identity and self-determination. If the Middle East is about to enter a further period of change and reconstruction, the position and contribution of the Christian population of the region needs to be carefully addressed.

Orthodox churches

The emergence of the modern state of Israel has created theological as well as political difficulties for Arab Christians. The Bible speaks of God favouring Israel against the Philistines. This has all too often been glibly equated with a 'God is on the side of the Israelis against the Palestinians' stance by certain (usually American) Christian groups. Use of the Psalms was easy when 'Israel' meant 'the people of God' in the sense of the Christian church. Now that a state called Israel actually exists (and is hostile to much of Arab culture and history), and Palestinians can be equated with the biblical Philistines, there can be a feeling that even the language of worship has been compromised for Arab Christians.

Before looking at the individual countries, it is important to remember that many of the nation states of the Middle East – Syria, Iraq, Saudi Arabia, etc. – are only of twentieth-century origin. They were created following the collapse of the Ottoman empire. The Western Great Powers who were largely responsible for defining the borders were influenced by many factors, including religion and ethnicity. The reality is, however, that the region is not composed of distinct groups in separate geographical areas. Instead, many different religious and ethnic communities have lived alongside one another for centuries. The proportions of the various groups have varied from place to place, but most groups are represented throughout the whole region. The imposing of borders on such a situation inevitably created anomalies. A clear example of this is provided by the (non-Christian) Kurds. The modern boundary between Turkey and Iraq cuts through an area where the Kurds form the majority of the population, with the result that the Kurds not only feel aggrieved at not having their own homeland, but live under two different governments, one Turkish and one Arab, neither of which reflects their own language and traditions.

The situation is further complicated by population movements, both voluntary and involuntary, that have taken place. The Assyrians, for example, migrated to Iraq following the Great War. The Lebanese Civil War of the 1970s resulted in significant displacement of Christians, as did the Turkish invasion of Cyprus in 1974.

The result is that Christians of the same ecclesiastical tradition may find themselves in different countries – for example, the Syrian Orthodox Church, whose members are now mainly divided between Turkey, Iraq and Syria. The different states may have different policies towards their Christian minorities. Even if the theoretical constitutional position is similar, the actual situation on the ground may differ greatly. The volatility of much of the region also makes generalizations dangerous.

All of this makes a country-by-country survey difficult and misleading.

A further immense complication is the lack of authoritative statistics. This is characteristic of the region generally, but especially so in relation to numbers of

Christians. Muslim governments often wish to play down the numbers of Christians in their countries. Equally, Christian communities themselves, after centuries of keeping a low profile, are often reluctant to advertise their presence lest they invite attacks at times of tension.

The presence of expatriate Christians working in the Middle East is an additional factor to take into account. These form a significant proportion of the Christian population in the Gulf States – and officially are the only Christian presence in Saudi Arabia. It is only in these contexts that the Anglican and Protestant presence rises above about 2%, and can be as high as 50%. It is important to note the existence of this element of the Christian presence in the Middle East, but its non-indigenous and frequently transient nature should not be minimized.

Egypt. Of all the Middle Eastern countries, Egypt has the largest number of Christians. By far the majority of these – estimated to be not less than 5 million in number – are Copts, belonging to the ancient indigenous church. The Roman Catholic (including various Eastern Catholic rites) and Protestant communities are much smaller, each numbering between 100,000 and 150,000, and together comprising only 5% of the entire Christian population of Egypt. Historically significant is the Orthodox Patriarchate of Alexandria, with a substantially Greek leadership. This has jurisdiction over Orthodox throughout Africa, but in Egypt itself members number only a few thousand. In total Christians make up perhaps 15% of the entire population of Egypt.

Lebanon. Lebanon has the highest proportion of Christians of any modern Middle Eastern country, with approximately 40% of the population, though the actual numbers (slightly over a million) are smaller than in Egypt. The largest single group are the Maronites, who number approximately half a million. The Orthodox and their Roman counterpart, the Melkites, together comprise nearly another half million, while the Armenian Orthodox are the next largest group with approximately 200,000. All the communities suffered substantial disruption during the Lebanese Civil War, which began in 1975, and substantial emigration of Christians has taken place.

Syria. Christians form just under 10% of the population of Syria, with approximately 800,000 faithful, half of whom are Orthodox of the Patriarchate of Antioch, whose headquarters are now in Damascus, the Syrian capital. There are also significant numbers of Armenians, Melkites and Syrian Orthodox.

Jordan. As in Syria, the largest Christian community (rather over 50%) is the Chalcedonian Orthodox, though in Jordan they belong to the Patriarchate of Jerusalem, rather than Antioch. Latin-rite and Eastern-rite Roman Catholics make up nearly 40% of the Christian constituency, with Anglican and Protestant groups numbering less than 3%. The Christian population as a whole is only about 5% of the entire population of Jordan.

Palestine. Palestinian Christians have suffered along with their Muslim neighbours in the warfare and displacements that have taken place since the establishment of the state of Israel in 1948. Together they now make up less than 4% of the population in the West Bank and Gaza, and the proportion is steadily falling. Most (50%) belong to the Orthodox Jerusalem Patriarchate. There is a significant Latin-rite Roman Catholic presence, and most Oriental Orthodox groups are represented. Anglicans and Protestants make up about 6% of the Christian presence.

Israel. The Christian presence in the state of Israel has declined sharply in recent decades and in places its very survival is in doubt. Instead of living communities, there is a very real danger that it will be reduced to what Archbishop Carey of Canterbury called a 'theme park' presence. Trapped between militant Islam and aggressive Israeli policy, Christians have felt themselves hated on all sides. Very many have emigrated. Those that remain represent a wide range of allegiances, with the Eastern-rite Catholics and the Orthodox of the Jerusalem Patriarchate comprising the majority.

Coptic Christianity ◀

Iraq. The more easterly situation of Iraq is reflected in the fact that over 70% of its Christian population is of the East Syrian tradition, rather than the Orthodox or Oriental Orthodox families. Of these, the vast majority are Chaldeans in communion with Rome and numbering perhaps 200,000. The Church of the East itself has about 45,000 members. Syrian Orthodox and Syrian Catholics have significant communities, as do the Armenians. The entire Christian population, however, only comprises about 2% of the total.

Middle Eastern Christianity challenges the strong identification of Christianity with Western European/North American culture, lifestyle and attitudes. It is ironic that Christian traditions that stress the authority and centrality of the Bible tend to be ignorant and dismissive of Christians who have lived continuously since New Testament times in the lands of the Bible, who use the languages of the Bible, and whose culture is far closer to that of the Bible than their own. A reassessment of much of Western Christianity in the light of this perspective could be extremely healthy. It could also inform contemporary debate on, for example, the role of women and homosexuality.

Bible

Women in Christianity
Homosexuality

CHRISTIANS IN THE MIDDLE EAST AT THE MILLENNIUM

Country	*Population*	*Roman Catholic*	*%*	*Independent*	*%*	*Protestant*	*%*	*Anglican*	*%*	*Orthodox*	*%*	*Non-Christians*	*%*
① Armenia	**3,520,000**	160,000	**4.5**	28,000	**0.8**	12,000	**0.3**	0	**0.0**	2,756,493	**78.3**	563,507	**16.0**
② Iran	**67,702,000**	16,400	**0.0**	80,000	**0.1**	13,800	**0.0**	1,200	**0.0**	202,290	**0.3**	67,388,310	**99.5**
③ Iraq	**23,115,000**	268,000	**1.2**	139,485	**0.6**	1,400	**0.0**	200	**0.0**	139,485	**0.6**	22,566,430	**97.6**
④ Israel	**5,122,000**	140,000	**2.7**	85,000	**1.7**	19,000	**0.4**	2,200	**0.0**	46,878	**0.9**	4,828,922	**94.3**
⑤ Jordan	**6,669,000**	48,000	**0.7**	77,000	**1.2**	9,822	**0.1**	7,200	**0.1**	131,330	**2.0**	6.395,648	**95.9**
⑥ Lebanon	**3,282,000**	1,395,000	**42.5**	118,000	**3.6**	20,000	**0.6**	200	**0.0**	535,000	**16.3**	1,213,800	**37.0**
⑦ Syria	**16,125,000**	325,000	**2.0**	100,000	**0.6**	30,040	**0.2**	4,000	**0.0**	798,289	**5.0**	14,867,671	**92.2**
⑧ Yemen	**18,112,000**	6,000	**0.0**	8,000	**0.0**	4,476	**0.0**	180	**0.0**	12,000	**0.1**	18,081,344	**99.8**

Independent is used here for Christians independent of historic, organized, institutional, denominational Christianity.

Source: David B. Barrett, George T. Kurian and Todd M. Johnson (eds), *World Christian Encyclopedia*, New York: OUP [2]2002

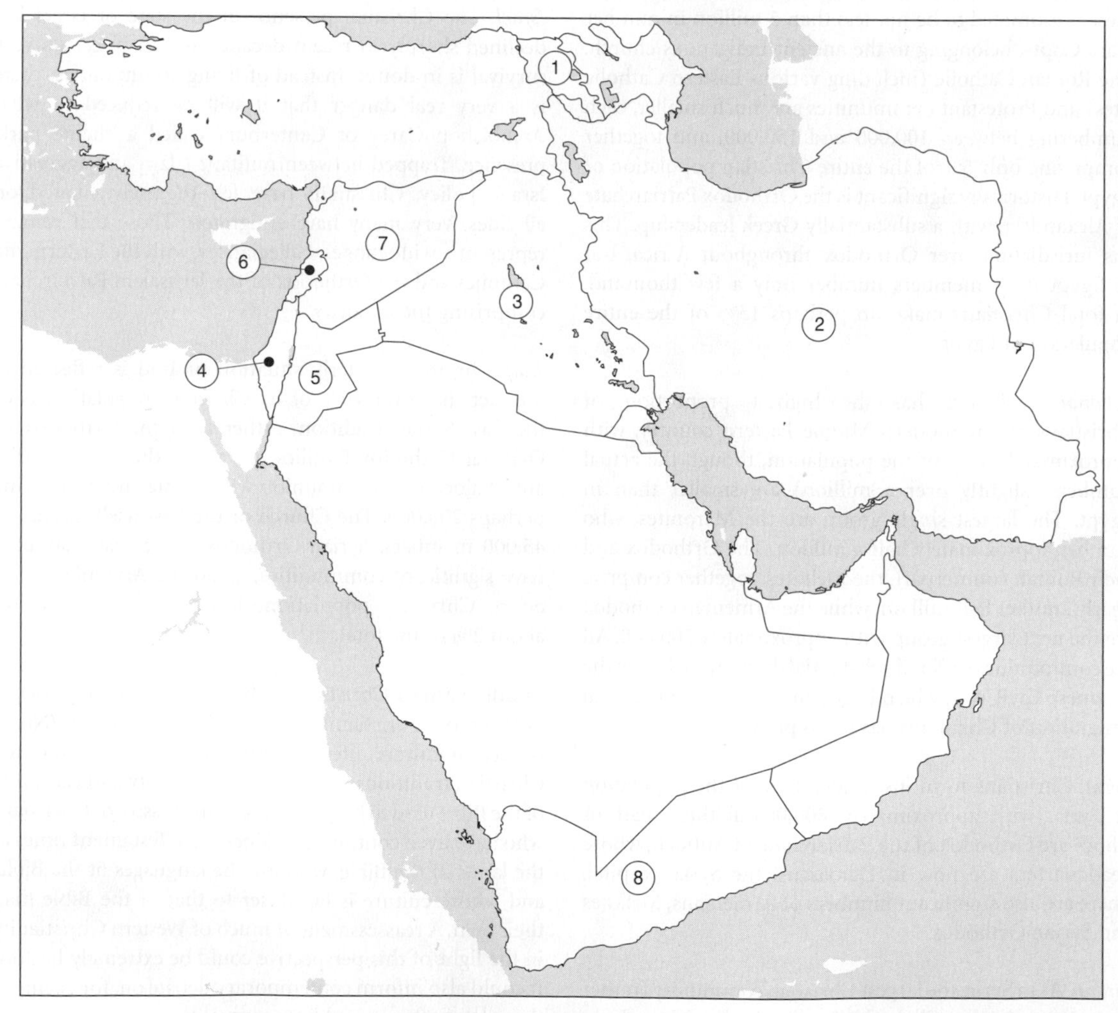

As the de-Christianization of Western culture continues, the experience of the Middle East may suggest some adjustments to be made by Western Christians – both in terms of their own expression of Christianity, and in terms of living as minorities in dominant cultures which are either not particularly supportive or may even be actively hostile. Middle Eastern Christians are survivors. The rapidly shrinking and increasingly beleaguered Christian communities in Europe could well learn some valuable lessons.

Middle Eastern Christianity challenges the individualism of the Western churches. The West tends to stress the one-to-one relationship of the believer with Christ. The Eastern churches have additionally a consciousness of the community's standing before God. The individual's faith is important, but it is understood in a wider context. This is a perception that might be profitably explored in the West, where even traditionally Christian families are losing their young people at an alarming rate.

Perhaps the greatest lesson would be to cease to view Middle Eastern Christianity as marginal, and to see it instead as central in the global understanding of Christianity. Sensitive support to enable the Middle Eastern churches to maintain their presence and witness in their own terms might help to ensure the survival of Christianity in its homelands.

JOHN FENWICK

Aziz Atiyah, *A History of Eastern Christianity*, London: Methuen 1968; Kenneth Cragg, *The Arab Christian: A History in the Middle East*, London: Mowbray 1992; Norman A. Horner, *A Guide to the Christian Church in the Middle East*, Eikhart, IN: Mission Focus 1989; Bat Ye'or, *The Decline of Eastern Christianity under Islam: From Jihad to Dhimmitude*, London: Associated University Presses 1996

Ministry and ministers

Ministry is one of the most frequently used words in descriptions of the activities of the churches. A cursory look on the internet immediately produces a youth ministry, a music ministry, a stewardship ministry, a social ministry, a health ministry, a deaf evangelism ministry, a family ministry, a small groups ministry, a counselling ministry and even a finance ministry – the list is seemingly endless. Churches in modern society are very different from the small groups of Christians who formed churches in the apostle Paul's day, but Paul, too, produces similarly comprehensive lists: to one is given the utterance of wisdom, to another faith, to another gifts of healing, to another the working of miracles, to another prophecy, to another the ability to distinguish between spirits, to another various tongues, to another the interpretation of tongues (1 Corinthians 12.8–10). Ministry in the broadest sense can be used of any work done by a member of the Christian community on behalf of that community.

However, the term 'minister' in the church is generally understood to refer to members of the clergy, men and women who believe that they have been called to special service in the church and have been officially accepted and set apart by the church through a public service of ordination. Not all Christian bodies have ordained ministers – the Religious Society of Friends (Quakers), for example, does not – and in the evangelical and Pentecostal traditions the emphasis is more on the spiritual gifts of the individual than on any form of church order; however, ordained ministers are characteristic of the majority of churches.

Christianity in Europe ◄

Quakers

There are various forms of ordained ministry: the Roman Catholic Church and the Orthodox churches, along with the Church of England, the Old Catholic churches and others, have an order based on the offices of bishop, priest and deacon, which go back to the early church. Some churches arising out of the Reformation, or standing in that tradition, have retained elements of this, though rejecting the term 'priest' because of its association with the view of the eucharist as a sacrifice, which they could not accept. Some Lutheran churches have bishops, and bishops were also appointed at a very early stage in the Methodist church in America. Other churches broke away more sharply: churches in the Calvinist tradition adopted a presbyterian form of ministry ('presbyter' means elder): the Presbyterian church takes its name from this, and, for example, the Baptist churches and the Reformed churches have a similar form of ministry.

Training for the ministry

Those offering themselves for ordination, like those seeking to join a religious order, are expected to feel that they have been called, that they have a vocation, and this sense of vocation is tested by the church in which they want to serve. Then follows training for the ministry. No trace of any special institutions for training the clergy can be found in the first centuries of the church; the training of priests was practical and personal, young men and boys assisting the bishop and priests of their church in discharging their duties and learning in the process. Pagan schools offered a liberal education and there were famous catechetical schools at Alexandria and Edessa, but these were meant to provide general, not vocational, Christian teaching. Augustine of Hippo had a house near his cathedral where clergy lived together and he would ordain only those who were willing to share this common life; the model was imitated elsewhere, in Italy and Gaul,

Religious orders

Schools

Education

Paul ◄

Monasticism

and these episcopal schools spread widely; monasteries also trained clergy to work in the world (so-called 'secular' clergy) as well as future members of their orders. By the eleventh century the schools were growing into universities, where famous teachers taught theology, philosophy and canon law. However, the negative aspect of this was that the universities drew the best teachers away from the cathedral schools and led to their decline; moreover only around 1 per cent of the clergy could attend university and generally speaking the average priest had little training, if any. Stories of illiterate or incompetent priests are legion.

University

Canon law

Reformation

The Reformation in the sixteenth century, with its emphasis on the need to return to the biblical sources, among other things produced a well-educated clergy, knowledgeable in Greek and Hebrew: in villages throughout Protestant lands for centuries to come the clergyman would be the best-educated citizen, and education would be a key to his authority. Seminaries were formed in many university towns and cities: the Evangelische Stift in Tübingen, founded in 1536, is one of the most famous. Harvard College, founded in 1636, was established for the training of clergy and became the prototype for American seminaries.

Patronage

The training given to Protestant clergy challenged the Roman Catholic Church to do the same, and so education and the training of clergy became an important issue at the reforming Council of Trent: a decree called for the establishment of a seminary in every diocese; the first seminary to open was the Roman Seminary in 1565. However, external factors in a variety of countries made it possible to implement the decree only to a limited extent. The first American seminary opened in Baltimore in 1791. The Second Vatican Council planned for major and minor seminaries, the minor seminaries providing education in arts and sciences, the major seminaries spiritual, pastoral and academic training for the priesthood.

Council

Attempts were made to found Anglican theological colleges in the seventeenth and eighteenth centuries, but the first permanent foundation was Edinburgh Theological College in 1810, followed by The Queen's College, Birmingham in 1828. A series of other colleges were founded during the nineteenth century. These represented a marked improvement on a situation in which men without any formal training, particularly the younger sons of landed families, could be ordained to a living offered by a patron – a practice attested to, for example, by the novels of Jane Austen.

The Orthodox churches also have seminaries for training priests. Despite a decline in their number because of the drop in candidates for the ministry, there are still seminaries and colleges all over the world.

Ordination

Ministers are given their status through ordination, but the forms of this differ. For example in Presbyterian and Reformed churches, new candidates are ordained by

APOSTLE

Apostle means 'someone who is sent' (from the Greek *apostellein*), an envoy bearing the authority of the one who sent him. Jesus is once called an apostle, in the letter to the Hebrews (3.1), but otherwise the term is used of those sent by him. It is a favourite word of the evangelist Luke: the second of the two books he wrote is called the Acts of the Apostles. For him the apostles are the twelve disciples chosen by Jesus from the beginning, and when their number is reduced to eleven by the death of Judas, a successor is appointed by drawing lots (Acts 1.15–26). The qualification is to be 'one of the men who have accompanied us during all the time that the Lord Jesus went in and out among us, beginning from the baptism of John until the day he was taken up from us'. Twice in Acts, Paul and Barnabas, who do not meet this requirement, are called apostles (14.4, 14). Elsewhere, though, for Luke Paul is notably not an apostle.

Paul himself in his letters differs vehemently: 'Am I not an apostle? Have I not seen Jesus our Lord?' (1 Corinthians 9.1). He claims to be an apostle like the other apostles. He also includes James the brother of the Lord among the other apostles (Galatians 1.19). The term clearly became a token of honour, but precisely who were apostles and who were not remains unclear. Nor are matters made easier by the way in which 'apostle' is now used of those who brought Christianity to a particular country, like Boniface 'the apostle to the Germans' or Patrick the 'apostle of Ireland'.

Creed

The earliest period of Christianity extending to the hypothetical date of 'the death of the last apostle' is now often referred to as the *apostolic age*, and the authors of a collection of writings contemporaneous with the New Testament or written soon after it are known as the *apostolic fathers*. Although now not thought to go back to the apostles, the Apostles' Creed also bears witness to the need to derive authority from the apostles, as does the *apostolic succession*, the belief that bishops today have been ordained in a constant chain of laying on of hands from the apostolic age. Documents attributed to the apostles but probably dating from the fourth century are the *Apostolic Canons*, the *Apostolic Church Order*, and the *Apostolic Constitutions*, all collections of church law. The *Apostolic Tradition*, an account of traditional practices in worship, is thought to have been written by Hippolytus of Rome in the third century.

Rather different from these are the terms *Apostolic See* to denote the Diocese of Rome, because of its associations with Peter and Paul, and *Apostolic Delegate*, an official appointed by the Pope to serve abroad.

existing presbyters, and in some churches ordination is administered by representatives of the congregation. But in the churches standing in the Orthodox and Catholic traditions (including the Anglican Church), ordination can only be administered by a bishop, who lays his hands on the candidates in a solemn service, praying for the gift of the Holy Spirit to them. The bishop is consecrated in a similar service by an existing bishop, accompanied by other bishops to represent the wider church. Collectively bishops are referred to as the episcopate, and a system of ministry to which bishops are integral is called episcopal, both terms from the Greek word *episkopos*, meaning overseer.

In some churches, great importance is attached to the belief that the chain of consecration of bishop by bishop extends right back to the apostles themselves, which is called the apostolic succession. The Roman Catholic Church and the Old Catholic churches, the Orthodox churches and the Anglican Church believe themselves to be standing in this succession, but the belief is not reciprocated in every case: the Roman Catholic Church does not recognize Anglican ordinations.

Just as the forms of ordination differ, so does the understanding of what is conferred by ordination. In the Reformation tradition ordination is formal appointment to service, but in the Orthodox and Catholic traditions (Roman Catholic and Catholic Anglican) it is something more. Ordination is thought to give the person ordained a permanent quality, known as 'character', which is indelible and remains for life.

In the Orthodox and Roman Catholic traditions only men are eligible to be ordained; in the Anglican Communion women may be ordained to the priesthood, and in some member churches women have been consecrated bishop, but this is a controversial matter. Candidates for ordination in the Roman Catholic Church must be celibate; in the Orthodox churches married men may be ordained but must not remarry if widowed, and unmarried candidates must remain unmarried. Only the unmarried or widowed may become bishops. In the Reformation churches both men and women are accepted for ordination.

The three orders of ministry, as they are called, are deacon, priest and bishop: in churches in the Catholic tradition ordination as deacon is followed relatively soon by ordination as priest. The deacon cannot celebrate the eucharist or give absolution, the two main functions of priests and bishops in worship. These three orders are often referred to as 'holy orders'; ministers would use 'clerk in holy orders' (the word clergy derives from clerk) in stating their occupation. They can be addressed as Reverend, Right Reverend (a bishop) or Most Reverend (an archbishop); as 'Father' or as 'Holy Father' (the Pope). Although there are only the three orders of deacon, priest, and bishop, by virtue of their responsibilities the clergy can take on a variety of other titles: archdeacon, archimandrite, cardinal, metropolitan, patriarch. Protestant churches are more sparing with titles, preferring to use terms like pastor or just plain minister.

Origins of the ordained ministry

Not only do the Orthodox and Catholic traditions (Roman and Anglo-Catholic) affirm the apostolic succession, but they also claim that the three orders of ministry in their churches – bishop, priest and deacon – were instituted by Jesus himself. In the light of the knowledge we now have that assertion is much more difficult to substantiate.

One problem is that there is so little information available from ancient sources about the origins of the threefold ministry, indeed of any form of ordained ministry at all. Scholars are generally agreed that the hierarchy of bishops, presbyters/priests and deacons had developed in essentials by the second half of the second century CE. By the beginning of the third century a single bishop stood at the head of each community, with presbyters and deacons under him, and this order was generally believed to be the will of God and in accordance with the tradition of the apostles. But precisely how all this came about is difficult to discover.

Jesus

p. 850

Jesus gathered around him a group of twelve disciples to symbolize the twelve tribes of Israel, but rather than indicating that they would be ministers in a future church, he told them that they would sit on thrones judging the twelve tribes of Israel (Luke 22.30); and while the Gospel of Matthew (and that Gospel alone) contains a famous saying of Jesus about Peter as the rock on which he will build his church (Matthew 16.18), there are no instructions as to the form that church is to take. To discover the orders of ministry in the very earliest church, we can only draw whatever inferences we can from the letters of Paul, the earliest source.

p. 851

Paul mentions ministries, but basically his churches are communities of individuals exercising different gifts that complement one another. There is no mention anywhere of presbyters in those letters that are undisputedly attributed to Paul; what we do find in the opening words of his letter to the Philippians are *episkopoi* (Greek overseer, hence the term episcopal, relating to the bishop) and *diakonoi* (deacons, usually understood to mean servants or ministers). However, *episkopoi* are mentioned in the plural: this is not the one bishop in charge of a diocese that emerges later (referred to as the monarchical episcopate). The office of deacon is generally thought to have developed out of the task of caring for the poor; Acts 6.1–6 mentions a group of seven, headed by Stephen, who became the first Christian martyr, as having been

p. 898

HOW TO ADDRESS THE CLERGY

It is by no means obvious how one should describe formally, address or write to the various members of the clergy. Here are some of the recognized usages:

Office	*Formal title*	*Written address*	*Formal verbal address*	*Social verbal address*	*Description*
			Roman Catholic Church		
The Pope	His Holiness the Pope	Your Holiness, or, Most Holy Father	Your Holiness	Your Holiness	His Holiness, or, The Pope
Cardinal Archbishops	His Eminence the Cardinal Archbishop of	Your Eminence	Your Eminence	Cardinal	His Eminence, or, Cardinal Smith
Cardinals	His Eminence Cardinal Smith	Your Eminence	Your Eminence	Cardinal	His Eminence, or, Cardinal Smith
Archbishops	His Grace the Archbishop of, or, The Most Reverend Archbishop	My Lord Archbishop, or, Most Reverend Sir	Your Grace	Archbishop	His Grace, or, The Archbishop of
Bishops	The Right Reverend John Smith, Bishop of, or, The Right Reverend Bishop Smith (for Irish bishops, 'Most Reverend')	My Lord, or, My Lord Bishop	My Lord	Bishop	His Lordship, or, The Bishop
Clergy	The Reverend John Smith, or, The Reverend Father Smith (Reverend without a Christian name or Father is incorrect)	Dear Father Smith	Father	Father Smith	Father Smith, or, Father John
			Religious		
Abbot	The Right Reverend the Abbot of, or, The Right Reverend John Smith with initials of the order	Right Reverend and Dear Father Abbot, or, Dear Father Abbot	Father Abbot	Abbot	The Abbot of
Prior	The Very Reverend the Prior of, or, The Very Reverend John Smith with initials of the order	Very Reverend and Dear Father Prior, or, Dear Father Prior	Father Prior	Prior	The Prior of

→

Office	*Formal title*	*Written address*	*Formal verbal address*	*Social verbal address*	*Description*
Heads of Women's Religious Communities	The Lady Abbess, or, The Reverend Mother Prioress, or The Sister Superior		Reverend Mother, or, Sister Superior		The Mother Prioress, or, The Reverend Mother, or, The Sister Superior
Church of England					
Archbishop of Canterbury and York	The Most Reverend and Right Honourable the Lord Archbishop of	Dear Archbishop	Your Grace	Archbishop	The Archbishop
Other Archbishops	The Most Reverend the Lord Archbishop of	Dear Archbishop	Your Grace	Archbishop	The Archbishop
Bishop of London	The Right Reverend and Right Honourable the Bishop of London	Dear Bishop	Bishop	Bishop	The Bishop
Other Bishops	The Right Reverend the Lord Bishop of (when retired, all bishops and archbishops are referred to by name)	Dear Bishop	Bishop	Bishop	The Bishop
Deans and Provosts	The Very Reverend the Dean/Provost of	Dear Dean/Provost	Dean/Provost	Dean/Provost	The Dean/Provost
Archdeacons	The Venerable the Archdeacon of	Dear Archdeacon	Archdeacon	Archdeacon	The Archdeacon
Canons and Prebendaries	The Reverend Canon/ Prebendary	Dear Canon/Prebendary (or Dear Canon/ Prebendary Smith)	Canon/Prebendary or Canon/Prebendary Smith	Canon/Prebendary or Canon/Prebendary Smith	The Canon/Prebendary or Canon/Prebendary Smith
Other clergy	The Reverend John/Jane Smith (Reverend without a Christian name is incorrect)	Dear Father/Mr/Mrs/Miss/ Ms Smith	Father/Mr/Mrs/Miss/Ms Smith, or, The Rector, The Vicar	Father/Mr/Mrs/Miss/Ms Smith, or, The Rector, The Vicar	Father/Mr/Mrs/Miss/Ms Smith, or, The Rector, The Vicar
Heads of religious communities					
Ordained members of religious orders are addressed as Father and lay members as Brother except in the case of the Society of St Francis, all of whose members are called Brother. Dom (from *dominus*, master) is a title given to monks of the Benedictine, Cistercian and Carthusian orders.					
Abbot	The Right Reverend the Lord Abbot, with initials of the order	Dear Father Abbot	Father Abbot		The Abbot

Office	*Formal title*	*Written address*	*Formal verbal address*	*Social verbal address*	*Description*
Prior	The Reverend the Prior, with initials of the order	Dear Father Prior	Father Prior		The Prior
Superior-General	The Reverend Superior-General, with initials of the order	Dear Father Superior	Father Superior		The Superior-General
Superior	The Reverend Superior, with initials of the order	Dear Father Superior	Father Superior		The Superior
		The Orthodox churches			
Ecumenical Patriarch of Constantinople	His All-Holiness the Patriarch of	Your All-Holiness	*Despota*/*Philostate* (Greek) *Vladyka* (Slav) *Sayidna* (Arabic) In English, forms of address like 'Your Serenity', 'Your Piety', 'Your Benignity' can be used		His All-Holiness the Patriarch of
Patriarch	His Holiness the Patriarch of	Your Holiness			His Holiness the Patriarch of
Primate Archbishop	His Beatitude the Primate Archbishop of	Your Beatitude			His Beatitude the Primate Archbishop of
Metropolitan Archbishop	His Eminence the Metropolitan Archbishop of	Your Eminence			His Eminence the Metropolitan Archbishop of
Archbishop	His Eminence the Archbishop of	Your Eminence			His Eminence the Archbishop of
Bishop	His Eminence the Bishop of	Your Eminence			His Eminence the Bishop of
Archimandrite	The Very Reverend John Smith	Dear Father Smith	Father		The Very Reverend John Smith
Priest	The Reverend John Smith	Dear Father Smith	Father		The Reverend John Smith

Protestant churches do not have this range of formal titles; in them 'Minister' and 'Pastor' are regularly used.

The following abbreviations are commonly used: Revd or Rev., Fr, Rt Revd or Rt Rev., Preb.
Reverend, Right Reverend, Very Reverend, Most Reverend and Venerable are always preceded by the definite article, whether abbreviated or not.

Quakers

CLERGY TITLES AND ORDERS OF MINISTRY

The members of most churches (the Religious Society of Friends, the Quakers, is one exception) are divided into laity and clergy. Laity, from the Greek *laos*, simply means people: originally *laos theou*, 'people of God', was used to denote those called by God as opposed to those who were not. Clergy, a collective of 'clerk', denotes those who have been appointed to special service in the church through ordination: 'clerk in holy orders' is one way they can describe themselves in the 'occupation' section in an official form.

Historically there are three degrees of these 'holy orders' in the church: deacon, priest and bishop, though in the Roman Catholic Church until 1972 there were further minor orders: doorkeepers, lectors, exorcists and acolytes. Subdeacons occupy a place between the major and the minor orders. In the early church there was also an office of deaconess: deaconesses looked after sick and poor women, instructed women members of the church and accompanied them to baptism. This office was revived in the nineteenth century, but has been abolished again with the admission of women to the diaconate and subsequently the priesthood in the churches where it existed.

Deacons are assistant ministers; as their name, 'servants', indicates, they were originally responsible for collecting and distributing gifts for the poor and needy. They may perform only limited functions in church worship, and are not allowed to celebrate the eucharist or give absolution. In the Church of England and the Roman Catholic Church, ordination to the diaconate is usually a step on the way to ordination to the priesthood, and the period served by a deacon is short. In the Eastern church there is a permanent diaconate, and this has also been proposed in the Roman Catholic Church to compensate for the shortage of priests.

Priests form the main body of the clergy in the historic Eastern and Western churches. The word comes from the Greek *presbyteros*, but this term actually means 'elder'. The Greek word meaning priest is in fact different, *hiereus*; hierarchy, a collective word for clergy, derives from it. A transliteration of *presbyteros* gives presbyter, and this is a term used in translations of the New Testament and adopted by many of the churches of the Reformation. The Reformers did not use 'priest' because the word was associated with a sacrificial view of the mass which they rejected. However, in Scandinavian languages, e.g. Swedish, the word *präst* can only be translated priest: it was never changed at the Reformation. The priest celebrates the eucharist, gives absolution and administers most of the other sacraments, functions which in earliest times were performed only by the bishop.

Bishop comes from the Greek word *episkopos*, which means 'overseer'. There are bishops in the Roman Catholic, Orthodox and Anglican churches, and also some Lutheran and Methodist churches. They are the focal point of the areas, dioceses, to which they are appointed, and from earliest times have met together to embody the unity of the church. In the Roman Catholic Church there are national Conferences of Bishops and a Synod of Bishops. Bishops oversee their dioceses and only they can administer the sacraments of confirmation and ordination. Roman Catholics and Anglicans attach great importance to episcopal succession, i.e. an unbroken chain in the line of bishops; however, in some churches, e.g. the Methodist Church in the USA, this line of succession is not claimed.

These three orders are fundamental to the structure of the ordained ministry and have a character all of their own. In fact *character* is a technical term in Catholic theology, denoting an indelible mark which ordination makes on a person: once a priest always a priest, once a bishop always a bishop.

All other titles given to clergy are of a different order. An ecumenical patriarch or an archbishop, for example, differs from a bishop only by his greater degree of responsibility; even the Pope is primarily a bishop: the Bishop of Rome.

Here are some of the great variety of titles given to clergy depending on the office they hold:

Apocrisarius: An envoy to one of the patriarchates of the Eastern Church appointed by the Ecumenical Patriarch or the Archbishop of Canterbury.

Archbishop: A bishop who holds a specially eminent position among other bishops; in the Church of England the head of a church province.

Archdeacon: An administrative officer appointed by the bishop to supervise the clergy and administer church property. While an archbishop is a bishop, an archdeacon is not a deacon (though the term derives from a time when he was chief of the deacons acting as servants of the bishop) but a priest.

Archimandrite: In the Eastern church the equivalent of an abbot; the term is also used as an honorary title for an unmarried priest.

Archpriest: In the Eastern church a priest who holds a specially eminent position among other priests.

The title *bishop* can be qualified in a number of ways:

Area bishop: bishop in charge of an area of a large diocese; there are five area bishops in the Diocese of London.

Coadjutor bishop: a bishop appointed to help a diocesan bishop; the term is mostly used in the Roman Catholic Church. In the Episcopal Church of America the title is used for an assisting bishop who will succeed as the chief bishop of a diocese when the incumbent retires.

Suffragan bishop: a bishop appointed to help a diocesan bishop; the term is mostly used in the Church of England.

Canon: One of the permanent ordained staff of a cathedral; these are known as residentiary canons. Canon is also an honorary title awarded to priests of a diocese. Canons regular were a body of canons observing a religious rule; from the twelfth century they came to be known as Augustinian (Austin) canons.

pp. 1022–3

p. 1220

Cardinal: A member of a college nominated by the Pope which meets in secret to elect a new pope. Cardinals hold senior administrative positions in the Roman Catholic Church, for example as heads of Vatican Congregations.

Chaplain: A member of the clergy appointed to serve individuals (e.g. monarchs or bishops) or institutions such as the armed forces, hospitals, prisons, universities, schools, etc.

Curate: Originally used to denote one who has the care ('cure') of a parish, but now normally used to denote an assistant to the incumbent of the parish. Strictly speaking, however, modern 'curates' are in fact assistant curates.

Dean: The head of the ordained staff of a cathedral. However, a rural dean or area dean is the senior priest in one of the areas into which an archdeaconry is divided.

General superintendent: Traditionally the highest office in one of the German Protestant churches.

Incumbent: In the Church of England used to denote, especially in legal documents, the priest in charge of a parish.

Metropolitan: A bishop with powers over an area greater than a diocese, like a province, but under the patriarch. In the Greek church, though, all bishops are called Metropolitans.

Minister: This term is widely used of the clergy in Protestant churches.

Parson: An old-fashioned term, used to denote a clergyman (not a woman priest!). It derives from the Latin *persona*, 'person', i.e. the person legally in charge.

Pastor: The title given by Lutherans and some other Protestant churches to their clergy, especially those in charge of a church.

Patriarch: A title given to the head of one of the great dioceses of the early church: Jerusalem, Alexandria, Antioch, Constantinople and also of Orthodox churches like the Russian, Serbian, Romanian, Bulgarian churches. The senior patriarch is the Ecumenical Patriarch of Constantinople.

Präses: A term now used in place of general superintendent in some German Protestant churches.

Prebendary: Equivalent to 'canon' and used as a title in some cathedrals, e.g. St Paul's. It derives from 'prebend', a specific part of the material resources of a cathedral which provided the salary for the prebendary.

Primate: The title used of an archbishop as head of a province.

Provost: A term generally used as the equivalent of dean, for the heads of newer cathedrals.

Rector: Originally the incumbent of a parish entitled to the tithes given by the parish, as opposed to a vicar, who was the representative of a monastery which controlled the parish. Since tithes are no longer paid in this way, the title has only historic significance. In the Roman Catholic church the title can be given to heads of seminaries or priests who do not have parochial responsibilities.

Vicar: From the Latin *vicarius*, representative. Originally vicars had a lower status than rectors, since they were merely representatives of a monastery in control of the parish, but now there is no real difference between vicars and rectors.

p. 245

appointed to serve tables. However, it has recently been argued that use of the terms *diakonia* and *diakonos* in Christian and non-Christian sources of the early period does not have connotations of humility or helping the needy; the term means 'messenger' or 'emissary'. That Paul makes no mention of presbyters, though, does not mean that there were none: the Acts of the Apostles speaks of 'elders' in Jerusalem from an early period (e.g. 11.30) and even has Paul appointing them (14.23, the one chapter where Paul is presented as an apostle). They also appear in other New Testament letters like 1 Peter and James, and 2 and 3 John are written by one who calls himself an elder (Greek *presbyteros*).

Just how fluid the situation still was at the end of the first century is shown by a letter attributed to Clement of Rome and written to the Corinthians. As usual, there is trouble in Corinth, where members of the church have removed some of their leaders from office. 1 Clement remarks how happy are the presbyters now dead, since they need not fear that anyone will remove them from office (chapter 44). Thus the church clearly by now has presbyters. But there are also, as in Philippians, *episkopoi* and deacons. At the same time the letter contains the first evidence of a distinction between the clergy and the laity, i.e. between those Christians who are ordained and those who are not (40.5).

With Ignatius of Antioch, in his letter to the Smyrnaeans, written at the very beginning of the second century, the threefold order which from then on was to be characteristic of the Catholic and Orthodox traditions is evident: 'See that you all follow the bishop, as Jesus Christ follows the Father, and the presbytery as if it were the apostles. And reverence the deacons as the command of God' (8.1–2). All that remains is for the presbyter to become the priest. Cyprian, Bishop of Carthage in the third century, plays a large part in this development, transferring much of the Old Testament imagery of priesthood and sacrifice to the Christian church.

Of the 'holy orders' now established, the office of bishop is by far the most important. Ignatius ends his letter to the Smyrnaeans by remarking that 'it is good to acknowledge God and the bishop; he who honours the bishop is honoured by God; he who does anything without the bishop's knowledge serves the devil' (9.1). From the second century onwards a chronology was constructed on the basis of the dates of bishops, in which the office (like that of pope later) was anachronistically projected back to the very beginning.

It was only comparatively late in the first millennium in the West that there was a steady development towards a celibate Roman Catholic priesthood, whose main task was to offer the mass. Along with this came an increasingly wide divide between clergy and laity, which the sixteenth-century Reformers rejected in their attempt to return to the early church. Against it they set the priesthood of all believers, a doctrine drawn from a phrase in 1 Peter 2.9, 'you are a chosen race, a royal priesthood', read as removing the possibility of any hierarchy among Christians. Orthodox Christians interpret this passage as making all Christians, both clergy and laity, responsible for the preservation of gospel and church, but do not set the clergy against laity or vice versa.

Ministry today

Reflection on the nature of ministry in the modern world continues; one of the most important documents of recent times is the so-called Lima Report on baptism, eucharist and ministry produced by the Faith and Order Division of the World Council of Churches in 1982. It discusses the church and the ordained ministry, the forms of the ordained ministry, succession in the apostolic tradition, ordination and the mutual recognition of ordained ministries. Much hard thinking and research has been done; whether it will be reflected in practice is another matter. Moreover, there are other factors at work that are creating a crisis for the ordained ministry in its traditional form.

First is the sharp decline over the past 50 years and more in the number of those offering themselves for ordination in the Roman Catholic Church and other churches and problems in deploying clergy to meet the shifts in patterns of population distribution. In many areas of Europe there are problems in having a regular celebration of the eucharist because there are not enough priests, and the pastoral work of priests is taken over by lay care workers, male and female.

Secondly, with the rise of other welfare agencies alongside the church and qualified specialists in counselling and caring, it is not always clear what contribution the ordained minister, perhaps without relevant training in those areas, can make. Moreover, with the laity, both men and women, taking a growing interest in theological and religious studies up to university level, lay people can have a better knowledge of Christian thought and tradition than clergy.

Thirdly, in the modern world the notion of the 'holy' has also become problematical in many ways. What does it mean to be 'holy', and what makes someone in 'holy orders' different from someone who is not? Should clergy live their lives in a different way from laity, and if so how? Is celibacy a particular form of holiness? Are not the signs of what most people would call a holy life evident in lay people as much as in clergy?

Holy

All these questions, together with the immense range of ministries called for in the modern world, make further reflection on the nature of ministry urgently necessary. The priesthood of all believers and Paul's kaleidoscope of ministries could provide important insights here.

JOHN BOWDEN

Baptism, Eucharist and Ministry (Faith and Order Paper 111 – The Lima Report), Geneva: WCC 1982; John Collins, *Diakonia: Interpreting the Ancient Sources*, Oxford: OUP 1990; Jan Kerkhofs (ed), *Europe without Priests?*, London: SCM Press 1995; Hans Küng, *Structures of the Church*, New York: Thomas Nelson 1964 and London: Burns & Oates 1965; Edward Schillebeeckx, *The Church with a Human Face*, London: SCM Press and New York: Crossroad 1985

Miracle

Ecumenical movement

p. 613

From the New Testament onwards, Christianity is full of stories about miracles. Jesus heals the sick, raises the dead, multiplies loaves and fishes, turns water into wine, stills a storm, walks on water. He is said to have been born of a virgin and to have risen from the dead and appeared to his followers in bodily form. The New Testament tells of the disciples being given power to perform miracles, and in the Acts of the Apostles Paul is said to have healed the sick also through the medium of handkerchiefs and aprons taken from his body; he even raised from the dead a young man who had fallen out of a third-floor window (having gone to sleep during Paul's preaching). Non-Christians are said to have sought to purchase or imitate such power: Jewish exorcists failed because the demons saw that they were neither Jesus nor Paul (see especially Acts 19).

Here already it is evident that miracle stories are of differing profundity. Some miracles have a deeply symbolic significance; others are little more than conjuring tricks (as with the story of the coin found in a fish's mouth to make Jesus' point over the payment of tax to the emperor, Matthew 17.24–7). Stories of the latter kind abound in the apocryphal Acts and Gospels written after the New Testament period. Jesus stretches a plank when his father Joseph has cut it too short and makes birds out of clay which then fly; the apocryphal Acts introduce talking animals, obedient bed-bugs and swimming kippers. Down the ages miracles of this kind have been a regular element of popular piety and often feature in icons of lives of saints.

Icon

Miracles involving healing the sick, raising the dead to life, miraculous deliverance and alterations in the course of nature abound in Christian literature and graphic art through the Middle Ages: they are particularly associated with holy persons and their relics, which have quite spectacular effects. The best-known miracles in modern times have been associated with the Virgin Mary, notably in the pilgrimage centre of Lourdes.

Mary

The ongoing interest in miracle in Christianity is not just confined to popular piety: in the Roman Catholic Church the performance of a miracle is still a necessary qualification for beatification and a further miracle is needed for canonization. The First Vatican Council declared: 'If anyone should say that no miracles can be performed … or that by them the divine origin of the Christian religion cannot be rightly proved – let him be anathema.' By contrast, after the Reformation the Protestant tradition questioned the role of miracle outside the Bible and its association with saints and holiness. However, here too a great interest in miracles and miraculous healings has arisen in modern times with the development of revivalist, charismatic and Pentecostal churches.

Kingdom of God p. 1077 Council Reformation Bible Saint Pentecostalism

Belief in miracles is not peculiar to Christianity. It is a feature of almost all religions, and reports of miracles are universal. The Hebrew Bible which became the Christian Old Testament is full of miracles: as the Israelites leave Egypt, the sea is turned back for them and at a crucial battle the sun stands still to provide longer time for them to slaughter the enemy. The Jewish historian Josephus, nearly contemporary with Jesus, reports an exorcism to which he was an eyewitness and the Talmud contains the story of a rabbi's wife whose oven produced bread from nothing. In the Hellenistic world miraculous cures and even virgin births and resurrections were reported for the sanctuary of Asclepius at Epidaurus, and the biography of the Pythagorean philosopher Apollonius of Tyana, another approximate contemporary of Jesus, contains numerous miracle stories including the raising of a dead girl. Although Muhammad refused to prove his vocation by signs and miracles, he is said to have made a miraculous journey to heaven; miracles came to be attributed to him and abound in Sufism. It is accepted in Hinduism that ascetics and yogis can attain the power to perform miracles, and Buddhist accounts say that not only the Buddha but also many of his monks had miraculous powers.

Critics of Christianity

It is possible, then, to talk about the occurrence of miracles in almost all religions. But what is a miracle? Nowadays a miracle is usually taken to be an action or event that apparently violates the accepted course of nature. But such a definition is far too simple, indeed unusable. First, the basic meaning of the word miracle is something that causes wonder and amazement (Latin *miraculum*, Greek *thaumasion*). The German word for miracle, *Wunder*, is used in a similar way. Secondly, ideas about nature and natural laws have varied too much down the centuries for the concept of their violation to be applied meaningfully. It is more useful to see miracles as remarkable happenings which are given a particular significance that relates to the agent through whom they are done and to a particular set of beliefs. Jesus puts his exorcisms and miraculous healings in the context of the kingdom of God: 'If I by the finger (or spirit) of God cast out demons then the kingdom of God has come upon you' (Luke 11.20; Matthew 12.28). What this kingdom of God is can be filled out from what Jesus says, for example, in his parables and other sayings, against the background of the Judaism of his time.

Although miracles appear in all religions, from antiquity onwards they were often disparaged. In the first century BCE the Roman orator Marcus Tullius Cicero went so far as to deny the possibility of miracles with an argument from cause and effect, but accepted that they necessarily formed part of popular piety. There were also arguments about how genuine miracles were: Christians claimed that their miracles were superior to those told of in the world around; the second-century CE pagan philosopher Celsus, a noted critic of Christianity, said that Christian miracles were improbable and not backed up by evidence as pagan ones were. Again, some people were more inclined to see miracles than others. Anselm, the famous Archbishop of Canterbury (1033–1109), was at one time accompanied on his travels by two companions: in their accounts one of these reported miracles regularly; the other did not.

The first major questioning of miracles came with the rise of modern science in the seventeenth and eighteenth centuries, when belief that the universe functioned as a closed system according to immutable laws seemed completely to rule out the intervention of divine power

THE MIRACLES OF JESUS

Miracle	*Matthew*	*Mark*	*Luke*	*John*
Man with a blind and dumb demon healed	12.22			
Blind man at Jericho healed (one)		10.46–52	18.35–43	
(two)	20.29–34			
Blind man healed with spittle		8.22–5		
Centurion's servant cured	8.5–13		7.2–10	
Coin in fish's mouth	17.24–8			
Cure at pool of Bethsaida				5.1–15
Deaf and dumb man healed with word 'Ephphatha'		7.31–7		
Dumb man possessed by a demon healed	9.32–4			
Epileptic boy healed	17.14–21	9.14–30	9.37–43	
Feeding of 5000	14.13–21	6.34–44	9.12–17	6.1–15
Feeding of 4000	15.32–8	8.1–9		
Fig tree blasted	21.18–22	11.12–25		
Gadarene swine and demons	8.28–34	5.1–20	8.26–39	
Jairus' daughter raised	9.18–26	5.21–43	8.40–56	
Leper healed	8.1–4	1.40–5	5.12–19	
Man born blind healed				9.1–38
Man with dropsy healed			14.1–6	
Man with withered hand cured	12.9–13	3.1–6	6.6–11	
Man with unclean spirit cured		1.23–8	4.33–7	
Miraculous catch of fish			5.1–11	21.1–14
Official's son at Capernaum cured				4.46–54
Paralytic cured	9.1–8	2.1–12	5.18–26	
Peter's mother-in-law cured	8.14–15	1.29–31	4.38–9	
Raising of Lazarus				11.1–44
Servant's ear healed			22.49–51	
Stilling of storm	8.23–7	4.35–41	8.22–5	
Syro-Phoenician woman's daughter healed	15.21–8	7.24–30		
Ten lepers healed			17.11–19	
Two blind men healed	9.27–31			
Walking on water	14.22–3	6.45–52		6.16–21
Water made wine at Cana				2.1–11
Widow of Nain's son raised			7.11–17	
Woman bent double healed			13.10–17	
Woman with flow of blood healed	9.20–2	5.24–34	8.43–8	

The miracles of Jesus can be divided into several groups: exorcisms, healings, a punitive miracle (the blasting of the fig tree), gift miracles (the feedings, the miraculous catch of fish) and deliverance miracles (the stilling of the storm and the walking on the water). There is discussion among scholars as to which miracles can be authentically attributed to Jesus: one common position is that he performed exorcisms, healings and punitive miracles, but that the other miracles are symbolic stories, composed about Jesus in the light of the early Christian community's faith in him. The miracles in the Gospel of John stand apart: they are a series of what the evangelist calls signs, beginning with the marriage at Cana and culminating in the raising of Lazarus.

Gerd Theissen, *The Miracle Stories of the Early Christian Tradition*, Edinburgh: T&T Clark and Philadelphia: Fortress Press 1983

Christ healing the paralytic and resurrecting the widow's son, from a twelfth/thirteenth-century Armenian Gospel

and the possibility of the miraculous. Doubts were cast on the credibility and authenticity of miracles. Evidence for miracles supposedly performed in the period after the Bible was dismissed as inadequate or unconvincing. As far as possible alternative explanations were found for the biblical material: Jesus did not walk on the water but on a half-submerged plank; the loaves and fishes were enough to feed so many people because Jesus' example of sharing proved infectious and others followed it.

Evidence

Jesus of history

Benedict de Spinoza, a pivotal seventeenth-century philosopher, wrote in his *Theologico-Political Treatise* that miracles were natural occurrences and had to be so explained as to appear neither new nor contrary to nature, but as far as possible in complete agreement with ordinary events. This view was pivotal because roughly speaking up to his lifetime miracles had been regarded as an argument for the authenticity of Christianity; after it they were regarded as a problem. Up to Spinoza's lifetime Christianity had had the benefit of the doubt; after it Christianity had to justify itself in the forum of reason. David Hume in his

An Enquiry concerning Human Understanding was more negative than Spinoza, concluding that 'whoever is moved by faith to assent to the Christian religion is conscious of a continued miracle in his own person, which subverts all the principles of his understanding, and gives him a determination to believe what is most contrary to custom and experience' (ch.10, part II).

As so often in the history of Christianity, during the eighteenth century, at the very point when miracles proved problematical, major attempts were made to prove Christianity on the basis of them. Miracles have continued to be defended strongly since then, influentially by C. S. Lewis, whose argument was that the ideas with which people approach miracle stories will determine what they make of them: 'Those who assume that miracles cannot happen are merely wasting their time by looking into the texts.' More recently, attempts have been made to use current views about the natural order and modern physics to support a new and more positive understanding of the possibility of miracle; but how on this basis miracles can be seen as acts of God, and more specifically acts of the God believed in by Christians, is still a major problem.

We are brought back to the question of the agent through whom miracles are performed, in Christianity above all Jesus of Nazareth, and the context of the particular set of beliefs within which these miracles are set.

An illuminating approach to the miracles of Jesus is to divide them into six types: 1. exorcisms, the driving out of demons; 2. therapies, healing by the transfer of a miraculous energy; 3. gift miracles, involving fish, bread and wine; 4. deliverance miracles, i.e. the stilling of the storm and the walking on the water; 5. epiphanies, or visionary experiences, as at the transfiguration and after the resurrection. 6. Jesus' cursing of the fig tree that thereafter withers (this stands in a category of its own). The Gospels present all these types of miracles as having been performed by Jesus during his lifetime, but the modern critical understanding of the Gospel accounts is that they combine words and actions of Jesus of Nazareth with beliefs about him after his death in such a complex way that it is almost impossible to determine what is to be attributed to him and what to the early church: they are portraits of faith. That Jesus was thought to have performed miracles is beyond question even on the most critical reading, and these miracles are most likely to have been healings and exorcisms. Other miracles, like the gift and deliverance miracles and the epiphanies, can be seen as mythical pictures of his work, poetic expressions of his significance in the light of the experience of his resurrection. (The resurrection, though often described as 'the greatest miracle of all', has so many dimensions that it is discussed in a separate article.)

If the miracles are approached in this way, the question whether they happened, or precisely what happened in them, is relativized. They are one way among several of expressing in terms of the Jewish – and Hellenistic – world of the first century CE what Jesus meant. The conflicts in which he became involved over the sabbath, often the setting for miracles, are closely related. Jesus' miracles were actions indicating that the end of the world was near, that the kingdom of God was about to dawn and change everything. In other words, the miracles have an eschatological significance.

Eschatology

Miracles are not just magic, though Jesus has been compared to contemporaneous magicians, for example when he uses specific formulae like '*Ephphatha*, be opened' or material like clay or spittle in his cures. What distinguishes them from magic is again the nature of the person who performs them and the set of beliefs within which they are done. The key feature of the coming of the kingdom of God is the bringing of deliverance, and for the Jews of Jesus' time living under Roman oppression deliverance was a powerful idea. So social anthropologists have discussed the miracles of Jesus against a political background; the fact that one demon tells Jesus that his name is 'Legion' because there are many of them is an enigmatic pointer here.

Science and theology

Some may find this approach to miracles helpful; others may feel it too negative. For there is, and probably always has been, a divide within Christianity over the understanding of miracle. That Christians of all traditions continue to believe in the possibility of miracles is indubitable. Many Protestants and Roman Catholics experience what they believe to be miracles today, whether at pilgrimage centres like Lourdes or in the spirit-filled Christianity of the southern hemisphere (and it is impossible to dismiss all of these occurrences out of hand as inauthentic or fraudulent), and this governs their views not only of what God can do but also of what God has done in the past, and hence of the biblical accounts. But there are also Christians with no experience of the miraculous and with a different perspective on the nature of God and the world. As things are, these two groups are likely to go on differing.

p. 1081

Geography

JOHN BOWDEN

David Hume, *An Enquiry concerning Human Understanding* (1690) ed Roger Woolhouse, Harmondsworth: Penguin Books 1997; H. C. Kee, *Miracles in the Early Christian World*, New Haven: Yale University Press 1983; Ernst and Marie-Luise Keller, *Miracles in Dispute*, London: SCM Press 1969; C. S. Lewis, *Miracles*, London: Geoffrey Bles 1947; C. F. D. Moule (ed), *Miracles: Cambridge Studies in Their Philosophy and History*, Cambridge: CUP 1965; Gerd Theissen, *The Miracle Stories of the Early Christian Tradition*, Philadelphia: Fortress Press and Edinburgh: T&T Clark 1983

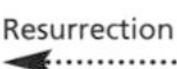

Resurrection

MISSION

Christianity in Africa, Latin America, North America, Asia, Australasia, Celtic Christianity, Chinese religions and Christianity, Coptic Christianity, Dutch Reformed Church, Ethiopian Christianity, Geography, Hinduism and Christianity, History, Islam and Christianity, Japanese religions and Christianity, Jewish Christianity, Journeys, Christianity in the Middle East, Moravian Church, Paganism, Paul

Although the words 'mission' and 'missions' have been in use to denote key activities of the church since the seventeenth century, they are not biblical terms. Indeed, they emerged in common parlance only when the Jesuits began using them in the sixteenth century to denote the assignments given to their rapidly growing fellowship. Used then to describe men sent (*missi*, past plural participle of the Latin *mittere*, 'to send') to Asia and Latin America 'on mission', ever since mission has been the shorthand term used to describe Christians sent to work among persons of other faiths as 'missionaries'. Missions became, in effect, the international marketing arm of the church. Since the use of the words began precisely when European colonialism was commencing, attitudes towards missionary activity have tended to rise and fall in synchronism with attitudes towards colonialism.

Religious orders

First a broad description; nuances will be added later. Christian mission is, first, the activities of the church among persons outside the Christian tradition, actions believed to be commanded by God and aimed at proclaiming Jesus Christ as teacher and saviour, the one to whom God wills that hearers of the message should entrust their lives in faith. In a second dimension, those carrying on these activities have generally seen the creation of local churches as one of the key objectives of mission. Third, in its extended meanings, Christian mission refers to activities of the church aimed at enriching the lives of its own members and of the followers of other religious ways. By such activities, Christians seek to alleviate human suffering, promote liberation, improve dialogue among peoples and their religious traditions, and to secure justice, peace, and the integrity of creation. Finally, 'mission' (in the singular) has been commonly used in recent decades in contra-distinction to 'missions' in the plural. The great Anglican bishop, missionary, and scholar Stephen Neill (1900–84) caught the importance of this switch in terminology in 1964 when he said, 'the age of missions is at an end; the age of mission has begun'. Neill said this to focus attention on activities that expressed the Christian mission to minister to the world in the spirit of the gospel, while encouraging honest research on ambiguous aspects of concrete Christian missions.

Church

That said, for many Christians and perhaps most non-Christians, Christian missions are synonymous with what they judge to be a five-century-long attempt by over-zealous and narrow-minded Christians to impose Western religious and cultural domination over peoples in Africa, Asia, Oceania, and the Americas. In the view of these critics, such peoples would have been better left alone, and present missionary efforts should be stopped.

In all that follows, several questions must be kept in mind. First, when one important component of the worldwide Christian communion holds the term mission in high regard, what do they understand by it? Why do other, equally sincere and committed members of the church and morally sensitive non-Christians condemn it? Is the term redeemable from complicity in the colonial-era presupposition that the West had the right to colonize the lands and minds of the rest of the world?

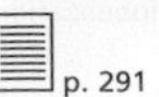
p. 291

Salvation

Putting the question theologically, if mission expresses essential Christian identity – as the Roman Catholic Church's Second Vatican Council puts it in saying 'The Church on earth is by its very nature missionary' (*Ad gentes*, 2) – are there defensible warrants for saying so? Are there examples of missionary activity, carried on in ways that morally sensitive persons can approve in at least some points in Christian history? Can the ideals of mission – founded in the conviction that Jesus as Christ is uniquely instrumental for the salvation of all – be squared with contemporary values holding that pluralism and respect for the religious and cultural ideals of all peoples are fundamental to peaceful human co-existence?

The modern period of Christian mission coincides roughly with the expulsion of Arabs and Jews from Spain in 1492, the same year that an Italian seaman in the employ of the Spanish royal house reached lands previously unknown to the West. Christopher Columbus was, of course, searching for a short-cut to China and had no idea that he was beginning the European conquest of the Americas and launching the missionary movement.

The modern missionary movement did not start as an organized programme. Instead, it began as questions first asked in the 1500s, when it became clear that the Spaniards – aided by diseases that killed untold numbers of Indians and weakened military organizations that had been enormously powerful before the colonial invasions – were achieving domination over the Americas. The conquerors' chaplains were confronted with the reality of uncounted millions of persons. Shocking as it is to modern ears, the question 'Are they human?' was asked. And it was not always answered in the affirmative. Even when the answer was 'Yes', the practical consequences were too seldom drawn by men whose hearts had been coarsened by the long toleration of slavery, the memories of centuries of conflict with Muslims, and the harshness and warfare of late medieval life. To the extent, nevertheless, that prejudices were overcome, the realization dawned that the Indians and their lands could not merely be exploited for the benefit of the invader. The attempt to bring Christianity to the original inhabitants of the conquered lands began.

The fruits of those efforts would for ever be judged by many not to be the result of free choice on the part of the Indians but fruit poisoned by its relation to colonial domination. Pablo Deiros' *Historia del Cristianismo en América Latina* shows that this is not the whole story of the evangelization of Latin America, but it is enough of the story that by the five hundredth anniversary of Columbus' 'discovery', few found much to celebrate.

In both Spanish and Portuguese settlements in the Americas and in Portuguese outposts in Asia, priests assumed the pastoral care of the voyagers and soldiers. Secular priests, Franciscans and Dominicans predominated at first. As the number of Jesuits (founded in 1540) available for work in the new lands grew, they were sent both to the Americas and Asia. The term mission as used by the Jesuits was rooted in the Roman military term *missio.* Just as the Romans sent soldiers on missions, so the Jesuits sent their men 'on mission' to achieve clearly defined goals. Since priests sent to Asia and the Americas accompanied soldiers and adventurers as the vanguard of the new colonies, the chain of association of missions with colonialism was forged so securely that it has never been broken.

In borrowing the term mission and its cognates from military parlance the Jesuits were conforming to the experience of their soldier-founder, Ignatius of Loyola (1491–1556). Both the military metaphors adapted by the Jesuits and the militant spirit of the *reconquista*, the recapture of Spain from the Muslims, that marked Iberian Catholicism portrayed the missionary as a soldier of Christ. He was involved in a spiritual warfare in which victory was to be achieved by overcoming belief in other religious traditions. Moreover, the Jesuits were becoming the

Globalization

paradigmatic international missionary organization just as the early phase of the process we now term globalization was getting under way. Jesuit structures and methods were copied by virtually every Roman Catholic order founded from the seventeenth to the twentieth centuries and by many Protestant missionary societies founded after 1792, when Protestant missions began in earnest. Lost in the oversimplification of that history, unfortunately, was the deeply evangelical training programme of the Jesuits which inculcated humility and devotion to Christ in the followers of Ignatius.

Though mission is a relatively modern term and not biblical in its roots, it is nevertheless used in contemporary documents of the World Council of Churches, the Lausanne Committee for World Evangelization, and the Roman Catholic and Orthodox Churches as a marker for essential Christian identity. This raises important questions. What are the antecedents of the modern term? Do some of these antecedents exemplify patterns of interreligious and intercultural interaction not burdened by complicity in the dominative practices of the colonial era?

'Mission' in the New Testament and the first five centuries of Christianity

Bible

p. 902

Attempts to identify in earliest Christianity what in the modern period is called missionary activity are beset by the classic conundrum of how much reliability one accords to the Bible and to what extent stories there conform to words and realities we use today to characterize them. In the modern era Matthew 28.19 ('make disciples of all nations') has been taken as the great commission to mission. And the missionary journeys of Paul are generally taken as the first missionary journeys. How valid are the connections?

Research into what was happening in the inner landscape of the peoples who became Christian in the first five centuries and how that corresponds to biblical portraits is hindered by the scant extra-biblical evidence about what early Christians were thinking. What was their motivation to become Christian? How strong was their conviction, for example, that there was salvation in 'no other name' (Acts 4.12)? Did they believe that non-believers in Jesus would be condemned (John 3.17–18)? Or are such texts rhetoric reflecting the bitterness of relations between Christians and Jews 50 to 70 years after the death of Jesus?

Biblical criticism

Canon

Jesus

Christology

Holy Spirit

The question of the message of first-generation gospel-transmitters and its relationship to the person and message of Jesus arises. For moderns the question is compounded by historical-critical studies of biblical and other early Christian literature. How reliable are they? How widely were they known and accepted? Biblical portraits of Jesus are of someone enigmatic, to be sure. Undoubtedly the books that coalesce into the New Testament canon by the middle of the second century testify to belief that a risen Jesus was uniquely related to God (Hebrew YHWH, Greek *theos* in the Old Testament). It is claimed that this testimony is confirmed by the activity of the Spirit, portrayed as empowering the church in a mystical but real way to become Christ's 'body' on earth, continuing his mission in history. And to become a member of that body is to attain salvation.

Origins and background

To what extent was this message of salvation understood and accepted? It is impossible to say. Many insist that the success of the new movement owed more to the attractive ethos of the communities founded in memory of Jesus than to doctrinal conviction. To some extent this is almost certainly the case, even if the evidence to prove it is fragmentary. Embodiment of the gospel in admirable individuals and communities, though, was almost certainly more important than verbal proclamation. To the extent the question can be resolved in modern sociological terms, it appears that the standard account of early Christianity – that it spread at first and primarily among the poor and dispossessed – is not true. Instead, it is likely that dissatisfaction with the traditional religions was greatest among the most educated, and that they embraced the Jewish ethical belief in one God and Christianity first.

Where the message spreads, communities celebrate the divine sonship of Jesus and the followers' incorporation into his church by the power of the Spirit. They do so in an open fellowship that over time is memorialized in baptism and the eucharist. These liturgies become steadily more elaborate and take on aspects of pagan mystery cults, but the centre of the celebration is acknowledgement of Christ in the mystery of his death and resurrection as the still-point, the central axis of cosmic history, including human history. What is occurring is the translation of the notion that Jesus is universal *kyrios* (Lord) into the many languages spoken between the Straits of Gibraltar and Persia and even India. Out of that translation process, in the Greek-speaking world, arises the question referred to earlier. Is Jesus divine? Is he some form of demi-god? A divinely anointed prophet, philosopher, or teacher?

Sacraments

Mystery cults

Language

Readers must make up their own minds whether they believe that the portrait of Jesus in the New Testament Gospels is reliable. And the implications of saying Yes are important. Some respected figures in contemporary biblical studies (the feminist scholar Elisabeth Schüssler Fiorenza, for instance) believe that this 'kyriological' aspect is responsible for erecting a patriarchal structure, whereas the preferable move would have been to embrace the spirit of Galatians 3.27–9 ('no longer male and female; for all of you are one in Jesus Christ').

What is certainly true is that by 451, the Jesus movement in a patriarchal form was dominant in the Mediterranean world and had spread far into Asia. It thrived as well in North Africa and in Africa below Egypt. That said, it existed with wide variations in doctrinal formulation and liturgical style. Oriental Orthodox churches (Armenian, Coptic, Ethiopian, and Syrian, once termed 'Nestorian' and erroneously considered heretical in the West) never adopted these formulae, yet they have believed and practised a vital form of Christian faith and life down to the present day. And despite the diversity in theological explanations of who Jesus was and is, the fundamental unity of Christians was unmistakable to followers of ancient traditions who watched those traditions being supplanted by the new movement. Finally, if we think that this movement was carried on in ways analogous to the highly organized nineteenth- and twentieth-century missionary movement, study of the evidence quickly suggests otherwise.

Orthodox churches

Diversity

Occurring alongside this growth is a split which became pivotal in emerging Christian self-understanding and proved immensely fateful in European and west Asian history. By the middle of the second century, Christians and Jews had bitterly parted ways. Two things are clear about the split. First, Jews and their communities outside Palestine in what is known as the 'Dispersion' (Greek *diaspora*) may have outnumbered Palestinian Jews by the beginning of the first century. These provided both the network through which Christianity spread in the first two centuries and many (perhaps the majority) of the converts to the new faith. Second, when the significance of the destruction of the second temple in the year 70 and their dispersion among the nations begin to be understood, Jews who remained faithful to the Mosaic covenant ceased to see Christians as just a wayward sect that would one day return to the house of Israel. And the church came to see itself as the new and true Israel.

Covenant

Jewish Christianity

The rupture between Jewish and Christian communities was bitter. But only in the shadow of clouds belching forth from the Holocaust of 1939 to 1945 would Christians begin seriously to reappraise the theology behind that rupture. Many have drawn the conclusion that the Christian 'new' good news does not mean that God's covenant with Israel has been abrogated. Much more can and does need to be said about this. Nevertheless, an honest account of Christian identity and mission must acknowledge that during most of their history, when Christians tried to explain to Persians, Indians, Chimbus, Masai, Celts, or Germans why they should abandon their old religions and become Christians, they told the Christian story as one of God's 'new' covenant which had superseded the 'old' one.

We have some idea how the message was shaped to present the gospel in forms which its hearers could understand in the Graeco-Roman world. In the first generation, Paul, born a Jew, translates an Aramaic message into Greek. His conceptual world is Jewish, but he moves beyond Jewish culture to express its significance. In the next century, Justin the Apologist (*c.* 100–*c.* 165), born of pagan parents, defends the new faith against both Jewish and pagan accusations of impiety. By the 200s, Origen (*c.* 185-254), born a Christian in a Christian family, is the son of a martyr. Thoroughly trained in Greek philosophy, he dedicates himself to assimilating the best of that philosophy in works which seek to show that all true knowledge brings the purified soul along the way toward divinization and union with Christ. Origen is perhaps the first great 'missiologist', the one who knew how radically the message had to be translated if the process of 'gospelling' were to bring about the transformation of the inner person.

Martyr
Philosophy

Buildings
Roman empire

In the Roman world, 'house-churches' appear to have been the first locus of the new faith. In the year 150, the Jesus movement was a marginal and heretical Jewish sect probably made up of no more than 40,000 persons, at best 0.7 per cent of the total population of the Roman empire. By the year 350, Christians were nearly 34 million, as much as 56 per cent of the population. They had become the dominant religion in the Mediterranean world. This happened in organic fashion because Christians had a plausible message understandable to the masses, a message made more plausible by the quality of their communities, whose members brought in neighbours to share the 'good news'.

Persecution

At the same time, Christianity was moving into Mesopotamia, Persia, Arabia and Ethiopia and becoming the most vital and fastest-growing religious force there. In addition, research today is restoring credibility to legendary claims that it reached India in the first century and finding evidence that it had almost certainly arrived in the second. Sources on what motivated the movement of large numbers of people to become Christian are varied and fragmentary. However, accusations that Christianity spread only because of favours granted by the dominant political and military power cannot be sustained. Indeed, the number of Christian martyrs in Persia probably exceeded those killed in the West. Persecutions continued there long after they ended in the Roman world. Nevertheless, Christianity continued to spread in Asia.

p. 788

It is important to realize that in this expansion, Christianity was not merely a creature of the Roman world. Oriental Orthodox Christianity, for example, was immensely vital and employed images of the Spirit as female. It went so far in some texts as to call upon God as Father and Mother to join the eucharistic celebration. Yet we find no organized missionary enterprise in the modern sense of the word in the Christian expansion eastwards in the first few centuries. Instead, there was an organic outreach and spread from local communities to their neighbours. Ranging further, whether through the agency of holy anchorites, wandering merchants or itinerants, Christianity was planted and grew.

What can be said in summary is that Christianity in the first to fifth centuries spread into diverse religious and cultural areas in western Asia, southern Europe and northern Africa because it filled real needs. On the one hand, it gave a credible account of what humanity could hope for transcendently because of Jesus. Equally important, its ethos created communities of men and women who took care of one another and reached out to their neighbours. It had a spirit and message that could be embodied and translated in vastly different contexts. The success of the church's mission on the transcendent level – helping individuals to come to faith in Jesus to attain their destiny in God – is, of course, invisible. On the historical level, the church contributed a plausible new 'philosophy' and way of life to a world that has been described by some historians as jaded and plagued by hopelessness.

Expansion in Europe, eclipse in Africa and the East (451–1492)

It is difficult to place what occurred next in the history of Christian mission on a tidy timeline. The Roman empire collapsed in the West in the fifth century. The next six to seven centuries become the story of the Roman world coming to terms with the Germanic tribes and the Germanic nations coming to terms with Roman civilization. With the rise of Islam in the mid-seventh century, Byzantine Orthodoxy centred in Constantinople was hemmed in to the south. Large communities of Oriental Orthodoxy survived in Muslim western Asia with various degrees of autonomy. On the other hand, Christianity virtually disappeared from North Africa, and by 732 the Islamic tide had reached Poitiers in Southern Gaul, where it met its first significant military defeat.

Middle Ages

In the early Middle Ages Christianity advanced significantly in western Europe. The growth of Christianity there is a familiar story. Less well known, but equally impressive, was the spread of Orthodoxy northwards into central and eastern Europe, the way led by the saintly brothers Cyril (826–69) and Methodius (*c.*815–85). In both East and West, the church began an inculturation or translation of its way of life in a variety of frontier settings. The pattern of evangelization might resemble what will later be called missions, but the differences are also important.

Monasticism

In the West monks paved the way, and the earliest evangelizers were planters of monastic enterprises, as is the case with Martin of Tours (*c.* 316–97), the founder of Gallic monasticism, and Patrick (*c.*390–460). In Ireland Patrick, although he was not himself a monk, founded a church in which monasticism became central. In that church abbots were holding sway over bishops by the time the Celtic Church emerged in mature form in the sixth century. Wandering Celtic monks brought the faith from Ireland to Scotland and to the continent of Europe. In their journeys they met nominally Christian Franks who traced their ancestry in faith to mass conversions in the age of King Clovis (*c.*466–511). They also met Christian communities expanding northwards in Britain, the result of monastic efforts sparked off when the Benedictine Pope Gregory I ('the Great', *c.*540–604) sent Augustine (of Canterbury) to England in 596.

The Benedictine form of monasticism, with roots in Italy and allegiance to the Pope as Bishop of Rome, emerged supreme in this stage of Christian expansion in the West. The dominant form of Catholicism was Roman or Latin. The Anglo-Saxon Benedictine monk and bishop Boniface (*c.*675–754) is a figure who can symbolize the multitudes of monks who carried on this task. He and his followers were midwives of the conversion of the Germanic (i.e., Frankish, Teutonic, Anglo-Saxon and Norman) peoples in the lands that form an arc from today's Austria through Czech and Slovak lands, Germany, the Netherlands and France. The pattern of evangelization, it must be stressed, was not centrally directed. Monasteries were planted and for a generation or more required the infusion of new monks from their mother abbey. Monks planted fields, cleared forests, introduced new plants and animals and had influence on their neighbours. Gradually the new monasteries attracted enough applicants to be self-sufficient. And eventually, when they matured, they founded daughter houses and themselves became fully-fledged abbeys. A map of Europe overlaid with the expansion of monasteries from the seventh to the fifteenth centuries shows dispersion and then a filling in of the empty spaces. Colour in the sites where bishoprics begin to rise. This brings out the way in which the Roman form of territorial dioceses and parishes develops. It also indicates the crossroad market centres that become the centres of European society by the sixteenth century.

The inner dynamic of that process was complex. It resembles what is today called 'inculturation'. Culture By that is meant the interaction between the gospel message and the culture in which the gospel is being presented, and the resultant changes in both the understanding of the meaning of the gospel in the new culture and the way the church is organized. Inculturation includes, then, changes in both the church and the host culture. The Western version of the process was pluralistic in form. It also brought unity by an increasing tendency to codify laws and purge abuses. The form of Christianity that resulted in the West has come to be called Roman Catholicism, but in fact it might as accurately be called 'Germanic' Catholicism. In the encounter with the Germanic world of miracles and warrior culture, the notion of salvation was individualized and the role of the church became one of providing the means to attain it. The church was pictured as the channel of grace by which one reached heaven, the goal of human life. The Roman liturgy brought north by the Benedictines was altered in the process. Princes and kings tried to shape the church and its message to meet their need to maintain order and extend their writ in turbulent times, just as the church attempted to tame warrior ideals in conformity with the gospel. Both had partial success. But the Roman form of Catholicism throughout Europe, including Italy, had been thoroughly Germanized by the twelfth century. Whatever misgivings early Christianity had about military service would be Society transmuted into attempts to mitigate its worst aspects, as Catholicism became part of a society that it could not totally transform.

The rise of Islam and the battles which Christians fought first to stem and later to roll back Muslim conquests from the eighth to the fifteenth centuries made Western Christianity highly War and peace militant. Although proponents of just-war theories would try to mitigate the worst aspects of war, the Portuguese and Spanish Catholic nations which became the vanguard of modern Catholic missions were tolerant of both war and violence as a means to attain an end sanctioned by the church. In terms of subsequent mission practice, it is important to note that principles developed by the North African bishops Cyprian of Carthage (died 258) and Augustine of Hippo (354–430) would be invoked to justify the idea of Christian mission as direct and indirect spiritual warfare waged against the religious other, now conceived as a quasi-enemy to be vanquished.

The process of Christianization was one in which Catholics struggled to present the gospel to peoples whose world-view was dominated by the centuries-old myths and ethos of nomadic warrior bands and who were coming to terms with the 'superior' culture of the peoples they had conquered. Individual salvation, the means necessary to obtain it, and a way of life modelled on Jesus Mary Jesus, Mary his mother, the saints, and the Ten Commandments were offered as a replacement for Saint an ethos based on kinship and the search for honour in battle. The tribes became Catholic, and Catholicism became, at least partially, Germanic. Liturgical norms and popular piety were adapted to peoples who expected practical results from the saints who took the place of departed ancestors and mythic tribal heroes. The landscape was gradually dominated by shrines to Jesus, his mother, and the saints, visual reminders that a new spiritual order prevailed.

That process of Christianization in both the Roman West and the Orthodox East in this period was not one in which formal ethical and doctrinal instruction transmitted the tenets of faith. Nor was it a process that demanded individualized personal commitment to Jesus. Lay Christian life became an omnipresent force throughout Europe. In both East and West – in a development which in the light of contemporary insights seems highly ambiguous – monks and contemplative nuns (and after the twelfth-century foundation of the Franciscan and Dominican communities, mendicant friars, who begged for their livelihood) took on the obligation to live out the full demands of the gospel. The laity's obligation was to follow the laws of God and the church. Missionary accommodation and inculturation had produced an altered form of Western Christianity.

In the East, during this same period, Byzantine ('Orthodox') expansion proceeded on somewhat different lines. As in the West, Byzantine developments involved the entanglement of church and state. But whereas in the West church and prince battled over who was supreme and in what realm, in the East the emperor was 'imitator of God' and his objectives and those of the church were virtually coterminous. It is not too much to say that the emperor and other kings were key figures in directing church expansion. Saying so, however, ought not to diminish our respect for the principles of Orthodox efforts. For despite the domination of the church by the emperor, the real conversion of peoples such as the Slavs took place over time, as the liturgy was celebrated and the worshipping community became the witnessing community.

p. 954

Orthodoxy spread northwards from Constantinople. In the East Slavonic liturgies spoke to and softened hearts, and the frontiers of Orthodox civilization pushed further and further east. Monasteries multiplied, and the Rus became Christian and then began to dominate the steppes. To the south, Oriental Orthodox communities became minorities in a Muslim sea. They were for many years sizeable minorities, but after having the bad luck of siding with the Mongols in their wars with the Muslims (Christians were numerous in the Mongol armies that sacked Baghdad in 1258), their prospects became bleak when Mongol fortunes went into decline in the fourteenth century. At roughly the same time, Franciscan missions to the Mongol and Chinese courts, which for a while held out a not unrealistic promise that Mongol rulers would become Christian and bring their peoples with them, came to nothing. Central Asia would become Muslim. In China, Christianity would never become numerically significant.

At the dawn of the age of Western exploration, Russian and other national Orthodox churches were consolidating in the lands from Poland to the Caucusus in the wake of imperial Russian victories over the Mongols. In world-historical terms, however, the next chapter in mission would be written by Roman Catholics. Their identity had been formed in the Middle Ages as the papacy developed and its primacy over all churches was accepted. It was the result of conflict with Islam, adapting to the Germanic world-view, in battles between the crown and the church, and in retrieving the classical tradition in the early Renaissance. By the end of the medieval era, the Roman Catholic Church saw itself as the sole divinely willed instrument through which the grace necessary for salvation could be obtained. Shut off from sub-Saharan Africa and West Asia by Islam and divided from Orthodoxy by a split that had been hardening since 1054, the Roman church had long had no scope for expansion. That was about to change.

Papacy

Renaissance

Early modern Christian missions and mission theory (1492–1792)

A radically new era in mission began when Asia and the Americas were opened up by Spanish and Portuguese sailors using improved methods of navigation and sailing technologies. In the light of contemporary developments, moreover, what resulted from these Spanish and Portuguese activities is far more important than the Reformation which began in 1517. While some of what follows may give the impression that Christian missions were fatally compromised by their relationship to the colonial enterprise, such a critique would have seemed strange to the missionaries who set out from Europe in the 1500s. Deep in their hearts lay the conviction that bringing them the gospel and the church was the only sure way to guarantee the salvation of those they encountered. If many regretted the brutality and death that accompanied the spread of the faith, it is important to realize

Reformation

The spread of Christianity, 1400–1800

Except where otherwise indicated, the date given is that of the creation of a Roman Catholic diocese; figures in brackets denote the date of the first Christian settlement. Places in CAPITALS are regions.

1 1404 Canaries
2 (1415) Ceuta
3 1511 San Juan
4 1511 Santo Domingo
5 1513 Panama
6 1514 Funchal
7 1517 Santiago
8 1530 Mexico
9 1531 Managua
10 1531 Caracas
11 1533 Goa
12 1534 Azores
13 1534 Cape Verde
14 1534 Cartagena
15 1534 Sao Tome
16 1537 Cuzco
17 1538 Chiapas
18 1541 Lima
19 1547 Asuncion
20 (1549) Kagoshima
21 1551 Bahia
22 1552 Charcas
23 1558 Cochin
24 1558 Malacca
25 1560 MOZAMBIQUE
26 1561 Santiago
27 1562 Timor
28 1564 La Imperial
29 1570 Cordoba
30 1576 Macao
31 1579 Manila
32 1596 (1491) San Salvador
33 1596 Masuanda Angano
34 (1601) GUINEA
35 1606 St Thomas
36 (1615) TONKING
37 1620 Buenos Aires
38 (1665) Reunion
39 1674 (1608) Quebec
40 1676 Recife
41 1676 Rio de Janeiro
42 1677 Sao Luis
43 1690 (1601) Peking
44 1690 Nanking
45 (17th century) Cape (Protestants)
46 (17th century) MADAGASCAR
47 (1706) Tranquebar (Protestants)
48 (1716) SENEGAL
49 1719 Belem
50 (1720) Mauritius
51 (1724) Irkutsk (Orthodox)
52 1745 Sao Paulo
53 1793 Baltimore
54 1793 New Orleans

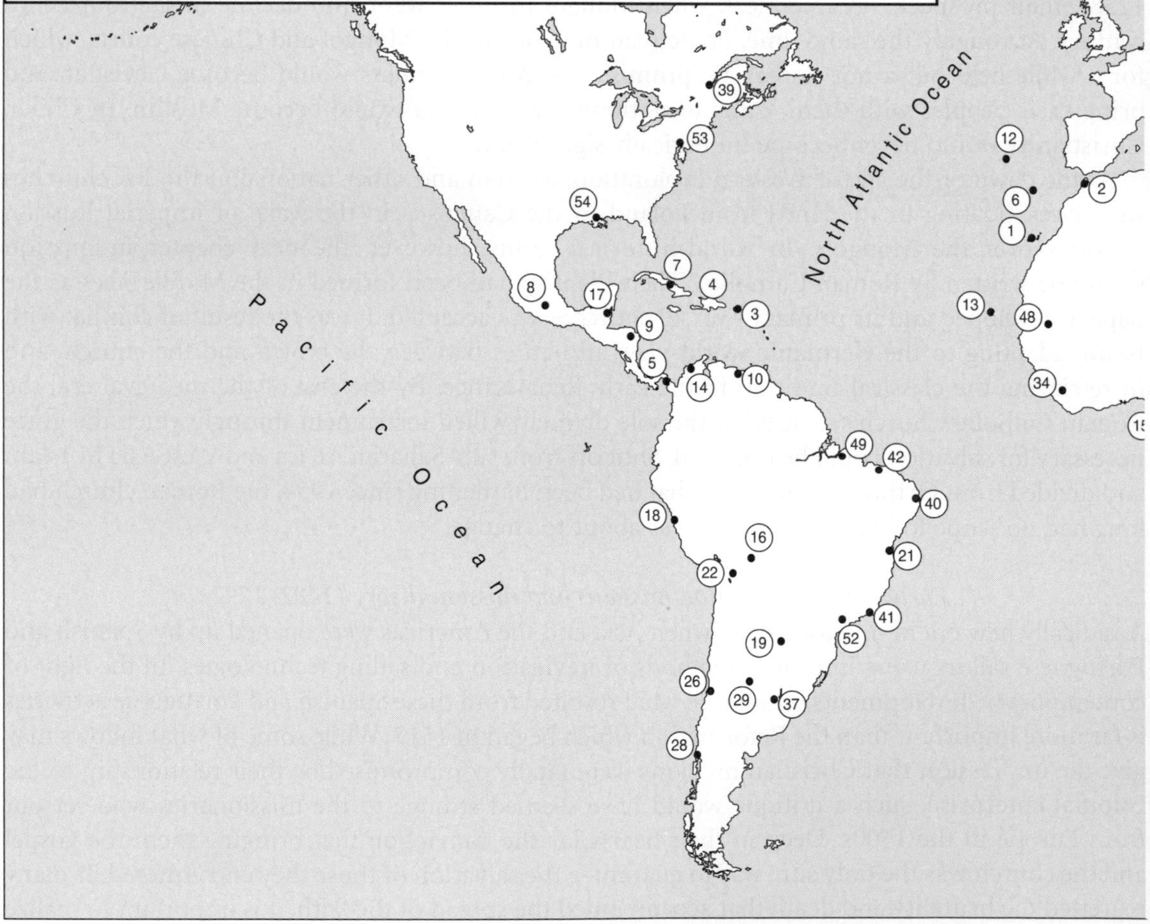

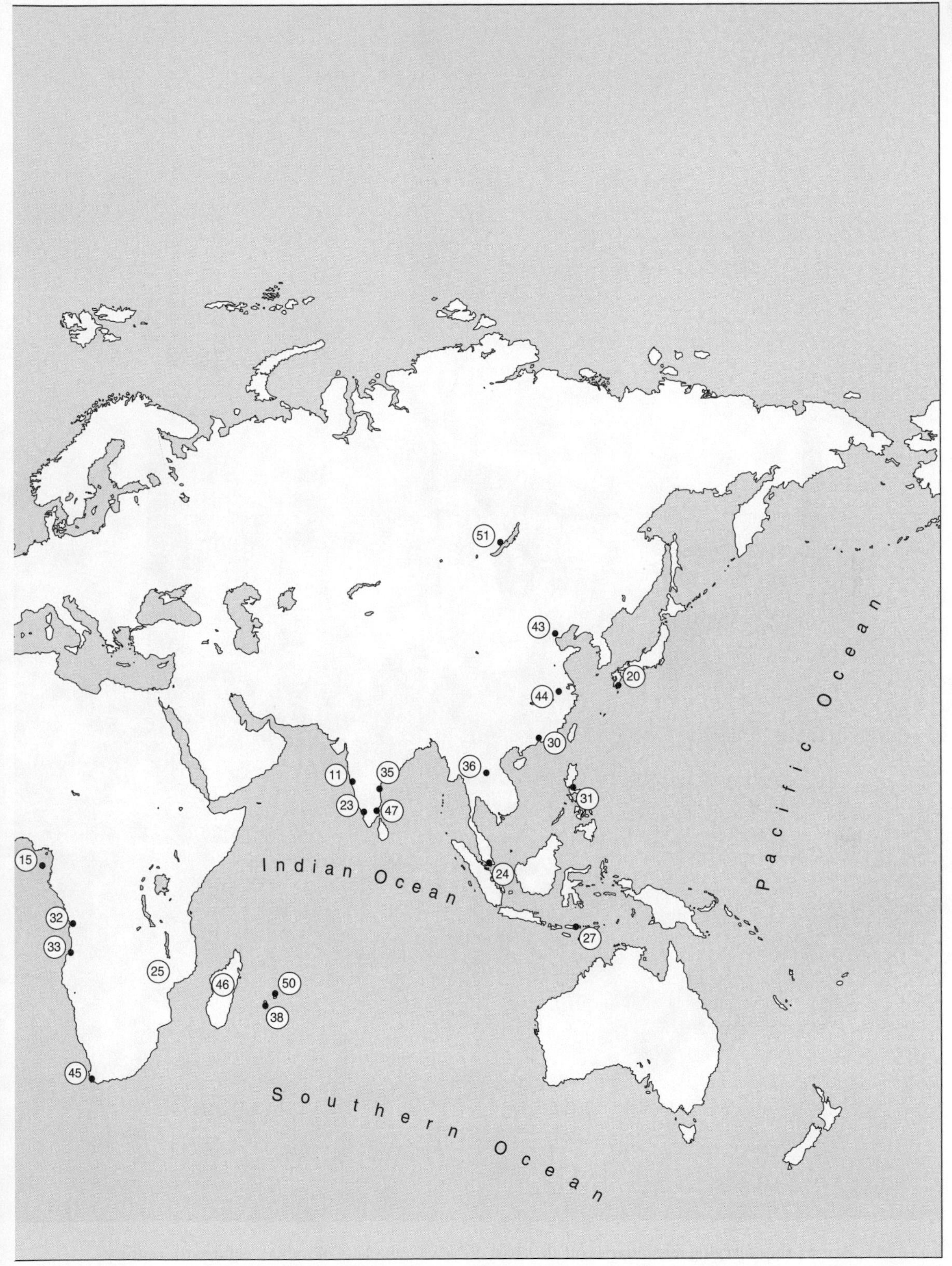
51
43
20
44
30
36
11
35
23
47
31
24
27
15
32
33
25
46
50
38
45
Indian Ocean
Pacific Ocean
Southern Ocean

MISSION

Armed ship carrying missionaries off the coast of New Granada (Colombia), eighteenth century that wherever one looks in missionary records and diaries one finds the conviction that even such evils served the higher good of bringing the means of salvation to peoples who lacked them. If this view seems grotesque to moderns, such convictions were both the motivation for and the theory behind the modern missionary movement.

In addition to this belief in the church's supernatural mission, a defining element in the experience of the Roman Catholicism that sent out missionaries evolved from battling with Protestants, using lessons learned during Spain's wars to expel the Muslims. The Hapsburg emperor Charles V (1500–58), the leader of anti-Protestant wars, was also King Charles I of Spain. Under his patronage the conquest of Latin America and Catholic missions advanced. Indeed, the training of Spanish, Portuguese, and Italian Catholic missionaries who went to Africa, Asia, and Latin America was suffused with the response to Protestantism that came from the Council of Trent (1545–63).

Protestantism

It is not necessary to labour the point that Roman Catholic missions in Africa, Asia and Latin America were carried out alongside and aided by European colonial efforts. What may need underlining is that in many cases, missioners struggled against royal officers to preserve freedom for the church and to seek just treatment of indigenous peoples. The result was that between 1492 and 1792, Iberian Catholic missions had achieved their primary goal. They had founded the church and had begun a process that would make America from the Rio Grande south to the Straits of Magellan Catholic.

Roman Catholic successes in the Americas are undeniable in numerical and institutional terms, but compromised by modern standards because of complicity in colonialism. It is impossible to argue with that judgement, at least in terms of the received picture. What is largely hidden from view, however, is the way in which a mulatto such as Martin de Porres (1579–1639) of Peru and Indian saints such as Juan Diego (1474–1548) in Mexico reveal that something other than the colonization of the Indian mind and land was also going on as Jesuits, Franciscans and Dominicans did their work. Contemporary research is unearthing evidence that Indians were discovering in Christianity a message of personal dignity and God's love, despite the indignities visited upon them. In the language of anthropology, while the structures of domination were being imposed, Christianity was being embraced because the image of the suffering Jesus and his mother's appearance to the impoverished also contained anti-structural, life-giving elements. God was on the side of the downtrodden and would reverse their fortunes. Although Spanish Catholic Christianity was embraced, the underlying faith was much more liberating than the vessel in which it arrived.

p. 733

Hispanic Christianity

In the person of missioners such as the Dominican Bartolomé de las Casas (1474–1566) and the Jesuit José de Acosta (1540–1600), Catholicism was planting seeds whose fruit transcended the dubious methods by which the message was being spread. It had results that chagrined those who brought it. For instance, in the 1680s the Brazilian black Catholic Lourenço da Silva presented an anti-slavery petition to the cardinals of the Congregation for Propagation of the Faith in Rome. It showed that the manner in which the buying and selling of slaves was carried on in Africa and the subsequent treatment of slaves in Brazil constituted 'the diabolic misuse of slavery'. The institution of slavery was not itself attacked. Rather, da Silva sought to show how its practice violated Christian norms. The cardinals of the congregation founded in 1622 to direct Roman Catholic missions agreed, and began a futile process of trying to end the abuses. The point here is not to justify colonial crimes in which missionaries were often complicit, but to bring into relief the fact that the crimes were recognized to be criminal. The history of these missions, in other words, gives evidence that dialectical processes were under way as liberating ideals found themselves in conflict with the structures of domination. The gospel, it can be argued, was subverting the principles of colonialism.

In West Africa and across the parts of Asia accessible from the sea, the results of Roman Catholic efforts in this early modern period were ambiguous and fleeting. If the standard of success is conversion statistics, the establishment of local churches, and achieving the power necessary to supplant other religious traditions, Portuguese and Italian Capuchins had fleeting moments of success in Congo and Angola. Over time, these missioners even discerned depths of similarities between African traditional religion and Christianity, but Christianity would be successful in Africa only when black Protestant ex-slaves freed in the aftermath of the American Revolution came on the scene.

In Asia Christian missions made enormous progress in Japan between 1549 and 1614, only to meet severe persecutions between 1614 and 1639, at least in part because Dominicans and Franciscans attacked Jesuits and gave Japanese rulers a breach they could exploit to rid themselves of bothersome foreigners. By 1650 Roman Catholicism was virtually extirpated, except for pockets of hidden faithful who, when discovered in 1865, had managed clandestinely to maintain their faith for over two centuries.

Between 1550 and 1650, missions in India, Indo-China (Vietnam), China and the Philippines were also undertaken. Only in the Philippines did such missions end in large numerical success or conversion percentages that would lead to a Roman Catholic majority. Three things must be noted here.

First, critics of missions in this era who say that Christianity in Asia was successful only when backed by military and political power are not entirely wrong.

Secondly, as in the Americas, Spanish missions in the Philippines did not succeed only because of that power. Schools, hospitals, orphanages and churches became beacons of hope and resistance in the midst of colonial encroachments that would have been far more debilitating had Jesuits and friars not come as missionaries.

Thirdly, four Jesuits, Alessandro Valignano (1539–1606), Matteo Ricci (1552–1610), Robert de Nobili (1577–1656) and Alexandre de Rhodes (1591–1660) epitomize an approach to mission in Asia that has proved more enduring and may deserve the accolade 'classic'. Valignano was the organizer of Jesuit missions in Japan and China and an Italian aristocrat. He insisted on the autonomy of missionaries and regarded Japanese and Chinese cultures as a positive base into which Christianity could be grafted. In effect, Valignano was advocating that these Asian cultures were in principle the equal of Graeco-Roman cultures in the early period of Christian origins. Did Valignano realize how deeply the Roman Catholicism he took for granted was also affected by Frankish-Germanic cultures? Probably not. Nevertheless, he set Roman Catholicism on a course in Asia which – with anti-inculturation zigs and pro-inculturation zags – it has continued down to our own day. This model of mission is marked by deep dialogue with Asian culture and the willingness to draw the consequences by rethinking the message and reshaping the church for Asia. It sunk roots in Roman Catholic mission theory and practice. It has also provoked profound opposition from some Vatican quarters, as well as from other Christians who judge that it compromises essentials. In other words, the debates between Antioch and Jerusalem, re-fought in the so-called Chinese rites controversies, have their counterparts in the modern period.

Japanese religions and Christianity
Chinese religions and Christianity
History

Of the three other Jesuits listed above, only Ricci worked directly under Valignano's direction (in China). Nevertheless, Valignano's policies influenced de Nobili's work among the Brahmins of India and that of de Rhodes in Vietnam. De Rhodes's *Catechism for the Vietnamese* bears studying even today as an example of profound engagement with Indo-Chinese culture, Buddhism and Confucian teaching. All four understood that lasting progress of Christianity in Asia depended upon deep understanding of and respect for Asian cultures and religious traditions.

In terms of the weight of Roman Catholic and later Protestant missionary work in Asia, however, the preponderance of effort was directed to traditional ministries aimed at creating charitable institutions, attempting to convert interested men and women to Christianity, and establishing the church. This was particularly the case when Roman Catholic missions recovered from the weakened state they fell into after the suppression of the Jesuits in 1773. The witness of these four men, however, assumed a mythic status for the Roman Catholic missionary ideal, even when Roman Catholic missions were dominated in the late nineteenth-century heyday of equating mission with the progress of European cultural ideals and colonial domination.

All four carried on their missions in Asia on terms set by Asians. Ironically perhaps, in the very area of the world where the missionaries had to work hardest to learn difficult languages and live on terms set by local cultures, their numerical success was the least impressive. And where it has begun to have its largest numerical successes in the second half of the twentieth century (in Korea and China, for example), the growth has occurred after most Western missionaries had departed.

Christian mission from 1792 to 1960

It is customary to note that the American Revolution of 1775–83 and the French Revolution of 1789 are pivotal in world history. While this is undoubtedly true, it is also worth noting that the results of the second phase of modern Christian missions are increasingly understood as having been of near-equal significance. 1960 marks the end of this period because by then the decolonization process begun by Mohandas K. Gandhi in India in the 1920s became irreversible. Ghana gained independence in 1957 under Nkrumah, and the rest of Africa followed quickly. Decolonization had an immense impact not just on international affairs but on the understanding and practice of Christian mission.

The main focus here is the history of Christian missions. Mission theology, a discussion of which follows later, was not monolithic between 1792 and 1960, but in both its Roman Catholic and Protestant versions it took its shape from the doctrine that faith in Christ and membership in the church were either the only way to achieve salvation or the normal way to attain it. In essentials Protestants agreed with Catholics on the necessity of faith in Christ for salvation. The chief differences between the two had to do with the nature of the church and the degree of intentionality that was necessary for faith. Catholics put more emphasis on the efficacy of grace operating through the sacraments as long as the recipient 'put no obstacle in their way' (Council of Trent, 'Decree on the Sacraments in General', canon 6). Protestants put much more emphasis on the individual act of faith, which itself – though Protestants would have denied it – acted as a functional equivalent to the sacraments. Such differences would play out in different practical ways as Catholics and Protestants battled with one another for ascendancy in African and Asian missions.

Salvation
Grace
Sacraments

Protestant missionary efforts are conventionally dated from 1792, when the English Baptist William Carey published *An Inquiry into the Obligations of Christians to Use Means for the Conversion of Heathens*; the Baptist Missionary Society was founded in the same year. The BMS is the prototype of the voluntary Protestant societies that would burgeon over the next several generations and attract thousands to leave home for missionary work. The success and numbers of these voluntary societies, indeed, became the spur for Roman Catholic orders founded in the nineteenth century along Jesuit lines to enter into mission, lest Protestants convert the world to their 'heretical'

MISSION

MISSIONARY SOCIETIES

In the Roman Catholic Church the religious orders, notably the Jesuits, were principally responsible for missionary work. Members of the Moravian Church had been as missionaries to all continents but Australia by 1760. Among Anglicans and Protestants, missionary societies played a key role. The first British missionary societies were founded at the beginning of the eighteenth century. A Society for the Propagation of the Gospel in New England had been founded in 1649; SPCK, the Society for the Promotion of Christian Knowledge, founded in 1698, had wider aims but did not begin missionary work until 1710.

Some of the more important missionary societies are:

1701 *SPG (Society for the Propagation of the Gospel in Foreign Parts)*
Founded in England by Thomas Bray to support missionary work in the British empire. In 1965 it united with UMCA to become USPG (the United Society for the Propagation of the Gospel).

1792 *Baptist Missionary Society*
Founded at the prompting of William Carey, who worked as its first missionary in India; it was also active in Jamaica, China, Zaire and Brazil.

1795 *London Missionary Society*
Founded by a group of Congregationalists, Presbyterians, Methodists and Anglicans for non-denominational work. It was active in Asia and the South Pacific; David Livingstone was its most famous representative in Africa.

1796 *Glasgow Missionary Society, Edinburgh Missionary Society*
In 1818 the Edinburgh Society changed its name to the Scottish Missionary Society; the societies did missionary work in West Africa, the Caribbean, the Caucasus and India.

1799 *CMS (Church Missionary Society)*
Arose out of the Evangelical movement. The first English missionary society to send missionaries to Africa and Asia.

1810 *American Board of Commissioners for Foreign Missions*
The first American society for foreign missions, founded by New England Congregationalists. It was particularly active in work on Hawaii.

A profusion of societies followed:

1813 *Wesleyan Missionary Society*
1814 *American Baptist Missionary Union*
1815 *Basle Missionary Society*
1819 *Missionary Society of the Methodist Episcopal Church*
1820 *Domestic and Foreign Missionary Society of the Episcopal Church*
1824 *Berlin Missionary Society*
1836 *Dresden Missionary Society* (it became the Leipzig Missionary Society in 1848)
1837 *Presbyterian Board of Foreign Missions* (though missionary work had been going on much earlier)
1857 *UMCA (Universities Mission to Central Africa)*
An Anglican organization founded in response to an appeal in Cambridge by David Livingstone and supported by the universities. In 1965 it united with SPG to become USPG (the United Society for the Propagation of the Gospel).

Some of these societies are still active, some have changed their names and others no longer exist.

 CMS: www.cms-uk.org; USPG: www.uspg.org.uk

version of Christianity. And the rise of these societies became one of the most characteristic aspects of church life in both church families, profoundly altering not just the way foreign missions were conducted but 'sending' churches as well. And there should be no mistake about it. The initiative and the greatest successes of mission in the nineteenth century were Protestant.

Women in Christianity

In a development that would have immense implications for Christian identity overall, women began working in mission in large numbers in the 1800s. In Protestant missions they began as wives of male missioners. In Roman Catholic missions, they came from the burgeoning ranks of newly-founded communities of religious sisters. These women all faced great obstacles that kept them from being considered full missionaries, since the archetype of both Protestant and Catholic missionaries was the ordained male. Indeed, the earliest of them had no idea that they were the vanguard of Christian feminism. Yet, from these pioneer female missionary cadres emerged a new form of vocational consciousness. At first they were confined to being auxiliaries of males, the 'true' missionaries, but distinctive insights unfolded and began to subvert the male domination of the church. These insights were threefold: that women's work in mission 1. was complementary to that of males, 2. was equally necessary, and 3. made Christian claims more plausible than if they were just backed up by the work of men.

The slow recognition of the integral nature of women's work and vocation is one of the factors that in the second half of the 1900s led to the expansion of lay consciousness and emphasis on what is essential if Christian missions are to embody God's love. From within the ranks of women missionaries came the push to acknowledge that improving the well-being of local peoples, whether they were likely to become Christian or not, was an essential dimension of mission. And with that would be abandoned the notion that mission is only about making converts and founding new churches. Equally important is embodying the love of God without regard to expanding the size of the church.

British Protestantism was not alone in sparking missionary activity, but in many ways it was the pioneer, and its methods of organization tended to be followed by missionaries of many nations. Several influences contributed notably to what began to happen after 1792. Two began as reform movements within Anglicanism. John and Charles Wesley's Methodist revival contributed to  fervour on both sides of the Atlantic. Their movement is especially important for having brought attention to social issues that would most noticeably affect the anti-slavery movement. George Whitefield (1714–70), influenced by the Wesleyan revivals, was one of the key progenitors of  the 'Great Awakening' in both England and America, where Jonathan Edwards (1703–58) was 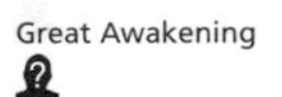 Great Awakening active. The ministry of Whitefield and Edwards would permeate and deepen Calvinist theology in American Protestant churches that would later become active in missions. Between 1787 and about 1825, a movement called the Evangelical Revival in England and the Second Great Awakening in Evangelicals America set the stage for the missionary movement.

Although missions in India were often established against the wishes of the British commercial companies that expanded both their own and British political interests, to Indians in the various small states into which missioners followed the flag, the mutual distrust of the East India Company and the missions was not apparent. In China, where the Portuguese, Germans, French and British competed to expand their areas of influence, both Roman Catholic and Protestant missions worked under the protection of European powers. Japan never fell under such domination, but both there and in the rest of Asia, one of the most common accusations against Asian Christians down to the contemporary era is that they have adopted a foreign religion. And, although Asian Christians are deeply committed to their faith, the accusation that they follow a Western religion still rankles. Whatever its relation to colonialism, Christianity had numerical successes in Asia, principally among the followers of 'local' religio-cultural traditions, many of whose followers felt themselves oppressed by Hindu, Buddhist, Confucianist or Muslim majorities. Among the Asian masses, followers of the traditions now called 'world religions' kept faith with their ancestors. That does not mean, however, that Asians did not become Christians. They did. Still, despite the vitality of

Asian Christian churches that arose from missionary activity, Christianity in Asia seems destined for minority status for the foreseeable future, although strong growth rates in Korea and among the Dalits (outcastes) and places such as north-east India, where large popular movements into Christianity are occurring, show that different futures could materialize.

In sub-Saharan Africa, something quite different occurred during this period. To bring it into relief, it must be realized that from the first Roman Catholic contacts in 1506 to the late 1700s, few positive results were gained. Whether this was because of too few personnel in Portuguese missions in Congo, the lax moral quality of the traders, or the difficulties which whites experienced in working in West Africa, the result was the same. And looming above all other obstacles was the slave trade, which was dominated by Portuguese Catholics. Granted that African domestic slavery was intolerable, the international slave trade introduced cruelty and degradation to an entirely different level, yet Portuguese priests and religious in Africa participated in it.

Freed black slaves from North America would be important in the next stage of African Christian mission. They were also important in carrying forward the work of the Englishman William p. 438 Wilberforce and the Clapham Sect. With the slave trade banned in 1807 by Britain and then slavery itself abolished in all British colonies in 1833, other European powers found it impossible to resist the anti-slavery tide. Eleven hundred slaves emancipated after the American Revolutionary War, when the British honoured their promise that those who fought the revolutionaries would be given freedom, settled from Nova Scotia to Freetown in Sierra Leone. These freed slaves had found liberation in Christianity even while enslaved by Christian masters. They yearned to share that freedom in their ancestral homelands.

Native-born Africans were also active in missionary successes. West African missions, for example, had foundered until a Yoruba lad named Ajayi was taken from a Portuguese slave ship to Sierra Leone by the British anti-slavery naval patrol in about 1820. He became a Christian and took the name Samuel Crowther. Quick to learn and an attractive leader, Crowther was ordained in London in 1843, after which he opened a mission in Yorubaland (in today's Nigeria). Crowther's character, achievements, and talents deepened the growing conviction of Henry Venn, secretary of the Church Missionary Society, that missions could and should become self-governing, self-supporting and self-propagating. Venn's so-called 'three-self' principle would in turn become a landmark in Protestant missiology, even if it took well into the twentieth century for all the consequences to be drawn from the theory.

In an important parallel development, an American black Baptist missionary society founded in Richmond, Virginia, had sent two preachers to Liberia in 1840. Others followed, and after the American Civil War (1861–5) many more would follow, including the founding of so-called 'industrial missions' under the inspiration of Bishop Henry McNeal Turner (1834–1915), a great proponent of the American 'back to Africa' movement. In another development on the initiative of former slaves, West Indian blacks settled down in Akrapong, 50 miles from Accra, along with other settlements in Port Clarence and Calabar in the Niger delta. Other black 'missionaries' took inspiration from Ethiopia as a Christian land that had not been dominated by whites. Henry Blyden (1832–1912), a West Indian black of Nigerian ancestry, may, at risk of oversimplification, be taken as the key to the attempt to found an Ethiopianized Christianity freed of white influence.

Much more could be said. The important thing to note is that many of the most dynamic initiatives in African missions were led by Africans. Although the numbers of European missioners in the years between 1860 and 1960 may have exceeded the number of prominent, ordained Africans, it was the life and work of persons like those named above, along with the efforts of untold

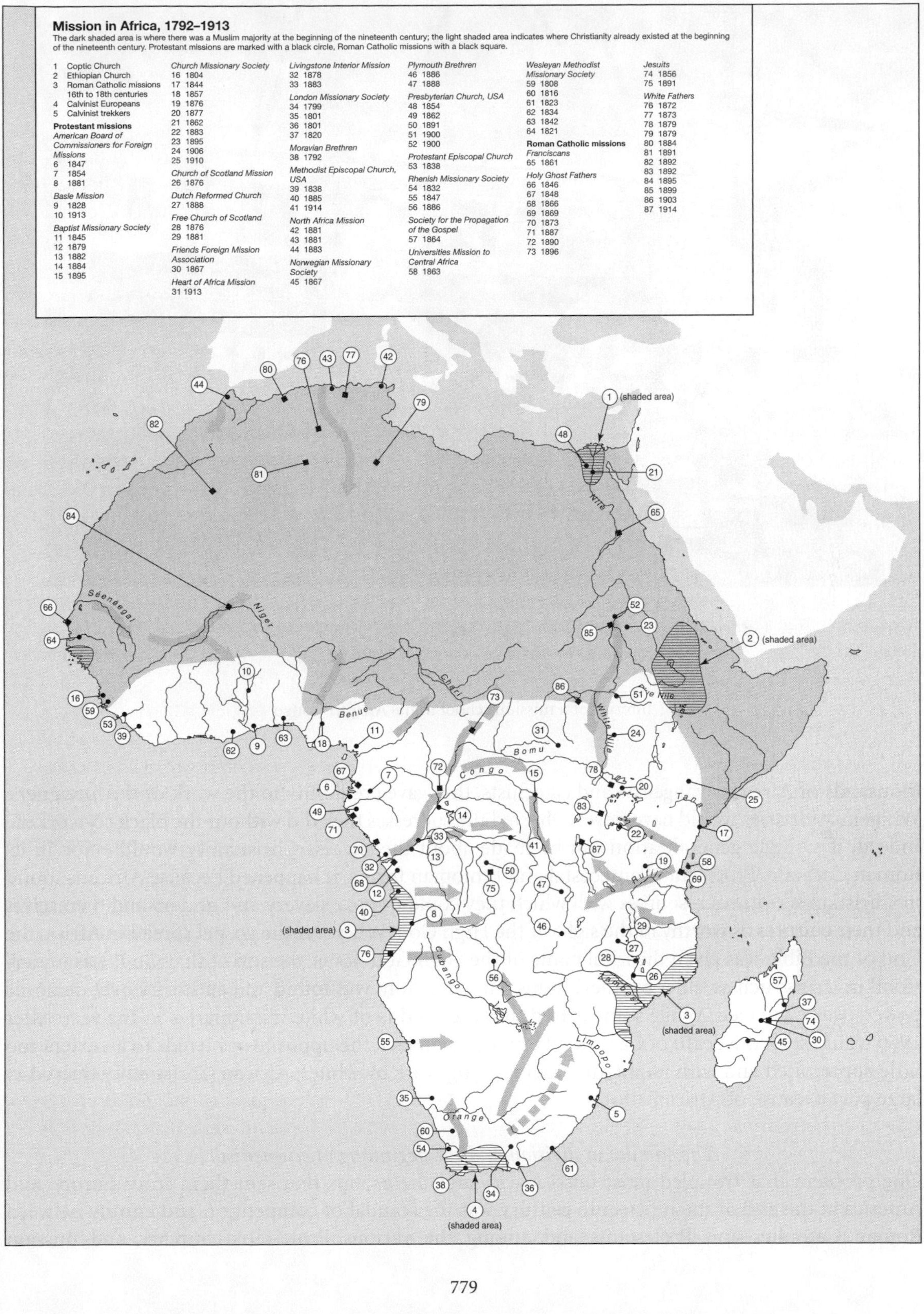

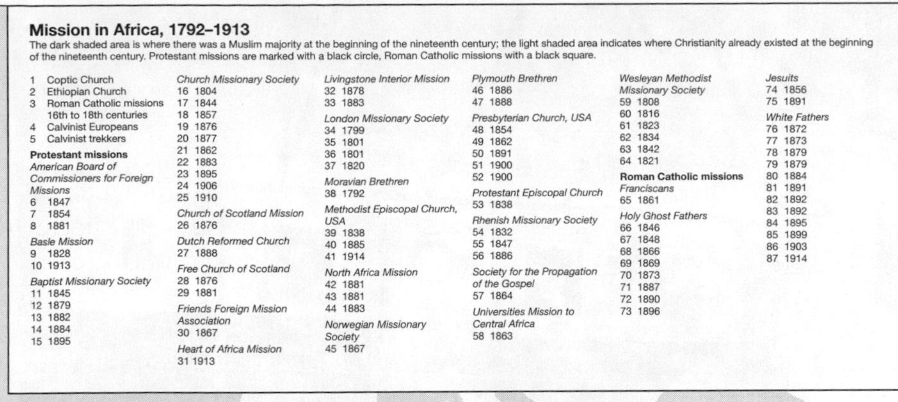
Mission in Africa, 1792–1913
The dark shaded area is where there was a Muslim majority at the beginning of the nineteenth century; the light shaded area indicates where Christianity already existed at the beginning of the nineteenth century. Protestant missions are marked with a black circle, Roman Catholic missions with a black square.
1 Coptic Church
2 Ethiopian Church
3 Roman Catholic missions 16th to 18th centuries
4 Calvinist Europeans
5 Calvinist trekkers
Protestant missions
American Board of Commissioners for Foreign Missions
6 1847
7 1854
8 1881
Basle Mission
9 1828
10 1913
Baptist Missionary Society
11 1845
12 1879
13 1882
14 1884
15 1895
Church Missionary Society
16 1804
17 1844
18 1857
19 1876
20 1877
21 1862
22 1883
23 1895
24 1906
25 1910
Church of Scotland Mission
26 1876
Dutch Reformed Church
27 1888
Free Church of Scotland
28 1876
29 1881
Friends Foreign Mission Association
30 1867
Heart of Africa Mission
31 1913
Livingstone Interior Mission
32 1878
33 1883
London Missionary Society
34 1799
35 1801
36 1801
37 1820
Moravian Brethren
38 1792
Methodist Episcopal Church, USA
39 1838
40 1885
41 1914
North Africa Mission
42 1881
43 1881
44 1883
Norwegian Missionary Society
45 1867
Plymouth Brethren
46 1886
47 1888
Presbyterian Church, USA
48 1854
49 1862
50 1891
51 1900
52 1900
Protestant Episcopal Church
53 1838
Rhenish Missionary Society
54 1832
55 1847
56 1886
Society for the Propagation of the Gospel
57 1864
Universities Mission to Central Africa
58 1863
Wesleyan Methodist Missionary Society
59 1808
60 1816
61 1823
62 1834
63 1842
64 1821
Roman Catholic missions
Franciscans
65 1861
Holy Ghost Fathers
66 1846
67 1848
68 1866
69 1869
70 1873
71 1887
72 1890
73 1896
Jesuits
74 1856
75 1891
White Fathers
76 1872
77 1873
78 1879
79 1879
80 1884
81 1891
82 1892
83 1892
84 1895
85 1899
86 1903
87 1914

1 (shaded area)
2 (shaded area)
(shaded area) 3
3 (shaded area)
4 (shaded area)
Séénégal
Niger
Nile
Benue
Chari
Bomu
Congo
White Nile
Blue Nile
Tana
Rufiji
Cubango
Zambezi
Limpopo
Orange

Africa - Kongo. Free State. Interior of Mission school.

Interior of a mission school in the African Congo

thousands of African evangelists and catechists, that gave credibility to the work of the foreigners. White missionaries would have never achieved the successes they did without the black co-workers. Indeed, if a single generalization can be made about the success Christianity would enjoy in its Roman Catholic, Protestant, Pentecostal and Ethiopian forms, it happened because Africans found in Christian scriptures resources with which they could oppose slavery and understand themselves and their cultures as worthy in the sight of the High God. Wherever the gospel spread in Africa, the God of the Bible was given the local name of the High God. Jesus, the son of that God, was understood in terms such as 'elder brother'. In his name freedom was found and authority over demonic powers was conferred. While some feared that the exodus of white missionaries in the years after 1960 would spell the death of Christianity in Africa, in fact, the opposite occurred. To an extent too little appreciated and with no intent of denigrating work by whites, African Christianity thrived in large part because of African efforts.

Ethiopian Christianity

The scandal of division and the beginning of ecumenism

One problem that troubled most missionaries and the groups that sent them from Europe and America at the end of the nineteenth century was the scandal of competition and enmity between Roman Catholics and Protestants and among the various Protestant churches and mission societies. The Edinburgh World Missionary Conference of 1910 was the fourth such conference, but the meticulous preparation that went into it made it the most important. While the Roman Catholics and the Orthodox took no official part (although there was one unofficial Italian Catholic observer), the 1200 Protestant representatives who took part under the chairmanship of the Student Volunteer Movement's John Raleigh Mott (1865–1955) laid down trails that would lead to the founding of the International Missionary Council, from which developed the World Council of Churches.

Ecumenical movement

Protestants and Catholics were both dealing with the same problem for 50 years after 1910. What should be the path from missions founded by and still largely led by missionary societies to the status of local churches? And in the light of the ecumenical problem, must divisions of the church that arose in sixteenth-century European quarrels be continued in the new churches?

Papal encyclicals were issued by Benedict XV, Pius XI and Pius XII that attempted to address the point of adapting the church in non-Western cultures. Much of the work of the IMC was similarly directed. Ideals such as Venn's three-self principle could offer practical guidance to Protestants. Catholics had greater difficulty putting into practice papal teaching, since few could imagine a Roman Catholic Church without its medieval and baroque accoutrements. The popes who wrote the encyclicals, if truth be told, did not understand the implications of their theories. In reality, neither Protestants nor Catholics found it easy to imagine the new churches surviving without direction and control from Europe and America. White racism and cultural bias judged itself benevolent and sought to maintain enshrined patterns of domination that lingered into the second half of the twentieth century.

p. 700

Developments in mission since 1960

As the 1960s began, among Roman Catholics and members of the World Council of Churches conversations switched from questions about how European and American societies could carry on missions whose goal was the expansion of the church to the language of 'mission'. Mission had been *missio ad gentes* ('mission to [foreign] peoples'). As the twentieth century drew to a close, however, mission was more and more an activity carried out as *missio inter gentes* ('mission among peoples'). Rather than going abroad to the religious 'other', local churches were seeking to engage in dialogue with neighbours, including their own family members, who followed 'other' religious traditions. The object of their dialogue was not to seek advantage, so that 'false' religions could be replaced by Christianity, so much as to seek ways to implement common concern for human liberation.

Feeding into these strands of mission thought were two important currents. The first was the rise of academically serious histories of religion. As insights from this discipline grew, Christian superiority over other traditions could no longer be genuinely proposed by any educated person. The great religions were on a level playing field. Moreover, in the eyes of humanists dedicated to alleviating human suffering, every religious tradition was shown to be highly ambiguous. All religions were under a cloud of suspicion generated by sincere people who saw in the concrete functioning of every religious way the dead hand of self-interest as much as a tradition passing on life-giving wisdom.

The second current – Marxism – took on many forms and existed in both Christian and anti-Christian forms. This family of criticism saw missions as the outposts of capitalism and capitalism as a system that required the subjugation of the Global South (usually called the 'Third World') to pay for the pampered lifestyle of the Global North (usually called the 'First World'). In many national liberation movements it became axiomatic that Christian churches were stooges for

Third World

European and American political and economic interests. Within the missions community such accusations sparked intense and often bitter debates, since many missioners believed that the accusations contained much more than a grain of truth.

With all this in the background, the WCC's Commission on World Mission and Evangelism (CWME), successor to the IMC, met in Mexico City in 1963 and attempted to articulate a path of dialogue that churches should follow in mission. At roughly the same time, the Roman Catholic p. 290 Second Vatican Council (1962–5) was debating the text of documents on the mission of the church in the contemporary world, *Gaudium et spes*, and on the relationship of the church to non-Christian religions, *Nostra aetate*. These documents were written in the context of the debates on global social justice and whether it was authentic Christian practice to seek to dominate and replace the world's religions. The Council's *Ad gentes* ('Decree on the Missionary Activity of the Church') was an attempt to bring insights from conciliar commissions that had worked on these documents and others to bear on the conduct of missions and the nature of mission. *Ad gentes* expresses the church's role as being a 'universal sacrament of salvation': a role that follows from the fact that the church 'is, by its very nature, missionary'. But it attempted to do so in the spirit of *Gaudium et spes*, which had insisted that the church 'offers to cooperate unreservedly with mankind in fostering a spirit of brotherhood ... to serve and not to be served'.

As WCC member churches and Roman Catholics debated the adequacy of such statements and tried to draw their consequences, two other forces were at work. First, the Cold War was still being waged between the capitalist First World and the Marxist Second. Each side would do anything to gain an advantage over its adversary, while the Third World peoples whom Christians had made the object of their missions since 1492 became the pawns in that game. Second, an independent, 'Evangelical' church movement, which also attracted theological conservatives from within WCC churches, coalesced around the 'Lausanne Covenant' (1975) to redouble efforts to reach unreached peoples with what Lausanne covenanters viewed to be the whole gospel. The implication, of course, was that liberal churches and missionaries had surrendered the absoluteness of Christ and the need to embrace him in faith as integral to the Christian mission message. Any account of Christian mission must bring into relief the fact that this argument was still raging at the dawn of the twenty-first century and shows no sign of abating.

In this context, John Paul II's (1990) encyclical *Redemptoris missio* ('The Mission of the Redeemer') insisted on the centrality of Christ for salvation of all the world and as the cause of saving grace that the Holy Spirit mediates to sincere followers of all religious ways. He was equally insistent that Christian mission involved alleviating human suffering. The adequacy of his position has been the focus of debates since the publication of *Redemptoris missio*. The seriousness with which John Paul's teaching has been taken by people on all sides of the conversation shows that understandings of mission and missions at the beginning of the twenty-first century are not reducible to one's church affiliation. Instead, a new phenomenon, called 'post-denominationalism' by many, has emerged.

Post-denominational understandings of Christian mission find persons and groups with similar views of the mission to which God calls the church banding together to carry out tasks without regard to the concrete church to which their potential allies belong. What becomes important is to achieve clarity on the so-called *missio Dei* (the 'mission of God') in a given context and to join as followers of Jesus to accomplish that mission. In one context, the primary mission may be alleviating famine; in another, replacing corrupt, enslaving political and economic systems with just systems; in another, overcoming environmental degradation and restoring the integrity of creation;

in another, reconciling social classes or helping make peace; in still another, furthering dialogue among religions and civilizations; in another, teaching seekers the way of Jesus and helping to plant new churches.

Implicit in this concept of mission is a shift in historical consciousness that has accompanied the rise of modernity. At least in the West, where they often wear post-Christian dress, but also prominent in the rest of the world, significant numbers of 'modern' people reject any hint that salvation can be understood as a spiritual reality transcending the world we know. While ancient and medieval world-views posited a gulf between the shifting, changing world of history on the one hand and the eternal, unchanging world of spirit on the other, many today find such distinctions implausible. Whatever Christian mission means, such moderns say, it is meaningless without work to overcome the many evils that keep both earth and human beings from achieving their potential. For such persons, the primary mission in which Christians participate is the struggle to overcome such evil forces.

Critics of such contemporary understandings of mission believe that those who advocate them (often termed 'theological liberals') misdiagnose the human situation and our need for radical forgiveness and conversion. The truest liberation, they maintain, involves accepting God's plan for the world embodied in Jesus, the proclaimer of the way to reconciliation with God and the first-fruits of God's final kingdom still to come. In that theological key, the primary mission that Christians join is the struggle to alert people to their inability to save themselves and to lead them to seek salvation in the gospel. Social consequences, they maintain, will follow.

Kingdom of God

This is not the place to settle such arguments. What is fruitful is to point to emerging understandings which offer the promise that Christians who occupy various places on the continuum between extremes can find common ground. It is possible to envision a viewpoint on Christian mission that sees mission as evangelization ('gospelling') and evangelization as a complex reality. Mission along such lines involves: 1. Presenting Jesus as way, truth, and life, inviting all interested peoples to consider following Jesus in faith, and founding new churches for those who wish to follow him; 2. 'Contextualizing' or 'inculturating' the church and translating the gospel into the languages of all peoples; 3. Promoting justice, peace and the integrity of creation; 4. Developing and practising modes of liturgy, prayer, study and contemplation that enable people to enter more deeply and intentionally into unity with God and to realize their rightful place in the cosmic order; 5. Enhancing intercultural and interreligious understanding through conversation, academic study and dialogue; 6. Striving to reconcile estranged peoples, religious, political and social traditions, as well as humanity and God.

Contextual theology

It goes without saying that persons who identify most with one or the other of these points will emphasize that point and put more weight on it. Christian mission is, when all is said and action begins, a multi-faceted, pluralistic enterprise. What bears underlining is that Christians today are about one third of the world's population, and the most vital sectors of the church are no longer in the West and North. Indeed, the centre of Christian gravity has moved south to Africa and Latin America. In Asia, the numbers are not as significant as in Africa and Latin America, but the phrase 'Pentecost in Asia' is not without meaning.

While northern and western churches hold the preponderance of material resources to carry on the kind of mission summarized in the six points listed above, the sense of participating in God's mission to attain these goals seems liveliest in the so-called Global South. Christian Indonesians 'in mission' among their fellow Indonesians, for example, are working with friends and neighbours. The tenor of their work differs from that of foreign missionaries in the classical era of modern mission.

Not without reason, then, is the changed reality of Christianity declared an emergence of 'world Christianity' or 'world church'. The modern missionary movement has not accomplished everything that those who resonated with the words of John Raleigh Mott had hoped for when at the end of the nineteenth century he called for the 'evangelization of the world in this generation', a phrase which was adopted by the famous 1910 Edinburgh Missionary Conference. The results of the Student Volunteer Movement, as of the modern missionary movement generally, have been more paradoxical. Christianity in the Europe that sparked the movement is now largely in recession in all its varieties, while African independent churches thrive. Conservative Third World Christians criticize First World permissiveness in sexual ethics and in some places seem prepared to enter into a new kind of war against the encroachments of Islam. Meanwhile, Pentecostalism spreads throughout Latin American and Africa, eroding Catholic predominance. Old and new northern Christian centres – Rome, Geneva, and Lausanne – witness a birth of mission spirit in a way no one predicted in 1492, and wonder about their futures.

Pentecostalism

WILLIAM R. BURROWS

Stephen B. Bevans and Roger Schroeder, *Constants in Context: A Theology of Mission for Today*, Maryknoll, NY: Orbis Books 2004; David J. Bosch, *Transforming Mission: Paradigm Shifts in Theology of Mission*, Maryknoll, NY: Orbis Books 1991; Jacques Dupuis, *Christianity and the Religions: From Confrontation to Dialogue*, Maryknoll, NY: Orbis Books and London: Darton, Longman & Todd 2002; Richard Gray, *Black Christians and White Missionaries*, New Haven and London: Yale University Press 1990; J. Andrew Kirk, *What Is Mission? Theological Explorations*, London: Darton Longman & Todd 1999 and Minneapolis: Fortress Press 2000; Dana Lee Robert, *American Women in Mission: A Social History of their Thought and Practice* (Modern Mission Era, 1792–1992), Grand Rapids: Eerdmans 1997; James J. Stamoolis, *Eastern Orthodox Mission Theology Today*, Maryknoll, NY: Orbis Books 1986; Andrew F. Walls, *The Missionary Movement in Christian History*, Maryknoll, NY and Edinburgh: T&T Clark 1996; Timothy Yates, *Christian Mission in the Twentieth Century*, Cambridge: CUP 1994

Modernism

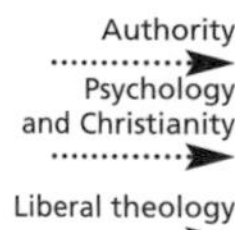
Authority
Psychology and Christianity
Liberal theology

The words 'modern', 'modernist' and 'modernism' can mean very different things in different contexts. Within modern theology 'modernism' is usually limited to a very specific movement of Roman Catholic thinkers whose key works were published in the last decade of the nineteenth century and the first decade of the twentieth. It is often said that the concept itself was really only brought into being by a papal encyclical of September 1907 which defined it as 'a synthesis of all errors' and in doing so brought under a single heading a number of loosely associated currents in contemporary Catholic thought. Whether or not modernism was 'invented' by its enemies in the church hierarchy, it was undeniably terminated by them, when the papacy imposed an oath abjuring modernism on all teachers of Roman Catholic theology (1910).

p. 700

Key issues in the modernist debate included the nature of authority, the role of history and historical research in doctrine and theology, and the psychology of the religious life. To a large extent the modernist agenda overlapped with that of liberal Protestant thought, but whereas the latter could plausibly claim to represent the Protestant mainstream, the course and fate of Roman Catholic modernism was determined by the nineteenth-century papacy's opposition to science, biblical criticism, democracy and modern thought in general. This opposition had already been clearly stated in the Syllabus of Errors (1864) and in the assertion of papal infallibility (1870). Although modernist currents were present in most European countries, it was in France and England that modernism's theological profile was chiefly defined, above all by Alfred Loisy (1857–1940), Baron Friedrich von Hügel (1852–1925) and George Tyrrell (1861–1909).

Loisy was the first to come to prominence. A biblical scholar, he had been dismissed from a teaching post in 1893, but in 1902 he wrote *The Gospel and the Church*, a response to the liberal Protestant Adolf von Harnack, whose book *The Essence of Christianity* had eliminated any idea of a church from the earliest Christian sources. Loisy argued that the calling of the apostles belonged to the core of the gospel. When he wrote that 'Jesus proclaimed the kingdom and it was the church that came', Loisy believed that he was defending Roman Catholic claims about the need for a visible church on earth. But by defending the apostolic ministry on historical grounds and allowing for a process of historical development and transformation he seemed to the hierarchy to undermine the church's claim that its forms of ministry had been established by Christ himself. Loisy also stated that the divinity of Christ was not itself a fact that could be proved by history. *The Gospel and the Church* and four other of Loisy's books were condemned by the Holy Office in 1903, and despite his submission Loisy was excommunicated in 1908. By then the anti-modernist encyclical *Pascendi* and the decree *Lamentabili* (listing 65 modernist errors) had unambiguously defined the church's agenda, and fellow modernists such as George Tyrrell were also in deep trouble with the church authorities.

Tyrrell, an Anglo-Irish Jesuit, had come to accept the idea of a historical development in religion, and strongly to oppose a view of faith couched in terms of a set of objective doctrinal assertions whose truth ultimately rested on the authority of the Pope. He saw this as a cowardly evasion of the truths of history, experience and science that were being opened up by contemporary thought. Doctrine, he insisted, was no more than a classifying and ordering of what first existed in the complex, protean ferment of life. The church's 'theologism' (as he called it) turned this upside-down and put theological definition first and living spiritual experience second. Like Loisy, Tyrrell saw his ideas as ammunition for Roman Catholic thinking. It was, he claimed, a virtue of Catholicism that it allowed the infinite variety of real religious life and the influence of living devotion to shape doctrine and organization, as opposed to Protestant attempts to reduce religion to a few fundamentals. Even its pagan elements and corruptions testified to Catholicism's deep realism. A powerful controversialist, Tyrrell asked his opponents in the hierarchy: 'How can the world imagine that you have faith in God, that you believe sincerely in the harmony of revelation and science, when it sees you so manifestly afraid of criticism, afraid of the light, afraid of liberty, afraid of outspokenness and moral courage?' From their point of view Tyrrell represented the attempt to place the individual conscience and judgement above the common mind of the church. From 1900 onwards Tyrrell's writing was progressively restricted. Dismissed from the Jesuits in 1905 and his right to function as a priest disputed, he was forced into increasing isolation. Though receiving absolution on his death-bed he was denied a Catholic funeral (1909).

For a long time Tyrrell had been encouraged and supported by Baron Friedrich von Hügel, a lay religious writer, whose chief work, *The Mystical Element of Religion*, attempted to vindicate the legitimacy of mystical experience and intellectual enquiry alongside religion's institutional element. Von Hügel was a keen follower of contemporary intellectual currents and strongly ecumenical in outlook. As a layman, and lacking Tyrrell's combative attitude, von Hügel largely escaped censure. At the same time his efforts to mediate and win some tolerance for the modernists completely failed. Even before von Hugel's own death in 1925, Maud Petre, a Roman Catholic laywoman and close associate of Tyrrell and of von Hügel, wrote that she was 'a solitary marooned passenger; the sole living representative of what has come to be regarded as a lost cause'.

The authorities could at that point be plausibly seen as having completely routed the modernists, and one current Roman Catholic website defines modernism as 'an exaggerated love of what is modern'. Nevertheless, modernist ideas were implicit in many of the reforms of the Second Vatican Council. Council

GEORGE PATTISON

A. Loisy, *The Gospel and the Church* (1903), reissued Amherst, NY: Prometheus Books 1992; A. Sabatier, *The Religions of Authority and the Religion of the Spirit*, London: Williams & Norgate 1904; N. Sagovsky, *On God's Side. A Life of George Tyrrell*, Oxford: Clarendon Press 1990; George Tyrrell, *Through Scylla and Charybdis. The Old Religion and the New*, London: Green & Co. 1907; A. Vidler, *The Modernist Movement in the Roman Church, its Origins and Outcome*, Cambridge: CUP 1934

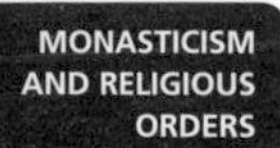

MONASTICISM AND RELIGIOUS ORDERS

Community, History, Mission, Monasticism, Orthodox churches, Religious orders, Roman Catholic Church, Spirituality

The terms 'monasticism' and 'religious orders' both describe ways of organizing the religious life, but they are not synonymous. The differences can to a large extent be explained historically, but it may be helpful to begin by explaining more precisely what is meant by the 'religious life' in a Christian context. At first sight, it might seem to signify nothing more than the moral and spiritual life lived by Christians in general, but it has in fact a more restricted and precise meaning: that is, the ways of life lived by men and women who have made a solemn profession of their intentions, sealed by vows (typically poverty, chastity and obedience) which bind them to their chosen course for life. This commitment may be to prayer and contemplation at one extreme, to active involvement in missions, medical work and teaching at the other. Whatever it may be, their way of life is governed by a rule, set down in writing and administered and interpreted by their superiors.

In the modern Western world, to adopt one of these vocations usually means joining a religious order, that is an organization, whether large or small, which possesses a centralized structure. All Roman Catholic orders look ultimately to the papacy as their supreme authority and they may have headquarters in Rome itself. However, this has not always been so. Historically the Christian religious life originated with contemplatives and solitaries, monks and hermits. For many centuries monks were organized only in autonomous communities, while solitaries were not organized at all. From the eighth century until about 1100, almost all monks in Western Europe may be described as 'Benedictine' (although this is not what they would have called themselves) because they followed the Rule of Benedict, but there was no such thing as a Benedictine 'order' which linked different abbeys together into a unified structure.

Organization

It can be said, however, that there was a monastic order. All monks and nuns, indeed every man and woman, belonged to an order in the sense in which the word *ordo* was understood for much of the Middle Ages, that is, a social grouping, almost a social status. The social order as a whole depended on the correct positioning of every man and woman in their particular *ordo*. Some thinkers went so far as to declare that Christians would be marshalled in their 'orders' at the day of judgement. One classic formulation, current in the tenth century, divided society into three 'orders': those who fought, those who worked, those who prayed. Reality was of course more complicated. 'Those who prayed' comprised a rich variety of people, monks (and nuns), hermits and recluses, bishops, priests and the lower orders of clergy. These were sometimes divided into two categories: the 'regulars', that is persons such as monks who lived under a rule (*regula*) and the 'seculars', clergy such as parish priests who lived in 'the world' (*saeculum*).

Middle Ages

It would be difficult to pinpoint a moment at which religious orders in the modern sense of the term came into being, but the concept can be seen as growing from twelfth-century roots. By about 1100 it was becoming obvious that different groups of monks, such as the Cistercians or the Carthusians, were following different interpretations of the monastic way of life (and were adopting distinctive modes of dress). The word 'order' could be conveniently applied to these groups, and certain features of their organization pointed tentatively in the direction of centralization. There were other significant new departures early in the twelfth century, for example the foundation of the Knights of the Order of the Temple, whose particular purposes required an international organization of a new kind. Groups of 'regulars' who were not leading a primarily contemplative life, as monks were supposed to do, also multiplied. Further developments took place early in the thirteenth with the Franciscan and, especially, the Dominican friars. In the sixteenth century, the Jesuits took to a further stage the concept that the recruit joined not a particular house where he could expect to spend his life, but an organization, a religious order. By this time, the period of the Roman Catholic Counter-Reformation, monasticism itself was increasingly organized along similar lines, and the preoccupation of the post-Counter-Reformation Catholic Church with the maintenance of unity and discipline, ultimately under papal direction, has helped to ensure that this has become the norm for the religious brotherhoods and sisterhoods of the modern age.

Counter-Reformation

DIANA WEBB

Monasticism

Although the picture most readily conjured up by the word 'monasticism' may be one of robed and cowled figures living together in an enclosed community, the word itself ultimately derives from the Greek for 'alone', *monos*, and monasticism in its widest sense has included not only religious communities but many types of solitary: hermits, recluses and anchorites. The historic origins of monasticism are to be found in the late Roman world, in fourth-century Egypt, Syria and Palestine. Groups and individuals detached themselves from the normal life of town and village and sought a closer union with God in the 'desert'. This self-distancing from ordinary human society was a penitential act. Physical suffering and privation embraced voluntarily have been historically closely associated with monasticism.

The result of withdrawal into the desert, however, was not necessarily or even usually a totally isolated existence. Men who lived as solitaries were often not far from one another and might have a weekly meeting, absence from which would be noticed; disciples lived close to a master and received instruction from him. The development of monasticism as it is now usually understood, that is 'cenobite' or communal monasticism (from the Greek *koinos bios*, 'common life'), in which monks live together in settled communities under a rule and under the direction of an abbot, was an overlapping rather than a later development. It is associated especially with the names of Pachomius (*c.*290–346) and Basil (*c.*330–79), whose rule, in an amended form, still provides the framework for the lives of monks in the Eastern churches. Among the hermits of the East, Antony (*c.*251–356) achieved special celebrity; the Life of him by Athanasius, Bishop of Alexandria, was rapidly translated into Latin and transmitted Antony's fame to the western Roman world.

Both the eremitical life (the life of the hermit) and the monastic life quickly appeared in Western Europe, where monasticism owed much to the work of John Cassian (*c.*360–435). Having travelled and studied monasticism in the East late in the fourth century, Cassian transplanted himself to the West, where he founded monasteries near Marseilles and distilled what he had learned into his *Institutes* and *Conferences*, which became staple reading for generations of monks. Monasteries multiplied in the West in the fifth century and Irish Christianity came to be organized to a very large extent around monasticism. Much of this early monasticism set severe standards of asceticism, but in the mid-sixth century Benedict of Nursia composed a rule which drew on earlier traditions but mitigated their more extreme demands. Benedict himself, according to the Life of him that was written by Pope Gregory the Great (died 604), graduated from a solitary life to become a monk and founder of monasteries, most notably Monte Cassino, south of Rome. He described his rule as 'a little rule for beginners' and sought to establish a balanced timetable in which worship (the *opus Dei*, 'the work of God') was of pre-eminent importance but manual labour and reading also had their place. Eventually, although by no means immediately, the rule became the basic handbook of Western monasticism, but the balance Benedict had envisaged between the different elements in the monk's life did not remain undisturbed.

p. 788

p. 889

The central purpose of monasticism, in East or West, was the salvation of the monk himself in an age when it seemed doubtful whether it was possible to lead a Christian life in 'the world'. Although monasteries were vulnerable to attack by predators, and were attacked during the Viking raids on the British Isles and France between *c.*800 and *c.*1000, in normal times they offered the individual a more secure and encouraging environment in which to pursue a life of prayer and penitence than could

Salvation

WORDS IN MONASTICISM

Here are some words used in monasticism. Strictly speaking, the entries on 'Friar' and 'Mendicant orders' should not be included here, since their activities were in the wider world and not in seclusion: it is wrong to call members of the mendicant orders such as Dominicans or Franciscans monks.

Abbey: A monastery governed by an *abbot* or an *abbess*.

Anchorite, anchoress: From the Greek *anachorein*, to withdraw. A man or a woman who chooses to live in strict confinement in a 'cell', never leaving it. In the early church the confinement was voluntary, but in the Middle Ages the anchorite would be bricked up in his or her cell. Sometimes these cells were attached to parish churches, with small openings through which the person inside could be offered food and drink.

Cenobite: From the Greek *koinos bios*, common life. Cenobites lived in communities, as opposed to anchorites, who lived alone.

Convent: A building in which a body of religious live together. It can refer to houses of religious of either sex, but in English tends to be used of the houses of women religious.

Friar: From the Latin, *frater*, brother. Used for members of the mendicant orders. Friars were distinguished by the colour of their habits: Grey friars = Franciscans; Black friars = Dominicans; White friars = Carmelites. Crutched ('crossed') friars were friars who carried a cross or had one sewn on their habits.

Hermit: A general term for someone who lives a solitary life for the sake of Christ: the first hermits appeared in Egypt at the end of the third century. There have always been hermits in the Eastern church since then; the practice died out in the West at the Counter-Reformation, but individuals have sought to revive it.

Mendicant orders: From the Latin *mendicare*, to beg. Orders whose members were not allowed to own communal property, originally the Franciscans and the Dominicans, and who relied on others to support them.

Monastery: Strictly speaking the generic term for the house of a community of monks or nuns. In English the term tends to be used of the house of a community of monks, while nuns are said to live in a convent.

Monk: A member of a religious community of men, living in a monastery, under vows of poverty, chastity and obedience, occupied mainly in prayer and worship.

Nun: A member of a religious community of women, living in houses (often called convents) under vows of poverty, chastity and obedience, occupied mainly in prayer and worship.

Priory: A monastery governed by a *prior* or a *prioress*. These generally do not have the same rank as abbots and abbesses, and in the Middle Ages priories were often dependent on abbeys. Those which governed themselves were known as conventual priories.

pp. 1022–3

Religious: Religious is used in a specialized sense to denote the member of a religious order who has taken public vows of chastity, poverty and obedience.

Stylite: Someone who lived on the top of a pillar. The most famous of these is Simeon Stylites (390–439). The pillars differed in height and would have a platform on the top, sometimes with a small hut on them. Stylites were mostly to be found in Greece and the eastern Mediterranean.

readily be obtained elsewhere. The provision of charity or education to the outside world was never more than a secondary concern, but monasticism in fact proved adaptable to a variety of other purposes. The space and time monks had for reading and book-copying was of the utmost importance in the history of European culture. Early medieval monks laboriously wrote out the works of pagan Roman authors, which sometimes survive only in their copies. Collectively they have been credited with the preservation of many other arts that had been cultivated by the Romans: gardening, beekeeping, viticulture, herbal medicine and basic surgery, drainage systems (a matter of some importance to communities living in close proximity on a permanent site). The settled, self-

Books

supporting community was, in economic terms, suited to the times, and as benefactors endowed monasteries with large quantities of land, many of them became centres of larger agricultural units which embraced peasant cultivators and became implicated in market exchange as they produced surpluses.

They also proved to be suitable bases for missionary activity. The missionaries sent to England by Pope Gregory I at the end of the sixth century were monks and organized themselves in monastic communities; Irish and English monks proceeded similarly in evangelizing the German lands in the seventh and eighth centuries. The missionary impulse was easily grafted on to Irish or 'Celtic' monasticism. In this tradition, the ideal of 'pilgrimage' (*peregrinatio*), the detachment of the self from home, kin and family in total reliance on the will of God, was a potent influence. Where the Eastern fathers retreated into the 'desert', the Celtic monk retreated to rocky coasts and islands, even the open sea, or transplanted himself to another land without thought of return. The stable way of life envisaged by Benedict and his predecessors among the lawgivers of cenobitic monasticism was still only one possible model, and an individual monk might during his lifetime move from one style of life to another.

Community

Alongside monks living a settled communal existence there were, from the beginning, solitaries. These can loosely be divided into two types: the recluse or anchorite and the hermit. The former sacrificed all freedom of movement in favour of total enclosure, which in the later medieval centuries was embraced in a solemn ceremony with its own liturgy. It followed that if recluses were to remain alive, they had to live in easy reach of people who could supply food and other necessities. Some medieval churches retain to the present day traces of 'anchorholds' in which such individuals lived, within or adjacent to the churches themselves. The hermit, by contrast, lived at a distance from his fellow men and women, but the distance was very variable, as was the style of life followed by the individual, a fact which attracted criticism from advocates of the stable cenobitic life. Some hermits performed useful social functions such as tending to bridges and fords; some were forest or mountain dwellers. Hermits appear as characters in medieval literature, providing counsel and hospitality to travellers and others in need.

Mission

Pilgrimage

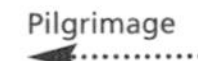

Celtic Christianity

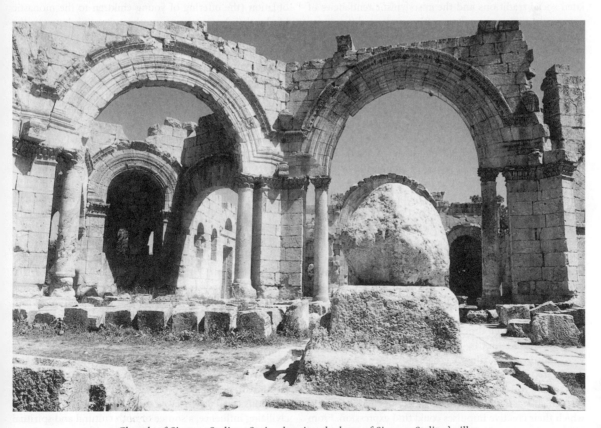

Church of Simeon Stylites, Syria, showing the base of Simeon Stylites' pillar

In East and West alike, withdrawal from normal social life and the willingness to tolerate, even to seek out, pain and discomfort was often thought to signify a greater closeness to God which fitted the ascetic to offer advice to his spiritual inferiors. The stylites (pillar saints) of Syria, who spent prolonged periods living on top of lofty columns, were sought out in this way. The role of hermits and anchorites (including women) as counsellors to the wider society is in fact historically well-attested. The number of individuals who lived in this fashion in town and country during the medieval period can never be computed, but they were clearly exceedingly numerous, and they were frequent objects of charity, on the part of rulers and urban governments as well as of ordinary individual Christians.

The hermit was more often male than female, but recluses were of both genders. Women were recruits to monasticism from the earliest times, and in the newly Christianized barbarian kingdoms of the early Middle Ages in the West women of royal and princely birth, sometimes widowed queens, played an important role as monastic founders and benefactors and as the abbesses even of mixed male and female communities. However, accumulated social traditions and the misogynistic tendencies of a masculine, priestly culture often made it difficult for women to embrace either the extremes of withdrawal and asceticism or the freedom of movement which were available to men. Concerns about the conduct of religious women was fuelled by the prevalent belief that women were innately more carnal and frail than men. If the preservation of chastity was both necessary and difficult for male religious, it was even more essential and difficult for women, requiring eternal vigilance. A succession of church councils and popes endeavoured (with mixed success) to enforce perfect seclusion on nuns. In principle the same strictures applied to the monk, but the anxiety generated by the nun was considerably greater.

Women in Christianity

Nuns could not be priests, and one of the reasons why they created anxiety in the ecclesiastical hierarchy was their constant need, if they were to make confession and take communion, for the ministrations of men. It is probably true overall that rather fewer female than male convents were distinguished for scholarship, a fact which reflected a prevailing ambivalence about the desirability of anything more than an elementary education for women, but there were at all times notable exceptions, and it must be remembered that by no means all male monasteries were centres of learning. Certain nunneries developed a special reputation for holiness and the prayers of their inmates were regarded as well worth having. For some women, at least, the convent provided an environment in which their creative impulses could find expression. From Hildegard of Bingen in the twelfth century to Teresa of Avila in the sixteenth, numerous female religious are still remembered as inspirational visionaries and mystics.

There has always been a tension in the monastic life between the demands of solitude and the demands of community. This could be a problem within monasticism: how much time and space was the individual monk to be permitted to have to himself? The relationship between the monastery and the outside world could also be problematical, and the shifts in this relationship form an important theme in the history of monasticism. It is clear that the community envisaged by Benedict was not totally isolated, for he laid it down that every house must have accommodation for guests. The guest house was to have its own kitchen, and the abbot was to eat with visitors. In the course of time, abbots (certainly of the larger houses) spent less and less time with the other monks and moved into separate lodgings of their own. Monasteries were often considerable landlords and the abbot and other officials of the community could be required to spend time transacting political and estate business outside the precinct.

Benedict also expected there to be boys in the monastic community, whose special requirements in terms of diet, health care and discipline had to be allowed for. Child oblation (the offering of young children to the monastic life by their parents) was another vital link between the monastery and the outside world. With the passage of the centuries monastic recruitment came increasingly to be from the upper classes of society. The monk was typically the son, brother and nephew of knights and lords; he was a specialist in prayer as they were in the arts of war. The placement of a son (or daughter) in a monastery may often have been regarded as an investment on which parents and kin expected a return, not so much in material terms as in terms of the spiritual benefits that could accrue from the prayers of religious professionals. There was of course no guarantee that the individual would be psychologically suited to the monastic life, but the choice made for him or her by parents or kin was regarded as binding, just as the promises made on his or her behalf at baptism were.

The emergence of more stable and developed systems of government in early medieval Europe had its impact on monasticism. The Frankish rulers of what historians call the Carolingian empire, which covered a wide area of northern and western Europe in the eighth and ninth centuries, valued monasteries highly for a number of reasons. Desiring to extend Catholic Christianity along with their own political authority, they favoured the activities of such missionary monks as Willibrord (658–739) and Boniface (*c.*675–754) in Frisia and Germany. Charles the Great (Charlemagne, died 814) and his successor Louis the Pious (died 840) viewed monasticism as an important civilizing influence, a source of both cultural and spiritual strength. This attitude entailed a concern for the life lived

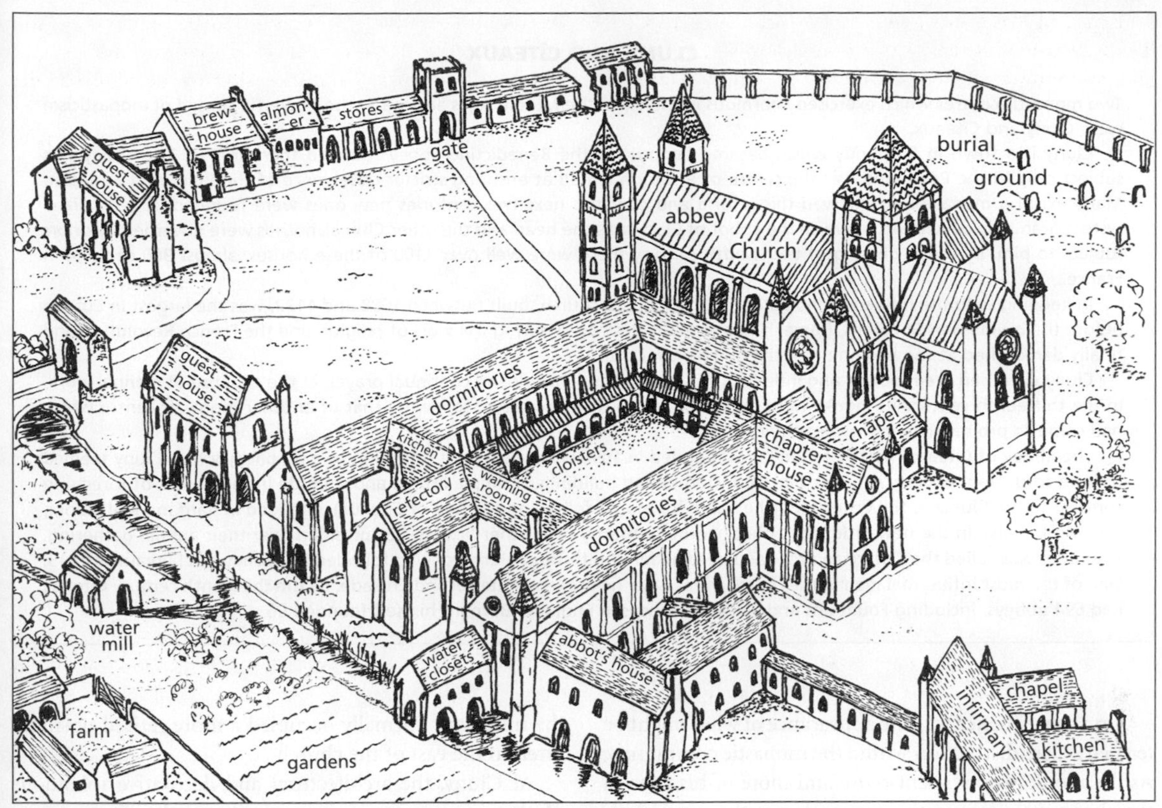

A typical medieval monastery

within the monasteries. Standardization of observance and discipline was thought important to ensure the quality of the prayer offered up by the monks. Charles and Louis accordingly lent their support to the reforming efforts of Benedict of Aniane (*c.*750–821), who developed from the Rule of Benedict a code of practice which was adopted for all the monasteries of the empire at a synod held at Aachen in 817. This was an important step towards making the rule the common standard for Western monasticism.

The tenth century witnessed further significant developments. Political authority in the French-speaking lands had become exceedingly fragmented since the Carolingian heyday; not only had many monasteries suffered from the raids of Vikings and others, but they had fallen increasingly into the hands of local power-holders. The abbey of Cluny, which was founded in Burgundy by William, Duke of Aquitaine, in 909, was important for several reasons. The founder and early abbots took steps to secure Cluny's independence by subjecting it to the sole authority of St Peter (that is, the Pope). The abbey became identified with a rigorous and physically demanding regime in which the monk spent hour after hour in the celebration of the liturgy. From Cluny these notions of monastic independence and liturgical discipline were exported to numerous monasteries all over Western Christendom. Christendom These houses, whether newly founded or 'reformed' by Cluny, recognized the abbot of Cluny as in a sense their commanding officer; their monks made profession to him and their heads were usually known only as 'priors'.

In the tenth century Cluny was in fact only one of a number of centres of monastic 'reform'. The abbeys of Fleury on the Loire and of Gorze near Metz were among others which exerted an influence not only in their own regions but in England, where monastic life needed reconstruction after the depredations of the Vikings. Broadly speaking, all these houses exemplified prevailing trends in male monasticism. One of these was the tendency for more and more monks to be ordained priests. This had not been the case in the earlier Middle Ages; Benedict appears to have envisaged that the monastery would have only a few priests among its members. This change accompanied the growing concentration on liturgical prayer and the celebration of masses as the central monastic activity. Papacy

CLUNY AND CÎTEAUX

Two monastic centres which exercised enormous influence in the Middle Ages and led to the powerful spread of monasticism were Cluny and Cîteaux.

Cluny is a town in Burgundy which became famous for the Benedictine abbey founded there in 910. The abbey was subject only to the Pope, and was the centre of a reform aimed at ensuring stricter observance of the Rule of St Benedict. Many existing monasteries followed this reform and over the next two centuries new ones were founded. A centralized system gradually developed, in which the abbot of Cluny was the head and the other Cluniac houses were governed by priors subject to him. By the beginning of the twelfth century there were well over 1100 of these houses, almost 900 of them in France.

In keeping with the influence and authority of Cluny, its church, built between 1088 and 1132, was the largest in Europe before the building of St Peter's, Rome. It was virtually destroyed during the wars of religion and the French Revolution and finally demolished at the beginning of the nineteenth century.

Cluny exercised great power and influence and emphasized liturgy and continual prayer, at the expense of manual work. In the thirteenth century its monks were organized into a religious order, following that of another monastic centre which had come to prominence in the meantime.

The abbey of Cîteaux, north of Cluny, was founded in 1098 with the aim of returning to a simplicity which Cluny seemed to have forgotten: poverty expressed in food, clothes and buildings, a simple liturgy and solitude in the depths of forests. In contrast to the Cluniacs, the Cistercians (the name for monks following the rule of Cîteaux), engaged in hard manual labour, clearing forests. In the new order the abbot had no authority over other houses, but presided over their annual gathering. The order was called the Cistercian order and became famous through Bernard, who founded the abbey of Clairvaux in 1115. One of the most influential men in the church of his time, he preached the Second Crusade. By the thirteenth century Cîteaux had 694 abbeys, including Fountains and Rievaulx Abbeys in England. Bernard himself founded 66.

One consequence was the appearance of what might be termed a class distinction within the monastic community. As the monk proper spent more and more of his time in the choir of the monastic church (hence the term 'choir monk'), it became necessary for the mundane tasks of kitchen, garden, orchard and workshop to be done by lay brothers. These second-grade monks often included men who had been recruited to the community as adults and were technically 'illiterate', that is, ignorant of Latin and unable to read the service books. The monk who had been offered as a child had been educated within the monastery with priestly ordination and service in choir in mind.

Architecture ➤

Even when reformed religious orders later set their face against child oblation, the lay brother remained a feature of monastic organization. The monastic lay-out which by the twelfth century had taken the definitive shape which is now familiar, even if only from ruins, typically included separate accommodation for the lay brothers (usually in the west range). The lay brethren celebrated a simplified version of the liturgy in the nave of the monastic church, while the full monks celebrated further east in the choir. The cloister, which tends to be thought of as the characteristic architectural feature of a monastery, was unknown to Benedict and probably did not exist before the ninth century, but in the standard monastic plan it provided an all-purpose space in which the monks could walk and meditate, and reading and other work could be done. The dormitory, the refectory and the chapter-house where the monks took counsel were arranged around the cloister; the infirmary normally occupied a more retired position, often to the east of the church.

At Cluny, the architectural and decorative splendour of three successive churches built on the site between the tenth and late twelfth centuries furnished a fitting backdrop for the all-important performance of the liturgy. The physical enlargement and elaboration of monastic churches was not, however, solely for the benefit of the monks. Many monasteries possessed valuable and greatly venerated saints' relics, and rebuilding was often designed to accommodate increasing numbers of lay pilgrims. The great royal monastery of St Denis, near Paris, as rebuilt under the direction of the great Abbot Suger (1122–51), is a particularly good example. Suger's own memoirs record how he identified the need for a bigger church because of the numbers of people who crowded into the church at great festivals. Once again we see that the monastery was not sealed off from 'the world'. By the twelfth century, also, a number of old-established monasteries had become centres of urban development. Domesday Book gives a particularly good description of the community which had grown up late in the eleventh century around the abbey at Bury St Edmunds in Suffolk.

In face of such developments, monastic reformers by the eleventh century were becoming increasingly preoccupied with the monk's lost 'solitude'. The appeal of the hermit's life, we have seen, had never died; now it underwent a major revival. In Italy Romuald (*c.*950–1027) retreated from conventional monastic life at Ravenna to embrace a more rigorous eremitical existence. He became the founder of a number of houses including Camaldoli, near Arezzo in Tuscany, but composed no rule. The original intention was to reinstate eremitical solitude at the centre of the monastic life, providing only the minimum of communal organization, but some of Romuald's later disciples reverted to a more conventional cenobitic model. John Gualbert (*c.*990–1073) followed a similar path, leaving his Florentine monastery to enter Camaldoli and later founding the abbey of Vallombrosa. Like Romuald, if less radically, he sought to make elements of the hermit life available to the monk, but he did not abandon the Benedictine Rule.

These initiatives remained confined to Italy. Much more influential and geographically widespread were two very different reforms which originated in France at the end of the eleventh century. In 1084, Bruno, a former cathedral schoolmaster at Reims, established a small community high in the French Alps near Grenoble. This became the Grande Chartreuse, and under Bruno's successors the mother-house of an order, the Carthusians, whose way of life has remained remarkably unchanged. Its original customs were approved by the papacy in 1133. Like the Camaldolese and Vallombrosans, the Carthusians sought to combine the eremitical with the cenobitic life, and they found an ingenious way of doing it, which can be explored by the visitor to the ruined Charterhouse (the English term for a Carthusian monastery) at Mount Grace in Yorkshire. Each brother lived, worked, studied and usually prayed and ate in a small detached dwelling, arranged around an unusually large cloister. The lay brothers, too, who brought food to the monk's window and performed other practical tasks, had their own self-contained apartments. The brethren came together only on Sundays and feast days to celebrate mass and to eat in community. There is therefore no dormitory and only a small refectory in a Charterhouse.

The Carthusians were never numerous, although they preserved an unblemished reputation for austerity and holiness. The Cistercians, by contrast, took the twelfth-century world by storm. Cîteaux was founded in 1098 by Robert of Molesme (*c.*1027–1111) near Dijon in Burgundy. Molesme, too, had been Robert's own foundation (in 1075), but divisions arose within the community and led to his temporary secession with some of his monks and the foundation of Cîteaux, although Robert then returned to Molesme. In 1112 a young nobleman called Bernard (1090–1153) entered Cîteaux with a large group of companions, including several of his own brothers. Three years later he was bidden to establish a new house and chose another Burgundian site, Clairvaux, where he became abbot. This was in fact Cîteaux's fourth daughter house; each of these daughters founded a family of affiliated houses which were subject to visitation by the abbot of the mother house. This system of affiliation, and the institution of General Chapters, regular meetings of abbots which legislated for all the member houses, were important pointers in the direction of the creation of a religious order. The network thus established spread over Christendom (including the recently reconquered Holy Land), and Clairvaux under Bernard was at the forefront.

The Cistercians propounded no new rule. Their stated purpose was to revive the proper observance of the Rule of Benedict, with its balance between prayer and manual work, and to create the conditions in which that observance could be carried out. As a basic precondition, Cistercian monasteries were to be built far from human haunts, and while the monks would necessarily accept gifts of land on which to establish their houses, they refused to receive parish churches for which they would then be responsible (as many Benedictine monasteries were). Because they aimed to exclude rather than attract pilgrims, their favoured style of architecture was severe and unadorned. Like the Carthusians, they set their face against child oblation, insisting that their recruits were capable of independent judgement. The Cistercians were visually distinguishable from the older Benedictines, who wore black habits, because they opted for habits of undyed wool, which were therefore (more or less) white. Historians therefore sometimes refer to the old-style Benedictines as 'Black Monks' and the Cistercians as 'White Monks'.

Bernard's own career can be taken to illustrate some of the paradoxes inherent in medieval monasticism. A fervent proponent of monastic seclusion and austerity, no man of his age was more thoroughly involved in the affairs of the world: he preached in favour of crusades and against heretics; denounced scholars, including Peter Abelard, whom he took to be heterodox; interfered in papal elections and exerted a widespread influence on other exponents of the religious life, including the regular (Augustinian) canons and the new Order of the Temple (Templars). His personality and magnetism undoubtedly helped to win the brightest and best recruits to the monastic life for the Cistercians. They were not universally popular, but they had many important admirers, including Pope Innocent III (1198–1216), who imposed their system of general chapter meetings on the Black Monks.

Crusades
Heresy

pp. 1022–3

Other movements of monastic reform in the twelfth century produced groups of houses which maintained a separate existence for varying periods of time. The abbey of Savigny (founded 1105) acquired a few daughter houses but in 1147 merged with the Cistercians. The Norman monastery of Grandmont, another product of the early twelfth-century impulse to incorporate elements of the eremitical life into monasticism, also acquired houses in England and elsewhere, but after a sometimes troubled

history became extinct at the French Revolution. The old idea of double monasteries for men and women underwent a revival in the Order of Fontevrault, founded by Robert of Arbrissel in 1100, and later in the Order of Sempringham, founded by Gilbert of Sempringham (*c.* 1083–1189), which remained confined to England.

By the early thirteenth century the age of new initiatives in monasticism seemed to be at an end. There were now several types of cenobitic monasticism, which itself was only one possible form of the religious life. The appearance of friars, in addition to regular canons and the military orders, added to the available diversity, and there was some hostility among the ecclesiastical hierarchy to the idea of any more new religious orders. A number of types of active apostolate were provided for, and it might well have seemed that henceforth the recruit to the religious life who sought a life of prayer and contemplation would enrol in one of the monastic orders. It would be a mistake, however, to underestimate the 'monastic' element which persisted in the lives of the newer orders. The Carmelite and Augustinian friars originated as groups of hermits, and it was not in the middle of a city but in prayer on a mountainside that Francis of Assisi himself received the stigmata, the marks of the wounds of the crucified Christ. For the Dominicans, too, the contemplative life was integral: the intellectual work to which they were dedicated was not supposed to be simply academic or functional. The recitation of the divine office was central to the daily lives of all these orders, and a female recruit to the full religious life had little choice but to be contemplative. Franciscan and Dominican nuns were not permitted to share the active apostolate, but were strictly enclosed. Even men and women who followed the less demanding and constrained path of the tertiary or Beguine were powerfully influenced by the contemplative and ascetic models enshrined in the traditions and literature of monasticism, as the lives of numerous saints vividly illustrate.

Religious orders

p. 966

Later medieval monasticism and indeed the religious life in general was subjected to a number of pressures. The world would not go away, and the close relationships which existed between some houses, especially of the older orders, and lay society could have potentially detrimental effects. Sometimes both male and female convents were used as dumping grounds or retirement homes for unwanted or incapacitated family members or for royal favourites. Abbots had long been persons of consequence in the outside world and were frequently taken away from their monasteries. More subtly there was the increasing expectation on the part of monks and nuns that they should be able to live up to the material standards that their kinsfolk (mostly members of the upper classes) enjoyed in the outside world. It seems clear that some lay observers, who tended to nurture the traditional idea that poverty and austerity were the hallmarks of true holiness, saw little justification for what could look simply like a rather comfortable existence which served no useful purpose. It is significant that in the later fourteenth century, when these sentiments were certainly burgeoning, several patrons, some of them persons of the highest rank, endowed new Carthusian foundations. This was the order of which it was said that it was 'never reformed because never deformed'. The Charterhouses of London and Mount Grace in Yorkshire, of Galluzzo near Florence and Pavia in northern Italy, and of Champmol near Dijon in Burgundy were all founded in the second half of the century, while a little later Henry V founded the Carthusian priory of Sheen in Surrey.

Another new initiative from this period is worth remarking. The Swedish noblewoman Bridget or Birgitta (*c.* 1303–73), widowed in 1343, a. few years later founded a female convent at Vadstena. In the course of time this became the mother house of the Brigittine order, which spread to England and elsewhere. Syon Abbey, founded near Isleworth outside London in 1415, became the largest nunnery in England and a place of pilgrimage. The appeal to patrons of novelty and renewed fervour was clearly not exhausted. To the majority of Christians, monasteries were part of the landscape and local pilgrimages to monastic shrines remained an established feature of popular religious practice.

Cenobitic monasticism suffered, as did the religious

BEGUINES

Beguines were women who in the Middle Ages lived pious lives but were not members of a religious order. They were to be found mostly in northern Europe, living in communities: in Germany they lived together as quite large groups in houses; in the Low Countries each had her own house and lived within a walled enclosure, as can be seen from the Great Beguinage in Louvain. They promised to remain celibate and live according to a rule while they were Beguines, but they could leave the community and marry if they so chose. They retained their private property. They worked to support themselves and engaged in charitable work in addition to their life of prayer and contemplation. Some famous Beguines were Mechthild of Magdeburg (c. 1207–82), Beatrice of Nazareth (1200–68) and Hadewijch of Brabant (mid-thirteenth century).

Their male equivalents, the Beghards, were fewer in number. They lived similar lives but held no private property.

MOUNT ATHOS

Mount Athos, also called the Holy Mountain, is on the easternmost of the three promontories of the Chalcidice Peninsula, projecting into the Aegean Sea from Macedonia. An area of great natural beauty, it is a self-governed part of Greece, politically subject to the Ministry of Foreign Affairs and in matters of religion to the Ecumenical Patriarch of Constantinople, and covers 130 square miles. It houses twenty monasteries, spread along the coast, each with its surrounding territory and dependent buildings like cells and hermitages. Eleven of the monasteries are conservative and nine liberal. The monasteries are governed by superiors and elect members of the Holy Council, executive power in which is held by a four-member council called the Epistasia. There are currently around 1500 monks on Mount Athos.

Although some of the monasteries first claimed to go back to the third, fourth and fifth centuries, it seems that the first monastery, Megisti Lavra, dates from 963; more monasteries were built in the eleventh century, and by the end of the thirteenth century there were 40. A period of decline set in during the fifteenth century under Turkish rule; the distinction between liberal and conservative monasteries also dates from this period. The move towards liberalism was countered by the formation of ascetic settlements, *skites*, around the monasteries. During the War of Greek Independence in the 1820s, many of the valuable libraries on Mount Athos were destroyed, but the monastic churches contain many precious icons and other works of art, and there are still libraries with ancient manuscripts.

Women and animals are banned from Mount Athos: only men are allowed to visit, 120 a day.

 www.inathos.gr

life in general, from the upheavals of the Protestant Reformation and later of the French Revolution and its aftermath. Although endangered by industrialization and secularization, it has also experienced some revival in face of the same challenges. The community founded in 1940 at Taizé, near the long-ruined site of Cluny in Burgundy, has attracted particular attention. The founder, Roger Schutz, was a Protestant, and Taizé is inter-denominational, its main objective being the promotion of Christian unity.

DIANA WEBB

Wolfgang Braunfels, *Monasteries of Western Europe: The Architecture of the Orders*, London: Thames & Hudson 1972 and Princeton, NJ: Princeton University Press 1973; Christopher Brooke, *The Monastic World*, New York: Random House 1974; new edition, *The Age of the Cloister*, Oxford: Oxbow Books 2003; David Knowles, *Christian Monasticism*, London: Weidenfeld & Nicholson and New York: McGraw-Hill 1969 and *The Monastic Order in England*, Cambridge: CUP 1940; C. H. Lawrence, *Medieval Monasticism: Forms of Religious Life in Western Europe in the Middle Ages*, London: Longman 1984

Money

The earliest Christians, attempting to live a simple community life and mindful of the warnings of Jesus against the dangers of riches, were not acquisitive. Generosity was the hallmark of the life of the individual believer and of the infant church communities. But the eventual success of the Christian mission and the expansion of the church in the ancient world, involving the erection of special buildings and the employment of full-time clergy, demanded that the acquiring of wealth and the spending of money be taken seriously.

Reformation
Secularization
p. 792

Today the mainstream churches have huge assets and equally large budgets. In Western Europe the Roman Catholic Church during the Middle Ages acquired vast landholdings and a great deal of money through practices such as masses for the dead and the sale of indulgences, as well as through generous gifts and legacies. Most of this capital has now been dispersed, though the Vatican still has considerable wealth and even its own bank. In Eastern Europe the close link between church and state led to the Orthodox churches being largely financed from public funds, a practice which continued in some countries during the Communist era and still exists today.

Roman Catholic Church
Vatican
Orthodox churches

Although the Church of England retained a substantial amount of its inherited wealth, the Protestant churches that came into being as a result of the sixteenth-century Reformation were required to pay their own way. They did this by imposing on their members the Christian duty of almsgiving, including strong financial support of their churches. In Scandinavia the state provided money for the upkeep of the Lutheran Church's buildings and the stipends of the clergy, and after the 1939–45 war the churches of Western Germany were, and remain, generously financed by a proportion of state-levied income tax.

Reformation
Christianity in Europe

In general, however, the churches in all but a few parts of the world are sustained financially by contributions from their members. This is achieved impressively by churches in the United States of America, where large and committed memberships dig deeply into their pockets

Community
Mission

and, aided by income tax concessions, contribute large sums to maintain fine buildings and to pay their clergy salaries near to those of other professions. The biblical principle of tithing (giving away one-tenth of net income) is still embraced by some small church communities, but Ministry most Christians believe this to be neither realistic nor even desirable in societies where high levels of taxation enable provision to be made for the sick, the poor and others who were once relieved by charity. The principle of Christian stewardship, which encourages individuals to consider carefully every year what proportion of their income should be given to the church, has, however, been widely accepted by Anglican and Protestant churches, though with less success in Britain, where questions have been raised about the validity of a method that directs all charitable giving to the church. There is a view that money given for the purpose of providing church facilities that are enjoyed by the donor is not so much giving as paying for a service.

Notwithstanding their substantial capital assets – £4,031 Church of England million at the end of 2001 in the case of the Church of England's main fund-holder, the Church Commissioners – and large regular incomes, none of today's churches can today be deemed wealthy. The financing of large networks of local churches, as well as educational and social institutions, and the employment of some hundreds of thousands of clergy, requires the available money to be spread widely and often thinly. The work of many churches is in fact seriously handicapped by lack of funds, and in some places the augmentation of direct personal giving by a variety of fund-raising activities absorbs an inordinate amount of time and effort, also leading to the complaint 'the church is always asking for money'. The amalgamation of Puritans small churches and the closure of ill-attended buildings is another consequence of financial difficulties. The stipends (salaries) of the clergy are generally at a level that requires p. 1131 a measure of sacrifice on the part of their recipients, and where there are married clergy the incomes of working wives contribute significantly to the finances of the clerical p. 700 households.

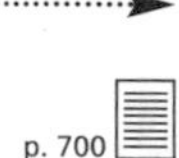

The expenditure of money by the churches is handled in a variety of ways. In the Roman Catholic Church it is controlled at every level from the Vatican to the local parish by the clergy, though in the United States in some instances lay groups do work with bishops and priests to advise them on financial matters. The accounts are not open to wider inspection. The laity of the Protestant churches have a much larger, sometimes an exclusive, role in all financial matters, and in the Anglican Church Liberation theology decision-making is normally shared. Financial policy is inevitably often a contentious issue and the determining of policy is closely related to the church's overall strategy – or lack of it.

During a period when the European churches are experiencing serious decline in numbers and influence, questions are now being asked with increasing frequency about the investment of large amounts of money in the maintenance of old buildings and the sustaining of traditional patterns of ordained ministry which appear to be a hindrance rather than a help to renewed mission. The flexibility displayed by growing churches in Africa and Latin America, and their dynamic use of relatively limited funds, suggests that the way in which money is spent is no less important than the way it is raised.

This has always been an accepted principle in Christian ethics. Jesus was deeply aware of the temptations that attend the acquisition and the use of wealth, in particular money-making's ability to claim priority over other elements in human life that contribute importantly to true happiness and fulfilment. Hence his severe warnings on the subject. A religious faith that claims to be concerned with the whole of human life cannot stand aside from the issues raised by the acquiring and spending of money, by individuals and by communities.

At various times in its history the church has made pronouncements about the right and wrong use of money. Generosity has always been urged on believers and the church was responsible for pioneering work among the sick, the poor and the uneducated. The medieval church regarded unrestrained usury as a source of evil in society and therefore sinful. During the eighteenth century a Church of England bishop wrote the first scientific treatise on Price, and a Surrey curate was also a professor of economics. John Wesley, the founder of Methodism, urged his followers to 'earn all you can, save all you can and give all you can', and during the eighteenth and nineteenth centuries the Puritan ethic was a significant element in the development of capitalism.

Since then, capitalism has sometimes been criticized by church leaders, and Christian Socialism has always attracted some adherents, of whom the British Prime Minister, Tony Blair, is the most notable example. During the twentieth century a number of papal encyclicals have seriously questioned the basis and consequences of capitalism. In 1943 the Archbishop of Canterbury, William Temple, addressed the Bank Officers' Guild in London on 'A Christian View of the Right Relationship between Finance, Production and Consumption'. Temple, who often spoke on economic and social matters, made it clear to the bankers that he was not telling them how to conduct their business; rather, he was enunciating the basic Christian ethical principles which should always determine their decision-making. More recently, liberation theologians in Latin America have, with considerable skill, used Marxist categories to criticize economic orders in which there is a wide gulf between a rich minority and multitudes living in dire poverty. The liberation of the poor from the shackles of poverty and political oppression is, they affirm, the primary task of the church in such circumstances.

A major problem now facing churches and individual Christians responding to this challenge is the sheer complexity of the factors that determine the course of the modern world's economic order. These require high technical skills for their understanding and therefore for credible criticism and proposals for change. Such skill is rarely available to church leaders, whose pronouncements therefore tend to carry little weight. Technically equipped lay people with a firm grasp of Christian ethical principles are urgently needed if the churches are to make a significant contribution to the debate about the creation of a just and sustainable society in an ever more closely integrated world.

TREVOR BEESON

Moral theology

Moral theology is a sub-discipline of systematic theology. Whereas systematic theology is the overarching discipline that tries to work out a coherent view of the world by integrating the truths of faith with all other truths we can know, moral theology focuses on how faith informs the way we live. In short, moral theology is the common term used in Roman Catholicism (Protestants use 'Christian ethics' or 'theological ethics') to name the project of discovering the meaning of discipleship.

Moral theology is also a species of ethics, or moral philosophy. This means that it shares an affinity with ethics in its formal interests and its structure. Both character and action constitute the formal range of interest of ethics and moral theology. The interest in character focuses on the interiority of the person, that is, the vision we have of life, the convictions we live by, the intentions we have, the dispositions that prepare us to act as well as the affections that move us to do what we believe to be right. The interest in action focuses on duties and obligations, moral principles or norms, the circumstances of the moral situation, and methods of making a decision.

The discipline of ethics might focus these interests with the questions 'Who should I be?' and 'What should I do?'. Moral theology, however, recasts them in terms of the challenge of discipleship and asks, 'Who should we be and what should we do because we accept the mystery of Christ as the full revelation of God?' As a philosophical discipline, ethics can reflect quite well on the nature of the moral life, moral character, and what constitutes right and wrong behaviour without any reference whatsoever to God's revelation, to Christian beliefs, or to the meaning of discipleship. Moral theology, however, as a theological discipline cannot, since it seeks to relate Christian faith to the complex realities of living in the world.

Poverty

In addition to sharing the same formal interests as ethics, moral theology also shares the same formal structure as this philosophical discipline – the interrelationship of theory (ethics) and practice (morals). While ethics and morals (or morality) are often used interchangeably in everyday speech, there is some merit in distinguishing them. Ethics, as theory, is like the grammar of morality. It gives the reasons to support or criticize different sorts of character and moral practices. That is, it tries to show why this sort of character is good and not that one, why this action is right and that one wrong.

Ethics is made up of three formal elements: 1. an understanding of the good that is the goal of the moral life and the basic reason for being moral; 2. an understanding of the human person as a moral agent; 3. the points of reference that serve as the criteria for a moral judgement. The practical aspect, morals, covers the interests involved in deciding what to do. It has four formal concerns: 1. fundamental convictions that influence the agent's interpretation of the situation; 2. the character of the moral agent who must decide; 3. the situation in which the conflict of values arises; 4. principles or norms to guide the agent by drawing on the accumulated wisdom of the moral community to protect moral values.

Theology

So moral theology is not distinguished from the discipline of ethics in its formal range of interest (character and action) or in its formal structure (the interrelationship of ethics and morals, or theory and practice). Every kind of ethics shares these formal elements, whether it is Jewish, Buddhist, Islamic or Christian ethics. Moral theology is distinguished as Christian ethics by its concern with clarifying the foundations of the moral life on the basis of Christian religious convictions and with interpreting how to judge and act in the light of those convictions.

Ethics

Moral theology appeals to sources of both faith and reason to give content to its formal elements. The principal sources of faith are the Bible and tradition, which includes not only theological writings and formal church teaching on the meaning of Christian life, but also the living wisdom expressed by people who foster the growth of the church by their lives. The sources of reason are moral philosophies, which include the whole tradition of natural-law reasoning in its various forms, and experience: not only an individual's own experience but the whole range of the social and scientific disciplines that help us to understand individual and collective human experience.

Bible
Tradition
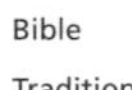
Christian life
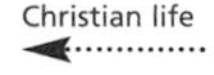

Moral theology is divided into fundamental and special moral theology. Fundamental moral theology is concerned with the overall nature of discipleship. This includes what it means to be a moral person, what makes things right or

Sexual ethics · Bioethics · Business ethics · Social ethics

wrong, and how to make decisions and to become a good person. It establishes the 'why' behind the 'what' of being a disciple in a particular setting, the focus of special moral theology, such as sexual relationships, medical practice, business relations and social living.

Church fathers · Thomas Aquinas

The interest of moral theology in discipleship has existed ever since Jesus called his first disciples and they tried to clarify in their own minds what shape their life would take in response to this call. But for most of our religious history, the term 'moral theology' was not used. There was no separate discipline of theology that made discipleship its focus. The project of exploring the shape of discipleship was integrated into the larger concern of theology generally, or the effort to understand Jesus and the God from whom he came. The integration of moral interests with the mysteries of faith is especially evident in the patristic literature and later in the great medieval works of theology such as the *Summa Theologiae* of Thomas Aquinas.

Forgiveness

However, the penitential books of the early Middle Ages (sixth to ninth centuries) represent a deviation from this norm. These books, though not theological works strictly speaking, did have an influence on the future development of moral theology. They were primarily lists of typical sins with a corresponding penance. These penitentials were designed as handbooks for confessors during the emergence of private, frequent, individual confession of sins. As such they had an influence on shaping the interest of morality in individual acts and turning moral reflection into an analysis of sin in its many forms.

Counter-Reformation Council · Ministry and ministers · Canon law

Moral theology emerged as a distinct sub-discipline of theology after the Counter-Reformation Council of Trent (1545–63), which sought to draw clear lines around Catholic doctrine to distinguish it from Protestant protest. To assure the continuation of teaching clear and consistent doctrine, the Council of Trent established the seminary system to train priests. As a result, theology shifted from the university to the seminary and became influenced by the pastoral agenda of priests. In the seminary, morality became closely allied with canon law and liturgical rubrics. These disciplines shared the common concern of determining clear and concise guides for right behaviour in church life, in worship and in human affairs.

Sacraments · Conscience

Perhaps the greatest influence on developing moral theology as a distinct discipline of theology was exercised by the decrees of the Council of Trent on the sacrament of penance. The requirement of an annual confession of mortal sins placed an emphasis on training priests to distinguish which actions were sins, and to use moral principles to solve cases of conscience. To this end, manuals of moral theology were developed with a focus on individual acts and the binding force of laws governing them. The manuals gave the impression that living within the law is really what discipleship is all about.

The sources of moral theology in the manuals were scripture, tradition and the magisterium, the teaching authority of the Roman Catholic Church. But these did not share equal authority. The method of the manuals separated moral theology from its integration with the great mysteries of faith by beginning a moral argument with the magisterial position, then finding scriptural support to confirm it, and finally drawing on theological writings from patristic and medieval theologians to show its further development. The overall moral perspective of the manuals was individualistic, act-centred, law-orientated, and sin-conscious. Other vital concerns of the moral life, such as the development of character and the life of virtue, were treated lightly, if at all.

The renewal of moral theology that began around the middle of the last century shifted the focus of moral theology from a discipline for confessors to one of a critical understanding of faith for Christian living. The primary tenet of this renewal has been that morality worthy of the modifier 'Christian' ought to be integrated with the Bible and the great mysteries of faith. No one contributed more to the renewal of moral theology than did the German scholar Bernard Häring. His collected works, beginning with his 'charter document' of renewal *The Law of Christ* (1954), show what a moral theology might look like when its focus is discipleship and its method integrates reason informed by faith.

The renewed moral theology has moved beyond the pastoral need to serve priests in the confessional. While pastoral interests remain, its focus has broadened to include the total human vocation of living in response to God's self-communication to human beings in creation, in history, and most fully in Jesus. In trying to clarify the human response to God, moral theology has entered into dialogue with other religions, and it has shown a critical openness to philosophical ethics and to the human and empirical sciences.

In this renewed moral theology, the fundamental value is the sacred value of persons as the image of God. In this light, the moral life becomes largely the matter of promoting positive human relationships which allow the full potential of one's own and another's gifts to flourish. With its attention to responsibility in relationships, the renewed moral theology is more socially conscious. It sees the moral life not as isolated actions but as the matter of appropriating values that promote positive moral character and life-giving human relationships. As such the moral life is a matter of an ongoing process of conversion so that who people are and what they do becomes more and more a response to the challenges of what being a disciple demands.

RICHARD M. GULA, SS

Charles E. Curran, *The Catholic Moral Tradition: A Synthesis,* Washington: Georgetown University Press 1999; Bernard Häring, *Free and Faithful in Christ* (3 vols), New York: Crossroad 1978, 1979, 1981; John Mahoney, *The Making of Moral Theology*, Oxford: Clarendon Press 1987; J. Philip Wogaman, *Christian Ethics*, Louisville, KY: Westminster John Knox Press 1993

Moravian Church

The Moravian Church is unique in the broader Protestant family since it has always been an international church. At present it consists of nineteen provinces worldwide and various institutions including a rehabilitation centre, formerly a leper home, in Ramallah, Israel. Each province governs its own affairs except for matters of doctrine, mission and interprovincial concern, which are decided by a Unity Synod of the whole church, meeting every seven years, and has its own tradition of liturgy and hymns, part of which it shares internationally. Each province faces unique issues which become issues for the international church and are explored in its Unity Standing Committee on Theology, some of the most important issues recently being the relationship of gospel and culture and the meaning of the charismatic movement.

Though the Moravian Church remains small in Europe, Great Britain and North America because of its historic policy of working with and through the territorial churches there, its worldwide membership is 800,000. It is of significant size in Southern Africa, Tanzania and the Caribbean.

What historians call the Ancient Moravian Church was founded in 1457 in what is now the Czech Republic. It had its roots in the movements inspired by John Hus, martyred at the Council of Constance in 1415. From its beginnings the church sought living relationships with other churches, in the fifteenth century with the Hussites and, as it developed, from the sixteenth century onwards with the Reformation churches. In the eighteenth century it sought relationships with both territorial churches and such movements as Pietism and Methodism. In the twentieth century the Moravian Church joined the World Council of Churches at its inception and became a member of various national councils and ecumenical dialogues.

The name Moravian was not used by the Moravian Church before the eighteenth century. Initially it called itself 'Brethren of the Law of Christ', affirming its special allegiance to Jesus' Sermon on the Mount as an expression of Christian life. It later gave itself the name *Unitas Fratrum* ('Unity of the Brethren'). One of the distinctive elements of the theology of the Ancient Moravian Church came to be a division of the elements of Christian faith and life into essentials, ministerials (that which serves the essential) and incidentals (the different ways things were done). The essentials (sometimes expressed in the singular because of the singular relational focus of its several elements) are the Triune God responded to in faith, love and hope, something which came to be affirmed throughout the church's history; church, sacraments and preaching are ministerials, serving the essential; while different styles of worship and organization are incidentals.

Trinity

When the Reformation began, the Moravian Church established relationships with its leaders, initially with Martin Luther, but later more strongly with the Reformed tradition. Though it had at first affirmed separation from the world, the nobility came to be welcomed, schools were established and ascetic attitudes were relaxed. Since in 1621 the Thirty Years War eliminated the right of the Moravian Church to exist legally in its home areas of Bohemia and Moravia, for a century it survived primarily as a 'hidden seed' in its homelands. In 1722 a group of refugees from Moravia were given permission to settle on the estate of Count Nicholas Ludwig von Zinzendorf in Saxony. Zinzendorf, a remarkable man, was educated at the Pietist school in Halle and the orthodox Lutheran University of Wittenberg. He was challenged by his exploration of Enlightenment views and inspired by contacts with religious leaders (including Roman Catholics) and reform movements to develop a vision of Christ for the world. These refugees formed, along with others, the beginning of what is called the 'Renewed Moravian Church'. Zinzendorf intended this church to be a 'little church within the church', according to a pietistic principle. For the latter half of the eighteenth century it came to be divided into three 'Ways': Moravian, Lutheran and Reformed. It accepted the various creeds of the churches with which it joined in mission.

Reformation

Martin Luther

Wars of religion

Culture

Pentecostalism

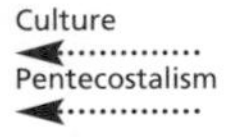

The Moravian orders of ministry date from 1467, when the first ministers were ordained from a Waldensian source and a priest ordained by Rome. Eventually an episcopacy was established which still exists, the first bishops of the Renewed Church being ordained by the last remaining bishops of the Ancient Moravian Church. Thus the continuity of ministerial orders was preserved. Though the members of the Renewed Church were at times called Herrnhuters (from Herrnhut, the village on Zinzendorf's estate where the church was renewed), they preferred the name 'Community of Brethren', which is virtually equivalent to their earliest name. 'Community' denotes the local congregation, the denomination, the ecumenical church and the heavenly church and also expresses the idea of holding something in common. All are constituted by fellowship with the Lord and each other. 'Community of Brethren' is still used in the European continental province of the Moravian Church, but in the

Pietism

Methodism

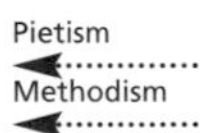

Ecumenical movement

Community

p. 385

English-speaking world 'Moravian Church' and 'Unity' are preferred.

Moravian congregations became examples of social reform; women were ordained and the laity played leadership roles, with congregations divided into age and status groups for the purpose of spiritual care. Ecumenical from the very beginning, Zinzendorf's concern for mission made it necessary to relate to churches serving potential mission areas, such as the Lutheran Church in Denmark and the Anglican Church in England. At the end of 1741 Zinzendorf paid a one-year visit to North America, particularly to Eastern Pennsylvania, where attempts were being made to address the religious needs of German-speaking settlers. This led to the formation of an ecumenical German-speaking church, the 'Congregation of God in the Spirit', in which Lutherans, Reformed, Moravians, Quakers, Mennonites and many others co-operated while retaining the identity of their traditions. However, opposition led to a restoration of traditional church patterns.

After the death of Zinzendorf the Moravian Church adjusted to more conventional norms. Radical social experimentation within Moravian communities ceased. Women and laity returned to more conventional social roles and synods established order and doctrine. By the mid-nineteenth century, after almost 100 years of control of Moravian churches from Europe, the mission provinces began to gain structures of their own and since the Second World War these provinces have been granted status equal to those in Europe, England and North America. The majority of Moravians are now in the developing world. Moravians are intentionally exploring the lessons to be learnt from the proclamation of the gospel in so many cultural contexts, and are developing distribution of the devotional *Daily Texts* (*Die Losungen*). These have been used since 1731 and now 1.5 million copies a year are published worldwide in 50 languages and dialects.

ARTHUR J. FREEMAN

Arthur J. Freeman, *An Ecumenical Theology of the Heart: The Theology of Count Nicholas Ludwig von Zinzendorf*, Bethlehem, PA and Winston-Salem, NC: The Moravian Church in America 1998; Gilliam Lindt Gollin, *Moravians in Two Worlds: A Study of Changing Communities*, NY: Columbia University Press 1967; J. Taylor Hamilton and Kenneth G. Hamilton, *History of the Moravian Church. The Renewed Unitas Fratrum 1722–1957*, Interprovincial Board of Christian Education, Moravian Church in America 1967; A. J. Lewis, *Zinzendorf. The Ecumenical Pioneer*, Philadelphia: Westminster Press and London: SCM Press 1962; Rudolf Ručan, *The History of the Unity of the Brethren*, Bethlehem and Winston-Salem: The Moravian Church in America 1992

Mormons

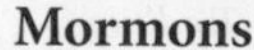

Founded by Joseph Smith in 1830, the Church of Jesus Christ of Latter-day Saints (Mormonism) had 11 million members by 2000 and is at present one of the fastest growing religions in the world. Some projections suggest a possible membership of over 160 million by 2080, leading to the possibility that Mormonism will be the first new world religion since Islam. With its headquarters in Salt Lake City, Utah, Mormonism is today a truly international church, having more members outside than within the United States, and the fastest growth occurring in Latin America. A church president and prophet presides over the membership, together with a quorum of Twelve Apostles and several Seventies (larger groups). The church is organized into areas, stakes (comparable to dioceses), and local congregations or wards presided over by bishops.

Expelled successively from two states in the mid-nineteenth century, later reviled in a vast media moral crusade for their practice of plural marriage, then declared in rebellion against the United States and marched upon by a federal army, Mormons are today a highly respected denomination, renowned for their clean living, their emphasis on strong families, an impressive work ethic, and a tradition of taking care of their own. Faithful members pay tithing (10 per cent of their income), and those monies fund the world leaders, or General Authorities of the church (local leaders are not compensated), a vigorous worldwide construction programme and numerous international humanitarian and welfare projects. A large missionary force (60,000 in 2000) fuels church growth, and is financially self-sustaining.

Mormons are Christians, although they are neither Catholic nor Protestant. They believe that Joseph Smith was chosen by God as a modern prophet to restore the fullness of gospel truth and priesthood authority to the earth. The office of prophet continues in perpetuity today, and Mormon belief in a literal, living prophet who receives revelation is a distinctive feature of the faith. Mormons believe in God the Father, in Jesus Christ and in the Holy Spirit, as do most Christians although, in contrast with trinitarianism, they believe that the first two are distinct, corporeal beings. 'The fundamental principles of Mormonism', according to Joseph Smith, 'are the testimony of the apostles and prophets, concerning Jesus Christ, that he died, was buried, and rose again the third day, and ascended into heaven; and all other things which pertain to our religion are only appendages to it.' Mormons affirm that Jesus was the son of God, and his atonement, or vicarious suffering for the sins of the world in Gethsemane and on the cross, makes human salvation and immortality possible. They believe that human souls are co-eternal with God, and come to earth to acquire

Atonement

a physical body that makes them more, not less, like their Heavenly Father. While here, they are to progress spiritually and morally, experience the vicissitudes of life, prove their faithfulness, and enter into covenants and sacred ordinances (performed in temples) that render marriage and family bonds eternal. In the distant future, Mormons believe, they may attain to a kind of divinity in emulation of, though never fully equal with, God and Christ.

Prominent among distinctive Mormon beliefs is acceptance of an open canon. Mormons accept the Bible as the word of God, but believe that God can and has revealed himself in other scripture as well. They also accept the *Book of Mormon* (see below), and the *Doctrine and Covenants* and *Pearl of Great Price* (comprising revelations received by Joseph and subsequent prophets).

Except for the repeal of plural marriage in 1890, and the cessation of a ban on men of African blood being ordained to the priesthood in 1978, church doctrines and practices have remained fairly stable over the years, and the church shows little disposition to engage in the kinds of liberalization common in other forms of Christianity. Mormon doctrine continues to emphasize chastity before marriage, is adamantly anti-abortion (in almost all cases), considers homosexual practices to be sinful, and maintains an exclusively male priesthood.

Smith insisted that 'only a religion that required the sacrifice of all things has power sufficient to generate the faith unto salvation'. Accordingly, Mormonism requires a life of uncommon commitment. In addition to tithing their income, members are expected to practise an abstemious health code (no coffee, tea, alcohol or tobacco), staff virtually all the positions in the church without compensation, give two years of unremunerated service as full-time missionaries (in the case of young men), and covenant to consecrate all time, talents and means to building up the church.

Mormons believe that Adam was already taught the gospel, and that other earthly dispensations have experienced the 'fullness of the gospel'. Following the death of Christ, Christianity fell into a period of corruption (the Apostasy), in which both core truths of the gospel and the authority to administer the ordinances of salvation were lost. In 1820, during the Second Great Awakening that swept the United States, a young boy named Joseph Smith, aged 14, was seeking to find a true church. In response to his prayers, God the Father and Jesus Christ appeared to him in what Mormons refer to as the First Vision. He was commanded to join none of the existing churches and to bide his time. Three years later he was visited by an angel who identified himself as Moroni, subsequently revealed to be a resurrected prophet who had lived in America in the late fourth and early fifth century CE. Moroni described a sacred history which he and his progenitors (Nephites) had maintained until their people were destroyed by kindred adversaries (Lamanites) in a civil war. Four years later, Smith was permitted to retrieve the gold plates on which this history had been recorded from a hillside in upstate New York. Employing both a seerstone and a sacred set of 'interpreters', he made a translation of the plates and published it in 1830 as the *Book of Mormon.* It chronicles the flight of an Israelite clan from Jerusalem to the western hemisphere around 600 BCE and its subsequent history. The record also includes several writings of Isaiah and of Nephite (and one Lamanite) prophets who prophesied of a coming Christ and taught a pre-Christian version of faith, repentance, baptism and receipt of the Holy Ghost. It also chronicles a visit of the resurrected Christ to the faithful Nephites soon after his ascension in Jerusalem.

Covenant

Canon
Bible

Shortly after publishing the *Book of Mormon*, Smith organized the Church of Jesus Christ of Latter-day Saints. He subsequently assumed the titles of prophet, seer and revelator, as well as president of the church. Subsequently, he chose twelve men to serve as apostles, which quorum continues today as the leading council of the church, second in authority only to the current prophet/president and his two counsellors, who form the First Presidency of the Church.

Finding hostility to his teachings in New York, and willing converts in Ohio, Joseph announced the principle of 'gathering', and believers flocked there. Internal dissension in Ohio forced Joseph to relocate to Missouri, which had by then been declared a new place of gathering. A combination of religious intolerance, political factors and the impolitic rhetoric of Mormons and old settlers led to brutal persecution of the Mormons in Missouri. They were expelled by order of the governor in 1838, after suffering pogroms and a bloody massacre. Fleeing to Commerce, Illinois, they found a warm reception and soon developed the thriving city of Nauvoo, which by 1844 rivalled Chicago in size. In that year, rumours of Mormon plural marriage, fear of Nauvoo's well-publicized militia of thousands, and hostility to Smith's perceived authoritarianism, followed by Mormon destruction of a dissident press, culminated in the murder of the prophet by an armed mob.

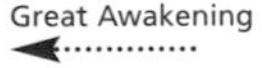
Great Awakening

After a period of brief uncertainty, with competing claimants jockeying for position, the vast majority of members accepted the leadership of Brigham Young. By 1847 he had led the first companies of Mormon pioneers to the Great Salt Lake Valley in a massive exodus. The city became the thriving hub of Mormonism, and a centre from which colonizing efforts spread throughout the inter-mountain West of America. Plural marriage, publicly announced in 1852, became a source of renewed

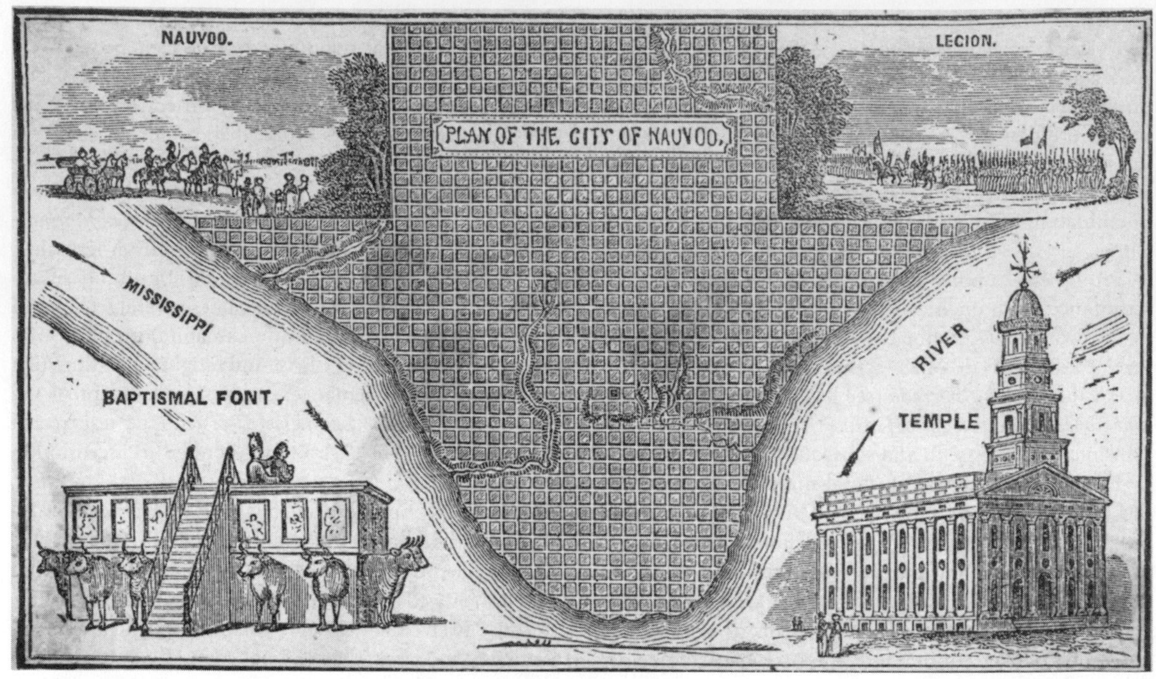

Plan of Nauvoo

persecution, carried out this time most effectively by federal legislation that eventually disfranchised Mormons, disincorporated the church, stripped it of its assets, and imprisoned many of its leaders. In 1890, the church announced the cessation of the practice of polygyny (commonly but inaccurately called polygamy), and a period of accommodation and Americanization could begin in earnest.

Church growth was strong and steady through the next decades, but became truly explosive as the church added vigorous missionary efforts to the process of internationalization in the second half of the twentieth century. The Church of the Latter-day Saints is now entering upon an era in which the challenges of multi-culturalism will be added to the pressures of liberalism and modernity. The fact that most devout Mormon young men, and many young women, spend two years (or eighteen months) abroad proselytizing, while immersed in a foreign language and culture, contributes to a healthy cosmopolitanism that bodes to serve the church well as it becomes increasingly international. At the same time, Mormonism's unflinching conservatism on moral and theological issues has obviously not impaired its demonstrable appeal and growth. The largest splinter group, the Community of Christ (formerly the Reorganized Church of Jesus Christ of Latter-day Saints, numbering 250,000) began a process of liberalization in the 1960s, diminishing the prominence in their church of unique Mormon scriptures and Joseph Smith's visions, and opening the priesthood to women. Their membership has been in serious decline ever since.

Mormonism is rooted in a concept of religion that makes ecumenism difficult. Joseph recorded that God had directed him to organize a true church precisely because Christian denominations were deficient in both truth and authority. Since Mormons believe that their prophet is called of God as his representative and that Jesus Christ literally directs his restored church, accommodation with other denominations would be a disavowal of its unique authority, historical origins and *raison d'être.* Furthermore, possessing a doctrine of revelation that emphasizes the literalness and immediacy of divine communication, Mormons effectively dismiss the efficacy of ecclesiastical committees or theological seminaries to advance spiritual knowledge. At the same time, recent decades especially have seen Mormons participate vigorously in interdenominational efforts aimed at humanitarian ends, and initiatives to further interfaith dialogue, tolerance and understanding.

TERRYL L. GIVENS

📖 Leonard J. Arrington and Davis Bitton, *The Mormon Experience*, Urbana, IL: University of Illinois Press

[2]1992; Richard Bushman, *Joseph Smith and the Beginnings of Mormonism*, Urbana, IL: University of Illinois Press 1984; Eric Eliason (ed), *Mormons and Mormonism: An Introduction to an American Religion*, Urbana, IL: University of Illinois Press 2001; Terryl L. Givens, *By the Hand of Mormon: The American Scripture that Launched a New World Religion*, New York: OUP 2002

Music

Church music

Most of the church most of the time has welcomed music. There are a few exceptions, but Martin Luther well expressed the church's instinct when he said that God has cheered believers through Christ so that they have to sing. Here are some glimpses of their song.

The first glimpse is at the church's *worship*. It has generally taken shape in two cycles: the central service on Sunday (mass, eucharist, Lord's Supper, holy communion, divine liturgy) and daily prayer on other days of the week. The weekly celebration on the day of Christ's resurrection is a word and table sequence derived from the Jewish synagogue and Jesus' meal with his disciples before his death. Daily prayer includes biblical readings, psalmody and hymnody in short morning and evening forms for the church in general and in up to eight longer services for members of religious orders.

As these cycles were lived out across the year, a liturgical calendar developed around annual celebrations of Jesus' resurrection (Easter) and God's coming in Christ (Christmas). Martyrs and saints were also remembered annually. A distinction developed between what ordinarily happens at each service and what changes with specific days and seasons – the former called the ordinary, the latter the proper.

The ordinary and proper of the mass as well as New Testament canticles (sung texts from the Bible, but not the Psalms) used at daily prayer have been set to both the simplest and the most complex music. Likewise, Old Testament Psalms in both cycles have prompted both simple psalm tones (musical formulas that accommodate different numbers of syllables per verse) and complicated musical compositions. Hymns (strophic texts), usually written in verses (technically known as stanzas) with regular metrical schemes on the model of Ambrose (*c.* 339–97), have found or stimulated tunes which have then inspired longer pieces. Ambrose, Bishop of Milan, wrote his texts for daily prayer. They are among the first hymns the church has deemed worth keeping, so he is often called the 'father of church song'.

The second glimpse sees *who sings what*. For much of the church's history, everything in worship except possibly the sermon has been sung. 1. Individual presiders and lectors sing versicles (short sentences), prayers and readings. 2. Congregations of believers sing responses to the versicles, amens or alleluias and hosannas, refrains, hymns and psalms. 3. Choirs help congregations to sing, and provide more complex music.

In general the ordinary of the mass has been sung in its simpler forms by the congregation and the proper in more complex forms by the choir, sometimes with congregational refrains. In the Middle Ages, however, choirs gradually took over the parts of the people. By the sixteenth century congregations were largely silent, as priests and choirs sang on their behalf.

The third is a view of *musical texture*, a term that refers to the horizontal and vertical elements of music. Music developed from a single line of successive pitches (monophony) to two or more independent lines (polyphony) to melodies with chords (homophony).

Worship

The singing of lessons and prayers, call-response patterns between leader and people, and the congregation's singing of the ordinary and of hymns and psalms stimulated the development of chant. Chant is vocal monophony, particularly suited to the needs of worship. It is grouped in families. Byzantine chant, dating from Constantinople in the fourth century, has been dominant in the East. Gregorian chant is most widely known in the West. Named after Pope Gregory I (540–604), it is actually earlier Roman chant altered by Frankish influences in the time of Pepin (died 768) and Charlemagne (742–814). Chant is closely related to the texts it carries and proceeds without strict metre.

Eucharist

p. 966

Calendar
Festivals and fasts
Martyrs
Saints

As choirs developed, they too sang chant, but of a more complex variety than the congregational stratum. In the ninth and tenth centuries polyphony called organum began: a second voice was added to chant melodies in various ways, and 'tropes' (the addition or insertion of words or music or words and music into pre-existent pieces) in organum were inserted into chants. The first composer whose name we know, Hildegard of Bingen (1098–1179), wrote monophonic music, but her period is better known for polyphony. Léonin (*c.* 1163–90) is reputed to have set parts of the proper in two-voice organum for the major festivals of the whole church year. Perotin (active *c.* 1200) is credited with improving Léonin's work while also writing up to four-voice organum.

Hildegard of Bingen

Hymns

In 1586 harmonizations by Lucas Osiander (1534–1604) with the melody in the soprano laid the groundwork for the homophony of J. S. Bach's (1685–1750) remarkable harmonizations and of most hymns in current hymnals.

MUSIC IN CHURCH

Anthem
A choral composition which is particularly characteristic of the Anglican Church, usually sung at the formal end of Morning or Evening Prayer. Anthems go back to the sixteenth century, and represent a significant body of music in their own right.

Antiphon
A short text sung before and after a psalm or canticle. In the early church the antiphon was repeated after every verse, and this practice is still followed in some modern forms of chant.

Canticle
Strictly speaking, canticles are musical settings of biblical texts other than those in the book of Psalms. There are four of these, the first two sung in the morning and the second two in the evening. They have Latin names:

pp. 692–3

Benedicite, Omnia Opera (O all ye works of the Lord, bless ye [the Lord]) from the Song of the Three Holy Children 35–66 (in the Apocrypha);
Benedictus (Blessed [be the Lord God of Israel]) (Luke 1.68–79);
Magnificat ([My soul] does magnify [the Lord]) (Luke 1.46–55);
Nunc Dimittis ([Lord], now lettest thou [thy servant] depart [in peace]) (Luke 2.29–32).

However, the *Te Deum Laudamus* ('We praise thee, O Lord') and other ancient Christian hymns are referred to as canticles, and some modern liturgies, notably the Roman Catholic daily office, include canticles from other sources. The Orthodox tradition has two famous canticles, *Phos hilaron* ('[Hail] gladdening light') and *Ho Monogenes Huios* ('The only-begotten Son').

Carol
A song associated with particular seasons of the church's year, notably Christmas and Easter. Originally it accompanied a dance and takes its name from the Italian *carola*, ring dance. The earliest carols date from the Middle Ages, and in England and America the words and tunes were kept in circulation by oral tradition; many of these were rediscovered in the folk-song revival at the end of the nineteenth century. The introduction of the Victorian Christmas saw the composition of many Christmas carols, and new ones have been written down to the present day.

Chant
From earliest times, services have been chanted: the practice goes back to Judaism, the music of the Jerusalem temple and the synagogue. At first the chant developed and was handed down orally. This monophonic music is commonly called *plainsong* or *Gregorian chant*, after Gregory the Great, who is said by legend to have composed it. At most, though, he is likely to have been involved in regularizing it. The chant used in the Eastern churches is known as *Byzantine chant.*

Anglican chant developed out of plainsong: the Psalms are sung to it. The chant is in four-part harmony and follows the distinctive bipartite form of the verses of the psalms. The first half consists of a reciting chord on which most of the verse is sung, ending with a cadence of three chords; the second half similarly has a reciting chord, this time followed by five chords including a final cadence.

Other forms of chanting have been used in modern times, notably that devised by Fr Joseph Gelineau for the Psalms, and the Taizé chant, short passages of scripture set to music and sung repeatedly as prayer.

Hymns

Hymn
A song of praise which has always been part of Christian worship. Hymns sung during the celebration of the eucharist are described according to the place they occupy in the service, e.g. the introit (entry) hymn at the beginning, the gradual hymn before the gospel (named after *gradus*, Latin for step, because it was sung as the reader ascended steps to read the gospel), the offertory hymn when the bread and wine are being brought as an offering, and the communion hymn during the communion.

Kontakion
The musical setting of an elaborate metrical poem sung in the Orthodox tradition. The most famous example is the Kontakion for the Departed.

Psalms

Psalm
Since earliest times, the Psalms of the Hebrew Bible have been part of Christian worship, often sung to some form of chant. *Metrical psalms,* psalms put into verse, were written from the time of the Reformation onwards and collections of them were made in French, German, English and Dutch. They were sung in Scotland from a very early stage, and also found their way to America. 'The Lord's my Shepherd', sung to the tune CRIMOND, is a very famous example.

Sequence or Prose
A text sung between epistle and gospel at the eucharist. It arose in the ninth century out of the florid vocalization of the alleluia sung there, to which words were added. The most famous of these texts are the *Veni Sancte Spiritus, Stabat Mater* and *Dies Irae*. The Anglican *English Hymnal* also contains Lent and Advent proses.

A fourth focus brings *voices and instruments* into view. Most of the church most of the time has sung without musical instruments. Chant is the unaccompanied medium by which people in all cultures can sing texts at worship. The Jewish synagogue knew this, and the church followed its practice. Chant has been remarkably durable and continues to be sung today. It has influenced music in and beyond the church, and individual chants have been the basis for new compositions.

The church also sang without instruments partly because in the first centuries of its existence they were associated with the immorality and idolatry of the circus and its clamour, lasciviousness and disregard for human life. For a thousand years the church in the East and the West followed this example of being purely vocal. The Eastern Orthodox Church still does. From origins in Byzantine chant it has produced a rich choral tradition seen in recent Russian composers like Alexandr Grechaninov (1864–1956), Sergei Rachmaninov (1873–1943) and Pavel Chesnokov (1877–1944). In the West the organ and other instruments gradually penetrated the church's musical practice.

In the early church the organ was as objectionable to Christians as other instruments. It was shorn of its associations by the end of the first millennium. It may have entered the church then as a visual aid: in pipes of different lengths one could see mathematical ratios. These gave access to the music of the spheres, sounds that could not be heard but were regarded as the most authentic music. The pipe organ became the instrument in the West most strongly associated with the church and with the largest repertoire of instrumental church music.

Once forms of worship, textural matters and the vocal preference of the church have been understood, one can perceive in a fifth glimpse the continuing growth of church music *up to the Reformation*. Sequences developed around the middle of the ninth century. These may have started as jubilant tropes on the final 'a' of 'Alleluia' which broke off as independent hymns. Sequences reached a peak with Adam of St Victor (died 1177 or 1192). By the sixteenth century there may have been as many as 5000 of them. After the Reformation the Council of Trent (1545–63) suppressed all but four for Roman Catholics. Lutherans pared them less extensively.

As choirs took over the congregation's singing, carols developed among the people. Their origins are obscure, but they were popular in England in the fifteenth century. They covered the whole church year and extra-liturgical topics, not just Christmas. A singer could tell a story in their stanzas, and the people could join in with refrains called burdens. Carols were sung at feasts and banquets, after mass in a dining hall, and in Italy at the church door before or after mass or as vernacular substitutes for parts of the mass.

Increasingly composers used more complex polyphony for the proper and the ordinary of the mass. Scriptural and devotional texts were written in the same style and called motets. A set of propers is found in the Jena Choirbooks which Frederick the Wise (1463–1525) assembled for the Castle Church at Wittenberg, Germany. Heinrich Isaac (*c.*1450–1517) composed settings of the proper for the entire church year for the cathedral in Constance. Other composers set parts of the proper, among them William Byrd (1543–85) and Giovanni Pierluigi da Palestrina (*c.*1525–94).

Most mass composition focused on the ordinary, so that 'mass' used today as a musical term refers to the ordinary (*Kyrie, Gloria in Excelsis, Creed, Sanctus* and *Agnus Dei*). Composers from the fourteenth century to the present have set it, especially between 1450 and 1600, when it was the chief compositional form. Guillaume de Machaut (*c.*1300–77) probably composed the first one. Attempts to pair movements were made by Leonel Power (died 1445), John Benet (active *c.*1420–50) and John Dunstable (*c.*1390–1453). Secular tunes were sometimes employed for such writing, as when Guillaume Dufay (*c.*1400–74) used *Se la face ay pale* and *L'homme armé.* Common musical figures were used to initiate movements, as in works by Johannes Ockeghem (*c.*1425–95) and Cristóbal de Morales (*c.*1500–53). Other important composers of masses and motets were Josquin Desprez (*c.*1450–1521), John Taverner (*c.*1490–1545), Orlandus Lassus (1532–94), Tomás Luis de Victoria (1548–1611), and Palestrina.

Orthodox churches ◄

A sixth glimpse shows us the *sixteenth-century Reformation and its aftermath.* Huldrych Zwingli (1484–1531) dismissed music altogether from worship in Zurich, Switzerland. Anabaptists did the same, though they produced martyr ballads and today embrace an eclectic range of hymnody and music. Some English Baptists did not sing at all until Benjamin Keach (1640–1704) 'repaired' the 'breach'. Other Baptists, influenced by John Calvin, sang psalms.

Huldrych Zwingli
Anabaptists
Reformation ◄
John Calvin

John Calvin (1509–64) and Reformed churches (Presbyterian and Congregational among them) included metrical psalm singing in their form of the Sunday word and table sequence. Clement Marot (*c.*1496–1544) and Theodore Beza (1519–1605) adapted the psalms into vernacular rhymed versions, while Louis Bourgeois (*c.*1510–60) fashioned tunes like OLD HUNDREDTH (psalm and hymn tunes are normally designated with upper case letters) for them in the 1562 Genevan Psalter. Many such Psalters followed. Calvinists sang psalms in unison without instruments, polyphony, harmony or choirs until the eighteenth and nineteenth centuries when choirs and instruments entered Reformed worship.

Council ◄

Roman Catholics, Lutherans and Anglicans were more respectful of their inheritance. Roman Catholics kept inherited forms of worship and their music, with choirs still substituting for the congregation and Palestrina's music the model. Pope Benedict XIV in his encyclical *Annus qui* of 1749 admitted orchestral music. This led to masses like those of Franz Joseph Haydn (1732–1809) and Wolfgang Amadeus Mozart (1756–91) – and to criticisms that these were too theatrical and operatic. In the nineteenth century the Caecilian movement in Germany and the monks at Solesmes in France worked to renew chant. The extensive research and chant editions from Solesmes influenced the 1903 *Motu proprio* of Pope Pius X (1835–1914), whose ideals remained in force until the Second Vatican Council (1962–5). After the Council, a plethora of congregational music was quickly produced for hastily-devised vernacular texts. Much of it was ephemeral, and in many places the historic choral repertoire was jettisoned. As Roman Catholics questioned their haste and iconoclasm, some late twentieth-century Protestants imitated their mistakes. Guitars and electronic equipment, sometimes employed creatively, were often used badly.

Martin Luther (1483–1546) kept the church's inherited forms of worship and their music with both Latin and vernacular texts. He also wanted to retrieve the people's singing and did so with marked success. New hymns and hymn tunes – known as chorales – and new choral, instrumental and organ music resulted, including J. S. Bach's cantatas. Johann Walter (1496–1570), Heinrich Schütz (1585–1672), J. S. Bach, Ludvig Lindeman (1810–87), Hugo Distler (1901–42) and Carl Schalk (born 1929) are some of the musicians in this stream. Lutheran congregations sang chorales in unison without accompaniment, while choirs and instrumentalists alternated stanzas with them. Either the congregation or the choir sang the ordinary of the mass. This strong musical embrace was renewed by a confessional and liturgical movement in the nineteenth century.

Pietism

Methodism

Oxford Movement

Anglicans also kept and enriched the church's liturgical and musical heritage. Christopher Tye and Thomas Tallis (*c.*1505–85) began a stream of settings of the Ordinary of the Mass, canticles for Morning and Evening Prayer, and anthems that was continued by many other English composers – like Henry Purcell (1659–95), Charles Parry (1848–1918), Charles Stanford (1852–1924), Ralph Vaughan Williams (1872–1958) and Benjamin Britten (1913–76). Congregations also sang metrical psalms. Thomas Sternhold's (died 1569) and John Hopkins' (died 1570) 1562 'Old Version' of the Psalter was the standard source for a century and a half and more. In the nineteenth century, Anglican liturgical renewal came in the Oxford Movement with a more Catholic practice at worship and music to go with it. *Hymns Ancient and Modern* of 1861 became the model of a modern ecumenical hymnal.

Nuns in choir, from a French illuminated psalter for Henry VI, early fifteenth century

Building on earlier influences, *nineteenth-century divisions* provide a seventh view. Seventeenth- and eighteenth-century rationalism curtailed the liturgy. Lutheran Pietism, reacting against rationalism and a wooden orthodoxy, also neglected the liturgy. With Reformed roots, the Lutheran Jacob Spener (1635–1705) and the Moravian Nicholas Zinzendorf (1700–60) influenced John (1703–91) and Charles (1707–88) Wesley in England. There, after Isaac Watts (1674–1748) had broken the hold of psalmody and paved the way for Calvinists to embrace hymns, Methodists – with Charles' hymns – split from the Anglicans. The upshot of these developments was an emphasis on individual heart religion, with a diminishing importance of confessions or liturgical structures. Congregational and choral music associated with the liturgy was slighted in favour of hymn-singing which in the modern world of professionalism somewhat paradoxically yielded silent congregations with choirs and soloists as emotional performers.

In the United States heart religion, the frontier and evangelism came together to form revivalism. Presbyterians gathered in 1800 at Cane Ridge, Kentucky, for an outdoor 'sacramental meeting'. The next year they jointly sponsored with Methodists what became known as 'camp meetings'. Such emotional revivals found a home among Baptists and influenced other denominations. The campaigns of Charles Finney (1792–1875), Dwight Moody (1837–99), and twentieth-century evangelical preachers followed.

Gospel hymnody was born with this movement and is especially associated with Moody's musician, Ira Sankey (1840–1908). Simple texts often included refrains. Singsong rhythms and little musical tension were common to tunes intended to appeal immediately to large gatherings, as in 'Blessed Assurance' by Fanny Crosby (1820–1915) with its tune ASSURANCE by Phoebe Knapp (1830–1908). At revivals massed choirs often gathered behind the preacher to lead throngs in choruses. These set the stage for the emotional 'altar' calls that Finney had begun and that pleaded for choosing Jesus. Music used as a tool of conversion here still causes profound polarizations with the historic church.

An eighth way to look at the church's music is to see its *ethnic flavours*. The church's music has been nurtured in families and cultures. Sometimes families have grown apart, even into separate confessional loyalties, as in Eastern Byzantine and Western Roman chant or those resulting from the breaks of the sixteenth and nineteenth centuries. Sometimes they have been forced together, as when Pepin and Charlemagne sought to enforce Roman chant but got a new thing with Frankish influences. The church's composers have often been most attentive to ecumenical contacts and to creative currents from various confessional bodies and cultures. For example, Heinrich Schütz brought Italian developments to bear on his German heritage.

In the twentieth century ecumenical and cross-cultural concerns have spread a wide array of musical materials throughout the church. African American spirituals grew out of the pain and horror of slave culture in the United States and broke out of their native context with concerts by the Fisk Jubilee Singers in the 1870s. From then on they influenced choral programming, with arrangements by composers like William L. Dawson (1899–1990). In the twentieth century their more original forms entered congregational singing among people who were not from an African American heritage.

In the nineteenth century white spirituals with 'shape notes' (pitches notated as shapes) were hidden away in rural areas in the United States. First published in oblong books – like *Kentucky Harmony* (1816), *Southern Harmony* (1835) and *Sacred Harp* (1844) – in the twentieth century these pentatonic (five-note) melodies entered mainstream hymnals and stimulated composers to base new organ and choral compositions on them.

Great Awakening

In the late twentieth century African, Latin American and Asian music contributed to the mix. Patrick Matsikenyiri (born 1937), Pablo Sosa (born 1933), and I-to Loh (born 1936) were important leaders. John Bell (born 1949) from the Iona Community in Scotland contributed music, served as a catalyst, and joined the cries for justice that much of this music exhibits. The French Reformed monastic community at Taizé used the meditative ostinatos of Jacques Berthier (1923–94), which spread throughout the world. The music of charismatics as well as praise choruses from evangelical and church growth groups added other genres. Their cyclical forms produced superficial resemblances that hid deep liturgical and ethical differences from the other groups.

p. 274

These glimpses, taken together, provide an overview, suggesting that the church proceeds by continual sorting. It tries out, discards, and then keeps what it judges worthwhile. The result is its remarkable and multi-faceted repertoire.

PAUL WESTERMEYER

Quentin Faulkner, *Wiser Than Despair: The Evolution of Ideas in the Relationship of Music and the Christian Church*, Westport: Greenwood Press 1996; Edward Foley, *From Age to Age: How Christians Celebrated the Eucharist*, Chicago: Liturgy Training Publications 1991; Paul Westermeyer, *Te Deum: The Church and Music*, Minneapolis: Fortress Press 1998; Andrew Wilson-Dickson, *The Story of Christian Music*, Minneapolis: Fortress Press 1996, originally Oxford: Lion Publishing Company 1992

Contemporary Christian music

The North American and UK churches include two tribes: one which is horrified at the very idea of the use of amplified guitars in church, and another which has never known anything else. Performers and writers of contemporary Christian music (whether for performance or for worship) have sometimes been accused of copying the world in an inappropriate way.

p. 808

This is not a twentieth-century phenomenon. Charles Wesley and his fellow hymn writers used popular tavern tunes during the Evangelical revival of the eighteenth century, while William Booth, the founder of the Salvation Army, did the same in the nineteenth, saying famously: 'Why should the Devil have all the best tunes?'

Evangelicals

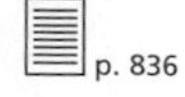
p. 836

SPIRITUALS

The spiritual is a religious song which originated in the American revivals that began in the eighteenth century. Although spirituals are popularly associated with black slaves (for a long time they were known as 'negro spirituals'), there are both black and white spirituals, the white spirituals being the earlier.

White spirituals

There are three kinds of white spiritual:

1. *Folk hymns*. These are religious verses sung to secular tunes. They arose out of the eighteenth-century Great Awakening and expressed personal experience in an exuberant way.
2. *Religious ballads*. These are narrative religious texts sung to secular tunes, and were used among other things for teaching children.
3. *Camp meeting spirituals*. These simple hymns made use of frequent repetition and refrains, sung with deep emotional fervour, like 'Glory Hallelujah', 'Hallelujah, praise the Lord', or 'Roll, Jordan, roll'. Many of the hymns were passed on orally.

Great Awakening

During the nineteenth century, in city-church Christianity, these white spirituals disappeared in favour of European-style hymns. However, gospel songs influenced by European music were written and published, and enjoyed some popularity.

Black spirituals

Black spirituals were first collected by W. F. Allen, C. P. Ware and L. McKim Garrison in a book called *Slave Songs of the United States*, published in 1867. That same year, Thomas Wentworth Higginson, colonel of the first regiment of freed slaves to fight in the American Civil War, transcribed 37 spirituals which were published in the journal *Atlantic Monthly*. Although some of these spirituals arose out of the songs sung at camp meetings, which blacks also attended, and were sung in churches, they were also work songs. As the songs of slaves, spirituals are very often about freedom from slavery, and the Christianity expressed in them can be covert as much as overt. The words and imagery often convey two meanings: home, for example, can be heaven, or it can be a free haven to which slaves can escape. It has been argued that spirituals like 'The Gospel Train' and 'Swing Low, Sweet Chariot', refer to the Underground Railroad, an informal organization which helped many slaves to flee.

After the war and the publication of collections of spirituals, interest in them spread throughout the North as well; more sophisticated harmonized versions were produced and performed in concerts, and in this form they also reached Europe. The English composer Michael Tippett used black spirituals in his oratorio *A Child of our Time* (1941). However, as black spirituals gained an increasingly wide audience, their popularity in black churches declined, and they were replaced by the gospel song, related to jazz, with clapped accompaniment. But hundreds of recordings of spirituals were made for the Folk Song Archive of the Library of Congress between 1933 and 1942, and they provide a lasting testimony to the tradition.

The Gospel Train
The Gospel train's comin'
I hear it just at hand
I hear the car wheel rumblin'
And rollin' thro' the land

Get on board little children
Get on board little children
Get on board little children
There's room for many more

I hear the train a-comin'
She's comin' round the curve
She's loosened all her steam and brakes
And strainin' ev'ry nerve

The fare is cheap and all can go
The rich and poor are there
No second class aboard this train
No difference in the fare

Eileen Southern, *The Music of Black Americans*, New York: W. W. Norton [3]1997

Texts of Wentworth's collections of spirituals, with audio clips, are available at www.xroads.virginia.edu

In practice the relationship between the church, rock music and other forms of contemporary popular music is more complex than the accusation of 'copying' implies.

All of the musical styles which have shaped the popular music of the last 60 years – blues, gospel, ragtime and jazz, and through them rock, soul and rap – were originally substantially shaped by the music of the church. From the eighteenth-century revival, the Great Awakening in America, the music of slaves and former slaves integrated their native West African rhythms with British hymnody, in particular the collection known as 'Dr Watts' (Isaac Watts). The resulting music is often known as spirituals. Although contemporary performances of songs like 'Go Down Moses' scarcely convey its original power, this music is the ancestor of blues, gospel, ragtime and jazz.

Great Awakening

As the music continued to develop in the black communities of the United States, the same revival influences led to the adapting of European folk traditions and hymnody to create the origins of country music. So the most distinctive American popular music of both black and white communities was shaped by the impact of the Christian message and developed in church. As black Americans moved from the country to the city, and electric instruments were developed, blues became rhythm and blues. When Elvis Presley, raised in the Assemblies of God, established rock and roll as more than a fad, it was said he sang rhythm and blues rhythms, to a country accompaniment, with the vocal technique of a gospel singer.

The early 1960s saw the emergence of soul music as the great popular music from black American culture. Soul music was gospel music with secular words. It was lifted straight out of the church, and all of the great first generation of artists, and many since, learned to sing in church choirs and gospel groups. Every British teenager dancing to the music of Tamla Motown was dancing to the gospel beat! When George Martin, producer of the Beatles, decided to retain their multi-vocalist style, rather than name Paul or John as lead singer, he allowed them to keep a call-and-response style which came straight from the black church. When the Eagles' country rock topped the charts in the 1970s their harmonies came straight from country gospel. The rap and hip hop artists who have dominated popular music for the last ten years derive their music indirectly from the black preaching tradition. The church may have copied the world, but as Mahalia Jackson used to say, 'The Devil stole the beat from the Lord.'

Why then was the introduction of rock styles into Christian witness and worship so controversial? In part because few church people knew the musicological history; in part because a dualistic approach which divided 'high' art, seen as inherently valuable, from cheap 'popular' art, was endemic in the church. This was as much a copying of the world as any imitation of popular styles; in part because the Catholic tradition of the church, shaped by the liturgical movement and the Oxford Movement, was focused on the renewal and retrieval of earlier styles; in part, finally, because many evangelicals saw it as 'the Devil's music'.

This expression had a history. Again it goes back to the black American church. Originally, as slave communities found faith, they retained the holistic spirituality which was part of their African inheritance. In the revivalism of the nineteenth century a more dualistic European spirituality took hold. Thus dancing was forbidden in worship, being deemed inappropriate for the sabbath. A sacred/secular divide was introduced which developed, after the abolition of slavery, into a split between gospel, as worship music, and blues as 'the Devil's music'. When gospel singers began to record as soul singers they were accused of betrayal and could no longer take part in the gospel circuit. As rhythm and blues became rock and roll, so 'the Devil's music' tag came with it. Many evangelical Christians shared this same dualistic world-view, and the view of rock which came with it. Since the 1960s this has led a section of evangelicals to regard rock as a corrupt music form, inherently incapable of bearing the Christian message.

Assemblies of God

Reformation

There is, however, another strand of evangelical spirituality which led in a different direction. Since the Reformation evangelicals have always been quick to use new forms of communication as opportunities to preach the gospel. From printing to steamships to published journals, advantage has been taken of any new development. So it is not surprising that in the 'beat group' era (early Beatles and Rolling Stones) of the early 1960s youth evangelism involved special Christian coffee bars with the music supplied by Christian beat groups. A band was formed by ministerial students at the Baptist Spurgeon's College in London, while the Salvation Army, in the spirit of the General, formed the Joystrings, and so on.

These two strands – one which rejected rock musical as, by its very form, inappropriate for the Christian message, and another which used it as a contextually appropriate vehicle to share the message – continued in conflict for many years.

But contemporary Christian music has one other important source. In the late 1960s, as the hippy movement and the 'summer of love' began to turn sour, there was a Christian revival in the United States, now known as the Jesus Movement. A number of new denominations, notably the Calvary Chapel movement, came into being at this time. From them would come John Wimber's Vineyard movement, which has made a huge impact on the worship music of both the North American and the British charismatic movements. Many of the hippy converts brought their musical tastes with them, and put them at the service of both witness and worship. Bands were formed, or continued after the members' conversion to Christ. Record labels were started. The Contemporary Christian Music movement and industry in the United States had begun. A new generation of musicians emerged, all entirely at home in the rock genre, the most prominent being the singer/song writer Larry Norman, who defended his art with a song based on General Booth's saying, 'Why should the Devil have all the best tunes?' Norman was an inspirational and very gifted artist. In his wake came a whole generation of musicians and albums. 'Jesus Festivals' were held in response to secular music festivals like that at Woodstock.

Oxford Movement

Dance

In the UK a number of Christian bands were still in existence following the coffee bar era, in particular Out of Darkness, After the Fire and All Things New. The key development came when a community from the Jesus Movement moved to Britain. Led by Jim Palosaari, and featuring a band called The Sheep, they settled in London and staged a rock musical called Lonesome Stone at the

Greenbelt Festival, Cheltenham, 2004

Rainbow Theatre, also touring the country. In Suffolk they met All Things New, a Christian blues band. Palosaari told them 'You have a band, you have a field, you have a festival.' As a result, in 1973, the Greenbelt Christian Arts Festival began. Thirty years later Greenbelt still makes a major contribution to the church in Britain. For many years its main stage concerts provided the major showcase for Christian bands. American artists were also featured, but there was a strong encouragement for the development of British artists.

Graham Kendrick, who has proved to be the most influential British Christian song writer, recorded his first album in 1971. For most of the 1970s he had a concert ministry, often working with an evangelist. By the beginning of the 1980s he had begun to major on worship songs for congregational use, and for musical witness in the streets – leading to the founding of the March for Jesus, which was to become an international movement.

The major difference between contemporary Christian music in the US and in the UK has always been a consequence of scale. The size of the US and the higher proportion of the population attending church allowed the growth of a huge Christian music industry. Any and every style – rock, blues, heavy metal, rap, reggae or soul – has its Christian version. The scale of the contemporary Christian market in the US has advantages and disadvantages. The advantages include the financial security that comes with scale, better budgets to assure a high production quality, the presence of Christian material in many mainstream record outlets and a truly contemporary music for young Christians, enabling them to see the relevance of Christian faith to their culture and contemporaries.

The disadvantages include a tendency to play safe and to be derivative. If the Christian faith is a transformative world-view, why do the non-Christians produce the most inventive music? The Irish band U2 are among the most original and innovative artists the rock world has seen, as is clear from their many imitators. They are explicit in their outlook, but have never been involved in contemporary Christian music. Finally, to a British eye, there is a substantial risk of creating a parallel Christian subculture which disables Christian young people from engaging with their culture and being agents of God's kingdom within it, including within its music.

In Britain there was no possibility of a market that size. Christian music would always be a niche market. But British Christians were also much more likely to resist a separate Christian subculture or parallel universe. Greenbelt encouraged Christian musicians to prove themselves in the musical mainstream. The public faith of Cliff Richard, Bob Dylan's explicit Christian years, and above all the huge success of U2, gave this approach some credibility.

As a consequence UK Christian music falls into three main sections.

First, there are a number of high quality Christian acts performing in the mainstream music industry. Some emerged in the church circuit. At the time of writing, the Celtic rock band Iona, the singer/song writer Martyn Joseph and the award-winning south London band Athlete are the best known. One band, Delerious?, has a high profile on both sides of the Atlantic. They began as a worship band before turning professional as a performance band. They have had records in the best-selling charts and can fill large concerts in Britain. However, they are most popular in the US, where they would be seen as part of the Christian music sector. At times, in the US, there has also been crossover from the contemporary Christian music scene to the pop mainstream. Amy Grant was a notable example, as are more recently 'Six Pence None the Richer' and P.O.D. (Payable on Death!). P.O.D are a highly successful Nu-metal band who gained a contract with a major record company because of the sales they achieved on their independent Christian label.

Secondly, there are full and part-time bands whose calling is primarily evangelistic. They perform at events arranged by local churches, and often work as staff members of youth evangelism organizations such as British Youth for Christ or Message to Schools.

Thirdly, there are the worship leaders, the largest group.

The British charismatic movement has probably had more impact on the wider church through its songs than in any other way. In particular the 'New Churches' (previously known as house churches) have used contemporary styles from their beginnings in the 1970s.

Songs by Noel Richards (Pioneer) and Dave Fellingham (New Frontiers) and other writers quickly entered the evangelical and charismatic mainstream. Graham Kendrick's songs, in particular, spread widely in the British churches. The regularly updated *Songs of Fellowship* song books, and a churches' copyright scheme have made this material easily available to the churches. The best of these 'soft rock' songs can now be heard in churches of all traditions, even in cathedrals.

In the early 1980s John Wimber, founder of the American Vineyard churches, began to hold conferences in Britain. He made close friendships with leaders in both the New Churches and the charismatic movement in the historic denominations, especially the Church of England. Wimber was a career musician, who had been the musical director of the hit group the Righteous Brothers. His songs and those of his worship leaders created a sense of intimacy in worship. American and British Vineyard song writers continue to be a major influence.

The final tributary for this river of new worship songs has been youth ministry. John Wimber's ministry inspired the creation of the New Wine summer events for 'worship, teaching and ministry in the power of the Holy Spirit'. The youth work at New Wine evolved into the Soul Survivor youth festivals. Here worship was led by a new generation of younger song writers, of whom Matt Redman became the best known. Together with Martin Smith of Delerious?, he has also had a significant influence in the US. A new generation, for whom the songs of previous decades were already old-fashioned, was being won for the gospel. But the better songs continued to spread to the adult church.

The old battles about 'the Devil's music' are largely laid to rest. The mainstream charts contain a sprinkling of artists who are known to be committed Christians. Youth (and adult) evangelism often has a concert-based approach. The dance music culture of the 1990s has led to the creation of a number of Christian night clubs. And why should the Devil have all the good (popular) music?

GRAHAM CRAY

📖 Steve Turner, *Hungry for Heaven*, London: Hodder & Stoughton 1995; Mark Joseph, *Faith, God and Rock 'n' Roll*, London: Sanctuary 2003

Music and Christianity

Music has been a part of nearly all religions. In Christianity the practice of singing hymns can be traced back to the lifetime of Jesus, and the traditions of church music go back to the first centuries of the church's existence. Outside the formal setting of worship there were popular traditions of carol singing in many English towns and villages – in pubs and public squares rather than in churches or chapels. In America spirituals, gospel music and revivalist songs are part of the same process. This is music performed largely by believers for believers, and the same could be probably be said of all 'Christian music' written up to the eighteenth century.

Hymns

Two great masterpieces of religious music, Handel's *Messiah* (1741) and Bach's *B Minor Mass* (1733–48), both written in the same decade, mark a new relationship between Christianity and music: music inspired by Christianity moved out into a wider world.

Handel's *Messiah* is an oratorio, a musical form with a long and complicated history which goes back to the great spiritual figure of Philip Neri in the sixteenth century. Oratorios, the dramatic setting to music of sacred texts, had long been performed in the oratories from which they took their name, private chapels for communities of priests which Neri founded. Handel's oratorios, however, were commercial enterprises. *Messiah* was first performed in Dublin to a paying audience in aid of charity. It is in fact unique among Handel's many oratorios in being a setting of scriptural texts with no dramatic action; the other oratorios were dramatic works on Old Testament subjects performed in the theatre: Saul, Samson, Belshazzar, Judas Maccabaeus, Solomon and Joshua among them. In many respects they resembled operas, but they were not staged and the chorus played a larger part.

Bach's *B Minor Mass* could never have been performed as music for the mass in any church: not only is it too long for liturgical use, but its form would not have been acceptable to either Protestants or Catholics – to Protestants because it set to music sections of the mass which Luther had rejected; to Catholics because it did not follow the official Latin text, and took liberties with the order of the final movements. The time Bach took to complete it shows how important it was for him: in it he transcended the church music that had gone before, including his own, and opened the way to a universal musical dimension.

Secularization

If we look at what happened to the oratorio after Handel and the mass after Bach we can see how what had once been church music became as it were secularized, and was integrated into the wider social and cultural world of music generally.

In England in the nineteenth century the oratorio was regarded as the supreme form of music and three great festivals provided an annual setting for performances. If the Three Choirs Festival, still alternating between the cathedrals of Gloucester, Hereford and Worcester, was a reminder of the Christian roots of oratorio, the famous festivals in Birmingham and Leeds, where the music was performed in splendid new Victorian town halls, had a far more secular background. Here the oratorios of Handel were performed, though now with massed choirs and at lumbering speeds. The oratorio had become an institution in itself. Franz Liszt even dreamed of religious music which would unite the theatre and the church on a colossal scale, though his own *Christus* (1862–7) is in fact far more intimate and personal; the same can be said of Hector Berlioz's *Childhood of Christ*, which contrasts vividly with his other choral works like the *Grande Messe des Mortes, Te Deum* and *Requiem*.

Hundreds of oratorios were written and performed during the nineteenth century, some of them, like Spohr's *Calvary*, immensely popular in their day, but few of them became established in the wider classical repertory. Haydn's *The Creation* and *The Seasons* and Mendelssohn's *Elijah* are the best known. Despite the festivals, which also spread to the United States, and the opportunities for performance they offered, the oratorio was in decline.

Only Edward Elgar (1857–1934) with his setting of Newman's poem *The Dream of Gerontius* reached heights of greatness; and his two biblical oratorios, *The Apostles* and *The Kingdom* show rare sensitivity and creativity in the choice of biblical texts on which they are based. Here again the influence of opera, notably the operas of Richard Wagner, made itself felt on musical language. Wagner was fascinated by Christian symbolism, and particularly that of the eucharist. At the beginning of his career he wrote a kind of oratorio, *The Love Feast of the Apostles* (1843), a 'biblical scene' for a massive chorus and soloists; at the end *Parsifal* has as a central scene the gathering of the knights of the Grail for a similar ceremony.

The twentieth century has seen some notable oratorios, William Walton's *Belshazzar's Feast* (1931) and Michael Tippett's *A Child of our Time* (1941), which are more in the tradition of Handel, and Franz Schmidt's *The Book with the Seven Seals* (1938) among them. Most recently, John Adams' *El Niño* (2000) is described as a 'nativity oratorio', with texts in Spanish, Latin and English from a wide variety of sources and music inspired by an equally wide range from Handel to pop. However, in a changed social setting, oratorios are rarely composed now.

Three great classical composers who followed Bach, Franz Joseph Haydn (1719–89), Wolfgang Amadeus Mozart (1756–91) and Franz Schubert (1797–1828), all wrote masses in their early days to be performed as part of church worship. But their attitude to these masses shows the change that was taking place.

Haydn wrote cheerful early masses in the 1750s and larger-scale festival masses in the 1780s until the Emperor Joseph banned complicated music, and was commissioned to write a series of meditations for orchestra on the *Seven Last Words from the Cross* (which he later rearranged for string quartet). But the masses which he wrote during his last years, along with *The Creation* and *The Seasons*, notably the *Nelson Mass* and the *Harmoniemesse*, move out into the wider world, influenced not least by what Haydn had learned from writing symphonies, and by Handel's dramatic precedent.

Mozart, too, wrote masses to be performed in church, but did so above all because he was well paid for his work. He did not compose church music when he did not have to. Two exceptions, the *C Minor Mass*, K 427, and the *Requiem*, K 626, both remained unfinished. These works move out from the narrower church context through their musical power and personal vision.

Like Mozart, Schubert wrote masses to earn money, and it is clear that his heart was not in them. But he too returned to the musical form of the mass in his last years, writing great masses in A flat and E flat. However, these are not liturgical compositions: they are more like romantic musical tone poems with chorus.

With Ludwig van Beethoven (1770–1827) the mass breaks free of its church setting. The *Missa Solemnis (*1816–23) was in fact planned for a great occasion, the installation of Beethoven's patron Archduke Rudolph of Austria as Cardinal Archbishop in Cologne Cathedral, but like Bach's *B Minor Mass* it took a long time to finish and the occasion passed without it. While it uses the Christian text of the mass, the mind behind it is far from being conventionally Christian. At the same time as finishing the composition of the *Missa Solemnis* Beethoven also wrote his *Ninth Symphony*; though he was, like Bach, a profoundly religious man, his religion was not one of dogma but of the universal fatherhood of God.

The other deeply religious composer of the nineteenth century was Anton Bruckner (1824–96). Because he spent his early years in rural Austria and then in monastic surroundings, he lacked Beethoven's revolutionary fervour, nor did he experience the tension between Christian faith and the modern world as others had done and did. A simple, indeed naïve, man of God, he wrote music to the glory of God, above all symphonies. That abstract music, without words, can give rise to experiences comparable to religious experiences is witnessed to still by those who go to concerts or listen to recordings today. How this comes about is a part of an ongoing discussion about music and its link with the emotions. It is easier to identify what music is saying when there are words with it; then analogies can be drawn between music with words and abstract music. Bruckner is a good illustration of this: he wrote both masses and symphonies, but they are of a piece, and the same motivation, the same quality, goes with both of them.

Gustav Mahler (1860–1911) was more of an agnostic than a believer, but the symphonies which he wrote are deeply spiritual works. He was a Jew who became a Roman Catholic, a move perhaps dictated to some degree by political motives, but his massive *Eighth Symphony*, 'The Symphony of a Thousand', contains a stupendous setting of the Catholic hymn *Veni, Creator Spiritus*, followed by a setting of the last scenes of Goethe's *Faust.*

Of course masses continued to be written by other performers during the nineteenth century, but few of them are still performed or recorded, and those that are are characterized above all by their sheer jollity. Rossini's *Petite Messe Solennelle* with piano and harmonium accompaniment and Puccini's *Messa di Gloria* are charmers, and Gounod's *Messe Solennelle de Sante Cécile* with its rollicking Credo could only have been written by the composer of the *Soldiers' Chorus* in Faust. The mass as a form suffered the same fate as the oratorio, though here too in the twentieth century isolated compositions gained popularity. Leonard Bernstein's *Mass* (1970–71), for example, subtitled 'Theatre Piece for Singers, Players and Dancers', combines rock, jazz, electronic music and Gregorian chant, and puts them in a context somewhere between Broadway and opera. Guido Haazen's *Missa Luba* was written before the reforms of the Second Vatican Council to a Latin text and combines it with modified African rhythms and polyphony. David Fanshawe's *African Sanctus* (1972) comes from the same background, conceived along the lines of the traditional Western mass and mixing media – voice, instrument, and audio tape – as it mixes styles, cultures and traditions.

However, one form of the mass, the requiem, did provide inspiration for a variety of compositions, some of them quite unconventional. Johannes Brahms was an agnostic and his *German Requiem* (1867), written in memory of his mother, does not use the traditional text but a series of biblical passages with an emphasis on consolation rather than judgement. Not so Verdi's *Requiem* which, like that of Berlioz, though originally planned for liturgical use, is operatic drama without the stage, its *Dies irae* cataclysmic in the same way as the storm which opens *Otello.*

Art and spirituality
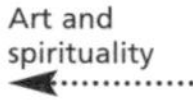

Benjamin Britten's *A War Requiem*, written for the reconsecration of Coventry Cathedral in 1962, also portrays cataclysms, the cataclysms of war, setting the traditional text of the Requiem Mass, including a *Dies Irae* quite as terrifying as Verdi's, against the poems of Wilfred Owen, and contrasting almost chamber-music-like passages with avalanches of sound. On an altogether smaller scale John Tavener's *Celtic Requiem (Requiem for Jenny Jones)* of 1969 also combines the text of the Requiem Mass with poetry and the words of children's singing games to produce a work of considerable dramatic force.

By contrast, a gentler form of requiem, sometimes with the *Dies Irae* omitted, has proved popular: after Gabriel Fauré's *Requiem* (1893) that of his fellow Frenchman Maurice Duruflé (1947), and in England that of John Rutter (1985). In addition to his musicals, Andrew Lloyd Webber, too, has written a *Requiem* (also 1985) in memory of his father.

At first sight the mainstream of classical music in the twentieth century appears to have little to do with Christianity. Austro-German composers such as Arnold Schoenberg (1874–1951) and French composers such as Claude Debussy (1862–1918) were strongly influenced by the expressionist and symbolist artistic movements

(Schoenberg was a painter as well as a composer), which had little time for religion. Schoenberg, who was Jewish (although he converted to Lutheranism between 1898 and 1933), did write a number of works on biblical themes, including his opera *Moses and Aaron.* These composers, along with Igor Stravinsky (1882–1971), were the dominant figures in European music in the first half of the century, and their successors among the composers growing up in after the Second World War, including Karlheinz Stockhausen (born 1928), Pierre Boulez (born 1925) and Luciano Berio (1925–2003), rejected traditional religion in their music even more thoroughly.

One towering exception to this trend is Olivier Messiaen (1908–92), who did briefly teach both Stockhausen and Boulez. His compositions, which include large-scale works for piano and organ as well as orchestral and choral works, are deeply affected by his Roman Catholicism. Some pieces, such as the piano suite *Vingt regards sur l'Enfant-Jésus* and the gigantic organ works like *La nativité du Seigneur* and *Le Livre du Saint-Sacrement*, have a clear Christian programme, but even those inspired by non-religious subjects, such as the large orchestral piece *Des canyons aux étoiles*, written to mark the bicentenary of the USA and depicting the canyons of Utah and Arizona, are rich in religious imagery. For over 60 years until his death Messiaen was organist of the Church of La Trinité in Paris.

On the edges of Europe, for a variety of reasons, the link between classical music and Christianity remained stronger. In England the Church of England supported (and still supports) a great number of church and cathedral choirs, some of which, along with a number of university-based choirs, have an international reputation. These choirs, which take boys in at an early age, but also provide positions for adults, have been the training ground for generations of English composers, who are as a result immersed in the traditions of church music from childhood.

A number of other factors had a powerful influence on the development of English music at the start of the twentieth century, including the presence of Charles Villiers Stanford, the composer of a large body of church music, as professor of composition at the Royal College of Music from 1883 to 1923, and a renewed interest at the turn of the century in both English folk music and the music of the fifteenth and sixteenth centuries. Ralph Vaughan Williams (1872–1958) was strongly influenced by all these things. Early in his career he was musical editor of two hymn books, *The English Hymnal* and *Songs of Praise*, as well as the *Oxford Book of Carols*, for all of which he arranged folk tunes as well as writing his own. The musical language of these hymns is distinctly audible in his symphonies, and in his settings of religious poetry. Similar influences can be found in the music of his friend and contemporary Gustav Holst (1874–1934), who was organist at Thaxted church, when its vicar, Conrad Noel, was engaged in reintroducing folk ritual into the church's liturgy; but Holst was also strongly influenced by the idea of Indian religion, as revealed for example by settings of words from the Rig Veda, and it is clear that his personal religious views were not traditional. Another composer who seems to have had a rather distant relationship with Christianity, but nonetheless composed a large body of works on Christian subjects, was Benjamin Britten (1913–76). As well as the *War Requiem*, his compositions include settings of English poets such as John Donne (*The Holy Sonnets of John Donne*), Christopher Smart (*Rejoice in the Lamb*) and William Blake (*Songs and Proverbs of William Blake*), whose spirituality is distinctly unusual.

The influence of the English choral tradition can be seen in composers whose own music is of a distinctive style, such as John Tavener (born 1944), all of whose music has Christian subject matter, from the avant-garde of *The Whale*, based on the story of Jonah, to his recent works which are rooted in Russian and Greek Orthodox traditions. Similarly popular, although utterly different in every other way, the composer of musicals Andrew Lloyd Webber (born 1948) is the son of an organist and choir-master, and he took religious subjects for two of his earliest successes, *Joseph and his Amazing Technicolour Dreamcoat* and *Jesus Christ Superstar.* To some extent the same tradition has influenced the Scottish composer James MacMillan (born 1959), but in his case it has been mixed with his deeply-held Roman Catholicism and his political views to produce a distinctly Scottish body of work which includes some church music, but also symphonies and concertos with titles relating to Christian subjects. John Rutter (born 1945) has written a large body of accessible choral music which is sung widely in churches.

The relationship between music and Christianity in the twentieth century is particularly interesting in Russia and the countries of the USSR. There was a long tradition of classical composers, including for example Tchaikovsky (1840–93), writing music for the Russian Orthodox liturgy, and this was maintained by composers exiled from Russia after the revolution of 1917, such as Sergei Rachmaninov (1873–1943). Stravinsky, another exile, wrote a number of works for church performance, although these are far less well known, and less influential than his secular music. Composers who stayed and composed in the USSR, of whom the most important were Dmitri Shostakovich (1906–75) and Sergei Prokofiev (1891–1953), had little to do with religion. This is as true of the works written for more private occasions as of the many official cantatas and other works that Soviet composers were expected to write. However, many composers of the generation that followed them, who lived into the period after the collapse of Communism, did write music with strong religious themes. These include Galina Ustvolskaya (born 1919), Sofia Gubaidulina (born 1931) and Alfred Schnittke (1934–98). Also from the former Communist bloc, above all the Estonian Arvo Pärt (born 1935) has become very well known. The Christian nature of the music of these composers varies considerably. Several of Ustvolskaya's works have religious titles, for example *Compositions I–III*, entitled '*Dona nobis pacem*', '*Dies irae*' and '*Benedictus qui venit*'; yet they are not vocal settings or liturgical works, but concert pieces for various unusual combinations of instruments. The same could be said of Gubaidulina's *Seven Last Words*, for cello bayan (a small accordion) and strings; these are very personal works, despite titles which appear to link them to the mainstream of liturgical composition. In contrast, Pärt, after he emigrated in 1980, has written a series of large-scale settings of texts including his *St John Passion*, *Te Deum*, *Miserere* and several masses.

In the United States Christian hymns had a marked influence on the innovative composer Charles Ives (1874–1954), notably in his Second Symphony and his two string quartets. However, subsequent composers, the occasional piece apart, have not added to the kind of repertory described here. 'Christian' music flourishes, but it is rather different in character.

HUGH BOWDEN AND JOHN BOWDEN

📖 Gerald Abraham, *The Concise Oxford History of Music*, London: OUP 1987; Wilfrid Mellers, *Man and his Music*, Vols 3 and 4, London: Barrie & Rockliff 1962; M. Oliver (ed), *Settling the Score: A Journey through the Music of the 20th Century*, London: Faber 1999

Mystery cults

Christianity is generally recognized as being rather different from the religion of the Graeco-Roman world into which it was born. The public ritual activity of the cities of the Roman empire mainly involved temples, cult statues, processions and animal sacrifice. It did not involve preaching or promulgating particular doctrines. One group of cults that appears to be an exception to this are 'mystery cults'. This term refers essentially to activity restricted to those initiated into a cult (the Greek word for 'initiate' is *mystes*), and it covers a somewhat disparate set of religious phenomena. Attempts have frequently been made to link mystery cults closely to Christianity, but these attempts are of questionable value.

Mystery cults are often thought of as particularly 'eastern', but while some of the deities worshipped in them have strong eastern associations, such as Egyptian Isis and Cybele from Phrygia in Anatolia – goddesses whose worship in mainland Greece cannot be traced back before the fifth century BCE – it is clear that such cults were part of Greek religion from at least the seventh century BCE. The most prestigious mystery cult was that of Demeter and Kore (Persephone) at Eleusis near Athens. The *Homeric Hymn to Demeter*, a poem from the seventh or sixth century BCE, tells the story of the rape of Demeter's daughter Persephone by Hades, lord of the underworld, and her eventual return to her mother for two-thirds of each year. The poem also tells how Demeter taught secret rites to the rulers of Eleusis, and adds: 'Blessed is he who has seen this among earthly men; but he who is uninitiated in the sacred rites and who has no portion, never has the same lot once dead down in the murky dark.' Initiation into the Eleusinian Mysteries was open to all who spoke Greek, male or female, slave or free, and by the second century CE initiates included even Roman emperors. Other Greek gods were worshipped by groups of initiates, including Dionysus, whose initiated worshippers were called *Bacchoi* (male) and *Bacchae* (female). The cult of Dionysus and of Cybele (also called the Mother of the Gods) was often characterized by wild behaviour, dancing and playing drums and other musical instruments.

Although widespread in the Roman empire, this kind of activity did not form a part of the religion of the Romans themselves. Although a cult of Cybele (or Magna Mater, 'the Great Mother of the Gods') was introduced to Rome at the end of the third century BCE, Roman involvement in her worship was restricted to public games, and her priests (who were required to castrate themselves) were drawn from non-citizens. Some forms of worship of Dionysus, long established in the cities of southern Italy, were also viewed with suspicion. It is this Roman perspective that has led to the misleading catch-all phrase 'oriental religions' being applied to both mystery cults and Christianity, thus linking them too closely together, although, as we shall see, there were indirect connections.

The one mystery cult whose roots do seem to lie in or around Rome is Mithraism. This cult, open only to men, and involving seven grades of initiation, appears to have emerged in Italy in the first century CE, and to have been spread, in particular by soldiers and merchants, across the whole empire. Despite the Persian name of its central god, Mithras, there is little evidence of a real connection with Persian religion. The relationship between Mithraism and Christianity is something else to which we will return.

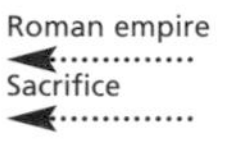

A further element of the religious activities grouped together as mystery cults was the existence in the Greek world of travelling individuals, apparently offering private initiations into mysteries to individuals and families. This kind of initiation was often associated with the mythical singer and poet Orpheus, and poems attributed to Orpheus, telling alternative myths about the creation of the universe and the gods, circulated in the ancient world. These included accounts of the underworld, and a number of burials have been found in Greece and Southern Italy containing texts written on gold leaf instructing the dead person what to do and say on reaching the 'House of Hades' in order to join the heroes and *Bacchoi* in a more blessed afterlife. In southern Italy, too, followers of the sixth-century-BCE Greek philosopher Pythagoras – who was in turn associated with the poems of Orpheus – formed communities of initiates who met together and, perhaps, followed practices such as vegetarianism, a dietary rule associated with Orpheus and Pythagoras.

Paganism
Church fathers

Pythagoras provides a link between cult practice and philosophy: the writings of his followers were known to Plato and later writers. The language of mystery cults, with references to initiation and mysteries, became part of the vocabulary of Greek philosophy, generally used metaphorically, and it appears in the work of the Hellenistic Jewish writers like the philosopher Philo of Alexandria, and in the letters of Paul (e.g. Romans 11.25; 16.25; 1 Corinthians 15.51; cf. Ephesians 3; Colossians 1.26–7). The use of words like 'mystery' and 'revelation' in these Christian contexts does not mean that Paul and his contemporaries considered Christianity to be in any sense a mystery cult: rather, they were using the kind of language in which contemporary non-Christian philosophers spoke about the divine.

Paul
Festivals and fasts

There were parallels between elements of Christian ritual and the ritual of mystery cults that encouraged ancient writers (and some modern ones) to make connections between the two. Baptism could be seen as a form of initiation, and baptism ceremonies in the early church which involved sudden illumination were probably similar to some acts of revelation in mystery cults. Mithraism involved shared meals of bread and wine. The sun was a central element in Mithraism, and its adherents celebrated festivals at the solstices and equinoxes, as Christianity came to do. And of course, the interest in the afterlife indicated in the 'Orphic' texts and the Eleusinian Mysteries can be compared to Christian teachings on the subject. Nonetheless, these similarities are more apparent than real, and in particular underplay the Jewish roots of Christianity. Baptism was a rite found in Judaism, even if its role in Christianity was different, and shared meals were also a feature of Jewish practice. Fixing religious festivals according to the solar year was a widespread phenomenon. Indeed, Roman emperors in the third century CE associated themselves with *Sol Invictus* (the Unconquered Sun), and Constantine, the first Christian emperor, saw the sign that led to his conversion in the sun: he appears to have recognized a close connection between the sun and the God of the Christians. Finally, the vision of life after death in mystery cults, which is essentially that found in other areas of Greek mythology and literature, has little in common with those developed by Christian writers.

Mary
Origins and background
Festivals and fasts
Constantine's 'conversion'

In the last attempts to defend what was becoming known as 'paganism' in the fourth century CE, non-Christian philosophers made much of mystery cults, emphasizing the wisdom they were supposed to teach. At the same time several of the church fathers mocked their rituals, revealing (or so they claimed) their great secrets as trivial or obscene. The final clamp-down on paganism in the late fourth century saw the end of these cults, along with almost all non-Christian religious activity.

HUGH BOWDEN

Walter Burkert, *Ancient Mystery Religions*, Cambridge, MA: Harvard University Press 1987; Robert Turcan, *Cults of the Roman Empire*, Oxford: Blackwell 1996

Mystery plays

Mystery plays were a form of drama on a grand scale which evolved at the end of the fourteenth century in England as part of the church's summer feasts and holy days: Corpus Christi in York and Coventry, and Whitsun, later Midsummer, in Chester. Their organization was delegated by the civic authorities in each city to the guilds, organizations which existed to protect the professional skills of craft or trade.

The plays presented their audiences with a dramatized summary of the highlights of the Christian story. The Old Testament is represented by the Creation, Fall and Expulsion from the Garden of Eden, the stories of Cain and Abel, Noah, Abraham and Isaac, and the Exodus. The focus in the New Testament is on a sequence of plays from the Annunciation of the birth of Jesus to Mary to the Epiphany; then, after a brief series of plays drawn from the life of Christ, there is a detailed Passion sequence. The cycles typically end with a Harrowing of Hell, Resurrection, Ascension and finally a spectacular Doomsday. Plays concerning the life of the Virgin Mary are threaded through the sequence, and many cycles contain a play about her Assumption.

Each guild produced its pageant on its specially constructed wagon, which stopped in sequence to perform at a number of 'stations' around a processional route. The wagons were elaborate vehicles, some requiring multiple stories and winches. The play texts were written by several different authors, almost certainly clerics, in a variety of forms. Yet the cycles cohere because of broad patterns drawn from popular worship and its representation in contemporary art. Like all medieval literature, the plays are in the dialect version of the language that predominated in the region to which they belonged, but the texts have great tonal variety, from high seriousness to knockabout farce. Not much is known of the performers, who were, according to any modern understanding, amateurs. All parts, including Eve and the Virgin Mary, seem to have been played by men. Contemporary records show that costumes, beards, wigs, haloes and gilded full-face masks, as well as elaborate sets, special effects and music, were usual.

Plays based on biblical subject-matter were popular across Europe in the Middle Ages. Mystery play cycles, such as those attributed to York and Chester, were just one of the forms that playing of this type took; many other groups, amateur and professional, from rural parish troupes to the parish clerks of London, are recorded as having staged plays based on stories from the Bible. Unfortunately most of the scripts do not survive, although records are numerous, varied and fascinating. The texts of surviving English cycles are very varied: the York cycle is genuinely medieval, whereas the manuscripts of the Chester cycle are post-Reformation. The so-called 'N-town cycle', from somewhere in East Anglia, is a composite designed for static performance, and the origins of the Towneley cycle and its connection with Wakefield are the subject of critical debate. Other survivors, such as the two Coventry plays, are mostly fragmentary and late in date, but support the view that the cycle form of organization was relatively widespread.

Ambitious cycles of plays appear to be linked to the emergence of the city as the focal point for conspicuous public forms of lay piety in the period after the Black Death. The York cycle in particular surfaces at a time when there was strong support for the church locally, and lay worship had become politicized in a backlash against the Lollards, who were opposed to the church and its institutions, condemning many practices as unscriptural. Modern scholarship no longer assumes that 'mystery play cycles' are a cohesive literary genre. There is common terminological confusion with 'miracle plays' about saints' lives, of which very few English examples survive. Mystery plays, where the tradition existed, served a number of social and cultural functions, the least of these being pious instruction. Cast and audience alike knew the story, but to take it out on to the streets and enact it splendidly on a holiday affirmed both the wealth and the piety of everyone involved and validated the commercial activity of the city in the eyes of God.

Mystery plays were long neglected in Britain because of conventions preventing the representation of the deity on stage. In 1951, however, the York cycle was revived as part of the Festival of Britain. Since then there have been a number of notable modern productions, in the form both of scholarly reconstructions and of reinterpretations aimed at the modern multi-faith and secular theatre audience. The most famous cycle, the Chester cycle, was presented in London to great acclaim in 1992; it was performed again in Chester in 2003 and the next performance will be in 2008.

PAMELA M. KING

Richard Beadle and Pamela M. King (eds), *York Mystery Plays: a Selection in Modern Spelling*, Oxford: OUP 1995; David Bevington (ed), *Medieval Drama*, New York: Houghton Mifflin Company 1975; David Mills (ed), *The Chester Mystery Cycle: a New Edition with Modernized Spelling*, East Lancing, MI: Colleagues Press 1992; Greg Walker (ed), *Medieval Drama. An Anthology*, Oxford: Blackwell 2000; Richard Beadle (ed), *The Cambridge Companion to the Medieval Theatre*, Cambridge: CUP 1994

Middle Ages
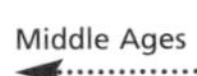

Mysticism

Mysticism is the study of ways in which the largely hidden aspects of God's nature have been approached and understood. Unlike other hidden areas of knowledge which have been made accessible by advances in scientific method, the nature of divine truths, which are both abstract and personal, tend to elude clear definition and objective research. The church, which has always had a rather ambivalent attitude to its mystics, has nevertheless always been challenged and fed by them, but now when the church is seen as an organization like any other, mysticism seems to have little or no part to play. Unlike the sixteenth-century liturgists who happily used the phrase 'the mystical body of Christ' to signify the church, the present church would see little sense in such an ill-defined image. Mystics have always seemed to exist on the margins of both church and society. The dominance of the secular, rigidly scientific model for understanding reality gives mysticism little room for manoeuvre in the modern world.

God

Church

Organization

p. 521

In modern usage 'mysticism' generally refers to claims of communion with Ultimate Reality as perceived in direct personal experience. The etymology of the word in English is very interesting. Mysticism and mystery share the same root word, which in English means to 'muzzle' or to maintain silence, to keep quiet, or to keep a tight mouth. The Greek word is *mysterion*. 'Mystic' appeared as an adjective after 1382, when John Wyclif used it to mean spiritual, allegorical or symbolic. In the early seventeenth century it came to mean 'pertaining to the ancient religious mysteries' and was also used as 'the distinctive epithet of that branch of theology which relates to the direct communion of the soul with God'. The word as

a noun, meaning 'a mystic doctor', did not appear until 1679, and 'mysticism' as 'the opinion or mental tendencies or habits of thought characteristics of mystics' was not used until 1736.

Symbol
Mystery cults

In the days of Greek philosophy, knowledge of the 'mysteries' was confined to a special group, and elaborate codes of conduct maintained that tradition in the mystery cults. Mysteries, to remain mysteries, had to be carefully guarded. Knowledge was power, and to disperse power too widely was to weaken it. Similarly, in the early church, matters of doctrine and liturgy could be known only by revelation, which were incomprehensible to outsiders and those insufficiently purified by faith, and moral conversion.

Revelation
Cinema
Philosophy
Kingdom of God
Music

The Christian understanding of the mysteries of the faith was much influenced by Greek philosophy and Jewish mysticism, and in the Gospels we see fascinating examples of an essentially open, public message about the kingdom of God, combined with certain restraints in the telling. So the proclamation of the Christian gospel had a paradox at its heart, and the history of Christian mysticism is described along this line of tension between secrecy and revelation. The mystery of God remains mysterious even in its revelation, with a need to 'hear the quietness' of Jesus as well as receiving his word, as the early Christian writer Ignatius observed in his letter to the Ephesians (15).

There are some particular problems associated with writing about mysticism. Over the past 100 years a lot of work has been done on the classification of the types of mystics, and the sorts of writings that have come from them. The essence of mysticism is its particularity and immediacy of vision. It has a freshness of feel when you get to the texts themselves, or when you read the personal accounts of revelations, both of which got lost in later digests or classifications of types of mystics.

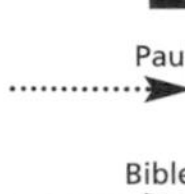

In addition to the problem of describing mysticism, there is also the subject-matter that mystics are dealing with. Often this is vague, paradoxical and difficult to put into words. Sometimes it involves the use of new combinations of words, or the use of familiar words in a new context. For example, the use of the word *milieu* by the French twentieth-century mystic Pierre Teilhard de Chardin has proved impossible to translate into English in such a way that it captures in one word both the environment and the central place in which God is present.

Paul
Bible
Poetry

Mystics often seem to be dealing with language at the full stretch of its meaning, and as such are close to the poets. Mysticism has often been the province of the poet. The poets have given themselves permission to write down their experiences of God, which is what mysticism basically is, using paradoxes, contradictions, phrases which state and contradict almost in the same breath. Above all, they have used the image. An image is a picture that assists hidden truths to be communicated as clearly as they can be in the human realm while acknowledging that it is only a representation of a hidden realm, where words simply cannot go. The film director Andrei Tarkovsky, writing about the difference between an image and a symbol, says that an image cannot be deciphered, unlike a symbol that can be decoded. 'The moment a viewer understands, deciphers,' said Tarkovsky, 'all is over, finished: the illusion of the infinite becomes banality, a commonplace, and a truism. The mystery disappears. Those of you who love music and poetry will understand what I am talking about.'

If we think of who might represent mysticism for the Christian church in the last 50 years we would probably think more of film makers, musicians and artists than of writers. The music of John Tavener (born in London in 1944) elevates the spiritual sense at the same time as speaking to the profound depths of human experience. The effect of music on the listener is more than one of 'audience'; it is of entering into the mystery without any desire to understand that mystery intellectually, but to give a sense of unity with God.

A familiar scenario in mysticism is the belief, or feeling, that God is unknowable in his essence, but knowable in so far as God desires to be experienced and understood. The paradox, or seeming contradictory glory, is part of our limitation as mere humans to know everything. The mystic glimpses the truth, or is given a revelation of the truth, and then does his or her best within the limited medium of language to communicate that. Words are often unable to speak of the glories that have been revealed.

At its root, and put as simply as possible, mysticism is the study of the ways in which humans have been in receipt of the knowledge of God. It is put in the passive tense, because the receipt of this knowledge has often seemed to come from outside the ordinary realms of knowledge, and directly from God. Such experiences have been described as revelations, or shewings, of God's nature.

The New Testament

It is to Paul and John that most commentators turn for the origins of Christian mysticism. The two are distinguished by the different emphasis on the place of Christ. Paul says, 'It is no longer I who live but Christ who lives in me' (Galatians 2.20), while John says, 'Beloved, we are God's children now; it does not yet appear what we shall be, but we know that when he appears we shall be like him, for we shall see him as he is' (1 John 3.2).

Albert Schweitzer (1875–1965), a German theologian, physician and organist, completed his work on *The Mysticism of St Paul* in 1930 (English 1931). It is built on the thesis that 'being in Christ', interpreted as the 'physical union between Christ and the elect', is the centre of Pauline teaching and is to be distinguished from 'God mysticism' which attains to God directly without the mediation of Christ. That Paul's thought had a deep element of mysticism in it shocked some of his Protestant readers, for whom mysticism was a bad word.

Paul, living in a world drenched in Gnosticism and neo-Platonism, saw the dangers of both for the Christian faith. However, he utilized the thought-world of both for creating his own particular insights into the nature of Christ, and for initiating a Christ-mysticism. The nature of discipleship was to be so identified with the new way of love and faith taught by Jesus Christ that the disciple actually shared the life of Christ. If the life, then also the death, and if the death then also the resurrection (Romans 6.4). The disciple becomes united with Christ. It is difficult to know always whether Christ is in us (Romans 8.10), or we are in Christ, but the idea of absorption or identification is very strong in Paul's thinking. The Holy Spirit connected with the believer's spirit, in unity with the church, superseded all bodily or physical distinctions. Unity lay in the realm of the Spirit.

In his teaching about death in 1 Corinthians 15, Paul reveals the mystery of the resurrection: 'Listen! I will unfold a mystery. We shall not all die, but we shall be changed ... this perishable body must be clothed with the imperishable, and what is mortal with immortality.' The revealing of mysteries was something his dependence on the victory of Christ gave Paul confidence to do, but he was also aware of the dangers of esoteric knowledge. 'I may have the gift of prophecy and the knowledge of every hidden truth, but if I have no love, I am nothing.'

John's Gospel is rich in Greek mystical thought. It uses a whole range of imagery. Jesus' earthly life is described in more exalted terms than in any other Gospel. The human life of Jesus is set between his home in God from where he came, and the place to which he longs to return. Jesus is the light in the dark world. He comes to bring light. He is the light and in him is no darkness at all. Outside Jesus, and those who belong to Jesus, there is darkness.

This use of darkness and light as metaphors for ignorance and knowledge, blindness and vision runs through all the vocabulary of mysticism. The story of Jesus and Nicodemus in John 3 is a classic example. It is in darkness that the meeting is held. Nicodemus has to relearn his faith by a meeting in a dark night before he can be freed to accept the heavenly things of being born again in baptism. These truths, Jesus says, are spiritual, and like the wind. 'The wind blows where it wills: you hear the sound of it, but you do not know where it comes from or where it is going. So it is with everyone who is born from the Spirit' (3.8).

The images in mystical writing are often mixed, and it is difficult to maintain a clear thesis when dealing with such deeply-packed poetic material. However, the insights into the spiritual world that John's Gospel evokes and which are so powerfully described in the primary images of light and dark, perceiving and blindness, pervade the entire history of Christian mysticism through the centuries. Often it borders on the realm of Gnosticism, a movement which Paul spent much energy rebutting, fearing that mystical knowledge would destroy the primacy and simplicity of Christ. This is a constant problem for mysticism, and one that Jesus himself countered by drawing attention to the child. The child is first in the kingdom of God because he is not learned in the schools, but holds on to the simplicity of faith. The 'learned and wise' depend on human wisdom and miss the dimension of simple trust.

Gnosis

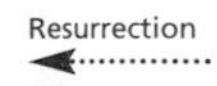
Resurrection

Philo

Philo (*c.* 20 BCE to *c.* 50 CE) was an Alexandrian Jew who made an important contribution to the history of mysticism by his development of the allegorical interpretation of scripture. This allowed him to discover much of Greek philosophy in the Jewish Bible, and to combine his respect for the Torah, the law contained in its first five books, with his aspiration towards a more spiritual interpretation of it. He accorded a central place in his system to the Logos, which was at the same time the creative power that orders the world, and the intermediary through which humans know God. It was the Logos who spoke to Moses in the burning bush, and who is represented in the Old Testament under the figure of High Priest. Philo wrote a *Life of Moses*, and a book on *The Contemplative Life.*

Holy Spirit

Death

The attention to the depths of meaning within scripture was at the heart of the concern of the earliest Christian mystics. The New Testament writers each in their own way were suited to the communities they were writing for, and were concerned for the fulfilment of Old Testament scripture in the life of Jesus. Post-scriptural writers searched the whole of scripture for levels of meaning beyond the straightforward factual account, to reach the details that provided spiritual truths. The blind are given their sight not only to see physically, but also to see spiritually.

p. 1197

Types of mystical theology

The understanding and application of varieties of mysticism are usually referred to in the phrase 'mystical theology'. To bring some order and clarification into this, certain generic titles or descriptions have arisen.

Apophatic (Greek *apophasis*, a denial or negation) is the term used of those theologians who experience the Christian journey as an entry into the darkness of unknowing. The glory of God is so great that it can be experienced in this life only in its negative form. Darkness is a hint or a foretaste of the greater glory to come.

Affective or *cataphatic* mysticism (Greek *kataphemi*, to say yes, assent to) is the journey that ends in assent to the love of God, having put aside on the way all intellectual operations. This end-point can be experienced as the result of the will or the affections, or, as in the case of Augustine, by love. Love itself, said Augustine, is our knowledge, superseding all intellectual operations. The Dominicans claimed that it was the ascent of the intellect enlightened by love which brought union with God.

Love

Experiential mysticism was the province especially of the late medieval writers. Some writers specified particular subjective experiences as constituting or indicating the attainment of mystical theology (generally identified from the sixteenth century onwards, with contemplation); this process reached its height in the Carmelite doctors, Teresa of Avila and John of the Cross, whose influence from then on was formative.

Trinity

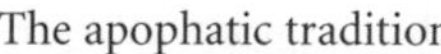

The apophatic tradition

Church fathers

Gregory of Nyssa (*c.*330–*c.*395). Gregory was Bishop of Nyssa, a Cappadocian father and the younger brother of Basil of Caesarea. He was a thinker and theologian of originality and learning, acquainted especially with Platonist speculation, as well as an outstanding expounder of scripture, an orator and an ascetical author. He was something of a bridge between Philo and Pseudo-Dionysius in the sixth century. His *Life of Moses* continued the interest in the revelatory quality of God's work in the experience of Moses, particularly in the stories of the burning bush and in the giving of the Law on Mount Sinai. It is his mystical understanding of scripture that makes him formative in the apophatic school of mysticism. This tradition saw God in the darkness, a negative theology, and was about the way of approaching God by denying that any of our concepts can properly be affirmed of him.

In his *Life of Moses*, at the moment where Moses enters the cloud on Mount Sinai, Gregory writes: 'What does it mean that Moses entered the darkness and saw God in it? (Exodus 20.21) … Leaving behind everything that is observed, not only what sense comprehends but also what the intelligence thinks it sees, it keeps on penetrating deeper until by the intelligence's yearning for understanding it gains access to the invisible and the incomprehensible, and there it sees God. This is the true knowledge of what is sought; this is the seeing that consists in not seeing, because that which is sought transcends all knowledge, being separated on all sides by incomprehensibility as by a kind of darkness.'

Pseudo-Dionysius. Mystical writing took a dramatic leap forward through the contribution of a sixth-century theologian who claimed to be the Dionysius the Areopagite mentioned in Acts 17.34. He was obviously not that person, and is now known as Pseudo-Dionysius or Denys/Dionysius the Pseudo-Areopagite. The Areopagite of Acts had listened to Paul speaking at Athens about 'the unknown God' being the God of Jesus Christ, raised from the dead. Some who heard this talk of Paul's 'became believers, including Dionysius a member of the Council of Areopagus'.

Dionysius took the identity of this first-century Areopagite and wrote *The Celestial Hierarchy, The Ecclesiastical Hierarchy, The Divine Names* and *The Mystical Theology*. These books were written in Greek, and were much influenced by the neo-Platonists. The short treatise *The Mystical Theology* is of enormous importance in the history of mysticism. It begins with a summarizing poem addressed to the Trinity, 'Higher than any being, any divinity, and goodness'. The Trinity is the guide for Christians, and the Trinity leads them to the mountain's summit. Here 'God's Word lies simple, absolute and unchangeable, in the brilliant darkness of a hidden silence'. At the summit 'God's Word' is still mysterious, it contains 'mysteries'. The mysteries emanate a revelatory light, and it is in, or by, that light that 'treasures beyond all beauty are received'.

In a further explanation of the poem, Dionysius draws on Psalm 18.11,'he made darkness his covering round about him', and Exodus 19 and 20, where 'Moses approached the dark cloud where God was'. The interplay of darkness and light, secrecy and revelation, seeing and not knowing, help to describe a setting, an experience, or a moment of revelation, but intellectually the content of that revelation is not made clear. 'Treasures beyond beauty are revealed', but this is as far, in human terms, as the author can go, except by way of making the nothingness, or the darkness, a reality. To the human mind 'nothing' is an absence, but confronted with the presence of God, as Moses was on the mountain, a human sense of nothingness gives way to a sense of God. Our natural faculties are striving to know, but it is in 'unknowing' that God finds room to be, and paradoxically it is in 'unknowing' that God allows himself to be known.

Dionysius broadly defines this process as the experience of three stages. First comes purification: 'It is not for nothing that the blessed Moses is commanded to submit first to purification.' Secondly, 'when every purification is complete, he (Moses) hears the many-voiced trumpets'. This stage is usually termed illumination. But then, thirdly, Moses breaks away from what he sees, and plunges into the truly mysterious darkness of unknowing. In this unknowing, he is united with God. This third stage is sometimes called 'participation in God', or 'unity with God'.

The Hesychasts in the Greek church. The Orthodox Church throughout the ages, with its very strong commitment to the historical persistence of the liturgy, and as its name suggests, with a concern for right thinking about tradition, has been very suspicious of mysticism. Perhaps there was also the thought that since the Roman Catholic Church had an intense interest in mysticism it was therefore per se heretical. However, the movement known as Hesychasm, the prayer of silence, stretched over many centuries.

The Dark Ages. It seems a large gap in the historical progression of the mystics to omit 600 years of Christian experience, from Pseudo-Dionysius to Eckhart, but the histories of mysticism tend to do just that. Perhaps the idea of mysticism as a logical study of types loses its way in this extremely fruitful missionary period of the church. The Anglo-Saxon poem *The Dream of the Rood* (early eighth century) is a visionary poem, rich in imagery, and full of levels with its dreams within dreams. It is alive with the elements of mystery and wonder, telling of the glory that lay in the victory of the cross. The imaginative art work and the illumination of manuscripts such as the Book of Kells (late seventh century?), dependent as they were on the mystical traditions of the Christian dispersion, breathe a mystical air. So much of the Celtic theology of the sixth to ninth centuries rested on a discourse between biblical texts and wider cultural motifs. These Christians wrote, prayed and were creative on the edge of the known world, and their creativity was inspired literally by views of eternity. The journeys of the sixth-century saint Brendan in search of an earthly paradise, related in the eighth-century Navigation of St Brendan, are understood to be largely a product of the imagination, though of course there was much sailing to and fro in the sixth century. The appearance and disappearance of islands is just one aspect of this deeply sophisticated, mystical work.

Meister Eckhart (*c.*1260–*c.*1328). The web of connections between many mystics from Germany and the Low Countries in the three centuries after the death of Thomas Aquinas and coinciding with the growing influence of the Dominican friars is complex. Suffice it to say that schools of mystical theology inevitably create a family likeness. The Dominican order took definite shape at the General Chapter at Bologna in 1220. Its intellectual life and involvement with public schools of theology, in which the writings of Aristotle were adapted to Christian theology chiefly by Albertus Magnus and Thomas Aquinas, could have been one major influence in producing a climate for mystical writings.

Religious orders

Mission

Eckhart was a German theologian and preacher who spent most of his life in Paris, and was drawn to the apophatic tradition of mystical thought. His brilliant, creative use of German makes him an author at once attractive and difficult. His readiness to exploit verbal ambiguities and dramatic paradoxes left him open to widely differing interpretations. For Eckhart abstractedness was the highest virtue, subsuming both humility and charity, because it produces the most intimate union with God. 'The soul, if she would work inwardly, must call home all

Books

Celtic theology

Journeys

THE HESYCHASTS

Hesychia is the Greek for quietness, and in the Eastern Church silent inner mystical prayer was practised above all by the monks of Mount Athos. It originated in the fourth/fifth centuries and is associated in particular with:

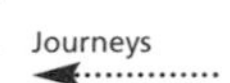

p. 795

Gregory of Nyssa (*c.* 330–*c.* 395)
Evagrius Ponticus (346–99)
Macarius/Simeon, author of *Homilies* (fourth/fifth century)
Diadochus of Photike (mid-fifth century)
John Climacus (*c.* 570–*c.* 649)
Maximus the Confessor (*c.* 580–662)
Simeon the New Theologian (949–1022)

Hesychasm in its fullest form finds its expression in the works of:

Gregory of Sinai (died 1346)
Nicephorus of Mount Athos (thirteenth century)
Gregory Palamas (*c.* 1296–1359)

They attached particular importance to the 'Jesus Prayer', 'Lord Jesus Christ, have mercy on me, a sinner.' The aim of this was to secure the union of the mind with the heart, so that this prayer became the prayer of the heart. This prayer leads eventually, in those who are specially chosen by God, to the vision of the Divine Light. It is often compared to the light at the transfiguration of Christ.

her powers and collect them from all divided things to one inward work. If a man would work an inward work, he must pour all his powers into himself as into a corner of the soul, and must hide himself from all images and forms, and then he can work. Then he must be in stillness and silence, when the word may be heard' (*Sermons*).

Bible

The Cloud of Unknowing. The author of this fourteenth-century work is unknown, but the book's final paragraph reveals him as a priest, dispensing 'God's blessing and mine'. We may guess that he was a country parson, perhaps in the East Midlands, with more than a nodding acquaintance of the religious life and a largish circle of souls under his direction. The greatest influence on the writing is definitely Pseudo-Dionysius. The author writes, 'By darkness I mean "a lack of knowing" – just as anything that you do not know or may have forgotten may be said to be "dark" to you, for you cannot see it with your inward eye. For this reason it is called a "cloud", not of the sky, of course, but of "unknowing", a cloud of unknowing between you and your God.'

The affective or cataphatic tradition

The notion of love. There is a very important connection between the notion of love and mysticism. Obviously this connection is not limited to one particular period, although notions of love do change their character through the ages and through particular cultural periods. John the evangelist was no stranger to the idea of love (Greek agape), nor were the Hebrews throughout their scriptures. Augustine of Hippo brought the love of God into the very heart of his life and his writings. Mysticism has hardly ever been inspired by the earning of great wealth, or particularly by the search for intellectual status. Rather, the life of the mystical experience, especially since the Middle Ages, has been a sense of 'falling in love with God', love in this case being a matter of the heart, as well as just a theological concept to do with the nature of God's being.

Mystics have felt God to be demanding the whole of their lives: emotional, mental and physical. There is a sense that the mystics have handed themselves over to the will of God to live in close, intimate relation with him. The offering of a life is not a planned matter, nor a scheme, though a way of life may assist the process. God

simply alights and says, 'Before this you did not know me, and from now on you will never not know me,' and this is experienced as the most comforting and creative thing that could happen. God becomes more real than many worldly things that previously had been taken to be real.

The cataphatic or affective tradition of mystical theology has love at its heart. It is a movement of the heart towards God. A converted heart becomes a powerful rudder to steer by. Mystics experienced amazing things because their hearts were in it.

Of a different complexion from the descent into unknowing is the ascent through the love of God into union with the Divine. The Old Testament book the Song of Songs has provided a text in which the relationship of lover to beloved, bride to bridegroom can flourish on both a literary and devotional level. Although both Origen (*c.*185–*c.*254) and Gregory of Nyssa wrote commentaries on this book; it was not until Bernard (1090–1153), Abbot of Clairvaux, and his *Sermons on the Song of Songs*, that the idea of using it as a mystical text comes into prominence.

Bernard of Clairvaux. With Bernard comes also a slight shift in understanding of what 'mysticism' might encompass. Bernard's sermons do not contain a sense of hiddenness or deliberate obfuscation. He uses the bride and bridegroom motif as a fairly straightforward allegory for the relationship of the devotee to God in Trinity, and as an opportunity to teach a quite simple morality. Taking the verse in the Song 'while the king reclines on his couch, my spikenard gives forth its scent' (Song 1.12), Bernard comments: 'the king's couch is the heart of the Father, because the Son is always in the Father ... and the fragrance of the spikenard is the fervour of your life, the good repute in which all men hold you' (*Sermon* 42.5, 6, 7).

Bernard describes the intention of his writing, again quite simply. 'Some other time we shall continue with the remainder of the text, provided that the Holy Spirit will be attentive to your prayers and enable us to understand the words of the bride, since he himself has inspired and composed them in a way befitting the promises of him whose Spirit he is, the Church's Bridegroom, our Lord Jesus Christ, who is God blessed for ever' (*Sermon* 42.7). It is the Holy Spirit who will lead his fellow monks into all truth. Bernard's way is one of enlightenment, matching text to text so that the way of Christ is seen as the constant thread. The mysticism is concerned with inwardness and the types of such an inward and individual piety.

The Victorines. The Abbey of St Victor in Paris in the twelfth century produced, among its canons regular (also referred to as Augustinian Canons), scholars and spiritual theologians of great ability and influence. Adam (died *c.*1185) was a composer of liturgical sequences; Hugh (died 1142) from Saxony was a prolific writer; and Richard (died 1173), who came from Ireland or Scotland, was the most mystical and ecstatic. Love was the theme of much of Richard's works. His *De Trinitate* presented a complex argument for a triune deity. His *Benjamin* provided the basis for the whole mystical psychology of Dante's *Paradiso*, and greatly influenced the Franciscan school, especially Bonaventure.

The Franciscan school. Francis of Assisi had a series of mystical experiences. His utter dedication to the poor emanated both from the practical experience of feeling compassion for the poor and the lepers, but also from a vision of one he called The Lady Poverty. Poverty is given a human form for him, dressed in rags, but showing the beauty of gospel poverty as a way of following the teachings of Christ. Francis' mysticism is not a literary one as such, although he sang out of his heart the Canticle of the Sun, in which the whole created order is cause for praise. His mysticism was in his direct contact with the suffering love of Christ, whose wounds became his own and showed on his body (the stigmata), and the joy of faithful service to the poor. His sanctity was of a unique order, but he shared with his followers much of the 'romantic' spirit of the times, and the mode of chivalry with which the soldiers fought their battles came out in his dedication for the souls of people of his age.

Bonaventure (*c.*1217–74) wrote a life of Francis approved in 1263 as the official biography of the founder of the Franciscan order. He emphasized that all human wisdom was folly when compared with the mystical illumination that God sheds on the faithful Christian, and this essentially mystical theology he set forth in his *Itinerarium Mentis in Deum* (Of the Journey of the Mind to God).

The medieval visionaries. There was a considerable openness to visionary experiences in such 'affective' mysticism, especially in the writings of female mystics such as Bridget of Sweden (*c.*1303–73), Catherine of Siena (*c.*1347–80), and Julian of Norwich (*c.*1342 to *c.*1420). Julian has taken a specific place in the history of English mysticism over recent years. Her *Revelations of Divine Love* have proved very popular, largely though her optimistic and comforting words 'all shall be well, all shall be well, and all manner of thing shall be well', and 'You would know our Lord's meaning in this thing. Know it well. Love was his meaning.' The mystical nature of the Shewings, or Revelations, indeed of God's love shown to her in her sickness, reveal the quality of her enjoyment in the mystery of Christ's death and victory.

Convergence in the experiential period

In the sixteenth century a remarkable outpouring of mystical fervour occurred when the two great mystical traditions, the one leading through the dark night and the other a reaching to glory through an intensity of the love of God, came together. This convergence was located in the Carmelite renewal in Spain, and is associated with the lives and writings of John of the Cross (1542–91) and Teresa of Avila (1515–82). The influence of the courtly romance tradition in literature gave the mystical experiences of these two, and many others, a language of the heart and of passionate love with which they could communicate their feelings. Indeed, the very idea of personal feelings, not new since they are expressed in the writings of Augustine, particularly in the *Confessions*, took on a fresh vigour and importance.

Teresa and John of the Cross were in many ways of quite different temperaments. John was an inward, reflective, scholarly poet. Teresa was an organizer, founding many houses for her sisters and for friars, a writer of letters, and of a spiritual autobiography, *The Life*. She was passionate, though, in her obedience to God and to what she saw as the gospel life. The two lives of John and Teresa were miraculously intertwined, and both had the tradition of Carmel at heart. The Carmelites looked back to the experiences of Elijah on Mount Carmel, scene of the contest between Elijah and the prophets of Baal (1 Kings 18). Teresa's mystical way was one of union with God, and the figures of bride and bridegroom are dominant in her writings. One of her books, *The Interior Castle*, describes seven dwelling places in which the soul can be with God, each with its own pitfalls and glories. Her writing is suffused with love for God, and it is described with great humility and a telling use of homely images. Bernini's famous sculpture of the ecstasy of Teresa is true to some aspects of her devotion to God, as when she speaks of 'the flames of that most vehement love of God that his majesty will have the perfect soul possess'. However, the baroque portrayal of ecstasy belies her essential pragmatism, her simple joy, and her practical genius. Her works also include *Foundations* and *The Way of Perfection*.

Sculpture

John of the Cross follows the mystic way largely through his meditation on *The Song of Songs*. His imprisonment in a small, unlit cell by opponents of the Carmelite reform has been seen as the time when his vision took fire. His works are largely the result of talks to the nuns among whom he sheltered for safety, after his dramatic escape from the cell in Toledo. He was a poet, and it is on his own reworking in verse of the biblical Song of Songs that he bases his commentaries. His writings are *Spiritual Canticle*, *Ascent of Mount Carmel* and *Dark Night of the Soul*. His poem, 'Song of the Soul', which begins in translation 'Upon a gloomy night', was translated by Roy Campbell in a seminal work published in 1951. The poem is in miniature a perfect example of John's mystical theology.

The Protestant mystics

Protestant mysticism was born out of the mysticism of the Roman Catholic Church and has been profoundly influenced by it throughout its entire course of development; but other influences can be detected too, giving it a particular character. The most important element was the New Testament, given added freshness through translation into the mother tongue. The Bible was felt to be the one

READING THE MYSTICS – AND OTHER BOOKS OF PRAYERS

The mystics are not difficult to explore: editions of their works in readable English are widely available, often in inexpensive paperback editions. Here are some of them, in alphabetical order, along with some other classic books of prayers.

Beguine Spirituality ed Fiona Bowie, London: SPCK 1989

The Cloud of Unknowing, Harmondsworth: Penguin Classics 2001

Lancelot Andrewes, *The Private Prayers* ed David Scott, London: SPCK 2002

Jean Pierre de Caussade, *Self-abandonment to Divine Providence*, London: Fontana Books 1971
– *The Sacrament of the Present Moment*, London: Fount Books 1981

George Herbert, *Complete English Works*, London: Everyman's Library 1995

Walter Hilton, *The Scale of Perfection*, modern English by John P. H. Clark and Rosemary Dorward, New York and Mahwah, NJ: Paulist Press 1991

John of the Cross, *The Dark Night of the Soul*, London: Hodder & Stoughton 1988

Julian of Norwich, *Revelations of Divine Love*, Harmondsworth: Penguin Classics 1998

The Book of Margery Kempe, Harmondsworth: Penguin Classics 1985

Richard Rolle, *The Fire of Love* ed Clifton Wolters, Harmondsworth: Penguin Classics 2001

Francis de Sales, *Introduction to a Devout Life*, New York: Vintage Classics 2002

Teresa of Avila, *The Interior Castle*, New York: Bantam Doubleday Dell 1990
– *The Way of Perfection*, New York: Bantam Doubleday Dell 1991

Thérèse of Lisieux, *Story of a Soul* translated by John Clarke OCD, Washington, DC: ICS Publications 1976

Thomas à Kempis, *The Imitation of Christ* translated by Leo Shirley-Price, Harmondsworth: Penguin Classics 1952

Thomas Traherne ed Denise Inge, London: SPCK 2002

The Complete Poetry of Henry Vaughan ed French Fogle, Norton Books 1969

Simone Weil, *Waiting on God*, London: Fontana Books 1959

The works of many other mystics are available in the series The Classics of Western Spirituality, published by Paulist Press, New York and Mahwah, NJ.

model of all religious experience and of all true piety. The rediscovery of the gospel, with its particular revelation of God and humanity and life, brought a new spiritualizing power to bear on people's minds. As a consequence, the new mysticism was far less negative in its way of approach to God, more practical and social in its outlook, and more eager to minister to people's lives in their entirety.

Martin Luther himself was an intense admirer of the *Theologia Germanica*, an anonymous medieval spiritual treatise, written in German by a priest of the Teutonic order at Sachsenhausen, near Frankfurt, and of John Tauler's sermons. A mystical depth is always in evidence in Luther's accounts of his own religious experience and in spiritual insight into the meaning of faith as the way of personal salvation.

Jakob Boehme (1575–1624). Boehme was born near Görlitz in Silesia, south-west Poland. Though an uneducated man, a shoemaker by trade, Boehme read much, and gathered into his meditative and original mind many strands of previous philosophies. Apart from the Bible, he absorbed the alchemical aspirations of the time, and inherited the baffling terminology of alchemy, astrology and theosophy. The core of Boehme's message sprang out of his own deep experience and his own vivid apprehension of the meaning of Christianity as a way of life. In 1600, as in a 'flash of lightning', he felt that 'the gate of his soul was opened' and that he saw and knew what no books could teach.

The main ideas were these. Behind the visible, material, temporal universe, there is an invisible, immaterial, eternal universe, which is the mother of the one that we see. This unoriginated matrix evolves into divine Personality within, and differentiates outwardly into visible and invisible worlds of matter, life and consciousness, through which the principles of light and darkness are revealed in temporal forms. The light, or love principle, the heart of God, has been perfectly revealed in the incarnation of Christ. To be saved is to be united with his life, to live in his love, to die to the isolated self, and to rise by a new birth into his Spirit and power and become a branch of Christ's tree.

George Fox (1624–91). Fox was the founder of the Quakers. Like Boehme, he went through a long period of baffling search, ending in a great mystical experience. The main religious ideas which formed his message, and which he delivered with great success in England and America, are these. There is a 'Light' or 'Seed' of God in the soul of every person. The soul, obedient to the divine endowment, increases its measure of light, triumphs over the innate tendencies to sin, and becomes a spiritual organ of the present, living, inward Christ, who is the only head of the true church. The best preparation for worship, as also for public service of any kind, is inward hush or silence, the suppression of self and selfishness, the inward reception of grace, and an attitude of waiting for a clear prompting of the Spirit's guidance.

William Law (1686–1761). In the writings of William Law, Protestant mysticism in the eighteenth century attained its most perfect expression. He shows throughout his life the influence of the Cambridge Platonists, Benjamin Whichcote, John Smith, Henry More and Ralph Cudworth, but early on he formed his own mind directly on the great models of mystical piety. In his first creative period, in which he produced *Christian Perfection* (1726) and *A Serious Call to a Devout and Holy Life* (1729), he strongly follows the line of classical, medieval mysticism, with much emphasis on self-denial and negation. These two books represent the culmination in England of the type of Christianity embodied in the sermons of John Tauler (died 1361), the *Theologia Germanica*, an anonymous medieval spiritual treatise, written in German, and *The Imitation of Christ* written by Thomas à Kempis (*c.* 1380–1471), though with less of a metaphysical cast and with more practical adjustment to life.

In the second period, which dates from 1733, Law was not so influential upon English thought, but his insights became far deeper and he was more conscious of a direct inward relation with a universe of invisible reality. In the group of the writings of this period, of which *The Spirit of Prayer* (1749), *The Spirit of Love* (1752) and *The Way to Divine Knowledge* (1752) are representative, we have the noblest English interpretation of Jakob Boehme's mystical message.

The mystical poets

A mystical element has run through poetry from the beginning. It is of course the ideal medium with which to capture the paradoxes and subtleties of thought with which mysticism challenges the writer. However, *The Oxford Book of Mystical Verse* has few poems written before the seventeenth century. It is with the 'metaphysical' poets of this century that the traditional themes of Christian mysticism re-emerge. George Herbert (1593–1633) wrote poems such as 'Love' and 'The Elixir' which reach great heights of homely exaltation. John Donne (1571/2–1631) is more philosophical, and deals with love and death in every aspect. The poem which begins 'Batter my heart, three-person'd God' takes the traditional mystical theme of lover appealing to the beloved. Henry Vaughan (1622–95), in his poem 'The Night', takes the familiar theme of the 'cloud of unknowing', as Nicodemus meets Christ by night. Thomas Traherne (1636–74) is best known as a prose writer. His work *Centuries* is a series of short pieces on the childlike vision of God as seen in the created world. Richard Crashaw (*c.* 1613–49) is the most conventionally mystical of them all, taking themes such as 'A Hymn to Saint Teresa', which is consciously written out of the tradition.

Since the seventeenth century, poets such as William Wordsworth, William Blake, Gerard Manley Hopkins, Francis Thompson, Emily Dickinson, Walt Whitman, and T. S. Eliot could all be described, in their different ways, as mystical poets.

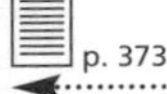

p. 373

The twentieth century

With the growing interest in psychology and the classification of knowledge, the early part of the twentieth century saw the appearance of a number of books on the evidence for mysticism. *The Varieties of Religious Experience* (1901) by William James looked at the psychological aspect behind mysticism. Evelyn Underhill's *Mysticism* (1911) gave a very broad overview of the writings of the mystics with classifications resonant of the time: Voices and Visions; Introversion; Ecstasy and Rapture; The Dark Night of the Soul; The Unitive Life. The book was subtitled *A Study of the Nature and Development of Man's Spiritual Consciousness.* For more accessible reading Underhill wrote *Practical Mysticism for Normal People* (1914).

Baron Friedrich von Hügel, a Roman Catholic living in London, wrote *The Mystical Element of Religion as studied in St Catherine of Genoa and her Friends* (1908). Von Hügel saw the institutional, the intellectual and the mystical as the three abiding elements in religion. William Ralph Inge (1860–1954), Dean of St Paul's, had great sympathy with Platonic spirituality, and this found its expression in a long series of devotional and theological writings, including *Christian Mysticism* (1899) and *The Philosophy of Plotinus* (1918).

Two writers, both French, stand out in the twentieth century as mystics of great note, and both were controversial. Simone Weil (1909–43), born a Jew, was moved

towards Christianity, but not to baptism, by reading George Herbert's poem 'Love'. The two books available in English, *Waiting on God* (1951) and *Gateway to God* (1974), give in selections the heart of her life and writings. Her mysticism is a radical combination of love and suffering. The other outstanding mystical writer is Pierre Teilhard de Chardin (1881–1955), a Jesuit priest, geologist and palaeontologist. He offered a fresh wisdom about the nature of the world, focused on the central image of fire and the dynamic of evolutionary change. His essay *Le Milieu Divin* (1917), written from the trenches, contains the seeds of his life's work in bringing creation into the centre of spiritual concern. Teilhard addresses the great problem for religion and mysticism in the modern world as they seek not to dispense with reality but to find in the real, the purposes of God.

Jalal al-Din Rumi, the Sufi mystic, said, 'The mystics speak in a hundred different ways, but if God is one and the way is one, how could their meaning be other than one? What appears in different disguises is one essence. A variety of expression, but the same meaning.' Continuous research into, and publication of, the texts of the mystical traditions of the great world religions have initiated a fresh impetus to the study and practice of mysticism. The writings of Thomas Merton (1915–68), the Cistercian monk, have done as much as any other to build bridges between disparate mystical traditions. His book *Mystics and Zen Masters* opened up to many the worlds of Zen, Taoism, the Russian mystics and the Shaker communities. In his lectures to the novices at Gethsemani Abbey in Kentucky he made the Sufi tradition accessible to modern Western mentalities by describing the links between Eastern and Western concepts. By his own alternative lifestyle, as a monk in an increasingly secular society, he was a prophet of hope. His correspondence with many of the great historians of Islamic mysticism such as Louis Massignon and Abdul Aziz gave a living reality to a sharing of traditions. He showed a generation new ways of relating to God, and described in his autobiographical writings the ways that he had experienced the love of God.

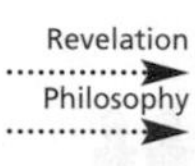
Revelation
Philosophy

Shakers
Trinity

A chapter in W. H. Vanstone's last book, *Farewell in Christ* (1997), with the title 'The Good Mysteries', points to the writings of the poet Dylan Thomas, the Russian novelist Fyodor Dostoievsky and the philosopher Ludwig Wittgenstein as fertile ground for a renewed understanding of mysticism in Christianity. At the very end he wrote more generally about the mysteries: 'When intellectual doubts assail me I turn my mind to the mysteries that enfold me. They are inexplicable, inconceivable, unimaginable yet undeniable – the mystery of existence, the mystery of my soul, the mystery of meaning. I find them unthreatening mysteries, welcome mysteries, good mysteries.'

p. 507

DAVID SCOTT

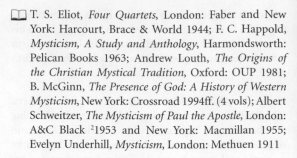

T. S. Eliot, *Four Quartets*, London: Faber and New York: Harcourt, Brace & World 1944; F. C. Happold, *Mysticism, A Study and Anthology*, Harmondsworth: Pelican Books 1963; Andrew Louth, *The Origins of the Christian Mystical Tradition*, Oxford: OUP 1981; B. McGinn, *The Presence of God: A History of Western Mysticism*, New York: Crossroad 1994ff. (4 vols); Albert Schweitzer, *The Mysticism of Paul the Apostle*, London: A&C Black [2]1953 and New York: Macmillan 1955; Evelyn Underhill, *Mysticism*, London: Methuen 1911

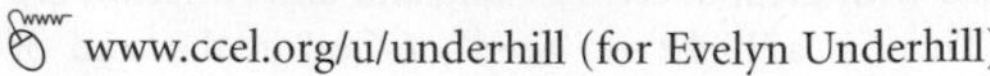
www.ccel.org/u/underhill (for Evelyn Underhill)

Natural theology

In Christian thought, natural theology has usually been considered to be the view that human reason can have knowledge of God and God's activity in the world without the aid of special revelation. Christian thought was influenced in this regard by earlier philosophical traditions which regarded the 'natural' as the rational; hence, many Christian thinkers adopted the assumption that a 'natural' theology entails 'rational' reflection on the possibility of God's existence and the evidence of divine activity in the natural order.

However, it was not until the Middle Ages that a systematic natural theology was formulated, in the work of Thomas Aquinas (1225–74). Most previous Christian thought on the subject had followed the lead of Augustine of Hippo (354–430). Augustine was influenced by the neo-Platonic view that the highest element of nature is human rationality. In his *De Trinitate* (On the Trinity) he applied this principle within a Christian framework and concluded that one could therefore expect to find traces of the trinitarian God within the structure of human rationality; this led him to a psychological theology of the Trinity. Even this limited natural theology, however, must be understood in the context of Augustine's unwavering principle that God can be known only with the aid of divine grace.

Thomas Aquinas departed from the Augustinian view by making a clear distinction between natural and revealed theology. According to Thomas, we can infer knowledge of God by reasoning analogously from the nature of the human mind and the nature of the world. Thus, reflection on the order of creation allows us to infer the existence of a Creator; we can further speak analogously of God's wisdom, goodness, etc. In this manner Thomas formulated his famous five 'ways' or 'proofs' for the existence of God. However, for Thomas, this natural theology must be complemented by special revelation, for there are many central Christian truths which reason cannot attain (the nature of God as Trinity, the doctrine of the incarnation, etc.).

While Martin Luther (1483–1546) and other Reformers were critical of this theological emphasis on the power of human reason, Protestant thought also found some space for natural theology. In his *Institutes of the Christian Religion*, John Calvin (1509–64) affirmed the possibility of a natural knowledge of God. All human beings have an inherent 'sense of the divine' (which can be experienced, for example, through an uneasy conscience). Moreover, the order and beauty of the creation allows any human person, Christian or not, to recognize God's activity and wisdom. Although this rudimentary knowledge of God means that no one can claim to be ignorant of the divine, it is also imperfect and inadequate knowledge, for God can truly be known only through special revelation. It is only in the divinely revealed Christian scripture that our natural knowledge of God is fulfilled in the encounter with God's redeeming activity in Christ.

Both Roman Catholic and Protestant natural theologies came under critical attack during the Enlightenment. The scepticism of the Scottish philosopher David Hume (1711–76) undermined many planks of classical Christian apologetics, including the principle that the very existence and the order of the world allows us to draw conclusions about its origin in a divine being outside the world. These attacks culminated in the world of Immanuel Kant (1724–1804). In Kant's view all a posteriori arguments (i.e. arguments from our experience of the world) for God's existence, such as those from causality or the ordered design of the world, are themselves founded upon an a priori argument (i.e. argument from rationality) which proceeds from our understanding what we mean when we think or say the word 'God'. Thus the teleological argument, which points to the apparent design of the elements of the creation for particular purposes, rests on the cosmological argument, which asserts that everything that exists must owe its existence to a Creator. But this in turn requires that we establish the necessary existence of a Creator God, the aim of the a priori argument. Kant believed that his critique of the a priori argument made this impossible. He argued that the a priori argument fails because 'existence' is a predicate which we cannot legitimately add to our definition of God; therefore it follows that the arguments dependent upon it also fail.

Kant's critique undermined confidence in classical natural theology, but this did not deter some Christian thinkers from defending it. Most notably, in the early nineteenth century the Anglican divine William Paley's *Natural Theology* (1802) argued that there can be no design without a designer. As Paley thought it evident that the world is designed, there had to be a Designer who achieved this. After all, he famously reasoned, if you found a watch upon the ground, would you not assume that it had been designed; how, otherwise, could it come to be so formed? As the world is far more complex than a single watch, should we not also assume that it too has a Designer? Paley was read with admiration by many at the time, including the young Charles Darwin, whose work was to further undermine natural theology.

Incarnation

Evolution

Darwin's theory of evolution through natural selection radically changed the nineteenth century's dominant metaphors for the natural world. Rather than evoking the sense of wonder and admiration for its benign design characteristic of Paley and many other Christians, nature in the mid-nineteenth century now came to be seen as 'red in tooth and claw', in Tennyson's memorable depiction. Rather than being the work of a wise and benevolent deity, nature was perceived by many as a battleground of waste and violence. In the Darwinian view the human species, too, became part of that natural world, and this was often taken to mean that humanity was not a special divine creation endowed with an immortal soul. Yet many theologians at the time sought to reconcile Darwinism with Christian theology. Some saw God as setting the evolutionary process in motion yet no longer interfering, but this viewpoint was dangerously close to deism. Others, emphasizing God's immanence in the world, sought evidence of divine activity in the evolutionary process itself rather than in interventionist acts of special creation.

Enlightenment

Karl Barth

In the twentieth century natural theology also came under attack from within Christian theology itself. Karl Barth (1886–1968) was a fierce opponent, seeing natural theology as inimical to God's free revelation. There is no 'point of contact' between human nature and God which would allow humans somehow to gain knowledge of God from their own powers; we know God only through God's revelation in Christ. When Barth's friend and colleague Emil Brunner suggested a revised natural theology, Barth reacted with a fury that broke their friendship. While Barth's criticism of natural theology was widely influential, one of its unintended consequences was the atheistic 'death of God' theology of the 1960s, which could find God neither in and through nature nor in Barth's positive theology of revelation.

Roman Catholic theology in the twentieth century sought a revised natural theology which would overcome the separation between natural and revealed truth characteristic of the prevailing interpretation of Aquinas. Henri de Lubac's (1896–1991) *Le surnaturel* (The Supernatural), published just after the Second World War, attempted to overcome this division by arguing against the idea of a 'pure nature' which has not been influenced by divine grace. This idea was expanded by others such as Karl Rahner (1904–84). Human beings are created with a desire for God and this desire is itself a gift of God's grace. There

is no gulf between the realm of nature and the 'supernatural' realm of God's activity; our 'natural' efforts to understand God are themselves gifts of God.

Paul
Reformation

Significant new interest in the question of natural theology has recently begun to emerge in the context of debates on science and religion: some contemporary theologians defend the so-called 'anthropic principle', arguing that there is something about the constitution of the universe that makes it seem prepared for intelligent life; some point to unresolved issues such as the problem of consciousness to defend the mysteriousness of existence; others have continued the attempts to reconcile Christianity with the theory of evolution, placing an emphasis on theologies of divine activity in the world (for example, the idea that God's activity could be understood as the input of information into the evolutionary process). These theologies no longer try to 'prove' the existence of God from features of the natural world but instead defend the rationality and coherence of religious belief or, more strongly, argue that the evidence of complexity and design in nature suggests a plausible cumulative case for theism. Prominent among such thinkers are Keith Ward, John Polkinghorne and Ian Barbour. They have, however, not been without their opponents, especially among scientists; Richard Dawkins, Stephen Hawking, Daniel Dennett and others have argued against the theologians that there is no need or role for God in the natural sphere and that 'natural theology' is thus a vacuous concept. Much like the universe itself, these debates are unlikely to end any time soon.

Science
Science and theology
Liberal theology

JAMES M. BYRNE

Ian G. Barbour, *When Science Meets Religion: Enemies, Strangers or Partners?*, San Francisco: Harper SanFrancisco 2000; Willem Drees, *Creation: From Nothing Until Now*, London and New York: Routledge 2001; John F. Haught, *God After Darwin: A Theology of Evolution*, Boulder, CO: Westview Press 2000; John Polkinghorne, *Belief in God in an Age of Science*, New Haven and London: Yale University Press 1998; Keith Ward, *God, Faith and the New Millennium: Belief in God in an Age of Science*, Oxford: Oneworld 1998

Neo-orthodox theology

'Neo-orthodoxy' was a major theological movement in the early and middle part of the twentieth century. Its impact and significance continue today. The principal figures associated with it included the great Swiss theologian Karl Barth (1886–1968), and his compatriot Emil Brunner (1889–1966) and in the United States the brothers H. Richard Niebuhr (1894–1962) and Reinhold Niebuhr (1892–1971). The prefix 'neo' indicates the movement's perceived return to 'orthodox' Christian teachings, especially the teachings of the apostle Paul and the sixteenth-century Protestant Reformers. Neo-orthodoxy never constituted a distinct school of theology, and the term itself was repudiated by Barth, yet it is a useful description of a particular form of theology which emerged in European and American Protestantism after World War I.

Karl Barth

Jesus of history

What the neo-orthodox theologians shared was a dissatisfaction with the prevailing theological liberalism. The movement's origins lie in Barth's criticism of the liberal German theology of the nineteenth century in which he had been trained. Following the impetus given by the philosophical critiques of Immanuel Kant (1724–1804) and the theology of Friedrich Schleiermacher (1768–1834), German liberal theology emphasized religious experience and the consequences for theology of the historical study of Christian development. However, for Barth, disillusioned with liberalism, any theology that compromised the Christian message by subjecting it to a worldly principle was a betrayal of true Christianity. He therefore set out to develop a theology that would present the gospel as standing over and against the assumptions of this world, including those inherent in liberal theology. This understanding of the Christian message as standing in judgement over the world was to give rise to what was termed the 'dialectical theology' of Barth and his followers. Any connection between God and the world can be only on God's terms, not ours. So the relation is always dialectical; every 'yes' from us also implies a 'no', for we can never claim to have fully grasped the divine revelation.

In 1922 the second edition of Barth's commentary on Paul's letter to the Romans caused enormous theological controversy, and divided theologians squarely into liberal and neo-orthodox camps. Barth's supporters saw themselves as putting theology on a whole new footing, one true to the original Christian message, to the theology of Paul, and to the 'otherness' of the God of the Bible. Their detractors perceived the new movement as abandoning historical criticism and as being inherently hostile to reason, culture and progress.

Under Barth's influence, the early criticism of liberalism by neo-orthodoxy was severe and wide-ranging, but it essentially focused on subjectivity and the question of historical consciousness. For the neo-orthodox there was no path to God from experience, culture, reason or religious practice; only the Word of God addressed to humanity and received in faith could bring us to God. No study of history, including the attempt to discover the 'historical' Jesus, could lead to faith; only God's own revelation gave the certainty that sinful humanity sought. Thus neo-orthodoxy repudiated liberalism's optimistic view of human culture, its emphasis on the ethical teachings of the man Jesus, its historical-critical reading of the Bible, and its appeal to the interiority of religious experience as a foundation for theology. Instead it emphasized the personal and social consequences of sin, the theological reading of the Bible from within a biblical perspective, a dialectical understanding of God who is revealed as the God hidden from the world, and a christology which appeals not to the Jesus of history but to the Christ recognized in faith.

In the 1920s differences emerged among some of the leading proponents of the dialectical theology. By 1930 Barth alone held firm to a full repudiation of any possible anthropological starting-point for theology. From this point onwards the early proponents of neo-orthodoxy followed a number of different, sometimes conflicting, theological trajectories.

As in Europe, theological concerns in the United States were changing in the 1920s and 1930s. Like their European counterparts, many American Protestant theologians became disillusioned with aspects of liberalism, especially its optimistic view of human nature and its attenuation of evil and sin. They demanded a more 'realistic' theology attuned to the needs of the times, and they found this neither in a strict Barthianism nor in the optimism of nineteenth-century liberalism. H. Richard Niebuhr's 1931 essay 'Religious Realism in the Twentieth Century' and Reinhold Niebuhr's *Moral Man and Immoral Society* (1932) marked the beginnings of this movement. Other significant figures included J. C. Bennett (1902–95) and W. M. Horton (1895–1966). While usually included within the broad neo-orthodox movement, these American theologians can be regarded as somewhat more sympathetic to the interests of classical liberalism than were their European counterparts, especially those closely associated with Barth.

H. R. Niebuhr was critical of the anthropomorphism of liberalism and its weak sense of human sinfulness, yet he did not abandon the importance it placed upon historical consciousness. Following Barth, Niebuhr emphasized the sovereignty of God and the sense of human sinfulness which had been absent in liberalism. In *The Kingdom of God in America* (1937) he famously castigated liberal theology: 'A God without wrath brought men without sin into a kingdom without judgement through the ministrations of a Christ without a cross.' Yet, influenced by Ernst Troeltsch and Max Weber, he retained liberalism's emphasis on history and the social construction of knowledge. This led him to a theology of divine revelation which was deeply personal yet mediated through historical communities. The meaning of human history is to be found not in the raw data of external or 'outer' events, but rather in their 'inner' significance for each person or community, and it is here that God's revelation is encountered. Niebuhr repudiated the charge that this emphasis on the personal results in subjectivism, for in encountering God's revelation we bring all personal experience under its judgement and thus avoid the egoism and immanentism which he perceived as characteristic of modernity. Rejecting metaphysical foundations, Niebuhr's theology eschewed apologetics as such, emphasizing instead Christianity's confessional nature.

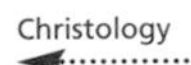

Reinhold Niebuhr combined theological reflection with social activism. During thirteen years as a pastor in Detroit he was widely involved in socialist and pacifist movements. He returned to academic theology in the late 1920s and in 1939 published his *magnum opus*, *The Nature and Destiny of Man*. Highly critical of secularist views of human nature, he defended Christian apologetics and emphasized the relevance of the Bible to contemporary social and political issues. Rejecting both philosophical pessimism and bourgeois optimism, Niebuhr argued that Christianity gives us a view of the human self that recognizes both its sinfulness and its capacity for self-transcendence. Sin is not the ignorance that liberalism thought, but is rather our attempt to deny or escape the finitude and contingency that is fundamental to the human condition. In denying our nature we place the relative in place of the absolute; this is most clearly seen in our moral pride and desire for power, whether personal, social or political. Yet, for Niebuhr, we can use power correctly in the service of love and justice. Thus he linked his theological anthropology with his social and political criticism.

One of Niebuhr's lasting contributions to modern thought is his subtle analysis of how we constantly shift the blame for our faults on to forces external to the self. Of course, for Niebuhr, this denial of personal moral responsibility is one of the marks of sin, and it demonstrates that we can never save ourselves. The self can only finally be redeemed through God's grace and judgement as encountered in the cross of Christ. This fundamental Christian anthropology provided the basis for Niebuhr's long career as a social critic and political commentator, tirelessly critical of the confidence which both Western bourgeois culture and Marxist eschatology placed in human nature and historical progress. An ethicist, moralist and theologian, Reinhold Niebuhr was the last great American Protestant public intellectual of the twentieth century.

The influence of neo-orthodoxy continues today in the work of diverse theologians whose over-riding concern is to reject philosophical or metaphysical foundations for Christianity. 'Postliberals' such as H. W. Frei, George Lindbeck and Stanley Hauerwas have all drawn on the neo-orthodox heritage to argue that the truth-claims of Christianity should not be dependent upon or subject

to various aspects of modern philosophy and theology, especially epistemological foundationalism. 'Radical orthodox' theologians, although often critical of neo-orthodoxy, share many of its concerns. John Milbank suggests that modernity, including much modern Christian thought, has disastrously reversed the correct relationship between social theory and theology. Modernity has lost its way through its tendency to naturalize the supernatural, yet a renewal of modern culture is possible through its recognition of its true theological origins. So rather than view the Christian message through the lens of secular thought, as so much modern theology has done, Christianity provides a framework from which to question many of the assumptions underlying the modern project. While these recent movements are currently of interest primarily to professional theologians, the increasing prevalence of conservative tendencies within the major Christian churches indicates that perhaps their time of greatest influence is still to come.

JAMES M. BYRNE

Karl Barth, *The Epistle to the Romans*, second edition, London: OUP 1933; George Lindbeck, *The Nature of Doctrine: Religion and Doctrine in a Postliberal Age*, Philadelphia: Westminster Press 1984; John Milbank, *The Word Made Strange: Theology, Language, Culture*, Oxford: Blackwell 1997; Reinhold Niebuhr, *Moral Man and Immoral Society: A Study in Ethics and Politics* (1932), Louisville, KY: Westminster John Knox Press 2002; Reinhold Niebuhr, *The Nature and Destiny of Man* (1951), Louisville, KY: Westminster John Knox Press 1996; H. Richard Niebuhr, *The Kingdom of God in America* (1937), New York: Harper & Bros 1959

New religious movements →

New Age movement

It is difficult to pin down any New Age teaching as held by a consensus of its devotees. One commentator has perceptively written that 'understanding the New Age is like trying to wrestle with a jelly', since it is so eclectic and amorphous a phenomenon. 'Movement' is a good name for it, given that it is in a state of continuous change. Nevertheless, like figures emerging from the mist, certain distinguishing features can be made out, including a particular division of religious time into a whole series of ages.

Ecotheology →

The New Age which gives the movement its name is that of Aquarius, the latest in a succession of astrological ages: Aries the ram (beginning *c.* 2000 BCE); Pisces the fish (beginning with the Christian era); and Aquarius the water carrier (from the very end of the second millennium). In this scheme the age of Aries was characterized by a notion of God as Father who presided over a patriarchal religion; that of Pisces has been described by the name Son and the religion is typically institutional; the age of Aquarius denotes transcendent reality as spiritual, and is a time when hierarchical and organized religion will give way to exuberant, unconstrained and creative spirituality.

Many strands from the past are eclectically pulled together: Hindu notions of *karma* and rebirth; astrology; pagan and wicca religions (witchcraft). However, these are torn from their original contexts and made to serve a point of view that reflects the malaise of late modernity. New Agers mostly deny the existence of a Creator God and believe in an enclosed universe, within which individuals have to create and live out their own spirituality. Interestingly, the roots of the New Age date from the 'experiences' of some people in Europe and North America after the Second World War. They investigated the phenomenon of Unidentified Flying Objects, and came to the conclusion that these were spaceships containing superior beings who came to offer a greater cultural, scientific, technological and spiritual development to humans.

Early utopian communities such as Findhorn in Scotland have often given way to a more postmodern spirituality of the self, encouraging spiritual consumers to pick and choose what fulfils them and makes them happy. This individualism marks New Agers off from members of new religious movements, whose religious reconstructions usually take communality and hierarchical leadership very seriously.

Christianity has not usually been the bearer of hope for New Agers. For them, the age of Pisces was characterized by injustice, hatred, bigotry, mistrust and even war, much of which can be laid at the door of organized religion, since it divided humankind into alienated and competitive institutions. The 1960s saw a burgeoning interest in religions from the East, especially Hinduism, which provide alternative visions of what it means to be human and how the transcendent is to be construed.

One aspect of Eastern religion that appeals to New Agers is that of 'Mother Earth', very important in some interpretations of Hinduism (though that religion's darker depiction of the feminine in, for example, the Kali cult has been ignored or played down). This emphasis upon reality as nurturing and female, rather than exploitative and male, has been widely disseminated through the Gaia hypothesis (Gaia was the Greek Earth goddess, also known as Ge). This sees Mother Earth as a living entity and organism, nurturing the whole environment. New Agers criticize the Jewish-Christian teaching in Genesis 1 about humankind as having dominion over the earth as the mastering and exploiting of creation by beings who regard themselves as a special and unique work of God; instead they believe that people should work harmoniously within nature, seeing themselves as part of it; part, as it were, of a great universal self, rather like the Hindu belief in the universal soul (*atman*) of and in which we all partake. Since Mother Earth is a self-contained entity, part of a self-contained universe, New Agers find the notion of a transcendent reality that reveals itself by breaking in from beyond wide of the mark. Christianity is sometimes portrayed as teaching about a male sky-god, invading the Earth and brutalizing women in particular.

New Agers are not impressed by traditional teaching about Jesus as the incarnate son of God: the notion that 'he came down to earth from heaven, who is God and Lord of all' hardly tallies with belief in an autonomous and self-sufficient universe. Many films of the last two decades demonstrate that New Agers can accept ghosts, witches, diviners and all sorts of emanations or functionaries of a spiritual reality, but they usually interpret these as this-worldly, not other-worldly. They are, as it were, another layer of the onion of reality which appears only when the present layer is peeled away. Jesus is sometimes seen as an enlightened teacher, but not as God's agent of salvation.

New Agers deny Christian belief in the fall of humankind: humans are not so much sinners needing salvation as seekers after enlightenment. So some New Agers interpret Jesus as a channeller of spiritual truth, or as an impressive mystic who taught (*inter alia*) vegetarianism and reincarnation. This means that they believe that mainstream Christianity suppressed such teaching: the Gospels are unreliable and other material (like the Gnostic Gospel of Thomas) is regarded as closer to their view of who Jesus should have been and what he should have done.

Much in the New Age movement is ephemeral, trendy and anti-intellectual, but it makes important criticisms of Christian faith, not least its attitude to the environment and the feminine.

MARTIN FORWARD

📖 J. Drane, *What is the New Age Still Saying to the Church?*, London: HarperCollins 1991; P. Heelas, *The New Age Movement: Celebrating the Self and the Sacralization of Modernity*, Oxford: Blackwell 1996

New religious movements

In one sense, 'new religious movements' are very old. For example, Christianity could be regarded as a new religious movement emerging from Judaism after the destruction of the second temple in 70 CE. But the term has come to be used to designate a phenomenon that has arisen since the late 1960s. New religious movements are counter-cultural movements, rejecting secularism and secularization, and promoting personal spiritual and moral growth. They are found in many countries, not just in the West, but wherever the tentacles of modernization and Westernization have spread. Yet they use modern technology to spread their message and to make links with other communities.

There are different families of new religious movements. Some have originated from Eastern traditions; others from Christianity; and yet more from within a particular country. An organization like the Unification Church falls within all these categories, illustrating that its members are fluid and open-ended. (The Unification Church is indebted to Far Eastern religious ideas, to an eccentric form of Presbyterianism, and to Korean nationalistic ideals.) Like many new religious movements, the Unification Church has a charismatic leader, the Revd Sun Myung Moon, who claims exalted status (since 1982 Moon has openly claimed to be the Messiah) and exercises a rigid control over the lives of his followers.

Incarnation

The sheer diversity and number of new religious movements means that it is difficult to point to specific traits held in common by most or all. However, as well as the similarities just noted, other characteristics of many new religious movements include: specific roles for women, which sometimes reinforce traditional gender patterns (e.g. in the Unification Church), but occasionally offer leadership positions (e.g. the Brahma Kumaris); authoritative texts (e.g. Moon's *Divine Principle*; and a particular translation and commentary of the Bhagavad Gita for members of the International Society for Krishna Consciousness); and an emphasis upon community rather than individualism, sometimes expressed in family terms with the leader as father or mother (e.g. Elizabeth Clare Prophet of the Church Universal and Triumphant is known as Guru Ma).

Gnosis

In the 1970s, many new religious movement members were young people who left family and education and joined community groups. Although they had an intense experience, statistically most became disillusioned and returned to 'mainstream' society. Less than 1 per cent of people in North America and Europe have been involved for more than two years with a new religious movement, and many have merely dabbled in one branch: for example, over a million people in the USA have taken a basic course in Transcendental Meditation, but only about 20,000 joined the movement.

Attitudes to new religious movements in society have mostly been hostile. In popular parlance, they are 'cults'. Many parents believe that when their children join new religious movements, they have been manoeuvred or even brainwashed into doing so.

Even more problematic has been the association of new religious movements with death and destruction. In November 1978, 922 members of Jim Jones' People's

Secularization

Temple apparently committed suicide in Jonestown, Guyana. There were other high-profile cases in the 1990s: the siege of the Branch Davidians at Waco, Texas, in 1993 by the FBI ended in tragedy; in 1994, 1995 and 1997, members of the Solar Temple were found dead; in 1995, Aum Shinrikyo perpetrated an attack on the Tokyo underground with the poison gas sarin; and in 1997, the bodies of 39 members of Heaven's Gate were found at Rancho Santa Fe in California. They died voluntarily, believing that a UFO would carry them off to a higher level of being.

It would be easy to react by restricting or even outlawing the activities of new religious movements. One such attempt was made in 1984, when a series of proposals, known as the Cottrell proposals, were laid before the European Parliament. These proposals would have monitored new religious movements, opening them up to inspection and limiting their freedom to make converts. But this attempt at legislating against new religious movements was not as appropriate a strategy as its proponents averred. These laws would have also infringed the liberties of older religious movements, such as the churches, and been in direct violation of the articles on religious liberty of the Universal Declaration of Human Rights and of the European Convention on Human Rights. The Strasbourg Parliament retreated from the brink of making a serious and unnecessary misjudgement, since the vast majority of countries already have legislation in place to punish those who commit acts of kidnapping or murder. When particular new religious movements or individual members break these and other laws, it is appropriate to punish them for this.

Papacy
Council

It would be folly to seek to chastize new religious movements for following strange doctrines, unconventional morality, authoritative texts and charismatic leaders. In their time, Christians have been ostracized and even penalized by wider society for these very reasons. It makes far better sense for the churches to engage in dialogue with new religious movements about issues between them and Christian belief and practices, rather than to marginalize them. One example of such dialogue in the United Kingdom is INFORM (Information Network Focus on Religious Movements). This was founded in 1988 with funding from the Home Office and the mainstream churches. Among those who contact it are relatives and friends of people who have joined new religious movements, ex-members, government departments and secular agencies, and the media. INFORM can give them information directly or put them in touch with a network of knowledgeable people who can help them with their enquiry.

Whether new religious movements will continue to flourish as they have done in recent years may well depend upon unforeseen factors. For example, who will provide the second-generation of leaders? Moreover, as its young members enter middle age, how many will feel that a new religious movement continues to meet their social, economic and spiritual needs? There have been a number of high profile cases of ex-members criticizing the new religious movement of which they were once a part. A serious issue for the churches is whether they can avoid the temptation of gloating over such lapses, and instead concentrate on offering hope and a home for such people as they explore other spiritual options.

MARTIN FORWARD

📖 James R. Lewis (ed), *The Oxford Handbook of New Religious Movements*, New York: OUP 2004; B. R. Wilson and J. Cresswell (eds), *New Religious Movements: Challenge and Response*, London and New York: Routledge 1999

Old Catholic churches

The Old Catholic churches of the Union of Utrecht are autonomous local churches. They consider themselves to be the Catholic church in each country as it used to exist before the dogmas of the infallibility and supreme jurisdiction of the Pope were promulgated at the First Vatican Council in 1870.

The Old Catholic Church of the Netherlands is the continuing church for which Willibrord was consecrated Archbishop of Utrecht in 695. In 1723 the then newly-elected archbishop was consecrated, but was refused recognition by Rome and consequently excommunicated. Since that time this church has officially existed as the 'Roman Catholic Church of the old episcopal clergy'. It began to call itself Old Catholic after 1870 when it entered into communion with the Old Catholic movement in other European countries.

Catholics in Germany, Switzerland and Austria-Hungary who were unwilling to accept the new Vatican I dogmas were forced, after they had been excommunicated by their bishops, to establish parishes of their own. These 'Old Catholics' (as distinct from the 'New Catholics' who would accept the Roman innovations) established synods in which the laity had a majority, and elected bishops (Germany in 1873, Switzerland in 1876, Austria electing a diocesan administrator in 1886). The bishops of Germany and Switzerland and the Dutch bishops (Archbishop of Utrecht, Bishop of Haarlem, Bishop of Deventer) joined forces in 1889 to issue the Declaration of Utrecht to the Catholic Church, to establish the International Bishops' Conference and to form the Union of Utrecht. This Union is a union of churches and the bishops governing them who are determined to maintain and pass on the faith, worship and essential structure of the undivided church of the first millennium.

The Union of Utrecht was later joined by other churches led by duly elected and consecrated bishops. The Polish National Catholic Church in the USA and Canada (PNCC) was established in 1897, also in response to quarrels with the Roman Catholic hierarchy (this time over matters of finances and property), and through the ordination of its first bishop by Old Catholic bishops this church joined the Union; because of major disagreements between the PNCC and the rest of the International Bishops' Conference, the PNCC left the Union of Utrecht in 2003. The Polish Catholic Church in Poland was set up in 1920.

The Old Catholic churches are not a centralized body (like the Roman Catholic Church) nor are they totally independent of each other. The link between the churches is the International Bishops' Conference of the Union of Utrecht. Members of the Union of Utrecht are the Old Catholic churches in the Netherlands (Old Catholic Church of The Netherlands; 8000 members, 2 dioceses), Germany (Catholic Diocese of the Old Catholics in Germany; 25,600 members, 1 diocese), Switzerland (Old Catholic Church of Switzerland; 13,000 members, 1 diocese), Austria (Old Catholic Church of Austria; 15,000 members, 1 diocese), the Czech Republic (Old Catholic Church in the Czech Republic; 1900 members, 1 diocese) and Poland (Polish Catholic Church in the Polish Republic; 22,000 members, 3 dioceses).

The Old Catholic Church in Croatia is recognized by the Union of Utrecht but does not have a bishop of its own. There are also parishes in France, Italy, Sweden and Denmark. These parishes come under the supervision of a bishop appointed by the International Bishops' Conference of the Union of Utrecht.

Each diocese consists of a number of parishes. It has a bishop and a synod. The bishop-in-synod governs the diocese, without any interference from outside the diocese. Where there is more than one diocese in a country, a general synod (under whatever name) has been established to legislate for the entire Old Catholic Church in that country. A presiding bishop (Archbishop of Utrecht in the Netherlands; Presiding Bishop in Poland) is responsible for executing the legislation of the general synod, without interfering in the internal affairs of each diocese. A standing committee of the synod legislates and executes necessary matters in the period between the sessions of the synod.

The bishop is elected by the synod and ordained (consecrated) by at least three other Old Catholic bishops. The Old Catholic churches in the Netherlands, Germany, Switzerland and Austria have legislated for the office of bishop also to be open to women; these churches already have women priests.

The International Bishops' Conference comprises the serving bishops of all dioceses. Its task is to take the necessary decisions in all organizational or disciplinary matters concerning the maintenance of communion and regarding joint projects.

Like all catholic churches, the Old Catholic churches cannot exempt themselves from the three foundational activities of the church without which it would not have the right to exist: witness to Christ crucified and risen (*martyria*), celebration of God's great deeds in the sacraments and other acts of worship (*leitourgia*), and care for those in need (*diakonia*). All the churches have organizational structures for these activities. The Western European Old Catholic churches have a reputation for a very careful celebration of the liturgy.

The communion of the Union of Utrecht confesses the catholic faith as expressed in the church in the East and West by the seven ecumenical councils. It approves of the historic precedence of the Bishop of Rome as first among equals, but rejects dogmas of his infallibility and universal jurisdiction and a number of other papal pronouncements in so far as they are at variance with the doctrine of the ancient church. It affirms its faith in the essence and mystery of the eucharist, and is aware of its obligation to do anything that will help to overcome the divisions in the church.

Eucharist

This view requires the autonomy of the local church, i.e. diocese, and its necessary link with other dioceses to make it truly a part of the Catholic church. The synod of each diocese or national church has the right to legislate in matters of organization and practice. This right of synods has been invoked to legislate in favour of, e.g., the introduction of the vernacular in worship and dispensation from compulsory celibacy for the clergy. In the 1980s and 1990s, the synods in the Netherlands, Germany, Switzerland and Austria regarded the matter of women clergy as one of practice, not of doctrine. Therefore they have opened the ordained ministry in all three orders (bishop, priest, deacon) to women as well. The church in the Czech Republic has ordained its first woman deacon.

Because of their origin, the Old Catholic churches of the Union of Utrecht have the same liturgical order as the other Western Catholic churches. They too recognize the supreme significance of the eucharist and the fundamental quality of baptism (of adults, children and infants) for the life of a Christian. The other sacraments, recognized as such by the Roman Catholic Church, are also celebrated. Ordination to the office of bishop, priest and deacon is recognized as 'valid' by the Roman Catholic Church. The shape of the liturgy is more or less the same as in the Roman Catholic and Anglican churches but slightly more concise. Full communion with the Anglican Communion has meant that recent revisions of the Anglican liturgy

Sacraments

Ministry and ministers

Anglicanism

have had a major influence on the liturgical revisions in the Western European Old Catholic churches in particular. One eucharistic prayer and the liturgy of ordination has been established communion-wide by the International Bishops' Conference.

A major difference from the liturgy, and therefore doctrine, of the Roman Catholic Church is the view that the entire eucharistic prayer, not just the words of Christ used at the last supper, 'This is my body, this is my blood', and repeated by the priest, make the bread the body of Christ and the wine the blood of Christ. Because this transformation is the action of the Holy Spirit, an exclusively male priesthood presiding at the eucharist as a mirror of (the maleness of) Christ is no longer seen to be necessary by the Old Catholic churches.

There has been a resurgence in recent years of forms of worship outside the eucharist, for instance morning praise, evensong (with a blessing of the light) and worship inspired by Taizé. But the regular parish eucharist each Sunday remains the central act of worship of all the Old Catholic churches.

p. 274

All the Old Catholic churches of the Union of Utrecht are full members of the World Council of Churches. However, dialogue with the Roman Catholic Church was non-existent before the Second Vatican Council. Since then, though, there have been national dialogue commissions in the Netherlands and Switzerland, and in 2003 the International Bishops' Conference established a Union-wide commission in response to a request by the Pontifical Council for the Unity of Christians. Dialogue with the Orthodox churches has been carried on since 1874; between 1975 and 1987 an official joint theological commission produced 23 common texts which could be the foundation for the re-unification of the Orthodox and Old Catholic churches. Since the Bonn Agreement of 1931/2 the Old Catholic churches of the Union of Utrecht have been in full communion with all the churches of the Anglican Communion, which includes joining in each other's consecration of bishops and joint presidency of the eucharist, and in 2001 the International Bishops' Conference established an official dialogue with the Lutheran World Federation.

Ecumenical movement
Roman Catholic Church
Papacy
Orthodox churches
Council

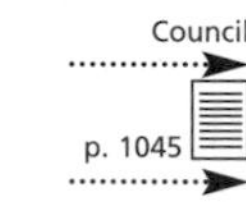

p. 1045
Lutheranism

THADDAEUS A. SCHNITKER

C. B. Moss, *The Old Catholic Movement: Its Origins and History*, London: SPCK [2]1964; Gordon Huelin (ed), *Old Catholics and Anglicans 1931–1981*, Oxford: OUP 1983

Vatican

Organization

Christianity began as a movement within Judaism, but its rapid growth made it inevitable that within a short space of time it should be expressed in institutional forms. As early as New Testament times it was found necessary to appoint and authorize some Christians to handle the movement's charitable work in Jerusalem (Acts 6.1–6). A council was also convened to determine conditions for entry to the Christian movement (Acts 15), and as Christianity expanded in the Mediterranean world, ministers with secular jobs were appointed to oversee newly-established groups. Arrangements were made for the methodical collection of money for the support of the impoverished group in Jerusalem (1 Corinthians 16.1–4).

Today the world's two billion Christians belong to a huge variety of churches, the organization of which has been determined partly by religious belief and partly by response to social and political pressures over a long period of history. In spite of the variety, however, it is possible to classify church organization in three main categories: 1. the centralized and hierarchical; 2. the federal and collaborative; 3. the independent and autonomous.

The *centralized and hierarchical* form is expressed powerfully and almost, but not quite, exclusively in the Roman Catholic Church, the organization of which has a pyramidal structure. At its apex is the Bishop of Rome, the Pope, who is believed by Roman Catholics to be the successor of St Peter and Christ's vicar (representative) on earth. He is elected by a college of senior bishops, known as cardinals, who owe their appointments to one of the deceased Pope's predecessors. Popes never retire. At different moments in history it has been asserted that the Pope is subject to the decrees of councils of the church, consisting of all the bishops, but recent times have seen a considerable increase in papal authority, including the power to make infallible pronouncements in particular circumstances and on particular subjects.

In theory, the Pope relates directly to around 3000 bishops, all of whom have been appointed by him and are responsible to him for the life and witness of the Roman Catholic Church in their territorial dioceses worldwide. In practice, and because it is impossible to administer so massive an organization in person, over the centuries various intermediate structures have been established to maintain unity and to communicate and enforce policy. Thus the Pope functions within and from a historic headquarters in Rome, known as the Vatican, where he is assisted by ten departments known as Congregations, which cover every aspect of the church's life. The members of the Congregations are all clergy and all are chosen, or at least officially appointed, by the Pope. Their function is advisory and they have no power other than that – often a great deal – delegated to them by the Pope.

For administrative purposes the dioceses are grouped together and their work is co-ordinated by national

CHRISTADELPHIANS

A Christian sect founded in America in 1848 by an Englishman, John Thomas (1805–71), who had originally been among the followers of Thomas and Alexander Campbell, founders of the Disciples of Christ. The group was originally called 'Thomasites', but adopted the name Christadelphians ('brothers of Christ') during the American Civil War when members organized formally to oppose military service; Thomas was opposed to the word 'Christian', which he believed had connotations of apostasy from the true faith.

Christadelphians are organized into ecclesias; there is no general overall organization nor is there a separate ministry. Each ecclesia is independent, but a member of the wider Christadelphian fellowship. They do not have buildings of their own but meet in rented buildings or private homes.

The central belief of Christadelphians is the return of Jesus Christ in power and glory to set up a visible kingdom centred on Jerusalem; they believe that the Bible is inspired and infallible, and attach great importance to the prophecies in it. They are anti-Trinitarian and believe that Jesus did not exist before he was born of the Virgin Mary. No statistics are available as to membership of the sect but it is thought that there are around 20,000 in Britain and around the same number in the USA.

H. Tennant, *The Christadelphians: What They Believe and Preach*, Birmingham: The Christadelphian 1986

bishops' conferences, presided over by one of the local bishops, who may or may not be the senior member of the local hierarchy. These conferences formulate national policy on a wide range of subjects, not involving fundamental matters of faith and order, but the individual bishop remains the supreme locus of power in his diocese. During the 1960s, when John Carmel Heenan was Bishop of Leeds (he later became Cardinal Archbishop of Westminster), the parish priests in that diocese received a letter from him one Monday morning instructing them to move to other parishes by the following Friday. Nothing could demonstrate more clearly that the Roman Catholic parish is seen as a branch of a diocesan structure and the parish priest as an assistant of the bishop, its manager.

However, the bishop does not lack personal oversight, albeit of a somewhat secretive kind. In every country where there is a significant Roman Catholic presence the Pope is represented by a nuncio or an apostolic delegate – a quasi-diplomatic post, the holder of which is normally an archbishop. He generally maintains a low profile and conveys through diplomatic channels the views of the Pope on secular issues, but he also keeps a wary eye on the affairs of the church, reporting regularly to the Vatican and sometimes conveying the instructions of the Vatican to the national hierarchy. His influence can be very considerable, not least over appointments.

The role of the laity in this large worldwide organization is minimal, and has been since the church's earliest centuries, when it was decreed that the role of the clergy was to rule and to teach. During the Middle Ages the clergy were in any case the only members of the church sufficiently educated to undertake administration. Attending mass, providing financial support and witnessing to the Christian faith in daily life are the obligations laid upon the non-clerical believer. The Second Vatican Council (1962–5) promulgated an important Decree on the Laity which envisaged a much greater role in church government for those who constitute the overwhelming majority of the church's membership, but although lay people now serve on parish councils and diocesan commissions, their influence is small. Clerical power remains largely unchecked.

This understanding of leadership has been reinforced by another factor. The broad pattern of the church's government was settled during the era of the Roman empire and there is a close parallel between the centralized, absolutist form of Roman government and that adopted by the church. The religious dimension of the church's life enabled it to survive the fall of the Roman empire and, largely through the self-contained, disciplined life of the monasteries, it had both stability and a degree of flexibility. During the later medieval period the universal character of its faith and administration also provided protection and power when nation states were emerging. The sixteenth century saw a mounting challenge to this power and to the faith which sustained it, but although this led to serious divisions in the church, the Roman-controlled, centralized institution survived, and as a result of the missionary opportunities provided by European colonization from the fifteenth century onwards, more than made up for these losses. The development of modern communications also enhanced the possibilities of control.

Roman empire

Monasticism

Mission

Communication

Whatever its merits, over the centuries this centralized, hierarchical system of organization has displayed some significant advantages. In an often threatening and sometimes fragmenting world, it has maintained a powerful sense of unity in the church. By prescribing the norms of belief and proscribing all deviations from these norms, and by defending traditional patterns of organization against innovation and experiment, it has

Middle Ages

SOCIETIES AND ORGANIZATIONS

Boys' Brigade: Founded in England by William Smith in 1883. The organization sought to transform traditional Sunday school into a volunteer band with the order, obedience and discipline of military volunteers, in a programme combining games and sport with hymns and prayers. The boys also were to wear a distinctive uniform of cap, belt and haversack. It has branches in many Commonwealth countries.

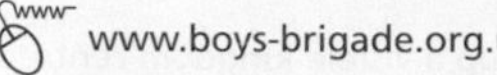
www.boys-brigade.org.uk

Church Army: Founded in England in 1882 by Wilson Carlile. An Anglican organization similar to the Salvation Army concerned with lay evangelism.

www.churcharmy.org.uk; www.churcharmyusa.org

Mothers' Union: Founded in England in 1876 by Mary Elizabeth Sumner. An Anglican organization aimed at preserving the sanctity of marriage and helping mothers to bring up children responsibly.

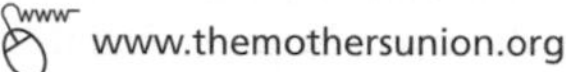
www.themothersunion.org

Opus Dei: Founded in Spain in 1928 by Josemaria Escrivá de Balaguer to promote Christian ideals in secular life. A Catholic organization, it is known as being right-wing and conservative.

www.opusdei.org

Salvation Army: Founded in England in 1865 by William Booth, concerned with evangelism and social work.

www.salvationarmy.org.uk;
www.salvationarmyusa.org

SCM (Student Christian Movement): Developed out of several student movements in Cambridge at the end of the nineteenth century and flourished particularly between the two world wars. It made a major contribution to the intellectual life of the churches, above all through its publishing house, SCM Press, which by the 1950s had become one of the world's leading theological publishers, a role which it kept until the end of the century. The movement was one of the few Christian organizations in which women truly had the same status as men. Sadly, it failed to adjust to the new conditions after the Second World War and went into decline. It still exists, but as a shadow of its former self.

www.movement.org

SPCK (Society for the Promotion of Christian Knowledge): Founded in England in 1698 by Thomas Bray. Essentially Anglican, it has a publishing house and a chain of bookshops and funds the provision of books in countries throughout the Commonwealth.

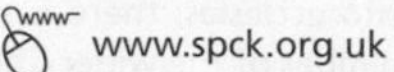
www.spck.org.uk

United Bible Societies: A world fellowship of national Bible societies founded in England in 1946. It aims to translate, produce and distribute the Bible in languages people can understand at prices they can afford. Its beginnings lie in the British and Foreign Bible Society, founded in London in 1804 and other early Bible societies in the Netherlands (1814), the United States (1816) and Russia (1821). Originally fully inter-confessional, and including the Orthodox churches (Greece and Russia) and the Roman Catholic Church (Malta, Russia, Germany), at an early stage pressure limited it to the Protestant churches. However, it does work closely with the Catholic Biblical Federation, and many translation projects now have Roman Catholic involvement.

www.biblesociety.org

WSCF (World Student Christian Federation): Founded in Sweden in 1895 under the leadership of John R. Mott, then student secretary of the YMCA, by students from Europe and the United States. It was instrumental in preparing for the important Edinburgh Missionary Conference of 1910 with its slogan 'the evangelization of the world in this generation'. The heyday of the Federation was in the inter-war years; after the Second World War it shared in the decline of the Student Christian Movement.

www.servingthetruth.org

YMCA (Young Mens' Christian Association): Founded in England in 1844 by George Williams. A non-sectarian organization which now welcomes young people of all faiths; it provides hostels and various forms of education.

www.ymca.net; www.ymca.org.uk

YWCA (Young Women's Christian Association): Founded in England in 1855 by Emma Roberts and Lady Mary Jane Kinnaird, to 'advance the physical, social, intellectual, moral, and spiritual interests of young women'. It provides hostels and other facilities.

www.ywca.org

provided security and inspired confidence. In time of persecution, of the kind experienced by Christians in Eastern Europe during the Communist era of the twentieth century, membership of an international church with its own powerful solidarity provided many with a buttress for faith and practice. In common with other absolutist regimes, the Roman Catholic system has in some respects operated with a high degree of efficiency. It has never had any difficulty in declaring its universally held beliefs, while its central control over its celibate clergy has often enabled it to respond to new challenges and opportunities. It is also to be noted that it has been extraordinarily

Persecution

successful in securing the financial resources essential to its institutional survival and expansion. The existence of a Vatican bank testifies to its financial acumen today, as do the magnificent cathedrals of Western Europe to its fund-raising skills in the Middle Ages.

The power acquired and expressed in unity and efficiency has, however, been purchased at a heavy price – too heavy for many Christians to bear. The imposition of uniformity of doctrine has seriously stifled openness to new insights in the field of religious thought and also in secular spheres, where new discoveries have sometimes been rejected because of their supposed threat to accepted beliefs. The history of the Roman Catholic Church is littered with examples of Christian explorers – spiritual and scientific – whose discoveries have been denounced by ecclesiastical authority and whose actions have all too frequently led to their excommunication from the church's fellowship. Later, sometimes centuries later, the church has been driven to revise its views on such matters and to find a subtle way of explaining that it had never been mistaken. In the meantime, the church's witness to the truth was seriously compromised and its spirituality impoverished.

There is also clear and unsurprising evidence that a worldwide organization of huge size is impossible to administer effectively by means of a single, personal authority. Although recent popes have undertaken frequent and extensive world tours, their personal knowledge of particular places and people can only be superficial. Their decision-making is bound to be influenced by the knowledge and advice of intermediaries and, since the organs of the central Curia (the name given to the Vatican administration) are responsible only to the Pope himself, the possibility of alternative power bases emerging is only too real. Thus many of the most important decisions of the Second Vatican Council, which at the time of their promulgation offered the promise of change and were a source of hope to many Roman Catholics, have been effectively blocked. Except in the religious orders, women play no significant part in Roman Catholic organization.

Another Christian community which displays some of the centralist character of the Roman Catholic Church is the Salvation Army. Founded in the mid-nineteenth century by William Booth to undertake evangelistic work among the poor of Britain's towns and cities, from almost its earliest days it was organized on military lines. The apostle Paul's talk of spiritual warfare and his injunction to Timothy to be 'a good soldier of Jesus Christ' were influential in the adoption of a hierarchical, authoritarian structure, as was the need for a highly-disciplined approach to Christian mission in testing environments. Thus the Salvation Army, today an international organization and especially strong in the USA, still has a General at its head and a hierarchy that includes brigadiers, colonels, majors, captains, lieutenants and sergeants. A semi-military uniform is worn. The most senior officers – men and women – form a High Council which *inter alia* elects the General. Subordinate units comprise territories, approximating to national boundaries, provinces, divisions and corps. All ranks are required to show 'unquestioning obedience', and the writing and publication by individuals of articles and books is subject to strict censorship. Adherence to the evangelical beliefs which brought the Army into being cannot in any way be compromised. Officers, who are permitted to marry only other officers, are posted, sometimes at frequent intervals, to units where they are most required. The apparently ruthless character of the administration sometimes surprises those who most admire and support the Army's outstanding compassionate work among the most needy members of society.

Money

Exploration

The federal and collaborative form of church organization is the most common. This attempts to combine the local and the universal character of the faith community. The most ancient example of this is provided by the Orthodox Church, which developed a distinct identity from the fourth century onwards, though its breach with Rome did not become formal until the eleventh century. It remains markedly different in ethos from that of any other Christian body. Although it is convenient to use the title Orthodox Church as a generic description, the church is in fact a family or federation of fifteen self-governing (autocephalous) churches which are usually, but not always, confined to particular countries in Eastern Europe and the Eastern Mediterranean region, for example, the Russian Orthodox Church and Greek Orthodox Church. These are united by adherence to a common understanding of the Christian faith and a common sacramental life.

Orthodox churches

The organization of the churches is not essentially different in structure from that of the Roman Catholic Church. Territorial parishes are served by priests and dioceses by bishops. At the head of each church is a senior bishop known as a patriarch, or in some less ancient foundations an archbishop. The Patriarch of Constantinople, usually known as the Ecumenical Patriarch, is a focus of unity for all. He has a primacy of honour, not of jurisdiction, and cannot interfere in the affairs of the patriarchates and dioceses. The difference between this role and that of the Pope was the primary cause of the early separation of the Eastern and Roman churches. A fundamental element in the organization of the Orthodox Church is the role accorded to its councils and synods. Each of the self-governing churches has its own synod attended by the bishops and representatives of the clergy and the laity. This is the decision-making body, which also elects bishops from the unmarried monastic clergy. Local councils are sometimes convened to deal with

p. 231

matters affecting one or more national churches. Over all is the ecumenical council, attended by all the bishops of the different churches, and concerned with matters of belief and church discipline, including canon law. Herein lies a problem. Inasmuch as ecumenical means worldwide, it has not been possible to convene such a council since the Orthodox and Roman Catholic churches became separated. Thus the last ecumenical council recognized by the Orthodox is that held at Nicaea, in modern Turkey, in 787. Councils convened since then are designated 'local', notwithstanding the fact that they were attended by representatives of all the Orthodox churches, and although these do not carry quite the same weight as their predecessors, some have had an influence on expressions of Christian doctrine. The last local council was held in Constantinople in 1923 and there now appear to be insuperable difficulties hindering the convening of a modern council. These include the fact that the Orthodox Church's long association with the Byzantine world requires a council to be convened by a secular prince, and no head of state in the world of the twenty-first century is likely to co-operate over this. It is also the case that the autonomous status of the different Orthodox churches has led to rivalry, jealously and disagreement, arising usually from nationalism or other political factors, and at the moment this precludes agreement over the calling of a council and over the subjects it might consider.

Discipline
Canon law
Church of England ➤
Reformation ➤

The Orthodox Church is not the only church in which the sharing of authority inhibits decisive action, but it is the one in which resistance to change has, in consequence, been most marked. Over the long centuries of its existence there has been no experience of reformation, so the Orthodox Church today is hardly different in its worship, beliefs, organization and even appearance from the church born into the world of Byzantium. This experience of continuity was of the utmost value in protecting the church against external assault during the long years of the Ottoman empire (sixteenth to early twentieth century) and more recently the Communist era. Ability to think in terms of centuries, rather than of years and decades, brings a different perspective to contemporary events. 'The river flows, but the stones remain, and we are the stones,' explained a Romanian bishop when asked about his church's survival during a period of particularly repressive Communist rule in his country. Churches under persecution are inevitably more concerned with survival than with change.

Byzantium
Anglicanism ➤

Yet for a church such as the Orthodox which emphasizes more than most the importance of the work of the Holy Spirit, and of the church as the chief locus of the Spirit's guiding and sustaining activity, an apparent inability to respond to those manifestations of the Spirit that lie beyond the church's own borders is bound to be a matter for concern among those of other Christian traditions whose admiration of Orthodoxy is great.

Holy Spirit
Presbyterian churches ➤

Many of these admirers are to be found within the Church of England, whose organization, particularly since the adoption of synodical government in 1970, is in some respects close to that of the Orthodox Church. The rejection in England of papal authority owed something to insights into the nature of the church gained during the sixteenth-century Reformation in Europe, but also to political factors related to national independence. In England, where the church has a strong territorial base, there is, however, sometimes disagreement as to whether the parish or the diocese is the basic unit of organization.

Those who emphasize the Catholic character of the Church of England are likely to favour the latter, pointing to the significance of the bishop as the focus of unity and the guarantor of continuity. On this view the parish priest is someone who shares in a ministry expressed in its fullness by his or her bishop. On the other hand, those who emphasize the Protestant character of the Church of England insist that its primary manifestation is expressed by the local faith community, which has its own spiritual autonomy and integrity and is not to be regarded as a branch of a larger diocesan unit. Both sides can raise theological arguments to support their case, but at the pragmatic level those who back the parish win hands down. Ask English Anglicans about the church and they will refer immediately to the local parish church and never to the diocese. The amalgamation of two or more parishes, driven by shortage of clergy and money, remains deeply unpopular. The bishop is a welcome visitor for special occasions, such as a confirmation or the blessing of a new organ, but the diocesan organization is seen largely as a bureaucratic body that makes unwelcome decisions and imposes heavy burdens of taxation. The General Synod has even fewer friends and is often regarded with scarcely-veiled hostility, even though since 1970 the laity have played a much more significant part in the church's decision-making at every level. The synodical structure inaugurated then now stands in urgent need of revision. The sharing of power does not necessarily make for popularity or efficiency when the locus of this power ceases to be local.

Over the centuries, the decentralized character of the Anglican Church has permitted and sometimes encouraged varieties of belief and practice but, as in the Orthodox Church, this has sometimes inhibited decisive action and strategic decision-making.

Some other non-Roman Catholic churches also have organizational structures which combine in varying degrees the federal and collaborative, the local and the universal. The government of the Presbyterian churches that emerged in the sixteenth and seventeenth centuries as a reaction against the authoritarian system of Roman

Catholicism and claimed to represent the New Testament model of church life has four elements. The local church is governed by a kirk (church) session consisting of the ministers and elected lay elders. Over a wider area the presbytery, consisting of ministers and representative elders, has the oversight of the local churches. Synods, responsible for an even larger area, are made up of ministers and elders elected by the presbyteries and exercise some judicial functions. The general assembly, usually covering a national area, has ministers and elders elected in equal numbers by the presbyteries and is presided over by an elected moderator who holds office for twelve months. However, the moderator has no executive power, and all Presbyterian ministers are of equal status. At every level of church government ministers and elders have an equal vote. The national and regional Presbyterian churches are linked by the World Alliance of Reformed Churches with a headquarters in Geneva, but with no power over any part of its constituency.

The Lutheran Church, another sixteenth-century Reformation creation, combines synodical and episcopal forms of government and, in common with the other Reformation churches, emphasizes the importance of the local church and the role of the laity. In Germany and Scandinavia, where it is particularly strong, it has a marked territorial basis and in these and some other countries the senior ministers who are responsible for the oversight of many local churches are known as bishops. Elsewhere they are superintendents. In neither case do they exercise authority apart from their synods, though powerful personalities among them sometimes exert considerable influence. The Lutheran World Federation, which also has its headquarters in Geneva, is, as its title indicates, a federal body which exercises no authority.

The Methodist Church, which began as an eighteenth-century reforming missionary movement in the Church of England but soon became a worldwide church with its own distinctive beliefs and practices, owes its basic organizational structure to the provisions made by its founder, John Wesley. He was concerned for the continuation of the movement after death had deprived it of his own dynamic and autocratic leadership. Thus 100 members of the movement were appointed to 'A Yearly Conference of the People called Methodists', the chief task of which was to appoint preachers to the 'Preaching Houses' (later to be known as chapels) which had been established by Wesley in the course of his unceasing travels.

Initially, Methodism was seen primarily as a lay movement, though Church of England clergymen could offer themselves as preachers. Few did. The hierarchical element in the Church of England, which was always an obstacle to Wesley's work, did not impress him and he was convinced that the Christian mission was a shared responsibility involving all the church's members. He believed also, however, that an authorized ministry was desirable and it was his decision, in the absence of episcopal leadership in America, to ordain ministers that led eventually to the movement's breach with the Church of England. Nonetheless, from the time of Wesley's death in 1791 until the Conference of 1836, appointment as a preacher, with authority to administer the sacraments of baptism and holy communion, required no ordination involving the laying on of hands but simply admission by Conference.

Eventually an organizational structure appropriate to a developing church emerged. Local congregations, known as societies, might be led by either a minister or a lay preacher, but always with a body of lay trustees and society stewards to share the responsibility. The societies are now grouped in circuits, under the leadership of an ordained superintendent minister and a lay steward. The circuits are grouped in districts which cover a large area, akin to a diocese, and these are supervised by a chairman whose pastoral and administrative role is similar to that of an Anglican bishop. In the USA the chairmen are known as bishops, though they lay no claim to apostolic authority.

Lutheranism

The elected national Conference, which consists in England of 288 ministers and 288 lay people, is the central locus of authority and has an annually-elected president, who is always a minister, and a vice-president, who is always a lay person. Although the Methodist Church has always taken its laity very seriously and has a generally participatory, collaborative structure, considerable authority is vested, as Wesley intended, in the Conference and, since this meets only annually, by delegation to the permanent departments which serve the Conference. The appointment of ministers to local societies and to district chairmanships, as well as major policy decisions, represents a concentration of power not found elsewhere, other than in the Roman Catholic Church and the Salvation Army. The World Methodist Conference is no more than a meeting place for representatives of the national conferences and has no authority.

Methodism

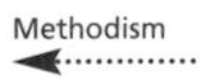

The independent and autonomous form of church organization again dates from the Reformation era and represents another reaction against the centralized and hierarchical character of Roman Catholicism. This was in some instances so radical that it led to the creation of Christian associations which prized the independence of the local congregation, eschewed all forms of centralized organization, and expected the local congregations to appoint their own ministers or pastors, with or without formal ordination. The Congregational and Baptist churches developed from this reaction and still reflect this sturdy independence, though in England and the USA the entry of Congregationalists into unity schemes

Congregationalism
Baptist churches

with Presbyterians and others has diluted their distinctive witness. The Baptist Church, however, remains staunchly independent, and its local communities, of which there are a very large number worldwide, are served by pastors and deacons appointed by local choice and will brook no outside interference in their affairs. This does not, however, lead to any wide variety of style or method, such is the conservative character of most Christian bodies. National Baptist Unions and Associations, which came into being towards the end of the nineteenth century, provide a means for mutual support, the sharing of common ideas and experience, and occasionally the expression of a common mind. The World Baptist Alliance, founded in 1905, has a similar function, and various Congregational Unions, which go back to the early years of the nineteenth century, ensure that their churches are not isolated.

Different again is the Religious Society of Friends, which was founded in the mid-seventeenth century and is commonly known as the Quakers. Emphasizing the essentially personal character of faith and reliance on the leadings of the Spirit, this body has never seen the need for church buildings and ordained ministers. Its basic unit of organization is the Meeting for Church Affairs, at which silent worship is offered but anyone present can speak, as guided by the Spirit. Elders are responsible for the development of the spiritual life of the Meeting and Overseers for the pastoral care of members. These are elected by the Meeting. In Britain the Monthly Meeting, which embraces a number of local gatherings in a particular area, is the primary assembly. General Meetings, held quarterly, cover a much wider area and a national Yearly Meeting is attended by representatives from the local Meetings. The Friends World Committee for Consultation is recognized by the United Nations, and a Quaker Council for European Affairs has been established in Brussels. None of these Meetings and committees has any jurisdiction over any of the others, and the Quaker organization remains simple and local.

Quakers

Fundamentalism ➤

Pentecostalism

The Pentecostal churches came into being during the early twentieth century as a reaction against heavily institutionalized Christianity, and during the second half of that century experienced phenomenal growth, especially in Latin America, Africa and other parts of the developing world. They exhibit considerable variety of organization and some local churches are affiliated to national or regional bodies such as the Assemblies of God and the New Testament Church of God, but independence and response to the Holy Spirit are their hallmarks. Their leaders are variously described as elder, pastor and not infrequently bishop, but they have no authority other than that granted to them by their own local communities. Most combine their role with secular employment, but some of the larger Pentecostal churches – which can be very large – employ full-time leaders.

Assemblies of God

More than any other Christian community, their life and organization is influenced by local cultural factors. The religious basis of their organization is, however, directly related to the belief that the patterns of church life in the earliest days of Christianity were intended to be retained until the end of time. A key New Testament text for all independent churches, whether or not they describe themselves as Pentecostal, is Matthew 18.20: 'Where two or three are gathered in my name, there am I in the midst of them.' Where Christ is, there is the church in its fullness, requiring none of the elaborate structures which have developed over the course of the centuries and which all too often have inhibited the Christian mission.

That most of the Pentecostal churches are dynamic Christian communities exhibiting the fruit of God's Spirit cannot be denied. In some parts of the world they have been responsible for spreading the Christian gospel in ways and on a scale that cannot be matched by the historic, traditional churches, whether centralized and hierarchical or federal and collaborative. Their independence does, however, foster a number of what other Christians regard as weaknesses. Among these is an understanding of the Holy Spirit's activity that does not permit illumination from sources other than those to be found in the text of the Bible, as interpreted in a particular fundamentalist tradition. This often leads to narrowly personal ethics and therefore a markedly conservative approach to social change. Independent churches seem least likely to challenge unjust and repressive political regimes.

In a world growing smaller as a consequence of modern communications and accumulations of international power, the Christian church needs more than ever before some sort of universal organization that facilitates the sharing of insights, the seizing of missionary opportunities, and the offering of mutual support. The fact that the best form of such an organization has yet to be found cannot justify the adoption of isolationism.

Throughout its history the church has, because of its origins and beliefs, found itself living in a constant tension between the local and the universal, and also between patriarchal and democratic understandings of community life. The organization of church life so as to take account of these complementary factors has yet to be accomplished.

TREVOR BEESON

Hans Küng, *Structures of the Church*, New York: Thomas Nelson and London: Burns & Oates 1964; Joseph C. M. McCann, *Church and Organization: A Sociological and Theological Enquiry*, Scranton, PA: University of Scranton Press 1993; Thomas J. Rees, *Inside the Vatican: Politics and Organization of the Catholic Church*, Cambridge MA: Harvard University Press 1998

ORIGINS AND BACKGROUND

Bible, Biblical criticism, History, Jesus, Jesus of history, Mary, Messiah, Ministry and ministers, Paul, Resurrection, Roman empire

Christianity developed out of Judaism, and for the first 70 years or so of its existence was not clearly distinguishable from it, either by Christians themselves, who claimed to offer the way forward for Jews, or by outside observers, such as the Roman authorities. The history and society of Palestine at the time of Jesus, the first half of the first century CE, provide the immediate background for the emergence of Christianity, but that area, and the other places to which Christianity spread in its earliest years, formed part of the Roman empire. Some understanding of the wider Roman world is therefore important to make sense of how Christianity developed. Judaism and Christianity

Some of the key institutions of Christianity were developed in the period between its emergence and the early second century CE. A lot of evidence survives from this period, including the writings of Jews, Christians and others, and remains of material culture found by archaeologists. Nonetheless, much of this evidence is limited in what it can tell us and is difficult to interpret. Very little of what follows, therefore, can be taken as absolutely certain, but it represents an attempt to make sense of current knowledge. Archaeology

The historical background

Christianity started in Judaea, a province of the Roman empire, in the 30s CE. The territory of Judaea, on the principal overland route between Egypt and Mesopotamia, was fought over constantly by rival powers from the third millennium BCE onwards. In 332 BCE it was taken over by the Macedonian king Alexander the Great in the course of his conquest of the Achaemenid Persian empire, and from then on came under the influence of the Greek culture of Alexander's successors, first the Ptolemies ruling from Alexandria, who controlled Palestine until 198 BCE, and then the Seleucids, who ruled Syria, Mesopotamia and what had been the eastern parts of the Persian empire.

In the second century BCE conflict within the Jewish community – in particular over Hellenization, the question of how far, if at all, they should adopt aspects of Greek culture – led to rebellion from Seleucid control in 167 BCE, and ultimately to the emergence of an independent Jewish kingdom in 142 BCE. The new ruling dynasty, the Hasmoneans, were also given the high priesthood, a decision that led to divisions within Judaism which, along with continuing tension over Hellenization, left their mark on the society of Judaea at the time of the emergence of Christianity.

The second century BCE also saw a decline in the power of the Seleucids, who lost territory to the Parthians in the east, and were increasingly under pressure from the Romans in the west. In the mid-60s BCE the Roman general Pompey put an end to Seleucid power altogether, and in 63 BCE took control of Palestine, including Jerusalem. The Romans usually avoided imposing direct rule on conquered territories if they could find loyal and reliable clients to work for them. Much of what had been Jewish territory was left under the control of the current high priest, Hyrcanus II (63–40 BCE), although after 49 BCE military responsibility was given to another Roman client, Antipater, an Idumaean from the area south of Judaea, whose inhabitants had been converted to Judaism when their territory was conquered by the Hasmoneans towards the end of the second century. In 40 BCE the Parthians seized control of Judaea, with Hasmonean support. The Romans responded by backing Antipater's son Herod, whom they named 'king of the Jews'. With Roman military backing he was able to reconquer Judaea and the surrounding area, which he ruled as a Roman client until his death in 4 BCE. As an Idumaean, Herod faced hostility from within Israel, where support for the Hasmoneans remained significant. Activities such as the rebuilding of the temple, which he started in 22 BCE, and his marriage to a Hasmonean, Mariamne (whom he later had executed), can be seen as attempts to curry favour with his subjects, and although their success was limited, Herod's military achievements, re-establishing a kingdom as great as that controlled by the Hasmoneans, and his ability to keep order, ensured his hold on the throne. After his death his kingdom was divided between his three sons, but Archelaus, whose territory included Judaea itself, was removed from his post by the Emperor Augustus in 6 CE, and from then until 66 CE, apart from a brief period 41–44 CE, the territory was governed on the emperor's behalf by Roman prefects, and later procurators (the difference was not significant), based at Caesarea. The Romans allowed the Jews some freedom, and the region remained generally peaceful.

In 66 CE Judaea revolted from Roman rule. The causes of the revolt appear to have been more economic than religious, and the Jewish élite involved themselves in it reluctantly. The revolt lasted four years and ended with the sack of Jerusalem and the destruction of the temple. These events were to have a profound effect not only on Jews, but also on Christians. A further revolt in 135 CE was put down by the Emperor Hadrian, who built a new Roman colony, Aelia Capitolina, on the site of Jerusalem, and forbade the practice of Jewish customs there.

Religion in the Roman empire

Our knowledge of the religious life of the citizens of the Roman empire is based partly on comments made by historians and other writers in the course of their accounts of major events, but mostly on the evidence of inscriptions, which include records of political decisions about religious activities, calendars listing the sacrifices communities were required to make through the year, administrative documents from sanctuaries and records of major dedications. Inevitably this kind of evidence tells us more about the activities of the élite, and about the major public aspects of religion, than it does about the actions and experiences of the majority of the citizen body.

The primary focus of public religious activity in the Roman empire was the city. The empire, in particular in the east, was administered as a collection of self-governing city-states, each with its own civil and religious calendar. Each city had its own cults, administered by priests drawn from the leading citizens, with sacrifices and festivals attended usually only by the citizens of that particular community. Festivals varied from major events involving athletic or musical or dramatic competitions, and the large-scale slaughter of cattle to feed the whole citizen body, to local gatherings without blood sacrifice of any kind. Divisions within the city would also have their own regular religious obligations, and each household would have its own shrines and rituals. Dedications to the gods, in thanks for good fortune of some kind, might be made by whole communities or by individuals. We have little evidence for the actual 'beliefs' of the vast majority of the inhabitants of the empire, but it is clear that religious ritual was a part of all areas of life in their communities.

Sacrifice

The religious understanding of the empire was based essentially on the idea of a contract between humans and gods, in which the people made offerings to the gods in return for their blessing, in the form of good harvests, military and commercial success and protection from external dangers. The will of the gods could, to some extent, be determined by the examination of the entrails of sacrificial victims or the consultation of oracles. An important feature of religious life was a recognition that mortals were to a large extent ignorant about the gods. There was no revealed scripture to provide an authoritative account of the nature of the gods, a circumstance which left plenty of room for philosophical discussion about religious matters on the one hand, and a need for care on the other. Tradition provided the best guide to what was acceptable to the gods, but communities had always to be open to the idea that there were unknown gods to whom they might owe reverence. One of the most important developments in the religious cults of the cities of what became the eastern part of the Roman empire in the last three centuries BCE was the practice of honouring powerful military figures, first Hellenistic kings, then Roman generals and finally the Roman emperors, as gods: this practice can be understood as a recognition of the enormous power wielded by these individuals, and of the communities' subordination to them.

It is sometimes suggested, as an explanation for the rise of Christianity, that the religion of the Roman empire was in some way unsatisfying for the majority of its inhabitants. It is no doubt the case that the subordination of the cities, first to Hellenistic rulers and then to Rome, reduced their autonomy, and therefore the role of their particular gods in the well-being of their cities. Nonetheless, cities continued to build new temples and restore old ones, and the evidence of archaeology does not support the notion of a general decline in religious observance. A more significant trend may have been a growing gulf between the élite members of communities, who were increasingly drawn into an empire-wide ruling class, granted Roman citizenship and the possibility of election to the Roman senate, and the rest of the population. Religion was one way in which this gulf could be bridged. A feature of life in the cities of the empire was the existence of groups of (usually) men who met regularly in clubs known as *collegia* (the word *collegium* was sometimes used to refer to synagogues – see below). These clubs usually had a specific purpose, for example burial clubs, whose members paid a subscription and received burial and commemoration on their deaths, or volunteer fire-fighters. They would have patrons from the élite, and would meet regularly for dinners typically on festival days of certain gods and on the birthdays of their patrons. Such groups might include slaves, who would generally be excluded, or at least marginalized, in the public religion of the community.

Mystery cults

Mystery cults were another form of religious activity which sometimes broke through the civic structures of the empire. The term covers a very wide variety of cults, from the Mysteries of Eleusis, celebrated near Athens, which were honoured by Hellenistic kings and Roman emperors, to much smaller local groups. What united these cults was the fact that they were open to initiates only. Some of these cults honoured gods from the eastern Mediterranean and beyond, including Mithras (a Persian name), Isis (Egyptian) and Cybele (Phrygian, from Anatolia), and this has led to the suggestion that they were part of a wave of 'oriental religions' that gradually overwhelmed the 'traditional' religion of the empire – an image into which the rise of Christianity might be fitted. The suggestion is, however, a gross oversimplification of the truth. There was, for example, little eastern in Mithraism beyond its name, and mystery cults in honour of Demeter and Dionysus, to mention but two, were part of the Greek mainstream of religion for centuries before the coming of Rome. Initiation, along with sacrifices, festivals and dedications, was an accepted element in the ritual life of the Roman empire.

An important aspect of some mystery cult groups, most notably those connected with the mythical figure of Orpheus and with the followers of the sixth century BCE philosopher Pythagoras, was the possession of special texts, which might include collections of spells and incantations, but also occult stories about the gods and other myths. Some of the works of Plato, who wrote  in the fourth century BCE, show the influence of these ideas, and much later Neoplatonist writers

Qumran

identified Pythagoras as the originator of some of the mystical ideas in their philosophy. Passing into the thought of Jews living in the Hellenistic world outside Palestine, the language of mystery and initiation was eventually to find its way, via Paul, into Christian ideas. Despite the attempts of Christian apologists to claim that certain mystery cults stole their rituals from Christianity, and the arguments of some modern writers that the theft was the other way around, many of the similarities in vocabulary between Christianity and Graeco-Roman mystery religion are probably best explained by this indirect transmission.

Stress on the common features of religion throughout the empire should not hide the diversity of religious practice. Cities, and in particular their élite citizens, continued to pride themselves on their religious heritage, and the unique importance of some of their shrines. In this sense, the claims made by the leading citizens of Jerusalem for their own cult and temple reveal both the differences and the similarities between Judaism and the other religions of the empire.

First-century Judaism

Our knowledge of Judaism within Judaea in the first centuries BCE and CE comes largely from the works of Josephus, a Jewish historian writing towards the end of the first century CE and, since Judaism stressed observance of Jewish laws and traditions, from some of the books of the Hebrew Bible. The evidence of archaeology, and above all the Dead Sea Scrolls, found at Qumran and belonging to a breakaway Essene community, provide glimpses of life in more marginal Jewish communities in the Judaean countryside.

THE DEAD SEA SCROLLS

In 1947, a young Bedouin shepherd by chance discovered jars containing scrolls in a cave on the western shore of the Dead Sea, about eight miles south of Jericho. Subsequently, additional material was found in ten further caves. While some scrolls were in good condition, there were also thousands and thousands of fragments which had to be put together painstakingly. All in all 813 documents have been discovered. These include twelve scrolls, eleven of leather and one of copper.

Near the caves where the scrolls were discovered is a complex of ruins known as Khirbet Qumran. It was occupied by a Jewish community, known as the Qumran sect, often identified with the Essenes mentioned by the Jewish historian Josephus, from around 150 BCE until 68 CE, when it was destroyed in the Jewish war with Rome. The scrolls are important for a number of reasons:

1. They offer texts of books of the Hebrew Bible far older than any previously known;
2. They contain fragments of many Jewish apocryphal and pseudepigraphical books, some of which were known previously only in translation;
3. They contain works produced by the community itself, including a disciplinary rule and commentaries on books of the Hebrew Bible which interpret them in terms of the history of the community.

The Qumran documents are referred to by the number of the cave, followed by the letter Q and letters or numbers denoting the particular work, e.g. 1QH is a scroll containing hymns from Cave 1; 11Q19 is the so-called Temple Scroll from Cave 11. These references make use of abbreviations of Hebrew terms, thus the H in 1QH does not represent 'Hymns' but the Hebrew for hymns, *Hodayot*; p stands for *pesher*, which means commentary.

The most important scrolls are:

Complete scroll of Isaiah (1QIsa[a])
Incomplete scroll of Isaiah (1QIsa[b])
Genesis Apocryphon (1QapGen)
Commentary on Habakkuk (1QpHab)
Community Rule (1QS)
Thanksgiving Hymns (1QH)
War Scroll (1QM)
Copper Scroll (3Q15)
Temple Scroll (11Q19)

Since the discovery of the Dead Sea Scrolls, a variety of studies have suggested that not all the Dead Sea Scrolls have been published because they contain material detrimental to Christianity, which could be disastrous for Christian beliefs if it were revealed. This view could point to the extremely long delay over making all the scrolls available, but that delay was caused partly by a complex set of political circumstances and partly by the way in which the reconstruction and editing of the scrolls was assigned, described by one scholar as 'set to become the academic scandal of the twentieth century'. Other writers have seen in the descriptions of the Qumran sect in the scrolls coded allusions to figures and events in early Christianity. However, the Dead Sea Scrolls contain no Christian documents, nor does the accepted chronology of them support such attempts.

The complete Dead Sea Scrolls are readily available in an edition by Geza Vermes, *The Complete Dead Sea Scrolls in English*, Harmondsworth: Penguin Books 1997. The story of the discovery of the scrolls and the problems connected with their publication is told in Geza Vermes, *An Introduction to the Complete Dead Sea Scrolls*, London: SCM Press and Minneapolis: Fortress Press 1999

Central to Jewish life in the period before 70 CE was the performance of rituals at the temple in Jerusalem, where regular sacrifices were made and festivals celebrated. Sacrifices were carried out by the priests, and in particular the high priest, and these positions were held by leading families in Jerusalem. In this respect Jewish cult activity was not very different from that of other inhabitants of the Roman empire, except that while in other cities there would be a great variety of temples to different gods, in Jerusalem worship in the name of YHWH, given by Jews to God but never pronounced, stood alone. The temple building in early-first-century CE Jerusalem had been started by Herod in 22 BCE and the result was a spectacular edifice, as impressive as any major temple in any of the cities of the empire, differing only, but fundamentally, in the fact that there was no cult image within it.

While ritual activity largely took place in the temple, synagogues were places for the reading and

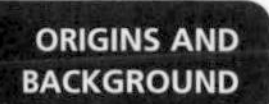

exposition of the so-called books of Moses, the Torah. There were a large number of synagogues in Jerusalem and Judaea, and throughout the Diaspora (dispersion), the term used to describe Jews living outside their homeland. The rabbis active in the synagogues were not usually from priestly families, and skill at interpreting the Torah might potentially give an individual a position of wider influence within his community. Thus the synagogues could be seen as an alternative source of status to the temple, and Judaism had a long tradition of criticism of the activities of the priests by men from outside the priestly families. This is not, however, to suggest that synagogues were in any way seen as challenging the role of temple ritual in Judaism: their functions were complementary.

Apart from their belief in one God, what struck contemporary observers as most distinctive about Jews was their observance of strict laws governing their way of life, in particular observance of the sabbath and strict dietary regulations. It would be wrong to suppose that these observers were struck because they themselves followed no such restrictions. It is inevitable that peculiar customs are visible as such only to outsiders. Graeco-Roman communities had great respect for their own laws and customs (*nomoi* in Greek, *mores* in Latin) and in particular for ancestral customs (*patrioi nomoi* or *mos maiorum*), but these did not take the form of an identifiable single text like the Torah, nor were they perceived to be as restrictive on the daily life of the people. Some other groups in the empire did impose restrictions on what their followers could eat or wear, including for example Pythagoreans who, among other things, were supposed not to wear wool or eat meat. It is not clear to what extent there were practising Pythagorean communities in the Roman empire, but their ideas were certainly known and discussed.

While reverence for the temple and the Torah created a common bond for all Jews, including those of the Diaspora, there was considerable diversity within Jewish thought. For the vast majority of Jews the debates between different trends within Judaism will have been irrelevant, but they are important for explaining how Christianity could emerge from Judaism. The three most important Jewish 'philosophies' identified by Josephus were the Pharisees, Sadducees and Essenes (*Jewish War* 2, 119–66).

The Sadducees were associated with the priestly families and the temple. Josephus has little to say about their ideas, except that they rejected ideas about fate and the persistence of the soul after death, but it was their links to the Jerusalem cult, rather than any common doctrine, that identified them.

The Essenes were founded in the late second century BCE by a man known as the Teacher of Righteousness and were isolationist, rejecting in particular the right of the Hasmoneans and their successors to hold the high priesthood and claiming as invalid much of the ritual of temple worship, while recognizing the importance of the temple itself. Essene ideas are characterized as more apocalyptic and messianic thought than other trends within Judaism, and were influential on the Diaspora. The Qumran sect which produced the Dead Sea Scrolls is thought to have been Essene.

The Pharisees, probably founded just before the second century BCE, were associated in particular with the interpretation of the law. Their influence was therefore felt more in the synagogues than around the temple, and after the destruction of the temple Pharisaic thought was particularly influential on the development of rabbinic Judaism. This fact leads to problems in identifying Pharisaic ideas in the earlier period, since the writers of the works containing the most detailed depictions of the Pharisees, the Gospels, keen to distinguish between Christianity and rabbinic Judaism at the time they were composed, emphasize their exclusivity and narrowness of thought.

A number of ideas can be identified within the debates between these groups that were to be particularly significant in early Christianity. In particular one can identify messianism – the expectation of the coming of 'the Lord's anointed', whatever that might mean in reality – and ideas about resurrection, again, a term that might mean a number of different things to different people. The Gospels, and in particular the Gospel of Matthew, emphasize the role of Jesus in fulfilling messianic prophecies found in parts of the Hebrew Bible. How far these passages were understood in this way before the rise of Christianity, and how important ideas of resurrection were to most Jews, is the subject of much debate.

Messiah

Resurrection

The relationship – or rather lack of one – between these debates within Judaism and the cult at the temple in Jerusalem is worth noting. Views about the correct way of carrying out many of the rituals of the temple, or about who had a right to perform these rituals, divided in particular Essenes and Sadducees, but no one denied that the rituals were of vital importance. Nor did any debate about the soul or the Messiah have implications for what should happen in the temple. Discussions about the nature of God or the soul were not seen to threaten the essential nature of Judaism. In the same way, in the wider Graeco-Roman world of the time, philosophical writings about religious questions, for example the Roman orator and philosopher Cicero's *On the Nature of the Gods*, written in the middle of the first century BCE by a man who was a leading politician and also, as a member of the College of Augurs, a priest, complemented rather than challenged the traditional religious rituals of the Roman state. What we know about the nature of Judaism, about which we are better informed than any other cults of this period, and the parallels between it and other religions of the empire, should encourage us to reject the view that Christianity succeeded because it filled an aching void in the lives of people whose religion had declined into a combination of empty ritual and sceptical philosophy.

Charismatic figures in Judaism

One feature of life in Judaea in the first centuries BCE and CE was the appearance of a number of charismatic figures advocating reform of some kind. In the period before Jesus' public activity such figures included the founder of the Zealots, Judas of Galilee, and most notably John the Baptist. Other similar figures appeared after the time of Jesus, including Bannus, whose disciples included, for a period, Josephus. Although Judaism could easily accommodate the variety of teachings offered by such individuals, they might be perceived as offering a threat to groups within Judaea, whether the priests, the local rulers or the Romans themselves, and thus it was not uncommon for them to be arrested and executed, as Herod did to John the Baptist. Commonly, too, the disciples of these men would carry on their teaching after the death of their leader. Although some figures were active outside the main areas of settlement in Judaea – John the Baptist was noteworthy for living and operating in the desert – it was the synagogues that provided the most obvious forum for offering new interpretations of the law and it was in synagogues that Jesus appears to have debated with other interpreters. Every aspect of Jesus' activity during the few years of his public ministry, debating the interpretation of the law in synagogues, speaking to large groups outside the cities, performing miracles and grand symbolic gestures such as his behaviour in the temple, can be paralleled in the actions of other charismatic figures, and can be seen as compatible with Judaism in the diversity of its first-century forms. It is the direction taken by Jesus' followers after his death that distinguishes Christianity from other strands within Judaism.

The Jewish Diaspora

Judaism was not, of course, limited to Judaea. There had been Jewish communities outside Palestine since at least the eighth century BCE, when significant parts of the populations of the kingdoms

JOHN THE BAPTIST

John the Baptist appears in all four Gospels as the forerunner of Jesus. A prophetic figure, he lived a solitary and ascetic life in the wilderness, and then attracted a circle of disciples. He proclaimed that God's judgement was near and that men and women should repent, receiving baptism and doing good works. In the Gospel of Mark he appears as Elijah brought to life again (chapter 9). He is closely associated with Jesus: in the Gospel of Luke a set of scenes from conception to birth presents him in parallel to Jesus. Even in his womb John recognizes the superiority of Jesus, and this is constantly stressed in all the Gospels; however, reading between the lines it seems that the situation was rather more complex than that. Jesus receives baptism from John, and the Gospels seem somewhat at a loss to explain this fact. Both Jesus and John had disciples and Jesus' disciples were aware of what John's disciples were being taught.

At some point after baptizing Jesus, John was imprisoned by Herod Antipas, ruler of Galilee. The reason was that John had denounced Herod's illegal (by Jewish law) marriage to Herodias, the divorced wife of his half-brother, after divorcing his first wife, who was of Arab descent. Politically, John's denunciation could have encouraged opposition to Herod from both Jews and Arabs, and in fact in 35–6 Herod was defeated by Aretas II, ruler of the semi-Arab Nabataeans. This was seen as a punishment for Herod's killing of John, made notorious by the story of Salome's request for his head on a platter, as a reward for dancing for Herod. It is said that John's followers took his body and buried it; the traditional location for his tomb is Sebaste, former Samaria.

John continued to be an influence and his disciples seem to have carried on for some time as rivals of Jesus' disciples. The Acts of the Apostles speaks of Apollos, 'who spoke and taught accurately the things concerning Jesus, although he knew only the baptism of John' (18.25), and a group of disciples who had never heard of the Holy Spirit but had been baptized with the baptism of John (19.1–5), both in Ephesus.

C. H. H. Scobie, *John the Baptist*, London: SCM Press and Philadelphia: Fortress Press 1964

of Israel and Judah had been deported to Mesopotamia, where many people settled permanently. In later centuries some Jews had settled abroad as traders or garrison troops, while others had been forcibly moved as a consequence of war. In particular Pompey's campaign of 63 BCE resulted in large numbers of Jews being brought to Rome as prisoners of war, to be sold as slaves. These communities made up what is referred to as the Jewish Diaspora. Glimpses of the life of the Diaspora communities come from writings of and about Paul (see below), but the most substantial source of information comes from the writings of the Jewish philosopher Philo of Alexandria, who wrote in the first half of the first century CE.

Language

Greek was the usual language of Diaspora Jews, and they would use Greek translations of the Torah in the synagogues. Along with Greek language came contact with the ideas of Greek philosophical schools. The writings of Philo, who favoured an allegorical interpretation of the Hebrew scriptures, probably represent an extreme example of the integration of Greek and Jewish thought, but other Diaspora Jews such as Paul, who came from the city of Tarsus in southern Anatolia, were clearly also influenced by Greek ideas.

Diaspora communities were to be found in a large number of cities throughout the eastern part of the Roman empire, including Rome itself. The Torah and the Jerusalem temple were central to their religious lives, and Diaspora Jews sent taxes to Jerusalem for the maintenance of the temple, and in many cases travelled there for major festivals They were organized around the synagogues, with their own councils of elders, and remained to some extent separate from the majority of the population. In western Anatolia, one of the areas of Paul's missionary activities, there had been significant Jewish settlement since the second century BCE, and in the picture of these communities in the Acts of the Apostles (chs 13–17) the observant Jews are surrounded by numbers of Gentile 'god-fearers', who attended the synagogues but did not observe Jewish law. It is these people who are presented as the chief recipients of Paul's teachings.

The Jerusalem community

Organized Christianity started in the early 30s CE with the resurrection of Jesus. What the resurrection was – whether indeed it is appropriate to treat it as a single historical event – is a complex issue. What followed from it was the establishment in Jerusalem of a group of followers of Jesus. Strikingly, leadership of this group belonged not to any of Jesus' disciples, but to his brother James (usually known as 'James the brother of the Lord', 'James the Righteous' or 'James the Just'). The fact that after James' death (see below) leadership passed to other relatives emphasizes that the early 'Jesus movement' was effectively seen as something inherited from Jesus by his family. A more or less separate group, led by Jesus' disciple Peter, seems to have existed for a decade or so, but after Peter's brief arrest in 44 CE, his authority declined.

p. 852

Although later Christian writers like Eusebius of Caesarea in the fourth century refer to James as Bishop of Jerusalem, and present him as leader of a church, these terms are anachronistic and probably misleading. References to James as 'the Righteous' emphasize his conformity with Jewish law, and the Jerusalem followers of Jesus continued to attend the temple, and to observe all the other activities associated with Judaism. Indeed James appears to have discouraged attempts to spread Christianity to Gentiles, or to recognize Gentiles as Christians unless they first converted to Judaism.

Some new rituals were practised by the followers of Jesus, such as the celebration of the resurrection each week on the day after the sabbath, the use of baptism to welcome in new members, and meeting regularly to eat together, but they did not use the term 'Christian', and would not have been easily distinguishable from the other Jewish groups which attended the temple. So closely was the Jerusalem group tied to the temple that with its destruction in 70 CE it effectively ceased to exist, and the future development of Christianity lay with communities which had up until this point been very much on the margins.

Initiation

Eucharist

Jewish Christianity

The earliest Christians outside Judaea

The first attempts to spread Christian ideas outside Judaea are associated with a group referred to as the 'Hellenists', whose leaders, known as the 'Seven', included Stephen, recognized as the first Christian martyr (Acts 6). The Hellenists travelled to the cities to the north of Judaea, including Tyre and Sidon, and above all Antioch: it was in Antioch that the Greek word *christianoi* was first used, as a result of their activity. Their message was directed exclusively to Greek-speaking Jews of the Diaspora, and they advocated abandonment of worship at the Jerusalem temple. Opposed by the majority within the Jewish communities, including the Christian groups within Judaea, but with no support from Gentiles, the Hellenists did not flourish, but they did lay the foundations of the more extensive activities of Paul.

Martyr

p. 538

The role of Paul in the development of Christianity is the central theme of the Acts of the Apostles, although both this work and Paul's own letters may give a distorted view of his activities. Paul's relationship with the Jerusalem community appears to have been strained, and his main area of activity was in the Roman provinces of Galatia and Asia in western Anatolia, and of Macedonia and Achaea in what is now modern Greece. Although he started by trying to work with Jewish communities in these areas, he was more successful in working with Gentiles. In contrast to the community in Jerusalem, Paul did not require Gentiles to convert to Judaism, and indeed he opposed the idea that Jewish law should apply to non-Jewish Christians. As a result Pauline Christianity had more features in common with the wider Graeco-Roman world than did that of the Jerusalem church. While Jewish law provided a guide to ritual and personal behaviour for

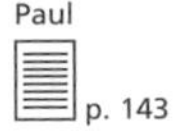
Paul p. 143

THE TWELVE

Matthew 10.2–4	*Mark 3.14–19*	*Luke 6.13–16*	*Acts 1.13*
The names of the twelve apostles are these:	And he appointed twelve, to be with him, and to be sent out to preach and have authority to cast out demons:	He called his disciples, and chose from them twelve, whom he named apostles;	And when they had entered, they went up to the upper room, where they were staying,
First, Simon who is called Peter,	Simon whom he surnamed Peter;	Simon, whom he named Peter,	Peter and
and Andrew his brother; James the son of Zebedee, and John his brother;	James the son of Zebedee and John the brother of James, whom he surnamed Boanerges, that is, sons of thunder; Andrew, and	and Andrew his brother, and James and John, and	John and James and Andrew,
Philip and Bartholomew; Thomas and Matthew the tax collector; James the son of Alphaeus and Thaddaeus (or Lebbaeus);	Philip, and Bartholomew, and Matthew, and Thomas, and James the son of Alphaeus, and Thaddaeus, and	Philip and Bartholomew, and Matthew and Thomas, and	Philip and Thomas, Bartholomew and Matthew. James the son of Alphaeus
Simon the Cananaean, and	Simon the Cananaean, and	Simon who was called the Zealot, and Judas the son of James, and	and Simon the Zealot and Judas the son of James.
Judas Iscariot, who betrayed him.	Judas Iscariot, who betrayed him.	Judas Iscariot, who became a traitor.	

In the Gospels Jesus is said to have chosen twelve disciples, as representatives of the twelve tribes of Israel, 'that you may sit on thrones in my kingdom judging the twelve tribes of Israel' (Luke 22.30). The Twelve are mentioned many times in connection with Jesus, and after the treachery of Judas Iscariot, one of them, a replacement, Matthias, is appointed to complete the number, the criterion for the candidates being that they should have been witnesses to the resurrection. However, they seem to have disappeared very early in the history of the church: James the brother of Jesus emerges as the head of the church in Jerusalem. The Twelve are listed four times in the New Testament, but with variations (see e.g. Lebbaeus and Judas the son of James).

p. 852

MARY MAGDALENE

The Gospel of Luke records among the women who followed Jesus along with his disciples the name of 'Mary, called Magdalene, from whom seven demons had gone out' (8.2). Her name suggests that she came from Magdala, a fishing village on the western shore of the Sea of Galilee. In Christian tradition she has often been identified with a prostitute who comes into a dinner which a Pharisee named Simon is giving for Jesus, washes his feet with her tears and pours a flask of precious ointment over them. However, for Luke these are clearly two different women, and although Mary Magdalene is traditionally portrayed as a fallen woman saved by Jesus, there is actually nothing in the Gospels to indicate this.

Mary goes with the other women to Jerusalem; according to Matthew she watches the crucifixion 'from afar' (27.55); according to John 19.25 she stands by the cross along with Mary, Jesus' mother, and the Beloved Disciple. In the first three Gospels she goes with other women to the tomb on the first day of the week; in Matthew and Mark she has noted previously where Jesus was laid. In the Gospel of John, Jesus appears first of all to Mary Magdalene alone in the garden in a moving scene (20.11–18). This incident has given rise to much speculation about the nature of the relationship between Mary Magdalene and Jesus, and novels have been written and films made about it; however, since this is the only information we have about her, nothing certain can be said.

PETER

Simon son of Jonas (or John), whom Jesus in the Gospel of John (1.42) once calls Cephas (this name occurs several times in the letters of Paul), is better known as Peter. Cephas in Aramaic and Peter *(petros)* in Greek have the same meaning, 'rock', and in a passage which occurs only in the Gospel of Matthew Jesus tells him, 'You are Peter, and on this rock I will build my church' (16.18). He was a married man, a fisherman working out of Capernaum with his brother Andrew, when he was called by Jesus. Thereafter he is presented as the leader and spokesman of the disciples; whenever the Twelve are listed, he comes first. He also comes first when there is mention of an inner group of three disciples, Peter, James and John, for example in the scene of the transfiguration of Jesus (Mark 9.2–8); they came to be known as the 'pillars'. In the first three Gospels Peter is the one who confesses Jesus as the Christ (Matthew 16.15–18; Mark 8.29; Luke 9.20); in Mark he is then rebuked when he protests at Jesus' prophecy of his crucifixion. Before the crucifixion he denies that he knows Jesus, but in Luke he is the first witness of the resurrection (24.34). In the Gospel of John, in which he appears less frequently, his prominence is challenged by the enigmatic 'Beloved Disciple', but in the final chapter he is told by Jesus three times in different words to 'Feed my lambs/sheep' (21.15, 16, 17).

In the Acts of the Apostles, Peter retains his prominent place in the early church, preaching at Pentecost when the Holy Spirit is given (Acts 2.14–36); he also acts as a judge in the case of two errant church members, Ananias and Sapphira (5.1–11). He engages in missionary preaching in Lydda, Joppa and Caesarea (Acts 9.32–10.1), and after a vision (Acts 10) is an advocate of admitting Gentiles (non-Jews) into the church. He is later arrested, but makes a miraculous escape from prison (Acts 12.1–17), after which 'he departed and went to another place'.

We get a slightly different perspective on Peter from the letters of Paul. Writing about his past in his letter to the Galatians, Paul records that three years after his conversion he spent fifteen days with Cephas in Jerusalem; James the Lord's brother was also present (1.18–19). Fourteen years later he went to Jerusalem again, in connection with a controversy over his preaching; the main figures at the meeting were James, Cephas and John (in that order, 2.9). In Antioch, Paul's base at the time, Cephas had been eating with the Gentiles without observing Jewish food laws, but when 'certain men came from James' (2.12) he withdrew, in fear of them. By now it looks as if the shadowy figure of James the brother of Jesus had become head of the church, but we know nothing of the circumstances.

p. 852

By the end of the first century there was a tradition that Peter had lived in Rome; he is supposed to have been crucified and buried there; this may be hinted at in John 21.18–19. However, evidence is very sparse; tradition that he founded the church of Rome or was its first bishop dates only from the middle to end of the second century.

There is an enigmatic reference to Peter in a document contemporaneous with the New Testament, Clement of Rome's first letter to the Corinthians, written around 96. In a long passage on jealousy, it speaks of 'Peter, who because of unrighteous jealousy suffered not one or two but many trials, and having thus given his testimony went to the glorious place which was his due' (5.4).

Two letters are attributed to Peter in the New Testament, but whether they were actually written by him is a matter of dispute; 2 Peter in particular seems to come from a much later date.

Oscar Cullmann, *Peter: Disciple, Apostle, Martyr*, London: SCM Press and Philadelphia, Westminster Press 1953

Jewish Christians, Paul's personal authority, as presented in the letters he wrote, took this role for the Pauline communities. Paul was also responsible for the appointment of overseers (Greek *episkopos*, conventionally translated as bishop) of the churches, providing a model for church organization that was later adopted universally.

The transformation in the 60s CE

The period of 62–4 CE saw the violent deaths of the three key figures of earliest Christianity, Peter, Paul and James the brother of Jesus. The death of James, possibly at the hands of the chief priest in Jerusalem, led to the rapid decline of the community he led: it seems that leadership passed to other more distant relatives of Jesus, but they lacked their predecessor's authority. The death of Paul in Rome, possibly in 62 CE, may have followed complaints against him from Jerusalem. Peter's death is often associated with the brief episode of persecution of Christians in Rome under the Emperor Nero, after a major fire which destroyed a large part of the city in 64 CE. Although the fire was probably started accidentally, Nero held Christians responsible. Christians had already once been expelled from Rome in 49 CE under the Emperor Claudius, but had returned under Nero.

Persecution

JAMES THE BROTHER OF JESUS

In Book 20 of his *Jewish Antiquities*, the Jewish historian Josephus reports the stoning of 'the brother of Jesus who was called Christ, whose name was James' for breaking the Jewish law in 62 CE. The Sanhedrin, the Jewish legal assembly which imposed the death penalty, was thought by responsible citizens to have acted in an illegitimate way and they complained to King Agrippa. Agrippa removed the high priest who had instigated the trial, but James was dead.

A James is mentioned in the Gospels of Matthew (13.55) and Mark (6.3) as one of four brothers of Jesus, and there is no reason to suppose that he was not the person stoned in 62. In his letter to the Galatians, written in 52, Paul mentions meeting James 'the brother of the Lord' in Jerusalem and James is named as the first of three 'pillars' of the church; in 1 Corinthians 15.7 Paul says that Jesus appeared to James. The Acts of the Apostles refers to an important James three times (12.17; 15.13; 21.18), but is not more specific about his identity. At the so-called apostolic council in Jerusalem reported in Acts 15, which lays down the conditions on which Paul may carry on his mission to non-Jews, Peter and the Twelve disappear from view. Some scholars argue that at this point the church of Jerusalem lost its primacy and the focal point of Christianity moved to Antioch and then to Rome. However, there is little evidence that the Jerusalem church lost its importance until the destruction of the city by the Romans in 70 CE: as its head, James would have become the most influential authority; he has even been labelled 'the first pope'.

In the early centuries of the Christian church James acquired a tremendous reputation for piety: he was said to have prayed so much that his knees were calloused like those of a camel; he was noted for his faithfulness to the Jewish law, and was also called 'the Just'.

Various reasons have been put forward to explain why it was James who became head of the mother church. Some scholars think that Peter designated James head when he had to flee Jerusalem; others see theological reasons behind his leadership: there was too much laxity in Christian observance of the Jewish law which had even led to the persecution of some Greek-speaking Christians, the Hellenists. However, James probably owed his position to his kinship with Jesus. Christianity would then resemble Islam and Mormonism in seeing the rise of a dynastic element after the death of the prophet.

Pierre-Antoine Bernheim, *James, Brother of Jesus*, London: SCM Press 1977

His death in 68 CE, and events in Judaea soon afterwards, will have led once again to the return of Christians to Rome.

It was events towards the end of the decade, with which Christians had no direct involvement, that were most important for the future development of Christianity. The Jewish revolt culminated in 70 CE with the sack of Jerusalem and the destruction of the temple there. The consequences of this for the development of Judaism were profound. With the failure of the revolt and the loss of the temple, it was the Pharisees whose influence became dominant in the development of what is known as 'rabbinic Judaism'. Reforms stressing the need for purity and stricter adherence to the Jewish law made it increasingly difficult for Jewish Christians to continue to worship with Jews in the synagogues. As Judaism worked towards creating a new identity for itself in a world without the Jerusalem temple, so Christians were forced to establish their own separate identity.

The establishment of Christian identity

Many of the major texts of the New Testament were composed in the period between the destruction of the temple and the early years of the second century, by authors attempting to offer a model for Christianity. Writing in Greek, their intended audience included Greek-speaking Jewish communities in the Diaspora, and in other cases those Christians expelled from the synagogues. The Letter of James (written *c.* 80 CE) and the Gospel of Matthew (90–95 CE) present Christianity as the next step for Judaism – a continuation of the religion now that the temple had gone. The Gospel of Luke and its sequel, the Acts of the Apostles (80–85 CE), written in one of the Pauline communities, seek to demonstrate that Pauline Christianity was part of the mainstream. Other literary works produced in these communities, including works attributed to Paul such as the Pastoral Letters and the Letter to the Ephesians (85–90 CE) can be read as reaching out to other Christian groups, perhaps those expelled from the synagogues, with advice on organization. The Gospel of John, probably written in the Pauline community of Ephesus in 100–110 CE, provides a developed christology that is compatible with the Pauline approach. Other Christian writing in this period reveals an increasing consciousness of the distinctiveness of Christianity, most obviously in the letters of Ignatius of Antioch (written 107–8 CE), who distinguishes between Christianity and Judaism.

Christology

Organization

From these documents it is possible to gain some idea of the organization of Christian communities. The synagogues clearly provided the basic model of organization, and churches were led by groups of elders (Greek *presbyteroi*, often referred to as 'presbyters'), one or more of whom might be designated 'overseer' (*episkopos* – see above). There was also a subordinate position of deacon (*diakonos*) (e.g. Philippians 1.1). As well as these administrative positions we also find mention of functional positions, including apostle (*apostolos*), prophet (*prophetes*) and teacher (*didaskalos*) (e.g. 1 Corinthians 12.28). The exact relationship between these different positions is not clear, and there may have been considerable variety. Formal organization of the churches into a single structure was a later development.

Being a Christian in the early second century

By the time of the Emperor Hadrian (117–138 CE) there were significant Christian communities in Rome, in Greece and Asia Minor, and in Antioch, and others about which less is known in Egypt and in Italy outside Rome. Christians nonetheless remained a small minority of the population of the Roman empire, and were little noticed by the rest.

Our knowledge of Christianity in this period is heavily dependent on literary works produced by Christians themselves, either at the time or in later years, and these are inevitably written by and from the perspective of its leaders. There is very little surviving material evidence of Christian activity from this period, and there are only occasional comments from non-Christian writers. One frequently quoted document is a letter written to the Emperor Trajan by Pliny the Younger, when he was governor of the Roman provinces of Bithynia and Pontus, in which Pliny describes how he dealt with those accused of Christianity (*Letter* 10.96). Although Pliny probably exaggerates both the scale of the problem as he perceives it, and the dramatic success of his policy, it seems likely that the attachment of many of those associated with Christian groups was not strong. While Jewish Christians might have understood Christianity as a development of Judaism, with the exclusive attachment to one God that that assumed, for non-Jews Jesus would have been one divine figure among many, and the notion that acceptance of Christianity meant the rejection of all other religious ties must have been slower in coming. The fact that Christianity spread through the Roman empire with relatively little persecution until the third century suggests that there must have been a certain level of compromise with the requirements of the civic religious practices of the time.

HUGH BOWDEN

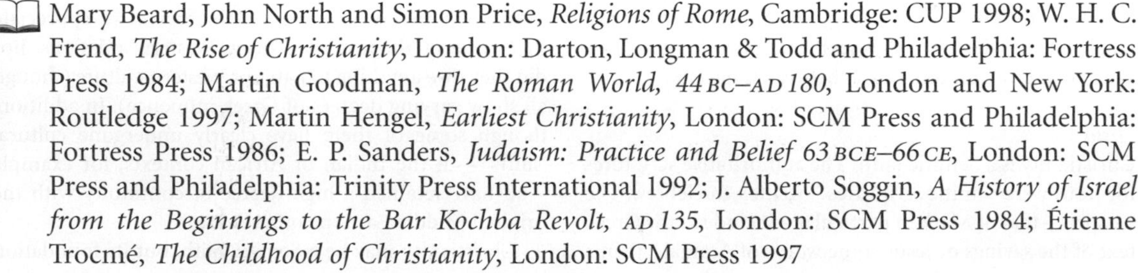

Mary Beard, John North and Simon Price, *Religions of Rome*, Cambridge: CUP 1998; W. H. C. Frend, *The Rise of Christianity*, London: Darton, Longman & Todd and Philadelphia: Fortress Press 1984; Martin Goodman, *The Roman World, 44 BC–AD 180*, London and New York: Routledge 1997; Martin Hengel, *Earliest Christianity*, London: SCM Press and Philadelphia: Fortress Press 1986; E. P. Sanders, *Judaism: Practice and Belief 63 BCE–66 CE*, London: SCM Press and Philadelphia: Trinity Press International 1992; J. Alberto Soggin, *A History of Israel from the Beginnings to the Bar Kochba Revolt, AD 135*, London: SCM Press 1984; Étienne Trocmé, *The Childhood of Christianity*, London: SCM Press 1997

Orthodox churches

Origins and background ➤
History ➤
Christianity in the Middle East ➤
Mission ➤

Christianity is widely perceived today as being a Western religion. It is associated with the standards and outlook of Western Europe and – perhaps supremely at the present time – of the USA. Thus, for example, many in the Muslim world see 'Western' lifestyles as 'Christian' lifestyles. Christianity, however, is not by origin a 'Western' religion. Its origins are undeniably in the region now commonly known internationally as the Middle East. And in the Middle East and adjoining regions there still exist Christian communities which reflect much of the culture, ethos and practice of the original heartlands of Christianity. These are the Orthodox churches.

Monasticism ➤

The word 'Orthodox' derives from two Greek words. *Orthos* means 'straight', 'right' or 'correct' – hence orthodontists and orthoptists who seek to straighten and correct teeth and eyes. *Doxa* relates to root meanings of 'teaching' and 'glory' – hence doxology, an expression of praise. 'Orthodox' therefore means 'correct teaching' and 'correct glory'. Orthodox Christians understand themselves as those who teach and transmit the truth of the Christian faith correctly and who glorify God in their worship correctly. Historically, the adjective was accepted by those who adhered to the doctrinal definitions of certain church councils – their opponents being described as 'heterodox' or 'heretical'. More recently it has become the generic term for a number of Christian jurisdictions.

Islam and Christianity ➤
Ethiopian Christianity ➤

The phrase 'the Orthodox Church' is usually used to describe a number of mainly nationally-organized churches in communion with each other and with the Patriarchate of Constantinople. These include a whole series of churches – the church of Greece, the church of Russia and the church of Romania, etc. which can all be described as 'Orthodox church*es*'. However, in addition a group of five churches is called 'Oriental Orthodox', though until recently they were not accepted as 'Orthodox' by the family of churches in communion with Constantinople. To complicate matters further, there is one church (the Church of the East or the Assyrian Church) which is not formally accepted as 'orthodox' by either the 'Orthodox' or the 'Oriental Orthodox', but which nevertheless is purely Middle Eastern in origin and ethos.

Here I shall use the word 'Orthodox' in its widest sense to denote all the above Christian communities, which have a family likeness that distinguishes them from other churches. We shall explore the differences between them later.

History

Bible

Christianity is a Semitic faith. The authoritative scriptures for Jesus were Semitic scriptures – written in Hebrew. The Gospels – that of Mark in particular – include in the Greek text of the sayings of Jesus some words of Aramaic, then a major Semitic language spoken over much of the eastern end of the Mediterranean, of which Syriac is the surviving descendant.

Part of the reason why this fundamental fact about the origins of Christianity is frequently lost sight of is that the Acts of the Apostles does not dwell on the Semitic communities, but very quickly deflects the reader's attention to the Greek-speaking world, which overlapped both with the Aramaic/Syriac-speaking areas in the East and with the Latin-speaking areas further West. By the end of Acts the focus has shifted from Jerusalem to Rome.

It is important to realize, however, that just as converts to Christ were won in Athens and Rome, so Christianity was gaining adherents in Damascus, Baghdad and further east. A 'snapshot' of Jerusalem in the fourth century CE shows us the sermons of a Greek-speaking bishop having to be translated for a Syriac-speaking local population. From the second century CE to the Arab invasions of the seventh century onwards there was a remarkable flowering of Syrian Christianity. Many movements which were to spread throughout the whole church – for example, monasticism – had their origins in the East in the period prior to the Arab invasions. A rich tradition of scholarship survived the rise of Islam and was to influence Islamic civilizations.

The expansion of the faith was impressive. By the second century there were Christian communities in Persia – modern Iran – and South India. Their descendants, many of them still worshipping in Syriac, are there to this day in considerable numbers. Further north Syrian traders took the gospel as far as China and Tibet, though these communities were wiped out in about the tenth century.

Expansion also took place to the south and east. The Arabian peninsula, now thought of as exclusively Muslim, was divided into Christian bishoprics by the sixth century CE. In Egypt Christianity spread rapidly after a period of intense persecution. To this day an estimated 10 per cent of the population of Egypt is Christian. Further south again, from the fourth century Christianity penetrated Ethiopia, taking on a unique blend of African culture with strongly Semitic features.

North-east of Jerusalem lay the kingdom of Armenia, which embraced the Christian faith in the early fourth century.

We shall be looking at each of these churches in more detail. For present purposes it is sufficient to appreciate that none of them derives from 'Western' missions, nor did they owe anything to Latin or Western culture (though all show varying degrees of Greek influence). In addition, though some of them have clearly undergone cultural 'shifts' – in the Indian or African contexts, for example – all have retained a high degree of continuity with the original Middle Eastern communities.

Christianity may be a Semitic faith, but its foundation

documents – the New Testament – are recorded in Greek. This was to be highly significant. It meant that the Christian good news could be disseminated rapidly through the Greek-speaking communities that encircled the Mediterranean in the first centuries CE – including, for example, Marseilles in southern France and Rome, where the church worshipped in Greek, not Latin, until the third century. It meant that the content of Christianity – the nature of God, the identity of Jesus, the meaning of his life, death and resurrection – was worked out and expressed in Greek terminology. The highly sophisticated language of Greek philosophy was pressed into service to explain the acts of God in Christ. The result has been described as 'a creative and life-giving cultural synthesis of a Hebrew religious awe and a Greek search for philosophical truth'. Consequently, in addition to the New Testament, a substantial corpus of material common to all Christians (including the Nicene Creed, the earliest texts of baptism and the eucharist, and fundamental doctrinal definitions about the Trinity and the nature of Christ) is preserved in Greek. For many modern (Western) churches this corpus is half-forgotten (for some it is irrelevant); for the Orthodox churches – some of whom still worship in Greek – it is a constantly-accessed source of teaching.

Following the toleration, then acceptance, of Christianity by the Roman empire in the fourth century CE, the opportunity arose for inter-church consultation on a scale previously impossible. A chief manifestation of this was a series of councils, which are extremely important in Orthodox thinking.

The councils – which saw themselves as perpetuating the tradition begun by the Council of Jerusalem described in Acts 15 – were gatherings mainly of bishops representing their communities. They were usually convened to deal with a particular problem, and they produced definitions and regulations which were supposed to be binding on the worldwide Christian community.

In the event, the councils were also to be the crystallizing points for a number of divisions which have led to the separate jurisdictions in Eastern Christianity to this day. In recent decades it has been increasingly acknowledged by the Orthodox themselves, as well as by Western historians, that cultural and political factors played an important (sometimes determinative) role in the outcome. The first council had been convened at Nicaea by the Emperor Constantine in the year 325 CE. From then on the emperors – who, after the collapse of the Western half of the Roman empire in the fifth century, were essentially Greek – saw it as their duty to secure the unity and good governance of the church. This caused problems for non-Greek populations, some of which lay outside the empire, others of which resented being ruled from the eastern capital of Constantinople/Byzantium.

The first substantial schism took place following the Council of Ephesus in 431 CE. This condemned the teaching of Nestorius, Patriarch of Constantinople, about the nature of Christ. Nestorius' teaching was held to be that of the Syriac-speaking churches which lay outside the eastern borders of the empire – though recent research has shown that much of the teaching of Nestorius was not translated into Syriac until a century later. Anathematized by the church further west, the Eastern communities reorganized themselves into what is now called the Church of the East, or the Assyrian Church, or simply the East Syrians. (The term 'Nestorian', often used in the past, is now seen to be both misleading and pejorative.)

The second substantial schism followed only twenty years later, after the Council of Chalcedon (451) sought to define how Jesus Christ was both God and man. The formula agreed was not accepted by the Copts, the Ethiopians and the West Syrians – nor, later, by the Armenians and the Indians. Collectively, these churches are therefore known as non-Chalcedonian or pre-Chalcedonian. The collective term Oriental Orthodox is now common in English-speaking contexts. (Once again, the former pejorative term 'Monophysite' is no longer used.)

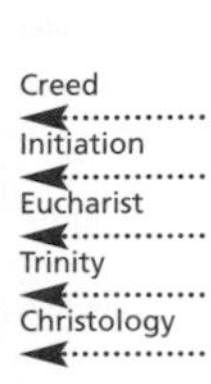

Attempts to heal these fifth-century divisions continued in the following decades. The whole situation was, however, 'frozen' by the Arab expansion of the seventh century CE. Most of the communities passed under Muslim rule, thus removing the opportunity for further development.

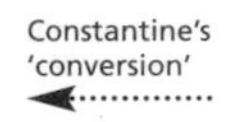

Although expansion to the east and south was substantially curtailed by the rise of Islam, there was rapid expansion north into the predominantly Slav lands. Countries now known as Russia, Ukraine, Bulgaria and Serbia – and some neighbouring non-Slav territories such as Romania – adopted Christianity in its Orthodox form.

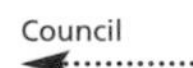

To the West lay the Roman patriarchate, recovering after the 'Dark Age' barbarian invasions. Its power – and that of the emerging Western European nation-states that supported it – was to grow at precisely the same time as the Eastern church weakened and fell under ideologically antagonistic domination. By the 'High Middle Ages' of the fourteenth and fifteenth centuries virtually all the Orthodox churches were under domination – of Arab Islam in the Middle East, Ottoman Islam in Asia Minor and Eastern Europe, the Mongol Tartars in Russia.

One consequence of this was that the Orthodox churches were unable to take part in the 'Age of Discovery'. There were no Greek or Syrian fleets, for example, searching for new lands across the Atlantic or, later, in Australasia. The Orthodox were 'hemmed in' – a situation perpetuated in the twentieth century by the subjugation of most of the European Orthodox under atheistic Communist regimes.

Exploration

A further effect of these centuries of enforced isolation

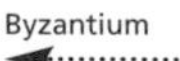

has been to create a Western perception of the Orthodox churches as inaccessible, archaic and incomprehensible. Another has been the cutting off of Western Christianity from its Middle Eastern roots.

Middle Ages

The separation between East and West became definitive in what the West calls the Middle Ages. The traditional date for the commencement of 'the Great Schism' is 1054. The Pope of Rome tried to force Greek congregations in southern Italy to use Latin-rite practices. In retaliation the Patriarch of Constantinople ordered the Latin churches in Constantinople to conform to Greek customs. The situation escalated and the papal legate in Constantinople, Humbert, issued a bull of excommunication against the Patriarch. In practice this incident did not bring about an irrevocable division: cordial relations continued in many places for long afterwards. The strained relationship was made much worse by the Crusades. Originally intended as Western aid to liberate the holy places and their Christian inhabitants from Muslim rule, the Crusades quickly degenerated into 'land grabs' by Western warriors. Orthodox Christians were often despised, maltreated or slaughtered along with their Muslim neighbours. The low point came in 1204 when the Fourth Crusade actually attacked and sacked Constantinople itself. Pillaging and desecration took place on an unprecedented scale in a situation which the East has never forgotten. It was not until 54 years later that a Byzantine emperor and a Byzantine patriarchate were restored in the city, which was left weakened and vulnerable to subsequent Turkish attack.

Crusades
Tradition
Reformation

This separation, created politically and by force of arms, was accompanied by increasing doctrinal differences. Chief among these was the growing insistence by the Roman papacy that its jurisdiction was of a theological nature. It was, argued the popes, intended by Christ, and not merely a reflection of the importance of the see. Submission to Rome was therefore an article of faith. This the Orthodox, who had far more apostolically-founded sees than the West, simply could not accept.

Papacy

p. 305
Globalization
Ministry and ministers
Holy Spirit

Another major focus of division, which persists to the present day, is the *filioque*. The word is Latin for 'and from the Son'. The original text of the creed used in both East and West had been defined by the Councils of Nicaea (325) and Constantinople (381), and confirmed by that of Chalcedon in 451. The agreed text stated that the Holy Spirit 'proceeds from the Father', echoing the language of John 15.26. The addition *filioque* seems to have originated in Spain and, after initially being resisted in Rome, was eventually introduced into the creed there in the eleventh century, under Frankish pressure. At issue was not simply who had authority to alter the agreed text, but the way in which East and West understood the nature of the Godhead itself. Nowadays some Western churches acknowledge that historically the Orthodox are right and that the *filioque* is an interpolation, though not all Western theologians agree that it is an illegitimate one. The issue remains a cause of division.

Despite a remarkable capacity for survival, in parts of the Middle East the Orthodox communities are now small and fragile. This is particularly true of the Greek and Syrian Orthodox in Turkey, the Church of the East in Iraq, and all communities in Israel/Palestine. In some places – the Arabian peninsula, for example – they have been totally extinguished. Direct or economic persecution has caused many to emigrate from their traditional homelands. Often Orthodox Christians have been blamed by their Muslim neighbours for the political action of Western 'Christian' states.

Living the tradition

'Tradition' is an important concept in Orthodoxy. It is not the same as 'traditions', which are a range of customs and practices of various ages. Tradition is the life of the Christian church in continuity from the apostolic community described in the New Testament. The Orthodox believe that they are the church. It will be appreciated that the very geography and history of most of the Orthodox churches as described above makes such a self-understanding possible. For some at least of the sixteenth-century Reformers the Reformation was an attempt to rediscover the authentic tradition of the early church which had become overlaid by the accretions of the Middle Ages with the encouragement of the papacy.

Subsequent Western theological debate has tended to contrast 'scripture' and 'tradition' as two separate sources of authority, leading, understandably, to a tendency to downgrade tradition by Protestants. Orthodox theology does not separate the two, but sees them inextricably intertwined.

For Orthodox, too, there are important questions about how much of their rich heritage is essential, and what can be changed to meet new situations and tensions. The debate is sharpened by the challenge of secular globalization.

The Orthodox churches have a traditionally structured ministry of bishops, presbyters and deacons. Alongside this there is a long tradition of lay ministries, from the boy acolytes assisting in worship to the *starets* of Russia, with his ministry of spiritual guidance. Orthodoxy also has a long tradition of lay theologians, unlike the West, where the clergy have tended to monopolize theological study. All ministries are seen as gifts of the Holy Spirit.

Among the range of ministries, the bishop occupies the central place. He is the shepherd and father of his people. His consecration in the historic succession connects him with the apostolic community, and his conferring with his brother bishops helps to maintain the unity of the church.

Russian Orthodox liturgy

In Orthodoxy the role of the bishop in safeguarding and teaching the deposit of faith is particularly important. Each bishop is responsible for a diocese, whose priests attend to the pastoral and spiritual needs of the local communities or parishes. There is a very strong sense of the priest being the bishop's representative, symbolized by the priest bowing to the (empty) bishop's throne before he begins to celebrate the eucharist.

The diaconate in Orthodoxy is not merely a short-term probationary period, but can be a long-term ministry in its own right. This ancient model is being increasingly explored by some Western churches. When a bishop celebrates the liturgy he will normally be attended by one or more deacons, as were the bishops of the early church. A bishop would never in normal circumstances preside at worship alone. Deacons have a distinctive role in Orthodox worship, frequently linking the clerical and lay participation.

For most Orthodox, gender is seen as part of the God-given image in humanity and as determining the precise forms that an individual's life of obedience may take. Patriarchy is seen as biblical and natural. No Orthodox church ordains women as priests or bishops, though there have been some tentative revivals of the order of deaconesses in recent years.

One result of the increased contact between Westerners and Orthodoxy has been a steady number of conversions. Many of these have been conversions to Christianity itself, others have been 'transfers' of members of Protestant churches or the Roman Catholic Church to Orthodoxy. The reasons for this latter phenomenon are complex.

Orthodoxy's claim to stand in continuity with the early church is clearly attractive. The problems of the papacy and the Reformation reaction are avoided. To become Orthodox is a way of being Christian without being caught up in that seemingly endless polarization.

Recent decades have seen a surprising number of evangelicals and charismatics become Orthodox. For the former, the Orthodox acceptance of the 'biblical world-view' as normative is congenial and contrasts with the 'demythologizing' and liberalizing trends seen in the nineteenth and twentieth centuries in the West. Christians with charismatic experience have found in Orthodoxy a much greater emphasis on the Holy Spirit (both in formal trinitarian teaching and in the experience of worship) than in more 'rationalistic' traditions. Recent years have

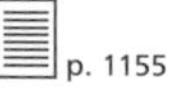

p. 1155

also seen a number of Anglicans who cannot accept the ordination of women to the priesthood or episcopate becoming Orthodox.

Orthodox jurisdictions in the West are learning to build bridges with aspects of the history of Western Christianity. Thus in Britain, for example, Celtic and Saxon saints who predate the Great Schism are accepted

Icon

as Orthodox. They are increasingly depicted in icons and churches are dedicated to them. English, Scottish, Irish or Welsh converts to Orthodoxy are therefore able to connect their Christian identity not merely with far-off Eastern patriarchates, but with the historic Christian communities of their own land and culture.

'Ecumenism' is an Orthodox word. It derives from the Greek *oikoumene*, meaning the inhabited (literally 'enhoused') world – originally the Christian empire. The Patriarch of Constantinople is, as we have seen, given the title 'Ecumenical Patriarch'. So ecumenism was a familiar word in Orthodoxy long before it entered the Western Christian vocabulary.

Ecumenical movement
Old Catholic churches →
Anglicanism →
Roman Catholic Church →

As might be expected, the Orthodox churches' attitude to the modern ecumenical movement is coloured by their treatment by other Christian traditions. There is, therefore, a strongly anti-Roman Catholic feeling in many parts of Orthodoxy. This has deep roots in Orthodoxy's sense of betrayal by the Roman Church, especially at the time of the Crusades. This feeling is so deep that recently Pope John Paul II felt it necessary to apologize for the sack of Constantinople by Western troops in 1204. Subsequent acts of aggression by Venice and other Mediterranean powers reinforced the sense of betrayal, culminating in the failure of the Western Church to come to the aid of Constantinople in her hour of greatest need in 1453.

Orthodox Christians do not accept the papal claims to universal jurisdiction. When, therefore, in recent years the Roman Catholic Church has sought to establish dioceses in former Soviet bloc countries (Russia in particular), this has been seen by the Orthodox as unwarranted aggression and an attempt to invade their lands. So seriously was this taken that it led to a suspension of the official dialogue between the Roman Catholic and Orthodox churches. Despite such setbacks, however, relations between these churches are considerably better than they have been for

Eastern-rite Catholic churches

a long time, though the Eastern-rite Catholic churches remain a continuing source of tension. The mutual anathemas whereby each church condemned the other in the thirteenth century were formally lifted by Pope Paul VI and the Ecumenical Patriarch Athenagoras in 1964. The two churches recognize each other's ministry and sacraments.

Christianity in Europe

The Orthodox in newly-liberated Eastern European lands have also experienced what they see as insensitive incursions by Western Protestant groups who often attack the Orthodox churches as corrupt or apostate. They see their ancient faith ridiculed and young people lured away by a presentation of the Christian faith accompanied by attractive Western culture and (as it is perceived) American money.

Despite the often sad experience of encounters with Western Christian traditions, for much of the twentieth century the Orthodox churches have nevertheless been deeply involved in attempts to seek the greater unity of the church. From its creation in 1948 the World Council of Churches has had Orthodox and Oriental Orthodox churches among its members. Some individuals from these churches had held important posts in the organization. In recent years, however, the Orthodox have become increasingly uneasy about what they perceive as a highly politicized liberal 'agenda' within the WCC. An important review is now being undertaken, exploring Orthodox concerns.

At the same time the Orthodox churches have been engaged in numerous dialogues with other families of churches. The Chalcedonian Orthodox, for example, have for many years been in dialogue with Old Catholics, the Anglican Communion and the Roman Catholic Church. Significant agreed statements have been produced, though none that have restored communion. With the Oriental Orthodox churches the advances have been, from a historical perspective, spectacular. A series of dialogues between 1964 and 1991 resulted in an agreement that the Chalcedonian and non-Chalcedonian Orthodox recognize each other to have preserved the same faith in Christ in spite of diverse formulations and resulting controversies. This means, in effect, that the schism caused by the Council of Chalcedon has been healed. In practice there remain many difficult issues to resolve – what to do about individuals whom one party honours as a saint and another has traditionally vilified as a heretic? What to do when a Chalcedonian and a non-Chalcedonian jurisdiction exist side by side – should one be disbanded? Some steps are being taken to admit members of the other family to receive communion. Despite the delay in implementation, the significance of the theological agreement after nearly one and a half millennia of division should not be underestimated.

Contradicting its caricature as an archaic organization, the (Byzantine) Orthodox Church has been very active in ecological issues in recent years. Particularly under the leadership of Patriarch Bartholomew I, the Ecumenical Patriarchate has sponsored a number of events which have brought together representatives of the scientific community and government, as well as theologians. One of the most recent was the symposium held in September 1997 under the joint auspices of the Patriarch and Jacques Santer, then President of the European Commission, under the title 'The Black Sea in Crisis'. This looked at a range of threats to the environmental balance of the Black Sea, which is bordered by a number of states and religious communities.

In its own Theological Institute at Halki, one of the islands in the Sea of Marmara near Constantinople itself, the Patriarch has organized a series of summer seminars on such subjects as 'The Environment and Religious Education', 'The Environment and Ethics' and 'The Environment and Justice'.

This concern for environmental issues and a holistic approach to them is deeply rooted in a Christian concern for creation. This is a theme that is perhaps more prominent in Orthodoxy than in Protestantism. In Orthodoxy there is none of the dualism or polarization between spirit and matter often implicit in Western Christianity, with its strong life-denying emphases, both in the Roman Catholic and Protestant traditions. While possessing some of the greatest ascetics, thinkers and theologians in Christian history, the Orthodox churches have never become 'cerebral'. Orthodoxy has simultaneously retained an 'earthiness'.

Part of the 'foreignness' of Orthodoxy in Western eyes is attributable to the appearance of its clergy. In all the Eastern churches these are required to be bearded. This is for a variety of reasons. At one level it expresses a different cultural heritage from the West. In the East hair is a sign of holiness (think of the 'holy men' in Hinduism), while in the West it is a sign of decadence (think of Cavaliers with flowing locks as opposed to short-haired Puritans; and hippies in the 1960s). Closely linked with this is the ascetic tradition: like Samson and the biblical Nazirites (see Numbers 6), Greek Orthodox monks do not shave or cut their hair. Partly it is after the example of Jesus and the apostles (of whom the ubiquitous icons provide a constant reminder). But there is also the influence of the holistic, incarnational approach already noted. The beard is part of the God-given 'image' in man. To remove it is to tamper with something that God has intended (as well as being a mark of vanity). The New Testament teaching that the Christian's body is a temple of the Holy Spirit has implications for one's appearance.

Among the various Orthodox and Oriental Orthodox churches there are a number of differences. Most of these are determined by culture and/or climate. Orthodox priests in India, for example, tend to wear a white cassock. Ethiopian Orthodox wear turbans, as did the Syrian Orthodox traditionally. Married Coptic priests wear a small 'pill-box' cap. This, in a stiffer and taller form, is the characteristic headdress of the Chalcedonian Orthodox: the 'stove-pipe', properly called the *kalymavki*. A pointed version of this is worn by the Armenians.

Also commonly seen is the monastic cowl, worn as a plain black covering over the *kalymavki* by the Byzantine Orthodox and the Armenians, but as a close-fitting headdress embroidered with crosses in the Syrian and Coptic traditions. Over this bishops wear a black turban.

Ecotheology
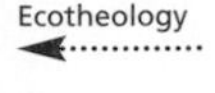

While outdoor dress is usually black, consisting of a cassock and loose gown or robe, liturgical vestments are normally highly coloured and elaborate.

pp. 354–5

Worship

The most characteristic activity of the Orthodox churches is worship. Indeed, for many of them at times it has been virtually the only activity they have been allowed to engage in – under both Islam and Communist regimes, education and mission, for example, have been severely curtailed or forbidden. Ironically, however, it is from the act of worship supremely that Orthodox draw their spiritual strength and sense of identity.

Worship

Creation

The dynamics of Orthodox worship differ in many ways from those of the Western churches. There is usually no seating (pews are a modern invention). The east end of the church, with the holy table, is usually divided from the rest by a curtain or wooden screen covered in icons – the iconostasis. At the eucharist, much of the action takes place behind this barrier, with priests emerging from time to time. Various clergy and laity have different roles to play. The entire service is sung. Incense will be used. The laity are relaxed – they do not necessarily arrive in time for the beginning of the service and during it they may move around. They will also frequently cross themselves and sometimes prostrate themselves with their foreheads on the floor. This biblical posture was almost certainly adopted by Islam from Christian practice.

Overall, the impression is usually very powerful. Frequently it is the experience of Orthodox worship that has begun an individual's journey to joining an Orthodox church.

A large element in the impact of Orthodox worship is that, even when one cannot understand the language or follow all that is going on, it is clearly God-centred. The whole dynamic is that of being in the presence of a powerful Being. Priest and congregation together worship the God of heaven and earth. Much of this stems from the theological understanding of worship as being eternally poured forth by 'angels and archangels and all the company of heaven'. Any human act of worship (corporate or individual) merely 'plugs into' this stream for a brief moment before the worshipper has to drop out again to resume life's other activities. In many Orthodox churches this sense of joining the worship of the heavenly host is accentuated by the icons of saints, apostles and angels painted on the walls and ceilings of the church. It is a physical reminder of the spiritual reality.

Body

Dress

The basic elements of, say, the eucharist in the Orthodox

Eucharist

churches are essentially the same as in an Anglican or Roman Catholic rite. The community gathers to songs of worship; there are then scripture readings, usually from an apostolic epistle, followed by a Gospel passage (in Orthodoxy great prominence is given to the reading of the Gospel – the words of Jesus himself are honoured with incense and candles); the Nicene Creed will be used; there will be intercessions for the church and world. The heart of the eucharist is the giving of thanks over bread and wine (introduced usually by 'Lift up your hearts') and a prayer that by the Holy Spirit the elements may be sanctified as the body and blood of Christ. After the receiving of communion (which is usually administered from a spoon, the bread having been placed in the wine) there are further hymns and prayers of thanksgiving before the people are dismissed with God's blessing.

Persecution

These core elements are woven into a drama meant to teach the faithful the essential features of the life and ministry of Jesus. The very division of the building by the curtain or screen symbolizes the juxtaposition of heaven and earth. The whole is a very powerful educational experience, especially in societies where, until recently, literacy levels have usually been low.

Nowadays many Orthodox churches face serious issues about their worship. In many the language is archaic, the years of oppression having made regular 'updating' impossible. Changing to a modern vernacular would create much opposition. Not only is the old form part of the tradition, but it is tied up with the sense of national identity. One practical problem is that most of the laity do not worship using service books, but know their parts in the liturgy by heart. This presents an enormous challenge to textual change.

Churches of the people

One remarkable feature of the Orthodox and Oriental Orthodox churches is the degree of identification between church and people. A number of factors contribute to this. One is simply history. A small people such as the Armenians, for example, with a distinctive language and culture, is strengthened in its sense of identity by having a national church. For most (though not all) Armenians, belonging to the Armenian Orthodox Church is part of what it means to be an Armenian. Most Greeks would feel the same about the Greek Orthodox Church. Part of this is a sense of national gratitude to the church for preserving the identity of the people in times of oppression. Thus, for example, prior to the recent introduction of the euro as the unit of currency in Greece, the 200 drachma note depicted The Secret School. This was a famous picture of an elderly Orthodox priest, during the years of Turkish occupation, teaching the Christian faith to some Greek children under the watchful gaze of some armed Greek adults. Importantly, what was also being taught was the Greek alphabet and language, and a sense of national identity. The Ottoman empire actually strengthened this sense of identity by dividing its Christian subject peoples into ethnic groups or *millets*, each headed by the senior ecclesiastical figure, usually the patriarch. Within their own communities such senior figures – ethnarchs – had the difficult task of trying both to improve the lot of their people and to please their Muslim masters. Many failed and were deposed or killed.

Christianity in Europe

In the twentieth century a similar sense of identification of church and people occurred in the Soviet bloc. In many Eastern European countries the church was the only organization with a different world-view from the Communist Party that was allowed to exist.

It is important for Westerners to understand the context of this. The world wars of the twentieth century lasted each about four or five years. Russia was under an atheistic Communist regime for approximately 70 years. The Turkish occupation of what is now Greece lasted four or five centuries. Arab domination of, for example, Egypt, has lasted nearly one and a half millennia. The experience of most Orthodox churches is vastly different from that of the West.

One consequence of this has been the link between Orthodox Christians and movements for independence. The revolt against the Turks in 1821 was precipitated by the raising of the flag of independence by the Bishop of Kalavryta in the Peloponnese. Christians were involved in the Ba'ath party's struggle for an independent Iraq. More recently a number of Russian Orthodox priests and laity – for example, Alexander Solzhenitsyn – protested against human rights violations in the Soviet Union.

This identification has resulted in some apparent contradictions. Orthodox churches have simultaneously claimed the allegiance of both leading intellectuals and of the mass of poorly educated people. Most Orthodox churches have been 'peasant' churches in a way which has not been true in Western Europe since the sixteenth century. Until recently there was no educational or class gulf between the clergy and the people they served. In recent years a gulf has appeared in some places, but it can sometimes be attributed to the fact that the clergy have been left behind as the population rapidly embraces mass education, which is a very different phenomenon from the Western experience of a clerical élite distanced by their education and professional status. Arguably, it is this very 'peasant' indigenization of the Orthodox churches which has helped them survive long years of persecution. A more 'cerebral' or middle-class church might not have fared as well.

In the changed circumstances of the late twentieth and early twenty-first centuries this strong ethnic identity of the Orthodox churches has created difficulties. In Russia, for example, there have been instances of the Orthodox Church being identified with a strong right-wing nationalism, sometimes at the expense of other Christian communities. There have been accusations of antisemitism in some quarters. In countries such as Britain or North America, where the Orthodox were originally communities of exiles, there is the problem of overlapping jurisdictions. For how many generations should, for example, the Serbs, Russians and Greeks maintain separate jurisdictions, rather than unite under a single episcopate? The situation is complicated by the natural desire to retain links with the ancestral homeland and one's ethnic identity. Sometimes, too, the mother church is financially dependent on members in the more prosperous West and so is unwilling to sever the link. All Orthodox admit that the situation is an anomaly – the Orthodox in any given place should be under a single bishop. There have been official condemnations of 'phyletism'. Some attempts have been made to address the situation: for example, the formation of the Orthodox Church of America (OCA) in 1970 from a number of jurisdictions, but the OCA has not been widely recognized, and long-term solutions are not yet in sight.

The churches

I shall not attempt a church-by-church description. Instead, here are brief notes on the three groups of churches, beginning with the smallest, followed by some general comments on the Chalcedonian family of churches.

1. The Church of the East (Assyrian Church)

The members of this church are sometimes described as 'East Syrians', as their liturgical language is the eastern form of Syriac (as opposed to the West Syriac used by the Syrian Orthodox). As we saw above, the centre of gravity of the church lay to the east of the Roman empire. The church's theological tradition has tended to emphasize the humanity of Christ (which was seen as being ignored by formulations which emphasized his divinity).

The lack of icons, together with the emphasis on the humanity of Jesus, led to the church being described as the 'Protestants of the East' by Western Protestants who came into contact with from the eighteenth century onwards. From the 1840s the Archbishop of Canterbury sponsored a mission of help to the beleaguered church in the Ottoman empire; it has sometimes been known as the Assyrian Church.

Already dwindling under Islamic rule, the Church of the East endured both internal schism and the loss of many of its members to Roman jurisdiction from the sixteenth century onwards. The community suffered further in the twentieth century. It was dislocated by the Great War and 'abandoned' (as they see it) in Iraq by the British after the Second World War. Rivalry over the office of patriarch has contributed to further fragmentation. More than half the present membership lives outside the Middle East, and in particular in the United States. In recent years there has been some tentative dialogue with the Oriental Orthodox churches.

Christianity in Europe

2. The Oriental Orthodox

Syrian Orthodox. This church can lay some claim to be the oldest expression of Christianity, having an unbroken Semitic tradition in the Middle East. Worship is in Syriac. Links with Jerusalem are traditionally strong. The form of the eucharist most commonly used is not only named after James the brother of Jesus who is credited with being the first bishop of Jerusalem; in addition parts of the very text can be shown to have been in use in Jerusalem in the fourth century CE.

p. 852

The Syrian communities did not generally accept the Chalcedonian Definition and for a century or so suffered some persecution from the Byzantine authorities. In 543 CE a monk named Jacob Baradeus was secretly consecrated by Patriarch Theodosios of Alexandria, a leading figure in the opposition to Chalcedon. For the rest of his life Jacob travelled extensively in the Middle East, from Egypt to Iran, consecrating bishops, ordaining priests and deacons, and helping the communities regroup as a single identifiable unit – the Syrian Orthodox Church. Jacob's reversal of this low point in the church's fortunes has led to the church often being called 'Jacobite'.

In the centuries following the Arab invasions Syrian Orthodox scholars were extremely influential. The frequently-cited absorption of Greek science by the Arabs was often through the medium of Syriac. Scholarship flourished in centres such as Antioch, Nisibis and Edessa. Gregory Bar Hebraeus (1226–86) is perhaps the best-known scholar in this tradition. Over the centuries the language has been largely replaced by Arabic and Turkish, though there are some Syriac-speaking villages in south-east Turkey/north-west Iraq.

Roman empire

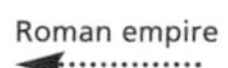

The church has suffered catastrophically in the upheavals of the nineteenth and twentieth centuries. There has been a long history of oppression by the Kurds, and the 'Pan-Turkist' policies of modern Turkey (following the collapse of the Ottoman Empire) have resulted in mass emigration from the traditional strongly Christian area of Tur Abdin, in the south-east of that country. Some villages that were predominantly Christian until the second half of the twentieth century now have no Christian inhabitants. The situation is slightly better in Syria, Iraq and Lebanon.

The patriarch is traditionally given the name Ignatius, after the famous bishop of that city at the end of the first century CE. While the patriarchal seat is nominally

Antioch, for centuries the patriarchs have lived elsewhere. From the thirteenth century their residence was at Deir Zafaran (the Saffron Monastery) near Mardin, but has been in Damascus since 1933.

Coptic Christianity

Indian Orthodox. The vast majority of Christians of Syrian ecclesiastical heritage live not in the Middle East but in South India. The Indian Church traditionally dates its own origins from a visit by the apostle Thomas in the year 52 CE. While there is no absolute proof that the visit took place, the known existence of Roman and Jewish trading posts in India in the first century CE makes such a visit a historical possibility.

Certainly, from the late second century onwards there is evidence of a Christian church in India, and by the time the Portuguese arrived in the late fifteenth century they found a numerous and well-established community in what is now the modern Indian state of Kerala in the south-west of the country. Although there are records of some migration of families from the Middle East, the community is totally Indian in appearance and culture. Until the nineteenth century the liturgical language was exclusively Syriac, and some Syriac remains in use today alongside the vernacular Malayalam.

Monasticism

The community was originally part of the Church of the East, but was forcibly united to Rome at the Synod of Diamper in 1599. In 1655 about one third of the community broke free from Rome and welcomed Syrian bishops again, this time from the Syrian Orthodox Church. The eighteenth and nineteenth centuries brought further disruptions, resulting in fragmentations that have lasted until the present day. There are five churches of Syrian Orthodox tradition. The Syro-Malankara are in communion with Rome. The Mar Thoma Church, while Oriental Orthodox in liturgy and tradition, has undergone a degree of reformation under the influence of Anglican missionaries in the nineteenth century. It is in full communion with the provinces of the Anglican Communion. Of the remaining three churches, by far the largest are the Orthodox Syrian Church (sometimes called the Indian Orthodox) and the Syrian Orthodox (sometimes called Jacobites). These are divided on the issue of their relationship with the patriarch in Damascus. The Jacobites accept him as their spiritual head, while the Indian Orthodox see themselves as an autonomous church. Both are headed by a catholicos (patriarch) in India, and are organized into a number of dioceses, some of which are made up of communities outside India.

Ethiopian Christianity

The third Oriental Orthodox Church in India is the Malabar Independent Syrian Church, which came into existence as a result of divisions in the late eighteenth century. A small, one-diocese jurisdiction, it is of historical significance, having at times consecrated bishops for both the Orthodox and Mar Thoma Churches when their episcopal successions have failed.

Coptic Church. The largest in the Middle East, it forms an estimated 10 per cent of the population of Egypt. (The name 'Coptic' is simply a derivation of 'Egyptian'.)

Its origins are very ancient, traditionally going back to the evangelist Mark. From early times the patriarchal see was Alexandria, and the patriarch had the title 'pope' (meaning 'father'; the title is not exclusive to the Bishop of Rome). After the Council of Chalcedon, the Greek-speaking section of the church tended to accept the decrees and remain in the same 'family' as Constantinople, while the Coptic-speaking majority gradually came to have an independent existence.

Monasticism has been extremely important in the history of the Coptic Church, with a number of important centres in the desert. In recent decades there has been a significant revival, with many educated young men embracing the monastic life. (Monks are distinguishable by their black cowls embroidered with white crosses.) Bishops are chosen from the ranks of the monks, as is the pope.

Ethiopian Orthodox Church. The first Ethiopian converted to Christianity was of course the eunuch whose story is told in chapter 8 of the Acts of the Apostles in the New Testament. The major Christianization of Ethiopia did not really begin until the ministry of Frumentius in the fourth century. Frumentius was a Syrian, but Ethiopia's main links were soon established with its northern neighbour, the Coptic Church. Until 1957 the Patriarch of the Ethiopian Church was consecrated by the Copts – a relationship with some similarities to that between the Syrian Orthodox and Indian churches. Since 1957, however, the Ethiopian Church has consecrated its own bishops.

Although its general practice follows that of Egypt, the Ethiopian Church is thoroughly indigenized in its African context. For many centuries it was closely connected with the ruling dynasty and suffered a period of persecution following the overthrow of the Emperor Haile Selassie (1892–1975) and the establishment of a Marxist regime. It has now recovered.

Following the break-away of the northern section of Ethiopia to form the independent state of Eritrea, the church there has been organized as the Eritrean Orthodox Church, for which the Coptic pope has consecrated bishops. It remains to be seen whether this will eventually become a sixth Oriental Orthodox church.

Armenian Orthodox Church. Armenians trace their origins back to the ministry of Gregory the Illuminator (*c.* 240–332), who brought the gospel, and under whose ministry King Tiridates accepted Christianity in 301 – a decade before the conversion of the Roman emperor Constantine. As with other countries since, the Armenian alphabet was created substantially so that the scriptures and liturgy might be translated into it.

The spiritual centre of the church is at Etchmiadzin in the recently independent state of Armenia. The church is much involved in the attempt at national reconstruction, following the hardships of the Soviet era.

Since then the identification between Armenians and their church has been strong, even despite massive relocations of people over the centuries. In the Middle Ages there was a substantial Armenian centre in Cilicia (now south-eastern Turkey) which brought the Armenians into contact with Western Christians in the context of the Crusades. As a result there are some visible 'borrowings' from the West, of which the mitre is perhaps the most visible. Both the Cilician and Etchmiadzin sections of the church are headed by a catholicos. During the years when Armenia was a Soviet republic, relations between them were strained, but have improved considerably since.

The Armenians have suffered greatly at the hands of the Turks, who seem for the last century or more to have pursued a policy that might be described as 'ethnic cleansing'. The forced removal and extermination of at least 1.5 million Armenians – with hardly a protest from the West – provided Hitler with a precedent for dealing with the Jews. There are reports that Armenian buildings in eastern Turkey have been destroyed in an attempt to remove any trace of their presence there.

3. The Chalcedonian Orthodox

Patriarchate of Constantinople. The actual Christian presence in Constantinople – modern Istanbul – is now extremely small. The city, however, still remains the seat of the Patriarch, whose office has survived the rise and fall of Byzantine emperors and Ottoman sultans. Located in the Phanar district, it is in some respects the equivalent of the Vatican, though in circumstances that could hardly be more different. Turkish nationalism and the continuation of bad relations between Greece and Turkey (particularly over Cyprus) make life very precarious for this ancient Greek community. Most of its members are now in exile, including, for example, the Greek-speaking jurisdictions in the UK and Australia. In Orthodox thinking, the Patriarch of Constantinople is the Ecumenical Patriarch – accorded a primacy of honour as the first among equals until the Bishop of Rome should return from his errors. The present Patriarch, Bartholomew I, is a well-educated and widely-respected individual.

Patriarchate of Alexandria. Descended from the predominantly Greek-speaking population of Egypt who separated from the Copts in the years following the Council of Chalcedon, its membership in Egypt itself has declined dramatically during the twentieth century. Its canonical jurisdiction includes the whole of Africa, and hence embraces both South African businessmen of Greek descent, and black Africans converted in Kenya and other countries as a result of primary Christian witness. There is also a bishop in Ethiopia.

Patriarchate of Antioch. Unlike the other ancient patriarchates, which are predominantly Greek in leadership, Antioch has had an Arab patriarch since 1899. This identification with the indigenous population has contributed to its success. It is the largest Christian community in Syria and has a sizeable presence in Lebanon.

There is also an important community abroad, helping to support the church in the Middle East. The Patriarchate of Antioch has shown itself capable of taking bold initiatives, such as recently receiving a group of former Anglican clergy, together with congregations, and permitting them to use a Western-derived liturgy.

Patriarchate of Jerusalem. Perhaps surprisingly, Jerusalem, though an important Christian pilgrimage centre from the fourth century CE, was only a suffragan (subordinate) see of Caesarea until the Council of Chalcedon elevated it to the status of a patriarchate on account of its historical significance. The Chalcedonian Patriarchate has remained very Greek in its leadership, though the 'lower' clergy are mainly Arab. The unsettled situation in Palestine/Israel has led to a serious loss of members through emigration.

These ancient patriarchates have a special place of honour in the Orthodox family of churches. Alongside them are a number of other churches and missions, which are self-governing to varying degrees. The list includes the churches of Russia, Romania, Greece, Serbia, Bulgaria, Georgia, Cyprus, Poland, Albania, Finland and Japan. Some of these are fully independent – 'autocephalous'; others still have a degree of dependence on another jurisdiction and are termed 'autonomous'. The situation is a fluid one, adapting to changing circumstances. Thus, for example, the collapse of the Soviet Union gave rise to an acrimonious dispute about the status of the Orthodox Church of Estonia, which in Soviet days had been under the jurisdiction of the Patriarchate of Moscow. Inevitably, the historical traumas have produced divisions. Following the Russian Revolution in 1917 a number of 'Russian Orthodox' churches have come into existence, divided on such issues as loyalty to the Patriarchate of Moscow, which exiles tended to see as a 'puppet' hierarchy, controlled by the atheistic state. Not all of these divisions have been healed. Though ancient, the Orthodox Church is very much engaged with modern realities.

Each of these Orthodox churches has its own history, saints and heroes. Each also worships in its own language. The Orthodox Church is thus a federation of local – though not necessarily national – churches. Their liturgical traditions are very similar, and they are in full doctrinal agreement with each other. Westerners, used to the all-pervading influence of the Vatican in the Roman Catholic Church, are often amazed how de-centralized the Orthodox Church is. The Ecumenical Patriarch of Constantinople has a primacy of honour and exercises a mediating role, but has no authority to interfere in the internal affairs of another Orthodox Church. In recent decades a common approach to issues has been sought via meetings of representatives of the different Orthodox churches. The Chalcedonian family usually form a team in international dialogues (as, for example, with the Anglican Communion or the Roman Catholic Church) with members drawn from most of the autocephalous or autonomous churches.

A church of contradictions

Despite increased contact, the Orthodox and Oriental Orthodox churches, together with the Church of the East, remain mysterious to most Westerners. This is in part because they display a mass of apparent contradictions. Here are churches of the Middle East with bishops in London, New York and Sydney. Here is a family of peasant churches which has produced some of the greatest Christian thinkers and theologians. Here are churches which can worship in dead languages yet address issues such as global warming. Here are churches which have at various times enjoyed enormous privilege and power and yet in the twentieth century have produced more martyrs than any other. In the case of the Chalcedonian Orthodox, here is a church with no centralized structure, yet a very strong sense of common identity which transcends ethnic, political and linguistic barriers.

In an international context where there is increasing talk of 'a clash of cultures', the Orthodox, expressing Christianity in non-Western forms, may yet have a significant contribution to make.

JOHN FENWICK

Aziz Atiyah, *A History of Eastern Christianity*, London: Methuen 1968; John Binns, *An Introduction to the Christian Orthodox Churches*, Cambridge: CUP 2002; J. F. Coakley, *The Church of the East and the Church of England*, Oxford: Clarendon Press 1992; Timothy Ware, *The Orthodox Church*, Harmondsworth: Penguin Books (1963) ^{2}1993

http://www.cnewa.org/ecc-introduction.htm for statistics

OTHER FAITHS

Buddhism, Chinese religions, Hinduism, Interfaith dialogue, Interfaith worship, Islam, Japanese religions, Judaism, New Age, Paganism, Traditional religions, Zoroastrianism

Religions: bearers of life or death?

Every time we open a newspaper, we are reminded that we live in a world in which we can no longer afford not to know our neighbours. We read not only of violence in faraway places, but also of the impact of that hostility upon our own societies. European and North American citizens who travel abroad are sometimes injured or killed, caught in the crossfire between competing groups. Aggression comes even closer to home. People in mainland Britain long ago became used to being the targets of indiscriminate bombings by factions who support a united Ireland. The tragic and shocking events of 11 September 2001 made North Americans aware that they are not isolated from the death and destruction that stalks much of the rest of the world.

As we look closer at places where there is great bloodshed, we note that there is often an inter- or even intra-religious component to the enmity between the conflicting groups. For example: the conflict in Ireland has something to do with Protestantism and Roman Catholicism; the Middle East crisis sets Jews and Muslims against each other; the simmering cauldron of Sri Lanka involves Buddhists and Hindus. We may suspect that religion is never the only issue. Indeed, social and economic factors are usually far more deeply responsible for the violence.

Sometimes, though, the rhetoric of religion is explicitly used to justify terror and slaughter. We are shocked by the fact that young Muslim men and women detonate bombs strapped to themselves, intending to create murder and mayhem among citizens of Israel, particularly when we are told that they believe they are martyrs in a good cause and will go straight to paradise. Although most people know about violence in the name of Islam, there are members of other religions who use their faith to justify aggression and cruelty and claim that it rewards those who choose the path of belligerence. Religious fundamentalism is on the rise, and some of its upholders will do anything to promote their own point of view. We live in a world of holy terror.

Fundamentalism

But the contribution of religion to violence is not the whole of the story. One of the great religious figures of the twentieth century was M. K. Gandhi, the *mahatma* or 'great soul' of modern Hinduism. The form of Hinduism where he grew up in west India owed much to the non-violence of the Jain religion. He was also deeply influenced by Christianity: by the pacifism of the Russian novelist, Leo Tolstoy, with whom he briefly corresponded; by his Quaker friends; and by the teaching of Jesus in the Sermon on the Mount. Gandhi's teaching of non-violent *satyagraha*, or truth-force, drew from these roots and deeply appealed to later Christians. Two have been very influential. The first, Dr Martin Luther King, Jr, a Baptist minister, was the visionary of the American civil rights movement of the 1960s. The second, Nelson Mandela, is a Methodist layman, whose commitment to peace and reconciliation helped to bring about the end of apartheid in South Africa in the 1990s in a remarkably non-violent way. It is an outstanding sign of hope in the world in which we now live that a Hindu, himself influenced by Christianity and Jainism, should have become an exemplary figure for two Protestant Christians. All three transformed the countries in which they lived.

Quakers
Jesus p. 385

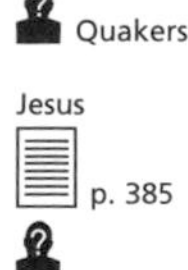

So, as we read the newspaper, we are brought into contact with a world of many religions, which bring about dreadful pain and cruelty but also produce good people and noble actions. When we have closed our newspaper, can we forget about them?

The changing religious landscape

Let us imagine one man who has just put aside his newspaper. His name is Richard. He goes into his garden to do some weeding, and over the fence he sees and greets his neighbour, Pritha Kaur. When she arrived last year, Richard went round to welcome her and her husband. He discovered that they were Sikhs. Pritha's husband, Ajit Singh, told him that Sikhs originated in the Punjab, nowadays split between India and Pakistan, but that many had emigrated to the UK, the USA, Canada and many other countries. From his new friends, Richard learned many things about their religion. For example, all Sikh men are designated Singh, meaning lion, and all women are named Kaur, meaning princess. He was told why Sikh men grow long hair, have a special steel bracelet on their wrist, carry a comb and a *kirpan* (a small sword), and wear a special pair of under-shorts. Richard and his family go regularly to a local church, so he was intrigued by how different his friends' religion was from his own.

At work, Richard told his friend Sam about his Sikh neighbours, and how fascinatingly different their religion was from his. Sam laughed and asked if Richard knew he was Jewish. Sam could see by the bewildered look on Richard's face that he did not. He teased Richard by saying, 'Because I'm white, you never even thought I'd be a member of another religion, did you? But what about Ali, who goes to the gym with us? He's white, too; obviously a convert to Islam. And think of Dalip, the Indian man who's often at the bar where we lunch. He's Christian and gets very cross with people who patronizingly assume he must be a Hindu because of his name and colour. In fact, he goes to your church, doesn't he?' Richard had to admit the truth of Sam's comments. 'OK,' he said, 'But I thought Jews ate special food. Yet you eat the same as I do.' Sam came back at him: 'You're right, to a point. Many Jews eat kosher meat, from animals slaughtered in a particular way and in the name of God. But not all of us do. I belong to a more liberal group. Still, I don't eat pork, and I don't mix milk and meat; but I don't insist on a kosher kitchen. I respect Jews who do, but I think it's just inappropriate in the modern world to cut ourselves off from sharing food with our friends in a normal way. Religions have got to update themselves, haven't they?'

Richard had become aware of a world that seemed quite different from that of his boyhood. Although he liked Pritha, Ajit and Sam, and had nothing against Ali and Dalip, whom he hardly knew, he was in two minds about whether he had the resources to cope with the changes he detected around him. It was one thing to enjoy the company of friends of other faiths. It was exciting and even exotic to taste new foods, walk past the local Asian store and take in its different smells and products, learn about others' customs. His uneasiness arose from his concerns about his two children, and the new religious opportunities open to them.

Matt was twenty years old. 'I'm more spiritual than religious,' he told his father. And to prove his point he was often seen in the new shop that had a jolly-looking sun and stars hanging outside. Inside it sold candles; lots of 'spiritual' artefacts; and books about witchcraft, recalling past lives, astrology and the occult. It was not at all like Richard's church's bookshop. In fact, when he had gone in to check up on it, the book he opened had told him that Jesus was a dispensable figure from the past, not part of the New Age. Although he hoped his son was going through a 'phase', he was uneasily aware that lots of the customers were at least his own age. He wondered what they found there that was lacking for them in Christian faith. He knew that Matt's friend Andrew had joined a new religious movement that venerated a still-living human being, and hardly ever saw his

New Age movement

family. Richard had a hunch that the New Age movement and the new religious movements were not the same thing, but he wasn't sure of the differences between them, and dreaded Matt getting too involved with any part of them.

New religious movements

An invitation Richard had been given to Pritha's niece's wedding stirred up his anxieties about his daughter. Although he was looking forward to going, he was aware that Susan, now eighteen years old, had come home talking endlessly about Aftar. He was, she said, wonderfully handsome. Richard expected that he was being softened up for an announcement that they had been dating for some time. What if they married? Would she have to become a Muslim, she asked, for that was Aftar's religion? He had heard stories that Muslim men treated their wives badly. Would Aftar be able to have other wives as well, and would he insist that they wear a veil? Richard had learned, from his friendship with his neighbours, not to believe everything that people said about members of other religions. But Susan was his only daughter, the apple of his eye. He was a good Christian, and could not cope easily with the thought that she would convert to Islam. 'I'd sooner see her as nothing at all,' he said to himself; and then felt a little ashamed of himself and his prejudices, and thought that maybe he was making a great big fuss about something that was unlikely to happen.

Richard was also puzzled by another issue. He knew from Pritha and Ajit that their Sikh religion had evolved out of Hinduism and Islam, and from Sam that Christianity had developed from Judaism. The occasional sermon he had heard about how Christians should regard other religions had lumped them all together. The preacher had said that Jesus was the answer for all people. But Richard now knew that different religions teach a wide range of beliefs and practices. Could there be one Christian response to all the religions? Surely Christian faith needed to respond differently to Jews and Hindus, to Sikhs and Muslims. He had picked up that Buddhism does not believe in a Creator God, so there were theological differences between Christianity and Buddhism which were not the same as those between his religion and Islam, which believes firmly in one Creator God, and regards the Trinity as a scandalous sell-out to polytheism, a belief in many gods. Moreover, there had been much talk in the news about 'Islamophobia', the Christian fear of Islam and Muslims that was far more pronounced than Christian uneasiness with most other religions. So it looks as though different histories as well as different beliefs about 'God' mean that relations vary between Christianity and the different world religions.

Trinity

God

Not so far away from Richard, Aftar's father Mohammed was also troubled about his daughter, Fatima. She was sixteen years old and had told him she intended to be a doctor. But there was no medical school nearby, so she would have to live away from home in a student hostel. Would he let her? He honestly didn't know. He had come from Pakistan to make a better life for his family, but had not counted on his children becoming so influenced by another culture. He had expected to choose their spouses, but he doubted if they or his wife would let him. Family honour was important to Mohammed, and he was genuinely troubled about what his brothers and sisters in South Asia would think. He knew that his wife Nasseem would always put their children's wants first, and gently challenge his old-fashioned views. 'We're in another country now, and we have to adapt our Islam to it,' she would say. 'We can't worry about what your family in the ancestral village think. How do they know the first thing about the changes we've had to face?'

If Susan and Aftar were to date and introduce their families to each other, Richard and Mohammed might be surprised to learn that both of them were troubled by all the new possibilities that previous generations of their families had hardly faced.

In the West, but not only there, there is a new religious landscape that would astonish our recent ancestors if they could return to see it. The rapid globalization of the world, its inter-connectedness

Globalization

by such phenomena as travel and the worldwide web, means that people are brought closer together than ever before. One aspect of our time is the many migrations of religious communities to Western Europe and North America. Muslims, Hindus, Sikhs and others now live and work there. Their children settle and most of them will stay, far away from the land of their origin. One major question that first-generation immigrants such as Mohammed face is whether their religion has the wherewithal to sustain them and flourish in a new environment.

For people like Richard, the question is rather different. It would be along the lines of whether his Christian religion has the resources to engage with people of other faiths in ordinary day-to-day living, being true to itself and yet without bearing false witness against others. Put this another way: does traditional Christian teaching have anything meaningful to offer for our inter-religious world?

Traditional Christian attitudes

Diversity

There has long been a variety of expressions of Christian faith, which have often been mutually antagonistic. In North America and Western Europe, Christians could nowadays be said to fall mostly under one of five headings: Roman Catholic; mainstream Protestant; evangelicals; charismatics; and liberals. (Of course, there are also Anglicans, Eastern Orthodox Christians and some other groups, but these five cover most Christians in these regions, though there is great diversity within each group.) How would members of each group tend to deal with religious pluralism?

Revelation
Holy Spirit

Although some liberals would dissent from this, the vast majority of Christians have believed and still believe that Christian faith is God's final revelation, brought by Jesus Christ and confirmed by the gift of the Holy Spirit. But there is a great deal of debate and difference about how this is so, and whether there is any hope at all for non-Christians.

Council
Church
Roman Catholic Church

Roman Catholics inherit a tradition that is not quite so straightforward as many believe it to be. Until the reforms of the Second Vatican Council (1962–5), the standard teaching was 'Outside the church there is no salvation,' which gave no value at all to other religions. By church was meant the Roman Catholic Church, so even Protestants and other forms of Christians could not hope to be saved unless they were in communion with the Pope as the successor of Peter, to whom Jesus gave the keys of the kingdom of heaven (Matthew 16.19). The council originally intended to address the specific issue of the church's relations with Jews, in the wake of the Holocaust of European Jews under Hitler, when six million perished. Hitler and his propaganda machine used Christian teaching about Jews to justify the slaughter. Something needed to be said by the church to counter this; its leader during the first part of the council, Pope John XXIII, had many Jewish friends and was keen to improve relations with them. However, during discussions, bishops in Asia and elsewhere made it clear that the church needed to speak not only to Jews, but also to Muslims, Hindus, Buddhists and other people of different faiths. Eventually the church produced an epoch-making document, *Nostra aetate*, which spoke warmly and with esteem of Jewish, Muslim and other forms of faith. Another document repaired relationships with non-Roman Catholic Christians, referring to them as 'separated brethren'.

p. 291

Tradition

The title *Nostra aetate* is significant. It means 'In our age …', and is the document's opening words. The Roman Catholic Church has always taken church tradition very seriously indeed, but had come to recognize that parts of that tradition were badly flawed and needed an *aggiornamento*, 'updating'. Not surprisingly, some Catholics think that the reinterpretation did not go far enough, whereas others feel that it went dangerously beyond the charitable and threatened the church's essential identity as the bearer of salvation. The reforms have proved to be work in progress, and more recent statements about the faiths of others have sometimes been more generous, though occasionally not. This is hardly unexpected: it is not easy to square the circle of 2000 years of traditional teaching with the new world of knowledge and diasporas in which we now live.

Ordinary Catholics will not know the details of these changes. They will, however, sense that they are heirs to two contradictory attitudes: the long-dominant one rejected other truth-claims and wanted only obedience to Rome, whereas the newer one seems to assume that Rome has the fullness of truth, but notes and affirms genuineness of faith and action elsewhere. Not surprisingly, many Catholics are people of goodwill towards others but of a quiet certainty that their church has more truth.

Mainstream Protestants are as certain as Roman Catholics of the truth of their position, though for different reasons. Whereas Catholics look to tradition and the teaching of the Pope and bishops for guidance, Protestants gaze back at the sixteenth-century Reformation for principles to guide them. They see it not only in a vernacular Bible, but in the ideas of inspirational figures such as Martin Luther. Luther's teaching that human beings are justified by faith in Jesus Christ alone and not by good works, based on a reading of the apostle Paul's letters, is core doctrine for many Protestants, not just Lutherans. Like Catholics, Protestants do not always or even often know the details of their history, but they are confident that faith in Christ is of paramount importance and that such a stance is their inimitable take on reality. Like Catholics, many mainstream Protestants may concede that members of other religions have some light, but others do not, thinking that Jews, Muslims and the rest are in darkness.

Protestantism
Papacy
Reformation
Martin Luther
Justification
Paul
Lutheranism

Evangelicals place great faith in the Bible as the means to know God's will for them and others. Some are literalists, and are persuaded that 'the faith [was] "once for all" delivered to the saints' (Jude 3). They deduce from this and other passages that the Bible condemns non-Christians to hell. Others have a more nuanced understanding of biblical texts, but often draw a distinction that is still damning for people of other faiths. On this view, non-Christians have some knowledge of God's will and may do their best to serve God, but the information they have is not saving, because they do not have a personal relationship with the Saviour Christ. Generous evangelicals may put the ball in God's court and say that God can save them if he wishes, but that Christians cannot know this. What they can know is that Jesus saves, so it is best for themselves and for others to come to terms with this (for them) fact.

Evangelicals
Bible

Charismatic Pentecostal Christians are the great Christian success story of the contemporary world. They are found in all parts of the world, especially the Americas and sub-Saharan Africa. Charismatic Christians emphasize the gift of the spirit. Many speak in tongues, and stress the need for lives of holiness: for these are gifts of the Spirit, and it is the life of the Holy Spirit that charismatics affirm in their own lives. Because the Spirit is the Spirit of Jesus, many such Christians will dismiss other faiths as misguided, even the works of the devil. Still, in Africa and among some Christian charismatics elsewhere, there has been considerable and imaginative borrowing from traditional faiths, whose emphasis upon healing and the importance of the spirits of ancestors have been accepted and 'baptized' into Christian faith.

Pentecostalism

Liberal Christians have been greatly influenced by many of the social revolutions of our day. They can be heard speaking up for women's rights and the environment, and against racism and the selfishness of big business. They feel that modern knowledge, particularly drawn from the natural and social sciences, makes many of the assumptions of the Bible and past Christians quite outdated. So they look for themes from Christianity that seem ever-fresh, love and justice being foremost among them. It seems evident to liberal Christians that God would not be either loving or just if God condemned other people to eternal death simply because they belonged, often by an accident of birth, to the wrong religion. Many have a gut feeling that Jesus was the perfect human being and so this makes his religion of Christianity the one they are glad to belong to. But, for them, he is not the saviour of those who trust in him, but a figure of hope and a symbol of God's compassion. There have been other such icons, like Moses, Krishna, the Buddha and Muhammad.

Are traditional Christian attitudes useful enough for a changing religious landscape? The attitudes just described are widely held among Christians in today's society. Discussion often centres upon which of them is true or more likely to be true than others. But that draws attention away from the really important question: are they relevant to our rapidly changing world? Of course they are compelling visions of reality; if they were not, they would not have so many followers. So we must not lightly set them aside. But maybe the traditional teachings are, of themselves, an inadequate compass to chart the new map of religious pluralism.

Representatives of all five positions assume that they are right: either completely accurate in their interpretation of and relationship to God, to the exclusion of all other interpretations, or at least more right than any other. Most of these positions are not argued for, but assumed and asserted. This is as true of the liberal position as of any of the others: the wrath of 'liberal fundamentalism' is sometimes amazing to behold, as many Muslims discovered when the Ayatollah Khomeini laid a *fatwa* (an Islamic legal 'opinion') upon Salman Rushdie in 1989, condemning him to death. Outraged appeals by liberals to freedom of speech and worship, as though these were revealed truths rather than human inventions, amazed and frightened many Muslims. They pointed up the fact that liberal Christians, along with other liberal-minded people, are often far more disposed to accept the inherent reality of secular values than religious truths revealed by God in scripture or church teachings.

We can most helpfully consider another range of criticisms of the traditional views by noting that Christians are deeply committed to answering the question, 'What sort of God is God?' Does God care for human beings, and for other of God's creations? How far does God's care extend? How can we know that God cares? In fact, much Christian language about other faiths seems in effect to deny God's love in any meaningful way. Although this could be illustrated from all five positions we have looked at, let us look at one of them through the beliefs and actions of Eric.

Eric is a Christian minister who works in an inner-city area where there are many Hindus. He chose to go there in particular, rather than take a better-paid position in the suburbs, because his vision of God's love fired him with the zeal to present the good news of Jesus to people who had not accepted it by joining a Christian church. He is an evangelical: not a biblical literalist, but he takes the teaching of the Bible very seriously indeed, and is committed to justice and peace issues. His local shop, which sells groceries, newspapers and just about anything, is owned by Subhash and his wife Rama. Eric has worked with them in a local political party to improve housing in the area. Another local clergyman, Kevin, also goes to the shop regularly and is good friends with the owners. One day Rama, somewhere between amusement, indignation and irritation, said to Kevin: 'Do you mind if I have a moan? It's about Eric. He's a good man. He's been really helpful to our community, working with us to get things done locally. Of course, he feels the need to tell us all about Jesus, and encourage us to go to his church. Fair enough! But ...'

What Kevin picked up from Rama was that Eric never listened to her and Subhash. He was so busy talking and telling that he never heard that Rama's mother's best friend was a Baptist preacher, so she knew lots about Jesus and would have converted long ago to Christianity if she had wanted to. 'I respect Jesus,' said Rama, 'but you have your church and I have my mandir.' Even more irksome to Rama was Eric's statement to her, just before he left the shop and Kevin walked in. He had said: 'Well, only Jesus can save, Rama. None of your gods can do that. You should become a Christian. If not, well, only God knows what will happen after you die. I'll pray for you.' Rama expostulated to Kevin: 'What does he know about my gods and what they can do? Has he ever taken the trouble to ask me or to find out in some other way? And I'm really angry at his comment that he doesn't know whether God loves me enough to accept me as I am. What sort of love is it that isn't given generously, that comes attached with so many strings? Mostly, he seems to know almost everything about God, almost to have God in his pocket. Yet, when it comes to the really big question, he doesn't know the most important thing of all: how far God's love extends.'

It is likely that in her exasperation Rama was not being entirely fair to Eric. Even so, she had focused on a number of interesting points. Do enough Christians, especially Christian leaders who formulate policy, listen to people of other faiths before they make statements about different religions? Why is it that so many Christians come across as condescending, even when they are trying to do God's work and help others? How odd it is that Christians who seem to know a great deal about God (too much perhaps, if we take seriously Paul's reminder in 1 Corinthians 13.12 that now we know only in part), all of a sudden become coy about the really important matter of the wideness of God's mercy!

Rama realized that she had been blowing off steam, giggled, and explained to Kevin: 'Eric's a cool guy. But he needs to lighten up. The thing is: I appreciate his commitment to what he believes. Many of you Christians seem embarrassed by your religion.'

Her comment got Kevin thinking about an incident at an interfaith peace march the previous week. One earnest young man from his church had been explaining to another marcher that all religions are paths up the same mountain, and was surprised when the woman said to him: 'How do you know? Are you a superior person who has been to the top yourself to see that this is so? If not, then give it a break. I'm proud to be a member of my faith. I don't have to trade in bits of what I believe to know that it's right for me to be here, and that God speaks to other sorts of people than me. It's OK to be different. We don't have to pretend agreement in order to respect and even learn from each other.'

Of course, members of other religions who try to 'place' Christians and Christian faith within their own universe of meaning, rather than taking us seriously by wrestling with our self-interpretations, are often as irritating to us as Eric was to Rama. But two wrongs don't make a right, so Christians are not absolved from the responsibility of trying to find a better understanding of other faiths, and of their own religion in relation to them, than mostly exists at present.

Jesus: the Christian gateway to God?

Some Christians seek to witness to their faith by putting stickers on their cars. A popular one reads: 'Thank God for Jesus'. In one sense, this is profoundly misleading. Christians should, rather, thank Jesus for God: it is in the incarnation that they see the fullness of God dwelling bodily and understand what he offers to and wants of them. Although Christians also interpret the world around them by focusing on the fatherhood of God or the work of the divine Spirit, it is Jesus who enables them to do this and who is the primary focus for beginning to intuit answers to the question: 'What

Incarnation

kind of God is God?' Any attempt to marginalize Jesus would seem doomed to either irrelevance or disaster or both.

One major recent reappraisal of Christian relations with people of other faiths deserves a mention because it bravely and cogently urges Christians to accept that all religions are appropriate vehicles of liberation and transformation for those who engage with them. Its most significant proponent is the British philosopher John Hick. He argues that True Reality lies behind the phenomena of all religions. In this world, we see its manifestations in Christianity and all the other religions. Jesus is the way for Christians, but the Torah is for Jews, and Islamic law based upon the Muslim scriptures, the Qur'an, is for Muslims. And so on. In so far as all religions promote justice and liberation, they are true ways of faith for their believers.

This is a different approach from the liberal one because there is an imaginative and hard-headed Christian vision behind it. But Hick is a philosopher rather than a historian and a theologian, and it is history and theology that undermine his case. Can you actually cut through centuries of religious development, dispute and compromise by this kind of philosophical argument? Although some religious sects are suspicious of philosophy as independent human reasoning, many accept its insights so long as they do not conflict with revelation. However, the basis for Hick's vision is the controversial teaching of the philosopher Immanuel Kant, who is certainly not going to be preferred by the vast majority of Christians, Muslims, Jews and others as a more profound religious genius than those found in their scriptures and traditions. Someone such as Richard, whom I introduced earlier, might at first be captivated by it, since it makes the religions of his non-Christian friends so much easier to accept. But as he searches his heart and asks how he really knows God, it seems to suffer a number of drawbacks. In particular, it does not take the Christian meanings of Jesus seriously enough.

Hick's insight has been developed by many contemporary religious scholars, but it (and the endless elaborations of it) now looks well worn and used up. Where, then, are resources going to come from for a relevant Christian restatement of its teaching about other faiths? We need to reassess christology, the study of the meanings of Jesus, so that it speaks faithfully yet relevantly to our world's needs.

Christology

We can put the problem that Jesus presents to advocates of good inter-religious relations in two ways. He has shown God's commitment to the world (not just to a few people) by entering it as one of us, helping us to see his love and compassion, his demand for justice and integrity. In worship, Christians hear and read and speak of him as the only Son of God, a special figure for everyone. How can Christians hold together the message of good news for all people with the belief that such grace was shown to us in one God-human, Jesus of Nazareth? Some Christians have emphasized that salvation comes through Jesus alone, to the point that they condemn those who believe differently to temporal or eternal punishment. Others have so stressed the grace of God in Jesus that they have played down claims made for the messenger as well as the message.

Crusades

The medieval crusades are a sad illustration of the failure of Western Christians to live out the teaching of Jesus. In his name, warriors went forth to liberate the Holy Land from Muslim rule. On the way, they massacred Jews and Eastern Orthodox Christians in Europe and West Asia. The crusaders took Jerusalem by force in 1099. Muslims were slain indiscriminately. When Raymond of Aguilers went to visit the temple area on the morning of 15 July, he recorded that he picked his way through corpses and blood that reached to his knees. The Jews of Jerusalem fled to their chief synagogue. They were held to have aided and abetted Muslims, so the crusaders burned the synagogue to the ground and the Jews were incinerated in it. This went some way towards achieving the ambition of the leader of the First Crusade, Godfrey Bouillon, who had sworn to avenge the blood of Christ and 'leave no single member of the Jewish race alive'. When Salah ud-Din (Saladin) retook Jerusalem for Muslim rule in 1187, few mourned Western Christian rule: not Muslims, not Jews, nor even the Christians of the area.

There are other ways of relating to other religions, even in those times. During the Fifth Crusade in 1219, Francis of Assisi, wanting to tell Muslims his version of the story of Jesus, crossed the battle lines in order to speak with Sultan Malik al-Kamil. The story is told that the Sultan was moved by Francis' words, spared his life and returned him to Italy. Possibly the story has grown in the telling. Nevertheless, Francis' non-violent, loving zeal for Jesus, not only giving others the chance to accept or refuse an offer to become Christians but also to engage in serious debate and to demonstrate their own grace, surely sounds a more authentic Christian note than the words and deeds of Raymond and Godfrey.

Another, more recent, example of someone living out the love of Christ, while being deeply committed to him as saviour of the world, is Mother Teresa of Calcutta (1910–97). She and her Missionaries of Charity have won the profound admiration of Hindus and other Indians for their work among the sick and dying of that city.

Both Francis and Mother Teresa made choices from their religious heritage, choices that have profoundly convinced many other Christians of their holiness. Such Christians have not usually wanted to embrace all their ideals: of poverty and chastity, for example. But these two people do illustrate that it is possible to attempt to hold together a belief in Jesus as the light of the world, and a love and commitment to wide sections of humanity. Not all recent Christian practitioners of dialogue have managed or even attempted that endeavour. Members of other religions such as Buddhism and Islam involved in interfaith dialogue have often been puzzled by and even suspicious of some Christians' willingness to sit loose to their major beliefs, and put it down to the baleful influence of secularism.

The question of truth

All religions have core commitments that for the vast majority of believers are non-negotiable. For example, Muslims will not easily give up their conviction that their scriptures, the Qur'an, are the exact words of God. But it is certainly possible to interpret *how* it is so, and *what* it means for contemporary Muslims. Likewise, since most Christians in the world place Jesus Christ centre-stage in their understanding of who God is and what God wants of God's human children, they should not jettison this conviction too quickly in the name of good inter-religious relations. But *how* they interpret him and his meaning is much more open-ended. The question of truth is important but often either ignored or crassly handled in interfaith relations.

Eric is full of goodwill towards his Hindu neighbours, but is far more hesitant than Richard or Kevin about really listening to them. He believes that religion is about truth, and he is convinced that the Bible tells him that Jesus alone is the way, and the truth and the life (John 14.6). He would be surprised, and maybe pleased, to discover that Kevin also takes religious truth seriously, but in such a way that enables him to listen seriously to what Rana and Subhash say and even, at least to some extent, affirm what they believe.

Kevin knows that the beliefs of the European Enlightenment emphasized the view of truth as factual accuracy, but that another range of meanings is to do with living a good life in God's power. In John's Gospel, Jesus talks of people 'doing the truth' (3.21), living by the light of God's presence. The Word of God, which became a person in Jesus, touches all human beings (John 1.1–18) and

Enlightenment

enables them to live the life of God. This could be interpreted to mean that Jesus is an icon through which we see God's nature and will. When people live lives of justice and peace, faith, hope and love, that accord with what Christians have seen is godly in Jesus, then Kevin rejoices that they are living in truth, not in spite of but by means of the religion that sustains them. For Eric, that would go too far.

Eric and Kevin, like Richard, are, to introduce a Chinese proverb, aware that they live in interesting times. Many Chinese use this proverb to indicate that change is threatening, unstable and to be avoided if at all possible. But we cannot turn back the clock on the late modern world. The changes that have faced Richard and everyone else are greatly different in degree, sometimes even in kind, than were faced by their grandparents.

By and large, religions are conservative institutions, in that they conserve past beliefs and practices that have survived because they have been winnowed by time and are found to have worked. So it is not surprising that Christian thinkers have not quite got hold of new ways of describing attitudes towards other faiths that make sense to someone like Richard of what he has been led to believe since he was a child, and also of his acknowledgement that Pritha and Ajit are goodly and godly people, whose religion is to be respected and in some ways affirmed. In our age of immense changes, religions will not flourish if they are on the one hand too gimmicky and on the other so anachronistic that they do not meet people's needs. They must tread a difficult course between the two.

Even some answers that do negotiate this route seem a little too glib. Richard once heard a sermon in which the preacher talked of Hindus, Jews and other non-Christians as 'anonymous Christians', living authentic lives out of their own traditions of good faith. Richard thought him generous; but condescending, so unhelpful. If the preacher had understood better what he was talking about, he could have explained that it was not intended to be patronizing. Among other things, it was formulated to help Roman Catholic lay people in the middle years of the twentieth century to understand that, if you define the church broadly enough, people of other faiths can be said to be within the ark of salvation. But these days, it sounds belittling and less helpful than it once may have been.

Richard is not looking for easy answers to the dilemmas that face him. In our changing world we are all explorers. But he would like some provisional solutions to problems he faces, and an idea of how he can get these.

Towards a new relationship

Richard would discover that such solutions may often best be reached by working with his friends of other faiths. He should not expect always to agree with them, but to work things out with them. So, for example, if Susan does go out with Aftar and marry him, he will learn that Muslims allow Christian women to keep their faith but expect the children to be brought up as Muslims. Richard (and Susan!) might take Mohammed up on this, and ask if it is just and right in the contemporary world for his religion to insist on this. He would be intrigued to learn that if Mohammed's daughter wanted to marry a Christian man, he would be expected to convert to Islam. But traditional expectations are not always met these days: there are a significant number of such weddings where the man does not convert, and Muslim women (like Christian feminists) in these relationships often work to change what they think is an out-of-date religious law. Some people in such situations are beginning to argue for, or simply instinctively to live out, what has been called hyphenated religious identity. Children of such relationships can be brought up to take part in both religious traditions, and may never choose between them. In China and other parts of East Asia, such practice has been common for generations, where people take part in, for example, Buddhist, Daoist and Confucian rituals and practices.

A few years ago, this mixing and even fusing of religions would have been dismissed as syncretism, a kind of religious mish-mash. Some people still think in this way, but growing numbers see it as a real choice for people willingly entangled in a net of relationships in our multifaith world; for them the religions form a 'salad bowl', in which each maintains a recognizable identity.

Especially in North America, scholars of different religions are beginning to meet together to talk about what their faiths have to say about important issues such ecology and women's issues. So the discipline of comparative theology is coming to birth. Another area of exploration is inter-religious conversation around the theme of the perennial philosophy. This depicts all the religions as having a common source. Their unity lies not in comparable concepts between them, but in their derivation from that source like streams going their several ways down a mountain, never meeting, but originating in the same lake. Nevertheless, common themes bubble up in every religion, and scholars are keen to ask how they are differently addressed in each religion.

p. 1186
Perennial philosophy and Christianity

Richard wryly notes that it is good that scholars are taking such topics seriously and trying to work at solving difficult issues together, but observes that he also has to muddle along and try to solve issues that a religiously-mixed society conjures up for ordinary people like himself.

All the characters mentioned above are convinced that it is an exciting if rather bumpy time to be a religious person. None of them is persuaded by the secular argument that God is entirely a human creation, and that people should have outgrown the need of God by now. They realize that each religion poses different answers to the question: what sort of God is God? And because the answers to that question matter, and often affect matters of birth, marriage and death, and so many other important activities, they each struggle to share their vision of reality, and to understand and appreciate the other. They are engaged in a process of discovery, and realize that things may look very different in a few years time than now they do. The story of Gandhi and his influence upon Martin Luther King, Jr and Nelson Mandela, recounted earlier, tells us that even if we do not change our religion (most people do not), taking others seriously can wonderfully shape our understanding of our own faith and its demands upon us. But Richard, Susan, Eric and Kevin recognize that Jesus must remain central to a Christian understanding of God, as he has always done. Whatever changes dialogue brings about, mainstream Christians affirm, as they have always done, that God has lovingly spoken through Jesus and the indwelling spirit. These are the notes they sound and interpret in order to live in harmony with others in this extraordinarily diverse world of ours.

MARTIN FORWARD

John Berthrong, *The Divine Deli: Religious Identity in the North American Cultural Mosaic*, Maryknoll, NY: Orbis 1999; Diana Eck, *A New Religious America: How A 'Christian Country' Has Become The World's Most Religiously Diverse Nation*, San Francisco: HarperSanFrancisco 2001; John Hick, *The Myth of Christian Uniqueness: Towards a Pluralistic Theology of Religions*, Maryknoll, NY: Orbis and London: SCM Press 1987; Paul F. Knitter, *Introducing Theologies of Religion*, Maryknoll: Orbis 2002; Alan Race, *Interfaith Encounter: The Twin Tracks of Theology and Dialogue*, SCM Press 2001

Oxford Movement

Three prominent features of Anglican church life over the last century have their roots in the Oxford Movement. First, a whole series of well-loved hymns, ranging from John Keble's 'Blest are the Pure in Heart' and 'New Every Morning is the Love', through John Henry Newman's 'Praise to the Holiest in the Height' to John Mason Neale's 'All Glory, Laud and Honour to thee, Redeemer King', 'Jerusalem the Golden' and many other hymns translated from early Latin and Greek texts. Secondly, the church of All Saints, Margaret Street, in London, with its flamboyant Victorian red-brick Gothic architecture, decorated with carvings, mosaics, gilt and stained glass, and its rich and colourful liturgy, together with countless other churches in English towns and villages. And thirdly, the Community of the Resurrection, an Anglican religious order with a house in Mirfield, Yorkshire, and a small priory in Johannesburg, which can list among its members names such as Trevor Huddleston, who did so much to abolish apartheid in South Africa, and Harry Williams, one of the great spiritual figures of the second half of the twentieth century, and alongside this the faithful work of countless Anglican priests in the worst slum parishes, such as London's East End.

The Oxford Movement brought about a wide-ranging revival of Catholicism in England and abroad. This is how it took shape.

John Henry Newman, John Keble, John Hurrell Froude and other high churchmen interpreted parliamentary reforms between 1828 and 1833 as representing a crisis for the church. The repeal of the Test and Corporation Acts in 1828 allowed for the full formal admission of Nonconformists into parliament; the Catholic Emancipation Act followed in 1829, and in 1833 the Bill to suppress ten Church of Ireland bishoprics was presented to parliament. To Newman, Keble and Froude, anxiously watching, it all smacked of a determined assault on the status and standing of the church, which to them and an impressive band of like-minded churchmen was a sacred institution founded by Christ and to be guarded as such. The parliamentary measures were viewed by these critics as merely the latest and most blatant expression of an ominous liberalizing tendency in political and church affairs. In their eyes such oppression of the church by the state was intolerable, and they could not stand by in silence. They felt compelled to protest.

They passionately believed that ever since the Reformation the Church of England had neglected its Catholic roots. The established church was Catholic and Reformed, and not simply Protestant. For a brief period in the seventeenth century the so-called Caroline Divines had moved in the right direction, but overall the post-Reformation years had seen a serious drift away from the church's true Catholic inheritance. It should now recognize and claim its rightful place and status. The way to such an end was through sound and orthodox teaching leading to personal holiness, and a re-assertion of the authority of bishops and clergy. The call of Newman and his friends was to help to restore the Church of England to a simple and apostolic vigour that was truly Catholic.

p. 303

The Oxford Movement, so-named from the university where it originated, was launched in 1833. The magnificent, exalted, and one might say visionary view of the church presented by the Oxford high churchmen burst upon contemporary Anglicanism with all the dynamic force of some new and surprising revelation. In September 1833 they set out their beliefs in the first of what was to be a long series of tracts, and they thus became known as the Tractarians. They taught people to give less regard to preaching than to the sacraments and services of the church. They stressed the value of inner and unseen self-discipline, the cultivation of industriousness, humility, self-distrust, obedience and, above all else, the need for individual and corporate holiness. The tracts were pungent and powerful utterances, and their effect was electric. They rang out like pistol shots.

During the twelve years of its Oxford phase the history of the movement was punctuated by dramatic headline-grabbing events. There was first the furore in 1836 when the Tractarians attempted but failed to prevent the election of the liberal theologian Dr Renn Dickson Hampden to the Oxford Regius Professorship of Divinity. Two years later, in 1838, a stir was created when Froude published the first of two volumes entitled *Remains*. Critics were horrified when they read his slashing and devastating condemnation of the leaders of the English sixteenth-century Reformation. His outspoken comments provoked a fierce and bitter reaction, and in Oxford the Martyrs Memorial was erected as a declaration of loyalty to the Reformation and all that it represented, and in order to embarrass the Tractarians. A further publication in 1844, W. G. Ward's *The Ideal of a Christian Church,* fuelled the heated debate over the perceived Romeward trend of some of the Tractarians. The sting in it was the claim by the author that he could keep his place in the Church of England while holding and teaching Roman Catholic doctrines.

In the meantime the major and most devastating crisis was looming. From as early as 1839 Newman's belief and confidence in the Church of England had been eroded, largely as a result of his own studies. Perhaps with more hope than expectation, in 1841 in Tract 90 he set out to prove that the Church of England was part of the Catholic Church, with its roots in antiquity, and that it was possible to hold all Catholic doctrines while assenting to the Church of England Thirty-Nine Articles of Religion.

THE OTHER 'OXFORD MOVEMENT'

For those unfamiliar with the difference between the two of them, it is easy to confuse the nineteenth-century Oxford Movement with a rather different movement which had its centre in Oxford, the Oxford Group.

The Oxford Group was founded by Frank Buchman (1878–1961), an American Lutheran of Swiss descent who was deeply influenced by the ecumenist John R. Mott and engaged in evangelical work among students, travelling to India and the Far East before visiting England, where he made a great impression in Oxford and Cambridge. In 1928 he took a party from Oxford to South Africa, and there they were given the name 'Oxford Group'. Buchman's aim was to promote a programme to produce personal, social, racial, national and supernatural change. Campaigns followed in Canada and in Europe, and between 1930 and 1937 what were called 'house parties' in Oxford drew students from all over the world. In Germany it was proscribed by the Nazis.

In 1938 Buchman called for 'moral and spiritual re-armament', and outside Britain, Moral Rearmament replaced Oxford Group as the title of the movement. The hope was that the spiritual awakening which it sought could prevent a war. In the United States the movement was launched by Harry S. Truman in 1939 and enjoyed its heyday after the Second World War with a programme for rebuilding the free world. With a simple philosophy, it aimed at converting the rich and influential, especially those whom the churches had failed to attract. Centres were established in many countries. However, with the deaths of its founder in 1961 and his successor, Peter Howard, in 1965 the movement fell into a decline.

The effect of the publication was immediate, widespread, violent and decisive. It set the whole university and much of the country ablaze with heated discussion and forthright condemnation.

Events were rapidly moving towards a climax. Finally, on 8 October 1845, Newman was received into the Roman Catholic Church.

The blow had fallen and Newman was gone. It was the end of the first stage of the movement, but not its demise. Under the leadership of Edward Bouverie Pusey, John Keble, R. W. Church, Charles Marriott and J. B. Mozley it continued and widened its geographical spread. Between 1845 and the end of the Victorian era it manifested itself in three particular ways.

There was the revival of religious communities, with perhaps more than 30 being founded or re-established. Of these, the most famous were the Society of the Sacred Mission begun by Father H. H. Kelly, which moved to Kelham in 1903, and the Community of the Resurrection, founded by Charles Gore in 1892, which moved to Mirfield in Yorkshire in 1898.

There was the development of a distinctive form of church architecture, which was part of a Gothic, neo-medieval movement most powerfully propagated by the Camden Society, later the Ecclesiological Society, and most successfully translated into the design of cathedrals and churches by Sir George Gilbert Scott and the devout high churchmen J. L. Pearson, G. E. Street and William Butterfield.

There was the high church ceremonial and liturgical revival in the Church of England in the latter part of the century, in which hymns by writers in the Catholic tradition played a major part.

The principles given prominence by the Oxford Movement, and perhaps the concern for a high standard of worship in particular, gradually percolated throughout the Church of England; and this high church impulse is still felt today.

KENNETH HYLSON-SMITH

Owen Chadwick, *The Spirit of the Oxford Movement*, Cambridge: CUP 1992 and *The Victorian Church* (2 vols), London: A&C Black 1966 and 1970; M. Chandler, *An Introduction to the Oxford Movement*, London: SPCK 2003; G. Herring, *What was the Oxford Movement?*, London: Continuum 2002; P. B. Nockles, *The Oxford Movement in Context. Anglican High Churchmanship 1760–1857*, Cambridge: CUP 1994

Paganism

The Latin word *paganus* originally meant 'country-dweller' or 'peasant', and was also used to distinguish civilians from soldiers. It was only in the fourth or fifth century CE that it came into common usage as way of referring to those who were not Christians, as a popular alternative to the word *gentiles*, usually rendered 'Gentile'. In the Latin translation of the Old Testament, *gentiles* is used to translate the Hebrew *goyim* and the Greek *ethne*, 'nations', hence its use as a designation for non-Jews. The fact that those who continued to observe religious practices that had been overseen by the emperors and senate of Rome in Jesus' lifetime could now be dismissed as mere peasants illustrates the transformation of the religious life of the Roman empire in the period between. Roman empire

In studies of the Roman empire the term 'pagans' is often used to refer to those who were neither Christian nor Jewish, but it can be misleading if it is taken to imply that these people were members of a single religion. The inhabitants of the Roman empire, and indeed those of the territories outside it, understood themselves as living in a world in which there were many gods and other supernatural beings. Religious activity involved honouring those gods who might be able to help you, or whom you wanted not to harm you. Much of this religious activity was carried on by communities on behalf of their members, and the question of which gods one honoured was largely determined by where one was born. Administration of religious matters was largely in the hands of the richer members of the communities, and usually priesthoods and magistracies were held by the same men; this meant that there was no clear distinction between political and religious affairs. To identify oneself as a citizen of Rome or of Ephesus was as much a religious description as a political one, and Augustine recognized this when he called his major work on Christianity *The City of God*.

Individuals might make prayers, vows and offerings to the gods, and might use divination to get advice from them, but it was the community – usually in the Roman empire the city, or sub-groups within it – that was central to religious activity. The form of festivals and public sacrifices was usually determined by the religious calendar of the community. Communities tended to be conservative in their relationship with the gods, which meant that festivals and sacrifices, once instituted, would tend to continue for centuries afterwards. Many of the religious activities carried out in the period of the Roman empire had origins lost in the mists of time, and while the rituals remained the same, the interpretation of them might well change over time. It is clear that many festivals were connected in one way or another with the agricultural cycle (for both grain and grapes), but in Rome in particular, commemorations or thanksgivings for historical events such as military victories were incorporated into the calendar. This indicates that conservatism did not prevent innovation: old rituals were carried on, but new ones could be added. As Roman power spread across the Mediterranean world in the last two centuries BCE, Roman gods – and even Roman generals – were made the recipients of cult activity in the cities the Romans came to rule. In the period of the Roman empire cities paid cult to the emperor, and the birthdays of members of the imperial family were often celebrated with festivals.

Constantine's 'conversion'

The emergence of Christianity associated with the conversion of Constantine led to a gradual change in non-Christian religious understanding. In the first three centuries CE Christianity had been generally a religion of the less wealthy members of society. The support of Christianity by Constantine, and even more by his son and successor Constantius II, encouraged the spread of Christianity among the social élite. But this was also a period when power was increasingly centralized on the emperors and their courts, and cities came to be seen more as sources of revenue and less as centres of administration. As the cities declined in importance, so did their gods: there was less incentive for the rich to pay for festivals and for the upkeep of temples, and so less interest by the rest of the city in attending. The growth of cults associated with the emperor such as that of the Unconquered Sun (*Sol Invictus*), and the worship of the (unnamed) Highest God (*Theos Hypsistos*) suggest that the increasingly monarchical nature of the government of the empire was paralleled by an increasingly monotheistic approach to religion, or at least an increasing focus on a supreme ruler god.

The brief reign of the last non-Christian emperor Julian (361–3) could do nothing to change this trend. Julian attempted to revitalize 'pagan' religious practices, and even tried to have the temple in Jerusalem rebuilt, but he was met by a combination of bewilderment and lack of interest even from the non-Christian inhabitants of the cities he visited. From his writings and actions it is clear that Julian was trying to promote a sort of unified alternative to Christianity – he was essentially trying to invent 'paganism' – but there was no realistic possibility of this working.

Even at the end of the fourth century there were members of the élite who were not Christians, most visibly in the senate in Rome. These men showed their attachment to Roman traditions through a love of classical Greek and Latin literature, and this brought with it a wish to hold on to traditional religious practices. But this did not amount to a serious opposition to Christianity. It is in the later fourth and the fifth centuries that the term 'pagan' becomes more common in Roman legislation, as emperors increasingly restrict their rights and actions. But the targets of this legislation do not seem to be the last few non-Christian senators. 'Pagans' are frequently put together with Jews and heretics in legislation that is more concerned with making sure that Christians toe the line than in attacking a rival religion.

It was the emphasis on establishing a clear doctrinal position that was crucial to the success of Christianity in the period from the reign of Constantine. To see the rise of Christianity as the victory of an intellectually coherent monotheism over superstitious polytheism, as some Christian writers did at the time and later, is to misunderstand the relationship between Christianity and the 'paganism' it came to replace within the territories of the Roman empire and beyond. Not only was 'paganism' not a single religious system; the understanding of non-Christians was that what they did know about their gods was considerably outweighed by what they did not. Because of this, cult activity, and even the identity of the gods who were worshipped, was always open to reinterpretation, and Christianity was able to benefit from this.

In the Acts of the Apostles there is a story of Paul referring to an altar to 'an unknown god' and claiming that he knew this to be the god of the Christians (17.23). From the fourth century onwards this kind of reinterpretation became one of the ways in which communities were Christianized. For example, the Parthenon in Athens was the temple of Athena the Virgin, and Athena was associated, among other things, with wisdom. In the fifth century CE the Parthenon was turned into a church dedicated to Holy Wisdom (*Hagia Sophia*) and then in the seventh century to the Virgin Mary. Cyzicus, a city near Constantinople, was a centre of cult to the Mother of the Gods, and it saw its temple become a church to the *Theotokos*, that is to Mary the Mother of God. Similar transformations occurred elsewhere, as the title of a god or goddess, or an aspect of their iconography made it open to reinterpretation. In many cases there is evidence that the older cult had declined before the transformation took place, and this might suggest that Christianity was in part revivifying the older cult and restoring its role as a centre of civic pride.

This practice of reinterpretation was not new with Christianity. As Roman power spread through northern Europe from the first century BCE onwards, the Celtic and German inhabitants of these areas became increasingly familiar with Roman religious ideas, and their cult activity became to some extent 'Romanized'. One example of this can be seen at Bath (Roman *Aquae Sulis*) in southern Britain, where a local deity, Sul, came to be identified with the Roman goddess Minerva, who had previously come to be identified with the Greek Athena. Pagan gods had complex identities, and this meant that finding equivalences was not always straightforward. The chief German god was Odin or Wodan, who was associated with war and death, wisdom and poetry. However, representations of him wearing a wide-brimmed hat, and tales of his wandering, led to an identification of him not with Jupiter, but with the Roman god of travellers, Mercury. The equivalence can be seen in the names of days of the week. French follows the Romans in naming the fourth day of the week Mercredi (Mercury's Day), while English has the Germanic Wednesday (Wodan's Day).

Almost everything we know about pre-Christian German and Celtic religion comes to us through a Roman filter. We have descriptions from Roman writers such as Julius Caesar, or the much later epic poetry, written by poets familiar with classical Greek and Latin poetic forms and inevitably influenced by them. There is a tendency to oversimplify interpretations, so that Celtic gods are particularly seen as 'nature gods', in contrast perhaps to Roman or German gods. But all societies that engage in agriculture have religious rituals associated with the agricultural cycle, and all societies that have political

Reconstruction of a Scandinavian pagan temple; many churches were built in this style

Paul ◄
Mary ◄
Iconography ◄

structures of any complexity reflect this in their religious hierarchies. The Germans and Celts within the Roman empire and beyond its borders had had centuries of exposure to Roman religious ideas, and these had influenced their understanding of their own practices. Thus when Christianity spread through Northern Europe in the centuries after Constantine, it was meeting forms of paganism that were already in flux.

The stories we are told about the spread of Christianity also need to be treated with care. They were often written long after the events they describe, and their authors were often writing to glorify their subjects. Nonetheless, it is possible to say something about the nature of the encounter between Christianity and paganism in northern Europe.

Mission

In general, Christian missionaries adopted one of two contrasting attitudes to the religions they found, represented by Boniface (*c.*675–754), known as 'the apostle to the Germans', and Pope Gregory the Great (*c.*540–604), the man who sent to England the abbot who became Augustine of Canterbury. Boniface's policy was to abolish the religion he encountered, destroying pagan temples. At a famous episode in Geismar in Hessen in 724, Boniface cut down an old oak dedicated to the god Donar, to the terror and amazement of the onlookers. His biographer relates that as he cut into the tree a mighty wind blew it to the ground and it split in the form of a cross. By contrast, Pope Gregory instructed Augustine not to destroy temples, but to sprinkle them with holy water and build altars containing relics in them. That these two approaches were not as far removed from each other as might be imagined is indicated, however, by Boniface's use of pieces of the oak to build a house of prayer dedicated to St Peter and the later legend that a small fir tree grew under its roots – the first Christmas tree.

Reformation

In Germanic areas a principle that was applied after the sixteenth-century Reformation seems to have been age-old: the ruler of a region determined its religion. So areas such as Scandinavia, to which Christianity was brought relatively early, remained pagan longest, until their kings became Christians.

Festivals and fasts

Just as many Germanic religious practices had been Romanized, so too they might be Christianized. Traces of Odin worship seem to have survived in connection with the feast of St Nicholas, a fourth-century Bishop of Myra in southern Turkey (who came to be known as Santa Claus). The feast took place on 6 December, the day of the coming of Odin, and Santa Claus was given Odin's grey beard and made to ride through the air and over the rooftops. He blessed trees and made the earth fertile for another year. Other attributes of Odin worship became associated with another fourth-century figure, St Martin of Tours, who gave his cloak to a beggar and was instrumental in destroying pagan temples. St Martin's Day, 11 November, became the time of the harvest festival, when Germans lit fires of joy on hills; this fire became St Martin's fire. The tradition of eating goose on that day also goes back to pre-Christian customs.

The *Heliand*, a Germanic epic poem which may date back to the ninth century, depicts the gospel story in a characteristically Germanic way, with Jesus as a prince going through the land accompanied by his knights, delivering people from the power of the devil and the wrath of God; the ship on the Sea of Galilee is described as a Viking ship and the marriage at Cana as a joyful drinking bout. These and other features were meant to communicate the story of Jesus to Saxons in terms and concepts that they could understand.

Celtic Christianity

North-western Europe was the land of the Celts. Celtic culture emerged in the period after about 800 BCE and spread over an area from the Atlantic to central Europe, including the area of Italy north of the Po valley. It is associated with distinctive forms of art and a strong warrior culture. In the third century BCE Celtic war bands engaged in raids taking them through Greece and into Anatolia. The southern parts of the Celtic world were in contact with Mediterranean societies from the middle of the first millennium BCE, but further north the influence was lessened, and some Celtic areas, most notably Ireland, never came under direct Roman control.

Calendar ➤

We know the names of more than 400 Celtic gods. Many of them relate to springs and rivers, and veneration of these places can be paralleled both in the Mediterranean world and in later Christian practice where wells are frequently associated with local saints. In Celtic mythology, recorded in later poetry, we find a more developed religious system, similar to that of other cultures, but with its own features. Tuatha De Danann is the name of the race of gods descended from Dana or Danu, the earth mother; among them Daghda was the highest of all gods, and has been called the god of Druidism. Daghda's daughter was Brigid, goddess of the hearth, of crafts and poetry, and seems to have been closely connected with an Irish saint, Brigid (*c.* 453–523), who became patron saint of teaching, healing and the domestic arts. The saint took over the portrayal and the mythology of the goddess, and her feast, on 1 February, is on the date of the pagan spring festival Imbolc. Moreover the convent that she founded and the neighbouring 'church of the oak' in Kildare are on the site of what was once a Druid settlement.

Little is really known about the Druids. They appear to have been the spiritual leaders and guardians of Celtic religion, functioning as mediators between the gods and the king. In the literature of their opponents, whether Roman historians such as Tacitus or later Christian commentators, they appear as implacable enemies. However, the links that appear to exist between Druid activities and later Christianity suggest a more ambivalent relationship. The schools that the Druids had created for training bards were preserved and even developed links with monasteries; the Christian foundation in Armagh is probably on the site of a former Druid place of teaching and worship. The Celtic tonsure, which consists of shaving all the hair in front of a line drawn over the top of the head from ear to ear, also probably goes back to the Druids.

The Celtic cross with the sun in the centre is likely to reflect a Celtic cult of the sun. Solar rites persisted in Ireland and even in modern times in parts of Ireland only water on which the sun had shone might be drunk. Christ became the 'Son of the sun', and in his *Confession* St Patrick compared Christ the true sun with the sun cult.

Celtic religion and Christianity also come together in the stories of King Arthur and his knights and the fourteenth-century legend of Gawain and the Green Knight, who may have links with the 'Green Man', a figure who can be found in many European fertility festivals.

Quite how much Christianity owes to the paganism it came to supplant is a question that has occupied scholars and others in particular since the reawakening of interest in 'paganism' in the nineteenth century. A constant battleground is the dates of the key Christian feasts, and above all Christmas. The German pre-Christian feast of Yule (*Jul*) was held on 24 December celebrating the revival of the dead, the renewal of vegetation and the solstice. This was a feast of Odin, but also of other gods: Thor, the strongest and bravest of the gods, and Freyr (or Fro), the god of light, warmth, peace, fertility and austerity. Many features of the pagan Yule, from the exchange of presents to the feasting, were transferred to Christmas. The tree was important in Germanic religion generally as the tree of life, as is evident from Boniface's dramatic action and its consequences. Yggdrasil, the evergreen ash, was the most important tree in Germanic religion, its roots in the underworld and its branches surpassing heaven. In Christianity this tree came to be associated with the cross. Meanwhile, however, 25 December was the date chosen by the Roman emperor Aurelian in the third century CE to celebrate the feast of the Unconquered Sun (*Sol Invictus*), and this date possibly derived from earlier solar festivals. Both dates are close to that of the winter solstice, which varied considerably in this period, centuries before the Gregorian calendar reforms. Was the date of Christmas deliberately chosen in an attempt to obliterate Yule? Was it chosen because Constantine identified the god of the Christians with the Unconquered Sun? There is unlikely ever to be a complete answer to such questions. All religions are subject to change and reinterpretation, drawing ritual elements from many sources. Modern Christianity is in many ways as much the heir of European paganism as it is of first-century Judaism.

HUGH BOWDEN

📖 Ken Dowden, *European Paganism: The Realities of Cult from Antiquity to the Middle Ages*, London and New York: Routledge 2000; Richard Fletcher, *The Conversion of Europe. From Paganism to Christianity 371–1386 AD*, London: HarperCollins 1997; Anton Wessels, *Europe: Was it Ever Really Christian?*, London: SCM Press 1994

Painting

Controversies at the end of the twentieth century in the press and in museum and academic circles, over Chris Ofili's *The Holy Virgin Mary* and Andy Warhol's *The Last Supper* have revived the debate that has now gone on for almost 2000 years over the question 'What is Christian art?' Traditional approaches in the defining of Christian art have been predicated on the faith commitment of the artists, and whether the work is used by a Christian community or has been commissioned by a Christian or for a Christian community. Other characteristics sought are whether it depicts recognizable Christian themes or is placed within a Christian structure such as a cathedral, church, convent or monastery.

Both Ofili's *The Holy Virgin Mary* and Warhol's *The Last Supper* series fit within the normative parameters of what has traditionally been termed Christian art: both artists are Christians (Ofili is a Roman Catholic, Warhol was a practising Roman Catholic familiar with Eastern Orthodox Christianity) and the subject matter of the work is identifiably Christian (Ofili depicts Mary, Warhol a major narrative event from the Christian scriptures). However, they stand at the end of a long and complex history.

Through the early and thus formative periods of Christianity, a series of recognizable if not clearly-defined characteristics emerged by which painting as a Christian art came to be identified. First, there are paintings which are didactic in theme or subject matter and so teach the faith, such as Simone Martini's *Annunciation* (1333). Secondly, there are paintings, including altarpieces, which are liturgical in function and were incorporated into liturgical ceremonies and sacramental rites, such as the *Wilton Diptych* (*c.*1395). Thirdly, there are paintings which are devotional in theme or subject matter, and which nurtured prayer and contemplation, such as Rogier van der Weyden's *Deposition* (*c.*1430). Fourthly, there are paintings – individual canvases, wall-narratives or altarpieces – which are aesthetic presentations whose beauty elevates the Christian spirituality of the soul, such as any of Fra Angelico's depictions of *The Madonna* (*c.*1437). Fifthly, there are those paintings whose symbolic forms – either representational, abstract or anthropomorphic – convey objective and subjective meanings, and are open to many interpretations, such as the fresco of *Loaves and Fishes* in the Catacombs of Callixtus. The majority of 'Christian paintings' are combinations of any or all of these categories: didactic, liturgical, devotional, aesthetic decoration and symbolic. One example is Hubert and Jan van Eyck's *Ghent Altarpiece* (1432). p. 325

All these paintings and others like them are counted as Christian art because of the way in which they present Christian theologies in visual form and were used in corporate worship; they bear witness to the religious inspiration of the artists and the way in which they expressed themselves by a gifted use of their central 'tools': colour, composition and form.

Typically in Western painting, the artist's primary element is *colour*, which is employed to evoke emotion, i.e., response within the viewer, and to beautify the surface. The evocative nature of colour is related to neurological responses within the human eye and through the eye to the other human senses. So, for example, the placement of a 'hot' colour such as red next to a 'cold' colour such as blue makes the eye seek relief from the red through the blue. The symbolic meanings associated with colours such as white for innocence and purple for royalty are culturally conditioned, so that the classical Mediterranean perceptions were 'baptized' into early Christian art and later transformed during the major cultural shifts identified as Byzantine, Medieval, Renaissance and so on, down to the twenty-first century. For example, black was transformed from being a colour of creative energy and power to being a negative sign of evil. Thus colour evokes our visual and emotional response to both the figures and the activity within the painting's frame, and so to our interpretation of Incarnation the painting. Painters who emphasize colour over composition or form in their art communicate emotionally to and with their viewers.

The painter's second major element is *composition*, which is the presentation and arrangement of elements within the painting's boundaries, or frame. As Christian painting moves beyond the simple compositions of early Christian art, such as the catacomb frescoes of the second to fourth centuries, which were minimal in figuration and with little or no detail, the arrangement of figures and objects within an architectural or nature setting became a crucial factor in the presentation of the meaning of a painting. The linear or circular pattern of composition of elements within the picture's frame delineated both the direction of the viewer's eye and the action within the depicted story. The viewer's interpretative response to the 'simultaneous' actions within the circular composition of Gentile da Fabriano's *The Adoration of the Magi* (1423) is distinctively different from the temporal progression of the linear composition found in Leonardo's *The Annunciation* (*c.* 1472). As the technical aspects of painting develop through the historical movement from Medieval to Renaissance, a major transformation in the 'reality' of composition, and thus of painting, occurs with the presentation of natural light and shadow, and aerial perspective (that is, a clear delineation of foreground, middle ground and background). Thus the presentation of persons and events within the picture's 'frame' is likened to our perceptions of persons, space and time in our everyday world. Painters who emphasize composition over colour or form in their art communicate intellectually to and with their viewers.

The painter's third crucial element is *form*, that is, the presentation of figures in either a representational or an abstract way. The presentation of the human figure in a naturalistic manner, i.e. with a recognizable body appropriate in size, shape and proportion to the categories of the society of its time (i.e. male or female, adult or child), is not found in Christian painting until the late Medieval and early Renaissance periods. The earliest renderings of Symbols the human body either as flat, that is, without the normal sense of mass and volume, or scaled, according not to gender or age but to importance in the depicted story, are credited to the early Christian and Byzantine fear of idolatry. The more naturalistically the human body is rendered, the greater the risk of idolizing whoever is being portrayed.

In the course of time certain Christian fears were challenged or defeated, especially when the Renaissance opened the way to the Classical (art and philosophy) and 'the new' (humanism and science). The human body was rendered in a naturalistic fashion and signified a transformed Christian understanding not simply of the human, but of the incarnation. What this meant can be seen by comparing the Christ figures found in Matthias Grünewald's *Isenheim Altarpiece* (1515) with Michelangelo's frescoes in the Sistine Chapel (1509–12). Without doubt, the human figure(s) within a painting become our entry points into the work of art and into our interpretation of the depicted story. Thus, painters who emphasize form over colour or composition in their art communicate relationality to and with their viewers.

Those painters who depicted representational human figures accepted the understandings of perspectives – foreground, middle ground and background – and the simultaneous visual connection to nature through light-shadow and figure-ground relations that had been created in traditional paintings. Traditional works of art were objective in their emphasis on the objects being seen and their presentation, which created 'reality' within the painting's frame. By contrast, those painters, including the Impressionists and the Abstract Expressionists, who incorporated abstract, non-realistic forms with shifting understandings of perspectives – two instead of three dimensions, or without any dimension at all – in a clear 'break' with nature as either the point of reference or basis for light-shadow and figure-ground relations, made non-traditional paintings. Non-traditional works of art were subjective in their emphasis on the process of seeing, in which the autonomy of the artist and the viewer authorized their individual creations of new worlds. The one constant in both traditional and non-traditional paintings was that the painter's orchestration of colour evoked emotions and emotional responses in the viewers.

Do any of the three fundamental elements of colour, composition and form in traditional and non-traditional art affect our recognition of a painting as Christian? Clearly they do, since painters' perspectives are shaped by their world-views, and one's world-view is affected by one's faith commitment. So the way in which painters use the fundamental and technical elements at their disposal determines their ability to communicate ideas visually. The development of a Christian understanding of colour symbolism, for example, becomes an effective mode of visual communication. Similarly, composition can clarify or obfuscate the meaning of the narrative, story or theological principle visually defined within a painting's frame. For painters, composition is a principal instrument in visual communication in their interpretation of the depicted event, person, story or doctrine. The last element in this triad, form, is employed most often to characterize the presentation of the human figure.

Top: Matthias Grünewald, central panel with Crucifixion, St John the Baptist and Mary Magdalene, *Isenheim Altarpiece*, *c.* 1515
Bottom: Michelangelo, The Creation of Eve, ceiling of the Sistine Chapel

Essentially, depictions of the human body parallel understandings of the God-human relationship, for Christians especially as found in the incarnation. The diversity of Christian views of the incarnation permit the variations of the human figure in Christian painting from the early Christian period to the present day.

Eucharist

Patronage

Typically, traditional art is said to be representative of Christian painting, and whether non-traditional art is Christian is either questioned or denied. However, the issue is neither so simple nor so clear. Much of early Christian and even some Byzantine art can be defined as non-traditional painting. Similarly, the consistent presence of aniconism (non-anthropomorphic imagery) throughout the history of Christian art would rule it out as traditional. Christian pluralism and the technical as well as stylistic advances in painting achieved over the two millennia of Christianity can be cited to support both traditional and non-traditional Christian painting.

Jesus Mary Saint Reformation Persecution Secularization

Three additional elements – subject matter, function and patronage – need to be mentioned in connection with the history of painting in Christianity. The subject matter of painting is derived from the scriptural and legendary narratives of the lives of Jesus, Mary and the saints, from the historical events and persons central to Christian history, and from aspects of Christian theologies and doctrines. Over the history of Christianity, painters such as Jan van Eyck, Sandro Botticelli, Rogier van der Weyden, Raphael, Lucas Cranach and Caravaggio formulated, retrieved and reconfigured the themes and motifs of Christian art. The re-presentation of a motif such as the Annunciation or the Last Supper reflected both the theological concerns and the art-style of the time of the painter. Before the Reformation, Christian themes dominated Western European paintings and identified them as 'Christian'. After the Reformation, this dominance continued only within the borders of Catholic countries, since other subjects, including landscape and portraiture, captured the attention of the painters within Protestant nations. From the eighteenth century onwards, Christian subject matter came to be marginalized in Western European and American art with the cultural process of secularization. Significant Christian themes continued to be painted – though often not by artists with either a Christian faith commitment or for a Christian purpose; rather, the challenge to paint the 'great themes' of the tradition influenced the artist's decision. This may have been the case with Pablo Picasso's fascination with the crucifixion or Warhol's with the Last Supper.

p. 1147

A painting's function, liturgical or didactic, helped to define it as Christian. For example, Grünewald's masterful *Isenheim Altarpiece* was designed for devotional and liturgical use in the chapel of a hospice dedicated to St Anthony. The painter took great care to develop an internal iconography related simultaneously to the Christian tradition and to the ailments treated at that hospice, so that the altarpiece 'functioned' as a Christian vision of religious and physical healing. Similarly, Michelangelo's arrangements of the scriptural episodes on the Sistine Chapel ceiling make visual connections with the meaning and unfolding of the eucharistic celebration within the Catholic mass of the time. Following the Reformation, and particularly in the nineteenth and twentieth centuries, critical questions have been raised about putting paintings with Christian themes by non-Christian artists such as Marc Chagall and Picasso in churches, or using them in connection with worship.

Before the Reformation, the church was the major patron of the arts, so the question of patronage was simple. Afterwards it became more complex. Clearly, a painting with.a Christian theme commissioned by an ecclesiastical authority from a Christian painter and to be put in a Christian building for a liturgical (or devotional) purpose was a 'Christian painting'. However, after the Reformation patronage was distinctively different; now a non-Christian could commission a painting with a Christian theme, to be put in a museum or private collection, from a painter who identified himself or herself as an agnostic or atheist.

Styles, techniques and themes of 'Christian painting'

Beginning with both the *acheiropoietoi* (from the Greek for 'not made by human hands'), otherwise identified as the Veil of Veronica and the Mandylion of Edessa, both of which are claimed to bear the imprint of Jesus' face, and the tradition that the evangelist Luke painted a portrait of the Virgin Mary holding the Christ Child, painting has played an integral role in Christianity. Some art and church historians have debated whether there was such a thing as 'Christian art' during the first 200 years because of Christians' adherence to the prohibition of images in the law of Moses, belief in the imminence of the second coming of Christ, continuing persecutions, and lowly economic status. Nonetheless, there is sufficient archaeological, documentary and visual evidence to defend the otherwise traditional position that graphic art was important in the establishment and formation of the Christian community.

The earliest cycles of Christian paintings are found on the ceilings and walls of both the church and synagogue in Dura Europos, in Syria (*c.* 240 CE), and in the Christian catacombs in Rome (late second century onwards). In these varied frescoes, painters have depicted events and stories from classical mythology and the Hebrew scriptures as foretypes of the Christian scriptures. These simplistic renderings of flattened figures reduce the story to its 'essence', i.e., simply the loaves and fishes, or a group seated at a semicircular table to signify through symbols, open to many interpretations, the many miraculous meals related in the Christian scriptures including the Last Supper (Catacombs of Callixtus, Domitilla and Priscilla). One of the earliest, if not the most common, forms of Christian painting was the technique of fresco, which is wall or ceiling painting with water-colour paints on plaster or mortar.

Prior to the fourth-century transformation of Christianity from a cult to the official religion of imperial Rome, the favoured themes found in Christian paintings were those of peril and salvation as imaged through the heroes and heroines of classical mythology and the Hebrew scriptures, as well as a series of important narratives from the Christian scriptures, e.g. the Good Shepherd and the Raising of Lazarus. If a human figure represented Jesus as the Christ, this identification was made through significant actions or gestures, not a stereotypical physiognomy. From the mid-fourth century onwards the attributes of court etiquette, activities and costume enter into Christian art, as does a normative physiognomy for Jesus as the Christ, and the earlier themes of peril and salvation are replaced by those of his power and grandeur. These changes within Christian painting are as much a result of the greater importance and wealth of the 'average' Christian, the development of 'Christian patronage' of the arts and the training of artists as of the new theological and liturgical emphases of an imperial religion.

Beginning with the founding of Constantinople in 324–6 and extending to its fall in 1453, that style of Christian painting identified as Byzantine is thought to be inseparable from the category of the icon and the tradition of Eastern Orthodox Christianity. There are, however, characteristics of the Byzantine 'style' that significantly influenced Western Christian painting. These include the belief that icons as a portrait of Jesus as the Christ, of Mary the *Theotokos*, or of an individual saint were derived directly or indirectly from 'originals' made in the lifetime of these individuals or shortly thereafter. This belief gave rise to the artistic convention of identifiable physiognomies for these persons, and the regularized employment of symbolic colours for their garments. Similarly, the artistic practice identifying these persons as ideals of doctrinal instruction and the minimal changes in depicted narratives is rooted in earliest Byzantine painting, as is the convention of flattened, elongated figures, rigid postures and gold backgrounds. Following the iconoclastic controversies of the seventh to the ninth centuries, the restoration of Byzantine painting brought a series of significant transformations, including the employment of architectural backgrounds, the continuous representation of narrative sequences and an expansion in narrative sources to include the apocryphal Gospels.

Medieval Christian painting is characterized by changes in topics and styles, and most importantly by advances in the techniques of tempera and oil painting. The historical evolution from Carolingian to Romanesque to Gothic styles during the Middle Ages is paralleled by shifts in the subject matter of Christian painting which result from the pilgrimages, the crusades, devotional literature and lay spirituality. Any theme or topic in which human interaction was emphasized, either figuratively or literally, came to be favoured by medieval Christian painters, who ranged from anonymous artisans, monks and nuns in the ninth to the twelfth centuries to known masters and named individual artists such as Duccio (*c.* 1255–1319), Giotto (1267–1377), van der Weyden (1400–64) and the van Eyck brothers (Hubert, *c.* 1370–1426, and Jan, *c.* 1390–1441). The birth of the altarpiece was a medieval phenomenon arising from both changes in liturgical action, especially the priest celebrating the eucharist with his back to the congregation (regulation of the Lateran Council of 1215), which led to the move of the frontal to behind and above the altar, and the technique of tempera painting.

Pilgrimage
Crusades
Constantine's 'conversion'
Furnishings

The colours of tempera are derived by mixing ground earth, mineral and vegetable substances with water and egg yolks. The latter serves to adhere the colour to the *gesso*, or plaster of Paris, surface, which is layered carefully on a wood panel. Given the restrictions of precise contour lines and colour within the technique of tempera, figures and other forms are presented as flat or modelled in relief. Later medieval painters, especially the van Eyck brothers, developed the technique of oil painting, in which the colours are mixed with oil, which produces rich luminosity and tonalities. Eventually the advance of oil painting would allow an artist to paint on canvas as opposed to wooden panels layered with gesso. Each of these technical developments would result in shifts in style, training and subject matter as well as affecting the portability, and thus the scale and function, of Christian paintings.

Icon

With the advent of the Renaissance, first in fifteenth-century Italy and later in northern Europe, the transformations in Christian painting were multiple: subject matter, scale, presentation of the human form and spatiality. The technique of oil painting was perfected by Renaissance artists, who were thereby enabled to create depth as opposed to surface and the effects of natural and supernatural light (and shadow). The Renaissance emphasis on 'the human', resulting from the retrieval of the ideal of the human form from Classical art and culture and the advance of modern medicine, combined with the Christian theology of the incarnation to undergird the Christian painters' fascination with anatomy. The 'discovery' of aerial, or one-point, perspective heightened the naturalism found in Renaissance Christian paintings, as the illusory creation of depth resulted simultaneously in a recognition of volume, so that the figures within the

Iconoclasm
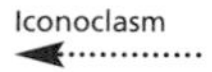

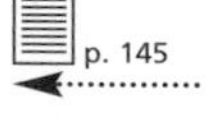
p. 145

picture appear to have 'stature' (weight and height). While the majority of Renaissance paintings were commissioned by or for the church and depict Christian subjects, these 'classical' Christian themes were revised through the growing interest in devotional and spiritual texts such as those of Bridget of Sweden, Jacobus da Voragine and Pseudo-Bonaventura. Paintings – whether individual canvases or wall surfaces – by Botticelli, Leonardo, Michelangelo and Raphael reflect the Christian tradition Humanism and the emerging humanism that define the Renaissance.

The revolution known as the Reformation created not simply new forms of culture, society, theology and the economy, but more significantly for Christian painting raised the problem of how to define Christian art. The once common religious foundation of Western Europe was shattered, and then divided, between Roman Catholicism, Lutheranism, Protestantism and Anglicanism. The result of this disintegration was more than theological redefinitions; it also led to cultural re-appropriations of art, artist and patron. A clearly identifiable and recognizable 'Catholic' art continued and was reinforced by the doctrinal decrees Council and definitions issued by the Council of Trent. New iconographies were developed by 'Catholic' artists in response to the teachings and practices questioned by the Reformers. So, for example, Titian, Rubens and El Greco Forgiveness visually explicated the sacrament of penance through new images of the weeping (and penitent) Mary Magdalene and Peter; and Murillo defended the Marian teachings of the Immaculate Conception and the Assumption.

Martin Luther recognized the importance of religious art as a didactic tool in teaching the faith. He argued against the use of violence in either the cleansing of Roman Catholic Church imagery from churches or other acts of iconoclasm. His theological views were defended visually in paintings by his friends, Lucas Cranach the Elder and his son, Lucas Cranach the Younger, and Albrecht Dürer. Protestant

Reformers, including John Calvin and Huldrych Zwingli, ultimately opposed the use and presence of the visual arts in religious worship while also opposing violent iconoclasm. As a result of these Reformed positions, the themes Vatican and patronage of art shifted in 'Protestant lands' away from Christian topics and the church to still life and genre scenes, with the rising middle class as 'the' patron.

Eventually the question arose among art and church historians as to the possibility of 'Protestant art', especially

with regard to Rembrandt, William Blake and Vincent van Gogh. On the larger issue of Christian painting, the parameter of the question shifted away from 'What is Christian painting?', 'What is Catholic painting?', or 'What is Protestant painting?' to 'What is religious painting?', and in the nineteenth and early twentieth centuries to 'What is spiritual painting?'. By the middle of the twentieth century, there was a recognized chasm between spiritual and secular painting which towards the end of the century led to paintings that parodied the great masterpieces of Christian art or re-appropriated Christian imagery with a deeply experienced nostalgia. Consequently, by the early 1980s, when Warhol painted his *The Last Supper* series, and in the mid-1990s, when Ofili painted his *The Holy Virgin Mary*, the explications and boundaries of Christian painting had not simply been redefined but had become complex, and perhaps indecipherable.

DIANE APOSTOLOS-CAPPADONA

Diane Apostolos-Cappadona, *Dictionary of Christian Art*, New York: Continuum 1994; Helen de Borchgrave, *A Journey into Christian Art*, Philadelphia: Fortress Press 2000; Jane Dillenberger, *Style and Content in Christian Art* (1965), New York: Continuum and London: SCM Press 1986; John Dillenberger, *A Theology of Artistic Sensibilities: The Visual Arts and Christianity*, New York: Continuum and London: SCM Press 1986; John Drury, *Painting the Word. Christian Paintings and their Meanings*, New Haven: Yale University Press and London: National Gallery Publications 1999; Margaret Ruth Miles, *Image as Insight: Visual Understanding in Western Christianity and Secular Culture*, Boston: Beacon Press 1985

Papacy

Unlike other world leaders who wear business suits or military uniforms, the Pope, the occupant of the office known as the papacy, who is the supreme head of the Roman Catholic Church, wears a white robe and a scarlet cape. When he is elected to the papacy, he chooses a new name for himself. From now on, he will be known to the world and to history by this new name, not by the one he was given at birth. The norms and procedures followed to elect him are public, but the actual twists and turns of the balloting are not. His electors, the cardinals, swear to reveal nothing of what happened in the conclave, the closed area of the Vatican in which they are segregated, until the voting is complete. The first sign of his election is a plume of white smoke from a small stove in the Sistine Chapel. Then a senior cardinal announces to the Roman Catholic Church and to the world the continuation of the papacy in the newly-elected Bishop of Rome. Tradition numbers John Paul II (elected in 1978) as the 263rd pope, linked in an unbroken line of succession with Peter, the head of the twelve apostles chosen by Jesus.

The Pope presides over the central government of the Roman Catholic Church, the largest of the three major branches of Christianity, which is administered through the Vatican. His authority is supreme and he is held to be infallible when defining a doctrine concerning faith or morals. He communicates with the church through encyclicals and other documents, hears reports from bishops all over the world who come regularly to Rome, and convenes synods; twice in the last 150 years popes have even convened councils of the whole church.

The term pope, applied exclusively to the Bishop of Rome only with Gregory VII from 1073 onwards, comes from the Latin *papa*, derived from the Greek *pappas*, 'father'. Originally it was used to describe any bishop in the West, and is still the title of the Patriarch of Alexandria. The pre-eminence of the Bishop of Rome was also slow to evolve. Initially the main weight of the churches lay in the East, and they were organized more as a network of independent dioceses under bishops, each managing their own affairs and meeting from time to time to settle differences. By the end of the second century, Rome began to emerge as a dominant force and to put forward its rulings, which were not always welcome. For example, Pope Victor (189–98) excommunicated bishops of Asia Minor for keeping Easter on the day of the spring full moon and not on the Sunday after it. Also, because the development of papal supremacy was gradual, many of the early popes are now little more than names on a list; virtually nothing is known about them.

At first, Rome appealed to its foundations in the preaching of both Paul and Peter to support its pre-eminence, but in the middle of the third century Pope Stephen appealed to Jesus' saying that Peter was the rock on which he would build his church (Matthew 16.18–19); from then on, this text played a decisive role in Roman claims to supremacy ('I will give you the keys of the kingdom of heaven, and whatever you bind on earth shall be bound in heaven and whatever you loose on earth shall be loosed in heaven'). The text was taken as proof of the authority given to Peter and passed on to his successors. Towards the end of the fourth and the beginning of the fifth century, Popes Damasus, Siricius and Innocent I further strengthened the power of the papacy and its administration, the Curia. Leo I, known as 'the Great', adopted the title *pontifex maximus* ('supreme pontiff': *pontifex* in fact means bridge-builder), formerly a title of the chief priest in Rome (the adjective is 'pontifical' and is applied to a variety of things associated with the Pope, from high masses to universities). He enhanced the papacy's prestige by his decisive contribution to discussions of the two natures of Christ at the Council of Chalcedon (451). In 495, Pope Gelasius was first to be hailed as 'vicar of Christ', a title which later became widely accepted. He put forward the doctrine of two powers that rule the world: the temporal power of the emperor and the higher spiritual power of the pope, another important step forward in grounding papal supremacy.

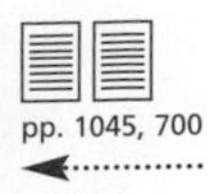
pp. 1045, 700

Council

Christology

Gregory I (590–604), also called 'the Great', was the first monk to become pope; faced with invasions from Germanic peoples from the north, the Lombards, he converted them to Christianity. However, this did not remove the long-term threat and in the 750s Stephen II appealed to Pepin III, the first king of the Carolingian dynasty, to drive them out. Stephen crowned Pepin king, and Pepin confirmed the Pope's right to what became the Papal States, areas in France and Italy which remained under papal rule until the French revolution in the eighteenth century and the establishment of the kingdom of Italy in the nineteenth century abolished them. In 800 Leo III crowned Charlemagne Holy Roman emperor. However, later emperors gained the upper hand in the balance of power in relations between secular and religious authority,

Paul

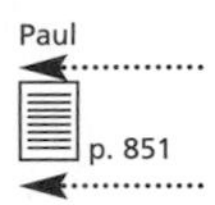
p. 851

Holy Roman empire

TWO FAMOUS FORGERIES

Donation of Constantine

A document from the late eighth or early ninth century, in which the Emperor Constantine, having been cured by Pope Sylvester I of leprosy, gives him supremacy over the churches of Antioch, Alexandria, Constantinople and Jerusalem and all the other churches in the world. The Pope is to have the same dignities as the Emperor; he is to be supreme judge of the clergy, of whom the senior have the rank of senator, and he is given rule over Rome and all the provinces, towns and cities of Italy and the West. Much use was made of the document by popes in their claims from the eleventh century onwards. It was demonstrated to be a forgery by Renaissance scholars in the sixteenth century.

Pseudo-Isidorian decretals (False decretals)

A collection of documents made in the ninth century under the name of Isidore of Seville (also known as Isidore Mercator), a Spanish historian and creator of encyclopedias. It contains a mixture of genuine documents and forgeries: letters from popes and decrees of councils. A whole series of letters from popes preceding the Council of Nicaea in 325 are forgeries, as are more than 40 letters from popes of a later period; the Donation of Constantine is included among council decrees. The forgers sought to protect the church from state interference and bishops against interference from archbishops, both with an appeal to papal authority. The decretals were widely appealed to from the tenth century on and seem to have had some influence. Their authenticity was challenged in the sixteenth century and their falsity established in the seventeenth.

THE POPES AT A GLANCE

Popes listed in square brackets are antipopes, i.e. rival popes appointed against the official holders of the papacy.

until c. 64 Peter
Linus
Anacletus

Church fathers

c. 96 Clement I
A letter bearing his name deals with disputes in the church of Corinth. This is the first instance of the church of Rome intervening in the affairs of another church.
c. 100–109 Evaristus
c. 109–116 Alexander I
c. 117–c. 127 Sixtus I
c. 127–c. 137 Telesphorus
c. 137–c. 140 Hyginus
c. 140–c. 154 Pius I
c. 154–c. 166 Anicetus
c. 166–c. 175 Soter
c. 175–89 Eleutherius
189–98 Victor I
He made vigorous attempts to settle the dispute over the date of Easter by calling synods throughout the church: an important step towards papal supremacy.
198–217 Zephyrinus
217–22 Callistus I
[217–c.235 Hippolytus]
Set himself up as an 'antipope' in view of the laxity of Callistus. The most important third-century Roman theologian, who provides important evidence about church life and worship of the time.
222–30 Urban I
230–5 Pontian
235–6 Anterus
236–50 Fabian
The first to suffer martyrdom when the Decian persecution broke out. He is said to have divided the church of Rome into seven church regions.

Christology

pp. 288–9

251–3 Cornelius
Tolerant to those who had lapsed in persecution so he was opposed by:
[251–257/8 Novatian]
an antipope who had a rigorist attitude.
253–4 Lucius I
254–7 Stephen I
Upheld the validity of baptism by heretics, leading to a split between Rome and North Africa/ Asia Minor. The first pope to appeal to Matthew 16.18 ('On this rock I will build my church') for his authority.
257–8 Sixtus II
259–68 Dionysius
269–74 Felix I
275–83 Eutychianus
283–96 Caius
296–304 Marcellinus
307–308/9 Marcellus I
310 Eusebius
310/11–314 Miltiades
Bishop of Rome when Constantine defeated Maxentius and issued the Edict of Milan. The first pope to enjoy government favour.

Constantine's 'conversion'

314–5 Sylvester I
336 Mark
337–52 Julius I
A firm supporter of orthodoxy in the Arian dispute, sheltering those condemned by Arian councils, including Athanasius.
352–66 Liberius
Ordered by the Arian emperor Constantius to condemn Athanasius, he refused and was banished. He later recanted and was restored.
[355–65 Felix II]
Appointed by the government to replace Liberius; for a period Rome had two bishops.
[366–7 Ursinus]
Appointed by the followers of Ursinus, but banished after popular protests and replaced by:
366–84 Damasus
Did much to strengthen the see of Rome and created a proper papal archive. In his papacy the emperor Theodosius made Christianity the official religion.
384–99 Siricius
Author of the first papal decretal.
399–401 Anastasius I
402–17 Innocent I
He so stressed the primacy of Rome that he is sometimes known as the first true pope.
417–18 Zosimus
418–22 Boniface I
[418–19 Eulalius]
422–32 Celestine I
432–40 Sixtus III
440–61 Leo I
Prevented the destruction of Rome when Attila the Hun attacked. Did much to strengthen the church by using Roman law. His Tome (a letter to the Patriarch of Constantinople) was an important contribution to the Council of Chalcedon.
461–8 Hilarus
468–83 Simplicius
483–92 Felix III (II)
His involvement in a dispute in the Eastern church over Monophysitism led to the first division (the Acacian schism).
492–6 Gelasius I
496–8 Anastasius II
498–514 Symmachus
[408–9, 501–6, Laurentius]
514–23 Hormisdas
An able diplomat who mended the Acacian schism.
523–6 John I
526–30 Felix IV (III)
530–2 Boniface II
[530 Dioscorus]
533–5 John II
535–6 Agapetus I
536–7 Severinus
537–55 Vigilius

556–61 Pelagius I
561–74 John III
575–9 Benedict I
579–90 Pelagius II
590–604 Gregory I
Became city prefect of Rome at the age of 30. Sold his property for the relief of the poor and founded seven monasteries. As pope he sent Augustine to Canterbury, revised the liturgy, developed church music (the Gregorian chant is named after him) and wrote what was to be the textbook for the medieval episcopate.
604–6 Sabinianus
607 Boniface III
608–15 Boniface IV
615–18 Deusdedit or Adeodatus I
619–25 Boniface V
625–38 Honorius I
640 Severinus
640–2 John IV
642–9 Theodore I
649–55 Martin II
654–7 Eugenius I
657–72 Vitalian
672–6 Adeodatus II
676–8 Donus
678–81 Agatho
682–3 Leo II
684–5 Benedict II
685–6 John V
686–7 Cono
[687 Theodore]
[687 Paschal]
687–701 Sergius I
701–5 John VI
705–7 John VII
708 Sisinnius
708–15 Constantine
715–31 Gregory II
731–41 Gregory III
741–52 Zacharias
752 Stephen II
752–67 Stephen II (III)
The first pope to preside over a papal state, territory including Ravenna and former Byzantine cities, donated to him by the king.
757–67 Paul I
[767–9 Constantine]
[768 Philip]
768–72 Stephen III (IV)
772–95 Hadrian I
795–816 Leo III
He crowned Charlemagne emperor in Rome.
816–17 Stephen V
He crowned and anointed Charlemagne's successor, the first pope to anoint an emperor.
817–24 Paschal I
824–7 Eugenius II
827 Valentine
827–44 Gregory IV
844–7 Sergius II
[844 John]
847–55 Leo IV
855–8 Benedict III
[855 Anastasius Bibliothecarius]
858–67 Nicholas I
867–72 Hadrian II
872–82 John VIII
882–4 Marinus I
884–5 Hadrian III
885–91 Stephen VI
891–6 Formosus
896 Boniface VI
896–7 Stephen VII
897 Romanus
897 Theodore II
898–900 John IX
900–3 Benedict IV
903 Leo V
[903–4 Christopher]
904–11 Sergius III
911–13 Anastasius III
913–14 Lando
914–28 John X
928 Leo VI
928–31 Stephen VIII
931–5 John XI
936–9 Leo VII
939–42 Stephen IX
942–6 Marinus II
946–55 Agapetus II
955–64 John XII
963–5 Leo VIII
964 Benedict V
965–72 John XIII
973–4 Benedict VI
[974, 984–5 Boniface VIII]
974–83 Benedict VII
983–4 John XIV
985–96 John XV
996–9 Gregory V
[997–8 John XVI]
999–1003 Sylvester II
1003 John XVII
1003/4–9 John XVIII
1009–12 Sergius IV
1012–24 Benedict VIII
[1012 Gregory]
1024–32 John XIX
1032–44 Benedict IX
1045 Sylvester III
1045 Benedict IX (for the second time)
1045–6 Gregory VI
1046–7 Clement II
1047–8 Benedict IX (for the third time)
1048 Damasus II
1048–54 Leo IX
1055–7 Victor II
1057–8 Stephen X
[1058–9 Benedict X]
1059–61 Nicholas II

1061–73 Alexander II
[1061–72 Honorius II]
1073–85 Gregory VII (Hildebrand)
Investiture Controversy
A leading reformer. He sought to centralize church authority and make alliances with secular rulers. However, his prohibition of lay investiture (the appointment of clergy by laity) provoked vigorous opposition in Germany, France and Italy. He is famous for forcing the emperor to do public penance at Canossa in 1077. His major contribution was to make the papacy a dominant force in Western Christendom.
[1080, 1084–1100 Clement III]
1086–7 Victor III
1088–99 Urban II
Crusades
He proclaimed the First Crusade but also sought to heal divisions between East and West.
1099–1118 Paschal II
[1100–1 Theodoric]
[1101 Albert]
[1105–11 Sylvester IV]
1118–19 Gelasius II
[1118–21 Gregory VIII]
1119–24 Callistus II
1124–30 Honorius II
[1124 Celestine III]
1130–43 Innocent II
[1130–8 Anacletus III]
[1138 Victor IV]
1143–4 Celestine II
1144–5 Lucius II
1145–53 Eugenius III
He commissioned Bernard of Clairvaux to preach the Second Crusade; he claimed that the Pope had supreme authority in secular as well as spiritual matters.
1153–4 Anastasius IV
1154–9 Hadrian IV
The only English pope (Nicholas Breakspear).
1159–81 Alexander III
[1159–64 Victor IV]
[1164–8 Paschal III]
[1168–78 Callistus III]
[1179–80 Innocent III]
1181–5 Lucius III
1185–7 Urban III
1187 Gregory VIII
1187–91 Clement III
1191–8 Celestine III
1198–1216 Innocent III

p. 345
The first regularly to use the title 'vicar of Christ' for the Pope, with an ideal of ruling the world as well as the church. He preached crusades against Islam and the Albigensians. He was a keen reformer. The Fourth Lateran Council set the seal on his efforts, banning new religious orders, requiring annual confession for Catholics, ordering distinctive dress for Jews and Muslims, condemning heretics, defining transubstantiation as eucharistic doctrine and calling for a new crusade.
Martin Luther
1216–27 Honorius III
Produced a first book of canon law; officially approved the Dominican, Franciscans and Carmelites.
1227–41 Gregory IX
1241 Celestine IV
1243–54 Innocent IV
1254–61 Alexander IV
1261–4 Urban IV
1265–8 Clement IV
1271–6 Gregory X
1276 Innocent V
1276 Hadrian V
1276–7 'John XXI'
1277–80 Nicholas III
The first pope to live in the Vatican.
1281–5 Martin IV
1285–7 Honorius IV
1288–92 Nicholas IV
1294 Celestine V
1294–1303 Boniface VIII
1303–4 Benedict XI
1305–14 Clement V
A Frenchman, he made his residence in Avignon: this arrangement continued for the next 70 years; critics termed it the Babylonian captivity of the church.
1316–34 John XXII
[1328–30 Nicholas V]
1334–42 Benedict XII
1342–52 Clement VI
1352–62 Innocent VI
1362–70 Urban V
1370–8 Gregory XI
The last French pope.
1378–89 Urban VI
Elected pope in Rome but ruled side by side with a pope in Avignon.
[1378–94 Clement VII]
1389–1404 Boniface IX
[1394–1417 Benedict XIII]
1404–6 Innocent VII
1406–15 Gregory XII
[1409–10 Alexander V]
[1410–15 John XXIII]
1417–31 Martin V
[1423–9 Clement VIII]
[1425–30 Benedict XIV]
1431–47 Eugenius IV
[1439–49 Felix V]
1447–55 Nicholas V
1455–8 Callistus III
1458–64 Pius II
1464–71 Paul II
1471–84 Sixtus IV
A Franciscan, he set up the Spanish Inquisition, confirming the famous Torquemada as Grand Inquisitor. Founded the Sistine Choir and built the Sistine Chapel.
1484–92 Innocent VIII
1482–1503 Alexander VI
1503 Pius III
1503–13 Julius II
Attacked by Martin Luther over his indulgences for rebuilding St Peter's.
1513–21 Leo X
Excommunicated Luther.

1522–3 Hadrian VI
1523–34 Clement VII
1534–49 Paul III
Commissioned Michelangelo to complete the Last Judgement in the Sistine Chapel. Excommunicated Henry VIII. Convened the Council of Trent, later broken off.
1550–5 Julius III
1555 Marcellus II
1555–9 Paul IV
The first of the Counter-Reformation popes.
1559–65 Pius IV
Reconvened and concluded the Council of Trent.
1566–72 Pius V
1572–85 Gregory XIII
Instituted the Gregorian calendar which replaced the Julian calendar devised by Julius Caesar.
1585–90 Sixtus V
Known as the 'iron pope', he reorganized church administration with a maximum of 70 cardinals and 15 congregations, an arrangement which lasted until Vatican II. He introduced the rule that bishops should visit Rome regularly to report on their dioceses.
1590 Urban VII
1590–1 Gregory XIV
1591 Innocent IX
1592–1605 Clement VIII
1605 Leo XI
1605–21 Paul V
1621–3 Gregory XV
Established the procedure for electing popes and also the central authority for mission, the Sacred Congregation for the Propagation of the Faith.
1623–44 Urban VIII
Chose Castel Gondolfo as the papal summer residence.
1644–55 Innocent X
1655–67 Alexander VII
1667–9 Clement IX
1670–6 Clement X
1676–89 Innocent XI
1689–91 Alexander VIII
1691–1700 Innocent XII
1700–21 Clement XI
1721–4 Innocent XIII
1724–30 Benedict XIII
1730–40 Clement XII
1740–58 Benedict XIV
1758–69 Clement XIII
1769–74 Clement XIV
1775–99 Pius VI
1800–23 Pius VII
1823–9 Leo XII
1829–30 Pius VIII
1831–46 Gregory XVI
1846–78 Pius IX
Stressed the supreme authority of the Pope in the church, promulgated the doctrine of the immaculate conception of the Virgin Mary after consulting the world's bishops; condemned almost all modern intellectual movements in the *Syllabus errorum*. Convened the First Vatican Council, which decreed papal infallibility.
1878–1903 Leo XIII
Set out to reconcile the church with modernity. Stressed the compatibility of Catholic teaching with democracy, issued a famous encyclical on social questions and gave limited encouragement to critical and historical study. However, towards the end of his reign his attitude hardened.

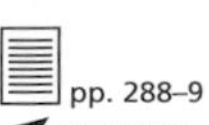
pp. 288–9

1903–14 Pius X
Condemned modernism and issued a revision of canon law. A good and holy man, he was revered as a saint in his lifetime.

Modernism

1914–22 Benedict XV
Sought to keep the papacy neutral in the First World War, and after it worked for reconciliation in the international world and the churches.
1922–39 Pius XI
Inaugurated Catholic Action, aimed at restoring Christ to society, and instituted a feast of Christ the King. Issued a famous encyclical on social problems, *Quadragesimo anno*.

Calendar

p. 700

1939–58 Pius XII
A diplomat after the First World War, he was instrumental in concluding concordats with Germany, which among other things gravely weakened Catholic opposition to Hitler. Whether he did enough against the evils of Nazi Germany has been much debated. After the war he issued an encyclical against modernist tendencies in Roman Catholic theology, *Humani generis*, and defined the doctrine of the Assumption of the Blessed Virgin Mary.

p. 954

1958–63 John XXIII
A saintly man, who became pope at the age of 77, he inaugurated a remarkable era of reform. He created the largest and most international body ever of cardinals and summoned the Second Vatican Council to bring the teaching, discipline, worship and organization of the church up to date. His 1963 encyclical on peaceful co-existence was a landmark.
1963–78 Paul VI
Continued and concluded Vatican II. However, his encyclical *Humanae vitae* condemning artificial birth control indicates his deep conservatism.
1978 John Paul I
Died within three weeks of taking office.
1978– John Paul II
The first Polish pope. Journeys all over the world have been the most distinctive mark of his papacy, and have made him internationally known as a symbol. As pope, though, he has been relentlessly conservative in theology, politics and ethics.

Lists of the popes of Rome traditionally begin with the apostle Peter. However, it took some time for papal authority to become established and it was only under Julius I, in 343, that the jurisdiction of the Pope over the Western church was officially recognized. Leo, Gregory VII, Innocent III and Boniface VIII represent further milestones in the growth of papal power. Little is known of many of the early figures, who are often no more than names in lists.

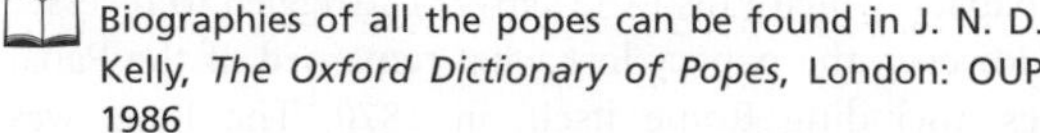
Biographies of all the popes can be found in J. N. D. Kelly, *The Oxford Dictionary of Popes*, London: OUP 1986

and the papacy went into decline until the middle of the eleventh century.

Investiture Controversy

It was revived above all by Gregory VII (born Hildebrand, 1073–85), who emphasized not only the Pope's holiness inherited from St Peter, but his supremacy over all Christians, including rulers, whom he had the right to depose. He prohibited lay rulers from giving bishops the ring and crosier, which were the sign of their office, as had been customary in the past; the resulting clash, known as the Investiture Controversy, saw King Henry IV of Germany deposing the Pope and the Pope excommunicating the king. It came to a climax in a famous scene at Canossa, in northern Italy, where the Pope was staying. Henry was forced to do penance before the Pope, kneeling in the snow. Innocent III (1198–1216) brought the papacy to the pinnacle of its medieval power, an accomplishment that was reflected in the decrees of the Fourth Lateran Council.

Renaissance

Reformation

However, the next century again witnessed a decline, with political conflicts and growing financial problems for the church. With Boniface VIII (1294–1303), the papal claims to universal power grew less and less credible. Corruption was rife; between 1309 and 1377 popes resided in Avignon, and after Gregory XI returned the papacy to Rome, popes were elected in both places. The so-called 'Great Western Schism' continued until 1417. This period also saw the beginning of the Italian Renaissance and a number of popes who did much to beautify the city of Rome, but led notoriously immoral lives. When Leo X (1513–21) granted indulgences to raise money for the rebuilding of St Peter's, he provoked a fierce attack from Martin Luther, then a Catholic monk in Wittenberg in Germany, and this was one of the factors which led to the Reformation.

Mission

Paul III (1534–49) saw the need for reform of the Roman Catholic Church and decided to hold a general council to renew it; however, this council, the Council of Trent, took place only under his successors. The sixteenth century also saw the Roman Catholic Church engaged in missionary activity all over the world, which many of the popes promoted.

p. 1043

Enlightenment

The beginnings of the modern world confronted the papacy with the rise of nation states and, consequently, opposition to the papacy's claims to universal power. Movements in France (Gallicanism) and Germany (Febronianism) promoted national churches' independence from Rome. Popes also had to contend with the Enlightenment and its hostility to institutional religion and, later, the French Revolution with its virulent hostility to the church. Hence this was another period of decline for the papacy, which Pius IX (1846–78) struggled to reverse.

However, the papacy lost what remained of the Papal States, including Rome itself, in 1870. The Pope was left only with the Lateran, the Vatican and a summer residence at Castel Gondolfo. From this time on, the papacy generally allied itself with conservative forces, despite notable efforts, like Leo XIII's encyclical *Rerum novarum*, to limit the sufferings caused by *laissez-faire* capitalism and industrialization.

Against this background, John XXIII and the Second Vatican Council that he convened sought to transform the church from the opponent into the partner of the modern world. This change was perhaps too great for his successors and the Roman Catholic Church as a whole to sustain. Certainly, since then Paul VI and John Paul II have been far more conservative in their leadership.

Numbered among the popes have been a wide range of personalities with all the strengths and weaknesses of human beings. Despite the failings of many of them, and the ups and downs of papal prestige, there can be no doubt that today all over the world the Pope is acknowledged as an important spiritual authority and advocate for global peace and justice, and not by Catholics alone.

Roman Catholics hold that a church cannot be completely Christian without the successor of St Peter. Thus, a fully reunited church of Christ will have a pope at its head, even though that title may no longer be used and the office exercised in a very different way. It is most unlikely that the papacy at the head of a reunited church will resemble the papacy of the past.

JON NILSON

John Eric, *The Popes: A Concise Biographical History*, London: Burns & Oates 1964; Christopher Hollis (ed), *An Illustrated History of the Papacy from St Peter to Paul VI*, London: Weidenfeld & Nicolson 1964; J. N. D. Kelly, *The Oxford Dictionary of Popes*, London: OUP 1986

Pastoral care

Pastoral care, or to use an old-fashioned term the cure (i.e. 'care') of souls, has always been part of the life of the church. Pastoral care involves helping men and women to find their complete selves. It is an educative process that has to take account of the brokenness, weakness and failings of human nature as well as its joys, hopes and creative potential. Pastoral care has been offered down the centuries to the present day in very different circumstances, from persecution to cultural dominance, and through varying expressions and means.

An influential modern definition of pastoral care is given by W. A. Clebsch and C. R. Jaekle in their *Pastoral Care in Historical Perspective*: 'The ministry of the cure of souls, or pastoral care, consists of helping acts, done by *representative Christian persons,* directed towards the *healing, sustaining, guiding* and *reconciling* of *troubled persons* whose troubles arise *in the context of ultimate meanings and concerns.*'

This definition takes the position that pastoral care is a specific dimension of ministry. It reflects common assumptions and practice. So in being given charge of a parish or congregation the minister is told not only to take up the ministries of evangelism, preaching and the sacraments but also the cure of souls. This responsibility is assumed to include caring for those in distress of body, mind or soul and being with people in life-shaping events such as birth, marriage and bereavement or decisions about family or work.

This will always be the central task of pastoral care, but to leave it there is to omit the wider context that gives shape and purpose and even suggests other dimensions to pastoral care. The pastoral task is for the building up of the whole community, which includes supporting the able and strong in their strengths, to enable community to grow and to help people have the vision and hope to face the challenges and opportunities of life. This also suggests that every ministerial activity has a pastoral dimension, because each contributes to shaping the life and witness of the Christian community. Conversely, the practice of pastoral care will feed into all the other facets of the life of the congregation, informing prayer and indicating teaching needs and so forth.

The definition also suggests that pastoral care is given by 'representative Christian persons'. This would imply, first of all, that pastoral care may only be offered by authorized persons. Issues of authority and power are raised here which can only be touched on in passing.

It has indeed been true that pastoral care has been the prerogative of the official, ordained ministry of the church. This responsibility is supposed to derive from Jesus himself, who is described as 'the good shepherd' (John 10.1–18). This image of the shepherd as the guide, defender and carer of the sheep, and therefore as a metaphor of leadership in the community, goes back into the Old Testament (Psalm 23; Ezekiel 34). Jesus is depicted as giving this charge to his disciples (John 20.19–23; 21.15–20). This is the image that most Christians still have of the parish priest or minister; and it is still true that for many, if the minister has not called, no one has come from the church! However, today many find the image too authoritarian and demeaning of the ability of the sheep.

The provisional definition, however, does not stipulate that pastoral carers are necessarily ordained. This reflects contemporary developments in the church. First, there has been a strong emphasis on the corporate nature of the church that has tended to blur the rigid distinction between the ordained and the laity in general. This has encouraged a much wider participation in various ministries, such as hospital and sick visiting. There has also been a strengthening and growth of specialized and auxiliary ministries in many areas, such as chaplaincies or counselling. Pastoral care has become much more diffused in practice.

Nevertheless, there have always been less formal resources for pastoral care, sometimes in tension with the legitimate authorities, in the wise and saintly men and women to whom people have turned for inspiration and advice. Classical examples may be found in the desert fathers of the fourth century, the mystics of the late Middle Ages and the *startsy* (plural of *starets*), the venerated spiritual counsellors of the Russian Orthodox Church. This, too, continues to the present, not least as an expression of the exploratory freedom that pertains in a pluralistic society.

Ministry and ministers
Monasticism
Mysticism
Orthodox churches

The definition seeks to limit pastoral care to Christian pastoral care. It is clear that the roots of pastoral care are in the Christian tradition and that normally the reference is to care in and through the church or its agencies. But in recent decades the term has been taken into secular contexts and can be used for almost any activity that offers guidance, support or therapy. So in schools pastoral care includes careers advice and supportive counselling for pupils under stress. Are these distinct activities, or are they linked? At one level there is a clear difference between them. But it has to be recognized also that much Christian care is open and generally accessible, and deals with everyday areas of life; and care offered in secular contexts has as its underlying aim the enhancement and strengthening of human lives and community. There may be differences, but they lie across a spectrum rather than being absolute distinctions.

Community
Authority

The characteristics of pastoral care

Four characteristics can be identified in pastoral care, each of which may be present at any time, though any one of them may be dominant in a particular instance.

Church
Jesus

1. *Healing.* The care and restoration of the sick has always been an important part of the church's service, through, for example, monasteries, nursing orders and, today, hospitals. It was assumed, until the era of modern medicine that has stressed the physical basis of illness, that there was a close integration of body, mind and the spiritual. In recent years this has begun to be recovered with a strong emphasis on the 'ministry of healing', parallel to the growth of holistic medicine and a cultural interest in the spiritual. Sometimes there have been extreme claims, but normally this is understood as a complementarity between the skills of the medical professions, social care and the spiritual dimension. This has resulted in the expansion of hospital chaplaincies, holistic health centres, centres for spiritual

Sickness and healing

healing and, in many congregations, an emphasis on the healing ministry of prayer and visiting, which can include sacramental acts (e.g. laying on of hands) and the regulated use of exorcism.

2. *Sustaining.* This points to the inevitable human need to accept that circumstances cannot always be changed. Healing may not be possible; or social conditions may not be alleviated; or the culture may be hostile to faith and even inflict persecution. There are times when all that can be done is to endure. The pastoral task here is to suffer with and to strengthen the afflicted. This is perhaps most evident in our society at times of bereavement and loss, especially as a result of disaster or criminal activity.

3. *Guiding.* Every tradition recognizes that there is a continuous educative process, helping people to grow and walk faithfully through the challenges and pitfalls of life. This has become radically true in our rapidly changing world, where both society and the church are having to respond to the advances of technology and the reality of a pluralist and mobile world.

Discipline

Roman Catholic Church p. 1045
Forgiveness
Persecution
Council
Celtic Christianity
Sacraments
p. 700

It is within Roman Catholicism that this has been most authoritatively expressed. The Pope and the bishops constitute the magisterium or teaching authority of the church, whose responsibility is to guide the faithful in matters of belief and practice. There are two principal ways that this is done. The first is through the teachings of a universal council. Modern Roman Catholicism has been shaped most significantly by the last council, Vatican II (1962–5), which introduced the vernacular liturgy, modified pastoral practice and opened ecumenical relations. However, it is through the pastoral letter that particular issues are discussed and such letters have the most direct effect. A papal encyclical naturally carries all the weight of the Pope's authority as the chief pastor of the church. The most contentious in recent years was Paul VI's *Humanae vitae* on sexual ethics, but this is just one among many on such issues as the economy, work, peace and culture. Regional and national colleges of bishops also may add their considered reflections on special local concerns, as in the case of the important pastoral letters on racism, war and peace, and social teaching issued by the US Conference of Catholic Bishops.

Reformation
Lutheranism
Anglicanism
Presbyterian churches

In other traditions the authority is more diffuse and the process more discursive. An important feature of the past 50 years or so, not least ecumenically, has been the publishing of reports arising out of a process of study and consultation with the intention of focusing on and drawing out the implications for Christians of key issues of the day. A British example would be the Anglican report *Faith in the City* (1985), which had widespread political repercussions as well as shaping church policy. Alongside such official processes there are other groups, institutions, publications and broadcasts that all contribute to the debate.

For most people, however, the teaching activities of the church are experienced through the sermon and study group or course. In a more explicit pastoral context this will be through such activities as preparation for marriage, baptism or church membership. At other times guidance is sought in relation to personal problems.

4. *Reconciling.* This is about building and mending relationships of people with themselves, between people, and between people and God. There has been a change from a more authoritarian pastoral discipline in earlier periods to one of discovering the caring love of God that embraces our weakness and sin in the modern period. However, this change should not be exaggerated.

The classical expression of the need to be reconciled with God has been the penitential discipline that has characterized the Catholic Church. From the beginning it has been necessary to deal with moral lapses and the breakdown of community in the church (Matthew 18.15–20). Over the early Christian centuries, there evolved a system of confession and penance designed to contain scandal and conflict and to encourage renewal and growth. The most formative influences for the Western pattern seem to have been the need to restore the lapsed in the age of persecution (250–312) and the Benedictine monastic practices on which Gregory I (540–604) based his treatise on pastoral care. At first confession was communal and public. In the Celtic tradition it was mutual, a practice that has recently been revived in modified form. It soon, however, became a private act of confession before a priest. By the Middle Ages penance was one of the seven sacraments. It formally became the nub of pastoral discipline at the Council of Trent (1543–63), confession being required before communion, which had to be received at least once a year, normally at Easter. However, as with all discipline, the aim was to restore and sustain the relationship between the individual and God. Such a model of spiritual guidance produced a tradition of great skills and insights, and noted confessor-guides, for example the Curé d'Ars, J. B. M. Vianney (1786–1859). However, the use of the confessional has steeply declined in recent years. This is possibly due to the greater participation in communion and the relaxation of rules, together with a greater sense of freedom from the traditional disciplines.

The traditions of the Reformation rejected sacramental confession but continued to recognize discipline as one of the marks of the church. Confession became central to public worship, although in Lutheranism and Anglicanism, where it has been accepted again by some as a sacrament, confession is a pastoral option. Among Presbyterians the practice was to visit each household before the (usually) quarterly communion to ascertain that they were in good standing. For Anabaptists and Congregationalists it was the church meeting that exercised discipline, though today that task is usually given to the pastor. Interestingly, John Wesley (1703–91) introduced the 'class' system of small groups into Methodism for both mutual support and discipline. Such groups have again become normal in many congregations as a means of sustaining and learning.

Perhaps the most characteristic form of pastoral care arising from the Reformation is the pastoral visit. Earlier, as we have seen, this was strongly linked with admonition, discipline and catechetical teaching; however, it was also always a means of building a personal relationship between pastor and people so that pastors could listen to and address the needs of the people in their particularity. This became the expected mode of pastoral care in the modern church. The tradition persists, though reportedly in a somewhat attenuated form. In a less authoritarian age there will be less formality and each minister will develop his or her own practice. A programme of regular visiting builds up a Christian fellowship and forms the basis of pastoral contact in times of crisis or conflict.

Since the Second World War there has been a widespread revolution in pastoral care. The rise of the human sciences and caring professions has put at the disposal of the pastoral ministry a new range of insights, perspectives and skills from the fields of counselling and therapy. This process has not been without tension. The modern secular approaches have tended to centre on the needs of the client, on personal self-fulfilment and self-determination, and play down external authority and tradition. Nevertheless there have been immense gains. Gradually a range of models of theory and practice have emerged that bring together the perspectives of faith and therapy. Perhaps the greatest influence has been the counselling methods based on Carl Rogers' 'client-centred therapy', but other voices may be heard, including those of Sigmund Freud, C. G. Jung and Viktor Frankl. At the same time there has been a rediscovery of the treasures of the pastoral tradition from the New Testament onwards. As a result pastoral care has moved closer to counselling and therapy. Even in the informal pastoral contacts of everyday, the emphasis will be on mutual exploration and personal development.

An important expression of this has been the development of pastoral counselling as a distinct practice. This has been more pronounced in the United States than in Britain. It has introduced the formal counselling model into pastoral care with its set times and place and client/therapist relationship. Some clergy will have this as one part of their ministry. Others have made it their speciality. There are also church-related organizations that specialize in pastoral counselling, and there are associations for such specialists.

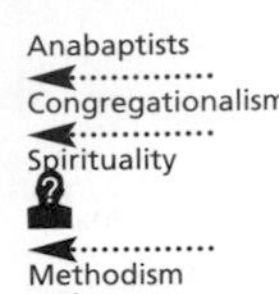
Anabaptists
Congregationalism
Spirituality
Methodism

This interest in therapeutic skills has more recently become related to the growing interest in 'spirituality'. In Christian circles this has produced a deepening interest in mysticism and contemplative prayer as well as in human well-being. It has revived an interest in spiritual direction whereby individuals seek to put themselves under the care of a director who works with them on their own spiritual pilgrimage. A less formal expression of this is that of a 'soul friend', where there is a sharing of a journey, a concept that can be traced to medieval monasticism. Similarly, there has been an increased use of retreats and spiritual exercises, like those of Ignatius Loyola. Others have linked Christian spirituality with insights taken from traditional native or Indian religions. There are also evangelical parallels, often informed by charismatic spirituality and building on traditions such as the Keswick Convention, an annual gathering of evangelicals that began in 1875, and Spring Harvest, another evangelical movement founded in 1979 that is active in the United Kingdom and Europe.

Journeys

p. 1143

Evangelicals

PAUL BALLARD

Paul Ballard and John Pritchard, *Pastoral Theology in Action – Christian Thinking in Service of Church and Society*, London: SPCK 1996; Wesley Carr, *Handbook of Pastoral Studies*, London: SPCK 1997; W. A. Clebsch and C. R. Jaekle, *Pastoral Care in Historical Perspective*, Englewood Cliffs: Prentice-Hall 1964; Howard Clinebell, *Basic Types of Pastoral Care and Counselling*, Nashville, TN: Abingdon Press and London: SCM Press 1984; G. R. Evans (ed), *A History of Pastoral Care*, London: Cassell 2000; Paul Goodliff, *Care in a Confused Climate – Pastoral Care and Post-Modern Culture*, London: Darton, Longman & Todd 1998; Roger Hurding, *Pathways to Wholeness – Pastoral Care in a Postmodern Age*, London: Hodder 1998; Stephen Pattison, *A Critique of Pastoral Care*, London: SCM Press [2]2000

Patronage

Patronage is an institution that dates from the time of ancient Greece and Rome. Those with wealth, power and status had their clients, dependents upon whom their patrons bestowed favours, particularly employment; the clients in return increased the prestige of their patrons. In addition to this general institution of patronage, which was a prominent feature of the ancient world, there was also specifically artistic patronage: in the fifth century BCE, wealthy citizens of Athens financed dramatic performances, and individual rulers, for example in Macedonia and Sicily, were patrons of writers and artists.

Saint
Martyr
Middle Ages

p. 792

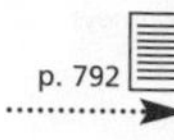

In Roman society, patronage was particularly highly developed: everyone was both client and patron in a chain which extended from the lowly to the emperor himself: the system has been described as a combination of an old boys' network, the Sicilian mafia, feudalism, and the 'machine politics' of some nineteenth-century American cities. Patrons granted favours to their clients in the form of loans, gifts, legal representation and protection, and clients gave political support and showed social deference. Some clients were totally dependent on their patrons for financial support, and were naturally more loyal to their patrons than to the government. In the literary world, Gaius Maecenas, who lived at the end of the first century BCE, provided a stimulating environment and financial support for a notable group of Latin poets, including Horace and Virgil. At the beginnings of Luke's Gospel and Acts of the Apostles, mention is made of one Theophilus; who he was is unknown, but he could well have been the patron who made production of these two works possible.

Sacraments

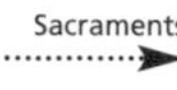

Architecture

Buildings

Investiture Controversy

Whether we should also regard as patrons the richer members of the early church who made it possible for Christians to worship in their homes is open to question, but they certainly played a similar role. When Christian people first gathered to worship, they did not build large buildings, but accommodated themselves in apartment houses and rooms. For the first two centuries of Christian history, these 'house-churches' were known as *tituli*, 'title churches', and were named after the families who owned the houses where they met. The *titulus* was a slab at the entrance bearing the owner's name. There were many such houses in Rome, and one of the most famous was found in the early twentieth century in present-day Syria, in the village of Dura Europos. It had been partially destroyed and over the years covered with desert sand. The person who saw to the extensive renovation of the private dwelling in order to house Christian worship was also a patron of the arts. One room for the ritual of baptism was decorated with paintings. But in the earliest period patronage was always that of family members who gave their property to Christian groups.

Church of England

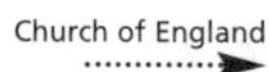

Constantine's 'conversion'

It was in the fourth century that the first patron in the traditional sense of the Christian church appeared, in the person of the Emperor Constantine, who had large basilicas constructed at major Christian sites. For example, his mother Helena, who was a Christian, went to Jerusalem and with the help of the bishop ascertained what was believed to be the site of the death and resurrection of Jesus. Constantine financed a great complex of buildings there, as well as others in Rome, Constantinople and in other places.

Renaissance
Reformation
Counter-Reformation

Under Constantine the hierarchy of the Christian church gained new influence and power, so the role of patronage passed to church leaders, primarily bishops. The names of church buildings changed from family names to those of saints and martyrs. In the early Middle Ages, bishops established themselves as powers over sacred and secular matters. They were the patrons of great cathedrals, the seats of power, and of other churches large and small. Their power of patronage slowly became wider as monastic centres grew. For instance, the monastic centre of Cluny, located in what was a remote area of France, became a focal point of patronage. The so-called Cluniac reform resulted in the construction of church buildings along the popular pilgrimage roads, even as far away as present-day Turkey and Israel. What emerges is a plurality of patrons, most of them church-related. At this time the power of the church, through the sacraments, to control the well-being and even the eternal state of souls was particularly great. There are many instances of royalty and wealthy merchants and families supporting the patronage activities of bishops, abbots and clergy.

One of the most influential abbots of the twelfth century was Abbot Suger of St Denis, near Paris. Suger was a patron who gathered artisans, architects and workers around the St Denis site to create a building in a new style which was to become known as Gothic. Out of that patronage grew a renewed aesthetic appreciation. Bernard of Clairvaux, who denounced it, was an opponent of Suger's efforts.

However, as was shown in the eleventh/twelfth-century dispute known as the Investiture Controversy, the role of the church in patronage more generally did not go unchallenged. In feudal society, lords had extensive control over churches in the lands under their control, and with it the right to appoint clergy to parishes or other ecclesiastical posts. This right was denoted by the technical term 'advowson' (connected with 'advoke' and 'advocate'). In the Roman Catholic Church it eventually died out, but it is more than a historical curiosity in the Church of England. Since advowsons could be given, bequeathed or even at one time sold (this was later prohibited), they have been handed on down to the present day. The patronage of many Church of England parishes is still in the hands of individuals, Oxford and Cambridge colleges and quite notably of evangelical societies, such as the Church Society and the Simeon Trust. Until 1986 anyone but an alien, an outlaw or a lunatic could be a patron, whether or not he or she was a Christian; now patrons have to be members of the Church of England. Theoretically bishops who refuse to accept patrons' nominees without due cause can be taken to court under civil law.

The time of the Renaissance, the Reformation and the Counter-Reformation saw the culmination of the kind of patronage typical of the ancient world. Pope Julius II had ambitious plans for building a new St Peter's in Rome (these were financed by his successor Leo X through a sale of indulgences which famously aroused the anger of Martin Luther) and was a great patron of artists, including Michelangelo, the young Raphael, and the architect and painter Bramante. So was Leo X, who also refounded Rome University. Although under the influence of the Reformation many traditional features of churches were abolished, with the destruction of windows, statues, altars, paintings, and so on, new works were produced which needed patrons. For instance, new 'Reformer' windows were made and new sculpture and new paintings were introduced. Martin Luther was a strong patron of the art of Lucas Cranach the Elder, and the results can be seen in the new altarpieces that were created.

The so-called Counter-Reformation (or Catholic Reformation) saw a renewed patronage of the arts throughout the Roman Catholic world. The artists were given a great deal of work to do by the church. Again, bishops were doubly active as patrons of the arts. The Roman Church latched on to the emerging Baroque style to renovate many spaces, so much so that this style was given great privilege and authority.

In the seventeenth century the Church of England was also an active patron. The Great Fire of London in 1666 gave the patrons of church architecture an enormous job to do. Out of that came the work of Christopher Wren, as he was given the task of rebuilding many of the parish churches in London. Eventually he was commissioned to design St Paul's Cathedral. His patron in all cases was both the Crown of England and the clergy of the Church of England. They had strong influence on the final design for St Paul's. Wren initially designed a Greek-cross shaped building, but the clergy patrons insisted that the design be changed to the form of a basilica. That form remains today.

A new form of artistic patronage took shape in the New World. In North America a strong role was played by early town organizations. The buildings that served the churches were also meeting places for a variety of town functions. Most often, the 'meeting house' was built on the town green. In South America the role of patronage remained for the most part with the bishops and clergy, as it had been established in Europe. They continued to use variations on the Baroque style, partly because of the success that it had had in Europe.

The churches in the New World became identified with great preachers, and the preachers became the patrons. In America, preachers such as Cotton Mather (1663–1728) and Jonathan Edwards (1703–58) were influential figures in patronage because of their powerful oratory. At the same time a lay leadership was emerging, as power and influence were equated with financial success. Many churches were built by lay leaders who became patrons by virtue of their money.

Today the role of patron is more diverse than ever before in the Christian tradition. Many influences shape the future of church patronage. Among these forces are strong religious leaders, influential wealthy persons, architectural expertise and democratic processes. The role of the clergy is slowly declining. Little in the education of modern clergy covers the role of good patronage, so the clergy are not prepared to take positions of leadership when patrons are needed. Two twentieth-century exceptions should be mentioned.

p. 476

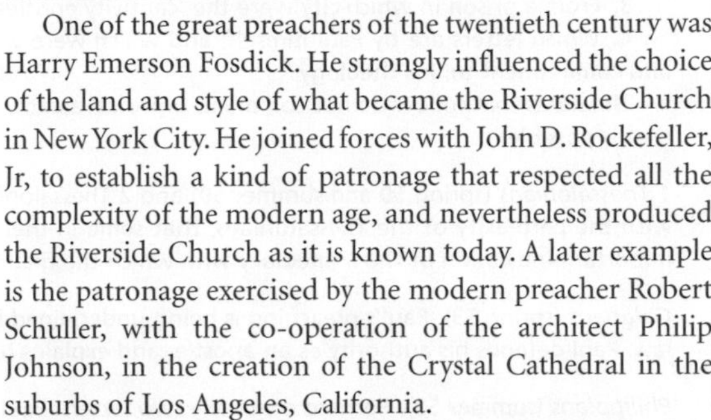

One of the great preachers of the twentieth century was Harry Emerson Fosdick. He strongly influenced the choice of the land and style of what became the Riverside Church in New York City. He joined forces with John D. Rockefeller, Jr, to establish a kind of patronage that respected all the complexity of the modern age, and nevertheless produced the Riverside Church as it is known today. A later example is the patronage exercised by the modern preacher Robert Schuller, with the co-operation of the architect Philip Johnson, in the creation of the Crystal Cathedral in the suburbs of Los Angeles, California.

The patronage of the Christian tradition today lies in the hands of many who exert influence on the material culture of the churches. Its rich diversity combines many of the economic and religious forces that make up modern-day Christianity. And as has always been the case, the divisions and strong opinions that strain the unity of the church have influence on patronage. One of the strongest new influences on patronage is best described as the secularization of the tradition. The adaptation of secular models for growing communities to Christianity is now emerging. Christian meeting places and Christian forms of worship are now being strongly influenced by what works in the secular culture. This process of integration is leading towards a new kind of patronage.

Secularization

JOHN W. COOK

A. F. Wallace-Hadrill, *Patronage in Ancient Society*, London: Routledge 1989; Evelyn Welch, *Art and Society in Ancient Italy*, 1350–1500, Oxford: OUP 1997

Paul

Paul of Tarsus, the zealous Jew and near-contemporary of Jesus who became a Christian, has sometimes been described as 'the real founder of Christianity'. Although this judgement is, at best, a half-truth, there is no question that Paul played a crucial role in the early development of the Christian faith: he can fairly be described as the most influential theologian of all time.

PAUL'S LETTERS

Reformation

It is difficult to overestimate the importance of Paul's letters in the history of Christian thought and practice – many episodes in the history of the church, not least the sixteenth-century Reformation, hinged on the interpretation of Pauline texts, especially the letter to the Romans.

Although Paul's letters can in general be dated more closely than most New Testament texts, composed as they were in the 50s, there is uncertainty in detail.

1. The letters as we have them may be consolidated versions of an originally more complex correspondence. How many letters did Paul write to the church in Corinth, and how are these embedded in 1 and 2 Corinthians as we now have them? Similarly, what pattern of correspondence lies behind 1 and 2 Thessalonians?

2. Was Galatians written to 'Galatians' in an ethnic sense (which would make it the earliest of Paul's letters), or to churches in the administrative region of Galatia (which would make 1 Thessalonians the earliest of his letters)?

3. From a prison in which city were the 'captivity epistles' (Philippians, Colossians, Ephesians, Philemon) written?

4. Which letters are by Paul himself, and which were written by other Christian leaders with a deep understanding of, and commitment to, his theology?

The dates that follow do not command universal assent, but indicate the kind of reconstruction of Paul's correspondence that is possible.

1 Thessalonians (spring 50 and summer 50) and 2 Thessalonians (late summer/autumn 50). Among other matters, Paul deals with the perplexity of the Thessalonians, that some in their church have died, and the Lord has not yet come in glory: an important indication of the immediacy with which the first Christian communities expected the end.

Galatians (spring 53). Paul's preaching is being undermined by rival teachers who insist that Christians must keep the Jewish law. Paul defends his authority as an apostle, and explains how Christians are justified in Christ through faith.

Philippians (summer 53). Perhaps originally two letters. Paul writes from prison (in Ephesus?) to reflect on his work and the possibility of his imminent death; the letter is remarkable for the sense of joy and thanksgiving which pervades it.

Colossians (summer 53). Pauline authorship has been contested. Paul reflects on Christ ('the image of the invisible God, the firstborn of all creation') and what it means to have died in Christ and have been raised with Christ.

Philemon (summer 53). Paul urges Philemon to take back a runaway slave, Onesimus, who is (or has recently become) a Christian.

1 and 2 Corinthians (54–6). Paul's Corinthian correspondence is rich in content, and complex in its history. He rebukes the Corinthian church for shortcomings in behaviour and community life, and touches along the way on issues of marriage and sexual ethics, the proper behaviour of women in the Christian assembly and the spirit in which the Lord's Supper should be celebrated. His meditation on the nature of love (1 Corinthians 13) and his thoughts on the resurrection of the dead (1 Corinthians 15) have been especially widely used in Christian worship. He urges the Corinthians to be generous in supporting the collection that he is making for the church in Jerusalem. His frustration breaks through in passages of passionate irony, which lead him to profound reflection on 'the foolishness of God'. The Corinthian letters therefore contain not only much that is important for Paul's thought, but also a vivid picture of the strains and pressures in an early Christian church.

Justification

Romans (56). This contains Paul's longest and most thorough statement of how God has reconciled us to him in Christ. He articulates his doctrine of justification ('being righteoused') through faith, and the new life that a Christian lives in Christ. The letter ends with a long series of greetings, which are helpful clues in reconstructing the sociology of the early Roman church.

Ephesians is generally thought to be by a colleague or disciple of Paul, although some defend Pauline authorship. If by Paul, it belongs to the same period as Philippians and Colossians. The letter returns to typically Pauline themes, of the working out of God's purpose in Christ, and the kind of response that Christians are called to make at the level of practical behaviour and in grasping their character as 'citizens with the saints and members of the household of God' (2.19).

Although the *Pastoral letters* (1 Timothy, 2 Timothy and Titus) are generally believed to be later than Paul's lifetime by one or two generations, they reflect a church whose ministry is much more structured and formalized than that in 1 Corinthians 12, in which definite officers exist (*episkopos* = 'overseer' or 'superintendent', later 'bishop'; *diakonos* = 'servant', later 'deacon'. It can be argued that 2 Timothy is by Paul – in which case it would be the last of his letters, written not long before his martyrdom in Rome (traditionally in 64 CE).

The order of the letters in the New Testament collections seems to be determined by length (longest at the beginning).

Jerome Murphy-O'Connor, *Paul: a Critical Life*, Oxford: OUP 1996

Attempting to reconstruct his theology is a difficult process, however, since his only writings are pastoral letters written to various Christian communities. These naturally deal with particular questions and problems, rather than spell out his beliefs. Only in his letter to the Romans do we have anything like a systematic account of the meaning of the gospel, but this, too, relates to a particular issue and concentrates on his conviction that the gospel was intended for non-Jews as well as Jews. Since Paul believed that the gospel was relevant to every aspect of life, however, his letters, even though concerned with 'practical theology', refer back constantly to the essentials of the gospel message. Indeed, the practical problems with which he had to deal may well have helped him to see the implications of his new faith.

Our knowledge of Paul's life and travels is very largely based on Luke's account in the Acts of the Apostles. Scholars are divided about the reliability of the information provided there, and prefer to rely on what Paul himself tells us. But whereas Paul is the central character in much of Acts, Paul himself is not concerned to relate his own story, and the information he provides occurs incidentally, when it is relevant to his argument. Any attempt to tell the story of Paul will therefore inevitably draw largely on the account given in Acts. It must always be remembered, though, that Luke was writing a number of years after the events he describes (how many is debatable), and that his knowledge of what happened was inevitably partial. It is, for example, notoriously difficult to reconcile what Luke tells us in Acts 15 about the so-called 'Council of Jerusalem' – called to discuss the question of whether or not Gentile (non-Jewish) converts should be required to be circumcised – with what Paul says about his dealings with the Jerusalem church in Galatians 2.1–10. Paul, embroiled in a heated discussion, saw the issues in a way that Luke appears not to have fully understood.

Luke tells Paul's story from his conversion (probably *c.* 33 CE) to his imprisonment in Rome. According to tradition, he was beheaded in Rome *c.* 64 CE. These dates are tentative, but a reference to Gallio, proconsul of Achaia, in Acts 18.12 suggests that Paul was in Corinth in 51–2 CE, when Gallio held office there.

Archaeology

It is Luke who tells us that Paul was born in Tarsus in Cilicia, but was trained in Jerusalem by Gamaliel, a famous first-century Jewish rabbi. It is clear from Paul's letters that he received the kind of Greek education that would have been available in Tarsus, and that he had been trained in rabbinic methods of expounding scripture. In the early chapters of Acts Luke refers to Paul by the Jewish name of 'Saul': 'Paul' would have been his Roman name, and Luke tells us that Paul was in fact a Roman citizen (Acts 16.37; 22.25–9). According to Luke, Paul was a tentmaker (Acts 18.3), and we learn from the letters that Paul continued to work at his trade to support himself (1 Thessalonians 2.9; 1 Corinthians 9.3–18). These details may well be correct, but what is important is the light they throw on the influences that made Paul what he was.

Bible

The incidental nature of the information concerning his own life with which Paul provides us is demonstrated by the way in which he refers to his Jewish heritage in Philippians 3.5–6 in order to demonstrate the overwhelming value of his faith in Christ, for which he has abandoned his former

PAUL ON HIMSELF

'But whatever anyone dares to boast of – I am speaking as a fool – I also dare to boast of that. Are they Hebrews? So am I. Are they Israelites? So am I. Are they descendants of Abraham? So am I. Are they servants of Christ? I am a better one – I am talking like a madman – with far greater labours, far more imprisonments, with countless beatings, and often near death. Five times I have received at the hands of the Jews the forty lashes less one. Three times I have been beaten with rods; once I was stoned. Three times I have been shipwrecked; a night and a day I have been adrift at sea; on frequent journeys, in danger from rivers, danger from robbers, danger from my own people, danger from Gentiles, danger in the city, danger in the wilderness, danger at sea, danger from false brethren; in toil and hardship, through many a sleepless night, in hunger and thirst, often without food, in cold and exposure. And apart from other things there is the daily pressure upon me of my anxiety for all the churches ... At Damascus, the governor under King Aretas guarded the city of Damascus in order to seize me, but I was let down in a basket through a window in the wall, and escaped his hands' (2 Corinthians 11.21–33).

'I know a man in Christ who fourteen years ago was caught up to the third heaven – whether in the body or out of the body I do not know, God knows. And I know that this man was caught up into Paradise – whether in the body or out of the body I do not know, God knows – and he heard things that cannot be told, which man may not utter. On behalf of this man I will boast, but on my own behalf I will not boast, except of my weakness. Though if I wish to boast, I shall not be a fool, for I shall be speaking the truth ... And to keep me from being too elated by the abundance of revelations, a thorn was given me in the flesh, a messenger of Satan, to harass me, to keep me from being too elated. Three times I besought the Lord about this, that it should leave me; but he said to me, "My grace is sufficient for you, for my power is made perfect in weakness"' (2 Corinthians 12.2–9).

privileges. Here we discover, among other things, that he had been a Pharisee, a persecutor of the church because of his zeal for the law, and blameless in his obedience to its commands. Elsewhere we learn something of his experiences as an apostle when he explains what has happened to him since he visited those to whom he is writing. These references tend to be vague, however: he writes, for example, of an 'affliction' he experienced in Asia, but does not explain what it was – only that it was life-threatening (2 Corinthians 1.8–9). He insists frequently that he is an apostle, called by God (Romans 1.1; 1 Corinthians 1.1; 2 Corinthians 1.1; Galatians 1.1), and says that he has seen the Risen Lord (1 Corinthians 9.1; 15.8–11) and was called to proclaim Christ to the Gentiles (Galatians 1.15–16; Romans 1.5), but never relates the dramatic story of his so-called 'conversion' on the Damascus Road which Luke records at length three times (Acts 9.1–19; 22.3–21; 26.4–18).

p. 750

That particular story illustrates well the different nature of our sources. In Galatians 1.13–17, Paul apparently refers to the same event: he describes his persecution of the Christian community, says that God had set him apart before he was born and called him to preach the gospel to the Gentiles, revealing his Son to him and through him. Following his call, Paul travelled to Damascus. Luke, the story-teller, relates the narrative in graphic detail, but the core of the story is essentially the same: Paul, zealous for the law, set off to Damascus intending to persecute the Christians there (Acts 9.1–2; 22.3–5; 26.5, 9–12; cf. 1 Corinthians 15.9; Philippians 3.6); he had a vision of Christ (described as a 'light', Acts 9.3; 22.6; 26.13), and was called by him to take the gospel to the Gentiles (9.15; 22.21; 26.17–18).

Paul the Jew

Origins and background ➤
Conversion
Messiah
Resurrection ➤
p. 1152

The emphasis on Paul's mission in all these accounts points to the fact that his 'Damascus Road' experience was essentially a call rather than a conversion. It is true that he was converted from a zeal for the law that had led him to persecute the followers of Jesus to a conviction that Jesus was in fact the Christ, or Jewish Messiah – i.e. God's 'anointed' one. For Paul, however, this was not a conversion from one religion to another. His God was still the God of his forefathers, who had revealed himself to his people Israel in the past, and called them to serve him, the God whom he had sought to obey all his life. God himself was faithful to his past promises (Romans 6.3–4; 9.6), but Paul now recognized what he had failed to see earlier, that the good news about Jesus Christ had been 'promised beforehand through the prophets in the holy scriptures' (Romans 1.2). As Luke graphically expressed it, the scales had fallen from Paul's eyes (Acts 9.18), and he saw God's purpose in a different way. Having previously vilified Jesus as a blasphemer, justly put to death, Paul was now convinced that God had raised Jesus from the dead and proclaimed him Lord. Having once believed Jesus to have been under God's curse, he now acknowledged that Jesus was the source of blessing for the whole world (Galatians 3.13–14).

Unknown artist, Paul being let down in a basket from the Damascus city wall (2 Corinthians 11.33), picture in National Museum, Damascus

Although Paul's conviction that Jesus was the Messiah changed his life, he never abandoned his hope in the God whom he had worshipped all his life. The belief that Paul was 'converted' from one religion to another was encouraged by subsequent developments. Paul's own mission to the Gentiles meant that large numbers of former pagans flocked into the church. Some time around the end of the New Testament period there came a 'parting of ways', when Christianity split from Judaism and became a separate religion; growing antipathy between Jew and Christian meant that Christians saw Jews as their opponents, even as enemies. The differences between them were stressed, and the break was inevitable.

It was Paul's belief in Jesus' resurrection that changed him from persecutor to disciple. Resurrection of the dead was part of Jewish hope, and was stressed by the Pharisees, but this general resurrection was expected at the end of time, on the Day of the Lord – the Day of Judgement. Now Christians were affirming that this future hope had been realized in the case of one individual, Jesus. The recognition that he was the expected Messiah, however, meant that his resurrection was seen as a representative one. Just as the fate of the king affected his subjects, so what happened to Jesus affected others. With Jesus' resurrection a new age had dawned, and the longed-for 'end-time' of Jewish expectation had in a sense arrived, like the first-fruits of harvest (1 Corinthians 15.20), even though final consummation still lay in the future.

Jesus' death and resurrection

The death and resurrection of Jesus, whom Paul now acknowledged as Christ, were thus seen as a crucial turning-point in history. How, then, was the death of Jesus to be explained? Paul used various images to express what it had achieved. He spoke of God 'reconciling the world to himself in Christ, not counting their trespasses against them' (2 Corinthians 5.19), and described Jesus' death as bringing redemption – i.e. release from slavery (Romans 3.24; Galatians 4.5). Elsewhere, he compared it to the sacrifice of the Passover lamb (the means by which God saved his people, 1 Corinthians 5.7). In Romans 3.25, he used the mysterious Greek word *hilasterion*, which is often translated as 'a sacrifice of atonement', but which is used in the Greek translation of the Old Testament to refer to the 'mercy seat'; this 'seat' covered the ark of the covenant in the Holy of Holies, the innermost sanctuary in the temple, and was sprinkled with blood by the high priest on the Day of Atonement. Paul seemed to be thinking of Christ as the place where God and his people were brought together and sins were annulled.

Christ's death, like his resurrection, was representative. Paul often referred to his death as being 'for us' (Romans 5.8; 1 Thessalonians 5.10), or 'for our sins' (1 Corinthians 15.3; Galatians 1.4). It was natural to link Jesus' death with sin: although crucifixion was a Roman punishment, the Jewish law had decreed that criminals who were executed should be exposed on a tree, as a sign that they had fallen under God's curse (Deuteronomy 21.23). The resurrection, however, was a clear sign of God's approval: by this action, God had declared Jesus to be righteous.

The resurrection was also a demonstration of God's own righteousness (Romans 1.17; 3.21–2), and so the fulfilment of Old Testament hopes that God would show himself to be righteous by setting things to rights. This hope included the expectation that God would save his people and punish the wicked. Now God had indeed put things to rights, through the death and resurrection of Jesus, not simply by raising him, but by 'setting-to-rights' ('justifying') sinners, restoring them to a right relationship with himself (Romans 5.6–11). Paul uses a Greek verb (*dikaioo*) that is related to the terms meaning 'righteousness' and 'righteous'; although normally translated by the verb 'to justify', it basically means 'to put right'. Astonishingly, Paul claimed that the ungodly and rebellious share in the verdict of 'not guilty' pronounced on Jesus at the resurrection, and have been restored to a relationship with God.

What, then, does Paul mean by saying that Jesus' death was 'for us'? The clearest explanation is found in Romans 5, where he compares and contrasts the figures of Adam and Christ. According to the story in Genesis 3, sin entered the world because Adam disobeyed God, so bringing the punishment of death upon himself and all his descendants, who also sinned. Paul was very much aware of human solidarity: to understand what he meant, we need only think of the way in which, in our modern world, every choice we make affects the welfare of others; whether we approve or not, we are all members of a society which is far from perfect, often unjust, cruel and repressive. Although Paul speaks of Adam, the name in fact means 'Man', and Adam is the representative of all humanity; all men and women share his status before God – he is in effect 'Everyman'. But Jesus himself, as Paul often emphasizes, was also a man (Romans 5.17; 1 Corinthians 15.21; Galatians 4.4; Philippians 2.7); although he did not sin, he was identified with sinful humanity (Romans 8.3; 2 Corinthians 5.21), even to the point of enduring the punishment for sin, death (Philippians 2.8). Christ's death, then, was the result of human sin: he died 'because of our trespasses' (Romans 4.25).

Sacrifice
Atonement
Covenant

In contrast to Adam, however, Christ was obedient to God (Romans 5.19; Philippians 2.8); working through Christ's obedience, God showed his overwhelming grace by reversing what had happened through Adam: Adam's disobedience had resulted in humanity sharing his sinfulness and condemnation, but Christ's obedience enabled humanity to share his righteousness and acquittal (Romans 5.15–21). Christ had shared our human life, identifying himself with our alienation from God: he had in effect been 'made sin', and had died. The resurrection had reversed the verdict, and the result was that, united with him, men and women now shared his acquittal and his status of righteousness before God (2 Corinthians 5.21; Romans 4.25). As our representative, he died 'for' us, and with his resurrection a 'new creation' had come into being (2 Corinthians 5.17); the longed-for new age had been inaugurated.

But how are men and women to share this new status before God? In order to do so, they have to identify themselves with Christ. This is done by baptism 'into Christ' (Romans 6.3). Baptism is clearly an appropriate rite, since in Jewish thought water symbolizes not only cleansing (Psalm 51.2; Isaiah 1.16) but new life (Isaiah 35.6–7; 41.15). In Paul's day, the candidate was immersed beneath the waters, so that baptism was also an obvious metaphor for death and burial, followed by resurrection. Baptism into Christ is thus seen as baptism into his death (Romans 6.3). Paul's experience of identification with Christ is so real and so important that he speaks of being crucified with Christ (Romans 6.6; Galatians 2.19), and so dying to sin (Romans 6.2, 10), and of living with him (1 Thessalonians 5.10). This new life has already begun: 'It

Initiation
Justification

PAUL'S MISSIONARY JOURNEYS

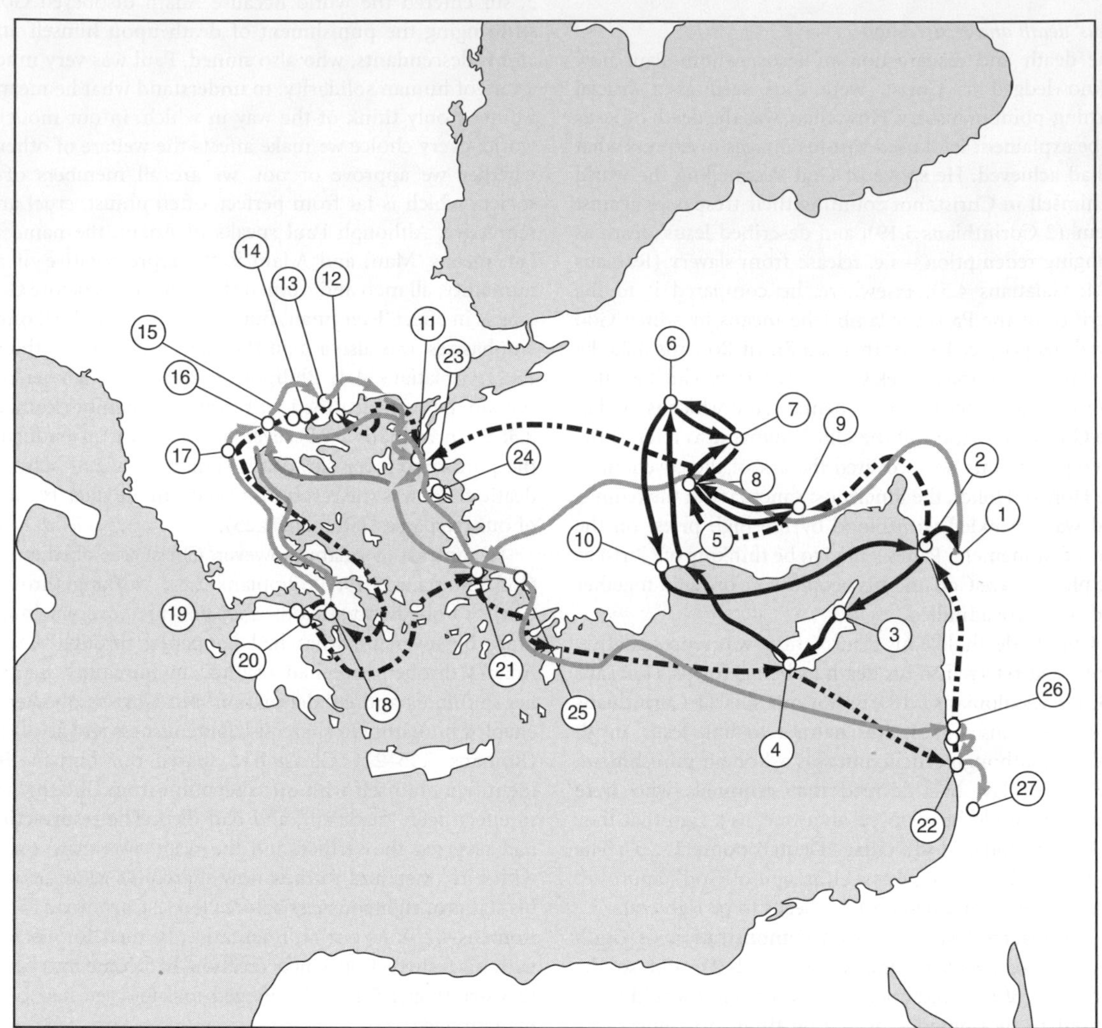

Paul was an indefatigable traveller in his zeal to preach the gospel all over the then known world. On the basis of the account of his activities in the Acts of the Apostles his travels have been divided into three journeys, as follows:

First missionary journey (Acts 13.2–14.28) (——————): Antioch (1), Seleucia (2), Salamis (3), Paphos (4), Perga (5), Pisidian Antioch (6), Iconium (7), Lystra (8), Derbe (9), Attalia (10).

Second missionary journey (Acts 15.36–18.22) (— · · —): Antioch (1), Derbe (9), Lystra (8), Troas (11), Neapolis (12), Philippi (13), Amphipolis (14), Apollonia (15), Thessalonica (16), Beroea (17), Athens (18), Corinth (19), Cenchreae (20), Ephesus (21), Caesarea (22).

Third missionary journey (Acts 19.21–21.17) (——————): Antioch (1), Ephesus (21), Thessalonica (16), Corinth (19), Philippi (13), Troas (11), Assos (23), Mitylene (24), Miletus (25), Tyre (26), Caesarea (22), Jerusalem (27).

Because the account in Acts cannot always be reconciled with what Paul says in his letters, these 'journeys' may contain some oversimplifications, and the dating of some events is not always clear. Be this as it may, his was a remarkable achievement.

is no longer I who live,' writes Paul, 'but Christ who lives in me' (Galatians 2.20). But though Christians already experience a new life, they continue to live an earthly existence, so that resurrection with Christ still lies in the future (Romans 6.4–5; 1 Corinthians 6.14; 15.12–57).

Faith

The identification of the believer with Christ clearly depends on a personal trust in what God has done through him. Summing up what this means, Paul writes: 'If you confess with your mouth that Jesus is Lord, and believe in your heart that God raised him from the dead, you will be saved' (Romans 10.9). Paul here uses a Greek verb (*pisteuo*) that is normally translated 'to believe' or 'to trust'. The noun related to it (*pistis*) means 'faith', 'trust', or 'belief'. Together, noun and verb express what Paul understands to be the appropriate human response to the gracious activity of God. Those who trust in what God has done through Christ are 'put right' with him.

This is a principle that Paul insists is set out in scripture. He appeals to Habakkuk 2.4, which links righteousness with faith (Romans 1.17; Galatians 3.11), and points to the example of Abraham, the great patriarch of the nation, who 'believed God, and it was counted to him as righteousness' (Genesis 15.6, quoted in Romans 4.3; Galatians 3.6). Those who trust in God are the true descendants of Abraham, and so inherit the promises of blessing that were made to him by God (Romans 4.16; Galatians 3.6–7, 14). The Genesis story tells how Abraham had trusted God to bring life out of Sarah's dead womb; for Christians, faith is centred on what God has done in raising Christ from the dead (Romans 4.18–21, 24) and in Christ himself (Galatians 2.16; Philippians 1.29).

On several occasions Paul uses an ambiguous phrase which translates literally as 'the faith of Christ', but which has traditionally been understood to mean 'faith *in* Christ' (e.g. Romans 3.22; Galatians 2.16). It is possible that Paul is thinking of Christ's own faith – his trust in God, even when his obedience to God's will resulted in his death. If so, then even the faith that Christians have is a sharing in the faith of Christ. Certainly, in all these passages he stresses the fact that Christians trust in God or in Christ.

Jew and Gentile

Paul's emphasis on faith is crucial in his argument about the position of Gentiles within the Christian community. Gentiles who wished to belong to the Jewish community had to accept circumcision (in the case of males) and agree to keep the commandments of the Torah, or law. When, following the resurrection, the early followers of Jesus proclaimed him to be the Messiah, they had no thought of founding a community outside Judaism. God had fulfilled his promises to Israel, and the natural way for Jewish Christians to respond was to worship him in the temple and in synagogues and to obey his commands. But then came an influx of Gentiles, responding to the gospel message. If they believed in Jesus as God's Messiah, and so wished to become members of God's people, was it necessary for them to become Jews? Many assumed that it was.

Surprisingly – since he had been a Pharisee, and exceedingly zealous in keeping the law – Paul argued differently. He may well have been persuaded by the evidence of changed lives. Gentiles had already responded to the gospel and been transformed by the Holy Spirit without becoming Jews – a fact to which Paul appeals when writing to the Galatians (Galatians 3.2–5). Clearly they had already received the blessing that God had promised to pour out on his people at the end of time (Joel 2.28–9). If the end-time had already dawned, and God himself had given these Gentiles the promised blessing, then they must already have been included among his people: there was no need for them to accept circumcision or undertake to obey the regulations of the law. Indeed, to do so would be to deny what God had already done.

Holy Spirit

Faith

Paul's argument is based on his conviction that, with the death and resurrection of Christ, the end-time has already arrived, even though the present era continues. He now sees the law as an interim arrangement, intended for the guidance of Israel until the era of faith arrived (Galatians 3.19–20, 23–6). The law is not destroyed by the gospel, but fulfilled (Romans 3.31), since what the law strove for – righteousness (Romans 9.31) – and what the law promised – life (Leviticus 18.5, quoted in Romans 10.5; Galatians 3.12) – had now been given by God, through Christ, to those who trust in him (Romans 10.4; 1.17).

The law, then, belongs to a temporary era. In contrast to the end-time, which is marked by the gift of the Spirit, the present era – in which men and women continue to live – is characterized by the 'flesh', that is, by humanity in its mortality, subject to pain, disease, death and sin. In the present age, creation is subjected to frustration and weakness because of Adam's sin. In the future age, which has already broken into this one with the resurrection of Christ, creation will be restored to what God intended for it (Romans 8.20–1). Moreover, the law, even though it had been given to Israel by God, was ineffectual because it operated in the realm of the flesh (Romans 7.12–20; 8.3). Its true purpose, then, was not to provide a way by which men and women might make themselves acceptable to God – as those who insisted that Gentile Christians must observe it implied – but to bear witness to what God fundamentally required from them – trust in his grace. God's righteousness has been revealed apart from law, in the person of Christ, but Law and Prophets both bear witness to it (Romans 3.21–2).

In Galatians, one of the earliest of his letters, Paul engaged in a heated argument with Gentile Christians who had apparently been persuaded that more was required of them than faith in God if they were to enjoy the full benefits of their new religion: they needed to accept circumcision, they had been told, and to keep all the regulations of the Jewish law, if they were to become members of God's people, Israel. Paul protested that they were already children of Abraham by virtue of their union with Christ, and had already received God's grace; to accept the law would have been to return to the past, and to exchange their status as God's children for slavery. It would be to deny that Christ's death and resurrection had transferred them from the present age into the new one (Galatians 1.4; 2.21). His argument was not with Judaism itself, but with the attempt to force Gentiles who were already Christians to become Jews. Like the man in Jesus' parable who sold everything he had to buy the pearl beyond price (Matthew 13.45–6), Paul saw his new relationship with God as being of far more value than the one he had had in the past (Philippians 3.7–8). What was being urged on the Galatians, then, was the equivalent of throwing away a priceless pearl for the sake of something inferior.

p. 506
Roman empire
p. 658

The metaphor that Paul himself uses is that of glory. Moses, when he received the law, saw something of what God was like; according to the story in Exodus, he caught a glimpse of God after he had passed by, but was unable to look on his face (Exodus 33.17–23). Nevertheless, what he had seen and heard meant that he reflected the glory of God, but this glory, great as it was, was only temporary. The glory that we see on the face of Jesus does not fade, and those who look at him reflect his glory, because he is the image of God himself (2 Corinthians 3.7–18; 4.4). Paul does not deny that the law was a revelation of God, but it was limited, because it was 'written on tablets of stone', not on 'human hearts' (2 Corinthians 3.3) – an image that Paul has taken from Jeremiah 31.33. Today, he might perhaps have compared a copy of a picture sent on a fax machine with the original.

Christology

Christology

Christ lies at the centre of Paul's teaching – hardly surprising, since Christ was the new element in his theology, and his death and resurrection had changed Paul's whole outlook. It has to be remembered, however, that it was God who sent Jesus, and God who raised him up; the gospel is about the power of God and God's salvation and righteousness (Romans 1.16–17). God was at work in what Jesus did (2 Corinthians 5.19). Whatever is said about Jesus is, for Paul, a way of glorifying God (Philippians 2.11).

Jesus

Who, then, *was* Jesus? Paul commonly referred to him as 'Christ' – frequently in conjunction with 'Jesus'. Although he used 'Christ' as a name, Paul could hardly have forgotten that it meant 'Messiah', or 'anointed one': God had worked through his Messiah to fulfil his promises to Israel. Paul's Gentile readers, however, would quickly forget its significance and treat it simply as a name.

An early Christian confession was 'Jesus is Lord' (Romans 10.9; 1 Corinthians 12.3; Philippians 2.11). In the Old Testament, 'Lord' is a name used of God himself. Although Paul applies some of these texts about the Lord to Christ, he never identifies him with God (1 Corinthians 8.6). Rather, Christ exercises lordship under the authority of God the Father (1 Corinthians 15.24–8; Philippians 2.11). The confession that 'Jesus is Lord' would, in time, bring Christians into conflict with the Roman empire, which came to demand that those whom it ruled acknowledged Caesar as lord.

Central to Paul's understanding of Jesus is his conviction that Jesus was 'the son of God'. His gospel, he told the Romans, concerned 'God's son' (Romans 1.3, 9; Galatians 1.15). The term is used in key texts where he sums up the content of his message: God sent his son (Romans 8.3; Galatians 4.4), and gave him up to death (Romans 8.32). The idea of sonship in the ancient world implied close likeness, identity of purpose, and obedience on the part of the son. Not surprisingly, then, we are told that the son gave himself up (Galatians 2.20). As son of God, Christ reveals what God is like and carries out God's will: he also enables men and women to be reconciled to God through the death of his son (5.10), and as a result of his death and resurrection (when he was openly declared to be God's son, Romans 1.4) they share his sonship (Romans 8.11–17; Galatians 4.5) and become like him (Romans 8.29). They share Christ's 'glory' (Romans 8.17–18, 30; 2 Corinthians 3.18). Another way of expressing this is to speak of Christ as 'the image of God' (2 Corinthians 4.4: Colossians 1.15). Christians are in a process of being conformed to his image (Romans 8.29; 2 Corinthians 3.18). Since Adam was created 'after the image of God, and in his likeness' (Genesis 1.26), Christians are being restored to what God intended for men and women from the beginning of time. In becoming like Christ, they become obedient to God's will (Romans 1.5; Philippians 2.12).

It is because of their close union with Christ that Christians become like him. Christ's death and resurrection are re-enacted in the lives of believers: they die to sin (Romans 6.10–11), die to the law (Galatians 2.19), and the life they now live they live 'in Christ' – or rather, Christ lives in them (Galatians 2.20). It is 'in Christ' that Christians are 'children of God' (literally 'sons', who share Christ's sonship), since in baptism they 'clothed themselves' with Christ (Galatians 3.26–7). It is because they are in Christ that they are now being conformed

Peter and Paul saying farewell, relief, third/fourth-century ivory buckle

into his likeness (Romans 8.29). The fact that they are 'in Christ' is the basis of Paul's appeal to his converts to make his manner of life their own (Philippians 2.1–5).

Ethics

This conformity to Christ leads to what Paul calls 'sanctification' (Romans 6.17, 22; 1 Thessalonians 4.3). At the heart of Judaism lay the command: 'I am holy, therefore you shall be holy' (Leviticus 19.2). God had saved Israel and made them God's own people; for that reason they were to serve God. In the same way, those whom God had made his own in Christ were expected to serve God (1 Thessalonians 1.9). They must become like God – and what God was had been revealed in Christ. Whereas the Jews had looked to the law for guidance as to how to live, Christians now looked to Christ. The qualities which Christians share are theirs because they are 'in Christ', and because the Spirit of Christ is at work in them. Writing to the Philippians, for example, Paul appeals to them to live as those who are 'in Christ'; reminding them that Christ was obedient, he urges them to continue to show their own obedience (Philippians 2.1, 5, 8, 12). In his letter to the Romans, after spelling out what it means to live 'in Christ' (Romans 8), Paul turns to the implications for Christian living (12.1–2). Christ died and lived again in order to be their Lord, and therefore Christians no longer live or die for themselves, but for him; whatever they do must be done for him (14.7–9). They must 'welcome one another, as Christ welcomed' them (15.7). The love shown by Jesus (Galatians 2.20) must be shown by the community (Galatians 5.13–14).

Ethics

Paul's insistence that Gentiles should not put themselves 'under law' was open to grave misunderstanding. Some of them assumed that freedom from the law meant that they were free to live as they pleased (Romans 6.15; Galatians 5.1, 13). Paul insisted that faith must be followed by obedience (Romans 1.5) – obedience not, however, to the law but to 'the law of Christ', which is love. Faced with a practical problem about how Christians should behave which was dividing the Corinthian church, Paul urged them to be concerned for the consciences of others, and to do nothing that might destroy the faith of others (1 Corinthians 8.7–13; 10.23–9). Those who live according to the Spirit and who love one another (Galatians 5.16–26) find that what the law requires is fulfilled (Romans 8.4; 13.8–10; Galatians 5.14). However, clearly many of Paul's converts found his advice impracticable, and required clear rules laying down what they should and should not do.

Apocalyptic

Those who belong to Christ are termed 'holy ones' ('saints', Romans 1.7; 1 Corinthians 1.2). Because they are all 'in Christ', they are said to be 'one body' in him (1 Corinthians 12.12–13). The Holy Spirit gives different gifts to each member for the benefit of the whole community, in order to unite and strengthen it (Romans 12.4–8; 1 Corinthians 12.14–31). Gifts of ministry are among these, but there is no hint of a structured ministry. The Christian community is also likened to a temple, sanctified by the Spirit of God living within it.

Community

Ministry and ministers

Canon

The Spirit – the power of God at work in the world – is given to all believers (Romans 8.9; 1 Corinthians 12.3). Love – which means concern for others (1 Corinthians 13) – is one of the 'fruits' of the Spirit (Galatians 5.22). The gift of the Spirit is seen as a guarantee of the life that will follow the final resurrection (Romans 8.23; 2 Corinthians 5.5). First, however, Paul expects Christ to return again (Philippians 3. 20; 1 Thessalonians 1.10). He uses typical Jewish 'apocalyptic' language to express his confidence that God will finally triumph (1 Corinthians 15.24–8, 50–7; 1 Thessalonians 4.14–17). Since Christ has been raised, Christians too will be raised: Paul insists that the Christian hope is for resurrection of the body (i.e. of the person), not a nebulous, bodiless existence, but this 'body' is spiritual, not fleshly (1 Corinthians 15.35–50). Finally comes the day of judgement (Romans 2.16: Philippians 1.10). When that arrives, Christians will fully share the likeness of Christ (1 Corinthians 15.49) and God's kingdom will finally be established (1 Corinthians 15.24–8).

Love

Paul's influence on later Christian thinking has been enormous, but he has frequently been misunderstood. Once his letters were recognized as part of the 'canon' of scripture they were treated as authoritative, and as having validity for all situations: Paul, who had insisted that righteousness was a matter of grace, not law, was thus turned into a lawgiver! Teaching addressed to particular

PAUL AND HIS LATER READERS

Paul's thought is clearly complex, and understanding is not helped by the way it is expressed in a series of letters written on different occasions; only his letter to the Romans is more systematic in its approach. But Paul has nevertheless had a tremendous influence on Christian thought and practice, not least in attitudes to women. Is there a central notion that lies at the core of his thinking?

Justification

Martin Luther famously focused on Paul's idea of 'justification by faith'; in doing so he was in the company of, among others, Augustine, John Calvin and John Wesley. According to this view human beings, though created good, have been so corrupted by sin that they are incapable of pleasing God and are therefore under condemnation. Their situation must be put right by divine grace, accepted in faith; it cannot be remedied by any works that they do. The law of Moses was given to make people aware of the need for divine grace, and those who are saved from condemnation need not bear the burden of observing its requirements.

However, with the rise of modern biblical criticism and the possibility of seeing Paul against the background of the Judaism of his time, this has increasingly been seen as an interpretation which distorts both Paul's thinking and the Judaism of his day. E. P. Sanders in particular has demonstrated that the Judaism of Paul's time was certainly not a joyless religion consisting of countless legalistic regulations to be observed, but is to be seen in a far more positive light.

This new approach, shared by many other scholars, has led to a change of perspective on Paul. It has been described like this:

Human beings find themselves in an ordered world which is not of their making. They can acknowledge or deny their dependence on the Creator, accept or reject the ordering of his creation. If they accept it they will find life; if they reject it they court disaster. The law is an appropriate human response to God, a divine gift to Israel. It contains regulations which are binding only on Jews. Humanity generally does not and cannot submit to this law, so it cannot be a way to life for them; indeed it emphasizes their plight. But God's righteousness revealed in Jesus is established quite apart from the law, though at the same time it fulfils the law.

This interpretation of Paul not only reflects his thinking better but also shows how many Christian understandings of Judaism are caricatures, which on closer acquaintance with Judaism past and present need to be replaced.

E. P. Sanders, *Paul and Palestinian Judaism*, London: SCM Press and Philadelphia: Fortress Press 1977; Stephen Westerholm, *Perspectives Old and New on Paul. The 'Lutheran' Paul and His Critics*, Grand Rapids, MI: Eerdmans 2004 situations took on new meaning when the letters were read out of their original context. When Christianity finally broke away from Judaism, arguments about what was demanded of Gentiles became irrelevant; growing antisemitism meant that Paul's teaching about the law was misinterpreted and seen as an attack on Judaism. Whereas Paul agonized over whether Israel would be saved, later generations were more concerned with the salvation of the individual. Martin Luther emphasized Paul's teaching about 'justification' by faith, but his attack on 'merit' led to the misconception that Judaism was a legalistic religion.

For Paul's teaching to be understood, he needs to be interpreted in the light of the social and religious structures of his own day. His importance lies, not only in the influence his teaching had on later generations, but in his profound grasp of the implications of the Christian gospel, and his ability to relate it to every aspect of life and behaviour.

MORNA D. HOOKER

C. K. Barrett, *Paul: An Introduction to His Thought*, London: Geoffrey Chapman 1994; Jürgen Becker, *Paul: Apostle to the Gentiles*, Louisville, KY: Westminster John Knox Press 1993; James D. G. Dunn, *The Theology of Paul the Apostle*, Edinburgh: T&T Clark 1998; Martin Hengel, *The Pre-Christian Paul*, London: SCM Press and Philadelphia: Trinity Press International 1992; M. D. Hooker, *Paul: A Short Introduction*, Oxford: Oneworld 2003; David Horrell, *An Introduction to the Study of Paul*, London and New York: Continuum 2000; Veronica Koperski, *What are they Saying about Paul and the Law?*, New York: Paulist Press 2001; Jerome Murphy-O'Connor, *Paul: A Critical Life*, Oxford and New York: OUP 1997; E. P. Sanders, *Paul*, Oxford and New York: OUP 1991; Krister Stendahl, *Paul Among Jews and Gentiles*, London: SCM Press 1977; John Ziesler, *Pauline Christianity*, revised edition, Oxford and New York: OUP 1990

Peace churches

The 'peace churches', a term used since the 1930s, are three communities descended from radical reform movements in Europe beginning in the sixteenth century. They have been given this name because non-violence was integral to their identity and mission. Placed chronologically, the first of these is the Anabaptists, whose most numerous descendants are Mennonites (the Hutterites and Amish are also of Anabaptist descent; representing a separatist interpretation of the Anabaptist vision, their focus has remained on the indirect influence of a non-violent lifestyle on society rather than direct engagement with it); the second is the Religious Society of Friends (Quakers) and the third the Church of the Brethren. While each of them has a separate theological and historical identity, the inspiration for and dynamics of their origin has substantive parallels.

Quakers
Brethren

p. 685

All of them protested against a church life that seemed to have lost its affinity for the teaching of Jesus and the life of the earliest church. The person of Jesus, his oneness with God, his teaching of love for neighbour and enemy, and his non-resistant death inspired these radical believers to do likewise. They believed that the Holy Spirit was present in the church of their day and in the life of every sincere believer no less than for the first Christians. Their dissent quickly attracted others wanting to live the life found in the New Testament, but also brought rebuke and then persecution from the established religious and political order. What had begun as a movement that was 'in the air' of that time soon developed into groups of believers, some of them in contention with others in the same movement for the 'true' interpretation of the original vision. Such organizational and theological divisions persist into the present; some groups participate fully in society, while 'old orders' preserve a separate, traditional existence. Large numbers of each community emigrated from Europe to North America in search of freer settings in which to live out their convictions. William Penn (1644–1718) invited all of them to take refuge in his commonwealth of Pennsylvania. There all of the peace churches developed a settled rural life characterized by simplicity, self-sacrifice and non-violence.

Jesus
Salvation
Holy Spirit

Through evangelistic and social mission, beginning late in the nineteenth century, they spread beyond the North Atlantic world to Asia, Africa and Latin America. In response to the carnage of World War I they mounted large-scale relief efforts in Europe. Brethren, Quakers and Mennonites began their institutional co-operation in North America in the aftermath of World War I as the 'historic peace churches' to press for the right of conscientious objection and its implementation in alternate service and for negotiation as an alternative to violence in the resolution of international conflict. After World War II they expanded their relief work, soon turned to development projects, and were pioneers in the field of conflict resolution, locally and internationally.

Mennonites

The Mennonites, named after one of their devoted early leaders, Menno Simons, emerged out of the Anabaptist movement of the early sixteenth century. Anabaptism, in turn, was a response to popular protest movements in German- and Dutch-speaking Europe aimed at restoring social and religious rights to ordinary people. Most of them concluded that the gospel could be faithfully lived

Anabaptists
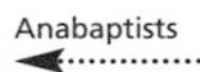

out only in freely-entered communities of disciples. They held that the state was ordained by God to restrain evil and promote good, but that it had no role in regulating religious belief and practice. For most Anabaptists this meant that Christians could not go to war and that the state could not impose the death penalty. This understanding of the church and its mission led them to reject infant baptism, which was administered to all infants born in 'Christian' countries, in favour of believer's baptism, which was given only to those who accepted Christ and his way (Romans 6). They taught that the Sermon on the Mount (Matthew 5–7) was the heart of Jesus' way: its apex is love of enemy and prayer for persecutors. Such a way of life was possible because of the transformative presence of the Holy Spirit in the church and each believer.

p. 385

The Anabaptists thought of themselves as orthodox, trinitarian Christians committed to living out the teaching of the New Testament in accord with Jesus' teaching and example. Persecution dispersed them across Europe, from the North Sea to Slovakia. Congregations met in secret, worshipped with simple forms, dispersed when they were discovered, and eventually negotiated with more tolerant local rulers to farm unarable land and quietly to practise their faith on condition that they did not evangelize or otherwise threaten the existing order of things. They continued their rejection of the oath and military service as defining dimensions of their identity.

War and peace

In the late seventeenth century Mennonites from regions where they were still discriminated against took refuge in Pennsylvania. In the late eighteenth century others sought religious freedom in South Russia. In both settings their pacifism was a chief reason – on their part and that of society at large – for a lifestyle of rural seclusion in which their goal was to be a 'city on a hill' (Matthew 5). This changed significantly only in the early twentieth century, when a combination of economic prospects and a renewed sense of evangelistic and social mission drew Mennonites into the mainstream of society in North America. They founded colleges that specialized in theology, education, nursing, social work and later peace studies.

Pietism

Quakers (The Religious Society of Friends)

The Quakers, so named because of their quaking under the inspiration of the Holy Spirit, emerged out of the profound religious and political dissent in England in the 1640s. Over against the hierarchical ordering of church and state, George Fox and kindred minds offered ordinary people a life-transforming indwelling of the Holy Spirit. They believed that the 'peaceable kingdom' was already at hand, making a new ordering of life possible within history. Jesus was not a far-off figure but 'one who had come to teach his people himself'. Life lived in his Spirit turned worldly conventions and institutions upside down: it was possible now to live as Jesus had lived, seeking 'that of God' in everyone and loving one's enemies. Among the most innovative of Quaker convictions was their insistence that in God's eyes butchers, bakers and candlestick makers had the same status as kings, nobles and clergy. Similarly, women were as blessed agents of the Holy Spirit as men.

Like Mennonites, Quakers were hounded for the intransigence of their conviction. William Penn was one of them. When he inherited vast tracts of land in the New World, many of his co-religionists joined him in establishing a social order based on 'upside-down' values. For two generations a Quaker-led government provided tolerance for all manner of dissenters and governed without a standing militia or capital punishment. Even after they ceased to govern Pennsylvania, Quakers continued to work for a society in which compassion and non-violence transform unjust structures, e.g., in the reform of prison life.

Because of their belief in 'that of God in everyone' Quakers worked in the confidence that sinful institutions could be reformed. After World War I this conviction was applied not only in providing relief to war-torn countries but also in working for the transformation of political institutions under the guidance of the British, American and Canadian Friends Service Committees. They were a benign background presence in the formation of the League of Nations, experimenting with the application of personal principles of peacemaking to international affairs. At the same time, conservative Quakers engaged in evangelism and built up churches in Latin America and Africa. Today there are 300,000 Quakers in the world, 200,000 of them outside the North Atlantic realm.

Brethren churches

In the 1690s in central Germany voices of alarm were raised about the brutality of life in a region which had been scourged by ongoing war for almost a century, and with it a lack of spiritual vitality in the established church. Alexander Mack was awakened by the heart religion of Pietism but radicalized it, under the influence of Anabaptist writings, to focus on following the 'hard sayings' of Jesus, including opposition to war.

The 'brethren' gathered in congregations of people whose lives had been changed by the experience of God's grace. Their refusal to conform to religious and political convention earned them harassment and even persecution. In 1708 most of them accepted Penn's offer of asylum. Their fresh vision of grace and discipleship enlivened their Quaker and Mennonite neighbours. Brethren were known for their peaceful relationships with indigenous people.

As they entered the American mainstream, Brethren joined the world missions mandate and began churches in India and Africa. Unique to the Brethren was their encouragement to indigenous believers to merge with other Christians there and develop their own identity. Thus, the majority of Brethren live in the United States, but churches they founded exist as part of ecumenical communities, especially in India. They total 350,000 in the US and 500,000 worldwide. Like the Mennonites, the various groups of Brethren founded colleges specializing in service vocations. Like both of the other peace churches, the Brethren were active in relief after World Wars I and II.

The role of the most progressive group, known as the Church of the Brethren, in the early formation of the World Council of Churches is noteworthy. It joined the quest of the large churches for reconciliation within the body of Christ but believed that such a quest was both futile and hypocritical without a renunciation of war. As a first step in the search for reconciliation, the Brethren delegate to the founding assembly of the WCC in 1948 tabled a motion that stated that the Christians of the world would henceforth refuse to kill one another. The motion died for lack of a seconder.

Co-operation among the peace churches

The threat of another war in Europe in the 1930s led to the co-ordination of local pacifist initiatives by Quakers, Brethren and Mennonites. In 1935 they formally structured their work as the 'historic peace churches' and together co-operated with the ecumenical Protestant Fellowship of Reconciliation. When war came, not only their mainline partners but sizable numbers of their own members joined the war effort. Afterwards, collectively and individually, the peace churches made non-violence central to their identity and mission in novel ways. They expanded their understanding of peace-making as a lifestyle to include participation in the movement for civil rights and international development programmes, linked conflict prevention and development, and experimented with applying micro-level (neighbourhood) conflict transformation skills to the macro-level (international conflict). Each denomination sponsors college-level peace studies programmes.

In the 1970s activists among peace church people banded together in a 'New Call to Peacemaking' with a challenge aimed at all the members of their churches. The call was to take the message of Christian non-violence into the social and political complexities of the day. In 1991, in *A Declaration of Peace*, this group renewed its appeal to its own people to live up to its pacifist conviction. The peace churches accepted an invitation from the Faith and Order Commission of the National Council of Churches in the United States to join a process, later called 'The Fragmentation of the Church and its Unity in Peacemaking'. In it, pacifist and non-pacifist churches would commit themselves to a self-critical presentation of their convictions. Their shared hope was that there might now be enough unity to recognize that peace is at the heart of the gospel and that an engaged pacifism and a stringent just war theory could both express faithfulness to the Gospel. Even though this level of agreement could not be reached, the conversations on peace helped make peace an indispensable part of future ecumenical dialogue and co-operation.

In 2001 the historic peace churches sponsored a week-long international dialogue aimed at forging common peace conviction and vision for a radically changed world among Brethren, Quakers and Mennonites from many countries. It marked a new era in the pursuit of a global theology and practice of pacifism.

Ecumenical movement

JOHN REMPEL

Peter Brock, *Freedom from Violence: Sectarian Nonresistance from the Middle Ages to the Great War*, Toronto: University of Toronto Press 1991; Fernando Enns et al. (eds), *Seeking Cultures of Peace: a Peace Church Conversation*, Geneva: WCC 2004; Jeffrey Gros et al. (eds), *The Fragmentation of the Church and its Unity in Peacemaking*, Grand Rapids MI: Eerdmans 2000; Cynthia Sampson, *From the Ground up: Mennonite Contributions to International Peacebuilding*, Oxford: OUP 2000

Pentecostalism

Pentecostalism takes its name from the outpouring of the Holy Spirit on the followers of Jesus at the feast of Pentecost, 50 days after Easter, reported in the Acts of the Apostles (chapter 2). It is a multi-faceted worldwide movement. Its adherents are held together by a common belief in the continuation of the gifts of the Spirit beyond the first century. Pentecostals are most strikingly known for the experience of baptism in the Holy Spirit with its accompanying sign of glossolalia, or speaking with tongues. The movement is one of the fastest growing within Christianity, with the largest percentage of its members living in the Third World; the events that gave rise to it are also known as the charismatic revival (charisms being a term for gifts of the Holy Spirit).

Holy Spirit
Festivals and fasts

While many of the distinctive phenomena found within Pentecostalism were exhibited within Christianity before the twentieth century, the movement traces its roots to the outbreak of tongues at a Bible school in Topeka, Kansas, in 1901. The Topeka revival and the teaching of its leader, Charles Fox Parham, on the baptism in the Holy Spirit, accompanied by the evidence of speaking in tongues, influenced William J. Seymour, an African

American holiness preacher from Texas. Seymour began to preach and teach on the experience of baptism in the Holy Spirit. His travels led him to Los Angeles, where under his leadership a revival began in 1906 at the Azusa Street Mission. Azusa Street is commonly known as the fountainhead of the worldwide Pentecostal movement. This revival was known not only for the phenomena of glossolalia, but also for inter-racial worship and gender inclusiveness.

Christianity in Latin America

The Azusa Street revival attracted thousands of people from around the world, and a wave of Pentecostal outpourings of the Spirit followed. The revival quickly took root in Scandinavia under the leadership of T. B. Barratt, a Methodist minister from Oslo. After receiving the baptism in the Holy Spirit in New York, Barratt took the message of the Pentecostal revival to Norway and Sweden. In addition, he was instrumental in bringing the movement to England. In Germany the Pentecostal message was pioneered by Jonathan Paul. During the early decades of the twentieth century Pentecostalism continued to spread in Europe, including countries in Eastern Europe.

Christianity in Africa

Christianity in Asia

The Pentecostal revival reached Chile in 1909 under the leadership of Willis C. Hoover, an American Methodist missionary. Here the movement experienced rapid growth. The Methodist Pentecostal Church in Chile became one of the largest churches in the world. The Pentecostal revival spread quickly throughout Latin America, especially in Argentina and Brazil, and at the dawn of the twenty-first century, Pentecostalism is the dominant form of Protestantism in Latin America. In Central America, in particular Guatemala, the movement's rapid growth is transforming Christianity from being predominantly Roman Catholic to being predominantly Pentecostal.

The Pentecostal movement began in South Africa in 1908 and spread rapidly throughout the African continent. As in Latin America, the growth of Pentecostalism within many African countries is transforming the religious landscape. In particular, indigenous African churches are exploding. These churches combine unique elements of traditional African religion with those of Pentecostalism.

The Pentecostal movement has flourished in Asian countries such as Korea. The Korean Yoido Full Gospel Church, pioneered by Paul Yonggi Cho, boasts a membership of over 700,000 members, making it the largest Christian congregation in the world. In countries such as Indonesia it is not uncommon to find Pentecostal churches with a membership over 10,000.

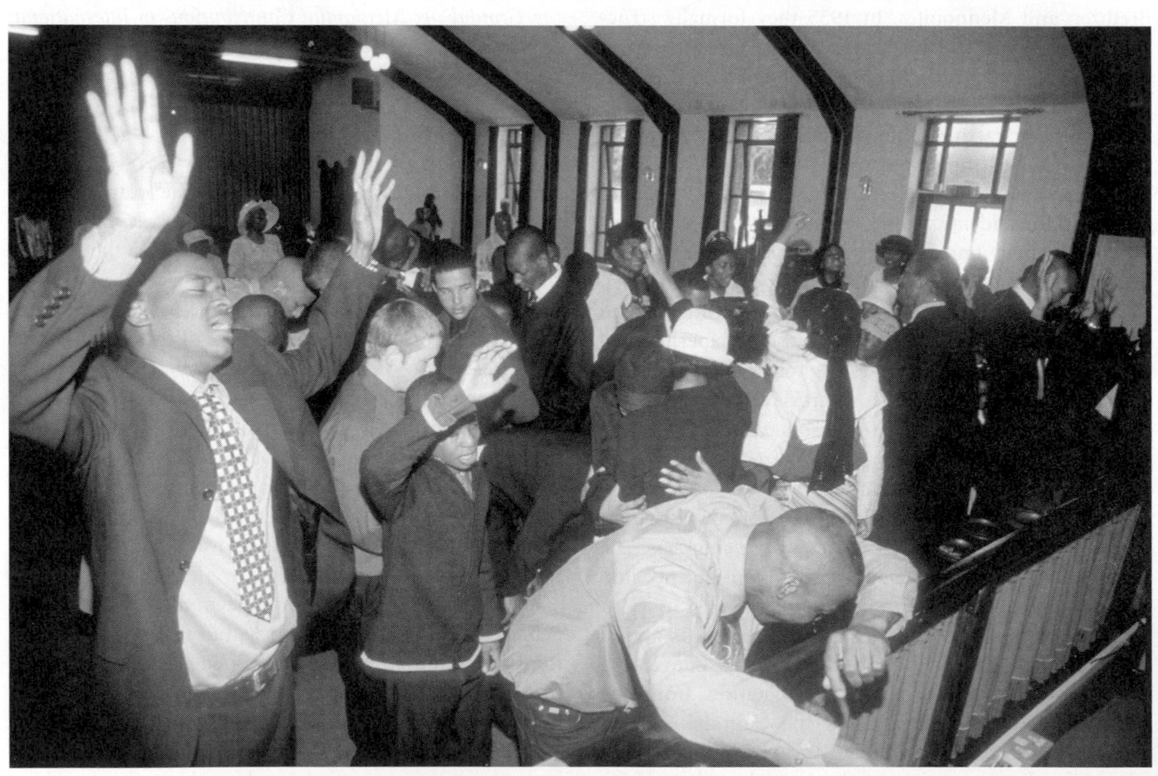

Possessed by the Holy Spirit, Apostolic Church, Beulah Hills, Birmingham

The experience of the baptism in the Holy Spirit began to emerge within mainline Protestant churches and within Roman Catholicism during the latter half of the twentieth century. Among the better-known leaders of 'neo-Pentecostalism' or the charismatic movement was Dennis Bennett, an Episcopal priest in Van Nuys, California. After being forced to leave his congregation in Van Nuys, Bennett was invited to lead an inner-city parish in Seattle, Washington. Under Bennett's leadership the church in Seattle experienced rapid growth. It became a major centre of charismatic spirituality in the United States.

The Roman Catholic charismatic revival began in 1966 at a weekend retreat at Duquesne University. The revival quickly spread to Catholic prayer groups at Notre Dame and the University of Michigan. A high point of the Catholic charismatic renewal movement was the 1973 gathering of some 30,000 Catholic charismatics at Notre Dame, Indiana, for a national conference. The Catholic charismatic movement has spread throughout the world with varying degrees of support from the Roman Catholic hierarchy. Pope John Paul II is noted for his encouragement of this renewal.

The Pentecostal renewal within mainline Protestantism and within Roman Catholicism is distinguished from 'classical Pentecostalism' by its adherents' attempts to remain within their churches and bring renewal to their denominations. There is also less of an emphasis upon glossolalia as the initial evidence of the baptism of the Holy Spirit.

The Pentecostal movement's theological roots can be traced to the holiness revivals of the nineteenth century. The holiness movement, as an outgrowth of Methodism, stressed the ongoing transformative nature of grace over against the Reformation's emphasis on the forensic nature of justification. This belief in the more specifically catholic tradition of transformation brought about an emphasis on the experiential and crisis nature of sanctification. Leaders within the holiness revival, such as Phoebe Palmer and John Inskip, emphasized a 'second blessing' experience of sanctification. British evangelicals also stressed a separate experience of grace in the Keswick Conventions beginning in 1875.

Alongside the belief in the 'second blessing' of sanctification, an emphasis on divine healing developed. Healing evangelists were popular in the late 1800s. In addition, leaders in the healing movement such as Charles Cullis, a Boston physician, built 'healing homes' for the sick where patients could be treated with prayer.

The teaching of the imminent return of Christ was also a strong part of the late-nineteenth-century holiness movement. An eschatological fervour dominated the movement as believers began to see themselves living in the last days. Corresponding to this fervour was a renewed emphasis upon the person and work of the Holy Spirit. Language conveying being 'baptized in the Holy Spirit' was part of the holiness movement prior to the Azusa revival.

Pentecostals who incorporated the basic tenets of the holiness movement spoke of preaching the 'full gospel'. By this they meant that the gospel contained the message of Jesus as Saviour, Sanctifier, Healer and Baptizer in the Holy Spirit and Coming King. This fivefold pattern was dominant in the early days of the movement and was part of the teachings of William Seymour, G. B. Cashwell, C. H. Mason and others.

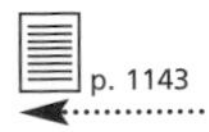
p. 1143

Two major theological controversies arose within Pentecostalism within the first half of the twentieth century. The controversy over the nature of sanctification emerged in Chicago in 1910 with the teaching of William H. Durham. Durham rejected the holiness movement's emphasis upon sanctification as a second work of grace, and began teaching a 'finished work' theory. This doctrine emphasized sanctification as progressive following conversion. For Durham, the experience of salvation marked a 'finished work' of grace. This would subsequently be followed by baptism in the Holy Spirit as a second blessing. Durham's emphasis upon sanctification as positional (imputed) and progressive led to the 'fourfold gospel' paradigm: Jesus as Saviour, Healer, Baptizer in the Holy Spirit and Coming King. The fourfold gospel is prominent within the non-Wesleyan wing of Pentecostalism. The Assemblies of God, which was organized in 1914, based its theology on Durham's teachings. Other groups advocating the fourfold pattern include the Pentecostal Church of God, International Church of the Foursquare Gospel and the Open Bible Standard Church.

Assemblies of God

Holiness movement
Reformation
Justification

The other major doctrinal controversy within Pentecostalism arose in 1911 with the teachings of Glen Cook and Frank Ewart. These men rejected the historic teaching of the Trinity in favour of an understanding of Jesus as being at the same time Father, Son and Spirit. In addition to this understanding of the Godhead, the 'Jesus Only' teachings included being baptized in Jesus' name only rather than with the historic trinitarian formula. In 1916 the 'Jesus Only' controversy led to a major schism within the Assemblies of God, out of which arose the United Pentecostal Church and the Pentecostal Assemblies of the World.

Trinity

Today worldwide Pentecostalism is multi-faceted in theological beliefs. It is therefore difficult to define the movement theologically. What generally holds together the multiple groups is a belief in the continuation of the gifts of the Spirit and the baptism of the Holy Spirit. While the movement is often identified with fundamentalism, this is a mistake. Whereas fundamentalism emphasizes

Eschatology
Fundamentalism

the letter of the law and a deductive, rational approach to scripture, Pentecostalism holds a dynamic view of scripture as Spirit-Word. Its adherents are encouraged to follow the leading of the Holy Spirit in a dynamic Spirit-filled journey of faith.

The rapid growth of the Pentecostal movement shows no signs of slowing. Its spread throughout the Third World is changing the face of Christianity itself. As a result, the centre of Christianity is shifting from the Northern hemisphere to the South and the East. The 'face' of Christianity is now distinctively non-white, poor and Pentecostal. These changes will continue to create challenges for traditional Christianity, whose centres of power are in the United States and Europe.

Geography

CHERYL BRIDGES JOHNS

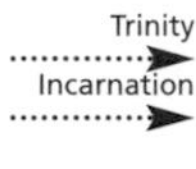
Trinity
Incarnation

Allan Anderson, *An Introduction to Pentecostalism*, Cambridge: CUP 2004; H. Cox, *Fire From Heaven: The Rise of Pentecostal Spirituality and the Reshaping of Religion in the Twenty-first Century*, Boston: Addison Wesley 1994; Walter Hollenweger, *The Pentecostals. The Charismatic Movement in the Churches*, London: SCM Press and Minneapolis: Augsburg Publishing House 1972; S. Land, *Pentecostal Spirituality*, Sheffield: Sheffield Academic Press 1973; R. Shaull and W. Cesar, *Pentecostalism and the Future of the Christian Churches*, Grand Rapids, MI: Eerdmans 2000

Perennial philosophy and Christianity

Theologians and philosophers of religion have understood the perennial philosophy in two distinct ways. Among Roman Catholic writers, those influenced in particular by the teachings of Thomas Aquinas, it is often associated with the classical heritage of ancient Greece and Rome and refers to beliefs about God, human nature, virtue and knowledge that church fathers and medieval scholastics share with pre-Christian philosophers, notably Plato and Aristotle. A translation of the Latin *philosophia perennis*, the phrase 'perennial philosophy' was probably first employed in this sense in the sixteenth century by Agostino Steucho, a Vatican librarian, and was given currency in the early eighteenth century by the philosopher Gottfried Leibniz. More recently, the phrase has been used in a broader way to refer to the idea that all of the world's great religious traditions are expressions of a single, saving truth. Comparing this truth to a perennial flower, a perennialist asserts that there is one divine Source of all wisdom, which has repeatedly blossomed forth throughout history. The major religions, including Hinduism, Buddhism, Taoism, Judaism, Christianity and Islam, are different forms of that wisdom and are sometimes referred to as paths leading to the same summit or dialects of a common language.

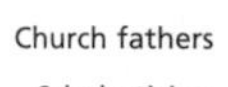
Church fathers
Scholasticism

Vatican

Understood in this second sense, the perennial philosophy was popularized in the twentieth century by Aldous Huxley in a book by that title (1946). Its best known and most authoritative exponents, however, are Ananda Coomaraswamy, René Guénon, and especially Frithjof Schuon, whose *Transcendent Unity of Religions* (1948) has been of signal importance in defining the contemporary perennialist viewpoint. According to Schuon and those of his school, a distinction must be made between the exoteric or outer and the esoteric or inner dimensions of religion. Outwardly the doctrines of the world's religions are clearly different, even contradictory, as can be seen in their theologies. The Hindu tradition, for example, includes many Gods, Judaism insists there is only one God, and Buddhism declares the question of God to be moot. Or again, Christianity believes that God is a Trinity and that the divine Son was incarnate as Jesus Christ, beliefs explicitly rejected by Islam. According to the perennial philosophy, however, such outwardly divergent teachings, providentially adapted to the spiritual, psychological and cultural needs of different peoples at different stages of history, can be inwardly reconciled by those who are sensitive to their metaphysical and symbolic meanings and prepared to follow the golden thread of the dogmatic letter to its deeper spiritual meaning. It is for this reason that one finds such a remarkable consensus among the greatest mystics and sages, such as Shankara in Hinduism, Ibn Arabi in Islam, and Meister Eckhart in Christianity.

The perennial philosophy may be classified as a kind of pluralism, though with two important qualifications. First, unlike many pluralists, perennial philosophers do not believe that every religious tradition is valid, but distinguish between true religions and their human or demonic counterfeits and, within authentic traditions, between orthodox and heretical forms. Some paths go all the way to the summit, but others circle aimlessly around the base of the mountain or lead away towards the desert. Second, where pluralism sees religion as resulting from human efforts to reach out to a divine Reality that can never be known in itself, perennialism teaches that the world's true or orthodox religions are directly revealed by that Reality, each of them corresponding to an archetype within the divine mind. In this way, the perennial philosophy honours the absolutist claims of the religions, especially those of the West. Revealed traditions do not communicate merely partial or complementary truths that must then be combined by the syncretist to achieve a complete understanding. Rather, each is fully true in the sense that it provides its adherents with everything they need for reaching the highest or most complete human state, a state in which they will be able to confirm the truth in their own experience through participation in the very nature of God.

It must be admitted that traditional Christianity is largely hostile to the perennial philosophy. In considering the claims of other religions, most Christians have been either exclusivists, denying the possibility of salvation to anyone outside the church, or inclusivists, extending the possibility of salvation only to those non-Christians who are invincibly ignorant of the gospel but who belong to the church by their desire for salvation and thus benefit from the redeeming work of the incarnate Son. But to say with perennialism that Christianity is just one among several revealed religions and that non-Christians can be saved independently of the events of the gospel has seemed to most Christians a contradiction to their faith. Since the Second Vatican Council (1962–5), the Roman Catholic Church, for example, has adopted a primarily inclusivist stance, acknowledging the presence of certain partial truths in other religions, yet in its declaration *Dominus Iesus* (2000) it explicitly repudiates the idea that there could be ways of salvation apart from Jesus Christ, whose historical passion, death and resurrection are said to be the essential means of redemption for all.

According to Schuon and other perennialists, this dominant attitude among Christians is not surprising, nor should its usefulness for the vast majority of believers be called into question. The entire point of any religion is to ensure the salvation of as many people as possible, and most people, whether Christian or otherwise, are able to take their tradition seriously only if they are persuaded that it is the best, if not the only, way to reach God. Critics have argued that the New Testament, taken as a whole, is opposed to the perennial philosophy, and this is largely true. Muslims could offer a parallel criticism, and they too would be correct in saying that the Qur'an, however positively it may sometimes speak about other people of the book, nonetheless gives priority to those who follow the example of Muhammad. But for the perennialist this simply shows that the primary aim of the world's religions, beginning with their scriptures and apostolic authorities, is to assist their adherents in remaining focused on a single form of saving truth, not to lay the foundations for interfaith dialogue. On the other hand, given the common origin of the religions in a transcendent Source which, as the traditions themselves all attest, infinitely exceeds even its own self-expressions, it is in the nature of things that the scriptural and dogmatic formulations of each religion should include certain openings or clues to the underlying validity of the perennial philosophy. These clues may be found not simply on the periphery of religious traditions, but in their most central and essential doctrines.

This is certainly the case with Christianity, where one of the most important openings can be found in the traditional understanding of the Person of Christ. Christians who believe that their religion is either uniquely or decisively true often support their position by quoting Christ's words, 'I am the way, and the truth, and the life; no one comes to the Father but by me' (John 14.6). According to perennialist theologians, however, an exclusivist, or even inclusivist, interpretation of this and other such passages is by no means necessary and may in fact betray a heretical christology. For in the developed doctrine of the ecumenical councils, the true person of Christ, that is, the subject who thinks his thoughts, speaks his words, and is the agent of all his actions, is the eternal Word or Son of God, the second person of the Trinity. Jesus Christ is not a man who was adopted by God, nor a man in whom God was the indwelling presence, nor an intermediate being created by God as the highest of creatures, nor again a composite being who was partly divine and partly human. Who Jesus is, is the divine Son, 'of one essence with the Father', 'by whom all things were made' (Nicene Creed).

God ◄
Salvation ◄

Christology

Council ◄

Of all the Gospels, John is the most emphatic in this regard, for the same person who says of himself that he is the only way to the Father also says that 'before Abraham was, I am' (John 8.58), a passage whose very tenses undercut the identification of Christ with a strictly temporal set of saving facts. Christian perennialists conclude that it is a mistake to confuse the uniqueness of the only-begotten and eternal Son of God with the alleged singularity of his historical manifestation in first-century Palestine. Without denying that there is only one Son of God, or that he alone is the author of salvation, or that Jesus Christ is that Son, they contend that there are no biblical or dogmatic grounds for supposing that this one Son has limited his saving work to his incarnate presence as Jesus. On the contrary, as Athanasius and other early church fathers insisted, though the Word 'became flesh and dwelt among us' (John 1.14), he was not confined by his body even during his earthly ministry.

It is sometimes objected that this line of reasoning drives a wedge between the two natures of Christ, diminishing the integrity and importance of the historical Jesus in favour of the Word or cosmic Christ. But this is to forget that a separate Jesus of history, understood as a particular man with a temporally conditioned psychology, is largely the invention of modern scholars, who are themselves often at odds with the very teachings that traditionalist Christians intend to safeguard. According to the church fathers, especially those who interpreted the Council of Chalcedon (451) along the lines established by Cyril of Alexandria, the Jesus of history *is* the cosmic Christ, for there is no historical person to be conceived alongside or in addition to the eternal Person of the only Son. Of course, the humanity of Christ cannot be denied. But in encountering this humanity, what one encounters is not

Jesus of history

an individual human being – some 'man of Nazareth' – but human nature as such, assumed into God and thus divinized.

Once this subtle point has been grasped, a number of other scriptural teachings begin to take on a more encompassing meaning. One reads in a new and fresh way that Christ is 'the true light who enlightens every man that comes into the world' (John 1.9), that he has 'other sheep who are not of this fold' (John 10.16), and that 'God shows no partiality, but in every nation any one who fears him and does what is right is acceptable to him' (Acts 10.34–5); and one notices that the events of Christ's passion and crucifixion are the working out at a particular time and place of a strictly timeless salvation, for the Lamb of God, whose 'act of righteousness leads to acquittal and life for all men' (Romans 5.18), is 'slain from the foundation of the world' (Revelation 13.8). Following the thread of such clues, one begins to sense that the Son or Word, far from being limited to a single religion, is the divine principle behind all revelation and the eternal source of salvation in every authentic tradition. Though truly incarnate as Jesus Christ in Christianity, he is operative in a saving way in and through non-Christian religions as well. In some he is present in an equally personal way, as in Krishna and the other Hindu avatars, in whom he was also 'made man' (Nicene Creed), while in others he appears in an impersonal way, as in the Qur'an of Islam, where he made himself book.

The concern is often expressed that a perennialist interpretation of Christianity has the effect of demoting Christ, making him only one among a variety of competing saviours. But if 'by their fruits' (Matthew 7.20) one may discern whether religions are valid and if the good fruit of sanctity often grows along non-Christian paths, it will perhaps seem instead that the power and scope of the Son of God are actually much greater than Christians had been led to believe, and the perennial philosophy will itself appear as a kind of inclusivism, but with an inclusivity no longer centred on Christianity or the church or its sacraments, but on Jesus Christ, the saving source of all wisdom.

JAMES S. CUTSINGER

James S. Cutsinger, *The Fullness of God: Frithjof Schuon on Christianity*, Bloomington, IN: World Wisdom 2004; Whitall N. Perry, *A Treasury of Traditional Wisdom*, Louisville, KY: Fons Vitae 2001

Persecution

The early centuries

It is a popular misconception that early Christian communities lived a hidden 'catacomb' existence and were subject to constant persecution by the Roman state until the conversion of Constantine introduced, in a complete reversal of fortune, a period of prosperity, privilege and establishment. This contrast is often expressed as one between a church that, though physically persecuted, was spiritually free, and a church that, though free from persecution, was in spiritual subjection. Neither side of this sharp contrast is justified by a study of the sources. Just as 'the conversion of Constantine' or 'the Christianization of the Roman empire' prove to be complex processes, with nuances which become more subtle the more closely they are studied, so the persecution of early Christians, far from being the universal experience of popular imagination, is a more varied reality.

Constantine's 'conversion' ➤
Roman empire ➤

There is in fact very little evidence for any official policy of persecution of Christians before the late third century. Our non-Christian sources do show that there were attacks on Christians from time to time, and that Christianity was considered to be an undesirable religious cult, but there was no concerted attempt to stamp out the faith until shortly before the time of Constantine, and even the so-called 'Great Persecution' was short-lived and taken seriously only in part of the empire.

Probably the best-known case of the persecution of Christians is that which took place in Rome in 64 CE, instigated by the Emperor Nero. This episode became the subject of several novels and films, most famously Henryk Sienkiewicz's *Quo Vadis* of 1895, filmed in 1951. This was a special case of local persecution, albeit one driven by the emperor, and it has to be understood in the context of a devastating fire of the city that preceded it. Christians might already have been a natural target for the city's traumatized need to find scapegoats, or were simply an outlet for anger and fear. The Roman writer Tacitus describes how they were burned as human torches to illuminate Nero's gardens.

Tacitus' account implies that Christianity was recognized – and despised – by many people in Rome, but too much weight should not be attached to this picture. It is often thought that Christians were easily recognizable because they were different: they were unable and unwilling to take part in the cults and ceremonies and the organizations which defined citizenship; obstinate for the same reason in refusing military service; insistent on the privacy of their worship; and they defied ordinary social custom in the roles that they allowed to slaves (and perhaps women) in the inner life of their community. In Nero's Rome, however, and in the cities of the Roman empire in the first two centuries CE, these differences would not have been obvious. The cities had large numbers of non-citizens living in them, including of course many slaves, who might well live away from their owners. Involvement in state religion and observance of social norms was much more the concern of the rich members of society than of the poorer.

For Tacitus' contemporary and friend Pliny the Younger, Christianity was much more of a puzzle. We have correspondence surviving between Pliny, when he was governor of Bithynia in 112 CE, and the Emperor Trajan, which gives a different impression from Tacitus' dramatic account. Despite a career in Roman public life, Pliny had apparently no personal experience of Christians or Christianity until he started to receive anonymous denunciations of individuals. Pliny claims to have executed those who persistently claimed to be Christians, although with no clear idea of what, beyond obstinacy, their crime was. He also indicates that most of the people accused of being Christians had either already ceased to be so, or were happy to do so when questioned. Trajan on his part, while content that Christians should be punished, discourages any attempt to seek out Christians, or to act on anonymous reports.

Eusebius' *History of the Church* contains an account that again might suggest that the authorities in the second century CE were more interested in keeping order than pursuing people for their religious beliefs. He quotes a letter describing the suffering of Christians in the cities of Vienne and Lyons in Gaul, in 177 CE, after an episode of civil disorder. This seems to have begun with antagonism between Christians and non-Christians, possibly made worse by accusations of cannibalism and incest levelled against Christians. Such accusations are part of a stock repertoire of outraged responses to groups about which little is known, but there were also certain features of Christian language and practice – such as the kiss of peace, the use of the terms 'brother' and 'sister' or the claim by Jesus in John 6 that one must eat his flesh and drink his blood to have any share in him – which may have encouraged fantasies about what Christians actually did behind their closed doors. The resulting riots in Lyons and Vienne forced the authorities to act to reimpose order. Although this action is presented as persecution of Christians, it is clear that non-Christians were also arrested and tried. As in Bithynia, it is also clear that some former Christians recanted. Again, as Pliny had done, when the governor discovered that some of the accused were Roman citizens, he consulted Rome on the principle of their case: they did not forfeit their rights as citizens because they were Christians. When sentence was eventually executed against the rioters, those of them who were Roman citizens were beheaded, while the others were thrown to the wild beasts.

In the course of the third century the nature of the Roman empire changed. Power was centralized, with the emperor taking more control of the administration of the provinces. Early in the century the Emperor Caracalla had extended Roman citizenship throughout the empire. As pressure on the empire's borders increased, the need for the emperor to maintain the support of the gods must have grown. This is the context in which the persecutions of the middle and later parts of the century need to be understood. In 250–1 CE the Emperor Decius demanded that all inhabitants of the empire sacrifice to the gods. Those who did so were to receive a certificate (*libellus*) to show that they had done so; those who refused to obey were to be punished. Whether Decius was responding to a specific danger, or possibly demanding recognition of his accession throughout the empire, is not clear. His action was not, apparently, explicitly aimed at Christians, but they were inevitably caught by it. In 257–8 CE his successor Valerian issued edicts that were more directly aimed against Christians, but were primarily intended to enforce loyalty to the emperor. Similar decrees were issued by Diocletian in 303 CE, and these were behind the last phase of official attacks on Christians, the 'Great Persecution', ended by the Edict of Toleration of 313.

Although an order might go out from Rome that all the people of the empire should be made to sacrifice to the traditional gods or to swear an oath to the emperor as a god, how far that order was put into effect would vary from one province to another. No emperor had the military resource or the communications to enforce his persecuting edict consistently. Much depended on the attitude of local governors, and on the kinds of relationship that already existed between the Christian community and its city. Several civic authorities were happy, either out of goodwill or possibly sometimes in return for a bribe, to issue the necessary certificate to people who had not actually done so. But in other places the persecution was carried through consistently. Christian scriptures and the equipment necessary for Christian worship were confiscated and destroyed, and Christians of different sorts – women as well as men, recent converts as well as bishops and leaders of long standing – were tortured and martyred. It is not possible to offer a realistic estimate of the number of Christians who were put to death, but that does not really matter. The importance of the persecutions lies in the stories that circulated about Christian courage under duress, the contribution that these made to the development of the Christian church's sense of itself, and the consequences that flowed from the persecutions for the distribution of power within the church.

Inevitably, then, in Christian texts persecution and martyrdom have a much higher profile than the events themselves might justify. Eusebius implies that persecution of Christians was the normal situation in the first three centuries, and descriptions of the trials and deaths of Christians became an important literary genre in their own right. *The Acts of the Martyrs* is the general

Martyr

Forgiveness

name given to a series of accounts of martyrdom under persecution. They typically take the form of a letter from one church to another, recounting the events that have recently taken place: the story of the heroic deaths in one church is good news to be shared with other churches by way of encouragement. The stories fall into the same general shape, and stock motifs are constantly repeated. The governor is initially courteous, but becomes increasingly hostile; the crowd is both amazed at the superhuman endurance of the Christians under torture and thirsty for blood. This element of stylized repetition means that we have to be cautious about reading these stories as simply the narratives of what any eye-witness might have related in the same way. These are stories told by Christians to Christians, for specifically Christian moral and exhortatory ends. It is only rarely possible to compare them with other kinds of sources, although in the case of North Africa the official transcripts of some interrogations have survived in the *Proconsular Acts*, and cast a vivid light on the dilemmas in which Christians found themselves. Even when read with caution, the acts of the martyrs are both horrifying and moving. There are details of great poignancy. Perpetua, a young and well-born martyr in Carthage at the beginning of the third century, awaiting her fate in prison, is anxious for the infant that she is still breast-feeding: as the Lord hears her prayer and takes away her anxiety, her breasts cease to be distended with milk.

pp. 666–7

Resurrection

Initiation

Often the story is deliberately shaped to recall the passion narrative of the Gospels, for the martyr retraces Jesus' own journey to the cross. To be martyred was to have an immediate share in his death and resurrection. Martyrdom was a baptism in blood, which made baptism in water unnecessary. The prayers of the martyr would be heard above others in heaven, and the cells of those condemned to death were crowded with visitors, anxious to load the soon-to-be-martyred brother or sister with commissions for the world to come. Even the confessors – that is, those who endured torture for their faith without being put to death – were clothed with enormous moral authority, and their intercessions were specially sought after.

Ministry and ministers

This moral authority precipitated a crisis in the mid-third-century church. By then a regular structure of church authority had been formed. The bishop was at the centre of a system of church government, and the college of presbyters, the deacon, the readers and the other authorized ministers stood in a defined relation to him. It was for the bishop to determine, in consultation with other bishops, the boundaries of Christian doctrine and the authentic exposition of scripture. It was for the bishop, in consultation with others within the diocese where necessary, to determine who did and who did not belong to the particular church that he governed, and how that church's resources should be spent. But now martyrs and confessors began to compete with the bishop for authority to determine who should and should not be included within the church. Those who had sinned could cut short the long and painful sequence of public penitence and restoration to communion by going to the confessors, who would, on their own authority and with the weight of their immense moral prestige, declare that so-and-so's sins were forgiven, and that so-and-so should be admitted to communion. The sins forgiven were often serious. The confessors seem to have issued written certificates of readmission, not just to individuals but also to whole households, and to groups of associates. This direct challenge to the position of the bishop drew from Cyprian of Carthage (died 258) a classic defence of monarchical episcopacy. Cyprian's account of a local church articulated around its bishop was immensely important for subsequent Christian history.

Cyprian's personal dilemma illustrates the problems which any Christian faced in time of persecution, but which the Christian leader faced in a particular way. One could obey the imperial edict, and swear an oath to the emperor: unthinkable for a bishop, perhaps, but evidently done by many ordinary Christians, because the question of what to do with these *lapsi*, those who had lapsed, became the subject of serious disagreement in the church afterwards. One could get a certificate to say that one had sworn the oath without actually having done it, or hand over impressive-looking medical treatises in exchange for a receipt for the sacred books. Was this apostasy or not? One could play for time, prevaricating about where the scriptures were to be found. ('They're not in church; the readers have got them at home, you don't need me to tell you who the readers are, because you have a list of them at the town hall,' and so on.) One could lie low in the countryside, and try to do one's best for the church while in hiding. One could openly resist the decree, and suffer glorious torture and death among the confessors and martyrs. The choice that was made would be carefully scrutinized when the persecution had subsided. Those who chose the way of heroic resistance were likely to be less impressed with those who went into hiding, or who let it seem that they had committed apostasy, or betrayed the scriptures into persecuting hands. Rigorists and laxists confronted one another, and it was easy for the rigorists to say that the laxists were not really proper Christians. And if a bishop himself gave way in the time of crisis, was he really a proper bishop to begin with, and could his actions as bishop be regarded as valid?

In the settling of accounts following a persecution, it sometimes happened that rigorists refused to recognize the bishop who had let them down, and appointed a bishop of their own. Thus the church in Alexandria went into schism at the end of the Great Persecution – an identical process can be seen at work in the schism that affected the Bulgarian Orthodox Church in the 1990s, after the fall of the Communist regime. Cyprian himself went into hiding at the beginning of the persecution under Decius, and was much criticized for it, although he defended his choice as the best way of continuing to serve his church. When a new persecution began under Valerius, Cyprian chose the way of martyrdom, and his prestige as a martyr did much – ironically – to ensure the success of his theory that it was the bishop and not the martyr who defined the boundaries of the church.

With the ascendancy of Constantine in the Western Roman empire from 312 CE, and in the Eastern empire from 324 CE, systematic persecution of Christians by the state became a memory. Constantine's official historian Eusebius in a number of works, and the Christian orator Lactantius in his *On the Deaths of the Persecutors*, were able to celebrate the way that God had liberated his people through Constantine. The memory may have come hauntingly close in the brief reign of Julian the Apostate (361–3), but his measures against Christianity did not have time to ripen into a full persecution. One of the reasons for the unique prestige that the Council of Nicaea (325 CE) has enjoyed in Christian tradition is that so many of the church leaders who gathered there had endured the Great Persecution. Among the other theological consequences of the persecution, it left the church with a sharpened sense of the boundaries of Christian scripture. If a priest or reader might be put to death for failing to hand over the sacred books, he would be very clear which books were sacred and which were not.

As the Great Persecution receded into the past, persecution at the hands of non-Christians became something that Christians experienced outside the boundaries of the old empire, rather than within it – under the Sasanians of Persia (sometimes), or within the caliphates and emirates of expanding Islam (sometimes), or as missionaries in distant China or Japan in the sixteenth centuries. Systematic persecution of Christians by the state did not re-emerge as a strong theme of Christian history until the twentieth century.

In the intervening period, persecution was largely an experience visited by Christians on each other in their competitive attempts to impose particular understandings of Christian faith and practice upon one another, or (to put it more sympathetically) to defend their own conviction of Christian faith against a perceived threat, or as princes co-opted churches to serve the emergent nationhood of early modern Europe. This new development can be seen as early as the time of Augustine, in the early fifth century. The Donatists had emerged as a rigorist movement in North Africa, following the Great Persecution. Their ruthlessness eventually persuaded Augustine that they must, and could only, be suppressed by the authority of government. The theological justification that he gave for this suppression in his anti-Donatist writings was deeply influential for subsequent Christian attitudes to other Christians defined as deviant, especially at the time of the Reformation. Thus violence against Christians continued to be a feature of Christian history, but it was now turned in a new direction, until the totalitarian regimes of the twentieth century returned the current to its original flow, and more devastatingly than in the early Christian centuries.

Reformation

ANDERS BERGQUIST

Bruno Chenu et al. (eds), *The Book of Christian Martyrs*, London: SCM Press 1990; Eusebius, *History of the Church*, translated by G. A. Williamson, Harmondsworth: Penguin Books 1965; Everett Ferguson (ed), *Church and State in the Early Church, Studies in Early Christianity*, Vol. 7, New York: Garland 1993 (contains the important article by G. E. M. de Ste Croix, 'Why Were the Early Christians Persecuted?'); Robin Lane Fox, *Pagans and Christians in the Mediterranean World from the Second Century AD to the Conversion of Constantine*, New York: Alfred A. Knopf and Harmondsworth: Viking Books 1986; W. H. C. Frend, *Martyrdom and Persecution in the Early Church*, Oxford: Blackwell 1965 and New York: Doubleday 1967

Council

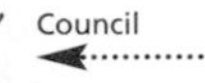

Canon

The twentieth century

Although it is difficult, perhaps impossible, to compare most aspects of the modern world with those of the distant past, it seems certain that the twentieth century witnessed the most violent and most sustained assaults ever endured by the Christian church. These were due not so much to widespread rejection of Christian belief, though atheistic ideologies were sometimes involved, as to the rise of several totalitarian regimes that dominated extensive territories and used modern techniques of control and brutality to subjugate large populations. In these places Christians rarely suffered more than members of other organizations that owed allegiance to alternative sources of authority. It is also important to distinguish between aggressive action against religious communities and, what is more common, restriction of their activities, with direct punishment confined to those who do not obey the regulations.

The most sustained and violent persecution occurred in the Communist empire that developed from the Russian Revolution of 1917. This was almost matched in intensity by the Communist regime that was established in China in 1949 and remains in power. The Fascist dictatorship that

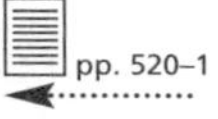

pp. 520–1

dominated Germany in the 1930s and extended its rule to most of the rest of Europe in the early 1940s was relatively short-lived and directed its instruments of terror mainly at the Jews, with catastrophic effect, but Christians were also firmly controlled and produced their martyrs. In Latin America, military dictatorships used ruthless methods from about 1970 onwards to suppress opposition that came mainly from within the Roman Catholic Church, while post-colonial Africa produced some particularly cruel dictatorships that cared nothing for human rights. The doctrine of apartheid employed for over 40 years to constrain the non-white population of South Africa was informed by a destructive, inhuman combination of Christian heresy and white tribal fear.

Icon

Appalling though these persecutions undoubtedly were, it is a matter for thankfulness that by the end of the twentieth century most of them – China being the notable exception – had ceased or been significantly modified. At the beginning of the new century, however, a number of new, albeit lesser, assaults on Christian freedom were sufficient to remind believers that following Christ may still involve suffering, and sometimes death.

The Soviet empire

The following statistics relating to the Russian Orthodox Church tell more eloquently than anything that might be attempted in words the story of what it endured when living under Communist rule:

Until 1911 the Russian Orthodox Church was the supreme embodiment and guardian of Holy Russia. Its membership embraced almost the entire population, and its close alliance with tsarism gave it a position of privilege and power. That made it a prime candidate for repression when the Communists seized power in 1917, though Karl Marx had never envisaged an all-out assault on religious institutions as necessary to the creation of a Communist order. He believed that they would wither when economic exploitation of the masses ceased. Lenin, the head of the new Russian state, saw things differently. He regarded a reactionary church as a serious obstacle to economic progress and, until it withered, in need of strict control. Resisters had to be treated severely

Lenin's first step was to separate church from state and then to apply laws restricting religious activities to church buildings. This brought resistance, and between 1917 and 1923 28 bishops and over 1200 priests were put to death. Many more fled, or adopted an underground existence in which icons and candles provided a focus of devotion. The death of Lenin in 1924 and his succession by Stalin only made matters worse, and a Law on Religious Associations promulgated in 1929 drew the net tighter. During the 1930s, Stalin exercised what can only be described as a reign of terror in which millions of Russian Christians were killed or deported to camps in Siberia. The church was virtually wiped out.

In 1941, however, there was a startling change of policy. Faced with a life-or-death struggle against Nazi Germany, Stalin took steps to ensure the unity of the nation and to win the unbridled loyalty of all its citizens. Restrictions on the church were relaxed, church buildings and monasteries were re-opened, bishops and priests came out of hiding, and although there could be no return to pre-Revolution days, the position of Christians was substantially improved. This continued until the death of Stalin in 1959, but then his successor, Khrushchev, initiated a vigorous anti-religious campaign that considerably reduced the church's resources and activities.

When Khrushchev was removed from power in 1964, the application of the laws was again relaxed, but only a little, with the church's activities restricted to worship and no possibility of running schools or holding missions. About this time the Patriarch of Moscow, Alexii, came

1917		1939	1947–57	1964	1980
163	Bishops in dioceses	4	74	63	64
51,105	Parish clergy	a few 100s	20,000	14,000	6,000
54,174	Churches	a few 100s	18,000	11,500	7,500
1,025	Monasteries and convents	0	67	32	16–20
94,629	Monks and nuns	unknown	10,000	5,000	unknown
4	Church academies	0	2	2	2
57	Theological seminaries	0	8	5	3
37,528	Parish schools	0	forbidden	by	law
291	Church hospitals	0	forbidden	by	law
34,497	Parish libraries	0	forbidden	by	law

under some criticism for his readiness to collaborate with the government over its church policy. This raised a question which cannot be avoided by any church leaders whose communities are facing persecution: Is it best to compromise and enter into a degree of co-operation with the persecuting power, so that the church might survive in some form and its members be cared for by their pastors? Or does Christian discipleship demand valiant confrontation with the persecutors, even at the cost of martyrdom? For much of the twentieth century and in many different parts of the world Christians had to make painful choices, and the evidence now, as then, suggests that differing circumstances and personal vocations validated different answers.

This dilemma was keenly felt by the minority Protestant churches in the Soviet Union, of which the largest is the Baptist. During the early years of the twentieth century the Baptist Church was tolerated and grew rapidly, but on the outbreak of war in 1914 it was identified with Germans and its activities were restricted. Many churches were closed and its leaders went into exile. After 1917, however, the Baptists were free to resume their corporate life and were not affected by the separation of church and state. Within the constraints of the time they flourished. But from 1929 onwards their fate was no different from that of all the churches in the Soviet Union, except that they became divided over the issue of collaboration with the government, and those who refused to register their congregations and obey other directives were very harshly treated.

The Roman Catholic Church in the Soviet Union was virtually annihilated in two extended waves of persecution – one began after the Revolution and the other followed a disastrous attempt by the Vatican to re-establish a hierarchy of bishops in 1926. Nor was there any relief during and after World War II, since Catholicism continued to be regarded as a hostile force – which it was. In Lithuania the Roman Catholic Church was very strong, and it flourished until 1945, when the nation was incorporated into the Soviet Union. It was then singled out for especially severe persecution and there were many hundreds of martyrs. This situation was eased slightly in 1964, but when the bishops refused to accept many of the state's requirements, the persecution continued.

After the end of the 1939–45 war the churches in all the other countries of Eastern Europe experienced in varying degrees the pattern of repression and persecution practised in the Soviet Union. Albania was declared to be a godless state and the church was driven underground. Romania had one of the most brutal regimes, yet the Orthodox Church, disdaining any form of social action, continued to attract the active support of over 90 per cent of the population and remained the chief expression of Romanian nationalism. In Poland the Roman Catholic Church remained numerically strong, and during the 1980s dockyard workers who were Catholics carried out a series of strikes which eventually secured democracy and religious freedom for a long-suffering nation.

This action in Poland is now seen as marking the beginning of the end of the Communist tyranny in Eastern Europe. Mikhail Gorbachev, who had been briefly in charge of the USSR economy before becoming head of state in 1985, recognized the need for urgent reform in every part of the Union's life, including greater freedom for religious and other institutions. The millennium of 1000 years of Christianity in the region was marked in 1988 by a great celebration, and two years later a new law guaranteeing freedom for all religions was passed. By 1991 the Soviet empire had collapsed and the long years of religious persecution were ended.

Martyr
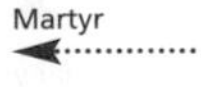

Baptist churches

Germany

When Hitler and his Nazi movement came to power in 1933 it was not their intention to persecute the church. They aimed simply to control it and incorporate its faith into the Nazi ideology. Thus their first move was to force the federally-organized Evangelical (Protestant) Church into a single structure and secure changes of leadership that would ensure compliance with the government's requirements. Reichsbischof Ludwig Müller – Hitler's confidential adviser on church affairs – was made the senior figure in what became known as the German-Christian Church Movement and devised a reform programme which forbade the use of the Old Testament, erased all Jewish references from the Gospels, and excluded Jewish Christians from the ordained ministry and other church offices. The church's youth organization was incorporated into the Hitler Youth.

Christianity in Europe

These steps were attended by a good deal of success, and until the end of the war in 1945 half of the Protestant regional bishops supported the new policy. But there was an almost immediate reaction against it, and towards the end of 1933 Martin Niemöller, who had been a wartime submarine commander before becoming a pastor, founded a Pastors' Emergency League. This attracted 2300 members, and led to the formation of the Confessing Church, dedicated to upholding the orthodox Lutheran faith and the priority of the gospel over the demands of the state. It soon had 800,000 lay members, and in May 1934 a synod held at Barmen issued a declaration that provided the theological basis for Christian resistance to Hitler.

Arrests, trial and imprisonments followed, and in 1937 Niemöller was himself arrested after reading the names of prisoners from his church pulpit. At the end of a secret trial he was sentenced to seven months in prison, all of which he had already served, but Hitler was so enraged by this 'lenient' punishment that he had him sent to a concentration camp where he remained until 1945, having spent four years in solitary confinement.

Following the outbreak of war in 1939 the comprehensive power given to the Gestapo made open resistance impossible except for those who were prepared to risk martyrdom. Among these was a young, courageous theologian, Dietrich Bonhoeffer, who was for a time an honorary member of the Army Intelligence and used his freedom to travel to visit and encourage Christian groups in German-occupied countries. In 1942 he contrived to get to Stockholm; there he had a secret meeting with Bishop George Bell of Chichester, who conveyed to the British Foreign Secretary some ill-received proposals for a negotiated peace. In May of the following year Bonhoeffer was arrested and imprisoned, and in April 1945 he was hanged, shortly before the American army reached his prison. His writings while in prison, and before, subsequently had a worldwide impact.

Christianity in China

Letters

The opposition of the Roman Catholic Church to Hitler was less well organized, though a few of its bishops spoke out against the growing repression of the population in 1937 – a year in which many Catholics were arrested and imprisoned. No attempt was made to get Catholic beliefs and practices changed in an Aryan direction, but in 1938 all the clergy were required to take an oath of allegiance to the Nazi state and thereafter the Gestapo ensured compliance. The German clergy were not exempt from military service, and a large number of them from all the churches were killed in action.

Mission

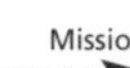

In the countries over-run and controlled by the Germans, the position was somewhat different, inasmuch as it was often impossible to separate religious faith from a wider resistance to occupation by a foreign power. In Poland, for example, by the end of 1942 some 200,000 of the largely Catholic population had been executed or sent to concentration camps. The fate of the Jews was even worse. Among the Catholic martyrs the best known is a Franciscan friar, Maximilian Kolbe, who was sent to the death camp at Auschwitz, where he volunteered to take the place of a young married man who had been chosen for death by starvation. Kolbe was canonized as a saint in 1982. In the Netherlands the Roman Catholic bishops protested against the deportation of Jews to death camps, and this led to severe reprisals against the Dutch Catholic community as well as further deportation of Jews who had become Christians. Worst of all, however, was the inter-Christian persecution carried out in Yugoslavia. An Independent State of Croatia was formed under Axis patronage in 1941 and ruled by a Fascist regime that declared its devotion to Roman Catholicism and its intention to 'purify' the state from Orthodoxy, this being the faith of the Serbs. At least 350,000 of them were killed, another 300,000 were deported or fled, while a further 250,000 were converted under duress to Roman Catholicism. The return of peace led to an often-heated discussion about the silence of Pope Pius XII, who, although aware of the atrocities being committed by Germans, Russians and others, made no public protest.

China and the Far East

Christians in China have never numbered more than one per cent of the huge population, and the twentieth century began badly for this small minority when many thousands of them, including missionaries from the West, were killed during the 1900 Boxer Rising. In this instance, however, as in later outbreaks of persecution, the violence owed more to anti-foreign sentiments that to religious conflict. Yet once the rising had been put down by Western intervention the churches were able to make significant progress Six Chinese Roman Catholic bishops were consecrated in 1926, and by this time more than 8000 missionaries of every Christian tradition were working in the country. In 1949 Protestant Christianity in mainland China had 15 universities and colleges, 240 middle schools, 322 hospitals and medical centres, 15 theological seminaries, more than 30 Bible schools and a variety of social work institutions.

All of this came to an abrupt end in 1949 when the Communist Party, aided by the army, took power and established the People's Republic of China. Missionaries were denounced as agents of Western imperialism and eventually obliged to leave the country. A number of churches were closed, the educational, medical and welfare bodies were taken over by the state, and Christians were required to conform to the government's restrictive demands. These included the breaking of connections with the West. A 'Three-Self Patriotic Movement' required the churches and other organizations to become self-supporting, self-governing and self-propagating, though their governance was always effectively in the hands of the state and evangelism was forbidden. Objectors were either imprisoned or exiled.

Worse was to come in 1966 when, as a consequence of the Cultural Revolution, all religions were banned and the churches were driven underground. Many church buildings were ransacked, others were turned to secular use, and although no Christians are known to have been killed, all suffered some degree of indignity and disadvantage. Meetings were now held in secret in private houses. In 1979, however, there was another change of policy: permission was given for a number of churches to re-open, and restrictions on religious activity were gradually eased; theological seminaries were also re-opened and the Bible was openly used and distributed; links with international Christian bodies were restored.

As Christians began to witness in public again, it seemed that the churches had survived quite well during the time of repression, and they continued to make modest progress. But the demonstration and massacre in Tiananmen Square in 1989, in which Christians were not involved, led to another crackdown on freedom of expression. The Three-Self Church survived, but by the end of the century it was estimated that as many as 80 per cent of Christians were once again meeting in homes and other unauthorized premises, and there were reports of persecution and imprisonment.

The Roman Catholic Church – always the largest Christian presence in China – experienced special difficulties because of its international character, and at different times endured severe persecution. By the end of the century it had become sharply divided between those of its bishops, priests and laity who were prepared, for the sake of some Christian witness, to work within the restrictive framework laid down by the state, and those who remained loyal to the uncompromising attitude of Rome. The former earned the deep displeasure of the Vatican.

Achille Beltrame, Firing squad executing peasants who converted to Catholicism in China, published in *La Domenica del Corriere*, 1900

Vatican

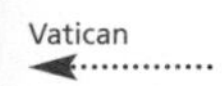

North Korea

During the first half of the twentieth century Christianity flourished in all parts of Korea, and still does, albeit with a very fragmented church, in the South of the country. But, since the division imposed in 1945, Christians in the Communist Republic in the North have been brutally persecuted. No churches or religious activities are allowed, and a very large number of Christians are known to have been killed. It is now virtually impossible to obtain information from this secretive society, so the present situation cannot be assessed.

Japan and South East Asia

Until Japan entered the Second World War at the end of 1941, Christians not only enjoyed freedom but also played a prominent part in public life, most notably Toyohiko Kagawa, a social reformer who achieved world fame. But as soon as the war started, all the European bishops and other clergy were dismissed, some of them enduring harsh imprisonment; others were simply interned. The government then tried, for administrative convenience, to bring all the Protestant churches into a single united church, and those that refused were dissolved. Their clergy and other leaders were imprisoned and a few of them were killed. Relief came when the war ended in 1945.

Singapore was over-run by the Japanese in 1942 and the Anglican bishop, Leonard Wilson, along with a number of clergy of all the churches, was subsequently incarcerated in what became the notorious Changi prison. It was fortunate that the Japanese army officer responsible for the oversight of wartime church life in the British colony was a Christian and displayed a degree of tolerance that was in the circumstances surprising. The prisoners, however, were less fortunate, and at one point Bishop Wilson was badly beaten.

Latin America

Until the seventh decade of the twentieth century the churches of Latin America were not subject to persecution, though the overwhelming majority of the population (90–95 per cent baptized Roman Catholics, the remainder Protestants, Jews and other religions) suffered greatly from the effects of a flagrantly unjust political and economic order. The Roman Catholic hierarchy, which enjoyed the closest possible relations with the governments of the time, was inevitably implicated in the injustice. From the 1960s the regimes in all but three of the South American and in most of the Central American countries were military dictatorships strongly supported by the United States, which saw them as bulwarks against Communism. Most of the leaders were devout Catholics of a conservative character, and weak economies were mercilessly exploited by multinational corporations.

Christianity in Latin America

The first signs of revolt came in Colombia, the most Catholic of the countries, and in 1966 Camilo Torres, a priest from a well-to-do family, joined the growing guerrilla movement fighting from the Andes mountains. He was killed in his first encounter with the Colombian army, and his death sent shockwaves through the Latin-American churches. To the great consternation of the bishops, other young Colombian priests shed their cassocks and joined the guerrillas.

The next significant development was a conference of the Latin American bishops held at Medellín, Colombia, in 1968. The bishops had been greatly challenged by their involvement in the Second Vatican Council, which had just concluded, and in particular by the discussions and the decree on the role of the church in the modern world. At Medellín they committed the church to the overthrowing of injustice and repression and to the liberation of the poor. Not all the bishops subsequently honoured this commitment, nor did it win universal support among the priests and the laity in the dioceses. But the influence of Medellín was sufficient to make it one of the turning points in the history of Latin American Christianity.

Community

Pentecostalism ►

Liberation theology

In the parishes educational programmes were started and many thousands of grassroots (base) communities were eventually established to help the poor to discover how social and political action informed by faith could transform despair into hope. Bishops and priests thundered from their pulpits against injustice and government policies. A new breed of scholars produced a dynamic liberation theology; this was disowned by the Vatican as being too much influenced by Marxism, but it had considerable influence worldwide.

The reaction of the governments to these developments was swift and brutal. They had earlier closed all secular agencies of protest and replaced the civil courts by military tribunals. Brutality and torture were normal methods of coercion. Thus during the period 1969–78, 935 bishops, priests, religious and lay people were arrested, 73 were tortured, 79 were killed, 37 were kidnapped or disappeared, 288 were exiled or expelled. Argentina killed the most: 18, including 2 bishops, followed by El Salvador: 15 including 4 priests. Brazil tortured the most: 31, of whom 23 were priests. In Chile 108 priests were forced to leave the country because of threats to their lives. In Colombia, where a popular uprising in 1977 led to ten years of civil war in which 75,000 people of all ages were killed, a widely-circulated handbill read 'Be a patriot, kill a priest'.

The persecution of Catholic activists continued well into the 1980s and the most notable of the martyrs was Oscar Romero, the political Archbishop of San Salvador, in Central America, who after a cautious beginning became one of the most powerful prophetic voices on behalf of the poor. On 24 March 1980 he was shot while celebrating mass in a hospital chapel and the widely-reported news of his death did more than anything else to alert the rest of the world to the injustice and oppression suffered by the majority of people throughout Latin America. In marked contrast to the situation in El Salvador, however, a socialist party took power in Nicaragua in 1979 and 4 priests held senior office in the new government, while another 20 had senior administrative posts. In 1981 the Nicaraguan bishops, under pressure from Rome, ordered them all to return to their vocations, and those who refused were forbidden to celebrate mass.

During the 1990s a number of factors contributed to a lessening of the conflict, except in Colombia, where early in the twenty-first century Christians who stood up against corruption were still being martyred, though now by bandits. American leaders, no longer enslaved by Cold War attitudes, withdrew their support for the dictatorships, and these were gradually replaced by more democratic and tolerant regimes. It was also the case that the leaders in the liberation struggle came to recognize that revolution in the social and economic order was likely to be long delayed and that in the meantime more effort was needed to alleviate the desperate plight of the poor who still comprise two-thirds of Latin America's population. This approach was shared by the minority Protestant communities, some of whose best scholars have contributed to the development of liberation theology. The Pentecostals, who became the fastest growing Christian community in Latin America, minister chiefly to the poorest of the poor, many of whom have a background in slavery, and their work with its non-political character has never attracted persecution.

Cuba is different again. The revolutionary forces led by Fidel Castro were welcomed by all the churches when they marched into Havana in 1959, but as soon as the Marxist-Leninist character of the new government was apparent they became in varying degrees hostile. A number of Christians were imprisoned for their political opposition, and many Roman Catholic priests were sent to forced labour camps. 400 priests (most of them Spanish) left the country and another 100 were expelled for 'counter-revolutionary activities'. An Anglican priest who later became the bishop spent ten years in prison, having been charged with conspiracy. Christmas was transferred to July to avoid clashing with the December sugar cane harvest.

In the late 1960s and early 1970s, however, relations between the government and the churches began to improve. Some Protestants aligned themselves with the revolution, while the Second Vatican Council and the Medellín Conference encouraged Roman Catholics to take a more positive view of socialist solutions to poverty and injustice. Castro was impressed by developments within the Catholic Church in other parts of Latin America and spoke of the need for a 'strategic alliance' with the churches in order to achieve social change. Yet while there was no official persecution of the church, Christians continued to be discriminated against and often found it difficult to get promotion in their careers. This ended after Castro declared in a book published in 1985, 'It is not anti-Cuban to be Christian.' Thousands flocked back to the churches in the 1990s.

South Africa

The persecution experienced by Christians in South Africa during the twentieth century took place in a broadly Christian context, albeit one grossly distorted by racism. Most of the suffering was institutionalized in a divided, unjust, repressive society, but some was deliberately inflicted on a small, courageous minority who sought to overthrow the racist order.

At the end of the Anglo-Boer war (1899–1902), the majority population of South Africa, many of whom had become Christian as a result of nineteenth-century missionary activity, hoped for a share in the wealth of their country and in some sort of democratic rule. But none of this materialized, and the Constitution of the Union of South Africa (1910) codified racial discrimination. The inferior status accorded to the black Africans and the severe restrictions imposed on their development amounted to a serious form of persecution, imposed tragically by a government claiming Christian authority. The black churches to which they were confined had no opportunities for declaring and witnessing to the universality of their faith.

Within the Anglican Church in South Africa there were always some among its leaders who were critical of this racist order, but they were rarely supported by their white congregations, and the white churches were not unfairly accused of aiding and abetting the repression and injustice. Chief among the white churches was the Dutch Reformed Church, which provided the descendants of the original Dutch settlers at the Cape, who were now known as Afrikaaners, not only with a spiritual home but also with what purported to be a biblical basis for a divided society. Conscious that they were only a tiny minority in the great continent of Africa, they were above all else fearful of losing their identity.

As British influence in South Africa waned, so Afrikaaner nationalism became the dominant force, and when the National Party, representing Afrikaaner interests, came to power in 1946, apartheid – the separate development of the black and white races – was made official policy. In practice this meant inferior development for the blacks, who had poor education, menial jobs, low wages and primitive housing, and whose movements were severely restricted by Draconian pass laws. Attempts were also made to relocate many of them in so-called Homelands, far removed from South Africa's chief sources of wealth.

Father Trevor Huddleston, an Anglican monk, exposed the evil of this regime in 1956 in a widely-read book, *Naught for Your Comfort*, and at Sharpeville in 1960 a local demonstration against school restrictions led to the deaths of 69 blacks (mainly women) and injury to 186 others, shot by the police. In spite of worldwide protests the repression continued, and severe punishment was meted out to those who disobeyed the apartheid laws or who protested against their inhumanity. Thousands were arrested, black leaders were imprisoned, and outspoken whites were either exiled or made subject to banning orders – a form of house arrest.

The conflict led to a sharp division between the Dutch- and English-speaking churches and also to disagreement in the latter between those who believed that public denunciation of apartheid was needed and those who believed that behind-the-scenes representations to the government were likely to be more effective. Among the most outspoken churchmen was the Anglican Archbishop of Cape Town, Joost de Blank, who described racial discrimination as a form of blasphemy, and among the most courageous was Beyers Naude, an Afrikaaner and former Dutch Reformed Church leader, whose Christian Institute offered a flicker of hope in the darkness until it was closed by the government and he was put on trial. After the Second Vatican Council the Roman Catholic bishops also spoke out boldly.

In the end, however, the most influential figure proved to be Desmond Tutu, the first black Archbishop of Cape Town, whose dynamic and courageous witness played a vital part in the dismantling of apartheid in the early 1990s. He and Nelson Mandela, who became South Africa's first black President after spending more than 25 years in prison, were both awarded the Nobel Peace Prize. Later Tutu organized and chaired a Truth and Reconciliation Commission that did much to secure a peaceful transition to a multiracial, tolerant society in South Africa.

Dutch Reformed Church ◄

Uganda

Unfortunately, no such peaceful ending of persecution was possible in Uganda. When Idi Amin seized power in 1971 and became President of a nation sharply divided on tribal lines, he immediately used the army to subdue all opposition to his dictatorial rule. During the first two years an estimated 90–100,000 Ugandans were murdered, including the Chief Justice, a Roman Catholic, who had called for the army's powers to be curbed. He was dragged from the High Court and dismembered alive in public. Two successive editors of the only Catholic newspaper were killed for bravely venturing to criticize.

The Anglican bishops were no less courageous, and as the brutal reign of terror intensified they became increasingly bold in their expressions of concern. Early in February 1977, following an attack on the home of Archbishop Janani Luwum, they addressed a joint letter to Amin in which they catalogued his regime's crimes and added, 'We have buried many who have died as a result of being shot, and there are many more whose bodies have not been found. The law has been replaced by the bullet.'

Amin summoned the bishops for 9.30 am on 16 February and they were surprised to find themselves arraigned before a parade of 3000 soldiers, together with some government officials and diplomats. After standing in the blazing sun for two hours they heard a man read out a document which purported to prove that the Archbishop had been involved in a secret arms deal with the President's toppled predecessor. The Archbishop denied this, whereupon the Vice-President, who was in charge of the event, shouted, 'What shall we do with the traitors?' The soldiers responded, 'Kill them, kill them.' The bishops were eventually allowed to leave, but the Archbishop was ordered to remain and later that day it was announced that he had been arrested. On the following morning Uganda radio reported that he had been killed in a car accident while trying to escape, but evidence collected from witnesses in the prison indicated that he had been shot the previous evening.

Orders were given over the radio that there should be no prayers for him and that a memorial service would not be allowed. Instead, thousands attended the normal service at Namirembe Cathedral the following Sunday morning, and this was described by many as an 'Easter experience'. Thereafter, regular church attendance throughout the country increased noticeably. But the persecution continued with no less intensity for another two years until Amin over-reached himself by trying to annex part of neighbouring Tanzania. This gave its President, Julius Nyerere, an excuse to send his army into Uganda, and after six months of bloody fighting Amin was deposed. Being some sort of Muslim, he was subsequently granted asylum, first in Libya and finally in Saudi Arabia.

Sudan

In Sudan a civil war between the Muslim North of this vast country and the South, where there is a significant Christian presence and influence, raged on and off for most of the second half of the twentieth century. This, combined with severe famine, brought great suffering to the population of the South, where the majority of Christians are either Roman Catholic or Anglican. At the end of the century it was estimated that two million Sudanese had been killed in the war and another four million displaced.

Fundamentalism ➤

When Sudan was an Anglo-Egyptian condominium, the North and the South were separately developed, but during the years preceding independence in 1958 attempts were made to integrate the two more closely. This proved to be to the great disadvantage of the economically weaker South, which found itself increasingly under Northern domination. Eventually the South rebelled and this led to a civil war in which religious differences and concern for the future of the country's oil fuelled the conflict.

In the North, Christian churches were closed, schools were taken over, missionaries were harassed, then expelled, and Christian activity was severely restricted, while on the battlefields in the South the government army, whose ranks included the most fanatical of Muslim soldiers, inflicted unspeakable atrocities on unarmed men, women and children. Many of these were Christians. In 1972 there was a lull in the violence, following an agreement signed at a peace conference held in Addis Ababa, and the churches began to rebuild their life under Sudanese leadership, including Roman Catholic and Anglican archbishops. The signs were encouraging.

But the agreement was not honoured for long by the central government in the North, in which Islamic extremists had gained influence, and hostilities were resumed, with further suffering for the heroic Christians in the South. After 1993 the fighting became more sporadic and was punctuated by cease-fires and further attempts to reach a negotiated settlement. In 2003 a government peace initiative stalled when church leaders in the South refused to support its approach to the rebel leaders. The Vicar-General of the Catholic diocese of Juba presented a government delegation with a three-page letter noting 'the planned programme of brutal Arabization, Islamization, oppression and persecution to the point of extermination carried out since 1990'. The government responded by demanding that church leaders confine themselves to 'religious' issues, refrain from involvement in political or security issues and abstain from inciting public opinion against the government.

The situation remained unstable, and the Southerners will not now be satisfied with anything less than self-rule. Christians continue to be persecuted whenever opportunity offers, but famine is now their chief enemy.

The second half of the twentieth century witnessed a major resurgence of the Islamic faith in Africa and many other parts of the world, and within this faith the emergence of a militant fundamentalism. Linked sometimes to extreme nationalism or to wholly legitimate feelings of injustice arising from the unfair distribution of the world's physical resources, this proved to be a highly dangerous mixture, with widespread terrorism taking the place of conventional warfare. The overwhelming majority of Muslims rejected this as a serious distortion and misuse of their faith, but in some countries national policy, or the actions of fanatical factions, made life difficult for Christian minorities, sometimes to the point of persecution.

Saudi Arabia provided an extreme example of this by forbidding all Christian activity except in the restricted spaces allocated to the housing of foreign nationals. Bibles and other Christian literature were routinely confiscated at the point of entry to the country. In Iran, the Anglican bishop, Hassan Dehqani-Tafti, escaped an attempt on his life in 1979 and was driven into exile. In May of the following year, his only son was murdered by government agents and later, in another incident, his English secretary was seriously wounded and left for dead. In Pakistan, Christian missionary activity was forbidden and from time to time Christians were attacked by fanatics and killed.

Thus the beginning of a new century demanded the highest priority for open conversation and deeper understanding between Christians and Muslims in the cause of religious toleration and world peace. The two are inseparable.

TREVOR BEESON

Trevor Beeson, *Discretion and Valour*, London: Collins Fount and Philadelphia: Fortress Press [2]1982; Trevor Beeson and Jenny Pearce, *A Vision of Hope: Churches and Change in Latin America*, London: Collins Fount and Philadelphia: Fortress Press 1984; J. S. Conway, *The Nazi Persecution of the Churches*, London: Weidenfeld & Nicolson and New York: Basic Books 1968; Jane Ellis, *The Russian Orthodox Church: A Contemporary History*, London: Croom Helm and Bloomington, IN: Indiana University Press 1986; John W. de Gruchy, *The Church Struggle in South Africa*, London: SPCK and Grand Rapids, MI: Eerdmans [2]1986; G. Hood, *Neither Bang nor Whimper: The End of a Missionary Era in China*, Singapore: Presbyterian Church in Singapore 1991; Penny Lernoux, *Cry of the People*, Harmondsworth and New York: Penguin Books 1982

Philosophy

Philosophy has deeply permeated Christian thought from the earliest days of Christians reflecting on what they believed. So it is impossible to understand Christian theology without having some idea of the philosophical background against which it has been done. A journey through the history of philosophy from the ancient to the modern world sheds much light on why particular issues were discussed at particular times and why, over the centuries, the agenda changed.

Ancient philosophy

Origins and background

When Christianity arose, philosophy was already well developed in the Graeco-Roman world. It encompassed most areas of theoretical knowledge and was divided into four areas of study: logic, natural philosophy (what is now called science), ethics and metaphysics ('first philosophy'). It was also divided into four chief schools, Platonism, Aristotelianism, Stoicism and Epicureanism, with some minor schools such as Cynicism. Although each school maintained a distinctive set of teachings, in the first century philosophy was eclectic as a result of continual interaction. The 'middle Platonism' of the period, for example, had absorbed numerous Aristotelian and Stoic arguments, fitting them into a larger, still recognizably Platonic framework. The educated general public had also absorbed a great deal of philosophy through works such as those of the Roman orator Cicero (106–43 BCE), which summarized and compared the positions of the schools; these were often the main means by which philosophical doctrines were known outside the schools. Philosophical terms and ideas, such as Aristotle's basic logic, were also part of higher education.

Philosophy within the schools was characterized by set discipline and questions. It was not, however, strictly a theoretical matter since virtually all schools aimed at making their students wise, and through wisdom to bring them to happiness (Greek *eudaimonia*), although they often differed on its precise nature. Ancient philosophy bore a spiritual and ethical character that made philosophy a way of life as much as a set of doctrines.

This link between philosophy as an intellectual discipline and a way of life attracted Christians of an intellectual bent to philosophy and certain philosophers to Christianity. The attraction of Christians to philosophy and the conversion of philosophers were quite natural, although hardly automatic. Christians sought to know God through God's word, which is wisdom. Significant portions of the Old Testament are concerned with wisdom; the New Testament, too, understands wisdom to be a goal of Christian life. Philosophy simply means 'love of wisdom'. For philosophers such as Athenagoras and Justin in the second century who were seeking wisdom, Christianity's promise of God's wisdom was attractive. The similarity was not just a verbal one. There was also a like desire of the heart, which remains dissatisfied with appearances, sensing an unhappy fit between itself and the world as commonly known, and therefore seeking a transcending 'really real' that alone can heal and satisfy the soul. The case of Augustine is an example. Augustine began turning from his dissolute younger life because he became inflamed by philosophy after reading Cicero's *Hortensius*; later it was the 'books of the Platonists' that set him on the final stretch of his journey to Christian faith.

God
Bible

p. 139

Theology

Philosophy played a crucial role in that journey, and in Augustine's own Christian thought.

Still, certain important steps were required before Christianity could absorb Greek philosophy. Christianity, Revelation like Judaism, is a religion rooted in revelation, that is, in specific historical events and the individual, personal will of God, as well as in the historical traditions of a community. It is not the result of general conceptual speculation. What was needed was a way to link the two. This was provided first within the biblical wisdom literature, which frequently hypostatized God's Wisdom (i.e. made it a separate figure; this was crucial later for treating Christ as Trinity God's Word, the second Person of the Trinity). Meditation on the Jewish law and obedience to it was called for as a matter of universal wisdom. Philo (*c.* 20 BCE–*c.* 50 CE), an Alexandrian Jewish thinker, capitalized on the tendencies in wisdom literature to develop a method of treating biblical material allegorically. Allegorical reading of the biblical material allowed its specificities to be dealt with in general categories: God's Word and Wisdom became the Logos which was so central to much Greek philosophy, especially Platonism and Stoicism. Philo's was probably the most important influence on the earliest Christian thinkers and mediated their contacts with the philosophical schools.

A century later, Clement of Alexandria (*c.* 150–*c.* 215) argued that Christ is the philosophical teacher *par excellence*, and further daringly argued that Gnosis the true Christian is a gnostic (*gnosis* = knowledge). But the most important thinker in making Greek philosophy fit conceptually with Christianity was Origen (*c.* 185–254).

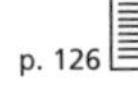

Origen was thoroughly instructed in Middle Platonism in Alexandria. A prolific biblical exegete, he developed the allegorical method of reading scripture to a point where it influenced biblical interpretation for over a millennium. p. 126 For him, the Bible contains a triple sense: literal, moral and allegorical. It was the allegorical which was the most important, containing the real spiritual meaning of a text. Origen in his *De Principiis* was also the first to put together systematically a wide range of doctrinal topics, although his taste for speculative venturing and philosophical consistency, often at the price of the literal, led him into views that were condemned after his death, perhaps less for the actual doctrines that he upset than the way he upset them, namely, by dissolving their concreteness and allowing philosophical reasoning to dictate the flow of meditating on scripture.

The relation between philosophy and early Christianity was largely one-way. Philosophy, explicitly and through general cultural absorption, took on life within Christianity, until the pagan philosophers disappeared and virtually all philosophy was done by Christians. However, Christian thinkers tended to work within only some of the main divisions of philosophy. With the exception of Boethius (*c.* 480–*c.* 524), they did not make contributions in logic or in natural philosophy, being content with the received science of their day. As was to be expected; their chief concerns were with issues such as the nature and knowability of God, the relation of God to the natural world; human nature and ethics; and the philosophy of religion. In his *The City of God*, Augustine, the most important Christian philosopher, also set out a political philosophy that was a dominant force for centuries after.

The most important source for Christian thinkers was *Platonism*. Platonism was the dominant philosophical school of the day (Stoicism was perhaps more popular, but largely as a personal philosophy, especially among the Romans); it also had certain similarities to Christian beliefs and forms of life, namely, that there is a God, one, wholly good and transcendent, approached and known through a virtuous life. Augustine notes approvingly that 'it is enough to remember that Plato asserted that the highest good is to live according to virtue; that only he can do this who has knowledge of God and imitates him; and that this is the only cause of happiness'. Platonic philosophical vocabulary and arguments became vital conceptual territory in the philosophical articulation of Christianity.

The chief elements of Platonism can be easily discerned in a few central texts. In the middle books of Plato's *Republic*, Socrates likens the Good, the most important of Ideas, to the sun. Like the sun it is the principle of all generation, and by being the source of light it is also the means of knowledge by letting things be seen as they are. The Good is thus the source of all that is and also the principle of all intelligibility. It is transcendent, the source of all being and not a being itself; it 'exceeds being in both power and dignity'. Plato's metaphysics of light and intelligence unfolds from this simile in 'the divided line'. Reality is graded according to its degree of intelligibility, which is in turn the degree to which it participates in the really real Good. This graded participation in and due to the Good is Plato's understanding of non-physical causality. It also allows the mind to work towards the Good, because each reality lower on the scale shows signs of the higher reality from which it is derived. If reality proceeds from a higher intelligible principle, by intelligence and learning to see things as they are the human soul can mount from a realm of shadowy reality to seeing the Good itself. This ascent is underlined in Plato's allegory of the cave, where he likens human life to that lived in a cave, lit only by artificial light and where shadows are mistaken for reality. The one who leaves the cave to live in the light of the sun outside can see things as they really are. Moreover, Plato argues, one can in time see the sun itself, and so see why things are through understanding what makes them. This escape from the cave and the progression of knowledge up the divided line are also linked to Plato's two dialogues on love, the *Symposium* and the *Phaedrus*, which treat love as a desire of the soul for truth and beauty in themselves that mounts from the love of a single body to a love of truth and beauty, where it finds its true home.

Plato's quasi-narrative account of creation in the *Timaeus* is also important. There a God, in an overflowing of divine goodness, creates a world by providing order to chaos through a careful mixing of mathematical forms which form a living World Soul that indwells and orders particular beings and governs their interactions, resulting in a harmony and beauty of the world which reflects its maker's perfection.

It is not entirely clear how all these elements go together for Plato. For example, the Creator God of the *Timaeus* looks to the perfect Forms or Ideas as a pattern by which to create, whereas the Good of the *Republic* would seem to be the generator of all being including the Forms. However, by the time Christianity appeared, Middle Platonism had assimilated the Good and the Creator God, and the Forms were considered as the god's ideas. Plotinus (*c.*205–70) and the Neo-Platonists further developed Plato's original insights into how a divine, non-physical source of being could cause a world and harmonize its interactions. In Plotinus the source of all reality was the One, whose transcendence can never be spoken of directly, since doing so would define its original and perfectly simple reality by concepts that properly belonged to its creation, containing an admixture of plurality. From the One all reality flowed through a series of *hypostases*, Intelligible Being (*Nous*), Soul (*Psyche*) and Matter, with each *hypostasis* showing marks of its original source in so far as it was unified and capable of unifying the *hypostases* under it. Each *hypostasis* bears traces of its proximate and remote origins. For Plotinus the goal of the human soul, which participates in Intelligible Being, was to find its own proper unity and to seek its home in the One from which all being sprang. Philosophy is this search.

Christian philosophers never adopted Platonism wholesale; at numerous points their commitment to biblical texts contravened Platonism, especially the creation of the world. They steadfastly maintained creation was in time, a gratuitous, willed act of God. God therefore could and did exist without a world. For Platonism, on the other hand, creation tended to mean ordering of something pre-existent, and not in time. Therefore the world could be and is eternal; the One is still part of nature – its highest part, but not separable. For example, in Neo-Platonism it seems that the emanation of reality from the One is an inherent process of the One: creation seems a natural necessity. Christianity's insistence on the distinction between God and creation, and thus on God's utter graciousness, ultimately demanded a stronger sense of God's transcendence than even Platonism could provide. Nevertheless, Platonism could provide a way by which God could be conceived non-physically (Augustine gives credit to the Platonists for getting him over this stumbling block) and, at the same time, a way by which God could be understood to create and order creation, especially through the mediating divine indwelling of the Logos (the Son of God) in creation. It also allowed a way to conceive moral life as having its source in God and its end in the vision of God, in so far as the search to understand God meant understanding the eternal law by which the world was ordered and ordering one's own life accordingly. Here Christianity also leaned, as did later Platonism itself, on arguments and concepts borrowed from Stoicism which also maintained that the world was a rationally ordered whole (although the Stoics were pantheists and materialists) permeated by the divine Logos and that human lives were perfected in knowing and being ordered by this reason.

Platonic Christian philosophy is often accused of intellectualism, i.e. of assuming that thought and vision alone constitute the way to the knowledge of God, and also of uncritically adopting an understanding of God in which God is impassible, unable to change in response to historical life, a picture opposed to the historically dynamic one of God in the Bible.

Early Christian philosophy should be evaluated in the broader context of what philosophy in general was in the late ancient world and in terms of its own religious goals. Ancient philosophy was theoretical, and did present a representation of the world that itself became the object of the mind. But it was also a way of life, a quest for wisdom and happiness; as such it was a therapy, especially a therapy of desire, that would reorientate and form the human subject, order its life, and return it to its true home. To look outwards at the universe was to find a model for life and for ordering the soul and the larger polity. When that order was instilled in the soul, one actually participated in a larger reality that was otherwise closed off.

Augustine (354–430) is an example of both the intellectualistic tendency and of treating Christian philosophy as a spiritual way of life. Shortly after his conversion he set out to write a series of treatises that would trace each of the 'liberal arts' (the basic intellectual disciplines) to its source in God, thus leading the knower by philosophical and intellectual means to the knowledge of God. He soon abandoned the project. This was in part because of his new ecclesiastical duties as bishop, but also because of his expanding biblical knowledge and his discovery of the will, a concept underdeveloped previously. At that point his project of leading the soul back to God was no longer a matter simply of thinking its way back, but of training it in all its parts – bodily, moral and intellectual. For

Creation

example, in *De Trinitate*, Augustine develops an analogy between the human mind and the Trinity, trying to show how both can be one and yet have three powers. Platonism had taught him to see in earthly reality the vestiges of divine reality, and therefore exploitable analogies. Yet, he was not trying so much to explain the Trinity by its likeness to the mind as trying to find a way by which the human mind could be healed of its fractured divisiveness by meditating upon the Trinity. The project was not a purely intellectual exercise, but one of taking an image of God (and, explicitly, the example of the incarnate Christ's life and death) sacramentally so that, being healed and ordered in the 'outer person', the soul might finally move inwardly and meet God. Healing outer life through knowledge, morals and discipline was essential to inner healing. Reflection upon doctrines was not divorced from everyday life, and doctrines were not simply a representation and map of reality; through their mediated images they made possible active spiritual and moral life.

Scholasticism

The unknown Dionysius the Areopagite (or Pseudo-Dionysius, *c.* 500) borrowed heavily from the Neo-Platonist Proclus (411–85). In a series of mystical treatises, Dionysius effects a thoroughgoing union of Neoplatonism and Christianity. God, utterly transcendent, is utterly unknowable by the creation and must be approached by a purgation of concepts and images belonging to creation. This is known as 'negative (apophatic) theology'. Thus, for example, it is proper to say that God is not good in so far as 'good' takes it meaning from anything we can conceive. Rather than annihilating the possibility of theology, Dionysius sees this negative theology as always linked with a positive (kataphatic) theology of naming. By a continual meditation that moves from positive to negative to positive, the soul ascends through the celestial hierarchy until union with God is achieved. Dionysius was highly influential throughout the Middle Ages, and Thomas Aquinas leaned heavily on him.

The Middle Ages

Christian philosophy continued within a Platonic mode until roughly the end of the first millennium. Speculation was conducted through allegorical readings of scripture, explicating the metaphysically linked essences of beings and their relation to God through biblical symbolism. Teaching was largely done within cathedral schools and monasteries. However, a number of changes in philosophical reasoning become apparent by the time of Anselm (*c.* 1033–1109).

Schools
Monasticism

With Anselm there is a new sense of a logical systematizing, as seen in his meditations, *Proslogion* and *Monologion*. Both give versions of his ontological proof of the existence of God ('God is that than which nothing greater can be conceived ...'). Within the Augustinian tradition, they are written as spiritual meditations. Anselm prays in the first chapter and clearly recognizes God as creator. He is not trying to convince himself of God's existence; he is trying to understand more fully what he has believed. His 'faith seeking understanding' deliberately builds on the Augustinian 'unless you believe you will not understand'. But he is also able to debate his proof with impressive logical rigour, and systematically draws out numerous conclusions about God's nature from it, such as God's unity, justice, etc. It is this systematizing, a new logical rigour, and deliberate debate, which are hallmarks of the scholastic philosophy of the high Middle Ages.

p. 507

The rediscovery of Aristotle (384–322 BCE) was at the root of scholasticism. Largely unknown except through ancient quotations and only his most basic logical works until the later Middle Ages, Aristotle became known to the West through its interaction with Islamic culture in Spain. The Arabs, particularly philosophers such as Avicenna and Averroes, had made considerable use of Aristotle, although they did not always distinguish sharply between Platonism and Aristotelianism.

Aristotle gave several important tools to medieval philosophy, including an expanded technical vocabulary in logic and in issues of causality. He also offered a way to deal with certain problems that plagued Platonism, especially concerning the Platonic essences.

In Platonism, the essences of things are the Forms or Ideas, and the reality of these Forms give reality to an individual under them. However, for Plato the Forms are separate from individuals. The form of human that makes each human a human exists separately from actual men. For Aristotle, however, while there are universal forms, they do not exist separately from the matter in which they are found, although they are separable in thought. (Indeed, they must be, since we know things by their forms, and through insight and logical deduction use them as the premises of argument. In this way we are able to gain new knowledge and understanding of them and their relations to other things; such knowledge is *scientia.*) Aristotelian *hylomorphism* (*hyle* = matter, *morphe* = form) thus allowed a far more sophisticated and obvious explanation of natural causality, since, for example, the transmission of human form, as from parent to child, could be a biological process and not entirely a metaphysical one. Moreover, with Aristotle's division of causality into formal, final, efficient and material causes, a schema applied across a nearly universal range of problems, there was a marked increase in philosophers' ability to deal with problems of motion and change.

The discovery of Aristotle was not, however, without its problems, not unlike those that the scientific revolution would present hundreds of years later and Charles Darwin after that. Aristotle gave more powerful explanations of nature than anything the early medievals had. Yet many suspected that his natural philosophy led to determinism, undermining the ability of God to act in nature. Earlier Christian thinkers thought that Aristotle was a materialist. Another problem concerned the nature of individuals, since according to Aristotle what makes a thing what it is is its form, and forms can be defined and reasoned about only as universals. Is there, then, only one human essence, making individuals simply examples of a universal form of humanity with no real difference between them? Moreover the Prime Mover, Aristotle's first cause and divine principle, was not a god worth worshipping. Yet with Aristotle's explanations so seemingly complete, it would appear that the claims of Christian faith, which were entwined with the older natural philosophy, must be ruled out of the court of reason, unless one held, as some Arab philosophers did, that truth came in two entirely different and contradictory versions, one theological and one natural.

There is no doubt that the greatest philosopher of the Middle Ages was Thomas Aquinas (*c.*1225–74). Thomas absorbed Aristotle and used him, but his overall vision still retains the larger Platonic metaphysics of participated reality that proceed from the ineffable, divine first cause, even while using Aristotelian logic and causality.

Benozzo de Lesse Gozzoli, Thomas Aquinas standing between Aristotle and Plato and over the Arab philosopher Averroes, from *The Triumph of St Thomas*, fifteenth century

The key to Thomas' achievement was to take essence to consist in 'activity' and 'actuality'. God on this account is still one, simple, transcendent, and the first cause of reality as in Platonism. But now these characteristics are defined in relation to God's complete activity. God does not change because God is fully active with no potentiality; nothing can be added or subtracted. Participated, created reality owes its activity to God's and can be graded by its level of actuality or activity. For Thomas, his 'five ways', his proofs of the existence of God, depend on showing that in every sense of 'cause' God is the first cause, and that all causality is rooted in and dependent upon the activity of the first cause, which, he notes, 'we understand to be God'. God's initiative and providence are thus maintained while at the same time allowing analysis of motion and change in Aristotelian terms.

Thomas also makes an important distinction between essence and existence, between a being and its being. For God alone does essence and existence coincide: as a being, being is his being. To be God is to be; God exists as an uncreated eternal being. Created beings in their concrete existence participate in an essence as their characteristic sort of activity, making them the sort of beings that they are. They also may live up to that essence or not. They are individuated by their specific matter, and thus in embodied life souls, which are the form of the body, are individual and known by their own history.

Thomas' philosophy allows room within natural causality for grace, and indeed since all activity is due to God's free giving of being to beings, creation itself is a gracious activity. Grace, moreover, does not undermine nature, but perfects it. Important as philosophy and science are, they must be ordered to the knowledge of God. By establishing a 'hierarchy of discourses', Thomas orders the philosophical discourses of physics, epistemology and metaphysics to theology which completes them, just as each completes the prior one and yet uses it. Philosophy is the 'handmaid of theology', which is the 'queen of the sciences'; now 'water is turned into wine'. Philosophy, if it cannot plumb the mysteries of God and must rely on revelation to be completed, is nevertheless vital within theology. 'Sacred doctrine makes use even of human reason, not, indeed, to prove faith … but to make clear other things that are put forward in this doctrine. Since therefore grace does not destroy nature, but perfects it, natural reason should minister to faith …'

Still, within Thomas one finds a sharper distinction between nature and grace, and hence philosophy and theology, than Christian philosophy had seen before, although the distinction was not unknown. Philosophy

Grace

finds itself in a more autonomous space than it had previously, a space that is expanded in coming generations when philosophy stands for only what human reason can know. It has a distinctive set of problems, and is a separate discipline now.

The concession of a separate, autonomous realm to philosophy and human reasoning has several important bases. First, at the end of the medieval period is the problem of universals and the rise of nominalism. Within both Platonism and Aristotelianism, the universal terms which mark out essences are held to define really what a thing is. If they do, then when combined logically they yield knowledge. Nominalism on the other hand holds that the universal premises needed in philosophical syllogisms to construct knowledge do not mark out things as they are, but are simply names (*nomines*). This doctrine goes back to the eleventh and twelfth centuries, but is best known in the form given it by William of Ockham in the fourteenth century, who argued that universals are only a human construct, and that substance is radically individual. If this is so, then we cannot be certain about knowledge derived from universal premises; there is no easy and natural passage from knowledge of nature to God. God's will and omnipotence are God's defining attributes. Our knowledge of God must rest entirely on faith and trust in authority. Martin Luther's demand for 'faith alone' and his imprecations against 'whore reason' are both very understandable in this light. Philosophy cannot lead to theological knowledge; however, if theology must rest on faith alone, then inevitably reason comes to occupy its own separate realm.

Evidence

Faith

Authority

A second way in which reason came to be regarded as autonomously separate from theology is a sociological and historical one. At the time of the Reformation and the ensuing wars of religion in the seventeenth century, religious authority had broken down, as different confessions each claimed the authority necessary for faith, and yet were opposed to each other. Some sort of neutral umpire was required to guide human belief and conduct safely. Reason came to play this role. Making faith reasonable was meant to undergird it, although in, say, Deism, religious forms did arise that would not confess anything more than a minimum allowed by reason. At this point, of course, metaphysics as the philosophical enquiry into questions beyond scientific determination is no longer merely a helpful discourse to think theologically; religion is understood exactly as a metaphysical doctrine, needing to be defended and approached as such. The possibility of doing so quickly becomes a problem.

Reformation

Wars of religion

p. 504

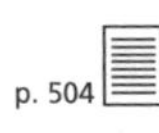

Miracle

Enlightenment

The Enlightenment

Reason was viewed as an overriding umpire in modernity because of its claim to universality. Also important was its indifference or neutrality over questions of method; it claimed that one needed to picture oneself as standing somehow outside any problem to be decided. One first considers reason, and then if, for example, the existence of God can be demonstrated, one can give assent. If it cannot be demonstrated, one either needs to withhold assent, or proportion the strength of one's belief to the strength of the evidence.

What, however, constitutes reason, and where does its universality lie? The repeated attempts to answer this question give modern philosophy a deep concern with epistemology (the study of knowledge) that has continually sought for two linked pillars: a reasonable method for discovering and guaranteeing truth and incontrovertible, public evidence. These serve as foundations for knowledge. The modern quest to prove or disprove Christianity on a purely reasonable basis depends on these pillars.

The beginnings of the quest for foundations and a universal method is usually credited to René Descartes (1596–1650), who found them in 'clear and distinct ideas'. Descartes has this confidence because by the ontological argument, already in Anselm and with roots in Augustine, God can be proved and thus ideas showing clarity (especially mathematical ideas) must be reliable, since God is not a deceiver. While Descartes is linked to the Augustinian tradition of an intelligible light proceeding from God, a very different way of approaching philosophy results from his *Meditations*. It is no longer 'faith seeking understanding'; rather, faith now starts to be understood as requiring rational proof. One upshot of his method is also that this rational basis of faith may be attacked while still maintaining the rational foundations of the clear and distinct ideas and universal method. Thus while Descartes hoped to put all human knowledge on a reasonable foundation, including morals and religion, his approach was particularly successful in science but far less so in morals and religion. The problem was that ensuing metaphysical discussions about the freedom of the will, the origins of the universe, the existence of God spawned any number of contrary arguments, despite seeming quite clear and distinct to those who offered them.

Clearly, some better sense of evidence was needed. This was provided in the British empiricists – John Locke, George Berkeley and David Hume – who, beginning with Locke (1632–1704), asserted that nothing is in the mind without having first entered through the senses. This did not preclude ideas such as 'God'. Locke thought that the existence of God could be demonstrated, and that in miracles God had provided credible evidence that he had spoken. Thus accepting God's word was rational. However, at this point a purely philosophical religion, Deism, appears, which refuses to believe anything more than can be rationally proved. Deism believed that God could be proved from the design of the universe, which after Isaac Newton (1642–1727) was shown to work with the same mechanical laws as machines, and thus appeared as a giant machine. Since machines have intelligent designers, it was reasoned that the universe must have one, too. But Deism did not think that God interfered with the universe's workings.

However, this optimism was soon dashed, as David Hume (1711–76) showed that any matter of fact, provided by empirical observation, could never give us what was needed to claim necessity for it, no matter how often we observed it. Because the sun has come up every day does not mean that it will necessarily come up tomorrow. We are entitled to think that it will, and Hume thought that we can reasonably stand on customary experience. But causality is no more than what we are accustomed to; conceptually, we cannot get to causal necessity from matters of fact, however often observed. The only necessity is logical necessity, but that is uninformative about the contents of the world; logical necessity is tautological and formal (as in mathematics). Hume's claims were extremely damaging to religious claims, particularly if they are regarded as strictly metaphysical claims. To argue for any metaphysical ideas requires reasoning beyond the merely observable. In order to demonstrate, for example, that God exists, the argument requires that causality is necessary, and hence universal, and thus extendable beyond the observable. Hume's empiricism denied that this could be done, arguing that just because everything in the world seems to have a cause does not entitle us to argue from causality in the world to a cause of the world; an orderly world does not necessarily imply a divine orderer. Moreover, he argued that miracles could not serve as good evidence either, since they are by definition rare and unusual, and we can only reasonably accredit what is usual and for the most part.

Hume's claims had another consequence, however, namely that scientific laws would, strictly speaking, not be laws because they would not be necessary. For Immanuel Kant (1724–1804) this was an unacceptable conclusion. His solution to the problem came by arguing that observation of empirical fact is never pure; rather, all observation is both from the outside and formed by the faculties of the mind. For example, one sees facts within a continuum of time and space, relates them by categories such as causality, and judges them according to logical form. Our minds contribute these things, and shape our observations. Thus our judgements can be necessary, because of the way we form and relate our observations. This solution, while guaranteeing necessity in empirical judgements, also means that we never see things as they are in themselves (*noumena*), since the world we see is in good part a world of our own making. Furthermore, since our faculties are meant to work on phenomena only, when extended beyond the phenomenal realm they create unresolvable contrary conclusions, each with the appearance of reason on its side. So even as empirical science is validated, metaphysical speculation cannot be, because it extends reason beyond its possible uses. Kant, who was not opposed to religion as Hume was, did not think that this discredited religion. If propositions about God cannot be proved metaphysically because reason is incapable of doing so, they cannot be disproved, either. Kant claimed that in limiting pure reason to science he was making room for faith. Indeed, by removing religion from the need to be grounded metaphysically and relating it to morality as he did, Kant was closer to how faith itself actually moves. However, he inverts traditional understandings of the relation of morality and religion, making religion depend on morals for its grounding rather than *vice versa*. The Kantian conscience's sense of right and wrong and obligation to do the good is generated by the self by reason alone, thereby guarding human autonomy. God is a reasonable postulate guaranteeing its success in this world and the next.

In this story philosophy is the acme of human reasoning; it is solely human reasoning, and it has very strict standards to keep it in its place. It is also work, as Kant claimed, and no longer the contemplative reception of truth of ancient and medieval philosophy. It transforms only by self-transformation, remaining within a world of common human experience. Nature, on which it works, is also a separate, neutral sphere.

The nineteenth century

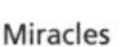

The questions that the philosophers from Descartes to Kant raise and with which they deal, and many of their assumptions, are like the trunk of a tree from which the branches of later modern philosophy develop. Those branches involve both positive and negative assessments of religion.

Hume set out to discredit the argument from design, that is, the use of an analogy that would allow one to infer from the workings of the natural world that those workings are the result and design of a divine mind. While devastating, Hume's argument did not go unanswered. William Paley (1743–1805) tried to answer many of Hume's arguments about the impossibility of arguing from nature to God through design. His *Evidences of Christianity* and *Natural Theology, or Evidences of the Existence and Attributes of the Deity Collected from the Appearances of Nature*, titles descriptive of their content, were immensely popular in the nineteenth century, and standard textbooks. In terms of sheer numbers, they probably had more contemporary influence than Hume's writings. While Paley's conclusions were opposed to Hume's, Paley had something of Hume's spirit of argument, assuming that in order to ground the knowledge of God philosophically one had to argue from empirical evidence and science. However, with the rise of Darwin's theories, which argued for non-purposive natural selection, the evidence turned against the plausibility of an analogy that depended on purposive design.

On the European continent, G. W. F. Hegel (1770–1831) sought to fill the gap Kant left between human thought and the *noumena*. Whereas for Kant the conceptual categories of the human mind by which it shaped and made its judgements were static and logical, by introducing a sense of history Hegel argued that they were far more dynamic. There is within human experience no pure subject or object; rather, in the human attempt to solidify its judgements it is continually modified by and builds on its experience. For Hegel, there is a logical evolution of ideas through the course of human experience from abstract to concrete, wherein the original abstract idea of a world actually comes to encompass the world not in thought alone but in actual experience. This Hegel sees as a world process wherein the Absolute Spirit becomes 'incarnate' in human thought and practice, which in the course of history becomes more genuinely universal and concrete. The Spirit unfolds and incarnates itself in the world through a series of dialectical struggles until all dualities are gone and mind is absolutely present with the object. Idealism, as it is called, since reality is the realization of ideas, was particularly relied upon in much nineteenth-century theology to combat the withering attacks of positivistically-minded scientists and philosophers. Hegel himself thought that Christianity was the highest religion, particularly since its doctrines of God and God's incarnation pointed the way to understanding the Spirit becoming concrete, although he claimed that taken literally Christian doctrines were only early, childish forms of what philosophy made explicit. Helpful as it might have been to make sense of the new evolutionary thinking and moral and spiritual aspirations in society, it tended to reduce religious knowledge to high cultural knowledge.

Incarnation

Evolution

Within Hegel's works, it is not entirely clear how this unfolding process takes place, since it involves both spiritual and material reality. The Idealists assumed that it was the unfolding of a spiritual reality. Others of Hegel's followers took it to be an entirely material process, and therefore thought that the notion of Spirit itself was historically contextual, and would be dissolved at the end of the process. Thus Ludwig Feuerbach (1804–72) argued that the idea of God was simply a projection of human aspirations into a hypostatized, eternal realm. This was further developed by Karl Marx (1818–83), who argued that the progress of history was strictly material and economic, and depended upon the struggle of the worker who had been alienated from matter and other humans through work. Human thought was the reflection of this economic history; ideas depended upon economic reality. The end of history would be the realization of all subjects in their work and in the unity of matter without 'false consciousness' such as found in religious ideas. Marx, however, in so far as he did see a movement towards a goal as inherent in this process, never did eliminate all spiritual ideas, since purposive behaviour is mental. Like many critics of religion in general and Christianity in particular during the nineteenth century, Marx's vision linked religion's hope for human transcendence with scientific knowledge and progress; Marx fully believed that his approach was purely scientific and empirical. In this way, he shared a strong commitment to scientific objectivity with his predecessors and most other nineteenth-century philosophers. Despite their wide differences, virtually all were committed to foundationalism, and a belief that philosophy was to follow a scientific method, or to justify it. Both critics and defenders tended to treat Christianity, since it involved ideas such as 'God', 'the soul', and final purposes as largely a metaphysical system that stood or fell on its philosophical underpinnings, even when they were mining its moral content which had its sources in something other than pure philosophy.

Critics of Christianity

There were, however, two major exceptions in the nineteenth century to these trends, namely Sören Kierkegaard (1813–55) and Friedrich Nietzsche (1844–1900). Both are often taken to be irrationalists. However, both, for very different reasons, thought that the philosophy of their age in seeking rational objectivity had ignored a crucial inner dimension of the human person. Kierkegaard did not think that one could ever simply think oneself into Christianity or be Christian by virtue of where one stood historically in the unfolding of the Absolute; faith took a certain, self-involving passionate 'leap of faith' which alone could bridge the gap between objective truth and the personal self-involving and self-transforming commitment that Christianity required. Nietzsche, no friend of Christianity, argued that his age had destroyed the individual and his relation to the nature from which he had sprung. Ethics, exemplified by Platonism and by Christianity, were simply the power of the mob that enforced its will on strong, original individuals. Both Kierkegaard and Nietzsche were forerunners of existentialist philosophy in the twentieth century, which put the individual's choice for or against life ahead of any general conceptual reflection.

The twentieth century

The modern quest for certainty through a universal rational method and based upon unassailable foundations can be described as a search for an ideal language which would refer to the real world without the ambiguities of natural language. The twentieth century is the century in which philosophy turns to the examination of language.

The high-water mark of the quest for a language that would be a perfect 'mirror of nature' came in logical positivism. Philosophy, for logical positivism, was not a quest for wisdom or even knowledge. Knowledge of the world, as Hume had dictated, comes only from empirical facts such as science provides. But since this knowledge is in propositions, philosophy is needed to give propositions a logical form. Ideally, this form is strictly logical and universal, like mathematics, neither adding nor subtracting content; it is a perfectly reflecting mirror of formal representation. Real knowledge is based on empirical observation that is transmitted into language in such a way that the transmission takes place by a series of logical equivalences. For example, 'atoms' are not seen, but talk about them is meaningful because they are the result of a purely logical translation of what is discerned in experiments. Here is the point of the 'verification principle', central to logical positivism, which holds that all meaningful statements are logical constructions from sense data. This principle was initially devastating for religious language, since it appeared that religious propositions such as 'God exists' or 'God is love' are not rooted in any verifiable fact about the world, or are compatible with contradictory ones. Religious language and ethical or metaphysical propositions were deemed meaningless.

Positivism, however, fell once it was realized that the verification principle itself was neither a construction from sense data nor a matter of analytical logical form. This had implications for philosophical reflection in general, since it indicates that there is no universal language which refers unambiguously to reality. The very dream of foundationalism is an impossible one.

One of the chief critics of positivism was Ludwig Wittgenstein (1889–1951), who in his early work was thought to have given the 'logical form of the world'. Wittgenstein, however, later argued that even if one could give such a form, one would still have to know how to apply it, which would require a set of prior rules. And even if one could give these rules, one would still have to have rules for the rules *ad infinitum*. Thus the sense of any language was in its use, including all its wide cultural context. So, far from seeking a universal language, Wittgenstein argued that 'All propositions of our colloquial language are logically fully in order, *just as they are*.' Natural language does not distort the world; it is precisely what we know about the world. The implication for religious language is that it does make sense, and does not need outside justification. To understand it, one needs to see how it is used, and should not lay a preconceived conceptual grid over it borrowed from elsewhere, such as science. This limits certain kinds of philosophical reflection on religion, and even suggests that earlier philosophical attempts to marry philosophy and religion may have mistaken religious language for something it is not. Properly, philosophy should seek to understand how religious language is used within its own life world. This has given rise to more sympathetic, contextual approaches to Christian claims, although some Christian philosophers have continued to seek a more objective basis for its claims than they think Wittgenstein allows.

Language

Similar attempts to free language from the dream of modern philosophy are also seen in the German philosopher Martin Heidegger (1889–1976) and his descendants. In his early *Being and Time* Heidegger first attempted an analysis of phenomena to show how they disclosed Being itself. Yet shortly afterwards he began to question the enterprise as 'too metaphysical', arguing that ultimate reality, Being, cannot be frozen into words and concepts. Only Being itself can disclose Being. Any attempt to say what Being is misfires since it hypostasizes it in particular beings. Heidegger's search to undo the metaphysical impulse to reify the disclosures of language has been followed by numerous continental philosophers who have been both positive and negative in their relation to Christianity, philosophers who have largely gone under the title of 'postmodernism'. In his later years, Heidegger also began to emphasize language in his philosophy. He called language 'the house of Being'. Because of this emphasis on language as it is used and transmitted, Heidegger has been an important source for hermeneutics, the study of interpretation, as has been Wittgenstein, since once the dream of an ideal language was dismissed, interpretation has come to the fore in philosophy.

Since about the 1970s, the term 'postmodernism' has been coined to describe certain recent trends in philosophy. The term is fluid, largely denoting the turn away from many of the assumptions of modern philosophy that came into prominence with Descartes and the philosophers of the Enlightenment. It has been largely used as an attempt to shake off many of the assumptions of modernism; as 'post'-modern, however, it does not claim to have settled on any new philosophical paradigm.

Among English-speaking philosophers, philosophy can be described as postmodern in so far as it is post-foundationalist and has taken a 'linguistic turn'. Much of the modern project since Descartes was an attempt to discover certain foundations on which to build the philosophical edifice. Originally, these were certain 'clear and distinct ideas'; from these, metaphysical ideas and systems could be built. After Hume, they were assumed to be empirical evidence, and there was a distrust of metaphysical systems, since, as Hume and Kant showed, metaphysical ideas went beyond what could be supported by that evidence. However, since much of the important work in twentieth-century philosophy came to conclude that even empirical data, including sense data, are never pure, but always mixed with cultural and social ideas, and especially are shaped by the languages in which they are used, this led to a bent in English-speaking philosophy towards analysing language. Wittgenstein was crucial in effecting this turn. So, too, was the English philosopher J. L. Austin (1911–60). This sort of post-foundationalism has had particular influence in the philosophy of science. It has also caused certain philosophers, such as the American philosopher Richard Rorty (1931–), to put much emphasis on the linguistic nature of reality, and to treat philosophy not only as chiefly analytical, but also as hermeneutical. Philosophy is not meant to build, but to interpret. With respect to the question of truth in philosophy, since there are no unassailable foundations, work such as Rorty's has drawn much from the American tradition of pragmatism, especially from John Dewey and William James, seeking truth in use and outcome.

Postmodern theology

There are certain broad similarities between the Anglo-American tradition and the European continental tradition in so far as both are post-foundationalist and both have been particularly interested in language. With some exceptions, though, continental practice has emphasized the hermeneutical nature of philosophy more than English-speaking philosophy. Postmodern continental philosophy, which chiefly derives from Heidegger and Nietzsche, has also been somewhat more self-consciously radical. It is frequently marked by its interest in deconstruction, i.e. in the attempt not simply to analyse but to unmask the social construction of reality. Two French philosophers, Jacques Derrida (1930–2004) and Michel Foucault (1926–84), are example of this approach. For Derrida, philosophy since Parmenides and Plato has been 'logocentric', i.e. centred on the use of language and logic to build coherent and smooth systems that demand unity, totality and sameness. The problem Derrida has claimed to recognize is that this is a 'tyranny of the logos', as it suppresses anything that does not fit within the dominant linguistic system. The hallmark of Derrida's thought has therefore been a concern with difference and heterogeneity. Seeking to reveal these in his work, he has argued that commonly accepted understanding is in fact largely a misunderstanding that excludes them. Foucault, on the other hand, argues that all intellectual systems ultimately have their roots in social power. For him, too, the task of philosophy is also deconstruction, in so far as it seeks to trace through the 'genealogy' of an idea (a method borrowed from Nietzsche) the structures of power which it really embodies and which gave rise to it. Like Derrida, this is meant to be in service of liberating the oppressed and excluded.

God
Miracles
Prophecy

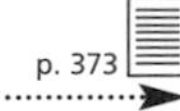

p. 373

Continental postmodern philosophy has not had much influence on professional philosophers in English-speaking countries, who, though sharing some broad continents with the European continent, largely eschew the term postmodern for themselves. However, continental philosophy has had significant positive and negative influence in theology and religious studies. Negatively, some postmodern thinkers, following Heidegger in seeking to unmask the reification of Being, i.e. the treating of Being as an object, have assumed that Christianity is another misguided attempt at metaphysics. A more radical strain, which has argued that culturally potent language is a construct of ruling power, has also sought to criticize Christianity on these grounds. Positively, however, some religious philosophers have seen in this 'postmodern' unmasking an opportunity to purify Christian thought just as Dionysius' negative theology did in an earlier time, and many thinkers have concentrated on the importance of Christian mystical thinking, since it is not open to the criticism of being centred on words.

ERIC O. SPRINGSTED

Diogenes Allen, *Philosophy for Understanding Theology*, Atlanta, GA: John Knox Press and London: SCM Press 1985; Diogenes Allen and Eric O. Springsted, *Primary Readings. Philosophy for Understanding Theology*, Louisville, KY: Westminster John Knox Press 1992; Louis Dupré, *Passage to Modernity*, New Haven: Yale University Press 1993; G. R. Evans, *Philosophy and Theology in the Middle Ages*, London: Routledge 1993; Eric O. Springsted, *The Act of Faith*, Grand Rapids, MI: Eerdmans 2002; Christopher Stead, *Philosophy in Christian Antiquity*, Cambridge: CUP 1994

Philosophy of religion

There are many religious questions that have been of interest to philosophy. From Plato on, philosophers have discussed the nature of God and of the soul, the possibility of miracles, the relationship between faith and reason, the meaning of prophecy. These questions, which are essentially about the meaning of religious terms, are an important part of the study of religion, but there is another area of even greater importance: the question of the truth of religious beliefs. This is the concern of 'philosophy of religion', a term first used by the Cambridge Platonist Ralph Cudworth in 1678. It has in the past been argued that 'philosophy of religion' should be used only to refer to the study of the logic of religious language, with the term 'philosophical theology' being used to describe attempts to apply rationality to the articles of Christian belief, and 'natural theology' to describe discussion of knowledge of the nature of God that is not dependent on specific religious beliefs or divine revelation. However, much recent philosophy of religion has been concerned with ideas and concepts internal to specifically Christian doctrines and concerns.

There is no consensus as to how the Christian faith and philosophy relate. And indeed Western philosophy has been deeply shaped by concerns and concepts found in Christianity. The ways in which personal identity has been understood have been influenced by differing understandings of the idea of an afterlife, and debates about freedom and determinism have been affected by the idea of predestination or divine fore-knowledge. William James has a useful distinction between what he calls 'tough-minded' and 'tender-minded' philosophers. The tough-minded who espouse a rigorous scientifically orientated reductionism have little sympathy for religious concerns. For those at the extreme end of the scientistic spectrum, 'philosophy of religion' is a fruitless exercise: the scientist Ernest Rutherford famously thought that 'there is physics and stamp collecting'. But when the more tender-minded philosophers try to give a more comprehensive and nuanced account of the relation between the mind and the world they find it as hard to exclude religion as it is to exclude ethics and aesthetics. Moreover, if theology wishes to distinguish itself from theosophy, superstition or consoling fantasy, it needs continually to face and consider the philosophical challenges that any living faith must answer.

God, the soul and salvation

The philosophical approach to religion is closely linked to monotheism, belief in one God. There are various different models of God. The theistic model envisages God as the transcendent source of all reality potential and actual, the agent of providence and judgement. Pantheism envisages God as the immanent principle of the world but denies that God is a transcendent cause. For the pantheist, God without the world is unintelligible and the pantheist denies the personal character of the deity (examples of this approach would include the Stoics or Benedict de Spinoza). Deism sees God as a transcendent principle but as essentially unrelated to the world and morally unconcerned with human action (this is the view, for example, of Aristotle). All of these models of God have their own specific strengths and weaknesses. Abrahamic theism, that is the understanding of God traditionally identified with Jewish, Christian and Islamic thought, in particular is much dependent on (Neo)-Platonic metaphysics. As a result, there are real problems in understanding how the austerely intellectual and absolutely perfect God, which patristic and medieval Christian theologians derived to some degree from ideas in the Platonism and Stoicism of late antiquity, can act in the world or even be aware of any imperfections in the world. Panentheism attempts to overcome this difficulty by envisaging the world as a part of the process of divine self-realization (the approach taken most significantly by G. W. F. Hegel).

Revelation

One of the most persistent and intractable questions in the philosophy of religion is how we can say anything about the supreme transcendent being. There is an ancient tradition of negation of predicates, or the *via negativa*. We cannot say what God is, but we can say what God is not. Closely linked to this is the idea that God-talk is metaphorical rather than literal. This is a huge and complex area. Much philosophical discussion is indeed metaphorical: the interesting question is the degree and/or philosophical validity of a given metaphor. To talk about the 'foundations' of knowledge is to use a metaphor, but anti-foundationalists have not won their case by pointing this out. Nor can a behaviourist win an easy victory by remarking that 'thoughts in one's head' is a metaphor. There is a long tradition of thinking of God-talk as neither literal nor metaphorical but 'analogical'. This is to claim that certain symbols express a higher reality in a lower form, but that there is some continuity between the language and the thing it refers to.

Life after death
Freedom
Predestination

If we accept the consistency and intelligibility of the theistic concept of God, we have to consider the likelihood of divine existence. There is a long tradition of proofs for the existence of God, which stretches back to Plato and up to the present day. At the same time, the existence of evil in a world may be thought to disprove the idea of a good and omnipotent creator. The apostle Paul seems to appeal to some version of the teleological argument, the argument from purpose, in Romans 1.20, and there is much cosmological speculation in the wisdom literature and the Psalms. The book of Job, the prophets and many passages throughout the New Testament show that the problem of evil is a common thread in biblical thought.

Evil
Paul

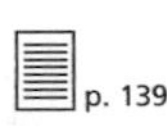

p. 139
Psalms
Bible

Until the renewal of interest in metaphysics within analytic philosophy, it was often thought that religious experience was a much more profitable direction in which to take the philosophical study of religion: empirically-minded philosophers in particular have been interested in the possibility of encounters with deity. This interest is linked to questions about revelation. Moses at Sinai or Paul on the road to Damascus claimed a vision or experience of God, and this was part of their purported revelation. Clearly, the idea of experience of God raises considerable problems concerning assessment of evidence.

Much traditional philosophy of religion was concerned with the soul's longing and experience of God. However, recent philosophy of mind seems determined to attack the idea of a soul – particularly in the guise of an immaterial 'I' as the agent of conscious experience. Sometimes

Philosophy

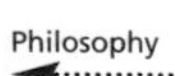

Christian theologians rejoice triumphantly in dissociating Christianity from 'dualistic' concepts that make a clear distinction between body and soul – concepts mainly derived from Plato – pointing instead to the biblical notion of the resurrection of the body. Such theologians, however, tend to be less lucid when explaining what the resurrection of the body is. Clearly, the coherence of the concept of the soul is of great importance for the philosophy of religion. If the idea of the soul is incoherent, it is not clear that appeals to the resurrection of the body for a communion with the purely immaterial God represent more than a rhetorical victory: the idea of salvation requires a soul to be saved. Moreover, Western, Latin Christianity has tended to employ legal models to describe the nature of salvation, such as the doctrine of substitutionary atonement, whereby Christ vicariously suffers for the sins of humanity. Such a model raises ethical questions that philosophers of religion have explored with particular urgency since the Enlightenment.

Thomism
Resurrection
p. 507
Salvation
Atonement
Enlightenment

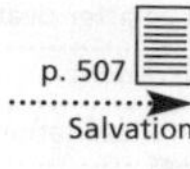

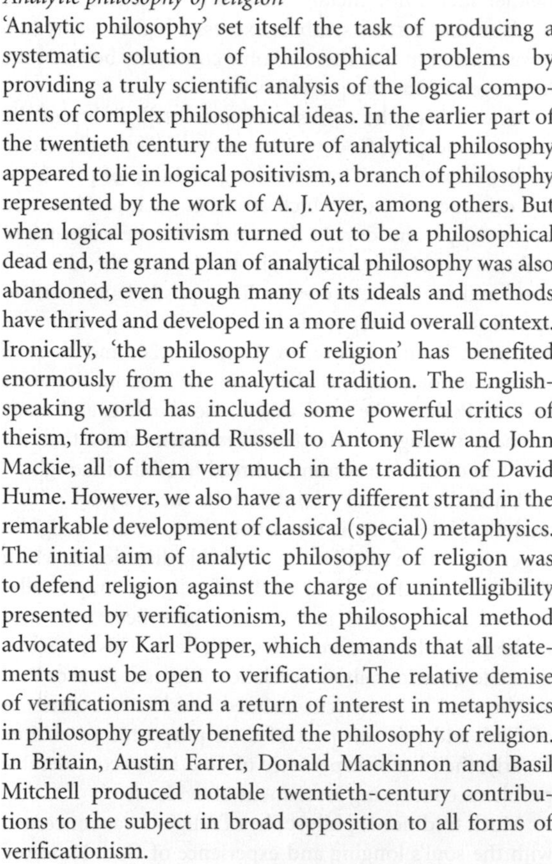

Analytic philosophy of religion

'Analytic philosophy' set itself the task of producing a systematic solution of philosophical problems by providing a truly scientific analysis of the logical components of complex philosophical ideas. In the earlier part of the twentieth century the future of analytical philosophy appeared to lie in logical positivism, a branch of philosophy represented by the work of A. J. Ayer, among others. But when logical positivism turned out to be a philosophical dead end, the grand plan of analytical philosophy was also abandoned, even though many of its ideals and methods have thrived and developed in a more fluid overall context. Ironically, 'the philosophy of religion' has benefited enormously from the analytical tradition. The English-speaking world has included some powerful critics of theism, from Bertrand Russell to Antony Flew and John Mackie, all of them very much in the tradition of David Hume. However, we also have a very different strand in the remarkable development of classical (special) metaphysics. The initial aim of analytic philosophy of religion was to defend religion against the charge of unintelligibility presented by verificationism, the philosophical method advocated by Karl Popper, which demands that all statements must be open to verification. The relative demise of verificationism and a return of interest in metaphysics in philosophy greatly benefited the philosophy of religion. In Britain, Austin Farrer, Donald Mackinnon and Basil Mitchell produced notable twentieth-century contributions to the subject in broad opposition to all forms of verificationism.

The work of Richard Swinburne and Alvin Plantinga deserves particular mention as developing specific metaphysical philosophies of religion. Swinburne's initial work was in the philosophy of science, and he has gone on to develop a sophisticated inductive proof for God's existence. He has mounted a highly ambitious project in natural theology, conceived of along broadly Thomistic lines, in order to prove the existence of God inductively; and has also produced a reasoned defence of the classic Christian doctrines. Plantinga, while averse to natural theology in the Thomistic sense, has also produced much highly sophisticated special philosophical theology: he has revived a version of the ontological argument (God is that than which nothing greater can be conceived) and an incompatibilist theory of divine and human freedom. Together with other colleagues at Calvin College, Plantinga propounded a version of epistemology known as reformed epistemology, the theory that theistic belief in the classical sense is 'properly basic', that is to say it does not require any inference from more basic beliefs, and that belief in God is not itself a form of explanation of other facts.

Reformed epistemology has something in common with a strand of philosophy of religion that has developed the ideas of Ludwig Wittgenstein, a strand of which the most distinguished and prolific representative is D. Z. Phillips. Wittgenstein did not write much on the topic of religion *per se*, but his followers have developed a distinctive position in insisting that religious propositions cannot be properly analysed independently of the forms of life of specific linguistic communities. While Phillips, in criticizing traditional interpretations of religious language as question-begging and naïve, appears to interpret Wittgenstein in a frankly non-realistic manner, William Alston interprets Wittgenstein in a distinctly and robustly realistic manner. Mention should also be made of such close associates of Wittgenstein as Elizabeth Anscombe, who have made significant contributions in the philosophy of religion. Peter Geach and Elizabeth Anscombe exemplify the force of a distinctly Roman Catholic contribution to the subject.

Contemporary philosophy of religion, through the innovating work of figures such as John Hick and Ninian Smart, has also moved into the sphere of comparative religion. Smart (1927–2001) in such works as *Reasons and Faiths* (1958) and *Doctrine and Argument in Indian Philosophy* (1964) was a pioneer of philosophy of religions, and he was responsible for the establishment of a Religious Studies Department at Lancaster University. John Hick's work in the multicultural and multifaith context of Birmingham led him to propose a 'Copernican revolution' in the philosophy of religion, whereby all the world religions are seen as different but complementary human responses to the one ultimate transcendent. Hick takes a 'Kantian' view of the religions. Though he retains a view of God as a real object, he sees the responses of living religions to God as necessarily determined by the cognitive frameworks of their interpretation of divine reality. Contemporary philosopher theologians of a cautious liberal stamp such as Keith Ward and Brian Hebblethwaite have done much to pursue philosophical dialogue between different religious traditions.

Continental philosophy of religion

The continental tradition has had the opposite effect. Initially it seemed much more hospitable to theology, but this is ultimately only in the sense in which the undertaker is an accommodating host. The effect of Nietzsche is so powerful upon the French avant-garde that there is little room for genuinely creative work in the philosophy of religion. The very term sounds strange in a tradition so accustomed to the 'death of God'. Yet whether 'cultural theory' or 'deconstruction' has much to offer in more theologically fertile terrain remains to be seen.

One might say that Friedrich Nietzsche (1844–1900) did not lack genuine insight when he diagnosed the general trend of Western thought from Plato to Hegel as being often closely linked to a basically theological perspective. This became the basis for Martin Heidegger's (1889–1976) critique of Western philosophy as locked into 'onto-theology', a theology of being. Continental philosophy of religion has been deeply influenced by Nietzsche and the later Heidegger's historiography and the attempt to talk about God without falling into the trap of 'onto-theology'. Here the move is either to employ some form of religious projectionism to redescribe Christianity in terms of purely human values (the approach of Don Cupitt), or to criticize inherited concepts of God as 'idolatrous' and to employ Nietzsche and Heidegger to cleanse the temple, as it were, before the epiphany of the true God (as Emanuel Levinas and Jean-Luc Marion have attempted to do). The influence of Levinas has been pervasive in the French theological tradition, and Jacques Derrida has exerted a pervasive influence upon those who wish to revive some form of apophatic, i.e. negative theology.

The influence of Heidegger on continental 'philosophy of religion' is not surprising because his early work was deeply indebted to 'religious' thinkers such as Augustine, Friedrich Schleiermacher and Søren Kierkegaard. Further, Jean-Paul Sartre's explicit identification of existentialism as the genuine atheistic humanism in opposition to Marxism in his *L'existentialisme est un humanisme* (Existentialism is a Humanism, 1946) was rejected by Heidegger in his *Brief über den Humanismus* (Letter on Humanism, 1946) in which he emphasizes that the object of philosophy is Being (*Sein*). However hard Heidegger attempted to distance his thought about being from theology, this period of his thought was interpreted by theologians as at least conducive to theological concerns, if not a form of crypto-theology. Hence in the figure of Heidegger the continental tradition has a most ambivalent reference point: is he a savage critic of inherited metaphysical theology, or a closet practitioner of the same? Or both? This to some extent explains the paradox that much 'continental' or 'phenomenological' philosophy of religion appears both hostile to philosophical theology and yet to be continually returning to the field. The work of John Macquarrie is an instance of a trained philosopher and expert Germanist using Heidegger to develop an 'existential ontological theism'. Whether such a synthesis can be sustained is debatable, but it is clear that Heidegger is open to such construals.

Paul Ricoeur identifies 'the masters of suspicion', Nietzsche, Marx and Freud, as employing a reductive hermeneutic. That is to say that all three can be interpreted as having elaborated unconscious motivations for the development of religion: the revenge of 'priestcraft' (Nietzsche), economic domination (Marx) or wish-fulfilment (Freud). Thus religious belief is unmasked as self-deception and self-interest. These 'masters of suspicion' remain a very powerful part of French philosophical thought about religion. And Michel Foucault (1926–84) has influenced much contemporary philosophy of religion: in particular he has had a deep influence on feminist theology, when he claims that the idea of a universal rational subject, as it is used by modernist thinkers, masks a focus on the privileged power-wielding male.

Critics of Christianity

Feminist theology

'Philosophy of religion' is a recent coinage, but the subject matter is as ancient as philosophy itself. The complexity of the relationship between Christianity and philosophy of religion is daunting. Few possess the verve and brio of Adolf von Harnack's attempt to define the *Essence of Christianity*, the title of a famous book written at the very beginning of the twentieth century; however, the significance of 'philosophy of religion' for Christianity depends greatly upon one's vision of the Christian religion. But Christianity cannot avoid questions of a philosophical nature. This is not to dwell excessively upon the more abstruse medieval metaphysical researches into dimensions of angels or the substance of the eucharistic host. One of the distinguishing marks of the Johannine and Pauline writings is a level of philosophical reflection that distinguishes them from the rest of the New Testament. This point becomes much more significant in the light of the explicit formulation of the Christian doctrines in the patristic period with philosophical concepts such as 'unity', 'person', 'trinity', 'consubstantial', etc. Hence any Christian reflection upon scripture or the doctrinal formulations of the Christian faith invites philosophical reflection. Christian theology has a long history of debate about the value or danger of pagan or secular philosophy. The rise of modern science and the increased awareness of the claims of other religions means that attacks on

Trinity

Christology

Science

Other faiths

the philosophical approach to Christianity as 'idolatrous' seem quite simply quixotic.

DOUGLAS HEDLEY

Brian Davies, *Philosophy of Religion. A Guide to the Subject*, New York: OUP 1993 and London: Cassell 1998; George Pattison, *A Short Course in the Philosophy of Religion*, London: SCM Press 2001; Charles Taliaferro, *Contemporary Philosophy of Religion*, Oxford: Blackwell 1998

Pietism

Quakers
Methodism
Historiography
Salvation
Conversion
Apocalyptic
Enlightenment
Humanism
Religious orders
Protestantism
Anabaptists
Reformation

Like seventeenth-century 'Quakerism' and eighteenth-century 'Methodism', Pietism (German *Pietismus*) originally was a nickname, derived from the Latin word *pietas* (English 'piety') and describing a person whose quest for a devout life was exaggerated and therefore a special trait. In general, Pietism stands for a Christian conviction that views Christianity as an individual way to salvation through personally experienced conversion and a moral seriousness, willing to forsake cultural and aesthetic values which society as a whole takes for granted. Broadly speaking, Pietism along with Enlightenment rationalism and humanism have been seen as the two basic modern interpretations of Christianity: both movements have in common a critical attitude to older Protestant orthodoxy; both state positively the rights of individuals as fundamental to religion; and both are more concerned about practice than theory in religious matters.

Lutheranism
Reformation
Justification
Holy Spirit

In a more narrow, historical sense Pietism is used to denote a multi-faceted religious movement of the seventeenth and eighteenth centuries within the Lutheran churches of Germany, whose common concern was to implement the ideas of Martin Luther and the Reformation of the sixteenth century. The beginning of the movement has been seen as the publication in 1675 of a religious tract or manifesto called 'Pious Wishes' (*Pia desideria*), written by Philipp Jakob Spener (1635–1705), then a senior minister in Frankfurt am Main, later in Dresden and Berlin. The manifesto was printed as a preface to an edition of 'True Christianity', an early seventeenth-century devotional manual by a Lutheran minister, Johann Arndt (1555–1621). Strongly inspired by pre-Reformation, Catholic traditions of devotion, Arndt had described an evangelical mysticism of the heart in contrast to the prevalent view on justification among his contemporaries, but without questioning the Lutheran doctrine or the frames of official church life. A strong admirer of Arndt, Spener, however, viewed established church forms and practices as cold and sterile, deeply in need of supplementing if the church was not to prove an obstacle to the pursuit of true spirituality, and become powerless to engage the larger groups of the population. In Spener's view the evangelical church that was a product of the sixteenth-century Reformation was marked by deep decay, conditioned by the fact that the evangelical faith of the Reformers had developed into religious formalism and their discovery of the gospel had turned into abstract doctrine.

In pietistic thinking this bleak view of the present state of Christianity was balanced by a view of the future course of history that allowed for the flourishing of Christianity geographically and numerically, with great spiritual depth and sincerity. This view of the historical potential for development and progress marked a decisive step towards modernity and stood in opposition to the mainstream Western Christian thinking about history, which went back to Augustine in the fifth century and had been adopted by the sixteenth-century Reformers. However, the view of history in Pietism was related to an older millenarian tradition, the most famous spokesman for which had been Joachim of Fiore, a twelfth-century abbot from southern Italy. Based on a detailed exegesis of biblical apocalyptic literature, Joachim taught that the church of the future would undergo profound changes, a message which became revolutionary during the latter half of the thirteenth century, when groups within the Franciscan order claimed that this era of a spiritual church had been inaugurated through the coming of Francis of Assisi. The ideas of Joachim even had their followers among the radical wing of the sixteenth-century Reformation.

In their views on specific doctrinal questions such as justification and sanctification, Spener and his followers reflected the innate complexity and discord of post-Reformation Lutheranism that had come to the surface during the debates over Arndt's books. This complexity was to a large part due to a tension between the theological terminology of the first Reformers (especially Martin Luther, whose authority remained unquestioned) and the development after the death of the first-generation Reformers of a more precise theological methodology and an academic theology among Lutherans. The main objective of this was to defend Lutheranism against both Roman Catholicism and other Protestant traditions (notably Calvinism). Caught between this confessional crossfire were theologians whose main interest was in pastoral matters, such as personal renewal, individual growth in holiness and religious experience. In doctrine, their main interest was to establish a terminology which could describe the subjective appropriation of redemption. Academic theology had worked out this topic in the terms of a pattern called the 'order of salvation' (*ordo salutis*), describing how the Holy Spirit worked in the individual believer. Spener and the Pietists put great emphasis on this doctrinal topic and developed it further towards a psychology of faith as experience that tended to blend the movements of the divine Spirit and of the human soul.

Besides this legacy of early seventeenth-century developmental traits within Lutheranism, what was new and special to the Pietist movement was the way in which a more positive view of the future of the church became a strong motivation towards church reforms, and human agendas based on principles drawn from the Bible were believed to make a difference as to how the Christian church actually would succeed. To achieve their goals, the spokesmen of German Pietism developed agendas for renewal and reform centred on new ideals of how the clergy should fulfil their ministry. Another central issue for the pietistic movement was to stimulate the practice of the so-called 'priesthood of all believers' through responsible lay participation in the mission of the church.

Spener's six proposals for reform in *Pia Desideria* may serve as a short summary of the mainstream Pietism of the seventeenth and eighteenth century. 1. The Word of God should be used more extensively among Christians, an agenda which was to stimulate publishing activities among the Pietists. 2. The 'priesthood of all believers' should be renewed in the sense that all Christians should take an active part in the work of the Christian ministry; this called for novel forms of religious societies, in Spener's case the organizing of so-called 'assemblies of piety' (*collegiae pietatis*). 3. 'The people must have impressed upon them ... that it is by no means enough to have knowledge of the Christian faith, for Christianity consists rather of practice.' 4. Restraint and charity should be shown in religious controversy; this had been emphasized in Arndt's writings. 5. A thorough reform of the study of theology and preparation for the ministry was needed, according to the principle that theology was a practical discipline, first and foremost introducing the students into the experience of faith. 6. The key to a new kind of ministry first and foremost meant a new kind of sermon which the people could understand, and which had an edifying purpose.

The main task of a true evangelical minister was to bring his congregation to a personal experience of salvation. Characteristically, Pietism thought it impossible to achieve this goal unless the inherited forms of religious life were at least supplemented by new forms of social interaction more capable of bringing the religious individual into focus. The insight that the basic forms of religious interaction expressed through the liturgy (the forms of which the Lutheran Reformers had kept intact, despite some alterations) stood in opposition to true religion was epoch-making and separated the pietistic movement from earlier forms of a theology of the heart, such as that upheld by Arndt and even that found among early seventeenth-century English divines and poets such as George Herbert.

Two key people carried the ideas of Spener further. Spener's close companion August Hermann Francke (1663–1727) turned the University of Halle (in Berlin) into a showcase for Pietism, with both a renewal of education for ministers and initiatives to help the poor, especially orphans. Count Nicholas von Zinzendorf (1700–60), who was the godson of Spener and a pupil of Francke, organized refugees from Moravia into kinds of *collegia pietatis*. This group was eager for missionary enterprises and brought pietistic ideas and ideals to several parts of the world, especially their concern for a personal spirituality based on the individual experience of Christ as saviour. These Moravian Pietists made a crucial impact on John Wesley, leading to his evangelical awakening. Moravian Church

Through considerable literary activity which produced prayer books, collections of sermons, devotional tracts and hymns, Pietism became influential beyond this period, especially in the Scandinavian Lutheran state churches. Here 'Pietism' in a broader sense has been used up to the twentieth century as a religious label for a specific kind of adherence to Protestant Christianity of the Lutheran Confession, which in an Anglo-American context would be called evangelical. The works of the German theologian Paul Gerhardt (died 1676), whose hymns permeate the passions, oratorios and cantatas of Johann Sebastian Bach, are outstanding examples of classic pietistic spirituality. The pre-Reformation inheritance in Gerhardt is most notable in what is perhaps his most famous hymn, 'O sacred head, sore wounded', which is based on the medieval poem *Salve caput cruentatum*, attributed to Bernard of Clairvaux, while Gerhardt's original hymn text, *Ich steh' an deiner Krippe hier* ('I stand here beside thy manger'), the first stanza of which is part of Bach's *Christmas Oratorio*, imparts perhaps better than anything else the spirit of Pietism.

JAN SCHUMACHER

P. Erb (ed), *Johann Arndt: True Christianity*, Classics of Western Spirituality, Mahwah, NJ: Paulist Press 1979 and *Pietists: Selected Writings*, Classics of Western Spirituality, Mahwah, NJ: Paulist Press 1983; J. Pelikan, *Christian Doctrine and Modern Culture (since 1700)*, Vol. 5, Chicago: University of Chicago Press 1989

Pilgrimage

Pilgrimage has been a universal feature of the religions of the world. The impulse to identify particular places as holy and to believe that a journey to such places brings with it a reward, whether this be physical healing or some Holy Journey

kind of spiritual benefit, has certainly not been confined to Christianity. Pilgrimages for healing and other purposes were familiar to the Egyptians, Greeks, Romans and the other peoples of pre-Christian Europe. The apparent
Constantine's 'conversion'
similarity between some aspects of the behaviour of pilgrims and of the modern tourist (including the appetite for souvenirs) has inevitably caused speculation about the underlying causes and motives of both phenomena. Like the pilgrim, the tourist hunts out places and objects associated with Shakespeare, George Washington, Elvis Presley or Princess Diana, and feels an indefinable
Buildings
Martyr

gratification at somehow being in their presence. That there is some common factor at work here which is deeply rooted in human psychology need not be denied, but it is doubtful whether modern tourists expect to derive all the benefits from their journeys that pilgrims, past and present, have expected to derive from theirs.

The adherents of the scriptural religions, Judaism, Christianity and Islam, have tended to sanctify places
Saint

with particular historical associations which God has proclaimed holy or where God is believed to have intervened in the lives of his people. In Christianity a special importance has always attached to the burial places of the heroes (and heroines) of the faith, foremost among
Jesus
Mary
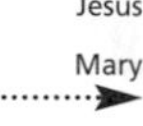
them the sepulchre of Jesus himself. There is some debate, however, about when (and indeed why) Christian pilgrimage can be said to have begun. Pilgrimage may have
Devotion

become a popular expression of Christian devotion, but it has never been obligatory for the Christian in the sense that the *hajj*, the pilgrimage to Mecca, is obligatory for the Muslim. There has in fact always been a powerful undercurrent of Christian criticism of pilgrimage. The belief that Christianity was quintessentially a spiritual religion, independent of physical location, proved enduring, drawing authority from texts such as Jesus' dialogue with the woman of Samaria as reported in the Gospel of John (chapter 4, especially verses 19–24). She thinks that Jesus has suggested that people must worship, not as her forefathers had done, 'on this mountain', but in Jerusalem.
Christendom
p. 1075

Jesus replies: '... the hour is coming when you will worship the Father neither on this mountain nor in Jerusalem ... God is spirit and those who worship him must worship in spirit and truth.'

It has also been suggested that in the early Christian period the belief that there was no specially favoured
p. 580

place for Christian worship drew strength from the desire to differentiate the new faith from its Jewish parent: holy land and holy city seemed essentially Jewish concepts. Only when Christianity was publicly triumphant could they be appropriated. In any case, it would presumably have been difficult for large numbers of Christians to
Persecution
make long journeys to holy places while persecution was still a threat. However, there is some evidence that already before the fourth century a few devout persons were making their way to Palestine in order to see the biblical sites, especially those associated with the life and death of Jesus.

With the conversion of Constantine the way was open for the transformation of the holy places of Palestine, Rome and elsewhere into shrines that could be openly frequented by Christian devotees. The emperor and his mother Helena led the way in their expenditure on buildings which provided models for subsequent imitation, among them the church of the Holy Sepulchre in Jerusalem and the basilica of St Peter at Rome. The latter was the most illustrious example of the martyrs' graves, which were now transformed by complexes of buildings that might include accommodation for pilgrims. Early Christian communities had more discreetly commemorated the martyrs in gatherings at their tombs, which, thanks to the standard Roman practice of burying the dead outside the settled area, might involve them in a short journey, miniature proto-pilgrimages. Those who later came to be regarded as saints were similarly commemorated and their tombs became, at least potentially, objects of pilgrimage. Birthplaces and places of residence have been less commonly sanctified, but the associations of Bethlehem, Nazareth and other places in Palestine with the earthly life of Jesus and indeed with other personages such as Mary, John the Baptist or the Old Testament patriarchs, were remembered (and even sometimes invented) for the benefit of pilgrims. Much later, the birthplaces of saints sometimes became shrines, those of Thomas Becket in London and Catherine in Siena among them.

With the dissemination of Christianity beyond the Mediterranean region and the appearance of local saints who were commemorated as the martyrs had been, potential pilgrimage sites multiplied. The ex-Roman soldier, monk, bishop and missionary Martin, who died in 397, rapidly became an attraction not only to the great church which was built at Tours over his remains but to many of the numerous churches which were dedicated in his name all over Christendom.

Over a period of centuries the movement of relics from place to place facilitated the multiplication of shrines. These relics did not always consist of bodily remains, although that came increasingly to be the case as early reservations about disturbing burial places broke down. There were of course no bodily relics of Jesus or the Virgin Mary to be had (with a few bizarre exceptions such as his foreskin or the Virgin's hairs or breast milk), but garments and fragments of the true cross (discovered by the Empress Helena in Palestine in the early fourth century) came to be scattered over Christendom, and these were a useful alternative. In the later Middle Ages Aachen drew pilgrims from all over central Europe to witness regular exhibitions of the smock the Virgin had worn at the nativity, and Jesus' swaddling clothes.

Any early Christian resistance there had been to the physical localization of devotion was thus overborne in favour of what seems to be the innate human propensity to accord holiness to particular places. Although it is true that these places were sanctified by association with holy persons, which could be acquired when a relic was acquired, as Aachen acquired the holy garments just mentioned, there can be little doubt that physical features such as hilltops and springs, which had been important in pagan religion, were often adapted to Christian purposes. The archangel Michael, a popular saint in the early medieval West, was frequently associated with hilltops and pilgrimages developed to his shrines on the Gargano peninsula in Apulia and to Mont St Michel on the Norman coast, to name only the most important: in England there was St Michael's Mount in Cornwall. More recently, the Virgin Mary has been venerated at hundreds of hilltop shrines. Holy wells, too, are innumerable. They are often especially associated with the 'Celtic' lands, but they are much more widespread than that; many saints and shrines have holy wells associated with them. Even a few caves became Christian pilgrimage centres. One of the most celebrated is St Patrick's Purgatory on Lough Derg, where the pilgrim used to undergo an ordeal of sensory deprivation by being enclosed for 24 hours in the cave. The association with Patrick was entirely fictitious.

In their associations with the founder and the co-founders of the faith, Jerusalem and Rome possessed the obvious credentials for a pre-eminence among Christian pilgrimage destinations that they have never lost. In the course of the seventh century, however, the Holy Land, with the rest of the Middle East, was overwhelmed by the forces of Islam. This did not mean the end of Christian pilgrimage to Jerusalem, although it may have added to the incidental hazards that the pilgrim had to confront. There is good evidence for a growing volume of Western pilgrimage to Jerusalem in the course of the eleventh century, which undoubtedly helped to prepare the psychological ground for the extraordinary armed pilgrimage launched at the end of the century with the aim of reconquering the holy places for Christianity. We call such expeditions 'crusades', but until at least the thirteenth century contemporaries referred to them as 'pilgrimages' (*peregrinationes*) and to the participants as 'pilgrims' (*peregrini*).

Ultimately the crusades failed, but the Muslim authorities in Egypt and Palestine, themselves familiar with the concept of pilgrimage, saw little reason to discourage a profitable flow of Westerners to the holy places, and the Venetians developed an equally profitable line in what can quite reasonably be called package tours to the East. The really thoroughgoing pilgrim either began or completed his tour by crossing the desert to the supposed burial place of Catherine of Alexandria on Mount Sinai.

Rome's fortunes as a pilgrim destination were and have continued to be conditioned by its standing as the papal city. By the twelfth century it was rapidly becoming established as the governmental centre of Latin Christendom. Even when absent at Avignon in Provence for much of the fourteenth century, the popes promoted pilgrimage to Rome. A third shrine, Santiago de Compostela in Galicia in north-western Spain, which was believed to be the burial place of the apostle James the Great, began to achieve prominence around the year 1000, and the journey to Santiago came to be ranked, along with those to Rome and Jerusalem, as one of the 'major' pilgrimages. In the later Middle Ages, vows to go to any or all of these places could be revoked only with the permission of the Pope himself. In the course of the twelfth century, a period of population and economic growth, a number of notable shrines joined the ranks of those that were capable of attracting pilgrims over considerable distances, including the shrines of the Three Kings at Cologne and of the murdered archbishop Thomas Becket at Canterbury, destination of Geoffrey Chaucer's famous tale-telling pilgrims (see colour plate 12).

Celtic Christianity

It is important to remember that however impressive the numbers of pilgrims who made the 'major' pilgrimages and other long journeys to holy places, Christendom was studded with shrines, new and old, which catered only for a local or regional market. Were it possible to count medieval pilgrims, it would doubtless be found that these minor places accounted for the greater part of the total pilgrimage traffic. The fifteenth-century English enthusiast Margery Kempe, who went in her time to all the major shrines of Christendom, also records going on pilgrimage to a church of St Michael 'two mile' outside her home town, King's Lynn.

Some pilgrimages, therefore, were (and are) small-scale excursions undertaken by groups of friends and neighbours, especially on major feast-days, and many were associated with fairs and markets. Where in the Middle Ages such parties walked or rode, the typical mode of conveyance in modern times is the coach. There is little doubt that women went on pilgrimage in large numbers; there is equally no doubt that although many, like Margery Kempe, did go on the 'major' pilgrimages, they were greatly outnumbered as long-distance pilgrims by men. On the other hand, women may well have been the mainstay of thousands of local shrines, not least because many of these were curative shrines and they went to seek cures for their children and other family members.

Crusades

Even if the journey involved was not a long one, it was an integral element of pilgrimage. Not all pilgrims even had a specific geographical destination. Irish monks in the early Middle Ages embraced a concept of pilgrimage as an open-ended journey, sometimes over the open sea, in which the traveller cut himself off from social and domestic ties and cast himself on the mercy of God. Pilgrimage of this type bore a certain resemblance to exile, and pilgrimages, sometimes even perpetual pilgrimages, were imposed on sinners as penance (or punishment) for a variety of offences. Repentant heretics and persons guilty of other offences were thus punished by a number of authorities in the later medieval period. While it is safe to say that involuntary penitential pilgrims were much more numerous in the Middle Ages than now, the species is not perhaps quite extinct. One travel writer records encountering two young Belgian tearaways, accompanied by a policeman, on the road to Santiago in the 1970s. They had been offered the pilgrimage (on foot) as an alternative to a custodial sentence.

Forgiveness

Given the physical rigours of pre-modern travel, almost any journey might have a penitential element. To go to Jerusalem of one's own free will was not merely to hope to see the places of Christian origins but to offer up the sufferings, privations and dangers one was highly likely to endure on the way in expiation of one's sins. To die there, or on the way there or back, might be thought particularly meritorious. Pilgrims might voluntarily embrace conditions, such as going barefoot or in fetters, which made the journey more difficult, or these could be imposed on them by higher spiritual authority. As a physically exacting activity, pilgrimage was a form of penance appropriate to ordinary men and women who lived in the world and were not, like monks and nuns, dedicated to the pursuit of perfection within the cloister. In fact efforts indeed were made to prevent monks and especially nuns from going on pilgrimage: they had other and better routes to salvation. Ascetic practices such as lengthy prayer, vigils, extreme fasting and flagellation were not, however, readily available to the man or woman in the street.

Monasticism

Something of this sense remains alive today even in an age of rapid and comfortable transport, indeed perhaps because of it: for example, a special value attaches to making the journey to Santiago on foot. At Knock in Ireland some pilgrims ascend the rocky hillside barefoot; at St John Lateran in Rome they climb the Scala Santa on their knees. Such rituals keep alive something of the penitential element which was much more powerful and pervasive in medieval pilgrimage. Given the prevailing assumption (which is still by no means extinct) that disease and misfortune were penalties for sin, this was true even of pilgrimages undertaken in order to obtain cures. Without penitence, there could be no remedy from God.

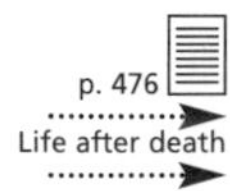

p. 476
Life after death
Sin

Have all pilgrimages, long- or short-range, been undertaken for the same reasons? In other pilgrimage cultures, for example in Hindu India, it has been observed that 'high-status' shrines are sought, often over long distances, in the hope of spiritual benefit, 'low-status' shrines probably over shorter distances and for more limited practical purposes, such as success in lawsuits or examinations. At many still-flourishing Roman Catholic shrines it is possible to inspect votive inscriptions that have been posted up by suppliants, who record their gratitude sometimes for reasons very similar to these, sometimes simply 'for benefits received'. Such benefits often include the cure of disease or injury, which many people probably think of as the chief object of pilgrimage past and present. However, pilgrimages to Jerusalem, St Peter's or Santiago have never been undertaken primarily in quest of cures. Their associations with Christ and the apostles have given them a 'high-status' character. Like their modern Hindu counterparts or like Mecca, they have been sought above all in the hope of spiritual benefit, which in Christian terms is likely to include the sense of the forgiveness of sin.

The motives of the earliest Christian pilgrims are hard to reconstruct in any detail, but they seem to have included the quest for spiritual enlightenment, a better inward understanding of the faith, rather as the modern historian may feel compelled to see at first hand the location of the historical events he or she is studying. The simple desire to behold with one's own eyes places so charged with spiritual associations has clearly remained an important part of the motivation of holy land pilgrims and indeed of pilgrims to other Christian shrines, such as those of Rome. The complex of emotions aroused by so doing is more easily experienced than analysed. The label 'devotion' is imprecise, but may conveniently serve to designate an emotional core experience from which other more specific motivations can sometimes be disengaged, among them, as already mentioned, the search for deliverance from the burden of sin.

Thanks to its association with Peter, the prince of the apostles, and his successors, Rome has historically been particularly identified as the place of forgiveness; certain penitents were specifically sent to the Pope to obtain absolution. It was in accordance with this special role that the popes made Rome the indulgence capital of Christendom. Indulgences, which awarded remission of the punishment Christians expected to undergo in purgatory, were granted to pilgrims to many shrines after 1100. In 1215 it was decreed that bishops other than the Pope could award only a maximum of 40 days' remission. In 1300, Pope Boniface VIII launched the first Jubilee or Holy Year, for the first time making a plenary indulgence available to pilgrims to Rome who fulfilled certain conditions. By the mid-fifteenth century it had been decided that a Holy Year would be held every 25 years, which is still the case. From time to time the popes used their prerogative to grant more generous indulgences, sometimes even plenary indulgences, to churches all over Christendom. As there were numerous other ways of earning indulgences, it is difficult to know whether they ever became the sole motive for undertaking long and dangerous journeys, however desirable they may have been. It seems likely that pilgrims expected them and eagerly collected them, but also continued to be moved by other considerations. Indulgences play little part in the modern pilgrimage experience.

The popular picture of pilgrimage gives a prominent place to cures. Much of our knowledge of medieval pilgrimage is derived from miracle collections, which mostly relate the relief of conditions both mental and physical. Close inspection of these stories shows that the sufferers usually did not travel all that far to reach the shrine, although they may well have come quite far enough for their discomfort. There were limits to the distance that a sick or injured person could be conveyed in pre-modern times by the available means of transport. It was, however, possible for a friend or kinsman to make a pilgrimage on behalf of a sufferer, and it seems that there was an increasing tendency in the later Middle Ages to make pilgrimages by way of thanksgiving after a cure had been received. The cure itself, that is, was earned by a vow of pilgrimage, not by the pilgrimage itself.

The advent of rail and, still more, air travel have eased these difficulties and enlarged the possibilities. In recent times, Lourdes has been particularly associated with the cure of disease, although officially authenticated cures achieved there are very few. In a novel published in 1894 Emile Zola described in minute detail the travails of a trainload of pilgrims on their way to Lourdes; it does not sound an inviting experience. The journey by air is presumably a little less purgatorial; like Knock in Ireland, Lourdes is served by what in effect is its own airport. Lourdes and Knock are among modern recruits to the ranks of pilgrimage sites that possess the power to attract pilgrims over long distances. Virtually all of these have been associated with Mary, the continuation of a trend already visible in later medieval Europe and now exported to the entire Catholic world. The shrine of Our Lady of Walsingham in Norfolk began to attract pilgrims (including royalty) in the thirteenth century and was probably the most popular in England on the eve of the Reformation; the Holy House of Loreto on the east coast of central Italy rose to prominence at a similar period.

The history of Christian pilgrimage exhibits some impressive continuities, but it is also possible to discern phases within it. Always the pilgrim seeks out a place where the earthly and the heavenly, the eternal and the temporal, intersect and which is therefore believed to be a source of enormous spiritual power. Until at least the thirteenth century such places were signposted above all by the presence of relics of all kinds – of the apostles at Rome or Santiago, of later saints such as Becket at Canterbury, of the True Cross or the Blood of Christ in a number of locations. The holy land looks like an exception, except that the holy places themselves were regarded as relics, and fragments of the holy sepulchre or dust from it were also so regarded. Relics never entirely lost their appeal and have never done so, but later medieval pilgrimage was increasingly characterized by a fascination with images.

Pilgrimage at Lourdes, 1936

Miracles

Images and the visual had always played a part in pilgrimage. Relics were not normally exhibited to the public as bare bones, but presented in shrines or reliquaries made of costly materials, and sometimes even enclosed in fully three-dimensional images. The tenth-century reliquary statue of the martyr Ste Foy (St Faith) at Conques in southern France is a rare surviving example (see colour plate 4). The late medieval growth was above all in pilgrimage to images of Christ and of his mother. The carved or painted crucifix, which might depict the human sufferings of Christ in a highly affecting form, or the statue of the Madonna which evoked her love for her child, or her sorrow at his death, brought vividly before the spectator the supreme personages of the Christian story. Crucifixes and images of the Virgin were not infrequently credited with

p. 1166

miraculous properties that were themselves apprehended visually: moving, bleeding, sweating, weeping. This was a development with its hazards, for ancient suspicions Protestantism of idolatry were lodged deep in Christianity and both the early Protestants and their forerunners, such as the English Lollards, accused pilgrims of confusing the images they beheld with the persons they worshipped. They also accused the ecclesiastical authorities of conniving at this confusion for profit. Hostility to pilgrimage and hostility to images were very closely associated and continue to be strongly felt by some Protestants.

In the Roman Catholic world, however, miraculous weeping Madonnas are still a devotional phenomenon and from time to time they generate popular pilgrimages. In the post-medieval period a different kind of experience, which often has both visual and aural components, has come to greater prominence: the vision, almost invariably of the Virgin. Such a vision, experienced by Bernadette Soubirous in 1858, laid the foundation of the shrine of p. 753 Lourdes; more recently the apparitions of the Virgin to some children at Medjugorje in Croatia, which began in 1981, have created a major pilgrimage. The Virgin continues to appear at Medjugorje and to speak, offering counsel to the faithful. This is to mention only two of many instances: Knock in Ireland and Fatima in Portugal also originated in Marian apparitions.

Christian pilgrimages in modern times obviously function in a wide variety of social and geographical contexts both in Europe and the wider world. Those which have been inaugurated or which have continued to flourish down to modern times in Europe have done so often in Secularization defiance of change, secularization and outright hostility in the surrounding social and political environment. The pilgrimage phenomenon in the modern West is, however, more than a matter of Roman Catholic resistance or revivalism, although these have been powerful forces that have created reverberations outside the strictly Roman Catholic world. The twentieth-century revival of pilgrimage to Our Lady of Walsingham, not only by Roman Catholics but also by Anglicans, illustrates the point. Undoubtedly a rather sentimental medievalism and hankering for 'the world we have lost' has played its part in such revivals, but it would be rash to make that the whole story.

More impressive still, perhaps, is the enthusiasm for the Santiago pilgrimage expressed in the activities of numerous national societies, in Europe and beyond, which offer advice and assistance to prospective pilgrims. The journey is undertaken – on foot, by bicycle, on horseback – by people of all religious affiliations and none, and to judge by the numerous memoirs that it has generated many experienced it as a voyage of personal self-discovery and spiritual healing. There is something here analogous to the inner experience of many devout pilgrims throughout history. The journey is both an obvious and a profound metaphor for the progress of the soul, from birth to death, from ignorance to enlightenment, from earth to heaven. Where critics of pilgrimage have thought of the physical journey as an unnecessary distraction from an essentially spiritual quest, its proponents have seen it rather as a way of enacting and reflecting upon that metaphor.

DIANA WEBB

Simon Coleman and John Elsner, *Pilgrimage Past and Present in the World Religions*, Cambridge, MA: Harvard University Press 1995; J. G. Davies, *Pilgrimage Yesterday and Today: Why? Where? How?*, London: SCM Press 1988; Mary Lee Nolan and Sidney Nolan, *Christian Pilgrimage in Modern Western Europe*, Chapel Hill: University of North Carolina Press 1989; Jonathan Sumption, *Pilgrimage: An Image of Mediaeval Religion*, London: Faber 1975; Diana Webb, *Mediaeval European Pilgrimage*, London: Palgrave Macmillan 2002

Poetry

Bible
Jesus
Worship

In these days, poets who call themselves Christians often find it difficult to say they are 'Christian poets'. They prefer to say they are poets whose poetry is imbued with many influences, the main one being their Christian faith. Rowan Williams (born 1950) put it this way: 'I dislike the idea of being a religious poet. I would prefer to be a poet for whom religious things mattered intensely.' What it actually feels like to be a Christian writing poetry is to be open to whatever offers itself as material for a poem. Whatever the poet considers to be right for shaping into a poem, be it a mood, a sighting, a relationship, an event, a conflict of interests, an object, a response to a book, a personality, a work of art, then becomes the raw material. R. S. Thomas (1913–2000) shaped his life in the Christian tradition as a priest in the Church of Wales, and so poems about the cross, prayer, matters of social justice and human integrity and the created world inevitably loom large in his published works.

Such a process was not always the case. The earliest poems written within the Christian tradition were more clearly a particular response to the scriptures, and to the nature of Jesus Christ. Sometimes, as in the letter to the Ephesians, Christ was the general subject of the work, and the poetry of other traditions, neo-Platonic and other classical models, were used to exalt his nature. Often such material was given a place in the church's worship.

As time has gone on, poetry within the Christian tradition, now probably referred to as religious or spiritual poetry, has absorbed more secular models. It will see the whole canvas of human experience as a resource, without feeling the need to relate it to the traditional doctrines of the church, or to serve the needs of its liturgy. It has become a resource for prayer and meditation, and more subtly a way of regenerating theological language and styles of discourse. A model for this would be e. e. cummings' *six non-lectures* and the writings of the Brazilian theologian Rubem Alves. Some things can only be told poetically. Some New Testament writers discovered that, and bear witness to it in their strong sense of imagery, emotional language and their delight in complex or cryptic references.

One significant area that helps draw secular and religious poetry into the same ring is the notion of 'inspiration'. Poets are born, not made. What is this 'inspiration', and would a theology of the Holy Spirit allow us to see wider connections and fewer boundaries? Would it help us to see deeper into the genesis of poetry? At this deep point, where 'things matter intensely', we might be able to understand the connections between different styles and traditions of poetry, and see that poets are all neighbours in the village of poetry. We may well find a God-given centre to this recurrent human desire to write, sing, recite and make poetry.

Poetry must come from somewhere. In thinking about how poems happen, there is always a story, always a poet: William Wordsworth (1770–1850) had been walking beside Ullswater with his sister Dorothy and they saw the daffodils, and a poem was born. For a long time T. S. Eliot (1888–1965) had been considering the nature of the Christian spiritual tradition; in the middle of the Second World War he visited Little Gidding, and *Four Quartets* took shape. Philip Larkin (1922–85) cycled to a church and went inside, and the poem 'Church Going' was begun. The actual moment of the conception of a poem may be difficult to discern, whether it is in the mind, or in the heart, or elsewhere, but it has to begin somewhere for the poem to get written. Dogs may inspire poems, but they don't write them. Poetic inspiration is a mixture of absorbing traditional methods of writing poetry, a poet's particular experience and knowledge of poetry, and the characteristic that unifies the influences and motivates the poet, which we could call 'inspiration'.

It is the 'inspiration' part of the process that is fascinating. Why should one person be a poet and not another, why that poem in that form, and how do the great poems happen? These areas of mystery have led the function of poet to be surrounded with a sense of awe, and sometimes given status. The prophets of the Old Testament who proclaimed 'the word of God' had a particular status in the community that was not always a comfortable one. The Greek philosopher Plato (427–347 BCE) recognized the value of poets, but gave them a lower status than the philosopher or statesman. Poets have a complicated relationship with the society of today. They are part prophet, part agitator, part conscience, part entertainer, living and writing often on the margin of institutions. In the Christian tradition the place of the poet has changed, too. Its most prolific times have been when the church itself has encouraged writers involved in liturgical matters in religious communities, such as Caedmon (died *c.*680) writing at Whitby, or have been sustained by the patronage of monarchs such as Charlemagne (*c.*742–814) in eighth-century Europe, or James I in seventeenth-century England. The individual poet writing independent thoughts about faith in the Christian tradition is a 'modern' phenomenon, reflecting the fragmentation of the church, and the growth of the individual as a creative unit separate from a community of faith. Much medieval and pre-medieval poetry was written anonymously. Today the poet is often more important than the poem.

p. 1037
Prayer

It is difficult not to be personal about poetry, because a large element of the interest of poetry is how a poet writes. Originality is of the essence. It may be that in previous eras poets could depend on a deeply and long-held tradition of writing poetry. Poets such as the Welsh bards would write in that tradition, and the sense of a personal style or contribution was minimal. Now that the essence of poetry is 'voice', the particular style or mark of a poet is all-important. So poetry within the Christian tradition is marked, not by schools of writing, but by individuals often hanging rather loosely to institutional structures. They write, in that sense, prophetically, often bringing the church back to an understanding of forgotten traditions. In the twentieth century, for example there are the Australian poets Les Murray (born 1938), and Kevin Hart (born 1954) who has edited *The Oxford Book of Australian Religious Verse*. American religious poets would include Denise Levertov (1923–97), Charles Wright (born 1935) and Thomas Merton (1914–68). From Ireland there would be John F. Deane (born 1943), Padraig J. Daly (born 1943), Paul Durcan (born 1944) and Seamus Heaney (born 1939). Jack Clemo (1916–94), the Cornish mystical recluse, who wrote out of a puritan, evangelical tradition, and R. S. Thomas, the Welsh priest, were mining the ancient contemplative tradition, both of them isolated individual voices. David Adam (born 1936) of Lindisfarne is restoring the treasures of the Celtic tradition. David Jones (1895–1974), another lone voice, gathered up a whole host of material, including Celtic sources, from his experience in the First World War, and from his membership of the Roman Catholic Church. Jones's Catholic faith helped him find in the Mass a unifying concept, gathering all the loose pieces up in a poetic offering. His major poetic work is called *Anathemata* (1952), which means 'things gathered up'.

Celtic Christianity

Prophecy
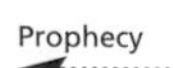

The church in its corporate life hasn't managed to handle this individualism, or to attract a sense of community among its writers. It seems that one can only write over against the established institution. Poets are outsiders. It could be that the manipulation of the tradition by such poets is hard to fit into traditional liturgical moulds. Psalms Contemporary poetry of a religious or even Christian nature is more welcome at funerals, memorial services, harvest festivals and special theme services. Contemporary Music music seems easier to manage, somehow, whereas poetry, being word, is under much greater scrutiny and is often less accessible to the majority of congregations.

The personal nature of much contemporary poetry, as distinct from poems which are of a much more solid traditional style, using obvious Christian biblical motifs, leads to a blurring of the edges about what is a 'Christian' poem. A poem imbued, dyed with the Christian spirit and ethos might not mention Jesus or Christ or God, but Incarnation be written out of a deep faith in the power and veracity of that tradition. So suffering love and compassion, and Resurrection a sense of the absence of God that, for example, were important elements of the poetry of the First World War, could be said to be helpful in understanding what it is to be Christ-like. When R. S. Thomas edited an edition of *The Penguin Book of Religious Verse* (1963) he had a special section titled 'Nothing'. This is how he justified his  choice: 'Poems such as the "terrible" sonnets of Gerard Manley Hopkins are but a human repetition of the cry from the cross: "Eloi, Eloi, lama sabachthani!" The ability to be in hell is a spiritual prerogative, and proclaims the Paul true nature of such a being. Without darkness, in the world we know, the light would go unprized; without evil, goodness would have no meaning. Over every poet's door is nailed Keats' saying about negative capability. Poetry is born of the tensions set up by the poet's ability to be "in uncertainties, mysteries, doubts, without any irritable reaching after fact and reason".' Poetry and Christianity is a tortuous, complicated and many-stranded subject.

There is inevitably a canon of names of poets writing in English. Within the Christian tradition there will be many others writing whose work is not so well known in the English-speaking world. To redress that is an important task of this century. This raises the question of translating poetry, and the access to many religious poets who have written within the Christian tradition but not in English. Although Geoffrey Hill (born 1932), himself a poet, has 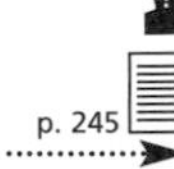 espoused the cause of Charles Péguy (1873–1914), Péguy's work is not very well known, and deserves much greater p. 245 attention, especially the three *Mysteries*, the *Tapestries of Our Lady, Saint Genevieve, Joan of Arc* and finally the great poem *Eve* which appeared shortly before his death. The Russian poets Boris Pasternak (1890–1960), Anna Akhmatova (1889–1966), Marina Tsvetayeva (1892–1941) and Osip Mandelstam (1891–1938), and the Polish poet Czeslaw Milosz (born 1911), are all well served with translators. Milosz writes fluently in English as well. Meanwhile, there is a long and distinguished heritage to unfold.

Much of the earliest Christian use of poetry is in quotation from Hebrew sources translated into Greek. The most popular texts are from the psalms, and verses from the prophets. The psalms are an archetypal form of religious poetry, and are very illuminating as models for a variety of forms of poetry in the Christian tradition. The subjects of the psalms are praise, lament, personal wrestling with faith and doubt, human failure, the beauty and majesty of the natural world. God is presented as king and shepherd, tyrant and lover, who abandons believers and supports them. The whole range of emotion and circumstance is traversed, and the use of metaphors to describe God provides an insight into the very nature of Christianity itself. Poetry was a tool with which to understand and to describe the nature of the incarnation, and its nature is at the heart of the discussion about how to understand the resurrection. To come at truth human beings have needed, and discovered, the gift of poetry. The psalms were not confined to liturgical use, but were the basis of private prayer too. Jesus imbibed both their spirit, and their words.

Some brief poetic pieces are embedded into the Gospel narratives. Few books of the New Testament lack a poetic reference: for example, 1 Corinthians 15.54, 55 is made up of the poetic writings of Isaiah 25.8 and Hosea 13.14. Freshly minted, credal acclamations take on a form of poetry in the letters of Paul, as in Philippians 2.6–11, and the letter to the Ephesians 5.14 has a three-line poem,

> Awake, sleeper,
> rise from the dead,
> and Christ will shine upon you,

but it could not be said that the New Testament sets out to work as poetry in the modern understanding of it. Poetry is not its primary style or purpose, and attempts to make Jesus a poet miss the mark. Jesus' use of parable or pithy statement are the poetic forms he seems to have been happiest with, preferring to use image and metaphor, but he did so in order to change lives rather than to be poetic.

It was when the earliest Christians came to writing their services of worship that the poetic traditions of the past came to their aid. In the Didache (second century) there is a section on the eucharist that contains this: 'As this broken bread once dispersed over the hills was brought together to become one loaf, so may thy church be brought together from the ends of the earth into thy kingdom.' There is a poetic mind at work here, and with the echoes of the feeding of the 5000 and the Last Supper we have the earliest stirrings of a poetic sensibility. The context of worship is one of the great seedbeds of Christian poetry. In Ignatius of Antioch's *Letter to the Ephesians* this hymn fragment occurs:

Very flesh, yet Spirit too;
Uncreated and yet born;
God and man in one agreed,
Very life-in-death indeed
Fruit of God and Mary's seed
At once impassible and torn
By pain and suffering here below:
Jesus Christ, whom as our Lord we know.

Poetry in the first three centuries of the Christian era was in Greek. But with the growth of the Roman empire in the fourth and fifth centuries, Latin became the predominant language of the church, and provided the literary basis of Christian poetry. The poems of Commodian (middle of the third century), a native of Gaza in Palestine, but later of Africa, are the earliest examples of Latin verse intended for and, we must assume, appreciated by uncultured members of the church. In his *Martyrium Volente* he addresses one of his acrostic poems to 'one who would be a martyr'. Each of the sixteen lines begins with a letter from the words of the title; the poem is in two verses and has rhythm but no fixed number of syllables. Poems are beginning to have a definable shape on the lines of their classical forebears. At the same time, Christian Latin poets of the third and fourth centuries learned their art in the schools of rhetoric. Poems such as the beautiful poem on the phoenix, attributed to the African Lactantius (*c.*250–*c.*325), making the bird a Christian reference to the resurrection, were written by the educated for the educated.

Augustine of Hippo's (354–430) *Psalm against the Donatists* has been seen as marking the beginning of a conscious poetic style, a 'Christian rhythm'. The lines are more or less composed of sixteen syllables, divided equally by the caesura; this is the only law observed beyond that of rough syllabic equality. In addition a regular accent falls on the penultimate syllable of each half line:

quisquis novit evangelium recognoscat cum timore

(whoever has known the gospel, let him understand with fear).

It has been claimed that rhythmical verse in the West was entirely a Christian possession, never employed by pagan writers. The origin of such verse has been thought to be Semitic, deriving in particular from Syriac hymns such as those of Ephrem the Syrian (*c.*306–373). The hymns of Ambrose (*c.*339–97) were written definitely for congregational purposes and soon found their way into the liturgies of Milan and elsewhere. One of the best known and most beautiful of Ambrosian hymns is the *Te lucis ante terminum* ('Before the ending of the day), sung daily at Compline in the Roman Office. The lyrical poems of Prudentius (348–*c.*410) are collected under the titles *Cathemerinon* and *Peristephanon*, and from the former comes the *Hymn for the Burial of the Dead.*

But for us, heap earth about him
Earth with leaves and violets strewn
Grave his name, and pour the fragrant
Balm upon the icy stone.

Two of the translations of Prudentius' poems have become famous as hymns: 'Of the Father's love begotten' and 'Earth has many a noble city'. Both of these translations, interestingly enough, continue in the tradition of the Augustinian rhythm.

A variety of schools of poets emerged in the middle of the first millennium. Around the court of Charlemagne (*c.*742–814), dominating the region of Gaul, Alcuin (*c.*740–804) and later Eriugena (*c.*810–*c.*877) were both writing in Latin. At the same time a native Irish Christian poetry was emerging with its early 'breastplate' poems, the most famous being St Patrick's Breastplate. Other loricas, or 'breastplate' poems, as they were called, were written by Lodgen (*c.* eighth century), and Mugron's poem (*c.*970) is particularly powerful, beginning:

Language

Christ's cross over this face, and this over my ear:
Christ's cross over this eye, Christ's cross over this nose.

Out of the Irish mission to Europe came poems in praise of Columba (*c.*521–97), the most important of which is the *Amra Choluimb Chille,* attributed to Dallan Forgaill and written about 575. A clutch of beautiful monastic poems celebrating the contemplative life and the harmony of spiritual fulfilment with the glories of nature have also been discovered from this time, some of them simple marginalia, written in a pause from the more exacting discipline of copying. In a more formal style, and much influenced by Virgil, is Walafrid Strabo's poem on gardening, *De Cultura Hortorum.* Strabo (*c.*808–49), having been tutor to the emperor's son Charles (the future king and emperor Charles the Bald), was rewarded with the abbacy of Reichenau, where the horticultural poem was written. The growth of the monastic life provided a setting in which these poems of wide-ranging subject matter flourished.

The third strand of this extension of poetry out of Latin into other languages is the Anglo-Saxon one. It begins with a masterpiece, the Anglo-Saxon *The Dream of the Rood.* The poem belongs to the early eighth century and uses the native Anglo-Saxon language and culture to present a noble, soldier Christ, as seen from the perspective of the cross, and all this within the context of a dream. It

Hymns

is a highly imaginative piece that allows the cross to feel the weight of Christ's body, and the quality of the Anglo-Saxon gives the subject a weight, a body and a depth of emotion quite new in Christian poetry. This poem usually stands at the head of all anthologies of Christian poetry reflecting the English tradition. The bridge linking *The Dream of the Rood* and the medieval Christian lyrics is not a long one. In the jewel-like intensity of the short poem 'Pity for Mary' (early thirteenth century), there are strong echoes of the *Dream*. Needless to say, most of these poems are anonymous.

Mary

The passion of Christ and the devotion of Mary is a central theme of medieval poetry: 'Stond wel, moder, under rode (the cross)', and 'Whanne ic se on Rode/ Jesu my lemman (lover)'. The place of Mary as an inspiration for poetry could well have emerged alongside a wider romance, or troubadour, movement. This has allowed Christian poetry to keep in touch with secular models and universal themes. The Franciscan poets such as Jacopone da Todi (1230–1306), who wrote many exquisite and deeply devotional poems (*Laude*) in Latin and in the Umbrian dialect, and Francis of Assisi (1181–1226) who wrote the Canticle of the Sun, are allowing the deep sources of human love to image the divine love. The tradition reaches its apogee with the Italian poet and philosopher Dante Alighieri (1265–1321), and in a modified and later form in the poetry of John Donne (1571–1631) and George Herbert (1593–1633). The Spanish Carmelite John of the Cross (1542–91) wrote his poems out of this tradition, weaving the sources of human and divine love so intricately together that they are in the mystical state almost indistinguishable. Dante in his love for Beatrice was inspired to create the most elaborate and extensive

Journey

structures of poetry, in his Christian journey from hell, through purgatory, to paradise. The name usually given to this sacred poem is *La Divina Commedia (The Divine Comedy)*. In it Dante describes his vision of these three realms, *Inferno*, *Purgatoria* and *Paradiso*. Dante travels for a week at Easter 1300 from a dark forest on the side of the world down through hell to Satan at the centre of the earth. Then he travels up the seven terraces of the Mount of Purgatory, an island in the antipodes opposite Jerusalem, to its summit, the Earthly Paradise, where Adam and Eve were created. So far Virgil has been his guide, but now he meets Beatrice, who conducts him through the nine planetary and stellar spheres to the Empyrean, where Bernard of Clairvaux takes her place. Bernard presents Dante to the Blessed Virgin Mary, at whose intercession the poet is granted a glimpse of the beatific vision. The poem was written during the first two decades of the fourteenth century. It has exercised a deep influence, and was particularly championed in nineteenth-century English literature.

The seventeenth-century English devotional writers, influenced by the Renaissance, and putting their learning at the service of the church, itself in the turmoil of revolution, produced a particular style of poetry. It has been called 'metaphysical'. Its feel is sinuous and intellectual. Here thinking and feeling come together, and by the extensive use of images the poets draw the things of this world into service for another. George Herbert is the most famous exponent of this style, and because of his sense of intimacy with the reader, and through his disclosure of his own spiritual state, his poems, as he originally intended, can be helpful for other, personal journeys in faith. John Donne, unlike Herbert, had given over his Roman Catholic youth to secular love poetry. The transition to divine poems involved a change of subject matter, but not a change of style. He became Dean of St Paul's in 1621. The nineteen *Holy Sonnets*, which include 'Death be not proud' and 'Batter my heart', still work on the metaphysical principles of a complex interchange of images. The poems, highly charged with a passionate faith, emerge as puzzles in which the working is left on show.

A different strain emerged with John Milton (1608–74), whose writings, more theological in a biblical sense, lost this movement of the heart behind a more classical style. *Paradise Lost* is written out of issues of faith, and dominated by the strong theological movements of the day. The Bible dominated his thought and his style, producing epics from what in contrast seem like quite frail biblical narratives. His own blindness gives an immediacy to *Samson Agonistes*, a poem on the biblical story of Samson, but also reflecting the agony of the loss of sight and vision, and the destruction of political power. Milton, in the English tradition, moves the story on into the eighteenth century.

Here the hymn begins to take pride of place, and what Milton did on the grand scale in his poetry, Isaac Watts (1674–1748), a Non-conformist, who wrote the incomparable passion hymn 'When I survey the wondrous cross', and Charles Wesley (1707–88), author of 'Hark! The herald angels sing', were to do in their hymns. William Cowper (1731–1800) contributed his finest work to *Olney Hymns*, published in conjunction with John Newton (1725–1807) in 1779. They include 'God moves in a mysterious way' and 'O for a closer walk with God'. Cowper's secular poetry, much of which has a religious bent, is marked by a love of nature and a tenderness that foreshadowed the romantics. The mystical strain continued in the writings of William Blake (1757–1827), who added a gospel of social outrage at poverty and the abuse of children. In Wales a very different writer, but equally inspired, was Ann Griffiths (1776–1805). She combined a strongly biblical sensibility with an innocent mystical strain, a reminder that poetry cannot really happen without some element of inspiration, which in earlier days was attributed to the Muse. The mystical strain was largely left to the romantic poets, who, rather than writing on Christian themes, developed a more wide-ranging spiritual philosophy, in which poetry itself became a major source of understanding over against a growing body of scientific knowledge. William Wordsworth was at his most powerful in poems such as 'Tintern Abbey' or 'Ode on Intimations of Immortality', where the specifically Christian or biblical content is overwhelmed by a more universal sense of the divine indwelling, in nature and in natural relationships. The nineteenth century did little to further a positive view of the Christian faith in poetry. On the contrary, it seems to have been a period famous for its doubt. Matthew Arnold (1822–88) caught the sombre mood with his poem 'Dover Beach' (written in 1831):

> The Sea of Faith
> Was once, too, at the full, and round earth's shore
> Lay like the folds of a bright girdle furl'd.
> But now I only hear
> Its melancholy, long, withdrawing roar,
> Retreating, to the breath
> of the night-wind, down the vast edges drear
> And naked shingles of the world.

The poems of Christina Rossetti (1830–94), marked by a great beauty and care in the selection of words, are the expression of a strong Christian faith. That tightness of expression that belies an intense and passionate spirit is best known in her poem, sung as a carol, 'In the bleak midwinter'. It is strange that some of the best religious poems are the poems of doubt. With the increasing sense of the loss of God in an industrial civilization, this is not surprising. It was not until Gerard Manley Hopkins (1844–89), a famous convert to Roman Catholicism, was prompted to write *The Wreck of the Deutschland* that poetry rediscovered its particularly Christian voice and rhythm, drawing together the theology of suffering, the cross, heroism and the church on earth. The revolution happened, as so often, through the form of the poem. Hopkins developed the concept of sprung rhythm, which is the rhythm of simple nursery rhymes. Based on an aspect of Duns Scotus' (*c.*1265–1308) theology, Hopkins also developed the idea of 'inscape', the internal landscape of things, in which, for example, the felled poplars of Binsey, near Oxford, about which Hopkins wrote, both felt the blow themselves and cause the reader to feel the blow. Francis Thompson (1859–1907), also a Roman Catholic, shares some of Hopkins' depth of anguish in 'The Hound of Heaven', but the poem seems monochrome in comparison.

By 1918, when Hopkins' poetry was first published, another group of poets, with experience of the First World War trenches, had expressed a challenge to faith in God. Wilfred Owen (1893–1917), a devout evangelical Christian as a child and young man, wrote about the 'pity' of war. His 'pity' is similar to the Christian *pietà.* It resonates with the crucifixion and also with the mother figure of the Virgin Mary.

The questioning of the place of God in the world of war opened up the next great change in religious poetry for other poets. This was focused on the poetry of the American-born writer T. S. Eliot. Eliot's popular contribution to Christian poetry was as much through his verse dramas, including *Murder in the Cathedral*, as through his poetry. The ability to think in a modern way through a reflective, free verse form, with internal echoes and rich imagery and an intellectual inner structure, gave *Four Quartets* its power and its popularity. It heralded the onrush of 'spirituality' as the main religious theme in the second half of the twentieth century.

Drama

Spirituality

W. H. Auden (1907–73) takes his place among modern religious poets as a complex mixture of devout Anglican and liberal intellectual. In a conversational way he talks through life's issues, seeing all round them with wide and urbane intelligence. 'Whitsunday in Kirchstetten' (1962), in which commitment to the Christian gospel is shrouded in understatement, is a good example of this.

A revival in the poetry of faith often comes as a result of a return to the foundation texts. David Jones's *Anathemata*, mentioned earlier, is prophetic in its rich vein of Celtic traditions. The Mass and the landscape, the crucifixion and the slaughter of the Great War are all poured into this extraordinary poem, which stands outside the general trend in twentieth-century poetry towards a bleak minimalism. The poetry of the 'modern' movement in Britain and America has tussled with God in line with much contemporary theology. R. S. Thomas is at his best when confronting God with the dehumanizing forces of modern society, and, paradoxically, as he finds consolation in prayer, silence and the wisdom of the natural world. The cross is his simplest and starkest image. The American poet, Ann Sexton (1928–74), in her book *The Awful Rowing Towards God*, writes out of the experience of mental illness, and works with God much as a patient might with his or her psychotherapist. Christ is no objective reality but is making both agenda and discourse in the mind of the poet.

The move towards the more general area of 'spirituality' as a subject for religious poets rather than the key notes of a specific Christian tradition gives us pause for thought about the future. There is an element of spirituality in all poetry, because at the heart of all good poetry is a spirit which refuses to be clearly defined outside the poems themselves. However, poems which are

Eschatology
Resurrection

written out of an authentic engagement with the truths of the Christian faith and ring true from what is known and experienced of Christ-like lives should continue to contribute to the wider world of writers and readers of poetry, and contribute significantly and uniquely.

DAVID SCOTT

Kingdom of God

Neil Astley (ed), *Staying Alive*, Newcastle: Bloodaxe Books 2002 (a very good anthology of general, mainly twentieth-century, poetry); L. William Countryman, *The Poetic Imagination: An Anglican Tradition*, London: Darton, Longman & Todd and Maryknoll, NY: Orbis 1999; Helen Gardner (ed), *The Faber Book of Religious Verse*, London: Faber 1972; Peter Levi (ed), *The Penguin Book of English Christian Verse*, Harmondsworth: Penguin Books 1984; David Scott, *Selected Poems*, Newcastle: Bloodaxe Books 1998

Political theology

Politics
Paul
p. 1155
Investiture Controversy
Liberation theology

Theology has had a political focus from the earliest days of Christianity, when Paul wrote to the Romans, 'Let every person be subject to the governing authorities, for … those that exist have been instituted by God', through the medieval arguments about the relationship of world power to sacred power embodied in the Investiture Controversy, to the liberation theology which came into being in the latter part of the twentieth century in Latin America and spread from there. However, the term 'political theology' has come to identify a particular movement that arose in Germany in the revolutionary situation of the 1960s.

The advocates of this theology, notably Jürgen Moltmann, Dorothee Sölle and Johann Baptist Metz, saw their political theology as being about the public dimension and social relevance of faith. Its emphasis was on promise and change. In the light of the future it saw everything that was going on in society and the church as being in need of change. It combined impulses from the Enlightenment and the Bible in a prophetic criticism of society. It set the biblical religion of the exodus, prophecy and apocalyptic over against middle-class modern religion.

Enlightenment
Bible
Prophecy
Apocalyptic

Jesus

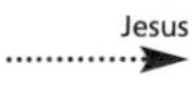

Taking up the Enlightenment in a critical way, these theologians saw the world as history, which has to be shaped by individuals and society. Their first concern was to de-privatize talk of God in Christian theology by relating it to the public world. And they saw the church as an institution that was free to criticize society on the basis of its faith.

Hope

Jürgen Moltmann introduced his theology of hope into political theology. Inspired by the Bible and based on it, this theology draws on the biblical promise that is rooted in the word of God and is universalized and intensified in prophetic eschatology. The Old Testament promise is not superseded in the gospel, but confirmed by God with the resurrection of Jesus. To this degree the background of the New Testament, too, is the horizon of the promised future. The theology of hope investigates the inner tendency of the resurrection of Jesus and its future and sees what happened to Jesus as the dawn of the all-embracing kingdom of God. The future of Jesus Christ is illuminated by the promise of the righteousness of God, of life from the resurrection of the dead and the kingdom of God as a 'new creation'.

The promise leads to criticism of existing circumstances and inspires forward-looking action that is in search of change. Christians live and act in expectation of God's future in a community that looks for future salvation. They engage creative discipleship, with a perspective that includes the realization of the hope of justice, the humanization of individuals, the socialization of humanity and the peace of all creation.

Dorothee Sölle arrived at political theology by grappling with the existentialist interpretation of the Bible of Rudolf Bultmann. She thought that the historical-critical method was liberating for theology, but that it was used in too narrow a way. So the demythologizing that Bultmann practised had to be supplemented by a criticism of ideology and taken further through political theology. If Bultmann's theology implies an insight into the historicity of any talk of God, political theology analyses the particular situation critically and thus spells out the concerns of existentialist theology. In contrast to the existentialist perspective, which is limited to the individual, its interest is in real history, the future to be realized and the authentic life of all human beings.

Johann Baptist Metz explains his approach in the 1970s as a political theology of the subject in society and history, the goal of which is for all men and women to become subjects in solidarity. He sees this political ideal indicated by the Christian idea of God. Here discipleship comes into the centre. Political theology recognizes that what Christians do is socially and historically governed; at the same time it emphasizes that this involves suffering. Christian faith understands itself as 'hope in solidarity for the God of Jesus as the God of the living and the dead'.

As the memory of his suffering and death, the memory of Jesus among Christians is always a dangerous and liberating memory. It breaks through the magical circle of evolutionist awareness. It evokes the history of the suffering of those who have failed and been annihilated. Faith mediated through the remembrance of suffering then means that the dead, those who have already been defeated and forgotten, have a claim that is still to be settled. Hope for the deliverance of the dead is made concrete in the expectation of an imminent end, which breaks the spell of evolutionist timelessness and first makes it possible to engage in radical discipleship. That makes the three concepts of memory, narrative and solidarity the leading categories of practical fundamental theology.

From the 1980s on, two basic challenges came to the fore. First, Metz drew attention to the history of the suffering of the Jews, which has to be remembered, and the history of Christian guilt, which cannot be suppressed or forgotten at any price. Both are indissolubly bound up with the name 'Auschwitz'. Auschwitz is a key factor for political theology, which recognizes in this catastrophe the end of all talk of God without a subject and all idealistic reconciliation. After Auschwitz, theology has to begin with the question of theodicy, the question how there can be a just God, in the form of the question, 'How does salvation come to those who suffer unjustly?' In the face of the incomparable horror of Auschwitz, theology must at the same time talk of a suffering in God.

Secondly, the challenge of the Third World increasingly came to light, the history of the suffering of the impoverished two-thirds of the world and the history of the guilt of European colonialist Christianity in a socially-divided world with many cultural centres. In the face of the privatized, apathetic and assimilated 'bourgeois religion' of the rich countries and churches of the north, what was beginning to happen in the poor churches of the south was seen as the birth of a political-mystical grassroots church.

As a counter-force to the spread of cultural amnesia, which wants to forget Auschwitz and leave the others out of account, political theology puts its weight behind a culture that remembers. Memory consists first of all in thinking of the suffering of others. The universalism that is an ineradicable part of belief in one God is articulated above all in a universal responsibility born of the memory of suffering. Theology has to bring to bear this universalism that is sensitive to suffering. It does so by arguing for a culture that recognizes others in their otherness.

Moltmann moved from the theology of hope to the theology of the cross, which he understood as the other, concrete, side of the theology of hope. In it both suffering and the cross come to the centre with reference to the crisis over the relevance and identity of Christian life and faith. Over against the religious cult of the cross, but taking up the mysticism of the cross, Moltmann was concerned with living out the discipleship of the cross as a Christian community. He understood his theology of the cross as a 'critical theory of God'. It takes up the history of human suffering. It recognizes God, whom it sees as himself suffering, in the godforsaken, accursed and crucified Christ. Through the history of the suffering God, which takes place in the event of the cross, men and women are called to become disciples of the crucified Jesus, to suffer with the suffering God. This opens up the way to psychological and political liberation from the vicious circles of poverty, violence, alienation, the destruction of nature, meaninglessness and godforsakenness. Such a political theology of the cross has the task of liberating the state from political idolatry and human beings from political alienation and servitude. But this liberation seems impossible unless theology liberates itself from the needs and demands of the dominant political religion.

Judaism and Christianity

In connection with his theology of the cross, conceived in trinitarian terms, Moltmann outlines a 'messianic' view of the church. He understands the church as a community of the exodus and the cross, which through fellowship with the crucified Jesus aims to bring together 'brothers and sisters without any domination'. As the church of the kingdom it becomes the critical catalyst in the economic, political and cultural process of the world. In the power of the Holy Spirit the church experiences itself as a messianic community in the service of the kingdom of God. It makes the story of Jesus Christ present, bears witness to it in its form and order, its practice and its messianic lifestyle. It lives and acts with a view to the coming kingdom.

Holy Spirit

Third World

Moltmann's political theology primarily sets out to offer a theological critique of a political religion that endorses government rule and stabilizes society, whether in a totalitarian form or in the liberal version constituted by civil religion. It is also concerned to provide a political interpretation of the gospel, bringing out its liberating potential and impetus towards critical resistance. And it is closely connected with political ethics, directed against economic exploitation and concerned for economic justice. In the face of racism and sexism it argues for a culture of solidarity and mutual recognition. All this takes place in critical solidarity with other approaches, including liberation theology.

Suffering

In Sölle's work, suffering and solidarity with victims is likewise given great emphasis. Sympathy shows itself first in the perception of suffering inflicted on others. Expressions of, and reflections on, non-repressive humanitarian religion are combined with criticism of authoritarian religion and the dominant theology. Resources can be found especially in the experience and language of mysticism. Here Sölle has moved on from political theology to a feminist theology of liberation. In the face of patriarchal religion orientated on God's power, God is to be thought of as a creative, liberating and enabling power, to be experienced in the conflicts and new beginnings of every day. From the mystic presence of this power of relationship, women and men can resist and oppose the social conditions in which they live and under which they suffer. So they can work to change all the unjust social structures, mechanisms of compulsion and oppressive social relations that destroy the fellowship and equality that should be part of creation.

Mysticism
Feminist theology
Community

EDMUND ARENS

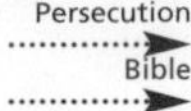
Persecution
Bible

📖 Johann Baptist Metz, *Faith in History and Society. Toward a Foundational Political Theology*, New York: Seabury Press 1980; Jürgen Moltmann, *Experiences in Theology*, London: SCM Press and Minneapolis: Fortress Press 1999; P. Scott and W. T. Cavanaugh, *The Blackwell Companion to Political Theology*, Oxford: Blackwell 2004; Dorothee Sölle, *Political Theology*, Philadelphia: Fortress Press 1974

Politics

Ancient alternatives

The tension between religion and politics arises not because the two are so different, but because in important respects they are so similar; not because they have nothing in common, but because in central areas of life they compete. Religious institutions and political ideologies have power and seek power. They both provide meaning in life, values by which to live and the promise of happiness – if always deferred. The tension exists at an institutional level of church and state, but also as an unresolved conflict within individual lives. The alternatives of conflict or collaboration have existed since the earliest days of the Christian church.

Origins and background

It is likely that the Herodians, mentioned in the Gospels, were supporters of Herod the Great, the Jewish king who collaborated with the Roman state, and subsequently of Herod Antipas, ruler of Galilee, whom Jesus described as 'that fox' (Luke 13.32). Jesus would therefore have been suspicious when they came with the Pharisees to ask him, 'Is it lawful to pay taxes to Caesar, or not?' His reply cleverly outmanoeuvred them: 'Render therefore to Caesar the things that are Caesar's and to God the things that are God's' (Mark 12.13–17). Throughout the centuries this has been taken as the compromise position of religion and politics, the balanced view of church and state. That is to ignore what Jesus did in calling on his questioners to produce a coin, the prescribed coin that was required for paying the poll tax. This coin was the Roman *denarius*, which bore the inscription *Tiberius Caesar Divi Augusti Filius Augustus*. It made the claim of the imperial cult: Tiberius is God. Jesus posed the counter-question: how do you give what Caesar demands when he requires obedience body and soul?

Jesus

Paul

Here is not collaboration, but the conflict of religion and politics, because politics has usurped the sphere of religion. Jews were not required to worship Caesar, but as soon as the early church left the protection of Judaism, Christianity became a new and therefore illegal religion. Christians were required to satisfy the imperial cult by taking the oath 'Caesar is Lord'. It was when they refused, confessing that 'Christ is Lord', that persecution began.

The persecution under Domitian, about 90 CE, is the context in which the New Testament book of the Revelation of John, or the Apocalypse, is written. Its images are as alarming as they are disturbed. There is war in heaven as Michael leads his angels to victory over the dragon. Victory sees the devil cast down to earth, but that only means that the dragon continues the war, now against those who 'bear testimony to Jesus'. The beast then arises from the sea and is given the blasphemous authority of the dragon (Revelation 13). This is the Roman empire; its demands are total and its persecution of the tiny defenceless church is bestial. The kings of the earth collaborated with Rome as it ruled the earth, but John foresees the defeat and downfall of 'Babylon the great mother of harlots and of earth's abominations'. Rome is 'drunk with the blood of the saints and the blood of the martyrs of Jesus'. The vision ends with grim satisfaction: 'Render to her, as she herself has rendered …' (18.6). Come, Lord Jesus, and indeed 'render to Caesar' what Caesar deserves! This is the earliest view of politics and religion in the Christian church. It is a conflict view that comes from Jesus himself and recurs whenever the state usurps the place of religion and requires that total obedience which can only be given to God.

This is not the only view of politics and religion in the New Testament: there could hardly be a greater contrast between Revelation 13 and Romans 13. 'Let every person be subject to the governing authorities. For there is no authority except from God, and those that exist have been instituted by God. Therefore he who resists the authorities resists what God has appointed, and those who resist will incur judgement.' For John, Rome was the creature of the devil: for Paul, the empire is by divine appointment. Written during the lifetime of those who witnessed the torture and crucifixion of Jesus and the stoning to death of Stephen, the teaching of Paul is that 'rulers are not a terror to good conduct, but to bad'. He urges Christians to pay their taxes, since 'the authorities are ministers of God …' Is this the same empire? No, and that is the whole point. In Acts 20, Paul decides to go up to Jerusalem: following in the footsteps of Jesus it is all but certain that he will die there. He was almost killed by the mob, almost scourged by the Romans, but in the end he was saved by playing a card that Jesus did not hold. 'Is it lawful for you to scourge a man who is a Roman citizen and uncondemned?' When finally brought to trial under Roman law he plays his final card, 'I appeal to Caesar' (25.11).

No, it was not the same empire. The Roman empire was the most efficient and powerful system the world had ever seen. It was organized in the interests of the few, the citizens, at the expense of the many (the enslaved). Paul was one of the citizens, and he experienced the fairness of Roman law towards its own, the protection of Rome against his persecutors the Jews, and safe passage at state expense as he travelled to Rome to stand trial. As he travelled, he was able to preach and establish churches. The will of God was furthered by the *Pax Romana*, the peace that the Roman empire had established. The authorities were ordained by God and the whole system must not be challenged. Generations of children have read passages of the Acts of the Apostles as a series of missionary journeys. In fact the book is an *apologia pro imperio*, a defence of the empire. It is addressed to Theophilus and tells of the favourable treatment that Paul received. The story ends with the relieved words, 'And so we came to Rome,' where Paul under loose house arrest received visitors and made converts. One man's dragon is another man's pussy-cat.

It is this view of religion and politics that prevailed within Christianity, that delivered a passive and compliant church and more importantly stayed the hand of rebellion against monarchy, even in the case of rulers who were by any standard servants of the dragon rather than the lamb.

The transformation from conflict to collaboration was brought about for sociological reasons. An even more astonishing transformation was to be effected for political reasons. Paul could tell the church that the state was the servant of God. Under the Emperor Constantine, Eusebius taught that by the will of God the church was the servant of the state. By the fourth century CE the Roman empire was still the most powerful in the world, but it was ruled by a system of four Caesars. When Constantine became a junior Caesar it was his ambition to reunite the empire under one single ruler, himself. Divine patronage was considered important at that time and he took the extraordinary step of declaring himself a devotee of the Christian God. There had been sporadic persecution of the church, but the church had continued to grow. The Christian religion was more dynamic than the old Roman cults; its adherents demonstrated their devotion, if need be to the death.

Constantine therefore made the strategic decision to end persecution and indeed to promote Christianity. He restored land and property that had been confiscated. He provided funds to rebuild damaged churches, paid for the building of new churches, and at imperial expense called an ecumenical council of all bishops. The Christians could not believe their luck: not surprisingly, they represented Constantine as the servant of God. In 336, 'on the thirtieth jubilee of the emperor's reign', an oration was delivered 'In Praise of Constantine' by Eusebius, scholar, theologian and Bishop of Caesarea in Palestine. In it he presents the emperor as the servant of God, friend of the divine Logos, who models his kingdom here on earth on that kingdom in heaven: 'the sovereign dear to God, in imitation of the Higher Power, directs the helm and sets straight all things on earth'. That is the theology of what happened. The political calculation was different. Constantine reckoned that the Christian church could help him to unify his divided empire, though of course only if the church was itself united – hence the ecumenical council. Christian leaders appeared in his court as aides and confidants. From that time they began to wear the royal purple. In time they adopted the feudal title Lord. The Bishop of Rome was housed in the Lateran palace. The church became the religious arm of the programme of imperial unification. In return the church interpreted his policies as the work of God.

Council

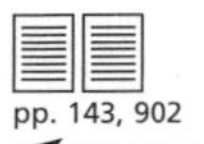

pp. 143, 902

This is a new relationship between religion and politics, the religious legitimation of the state. It assumes a commonality of interest between church and state: the servant of God recognized by the servants of God. Or is it simply that one beast recognizes another?

Modern equivalents

It is convenient to use the above typology when considering modern examples of religion and politics.

The most famous example of the conflictual relationship of religion and politics in modern times was the German church struggle of the 1930s. Indeed it forms a close parallel to the situation of the early church, closer than should have been possible in the middle of the twentieth century. At a time of the secularization of consciousness and the rationalization of society associated with industrialization, it seems incredible that such a regressive model should reappear. National Socialism was not simply a secular regime oppressing the church. The Nazi ideology had about it a conscious and deliberate aura of ancient pagan religion: the church was indeed facing something akin to the ancient imperial cult.

Secularization

Constantine's 'conversion'

In the nineteenth century, Richard Wagner had sought to turn Germany away from Romanized, capitalist, Western civilization by a return to ancient Nordic myths in which Volk legend was preferred to science, the organic to the atomistic, instinct over reason. Parliamentary democracy was rejected in favour of a Führer who embodied the Volk-will. The leader would be a divine hero, a third incarnation of the Nibelung warrior Siegfried and the medieval Kaiser Frederick Barbarossa. Such a one – unlikely as it now seems – was Adolf Hitler.

Given the deep attachment to Christianity in Germany, in both its Protestant and Catholic forms, National Socialism did not openly reject Christianity. Instead, it presented itself as 'positive Christianity'. Alfred Rosenberg, author of *The Myth of the Twentieth Century* (1930), was appointed Director of Education and World-View. The myth refers to the worldwide revolution of the Aryan race. To purify the race for its task all alien races must be eliminated, especially Slavs and Jews. The Jewish elements were omitted from the history of positive Christianity. Jesus was

CHURCH AND STATE

The relationship between church and state differs from country to country and church to church. For example, the First Amendment to the US Constitution states that: 'Congress shall make no law respecting an establishment of religion, or prohibiting the free exercise thereof', whereas in England there is an established Church of England. Relations between church and state were a constant issue in the Middle Ages, as symbolized by the Investiture Controversy. In the Orthodox churches the link between state and church is very close. The Baptist Church insists on the separation of church and state as a matter of principle.

Investiture Controversy

In this context a number of specialized terms are used:

Caesaro-papism: The situation in which a ruler has absolute control over the church, even in church matters. The term is generally applied to the rule of the Byzantine emperors over the Eastern patriarchates towards the end of the first millennium.

Concordat: A concordat is an agreement binding in international law between church and state, especially between the Pope as head of the Roman Catholic Church and a head of state. The earliest concordats were made during the Investiture Controversy, most notably the Concordat of Worms (1122) between Pope Calixtus II and Emperor Henry V, which resolved this controversy over appointment to church offices. Napoleon and Pope Pius VII concluded a concordat for France separating church and state in 1801; the Lateran Treaty (1929) between the Vatican and Mussolini recognized papal sovereignty over Vatican City; in a later concordat (1985) Roman Catholicism ceased to be the state religion of Italy. In 1933 Eugenio Pacelli, later to become Pope Pius XII, concluded a notorious concordat with Nazi Germany which led to the disbanding of the Catholic Centre Party, at the time the only obstacle to Hitler's one-party rule.

Erastianism: The view that the state is superior to the church in ecclesiastical matters. It takes its name from a sixteenth-century Swiss professor, Thomas Erastus, but Erastus himself was not an Erastian. He wrote a book arguing that where all citizens professed the same religion, the state had the right and duty to punish all offences, whether religious or secular. Erastianism developed out of this through the writings of the Anglican theologian Richard Hooker (1554–1600), who argued for the supremacy of the state over the church in his *Ecclesiastical Polity*.

Establishment: An established church is a church recognized by law as the official church of a nation. From the very beginning, the Church of England has been an established church. In 1534 the Act of Supremacy made Henry VIII its 'only supreme head on earth', and the monarch is still its titular head. Bishops sit in the House of Lords and parliament has a say in church affairs. In some Scandinavian countries the Lutheran churches are established churches (though the Church of Sweden was disestablished in 2000), as is the Roman Catholic Church in Italy and Spain. It has long been argued that in today's pluralist society establishment is inappropriate and the Church of England should be disestablished, but the process would be so complicated that this has never been attempted. Other churches have, however, been disestablished: the Roman Catholic Church in the Netherlands in 1848 and in France in 1910, the Church of Ireland in 1869 and the Church in Wales in 1919.

Symphony: The Orthodox churches speak of 'symphony' between church and state. Symphony essentially means co-operation, mutual support and mutual responsibility without one side intruding into the exclusive domain of the other. The bishop obeys the government as a subject, and not because his episcopal power comes from a government official. Similarly, a government official obeys his bishop as a member of the church, who seeks salvation in it, and not because his power comes from the power of the bishop. Ideally, in such a symphonic relationship the state has the support of the church while the church enjoys support from the state in creating conditions favourable for preaching and for the spiritual care of its members. Of course in Byzantium and in Russia this symphony was more a dream than a reality.

pictured as an Aryan. National Socialism was presented as a faith by which the German people – so broken and humiliated by the Treaty of Versailles – could be rebuilt, re-armed, made self-confident and proud once more. The saviour of the German people was now Adolf Hitler. National Socialism had its rallies, symbols, initiations, creeds and hymns. It also had the evangelical, prophetic speeches of the Führer. More ominously, it sought to capture German youth not only through organization but also through special prayers addressed to Hitler:

Führer, my Führer, bequeathed to me by the Lord,
Protect and preserve me as long as I live:
Thou hast rescued Germany from deepest distress,
I thank thee today for my daily bread …

It is as though Hitler was omnipresent, to hear but also to observe.

There could hardly be a closer parallel with the conflict between the Roman empire and the early church: 'Hitler is Lord' versus 'Jesus is Lord'. The resistance from the Christian churches was surprisingly weak. On the Protestant side 'The Guiding Principles of the Faith Movement of the "German Christians"' was published the year before National Socialism came to power in 1933, advocating 'positive Christianity'. The Vatican signed a concordat with the Third Reich in July 1933. A year later the Confessional Synod of the German Evangelical Church met in Barmen. The Barmen Declaration represents the most significant statement of opposition to the religious pretensions of the state and the collaboration of the German Christians. The fifth paragraph is particularly interesting in this context. 'Fear God. Honour the emperor' (1 Peter 2.17). It acknowledges the Pauline position on the divine source of the authority of the state, but goes on to qualify obedience in a way that Paul did not. 'We reject the false doctrine, as though the state, over and beyond its special commission, should and could become the single and totalitarian order of human life, thus fulfilling the church's vocation as well.'

In the German church struggle we have both conflict and collaboration. The religious elements in the ideology of National Socialism were already alien to the modern world. It is unlikely that we shall see such a conflict again.

The classic case of collaboration between Christianity and the state is the case of the United States. The Declaration of Independence of 1776 was concerned with separation from the abusive relationship with the imperial power, Great Britain. Eleven years later the Constitutional Convention concentrated on the organization of the new federation and with the separation of powers of the legislature, the executive and the judiciary. But did this mean that the citizenry exchanged one oppressive regime for another? Not surprisingly, in 1789 ten amendments to the Constitution were passed, known as the Bill of Rights, mainly concerned with individual liberty in relation to the state. What is surprising is that the first amendment concerns not self-defence or fair trial, but religion. 'Congress shall make no law respecting an establishment of religion, or prohibiting the free exercise thereof ...'

However, the colonial population was sufficiently monocultural for Protestant Christianity to become the established religion of the USA – though not by law. As early as 1831 Alexis de Tocqueville commented on the separation of church and state, observing that if religion in America takes no direct part in government, yet 'it must be regarded as the first of their political institutions ...' The early church was too insignificant to influence the Roman empire, but Christianity had a unique opportunity to influence the development of the USA from its earliest days.

Where religion counts, it can inspire political action, but it can also be used to legitimize political interests. An example of this was to be found in the process by which in South Africa traditional racial discrimination was transformed into apartheid, the legal separation of the races. In the 1940s Afrikaner leaders, such as H. F. Verwoerd, B. J. Vorster and Piet Myer, specifically allied Afrikaner nationalism in South Africa with National Socialism in Germany, seeing the Afrikaners as part of the Aryan race. However, it was as Christians, members of the Dutch Reformed Church, that they attributed the separation of the races and the dominance of the white race to God's great plan for the world.

Vatican
p. 302
Dutch Reformed Church

It was no accident that D. F. Malan, who is credited with being the founder of apartheid as a political programme, as a young man studied theology first at Stellenbosch and then at Utrecht. His presentation of the case for apartheid represented the 'theologizing of politics'. It was not that the Dutch Reformed Church was the National Party at prayer. The National Party itself was becoming a church, speaking the language of religion, mission and the necessity of saving the world. Apartheid was not just a policy. According to D. F. Malan, 'Afrikanerdom is not the work of man but the creation of God.' He added that 'our history is the highest work of art of the Architect of the centuries' (*Pro Veritate*, 1971) Nicolaas Diederichs saw apartheid as the task and responsibility that God had laid upon his (white) nation. Theologians of the Dutch Reformed Church followed on with biblical justifications of the policy. In this they provided a religious legitimation of politics. However, the real religious legitimation of politics was carried out by the politicians themselves, acting as 'believers' in apartheid as a divine order. The 'Milanazis' not only theologized politics, but Christianized National Socialism.

The interaction of politics and religion today is seldom a matter of church and state. It is more often a case of Christians, individually or as groups, allying themselves with a cause which has been raised by secular groups and parties: the women's movement, gay and lesbian rights, international debt cancellation, ecology, racial discrimination, fair trade. This fragmentation is to be expected in a postmodern culture: Christian values are no longer part of a social consensus. There is, however, a notable exception. The Christian concept of reconciliation has been accepted pragmatically as the basis for long-term healing in divided societies: El Salvador, South Africa, Bosnia, Northern Ireland. When Christians enter politics they have a long and rich tradition upon which to draw, but their influence lies not in the authority of that tradition but on the efficacy of the programmes and solutions they propose.

Protestantism
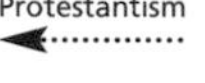

ALISTAIR KEE

Paul Gifford, *Christianity and Politics in Doe's Liberia*, Cambridge: CUP 1993; Michael Lienesch, *Redeeming*

America: Piety and Politics in the New Christian Right, Durham, NC: University of North Carolina Press 1993; Graham Ward, *Cities of God*, London: Routledge 2000

Postmodern theology

A variety of theologies are on offer today; not all of them can be called 'postmodern'. 'Postmodern theology', then, is not synonymous with 'contemporary theology'. Postmodern theology is theology being undertaken and composed with reference to both 'postmodernity' and 'postmodernism'.

Most sociologists use the term postmodernity to describe a certain period in Western history. This is frequently documented as beginning in the mid-1970s, though some relate it more specifically to the student uprisings in the late 1960s. Certainly, by the mid-1970s the economic situation in the West was changing because of factors such as the oil crisis, the detachment of the American dollar from the gold standard and new forms of banking and financial services. This makes it sound as though postmodernity was the product of economic transformation, and some Marxist interpretations of postmodernity (such as David Harvey's) would associate it with post-industrialism and the rise of consumerism.

But whatever the nature of the historical changes, postmodernity describes the emergence of certain cultural values and phenomena that become dominant from the 1970s onwards. These values and phenomena were not only seen to differ from the values and phenomena that defined modernity but were critical of the cultural ethos of modernity. Architecture is a case in point, because it is frequently pointed to as an indicator of cultural change. In the 1970s Robert Venturi saw a new trend in architectural design. Modernism had been characterized by the geometric cubes and oblongs of Bauhaus, Mies van de Rohr and Le Corbusier. With their use of glass and steel they aimed at a transparency of design, giving form to light and space as such, rendering concrete certain transcendental or utopian ideals. But Venturi saw in the buildings along the Strip at Las Vegas a new set of aesthetic values that prized the superficial and the kitsch. These buildings were expensive air-conditioned façades backing on to the Nevada desert; they were like film sets: fabulous and ephemeral.

Postmodernity in distinction to modernity values irony above reason, paradox and sharp juxtaposition above light and logic, ambivalence above certainty, the hybrid above the purified, the fragment above the completed, surface rather than profundities, monism rather than dualism. As such, postmodernity both resonated with and produced social and cultural theories that drew upon the monistic philosophy of Benedict de Spinoza (1632–77), the nihilism of Friedrich Nietzsche (1844–1900), language as a semiotic system in Ferdinand de Saussure (1857–1913), and the different forms of non-foundationalism in Ludwig Wittgenstein (1889–1951) and Martin Heidegger (1889–1976). Postmodernism is the term used for this theorizing and thinking that seeks to counter and render problematic the philosophical and metaphysical trends of Enlightenment figures such as John Locke and Immanuel Kant and the romantic reasoning of G. W. F. Hegel and hermeneutics.

On the whole, postmodern theology has been Christian in either its character or its ethos, though there have been significant Jewish and Buddhist postmodern theologies. Postmodern theology responds to both postmodernity and postmodernism. In fact, it not only responds to them but also is in tune with them. For a number of cultural analysts have drawn attention to the 're-enchantment' of reality that postmodernity fosters. Since the mid-1990s increasing use has been made of the term 'post-secular' to describe postmodern culture. No theological thinking takes place in a vacuum. All thinking is historically and culturally embedded; it draws upon, reproduces and modifies what is available in any given context. Of course, theology has its traditions, its teachings, its sacred texts, its liturgies. But in postmodern theology all these are rethought in response to the culture of postmodernity or to the body of theory resonating and issuing from that culture. Here it has to be noted that social scientists and sociologists of religion have seen the various forms of fundamentalism – most particularly Christian, Jewish and Islamic – and the appeal of fundamentalism globally as phenomena not unrelated to postmodernity. The theologies produced by such fundamentalisms are not postmodern, but might be understood as counter-cultural moves against the rampant pluralisms, hybridities, potential nihilisms and superficialities of postmodernity.

Postmodern theology itself seems to have taken two main directions. A number of highly individual figures are doing distinctive work between them: they include feminist postmodern theologians such as Grace Jantzen, Mary McClintock Fulkerson and Sharon Welch.

The first direction is the continuation of liberal theology developed, according to Karl Barth, from Friedrich Schleiermacher and G. W. F. Hegel onwards. In the twentieth century this theology focused on the work of Paul Tillich and the demythologizing of scripture undertaken by Rudolf Bultmann. Its postmodern form began in the 1960s with the death-of-God theologians such as Thomas Altizer and William Hamilton, who took their bearings from the Christian doctrine of kenosis and the death of God as it was proclaimed first by Hegel

Enlightenment ➤

Fundamentalism ➤

Christology ➤

(referring to the kenosis, or self-emptying of God in Jesus Christ) and later by Nietzsche. Altizer, in particular, drew a number of figures around him who began to call themselves postmodern theologians and who were explicitly developing postmodern theorizing into Christian theology – often becoming post-Christian in the process. Mark C. Taylor and John D. Caputo were developing the ideas of the French thinker Jacques Derrida; Charles Winquist worked productively with both Derrida and Jacques Lacan; Edith Wyschogrod engaged the thought of Emmanuel Levinas. Theology began to appear in the wake of Gilles Deleuze and Michel Foucault. Insights from these thinkers were used in developing what Taylor called a/theologies and have more recently been called 'secular' theologies.

These self-named postmodern theologies share certain characteristics. First, while Christianity remains their loose frame of reference, they are post-Christian in their sentiments. That is, the Christian faith offers metaphors for certain kinds of religious experience. These experiences are not positive encounters with the presence of God (as can be found in William James's *Varieties of Religious Experience*); they are negative experiences of aporia or the unpresentable. Furthermore, they do not concern themselves with communities or practices of the Christian faith. The pieties they sketch are intellectual, individual and existential. They are theologies of the academy, not theologies of the church. Secondly, they are nominalist in their orientation. That is, they focus on representation, on writing, on aesthetic forms in order to point to an absence or silence that fissures while remaining the condition for the possibility of that representation, writing or aesthetic form. They work, then, with the dualism of representation and the ineffable. Thirdly, these theologies – like the existential theologies of Tillich and Bultmann that drew upon the early work of Heidegger – tend to be uncritical of their postmodern philosophical foundations. They work within the framework of ideas presented by Derrida, say, or Lacan or Levinas, and the framework is not challenged. The 'theology' is an outworking or the product of the governing ideas.

The second direction postmodern theology has taken has been in terms of defining a contemporary orthodoxy for those who practise a faith, whether Christian or Jewish. These theologies situate themselves with respect to the tradition and engage critically with both postmodernity and postmodernism without becoming simply countercultural. They may employ some insights from postmodern thinkers, but criticize the nihilistic trajectories or the perceived ethical and political inadequacies of such thinking. They are not just theologies of the academy, since they concern themselves with not only the teachings of the faith but its implications for the church or the reading of a sacred text. Frequently, they deepen and develop the postmodern criticism of modernity. Some might say they develop an account of modernity that they characterize as antithetical to theology because of its secular modes of thinking, its perpetuation of a number of dualisms, its monistic or empirically reductive philosophies. These theologies then attempt to retrieve some of the tradition to which modernity gave so little heed. A Roman Catholic theologian such as Jean-Luc Marion, for example, will critically engage with Heidegger, Derrida and Levinas while simultaneously developing a theology with reference to Pseudo-Dionysius and Thomas Aquinas. Anglo-Catholic theologians, such as several who work under the aegis of radical orthodoxy, point to worrying trends in postmodern thinking (its gnosticism, its aestheticization of politics, its underlying nihilism) while creating contemporary theologies on the basis of Augustine or the Cappodocian fathers.

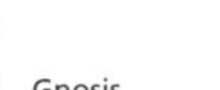

Gnosis
Church fathers

These postmodern theologies also share certain characteristics. First, they are conceived within the framework of a faith they seek to explicate. As such they view themselves as continuing the tradition by engaging it with the contemporary *Zeitgeist*. They think on the basis of the credal grammar and liturgical offices of Christianity (Jean-Luc Marion, John Milbank, Catherine Pickstock, Graham Ward) or Judaism (Robert Gibbs, Elliot R. Wolfson, Peter Ochs). Secondly, while philosophical in their orientation, they frequently appeal to the foundational documents of the scriptures. Thirdly (and this is particularly so in those who write from the Christian perspective), they reject nominalism and dualism, in an emphasis upon incarnationalism. They are realist theologies. That is, they foster an understanding of the sacramental and non-reductive view of the world, a world that participates in the operations of the divine because it is maintained in its being by the divine. As such, it is not absence they extol but sacramental presence.

GRAHAM WARD

📖 Fredric Jameson, *Postmodernism or The Cultural Logic of Late Capitalism*, London: Verso 1991 and *The Cultural Turn: Selected Writings on the Postmodern, 1983–1998*, London: Verso 1998; Jean-François Lyotard, *The Postmodern Condition: A Report on Knowledge*, Manchester: University of Manchester Press 1984; Graham Ward, *The Blackwell Companion to Postmodern Theology*, Oxford: Blackwell 2001

Poverty

The Bible talks about poverty almost as much as it talks about sin, and one serious sin is to mistreat the poor. The

Bible
Sin

Old Testament writers rarely, if ever, criticize the poor, but regard them with sympathy. Their poverty is mainly material: they are often referred to as 'the poor and needy'. They lack food and shelter and what today we might call secure livelihoods. Not only are the writers of the Psalms Old Testament on their side; so is God. Psalm 72, which celebrates the accession of a new king, prays that God will judge the poor with justice, defend the cause of the poor and give deliverance to the needy.

There are frequent references to God's concern for the poor and God's determination to rescue them out of their humiliation, though sometimes, in the Psalms for example, the poor can sound impatient at the apparent delay.

But poverty can be a consequence of sinful behaviour, as Job's friends point out, either of the poor themselves, as in Job's case, or because of the wickedness of others. Prophecy When castigating Israel and Judah, prophets such as Amos and Jeremiah never tire of stressing that if God's people oppress the poor, punishment will follow. Judgement will come upon those who sell the needy for a pair of shoes and trample the poor into the dust of the earth (Amos 2.6–7).

The Old Testament makes no positive case for poverty, while wealth is unashamedly regarded as a good thing and a blessing from God. The wealthy are not called to give up their wealth, but to treat the poor and especially their own kith and kin with kindness and justice by not robbing them, for example of their meagre earnings or the left-overs or gleanings from the harvest. Attempts were even made in Old Testament times (Leviticus 25) to build anti-poverty measures into the social system so that every 50 years, at the time of Jubilee, the poor were to be given back their freedom (if they had fallen into slavery) and their land (if it had been sold to pay their debts) and their debts were to be cancelled.

Some of these themes can be found in the New Mary Testament. Mary's Magnificat (Luke 1.46–55) echoes Hannah's song (in 1 Samuel 2) and reflects the continuing hopes of the poor in God's promise to reverse their Jesus fortune. Jesus' inaugural sermon in Nazareth (Luke 4.18f.) is almost entirely focused on bringing good news to the poor and can be understood as referring back to the old Kingdom of God practices of the Jubilee as if, in God's kingdom now at Religious orders hand, they are about to become a permanent reality. Jesus seems to confirm God's special concern for poor and Paul socially marginalized people. One of Paul's main concerns  was to make a collection for the poor of the Jerusalem church (2 Corinthians 9), so continuing the long-established traditions of caring for them, and Stephen and six others are responsible in the Jerusalem church for the welfare of widows, along with orphans and the poor (Acts 6.1–6). Those who fail to care for the poor will, as of old, reap the consequences (Luke 16.19–31).

However, the New Testament strikes one or two different notes. First, it is much more cautious in its attitude to wealth. Wealth can preoccupy us far too much and replace God in our affections. We cannot serve both. Secondly, material poverty is not simply justified in certain circumstances but actively advocated. Voluntary poverty, chosen not imposed, is a way of discipleship following the example of Jesus himself. He had no place of his own to lay his head during his ministry, but that for him was probably a matter of choice. Contrary to the impression given by some Christmas story-telling, he may not have come from the poorest of families, but during his ministry he sat light to material possessions and, to put it in the grander and more theological terms of Paul (2 Corinthians 8.9), 'though rich for our sakes became poor'. Rich people are certainly not beyond his or God's caring love and they are not denied the possibility of salvation, but being saved is very difficult for them (Luke 18.25) and they are called to give away their riches to follow Jesus. Thirdly, although the idea is not entirely absent from the Old Testament, the New Testament speaks not only of material poverty but of spiritual poverty or 'the poor in spirit', who perhaps are more accurately described as spiritually rich! Rich or poor in material goods, they are humble before God.

These biblical themes of wealth, material and spiritual poverty, and the personal and social responses to them, more or less set the agenda for all the debates that have followed.

Wealth soon became an issue, even in the early church. If Christianity began among poor people like those who sang the Magnificat with Hannah and Mary, and among communities of which not many were powerful (1 Corinthians 1.26), rich people were associated with the church from the beginning and they rapidly grew in number. But from an equally early date there are signs of unease. At the turn of the third century, Clement of Alexandria addressed the question, 'Can the rich man be saved?' He concluded that though salvation was hard to achieve, the rich should not be discouraged from seeking it, and that a rich man's attitude to his riches, not the riches themselves, was crucial. The monastic movement, dating from much the same time, was not so sure and exchanged a worldly life for the desert and the austere disciplines of poverty, chastity and obedience. As the religious orders themselves amassed great wealth, a further protest came from Francis of Assisi in the thirteenth century with his followers and their sisters, the Poor Clares. Francis literally gave away everything he had – and he had a great deal to give away. Radical renunciation like his is still practised. More widespread, however, especially among better-off Christians, is the practice of tithing (giving back to God a tenth of one's income) and of stewardship; in other words, using money well rather than giving it up.

Material poverty has not been universally opposed by Christians. Some, both poor and rich, have been fatalistic about it. It is the way of the world. They have generalized Jesus' saying, 'You always have the poor with you' (Mark 14.7), totally disregarding its context, which is that of an extraordinary act of generosity towards Jesus' person. Some poor people have comforted themselves or been comforted by their spiritual, sometimes more prosperous, leaders and guides with the thought that their turn will come and they will have riches in heaven. A vivid, colourful and emotional liturgical life can meanwhile compensate for the drabness of poverty. The novels of Charles Dickens reveal the harsh attitudes of the 'Hard Times' when poor people were barely distinguished from criminals, few were regarded as 'deserving', and the poor laws made sure that when parish councils and the authorities of the day made provision for the poor it would be of a kind that would encourage no one to lean on their charity too often. Christians, among others, can still be found who regard the poor unemployed, or people on social security benefits, or the poor of the so-called Third World as largely to blame for the state that they are in.

In modern times Western Christianity has been perceived as the religion of rich and powerful people, many of whom have seen no need to apologize for their good fortune. Indeed wealth has been accepted as the due reward of a Christian way of life, whether characterized by hard work (sometimes known as the Protestant work ethic), or frugal spending and careful saving (commended, for example, by John Wesley), or by the belief expounded in the Prosperity Gospel, namely that faith in Christ will bring material blessings to rich and poor alike.

Perhaps Western culture has lost the knack of being challenged by prophetic teaching about riches and poverty, Western Christianity in particular because of an excessive individualism that fails to take seriously the social implications of Christian faith or even to see that aspect when reading the Bible.

Karl Marx was dismissed by many as an anti-Christian atheist, but he had a good deal of Jewish prophetic blood in him. He gave good reason to be suspicious of all attempts to justify material poverty or encourage the poor to acquiesce in it. Such ideas tell us more, he suggested, about the interests of the rich than the nature of poverty. What look like vaguely moral and spiritual arguments in its favour are spurious attempts to maintain a status quo that benefits the rich and powerful people who put these arguments forward.

A similar critique, partly inspired by Marx but fuelled by the enormous scale of poverty, especially in the Third World, and its persistence, not to say intensification, has come from some Latin American and other churches of the South in the form of liberation theology. These churches became wary of a gospel that focused on personal sin and private spiritual problems and neglected to tackle social issues. For the liberation theologians, poverty was not the fault of the poor and it did not have to be tolerated. Its causes could easily be demystified. People were made poor and kept poor largely through no fault of their own (just as many were rich through no virtue of their own). Natural disasters and misfortunes played their part. The main culprits, however, were the political and economic systems that had been constructed by human hands and were now maintained to benefit the rich and powerful who presided over them. They are man-made disasters, bringing in their wake not only riches for a few and poverty for many, but conflict and environmental damage that in the end are a threat to everyone. The only solution was to change them and so free or 'liberate' poor people from the exploitation, oppression and humiliation of which these systems were the instrument. The talk often echoed the inspiring stories of the Israelites' exodus from Egypt. It was not surprising that many Christians, used to the idea that their faith was a private matter between themselves and God which had little or nothing to do with politics, found such ideas revolutionary and alarming.

Third World

Maybe the one thing that does become clear in the course of this long debate about the merits or demerits of wealth and the justifiable or unacceptable nature of poverty is that a yawning gap between the haves and have-nots, rather than an equitable distribution of what Christians believe God has given all to share and enjoy, is indefensible if God is believed to be a God of love and justice.

Modern responses to poverty in some ways run parallel to the earlier biblical responses. Like them they can be both personal and social. On the personal and individual level the Bible calls for simple kindness and generosity towards the poor. They are to be fed and cared for. Collections are to be taken for them. Charitable giving, which can be condescending but also warm-hearted, is the obvious modern counterpart. It may be direct to beggars on the streets or through the poor funds of the churches or through charities that try to channel donations in a more professional way. Some, such as the Salvation Army, focus their attention on needy people close to home; others, such as Christian Aid and Tearfund from the UK, Caritas from Europe, and Bread for the World and the Church World Service in the United States, focus attention on poverty overseas, offering among other things immediate relief to famine victims and refugees. There are similar church relief agencies in many countries.

Critics of Christianity

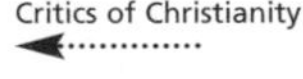

Christians normally give to charities out of what is surplus to their own requirements. When they begin to dig deeper into their pockets it can affect their lifestyles, as those who gave up everything to follow Jesus found

Liberation theology

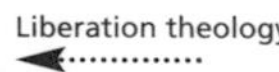

CHRISTIAN SERVICE AGENCIES

Helping the poor and needy has always been a priority for Christians. Since the Second World War in particular, the need for aid on a worldwide scale has been massive, and Christian service agencies have made a major contribution towards providing aid, education and skills for development. Here are just some of them, from the United States and Britain; there are of course countless others in other countries. There is also widespread Christian concern and action over the HIV/AIDS pandemic.

Bread for the World: Founded in 1974 by Arthur Simon, Bread for the World is a US national Christian movement seeking justice for the world's hungry people by lobbying the nation's decision-makers. Its institute seeks justice for hungry people by engaging in research and education on policies related to hunger and development.

www.bread.org

Caritas Internationalis: Founded in Germany in 1897 by Lorenz Werthmann, Caritas Internationalis it is the official Roman Catholic welfare and aid organization, with branches in many countries around the world.

www.caritas.org

CAFOD (Catholic Association for Overseas Development): Founded in 1962, CAFOD is a British charity which fights Third World poverty. It is the English and Welsh arm of Caritas Internationalis.

www.cafood.org.uk

Catholic Relief Services: Founded in 1943 by the Roman Catholic bishops of the United States to assist the poor and disadvantaged outside the country, Catholic Relief Services provides direct aid to the poor, involving people in their own development and helping them to realize their potential. It also educates the people of the United States to fulfil their moral responsibilities towards their brothers and sisters around the world by helping the poor, working to remove the causes of poverty, and promoting social justice.

www.catholicrelief.org

Christian Aid: Starting in 1945 as Christian Reconciliation in Europe to respond to the needs of refugees and churches in Europe in the aftermath of the Second World War, in 1949 it became an integral part of the British Council of Churches, involved with world refugee settlement and justice issues. Christian Aid took its present name in 1964. It is an ecumenical organization working on long-term development projects where the need is greatest, co-operating with people and communities regardless of race or creed, in over 60 of the world's poorest countries.

www.christian-aid.org.uk

Church World Service: Founded in 1946, Church World Service is the relief, development and refugee assistance ministry of 36 Protestant, Orthodox and Anglican denominations in the United States. Working in partnership with indigenous organizations in more than 80 countries, it is active worldwide in meeting human needs and fostering self-reliance for all whose way is hard.

www.churchworldservices.prg

Lutheran World Federation, Department for World Service: This is the largest department in the Federation and operates programmes throughout the world. It includes a large Community Development Service with many projects. Lutheran World Relief is a related US-based agency.

www.lutheranworld.org; www.lwr.org

Tearfund: Founded in the 1960s, Tearfund is an evangelical Christian relief and development charity working through local partners to bring help and hope to communities in need around the world. At present it is operating in over 80 countries.

www.tearfund.org

UMCOR (United Methodist Committee on Relief): Founded in 1940, UMCOR is the not-for-profit humanitarian agency of the United Methodist Church. It provides relief in disaster areas, aids refugees and confronts the challenge of world hunger and poverty, working in nearly 100 countries.

www. gbgm-umc.org/umcor

World Vision International: Established in 1950 to care for orphans in Asia, World Vision is an international evangelical Christian relief and development organization working to promote the well-being of all people, especially children. It is active in 99 countries.

www.wvi.org

it affected theirs. There are several reasons for this more radical response. Voluntary poverty can be embraced so that the poor can benefit directly; or as an act of solidarity with the poor; or to be free from an over-preoccupation with wealth; or, as in recent years, to reduce consumption and make sure that resources are more fairly shared out and the earth itself is not exhausted: 'live simply that others may simply live'.

Charitable giving and a sacrificial lifestyle both have their merits, but both run the risk of evading any fundamental change to the structures that make and keep people poor. The hungry are fed out of charitable donations when what they really need is the chance to feed themselves. Some may give away almost everything, but realism suggests that very few other Christians will do the same, and a readiness to have less will have little effect, given the scale of the problem. Here as elsewhere, Christian responses can come close to empty gestures that have more to do with sentiment than intelligent love. However, that is not necessarily the case.

The biblical writers, especially in the Old Testament, looked for a social or structural response to poverty as well as a more personal or individual one. The Jubilee is a social mechanism for reversing the relentless drift of resources from poor to rich. Prophets such as Amos and Isaiah demand fair trading practices. The ideology of the kingship expressed in the Psalms calls for good governance. A whole variety of 'social' responses aimed at fundamental change in favour of justice and the poor have been advocated and supported by Christians in the second half of the twentieth century and the early years of the twenty-first. Here are four. It may be wise not to see them as mutually exclusive.

1. Christians are to work for worldwide economic growth and wealth creation so that there is more than enough for everyone. Some rich people may grow even richer in the process but 'all the boats will rise' and even the poorest will benefit. The means by which growth will be brought about is the free-market, capitalist system and the aim is to make it work everywhere and for everyone, in Africa for example as well as in Europe and North America. This is a central feature of the phenomenon called 'globalization'. This response has many resonances with Christianity. It takes a positive view of 'God-given' wealth. It seeks to eradicate poverty and does not put all the blame for it on the poor. And it has deep roots in a Western tradition where the ethical teachings of reformers such as John Calvin, who saw daily work as a vocation and hard work and financial prudence as Christian virtues, and where the church's change of mind about usury (or loans with interest, see Exodus 22.25 and Deuteronomy 23.19f.) are thought to have provided fertile soil for the growth of capitalism.

2. The distribution or the redistribution of wealth is more important than simply creating more of it. Opportunities for poorer people to create some wealth for themselves must be distributed more evenly. One strategy is to look for modern counterparts to the biblical Jubilee mechanisms for redistribution in which all debts were forgiven every 50 years (Leviticus 25), such as cancelling the debts of the poorest countries, and imposing taxes on the speculative movement of capital or on environmentally damaging international air flights, and using it for poverty reduction and human development. Fairer trading systems are also proposed where smaller producers and smaller countries as well as large international companies can find markets to sell their goods at reasonable prices. Credit unions at home and abroad providing loans at low rates of interest redistribute opportunities for investment to poor people who otherwise would never get a mortgage or a bank loan. Higher levels of official government aid from rich countries to poor can also be seen as redistributive. By supporting these and other measures, Christians fulfil the biblical injunction to share what we have and to seek God's justice or righteousness rather than to allow relatively few to win all the prizes.

3. What might be called 'Christian realism' recognizes that most people most of the time, Christians included, tend to act in their own self-interest. This means that rich people are not likely to make decisions in favour of poor people if those decisions have an adverse effect on themselves. Rich nations are even less likely to do so. Ways have to be found, therefore, by which the poor do not have to wait for the goodwill of the rich to do something for them, but increasingly have the power and ability to act in their own self-interest. This is another way of seeking God's justice, taking full account of the darker or 'sinful', egotistic side of human nature. It is not at all easy, since attempts at training, education, capacity building, giving people a greater say in their own affairs, encouraging participation, political and economic empowerment, can all involve those who already have the capacity and the power of giving something of themselves away. Empowering the powerless is hard to achieve without the co-operation of the powerful! However, human nature does have a creative and generous side to it, and for poor people and poor communities and nations to be in solidarity with one another is a crucial way of increasing their strength and lessening their dependence.

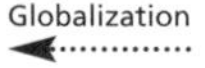

4. All of these responses may seem too like the response of a Christianity that has compromised too much with the ways of the world. Some radical alternatives, even if they are only islands of resistance in a great sea, are surely needed as an antidote, turning our present world upside down. As a result efforts are made, for example, to create communities built on a different set of values from those

of the competitive and materialistic market place, emphasizing a more co-operative spirit and a more holistic vision of wealth that involves the flourishing of relationships and of cultural and spiritual as well as economic life.

These four responses to poverty indicate that the more personal responses of 'charity' and 'lifestyle' and action to eradicate the roots of poverty can go together. And there are possibilities open to Christians living in twenty-first-century democracies that were not open to the early Christians.

Attitudes to poverty and wealth are also influenced by the circumstances of those advancing a particular opinion or biblical interpretation. This is sometimes called 'hermeneutical suspicion'. People's poverty or wealth are bound to govern their sympathies and colour their views. Who, for example, says that the Bible is really interested in 'spiritual poverty'; and who says that it would be better if those at present in charge were replaced by the humble poor?

Christianity has an ambiguous record with respect to the poor. Morally speaking, it has found reason to be their champion, but it has also been very hard on them indeed. It has raised them up (as when for example evangelical Christians fought hard for the abolition of slavery) and trampled them under foot (reducing some indigenous peoples, for example, from sustainable livelihoods to abject misery). It has often proclaimed good news to the poor and been confident that justice will be done and a sinful, unjust world be put to rights. But its achievements have hardly come up to its self-confessed expectations. The ability of Christianity to overcome poverty is debatable. The claim of the poor on those who follow Christ is beyond question.

MICHAEL H. TAYLOR

📖 Ronald J. Sider, *Rich Christians in an Age of Hunger*, London: Hodder and Dallas: Word 1978; Charles Dickens, *Hard Times*, first published London 1854; Gustavo Gutiérrez, *A Theology of Liberation* (1974), Maryknoll, NY: Orbis and London: SCM Press ²1988; Michael Taylor, *Poverty and Christianity*, London: SCM Press 2000 and *Christianity, Poverty and Wealth*, London: SPCK and Cleveland, OH: Pilgrim Press 2003

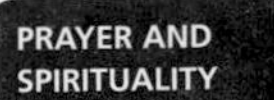

PRAYER AND SPIRITUALITY

Art and spirituality, Christian life, Devotions, Eucharist, Festivals and fasts, Forgiveness, Monasticism, Mysticism, Pietism, Prayer, Spirituality, Worship

Of these two terms, prayer, though hugely significant in the Christian life, has a narrower range than spirituality. Prayer is the more ancient, known in English since 1300 as 'a solemn and humble request to God, a supplication, petition or thanksgiving usually in words'. It is a more closely-defined term and more widely understood, though not necessarily more widely practised. It is generally understood to include both the saying of prayers in church or at home, with the Lord's Prayer as its most basic form, and as an attitude of body and soul in which Christians present their most holy thoughts before God in adoration and ask for God's help. p. 967

The picture of Jesus praying is vivid in many minds from childhood, solitary, high up on the mountain and with arms outstretched. That was certainly part of his way of saying prayers, but he was also involved in the synagogue prayers, chanted and, as the Psalmist says, ascending to God like incense. Prayers of intercession, or asking God for things, initiate deep discussion and open up large areas of difficult theology, but for many these are the most natural prayer of all, and certainly the most immediate. Such prayers are also encouraged in the Gospel of John: 'God will grant you whatever you ask of him' (11.22), and more circumspectly in the first letter of John: 'if we make requests which accord with his will, he listens to us' (5.14). Jesus

However, as T. S. Eliot wrote in *Four Quartets*, 'prayer is more than an order of words, the conscious occupation of the praying mind, or the sound of the voice praying'; it is something which engages the heart, and thus the whole of one's being. Without that close and deep relationship with God, the Christian commitment becomes an empty one. Prayer fuels the engine of the Christian life, and therefore it becomes a matter of constantly renewing this source by a conscious turning to God. God is understood to be the greatest help in this relationship of prayer, and to assume that it is a one-sided affair is to be blind to its only real source. So, waiting on God with an attentive stillness, 'be still and know that I am God' (Psalm 46.10), is an essential part of maturity in the life of prayer.

This opening up of the whole area of listening to God, as in meditation and contemplation, has meant that the definition of prayer has lost its clarity and begins to impinge on studies of prayer of a whole realm of religious experience. Prayer can no longer be simply classified as something in a book that is said; it becomes a way of living, an orientation in the style of relating to God. When this widening of the field of the ways in which people are understood to communicate with God coincided with the 'Enlightenment' desire to categorize knowledge in an objective manner, then the science of prayer, so called, needed a new word. That word is 'spirituality'. Enlightenment

Spirituality has no fixed definition. It embraces the widest of activities and sensibilities, ways of prayer, and writings on the 'spiritual life'. Contemporary books on spirituality usually begin by making this point. In the latter part of the nineteenth century, and in the early twentieth century, writers on spirituality, most of whom were French authors, were quite bold in their definitions. For example: 'Spirituality is that part of theology which deals with Christian perfection and the ways that lead to it.' It was seen to be separate from, though dependent on, dogmatic and moral theologies, and was itself divided into ascetic theology and mystical theology. The monumental

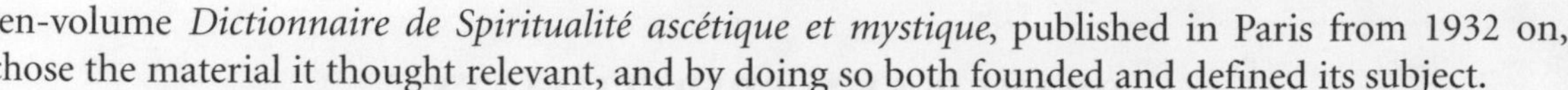

ten-volume *Dictionnaire de Spiritualité ascétique et mystique*, published in Paris from 1932 on, chose the material it thought relevant, and by doing so both founded and defined its subject.

Music
Poetry
Art and spirituality
New Age movement

Spirituality continues to draw to itself kindred disciplines and activities such as music, poetry and the arts in general. It is also felt to be home to ecologists and those who care for the natural world, and for the new science at the point where the known facts dissolve into mystery. New Age books on spirituality deal with a wide range of religions and experiences from Shamanism to psychedelic drugs, and from personal growth to mystical union. Interest in 'spirituality', so defined, has grown rapidly in the last half of the twentieth century. Popular authors such as Aldous Huxley, and the Trappist monk, Thomas Merton; the music of the Beatles; contemplative religious traditions such as Buddhism and Sufism; and the rediscovery of the body as a part of spiritual wholeness have helped to make the subject extremely accessible and popular. Spirituality is understood to have broad and flexible boundaries, and to welcome new connections and discoveries.

Prayer would now most naturally come under the umbrella of 'spirituality' in the minds and lists of libraries, booksellers and teaching courses. However much Christian spirituality stands above the mundane matters of history, it is rarely dealt with as a subject except in its historical progression. This is paradoxical, because the spirit of religion somehow defies traditional time sequences. This paradox has been most tellingly worked on in Eliot's *Four Quartets*, which provides as sympathetic a description of what we have come to understand as 'spirituality' as any guide or history could do. Eliot weaves the historical and the eternal viewpoints powerfully, and calls on potent images to cast their particular spell. However, the history of the ways that traditions have influenced each other is both fascinating and ongoing.

Monasticism

Today, in the church, spirituality poses problems of definition, causing it to be separated from all that it could best influence and regenerate. So, administration and structures, legal and financial matters, ethics and doctrine, everything that comes broadly under the title of mission, and the general ethos of church life, seem to have little to do with spirituality. In the light of this the Benedictine tradition has brought great insights and provides a bridge between the apparently mundane matters of routine work and the mystical flights of the alone to the alone. The Rule of Benedict grounds spirituality in a balanced life of prayer, study and manual work, is attractive by its attention to the rhythms of Christian life, and through it many are finding a sane space to assess the range of 'spiritualities' that are now on offer. The language of the supermarket is not inappropriate for the perceived nature of contemporary 'spirituality', and many are wary of it because of that. Because 'spirituality' is developing so fast and attracts the interest of so many, the challenge is to find rootedness in God and to discern truth and value from that point.

DAVID SCOTT

Prayer

A definition

God

One starting definition for prayer is 'communicating with God'. At the simplest level of popular understanding, prayers are said to God. God is generally understood to be beyond us, waiting to receive our prayers. As a rule the child, the untutored, and the simple unreflecting mind, seek God above, not within. Prayers are sent up to God, and God is understood to receive them. Prayer is often just felt to be the right thing to do. That instinctive trust has come largely from a tradition of prayer communicated in a very early stage of life. This childlike, primitive sense of the rightness of prayer presupposes a belief in God, but not one which is necessarily worked out intellectually. Often, this belief is a simple intimation of the presence of God. It is unclear exactly what God is like. Trust is put in God, and prayer becomes the language of that trust.

The seventeenth-century Anglican devotional writer Jeremy Taylor wrote that prayer is 'an ascent of the mind to God'. All forms of such ascent – adoration, confession, thanksgiving, and supplication (the acronym ACTS is a well-known *aide-memoire*) – can be included in the umbrella word 'prayer'. Prayer is, in general, the communion of the human soul with God. A century earlier Taylor's fellow Anglican George Herbert, in his poem 'Prayer', describes prayer in many ways and concludes with the phrase, 'something understood'.

Spoken prayers to God have been handed down through generations of believers, and it is in such a way that the Lord's Prayer, the basic Christian prayer, has been transmitted. The tradition of prayer, though, stretches much further back than the Gospels. The Hebrew Bible, the Christian Old Testament, has many examples of prayers.

The Old Testament and prayer

Prayer to God in its pre-Christian form reaches its greatest heights in the Old Testament. All the forms in which humans can address and converse with God are found there in abundance, striking and profound. The principal elements which distinguish prayers of the Old Testament are a vivid sense of God as a living, personal presence and one with supreme power and an unfailing comprehension of God's holiness, which involves the conviction that it is only through moral goodness that human beings can become acceptable. An excellent example of this is in Psalm 139, 'O Lord, you have searched me out and known me; you know my sitting down and my rising up; you discern my thoughts from afar.'

The story goes that when Moses was leading the Israelites through the desert they became recalcitrant, disobeying the will and laws of God. Moses knew that the Lord was becoming impatient with the people of Israel. So Moses prayed: 'Lord, long-suffering, ever faithful, who forgives iniquity and rebellion ... You have borne with this people from Egypt all the way here; forgive their iniquity, I beseech you, as befits your great and constant love.' The Lord said, 'Your prayer is answered and I pardon them' (Numbers 14.18–20).

When Daniel was in exile among the Chaldeans he wrote: 'I, Daniel, was reading the scriptures and reflecting on the seventy years which, according to the word of the Lord to the prophet Jeremiah, were to pass while Jerusalem lay in ruins. Then I turned to the Lord God in earnest prayer and supplication with fasting and with sackcloth and ashes. I prayed and made this confession to the Lord my God.' A long prayer follows in which Daniel, on behalf of his exiled people, prays for forgiveness for the wrongs that he and his people have committed. The prayer concludes: 'Lord, hear; Lord, forgive; Lord, listen and act; God, for your own sake do not delay, because your city and your people bear your name' (Daniel 9.19). It is a classic example of faithful address to God. God is believed to have the power to change individual souls and even political situations. It is also interesting to note that the prayer arose from meditation on the scriptures of Daniel's own day, the writings of Jeremiah.

After the capture of Jerusalem, Jeremiah himself was requested by the armed forces to pray to God. He answered: 'I have heard your request. I shall pray to the Lord your God as you ask, and whatever answer the Lord gives, I shall tell you, keeping nothing back' (Jeremiah 42.4f.).

The literary form of these descriptions of prayer is of great interest. Prayer often takes place in the privacy of a room, or when individuals are on their own. The author of the Book of Numbers writes as if what Moses said in secret to God is clearly known. In this case, a prayer is followed by a response, and so the writer is also describing a conversation. God is not giving comfortable answers to Moses. God is forthright and judgemental in his response. There Bible is a sense in this apparently straightforward description of an act of prayer that more, in the literary sense, is going on. The literary form of prayer is being used as a means of communicating a nation's understanding of the way God works. There is more than simple devotion here. This is theology couched in the form of prayer. The threads of original prayer and literary editing are not easy to disentangle. Such a process of editing, though, has gone on, and books of prayers from the Old and New Testaments have provided a fundamental source for the prayer books of the church, and for the praying experience of individuals.

Psalms could be called the prayer book of the Old Psalms Testament: 'O God, you are my God; eagerly I seek you; my soul is athirst for you' (63.1); 'Like as the deer longs for the water-brooks, so longs my soul for you, O God' (42.1); 'My God, my God, why have you forsaken me and are so far from my salvation, from the words of my distress?' (22.1). The outpouring of praise from joyful hearts at the rebuilding of the Jerusalem temple provided the occasion for the prayers we find in Psalms 95–100: 'O come let us sing to the Lord' (95.1), and 'The Lord is King, let the earth rejoice' (97.1). Among the psalms, as we have seen, there are also private prayers of lamentation (22), and reflective meditative prayers in which a variety of emotions are transformed into prayers. Psalm 43 is an example of this. Here the psalmist prays to God in his distress, and then receives from God a message of hope: 'O put your trust in God; for I will yet give him thanks, who is the help of my countenance and my God' (43.5). One verse of the long Psalm 119, with sections based on the letters of the Hebrew alphabet, which speaks of praising God seven times a day, provided the basis for the Western monastic order of daily prayer. The Psalter is a complete treasury of prayer unequalled in its range and power in the Jewish and Christian traditions, and the influence the Psalms have had on the prayer of the church cannot be underestimated. They have fed people in their private prayers, as well as providing the inspiration for a major part of public worship. They contain a great variety of different moods and emotions in the believer's relationship with God, so when people need to find words to express their own feelings, the Psalms provide the words. Perhaps Psalm 23, 'The Lord is my shepherd', through its rich imagery of shepherd and sheep, wine and oil, and streams of living water, has captured more than any other psalm archetypal patterns which resonate in the human soul and assist prayer.

Prayer in the New Testament

Jesus, according to the Gospels, seemed to prefer the quiet, desert places for prayer where he could escape from the crowds, and remain alone with God. He liked to pray at night. This allowed him to concentrate, to listen for God's voice, and to hear his own heartfelt feelings. These he could share with God. In this practice, he was following the way of Moses on the mountain, Elijah in the cave, and Daniel in his room in exile. Each fostered a personal relationship with God, in secrecy: 'When you pray, go into a room by yourself, shut the door, and pray to your Father who is in secret; and your Father who sees what is done in secret will reward you' (Matthew 6.6).

Kingdom of God ➤

Jesus' prayer became focused on God as Father (in Aramaic, *Abba*). Abba indicated an intimate but respectful relationship, suitable for private prayer. In prayer the soul is to approach God as a child drawing near to his father, with perfect simplicity and directness, in trust and love: 'Your Father knows what your needs are before you ask him' (Matthew 6.8).

For Jesus, prayer had to have a spiritual reality. This truth was reinforced by warnings against hypocrisy. We learn as much about what Jesus did in his times of prayer by what he warned against as by what he positively recommended. For example, he warned against too lengthy public acts of prayer (Matthew 6.7), showing off in prayer, and hypocrisy. An admonition to prayer is often coupled with a request to fast, and prayer is to be earnest, expecting a response from God. Prayer is also to be used in times of difficulty and danger.

The Lord's Prayer, the prayer that Jesus taught his disciples, also known as the 'Our Father' after its opening words, has become a model prayer for the Christian church (for centuries it was prayed in Latin, in which form it was called the Paternoster). Its shape and content cover five main areas. The first is that God opens himself as a reality to be adored. The prayer of adoration becomes an opening up of those who pray in an act of loving obedience to the God who is worthy of all praise: '*Our Father in heaven, hallowed be your name.*' God is holy, and this holiness deserves praise and fervent acknowledgement. The kingdom of God was both a present and a future reality for Jesus. In the urgency of the times it was to be prayed for most earnestly. For as long as it takes to become a present reality in our own day, it is prayed for still. '*Your kingdom come.*' God's kingdom is to replace all worldly kingdoms, and God is to be all in all. '*Your will be done.*' The will of God is to replace human wills, both personally, as with individual wishes, and corporately, through the schemes and policies of nations. Those who pray acknowledge their human needs, such as food, health, security, friendship, and work and pray that these may be obtained, for themselves and for others, and so they pray, '*Give us this day our daily bread.*'

The final sections of the prayer, not including the

CANONICAL HOURS

Canonical hours is one of the terms used to denote the times of prayer officially laid down by the church and to be observed especially by priests and members of religious orders. They are grounded in a phrase from the Psalms, 'Seven times a day will I praise you' (119.164). They are also known as the divine office, and the prayers said can also be referred to as the offices. The Second Vatican Council changed the term to 'Liturgy of the Hours', and in 1971 the whole system was simplified in the Roman Catholic Church, Traditionally it comprised:

Matins/Lauds	The middle of the night
Prime	About 6 a.m.
Terce	9 a.m.
Sext	12 noon
None	3 p.m.
Vespers	Evening
Compline	Said before retiring for the night

These hours of prayer are still observed in many monastic communities.

THE LORD'S PRAYER

Traditional form	*Matthew 6.9–13*	*Luke 11.2–4*	*Modern form*
Our Father, which art in heaven, Hallowed be thy name; Thy kingdom come; Thy will be done; In earth as it is in heaven. Give us this day our daily bread.	Our Father in heaven, hallowed be your name. Your kingdom come. Your will be done, on earth as it is in heaven. Give us this day our daily bread.	Father, Hallowed be your name. Your kingdom come. Give us each day our daily bread.	Our Father in heaven, hallowed be your name, your kingdom come, your will be done, on earth as in heaven. Give us today our daily bread.
And forgive us our trespasses, As we forgive those that trespass against us. And lead us not into temptation; But deliver us from evil.	And forgive us our debts, as we also have forgiven our debtors. And do not bring us to the time of trial, but rescue us from the evil one.	And forgive us our sins, for we ourselves forgive everyone indebted to us. And do not bring us to the time of trial.	Forgive us our sins as we forgive those who sin against us. Lead us not into temptation but deliver us from evil.
For thine is the kingdom, the power, and the glory. For ever and ever, Amen.			For the kingdom, the power and the glory are yours now and for ever. Amen.

In the New Testament, the Lord's Prayer appears in the Gospel of Matthew in the Sermon on the Mount, in Luke in answer to a request by one of Jesus' disciples who asks him to teach them to pray. The two versions are different, not just in wording, but in poetic form, a difference which is even more striking in the original Greek, so it cannot just be said, say, that Luke's simpler version is the earlier which has been elaborated by Matthew. It should be noted that the meaning of the Greek word for 'daily', *epiousios*, is uncertain: it appears only here and has otherwise been rendered 'necessary for today' (a modern Swedish translation for use in worship says 'the bread we need'), or 'for tomorrow', perhaps an allusion to the story of the Israelites in the wilderness who are given each day sufficient manna for the next. The original prayer foresees a time of trial for those who pray it, the tribulations of the end time described, for example in Matthew 24. In subsequent usage in the church, this reference has been generalized into a prayer to escape temptation and evil. A variant of the doxology in the traditional version, 'For thine is the power and the glory', appears in another text of the Lord's Prayer in an early Christian writing, the Didache (The Teaching of the Twelve Apostles); other forms have been added in some New Testament manuscripts, but it did not form part of the original. Attempts have been made to introduce into worship a form of the prayer which follows the Gospel texts very closely, as in Church of England liturgical reform during the 1970s; however, there were strong objections from congregations and it was dropped.

C. F. Evans, *The Lord's Prayer*, London: SCM Press 1997

words, '*for yours is the kingdom, the power and the glory for ever and ever. Amen*', which are a later addition (known as the doxology, from the Greek for ascription of glory), are to do with human conduct. In the sight of God, men and women fall short in the way they live their lives. They break the commandments of love, to God and to neighbour, and so they pray for forgiveness. '*Lead us not into temptation*' has both a moral and an apocalyptic sense. God is asked to '*deliver us from evil*' in the form of making wrong moral Paul decisions, but he is also asked to give protection from the final destruction of the universe as we know it. This sense of apocalyptic judgement was very strong in the time of Jesus, although it is not something which modern science confirms for us in our day. However, in its moral sense it Evil has significance for us, and the notion of evil is well understood in many areas of life, even by those with little formal moral education.

The resilience of the Lord's Prayer in a largely unbelieving generation is partly to do with the resilience Tradition of tradition itself, but its nature is such that it appeals very generally to Christians and non-Christians alike. Its propositions are extremely general, and do not depend on specifically 'Christian' interpretations. The intensity with which each sentence is observed can depend largely on the devotion a person has to the stated author of the prayer, Jesus himself, but the concepts of holiness, the kingdom, the will, daily bread, sin and mutual forgiveness, have a universal appeal and relevance.

More general prayers of thanksgiving express gratitude not only for the small details of daily life, but also for the great acts of salvation that God has performed through Resurrection history, culminating in the death and resurrection of Jesus. Eucharist In the eucharist, the central service of thanksgiving in the church, the wonderful deeds of God are recounted with praise and thanksgiving. The eucharistic prayer, which means 'prayer of thanksgiving', is the central prayer of Christian worship. It gathers up the history of salvation from earliest times through to Jesus' actions on the night Creed of the Last Supper, and beyond to his saving actions, and the hopes of the Last Day when he will come again to gather all things to and in himself.

The so-called 'high-priestly prayer', an elaborate and intricate prayer attributed to Jesus in the Gospel of John (chapter 17), gives a picture of his relationship with God, the disciples and the world. Archbishop William Temple wrote in his classic *Readings in St John's Gospel*: 'This is, perhaps, the most sacred passage even in the four Gospels – the record of the Lord's prayer of self-dedication as it lived in the memory of His most intimate friend.' Jesus prays for unity among believers and for protection for the disciples remaining in the world. It is a profoundly theological prayer, but as so often in John's Gospel, there are flashes of simplicity and of an authentic voice: 'I in them and you in me, may they be perfectly one. Then the world will know that you sent me, and that you loved them as you loved me' (John 17.23).

It was this chapter of John's Gospel that inspired Abbé Paul Couturier (1881–1953) to start the Week of Prayer for Christian Unity in 1934. The week runs from 18 to 25 January, the feast of the conversion of St Paul, and still provides opportunities for the church to find its essential unity in Christ.

In chapter 8 of Paul's letter to the Romans there is an impassioned description of his experience of prayer. The cry 'Abba, Father' is a response to God's receiving a believer by 'adoption'. The connection seems almost automatic, inspired by what God is doing, rather than the believer. 'In the same way the Spirit comes to the aid of our weakness. We do not know how we ought to pray, but through our inarticulate groans the Spirit himself is pleading for us.' Prayer is not just requesting God's help for things we want, but a movement of the Holy Spirit in the one praying, which may emerge simply as a cry or a groaning. However, Paul does also say that the church in Rome is 'in his prayers continually' (Romans 1.9; see.12.12; 1 Thessalonians 5.17, 'Pray without ceasing'). He also asks the church to pray to God for him that he may 'be saved from unbelievers in Judaea' (Romans 15.31; see 1 Thessalonians 5.25). For Paul, prayer is a matter of daily necessity as well as part of the process of becoming united with Christ through the Holy Spirit.

The letter to the Ephesians (3.20, 21) provides a further example of this development in the use of prayers from scripture: 'Now to him who is able through the power which is at work among us to do immeasurably more that all we can ask or conceive, to him be glory in the church and in Christ Jesus from generation to generation for evermore.' Here the prayer is not a direct conversation with God, but a proclamation of the attributes of God for the early church to use, as a reminder of the type and nature of the God they believe in. It is a prayer which comes from a creed or statement of belief, rather than a prayer as a dialogue with God. This is a process that went on in the history of biblical texts, and what follows is an increasing sense of objectivity in the tone of the prayer. A growing sense of formalization occurs, as the church needed more public prayers to feed its liturgical and worship life.

For example, in the Revelation of John, we read what seems like a prayer, although it is called a song (Greek *ode*), and it has the feel of a prayer written particularly for the worship of the church: 'Great and marvellous are your deeds, O Lord God, sovereign over all; just and true are your ways, O King of the ages. Who shall not fear you, Lord, and do homage to your name? For you alone are holy. All nations shall come and worship before you, for your just decrees stand revealed' (15.3, 4). It is easy to see the difference between a song-prayer such as this and the spontaneous prayer of Paul in Romans 7.24: 'Wretched creature that I am, who is there to rescue me from the state of death? Who but God? Thanks be to him through Jesus Christ our Lord.'

Finally, from the Jewish traditions of prayer also comes a rich tradition of the prayers of blessing, from the classic blessings of the patriarchs on their children to the blessing of creation, and from the blessing of children in every generation to a blessing on the food that is set before the family. Such prayers ask God to show a particular favour on someone, or something, or some event: for example, on a marriage, or on a congregation at the conclusion of an act of worship, or on the crops at Rogationtide.

So we can begin to discover varieties of prayer within scripture. They range from the intimate use of psalms by Jesus on the cross, and cries to God for help in the Garden of Gethsemane, to the equally intimate revelations of the state of Paul's soul. These intimate prayers lead on to the more objective prayers that came to be used for the formal liturgies of the church. These formal liturgies along with the creeds, sections of scripture, hymns, and prayers in the form of a direct address to God, make up the treasury of prayer available to all.

As the church developed its life and witness it also developed a pattern of daily prayer based on scriptural hours of prayer. These became known as 'hours', and *Books of Hours*, many of them elaborately decorated, became popular in the Middle Ages.

Difficulties with prayer

Not only Jews and Christians but also Muslims and members of countless other faiths pray to God. Prayer seems to have been an essential part of any faith that depends on another and greater being, but where there is no faith, there seems to be no real need for prayer, and certainly no sense of the efficacy of prayer. In a secular system, events and decisions are organized by a social dynamic and structure. The society is responsible for the outcome of its decisions. Humankind is the limit of its own power. God is not seen to be part of that, no communication with God takes place, and prayer is seen to be nonsense. This highlights the role that prayer has in a life of faith. It shows how important it is as a means of communication along the pulse and heart of religious life. To believe in God and not to have any means of communicating with God spells death to the relationship, but similarly it is this spiritual relationship with God that makes prayer valid, something of worth.

For those who pray and yet do not receive answers there can be great frustration. God seems not to hear, or at least not to act. These problems sometimes seem insurmountable. It is slow and patient pastoral contact, and teaching about the human relationship with God that can sometimes allow people to trust God even in the dark. Or, advice can be given on how to reshape a picture of God from the idea of a God who simply makes automatic responses into a loving and caring God who suffers alongside humanity.

The prayer of healing, along with the laying on of hands, was an important part of the ministry of the early church. In the Anglican Book of Common Prayer there is a service of prayers and collects including a confession of sins and an absolution, and a blessing. In our more openly tactile age and culture, the importance of touch, associated with prayer, comes close to the method that Jesus used when he touched the sick, and sighed, and looked towards God and said some healing words.

Sickness and healing

Forgiveness

Festivals and fasts

Praying alone and praying together

'When you pray, go into a room by yourself, shut the door, and pray to your Father who is in secret; and your Father who sees what is done in secret will reward you' (Matthew 6.6). How a person prays alone depends very much on the inclinations of the one praying. By its very nature, 'solitary' prayer doesn't allow for easy copying, so it is likely that those who pray will have to make things up as they go along, and be courageous enough to follow the movement of the Holy Spirit. Books by solitaries and those who understand the value of private prayer usually suggest a period of quietening down, and a physical posture that suits the mood of the prayer. Adoration may involve an opening out of the heart with the stretching and raising of the arms. Confession may call for a prostration, or a beating of the breast. Both of these may just as well be achieved by sitting still in a chair, but many people need to be given permission to experiment.

Holy Spirit

It is very easy in one's own room to be distracted, or to be anxious about someone coming in by accident. The nervous need to be sure of privacy. Telephones can be switched off, and times of the day when there is less moving about by others are also important. The creating of a prayer-space is helpful. This can be part of a room where it is possible to place a statue, a candle, an icon, stones or water, or a crucifix. A prayer mat can give rootedness to a special place. A prayer stool assists prayer in a kneeling position, by taking pressure off legs, ankles and feet.

The environment is one thing; the will or desire to pray is another. The success of such places and times for prayer will certainly be helped by these aids to prayer, but the intent is all-important. The offering of oneself to God at the beginning of a time of prayer allows the one praying to accept whatever comes, even if it is long periods of apparent nothingness. The meaning is often in the waiting. However, the image of Mary, the mother of

Pastoral care

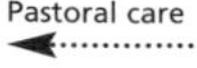

Jesus, sitting in a small room, being visited by the Spirit, is a powerful icon of what prayer can be.

Unfortunately, churches are all too often not conducive to private prayer, but when they are they are a great blessing. Praying in a church or a chapel has the added benefit of allowing people to feel surrounded by the prayers of others that have been accumulated over the years. The prayer seems to get into the walls, and it is quite common to feel drawn into prayer by the sense of the presence of God. Groups meeting for silent prayer have become increasingly popular. They begin with a short reading or thought by a member of the group and then there is a period of silence for about half an hour, and the time is concluded with a prayer. Julian Groups, inspired by the life and writings of Mother Julian of Norwich, often use this pattern of prayer.

The Orthodox tend to stand to pray and spend time in front of an icon, a holy picture of the Mother of God with the child Jesus, or of a saint, or of a biblical scene. It is the custom to light a candle and place it before the icon, to make the sign of the cross, and to kiss the icon. The sign of the cross is made on the front part of the body, from forehead to the heart and then from shoulder to shoulder, and then back to the heart, thus tracing the shape of the cross of Christ on a person's physical and living being.

Icon

Praying in groups sets up a different dynamic in which it is possible to remain quiet, or to speak out, and to be nourished by the spoken prayers of others. Prayer groups can be nerve-racking when people are embarrassed to speak out, but they can also be very supportive. Spontaneous prayer (also known as extempore prayer), spoken aloud among fellow Christians, is very popular among some groups. With Pentecostal prayer spontaneity, exuberance and joy are the hallmarks. Alongside more traditional expressions of worship such as kneeling and clasped hands, there is clapping, dancing and the raising of hands in praise. Tongues, interpretations, prophecy, visions, words of wisdom and knowledge and healing all find their place, with a centrality being given to the Bible as the sword of the Spirit.

p. 1253

Pentecostalism

Contemplative prayer

Contemplative prayer is a hidden form of prayer and is therefore difficult to describe systematically. It eschews words, and concentrates rather on listening to God. It involves being open to the Word of God, of being aware of the presence of God, of resting in the silence for as long as it seems right to do so. Such prayer affirms the priority of God. It is a waiting on God to speak or communicate, and as such follows a strong theological and biblical principle defined by the first words of Genesis, 'In the beginning, God.' Those praying wait on God's initiative. They offer themselves in obedience and receptivity for whatever God may wish to communicate. Such a form of prayer has always been part of Christian prayer, particularly in the desert or monastic traditions.

p. 1143

Contemplative prayer has received fresh impetus in our own day by two things. First, in a world where there is so much verbal communication and noise, silence has become an essential antidote. Silence has also taken on the aspect of healing as well as prayer. Secondly, words themselves have become a way of avoiding God rather than meeting God, and if prayer is to be a meeting with God then something has to go deeper than words. *Waiting on God*, the title of a book by the French spiritual writer Simone Weil, describes this attentive waiting in expectant silence.

Meditation

As with contemplation, meditation has become more well-known over the last half century through increased contact with Eastern religions. Buddhists practise walking meditation. The Chinese practise mirroring, a form of meditation called Tai Chi. It helps to develop a spacious, meditative awareness in which one starts to perceive directly with the body, rather than through mental processing. From the Hindu tradition comes 'yoga' which means 'union'. Many of these ways are being absorbed into Christian prayer, but the resistance in Christianity to allowing the body to play its part, at the expense of the mind and will, has made it difficult for many to accept even the simplest new methods. However, the stilling of the mind and the body, prayer walks, and experimental body positions in prayer, such as prostration, raised hands, and regular breathing patterns, are beginning to be valued.

The monastic tradition of reflecting on biblical readings as a way of praying, known as *lectio divina* (divine reading), is also a way of deepening a sense of the presence of God. This method allows time for a passage of scripture to go beyond just mental acceptance, and into the heart, where all true prayer begins and ends. Daniel was reading the scriptures when he was overwhelmed with the need to pray.

One of the classic forms of Christian meditation is found in the *Spiritual Exercises* of Ignatius Loyola. These originated from Ignatius' spiritual experiences at Manresa, near Barcelona, in 1522–3, and were substantially completed by 1541. The book is a manual for those giving retreats. It provides for a structured, individually guided programme of mainly imaginative prayer lasting, in its full form, for about a month. After an initial retreat reflecting on sin, the exercises concentrate on the life, death and resurrection of Jesus Christ. Those directing the retreat make substantial allowances these days for the needs of individual retreatants. Gerard Manley Hopkins (1844–89), the Jesuit priest and poet, was much influenced in his writing by this form of meditation, and more recently the writings of Gerard Hughes, SJ, and the work of St Beuno's House in North Wales have made the *Exercises* well known to many clergy and laity.

Words at their best, and used in manageable amounts, can provide a springboard for prayer. Further, scriptural texts have a numinous or prayerful quality that, if used in the right frame of mind, can provide a way into the presence of God.

Praying to Jesus

In the Orthodox tradition Jesus is invoked primarily by the 'Jesus Prayer' or 'Prayer of Jesus'. This practice has become a way of entering into prayer more fully, by the constant repetition of the phrase 'Jesus Christ, Son of the Living God, have mercy on me, a sinner'. The idea is that through repetition the prayer moves from the head into the heart, and so can become a permanent prayer not said so much as felt, as if it were being said with the whole body, and with all of one's intent or will. Essentially this is an adaptation of the prayer of the blind man outside Jericho (Luke 18.38); compare also the prayer of the publican (Luke 18.13). The origins of the Jesus Prayer are to be found in fourth-century Egyptian spirituality. The desert fathers of Nitria and Scetis laid special emphasis upon inward mourning, and upon the need for God's mercy. They also recommended the use of a short phrase, frequently repeated, similar to 'arrow prayers', as a method of maintaining the continual remembrance of God. So it also became known as the 'Prayer of the Heart'.

The Jesus Prayer is just one manifestation of the concept of praying to Jesus, or through Jesus, which delineates a particularly Christian way of praying. The New Testament centrality of Jesus, the love and faith he evoked in people, his power to heal and bring new life, his charisma, all combined to make him one who was perceived as having a special way through to God.

The devotion to Jesus and the use of the name in prayer can also be traced to the poetic and mystical writings of Bernard of Clairvaux (1090–1153). In his long series of sermons on the *Song of Songs*, he speaks of Jesus like this: 'None other, whether angel or man, but Himself I ask that he kiss me with the kisses of His mouth.' 'Jesus is honey to the lips, in the ear melody, in the heart joy. Medicine also is that name. Is any sad? Let Jesus come into his heart, and thence leap into his tongue.' This same devotion is reflected in a series of verses whose beauty caused them to be attributed to Bernard, though this is now disputed. His famous *Jesu dulcis memoria* is the basis of the hymn 'Jesus, the very thought of thee', translated by E. Caswall.

Francis of Assisi (1181/2–1226), like Bernard, brought a new personal element into Catholic devotion, and a mysticism based on the direct experience of God's love as revealed in his Son. Francis showed a particular devotion to the cross of Christ, and in his writings used prayers of adoration to Jesus: 'We adore you, most holy Lord Jesus Christ, here, and in all your churches throughout all the world; and we bless you, because by your holy cross you have redeemed the world.'

p. 821

The hymns of Charles Wesley (1707–88) continue this tradition of addressing Jesus in terms of deep affection, in a way that might be used in personal or vocal prayer: e.g. 'Jesu, lover of my soul'; 'Jesus, all-atoning lamb'; 'Jesus thy name, high over all.' In this discourse of deep emotion, praying to Jesus with the name spoken out loud bears a close relation to the human desire to repeat a loved one's name. The hypnotic repetition of the name can induce frenzy as well as devotion, and the test of authenticity may well come under the scrutiny of the very name that is being used: 'Why do you call me Lord, Lord, and never do what I tell you?' (Luke 6.46; Matthew 7.21).

Intercessory prayer

One of the best-known forms of prayer, but the one that gives rise to the most perplexity and discussion, is 'intercessory prayer', asking prayer. The popular picture is that whatever we ask of God he will, out of his huge bounty, give us. Indeed, Jesus is reported as having said, 'Whatever you ask in my name, I will give you.' Jesus is seen to be the one who intercedes for us with God, pleads

Devotions

ARROW PRAYERS

Arrow prayers were first commended by the desert fathers and have been used by Christians ever since as a way of continually remembering the presence of God. They consist of a short phrase which is easy to memorize and can be particularly useful as people go about their busy lives. Some classic ones are:

Be still and know that I am God.
Come, Lord Jesus.
Lord, have mercy.
My Lord and my God.
Jesus, remember me.
Abba, Father.
Father, forgive.
Lord, I am not worthy.

our cause, and enables things to happen. With this in mind people set to in their asking, and the outcome is not always what they would want. The asking does not always issue in an automatic answer, and God is accused of being deaf to requests, or worse unconcerned, disinterested, or impotent. This puts the efficacy, and indeed the very existence, of God in doubt.

Intercession is a form of prayer that has much to do with the pastoral work of the church and is closely allied with it. As such, it is important that, on the level of care and concern for people, visiting, giving advice, and conveying a sense of hope and belief in God, the prayer of intercession receives the attention it deserves and demands. People want to know whether or not God listens and has the power to act. Those involved in the pastoral work of the church need to know how to respond to questions about this. But although it is easy to see the problem, the question is the most difficult to answer easily and simply.

Calendar

Incarnation

The incarnation of God in Jesus allows some inroads to be made in this complicated area. Many prayers for the healing of illness and prevention of death must be set, not just alongside Jesus' own miracles but against his experience of the inevitability of pain, suffering and death. God in Christ suffered physically and mentally, and so the human experience is bound to contain such suffering. Yet there are powers and possibilities within that general picture which can alleviate unfairness, reduce pain, focus love, and open up possibilities of release and forgiveness. To call on the Holy Spirit to be an agent of change in certain situations is entirely valid, and the healing ministry of the church harnesses that resource to the utmost of its power.

Miracle
Suffering
Death

The voluntary offering of Jesus on behalf of others is an example of the way prayer can be effective. Certain individuals and communities dedicate their lives to prayer on behalf of others, so that in the 'spiritual realms' a process of exchange or substitution can take place. The sacrifice of one becomes the means of blessing for another. Some pray for others who cannot or do not pray. Some take on the pain of another so that it relieves a portion of another's pain. With intercessory prayer there is always a level of obscurity. Its ways are not always scientifically or mathematically accountable, but that is not to say that the benefits of prayer are not experienced or felt realities. The power of prayer is undoubtedly felt, and there are countless examples of answered prayer. Those who have damaging experiences of unanswered prayer need the sympathetic and wise counsel of those who understand the ways of God and can communicate them in pastoral situations of great sensitivity.

Often the formal words of a collect can help to deepen intercessory prayer. The collect (the word denotes a prayer which collects a number of petitions into a single prayer) is a short form of prayer, made up (with many varieties of detail) of an invocation or a calling on God, a petition or a request to God, and a pleading of Christ's name or an ascription of glory to God. The collect is one of the most characteristic items in the Western liturgy. Many of Thomas Cranmer's collects, largely translations from the Latin of the Roman rite, and placed in the 1549 Book of Common Prayer, have survived through the centuries and are much loved. There was a tradition at one time of learning by heart the collect of the week. These prayers cover the Sundays of the church's year, and saints' days, and some of them are classics. Take, for example the collect for the twelfth Sunday after Trinity in its original wording:

> Almighty and everlasting God, who art always more ready to hear than we to pray, and art wont to give more than either we desire, or deserve; Pour down upon us the abundance of thy mercy; forgiving those things whereof our conscience is afraid, and giving us those good things which we are not worthy to ask, but through the merits and mediation of Jesus Christ, thy Son our Lord.

The conciseness and internal balancing of phrases and rhythms of the collects have given them a special place in the history of devotional literature. Nor should that most characteristic of endings to prayers, 'Amen', which is the Greek word for truly, or 'yes, indeed', be forgotten.

Another form of intercessory prayer, which is particularly helpful in praying together, is the litany, which consists of a series of petitions said by one person and responded to by the rest of the group with a fixed phrase like 'Hear us, good Lord' or 'Lord have mercy.' Cranmer's litany for the Book of Common Prayer is a classic, and new litanies have appeared in revised prayer books, some of them for use at the eucharist.

Teaching prayer

Because prayer is such an enigmatic and ill-defined area of human experience, the teaching of its ways, and guidance along its paths, has given rise to its own helpful and fascinating traditions. Jesus taught his disciples to pray, and women and men throughout Christian history have taken on the responsibility to continue that tradition. Spiritual mentors, those involved in spiritual direction, teachers of prayer, and scholars in the traditions of prayer have all played their part in helping people come to know and experience deeper levels of prayer.

With an ever-increasingly mechanistic view of the world, and with ministry in the church selling itself to a more administrative and organizational model of its task, prayer must now be seen to have a crucial role to play in the building up of spiritual resources in the life of Christian ministry. Prayer is the hidden strength of an active ministry. A lively relationship between God and the believer, open and effective means of communication between the human and the divine spheres are the essence of prayer. The different emphases within the Christian church on this matter lead us into the area now commonly called spirituality. It was out of the spiritual tradition of Benedict that Dom Cuthbert Butler (1858–1934) coined the phrase 'pray as you can, not as you can't'. It was from the spiritual tradition of the Carmelites that John of the Cross taught the nuns in his care to pray in and from 'the dark night of the soul'. Such spiritual wisdom in the matter of prayer is receiving a much-needed renaissance in our own day. The sale of books on prayer and prayer methods bears a modest witness to this. The real benefits are, as ever, known to God alone.

DAVID SCOTT

Books about prayer: Jean Pierre de Caussade, *On Prayer* (1931), London: Burns & Oates 1960; Francis de Sales, *Introduction to a Devout Life*, New York: Vintage Classics 2002; C. S. Lewis, *Letters to Malcolm. Chiefly on Prayer* (1948), London: Collins Fount 1998; W. Lowther Clarke (ed), *Liturgy and Worship*, London: SPCK 1959; *David Scott, Moments of Prayer*, London: SPCK 1997

Books of prayers: Lancelot Andrewes, *The Private Prayers*, Cleveland, OH: Pilgrim Press 2002; Angela Ashwin (ed), *The Book of a Thousand Prayers*, Leicester: IVP 2002; John Baillie, *A Diary of Private Prayer*, Oxford: OUP 1980; Eric Milner-White, *A Procession of Passion Prayers*, London: SPCK 1956; Esther de Waal, *The Celtic Vision. Prayers and Blessings from the Outer Hebrides*, Petersham, MA: St Bede's Publications 1990

Preaching

Through long millennia, news of God has spread by word of mouth. In Israel, story-tellers told of a God who made a covenant with the patriarchs Abraham, Isaac, and Jacob: God would be their God; they would be God's people. Story-tellers told how God had set people free from bitter slavery in Egypt and led them to a promised land. Story-telling was part of the Passover feast as well as temple rituals, rituals that re-enacted the shape of covenant.

In addition to story-tellers, there were prophets. Prophets were messengers who delivered 'the word of the Lord' to Israel. Kings might govern, but the word spoken by prophets overruled every ruler. Thus long before Christianity there was preaching. Preaching was institutionalized in Israel with court prophets like Habbakuk. There were also prophets like Amos, a shepherd from tiny Tekoa, who was stirred to express God's outrage against profiteering in Israel. The Hebrew Bible is a record of the 'word of the Lord'.

Israel had preachers and a theology of preaching. According to the story-tellers, God created the heavens and the earth by speaking words. God commanded and, day by day, a world happened. Whatever God spoke, would be. Just like rain that falls from heaven to make seeds grow, so God's word is never fruitless but, once spoken, will accomplish what God intends (Isaiah 55.10–11). In the Psalms, God's word is guidance, like a lamp shining ahead of itself – a light to walk by, a word to do (Psalm 119.105). Israel's preachers spoke between memory and hope. They recited wonderful works of God and thus shaped Israel's covenant memory. They looked to God's future promises, and prophetically called Israel to obedience. But preaching was always God's word. 'The word of the Lord' came to preachers – leaders like Moses, prophets such as Jeremiah – and they were commissioned to speak.

Creation

Psalms

After their exile in Babylon, the Jews dispersed over the Near East and elsewhere kept preaching alive in synagogues. Preaching became a professional task and sermons interpreted scriptural passages. Customarily, there were readings from Torah and *haftorot* (the Law and the Prophets), followed by discourse that began with the explanation of a text but soon moved to application. Preaching served to pass on tradition and urge ethical obedience; its style was wisdom teaching. In the two centuries before the birth of Jesus, story-telling and prophecy moved into the pulpit.

Bible

p. 139

Christianity began as a word of God when Jesus came preaching (Mark 1.14). From the beginning, Christianity announced a new state of affairs; the 'kingdom of God', a prophet's dream, was *happening*. Jesus' preaching seemed to draw on Israel's speech legacy, for he embodied the story-tellers by posing paradoxical parables and echoed the prophets by taking on religious hypocrisy. Jesus' parables often began with here-and-now detail, but became revolutionary with symbols of the kingdom. His teachings were equally edgy: 'Blessed are the poor', 'Blessed are the persecuted', 'Do not oppose evil', 'Love your enemies', 'You can't serve God and Money'. With wisdom aphorisms Jesus spoke ethics for a new social world. In a stratified society where the religious rich got richer and poverty multiplied, he feasted with poor and outcast people; he cared for the sick and announced an egalitarian 'kingdom of God'. Apparently he gathered disciples to share the preaching of his message. They spread word of kingdom come, God's promised social order, and urged people to live in God's future ahead of time. Though the message was a reiteration of Israel's covenant faith, within a repressive

Jesus

Kingdom of God

p. 1152

Covenant

Story

Prophecy

occupied land, the call to live in the kingdom was heard as liberation.

According to the Gospel record, Jesus' preaching, like that of the prophets, stirred opposition. Institutions based on the status quo were troubled by sermons urging people to live free in God's social order. Jesus' story ends abruptly: he is stripped, nailed to a cross and crucified during Passover week in Jerusalem. The Jesus movement ended as abruptly and disciples scattered. If people had hoped for social change, hope ended. Jesus' cruel death was a sign of God' disapproval; the kingdom message was evidently a sad, visionary hoax.

Resurrection

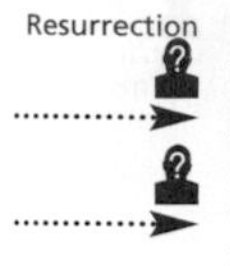

Then, with the resurrection, true Christian preaching began. For if God raised up Jesus, though he was executed, then his message of God's kingdom was certifiably true. Disciples of Jesus came together again to preach with renewed vigour. Their message was the faith of Israel, Jesus' faith, but declared to the entire Roman empire. To certify their gospel, they told of Jesus' repudiation by the powers that be, and of God's raising him up as 'Lord'. So the gospel message became a message of God's new order and of Jesus Christ the Lord.

Roman empire

We know little of earliest Christian preaching. In Acts, Luke provides samples, but they are likely to be Luke's own work, more Greek rhetoric than Hebrew in style. The rhetoric of Paul's letters may be a better clue, for though writing to Gentiles, Paul speaks as a Jew. From the beginning, there would be a difference between the gospel rehearsed when Christians gathered for worship and the gospel declared in broader contexts. Early Christianity was a Jewish sectarian movement, so preaching was concerned to establish Jesus' messianic credentials and, by drawing on Isaiah's 'servant songs', define his brutal death as a fulfilment of prophecy. Models for Christian preaching were drawn from synagogue practice. But as Christianity moved into the pagan world, preachers, speaking in impromptu settings, would have developed rhetorical savvy and sophisticated cultural awareness. We must assume that Christianity learned to preach by putting together Jewish speaking – the story-tellers, prophets and wisdom teachers – with the Greek rhetorical tradition.

University

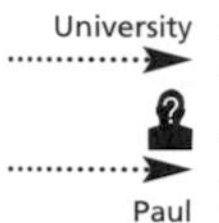

Paul

Religious orders

Church fathers

Down through the centuries we can pick out preaching styles as well as noted preachers. In the third century Origen, using analogy and imagination, set a pattern for early Christian preaching. A century later, Eastern Christianity featured the remarkable Cappadocian trio, Basil and the two Gregorys, and above all the great John Chrysostom (347–407). In the Western church, Augustine (354–430), trained as a teacher of rhetoric, was not only a powerful preacher but produced the first text on preaching, *De doctrina christiana*. By the fifth century, preaching had developed many different modes: impromptu 'preaching' by the laity reached out evangelically and drew people into faith; catechetical preaching trained those being baptized; mystagogical preaching introduced those newly baptized to eucharistic liturgy; and, week after week, preaching opened scripture to members, urging their moral courage in the world. Within these several modes, preaching still told stories, spoke prophetically, and offered Christian wisdom to the faithful.

Renaissance

Reformation

After the Roman empire fell to barbarians, preaching no longer functioned within patterns of Roman culture. Instead, preaching had to move in two directions at the same time, reassuring the faithful under siege and converting invaders. During this period, sermons (many by Gregory the Great) and sermon helps, 'Homilaries', were circulated to aid local priests. In the eighth century, Charlemagne was instrumental in promoting an educated clergy and a restoration of the preaching office. Preaching was required every Sunday and feast day in the language of the people. Though Augustine's text on preaching still circulated, sometime after 1084 Guilbert of Nogent produced 'A Book about the Way a Sermon Ought to be Given'. Then, a century later, Alan of Lille's *The Art of Preaching* shaped a set pattern for preaching. Sermons should begin with theological authority, namely, a biblical text from which a theme could be drawn and substantiated. Though preaching was taught in universities, it was nourished by monasteries. Bernard of Clairvaux (1090–1153), a Cistercian monk, published several collections of sermons on the lectionary, the Bible readings for the church year.

In medieval years preaching may have been erratic and, at times, unwanted, but in the thirteenth and fourteenth centuries it flourished with Franciscan and Dominican friars. Though they begged for their living, those who went out to preach were often university trained. Sermons usually began with a single biblical verse from which a theme might be distilled, then exposition was developed in subordinate sections, each supported by scriptural citation and illuminated by *exempla*. To support practice, a number of textbooks on the art of preaching, *Ars Praedicandi*, were produced, as well as collections of sermonic material. The Dominicans and those Franciscans authorized to preach merged rhetorical skill with biblical texts. But preaching, after the friars (and in part, because of the friars), moved towards allegorical spirituality in the sermons of Meister Eckhart and John Tauler, critical revision in the practice of John Wyclif (*c.*1330–84), and apocalyptic fervour in the declaiming of Girolamo Savonarola (1452–98). The medieval synthesis was unravelling.

During the Renaissance and Reformation there was a renewal of pulpit tradition in both Catholic and Protestant communions. The Catholic humanist Desiderius Erasmus wrote *Ecclesiastes*, considered a great watershed in the history of sacred rhetoric. The work was a theoretical and

HOMILY AND SERMON

When referring to the words preached during worship, Protestants and Anglicans now tend to speak of the *sermon* and Roman Catholics of the *homily*. Today the terms have come to be equivalents, but there was originally a difference between them. A homily is defined as a simple religious address, less elaborate than a sermon, and confining itself to the practical exposition of some ethical topic or some passage of scripture. The term comes from the Greek verb *homilein*, which means to speak with a person (ironically, perhaps, in Acts 20.11 it is the word used of Paul when he talks with a group in Troas during a celebration of the eucharist and goes on so long that a young man sitting in the window of the house where the meeting takes place goes to sleep and falls from the third floor to his death, immediately to be cured by Paul!). *Sermo* is the Latin equivalent.

Origen in the third century was the first to distinguish between homily and sermon, translating *homilia* into Latin not as *sermo* but as *tractatus*, and translating *sermo* with the Greek word *logos*, word. For him the homily was a commentary and explanation of some part of scripture. Collections of homilies for reading at the daily office of Mattins were compiled in the Middle Ages; they are known as *homiliaries*. Two books containing 23 homilies in all were issued in the Church of England in 1547 and 1571, intended for unlearned clergy; although they seem to have been used for little over a century, they became a source of Anglican doctrine alongside the Thirty-Nine Articles and the Book of Common Prayer.

The study of the art of preaching is called homiletics. The term has never taken on the negative connotations of 'sermonizing'.

There is an old Lutheran tradition, German and Nordic, of 'church postils'. These were brief sermons, commentaries on texts, which were often subsequently published for the edification of the laity.

In many churches today the homily or sermon has given way to a 'talk' or 'address'.

Church fathers

technical homiletic applying classical rhetoric to the task of preaching. The Reformer Martin Luther (1483–1546) also had huge influence on the practice of preaching. To Luther, preaching was the 'Word of God'. Inasmuch as the Bible contained preaching, it also could be labelled 'Word of God'. Preaching was an essential part of God's great plan of salvation because it delivered news of God's mercy to sinners. Luther saw sermons as 1. articulating the moral demands of God's law, followed by 2. the message of God's free, justifying grace through Jesus Christ, a pattern still featured in Lutheran proclamation. Though Luther preached thousands of sermons, he wrote no treatise on preaching; but his associate, Philipp Melanchthon, drawing on the work of Erasmus, produced three books on sacred rhetoric as well as his influential *Loci communes theologici*, a guide to theological themes and issues for interpreters.

John Calvin (1509–64) was the other Reformer who influenced the Protestant preaching tradition. Calvin, like Luther, was prolific, delivering more than 2000 sermons in Geneva. He also developed a theology of proclamation, arguing that preaching is the will of God for the church. Actually, Calvin seems convinced that when the gospel is truly preached, the voice of God addresses the church. Thus, preaching is a sacrament of God's presence. Sermons are human products demanding intelligence and skill, but by the power of the Holy Spirit, the human product becomes 'a means of grace'. Like the reformer Huldrych Zwingli, in nearby Zurich, Calvin preached at least five times a week, working through whole books of the Bible.

Within the 'radical Reformation', in evangelical Anabaptist communities preaching was impromptu and was a shared activity based either on a literal interpretation of scripture or on the inspiration of the Holy Spirit among members. Communities assumed that they were replicating the apostolic age before the time of Constantine. Thus they rejected infant baptism and an ordered priesthood, as well as the authority of secular governments. Preaching was mostly mutual exhortation and admonition.

Anabaptists
Martin Luther
Constantine's 'conversion'

The Roman Catholic renewal of preaching, presaged by the work of Erasmus, was carried on with the founding of the Jesuit order by Ignatius Loyola. The missionary preaching of Jesuits was both evangelical and biblical. In 1545, the Council of Trent declared that preaching was the principal duty of bishops. The Council also required preaching every Sunday and feast day, and provided for the homiletic training of priests. Bishop Charles Borromeo of Milan was a leader in the Catholic renewal of preaching.

Council

John Calvin

Preaching during the English Reformation is difficult to assess because of the changing positions of the monarchy. Henry VIII did little more than replace papal with royal authority. Edward VI tipped the church in a Calvinist direction. Under Mary Tudor papal obedience was reinforced. Only the long reign of Elizabeth I offered stability to religious life. Even then, there was a brief uprising of Puritanism. During the period, both Erasmus and Luther were influential. There were great Anglican preachers: Hugh Latimer, John Donne, Lancelot Andrews. Among Puritan figures, William Perkins produced an important guide, *The Arte of Prophesying* (English version, 1607), in which he argued for a plain reasoned style in

Church of England
Sacraments
Puritans

Huldrych Zwingli preaching in Zurich, fresco

preaching. Perhaps the most influential Anglican figure was John Tillotson (1630–94), who championed a neo-classical, topical pattern of rational discourse in plain style. Such sermons tended to be short on theology (as well as biblical reference) and could tumble into somewhat pedantic moralism. Sermons began to be circulated in published form and sold widely.

Publishing

At the same time, the rise of continental Pietism produced evangelical preaching that appealed to the heart rather than reason, scripture or tradition. Such preaching, conversionist in character, was apt to be both individualistic and affective. The rise of Pietism eventually prompted the eighteenth-century evangelical awakening promoted by John Wesley in England and by Jonathan Edwards in America. George Whitefield was the great preacher of the evangelical movement. His homiletic skill (not to mention showmanship) was undeniable. He developed a basic form for evangelistic preaching; his sermons began with conviction of sin and acknowledgement of human helplessness, before declaring the free gift of God's unmerited mercy. In America, the Great Awakening was followed by a second Awakening at the start of the nineteenth century. Evangelistic preaching became stylized with a procession of famed revival preachers: Charles Finney, Dwight Moody, and in the twentieth century, Billy Sunday and Billy Graham.

Romanticism
Pietism
Great Awakening
Evangelicals

Preaching in the modern age can be studied by tracing alternating currents of rationalism and Romanticism. Though revivalism was a movement in Great Britain and America, most sermons during the nineteenth century were shaped by Enlightenment rationalism. Hugh Blair, George Campbell and Richard Whately were leading theorists in England. Their influence is evident in the noted preachers John Henry Newman and Frederick W.

Robertson. In America, the major homiletic figures were John Witherspoon, John A. Broadus and the Swiss scholar Alexandre Vinet. The theoretical struggle was how to draw reason and feeling together in order to persuade.

During the twentieth century, four movements have been influential:

1. *The rise of a biblical theology.* P. T. Forsyth led the way with his 1908 Beecher Lectures, but the publication of Karl Barth's *Letter to the Romans* (1922) and *The Word of God and the Word of Man* (1928) inaugurated neo-orthodoxy along with a return to biblical preaching. For Barth, sermons should be no more than reiteration of scripture; cultural thought as well as rhetorical wisdom were excised.

2. *The emergence of pastoral care preaching.* In 1928, Harry Emerson Fosdick urged what has been termed 'life situation' preaching. Every sermon, he argued, should address some human problem, 'puzzling minds, burdening consciences, distracting lives'. For Fosdick the test of any sermon was how many persons asked for pastoral counselling. Leslie Weatherhead preached from similar concern at London's City Temple.

3. *The liturgical movement in the Roman Catholic Church* that ultimately led to the revisions of worship which followed the Second Vatican Council. The movement urged a liturgical interaction of word and sacrament. Documents of Vatican II restated that a bishop's first concern is with the proclamation of the gospel and urged a renewal of preaching in parish life.

4. *A concern for the social relevance of the gospel message.* Walter Rauschenbusch asked for a 'social gospel' during the first decades of the century, an emphasis maintained by Fosdick, Reinhold Niebuhr, and by the stunning oratory of Martin Luther King, Jr. Similar concern has been voiced by liberation theologies.

In America, two important social groups have altered the preaching tradition. The black church, inheriting cadences of slave religion, has seen a host of brilliant preachers. After the civil rights struggle of the 1960s, African American preaching began to influence all pulpit discourse. In 1970, Henry Mitchell wrote his significant *Black Preaching.* Sermons of formidable African American preachers, such as Adam Clayton Powell, Samuel Proctor and Gardner Taylor, have received deserved attention.

The number of women entering the ministry has had an impact. Women, supported by feminist and womanist literature, have turned attention to the task of preaching. The first woman ordained to ministry in America was Antoinette Brown in 1853. But without ordination women have been preaching since biblical times, when the prophetess Miriam celebrated Red Sea deliverance (Exodus 15.1–18): women as different as Hildegard of Bingen (1098–1179), Sojourner Truth (*c.*1797–1883) and Aimée Semple McPherson (1890–1944). Christine Smith's *Weaving the Sermon* (1989) prompted a number of subsequent works. The influence of women on preaching in terms of biblical interpretation, inclusive language and style has been revolutionary.

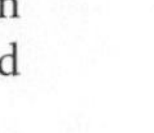

Of late, literature on preaching has grown enormously. There seems to be a search for a new way of preaching. Theorists are asking for narrative sermons, or for 'inductive' preaching. Some are asking for a partnership with contemporary rhetoric.

Karl Barth
Neo-orthodox theology

Over the centuries there have been different understandings of preaching. For Gregory the Great, preaching was formational. For Alan of Lille, preaching began with the authority of a biblical text. Luther associated preaching with justification, John Wesley with sanctification. Calvin insisted that preaching should glorify God. The revivalists supposed emotion generates decision. There are unresolved theological issues.

What is preaching? The split between reason and feeling seems to have limited preaching to instruction and/or conversion. But from the beginning, Christian preaching has functioned in many ways both in and out of the church.

What is the gospel message? Jesus preached the kingdom of God. After the resurrection, the gospel was news of God's social order, but now certified by the symbol of Christ crucified and risen. After Christianity became a permitted religion in the Roman empire under Constantine, the focus was primarily on Jesus Christ, Lord and Saviour. But in periods of social change such as our own, the theme of the kingdom returns.

p. 291

Is preaching recital or prophecy? Are sermons all about what God has done in past generations? Or do sermons look towards the future of God? Of late, preaching seems to have been preoccupied with historical revelation. Theology has been turning towards the future, towards eschatology; preaching must follow.

p. 1132

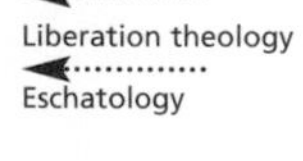

Liberation theology
Eschatology

Must every sermon begin with a biblical passage? Christians should be aware of biblical tradition, but sermons bridging biblical texts and contemporary life are often strained. Biblical passages are read liturgically, but must sermons always be about the Bible? Faith seeks understanding, and may need to explore theology and social ethics, as well as recall the story of the church.

African American Christianity

DAVID G. BUTTRICK

Women in Christianity

Y. Brilioth, *A Brief History of Preaching,* Philadelphia: Fortress Press 1965; D. Buttrick, *Homiletic,* Philadelphia: Fortress Press and London: SCM Press 1987; W. Willimon and R. Lischer (eds), *Concise Encyclopedia of Preaching,* Louisville, KY: Westminster John Knox Press 1995

Predestination

Life after death

'Predestination' means literally the determining of a destination in advance. In religious and theological usage it is generally related to an ultimate human destiny in the blessedness of heaven (for the 'elect'), and in some versions also to the destiny of the damned in hell (for the 'reprobate', i.e. those rejected by God). The 'pre-' emphasizes that the destiny in view has been decided in advance by God. The theme of predestination is commonly associated with

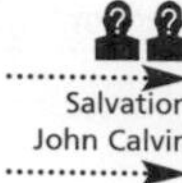

Salvation
John Calvin

three other convictions: 1. that only some of humankind will be saved; 2. that salvation is a gift of divine grace rather than a human achievement; 3. that the divine decision is not dependent on the accidents of historical events, but stands fast from the beginning. At the same time, defenders of the doctrine also generally distinguish it from fatalism or determinism and insist 1. that there is a real human freedom within history even though everything is foreordained by God; and in particular 2. that the reprobation of the damned is the justly deserved punishment for their sin and guilt for which they are themselves responsible.

p. 302

The issues involved here surface in many religious traditions including the Jewish – e.g. in some of the writings found at Qumran and broadly contemporary with the New Testament. However, the topic of predestination has been especially frequently and controversially handled in Christian theology. This is not surprising, for it lies very close to the New Testament themes of the divine plan of salvation and the last judgement. Several biblical texts are important for the debate; the most prominent is a statement of Paul: 'For those whom he foreknew he also predestined to be conformed to the image of his Son, in order that he might be the firstborn within a large family. And those whom he predestined he also called; and those whom he called he also justified; and those whom he justified he also glorified' (Romans 8.29–30).

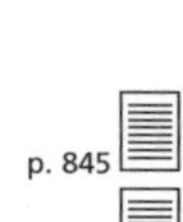

p. 845
p. 1016
Paul

Three broad types of predestinarian doctrine (though there are numerous further variations in detail) developed in the history of Western Christian theology. The first was originally drafted out by Augustine. He stressed that human nature is corrupted by the fall and that all human beings consequently constitute a 'mass of perdition'. However, God graciously chooses out of this mass certain individuals and predestines them for salvation while the rest remain headed for damnation. (The focus thus lies here on God's gracious predestination of the elect; a question remaining unanswered is why God should elect only some and not all, as the elect are in themselves in no way better than the others.) This position, focusing on the predestination of the elect, was subsequently affirmed by the Second Council of Orange (529) and generally maintained through the scholastic theology of the Middle Ages, for example by Thomas Aquinas. The doctrine was given quite a lot of attention in medieval theology, but generally only as one topic alongside many others of theological interest.

Scholastic theology

The second type goes beyond the first in explaining the condemnation of the damned by appeal to a parallel divine 'decree of reprobation'. Here, other than with the first type, it is possible to speak of 'double predestination'. Statements leaning in this direction can already be found in Augustine and later theologians including Martin Luther in his controversy with Erasmus on the 'bondage of the will'. It was John Calvin, however, who most systematically developed and most vehemently defended what he believed to be the true biblical teaching of a twofold predestination of all individual human beings to salvation or damnation. Leading Calvinist theologians in the Netherlands, England and Scotland went on to make the doctrine a main cornerstone of their entire system of theology. The prominence thus given to the doctrine was enshrined in the decrees of the Synod of Dort (1618–19) and the documents of the Westminster Assembly meeting in the 1640s, and so became for centuries a distinguishing benchmark of 'reformed orthodoxy'. (A similar position was also maintained in seventeenth-century Roman Catholic theology by the Jansenists. They too saw themselves as following Augustine, but their views were eventually condemned by Rome.)

The third type has generally tended to emerge in reaction against the harsh implications of the second. It characteristically inclines to weaken the idea of predestination to salvation by basing it on God's foreknowledge of people's faith or merits. This approach was rejected by the more consistent representatives of the first or second types. They saw it as incompatible with the divine sovereignty and as making the divine 'decision' a mere reaction to human behaviour foreseen by God. This third type appears in some reactions to Augustine in the ancient church, in some forms of medieval Nominalism, and then especially in reaction against Calvinist orthodoxy. Its reformed version was upheld by the Dutchman Arminius at the beginning of the seventeenth century and is still known as Arminianism. This was the position rejected by the Synod of Dort, which asserted against it what came to be called the 'five points of Calvinism', traditionally summarized under the acronym TULIP: Total Depravity; Unconditional Election; Limited Atonement; Irresistible Grace; Perseverance of the Saints.

In most Reformed theology in the last 150 years the whole tradition of predestinarian thought has been either silently ignored or sharply criticized. It is indeed weak at many points which cannot be developed here: for example, in its implied view of God's sovereignty and judgement; its understanding of human sinfulness; its focus on the election or reprobation of individual persons; the restricted attention it gives to the impact and effects of God's will to save through Jesus Christ; and the whole framework of thinking in which it uses and interprets the Bible. These implications have also been exposed to biting parody, for example by Robert Burns in his poem 'Holy Willie's Prayer'.

The most sustained and radical attempt in recent Reformed theology to correct and rework the theme of predestination in a positive way can be found in part II/2 of Karl Barth, *Church Dogmatics*, chapter 7, 'The Election of God'.

ALASDAIR HERON

Karl Barth, *Church Dogmatics, II/2, The Doctrine of God*, Edinburgh: T&T Clark 1957

Presbyterian churches

Presbyterian churches form a major branch of the Reformed family of churches that emerged from the sixteenth-century Swiss Reformation. But while Presbyterians have a historical and theological affinity with all Reformed churches, they have a particular understanding of the nature of the church and the way it should be governed. As the name indicates, Presbyterian churches are governed by presbyters – both ministers (teaching elders) and ruling elders – chosen by the congregation. Presbyterian ministers and elders serve together in a system of representative assemblies at the congregational, regional and national levels.

The place of Presbyterians within the larger Reformed family is suggested by the composition of the World Alliance of Reformed Churches, an association that includes churches calling themselves Reformed, Presbyterian, Congregational, Evangelical, Protestant, Free and United. These churches have differing forms of government, from episcopal to congregational, but the majority of them are led by presbyters. Those with English-speaking origins are called 'Presbyterian', while those with continental European origins are identified as 'Reformed' or simply 'Protestant'. Despite their diversity, though, the churches share a broad historical and theological heritage.

The different terms used to describe churches in the tradition reflect different realities in them; the Reformed tradition is the most diffuse of those emerging from the sixteenth-century Reformation. A 1999 survey, *The Reformed Family Worldwide*, lists over 700 Reformed churches, including 96 Presbyterian denominations in the Republic of Korea and 22 in the United States! Reformed fragmentation is so extensive that a large number of churches with Reformed antecedents, including many Baptist churches, are no longer self-consciously or identifiably Reformed.

Reformed churches were diverse from the beginning: Zurich and Huldrych Zwingli on the one hand, Geneva and John Calvin on the other. Churches of the Reformed tradition have not only different forms of church government but also different forms of worship, liturgical or free; different attitudes towards the sacraments; and different views on the value of precise doctrine and individualistic convictions. Most Reformed churches embody these tensions in some forms: churches with Dutch and Scottish roots are likely to be Calvinist and inter-connected, while churches with English roots are more often Zwinglian and congregational. Present-day Presbyterian churches emerged from the Scottish appropriation of the Swiss Reformation and the theology of the Westminster Confession of Faith (1647).

Huldrych Zwingli
Bible
John Calvin
Worship
Sacraments
Karl Barth
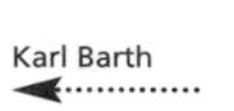

p. 302

During his exile in the 1550s, John Knox of Scotland spent several years with Calvin in Geneva, ministering to the city's English-speaking refugee community. Knox's exposure to Calvin's theology, liturgy and church order had a profound and lasting effect. 'In other places, I confess Christ to be truly preached,' Knox exclaimed, 'but manners and religion to be so sincerely reformed, I have not yet seen in any other place.' The linking of 'manners and religion' – life and faith, discipline and piety, ethics and theology – has been a hallmark of Reformed church life, and their embodiment in Geneva shaped Knox's view of the church and the distinctive Scottish form of Presbyterianism.

Reformation
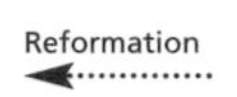
Church of Scotland
Ministry and ministers

John Calvin is important to Presbyterian churches, not simply as the founder of a theological tradition, but because his approach to the church and its ministry has influenced Reformed church life for centuries and is clearly evident in current Presbyterianism. Together with other sixteenth-century reformers, Calvin understood the church as *creatura verbi* – the creature of the Word. The Theses of Berne (1529) typify the Reformed doctrine of the church: 'The holy Christian Church, whose only head is Christ, is born of the Word of God, and abides in the same, and listens not to the voice of a stranger.' In continuity with this basic conviction, Presbyterian churches understand themselves as communities called into being by the incarnate Word and shaped by witness to that Word in the word of scripture. Thus the church's faith, worship and order must obediently proclaim and reflect the Word. Cultural forms and institutional structures are not signs of the church; even at their best they are only evidence of the power of the Word to transform corporate and personal life. The ordering of church life, its ministry and form of government, must be tied to the church's origin, mission and goal.

Reformed Churches

The influence of Knox's contact with Calvin and his

Grace

observation of the Geneva church's order are evident in the Book of Discipline and the Scots Confession (1560) and the Book of Common Order (1564), all largely composed by him. Yet it fell to another Scot who spent time in Geneva, Alexander Melville, to shape the Scottish Kirk's distinctive presbyterian form. The Second Book of Discipline (1581) firmly rejected episcopacy in favour of a thoroughly presbyterian system of representative church assemblies at local (kirk sessions), regional (presbyteries) and national (the general assembly) levels. This pattern, adapted to the needs of particular churches in other places and times, has characterized Presbyterian churches ever since. However, Presbyterian church order cannot be understood apart from its grounding in Reformed perspectives on theology, the nature of the church and the ordering of ministry.

Faith

From the cities of Switzerland, Reformed approaches to faith and life spread to France, Italy, Hungary, Poland, the Netherlands, Scotland, Ireland and America. These expressions of Reformed church life were never uniform, however, for it is an essential conviction of Reformed churches that the people of God are called to confess their faith anew in each time and place.

Predestination
Salvation
Covenant

Freedom and the need to express the faith locally has always led Reformed churches to be confession-making churches, giving present testimony to their faith and action. In the sixteenth century alone, more than 60 confessions were produced by Reformed churches. The World Alliance of Reformed Churches has published a representative sample of more than 25 Reformed confessions from the twentieth century. Each church is responsible for its own confession, and no church is bound by the confessions of other places and times unless it chooses to be.

This confession-making characteristic of Reformed churches distinguishes them from churches that look to a particular credal era, churches that hold to one formative confession of faith, churches that reside in a continuous development of doctrine. Reformed confessions are public declarations of who and what a church is, what it believes, and what it resolves to do. The occasion for framing a confession may be an internal danger that threatens the church's integrity, an external threat to the gospel, or an insight into the gospel that is needed by the church and the world.

Bible
Holy Spirit
Church
Community

However, Reformed confessions are always subordinate and accountable to the Bible. The Westminster Confession of Faith (1647), the most widely embraced confession among Presbyterian churches, acknowledges that 'All synods and councils ... may err, and many have erred; therefore they are not to be made the rule of faith or practice, but to be used as a help in both.' Creeds, confessions, and catechisms are vital, but scripture is the only infallible rule of faith and obedience. A Reformed principle, *ecclesia reformata semper reformanda secundum verbum Dei* (the church reformed, always being reformed according to the word of God), expresses both the confidence and the modesty of Reformed confessions and theological thought. The church is being reformed continuously, not by its own insights or efforts, but by the action of God's Spirit leading the church into truth through the witness of scripture.

The pre-eminence of scripture is accompanied by distinctive Reformed perspectives on Christian faith and life. These perspectives are not unique to Reformed churches, but are understood as particular angles of vision on the faith of the Church catholic and the affirmations of the Protestant Reformation.

Within the Reformed tradition, grace is at the centre of all that is known and experienced of God. The distance between God and humankind is bridged by God alone, setting people free from anxiety about the adequacy of their lives and the depth of their belief. Neither faith nor works can save; neither is a precondition of God's love in Christ. Instead, both faith and works are expressions of gratitude for the grace of the Lord Jesus Christ. The priority of grace is articulated as God's free election of a community for salvation and service. Election has sometimes been formulated as a double predestination to eternal salvation or damnation, but this has been more often rejected as unnecessary speculation. Instead, Presbyterians have emphasized the doctrine of election as an expression of God's unmerited grace. They generally understand the priority of grace in terms of covenant, God's gracious promise of saving care for his people. The covenant of grace is sealed in baptism, nourished in the Lord's Supper, and lived out in vocation.

A central conviction of Reformed theology is that the creator of heaven and earth is powerfully present in the world, sustaining and governing all things in the accomplishment of his holy purpose. At its best, Reformed theology has paired the sovereignty of God with God's gracious love, and the holiness of God with God's providential care. Reformed theology never sentimentalizes God's love, however, for it knows that the Lord is God, not human, the Holy One in our midst. Reformed emphasis on the sovereignty of God leads to an acute awareness of the dangers of idolatry.

Reformed Christians have emphasized that faith is not individualistic, but rather originates and is lived out in a community called, formed, equipped, and maintained by the Holy Spirit. The Spirit calls the church to be one, holy, catholic, and apostolic – a distinctive community of obedience and service. The church is to be a sign in and for the world of the new reality that God has inaugurated in Jesus Christ. The church's response to its calling is always ambiguous, yet the Holy Spirit continues to lead the community into the truth of the gospel. Complete realism about the church and confidence in the Spirit's presence result in church structures that engage the whole people of God. Ordinary people are chosen by the community to serve as ministers, elders and deacons with the confidence that through them God distributes spiritual gifts to the church. Presbyterian concern that everything be done 'decently and in order' reflects a resolve to shape church life in ways that keep the church open to the Spirit's leading and open for faithful witness in the world.

Presbyterian churches are committed to a particular pattern of church government because they understand that church order and an ordered ministry are indispensable in ensuring the church's fidelity to the Word. It is well known that Calvin commended four offices of ministry: pastors, teachers, elders and deacons; however, he understood these as plural expressions of the church's one undivided ministry.

This understanding of the church's ordered ministries signal two key features that endure in current Presbyterianism. First, clericalism is resisted. Most continental Protestants rejected the Roman Catholic Church's pattern of holy orders, replacing it with a pastoral office centred on proclamation. Calvin, on the other hand, constructed a pattern of ministry that breaks down the distinction between clergy and laity by instituting two 'lay' church ministries: deacon and elder. In many Presbyterian churches, elders and deacons, like ministers, are ordained to their office. Second, the church's various ministries are corporate, not only within each order of ministry but among the orders. No person can exercise an ordered ministry independently, and no order of ministry can function apart from its essential relationship to other orders.

The communal character of Presbyterian orders of ministry is evident from the way in which they are exercised within corporate assemblies. Ministers and elders serve together in sessions, presbyteries and general assemblies. In assemblies beyond the congregation, ministers and elders are usually represented in equal numbers. In congregations, shared presbyterial responsibilities include providing for the proclamation of the word, administering the sacraments, instructing the faithful in sound doctrine, and structuring discipline that ensures free space for word and sacrament to take root in the life of the church and its members.

Presbyterianism expanded beyond its Scottish roots in two ways: migration and mission. Presbyterian churches in the United States and Canada have their origin in emigration from Scotland and Northern Ireland. Scottish immigrants also established Presbyterian churches in Australia and New Zealand. The largest Presbyterian expansion came from the missionary movement of the nineteenth and twentieth centuries. The Church of Scotland and several American Presbyterian churches were particularly active, establishing churches in Asia, Africa, and Latin America. Particularly vigorous Presbyterian churches were founded in Korea, China, Kenya, Southern Africa, Brazil and Mexico. While statistics for distinctly Presbyterian churches are unavailable, the World Alliance of Reformed Churches reports in its membership alone more than 75 million Reformed Christians in over 100 countries.

At the beginning of the twenty-first century, once-dominant Presbyterian churches in Scotland and North America are experiencing numerical decline as they adjust to their 'cultural disestablishment'. Debilitating splits over doctrinal and moral issues continue to plague Presbyterians of the West, especially in the United States. Many Presbyterian churches in Africa, Asia and Latin America are growing, although they are challenged by the dramatic rise of Pentecostalism. Presbyterian churches worldwide continue to embody a vision of the church which is characterized by commitment to scripture, the responsibility to articulate contemporary confession of faith, active engagement with the social order, ministries that are shared by clergy and laity, and structures of governance that are representative of the whole church.

Organization ◄

Pentecostalism

JOSEPH D. SMALL

📖 Jean-Jacques Bauswein and Lukas Vischer (eds), *The Reformed Family Worldwide*, Grand Rapids, MI: Eerdmans 1999; John H. Leith, *Introduction to the Reformed Tradition*, Atlanta: John Knox Press 1977; John T. McNeill, *The History and Character of Calvinism*, London: OUP 1954; James H. Smylie, *A Brief History of the Presbyterians*, Louisville, KY: Geneva Press 1996

Professional ethics

Professional ethics is a branch of ethics that applies the methods and standards of moral evaluation to the character and action of professionals, as in medicine, law, business, ministry, education, etc. It addresses three levels of concern: the general level of being a professional person, the specific responsibilities of the profession in question (business, ministry, medicine, etc.), and the personal character and actions of the professional individual within the specific profession (this salesman, this minister, this physician, etc.).

Ethics

At the general level of what it means to be a professional, there is no uniform portrait of what constitutes a professional. However, at least four characteristics are generally recognized as minimally distinguishing marks:

Mission ◄

1. training and certification in specialized knowledge and skills; 2. serving a human need; 3. the commitment to act in the best interest of those seeking the professional service; and 4. structures of accountability to evaluate performance and control entry into the profession.

At the level of the responsibilities of a particular profession, the duties that correlate with each of these distinguishing marks can be developed to identify the specific obligations that belong to the profession in question. For example, in ministry the obligation to be competent in theological reflection correlates with the duty to be trained in theology as a specialized field of study. The obligation to provide religious services according to the norms of one's religious tradition correlates with the duty to serve human need. The obligation to be self-sacrificing correlates with the duty to act in the other's best interest. The obligation to follow the standards of practice of one's religious tradition correlates with the duty to be accountable.

Jesus ▸

Christian theology can offer a perspective on two issues of professional ethics that every professional must face: the nature of the professional relationship itself, and managing the imbalance of power between the professional and the client.

Covenant

Contract and covenant are two dominant models of the nature of the professional relationship. They are close cousins, but they are not the same. Both include agreement and exchange between parties and obligations that protect human dignity and block the tendency of one to exploit the other. Contracts work well if the necessary services and fees can be clearly spelled out in advance. Covenant, however, differs in spirit. The biblical witness to the covenant informs the basic structure of the professional relationship as one based on freedom, motivated by love, respectful of the dignity of the person as grounded in God, and held together by trust. Partners in a covenant are willing to go the extra mile to make things work out. It makes room for the gratuitous, not just the gratuities. Covenantal thinking wants to know what is the most one can do in grateful response to what one has received.

The act of entrusting something of oneself to a professional and the professional's accepting entrustment make the relationship one of unequal status and put the professional in a position of power over those seeking the professional service. Managing the imbalance of power is a major moral challenge for the professional person. Power in the professional is the capacity to influence the client for good or ill. Since power and vulnerability are always relative to resources, the professional is always the one with the greater power because the professional has the resources that the client needs. The primary covenantal obligation for the professional in this position of 'power over' is the fiduciary responsibility to respect the dignity of others by acting at all times in the best interest of the client, even if it demands that the professional sacrifice self-interest. The covenantal model resists an easy accommodation to standards of individualism, self-glory, or greed. It favours service, self-discipline and generosity.

Any professional ethic will have to contend with the inevitable inequality of power in the professional-client relationship. The professional's knowledge and skill foreordain a power-over relationship with the client. Power-over relationships acknowledge a real difference in status and authority, and they have a great potential for the more powerful professional to misuse this power in ways that manipulate, exploit or dominate the client. While these abuses of power are always possible, the power-over relationship is not evil in itself and so inevitably abusive. Power-over can be a loving influence that enables and liberates the client. It need not always exploit the client's vulnerable dependency.

Christian professionals have a model on the right use of power in the ministry of Jesus. A collage of Gospel stories gives us a picture of what acting in the spirit of Jesus' liberating use of power might be like. Jesus as seen by Matthew's community, for example, instructed his disciples to avoid all techniques that would secure positions of superiority that could lead to domination in the name of service (Matthew 23. 5–10). In short, the way of Jesus is the way of 'servant leadership': leading without lording it over others, and inviting people to change without forcing them to think the way he did. Jesus did not have to abuse his power to influence change. Rather, he knew that whatever power he had was rooted in God. He expressed this power of divine love through his life of service and setting people free. His miracles are signs of liberating power and his parables are often judgements about reversals in power relationships: the first become last, and the last first; the great are made humble while the humble are made great. He was free in himself so that he could be free for a great variety of people despite the features that made many of them outcasts to their own people. Professional relationships informed by the spirit of Jesus are ones which are all-inclusive, which deal with others as persons and not as customers, and which exercise nurturing and liberating power in the imitation of God's ways with us through Jesus. He manifests in his life what professional relationships might be today: centred in God, inclusive of all people, liberating, and standing in right relationship with everyone.

Professional ethics holds that the power gap places the greater burden of responsibility on the professional to avoid harming the vulnerable client. Even if being manipulated or seduced, the professional is to be guided by the principle of not only doing no harm but of doing good. These principles are enshrined in the professionals' fiduciary responsibility towards their clients. This means that professionals are to give greater preference to satisfying the needs of their clients over their own personal interests. To do this, professionals are to uphold the highest standards of trustworthiness.

At the level of the individual professional, trustworthiness remains the central virtue in any covenantal relationship and coherent ethic of the professions. It is unthinkable that one could be a professional without being trustworthy because of the covenantal action of entrusting and accepting entrustment in the professional relationship. Without trust, the professional relationship cannot attain its goal of serving the best interest of the client. The relationship becomes a means of exploitation rather than of liberation. The core of professional ethics at the individual level revolves around this obligation of fidelity to trust.

But an ethics of trust must go beyond a duty-based ethics to an ethics of virtue. More attention to character formation in the process of becoming a professional is essential, since virtue is taught by practice in the presence of teachers who themselves are models of virtue. For the Christian professional, Jesus is the supreme mentor, or exemplary role model. The most illustrative image of the character and virtue of professional life that can be derived from the life of Jesus is the scene in which he washes his disciples' feet (John 13.6–10). When Jesus deliberately reverses social positions by becoming the servant, he witnesses to a new order of human relationships in the community whereby the desire to dominate has no place in the professional life.

Common professional boundaries are boundaries of time, place and person. Boundaries of time give the security of respecting the other's interests by starting and stopping meetings on time, by setting enough time to complete a project, by taking on a limited number of projects that suit one's emotional, spiritual and physical health. Boundaries of place help to clarify the role and purpose of the relationship by meeting in an environment that fits the task and protects the privacy of the meeting. Boundaries that respect the person maintain a safe haven so that the client can be vulnerable without fear of being exploited. Personal boundaries include such things as being aware of the problems of physical closeness and the use of touch as a gesture of concern; steering clear of giving and receiving gifts; keeping secrets and not contributing to gossip; and avoiding dual relationships that only confuse roles.

Dual relationships are a great threat to boundary violations because they put the professional at risk of exploiting the dependency of the client. In dual relationships the professional relates to the client in more than one capacity, such as a business partner, a friend and an employee, all at the same time. Such relationships put the professional at risk of taking advantage of role and power to get special personal favours, or of impairing professional judgement of what the other needs because of being so emotionally enmeshed in the client's life, or of creating a conflict of interest by confusing whose needs are the primary ones being met in the relationship.

Maintaining boundaries and avoiding dual relationships as far as possible are essential to a professional ethics of trust. Without trust, the professional relationship degenerates into a relationship of mutual self-defence. Professionals no longer under any obligation of their fiduciary responsibility will feel free to pursue their own self-interest at the expense of the vulnerability of their clients. Such a scenario will only destroy the professional relationship and undermine the ethics upon which it is built.

RICHARD M. GULA, SS

📖 Paul F. Camenisch, *Grounding Professional Ethics in a Pluralistic Society*, New York: Haven Publications 1983; Edmund D. Pelligrino, Robert M. Veatch and John P. Langan (eds), *Ethics, Trust, and the Professions: Philosophical and Cultural Aspects*, Washington, DC: Georgetown University Press 1991; Marilyn R. Peterson, *At Personal Risk*, New York: W. W. Norton 1992

Prophecy

Prophecy is linked with either prediction (telling of divine mysteries beforehand) or mediation (speaking on behalf of God about past, present and future). Both elements are found side by side in the Bible. The main prophetic texts Bible are cast in a form in which a human medium acts as a mouthpiece for God. Words on a variety of issues, some more easily pinned down than others, are preceded by phrases such as 'Thus says the Lord'.

Prophetic writings take up a large part of the Hebrew Bible (the Christian Old Testament), and prophecy is a frequently mentioned theme in the New Testament. The origins of this remarkable phenomenon in ancient Judaism are not easy to discern. The fact that there is often recourse to some ethical tradition in the critique (e.g. Isaiah 1.24) may indicate that in part the prophets may be bringing out aspects of the religious tradition that have either been neglected or overlaid. One of these aspects may well be the Mosaic traditions which were perhaps marginal to the pomp and ceremony of the Jerusalem temple set up by Solomon. A significant part of the words spoken by the prophets as the words of God are about outrages of a theological or social kind: rejection of

THE PROPHETS

Following the New Testament and especially the Gospel of Matthew ('All this took place to fulfil what the Lord had spoken by the prophet, "Behold a virgin shall conceive and bear a son"', 1.22–3), the Christian tradition has seen the prophets as figures foretelling Christ, and it is in this p. 1197 capacity that they are depicted in statues and stained-glass windows. However, this interpretation is an illustration of how Christians took over the Jewish tradition and reinterpreted it for their own ends.

The prophets whose activities and writings are celebrated in the Old Testament are part of a wider spectrum of prophetic activity which is found among several ancient Near Eastern cultures and was not unique to Israel. The great prophetic teachers, with their vivid criticisms of contemporary politics and society, can be contrasted with the institutional prophets who, we learn, were sometimes wheeled out to support the policy of the ruling groups. 1 Kings 22 tells a lively story of the contrast between the prophet Micaiah, prophesying defeat for the king of Israel's proposed expedition against Damascus, and the 400 or so prophets prophesying success. The conflict between Jeremiah and Hananiah in Jeremiah 28 is in a similar vein.

The first prophets have left no writings; they are portrayed as formidable religious figures with remarkable powers; the later prophets are represented by books bearing their names which contain collections of their sayings, sometimes made by disciples: their message is essentially one of judgement, and has a marked ethical dimension. These sayings were not only treasured and handed down but reinterpreted, particularly after the exile, when their message seemed to have been vindicated. At that time the original sayings were put in a context which also conveyed optimism. The prophetic books as we have them now are thus the product of a long process of growth and reflection.

The earliest prophets

Several are mentioned as anonymous individuals (e.g. 1 Kings 13.11–32) or groups (1 Samuel 10.9–13), and one or two by name, but the most famous are:

Elijah (active *c.*869–39 BCE): He first appears in a garment of haircloth with a leather girdle, and is a resolute opponent of Ahab, king of Israel and his wife Jezebel. He revives the dead son of a poor widow (1 Kings 17); he champions the one God and defeats the prophets of Baal in a trial of power on Mount Carmel by bringing down rain (1 Kings 18); he goes into the wilderness for an encounter with God who comes not in wind or earthquake but in a 'still small voice' (a gentle breeze, 1 Kings 19); he announces that Ahab and Jezebel will die bloody deaths because they have killed one Naboth to get possession of his vineyard (1 Kings 21); and he is transported to heaven in a chariot of fire (2 Kings 2). As he ascends, his mantle falls on:

Elisha (*c.*850–800 BCE): He does not have the weight of Elijah, and the stories about him come from a cycle of legends describing miracles. Some of these are quite trivial, as when Elisha retrieves an axe head from the water by throwing in a stick which makes the iron float (2 Kings 6.1–7). He too revives the dead son of a widow (2 Kings 4) and cures Naaman, a Syrian commander, of leprosy by telling him to bathe in the Jordan (2 Kings 5). He has dealings with kings which are not as antagonistic as those of Elijah; they clearly set great store by his predictions.

The writing prophets (in chronological order)

Amos (*c.*750 BCE): Active in the northern kingdom of Israel. Originally a herdsman, his words are sharply critical of the social injustices which he sees around him, and which are a profound contradiction of the holiness and justice of God. The nine chapters of his book are full of the most vivid imagery about the 'day of the Lord' which is to come:

'Let justice roll down like waters,
and righteousness like an everflowing stream' (5.24).

Hosea (*c.*750 BCE): Probably active in the northern kingdom. He is told by God to marry a prostitute, who continues to be unfaithful to him; he sees this relationship as a parable of the relationship between Israel and God. The most powerful passages in the book of fourteen chapters speak of God's love for his unfaithful people:

'When Israel was a child, I loved him, and out of Egypt I called my son.
The more I called them, the more they went away from me' (11.1–2).

Isaiah (*c.*740–700 BCE): Receives the call to be prophet in the Jerusalem temple in an awesome scene (chapter 6). This leads to an encounter between Isaiah and King Ahaz in which Isaiah tells the king, under threat of attack from Assyria, not to make alliances with his neighbours, but to trust in God and all will be well. This is the context of the famous prophecy about a young woman (thus the Hebrew; only the Greek has 'virgin') conceiving: before the child can distinguish between evil and good, neighbouring lands will be devastated. Isaiah emphasizes the holiness of God, who will therefore bring judgement. (Only) a remnant will survive – the sayings about this are ambivalent.

'Holy, holy, holy is the Lord of hosts;
the whole earth is full of his glory' (6.3).

There are 66 chapters in the book of Isaiah. The material thought to go back to Isaiah of Jerusalem is to be found in chapters 1–39. Chapters 40–55 reflect a completely different period, the time of the impending return from exile, and are therefore thought to come from an anonymous prophet of that period, who is known as *Second Isaiah* or *Deutero-Isaiah.* These chapters are a hymn of promise and hope, made familiar by Handel's *Messiah*: 'Comfort ye my people'; 'Every valley shall be exalted and every hill made low' (40.1, 4), so that the returning exiles will have a swift journey home. A different tone is struck by four 'Servant Songs' contained in the chapters, which depict someone chosen by

God to suffer for the people, again familiar from *Messiah*: 'He was despised and rejected by men; a man of sorrows and acquainted with grief' (53.3).

Chapters 56–66 seem to reflect yet another period, reflecting a time when the Jerusalem temple has been rebuilt. Scholars sometimes call this section *Trito-Isaiah* or Third Isaiah, although it is not connected as closely with a particular prophetic mind as First Isaiah or Second Isaiah.

> 'Arise, shine; for your light has come,
> and the glory of the Lord has risen upon you' (60.1).

Micah (c. 660 BCE): We know nothing at all of his life; like his contemporary Isaiah he seems to have been active in Jerusalem. Some passages in the seven chapters of his book also appear in Isaiah. He too preaches judgement and a powerful ethic:

> 'He has showed you, O man, what is good; and what does the Lord require of you but to do justice, and to love kindness, and to walk humbly with your God?' (6.8).

Zephaniah (c. 630 BCE): A prophet of judgement, proclaiming the coming of the day of the Lord. We know nothing about him, and the three chapters of his book contain a mixture of oracles. 'A day of wrath is that day, a day of distress and anguish' (1.15) in Latin provides the text for the *Dies Irae* of the Roman Catholic requiem mass.

Nahum (c. 625 BCE): A series of invectives against Assyria and its capital Nineveh: 'Woe to the bloody city!' (3.1).

Jeremiah (625–587 BCE): Jeremiah lived in the period between the last years of the southern kingdom and the beginnings of the exile; when Jerusalem was captured for the first time he was taken to Egypt, where he died. His book, of 52 chapters, comes across as the most personal of the prophetic books partly because of the passages between chapters 11 and 20 which are known as the 'Confessions' of Jeremiah – written in the first person they express the prophet's suffering as a result of his calling – and partly because of the quantity of apparently biographical incidents included in the book. Again his message is one of judgement on the abuses in the worship of his time and contains a vision of what God wants:

> 'This is the covenant which I will make with the house of Israel after those days, says the Lord: I will put my law within them, and I will write it upon their hearts, and I will be their God, and they shall be my people' (31.33).

Habakkuk (c. 600 BCE): Nothing is known of this prophet, who sees the Chaldeans being used as an instrument of God's judgement. The Dead Sea Scrolls contain a commentary on the short book (3 chapters), reinterpreting it for the time of the sect.

Ezekiel (593–570 BCE): A near contemporary of Jeremiah, he went into exile in Babylon. He is the most 'priestly' of the prophets, and the last chapters of his long book (40–8) describe a vision of the restored Jerusalem, temple and city. He was clearly a well-known public figure in Jerusalem immediately before the exile, and performed a number of symbolic actions, lying on his right side for 40 days to symbolize the duration of the exile, going around naked, and not observing mourning for his wife. Chapter 37 of his book depicts symbolically the resurrection of his nation with a valley of dry bones which are given flesh. The vision he had at his call was of a marvellous chariot of fire; the term 'wheels within wheels' comes from it.

Obadiah (c. 580 BCE): A single chapter by an unknown prophet, reflecting on the fate of Israel's neighbour Edom and the coming of the 'Day of the Lord'.

Haggai (c. 520 BCE): Active in Jerusalem after the exiles returned from Babylon. He is also mentioned in the book of Ezra (5.1; 6.14). The two chapters of the book express concern over the delay in rebuilding the temple.

Zechariah (c. 520 BCE): A contemporary of Haggai, who is also concerned with the rebuilding of the temple. The book has fourteen chapters, with a clear break after chapter 8. The first half contains a series of eight visions which are interpreted by an angel, referring to Jerusalem and the key figures in the restoration of city and temple. Judgement, kindness and mercy still predominate.

Chapters 9–14 seem to come from a later date. They were used by Matthew in particular in his account of the passion and crucifixion of Jesus: for example the 30 pieces of silver paid to Judas come from here (11.12–13), as does Jesus' remark about the shepherd being struck and the sheep scattered (13.7).

The book of Zechariah marks a transition between prophecy and apocalyptic.

Malachi (c. 400 BCE): Malachi is not a proper name: it means 'my messenger'. Much of the book is concerned with failures to fulfil the precepts of the law. It ends with the words 'Behold, I will send you Elijah the prophet before the great and terrible day of the Lord comes' (4.5); this passage led to the Jewish practice of leaving a chair empty at the Passover meal for Elijah to occupy.

Joel (impossible to date): Another unknown prophet. The first half of the three chapters of his book are dominated by the image of an attack by a swarm of locusts. The second half contains promises of a new time when 'I will pour out my spirit upon all flesh; your sons and your daughters shall prophesy, your old men shall dream dreams' (2.28).

Jonah: The book probably dates from the fourth to second centuries BCE. It is a story about an eighth-century prophet and his reluctance to preach to the people of Nineveh.

p. 845

Daniel (c. 164 BCE): Although this book is included among the prophets, Daniel is not really a prophet. The first six chapters portray him as a pious exile in Babylon, living under Nebuchadnezzar and Belshazzar, for whom the 'writing on the wall appears'. The last five chapters contain visions characteristic of apocalyptic. They are the only instance of this genre in the Hebrew Bible.

Apocalyptic

idolatry and the oppression of the poor and vulnerable. The language is frequently strong, nowhere more so than in the case of Jeremiah's stunning critique of the Jerusalem temple in Jeremiah 7, where he famously calls it a den of robbers: what he says is so negative that it would inevitably have been offensive to his hearers. No wonder that he was persecuted and imprisoned.

The prophetic critique of the present and the threat of judgement also produced a future hope of a return to the conditions of paradise. Although this hope is one which is deeply rooted in the human race, what is much more remarkable is the consistent streak of self-criticism evident in the prophetic literature.

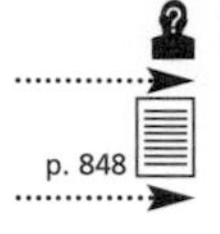
p. 848

The prophetic religion of the Bible also resembles similar movements in other religions in another way. Prophets such as Elijah and Elisha and their predecessors, such as Samuel, behave eccentrically. Samuel pronounces the downfall of King Saul because Saul has not waited for him to arrive before offering a sacrifice (1 Samuel 13.8–15); Elijah calls down fire from heaven on messengers from King Ahaziah (2 Kings 1); and after a curse by Elisha, bears devour children who call him 'Bald head' (2 Kings 2.23–5). This suggests that these figures were not learned scribes or social critics but religious ecstatics, akin to the shamans who are to be found in different religious traditions throughout the world. Such behaviour tends to be less to the fore in the 'classical' prophets such as Isaiah, though Jeremiah's tortured relationship with the divine and Ezekiel's strange visions and peculiar behaviour remind us of this ecstatic element in prophetic religion. That element has a long tradition in Judaism and Christianity and is closely linked with mystical currents in both religions. In Judaism Ezekiel's vision of the divine throne chariot (Ezekiel 1) prompted a long tradition of ecstatic religion in which adepts believed that they could ascend to heaven, see the glory of God, and have divine mysteries revealed to them. This is hinted at briefly by the apostle Paul in 2 Corinthians 12.2–4.

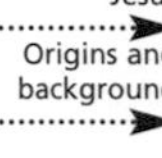
Jesus
Origins and background

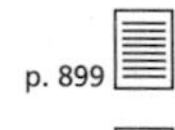
p. 899

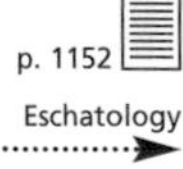
p. 1152
Eschatology

There was a great burst of literary activity during the exile of the Jews in Babylon in the sixth century BCE, when ancient traditions were codified and reflections on recent experience took place. The vindication of the prophetic message of judgement meant that the prophetic oracles were treated with great reverence and set alongside the original deposit stemming from Moses as the bedrock of the Jewish faith. The return from exile saw the gradual waning of the prophetic movement. Possibly it may have been discredited by the fervent support given to the messianic movement centred on Zerubbabel by the prophets Haggai and Zechariah, but apart from a few cryptic passages (e.g. Zechariah 13.1ff.), little is known about the fate of the movement. It is difficult to believe that it vanished without trace: it may either have been forced underground during a power struggle in the post-exilic community or have become connected to the emerging apocalyptic literature. Nevertheless, prophecy became not the living words of the contemporary individual but the written deposit of past ages whose words were looked to as a means of ascertaining the divine will in the present. Biblical interpretation became more important than attention to the living voice of prophecy. Although it is not possible with any degree of certainty to trace the history of prophecy after biblical times, it is likely that on the fringes of a Jewish religion increasingly orientated on temple and book, there were groups of spiritual visionaries and seers. Such individuals make their appearance from time to time in the account of temple worship given by the Jewish historian Flavius Josephus of Second Temple religion in his *Antiquities* and *Jewish War*.

Paul

The appearance of a prophet like John the Baptist and his contemporary Jesus would not have been at all surprising, even if their social effects were viewed with suspicion by the political authorities. Jesus resembles both the holy men who frequented Galilee in the first century CE and the prophetic figures described by Josephus. John the Baptist was executed for subversion by Herod Antipas, and appears to have seen himself as the herald of a decisive moment in God's purposes. This seems to have provided the context for Jesus' own activity. Jesus had a prophetic-type call (there is an echo of Ezekiel 1.1 in Mark 1.10). Like the prophets before him (compare Hosea 6.6 with Matthew 9.13; 12.7), Jesus condemns the religious obligation which lays such great weight on narrowly-conceived religious acts and neglects the more important aspects of the demand of God's righteousness in practice of one human towards another (see Luke 11.42). Jesus seems to have predicted the downfall of the Jerusalem temple (Mark 13.2), and contemporaries seem to have considered that he thought of himself as a prophet (Matthew 12.39; 13.57; 21.11, 26; Luke 7.16; 13.33f.; John 6.14).

The prophetic is a crucial element in the rise of Christianity. However, the early Christians believed that the eschatological salvation was not wholly in the future, particularly since the new age had broken into the old in the resurrection of Jesus. The belief in the return of the prophetic Spirit, such a dominant feature of early Christian religion, cannot be understood apart from this eschatological perspective. While there was no unified view of the Spirit's activity in contemporary Judaism, there is evidence that some Jews thought of it as part of the past experience of God's people. Visions also are central to early Christianity. Paul makes much of the centrality of the prophet even in his Greek-speaking church (1 Corinthians 12–14). The return of the Spirit was believed to coincide with an outburst of prophetic activity, and such activity was characteristic of the Pauline communities. In the account of the origin of the church in Acts Luke places prophetic and ecstatic experience at the centre, and this element makes its appearance throughout the account he offers of Christian origins. Some of Paul's problems with the church at Corinth could have been alleviated had there not been other Christian missionaries in the Corinthian church with different approaches.

The major prophetic text in the New Testament is the Book of Revelation. This too has both prediction and social criticism. It predicts the coming of a new world in which God's dwelling will be with humanity and uses images from the book of Daniel to mount a strong critique of the politics and economics of the Roman empire (Revelation 13 and 17). It also predicts the overthrow of the empire and places early Christianity's understanding of political hope firmly at odds with the empire as the tool of the fulfilment of God's promises.

Whether prophetic movements of any kind are authentic, despite their disruptive qualities, is decided by the test of time (cf. Acts 5.39). Like the test of prophecy in Deuteronomy 13, the validity of such claims depended on whether they actually were fulfilled. As in Judaism, so too in Christianity there was suspicion of the prophetic as something unpredictable, tending towards the extravagant and eccentric. The continued existence of the church necessitated the regulation of prophetic activity.

In Phrygia in the middle of the second century CE the Montanists claimed that they were the true heirs to the early Christian experience, emphasizing the importance of prophecy and the activity of the Spirit. That indicates that this form of activity was deeply ingrained within the Christian experience. Such prophetic movements have been a constant feature of the church, particularly since the late medieval period. The book of Revelation has provided a stimulus to prophetic activity among women as well as men. At the Reformation the early Anabaptist movement was marked by the kind of ecstatic prophecy which was typical in the early church; the same was true in the early years of the Commonwealth in seventeenth-century England, as women found a voice through the permission given them to speak by Paul's words in 1 Corinthians 11.5. While prophecy as a prediction has always been a feature of Christianity, alongside this there has been the dimension of prophecy as 'forthtelling', or speaking on behalf of God. It is this latter dimension that characterizes modern understandings of the prophetic in Christian theology.

CHRISTOPHER ROWLAND

D. Aune, *Prophecy in Early Christianity and the Ancient Mediterranean World*, Grand Rapids, MI: Eerdmans 1983; N. Cohn, *The Pursuit of the Millennium*, London and New York: OUP 1970; J. J. Collins, B. McGinn and S. Stein (eds), *Encyclopedia of Apocalypticism* (3 vols), New York: Continuum 2000

Protestantism

Protestantism is the term used to describe the churches and more generally the religious culture that grew out of the Reformation of the early sixteenth century, a movement that sought the reform of Western Christianity in a variety of ways, all of which resulted in breaks with Catholicism. The term 'Protestant' emerged following the second imperial council of Speyer (1529), which outlawed Lutheran teachings and practices. In reaction to this development, a group of princes and representatives of free imperial cities withdrew and protested. They were referred to as *protestantes* ('protesters'), hence the origin of the terms 'Protestant' and 'Protestantism'. The Protestant movement can be seen as growing out of the European Renaissance, which emphasized the renewal of culture based on a return to classical (Greek and Roman) patterns in conscious opposition to cultural patterns inherited from the 'middle age' (*media aetas*, the term coined in the Renaissance as a way of making this distinction; nowadays this term is always used in the plural, Middle Ages).

Reformation
Roman empire
Renaissance
Middle Ages

The Protestant Reformation was also preceded by a number of reforming movements within Catholicism, including the work of such reformers as John Wyclif (England), John Hus (Bohemia) and Girolamo Savonarola (Italy), the conciliar movement that had sought the reform of the papacy by church councils, and the spiritual renewal brought about by the late medieval *Devotio moderna* ('modern devotion', represented by Thomas à Kempis and others). The Protestant Reformation was closely tied to the development of northern European commerce, political states, and especially the free imperial cities technically within the governance of the Holy Roman empire, but which were seeking greater independence from the empire in the early sixteenth century. It is often associated with the development of printed books (from the middle of the fifteenth century) and growing literacy among the *bourgeoisie* of northern European cities.

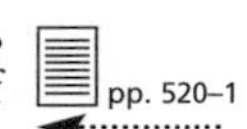
pp. 520–1
Papacy
Council
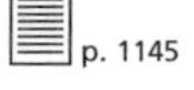
p. 1145
Reformation
Anabaptists
Books

On closer examination, Protestantism can be seen as embracing a variety of church traditions.

The *Lutheran* pattern of Protestant culture and church life originated with the reforms of Martin Luther (1483–1546), an Augustinian monk and scholar of biblical languages, whose 95 Latin theses for debate (October 1517) questioned fine points of traditional Catholic theology related to the practices of penance and indulgences. Ensuing controversy seems to have led Luther to question more broadly certain historic Catholic teachings.

Lutheranism
Martin Luther
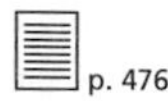
p. 476

PROTESTANTS, DISSENTERS AND NON-CONFORMISTS

From the sixteenth century onwards, many Christians came to be referred to by terms which did not indicate the positive aspects of the faith but the fact that there were things that they were against. Here are some of them:

Protestant: This term was first used of a group of princes and representatives of free imperial cities who after the Second Imperial Council of Speyer in 1549 protested against the banning of Lutheran teaching and practices. It came to be used generally of those churches which arose out of the Reformation, as opposed to the Roman Catholic Church. The Anglican Church is sometimes included among them, but occupies a middle position between Protestantism and Roman Catholicism.

Dissenter: Used first of those who excluded themselves from the Church of England, including Roman Catholics. Now, however, it is used only of Protestants. A difference from Non-conformist is that it indicates not only dissent from the Church of England but also the rejection of the principle of established churches.

Non-conformist: The term was first used in the seventeenth century of those who, while initially agreeing with the doctrines of the Church of England, rejected its discipline and forms of worship as laid down in the 1662 Act of Uniformity. It is now used of Protestants generally, but particularly of Presbyterians, Congregationalists, Methodists, Quakers and Baptists.

Non-juror: Literally, refusing to take an oath. The oath in question was the Oath of Allegiance and Supremacy to the English monarchs William and Mary in 1688. A number of bishops, priests and laymen refused to take the oath because in so doing they would break a previous oath to King James II. The bishops and priests were dismissed and others appointed in their place, but they and the Non-juror laity refused to accept this action as legitimate and so for more than a century there was a split in the Church of England.

Schismatic: The term is used of those who are involved in a schism, i.e. formal division in or separation from a church body. Major schisms were that between the Eastern and Western Churches from 1054 onwards and the Great Schism, the division within the Roman Catholic Church from 1378 to 1415 when there were two popes, one in Rome and another in Avignon. Unfortunately schism has been all too frequent in Christian churches.

Authority

Sacraments

Justification

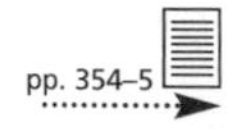

pp. 354–5

John Calvin

By 1520 he openly questioned traditional teachings about papal authority and the authority of church councils, about the seven sacraments, and about justification, on which point he insisted on the teaching that justification is by 'faith alone' (*sola fide*) on the basis of 'grace alone' (*sola gratia*). By this year a number of his teachings had been formally condemned by papal decree and in the following January he was excommunicated.

p. 302

Luther gathered supporters through the 1520s. Following the second imperial council (or 'Diet') of Speyer in 1529, he was placed under ban of empire, a marked man, and representatives of Lutheran churches gathered in his absence in Augsburg in the next year (1530) to adopt the Augsburg Confession, a very moderate statement of Lutheran doctrinal concerns addressed to the emperor in the hope that the empire might be persuaded to adopt Lutheran reforms or at least to tolerate Lutheran teachings. Throughout the 1530s and beyond, Lutheran churches were organized in specific principalities and cities in German-speaking areas of the empire.

Reformed churches

Huldrych Zwingli

A second distinct pattern of Protestant culture is represented in the *Reformed* tradition, a first example of which is the work of Martin Luther's contemporary, Huldrych Zwingli (1484–1531). As priest of the Great Minster in Zurich from late 1518, Zwingli began a series of daily sermons commenting on the New Testament, starting with the Gospel of Matthew, in which he made specific suggestions for the reform of the church in the city. He simplified the church services and began holding services in German. Eventually he did away with the practice of making confessions, religious images, priestly vestments and the church's organ. His reforming work was carried on by John Calvin (1509–64), who in 1536 was forced to assist William Farel in his work of reforming the church in Geneva. Calvin's systematic mind had already led him to issue a first edition of his *Institutes of the Christian Religion*, which was to go through numerous revised and expanded editions in his lifetime. Though Calvin and Farel met strong opposition and Calvin was forced to flee from the city in 1538, he returned in 1541 and had general support from the city council from that time to the end of his life. Under his leadership Geneva became a model for reform, attracting Protestant exiles from other European nations. The city reformed not only church practices but also educational systems and even public works. As a result of the Geneva reform, the patterns initiated by Calvin and Zwingli were emulated in other cantons of Switzerland (leading to Swiss Reformed churches), in some German states and cities (German Reformed churches), in the Netherlands (Dutch Reformed churches), and in some areas of France (where Reformed Christians were referred to as 'Huguenots') and Britain (English and Scottish Presbyterians and Congregationalists).

A third distinct pattern of church life and culture is represented in the *Anglican* tradition, the evolution of which was tied more to the religious policies of reigning monarchs than to particular theologians. In the latter years of Henry VIII (reigned 1509–47), the church in England was separated from continental church courts and the hierarchy of continental Catholicism, although its doctrine and worship remained essentially Catholic. The regents of the boy king Edward VI (reigned 1547–53) moved the English church in a much more clearly Reformed direction, with a revised English liturgy and Articles of Religion affirming Reformed doctrine. Under Mary Tudor (reigned 1553–58) the nation was received back into the fold of European Catholicism and Protestant ministers were suppressed – some were executed and some fled into exile in Europe (many to Calvin's Geneva). The religious policy of Mary's half-sister, Elizabeth I (reigned 1558–1603), set the truer foundations of the Anglican tradition. Under Elizabeth the English church adopted a set of Thirty-Nine Articles of Religion expressing Protestant principles in moderate but recognizably Reformed language. At the same time, the church adopted an English prayer book that retained much more of ancient and medieval liturgical traditions than continental or Scottish Reformed churches had maintained. This balance is sometimes described as reflecting a *via media* ('middle of the way') between Catholicism and the Reformed tradition in the Elizabethan settlement of religion. Despite the settlement that Elizabeth advocated, however, the English church in her reign was seriously divided between those Anglicans who favoured her *via media* and those who sought a more thorough reform of the church modelled on Geneva and the Reformed tradition – the latter came to be known as 'Puritans'. This division would lead in the seventeenth century to the English Revolution and its aftermath.

A fourth very distinct pattern of Protestant culture is represented by the so-called *Radical Reformation* and is represented in a variety of Anabaptist church traditions that originated in the sixteenth century. The 'Zwickau Prophets' associated with Thomas Müntzer were allied with the Peasants' Revolt (1521) against state authority. A very different group emerged in the vicinity of Zurich during Zwingli's time there (*c.*1525); unlike the Zwickau Prophets it took a pacifist stance that would characterize almost all Anabaptist groups after the attempt of some Anabaptists to take the city of Münster by force (1534–5). Later in the sixteenth century Bohemian groups identified as Hutterites and then the followers of the Dutch teacher Menno Simons (1496–1591), 'Mennonites', became the largest Anabaptist communities. The various Anabaptist groups not only rejected infant baptism and insisted on baptizing those who had previously been baptized as infants (hence the accusation that they were 're-baptizers', the literal meaning of 'Anabaptist'); they also rejected church-state collaboration and adopted communal lifestyles. Anabaptists were generally persecuted during the sixteenth and seventeenth centuries.

These varied traditions have some marks of Protestant belief and cultures in common. It is characteristic of historic Protestant churches to insist that the Bible is the sole, final authority for faith and for the reform of the church (thus *sola scriptura*, 'by scripture alone'), rejecting traditional Roman Catholic teachings about church councils and the interpretation of the Bible by bishops (including the Bishop of Rome). Lutherans and many Anglicans allowed that later Christian traditions not condemned in scripture could be observed in churches (for instance, the use of liturgical vestments), although the Reformed tradition tended to insist on a positive precedent in scripture for the reform of the church. Anglicans and Lutherans valued the early traditions of the Christian church, including the creeds and doctrinal statements of the early councils and (for Anglicans and some Lutherans) the episcopal constitution of the early churches.

Almost all of the churches of the Protestant tradition affirm the doctrines of the Trinity and the full divinity and humanity of Jesus Christ defined in the early councils of the Christian church. The only exceptions to this would be a small minority of Socinians, followers of Fausto Sozzini (1539–1604), who rejected the traditional doctrine of the Trinity, and are sometimes classified, along with Anabaptists, as comprising the 'Radical Reformation', though this identification is suspect because Socinians and Anabaptists had very little in common. Reformation churches in general did not define traditional Roman Catholic doctrines about Mary the mother of Jesus, although individual Reformers such as Luther and Calvin continued to believe in the doctrine of her perpetual virginity.

In their teachings about human nature and salvation, Protestant churches generally insist on human depravity and consequently the need for salvation by divine grace alone (*sola gratia*) on the basis of faith alone (*sola fide*). Most Reformation churches defined doctrines of predestination, although in a number of different forms, as ways of emphasizing the priority of God's work in salvation. A minority of Protestants (Remonstrants or Arminians) would later reject doctrines of predestination, and over the last 150 years these doctrines have tended to be either ignored or criticized.

Classic Protestant doctrinal standards defined the church as constituted by faith, the preaching of the gospel, and the administration of the sacraments of baptism and the

Anglicanism
Church of England
Bible
pp. 288–9
Trinity
Mary
Puritans
Anabaptists
Predestination
Salvation
p. 1016
Peace churches

eucharist. To these elements, the Reformed churches added the need for discipline in the church, which Anabaptists also maintained in their own ways. Sacramental teachings within the Reformation churches varied considerably. Lutherans and many Anglicans insisted that baptism brings about the 'new birth' (regeneration) in Christ and that Christ was bodily present in the eucharist (though rejecting medieval formulations of the Roman Catholic understanding of transubstantiation). The mainstream of the Reformed tradition, following Calvin, asserted a close but not quite necessary relationship between baptism and the new birth and asserted that although Christ's literal, material body is not present, Christ is present as a distinct power (*virtus*) to those who receive the eucharist with true faith. The left wing of the Reformed tradition, following Zwingli, tended to believe that baptism is a symbol of the faith by which we are saved and that the bread and wine of the eucharist are appropriate and scriptural symbols of Christ's presence, though this presence is not unique to the eucharist. Anabaptists advocated similar ideas, with the further nuance that baptism is appropriate for adult believers only, since only adults could place themselves under the discipline of the Christian community.

Discipline

p. 1068

Ethics

A significant aspect of Protestant culture is that Lutheran, Reformed and Anglican churches were established as state churches in European countries. Anabaptists, on the other hand, rejected the conception of co-operation between church and state, military service on the part of Christians, and in some cases the participation of Christians in governmental offices or even their taking oaths in civil courts.

Protestant churches differed considerably in the forms of church governance or polity that they adopted. Churches of the Anglican tradition and some Lutheran churches maintained a form of episcopal polity (governance by bishops in association with church councils) inherited from the Middle Ages and modified somewhat during the Reformation. Reformed churches are divided between those that favour a presbyterian or synodal polity (governance is shared between local congregations and a representative presbytery or synod) and those that favour a more strictly congregational polity (church life is governed by a congregational assembly with relatively little connection to larger church bodies). Some Protestant churches later developed hybridized versions of these three historic forms of polity, and Lutheran churches have never adopted one form of polity, so that some Lutheran churches are episcopal, some synodal, and some nearly congregational in their governance.

Organization

Pietism

Evangelicals

Methodism

In its moral teachings Protestant culture has strongly inculcated the need to follow the 'great commandments': to love God and one's neighbour with one's whole being. Protestants have also taught the Ten Commandments of the Hebrew scriptures. There were some significant divisions within Protestant culture over moral issues, for example, the Reformed tradition's strong insistence on observing Sunday as the Lord's Day and the fulfilment of the sabbath spoken of in the Ten Commandments. Neither Lutheran nor Anglican cultures developed this same emphasis on the Lord's Day. Since the time of Max Weber in the early twentieth century, Protestants have been seen as closely allied to the beginnings of mercantile economies, hence Weber's attempt to identify a 'Protestant work ethic', although his identification of this ethic with Protestant culture has been contested: it can be argued that it reflects a culture of modernity of which Protestantism was but one expression.

pp. 384–5

Since the time of the Reformation, Protestant churches have undergone a number of significant changes. In the seventeenth century, corresponding to the period of inter-confessional wars in Europe, there was a trend towards Protestant scholasticism, the attempt to define and defend systematically the teachings of national churches. Both Reformed and Lutheran scholars undertook large-scale systematic theological treatises designed to interpret and defend their versions of Protestant culture. Although Anglicans did not develop the same kind of scholastic theology, in the seventeenth century they developed a historical defence of Anglicanism, arguing that their traditions represented a revival of early Christian practices and beliefs, purified of the later embellishments of medieval Catholicism.

The later seventeenth century saw the rise of Pietism (in Lutheran and Reformed churches), emphasizing a 'religion of the heart' and the need for heartfelt repentance and faith. Early Pietists also stressed the need for Christian learning (Halle University was a centre for Pietist culture), social engagement (for example, the 'Franckean institutions' organized by August Hermann Francke at Halle), and mutual understanding between Christian communities.

A British parallel to Pietism was offered in the evangelical revival, associated with the preaching of George Whitefield, John Wesley, and others and beginning in the early eighteenth century. One significant outgrowth of the evangelical revival was the Methodist movement, led by the Anglican priests John and Charles Wesley in the eighteenth century. The spread of the Methodist movement led eventually to the organization of independent Methodist churches in the United States (1784), in the United Kingdom (1795), and eventually throughout the world. The Methodist churches adapted the polity and doctrines of the Church of England, and emphasized the preaching of the 'way of salvation' (repentance, faith, and holiness) and direct engagement with the social concerns of displaced populations in England (due to the industrial revolution) and in the United States (following the westward expansion of the American frontier). The eighteenth century also saw the Great Awakening in the United States.

In the nineteenth century, the Great Awakening and the evangelical movement would result in a wide variety of new movements and churches, for instance, the rise of Dispensationalist groups and independent evangelical congregations in Britain and North America, the rise of holiness revivals and holiness churches, and the prominent development of Baptist evangelicalism in the nineteenth and twentieth centuries. Camp meetings, Bible conferences, and urban revivals all contributed to the spread of the evangelical movement in the nineteenth century.

The nineteenth century also witnessed the rise of Protestant liberalism, an attempt to interpret traditional Christian beliefs in the light of modern scientific culture. Emphasizing a positive evaluation of humankind and its own version of progressivism, Protestant Liberalism embraced Enlightenment theories of knowledge and modern biblical criticism.

The early nineteenth century also saw a series of new conservative movements within historic Protestant traditions, such as the Oxford Movement (sometimes called the Tractarian Movement) within the Church of England, the New Lutheranism and Old Lutheran churches in German states, and the Mercersburg theology among Reformed churches, especially in the United States. Though rejecting Protestant liberalism, these movements all also rejected Pietism and Evangelicalism, reviving the sacramental and liturgical life that had characterized Anglican, Lutheran and Reformed life in the sixteenth and seventeenth centuries.

Protestants became significantly involved in missionary activities from the 1790s, with the arrival of William Carey in India. The nineteenth century was 'the great century' for Protestant missionary work, with significant missionary enterprises in Africa and Asia (especially India and China) and some work (beginning late in the nineteenth century) in Central and South America. By the end of the nineteenth century Protestantism had developed an elaborate infrastructure of churches, schools, hospitals and other institutions throughout the world.

The emergence of Pentecostalism in the very early years of the twentieth century represents a new direction for Protestant churches. Growing out of the holiness movement of the nineteenth century, Pentecostals taught believers to expect a 'baptism of the Holy Spirit' accompanied by the initial evidence of speaking in unknown tongues. The Pentecostal movement grew in the early twentieth century among the poor and the working classes in social situations where there was considerable population displacement because of rising industrialization. After the middle of the twentieth century, its influence in older, liturgical churches could be seen in the charismatic movement. Pentecostalism became such a huge global phenomenon by the end of the twentieth century that many interpreters understand it to be a phenomenon distinct from its Protestant roots.

Great Awakening

The neo-orthodox movement of the twentieth century marked a renewal of Reformation themes, but refused to embrace either the liberal or the conservative movements of the nineteenth century. Associated with the seminal theologian Karl Barth, it emphasized divine sovereignty, the fallen state of humanity and the need for divine grace. The movement was also associated with overt opposition to the Third Reich in Germany (for example, in the person of Dietrich Bonhoeffer), and lay in the background of some civil rights activism in the United States.

Neo-orthodox theology
Holiness movement
Karl Barth

Liberal theology
Ecumenical movement

Protestant involvement in the ecumenical movement in the twentieth century led to significant church mergers and rapprochement, as well as noteworthy changes in forms of worship grounded in ecumenical discoveries of common liturgies from the early Christian church. Ecumenical exposure called on Protestant churches to re-consider many of their historic teachings and practices in the light of their exposure to Orthodoxy and Roman Catholicism, and would lead to very significant doctrinal and practical developments, exemplified in the World Council of Churches Faith and Order study of *Baptism, Eucharist and Ministry* (1982) or the Lutheran-Roman Catholic *Joint Declaration on Justification* of 31 October 2000.

Oxford Movement

p. 1186

Protestantism has entered the third Christian millennium with signs of stagnation and decline in Europe and North America and signs of renewal and growth in Africa and Asia and (to a lesser degree) in Central and South America. The older Protestant communities of Europe and North America witnessed very significant declines in church membership and some decline in church activity in the later twentieth century. Declines in membership could be attributed to the fact that European and American cultures in general no longer value church membership, and consequently a large number of formerly nominal church members no longer appear as members of these denominations. Declines in church activities (e.g. attendance at worship and participation in educational and service activities) have not been as serious as declines in membership; indeed in some cases churches have even shown small increases. In contrast to these European and North American patterns, Protestant churches in Africa and Asia have experienced very strong growth both in total memberships and in participation in church-related activities in the later decades of the twentieth century, so that in many cases Third World Protestants outnumber those in the so-called First World (so, e.g., there are now more Anglicans in the southern

Mission

Pentecostalism
Third World
Geography

hemisphere than in the northern hemisphere). Combined with the explosive growth of Pentecostalism and other independent evangelical movements in the twentieth century, these Pentecostal and indigenous evangelical churches of the Third World are sometimes seen together as a distinctive form of Christian faith alongside the conventional categories.

TED CAMPBELL

Ted A. Campbell, *Christian Confessions: A Historical Introduction*, Louisville, KY: Westminster John Knox Press 1996; John Dillenberger and Claude Welch, *Protestant Christianity Interpreted through its Development*, New York and London: Macmillan [2]1988; Carter Lindberg, *The European Reformations*, Oxford: Blackwell 1996; Hans J. Hillerbrand, *The Protestant Reformation*, New York: Harper Torchbooks 1977

Psalms

Christian use of the psalms

It is impossible to overstate the importance of the Psalter (i.e., the biblical book of Psalms as used in various translations during church worship) for the prayer and worship of Christians. It is the one book of the Old Testament that is commonly bound in on its own with a New Testament, and the regular recitation of psalms has been an essential part of structured Christian prayer from the beginning, as it was of Jewish prayer. Early Christian ascetics in the deserts of Egypt or Syria were reputed to say the entire Psalter in a day. Benedict, in his Rule, provides for a gentler rhythm, in which the whole Psalter is to be distributed across a single week. In the Book of Common Prayer, Thomas Cranmer, reshaping the medieval monastic scheme of daily prayer for the use of Anglican clergy and congregations, provided for all the psalms to be recited 'in course' (i.e. consecutively) once each month. This Anglican tradition of continuous reading now co-exists with schemes that allocate particular psalms to particular days or seasons, but the principle that the Psalter should be used systematically in daily prayer and (to a lesser extent) the eucharist is very widely adhered to. So is the association of certain psalms with certain occasions in the Christian year, e.g. of Psalm 51 with Ash Wednesday or of Psalm 22 with Good Friday.

Bible
Prayer
Calendar

The translation of the Psalms that Cranmer included in the Book of Common Prayer, by Miles Coverdale, is a very early one, dating from 1535. Although Coverdale did not know Hebrew and did much of his translation from the German Bibles of Martin Luther and Huldrych Zwingli, he did have second-hand access to the Hebrew text by way of literal Latin versions that had been prepared for translators. The many differences of substance between Coverdale's translation and a modern Psalms translation reflect the enormous advances that have been made by Hebraists in understanding the text and meaning of the psalms since the sixteenth century. However, so picturesque are many of its phrases, and so embedded in the English language, that it has taken on a life of its own.

Reading the psalms

The poetical form used throughout the psalms is parallelism, in which a short statement is balanced in some way by another short statement. The second statement can reinforce the first by reiteration, e.g. 'O come, let us sing to the Lord, let us make a joyful noise to the rock of our salvation' (95.1), or by contrast, e.g. 'For the Lord knows the way of the righteous, but the way of the wicked will perish' (1.6); it can also develop the first, e.g. 'To God belongs victory, upon your people may your blessing be' (3.8). These simple forms can be developed into quite complex structures, as in Psalm 121: 'I lift my eyes to the mountains. Whence comes my help? My help comes from God, maker of heaven and earth. He will not let your foot slip, nor will your guardian sleep. No he will not sleep, will not slumber, the guardian of Israel' (1–4). Here two sets of couplets are each linked by the repetition of a single word: in the case of the first couplet 'help' and in the case of the second 'sleep'. Studying how the psalms are built up in this way can be endlessly fascinating.

However, all down Christian history, the psalms have been read in a rather less dispassionate way. They are unique in the prayer literature of the world in the depth of the emotion they express – doubt, despair, hopelessness, anger, all directed against God. The accounts of the crucifixion of Jesus in the first three Gospels show him dying with the words, 'My God, my God, why have you forsaken me?' upon his lips. These are a quotation of the beginning of Psalm 22 and such words appear time and again elsewhere in the Psalter. 'I am weary with my crying; my throat is parched. My eyes grow dim with waiting for my God' (69.3). The psalmists are experts in depicting human distress: 'I lie awake, I am like a lonely bird on the housetop. All day my enemies taunt me, those who deride me use my name for a curse. For I eat ashes like bread, and mingle tears with my drink, because of your indignation and anger; for you have taken me up and thrown me away' (102.7–10). And they are not afraid of savage hatred: 'O daughter of Babylon, you devastator! Happy shall he be who requites you with what you have done to us! Happy shall he be who takes your little ones and dashes them against the rock!' (137.8–9).

At the same time the psalms are unparalleled in their exuberant trust and praise: 'God is our refuge and strength, a very present help in trouble. Therefore we will not fear

Choir of monks singing from the Psalter of Stephen of Derby, fifteenth century

though the earth should change, though the mountains shake in the heart of the sea' (46.1–2). 'Praise the Lord from the heavens, praise him in the heights! Praise him, all his angels, praise him, all his host! Praise him, sun and moon, praise him all you shining stars! Praise him, you highest heavens, and you waters above the heavens!' (148.1–4). And they paint some of the most vivid pictures of the glories of God's creation, which are enumerated in loving detail, e.g., in Psalm 104.

All this makes the book of Psalms a unique prayer book to be explored. However, today it is largely unknown territory. Of all the psalms, only Psalm 23 has maintained a particular hold on the affection of Christians, and is one of the very few texts – alongside the Lord's Prayer and 1 Corinthians 13 – of which some clear memory survives in a culture which has mostly forgotten its Christianity.

Performing the psalms

Christians have developed a variety of ways of performing the psalms musically in worship. The origins of plainsong, or 'Gregorian' chant (after a traditional but unsubstantiated connection to Pope Gregory the Great at the beginning of the seventh century), lie in the first millennium CE and are not well understood; it continues in current use, especially in the Roman Catholic Church, and since the restoration of the medieval tradition of plainsong led by the monks of Solesmes in the second half of the nineteenth century. At the end of the seventeenth century, English church musicians began to develop a system of harmonized 'Anglican chant' for the singing of psalms, which was expanded in the nineteenth and twentieth centuries, and continues in use today, especially in Anglican cathedrals. Under the influence of the conti-

Music

nental Reformation, metrical versions of psalms were produced in England from the mid-sixteenth century onwards, those by Sternhold and Hopkins and by Tate and Brady enjoying a wide currency. A few of their metrical psalms have found their way into current English hymn books, e.g. 'As pants the hart for cooling streams' (Psalm 42) or 'Through all the changing scenes of life' (Psalm 34), but their greatest success was in Scotland, where metrical psalmody became a characteristic feature of worship in the Presbyterian church.

Hymns

Presbyterian churches

Messiah

Council

In the liturgical reforms following the Second Vatican Council, a new system of simple harmonized psalm chants was developed by Fr Joseph Gelineau (born 1920). Gelineau chant is less formal than Gregorian chant, and easier for congregational use; it has encouraged the development of the responsorial psalm, i.e. a performance in which the verses are sung by a cantor, and interspersed by a simple, repeated congregational response. Responsorial psalmody is widespread today at sung eucharists, especially Anglican and Roman Catholic, and several complete sets of chants and responses have been written by contemporary church musicians, such as Michael Mizgailo-Cayton (born 1961). In contrast to this variety of Western uses, the Orthodox churches, whose liturgies make equally extensive use of psalms, have consistently used and developed Byzantine psalm tones.

Origins and background

The Psalter in its original setting

The Christian use of the Psalter should not displace a recognition of its original use when set in the context of the history of Israel. The 150 psalms of the biblical Psalter encompass a great variety of genres, and were composed and revised over a period of many centuries. It is not certain when the collection was gathered together in the form in which we now have it. A manuscript from Qumran (1 1QPs[a], dated 30–50 CE) contains roughly the last third of the Psalter, but with important differences of content and order from the biblical book. Scholars debate whether this scroll represents a stage towards the making of the biblical Psalter, which would then have been finalized at a surprisingly late date, or whether it represents a collection of psalms extracted from the already existing biblical Psalter and put together for some other purpose, in which case the Psalter could date from almost any of the last few centuries BCE.

p. 139

p. 845

The oldest stratum of psalms goes well into the period of the first Jerusalem temple, which was destroyed by the Assyrians in 587 BCE. Psalm 82, where Israel's god Yahweh takes his seat at the council of the gods, reflects an early stage in Israelite religion; Psalm 29 celebrates 'the voice of the Lord' in ways that find analogies in ancient Near Eastern cult-texts. It is plausible to suppose that a good deal of psalms material originated in the liturgical practice of the first temple, even if doubt is now cast on a celebrated theory of the Old Testament scholar Sigmund Mowinckel (1884–1965), that a group of psalms (e.g. 24, 96–9) could be used to reconstruct a ceremony of the enthronement of Yahweh, as part of the autumn festival. The Davidic monarchy was closely connected with the temple, and it is not surprising that many psalms reflect the ideology and ceremonies of kingship. These royal psalms often refer to the king as the Lord's anointed, i.e. 'Messiah'. Psalm 45 was clearly written for a royal wedding (perhaps in the northern kingdom based at Samaria until 722 BCE, rather than for a Davidic king at Jerusalem).

Several psalms reflect the defeat and destruction of Jerusalem and its temple and the exile that followed. Psalm 89 celebrates at length the everlasting covenant that Yahweh has made with David, and then reflects, with bitterness and perplexity, that he seems to have brought it to an end. This is one of the clearest examples of the way in which a psalm could be rewritten, as new historical circumstances caused old ideas to be questioned. Psalm 74 gives a vivid picture of the destruction of the first temple; Psalm 137 evokes the nostalgia of exile. Other laments of this kind may originate in subsequent misfortunes. Psalm 44 insists that suffering has come upon God's people precisely because they have been faithful to him, which locates the text in the lead-up to the Maccabean revolt in the second century BCE.

An important strand of the Psalter celebrates the law, in ways that are characteristic of the wisdom tradition: e.g. Psalm 19 (where an ancient piece of hymnody has been recycled into a celebration of the law as grounded in creation) or Psalm 119. Psalm 137 reflects the wisdom tradition's interest in the study of the natural world, Psalm 37 its sometimes limited approach to issues of theodicy.

Within this large body of material, of varying dates and historical circumstances, scholars have sought to identify different genres: thanksgivings, individual laments, communal laments, etc. These categories are useful up to a point, but they can obscure the extent to which psalms were re-used and reshaped from one circumstance to another. Psalm 89 has already been mentioned. Psalm 51 originated as a communal lament after the destruction of Jerusalem (cf. v. 18), but a superscription has been added to make it an individual lament of David, after Nathan the prophet had rebuked him for his adultery with Bathsheba.

The superscription of Psalm 51 is one of a large number of such 'titles'. These are not fully understood, but apparently include indications of (reputed) authorship, and musical and performance directions, as well as the location of several psalms in the biography of David. The superscriptions do not appear in the psalms as they are printed in Christian prayer books, but normally appear in English versions, as they form part of the biblical text.

The motive for the composition of the Psalter as a whole is much discussed. The collection begins with Psalm 1 – a meditation on the law, in the wisdom tradition – and this, together with the fact that it is divided into five books (cf. the five books of the Law?), has encouraged a view that the Psalter originated as a prayer book, for use in meditation, more than as a liturgical resource, for use in worship. But it ends with Psalm 150, an unrestrained expression of musical joy, and the Christian use of the Psalter for both collective worship and individual meditation shows how hard it is to maintain the distinction. The fact that the Psalter is a deliberate selection from a larger body of psalms material is shown by the appearance elsewhere in the Old Testament of psalms and canticles that are not in the Psalter (e.g. the song of Moses and Miriam in Exodus 15).

ANDERS BERGQUIST

Peter R. Ackroyd, *Doors of Perception: A Guide to Reading the Psalms*, London: SCM Press 1983; Walter Brueggemann, *Israel's Praise: Doxology against Idolatry and Ideology*, Philadelphia: Fortress Press 1989; John Day, *Psalms*, Sheffield: JSOT Press 1990; John Eaton, *The Psalms*, London: T&T Clark 2003; S. E. Gillingham, *Poems and Psalms of the Hebrew Bible*, Oxford: OUP 1994; N. Temperley, *The Music of the English Parish Church*, Cambridge: CUP 1979

Pseudepigraphy

Pseudepigraphy is the name given to texts that contain a false claim of authorship. Thus pseudepigraphy can appear to be a euphemism for 'forgery'. Many Jewish texts from around the period when the New Testament was written are pseudepigraphy, like the Book of Enoch and the Psalms of Solomon, and some scholars also argue that the New Testament Gospels and some of the New Testament letters, like the letters to Timothy and Titus, 1 and 2 Peter and James, are pseudepigraphy also. With biblical texts, difficult moral questions immediately arise – is Christianity based on forgeries? The seriousness of the implications of such a conclusion ensures that pseudepigraphy remains a controversial topic in the study of Christianity.

However, not all pseudepigraphy is forgery. For a 'forgery' is a text created with the intention to deceive its readers concerning its authorship. Thus for pseudepigraphy to be forgery 1. there must have been an intention to deceive about authorship and 2. this must have been the intention of the text's creator. The second of these criteria is necessary because both the texts themselves and the way they are read can change after they left their authors' hands. For example, scribes frequently attributed anonymous writings to 'appropriate' famous authors, whether for good motives ('I am sure that this is by this person and it will help later readers if I point it out') or bad ('This will be worth more if it is by someone famous'). However interesting this phenomenon is, it says nothing about the origins of the text itself. The first of these criteria, 'intention to deceive about its authorship', is more difficult to investigate: uncovering someone's intentions is, strictly speaking, impossible. However, generally (e.g. in a court) one infers intentions from actions and statements ('you would only do X if you were intending Y'). Such judgements, however, are culturally conditioned. In inferring intention to deceive we need to be asking, 'How would the production of this text have seemed to people at the time?' not, 'How does it seem to us?' This is further complicated by the fact that the Bible was written in at least two very different cultural worlds: the New Testament between 50 and 100 CE by (mainly) Jewish believers in Jesus in the Greek-speaking Roman empire, and the vast majority of the Old Testament between perhaps 700 and 350 BCE by Jews in Hebrew and Aramaic within Near Eastern cultures. Questions of 'How would it have seemed at the time?' need to be asked separately of these very different cultures, hundreds of years apart.

Bible
Origins and background

The Old Testament

Few texts in the Old Testament actually contain a claim of authorship. This itself points to the nature of the culture from which it emerged: 'authorship' seems not to have been a strongly developed concept. This is natural in a predominately oral culture, for the very nature of oral transmission makes it impossible to compare the version of an account that someone received with the version they passed on. Indeed the transmitters themselves may be unaware of changes they make. This is not to deny the importance given to the names, such as Moses, associated with Old Testament material. But it is impossible for modern scholars to identify the way in which this material developed, and at what points and with what intention the name Moses was used. For example, it is likely that the final compilers of the five 'books of Moses' were editing material that they had received as being from Moses – the origin and meaning of such a claim being lost in the shadows of time. Thus even if some Old Testament texts could be seen as pseudepigraphy, it would be impossible to move from this to label them forgeries.

The New Testament

The Gospels and the letters need to be considered separately from each other for two reasons. First, the Gospels make no explicit claim of authorship. The names associated with each Gospel are only found in the titles, not in the

OLD TESTAMENT PSEUDEPIGRAPHA

Pseudepigrapha is the term used by scholars to denote Jewish writings from around the second century BCE to the second century CE whose authors assume the name of an important figure of the past to give them added authority (this practice is known as pseudepigraphy). Many of them take the form of apocalypses.

There is no agreed list of Old Testament pseudepigrapha, but the following are the most important works:

Apocalypse of Abraham
Testament of Abraham
Life of Adam and Eve
2 Baruch (Syrian Apocalypse)
1 Enoch (Ethiopic Enoch)
2 Enoch (Slavonic Enoch)
Martyrdom and Ascension of Isaiah
The Paraleipomena of Jeremiah
Testament of Job
Joseph and Asenath
Jubilees
Testament of Moses
Pseudo-Philo, Book of Biblical Antiquities
Lives of the Prophets
Sibylline Oracles
Psalms of Solomon
Testaments of the Twelve Patriarchs

The pseudepigrapha are important evidence for the thought-world in which Christianity came into being.

The standard collection of these writings is James H. Charlesworth (ed), *The Old Testament Pseudepigrapha* (2 vols), New York: Doubleday and London: Darton, Longman & Todd 1983, 1985

texts themselves, and the titles are not 'by/of/from X' but 'according to X'. Perhaps this is just because the Gospel is 'by/of/from' Jesus and so any human author needs to be designated in another way. Equally plausibly, however, it is because the named people were not seen as authors but as the original source of the tradition contained in the Gospel. Secondly, the Gospels are to a greater or lesser extent the product of oral transmission, the text being produced by a compiler/editor, not an author. Thus even the term pseudepigraphy is probably inappropriate for the Gospels, since they carry no ascription of authorship that could be deemed false. It would be even more difficult to consider them forgery.

The New Testament letters are different. Here, other than in the letter to the Hebrews and the Johannine letters, the text itself contains a clear claim to authorship. Indeed, generally it is not just that the author's name is given, but the author's presence recurs throughout the text, through direct commands, personal notes and autobiographical elements. To modern eyes, these letters claim and present themselves as having been written by Paul, Peter, James or Jude. However, many scholars judge that a number of these texts were not written by their purported authors. Should they then be considered forgery? Traditionally scholars have answered 'no' to this question, though their justification is weak. The argument is based on a claim that it is only to modern eyes that the texts appear to claim an authorship which is false: the original recipients of the Paul texts would not have thought the texts were claiming Paul, for example, as their author but merely that they contain 'Pauline material' or 'what Paul would have said in our day'. This is a claim about the way in which texts were viewed within early Christianity.

Evidence for how early Christians viewed texts is limited. Four strands emerge.

1. The attitudes towards texts within the broad Greek culture in which the early Christians lived are well documented. This culture had highly developed understandings of texts, being well aware of the dangers of forgery, creating devices to protect against it or detect it, investigating texts to remove spurious additions, or identifying texts wrongly attributed to famous authors.

2. Evidence is available about how Christians around 200 CE viewed texts. It is clear that by this point at least, the Christians closely connected the author of a text to its value, and hence were concerned about false authorship claims.

3. There are snippets of information within the New Testament itself; for example, in 2 Thessalonians 3.17 the author indicates that his distinctive signature proves that the letter is genuine. This suggests that the possibility that letters were forged was well understood, and that it mattered whether the text was thought of as by Paul or not.

4. The attitudes to texts among Jews in the first-century CE are disputed. However, it is clear that most Jews (particularly perhaps those writing in Greek) shared the views about texts held in the wider Greek world of which they were a part. This position is complicated, however, by the existence of a number of texts from around the first century (called 'apocalypses' or 'testaments'), which purport to have been written by the great heroes of Israel's

past such as Enoch. It has often been assumed that these attributions were never intended to be taken literally, nor were they. However, there is no evidence to support this assumption. In truth we understand very little about the meaning of the attributions in such texts; views range from them simply being deceptions to lend authority to the text to their being 'truthful' in the sense that the writer underwent a trance in which he experienced the ancient figure speaking or acting through him. But such Jewish apocalypses and testaments are very different in content and genre from the New Testament epistles.

Thus, overall, while our understanding of the way in which the early Christians would have viewed claims of authorship is hazy, the balance of the evidence suggests that the original recipients of the letters in the New Testament would have thought they were written literally by their purported authors, and would have been unhappy if this were not true. Thus, it appears that any pseudepigraphy among the New Testament letters should be considered as forgery.

The importance of such a conclusion depends, naturally, on whether there is pseudepigraphy among the New Testament letters. However, our methods for determining whether, say, Paul wrote Ephesians are rather faltering because different letters of his are responding to different circumstances, the texts are brief, and scribes, secretaries and in the case of Paul's letters often co-authors were involved. This makes comparison difficult. If one did conclude that a text's claims are false, and thus it is pseudepigraphy and (given the conclusion above) forgery, this would have widespread implications. Many would feel that an intentionally deceptive text cannot function as part of Christianity's scripture. Furthermore, even if such moral arguments are overcome, it is difficult to interpret a text which claims one historical context for itself, but which came from a different one. Against which background, the claimed one or the real one, do you interpret it?

JEREMY DUFF

📖 Most of the discussion of pseudepigraphy occurs in the introductions to commentaries on New Testament letters whose authorship is disputed. But see J. D. G. Dunn, *The Living Word*, London: SCM Press 1987 and Minneapolis: Fortress Press 1988

Psychology and Christianity

The relationship between psychology and Christianity is complex and opens up many historical and interpretative problems. It would be wrong to assume that the relationship between a modern discipline and a religious tradition is one-way traffic, as if we are faced with the simple problem of the science of psychology studying the behaviour of a religion. The relationship is a twofold process and understood in a variety of different ways.

Psychology is a modern discipline developed in the 1870s and relates to Christianity in various ways over the last 130 years or so. There are two broad concerns in understanding this engagement. First, the historical emergence of psychology from Christianity and the relationship between Christian introspection and psychological measurement; secondly, the attempt by psychology to provide a descriptive or interpretative reading of the Christian message and life through its diverse methods. The portrayal of the history and the understanding of the methods of psychology will vary according to how those engaged in the field of enquiry known as 'psychology' understand it, and how such knowledge is embedded in the culture of scientific enquiry. Psychology covers a range of ideas from scientific experimentation and empiricism to case studies and imaginative models of being human. In this sense there is a spectrum of methods, ranging from scientific to non-scientific psychology. What we find, therefore, is that psychology and Christianity inter-relate according to different methods and theological positions.

Apocalyptic ◄

There is also a different understanding among psychologists and Christian thinkers as to the level of threat to either the scientific or the doctrinal purity that the other group wishes to preserve. There is no common agreement about how psychology and Christianity inter-relate; rather, there is a series of competing views about the nature of the discipline and the nature of the tradition. What we find is a series of fluid interactions from two different discourses that seek to describe the world and human beings in different ways. We can unpack this relationship through a series of questions.

What is the relationship between the history of Christianity and psychology?

The encounter of psychology and Christianity is the engagement between a technical knowledge of the self and a range of different traditions of Christian culture. However, the knowledge of being human which has been developed in psychology is not unrelated to the history of Christian thinking, and contemporary Christian thinking is not unrelated to modern ideas from psychology. This is the twofold process again. Psychology and Christianity are entwined in terms both of the formation of psychology and of the subsequent utilization of psychology to develop Christian thinking. Unlike the relationship between the hard sciences, like chemistry and physics, the relationship with psychology is not overridden with conflict but shaped by fascinating alliances. We find numerous interactive configurations in the relationship between Christianity

Culture

and psychology, including the psychology of religion, religion and psychological studies, religious psychology, pastoral psychology and, more recently, neuro-theology. These points of engagement reflect different relations of power between the two fields. The first reflects a domination of psychology examining the subject-matter religion, which can be either reductive or descriptive. The second reflects a dialogical model, an equal partnership in exploring the nature of being human, using insights from both fields of enquiry. The final three areas reflect the different confessional utilizations of psychology to promote the Christian faith, where for example God's creative power is found in the mystery of neurology.

We may also note that psychology to some extent would not be possible without Christianity, and some may wish to argue that psychology is a development of Christian ideas about the self, which are carried into science. The early history of psychology is based on methods of introspection echoing the Christian tradition. From Augustine's *De Trinitate* in *c.* 420, where we find models for the Trinity based on ideas about the mind, such as memory, understanding and will, to such thinkers as Jonathan Edwards (1703–58), Friedrich Schleiermacher (1768–1834) and Søren Kierkegaard (1813–55), who focus on the inner religious world of the passions or feeling, we find introspective ideas that inform the history of psychology. It is also possible to argue that psychology was born out of German Protestant theological traditions, where the individual's relationship with God generated an inward evaluation of the self. In this sense, it is possible to see some continuity between Christianity and some versions of psychology.

Trinity

Protestantism

The idea of self-examination is very much part of the Christian monastic life from the influential *Institutes* of John Cassian (*c.*360–435), which sets out rules for the monastic life, onwards. If psychology can be seen to carry forward Christian ideas about the self, we can also see that from the 1890s it at times enters theology. This is evident in the advent of pastoral psychology and, for example, in the work of Paul Tillich (1886–1965), who used psychoanalysis as part of his theological understanding. Psychology and Christianity, therefore, have a close relationship, even though it is denied in some areas of the scientific world. The very philosophical assumptions behind scientific experimentation can reflect Christian cultural values about the self. This raises a problem about the nature of psychology.

Monasticism

What is psychology?

Psychology is not a unified field of study, but rather a multiple set of ways of examining the human person. It ranges from physiological psychology to social psychology, and in that respect uses different methodologies. It is broken up according to loose definitions of scientific and non-scientific approaches, but such a distinction is itself questionable by the criteria of what constitutes science. Psychology is a modern discipline of thinking developed in Western society on the boundaries of physiology, philosophy and the politics of the self and often confuses these three realms of knowledge.

Historically, the field of psychology is seen to begin with the development of the first experimental laboratory established by Wilhelm Wundt (1832–1920) in Leipzig, Germany, in 1879, although William James (1842–1910) had established a similar laboratory in 1875 in Boston, USA. The key factor in the emergence of psychology at this time was the establishment of a methodical analysis of the individual. Prior to the birth of psychology there had been no such systematic analysis. Psychology can therefore be seen as a distinct field, separate from other forms of introspection, in so far as it uses a methodical approach in understanding the human being. It is the process of bringing measurement and calculation into the understanding of being human. However, the key problem is to what extent this measurement also carries hidden philosophical assumptions about the nature of being human and whether calculation is possible. This can be seen in the problem of terminology and the diverse language of brain, mind and psyche. It is possible to measure brain tissue, chemical and electrical activity, but much more difficult, if not impossible, to measure ideas and imaginative constructions of the mind or psyche. The slippage between these terms in psychology is often reason for critics to question the limits of psychology in its engagement with Christianity.

What are the different types of psychology and how do they relate to Christianity?

Different methods are employed in the broad field of psychology. We find developmental, behavioural, psychoanalytical, cognitive, evolutionary and neuro-physiological types of psychology. The engagement of these different types of psychology with Christianity fluctuates according to the receptivity of the field and the politics of reductionism: the desire to explain away and control, rather than acknowledge limitations. There was, for example, little engagement between behaviourism and Christianity in the 1930s, but positive engagement between psychoanalysis and Christianity after the Second World War, principally because Christian pastors needed new insights to deal with a traumatized population.

The encounter between the discipline of psychology and Christianity begins in the 1890s. The first psychological engagements reflected the use of positive descriptive surveys and confessional models of understanding the self. The early psychologists of religion were very much influenced by Protestant Christianity and their work reflected this bias. The first major studies were carried out at Clark University in the USA under the direction of Granville Stanley Hall (1844–1924). Hall tried to show the value of psychology for Christianity and wrote *Jesus, the Christ, in the Light of Psychology* in 1917, a work that promoted the relevance of Christ for each new generation. Hall's study of Christ was largely ignored, but his earlier work on adolescence provided the foundations for later biological and evolutionary models of religion.

Most of the early studies were concerned with conversion in Christianity and belief in God. In 1899 Edwin Starbuck wrote the first textbook on the psychology of religion and gathered questionnaire data about belief, which showed a distinctive Protestant inclination towards aspects of religious belief rather than practice. These early studies sought to show that Christian conversion occurred around the time of puberty. Unfortunately, they assumed a false model of development that saw the individual progressing in a similar manner to the development of the species, so that adulthood reflected the development of Christian civilization. While much of the early work was flawed, it attempted to offer a scientific understanding of Christian belief.

One of the key foundations of the Christian engagement with psychology in the twentieth century can be seen in William James's *The Varieties of Religious Experience* (1902). James provided extensive documentation of religious experience; some have argued that his organization of the material reflects a bias towards a Protestant conversion experience, with a pattern moving from sick soul to conversion to mysticism. The data he gathered, some 214 documents, relied on work by colleagues, such as Starbuck, and offered one of the finest collections of religious experiences, including accounts of Ignatius Loyola, Teresa of Avila and John of the Cross. James is important for the way he shapes and transforms Christian experience into psychological events. For example, he understood mysticism as a psychological phenomenon consisting of short, intense and ineffable experiences. While he used many figures from Christian history to illustrate his point, his work subsequently reshaped the history of Christian experience according to psychological registers. James's understanding of Christian experience reflected the Swedenborgian background of his father and established an important phenomenological basis for reading Christian experiences as inner events. He argued that religious experience resulted from engagement with the margins of consciousness or the subconscious. He was influenced by work in psychical research, especially by the British psychical researcher Frederick Myers (1843–1901) and the Swiss psychologist Theodore Flournoy (1854–1920). It is important to recognize that early work in the psychology of religion was very much concerned with exploration of mediums and séances, as psychologists tried to identify the underlying mysteries of the mind. This work continues today in the examination of near-death experiences.

The psychoanalytical work of Sigmund Freud (1856–1939) and Carl Jung (1875–1961) carried forward the psychological insights about a subconscious reality, but with the new language of the unconscious, Christianity faced an ambivalent history. While the world of dreams and visions had always played an important part in the Jewish and Christian traditions, Freud's psychoanalytic theories of religion as infantile wish-fulfilment and the idea of God as a father figure caused confusion over whether this was a useful pastoral insight or an attempt to reduce God to a projection of unconscious needs. However, after initial anxiety, the reception of psychoanalysis was on the whole positive and allowed for an appreciation of the ways in which personal history and unconscious fantasy influence theological understanding. The development and refinement of Freud's psychoanalytical theories also offered Christianity resources for understanding religious experience in relation to the early infant relationship to the mother. These studies were known as object-relations theory and developed from the work of Melanie Klein (1882–1960). Here the oceanic feeling of union was explored in relation to mysticism and from this basis feminist revisionists investigated how feminine dimensions of God or the Goddess were rooted in childhood fantasy.

Conversion

Feminist theology

Jung's analytical psychology, while raising concerns about reducing God and Christianity to the psyche, provided Christianity with a new understanding of religious images as powerful and important unconscious realities. Jung allowed for a new reading of the Christian message as a vital channel into collective structures or what he called the archetypes (or dominant images) of the collective unconscious. Jung believed God to be a fundamental reality of psyche, and the religious attitude a vital symbolic system for mental health. This psychological understanding provided Christianity with a rich resource for invigorating the Christian message in uncertain times. Jung offered Christianity useful pastoral models to understand the religious journey and identified personality types which later thinkers mapped to prayer and spiritual typologies.

Mysticism

The sense that religious images were positive for mental health was also promoted in the development of humanistic psychology in the 1950s and 1960s in the United States. In the work of Gordon Allport (1897–1967) and Abraham Maslow (1908–70), Christianity was offered a way of seeing spiritual development as a positive psychological event, through which individuals could reach their full potential. In contrast to the psychoanalytical view that saw religion as a neurosis, or the behaviourist view that saw religion as a form of conditioned behaviour, Paul humanistic psychology appeared to offer the view that a mature religious position could bring about a full realization of human potential. While Western society celebrated Maslow's theories of peak-experiences (ecstatic moments of intense meaning) and plateau-experiences (the experience of life having reached higher levels of cognition) as part of a new psychological profile of religion, Christianity received these insights with mixed feelings. For some critics humanistic psychology was nothing other than the worship of self and a reflection of American affluence, while for others it provided yet another resource for understanding the Christian message. However, much of humanistic psychology also sought to find ways of Spirituality developing an understanding of 'spirituality' outside the institution of the church and, in consequence, rejected the authoritarian dogma of Christianity. This resulted in a privatization of religion and raised significant questions about the way in which psychology turned religion into an individual rather than a social reality.

While the early psychologists in the 1890s had been concerned with religion and pedagogy, it was not until the work of Jean Piaget (1896–1980) that the question of Education religious development and education took on a sharper focus. According to Piaget's psychology, the child understood the world through different stages of cognition. This provided Christian educators with a deeper appreciation of human development. Psychology was here seen as an important companion for religious teaching and opened the way for a whole range of cognitive models for Christian education. However, the emergence of cognitive psychology in the 1950s was to provide both a challenge and support for Christianity. Contemporary cognitive theorists often want to explain religion as patterns of habitual or ritualized memory, and evolutionary psychologists try to find ways of showing the genetic importance of Christianity. It was thought that the persistence of Christianity showed it held genetic or what has become known as 'memetic' (the survival of strong ideas through culture) importance. What all these engagements demonstrate is that the Christian community seeks to use the developments within psychological theory as positive ways of refreshing the meaning of Christianity, rather than seeing them as a threat. This can be seen particularly in the world of contemporary neuroscience.

While some neuroscientists wanted to reduce God to electrical activity in the temporal lobes, the parts of the brain inside from the ears, others saw this as the physiological correlate of God's engagement with humanity. Research into temporal lobe epilepsy – a disorder not associated with convulsions but with electrical activity in the brain connected with intense and vivid sensations of light, sound or smell – has found a link with religious experience. It was, for instance, thought that Paul was suffering from temporal lobe epilepsy on the road to Damascus. While neuroscience provided all sorts of theories about religion, it easily became a site for both believers and non-believers to argue for and against the reality of God. While for some neuroscience could explain religion away, for others, following James's early insight on the matter, neurology could only provide information about the brain, not religious truth. As human beings had physical bodies and brains, Christian thinkers argued that God was revealed in the world of neurology, and they created a neurotheology to illustrate this expression of God's created order. It is precisely here we see the limits of psychology in providing value for Christian understanding and the way in which psychology is a contested site for Christian and non-Christian world-views.

How does psychology shape Christian experience?

From the time of psychology's origins in the 1870s, Christianity has always engaged with all its different branches. Some of these engagements have been successful and others not, but on the whole Christianity has seen psychology as a companion for its message rather than an enemy, particularly in the field of pastoral care. However, the question remains as to how psychology shapes Christianity. Psychology offers a way not only of explaining religious ideas but of representing Christianity. The tension for the Christian community is whether this is a distortion or an elaboration of Christian truth. What is important to realize is that psychological knowledge is always provisional and always evolving. Many psychological theories have been shown later to be not only false but also oppressive. With the advent of critical psychology in the 1990s, it was shown how questions of race, gender and social class were silenced in psychological theory. It was also shown how psychology reflected Western cultural values about the self and supported political values of individualism. This critical evaluation of psychology opened up the question whether Christian models of being human have an equal value to those offered by psychology. It is in the light of these tensions that a more dialogical model between Christianity and psychology has emerged. The authority of a so-called 'science' of psychology is now placed in the critical context of the limits of such knowledge, and the relation between what is measurable and what is beyond measurement becomes central to the Christian understanding of what it is to be human. Psychology can be both friend and enemy to Christianity, but in the end the limits of psychological knowledge and the imagination of Christian theologians have shown the enduring mystery of being human.

JEREMY R. CARRETTE

William James, *The Varieties of Religious Experience* (1902), Centenary Edition, London: Routledge 2002; Diane Jonte-Pace and William Parsons, *Religion and Psychology*, London: Routledge 2001; David Wulff, *Psychology of Religion*, New York: John Wiley 1997

Publishing

Publishing books in the modern world covers a wide variety of activities, from recruiting authors, through editorial preparation and production, to promotion, distribution and sales. It is a business, and even the publication of new translations of the Bible and new prayer books is not free from financial pressures. Indeed from the invention of printing onwards, liturgical, devotional and morally edifying books have played a major role in commercial publishing.

The complex network which makes up the world of publishing, involving printers, binders, publishers and booksellers, took a long time to develop, but the commercial book trade goes back to antiquity; it flourished in Athens and in Rome. However, the book may be said to be essentially a Christian invention; the Greeks and Romans had used rolls. Between the fifth and thirteenth centuries manuscripts were copied only within the church, and this situation to a large degree determined precisely what works by ancient authors were handed down.

The invention of typographic printing by Johann Gutenberg in the fifteenth century is a landmark in book production; the first dated printed book, printed in 1547, was a copy of the Psalter. The Reformation saw a flood of books in Protestant countries, in particular on Bible reading and sermons, religious propaganda and instruction, and indeed religious books were the backbone of the early printers. Outside Europe, Roman Catholic presses were established during the sixteenth and early seventeenth centuries in Goa, America, Japan and the Congo.

From then on three strands developed in publishing. First, during the sixteenth century in Britain the first real university presses produced books, at Cambridge in 1584 (though the press was founded in 1534!) and in Oxford in 1586. Secondly, there were as ever the trade publishers, established by individual entrepreneurs: Vandenhoeck & Ruprecht was founded in Göttingen (1735), J. C. B. Mohr in Tübingen (1801), Harper in New York (1817) and T&T Clark in Edinburgh (1828). Thirdly, at the beginning of the eighteenth century the newly developing religious societies saw the value of publication for the work of education and evangelization. They were led by the Society for Promoting Christian Knowledge (founded 1698) in England and the Canstein Bibelanstalt in Germany (1710). The British and Foreign Bible Society, founded in 1804, gave rise internationally to many other Bible societies, promoting the translation and publication of the Bible into many languages, and the best possible scholarly editions of the original texts. The spread of the churches in the United States led to the foundation of church publishing houses, the first by the Methodists in 1789. Roman Catholic publishing really began to develop only during the nineteenth century with the revival of the papacy and the church. By the end of that century most churches and religious denominations had their own publishing houses and bookshops.

Books

The time of the Enlightenment also saw the birth of the periodical: pamphlets, newspapers and journals, many of them polemical. Polemic had long been a feature of publishing and the relatively free dissemination of printed material regularly attracted the attention of censors in both state and church, since religious polemic was often closely connected with political polemic. The Inquisition instituted the first Index of Prohibited Books in 1557, and at times the state imposed very severe restrictions on publication, notably in England during the time of the French Revolution. However, the degree of freedom for the printed word was particularly striking.

Enlightenment

p. 345

The heyday of publishing, and particularly religious publishing, was probably between the publication of the controversial *Essays and Reviews* in 1860 and of John A. T. Robinson's *Honest to God* in 1963. The industry was fully developed, and despite the havoc caused by two world wars, it had a very broad scope. The threats from other media were still barely in the making, and the giant organizations that dominate the scene today had not yet been formed. Towards the end of this period the paperback revolution promised an even wider spread of books.

Reformation

More recently, however, pressures have been mounting. First and foremost has been the increasing secularization of society and a sharp decline in church membership, reducing the potential audience. Secondly, the demands of the academic research assessment by universities and colleges, which is an essential element in job tenure and promotion, have favoured the writing of highly-specialized academic monographs rather than books addressed to a wider readership. And thirdly, the increasing involvement in publishing of conservative evangelicalism, often financed by major funding from the United States, has produced a whole sector of publishing and bookselling which calls itself 'Christian', though it represents only a very narrow form of Christianity and practises its own internal censorship. This, too, addresses only a small segment of the general public.

Secularization

Despite all these problems, good books on Christianity are still being published in Britain, the United States and continental Europe. However, there is also a tremendous amount of dross, and at a time when informed writing about religious issues of all kinds is more urgent than ever, it is a tragedy that communication through publishing between the churches, academic institutions and the world outside is not wider and more effective.

JOHN BOWDEN

John Calvin

Asa Briggs, *Essays in the History of Publishing*, London: Longman 1974; Eugene Exman, *The House of Harper. One Hundred and Fifty Years of Publishing*, New York: Harper & Row 1967; John Feather, *A History of British Publishing*, London: Croom Helm 1988

Puritans

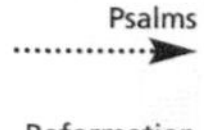

Psalms
Reformation

The Puritans were English Reformers of the sixteenth and seventeenth centuries frustrated by the slow progress of the Reformation in the English church. They take their name from their view that the church had not been purified enough and still had much corruption in it.

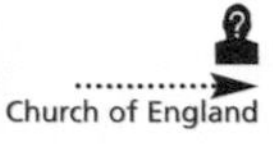

Church of England
Presbyterian churches
Papacy

By the 1570s, just over a decade into the reign of Elizabeth I, there was a new and contrasting religious landscape in England. Gone were all of the distinctive features of Roman Catholic church life, including the mass as the most treasured act of worship, the adoration of saints, the honour accorded to relics, pilgrimages and the acknowledgement of the Pope as the head of the church. These beliefs and practices were things of the past for everyone bar a few remaining loyal Roman Catholic subjects, who by then were a beleaguered minority. In their place was the Bible in the vernacular, available for all to read, and the 1552 Book of Common Prayer. Church services were in the mother tongue, and at their heart was the exposition of the scriptures. In place of the mass there was the holy communion, no longer primarily an act of sacrifice in which the bread and wine were considered as the very body and blood of Christ, but rather a corporate celebration of the saving death of Christ.

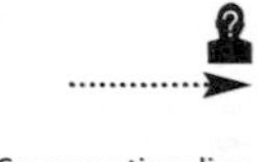

Congregationalism
Eucharist
Sacrifice

All this represented a bewildering array of changes. Nevertheless, the unprecedented religious transformation did not satisfy everyone. There was a minority movement that sought further reformation and renewal. These so-called Puritans believed that the process of Protestant Reformation had been arrested before it had reached its full and desirable extent and potential. They opposed church ornaments, vestments and other traditional forms of clergy dress, organs, the sign of the cross and ecclesiastical courts. They were fiercely antagonistic to any remaining trace of papal influence, and alert to detect the slightest evidence of such blemishes.

Protestantism

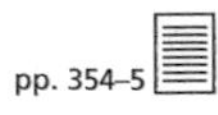

pp. 354–5
Church of Scotland

Within a few years they began to build up a common body of pastoral, evangelistic and didactic literature that had its own distinctive style and an experiential emphasis. Among the early authors, William Perkins was prominent; and among those in the seventeenth century Richard Baxter and John Bunyan are outstanding. John Milton also upheld the Puritan outlook on life, and his poetry is redolent of the Puritan concern to honour and expound the sovereignty of God.

The Puritans were identifiable because of their fervent, Calvinistic, brand of Protestantism. They were distinguished from the general mass of those who merely conformed to the new established religion, and indeed were known as the 'godly'. Most of them attended their parish churches and mingled with other worshippers at church services, but otherwise they almost exclusively sought the company of fellow Puritans. They met together in private homes to study the Bible, habitually walked around together singing psalms, and made excursions to hear their favourite 'godly' preachers.

It was not long before some of these reluctant and uneasy Puritan conformists rebelled against the Church of England of which they were unenthusiastic members. From the 1570s onwards Thomas Cartwright, John Field and William Travers headed up an attack on the institution of episcopacy and the whole hierarchical system of the established church. They advocated, and took steps to establish, Presbyterianism, in which presbyters were the key figures in the governance of the church: locally, regionally and nationally.

By the end of the sixteenth century and into the early years of the following century a further group of Puritan separatists, led by Robert Browne, Henry Barrow, John Greenwood and John Penry, founded the Independent (later to become the Congregational) Church. This adopted a form of church government and life that rested on the independence and autonomy of each local 'gathered' body of believers.

Queen Elizabeth (1558–1603) was bitter in her opposition to the Puritans. She trod a middle course (*via media*) in all ecclesiastical matters, and she abhorred any form of extremism. She was not satisfied with the somewhat lukewarm and qualified support for such a policy that she received from Archbishop Edmund Grindal (1575–83), but his successor, John Whitgift, was at one with her. He was a strict disciplinarian and thoroughly anti-Puritan, and during his episcopacy (1583–1604) Puritanism withered.

The Puritans had high hopes that they would fare better when James I replaced Elizabeth in 1603. They anticipated that the reforms for which they longed would be promoted by a king who had been nurtured in the Presbyterian Church of Scotland, one of the most notable of the Reformed churches. They promptly made their requests known by presenting him with a Millenary

Petition. The conference called by James to discuss the issues raised was held at Hampton Court in January 1604. It failed to produce any resolutions that remotely satisfied the dissenters, with one gigantic exception of lasting significance for them and for the country as a whole, for it set in motion the preparation of the Authorized Version of the Bible that appeared seven years later.

By the early seventeenth century there was much discontent among Puritans about the severely limited response to their pleas. There were several localized secessions from the Church of England. In 1608 a number of these more radical, separatist, Protestants emigrated to the Netherlands. They hoped that they would escape from the harassment and persecution they had encountered in England and find a hitherto unknown joy and fulfilment in a harmonious and unfettered life of spiritual unity and fruitfulness. Unfortunately for them this was not to be. Their fellowship was soon rent by controversy.

In September 1620, in their desperate search for freedom to pursue their chosen way of life, some of the Puritans, later to be designated the Pilgrim Fathers, took flight in the *Mayflower* and founded the colony of Plymouth, Massachusetts, in the New World.

Meanwhile in England, separatism, in the form either of the Presbyterians, the Independents or the Baptists, who trace their origins in modern times to the action of John Smyth in Amsterdam in 1609, made little headway in attracting new members. The total membership of such congregations during the reign of James I (1603–25) was never more than a few hundred: they were scattered, and they had little impact on the life of the nation.

The accession of Charles I to the throne in 1625 heralded a major shift in the political and religious life of the nation and brought the separatist Puritans into ever more dramatic prominence. In his religious upbringing Charles had emerged as a convinced and unswerving Church of England Arminian, resolutely opposed to the predestinarian Puritans. Politically, he inherited and enthusiastically embraced a belief in the divine right of kings. He declared that he owed an account of his actions to God alone. Thwarted in some of his intentions by what he viewed as recalcitrant politicians, in 1629 he decided to dispense with Parliament and conduct affairs in a prolonged period of personal rule.

In the propagation of his religious policies, Charles worked in close collaboration with the ultra-high-churchman William Laud, who from 1633 was Archbishop of Canterbury. The primate had demonstrated his strong anti-Puritan attitude as chancellor of Oxford University, and he developed this in his role as archbishop. Laudianism, united with the insensitive, assertive and single-minded ambitions of Charles, inevitably resulted in conflict, including a running battle with the Puritans both within the established church and in the dissenting congregations. Nevertheless, few would have anticipated such a fearful and devastating outcome as the violence, divisiveness and trauma of the Civil War, the execution of Charles and Laud in 1649, the Protectorate, the Commonwealth and the Restoration of 1660.

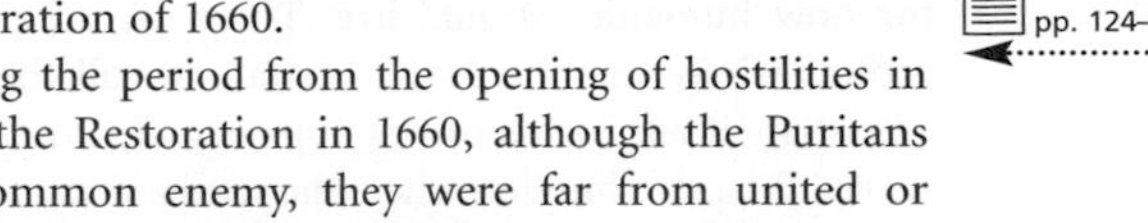

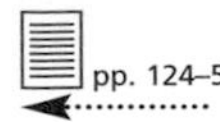

pp. 124–5

During the period from the opening of hostilities in 1642 to the Restoration in 1660, although the Puritans had a common enemy, they were far from united or at one in their political and religious views. The two main contending groups were the Presbyterians and the Independents, with their differing opinions on church government. But in addition, an alarming number of sects appeared, of which the foremost were the Muggletonians, the Family of Love, the Grindletonians, the Ranters, the Seekers and the Religious Society of Friends (Quakers). Only the last of these have survived to the present day.

Quakers

The overwhelming majority of the English parish clergy welcomed or endured the Restoration changes introduced in 1660–2. Nonetheless, between 1660 and 1663, 1760 priests were forced by conscience to leave their parishes because they could not accept the terms required of them to remain as churchmen. The Act of Uniformity of 1661, and the other policies imposed in these years, drove them out of the established church and into one of the dissenting bodies. This was the period that marked the consolidation of dissent. The various denominations were recognized as a permanent feature in national life.

Baptist churches

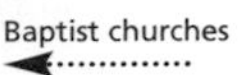

Perhaps the term 'Puritan' never had a single precise meaning. Nevertheless, in every generation since 1660 there have been those in all the Protestant churches throughout the world for whom 'Puritanism' represented a theological ideal and a pattern for both church life and daily conduct which was to be cherished and emulated. This continues to be so in the twenty-first century.

KENNETH HYLSON-SMITH

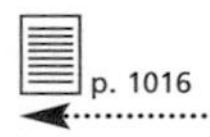

p. 1016

Patrick Collinson, *The Elizabethan Puritan Movement*, Oxford: Clarendon Press 1967; Christopher Hill, *Society and Puritanism in Pre-Revolutionary England*, London: Secker & Warburg 1964 and *The World Turned Upside Down. Radical Ideas during the English Revolution* (1972), Harmondsworth: Penguin Books 1991; Geoffrey F. Nuttall, *The Holy Spirit in Puritan Faith and Experience* (1946), Chicago: University of Chicago Press 1992

Quakers (Religious Society of Friends)

Quakers (or members of the Religious Society of Friends, known also as Friends) are members of a worldwide religious movement whose origin goes back to religious

Jesus

radicals living in mid-seventeenth-century England. They currently number about 340,000. There is no overall creed or statement of beliefs. Quakers vary widely on how they understand the role of Jesus, some believing him to be Lord and Saviour, others seeing him as a great prophet or model for how humanity should live. There are some Quaker groups whose members may hesitate to call their beliefs Christian at all. Forms of worship also vary, from pastor-served Friends' churches where the services resemble other Protestant congregations to the silent worship of the liberal and Conservative Friends' meeting houses. In spite of these differences, Quakers from all traditions trace their origins to George Fox (1624–91) and the early Quakers, men and women of great religious fervour, who saw their role as reviving primitive Christianity.

Creed
Kingdom of God
Bible
Holy Spirit

The key to the Quaker movement is its emphasis on the direct relationship possible between God and ordinary men and women. Early Quakers were people who felt that lives could be changed as they turned to the light of God, or of Christ, within them. They avoided creeds as human inventions: they stressed the experience of the Seed or the Light or the Voice (as they called it) within their hearts. This inward power could show them their darkness and could also lead them to live transformed lives. As men and women met together in this power they could also change the society in which they lived and thus usher in the kingdom of God. For them there was no difference between the religious life and the political realm. Their whole lives were based on an openness to the leadings of the Spirit of God. This Inward Light, as it was called, was their primary source of authority. It was the word of God speaking in their lives. The Bible was a secondary authority known as the words of God. The believer interpreted it under the guidance of the Spirit and with the help of others from his or her religious community. For these convictions Quakers were persecuted and imprisoned, and many died as a result of their sufferings.

This emphasis on experience is still at the core of the Quaker movement today. It is, however, interpreted differently in the diverse trends of world Quakerism. In North America, there are four main groupings of Quakers: 1. the evangelicals or Evangelical Friends Alliance, who call their places of worship churches and who have pastors and a strong emphasis on the Bible and on mission; 2. those Friends of Friends United Meeting, who comprise both evangelicals and liberals, and who meet in either meeting houses or churches; 3. conservative Friends with strong Christian convictions and silent meetings for worship in meeting houses without pastors; 4. Friends General Conference and various independent groupings, made up of liberal Quakers mostly without pastors, whose meetings for worship take place in the context of silence.

Quakers in Europe and those in Australia and New Zealand tend to resemble those of Friends General Conference, as do a few in Asian countries, though there are an increasing number of evangelical Friends in Taiwan, Indonesia and the Philippines. There is also an evangelical Quaker group in India. Most of those in Africa and South America are similar to the Friends in Evangelical Friends Alliance and Friends United Meeting, though there are a few silent liberal meetings there also.

With such diversity it is quite difficult to describe exactly what all Quakers believe or do, or how they worship and live out their lives. Early Quakers found that they could best be receptive to the Inward Light of God or of Christ by waiting in silence. As they let go of their human strivings, they could listen to the voice of God speaking in their hearts. This listening also led them to proclaim what they believed was the message of Christ both for themselves and for a world in need of redemption. This listening was the foundation of the Quaker meeting for worship as it is still practised by liberal and conservative Quakers.

In the early days worship took place in 'meeting houses' rather than churches, as it was believed that the word 'church' referred not to the building but to the people of God. Liberal and conservative Friends still call their places of worship meeting houses. The word 'church' was introduced by American Quakers of the more evangelical tendency in the nineteenth century under the influence of other Christian denominations. The more evangelical Quakers have prayers, sermons and hymns, though some do have times for silent worship also and extempore ministry.

Quakers do not have a set-aside ordained ministry: all people have a role in the meeting for worship and there is a strong stress on the equality of men and women in most Quaker gatherings. When there is a pastor, as in the evangelical tradition, he or she functions as a preacher and administrator, rather than as someone with greater spiritual authority than the rest of the congregation.

Friends of the silent, liberal traditions usually meet for about an hour on a Sunday morning for worship. Their simple meeting houses have no obvious religious symbolism. Their meetings are open to the public. During the time of worship, worshippers may be praying silently, reflecting on their lives, or otherwise opening themselves to the promptings of the Spirit. It is said that meeting for worship begins when the first Friend sits in the meeting room. After some time anyone present, member or attender (that is a regular worshipper who has not yet decided to take membership) may rise to speak, if he or she feels inspired or moved by the Spirit to do so. This is called 'vocal ministry'. Ministry may consist of a Bible reading or a reading from another inspiring book (reading from books being less common in the United States than

Engraving of a Quaker Meeting

in Europe), a quotation, or an anecdote or reflection from the speaker's experience. It may also be an extempore prayer. Some meetings may remain silent for the full hour; in others there may be up to four or even more ministries. The meeting closes when elders shake hands. It is now usual for each worshipper also to shake hands with those sitting near him or her.

Because of the early emphasis on the inwardness of the divine presence, Quakers were mistrustful of any outward form. God was to be worshipped in spirit and truth, as John's Gospel has it. Baptism and communion were also seen as spiritual events not needing outward symbolism. In spite of some attempts to introduce baptism with water and a communion service with bread and wine, these rites remain, with some rare exceptions, foreign to Quaker practice. This inwardness was extended to the church calendar. Quakers today, especially of the liberal tradition, do not celebrate Christmas and Easter as special festivals. These are seen as events in the soul: the birth and the crucifixion of the divine within. However, it must be said that many Quakers are affected by local customs and references are made to these festivals in Quaker worship.

Festivals and fasts

Business meetings are likewise held in a spirit of worship. Quakers do not vote. Matters which need to be discussed are brought by Friends to the business meeting, the 'meeting for worship for church affairs'. All members may attend these meetings. An agenda will have been put together by the clerk of the meeting. Friends will speak to the matter at hand when they feel led to do so. It is not a matter of one point of view being imposed on the gathering. The community is trying to find the right thing to do which it sees as an expression of the will of God. It is the role of the clerk to discern the sense of the meeting and record it in a minute agreed by the group while still in session.

Each meeting will have elders and overseers or some committee which is responsible for watching over the spiritual education of worshippers and for ensuring that any member or attender who is in difficult circumstances is supported in some way.

Ecumenical movement

Quaker spirituality is based on the empowerment by the Spirit of ordinary men and women as they live out their daily lives in the world. The Quaker way has been described as one of practical mysticism. Testimony, as Quakers use the word, is an act of witness, a way of living one's life in the world that shows that the whole of life is sacramental. Testimonies can be seen today in terms of clusters of values: equality, peace, truth and simplicity, with an ever stronger emphasis on care for the environment. Evangelical Friends see evangelism, bringing people to Christ, as their foremost testimony.

Mysticism
Sacraments

The equality of men and women has already been mentioned. Equality was a revolutionary act as it encompassed all people, of all races, and it has been a force for social reform throughout its history. Quakers were among the earliest groups demanding the abolition of the slave trade and still work against racism. In some meetings this inclusivity is extended to diversity in matters of sexual orientation. They are perhaps best known for their peace testimony, which led to two Quaker agencies being awarded the Nobel Peace Prize in 1947. As there are no creeds among Quakers, the peace testimony is not seen by Quakers as a simple synonym for pacifism. Although many Quakers are pacifists, others interpret their understanding of the peace testimony in other ways such local mediation, reconciliation of communities and working with international relief agencies. There are Quaker offices to implement the practical consequences of this testimony at the United Nations and the European Community and in several capital cities.

Peace churches

Truth or integrity in personal relationships and in business is fundamental to the Quaker way. It was the Quaker way of commerce that led to the fixed price of goods without haggling, and their trustworthiness led to the establishment of a number of Quaker banks such as Lloyds and Barclays. Simplicity likewise has been a characteristic of Quakers, whose attitudes tend to be anti-materialistic. This has led to their concern about the exploitation of the earth's resources.

Environmental ethics

Quakers are divided into regional or national groupings known as yearly meetings. There are 85 of these, together with several smaller groups. Each has its own decision-making process. Depending on the region, the yearly meeting is divided into local congregations known as Friends churches, monthly meetings, or preparative meetings. There are also local groupings of congregations that meet together for business and spiritual uplift. An international body of Quakers, the Friends World Committee for Consultation, has the role of liaising between many of the yearly meetings and is in touch with others who do not have formal membership of it.

Many Quakers, especially those from the liberal tradition, are open to insights from other spiritual and religious paths. Yearly meetings belonging to Friends United Meeting and Friends General Conference, as well as Canadian Yearly Meeting, are members of the World Council of Churches. Other yearly meetings are also involved with their national council of churches. Many Quaker groups are also involved in interfaith activities.

HARVEY GILLMAN

📖 Margey Post Abbott, *A Certain Kind of Perfection*, Wallingford, PA: Pendle Hill Publications 1997; Hugh Barbour and J. William Frost, *The Quakers. A History from an American Perspective*, Richmond, IN: Friends United Press 1994; A. Wilmer Cooper, *A Living Faith, A Historical Study of Quaker Beliefs*, Richmond, IN: Friends United Press 1990; George Fox, *Journal* ed Nigel Smith, Harmondsworth: Penguin Books 1998; Harvey Gillman, *A Light that is Shining*, London: Quaker Life 2002; John Punshon, *Portrait in Grey: A Short History of the Quakers*, London: Quaker Home Service 2001

Radio

Within a single century radio transformed the world's and its peoples' understanding of each other. Even in the solitary, undeveloped regions of the earth, with the help of the sun's energy or with a simple clockwork motor, voices carried on wireless waves have linked the richest and poorest peoples of the globe.

Wireless waves had always existed, but until an invention by a young Italian in 1895 they meant nothing to anyone. Aged only 21, Guglielino Marconi brought together various scientific theories which had until then proved more interesting than useful, and found a way of combining them to use electricity to transmit intelligible signals across space. Popular history gives Marconi all the credit, but without the earlier work of a German, Heinrich Hertz, the French scientist Edouard Branly, a Russian named Popoff and a Scotsman called Clerk Maxwell, broadcasting as we know it would not have been developed.

Marconi's invention particularly fascinated amateur engineers and scientists who, with the developing conveniences of modern life early in the twentieth century, had more leisure to spend on hobbies. Clergymen were among the first to construct vast aerial systems in their homes, using primitive receivers to listen in, logging the dots and dashes of Morse, and vying with each other to decode the most distant signal.

As the world was recovering from war, in the early 1920s radio was already developing rapidly in North America, chiefly due to a far-sighted former office boy from the Marconi Company, the entrepreneur David Sarnoff. He saw radio's potential for 'entertaining, informing and educating the nation'.

In the United States the first religious programme was broadcast less than two months after the first licensed station went on the air. On 2 January 1921 station KDKA, Pittsburgh, provided a remote broadcast from Calvary Episcopal Church by the Revd Edwin Jan van Etten, the assistant minister, who spoke because the rector of the church was 'too busy'.

Within a short time ministers seized upon radio as a tool for evangelism. In 1923, Walter A. Maier, a professor of Old Testament at the Lutheran Church Missouri Synod's Concordia Seminary, wrote an editorial entitled 'Why not a Lutheran Broadcasting Station?', and on 14 December 1924 KFUO ('Keep Forward, Upward, Onward') became the first religious station, broadcasting from the Seminary's attic in South St Louis, Missouri.

By 1925 at least 63 stations were owned by church institutions. As frequencies became more valuable, churches sold out to commercial groups, in many cases accepting a promise of free broadcast time in lieu of cash. By the 1930s the rash of church-owned stations had all but vanished, but many local stations continued to broadcast Sunday worship, either remote from the sanctuary itself, or delivered from the station's studios.

Broadcasters soon recognized the need for religious advisory committees to guide them in dealing with the increasing number of denominations requesting time. The Federal Council of the Churches of Christ (FCCC), representing 25 denominations, encouraged councils of churches in local communities nationwide to develop co-operative broadcasting, and the idea caught on in most urban areas.

In 1923 Frank C. Goodman developed three weekly religious programmes on New York stations, and in 1924 the Greater New York Federation of Churches began 'The National Radio Pulpit' on WEAF. That station became WNBC when the NBC network was born in 1926, and 'Pulpit' became the first national network religious programme. It has been on the air every week since then, with preachers such as Harry Emerson Fosdick, Ralph Sockman and David H. C. Read.

In 1927 the Columbia Broadcasting System became the second network. At first it sold time to religious groups, including the Lutheran Church Missouri Synod and Father Charles E. Coughlin. But controversy surrounding Coughlin's fiery political and racial statements brought about a change in policy, and from 1931 CBS joined NBC in refusing to sell network time for any religious programmes, instead making time available as a public service. For example, the Mormon programme 'Music and the Spoken Word', featuring the Tabernacle Choir, was carried every Sunday by NBC from 1929 to 1932, and from then on by CBS. When the FCCC became the National Council of the Churches of Christ in 1950, its Broadcasting and Film Commission, later renamed Communication Commission, represented the broadcasting efforts of some 32 member denominations.

However, many denominations and independent evangelists not related to the NCCC purchased time from non-network stations. The Lutheran Missouri Synod began syndicating 'The Lutheran Hour' in 1930. The Seventh-day Adventist Church began its radio broadcasts in 1924, and its first regularly scheduled programme, 'The Voice of Prophecy', in 1930. Several Roman Catholic dioceses and religious orders and hundreds of local preachers sought time on local radio. Independents such as Charles E. Fuller, Aimée Semple McPherson, M. R. De Haan and H. M. S. Richards put most of their funds into buying time. By 1933, conventional Protestant broadcasting accounted for only 28 per cent of the total religious radio output.

A basic policy difference developed among religious broadcasters. The larger, established, 'mainline' denominations generally held the view that broadcasters should provide time on the air for a balanced presentation of religious views, involving representative groups in the community, even if this required stations to supply the time without charge. The smaller, more 'sect-type', groups believed that they were being ignored, and accused the co-operative groups of attempting to silence them. They chose to purchase time and to make financial appeals on air.

In the UK, a young Scottish Presbyterian engineer named John Reith was appointed on 13 December 1922 to a post managing the newly-formed British Broadcasting Company (in 1927 it was granted a royal charter and became the British Broadcasting Corporation). This marked a turning point in broadcasting throughout the world. The technical gadgets and the pioneering engineers and performers would now work together as a public service.

John Reith understood broadcasting as a high moral responsibility. He believed that radio broadcasting could be the salvation of a society still shocked in the aftermath of the First World War. Families would be united around the radio as once they had gathered around the hearth.

Wherever new technologies were in place, there were always a few preachers keen to enlist its support, especially in the revivalist days of the end of the nineteenth century. Even before Marconi's first radio broadcasts, telephone subscribers were listening in to 'electro-phoned' church services. On summer Sundays on the eve of the First World War, telephone exchanges connected homes to a London church where Wilson Carlile, founder of the Church Army, preached. One of his favourite sermon themes, 'God's wonderful radio', seems to have prophesied a Sunday early in 1922 when the congregation of Peckham Baptist Church in South London heard Mr Boon, their pastor, preaching his sermon from the Burndept Aerial Works several miles away.

Radio religion had arrived, with enormous potential for outreach and evangelism, but apart from a few individuals, the British churches as a whole were, and have remained, slow to recognize it. Although a son of the manse, John Reith did not see his own role as that of an evangelist. That was the churches' task, and he was later to express his disappointment at their response to the new medium. Religion (meaning Christianity) was naturally included in the BBC output because the king of England was a Christian. Reith prescribed a 'thorough-going, optimistic and manly religion' with programmes applying 'the teaching of Christ to everyday life'. By far the greatest impact in the early years was made by the Revd H. R. L. 'Dick' Sheppard, vicar of St Martin-in-the-Fields in the heart of London. His was the first congregation to host a live Sunday evening broadcast, early in 1924, and carefully scheduled by Reith so as not to clash with the radio audience's first duty: to attend evensong in their own churches.

Eighty years on, the churches and the broadcasters in Britain still have an uneasy relationship. Some believe that radio is an obvious but undeveloped evangelistic tool, and blame the BBC for blocking their access to it. Others seem to think that the most that can be expected of it is the possible stimulation of a natural religious impulse in a few listeners and they despise the medium as pointless. Meanwhile, the BBC employs a team of professional radio producers to maintain the output, who are not required to have any religious affiliation. Few are clergy, and today's Head of Religion and Ethics is a self-declared agnostic.

A major controversy between the churches and the broadcasters in Britain arose in 1941 when it was discovered that the BBC intended to broadcast *The Man Born to Be King*, a play by the novelist Dorothy L. Sayers, in which for the first time an actor was to portray Jesus Christ. There was uproar, and it was even suggested that Britain would lose the war if it were broadcast. The whole saga was a good example of the protests of blasphemy that often precede any change or innovation in religious broadcasting.

In the third millennium, religion is broadcast daily in Britain on all the BBC's analogue radio channels. Radio religion is now an area of programming where questions are asked. Disturbance of the comfortable is scheduled alongside comfort for the disturbed. All major faiths are reflected in the output.

In the rest of Europe, religious broadcasting also developed in the early 1930s. Today it reflects the distinctive religious and political make-up of individual nations. Germany has a rich diversity of programming on both national and local channels, with worship services, church news, information programmes, drama series, meditations, talk shows and documentaries parcelled out evenly between Protestants and Catholics, and with time also available for the Free Churches. Stations support substantial religious departments, and there is an elaborate advisory system. In Austria, ORF divides its time between Catholics and Protestants, plus several programmes a year to serve the Old Catholics, Muslims and Jews. Switzerland provides a wide range of formats and subjects under the auspices of the Reformed, Catholic and Free Church groups.

On 12 February 1931 a new station, Vatican Radio, began broadcasting. Unlike most other national stations, its aspirations were global. Built by Marconi himself, it had a simple objective: to broadcast the voice of the Pope to all people. Pope Pius XI began with words of peace and blessing in the Roman Catholic Church's universal language, Latin: 'We address ourselves to all things and to all men. May the earth listen to the words of my mouth; pay attention, remotest people!'

Outside North America and Europe the amount of religious broadcasting is much less and varies considerably country by country. In Africa, for example, both Christian and Muslim groups have their own studio facilities and broadcast regularly through the Ghana Broadcasting Corporation, while in Liberia Protestants produce a weekly programme for rebroadcast via short wave into the Ivory Coast, since they cannot get time on local stations. In Burundi, which is more than half Roman Catholic, the churches participate in the national 'Voice of the Revolution' station, while Protestant station RVOG in Ethiopia was taken over by the revolutionary government in 1977. In Kenya religious groups have an impressive broadcasting programme, including a training centre and several recording studios, with the government providing time on the Voice of Kenya.

When short wave radio became a reliable means of communication, Christian groups immediately grasped its potential for proclaiming the gospel. On Christmas Day 1931 the World Radio Missionary Fellowship went on air in Quito, Ecuador, with station HCJB, which was then a carbon microphone in a wooden box, a 250-watt transmitter in a sheep shed, and an antenna wire strung between two eucalyptus poles. Since then HCJB has grown to 10 studios, 12 transmitters, 28 antennas supported by 50 towers, and a staff of 200 North Americans, broadcasting 24 hours a day in 13 languages and reaching virtually every corner of the globe.

HCJB is but one of a half-dozen large short-wave evangelistic efforts. The Far East Broadcasting Company, with offices in 13 countries, broadcasts in 90 languages and dialects for a total of about 8000 hours per month. Trans World Radio, established in 1952, broadcasts from sites in Monte Carlo, the Netherland Antilles, Guam, Swaziland, Sri Lanka, Evangelium Rundfunk (its German branch), plus purchased time on Radio Cyprus, claiming an audience potential of more than 80 per cent of the world's population. Seventh-day Adventists support programming on more than 3900 radio, television and cable stations in 90 countries, in addition to some 300 local pastors and lay persons broadcasting on local stations in the USA.

By the 1930s radio was penetrating every corner of the globe. Many countries followed North America, where programmes including religious broadcasting were sponsored or funded by advertising, but in India, Australia, New Zealand and South Africa radio stations followed the BBC by being funded by licence fee. With the rise of Hitler, German broadcasting came increasingly under government control during the 1930s. In wartime and after, the BBC's World Service became the one trusted voice of the free world for billions of listeners worldwide, with its famous motto: 'Nation shall speak peace unto nation.'

Today's BBC radio competes with many popular commercial stations, and the mass audiences of the past are fragmenting. However, radio itself is more than holding its own against the proliferation of television channels in the UK, and new technology has brought overseas audiences. Some listen in via digital satellites and others go on-line with a home computer. Listeners can now instantly interact with live radio by emailing presenters, adding a global development to that long-running and most successful low-cost radio programme, the 'radio phone-in'.

Many of the commercially funded stations now provide for special interests such as jazz and sports. Some Christians have campaigned for specifically Christian stations. In the 1990s Premier Christian Radio was licensed in the London area. One hundred per cent Christian-based both in leadership and programme policy, it is motivated by the potential of radio for evangelism, but as Premier works to build its support through local churches, there is always the risk – spelt out by the world's best-known evangelist, Dr Billy Graham – of 'preaching to the choir'.

The 2003 Communications Act, intended to loosen the reins of regulators in order to allow for the growth of broadcasting for the business benefit of Britain, removed only some of the restrictions on religious ownership. It is a puzzle to many Christians in the UK, and for some an outright affront in a society committed to human rights, that the arguments against religious ownership of special-interest radio stations still prevail. In his day the BBC's first Director General feared the same sort of thing, from the sectarianism and conflicts that have blurred Christian communication throughout its history. Today, in multi-faith Britain, some believe that religion has a new potency to cause disharmony and rupture community life, as evidenced by its frequent appearance as sad and bad news headlines.

In the radio of the future, religion needs to keep its position in the market place of ideas, within all channels that provide a public service. The hard-pressed churches of the Western world, facing declining membership, could never fund the talent that still provides the broad rich mix of programming on which so many listeners still rely. They can and should, however, be critical friends to the religious broadcasters, realizing that in their role as missionaries and community leaders it is worth understanding the ingredients and skills that make for successful broadcasting.

In Britain there are small, hopeful signs for religious broadcasting in the future. Local Muslims in cities like Bradford and Glasgow now provide Radio Ramadan to support listeners through the long weeks of fasting. Christians within the 55-year-old Gospel Radio Fellowship – now GRF Christian Radio – have volunteer teams to make radio programmes and place them at very low cost on 'audiopot', a purpose-built computer server available to the growing number of small, community-based radio stations all over the world.

High-quality digital radio, in which wave-form transmission has been replaced by signals encoded in streams of billions of numbers, has become affordable by all and is readily available. It is creating new technical possibilities every day. In 1924 John Reith told listeners: 'One might venture to say that nothing is too fantastic for realization sooner or later. Voices from the ends of the earth will cease to be a marvel; wireless disregards the barriers of nature and man's device; it is super-natural, and when upon it is superimposed the burden of music, when it is the carrier for the interchange of achievements in all the arts and sciences, it may well become the vehicle of an understanding that will embrace all men and nations.'

Eighty years on, radio voices from around the world tell us that there is still a long way to go.

ANDREW BARR AND WILLIAM F. FORE

📖 Erik Barnouw, *A Tower in Babel: A History of Broadcasting in the United States*, New York: OUP

1966; Asa Briggs, *The History of Broadcasting in the United Kingdom* (3 vols), London: OUP 1962–5; Stephen Kern, *The Culture of Time and Space 1880–1916*, London: Weidenfeld & Nicholson 1983; Jolyon P. Mitchell, *Visually Speaking*, Edinburgh: T&T Clark 1999; Kenneth Woolf, *The Churches and the British Broadcasting Corporation 1922–1956*, London: SCM Press 1984

Papacy

Reformation

The term Reformation traditionally describes a period of European history, covering the sixteenth century, a tumultuous era marked by a diverse series of movements aimed at the religious reform of church and society. Historians have recently pointed out that movements of reform were endemic to later medieval Western Christianity. Viewed in the context of this long tradition of reform, the Reformation clearly represented the extension of energies already long at work. Unlike previous reforming movements, however, the Reformation led not to the internal renewal of a still more or less united 'Roman' Catholic Church, but to the fragmenting of Western Christendom itself. The end result was the establishment of a number of alternative forms of Western Christianity, each of which eventually codified its beliefs and practices in its own distinctive 'confessions'. In short, the Reformation simultaneously shattered the unity of Western Christendom in the Catholic Church and released centripetal energies that led to the establishment of competing and, to a certain extent, mutually exclusive confessional forms of Christianity.

Christendom

Germany

The beginnings of what eventually became the Protestant Reformation are usually traced to the protest of Martin Luther (a pious Augustinian friar in Erfurt, Germany) against the practice of selling 'indulgences'. Indulgences were certificates vended to the faithful by preachers specially deputed for this task by church authorities. The indulgence offered to its purchaser the remission not of the guilt of sin, but of part or all of the punishments owing on account of sin, particularly those that would otherwise have to be remitted through the pains of purgatory.

Martin Luther
p. 1068
Sacraments
Justification
Life after death

A properly confessed and absolved Christian was thought to stand in a 'state of grace' before God; in this state, he or she could perform 'good works of satisfaction' and thereby earn merits that could be used to offset the punishments due for previous sins. The 'sale' of an indulgence presupposed that by means of heartfelt confession and priestly absolution the buyer had previously been forgiven the guilt of sin. Giving money to the church (almsgiving) was itself considered one of these good works, and it could be rewarded out of the 'treasury of merits' (the infinite supply of merit earned by Christ and the saints) thought to be under the control of the Pope as head of the church. These merits could be applied, moreover, not only to the living but also to the dead, making it possible for the faithful in effect to buy the release of their departed families or friends from the pains of purgatory. Understood in this way, indulgences occupied a prominent place in the penitential discipline and popular piety of the late medieval church.

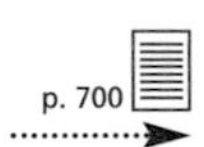

p. 700

In practice, however, the fine theological distinctions made in constructing the church's penitential teaching tended to blur, especially when the sale of indulgences became an important method of fund-raising for the church. In their zeal to promote a successful sale, in 1510 the preachers of a special 'plenary indulgence' (which guaranteed release from all punishments owed) for the construction of the new St Peter's basilica in Rome could go so far as to claim that 'when the coin clinks in the coffer, the soul flies to heaven (i.e., from purgatory)'. Luther was serving at that time as professor in the newly-founded university in Wittenberg, Germany, and as pastor in the city's church. He became alarmed when he observed his parishioners focusing their hopes on indulgences rather than dedicating themselves to lives of authentic repentance and faith. He expressed his concerns in the so-called Ninety-Five Theses, a document originally intended for debate with other learned scholars. When it became clear that the theses would cause a public sensation, however, enterprising printers made them widely available across Europe.

The ensuing controversy swiftly radicalized Luther's views, and a flurry of ingenious treatises flew from his pen. By the end of 1520 he had argued for the superiority of scripture to the teachings of pope or tradition, rejected both the sacrificial understanding of the mass and the related notion of transubstantiation, insisted on the validity of the marriages of priests, and reduced the number of sacraments from the traditional seven to two (baptism and eucharist) or perhaps three (penance). Perhaps most importantly, he argued that the justification of the sinner before God should be understood as a pure gift given by divine grace through faith alone, entirely apart from meritorious good works.

In 1520, Luther's views were examined and condemned in Rome, and he was threatened with excommunication in a papal bull entitled *Exsurge domine* ('Arise, O Lord', its opening words). However, Luther's prince, Frederick the Wise (who was also one of the seven 'electors' with power to choose an emperor), resolutely refused to allow his deportation to Rome for trial. Thus the 'Luther affair' became entangled in imperial political wrangling at the highest level. Eventually, Luther was offered a guarantee

Claude Joseph Vernet, Pope Julius II orders the building of the Vatican and St Peter's

of safe passage to a meeting of the imperial congress (Diet) that was to be held in the German city of Worms in 1521. Interviewed before the Diet (in the presence of the young emperor Charles V), Luther refused to recant his views. 'Here I stand, I can do no other.' As a result, he was immediately placed under the so-called 'imperial ban' and became a wanted outlaw.

Luther was protected, however, by Frederick, whose unwillingness to enforce the ban led to considerable tension with the emperor and the Pope. Together with other sympathetic princes, Frederick and his successors permitted 'evangelical' reforms within their territories along the lines envisioned by Luther and like-minded theologians. Initially, the imperial authorities tolerated these reforms, but at the Diet of Speyer in 1529 this toleration was rescinded. The evangelical princes protested against this decision, and were consequently labelled 'Protestants'. At the Diet of Augsburg in 1530 they presented a summary of their faith, the so-called Augsburg Confession (written by Luther's younger academic colleague, Philipp Melanchthon). Afterwards they formed a defensive military pact, the League of Smalcald, to protect their interests. This task was made easier, at least up until the time of Luther's death in 1546, by ongoing military demands and political intrigues that pitted the emperor not only against an aggressive Ottoman empire (under the capable leadership of Suleiman the Magnificent), but at various times also against the French king, Francis I, and the Pope himself.

Protestantism

In 1547, Charles V was finally free to take military action against the Protestant princes and attempt to restore the religious unity of the empire. Following the defection of a Protestant prince, Moritz of Saxony, Charles won a decisive victory at Mühlberg in 1547. His attempt to reimpose the Catholic faith in previously Protestant territories failed, however, when Moritz defected back to the Protestant side in 1552. Afterwards, the emperor was forced to recognize the Augsburg Confession as licit within the empire, a policy that was codified in the Religious Peace of Augsburg in 1555.

Switzerland

At nearly the same time as Luther was attacking indul- Huldrych Zwingli gences in Saxony, Huldrych Zwingli began a substantial movement of reform while serving as a priest, first in Einsiedeln and later in Zurich. He, too, attacked indulgences (as had others before him), but favoured a version of reform inspired by the 'philosophy of Christ' taught by Erasmus of Rotterdam. In 1523 he successfully defended 67 Reformation theses before the city council; afterwards, he oversaw the city's reform of faith and practice. Like Luther, he emphasized scriptural authority, argued for Predestination clerical marriage, and attacked monasticism. Additionally, Zwingli promoted a version of reform that would purge from the church's faith and worship all elements that were not specifically commanded in scripture. This led to his rejection of the liturgical use of musical instruments, as well as to the removal of images from the churches Iconoclasm (iconoclasm).

Even more radically, he adopted a symbolic understanding of the eucharistic meal (suggested by a Dutch theologian, Cornelius Hoen). Under considerable political pressure, Protestant leaders sought in 1529 to forge an alliance between the reform movement in Switzerland and the one in Germany. The so-called Marburg Colloquy failed, however, when Luther insisted on a more literal understanding of the eucharistic elements as the true body and blood of Christ and not an empty symbol. Two years Apocalyptic later, tensions between Zurich and the other Swiss cantons Holy Spirit led to war, and Zwingli was killed at the second Battle of Kappel. Zurich remained a centre of reform, however, Heinrich Bullinger under the leadership of Zwingli's successor there, Heinrich Bullinger.

John Calvin In 1536 the Frenchman John Calvin – a refugee from Catholic persecution of Protestants in France – was persuaded by the reformer Guillaume Farel to lend his efforts to the leadership of the reform of the city of Geneva. In 1538, however, the city council banished them, and Calvin went to Strasbourg where, under the guidance of Martin Bucer, he laboured contentedly as a pastor. Anabaptists There he also met and married the widow Idelette de Bure, who predeceased him in 1549. At the invitation of the Genevans, Calvin returned to the city in 1541 and remained there until his death in 1564. With Calvin's help and inspiration, the city of Geneva developed a version of reform that embraced not only doctrine and worship, but city life as well. Pastors preached and led the church, teachers taught the faith, elders assisted the pastors, and deacons took care of the sick and needy. The Consistory (a council composed of six clergy and the twelve elders) heard morals cases, and attempted to ensure that the people of the city should live in a manner consistent with their newly-reformed faith.

Formally trained as a lawyer, Calvin taught himself theology, along with the Greek and Hebrew languages. In 1536 he published the first edition of the *Institutes of the Christian Religion*, his summary presentation of Christian belief. Over the years he revised and expanded the book several times (in Latin and French) until it reached its final form in 1559. Calvin was perhaps the greatest of the systematizers of 'Reformed' theology. The *Institutes* provided textbook Reformed solutions to the most pressing theological issues of the day. Calvin's thoroughgoing biblicism, his emphasis on God's gracious providence, and his insistence that human salvation depends ultimately on divine election and predestination alone became some of the hallmarks of Reformed theology. His doctrine of the 'spiritual presence' of Christ in the elements of the Lord's Supper was an attempt to bridge the gap between Luther and Zwingli, but it did little to resolve the controversy. In 1559, at Calvin's urging, the city council established the Academy of Geneva (later the University of Geneva). Hundreds of young Protestant theologians studied there, and Calvinist teaching thus spread throughout Europe and, eventually, to the 'new world' of the Americas.

Radical reforms

While Luther and Zwingli initiated movements that relied on the support of the established political authorities, reformers such as Andreas Carlstadt, Nicholas Storch and Thomas Müntzer argued for even more radical reforms. Müntzer interpreted the events of his age in apocalyptic terms, and looked to the internal guidance of the Holy Spirit in order to interpret them. Eventually he became one of the leaders in a popular uprising, the so-called Peasants' War. After the peasants' defeat at the battle of Frankenhausen in 1525, he was captured and beheaded.

In Zurich, some of Zwingli's parishioners concluded on the basis of Zwingli's own preaching that baptism should be administered only to believing adults. When they proceeded with plans to do so (over the objections of Zwingli and the city council), Conrad Grebel, Balthasar Huebmeier, Georg Blaurock and Felix Manz initiated the non-conformist 'Anabaptist' (rebaptism) movement. These so-called 'Swiss Brethren' were persecuted severely: Manz was executed in Zurich in 1527; Blaurock was burned at the stake in 1529. The Schleitheim Articles, the first Anabaptist confession of faith, were published in 1527 and were apparently written by Michael Sattler.

Similar movements sprang up all over Europe, but it

THE REFORMERS

The principal figures in the Protestant Reformation and where they were active:

Germany	
Martin Luther	(1483–1546) Wittenberg
Philipp Melanchthon	(1497–1560) Wittenberg
Switzerland	
John Oecolampadius	(1482–1531) Basel
Huldrych Zwingli	(1484–1531) Zurich
William Farel	(1489–1565) Geneva
Heinrich Bullinger	(1504–75) Zurich
John Calvin	(1509–64) Geneva
Theodore Beza	(1519–1605) Geneva
France	
Martin Bucer	(1491–1551) Strasbourg, later Cambridge
England	
Thomas Cranmer	(1489–1556)
Hugh Latimer	(1490–1555)
John Hooper	(c. 1495–1555)
Nicholas Ridley	(1500–55)
Scotland	
John Knox	(c. 1513–72)

is difficult to identify their common features. All held to believers' baptism, and most emphasized separation of church and state, refused to take oaths, found a role for human free will in conversion, appealed to the inner light of the Holy Spirit for direct revelation, and saw the church as a voluntary society composed of believers only; many also used the so-called ban (total exclusion from the church or community) as a means of church discipline. Still, there were important variations. The German city of Münster, to take one regrettable example, descended into excess inspired by religion following its adoption of an Anabaptist church order in 1533. Leaders christened the city a 'New Jerusalem', and along with mandatory believers' baptism they forcibly instituted a community of goods, burned all books except the Bible, and declared polygamy legal. The Catholic and Lutheran authorities were scandalized and co-operated in a horrific siege against the city; following their victory, they tortured and executed the Anabaptist leaders and the city reverted to Catholicism. In south Germany, on the other hand, the capable Jacob Hutter, who followed Blaurock as leader of the Anabaptists in Tyrolia, moved to Moravia and developed a communal form of Anabaptism, the Moravian Brethren or Hutterites. Eventually, these Anabaptists became respected agrarian pacifists. The Hutterites prosper today in North America.

England and beyond

Movements of reform also took hold in eastern Europe, Scandinavia and the British Isles. In England, religious reforms were confused by the vacillation of the Tudor king, Henry VIII. Inspired by Erasmus, Christian humanists like Cambridge's John Colet helped to create an intellectual and cultural atmosphere favourable to religious change. At Cambridge's White Horse Inn, the men who would soon make up the first wave of England's Reformation met: Robert Barnes, Hugh Latimer, Nicholas Ridley, John Foxe, John Frith and others. Many were later put to death for their role in bringing Reformation to England, and their inspiring stories were told with partisan sympathy and pathos in Foxe's *Book of Martyrs*.

Church of England

Early on, prospects for a Reformation in England seemed poor. The young English king (who had been thoroughly trained in theology) even took up the pen himself against Luther. His 'Assertion of the Seven Sacraments' of 1524 (written against the attack on the sacramental system contained in Luther's 'Babylonian Captivity of the Church' of 1520) earned him the title 'Defender of the Faith' from the Pope. Faced, however, with a childless marriage to his dead brother Arthur's wife, Catherine of Aragon, and concerned to provide an heir for the Tudor line, Henry appealed to the church for a divorce, a case that soon wound up before Pope Clement VII. Clement refused to grant the divorce, at least as much for political as for religious reasons, but Henry would not give up. In the ensuing controversy, the Archbishop of Canterbury lost his job (Thomas Wolsey) and the Lord Chancellor lost his head (Thomas More); in time, the king got his divorce, and two of his total of six wives (Anne Boleyn and Catherine Howard) lost their heads as well. Henry then broke with the papacy, and in 1534 parliament's Act of Supremacy declared the English king 'supreme head on earth' of the Church of England. Although Henry himself remained decidedly Catholic in theology, he did much to de-catholicize England, not least in closing and expropriating the properties of England's religious houses (monasteries and convents).

Discipline

The task of reforming the English church after Henry's death fell to Thomas Cranmer, who had been named Archbishop of Canterbury in 1533. During the reign of Henry's lone male heir, Edward VI, Cranmer and his supporters carried out a moderate reform. Cranmer's Book of Common Prayer (1549, 1552) decisively shaped English faith and worship for generations. His work was temporarily reversed, however, when Mary, the daughter of Catherine of Aragon and therefore a Catholic, succeeded her half-brother in 1553. Mary's reign – during which many English Reformers (including Cranmer himself)

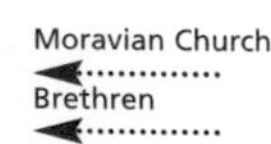

Moravian Church
Brethren

were burned at the stake – ended after only five years. It was not until the long reign of her half-sister, Elizabeth, that the Reformation in England assumed its final form. The Reformation also met with success in Scotland, where the church was reorganized under the leadership of 'elders' or 'presbyters'; hence the name Presbyterian.

Church of Scotland Reformation
Presbyterianism
Christianity in Europe
Lutheranism
Anglicanism

Scandinavia, too, adopted the Reformation, as did the Baltic states. Denmark was reformed first, with the assistance of the Wittenberg pastor and churchman, Johannes Bugenhagen. Soon Norway and Iceland, ruled by Denmark, also came over to the Reformation. Sweden was reformed under the rule of Gustav Vasa in 1527, a process guided by Olaf and Lars Petri, churchmen who had studied in Wittenberg. Similarly, the Finn Michael Agricola brought the Reformation to Finland after study in Wittenberg from 1536–9. Reform movements also met with varying degrees of success in Poland, Bohemia, Moravia and Slovakia.

Catholic Reformation

Council
Martin Luther
Roman Catholic Church
Counter-Reformation

The Church of Rome was initially slow in recognizing the need for internal reform; the Fifth Lateran Council had completed its modest reforming work in 1514 and few were prepared to heed Luther's call only a few years later for a new council to consider his views. Many recognized the need for additional reform, however, and once the process received official sanction under Pope Paul III (1534–49) it proceeded with energy. Meeting at various times from 1545–63, the Council of Trent provided a thoroughgoing reform. It clearly articulated Roman Catholic teaching, offered a new catechism, promulgated the Latin Vulgate as the church's official text of the Bible, and composed a revised liturgy and breviary. The Society of Jesus (Jesuits), founded by Ignatius Loyola in 1540, provided the church with a dedicated and able contingent of men dedicated specially to the Pope; they spear-headed the Counter-Reformation, and at the instigation of Francis Xavier inaugurated a new Roman Catholic mission movement. Ironically, the Roman Catholic Church ended the century strengthened and newly confident, even after nearly a century of Protestant reforming.

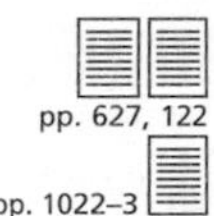

pp. 627, 122
pp. 1022–3
Counter-Reformation

Mission

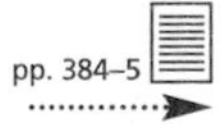

pp. 384–5

MICKEY L. MATTOX

p. 1068

Euan Cameron, *The European Reformation*, Oxford: Clarendon Press 1991; Carter Lindberg, *The European Reformations*, Oxford: Blackwell 1996; Diarmaid MacCulloch, *Reformation: Europe's House Divided, 1490–1700*, Harmondsworth: Penguin Books 2003; Steven Ozment, *The Age of Reform, 1250–1550: An Intellectual and Religious History of Late Medieval and Reformation Europe*, New Haven: Yale University Press 1980; Lewis Spitz, *The Protestant Reformation, 1517–1559*, New York: Harper & Row 1985

Reformed churches

The Reformed churches make up one of the largest families of Christian churches stemming from the European Reformation in the sixteenth century. Today the World Alliance of Reformed Churches (WARC) includes more than 200 churches numbering some 75 million members in almost every country in the world. It is numerically larger than the Lutheran and Anglican communions (who each have some 60 million members), but is also much more diverse in church order, theology and liturgy. At present, Reformed churches are growing and spreading particularly in the Third World; like other mainstream denominations in Europe and North America, the Reformed there are generally experiencing a slow but recognizable decline in numbers and influence.

The roots of the diversity of the Reformed churches lie in their origins and subsequent history. In the sixteenth century there emerged distinctive Swiss, German, French, Dutch, English, Scottish, Bohemian and Hungarian Reformed traditions, to name only the most prominent at that time in Europe. They had in common the principles of the Reformation unleashed by Martin Luther. They disputed the claim of the Roman Catholic Church to be the divinely instituted means of grace and salvation, insisted on holding to the Bible alone to be the authentic Word of God, and aimed to reform both church and society accordingly. If anything, they stressed the sovereignty of grace and the divine lordship even more than other Reformation traditions. This found particularly sharp expression in the Calvinist doctrine of 'double predestination', though it should be added that most Reformed churches today no longer affirm this teaching.

The Reformed Reformation was more radical than the Lutheran in regard to liturgical forms and expressions of piety. This was very markedly shown in a renewed allegiance to the second of the Ten Commandments in Exodus 20.4–6: 'You shall not make or worship idols.' This injunction had been suppressed by the medieval church (which compensated for the loss by dividing the tenth commandment into two) and Luther, though in other ways so radical, had here simply accepted the medieval tradition unaltered. A related point was the general rejection by the Reformed of the Lutheran understanding of the 'real presence' of the body and blood of Christ in the Lord's Supper. These controversies have today been largely resolved by the Leuenberg Concord of 1973, but are important for understanding the historical divisions between Lutheran and Reformed Churches in the sixteenth century. Lutheran Protestantism at that time was dominant in Germany and Scandinavia, while the Reformed spread east and west of that area. The two leading influences in the century of the Reformation were those of Zurich (Huldrych Zwingli and his successor, Heinrich Bullinger) and Geneva (John Calvin). Calvin's immense stature has led to the common equation of 'Reformed' with 'Calvinist', but Calvin was not the only shaper of Reformed belief, and there are also significant differences between Calvin and the 'high Calvinism' of the seventeenth century as reflected in the Decrees of Dort (1618) or the Westminster Confession (1647).

A further characteristic was that the Reformed for the most part broke more radically with the liturgical traditions and patterns of the medieval church. In general they greatly simplified the forms of worship, particularly the form of celebration of the Lord's Supper. Here the Reformed quite consciously departed further than the Lutherans or Anglicans from the medieval form of the mass and followed instead the late medieval pattern of the 'prone' or preaching service. In the Zurich Reformed tradition, music – both sung and instrumental – for a long time found no place in worship. In Geneva, by contrast, Calvin introduced the Psalms of David in verse form for congregational singing. Calvin's own attempts to put some psalms into rhyme were not particularly successful, but he soon found others who were better equipped, poetically and musically. The versified Psalter on the Geneva model rapidly made an abiding mark on the Reformed tradition and for centuries was the only form of hymn book in many Reformed churches. Some of the best-known psalm versions today come from that source – e.g. 'All people that on earth do dwell' to the Geneva melody known in the Anglo-Saxon world as OLD HUNDREDTH. Only gradually did scripture paraphrases (e.g. 'O God of Bethel') and then hymns (which from the beginning had been central in Lutheran practice) find their place in Reformed worship.

Yet another prominent feature has to do with church order and patterns of office. Here, too, the Reformed tradition broke more radically with the medieval heritage. In Geneva, Calvin introduced the 'fourfold office' of pastors, elders, teachers and deacons. This structure was adopted and modified in various ways in the Reformed traditions. It generally led to a pattern of church government based on co-operation between ministers and elders. In particular it came to replace the previous bishops and the theory of episcopal apostolic succession – both of which were preserved in Anglicanism and in Scandinavian Lutheranism – with a system of church government by regional and national synods. (Some Reformed churches did combine this model with a modified episcopal system, but generally saw their 'bishops' or 'superintendents' as administrators rather than as specially profiled or sacrally consecrated 'successors to the apostles'. The chief 'apostolic office' was that of the minister ordained to preach the Word of God and dispense the sacraments of baptism and the Lord's Supper.) This model, combining ordained ministers with 'ruling elders', may justly be described as the only effective alternative developed in the Reformation to the medieval episcopal system. It is to be found today – in varying forms – in virtually all Protestant churches. It may be added that in modern times the episcopal churches stemming from the Reformation have also adopted elements of this system and so complemented their emphasis on the office of the bishop.

Huldrych Zwingli
Heinrich Bullinger
John Calvin

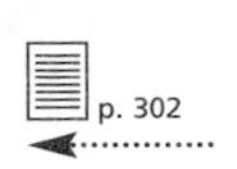

p. 302

Reformed churches in their different countries underwent very diverse histories in the centuries following the Reformation. Those in Bohemia and Western Hungary suffered 150 years of Austrian suppression following the Thirty Years War, though those in Central and Eastern Hungary were to some extent protected under Turkish rule. The Reformed Church in France experienced especial hardships under the despotic regime of Louis XIV. Following his revocation of the Tolerance Edict of Nantes in 1685, some 200,000 Huguenots (as the French Reformed were called) left their homeland and settled as exiles in Switzerland, Germany, the Netherlands, Britain, America and South Africa. By contrast, the Swiss, West German, Dutch and Scottish Reformed churches (and for a time to some degree the English) generally found acceptance, frequently becoming the established church of their region or nation; they achieved social and political influence, worked to raise standards of education and produced a very considerable number of outstanding intellectuals, scientists, lawyers and other academic, cultural and political leaders, who made lasting contributions to the shaping of Western democratic society. (There is also some truth in the often alleged connection between the Calvinist ethos and the beginnings of capitalism, but the point should not be pushed too far.)

Worship
Eucharist
Wars of religion

Music
Psalms

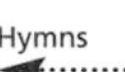

Hymns

Along with this geographical and historical diversity may be set the fact that, unlike Lutheranism with its Formula of Concord, the Reformed did not establish a closed and complete canon of confessional writings to serve as the norm of Reformed belief: there are Reformed confessions from the most varied places and dates between the Reformation and the present but there is no single universal confessional standard to which all Reformed even theoretically subscribe.

Ministry and ministers
Creed

Especially important for the further development and diversification of the Reformed tradition was its anchoring in England and Scotland in the sixteenth and seventeenth centuries. This anchoring was accompanied by religious, social and political conflict. It was in fact a major factor in the century and a half of upheaval that racked the British Isles from the Reformation until late in the seventeenth century. As it ran its course it brought further social, religious and political divisions. The British Reformed were united in opposition to the Anglican

Organization

TWO CONTROVERSIAL THEOLOGICAL MOVEMENTS FROM THE NETHERLANDS

Arminianism

Arminianism was a liberal reaction to some of the harshest features of Calvinism. It takes its name from the Dutch Protestant theologian Jakob Hermandszoon (in Latin Jacobus Arminius, 1560–1609) of the University of Leiden. Arminians are also called Remonstrants because Arminianism was expounded in the Remonstrance (1610), a theological statement drawn up and submitted to the Synod of Dort (1618–19), which states five principles:

1. Those who believe will be saved;
2. Christ died for all, but works salvation only for those who believe;
3. No one can respond to God's will without the aid of the Holy Spirit;
4. Saving grace can be resisted;
5. Believers can fall from grace.

The crux of all this is to assert that God's sovereignty and human free will are compatible and human dignity requires free will.

Methodism
Unitarians

The Arminians were condemned and subsequently persecuted for a while, but they proved influential. Arminianism was an important influence on John Wesley and Methodism, and also on American Unitarianism.

Jansenism

Jansenism takes its name from the Dutch Roman Catholic theologian Cornelius Jansen (1585–1638), who taught at Louvain. He was the author of a book, published posthumously under the title *Augustinus*, which emphasized the degree of human sin (human beings cannot keep God's commandments by their own efforts) and the irresistible character of grace. As the title of his book indicates, Jansen was appealing to Augustine, and he was writing against the Jesuits in particular. The Jansenists concluded that the sacraments of the church were effective only when God had already transformed those who received them by his grace. This grace was limited to the elect, so there was no need to be concerned with the salvation of outsiders. Rather, it was important to lead a life of strict discipline and asceticism. These views were not unlike those of John Calvin and shared his pessimism.

Church fathers

John Calvin

Although Jansen was Dutch, French Catholics were the ones who took up his cause: Blaise Pascal's championship of it in his *Lettres Provinciales* made it famous. The Jansenists had their centre at Port-Royal, a nunnery in Paris, headed by the Abbess Mother Angélique Arnauld, whose sisters led lives of deep and rigorous devotion.

The Jansenists were condemned in the bull *Cum occasione* ('With occasion', 1653) of Innocent XI and the constitution *Unigenitus* ('Only begotten', 1713) of Clement XI and at times were persecuted; however, the French hostility to the Jesuits helped them, and those who fled to the Netherlands found more tolerance there. Jansenism effectively died after the French Revolution and the concordat drawn up by Napoleon in 1801 which allowed the restoration of the French Catholic church; however, its principles continued in some circles as a source of inspiration.

establishment, in particular to the rule of the church by bishops, especially when the bishops were appointed by the crown. They came to differ on other matters relating to church government and order. Early in the seventeenth century there emerged among the Reformed in England Baptist congregations, which rejected infant baptism. Soon after, differences between the congregational (or 'independent') and presbyterian views of church order came into the open. The Church of Scotland and the Presbyterian Church in Ireland followed the presbyterian system; the English Reformed inclined rather to congregationalism. Both systems were exported in the first instance to North America through the settlement of New England. North America experienced at the same time an influx of Dutch Calvinists bringing their own traditions and understanding of a proper church order. All these traditions, added to by later immigrants from other Reformed churches, helped to shape North American Reformed church diversity. The subsequent missionary endeavours of these Dutch, British and North American churches, often going hand in hand with extensive colonization by these same countries, are reflected in the great variety of Reformed churches in the Third World today.

Baptist
Congregational
Church of Scotland
Architecture

p. 274

Preaching

Christianity in North America

In today's world it cannot be assumed that a Reformed church will necessarily be as liturgically simple as in the beginnings in Zurich or Geneva. The presbyterian tradition in particular experienced in the nineteenth century a liturgical revival, a renewal of hymns and liturgical forms and a rediscovery of neo-Gothic church architecture. More recently still other Reformed traditions have seen a return to liturgically richer forms of worship and (e.g. in centres such as Taizé in France) an attempt to recover some of the values of monastic life and worship. These go a long way to offset the traditional liturgical spareness of the Puritan tradition. In contemporary Reformed worship music plays a significant part, as do carefully worked-out forms of prayer. In principle, however, Reformed theology and custom still stress the importance of the sermon as living speech, as engaged interpretation of the Bible, as vivid interpretation of the Word of God in and for the gathered congregation, and as a 'Word from the Lord', a 'Word for our time' and a 'Word for us'.

The history of the Reformed churches up to the nineteenth century was often one of diversity, division and sub-division. More recently a new spirit manifested itself: that of a search to recover unity. In the last 200 years a number of Reformed churches in various parts of the world have entered into union with churches from other confessional and denominational backgrounds. Similar impulses led to the founding of both the World Alliance of Reformed Churches holding the Presbyterian System (1875) and the International Congregational Council, which held its first assembly in 1891. These bodies merged in 1970 to form the present World Alliance of Reformed Churches, based in Geneva. A characteristic emphasis from the beginning of this new inner-Reformed ecumenical activity was that it should also be outward-looking and concerned for a wider ecumenism. Throughout its history, and especially since the founding of the World Council of Churches in 1948, the WARC has tended to keep a relatively low profile (reflected in a small staff and shoe-string budget) and to encourage its members to work actively within the WCC and in other ecumenical partnerships. Its aim is not to build up a distinct Reformed block within the ecumenical world, let alone turn the WARC into a kind of centralized, uniform and organically united worldwide Reformed church. In terms of today's ecumenical diplomacy this stands in marked contrast, for example, to the goals of the World Lutheran Federation, or indeed of the Anglican Lambeth Conference.

At the same time the WARC has for many years conducted its own programme of ecumenical meetings and dialogues with other communions, including the Orthodox, the Roman Catholic, the Lutheran, the Anglican and other Protestant and charismatic churches. The WARC has been more openly critical of some recent tendencies within the Roman Catholic Church (such as the reassertion of papal claims or the renewed emphasis on indulgences in the context of the Jubilee Year 2000) than either the Anglican or Lutheran world bodies. Reformed enthusiasm for the statement by the Faith and Order Commission of the World Council of Churches on baptism, eucharist and ministry at their conference in Lima in 1982 (the 'Lima Declaration') was also generally restrained, particularly perhaps because of the way the statement advanced the predominantly Anglican/Orthodox theory of the 'threefold ministry' (bishop, priest and deacon) as the model for a future ecumenical doctrine of the church.

This does not mean that Reformed churches are necessarily anti-ecumenical, though some (particularly some which do not even belong to the WARC) may fairly be said to be so. It is rather that since the sixteenth century matters of church order and in particular of the order of forms of ministry and church administration have been a central Reformed concern. Conviction reinforced by experience has led Reformed churches to be sceptical of claims made by ecclesiastical hierarchies. In recent decades the WARC programme has also seen a partial shift from the classical topics of ecumenical exchange in the 'Faith and Order' mould to greater concentration on ethical, economic and ecological issues, especially as these affect the Third World.

Ecumenical movement

ALASDAIR HERON

Jean-Jacques Bauswein and Lukas Vischer (eds), *The Reformed Family Worldwide*, Grand Rapids, MI: Eerdmans 1999; John H. Leith, *An Introduction to the Reformed Tradition*, Atlanta: John Knox Press 1977; Donald K. McKim (ed), *Encyclopedia of the Reformed Faith*, Louisville, KY: Westminster John Knox Press and Edinburgh: St Andrew Press 1992; Alan P. F. Sell, *A Reformed, Evangelical, Catholic Theology: The Contribution of the World Alliance of Reformed Churches, 1875–1982*, Grand Rapids, MI: Eerdmans 1991

http://www.warc.ch

Religious orders

The monastery of the centuries before 1100 was typically an autonomous community that lived under the direction of its abbot and might be exempted from the authority of the diocesan bishop. It was not unknown for there to be links between houses, but these were informal rather than constitutional. Pachomius in fourth-century Egypt and Benedict in sixth-century Italy, among others, founded a number of communities for which they legislated and over which they exercised a personal supervisory authority. An important impulse towards a greater degree of system came from reformers, supported or even inspired by rulers and other lay patrons, who identified the need to raise standards of observance among monks over a wide area, as the Emperor Charlemagne and his successor did when they supported the reforms of Benedict of Aniane. The means employed were, however, still primarily legislative: reforming measures were approved at church councils or synods, but there was no real system of 'follow-up', visitation or reporting back.

p. 476

Council

A new departure between the tenth century and the twelfth at first sight seems to have heralded the birth of the religious order proper. The many monasteries that were founded or reformed from Cluny in this period were regarded as dependencies of the mother house. They were designated 'priories', and their superiors were mere 'priors',

p. 792

not 'abbots'. Furthermore, every Cluniac monk made his profession to the abbot of Cluny and not to his own prior. This subordination was a sign that the Cluniac house and the Cluniac monk accepted that their lives would conform to the norms dictated by Cluny itself. The abbot of Cluny in this sense looks like the head of an order. However, this subordination was not translated into a real centralized organization. There was, for example, no division of the Cluniac commonwealth into provinces, and there were no regular 'chapters' (meetings) of representatives of member houses. Both would become hallmarks of later orders.

The wave of monastic reforms that occurred in the later eleventh century had more far-reaching effects. In the early twelfth century both the Cistercians and Carthusians had adopted general chapter meetings that brought the heads of member houses together on a regular basis. A prime purpose of the general chapters was to maintain vigilance over the quality of life lived in individual houses. The chapters could and did legislate on the interpretation of the rule and codify the 'customs' by which the monks were to live. In addition, each Cistercian house was 'visited' annually by the abbot of the house from which it had been founded. Thus families of affiliated houses (rather than geographical provinces) came into being. These arrangements represented a considerable advance in sophistication on the relationship of Cluny with its dependencies. The autonomy of the individual monastery and its abbot was modified but not abrogated. For day-to-day purposes every monastery, Cluniac, Cistercian or Carthusian, remained a self-contained community, as of course did the old 'Benedictine' houses such as St Denis near Paris or (in England) St Albans or Bury.

The twelfth century witnessed a very considerable diversification of the basic principles of the religious life to serve new purposes, and this was accompanied by a number of novel organizational expedients. The foundation of the Knights of the Temple (Templars) in 1120 was an example. What seems to have originated with an oath taken by a small group of knights to protect pilgrims to the Holy Land became within a generation an organization with a rule and a growing Christendom number of estates scattered across Christendom, on some of which 'preceptories' were established. Like the analogous 'commanderies' of the Knights of the Hospital (Hospitallers), who originated slightly earlier, these were more like 'branches' than autonomous centres. They came into being not so much to provide local focuses of the religious life as to administer the order's possessions. At least until the final loss of the Holy Land, both the individual members of these orders and their widely scattered resources were in principle dedicated to a single objective, the defence of Christendom in the East. Both orders were headed by a grand master.

The individual brother of the Temple or the Hospital in effect joined an order rather than a particular religious house. His career was much less likely to be spent within the confines of a single locality or a single convent than a monk's was. (It was in fact possible for a man to serve in the Order of the Temple for a limited period, returning thereafter to secular life.) Numerous other military brotherhoods came into being. The Teutonic Order of Knights also originated in the Holy Land, in 1190, but soon became dedicated instead to the wars against the heathen in Prussia and the Baltic region, while the special circumstances of the struggle against Islam in Spain produced orders native to the Iberian peninsula, notably those of Santiago, Calatrava and Alcántara.

The military religious orders represented one response to a contemporary need to provide forms of religious organization that could serve the world outside the cloister. The best way of doing this, it was widely believed, was to provide the individual brother with the spiritual and material support system of a community life. It was an ancient principle that had found expression centuries earlier in the use of monks as missionaries. In the early fifth century, Augustine as Bishop of Hippo in North Africa had sought to organize his clergy on quasi-monastic lines; what was known as the Rule of St Augustine was derived from a letter of instruction which he had addressed to a religious community. It provided very general guidance on the living of the common life, a core to which each congregation could add its distinctive customs.

One of the uses to which the Augustinian rule was put in the twelfth century was the reform of cathedral chapters, but it could also be used to provide the framework for a modified form of the monastic life. The communities of 'regular canons' which multiplied in Christendom in the course of the century are often collectively referred to as 'Augustinian', but they had no single umbrella organization. They served a variety of purposes and developed a variety of specialisms, from the pursuit of learning (as at the famous house of St Victor in Paris) to the service of hospitals (St Bartholomew's in London originated as an Augustinian foundation). Many regular canons lived a community life virtually indistinguishable from that of contemporary monks, and many were deeply influenced, in spirituality and in organization, by the Cistercians. This was particularly true of the Premonstratensians or 'White Canons', who had houses all over Europe but became much involved in missionary work in the newly-Christianized lands of eastern Europe. At the very end of the century, another 'Augustinian' group, the Trinitarians, originated with the particular purpose of ransoming prisoners, and they too spread widely.

The regular canons and the Rule of St Augustine had their importance for the future development of the religious

MILITARY ORDERS

Institutions which combined war and religion were highly popular in the Middle Ages, and a complete list would probably number around 100. However, three stand out above the rest; two of them still exist.

Knights of Malta

Also known as Hospitallers or Knights Hospitaller. The order originated in a group of Italians who cared for sick pilgrims in a hospital in Jerusalem. After the capture of Jerusalem by the Crusaders, Gerard, the monk who was in charge, extended the work and provided hostels on the route to the Holy Land. The order was recognized by the Pope and given its name in 1113. It became rich and powerful and not only cared for the sick but waged war on Islam, becoming a formidable military force. In 1309 the Knights conquered Rhodes and ruled it as an independent state, but they were driven out by the Muslims in 1530. In 1530 the Holy Roman Emperor Charles V gave them the Maltese islands, which they ruled until the islands were conquered by Napoleon in 1798. By now the Knights had given up their warlike activities, From 1834 they have been based in Rome. Membership is restricted to Roman Catholics and the order is controlled by aristocrats. It founded the St John Ambulance Brigade in 1888.

Symbol: White Maltese cross on a black background

Crusades

Knights Templar

Also known as Templars. The order was founded after the Crusader capture of Jerusalem by a group of knights who formed a religious community and devoted themselves to protecting pilgrims from attack. They were given quarters in the temple, hence their name, and took vows of poverty and chastity. Their rule was written by Bernard of Clairvaux and in 1139 they came under the Pope's sole authority. The Templars became rich and powerful, owning property all over Europe, and became specialists in transporting bullion and in banking. This led to rivalry with the Hospitallers, and at the end of the thirteenth century, when the Crusaders no longer had any strongholds in the Holy Land, there were proposals to merge the two orders. This came to nothing. Instead, in 1307 Philip the Fair of France arrested all the French Templars and confiscated their property. Rumours of sodomy, heresy and blasphemy circulated round Europe and Templars were tortured and executed. The order was disbanded by Clement V in 1312. The Temple church in London, circular after the Church of the Holy Sepulchre in Jerusalem, was once the Templars' headquarters in England.

Dress: White cloak with a red cross

Teutonic Order

An order of German knights which grew out of a fraternity of German merchants caring for the sick in a hospital in Acre after its capture by Crusaders. It was made a military order in 1198 with papal approval. Early in the twelfth century the knights transferred their activities to Eastern Europe, conquering Prussia and extending into Lithuania. Though essentially engaged in Christian mission, they became a threatening political power and in 1410 were defeated in battle by the combined forces of Poland and Lithuania. The order was dissolved in Prussia in 1525, and subsequently lost other territories, being abolished by Napoleon in 1809 in his war with Austria. Austria retained the order, however, though it was limited to charitable activities. It still has headquarters in Vienna.

Dress: White habit with a black cross

orders. As a member of the cathedral chapter of Osma in Castile, Dominic (1170–1221) was an Augustinian canon. With his bishop, Diego, he was diverted from an original ambition to preach to the heathen in the Baltic into the campaign against the Cathar heresy in southern France. Dominic soon identified the need for a brotherhood dedicated to preaching and religious instruction. His intentions were approved, but in the wake of the significant decision by the Fourth Lateran Council (1215) that no new religious rules should be permitted, he was compelled to adopt one of those already in existence. It was no surprise that this should be the Rule of St Augustine, but this was only the beginning of the most highly-organized religious order that had yet been devised.

Dominic and his successors applied to the organization of the Order of Preachers (to give it its proper name) every good idea that anyone had ever had on the subject and some that no one seems to have had before. One distinctive feature was the geographical division of the order into provinces, each of which had an elected prior, and the institution of annual provincial general chapters, to which every house sent its prior and another elected representative. The provincial chapter in turn elected representatives to the general chapter, which legislated for the order and when necessary elected the master general. The general chapter was composed somewhat differently, according to what function it was to perform in a given year, for example, whether or not a new master general was to be elected. Election was very important in the life of the order; for example, the provincial chapter was

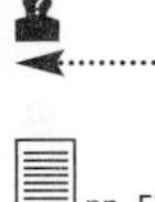
pp. 520–1

Franciscans caring for lepers, from the fourteenth-century manuscript *La Francheschina*

attended by representatives elected from among the body of the conventual friars, who afterwards returned to their ordinary lives. The conventual prior was not elected for life or for a fixed term; he held office until he resigned, was 'absolved' by superior authority or was moved on to a higher post elsewhere. The provincial prior similarly held office for an indeterminate period; the master held office for life but could resign or be 'absolved'.

Educational provision was a hallmark of the Order of Preachers, and here too there was an organized hierarchy. Every convent had its school; there were provincial schools of theology and also of the humanities; and at the summit there were 'general schools', *studia generalia*, the order's University universities. The first of these was at Paris, already the greatest centre of learning north of the Alps; in 1248 the order was given for the institution of another four, at Cologne, Oxford, Montpellier and Bologna, and more followed later.

The Order of Friars Minor (more familiarly known as the Franciscans) grew from rather different spiritual roots but rapidly experienced a convergent development that gave it an organization (and a system of schools) in many ways very similar to that of the Order of Preachers. The Franciscans were not, however, compelled to adopt an existing rule. Francis (*c.*1181–1226) produced a very basic rule for his brotherhood in 1209, and this was approved by Pope Innocent III, but a simple collection of gospel precepts did not provide the guidance required by a rapidly growing international order, and it had to be substantially amplified in 1221.

For Francis himself the gospel remained the rule. His call and that of his first followers was to the imitation of Christ in their own daily lives and voluntary poverty, both individual and collective, was a vital part of their way of life. In this particular, the Franciscans seem to have influenced the Dominicans, at least to the extent that the latter adopted poverty not only as an element of personal holiness but as a part of their pastoral strategy. It would help them to compete with heretical holy men who looked impressively ascetic and impoverished. An uncompromising insistence on real poverty was soon to lead the more radical Franciscans into conflict with the majority of their own order and even with the papacy. The majority continued to be inspired by the distinctive image of their charismatic founder, but in practice they settled for a modified vision of his ideals. The popes underwrote a legal fiction whereby the papacy owned the order's property, the brethren merely having the use of it. Property meant, among other things, the large churches and permanent conventual buildings which Francis had never intended his brotherhood to have.

These churches and other buildings, major landmarks still in many European cities, are reminders that although the friars were individually mobile, they also had a powerful local presence wherever they settled. Indeed, it was essential to their success that they did. The Franciscans and Dominicans established themselves in towns, because it was their intention to live on gifts, not on rents from landed property, and only in the urban environment was a sufficient surplus of foodstuffs and other necessities to be had. The fact that originally at least the friars lived by begging gave rise to the label 'mendicants', by which they are often known. The typical mendicant settlement was in the 'suburbs' of a town, that is outside the Roman or earlier medieval wall, but with the continued demographic growth of the thirteenth century not only did the friars themselves build bigger churches, but their convents often came to be enclosed in newly-enlarged circuits of walls. Within the walls or without, they often established a particularly strong influence over their immediate neighbourhood, effectively building up a kind of 'parish' and rivalling the parish clergy proper and other older established urban churches. Not surprisingly, the tendency of townsfolk, male and female, not least the wealthier ones, to opt for burial with the friars and to remember them favourably in their wills gave rise to conflicts in which popes on several occasions endeavoured to intervene. Conflict was not, however, invariable and the orders not infrequently co-operated with bishops and other clergy in initiatives designed to promote popular devotion.

Unlike Dominic, Francis was a layman, and many of the early Franciscans were not priests, although this changed by the second half of the thirteenth century. Like the monks before them, the mendicants realized that gardens, cellars, kitchens and workshops had to be tended if the priests, teachers and contemplatives were to be free to pursue their calling, and as a result they too embraced persons of differing status within their ranks. Both Franciscans and Dominicans imposed restrictions on the admission of lay brethren, but the Franciscans seem to have been the more draconian in their approach, preferring to authorize the employment of servants. Among the Dominicans, it was possible, if not common, for a lay brother to transfer to clerical status.

The Franciscans rapidly became and remained much more numerous than the Dominicans, but both established themselves all over Christendom. In England the distinctive colours of their habits earned them the names, respectively, of Greyfriars and Blackfriars, still commemorated in a number of street names. By the end of the thirteenth century other orders of friars had also established themselves throughout Europe. The word 'friar', it should be remembered, means nothing more than 'brother' (Latin *frater*, French *frère)*, and it came to be applied to a number of groups which placed their emphasis on different aspects of the religious life. The Carmelites, or Whitefriars, originated as a group of hermits in the Holy Land in the twelfth century, but reorganized themselves on the mendicant model when they were forced to transplant themselves to the West. Another new order of friars grew from earlier eremitical beginnings in Italy: the Augustinian Hermits (Austin Friars) were so-called because they adopted the Rule of St Augustine, and they have to be distinguished from the Augustinian canons already mentioned. The Servites, or Order of the Servants of the Blessed Virgin Mary, resembled the Hermits in their Italian origins, their adoption of the Augustinian rule and the influence the Dominicans had on them. They remained principally an Italian order. Other orders of 'friars' were still more restricted in their geographical range and in some cases short-lived. The overlap between regular canons and 'friars' is illustrated by the designation 'Crutched Friars' ('crutched' means 'bearing a cross') which has been applied to a number of different groups, mostly of regular canons, which have flourished in different areas of Christendom.

The friars collectively had a further contribution to make to the diversification of religious orders. There were Dominican and Franciscan 'second orders', that is, nuns, almost from the beginning. The Franciscan nuns were, and some still are, known as 'Poor Clares', taking their name from Francis' friend and disciple Clare of Assisi (died 1253). These women were not, however, permitted to embrace the active life of mendicancy and preaching, but were committed to a strict regime of penitence and contemplation. Other mendicant orders developed female branches either later (the Carmelites in the fifteenth century) or not at all.

In addition to these 'second orders' there were 'third orders', of 'brothers and sisters of penance', who came also to be known as 'tertiaries'. These were lay enthusiasts who wished to give expression to the need for penance

RELIGIOUS ORDERS

There are so many religious orders that a whole dictionary has recently been published (Peter Day, *Dictionary of Religious Orders*, London and New York: Continuum 2001) listing over 1450 of them. Many were founded from the eighteenth century on; a few stand out for their antiquity and pre-eminence, and they are listed here. Names of members of religious orders are customarily followed by initials denoting the order.

Augustinians (also called Austin)

A number of religious communities of men and women Augustine have constitutions based on the Rule of Augustine of Hippo (354–430). The two main ones are:

Augustinian Canons (Austin Canons or Black Canons):  communities of clergy in the middle of the eleventh century who gave up their possessions to live a monastic life. The number of these communities steadily grew until the Reformation. Notable among them were the *Victorines*, founded in 1113 by William of Champeaux, Abelard's  teacher, whose number included the famous scholars Adam, Hugh and Richard of St Victor, and the Premonstratensians (White Canons), founded by Norbert at Prémontré, near Laon, in 1120.

 *Augustinian Hermits (Austin Friars: The Order of the Hermit Friars of St Augustine, OSA)*. One of the great mendicant (begging) orders of the Middle Ages along with the Franciscans and the Dominicans. The members were originally hermits living in Italy who were made into an order by Pope Innocent IV in 1244 and subsequently called to work in the cities. They were also involved in Martin Luther university and church affairs: Martin Luther is their most famous member. The order still exists and does educational, missionary and pastoral work.

Benedictines

The Order of St Benedict (OSB)

Monks who follow the Rule of Benedict (c. 480–547), which prescribes a routine of prayer, manual work and study. Between around 800 and 1100 Benedictine monasteries, which were self-governing, became large and rich, so that p. 792  they were in need of reform. Cluny, in Burgundy, led the way in this and more than a thousand monasteries were formed under its influence, following its customs. However, from the twelfth century onwards decline set in, and during and after the Reformation Benedictine monasteries almost disappeared. There was a revival in the nineteenth century  which saw the foundation, among others, of the abbey of Solesmes in France and Beuron in Germany, both of which played an important part in liturgical reform. In 1893 Pope Leo XIII created a confederation of Benedictine monasteries, headed by an abbot primate. Benedictine communities of women nuns existed from a very early stage, and there are also Benedictine sisters who work as missionaries, in caring for the sick, and in education.

Carmelites

Order of Brothers of the Blessed Virgin Mary of Mount Carmel (OCarm)

Order of Discalced Brothers of the Blessed Virgin Mary of Mount Carmel (OCD)

(White Friars)

Founded in the twelfth century when some former pilgrims and crusaders began to live as hermits on Mount Carmel in Palestine, near what was claimed to be Elijah's fountain. A rule of life was written for them by Albert, Latin patriarch of Jerusalem, and approved in 1226 by Pope Honorius III. When the failures of the crusaders made life in Palestine difficult they moved out to Cyprus, to Sicily, to France and to England and adapted their rule: now they became a mendicant order. From 1452 women also joined the order. The most famous of these women was Teresa of Avila (1515–82). She founded a small convent with a stricter rule of life. Because the sisters wore sandals instead of shoes and stockings, they came to be called 'discalced', barefooted Carmelites. Through John of the Cross, she extended the reform to the male order; the Discalced Carmelites later became a separate order. The original order works primarily in preaching and teaching, the discalced order in parishes and foreign missions. They have a special devotion to Mary. Thérèse of Lisieux and Edith Stein were both Carmelites.

Carthusians

Order of Carthusians (OCart)

Founded in 1084 by Bruno of Cologne in the Chartreuse valley, near Grenoble in France. It is a contemplative order, vowed to silence, and members live the lives of hermits in their own cells, meeting only for the daily office, the eucharist, and meals on feast days. They wear hair shirts, abstain from meat and on Fridays have only bread and water. There are also Carthusian nunneries. This is the strictest of all the orders, but had spread through Europe by the sixteenth century. The famous Bishop Hugh of Lincoln (c. 1140–1200) was a Carthusian.

Cistercians

Sacred Order of Cîteaux (SO Cist) (White Monks)

Founded in 1098 by Robert of Molesme at Cîteaux in Burgundy, after which it is named. The order was a stricter form of the Benedictine order and manual labour was an important part of it. Cistercian houses all followed the same rules, and there were annual meetings of all the abbots and visitations by the founding abbot to ensure this. Bernard of Clairvaux (1090–1153) was the force behind a tremendous increase in the number of monasteries; by his death there were almost 350 and this number doubled by the end of the thirteenth century. From the end of the twelfth century there were also communities of nuns. However, this success and the wealth that it brought led to relaxation of the rule and decline set in. The Cistercian houses in Europe largely disappeared at the Reformation.

A new development began at the monastery of La Trappe, near Soligny, in 1664 when the abbot, Armand-Jean le Bouthillier de Rancé, introduced a new and strict rule of silence, prayer, manual labour and seclusion. Those who followed the rule were given his name, and called *Trappists,* formally the Order of the Reformed Cistercians of the Strict Observance (OCSO). Cîteaux was destroyed during the French Revolution, and La Trappe was the only French monastery to survive. Thomas Merton (1915–68) is the best-known modern Trappist, and exemplifies the Cistercian interest in literary work.

Dominicans

Order of Preachers (OP) (Black Friars)

Founded by Dominic (1170–1221) in 1215. The order was formed as a group of preachers to convert the Albigensians, and was approved by Pope Innocent III. It was a major innovation, in that previously preaching and teaching had been the task of bishops and those delegated by them. To further this aim, brothers went to the great schools of the time, in Paris, Oxford, Bologna and Cologne; from their number arose the great figures of Albertus Magnus (1193–1280) and Thomas Aquinas (1225–74). As well as preaching against heretics, Dominicans engaged in missionary work in Europe and further afield; they were also entrusted with implementing the Inquisition. In France they were known as Jacobins.

Even before founding the order, in 1206 Dominic founded a nunnery at Prouille, in southern France, and women too have played an important role. The Maryknoll Sisters are just one of a number of congregations in modern times engaged in mission, teaching and nursing. The best-known Dominican theologian of today is Edward Schillebeeckx of Nijmegen, the Netherlands.

Franciscans

Order of Friars Minor (OFM) (Grey Friars)

Founded by Francis of Assisi in the early thirteenth century. The Franciscans are the largest order in the Roman Catholic Church. They are in fact made up of three orders:

First Order: Friars Minor (OFM), Friars Minor Conventual (OFM Conv) and Friars Minor Capuchin (OFMCap). These three groups arose out of controversies over the nature of Franciscan life in the fifteenth and sixteenth centuries: the Conventuals propagated a more moderate rule than that upheld by the Friars Minor, suitable for those engaged in study and preaching. The Capuchins, named after the hood (*capuche*) that they wore, were the strictest in matters of prayer and austerity. All three orders are made up of priests and laymen who have taken vows to lead a life of preaching and prayer.

Second Order: Order of St Clare (OSC) known as Poor Clares. This consists of nuns living in nunneries.

Third Order: Secular and Regular. The Third Order Secular is made up of men and women living in the world without having made vows; the Third Order Regular is made up of men and women in religious communities. Both seek to follow the spirit of St Francis in teaching and caring.

The Franciscans introduced the Christmas crib, the Angelus and the Stations of the Cross into the Roman Catholic Church. There has also been a community of Anglican Franciscans near Cerne Abbas, in Dorset, since the 1920s.

Jesuits

Society of Jesus (SJ)

Founded by Ignatius Loyola (1491–1556) in 1534 and approved by Pope Paul III in 1540. The order was innovative in many ways: it has no female branch, has a firm centralized authority demanding strict obedience, and requires its members to serve a long period of probation. Its members vow to travel to any part of the world to which the Pope commands them to go and in fact an early member, Francis Xavier (1506–52), was a famous missionary to India and Japan. Jesuits are also particularly active in education and founded three important institutions in Rome: the Gregorian, the German College and the English College. In addition they work among the poor and outcast of society, and do important welfare work. Because of their loyalty to the Pope they have not been uncontroversial, and for 40 years during the Enlightenment, from 1773–1814, the order was abolished in some European countries, though it continued in Germany, Austria, England and North America. The Jesuits were attacked for lax doctrine by the Jansenists, and their assimilation to local custom in the Chinese Rites controversy was also held against them. There are now 20,000 Jesuits working in 112 countries on six continents in their traditional roles.

p. 1016

and to lead a religious life without totally abandoning the world. Francis himself is said to have composed a rule for the guidance of such people, but it has not survived in its original form. The earliest known version shows that there was some degree of organization. Each community had officers including a bursar, there were to be regular chapter meetings, and there was provision for spiritual guidance, for external visitation, and for arbitration by the bishop in cases of dispute. It seems that these groups were not at first decisively affiliated to any particular order, but sometimes the simple fact of neighbourhood disposed them to turn to the Franciscans or Dominicans, as the case might be, for guidance, and by the end of the thirteenth century the two orders each had their 'own' tertiaries, specifically assigned to the guidance of the friars of the first order.

In its origins the 'third order' must be seen in the context of the proliferation of confraternities of all kinds, secular and religious, which characterized the period. Similar groups had developed already before 1200; the men and women in north Italian cities who were known as 'Umiliati' predated the friars. The friars in their turn encouraged all kinds of spiritual activity, from active opposition to heresy to ritual flagellation, hymn-singing and works of charity such as the distribution of food to the poor, visiting the sick and imprisoned, and providing burial for paupers. It is important to remember that despite the contemporary enthusiasm for organization and regulation, and the church's increasingly keen desire to bring the spiritual life of the laity under closer supervision, many forms of religious life remained fluid. Some of the religious women known as Beguines, who were numerous in the towns of northern France, the Low Countries and Germany, were closely associated with the Dominicans, Cistercians or other orders, but others seemed to contemporaries to be exempt from any control at all.

p. 794

Pope Innocent III (1198–1216), an early supporter of both Francis and Dominic, was also a great admirer of the Cistercians. In 1215, the Fourth Lateran Council, under his presidency, passed a measure (canon 12) which imposed some degree of collective organization on the hitherto unorganized 'Black Monks'. It was decreed that every three years, in each province of the Roman church, there should be a general chapter 'of abbots and of priors having no abbots [this covered both Cluniacs and regular canons] who have not been accustomed to celebrate such chapters'. Significantly, the first such meeting was to be attended by two neighbouring Cistercian abbots, who were clearly identified as experts on 'good practice'. They were to advise on the basis of their long-standing experience of such meetings, and they were empowered to co-opt from those present two persons with whom they would then preside over the assembly.

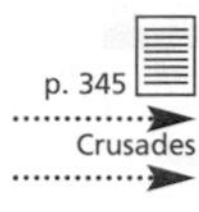

p. 345
Crusades

The ecclesiastical province provided a convenient pre-existing framework within which these meetings could be organized, even though many monasteries were exempt from ordinary episcopal supervision. There was no provision for meetings at any level above that of the province; an organizational principle would have had to be invented for that purpose, and the decree therefore did not and could not transform the 'Benedictines' into an international order of the kind the Dominicans were to be. One important function of the chapters thus instituted was the appointment of visitors who would then carry out a triennial visitation of the monasteries of the province. In addition, the decree enjoined bishops to see to the reform of those monasteries that were under their jurisdiction, so that they would be presentable when the visitors came around. Non-exempt houses might therefore now expect visitation from time to time by the diocesan bishop, by the metropolitan when he was carrying out a visitation of his province, and by the monastic visitors appointed by the provincial chapter. The hope was that the traditional spiritual values of monastic life could be renewed and maintained by the concerted efforts of chapters, visitors and bishops.

Reformation

Anglicanism

Already with the military religious orders and some of the regular canons it can be seen how the ancient monastic requirement of physical stability within the precinct was breaking down in face of new demands. Mobility at the command of religious superiors was essential for the Templar knight, and it was essential for the friar, who might be required not only to go about preaching but also to live far from his homeland as a university master or to conduct investigations into heresy as an inquisitor. This mobility and amenability to command reached a still further point of development in the sixteenth century with the Society of Jesus, founded by Ignatius Loyola in 1534. The Jesuits, as missionaries and guardians of theological orthodoxy, in many respects resembled and rivalled the Dominicans. In addition to the three normal monastic vows the Jesuit vowed to put himself totally at the disposal of the Pope, to do his bidding and go where he commanded at a moment's notice. Without taking so specific a vow, the orders of friars had not infrequently been used for the Pope's purposes: manning the Inquisition, preaching a crusade, undertaking missions of all kinds. The Dominican friar on the road was enjoined by the early constitutions of the order to recite the office as best he could and to be content to join in the office as it was said in any church he came across. The Jesuit was permitted to omit the office altogether if some more pressing necessity overcame him.

The consciousness of direct obedience to the directives of Rome may be regarded as one of the hallmarks of many of the religious orders as they have developed since the sixteenth century, and especially in most recent times, but generalization is hazardous. The history of the religious life has been at least as complicated in the last four centuries as it was in the preceding twelve, if only because of the violent upheavals which have afflicted the Roman Catholic world, often resulting in prolonged breaks of continuity in the lives of many orders if not their outright disappearance. Even before the Protestant Reformation, several of the religious orders were thrown into upheaval by internal pressures and the recurrent belief that the standards of their spiritual life and discipline left something to be desired. The French Revolution and the waves of secularizing activity on the part of governments that followed it destroyed or came close to destroying many orders that had already changed very considerably since the medieval period. In a kind of reflex movement, however, a Catholic or catholicizing reaction in many parts of Europe, including Britain, has led in the past century and a half to the re-establishment or revival of the religious life, to the extent that not only are there houses of the Roman Catholic religious orders all over the world, but there are Franciscans and other orders to be found within the Anglican Communion.

Only a few examples can be given here of the sometimes very complicated post-medieval histories of the orders. Some, among them the Dominicans and the Carthusians, have suffered relatively little internal upheaval. By contrast, the Franciscans, troubled almost from the beginning by internal differences on the observance of the rule and of Francis' intentions for the order, have an exceptionally long history of division and reformation. A movement for stricter observance gained momentum in the later fourteenth century, originally in Italy, drawing some of its inspiration from the radical 'Spiritual Franciscans' who had been persecuted and outlawed earlier in the century. By 1517 the Observants were constituted into a separate Franciscan order, distinct from the 'Conventuals' who followed a modified way of life. Even then the aspiration to recreate the austerity and fervour of the original Franciscan regime was not satisfied, and within a few years another offshoot, which has survived to the present day as the Capuchins, had acquired its own rule. The Observants underwent further divisions later, until in 1897 Pope Leo XIII reconstituted them as a single Order of Friars Minor. The Franciscan second order, the Poor Clares, became similarly divided in the fifteenth century between the mostly French 'Colettines', reformed by Colette according to strict and austere principles, and the so-called 'Urbanists', who continued to live according to a mitigated version of the rule approved by Pope Urban IV in 1263.

The Cistercians experienced a movement for stricter observance somewhat later, in the seventeenth century, when the order's central control mechanisms disintegrated and it resolved itself into a number of national congregations. The Strict Observance took root especially among the French Cistercians, and the monastery of La Trappe (in fact founded from Savigny in the twelfth century) has given the whole movement its popular name, 'Trappist'. Along with the rest of French monasticism it suffered shipwreck in the Revolution, but the monks preserved their community in exile and returned in 1817. Cîteaux in turn was restored in 1898 and took its place at the head of the Strict Observance. Meanwhile the Cistercians of the 'Common Observance', who had not embraced the reforms, found refuge in the Austro-Hungarian empire and survived by moving out into the world, undertaking pastoral and educational tasks. In more recent times they have expanded in Europe, the United States and elsewhere. There are now two distinct Cistercian orders; both, significantly, have an abbot-general who is resident in Rome.

Although the Protestant Reformation led to the outright destruction of monasteries and friaries in many parts of Europe, its effects were by no means entirely negative, for religious orders were the chosen vehicle for many initiatives of revival and reform within Roman Catholicism. The Jesuits have already been mentioned. They have had as turbulent a later history as any of the older orders. Apart from getting involved in theological controversies within the church, they aroused the suspicions of many secular governments as agents of Roman influence; they were expelled from France in 1764 and in 1773 the Pope was prevailed upon to suppress the Society altogether; however, it was reconstituted in 1814. The Jesuits have been distinguished for intellectual activity; the Brussels-based Société des Bollandistes, which was founded by Jesuits in the seventeenth century, specializes in publishing the lives of the saints of all periods.

Many other orders originated in the sixteenth century, some of them remaining restricted in geographical scope, some eventually achieving a worldwide extension. The Ursulines, for example, were founded in 1535 by Angela Merici, and have gone through a number of stages of evolution, surviving the French Revolution to become, now, a widely-distributed female teaching order. The Oratorians were a product of the Counter-Reformation. Both the Oratory of St Philip Neri, founded in Rome in the 1560s, and the French Oratory, founded in Paris in 1611, originated as a means of promoting the spiritual life of the priesthood, but they went on to develop different specialisms. The former gave its name to the oratorio, thanks to its enthusiasm for the devotional use of music, while the latter has been distinguished for its educational work and promotion of popular devotion in France. Both have produced notable scholars. Having both revived after the revolutionary epoch, they differ in that the French Oratory has a central organization and a superior general, while St Philip's Oratory (introduced into England by Cardinal Newman) does not require vows of its members, who are priests living in community.

Since the nineteenth-century Catholic revival, more religious orders have been founded than in all the preceding centuries, many of them small and localized. Organization, purposes and composition have been very varied. Many modern orders consist of priests and lay brothers rather than of monks and friars. Teaching orders have been prominent among them, for example the Salesians (or Society of St Francis de Sales), founded in 1859 and taking its name and inspiration from a leading Counter-Reformation saint (1567–1622). The Society of Missionaries of Africa, popularly known as the White Fathers, founded in 1868, have been devoted to the task their proper name suggests. Opus Dei, founded in Madrid in 1928 by Josemaria Escrivá de Balaguer, originated as a kind of updated 'third order' for Roman Catholic laymen, intended to promote the application of Christian principles in daily life. Provision has been made more recently for women, and priests too are now admitted. Opus Dei has been both influential and controversial.

The medieval period bequeathed to post-Reformation Western Christianity numerous types of religious organization. In modern times this diversity has grown, and the sense that life in community lends strength to men and women who seek to fulfil a variety of purposes has commended itself even to non-Roman Catholic Christians. In one respect the modern religious life differs significantly from its medieval counterpart. In the medieval period it is certain that male religious outnumbered females; in the modern world the reverse is true.

DIANA WEBB

Peter D. Bay, *A Dictionary of Religious Orders*, London and New York: Continuum 2001; Richard DeMolen (ed), *Religious Orders of the Catholic Reformation*, New York: Fordham University Press 1994; Alan Forey, *The Military Orders from the Twelfth to the Early Fourteenth Centuries*, London: Macmillan 1992; David Knowles, *The Religious Orders in England* (3 vols), Cambridge: CUP 1948–59; C. H. Lawrence, *The Friars: The Impact of the Early Mendicant Movement on Western Society*, London: Longman 1994

Renaissance

Humanism
Painting
Architecture
Culture

People use the capitalized word 'Renaissance' to refer to one of two things. It may denote the period of time in European history that extends roughly from the mid-fourteenth century until the end of the sixteenth century. Or it may denote, within that period, a certain set of cultural developments that began to appear first in Italy in the fourteenth century, and then north of the Alps in the century following. The second sense is the one that concerns us. Those developments, at first sight anyway, do not have to do with theology or religion so much as with other aspects of the culture, especially literature, the visual arts and politics. But since the culture was a deeply Christian one, these can be seen as developments within, and with major long-term implications for, Christianity. The Renaissance marked a shift in sensibility that permanently changed the way Western Christians experienced the faith.

Although, as the enormous scholarship on the subject has shown, the Renaissance was a complex phenomenon that resists any precise definition, still we would not go far wrong to say that it marked a reconceptualizing of the relations of human beings to the world around them. We see the first inklings of that reconceptualizing in the fourteenth and early fifteenth centuries in Florence and the other Italian city states, where a new kind of urban life was taking shape, commercially active and politically self-determining. It was in that milieu that the 'humanist' poet and scholar Francesco Petrarch (1304–74) began looking to ancient Roman models, especially the orator and philosopher Cicero, to create a literary style that put a strong new focus on the experience and selfhood of the writer. In the process he became the first celebrated 'humanist' – a term that, in the Renaissance context, refers to both a profession of literary scholarship and an approach to literature and life that valued rhetoric, the dignity of human beings and the particularity of human experiences, as well as the heritage of classical antiquity.

At roughly the same time the artist Giotto di Bondone (*c.*1226–*c.*1337) and a few others were pioneering three-dimensionality in painting, creating the powerful illusion – brought to a high degree of perfection by such successors as Leonardo da Vinci (1452–1519) – of a distinct and self-sufficient space within the picture itself. Such an approach to painting was able to represent figures in their own particular time and space, clearly separated and in a sense freed from the time and space of the viewer. Architects such as Filippo Brunelleschi and Leon Battista Alberti (1404–72), influenced by the ancient Roman theorist Vitruvius, designed buildings that conformed to the proportions of the human body and thus took as their point of reference humanity itself rather than (as in late-medieval Gothic architecture) the transcendent order of the cosmos. And historians like Leonardo Bruni (1369–1444), who wrote in the context of the conflict of republican Florence with autocratic Milan, argued for the central human importance of active political engagement, in contrast to the more transcendental values of medieval Christian culture.

The influence of ancient classical, particularly Roman, culture upon those fourteenth- and fifteenth-century writers and artists was not itself unique, but it was nonetheless a crucial element in the shift of sensibility that the Renaissance entailed. The term 'Renaissance' of course refers to a 'rebirth' of the culture of antiquity, and although the word did not enter the standard vocabulary of historians as a comprehensive term for these developments until many centuries later (roughly 1850), contemporaries themselves did often speak of their own relation to antiquity in terms of rebirth or revival. However, it is important for us to remember that European culture had never really lost touch with the cultural inheritance of classical antiquity. In fact in the Carolingian era of the eighth and ninth centuries, and again amid the cultural ferment of twelfth century, interest in ancient arts and letters had been of an intensity comparable to that of the Renaissance, so that one can speak of those periods, too, as times of rebirth or revival of the antique. What was new in the Renaissance interest in antiquity was therefore not the subject-matter but rather the mode in which that subject-matter was approached.

The Carolingians had made use of ancient texts or images in the form in which they found them, as when, for example, the sculptor of an ivory inserted at the bottom of a crucifixion scene the classical figure of Atlas shaking the earth. Twelfth-century writers and artists tended instead to assimilate ancient texts and images to Christian content and purposes, as when writers of that time invented Christian allegorical meanings for the poetry of Ovid, or artists modelled their figures of Christ on ancient images of Orpheus. In contrast to both of those earlier approaches, the writers and artists of the Renaissance kept antiquity at a certain distance, in spite of, or perhaps rather as a symptom of, their very devotion to it. For viewed with the newly-discovered tool of perspective, antiquity appeared to them as a coherent cultural system within which all things belonged together. It was no longer something that one appropriated or assimilated, but rather something that one observed and emulated in its own discreteness, maintaining awareness of the coherence of one's own culture as well, i.e., of the particularity of the 'place' from which one was observing.

What then did this shift in sensibility have to do with religion, with Christianity?

It has often been assumed that the shift signalled, in effect anyway, a move away from religion. This was in essence the view of the great nineteenth-century historian Jakob Burckhardt (1818–97) in his *Civilization of the Renaissance in Italy* (1860), a work that brought into being the modern field of Renaissance history. Burckhardt placed particular emphasis on the spirit of individualism encouraged by the ambitious Italian city states of the Renaissance, and consequently on the ideal of the cosmopolitan 'many-sided man', who displayed a wide learning and a varied expertise and had an insatiable desire for fame. In Burckhardt's view such encouragement of egotism paved the way for the rampant scandals of the period, of which the crimes of the Borgia family are a famous but hardly unique example. Furthermore, the ecclesiastical hierarchy behaved in a such a way as to undermine public confidence in itself, and one can say the same of the major religious movement in the cities, the mendicant friars (Dominicans and Franciscans), in spite of the allure of a few popular preachers like the Dominican Girolamo Savonarola (1452–98).

So too, in Burckhart's view, the Renaissance interest in the culture of ancient Rome, which was after all a pagan culture, constituted an obvious encouragement to a decline of Christian faith at the time of the Renaissance: not only did ancient texts provide support for pseudo-religious superstitions and belief in astrology that undermined orthodox practice, but also the reading of such Roman authors as the Epicurean Lucretius encouraged a general scepticism in matters of belief. All of this suggests a picture of the Renaissance as at heart a movement that was indifferent or even hostile to Christian belief and that stands, in any event, as a milestone in a long-term erosion of religious authority that was to become famously evident in the Enlightenment of the eighteenth century. The Renaissance was in this sense a harbinger of secular modernity.

Enlightenment

Although Burckhardt's views have been highly influential and many people still habitually think of the Renaissance as essentially secular or even downright anti-religious, research in recent decades has begun to suggest a different picture. Burckhardt himself would not have denied, of course, that the culture of Europe in the period from the fourteenth to the sixteenth centuries was still a fundamentally Christian culture, nor that the great writers, artists and statesmen of the Renaissance at least nominally professed the Christian faith. But what has now become clearer is that as a movement within a Christian culture, the Renaissance itself defines an important episode in the history of Christianity. It does so in two ways. First, the shift in sensibility that we have noted can itself be understood in part – and was understood at the time – as a response to a crisis in the Christian faith. Secondly, in its very response to that crisis the Renaissance displays such a profound connection to the explicitly religious movement that we know as the Reformation, with which it overlaps in time, that Renaissance and Reformation indeed can be seen as representing two aspects of a single phenomenon.

Reformation

In what sense was the Renaissance a response to a crisis in Christian faith? Let us return for a moment to the early years of the movement, and the seminal humanist figure Petrarch. The first-time reader with a general awareness of the Renaissance as a secular phenomenon may be surprised to discover how devout a Christian Petrarch was, and moreover how central a role his Christian devotion played even in his interpretation of pagan writers. In his late treatise *On His Own Ignorance and That of Many* (1370), for example, Petrarch displays his erudite knowledge of classical Latin literature and explains his affection for the writings of Cicero specifically in the context of lamenting the influence that the thought of Aristotle had exerted on Christians through the medium of scholastic theology. Petrarch's self-consciously Christian objections to Aristotle are both substantive and practical: that the ancient philosopher's view of the world as eternal subverted the Christian doctrine of creation, and that his thought in general did not lead to virtue. In Cicero, by contrast, Petrarch claims to find not only an explicit belief in creation (as inspired by Plato, in whom Petrarch, self-consciously following the lead of Augustine, found profound support for Christian belief) and a sound doctrine of divine providence, but also an ability to move the reader to virtue, without which, he believes, any wisdom would be useless. Petrarch does not ignore Cicero's belief in the pagan gods; in fact he goes out of his way to deplore it. His care to do so is much to

Scholasticism
Religious orders

Creation

the point of his spirituality: his desire is for a viable and accessible Christian piety, and it is only with that desire in mind that he makes his use of the beloved Cicero. That is to say, Petrarch did not 'baptize' Cicero, i.e., assimilate him to Christian culture as in the approach to the classics that had been in fashion two centuries earlier, but rather observed him in all his particularity, and imitated only what, in his view, merited imitation.

This use of the resources of classical antiquity for the purposes of a viable and accessible Christian piety, in marked and often self-conscious contrast to the tendencies of scholastic theology, is not limited to Petrarch; we find it everywhere in Renaissance thought. Petrarch's admirer, the Florentine poet Giovanni Boccaccio (1313–75), for instance, in his treatise *Genealogies of the Gentile Gods*, attempted a thoroughgoing investigation of the Christian truths discernible within the ancient Graeco-Roman myths, and Leonardo Bruni's philosophical *Dialogues* further cultivated Plato and Cicero for Christian ends along the lines set out by Petrarch. Lorenzo Valla (*c.* 1407–57), famous for taking the philological tools that the humanists had been developing in their study of pagan texts and applying these to the study the New Testament, combined these philological interests with strong critiques of scholastic Aristotelianism. He began to envisage a scripture-based piety that rejected high-flown speculation and was reasonably within the reach of normal human beings. Marsilio Ficino (1433–99), in his *Theologia platonica* (1482), developed a full-scale Christian theology heavily dependent upon the thought of Plato and the ancient neo-Platonist Plotinus as sanctioned by the authority of Augustine, and specifically as a superior alternative to what Ficino regarded as the spiritually ineffectual speculations of the Aristotelians. When, moreover, these Italian writers are examined in relation to each other, it becomes apparent that the Renaissance made a substantial contribution to the Christian theological tradition, especially in its understanding of the nature and potential of human beings. And there were other important figures from countries north of the Alps, who, significantly influenced by the Italians, developed ideas along similar lines in their own settings – among them, for instance, the French biblical exegete Jacques Lefèvre d'Étaples (*c.* 1455–1536), the English cleric and educational reformer John Colet (*c.* 1466–1519), and, above all, the peripatetic scholar and man of letters Desiderius Erasmus (*c.* 1469–1536).

What, then, of the relation of the Renaissance to the famous Reformation of the sixteenth century? The influence of Renaissance humanism on the Reformation is very well known. Here the brilliant Erasmus played a pivotal role. Erasmus never embraced the Protestant cause, and in 1523 came out decisively against Martin Luther's denial of free will, his interpretation of scripture and above all his separation from the Church of Rome. But there was truth in the popular view that Erasmus had 'laid the egg that Luther hatched'. Not only had Erasmus, in his advocacy of a simple and sincere Christian piety based upon the New Testament, unsparingly criticized the follies and abuses of the church and popular religion; he also, picking up where Valla had left off, had applied the tools of humanist scholarship to the New Testament to make it directly accessible in its original language, publishing the first critical edition of the Greek text, entitled *Novum Instrumentum*. This edition appeared in 1516, on the very eve of Luther's emergence to fame, and the Protestants embraced it wholeheartedly for the directness of its witness to the authority that they placed decisively above that of the church. The Protestant motto 'by scripture alone' (*sola scriptura*) was closely related in spirit to the humanist motto 'back to the sources' (*ad fontes*); the Reformation, like Renaissance humanism, aimed for a direct encounter with the ancient texts, in this case those of the Bible, so as to 'hear' them in their own integrity apart from any intervening authorities. And this is clearly a matter not simply of similarity but of influence, that is, an influence of Renaissance on Reformation. It is not incidental that several of the leading early Protestant leaders – including, not Luther himself, but his Wittenberg associate Philipp Melanchthon (1497–1560) and the Swiss reformers Huldrych Zwingli (1484–1531) and above all John Calvin (1509–64) – were lifelong humanists in the Renaissance sense, both in training and in conviction.

Martin Luther

If there was, therefore, an obvious influence of the Renaissance upon the Reformation, we can go even further in seeking the connections between the two. For if, as we have seen, the Renaissance itself contained or even constituted a response to a religious or theological need – the need for a form of Christian piety that was meaningful, admirable and attainable in the real world, in contrast to the teachings of the theologians of the schools – then it may be that the two movements were related not only by the influence of one upon the other but, more profoundly, by the fact that they represented responses to the same fundamental problem or crisis in the Christian faith. For the religious need that motivated the humanists is also to be seen in Luther's famous question, 'How can I find a gracious God?' Luther, it is true, was trained not as a humanist but as a scholastic theologian; yet the fact that he came to his own solution of the problem of an accessible faith in the very context and language of the theological traditions that had made that problem so pressing suggests that the nature of the problem was fundamentally no different from what the humanists saw it to be. It is also true that the Renaissance in Italy did not lead to that separation from the Roman Catholic Church that was such an essential component of the Reformation, and that the theological insights of the humanists in general stopped short of Luther's radical vision of the Christian as utterly reliant on grace in such a way as to be *simul justus et peccator* ('saved and a sinner at the same time'). Whether or not we ourselves find Luther's answer to the question of how to find a viable faith (in so far as we too experience that question as problematic, in terms suited to our own day) a satisfactory one, it is well to remember that it did not suit everyone in the sixteenth century. The validity of the question itself, though, seems to have been very widely recognized.

JOHN W. COAKLEY

Jakob Burckhardt, *The Civilization of the Renaissance in Italy*, revised and edited by Irene Gordon, New York: Harper & Row 1960; Wallace K. Ferguson, *The Renaissance in Historical Thought. Five Centuries of Interpretation*, Boston: Houghton Mifflin 1948; Anthony Levi, *Renaissance and Reformation: The Intellectual Genesis*, New Haven: Yale University Press 2002; Charles Trinkaus, *In Our Image and Likeness: Humanity and Divinity in Italian Humanist Thought*, Chicago: University of Chicago Press 1970

Resurrection

That God raised the crucified Jesus of Nazareth from death to new life is the central belief of Christianity, celebrated at its major festival, Easter. Paul, whose writings are the earliest testimony to the resurrection of Jesus, remarked: 'If Christ has not been raised, then our preaching is in vain and your faith is in vain' (1 Corinthians 15.14). Virtually every book of the New Testament reflects this faith in the resurrection of Jesus, which is believed also to shape the lives of believers, linking it to ethical questions, life in the Spirit and hope for the future. The resurrection is seen as a present reality. 'If then you have been raised with Christ ... set your minds on things that are above ... put to death what is earthly in you' (Colossians 3.1–5).

The resurrection of Jesus: the evidence

The evidence for the events described as the resurrection of Jesus is to be found in Paul's first letter to the Corinthians and in the Gospels. It is claimed that the tomb in which Jesus had been laid was empty and that Jesus appeared to a variety of men and women after his death.

Paul in fact makes no specific mention of an empty tomb but he mentions a series of appearances: to Cephas (i.e. Peter); to the Twelve; to 500 brethren all at once, some of whom have since died (Paul is probably writing about twenty years after the crucifixion of Jesus); to James; to all the apostles and finally to himself (1 Corinthians 15.5–8). The Acts of the Apostles (chs 9, 22, 26) three times reports an appearance of the risen Jesus to Paul on the road to Damascus, as a result of which he is blinded, healed and converted, twice putting the account on the lips of Paul, but in his letters Paul himself gives no details of the circumstances of the appearance to him.

p. 668

All the Gospels agree in reporting that the tomb in which Jesus was laid was empty, but differ slightly over precisely who first found the empty tomb. Mary Magdalene is always mentioned, but in one Gospel (John) she is alone; in Matthew, Mark and Luke the number of her companions varies. The Gospel of Mark as we have it mentions no resurrection appearances: after discovering the empty tomb the women say nothing to anyone because they are afraid, and there the Gospel breaks off (the verses after 16.8 found in some Bibles are a late addition thought not to be original). Matthew mentions briefly an appearance in Jerusalem and then a concluding one in Galilee. Luke mentions appearances only in Jerusalem, culminating in an ascension of Jesus to heaven (narrated twice, once at the end of the Gospel and once at the beginning of the Acts of the Apostles, in slightly different forms). John has appearances in both Jerusalem and in Galilee. In Luke the risen Jesus spends 40 days with his disciples before leaving them and sending down the Holy Spirit; in Matthew and John the period seems to be shorter; and in John Jesus himself breathes the Spirit on the disciples.

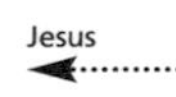
Jesus

No attempt is made in the New Testament to portray the resurrection itself; it happens, as it were, 'off-stage'. The earliest description of the event comes in the apocryphal Gospel of Peter, which depicts three men emerging from the sepulchre, two leading the third, whose head is towering above the heavens, with a cross following them.

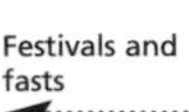
Festivals and fasts

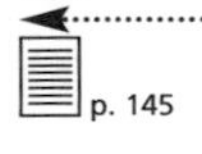
p. 145

Attempts have been made to reconcile all the variant details in the resurrection tradition and to argue that it forms a consistent and persuasive whole, most notably by the lawyer 'Frank Morison' (a pseudonym for Albert Henry Ross) in his immensely popular *Who Moved the Stone?* (1930). However, this is to overlook the fact that the Gospel accounts are all testimonies of faith and in each case are deeply stamped by the theology of the evangelist who wrote it. For example Matthew, whose Gospel contains the Sermon on the Mount, has Jesus appear finally on a mountain to which he has sent his disciples, and commands them to make disciples of all nations; Luke has the risen Jesus joining two disciples leaving Jerusalem disillusioned at what they have seen, and explains to them that all this was 'in accordance with the scriptures', subsequently opening their eyes so that they recognize him in the breaking of bread. What we have in fact is a complex interpretation in the light of a formative experience of events the precise nature of which it is no longer possible to ascertain.

Holy Spirit

p. 385

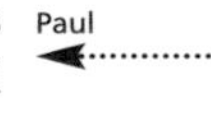
Paul

The character of the resurrection tradition also means that objections made from the beginning to the claim that Jesus had been raised by God likewise cannot be substantiated. Various critics have argued that the women at the tomb were hysterical and unreliable or must have gone to the wrong tomb; that the body of Jesus was stolen by the disciples; that Jesus did not really die but returned to life and was looked after by a secret society until he recovered; that the resurrection 'appearances' were subjective visions with no grounds in reality. However, there is no firmer basis for these objections than there is for a harmonization of the tradition into a single account.

The resurrection of Jesus: its significance

Kingdom of God

Jesus is said to have raised others from the dead during his lifetime, e.g. the son of the widow of Nain (Luke 7.11–17) and Lazarus (John 11), and he mentions raising the dead among his actions that are to be reported back to John the Baptist (Matthew 11.5; Luke 7.22). There are also accounts in several ancient authors of the dead being raised to life by miracle-workers, for example by the Pythagorean holy man Apollonius of Tyana. However, the resurrection of Jesus is more than this. From the start it is seen by the New Testament as a vindication of Jesus' person, life, actions and teachings. What is important is not that someone has been raised from the dead but that *Jesus* has been raised from the dead, with consequences not only for him but also for the whole future of the world.

Time and again throughout the New Testament the resurrection of Jesus is said to be 'according to the scriptures' and it is dated to 'the third day' after the crucifixion. However, it is very difficult to find actual passages in the Old Testament that refer to a resurrection or to three days. Ezekiel 37 presents the vision of a valley full of dead bones that are raised up and given new flesh, but this relates to the people of Israel being given new life after the devastation of the exile to Babylon. Hosea 6.2 has the passage 'on the third day he will raise us up, that we may live before him', but there is no evidence of this being applied to the resurrection of Jesus until the second century.

Life after death

p. 845

Origins and background

Martyr

In fact the notion of resurrection is a relatively late one in Judaism; at the time of Jesus neither the Sadducees nor the Dead Sea sect, the Essenes, seem to have believed in it. In the Old Testament the dead are thought either no longer to exist or to lead only a shadowy life in the underworld (Sheol). Resurrection is mentioned only in the late book of Daniel (12.2) and in the apocryphal books of Maccabees. Here it appears in the context of the Maccabean resistance to attempts to Hellenize Judaism and abolish its distinctive practices, one of the most traumatic events in Jewish history. It is felt intolerable that those who suffer martyrdom for their faith should simply perish and have no reward. They must be vindicated. Hence it came to be believed that God would raise up the dead. However, this belief in resurrection was by no means uniform: it took many forms, for example that the faithful would be raised to new life and those who had abandoned the faith to condemnation and death. In some traditions only righteous Israelites are raised; in others both the righteous and the unrighteous; in yet others all human beings. What they will be raised to and how they will be raised also varies: with or without a body, to earth, to a transformed earth or to paradise. But along with resurrection comes judgement: the ethical assessment in the eyes of God of the one who has died.

It is from this background that the resurrection of Jesus derives its meaning. It is the vindication of one whose life, brutally cut short, cries out for resurrection. Moreover, because during his lifetime Jesus proclaimed that his actions were instrumental in bringing in the kingdom of God, God's kingly rule, his resurrection was given an eschatological significance: in other words it marked a decisive turning point after which everything would be different. It ushered in a new world, in which Jesus would have a prominent place, indeed in which attitudes to him and his values would be the criteria for judgement.

The resurrection of Jesus and the resurrection of others

From the start the resurrection of Jesus was seen as bringing a new quality to the life of his followers. It was also believed that what had happened to him would happen to them: it was a foretaste, a pledge, of their final destiny.

To begin with, the interval between Jesus' resurrection and the realization of this final destiny was expected to be short. 1 Corinthians ends with an Aramaic prayer, *maranatha*, 'Come Lord!', and Paul clearly felt himself under pressure to complete his work before the second coming of Jesus. Paul plainly thinks that this will take place imminently and will bring resurrection. In 1 Thessalonians 4.16–17 and 1 Corinthians 15.51–2 he depicts a complex scenario in which at the sound of a trumpet first the dead will be raised, and then those who are still alive will be caught up with them in the clouds 'to meet the Lord' in the air: 'and so we shall always be with the Lord'.

However, as a second coming of the Lord failed to materialize, resurrection ceased to be closely linked with a turning point in history and lost its initial eschatological colouring.

Whereas the first Christians had hoped for bodily resurrection to a renewed and restored world which would come very soon, by the Middle Ages resurrection was a remote prospect in another space and time. And whereas the first Christians simply believed that between death and resurrection the dead slept in the dust, over the course of time ideas about their future came to be different:

Matthias Grünewald, The Resurrection of Christ, *Isenheim Altarpiece*, *c.* 1515

Christian hope was focused on heaven, to which the soul might go while the body was still buried in the ground. Moreover the judgement on people's deeds came to be thought of as taking place, not at the end of time, but at the point of death. And the rise of the doctrine of purgatory introduced the notion that change was possible even after death.

The resurrection of the body

Paul is insistent that at the resurrection the body is raised; however, this is not the perishable body, but a transformed, imperishable body (flesh and blood cannot inherit the kingdom of God). He uses the image of the grain of seed which when it is sown in the ground dies, but God gives it a new body, and compares the physical body and the spiritual body, the man of dust and the man of heaven. From the second century CE until the rise of the modern world the nature of the risen body was the subject of intense and detailed debate. This debate could not be other than speculative, but it proved the focal point for a whole series of questions which still preoccupy philosophers and theologians today. What constitutes the self? How can personal identity be maintained through change? What makes the individual unique?

Although as the discussion went on, immortality came to feature alongside resurrection, the soul alongside the body, and it began to look as if the immortal soul constituted the self, there was always an emphasis on the body as being integral to self. And the body was thought of in the most materialistic of terms. Resurrection of the body was resurrection of the flesh, human flesh that is subject to mutilation and decay.

Church fathers

The church father Tertullian, one of the first to write on resurrection in his *The Resurrection of the Flesh*, insisted that resurrection consisted of the reassembling of the parts of the dead person, and this view of resurrection continued for 1000 years, despite all the problems associated with it, which were regularly discussed. These parts were thought to constitute identity, and throughout discussions of the resurrection there is a fear of change, which threatens identity. However, Paul used images of change, and there were others who did not hesitate to follow him, notably the Alexandrian theologian Origen. The original text of Origen's treatise on the resurrection is lost, but it seems that he argued that just as the body changes in life, so it certainly changes after death: this change was real and good.

Continuity and change form the two poles in the complex discussion of the nature of the relationship of the risen body to the earthly body, and some theologians sought to hold the two together, sometimes in what now seem inconsistent arguments. Augustine of Hippo was a third figure who set the agenda for discussion by considering in detail how the earthly body would reappear in heaven. Will everyone be the same sex, the same height? Will they be able to eat? Will they see in heaven only when their eyes are open? What age will they be? Among his answers were that we would rise with gender, and our age would probably be around 30 (a mature age).

The ongoing discussion took place against changing social conditions and religious events and practices that shaped thought. Some theologians would be thinking about the bodies of martyrs, others of saintly women and ascetics, yet others of the practice of collecting relics and the dissection of bodies that went with that. But the discussion was always about the *body*, and the actual body which had lived on earth.

Body 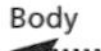

The modern period

At the beginning of the modern period, attention was focused on the resurrection of Jesus, and the old objections to it as deliberate deceit by the disciples or a misunderstanding of what had actually happened were revived and refined. The pioneering New Testament critic H. S. Reimarus denied a resurrection on the basis of his examination of the Gospels; for the Scottish philosopher David Hume it fell under his blanket rejection of the possibility of miracle. In this context, speculation on the nature of the risen life had no place; moreover, essential identity had come to be located in the mind, so the immortality of the soul rather than the resurrection of the body came to the fore.

Miracle

However, in the middle of the twentieth century an influential group of theologians stood the objections to belief in the resurrection on their head. The German Protestant theologian Rudolf Bultmann simply took it for granted that modern men and women could not accept miracles; moreover it was illegitimate to look to miracles to provide a basis for belief. Resurrection is the sheer unmerited and sovereign act of the God who can create out of nothing. In similar vein, Karl Barth argued that the resurrection is a historical event, but not the kind of event that historians could deal with, because the techniques that they use are incapable of grasping it. Historians work by analogy, and there is no analogy to the resurrection.

To later German theologians of this period, notably Wolfhart Pannenberg, this position was unsatisfactory: the resurrection had to be demonstrably a historical fact, and its meaning had to relate to history. So attempts were made to revive the early Christian belief in the resurrection as a foretaste of the end of history. However, both the Barth/Bultmann and Pannenberg discussions proved to be very much of their time and did not have lasting influence.

Faith

Belief in the resurrection today

Tradition

Community

Discussions of the resurrection today are likely to emphasize a dimension of the resurrection which was there from the start and which does not bring with it problems of miracle or speculations about a future state, namely the impact that the resurrection has on life in the present, for both individuals and communities. Resurrection is here and now, and eternal is a quality of life, not an indication of duration. Some of these theological interpretations are all too superficial and over-optimistic, and their easy assertions might be thought to fit badly with some of the characteristics of church life today.

Prophecy
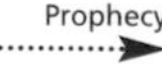

More convincing are those who insist on the ethical dimension of the resurrection and see it as the vindication of the victim, the event in which God identifies himself with the poor and the oppressed, who apparently have no hope. Here we have the equivalent of the early Christian theologians who located hope in the raising of putryfing, mutilated or tortured bodies to glory, despite all the difficulties in envisaging such a thing. The restoration of the outcast to love and community and joy may seem equally impossible, but it is the same hope, and the same answer to the problem of human nature and destiny.

Paul

JOHN BOWDEN

Rudolf Bultmann, *Jesus Christ and Mythology*, New York: Charles Scribner and London: SCM Press 1958; Caroline Walker Bynum, *The Resurrection of the Body in Western Christianity, 200–1336*, New York: Columbia University Press 1995; C. F. Evans, *Resurrection and the New Testament*, London: SCM Press 1970; Wolfhart Pannenberg, *Jesus – God and Man*, Philadelphia: Westminster Press and London: SCM Press 1977; Rowan Williams, *Resurrection* (1982), London: Darton, Longman & Todd 2002

Revelation

The claim that God has made 'himself' (the symbolism is mostly personal and masculine, but not to be taken literally) and his will known is as basic to Christian as to Jewish self-understanding and talk of God. The words best translated 'reveal' and 'revelation', and referring to divine self-disclosure, are relatively rare in the Old and New Testaments, and refer to specific acts vouchsafed to particular individuals (e.g. 2 Corinthians 12.1; Revelation 1.1), but the idea that God has taken the initiative and that all human knowledge of God is response to that revelation is everywhere assumed. The concept refers primarily to God who remains hidden even in his self-revelation, and only indirectly to anything said (always inadequately) about the mystery, or to the medium through which faith and a knowledge of God are communicated in the present. This present conviction is based on a past foundational event mediated by a tradition and actualized in a religious community. In faith, revelation is experienced as incomplete (e.g. 1 Corinthians 13.9); it therefore includes the dimension of hope.

Belief in one God as creator of heaven and earth is clearly expressed by the sixth-century BCE prophet who wrote Isaiah 40–55, in some psalms, and in the first creation story in the book of Genesis. Earlier writers and traditions took a more restricted view of the nation's God, but the Hebrew Bible in its canonical form assumes the universal scope of its later strands. God created the world and humanity, and can be known from nature sufficiently for humans to be held accountable for rebellion against God's will. The universality of this 'general' (as it has sometimes been called) or 'natural' revelation is implied by the prophetic criticisms of the nations' cruelty (e.g. Amos 1–2). In the New Testament it allows Paul to echo the language of Stoic natural theology in Romans 1.19f.; 2.14f. when he argues that all are morally accountable. However, Amos and Paul make these accusations and claims from the perspective of their own particular traditions of God-talk, based as these are on the conviction that God has spoken and declared 'his' will and glory and power at particular times and places, and that a divine event on the stage of history is foundational for their own religious practice and belief. A religious community's claim to a foundational revelation is simply part of its members' religious discourse. It can be rationally questioned and criticized by anyone, but cannot be verified from outside its own particular religious circle. It is (arguably) reasonable to believe in divine revelation, but the truth of any particular claim is verified (if at all) in the experience of those whose spiritual and moral practice confirms the authenticity of their belief.

In the case of Judaism, this 'special' foundational (in contrast to 'general') revelation is located in the cluster of events associated with Moses narrated in the book of Exodus. It includes God's revealing his name, YHWH (6.2–7; cf. 3.14), the exodus liberation itself with its attendant wonders, notably at the Red Sea, and the Sinai covenant, including the Ten Commandments, the Decalogue. This covenant made by God is Israel's founding event, based on the revelation of God in a set of supposedly historical events written down much later, and partly re-enacted liturgically in the Passover. Those historical memories embroidered in texts and retold within the community remain constitutive of Israel's identity as God's chosen people.

If phenomenologists of religion call this Israel's 'foundational revelation', they are borrowing a theological term more common in Christianity, and doing so to emphasize all participants' belief in the divine initiative in the origins of their religion. Jews use the word less and would more naturally apply it to Torah (written and oral) or (like Christians) to their scriptures, the Hebrew Bible. This authorized version of Israel's election, the God-given basis of its religious life, consists of both narratives and laws believed to stem from God through Moses, the supposed author of the Torah. It is prefaced by creation myths, primeval stories, and accounts of the patriarchs, all correlated with the foundational revelation through the later assumption that God the creator was YHWH, and that it was YHWH (not yet known by this name) who called Abraham and made him the promise of descendants and a land. The story of the nation's uneven response to God's law is continued to the Babylonian exile. In the oracles of the writing prophets God is heard speaking to subsequent generations, and the Psalms both recapitulate the history of salvation and express the people's joyful response, hallowed by centuries of liturgical use in the temple, and by private devotion. In the Hebrew Bible's limited inclusion of wisdom literature ideas of general revelation and of YHWH's self-revelation to Israel are pre-supposed. Revelations to seers are constitutive of the apocalypses, but this genre is marginal in the Hebrew Bible. The idea of revelation became attached to texts considered inspired by God in every letter; Judaism became the people of the book.

p. 139

Apocalyptic

The concept of divine revelation can nevertheless also be applied analytically to Judaism's view of the exodus event. Christians make a stronger connection between their founding revelation and their present experience of God in Christ. The biblical witness is essential, and is a source and norm of Christian faith, but is only indirectly called revelation. When in doctrinal disputes the problem of interpretation is short-circuited and appeal made to scripture as though selected texts were immediate revelation, this misrepresents Christians' engagement with the Bible in their ongoing response to God in Christ. Locating revelation in a person rather than in texts requires a doctrinal superstructure, and this requires scriptural support; that has sometimes led to un-Christian doctrines of scripture, but Christianity is less directly a religion of the book than Judaism or Islam. In Judaism the covenant and what it requires of God's people makes the written word primary, and the tradition of its interpretation central. The divine origin and content of Torah requires fewer supporting arguments than Christian belief in the divinity of Christ, but is functionally equivalent to the revelation of God in Jesus in Christianity. Here scripture is essential witness to the revelatory event in Christ that is actualized in the present. God's Spirit is expected to inspire hearts and minds as scripture is read in the community's process of discernment, and in this dialectic between the gospel and scripture individual texts are related to a sense of the whole.

p. 131

Covenant

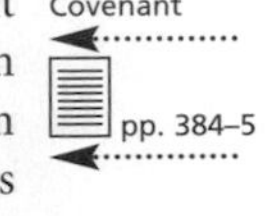
pp. 384–5

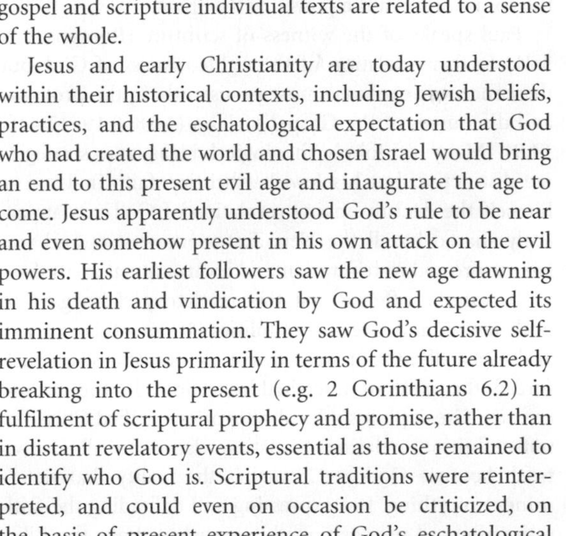

Jesus and early Christianity are today understood within their historical contexts, including Jewish beliefs, practices, and the eschatological expectation that God who had created the world and chosen Israel would bring an end to this present evil age and inaugurate the age to come. Jesus apparently understood God's rule to be near and even somehow present in his own attack on the evil powers. His earliest followers saw the new age dawning in his death and vindication by God and expected its imminent consummation. They saw God's decisive self-revelation in Jesus primarily in terms of the future already breaking into the present (e.g. 2 Corinthians 6.2) in fulfilment of scriptural prophecy and promise, rather than in distant revelatory events, essential as those remained to identify who God is. Scriptural traditions were reinterpreted, and could even on occasion be criticized, on the basis of present experience of God's eschatological activity.

Bible

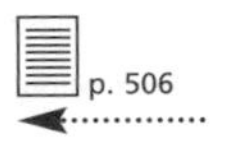
p. 506

Psalms

Resurrection
Enlightenment
Liberal theology

All the New Testament writers were convinced that in Jesus' activity and death and vindication God was decisively at work on behalf of his people, and that in responding to Jesus as communicated by those who had known him on earth they were responding to God who had sent him. The belief that Jesus spoke and acted with the authority of God, more directly than any prophet or teacher, had its roots in his own self-understanding and was strengthened after his martyr's death by mysterious experiences of his presence.

Karl Barth

This early Christian belief in Jesus as himself the decisive eschatological revelation of God, making him the foundational revelation of the new sect, led to a break with the parent religion over what was fundamental and what merely more or less valuable tradition. Within about twenty years of Jesus' death, in Antioch and soon after in Galatia, there was a conflict which in retrospect seems to imply competing claims to revelation. Paul insisted against Peter (Galatians 2.11–14) that only faith in Christ was now constitutive of their identity. Gentile converts did not therefore have to obey the Torah, the Jewish law, as a whole. Scripture remained foundational for knowledge of God, and Paul himself saw much of its moral content as a true expression of God's holy will. But by judging much of the law non-essential he in effect denies that it is revelation. Only Christ, communicated by his representatives and known through the Spirit, can be called revelation now. The foundational revelation of what was emerging as a new religion was the crucified, risen, and expected Lord Jesus Christ whom Paul could speak of in close association with 'God our Father' without infringing his Jewish monotheism. This revelation was actualized in the present in word (proclamation) and sacrament within the community in the power of the Spirit.

Philosophy of religion

Paul speaks of the witness of scripture (Romans. 1.2; 3.21) to this revelation of the righteousness of God, but the concept is explored most persistently in the prologue and discourses of the Gospel of John (1.18; 8.19; 12.44f.; 14.9). Many of John's theological ideas and strategies are distinctive, but his Jewish-Christian faith in Jesus as himself the decisive saving revelation of God was apparently shared by all the New Testament writers and was later expressed in trinitarian and incarnational formulae.

Trinity
Incarnation

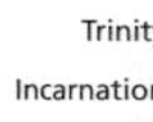

It was the offence that this revelatory claim gave to both Jewish and Greek sensibilities (1 Corinthians 1.18), and especially its apparent threat to monotheism, which forced the pace of doctrinal reflection. In the second century, Greek philosophical categories clarified Christian self-definition, relating Christian claims to all known truth because God as Creator is the reality that determines everything. But expressing and defending the faith rationally and propositionally seemed to make the Bible a source of doctrine and a revelation of the 'faith which is believed'. That confusion presented an easy target for rational criticism in the European Enlightenment. Some beliefs might be defended as beyond reason, but many were clearly contrary to new knowledge, and their biblical source was evidently fallible.

The response of modern liberal theology was to recover Paul's distinction between the Bible and the gospel revelation. Rationalist theologians first tried to identify the reasonable and moral parts of the Bible with divine revelation, but that destroyed the concept by making reason its judge. German idealists found God's self-revelation in the totality of the historical process. This failed to express the uniqueness and finality of the incarnation. Friedrich Schleiermacher made this again foundational, but failed to combine it adequately with his historical perspective. His liberal successors expanded historical knowledge of Christianity but scarcely did justice to the traditional belief in Jesus as himself the revelation of God. In reaction, the neo-Reformation strategies of Karl Barth and dialectical theology emphasized the witness of the biblical 'word of God' to the revelation of God in Christ. The reception of revelation in the response of faith to Christian proclamation was preserved, but its future and cosmic aspects were under-emphasized in kerygmatic theology. Jürgen Moltmann and Wolfhart Pannenberg corrected this by retrieving biblical eschatology and in different ways making it central to their accounts of revelation in Christ.

It remains clear that talk of revelation is 'insider' talk by participants, even though the concept has been borrowed by phenomenologists describing the language of believers. Its prominence in modern theology stems from the restriction of meaningful talk of God in the modern world to religious groups where God is worshipped. If God is not 'known' by human reason, but only in contexts of religious practice, it is to these religious communities themselves, and their distinctive traditions of God-talk, that philosophers and social scientists must turn to understand the idea of revelation. As the Christian example shows, it refers to the past (foundational), present (experiential) and future (eschatological) aspects of believers' talk of the divine.

ROBERT MORGAN

Karl Barth, *Church Dogmatics I/1, The Doctrine of the Word of God*, Edinburgh: T&T Clark 1956; H. Richard Niebuhr, *The Meaning of Revelation*, New York: Macmillan 1941; Wolfhart Pannenberg, *Systematic Theology*, Vol. 1, Edinburgh: T&T Clark 1991, pp. 189–257; Karl Rahner et al. (eds), *Sacramentum Mundi*, London: Burns & Oates 1970, pp. 342–59; Paul Tillich, *Systematic Theology*, Vol. 1, Chicago: Chicago University Press 1950 and London: SCM Press 1978, pp. 118–77

RITUAL AND WORSHIP

Eucharist, Festivals and fasts, Hymns, Interfaith worship, Music, Pentecostalism, Preaching, Psalms, Ritual, Sacraments, Worship

In a German home, before the family begin their evening meal they bow their heads and the father of the family says a prayer of thanksgiving for the food that they are about to eat.

A child comes forward in a packed English church to light a candle. But this is no ordinary candle. Its holder is an orange into which pointed sticks have been stuck, with nuts, raisins and sweets on them, and this symbol, the christingle, represents Christ in the world and all its good things.

In a city in the United States a group meets for worship. Each member brings a flower, which is put into a common vase. Towards the end of the service the vase of flowers is blessed, and as they leave, the members take away a different flower from the one they brought. They call this Flower Communion. Unitarians

In a shanty town in Venezuela a dozen people meet in the twilight to sing hymns, pray and study the Bible. Some can read, some cannot. All are free to contribute, and though theoretically unstructured, their gatherings take on a form of their own. Christianity in Latin America

In St Peter's, Rome, scarlet-clad cardinals gather in solemn assembly to hear the formal proclamation of the names of church dignitaries who will be added to their number. Vatican

In London's Westminster Abbey monarchs are crowned with time-honoured splendour in a rite which goes back well over a thousand years.

There is a wealth of ritual of every kind in Christianity, from the pomp of public ceremony in the presence of large numbers of people, to intimate private ritual involving only a handful. Ritual behaviour is one of the most ancient of all recorded human activities. In every culture throughout our history we can find people engaging in complex patterns of action by which they celebrate births, marriages and deaths, lament loss, and negotiate changes in social status within a community. By definition, ritual is an agreed-upon form of coded communication using the language of significant action, objects and formalized speech to convey meaning. Whatever its shape and intention, ritual plays an essential role in constructing our personal, social, and cultural identity as human beings.

Effective ritual functions in a number of different ways. It gives shape to the depths of emotion so often experienced in the various forms of concrete human encounter, enabling us to come to terms on an intuitive level with facts and feelings whose literal significance we may not yet be ready to face. In addition, ritual can hold together multiple meanings without forcing us to choose between and among them. More importantly, through ritual we are able to articulate those human realities that we find most difficult to express in words, such things as our deepest values, ideals, hopes, loyalties, fears and affections. And finally, ritual properly enacted has the qualities of 'performance'. In other words, it is understood to create the state of affairs which it represents: a wedding rite with the words 'I will' effects a marriage between two people; breaking a bottle of champagne over the bow of a ship gives the ship its name; a handshake seals an agreement.

Some human ritual behaviour is specifically intended to function as a form of communication within the divine-human relationship. In addition to those qualities described above, religious ritual helps participants to place their immediate and local concerns on a wider canvas, and to open themselves to spiritual insight. In many religious traditions, including some Christian traditions, ritual is understood to have been given to the community of faith by God, as a means by which God's bond with humanity can be maintained in the face of human frailty and sin. For many Christians, this is most clearly true of the core Christian rites, baptism and the Lord's Supper, as well as penance (the rite by which sins are declared absolved), and anointing of the sick. In some communities of faith, however, ritual is understood as an essentially human construct, designed to evoke in participants memory, hope and faith. A number of Christian traditions view worship as something which humanity owes to God, a duty to be performed in grateful obedience to the One who is the author of life and salvation. We see a reflection of this understanding whenever a meeting for worship is described as a 'service'. But at various times religious ritual has also been viewed with deep suspicion by Christians, who become concerned that the nature of ritual as a performance might lead us to believe that we somehow control God's action and our destiny through the enactment of proper rites.

Christian worship is a constellation of ritual words and actions through which the company of Christian believers praises and prays to God, listens for God's voice, initiates new members, confesses sin, intercedes for others, and asks for God's blessing on events in the human life-cycle (birth, maturity, marriage, sickness and death). From the time the earliest Christian communities were established, gathering for worship on 'the first day of the week' (Sunday) for 'the fellowship, the breaking of bread, and the prayers' (Acts 2.42) has been one of Christianity's most persistent and identifiable features. For some Christians, public worship on Sundays is augmented by meetings for daily prayer morning, noon and evening, on feast days and on the occasion of special commemorations. Christians have also worshipped privately in their homes, but domestic worship has usually been understood to be rooted in and patterned after the corporate worship that takes place in public settings.

Christian worship has not only been a highly significant source of spiritual nourishment for Christians, but also of Christian theological reflection and doctrinal formation as well. The liturgical hymns, prayers, exhortations and meaningful gestures both reflect and shape the theology of those who use them. This phenomenon is described in a Latin phrase from the sixth century CE: *lex credendi legem statuat supplicandi* ('the law of believing stands on the law of praying'). Certainly many of the most important Christian theologians, as well as governing bodies and other church institutions, have worked towards doctrinal clarity through an analysis of the content and intention of services of Christian worship. As early as the New Testament period, there was important debate about whether Jesus Christ was an appropriate object of worship for Christian believers, or whether worship is always to be directed to God the Father, through the Son and in the power of the Holy Spirit. Again, the tradition of common prayer has been employed in arguments on both sides of this issue.

Christology

Worship has also been instrumental in the formation and maintenance of the Christian codes of behaviour. Core values of hospitality, a concern for justice and peacemaking, generosity, mutual love and care for the poor and marginalized in society are embedded in forms of Christian worship and are given ritual expression in various ways. As they are practised over and over again in the context of the worship of God, these ritual behaviours become embodied, and thereby inform our action in the wider world. That is to say, through the words and actions of worship, Christians expect gradually to be transformed into what they proclaim.

Several accessory terms are associated with these dual categories of ritual and worship. The

LITURGY

The word liturgy and its adjective liturgical are used a great deal in Christianity in connection with worship. What they refer to are not always the same. Liturgy comes from the Greek word *leitourgia* (literally 'people's work'), and in classical Greek denoted the fulfilment of a public duty, often an onerous public office which the holder discharged at his own expense. In the Greek translation of the Hebrew Bible it came to be used of services held in the Jerusalem temple.

In Christianity liturgy it is first used to describe the prescribed services, i.e. forms of worship, of the church, including what are referred to as the daily offices or canonical hours, worship engaged in at specific hours of the day and night, e.g. Prime, Mattins, Lauds, Compline or Morning and Evening Prayer. The current Roman Catholic term in use is Liturgy of the Hours. The calendar observed by churches throughout the year, from Advent to Pentecost and beyond, is referred to as the liturgical year.

Secondly, the liturgy, with the definite article, is taken to refer to the Lord's Supper, the eucharist, the mass. The term is particularly widely used in the Eastern Orthodox churches. Consequently various forms of celebrating the eucharist are called 'The Liturgy of ...' There is for example *The Liturgy of St John Chrysostom*, dating from around the eighth century, which is the liturgy used on all days in the Eastern Orthodox Churches, except on the first five Sundays in Lent, Maundy Thursday, the eves of Easter, Christmas and Epiphany and the feast of St Basil, when *The Liturgy of St Basil* is used. This liturgy is the regular liturgy of the Coptic Church. The Syriac Church uses *The Liturgy of Addai and Mari,* which in parts may go back to the third century. There are also *The Liturgy of St Cyril*, *The Liturgy of St Gregory* and *The Liturgy of St James*, used in the Armenian and Georgian Churches. The books used in the eucharist are called liturgical books and the vessels liturgical vessels.

The *Liturgical Movement* is a twentieth-century movement which sought to revitalize the church by renewing its worship: it began in the Roman Catholic Church, notably in monasteries in France, Germany and Belgium and expanded over the world, also drawing in other churches.

Liturgical reform is the revision of patterns of worship and the production of new forms and new prayer books: in the Roman Catholic Church after the Second Vatican Council this included the celebration of the eucharist in the vernacular, local languages, rather than Latin; in churches already using the vernacular it led to the replacement of traditional archaic language with contemporary, inclusive language, along with new music and art forms.

The word 'liturgy' is also used to denote the study of worship as shorthand for the longer 'liturgiology'.

Paul F. Bradshaw (ed), *The New SCM Dictionary of Liturgy and Worship*, London: SCM Press 2002 (US title: *The New Westminster Dictionary of Liturgy and Worship*, Louisville, KY: Westminster Press 2003)

word 'liturgy' often implies a form of worship that is highly stylized, with elaborate ceremonial and formal speech patterns. But the ancient origin of the English word 'liturgy' does not bear this interpretation, rooted as it is in the Greek words for people (*laos*) and work (*ergon*), and carrying an understanding that somehow the gathering for the worship of God is a 'public work', undertaken for the sake of the redemption of the world. For this reason there is increasing ecumenical agreement on the use of 'liturgy' as the ordinary description of any form of Christian corporate prayer. In the same way, some commentators speak of 'high church' and 'low church' worship, distinguishing again between church services that are rich in sensory experience and those that are more spontaneous or that rely more heavily on the spoken word. This, however, is not always a helpful distinction, since even in gatherings that display little overt formalized behaviour, there can exist a more subtle, underlying ritual structure that is apparent to participants. Ritual is intended to point beyond itself to a deeper reality, and in the case of religious ritual to a divine reality. But ritual can be deformed into 'ritualism', which denotes a form of ritual done for its own sake, without reference to the transcendent.

In many ways, worship is the principal marker and shaper of Christian identity; to worship is to call oneself a 'Christian', to claim a place in a particular worshipping community, whatever form it takes, and to place oneself in the context of the symbols and rituals peculiar to Christianity.

SUSAN J. WHITE

Ritual

Holy · Devotions

Human beings are, by nature, ritual-making creatures, and ritual clearly plays an essential role in constructing our personal, social and cultural identity. Religious ritual, ritual which has meaning within the divine-human relationship, has always been understood as making an indispensable contribution to the deepening of spiritual insight, the internalizing of ethical values and doctrinal norms, and the appropriation of patterns of holiness. This is certainly true of the ritual patterns employed by Christians. From the smallest gesture performed as an element in private devotion to the most elaborately-constructed public rite, the rituals which have found their place in Christian life and worship are all somehow directed towards communicating the love and mercy of God to faithful believers.

Worship · Eucharist · Sacrifice · Community

Unfortunately, the word 'ritual' has come to have a negative connotation for many Christians. An 'empty ritual' is something devoid of real significance and sincerity, and 'ritualism', the obsessive or rigid formality sometimes experienced in worship services, is something which is viewed as a perversion of true worship of God. Both of these perceptions signal a very real danger in the use of ritual as an expression of the Christian faith, namely that it may become detached from the experience of faith, from its symbolic meaning, from the memories and aspirations of the community that uses it. But the word ritual itself is derived from the Latin work *ritus*, which simply means 'the form and manner of religious worship', 'a religious ceremony or custom'. This more neutral definition implies that all Christian worship, from the most formal and the most elaborate to the most simple and spontaneous, is actually 'ritual'. Christians worship in patterned ways, and know immediately if those patterns are being violated.

Reformation

To describe ritual as an established and patterned sequence of movements highlights a number of aspects of the nature and purpose of ritual. It is an action of the human body, and the interaction of human bodies with one another. Ritual takes various forms, but it is always composed of predictable patterns of activity that are repeated by participants at particular times and in particular circumstances. Both individuals and groups engage in ritual behaviour, and not all rituals are religious. Men and women have rituals for going to bed or exercising, and families have rituals for celebrating birthdays and anniversaries. Rituals in schools govern the conduct of sports days and graduation exercises, and communities and nations ritualize significant events in their history. But both religious and non-religious ritual have the same capacity to shape and renew those who use them, to give stability to life, to order and convey meaning, and to transmit to future generations the most deeply-held values and ideals. In Christian worship, ritual serves all of these important functions.

All Christian worship is a creative dialogue between form and freedom, between those elements that are stable and those that change according to the occasion. In worship, Christians seek to ensure both that they do not 'quench the Spirit' (1 Thessalonians 5.19) and that things are done 'decently and in order' (1 Corinthians 14.40). But the repeated elements of worship not only give participants the sense that things are being done properly, they also become known and trusted patterns which they depend on to give the sense that worship is being done 'rightly'. Ritual has the power to draw worshippers into a mode of human communication in which words diminish in importance. At their best, rituals speak for themselves; and they speak volumes. When a person places a wreath on the Cenotaph or the Tomb of the Unknowns, how many words would it take to express fully the love, devotion, gratitude, respect and sadness which is embodied in that single ritual gesture? When Christians break bread at the eucharist, the ritual action speaks all at once of sharing, of sacrifice, of communal nourishment at the hands of Jesus, and of hope for the future transformation of all creation. The ritual breaking-of-bread reinvigorates the common memory of Jesus' last meal with his friends, and of all the previous gatherings of the community around the common table. All rituals are actions that point to a deeper reality, but whenever a ritual needs to be 'explained', it is a sign that the rite has lost much of its inherent communicative power.

Many specific rituals have found their home in Christian worship during its nearly 2000-year history. Some currently-practised rituals have been essential to corporate worship since the earliest Christian communities gathered for 'the apostles' teaching and fellowship (*koinonia*), the breaking of bread and the prayers' (Acts 2.42). Others have developed later, but remain a part of contemporary liturgical experience; still others have become extinct over the centuries, or continue to flourish only in small branches of the Christian family.

Many rituals have also changed their meaning over time. One good example of this is the early Christian 'kiss of peace', given and received as a sign of reconciliation, love, and unity in the body of Christ before partaking of communion. Attested to in the New Testament letters (for example in Romans 16.16 and 1 Peter 5.14), the ritual kiss of peace persisted as a normal feature of Christian worship for several centuries after Jesus' death. Gradually this significant rite became truncated into a bow exchanged between the presiding ministers in a service. And in the churches that came into being after the sixteenth-century Reformation, the passing of the peace largely disappeared

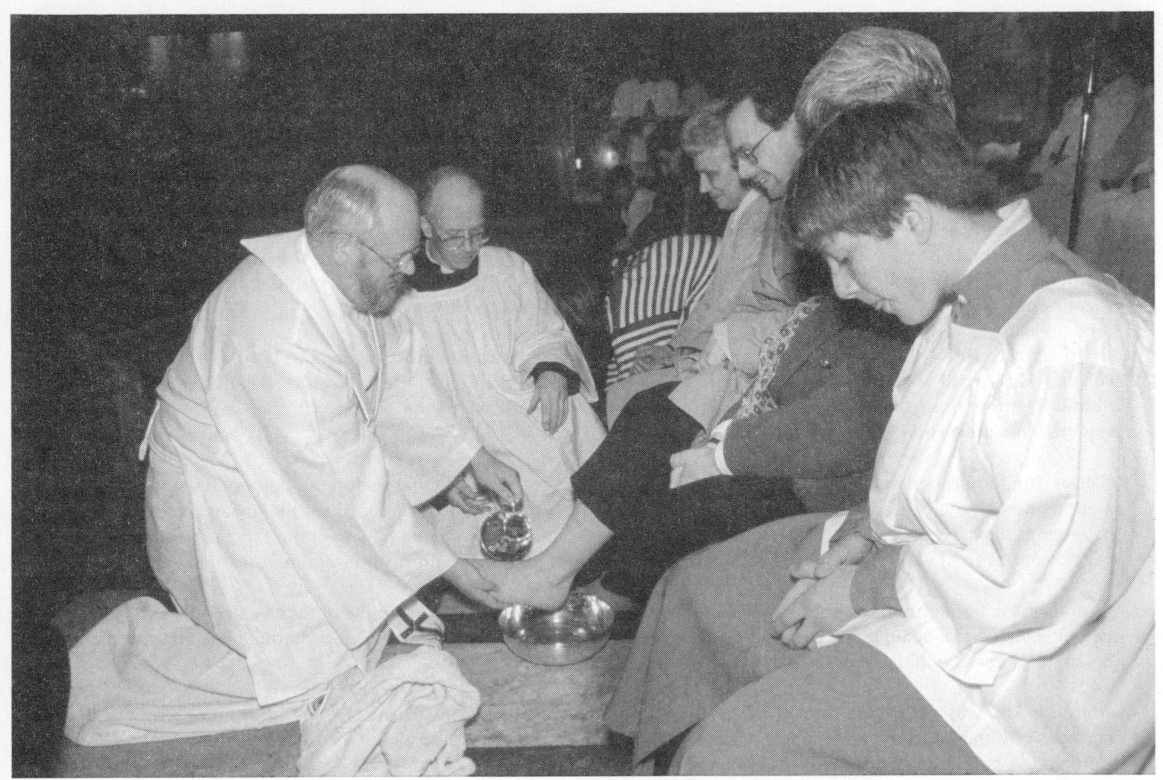

Foot-washing in a Roman Catholic Church in South London

for over 400 years. Recently, however, the more ancient practice of sharing a Christian greeting among members of the congregation during the Lord's Supper has been restored in many Christian denominations, and established as a meaningful part of preaching services as well. Unfortunately, the peace (now usually expressed in a handshake) is sometimes viewed today not as a ritual of reconciliation, a deeply significant gesture that proclaims that baptismal unity in Christ should never be divided by anger and resentment, but rather as a secular greeting, a way of saying 'hello' to members of the congregation who have not been seen since the previous week. So, even though this ancient ritual action has been restored to Christian worship, there is no guarantee that its original meaning has been restored with it.

Many other rituals from the early church have also been reintroduced to contemporary services of Christian worship. Some of these had been lost to Protestant Christians in the sixteenth century, when deep suspicion that ritual might lead to idolatry marked the reformed theological agenda, but retained in the Roman Catholic, Orthodox and Eastern-rite traditions. Others have been simply lost or seriously deformed in the intervening centuries. The ritual of foot-washing, commanded by Jesus to be observed as a part of the Lord's Supper as a sign of mutual servanthood (John 13.2–18), is one example. In the early centuries of the church, foot-washing came to be included among the rites for Maundy Thursday as a part of the commemoration of the institution of the eucharist. But although the ritual washing of feet may have been originally intended as an act to be exchanged among all members of the congregation as a mark of their discipleship, gradually only clergy (and later only bishops) celebrated the rite, and the Protestant purging of 'unnecessary' rites and ceremonies completed the removal of foot-washing from many traditions of Christian worship. In the past few decades, however, the attempt has been made to restore congregational foot-washing as part of the rites for Maundy Thursday in Christian churches of all denominations.

This kind of renewed attention to meaningful rituals and ceremonies is rooted in the recognition of the powerful role ritual plays in the shaping of the human religious imagination. Christians have believed that, as they rehearse the rituals week after week and year after year, the values and attitudes embedded in the rituals

Roman Catholic church
Orthodox churches
Eastern-rite Catholic churches

RITES

Rite is the term used to denote the order of service followed in the eucharist, the daily offices and other forms of worship and ceremonial. In the first millennium there were a number of ancient rites, each differing slightly from the other, used in different regions; these were gradually almost all replaced by the Roman rite.

Roman rite: This is the earliest and most widespread rite, in Latin, which evolved gradually; its fully developed form can be seen in the Leonine and Gelasian sacramentaries. Originally it was used only in the province of Rome, but by the twelfth century it was used almost everywhere in the Roman Catholic Church, except in Milan, where the Ambrosian rite survived. It determined forms of worship up to the Second Vatican Council, when it was replaced by worship in the vernacular, but the evocative power of its Latin mass has led to that mass still being celebrated.

Ambrosian rite: This is the rite used in the province of Milan, named after Ambrose, its famous bishop, though there is no evidence that he had anything to do with it. It has survived alongside the Roman rite and was revised at the Second Vatican Council. It differs from the Roman rite, among other things, by the place of the offertory in the mass before the creed, presented in a procession.

Gallican: The term is generally used to denote the forms in which the eucharist was celebrated before Charlemagne's reign, when the Roman rite was adopted. There were a variety of these, some more elaborate than the Roman rite, some shorter. The order of the mass contained a whole series of variations, including the repeated singing of the *Sanctus* ('Holy, Holy, Holy') in Greek and Latin at various points and a eucharistic prayer which changed with the liturgical seasons.

Mozarabic: The term is used to denote the forms of worship used on the Iberian peninsula until the eleventh century. On the Roman reconquest of Spain it was replaced by the Roman rite, but is still celebrated in Toledo Cathedral. It is richer than the Roman rite and has additional prayers and chants; the Sanctus is said in Greek.

Sarum rite: This was a modified form of the Roman rite used in Salisbury from around the twelfth century onwards. It was enormously influential, and by the middle of the fifteenth century was being used almost all over England, Wales and Ireland. It formed the basis for the first Book of Common Prayer in the Church of England (1549).

Byzantine rite: The rite of the Eastern Orthodox churches.

Revised forms of the eucharist are still called rites: in modern prayer books they are prosaically referred to as Rite A, Rite B, Rite 1, Rite 2, etc.

become a part of their lives and actions. In other words, they gradually become what they ritualize. Rituals in the life of the Christian church are understood as effective means of deepening and enriching the Christian corporate life by expressing those things that bind the community together (shared values, hopes, concerns, and ideals), and thereby strengthening human bonds of fellowship.

But, as indicated earlier, rituals can go wrong, and when they go wrong their inherent communicative power can deform the Christian community and misinterpret the essential redemptive core of the Christian message. Since the early sixteenth century, this has been the central Protestant critique of the extensive use of ritual in worship: that it may lead to idolatry by encouraging participants to confuse their rituals with the God who is alone to be worshipped. With the growth of both the ecumenical movement and the liturgical movement in the twentieth century, some of the Protestant suspicion of Christian ritual has abated, and although emphasis on the Word of God proclaimed and on preaching remains strong in Protestant worship, the recovery of a number of key ritual activities has also begun to occur.

Ecumenical movement

Some students of Christian worship wish to make a distinction between 'ritual' and 'ceremonial', although it is common to find the terms used interchangeably. If there is such a distinction to be made, the more central term is ritual, describing the core Christian sign-acts that carry some meaning related to redemption. Ceremonial, on the other hand, is the complex of peripheral symbolic actions that elaborate and expand upon the central rites. So, for example, the eucharist is usually spoken of as a 'ritual' action, while honouring and purifying the presiders at the altar-table with incense might be considered 'ceremonial' action. Other ceremonial actions are processions, the lighting of candles, and the formalized kissing of books and other objects used in the liturgy. Often the term 'rite' is also used to describe a constellation of rituals that centre on a common meaning. So the 'rite' of Christian baptism is composed of rituals of washing with water, anointing with oil, and patterns of formalized speech; the 'eucharistic rite' consists of the separate rituals of taking bread and wine, breaking bread, blessing the elements, and sharing them among participants.

Other terms that are frequently associated with specific kinds of Christian ritual are 'sacrament' and 'ordinance'. Again, these are symbolically-charged words, carrying with them an array of theological and historical associations for those who use them. The definition of precisely which church rituals were to be considered sacraments was late in developing, and in the earliest centuries of the church's life the term ritual could be used for any rite which carried redemptive meaning for participants. In the writings of Augustine of Hippo (354–430 CE), for example, as many as 35 different ritual acts are described as a *sacramentum*, including the imposition of ashes on the forehead of believers on Ash Wednesday, anointing for exorcism of candidates before their baptism, and the tonsuring of a monk. But by the early years of the twelfth century, the conditions under which a ritual could be described as a sacrament had narrowed. A sacrament was defined as a rite which had been ordained by some word or action of Jesus, and which, when performed properly and with the right intention on the part of the ministrant, conveyed saving grace to individual believers. The number of actions that conformed to this definition was seven: the eucharist, baptism, confirmation, penance, anointing of the sick, ordination and marriage.

This kind of definition presumes that God is active and working in the ritual action. For many Christians who would naturally speak of these ritual actions as 'sacraments', these acts are gifts of God to human beings, given as a means of establishing and maintaining the divine-human relationship. Because it was the exactitude with which the rite was performed that guaranteed saving grace, and not the interior disposition of the individual, there was always some danger that the proper enactment of the ritual might be understood as having the ability to compel God into some particular action.

This danger of treating rituals as if they had 'magical' or coercive power led many post-Reformation Christians to emphasize the absolute necessity of faith on the part of the recipient for the grace promised in the ritual to be released. In addition, they wished to make certain that there was a direct commandment of Jesus for the establishment of a redemptive rite. Under these conditions, only two church rites, baptism and the Lord's Supper, qualified as sacraments. These two were understood to have specific redemptive promises of God attached to them (as attested to in scripture) that were activated by the performance of the rite. Over the next several centuries, the purging of all 'undue ceremonies' of the church proceeded, anxiety over the worthiness of the sinner to appropriate sacramental grace increased, and there was a heightening of suspicion that human beings might see ritual action as a way of manipulating divine favour. The term 'ordinance', used by Puritans, Baptists and others desiring a more radical pruning of ritual elements from Christian worship, goes back to the necessity of a direct mandate of Jesus for any form of ritual to continue. The implication is that the Christian community enacts the rite in obedience to the mandate of Jesus, and not because of any expectation that God's grace will be decisively activated in and through the ritual action.

Puritans
Baptist churches
Sacraments
Jesus

A ritual action which is described as a 'sacramental' is usually a ceremonial act which, by its performance, turns an individual towards the knowledge and love of God, but which has no direct saving promise attached to it. Devotional aids such as making the sign of the cross during prayer, kneeling, lighting candles, using rosary beads to count out certain numbers of prayers are all described as sacramentals, helpful to spiritual growth but not essential. It is important to recognize here that for many Christians ritual has a place not only in the public worship of God, but in their private devotions as well.

p. 342

In addition, ordinary family rituals (the celebration of birthdays, putting children to bed, honouring a particular achievement, for example) are often given added meaning by overlaying them with forms of religious ritual. When a Christian parent leads a small child to kneel for prayer by her bedside and then marks her forehead with the sign of the cross before she goes to sleep, the bonds of love between parent and child are set into a larger, indeed a cosmic, frame as they embody their mutual submission to God.

p. 193

Ritual creates, almost by definition, 'insiders' and 'outsiders'. So, while ritual is a natural and necessary part of the Christian tradition, it bears within it the seeds of difficulty for a religious path that values unity and peace among its members. That being said, however, ritual clearly has a defining function in Christian faith and life. It may be possible, and even wise, to identify and delimit the various forms Christianity takes, not by their respective ethical stances, nor by their interpretation and appropriation of biblical texts, nor even by their particular theological approaches, but rather by the differences in the ritual patterns they adopt. Communities of believers and individual Christians make visible their most basic religious needs, values and aspirations through ritualizing them. And when Christians fail to recognize one another as members of one family in Christ, it is often because they fail to recognize the validity of one another's forms of ritual expression.

Grace

SUSAN J. WHITE

Michael Aune and Valerie DeMarinis (eds), *Religious and Social Ritual: Interdisciplinary Explorations*,

Jesus

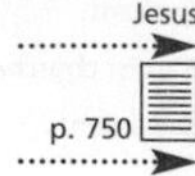

p. 750

Albany, NY: State University of New York Press 1996; Jensine Andresen (ed), *Religion in Mind: Cognitive Perspectives on Religious Belief, Ritual, and Experience*, Cambridge: CUP 2001; Tom Driver, *Liberating Rites: Understanding the Transformative Power of Ritual*, Boulder, CO: Westview 1998; David Hogue, *Remembering the Future, Imagining the Past: Story and Ritual and the Human Brain*, Cleveland, OH: Pilgrim Press 2003; James D. Shaughnessy (ed), *The Roots of Ritual*, Grand Rapids, MI: Eerdmans 1973

Roman Catholic Church

The news media loves the Roman Catholic Church. It not only makes great copy but it is also quite photogenic with its images of ornate churches, dramatic statues, and splendid processions. Then there is that white-robed figure with a gold cross on his breast, his right hand raised to bless cheering crowds, to form the backdrop for the news stories. No wonder that those who are not Roman Catholics tend to equate the church with its eye-catching but accidental features.

p. 291

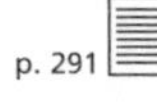

Appearances are deceiving; the church is not its pageantry. As its epoch-making Second Vatican Council declared, '… the Church is a kind of sacrament, that is, both a sign and a means of intimate union with God and of the unity of the human race …' (Dogmatic Constitution on the Church, *Lumen gentium*, no.1). So, according to its own self-understanding, the church is more truly visible in the nurse tenderly bathing a dying AIDS patient, the nun testifying on tax reform before the US Congress, the Brazilian peasant leading fellow villagers in discussion and prayer over the meaning for their lives of a Bible text, and priests celebrating the eucharist with their people on Sundays in thousands of places around the globe.

Papacy

Orthodox churches

Reformation

Anglicanism

This church is called 'Roman' because it is headed by the Bishop of Rome, better known as the Pope. It is also called 'Catholic' because of its claim to be the original universal church, distinct from the Orthodox churches of the East, which broke with Rome in 1054, and from the churches, Protestants and others, which broke with Rome during the Reformation of the sixteenth century. There are Christians, such as Anglicans and Orthodox, who are uncomfortable when they hear 'Catholic Church' and 'Catholicism' used to designate the Roman Catholic Church. They argue that they, too, are 'Catholic' because they maintain the essentials of the undivided church, which existed until the split of 1054. Yet 'Catholic' and 'Catholicism' prevail as verbal shorthand for the Roman Catholic Church.

Resurrection

All Christian churches and groups trace their origin to the ministry, preaching, death and resurrection of Jesus of Nazareth. The Roman Catholic Church goes further. It claims an unbroken corporate unity and continuity from its present condition back to Jesus himself and to the group of twelve men called 'apostles' (or 'ones sent') whom he gathered around him as the nucleus of a renewed 'people of God'. Jesus' earliest followers thought that Jews alone could belong to this people. Soon they understood that membership was open to the whole human race. So 'Catholic' also means 'universal'. No corner of the world and no ethnic group or race falls outside the church's care and concern. There is a Roman Catholic bishop charged with responsibility for the welfare of people living on every square inch of this earth. *The Sparrow*, a novel by Mary Doria Russell about a Catholic missionary expedition in 2054 to a planet newly discovered to be inhabited, is thoroughly Catholic in its inspiration.

Catholics are found nearly everywhere. They number about 17 per cent of the world's population, just over a billion. Almost half of these are North, Central and South American. A little over a quarter are European. Africa has 12 per cent, Asia 10 per cent, and Oceania the rest.

The claim of corporate continuity with Jesus' twelve apostles is not based upon meticulous historical evidence. In fact, the careers and fates of most of the apostles are lost to us. Instead, the lineage is grounded in the conviction that Jesus' life, execution and resurrection constitute the unconquerable beginning of God's full and final triumph over evil and death. Since the 'Jesus event' is God's decisive act, its ongoing influence on the world cannot be erased or destroyed by any other power. Nothing is stronger than God.

Contrary to popular belief, the Roman Catholic Church does not consider itself to be the single and exclusive true church of Christ. Vatican II also stated that '… the one Church of Christ, which in the Creed we profess as one, holy, catholic, and apostolic … subsists in the Catholic Church, which is governed by the successor of Peter [i.e., the Pope] and by the bishops together with him …' (*Lumen gentium*, no. 8). So the whole church, and not just the Roman Catholic Church, is understood as 'one, holy, catholic, and apostolic': one in its founder who called for unity among his disciples (which is why the existence of many Christian churches remains a troubling anomaly); holy not on account of the lives of its members but of God active among them; catholic because God's salvation in Christ is offered to every single human being; and apostolic because it is rooted in the apostles' preaching and witness to Jesus.

Modern Roman Catholicism

For its first millennium, Christianity was basically united, despite great diversity in language, worship, theology and traditions. But Christian unity was sundered in the final

THE CHURCH OF ROME AND NATIONALISM

Gallicanism: In England, the national church broke away from Rome at the time of the Reformation and became the Church of England; in France it did not, but nevertheless there were tensions between nationalism and allegiance to Rome. The term Gallicanism denotes these tensions, which go right back to the end of the thirteenth century, when King Philip the Fair of France and the powerful Pope Boniface VIII were in conflict over papal powers. Conciliarism, the view that the Pope is subject to a council, subsequently played a part: in 1438 King Charles VI of France issued the Pragmatic Sanction of Bourges, which affirmed this and also that the Pope's jurisdiction was limited by the will of the King.

p. 303

The Gallican Articles of 1682 are a first landmark of Gallicanism in the church; they were drawn up by Bishop Jacques-Bénigne Bossuet and stated:

1. The Pope has supreme spiritual but no secular power;
2. The Pope is subject to ecumenical councils;
3. The Pope must accept the traditional customs of the French church, e.g. the right of secular rulers to appoint bishops;
4. Papal infallibility in doctrinal matters has to be confirmed by the whole church.

Rome condemned the articles and they were revoked by Louis XIV.

Because there were also those in France, like the Jesuits, who did not share these views, Gallicanism was never formally strong, and though it was favoured by Napoleon, it had to give way to another tendency with a long history, Ultramontanism.

Ultramontanism: The tendency takes its name from the Latin *ultramontanus*, 'beyond the mountains'. It emphasized papal authority and centralization, and shaped the French Catholic church after the Restoration. Ultramontanism triumphed at the First Vatican Council (1870) with its definition of papal infallibility.

Febronianism: Febronianism is in many respects the German equivalent of Gallicanism. It takes its name from Johann Nikolaus von Hontheim (1701–90), a historian and theologian who wrote under the pseudonym of Justinus Febronius. His most important book, 'Concerning the State of the Church and the Legitimate Power of the Pope in Rome', appeared in 1763. In it he argued that the Pope's power should be limited and that the Pope should be subject to bishops and general councils, seeking to dispel the fears of German Protestants about the papacy. The book was condemned by Rome and put on the Index of Prohibited Books, though it did receive some official support in Germany. Febronianism collapsed with the French Revolution and a lack of support from German bishops.

Josephinism: This is the Austrian version of Febronianism, the name given to the principles behind the church reforms of Joseph II, Holy Roman Emperor from 1765–90. They included the right of the state to reform the church and to regulate church affairs, and a limitation on the powers of the Pope. However, promotion of the principles did not survive the Emperor's death.

split between the Eastern and Western churches in 1054 and again in the Reformation of the sixteenth century. The trauma of European Catholicism was compounded with declarations of independence from church authority by science (symbolized in Galileo) and philosophy (symbolized in René Descartes), the eighteenth-century Enlightenment, and finally the French Revolution of 1789 with its all-out assault on the church's teachings, privileges and property.

Over the next 80 years, the church adopted a separatist and defensive stance against this new age of enlightenment and liberation. Its strategy culminated in the First Vatican Council, 1869–70. This meeting solidified the church in its adversarial posture against modernity, which was often virulently anti-religious. Its teaching about the Pope made Catholic and non-Catholic alike see him as a quasi-absolute monarch. For nearly a century thereafter, the church recreated itself as a self-enclosed and self-sufficient fortress. In its own view, it was the repository of all religious truth, the custodian of all the perennially valid truths and values in the Western cultural heritage. The Catholic way was normative for a truly human life. Every other way led to grief.

Enlightenment

In 1958, Pope Pius XII died after a reign of nearly twenty years – from the dawn of the Second World War to the first earth-orbiting satellite. It was not clear what sort of pope the church needed in this new world. So an elderly cardinal, Angelo Roncalli, was elected as Pope John XXIII. He would be a 'transitional pope', living for just a few years, while the church decided on its long-term future. But Roncalli had a clear, particular vision of how the church should engage with the world. The church needed to engage in dialogue with the world about the issues facing humanity – after all, he pointed out, God had never abandoned this world – and to make the changes needed to 'bring light kindled from the gospel' to the tasks of human renewal. So he convened the Second Vatican Council (Vatican II), a gathering of the church's bishops

Council

and intellectual élite, to bring about this epoch-making change.

Paul
Martyr
Pilgrimage

Initially, the bishops at the council felt, 'If it ain't broke, don't fix it' – and the church was not broken! Gradually, however, most of them came to see the wisdom of John's vision and acted accordingly. The council terminated the church's policies of denying the legitimacy of other Christian churches and of distancing itself from many features of the modern world. Instead, it called for dialogue with other Christians in hopes of restoring the unity of the Church of Christ and for collaboration with all people of good will to deal with the crises facing humanity. Vatican II is the defining event for Roman Catholicism's last 40 years and for its foreseeable future.

Vatican

In the council's final sixteen documents, however, some serious differences of opinion were sometimes papered over. The bishops adopted compromise wordings in order to gain a commanding consensus for the final text. This strategy left the conflicts to simmer unresolved ever since. The Roman Catholic Church is at present polarized. Some Catholics argue that Vatican II mandated major changes and that even more changes are necessary today. Others maintain that certain groups have pushed reform far beyond what the council intended. Now it is time to pull back, to 'reform the reform', as they say. Specific elements of the new course set by the council will continue to be debated and played out for the foreseeable future. Meanwhile, a new generation of Catholics has come to maturity with no living memory of Vatican II and its dramatic achievements.

The papacy

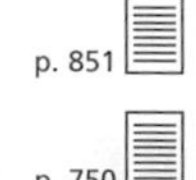
p. 851
p. 750

Among its actions, Vatican II tried to mitigate the tendency to identify the church with the Pope. Yet the tendency has validity, since the papacy is unique to Roman Catholicism. No other Christian body has an office comparable in its responsibilities, functions, and history. The Pope is the Bishop of Rome and successor to Peter, chief among the apostles. Pope John Paul II is deemed to be his 263rd successor. For Roman Catholics, the Pope symbolizes the unity of their worldwide diverse community. He is charged with promoting their fundamental unity of belief and worship, even while he encourages a legitimate and enriching diversity of thought and practice. Participating in the high point of Catholic worship, the mass, or the eucharist, should be a very different experience in rural Zimbabwe, downtown New York, and the barrios of Tegucigalpa.

Roman Catholics hold that the papacy is not just a convenient organizational arrangement. Rather, it reflects the will of Jesus himself for his church. New Testament texts show that one of his closest followers, Simon Peter, held a leadership role in the early Christian community. He was pre-eminent among the apostles. Solid (though not conclusive) historical evidence shows that Peter came to Rome in the mid-first century and was killed there (or 'martyred') under the Emperor Nero. Likewise, Paul of Tarsus, author of many of the influential letters preserved in the New Testament, was brought to Rome as a prisoner. He, too, was martyred there.

So Rome became a place of pilgrimage and a 'court of last resort' when it came to resolving disputes over the meaning of Jesus' mission for new problems and circumstances. Christians thought of the community at Rome with its leadership as a reliable arbiter because the Romans had received Jesus' message from the two giants, Peter and Paul, and had kept it intact. For Roman Catholics, this development of Roman primacy was not accidental but belonged to God's design for the church. Even though the papacy is a tremendous obstacle to the reunion of Christianity (no other Christians accept the Pope's authority), it is not a negotiable item for Catholics. Reform may be necessary and desirable, but the papacy cannot be dispensed with altogether.

Organization

Two groups assist the Pope in fostering the unity of the world's billion Catholics and advancing the church's multi-faceted agenda. One is the Pope's administrative staff, the bureaucracy known as the Curia, which is located in Vatican City, the independent city-state in the midst of Rome. The other is the 'College of Bishops', the approximately 4000 bishops all over the world, considered here as a group (or 'collegium').

Catholics hold that the apostles' continuance of Jesus' work continues up to the present day in the bishops, who are deemed their successors. The bishops are key figures in the church. They are its official teachers. They preside at the church's official worship. They govern the local community committed to their care, organizing and directing its internal life and external relations. Together with the Pope, they are responsible for worldwide Catholicism.

Vatican II attempted to strengthen the governing power of the bishops by recommending a Synod of Bishops. The Council envisaged regular meetings of elected representatives of the bishops throughout the world. They would advise the Pope on issues facing the church and, in some cases, make policy. Some commentators even proposed that the Synod might elect the Pope.

While the Synod meets regularly and has an ongoing co-ordinating committee, it has not fulfilled expectations. Its agenda is tightly controlled by the Curia. In its sessions, more time is spent in speech-making than in real give-and-take discussions. Its topics often focus on questions that few are asking and the results of the sessions are

MAGISTERIUM

Other Christians, and even more so non-Christians, may be puzzled when they hear Roman Catholics talking about the magisterium. The term magisterium, from the Latin *magister*, master, denotes the teaching authority of the church. This magisterium has two levels, the extraordinary (or solemn) magisterium and the ordinary magisterium. It is exercised as follows:

Teacher	*Level*	*Degree of certitude*	*Assent required*
Pope *ex cathedra*	Extraordinary/solemn	Infallible	This is the Catholic faith which requires definitive assent
Bishops in union with the Pope proclaiming doctrine at a General Council	Extraordinary/solemn	Infallible	The Catholic faith
Bishops in union but not assembled	Ordinary	Infallible	The Catholic faith
The Pope	Ordinary	Authoritative	Submission
Bishop	Ordinary	Authoritative	Submission

'Extraordinary teaching' is also referred to as teaching *de fide* ('of the faith'); definitive assent means unconditional assent. Someone who denies extraordinary teaching is a 'heretic'; someone who denies ordinary teaching is 'in error' and commits a grave sin. The Pope's teaching is *ex cathedra* ('from the throne') when it is made in his capacity as infallible guide and teacher of the faithful. An encyclical does not necessarily constitute an *ex cathedra* pronouncement invested with authority. The extraordinary magisterium is exercised only rarely; the ordinary magisterium is exercised regularly by the church in teaching about faith and morals, particularly as expressed by the church fathers, theologians and the decisions of Roman Congregations concerning faith and morals, and the 'sense of faith' of the whole body of believers.

An authoritative statement about the magisterium is to be found in the Vatican II document *Lumen gentium*, chapter 25. p. 291

never made public. Instead, they are passed to the Pope. Some time later, he issues a lengthy statement purporting to synthesize the work of the Synod and encouraging its incorporation into the life of the church. Though it is currently moribund, the Synod remains a potential instrument for re-vitalizing the church in the hands of a new pope, who may have a different vision for the church.

In theory the Pope and the College of Bishops govern and guide the church. In practice the Curia is more influential than the College because the bishops are dispersed all over the globe. Rarely do they meet together (about once a century) for concerted action and decision-making in a council. The Curia, by contrast, is always on the scene in Rome and its main department heads meet regularly with the Pope for planning and approval of their policies.

Like other bureaucracies, the Curia has offices, departments, supervisory and staff positions. Its personnel, priorities and placements change over time to cope with evolving needs. Its organizational chart is not the product of management theory but of age-old traditions and contemporary experience.

For instance, before Vatican II, the church had no special department to direct and co-ordinate its relationships with other Christian churches, taking the attitude that the 'one true church' had no need of such a thing. Now the Pontifical Council for Promoting Christian Unity has that responsibility. For years after Vatican II, responsibility for Catholicism's relationships with the Jews fell to this office, despite its name, because Jewish leaders knew and trusted the Pontifical Council's personnel and wanted to continue to work with them.

There are two main divisions to the Curia itself. One deals with the church as a religious institution. It includes the offices that have responsibility for Catholic education, inter-religious dialogue, regulation of worship, etc. The other division reflects the church as an independent political entity, Vatican City.

Vatican City is a city-state because the papacy was the largest property owner and ruler in Italy for centuries, with its dominions lying across the centre of the peninsula. Nineteenth-century Italian nationalism stripped the papacy of these territories. So the popes refused to set foot outside the Vatican's boundaries and to recognize the new nation. In 1929, however, the church signed the Lateran Treaty with the Italian government. The treaty

Christianity in Europe

indemnified the church for its lost lands and established the political independence of the Vatican. Yet there are no checkpoints or border crossings between Italian and Vatican territories in Rome. A pickpocket can be pursued from the Via Della Conciliazione and arrested in the Piazza San Pietro, in the heart of Vatican City, by Italian police.

Ministry and ministers

Though its sovereign territory covers only 108.7 acres, the Vatican sends ambassadors (nuncios) to other nations and the Pope receives the credentials of their new ambassadors to the Holy See (a term for the official throne of a bishop and thus extended to his whole headquarters). The Vatican grants or withholds recognition of nations. It also sends representatives to the United Nations and to special UN conferences. This gives the church a voice in the world's forum on women's issues and family planning, which some other groups deeply resent.

Besides the College of Bishops and the Curia, a third group has become increasingly influential in the church, the College of Cardinals. Pope John Paul II expanded their role by calling on them – and not the Synod of Bishops – for advice and counsel on certain key issues, like church finances and the child abuse crisis in the US.

Normally, the title of cardinal comes with certain positions in the church. When a man is appointed Archbishop of Westminster, New York or Milan, he soon will become a cardinal. Certain departments in the Curia are always headed by cardinals. Sometimes, the title is conferred for distinguished service to the church; e.g., John Paul II has named some aged priest-theologians as cardinals.

Cardinals under the age of 80 have the unique responsibility of electing the new pope when a pope dies. (In theory, a pope may resign, but this has occurred only once in the church's history.) Originally, the Pope, the Bishop of Rome, was elected by the senior priests of Rome. Now the 120 or so cardinal-electors come from every race and nation, but each has a church in Rome assigned to him as his 'titular' church. This is in deference to the tradition that the clergy of Rome elects its bishop, the new pope. By church law, the cardinals can choose any adult male Catholic as pope. In practice, they always elect the new pope from among their own.

Religious orders

Roles and responsibilities in the church

When people say 'The church should do this or that', they mean the church's leadership. This tendency to identify the church with its leadership is understandable. At Vatican II, however, the decline of monarchy and the spread of the democratic ethos prompted the rediscovery of a traditional Christian conviction: every member of the church is fundamentally equal in dignity, destiny and rights. Vatican II reclaimed this truth and wanted it to infuse the church's life and thinking. So the Council re-framed the roles of the Pope, bishops and priests from superiority to service. The leaders of the church, insisted the Council, are actually servants of the people of God. Nonetheless, the church maintains a differentiation of responsibilities for persons within the church.

The first and most numerous group is the 'laity'. These are the ordinary Catholics, men and women, who attend mass on Sunday, more often than not, and live lives like their non-Catholic friends and neighbours. Theirs is a crucial role because they are to proclaim the Christian message and exemplify the Christian way of life in their homes, neighbourhoods, offices, factories and fields. In them, the church's presence and influence can be felt everywhere. Without their witness, the church's outreach and transformative power is crippled.

At the service of the laity is a second group, the official ministers, those in 'holy orders'. First among these are the bishops who, with their collaborators, the priests (and their collaborators, the deacons), teach the laity and help them grow as Christians by preaching and presiding over Catholic worship. A male adult becomes a deacon or priest by 'ordination' and bishop by 'consecration'. Ordination is a rite deemed to change a man in an essential way. The Catholic saying 'Once a priest, always a priest' reflects this conviction.

A bishop is normally responsible for a certain territory, called a diocese. Within the diocese are parishes, or smaller local congregations of Catholics, served by priests assigned or deputed by the bishop. (An archbishop is a bishop who has supervisory responsibility over other bishops within a region, like a small country, province or state.) In large dioceses with thousands of Catholics, such as New York, Catholics might rarely, if ever, encounter their bishop face to face. For them, the meaning and truth of Catholicism, therefore, are mainly shaped by their priests and fellow Catholics in their parish.

The third main group in the church is made up of the 'religious'. These are men and women who have felt a special attraction to a particular way of life and service in the church. They join a religious order whose members have taken certain vows to deepen their commitment and undertake this service. The oldest religious order in the Roman Catholic Church is the Order of St Benedict, or Benedictines, who are committed to prayer and study. Education is the chief calling of the most well-known order, the Society of Jesus, the Jesuits. Throughout the history of the church, human needs have drawn Catholics to join religious orders or even to found them, as Mother Teresa of Calcutta did in founding the Missionaries of Charity to care for India's poorest of the poor.

After a period of probation and formation, members of religious orders normally take three promises, known as

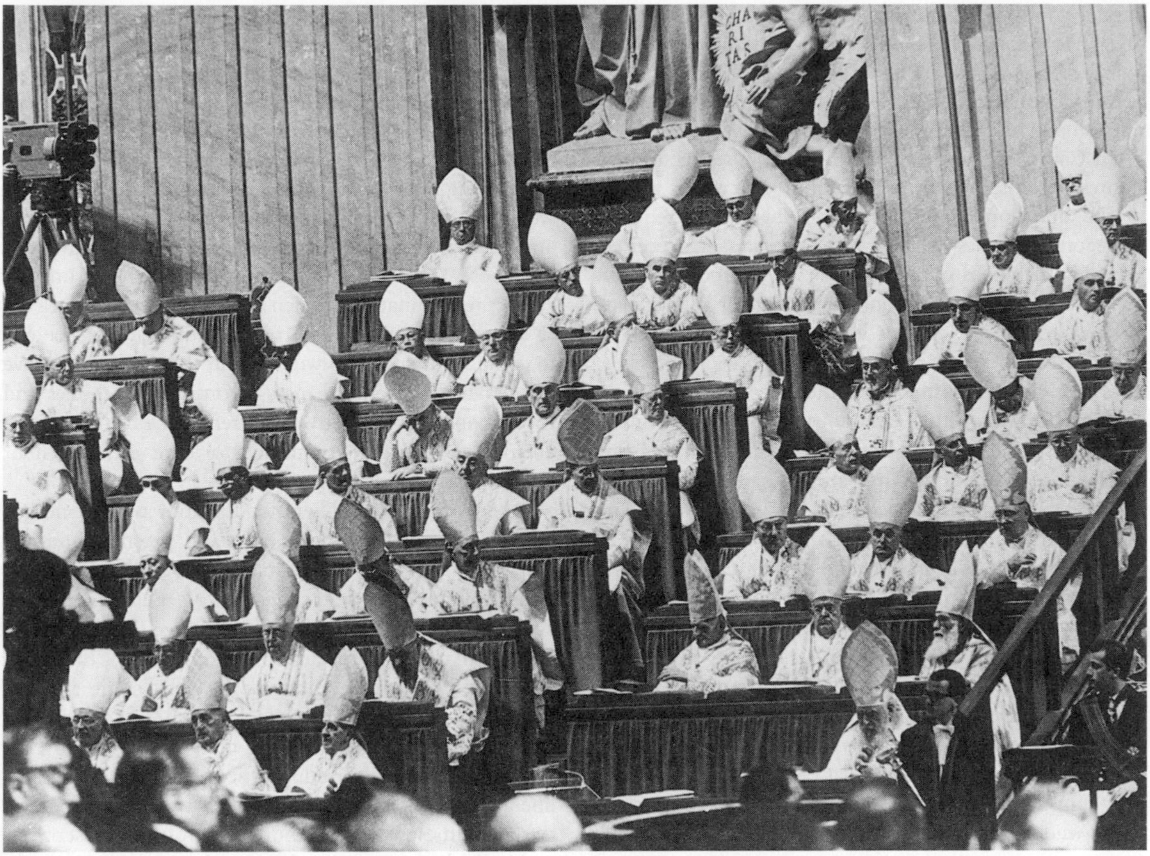

Bishops at the Second Vatican Council

the 'vows' of poverty, chastity and obedience. To outsiders, these vows look like deprivations. To those called to this way of life, the vows bring freedom. The vow of poverty frees one from enslavement to greed and materialism. The vow of chastity (or, more accurately, celibacy) makes one available to serve many more people than one could with a spouse. The vow of obedience loosens the grip of ambition and prepares people to serve where they are most needed. So the lives of faithful religious are truly counter-cultural. They remind their fellow Catholics that the ideals and values they embrace can be lived in the world of the here and now.

Worship

However different their lives and responsibilities may be, Catholics are all one around the 'Lord's table' in the celebration of the mass or the eucharist (the word means thanksgiving). This rite is the summit, source, and centre of Catholic life, according to the Second Vatican Council. Catholics gather on Sunday, the day of Jesus' resurrection, in obedience to the command he gave at his last meal with his followers. There Jesus took bread and wine and gave it to them, saying, 'Take this and eat it; this is my body which is to be given up for you. Take this cup and drink it; this cup is the new covenant in my blood. Do this to remember me.'

p. 665

This remembrance is not a vague recollection of an event in the past, but it makes that event present here and now. At mass, readings from the Bible are proclaimed and explained as God's word to this congregation at this time. Then, in a prayer of praise and gratitude to God for Jesus' saving mission, bread and wine, declared and believed to be Christ's body and blood (an intensified form of his intimate presence), are consumed.

Catholicism is among the most materialistic of the Christian churches. After bread and wine, water is the most important element. It is used in baptism, the rite by which one becomes a Catholic Christian. An adult is sometimes immersed in a pool, but more often the water is poured over the head by the priest with the words, 'I

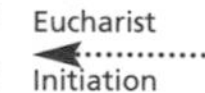
Eucharist
Initiation

baptize you in the name of the Father, and of the Son, and of the Holy Spirit.' This too accords with Jesus' command to his disciples: 'Go therefore and make disciples of all nations, baptizing them in the name of the Father and of the Son and of the Holy Spirit ...' (Matthew 28.19).

Saint Mary
Women in Christianity

In Catholic churches banks of lit candles in front of statues of the saints and of the Virgin Mary bear witness to the devotion of Catholics and their deep religious sense; often plaques will bear witness to blessings received. Popular Catholicism includes the observance of many festivals with local ceremonies, and regular pilgrimages, not just to famous shrines like Lourdes or Santiago da Compostela but to nearby centres.

Liberation theology
Spirituality
p. 1143

Other sacraments mark the rites of passage: baptism, marriage and anointing with holy oil during a terminal illness. The material and the spiritual are seen as being interwoven. Catholicism has always had an earthiness about it, an appreciation of the joys of creation, and alongside that an understanding of the need to cultivate the spiritual, by both private and communal prayer, and through particular forms of spirituality, which can include spending time apart in silence, in some form of retreat.

Kingdom of God
Schools
University

Care of the poor, the needy and the oppressed is more than a principle: all over the world there have been and are Catholic welfare organizations looking after orphans, the sick and the elderly as well as victims of war and natural disaster. The Catholic Church has been prominent, too, in providing schools, colleges and universities with concerns far beyond training priests and religious.

Challenges of the twenty-first century

In every era of its 2000-year-old history, the church has faced and dealt with major challenges, more or less successfully. The new millennium, however, presents five that are unprecedented.

Ecumenical movement

A concerted effort to reunite the churches (the ecumenical movement) began early in the last century, but the Roman Catholic Church remained aloof from it. It stood firm in its belief that it was the one true church, and that the others who broke away must return.

The Second Vatican Council changed this attitude. It no longer simply identified the one true church with the Roman Catholic Church, but recognized other Christians as true sisters and brothers. The council also avowed that a divided church of Christ is not a credible witness to the Jesus who prayed that all his followers be one 'so that the world may believe'. It admitted the church's own guilt for the divisions which plague Christianity and committed Catholicism to ecumenism. It vowed not to rest until the complete visible unity of the church was restored.

Sin Grace
Salvation

Vatican II energized the ecumenical movement. At that time, knowledgeable observers predicted that Christian unity might be reached within a generation. That optimism was defeated by mass inertia, and by fear and lack of imagination on the part of leaders in most churches. Now observers wonder if the moment of opportunity for ecumenism has passed, and whether a sense of hope and urgency can ever be regained.

Meanwhile, Catholics worldwide, women and men, are arguing for and demanding more prominent roles for women in the church. Why not, they ask, women priests and bishops in the Roman Catholic Church, as in other churches? The Vatican put forward its own reasons for restricting ordination to men in 1978. In 1994 John Paul II declared that the church has no authority whatsoever to confer ordination on women. But these initiatives have not persuaded a critical mass of ordinary Catholics and theologians. The role of women remains a burning issue, and women and men continue to leave the church or mitigate their loyalty because of it.

A third challenge is liberation theology, which emerged after the Council. This was born and promoted among deprived and oppressed Christians in the United States and Latin America, who reacted against a hyper-spiritualized, ethereal interpretation of Jesus' message. The kingdom of God that Jesus proclaimed and embodied, they said, is meant for life here and now, not just some afterlife. God's reign means human life transfigured according to God's will and design. God does not will hunger, poverty, ignorance, oppression and injustice for human beings. So, liberation theology asks, what does the gospel demand in the face of these assaults on human dignity? Not just prayer and individual conversion, but social transformation.

Fearing that liberation theology might reduce Christianity to a social movement or, worse, a version of Marxism disguised as the gospel, the church's leadership has accepted it only tentatively and gingerly. Men known to oppose it have been appointed bishops in Latin America. Yet no religious message that leaves children hungry and the poor powerless can still hope to be credible.

For most of its history, the church has been European. Its teachers have included not only Jesus, but also the Greek philosophers Plato and Aristotle. Its legal and social models have been Roman and Germanic. With the collapse of colonialism after the Second World War and the development of high-speed air travel and satellite communications technology, the church now encounters peoples and cultures in Africa and Asia who are not only unfamiliar with the West's heritage of Greek philosophy, the Reformation, the Enlightenment and the democratic revolutions, but also speak languages which may not even have verbal equivalents for such key Christian terms as sin, grace and redemption. These cultures do, nonetheless, have religious traditions as rich and ancient as Christianity itself.

How can Christians continue to present their claim

that Jesus Christ is the sole saviour of the world, when millions upon millions of people are born, live and die with no knowledge of Jesus whatsoever? How are Christ and the Holy Spirit present in non-Christian religions? To find the ways and means of encounter with these cultures and religions and then to forge the language needed to make dialogue intelligible are two of the most formidable problems facing the Roman Catholic Church – and, indeed, all of Christianity – in the new millennium.

The technologies made possible by genetic research, the transformation of consciousness by computers and the impact of globalization are also phenomena unlike any that the Catholic Church has ever faced before in its history. For most of the history of the West, tradition and stability have been the prized values – and the Catholic Church has offered these in abundance. Now novelty and change seem to be the hallmarks of today's global societies. How can the Roman Catholic Church, shaped by tradition and nurtured in stability, adjust to the new world that it finds itself in?

Faithful Catholics do not know how their church will adapt. But they are confident that it will, not only because of its 2000-year-old track record but also because of Jesus' assurance: 'Look, I am with you always, even to the consummation of the world' (Matthew 28.20).

JON NILSON

📖 Adrian Hastings (ed), *Modern Catholicism. Vatican II and Beyond*, London: SPCK 1991; Richard P. McBrien, *Catholicism*, New York: HarperCollins [2]1994; Peter C. Phan (ed), *The Gift of the Church*, Collegeville: Liturgical Press 2000; Francis A. Sullivan, *The Church We Believe In: One, Holy, Catholic, and Apostolic*, New York: Paulist Press 1988

Roman empire

Christianity was born under the Roman empire, and the nature of that empire had a major impact on the way the new religion developed and the forms it took. The geography, history and social and political structures of the Roman empire all affected how Christianity spread, how its doctrines were formed, and how its institutions developed. The expression 'the Roman empire' is used to refer to two distinct, but related things: the territory controlled by the city of Rome, which was mostly acquired in the last two and a half centuries BCE, and the autocratic system of government that was created to administer this territory, which came into being in the last few decades BCE, and lasted until the fifth century CE in the western part of the empire, and, with considerable modifications, until 1453 in the east.

Growth

Roman expansion into the Mediterranean world was the result of conflict with the other major imperial powers of the region: first the Carthaginians, and then the Hellenistic rulers of the eastern Mediterranean. By the middle of the first century CE Roman power reached as far east as the river Euphrates. The eastern territories they now governed, including Palestine, had been under the control of Graeco-Macedonian monarchs since they were conquered by Alexander the Great in the late fourth century CE. Before that they had been part of the Persian empire founded by Darius I (died 486 BCE). The Romans largely took over the existing political organization, and Greek remained the language of administration, and the language generally spoken by the inhabitants of the cities of this part of the empire. Greek ideas were influential on their Roman rulers, and the second century CE saw a flowering of Greek literature and culture, sponsored by emperors such as Hadrian (117–38) and Marcus Aurelius (161–80).

By the time of the birth of Jesus, territory under Roman control stretched from the Atlantic to the Euphrates, and from the Rhine and Danube rivers to the edges of the Sahara. This empire had been gained in a haphazard way: large territories such as Gaul (roughly modern France), conquered in the 50s BCE, had been incorporated into the empire as a result of the actions of individual military commanders, acting with minimal central control. The Roman system of government, designed for running a city-state, was not well equipped to control such a vast territory, and after a series of civil wars, the republican system of government was effectively replaced by an autocracy. The first Roman emperor (this is the word generally used nowadays, although there was no formal title for the post), Augustus, gained sole power after defeating his rival Mark Antony at the battle of Actium in 31 BCE. In 27 BCE his position was formalized, and most importantly, the Roman senate gave Augustus command over the territories of the empire, and hence of its army, for five years initially, but effectively for the rest of his life. After his death, these same powers were granted to his heir, Tiberius (14–37), and this created a pattern of the emperor choosing an heir, often by adoption, who was formally given his powers by the senate.

Although the emperor had other responsibilities, it was his military role that was most important. Emperors stood or fell on the basis of their military ability: in the mid-third century, when pressures on the frontiers of the empire grew particularly strong, there was a rapid turn-over of emperors until a new order emerged under Diocletian (284–305). At the same time, military achievements could enhance the standing of an emperor, and there was therefore a continuing desire among emperors

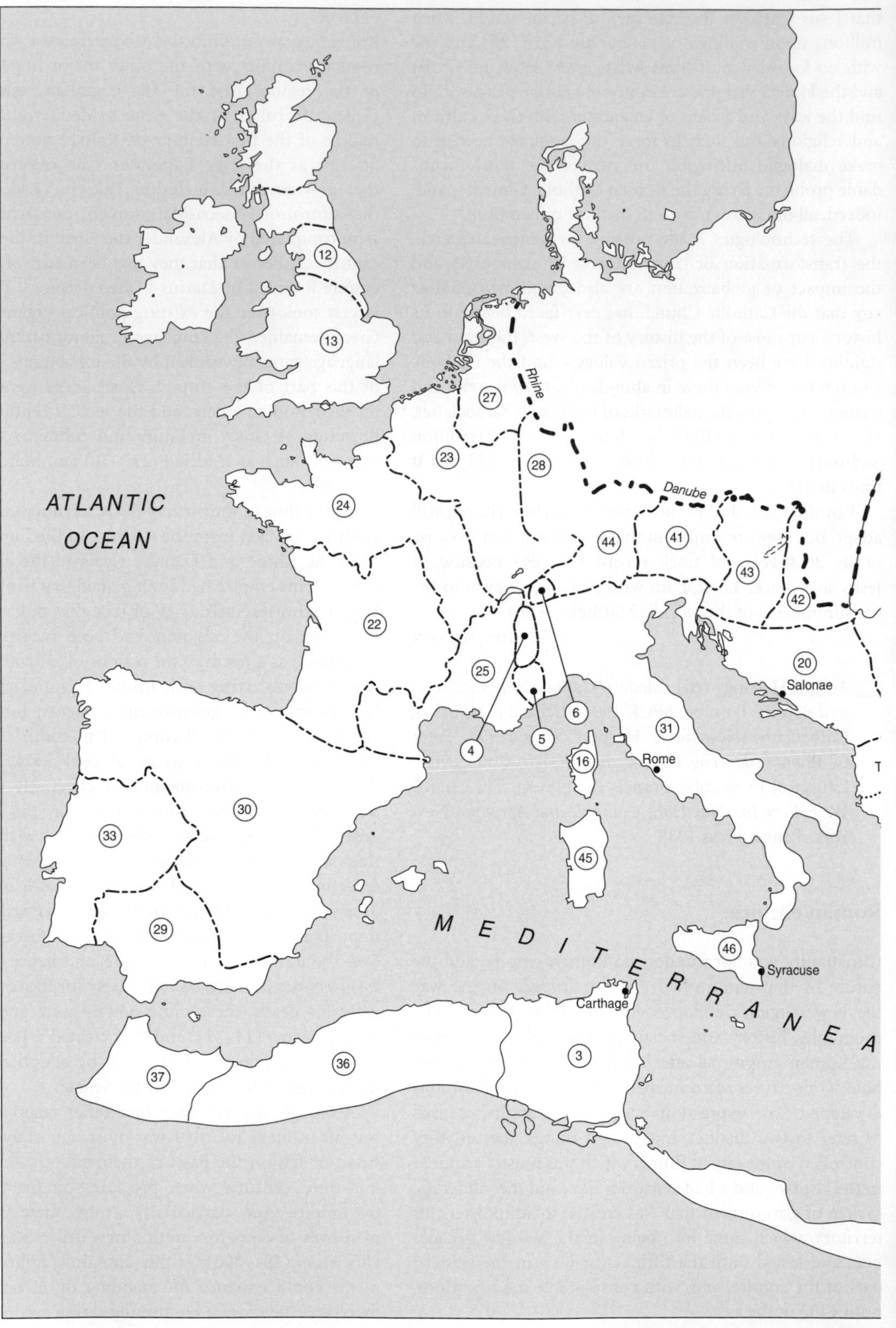
ATLANTIC
OCEAN
MEDITERRANEA
Rhine
Danube
Salonae
Rome
Syracuse
Carthage
12
13
27
23
28
24
44
41
43
42
22
25
20
6
4
5
31
16
30
33
45
29
46
37
36
3

The Roman empire in 116 CE
Under Trajan, by 116 the Roman empire had reached its greatest extent. It comprised the provinces listed below (Crete and Cyrenaica were combined as a single province). The new provinces of Armenia, Assyria and Mesopotamia were abandoned very soon afterwards, by Hadrian.
1 Achaea
2 Aegyptus
3 Africa
4 Alpes Cottiae
5 Alpes Maritimae
6 Alpes Penninae
7 Arabia Petraea
8 Armenia
9 Asia
10 Assyria
11 Bithynia and Pontus
12 Britannia Inferior
13 Britannia Superior
14 Cappadocia
15 Cilicia
16 Corsica
17a Creta
17b Cyrenaica
18 Cyprus
19 Dacia
20 Dalmatia
21 Epirus
22 Gallia Aquitania
23 Gallia Belgica
24 Gallia Lugdunensis
25 Gallia Narbonensis
26 Galatia
27 Germania Inferior
28 Germania Superior
29 Hispania Baetica
30 Hispania Tarraconensis
31 Italia
32 Judaea
33 Lusitania
34 Lycia and Pamphylia
35 Macedonia
36 Mauretania Caesariensis
37 Mauretania Tingitana
38 Mesopotamia
39 Moesia Inferior
40 Moesia Superior
41 Noricum
42 Pannonia inferior
43 Pannonia superior
44 Raetia
45 Sardinia
46 Sicilia
47 Syria
48 Thracia
CASPIAN SEA
BLACK SEA
Nicomedia
Thessalonica
Ephesus
Athens
Antioch
Euphrates
N SEA
Cyrene
Alexandria
Nile
RED SEA

ROMAN EMPERORS

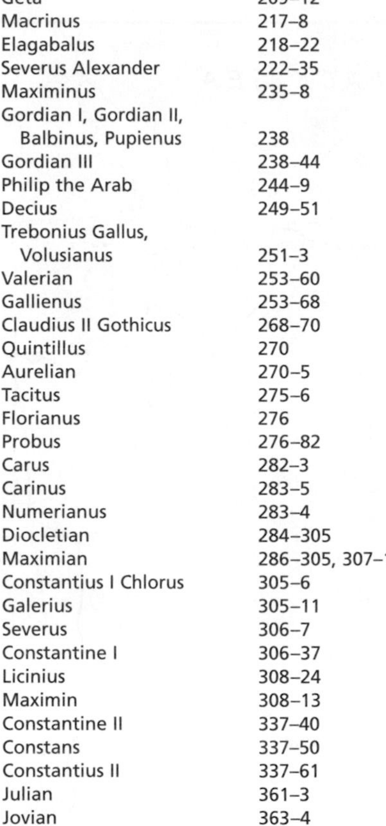

Augustus	27 BCE–14 CE
Tiberius	14–37
Gaius (Caligula)	37–41
Claudius	41–54
Nero	54–68
Galba	68–9
Otho, Vitellius	69
Vespasian	69–79
Titus	79–81
Domitian	81–96
Nerva	96–8
Trajan	98–117
Hadrian	117–38
Antoninus Pius	138–61
Marcus Aurelius	161–80
Lucius Verus	161–9
Commodus	178–93
Pertinax, Didius Julianus	193
Septimius Severus	193–211
Caracalla	198–217
Geta	209–12
Macrinus	217–8
Elagabalus	218–22
Severus Alexander	222–35
Maximinus	235–8
Gordian I, Gordian II, Balbinus, Pupienus	238
Gordian III	238–44
Philip the Arab	244–9
Decius	249–51
Trebonius Gallus, Volusianus	251–3
Valerian	253–60
Gallienus	253–68
Claudius II Gothicus	268–70
Quintillus	270
Aurelian	270–5
Tacitus	275–6
Florianus	276
Probus	276–82
Carus	282–3
Carinus	283–5
Numerianus	283–4
Diocletian	284–305
Maximian	286–305, 307–10
Constantius I Chlorus	305–6
Galerius	305–11
Severus	306–7
Constantine I	306–37
Licinius	308–24
Maximin	308–13
Constantine II	337–40
Constans	337–50
Constantius II	337–61
Julian	361–3
Jovian	363–4
Valentinian I	364–75
Valens	364–78
Gratian	367–83
Valentinian II	375–92
Theodosius I	379–95

WEST		*EAST*	
Honorius	393–423	Arcadius	383–408
Valentinian III	425–55	Theodosius II	408–450
Avitus	455–7	Marcian	450–7
Majorian	457–61	Leo I	457–74
Libius Severus	461–5	Zeno	474–91
Anthemius	467–72	Anastasius	491–518
Glycerius	473–4	Justin I	518–27
Nepos	474–5	Justinian	527–65
Romulus Augustulus	475–6	Justin II	565–78
		Tiberius II	578–82
		Maurice	582–602
		Phocas	602–10
		Heraclius	610–41

Christianity was born in the Roman empire, and in its first five centuries the vast majority of Christians lived in territories ruled by the Roman emperor. At its height, under Trajan, this territory stretched from the Atlantic to the Persian Gulf, and from the Sahara almost to Scotland. The absolute power of the emperor was expressed by the presence of his image visible throughout the empire, above all on coins. When Jesus was asked about whether it was right to pay taxes he illustrated his response with a coin, telling the Pharisees to 'give to Caesar what is Caesar's' (Matthew 22.21).

While Christians were constantly aware of the presence of the emperor, it is less clear that the emperors took much notice of them. There was a brief episode of persecution under Nero, and we have correspondence between Trajan and one of his governors, Pliny, about the punishment of Christians. Decius required all the inhabitants of the empire to sacrifice to the gods, and those Christians who refused to do so were severely punished. There was a further episode of persecution under Diocletian and Galerius, before Licinius and Constantine introduced a policy of religious toleration. For the rest of the time, until the reign of Constantine II, Christianity appears to have been ignored. From then on all the emperors were Christian, with the exception of Julian, whose brief reign saw an attempt to reintroduce the previous cults of the empire. Under Theodosius I non-Christian religious practices were effectively brought to an end.

Marcus Aurelius was the first emperor formally to rule with a co-emperor, a practice that grew more frequent. The principle of co-rulership became formalized in the reign of Diocletian, and from then on it was usual for different emperors to take responsibility for different parts of the empire. Until the end of the fourth century the way the empire was divided varied, but after the death of Theodosius I it was effectively split in two. After this the eastern emperors, ruling from Constantinople, tended to dominate. In the fifth century they imposed some of the emperors on the west, and in the sixth century under Justinian took back control of parts of Italy and North Africa.

The last western emperor was deposed in 476. The rise of Islam in the early seventh century led to the rapid shrinking of the territory controlled by the eastern emperors. Heraclius' successors ruled Constantinople until its final fall in 1453, but they had less and less of an empire to govern.

to extend the empire. Most of Britain was brought under Roman control in the first century CE and remained so until the fifth; Dacia (roughly modern Romania) was conquered early in the second century, but lost in the third. Mesopotamia was briefly added to the empire under Trajan (98–117), but given up by his successor Hadrian.

Transformation

There was no clear distinction between civilian and military power in the Roman empire. Up until the middle of the third century CE legionary commanders and the imperial legates who led campaigns were normally senators. In the second half of that century senators played less and less of a role in the administration of the empire, returning to their primary function as the city councillors of Rome itself. Under the new system of government, fully developed in the reigns of Diocletian and Constantine (306–37), and sometimes referred to as the 'Later Roman empire', the emperor was no longer granted powers by the senate but claimed them directly from the gods, or God. Imperial power was shared between a number of emperors, and the cities which they made their bases, including Milan and Trier in the West and Constantinople and Antioch in the East, developed imperial courts with elaborate protocols and hierarchies with their roots more in the army camp than the emperor's house on the Palatine in Rome.

The fourth century CE saw the reigns of a series of influential emperors including Constantine, Constantius II (337–61) and Theodosius I (379–95), ruling some of the time with others, some of the time alone, but after Theodosius' death there were always two emperors, and a division gradually grew up between the western and eastern halves of the empire. In the West the Romans relied increasingly on 'barbarian' troops, Goths and Huns

among others – and responsibility for military affairs was increasingly put into the hands their leaders. In 476 the Hunnic leader Odoacer deposed the emperor Romulus Augustulus, and this event is taken to mark the end of the Roman empire in the West. In truth, since most aspects of life continued regardless of who was actually in power, the absence of an emperor made remarkably little difference. Meanwhile in the East, the empire continued for a further Byzantium 1000 years as what is generally referred to as Byzantium.

Administration

Despite its size, the empire was governed by a very small number of officials. Even after the reforms of Diocletian and Constantine, which historians have seen as creating a much more 'bureaucratic' state, there were far fewer centrally appointed officials than in any modern system of administration. Before the mid-third century there were fewer still. Each province had a governor, usually drawn from the senate, and a financial official. The governor was the ultimate judicial authority within the province, and in less settled areas he might also have legions of soldiers serving under him. Throughout the empire there were also imperial procurators, men employed by the emperor to look after his property. The smooth functioning of the empire required the co-operation of the local communities, and above all their leaders. In some places the local ruler might continue to govern as a 'client king', as Herod Antipas did in his small territory, called the Tetrarchy, which included Galilee. In the eastern part of the empire city councils set up under the Hellenistic kings carried on their administration, and similar organizations were set up in the west. In some cities the priest of the city's principal temple would also be the chief magistrate. Jerusalem, which was administered by the chief priest and the council of the Sanhedrin, was not untypical in this respect. Roman officials usually intervened only p. 662 when serious problems arose. Jesus' trial and crucifixion were conducted by the Roman procurator, Pontius Pilate, because the city authorities in Jerusalem did not have the power to execute wrongdoers.

To the inhabitants of the provinces the Romans might appear as unwelcome occupiers, but more commonly they were seen as guarantors of order. Appeals against injustices could be made to the governor, or beyond to the emperor himself, either through the governor or an imperial procu- Paul rator. Paul famously appealed to Caesar after he had been arrested in Jerusalem, although it is not clear how typical his position was.

Taxation

The provinces paid tribute to Rome, and this was a cause of tension. The task of collecting tribute was contracted out to 'tax farmers', who would usually subcontract the task to local tax collectors. The frequent coupling of tax collectors (that is the men at the bottom of the administrative pyramid who actually collected the money from taxpayers) with sinners in the Gospels is probably a fair indication of their unpopularity throughout the empire. This system meant that a relatively small proportion of the money paid by the inhabitants of the empire actually reached the Roman treasury, since much was kept by the men through whom the money passed on its way up the collecting chain. Pressure to increase imperial revenues led to increased pressure on the taxpayers, and increased resentment. Jesus was accused of opposing the payment of taxes (Luke 23.2), although elsewhere he is presented as saying the opposite (e.g. Luke 20.25). Paul advises the Christians in Rome to pay their taxes. Much of the money collected in the end found its way back to the provinces as pay for the soldiers there. Coinage, mainly bronze and silver, was used more for these official transactions than for day-to-day trading, which worked more on exchange. At the same time the coins, with the head of the emperor on one side and a design and a slogan on the other, were used to transmit images of the emperor and his achievements across the empire.

Social hierarchy

The society of the Roman empire was very stratified. There was a fundamental division between slaves and freemen, but also between Roman citizens and non-citizens. Roman citizenship had been extended throughout Italy by the time of Augustus, and in the first centuries CE it was granted to increasing numbers of inhabitants of the provinces, either on an individual basis or to whole communities. Roman citizens in the provinces had higher status than their fellow inhabitants, and were in theory at least entitled to better treatment by the Roman authorities. For the rich, citizenship also opened up the possibility of a political career in Rome itself. However, as citizenship was spread more widely through the provinces its value declined. In 212 CE the emperor Caracalla granted citizenship to almost all inhabitants of the empire, and by this time differences in wealth had become the most important indicators of rank. Most of the inhabitants of the empire were categorized as *humiliores*, the poor, in contrast to the *honestiores*, the better-off; to be poor was to be excluded from much of the protection of the law. The better-off included legionary soldiers and those who were rich enough to hold public office, whether as city councillors or as members of the equestrian order, which was made up of rich landowners, some of them in the lower ranks of imperial service. At the top of the social hierarchy sat the senators, between 600 and 1000 men who governed the empire on behalf of the emperor. Although these social divisions were emphasized in various ways – decorations on clothing, reserved seating in theatres and circuses – they were permeable. It was possible for individuals to move rapidly up the social ladder, and in the second and third centuries very few generations might separate a peasant farmer or even a slave from a senator. The fastest route for social advancement was the army.

The Roman army

Before the time of Augustus Rome had no standing army. The armies that conquered the Mediterranean were conscripted each time a campaign was begun, and then disbanded at its end. The combination of wars of expansion and civil wars in the first century BCE meant that there was no shortage of work for those who wanted to be soldiers, but it was only when Augustus and his successors were given permanent responsibility for all military campaigns that Rome ended up with a permanent standing army, and military service became a professional career. In theory only Roman citizens could serve in the legions – non-citizens served as auxiliaries, and were given citizenship on retirement – but for poor citizens it promised an increase in status. By the middle of the second century a peasant farmer who enlisted as a private soldier and rose to the non-commissioned rank of centurion would retire after 25 years' service with equestrian status and the possibility of further advancement after that.

Religion

Religion was in many ways fundamental to the thinking of the Roman empire. Most of the inhabitants of the empire were polytheistic. They worshipped a large number of gods: some local, and some with wider powers. Each community had its own gods, so that, for example, there was not one pantheon of Greek gods worshipped by all the inhabitants of the province of Achaea (roughly modern Greece), but every city – and some were little more than villages – had its own set of gods, with their own temples and festivals. Some cults had wider recognition – Olympian Zeus, at whose sanctuary in the Peloponnese the Olympic Games took place, received worshippers from all over the Greek world – but in general each city chose which gods it felt it was worthwhile to worship. The Romans attributed their success in war to the support of their own gods, and this was acknowledged by the communities they conquered, which often adopted some of the cults of their conquerors. This religious system is often referred to as 'paganism': the term 'pagan' – literally 'country-dweller' – was used after Christianity had become dominant in the empire to describe the rural poor who had not become Christian. However, the non-Christian inhabitants of the empire would never have considered themselves as having a particular 'religion': their religious identity was totally bound up with their political identity. To call oneself a Roman or an Athenian was as much a statement about religion as it was about politics or geography.

Although the Romans had their own gods, they were prepared under certain conditions to accept new gods and new practices, for example mystery cults, in particular those from the Greek world. From the eighth century BCE Greek communities had honoured their founders – historical as well as mythical – as heroes, and made sacrifices to them. Such honours were very occasionally extended to living men, and from the third century BCE Greek cities had frequently worshipped their living Hellenistic rulers as gods, setting up festivals and priesthoods to them. Such practices have been criticized as signs of decadence or dismissed as empty flattery, but that is a misunderstanding. Worship of a ruler, like the worship of a god, is in part a way of acknowledging the vast difference in power between the worshipper and the object of worship, and the dependence of the one or the other. The Hellenistic kings, with their armies, were far more powerful than any single community.

Mystery cults

As the Romans became involved in Greek affairs in the second century BCE, Roman generals were also offered divine honours of various kinds. When he emerged victorious at the end of the civil wars Augustus was careful to control this practice, although he did not discourage it, allowing non-citizens to worship him, but not citizens. In the western parts of the empire, in centres like Lyons and Cologne, he actually encouraged the erection of altars in his honour, and regular festivals. The imperial cult, as it is often known, spread rapidly throughout the empire. Being a priest of the imperial cult was a source of prestige. In a few places the cult did cause problems: in Judaea attempts by the Emperor Caligula (37–41) to have a statue to himself erected in the Jerusalem temple were bitterly resented, and in Britain the temple of Claudius (41–54) at Colchester was the first target of the revolt of Boudicca in 60 CE.

In Italy itself temples were not erected to living emperors in the first two centuries CE. Roman religion was under the authority of the senate, which included in its membership all the members of the major priestly colleges. The emperors maintained the notion that they were also members of the senate, so could hardly be worshipped in Rome. Dead emperors might be considered as gods, however, and living emperors were always at the centre of Rome's religious life. Augustus was elected to the position of Pontifex Maximus (chief priest) in 12 BCE, and this post was inherited by his successors. The emperor was also a member of all the priestly colleges of Rome, so that he had a role in all major religious activities. Several temples were even incorporated into the imperial palace, blurring the distinction between public religion and the emperor's religious position. Prayers for the health of the

Paganism

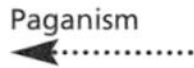

emperor were an important feature of all religious rituals, and it is clear that although formally he did not receive worship, even in Rome he was treated as a divine figure.

In the second half of the third century, as the emperor became less and less associated with the city of Rome, so his religious image also changed. Cults associated with the person of the emperor became more prominent, and in particular the cult of *Sol Invictus*, the Unconquered Sun. The sun, like the emperor, looked down on all the empire alike, and brought health and prosperity to all. It was therefore an appropriate cult for the emperors, who often depicted themselves on coins surrounded by the rays of the sun.

Judaism and Christianity

The one area of the empire where religion operated differently was Judaea, where the Jews were not expected to pay cult to the emperor, although they did pray for his health. Jewish monotheism, especially with its absence of an impressive cult statue, was apparently looked down on as a rather poor religion. Christianity in its early days resembled Judaism, although elements of the vocabulary and imagery of the imperial cult were applied to Jesus in early Christian writings.

Origins and background

Persecution

Although the Romans have a reputation for persecuting Christians, Christianity was generally tolerated, or more commonly ignored altogether. Christians were blamed for the burning of Rome in 64 CE, and were punished by the Emperor Decius in 251 if they refused to offer sacrifice to the gods at a time of crisis. A further period of persecution occurred in the early fourth century. Between these times, however, persecution was rare, and the presence of Christians in the Roman army and in other parts of the administration of the empire suggests that little notice was taken of the religious practices of most Romans most of the time.

Constantine's 'conversion'

The conversion of Constantine marks the beginning of the transformation of the empire into a Christian organization, although it took many decades for Christianity to become completely dominant. The last non-Christian emperor was Julian (361–3). The already existing association of the emperor with one particular god, *Sol Invictus*, made the transition from 'paganism' to Christianity in some ways almost imperceptible.

Influences

It is a commonplace that the *Pax Romana*, the peace brought to the Mediterranean world by Roman rule, was one of the factors that allowed Christianity to grow and spread in its earliest years. It is also true that the power structures of the empire had a profound effect on the development of church hierarchy, especially from the time of Constantine. Christianity also took other things from the Roman empire. The ideas of Greek philosophers became part of Roman aristocratic values, and then of Christian thought. Along with traded goods Christianity spread beyond the frontiers of the empire to the north and the east. Centuries after the end of the last Roman emperor in the west, when Islam was becoming the dominant religion of the Mediterranean, the Latin language and Roman civic institutions continued to underpin the society of Western Europe.

HUGH BOWDEN

Cambridge Ancient History, Vols 10–13, Cambridge: CUP 1995–8; Averil Cameron, *The Later Roman Empire*, London: HarperCollins and Cambridge, MA: Harvard University Press 1993; Martin Goodman, *The Roman World 44 BC–AD 180*, London and New York: Routledge 1997

Romanticism

Romanticism is not known primarily for its connection with Christianity; it is seen more as a movement that charted the development of philosophy, the arts and social revolution. However, perceptions of Christianity are always affected by currents in society and by the works of philosophical commentators. Romanticism manifested itself first in a challenge to eighteenth-century establishment values, and then through the artistic endeavours of poets, architects, painters and composers; both these influences posed important challenges to Christianity. For some the romantic movement meant a return to forgotten values of the past; for others the writing of hymns and the outpouring of oratory; and for yet others a visionary concern for the future. For all it meant coming to terms with a post-revolutionary society, particularly in France and America, with radical changes of outlook and a reassessment of the place of Christianity at the beginning of a 'modern' world.

One major difficulty with cultural definitions is that they tend to run after the realities they are describing. 'Romanticism' happened in a variety of ways un-named, if one can put it like that. Only later did cultural historians, for clarity's sake, label a cluster of ideas, or a group of like-minded poets, by that term. To go to the dictionary is to read 'romanticism' in retrospect. It is unlikely that William Wordsworth (1770–1850), Samuel Taylor Coleridge (1772–1834) or Johann Wolfgang von Goethe (1749–1832) acknowledged themselves as 'romantics' at the time. The pre-Raphaelites, however, self-consciously painted in a particular way to renew the ancient styles; Gothic architects were self-styled copiers of their medieval forebears and named themselves accordingly.

Many of the writers whom we now call 'romantics' did feel that they were doing something new. Wordsworth writing the *Lyrical Ballads* (1798) set out his philosophy to speak of the ordinary and humble characteristics of Cumberland life. Coleridge assisted him in that, writing poems 'directed to persons and characters supernatural or at least romantic', but the idea that that they were creating a 'romantic movement' as such would have been strange to them. 'Romantic' was a word Coleridge used in his poem *Kubla Khan* (published 1816) to describe 'the deep ... chasm which slanted down the green hill athwart a cedarn cover!', but not usually as a term that denoted a movement in which he was personally involved.

Romanticism is therefore an essay in looking backwards, a way of interpreting a variety of books, ideas and personalities that were proposing similar thoughts and styles. The period that the movement is usually meant to cover is *c.* 1780–*c.* 1820, but with music it covered the later period of *c.* 1820–*c.* 1860. There was also what may be called a second-generation romanticism between *c.* 1840–*c.* 1890.

'Romance' is the vernacular language of France, as opposed to Latin, that in later usage was extended to related forms of speech such as Provençal and Spanish. However, it is the popularity of tales in verse in the 'romance' language embodying the adventures of some hero of chivalry that links the medieval use of the word with later conceptions of the 'romantic'. It was in the middle of the seventeenth century that the idea of a project being fantastic, extravagant, quixotic, going beyond what is customary or practical, hints at the use of the word in what we might call the high period of romanticism as a cultural form between 1780 and 1820. In 1671 Sir William Thompson talked of the romantic and visionary scheme of building a bridge over the river at Putney, and Samuel Pepys in 1666 used the word romantic as meaning invested with imaginative appeal. These seventeenth-century usages are a reminder that the romantic movement had its seeds in the Enlightenment movement of the seventeenth and eighteenth centuries. The latter was above all a movement that sought to emancipate humankind, regardless of political frontiers, from the triple tyranny of despotism, bigotry and superstition.

Most particularly, the term 'romantic' became attached to the movement in literature and art that set itself against the classicism of the eighteenth century, a dichotomy that Ralph Waldo Emerson (1803–82) denied in 1841 when he wrote that 'the vaunted distinction between classic and romantic schools seems superficial and pedantic'. Emerson, born in Boston, Massachusetts, was a man of strong religious and spiritual tendencies, and in 1833 he visited England, meeting Coleridge and Wordsworth, who were seminal characters in the English romantic movement.

The first use in English of the word 'romanticism' meaning 'the distinctive qualities or spirit of the romantic school in art, literature and music' was in 1844, and it was used of the music of Franz Liszt (1811–86). The romantic movement as such had got under way long before 1844, but music, it seems, was a late starter, picking up the 'romantic' momentum in the middle of the nineteenth century. Liszt was a virtuoso pianist, flamboyant in style and taste, the friend of Hector Berlioz and Frederic Chopin. He was the noblest and most powerful champion of Richard Wagner, who was perhaps in musical terms the finest example of German romanticism. It was in Germany that many of the ideas of romanticism began: in philosophy with the writings of Friedrich von Schlegel (1772–1829), the idealism of Immanuel Kant (1724–1804) and the works of Johann Wolfgang von Goethe (1749–1832), particularly *The Sorrows of Young Werther* (first published 1774).

Music

Not long after that first use of the word 'romanticism', a second in 1856 refers to German romanticism in a book on mysticism. Romanticism therefore seems to be the word that is used to convey the ideas, thought forms and lifestyle of those involved in the romantic movement. Romanticism is a way of knowing, of coming at the truth, and the particular way the romantics came at the truth was by way of the feelings, or of intuition. That is not to say that they lacked a rigorous intellectual streak, but they took bold chances. They risked reputations, they shocked, they were concerned with 'the new', and that often put them outside conventional and ordered patterns of society. In the long view of cultural trends, romanticism often follows a period of stable classicism. The one reacted against the other, the one needed the other. The romantics of the late eighteenth and early nineteenth centuries were reacting against a century of comparative stability.

Mysticism

It is the European romantic movement of the early nineteenth century that has given cultural historians the most material for theorizing. It is recognized as a major movement, and the term romanticism has been found by historians to be both indispensable and embarrassing, but they cannot do without it. Something is needed to distinguish Wordsworth's 'Ode, Intimations of Immortality' (1805) from Alexander Pope's 'Essay on Criticism' (1711). The same might be said of the need for a distinction between the philosophers Edmund Burke (1727–97) and Jean-Jacques Rousseau (1712–78), or in the theological world between Charles Kingsley (1819–75) and John Henry Newman (1801–90) or William Paley (1743–1805) and Samuel Taylor Coleridge (1772–1834). There is a shift of sensibility. Something new is happening.

First stirrings

The defining moments of the beginning of romanticism were events as disparate as the French Revolution of

1789 and Wordsworth hearing the River Derwent and realizing it was turning into poetry in his inner being. The American War of Independence of 1775–6 signalled the first stirrings of the worldwide spirit of revolution that was to galvanize the romantic age. It was a change conceived as fully compatible with the rationalist and Enlightenment common-sense principles of the Enlightenment, and was significantly less radical than the French Revolution.

Rousseau attracted attention at an early stage by the works in which he expounded his revolt against the existing social order. The first of these was a *Discourse on the Influence of Learning and of Art* (1750), and *Émile*, his views on education, in 1762. Instead of attending to the doctrines of the philosophers, he wrote, we should listen to our own intuitions, which tell us that there is a benevolent divine spirit who rewards virtue and punishes crime, and that the human soul is free and immortal.

Since the revolutionary spirit was essentially a reaction to what is perceived as order and reasonableness, tradition, hierarchy and organization, the eighteenth-century church was hardly in a state to contain the revolutionary spirit. The romantics experienced the divine as a living force and did so as a direct result of freeing themselves from the moral codes of the established church. The atheism of Shelley (1792–1822), the sexual liberation of Byron (1788–1824), the mystical radicalism of Blake (1757–1827) and the incipient pantheism of Wordsworth all left traditional Anglicanism and faithful church-going well alone. Growing numbers of 'Dissenters' became the backbone of radical political and social movements of renewal. Earlier Methodism in the eighteenth century the Methodist movement was a revolution of the Spirit, and could in some ways be seen as 'romantic'. Acts of individual heroism, freedom to worship wherever and whenever the Spirit moved, the outpouring of poetry and oratory, a radical overhaul of attitudes to society, especially in a concern for the poor and for slaves, were all echoing a wider movement in society for freedom of the individual spirit.

It was Samuel Taylor Coleridge who did most in this period to bridge the gap between a romantic culture and a serious theological critique. His knowledge of German theology and philosophy, the influence of the pantheism of Jakob Boehme and Benedict de Spinoza, and his sympathy with the Anglican divines of the seventeenth century, Bishop Jeremy Taylor in particular, made him a great apologist for the integration of romanticism and Christianity. His placing of the imagination as an important part of the fabric of belief was the bridging concept. He preached the human need for a spiritual interpretation of life and the universe against a fossilized Protestant orthodoxy as well as against the materialistic and rationalist trends of his time. His ideas were propagated as much in his poems, notebooks and conversation as anywhere else. However, his book *Aids to Reflection in the Formation of a Manly Character on the Several Grounds of Prudence, Morality, and Religion* (1825) through responses and glosses on the works of Archbishop Leighton (1611–84), Archbishop of Glasgow, and Bishop Jeremy Taylor, was at pains to show the validity of religious belief within the context of early nineteenth-century scientific thought. He believed passionately that the two could co-exist. Coleridge wanted his readers to reject the scepticism of the Enlightenment. But he urged that calm and serious reflection on man's place in nature led logically to a belief in the divine that was wholly compatible with scientific rationalism.

The imagination, distinguished from something altogether more lightweight, 'the fancy', was the mental faculty that in Coleridge's understanding absorbed the whole of a person and created new thoughts, new relationships, new connections with the things of God. He studied the German idealists Immanuel Kant, Johann Gottlieb Fichte (1762–1814) and Friedrich Wilhelm Josef von Schelling (1775–1854), and found in them a way of uniting the imagination and the reason. Poetic truth, or insights gained by the poetic imagination, held their own with those truths that had been the sole result of reasoning.

Feelings

Friedrich Schleiermacher, in his *Speeches on Religion* (1799), maintained that religion has its origin not in scientific thought, nor in morality, but in the feeling of absolute dependence upon God. Early in his career Schelling identified religion and art. G. W. F. Hegel described Christianity as a religion of images whose content could not be superseded, but whose proper form was the evolving philosophical idea. Emerson reformulated Christian experience into an American religion of nature, a sense of supreme beauty that ravishes the soul. If Emerson could see sermons not only in stones but also in 'mud puddles on Boston Common', Horace Bushnell (1802–76), an American Congregationalist divine, viewed religious nurture as a way to invoke innate Christian goodness through a process of naturation. He believed that the appropriate mode of religious education was in symbolic, organic and literary language.

One of the main characteristics of romanticism which transcended disparate centuries and individuals was an interest in the past as a way of revitalizing the future. This took various forms from a safeguarding of orthodoxy, a model for heroism, and what Stephen Heppell called a 'criterion for determining truthful faith in the authentic human subject'. This was a call for personal experience, or religious experience, to take precedence over doctrines, and the biblical as the foundation upon which human life was based. At one end of the spectrum it was a movement to regain the place of the saints as models of human aspiration, and the whole Catholic apparatus of monasticism, prayers for the departed, and the return to Gothic forms of architecture. At the other end of the spectrum was a creative vision disclosing a religious transcendence ambiguously unacquainted with Christianity. It was to nature that people went for inspiration. Wordsworth became the high priest of the romantic movement, finding in the beauties of the natural world, hills, lakes, flowers, mountains and the affecting simplicity of human nature untainted by the urban scene (*The Solitary Reaper,* 1803) a way into a deeper truth than ever Christianity could furnish. This was a religion of wonder and feeling. It laid claim to truths which children and the simple might discover, but which were hidden to those who laid claim to reason alone.

The second phase

The romantic period produced some distinct works of art. William Blake was trained as an engraver but evolved into a mystic, philosopher and priest, compelled to set his visions before the world. They took the form of epic quasi-biblical dramas of spiritual redemption, addressed above all to his own nation, of whose contemporary condition he offered a robust critique. He increasingly eschewed conventional media and published his own 'Prophetic Books', written and illuminated himself by processes of colour printing. Much of his work had strong biblical connections, especially his *Illustrations to the Book of Job* (1821–5, published 1826), but his mythology stretched far beyond the bounds of Christianity. In 1804 he published his poem *Milton,* the proem of which consists of his famous lines 'Jerusalem'.

A disciple of Blake, Samuel Palmer (1805–81) gathered round himself a group called the 'Ancients' in recognition of their loathing of modern life and art, and retreated to the secluded village of Shoreham in Kent. The Ancients were intensely moved by a set of tiny wood engravings Blake had made to illustrate a school edition of Virgil's *Pastorals* (1820): tender, elegiac, visionary, these struck Palmer with a mystic and dreamy glimmer 'as penetrates the inmost soul ... unlike the gaudy daylight of this world'. Palmer was but one of a number of artists who worked in the romantic tradition. Others were Caspar David Friedrich (1774–1840), who painted the heroism of the isolated individual ('Monk by the Sea', 1809; 'The Cross in the Mountains', 1808); J. M. W. Turner (1775–1851), who sought to harmonize the material and the spiritual worlds ('The Angel Standing in the Sun', 1846) and Benjamin Robert Haydon (1786–1846), who portrayed the issue of doubt and faith, assembling both Voltaire and Wordsworth among the crowd for his painting of 'Christ's Entry into Jerusalem' (1814–20).

With many of these works of art and cultural movements we are looking at what may be called a second-phase romanticism. Certainly this was the case with architecture, where because of the nature of the work, the design and construction of buildings take longer to bring to completion. Architecture in the Gothic revival looked back to the glories of the medieval period, with its soaring arches and its use of space to create a sense of wonder, awe, and mystery. So what J. M. W. Turner saw in the waterfalls of the Alps, A. W. N. Pugin transposed into stone and space. He was the chief inspirer of this revival. Among his numerous works is St Chad's (Roman Catholic) Cathedral, Birmingham (1839–41). He also collaborated with Charles Barry in his designs for the Houses of Parliament. His philosophy emerged in his writings, too, in books such as *A Parallel Between the Noble Edifices of the Fourteenth and Fifteenth Centuries, and Similar Buildings of the Present Day* (1836) and *The True Principles of Pointed or Christian Architecture in England* (1843).

Monasticism
Architecture

A towering figure in this second phase of the romantic movement is John Henry Newman. Newman was a solitary figure, the romantic individualist fighting against the prevailing ethos of his day. Although he began the Oxford Movement with a few friends, particularly Edward Bouverie Pusey (1800–82) and John Keble (1792–1866), through the writing and dissemination of tracts that were instituted to reform the theology and practice of the Church of England, he left that church in 1845 and joined the Roman Catholic Church. This was a great shock for the Church of England, and it had all the hallmarks of a romantic gesture. Newman was concerned, as was Pusey, to restore the priorities of the early church, both its theology and its spiritual practice. Elements of medievalism, such as monastic orders and devotion to the saints, played an important part in his writing and practice and to a large extent this was mirrored in the emergence of the pre-Raphaelite painters and the poetry of John Keats (1795–1821). Deep emotion, strains of melancholy, unrequited love and a fascination with death all reflect the Victorian bent for romanticism.

Oxford Movement

Religious orders
Devotions

The fact that we can isolate individuals within the romantic movement is of the essence of the movement itself. It was a movement of individualists and individualism, and of the artist in isolation; as Rousseau said, 'I am not made as others I have known. But if I am worth less, at least I am different.' The path is lonely to the top of the high mountain.

The twentieth century

Although as a literary and artistic movement romanticism is set in the nineteenth century, elements of romanticism permeate every generation. Frank Kermode, the literary critic, in his book *The Romantic Image* (1957), traces

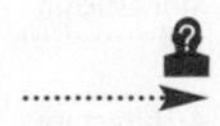

romanticism in the writings of W. B. Yeats (1865–1939). In the Christian tradition, Father Cuthbert, OSFC, a Franciscan Capuchin, wrote a book on *The Romanticism of St Francis* (1915), charting that quintessentially romantic saint's influence on twentieth-century Franciscans. The presence of 'idealists' in the church is a continuing witness to the strength of the romantic way. The renaissance of the community centred on the abbey on Iona under the inspiring leadership of George Macleod (1895–1991) and the rediscovery of an authentic Celtic spirituality within the Church of Scotland can be seen as a romantic adventure.

Celtic Christianity

The 1960s produced an ideological revolution in which theology, morality, music, art and literature underwent a radical change: 'Back to nature', 'Do your own thing', 'How does it feel?', 'Sit-ins', were all underlying romantic themes and strategies. 1960s culture was reacting against the austerity of the war years and the post-war years, which inevitably gave way to a new conservatism. Others would argue that conservatism is romantic, too. The Oxford Movement could be seen as a refusal to accept a new liberalism, and emotionalism in religion often has a right-wing political agenda. It is interesting to note how what is radical in one century and one setting can be conservative in another. With romanticism touching the deep core of what it is to be human, free yet bound, individual yet dependent on community, imaginative yet limited, idealistic yet committed to self-preservation, there will be paradoxes in its practical working out in shifting societies and variable cultures. Yet as an archetype of collective consciousness it is likely to remain a feature of the human experience, and at particular periods to be volcanic in its activity.

Festivals and fasts

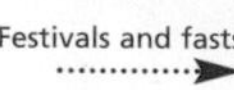

Scholasticism

DAVID SCOTT

Karl Barth, *Protestant Theology in the Nineteenth Century*, London: SCM Press and Atlanta: John Knox Press 1972; James D. Boulger, *Coleridge as a Religious Thinker*, New Haven: Yale University Press 1961; Samuel Taylor Coleridge, *Aids to Reflection* ed Douglas Hedley, Cambridge: CUP 2004; Laura Dabundo (ed), *The Encyclopaedia of Romanticism*, New York: Garland 1992; David Morse, *American Romanticism* (2 vols), London: Palgrave Macmillan and New York: Macmillan 1987

Sacraments

Ritual

In most Christian churches, certain important rituals are referred to as sacraments. The word itself derives from the Latin *sacramentum*, meaning a sacred sign or symbol. In ancient Rome, for example, the initiation ceremony in which a soldier swore allegiance to the emperor was called a *sacramentum*. Around the year 210 CE a Christian apologist named Tertullian, noting the similarity between the military ritual and the ritual of baptism through which Christians swore fidelity to Christ, was the first to use the word in reference to a Christian ceremony.

Until the Middle Ages there was no perceived need to decide which religious symbols and rituals should be designated sacraments. Augustine of Hippo around the year 500 had defined *sacramentum* simply as a sign of something sacred, and under this rubric anything that reminded one of God or signified a sacred mystery could be called a sacrament. Indeed, during Christianity's first millennium, not only baptism but also the liturgy of Easter and the dedication of churches were sometimes referred to as sacraments, as were ritual items such as blessed ashes and holy water. Well into the twelfth century, lists of sacraments compiled by scholastic theologians contained as few as six and as many as 30.

Around 1250, a scholastic theologian named Peter Lombard, at the influential University of Paris, published a four-volume compendium of theological texts and opinions known as *The Book of Sentences*. Lombard's work rapidly became widely used by students of theology, and his list of seven sacraments came to be regarded as standard (some religious practices which had previously been regarded as sacraments came to be known as 'sacramentals'). Sacraments marked the lives of Christians from cradle to grave and, since seven was considered symbolic of wholeness or completeness, this list seemed most appropriate.

The seven were baptism (performed in most cases for infants), confirmation (usually for children), penance (for forgiveness of sins committed after the age of discretion, about seven years old), eucharist (first received in adolescence), matrimony and ordination (a young person's entrance into marriage on the one hand or celibate priesthood on the other), and extreme unction (an anointing received close to death). The principal churches that retain these seven in one form or another are the Roman Catholic Church, the Orthodox churches and some currents within the Anglican Church.

Roman Catholic Church

Orthodox churches

Anglicanism

Unlike many other church ceremonies, these seven were understood to produce spiritual effects, and the scholastic theologians were eager to work out how this happened. Six of the seven were what modern anthropologists call rites of passage, and in the eucharist bread and wine were changed into the body and blood of Christ. All seven were therefore appropriate objects of theological investigation.

The only theoretical concepts available in the Middle Ages were those that had been inherited from the ancient Greek philosopher, Aristotle, whose works had recently been recovered and translated into Latin. Using pairs of terms such as matter and form, substance and accidents, essence and existence, the scholastics analysed what occurred in the various rituals.

The scholastics also inherited solutions to theoretical problems that had been resolved by earlier church practice or by earlier theologians. For example, since the days of the controversy with the Donatists, who argued that sacraments administered by those who had betrayed the church in persecution were invalid, it had been agreed that one could be baptized only once. Augustine had provided a theoretical underpinning for this practice by saying that baptism produced an indelible character on the soul, and his authority ensured that this explanation was readily accepted in the Middle Ages. Likewise, the status of the eucharist as consecrated bread and wine had been resolved during earlier medieval controversies that had dealt with the question of whether they were a sign of Christ's body and blood or were really his body and blood. The theological community agreed that the latter interpretation was correct.

Earlier thinkers had distinguished between the sacramental sign and the spiritual reality that it signified, but the medieval scholastics found it necessary to introduce a third aspect. Augustine had already done so in developing the concept of the baptismal character; the scholastics expanded on this idea and applied it to all seven sacraments. In their analysis, each sacrament had not two but three distinguishable aspects: the visible ritual that was a sign only or *sacramentum tantum*; the invisible reality to which the sign pointed, which was not a sign but a spiritual reality only or *res tantum*; and a third aspect that was both sign and reality, *sacramentum et res*, which mediated between the visible and the invisible, between the sign and what it signified, between the material and the spiritual, between the external ritual and the internal mystery to which it referred. The Latin term *sacramentum et res* is usually translated into English as 'sacramental reality', but it is important to keep in mind that this 'reality' was a hypothetical entity, a theoretical construct introduced to help to explain, in an Aristotelian intellectual framework, how the medieval sacraments produced the effects that they were supposed to produce.

Nevertheless, the *sacramentum et res* was quite real to the scholastics, once the concept became generally accepted in theological schools. Indeed, belief in its reality continues to linger in people who speak about 'receiving the sacraments', or who think that the purpose of attending one of the church rituals named above is to 'receive a sacrament'. The sacrament referred to in these phrases is clearly not the ritual but something else, namely, the sacramental reality postulated in the Aristotelian-scholastic explanation of how these rituals worked.

The *sacramentum et res* of baptism was said to be an indelible character on the soul, but this image presented a problem for medieval metaphysics, which regarded the soul as a purely spiritual entity on which nothing could be written or stamped. The rather material image of a written symbol or character was therefore interpreted to be a spiritual *habitus*, a habit or predisposition to act in a certain way. Through baptism Christians were said to receive the virtues of faith, hope and Christ-like love or charity, and the scholastic theory of three sacramental aspects was able to combine the Augustinian image with this Christian belief to produce an Aristotelian interpretation of what happened when a person was baptized. According to the scholastic theory, certain habits or abilities were bestowed on the soul when the ritual was properly performed. The abilities or powers received through baptism were a sacramental reality that could never be lost – the ability to have faith in the one true God, the ability to hope for glory in heaven, and the ability to love in a Christ-like manner.

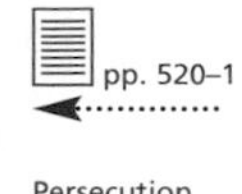
pp. 520–1

Persecution

p. 1068

Similarly, when a person was ordained, he received a set of priestly powers: the ability to turn bread and wine into the body and blood of Christ, the ability to forgive sins in God's name, the ability to prepare the soul of a dying person for heaven, and so on. According to the theory, once these priestly powers were received into the soul, they could never be lost, and this provided a theoretical explanation for the church rule against reordination, for once a soul received the priestly character, repeating the ordination ceremony would be a pointless ritual.

The same theory explained the church's rule against rebaptism, for once a soul received the Christian character, its spiritual powers could not be lost – although, admittedly, they might not be used very much if a baptized person lost faith in God, stopped believing in heaven and hell, and behaved in self-centred and even hateful ways. The theory was therefore extended to confirmation which, like baptism and ordination, could be 'received' only once.

Matrimony was similar to the above sacraments in that one could be married only once, or at least once at a time. Religious and civil tradition spoke about a marriage bond that was created by the wedding ritual, and the scholastics were able to interpret this too as a sacramental reality. Like the characters bestowed by baptism, confirmation and ordination, the marriage bond was permanent, which provided an explanation for the church's prohibition against divorce. Unlike the three sacramental characters, however, the bond was dissolved when one of the spouses died, which explained why widows and widowers were allowed to remarry.

Marriage

Eucharist as well benefited from the theory of the sacramental reality. Since the early Middle Ages, the status of the consecrated bread and wine had been hotly debated. Calling them a symbol of Christ's body and blood seemed to contradict the long-standing tradition of referring to them simply as the body and blood of Christ. At the same time, insisting that they really were what the tradition called them seemed to contradict the senses, for they did not look or taste like flesh and blood. Calling them either a sign or a reality was problematic.

Council

Scholastic sacramental theory came to the rescue with the introduction of the notion of *sacramentum et res*, the concept of something that was both sign and reality. The consecrated eucharistic elements seemed ideally suited to this interpretation. Regarded as a sacramental reality, they could be said to be truly Christ's body and blood, thus preserving the church's liturgical tradition. At the same time, they did not look or taste like flesh and blood, thus allowing them to be perceived as symbols pointing to the spiritual reality of union with Christ. This explained why, when devout Christians received the eucharist, they could experience spiritual communion with their Lord and Saviour.

Scholastic theology had a harder time with penance and extreme unction, for it was difficult to specify a sacramental reality for these sacraments. Nonetheless, the theory of three aspects to each sacrament helped explain the beliefs and practices associated with five of the seven sacraments. The absence of agreement about two of the sacraments gave Catholic theologians something to write and debate about well into the future.

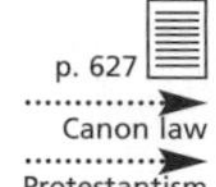

p. 627
Canon law
Protestantism

Medieval sacramentalism was prone to superstition and abuse, and in the late Middle Ages the Catholic sacramental system came under attack as symptomatic of corruption in the church. Eventually known as Protestants, the Reformers lost confidence that the church had preserved the true teaching of Jesus, and so they turned to the Bible for help in determining the number and nature of Christian sacraments. Accepting the scholastic understanding that a sacrament is a church ceremony instituted by Christ, most Protestants rejected five of the medieval seven because they lacked a sufficient scriptural foundation, retaining only baptism and eucharist, more commonly called the Lord's Supper or holy communion.

Initiation

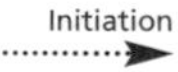

Protestant theologies of these two sacraments ranged from being close to the Catholic understanding to being far from it. Martin Luther's was the closest, with his acceptance of infant baptism and of the real presence of Christ in the eucharist. Huldrych Zwingli's was the most radical in so far as it rejected all sacramental effectiveness and regarded the sacraments as purely symbolic of Christian beliefs and values. Indeed, the so-called radical Reformers (of whom today's Baptists are descendants) rejected even the name 'sacrament', preferring to call the two rituals 'ordinances' because they believed that the scriptures proved that Christ had ordered his followers to perform them.

Anabaptists

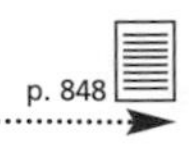

p. 848
Paul

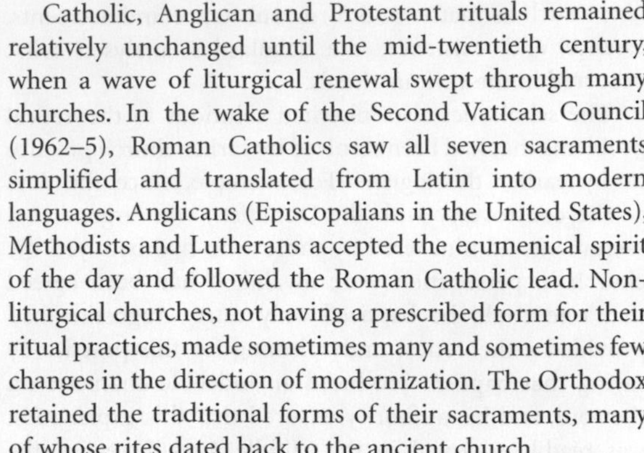

Catholic, Anglican and Protestant rituals remained relatively unchanged until the mid-twentieth century, when a wave of liturgical renewal swept through many churches. In the wake of the Second Vatican Council (1962–5), Roman Catholics saw all seven sacraments simplified and translated from Latin into modern languages. Anglicans (Episcopalians in the United States), Methodists and Lutherans accepted the ecumenical spirit of the day and followed the Roman Catholic lead. Non-liturgical churches, not having a prescribed form for their ritual practices, made sometimes many and sometimes few changes in the direction of modernization. The Orthodox retained the traditional forms of their sacraments, many of whose rites dated back to the ancient church.

Sacramental practices have continued to evolve slowly. Churches in Africa, Asia and Latin America have introduced non-European elements to their liturgical celebrations. In Europe and North America, contemporary music and art have been blended with traditional practices. Lay people, especially women, increasingly join ordained clergy in sacramental ceremonies, and some churches have allowed the ordination of women.

Contemporary explanations of the sacraments tend to be scriptural and doctrinal rather than philosophical. Churches without a strong intellectual tradition, especially those with only baptism and communion, usually appeal to biblical texts and standard church teaching without much further elaboration. The Roman Catholic Church retains many scholastic elements in its catechism and its code of canon law, but its theologians also utilize ideas from contemporary philosophies and liturgical studies in discussing the sacraments. Sacramental theology today is therefore somewhat pluralistic and eclectic.

Baptism

Since New Testament times, the primary initiation ritual for Christians has been baptism. The name is derived from the Greek word meaning to immerse, and early Christian baptisms were either full or partial immersions. As time went on, partial immersion combined with pouring water over the head became acceptable, and even simply pouring. While the action was being performed, the one baptizing recited a short formula such as 'I baptize you in the name of Christ.' Later, the words found at the end of Matthew's Gospel became standard, and Christians were baptized 'in the name of the Father and of the Son and of the Holy Spirit' (Matthew 28.19).

In adopting baptism, early Christians were probably following the example of John the Baptist, who is mentioned in all four Gospels, although they may also have been influenced by the Jewish practice of baptizing proselytes. The apostle Paul was the first to offer a theological interpretation of the ritual, explaining that going into the water meant participating in the death of Christ, and coming out of it meant sharing in his resurrection from death (Romans 6.1–11).

By the third century, Christian initiation had become a process that culminated in the water bath and led to a first participation in the eucharistic supper. It was preceded by a one- to three-year period of preparation during which initiates learned the Christian way of life and were helped to stop behaving in ways that were self-destructive and socially harmful. The initiation process was therefore an immersion into a new community, its beliefs and values; baptism aptly symbolized that experience and celebrated the start of a new life. Since the process helped people to convert from immoral to moral living, baptism was said to bring the remission of sins, to bestow God's spirit, and to be the start of salvation.

In Christian communities throughout the Roman empire, baptisms were generally performed once a year in conjunction with the celebration of Easter or Pentecost. Those who went through the initiation process were primarily adults, although children could also be baptized with their parents. Moreover, the number of initiates remained relatively small as long as Christianity remained an illegal religion. Christians gathered for worship in private homes, and baptisms were performed in pools and cisterns as well as in natural bodies of water.

This picture began to change in 313 when the Emperor Constantine lifted the ban on Christianity and began favouring the new religion in the hope that it would become a force for morality and a source of religious unity in the Roman empire. As the ranks of initiates began to swell, the preparation period began to shrink, since church leaders reasoned that people could be baptized first and instructed in the faith afterwards. Basilicas were constructed for the larger crowds that attended Sunday eucharistic worship, and baptisteries were built for the annual baptisms.

By the end of the fourth century, Christianity was declared the official religion of the empire, and virtually all adults had been brought into the church. Although the process of initiation had changed, the theology of baptism remained the same: baptism was regarded as bringing about the remission of sins, as bestowing the Holy Spirit, as conferring a new life of grace, and as being needed for salvation. Now, however, the focus was on the ritual rather than on the process, and baptism was viewed rather magically as a cause of spiritual effects.

This being the case, Christian parents sought to have their children baptized younger and younger, and by the turn of the fifth century it was not uncommon for children to be baptized at a fairly early age. This change in practice gave rise to further theological questions. For example, if baptism was for the remission of sins, what sin was removed when a young child – presumably incapable of committing a serious sin – was baptized? And if baptism was necessary for salvation, what happened if a child died before it was baptized?

Augustine of Hippo, a brilliant African bishop who had been educated in Italy, addressed these and other theological questions in the Roman church. He reasoned that if the church is guided by the Holy Spirit, the baptism of children must have divine approval, and that if baptism is for the remission of sins, there must be some sin that is forgiven even when an infant is baptized. Searching the scriptures, he concluded that the original sin committed by Adam had tainted all of humanity, and that this sin is washed away by the water of baptism. (Of course, when an adult is baptized, personal sins are also forgiven.) Augustine reasoned further that if baptism is truly necessary for salvation, as the tradition affirmed, then dying without baptism implies eternal perdition, even for the souls of children.

Salvation
Roman empire
Life after death
Festivals and fasts

As Augustine's theory of original sin became more widely accepted, especially in the Western or Latin-speaking church, parents brought their children to be baptized earlier, especially when a child was sick and in danger of dying. Indeed, clergy sometimes preached that if children died without baptism, their souls would be lost, and eventually the practice of baptism for all once a year was replaced by the individual baptism of infants soon after birth.

Constantine's 'conversion'
Scholasticism

Scholastic theories of baptism reflected the medieval practice of infant baptism while incorporating much of what had originally been written about adult baptism. Baptism was said to be necessary for salvation, offering new life to the soul and infusing the grace of God. Original sin was washed away, and the soul received an indelible character that both marked it as Christian and gave it supernatural virtues of faith, hope and love. Having thus received this sacramental reality, the soul was enabled to receive other sacraments as the person grew older and needed the spiritual help that they offered.

Buildings
Faith Hope Love

Reformers in the sixteenth century took issue with either the medieval theory or practice or both. Martin Luther accepted infant baptism but argued that the grace through faith in which it was received was dormant until the recipient was old enough to confess it. John Calvin regarded baptism as a sign of salvation but not a cause of salvation, since God's elect were predestined for glory irrespective of any ritual. The Anabaptists rejected infant baptism as unscriptural since only adult baptisms are recorded in the Bible, and insisted that people baptized as children be baptized again after professing faith in Christ. Roman Catholics at the Council of Trent rejected all of these Protestant innovations as heretical, and insisted that the medieval practice and theology were correct.

Holy Spirit
Ritual
Predestination

Sin

Christians today are united in the acceptance of baptism as a ritual of initiation that is rooted in the New Testament, but they are divided when it comes to baptismal practice and theology. Roman Catholics and Orthodox regularly baptize children of church members, and they regard it as a ritual that leads to salvation. Anglicans and mainline Protestants likewise retain infant baptism, but they are not in agreement about the spiritual effectiveness of the ritual. Nevertheless, most of these churches regard each other's baptisms as valid and do not rebaptize converts. Baptists and evangelical Christians, however, deny any effectiveness to infant baptism and insist that converts from other churches be baptized as adults.

Holy Spirit ➤

Common recognition of the importance of baptism, combined with an obvious disarray regarding its interpretation, has fostered ecumenical discussion among the churches for the purpose of mutual understanding. It is unlikely that historical differences will diminish in the future, for Christians in an ecumenical age are learning to have greater respect for diversity. Moreover, dialogue with non-Christian faiths has even moderated the traditional insistence on baptism as necessary for salvation.

Confirmation

Initiation
Scholasticism ➤

Confirmation is a ceremony of initiation, the primary symbolic gesture in which is a laying on of hands, an anointing with oil, or both. The name of the sacrament derives from the fifth century, when the ritual was used by bishops to confirm baptisms that had earlier been performed by priests.

Festivals and fasts

In the early church the liturgy of baptism included a number of symbolic elements including anointing with oil, immersion in water, ritual embrace or symbolic kiss, and placing one or both hands on the head of the initiate. Baptisms were customarily performed once a year at Easter or Pentecost, and they were presided over by the local church leader or bishop. When communities grew so large that the annual initiation ceremony had to be conducted in more than one locality, a way had to be found to signify the bishop's approval and reception of the individual initiates.

Roman empire

Reformation ➤

In the Eastern or Greek-speaking half of the Roman empire, the problem was solved by having the bishop bless the oil with which the initiates were anointed after having been bathed in water and clothed in white garments. The bishop's blessing was thus symbolically given to each initiate, even though he himself was not present. In the Western or Latin-speaking half of the empire the solution was to leave the blessing out of the baptismal ceremony and have the bishop give it in person at a later date. Either the newly baptized were brought to the bishop's cathedral or he travelled to each of the parishes in his diocese.

Liturgies at this time were not uniform, so in some localities oil was placed on the forehead in the sign of the cross, and the rite was call consignation. In others it was called simply an anointing or blessing, and, in places where the blessing was bestowed through a laying-on of hands it was called the perfection or consummation (meaning the completion) of baptism. Eventually in the West the ceremony came to be commonly referred to as confirmation.

Baptism was understood as necessary for salvation, but there appeared to be no such urgency for confirmation. When it became common for children and even infants to be baptized, parents often postponed or neglected to have these baptisms confirmed. In response, bishops exhorted parents not to neglect this ritual, giving various theological reasons for it. Faustus of Riez, for example, around the year 460, suggested that in confirmation the Holy Spirit bestowed the additional strength that Christians needed to combat temptation and live in accordance with God's commandments.

Four centuries later, what Faustus had written was incorporated into a collection of church documents and attributed to early popes. His ideas were thus given the authority of venerable tradition, and in this form they were circulated throughout Europe. Then in the twelfth century, when scholastics were compiling lists of sacraments, they often included confirmation among them.

The medieval theology of confirmation both reflected the practice of the day and influenced that practice. Since Christians went through the ritual only once in a lifetime, confirmation was said to bestow an indelible character on the soul. Since some versions of the rite did not contain the laying on of hands, only the anointing with oil was regarded as essential. Since confirmation was believed to strengthen the soul for spiritual combat, the bishop's ritual embrace of initiates, long since replaced with a caress on the cheek for infants, was transformed into a ritual slap. And since the grace of confirmation was deemed necessary in adulthood, the age for confirmation moved upwards from infancy to late childhood.

In actuality, however, not many Christians were confirmed. Unless parents lived close to the bishop's cathedral, they did not undertake to bring their children to him for the sacrament. And unless bishops were vigorous in the fulfilment of their pastoral responsibilities, they did not journey out to the countryside to confirm new additions to their flocks. When they did, the anointing could be a rather perfunctory performance amidst a show of episcopal pageantry.

It was therefore almost inevitable that confirmation was rejected by the Protestant Reformers. There was no place in the scriptures where Jesus clearly instituted the sacrament. The New Testament described the apostles laying on hands to impart the Holy Spirit, but the medieval rite was an anointing with oil. The scholastic theology of the sacrament talked about the gifts of the Holy Spirit, but the Spirit had already been received in baptism. Baptism was obviously needed for salvation, but no such necessity could be claimed for confirmation.

Just as inevitably, the Roman Catholic bishops at the Council of Trent (1545–63) rejected the Reformers' rejection and retained confirmation as one of its seven sacraments. Rome also persuaded the Orthodox to regard the anointing after baptism (called chrismation in the East) as a separate sacrament, even though that anointing had never been detached from baptism, as it had in the West. Anglicans (and later, Methodists and Episcopalians) retained confirmation as a sacrament of the church, but not as one instituted by Jesus.

Today the practice of confirmation among the churches is quite varied. The Orthodox retain chrismation as part of the rite of baptism, whether for infants or adults. Roman Catholics in different parts of the world are confirmed in childhood or adolescence according to local custom. Converts are confirmed at the time of their baptism or, if they are already baptized, at the time of their reception into the Roman Catholic Church. Orthodox and Roman Catholics regard the ritual as having a permanent spiritual effect, so they allow participation in the sacrament only once in a lifetime.

Anglicans and Episcopalians have retained confirmation as a minor sacrament, performed usually when adolescents formally accept membership of the church into which they were baptized as infants. Adults who were confirmed earlier in their lives, however, can participate in the sacrament again if and when they desire to make a public affirmation of their baptismal commitment. Lutherans practise adolescent confirmation and, like Roman Catholics, use the confirmation ceremony to celebrate the reception of the already baptized into the church, but they also allow the reconfirmation of once-confirmed individuals who have left the church and later seek readmission. Methodists, Presbyterians and other Protestant denominations have ritual affirmations of baptism for adolescents or adults, but practices and interpretations vary widely.

Penance (Reconciliation)

Christians have had sacraments or rituals of repentance and reconciliation since the earliest centuries, but these rituals have taken a wide variety of forms. Roman Catholics currently have three rites of reconciliation, although only one of these is in wide use.

The Gospels record that Jesus began his ministry with a call to repentance, and during his ministry he both forgave sins and exhorted his followers to forgive one another (see, e.g., Mark 1.15; Matthew 9.2; Luke 17.3–4). Jewish rabbis followed a practice called binding and loosing, first restricting a sinner from normal relations with a community and later lifting the restriction if and when the sinner repented, and Paul seems to have recommended this practice to the Gentiles in Corinth (see 1 Corinthians 5.11; 2 Corinthians 2.6–8). The only Christian ceremony that spoke explicitly of the forgiveness of sins, however, was baptism.

Paul

Counter-Reformation

Church leaders faced a pastoral problem when individuals who had left the community asked to be readmitted, and in some places such persons were put through the process of baptism a second time. An early second-century writer named Hermas envisioned an alternative, namely, the reconciliation and readmission of repentant sinners – a process that would be available only once in a person's lifetime, lest people think they could sin and be forgiven as often as they liked. By the end of the second century, a process of public repentance was available throughout the Christian world.

p. 245

Sometimes called canonical penance, because it followed certain canons or rules, public repentance was meant primarily for notorious sinners whose behaviour had scandalized the community. An outward display of repentance was always required for apostasy, murder and adultery; local regulations required the process for various other sins as well. Except in times of persecution, however, when a noticeable number might renounce their faith, this procedure was not utilized very often.

The regulations, called canons, required sinners first to admit their guilt to the bishop, who then assigned public works of penance that would show their admission of sin and signify their willingness to repent. Penitents wore sackcloth and ashes, for example, or they fasted and and begged forgiveness of the faithful. They had to stand or kneel apart from the community during the eucharist, and they were not allowed to share communion. This period of repentance might last a few months to a few years, depending on the case and on local custom. When the bishop was satisfied that the penitents were reconverted to the Christian way of life, they were ceremoniously welcomed back to the ranks of the faithful and readmitted to the eucharistic table.

This severe regime worked well when Christians were few in number, but when Constantine first tolerated their religion and then promoted it in the Roman empire, the system began to fail. More Christians meant more backsliders, and more sins were added to the list of those that required public repentance. In some places penances were made more severe, in others more lengthy. In reaction, people postponed becoming public penitents until later in life, when the penances would necessarily be shorter, or even until they were dying, when they could ask the bishop to be merciful and forgive them.

Constantine's 'conversion' Roman empire

Jesus

Sin · Scholasticism · Eucharist · Life after death · Atonement · p. 476 · Crusades · Paul · Resurrection · Sacrifice

With the fall of the Roman empire this penitential system fell into disuse and was eventually replaced. Private, repeated confession of faults to a spiritual adviser was a common practice in monasteries, and when monks were ordained and sent as missionaries into the heart of Europe they brought this monastic practice with them. Gradually the practice was extended to the faithful, and by the tenth century it was accepted as a normal part of church life.

The rite of penance discussed by scholastic theologians in the Middle Ages was therefore private confession to a priest, which was repeated as often as was needed. The priest's words were understood to bestow God's forgiveness, but the mild penances that were assigned seemed insufficient to satisfy God's justice, so these theologians theorized that most souls would have to undergo a painful purgation before being allowed to enter heaven.

The theory of purgatory led to abuses, which in turn led to calls for reform in the church. Satisfaction had to be made for sins, but in the medieval mind this could be done by the sinner or by someone else, rather like a debt being paid by a third party. Indeed, the scriptures proclaimed that Christ had paid the debt of sin for all (see Romans 5.15–21), so the scholastics reasoned that what was needed was a way to apply the merits of Christ's death to individual sinners. According to the theory of indulgences, Christians could obtain merit for themselves or others by doing good works such as going on a crusade, giving alms to the poor, performing religious rituals or donating to the church. By the sixteenth century the sale of indulgences was being used to increase the church's wealth by appealing to the belief that people could in effect buy salvation for their departed loved ones.

Martin Luther was the first of the Reformers to attack indulgences and other abuses in the penitential system, and eventually all Protestants rejected the view that penance was a sacrament that had been initiated by Christ. Churches in the Anglican Communion retained it as a minor sacrament that could be used for spiritual growth. Within decades of the start of the Reformation, the Roman Catholic Church eliminated the sale of indulgences and curbed other abuses, but it continued to maintain that private confession was a sacramental practice that came from Jesus himself.

In the mid-twentieth century, the Roman Catholic Church made sweeping changes in its sacramental rites, based on decades of research into early liturgical history and on a more critical interpretation of scripture. The name of this sacrament in English was changed to reconciliation and three new rites were devised: a more open form of private confession, a penitential service with an opportunity for private confession, and a form for use in emergencies in which there was no time for private confession. New insights from biblical scholars and social scientists led theologians to move away from a legalistic to a more personalistic understanding of sin. The Roman Catholic laity in turn began using the sacrament less to confess lists of individual sins and more to receive moral guidance and assurance of God's forgiveness.

These changes prompted revisions in Anglican and Episcopalian rites, but not much change in pastoral practice. Eastern Orthodox churches have always had private penitential rites, but their theology and pastoral practice have remained fairly consistent through the centuries, without the dramatic vicissitudes seen in the West.

Eucharist

Eucharist is the primary form of public worship in the so-called liturgical churches (Orthodox, Catholic, Anglican or Episcopal, and some Lutheran). In non-liturgical churches (mainly those in the Calvinist and evangelical traditions) it is regarded as an important memorial of Jesus' last supper, but it is used as part of worship only monthly, quarterly, or even only once a year.

The name 'eucharist' comes from a Greek word meaning to give thanks, and it was the most common name for this ritual in the early church, for its central prayer is one of giving thanks to God. In New Testament times it was referred to as the breaking of bread or the Lord's Supper, which is a name often used by Protestants today. In the Middle Ages it came to be referred to as the mass, which is the name commonly used by Catholics. Since receiving the bread and wine symbolizes spiritual union with Christ, communion, receiving these elements is commonly referred to as receiving communion or holy communion.

The synoptic Gospels (Matthew 26.26–9; Mark 14.22–5; Luke 22.14–20) depict Jesus' last meal as a Passover meal, the *seder*, during which he blessed bread and wine, identified himself with these elements, and told his disciples to eat them. According to Acts 2.42, followers of Jesus gathered regularly to share meals that enhanced their unity with one another and with their Lord. Paul referred to this practice as the Lord's Supper (1 Corinthians 11.20), describing it as a full meal for which the church in Corinth gathered, probably weekly.

By the end of the second century, the eucharist had evolved from a full meal to a symbolic meal consisting of prayers, scripture readings and communion. Increasingly Christians gathered not in the evening but in the morning of the first day of the week, the day of Christ's resurrection from the dead. Partly because of its association with Christ's sacrificial death on the cross, and partly because of its similarity to the sharing of food sacrificed in temple worship, the eucharistic meal came to be regarded as a sacrifice and its leader as a priest.

In the fourth century Constantine legalized Christianity in the Roman empire and made Sunday a pubic holiday. This enabled church leaders to expand the eucharist into a formal liturgy or ceremony of public worship, sometimes lasting for hours. Many of the ritual trappings associated with the eucharist in the liturgical churches date back to this time: stylized vestments and sacred vessels, a prescribed written rite, assigned scripture readings followed by a homily or sermon, psalms and hymns sung by a choir.

Basing their belief on Jesus' words, 'This is my body ... This is my blood' (cf. Mark 14.22–4), Christians commonly referred to the eucharistic elements as the body and blood of Christ. In the early church, bishops emphasized this belief as an important Christian doctrine, while at the same time affirming the divinity of Christ in their fight to defend orthodoxy against a variety of heresies. However, this combination of beliefs gradually deterred ordinary Christians from receiving communion, since they considered themselves unworthy to have close contact with the divine.

The fall of the Roman empire in the West led to drastic changes in worship there, while churches in the East continued the tradition of having forms of eucharistic worship, liturgies, that had been composed by gifted fathers of the church. Except for the city of Rome, where papal liturgies continued in the ancient ceremonial tradition, eucharistic worship in the West was reduced to a ritual that could be performed by a single priest. An abbreviated rite was needed by missionary monks who carried the gospel of Christ and the sacraments of the church into continental Europe for the conversion of the barbarian tribes whose attacks had hastened the empire's collapse. Charlemagne in the ninth century proclaimed his to be a Holy Roman empire, and the medieval mass became the standard form of Christian worship throughout Europe, even in Rome, through the exchange of liturgical books during this period.

Christians had worshipped in Greek when it was the universal language of the Roman empire and in Latin when that language became more common in the West. The tribes of Europe, however, spoke a myriad of Germanic dialects, none of which were written languages. Liturgical books therefore remained in Latin, and this transformed the experience of eucharistic worship from participating in a public ritual to watching a performed ritual.

The European understanding of worship reflected this change in experience. It was now regarded as a ritual performed by a priest for the benefit of the church. The mass, as it was increasingly called, was thought of as a sacrifice that mystically made Christ's redeeming sacrifice on the cross present to those who attended. Through the priest's recitation of Jesus' words at his last supper, the bread and wine were transformed into his body and blood, making Christ himself really present on the altar to be adored by the faithful and received in communion.

Scholastic theologians in the high Middle Ages attempted to understand their faith using concepts derived from the Greek philosopher, Aristotle. In fact, three different theories were introduced to explain the change that medieval Christians believed and experienced. The theory of consubstantiation proposed that the consecrated elements continued to be bread and wine after they became the body and blood of Christ. A second theory suggested that the reality of bread and wine was removed and replaced with the reality of Christ's body and blood. According to the theory of transubstantiation, such a change in reality(*substantia*) did occur, but the appearances (*accidentalia*) of bread and wine remained. Nevertheless, the change remained a mystery, for Aristotelian philosophy could not explain how this happened.

For all the sophistication of scholastic theologizing, peasant faith was riddled with superstition. The consecrated bread or host (from the Latin *hostia*, meaning sacrificial victim) was believed to be capable of warding off evil, and even gazing upon it was thought to bring good fortune. Reverence for the Blessed Sacrament, as the eucharistic elements came to be known, was so intense that most people considered themselves unworthy to receive communion. In response, the church mandated that all the faithful had to receive communion at least once a year.

The mass was believed to re-enact Christ's sacrifice on the cross, and the spiritual merits of that sacrifice were thought to be available to anyone for whom the priest prayed. Eucharistic piety was therefore open to corruption by priests who willingly accepted donations in exchange for the blessings at their disposal. In fact, some priests earned their living by reciting a number of quick masses every day for people who were in effect attempting to buy salvation for themselves and their loved ones.

Reformers in the sixteenth century, such as Martin Luther and John Calvin, pointed to such superstitions and corrupt practices as evidence that the church had lost the original meaning and purpose of the eucharist. Luther translated the mass into German, introduced hymns that people could sing, and insisted that they receive communion more often. Calvin thought it better to eliminate the mass entirely and replace it with a service that put more emphasis on scripture, with times for communion to be determined by the local congregations.

The Council of Trent (1545–63) defined Roman Catholic doctrine largely in reaction to what it perceived as Protestant errors, but it also addressed blatant abuses in eucharistic practice. The council's teaching reiterated the medieval understanding of the mass as a sacrifice in

Constantine's 'conversion'
Scholasticism

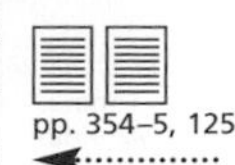
pp. 354–5, 1257
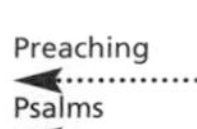
Preaching
Psalms

Hymns

Heresy
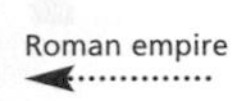
Roman empire

Mission

Holy Roman empire

Books

Worship

Counter Reformation

TRANSUBSTANTIATION AND REAL PRESENCE

Transubstantiation is the doctrine that the substance of the bread and wine consecrated at the eucharist become the body and blood of Christ, though their appearance remains the same. The verb 'transubstantiate' was first used officially at the Fourth Lateran Council of 1215, and subsequently the doctrine was developed on the basis of Aristotelian philosophy, which distinguished between substance, the permanent underlying reality, and accidents, qualities which inhere in the substance like colour, shape, taste, etc. The classic statement of the doctrine of transubstantiation was made by Thomas Aquinas, and it was reaffirmed, but without reference to accidents, by the Council of Trent. Transubstantiation was rejected by the Reformers. Martin Luther spoke of 'real presence', saying that to understand 'this bread *is* my body by no means implies transubstantiation but simply a 'sacramental union' analogous to the union of natures in the person of Jesus: 'a religious affirmation that the God-man Jesus Christ has graciously bound his presence to this celebration as a special instance of his self-impartation'.

Thomas Aquinas

Martin Luther

Some modern Roman Catholic theologians, recognizing that Aristotelian philosophy can no longer be used unquestioningly in theological definitions, have attempted to restate the doctrine in other terms, focusing rather on a change in the meaning of the bread and wine. The terms used are transfinalization, transfunctionalization and transsignification. The Dutch theologian Edward Schillebeeckx has focused above all on the existential dimensions of the eucharist, as what happens when men and women meet before God to commemorate the crucified and risen Jesus through bread and wine. However, in his 1965 encyclical *Mysterium fidei*, Pope Paul VI reaffirmed the doctrine of transubstantiation and the traditional terminology.

Anglican tradition, too, was concerned to affirm that Christ is really, as opposed to symbolically, present in the eucharistic bread and wine, without formulating any doctrine about the nature of these elements. Instead, it came to teach the real presence of Christ. The famous seventeenth-century bishop Jeremy Taylor wrote a book entitled the *Real Presence and Spirituall of Christ in the Blessed Sacrament Proved against the Doctrine of Transubstantiation.* Charles Wesley gave expression to the doctrine in his 1745 *Hymns on the Lord's Supper*, for example:

His presence makes the feast;
And now our spirits feel
The glory not to be expressed,
The joy unspeakable.

In the Roman Catholic tradition today the real presence is closely linked with the doctrine of transubstantiation.

Edward Schillebeeckx, *Christ the Sacrament*, London: Sheed & Ward 1963

which, through the action of the priest, Christ offered himself to God the Father for the salvation of the world, just as he had on the cross. The consecrated elements were the sacrament in which Christ was truly present under the appearances of bread and wine. Although it was spiritually beneficial to receive communion, one could also receive benefits from participating in the sacrifice.

To curb the abuses in Catholic worship, Rome published a missal that priests had to follow meticulously in reciting the mass, and it drastically reduced the number of masses that priests could say on any given day. The Roman Catholic liturgy thus remained the same for four centuries, and transubstantiation became that church's official explanation of eucharistic change. Protestant worship, after some initial creativity, settled into patterns that quickly became traditional, and Protestants in general rejected transubstantiation as a theological explanation.

Ecumenical movement

All this began to change in the twentieth century, when the liturgical renewal movement and the ecumenical movement culminated with the Second Vatican Council (1962–5) on the Roman Catholic side and with increased exchanges through the World Council of Churches on the Anglican and Protestant side. Rome mandated new eucharistic rites that would be celebrated not in Latin but in modern languages, and it permitted adaptations that took local custom and culture into account. Its transformed worship style reflected that of the patristic era, and it spoke of the mass as a eucharistic liturgy, as the Greek fathers of the church had. While the Roman Catholic Church continued to insist that transubstantiation is a valid explanation of eucharistic change, it allowed the consideration of other philosophical explanations as well.

Anglican and Protestant churches in the liturgical tradition modernized their eucharistic worship as well, and they often agreed to use common translations of prayers composed by ecumenical committees. Orthodox churches continued to use patristic liturgies, although these were often shortened through the abbreviation of non-essential prayers, in accommodation to the sensibilities of modern worshippers.

In the 1992 *Catechism of the Catholic Church*, the eucharist is regarded as 'the source and summit of the Christian life' (no. 1324). Nevertheless, there is a growing shortage of ordained priests due to both external cultural

Ministry and ministers

factors and internal church policies, and priests are the only ones who are allowed to preside at the mass. As a result, Roman Catholics increasingly have to make use of forms of worship built around scripture readings and a sermon, not unlike Protestant worship.

Matrimony (Marriage)

Marriage is regarded as a sacrament in the Roman Catholic, Orthodox, Anglican and Episcopal churches, although there are differences in their wedding ceremonies and in their understanding of the sacrament. Other Christian churches have wedding ceremonies, but they regard neither these rites nor the marital relationship as sacramental.

Christian wedding ceremonies first evolved in the eastern part of the Roman empire from a priestly blessing in the fourth century to a full liturgical rite in the seventh century. In the Western church this development was much slower, and the sacramental nature of marriage was not fully recognized until the twelfth century.

Marriage in the ancient world was primarily an arrangement between families, with heads of families presiding at the nuptial rituals. In the pre-Christian Roman empire, marriage could also be contracted by two individuals without any public ceremony. Both of these possibilities existed for Christians during the early centuries of their religion.

After the fall of the Roman empire in the West, ecclesiastical courts were increasingly called upon to decide marriage cases, which had previously been heard by civil courts. One important source of contention was the difference between the Roman tradition, which allowed for marriage without parental consent, and the Germanic tradition, in which the consent of the parents was essential. In addition, while Roman law considered the giving of mutual consent as the factor that made the marriage binding, Germanic custom did not consider the marriage binding until the first act of sexual intercourse had taken place. The matter was resolved to some degree in the twelfth century, when Pope Alexander III decreed that the consent of the couple created the marriage contract, and the first act of intercourse made the marriage binding for life.

If mutual consent created a valid marriage, however, couples could legally marry in secret, without any witnesses. To combat the problem of clandestine marriage the church demanded that all marriages be witnessed and blessed by a priest. Over the course of four centuries weddings began to be celebrated near a church, then in a church, and finally were presided over by the priest instead of the spouses' parents. By the twelfth century, church weddings had become an established custom.

But was this ceremony a sacrament? Medieval theologians (mostly celibate monks) objected on the grounds that marriage entailed sexual activity, which was generally regarded as impure. In their Latin translation of the Bible, however, Ephesians 5.32 said about marriage, *Hoc est enim magnum sacramentum*, which the scholastics took as meaning, 'For this is a great sacrament.' Moreover, no less an authority than Augustine had argued, centuries before, that a crucial difference between pagan marriage and Christian marriage is that the latter is sacramental: a sign of the indissoluble relationship between Christ and the church (see Ephesians 5.21–33).

Marriage ◄

In the end, both the wedding ceremony and the marriage itself were regarded as sacramental, following the scholastic distinction between the visible ritual (an outward sign) and the marriage bond (an inner reality) that was invisible but no less real. In practice, however, when theologians and canonists spoke about the sacrament of marriage, they meant the spiritual union between the spouses.

Protestant Reformers in the sixteenth century regarded marriage as sacred, but sacraments were supposed to be instituted by Christ, and marriage had obviously existed prior to Christ's coming. The Roman Catholic bishops at the Council of Trent (1545–63) responded that Christ had raised marriage to the dignity of a sacrament, and that marriage had always been a sacrament in the church. In addition, the bishops declared that marriages that were not contracted in the presence of a Roman Catholic priest and two witnesses were invalid, in effect making all Protestant marriages sinful unions.

Counter-Reformation

Roman empire ◄

The Roman Catholic Church also taught that marriage is indissoluble, so divorce was impossible. If Roman Catholics disobeyed their church's laws and obtained a civil divorce, the church regarded them as still being married to each other. The only possibility of separation and remarriage was through annulment, a declaration by an ecclesiastical court that what appeared to be a marriage in fact had never existed because something needed for validity at the time of the wedding had been lacking. There were few grounds for such a declaration, however, and so annulments were rare.

The bishops at the Second Vatican Council (1962–5) acknowledged that the purpose of marriage in the modern world was not only the procreation of children but also companionship and even intimacy between the spouses. Canon lawyers interpreted this shift as an expansion of the grounds for annulment to include psychological factors, and consequently the number of annulments granted in the church rose significantly. Nevertheless, the majority of Roman Catholics who divorced did not bother to seek an annulment before remarrying, and this anomalous situation holds true today, when the divorce rate among Roman Catholics is the same as in the general population.

Council

Canon law

Although the Orthodox look upon marriage as a

sacrament, they do not consider it indissoluble. Nevertheless, divorce is undesirable, and a marriage after divorce is not regarded as sacramental. Protestants, including Anglicans, also believe that divorce is undesirable, but having few if any church laws about marriage, their approach to marriage and marital problems is almost exclusively pastoral.

Ordination

Ministry and ministers The formal ritual of initiation by which clergy take office in the church is called ordination. Although many churches have ordination rituals, only Roman Catholics, Anglicans (Episcopalians in the United States) and Orthodox regard Scholasticism it as a sacrament and refer to the ordained as priests. The official Roman Catholic name for this sacrament is holy orders, referring to the three ranks or levels of ordained ministry, namely, deacons, priests and bishops.

Although the New Testament speaks about a laying on of hands for those about to serve in the church (e.g. Acts 6.6; 1 Timothy 4.14), this may have been a gesture of blessing rather than a ritual of ordination. The earliest reference to an ordination ritual comes from the early  third century, when Hippolytus of Rome wrote about three distinct ceremonies for the initiation of bishops, elders (presbyters) and deacons.

Bishops were the first to be called priests, because of the parallels between their role at the Christian eucharist and the role of pagan priests at temple sacrifices. When elders began to substitute regularly for bishops at Sunday eucharists, they too came to be called priests. Since deacons never had a presiding role in Christian worship, theirs was not regarded as a priestly ministry.

When in the fourth century Christianity came to be favoured by the Roman government, the church swelled with new converts and Sunday worship expanded into a formal liturgical service with many ministers, presided Reformation over by a bishop or priest. Additional orders of ministry  performed various functions in the church, and progress through the ranks provided training in ministerial duties. Initiation into each order was accomplished through a ritual that conferred rights and responsibilities on the ordained. 

Christian ministers during this period were normally Monasticism married, in contrast to monks who lived together in communities and remained celibate. After the collapse of Roman empire the western half of the Roman empire in the fifth century, however, monks were often ordained as priests and sent Mission as missionaries to convert the barbarians of central and northern Europe. Since monks were celibate, celibacy came to be associated with priesthood, and since celibacy was regarded as holier than marriage, priests who were not monks were encouraged to refrain from sexual activity with their wives.

Developments in Eastern Christianity took a different turn. Married men were ordained to the priesthood, but only celibates (usually monks) were ordained as bishops. Since bishops controlled the wealth of the church, this practice ensured that church property was not given to heirs. Orthodox churches continued to have married priests and celibate bishops.

Although celibacy was gradually becoming a norm in the West, it did not become an ecclesiastical rule until the twelfth century, when the church gained full control over marriage. Henceforth only celibates would be ordained, and priests who went through a wedding ceremony were not regarded as validly married.

Scholastic theology reflected the experience of priesthood in the Middle Ages. The seven stages in clerical training were regarded as seven holy orders. Each stage conferred certain duties and the power to carry them out, so ordination was conceived as a ritual that conferred power. Priests were perceived as having the power to offer the sacrifice of the mass, and in doing so to change bread and wine into the body and blood of Christ. They also had the power to absolve the sins of penitents in confession and to prepare the souls of the dying by bestowing extreme unction. Since the ordained remained priests for a lifetime, ordination was thought to imprint an indelible character on the soul.

Bishops could confirm and ordain, which ordinarily priests were not allowed to do. But bishops had earlier been ordained as priests, and their power to administer these two sacraments was believed to come with ordination. Bishops, however, had authority that priests did not have, and so the distinction between priests and bishops was conceived in terms of authority rather than in terms of spiritual power. This explained why bishops could sometimes give priests permission to administer confirmation.

The Protestant Reformation rejected the Roman Catholic concept of priesthood and the medieval understanding of priestly power. Martin Luther believed in the 'priesthood of all believers', based on 1 Peter 2.5 and other texts, and he doubted that ordination bestowed any special powers. John Calvin's reading of the scriptures led him to rethink the notion of ministry in the church, and since the New Testament does not mention priests, he did not include them in his reorganized church structure. Protestants today do not speak of their ministers as priests, with the exception of Anglicans and Episcopalians, although many continue to have a formal ritual of ordination.

The Roman Catholic Church reasserted the existence of holy orders, but it acknowledged the existence of clerical abuses that needed to be reformed. It instituted seminaries for the training of priests, mandated their intellectual and spiritual formation, and promoted monastic piety as a model for all the ordained. By selecting only reform-minded priests to be bishops, it gradually eliminated most incompetence and corruption from the hierarchy.

The Second Vatican Council (1962–5) reaffirmed the importance of priesthood, but it reduced the number of holy orders to three, calling episcopacy an order rather an elevation in authority. Neither the council nor subsequent popes changed the rule of priestly celibacy or admitted women to ordination. Changes in the church and in society, however, have led to a decline in the number of priests, and today most Roman Catholics serving in the ministry of the church are not ordained, are married and are female. The role of priests has been largely reduced to the performing of sacramental rituals, and lay ministers hold many of the positions once held by priests.

Extreme unction (Anointing of the sick)

Churches that practise anointing of the sick or the sacrament of unction trace its origin to the letter of James, which recommends that church elders anoint and pray over the sick (James 5.14–15). Historically speaking, however, there is no evidence of a church ritual for anointing the sick until the middle of the ninth century.

Jesus himself cured the sick, and the New Testament records that he enjoined his disciples to do likewise (e.g., Luke 10.9). Moreover, there is ample evidence that laying hands on the infirm and praying over them for healing was a charismatic practice in early Christianity. The Acts of the Apostles credits Peter and Paul with this charism, and 1 Corinthians 12.8–10 mentions it as a gift that some in the community are given for the benefit of others. Some early liturgical books contain prayers for the blessing of oil to be used in anointing the sick, and other writings indicate that blessed oil was used by both laity and clergy in ministering to the ill and suffering.

During the ninth century, bishops in Charlemagne's Holy Roman empire introduced a rite of anointing to be performed by priests and forbade anointing of the sick by lay people. Through the copying and lending of liturgical books this rite made its way into the Roman sacramentary, the book of sacramental rites, and eventually it was assumed to be as old as the other sacramental rites described there. The rite's prayers asked for healing, but it had to be performed in a church, and some versions of it called for the attendance of three or more priests. Most people never sought this anointing, and those who did were often close to dying.

By the twelfth century the rite's prayers had become adapted to its actual use, and instead of asking for healing they asked for forgiveness and salvation. Likewise, oil was placed not on the parts of the body that were suffering but on the eyes, ears, mouth, hands and feet, through which the dying person might have sinned. Moreover, the rite had been simplified so that the sacrament could be administered by a single priest. Since this was the last anointing that people received before death, it came to be known as *extrema unctio*, extreme unction.

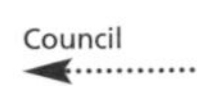

Medieval theologians scrutinized the words of the rite in order to determine its effects. The prayer said during the anointing asked for God's forgiveness, but since forgiveness of sins was also the purpose of the sacrament of penance, the precise purpose of this sacrament was not clear. Some scholastics theorized that it removed lesser sins that had not been confessed during the dying person's lifetime, since church law required the ritual absolution of only grave sins. Others thought that it removed the effects of sin, or sinful dispositions, with which the soul could not properly be admitted into heaven.

Protestant Reformers compared the Roman Catholic rite with James 5.14–15 and concluded that it could not be the scriptural foundation for extreme unction, for the apostle had recommended anointing the sick and praying for healing, not anointing the dying who had no hope of recovery. Catholics pointed out that the institution of the sacrament was supported by Mark 6.13, which said that disciples sent by Jesus anointed the sick, and they doubted that James would have recommended a practice that had not been ordained by Christ.

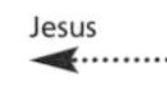

Modern historical research eventually unearthed the history of the rite, and the Roman Catholic Church revised the sacrament to bring it more into line with its original purpose. The name was changed to anointing of the sick, and the oil was to be administered not just to the dying but to anyone who was seriously sick, even the aged who were chronically ill. The revised rite also allowed for communal anointing that could be performed in a church or a nursing home, and this has become a common form of the sacrament today.

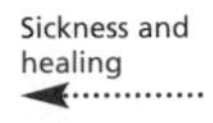

Orthodox churches have a sacramental anointing for the sick, and churches in the Anglican Communion call it the sacrament of unction. Administration of the sacrament is restricted to priests, and the shortage of such ministers in the Roman Catholic Church has diminished the availability of individual anointing, especially in hospitals, which increasingly rely on Roman Catholic chaplains who are not ordained.

JOSEPH MARTOS

Philippe Béguerie and Claude Duchesnau, *How to Understand the Sacraments*, London: SCM Press and New York: Crossroad 1989; J. D. Crichton, *Christian Celebration: The Sacraments*, London: Geoffrey Chapman 1973; Joseph Martos, *Doors to the Sacred. A Historical Introduction to Sacraments in the Catholic Church*, New York: Doubleday and London: SCM Press 1981

Sacrifice

Death → Suffering → Jesus Origins and background → Sin Martyr →

Anyone who throws a coin into a wishing-well might be said to stand on the edge of the sacrificial system, seeking some sort of supernatural favour. The word 'sacrifice' is still meaningful today in the sense of a costly gift, and this ties in with Christian beliefs about Jesus' giving up his life to reconcile humanity to God. However, some account of the origin and development of sacrificial language will help to illuminate its deeper significance and to judge its adequacy in relation to the objective act of God in Christ dealing with sin, and the inner, subjective transformation of the sinner.

p. 306

Whatever lay in the background in the way of offerings to spirits or deities to appease their anger or win their blessing, by the time the Old Testament was written, sacrificial worship was concentrated exclusively on YHWH (the Hebrew name for God). Not all sacrifice involved the death of an animal; offerings of grain, oil, wine or incense could be made. However, the offering of a physically unblemished animal had particular significance, especially the shedding of its blood. This was thrown against the altar or collected in a bowl at its base or disposed of with other rituals. The reason for this may be found in Leviticus 17.11, 'The life of the flesh is in the blood; and I have given it to you for making atonement for your lives on the altar; for, as life, it is the blood that makes atonement (reconciliation).' By laying a hand on the head of the sacrificial victim, the worshipper in some way identified with it as an offering to God. Apart from whole burnt offerings (holocaust), portions of sacrificial offerings were shared by the priests and worshippers.

Atonement Paul →

Covenant

In the Old Testament, sacrifices were associated with many aspects of life: covenant-making, family gatherings shared with God, the offering of gifts, praise or thanksgiving to God, and the Passover. After the Babylonian exile (following the destruction of Jerusalem in 586 BCE) sacrifices dealing with sin and guilt predominated, with the climax on the Day of Atonement (see Leviticus 16), when the Israelites' ritual uncleanness and acts of rebellion were purged. The Hebrew word *kippur*, meaning 'expiation', points to sacrifice as the God-given means to 'cover' or wipe out sins in contrast to 'propitiation' (aiming to appease an angry deity and so looking for change in God rather than in human beings).

On the Day of Atonement the sin of the nation, not just individual sin, was addressed. Two goats were selected. The blood of one was sprinkled on the 'mercy seat' (the cover of the ark) in the Holy of Holies at the heart of the atonement ritual. The other, the scapegoat, in a unique ritual (Leviticus 16.20–2) was driven into the wilderness after the sins of the people had been laid on its head. Though not strictly a sacrifice, like blood sacrifice it served to dispose of sin.

The 'spiritualization' of sacrifice occurred when attention moved from the physically unblemished animal to the offering of a spiritually unblemished, holy life (cf. Psalm 51.16). But when such a life met suffering or death, the belief that suffering was punishment for sin posed an acute problem (cf. Job). The solution that emerged, especially at the time of the Maccabean rebellion (*c.* 166 BCE, see 4 Maccabees 6.28–9, also Isaiah 53), was that the righteous were suffering penalties for the sins of others, not their own, thus satisfying God's judgement on sin and making reconciliation possible. As a means of atonement, martyr death could then be associated with sacrifice, but it introduced an idea of penalty previously absent in animal sacrifice (where the victim was not punished and where the shedding of blood but not suffering was significant).

It is against this rich and varied background that sacrificial language in the New Testament should be understood. The first Christians were bound to resort to it to express their conviction and experience that through the life and death of Jesus they were reconciled to God. According to the New Testament, Jesus himself at the Last Supper associated his death with the Passover and the making of a new covenant. In the letter to the Hebrews and the book of Revelation he is portrayed as both priest and victim, interceding on behalf of sinners and representing them before God. Paul writes of Christ as an atoning sacrifice, the God-given means to expiate sin (Romans 3.25; 5.9; 1 Corinthians 5.7).

Such allusions are enriched by the sacrificial significance of martyr death, but whereas the Maccabean martyrs died for the Torah, the Jewish law, and so reinforced its claims, Jesus, rejected by all, died for the unique vision of God by which he lived. His followers were challenged to decide whether his death was punishment by God, or a sacrifice acceptable to God to atone for sin. Responding in faith to Jesus, they saw not only God in a new light, but themselves also, in a new relationship reconciled to God. The objective fact of Jesus' death on the cross thus effected or rather set in motion an inner transformation. The intention of traditional sacrifice was fulfilled and no further sacrifice was needed.

In the early church, 'sacrifice' was one of many metaphors used to illuminate the saving work of Christ. Though implying an offering to God, it often stands alongside the image of 'ransom' offered to the devil to secure humanity's release from evil. By appearing side by side, such images may point to underlying truths that are obscured when imagery is taken too literally. However, words can change their meanings. In a cultural context in which sacrifices were commonly offered to placate the gods in the face of disasters, it is not surprising that the biblical concept of expiation yielded ground to propitiation. A chasm could then open up between the loving Son and the angry Father he dies to appease – with sacrifice being understood as the penalty demanded by the Father rather than being provided by him.

The worst outcome is avoided when, as with Origen, we encounter a God who is at once appeased by Christ's sacrifice, but who at the same time reveals his love in delivering Christ up for our salvation. By removing sin, Christ cleanses the soul and so makes possible the offering of spiritual sacrifices. Thus the objective and subjective aspects of Christ's sacrifice are held in balance (as in different ways with Athanasius and John Calvin).

Not surprisingly, sacrifice came to be focused on the eucharist, celebrated as a thank-offering to God for redemption in Christ and the means for participating in that redemption, but it was over the eucharist that the Reformers were to diverge from the Roman Catholic tradition. The Council of Trent declared that 'in this divine sacrifice which is celebrated in the mass, that same Christ is contained and offered in an unbloody manner, who once offered himself in a bloody manner on the altar of the Cross; ... this sacrifice is truly propitiatory'.

In contrast to any idea of believers adding anything to Christ's sacrifice, the English Reformer and Archbishop of Canterbury Thomas Cranmer wrote: 'One kind of sacrifice there is, which is called ... propitiatory ... such as pacifies God's wrath and indignation, and obtains mercy and forgiveness for all our sins ... Another kind of sacrifice there is which does not reconcile us to God, but is made of them that be reconciled by Christ ... sacrifices of praise and thanksgiving. The first kind of sacrifice Christ offered to God for us; the second kind we ourselves offer to God by Christ' – words echoed in his Book of Common Prayer.

Differences on this issue continue to divide the Western church, perhaps because of over-reliance on a single interpretative metaphor, excluding illumination from others. This happens when sacrifice is tied too closely either to the theory put forward by Anselm in the eleventh century that Christ's death satisfied God's justice or to the Reformers' theory that Christ suffered the penalty for sin as our substitute, or to any other particular interpretation. There is a danger, too, of sacrifice being interpreted too narrowly in the light of Old Testament animal sacrifice in ignorance of its later enrichment. It is therefore vital to remember that metaphors like sacrifice gain their full weight and meaning not from human interpretations but from Christ's atoning work, in other words, from what God is seen to have done in him and from the transformation and healing experienced in living relationship with him, not the other way round. The value of sacrificial imagery lies not only in its diversity as a rich resource for illuminating Christ's reconciling work, but as drawing his followers into sharing in his life and work.

TREVOR WILLIAMS

Godfrey Ashby, *Sacrifice: Its Nature and Purpose*, London: SCM Press 1988; R. J. Daly, *The Origins of the Christian Doctrine of Sacrifice*, London: Darton, Longman & Todd 1978; Frances M. Young, *Sacrifice and the Death of Christ*, London: SPCK 1975

Saint

In the New Testament, the word saint (Greek *hagios*, 'holy', hence hagiography = writing about the saints) refers to everyone who possesses the Spirit of God in Christ. A person's saintliness derives from the holiness of God: 'Indeed, as he who called you is holy, be holy yourselves in all your conduct, for it is written, "You shall be holy, for I am holy"' (1 Peter 1.16). Paul assures non-Jewish, Gentile Christians that they have a share in God's holiness by their call to faith: 'So then you are no longer strangers and aliens but you are citizens with the saints (*hagioi*) and also members of the household of God' (Ephesians 2.19).

Holy

Council

The Catholic tradition of Christianity acknowledges that broad understanding of the saint when it confesses in the Apostles' Creed a belief in the 'communion of saints'. The *Catechism of the Catholic Church* (no. 948) notes that this confession has two intimately related meanings, namely that all share in the holy things that the church provides and that this sharing is for all holy people. As the Second Vatican Council taught, there is a universal call to holiness that means, briefly, that everyone is called to be a saint. The completion of that call to holiness comes when a person passes from this life to enjoy light, happiness and peace in the presence of God.

Creed

p. 627

From the early centuries of Christianity, however, the church singled out certain people to commemorate by name as exemplars of the Christian faith. That practice developed out of the intense admiration for those who died in defence of the faith during the period of the Roman persecutions. This period did not end until the early fourth century. Looking back on the honour paid to the early martyrs we can detect a whole complex of customs that were normative for shaping the practice of venerating saints in the tradition. That complex of customs would include the annual commemoration of the person's death date (also called their 'birthday', for it was then that they were [re]born into heaven), honour paid at the person's burial site, safeguarding relics connected to the martyrdom of the person, and the development of a literature about the person's life, trials in persecution and exemplary death.

Persecution

Martyr

Miracle

St Ursula, sixteenth-century woodcut

A number of assumptions were implicit in the development of the veneration of these martyrs. First, the memory of them served as a kind of model to describe an exemplary form of Christian living. Hence it is not surprising that many of the descriptions of early martyrdoms made conscious allusions to the suffering and death of Jesus. Secondly, the belief that these persons were crowned in heaven by God made them natural intercessors for those who were on earth. Thirdly, their tombs and/or materials connected to them were the seat of supernatural power; thus, praying close to their tombs or touching relics connected to them were efficacious means of obtaining their grace or favour.

The desire to honour such saintly persons did not end when the persecution of the church was over. Christian communities found their attention turning to holy men and women who made themselves conspicuous by the austerity of their lives and their total devotion to the spiritual life. Saints then became venerated after their deaths, not because they died for their faith but because their lives were such conspicuous examples of Christian heroism. They took on the role of martyrs in the etymological sense of the term: as witnesses of the faith. One of the earliest and most popular of such saints in the West was Martin of Tours (died 397), who was famous as an ascetic, evangelizing bishop and a reputed miracle-worker in his own lifetime.

The saints played a major role in the everyday life of the Middle Ages; their festivals proliferated and they were prominent in folk religion, their shrines becoming the focal points for pilgrimage. Numerous lives of saints were written from the ninth century on, many of them more fiction than fact. The *Golden Legend*, a collection of them completed in the thirteenth century, was immensely popular.

There was no consistent formal process for 'naming' such saints in the first millennium of the church's history. The cult of the various saints evolved from the reputation of the saints as powerful intercessors whose power was such that favours were granted or miracles performed through their prayers, especially at their shrines. The legitimacy of such localized cults was certified by the local bishop or abbot of the place in question. Researches in hagiography have demonstrated that many such venerated saints had dubious historical pedigrees.

The response to this rather informally spontaneous evolution of the veneration of the saints came through a process known as canonization, i.e. a procedure by which a person became formally recognized by being added to a list (a canon) of those who could receive formal liturgical honours either in the church as a whole on a particular day or in a particular place or within a particular religious community.

In the West, Pope John XV in 993 was the first pope to canonize a person who lived and died outside Rome itself. In 1234 Pope Gregory IX established a law that prohibited any canonization without the approval of the Bishop of Rome. It was only in the fourteenth century that procedures for canonizations were put into place. Pope Sixtus V established the Congregation of Rites to oversee canonizations and the authentication of relics in 1588. Pope Urban VIII (died 1644) stipulated that any unauthorized cult of a person would automatically disqualify that person from consideration for canonization. The canon lawyer and later Pope Benedict XIV published a five-volume work on the canonization of saints between 1734–8 that would be normative in the church until the papacy of John Paul II. The steps in the canonization process were highly juridical and adversarial (they include the office of the 'devil's advocate' who argued against the case), but were, in the main, included in the old code of canon law (1917).

The apostolic constitution published by Pope John Paul II under the title *Divinus perfectionis magister* (The Divine Teacher of Perfection, 1983) now stands as the normal process for beatification and canonization in the Roman Catholic Church. The stipulations of that constitution greatly streamline the procedures for canonizations; it is less a juridical procedure and more a matter of historical

RELICS

The veneration of relics is particularly characteristic of Roman Catholicism but the practice goes back almost to the beginnings of the Christian church. Relics are, strictly speaking, preserved remains of the bodies of saints, but the term is extended to objects which have been worn or touched by a saint. The most famous relics of all are the fragments of the supposed true cross on which Jesus was crucified, discovered according to legend by the Empress Helena, wife of the Emperor Constantine, in 326.

The cult of relics originated with the veneration of martyrs; the account of one of the earliest Christian martyrs, Bishop Polycarp of Smyrna, describes his bones as 'more precious than precious stones'. Its popularity derived from the belief that even the tiniest fragment of a holy person conveyed the fullness of that person in the place where the relic was kept. As well as pilgrimages to holy places, and often even before these developed, the transportation of relics all over the world, particularly from the East, where Christianity had its beginnings, and the establishment of shrines to contain them, brought the holy within reach of large numbers of people. Relics were placed in reliquaries of various sizes, of valuable material and richly decorated, or within altars. Sometimes, as with the consecrated host at the eucharist, they were put in monstrances so that they could be displayed to the faithful. Miracles were attributed to relics.

Martyr

As demand grew, so the bodies of saints increasingly came to be dismembered at death and sometimes there was an unseemly rush to get hold of such bodies and process them. As early as the fourth century sermons were being preached against this and there were laws against it. However, the practice was still going on in the time of Thomas Aquinas, who himself sanctioned the cult of relics, following Jerome and Augustine earlier.

The time of the Crusades saw a vast increase in the importation of relics from the Holy Land. This also increased the problem of the authenticity of relics, which had been there almost from the start. John Calvin pointed out that the extant fragments of the true cross, if put together, would fill a large ship.

Thomas Aquinas
Church fathers
Crusades

The Reformers condemned the cult of relics, but it was endorsed by the Council of Trent.

investigation. Such processes typically begin at the local level, where investigation into the virtues, holiness, orthodoxy, and life of charity of the person is carried out. The dossier of the person, including all research into his or her life and a complete biography, goes on to Rome, where the merits of the case are discussed by the prelates in the Congregation for the Causes of the Saints. A separate dossier on the attestation of miracles (one for a beatification; another for canonization) is judged. The Congregation sends its final report to the Pope, who alone judges if a person is to be beatified or canonized. Beatification permits a person to be honoured on a local basis, while canonization, in the words of the declaration of canonization, allows that his or her 'memory shall be kept with pious devotion by the universal church'.

The Orthodox Church does not follow any official procedure for the recognition of saints. Initially the church accepted as saints those who had suffered martyrdom for Christ. The saints were believed to be saints by the grace of God, and to need no official recognition. The Christian people, reading their lives and witnessing their performance of miracles, accept and honour them as saints. John Chrysostom, persecuted and exiled by the civil and ecclesiastical authorities, was accepted as a saint of the church by popular acclaim. Basil the Great was accepted immediately after his death as a saint of the church by the people. Recently, in order to avoid abuses, the Ecumenical Patriarchate has issued special encyclical letters (*tomoi*) in which the Holy Synod recognizes or accepts the popular feelings about a saint. One such example is Nicodemos of the Holy Mountain (1729–1809), who spent his life as a monk on Mount Athos and in addition to writing a classic book, *Unseen Warfare*, edited the *Philokalia*, a collection of ascetic and mystical writings of the fourth to the fifteenth century. He was canonized in 1955.

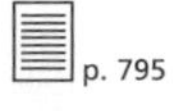
p. 795

Orthodox theologians group the saints into six categories: the apostles, the prophets, the martyrs, the fathers and leaders of the church, the monastics and the just, those who lived in the world, leading exemplary lives as clergy or laity with their families, becoming examples for imitation in society.

The veneration of the saints has not been without critics; indeed, their invocation, the veneration offered to their relics, and honours paid to them in the liturgy have been rejected by most of the churches that evolved from the Protestant Reformation of the sixteenth century. By contrast, Roman Catholics, Orthodox, Anglicans and some Lutherans have honoured the saints from time immemorial. What are the main theological and pastoral reasons for this practice?

Reformation

Named saints, in the first instance, are a reminder that while Christian spirituality consists in following Christ who is the one Way, there are, in fact, many ways of following that one Way. The lives of the saints show how people have had insights into gospel living that reflect their own age and the intuitions that come from a particular age. They demonstrate that it is possible to live the gospel in a particular fashion. In some cases, the

SAINTS AND THEIR SYMBOLIC REPRESENTATIONS

Down the centuries, Christians have been edified and entertained by the stories of saints and their martyrdoms, and have chosen them as patron saints. Symbolic representations can be found in churches in many forms. Most of the the stories are legends, and the saints are no longer officially recognized by the Roman Catholic Church. However, they are still objects of popular devotion. Here are some of them.

Agatha: Died in Sicily *c.*250. A rich young woman, under persecution she was sent to a brothel but refused to accept customers. She was tortured and her breasts were cut off. She was martyred by being rolled on hot coals.
Symbol: dish containing her breasts

Catherine: Died in Alexandria *c.*310. Engaged in debate with pagan philosophers many of whom she converted. She was ordered to be broken on the wheel, but when she touched it, it fell apart. She was beheaded.
Symbol: wheel

Cecilia: Died in Rome *c.*117. A Roman noblewoman, she converted her husband and his brother who developed a ministry of giving burial to martyred Christians. They were martyred and she was in turn martyred for burying them. Patron saint of music.
Symbol: garland of roses and musical instruments

p. 217

Christopher: Martyred *c.*251. A powerfully built man who travelled the world in search of adventure. He spent some time carrying travellers across a dangerous stream. One day he carried a small child across, but as they went the child grew heavier and heavier. On the other side the child explained that he was the Christ bearing the sins of the world, and he baptized Christopher. Patron saint of travellers.
Symbol: man carrying child

George: Beheaded *c.*304 in Lydda, Palestine. Killed a fierce dragon in Libya which was being offered maidens, and even a princess, for food by the terrified locals. Chivalrous to women and generous to the poor.
Symbol: spear and dragon

Lawrence: Died 258. Archdeacon of Rome at a time of persecution. When ordered to appear for execution bringing the treasures of his church he brought along the crippled, blind and sick. He was roasted to death on a gridiron.
Symbol: gridiron

Lucy: Lived in Syracuse *c.*283–304. A devout Christian, she refused an arranged marriage with a pagan who denounced her to the authorities. Her eyes were torn out in torture and she was stabbed to death.
Symbol: eyes on a plate

Nicholas: Died *c.*346. Bishop of Myra, he was a protector of the poor and wronged. He gave three bags of gold to a poor man about to sell his daughters into prostitution and raised to life three boys who had been murdered and pickled in a barrel of brine. He became Santa Claus. Patron saint of pawnbrokers.
Symbol: three golden balls

Sebastian: Died *c.*288. A senior Roman officer, he visited Christians in prison at a time of persecution and brought them food. Suspected of himself being a Christian he was tied to a tree and riddled with arrows. He survived, but was beaten to death.
Symbol: naked young man pierced with arrows

Ursula: Travelled around Europe with either 11 or 11,000 virgins; all of them were tortured to death in an attempt to persuade them to renounce Christianity. She inspired the Ursuline order, founded for the education of young Catholic girls.
Symbol: arrow

Vitus: Died *c.*303. Son of a pagan senator in Sicily, who became a Christian at the age of twelve and was constantly persecuted. He was thrown to the lions but they would not touch him so he was boiled in oil along with a rooster, as part of the ritual against sorcery. In the sixteenth century Germans believed that they could gain a year's good health by dancing in front of his statue.
Symbol: rooster

David Hugh Farmer (ed), *The Oxford Dictionary of Saints*, Oxford: OUP 2003

Spirituality

lives of individual saints take on 'classic' status in the sense that their lives have an overflow of meaning that can be drawn on by subsequent ages. Some classic saints, Francis, Dominic, Francis de Sales and Ignatius Loyola, either through their own writings or those of their disciples, go on to define a 'school' of spirituality which often bears their name: Franciscan, Dominican, Salesian, Ignatian, etc.

Secondly, recalling the memory of the saints either formally in the liturgy or informally in everything from taking a saint's name to dedicating churches in their honour helps the Catholic community to realize that the church is not just the body of congregations that exist in this particular moment of history; it is also formed of the large numbers of those who have followed Christ through the ages as this is described in the New Testament: 'we are surrounded by so great a cloud of witnesses' (Hebrews 12.1). The saints show just what a wide variety there is

THE MAKING OF A SAINT

In the early church, there was no formal process of officially recognizing a saint. There was widespread veneration of martyrs, whose remains would be placed in a church; this amounted to formal acknowledgement of their sainthood. However, from the tenth century onwards, reference was increasingly made to the Pope over the process of *canonization*, as it came to be called, and Pope Gregory IX in the thirteenth century ruled that all cases for canonization should be referred to Rome.

Martyr

A preliminary process of *beatification* was introduced in the sixteenth century and the responsibility for these two processes was given to the Congregation of Rites. In the seventeenth century, Pope Urban VIII laid down procedures which were to become the canon law of the Roman Catholic Church until the 1960s, when Pope Paul VI decentralized and shortened the processes. They are now carried out by courts from diocesan to regional level and then by a new congregation, the Congregation for the Causes of Saints.

p. 1220

Beatification begins by bringing together all available information about the candidate for sainthood, including miracles performed before or after the candidate's death. An advocate is appointed by the bishop concerned (popularly known as the 'devil's advocate') to make sure that everything is brought out. After all the evidence has been examined, if there is to be a beatification it is pronounced by the Pope. A person who has been beatified bears the name 'Blessed'.

Canonization follows the same course, except that there has to be evidence of two further miracles after beatification, performed after prayer has been made to the candidate.

Becoming a saint means that new saints' names are included in the list of saints and called on in the prayers of the church; festivals are celebrated in their name and churches named after them; and their relics are preserved and venerated.

In the Eastern Orthodox churches canonization arises out of spontaneous devotion and veneration by the faithful. A request for a person to be recognized as a saint is presented to the bishop, and then examined by a commission.

In other traditions which have no formal process of canonization, the list of 'saints' commemorated in the church's calendar does expand. For example the US Lutheran Book of Worship now has days commemorating such persons as Dietrich Bonhoeffer and Dag Hammarskjøld, and the Church of England calendar includes commemorations of Florence Nightingale, Charles Gore and Oscar Romero, among others.

among those who follow Christ, and in so doing become our contemporaries. In short, they help to expand our understanding of the church beyond the merely sociological dimension. The Second Vatican Council (1962–5) has illustrated this truth in various places in its declarations. The Dogmatic Constitution on the Church (*Lumen gentium*) asserts that 'just as Christian communion among wayfarers brings us closer to Christ, so our companionship with the saints joins us to Christ, from whom as from their fountain and head issue every grace and the life of God's people' (§ 50).

Pope John Paul II has been notably active in his papacy in promoting the cult of the saints. He has beatified or canonized more persons in his papacy than any other pope in the history of the church. In his pastoral visits to various parts of the world he has made it a practice to canonize someone whose roots were in that area of the world. The purpose behind these activities seems to derive from two intentions. First, the Pope has tried to single out those persons who stand for Christian fidelity in the face of the moral evils that face the contemporary world; hence his interest in persons who suffered under totalitarian regimes, such as Maximilian Kolbe and Edith Stein, who died at Auschwitz, or the Ukrainian martyrs who suffered at the hands of Stalinists. Secondly, he aims to emphasize the witness of holiness that can be found throughout the church in its various localities. For both reasons the Pope sees the raising up of saints as an instrument of evangelism. In using that strategy the Pope echoes in practice an observation made by the late Pope Paul VI who, in his apostolic exhortation *Evangelii nuntiandi*, wrote: 'Modern people listen more willingly to witnesses than to teachers, and if they listen to teachers it is because they are witnesses.'

p. 700

LAWRENCE S. CUNNINGHAM

Peter Brown, *The Cult of the Saints*, Chicago: University of Chicago Press and London: SCM Press 1982; Lawrence S. Cunningham, *The Meaning of Saints*, San Francisco: Harper & Row 1980; Elizabeth A. Johnson, *Friends of God and Prophets: A Feminist Reading of the Communion of Saints*, New York: Continuum 1998; Richard McBrien, *Lives of the Saints. From Mary and Francis of Assisi to John XXIII and Mother Teresa*, San Francisco: HarperSanFrancisco 2001; William Thompson, *Fire and Light: The Saints and Theology*, Mahwah, NJ: Paulist Press 1987; Kenneth Woodward, *Making Saints*, New York and London: Simon & Schuster 1990

SALVATION

Apocalyptic, Atonement, Body, Church, Conversion, Death, Destiny and purpose, Eschatology, Evil, Faith, Forgiveness, Holiness movement, Hope, Initiation, Jesus, Justification, Kingdom of God, Life after death, Mission, Predestination, Sacraments, Sacrifice, Sin

'What must I do to be saved?' This cry, uttered by a jailer in Philippi when his prisoners, including Paul the apostle Paul, are miraculously released (Acts 16.30), and by John Bunyan's Pilgrim right at the beginning of his progress, expresses a concern which lies at the heart of Christianity. The salvation (another word used is redemption, meaning deliverance from sin, suffering and death) that it looks for may be understood as the fulfilment of the deepest yearnings of human beings for peace, healing and harmony within and between themselves and their world. Christians believe that this goal can be reached through faith in Jesus Christ, through whom humanity is released from all that obstructs fullness of life, and is reconciled to God. Beyond this point, wide differences in the understanding of salvation arise, over whether it may be found only in the Christian church, or Other faiths through other faiths; only in this world or in some heavenly realm; and whether it is already a fact, or rather a process, or a goal to be hoped for, or perhaps some combination of all these.

The Latin *salvare* means 'save' or 'heal'. What salvation means will largely depend on different perceptions of the problem that needs to be overcome. This may be the fear of death; the burden of sin and guilt; the threat of evil powers, natural or supernatural; a sense of condemnation in the face of divine justice, or of worthlessness arising in oneself or imposed by others; or a sense of meaninglessness.

Bible In the face of all such threats, burdens and failures, the New Testament proclaims salvation stemming from and grounded in the love of God revealed in Christ and his atoning work. The pervasive theme of hope points to victory over meaninglessness, even if that term is not employed. Forgiveness Sin and guilt are met with love and forgiveness, condemnation with acquittal, fear of death by the Satan power of life, the power of the devil by the victory of Christ. The outcome looked for in each case is life in loving relationship with God. But this cannot be without cost: the abandonment of false idols, of godless self-centred or world-centred existence.

However, this is not the whole answer. The power of evil is still all too real in the lives of individuals and nations, in the church as well as in the world. In the face of this challenge, Christianity has traditionally emphasized that although salvation has already been won in Christ, it is not yet complete in Christians. Therefore the fulfilment of God's purposes for humanity and the whole creation lies in some sense beyond the world as we know it, and will be revealed at the *eschaton,* or 'last day', symbolized by the second coming of Christ. In the meantime, faith believes Holy Spirit that in individuals and communities the Holy Spirit is at work healing broken lives and restoring broken fellowship.

The problem for many today is that talk of the devil, sin and guilt, of Christ's second coming and even of God, means little. Rather than persisting with such language, some theologians have attempted to reinterpret it symbolically in terms they hope will still make sense. Existentialists such as Rudolf Bultmann speak of human beings uniquely aware of death, and hence of their finitude; tempted to hide from it, they lose themselves in the world of things or in the crowd and so fall into inauthentic existence. Similarly, Paul Tillich speaks of turning away from the ground of being and so falling into estrangement by turning to what is finite and creaturely instead of to God, with demonic and destructive consequences. Salvation will then mean the overcoming of inauthentic existence or estrangement, not by human effort but by the gift of grace given through Christ and received in faith.

In recent years the question of salvation has arisen in new forms out of various experiences of negation. Liberation theologians especially have criticized the existentialist approach for its typically Western individualism. In the face of abject poverty in Latin America they have drawn on Marxist analysis and emphasized the conditioning of human life by social and economic forces and the reality not only of personal sin, but also of structural sin, as it is entrenched through capitalism. In this context salvation is seen largely in the liberation of the oppressed through the overcoming of alienated and alienating political and economic conditions in the present world.

Liberation theology

A problem is that without the hope of heaven (however that is understood), a fundamental Christian belief that humanity's salvation is ultimately in God's hands, not its own, is put in question; but with that hope, commitment to salvation through liberation from injustice and poverty in this world may be weakened (as Karl Marx maintained in his criticism of Christianity as the 'opiate of the people'). Yet the doctrine of the incarnation points to God in Christ present and active in the world here and now, and the New Testament portrays Jesus on the side of the weak and poor against worldly powers, and as engaged in the work of healing in the present as well as proclaiming the coming of the kingdom of God.

Critics of Christianity
Incarnation

Poverty

In distinct but comparable ways the question of salvation is raised in feminist and black theology, as it arises out of different experiences of estrangement or the denial of human worth. However, critics point to the danger of letting different cultural circumstances determine the understanding of Christ's saving work, instead of letting his life and work reveal humanity's true need.

Feminist theology

African American Christianity

A difficulty remains over the understanding of time and eternity. Traditionally, the goal of salvation has been understood in terms of life after death in a manner that somehow involves continuity and at the same time radical discontinuity with present existence, for good or ill (in other words, the hope of heaven has been matched by the threat of hell). The problems posed by philosophy, science and ethics to these beliefs have led some theologians (such as Bultmann and Tillich) to reject the idea of eternity as endless life and to reinterpret the Christian hope of eternal life in terms of a transcendent quality and way of life in the present in which believers can participate here on earth, while 'hell' stands for the negative consequences of not doing so. Objections arise here over the apparent watering down of heaven and hell and the seeming loss of human responsibility before God to which the Bible witnesses. Yet the other difficulties remain, and even certainty of heaven can have demonic consequences when claimed as a reward for crime and murder.

Time

Eternity

The Christian hope of salvation, as present gift and future hope, is grounded in the revelation of God's love and the experience of healing already begun. The beliefs that flow from this are fundamental to Christian faith, but human language, understanding and experience cannot expect to measure up to the ultimate mystery of salvation as the fulfilment of God's purposes.

Sickness and healing

TREVOR WILLIAMS

Anglican-Roman Catholic International Commission II, *Salvation and the Church*, London: Church House Publishing 1989; Doctrine Commission of the Church of England, *The*

Mystery of Salvation, London: Church House Publishing 1995; Jürgen Moltmann, *The Spirit of Life*, London: SCM Press and Philadelphia: Fortress Press 1992; Karl Rahner, *Foundations of Christian Faith*, New York: Seabury Press 1978; Paul Tillich, *Systematic Theology*, vols 1 and 2, Chicago: University of Chicago Press 1951, 1954 and Welwyn: James Nisbet 1953, 1957, reissued London: SCM Press 1978

Satan

Satan is one of the most intriguing figures in the Christian religion. In modern times he has been largely ignored or discounted in more 'liberal' churches, but he is still the object of strong belief and fearful attention in many Christian denominations. He is accepted not only as the chief spiritual opponent of God, determined to procure the damnation of as many human souls as he can, but also as one who torments men and women by 'possessing' their bodies. Moreover, there is a widespread belief that there are 'Satanists' in our midst, who worship Satan and perform obscene rites in his honour.

Jesus

Most people who talk about Satan, whether believers or sceptics, are agreed on his history: he was originally one of the highest angels in heaven, named Lucifer, who rebelled against God and was cast out. He subsequently caused Adam and Eve to sin, and ever after he has sought to enlarge his kingdom of hell.

This history, however, is not biblical, but rather is an account based on conjectures, mainly made by the early church fathers. What the Bible actually says about Satan is considerably different.

Bible

The Hebrew word *satan* means 'adversary', and we find it used of human adversaries in the Hebrew Bible. Hadad the Edomite is said to be an adversary (*satan*) of King Solomon (1 Kings 11.14–25). But in the story of Balaam and his ass in the book of Numbers the way is blocked by an angelic *satan* (22.22). In the opening of the book of Job, 'the satan' seems to be identified with other 'sons of God', angelic figures who assemble in God's court. The satan's duty is to patrol the earth, spying out what is happening. He thinks that Job's fidelity needs to be tested, and God agrees to the tests. In the book of Zechariah (3.1–5) another *satan* acts as a prosecuting attorney against the high priest Joshua, while the angel of the Lord acts as defence attorney.

The Jewish rendering of the Hebrew Bible into Greek, called the Septuagint, translates *satan* with the word *diabolos* (hence the English word 'devil'); this means 'adversary', but sometimes has the connotation of 'slanderer'. It is usually a common noun, 'a devil', but in the book of Job, the common-noun *satan* becomes a proper noun, *ho Diabolos*, 'the Devil'.

p. 1152

In the books of the New Testament 'the Devil' is also a proper name, and it alternates with the proper name *Satanas* (from the Aramaic form of *Satan*). The big question is: is Satan still an agent of the divine government, as he was in the Old Testament? The answer seems to be yes. Jesus calls him the ruler of the world (John 12.31), and Satan explains to Jesus that he has been given authority over all of the kingdoms of the world, and that he can delegate it to whomever he wishes (Luke 4.5–6). Jesus later acknowledges that Satan acts with authorization: he has asked for and received permission to test the apostles (Luke 22.31–2). In the New Testament letters Satan and his associates (the principalities and powers) also have authority over the law of Moses and the astrological and natural forces of the world. Satan is in charge of disciplining even Christian offenders (1 Corinthians 5.5; 1 Timothy 1.20), and he functions as the angel of death (Hebrews 2.14; Jude 9).

Though Satan's methods have always been brutal and immoral (John 8.44), he can be seen as insisting on strict standards for the human race, and as being defensive about change, especially the innovations preached by that alleged son of God, Jesus. Jesus predicts that Satan's position as ruler of the world will soon come to an end. But in the Book of Revelation, at a time when Jesus is established in heaven as the divine lamb, we hear that Satan has continued his traditional role as celestial prosecutor: he accuses 'our brothers' night and day before God (Revelation 12.10). This function will continue until his eventual expulsion from heaven at the hands of Michael (12.7–9).

Satan is also called Lucifer, but where did the Lucifer story come from? The name 'Lucifer', which means 'Light-bearer', is the designation for the planet Venus when it appears as the Morning Star, just before the rising of the sun. In the New Testament, only Jesus is spoken of in this way. For instance, on the last page of Revelation, we read: 'I, Jesus … am the root and descendant of David, the bright Morning Star' (22.16).

Now there is one person in the Old Testament who is called the Morning Star, namely Nebuchadnezzar, king of Babylon, who has been holding the Jews captive. When it seems that the captivity is finally coming to an end, a prophecy is put into the mouth of Isaiah: 'See how you are fallen from heaven, O Morning Star, Son of Dawn!' (14.12). Christian interpreters, beginning with Origen of Alexandria (*c.* 158–254), while acknowledging that the passage literally applied to Nebuchadnezzar, argued or assumed that it applied allegorically to Satan, and they re-located the future battle between Satan and Michael, which was to terminate his function as heavenly accuser, to before the creation of the world.

The idea that Satan was connected to the serpent who deceived Eve in the Garden of Eden may have become current in the time of Jesus. But once Satan was envisaged as the Luciferian rebel against God, his intervention in human affairs became much more sinister, with motivations of revenge and envy added to or replacing those of law enforcement and over-zealousness in testing.

The demons or unclean spirits who appear in the Gospels are portrayed as being under the control of Satan, like all illnesses. They seem to belong to a comparatively low level of being, like parasitic microbes, with no motivation other than self-preservation. But they were eventually interpreted as angels who fell in Satan's rebellion, like the principalities and powers, and while they are rarely called 'satans', they are often called 'devils'. Thus 'devil' reverted to its original status as a common noun, while the proper name of 'the Devil' continued in use.

In early texts the underworld has no one in charge, except for the personifications of Hades and Death, and in the first Christian centuries the Devil has no role as the guardian or punisher of souls at the time of Christ's death. Fire is prepared for the Devil and his angels (Matthew 25.41), but only in the future, and perhaps not for their own punishment, or not only for their punishment, but as a means for them to function as the punishers of men.

Tertullian and Augustine argued that the Devil was cast down to the air above the earth, but there was an alternative view that the fallen angels were punished in the hellish underworld. Thomas Aquinas approved of the view that Lucifer was originally the highest angel in heaven who caused the other angels to sin; and he holds that, no matter where they are, even while operating on earth, they are constantly tormented spiritually by hell-fire.

By the second century CE, Satan and the other angels or demons were associated and identified with the gods of paganism, and a formal rejection of paganism was incorporated into the ritual of baptism in the form of a renunciation of Satan. Elaborate preliminary exorcisms, the driving out of evil spirits thought to be responsible for causing people to sin, also became part of baptism from early on. These rites were soon interpreted metaphorically to refer to the malign influence of Satan and his subordinate angels. Beginning in the sixteenth century, Protestants for the most part eliminated the exorcisms, but they remained in the Roman Catholic ritual until the new rites of 1969 and 1972, when all direct addresses to the Devil were eliminated.

Paganism
Initiation

EXORCISM

The first three Gospels are agreed that the casting out of evil spirits was an important activity of Jesus and exorcisms, as these are called, appear in all strands of the tradition. Jesus' followers were also expected to cast out demons in his name (Mark 16.17). Exorcism was also practised in Judaism; in one of the few humorous stories in the New Testament, itinerant Jewish exorcists in Ephesus attempt to cast out an evil spirit, but the spirit retorts: 'Jesus I know, and Paul I know, but who are you?' (Acts 19.15).

Exorcism was practised in the early church, and came as it were to have two degrees. Those thought to have an evil spirit were exorcised, usually by a bishop or a priest appointed by him; this was known as solemn exorcism. However, exorcism also formed part of the rite of initiation, and new members of the church, catechumens, were exorcised before they were baptized. Such exorcisms are preserved in the modern Roman Catholic order of baptism. In the middle of the second century an order of exorcists was created in connection with exorcisms at baptisms, as one of the minor orders: it was abolished in 1972.

Over the centuries exorcisms have taken many forms and have involved the use of holy oil, holy water and salt, herbs and incense, along with prayer and adjurations. In the 1960s and 1970s, with the rise of the charismatic movement, there was considerable interest in solemn exorcism, not least in the Church of England, and exorcists were appointed in many dioceses. The first new Roman Catholic ritual for exorcism since 1614 was issued in 1999; it includes prayers, the blessing and sprinkling of holy water, the laying of hands on the possessed and making the sign of the cross and continues with appeals to Christ, the Holy Spirit and the saints of the church. The fact that the Roman Catholic Church has had to issue instructions against illicit exorcisms indicates their growing frequency. This increased frequency may also have resulted from William Peter Blatty's 1971 novel *The Exorcist* and William Friedkin's 1974 film of it, which created widespread public interest in the practice of exorcism.

Michael Cuneo, *American Exorcism: Expelling Demons in the Land of Plenty*, New York: Doubleday 2001

The traditional formulas of pre-baptismal exorcism had long been used outside baptism, for persons who showed symptoms of literal physical 'possession' (seizure and internal occupation) by Satan or one or more of his fellow evil spirits. The use of such rituals was severely restricted in the Roman Catholic tradition with the publication of a new priest's manual, the *Roman Ritual*, in 1614. Any exorcizing had to be authorized by the bishop, and only in cases in which the Devil's agency was verified by otherwise unexplainable signs, such as superhuman strength, suddenly acquired knowledge of foreign languages, or clairvoyance. The result of these rules was a dramatic decrease in alleged instances of possession. But belief in diabolical possession remained, and in 1999 the Vatican issued a slightly updated version of the rules and formulas.

Canon law

p. 345

Few such precautions are taken in many evangelical and charismatic circles, where demon-expellings, along with other forms of faith healing, remain in practice. They often take place in public gatherings and consist in the laying on of hands and prayers. It is often necessary to restrain the writhings of the perceived victims of the Devil's torments.

Heresy

Those who believe in the active interference of the Devil in human affairs find it easy to attribute all obstacles or difficulties to him. And the idea readily suggests itself that one's enemies are supported by the Devil, with or without their knowledge, even though, as in the case of possession, diabolical deeds can be 'proved' to be such only when they are seemingly miraculous. If certain actions or manifestations are beyond human power they can only be caused by a superhuman agency; and if they are malign, that leaves only the Devil and his angels. Augustine summed it up like this: non-Christian miracles ('wonders') are either false, or they are the result of compacts between men and demons. This explanation became part of medieval canon law. And in the year 1254 Pope Alexander IV warned the newly-appointed heresy-prosecutors (Inquisitors) not to deal with alleged sorcery cases unless they were specifically connected with heresy. But eventually the implicit

THE WITCH CRAZE

The witch craze is a strange phenomenon in Christianity. From the fourteenth century onwards, in parts of Europe – above all in France, parts of Germany, in Switzerland and northern Italy, the Low Countries and Scotland, but less so in southern Italy and Spain, England, Ireland, Scandinavia and eastern Europe – individuals, the vast majority of them women, were hunted down, tried and killed on suspicion of being witches. They were supposed to have made a pact with the devil which they sealed by sleeping with him, to have conjured up the devil and danced with the devil. They were accused of unspeakable activities, often desecrating the crucifix and bread and wine of the eucharist.

The first trials of witches took place in the fourteenth century; then at the end of the next century two momentous documents were published: Pope Innocent VIII's bull *Summis desiderantes affectibus* ('Desiring with the utmost ardour', 1484), condemning witchcraft as Satanism, and the *Malleus maleficarum* ('The Hammer of Witches'), a handbook on witchcraft by two German inquisitors, Heinrich Institoris and Jacob Sprenger, which was reprinted around 30 times in the next two centuries and became the standard work on the subject. It included guidelines for punishment. The witch craze in Europe reached its height at the end of the sixteenth and beginning of the seventeenth century, but there were still mass burnings of witches in Brandenburg in 1786. The first hanging of a witch in North America was in New England in 1647; the famous 'witches' of Salem were hanged in 1692. All in all, scholars reckon that there were at least 100,000 executions of witches.

The hunt for witches began with rumours or suspicions that certain people were in league with the devil; they would then be interrogated and subjected to ordeals based on popular suspicion. Did they suffer pain when pricked (the devil made them immune to pain)? Did they float when 'ducked' (the devil kept them afloat)? Did they have 'the devil's mark'? Denunciations began at a local level and were investigated in local courts: these were the most brutal; strangely enough the Inquisition with its strict rules was a mitigating factor. Women seem to have been the main victims, but recent research has shown that between a fifth and a quarter of those executed for witchcraft were men.

The Reformation and Counter-Reformation did not affect the witch craze; belief in witchcraft was common to Catholics and Protestants alike. Opposition to the witch craze began with the Jesuit Friedrich von Spee's *Cautio criminalis or Legal Objections to the Witch Trials* (1631) and the legal works of the Protestant Christian Thomasius (1655–1728), who was instrumental in founding the University of Halle. The Enlightenment finally brought it to an end.

Why the witch craze developed has yet to be explained satisfactorily. There are many partial explanations, from the sexual obsessions of celibate inquisitors and women as scapegoats for crop failure, disease and death to social or economic changes, but none is satisfactory. *That* it developed, though, cannot be forgotten, any more than can the parallel anti-Judaism in Christianity.

p. 685

Lara Apps and Andrew Gow, *Male Witches in Modern Europe*, Manchester: Manchester University Press 2003; Ian Bostridge, *Witchcraft and its Transformations*, Oxford: OUP 1997; Norman Cohn, *Europe's Inner Demons. The Demonization of Christians in Medieval Christendom*, revd edn, Chicago: University of Chicago Press 2000 infidelity that was detected in all sorcerers was considered to be the equivalent of heresy, even if there was no explicit pact with the Devil.

It is unfortunate that the English term 'witchcraft' has been used by historians to speak of this development, because in general accusations of magic in the British Isles were usually free of diabolical interpretations until the late sixteenth century. European ideas of diabolic sorcery were denounced by Reginald Scot in his *Discovery of Witchcraft* (1584), but his denunciation had the effect of stimulating others, notably King James VI of Scotland in his *Demonology* (1597), to defend and promote such notions.

The number of sorcery persecutions has been exaggerated by earlier historians. Even in the most intense period of the anti-sorcery movement, from about 1550 to 1630, witch-hunting and prosecution was limited to a few specific places. All prosecutions ceased by the eighteenth century, thanks in great part to a greater insistence on the rules of evidence.

Liberal Protestant doubts about the existence of the Devil began with the de-literalizing analyses of Friedrich Schleiermacher, especially in his *The Christian Faith* (1821–2). Existential doubts about the Devil did not surface in Roman Catholic circles until the 1960s. The usual question in this regard is whether there is a real supernatural person named Satan. Sceptics tend to conclude that the biblical satans are fictitious characters developed in the world-view of the Hebrew imagination. Modern believers in the reality of the Devil are invariably thinking of the post-biblical story of the rebellion and fall of Lucifer as outlined above, and rarely consider the possible existence of unfallen 'diabolical' ministers such as the biblical satans who are authorized to enforce divine mandates or to test the virtue of human beings (as in the case of Job).

Satanism
Worship of Satan and other devils or demons was taken for granted in the early church, when pagan gods were identified with the fallen angels of Christian thought. Even in later times the idea persisted that the heathen were under the sway of the Devil, and if their gods were thought to exist at all, they were judged to be diabolical spirits, that is, fallen angels.

It is doubtful whether there were ever any worshippers of Satan under his own name until recent times. Historians consider medieval rumours or charges of such worship to be groundless. Accusations of black masses in the late seventeenth century were as imaginary as the literary portrayals of them two centuries later. The same is true of more recent suspicions connecting child abuse with Satanism.

Persons who profess themselves as Satanists in the modern world usually do not worship Satan in any traditional Christian sense, but rather take Lucifer as a symbol of divine force (this is true of the Church of Satan in 1960s San Francisco) or of rebellion, or else they claim to be devil-worshippers for its shock-value.

HENRY ANSGAR KELLY

G. B. Caird, *Principalities and Powers: A Study in Pauline Theology*, London: OUP 1956; H. A. Kelly, *The Devil, Demonology, and Witchcraft* (1974), reprinted with new appendix Eugene, OR: Wipf & Stock 2004, *The Devil at Baptism* (1985), reprinted Eugene, OR: Wipf & Stock 2004 and *Satan: A Biography*, Cambridge: CUP 2005; Jeffrey Burton Russell, *Satan: The Early Christian Tradition*, Ithaca: Cornell University Press 1981, *Lucifer: The Devil in the Middle Ages*, Ithaca: Cornell University Press 1984 and *Mephistophiles: The Devil in the Modern World*, Ithaca: Cornell University Press 1986

Schleiermacher, Friedrich

Friedrich Daniel Ernst Schleiermacher (1768–1834) was the most important Protestant theologian after John Calvin. Through a theological 'turn to the self' he revolutionized Christian theology as Immanuel Kant had revolutionized philosophy by pointing out the impossibility of knowing 'things in themselves'. Towards the end of the Enlightenment, at a time when the very possibility of theology was in question, Schleiermacher set Christian thought on a new course which marked the beginning of modern theology. Indeed, he could be called the 'father' of liberal theology.

Philosophy
Enlightenment
Liberal theology

Schleiermacher was born into the Reformed tradition, but following his parents' conversion to the Herrnhuter Brethren he attended Moravian schools. The Pietism which he encountered there was to have a lasting impact on his understanding of Christianity, particularly through its emphasis on personal religious experience. Finding these schools too intellectually constricting, he moved to the University of Halle. In 1796 he went to Berlin to take up a preaching position and there he came under the direct influence of the romanticism of Friedrich von Schlegel (1772–1829). His thought developed in a context in which the attacks of David Hume and Immanuel Kant on the old theory of knowledge and metaphysics had undermined the dogmatic certainties of Christian orthodoxy. The Enlightenment's attention to history as well as its enthusiasm for cross-cultural comparison had removed from the Bible the special air of divine authority that it once had. For many, God was at best the deists' distant creator, at worst a non-existing human construct;

Moravian Church
Pietism

Romanticism
Biblical criticism

p. 504

the Bible was a historical document to be studied like any others; and Christianity merely one religious culture among many. If Christian theology was to survive these new challenges, its foundations had to be radically rethought. Schleiermacher's theology must be understood as fundamentally an attempt to overcome this separation between God and the world, including the world of human consciousness, which was the religious legacy of one branch of the Enlightenment.

The young Schleiermacher's response to this situation was not to attempt a reformulated dogmatic metaphysics or to follow Kant into viewing religion as a correlate of morality, a step that he explicitly rejected. Rather, he sought to re-position theology on the intellectual spectrum as a valid activity which recognized the autonomy and achievement of the new sciences, yet also claimed a legitimate role for religion in human life. His first and most influential articulation of this position is to be found in *On Religion: Speeches To Its Cultured Despisers* (1799), a series of five 'speeches' aiming to persuade the anti-religious intelligentsia to think again about Christianity. In the *Speeches* Schleiermacher presents the human mind under three headings: perception, activity and feeling. Perception gives rise to knowledge; activity is the sphere of ethics and morality; feeling is the domain of religion. For Schleiermacher, our understanding of the human person is not complete without the recognition that religious feeling (*das Gefühl*) is integral to humanity.

Schleiermacher has been much criticized for calling this religious consciousness 'feeling' (Paul Tillich later attributed the decline in male church attendance in nineteenth-century Germany to a sentimentalist misunderstanding of the term), yet such sentimentalism is not what Schleiermacher meant. *Das Gefühl* here is not to be taken as a fleeting emotion or as something merely superficial to the human person, but rather as our deepest direct experience of the world, of the infinite or, in religious terms, of God. It is bound up with the 'heart', with intuition, with self-consciousness, with the imagination, with our experience of there being always something greater. It is this experience which Schleiermacher was later to describe as 'the feeling of absolute dependence', an experience which opens the finite human creature to the infinite God and provides the basis of religious reflection: 'To be one with the infinite in the midst of the finite and to be eternal in a moment, that is the immortality of religion.' Schleiermacher's stress on the immediacy and validity of this primary religious experience, prior to all reflection and rationalization, circumvented the empty debates over the rationality of belief and re-positioned theology as the essential exploration of human religious practice.

Salvation

Trinity

It follows from Schleiermacher's emphasis on the priority of religious 'feeling' that the doctrines and dogmas of historical Christianity are simply the community's articulation of this fundamental experience; believing in doctrines as an intellectual activity does not make one truly religious. But, again, this does not mean that the experience is merely subjective and individualistic. It is always an experience of something 'objective' that is greater than the self. Further, we recognize our common dependence on the Absolute in and through our social interaction with like-minded people. There is therefore a rightful role for our historical religious communities, the churches. While no one is bound to belong to a church, a purely formal or abstract religion does not exist independently of human society. The churches, for Schleiermacher, provide a space within which the truly spiritual nature of religion may be manifest, a position that he lived out by continuing his preaching activity throughout his academic career. Needless to say, the existing churches are far from this high spiritual ideal, but by so emphasizing the social nature of piety Schleiermacher gave a new impetus to the Protestant doctrine of the church.

Schleiermacher spent three years teaching at the University of Halle and then returned to Berlin, where he became professor of theology in 1811. His work in the following years resulted in his *magnum opus*, *The Christian Faith* (1821–2; revised second edition 1830). For the later Schleiermacher, Christianity is to be understood essentially as a monotheistic faith, distinguished from other such faiths by its emphasis on the salvation brought by Jesus Christ. Christianity is a teleological religion, in the sense that God is the goal (*telos*) of our religious and moral life. Theology is reflection on the concrete reality of Christian life lived in the framework of Christ's work of salvation, and is thus closely related to ethics and to the pastoral activity of the church. It is an activity internal to the Christian faith as given, and is not an attempt to prove or demonstrate its veracity. That is why Schleiermacher called his major work *Glaubenslehre* ('The Doctrine of Faith') rather than the 'doctrine of God' implied by the word 'theology'.

Schleiermacher understood salvation not as something other-worldly or as the continuation after death of one's personal existence, but rather as a fully-developed consciousness of God in the here and now, without falsity, distortion or limit. This salvation comes through Christ, who is not simply an example to us; as the one in whom the consciousness of God is most fully present he becomes the saviour for us. In Christ we see God for us, and it is only in this 'for us' that Christianity has its meaning. One consequence of this perspective was that Schleiermacher relegated his discussion of the Trinity to an appendix to *The Christian Faith*, on the grounds that it is a derived doctrine that arises out of the lived experience of Christian faith and is not a constitutive part of the immediacy of religious feeling.

Schleiermacher's notion of sin is also an important element of his theology. While we can encounter the divine through the natural world as we experience it, we encounter God primarily through our experience of guilt, sin and redemption. Sin, for Schleiermacher, is the tension between our awareness of God as absolute and the demands made on us by our human condition, between our consciousness of the infinite and our inescapable nature as finite beings. It is the space between what we are and what we could be, and our awareness of this disjunction causes the unhappiness and guilt of a distorted conscience. In Christ the saviour we see the possibilities of what we could be if our human consciousness were imbued with the consciousness of God. Christ is thus the new Adam, the archetype of perfect humanity who, as the one whose nature is permeated with the consciousness of God, shows us the path to redemption. Salvation from sin is the overcoming of our natural estrangement; it is the abiding presence of the infinite (God) in the finite (humanity). Yet this salvation does not come from our own efforts but is mediated to us by the communication of God's grace through Christ's own God-consciousness. This is God's gratuitous offer of salvation, which we can only receive as a truly miraculous gift.

Schleiermacher's impact on modern Christian thought has been enormous. He freed theology from the burden of competing with science and placed it in an autonomous sphere of its own, namely, the analysis of human religious feeling. In so doing he provided the basis for all subsequent theologies of experience. His emphasis on the immediacy of the infinite in the finite helped to heal the breach between the world and the divine left by the Enlightenment, and dealt a severe theological blow to naïve and supernatural understandings of Christianity. His influence on areas such hermeneutics ('the art of understanding'), comparative religion and the psychology of religion have been profound. Although Schleiermacher was severely criticized by twentieth-century neo-orthodox theologians such as Karl Barth, it is his influence that is most likely to endure. He was truly the 'father' of modern theology.

JAMES M. BYRNE

Keith W. Clements, *Friedrich Schleiermacher: Pioneer of Modern Theology*, London: Collins and Minneapolis: Fortress Press 1991; B. A. Gerrish, *A Prince of the Church: Schleiermacher and the Beginnings of Modern Theology*, Philadelphia: Fortress Press and London: SCM Press 1984; Martin Redeker, *Schleiermacher: Life and Thought*, Philadelphia: Fortress Press 1973; Friedrich Schleiermacher, *On Religion: Speeches to its Cultured Despisers* translated by Richard Crouter, Cambridge: CUP 1988 and *The Christian Faith* ed H. R. Mackintosh and J. S. Stewart, Edinburgh: T&T Clark 1948

Sin 

Scholasticism

The main goal of scholasticism is to offer an orderly treatment of the multifarious questions entertained by a particular culture. Western scholasticism, which is the best-known form, marked a change from giving 'lectures' on texts to raising 'questions' about how to relate the numerous positions presented by those texts to one another. Were these various positions reconcilable or irreconcilable? However, for all its distinctness, Western, Latin scholasticism is not a unique phenomenon. There are also forms of Jewish, Arabic, Hindu, Tibetan and Chinese scholasticism.

The cultural setting

During the twelfth century, in the French cathedral schools, the cleric in charge of education was called a *scholasticus*. *Schola* is used to designate a group: military, monastic or academic (the teacher and his students). The derivation of the Latin word from the Greek *schole*, which means leisure, suggests the resurgence of the Socratic desire to know truth for its own sake. The *scholasticus* gave his name to scholasticism, a development in thinking which comes between the world of the church fathers and the rise of the modern world.

Schools

Grace 

Science

Among the major unifying factors that shaped Latin scholasticism, one ought to include the Bible, the liturgy, the role of symbols and the educational customs inherited from the ancient world.

Bible

Symbols

Education

The Bible fashioned the outlook on the world of medieval people, their spontaneous responses to events, their social relations and their intellectual life. They thought that both their biblical ancestors and the Graeco-Roman sages were engaged in the quest for wisdom. Accordingly, they quietly assumed that there could only be one basically coherent world. This sense of overall harmony, which consisted of the multiple correspondences that could be deciphered in the universe, not only permeated learning but also expressed itself in the complexity of the cathedral.

Hermeneutical theology 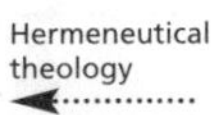

Psychology 

Cultured people had access to biblical interpretations given either in homilies based on the works of the church fathers, which were usually chanted, or in sermons on the Bible delivered by the bishop, the abbot or a designated cleric. These liturgical texts presented history as a single whole, giving pride of place to the book of Genesis (creation, fall, promise, covenant and providence), the Psalms, the Song of Songs (love between God and humankind), the Gospels (incarnation, passion

Preaching

and resurrection) and the letters of Paul (law, sin and redemption).

This biblical-liturgical mould produced a cast of mind that thought first and foremost in terms of symbols. As both the Bible and the world were read allegorically, not only words but also things themselves became signs. Everything that was heard or read affected the whole of the human person: imagination, intellect, heart. So rational thought was balanced by a religious and emotional receptivity that we rarely find in modern philosophy.

Philosophy

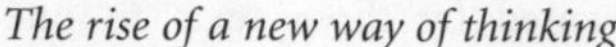

The rise of a new way of thinking

Stepping stones that made the development of scholasticism possible were put in place at the very outset of the Middle Ages. The disciplines of grammar and logic were adopted from the Greeks and Romans. Understanding scripture required the solution of problems of interpretation through a mastery of poetry, rhetoric and other literary genres (scripture was understood to have several senses). The expansion of scholarship also demanded a more frequent recourse to logic, later called dialectic, for greater precision.

In the twelfth century the Laon school, in France, produced the first 'sentence literature', collections of 'sentences', i.e. statements from the Bible, early Christian writers and contemporary scholars, to which were subsequently added reflections from Greek, Roman, Arabic and Jewish thinkers. All such assertions (the texts, not the authors themselves) were treated as 'authorities', that is, as worthy of respectful consideration. The best-known compiler is Peter Lombard (*c.*1095–1169), who also commented on the sentences he had put together.

Church fathers

This ever-growing body of diverse assertions exposed the inconsistencies and gaps in the Christian tradition. By being placed alongside divergent or contrary affirmations, each singular doctrine could be doubted or at least relativized. In response to this uneasy situation, the best minds felt compelled to highlight the contrasts between discordant opinions and to come up with satisfactory solutions. For them, the resolution of a problem could be obtained by marshalling the unequal 'authorities', introducing definitions, distinctions, classifications, using worldly concepts as analogies, advancing a reason or a cause, and eventually situating the issue within an explicit theory of knowledge or a full-blown metaphysics.

In this way the problem-solving mentality characteristic of scholasticism asserted itself. It entailed a revolutionary treatment of the Bible: no longer the purely symbolic approach which consists in expounding the various levels of meaning, but an increasingly systematic endeavour to tackle interpretative problems. More and more twelfth-century scholars began to write personal, more flexible and innovative commentaries, later to be followed by disputed questions and summas (systematic theologies). The problems they grappled with had to do with the shifts of meaning that took place in the encounter of very different cultural contexts. For example, what was to be made of an Old Testament writing in an interpretative setting framed by the New Testament? Or, how was a Christian doctrine to be construed in an intellectual cast of mind heavily influenced by Neoplatonism and Aristotelianism?

Prior to this strictly scholastic period, three geniuses had approached the Bible with that new attitude. The ninth-century John Scotus Eriugena, who knew Greek, wrestled with conflicting statements expressed by such writers as John the Evangelist, Augustine and Dionysius. In the eleventh century, Anselm of Canterbury departed from his contemporaries' style in that he did not offer a continuous reading of biblical texts, but selected a few excerpts as a springboard in order to launch into discussions based on logical rules set down by the sixth-century philosopher Boethius (*c.*480–*c.*524). A few years later, the powerful dialectician Peter Abelard enunciated hermeneutical rules in the Preface to his *Sic et Non* (Yes and No), and proceeded to list antithetical opinions to be discussed, with several remaining unresolved.

In the second half of the twelfth century, Western scholasticism became genuinely comparative. It had long grappled with books originally written in Hebrew (the Bible) and in Greek (the church fathers). As early as the eighth century, a few monks could read those languages. But the novelty of the twelfth-century renaissance was the large-scale enterprise of translating (or retranslating) non-Latin texts: hitherto unknown or poorly translated works by such authors as Aristotle; the church fathers; Byzantine thinkers such as Dionysius, Maximus the Confessor and John of Damascus; the Jewish scholar Maimonides; and several Arabic figures including Avicenna and Averroes. Thanks to this vigorous project of translation, a good number of foreign voices were allowed to speak for themselves and the circle of participants in the intellectual conversation was considerably widened.

Latin scholasticism emerged from the commentaries on the Bible and on the sentences. The linchpin was the *question*. The running exposition of the sacred text was interrupted by questions suggested by the text in connection with current and varying positions on the topic. Thus theological discussions were inserted into the simple line-by-line explanation of the text. They reflected the practice of the *lecture*, in which brief discussions would alternate with the exposition of biblical passages. The next stage in the development of scholasticism was the extraction and the circulation of longer discussions apart from their original exegetical framework. Along with this later custom goes the establishment, around 1200, of

SCHOLASTIC DOCTORS

In the high Middle Ages the leading representatives of scholasticism were given special titles. The best known of these are:

Doctor angelicus	Thomas Aquinas (*c.* 1225–74)
Doctor authenticus	Gregory of Rimini (died 1358)
Doctor christianissimus	Jean Gerson (1363–1429)
Doctor ecstaticus	Jan van Ruysbroeck (1293–1381)
Doctor invincibilis	William of Ockham (*c.* 1285–1347)
Doctor irrefragabilis	Alexander of Hales (*c.* 1186–1245)
Doctor melifluus	Bernard of Clairvaux (1090–1153)
Doctor mirabilis	Roger Bacon (*c.* 1214–92)
Doctor profundus	Thomas Bradwardine (*c.* 1295–1349)
Doctor seraphicus	Bonaventure (1217–74)
Doctor solidus	Richard of Middleton (*c.* 1249)
Doctor subtilis	Duns Scotus (*c.* 1265–1308)
Doctor universalis	Albertus Magnus (died 1280)

Thomas Aquinas

the *disputed question* (also called *disputation*), held in the afternoon, which complemented the morning lecture on the Bible. The unitary vision of medieval scholars spontaneously displayed an encyclopaedic propensity which was to culminate in the thirteenth-century summas.

The thirteenth-century scholar Albertus Magnus (Albert the Great) ranks as a model of ecumenical commitment. He exemplifies the comparative method in his commentaries on the Greek Aristotle, on the Muslim author of the *Book of Causes*, and on the Byzantine Dionysius. He is concerned with the adequacy of the translations he uses. He discusses ideas expressed by many non-Christian authors.

Albert's scholastic penchant is noticeable all through his commentaries on Dionysius the Pseudo-Areopagite, as he tries to systematize the often fragmentary thoughts offered by the author. Evidently, in the course of this recasting of Dionysius' vision, much of the imaginative and rhetorical forcefulness of the original writing is lost. However, another kind of beauty is gained: the luminosity of clear definitions systematically correlated in an overall metaphysical synthesis. Albert's commentaries on Dionysius do not purport to replace the original religious experience of hearing the word of God in a liturgical setting, of interpreting it in a symbolic context, of appreciating the literary suggestiveness of Dionysius' writings, and of being challenged by their profundity. Albert's desire to know raises questions that require for their answers the epistemological and metaphysical conceptuality he has himself painstakingly worked out in dialogue with Christian doctrine, Aristotle, Neoplatonism and Jewish and Arabic philosophy.

Similarly, Thomas Aquinas, Albert's greatest disciple, goes beyond Paul's paradoxes as he comments on the famous first chapter of Paul's First Letter to the Corinthians. Thanks to a set of distinctions, the 'folly of the cross' is construed as being not against human reason but beyond reason's capacity to grasp it fully. In Thomas' writings, one can observe a genuine attempt to get a glimpse of the truth from any 'objection', because there is always a sense in which the objector is right (to the extent that the objection conveys a resistance to some caricature of truth). He exemplifies a listening disposition towards non-Christian sources that struggles to resist the temptation of proving them wrong too expeditiously.

To sum up: Latin scholasticism was shaped in a biblical, liturgical and symbolic matrix. The factor that allowed it to emerge out of that matrix, without ceasing to be nourished by it, was the logical inquisitiveness inherited from the Greeks, coupled with the exposure to a great amount of conflicting religious and philosophical assertions. This prompted an ardent quest for intellectual consistency by the most brilliant minds of that epoch, namely those who were convinced that faith and reason could be reconciled in an attitude of discriminating openness to all expressions of truth.

Various brands of scholasticism

There have been several brands of Western scholasticism: high-medieval, late-medieval, Baroque, neo-scholasticism and historical scholasticism.

The mind-set of high scholasticism (twelfth and thirteenth centuries) aimed at an integration of all the available knowledge. It remained in direct contact with its sources: the Bible, the church fathers, Christian spirituality, Greek thought mediated by the Arabs and the Jews. The great thirteenth-century theologians (Albert, Bonaventure, Thomas, to name just three) all performed the three tasks

Thomas Aquinas

of commenting on biblical writings, discussing questions and preaching to the university body.

In the early fourteenth century a new mentality developed: logic totally overrode the sense of the symbolic. John Scotus Eriugena and William of Ockham did not put a high premium on writing biblical commentaries (if they wrote any, none of them is extant). Debates then displayed an excess of logical virtuosity, at the expense of a pious attentiveness to the divine Word. Moreover, Thomism Thomists started commenting, no longer on the sources of theology, namely the Bible, the pre-scholastic writings and Peter Lombard's *Sentences*, but on Aquinas' *Summa Theologiae.* Thus the systematic end-point became the starting point. Thomas' synthesis, which was meant to throw light on Christianity's founding documents, was received by the commentators in a static manner, with a host of excessively refined distinctions that proved irrelevant to the challenges of the times (for example, the Renaissance humanism of the Renaissance or Martin Luther's reliance on religious experience). We may call this mind-frame Baroque scholasticism.

Its relentless insistence on comparing the relevant sources and asking questions is the characteristic that distinguishes medieval Latin scholasticism from the thesis approach typical of modern Roman Catholic apologetics. In the seventeenth and eighteenth centuries the key role of Education the questions was replaced by theses, the function of which consisted in marshalling assertions, supported by proofs, Protestantism against the opinions of Protestants and Enlightenment Enlightenment thinkers. In the early twentieth century, Roman Catholic theology came to be dominated by the use of manuals.

In the nineteenth century, neo-scholasticism retained the immoderately logical cast of mind of its predecessor and ignored the romantic insights of the Catholic

Tübingen School. Still, neo-scholasticism made a useful Council contribution to the First Vatican Council. It helped many Roman Catholics to keep at a safe distance from René

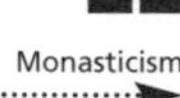

Descartes' rationalism and Immanuel Kant's idealism. In Monasticism this respect, the critical stance of thinkers like Jacques Maritain *vis-à-vis* modernity is currently being vindicated Psalms by the postmodernist philosophers.

In the first half of the twentieth century, scholars such as Pierre Mandonnet, Odon Lottin, Artur Michael Landgraf, Etienne Gilson and Marie-Dominique Chenu began to apply the methods of modern historiography

to medieval texts. At the same time, Pierre Rousselot and Bernard Lonergan went beyond the conceptualism of late-medieval thought.

Modern scholasticism is an ambiguous heritage. Its

conceptualism and its classicism run counter to our historical mind. It is not a complete system. While it is true that many modern scholastics operated within a closed intellectual scheme, any serious acquaintance with medieval scholasticism cannot fail to persuade unbiased readers that it represents a dynamic and yet modest search for understanding, entirely open to an enormous diversity of perspectives, continually on the move and aware of its limitations.

LOUIS ROY, OP

José Ignacio Cabezón (ed), *Scholasticism: Cross-Cultural and Comparative Perspectives.* Albany, NY: SUNY Press 1998; G. R. Evans, *The Language and Logic of the Bible: The Earlier Middle Ages*, Cambridge: CUP 1984; Gerald A. McCool, *The Neo-Thomists.* Milwaukee: Marquette University Press 1994; Josef Pieper, *Scholasticism: Personalities and Problems of Medieval Philosophy*, New York: McGraw-Hill 1964

Schools

The first Christian schools were the monastic schools of the fifth century. Of course, before that Christians had been concerned that their children should learn the faith as they grew up, but this learning will initially have been a familiarization with beliefs and practices through experiences in their homes and local communities. When boys and girls were old enough, they will have received formal instruction in the catechumenate. In addition, those whose parents were in a position to enrol them will have attended the classical secular schools in the Graeco-Roman tradition, where they will have been taught to read and write and will have studied philosophy. The majority of pupils will have been boys, but girls too attended schools.

Not all Christians approved of classical education. The late second-century church father Tertullian famously asked, 'What has Athens (the symbol of learning) to do with Jerusalem?' This criticism was voiced even more strongly in the fifth century when monastic schools provided a viable alternative. While these schools were mostly to train adults, they also accepted children and adolescents, teaching them to read and write and memorize the Psalms; after the fall of Rome and the barbarian invasions this alternative had become the norm, which was maintained until the fifteenth century. There were also episcopal and parish schools, which accepted some children.

In the ninth century, the Emperor Charlemagne presided over a campaign to increase literacy in the West. He decreed that each monastery and cathedral should establish a school. The English Benedictine monk Alcuin was a key figure at Charlemagne's court in Aachen, introducing the study of grammar, rhetoric and classical literature. As well as educating potential monks, the schools also catered for boys who were to have a career

William of Wykeham, founder of Winchester College, from the Chaundler manuscript, *c.* 1464

in public service. However, it was not until the eleventh century that cathedral schools became a powerful force. In the thirteenth century these schools gave birth to universities.

That in England there was interest in both schools and universities at the highest level can be seen from the foundation by William of Wykeham, Bishop of Winchester and Chancellor to Richard II, of both a university college and a school: New College, Oxford in 1379 and Winchester College in 1382. These became the models for two later foundations by King Henry VI: Eton College in 1440 and King's College, Cambridge in 1441.

The early sixteenth century saw the rise in England of grammar schools, created to meet the educational and vocational needs of the new commercial classes. They promoted the humanism of which Erasmus was the most prominent representative, though he himself did not put his views on education into practice. Here a more significant figure was John Colet (*c.* 1466–1519), Dean of St Paul's Cathedral in London, the son of a rich merchant who had twice been Lord Mayor of London. In 1509 he founded St Paul's Grammar School, with places for 153 boys.

Renaissance humanism also influenced the Reformers, though of course emphases were different. Martin Luther and other Reformers tried to make the education of both boys and girls compulsory and played a part in developing the first national education system since Roman times. Luther saw education as a way of breaking the power of the Roman Catholic Church and producing obedient citizens. His school day was planned to be one of two hours, so that pupils would also have time to learn a trade; the curriculum was based solely on the Bible. As a result of Luther's campaigning, schools were established all over Saxony.

In 1528 a grammar school or gymnasium was founded in Strasbourg. In it the classical curriculum had a place alongside the Bible. The gymnasium became a model for schools all over Europe. John Calvin taught there for four years and went on to establish schools in Geneva; while the classics were taught in them, Calvin's own interest was primarily in the teaching of the Bible.

Church of England

With the establishment of the Church of England in the sixteenth century and the dissolution of the monasteries, the whole pattern of education changed. Under Elizabeth I education became the instrument for making the nation observe one faith. All schoolmasters and university graduates had to take an oath of allegiance to the sovereign, all school textbooks had to be officially approved, and children had to learn the Catechism in the Book of Common Prayer. Although there was resistance and opposition from Puritans, Quakers, the Calvinist Church of Scotland and churches in Wales and Ireland, the Church of England gained a dominant position in education that it was to maintain for three centuries.

Counter-Reformation
Religious orders

Responding to the work of the Reformers, in the context of the Roman Catholic Counter-Reformation the Society of Jesus established schools and colleges all over Europe; this earned the Jesuits the title of 'schoolmasters of Europe'; by the eighteenth century there were 700 Jesuit schools and seminaries. First founded for would-be members of the order, they soon accepted other boys. While piety was thought important, the schools followed the classical curriculum. Other religious orders followed suit. The Ursulines (founded in France by Anne de Xaintogne in 1609) set up schools for girls on Jesuit lines in France and Canada. The Oratorians, founded by Philip Neri and sanctioned as an order in 1612, and the Piarists, sanctioned as an order in 1621, set up schools in France, Italy and Spain that were more specifically focused on the poor. The Piarists derive their name from the 'Pious Schools' or free public schools for which they were responsible, the first being opened in a poor district of Rome by Joseph Calasanctius in 1597.

The Brothers of the Christian Schools founded by Jean Baptiste de la Salle (1651–1719) are particularly important here. They pioneered elementary schools with classes 100 strong to teach reading, writing, singing and religion. They also pioneered in educating children with special needs. De la Salle founded the first teachers' training college at St Sulpice, Paris. Under Napoleon these schools were integrated into the French national system and they have spread all over the world. Over this period girls tended to be educated in convents.

A Moravian bishop, John Comenius (1592–1670), in the tradition of the martyred Reformer John Hus, made a tremendous impact on religious and secular education in schools in Protestant Europe. He proposed an approach to education based on the development of a child's mind rather than on the logical structure of disciplines. Far in advance of their time, his views finally gained real appreciation from the beginning of the twentieth century on.

Secularization

The first schools in America were established by the Church of England in New York and New Jersey in the sixteenth century; by Quakers, German Lutherans and Pietists in Pennsylvania in the seventeenth century; by Presbyterians in New Jersey in the eighteenth century; and especially by Puritans in Massachusetts in the seventeenth century. Education was firmly focused on the Protestant faith. In New England the most prominent educationalist was Cotton Mather (1663–1728), and the most important educational tool *The New England Primer*, which contained an alphabet, the Lord's Prayer, Creed and Ten Commandments, and a catechism.

During the early eighteenth century the Society for Promoting Christian Knowledge, which had been set up by royal charter in 1689, was very active in opening schools for the poor, and they received a charter to do the same in the American colonies. After the Revolution the Quakers were prominent in founding charity schools and also set up schools for Negro pupils. In them older children, taught by instructors, went on to teach younger children. From the beginning of the nineteenth century the Sunday school, founded by Robert Raikes in England and Robert Owen in Scotland, which soon spread all over the world, was another important means of providing education for underprivileged children; with the industrial revolution the number of such children had increased enormously.

Quakers

Industrial revolution

The Enlightenment and the spread of its ideas marks the beginning of the end of the virtual monopoly in the provision of education by Christian schools, in both Europe and the United States. From this point on, schools increasingly came under state control. In France, from the time of Napoleon, constant pressure was put on Roman Catholic schools, and in 1879 primary education was made compulsory and secular; in England the Anglican grip on education was markedly loosened, not least by the creation of charity schools. In the United States the power of religious denominations was weakened by increasing support, first for charity schools and then for common schools under public control. The curriculum of these schools so offended Roman Catholics that they set up a school system of their own.

Enlightenment

Science and theology

Today in a number of countries church schools and state schools exist side by side. Conditions vary from country to country and a detailed account of the overall situation would be enormously long and immensely complex. The role that Christianity has played in the creation of schools and the provision of education is tremendous, and the desire of churches to maintain what they have taken so long to develop is quite understandable. But in a world that has been so widely secularized, the desire to maintain a special place for Christian schools comes up against a whole series of difficult questions. In some countries, notably the United Kingdom, Christian schools, Jewish schools and Muslim schools are accepted as part of the system, but how sound is the basis for them? How far should religious education be part of the school curriculum, and if it is, how should the subject be taught and how far should Christianity be part of it? These are urgent questions for the beginning of the twenty-first century.

JOHN BOWDEN

John L. Elias, *A History of Christian Education. Protestant, Catholic and Orthodox Perspectives*, Malabar, FL: Krieger 2002

Science

The natural sciences as they have developed since the seventeenth century have had a major influence on religious life and theological reflection. Science-driven technology has changed our lives, including our sense of dependence. New information has changed our ideas about our place in the universe and in natural history. And the success of the sciences has changed ideas about appropriate methods of acquiring reliable knowledge. However, there is widespread misunderstanding about precisely what science is, what scientists can say with authority and what they cannot. Before exploring issues relating to science and theology, it is therefore important to look at the role of science in the modern world, and that is what we shall be doing here.

Diversity in the sciences

While we may speak about 'science' in the singular, the term refers to a variety of disciplines. Physics concentrates on underlying laws, entities and processes, whereas biology faces the variety of organisms as fruits of those processes. Chemistry is typically a laboratory science, whereas geology is primarily a field science. Those interested in causal explanations will often focus on physics. When the prime interest is in human experience, there will be a greater interest in relations between psychology, the neurosciences and biology. When we focus on human responsibility, we might pay attention preferably to sciences that transform reality, such as chemistry and engineering, rather than to descriptive sciences such as geology or astronomy.

There are not only different disciplines. Within each discipline there are theories of different standing. Some have withstood tests under a wide range of conditions. A good example might be the ideas expressed in chemistry in the Periodic Table of the Elements, describing similarities and differences between hydrogen, helium, lithium, carbon, oxygen and so on. Like any scientific theory, this theory is in principle provisional. However, there is no serious challenge to the validity of its description of matter at ordinary temperatures and pressures. Its acceptance is not typically 'Western'. Ideas about atoms and their properties are used daily in pharmaceutical and industrial contexts. The scheme is intelligible in relation to the physics of nuclei and electrons. Hence, in relation to other theories and a wide variety of practices, the idea that matter consists of atoms of various kinds is extremely well established. As other examples of consolidated knowledge one might think of neo-Darwinian evolutionary theory and of the idea that the earth is more or less spherical.

Alongside such well-established knowledge, there are ideas that are corroborated only to a certain extent. That is what current research is about: ideas that may be adequate, but about which there is as yet no certainty. In science there are also more speculative ideas and wild guesses. They may be abandoned without leaving a trace, but may also become part of more consolidated knowledge. Often, theological reflection is interested in areas where ideas are of a speculative kind – for instance in ideas about 'the beginning' of our universe or the nature of substance and causality. Those are issues where science may be most relevant for metaphysical reflection – but these particular areas of science are also most speculative; here the interpretation of findings and ideas is least certain.

Such areas of metaphysical interest are less secure than others because of the way science works. The methodological core of modern science is found in a persistent interaction between rational and empirical approaches. Science aspires to be about the world, so we need to observe the world. Indeed we need to do even more than merely observe, since the world is confusingly complex. We aspire to experiment, to arrange situations in such a way that we can see how 'nature' behaves if we do things this way and how it behaves if we do things slightly differently. By creating small known differences in conditions and observing carefully different outcomes, we get a sense of what influences a certain process. A good example is in testing pharmaceutical options. When we want to know whether a certain drug has therapeutic value, we give the drug to some and not to others, and compare the two groups. We try to get rid of other sources of differences, such as age or sex. And, to exclude psychological influences, we do the trial 'double blind', by giving an alternative pill to the others and not telling them or even the one who hands out the pills who gets what. Experimentation is obviously easier in chemistry, where we can manipulate matter in earthly laboratories or even at the kitchen table, than in astronomy, where distances and sizes are so vast as to surpass human capacities. And some areas of science seem to be far beyond experimentation, such as the beginning of our universe.

Science is not only about observations and experiments, but also about mathematics. Mathematics itself is not science, as it is not about the world. Rather, mathematics is a tool for science, a tool that allows us to describe possible ways the world might be. Theoretical work in science has at least two interests beyond capturing observed regularities. One is in generating explanatory models of causal processes that might have created observed phenomena. Thus, we see certain relations between the pressure, volume and temperature of a gas, and this can be described by an equation (p.V/T is constant, the Boyle-Gay Lussac law); that is a way of describing the observations. This observed relationship may be explained by a model which describes a gas as consisting of many minute 'balls' moving in all directions, 'balls' which have a certain velocity (related to temperature) and thus have a certain impact on the walls (generating pressure). Alongside its interest in explanatory models, theoretical science is also interested in linking phenomena and explanatory models from different areas. Theoretical unification has been very fruitful and successful; chemistry and physics are now fundamentally thinking along the same lines about the nature of matter, and cell biology has become intertwined with chemistry.

Evolution ◄

What makes science science?

Science has an observational and experimental side as well as a theoretical one. The ideal is the combination and confrontation of these two. One view of science has been inductive: observations come first, and from the observations we conclude to a general regularity, a law of nature. Thus, experiments with gases may be summarized in the Boyle-Gay Lussac law mentioned above. However, induction leads only to generalizations. Modern science has moved further, towards ideas about possible underlying mechanisms. These cannot be found by induction from the phenomena, as they may well refer to entities and relations that do not correspond to variables used in the experiments. Science is also about imagination, about proposing explanatory theories. If a theory is proposed, the immediate question is: 'If this were to be true, what would follow that would be observable?' That is, a hypothesis is followed by the deduction of consequences, of predictions. It is these predictions that can be put to the test: by performing experiments where the outcome would correspond to the prediction if the theory were right. If experiment and theory agree, we may have some confidence in the theory, but it still remains a hypothesis, a guess about nature. If experiment and theory disagree, the theory must be wrong and has to be abandoned.

This understanding of science, as creative ideas which can be falsified, has become associated especially with the philosopher Karl Popper (1902–94), who made it the prime criterion for deciding what ideas were to be considered as science at all. If ideas are presented which are immune to falsification, e.g. the integration into one's view of the world of a conspiracy theory that would see any falsifying result as the forgery of an enemy, they are not science. For Popper, the prime example of such an ideology masquerading as science was the Marxist, Communist view of historical development. However, similar objections can be made to various religious and metaphysical ideas, both within mainstream traditions and in the New Age movement. If we cannot say what would refute the theory, the theory is meaningless. Unfalsifiable approaches are, on Popper's view, pseudo-scientific.

New Age movement

Though the emphasis on falsification catches a major characteristic of science, namely the authority of the world to judge our ideas, it is not totally adequate to real science. What happens when a researcher has invested a lot of intellectual effort in a certain theory, and now is confronted with an observation that would falsify the theory? Often, theoreticians will question whether the experiment has been set up properly and measures what it is supposed to measure. Or there may have been a mistake or dubious assumption in the calculations that derived the problematic prediction from the theory. Falsification means that the world says 'No', but it will not be clear to what specific element this 'No' is being said. This insight is named after Pierre Duhem (1861–1916) and Willard Van Orman Quine (1908–2000) as the Duhem-Quine thesis: ideas are never tested in isolation, but in larger wholes of assumptions in models and in experimental set-ups, so one can never be sure what aspect of the larger package precisely has been falsified.

Challenges to the standard understanding of the rationality of science have also come from the study of the history of the sciences. In the hypothetical-deductive view of scientific theories and testing, rationality is concentrated in the testing of hypotheses. Hypotheses may have been inspired by poetry, dreams, ideologies or whatever: what makes them scientific is their testability. Thus, there is a strong separation between 'the context of discovery' (which can be as irrational and creative as anything) and 'the context of justification', where ideas are put to the test. However, historical cases show that the distinction between these two contexts is not as clear as it seems. In the context of justification, assumptions may be present that are ideological or metaphysical, a matter of worldview. A classic example is the shift from a geocentric to a heliocentric view of the solar system that occurred with Nicolas Copernicus (1473–1543), Galileo (1564–1642) and others. It was not merely that one model made predictions that were falsified, whereas the other had only successful predictions. The clash was also about the criteria for judging theories and observations. Consequently, in *The Structure of Scientific Revolutions* (1962), Thomas Kuhn argued that the development of science takes place within a larger framework of understanding the world and science, a 'paradigm'. Alongside normal, piecemeal development in science along the ways described above, there are occasional 'scientific revolutions' in which a 'paradigm shift' takes place. Thereafter, ideas are seen in a new constellation; the old and the new are 'incommensurable', as there is no neutral perspective from which to evaluate the merits of the one paradigm relative to those of the other. Since Kuhn, historians and sociologists have shown extensively the social, ideological and human character of science, not only for 'the context of discovery' (where the human, constructive and creative character always had its place) but also for practice as a whole.

Such developments have stimulated the consideration of other ways of understanding the development and testing of scientific theories. Basically, two approaches may perhaps be distinguished. On the one hand, there are forms of coherentism. They emphasize the insight that ideas are never tested in isolation, and even that words do not have meaning in isolation from a wider context of use (a view which is often inspired by the later writings of Ludwig Wittgenstein). Thus, Quine suggested that all knowledge is to be seen as 'webs of belief', confronted with reality only at its edges. He claims that any particular belief may be held true as long as one is willing to make sufficient adaptations elsewhere in one's set of beliefs. This option has attractive possibilities for theologians, since they can seek to present religious ideas as part of a large 'web of beliefs' while denying the possibility of any immediate test of the claim that God exists. Rather, the coherence of the belief system as a whole could be the feature that makes it reasonable (or at least not unreasonable) to accept it.

On the other hand, there has been emphasis on competition between hypotheses or theories rather than coherence. We compare different possible explanations or competing hypotheses and opt for the more plausible one – even though both may have survived various tests, or may have been confronted with counter-examples which have not yet been handled successfully. A combination of the emphasis on coherence and on competition is found in Imre Lakatos' understanding of scientific research programmes. Scientists working in a certain field may have become convinced that one particular understanding is the right one. In their daily work a 'core' of theories and methodological beliefs is supplemented with all kinds of additional hypotheses about the situation: how it can be modelled, how calculations can be simplified, irrelevant or relevant additional factors, and so on. This combination of hard core and additional hypotheses results in predictions. If predictions do not fit observations of novel data, researchers will modify their additional hypothesis, while sticking to the core of their approach. Thus a research programme is flexible, while also being resilient with respect to the hard core of beliefs involved. It has to prove itself, however, in a world with competing research programmes – others with a different idea about the central issues. In this competition, it may turn out that one programme has more difficulty in responding to novel data than another, making more arbitrary, *ad hoc* moves to protect its core. While it is rational to stick to a programme for some time, it may then become rational to abandon a research programme and opt for its competitor.

Though at the moment there may not be a generally accepted single understanding of the rationality of science, it seems to me that extreme relativism is not justified. Both understatement and overstatement need to be avoided. The demise of the idea that science delivers undisputable truth in an ahistorical way saves us from seeing science in absolutist or even miraculous terms. However, once overstatement has been avoided, there is the risk of understatement. If science can be understood as a phenomenon which arose and developed through a natural process, and in which judgements arise through social interactions and interactions with nature without reference to some absolute rational principles, its special status in comparison with other practices needs to be justified.

The development of precision tools may be an analogy. Can one envisage making a precision tool for measuring lengths in microns (a thousandth of a millimetre), even if one has to start with a shed which contains only large and imprecise tools? The answer is: Yes. We can trace the history of technology, and from it come to see how new instruments have been made by means of a preceding generation of instruments. It would be impossible to construct a precision instrument at the level of microns in one step from scratch, say with only plain hammers and screwdrivers. Our current generation of tools is the fruit of a long chain of technological achievements. The history of technology resembles an ascending spiral rather than a jump from the bottom to the present level. Similarly, a long and convoluted road of perpetual modification of methodological norms, techniques and results characterizes the development of science.

An adequate view of science will need to pay attention to the variety of persons and procedures within science, rather than sticking to a general statement that science is judged by science. Some scientists evaluate the claims of others via procedures that are currently part of the accepted consensus; other scientists propose new instruments; yet others propose a modification of accepted procedures since they do not account properly for results obtained and accepted as part of the current consensus, etc. Science is an interplay of theories, concepts, criteria of credibility, instruments, sets of questions considered significant, sets of explanatory schemata, and so on. As analysed by Philip Kitcher in *The Advancement of Science* (1993), such aspects have their place in the practices of individual scientists and in the consensus at any moment. When a theory is replaced by a different one, a norm applied to both theories is stable during that evaluation. On some other occasion major concepts may change, or the division of labour, or the set of questions deemed significant, or the norms for credibility. These changes occur at the level of individual scientists with their individual practices and also affect the consensus practice. Thus a temporary consensus shapes subsequent work in individual practices, which in turn shape a new consensus. All the work is done at the level of individuals interacting with each other and with nature. In such a way, science may be presented as a thoroughly human enterprise of individuals in interaction.

That science is understood as a natural enterprise does not imply that epistemology (the philosophical consideration of knowledge) can be eliminated in favour of psychology. We appeal to criteria that surpass the criteria that human beings are naturally inclined to use. Logical and mathematical analysis, criteria such as universality and coherence, and the variety of ways of experimenting and testing claims, for instance by 'double blind' experiments, are important for the credibility of science, precisely because they surpass and correct the conclusions of ordinary psychological mechanisms. Our understanding of science has to combine social, empirical and rational aspects in the interplay of various aspects (theories, techniques, questions, etc.) in a variety of interacting individual practices.

If science can be understood along such lines as a natural phenomenon, based on the variety of cognitive practices of individual scientists and the social interactions by which they modify the consensus about claims, questions, procedures, criteria, instruments, assessments of authority, and the like, we avoid an overly pretentious understanding of science. However, we then have to make clear why such a human practice deserves pre-eminence over other human practices, such as astrology, sport, politics or art.

A preliminary element in the defence of the importance of science should be to note the limited character of the claim. Health may be improved more by physical exercises than by exercises in physics. Emotional satisfaction may be a prime effect of music or of gastronomy, rather than of science (though it is not absent from scientific practices). Social relations require something different from knowledge, and feelings may be expressed and recognized on many occasions in non-discursive ways. Practices such as those in the arts are guided by a different goal from the sciences, and thus are governed by different notions of excellence. Science is not the sole practice in which we pursue some form of excellence. Rather, science deserves to be appreciated as our major cognitive enterprise. There are other human practices that result in cognitive claims. An astrologer, for example, might claim the ability to inform us about a person's character or about opportunities which will come up next week for finances or intimate relations. The claim is that such cognitive enterprises do not deserve the same authority as the natural sciences.

The study of some extraordinary claims outside the current consensus, e.g. on telepathy, may well be scientific (even when claims regarding results have not been supported by science). Whether one considers the study of such claims worthwhile will depend on one's assessment of the utility of pursuing such a project, given what others have been doing so far, what other projects one might engage in, and expectations about the feasibility and fruitfulness of such research; there is in principle no external constraint on the projects to be explored. Such a liberal attitude in no way entails that all projects deserve equal funding or equal status in curricula; many would-be scientific ideas conflict with experiences and experiments, are inconsistent or imprecise, stand in isolation from other knowledge or introduce *ad hoc* elements which seem artificial or superfluous. Some cognitive projects that aspire to be recognized as scientific fail not so much because of the beliefs they advance as because of their lack of proper development; they do not respond adequately to new discoveries. For example, creationists advance positions that were part of the scientific consensus in geology and palaeontology some 200 years ago. So one cannot say that these beliefs as such could not be part of science at some stage. However, research has moved on, and scientists have abandoned them for good reasons. Repeating previously held positions without accommodating more recent discoveries is not likely to promote advance in knowledge, though it might promote the well-being of certain religious groups. There is no global criterion which delineates the proper sciences and excludes all other practices which compete for cognitive credibility, but consistency, precision, fertility, avoidance of *ad hoc* elements and coherence with other knowledge are among the general criteria which we use to evaluate cognitive practices.

Scientific and manifest images

Scientific theories offer us scientific images of the world, that is, images that differ from our manifest images. We see the sun rising, even though scientists tell us the earth is rotating. This distance between scientific understanding and common-sense images is especially relevant when we consider religion, since religion is in general intimately related to manifest images. This has to do with the importance of tradition for religion, and hence that of symbols and myths from earlier times. It has also a 'public relations' side, since most religions reach out to a wide audience that understands and relates to manifest images more easily.

At some points the distance between our manifest and scientific images may be minimal; at others it may be more significant. If we find ourselves with two images, which is more important? That depends on the purpose. It may well be that manifest images which are close to the richness of experiences are more important when we deal with one another as human beings, when we long for consolation, or for a sense of beauty. The scientific image, however, has gone through a critical process of articulation with precision and testing, and is therefore more adequate when we are after 'intellectual adequacy', since that is what it has been selected for.

In and through the sciences we have come up with all kinds of scientific images that differ significantly from the way we experience the world, our manifest images. This can be explained further when we consider two different ways of using the word 'experience'. 'I experienced a tree' can be said in two ways. It can be a description about how something seems to me, without regard to the accuracy of that seeming. I may say 'I experienced a tree, but then I realized I was mistaken.' But experience is also used as an achievement word; 'I experienced a tree' if it not only appeared to me that there was a tree, but there was a real tree which I saw or felt. We cannot and should not seek to explain away experiences as people have them – 'experience' in the first sense indicated above. However, it is fair game for science to offer explanations that differ from the person's initial explanation. No one is infallible with respect to the underlying processes, even if they are honest in reporting what they believe they have seen. We know all too well how we can be fooled by illusions, triggered by clues that we do not take into account consciously (this is exploited very well in advertising). We can easily fool ourselves, intentionally or unintentionally, by creating explanations that seem to make our actions seem rational and justified.

Reduction is not elimination, but rather affirmation

The combination of diversity and coherence in the sciences seems to reflect properties of reality. There is a variety of different levels of complexity, while there are also relations between those levels. These relations that suggest integration of one kind or another, an integration often labelled 'reductionism'.

Some are worried by reductionist explanations, since they fear that successful reduction eliminates the phenomena considered. However, this is mistaken. Discerning the physiological basis for a trait rather affirms its reality. Genes are no less real for being understood as strands of DNA, and pain is no less real if understood physiologically. Rather the opposite: if the doctor can locate bodily process underlying my pain, friends will take my complaints more seriously. Any scientific description of a table – even when understood as mostly empty space with a few electrons and nuclei – will have to incorporate the fact that I cannot put my hand through the table, unless I do so with considerable force and with major consequences for the table and for my hand. We may have to give up some philosophical notions about substance, but we do not eliminate common-sense solidity.

Tables and trees, humans and bees; we all consist of atoms: hydrogen, carbon, oxygen and the like. If we take anything apart, we will not find additional substances. This has led some to make a negative statement of human worth. If we were to buy most cheaply the ingredients necessary for a human being, we would not need to spend much. We would need water, some rusty nails (for the iron in our blood), some matches for the phosphorus, some charcoal for the carbon, etc. A human being does not add up to much. That may seem to be a 'reductionist' message from the sciences. However, if one continues this assessment of the economic worth of humans, there is something else – the cost of the labour needed to put it all together in the right way. Labour has been invested in us, by our parents, partners, friends and teachers and by ourselves, from embryological development to reading dull books. Labour has also been invested in the construction of human beings during our whole past cultural and evolutionary history. That, too, is part of the 'value' of a human being – and that drives up the price enormously. One could quite easily reconstitute a simple chemical substance out of the constituent parts (e.g. water out of hydrogen and oxygen), but to reconstitute a human from matter is way beyond what is, or will become, feasible.

On the one hand, science suggests reductionism. Everything is composed of substance as studied by physics. What this substance is, is known in many ways – atoms and molecules, photons, quarks, etc. – but deep down we do not have the ultimate foundation as we develop physics from our range of experiences and delve deeper and deeper. This unfinished quest within physics brings us to the issue of limit questions (see below). In considering the relation between 'higher levels' of reality and descriptions given by physics, there are good grounds for objecting to certain forms of reductionism.

Here is a simple example: paying someone some money. Would that be an activity that we could describe in terms of physics? Every time we pay someone, there is a change in the physical world – coins or paper money change place, bytes in the computer of the bank are set differently, and so on. However, it would be very odd to describe monetary transactions in terms of physical changes, as it is not just some atoms of copper, some pieces of paper, or some magnetic states that have changed. Nor would all transfers of paper or metal count as paying. The categories that are fruitful in understanding our world are not the same for economics as they are for physics. When it comes to money, the environment (and thus the 'higher level' of culture) also plays an important role: the bytes are money only when the employees of the bank are willing to interpret the state of the computer as money. There is an even stronger form of non-reductionism. When two atoms of hydrogen form one hydrogen molecule, there is a genuine new entity with new properties. It is not a bag with two balls in it. It would be rare to find someone who argued that current entities are not real, since they emerged from past ones. Why then deny the reality of higher-level entities if they have emerged out of more elementary systems?

This, in a nutshell, is an understanding of reality inspired by the sciences. Everything is 'nothing but the stuff studied by physics', atoms and the like. But more complex entities, including us as human beings, are not adequately described by physics; we need concepts and explanations of many other kinds to do justice to the rich possibilities of nature. In these reflections on reductionism I have combined two moves. A good case can be made against certain forms of reductionism. Higher levels are real, and they need their own concepts in order to be described adequately. Pain does not become less real or painful when its physiological basis is unravelled. At the same time, some forms of reductionism seem to hold true; more complex entities are made out of more simple ones. There are underlying processes. Such a form of reduction is not elimination; rather, it is integration of these phenomena into our picture of the world. Such a reductionism might even be considered a form of holism. It upgrades our view of what matter is capable of.

Technology: beyond nature towards the artificial

The standard view of the place of technology in relation to 'religion and science' can be illustrated well with the titles of two books by Ian Barbour: *Religion in an Age of Science* and *Ethics in an Age of Technology.* This may seem an obvious pair of titles, but it is nonetheless a way of dividing the field that also has particular consequences. Why not also *Religion in an Age of Technology*? And does the absence of *Ethics in an Age of Science*, to take the fourth combination of the pairs (science/technology and religion/ethics), imply that there are no moral issues in relation to scientific knowledge, but only in relation to technological applications?

The underlying issue is in part the understanding of 'science'. There is a serious interest in the religious implications of cosmology and fundamental physics: our attempts to understand the nature and origins of physical reality. But science is not only about understanding reality. Science is also about transforming reality. That may not be obvious when cosmology is the prime example, but it is clear when one thinks of chemistry with its roots in alchemistic practices, seeking to purify reality, to transform elements, to create new substances. Disciplines like the material sciences are clear examples of this active, reality-transforming side of science. The case for including engineering among the sciences has become far more serious over time, with a fundamental transition somewhere in the eighteenth and nineteenth centuries with the rise of chemistry and the control of electromagnetism. Modern technology is interwoven with science; the computer would not be possible without the understanding provided by quantum physics; and genetic engineering depends on understanding the double helix of DNA. And vice versa: progress in understanding depends upon progress in construction.

The underlying issue is in part also the understanding of what 'religion' is about. If the interest in religion, in the context of 'religion and science', is defined by an apologetic interest in arguing for the plausibility of God's existence, approached as 'the best explanation' of reality and its order, or by conflicts between religious and scientific explanations, then the prime interest in science is for the understanding of reality it aspires to offer. However, religious traditions have not only this 'explanatory' function, but often also a transformative interest: calling people to work for a better world or to make this world better, seeking to liberate beings from bondage. Such liberation theologies certainly should have an interest in the way we humans transform reality, for better or for worse. And more metaphysically-orientated theologies and world-views, too, need to accommodate the fact that our world turns out to be as flexible, as malleable as technology reveals it to be.

God

Liberation theology

When speaking about technology, most people at first refer to devices such as the telephone, the car and the refrigerator. We live in the midst of such technological artefacts. But technology is more. These devices cannot function without infrastructure. Think of telephone lines, receivers and transmitters, electricity and petrol stations, and behind those more infrastructure: refineries, ships and pipe lines, oil wells – and there the sequence ends, as the oil deep down in the ground is not itself a product of human technological activity. That is where we touch upon natural resources, at the beginning of the line. And in using oil as fuel we also have to get rid of excess heat and waste products, and thus need not only a well but also sinks to dispose of what we do not use, generating ecological problems for atmosphere and soil.

'Devices' and 'infrastructure' may still be imagined as hardware, the material manifestation of technology, but infrastructure is also organization. Technology is a social system, both for the kind of actions it requires and for the services it provides. And technology depends on skills (and thus on educational systems) as much as on hardware. Highly technical medical disciplines such as surgery are also about skills of the humans involved. And skills are also involved for ordinary people; driving a car is a technical skill. Technology is a much wider notion than the devices of metal and plastics that may come to mind first.

So far, we have considered two 'layers' of technology: the material manifestations of technology in devices and infrastructure, and the social, human dimension of organization and skills. There is a third layer when we consider the psychological level. We can also consider particular attitudes 'technological'. It refers to a way of life in which a problem, whether a leaking roof, illness or miscommunication, is not the end of a story, to be accepted as a facet of life, accepted as fate, but rather as a problem to be addressed. An active attitude, sitting down to analyse a problem in order to solve it by practical means, is part of our lives. To us this is so natural that we sometimes find it hard really to understand cultures in which a tragic or fatalistic attitude is more common. The 'technological attitude' raises issues for some theological questions: do we wait for God to rescue us, or should we do it ourselves? How do we see human action in relation to the wider understanding of reality?

Last but not least, technology is more than devices and infrastructure, organization, skills and attitudes. We live in a technological culture. Technology is not a separate segment of our lives, but pervades and shapes our lives; it is the world in which we live. Antibiotics, sewage systems, contraceptive pills, refrigerators and central-heating systems are more than new means. Antibiotics and sewage systems changed the sense of vulnerability (limiting enormously the number of parents who had to bury their own infants). The pill changed relations between men and women and between parents and their children. Thanks to the refrigerator and the microwave, we can eat whenever it suits us, individually, and each according to his or her taste, with the result that the common meal as a major characteristic of the day has lost significance. Central heating has made the sitting room with the fireplace less important; we can each spend our time in our own rooms in the way we like. Technology makes life easier and more attractive; music is available for the listener with no effort beyond switching on the stereo. Such developments were considered by the philosopher Albert Borgmann in his *Technology and the Character of Contemporary Life* (1984). His concern is that while consumption has become easier, some of the more demanding but meaningful and rich experiences are lost from sight.

Technology also influences our self-understanding. Who has never been 'under stress', feeling 'huge pressure'? Do you occasionally need 'to let off steam'? These are images from the steam age. We may consider ourselves as made in God's image, but we speak of ourselves as if we are in the image of machines. This is not exclusive to the steam age. The early radio receivers left their own traces in our language – we need 'to tune in' – and computers and the net are modifying our vocabulary and self-understandings at this very moment.

Science, scientism and ultimate questions

Valuing science is sometimes dismissed as scientism. Scientism is a critical term to indicate that science is used inappropriately as an authority. Indeed, it is important to realize that science is not able to answer all our questions. Some are questions of everyday life, e.g., 'What is your name?' That is not a scientific question because it is too particular. Others are of a moral nature. Even if some kind of behaviour is discovered to be natural (among primates, for instance), it is not thereby judged to be morally right. The proper claim is that in the case of those questions which for which science is adequate it is more adequate than any alternative, whether relying on intuition, consulting tarot cards, a horoscope, or a religious authority.

There is one kind of limitation of the sciences that is important to note here, as it is of some interest to theological or metaphysical reflections. In the natural sciences, research may be orientated in two 'opposite' directions. Some speculative thinkers, also outside the professional communities, are attracted to the quest for an understanding of the most fundamental laws and constituents of reality, while most scientists work on the understanding of phenomena and on the discovery and construction of new phenomena, assuming that the constituents and laws relevant to their purposes are sufficiently well known. This division of work among scientists is successful. Chemists can go on with their work, even though particle physicists may lack consensus on the most fundamental theory (quarks, superstrings, quantum gravity). While fundamental physics is essential as enquiry about the basic ontology of the world, it is the most speculative of the sciences, the pinnacle rather than the foundation of the building of scientific knowledge. Fundamental physics shares this status with cosmology, the study of our particular universe in relation to the possibilities relative to the fundamental laws and constituents.

While one may consider humans as 'inventions' of the evolutionary process, the question arises 'whose invention' that process itself is. The intentional language is a metaphor conveying an insight: reductionistic explanations within a naturalist framework do not explain the framework itself, as a thumbnail sketch of the sciences may illustrate. A biologist may refer to the biochemist in the next office for the properties of genes. When asked 'when and where did the 92 elements arise?', the chemist can refer to the astrophysicist. The astrophysicist might answer that question in terms of nuclear processes in stars and in the early universe, referring for further explanations to the nuclear physicist and the cosmologist. This chain of referring to 'the person in the next office' ends, if it ends successfully at all, with the cosmologist and the elementary particle physicist, the one concentrating on the ultimate historical questions and the other on the most basic structural aspects of reality. Physicists and cosmologists cannot refer to a 'person in the next office'. Because of this particular situation they sometimes engage in philosophical and theological speculation with much less embarrassment than scientists from other disciplines, though not necessarily with greater competence.

Fundamental physics and cosmology form a boundary of the natural sciences, where speculative questions with respect to a naturalist view of our world come most explicitly to the forefront. The questions that arise at the speculative boundary might be called limit-questions. The questions that are left at the metaphorical 'last desk' are questions about the world as a whole, its existence and structure. Such limit questions are persistent, even though the development of science may change the shape of the actual ultimate questions considered at any time. Relying on science need not imply the dismissal of such limit questions as meaningless, nor does it imply one particular answer to such limit questions. There is in principle no tension between a scientific understanding of processes in the world and religious views which understand the natural world as a whole, with its laws and regularities as a creation dependent on a transcendent Creator.

Creation

WILLEM B. DREES

Willem B. Drees, *Religion, Science and Naturalism*, Cambridge: CUP 1996; Philip Kitcher, *The Advancement of Science*, New York: OUP 1993; W. V. O. Quine and J. S. Ullian, *The Web of Belief*, New York: Random House [2]1978; Mikael Stenmark, *Scientism: Science, Ethics and Religion*, Aldershot: Ashgate 2001

Science and theology

Science

Religion and science are two of the most powerful forces that have formed our current culture. Religion has not only shaped our sense of what is sacred, our values and social structures. Much of our finest music, literature and art are imbued with religious motifs. Science and technology have not only taken humans to the moon, they have come to be involved in almost every aspect of life. Therefore, it seems natural that these two forces should have a mutually critical relationship. So for the last few decades, theology as reflection on the Christian religion has become increasingly involved with natural science.

Theology

The history of the relationship between theology and science is not unlike the dynamics of a growing family. In medieval times, theology was the queen of sciences. In  the thirteenth century, the theologian Thomas Aquinas created a powerful synthesis of the best knowledge about religion, philosophy and nature. His principal resource  was the philosophy of Aristotle, which had come to Christian Western Europe thanks to Muslim scholars. Christian theology in and of itself inspired scientific enquiry. Where God is understood as the creator who has endowed nature with order and humans with creative rationality, enquiry into how nature works can indeed become a way of worship. Reading and understanding both 'the book of scripture' and 'the book of nature' can be noble and necessary enterprises. In that sense, early modern science was indeed a child of theology and the church. Quite a number of the pioneers of modern science were close to theology or the church (Johann Kepler,  Nicolas Copernicus). Just as children have to struggle their way through adolescence, the natural sciences had to strive for their emancipation and autonomy. This dynamic has created notions of a clash between theology and  science (Galileo, Charles Darwin). The late nineteenth-century writers John William Draper and Andrew Dickson White spoke of conflict and warfare between science and theology. However, more recent research has shown that these are not adequate metaphors for relationships that are far more complex. Nevertheless, notions of inevitable conflict between science and religion have prevailed in popular understanding.

Evolution

During the twentieth century, theology and science reached a more mature relationship. Some of the most powerful obstacles against a constructive engagement were at least partly overcome. Scientific positivism or scientism, a position that seeks to reduce all knowledge to scientific explanations, was successfully challenged. Likewise, attitudes of theological indifference or the theological domination of science and culture were widely shown to be inadequate. Thinkers such as Alfred N. Whitehead, Pierre Teilhard de Chardin and Karl Heim inspired new forms of interaction between theology and science.

During the latter half of the last century a number of programmatic approaches to a good relationship between theology and the natural sciences were developed by thinkers such as Ian Barbour, Arthur Peacocke, John Polkinghorne and Thomas Torrance. Simultaneously, a number of academic societies and centres for religion/theology and science were created, e.g. the European Society for the Study of Science and Theology (ESSSAT), the Ian Ramsey Centre in Oxford, the Zygon Centre for Religion and Science (ZCRS) in Chicago, the Centre for Theology and the Natural Sciences (CTNS) in Berkeley, CA, the Society of Ordained Scientists (SOSc) in the UK and the International Society for Science and Religion (ISSR). Major journals in the field are *Zygon: Journal for Religion and Science* (since 1966) and *Theology and Science* (since 2003). Interdisciplinary working groups have emerged in many countries. There are academic chairs in theology/religion and science, for example, in Oxford, Cambridge and Princeton.

Fresh starts for dialogue between theology and science during the last century often struggled with a constructive understanding of the theory of evolution. The outcome of these efforts has taken two contradictory directions. On the one hand, the evolutionary perspective is today taken for granted in many respects and applied in many different areas, including epistemology, psychology and religion. Occasionally it seems so well integrated that critique is called for: the process of making evolution a commonplace concept runs the risk of ending up with watered-down ideas that equate evolution with a general notion of development. In that sense, evolutionary theory has come to be almost too successful. On the other hand, we still see – in the US much more than in Europe – considerable energy invested in promoting creationism and design theories, often based on fundamentalist understandings of the Bible. Both science and theology have moved on since early conflicts about evolution. The concept of 'God at the edges of the universe' is experiencing strong competition from discussions about 'God in the messy middle of life in the world'.

In many places, the focus on evolution was followed by a special interest in physics and religion. In the wake of an attempt to understand the implications of the theories of relativity and quantum physics, questions about time, cosmology and God's action in the world came to the fore. This was a phase of the dialogue that interested philosophers and physicists and theologians alike. It resulted in systematizations of the history of the interplay between scientific and religious world-views, and it has provided a number of typologies. Ian Barbour, for example, has proposed four types of relationship, namely conflict, independence, dialogue and integration. These categories have proved useful, especially in connection with education.

More recent developments suggest a shift of interest back to biology and the human sciences. The Human Genome Project, biotechnology, bioethics, genetically modified organisms (GMOs), stem cell research, cloning, neuroscience and evolutionary psychology all raise issues that call for ethical discussions that include theological perspectives. A satisfying understanding of human nature in its relationship with the rest of nature needs to include knowledge from many disciplines, including theology.

The dialogue between theology and natural science finds itself challenged to deal adequately with conceptual questions of world-view as well as ethical issues. Increased knowledge about the nature of understanding itself – also called hermeneutics – both enriches and challenges this dialogue. It disperses naiveté about the crystal clarity of facts, and it provides methods that allow handling the process of understanding and interpreting in rational, intelligible ways. Hermeneutical reflection sharpens the awareness of the risk of ideological distortions in scientific and religious concepts and it takes seriously the impact of social and economic factors on intellectual endeavours. For example, in the early seventeenth-century world of Francis Bacon, science was presented as the saint who gathers her followers in monastery-like noble communities, whereas nature was the wild woman who needs to be forced into submission. Historical examples as well as current scientific conceptualizations indicate that beliefs in the inferiority of woman still form part of our inherited scientific, religious and philosophical framework.

Feminist scholarship has challenged theology and natural science in at least three ways: it has raised issues of ethics and politics that are basically human issues, equally involving women, men, children and the nature we all relate to; it has addressed issues of exclusion and inclusion of women and their work, and of minorities and their cultures; and, demonstrating how gender categories are informing and biasing both research agendas and the interpretation of data, it analyses and suggests different ways of doing science and theology.

Postmodern thought has also opened interesting perspectives for theology and natural science. In spite of the fear that postmodernism might lead into relativism, precious insights can be gained from a constructive engagement with postmodern thought. Postmodernism questions at least two myths of modernity, the myth of progress and the myth of secularization. It is not true that every development is progress, and it is not true that wherever science and modernity go in, religion goes out. Criticizing these myths does not make research impossible. Rather, it makes research more complicated, but maybe even better. Such thought does not embrace an extreme form of constructivism that suggests that everything is social construction, but it will have to acknowledge that everything comes along with construction. This does not deny the value of so-called hard data, but it realizes that our representation of data is always embedded in construction, a construction that informs how theology and natural science are taught, carried out and talked about. Such a postmodernism offers an exciting way between the Scylla of boundless relativism and the Charybdis of rigorous non-ambiguity, of totalization, of reduction to sameness. It opens a path to a mutual, critical and self-critical correlation between disciplines that are indispensable for an adequate view of world, life and faith.

Postmodernism
Secularization
Bioethics

Yet, dialogue alone is not enough. There is a need for taking the step from a policy-orientated approach towards one that is more problem-orientated.

Taking these challenges seriously will help successfully to develop the relationship between faith in knowledge (as expressed in trust in science and technology), the knowledge of faith (as expressed in various theological concepts and religious wisdom) and the common responsibility of these two for the world.

ANTJE JACKELÉN

Ian Barbour, *Religion and Science*, New York: HarperCollins 1997; Philip Hefner, *The Human Factor*, Minneapolis: Augsburg Fortress 1993; Arthur Peacocke, *Theology for a Scientific Age*, Minneapolis: Augsburg Fortress and London: SCM Press [2]1993; John Polkinghorne, *The Faith of a Physicist*. Princeton, NJ: Princeton University Press 1994; J. Wentzel van Huyssteen et al. (eds), *Encyclopedia of Science and Religion*, New York: Macmillan Reference 2003

Feminist theology

Sculpture

In the Jewish tradition, which was initially followed by Christianity, sculptures are associated with idolatry, and the larger the sculptures, the more threatening they are. They are a source of offence to the faithful, and are to be opposed. The sacred ark of the Israelites causes the Philistine statue of the god Dagon in Ashdod to fall to the ground (1 Samuel 5.1–5) and Jews are prepared to be thrown into a burning fiery furnace rather than prostrate themselves before an enormous gold statue set up by Nebuchadnezzar (Daniel 3). This raises the question of the role of sculpture within a monotheistic religious tradition. In the Christian hierarchy of the arts, sculpture traditionally ranks very low. The question is whether this apparent distaste for sculpture is theologically or culturally conditioned.

Within the history of Western culture, sculptural monuments such as the equestrian statues of Marcus Aurelius and Donatello's *Gattamelata* have been the preferred artistic form of celebrating military and political victories. These larger-than-life-size figures of the rider and his horse, and the siting of the sculptures in prominent public places, denote not simply the sign of victory but the power accorded to the victor. There are parallels between the presentations of the human figure in these otherwise 'secular' works and those found in contemporary religious images, for example statues of Zeus as the Ruler of Olympus as a visual metaphor for the Roman emperor and general, or statues of military Christian saints, such as George or the Archangel Michael, for the Renaissance general. These visible similarities are a pointer towards the problems of Christian sculpture.

Iconoclasm
Roman empire
Paganism
Body

Christianity inherited the prohibition of making images from the tradition and teaching of Judaism, and a recognition of beauty, especially the beauty of form as a metaphor for the divine, from the Hellenistic culture of the Roman empire. The tension between these two opposites becomes particularly great in sculpture, because of the singular correspondence between the art of sculpture and the human body; encountering a sculpted work, especially one that is life-sized or monumental, suggests the experience of encountering another human person. Thus fear of paganism and idolatry combined with a theological denial of the body motivated a negative Christian attitude towards sculpture, while the acceptance of a role for art combined with a theological recognition of the beauty of the human body as an optical metaphor for the divine prompted a positive one.

Painting

Traditionally typified by the action of the carving, incising or cutting of a hard substance such as wood, stone or marble rather than the moulding of clay, sculpture has a series of identifiable characteristics that distinguish it from the other visual arts such as painting and photography. A sculptor's employment of colorations from alabaster-toned or variegated marbles to single- or multi-coloured bronzes to stained or untreated woods, and of surface handling from the smoothness of polished marble or the patinas of bronze to the roughness of hewn woods or unpolished stones, offers specific sensibilities and bodily references for a viewer. The elements of colour directly evoke an emotional response, while the surface qualities evoke a tactile reverberation, and the sculptor's mastery over mass, volume and form elicit an intellectual reaction. Perhaps just as significant is the sculptor's use of scale, which has traditionally been the single most effective element in the way in which sculpture conveys ideas or sentiments.

Sculpture is differentiated by its ability to express scale and form, to accept and display movement, and to affirm freedom even as it remains motionless; thus a sculpture can be said to dominate its environment in a manner similar to a human being. The style in which a sculptor creates, either representational, i.e. projecting a sense of recognizable figural forms through mass, volume and scale, or non-representational, that is, abstractly or symbolically, further characterizes sculpture in terms both of historical period of creation (Classical, Renaissance, Modern) and viewer reception. As with a painting or a photograph, the representational human figure provides both a horizon line and an entry point into the world of the artwork for the majority of viewers; sculpture is an aesthetic method of communicating ideas, messages and values.

Characteristics of Christian sculpture

How, then, does a sculpture become identified or 'named' as Christian, and more significantly, does the Mosaic proscription of graven images constrain or deny the possibility of 'Christian sculpture'? One can categorize as Christian sculptures those works of art which are: clearly didactic, i.e. the visual depiction of Christian narratives or doctrines which teach the faith such as the fourth-century Sarcophagus of Junius Bassus (a stone coffin, the name of which derives from a Greek term meaning 'flesh-eating'); liturgical, i.e. objects which are incorporated into the ritual and ceremony of corporate worship such as the carved reliefs on the Episcopal Throne of Maximian; devotional, i.e. images which nurture prayer or contemplation such as Michelangelo's Vatican *Pietà*; decorative, i.e. beautiful entities or designs which elevate the soul to the spiritual such as medieval tympanum reliefs of Christ in majesty, the *Majestas Domini*; symbolic, i.e. representational, forms with objective and subjective meanings such as the early Christian statuettes of *The Good Shepherd* or *Jonah*; and any combination of these recognizable categories, as evidenced in Gian Lorenzo Bernini's *Cathedra Petri*, the Chair of Peter in St Peter's Rome. The majority of artworks identified as Christian sculpture can be classified as traditional artworks that are objective in their emphasis on the objects being seen and a presentation that creates a 'reality' within the parameters of sculpture. And typically, the central component of a 'Christian sculpture' is the human body.

The prohibition against making 'graven images' is meant to secure the integrity and singularity of the one God: they were associated with idolatry and paganism. Consequently, early church fathers such as Tertullian and Clement of Alexandria questioned the appropriateness of any form of Christian art, but specifically singled out as troublesome 'Christian sculpture' which in presentation was too close to the pagan idols which the emerging Christian collective encountered on a daily basis in Jerusalem, Damascus, Athens and Rome. Their concern was simple and obvious: how does a child or a catechumen, or even a baptized Christian, distinguish between these carved pagan idols and a carved image of God? How do you render God in human form without impinging upon either the integrity or singularity of God's divinity? How do you prevent the Christian collective from being 'enchanted' by the pagan philosophy or religious teachings that these idols represent?

Ideas of what Christian sculpture can be were directly related to cultural attitudes and to theologically-directed artistic principles. The cultural shift from the God-centred universe that dominated Christian consciousness from its earliest period to the High Middle Ages to the human-centred universe that has ruled from the Renaissance to the present time has theological and artistic ramifications. These cultural perspectives, God-centred and human-centred, signify as much modes of action in the everyday world of politics, economics and moral values as they do religious creeds; all of this directly relates to the Christian collective's acceptance or rejection of Christian sculpture.

The historical periods – early Christian, Byzantine and medieval – led by a God-centred world-view were traditionally the least open to the art of sculpture. If required by necessity, such as function or placement, sculptures created during these periods were carefully regulated and fixed to a building or furnishing; they emphasized the 'unreality' of the human body through the sculptural absence of naturalistic mass, volume, form and scale. Periods from the Renaissance onwards may be said to have championed the art of sculpture in function, form and scale as either Christian or secular. Such sculptural works were created in an environment of artistic freedom; they were realistic, free-standing and often monumental in form, and stressed the human body as beautiful form and free agency.

Here lies the second great challenge that sculpture makes to a monotheistic tradition, especially in modern times. Given the fundamental nature of sculpture, especially as the classical presentation of the idealized human form on a monumental scale, the sculptor followed through with the essence of creativity: the human impulse to create an animate body and thereby to allegorize the creative act of God. Ironically, the result of sculptural creativity is an ambiguous entity. The sculpted form, the body, appears to reside eternally in a nebulous region between life and death. When we stand before a sculpture, especially a life-size or monumental work, we have the same response(s) as if encountering another living creature: one with whom we can communicate or by whom we can be overwhelmed.

Case studies

A detailed survey of the history of Christian sculpture would prove too incoherent to be useful. Historians of sculpture in fact have a variety of assumptions about such an overview: that all identifiable periods of Western cultural history include equally identifiable works of Christian sculpture; that an obvious Christian sculpture does not exist throughout all eras of Western cultural history; that because it is required to produce figures, Christian sculpture flourishes during periods of realism and representation and diminishes or disappears during periods of abstraction; or that if sculpture is seen as equivalent to idolatry, there is no such thing as Christian sculpture.

The conventional reading of early Christianity offers a socio-economic-cultural matrix in which there was a minimal place for the arts, if any. The significance of the prohibition against graven images and the inherent fear of idolatry among the earliest Christian community cannot be overestimated. Moreover, the influence of the terror of religious persecution at the time, the apparent poverty of the majority of the earliest Christians, and the expectation of an imminent Parousia or Second Coming heightened this denial of Christian art. However, archaeological discoveries made from the middle of the twentieth century onwards have provided a new way of seeing the early Christian community from the perspective of art and architecture. The reality may have been that Christians did not deny the visual but presented it in a 'disguised' way, so that Christian art and architecture were indistinguishable from that of the wider culture, except to those who belonged to the community and were able to read the clues.

Byzantium
Archaeology

Renaissance

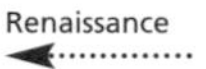

Among the earliest works of Christian art are sarcophagi, reliquaries, liturgical objects and jewellery, all of which can be classified as Christian sculpture. As with Christian painting, these carved images, which ranged in size from miniatures and small, portable pieces to life-sized sarcophagi, bore a series of encoded geometric, animal and anthropomorphic symbols that were allegories or metaphors intelligible to the average Christian. This presentation of Christian symbolism was dependent upon

Symbols

Sarcophagus of Junius Bassus

p. 1197 the writings of the early church fathers, who initated a process of analogy known as 'typology', in which the categories of foretype and type came to identify Jesus as the Christ, the fulfilment of what was promised or prophesied in the Hebrew scriptures. As Christianity flourished across the Mediterranean, this typology expanded to include the motifs and images of classical mythology and philosophy.

Jesus

The reluctance, if not downright refusal, to depict Jesus as the Christ in human form and especially the development of an identifiable physiognomy in both painted and sculpted figurations was based as much on the socio-political situation in which early Christianity was established as on a devotional or theological rationale. As Christianity was transformed from a persecuted cult to the official religion of the Roman empire during the crucial period of the fourth century, so too Christian sculpture, as the themes of peril disappeared, was to be replaced by motifs signifying the power and grandeur of Jesus as the Christ, especially as his imagery became synonymous with that of the emperor in dress, manner and facial type. Christian art, and with it Christian sculpture, began to exhibit distinctive characteristics and elements. Simultaneously, the quality of both materials and craftsmanship improved as the higher classes, including persons of taste and substance, converted to Christianity.

Constantine's 'conversion'

Ironically, the fundamental visual cues of early Christian sculpture which may be the initial marks of Christian sculpture remained constant as distinguishing marks from paganism and idolatry: small-scale as opposed to the monumentality favoured by the Greeks and Romans; a flatter rendering of mass and volume; the absence of human individuality expressed through a particular physiognomy; and the affixed character of Christian sculpture prior to the Renaissance. Typical works of imperial Christian sculpture ranged from the raised reliefs found on liturgical objects and furnishings, book covers, reliquaries and pilgrimage souvenirs to the doors and capitals of ecclesiastical buildings and the sides and tops of sarcophagi. Monumental and/or free-standing pieces were deemed too close to the pagan idols of the pre-Constantinian era.

Perhaps the finest example of this imperial early Christian sculpture is the famous Sarcophagus of Junius Bassus (*c.*359). The prefect of Rome, and scion of a patrician Roman family, Junius Bassus became a Christian in 359 and died later that same year. His elaborately decorated sarcophagus is an extraordinary example of the initial integration of classical art with the emerging visual art of the recently established imperial Christianity. Even to the learned eye, this elegant marble casket was similar in design and stylistic form to the high relief carvings of late antique Roman art in terms of bodily presentation, dress, proportion and perspective. However, thoughtful examination of the ten carved panels disclose specific Christian narrative episodes arranged in two registers, demonstrating the typology favoured by the early church fathers and Christian artists. From the viewer's left to right, the lower-register depictions include the Story of Job, Fall of Adam and Eve, Entry into Jerusalem, Daniel in the Lions' Den and Paul being led to his Martyrdom, while the upper-register depictions are of the Sacrifice of Abraham, Arrest of Peter, Giving of the Law, Arrest of Christ and Christ before Pilate. Here images of peril are interwoven with images of salvation.

This singularly refined and elaborately decorated sarcophagus can be characterized as 'Christian', as it fulfils five of the six categories of Christian art (didactic, devotional, decorative, symbolic and a combination of these, lacking only the liturgical dimension) and an almost similar number of the six classifications of Christian art (commission, patronage, function, theme and a combination of these); perhaps it also incorporates placement, as the Christian catacombs may have served as liturgical centres, but since the work is anonymous we cannot be confident of the credal identity of the artist. It is also a work of Christian sculpture by virtue of the media and craft employed in its creation – a carving or incising of marble – and the representational renderings of the human form. The combination of the small scale of the human figures, the lack of individuality and the naturalistic presentation of mass and volume, and the 'fixed' nature of both the plaques and the figurations, complete the identification of the Sarcophagus of Junius Bassus as Christian sculpture.

Other novel sculptures typify artistic and theological innovations in the history of Christian sculpture. These include the thirteenth-century statues of *Synagoga* and *Ecclesia* (Synagogue and Church) by Sabina von Steinbach, the first known woman sculptor, Michelangelo's early sixteenth-century Vatican *Pietà*, and Gian Lorenzo Bernini's seventeenth-century *L'estasi di Santa Teresa*. Each of these works shows significant signs of maturing in style and theology, from Sabina's naturalistic renderings of body mass, volume, proportions and pleated garments in her almost 'freed-from-the-cathedral-portal' sculptures to Michelangelo's sculptural meditation on mariology, devotionalism and human dignity in his transfixing and 'freed' vision of the physiognomic range of figure and form. Bernini's visualization of the transverberation (piercing of the heart) of St Teresa is a fusing of contemporary Roman Catholic categories of sacramentality with eros and agape in his 're-affixed' central element, in an integrated ensemble of painting, sculpture and architecture.

Gian Lorenzo Bernini, *The Ecstasy of St Teresa of Avila*

However, the cultural revolution of the sixteenth-century Reformation created the problem, for sculpture as well as for the other arts, of how to redefine Christian art. Once the common religious foundation of Western Europe was shattered, the questions of the relationship between sculpture and Christianity, Christian sculpture and idolatry, and sculpture and human autonomy reappeared. Reformation

Education

The previously normative category of Christian sculpture was then translated initially into Catholic sculpture and Protestant sculpture, and more recently into spiritual sculpture. The conundrum of defining and promulgating Christian sculpture was exacerbated by the late nineteenth- and early twentieth-century stylistic move from figuration to abstraction, and the redefining of art and artist that went with it. By the time Pablo Picasso created his semi-figural, semi-abstract, life-size sculpture entitled *Man with* a *Lamb*, the question whether this is a revival of classical imagery, of Christian sculpture, a modernist idol, or perhaps a combination of all three, is not central to critical discussions of style and technique. Nevertheless, what distinguishes sculpture – the principle of freedom as individuation, figural and thereby human – continues to challenge religious values even into modern culture, as it resurrects the Mosaic prohibition of images and the inherent claims of idols, idolatry and paganism.

Christianity in Europe

DIANE APOSTOLOS-CAPPADONA

Ruth Butler, *Western Sculpture: Definitions of Man*, Boston: New York Graphic Society 1975; Victor H. Debidour, *Christian Sculpture*, New York: Hawthorn Books 1968; Tom Flynn, *The Body in Sculpture*, London: Weidenfeld & Nicolson 1998; Kenneth Gross, *The Dream of the Moving Statue*, Ithaca: Cornell University Press 1992; Herbert Read, *The Art of Sculpture* (1956), Princeton: Princeton University Press 1969; Hubert van Zeller, *Approach to Christian Sculpture*, New York: Sheed & Ward 1959

Secularization

Secularization has become a term used to denote the decline of religion and religious values within a culture. However, the word was first used in the seventeenth century in a rather different and quite specific way: for the transfer of assets and institutions from religious control to control by the *saeculum*, the worldly authorities. At the talks leading to the Treaty of Westphalia in 1646, which put an end to the disastrous wars of religion and replaced religious conflict with an era of toleration, the Elector of Brandenburg was compensated for ceding some of his territory to victorious Sweden by the secularization of various assets that had previously fallen under church jurisdiction.

Wars of religion

Many basic institutions in society, such as hospitals, schools and universities, have their roots in Christianity, and were first established by Christians. There are still Christian hospitals, schools and universities today, but as early as the Middle Ages, and particularly with the rise of the modern world, the role of providing care for the sick and education was increasingly removed from religious to secular control. This process, which can be documented through history, represents a specific form of secularization.

Schools
University
Middle Ages

However, secularization was soon used for more than the transfer of the control of property and institutions, and became a programme. By the middle of the nineteenth century it had come to mean giving a secular or non-sacred character to study or art, putting morals on a secular basis, and restricting education to secular subjects. It was also used widely as a blanket term to describe what was happening in Western society, particularly the falling membership of religious bodies and declining religious practices, a much reduced role of the church in national and social life, and so on. The extent of this process was demonstrated by statistics: lower church attendance, fewer baptisms and church marriages, a drop in the number of clergy being ordained, and so on.

If secularization is basically a neutral term indicating an actual process of change in particular societies, which could also be a programme, in the 1960s it became a theory denoting how the world was going to develop, put forward both by theologians and by sociologists.

The theological discussion was prompted by the publication in the 1950s of *Letters and Papers from Prison*, by Dietrich Bonhoeffer, a talented theologian executed by the Nazis for his involvement in a plot against Hitler. He had described the process of God being forced out of the world and argued that God had to be rediscovered in human worldliness. What this meant was spelt out by three influential books of the 1960s: Harvey Cox, *The Secular City*; Paul van Buren, *The Secular Meaning of the Gospel*; and Ronald Gregor Smith, *Secular Christianity*. Common to them, and to many others, was a tendency to write off the supernatural dimension of Christianity and religion generally, to glorify excessively the achievements of technology, and to have an over-optimistic view of human nature. They argued that the process of the secularization of religion would continue and that ultimately the world would become completely secular, a development that nevertheless had to be welcomed. Cox praised the freedom offered by the secular city as opposed to the ties of tribal society and the small local community. Van Buren and Gregor Smith both embarked in different ways on what they argued was the necessary process of translating Christianity into the terms of this world without abandoning it altogether, a translation which reduced Christian faith to its historical and ethical dimensions.

At the same time sociologists, notably Bryan Wilson in his *Religion in Secular Society*, argued that it was a general characteristic of modern societies for religious observances to become irrelevant, even if they still continued:

religious claims, practice and institutions had lost social significance.

However, there were also challenges to the idea of secularization, both as a process and a theory. Religious observance in the United States, constitutionally a secular nation in which religion cannot be taught in state schools, was always a problem for the theory of secularization. At the very time this theory was being propounded, conservative, indeed fundamentalist Christianity was becoming increasingly prominent in American public life. At the same time it was argued that changes in patterns of social behaviour did not necessarily reflect changes in religious belief: a decline in religious social behaviour did not necessarily mean that individuals were no longer religious; they might just be religious in a different way. It was also argued that the claim that there was an overall process of secularization was based on an unrepresentative selection of data, and had been distorted by an excessive concentration on what has been happening in Europe. Elsewhere, the scene looked very different.

In the last two decades of the twentieth century, the religious dimensions of conflicts at every level, between different faiths in areas such as the Balkans, the Middle East and the Indian sub-continent, and also the religious tensions within individual nations, not least in Europe, have shown that the idea of a steady advance of secularization is simplistic and naïve. Religions are a more powerful influence than has been supposed. Moreover, in an influential article 'The Clash of Civilizations?', developed into a book, Samuel P. Huntington argued that the next conflicts would be on the fault-lines between religions, notably between the Christian West and Islam. The continuing role played by religion is also highlighted by the enormous and rapid growth of Christianity in the southern hemisphere, to the degree that the numerical strength of southern Christians is proving to be a major force.

However, the spread of commercialism and scientific technology, neither of which has a foundation in religion, continues inexorably, and the impact that these will have on the developing world is still to be seen. Moreover, the conservative character of those churches that are growing, and their opposition to so much of modern thought, raise questions about their capacity to relate to the crucial global issues of today. Complex though the evidence is, that there has been a process of secularization and that this is not yet at an end seems hard to deny.

JOHN BOWDEN

Harvey Cox, *The Secular City*, New York: Macmillan and London: SCM Press 1965; Ronald Gregor Smith, *Secular Christianity*, London: Collins and New York: Harper & Row 1966; Samuel P. Huntington, *The Clash of Civilizations and the Remaking of the World Order*, New York: Simon & Schuster 1996; Paul van Buren, *The Secular Meaning of the Gospel*, Philadelphia: Westminster Press and London: SCM Press 1963; Bryan Wilson, *Religion in Sociological Perspective*, Oxford: OUP 1982

Christianity in North America

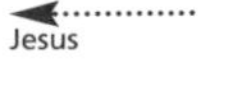

Sexual ethics

Fundamentalism
Jesus

According to the Gospels, Jesus himself had little to say about sexuality, and nothing is known about his sexual identity or experience. His earliest followers, as Jews, accepted the ethical prescriptions within the Jewish law. That ethic limited permissible sexual activity to heterosexual marriage, and included penalties for those who went beyond this limit: partners caught in adultery were stoned to death; rape claims within cities were disbelieved and treated as adultery, while rape claims in the fields were believed; unmarried rapists of virgins were forced to marry their victims and pay bride-price, and were forbidden to divorce them. Sexual ethics for women under Jewish law also included observing *niddah*, ritual purity rules concerning menstruation and childbirth. Women were considered unclean during and for one week after their monthly period and again during pregnancy and childbirth; they were required to immerse themselves in the *mikvah*, a ritual bath, before resuming marital relations, entering the temple precincts and other normal activities, lest they contaminate all persons and things that they touched.

Geography

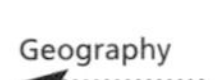

Origins and background

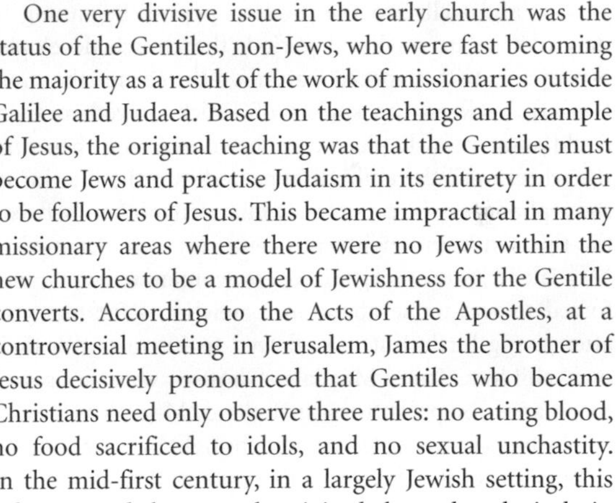

One very divisive issue in the early church was the status of the Gentiles, non-Jews, who were fast becoming the majority as a result of the work of missionaries outside Galilee and Judaea. Based on the teachings and example of Jesus, the original teaching was that the Gentiles must become Jews and practise Judaism in its entirety in order to be followers of Jesus. This became impractical in many missionary areas where there were no Jews within the new churches to be a model of Jewishness for the Gentile converts. According to the Acts of the Apostles, at a controversial meeting in Jerusalem, James the brother of Jesus decisively pronounced that Gentiles who became Christians need only observe three rules: no eating blood, no food sacrificed to idols, and no sexual unchastity. In the mid-first century, in a largely Jewish setting, this rule assumed that sexual activity belonged exclusively in heterosexual marriage.

pp. 143, 852

A second change in Christian sexual ethics occurred in the second century with the emerging monastic movement, which developed quickly in succeeding centuries until by the medieval period one in every twelve to fifteen persons in Europe was a monk or nun vowed to celibacy, recognized as the superior vocation for Christians. A combination

Monasticism

of circumstances and developments surrounding the monastic movement over its first eight centuries helped to create a sexual ethics within Christianity that distrusted human sexuality, encouraged abstinence, and blamed women for the human temptation to sexual pleasure, which was understood as the centre of sexual sin.

Religious orders
Holy
Sin
Church fathers

Ministry and ministers
Feminist theology

In the beginning of monasticism, monks retreated to desert communities, which, while known to the urban churches, were cut off from them. But as the few early male hermits developed into male and female orders with huge complexes and lands throughout Europe, their model of Christianity became more and more normative. Celibacy became associated with holiness, and sexual activity with sin. For many of the church fathers, sexual activity was justified only by the intention of producing children, and they were suspicious of many marital claims to this. Augustine went so far as to argue that even marital sex with the intention of procreation was venially sinful, because it was virtually impossible to avoid pleasure in sex. During the second half of the first millennium the bishops of the church tried to impose on the secular clergy the view that holiness required celibacy, an attempt that met much opposition; the imposition of priestly celibacy was not successful until the end of the first millennium.

Reformation
Homosexuality
Bioethics

There has always been some difference between official teachings on sexual ethics and the behaviour of Christians. Church restriction of sex to heterosexual marriage for purposes of procreation was not observed by many lay persons, as demonstrated in high illegitimacy rates throughout Europe in the medieval and Reformation periods and well into the modern period. Beginning in Italy in the late medieval period, the church developed orphanages with a special feature on the corner, the *ruota* (wheel), between the spokes of which unwed mothers could anonymously place their newborns, and then turn the wheel until the child disappeared into the interior of the orphanage to be cared for. Unmarried mothers between the thirteenth and eighteenth centuries were detained in Magdalene houses organized by women religious, and forced to wet-nurse abandoned newborns for one year after giving birth, but not allowed to interact with their own children. Later Magdalene houses were houses of repentance for prostitutes. In Ireland, Magdalene houses run by nuns incarcerated women thought by their families, pastors, or local police to be delinquent; they closed only in the 1990s.

Protestantism
Marriage
Revelation

Reformers targeted priestly celibacy for rejection; otherwise they accepted the restriction of sex to heterosexual marriage and procreative intention. However, early in Protestantism social and economic shifts connected to modernity gradually produced two changes in teaching on sexuality: a shift from marriage as contract to marriage as companionship, gradually understood as based in love and intimacy, and an acceptance of marital sex for other than procreative purposes. The shift towards marriage as companionate partnership emanated in the commercial class in which early Protestantism was strong; this shift supported an acceptance of sex in marriage for purposes of bonding through shared pleasure. This de-centring of procreation in marital sex also supported contraception, to which the middle and upper classes in Europe were turning in the late eighteenth and early nineteenth centuries as the demographic transition in Europe produced large families and intense population growth as a result of continuing high birth rates, combined with increased control of epidemics and consequently lowered death rates.

Both these shifts, towards marriage as intimate partnership and marital sex as supporting bonding between spouses and as open to contraception, took over a century to penetrate all the classes in Europe and North America thoroughly, first in mainstream Protestant denominations and then in Roman Catholic and evangelical/Pentecostal denominations; this shift is still occurring among Christians in the Third World. The insistence in the twentieth-century women's movements on women as subjects, not objects, of religious teaching and on women's experience as critical to social ethics has both supported and been supported by this shift in marriage and contraception.

Artificial forms of contraception are not yet accepted today in the Roman Catholic Church, although the vast majority of Catholics of child-bearing age all over the world use them. On the other hand, official Roman Catholic documents on marriage have increasingly adopted language on marriage that reflects personalism and intimacy.

Contemporary Christian sexual ethics are disputed within virtually every denomination. While many denominations have accommodated or begun to accommodate gender equity changes as well as contraception, they are deadlocked on other issues. Among mainstream liberal Protestant churches, governing bodies are torn over issues such as whether or not openly gays, lesbians and transgendered persons should be ordained, whether abortions can be moral and therefore should be legal, and whether sexual activity for unmarried adults is always sinful.

The academic circles that inform these intra-church debates are divided over related but even more fundamental issues. Many scholars argue that sexual ethics are not merely a matter of discerning either what scripture says about sexuality or what examination of human bodies can tell us about God's will for sexuality, but that sexuality itself, including sexual ethics, is socially constructed, and is therefore open to change. Other scholars deny this, arguing for traditional moral norms in sexuality as based in sacred revelation and as corresponding to essential human nature, and insisting that to move beyond these norms is to open church teaching to complete relativity, to moral chaos amid historical change.

Knowledge of sexuality in other cultures has increased exponentially in the last century, making it very clear that gender is socially constructed. Since Alfred Kinsey's in the 1940s and 1950s, research has strongly supported sexual orientation as also socially constructed. More recently, it has been argued by scientists that categories of male and female previously thought to be biological are also constructed. Perhaps the most basic shift in Christian sexual ethics today is that they are no longer exclusively male in perspective, no longer the sole province of clerical élites in homogenous European cultures, and no longer based on commonly accepted understandings of human sexuality.

CHRISTINE E. GUDORF

📖 John Boswell, *The Kindness of Strangers: The Abandonment of Children in Western Europe from Late Antiquity to the Renaissance*, New York: Vintage Books 1988; Lisa Sowle Cahill, *Sex, Gender and Christian Ethics*, New York and Cambridge: CUP 1996; Christine E. Gudorf, *Body, Sex and Pleasure: Reconstructing Christian Sexual Ethics*, Cleveland, OH: Pilgrim Press 1994; Patricia Beatty Jung and Ralph F. Smith, *Heterosexism: An Ethical Challenge*, Albany, NY: State University of New York 1993; Eleanor E. Maccoby, *The Two Sexes: Growing Up Apart, Coming Together*. Cambridge, MA: Belknap/Harvard University Press 1998; Rosemary Radford Ruether, *Christianity and the Making of the Modern Family: Ruling Ideologies, Diverse Realities*, Boston: Beacon Press 2000; Kathleen M. Sands, *God Forbid: Religion and Sex in American Public Life*, New York: OUP 2000

Sexuality

There is a profound ambivalence within Christianity about sexual desire. On the one hand, passion for sensual pleasure and erotic intimacy can be seen as God's good handiwork. According to the biblical account of creation in the book of Genesis, built into human being is a deep longing to live in harmonious relationship with God, one another and the earth. Sexual desire incarnates this yearning for companionship. It inclines people towards passionate attachments and empowers the maintenance of such bonds. It draws humans into each other's arms. Since it is by God's design that people so love, it can be affirmed that the many expressions of human sexuality – the ache of loneliness, the attraction of desire, the heat of arousal and the joy of genital pleasure – are good and gracious gifts of God. Human partners can become 'one flesh' through their sexual coupling. Sexual partners can become so connected that the other's concerns, interests and agendas become their own. When loving, sexual activity can be mutually de-self-centring.

On the other hand, that same biblical account of creation makes it clear that sexual desire, like all that is human, is tainted by sin. Sexual ardour can be a source of lustful, as well as loving, relationships. All sexual contact is boundary-blurring, but when such contact is disordered, it is boundary-violating. Sexual appetites can be addictive and compulsive. Passion can seduce, instead of serve, people, forging relationships that are abusive and destructive of human dignity. Sexual desire can fuel relationships wherein people take, rather than share, pleasure and thereby fail to embody love. It can draw and bind people into relationships that are marked by possessiveness and domination. Our bodily availability to one another and our longing for such intimate engagement leaves us extremely vulnerable to sexual forms of aggression and humiliation.

Sexuality

As a result of this ambivalence, chastity has been a prime virtue in the history of Christianity. It has been commended to all people, regardless of their gender or sexual orientation and regardless of whether they are married or celibate. It is understood to be both a grace and a moral virtue. As a virtue, it is a learned way of channelling sexual passion that (re)forms erotic desire, integrating it within the person and ordering it to its proper purpose(s), so that the respect due every body and the dignity inherent in all persons is reverenced in every relationship.

Chastity is a matter of personal integrity, if not honesty. It is about the integration, as appropriate, of sexual thoughts, feelings and actions into a person's life. It aims to bring body language into harmony with what is in on a person's mind or tongue. Despite connotations to the contrary, chastity is not exclusively, or even primarily, about the suppression or denial of sexual passion. Of course, sometimes living chastely requires a degree of continence. But chastity is about the cultivation as much as the containment of sexual desire. It is about integrating sexuality into personal relationships, but not going so far as sharing the delights of intimate companionship and genital pleasure with just anyone.

Creation

Sexual ethics

For most of its history, the church taught that sexual activity, even in a just and loving marriage, could be chaste if, and only if, it was intended to be reproductive. For the church father Augustine of Hippo, a procreative intention excused the desire for sexual pleasure, while for the Protestant Reformer Martin Luther, such desire was part of God's general plan to propagate the species. To 'indulge' in sexual activity which was not intentionally

procreative, even if done not to satisfy one's own desires, but simply to 'remedy' the lustful desires of one's spouse, was sinful.

Historically, this emphasis on procreativity had tremendous effects on Christian sexual norms. First, it blurred the distinction, if not separation, between reproductive and sexual activity. Consequently most Christian denominations condemned contraceptive activity until the twentieth century. Secondly, all non-coital forms of sexual activity – digital, oral, and anal sexual activity, whether practised by same-sex or other-sex couples, along with masturbation and the sexual activity of post-menopausal women – were condemned. They were seen as perverted because they were non-procreative. Thirdly, since procreative activity entails the responsibility to rear children properly, it followed that all sexual activity outside the stability of heterosexual marriage should be forbidden. Fourthly, Christianity endorsed the punishment of all those whom most in Western society would recognize today to be transgendered or homosexual in orientation. Indeed, feminist challenges to the theory of gender complementarity that stems from this emphasis on procreativity are met with great resistance. Many Christians today commend to those who are gay or lesbian either sexual reorientation via so-called reparation therapy, or total, life-long abstinence. Fifthly, this emphasis on procreativity privileges male sexual pleasure, since his delight alone is requisite for coitus.

Homosexuality
Feminist theology

In the ancient Mediterranean world, Christians were notable for the way they welcomed and nurtured children. Yet this traditional emphasis on procreativity first as the sole, then the primary, and now as a necessary, justification of sexual activity finds its clearest rationale in male sexual experience, particularly the natural coincidence of orgasm and ejaculation in male sexual physiology. Certainly, there is no necessary link between ovulation and the experience of sexual desire, erotic activity and orgasm in women. The association between the reproductive potential of women and coital activity is much more fluid. It is at most a link established only for a few days, on a monthly basis, and then only for that season of the adult woman's life prior to menopause. Indeed, the active role of women in human conception was not clearly understood until the ovum was discovered in the nineteenth century. Consequently, for most of Christian history, the church treated male sexual experience as normatively human.

Body

In the modern era, there has been a genuine revolution in regard to the normative place of procreativity in Christian sexual ethics. Artificial forms of birth control have been legitimized by most Protestant denominations. 'Responsible parenthood' has been endorsed and methods of natural family planning have been approved by the Roman Catholic Church. Correspondingly, Christians, especially those from countries bordering the North Atlantic, increasingly debate public and church policies that discriminate against persons on the basis of their gender or sexual orientation. The unitive bonds that are forged through the sharing of pleasure are no longer seen as 'secondary' to the procreative meaning that might well accompany sexual activity.

Sexual activity required justification in Christianity because the distinction between the desire for sexual pleasure and lust became blurred. For much of its history, the church misidentified sexuality as impure. Traditionally, sexual passion and pleasure (even in marriage) were thought morally suspect. In the Middle Ages temporary forms of continence were often commended to married couples.

The story of how the distinction between lustful and graceful experiences of sexual desire became blurred in Christianity is quite complex. For the richer members of the ancient Mediterranean society in which Christianity arose, sexuality was not confined to marriage, and marriage was not associated with sexual pleasure. Sexual slavery and sex trade were fairly commonplace. Maternal and infant mortality rates were high. Along with emotional indifference and control, detachment and autonomy were considered morally ideal. The teachings of many philosophical schools condemned not only the 'intemperance' of sexual passions, but also even the tender affections sometimes shared by lovers. In this philosophical tradition the material world, including the body and its sexual passions and reproductive functions, especially as evidenced in women, was thought to be a threat to the purity of the soul.

Furthermore, wealth, power and pleasure were tied to and transferred through marriage and kinship systems. In this historical context, sexual continence vividly signalled the renunciation of such worldly pursuits. The endorsement, and eventual idealization, of virginity, celibacy and widowhood signalled the refusal to prioritize such concerns. It has never been part of Christian belief that personal continuity is established through reproduction or ensured by ancestor worship. Hence, procreation has never been seen as essential to the Christian life.

In view of the expectation that everything – including the body – would be transformed in the life of the world to come, it is not surprising that many early Christian theologians argued that in the new creation the body would be 'spiritualized' or gutted of all its visceral emotions. Consider the comparatively moderate views of Augustine of Hippo. He argued that marriage along with sexual differentiation and reproduction (though devoid of desire) were part of God's original blessing in paradise. Even so, as Augustine saw it, these dimensions of sexuality, along with passion and pleasure, would have no place in the world to come.

The absence of sexuality in the visions of the new heaven and new earth that prevailed in the early church explains the idealization of celibacy within Christianity. In the 'culture of celibacy' that emerged, sexual lifestyles were ranked in descending order of acceptability. Virginity was best, then perpetual celibacy, followed by widowhood, temporary continence within marriage, and finally procreativity within marriage.

From the third to the sixteenth centuries, the notion that celibacy was a superior path of discipleship went virtually unchallenged. Then, in the context of the Protestant Reformation, Martin Luther argued that while the gift of celibacy might be given 'for the sake of the kingdom' to a few, such a special calling was quite rare. Most who attempted to travel this path were self-deceived. They were most likely in denial of God's remedy for human lust graciously provided in the holy estate of marriage. As Luther saw it, efforts to live a celibate life usually ended in promiscuity. Though he did not condemn celibacy, John Calvin argued that this state of life has no greater spiritual or moral value than marriage.

Today, celibacy in Christianity is no longer understood as being rooted in suspicions about sexual desire. Instead, the choice not to marry is seen as a vivid witness to the centrality of God in the Christian life. From this perspective, celibacy dramatically models the subordination of the real goods associated with marriage and family life to God, the centre of all value for Christians. Celibacy also serves as testimony that life is not all about the pursuit of pleasure, the acquisition of wealth and/or the establishment of power and status over others. But whether or not celibacy is chosen, the prime understanding of sexuality in Christian tradition remains that it should be rooted in love.

Whether sexuality rooted in love can also be extended to homosexual relations is, of course, one of the most hotly-debated issues of the present day. Here there has been no long-lasting ambivalence in the Christian tradition but rather, until very recently, indeed an attitude of total rejection. It is unlikely that any agreed position on the issue will be reached easily or soon.

PATRICIA BEATTIE JUNG

Peter Brown, *The Body and Society: Men, Women and Sexual Renunciation in Early Christianity*, New York: Columbia University Press and London: Faber 1988; Gareth Moore, OP, *The Body in Context: Sex and Catholicism*, London: SCM Press and New York: Continuum 1992; Adrian Thatcher and Elizabeth Stuart (eds), *Christian Perspectives on Sexuality and Gender*, Grand Rapids, MI: Eerdmans 1996

Shakers

The United Society of Believers in Christ's Second Appearing, more commonly known as the Shakers, is arguably the most successful experiment in community living in the United States. Ann Lee, founder of the sect, began her public ministry near Albany, New York, in 1780. Her message spread quickly, and the movement survived a period of persecution to gain popularity in the early nineteenth century. At Shakerism's peak in the 1840s and 1850s, Shaker villages spanned the United States from the east coast to the Ohio Valley. By the late-nineteenth century, however, increasing economic opportunities and changing cultural sensibilities rendered the Shaker message less appealing to outsiders. Fewer people joined the group and young Shakers left, forcing the gradual closure of all but one village. Today a handful of Shakers still live and worship at Sabbathday Lake, Maine.

Community

Although the Shakers are considered an American religious sect, Ann Lee was born into a working-class family in Manchester, England, and baptized in 1742. Poor and illiterate, she worked in the factories and married Abraham Standerin, against her wishes as she later claimed, in 1762. She found solace in religion. Lee joined a small group of Shaking Quakers, so-called because they danced and cried out in strange tongues, but eventually left when she clashed with the group's leaders over her claim that God had revealed to her that celibacy was essential for salvation. She based this teaching, which became the cornerstone of the Shaker faith, on her assertion that lust was the sin responsible for Adam and Eve's expulsion from the Garden of Eden. The only way to reclaim the purity of Paradise was to live a celibate life free of all desires.

Quakers

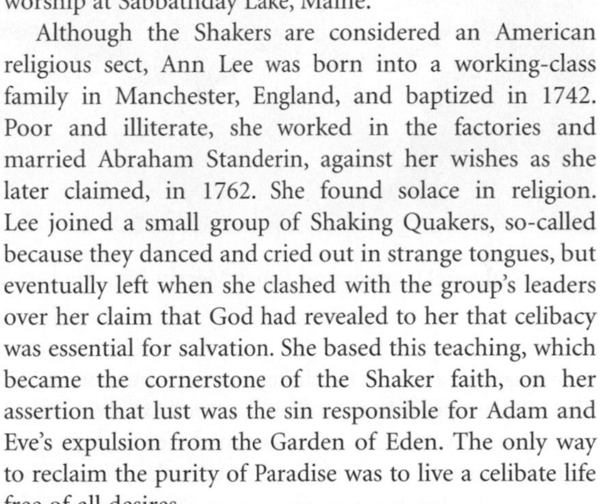

In 1774 Ann Lee, her husband, and a few followers sailed for America after Lee claimed another revelation directed her there. The group landed in New York City, where they worked at their various occupations while Lee waited for the right time to 'open the gospel'. Several years later, the group moved to Niskeyuna outside Albany, New York, and Lee began to teach publicly her views on celibacy and right living. Encouraged by this early success, Ann Lee, her brother William Lee, and James Whittaker, one of her English followers, conducted a missionary tour through New England from 1781 to 1783 and gathered the nucleus of what would become the major Shaker villages of the nineteenth century. From all accounts Ann Lee was a charismatic personality and attracted large crowds. Much of her teaching – frugality, simplicity, meekness, and hard work – was amenable to the Yankee mind-set. Nevertheless, her insistence on celibacy stirred up angry mobs that physically attacked the Shakers when they gathered to worship. Worn out from their travels, the

Nathaniel Currier and James Merritt Ives, *Shakers dancing near New Lebanon, New York*, lithograph, *c.* 1890

missionaries returned to Niskeyuna in September 1783. The following year both William Lee and Ann Lee died.

Fortunately, those who assumed leadership after Ann Lee's death were able to sustain the momentum generated by the missionaries. James Whittaker was the first to take command of the fledgling movement. A devout and zealous Shaker, Whittaker reinforced the teachings of Ann Lee. He also visited the clusters of Shakers and promoted communal ownership of property among them. It was American-born Joseph Meacham, however, the male successor upon Whittaker's death in 1787, who developed the blueprint for gathering Shakers into communal villages. Under the guidance of Meacham and Lucy Wright, co-leaders of the Central Ministry, Shakers in New York, New Hampshire, Massachusetts, Connecticut and Maine organized themselves into eleven villages. Upon Meacham's death in 1796 Lucy Wright assumed primary leadership of the movement. During her tenure a group of Shaker missionaries travelled west in 1805. Their labours sparked the formation of Shaker villages in Ohio, Kentucky, and for a brief time, Indiana.

The Shaker village formed the foundation of the movement. Each village was divided into several families or orders based on the spiritual maturity of its members, from the gathering order, for those first setting out to learn about Shakerism, to the church order, for those who had decided to commit themselves fully to a Shaker life. To enter the church order an individual signed a covenant and turned all property over to the Shakers. The strength of the Shaker village was its ability to provide emotional support for its members by replacing the biological family with a spiritual family. To facilitate the maintenance of celibacy, men and women, married or single, lived separately in dormitory-like settings while children were raised in their own order, prompting some detractors to accuse the Believers of destroying families. In place of biological ties, however, the Shakers stressed the importance of spiritual ties. The Shakers called each other 'Brother' and 'Sister', and in the formative years of the movement Shaker leaders, including Ann Lee, were called 'Mother' or 'Father'.

The communal nature of a Shaker village enhanced this feeling of family. No one received a wage, but everyone's needs were cared for, from food and clothing to health care and entertainment. The Shakers emphasized the importance of manual labour and expected everyone to work in some capacity. They did not, however, believe in drudgery. Work assignments were rotated among members, and the

Believers became known for their inventions, including the circular saw and a washing machine patented by the Canterbury, New Hampshire, Believers.

In addition to their inventions the Shakers were also known for their business acumen. Although farming formed the basis of each village, the Shakers strengthened their economic position by trading with the outside world. Meticulous and hard working, the Shakers earned a reputation as honest dealers in high-quality products ranging from furniture and brooms to seeds, herbs and apple sauce. They marketed their products through peddling trips as well as in stores that they operated in their villages.

Despite their economic success, Shaker villages were essentially religious communities, and theology played an important role in their development. Theology, for example, grounded the Shakers' efforts to create one of the most gender-equal communities in nineteenth-century America. The Shakers believed in a dual godhead – God as both male and female – and believed that all creation reflected this duality. Thus they taught that the Christ spirit, first manifested in the man Jesus, was later manifested in the woman Ann Lee. They also modelled their leadership structure on the notion of duality, seen in the dual leadership of Joseph Meacham and Lucy Wright. For every leadership position in a Shaker village the hierarchy appointed both a male and a female. Elders and eldresses, deacons and deaconesses, and trustees and office sisters worked side by side to maintain the functioning of their villages. Celibacy also contributed to the equalization of the sexes. Because women were not expected to channel their energies into numerous pregnancies and endless child-rearing, they had more time and energy to devote to learning new skills and developing other sides of their personalities.

Although they had enlightened views, the Shakers divided work along traditional gender lines. Women cooked, cleaned and laundered. Men performed agricultural work and craft-work such as blacksmithing, shoemaking and cabinet-making. This traditional division of labour has been criticized, but Shaker communities did not view labour as the outside world did. Society, generally, treated male occupations as more important than women's work, which was devalued because it centred on the home and child-care. The Shakers, however, understood all labour as equally important and refused to consider some types of work as more important than others, thus removing one major barrier to the equal treatment of men and women.

Because the Shakers were a religious community, worship was a central feature of their life together. In the earliest years of the movement Shaker worship was wild and exuberant as people danced and shouted under the power of the spirit. Once the Shakers organized into villages, however, they toned down their activities. They abandoned spirit-led dancing for intricate and choreographed dance steps that all members were expected to learn. They also developed a repertoire of songs that taught Shaker history and theology. The Shakers sang and danced, without the accompaniment of instruments, in weekly sabbath meetings that were open to the public and drew large crowds. From the late-1830s to the 1850s, they experienced a period of revivalism in which they reverted to the charismatic activity of earlier years. During this time they closed their meetings to outsiders but reopened services when the revival passed and worship resumed an orderly fashion.

Dance

The Shakers' need to monitor observation of their worship is indicative of their relationship with the outside world. They walked a fine line between maintaining their integrity as Shakers and developing a good relationship with outsiders. The persecution of the early years disappeared when the Shakers gathered into villages, and non-Shakers discovered that they made good neighbours. The Shakers kept their villages neat and tidy; they were honest and industrious. But they were also noticeably different, in their dress, their lifestyle and their celibacy, and lurking beneath the surface of the world's acceptance was always the fear that Shakers were different. Their constant struggle to maintain their beliefs while minimizing points of contention with non-Shakers, to be in the world but not of it, constituted the central struggle of Shakerism.

SUZANNE R. THURMAN

Edward Deming Andrews, *The People Called Shakers*, New York: Dover Publications 1963; Priscilla Brewer, *Shaker Communities, Shaker Lives*, Hanover, NH: University Press of New England 1986; Sister Frances A. Carr, *Growing Up Shaker*, Sabbathday Lake, ME: United Society of Shakers 1994; Daniel W. Patterson, *The Shaker Spiritual* (1979), New York: Dover Publications [2]2000; David R. Starbuck, *A Shaker Family Album: Photographs from the Collection of Canterbury Shaker Village*, Hanover, NH: University Press of New England 1998; Stephen J. Stein, *The Shaker Experience in America*, New Haven, CT: Yale University Press 1992; Suzanne R. Thurman, *'O Sisters Ain't You Happy?': Gender, Family, and Community among the Harvard and Shirley Shakers*, Syracuse, NY: Syracuse University Press 2002

Work

Sickness and healing

Health is one of the most important considerations occupying modern society, as we search for a lifestyle that offers the alluring elixir of a long and healthy life.

Pastoral care

As we live longer so we will also suffer many more years of ill health, and therefore the search for healing will gather momentum. Some will seek out Christian resources to alleviate their suffering, and many churches today offer healing services, prayer ministry, pastoral care and counselling, and other such support.

Jesus

Although Christians recognize that much healing comes through medical and nursing care, there are many churches today that minister to the sick in the expectation and faith that Jesus Christ, who came to save and heal, continues to do so through the church in the power of the Holy Spirit. So an exploration of sickness and healing in the Christian tradition needs to begin with the ministry of Jesus.

Jesus

Miracle
Kingdom of God
Sin
Evil

Nearly 40 per cent of the narrative verses in the Gospels are devoted to describing Jesus' healing activity. These miracles brought physical health, wholeness and peace to sufferers and allowed them to take their place in the community once again. At the time, and still today, there was and is no obvious naturalistic explanation for these mighty deeds. These supernatural displays of power were signs that the kingdom of God (that is the rule and reign of God) had invaded human history in the person and mission of Jesus who, as the human face of God, had come to save and heal and deliver people from the power of sin and evil.

Sacraments
Forgiveness
Suffering
Eucharist
Worship

The world still continues, however, to witness a conflict between God's kingdom and the hostile opposing forces of evil that seek to frustrate God's rule. Sickness and suffering may hold us in their grip now, but the New Testament promises an end to these with the final establishment of the kingdom of God, when there will be a new heaven and a new earth in which hurt and pain will be a thing of the past. The consummation of God's kingly rule will be beyond history in the life of the age to come, when creation will be restored and suffering and evil are finally defeated. Jesus' healing miracles offer glimpses of that future kingdom of perfect health and wholeness.

Attitudes to healing

Faith
Holy Spirit

The question arises whether Jesus' healings are to be seen as a unique phenomenon, or whether they are models for his followers to emulate. Should there be an expectation that these healings can be repeated today, as Christians seek to continue the healing ministry of Jesus in his church in the power of the Holy Spirit?

Those who hold a liberal view are suspicious of any kind of supernatural miraculous healing, expecting God to work through normal means. The idea that God intervenes directly in the physical world seems to them to be incompatible with what is known scientifically about the universe, and so they find it difficult to call Jesus' healings miraculous. They may be attributed to medical or psychological causes.

Yet other Christians take a cessationist or dispensational view of healing miracles that holds that miracles ceased after the apostolic age. In order to launch the church, the apostles were granted a special temporary dispensation to perform signs and wonders. Once the Christian church was established, healings and other miracles were no longer required. God has now withdrawn the power to heal, and modern medicine fulfils the New Testament promises about healing today. There does not appear to be any support for this view in the New Testament.

Many Christians have concluded, however, that the mission of the church today is nothing less than the continuation of Jesus' own mission of proclaiming the good news of the kingdom of God and healing the sick. Charismatic churches, in particular, often see the healing ministry as part of the evangelistic mission of the church. Jesus sent out his disciples to preach and to heal, and as the church continues his healing ministry we should expect miracles of healing today. There is a direct line between Jesus' practice and contemporary healing, for his healing is made available to believers through his Spirit working in them.

The healing ministry is carried out within the Christian church today in a variety of ways ranging from a sacramental approach through penance, the eucharist, prayer with the laying on of hands and anointing of the sick, to a charismatic setting through gifts of healing, 'words of knowledge' and 'deliverance' ministry. Worship, the sacraments and the proclamation of the word of God are often intertwined in seeking healing. Throughout history the church has cared for the sick and anxious in many different ways, whether through the establishment of Christian hospitals or by providing various pathways to wholeness such as those referred to above.

Faith and healing

A further important consideration in healing is that of faith. The basic meaning of faith in the Gospels equates it with belief and trust in the person of Jesus, his mission and his ability and willingness to grant healing. Faith is a common ingredient in the healing accounts in the Gospels, as can be seen from the number of narratives containing such phrases as 'your faith has made you whole'.

Faith is also a live issue in the contemporary church. Today, the relationship of faith to healing is a complex one. Those who see Jesus' healings as something to be emulated tend to stress that it is only through faith that God releases his power to heal. There is a direct link between a person's level of faith and the chance of miraculous healing. Lack of healing is indicative of lack of faith. However, an

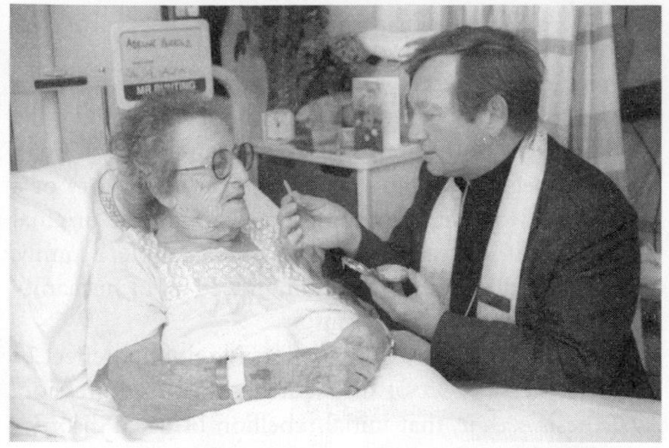

Hospital chaplain giving communion

insensitive application of this approach to people with disabilities can sometimes have the reverse effect and destroy faith.

An overemphasis on faith can also have the effect of making Jesus a servant of such a faith, whereby he can be manipulated and coerced into healing through it. This is a corruption of the gospel. It can also tend to set up an artificial opposition between medicine and faith, between believing in the doctor or the preacher, sometimes with tragic results. There are of course some disabilities such as an amputated leg that cannot be cured, no matter how much faith one has. Nevertheless, many have found faith to be a vital ingredient in healing. The faith of persons with disabilities sustains many in their daily existence and is a healing element in their lives.

Sickness as a punishment for sin

In Jesus' day Jews saw a link between sickness and sin. Physical problems were thought to be caused by human sinfulness. It would appear that Jesus would have us reject that notion. It is true that in Mark 2 and John 5 Jesus appears to acknowledge the inter-relationship between sickness and sin and to heal by proclaiming the forgiveness of sins. In the healing of the blind man in John 9, however, Jesus went against the popular belief of his day that sickness and sin were related.

The theology expressed in the 'Order for the Visitation of the Sick' in the 1662 Anglican Book of Common Prayer regards sickness as 'God's visitation', 'the chastisement of the Lord' and 'our Heavenly Father's correction'. Even today there are Christians who see conditions such as HIV/Aids as a judgement of God on our permissive society. Liberals regard this as a pre-scientific view of the world, and do not see God intervening directly in his universe to send illness upon people.

Nevertheless, there is often a relationship between sickness and sin. Sinful attitudes and actions can contribute towards or cause much sickness and suffering. Certainly contemporary preachers involved in the ministry of healing stress the importance of forgiveness of sins in healing. They also see some sickness as serving a higher purpose. Sometimes it serves to chastise us or to bring us to our senses. At other times, it may turn us around and redirect our lives in a better course.

The power of evil

Belief in the existence of evil spirits was widespread in Jesus' day. On several occasions the Gospel writers link Jesus' healings with casting out demons or unclean spirits. The question is how far his attitude was sociologically determined as part of his Jewish culture. For some, Satan and deliverance from demonic oppression or possession feature prominently in advocating a theology that depicts the kingdom of God and the realm of Satan permanently at war with each other. Others tend to dismiss the demonic elements in Jesus' healings as being a product of a world-view which no longer has a place in modern society. There are differences of opinion among Christians as to whether evil spirits actually exist as real entities or whether they are just nameless forces or personifications of evil.

Satan

Nevertheless, Christians emphasize spiritual evil as a reality which cannot be ignored, because such evil can dominate the lives of some people who need the church's authority and power in Christ to liberate them. Others emphasize the demonic in social and political structures such as apartheid and Nazism, to which the church needs to bring Christ's healing and deliverance.

Evidence for healing

While there are many in the world today who sadly do not experience healing and are not cured of their disabilities when they seek God's help, there are many others who do bear witness to God's healing power in their lives.

Charismatic Christians report a plentiful supply of healing miracles, particularly in African and other Third-World countries, where they are attributed to the greater faith of Christians there who are dependent upon God healing directly because of limited medical resources. But critics will ask, 'Is this not rather due to a lack of accurate verifiable reporting?'

Over the 100 or more years of the International Medical Bureau at Lourdes, 66 cases have met the rigid criteria for miraculous cures. In addition, thousands of other claims of healing have been registered at this shrine which are beyond medical explanation but do not meet these criteria.

Various scientific research projects, particularly in the USA, have also been carried out to ascertain the effects of religion on health. Some research has shown the positive effects of spiritual activities on health and physical well-being that affect both quality of life and longevity.

Bible

Stories continue to persist of alleged remarkable physical healings throughout the world. Healings are experienced in various ways ranging from extraordinary cures, to recoveries more rapid than expected, to those who experience God's sustaining strength in human weakness to help them cope with prolonged suffering.

Health and wholeness

Salvation

Christian healing is not just about recovery from physical illness. A biblical understanding of health involves a close relationship between healing, wholeness and salvation. The New Testament word for salvation (*soteria*) conveys the idea of soundness of health in body, mind and spirit. So much unhappiness and ill health is connected with our own mental well-being and the state of our relationships with each other, our environment, and with God. Health is, therefore, a state of complete physical, mental, social and spiritual well-being.

God

Creation

For Christians, health and wholeness extend, however, beyond the individual's need for health to bringing healing to a sick society through addressing the social, moral, economic and environmental issues that give rise to the wider causes of ill health. It involves Christians addressing the deep-rooted sicknesses and social evils in local and national life. It involves the righting of wrongs by combating poverty, injustice, violence and the exploitation of the environment in order to bring about a healthier world in anticipation of seeing creation finally healed.

Poverty

CHRISTOPHER GOWER

📖 *A Time to Heal. A Report on the Healing Ministry for the House of Bishops of the General Synod of the Church of England*, London: Church House Publishing 2000; Christopher Gower, *Speaking of Healing*, London: SPCK 2003

Sin

While the word sin may seem very familiar to us in the twenty-first century, over the years its meaning and ethical content have become somewhat elastic. Sin is synonymous with life's little luxuries: gourmet food, designer clothes, refined perfumes, deluxe automobiles and so on. Of course, the older religious meaning endures, but often this becomes a caricature in the popular mind in the form of the 'sins of the flesh' and such like. So if we want a more focused account of what sin means today, like a restorer, we must peel away the layers of varnish and overlay that distort the original picture. This task has been greatly aided by the enormous flowering in biblical scholarship and enquiry over the last century.

p. 1152

Biblical criticism

The biblical background

If we turn to the Bible and look at it in its own terms, the picture that emerges is an integral one, giving a multi-dimensional picture of humankind. Right from the opening pages of the book of Genesis, the story of human weakness begins to unfold. Chapter 3 tells the story of a man and a woman, Adam and Eve, who are the original sinners, but if we read on we soon find a couple, a family, a dynasty, a city, an entire nation, indeed all of humanity described as in some sense sinful.

The effect is to chart the irreversible domino effect of sin after the first act of disobedience and transgression. As Genesis sees it, that initial rebellion brings a disorder into the relationship between God and creation because creatures try to become like their creator. The nub of the issue is that human beings reject the truth about themselves, they overstep their status as creatures, and sin puts a separation between them and God. The ultimate effect of sin is alienation and isolation.

Yet in the earliest scriptural accounts it is not just the relationship with God that has been disordered; life itself takes on a very different complexion. Chaos enters the web of human relationships and even the relationship with the natural world is upset. Sin no longer simply concerns the lives of the first parents (Adam and Eve); it begins to cast its shadow over the entire human race and all creation. The emphasis here is on the universal; the consequences of sin have rebounded not just on Israel and the Hebrews but on all of humankind. All humanity is represented in the symbolic name 'Adam'. Recriminations and rationalizations abound, but despite the best efforts, the consequences of sin cannot be undone (Genesis 3. 14–24). Adam is henceforth to be a tiller of the soil; he and his descendants will have to engage in a silent combat between man and soil in order to win their livelihood. Eve, in turn, is destined to suffer in giving birth, and the story of Cain and of the subsequent generations down to the tower of Babel in the chapters of Genesis that follow is a litany of jealousy and envy, giving rise on occasion to violence, bloodlust and even death.

These mythical narratives attempt to account for the replication and reproduction of sins from one generation to the next. The estrangement of Adam and Eve is mirrored in Genesis 4 in the life-story of Cain, who becomes the archetypal fugitive. Here, in this narrative of origins, we can already discern some key elements of the underlying understanding of sin. A first element is the damage which sin does to the relationship between God and God's people, a relationship that set Israel apart from the other nations. Here, human pride and rebelliousness are not simply the hubris of Greek tragedy, which brings about the downfall of the flawed hero through the blind forces of fate. They are an expression of rebellion against

God: the Lord who has loved his creatures into being. Sin is a wilful breaking off of the loving dialogue through which God converses with God's creation and calls it to fullness of life. This dialogue will later take the form of a covenant – the pledge of intimate love, which God calls upon God's people to reciprocate.

For the Hebrew prophets in turn, the essence of sin is the deliberate rupture of personal relations between humankind and God. God 'knows' God's people with an irrevocable love (Amos 3.2; Hosea 13.5); Israel must therefore 'know' God (Hosea 13.4). The expression to 'know' here has a profound conjugal sense of mutual gift and intimacy. Sin is the rejection of this intimacy with God, the refusal of the dialogue, the rebuff of the call. It is the injury done to the heart of God and a damaging of the conjugal bond. This understanding of sin is also the backdrop to the prophets' frequent use of the figurative vocabulary of adultery and prostitution (Hosea 3; Jeremiah 3.1–5, 19–25 and 4.1–4 as well as Ezekiel 23). Sin therefore brings about a rupture and a separation between creature and creator (Isaiah 59.2). But God never leaves the sinner without hope. Consciousness of sin is the first step to conversion. To the Hebrew mind, this awareness can only be born out of a sincere acknowledgement of the truth, a frank confession of one's recognition of the unlovely spectre of sin before the blinding holiness of God. In the words of the psalmist, 'My sin is always before me' (Psalm 51.5)

So in the Old Testament we find a searingly realistic view of humankind and of its fallibility. We find here a truthful anthropology, a view of human beings that is credible. There is no pretence that human beings are anything other than creatures prone to all the foibles and frailties of the human condition. Nevertheless, they are loved by a God who will never abandon them, no matter how great their sins may be. New Testament thought and its understanding of sin is also dominated by the horizon of covenant. This covenant continues to be understood in terms of God's loving intimacy, but now it finds its most vivid expression in the gift of God's only-begotten Son.

As depicted in the Gospels, the earthly ministry of Jesus too is consistent with the Father's loving care. The Gospels are replete with examples of his tenderness and compassion towards all who encounter him, especially those who are publicly identified as sinners. On numerous occasions this attitude is a source of scandal to the civic and religious leaders of the day, notably many scribes and Pharisees, who (not unreasonably perhaps) considered it entirely inappropriate that a rabbi should have such familiarity with tax-collectors, women and foreigners without first insisting that they repent. Nevertheless, the world in which Jesus lived tended to make a marked separation between respectability and sinfulness, so that some states of life were seen as sinful in themselves. It is this judgemental, human tendency, which is of course by no means limited to first-century Palestine, which Jesus seeks to challenge and to change.

Covenant

Prophecy

Thus Jesus is pictured as having overstepped the rigid conventions of his society and disregarded many of the traditional taboos. In so doing he also demonstrated his wish to move beyond the prevailing cultic notions of sin. External impurities that could be washed clean, omissions in the ritual prayers and sacrifices, eating proscribed foods, all of these understandings of sin, though having a valid cultic basis, were not in themselves capable of encapsulating the moral meaning of sin. Even though the prophets had already struggled against deficient conceptions of sin, Jewish morality at the time of Jesus (in common perhaps with much of human morality before and since) still tended to measure guilt by the external material act rather than the internal disposition towards good or evil. By contrast, Jesus taught that sin, like goodness, is a quality of the inner self, for it is from within the human heart that all good and evil thoughts and deeds come (Luke 6.45; Mark 7.21f.). Jesus therefore demands interior disposition as the decisive factor in moral action. And so, for example, by way of a lustful look at another, the sinner is deemed to have already committed adultery 'in the heart' (Matthew 5.27). In this way Jesus radically redefines sin, not by revoking what went before but by drawing out the full implications of a morality centred on the 'heart'.

Since sin is a failure in a relationship of love, it necessarily involves the 'heart'. For Jesus, as for the prophets before him, the response to God is rooted in the heart and to sin is really to 'harden one's heart' to God's love. This is a metaphorical vocabulary that emphasizes the inward thrust of the New Testament message. For Jesus, this table fellowship with sinners is central to ministry. 'I came not to call the righteous but sinners' (Mark 2.17). The righteous here are those who, like the elder son in the parable of 'the prodigal son' (Luke 15.11–32), are too concerned with their own status and standing to appreciate their sinfulness and need of salvation. Self-absorption and excessive self-preoccupation are the sinful pitfalls for the 'righteous'. These are diametrically opposed to the call to discipleship, which is a call to love one's neighbour and to take up the cause of the 'poor, the widow and the orphan'.

Jesus

Jesus' parable of the Pharisee and the tax-collector (Luke 18.9–14) demonstrates the point lucidly. A Pharisee enumerates all the religious actions he has performed; the tax-collector can only beat his breast and ask for mercy. The proud and self-satisfied 'holy man' is so infatuated with his own exemplary but purely external generosity that he loses the measure of true justice. The humble tax-collector by contrast knows his sins, and in that acutely painful self-knowledge is profoundly aware of his need.

Origins and background
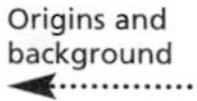

God is therefore like the loving and compassionate father who seeks an errant child, the good shepherd who searches for a lost sheep and the woman who combs the house for a lost coin. There are to be no limits to love.

For the authors of the first three Gospels, all human failure and personal sin are to be seen in the light of the Great Commandment, to love God with all one's strength and to love one's neighbour as oneself. Sin can therefore be understood as a betrayal or a neglect of love. For the evangelists, this manifests itself in negative stances and attitudes towards others and is seen especially in the insensitivity, selfishness, vengefulness and coldness of the Pharisees.

Council

Here, though, we must be on our guard. When the evangelists paint their negative picture of the Pharisees, they are influenced by the rift between the Jews and the followers of Jesus that was taking place in their time. Modern New Testament scholarship has taught us to distinguish between the reality of the Pharisees in Jesus' day, who often represented the best in contemporary Jewish religious practice and ethical seriousness, and the presentation of the Pharisees in the New Testament, where they unfairly come to represent an approach to religious practice that can be found in almost any religion.

Justification

Given that all sin is an offence against God's love and providence, which seeks humanity's own good, refusal to acknowledge the power of God working in Christ is seen as the unpardonable sin. This is the sin against the Holy Spirit, because it is a closing of oneself to the very source of love and of life (Matthew 12.30–2). It is also a refusal to grow, to interact, to live in communion and to give of one's self. It is undeniably a refusal of God, but also a refusal of the truth about oneself. As such it is the most radical form of revolt open to humankind. It represents the deliberate abandonment of good and the choice of evil under the influence of what Matthew and Paul were to call *anomia,* that iniquity which can make its way into the heart and gnaw away there like a disease.

Holy Spirit

Viewed thus, sin eventually cuts the individual off from God as a branch is cut from the vine. The sinner's heart is hardened so that he or she refuses to be receptive to God's love. Sin becomes a refusal of the Father's love, a refusal rooted in the free, self-determining choice of the sinner. In the end the starkness of this choice is as striking as the difference between light and darkness, and this imagery is taken up by the Gospel of John to describe sin's mysterious and pervasive presence in the world.

Ministry and ministers

Forgiveness

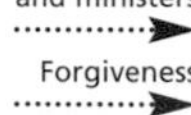

Original sin

If Adam and Eve were not historical figures, clearly original sin cannot simply be about eating a piece of fruit offered by a serpent. Nevertheless, Christian tradition has always insisted that the sinful inheritance of Eden affects the very being of men and women and is not just symbolic in a narrow way. It is through the new Adam, Christ, that the human heart is re-orientated towards the infinite love of God.

Augustine, despite his certainty about the power of baptism, recognized the reality of sinful inclination. Baptism in a sense was a down payment on a new life, which would be experienced fully only in the hereafter. Many centuries later, Martin Luther was to pick up on this point. Unlike Augustine, he came to identify concupiscence and original sin as one and the same thing. For him, original sin was no longer simply a question of a sinful disposition but of 'a profound and total upset in the human economy, whereby … man is constituted in a permanent state of sin'. The Council of Trent disagreed. It was not simply a question of original sin not being imputed; rather, in baptism the sinner was buried with Christ, and so the 'old man' was thrown off and the 'new man' emerged. The merits and demerits of the respective positions of Luther and Trent were to be the subject of much lengthy and detailed historical analysis. That episode in the gradually unfolding theology of sin is richly expressive of a conundrum that is at the very heart of the human condition. Human beings are at once free and yet somehow slaves to themselves. They are convinced of a call to the greatness of God and to partnership with God, yet everywhere they are confronted by the signs of their own fragility and finitude. The nature of original sin therefore resonates with the fundamental realization that as well as individual transgressions and acts of rebelliousness, sins also have a kind of transpersonal and even cosmic dimension. As well as being evidenced in categorical acts, sin at another level also represents the very ground from which these acts spring.

Contemporary accounts of sin

What is our understanding of sin today? Gradually, a more biblically based account of sin has begun to replace the legalistic and narrow understandings of sin that dominated much of Western Christian thought for the better part of four centuries. Chief among these was an unhealthy preoccupation with sin and an excessive casuistry aimed at avoiding punishment. Sin had come to be seen as infringement of the law. Further, there was often confusion between positive (man-made) law and moral law, as well as a tendency to neglect the Bible and to emphasize individual rectitude over social awareness.

Some of the reasons for this are obvious. From the time the church began to regularize the formation of clergy and train them for the confessional, it had become imperative that pastors should also be equipped to deal with the practicalities of sin as manifest in the concrete lives of penitents. This probably tilted the balance, especially in the Roman Catholic tradition, away from a dynamic approach and towards the more static understanding of sin expressed in the manuals of moral theology as failure before the law.

With the development of psychology and the human sciences in the twentieth century the need was increasingly felt for a theology of sin which could combine the dynamic account by the church fathers with precise applied pastoral, ethical and human wisdom. The stage was set for a thoroughgoing renewal of the theology and language of sin. Gradually, the Great Commandment with its inescapable link between love of God and love of neighbour became central to moral theology. Rediscovery of Jesus' interpretation of neighbourly love in an absolute and universal sense brought with it inevitable criticism of a theology of sin which was legalistic and minimalist. Renewal of moral theology in favour of a positive accentuation of discipleship and the imitation of Christ also re-awakened interest in the virtues, vices and 'tendencies of the heart' which underpin human action. Understanding the roots of sinful behaviour was now more important than precise enumeration of misdeeds. This approach also re-focused scrutiny on sins of omission as well as commission. Sin was no longer merely the contravention of law and the transgression of boundaries. The sins of not doing enough, of not caring enough, of not serving enough and ultimately of not loving enough re-emerged.

Influenced by a strong renewal of interest in personal relations, contemporary theologians have described how the call to life and the call to love are fundamentally a call to relationship with God and with one's fellow human beings. The meaning, substance and consummation of life are summed up in love of God and love of neighbour, and the entire force of the Great Commandment insists that these two loves may not be separated. It therefore follows that the path towards discovering that meaning, substance and consummation is to be found in human relationships and the virtues such as justice, tolerance, fraternity, respect and forgiveness which sustain them. For Paul, Christ showed true love, self-denial and self-emptying. For humankind he therefore becomes the new creation, the personification and incarnation of the call to love. In future all human actions are to find a reference in Christ; every moral failure is to be viewed in the light of this new ethical criterion: the call to love as Christ loved. Consequently, Christian morality is more intensely personal, for it takes place within the framework of relationship with Christ.

The struggle against sin here loses some of the negative character that served to fossilize its true meaning. It is no longer simply a question of fleeing from a taboo or 'avoiding occasions of sin' as if treading through a minefield. Instead sin is now conceived as all that keeps the individual (or community) from making real that 'newness of life' (Romans 6.4) which is their fundamental calling. In other words, it is a failure to do the good that one could do in order to develop one's own insight, sensitivity, freedom and creativity. Sin is a refusal to grow a refusal of responsibility and co-responsibility.

Moral theology
Psychology and Christianity
Church fathers

Sin thus understood presupposes a certain freedom and ethical awareness. It takes for granted an adequate internalization of moral principles and beliefs. Without such internalization the capacity to act morally is significantly impaired. As a result, a basic understanding of the process of human growth towards psychological maturity is central to the new vision. The internalization of moral responsibility also presupposes the capacity conscientiously to weigh moral values and to embrace them by personal choice. If, as psychologists have suggested, in the early years human conduct is regulated from outside by means of taboos and promises of reward or punishment, it then becomes paramount for the individual will to attain a sufficient level of personal maturity to achieve moral autonomy. Where such autonomy has not been achieved, the capacity to sin will also be significantly reduced.

There is always, of course, the danger of regression towards a Pharisaic concept of sin. As in the attitude of the prodigal son's mistaken elder brother in Jesus' famous parable, the emphasis can too easily be placed on obeying orders and observing law to the detriment of deepening the relationship with the Father.

The renewal of biblical scholarship, spearheaded by the Reformation tradition, has also led to an increased emphasis today on the corporate or collective dimension of sin. Some of the great prophetic texts in scripture such as Isaiah 1–5; Deuteronomy 4–7; and Matthew 23–7 are clearly about the totality of humanity in both its personal and social dimensions. Careful emphasis is laid here on the responsibilities held by people in different roles and functions: heads of families, civic leaders, parents and religious leaders. Similarly, the misdeeds and uncharitable dispositions of all manner of groups and assemblies are denounced. Gently, the people of God are led to assume, distinguish and articulate the responsibilities that belong both to individuals and to groups and indeed to the multiple collective expressions of humankind: families, tribes, tongues, peoples and nations. Amid this great diversity of historical and social forms the preaching of the law of the covenant is designed to engender both individual responsibility and community solidarity.

Reformation
Paul

The Gospels make clear the close parallel between 'hardness of heart' and the 'perversity of the world'. This double symbolism lies at the heart of their concept of sin, sometimes referred to as 'the sin of the world'. The animated debates about the sabbath, what is clean and unclean, the precepts of the law and table fellowship with sinners, are all directed against a collective hardness of

Scholasticism

heart. It is sin born in the human heart, born in the hearts of the learned, those who 'know' much but 'understand' little. It takes expression in the life of the group.

Although the refusal to open one's eyes and one's heart to Jesus' saving message is individual, the structures, the social ties and pressures are such that this refusal appears to be the embodiment of a single attitude. Sin is therefore more than the accumulation of individual acts of sinfulness; it is, as Paul writes, a power that seeks dominion over our lives. 'Sin abounded ... sin has reigned' (Romans 5.20–1). The inward disruption of the sinner is mirrored in the dismemberment of society. For Paul, sin has a very real corporate dimension. Because through baptism the individual is admitted to the community, the *koinonia* of the body of Christ, thenceforward he or she cannot be considered a mere individual, nor can their acts, attitudes and dispositions be solely private. 'None of us lives to himself and none of us dies to himself' (Romans 14.7). All are members of the body of Christ.

Initiation
Community

This does not mean that traditional distinctions such as capital, mortal and venial sin are dispensed with. The notion of capital sin has been with us since the time of the church fathers. The spiritual writer Evagrius Ponticus (346–79) drew up a list of eight generic malevolent thoughts that he maintained were at the root of every sin. This list became a classic text of Eastern Christianity. It explains that 'there are eight generic thoughts: gluttony, fornication, avarice, sadness, anger, sloth, vainglory and pride'.

p. 216

One can see a similarity here with the Western idea of the seven vices. In fact these were a version of Evagrius' list taken up later by Gregory the Great. The order was inverted to take account of the prophet's view that 'pride is the beginning of all sin' (Sirach 10.13). He also reduced the number of vices by combining vainglory and pride and replacing sadness with envy, i.e. destructive and selfish sorrow. Evagrius' list may have been inspired by the three temptations of Jesus, to which the others were added. Noting that Jesus responded to each of the devil's temptations with admonitions from holy scripture, Evagrius later set out to provide a compendium of scriptural passages which would equip the follower of Christ to combat every temptation. This text, too, was divided into eight parts according to the eight generic vices, and this scheme has become a regular feature of subsequent classifications of sin.

Augustine is largely credited with the introduction of the mortal sin/venial sin vocabulary. He sought to make a distinction between sins *ad mortem* (mortal sins) that broke the bond of communion, and more easily pardoned sins (*veniabiliora*). This division laid the foundation for the classic distinction between mortal and venial sin that has largely remained, although it was later taken up and developed into a coherent system by the scholastics. With the gradual sophistication of theological enquiry, the subjective condition of the sinner was open to ever-greater scrutiny. In time venial sin came to be seen as a transgression of God's law without 'complete commitment to the evil end' in comparatively unimportant matters or in important matters that were carried out with imperfect knowledge or imperfect consent. By contrast, mortal sin was viewed as a decision in radical contradiction to God's will, which always presupposed full knowledge and full consent of the will.

Doctrine traditionally argued, therefore, that three conditions had to be verified for mortal sin: grave matter, full knowledge and full consent.

In more recent times the shift to a personalist focus has led to a re-evaluation of this traditional doctrine. In particular, the previous emphasis on 'the gravity of the matter' was called into question. Was there not a danger that the manualist method had to some extent 'materialized sin', thus glossing over the personal component and interior disposition? Moreover, were not categorical acts expressive of interior attitudes which ultimately determine whether or not sin is present? The theologian Karl Rahner among others had argued that actions spring from different levels of our being. Not everything we do emerges from or is expressive of our deepest core. The human decision-making process is constructed in layers starting at that core and becoming more and more external. Thus it is possible to do one and the same thing and have several motives and intentions for it, contradictory in themselves. The difficulty for Rahner and others was the traditional insistence on identifying mortal sin with one specific act. Was it possible for one specific decision or deed at the outer level completely to alter the moral orientation of one's existence?

And so the theory of the fundamental option was advanced, as giving a more credible anthropological basis to this aspect of the moral life. Mortal and venial sin are held to be expressive of the basic disposition of the sinner. They cannot simply be considered in themselves, because choices and deeds alone are ambiguous. Mortal sin is to be understood as any action or series of actions or attitudes that change, or are equivalent to changing, one's fundamental option towards God. Venial sin, however, on the other hand, does not concern one's fundamental option at all. It is a step off the right path, but still generally headed towards God.

There is a danger that in attempting to correct an overly materialist conception of sin one can unwittingly encourage the opposite fallacy, namely an excessively spiritualized notion. Certainly, the fundamental option defines a person's moral disposition. But it can be completely changed by particular acts, especially when, as often happens, these have been prepared for by previous more superficial acts. Thus it would be wrong to say that particular acts are not enough to constitute mortal sin. The usefulness of the fundamental option theory is therefore often counter-balanced today by an insistence on the importance of evaluating sins according to their gravity and of not underestimating the consequences of losing sight of the sinful character of particular acts.

Modern correctives to the theology of sin

The contribution of political, ecological, liberationist and feminist writers has been central to recent efforts to move away from mono-dimensional accounts of enquiry towards a more representative, synthetic and holistic approach development.

While feminists have tended to concentrate less on the theme of sin and more on the patriarchal identification of women with sin, their work has on occasions lucidly demonstrated how prone our religious imagery and theological paradigms are to distortion and bias. Such bias may also express itself in ethical theory and in the basic understanding of the moral life. Spiritual and moral machismo may be found in inordinate preoccupation with victory over individual sins to the neglect of responsibility for nourishing and nurturing relationships. Some critiques go further and argue that there is a tendency within traditional conceptions of morality to legitimate so-called 'feminine virtues', thereby perpetuating injustice and oppression. Whatever the validity of these claims, there is no doubt that feminist thinkers have done a service in highlighting the 'sin' of sexism. The blatant dishonesty at the root of a belief that gender is the primary determinant of human characteristics, abilities and talents and that sexual differences produce an inherent superiority of one sex has been clearly exposed.

This critique also raises questions about the accuracy of hubris as a type for universal sin, as this very concept mirrors chiefly the experience of men who aspire to positions of power and influence. It argues that patriarchal structures and sexist attitudes are still a reality in society generally, and in Christian churches and communities more particularly. Like liberation theologians, feminists have drawn inspiration from the prophetic tradition of Jewish and Christian ethics, which emphasized God's defence of the oppressed, as well as the need to criticize oppressive power structures and to recognize ideological elements in religious belief. They have also criticized an overly spiritualized account of original sin that fails to respect the bodiliness of human life. Such reflections have made an invaluable contribution to unmasking the dehumanizing side of sin. In doing so they are broadly at one with theologians who argue that sin is essentially about refusing the invitation to play our part in the human family's journey towards becoming more fully human. The fact that Christian theology and in particular its reflection on sin and evil has until recently been constructed predominantly by men, to the near exclusion of the experience of women, means that there is corrective work to be done.

Ecotheology

Environmental ethics

A new awareness of the fragility and delicate ecological balance of the environment has led to increased reflection on the duty of stewardship for all creation and what this means in terms of concrete individual and collective moral responsibility. Here there are ready parallels with the classical Christian view of justice as right relationships. Ecological sin is a refusal or neglect to share these resources with those who are most in need of them. It is also a failure to recognize the inherent goodness of the natural world. That goodness is a deeply-rooted scriptural conviction. After each of God's acts of creation, 'God found it very good'. Similarly, the psalms proclaim that 'the earth is the Lord's and all that is in it' (Psalm 24.1–2).

Feminist theology ◄

There is a pervasive recognition here that the world is not ours and that human beings are a part of the created world. Made in the image and likeness of God, human beings are to reflect God and to look after and care for the world and its resources. There is the implication here of a care-taking role, a duty of stewardship, which is part of a respect for the integrity of all creation. Such an attitude is directly opposed to the purely utilitarian stance, which considers natural resources to be expendable and disposable commodities. It is also a relational attitude, an attitude that calls for a rediscovery of our dependence on the earth. This sense of justice towards all creation had once found expression in the ancient Jewish tradition of the sabbath law and the jubilee year. There was a sense of allowing the earth to replenish its resources and restore its energies during a fallow period. One can speak, meaningfully, therefore of ecological sin and of the need to encourage awareness of sustainability.

Reverence for the earth is an ethical and religious imperative that touches our self-understanding in a profound way and asks searching moral questions of our individual and collective lifestyles. In so far as we refuse to recognize these questions or reject their import or fail to answer them, we also disregard the perennial summons to 'act justly, love tenderly and walk humbly with our God'. This rejection is what we have learned to call sin.

Liberation theology ◄

Political theology

The fields of political theology and liberation theology are the context of some other recent attempts to contextualize the concept of sin. In large measure the preoccupations of these theologies are those connected with 'social sin'. 'Political' theologies have sought to develop theological reflection on sin and guilt in the context of contemporary social relationships in the modern world. Their approach sets out specifically to challenge and

Bioethics
Roman empire

criticize the individual bias, which is part of modern Western culture. Some of this theology has been influenced by the traumatic experiences of the Second World War. These raise the question of the suffering of innocent victims and of the large groups of people who are denied the opportunity of becoming 'subjects' due to political and social repression. People need to liberate themselves from the structures that impede their integral growth and development. A collective conversion, an 'anthropological revolution', is required whereby people emancipate themselves from the influences of 'privatism' and from the sinful tendencies of consumption and domination. This can only be achieved by a collective abandonment of the competitiveness and egotism of the 'success ethic' and a realization of the full implications of the status of men and women as social beings who accept responsibility for the human family, the world and themselves.

HUGH CONNOLLY

Paganism

R. E. Coll, *Christianity and Feminism in Conversation*, Mystic, CT: Twenty-Third Publications 1994; H. Connolly, *Sin*, London and New York: Continuum 2002; S. Fagan, *Has Sin Changed?*, Dublin: Gill & Macmillan 1978; R. Gula, *To Walk Together Again*, New York and Mahwah, NJ: Paulist Press 1984; P. Kierans, *Sinful Social Structures*, New York and Mahwah, NJ: Paulist Press 1974; P. McCormick, *Sin as Addiction*, New York and Mahwah, NJ: Paulist Press 1989; G. Müller-Fahrenholz, *The Art of Forgiveness*, Geneva: WCC Publications 1996; J. P. Theissen, *Community and Disunity: Symbols of Grace and Sin*, Collegeville: St John's University Press 1985; P. Schoonenberg, *Man and Sin*, London: Sheed & Ward 1965

Social ethics

War and peace
Environmental ethics
Globalization
Sexual ethics

pp. 666–7
Ethics
Bible

Christians today attempt to address a wide variety of social issues, including war, economic justice, race relations, international trade, increasingly powerful technology, the environment and globalization. Often a distinction is made between such social issues and more personal ethical issues such as sexuality or individual honesty, although in reality these issues are difficult to separate entirely within most accounts of Christian ethics. There is widespread agreement today among exponents of Christian ethics that the discipline should seek to address both personal and social issues.

Nevertheless, despite this widespread agreement, Christians remain divided on most ethical issues, whether they are considered to be personal or social. More worryingly, on face value the New Testament does not seem to be directly concerned with most issues that are now considered to be important within social ethics. For example, it offers no direct teaching on the proprieties of war, international trade or environmental destruction. And obviously it offers no direct teaching about ethical issues raised by modern technology, biotechnology or globalization. Indeed, despite the huge ethical problems raised by the Roman empire, the New Testament appears to be remarkably quiescent about them. Notoriously, it does not condemn slavery, conquest and occupation, patriarchy, or even the extraordinary cruelty that characterized this empire.

There is nothing particularly new about this observation. It was felt keenly by Augustine in the fourth century and even by Martin Luther in the sixteenth. Each struggled in his own way to derive teaching in social ethics from the New Testament, but in reality each used additional non-biblical resources to do so.

One of the issues in social ethics that particularly troubled Augustine was the legitimacy of Christians taking part in warfare. He was well aware of the jibe that Christianity had contributed significantly to the demise of the Roman empire. Indeed, his fellow North African, Tertullian, writing two centuries earlier, had argued that Christians should not become soldiers even to defend the state. For Tertullian, Christians should not be involved in the taking of human life in any form (whether in war, capital punishment or even abortion), nor should they be involved in the 'pagan' rituals that were an essential part of military life.

Before he became a mainstream Christian, Augustine as a young man had agonized about how to understand the Bible on the issue of war. He was frankly appalled by some of the cruelties evident in parts of the Old Testament and did not know how to respond to the apparent silence of the New Testament. However, under the influence of Bishop Ambrose he finally 'resolved' this tension by reading the Bible through the perspective of Roman just-war theory. According to this a 'just' war, or a 'just' use of violence, was deemed to be one that was properly authorized, whereas an 'unjust' war or act of violence was one undertaken with no such authority. On this understanding, just wars in the Old Testament were (despite being wars of conquest against the resident Canaanites) wars authorized, even commanded, directly by God. However, Peter's act of violence against the slave of the high priest in Gethsemane was unauthorized by Jesus and, on that account, condemned.

Augustine's use of the extra-biblical concept of 'just war' had a profound influence upon Aquinas and upon subsequent Christian history. It has remained a contentious legacy, with some Christians regarding it as an important means of limiting warfare and other Christians considering it to be an illegitimate, even 'pagan', borrowing that distorts Jesus' message of non-violent action. But it does illustrate the point that this key area in social ethics still divides Christians and cannot easily be resolved by appealing directly either to the New Testament or to the Bible as a whole.

A social issue that particularly vexed Luther was that of trade. He was well aware that some form of trade in a complex society is an essential requirement for Christians and non-Christians alike. He also believed that merchants all too often became greedy, attempting to sell their goods as expensively as possible to the detriment of purchasers (Luther was still committed to the medieval notion of the 'just price'). He attempted to set out four biblical ways in which Christians might exchange goods. The first was for Christians to let other people simply steal their property. The second was for Christians to give to anyone in need. The third was for Christians to lend but expect nothing to be returned. Luther was aware that each of these methods was unlikely to promote effective trade! So, fourthly, he suggested that it was biblical for Christians to buy and sell in cash, provided that they did not rely upon credit at all or, of course, seek to sell their goods expensively. However, even as he gave this advice (and even supposing that the fourth suggestion is properly 'biblical'), he seemed to be aware it would be extremely difficult for Christians to keep to it.

Examples could be replicated from any of the major areas of social ethics. Both today and in the past, Christians tend to disagree with each other on specific issues and also on the way that the Bible might be used as a key resource. One way to resolve the latter is to follow the contextual path of biblical interpretation. According to this it is assumed that the Bible is always read and interpreted by particular interest groups (whether they are aware of it or not). A generation ago it might have been assumed even by many scholars that the Bible could be read dispassionately and that a particular ethical issue might be resolved through careful analysis of biblical texts. However, those following the contextual path of biblical interpretation have argued that such a 'dispassionate' approach was often a mask adopted by Western, male, privileged biblical scholars (or by their counterparts in conservative, fundamentalist Christian groups today). Once read instead through the eyes of the poor or the marginalized, the Bible appears very differently, especially on social issues.

Liberation theologians have been among the most articulate defenders of this contextual approach. Characteristically, they do not claim to be reading the Bible 'dispassionately' or even the Bible as a whole. Rather, they find certain themes concerned with liberation – notably the story of the exodus in the Old Testament and the theme of new life to be found in Jesus – to be especially relevant to those living in areas of political oppression around the world. In parts of South America and in South Africa under apartheid, liberation theology was able to generate radically politicized forms of Christian practice and opposition to repressive states. In India it has also been formative among Dalit (or 'outcast') Christians.

Feminist theology

Feminist theologians, especially in Western countries, have also been deeply influenced by this contextual approach. For some it involves a rejection of traditional churches altogether, whereas for others it involves a radically changed perspective, albeit within these churches. While recognizing that the Bible was characteristically written by men, many feminist theologians argue that it can still be interpreted afresh by women in a way that enriches their life and practice as women.

Another influential approach within recent social ethics has argued that although the Bible should not be used to determine specific social issues (especially since it assumes the legitimacy of, say, slavery and wars of conquest), it nonetheless still contains virtues that can properly be applied to modern-day social issues. For example, parts of the Old Testament assume a strong notion of 'justice' and 'fairness' that can contribute significantly to modern arguments about welfare and resource allocation. The Old Testament notion of 'stewardship', or better 'trusteeship', has been used effectively by some Christian environmentalists. Or again, there are important notions of 'reconciliation' and 'restoration' in the New Testament that have been used by Christians working in modern criminology. And in both the Old and New Testaments there is a distinct emphasis upon 'compassion' that again has been used by Christians involved in modern health care ethics. None of these biblical virtues leads to easy resolutions of complex social issues in the modern world, yet, so it is argued, they can still make an effective and distinctively Christian contribution.

ROBIN GILL

James F. Childress and John Macquarrie (eds), *A New Dictionary of Christian Ethics*, Philadelphia: Westminster Press 1986 and London: SCM Press 1987; Robin Gill, *A Textbook of Christian Ethics*, Edinburgh: T&T Clark [2]1995; J. Philip Wogaman, *Christian Ethics: A Historical Introduction*, Louisville: Westminster John Knox Press 1993 and London: SPCK 1994

Fundamentalism

Liberation theology

SOCIETY

Christendom, Church, Community, Culture, Globalization, Kingdom of God, Law, Liberation theology, Persecution, Politics, Social ethics, Sociology of religion, World

According to the tradition stemming from the Greek philosopher Aristotle, human beings are social animals. They come together for mutual support and can realize their full potential only within the network of institutions and relationships that forms human society. Up until the eighteenth century the term 'society', which comes from the Latin word for 'companion', was synonymous with cognate words including community, mutuality and fellowship. On this understanding, society is simply an aspect of the natural constitution of human beings.

The American political philosopher John Rawls writes, for instance, that society is 'a system of cooperation designed to advance the good of those taking part in it. [It] is a cooperative venture for mutual advantage.' Through the course of human history there has been a huge variety of such co-operative systems, consisting of very different rules and regulations which have been established to ensure (at the very least) a minimum of social provision and order. The need to regulate conflict and to ensure social order forms the basis for the various methods of government: this means that politics, as the art of governance of society, and law, as the regulation of justice, become equally necessary parts of human life. An analysis of Christianity and society will of necessity have to discuss ideas developed by political theorists, lawyers, ethicists and sociologists, as well as theologians. All this leads to important ethical questions: to what extent should Christians obey the law, even when that law might be unjust or result in evil (as, for instance, in war)? How far should Christians participate in the political process, even when that process is manifestly corrupt?

Ethics

Christianity cannot but be involved with politics and law, and much of its language has made use of analogies drawn from political institutions and the law courts, as well as other social institutions. Christianity has thus been concerned with society from its very beginnings: Jesus himself proclaims the kingdom of God, with its much-disputed political and social connotations, as the heart of his preaching. The wider society made an obvious impact upon the nature of early Christianity: it started within an occupied territory set on the margins of the Roman empire. Some of the characters in the Gospels are political rulers, such as Herod the Great at the time of Jesus' birth and Herod the Tetrarch at his death. Others are government officials, such as Pontius Pilate, procurator of Judaea.

Jesus

Roman empire

Origins and background

At the same time, however, there is another dimension of Christian teaching on society. Again from the beginnings, Christians have sought to organize themselves into distinct societies or 'churches', which existed within the broader societies in which they were located. These too have been guided by distinctive rules and regulations. Fundamental for the relations between Christianity and society has been the maintenance of the boundaries between the one divine society and the other secular society. Crossing from the one to the other was one of the most hotly contested issues in the early churches, and it has continued to be of central importance to Christian self-identity until the present day. There is thus a particularly complex set of relations between church and society: sometimes the church sees itself as opposed to and set against society (which sociologists have termed the 'sect-model'), while at other times it sees itself as virtually identical to the wider society (which has been termed the 'church-model'). Similarly, the attitude of the society outside the church towards Christianity has sometimes been hostile, sometimes indifferent, and sometimes all-embracing.

Christianity and society in the New Testament

The Gospels. Many of the earliest texts of the New Testament are permeated by the expectation of the end of the world and the coming reign of God. Jesus' proclamation of the kingdom of God most probably relates to the idea of the imminent restoration of God's rule over Israel, which would eventually be universally applied to all peoples; his band of apostles were perhaps those who were to be entrusted with the rule of the coming kingdom (symbolized by the number twelve, which possibly referred to the twelve tribes of Israel). In the light of this proclamation of total social transformation it is hardly surprising that the Gospels contain few detailed injunctions about how to relate to the wider society. Those who gather behind Jesus might be expected to behave in certain ways, along the lines of the Sermon on the Mount (Matthew 5–7), but how they were to relate to others outside is simply not discussed with any degree of precision. While Jesus undoubtedly wanted to purify his own religious tradition, he seems scarcely concerned with the structures of Roman society. His elusive response to the Herodians, 'Render to Caesar what is Caesar's' (Matthew 22.21), can hardly be considered detailed social theory. Given the superhuman level of commitment expected of disciples, who should even be prepared to make themselves eunuchs for the sake of the kingdom of heaven (Matthew 19.12), it is likely that the first disciples were a close-knit community of like-minded people who consciously separated themselves from the wider society, who perhaps lived by begging (Luke 10.4) and who embodied a quite distinct form of life. If modern sociological categories can be applied to the New Testament, then this is far closer to the 'sect-type' of social organization than the 'church-type'.

p. 850

p. 385

Paul. Similarly, there was little detailed discussion about how to deal with the wider society in the letters of Paul. As with the Gospels, his writings are soaked through with a sense of the expectation of the imminent return of Christ. He wrote in 1 Corinthians: 'the appointed time has grown very short'. Consequently the structures of society – including marriage – would soon pass away: 'from now on, let those who have wives live as though they had none, and those who mourn as though they were not mourning, and those who rejoice as though they were not rejoicing, and those who buy as though they had no goods, and those who deal with the world as though they had no dealings with it. For the form of this world is passing away' (7.29–31). Similarly, the notorious passage in Romans 13 ('Let every person be subject to the governing authorities. For there is no authority except from God, and those that exist have been instituted by God', v. 1) needs to be read alongside the hope for Christ's return expressed at the end of the chapter: 'Besides this you know what hour it is, how it is full time now for you to wake from sleep. For salvation is nearer to us now than when we first believed' (v. 11).

Paul

Christian conduct seemed more directed towards the ethics of preparation for the future than towards detailed prescription about how to relate to the wider society. Again, Paul's ethics are more like those of a sect: his churches were groups of highly-committed and devout people who had gathered together to form close-knit communities with strict entry criteria (death to the 'old self', Romans 6.6). They were to wait together in the expectation of the return of Christ. Fellowship (*koinonia*) and community were experienced to as great an extent as possible apart from society. Elsewhere in the New Testament society is condemned through pejorative (and virtually dualistic) use of the term 'the world' (especially 1 John 2.15–17).

The ethical injunctions of the Pauline letters are consequently almost entirely inward-looking and focused on building up the community of believers, who were even commanded to hold all things in common so that no member was to remain in material need (Acts 4.32–5). On this basis mutual support was offered to all members of the community, who lived together organically as 'one body'. This offers an example of what Gerhard Lohfink terms 'contrast-societies': the primitive communism of the early chapters of the Acts of the Apostles, as well as the redefinition of family and social hierarchy in the Gospels (e.g. Mark 10.42–5: 'The Son of man came not to be served but to serve'), sets the Christian communities apart from the wider society. But whether this alternative form of ethics, with an emphasis on non-violence, non-discrimination and apartness, was perceived as a critique of the political and social structures of the wider society needs to be questioned. The expectation of the imminent end of the world meant that the primary focus was always on the community itself, but with the hope that others might be invited to share in God's reign.

At the same time, however, it is also possible to see the beginnings of what might be termed 'catholic networks' of organization which gradually lead to the church becoming an alternative society. As Paul makes clear in 1 Corinthians 16.1–4, financial and material assistance was not to be restricted simply to the local community or congregation, but was to be redistributed from one part of the world to another. This meant that the church was gradually becoming in some sense an alternative international 'society' with its own rules and regulations, and its own system of internal organization.

Organization

The early church

As time moved on and the hopes for the return of Christ became increasingly frustrated, it was necessary to work out in greater detail how to live as Christians in the world and how to relate to the wider society. In the writings of the second and third centuries there are frequent references to how Christians should deal with the broader institutions of society. These often reveal an underlying paradox that was noted by many: although Christians are in the world they are not of the world. They are 'resident aliens'. In the words of the Letter to Diognetus, written in the second or third century, 'Christians cannot be distinguished from the rest of the human race ... they do not follow an eccentric manner of life ... At the same time they give proof of the remarkable and admittedly extraordinary constitution of their own commonwealth. They live in their own countries, but only as aliens ... Every foreign land is their fatherland, and yet for them every fatherland is a foreign land ... To put it simply: What the soul is to the body, that Christians are in the world.'

p. 245

The Christian is thus a citizen of two worlds: the questions which emerged in the early church, and which have recurred throughout Christian history, are over how the two worlds connect to one another. As Ernst Troeltsch, one of the most important historians of Christian social teaching, remarked: the Christian ideal of neighbourly love 'requires a new world if it is to be fully realized; it was this new world order that Jesus proclaimed in his message of the kingdom of God. But it is an ideal that cannot be realized within this world apart from compromise. Therefore the history of the Christian ethos becomes the story of a constantly renewed search for this compromise, and of fresh opposition to this spirit of compromise.' Different forms of compromise quickly emerged: on the one hand, many continued in the tradition of the world-denying sectarianism of the New Testament, which was often marked by a strong asceticism. Ignatius of Antioch provides a good example of such an approach: the 'greatness of Christianity' lies in 'its being hated by the world, not in its being convincing to it'. This tendency towards separation from the world formed one of the chief impulses towards the formation of the early monastic movement.

Monasticism

On the other hand, some thinkers adopted a more positive approach to the world outside the church, seeing the institutions of human society as in some sense ordered by a divinely-given natural law. Such an attitude can easily be detected in the first letter of Clement, where there is a prayer that speaks of God conferring 'imperial power' on 'our rulers and governors'. The argument was simple: because the whole world – both Christian and non-Christian alike – was made by God, Christians were to submit to the divinely-appointed civil authority. In justifying such a position it was natural that Christian thinkers should make use of the philosophical resources of the ancient world. There was an evident desire among many writers to bring Christianity into the mainstream of civilization, in order to make it socially acceptable, against the alternative conception of Christianity as a counter-cultural community. As increasingly sophisticated connections were made between Christianity and Graeco-Roman philosophical thought by such thinkers as Clement and Origen in Alexandria, so questions were raised about the relationships between Christianity and the wider society. The whole range of social activity was explored, even including such matters as table manners and the 'useless art of making pastry'. The emphasis was on understanding Christ as the Word (*Logos*), or Reason, a concept which was shared with many outside the Christian community, especially those influenced by Stoic philosophy. While Origen remained pacifist, thinking it improper for Christians to bear arms for the state, he nevertheless thought that Christians formed 'another rational organization, founded by the Word of God' within a state which was itself also part of an order established by God.

Tertullian, writing at the turn of the second century, offers a good example of the paradox of the relationships between Christianity and the wider society. In his *Apologeticus*, he saw Christians as a close body 'knit together by our common religious profession, by unity of discipline', not hesitating 'to share our earthly goods with one another'. There was a strong corporate identity for Christians who were tied together in a community which witnessed to the wider society that had been debased by 'the atrocities of the arena' and the 'madness of the theatre'. For Christians, citizenship was derived from the church of Christ: 'You are an alien in this world, and a citizen of the city of Jerusalem that is above.' At the same time, however, Tertullian displayed a remarkable respect for the authorities of the world outside the church, speaking of the 'reverence and sacred respect of Christians for the emperor, whom we cannot but look up to as called by our Lord to his office'. Christians, he went on, are enjoined to pray for the emperor, 'for protection of the imperial house; for brave armies, a faithful senate ... The emperor gets his sceptre where he first got his humanity; his power where he got the breath of life.' Even though later he became far more uncompromising, what this reveals is a strong sense of the legitimacy of the institutions of government, law and order of the wider society, even where that society made no pretence towards being Christian.

The Constantinian revolution

Constantine's 'conversion'

The turning point in the relationship of Christianity and society came in 313 CE, after Constantine had become undisputed emperor of Rome under a Christian banner. Following the so-called Edict of Milan, Christianity was transformed from a frequently persecuted sect into the dominant religious force of Roman civilization. The relationship between the church and the wider society quickly changed. From being a more or less tolerated minority primarily seeking the purity of lifestyle of its own members, Christianity and the clergy were brought into the corridors of power. Church officials became involved with political bureaucracy and the administration of justice, and

Christianity was forced to come to some accommodation with the culture of the wider society. Christians were no longer 'aliens' but were now citizens of a Christian society that embraced both church and state. The effects were rapid and profound. Lactantius, for instance, tutor to Constantine's son, wrote of the importance of 'serving justice' as the highest Christian duty. This implied the common brotherhood of all people, 'since God alike is a Father to all'. The law of God was applied not simply to the church as a community set apart from the world, but to all people living under a universal order created by God. Similarly, Ambrose, Bishop of Milan from about 374, understood justice as a universal concept applicable to all people: it 'exists for the good of all and helps to create unity and society among us. It is so high that all else must fall under its authority.' The church was thus changing: its boundaries were being redrawn and its membership was becoming co-terminous with citizenship of the wider society.

The most developed thought on church and society in the late Roman period came from Augustine, Bishop of Hippo in North Africa from the end of the fourth century until his death in 430, who had probably been converted to Christianity under the influence of Ambrose. His *City of God* was written in 410 as a vindication of Christianity against pagan critics who were inclined to blame the decline of Rome on the Christian virtues including love and kindness. It is a massive work that aims in part to demonstrate the illusions upon which Roman society was based. Augustine contrasts the city of this world with the city of God, which he understands as the only true commonwealth founded by Christ and ruled by him. The worldly city is based on what he calls 'self-love', whereas the city of God is based on the love of God. 'In the one,' he writes, 'the princes and the nations it subdues are ruled by the love of ruling', whereas in the other 'the princes and the subjects serve one another in love'.

The most important question for Augustine was over the connections between the two cities: to what extent, he asked, could the city of God be realized on earth? His solution is complex: the city of God existed within the city of this world as a foretaste of the city that was to come. The Christian consequently existed as a pilgrim on the way to the heavenly society. Against the disorder so obvious in the world during the breakdown of the Roman empire, the heavenly society, like the well-ordered household, was one in which order and stability were dominant. 'The orders,' wrote Augustine, 'are given by those who are concerned for the interests of others.' In turn, the maintenance of order became the main duty of the rulers. In a provocative phrase he could thus write: 'What is more horrible than the public executioner? Yet he has a necessary place in the legal system, and he is part of the order of a well-governed society.' This leads Augustine into a discussion of the importance of peace with justice which applies to all people, including earthly rulers: the happy emperor is the one who thinks of sovereignty as a 'ministry of God'. Consequently, where the earthly city promotes justice and is not simply guided by selfishness, it 'cannot justly be said to be evil, for it is itself, in its own kind, better than all other human good'. This need for peace with justice leads him to develop his famous doctrine of a just war: 'For [the earthly city] desires earthly peace for the sake of enjoying earthly goods, and it makes war in order to attain this peace … These things, then, are good things.'

Social ethics

War and peace

In some senses, Augustine's understanding of the two cities pointed to the role of the church within society. It was to serve the worldly city as a signpost to the virtues of the love of God. Nevertheless, he was well aware that even within the church the love of self was often dominant. Consequently he could write: 'On earth, these two cities are linked and fused together, only to be celebrated at the last judgement.' Crucially both the city of this world and the city of God are understood as universal societies, the church being the expression of society as it is intended by

God, but never fully realized until the end of the world. In Western theology Augustine's model has been profoundly influential on all subsequent thought about church and society.

In the Eastern churches, the relationships between church and society continued in the mould set in the fourth century. As the influence of Constantinople increased, emperors were keen to ensure religious uniformity throughout the empire. By Justinian's time (527–65) the law code was systematized, which affected everything, including the church. Considered to be 'divinity walking upon earth', Justinian sought to enforce religious conformity: 'If we strive by all means to enforce the civil laws, whose power God in his goodness has entrusted to us for the security of our subjects, how much more keenly should we endeavour to enforce the holy canons and the divine laws which have been framed for the salvation of our souls.' This understanding of Christianity and society took the 'church-model' to the extreme: the church was understood as a department of state, the civil ruler having absolute authority except in sacramental matters.

Christendom: medieval Catholicism and the church model

Things developed differently in the Western church. Following the collapse of the Western empire, the survival of Christianity was under threat from the onslaught of the Germanic peoples from northern Europe. Nevertheless, the fact that Christianity preserved a culture of learning and administration meant, perhaps ironically, that it became increasingly more closely tied to the wider society, especially after the adoption of Christianity in a significant proportion of hitherto pagan territories. This helped to consolidate the authority of bishops, giving them increasing secular power, so that in many parts of the world they were elevated to the ruling classes and often became responsible for the administration of justice: many high offices of state were held by churchmen through the Middle Ages.

History

Not surprisingly, there were frequent conflicts between the church and the secular rulers. The most important was the Investiture Controversy of the eleventh century, when during the reforming papacy of Hildebrand (Gregory VII) there were successful efforts to reduce the power of the lay rulers, including the Holy Roman emperor, over the church. The monarch, it was held, had duties towards – but not rights over – the church. While some thinkers were more inclined to limit the powers of the state over the church, others moved in the opposite direction, questioning the increasing sovereignty of the papacy. Most importantly, in his influential work, *Defender of the Peace*, Marsilius of Padua (*c.*1275–1342) sought to increase the authority of the people, although in practice this was equated with the will of the monarch as 'representing' the people: such ideas were later to be influential on the political thought of the Reformation. However, although there were frequent disputes, it is also important to note that in general both church and state were seen as two aspects of a single overarching system.

Investiture Controversy

Holy Roman empire

Papacy

Reformation

The social thought of the Middle Ages reached its climax in the scholasticism of the thirteenth century, particularly in the thought of Thomas Aquinas. Like the church, the state was elevated into a 'perfect society', existing for the preservation of peace and justice, as well as the restraint of evildoers. 'It is natural to man,' Thomas wrote, imitating the recently-rediscovered Aristotle, 'that he live in partnership (*societate*) with many … It is therefore necessary, if man is to live in association, that one should be helped by another, and that different people should be occupied in discovering different things through reason.' More positively, the state existed to promote the 'common good' – the authority of the political system was grounded in the natural law established by God. This led to a conception of universal rights and of equality before the law, which was to treat all people, including rulers, in the same way: justice became the key theme in Christian thinking.

Scholasticism

In many ways this was a revitalization of the Roman understanding of 'civil society', where all individuals were seen as equal under the law. As the Roman orator Cicero wrote: 'legal rights at least should be equal among citizens of the same commonwealth'. The concept of private property and other forms of human autonomy, including the freedom of children from rule by their fathers, were also developed out of Roman law. For the medieval humanist John of Salisbury (*c.* 1115–80), for instance, virtue or sanctity could not be 'perfectly achieved without liberty, and the loss of liberty shows that perfect virtue is lacking'.

Throughout the Middle Ages one of the duties of the state was to uphold the church so that it could pursue its divinely-appointed ends. There was no great separation between society and Christianity, the two interacting so intimately that they were frequently indistinguishable. Both were grounded in God himself. This great 'compromise' between church and society based on natural law has often been referred to as 'Christendom', which Ernst Troeltsch called a 'unity of culture'. However, the scholastic form of social thought was not the only way of thinking about society in the Middle Ages. An alternative form was associated with the guild system of Germany, which sought to develop the Christian virtues within the confines of a distinctive participatory community, often composed of those engaged in a particular trade.

At a more popular level, medieval society can be described as 'Christian' in the sense that virtually everybody shared a common understanding of the world in which they lived, based on Christian premises. This 'church model' describes a form of Christian organization into which one is simply born, and in which there is a virtual conflation between the natural and supernatural: the sense of dualism that survives in Augustine, where church and society remain separated in virtue of the impossibility of the full realization of the city of God in the here and now, is overcome in the synthesis between church and worldly society bolstered by a high doctrine of natural law. Nevertheless, despite this all-embracing unity there were always strands, in particular what Troeltsch called the 'safety-valve' of monasticism, which aimed to represent the Christian ideal in its purity and which stood in marked contrast to the values of everyday society.

The Reformation

Although there were significant changes in the organization of the Western churches following Martin Luther's break with Rome and the formation of independent national churches, the connections between church and society remained extraordinarily close. Indeed, the church model could equally be applied to the churches of the Reformation, and it is fair to say that in most places the authority of the secular power over the church was strengthened. Far from being the first triumph of individual liberty, the Reformation did not fundamentally challenge the structure of medieval

Christendom

Christendom. It was again the natural law that provided the basis for the Christian understanding of society, even though it was often considered to be a by-product of the human state of sin, and thus reminiscent of Augustine. This is clear in Luther's doctrine of the two kingdoms, the one a kingdom of love, but the other a kingdom of this world that was forced to legislate for the world of sin. Rule over such a world could never be wholly Christian, 'since', as Luther wrote, 'the world and the masses are and always will be un-Christian, although they are all baptized and nominally Christian'. The two worlds were both important, but needed to be sharply distinguished. The one, the spiritual kingdom, existed to produce piety, while the other was there to 'bring about external peace and prevent evil deeds'. Luther's famous diatribes against rebellion are rooted in the notion of a fallen humanity requiring discipline and a firm sense of order to prevent the triumph of sin. At the same time, however, the social order itself was understood by Luther to be a given: each person was to fulfil a divinely appointed vocation, almost as a religious duty. The result was that the seriousness of the life of medieval monasticism was transferred into the sphere of everyday life.

For John Calvin, too, the secular leaders were to ensure that piety was defended and behaviour was adjusted by the need to live together with other people, which required the 'promotion of peace and tranquillity'. Calvin distinguishes between 'Christ's spiritual jurisdiction' and 'the civil jurisdiction' as between the soul and the body. Civil government is primarily a remedy for evil, to prevent the great excesses which would emerge if people saw 'that their depravity can go scot-free – when no power can force them from doing evil'. Civil magistrates thus have a 'mandate from God, [having] been invested with divine authority … [They are] wholly God's representatives, in a manner, acting as his vice-regents.' Even unjust rulers, he thought, should be respected, since they would be punished for their misdemeanours at the divine tribunal. Again the doctrine of vocation was important, but was radicalized in comparison with Luther's. Whatever one's sphere of life, there was the need to perform the duty of glorifying God: 'Each man', wrote Calvin, 'will bear and swallow the discomforts, vexations, weariness, and anxieties in his way of life, when he has been persuaded that the burden was laid upon him by God.' Everything was thus approached with a sense of seriousness and sobriety, leading to what the German sociologist, Max Weber, called 'inner-worldly asceticism'. An interesting illustration of a similar teaching comes from the Strasbourg Reformer Martin Bucer, who wrote that the 'most Christian stations and occupations' are not priesthood and politics but 'farming, raising cattle and the handicraft trades'.

Something similar can be seen in the writing of the most important English theologian of the period, Richard Hooker (*c.*1554–1600), whose *Ecclesiastical Polity* amounts to a theology of law and sovereignty, both secular and sacred. In Hooker's theology, however, power and sovereignty are redirected away from the church towards the state in the person of the monarch, the 'common parent' in whom all authority (apart from the strictly supernatural authority connected with the sacraments) is ultimately invested. The church model still characterizes his thought. Indeed, he could write: 'There is not any man of the Church of England but the same man is also a member of the commonwealth; nor any man a member of the commonwealth which is not also of the Church of England.' Furthermore, the rigid hierarchy of the social order is emphasized by Hooker in a manner resembling Thomas Aquinas. Marsilius' theory, which invested all authority in the civil power and had justified the separation from Rome under Henry VIII, was elevated into an absolute principle. The most important social doctrine of the English Reformation was the divine right of kings. For those less enamoured of the supernatural aspects of the church (which, as in the Byzantine model, was the only independent sphere left to it), it was but a short step, partly taken in the late seventeenth century by Thomas Hobbes, to see the church as little more than an organ of social control.

The breakdown of unified culture

Despite the persistence of the church model at the Reformation, it nevertheless marked the first major stage in the breakdown of a unified conception of church and society. The logic was simple: if there was more than one church, this meant more than one claim on absolute truth. Yet they could not all be true. Religious diversity – at least on the international stage after the Peace of Westphalia in 1648 that brought the wars of religion to an end – was a matter of fact. This became even more obvious when there was toleration of more than one version of Christianity within the confines of the one state. Again, following the Reformation, a number of radical religious sects developed alongside the official church. While they might claim the whole of the truth, they defined themselves against the world (and often the church) outside and often were radically

Wars of religion

world-rejecting. Frequently in conscious imitation of New Testament models, they displayed in practice a tendency to tolerate the outside world even where they despised it. As in the early church, there was a concentration on purity within the group: boundaries were no longer co-extensive with the state, but required a great commitment on the part of the believer. However, although requiring absolute obedience, membership of the sect was voluntary. Thus, however absolute the claims of sectarian religion, allegiance was ultimately a matter of choice. This led, following the English Bill of Rights of 1689, to a de facto separation of religion from the system of government. Such limited toleration marks a fundamental change in the relationship between Christianity and society.

It was but a short step to the more contractual theories of social organization that developed in the seventeenth and eighteenth centuries, based on the theory of individual natural rights. Politics was a matter of individuals negotiating their own goals: as the English philosopher John Locke put it: 'That which makes the community, and brings men out of the loose state of nature, into one politick society, is the agreement which every one has with the rest to incorporate, and to act as one body, and so be one distinct commonwealth.' The notion of an autonomous sphere for society apart from the church and upheld by an alternative theory of sovereignty – the authority given by natural rights and democratic accountability – meant that the unified concept of church and society was seriously threatened. Since the eighteenth century there has thus been a constant renegotiation of the church's relationship with the rest of society. Indeed, the rise of the 'secular' has threatened to remove the role of the churches altogether.

It becomes virtually impossible for any church to claim a unified vision of church and society or to be a 'national' church in a situation where religious practice has sunk to unprecedentedly low levels. The rate of change is rapid: for instance, at the 1851 English religious census about 27 per cent of the population were members of churches compared with a mere 7 per cent in 1990. Similarly, in France, the numbers of parents bringing babies for Roman Catholic baptism fell from 92 per cent as late as 1958 to 58 per cent in 1993. The decline of religion can be explained in several ways. Changed leisure pursuits, the ending of taboos on Sunday activities and the rise of sport, for instance, all challenged the dominance of the churches. Furthermore, the form of hierarchical society that had been upheld by Christianity began to collapse along with the enfranchisement of the working classes and rise of meritocracy.

Similarly, what Max Weber loosely termed 'rationalization' meant that there was far less space left for the sacred: the single 'sacred canopy' which covered the pre-modern world was removed. Men and women lived out their lives in a society increasingly dominated by technology, and no longer amenable to religious and supernatural explanation: God had less and less to do. Christianity thereby became a leisure-time activity that made little direct impact on society.

By the end of the nineteenth century some church leaders in Britain, Germany and the USA had become so anxious about such a situation that they undertook research into the problems of the industrial poor, seeking methods for alleviating social hardship in the hope of bringing people back into the church. This led to the Evangelical Social Congress in Germany, for which Max Weber undertook his first important work, as well as the Christian Social Union in England which, under the influence of Charles Gore and Henry Scott Holland, developed strategies for moderating some of the worst effects of capitalism. As with earlier forms of Christian Socialism, there was often a desire to create communities of co-operation against unbridled competition. Something similar developed in the USA which was expressed by Shailer Mathews and Walter Rauschenbusch in the Social Gospel movement: it was possible to 'Christianize the social order' through the removal of privilege and by encouraging economic and social equality.

p. 1132

CHRISTIAN SOCIALISM

The term is used of any movement which seeks to combine the aims of socialism with Christian belief and practice, but it was originally used to describe a movement for social reform among a group of Anglicans in the mid-nineteenth century.

The best-known members of this group were F. D. Maurice (1805–72), professor at King's College, London; Charles Kingsley (1819–75), a clergyman-novelist who wrote *The Water Babies*; and J. M. Ludlow (1821–1911), who was its real founder. He had made the acquaintance of French socialists before becoming a barrister in London, and was perhaps the only really convinced socialist among the varied leaders of Christian Socialism. Together with Maurice, Ludlow founded a Working Men's College, where he taught for many years.The movement began after the wave of revolution which swept Europe in 1848 and which in England took the form of the Chartist riots, the Chartists being the first mass working-class revolutionary movement in Britain, named after the People's Charter which they produced. Initially it sought to provide an alternative to Chartism; subsequently it tried to introduce radical socialism into the church. Though it proved a failure, it did a great deal to prevent the hostility between Christianity and socialism which developed in other European countries.

Christian Socialism continued in England with the launching of the Christian Social Union by Henry Scott Holland, a canon of St Paul's Cathedral, in 1889. This attracted the largest number of members of any organization for social reform in the history of the Church of England and created a tradition which includes great figures like William Temple. It came to an end after the First World War, in 1919, and is contemporaneous with the height of the Social Gospel movement in the USA. At the same time a 'religious socialism' was being propagated in Germany, associated with Paul Tillich, Leonhard Ragaz and others. It was an important influence on Karl Barth in his early days.

p. 1132

Karl Barth

R. H. Tawney (1880–1962), the great economic historian and educationalist, was deeply influenced by the Christian Social Union and in turn was a major influence on Archbishop William Temple, whose *Christianity and Social Order*, published as a 'special' by Penguin Books during the Second World War in 1942 and immediately a best-seller, became a classic. The story of Christian Socialism continued in Britain in the post-war period against the background of largely Conservative governments; in Tony Blair, Prime Minister from 1997 on, it found yet another representative who was prepared publicly to acknowledge his antecedents.

Alan Wilkinson, *Christian Socialism: Scott Holland to Tony Blair*, with a Foreword by Tony Blair, London: SCM Press 1998

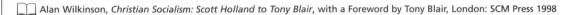

However, in most countries the churches became minor players in the alleviation of the problems of industrialization. Instead, 'secular' solutions to social inequality were undertaken by most Western states, which began to take on many of the welfare functions hitherto reserved for the churches. Similarly, social institutions (like marriage), which had been the monopoly of the churches, were opened up and liberalized. Some Christian leaders, represented by William Temple in England, became theorists of the so-called 'welfare state', seeing the role of Christianity in the formulation of basic moral principles rather than in detailed legislation. Although Temple's vision remains dominated by a conception of the social whole, it was the 'nation' and the 'family', rather than the church, which were perceived to function as the main upholders of a common good. Christianity appeared to be reduced to a set of moral values alongside the wider society: it seemed almost as if the church had been quietly removed from the church-model.

Marriage

Ironically, however, as José Casanova has shown, the greatest decline in church membership comes in those churches that have not sufficiently differentiated themselves from the secular world as, for example, in the mainstream liberal denominations in Europe and the USA. Yet even where practice remains high, Christianity has often become a voluntary activity that makes little direct impact on the wider secular society. Only in those places where Christianity is part of a wider form of social identity (as in Poland or Northern Ireland) does it continue to be a major factor in politics and society. For the most part, however, Christians behave in much the same way as most other people, even where they are highly committed to a particular church. It can thus be claimed that the sphere for a 'Christian' theory of society has declined as the scope of the secular society in which people are forced to live has increased. As Charles Taylor has noted, theology has become a personal discourse rather than a public discourse.

SOCIAL GOSPEL

Kingdom of God

Social Gospel is a term which began to be used at the very beginning of the twentieth century for a movement in the United States which protested about the inhuman conditions imposed on the working classes and the problems caused by urbanization, finding inspiration in socialist views and the rising discipline of sociology, along with the biblical principles of charity and justice and Jesus' vision of the kingdom of God, seen as a process immanent within history. The liberal Christians who were its representatives differed radically from evangelicals with their individualism and acceptance of the social order as God-given and the Roman Catholic Church, which as an institution had too much of a stake in capitalism.

Proponents of the Social Gospel were concerned for social reforms, including a fair wage, a shorter working week and the abolition of child labour, and to this end were in favour of the formation of trade unions. Although they did not all share the same theological views, they were agreed on a high regard for human nature, the Fatherhood of God and the brotherhood of man, and the teaching of Jesus as the basic source of ethics.

Perhaps the earliest representative of the movement was Washington Gladden (1836–1918), a prominent Congregationalist minister from Pennsylvania, who spent most of his life in Columbus, Ohio. Josiah Strong (1847–1916) was also a Congregationalist, from Illinois, who in 1886 became Secretary of the Evangelical Alliance; his *Our Country*, published the previous year, was a best-seller. Richard T. Ely (1854–1943) was an economist who taught at Johns Hopkins, the University of Wisconsin and Northwestern University and wrote an important *Social Aspects of Christianity* (1889). Shailer Mathews, founder of the Chicago school of theology, wrote *The Social Teaching of Jesus* (1897). However, by far the most important figure in the movement proved to be Walter Rauschenbusch, from a German Lutheran family, whose approach grew out of the social problems he encountered in New York; his major work was *Christianity and the Social Crisis* (1907).

The movement lost a good deal of its vitality after the Second World War, but many of its ideals were realized during the 1930s with the rise of organized labour and Roosevelt's New Deal. The Social Gospel movement is contemporaneous with Christian Socialism in England, which reached its height at about the same time.

p. 1131

Recent theories of Christianity and society

Against such a background, many twentieth-century writers have sought to re-invigorate Christian teaching on society by drawing on different aspects of the tradition. Some have adopted a more sectarian approach, whereas others have tried to breathe life into the 'church-model' with its unified vision of Christianity and society. The American theologian Stanley Hauerwas, for instance, has consciously adopted a sectarian understanding of Christianity: the 'primary social task of the church is to be itself'. It bears witness to its promise of redemption over and against all social and political systems: 'The church does not exist to provide an ethos for democracy or any other form of social organization, but stands as a political alternative to every nation, witnessing to the kind of social life possible for those who have been formed by the story of Christ.' The church is a 'contrast society'.

p. 700

Other Christians have been less sectarian: recent Roman Catholic encyclicals, for instance, have returned to a sense of natural law to develop a theory of society, often using the concept of the 'common good' to express the shared interests between the church and the wider society. Christians are called on to participate in the structures of society, and to build alliances with others with whom they share common ground. Thus the Second Vatican Council proclaimed that the Roman Catholic Church 'looks with sincere respect upon those ways of conduct and of life, those rules and teachings which, though different in many particulars from what she holds and sets forth, nevertheless often reflect a ray of that Truth which enlightens all men'. Similarly, many Protestant thinkers have been prepared to engage in the political process. Some have tried to revitalize the Augustinian tradition with its often conflicting interests of the two cities. Reinhold Niebuhr, for instance, recognized the need to constrain the natural tendency to evil through social regulation, participative democracy and human rights: 'Man's capacity for justice makes democracy possible, but man's inclination to injustice makes democracy necessary.' Such 'Christian realism' has been particularly influential in the USA.

Council

Other thinkers have moved in different directions. The liberation theologians from Latin America have seen Christianity as inherently biased to the poor, often drawing on Marxist social analysis to explain the conditions of their society. Similarly, for Charles Davis, critical secular theory becomes a means for exposing the church's culpability in systems of domination. Other more conservative thinkers, including the American theorist of 'civil religion', Robert Bellah, have seen churches as communities which seek to promote the common values of citizenship, without which society cannot function: 'Perhaps enduring commitment to those we love and civic friendship toward our fellow citizens are preferable to restless competition and anxious self-defence. Perhaps common worship, in which we express our gratitude and wonder in the face of the mystery of being itself, is the most important thing of all.' Some thinkers, including John Milbank, have even sought against all the odds to revive a Christendom model of church and society, and are deeply critical of theories of secularization.

Secularization

Such a variety of responses, however, merely indicate the extent to which the relationships between Christianity and society are no longer as straightforward as they once were. The all-pervasive secularism of the modern world, coupled with the multiculturalism of many societies, mean that Christianity must co-exist with many other forms of voluntary organization. New compromises and new forms of religious organization may well be necessary if Christianity is to retain any influence on society at all.

MARK D. CHAPMAN

Robin Barbour (ed), *The Kingdom of God and Human Society*, Edinburgh: T&T Clark 1993; José Casanova, *Public Religions in the Modern World*, Chicago: University of Chicago Press 1994; Charles Davis, *Religion and the Making of Society*, Cambridge: CUP 1994; R. A. Markus, *Saeculum: History and Society in the Theology of St Augustine*, Cambridge: CUP 1970; Wayne Meeks, *The First Urban Christians*, New Haven: Yale University Press 1983; John Milbank, *Theology and Social Theory: Beyond Secular Reason*, Oxford: Blackwell 1990; Reinhold Niebuhr, *Moral Man and Immoral Society* (1932), Louisville, KY: Westminster John Knox Press 2002; Charles Taylor, *Sources of the Self*, Cambridge, MA: Harvard University Press 1989; Ernst Troeltsch, *The Social Teaching of the Christian Churches*, London: Allen & Unwin 1931; Max Weber, *The Protestant Ethic and the Spirit of Capitalism*, London: Routledge 1992

Sociology and Christianity

The relationship between sociology and Christianity can be considered from two perspectives: the nature and development of sociology as a social science and the broader perspective of the sociology of religion as a sub-field of theory and research. In both cases it is clear that for much of its history, the key preoccupation of sociology was 'modernization': the nature and problems of becoming a modern society. It is also clear that the early sociologists regarded the way in which religion functioned as being extremely revealing of the processes that bind individuals together in communities. Of course, this should not be surprising, as the term 'religion' is derived from *religio*, which can be interpreted as the bond of social relations between individuals. Correspondingly, the term 'sociology' is derived from *socius*, the bond of companionship that constitutes societies. Following the French sociologist Emile Durkheim, many sociologists of religion adopted his definition of religion as a set of beliefs and practices, relating to the sacred, which create social bonds between individuals. They might also have been prepared to define sociology, however naively, as the 'science of community'. As the contemporary sociologist of religion Bryan Turner puts it: 'Sociology in general and the sociology of religion in particular are thus concerned with the processes which unite and disunite, bind and unbind social relationships in space and time.'

Sociology began to emerge as an aspiring science of society in the middle of the nineteenth century. It was given its name by the Frenchman, Auguste Comte (1798–1857). Both Comte and the other great figure in the early development of sociology, Herbert Spencer (1820–1903), couched their discussions of religion in social evolutionary terms. In fact, they developed their evolutionary conclusions before Charles Darwin arrived at them in the sphere of natural science. In the case of Comte, we find a social evolutionary scheme developed in writings published in the 1830s, well in advance of Darwin's *The Origin of Species*, which was not published until 1859. Comte's emphasis, in line with the Enlightenment philosophers of the eighteenth century, was on the development of the human intellect and its mode of thinking. His Law of the Three Stages of Intellectual Development maintained that human thought had gradually evolved from a theological mode of explanation of all phenomena in which there was constant reference to supernatural beings, through a metaphysical stage which involved reference to 'essences' that resided in objects and caused them to behave as they did, to a final stage in which the most advanced mode of thought predominated: that of science, which made reference solely to immediately preceding events as causes of phenomena and analysed interconnections on the basis of general abstract laws.

Enlightenment

The general sociological framework adopted by Comte and Spencer was both 'functionalist' and evolutionist: concerned with the relations between the parts of the social organism and with the gradual evolution from simple to complex social structure. Consequently, both writers focused attention on the interconnections of religion with other components of the social system at various stages of social development. Thus Comte devoted a great deal of attention to discerning parallel changes in religion and other aspects of society such as the mode of political organization. Unlike the Enlightenment philosophers, he emphasized the positive functions of religion. For example, with regard to cognition, he paid tribute to the role played by theologians, as the first class of theorists, in developing human capacities. He stated that but for the theologians, human society would have remained in a condition much like that of a company of superior monkeys. The abstractions and conceptualizations of religious thinkers paved the way for scientific thinking.

But Comte saw more important social functions being served by religion than simply acting as an intellectual precursor of science. Although he used a biological analogy, comparing society in its relations of parts to whole with similar relations in a biological organism, he drew out the difference between the social organism and the biological organism. He noted that whereas the biological organism is separated off and unified by its encasing skin, the social organism has to depend primarily on 'spiritual' (cultural) unifying factors. It was for this reason that Comte emphasized the functions of language and religion. Much of the sociological tradition he founded was about the binding nature of culture. Religion and morals were viewed as supplying the 'cement' that binds society together in a common 'cult', excites affective attachments to the social order, and supplies beliefs that legitimize the social order.

Spencer's social evolutionism differed significantly from that of Comte, even though he had been greatly influenced by Comte's ideas. Spencer placed less emphasis on intellectual development and paid more attention to other factors such as population pressures and structural differentiation: the increasing specialization of functions in society. Spencer believed that the origins of religion were to be found in the worship of ancestors: propitiation of the dreaded dead gave rise to religious ritual, and the ghosts of the ancestors were made into gods. Later sociologists were to reject all such speculative and unverifiable theories about the origins of religion, but they maintained an interest in the second element of Spencer's theory of religion, which dealt with the relationship between the religious and political spheres. Spencer pointed out that as societies moved up from the patriarchal stage where the father both ruled the group and propitiated the dead, the specialization of functions gave rise to more elaborate social hierarchies, and these were paralleled by more clearly differentiated and specialized deities. The sociologist Guy Swanson, on the basis of a comparative analysis of religion and political structure in a large number of societies, found support for the theory of a transition to monotheism with the growth of more elaborate forms of political organization. Robert Bellah, another contemporary American sociologist, has developed a sophisticated evolutionary scheme in which stages of development in social organization are paralleled by similar developments in religious belief and organization.

There can be no doubt that the evolutionary schemes used by sociologists such as Bellah represent an improvement over those of their predecessors in the nineteenth century, even though social evolutionary theories, like modernization theories, are now out of fashion in sociology. Although Bellah's definition of evolution is similar to Spencer's in its stress on increasing differentiation and complexity of organization, his description of the corresponding evolution of religion is significantly different. For the nineteenth-century evolutionists the history of religion was essentially one of progress out of 'superstition' and error up to the 'enlightened present' of their own intellectual circle. Bellah makes no such judgement, but rather concentrates on the evolution within religious symbolization from 'compact' to 'differentiated'. Secondly, he relates this change in symbolization to associated changes in religious action and religious organization. Finally, he relates those changes in religion to similar changes in other social spheres. He divides the developments into five stages: primitive, archaic, historic, early modern and modern. There is nothing hard and fast about the stages, but they are intended to help in ordering empirical examples in this sphere in the same way as the concept of stages of the life-cycle is used in the study of personality development. Whereas for Comte it was the Roman Catholic Church that represented the kind of complex organization that could serve as a model for a new secular religion to bind modern society, Bellah identified Protestant Christianity as the epitome of the early modern period, in which religious symbolism and organization involve the collapse of hierarchical structuring and a concentration on the direct, unmediated relation between the individual and transcendent reality. In the mature modern stage, he claimed, Christian symbolization was becoming increasingly fluid and 'demythologized', just as the denominational form of religious organization entailed the development of more open and flexible patterns of organization.

Despite Bellah's attempt to separate his evolutionary approach from that of his nineteenth-century predecessors, as in his statement that there is no assumption that evolution is inevitable, irreversible or must follow any single particular course, there is still a suggestion of ethnocentrism: he is very much focused on his own American society. (A similar tendency was evident in the work of the most influential of post-war American sociologists, Talcott Parsons.) The most advanced stage of evolution seems to coincide with Bellah's own society, and in the religious sphere the advanced prototype sounds like the intellectualism of the most liberal version of Protestantism. In the heyday of sociological theories of modernization – the immediate post-Second World War period – such assumptions may have seemed well founded. Since that time, sociologists have become more critical of such ideas. Liberal Protestantism has been in decline even in America, and the upsurge of sects, fundamentalism and New Age cults has led sociologists to look elsewhere for their theories of religious development. Some sociologists have developed ideas derived from the 'classical' sociologists of the late nineteenth and early twentieth centuries, especially Max Weber and Emile Durkheim. Others have turned to theories of postmodernity to explain these religious developments, sometimes combining these postmodernist theories with elements drawn from the works of Weber and Durkheim, such as Weber's concept of charismatic leadership and Durkheim's concept of 'collective effervescence' (emotional feelings generated in certain social assemblies).

Max Weber (1864–1920) is perhaps the best-known example of a sociologist whose work on aspects of Christianity gained widespread attention. Weber has often been described as being engaged in a critical dialogue with the ghost of Karl Marx (1818–83). Marx argued that the form of religion and its functioning were determined by the structure of economic relations. Thus, he maintained, the Christianity of his own period was ideally suited to the needs of the capitalist economic system because it was an ideology that disguised the exploitative nature of the relations between capitalists and workers, while at the same time legitimizing the inequalities. For the individual, it provided consolation and comfort; as Karl Marx put it in 1844, it was 'the opium of the masses'. Religion would inevitably decline because it was a 'false consciousness', but this decline would be completed only when the social structure that produced it (e.g. capitalism) disappeared. Some sociologists followed Marx's line, especially in viewing Christianity as an ideology that legitimized inequality and distracted disadvantaged groups, such as the working class, from developing a consciousness of their economic and political interests. In contrast to Marx, Weber gave more independence to religious culture in relation to social structures, especially at the point when a new religion first began. The founders of a religion, such as Christianity, were often drawn from a variety of social strata and their beliefs did not simply reflect their social position. However, Weber went on to argue that the subsequent development of a religion was often influenced by the needs of the social group (or 'stratum') that became its main carrier – small traders and urban artisans in the case of Christianity.

Symbols

p. 1155

In his most famous work, *The Protestant Ethic and the Spirit of Capitalism* (1904), Weber traced the way in which the Calvinist version of Protestantism was a causal factor in the development of capitalism. According to popular belief among Calvinists in the sixteenth and seventeenth centuries, business success deriving from conscientious work and the investment of savings could be a sign of being predestined to salvation, of being one of God's elect. This Protestant ethic was ideally suited to the development of early capitalism, especially by virtue of its emphasis on individual responsibility and striving, combined with a compulsion to save and not spend. The only problem for religion was that, once this religious ethic had done its work, it became absorbed into the general spirit (or culture) of capitalism. Weber quoted Benjamin Franklin's statement 'Time is money' as an example of an essential element of the spirit of modern capitalism and of the Protestant ethic, but by Franklin's time this ethic had begun to lose its religious basis. However, Weber also found traces of the same Protestant ethic in Methodism, as in John Wesley's statement that 'we must exhort all Christians to gain all they can, and to save all they can;

Protestantism

Liberal theology

Fundamentalism

New Age movements

Methodism

that is, in effect, to grow rich'. Wesley went on to exhort his followers to give away their riches, but he feared that after the peak of religious enthusiasm was over it would pass into sober economic virtue.

Weber's key idea about modern society was that it was subject to increasing rationalization. This brought about a 'loss of enchantment' (disenchantment) of the modern world. Disenchantment and rationalization would inevitably result in the decline of religion: secularization. The only exceptions he foresaw would be occasional breakthroughs in the form of new movements led by charismatic leaders, such as new religious cults and sects. Weber followed his colleague, the sociologist Ernst Troeltsch, in using a typology of the different forms of religious organization: church, sect and cult. The church is defined as a large-scale organization with a broadly inclusive membership, as in the Roman Catholic Church, possessing a hierarchy of professional office-holders (priests, bishops, archbishops, cardinals and pope). The sect sets itself apart from the social and religious mainstream and is less hierarchical and more exclusive in its membership. The cult is even more dependent on personal experience and lacks any permanent form of organization.

Secularization

New religious movements

Much of the sociology of religion as applied to Christianity has been framed by Weber's theory of secularization, with the implication that periodic reactions against this master trend would usually be in the form of sects or cults (now usually referred to as new religious movements). Even when the evidence seemed to be to the contrary, as in post-war America, sociologists were inclined to interpret apparently high rates of religious involvement as simply a kind of community attachment. In his best-selling book *Protestant, Catholic, Jew* (1956), Will Herberg suggested that religious participation in America was largely a way of identifying with a wider community and of being American. The implication was that people had worldly motives for their religious involvement, such as the desire for respectability, and that the churches were being secularized from within. A weakness of this argument is that it is difficult to produce evidence of such worldly motives. One type of evidence that has sometimes been offered is that contained in surveys of religious knowledge, which often reveal widespread ignorance in response to factual questions concerning the Bible. But this kind of ignorance is not confined to religion and is just as evident in other spheres, such as politics. George W. Bush, Jr, when running for the Republican Party nomination, was unable to name the heads of state of several major countries, and other candidates revealed similar ignorance.

In recent years sociologists have begun to revise their ideas about secularization. A persistent problem has been how to explain the apparent high levels of religious participation in America, the most advanced society in terms of modernization. One tactic employed by secularization theorists has been to suggest that American religious practice is superficial and simply a form of community attachment. But, as we have seen, this is hard to substantiate. The secularization thesis that the decline of religion is linked to the process of modernization has also been disputed with respect to the period of urbanization and modernization in the nineteenth century, where there is some evidence of religious revival having occurred, rather than steady decline. In the case of Britain, it has been demonstrated that between 1840 and 1920 indexes of urbanization and church attendance increased alongside each other, but that after 1920 the latter falls off markedly while the former does not. Some secularization theorists have conceded the point that industrialization, especially in the early stages in which traditional communities and ways of life are seriously disrupted, may indeed stimulate a temporary religious revival. Other supporters of the secularization theory take the view that secularization is a product not so much of modernity as of advanced modernity, since the decline in religious activity in the more apparently secularized countries is very much a twentieth-century rather than a nineteenth-century phenomenon.

Critics of the secularization thesis go even further and question whether there is any uniform relationship between modernization and secularization. They point to the variations brought about by a number of key variables, such as the degree of religious pluralism, the strength of religious minorities and their geographical dispersion, the relationship between religious groupings and the dominant élites. The prominent British sociologist of religion, David Martin, describes the different trends according to the main types of situation: total monopoly, where the tradition is Roman Catholic; the duopolistic type, where a Protestant church is the major organization, but with a large Roman Catholic minority; the still more pluralistic situation, exemplified by England, with a large state church and a wide range of dissenting and other groups; the fully pluralist, but Protestant-dominated case, such as the United States; and, finally, those countries that have no substantial Roman Catholic presence, including Scandinavia and the Orthodox countries. Martin goes so far as to question the usefulness of the secularization theory in the light of his conclusion that secularization is largely a European phenomenon, related to the struggles between the churches and secular forces in early modern Europe, which discredited religion to a degree not experienced elsewhere.

Martin's insistence on looking at social and cultural differences has its equivalent in American sociology of religion, where 'rational-choice' theory makes reference to different religious 'markets', in which individuals make rational choices about available beliefs and practices to satisfy needs that are not otherwise capable of being satisfied. The rational-choice approach to religion rejects the idea that America will eventually follow the European pattern of secularization, and insists that there is no reason why the European societies could not come to resemble the American religious market over a period of time, if the same range of religious choices is supplied. The persistence of relatively high levels of belief in the face of low religious participation in parts of Europe – what Grace Davie has called 'believing without belonging' – is taken as evidence of potential demand.

A growing body of contemporary sociologists has largely lost interest in the once dominant theories of modernization and secularization, and this has had a knock-on effect on the preoccupations of sociologists of religion. Now there is more interest in theories of globalization, cultural differentiation and identity (e.g. the hybrid cultures and identities of ethnic diasporas, brought about by immigration), and postmodern cultural trends that reveal people picking and mixing supposedly incompatible combinations of 'rational' and 'irrational' beliefs and practices. According to secularization theorists this kind of picking and mixing reduces religion to part of a range of stylistic options and is itself an indication of secularization. Critics respond that this is a value-judgement about what constitutes authentic religion. For example, does Christianity have to operate at both the public and private levels in a cohesive way? In some cases it may continue to do so. For example, the impact of globalization on religion in some societies seems to be less in the direction of secularization and more towards promoting a revival of 'fundamentalist' versions of religion and even, in some cases, a greater role for religion in the public sphere (the New Christian Right finds its counterparts in Islamic revivalism, Hindu nationalism, and militant Zionism). But, as the American sociologist Peter Berger notes, societies in late or postmodernity are generally characterized by 'unstable, incohesive, unreliable plausibility structures'. In contrast to earlier phases in the sociology of religion, it may be no longer essential to link systems of belief that provide personal meaning with the institutions of public regulation and legitimization.

To sum up: sociology was born in Europe and focused on issues concerned with modernization. Social institutions would become more differentiated and specialized, which would entail a decline in the scope of the functions performed by religion as an institution. The process of secularization in Christian Europe seemed to bear out this prediction. The sociology of religion was mainly concerned with this scenario until quite recently. Even the higher level of religiosity in America was explained away as being due to special factors that would eventually recede. The fatalism of this view, as far as the sociology of religion was concerned, was only partly mitigated by disputes among sociologists about whether the evidence really did point to the inevitable and universal decline of religion in the longer term. Recently, other more urgent social issues have attracted the attention of sociologists and these have caused them to give fresh attention to religion. The result is that a whole range of sociological perspectives and theories are beginning to breathe new life into the sociology of religion. This may mean that Christianity will have to share the stage with other sets of beliefs and practices vying for attention.

KENNETH THOMPSON

P. Berger, *The Social Reality of Religion*, Harmondsworth: Penguin Books 1973; R. Bocock and K. Thompson (eds), *Religion and Ideology*, Manchester: Manchester University Press 1985; A. Comte, *Positive Philosophy*, translated and condensed by H. Martineau (3 vols), London: Chapman 1853; G. Davie, *Religion in Britain Since 1945*, Oxford: Blackwell 1994; E. Durkheim, *The Elementary Forms of the Religious Life* (1912), New York: Free Press of Glencoe 1995; P. A. Mellor and C. Shilling, *Re-forming the Body: Religion, Community and Modernity*, London: Sage 1997; R. Robertson (ed), *Sociology of Religion*, Harmondsworth: Penguin Books 1969; H. Spencer, *Principles of Sociology* (3 vols), London: Williams & Norgate [3]1893; R. Stark and W. S. Bainbridge, *A Theory of Religion*, New York: Lang 1987; B. S. Turner, *Religion and Social Theory*, London: Heinemann Education (1983), revised edition 1991; R. Wallis and S. Bruce (eds), *Religion and Modernization*, Oxford: Clarendon Press 1992; M. Weber, *The Protestant Ethic and the Spirit of Capitalism*, London: Allen & Unwin 1930

Globalization

Spirituality

Spirituality is a word commonly used for an area of relationship between the human spirit and the Spirit of God. It is a wide and ill-defined area, dealing with intangible ideas and often hidden practices. Rather like the definition of a sacrament as an outward and visible sign of an inward and spiritual grace, so spirituality deals in internals and externals, and the relationship between the two. With regard to spirituality, 'the wind blows where it wills, and you hear its sound, but you cannot tell where it is coming from or where it is going to: so is everyone that is born of the Spirit' (John 3.8).

Sacraments

In the seventeenth century, the word 'spiritualities' referred to the items of the church building that were

Prayer Evangelicals

the property of the incumbent, but the word 'spiritual' has long been used to distinguish the holy from the crudely material. The word 'spirituality' derives from French Catholicism, and the French more generally used the name for the finer perceptions of life. Evangelical Christianity has used the term to indicate the warmer, religious emotions; and for many its proper use is to describe the distinguishing quality of New Testament believers.

The concept of the spirit has a very ancient history, as old as the history of human beings. Indeed the spirit has been understood to be a defining characteristic of humanity, and spirit and life are intimately linked. In this context spirit is often set over against matter, dealing with essentially non-physical areas of life such as dreams, life beyond death, and experiences out of the body. The spirit has a place in musical and poetic inspiration, and in abstract qualities such as courage, beauty, intelligence and intuition.

Mystery cults

Because the spirit often has to do with secret and ill-defined areas of life, described by the Greek word 'mysteries', the discussion of the subject itself often calls forth great attempts of human creativity. The artist, the healer, the holy person are frequently seen to be those with particular gifts connected with the spirit, the spirits, or the spiritual world. They are thought to have greater insight into unseen things than ordinary mortals, and in many societies are revered for this. Most religions deal with the spiritual side of human life, and are understood to be in possession of secret knowledge, not easily communicated to those outside the defined group.

Evil Jesus Satan Bible

In the spiritual world, spirits tend to be categorized as good and evil. Good spirits are benign, bring good human benefits and rewards, and are associated with light. Evil spirits, on the other hand, initiate disasters, evoke fear, and are associated with darkness. Certainly in the biblical period these opposing forces of good and evil took on a metaphorical life as good and evil spirits. Jesus spoke with the devil, and Jacob wrestled with an angel. The ministry of Jesus dealt in depth with the world of evil spirits, and his power over such forces, through his intimacy with God, was seen to be one aspect of his divinity.

The spirit world, so much the background of the biblical literature, was understood to have its place in the ordinary world of men and women. Spirits took up residence in particular places and people, transmitting a particular benign or frightening character, and many myths grew up around those basic human experiences. Around the myths developed rituals, customs, writings and groups of people defining themselves in relation to the spirits they knew and to a certain extent cultivated. The ministry of deliverance in the church today, as exorcism is now called, associates itself with those whose illness or distress seems to be intimately bound up with this world. Prayer, the sacraments, the laying on of hands and the casting out of spirits are some of the means by which healing is brought.

To believe in God is to enter a thought-world that opens up the inevitability of spirits. They are often seen to be the mediators between the distant unattainable God and ordinary human mortals, God's agents or deputies. They are sometimes depicted as angels, and the wings of angels indicate that they are able to travel between the spiritual world and the human world. Luke's Gospel delights in the play of angels as he describes the birth of Jesus Christ. In William Blake's paintings such creatures are vividly depicted, and more recently we see the same delight in the paintings of Cecil Collins.

The study of this area of experience is usually covered by the word 'spirituality'. It is a helpful defining word that covers a huge area of human experience and exploration. Christian spirituality focuses all this into a still vaster area of concern and interest. Prayer and spirituality are seen to be closely linked, and sometimes almost synonymous, but prayer needs to be understood as more than just a simple asking, however valuable that may be. It is a whole relation to God, and so spirituality concerns the way in which prayer influences conduct and behaviour, manner of life, and attitudes to other people.

Belief in God so motivated by a thought-world dependent on the understanding of a spiritual world like this takes an interesting turn when that world is challenged by secular materialism. The concept of spirituality depends so much on the picture of a world other than the material one. Notions of spirituality become fragile when people have little or no idea of how another world supports it. Put rather simply, the result is that people either turn from Christianity to religions that have maintained a confidence in their spiritual roots, or they remain within Christianity and seek to identify links across the ages and cultures.

The Old Testament

Old Testament spirituality is concerned with the way in which God enters into the world as creator, and gives the created order dignity and a moral foundation, evoking respect and responsibility within human beings to understand their place in its overall harmony. The writings create a sense of wonder, and even in the language itself words and individual letters bear the nature of God, and God uses speech to be present and authoritative in the dealings of the community. This is vividly seen, for example, in the giving of the law on Mount Sinai, and in the dialogues between God and Moses in Exodus.

The link between 'breath' and 'spirit' (one word, *ruach*, in Hebrew), between the physical and the incorporeal, provides the seedbed for the Old Testament understanding of the nature of 'spirit'. When in Genesis the writer speaks of 'a wind from God' that 'swept over the face of the waters', the word translated 'wind' or 'breath' could easily be translated 'spirit'. Gordon Mursell, in his prologue to *The Story of Christian Spirituality*, writes: 'Hebrew knows no absolute distinction between the physical, material world and a wholly separate "spiritual" world. The two are inextricably linked. The wind or "spirit" of God works together with the "word" of God ... what God says, comes to be, comes alive. So spirituality in the Hebrew tradition of scripture is that process by which God seeks continually to work upon, or address, the raw unstable chaos of our lives and experience, and of our world, drawing forth meaning, identity, order and purpose.'

The poetic and prophetic traditions of the Old Testament lead us into a spirituality that sees a profound communication between God and his servant people. This intimacy of communication, both tender and, in difficult times, tense, could be defined as filial. God works with his people as a father to his children. It is a spirituality that acknowledges suffering and a way of faithfulness, particularly in the Book of Job and in the Servant Songs of Isaiah. It is also a spirituality of place, in which there is a devotion to those particular places where God has made himself felt most strongly. 'The spirit of God', said Jacob, 'is in this place,' and he named the place of his spiritual awakening Bethel, the House of God. Jerusalem, or Zion, becomes the spiritual centre of the Judaic faith.

Closer to the New Testament period we see a spiritual awakening in the history of Judaism, described in the form of apocalyptic. The Spirit inspires visions and oral communication between God and individuals. The book of Daniel has examples of this, as well as the non-scriptural book of Enoch, and in the New Testament it is found in the Revelation of John: 'On the Lord's Day the Spirit came upon me' (Revelation 1.10).

Spirituality and theology

It will be useful to pause and note what the distinction might be between spirituality and theology. Are they not one and the same thing? They do seem to have great similarities, but the tone of each is slightly different. Theology charts the understanding of God throughout the centuries. Spirituality focuses more on what those understandings and insights have encouraged in the way of active responses. So, for example, theology would be interested in the evidence that God gave the law to the Israelites in the desert. Spirituality would focus on the way in which that law-giving created a way of life, or a way of worshipping which then became distinctive. Spirituality is concerned with the lifestyle that is opened up as a result of the interaction between God and human beings. Prayer, worship and life in community would be matters covered in the study of spirituality.

Worship
Community

How did Moses pray? How was his life shaped round his experience of God and what was the nature of the community life inspired by the presence of God among the Israelites? Lifestyles, ethos, traditions of prayer, the cultural life which an understanding of God helps to develop, the spirit of a thing, are all issues which spirituality in particular would focus on. In a world where choice is opening up on so many fronts, it is hardly surprising that it is also affecting the world of religion. Spirituality has found itself in an important position with regard to the matter of choice. If spirituality is a study of the outworking of faith, then there is a great deal of material to deal with. Some say that spirituality suits our 'pick and mix' culture, and its popularity among a searching people knows few bounds.

Spirituality and Jesus

Intimacy with God, the understanding of God as someone who is close and with whom one can communicate, is a spiritual matter that slips easily and excitingly into Christianity from the generations of Old Testament experience. The spirituality of Jesus, how he prayed, how he worshipped, and how his values helped to frame a Christian way of life closely follow the principles we have seen developing in the Old Testament.

First, we can see the intimacy with God that was fostered in the desert, immediately after Jesus' baptism. This relationship continued intensely in the three-year period of Jesus' ministry. He addressed God as *Abba* (Father). He prayed to God early in the morning and sometimes through the night, and when he could escape from the press of the crowds. He understood prayer to be a guard against the temptations of the devil, and a means of building up spiritual power. It was on this power that he drew in his healing ministry. It was this power that allowed him to prepare for the imminent coming of the kingdom. It was prayer that helped him make decisions according to the will of God, and consequently gave him the strength and purpose to meet the challenge of the cross.

Apocalyptic

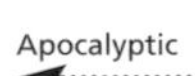

Jesus encouraged his disciples to pray, and gave them the Lord's Prayer as a model prayer. In the disciples' experience, prayer was a real strength, helping them to live a hard and challenging life. Jesus also gave the disciples the Beatitudes (Matthew 5). These are a series of profound ethical statements consisting of very high demands and unusual categories of holiness. The blessed are to be poor in spirit, sorrowful and gentle. They are to hunger and thirst to see right prevail. They are to be merciful, peace-loving, and ready to be persecuted in the cause of right. To ask those who wished to follow the ways of God to live the Beatitudes was to ask a great deal of them. The spirituality

p. 967
Theology

that Jesus demanded was of the highest order, and its authenticity was confirmed by the way that Jesus lived out the things he taught. He practised what he preached. The relationship between Jesus and his disciples was of such intimacy that his spiritual power transferred itself to them. However, the Gospels record that the disciples found it difficult to access that power in the latter part of Jesus' ministry and at the time of the crucifixion they deserted him.

p. 385

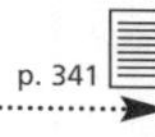

p. 341

There are various key moments or experiences in the life of Jesus. The Sermon on the Mount is one, upon which the Christian church in later periods has found a focus for its spirituality. And here 'spirituality' means the church's defining purpose, what it is in particular that no other religion or system has in quite the same way as Christianity. So Christian spirituality, in the case of Jesus' teaching in the Sermon on the Mount, could be said to be a highly moral spirituality, testing in its demands and pure in its intent. A parallel could be drawn with the Methodist movement founded by John Wesley (1703–91). Methodism grew out of the desire to increase the holiness of the church and to link faith to a rigorous concern for moral purity as set out in the Gospels. Similarly, the writings and life of the Lutheran pastor Dietrich Bonhoeffer (1906–45) are a shining example of a life lived closely to the tenets of the Sermon on the Mount, and where 'spirituality', most accessible in his *Letters and Papers from Prison*, is one founded on strong ethical principles.

Methodism

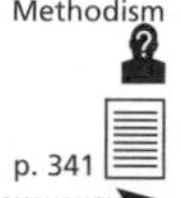

p. 341

Four other key moments in Christian tradition have also helped to focus this complex notion of 'spirituality'. They are the incarnation, the crucifixion and the resurrection of Jesus, and the gift of the Holy Spirit at Pentecost.

Incarnation

Incarnational spirituality. The birth of Jesus into the world as a poor and vulnerable child, in a society fraught with ethnic tensions and religious strife, has been the inspiration for spiritualities of involvement. God has shown a willingness to care for ordinary people by living among them and caring about them, healing their diseases and opening up a new vision of what being human can mean. This has been an encouragement for the way in which Christians can show the compassion of Jesus in their own day. The work of agencies such as Caritas Worldwide, Christian Aid and the Catholic Association for Overseas Development in Britain and the Church World Service and Catholic Charities USA in America, along with many others, are the outward and visible sign of a spiritual grace within people who care about others. It is a spirituality that combines love and practical action. It tries to incarnate the spirit of God's love for the world by dealing with contemporary situations of need. Mahatma Gandhi, much inspired by the Sermon on the Mount, and Mother Teresa of Calcutta and her worldwide communities of sisters, are well-known examples of incarnational spirituality.

Resurrection

p. 960

The spirituality of the cross focuses Christians on the idea of dying, in order to live. It follows Jesus' pattern of going through death in order to be raised to new life. The cross as an object of contemplation has become the defining symbol of that pattern. Christians put crosses in all sorts of places in order to say: 'This is what we are about. We follow Christ crucified.' It is also a reminder of the need to make daily sacrifices and to become more like Christ, more loving and peaceful, less centred on oneself and more occupied with caring for the neighbour.

The Stations of the Cross are an act of devotion in which the passion and death of Christ are re-enacted.The *Via Dolorosa* in Jerusalem is a route to the cross which many pilgrims and travellers follow. Simpler versions of this route are followed weekly in churches throughout the world. Similarly the practice of keeping the Three Hours, the time Jesus was on the cross, continues as a spiritual devotion, particularly on Good Friday, but other groups and communities keep those hours more regularly.

'Dark Night' spirituality emanated from the experience of Jesus in Gethsemane and on the cross. It emerged in the writings of Dionysius the Areopagite (*c.*500), and later in the anonymous English medieval writer of *The Cloud of Unknowing*. The seventeenth-century Spanish writer John of the Cross wrote of 'the dark night of the soul', and more recently the spiritual tradition has continued under the influence of the Holocaust. The Carmelite nun Edith Stein (1891–1942) was much influenced by the Spanish mystics, and by the times in which she was living. She was captured by the Nazis, taken to Auschwitz and was killed in the gas chambers. The diaries of Etty Hillesum and the poetry of Primo Levi, both written from outside the Christian tradition, have shared very similar universal themes of compassion, and faith within suffering.

The resurrection as a stimulus for a particular spirituality focuses on joy, celebration and new life. We can sense its power in the writings of the Herefordshire priest Thomas Traherne (1636–74). Glory and beauty are key themes, and light is the image that shines very strongly through his writings. Archbishop Michael Ramsey's book *The Resurrection of Christ* is in this tradition, but is keen to point out that we can only really understand the resurrection through the eyes of the crucifixion. Maximus the Confessor (580–662), the Greek theologian, wrote about the glorification of human beings in the light of a resurrection faith. In his *Commentary on the Lord's Prayer* he wrote: 'Christ having completed for us his saving work and ascended to heaven with the body which he had taken to himself, accomplishes in his own self the union of heaven and earth, of material and spiritual beings, and this demonstrates the unity of creation in the polarity of its parts.' H. A. Williams, the Cambridge theologian who later became a member of the Anglican Community of the Resurrection, did major work in existentializing this spiritual tradition in his book *True Resurrection*.

The Holy Spirit and being 'born again'. As the time approached for Jesus to fulfil an inevitable destiny to suffer and die and be raised again on the third day, he promised another presence, the Comforter, who would maintain this union. Life in Jesus was not to dissipate as a fond memory, but would be sealed in the Spirit. Communication would be maintained, and the continuation of the spiritual life would live on in the faithful believers. It is John's Gospel that most vividly charts the spiritual story of Jesus. His insistent demand is, 'You must all be born again' (3.7; cf. v. 3). To enter the kingdom of heaven means a significant change in a person's way of life. The new birth is also described as being 'born from water and spirit' (John 3.5).

The heart is mysteriously moved towards the ideals of the kingdom of heaven, and the decisive moment is also a movement from what might be called the natural life into a sphere which seems infinitely more glorious, because more spiritual. It is experienced not just as a heightening of the moral quality of life, but as entering a completely new sphere of reality, and felt as an entering into a new form of being. Mysterious in its origin, there is a definite link with ordinary life and the workings of the human faculties. The mind, the heart and the body clearly function in one way as they did, but the mind is sharpened, the heart is softened, and the body given a new urgency to carry the person where the spirit would have it be. John Henry Newman described it like this: 'The Holy Spirit pervades us (if it may be so said) as light pervades a building, or as sweet perfume the folds of some honourable robe; so that, in Scripture language, we are said to be in Him, and He in us.'

The effects of the Holy Spirit on the believer are felt to be overwhelmingly gracious, and could be simplified into three main areas. First, when the Holy Spirit comes in all its fullness it is present as a moral power in the heart: 'he will prove the world wrong about sin, justice and judgement' (John 16.8). The effect of the Spirit's illumination is to heighten a person's moral sense in his involvement with the issues of the day, and their actions and decisions would then be in line with the intentions of Jesus as he outlined them in his human life in the world. So a person understands the moral relation between human action and the universe through entering into Jesus' frame of mind. The conscience takes on a new life and becomes more central and authoritative in the life of the Christian.

The second effect of the Spirit's presence will be a new possession of truth: 'he will guide you into all the truth' (John 16.13). The 'truth' that Jesus was thinking of was not just an academic grasp of facts, but of a relationship with God that would allow the believer to understand 'the mind of Christ', and 'the truth will set you free' (John 8.32). The spiritual mind would be a combination of delight in moral truth, and also an eagerness to pursue knowledge in so far as it encourages a greater understanding of human nature and of the human predicament.

Holy Spirit

Thirdly, the Holy Spirit will glorify Jesus. Jesus is at the heart of Christian spirituality, the source and an inspiration for any attempt at living a spiritual life within the Christian tradition. It is the Holy Spirit who has the immense privilege of being Christ in the heart of the disciple: 'when the Advocate has come, whom I shall send you from the Father – the Spirit of truth that issues from the Father – he will bear witness to me' (John 15.26). The spiritual life of Christians depends on a calling on the Spirit to glorify Jesus within them, and the perceived effects of that will be a daily experience of what God can do even within our frail human frame. There will inevitably be limits to the extent of this relationship while the disciple is on earth. The incarnation of Christ is the model for those limitations, and any judgement of spiritual claims that are made will best be made in the light of Jesus' experience.

Taking one aspect of the experience of Jesus and making it the centre of a personal spirituality has the disadvantage of neglecting a wider range of experience, or a wholeness of experience, of who Christ was and what he did. It is in following the church's year that the breadth of Christian spirituality can be focused. The church helps Christians by its liturgical round of Sunday services, and particular festivals, to enter into the life of Jesus in all its aspects. That is why the Book of Common Prayer within the Anglican spiritual tradition has been such a rich spiritual resource, and the prayer books of other traditions have played and can play a similar role.

Calendar

Paul and the early church

Paul

Attention to the history of the New Testament documents leads us to be wary about definite historical progression in the forms of 'spirituality'. John's insight into the relationship between the Holy Spirit and Jesus could be as late in formation as any of Paul's thinking about the same matter. Different cultures and languages have their effect, but in all the writings, it is the Holy Spirit who makes the significant connections between the earthly Jesus and the risen Christ, and between the risen Christ and the believers who constituted 'the early church'.

Paul's immense task of working out a spirituality for the Christian communities he founded and for which he had such a passionate responsibility is seen in the raw in his letters. The main tenets of his spirituality have their roots in the priorities of Jesus. The moral quality of a spiritual life influenced by the Holy Spirit is described in Paul's letters to the Romans (chapter 8) and Galatians (chapter 5). A spiritual life is inevitably beset by the struggle between the passions of the lower nature and the exalted demands of the Holy Spirit, and it is 'in Christ

Celtic Christianity

Jesus that the life-giving law of the Spirit sets you free from the law of sin and death'. Life 'in Christ' is the cornerstone of Paul's spirituality. The result of that life 'in Christ' gives a clear and dramatic picture of spirituality in the early church. In one famous sentence Paul lets us understand his sense of the moral sufficiency of the Holy Spirit in a Christian: 'where the Spirit of the Lord is, there is liberty' (2 Corinthians 3.17).

A Christian in Paul's understanding was not meant to be intellectually brilliant, but enlightened by the indwelling grace of the Holy Spirit (1 Corinthians 14.15). Boldly, Paul claims that a humble believer is better informed than the wisest teachers of the schools (vv. 10–13). So truth is

Monasticism

practical wisdom, relating to conduct as it touches God and as it affects human beings. In the light of that, the spiritual people may set themselves up to judge all things: 'a spiritual person can judge the worth of everything, yet is not himself subject to judgement by others' (2. 15).

Christian spirituality as taught by Paul is that the Spirit should speak of Jesus. The Lord is the Spirit, 'and because for us there is no veil over the face (as there was in Moses' day), we all see as in a mirror the glory of the Lord, and we are being transformed into his likeness with

p. 792

ever increasing glory, through the power of the Lord who is the Spirit' (2 Corinthians 3.18). The final result of the Spirit's influence in the heart is that Christ is formed in the believer (Galatians 4.19).

Finally, in his letter to the Galatians, Paul consciously and definitely describes the conduct of 'spiritual' persons (Greek *pneumatikoi*). They are to bear one another's

p. 274

burdens, to communicate their knowledge to the ignorant, and never to weary in doing good (chapter 6). But it is in 1 Corinthians 13 that Paul crowns love and sets it on the throne of the Christian character. So the ground rules of the spiritual nature of the Christian were set in this early period. It is to these insights, challenges and promises that spiritual persons turn for maintaining the quality of their Christian lives. They are marked by it, and in times of persecution are judged by it. The period of the martyrs in the early church, and brave souls ever since who have died for their faith, have proved the strength of their spirituality.

Martyr

Later spiritualities

Religious orders

With the windings of the stream of Christian history, there have inevitably been varieties of emphasis within the communities of Christians. The varieties have often caused friction and dissent on major and minor scales, as people have clung to the familiar ways of being the church in their place. Any description of the glories of one way of living a Christian life also needs to contain reflection on what other way of being Christian has been rejected. The choice of spirituality is often geographical, and to do with the culture of the places where those involved in mission found themselves. Such was the individuality of the Celtic church, and with the church involved in different cultures came variations in ways of worship and prayer, with differing notions of authority and organization. Very often we can trace the sources of these streams in the life and teachings of Jesus, and in the experience of the early church, but human nature has its influence too and the spiritual is mixed with the worldly.

Monastic spirituality. Inspired by the desert experiences of Elijah (1 Kings 17.3f.), and of Jesus in the desert (Mark 1.12f.) and under the influence of the way of the desert fathers in Egypt, Antony (*c.*251–356) and John Cassian (*c.*360–435), monasticism developed in different streams. The communities of monks under the Rule of Benedict (*c.*500) had an enormous influence on the life of Western Europe. The simple rule became the foundation stone of a great many monasteries, each under the leadership of an abbot and organized to enable an ordered and prayerful life. The day was divided into set times for prayer, work, study and recreation.

Other foundations came from the original Benedictine system, including the Cistercians, founded by Robert of Molesmes at Cîteaux in 1098. Bernard of Clairvaux was a novice there in 1112. These communities have sustained their life and worship through many centuries, and in the twentieth century the writings of Thomas Merton (Fr Louis) of the Cistercian monastery of Gethsemani, Kentucky, have been very influential in the regeneration of interest in the monastic, or contemplative, life. The ecumenical community at Taizé, in France, founded in the Second World War by Brother Roger, has brought to many young people a love of silence and meditative chanting, combined with a deep involvement in social and political justice.

The spirituality of the desert has had a rebirth in our own times in movements such as the Little Brothers and Sisters of Jesus, inspired by the desert writings of Charles de Foucauld (1858–1916). Many of these brothers and sisters have found their 'desert' in the inner cities of the modern world, and wherever there is material and spiritual poverty. Each monastic development has given rise to different forms of spirituality. There are also the Augustinian, the Franciscan, and the Carmelite communities and the members of the Society of Jesus (founded by

RETREATS

A retreat is a period of time with intervals of silence, spent in a house appropriate for this, usually in country surroundings, with comfortable accommodation, simple meals, a chapel for prayer, a library and grounds to walk in. Retreats vary in character and length. Although they have traditionally been attended mainly by clergy, especially before their ordination, they are in fact for anyone who wishes to go on one.

Conference-type or *preached retreats* are more formal and are led by a conductor who leads worship, gives addresses and is available to those on retreat who want to talk privately. They often centre on a particular theme: aspects of the Bible, the life of Jesus, exploring a particular form of spirituality. In *guided retreats*, smaller groups have a daily meeting and are then on their own for the rest of the day. In *directed retreats* individuals meet daily with a director who helps them with prayer and spiritual growth. Or individuals may simply spend time at a retreat house by themselves and make their own times for silence, prayer, meditation and study.

Retreats can last for a single day or a weekend to a month or more, depending on the time available to individuals and groups. Although they are characteristic of the Catholic traditions of Christianity, they have become increasingly popular among all Christian denominations. There are more than 600 retreat houses in the United States and Canada and a correspondingly large number in the United Kingdom.

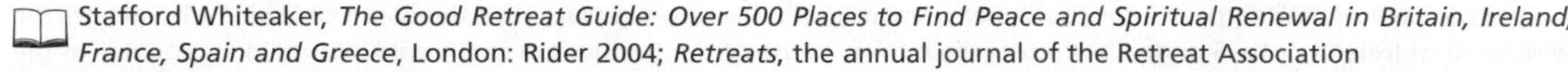
Stafford Whiteaker, *The Good Retreat Guide: Over 500 Places to Find Peace and Spiritual Renewal in Britain, Ireland, France, Spain and Greece*, London: Rider 2004; *Retreats*, the annual journal of the Retreat Association

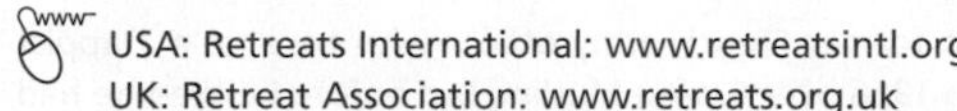
USA: Retreats International: www.retreatsintl.org;
UK: Retreat Association: www.retreats.org.uk

Ignatius Loyola). Each has a different style and rule of life, but all come within the broad heading of monastic, with their commitment to the three vows of poverty, chastity and obedience, and a desire to serve God in all things. Monasteries and small monastic houses have become the focus today for spiritual retreats.

Celtic monasticism. A monastic tradition in the Celtic areas of the West grew up essentially separate from the influence of the Rule of Benedict. A strong monastic life existed in Ireland, Scotland, Wales, Northern England and Brittany. It was again fired by the desert communities of the second century and by the desire of men and women to seek a solitary and ascetic life in touch with the numinous of the natural world and with a desire to meditate on God in Trinity without distraction. Thus Samson finally settled in Brittany and Columba settled in Scotland, establishing the monastery of Iona. The spiritual quality of such movements was seen in the blossoming of an artistic tradition. The high crosses that were set up provided a picture book of the Christian faith, and the decorating of the Gospel books (the Book of Kells and the Lindisfarne Gospels) indicates a spirituality centred on the scriptures in the battle against a pagan world. The love of solitude, of being alone within the small community, is dramatically seen in the beehive huts and oratories of western Ireland. The Celtic monks were first and foremost athletes for Christ.

Anglo-Saxon spirituality. Under the influence of the great upsurge in Christian culture, education and artistic endeavour in the court of Charlemagne (768–814), the liturgical work of Alcuin (740–804) and the theological writings of John Scotus Eriugena (810–77) set the tone for centuries to come. It was a time of translation, history, poetry and cosmology. Alfred the Great (849–99) translated Bede's *Ecclesiastical History* and Gregory's *Pastoral Care* into Anglo-Saxon. Celtic and Anglo-Saxon spirituality ran side by side, and led the church into a renewed strength, and the Benedictine tradition at Winchester and the influence of Dunstan at Glastonbury in the tenth and eleventh centuries brought a renewed sense of learning and holiness to the monastic tradition. The spiritual intellect of Anselm of Bec (1033–1109) and the mystical theology of Bernard of Clairvaux (1090–1153) were high points in the early medieval period. Bernard was a monk of the Cistercian order. This order had wanted to deepen its Benedictine roots in the direction of simplicity. The architecture of the Cistercian order is particularly resonant of this desire for a greater simplicity in the worship of God, and in the environment of Christian living.

The Middle Ages saw this ascetic priority taking an interesting course. Devotion to God in silence and contemplation was both fuelled by, and resulted in, a mystical theology that had its main inspiration in the biblical book of the Song of Songs. This one book gave rise to an enormous spiritual literature that did not abate until its greatest exponent of all, John of the Cross (1542–91), had completed his poems and commentaries. The idea that the love of God gathered together the very best of human

DESERT AND WILDERNESS

There is no completely appropriate term to describe the arid, unfertile land of the Middle East. 'Desert' conveys vast tracts of sand, crossed by caravans of camels and inhabited only by fierce nomads, whereas the 'deserts' of Syria and Palestine are sometimes mountainous, produce vegetation after rain, and even sustain communities, like that beside the Dead Sea at Qumran (in fact there are no fewer than six terms for such land in the Hebrew Bible). Hence the alternative term 'wilderness' is also used to describe this barren area.

The wilderness has great importance in the Bible. It is through the wilderness that the Israelites travel to reach their promised land, and in the wilderness that Moses encounters God and receives the Law. Prophets like Elijah withdraw into the wilderness to commune with God, and it is a place from which divine messages come: John the Baptist is introduced as 'a voice crying in the wilderness, "Prepare the way of the Lord"'. Abraham drives his concubine Hagar into the wilderness, and throughout the Bible the wilderness is a place of refuge for fugitives. The wilderness is also a place of temptation and demons: the Israelites are tempted there to worship the golden calf, and Jesus goes into the wilderness to be tempted.

Monasticism began in the desert (the word 'desert' is always used in this context; one group of monks is known as the 'desert fathers'): at the beginning of the third century Antony, Pachomius and Basil pioneered this way of life, with men seeking to come nearer to God, either as individuals or in groups, in these austere surroundings. The temptations of Antony are legendary. Life in the wilderness continued to be an ideal for monks, and explains why they built their monasteries in such remote places. 'Wilderness' later could mean any wild and inaccessible place, like the island of Skellig Michael off the west coast of Ireland or La Grande Chartreuse, the mother house of the Carthusians in the wild mountainous country of the French Alps north of Grenoble.

At the beginning of the twentieth century Charles de Foucauld, a former French army officer who became a Trappist monk, went into the desert to live the life of a hermit. He was killed in 1916 by a Tuareg Muslim, but before he died he had written rules of life for men and women and in 1933 René Voillaume founded the first of what were to be several orders, the Little Brothers of Jesus in the Sahara.

There is also an 'inner wilderness', an inner disorder and darkness which Christians deliberately choose to enter to find a deeper relationship with God, particularly during Lent. It, too, plays an important part in Christian spirituality.

H. A. Williams, *The True Wilderness*, London and New York: Continuum 2002

desire and beauty, and in a sense made that a metaphor for divine love, gave a very powerful stimulus to prayer and spiritual writing. The Blessed Virgin Mary as incarnating the principle of divine beauty, and the image of Christ as the bridegroom and the soul as his bride, were themes that entered into the Christian spiritual tradition in a very creative way. Much of the spiritual writing of the Middle Ages was influenced by these themes. This is seen in the English mystic Richard Rolle (*c.*1300–49), and in the anonymous author of the *Cloud of Unknowing* (fourteenth century), in Julian of Norwich (*c.*1342–*c.*1420), and in the poetry of Dante (1265–1321). Even Francis of Assisi (1181–1226) can be seen not only as 'the poor man' but also as a 'divine lover' pursuing the hand of Lady Poverty, prepared to give up all for the sake of love.

Mary

Contemporary with St Bernard was Hildegard (1098–1179), the abbess of Rupertsburg, near Bingen. The basis of her writings was an awareness of her divinely- inspired office as a prophetess, in the conception of which she was indebted to Dionysius the Pseudo-Areopagite and John Scotus Eriugena. Her book *Scivias* is a remarkable series of 26 visions, which includes a body of dramatic songs and some highly original illustrations. Her spiritual influence has been widely espoused in recent years by those seeking to extend the use of the imagination in the life of prayer.

Hildegard of Bingen

Roman Catholic, Orthodox and Protestant spiritualities. From the sixteenth century onwards there has been something of a polarization in spirituality relating to the three main divisions in the churches. Pierre de Bérulle (1575–1629), along with Mme Acarie (Blessed Marie de l'Incarnation, 1566–1618) and others, worked in the face of great opposition to introduce the reformed Carmelites of St Teresa into France. De Bérulle also helped to bring renewal into the priestly life in general. The French Catholic devotional tradition has been rich in spiritual teaching. Francis de Sales' *Introduction to the Devout Life* (1608) gives homely advice on prayer to 'dearest Philothea'; Jean-Pierre de Caussade (1675–1751) wrote *Letters of Spiritual Direction.* The lives of the Curé d'Ars, Jean-Baptiste Marie Vianney (1786–1859) and of the Abbé Huvelin (1838–1910) are lessons in themselves on what it is to have spiritual discernment and to spend oneself in sacrificial listening and guiding. The French Catholic tradition is very much one of direction of people in the art of prayer and guidance in the spiritual life, but it also produced saints whose spirituality was one of service. Vincent de Paul (*c.*1580–1660) founded the Lazarist Fathers and the Sisters of Charity, and John Eudes (1601–80) founded the 'Order of our Lady of Charity', to care for fallen women.

DEVOTIO MODERNA

Devotio moderna was a movement characterized by a mystical piety, which originated in the Netherlands in the fourteenth century and spread from there to Germany and northern France and on to Spain and Italy. The Latin term, 'modern devotion', needs some explanation: the word devotion means 'service of God' and the practice was modern by comparison with the mysticism of the piety of the Benedictines and great German mystics like Meister Eckhart and John Tauler.

The most famous representative of the movement is Thomas à Kempis (1380–1471), who wrote the *Imitation of Christ*, one of the classics of spirituality. The characteristics of this book are the characteristics of the movement as a whole. Rather than being speculative, the *Imitation of Christ* is down-to-earth and practical, emphasizing obedience, and a conforming of the will of the disciple to the will of God by imitating Christ, putting love above all things and practising the virtue of humility.

The founder of the *Devotio moderna* was one Geert Groote (1340–84) from Deventer in the Netherlands. He was trained in canon law but gave up that career in 1374 and retired to a monastery. He was never ordained priest, but became a deacon so that he could preach, until he was banned by the authorities the year before his death.

He gave his home to a group of women who became the first 'Sisters of the Common Life'; a house for men was also established in Deventer. The way of life of these brothers and sisters resembled that of the Beguines and Beghards. Members lived together but not under any vows, so that they could leave the community at any time. Their life centred on regular periods of meditation but they also ran schools and copied manuscripts; later they started printing firms. They were thus a force in education. Their influence was wide, but first the Reformation and then the formation of new universities led to a decline, though the last house did not close until the nineteenth century.

p. 794

John H. van Engen (ed), *Devotio Moderna: Basic Writings*, Classics of Western Spirituality, New York and Mahwah, NJ: Paulist Press 1993

QUIETISM

Anyone reading much about spirituality is bound in due course to come across the term 'Quietism' and to wonder what it refers to. However, explanations are by no means easy to come by. The term is used so sweepingly that the Cambridge historian Owen Chadwick was led to remark that 'it sometimes seems to be used of any author when teaching about contemplation what another author approves'. Older Roman Catholic textbooks are quick to condemn it as heretical, but when one sees mentioned among its representatives such different figures as the Hesychasts, the Beguines, Martin Luther and the early Methodists and Quakers, one begins to doubt whether it can mean anything much at all.

pp. 821, 794

In the narrowest and most specific sense Quietism is a form of mysticism developed by the Spanish priest Miguel de Molinos (*c.* 1640–97). In his *Spiritual Guide* he taught that the soul must abandon itself entirely to God, thinking neither of reward nor of punishment, of heaven or hell, and let God work out his will without any action on the part of the soul. Those who commit themselves in this way to God must neither ask anything of God or thank God, simply abiding in the divine presence in adoration and love without performing any actions arising out of this state.

From Spain, Quietism (which also came to be known as Molinism) spread to France where its most influential exponent was Jeanne-Marie Bouvier de la Motte, known as Madame Guyon (1648–1717), a wealthy widow who promoted it among the French aristocracy, including Louis XIV's consort Madame de Maintenon and Archbishop Fénélon, among other things tutor to the king's grandson. Molinos was condemned by Pope Innocent XI in 1687; Madame Guyon was condemned by the church and twice imprisoned; and Fénélon was deposed.

That an excessive form of Quietism could be pernicious is evident; however, against a wider background the resemblances between the controversy over it and the controversy from Paul onwards over the relationship of faith to works and justification by faith alone is all too evident. So at the very least Quietism is a term not to be used lightly as a form of denigration.

Justification

During the twentieth century, the term Quietism came to be used in connection with ethical and political matters, of those who remained inactive in situations like that of Nazi Germany for theological reasons.

In seventeenth-century Spain, Ignatius Loyola (1491–1556), once a soldier and then wounded, underwent a series of profound spiritual experiences, and eventually founded the Society of Jesus in 1540. He wrote the *Spiritual Exercises*, a form of teaching that was based on a series of meditations to be used over a period of weeks, and months. The Jesuits, as they are known, have rediscovered the power and value of this method of meditation for members of the church, and Ignatian spirituality has become a real source of renewal for those beyond the monastic community.

The Orthodox Church has taught mystical theology

Orthodox churches

ESOTERIC SPIRITUALITIES

A number of types of spirituality stand on the very edge of Christianity and have been regarded as heretical or highly suspect. Here are some groups associated with them.

Alumbrados: Also known by the Latin name *Illuminati*; both mean 'enlightened'. These were mystics in sixteenth-century Spain who are supposed to have claimed that when the soul had reached a certain degree of perfection, it enjoyed the vision of God and could communicate directly with the Holy Spirit. No outward observances were needed by those who were thus 'enlightened'. They were persecuted and because some of the information about them comes from their opponents, which included the Inquisition, it may be distorted. Some were certainly saintly people and were canonized.

Rosicrucians: The name of seventeenth-century secret societies similar to the Freemasons who venerated the rose and the cross as symbols of resurrection and redemption. Their origin is obscure; they are first mentioned in a work entitled *Fama Fraternitatis* (Account of the Brotherhood), which describes the journeys of one Christian Rosenkreutz, supposed to have been born in 1378 and to have died in 1484; he allegedly travelled to the East and brought back secret wisdom which he passed on to disciples. Theophrast Bombast von Hohenheim (1493–1521), better known as Paracelsus, a Swiss physician and alchemist, is also associated with Rosicrucianism.

Theosophists: Theosophy (Greek *theosophia*, wisdom about divine things) is a word that occurs in Greek magical papyri and was used in the seventeenth century to describe the spirituality of figures like Jakob Boehme (1575–1624). Since the nineteenth century the term has been associated with the Theosophical Society, founded in New York in 1875 by Helena Blavatsky, a Russian woman who had spent many years investigating the occult in Europe, and Colonel Henry Steel Olcott, an American lawyer. The society set out to investigate unexplored dimensions of nature and of human powers. Among other things it claimed that there is a brotherhood of Great Masters or Adepts who have perfected themselves. Since it was much inspired by Indian thought, Madame Blavatsky and Colonel Olcott established a headquarters in India. The movement proved influential within Buddhism and Hinduism and in the West influenced a series of new religious movements.

Anthroposophists: Anthroposophy is a philosophy based on the premise that the human mind can of its own power contact the spiritual world. It was developed by Rudolf Steiner (1861–1925), an Austrian Catholic scientist and editor who for a time was a Theosophist, but in 1913 founded the Anthroposophical Society, with headquarters in Switzerland, near Basle. He aimed to develop faculties inherent in ordinary people so as to put them in touch with the spiritual world. Christ plays a part in his system, but as a 'sun being' incarnate at the turning-point of human spiritual evolution.

Antoine Favre and Jacob Needleman (eds), *Modern Esoteric Spirituality*, London: SCM Press and New York: Crossroad 1992

Trinity

largely through its liturgy, but also in its visionary understanding of the nature of God as Trinity. The unity of its theology and its spirituality is one of the greatest gifts of Orthodoxy. Theology, for the Orthodox, is prayer. The writings of the *Philokalia* (love of what is beautiful) are anthologies dealing with Hesychasm (a form of inner mystical prayer) and the Jesus Prayer. This prayer involves the internalizing of the short phrase 'Jesus Christ, Son of God, have mercy on me a sinner' until such time as it becomes part of one's inner being.

p. 821

The Reformed or Protestant tradition of spirituality, of which the Anglican Church would be a part, had its roots in dissent from the Roman Catholic Church and in a strong commitment to scripture. The seventeenth-century Caroline Divines, George Herbert (1593–1633), John Donne (1571/2–1631), Bishop Jeremy Taylor (1613–67) and Bishop Lancelot Andrewes (1555–1626), among others, rooted their spirituality in scripture and in the traditions of the church. Their writings were of a high literary quality. The King James Bible of 1611 is a version of the Bible that shows the spiritual nature of language at its best. Another jewel of the Protestant tradition is *The Pilgrim's Progress* (1678) by John Bunyan. Also within this tradition are the writings of Richard Baxter (1615–91), and the hymns of Isaac Watts (1674–1748) and Charles Wesley (1707–88). The Catholic revival within the Church of England gave rise to a restoration of a concern for prayer and the sacraments, a renewal of the monastic life, and through the influence of Edward Bouverie Pusey (1800–82), John Henry Newman (1801–90) and John Keble (1792–1866), a renewed interest in the writings of the early church.

Contemporary spiritualities. In the late twentieth century the popularity of Celtic spirituality and creation spirituality can perhaps be accounted for by the strains and stresses of contemporary suburban and city living. Both forms of spirituality breathe the fresh air of the wilder parts of the world. American-Indian wisdom and the Green movement encourage people not only to campaign for changes to the industrial society but also to seek refuge in nature, the sea, the sky, the forests and the mountains. Creation is understood to be an 'original blessing', and its destruction in the felling of the rain forests, through acid rain and pollution of all kinds has given both a political and spiritual drive to preserving the creation. It is also something of a reaction to the domination of a theology centred on Christ that leaves the natural world sidelined. The cosmic Christ, a Christ in many ways resonant of the teaching of John Scotus Eriugena, but popularized by Matthew Fox, is the product of a reaction against a simplistic Jesus cult. The need to embrace a wider spiritual culture with insights from a variety of religious faiths has become the dominant spiritual culture of the day. The place of Jesus in contemporary spirituality, apart from its obvious place in the faith of the church, may well reside in the unfashionable attention to the earliest texts of the Christian faith. In the restoration of the immediacy of the teaching and life of Christ, as in the literary scholarship of Austin Farrer (1904–68), in the writings of W. H. Vanstone (1923–99), Alan Ecclestone (1904–92) and J. C. Fenton (1921–), there are seeds of a highly creative partnership between scholarship and Christianity.

These simplified divisions between the spirituality of the churches do not mean that there has never been a sharing of traditions. On the contrary, over the last 100 years the ecumenical movement and the individual enthusiasms of many Christians have opened up ways into the traditions of others. So spirituality has become a matter of openness, *sobornost*, that untranslatable Russian word for unity in love and grace and reconciliation. There are now a great many 'spiritualities', as many as there are groups who respond to God in ways that reflect their own culture and speak to their own roots. Spirituality, in the end, is perhaps best defined as the way in which the inner reality of God is perceived, and then made real, in the human context.

DAVID SCOTT

📖 Dietrich Bonhoeffer, *Letters and Papers from Prison. The Enlarged Edition*, London: SCM Press and New York: Macmillan 1971; Gordon Mursell, *The Story of Christian Spirituality*, Oxford: Lion Publishing and Minneapolis: Augsburg Fortress 2001; A. M. Ramsey, *The Resurrection of Christ*, London: Geoffrey Bles 1945 and Philadelphia: Westminster Press 1946; Gordon Wakefield, *A Dictionary of Christian Spirituality*, London: SCM Press 1983 (US title *The Westminster Dictionary of Christian Spirituality*, Philadelphia: Westminster Press 1983); H. A. Williams, *True Resurrection*, London: Mitchell Beazley and New York: Holt Rinehart & Winston 1972

Stained glass

Stained-glass windows act, in the United Kingdom at least, as a shorthand for churches, whether in calendar illustrations or newspaper cartoons. This perception is deeply founded, even though, like organs, stained glass is not confined to churches, being found also in schools, town halls and even houses of various dates and sizes.

The use of coloured glass in church windows seems to have become established by late Roman times and it developed into such a desirable feature that, when in the seventh century Benedict Biscop wanted to build churches of the highest quality and latest fashion in his native Northumbria, he brought not just skilled masons but also stained glass makers with him from continental Europe. Excavations at his church at Jarrow have uncovered evidence of their work.

These early windows were decorative rather than figurative, set into wooden or plaster frames, not dissimilar from contemporary mosaic panels. During the succeeding centuries, a technique developed of joining the pieces of glass with lead, thus permitting much larger and more coherent designs. By the High Middle Ages, glaziers had developed both their practical expertise and their artistic skill to the extent that they could create both monumental figures which could make their effect even from the highest windows of a great church's clerestory and also small jewel-like compositions telling the life of Christ and his saints with elegance and economy. The colours are integral to the glass itself, and their rich blues and reds would have blended with the wall paintings and polychrome statuary which would have covered the rest of the interior, but the modelling of features and drapery were painted on to the glass. Chartres cathedral is perhaps the most perfect surviving witness to the artistic power and technical brilliance of the glass of this period.

Ecumenical movement ◀

Later in the Middle Ages, particularly in England, taste turned away from this rich palette towards paler glass, often washed with yellow stain, which was more suitable for the large windows of many lights typical of the Perpendicular style now to be found in churches great and small. The laity as well as the clergy were involved as patrons, often using heraldry and donor figures to link themselves with the sacred scenes.

Patronage

The Reformation virtually destroyed the development of this flourishing craft and in time led to the removal of much existing glass, sometimes in order to censor scenes or figures that were deemed superstitious, such as God the Father wearing a papal triple crown, but also in order to

Reformation

allow more light into the buildings, much more important once the congregation was expected to follow the services from their books. Protestantism created a conscious preference for the clear light of the Reformed gospel over the murk and mystery of traditional stained glass. However, pride in family descent and thus in heraldry continued, and by the early seventeenth century Flemish immigrants reintroduced figurative glass of those saints and holy stories guaranteed by scripture, not created by legend.

Protestantism

All over Europe, the century-old techniques of stained glass were being abandoned and replaced by windows where the designs were enamelled or even simply painted on to clear glass, thus allowing a much closer relationship with easel paintings. Nineteenth-century criticism denounced such work as false to the true principles of stained glass and thus unworthy of study or even preservation, but an example like Sir Joshua Reynolds' west window at New College chapel in Oxford shows the delicacy of which the style was capable.

In the nineteenth century, the medieval techniques were revived and adapted for mass production, thus creating an industry that could satisfy the extraordinary demand for stained glass to furnish churches of every size or shape, whether newly built or ancient. The conventions of family commemoration that had prompted stone tablets in previous generations were diverted towards memorial windows instead, as more useful and more demonstrably Christian, without the pagan imagery of much funerary art. Thanks to Victorian technology, artificial illumination by gas or oil lights was now available cheaply, so the loss of clear glass, and so of natural light, did not matter.

This insistence on stained glass affected churches of every denomination, even those such as the Church of Scotland that had hitherto distrusted these adornments as frivolous or even superstitious. The major firms achieved much work of quality but the sheer volume of demand meant that there were also many examples of routine design and feeble draughtsmanship. Demand continued at a high level into the twentieth century, not least to give expression to the grief caused by the world wars, but different techniques were introduced, for instance using thick slabs of glass. In more recent times, modernism in art and architecture has brought yet further changes, both in technique, to suit concrete construction, and in style, with abstract designs in complete contrast to traditional iconography. The vivid glass installed in the 1960s cathedral in Coventry set a seal of official approval on these innovations.

Church of Scotland

The Millennium commemorations in 2000 stimulated hundreds of stained glass projects all over Britain, thus proving how widely people still consider the installation of stained glass in a church an appropriate public memorial, even if the quality was disappointing. It is striking that an art form so ancient and so laden with history can still inspire both artists and patrons in the twenty-first century.

This enduring delight in stained glass is not confined to Britain or even Europe. Twentieth-century glass in the USA has been every bit as inventive and innovative, and both Japan and the Middle East have seen a great interest in the medium, though of course in secular rather than religious contexts. In France, despite the separation of church and state, there have been major schemes involving the installation of contemporary glass in ancient churches, and in Germany the impetus arising from post-war rebuilding has not slackened; Johannes Schreiter's designs in the Holy Spirit Church in Heidelberg are a particular fine example of imaginative and innovative modern work.

THOMAS COCKE

📖 John Harries, *Discovering Stained Glass*, Princes Risborough: Shire Publications 1980; Lawrence Lee, George Seddon and Francis Stephens, *Stained Glass*, London: Mitchell Beazley 1976

STORY

Bible, Biblical criticism, History, Jesus, Literature, Tradition

Christianity is full of stories. It has a story book as its Bible, and all through its history Christians have told stories about martyrs and saints, popes and bishops, miracles and healings, conversions and visions.

Generations of people have summed up their experiences, convictions, idealism, faith and views of life in these stories. The Hebrew Bible, which was written by Jews and which Christians took over and used as their own, tells a story that begins with the creation of the world and the first human beings. It tells of the generations of their children and how they were divided into different peoples spread all over the world. Then one man, Abraham, is chosen to fulfil God's purpose. Out of Abraham comes the people Israel, the ups and downs of whose story continue down to the birth of Jesus and the beginnings of the movement that he founded. Along the way we hear about Eve persuading Adam to eat an attractive fruit, with enormous consequences (Genesis 3); Cain killing Abel (Genesis 4); Noah escaping the flood with an ark full of animals (Genesis 6–8); Abraham being prepared to kill his own son as a sacrifice (Genesis 22); Jacob cheating Esau of his birthright in exchange for a bowl of stew (Genesis 27); Joseph with his multi-coloured coat being sold into slavery by his brother and rising to become right-hand man to the Pharaoh of Egypt (Genesis 37–50); Moses leading the Israelites out of Egypt by a series of miracles including a parting of the sea (Exodus 2–15); Joshua demolishing the walls of Jericho with a mighty trumpet blast (Joshua 6); Samson the strong man being seduced by Delilah and losing his hair and his strength (Judges 14–16); David the shepherd boy killing the Philistine giant Goliath, rising to be king of Israel, but seducing Bathsheba and losing his dear son Absalom, whose long hair gets caught in the trees, pulling him off his horse to his death (1 Samuel 17–2 Samuel 18); the fabulous King Solomon with his host of wives and his unrivalled wisdom, visited in all his splendour by the Queen of Sheba (1 Kings 4–10); Elijah calling down rain and defeating the prophets of Baal (1 Kings 18); the framing of Naboth the Jezreelite by King Ahab and Queen Jezebel so that they can seize his vineyard, their denunciation by Elijah, and their fate (1 Kings 21) ... The classic stories are not only read over and over again in their original form but have become novels, oratorios, operas and films attracting audiences of millions.

p. 131

Jesus was one of the world's great story-tellers; his teaching was in parables, which vividly depict the life of the countryside through which he travelled and the society in which he lived. His own life, itself narrated in the vivid stories of his birth (Matthew 1–2; Luke 1–2) to the accounts of his suffering, execution and resurrection (Matthew 26–8; Mark 14–16; Luke 22–4; John 18–21), is told and retold year after year as Christians celebrate the cycle from Christmas to Easter; a 1965 film of the life of Jesus could not think of a better title than *The Greatest Story Ever Told*.

p. 658

Calendar

In the New Testament what happened to Jesus, his message and its fatal consequences, is presented as a continuation of the Jewish story in the Hebrew Bible, which from then on was understood as the Old Testament. Jesus' story is continued in the adventures of Peter and Paul in the Acts of the Apostles; thereafter this story continues in the stories of many narrators, as Christians spread across the globe and explore every aspect of their faith. Not only do Christians tell stories about the heroes of the faith, men and women; they too describe their faith in stories,

Literature

from John Bunyan's *Pilgrim's Progress* to C. S. Lewis's Narnia chronicles, which enliven the imagination and stir the spirit.

In all these stories experience is solidified and, as a store of such experience, stories, and above all the biblical stories, have come to be regarded as a source of inspiration. Even the best stories remain dead things unless they are told or read, and so the life of Christians has been characterized by storytelling: in teaching, in worship and in conversation when they have been gathered together. The Bible, of course, has a special place; however, it is not the reference to past experiences which makes the Jewish and Christian stories in the Bible unique or meaningful, but the dynamic processes in history in which these have been performed over and over again. This performance opens up the understanding and the senses; the utterances in the text do something with present-day hearers and readers, as they did with past hearers and readers: they perform an act that produces an event or an experience, a belief or emotion. It is this dynamic openness of the biblical stories which makes them so powerful and attractive, the power to become events in our daily lives.

The primary goal of hearing and reading stories in Christianity is not reconstruction of the past but a recognition of the presence of the past. For example, when we hear in the exodus story about God's liberation of Hebrew slaves from Egypt, we are invited to recognize the uniqueness of this God. Knowing that in the ancient Near East deities were closely related to kings and were described as defending these powerful men's positions, we discover how the God of Israel is sometimes described in similar terms and at other times is viewed from a completely different perspective. This is when the God of Israel is described in the book of Exodus as the one who cares for powerless people, as the one who pays attention to the poor and to the lowest social class at the time, the slaves. These people, who are generally not considered to be human and belong to a class in between animals and human beings, are liberated by Israel's God. Thus the exodus story tempts one to share its view, to adhere to this most powerful of all gods who cares for the most powerless of people. It asks for an adequate dynamic response: a God whose identity consists of this unique devotion to the powerless asks readers to commit themselves to him.

Story and history

A story is not the same as a history and a story does not present a historical account. Nevertheless a story originates in a certain historical background and functions against it, and may refer to historical persons or events. History, on the other hand, is often misunderstood to mean 'the past', although a more correct definition is 'a narrative that presents a past'. That is to say, history is not what happened; it is what a narrator reports to have happened. For example, a history can be entirely false. Fascist governments frequently publish histories that falsify the past in order to put the government in a positive light. There are many varieties of history because there are many ways of narrating a past and various reasons for doing so. True history is therefore a matter of degree, and the truth-value of a history lies not in its facts but in its treatment of the facts. All of this is to say that history is always an interpretation; it is the past as narrated, and the narration will confirm to the interpretational assumptions of the narrator. There is no such thing as an objective or unbiased history, since interpretation is the imposition of biases on the topic under scrutiny. Therefore it is important to be aware of precisely which kind of biases are operating in a given history. Some biases are more reasonable than others. As a result, some histories are more reasonable than others.

Historiography

Having said this, the question is what the difference is between history and story. History is generally written by a historian who transforms facts and events in the past into an overall picture, usually by imposing a sequential line on them. An explanation is given by means of a process of deduction in which the causes and effects are established. In other words, the sequence in time is presented as a logical order. By contrast, a story is not necessarily arranged logically. A temporal linear sequence is often there and it functions within a created spatial realm. The author sometimes takes up a omniscient position, but very often hands over his words and perspectives to various characters and lets them speak, see and think; readers are invited to read through the eyes of these characters, whereas in history-writing this is seldom the case. In stories, even imaginary worlds may have been created. Thus, a great number of different types of history and story exist which can be viewed as a continuum or continuous line. At one extreme of this line one can find the academic form of history-writing, in which the sources used for the narration are provided (in notes) together with the narrated past (in the text); the sources are verifiable and originate from as many different angles as possible, so that the information in the historical narration may be verified or falsified. At the other extreme is the fantasy story, in which an imaginary world is created with only minor perpendicular lines to the real world in past or present, if there are any at all. However, most stories take up a position in between both extremes.

It turns out that biblical stories prove to be very dissimilar. In the Hebrew Bible more verifiable historical texts can be found alongside complete fantasies. The latter include the apocalyptic texts in the book of Daniel or the legendary 'didactic' tales like Jonah in the whale. Examples of the former are the books of Chronicles, Ezra and Nehemiah, although even these show a strong interpretative bias. Compare, for example, the books of Samuel and Kings with the books of Chronicles, and the differences are obvious: in the older books, like 1 and 2 Samuel, King David is described as a normal human being with a number of shortcomings; in the later books of Chronicles he is idealized as the perfect king. All these so-called 'historical books' in the Hebrew Bible are narrations of the past. However, because we have virtually no ancient Near Eastern sources that mention the kings of Israel and Judah, it is not possible to confirm the historical reliability of the biblical stories. And even if we did have Egyptian, Assyrian, Babylonian or Persian sources, these, too, would be interpretations, narrations of the past written from their own perspectives and with their own aims. No history is unbiassed. To check biblical stories against ancient Near Eastern texts thus remains a difficult task.

Apocalyptic

p. 137

Another feature of the biblical stories, and of the Christian stories narrated in later times, is the way in which they are firmly tied to male perspectives. Even in the Ten Commandments embedded in the story of Israel's escape from Egypt, which are often declared to be of a 'universal' and therefore unbiased character, the perspective is male. They are written for and by men. They are intended to be read by the head of the household, as can be deduced from the last commandment, in which we can read about the man's desire for his neighbour's wife. Surely it isn't addressed to the woman in this household? The idea that she might desire her neighbour's husband is unthinkable. History and story alike ask for a critical attitude in us readers: we can be inspired, seduced or carried along, but we do not have to share the text's bias and vantage point.

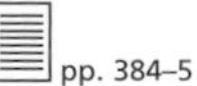
pp. 384–5

Gospels: story and history

The need to determine the historical reliability of a story is felt particularly strongly when personal beliefs and the faith of a community of believers are involved, and it seems to be crucial to establish firmly the relationship between what is told and what really happened. For Christians at least, this is true with regard to the Gospels in the New Testament. And the question arises whether Jesus actually lived, spoke and acted in the way narrated in the four Gospels (the one extreme),

ISRAEL AND ITS STORY

The story

Like Jesus, the first Christians were Jews and used the Jewish Bible, which later became their Old Testament. With the Jewish Bible they took over the story of Israel and made it their own. (The books of the Bible in which the story is told are given in brackets.)

The story begins with the creation of the world by God, its corruption by sin, a devastating flood and a new beginning, which once again goes wrong as humankind builds a tower to reach heaven and God confuses their languages (Genesis 1–11).

Against this background Abraham appears, and is summoned by God to go out in faith from Mesopotamia to seek a new, promised land. Abraham sets out and settles in Canaan; he has a son, Isaac, who in turn has two sons, Jacob and Esau. Jacob, though the younger, is the favourite, and receives the blessing. He is also given the name Israel. He has twelve sons, the twelve tribes of Israel. Joseph, the second youngest, is sold as a slave to Egypt by his brothers out of jealousy. But disaster turns to great success and Joseph becomes right-hand man to the Pharaoh. When famine strikes in Canaan, Egypt prospers because of his foresightedness, and his brothers come for help. Eventually there is a reconciliation (Genesis 12–30).

Joseph has prospered in Egypt, but rulers change, and under a new Pharaoh the Israelites are conscripted for slave labour. However, a leader emerges among them, Moses, who calls down plagues on the Egyptians including the slaughter of all their firstborn. The Israelites celebrate a feast, Passover, on this night, because the angel of death passes over them, and escape through the Red Sea, which miraculously opens (Exodus 1–15). They spend 40 years wandering through the wilderness, during which Moses receives God's Law on Mount Sinai; they cannot enter the promised land directly because of their sin, and Moses can never enter (Exodus 16–end; Leviticus; Numbers; Deuteronomy).

On Moses' death, Joshua leads the Israelites into the promised land, which they occupy with fire and sword; territory is allotted to all the tribes (Joshua). After a period of tribal government, in which the main figures are judges (Judges), the tribes want a king. The first king, Saul, is a tragic figure, who dies in battle; however, after him David and Solomon create a great kingdom, which takes in all Israel (1 and 2 Samuel).

Because of internal tensions, the kingdom does not last and splits into two: Israel in the north, which comprises ten of the tribes, and Judah in the south, which comprises the other two. From now on 'Israel' is used to denote only the northern kingdom. Kings come and go, some good, some bad, but the pattern is one of decline. The kings and their people are sinful, and prophets denounce their sins and threaten judgement. This comes about. First Israel is conquered by the Assyrians: its inhabitants are deported and replaced with people from various parts of Mesopotamia. The ten tribes disappear for ever. Then Judah is conquered by the Babylonians; it fares slightly better: the ruling classes are deported to Babylon; the remainder live out a wretched existence in their tiny state (1 and 2 Kings).

The exile lasts for almost 70 years; then those who have been deported are allowed by the Persians to return and build their temple (Haggai and Zechariah). However, they are no longer a state, but a religious community within an imperial province (Ezra and Nehemiah). This period sees great changes to the Israelite way of life, so much so that the term used from now on is no longer Israelites but Jews. The books which tell the story are brought together and the Law is re-established (Genesis–Deuteronomy, known as the Torah or the Pentateuch). Now that the judgement which the prophets proclaimed has come about and has been endured, there is a feeling that a new beginning is possible, that there can be a new people under God.

But although there is a brief period when pious Jews revolt against attempts to impose Greek customs on them and are so successful that for a while they set up a kingdom (1 and 2 Maccabees), the Jews live in occupied territory under foreign rulers, and after a final revolt against the Romans they are driven from their land.

Israel

For Jews, the end of the story of Israel, or rather its new beginning, lies in the creation of the State of Israel in 1946, when for the first time they have a land of their own and a state of their own.

For Christians, the story takes a rather different turn. Jesus seems to have envisaged the restoration of Israel: he appoints twelve disciples, and promises them that they will sit on thrones judging the twelve tribes of Israel. But this more literal expectation fades, and instead, when Christians take over the story, they see it all as leading up to Christ. Above all it is interpreted by means of typology, the main characters and events of the story no longer existing in their own right, but as prefigurements of Jesus and the church. Joshua in Greek is 'Jesus'; the miraculous deliverance from Egypt figures in Easter imagery of death and resurrection, particularly in Easter hymns and prayers; Jesus, said to be descended from David, is 'great David's greater son', and so on. Above all Christians come to believe that they are the 'true Israel' (not the 'new Israel', a term which never appears in the New Testament). And perniciously, they infer from this that God has rejected his former people, the Jews.

p. 1197

The story and history

What the Hebrew Bible tells is a story, not a history in the modern sense; scholars today setting out to write a history of Israel would produce strikingly different versions, indeed some would argue that it was impossible to write a history of Israel in the modern sense at all. But they have been able to produce this alternative version only since the archaeological discoveries of the last two centuries gave them evidence. Down through the history of the Christian church it has been the biblical story which has shaped people's minds. The images derived from it, particularly those of judgement and liberation, have been particularly influential. However, it should never be forgotten that in the political realm another Israel exists, and cannot be ignored.

or whether these are merely stories (the other extreme). It can be deduced from the explanation of the characteristics of history and story given above that the first extreme, the existence of pure, 'objective' history, history as something that happened and not as something that is told, can be and should be excluded. A weaker option, that in the New Testament a verifiable history is presented, should also be questioned, because we have no reliable historical data about Jesus from a non-Christian source and therefore verification or falsification of the New Testament texts is impossible. The other extreme can be excluded as well. The flavour of the world as evoked in the Gospels, the words used and the references made, indicate that these texts originated in and functioned against the background of the first century CE. But does this mean that what is said to have happened actually did happen the way it is told? In order to answer this question we should leave our receivers' point of view and look at the material from the Gospel writers' point of view.

Suppose you are confronted with an impressive human being. This person shows you who God really is and what God might mean to you. He makes a tremendous impression which changes your life completely. How do you find the words to tell other people? How will you convince them of the uniqueness of this person, that he is the one announced by the prophets, the saviour of humankind, and the son of God? Jesus' disciples were confronted with these and other problems. Mark was the first to answer the question: he wrote a Gospel, i.e. a mixed form of story-telling, history and biography writing. He wanted to communicate the message that Jesus of Nazareth is the Christ and that this breaking 'good news' (Greek *euangelion*) could change his readers' lives. In order to convince his readers, Mark made a selection of some events in Jesus' life, while neglecting others. He described some of Jesus' words and deeds as presented by and handed down in the tradition, and built them into a sequential series of actions. He created a time-frame and a spatial realm in which the characters could move around. In short, he constructed a story-world and a story-line. Mark also gave shape to the characters and made them speak. He chose the perspectives from which the material was presented. He omitted some things and left others open, building up ambiguities and complexities. His story-line started with Jesus' baptism by John the Baptist in the river Jordan, then continued with the miracle stories alternated with Jesus' speeches. Mark arranged these words and actions in a meaningful order. For example, before and after the miracle stories about Jesus' healing of blind men Mark put speeches in which Jesus tried to make clear that he wanted to open the eyes of his disciples so that they would understand who he, Jesus, really was. Thus the words clarified the actions, and the actions the words. After the series of miracle stories and speeches Mark came to his main part, the narrative about Jesus' suffering and death on the cross. And he wanted to demonstrate that this is not the end: the empty tomb with an angel or divine messenger told the women in the graveyard and the readers of Mark's book what to do, namely to follow this person, Jesus Christ, and to take this Gospel as a new starting point in their lives.

p. 848

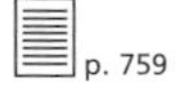
p. 759

p. 668

Later on Matthew and Luke wrote their Gospels, inspired by Mark's. They followed the story-line of Mark's Gospel, but extended it, supplied their own perspectives and accents, and added their own interpretations. Still later a fourth, more philosophical Gospel was written by John. Thus we have four Gospels presenting Jesus in the same mixture of biography and story. Their writers, Mark, Matthew, Luke and John, are comparable with portrait painters who have painted a picture of one and the same person, say, Queen Elizabeth I. Each portrait painter has used his own technique and his own style and depicted her in his own way, thus providing a unique view of this queen. We spectators who live in the twenty-first century look at these pictures and create our image of her. Had these been pictures of Queen Elizabeth II, we would have been able to compare the four pictures with a real-life image of her, presumably an image constituted by a mixture of television images and pictures in newspapers. But we have no access to Queen Elizabeth I other than through paintings. We would be very surprised indeed if we discovered that she had dark hair cut in a punk style, and not long ginger hair as in her portraits. We consider this hair to be a fact, shared as it is by all extant paintings of her. We cannot reach beyond these pictures to compare her with the way she really was. That is all we have, together with the texts about her.

We have four portraits of Jesus, painted by writers who narrated his life. In each narrative the Gospel writer has presented his own view of Jesus in his own style, with his own selections and accents. We do not know what Jesus looked like, nor do we know what he thought of himself or what his self-image was. All we know of Jesus is through these Gospels and other writings in the New Testament. Reaching back behind the text to the facts of real life is impossible: we cannot touch Jesus in the flesh, we cannot scratch things away and say 'this is the real Jesus', the person who lived then and there. Because the four Gospels, these stories laden with a message, are the only material we have, we should devote all our attention to them. Only in this way can we get an idea of who this Jesus was and what his message was.

Jesus of history

In the second half of the twentieth century there was a tendency in biblical studies and theology to make a distinction between the historical and the kerygmatic Jesus, i.e. between the Jesus who lived in real life and the message of Jesus, the way he is proclaimed. Most people preferred the former. It was also called 'demythologizing', scratching away the myth or mythical and narrative aspects. However, the very structure of the gospels, i.e. as biographical stories or narrative history writing, makes it impossible to suggest that we can scratch away the paint, the language, the literary form, the perspective, the selection, the choice of words, and still have anything left. Take a Van Gogh painting, scratch away the colours, the paint, the canvas, and you are left with an empty frame. Jesus' picture is to be found only in the narration; only in the performance, the reading and living by readers later in history, can he be heard. Demythologizing is doomed to fail, and its fallacy should be faced. Jesus' life is told and lived in story form. A story is not the same as life, it is not life. Life itself can only be lived, and a story's meaning is there only in the telling. And a religious story is there only in being told and lived out.

Story and canon

Canon

The cultural and historical significance of the great stories in the Bible results from the fact that the Christian Bible functions as a canon, i.e., a collection of texts, deeply studied, the forms, values and norms of which are thought important. The canonical status of these texts leads to an ongoing process of reinterpretation and actualization, during which the biblical stories are read selectively and combined with reservoirs of images, ideas and insights in various historical periods. Because the Bible is an authoritative document, the stories have been an inspiration in church history and art history, a legacy in culture and doctrine. However, the plurality of perspectives, the multiplicity of meanings and the dynamic interaction between text and reader which are now acknowledged to be the main characteristics of the biblical texts raise the question how we can handle these canonical and authoritative claims.

On the one hand, canonicity has turned out to be a piece of great historical good fortune. Most of the texts which were not canonized in the first centuries have disappeared; they were no longer copied and therefore were bound to disappear and be blotted out of the collective memory, whereas canonized texts have survived to the present day after two millennia of transmission. This having been said, the normativity and authority of the canon has also proved to have had some negative consequences. Down history to the present day, all over the world, inside and outside

DEMYTHOLOGIZING

At one time the words 'myth' and 'mythical' were taken to mean a purely fictitious or imaginary narrative, event or person. The terms could even be used as a synonym for 'falsehood' and 'false', as in the 'myth' of the superiority of a particular race. In the debate at the beginning of the twentieth century over whether Jesus ever existed, the alternative could be presented in terms of 'myth or history?'. This disparaging use of the term goes right back to the New Testament, where Timothy is told to have nothing to do with godless and silly myths (1 Timothy 4.7).

Such negative connotations of the word myth still persist, but myths are now taken much more seriously by scholars. Myths as told in fables, fairy tales, sagas and epics seem to have existed in every society and are an important part of the way in which peoples understand themselves and the world in which they live.

How far myth in this sense plays a role in Christianity has also been a topic of much discussion. The situation is complicated by the vagueness of the concept of myth: how, for example, do narratives bordering on myth or alluding to myths differ from legend bordering on history and history bordering on legend? To call, say, the accounts of the creation in Genesis myths is not particularly helpful; the term is better used of other fragments of creation stories like Isaiah 51.9 ('Did you not cut Rahab in pieces and pierce the dragon') or Psalm 74.14 ('You crushed the heads of Leviathan, and gave him as food for the creatures of the wilderness').

Nevertheless since the middle of the twentieth century the term 'demythologization' has often appeared in accounts of attempts to reinterpret the Bible for the modern world. It owes its name to the German New Testament scholar Rudolf Bultmann, concerned that the Bible should make sense to 'modern' men and women. For him, the New Testament view of the world as a three-storied structure with the earth in the centre, the heaven above and the underworld beneath, with angels and demons, miracles and supernatural forces, was mythological, and incredible to 'modern man' because it was obsolete. It could not be accepted as true as it stands and had to be reinterpreted. It is impossible, Bultmann said in a famous remark, 'to use electric light and the wireless and to avail ourselves of modern medical and surgical discoveries, and at the same time to believe in the New Testament world of demons and spirits'.

Bultmann thought it illegitimate to solve the problem by choosing to retain some features of the New Testament and to drop others; rather, the whole of the New Testament had to be reinterpreted. To do this he chose the means of existentialist philosophy, particularly that of Martin Heidegger: the New Testament is about a transition from 'inauthentic' to 'authentic' life, brought about by a decision made in an act of faith in Jesus Christ. The central message of the New Testament can be interpreted in these terms and when it is, it makes sense for the modern world.

Bultmann's proposal immediately gave rise to a lively debate in continental Europe, Britain and America. It was ultimately found wanting, and with the decline of interest in existentialism it disappeared from the scene. However, it represents a fascinating attempt to make a set of ancient writings directly comprehensible in a very different culture, and therefore has rightly not been forgotten.

Rudolf Bultmann, 'The New Testament and Mythology' in H. W. Bartsch (ed), *Kerygma and Myth*, London: SPCK 1953 and New York: Harper Torchbooks 1961; John Macquarrie, *The Scope of Demythologizing*, London: SCM Press and New York: Harper & Row 1960

church communities, many people have regarded the biblical stories as the normative 'Word of God' – which very often means that they have been applied almost literally as moral guidance in every time and place. This has extended to their patriarchal culture, gender stereotyping and social stratification. Slavery and apartheid, the denial of an autonomous role for women and many other attitudes were, and sometimes still are, defended with an appeal to the Bible as the 'Word of God'. Another consequence of this is the use of the biblical stories in a one-sided model, that is, taking only their spiritual or theological dimension into account. With a one-sided approach to these stories, biblical truths or specifically selected verses are often absolutized and treated as casuistic laws and principles, or even worse, as direct imperatives from God, applicable in the same way at all times and in all circumstances. Such an approach is not only unsatisfactory; it is ethically irresponsible, because it does not take the concrete circumstances of the texts and of the present readers seriously. A sensitivity to the linguistic, literary, socio-historical and cultural aspects of these documents is often totally absent. In this way the dynamic and complex, multi-faceted nature of biblical stories is either ignored or played down, and critical discussion is totally absent.

Considering these two sides of canonicity forces us to reflect on our own responsibility in reading the biblical stories and other stories which function in Christian tradition.

The relationship between canon, history and story is difficult to trace. However, the main question it raises is clear: what is the relation between past and present, what is its cultural and religious legacy for us? If we recognize that, we shall not concentrate on the historical aspects of the religious story for its own sake, nor on the authority of the canon in itself, but try to understand where our inspirations and convictions come from. We can realize how what we assume simply to be there in contemporary culture is the product of an ongoing transformation. The biblical and other religious stories are cultural objects which are not only narratives themselves but exist in historical time. They are not linear, but make bends and turns; they zoom in and out on specific details. And the place where we are standing now could be seen to be on the same prolonged historical line, zooming in on certain questions, doubts or commitments, viewed from our contemporaneous points of view. As such, these religious stories can help us to become aware of our own choices and selections, and of our own historically conditioned perspectives.

Story and the ethics of reading

Religious stories exist in being told and lived out: their function in our world is not only to interpret the world and our position in it, but also to change it. However, we will change too little if we do not at the same time change our understanding of what we mean when we so easily claim to interpret the world. The act of reading, therefore, can be regarded as an ethical choice, decision and responsibility. And the question arises: a responsibility to whom or to what? The answer: a responsibility to both the community and the world in which we live and to the nature of the material, i.e. the ancient stories.

The ethics of reading necessitates not only an ethics of responsibility, but also an ethics of accountability which holds the reader responsible for the consequences of reading the religious stories in Christianity. What has to be appropriated is the meaning of the text itself, conceived in a dynamic way as the direction of thought opened up by the text. In other words, what has to be appropriated is none other than the power of disclosing a world that constitutes the reference of the text. The genuine referential power of a text is the disclosure of a possible way of looking at things.

Narratives, the old stories, give form to experience in ways which tie the past to the present and anticipate the future. Or, narratives disclose an order which may already be there, but which comes to expression as we tell of it. Powerful religious stories mould people's identities and their sense of the world and reality. They create a basic orientation for those who are drawn into them. They help form commitments and convictions. They yield insight, and inspire; they can change people's way of looking at life and their modes of behaviour. This is the transformative potential of textual communication. In short, the communicative power of the story is its ability to disclose an alternative moral world, a new perspective on reality.

Communication

ELLEN VAN WOLDE

N. Frye, *The Great Code. The Bible and Literature,* New York: Harcourt Brace Jovanovich 1981; E. Mouton, *Reading a New Testament Document Ethically,* Atlanta: Society of Biblical Literature 2002; K. Noll, *Canaan and Israel in Antiquity: An Introduction*, Sheffield: Sheffield Academic Press 2001; P. Ricoeur, *Interpretation Theory. Discourse and the Surplus of Meaning,* Fort Worth: Texas Christian University 1976; Ellen van Wolde, *Stories of the Beginning. Genesis 1–11 and Other Creation Stories,* London: SCM Press 1996

Suffering

The season before Christmas, the feast of the Nativity, when Christians await the King, Jesus Christ, whom they believe was God become man, is also the time of darkness in the northern hemisphere, when the nights close in and the dark begins to trap us, and we are cold. The spring becomes unimaginable. But the darkness of winter also symbolizes other sorts of darkness for us: the darkness of physical pain, of despair, of mental illness, of grief.

I have been asked to write about suffering and the Christian belief in its redemption, the rising of light in the darkness, the coming of the Lord, because I have some personal experience of darkness of these kinds. I have a bone disease myself, which was eventually diagnosed when I was in my early thirties, and which, when it was unstable, led to a lot of spinal fracture and acute pain. I know quite a lot about fear, as a result – and I am not a brave woman. Secondly, and more importantly, we had a daughter who died when she was 22. She was born with a rare genetic illness, which was diagnosed when she was a year old, so I spent an enormous amount of time with her – over a year – in the wards of the big children's hospitals in London, far away from where we lived. There I watched lots of other parents and children in similar situations. In the end, after two kidney transplants, she died of neurological failure, which is very unpleasant. So, one way and another, I know a little about the dark, and about what help faith is, and what help it isn't, in the middle of suffering. And that phrase 'what help it isn't' is important: for we are only ever helped by the truth.

I remember an occasion when a pious friend came to see me in the middle of that long year on the ward of the magnificent children's hospital where our daughter was. Because it was so good, this hospital collected up, as a last resort, cases other hospitals had despaired of. Oddly, the British only get any approach to Third World mortality in the most sophisticated hospitals of this country, because they gather cases local hospitals can't deal with. So children were dying, in the ward I was on. The day my friend called, I had reached some kind of emotional rock-bottom, when I had tried to comfort an anguished tiny child (words are useless, only touch will do) and as I reached out to stroke his head, a nurse said hastily, 'Don't touch him, his skull might fracture.' And my friend said, enviously, 'Your faith must be such a comfort to you.'

Well, it wasn't. Belief in an omnipotent and all-loving Creator who is capable of producing results such as those I was observing produced for me at least as many problems as it solved. That experience led me to question, in a very fundamental way, whether Christianity had any valid application at all to this very real and painful world in which I found myself. For, you see, Christianity isn't an insurance policy. It doesn't mean that you, or your family, won't get cancer, that my bones won't break, that our daughter didn't go into neurological failure. Those people to whom it is an insurance policy, who think that it means that the feared thing won't happen, perhaps even that they should prosper and own the flocks and herds of Job, are in for trouble. They are thinking of magic, and then, when the magic doesn't work, when they meet disease, or poverty, or death, they think that they have perhaps lacked faith themselves, and that is why God has failed them too, as they see it.

Festivals and fasts ◄

But if Christianity has a meaning, it is a much deeper and more subtle one than 'as an insurance policy', or magic. As I thought about these things on those terrible wards, in that darkness, I thought also about the incarnation. Isaiah said of the suffering servant who was to come 'a bruised reed shall he not break'. Well, true – Jesus never broke those who came to him. He healed, accepted, forgave them. But he was broken himself, instead. The people of Israel, who were waiting for the Messiah, didn't expect this sort of Messiah. They wanted a triumphal leader; the 'promise of his glory' to them was regal glory, full of power. They wanted, as we all want, to be delivered from their enemies in the most obvious way possible. What they actually got was the birth of a baby, as vulnerable and helpless as all babies, but perhaps a little more so because his social background wasn't quite right for his own time: indeed, there was some considerable doubt about who his father was. For his mother, the waiting time of Advent, which was for her the preparation for the birth of her first child, must therefore have been more difficult, and sometimes dark, even than usual. No young woman looks forward to the birth of her first child only with eager anticipation. There is the fear of the unknown, as well as the knowledge of possible pain, and even, for very many centuries, the common reality of death in childbirth. This particular girl, who was Mary, Mother of God, depended even more than usual on the goodwill and acceptance of her new husband: for the penalty in Jewish law for pregnancy outside marriage was stoning to death. So when Mary replied to the angel, the messenger, 'Be it unto me according to thy word', she was accepting that risk. I don't think we always realize that. She must have been terrified.

Incarnation

Messiah

Mary

This fragile baby, born on the margins of society, in a country occupied by the Romans, then became a refugee along with his parents. And refugees, or asylum-seekers, then and now, have never been very welcome people. He grew up to associate with all sorts of peculiar people, marginal people, collaborators, lepers, women – and indeed died as common criminals did, tortured to death. It took some time for the disciples, and perhaps for his mother, to realize that this man, who knew pain and such distress, was also fully God, who had come to them

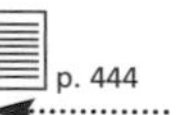
p. 444 ◄

and shared their dark, so fully that he, too, knew even despair. And because he knew despair and death, and there is nowhere he has not been, he brings us hope.

Theologians write that the crucifixion, God incarnate being tortured to death in the form of Jesus Christ, and the resurrection when, three days later, the Lord rose from death, are to be understood as one event. He was so glorious that his first words to a group of his followers, who had almost all run away or betrayed him, were not the words of a terribly injured, damaged man, but the affirming, healing greeting, 'Peace be with you.'

Resurrection

It is indeed a paradox, as Christianity is the religion of paradox. But if Jesus Christ had only died tortured to death, and not risen in another subtly different body, which yet still bore the marks of his pain, we would neither remember nor worship him. His followers would have grieved, some of them to their lives' end, but no religion would have been founded in his name. His death, and his rising, are the reverse and the obverse of one coin, one event.

Yet this unity has to be qualified for his followers. In our suffering, if it is bad enough, we lose hope. This means we have literally no hope of coming through. We are broken. We despair. It may be that we remember the words of Jesus, dying on the cross. He lost all comprehension of what was happening to him, despite his own earlier knowledge that he was to suffer, and die, and rise again.

Jesus himself in his pain on Good Friday lost the conception of Easter Day. That is part of the point of Good Friday. If everyone had been able to retain a cosy, reassuring memory that something else was supposed to happen afterwards, it wouldn't have been Good Friday. Nor would it have been redemptive. We may only have hope because Jesus lost it, and therefore totally shares our dark. There is nowhere we can go where he hasn't been, no abyss where he cannot be encountered at the bottom. On the cross, he, too, forgot that Good Friday and Easter Day were one event.

Hope

He also lost all knowledge of his relationship and, indeed, his identity, with God his Father. This knowledge seems to have been growing in him at least since he was twelve, and became so absorbed in 'being about my Father's business' that he got left behind in the temple in Jerusalem. On the cross, in his physical pain, he lost this experience of unity, which was the most fundamental thing in his life. This loss was to him the ultimate dereliction. All his life and his purpose became non-sense. He was mistaken. He was rootless, Fatherless, fallen into an abyss which was truly bottomless. And he cried, 'My God, my God, why hast thou forsaken me?' If those words reach us in our own dereliction, so may also a glimmer of hope reach us.

It is precisely and exactly because the Lord experienced this bottomless despair that we can worship him. There is nowhere he has not been before us. It is precisely because of his agony, the fringes of which may touch us, that we may have hope.

'Only a suffering God can help us,' the German theologian Dietrich Bonhoeffer wrote in 1944 from a prison cell from which later he was to go on to his execution for involvement in a plot to kill Hitler. Yet, if we can only worship a God who has suffered with us, we also could not worship a God who had not then risen and triumphed. Visionaries write occasionally of their glimpses of this Lord of Christianity, in his beauty, his glorified humanity and dynamism, his delight in his creatures, and his amusement. The evangelists wrote a good deal more in their account of his post-resurrection appearances, trying to convey the unconveyable, as they are. The image of the double-faced coin must stay with us. Yet it is inevitable that we constantly lose either the one comprehension, or the other, as we live through our confused and muddled lives.

Julian of Norwich, that very special saint, who lived through the most horrible waves of fourteenth-century plague, and who brimmed over with warmth and loving-kindness, was led to reflect on the tenderness and love of Christ for humankind. She called Christ our true mother, 'for', she said, 'a mother's caring is the closest, nearest and surest, (yet) our own mother bore us only unto pain and dying. But our true mother, Jesus, bears us into joy, and endless loving … A mother feeds her child with her milk, but our beloved mother Jesus feeds us with himself.'

It seemed to me on those children's wards that it was only because of the incarnation that there was any hope. If God had not made himself vulnerable and fragile too, and cared enough to come and share the pain of his world, I couldn't have worshipped him. The incarnation is telling us that God is very near us: it is telling us he comes to us, is touching us, just as he touched the leper in Mark – that there is no one who needs him whom he rejects. He isn't an insurance policy: he doesn't solve the mystery of pain and dark for us, or take it away. He chooses not to represent power. Instead, he shares our dark. He lives through it with us and, by so doing, he transforms it. The trust we have to have in him lies far deeper than belief in his power simply to remove the problem. It is trust that he will be present to us in the deepest waters, and the most acute pain, and in his will to transform these things.

Christmas is the feast of his coming, and the word 'coming' and the word 'presence' are the same in Greek, the language that the New Testament was written in. So his coming is also his being with us now. And his presence is light in the darkness, not taking it away, but transforming it. The Gospel of John sums it up for us: 'The light shineth in darkness and the darkness comprehended it not … And the Word was made flesh, and dwelt among us, and we beheld His glory, the glory as of the only-begotten of the Father, full of grace and truth' (1.5,14).

Here I have concentrated on fundamental malformation and genetic evil for which no human agency can be blamed, which I have been brought to observe. Some authors feel that man-made suffering, exemplified for us in the suffering of the Armenian massacres, and the horror of the Holocaust, and endlessly continued in Sierra Leone and the Congo, Kosovo and Chechnya, Israel and Palestine, Afghanistan and Iraq, are more incomprehensible than this sort of innate evil. They may be right, but I am not entitled to write of this sort of suffering at all, for I have not had to observe it at close quarters. Further, I am a historian, and humanly caused disaster, from Ghengis Khan to Belsen and beyond, is unfortunately familiar to any trained historian. To explore this issue further, you should turn to the article on Evil in the *Guide*, or read some of the books mentioned below.

MARGARET SPUFFORD, OBE, FBA

📖 Julia de Beausobre, *The Woman Who Could Not Die*, London: Chatto & Windus and New York: Viking 1938; Ladislaus Boros, *Pain and Providence*, New York: Seabury Press 1956 and London: Burns & Oates 1966; Harold S. Kushner, *When Bad Things Happen to Good People* (1981), New York: Schocken Books and London: Pan Books 2001; Geoffrey Lay, *Seeking Signs and Missing Wonders: Disability and the Church's Healing Ministry*, Crowborough: Monarch 1998; Margaret Spufford, *Celebration* (1989), reprinted London: Mowbray and Cambridge, MA: Cowley Publications 1996; W. H. Vanstone, *Love's Endeavour, Love's Expense: The Response of Being to the Love of God*, London: Darton, Longman & Todd 1977; Elie Wiesel, *Night* (1960), Harmondsworth: Penguin Books 1981; Rowan Williams, *Resurrection*, London: Darton, Longman & Todd [2]2002

Evil ◄

SYMBOLS

Arts, Icon, Iconoclasm, Iconography, Painting, Sacraments, Saint, Story

Among the reasons for the emergence and current popularity of the new literary genre of 'art thrillers' most successfully represented by Dan Brown's novel *The Da Vinci Code* are the leitmotif of the Christian but otherwise 'secret' vocabulary of signs and symbols and the current fascination of Christian art. We have been regularly reminded by philosophers and scientists since the Enlightenment that the human mind despises mystery; rather, it seeks clarity, reason and empirical fact. That 'grey' realm of shadows, secrets and the suspense of 'unknowing' is best left to the sphere of mystery writers such as P. D. James, and to religious mystics. However, the popular infatuation with the historical legends of secret codes predicated upon special knowledge combines with religious scepticism and the everlasting whiff of sexuality and scandal to create a contemporary audience receptive to an explanation, like Brown's, of the sacred mysteries, secret codes and symbolic discourses of Christianity.

Enlightenment

Symbols, whether verbal or visual, are complex; they cannot be identified unequivocally on a one for one basis. They are not like traffic signals where red denotes 'stop', yellow 'proceed with caution' and green 'go'. Rather, in the realm of Christian symbolism red, yellow and green have multiple and often contradictory meanings: red has connotations of anger or emotional passion; yellow of treason or divine illumination; and green of jealousy or fertility. As fluid entities open to multiple meanings and to the immediate transfer of ideas, symbols function as gateways to exploration and speculation, as well as to knowledge and identity.

The dynamic correspondences between the symbol and what is symbolized transcend the traditional boundaries of human reason, and call for trust in intuition and comprehension. The significance of individual symbols employed systematically as communicators of meaning and value (political, religious or social) depends on both an identifiable context and a specific culture. Symbols are culturally conditioned; the interpretation of symbols is a trained skill acquired through the process of socialization involved in becoming a member of a particular culture or cultural group, and at its highest levels is like that of a iconologist or iconographer whose knowledge of how to interpret symbols has been gained through disciplined training. Symbols, individually or as a 'symbol set', do not communicate by direct transference of information on to a blank slate, but rather by a collective progression of information filtered through life experiences and communal history. Although the basic understanding of a symbol, especially of a visual symbol, is predicated upon its ability to communicate with an intuitive immediacy, the reality is a combination of instinctive and learned responses to the exchange of ideas.

Symbols, then, as instruments of knowledge, reveal dimensions of reality inaccessible through other modes of expression. Their fluidity transcends the structured conventions of words and texts, numbers and formulae, and mental constructs and intellectual exercises. Symbols operate as a communications network based on the abstraction and re-presentation of meaning in communicable forms, verbal or visual, which breathe new life, provoke introspection, and establish the relevance to life of a concept or ideal. The etymology of the otherwise modern concept of abstraction provides a critical edge to a discussion of symbolism: the Latin root for the English word abstract translates 'to extract the essence from', or simply 'to get to the heart of the matter'.

The symbol is about the essence of an idea or an event, so that symbolic discourse, whether visual or verbal, strips away all the unnecessary detail to express the essential message.

Symbols are most often associated with the visual arts, so we need first to consider a series of factors that may distinguish or characterize visual symbolism, especially in distinction from the process of verbal symbolism. There is a saying that 'a picture is worth a thousand words'. More information may be disseminated and apprehended within the frame of one painting than in the most eloquently written paragraphs or text pages. The visual arts, especially painting, may be best understood as an image map with a series of discernible clues about how to read not only the image displayed but also its potential internal meanings. The visual artist skilfully employs several – size, perspective, figuration, gesture, costume, location, function and colour – to guide the viewer's eye in and through the frame. Symbols included in this discipline of internal patterns can communicate moral lessons, cultural values and religious ideals.

One classification of 'culturally conditioned symbolism' is religious symbolism, the use of symbols in forms as varied as archetypes, works of art, ceremonies, events and natural phenomena to identify a religion. Symbols emerge from and come to represent those ideas and ideals that a religion identifies as compelling and formative for its individual world-view. At the same time, specific symbols become incorporated within the texts, rituals and arts as distinctive forms of symbolic discourse particular to a religion; they help to give a public definition of that religion and identify those who have been 'socialized' into this particular symbolic language as believers or members.

Religious symbolism has a variety of applications within a religious tradition or a cultural environment. This identifiable set of religious symbols becomes a vernacular language with which individuals can be initiated into the ethos of a religion and believers instructed in its history and doctrine. Religious symbolism resonates with the stories that express the moral values of a religion and affirms and endorses those values within the larger cultural community and to the world. It also contributes towards identity and solidarity among members of the same faith tradition. So during periods of persecution or alienation from society, individual adherents come to discern and communicate with one another by means of symbols, visual and verbal. On an individual plane, religious symbols nurture personal devotion and faith and could be described as bringing the believer closer to God.

Christian symbolism is not merely an identifiable form of religious symbolism or 'namebrand religion'; it stands at the beginning of symbolic discourse in Western culture. So closely is this symbolic discourse integrated into Western culture that it is sometimes impossible to separate it clearly from that culture.

Unfortunately, when it comes to the central principles and features of Christian symbolism, most people today – you and I included – remain children of the Enlightenment. We have suspended what was an earlier cultural 'trust' in the visual and replaced it with a cultural faith in the word, the printed text. Since we most commonly associate the term Christian symbolism with the visual arts and perhaps with the variety of Christian liturgical expressions in our contemporary world, we no longer recognize these signs and symbols and have lost our ability to read them. Nonetheless, we have retained our recognition of the cultural value of art as an expression of aesthetic taste and social class. So we visit art museums or churches and stand before paintings such as the early Christian catacomb frescoes, Hubert and Jan van Eyck's *Ghent Altarpiece*, Mathias Grünewald's *Isenheim Altarpiece* or Leonardo da Vinci's *The Last Supper*, admiring the artistic technique, the artist's creative genius and the depiction of the symbolic forms, human figures, gestures and

p. 325

costume. Similarly, well-trained and articulate art educators recognize the importance of such paintings in terms of the historical evolution of Western art, the techniques of oil or fresco, and the critical evaluation of individual painters.

However, we do not necessarily recognize that the meaning and relevance of all the objects and persons in the arrangement and the presentations of each individual painting provide both clues to and clarification of the Christian theme or scriptural reference. The art educator may not be able to understand that the inspiration and creative drive behind such masterpieces was something more than the individual artistic ego, the demands of a patron, or a technical advance. Nonetheless, the viewer may wonder why the lamb and its banner are so centrally placed, especially in relation to the depictions of Adam and Eve, in the *Ghent Altarpiece*; why the red rose bush is without thorns as it grows in the enclosed garden in which Mary and the Christ Child sit in the *Isenheim Altarpiece*; and why Leonardo is so concerned about the individual groupings and gestures of the disciples present at *The Last Supper*. We – the viewing public and the art educators alike – know there is a 'more' which appears to be hidden or unavailable to us. Thus the myth of secret codes and Christian special knowledge re-emerges and is reinforced. The reality is much simpler, perhaps too simple for our post-Enlightenment minds to accept. There is both a history and a purpose to Christian symbolism in all of its forms: visual, auditory, sacramental, liturgical and theological.

An overview

Renaissance

From its beginnings to the Renaissance, Christianity existed and flourished in the highly-charged symbolic universe of Western European culture. This Christian culture operated through a complex symbolic system that assigned certain attributes to specific things such as animals, plants and objects, and extended even to the weather and to abstract concepts. Moral lessons, cultural values and Christian ideals were communicated through the verbal and visual allegories, analogies, images, metaphors and symbols of Christian symbolism to Christian believers regardless of class, gender, age or education. The vitality of Christian symbolism communicated the tenets and narratives of faith that supported further the presentation of Christian art, literature and ritual and helped it to flourish.

Whether in word or image, signs and symbols taught and presented religious truths in modes of 'conversation' accessible to all believers. For in the ubiquitous acceptance of visual discourse and symbolism it was possible on the widest plane to give voice to realities that words often fail either to express or to communicate. Within such a culture, the symbol illustrates what it stands for while adding both beauty and mysticism to the spiritual life of individual believers, and affirming the unseen world and supernatural qualities of faith that sustained Christianity.

Initiation

Signs and symbols caught the attention of catechumens, those being initiated into Christianity, and helped believers to elucidate their otherwise silent thoughts. The intuitive transfer of knowledge through Christian symbolism was an aid to education, inspiration and devotion. Nonetheless, debates raged within Christianity over the purpose and existence of images and symbols. While many theologians will argue that the fundamental issue was that of idolatry, there were two other issues that may be even more basic. First, the character of the openness of the symbol, which distinguishes it from a sign: a symbol can be explained in manifold and sometimes contradictory ways, so that for example when green can signify jealousy *and* fertility, a dog fidelity *and* lust, or the triangle female sexuality *and* the Trinity. Secondly, flexibility and diversity are critical characteristics of symbols.

These fundamental qualities of symbols – ambiguity, resilience and paradox – complicate further the acceptance of Christian symbolism by certain theologians and the ecclesiastical hierarchy over the centuries. The dilemma is predictable, for if the dynamism of symbols is derived from inherent but variable and enigmatic connotations, then symbols are unpredictable and thereby uncontrollable. Theological anxieties about the emotive and intuitive properties of the visual were exacerbated by this suspicious nature. By contrast, the word and the text, composed of verbal metaphors, analogies and symbolisms, were trustworthy and safe, for the written text was 'fixed', thereby appearing to be controllable, clear and unchanging.

Origins and definitions

From its beginnings, Christianity was a religion of both the word and the image, so it was accessible to all: to those who could read and those willing to see. It was also a religion committed to evangelization and thus to mission. Its historical founder, Jesus of Nazareth, employed allegories and analogies in his stories, parables and sermons. He taught both by his own example and by narrative examples accessible to all who could hear. His initial followers, among whom I would include the apostle Paul, and the first generations of church leaders understood that the future of Christianity in terms of influence and geographical expansion depended upon the continued accessibility of his teachings to the multitudes in foreign cultures and lands. Thus it became the practice of Christian evangelization to incorporate indigenous stories, personalities and images into the explanation of the new religion, and these were eventually baptized and assimilated into a Christian system of symbols and symbolism.

Mission

Jesus

Paul

As Christianity expanded its geographical borders and cultural boundaries – even from its earliest origins within the Jewish culture of the Roman empire into the Hellenistic culture of the Mediterranean – it found itself encountering and continually expanding its vocabulary of symbols and symbolic discourse. So the moral narratives and the heroes and heroines of classical mythology, like those of the Hebrew scriptures before them, became elements within the 'Christian symbol system' that helped to explain the meaning and teachings of Christianity to a new audience. Jesus was presented both in word and in image as the Christ through the Hebraic figure of the Good Shepherd, the Hellenistic figure of Orpheus, and the Roman figure of the philosopher-teacher. This process of explanation by cultural adaptation has survived throughout the centuries and varieties of Christianity – Eastern Orthodox, Roman Catholic, Lutheran, Protestant and Anglican – down to the New Age spiritualities of the late twentieth century.

History

New Age movement

p. 1197

Those who initiated the process of visual analogies which became the foundation for Christian symbolism and that we identify as typology, especially church fathers such as Clement of Alexandria and Origen, were aware that the Bible, especially the Hebrew Bible, was the wellspring of narrative allegory and symbolism. We find the two categories of the foretype and type through which the viewer identified Jesus as the Christ, and later Mary of Nazareth as his mother, as the fulfilment of what was promised or prophesied in the persons and motifs of the Hebrew scriptures. So, for example, the motif of Jonah swallowed by the sea monster and lying in its belly for three days and nights before being spewed out into a 'renewed' life was a foretype of the entombment and resurrection of Jesus as the Christ. When motifs and images of classical mythology and philosophy came to be incorporated into Christianity, Orpheus, whose beautiful music soothed the savage beasts while bringing them to civilization, was a foretype of Jesus, whose sweet voice calmed pagans while leading them to Christianity.

Mary

Resurrection

The earliest forms of Christian symbolism, then, were scripturally based and advocated by the church fathers. This fundamental visual symbolism included the dove, the anchor, the ship, the

Church fathers

SYMBOLS

Christianity makes widespread use of symbols, and learning to read them is an art in itself. Here are some :

Symbols using letters

Alpha and Omega (A Ω): The first and last letters of the Greek alphabet, symbolizing the eternity of God. They are mentioned in the book of Revelation (1.8) and appear in paintings, icons and on the Easter candle.

Chi-rho: A monograph made up of the two Greek letters X P. It is also known as the labarum, a Latin term for a military standard, and is the sign which Constantine is said to have seen in a dream promising him the victory that would make him emperor of Rome.

IHS: Originally an abbreviation of the Greek word for Jesus (the last letter sometimes appears as a C since the Greek letter sigma, equivalent to our s, has variant forms). In the Latin world it was read as the initials of three words, *Iesus Hominum Salvator*, 'Jesus saviour of humankind'. It is used as decoration on church furnishings, eucharistic vessels and vestments.

INRI: The initial letters of the Latin *Iesus Nazarenus Rex Iudaeorum*, 'Jesus of Nazareth King of the Jews'; the wording of the placard affixed to Jesus' cross. Like IHS it is used in many church contexts.

Pictorial symbols

Symbols of the evangelists: These derive from the four living creatures seen in a vision of God's throne in the book of Revelation: 'the first like a lion, the second like an ox, the third with the face of a man and the fourth like a flying eagle' (4.7).

When these are used to symbolize the evangelists, Matthew is the man, Mark the lion, Luke the ox and John the eagle.

Anchor: A symbol of hope.

Apple: A symbol of the Fall, often appearing in paintings in the hand of the infant Jesus, to indicate that he is the redeemer from the Fall.

Dove: The symbol of the Holy Spirit, which in Luke 3.22 is said to have descended on Jesus 'in bodily form, as a dove'. It is always present in pictures of the annunciation to Mary of Jesus' birth.

Fish: One of the earliest Christian symbols: the letters of the Greek word for fish, ICHTHUS can be read as the initial letters of IESOUS CHRISTOS THEOU UIOS SOTER ('Jesus Christ Son of God Saviour').

Instruments of the passion: The objects associated with the crucifixion of Jesus: crown of thorns, reed, nails, hammer, pincers, ladder, cross, scourge, pillar, sponge, spear, seamless robe, dice.

Keys: The symbol of St Peter and thus the papacy, from Jesus' words to Peter, 'I will give you the keys of the kingdom of heaven' (Matthew 16.19).

Lamb: The lamb represents Jesus as the sacrifice for the sins of the world. It is often depicted with a halo and a banner with a cross, denoting the resurrection ('lamb and flag').

Peacock: A symbol of immortality, because the bird was thought to have incorruptible flesh. It is particularly associated with the Virgin Mary, believed not to have died but to have been taken up into heaven.

Pelican: The image of unselfish love, and thus of Jesus' love for the world. The pelican was thought to pierce her breast to provide blood for her young; the depiction of this is called a pelican 'in her piety'.

Phoenix: Used from earliest times, especially in funeral art, to symbolize the triumph of life over death, because legend has it that the bird rises from its own ashes.

Jennifer Speake, *The Dent Dictionary of Symbols in Christian Art*, London: Dent 1994

Fourth-century fresco, Catacomb of St Callistus

vine, the winepress and the lamb as well as the alphabetical monogram consisting of the Greek letters *chi* and *rho*, the first two letters of *Christos*, Christ. The symbolism could easily be referred back to biblical texts. The use of the acrostic form was more complex: the Greek word for fish, *ichthys*, made up of the initial letters of one of the earliest Christian liturgical refrains, 'Jesus Christ, Son of God, Saviour', when depicted graphically in the form of a fish, became one of the

CROSS AND CRUCIFIX

Cross

Early Christians did not use the cross as a symbol, because of its associations with a shameful death. There are no undisputed instances of symbolic Christian crosses before the fourth century, and the famous labarum, the military standard of Constantine, topped with a combination of the Greek letters *chi* and *rho*, which may be interpreted as the first two letters of the name Christ, is one of the earliest pieces of evidence. Subsequently, a variety of types developed:

The *Tau (T-shaped) cross*, known as the *crux commissa* ('put-together cross'), is Roman and Egyptian and probably depicts the type of cross on which Jesus was crucified.

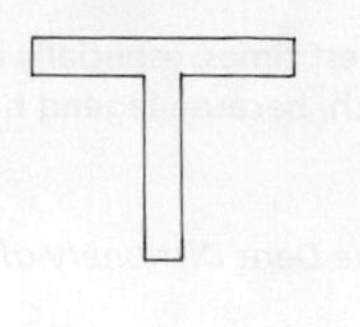

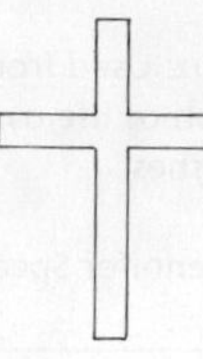

The *Latin cross* (*crux immissa*, 'inserted cross') is the most common, with a short horizontal bar one-third of the way down a longer vertical member.

The *Greek cross* (*crux quadrata*, 'square cross') has four equal arms. It is also known as St George's cross.

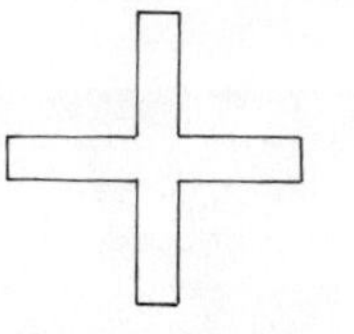

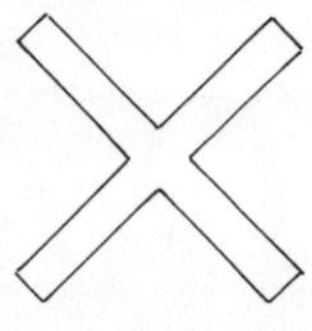

The Saltire or St Andrew's cross (*crux decussata*, 'divided crosswise') is X-shaped. Legend has it that Andrew did not think himself worthy to be crucified on the same type of cross as Jesus.

These basic forms came to be ornamented. Some examples are:
The *Egyptian cross* consists of a Tau cross surmounted by an oval, known as *crux ansata* ('handled cross').

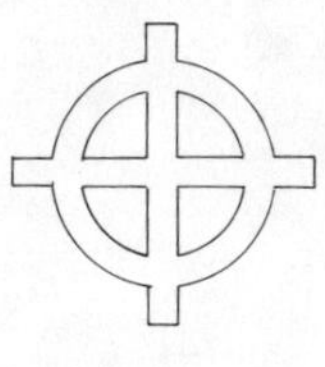

The Celtic cross is a cross with a circle, representing eternity, at the intersection of the two arms.

In the West, the 'Latin' cross appears with one extra shorter bar (*cross of Lorraine*, cardinal's cross)
or two extra shorter bars (*papal cross*) above the main horizontal bar; here the bars have come to represent seniority.

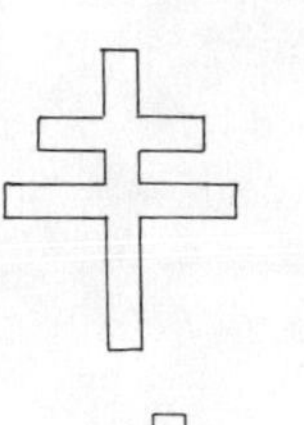

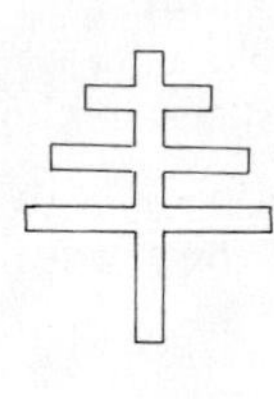

In the East, shorter bars are added above and below the main horizontal bar to indicate a deeply held faith;
an oblique stroke is also sometimes added at the foot to indicate the death of Christ (*Russian cross*).

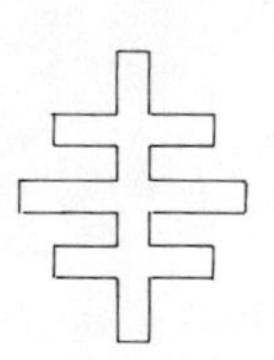

In the *Germanic cross*, short bars are added to all four arms of the Greek cross;
in the *Jerusalem cross*, the sign of the crusades, small crosses are added in the spaces between the arms.

The *Maltese cross* consists has four spearheads with their points together at the centre.

Other developed forms of the cross are found in Latin America in the *Aztec cross*, a Greek cross with arms which become wider towards their extremities,

and the *Pueblo cross*. Sometimes the sharp angles are rounded.

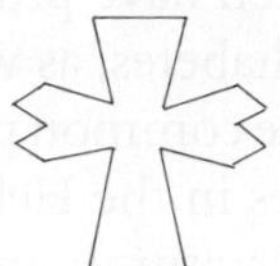

Because of its symmetry, the cross can be ornamented in countless ways, depending not least on the contexts in which it appears, of which there are many. For example, clergy wear crosses suspended from a chain round the neck known as pectoral crosses, and crosses are embroidered on vestments and altar linen. They are placed on the altar and carried in procession; they are carved into church buildings to mark the points at which they have been consecrated, and they are used as monuments in cemeteries.

Crucifix

The first use of the image of the crucified Jesus seems to have been in Rome in the fifth century; before this Jesus was commonly depicted in the form of a lamb. Moreover, Christians of the first millennium, especially in the East, focused more on the divinity of Christ than his humanity. Consequently, it was not until the Middle Ages that the crucifix was widely introduced, in the form of paintings or reliefs. The earliest versions show Christ on the cross alive and clothed in a long garment; moreover in the early Middle Ages, Jesus on the cross tended to be depicted with open eyes and no trace of suffering. With the introduction of the suffering Jesus, other figures appear alongside him, notably Mary and the Beloved Disciple, as on the rood screen which divided choir from nave in churches ('rood' is Anglo-Saxon for cross). From the thirteenth century onwards the suffering was depicted in increasingly harrowing ways: this development is shown at its extreme in the early sixteenth-century *Isenheim Altarpiece* by Matthias Grünewald, where Jesus is depicted as ravaged by the plague, his body covered with bleeding sores and a sickly green. Painting

At the Reformation, Protestant churches banned the crucifix (Calvin even banned the cross), and since then it has appeared mainly in churches in the Catholic tradition.

earliest identifying symbols of the individual Christian, of Christianity, and of Jesus as the Christ. Like all good symbols, *ichthys*/fish had multiple references in both the Christian scriptures and in Christian practice, from its scriptural reference as a metaphor for the apostles as 'fishers of men' to its symbolization of the miraculous Loaves and Fishes or the Last Supper or Tobias, with connotations of baptism, sacred food and immortality.

Ironically, what the twenty-first-century reader has to have explained was recognized easily and immediately by the fourth-century Christian. We have lost the direct visual, scriptural and cultural process of referencing by which the Jonah story or the imagery of the *ichthys* communicated so succinctly and immediately. That is not to say that every Christian symbol was promptly understood without any educational or interpretative tools. All catechumens had to be instructed, as in later centuries had all Christian children, who were initiated both visually and verbally into the meaning and reality of the Christian message through the Bible, worship and the image.

Developed Christian symbolism evolved from a series of identifiable sources which were an amalgam of religious and cultural practices, such as the forms of costume, gesture and etiquette and the rituals and ceremonies of Hebraic and classical cultures; the oral, ritual and written traditions of indigenous 'folk' religions; the oral and written traditions of classical myths and legends; the written traditions of the Hebrew and Christian scriptures, devotional and spiritual texts, hagiographies, histories and chronicles. This means that any careful study of Christian symbols, especially visual symbols, can provide information of more than theological or religious significance. The observant 'reader' can gather information about ceremonial rites, social class, manners, gender definitions and human relationships as well as cultural attitudes to dress, furnishings, food, magic, medicine and the body. Late twentieth-century interpretations of Christian art by such master painters as Mathias Grünewald, Sandro Botticelli, Leonardo da Vinci and Rogier van der

Weyden have provided substantive information on a variety of physical ailments such as arthritis and diabetes, as well as references to the medical treatments of the time.

The common perception of Christian symbolism presumes that its references are to metaphorical figures in the Hebrew and Christian scriptures and Christian teachings; to events and artefacts in the scriptures; and to the history and acts of worship in the Christian church. However, detailed and careful analyses of Christian symbols prove that the boundaries of influences and foundational sources must be expanded to incorporate those larger frames of reference known to the Christian cultural world and its inhabitants, including epics, romances, manuals of behaviour, astronomical and mathematical texts, and medical guides from non-Western cultures. The correspondences between these multiple source materials and Christianity have arisen from the combination of a shared human experience and the Christian commitment to evangelization.

Similarly, the presentation and depictions of Christian symbolism have been subject to simultaneous and multiple readings or interpretations including historical and cultural transformations and theological and doctrinal pronouncements. The fundamental use of Christian symbolism, especially visual symbols, was as a mode of communication through the 'secret code' of signs and symbols known to the faithful during periods of persecution, military strife and missionary expansion; as visual aids to teach the faith to multitudes who were textually illiterate; as a mode of visual remembrance of God's divine action in human history; and as a historical chronicle of Christianity. Additionally, these 'readings' included depictions, for example, of liturgical rites, such as baptism and the eucharist, and could be used to explain the ritual actions, to prepare believers to share in the rite, or to examine the story and transformations of worship throughout Christian history. By embodying the shared memory that is the foundation of religious and social identity, Christian symbolism operated as a series of visual connectors in the formation and experience of the Christian life. This once-common vocabulary of Christianity was a pictorial tradition based on the principle that Christianity must be communicated and accessible to all.

Historical considerations

The initial status of Christianity as a proscribed religion at first supported the development and use of Christian symbolism as a mode of discourse between believers as a form of both identification and communication. Consider for a moment the rendering of an open basket resting upon a fish from the third-century Catacomb of Callixtus in Rome (see page 1165). The simplicity of both design and objects are extraordinarily deceptive, as there are countless possible interpretations of this image. If the round objects placed in the basket are thought to signify bread, the initial visual connection would be to scriptural episodes such as Jesus' Feeding of the Multitude, the Last Supper, and the Vocation to the Apostles to become 'fishers of men'. Additionally, these bare essentials of imagery connote the sacraments of baptism and eucharist, a sacred meal, and the Christian missionary movement. However, if you suppose that what appears to be bread may in fact be something else, the interpretation of the image moves from a scriptural or theological reference to a cultural one. What if these round shapes with their apparent centre 'holes' are not the early Christian form of bagels or doughnuts but rather rolled up pieces of papyrus, a set of scrolls in a basket? If there were scrolls in a basket, what would they signify?

Sacraments

Within the Graeco-Roman cultural world the role of the philosopher-teacher was well known; he was characterized by gestures such as counting on his fingers, or by the basket or bag of scrolls placed at his feet, alongside his chair or held in his hands as he walked to or from the academy. The large fish in this fresco is clearly a Christian symbol, that of the *ichthys*, and signifies Jesus as the

Christ. So following the then accepted view that Christian philosophy had been brought by Jesus of Nazareth to complete and thereby supersede classical philosophy, we can interpret this simplistic image of a basket of scrolls resting upon the large fish as a visualization of Jesus as the philosopher-teacher. It could also be suggested that the principle that Christian philosophy was contained in the scriptures, that the scriptural connection between knowledge and food can be found in several biblical episodes, including the Sermon on the Mount and the Feeding of the Multitude, and that this connection is made visible in this catacomb fresco. Similar multiple readings – scriptural, cultural, liturgical and sociological – can be made of other early Christian symbols including the anchor, the ship, the vine, the winepress, grapes, the *chi-rho*, the lamb, the dove and the star as well as the two most popular symbolic episodes in the art of the catacombs: the Good Shepherd and the Raising of Lazarus.

Middle Ages
Pilgrimage
Crusades
Architecture
Mysticism
Scholasticism
Devotions

For many art educators and church historians, the Middle Ages are the high watermark of Christian symbolism. The medieval synthesis was the world of the pilgrimage, the crusades, the courtly romance, and the Gothic cathedral as well as of mysticism, scholasticism and devotion. Medieval Christianity was fascinated with the connectors between the spiritual and the secular. This highly-charged symbolic universe easily incorporated everyday life in all its activities and frailties as well as nature and the natural order into the visual and verbal modes of Christian symbolic vocabulary. During the Middle Ages, then, Christian symbolism incorporated the realms of devotional texts and practices, lay spirituality, texts and legends of the natural order including animals and vegetation, epics and chronicles, and poetry, as well as the growing influence of Islamic art, culture and spirituality. Medieval Christian symbols and images were an amalgam of the secular, cultural, scriptural, literary and social significations which had been transformed into an identifiable symbolic language of faith. The medieval Christian clearly saw symbolic meanings in everything and experienced life within the context of symbols and images.

Incarnation
Salvation

Consider, for example, the depiction of the rose bush placed directly behind the Virgin and Child in the central panel, *Allegory of the Nativity* (or *The Mystic Nativity*), of the second opening of Matthias Grünewald's masterpiece, the *Isenheim Altarpiece* (see colour plate 8). Without doubt, this polyptych is an extraordinarily complex presentation of Christian symbolism reflecting the then current understandings of the theology of incarnation and redemption; of the significant events in the life of Christ; and the interconnection between physical and spiritual healing. Further, the images and symbols presented in the *Isenheim Altarpiece* explore the homeopathic and natural symbolism of stories, plants and flowers, discern the visual connections between the natural and supernatural realms, and advocate the primordial role of the visual.

The Virgin Mother is seated in the foreground of the (viewer's) right hand side of this second central panel. On the left-hand side of this same panel, Grünewald depicts music-making angels in an elaborately decorated ecclesiastical structure. This celestial concert is in homage to the Virgin and Child, as signified by the connecting figure of Ecclesia (the church) who stands at the threshold of the 'church' and points towards the enclosed garden on the right. The largest angelic figure sits playing a cello in the left foreground as a paralleled contrast to the more monumental figurations of the Virgin and Child on the right. Bridging the foreground between sacred structure and secular garden are a wash tub, a clear-glass ewer filled with oil, a chamber pot and a birthing bed – all common objects from daily life – symbolically charged here with references to this special child, his unique birth, and Christian liturgical ceremonies.

Among the natural objects in the garden are a fig tree, a small mountain and a rose bush. It is this last which captures our attention, as it is positioned directly behind Mary, and on a plane continuous to the diagonal line created by this, especially as Jesus' mother's raised right hand holds his head, his torso touches hers, and her left hand supports his lower body as his feet dangle over her left thigh. The viewer's eye is led from those little feet to the ragged swaddling cloth and to the curve of Mary's mantle, which is deep blue with a rosy-coloured lining – obviously a visual symbolic pun on the rose bush, which is the next object coming into sight as the viewer's eye continues on this vertical path towards the right-hand corner.

Grünewald has carefully situated the rose bush to catch the viewer's attention. The red roses bloom in complement to the green foliage and as a parallel to the colours of the Virgin's garments. The symbolic values of the colours and of the rose are not lost on the attentive viewer. However, one must ask why Grünewald positioned his rose bush on this dramatic vertical line. If we are aware of the medieval way of seeing, we look extra carefully at this rose bush and notice that the leaves, the branches and the flowers are depicted in a natural manner. Then, the unnatural element becomes apparent: there are no thorns. Every gardener knows that it is impossible to have a rose without thorns, so we must ask ourselves why Grünewald would paint a rose bush without thorns, especially one so intentionally positioned.

For the medieval Christian, educated not simply in the symbolic language of flowers or in the Christian scriptures, the answer is obvious and derived from folk traditions as well as from devotional texts. The Virgin and Child are not sitting in just any garden; rather Grünewald has situated them within a symbolic Garden of Eden, that paradisal site to which Mary initiates our return when she assents to be the mother of this most special son. In this paradise garden – an enclosed rose garden as it is described in Islamic poetry and devotional literature – roses have no thorns because those unpleasant and pain-inducing protrusions draw blood, and no more blood needs to be spilled after the sacrificial death of Jesus as the Christ. Rose bushes have thorns, popular legends report, only after the Fall, as a reminder of human frailty, finitude and guilt. Having seen that this natural object, the rose bush, is so layered with theological, devotional and legendary values, the astute eye can now perceive a similar process of symbolization in objects, instruments, elements and figurations throughout the nine panels of this polyptych and elsewhere in medieval art.

The Renaissance was an extraordinary moment in human history, as the traditional world of Christian faith was balanced by the 'new' cultural ethos of science, the arts, and politics. New world-views were to emerge from this distinctive blending of Christianity and humanism. Perhaps no work of art presents this balance more directly than Leonardo's masterful *The Last Supper*. Our initial view of this fresco shows a simplification of the complex and highly symbolic world of an artist such as Grünewald, as this scripturally-based topic has an established visual tradition from the early Christian period onwards. However, if we accept the premise of a symbolic universe, then even the most naturalistic and direct presentation, whether in words, tones or figures, is neither simple nor one-on-one in correspondence.

Humanism

Recent discussions of this masterpiece of Western art have focused on the details discovered, or in some instances lost for ever, as a result of its recent cleaning and conservation. Many art-historical analyses have centred on the technical advances of perspective, *in situ* architectural co-ordination, and presentation of the human body. Those interested in the iconography and the iconology of this fresco recognize the symbolic importance of the varied hand gestures, and their importance in the study of the history of the liturgy, especially of the eucharist. Most recently, the central clue in solving both the murders and the thefts in Dan Brown's *The Da Vinci Code* is the spatial relationship between the figures of Jesus of Nazareth and the disciple to his immediate right:

an individual whom Brown 'decodes' as Mary Magdalene. The potential for these many interpretations of Leonardo's fresco lies in his artistic ambiguity: not as in 'he doesn't know what he is doing', but rather in his careful presentation of symbols and symbolic connectors, which as with all good symbols are open ones.

So the etymology of the word 'symbol'– it is made up of two Greek words meaning 'throw' and 'together' – can be seen as appropriate to a symbol's multivalent nature and the practice of informing by visual and verbal analogies. Eventually a vocabulary of symbols, i.e. an identifiable symbol system or symbolism, was created to meet the individual needs of each secular, social and religious group. As part of the process of initiation, or entry, into that group an individual was 'trained' in its singular symbolic language. Simultaneously, transformations in meaning and presentation have ensured the continuing symbolic life of Christianity – a life which has been challenged by the internal divisions and variety of attitudes that comprise contemporary Christianity. For all the current fascination with and fear of 'secret codes', Christian symbolism is the embodiment of that shared memory that is the foundation for social and religious community identity.

DIANE APOSTOLOS-CAPPADONA

Diane Apostolos-Cappadona, *Dictionary of Christian Art*, New York: Continuum 1994; David R. Cartlidge and J. K. Elliott, *Art and the Christian Apocrypha*, London and New York: Routledge 2001; John Drury, *Painting the Word: Christian Pictures and Their Meanings*, New Haven: Yale University Press and London: National Gallery Publications 1999; George Wells Ferguson, *Signs and Symbols in Christian* Art, New York: OUP 1959; André Grabar, *Christian Iconography. A Study of its Origins*, Princeton: Princeton University Press 1968; Neil MacGregor and Erika Langmuir, *Seeing Salvation: Images of Christ in Art*, London: BBC Publications 2000; Coileen McDannell, *Material Christianity: Religion and Popular Culture in America*, New Haven: Yale University Press 1995; Margaret Ruth Miles, *Image as Insight: Visual Understanding in Western Art and Secular Culture*, Boston: Beacon Press 1985; Jennifer Speake, *The Dent Dictionary of Symbols in Christian Art*, London: J. M. Dent 1994

Television

'Well, sir, you will be pleased to hear that I have invented a means of seeing by wireless.' In 1924, a Scotsman, John Logie Baird, told a friend that his successive primitive experiments incorporating research done by French, Russian and American scientists since the beginning of the twentieth century had met with success. It was the beginning of the world's most pervasive and persuasive form of electronic communication. The development of television might have gone hand in hand with radio had it not been for Baird's commercial insecurity, his secrecy and the outright opposition to television of his fellow Scot, John Reith, who as the first Director General of the BBC in the UK insisted on the supremacy of sound radio.

In the UK and even in the USA, where television spread with greater success in the 1930s, the industry was hampered by incompatible technology, commercial rivalry and unreliable equipment. Yet even in its infancy in the USA, television was recognized as a force that would transform the world.

In the UK, the Second World War brought an abrupt end to TV transmissions to the few thousand viewers in the London area, and when BBC television broadcasting resumed in 1946, it simply picked up where it had left off in 1939. Francis House, post-war Head of BBC Religious Broadcasting, was told by the Controller of Programmes that television was for entertainment and hence not suitable for religion. Eventually, he was permitted to make a dozen 'live' TV broadcasts of church services each year. The church establishment represented on the Central Religious Advisory Committee (CRAC) set up by the BBC in 1923 advised cautiously that holy communion should not be televised.

Radio

A huge leap was taken in 1953 with the coronation of Queen Elizabeth II. At first, both church and government opposed the cameras being allowed into Westminster Abbey, but at the last minute the new monarch gave her consent. Even so, the most sacred moment, the anointing of the Queen, was hidden from viewers by a silk canopy. For a whole generation, the Coronation became the defining moment for the new experience of watching TV.

From the outset, CRAC insisted that no TV should be transmitted at the time of Sunday evening church services. During what was dubbed the 'closed' period, the only exceptions allowed would be programmes for the deaf, live sports events and broadcasts in the Welsh language. A big change in the UK occurred in September 1955 with the launch of independent commercial television. The 1954 government legislation setting it up did not oblige the ITV to show religious programmes, but the regulator took the view that they were important in providing 'a proper balance'. At first the new ITV transmitted weekly a live outside broadcast from churches and chapels, including the communion service, following a pattern established in France in 1949, when a weekly mass and a religious news feature, *Le Jour de Seigneur*, began. (This programme was still the main public service television religious broadcast in France in 2004.) ITV's programming was accused of being dictated by convenient proximity to horse-racing coverage on Saturday afternoons, and no attempt was made to 'produce' broadcasts of worship.

Another significant development on ITV was the launch of Sunday evening broadcasts intended to attract a non-churchgoing audience. The *Sunday Break* was created not only for a young audience, but to be made by young people, such as the 'cricketing parson', David (now Lord) Sheppard. The BBC soon followed, and stiff competition resulted as audiences were drawn to programmes that asked questions rather than preached answers.

In 1961 this pattern was dislocated by the introduction of a BBC series which is still being transmitted and whose programmes are now sold to countries around the world including Australia and New Zealand, as well as to the cable networks of the USA and Canada. *Songs of Praise* was the brainchild of Donald Baverstock, a Welsh current affairs producer. The Head of Religious Broadcasting, Roy McKay, was dubious of the value of broadcasting congregational hymn singing. His objections were over-ruled by his television programme head, Stuart Hood, an agnostic, and in 2004 *Songs of Praise* was still attracting 5 million viewers each week against intense competition from the multi-channel TV environment in the UK. *Songs of Praise* has escaped from local churches and chapels to almost every conceivable alternative setting, save the moon. The uniquely British musical celebration of faith has been made in China, Russia and Africa, as well as in all the countries of the Western world that show the series. It is claimed by the BBC to be the most popular religious programme in the world, and is certainly the only religious TV to be transmitted at peak-time in Europe.

In the 1970s, religious television changed dramatically when both the BBC and ITV developed programming which was to influence religious broadcasting in much of Europe. A new strand of factual television, with programmes such as *Everyman* and *Heart of the Matter* from the BBC and *Credo* from ITV, approached faith communities and issues of faith journalistically. While the world would still be shown through the lens of faith in church services, the new objectivity of the factual output resulted in programmes that were critical and controversial. The multi-part *Sea of Faith* made by Don Cupitt began with the radical theologian on Dover beach listening to the 'melancholy, long withdrawing roar' of the tide described in Matthew Arnold's poem. This and similar programmes were accused by the churches of attacking 'the faith of simple people'.

The editorial change to open and sometimes searching criticism of the faith communities and their ideas coincided with the UK government's Annan Commission into broadcasting. The then wholly Christian membership of the Central Religious Advisory Committee in their evidence proposed that religious broadcasting should reflect all of the world's principal faiths, in keeping with the multi-cultural Britain of the 1970s. This liberal, open policy was adopted across Western Europe, and remained in place to be expressed in the 2003 Communications Bill passed by the UK parliament. For some Christians it was an invitation to an unacceptable relativism and bolstered their campaign for religious ownership of TV channels, which the UK government continued to oppose.

In the third millennium, television religious broad-casting in Britain is in slow decline. Regular Sunday services have been replaced by occasional 'blockbuster' specials like the 'live' global link-up in 2004, 'What the World thinks of God', and so-called 'landmark' programmes such as *Son of God*, co-produced with the USA's Discovery Channel. Critics of the latter programmes, which attracted almost six million viewers, questioned the editorial emphasis on science, biology and archaeology at the expense of theology.

In 2004, the weekly diet of worship from churches is left to ITV, and even though half-a-million viewers watch, many of whom write with prayer requests for one another, increasing competition from satellite channels threaten its future. Critics, including theologians and church members, argue that fly-on-the-wall camera coverage of ordinary Sunday worship is unattractive and intelligible only to former church-goers. Ironically, such audiences, described as 'shut-ins', confined to home or hospital, are the very constituency for which religious television throughout much of Western Europe was originally developed. For example, such output had begun in 1954 in Italy, where it was not until 1973 that Protestant programmes were added to the weekly transmission of the mass.

Religious broadcasting in the United States is distinct from that in Europe in two ways. First, the constitutional separation of church and state prevents any church from having governmental guarantee of access to broadcasting. Secondly, although broadcasters, in meeting their public service obligation, provide some time without charge to local and national church groups, they also sell time for religious programmes on a strictly business basis.

Very early in the development of television, each of the three networks provided time for religious television programmes. During the 1950s and 1960s CBS offered two half-hours a week: *Lamp Unto My Feet* (1948) related to general topics and the interests of religious groups not affiliated with the National Council of Churches, US Catholic Conference or the national Jewish organizations; *Look Up and Live* (1952) was primarily related to the mainline church groups. In 1951 NBC began giving a half-hour to each faith group, variously titled *Frontiers of Faith*, *The Catholic Hour* or *The Eternal Light*, depending on the faith group being served. ABC provided *Directions* (1960), also a half-hour weekly, divided among the faith groups.

These programmes were shown all round the year, in most cases during late Sunday morning or early afternoon. They were carried on an average of 90 stations per network, reaching an estimated weekly audience of 1.5 million through each of the four series, or approximately 4 million persons (taking into account some overlap of viewers). The programmes themselves were diverse, presenting Bible study and Christian ethics, religious instruction and current events, analysis and the arts, plays and musical events, as well as documentaries on current events and commentaries from a religious perspective.

During this same period, a number of denominations and church groups maintained extensive syndication of religious programmes. Some of the largest included the Lutheran Church – Missouri Synod's *This is the Life* (52 per year); the Lutheran Church in America's *Davey and Goliath* programme for children; the Paulist Production's *Insight* dramatic series (30 per year); the Seventh-day Adventists' series *Faith for Today*, *It Is Written* and *Westbrook Hospital* (all 52 per year); plus innumerable TV spots produced by virtually all mainline Protestant and Roman Catholic groups.

However, by the mid-1980s the number of mainline programmes had been reduced to an annual schedule of 4 one-hour specials on ABC, 8 one-hour specials on NBC, and 39 half-hours on CBS – plus, in each case, 'liturgical' programmes covering the major religious observances. Station acceptance of these programmes had dropped to half of the earlier figures or even less, and the programmes slowly moved into increasingly 'fringe' time, sometimes before 8 am on Sundays. In 1986 NBC eliminated its religious production unit entirely, and offered to donate $1 million to the four faith groups for them to produce four programmes each year to be carried on the network. In response, the religious groups formed the Interfaith Broadcasting Commission, to co-ordinate the productions. A year later ABC took a similar action, although both networks still carry 'liturgical specials' in addition to the church-produced programmes.

Evangelical churches and ministries had begun producing programmes as soon as television began. Evangelists such as Rex Humbard and Oral Roberts had weekly programmes in the early 1950s. As more stations sought to sell time for religion, televangelists flocked to the opportunity, and by the mid-1980s there were more than 20 'electronic church' programmes on the air 52 weeks of the year. Several, such as *The 700 Club* and *The Jim Bakker Show*, were on daily. Many televangelists reached out to cable TV as well as over-the-air television, and both Pat Robertson of CBN and Jim Bakker of PTL established their own satellite-to-cable networks. The audience for these programmes peaked during the late 1970s at about 2.5 million for the most-watched evangelists, and since then the increasing costs of airtime, together with the fact that many more evangelists have entered the field, has resulted in the most-watched programme, *The Hour of Power*, having an audience of no more than 1.2 million.

Many mainline church leaders began to raise questions about the effects of the 'electronic church', so in 1980 the NCC's Communication Commission, representing main-line Protestantism, and the National Religious Broadcasters, representing the televangelists, jointly undertook a major research project to get at the facts. The group spent more than a year agreeing on what questions needed to be asked, then it hired the Annenberg School of Communication at the University of Pennsylvania and the Gallup Organization to conduct the research.

On 16 April 1984, the results were announced at a heavily attended press conference. The audience was discovered to be far smaller than many had claimed. Less than 5 million persons, or 2.17 per cent of the population, watched an hour or more of religious TV per week. The programmes were acting essentially as a reinforcer of existing religious beliefs, not as an outreach to non-Christians. Most religious TV viewers were already regular church members, and their giving to the electronic ministries was in addition to their support of their local church.

Finally, the researchers concluded that 'as for matters

of religious importance, experience, participation and dollars, the churches' principal competition is not the television ministry but general television'.

God
Jesus
Language

By the end of the twentieth century there was almost no broadcasting through the 'lens of faith' on the six 'over-the-air' (as opposed to cable) networks in the USA. Some of the famous 'anchors' of the nightly news broadcasts would assume tones of personal Christian piety at times of crisis or at Christmas time, but there was very little news coverage of the churches and absolutely no coverage on mainstream TV of the beliefs of Islam. One notable exception was the annual appearance of the distinguished news 'anchor' and senior commissioning editor at ABC, Peter Jennings, with a major factual enquiry into such subjects as the resurrection of Christ.

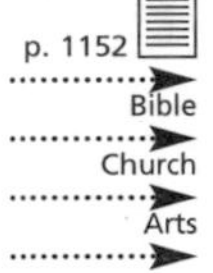

p. 1152
Bible
Church
Arts

The historic concept in the USA of 'sustained time', whereby the major broadcasters made time and resources available for religion, vanished when the broadcasting regulators declared that broadcasters no longer were expected to provide religious programming as a public service. Those who were prepared to pay to have their programme aired on a local network were free to do so and even to acquire and operate their own channel. Today there is only one regulatory requirement on some local 'access' TV channels in the USA, namely that religious programmes must be transmitted in the order that they arrive at the transmission suite. The result resembles a latter-day Tower of Babel. There is little evidence that anyone watches.

The 'electronic church' remains, as it always had been, a small and vociferous sector in the USA and elsewhere. In the 1980s viewers, often elderly and on low incomes, were drawn into single-issue politics so that they supported the right-wing policies of the Reagan era as they have more recently supported the administration of George W. Bush.

Culture

From 2000 onwards, religion has increasingly been featured as a personal lifestyle choice in daytime television, both in the UK and the USA. Orthodoxy and dogma have been given short shrift in the exploration of 'spirituality', with equal consideration given to spiritualism and foot massage. Such palliative programming marked the treatment of religion as a commodity, and a general move in secular society from community to consumer.

Increasingly polarized arguments contrast the demands for 'niche' channels on which programmes make plain by TV that all people can find meaning for their lives in Christ with the coverage of faith as an interesting option. Neither approach does justice to Christianity, and there is a danger that in the third millennium, TV audiences will have to switch off and look elsewhere for the 'footprints of God'.

ANDREW BARR AND WILLIAM F. FORE

Theology

When Christian women and men reflect upon any aspect of their faith, they are engaged in theology. Christian theology arises out of faith in God, as shown in Jesus of Nazareth. With the help of language and reason this faith is explored and discussed. Theology is not the privilege of a few professional thinkers, but part and parcel of a critical Christian faith. However, it is the special duty of those engaged professionally with teaching, research, church leadership and pastoral responsibilities to present a critical and self-critical understanding of Christian faith both to their own church communities and to a wider interested culture.

The word theology is a combination of the Greek words for God (*theos*) and for talking/meaning (*logos*). In a minimalist definition, theology therefore can be said to mean God-talk. But in Christian tradition it has come to mean much more: it involves thinking about all aspects of faith in God and how that faith inspires the human desire to enter more deeply into the mystery of God's self-revelation in our world and thus into the mystery of God's own nature and into the mystery of our own human existence. Theology deals with the experiences of God's presence in the world, in the history of Israel, in Jesus Christ, in scripture, in the church and its continuing development, in other religions, in nature, in the arts, and in every individual human being. Ultimately, all theology is concerned with truth: the truth of human existence in a universe created and sustained by God.

As a professional exercise, Christian theology seeks to serve three publics at once: the church, the academy and society at large. Thus theology never occurs in a vacuum; rather, it emerges at the interface of many human interests (religious, philosophical, social, political, economic and cultural, and so on). Faced with the particular questions and scientific methods of any given time, theology seeks to interpret the texts, traditions and implications of Christian faith within changing historical contexts. Since the beginning of historical consciousness in the nineteenth century, the task of theology has involved even the very way in which theology has been done previously throughout the history of the church.

When, for instance, a culture, such as our postmodern culture, is in the process of redefining its views on and approaches to both the potential and limits of human reason and on the understanding of the human subject, this process presents a challenge to theology. Should theology follow these reconceptions of reason and subjectivity, or should it resist them in the name of a previously established way of thinking and acting? Whatever the answer to this question might be, theology must react to cultural developments and changes. It must try to explain anew, in critical and self-critical discussion with the emerging concepts of postmodern reasoning, how Christian faith can be understood now in view of this shift in cultural horizon. At the same time, theology must itself actively participate in the discussion of what human reason is, can do and cannot do, and of how to understand the human subject and intersubjective relations. Theology ought not to apply traditional, changing or emerging concepts and paradigms uncritically to its own tasks. It is by no means condemned to be a mere passive player in the concert of academic disciplines. Rather, contemporary theology understands itself as one among these disciplines, as one among the different, though necessarily related human efforts to reflect upon life, its origin, its vocation, its plurality, its interconnectedness and its destiny in our complex universe.

Theology, then, must always be sensitive to the surrounding context and to its questions, concerns, values, expectations and fears. This is, once again, not to suggest that theology must submit its own experiential and intellectual horizon to that of its surrounding culture. However, a theology that does not engage critically with the culture of its time runs the risk of talking either only to itself, and thus to nobody else, or at best to those members of the Christian community who do not want to confront any change in church and society. Such a theology would run the risk of moving into a ghetto existence and thus betraying its vocation to think about God. For Christians have always confessed that they worship the one and only God, the creator and redeemer of this universe, and not some kind of (Christian) tribal deity. Hence worship of the one and only true God as well as critical and self-critical reflection on the worship of God must by nature be public exercises, accessible to everybody who asks about their nature, aims and traditions. Theology is thus necessarily a public endeavour.

Theological thinking in the church always occurs within a living tradition of thinking. This was already the case when Christians were engaged in the painful process of parting from their Jewish roots. Originally, all Christian reflection on the significance of the coming, proclamation, death and resurrection of Jesus Christ occurred within particular traditions of Palestinian Judaism. Early Christian theology was a form of Jewish theology. The New Testament texts can be read as early Christian commentaries on central texts of Jewish scripture in the light of particular experiences of Jesus as the Christ. Christians interpreted the emerging New Testament and Old Testament collections of texts within the horizon of their respective communal experience of the risen Lord. This practice points to the important fact that in Christian tradition the task of theology was always understood to be a communal task, a corporate activity, a responsibility of the entire church.

However, the corporate nature of Christian theology does not suggest that there once was a time when all Christian believers agreed on one theology. Rather, a quick look at the diversity of biblical theologies already shows that theology has always been in process, motivated by the dynamics and concerns of particular Christian communities, facing and reacting to particular challenges from inside the churches and from the outside world. Theological thinking has been and must be pluralist by nature. There has never been a single and universally accepted Christian theology. Eastern Orthodox theologies, Armenian theologies, Coptic theologies, Ethiopian theologies, Roman Catholic theologies, Anglican theologies, Protestant theologies, Pentecostal and charismatic theologies, all of these and many more theological developments claim to offer valid interpretations of and reflections on authentic Christian faith and tradition. But even within particular confessional movements we can observe a great diversity of theological approaches, methods and forms of expression. Theology is pluralist and always will be. The challenge to all of the different strands of theology, now as ever, is to remain engaged in an honest and public conversation. The unity of theology does not lie in its particular approaches, methods and forms of expression; rather, it lies in the critical and self-critical effort of theologians and theological communities to explore the mystery of God's presence in this universe. The unity of theology arises from its task and spirit, not from its methods and contexts.

Biblical theology

Worship

Within the biblical writings themselves we can detect many levels, approaches and forms of theological reflection. Three examples demonstrate this.

The story of Moses' meeting with God at the burning bush in Exodus 3 offers a very profound reflection on the mysterious nature of God. First of all, God is identified as the God of Israel's patriarchs, i.e. Abraham, Isaac and Jacob. Secondly, the story adds that this God who reveals himself to Moses is the One who wishes to be known as the One who is present: 'I shall be with you as the one who shall be with you' (Exodus 3.14). Thirdly, God expresses his intention to liberate Israel from slavery. Thus the theology of this biblical tradition invites readers to think of God in terms of historical continuity, mysterious presence in history and concern for human freedom and liberation. In short, this God is fervently involved in concrete human lives and circumstances.

Origins and background

Psalm 42 offers a passionate act of contemplation on the human desire for the intimate experience of God's presence. 'As a deer longs for flowing streams, so my soul longs for you, O God. My soul thirsts for God, for the living God. When shall I come and behold the face of God?' (Psalm 42.1–2). Ardent expressions of the human desire to meet God, such as this one, cannot be found in

Mysticism
Monasticism
Mystery cults
Gnosis
Love
Story
Prayer
Preaching
Letters
Hymns
Prophecy
Constantine's 'conversion'
Creed
Philosophy
Heresy
Church fathers
Canon
Faith

the New Testament. However, they return into Christian faith and theology most prominently with Augustine (354–430), and later on with the Christian mystics.

The Johannine texts in the New Testament, i.e. the Gospel of John and the three letters of John, reflect on God in view of God's revelation in Jesus Christ, the Word of God. The theological reflection of the Johannine community culminates in the definition 'God is love' (1 John 4.8 and 16). This profound theological formula summing up Christian faith in God has needed to be unpacked anew by every generation of Christians. Theologians have had to tackle and explain the meaning of love. Moreover, the theological reference to Christ as the Word of God (God's Logos) in the opening of John's Gospel has inspired the theological imagination of many generations of Christian thinkers.

These three examples show how theological thinking within the scriptures themselves employs various forms of reflection: narrative, prayer, image, philosophical definition, etc. Different forms of theology, many inspired by Jewish sources, emerged in the early church: sermon, letter, gospel, biblical commentary, liturgy, hymns, moral exhortation, prophecy, legal provisions and definitions, etc. These forms witness to the practical nature of theology: the demands of organizing Christian worship and community life have always promoted theological reflection and imagination in the Christian movement. Moreover, in the fourth century, when the Christian church was established as an accepted faith community within the Roman world, it felt an increasing need to express its faith in collections of concise definitions, such as the creeds, which could be used in the context of worship and religious training, but also in order to define who is part of the Christian community and who is not. Theological reflection was expected to clarify the contents and limits of Christian faith against heretical convictions inside the church or against non-believers, such as Jews, Gnostics, Greeks, Romans and others who were perceived to be a threat from outside. Thus, the task of theology to provide a rational and ordered account of Christian faith has since been instrumentalized also in order to define Christian identity at times of crisis and to offer criteria for determining who might be said to belong or not belong to the church. In this sense, theology could assume a defining and limiting role within the church.

The early church

For more than 1000 years, Christian theologians understood themselves predominantly as expositors of the Bible. The emergence of a canon of scripture, comprising the Old and New Testaments, soon produced a primary source of faith and theology. Though faith was a gift of God, scripture alone was able to offer trustworthy and reliable information on God's creation, God's incarnation in Christ, and God's coming reign on earth. The Old Testament was read in the light of the New, and the theological task of biblical interpretation was usually carried out by leaders of Christian communities, i.e. by bishops, priests and members of the monastic movement that quickly developed. Theology was an exercise of the church. However, the church needed to explain to a hostile, indifferent or competing religious, multicultural and political environment that Christian faith was neither a new form of mystery cult, nor a Jewish sect, nor another Gnostic faction, nor a new and therefore discredited form of philosophy. In the Graeco-Roman world any genuine philosophy was expected to be able to demonstrate its ancient origin. Hence, the first theological works to appear were so-called apologetic theologies. Their aim was to refute wrong accusations about Christian faith and lifestyle and to establish the intellectual integrity and religious superiority of both. Thus these theologies, written first in Greek and soon even in Latin, were directed primarily towards the educated among the non-Christian sections of the Graeco-Roman world. However, their effects also included an intensified reflection on theological issues within the church.

Justin (*c.*100–*c.*165), for instance, attempted to demonstrate how both the Christian concept of God and Christian lifestyle are superior to the religion and lifestyle of Greeks, Jews and other peoples in the Roman world. In two *Apologies* and a *Dialogue with the Jew Trypho* he set out to show how the biblical understanding of Jesus as the divine Word (Logos) was in fact prepared and prefigured in the Old Testament and in Greek philosophy. Logos speculation was also common in Stoic and Platonic thinking. In the Bible, it could be found most prominently at the beginning of John's Gospel. This Logos, Justin argued, is truth itself. He is fully incarnate only in Jesus, though seeds can be found in every human person, even before the birth of Jesus, for instance in biblical figures such as Abraham and Moses, but also in major Greek philosophers such as Socrates and Heraclitus. To the Jew Trypho Justin explained that worship of Jesus Christ did not violate monotheism, belief in one God. Justin's theological strategy was to establish connections and analogies between Christian faith and aspects of the surrounding philosophical and theological thinking. The apology, i.e. the defence of Christianity, as a theological form of expression can be found in many works written by the fathers of the church, especially Clement of Alexandria, Irenaeus of Lyons, Origen, Tertullian and Augustine; and even modern theologians, such as Friedrich Schleiermacher, have used this genre of expression in order to converse with the culture of their time.

Irenaeus of Lyons (*c.*130–*c.*200) and Origen (*c.*185–

*c.*254) helped to develop theological thinking in more systematic ways. In response to Gnostic movements that claimed to be able to offer plausible knowledge (Greek *gnosis*) about God, the Bible and the origin of evil, Irenaeus developed a defence of biblical theology. Only those who are in touch with the uninterrupted and ancient tradition of the church (going back in fact to Adam and Eve) and who possess the church's own criteria of truth, the so-called rule of faith, he argued, can interpret the Bible with authority. Against the Gnostic theory of interpretation Irenaeus elaborated a first set of criteria for appropriate biblical interpretation, based on tradition and theological authority. Origen, too, was concerned with proper biblical interpretation. He presented an intricate theory of biblical hermeneutics, suggesting that every reading of the text needed to pay attention to three levels of meaning: the literal sense, the moral sense and the spiritual sense. This approach thus distinguished clearly between a literal level of meaning in the text and an allegorical level. Since the scriptures contain the ultimate mystery which can never be expressed other than in symbols, and since symbols can never be properly understood when taken literally, only an allegorical approach to the text can provide the key which is needed to unlock the sacred mystery hidden in the text. Like Irenaeus and all the other theologians of the early church, Origen affirmed the need for the interpreter to be guided by the church's rule of faith.

The greatest theologian in the early church – from a Western perspective – was Augustine, bishop of the North African city of Hippo. To a greater degree than any other Christian thinker before him, he developed theological reflection and influenced all future theology, especially in the West (he wrote in Latin). For him scripture was the undisputed source and authority for Christian thinking. However, with the help of a carefully worked out theological hermeneutics he treated an immensely rich spectrum of themes covering nearly every conceivable aspect of Christian faith. In his work we find the first systematic treatment of the Trinity; a fully-fledged theology of history; a first kind of textbook introduction to theology containing his remarkable hermeneutics; a spiritual autobiography that describes the author's intricate path to accepting the Christian faith and has been fascinating readers ever since; a corpus of biblical commentaries; a collection of sermons; a rich collection of letters; and a huge amount of texts dealing with acute practical or theological problems within his orbit. Augustine's thought led to a first constructive attempt to develop a synthesis between (Neoplatonist) philosophy and Christian thinking. Theology and human reason are no enemies, but potential partners. Augustine made Christian theology into a way of thinking respected universally (i.e. throughout the Roman empire), and introduced a great variety of theological genres. Theology during the following centuries both benefited from Augustine's work and in one way or other related to it. Alongside scripture and the rule of faith, Augustine himself was soon to be regarded as a major authority in Christian thinking.

Evil

The rule of faith to which all early theologians referred was made somewhat clearer through the doctrinal decisions of the early councils. Between the Council of Nicaea in 325 and the Council of Chalcedon in 451, theologians in the church (mostly bishops) debated a number of central questions of faith within an at times tumultuous context marked by shifting socio-political interests and divisions as well as by religious diversity. Two major schools of theology, one at Alexandria and the other at Antioch, inspired theological discourse before and after the councils and provided an intellectual matrix for theological minds. Especially questions about the divinity of Christ the Logos, the Trinity, but also the two natures in Christ, the human and the divine, as well as the nature of divine grace were at the forefront of theological debate at that time. These questions all concerned the nature of divine salvation and therefore were deemed to be of great significance for all of society. Trinitarian thinking was developed especially by a group of theologians called the Cappadocian fathers, after their region of origin.

Tradition
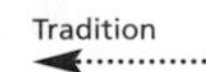
Council
Authority
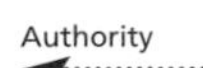
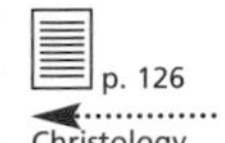
p. 126
Christology
Symbols

Salvation

At the end of the Roman empire and the beginning of what we now call the Middle Ages, theology had been firmly established throughout the urban centres of Europe. Theology was written in Greek in the Eastern part of the empire, and in Latin in the Western part. The agents of theology were mainly clerics and monks. Their first great debates led to conflicts adjudicated at the councils under the presidency of state authorities. In the Roman empire, as indeed in subsequent periods of Western history, it was taken for granted that a state could have a future only if it was firmly built on one religion. As long as Christianity was persecuted, its theology remained merely apologetic in orientation. As soon as Christianity had become the state religion, some of its theology developed triumphalist ambitions and expressions.

Middle Ages

Persecution
Trinity
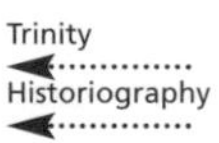
Historiography

The Middle Ages

During the difficult process of restructuring Europe after the fall of Rome in 410, theological thinking could flourish chiefly in monastic centres where books were collected and composed and intellectual skills promoted. The interpretation of the great authorities of Christian faith, i.e. the scriptures and the fathers of the church, was at the centre of early medieval theology in the West and of Byzantine theology in the East. Speculative thinking and the broader academic development of theology became concerns in high medieval thinking.

Books
Byzantium
Roman empire

Under the lasting influence of Neoplatonic philosophy,

Byzantine theologians continued both doctrinal work and mystical reflection within the cultural horizon of the Greek tradition. Doctrinal issues of christology, trinitarian thinking and cosmology dominated the agenda. Maximus the Confessor (*c.*580–662) developed a cosmological approach to the doctrine of the incarnation. Only the Son of God could redeem humankind through becoming human himself and thus restore the God-created harmony that was destroyed by human sin. As a result of the work of Christ, every human being could now be reconciled with God and empowered to embark on the spiritual journey of deification (*theosis*) within the church. Both Maximus and John of Damascus (*c.*675–749) were influenced by the mystical theology of the fifth-century Dionysius the Pseudo-Areopagite, whose apophatic (i.e. negative) theology has been identified since as the most important source of mysticism in both Eastern and Western Christianity. In the work of John of Damascus, who lived within an Islamic context, we see a combination of Platonic and Aristotelian influences, the mystical tradition, a detailed knowledge of Greek patristic theology, the cosmological vision of Maximus and an urge to present a reliable and comprehensive treatment of orthodox faith. His summary of faith, the *Fount of Wisdom*, was translated into many languages and exerted great influence throughout the entire church, even in the West, where it helped to inspire the theological form of the *summa* (systematic theology) and facilitated access to the dogmatic tradition of the church fathers. Moreover, John was involved in the iconoclastic controversy. He defended the veneration of religious images as a way of venerating what they represent rather than venerating the images themselves.

Iconoclasm
Scholasticism
p. 821
Thomas Aquinas
Revelation
University

In the fourteenth century, the interpretation of Dionysius' theology led to the so-called Hesychast controversy, over the nature of prayer and the potential of the spiritual relationship between the human being and God. Can human beings reach a vision of the divine light, i.e. a form of deification, through a particular form of prayer, as the Hesychasts believed (*hesychia* means quietness), or is the radically transcendent God only 'knowable' through negations of all statements about God, as their opponents believed? Hence this controversy touched ultimately on the potential and limitations of theological insight. The theologian Gregory Palamas (*c.*1296–1359) defended the Hesychasts by offering a distinction between the essence and the energies of God: both God's essence and God's energies are fully God and uncreated; but while God's essence is unknowable, God's energies are knowable. They permeate everything and can be directly experienced by human beings in the form of deifying grace. After the fall of Constantinople to Muslim rule in 1453, Byzantine theology continued in its monastic settings, where its heritage was preserved in relative, though never total, isolation from Western theology.

Speculative thinking and the broader academic development of theology became concerns in high medieval thinking in the Latin culture of the West. In the words of Anselm (1033–1109), Benedictine monk and later Archbishop of Canterbury, theology was 'faith seeking understanding'. Reason was employed to expose and explain faith. Moreover, Anselm introduced the method of dialectical thinking into theology, thus encouraging a wider use of reason beyond the traditional attention of theology to biblical interpretation. Different views in theology could now be contrasted with regard to their inherent logic. Theology thus developed beyond the mere contemplation of the divine mystery inspired by scripture and the fathers into an academic discipline driven by an optimistic appreciation of human reason.

The entry of dialectics, investigation and argument by means of dialogue, into theology; the simultaneous development of monastic schools as a particular space for theological discourse; the reintroduction of Aristotelian philosophy into Western thought; and the accompanying emergence of an independent philosophy revolutionized theology and promoted its career as a professional discipline.

Theology now approached the mysteries of faith through reason, methodologically independent of both revelation and the tradition of the church, although in theory always aiming to reconcile human reason with the content of revelation and the authorities of the church. Aristotle's metaphysics offered the framework for this emerging scholastic theology that preferred to express itself in the genre of the *summa* and through the method of formulating a question (Latin: *quaestio*) then to be discussed rationally from all conceivable aspects. The Dominican scholar Thomas Aquinas (1225–74) produced the greatest medieval theological work, the *Summa Theologiae*, in accordance with these principles. Thomas always insisted, though, that theology done in this rational manner must be subordinated to divine revelation. However, he also held the belief that there was no conflict between truths arrived at through revelation or those arrived at through discursive rational thinking and that God has to be thought both in the light of reason and the light of revelation.

Scholastic theology is yet another example of a theological effort to approach faith according to the best available knowledge of the time. This theology reflects the emerging academic contexts (such as the medieval university) and cognitive optimism of thirteenth-century Europe. However, scholastic theology, promoted chiefly by Dominican thinkers, was not the only paradigm in high medieval theology. Retrieving aspects of Augustine's theology and its Neoplatonist philosophical background, and criticizing scholastic learning at the expense of Christian spiritual development, a wisdom-type theology was developed by Franciscan scholars such as Bonaventure (*c.* 1217–74). Moreover, the Western-style scholastic approach to theology was never adopted by the Christian churches in the East. Instead, they maintained their ancient traditional theological practice – reflecting on scripture and the fathers in view of emerging liturgical, pastoral and spiritual needs.

The cognitive optimism of scholastic theology was never shared by all Western theologians either, and was to be more widely challenged in the following centuries. New attempts to retrieve the basics of Christian faith, i.e. scripture and tradition, emerged in critical reaction to the scholastic trust in the independence of human reason. In spite of a number of efforts to defend the Thomistic synthesis between reason and revelation, from the Council of Trent to Roman Catholic Neo-Thomism, in approaching faith and reason theologians have more often highlighted their critical tension than defended their mutual harmony.

The main agents of medieval theology were male scholars belonging to different religious orders. However, a few women religious, such as Hildegard of Bingen (1098–1179) and Julian of Norwich (*c.* 1342-*c.* 1420), used the monastic potential for education and developed their own distinctive voice in church and theology supported by references to direct visions of God. Although the new scientific and professional paradigm of theology favoured an encyclopaedic approach to all conceivable theological topics, all medieval theologians paid particular attention to the question of human salvation by God through Christ. At the same time Anselm's theory of satisfaction and its transformation in the theology of Thomas Aquinas reveal the affinity of theology to the contemporary cultural and religious imagination.

The Reformation

Martin Luther (1483–1546) criticized scholastic theology and developed a new approach to theology. Against cognitive appraisals of human reason in philosophy and theology he interpreted the human situation in terms of estrangement from God, i.e. in terms of sin and death. Only God can justify the human being and God has done so in the cross of God's Son. Against the scholastic *theologia gloriae*, the theology of glory, Luther develops his *theologia crucis*, his theology of the cross. For him, knowledge of God and thus theology are possible only because of Jesus Christ. Accordingly, Luther vehemently rejects any form of natural or philosophical theology. Over against the rational and philosophical approach to theology by the scholastics, Luther favours a biblical, personal and existential approach to theology. The human being is justified by faith alone (*sola fide*). Knowledge of faith is mediated by scripture alone (*sola scriptura*). However, even Luther's biblical theology reflects the new Renaissance interest in retrieving the texts of Christian antiquity as well as the emerging turn to the human subject in Western humanism.

Thus Reformation theology, too, responded to significant cultural shifts and developments. Luther's personal self-understanding allowed him to confront contemporary institutionalism in church and society and to castigate certain spiritual and theological developments. Hence it would not be correct to say that Luther merely returned to a pre-scholastic theological paradigm. Rather, he promoted an alternative theological approach to God, to faith, to the understanding of the human being and of human salvation, to the scriptural sources of Christian faith and to the nature of the priestly office in the church, though he never questioned the importance of theological thinking. Quite the opposite: Luther was a thinking Christian individual and accepted self-consciously the role of a theological leader whose duties included rigorous theological work.

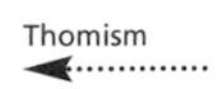

Similarly, John Calvin (1509–64) demonstrated the significance of systematic theology for the practice of the Reformed faith through his writings (especially his *Institutes*) and political activity on behalf of the reform of Geneva. Like Luther, Calvin was a gifted biblical interpreter and knew the church fathers well. However, the scriptures represented the only formal authority, even though there were different interpretations of them. For Calvin, faith rests on the word of God in Christ as encountered in the gospel. Faith is a gift from God that reaches men and women through the word as preached and made visible in the sacraments. Like the other Reformers, Calvin criticized Roman Catholic sacramental theology and practices for reducing the mass to a human act by a priest, thus downgrading the community of the faithful. As far as justification by faith was concerned, Calvin emphasized that God meets human beings as a gracious Father rather than as a judge. Moreover, ultimately, only people redeemed by Christ can appreciate the graciousness of God the creator. The further development of these Reformation churches and the emergence of new movements within Protestantism have added fresh expressions to the wider theological tradition within Christianity.

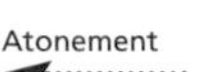

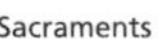

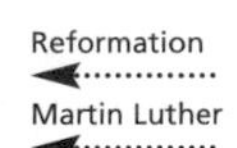

Theology changed dramatically as a result of the Reformation. Aristotelian thinking no longer provided theology with a self-evident approach and unifying set of principles. Moreover, the rapid differentiation of human thinking led to the autonomous development of academic disciplines and thus confronted theology with new challenges. Neither the church nor Aristotle could continue to guide and control human thinking and its evolution. Questions concerning the nature of the discipline and its authority have remained open questions in theology ever since. No single paradigm of theology and of theological authority was accepted any longer by all Christian thinkers in the West. Hence, theology had to reconsider its role now as one among many disciplines and to enter the broader discussion of possible paradigms and methods of human thinking.

Roman Catholic reactions to the Reformation led to a number of efforts to reconfirm scholastic paradigms, although the spirit of the time influenced even such attempts in more or less visible ways. The synthesis between reason and faith worked out at the Council of Trent (1545–63) was simultaneously directed both against Protestantism and against some of the aberrations in the Roman Catholic Church itself that had been exposed by the Reformers. While the officially accepted method in theology remained scholastic, though significantly developed in particular schools, e.g. the school of Salamanca, the reinterpretation of the texts of the Bible and the church fathers preoccupied even Roman Catholic theologians. Nevertheless, the polemical tone of much Roman Catholic theology originally aimed at Protestant theologians was soon to be extended even against the voices of the emerging Enlightenment. Thus reason was appealed to in theology, but rejected when appealed to by modern thinkers critical of institutional Christianity and theology.

Enlightenment
Liberal theology

In spite of confessional differences, the emerging theologies on both sides of the confessional divide had to deal with the same fundamental challenges: the relationship between faith and reason, between faith and culture, between the individual believer and the church, between mystical experience and mediated faith, between theological system and personal experience, and between the claims of the emerging sciences and the claims of traditional theologies. Thus it comes as no surprise that theologians on both sides attempted to erect scholastic or rational systems in order to structure and defend the orthodox positions of their respective confession. This new combination of theological rationalism and church orthodoxy provoked the critical reactions of mystical and pietistic voices in church and theology, thus showing that no theological system will ever be able to incorporate the natural diversity of religious experience and theological reflection.

Pietism
Modernism

Modernity

Humanism
Renaissance

Propelled by humanism and the Renaissance, the Enlightenment espoused a new optimism about human reason: the only formal authority to judge human experience, action, belief, scriptural interpretation and morality was autonomous and critical reason. This view of the human potential included a strong distrust of all formal authorities and unsubstantiated appeals to tradition. Belief in anything not immediately evident to ordinary human capacities was met with suspicion. This new paradigm of thinking presented theology with significant challenges: divine revelation, scriptural authority, claims to tradition and references to divine authority and holy offices were all now subjected to human reason. Moreover, the growing historical consciousness demanded comprehensive rationalist readings of all the sources of theology. Hence the norms, methods, sources, critical self-understanding and traditional agents of theology were all submitted to systematic and public doubt. This cognitive crisis of theology provoked three very different responses.

First, a tendency to agree with the spirit of the Enlightenment led to the development of an equally rationalistic and optimistic theology within the limits of reason alone as defined by Enlightenment philosophers. Christian faith was presented as a rationally based moral attitude to life, thus incorporating what counted as the principles of the universal natural religion. No conflict between reason and revelation need arise. Doctrines seen to conflict with this rationalistic paradigm of theological thinking were either discarded or toned down. Culture and faith formed a union. So-called liberal theologians such as Albrecht Ritschl and Adolf von Harnack during the latter half of the nineteenth century did not see or accept any radical opposition between God and the world. Rather, human experience provided the only adequate source for the understanding of God. The essence of Christianity was seen to consist in God's kingdom as the infinite value of the human soul (thus Adolf von Harnack). God's reign was thus relocated to the inner life of the believer and no longer represented a counter-cultural challenge. Sin could accordingly be reconceived in terms of a lack of knowledge.

Secondly, a radical defence of traditional theological paradigms, both Roman Catholic and Protestant, rejected the terror of reason and emphasized the supernatural gift of revelation and scriptural truth respectively. Roman Catholic Church authorities wanted theologians, understood as mediators of a central doctrinal authority, to reject any liberal, revolutionary and modernist thinking and to rally behind a unifying Neo-Thomist methodology. Those theologians who saw the need to engage critically, but constructively, with modernity and expressed their dissatisfaction with the uniformly administered paradigm for theology were persecuted, some even excommunicated. Only since the Second Vatican Council (1962–5) has Roman Catholic theology been officially encouraged to enter into a critical dialogue with all important intellectual currents and signs of the time. Protestant apologetics of Christian orthodoxy aimed at safeguarding scriptural truth, sometimes even scriptural inerrancy, over against any espousal of natural religion. Here scriptural authority was seen as the only guarantee for the authenticity of faith. A radical wing in the Protestant denial of modernity has developed a biblicist and at times even fundamentalist attitude to faith, while a radical faction in Catholicism has favoured an attitude of blind obedience to the authorities and selective traditions of the church. The doctrine of papal infallibility pronounced in 1870 at the First Vatican Council can be interpreted against this background.

Thirdly, a number of theologians were dissatisfied with both the lack of self-criticism in some modern philosophy and the uncritical appeals to scripture or/and tradition in conservative theologies. Their search for a critical and self-critical theology called for a responsible hermeneutics, i.e. a critical theory of interpreting the texts of the Bible and tradition. Theologians such as Friedrich Schleiermacher (1768–1834) concentrated on rehabilitating Christian experience in prayer, liturgy, the interpretation of texts and life as the ultimate source of Christian religion and theology, yet at the same time protested against the dissolution of religious experience into either philosophy or morality. Thinkers such as John Henry Newman (1801–90) examined the historical dimensions of both faith and church and demanded reform, not least with regard to the vocation and spiritual authority of the laity. In addition, the emerging liturgical and ecumenical movements attempted a renewal of Christian life, worship and thought, and both implicitly and explicitly challenged the absoluteness of confessional boundaries between the Christian churches. Renewed attention to biblical, patristic and archaeological studies helped to soften a controversialist outlook and approach. Presented with the claims of modernity, confessional differences between the various theologies began to lose importance, although many universities in Europe still retain parallel faculties of Roman Catholic, Protestant or Orthodox theologies.

The experience of two devastating world wars, the rise of nationalist and Communist ideologies, the Holocaust, the Cold War between East and West, the recognition of the ambiguity of the rapid scientific progress, and the increasing split in opportunities and welfare provisions between rich countries in the northern and poor countries in the southern hemisphere have further challenged any modern optimism with regard to human nature, reason and progress. A theology incapable of confronting human evil, sinfulness, injustice and limitation lacked persuasion for many twentieth-century theologians. Representatives of what are now often called neo-orthodox theologies, including Karl Barth, Emil Brunner, Paul Tillich, H. Richard Niebuhr and Reinhold Niebuhr demanded a clearer distinction between God and God's reign on the one hand and the world and human nature on the other. They strongly emphasized both the transcendent nature of God and the brokenness of all human beings. This theology came to be called dialectical theology, because its advocates argued that God could be spoken of only by statement and counter-statement, dialectically. Though not subscribing to anti-modern searches for Christian orthodoxy, these theologians rejected nineteenth-century liberal theology and argued that a broken world can be healed only by God's gracious intervention in Jesus Christ. The Word of God transmitted through a faithful attention to the biblical witness requires of each Christian a radical decision for or against God and divine grace and forgiveness. Hence Protestant neo-orthodox theologians attempted to ground theology again on the principles of the Reformation. Nevertheless, they took human experience seriously, but judged it either ambiguous (Tillich, the Niebuhrs) or mostly negative (Barth).

Fundamentalism

At the same time, and some would say at the other end of the neo-orthodox spectrum, Karl Rahner (1904–84) developed his transcendental theology. He saw the human journey towards God as always already inspired by God's universal grace. He thus linked God and the human person much more intimately than Barth. Rahner's anthropology provided for him and many of his followers a bridge between traditional Neo-Thomist theology and the challenges of much modern humanist thinking. Moreover, it opened the way for a constructive and critical encounter with other religions, with atheism and with modern philosophies. Rahner's transcendental theology reckoned with the mysterious presence of God's spirit everywhere in the world and thus helped to open the horizon towards a global theology. However, his theology was criticized for its lack of political and contextual concerns. It remained more committed to issues of theological theory than to the demands of a critical and transsformative pattern of action in society and the church.

Ecumenical movement

In view of the Christian belief in the ultimate renewal of the universe by God, all Christian theology can be said to include a political dimension that transcends the concern for individual salvation. The relationship between the worldly realm of political action and the spiritual experience and expectation of a new heaven and a new earth has led to a rich and varied history of political thinking in Christian theology. When we speak today of political theologies, however, we refer to specific theological programmes which have emerged in Europe since the 1960s and which have had a strong impact on liberation theologies throughout the world. Inspired by Dietrich Bonhoeffer's (1906–45) theology and his costly resistance to the Hitler regime in Germany, Jürgen Moltmann (1926–) and Johann Baptist Metz (1928–) have each developed theological programmes that bring

Political theology

Neo-orthodox theology

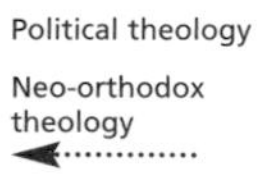

social and political realities into their reflection upon the nature of God, the vocation of the church, and the hope for salvation. Both theologians have thus protested against forms of neo-orthodox theologies that have sharply separated between God and world, though they have also insisted on the necessary distinction between God and world. They have argued that Christian faith concerns the entire world and not only some carefully demarcated realms of belief and spiritual existence.

Hermeneutical theology

The renewal of hermeneutical thinking in the field of theology since the time of Schleiermacher regained a new dynamic in response to a number of significant philosophical developments. Philosophers such as Wilhelm

Dilthey, Martin Heidegger, Hans-Georg Gadamer, Paul Ricoeur, Jürgen Habermas, Jacques Derrida and Gianni Vattimo have attempted to explore the universal claims of a hermeneutical approach to the understanding of texts, traditions, actions and experiences. Moreover, they have helped to expose the intimate relationship between thought and language. Three stages in the theological reaction to this turn to hermeneutics can be observed so far.

Rudolf Bultmann (1884–1976) recognized that no theology is ever free of presuppositions. Rather than regretting this hermeneutical predicament, Bultmann demanded that theologians become aware of their particular presuppositions, their specific starting points and interpretative methods as well as their existential and implicit or explicit philosophical agendas when they attend to the text's own message, its kerygma. For Bultmann, the significance of biblical interpretation concerned the text's existential claim on the reader. He suggested a method that would do justice both to the 'mythological' content of the text and the existential expectations of the modern enlightened reader. Bultmann's approach came to be known as the demythologization of the New Testament.

p. 1155

Liberation theology

The advocates of the so-called new hermeneutic (e.g. Gerhard Ebeling, Ernst Fuchs and others) agreed with the later Heidegger's claim that language possessed an ontological primacy, i.e. came first in the order of being, and a self-revelatory nature. Thus a theological hermeneutics was necessary in order to do justice to the event character of the Word of God that wishes to make itself heard through human language. These theologians wished to free the process of the Word's communication of itself from all obstacles in order to facilitate a hermeneutics of agreement with the very Word of God. Here modern hermeneutical insights into the significance of language were used to strengthen traditional Reformation beliefs in the Word of God. Hermeneutics became a tool to make way for God's Word to be heard anew by modern men and women.

The ongoing concern about hermeneutics in theology has promoted a greater sensitivity to all aspects of communication and their significance for Christian talk about God. Efforts have been made to include reflection on textual linguistics, semantics, pragmatics, sign theory, gender presuppositions, analogical imagination and anti-colonial aspects as well as political and cultural considerations in a comprehensive framework for theological hermeneutics. Gadamer's exploration of the role of a text's history of effects, Ricoeur's insistence on the need for a combination of hermeneutical theory and critical and self-critical explanatory strategies, Habermas' stress on the demands of unrepressed communication, and postmodern reflections on the production and function of communicative systems have all helped to inspire the development of theological hermeneutics. The crucial question for theological method remains how to establish a bridge in communication between the texts of the Christian tradition and their reception by contemporary men, women and children.

The connection between faith and contemporary culture has also been the primary focus of a number of correlational methods in recent theology. Paul Tillich (1886–1965) first formulated the programme of a 'method of correlation': philosophical analysis was to determine the existential concerns of modern men and women and theology was to provide the answers in terms of how the New Being offered in Christ could shape human life. David Tracy (born 1939) has developed Tillich's method by insisting on the need for a mutually critical correlation between the interpretation of the Christian tradition and the interpretation of contemporary ways of being in the world. Thus, for Tracy, any approach to truth must include a commitment to listen again both to one's own tradition and to the plurality of present interpretations. In sum, his correlational approach demands a radical openness for continuous revision of one's position as well as a commitment to the public nature and plurality of theological discourse. Langdon Gilkey, Hans Küng, Edward Schillebeeckx and many liberation theologians have promoted similar forms of correlational theology.

A debate has arisen between correlational and narrative theologians. Narrative theologians such as Hans Frei, George A. Lindbeck and Stanley Hauerwas have claimed that the correlational theologians seek to ground their theologies in a framework of contemporary philosophical rationally and not on the tradition's own internal description of divine and human reality. Hence, narrative theologians have called correlational theologians 'foundationalist' (not to be confused with fundamentalists) because they are seen to favour rational foundations for their theological thought. In contrast, narrative theologians see themselves as working in a non-foundationalist way, as they do not search for universally acceptable rational criteria for authentic theology. Rather, they offer 'thick descriptions' of their own particular faith tradition, especially of the biblical witness to God's own Word. The question at stake between both paradigms is whether or not the Bible creates its own community of listeners and disciples or whether that community always already finds itself in tension between the demands of biblical witness and the demands of a modern and postmodern interpretation of Christian faith.

Narrative theology also denotes approaches developed by disciples of Karl Barth (e.g. Eberhard Jüngel, David Ford) who wish to defend the primacy of God's Word over against rational considerations of the human condition that are also necessary. Finally, narrative theology is also the name for a programme advocated by Jewish and Christian thinkers who wish to retrieve the original and emancipatory power of biblical and post-biblical stories in the specific situations of the respective faith communities. Narrative theology has thus become a way of identifying as Christian a number of Christian approaches in our postmodern world.

Eastern Orthodox theology has had an increasing impact on Western theological discussions during the twentieth century. Although there had always been contacts between Western and Eastern theologians, since the early nineteenth century Orthodox thinkers in Russia had been able to develop theological thinking in the Eastern tradition outside Ottoman rule in a climate of increasing exchange with Western philosophy and theology. When, after the Russian Revolution of 1917, a number of significant Russian theologians in exile congregated in Paris, their presence inaugurated a uniquely challenging theological encounter between East and West. George V. Florovsky (1893–1979), Vladimir Lossky (1903–58) and others attempted to develop theologies both hostile to Slavophile approaches to a typically Russian theology and critical of many Western theological programmes. Instead, they propagated a retrieval of the theological wisdom of the Greek fathers, Florovsky going so far as to advocate a new Christian Hellenism. (In Eastern Orthodox thought the period of the Greek fathers ends in 1453 with the fall of Constantinople.) This reassessment of the patristic mind and the prominent retrieval of the theologies of Dionysius and Gregory Palamas did not entail romanticizing a long-gone theological past, but represented a conscious hermeneutical effort to develop the Eastern theological approach to God's presence in the universe and reflect upon the consequences of Eastern cosmological theology for the understanding of prayer, love, liturgy, mystical experience, christology, the Trinity and the church.

As a result of the ecumenical movement; the changing political and cultural conditions in Central and Eastern Europe since 1989; the emergence of new Orthodox theologies in Russia, Romania, Greece and elsewhere; and the work of new generation Eastern Orthodox thinkers in the West, Orthodox theology continues to flourish and to influence Western theological thought and vice versa. Current debates on the theology of the Trinity, on the nature of personhood, on the vocation and nature of the church, on ecology, and on ministry in the church are increasingly enriched by contributions from all the four major traditions (Eastern Orthodoxy, Anglicanism, Protestantism and Roman Catholicism) and their distinctive theological presuppositions, spiritual and intellectual interests, and methodological agendas.

Ecotheology
Ministry and ministers

Liberation theology has passed through a number of stages since its original conception in the early 1970s. Its basic inspiration and concern, however, has not changed. The liberating power of the Christian understanding of a compassionate God who is involved in this world on behalf of the oppressed, the poor and the victims of injustice is brought to bear on a world whose many forms of oppression, poverty and injustice are critically analysed. Thus this form of theology critically correlates human experiences of suffering with the liberational strength and vision of the gospel. The modern emphasis on individual experience, however, is mediated here with a concern to uncover systemic forces of evil. Though initially arising out of Latin American theology (Gustavo Gutiérrez, Juan Segundo, Jon Sobrino and others), liberation theology today has developed into a theological paradigm applied to most geographical contexts associated with oppression, injustice, torture, famine and exploitation.

Orthodox churches

Black theology can be understood as an independent development within the broader spectrum of liberation theology. It has arisen both as a critique of Western theology that had ignored the scandal of slavery and colonialism in Christian history and as a constructive enterprise by African American theologians, including James H. Cone, J. Deotis Roberts and Gayraud S. Wilmore, who wished to develop an emancipatory theology concomitant with the struggle for justice and freedom in the Civil Rights and Black Power movements in the US. Black theology also spread to South Africa and other countries in Africa and thus helped to inspire the emergence of an African theology. African American women, however, came to criticize black theology for ignoring the specific experience of black women, and drew theological attention to the perspective of women of colour and their experiences of marginalization and oppression in American history (and not just American history), society and Christianity. Moreover, since white and black theology have both participated in the oppression of black women, a womanist theology was developed by theologians such as Jacquelyn Grant, Katie Cannon and Delores S. Williams, who have been explicitly

African American Christianity

addressing the pressing questions of race, gender and class in their reflections on how black men and women can understand themselves as whole people created in God's image.

Feminist theology

The many different shapes of feminist theology since the late 1960s can also be said to represent forms of correlational and liberation theology. These theologies are centred on experience of the contrast between God's creative and redemptive presence in the lives of every human being and the systemic distortion of Christian tradition by patriarchal and sexist reductions (Mary Daly, Elisabeth Schüssler Fiorenza, Anne Carr, Elizabeth A. Johnson, etc.). The analysis and strategies of overcoming implicit and explicit dimensions of sexist oppression in Christianity give rise to a demand for radical reform of Christian faith and discipleship. Feminist theology is by no means the sole prerogative of women; rather, it concerns all aspects of the critical and self-critical reconception of Christian faith in church and society. It is difficult to imagine a critical theology that does not pay attention to the need to overcome patriarchal structures and reductions. However, some feminist theologians, e.g. Daphne Hampson, consider the Christian church to be incapable of reform and therefore have begun to advocate a post-Christian feminist theology and spiritual praxis.

Globalization

The recent rise of gender studies has provoked Christian theology into becoming more aware of the complex connections between gender, body, culture, religious imagination and faith. No aspect of human existence and the shaping of human imagination and praxis can be excluded from theological reflection. Moreover, the relationship between the development of sexual identity and Christian faith has taken on a place of primary attention in much theology.

Body

All of these forms of correlational theologies combine methods of critical analysis of particular cultural circumstances with methods of critical and self-critical interpretation of the transformative potential of Christian faith. Neither human reason nor appeals to tradition are accepted uncritically. Rather, a multi-disciplinary cultural analysis is made fruitful for theological thinking and vice versa. The different correlational theologies seek to ground theological discourse in the actual practices of life and discipleship, whereas neo-orthodox theologians are often accused of again separating theology from the world.

By now, theology has not just become interested in relating all aspects of human experience to faith in God the creator and redeemer and vice versa. The self-understanding of who counts as a theologian also changed radically during the twentieth century. Not without analogy to the Reformation insistence on the priesthood of all believers, theology has become socially and academically accessible to all women and men who seek to be educated in critical reflection on Christian faith. In principle, anyone with access to education now can become a professionally trained theologian. Many universities and other institutions of higher education offer courses in theology and religious studies. The increase in theological education has increased the pressure within all Christian movements for change and ongoing reform. This in turn has challenged traditional forms of theological authority and power and helped the emergence of a more public debate on theological issues in all contemporary media.

Towards a global theology?

Contemporary theology is faced with many challenges. In our time, which has been labelled postmodern, the rise of modern subjectivity and the development of scientific and technical reason continues with perplexing speed. However, emerging experiences of globalization, not only in economic but also in cultural terms, the daily encounter of a plurality of religious experiences and traditions in many places, and a radical cultural openness and potential coupled with individual uncertainty and a new longing for firmer social identities have given rise to a new set of theological questions, concerns and approaches. Christian thinkers have become aware of the need to develop theologies of religion in order to clarify what religious belonging or identity might mean in a globalized world and in a postmodern cultural context. At the same time, universal claims of any kind of theology are met with suspicion. Should theologians attempt to work out models for a global theology, or should they concentrate on local theologies designed for particular cultural contexts in this world? Should they understand their vocation more in terms of providing critical reflections on the ongoing practice of faith in particular social, political and cultural contexts, or should they challenge any form of Christian practice in order to promote a dynamic relationship between Christian practice and the continual rethinking of it?

While social, political and cultural circumstances differ, sometimes dramatically, and thus demand local approaches to the transformative potential of Christian faith, there can be no doubt that all human beings on earth are affected by cultural, religious, political, scientific and technical developments. Issues of peace and the overcoming of all sorts of violent conflicts and of natural and man-made disasters on earth concern all Christians as much as developments on the biogenetic and other related scientific and technological fronts. New questions arise, and some older questions assume a new urgency: What kind of human beings do we want to be in the light of both God's creative and redemptive presence in Jesus Christ and the possibilities of postmodern bio-technical possibilities? What kind of church community should we

A PLETHORA OF THEOLOGIES

To judge from the titles of current books and courses, in Christianity there is a theology of just about everything, from a 'death of God' theology to a theology of the musical, and it sometimes looks as if theology as a word is becoming almost meaningless. On the other hand if, as its etymology indicates, theology is talk (perhaps better, rational discourse) about God, then it is only to be expected that this rational discourse about God in relation to human beings and the world in which they live should take many forms and be done over many periods and in many contexts, and therefore require a great number of names to describe it.

A degree of order can be brought into the many types of theology which appear. Some of them are described at length elsewhere in *The Guide*, in other cases a book (or books) is indicated for further reading.

First comes a series of –ologies which have the same verbal form as the word theology itself and all of which derive from the Greek.

Christology: rational discourse about the person of Jesus as the Christ; Christology
Ecclesiology: rational discourse about the church; Church
Hamartiology: rational discourse about sin; Sin
Heresiology: rational discourse about heresy; Heresy
Mariology: rational discourse about the Virgin Mary; Mary
Soteriology: rational discourse about salvation. Salvation

Next comes a series of traditional divisions of theology grouped according to their subject matter:

Apophatic theology: 'Negative theology', a theology which denies that God can be conceptualized in any way and thus emphasizes the inadequacy of human understanding. It is characteristic of the Eastern churches; the term is first used by Dionysius the Areopagite. Church fathers
📖 Vladimir Lossky, *The Mystical Theology of the Eastern Church*, London and Cambridge: James Clarke 1957, reissued Crestwood, NJ: St Vladimir's Seminary Press 1976

Ascetical theology: concerned with the efforts of believers to live a life of grace by means of prayer, fasting and a disciplined lifestyle. It can also be called spiritual theology. In the Orthodox tradition this is now called *neptic theology* (from the Greek *nepsis*, watchfulness, i.e. in prayer).
📖 F. P. Harton, *The Elements of the Spiritual Life* (1932), London: SPCK 1964

Biblical theology: the theology or theologies contained in the Bible. Biblical theology

Dogmatic theology: also referred to as dogmatics. The term is often used as a synonym for systematic theology; if there is a difference it is that systematic theology has a wider range including, say, moral theology. Dogmatic theology examines systematically all the major Christian doctrines. Many theologians have written *Dogmatic Theologies* or *Dogmatics*, most notably Karl Barth. Karl Barth
📖 Karl Barth, *Church Dogmatics*, Edinburgh: T&T Clark 1936–69

Eucharistic theology: the theological interpretation of the eucharist. Eucharist
📖 David N. Power, *The Eucharistic Mystery: Revitalizing the Tradition*, New York: Crossroad and Dublin: Gill & Macmillan 1992

Fundamental theology: concerned with the basic issues of Christian theology, especially how the Christian faith was revealed, to whom, to whom it was handed down and whence its authority derives.
📖 Gerald O'Collins, *Fundamental Theology*, London: Darton, Longman & Todd and New York and Mahwah, NJ: Paulist Press 1981

Liturgical theology: concerned with the content and structure of the liturgy in the light of its history and present-day cultures.
📖 Geoffrey Wainwright, *Doxology*, London: Epworth Press and New York: OUP 1980

Moral theology: concerned with normal acceptable behaviour for the Christian life. Moral theology

Mystical theology: in the Eastern churches an approach which relates doctrinal and theological teaching to the spiritual life and experience of God.
📖 Vladimir Lossky, *The Mystical Theology of the Eastern Church*, London and Cambridge: James Clarke 1957, reissued Crestwood, NJ: St Vladimir's Seminary Press 1976

→

Natural theology

Natural theology: concerned with the knowledge of God that human reason can arrive at without the help of revelation.

Pastoral care

Pastoral theology: traditionally concerned with the nature and role of the ordained clergy and their work of pastoral care and counselling.
📖 James Woodward and Stephen Pattison (eds), *A Reader in Pastoral and Practical Theology,* Oxford: Blackwell 2000

Practical theology: concerned with the relationship between belief and behaviour. Traditionally it reflected on training for the ministry and related topics – preaching, celebrating the eucharist, catechizing – but now its scope is much wider and it is closely related to pastoral theology.
📖 James Woodward and Stephen Pattison (eds), *A Reader in Pastoral and Practical Theology,* Oxford: Blackwell 2000

Sacraments

Sacramental theology: concerned with the theology of the sacraments.
📖 Joseph Martos, *Doors to the Sacred*, New York: Doubleday and London: SCM Press 1981

Systematic theology: related to dogmatic theology, but with a much wider scope and often concerned to correlate Christian thought with other disciplines. It is particularly interested in the way in which theology is done. Many theologians have written systematic theologies, most influentially Paul Tillich.
📖 Paul Tillich, *Systematic Theology* (3 vols), Chicago: University of Chicago Press and Welwyn Garden City, James Nisbet 1951–64, reissued London: SCM Press 1978 and 1997

Theologies have also been named after the particular periods in which they were practised, for example:

Church fathers
Reformation
Enlightenment

Patristic theology: also referred to as patristics, the theology of the church fathers.
Reformation theology: the theology of the sixteenth-century Reformers.
Modern theology: usually taken to begin after the Enlightenment.

or by church traditions:

Anglican theology, Baptist theology, Lutheran theology, Orthodox theology, Methodist theology, Roman Catholic theology. There is also an *ecumenical theology*.

Theologies are named after the places where they were practised, for example:

Alexandrian theology: a theology which emphasized the spiritual aspects of the Bible, the unity of the person of Christ and the role of his divine nature.

Antiochene theology: a theology which emphasized the literal and historical sense of the Bible and the humanity of the person of Christ.

Mercersburg theology: named after a German Reformed Church seminary in the Appalachian foothills in the mid-nineteenth century and associated with John Nevin and Philip Schaff. It opposed both emotionalism and rationalism and emphasized doctrine and sacramental theology.
📖 J. H. Nichols (ed), *Mercersburg Theology*, New York: OUP 1967

Princeton theology: a conservative, Calvinist theology which flourished in the United States over much of the nineteenth century which emphasized common sense and stressed the infallibility of the Bible. Its two main protagonists were Charles Hodge and Benjamin Warfield. In the end it came to grief over the fundamentalism issue.
📖 Mark A. Noll (ed), *The Princeton Theology 1812–1981*, Grand Rapids: Baker Academic 2001

Some theologies can be grouped by the method that they adopt:

Comparative theology: a comparison of theologies, reflecting on theological themes in various traditions which seeks to build up a specific theology by this method.
📖 Michael Barnes, *Theology and the Dialogue of Religions*, Cambridge: CUP 2002

Dialectical theology: also called crisis theology. Karl Barth and other like-minded theologians claimed that the only valid way of talking about God was to use dialectic, yes and no, statement and counter-statement, thus holding together opposites.
📖 James M. Robinson (ed), *The Beginnings of Dialectical Theology*, Richmond, VA: John Knox Press 1968

→

Hermeneutical theology

Hermeneutical theology: theology concerned with interpretation and understanding.

Kerygmatic theology: an alternative name for crisis theology or dialectical theology, concerned to understand theology as proclamation (Greek *kerygma*).

Story

Narrative theology: concerned to relate the impressions made by narratives, particular biblical narratives, and the insights out of them to theological questions.

George Stroup, *The Promise of Narrative Theology,* Atlanta: John Knox Press and London: SCM Press 1981

Neo-orthodox theology

Neo-orthodox theology: the term is sometimes used of the conservatism which developed in the Christian churches in the 1980s and 1990s, but more specifically refers to theologies after the Second World War, represented by Karl Barth on the Protestant side and Karl Rahner on the Catholic, which sought to present classical doctrines in a new way.

Postmodern theology

Postmodern theology: theology done with reference to 'postmodernity' and 'postmodernism'.

Some are named after a related philosophy:

Existentialist theology: theology which uses existentialist philosophy in its interpretation of Christianity. Rudolf Bultmann in particular used the thought of Martin Heidegger to interpret the Bible and Christian doctrine in terms of authentic and inauthentic existence and the call to decide in favour of authentic existence in his programme of 'demythologization'. But Blaise Pascal, Søren Kierkegaard, Nikolai Berdyaev and Gabriel Marcel can also be seen in the tradition of existentialist theology.

p. 1155

John Macquarrie, *An Existentialist Theology,* London: SCM Press 1960

Marxist theology: theology growing out of the Christian-Marxist dialogue of the late 1950s, and grappling with the Marxist critique of religion. At a later stage it was practised by Christians who accepted the basis of Marxism and sought to reinterpret Christian faith in the light of it.

J. P. Miranda, *Marx against the Marxists: The Christian Humanism of Karl Marx*, Marykoll, NY: Orbis Books and London: SCM Press 1980

Process theology: theology which draws on process philosophy, notably as represented by A. N. Whitehead, to take account of change and development in the world and indeed in God. Its pioneer was Charles Hartshorne.

John B. Cobb Jr and David Ray Griffin, *Process Theology. An Introductory Exposition*, Philadelphia: Westminster Press 1976.

Some theologies are issue-related, for example:

Crisis theology: An alternative title for dialectical theology, indicating the sense of crisis with which that theology arose.

Ecotheology

Ecotheology: theological reflection on ecological issues and the global crisis of the environment.

Feminist theology

Feminist theology: this calls into question theological assumptions which justify male dominance in society. It has two variants:

Mujerista theology: a feminist liberation theology which seeks to show Latinas how they are oppressed by the system under which they live and how they can be liberated from it.

Ada María Isasi-Díaz, *Mujerista Theology: A Theology for the Twenty-First Century*, Maryknoll: Orbis Books 1996

Womanist theology: critical reflection on black women's place in the church and society, criticizing the negative attitudes of the church and the black community towards them and affirming positive values.

Alice Walker, *In Search of Our Mothers' Gardens*, New York: Harcourt, Brace, Jovanovich 1983

Gay and lesbian theology

Gay and lesbian theology: reflects on the attitudes to homosexuals of both sexes in the Christian tradition and puts forward proposals for change.

Liberation theology

Liberation theology: a form of theology originating in Latin America which seeks to ensure that theology does not identify with the interests of those who benefit from structural injustice in society and shows ways to intellectual and social liberation from these structures. It also has local variants in other parts of the world. These can also be seen as *Contextual theology* or *Indigenous theology:*

African American Christianity

Black theology: this theology was prompted by the civil rights movement in America in the 1950s and 1960s, the black power movement, and the publication of Joseph's Washington's book *Black Religion* (1964). It is discussed at length in the article on African American Christianity.

📖 Gayraud S. Wilmore and James H. Cone (eds), *Black Theology, A Documentary History 1966–1979*, Maryknoll, NY: Orbis Books 1979

Burakumin theology: a Japanese liberation theology named after the 'Burakumin', a class regarded as unclean because of their occupation as leather-workers, skinners or grave-diggers, living on the edges of towns and cities.

Dalit theology: named after the Dalits, the Indian outcastes, and influenced by black theology.

📖 M. E. Prabhakar (ed), *Towards a Dalit Theology*, New Delhi: Printsman 1989

p. 394

Dread theology: the theology of the Rastafarians, who believe that they are exiles from Ethiopia and for whom Ethiopia is heaven on earth and the emperor Haile Selassie a god.

📖 William David Spencer, *Dread Jesus*, London: SPCK 1999; Robert Beckford, *Dread and Pentecostal*, London: SPCK 2000

Minjung theology: a Korean liberation theology named after the 'Minjung', 'the ordinary people', who in Korea have been and are oppressed and discriminated against.

📖 *Minjung Theology. People as the Subjects of History*, Maryknoll, NY: Orbis Books ²1983 (conference volume)

Neurotheology: a new interdisciplinary study which seeks to establish the biochemical origins of religious experiences.

📖 Laurence O. McKinney, *Neurotheology: Virtual Religion in the Twenty-First Century*, Arlington, MA: American Institute for Mindfulness 1994

Political theology

Political theology: a movement in the 1960s associated with Jürgen Moltmann, Johann-Baptist Metz and Dorothee Sölle which saw the need to deprivatize theology and engage in social issues.

Evolution
Other faiths
Eschatology
Cinema

develop in order to respond best to God's call in Christ to help build God's reign? How should Christians relate to other religions? Is the affirmation of Christian faith open to a rational and universal theological discourse, or does it require the closed circuit of a community shaped by its own Christian language and imagination? In what way can Christian theology participate in a universal conversation on truth?

Theological disciplines

Communication

Although the current organization of theological education and the disciplines of theological research continue to reflect many of the concerns of modernity, some changes and new developments can already be observed, and many calls for a renewal of theological thinking can be heard today.

Community

Creation
Science and theology

There seems to be a general acceptance that no realm of human experience can be excluded from theological thinking. Believing in God the creator and redeemer implies taking all aspects of divine creation seriously and reflecting on their theological significance. Hence, efforts are being made to introduce a consideration of the potential and ambiguity of the natural sciences into theological discussion, beyond the concern for tackling the increasingly difficult moral dilemmas presented by the rapid scientific and technological progress. Nature as such is seen as an integral part of God's concern. Therefore evolutionary, ecological and cosmological theories need to be discussed within the framework of Christian eschatology and brought into a mutually critical and enriching conversation with theological thinking in general.

The emerging dialogue between theology and the arts has also facilitated new insights and areas for research. Contemporary media such as film, computerized images, virtual reality productions, etc. have an impact on the religious imagination and thus need to be explored by a critical theology. Moreover, media studies are urgently needed in theology in order to assess in what way the rapid development of human communication is affecting the nature of the relationship between human beings as well as the religious formation of children. The ongoing transformation of human social reality makes the development of radically new ways of approaching Christian community all the more urgent. Christian life is necessarily connected with this world and its development. Hence, theology can never afford to ignore the state and transition of this world if it wishes to be faithful to its vocation, namely to reflect upon all aspects of Christian faith in this complex universe.

Even the internal organization of theological thinking is in the process of changing. The increasing differentiation of theology throughout modernity has allowed a closer focus on specific areas of Christian faith through biblical, dogmatic, fundamental-theological, philosophical, sociological, psychological, liturgical, canonical, historical, hermeneutical, ethical, feminist, liberationist, gay and lesbian, gender studies, mission studies, history of religion and other approaches. The price for this detailed focus on particular phenomena and areas of Christian faith, life, experience and teaching has been an increasing loss of a holistic perspective on faith and discipleship in theology. The distance between biblical exegesis and systematic theologies has been widening for decades and, as once before in scholastic theology, now again threatens to separate theological thinking from its biblical foundations and challenges. Likewise, biblical scholars are increasingly in danger of overlooking the fact that the texts they study involve religious imagination, theological dimensions and truth claims beyond their undoubtedly linguistic, historical, social, cultural and literary significance. A new integration of all approaches to the different aspects of Christian faith is needed, but without endangering all particular approaches to phenomena of Christian faith.

Theology always needs to balance the concerns of its particular sub-disciplines and overall tasks, and it needs to link its local horizons and universal aspirations if it wishes to continue to serve the many needs of church, society, academy, and individual Christian discipleship.

WERNER G. JEANROND

Roger A. Badham, *Introduction to Christian Theology*, Louisville, KY: Westminster John Knox Press 1998; David F. Ford (ed), *The Modern Theologians: An Introduction to Christian Theology in the Twentieth Century*, Oxford: Blackwell [2]1997; Werner G. Jeanrond, *Theological Hermeneutics*, London: SCM Press 1994; Hans Küng, *Christianity*, London: SCM Press and New York: Crossroad 1995; Johann B. Metz, *Faith in History and Society: Toward a Practical Fundamental Theology*, New York: Crossroad 1980; Letty M. Russell and J. Shannon Clarkson, *Dictionary of Feminist Theologies*, Louisville, KY: Westminster John Knox Press 1996; Robert J. Schreiter, *The New Catholicity: Theology between the Global and the Local*, Maryknoll, NY: Orbis 1997; David Tracy, *The Analogical Imagination: Christian Theology and the Culture of Pluralism*, New York: Crossroad and London: SCM Press 1981; Graham Ward (ed), *The Postmodern God: A Theological Reader*, Oxford: Blackwell 1997

Third World

The Third World (first given that name by Alfred Sauvy of France in 1952) can be defined negatively by what it is not. It is not the First World of the capitalist West and it is not the Second World of what until the late 1980s was thought of as the socialist East. It is not those parts of the world that have taken centre stage in modern history, but those that have been pushed to the margins.

Gay and lesbian theology ◄

More positively, the Third World can be defined by what it is. It is varied and vast, spread across Asia, Africa, Latin America, the Caribbean, the Pacific and the Middle East. It contains up to 75 per cent of the world's population, so that it is sometimes referred to as the 'Two-Thirds World'. It comprises peoples with a world of their own, with their own long histories and cultures. Above all, it is united by a common heritage of capitalist and colonial exploitation. That exploitation, first at the hands of imperial powers such as Britain who grew rich at the expense of Third-World countries, is now perpetuated in many eyes by the neo-colonialism of globalization which, for good or ill, tends to impose not only free-market capitalism but a creeping cultural conformity on all parts of the world. The countries that are the source of these developments continue to prosper, while poorer countries, most notably in Africa, which has been called the Fourth World, become poorer. It is from these oppressive political and economic forces that Third-World countries struggle to be free.

Globalization

This definition of the Third World, focusing on the common problems and needs and aspirations that unite it, seems to be acceptable to Third-World peoples themselves. It is not yet another imposition but reflects their own self-understanding.

Third-World theologies, which again vary according to the many contexts and cultures of Third-World peoples, are inspired and informed by the same shared history of oppression and exploitation and the struggle for liberation. They understand sin as embedded in social and economic structures, such as colonial rule and capitalism, and not just as personal disobedience. They see Christ's work as setting captives free as well as forgiving individuals their sins. The exodus from slavery to a new life of dignity and self-determination for God's people, and God's special concern for the poor and downtrodden, are for them key sources of inspiration.

Sin

Third-World churches can also be defined against this background as churches that have asserted their independence from Western influence and control and have supported movements for liberation. African Indigenous Churches, founded in Africa by Africans, would be one example, and the base Christian communities of Latin America, relating faith to social issues, another, though as other opportunities or 'spaces' for political activity have opened up, they are less prominent than they used to be.

Community

This acceptable understanding of the Third World as sharing a common history helps to deal with some of the problems that can be associated with the term. One of

Geography them has to do with geography. With the end of the Cold War and the demise of the socialist economies, and even beforehand, some have suggested that the language of Poverty North-South and two worlds would be more accurate than the language of three worlds. Again, if we think of Third-World countries as characteristically poor in economic terms, there are countries in Asia especially, sometimes known as Newly Industrialized Countries (NICs) or 'Asian Tigers', which are prosperous; and with ever growing numbers of migrants heading north, significant numbers of Third-World peoples are to be found in Europe and North America.

Third World, however, need not be thought of only as a geographical term, though broadly speaking it has had a not misleading geographical reference: it describes people, wherever they may be, who have suffered the consequences of colonialism and neo-colonialism, and in all too many cases still do.

It is more important to steer clear not just of inaccuracies but also of misrepresentation, prejudice and racism. 'Third World' all too easily becomes a pejorative term and is frequently used to imply inferior peoples, cultures, economies and churches. Third-World societies have been described as 'backward' and, by Christian missionaries, as pagan, savage and barbarian. Third-World countries have been called 'dark continents', not because they were unknown to many but because they needed the light of the gospel and the enlightenment of Western civilization. The Third World is thought to be under-developed, not just as an industrialized economy but in every respect. A lack of Western education is equated with a lack of intelligence. Non-Western can mean 'primitive' and in need of modernization, and non-Christian can mean devoid of spirituality. Third-World churches have been treated paternalistically as 'younger churches' that have yet to grow up and mature and learn to take care of themselves. Protest and struggle have been looked on as youthful exuberance and rebelliousness.

While it is as unhelpful to romanticize the Third World as it is to romanticize the First, it is important to avoid all forms of disrespect and misrepresentation. Third-World cultures are both ancient and rich. Third-World economic systems, before Western influences undermined them, were often sustainable. First-World countries have plenty of room left for human development, as a growing Religious orders hunger for spirituality and community among their peoples suggests. The vast majority of Christians in the twenty-first century are to be found in the Third World, which in any case has harboured for centuries Christian  traditions as old if not older than Western Christianity. And some would argue that it is to the churches of the Third World that Western Christians must now look  for fresh understandings of the gospel, for vibrancy in worship and discipleship, and for the renewal of their faith and life.

Maybe the easiest and most unfortunate misuse of the term Third World is to equate it with 'poor'. For example, badly-run hospitals in England in the early 2000s were described as 'Third-World' hospitals, as if everything in the Third World is of poor quality, inferior or third rate.

It is obviously true that there is a great deal of abject, material poverty in the Third World, which certainly includes among other things a lack of health care and hospitals without doctors and medicines. Oppressed, exploited and marginalized people are not likely to be well-off. Though poor in things, however, they may be rich in soul, and those who are rich in things may be poor in soul. The materially poor may well be rich in their courage, endurance, wisdom, skills and faith. They may have much to teach and much to give. Third-World people have given a great deal to the First World in the past. Cheap raw materials and cheap labour are two examples. They have continued to give in more recent times as they have migrated to live in First-World countries as manual workers and professionals and opened these countries up to more varied and interesting cultural realities. And Third-World people have much to give in the future to the church communities of the Western world, and indeed to the whole world as it now struggles to liberate itself from some of the more dehumanizing and environmentally damaging effects of globalization.

MICHAEL H. TAYLOR

North-South: A Programme For Survival. The Report of the Independent Commission on International Development Issues under the Chairmanship of Willy Brandt, London: Pan Books 1980, US title: William K. Brandt and Anthony Sampson (eds), *North-South: A Programme for Survival*, Cambridge, MA: MIT Press 1980; Virginia Fabella and R. S. Sugirtharajah (eds), *Dictionary of Third World Theologies*, Maryknoll, NY: Orbis 2000 and London: SCM Press 2003

Thomas Aquinas

Born in Italy, in the region of Naples, Thomas Aquinas lived from 1225 to 1274. His parents had taken it for granted that he would be a Benedictine abbot, but he resisted their pressure to become a monk and joined the Order of Preachers or Dominicans. He was quite cosmopolitan. He studied in Italy, France and Germany. His apprenticeship in Cologne took place under a renowned scholar, Albertus Magnus (Albert the Great). Both commented extensively on the newly-translated *Nicomachean Ethics* as well as on many of Aristotle's other works. There was a lot of

THOMAS AQUINAS, *SUMMA THEOLOGIAE*

Thomas Aquinas' *Summa Theologiae* (now the preferred title; it used to be called the *Summa Theologica*) is beyond doubt the greatest work of Catholic theology. However, its sheer size can be forbidding and the way in which scholars refer to it perplexing. What is one to do when asked to look up *ST*, Ia, 2, 3 *ad* 1? On the other hand, the English text is easily available (in book form or on the internet), and when the structure of the work is explained, the problems disappear.

The *Summa Theologiae* consists of three parts with an added supplement, each of which covers a variety of topics as indicated below; the second part is divided into two parts (the Latin titles are usually preserved).

Prima Pars
Sacred Doctrine. The One God. The Blessed Trinity. Creation. The Angels. The Six Days. Man. The Government of Creatures.

Prima Secundae Partis
Man's Last End. Human Acts. Passions. Habits. Vice and Sin. Law. Grace.

Secunda Secundae Partis
Faith. Hope. Charity. Prudence. Justice. Fortitude. Temperance. Acts Which Pertain to Certain Men.

Tertia Pars
The Incarnation. The Life of Christ. Sacraments. Baptism. Confirmation. The Holy Eucharist. Penance.

Supplementum Tertia Partis
Penance (continued). Extreme Unction. Holy Orders. Matrimony. The Resurrection. Appendices

Each part is subdivided into 'questions', and most questions contain several 'articles'; for example, question 2 of part I is 'The existence of God', and there are three articles: '1. Is the proposition "God exists" self-evident?', 2. 'Is it demonstrable?', 3. 'Does God exist?' In each article Thomas first quotes objections against the doctrine he proposes (there are two in the article 'Does God exist?'). Then he expounds his doctrine in what is known as the body of the article (in this case outlining his famous 'five ways'). Finally, in many articles he replies to objections (here to both). The numbering of questions begins afresh with each part (or sub-part), and the numbering of articles begins afresh with each question.

We are now in a position to understand the perplexing reference *ST*, I*a*, 2, 3 *ad* 1. *ST* stands for *Summa Theologiae*. I*a* denotes the first part (the *a* after I represents the Latin *prima*, first; II*a* would denote the second part, but since this is divided into two further clarification is needed, i.e. II*a* I*ae*, the first division of the second part. The next figure, 2, denotes the question and the next, 3, the article. If the reference stopped there it would be to the body of the article, but there is also the *ad* 1. The *ad* indicates that the reference is to Thomas' answer to one of the objections, here the first. In short, the reference is to *Summa Theologiae*, first part, question 2, article 3, objection 1.

The classic text is Thomas Aquinas, *Summa Theologiae*, Latin text and English translations by the Dominicans of the English-speaking provinces (60 vols), London and New York; Blackfriars in conjunction with McGraw Hill and Eyre and Spottiswoode 1964–76 (known as the 'Blackfriars Edition'). An earlier translation is *Summa Theologica*, translated by Fathers of the English Dominican Province (second revised edition 1920) (5 vols), Notre Dame, IN: Ave Maria Press 1981.

The text is available online at: http://www.newadvent.org/summa

excitement and controversy over the opportunity to learn important things from a pagan philosopher and scientist.

Because Thomas was both big and silent, he was dubbed 'the dumb ox'. His mind was unusually inquisitive. As a child, he used to annoy his entourage by repeatedly asking, 'What is God?' Because he was almost continually getting insights, people compared his mind to that of an angel and called him 'the angelic doctor'.

He gave homilies, composed hymns and prayers, lectured on the Bible, took part in debates, replied to intellectual queries, and wrote commentaries, treatises and two long syntheses of Catholic thinking, the *Summa Contra Gentiles* and the *Summa Theologiae*. Ironically, the man who was one of the best metaphysicians in the West, though he had said that one could not be an accomplished metaphysician before the age of 50, died at the age of 49!

Thomas' world-view reflects the universe of Plato, Aristotle and the Neoplatonists: a cosmic hierarchy, a multi-dimensional universe in which unequal beings participate in one another – inanimate things, plants, animals, humans, angels, God. This is not a mere physics, but a metaphysics, namely the kind of reflection that comes after physics. Philosophy

Apart from simple observation, which tells us that we can expect more from higher beings than from lower beings in terms of their activity, the key to this gradation of beings is self-knowledge. Like Plato, Thomas knows that understanding is more than perceiving. Like Aristotle, he knows that judging is more than perceiving and understanding. Keeping in mind the sense data, humans reflect upon their insights, and pronounce them to be correct or incorrect. In both of these acts – understanding and judging, which Thomas calls the first and second intellectual operations – human beings stretch to a level of thinking that is higher than animal knowing.

Cognitional theory is one of the ways in which Thomas brings together faith and reason. The man of faith wants to understand what he believes. In the human capacity to raise questions, he discerns a basic openness to the infinite, God a natural desire to see God. This natural desire to under- Grace stand everything is elevated by grace to a supernatural level. The natural and the supernatural must be distinguished, not separated, since they are two aspects of a single human life. Reason, which sets the philosophical quest in motion, is elevated by faith and becomes theological reason.

Thomas totally respects the capacity of human reason. Having a built-in sense of unlimited truth, our intelligence should naturally recognize its limitations and acknowledge that its very tendency to seek truth comes from an infinite p. 507 Source. For instance, among his ways of proving the existence of God, in the fourth one he shows that there exists a highest Perfection, or greatest Truth, which is the cause of all finite 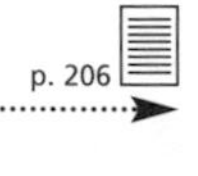 p. 206 truths. This way to God is a natural one, based on intellectual self-knowledge. Nevertheless, when someone comes to assent to God's self-revelation, this sense of a First Truth Jesus is supernaturally raised to a higher level, where Jesus Christ, Holy Spirit  incarnate Truth, illumines the human mind in a special manner. For Thomas, faith is more than a religious opinion, a wager, or even trust in God: it is knowledge too.

Thanks to this intertwining of faith and reason, there is nothing purely philosophical in Thomas' works. Of course, most of what he writes philosophically can stand on its own by the criteria of reason. Still, he experiences the light of faith as liberating and stimulating human  reason. For instance, the definition of God given in the book of Exodus, 'He Who Is', helps him to appreciate the distinction between essence and existence made by  the Arab philosopher Avicenna (980–1037), who was a key figure in mediating Aristotle's thought to the Middle Ages. When we consider a thing, we realize the difference between understanding what a thing is (its essence) and asserting the fact that it is (its existence). The existence of finite beings is particularized and hence limited by that Law which they are, namely their essence. Accordingly, there is 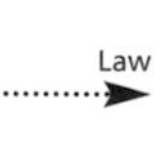 a real distinction between essence and existence. But in the One who simply Is, the essence is the existence.

This is the context in which the arguments for the existence of God, the five ways, of the *Summa Theologiae* function. (We find many other proofs for the existence of God in the rest of his writings.) In each case, he examines a certain kind of effect requiring a causal explanation. Salvation Reason remains dissatisfied until a first cause is posited.  Thus we can affirm the latter's existence, but we cannot imagine or picture how this first cause operates. The first cause remains unknown. We cannot grasp its essence.

Another feature of Thomas' universe is what he calls 'Providence', the overall cause of purpose. For him, Providence is rational and almighty, benevolent and beneficent, caring for both the universe as a whole and individuals in particular. Furthermore, as the creator of time, God is above time. Strictly speaking, Providence does not foresee, does not decide beforehand what will take place. In his eternity, God always knows and loves the creatures, especially the intelligent ones, to whom he grants the capacity to act freely. Because God's causality is not on the same level as human action, since the former sets the latter in motion, this free action must be permanently sustained by the Creator.

Thomas adopts as much of Greek knowledge as possible. Thus, his ethics is an ethics of virtue, or excellence. Given the basic aptitude of the human mind, the skills called virtues can be acquired, either by learning in the case of the intellectual virtues or by practice in the case of the moral virtues. However, for him, the intellectual and moral virtues are insufficient. He complements them with a third category, the theological virtues of faith, hope and charity. Their role is to place each believer in a personal relationship to God. Pure gifts from the Holy Spirit, the theological virtues nonetheless become ours; they function as principles of our activities and we can co-operate in increasing their strength.

In addition to virtues, the end is central. Virtues are enfeebled if they are not cultivated for the sake of true happiness, which is our ultimate end. For Aristotle, happiness consists in virtuous activities, in the noble acts performed by reason, both speculative and practical. Confronted with the conflict between Aristotle's optimistic and Augustine's pessimistic views on happiness, Thomas Aquinas the synthesizer reconciles them by subordinating the natural to the supernatural. He calls the earthly happiness envisaged by Aristotle 'imperfect happiness'. He calls 'perfect happiness' the heavenly happiness pointed to by Augustine. Basing himself on the authority of the New Testament, he boldly asserts that perfect happiness, promised by Christ, is nothing less than the vision of the divine essence – something unattainable on earth.

Thomas sees law as a work of reason. For most modern thinkers, law is a decree issued by someone who exercises power. It is an act of the will, and so it may easily become arbitrary. Moreover, because people's instincts are seen as selfish, law is enacted for the sake of imposing and maintaining order in society.

For Thomas, law derives from wisdom and aims at rendering humans more virtuous. Because he believes in the actuality of salvation, on the one hand he is hopeful that some citizens can become virtuous. On the other hand, he is realistic enough to admit the necessity of coercion, but only for non-virtuous people. Finally, natural law is what enables people to assess positive laws. Unfortunately, to a certain extent natural law has been defaced by sin. Consequently revelation is required if humans are to retrieve natural law and interpret it correctly.

In his approach to salvation, Thomas takes account of two facts. First, we cannot attain our ultimate end by our own efforts. Secondly, we are endowed with free will and therefore with the capacity to heed Christ's calling. In the light of these two facts, Thomas divides grace into operative and co-operative. In the former, only God operates; in the latter, God and the person work together. Operative grace consists in inserting into the human heart an inclination towards the supernatural end; co-operative grace enables the human agent to will and choose the means that lead to that end.

There is no coercion of the human will here. Whereas the will of the sinner is frustrated because it cannot will the truly good, the will of the redeemed recovers not only its natural tendency towards the good in general, but is also empowered to respond to divine love. Grace is not something extrinsic, tacked on to our soul.

When he talks about charity, or divine love, Thomas draws from what Aristotle wrote on friendship. Whereas the Greek philosopher was of the opinion that no friendship could obtain between such unequal parties as God and man, the Christian theologian affirms that God does establish a certain equality and bestows his friendship. This relationship makes the believer already possess and enjoy God's presence in this life.

Another theological virtue, hope, makes the believer count on God and look forward to complete beatitude in the resurrection. Both the virtues of charity and hope are given to the human heart, or the will (the same word in Latin: *voluntas).* But faith is given to our intelligence, illuminating it and enabling it to begin thinking as Christ thinks and to receive revelation regarding the mysteries of Christianity such as the incarnation, redemption, the Trinity, the sacraments. Besides the three theological virtues, the Holy Spirit grants the seven gifts, which render people responsive to his particular promptings.

Thomas Aquinas' contribution is typical of a great synthesizer. Most of the concepts he employed had already been coined by others. His genius consists in having brought them together into a coherent unity.

LOUIS ROY, OP

Thomas Aquinas, *Summa Theologiae* ed Thomas Gilby, London: Eyre & Spottiswoode and New York: McGraw-Hill, 1964–74 (60 vols, Latin and English texts, with translators' introductions and appendices); Marie-Dominique Chenu, *Aquinas and His Role in Theology*, Collegeville, MN: The Liturgical Press 2002; Brian Davies, *The Thought of Thomas Aquinas*, Oxford: Clarendon Press 1992; Etienne Gilson, *The Christian Philosophy of St Thomas Aquinas,* Notre Dame, IN: University of Notre Dame Press 1994; Fergus Kerr, *After Aquinas: Versions of Thomism*, Oxford: Blackwell 2002; Aidan Nichols, *Discovering Aquinas: An Introduction to His Life, Work and Influence*, London: Darton, Longman & Todd 2003; Jean-Pierre Torrell, *Saint Thomas Aquinas*, Washington, DC: The Catholic University of America Press 1996–2003 (2 vols)

www.newadvent.org/summa for a list of Aquinas' writings in Latin and in English and an English translation of the *Summa Theologiae*

Revelation

Thomism

The term 'Thomism' encompasses a range of philosophical and theological viewpoints developed out of the thought of Thomas Aquinas (1225–74). The term has been used to refer both to the work of Aquinas himself and to that of his followers, who claimed him as both their source and their authority. It is in this latter sense that it is most commonly used today.

Thomas Aquinas
Love
Friendship

Despite Thomas' prominence during his lifetime, both as a teacher in Paris and as a theologian at the papal court, initially his work was not well accepted and he was condemned by the universities of Oxford and Paris in 1277, only three years after his death. Nevertheless, the sheer power and range of his thought ensured that his ideas could not be ignored. The Dominican John Capreolus (*c.*1380–1444) was the first great commentator on Thomas' thought, producing four detailed commentaries which defended his fellow Dominican against Duns Scotus and William of Ockham, among others. This dedication earned him the sobriquet 'Prince of Thomists'. Capreolus' mastery of Aristotle enabled him to reaffirm for subsequent Thomists the attempt to balance faith and reason, which is Thomas' lasting legacy to Roman Catholic thought.

Hope
Faith
Incarnation
Trinity
Sacraments
Holy Spirit

Thomas de Vio (1469–1534), Cardinal Cajetan, was the most prominent Thomist in the early Reformation period. His *De nominum analogia* ('The Analogy of Names', 1498) stands as one of the most important of Thomist texts. Cajetan developed Thomas' theory of analogy beyond Thomas' own position, arguing that there are various ways in which analogy may be understood, but that only an analogy of proportionality is analogy strictly speaking. Cajetan applied this idea to talk about God. Thus, to use an analogy in speaking of God (as in references to God's goodness) is to say that the goodness of God is proportional to God's nature, just as human goodness is proportional to human nature. Whether Cajetan correctly

God

interpreted Thomas' views on analogy is open to dispute, but his aim was to clarify the meaning of analogy and also to help remove the theological difficulty which arises from speaking anthropomorphically of the divine. Cajetan's commentaries on Thomas were greatly influential, so much so that Pope Leo XIII, the nineteenth-century reviver of Thomism, ordered that they should be included in his edition of the *Summa Theologiae.*

Council

In the post-Reformation period, differences between Dominicans and Jesuits on the nature of grace and freedom led to bitter disputes. The issue centred on the question whether or not human acts were determined in advance by divine grace, including the question whether humans have the capacity freely to accept God's saving grace, or whether this acceptance is an act of God. In defence of human freedom, Luis de Molina (1535–1600), the first Jesuit to write a commentary on Thomas' *Summa Theologiae*, rejected the idea that God determines the human act of accepting grace. The Dominicans defended what they perceived as Thomas' view, namely that human beings cannot accept grace unless moved to do so by God. The most notable Dominican Thomist was Domingo Bañez (1528–1604), professor of theology at Salamanca and confessor to Teresa of Avila, who claimed never to have deviated from Thomas' teachings, not even by the breadth of a finger-nail. This dispute had no clear victor.

Another dispute between the Jesuit critics of Thomism and Thomas' more conservative Thomistic interpreters was over the moral teaching of probabilism. The Spanish Dominican Bartholomew de Medina (1527–81) stated the principle, 'If an opinion is probable it may be acted upon, even though the opposite opinion is more probable,' a view that he claimed to find in Thomas. Thomists have endlessly disputed whether Medina taught this doctrine himself or merely discussed it, but it nevertheless gave rise to fierce arguments over moral standards. Its relevance was that an opinion in favour of freedom could be held even if an opinion in favour of the law was more probable, and the Jesuits, eager to keep the leading aristocratic families of Europe within the Roman Catholic Church, used the teaching in the confessional to promote moral freedom. Their opponents, among whom were the strict Jansenists of the seventeenth century, taught that probabilism led to moral laxity and that in cases of doubt the decision should favour the established moral precedent.

Political theology
Other faiths
Ecotheology
p. 1016

The influence of Thomism declined in the Enlightenment period as theology came under the influence of the new thinking of René Descartes and others. However, it was revived among Roman Catholic theologians in the nineteenth century as they attempted to counter what they saw as the corrosive effects of Enlightenment rationalism. This revival was given a major impetus by Pope Leo XIII's encyclical *Aeterni patris* (1879), which encouraged Roman Catholic scholars to respond to what Leo saw as the errors of modern thought by drawing on their heritage of medieval philosophy and theology. Leo effectively declared Thomas Aquinas to be the official theologian of the Roman Catholic Church. This Neo-Thomist revival waned only with the changes brought about by the Second Vatican Council (1962–5).

Enlightenment
p. 700

In this period Roman Catholic philosophers such as Étienne Gilson (1884–1978) and Jacques Maritain (1882–1973) saw in Thomism the possibility for a revitalized dialogue between Roman Catholic thought and modern culture. In theology the most influential Neo-Thomist movement of the twentieth century was the so-called 'transcendental Thomism' initiated by Pierre Rousselot (1878–1915) and Joseph Maréchal (1878–1944) and developed by their younger Jesuit confrère Karl Rahner (1904–84), among others. These thinkers drew upon Thomas' fundamental teaching on the relationship between grace and nature to respond to the challenge issued to religious belief by Immanuel Kant and other Enlightenment thinkers. Rahner's fundamental thesis was that the depth structures of human experience allow us to think of a transcendent horizon of experience that is Absolute Mystery (in theological terms, God). This argument is considered 'transcendental' because it works not from dogmatic or metaphysical premises to further theological truth, but rather from an analysis of human experience to a transcendent religious possibility; the transcendent, argued Rahner, was the condition of the possibility of human knowledge, freedom, willing and love. This approach gave a new sense to the classical Catholic theological dictum that 'grace builds on nature', and provided an epistemology which allows for knowledge of God in and through human experience.

Rahner's revitalized Thomism has been of immense significance in modern Roman Catholicism, so much so that it has seeped into the fabric of Catholic thinking on a wide range of issues, including political theology, the theology of religions, and ecological theology. While Neo-Thomism as a movement declined in the face of the new theological pluralism of the 1960s and 1970s, essential aspects of Thomas' own thought were thereby preserved in a new, innovative and, for Roman Catholic theology, quite modern way.

JAMES M. BYRNE

Norman Kretzmann and Elenore Stump (eds), *The Cambridge Companion to Aquinas*, Cambridge: CUP 1993; Ralph McInerney, *Aquinas on Analogy*, Washington, DC: Catholic University of America Press 1996; Karl Rahner, *Foundations of Christian Faith: An Introduction to the Idea of Christianity*, New York: Crossroad 1978

TIME

Apocalyptic, Calendar, Eschatology, Eternity, Evolution, Festivals and fasts, Future, Kingdom of God

The history of Christianity and the history of human time are closely connected. Even now, many of our fundamental ideas about the shape, measurement and meaning of time derive from Christian beliefs and practices. Our week, for example, with its pattern of days at work and rest, derives from the ancient Jewish and Christian belief that the world was created in six days. On the seventh God took a 'day of rest'. Furthermore the date today, whatever it is, is still counted forward from the year of Jesus' birth. Christianity was not the only influence upon the Western understanding of time, but it has certainly been the most dominant one.

The central place of the church in the life of medieval Europe meant that the first public clocks were erected in churches and cathedrals. The church was one of the few organizations wealthy enough to purchase such rare and expensive items, and it also had grand buildings in which to house them. Before the mass production of watches the sounding of church bells (such as the morning, midday and evening 'angelus', which is a summons to recite the 'Hail Mary') gave structure not only to church worship, but also to the life of the whole community. The church clock was symbolic of order and authority, a reminder to Christians that God is in charge of time and human destiny.

More importantly though, Christianity has provided the West with many of its basic ideas about the meaning and purpose of time. For example, the idea that humanity is progressing through time towards a perfect future – which has been the dominant myth of the industrial age – can be seen as a secular version of the Christian belief that God is guiding human history to a 'kingdom of God'. Even Karl Marx's aggressively anti-Christian view of history can be read as a story of 'fall' and 'salvation' that has its roots in Jewish and Christian beliefs about God's activity in time. In very many apparently secular ideas about time we can find remnants of Christian thinking.

Critics of Christianity

The question of the meaning of time takes us to the centre of the Christian message. At the heart of Christianity is the belief that on a particular day in world history God became human in Jesus Christ. Christians believe that this event, the incarnation or becoming-flesh of God, gave structure to all prior and subsequent time. According to Christian doctrine, Jesus' death made it possible for humanity to overcome 'original sin'. As a result, Jesus gave his followers the hope of a perfect heavenly future without violence, misery or injustice. In this way the passage of time itself took the shape of a path towards heaven. This is why Christianity is often credited with a purely 'linear' view of time.

Incarnation

Sin

Linear and circular views of time

The Christian linear view was a radical new idea, quite different from the circular views of time that were popular among the ancient philosophers. Plato, for example, saw time as a way of ordering the world by giving life a regular, repeating structure of days, seasons and years. Aristotle connected time with ideas of circular planetary motion and the human cycle of life and death.

To the ancient world, the idea of the 'circle of time' was an obvious truth. So the Christian idea that time does not repeat itself, but moves down a one-way street towards a final conclusion, must have seemed very strange and controversial. Augustine (writing in the early fifth century CE) felt 

it necessary to launch a defence of the linear view of time. In his *City of God* (Book 12) he argued – against Plato and Aristotle – that circular views of time were 'miserable' and 'prevented the appearance of anything new'. By contrast Christianity offered the possibility of renewal, growth, Salvation personal change and salvation.

Augustine made the case for the linear view very well, but he did not acknowledge the complex character of the Christian understanding of time, which includes other non-linear concepts. In Jesus particular, Jesus taught his disciples about the importance of special openings or turning points in time. Jesus used a Greek term for this: *kairos*, a word meaning 'opportunity' or 'the right time'. *Kairos* is distinct from *chronos*, the usual Greek word for time, which refers to the mere passage of events. In *kairos* the linear movement of time is less significant than the power and potential of every given moment. From this, time is not so much a 'line' as a pattern of dots, where each dot represents a unique historical opportunity.

In Greek culture, Kairos was the name of a god, a young man with winged feet and long hair. Kairos represented life's fleeting opportunities that are either seized or lost for ever. Ancient pictures of Kairos show people reaching up to grasp him by the forelock before he speeds away. The concept of *kairos* was used mainly by rhetoricians, who stressed the importance of 'decorum', or saying the right words at the right time. Isocrates (a Greek philosopher of the fourth century BCE) developed the rhetorical theory of *kairos* into a more general theory of life. He believed that there was a time for every human action and that true happiness could come only from acting appropriately in every situation.

In the New Testament, the concept of *kairos* is used in a special theological sense, to speak about the timing of salvation. Jesus describes his own appearance and the coming of his kingdom as Paul moments of *kairos*. Paul tells us that Jesus died at a moment of *kairos* and that his second coming will be another. To see *kairos* moments, said Jesus, we need to be able to 'read the signs of the times' by looking at the world with the eyes of faith. Only then does the array of religious opportunities become visible. Paul urges his fellow Christians to seize the *kairos* and put their lives right, before Jesus' second coming and the final judgement.

Thinking of time as *kairos* has been an important counterpart to the tradition of linear 'salvation history'. This view of time has been popular among Christian mystical thinkers. One of the classic expositions of it was given in the seventeenth century by Jean-Pierre de Caussade, who spoke about the Christian experience of time as 'the sacrament of the present moment'. The Christian poet T. S. Eliot also advanced a view of time as *kairos* in his *Four Quartets*, where all the dimensions of time are seen to converge on the present moment.

The idea of *kairos* also played an important part in shaping the existentialist philosophies of Søren Kierkegaard, Martin Heidegger and Karl Jaspers. Broadly speaking, the existentialists argued we must seize the opportunity presented by our own present existence. We must decide to engage with our lives here and now, as they happen. Only then can we uncover the real nature of human existence, which otherwise gets overlooked. These existentialist ideas of time had a considerable influence on a range of twentieth-century theologians, including Rudolf Bultmann, Paul Tillich and Karl Rahner.

The tension between the linear and non-linear views of time is not resolved within the Bible. Indeed the Bible contains further ideas of time. For example, the Bible also describes time as a circular repetition of 'types': the Garden of Eden (where Adam was tempted) is repeated in the Garden of Gethsemane (where Jesus was not). Eve is repeated anew in Mary and Adam is repeated anew in Jesus. This typological view sees time as a spiral in which different themes are re-worked Eucharist and developed. The central act of Christian worship, the sharing of bread and wine at holy communion, works in this way. Communion is a ritual of repetition in which the same words and

TYPOLOGY

Typology is a method of interpretation which uses the story of a figure from an earlier time as a 'type' which foreshadows a later person or event in a different context. It became commonplace among the church fathers as a way of interpreting the Old Testament, but actually begins with Paul, who in his letter to the Romans speaks of Adam as the 'type of the one to come' (5.14). The 'type' in the Old Testament foreshadows an 'antitype': this term is used in 1 Peter 3.21 where baptism is the antitype to the salvation of Noah and his family in the ark.

Church fathers

In the New Testament, the mysterious priest king Melchizedek (Genesis 14.18/Hebrews 6.20) and Aaron (Exodus 28/Hebrews 9) are also types of Jesus, and so was the supernatural rock which followed the Israelites fleeing from Egypt (Exodus 17.6/1 Corinthians 10.4). The Jewish Passover lamb is a type of Christ (Exodus 12/1 Corinthians 5.7), as is the brazen serpent which Moses lifted up in the wilderness to heal the people (Numbers 21; John 3.14–15).

This method of interpretation begins from an approach first found in the Dead Sea Scrolls, in the commentaries on Habakkuk and Nahum. The members of the Qumran sect believed that these two prophetic books, like others, were written with them in view; once that was recognized they had the key to true understanding. Christians read the Hebrew Bible, their Old Testament, in the same way. Typology gave them the key to understanding it, and moreover taking it over and establishing a unity between it and their New Testament. This was a useful argument against their opponents; it also turned the Old Testament into a rich source of deepening knowledge about Jesus.

 p. 845

Sometimes the boundary between typology and allegory is difficult to draw; typology takes the dimension of past and present and developments in time more seriously. However, they are very closely related. The highly complex system of typological relationships which became established is expressed in Christian symbolism and in Christian worship, from paintings and stained-glass windows to hymns and prayers. Once understood, it provides a new dimension in appreciating them.

Symbolism
Paintings
Hymns

actions are re-enacted monthly, weekly or even daily in order to connect the believer with Jesus himself. In this way, holy communion affirms a strongly cyclical view of human time. So too does the constant cycle of the Christian year, with its calendar of festivals.

There is no one, simple Christian view of time. Instead we find, within the Bible and Christian tradition, a collection of insights about time's shape and meaning. For the Christian, time has an important linear dimension, but the non-linear dimension of the *kairos* experience is important too, as is the dimension of cyclical repetition. These differing perspectives cannot be woven together into a tidy Christian doctrine of time.

The end of time

A concept that is crucial to Christian theology is the idea that there will be an 'end of history' when the present time-bound world will give way to an eternal 'kingdom of God'. The idea has its roots in pre-Christian Jewish ideas of the apocalypse. The Greek word apocalypse literally means 'revelation' or 'uncovering' and refers to the divine closure of human history and the uncovering of God's kingdom.

Kingdom of God

The Jewish ideas of apocalypse grew out of the failure of the so-called 'prophetic' understanding of time. The Old Testament prophets – such as Isaiah and Jeremiah – believed that human history could have a positive future if people would only be more faithful to God. They believed that the problems of human history could be mended if people were given the correct warnings and guidance. It was the prophets' role to hand out this advice along with reassurances that future times would be better. When things did not get better, however, the prophetic view of time lost favour, and the prophets were replaced by a new breed of radical, apocalyptic thinkers. The foremost of these was Daniel, who argued that human history had failed, that prophetic guidance was pointless, and that God must now bring it all to an end.

Prophecy

The influence of Jewish apocalyptic ideas on Jesus is unmistakable. At many points in the Gospels he speaks graphically about the apocalypse and what he calls 'the close of the age'. As a consequence, the early Christians were captivated by the belief that the world would end in their own lifetimes, and we can see this expectation expressed powerfully in Paul's letters, particularly his letter to the church in Rome. Paul saw time as a process of decay and corruption and looked forward to the new kingdom in which the faithful would be given incorruptible bodies that would last for eternity.

The fact that the world did not end provoked a major crisis in the mind-set of the early church. This was not only a crisis of timing, but a fundamental crisis in the Christian thinking of time. If the apocalypse was not going to happen for decades or perhaps centuries, this posed the problem of what to do with all the time between now and then. When the church was just waiting for the apocalypse, the purpose of time was relatively straightforward: Christians should get themselves ready for the 'time of the end'. Now Christians would have to think through the long-term role and purpose of the church. We see an example of this new thinking in the letter to the Ephesians, where the future kingdom is described in more 'prophetic' terms, as the outcome of a long-term 'plan'. The role of the church, argued Ephesians, is to work as a unified body to assist in the realization of the 'plan'. In the Gospels there are also many hints that the kingdom of God is not only waiting in the future, but mystically present in people's hearts. So the Christian thinking of time became more complicated: the apocalypse was in the future, but there was nevertheless a 'plan' that could engage Christian efforts in the meantime; furthermore Christians believed themselves to be mystically connected with the kingdom before its full arrival. Thus the 'end of time' was thought, all at once, to be a hope, a task and present reality.

Over the centuries there has been much Christian speculation about the date for the future apocalypse. Early Christian theologians such as Justin Martyr and Irenaeus adopted the 'millenarian' view that 1000 years would pass between Jesus' birth and the end of time. Since then, millenarian beliefs and anxieties have surfaced from time to time in history, notably among the sects of the radical Reformation such as the Anabaptists. Few in the mainstream churches would now bother to try to put a date on the apocalypse, and many would regard the idea of an apocalypse as a colourful myth. The literal belief that 'the end of the world is nigh' is generally seen as eccentric and extreme. This is ironic when we consider the importance of a literal apocalypse to the first Christians.

Anabaptists

History and progress

In the modern period Christian philosophers and theologians have conceived of 'the end of history' in terms of the progress of human society. The most famous of these thinkers was the early nineteenth-century German philosopher G. W. F. Hegel, who argued that history was the outworking of logical social processes that would bring about the kingdom of heaven on earth. Hegel argued that time was divided into three ages: the 'age of the Father' (before Jesus' birth); the 'age of the Son' (when Jesus set out the principles of Christian society); and the 'age of the Spirit' (in which the principles of Christian society would become a concrete reality). Hegel influenced not only secular thinkers such as Karl Marx, but many generations of Christian activists, who have believed that the church must work towards the end of history by changing society and eradicating suffering. In the 1980s the American thinker Francis Fukuyama argued Hegel's case afresh in his highly influential, but controversial book *The End of History and the Last Man.*

The belief in the progress of history towards an end had a profound impact upon thinking about time in the modern period. Time was thought of as a human resource which could be 'organized'. So people started to talk about 'time management'. Time could be 'saved', 'spent', and 'wasted'. Time was thought of as something to be 'used' to realize human ends. Such ideas would have seemed bizarre to Paul, who believed that God was the only person who could manage time.

The abject failure of modern Western societies to bring about a perfect future has corroded both Christian and secular confidence in 'the end of history'. Our contemporary attitude is often called 'postmodern' and is defined by a radical uncertainty about the meaning of time and a deep scepticism about the human capacity for self-improvement. This has lead to the increasing popularity, within the churches and outside them, of the *kairos* view of time as a spirituality of the present moment. There is now a burgeoning industry in spiritual literature of all kinds designed to connect people with moments of religious experience.

The puzzle of time

Augustine was the first Christian thinker to give serious philosophical consideration to the question of time. In his *Confessions* he tackled the issue head-on, asking the very simple question, 'What is time?' He expected a simple enough answer – after all, he said, the word 'time' is one that we use every day without any difficulty. But the more Augustine thought about the exact nature of time, the more perplexed he became. 'What then is time? I know well enough what it is, provided that nobody asks me … "Time" and "times" are words forever on our lips … No words could be plainer or more commonly used. Yet their true meaning is concealed from us. We have still to find it out.'

Augustine argued that time cannot exist in the 'past' because that time has disappeared. Similarly, time cannot exist in the 'future', because that time has yet to appear. This means that time can only be real in the 'present'. But here Augustine encountered a further problem, because he could not determine the duration of the present. However long we say the present lasts, we can always imagine it being shorter. In this way the duration of the present keeps shrinking until it becomes almost nothing at all. So time may be real in the present, but we cannot say what the present is.

The problems identified by Augustine – particularly the question of the 'present' – have puzzled theologians and philosophers ever since. Indeed further problems have been thrown up. We say that time flies or moves, but in which direction and relative to what? We say that we live in time, but in what sense are we 'in' time? And so the difficulties multiply. 'Don't even ask me [what time is] …' said the modern physicist Richard Feynman, 'it's just too hard to think about.' In 1995 another scientist, Paul Davies, listed twelve 'oustanding puzzles' of time. The study of time – in theology, philosophy and science – has been dominated more by problems than solutions.

One radical solution to the problem of time is to argue that it does not really exist. Although this goes against our common sense, it is a point of view that needs to be taken seriously. We certainly appear to live in a universe where time 'moves' through the tenses of 'future', 'present' and 'past', but appearances can be deceptive. After all, the sun appears to go around the earth, even though the opposite is true. Some philosophers – Benedict de Spinoza and J. M. E. McTaggart, for example  – have argued that our universe is really a static system. Many Christian theologians, particularly those influenced by Plato, have also argued that our universe of time and change is just an illusion, and that the 'real' world is a static dimension in which there is no time or change.

For all the intellectual and scientific advances of the past 1600 years, the truth is that we are not very much further on in our understanding of time than Augustine. The constitution of time is still a puzzle and the meaning and purpose of time is still a topic of Christian argument and discussion.

HUGH RAYMENT-PICKARD

Oscar Cullmann, *Christ and Time*, London: SCM Press and Philadelphia: Westminster Press 1949; Paul Davies, *About Time: Einstein's Unfinished Revolution*, Harmondsworth: Penguin Books 1995; Hugh Rayment-Pickard, *The Myths of Time: from St Augustine to American Beauty*, London: Darton, Longman & Todd 2004; Charles M. Sherover (ed), *The Human Experience of Time: The Development of Its Philosophic Meaning*, Evanston, IL: Northwestern University Press 2001

TRADITION

Authority, Bible, Church fathers, Council, Creed, Ecumenical movement, History, Jesus, Orthodox churches, Roman Catholic Church

From the very beginnings of Christianity, how the faith is handed on from one generation to the next has been a principal concern. In this process it has always been shaped and reshaped. The concept of 'tradition' (Latin, *traditio*; Greek, *paradosis*), which simply means 'handing over', is thus central to Christianity. However, the precise content and authority of what is handed on, together with the claims made by the institutions involved in the process of transmission, make the problem of tradition one of the most disputed of all areas of theology.

The notion of tradition does not begin with the emergence of Christianity. Jesus' own life and activity are characterized by disputes about the nature and authority of his own Jewish tradition: the most frequent use of the word tradition (*paradosis*) in the New Testament refers to the traditions of the elders, the *halakah* or the rabbinic elaboration of the law. In many places Jesus challenges his disputants with arguments about tradition. In the process of transmission, he claims, the traditions of the rabbis have begun to distort the tradition of Moses. Particularly instructive is the dispute in Mark 7.9–13, where Jesus claims that the fifth commandment, 'Honour your father and mother', has been displaced by the tradition of the elders that vows made to God (Deuteronomy 23.21–3) should always be kept. Jesus is thus using a central theme of the Law (one's obligations to parents) to interpret the traditions of the rabbis. So he says to the scribes and Pharisees, 'You are making void the word of God through your tradition that you hand on' (Mark 7.13). Jesus' method is to search for a principle of interpretation whereby those traditions which are handed down by the elders are subordinated to what he sees as the divine intention underlying the traditions. An understanding of tradition is therefore absolutely vital for assessing the relationship between Jesus and Judaism.

Elsewhere in the New Testament a similar method is displayed, but with one crucial difference: the figure of Jesus supplants everything else as the centre of the tradition, becoming the key to interpretation of scripture and the criterion for assessing everything that affects salvation. Just as Jesus applies a critical principle derived from the Hebrew scriptures to judge the validity of the tradition of the elders, so Paul begins to use the tradition of the life, death and resurrection of Christ as the interpretative key to scripture: the law of Moses gave way to what was 'received from the Lord' (1 Corinthians 11.23). This idea of a central core of tradition – the tradition of Christ – which is used to judge other human traditions is of the very essence of Paul's understanding of tradition, having its roots in the proclamation of the first Christians of the saving events of the life, death and resurrection of Jesus Christ. In 1 Corinthians 15, for instance, Paul speaks to the Corinthians of the message 'which you received, in which you stand, by which you were saved' (vv. 1–2). He 'delivered' to them what he had himself 'received', outlining what he sees as the core of the tradition: 'that Christ died for our sins in accordance with the scriptures, that he was buried, that he was raised on the third day, in accordance with the scriptures'. As an apostle, Paul felt himself entrusted with transmitting the gospel message, the tradition, which had previously been passed to him, and which was central to his new-found identity in Christ.

Salvation

Resurrection

At the same time, however, there were other traditions that were handed down along with this tradition of Christ, but which did not seem to be of such significance for salvation. Paul speaks of receiving other 'traditions', writing, for instance, to the Corinthians: 'To the married I give charge, not I but the Lord, that the wife should not separate from her husband ... and that the husband should not divorce his wife' (1 Corinthians 7.10–11). Again he talks about having 'received from the Lord what I also delivered to you' concerning the origins of the eucharist (1 Corinthians 11.23). Eucharist Elsewhere it is clear that there was a moral core to these traditions: 'as you received from us how you ought to live and to please God, just as you were doing, you do so more and more. For you know what instructions we gave you through the Lord Jesus' (1 Thessalonians 4.1–2). Such traditions are very different from confessions of faith in salvation through Christ and point to one of the central problems of the theology of tradition: how to distinguish between the central narrative at the heart of proclamation which forms the tradition of Christ, and the many other traditions which are handed down alongside. What is crucial in theology is to have some criterion to ensure that what is of central importance – what affects salvation – can be distinguished from what is merely accidental.

Two types of tradition

There are thus two strands of tradition in the New Testament letters: confessional statements about the saving significance of Christ and the many ethical and liturgical injunctions that were also taught as part of the tradition. Both were often confused, and both could easily be elevated to the same status. Paul himself seems to have elided both types of tradition: 'So then, brethren, stand firm and hold to the traditions which you were taught by us, either by word of mouth or by letter' (2 Thessalonians 2.15). The same holds true in some of the later New Testament writings, where although several passages point to a fixed form of the 'tradition', the precise content of 'the faith which was once for all delivered to the saints' (Jude 3) is far from clear. Similarly Timothy is twice enjoined to 'guard the deposit' which has been entrusted to him (1 Timothy 6.20; 2 Timothy 1.14) and which he is to hand on to 'faithful men who will be able to teach others also' (2 Timothy 2.2); the limits of this deposit, however, are ill-defined.

In the New Testament the concept of tradition – of something which has been handed over to the next generation, and which the present generation is expected to transmit – lacks precision. Although there was undoubtedly a body of tradition that was handed down orally (and perhaps secretly) alongside the public tradition of the saving events of Christ, its extent cannot be known. Very quickly, however, the validity of such unwritten traditions and teachings was guaranteed by the authoritative voice of the bearer of the tradition. This is clear even in Paul: 'What you have learnt and received and heard and seen in me, do' (Philippians 4.9). The authority of the transmitter of the tradition becomes as crucial as the content of the tradition itself. In post-New Testament times such an understanding of tradition develops as the church increasingly asserts its own authority: the truth came to be seen as revealed partly through the scriptures understood in the light of Christ, and partly through the unwritten traditions of the church.

This issue has become a focal point in modern ecumenical discussion between the churches. At its 1963 Montreal Conference the Faith and Order division of the World Council of Churches made what is now a famous distinction between Tradition (with a capital T) and traditions. Tradition is the transmission of the gospel as a whole (including the Bible); traditions are authoritative traditions of the church.

The rule of faith

In the generations following the New Testament, the tradition of the saving events of Christ gradually came to be used as a method for distinguishing truth from falsehood. The tradition of

Christ – what was believed by all Christians – was formulated into the 'rule of faith'. Brief statements of the Christian tradition about Christ frequently appear as rules or criteria, 'canons', to establish the integrity or orthodoxy of Christianity against opponents: to survive, the Christian faith required such summary statements to ensure that it could maintain its identity. The first use of such a method was by Irenaeus, who was active in Lyons at the end of the second century. In his work *Against the Heresies* he spoke of a rule of truth (*regula veritatis*) which embodied the 'true knowledge, the teaching of the apostles'. As a test of orthodoxy it was particularly suitable for those who could not read the scriptures: 'All teach one and the same God as Father and believe the same economy of the incarnation of the son of God and know the same gift of the spirit and take to heart the same commandments and preserve the same shape of the ordinances which is towards the church and wait for the same coming of the Lord and uphold the same salvation of the whole man, that is of soul and body.' The rule of faith conferred an identity on Christians, both literate and illiterate, throughout the whole world: 'The force of the tradition is one and the same. For the churches planted in Germany have not believed or handed down anything different, nor yet the churches among the Iberians or the Celts, nor those in the east, nor yet in Egypt and Libya, nor those established in the centre of the world (i.e. Rome).'

Heresy

Other fathers adopted a similar method: Hippolytus, for instance, speaks of a 'definition of truth' or 'word of truth' and the 'canon (rule) of the church', and Tertullian of the 'rule of faith' (*regula fidei*) or 'rule of God' (*dei regula*), while Origen uses the term 'rule of faith' or the 'ecclesiastical rule'. Such rules clarified what was central to the faith in testing for orthodoxy, but also became the central focus for interpretation of scripture. The rules were obtained from the scriptures, but were then re-applied to scripture. Authentic Christianity and authentic interpretation were both maintained through the priority of the tradition of Christ enshrined in the rule of faith. Thus Irenaeus could write against the heretics: 'They indulge in spurious fantasies and by their inventions they destroy the proper construction of the scriptures … but the man who maintains undistorted in his own mind the rule of truth which he has received through baptism will recognize the words and passages and the parables from scripture, but he will not recognize this blasphemous construction.' For Irenaeus the scriptures took on authentic meaning when they were read properly in the light of the tradition of Christ.

In interpreting scripture and in solving doctrinal disputes the church was appealing to a central truth behind scripture: the rule of faith as used by the fathers was intended to express what might be called the 'drift' of scripture. Tertullian went so far as to rank the rule of faith above scripture. He was forced to this conclusion, as he realized that appealing to scripture would never convince the heretics. A concept of tradition was thus necessary to hold the Bible together, to unify it, in the sense of applying the main body of truth confessed in the rule of faith as an interpretative system. A similar idea can be found as early as the time of Ignatius. In his letter to the Philadelphians he wrote: 'My archives are Jesus Christ; the inviolable archives are his cross, his death, his resurrection, and the faith which is exercised through him' (8.2). Such a method survived throughout the history of the church.

Secret tradition and public tradition

The development of the rule of faith needs to be considered alongside other forms of tradition, including the secret or mysterious traditions given to initiates that are mentioned by some writers. Such secret traditions are rare, most fathers understanding the Christian faith as public and open for all to see. Irenaeus, for instance, rejected the hypothesis that the apostles reserved some teaching for the initiates and some for the public domain and Tertullian wrote that although the apostles 'used to converse about some subjects among their intimate friends … we are not to believe that these subjects were any which should impose another rule of faith different from and opposite to that one which they were publicly representing to the Catholic Church'. Others, however, show evidence of an esoteric unwritten tradition in Christianity, which Clement of Alexandria calls *gnosis*. The *Apostolic Tradition* notes that at baptism there were various aspects of the faith which were only to be communicated secretly. Even here, however, it is likely that the doctrine was public among the initiated. Using such scanty evidence, however, some later interpreters, particularly in the Roman Catholic Church, have emphasized the notion of a *disciplina arcani*, the deliberate concealing of traditions to avoid profanation, where the substance of later doctrines, including the Trinity, the mass and the cult of the saints, was imparted secretly at baptism.

The oral tradition

Alongside the understanding of tradition as rule of faith and the secret tradition was that understanding of tradition frequently alluded to in the New Testament which consisted in the authoritative teachings of the church which had been handed down through the apostles from Christ himself. This understanding of tradition has its roots in the oral traditions of the early church. In the ancient world there was a prejudice against writing in favour of the spoken word, which was frequently given far greater authority than the text: Clement of Alexandria, for instance, had to give an elaborate justification for producing written texts, which he saw as a 'remedy for forgetfulness, nothing but a rough image, a shadow of those clear and living words which I was thought worthy to hear, and of those blessed and truly worthy men'. Eusebius reports that Papias, writing in about 130 CE, sought to collect the largest number of traditions about Jesus as he tried to find the *viva voce*, the living surviving voice handed down orally from the Lord himself. What Papias produced, however, was a collection of extraordinary sayings of the Lord, which he considered authoritative on account of the status of those handing on the tradition. Indeed, he preferred the oracles he had acquired from 'those who recall the commandments given by the Lord to faith' to Matthew's Gospel (which he knew) and Mark's supposed transcription of Peter's reminiscences. 'For I supposed that things out of books did not profit me so much as the utterances of a voice which *lives and abides*.'

A survey of the contents of such oral traditions, however, does not disclose much of consequence for the Christian faith. Origen, for instance, is able to write that the manger where Jesus was laid was in a cave and 'everybody knows this', while Eusebius on many occasions uses phrases like 'the story goes' or 'it is said', for instance, that the Jewish philosopher Philo conversed with Peter in Rome. A list of oral traditions from Tertullian to the sixteenth-century Council of Trent amounts to little more than facing east during the creed, the use of the sign of the cross at infant baptism and praying on the knees. It would seem that some fathers tended to attribute anything to the apostolic tradition which could not be found in scripture and which appeared to be older than living memory. Nevertheless, oral tradition became of central importance, not so much in its content as in the growth of the authority of the office of transmission of the tradition, and in particular the rise of the doctrine of apostolic succession: the word of God handed down orally became the basis for the teaching office of the church.

The two-source theory

The continued survival of a parallel tradition of teaching and practice gradually became identified with the authority of the church: equal respect came to be paid to the written tradition enshrined in scripture and the creeds and to the unwritten traditions preserved by the church. Indeed, where the traditional practices and teachings of the church could not be grounded in scripture or creed, there was an obvious need for an apostolic authority to guard a 'parallel tradition', which became a second source for doctrinal norms. By the Middle Ages a two-source theory of scripture and tradition had become normative and embodied the idea of proof from tradition. The claim was that the traditions and teachings of the church had come down in a parallel fashion from the apostolic age through the bishops as guardians of the faith and successors to the apostles. Scripture interpreted in the light of the rule of faith (the creed) ceased to be sufficient for proving all the doctrines of the church.

Reformation

Tradition and the Reformation

It is not difficult to interpret the Reformation as a conflict over the understanding of tradition. The question focused on the authority of the church to add to tradition or to insist on traditions which could not be grounded in and proved by scripture: apparent non-essentials (like ecclesiastical dress) thus became major points of conflict. For Martin Luther, although the church had to interpret scripture using a rule of faith, it could never have the authority to add its own traditions to scripture as necessary to salvation: the Bible was always sufficient. In the Reformers there is a high regard for the tradition of what Luther called the 'living word' – the criterion for Luther's interpretation was 'that which drives to Christ' – but little admiration for the parallel traditions of the church, which needed to be weighed up and justified in the light of the gospel, the tradition of Christ. The church could add nothing to scripture, even though it was always required to weigh up scripture in the light of faith.

Martin Luther

The church as authoritative interpreter

Against this effort to reduce the influence of the traditions of the church, the Council of Trent formulated a clear expression of the two-source theory: the gospel was proclaimed by Christ to the apostles and from them it came down to the present and was contained both in the written books and unwritten traditions. All the traditions concerning faith and morals were elevated to the same status as scripture and were held to be inspired by the Holy Spirit and preserved in continuous succession in the Roman Catholic Church. This was maintained in the nineteenth century at the First Vatican Council, but with a more specific definition of the authority of the teaching office of the church: all those things are to be believed which are contained in the word of God, written or handed down, and are said to have been divinely revealed by the church, either in solemn judgement or through its teaching office (magisterium). The traditions of the church are thus elevated to the same status as the written scriptures, and, furthermore, the traditions of interpretation ensure that scripture is understood in the correct fashion. In 1976 Paul VI confirmed this idea, noting that since scripture is handed down by the church and in part came into existence within the church, it has to be read and understood in the light of the church's tradition. Even though in many ways the Second Vatican Council was to moderate the claims of the magisterium, it still maintained a doctrine of the word of God, whether written or handed down.

p. 1045

Some Roman Catholic theologians developed a theology of tradition on such a basis. Yves Congar acknowledged the primacy of scripture but also emphasized the traditions that grow in the process of transmission, comparing them to an accrual, a 'compound interest'. For him there is a kind of vitality in the very passing on of tradition (the primary sense of tradition), a living spirit, which takes on a life of its own and develops new traditions. Traditions thus develop through the living power of the spirit at work in the church.

A third type of tradition

In the nineteenth century a development in the teaching office of the Roman Catholic Church allowed for the possibility of increasing the body of what was necessary for salvation, even where this could not be proved from scripture or universal tradition. What was primarily an office, a 'norm' for interpreting the sources of doctrine, especially scripture, began to function as itself a source of dogma, gaining a declaratory power in its own right. Thus the Apostolic Constitution in which the bodily assumption of the Virgin Mary is defined refers to the unique consensus, not of the church throughout all ages (the so-called Vincentian Canon), but of the present. A dogma becomes not simply a teaching of the church, but an article necessary to salvation and depends on the authority of the office which defined it.

Conclusion

There are thus three aspects to tradition:

1. In the tradition of Christ, truth is grasped by reflection on the saving activity of Christ witnessed to in scripture and particularly the New Testament; this form of tradition is formulated in creeds and summaries of the central features of faith in Christ. While never supplanting the final authority of scripture, it nevertheless acts as a constant check against literalism and focuses on the saving acts of Christ: scripture and tradition always interact.

2. There are also the parallel traditions of the church which are seen as a commentary on the first understanding of tradition and which are themselves weighed up in the light of the creeds as expressions of that tradition. These primarily liturgical and ethical traditions of the church have often been regarded as having an authority guaranteed by the office responsible for handing on these traditions. Without the constant check of such traditions by the tradition of Christ, however, the church can easily render its own traditions beyond criticism, a problem that led in part to the Reformation of the sixteenth century.

3. The declaration of a new dogma as an article of faith is even more clearly focused in the authority claimed by the teaching office to define the content of faith beyond all criticism. However, this represents a departure from the concept of tradition developed in the early church.

MARK D. CHAPMAN

F. F. Bruce, *Tradition Old and New*, Exeter: Paternoster Press 1970; F. F. Bruce and E. G. Rupp (eds), *Holy Book and Holy Tradition*, Manchester: Manchester University Press 1968; Yves Congar, *Tradition and Traditions*, London: Burns & Oates 1966; J. R. Geiselmann, *The Meaning of Tradition*, London: Burns & Oates 1966; R. P. C. Hanson, *Tradition in the Early Church*, London: SCM Press 1962; George Tavard, *Holy Writ or Holy Church*, London: Burns & Oates 1959

Traditional religions and Christianity

Traditional religions are usually defined as the religions of the 'first peoples' of tropical Africa, Australia, the Americas, the Pacific Islands and other parts of the world (often remote, like Siberia) before outsiders arrived with their own religion. These outsiders could be Muslims in Asia and Africa, or even Buddhists in China. Often, however, they were Europeans in the modern period who settled and largely displaced 'first peoples' in many areas, and imposed various forms of Christianity upon those that remained. In some cases, elements of these traditional beliefs and practices were grafted on to Christianity, and influence them to this day. So, for example, Latin

American Catholicism is deeply influenced by certain pre-Christian customs, as are Pentecostal and other forms of Christianity in sub-Saharan Africa.

But traditional religions do not only exist in a residual way. Indeed, there is a resurgence of interest in and even a return to them in our post-colonialist world. Many people in the US who identify themselves as Native American have reverted from Christianity to what they see as their religious origins, or else have consciously integrated them into their Christian faith. A number of black Africans have resisted the missionary endeavours of Christians and Muslims, or else, as Christians or even as Muslims, are deliberately incorporating old customs into their new faith. In India, many Dalits, outcaste people crushed by what they see as the burden of mainstream Hinduism and its caste system, have gone back to pre-Hindu faith and practices. Some have incorporated them into Christianity, Buddhism, Islam or even Hinduism; but others completely identify themselves with this rediscovered faith of the original inhabitants of the land.

Paganism

Many practitioners and some scholars of traditional religions detect certain common features among this faith of 'first peoples'. Mostly there is no scripture, because these world-views grew up in pre-literate societies, or else in cultures where stories and other oral communication were more important than the written word. Other widespread characteristics include: an emphasis upon care for the environment; a sense that human beings are a part of the web of life and not in competition with or in mastery of it; a view of human relations that, though hierarchical, may yet be less competitive and more consultative than in Western societies; different attitudes to sexuality and sexual roles. An example of this last feature is the *berdache* tradition of certain Native American nations: the *berdache* is often regarded as a third sex and is accorded an honoured place in the group, often as an intuitive person powerfully in touch with supernatural power on behalf of others.

Since most of the study of 'first peoples' was initially done by agents of European imperial powers, particularly by anthropologists and missionaries, this area of scholarship has been fraught with problems. Anthropology has been far from an objective discipline: in its earliest days in the nineteenth century it perpetrated a nonchalant racism. For example, in 1863 James Hunt, the President of the newly formed British Anthropological Society, read a paper entitled 'The Negro's Place in Nature', arguing 'that the Negro is intellectually inferior to the European, and that the analogies are far more numerous between the ape and the Negro than between the ape and the European'. Moreover, many anthropologists espoused or at least assumed Western dualistic notions, seeing people (so they believed) as the focus of objective study, objects under the microscope. Such study was in fact far from dispassionate and detached. At first, many anthropologists were naïve enough to assume that people would tell them the truth rather than feed them false information about the meaning of their public rituals and private lives; and they tended to interpret others' behaviour by the standards of their own, so their conclusions were often disastrously in error. Moreover, early anthropologists were often agnostic or atheist, and accepted the now outdated notion that if they could find the origin of religion in the rituals of so-called 'primitive' first peoples, they could explain religion away, interpreting it by societal rather than transcendental categories.

Christians, whether missionaries, politicians, bureaucrats or just visitors, were inclined to dismiss traditional beliefs as paganism, and their worshippers as either entirely misguided or else at an early stage of religious development. One example can serve to illustrate this. As late as 1930, the distinguished Primitive Methodist minister Edwin Smith met the biographer Emil Ludwig, who asked him: 'How can the untutored African conceive God?' Ludwig could not believe Smith when he told him that Africans knew of God as a living power. Smith observed that: 'He was frankly incredulous. "How can this be?" he said. "Deity is a philosophical concept which savages are incapable of framing." I doubt whether I convinced him.'

More recent Christian engagement with practitioners of traditional religions has had to deal with the entail of such colonial *hauteur*. It has proved hard to find a language for describing that faith freed from the prejudices of outside observers. Anthropologists, especially Lucien Lévy-Bruhl (1857–1939), can be credited with creating and reinforcing the notion of a universal 'primitive religion' held by (in his view) backward peoples everywhere. Even words like 'first' and 'primal' have been used to affirm or at least imply that such faith, and its practitioners, are low on the evolutionary chain. Only in the second half of the twentieth century, after two world wars had blown holes through the Western belief in the progress of the natural order up to the heights of the white man and his beliefs (whether religious or otherwise), have less superior terms been tried and tested, or original terms been interpreted in less patronizing ways.

Furthermore, it remains an open question whether all or most pre-literate and oral faiths can reasonably be compared with each other. Maybe the construction of a universal category of traditional religions has been yet another arrogant Western tendency to over-simplify complex phenomena by making them fit a category that is mostly meaningless. Can Dalit world-views and practices usefully be compared with Latin American ones? Can even one African group's views and practices profitably be compared to those of a neighbouring people?

Ironically, perhaps the universally-held features detected by many outsiders (care for the environment, and other factors outlined above) exist as much in the beholder's mind as in reality. The capacity for both outsiders and insiders to over-theorize about and romanticize traditional religious world-views and practices is great; both groups tend to ignore the actual practices of holders of traditional world-views. This raises serious academic and religious questions about truth. For a pertinent and delicate example: much of the debate about Dalit spirituality by both Dalits and others is often located more in an understandable desire for empowerment of the underprivileged than in any careful historical investigation of pre-Hindu religion in India. Another associated and equally delicate area has been whether outsiders can fairly criticize traditional religious practitioners' views about the faith of their forebears, given that many of them were brought up as Christians and learned their ancestral faith from European teachers.

Some Christians have seen the major challenge of traditional religions to be how to avoid syncretism: diluting and even poisoning pure Christian faith with beliefs and practices from pre-Christian world-views. In fact, recent theories of inculturation have revealed that this is a naïve stance that fails to see how much Christianity has always been a religion that translates and adapts itself to different settings. Far more intriguing a challenge for Christians is how to deal with the ironies of a category of traditional religion that was created by outsiders, accepted and adapted by insiders, and has since become fascinating to many contemporary Christians and ex-Christians, even if it has been somewhat sentimentalized by them.

MARTIN FORWARD

D. L. and J. T. Carmody, *Native American Religions: An Introduction*, New York and Mahwah, NJ: Paulist Press 1993; S. Jayakumar, *Dalit Consciousness and Christian Conversion*, Delhi: ISPCK and Oxford: Regnum 1999; John V. Taylor, *The Primal Vision*, London: SCM Press 1963, 2001

Trinity

The doctrine

The Christian doctrine of the Trinity is that there is one God, who exists in three persons, Father, Son and Holy Spirit. These three persons together share the one divine nature. They are equal, co-eternal and omnipotent. They are distinct from one another: the Father has no source, the Son is born of the substance of the Father, the Spirit proceeds from the Father (or from the Father and the Son). Though distinct, the three persons cannot be divided from one another in being or in operation.

The doctrine of the Trinity emerged from the early church's commitment to four articles of faith. God is all-powerful and transcendent. Jesus, who lived in first-century Palestine and died and was raised by the power of God, is also God. The Holy Spirit, received in abundance by the church at Pentecost, is likewise also God. Yet there is only one God.

Jesus
Resurrection

The doctrine is a mystery, which can only be fully entertained in faith. But the heart of the doctrine is that the God who makes himself known in revelation is identical to the God who exists in eternity. In other words, there is no 'secret' God, so holy that he cannot be revealed. The doctrine of the Trinity emerges as the Son and the Spirit are experienced in the 'economy' of Christian history, and what is vital is the conviction that this experience reveals the true, 'immanent', character of God.

Revelation
Eternity

The origins of the doctrine

The Bible

Bible

The doctrine of the Trinity emerged as theologians of the early church tried to reconcile the revelation of God in Jesus Christ with the conviction of the unity of God that dominates the Hebrew scriptures.

The books of the Old Testament are practically unanimous in the determination that the God of Israel is, sometimes despite appearances, the Lord almighty of the heavens and the earth. Three ways of talking about the activity of God emerge, each of which becomes significant for New Testament and later understandings of God. One is wisdom. In Proverbs, for example, wisdom is regarded as a divine person, yet not identical with God, and particularly active in the creation and ordering of the world (1.20–3; 9.1–6). A second is word. The Word of God emanates from God, but having been spoken, retains an existence of its own, dependent on, yet not reabsorbed into, God. This is particularly evident in the Psalms (119.89; 147.15–20). A third is spirit. The Spirit (or 'breath' or 'wind') of God hovers over the deep at creation (Genesis 1.2) and is expected to bring about a new creation at the end of time (Ezekiel 37.1–14). These three denominations of God may be seen as embryonic members of the Trinity. The early church theologians found disclosures of the Trinity elsewhere, particularly in the appearance of three men to Abraham by the oaks of Mamre (Genesis 18).

In the New Testament the reality of Jesus as equal with God pushes at the boundaries of the Jewish insistence on the singularity and unity of God. For example, in the Fourth Gospel Jesus says, 'I and the Father are one,' and 'I am in the Father and the Father is in me' (10.30; 14.10). Later Jesus says to the disciples, 'I will ask the Father, and he will give you another Advocate, to be with you forever. This is the Spirit of truth,' and later again he breathes on them and says, 'Receive the Holy Spirit. If you forgive the

God

sins of any, they are forgiven them; if you retain the sins of any, they are retained' (14.16–17; 20.23). These are clear statements that the different aspects of the one God are becoming more distinct. The best-known reference in the Gospels comes in Jesus' closing words in Matthew's Gospel: 'Make disciples of all nations, baptizing them in the name of the Father and of the Son and of the Holy Spirit' (28.19). But there are many other implicit references, for example at Jesus' baptism, where the Father speaks from the cloud and the Spirit descends as a dove upon the Son (Matthew 3.16–17).

Paul

In Paul's letters there are many examples of Father, Son and Spirit being closely linked in their activity. Paul refers to the varieties of gifts, services and activities, but the same Spirit, Lord and God (1 Corinthians 12.4–6). Similarly in Ephesians he speaks of 'one Spirit ... one Lord ... one God and Father' (4.4–6). In 2 Corinthians he speaks of God establishing us in Christ and giving us the Spirit as a first instalment (1.21–2). He says to the Galatians that 'God has sent the Spirit of his Son into our hearts, crying, "Abba! Father!"' (4.6). Most explicitly, he completes his second letter to the Corinthians with the formulaic expression, 'The grace of the Lord Jesus Christ, the love of God, and the communion of the Holy Spirit be with all of you' (13.14).

Master GH, *The Trinity*, fifteenth century

The early church

Gnosis

Philosophy

Doctrinal terms

The second-century apologists set about understanding this first-century faith in the light of existing (largely Greek) conceptuality, particularly concerning the 'Logos' or word. Stoics saw the Logos as the rational principle that imposes order on the otherwise shapeless universe, and is most fully realized in the human soul. They distinguished between immanent (unexpressed) reason and outward thought. Justin Martyr (*c.*100–*c.*165) adopted this Stoic distinction. He began to speak of God the Father as immanent reason and God the Son as expressed thought. Meanwhile, in relation to Platonism, Middle Platonists of the second century such as Athenagoras and Tatian, inspired by the Jewish theologian Philo of Alexandria (20 BCE–50 CE), had started to go beyond Plato's Supreme Being (the 'One') to perceiving his Demiurge (or Architect of the Universe) as the Logos, and to begin to speak of a third entity, a World-Soul or Psyche, rather like a Holy Spirit figure. The one was becoming the three.

The key figure bridging the New Testament accounts of the first century and the philosophical and political debates of the fourth century is the Latin theologian Tertullian of Carthage (*c.*160–225). The Greek theologian Theophilus of Antioch spoke of the 'triad' of God, Word and Wisdom around 180. But it was Tertullian who coined the word 'Trinity'. He introduced the term *persona* (role) as a Latin rendering of the Greek term *hypostasis*. This offered a language in which to express the distinctiveness of the three persons. And he proposed the term 'substance' to convey the reality shared by all three members of the Trinity, thus offering a language in which to express the unity of the persons. Meanwhile Irenaeus of Lyons (*c.*130–*c.*200) talked of the 'economy' of salvation, meaning the ordering of God's saving acts in history, and insisted (against some Gnostics) that the God who redeemed was identical with the God who had created. In the ordering of salvation history, he said, the Father's primary role is to create, the Son's to restore, and the Spirit's to renew. The Son and the Spirit were the 'two hands' of the Father. Thus by the early third century there comes from Irenaeus and Tertullian an account of plurality without division – three persons distinct yet not divided, different yet not separate, and each with a particular yet complementary role to play in salvation.

The Greek theologian Origen of Alexandria (*c.*185–*c.*254) set the terms of the debate that was to follow in the fourth century. On the one hand he developed the notion, implicit in Tertullian, of the eternal generation of the Son (like light from the sun) and the eternal procession of the Spirit. He used a telling phrase concerning the Son, 'there never was when he was not'. Thus he abandons the Stoic distinction between the 'immanent' God-in-himself and the 'economic' God-for-us-in-salvation. This was a decisive move. Similarly he regards the Holy Spirit as 'united in honour and dignity with the Father and the Son'. On the other hand, however, there remains a hint that the Son is still in some sense subordinate to the Father. The Son is *theos*, God, but the Father is *autotheos*, absolute God.

The fourth-century debate had a much higher profile, largely because the first Christian emperor, Constantine, took a close interest in the church and its doctrine. The debate began in 318, when Arius, a priest of Baucalis, in Alexandria, began to propound such a strong doctrine of the impassibility of God that a full understanding of the incarnation became unsustainable. Jesus must be a creature, albeit one who was exalted and achieved union with God. Reversing Origen's assertion, Arius insisted 'there was when he was not'. Arius was simply fulfilling the Stoic-shaped logic of trinitarian reflection prior to Origen, for he assumed that the expressed word of God (the Son) was inferior to the inherent reason of God (the Father). He forced the church to break decisively from Jewish and Greek assumptions that saw the incarnation as diminishing God.

A flurry of controversy led Constantine in 325 to call a council of over 300 bishops at Nicaea, near Constantinople. The council stated clearly that the Father and the Son are both God in exactly the same sense of the word 'God'. It did this by agreeing phrases such as 'true God from true God', 'begotten, not made', and 'of the same substance as (*homoousios*) the Father'. This last term, *homoousios*, caused considerable disquiet because it was new to theology and absent from scripture, and went so far in the direction of asserting the unity of Son and Father that it appeared to make the Son little more than a mode of the one God's existence. However, for Athanasius of Alexandria (*c.*296–373), who emerged as the arch defender of Nicaea, the issue was about salvation: the Son could only save if he was fully divine, for no creature could save.

The Nicene agreement did not retain its dominance throughout the fourth century. Four positions emerged, and jostled for pre-eminence. The Nicenes, led by Athanasius, advocated *homoousios* (of the same substance as the Father); the neo-Arians advocated *anomoios* (unlike the Father); and in between were two compromise parties, those nearer Nicaea proposing *homoiousios* (of a like substance to the Father), and those nearer Arius proposing *homoios* (like the Father). The *homoios* party achieved the ascendancy by the decree of the Emperor Constantius in 360.

Only at this stage did the debate begin to include the Holy Spirit, and thus become truly trinitarian. Three Cappadocian bishops, Basil of Caesarea (*c.*330–79), his brother Gregory of Nyssa (*c.*330–*c.*395), and Gregory of Nazianzus (329/30–389/90), began to elaborate how God could be one substance (*ousia*) in three persons (*hypostases*). They saw the 'substance' as a universal nature, common to the three persons, whereas the 'person' referred to a particular characteristic of each one. This personal characteristic refers to their respective origin. The Father is the Unoriginate (or Unbegottenness); the Son is Generation; and the Spirit is Mission (or Procession). The three exist in pure relation to one another. A later term that came to be associated with the Cappadocian understanding of the Trinity is mutual indwelling, or *perichoresis*. This profound sense of the community of relationship is perhaps best portrayed in Sergei Rublev's famous icon portraying Abraham's three visitors (see colour plate 16). The Council of Constantinople, called by the Emperor Theodosius in 381, largely endorsed the Nicene Creed, while expanding the article on the Holy Spirit considerably. The faith that emerged from the council was a Cappadocian one – of three divine persons united in one divine substance.

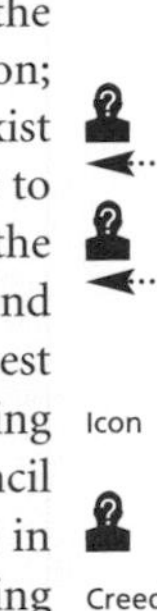

If Eastern, Greek theology, influenced by the Cappadocians, tended to emphasize the threeness of God, then Western, Latin theology, tended to stress the oneness. The strongest influence here was Augustine of Hippo (354–430). In his hugely influential work *On the Trinity*, Augustine departs from the tendency in Latin theology since Tertullian to identify the one God with the Father. Instead, Augustine sees the one God as primarily the divine substance, which is only secondarily distinguished as Father, Son and Spirit. Indeed, Augustine is generally uncomfortable with the notion of the three being 'persons' at all, since it suggests too close an analogy with human persons. Whatever is said about the divine substance must be true of all three persons. The only thing that can be said exclusively about a person is the relation this person has to the other persons, such as 'Only-Begotten'. The persons are inseparable in what they are and in what they do. This leads to the principle of appropriation. While every person of the Trinity is involved in every outward action of God, it is appropriate to think of creation as the work of the Father, and redemption as the work of the Son. Appropriation is the way Augustine (and his successors) reconciled the language of scripture and the experience of believers with his own conceptual requirements.

Augustine talked of the two key activities (or 'processions') of the divine life in psychological terms. Thus he described the begetting of the Son (what Thomas Aquinas later called 'filiation') as like human self-knowledge, and the sending of the Spirit (later called 'spiration') as like human self-love. This creates the language of the well-known idea of the Trinity as Lover, Beloved and the Love between them. Augustine looked for an imprint of God's character in what he took to be the height of creation – the human mind. Hence he developed

DOCTRINAL TERMS

In the early church, in debates about doctrine which gave rise to the definition of orthodoxy over against heresy, a number of common Greek and Latin words came to play a crucial role both in the debates themselves and in the resultant credal definitions. This was particularly the case with the doctrines of the Trinity and of the person of Christ (christology). In modern discussions these key words are often left untranslated (being simply transliterated into English script in the case of Greek words). This is done because the words do not all have exact or agreed equivalents in English, and, if one is to follow the course of particular arguments, it is often essential to know which terms were used in the original Greek or Latin text. It is important to recognize that such words were not always intended or understood in precisely the same sense at different times or by different people. Such differences in the understanding of key terms were especially likely to occur in the case of a creed or agreed statement drawn up at a church council with the express purpose of reconciling groups who had been in disagreement about the particular issue in question.

The list of words that follows is divided into two categories: basic terms, and more complex terms (mostly describing differing groups of believers).

Basic terms

Hypostasis: A Greek word, which etymologically means that which stands underneath (Latin and English etymological equivalents *substantia* and substance). It indicates that which gives to a particular thing its separate, individual identity. The best overall English equivalent is perhaps an 'entity'. In christological doctrine it refers to the person of Christ (in contrast to his two natures or *physeis).* In trinitarian doctrine it is used to refer to the three persons of the Trinity (in contrast to the one Godhead or *ousia*). But, although later carefully contrasted in these ways, sometimes in very early Christian writers *hypostasis* and *ousia* are used interchangeably.

Ousia: A Greek word, a noun derived from the basic word for 'to be'. Its natural English equivalent is 'being', either in a more abstract sense where it might be translated 'essence', or in the more concrete sense of 'a being', 'an existent'. In the traditional translation of the Nicene Creed, however, it is rendered as 'substance'. Whatever translation is used, the intention is to indicate the most fundamental level of existence. What the nature of that fundamental level of existence is understood to be (e.g. material or immaterial) will, of course, depend on the particular philosophical beliefs of the speaker or hearer.

Persona: A Latin word regularly used to refer to the three 'persons' of the Trinity and to the one 'person' of Christ. It therefore fulfils the role in Latin theology performed by *hypostasis* in Greek. The natural translation into 'person' in English is misleading. *Persona* originally meant a 'mask', and then a 'role'. It is used to indicate an individual in his or her external presentation, and does not convey the idea of selfconsciousness or the internal psychological content suggested by the English word 'person' with its close link to the word 'personality'.

Physis: The Greek word for 'nature'. It was normally intended and understood in a purely conceptual sense, but was sometimes given a more concrete meaning, with subsequent confusion.

Prosopon: A Greek word, primarily meaning 'face', but also carrying the same meanings of 'mask', 'role' or 'individual in his or her external presentation' associated with the Latin word *persona*. When used of the persons of the Trinity or of the person of Christ, it was often understood (though not necessarily intended) to convey that the persons of the Trinity are temporary roles rather than eternal and distinct entities within the Godhead, or (in the case of christology) that the divine and human natures of Christ are less than fully united.

Substantia: A Latin word regularly used to refer to the single reality of the divine Godhead. The fact that its etymological equivalent in Greek, *hypostasis*, was used to refer to the three distinct divine realities within the Godhead was sometimes a source of misunderstanding between the two linguistic communities of East and West.

Complex terms

Apophatic: Using negative terms to indicate indirectly the nature of God, e.g. 'immortal', 'invisible'.

Dyophysite: Having two natures. The belief that Christ has both a human and divine nature; one who holds that belief.

Dyothelite: Having two wills. The belief that Christ has both a human and a divine will; one who holds that belief.

Homoian (sometimes spelt Homoean): One who affirms simply that the Son is like the Father. From a Greek word, *homoios,* meaning 'similar' or 'like'.

→

Homoiousios (Homoiousian): A Greek word meaning 'similar in essence' (one who holds the view that the Son is like in essence to the Father). The word played a smaller role in the debates of the fourth century than is sometimes implied by suggestions that it was a widely championed alternative to *homoousios.*

Homoousios (Homoousian): A Greek word meaning 'identical in essence' (one who holds the view that the Son is of the same essence as the Father). The word came to prominence by its inclusion in the Creed of Nicaea in 325 CE. Its central importance as the touchstone of orthodoxy only developed as a result of Athanasius's insistence some decades later in the 350s and 360s.

Kataphatic: Using positive terms as pointers towards an understanding of the greater and mysterious reality of God (e.g. God is 'Father'; God is our 'rock').

Monophysite: Having one nature. The belief that Christ has only one (divine) nature. One who holds such a belief. Separate monophysite churches sprang up after the Council of Chalcedon in 451 CE, at which a belief in Christ's two natures was declared to be the orthodox view.

Monothelite: Having one will. The belief that Christ had only one will. One who holds such a belief.

analogies that illustrate the interrelationship of the three persons of the Trinity. Notable among these psychological analogies are mind, knowledge and love, and memory, understanding and will. Augustine's underestimation of person and relationship in both his understanding of substance and his analogies dominated Western theology through Thomas Aquinas to John Calvin, and it has become fashionable in contemporary theology to see it as the source of many ills.

What the doctrine seeks to avoid

The doctrine of the Trinity sets out to avoid a number of pitfalls, the first and second of which can be broadly gathered under two extremes.

To one side lies such a strong emphasis on the one God that the threeness of God is obscured. This is given various names in different eras, including Sabellianism, Modalism, Monarchianism, Patripassianism, Socinianism and Unitarianism. In its milder form, this assumes that Father, Son and Spirit are simply modes of expression, and that God initially revealed himself as creator, later as redeemer, and later again as sanctifier. The one God has three pseudonyms. In its extreme form it may suggest that the whole of God was, for example, present in Jesus – that heaven was empty when Jesus walked on earth. In relation to the cross, it may imply that, because there is no distinction between Father and Son, the whole of God suffers equally as Jesus dies, and indeed God dies entirely on the cross – leaving a large question as to how the resurrection can come about.

A more general form of Unitarianism is found in an overemphasis on one person of the Trinity, to the detriment of the others. For example civil religions tend to concentrate on the Creator, with little sense of sin or the need for reconciliation. Pietism tends to concentrate on a relationship with Jesus, to the exclusion of wider human or environmental issues. Some aspects of the charismatic movement can concentrate on experience of the Holy Spirit and neglect other aspects of revelation.

To the other side lies such a strong emphasis on the threeness of God that there seem to be three gods. Tritheism arises whenever the unity of the three persons in God is weakened. For example, the Italian Cistercian mystic Joachim of Fiore (1135–1202) developed an elaborate trinitarian view of history. The Age of the Father lasted (under Law) until the end of the Old Testament era; the Age of the Son lasted (under Grace) from the coming of Christ for 42 generations; the Age of the Spirit was just beginning, during which religious orders would convert the whole world. Joachim's notion of unity concentrated on the love the persons bore each other, like citizens making up a country. Joachim's approach has no trace of Augustine's principle of appropriation, or the Cappadocians' coinherence. It is almost a doctrine of three gods.

Heresy

The third pitfall in some ways resembles the first. It is to suggest that the Father is somehow prior to the Son and the Spirit. This is known as Subordinationism. It was this tendency, pursued by Arius and others, which the Nicene and Constantinopolitan creeds set out to avoid. A variation on the idea that Jesus is somehow less than God is Adoptionist Subordinationism. This takes the view that Jesus, either because of his quality of character or because of his remarkable deeds, was adopted into God at a certain point in history – his baptism, say, or his resurrection. Such approaches often make a healthy place for the role of the Holy Spirit in Jesus' life; but they dispense with any meaningful unity between Jesus and the Father. As Athanasius said, this makes all Christians who worship Christ into idolaters.

Pietism

The divine processions

The difference in emphasis between the Eastern view of the Trinity chararacterized by the Cappadocians and the Western approach represented by Augustine grew through the centuries of the first millennium. By the ninth century it was common in the West to regard the Holy Spirit as proceeding 'from the Father and the Son'. This 'double procession' of the Spirit was a departure from the creeds of the fourth century. The original creeds contained no phrase *filioque* ('and from the Son'). This issue still divides the churches today.

p. 305

The Greeks were concerned about two problems. One was that there not be two Sons. Hence the insistence that whereas the Son is begotten, the Spirit proceeds. The same divine source is the origin of the two other members of the Trinity, but in different ways. The Spirit is not a second Son. The Spirit is breath, whereas the Son is word. On the other hand, it is equally important that there not be two Fathers. When the Western theologians began to stress that the Spirit had two processions, from the Father and from the Son, the Son began to look suspiciously like another Father.

Friedrich Schleiermacher

But Augustine and others who advocated the double procession of the Spirit from the Father and the Son had plenty of scriptural support. In the Fourth Gospel Jesus says the Spirit will 'take what is mine and declare it to you' (16.15), and later he breathes on the disciples and says 'Receive the Holy Spirit' (20.22). Paul calls the Holy Spirit 'the Spirit of the Son' or the 'Spirit of Christ' (Galatians 4.6; Romans 8.9; Philippians 1.19). Augustine moderates his position when he acknowledges that the procession of the Spirit is something 'given by the Father to the Son', but since this is given in the act of begetting, it is an eternal gift. Because Augustine has such a strong notion of the Holy Spirit as the bond of love between Father and Son, he sees the relations in God as more significant than the processions. God is not simply three persons who relate to one another: God *is* the relations. So one can see the controversy as lying in a difference in emphasis regarding relations and processions within God.

Karl Barth

Contemporary reformulations

The doctrine of the Trinity received little development either in the medieval period, when Thomas Aquinas largely accepted the tradition of Augustine, or from the Reformation theologians, who did not find in it the origin or pretext for the controversy they found elsewhere. The Enlightenment presented the same series of challenges here as in most other parts of theology. It assumed experience as the testing ground for truth, it turned from external authority to the individual subject as the centre of philosophical and moral reflection, and thus it placed on traditional authority the heavy burden of proof.

Enlightenment

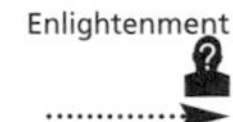

William Blake, *The Trinity*

Friedrich Schleiermacher (1768–1834) was the first to respond to these challenges. He saw faith as 'neither knowledge nor action, but a determination of feeling or immediate self-consciousness' of 'absolute dependence' on God. All statements about God are at the same time statements about personal existence – otherwise they are, in characteristic Enlightenment terms, speculation. The Trinity is not essential, because it is an assemblage of statements about Christian self-consciousness. It therefore appears in Schleiermacher's account at the end. This approach dominated nineteenth-century theology.

Karl Barth (1886–1968) set out to reverse Schleiermacher's ordering of theology. He begins his account of Christian doctrine with the Trinity, because the whole ground of theology is God's determination to reveal himself through himself. The question is, then, what kind of God could have revealed himself in this way? Given the character of humanity as sinful, and thus incapable of hearing God, how could God ensure that he could nonetheless communicate with humanity – for he clearly has. The shape of the Trinity can be derived from the correspondence between the revelation made and the one who reveals. In other words, the Son reveals the Father. The intransigence of humanity in receiving this revelation is overcome by the Holy Spirit, who both gives humanity the capacity to hear and does the hearing itself. 'He alone is the revealer. He is wholly revelation. He himself is what is revealed.'

Karl Rahner (1904–84) sought to correct the tendency of Roman Catholic theology to make too great a distinction between the differentiated union of God's ('immanent') inner life and his diverse but unified ('economic') revelation in history. For Rahner, they were identical – the economic is the immanent and the immanent is the economic. Reflection on the nature of the Trinity begins with the history of salvation, the story of the Bible. The diverse unity experience in this history corresponds to the diverse unity of the Trinity itself. The Trinity is God's threefold self-communication. The Spirit represents the arrival of salvation in the centre of the person, the Son is the same God in the historicity of our existence, and the Father is the ground and origin of the coming of Son and Spirit.

Jürgen Moltmann (1926–) rejects Barth's portrayal of the Trinity as tautologous and Rahner's as superfluous. He sees both theologians as broad Modalists. Instead he insists on a social doctrine of the Trinity, in a move that is also taken up by the liberation theologian Leonardo Boff (1938–). Moltmann concentrates on the significance of reciprocal relations in harmonious partnership with creation. The unity of God is the communion of persons. The missions of the Son and the Spirit have brought creation within the trinitarian process. At the end of time, all will be folded into the Trinity. The history of salvation is the story of the inclusion of creation into the perichoretic relationship (mutual indwelling) of the persons of the Trinity. Boff endorses this approach, pointing out that it prevents any totalitarianism based on monotheism and any paternalism based on the monarchy of the Father. Domination is replaced by communion, conquest by participation. Such perspectives highlight the interaction between an understanding of God and an understanding of human social relations.

Increasing numbers of theologians have found fault with the masculine language of Father and Son. Some of these criticisms derive from the social consequences of such language. For example, Mary Daly points out that 'Where God is a male, the male is god.' Others point out the variety of names and portrayals of God in scripture and church history. For example, God refuses to disclose a specific name to Moses, calling himself the One (Exodus 3.15); Isaiah 49.15 and Matthew 23.37 speak of God in feminine terms; the Council of Toledo in 675 speaks of the Son being born from the womb of the Father; and Julian of Norwich speaks around 1400 of 'Mother Jesus'. New triads such as Creator, Redeemer, Sustainer have been coined, although most suffer from a difficulty in retaining the full personal quality of the traditional formulation. An alternative is to develop more explicitly feminine designations, such as Mother, Lover, Friend, or to bypass personal notions altogether, for example to reconceive God as a verb rather than a noun. Further approaches are to treat the Spirit as feminine, following the gender of nouns such as the Hebrew *ruach* (breath) or the Greek Sophia (wisdom); or to bring out both feminine and masculine in God, with phrases like paternal Mother and maternal Father.

What the doctrine affirms today

It is easy to get lost in either the debates of the early theologians or the later language of persons, missions and processions, or again the contemporary misgivings about the knowability of God and the significance of apparently sexist language. So it is worth briefly restating some broad principles affirmed by most theologians concerned with the doctrine of the Trinity today.

The heart of all things is love, and the manifestation of love is self-offering and other-receiving relationship.  The significance of this statement for trinitarian theology is that it puts the emphasis on the dynamic relations between the members of the Trinity, rather than on the rather more static notion of the shared divine substance or  the members in their processions and missions themselves. The significance of the statement in contemporary life is that it emphasizes a perception of person that is inseparable from relationship, rather than an assumption that a true individual is an atomized, autonomous compound of impressions, choices and desires.

That this kind of love is at the heart of all things is a conviction based on the centrality of the cross and the compassion that it embodies, together with the transformation of the resurrection and its promise of a force stronger than death and despair. The picture and character of God disclosed in Jesus' birth, life, death, resurrection and ascension are taken to epitomize the whole nature of the Trinity, and thus the ultimate truth about all things, which will be finally visible on the last day.

To what extent this understanding of the Trinity shapes a Christian understanding of community is a controversial area. Some theologians fear the doctrine is being asked to do too much work by being invoked in favour of one kind of model of society over others. Others happily see the Trinity as embodying mutual hospitality and an inclusive dance of love, and as a paradigm of partnership of equals subverting the prevalence of relationships of domination and oppression to be found the world over. Less controversial is a recognition that differentiation and otherness are intrinsic to God, and assumed in the creation of a world full of diversity and creaturely interdependence.  Even those most suspicious of social notions of the Trinity generally acknowledge that those who seek homogenization of human variety – of culture, gender, and race for example – can find no foundation for their convictions in the doctrine of the Trinity.

There seem to be two contrasting traditions – the 'West' with its psychological analogies, commitment to the double procession of the Spirit from the Father and the Son, and concern with the unity of God (Augustine, Barth and Rahner), and the 'East' with its social analogy, maintenance of the single procession of the Spirit from the Father alone, and concern for the full exploration of the communion of God, on earth as in heaven, with a more open understanding of feminist concerns (the Cappadocians, Moltmann and Boff). But the liveliness of the contemporary debate most amply represents the fascination of this doctrine, which begins and ends with the discovery of Jesus as being at the heart of the one true God.

SAMUEL WELLS

Karl Barth, *The Doctrine of the Word of God: Church Dogmatics* I/1, Edinburgh: T&T Clark 1975; Leonardo Boff, *Trinity and Society*, London: Burns & Oates 1988; David Cunningham, *These Three are One: The Practice of Trinitarian Theology*, Oxford: Blackwell 1998; Elizabeth A. Johnson, *She Who Is: The Mystery of God in Feminist Theological Discourse*, New York: Crossroad 1992; Eberhard Jüngel, *The Doctrine of the Trinity: God's Being is in Becoming*, Edinburgh: Scottish Academic Press 1976; Walter Kasper, *The God of Jesus Christ*, New York: Crossroad and London: SCM Press 1984; Catherine Mowry LaCugna, *God For Us: The Trinity and Christian Life*, San Francisco: HarperCollins 1991; Thomas Marsh, *The Triune God: A Biblical, Historical and Theological Study*, Dublin: Columba 1994; Jürgen Moltmann, *The Trinity and the Kingdom of God: The Doctrine of God*, London: SCM Press and New York: Harper & Row 1981; Karl Rahner, *The Trinity*, New York: Herder & Herder 1970; Gerard Watson, *Greek Philosophy and the Christian Notion of God*, Dublin: Columba Press 1994

Bible

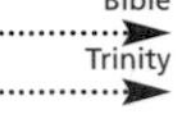

Trinity

Unitarians

The Unitarian movement owes its origins to no single founder, communities having been established in different countries mainly by internal processes of development rather than missionary activity by any central organization.

Puritans

The oldest Unitarian congregations, dating from the second half of the sixteenth century, are Hungarian-speaking and located in Transylvania, now part of Romania. The key figure was Francis Dávid, a Reformed bishop who became anti-trinitarian in his views. He was a persuasive speaker, and following a ten-day debate in 1568 between trinitarians and anti-trinitarians the king of Transylvania, John Sigismund, became an anti-trinitarian. He then proclaimed the Declaration of Torda, one of the earliest edicts of toleration in European history, declaring the new anti-trinitarian faith one of the four recognized denominations of the country, the others being Roman Catholic, Lutheran and Trinitarian Reformed. There are around 80,000 Unitarians in Transylvania today, with some thousands more in neighbouring Hungary.

A sizeable proportion of Unitarian congregations in England have their origins in the Great Ejection of 1662, when around 2000 Church of England clergy were ejected from their pulpits for refusing to comply with the Act of Uniformity, which required public assent to the Anglican Book of Common Prayer. Some of these ministers formed dissenting congregations that met in secret until the passing of the Toleration Act of 1689. This Act permitted freedom of worship, but not of doctrine. The ejected groups of 1662 fell broadly into two camps, the Independents (later to become the Congregationalists) and the Presbyterians, and it was a sizeable number of congregations from this latter group, believing in the right of private judgement and rational dissent, which were leaning towards a Unitarian theology by the end of the eighteenth century.

The first avowedly Unitarian congregation in England was founded by Theophilus Lindsey as late as 1774 at Essex Street, off the Strand. Lindsey, the scientist Joseph Priestley and other dissenters, rejecting creeds, argued that the Bible did not support the doctrine of the Trinity but instead emphasized the oneness of God. In the nineteenth century, however, under the influence especially of James Martineau, Unitarians moved away from the principle of scriptural authority in favour of an emphasis on the individual exercise of reason and conscience.

Although James Relly established a congregation in London during the 1750s which was universalist in outlook, Universalism did not spread in Europe. It did, however, take hold in America, where the first congregation was established in Gloucester, Massachusetts, in 1779 by a follower of Relly, John Murray. The main belief of Universalism was the salvation of all men and women after death. The movement grew, and after the Civil War spread throughout the United States.

Many of the earliest surviving Unitarian congregations in the United States can trace their history back to New England, to the Puritans there. Originally Calvinist in theology, these churches rejected the imposition of statements of faith upon members. Gradually, a liberal wing of the church developed in contrast to the evangelical mainstream. Critically, in 1819 William Ellery Channing, a liberal Boston Congregationalist minister, preached a sermon on Unitarian Christianity, accepting the Unitarian label and demonstrating the willingness of the liberals to make their distinct position known. The American Unitarian Association was founded in 1825, coincidentally on the same day as the British and Foreign Unitarian Association.

The Unitarians in the United States merged with the Universalists in 1961 to form the Unitarian Universalist Association (UUA). The present membership is around 225,000. Canadian congregations belong to the Canadian

Unitarian Council (CUC), which has close ties with both the UUA and the Unitarian movement in Britain.

A focus on Jesus' life and teachings led many Unitarians to be active in campaigning for social reform in fields such as education, health and women's equality. The concern for social justice and civil liberty continues to this day.

There are presently a little over 5000 Unitarians in Britain, constituent congregations being in membership of the General Assembly of Unitarian and Free Christian Churches. There are nearly 150 congregations and fellowships in England, four in Scotland and over 20 in Wales, mostly Welsh-speaking. There are also historic ties with the Non-Subscribing Presbyterian Church of Ireland (NSPCI), the majority of whose churches are located in Ulster.

Rooted in the Jewish and Christian traditions, the Unitarian movement in the English-speaking world is today religiously pluralist in character. Only a minority of Unitarian Universalists in North America regard themselves as Christian. In Britain probably a majority still affirm a liberal Christian identity. Yet even here many members claim their primary inspiration from other sources – from humanist ideas, or earth-centred spirituality, for example.

Free from credal restrictions, Unitarians are not expected to share identical religious beliefs. Rather, they are helped to find strength for a personal spiritual quest alongside others who value a liberal religious environment. Thus Unitarians sometimes speak of striving for 'unity in diversity'.

Unitarians are sceptical of claims that either church tradition or the Bible can provide an inerrant basis for religious truth. Instead, church members are expected to look to their own reason and conscience as a guide. Truth may be gleaned from scripture, science, the world, the arts, personal experience and intuition. Recognizing the dangers of individualism, the continued willingness of Unitarians to gather in congregations, chiefly on Sunday mornings, is mainly a recognition of the need for a community context for the shaping of one's own thoughts and theology.

For Unitarian Christians, the figure of Jesus remains of central significance. However, the emphasis is on his life and teachings rather than belief in his resurrection. Unitarians are struck by Jesus' concern for the poor and needy and his call to forgive others. They stress his essential humanity, pointing to Bible passages that suggest that God is within everyone – that men and women are all sons and daughters of God. Some Unitarians, however, question the validity of words such as 'worship' and 'God', perhaps preferring the phrase 'celebration of life'.

Sunday services typically consist of prayers, hymns and readings followed by a sermon from the minister or lay worship leader. There is complete freedom as to the selection of readings, which may be drawn from the widest possible range of sources. Newer features of Unitarian worship may include the lighting of a flaming chalice – the recognized symbol of the Unitarian movement – and the sharing of 'joys and concerns' by members of the congregation. Communion takes place in only a few churches, while the Flower Communion, invented by a Czech Unitarian before the Second World War, is increasingly popular. Church members each bring a flower to church and these are placed in a common vase. Towards the end of the service the flowers are blessed and redistributed so that each person takes away a different flower.

Unitarians have a long history of working for interfaith understanding, being founder members in 1900 of what is known today as the International Association for Religious Freedom (IARF). Unitarian communities around the world – including those in India, Australasia and Africa – are united through membership of the International Council of Unitarians and Universalists (ICUU).

MATTHEW F. SMITH

📖 John A. Buehrens and Forrest Church, *A Chosen Faith: An Introduction to Unitarian Universalism*, Boston: Beacon Press 1989; Andrew Hill, *A Liberal Religious Heritage: Unitarian and Universalist Foundations in Europe, America and Elsewhere*, London: Unitarian Information Department (undated); Charles A. Howe, *For Faith and Freedom: A Short History of Unitarianism in Europe*, Boston: Skinner House 1997; Cliff Reed, *Unitarian? What's That? Questions and Answers about a Liberal Religious Alternative*, London: Lindsey Press 1999; Matthew F. Smith (ed), *Prospects for the Unitarian Movement*, London: Lindsey Press 2002; Ruth Watts, *Gender, Power and the Unitarians in England 1760–1860*, Harlow: Longman 1998

United Reformed Church

In 2003 there were 1719 United Reformed Church congregations in the three nations of England, Scotland and Wales, organized in thirteen synods (including the two national synods of Scotland and Wales). The church had a membership of 87,732, its work financed entirely by the giving of its members. Doctrinally it honours its Reformed heritage, and in its Basis of Union of 1972 confesses that obedience to the Holy Spirit may require it to '... make such new declarations of its faith and for such purposes as may from time to time be required by obedience to the same Spirit'.

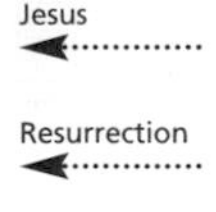

The United Reformed Church was formed in 1972 from the union of the Congregational Church in England and Wales and the Presbyterian Church of England. Its formation needs to be understood in the context of the

Congregationalism
Presbyterian churches

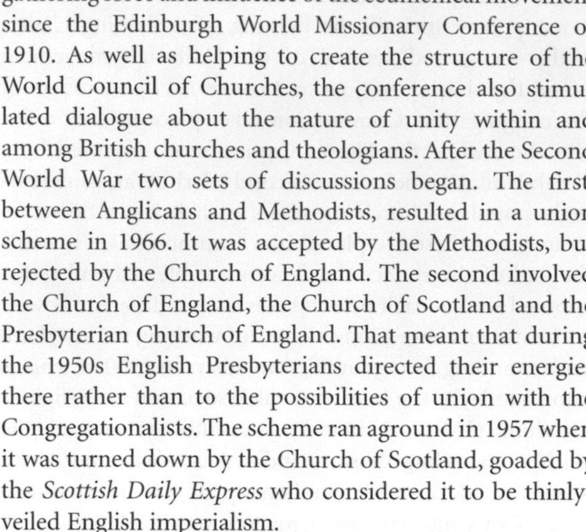

gathering force and influence of the ecumenical movement since the Edinburgh World Missionary Conference of 1910. As well as helping to create the structure of the World Council of Churches, the conference also stimulated dialogue about the nature of unity within and among British churches and theologians. After the Second World War two sets of discussions began. The first, between Anglicans and Methodists, resulted in a union scheme in 1966. It was accepted by the Methodists, but rejected by the Church of England. The second involved the Church of England, the Church of Scotland and the Presbyterian Church of England. That meant that during the 1950s English Presbyterians directed their energies there rather than to the possibilities of union with the Congregationalists. The scheme ran aground in 1957 when it was turned down by the Church of Scotland, goaded by the *Scottish Daily Express* who considered it to be thinly-veiled English imperialism.

Unitarians

Church of England Church of Scotland

The English Presbyterians were faced with a dilemma that had recurred many times in their history. Should they seek closer relations with the Church of Scotland, or direct their energies to the English scene? The English Presbyterians eventually decided to turn to the Congregationalists, and discussions began in 1963, leading to the union of 1972, against a background that was far from conducive to church unity.

Peace churches
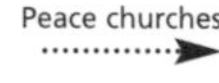

In 2000 the United Reformed Church, committed to the quest for visible unity by its foundation document, the Basis of Union, united once more, with Congregationalists, namely with the Congregational Union of Scotland. As the focus of ecumenical activity has turned from union schemes to local partnerships in mission, the United Reformed Church has maintained its commitment, and some 10 per cent of its congregations are in partnership, mainly with Methodists, but also in places with Anglicans, Baptists and members of the Church of Scotland and Presbyterian Church in Wales.

The United Reformed Church is a united church, but it is also a Reformed church. Each of its traditions was either a product of, or looks back in veneration to, the work of the Reformers of the sixteenth century.

Reformed churches p. 1016

Presbyterianism as a system of church government was given its definitive shape in Calvin's Geneva. It means the government of the church by presbyters (ministers and elders) in a series of graded courts (presbyteries, synods, assemblies). It knows of no hierarchy of ministry. Presbyterian theory was first propounded in England by the Cambridge theologian Thomas Cartwright (1535–1603) in his lectures on the Acts of the Apostles in 1570. Such views were rapidly outlawed by the Elizabethan regime, but never totally extinguished, and an undercurrent of 'Puritan' radicalism was a permanent feature of English church life until the civil wars and the establishment of the republic. After that, Presbyterianism faded rapidly and most Presbyterians were (like the great spiritual and pastoral theologian Richard Baxter 1615–91) 'mere Puritans' who simply sought a more inclusive national church. By the early decades of the eighteenth century most Presbyterian congregations had slid into 'advanced' Unitarianism. The exceptions were to be found in the far north, for the religious boundary between England and Scotland should have been drawn at the Tyne, not the Tweed. The Presbyterian Church of England that became part of the United Reformed Church in 1972 included some of those congregations, but the majority of its churches had been founded in the nineteenth century by migrant Scots. Although deeply committed to mission in England, English Presbyterianism placed a high premium on its close relationship with the Church of Scotland.

Christian Church (Disciples of Christ) Puritans

One of Congregationalism's finest theologians, P. T. Forsyth (1848–1921), argued that the essence of Congregationalism was a fusion of Calvinism with the free leading of the Spirit that was characteristic of the Radical Reformation. It was far more eclectic in its origins than Presbyterianism, formed from the radical ground of the left-wing of the reformation which also gave rise to Conrad Grebel and the Swiss Brethren, the Anabaptists and the Mennonites. If Presbyterianism was about 'godly order', Congregationalism was about the freedom of the Spirit and the autonomy of the local congregation under Christ. Echoing earlier traditions of monasticism, Congregationalism emphasized the significance of being gathered 'out of the world' into the fellowship of Christ. Decision for Christ was literally of eternal significance, so confessing the faith, becoming a member of the church and accepting the responsibilities of that membership, were of crucial importance. Believers covenanted together under God to be the church in a particular place. For Congregationalists the local was the catholic.

Presbyterianism and Congregationalism were profoundly different understandings of church order. Theologically, however, they were close cousins. They shared a common Calvinist heritage, duly tempered (albeit at different speeds) by first Arminianism and then liberalism. Their instincts were suitably Reformed – the authority of the Bible interpreted by the Spirit as the rule of life, a ministry of word and sacraments duly honoured but non-hierarchical, worship theoretically maintaining a balance between word and sacraments but in practice leaning to the supremacy of the word, rule by theocratic councils seeking to discern the mind of Christ.

Another strand within the United Reformed Church, the Churches of Christ (known at the Disciples in the United States), is a small body whose origins are to be found in the 'restorationist' movements of the nineteenth century. Its roots are to be found in the work of the

Campbells, Thomas (1763–1854) and his son Alexander (1788–1866), Presbyterian dissenting ministers who sought to heal the divisions between Presbyterians in Ireland and America, the Scottish Baptists, and some other tiny groupings in nineteenth-century England. They were united by 'restorationist' ideas – the attempt to 'restore' the primitive church of the New Testament, and by so doing to reform and renew church life. You can hear there the authentic voice of the Reformed tradition.

Although a relatively modern movement, its various founders adopted the same theological method as the Reformers of the sixteenth century – 'restoring' the nature of the primitive church. The emotional and intellectual roots of the churches are to be found in the quest of the Reformers for a church faithfully biblical. It was that attempt which led to the significant features of the churches' witness: communion as the normative act of Christian worship, believers' baptism, the ministry of settled elders and itinerant evangelists (who later became ministers) and closed communion (i.e. only those baptized as believers could communicate).

During the twentieth century the churches' theological self-understanding developed, most notably under the guidance of William Robinson (1888–1963), the Principal of Overdale College (the churches' theological college in Selly Oak, Birmingham). He sought to show how their distinctive contribution to British church life was to be a church that was neither Protestant nor Catholic but Christian. The essentials of Protestantism – freedom, an emphasis on the priesthood of all believers, personal faith in Christ and the centrality of scripture – were united with the fundamental aspects of Catholicism: a hatred of schism, the centrality of the eucharist and a respect for reason and tradition. That in turn led the churches to re-evaluate the issue of closed communion and believers' baptism and to admit those baptized as infants in other denominations to their communion celebrations. The way was thus prepared for them to move towards an ecumenical future, and in 1981 the Re-formed Association of the Churches of Christ in 1981 united with the United Reformed Church.

The United Reformed Church brings together three traditions. Its life is crafted from creative tension, for example honouring both infant and believer's baptism, and allowing national autonomy within a supranational assembly. As it lives with this tension, it does so in the belief that respecting difference is part of the gift that it will be able to offer to any future united church in the nations it serves.

DAVID CORNICK

David Cornick, *Under God's Good Hand*, London: United Reformed Church 1998; A. H. Drysdale, *History of the Presbyterians in England: Their Rise, Decline and Revival*, London: Publication Committee of the Presbyterian Church of England 1889; R. Tudur Jones, *Congregationalism in England 1662–1962*, London: Independent Press 1962; David Thompson, *Let Sects and Parties Fall: A Short History of the Association of the Churches of Christ in Great Britain and Ireland*, Birmingham: Berean 1980 and *Stating the Gospel*, Edinburgh: T&T Clark 1990

University

The relationship between Christianity and education is a rather tangled one, and this is particularly true in the area of 'higher education', that is, in universities. In the modern world universities are expected to be places in which learning is pursued to the highest possible level, free from external pressures. They are supposed to be repositories of wisdom and knowledge: many of the contributors to this *Guide* have worked in universities, and nearly all have studied at them. It is the possession of both knowledge and scholarly independence that gives universities their claim to authority, and they have used this claim in different ways in different periods. In the twenty-first century universities, with their scientific laboratories on the one hand and their often liberal theological studies on the other, are often seen as leading the attack on religious traditions and religious authority, and this view of their role was already being put forward at the time of the Reformation, but on occasions their effect was the opposite. In the period before the Reformation and during the Enlightenment, the theological libraries and clerical academics in universities put them in a powerful position to lead the attack on what could be seen as suspect science and dangerous humanism.

Reformation

Enlightenment

The university was a Christian creation. The beginnings of the oldest universities, Bologna, Paris and Oxford, are obscure, and until modern times legends circulated that Bologna was founded by the fifth-century Roman emperor Theodosius, Paris by Charlemagne and Oxford by King Alfred. However, the more prosaic story is that the university arose in the Middle Ages out of a type of school called the *studium generale*: these schools were open to students from all over Europe and were intended to give a better education to clergy and monks than the schools attached to cathedrals and monasteries. The term 'university', from the Latin *universitas*, did not mean the whole range of academic disciplines but the whole body of those engaged in work in them.

Middle Ages

Schools

The first university was founded at Bologna at the end of the eleventh century and was famous for its teaching of civil law and canon law. This was followed by the

University of Paris, founded between 1150 and 1170, which was famous for its theology and became a model for other universities, notably Oxford, founded towards the end of the same century. In Paris the teaching of theology was dialectical, i.e. through rational discussion; Scholasticism this method developed into scholasticism and the genre of great systematic theologies, called *Summa*, the most Thomas Aquinas famous of which is by Thomas Aquinas, who studied and taught there.

Three factors were crucial to the formation of the first universities. First, they had to be popular and attract large numbers of students and the best teachers. Secondly, the physical safety of students and teachers who came from foreign lands, and freedom of discussion, short of atheism or heresy, had to be guaranteed; this eventually led to charters from rulers or from the Pope. And thirdly, they had to develop an internal organization. In Paris the university was formed from three schools, the most famous of which was the cathedral school of Notre Dame.

The subjects taught in Paris were theology, philosophy, Religious orders medicine and law. Teachers of these subjects tended to group together, and early in the thirteenth century these groups were called 'faculties', from the Latin *facultas*, a term which originally meant a discipline or a branch of knowledge. The universities had little corporate property and teachers had to charge fees. This meant that they had to supply the demands of the students or risk losing them; it was dissatisfaction with the teaching at Oxford that led Humanism

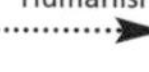

to the establishment of the University of Cambridge in 1209. From an early stage in Paris students, too, organized themselves into groups, based on nationality; these groups were called the 'Nations', originally the French, the Picards, Renaissance

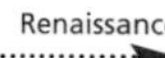

the Normans and the English. Each of the Nations elected a proctor, and the four proctors elected the rector of the university. The head of the university, though, was the chancellor, elected by the Pope. Oxford followed the same pattern, but with just two nations, the Boreales (the English and Scottish students) and the Australes (the Welsh and Irish).

Universities came to be established in many of the major cities of Europe: Salamanca (1218), Montpellier (1220), Padua (1222), Rome (1303), Florence (1321), Prague (1348), Vienna (1365), Heidelberg (1386), Aix-en-Provence (1409), Leipzig (1409), St Andrews (1413), Louvain (1425), Glasgow (1451), Freiburg (1457) and Tübingen (1477). Many of these were also modelled on the University of Paris.

Students ranged in age from around twelve to twenty. How many there were at a particular university in the early days is difficult to establish: it is reckoned that Paris and Bologna had a maximum of 6000 and Oxford 3000; in the fourteenth century Prague had around 1000 and in the fifteenth century Leipzig had under 500. The pattern of an academic year from October to June with breaks at Christmas and Easter goes back to the fourteenth century; the two-semester year was established in Leipzig in the middle of the fifteenth century, and spread widely from there. Degrees (Latin *gradus*, 'grade', 'step') were awarded to mark the student's progress from simple scholar to doctor; they developed out of the need to establish firm rules about who might or might not teach at the university. Teaching was initially based on books and lectures, but this changed through the institution of colleges. These were originally established by bishops or other church figures to provide accommodation for the poorer students: between 1200 and 1500 Paris had six colleges, Oxford eleven and Cambridge thirteen. However, the system steadily grew, and with it the system of tutoring. Colleges provided students, usually studying the arts or theology, with tutors to supervise their work on a more individual basis and this came to be regarded as more important than university lectures. Until the fifteenth century the teachers were required to be celibate, though this rule was not always enforced. Here the religious orders played a particularly important role: the Dominicans came to Paris in 1217 and to Oxford in 1221; the Franciscans to Paris in 1230 and to Oxford in 1224. At both universities the Carmelites and Augustinians also had their convents.

The areas of study other than theology came in the fifteenth century to be referred to as *litterae humanae*, 'human literature', in contrast to the word of God that was the subject of theology. The modern term 'humanist' comes from this phrase, but its meaning has always been broader than just denoting those who promulgate an atheistic world-view. The original humanists came to prominence with the Renaissance and the renewal of interest in the Greek and Latin literature of classical antiquity. Over time, the study of classical languages and literature came to be a central pillar of university education, but initially its path was not so smooth. When humanist scholars began to turn to Christian texts with the same critical approach that they applied to secular ones, they found considerable resistance within universities, and scholars such as Erasmus did most of their work outside them.

On the other hand, for some people the 'scholastic' approach to theology favoured within universities was also attacked as harmful to Christianity. In Germany Martin Luther denounced the universities as 'devil's workshops' and would have abolished them, and Philipp Melanchthon declared that philosophy was idolatry and that knowledge of the Bible was all a Christian needed. But wider counsels prevailed. In the German states which went over to Protestantism, the old universities were taken over by Protestants and new ones founded; Roman Catholic universities became strongholds of the traditional teachings of the church. But a concern with defending the truth of religion meant that the universities were not open to the increasing interest in science and new forms of learning. The new situation also meant that the universities, now under the patronage of local rulers, lost their international character.

Meanwhile, across the Atlantic, the earliest university to be founded was that of Santo Domingo in 1538, ante-dating by a century the earliest American foundations: Harvard (1636), William and Mary (1693), Yale (1701) and Princeton (1746). Santo Domingo was a Roman Catholic university; the others owe their origin to Protestant denominations. Here too, Christian influence was still predominant.

A crucial change in the nature of the university was marked by the foundation of the University of Halle in Germany in 1694, which rejected religious orthodoxy in favour of rational and objective investigation. Above all, teaching was no longer in Latin, as had been customary, but in German. The date of the foundation of the university is important. 1648 was one of the great watersheds of European history, the Peace of Westphalia, which put an end at last to the wars of religion. The disillusionment with religion which these wars had brought led to an emphasis on reason as the leading cultural value. The new developments at Halle were followed by the University of Göttingen (1737) and spread elsewhere in Germany. The University of Berlin, founded in 1809, became a model as influential as Paris had been in its day, leading to the spread of the idea of the university as a complex of graduate schools engaged in research. From the beginning of the nineteenth century, Americans began to study in Germany and under their influence new colleges and universities in the expanding United States followed the Berlin pattern; in Europe, especially in Italy, Spain and France, universities came to be secularized. In Britain a group of men including the philosopher Jeremy Bentham and the historian George Grote set up what was to become University College London as an explicitly non-religious English university.

It is, however, easy to overestimate the change in the nature of the university. While it is true, for example, that Isaac Newton (1642–1727) studied at the University of Cambridge, and wrote his major scientific works while he held the Lucasian Chair of Mathematics there, his presence would have had no effect on the syllabus taught to students, and many of his fellow scientists worked entirely outside the university system. Nor did Newton's eighteenth-century successors contribute much to the progress of learning. The hold of the churches on the universities proved tenacious, and it was only in the nineteenth century that what could be considered modern universities came to be the norm. In England up to around 1850 only members of the Church of England could attend the University of Oxford, and even when after Acts of Parliament in 1854 and 1856 the university was opened to members of any religion or none, the government of the university and its college and the teaching in them was reserved to members of the Church of England. Not until 1871 were all degrees and offices (except offices specifically related to ordained clergy) opened to all men of any religion or none. Admission of women came much later, towards the end of the century. All this was brought about only after a bitter and long-drawn-out fight with the church.

Surprisingly, although the ideal of the German university became so influential throughout the Western world, in Germany today the battle which was fought and won by the secular side in England in the nineteenth century is still going on in the area of theology. This is not least because a church tax is paid to the state by all Protestants and Roman Catholics who do not choose to opt out of it, and the proceeds from the tax keep denominational divides institutionally alive. In theology, German universities have separate Protestant and Catholic faculties, teaching different curricula, and admission to them is strictly regulated. Those doing doctorates in theology have to be baptized Christians. This makes it impossible for, say, a Jew to do a doctorate on the life of Jesus, though Jesus himself was a Jew.

Wars of religion

There are still 'private' religious universities, especially in the USA, and universities like Yale and Harvard have their divinity schools, but the trend in universities is clear. Having begun as church institutions they are now secularized. And outside Germany there have been vigorous discussions about how far theology, once the major discipline of the university, is an appropriate subject to be taught at university at all. Should not teaching and research in connection with religion be designated 'religious studies' and practised in the way that might be expected from that term?

Secularization

HUGH BOWDEN AND JOHN BOWDEN

L. J. Daly, *The Medieval University 1200–1400*, New York: Sheed & Ward 1961; Jaroslav Pelikan, *The Idea of the University. A Reexamination*, New Haven and London: Yale University Press 1992

Vatican

Visitors to Rome can enter Vatican City simply by walking into St Peter's Square, the Piazza San Pietro. Though they do not have to obtain a visa or present their passport, they can step across an international border into the smallest sovereign state in the world, located in the north-west corner of the city.

They will not enter or see, however, the other Vatican, the vast and complex array of agencies which assist the Pope in meeting his many responsibilities as Bishop of Rome, sole ruler of the state of Vatican City, Primate (or chief bishop) of Italy, and supreme teacher and governor of the worldwide Roman Catholic Church.

Papacy

Roman Catholic Church

The territorial expanse of Vatican City, 108.7 acres, is all that is left of the Papal States, once a realm of about 16,000 square miles and 3 million inhabitants, lying across the middle of the Italian peninsula. For centuries, the lands of the Papal States provided the church with the revenues it needed for its work. With the rise of Italian nationalism in the mid-1900s, these lands became a major obstacle to the dreams of patriots for a united country, from the Alps in the north to Sicily in the south. In 1870, therefore, the Kingdom of Italy simply expropriated them from Pope Pius IX.

In response, Pius IX and his successors remained

THE VATICAN

The Vatican, the complex of agencies which assist the Pope in his government of the Roman Catholic Church, is made up as follows:

Pope

College of Cardinals

Synod of Bishops

Roman Curia
Secretary of State
Council for the Public Affairs of the Church

Congregation for the Doctrine of the Faith
Congregation for Bishops
Congregation for the Oriental Churches
Congregation for Divine Worship and the Sacraments
Congregation for the Clergy
Congregation for Institutes of Consecrated Life
Congregation for the Evangelization of Peoples
Congregation for the Causes of Saints
Congregation for Catholic Education

Courts
Apostolic Penitentiary
Rota
Apostolic Signature

Pontifical Councils
Pontifical Council for the Promotion of Christian Unity
Pontifical Council for Inter-religious Dialogue
Pontifical Council for Culture
Pontifical Council of the Laity
Pontifical Council on Justice and Peace
Pontifical Council for the Interpretation of Legislative Texts
Pontifical Council for Social Communications
Pontifical Council for Migrants and Itinerants
Cor Unum Pontifical Council
Pontifical Council for the Family
Pontifical Council for Health-Care Workers

Papal representatives
Nuncios
Pro-nuncios
Apostolic delegates

within the confines of the Vatican, refusing to set foot even in the city of Rome, though the Pope is its bishop. In 1929, however, the long-vexed issues between the church and the Italian government were settled by the Lateran Pact. This treaty guaranteed the Pope's sovereignty over an independent Vatican City and compensated the church for the territories taken in 1870.

The Pope is unique among all the leaders of the Christian churches because he is the supreme governor, legislator, and judge of a state which operates like other states in many respects. The Vatican sends and receives ambassadors. It recognizes or withholds recognition from other national governments. It sends a representative to the United Nations and participates in certain international conferences under UN sponsorship. Until the adoption of the euro as the single European currency, the Vatican even had its own money. It still has its own postal service, which knowledgeable foreigners in Rome always use, instead of the less efficient Italian mails.

Most often, the term 'Vatican' refers not to the city state, but to the massive network of offices and personnel that the Pope needs to fulfil his many responsibilities. The organization and procedures of this bureaucracy do not reflect business-school textbooks on management. Rather, the Vatican is shaped by its own centuries-long traditions, the personality and priorities of the Pope himself, Italian culture, and the contemporary needs of the church. Managing the Curia, as it is also called, so that it serves him and the whole church (and not vice versa) is always one of the Pope's main tasks. Thus, Pope Paul VI ordered a re-organization of the Curia in 1967, shortly after the close of the Second Vatican Council, so that it could carry out the conciliar agenda more effectively. In 1988, Pope John Paul II fine-tuned Paul VI's design.

The Secretariat of State stands at the top of the Vatican flow chart, since it manages most of the bureaucracy's work. The Secretary of State is comparable to a chief of staff or a prime minister to the Pope. The Secretariat has two main departments. Its Section for General Affairs helps the Pope to conduct the ordinary business of the church and of Vatican City. Its Section for Relations with States is responsible for Vatican City's diplomatic relations with other nations and governments.

The rest of the Curia comprises nine congregations, eleven councils and three tribunals. Congregations deal mainly with internal church matters, such as worship, missionary activity, education, the life of priests and the appointment of bishops. Each is headed by a cardinal. Councils deal mainly with matters of church outreach, such as promoting Christian unity, furthering the causes of justice and peace, and maintaining the church's relationships with non-Christians. Yet the chief distinction between a congregation and a council is age. A council is

Vatican conclave in August 1903 to elect a new pope after the death of Leo XIII, engraving from *Le Petit Journal*

a relatively new agency, while a congregation can trace its history over centuries. Obviously, some issues require consultation and collaboration among curial agencies.

One of the three tribunals is the Rota. It deals mainly with judgements on the validity of marriages. Another, the Apostolic Penitentiary, deals with absolution for grave crimes and dispensations from vows and other religious obligations. The cardinal who heads the Penitentiary is one of the few curial officials who does not lose his job when the Pope dies, since forgiveness cannot be delayed when it is sincerely sought and warranted. The third, the Apostolic Signatura, is a sort of supreme court for the church, although its decisions, like any other curial decision, have to be ratified by the Pope.

The most influential congregation is the Congregation for the Doctrine of the Faith. It originated in the early thirteenth century as 'the Holy Office of the Inquisition' with a mandate to combat heresy. Paul VI's reorganization gave it a more positive task. Besides being the guardian of orthodoxy, the Congregation was also to promote sound theology and teaching in the church. Yet the Congregation continues to investigate theologians suspected of deviating

p. 345

from the fullness of Catholic faith. Its procedures have often been criticized for failing to protect the rights and good name of those theologians. In 1988, John Paul II significantly increased its power by directing that any curial decision involving church doctrine had to be first approved by the Congregation.

Catholics outside the Curia have a love-hate relationship with it. On the one hand, no one denies the need for the work that it does. On the other hand, criticisms of the Curia's high-handed dealings with bishops and theologians, of its policy-making for situations it knows too little about, and of its pre-empting the rightful role of bishops in governing the church have been loud and frequent ever since they first surfaced at the Second Vatican Council. Critics hope that the Synod of Bishops, a representative body of the world's bishops, might yet become vigorous enough to serve as counterweight to the Curia. Supporters of the Curia agree that it is not perfect, but maintain that it does a remarkably good job, given the scope of its responsibilities and the limitations of its resources.

Heresy
Council

JON NILSON

Peter Hebblethwaite, *In the Vatican*, Bethesda: Adler and Adler 1988; Bart McDowell, *Inside the Vatican*, Washington: National Geographic Society 1991; Peter Nichols, *The Vatican*, Dublin: Gill & Macmillan 1980; Thomas J. Reese, *Inside the Vatican: The Politics and Organization of the Catholic Church*, Cambridge, MA: Harvard University Press 1996

Waldensian Church

Waldensians form the Protestant population of four valleys in Piedmont in Italy, west of Turin. The Waldensian Church is the Presbyterian Reformed Church of Italy, with communities in Uruguay and Argentina which were formed following emigrations in the second half of the nineteenth century. Evangelization carried out in Italy in the second half of the nineteenth and first half of the twentieth century led within a few years to the church being spread throughout the Italian peninsula.

Sacraments
Life after death

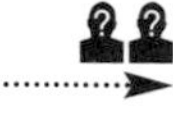

The origin of the Waldensians is usually connected with the conversion of a merchant from Lyons known commonly as Waldo (whose name is spelt in many different ways). There are various legends about his conversion around 1170, but his friendship with a canon of Lyons cathedral seems to have led him to discover the New Testament. The Bible and texts from some church fathers encouraged him to sell his possessions and give the proceeds to the poor (after seeing that the family which he left were adequately looked after), and with some disciples he devoted himself to itinerant preaching. For this purpose he commissioned a translation of the New Testament into Provençal, which was in use until the Reformation. The group supported itself by alms, so it was known as the 'Poor of Lyons'.

Reformation

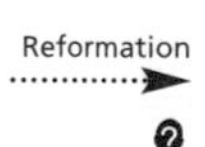

The doctrine of the primitive Waldensians does not seem to have been substantially different from that of the rest of the Western church. It stood out, however, for its use of scripture in the vernacular, its poverty and its preaching (this was also extended to women, but preaching did not imply aspirations to the priesthood). Consequently the Waldensians clashed with the Roman Catholic Church, all the more so since their sermons contained criticisms of the clergy, who were considered corrupt and avaricious. So they were not heretics but schismatics.

Disregarding a call from the Bishop of Lyons to stop preaching, the Waldensians were excommunicated and expelled from the diocese. What happened next is difficult to discover for lack of sources, but the movement rapidly spread. An important group formed in Lombardy with a structured community life governed by a fixed rather than a charismatic rule: these 'poor Lombards' were artisans, largely wool-workers. This led to a split between Waldo (an extant confession of faith demonstrates his Catholic orthodoxy) and his successor Durando and the Lombards. Part of the original Lyons group eventually rejoined the official church. During the twelfth century the movement continued to expand and soon traces of it could be found from Flanders to the Baltic, in Poland, Hungary, Bohemia, Germany, Austria and Switzerland; in Italy the movement extended as far as Calabria. But everywhere it was harshly repressed, in contrast to the contemporaneous Franciscans and Dominicans.

The Bergamo Conference of 1218 brought together the two branches of the Waldensians and at the same time established differences from the Roman Catholic Church. Heretics were not to be suppressed but to be admonished and persuaded; the sacrament was not a visible sign of the unity of the church but a sign of apostolic mission and love; oaths and the doctrine of purgatory were rejected.

Persecution intensified, and to escape it a nucleus took refuge in a sparsely populated area of the Alps. However, even here they were persecuted in what amounted to a crusade. By the end of the fourteenth century the movement seemed almost dead, but their aims were pursued in similar movements led by John Wyclif in England and John Hus in Bohemia.

However, Waldensians lived on and in the early sixteenth century made contact with the leaders of the Reformation, after much debate endorsing the main principles of John Calvin's reform in Geneva. This brought them into the political conflicts that accompanied the Reformation, and as a Protestant enclave in a Catholic territory they were again the subject of attack. This led them even to renounce their traditional pacifism. Their plight is the subject of a famous sonnet by John Milton, 'Avenge, O Lord, thy slaughter'd Saints, whose bones lie scattered on the Alpine mountains cold'.

It was not until the end of the seventeenth century that the Waldensians were left in relative peace, but at the same time they were isolated in their mountain ghetto. Their fortunes improved further at the time of the French Revolution, and a number held office in the revolutionary government. Pastors were even paid by the state. But this period was short, and persecution struck yet again.

In 1848 the king of Sardinia and Piedmont, Carlo Alberto, granted civil and political rights to the Waldensians (at about the same time as the Jews), and their situation steadily improved with the ongoing democratization of the state. A college for training pastors was established in Rome, and a publishing house, Editrice Claudiana in Turin, which still exists. The Waldensians, like other Protestant churches, also attracted converts from Roman Catholicism, particularly liberals who could not accept the conservatism of their church under the Pius popes.

There were difficult years again under Fascist rule from 1922 onwards, and during the Second World War Waldensians joined the resistance. After the war, the reconstruction of the Waldensian Church began along with the reconstruction of Italy. The church took part in the first assembly of the World Council of Churches in Amsterdam in 1948 and is now part of a federation of Italian Protestant churches; it has a faculty of theology in Rome and an Agape Centre at Praly. Relations with the Roman Catholic Church have developed since Vatican II and Waldensians are often invited to Catholic meetings and congresses.

J. ALBERTO SOGGIN

G. Tourn, *The Waldensians: The First 800 Years*, Turin: Claudiana 1980

War and peace

According to some historians, the early church was pacifist by conviction until the era of Constantine, during which it became increasingly corrupted by close links to the Roman state, thus opening the way for the development by Augustine of the view that in some circumstances wars could be just. On this view the just war tradition is the product of a corrupted Christianity; true Christianity is properly pacifist.

There are a number of problems with this view. Clearly the first-century church did reject military service, but this rejection must be understood in the context of its more general effort to hold itself aloof from involvement in the affairs of this age so that Christians could devote themselves to preparation for the imminent second coming of Christ. Nevertheless, in many areas there were compromises: for example, while recommending celibacy, Paul allowed Christians to marry rather than 'burn'; in the same vein, there are stories of individual Christians who belonged to the Roman military.

Paul

Early in the second century, as Christians increasingly decided that the second coming was not imminent after all, they began to move into closer relations with the wider society around them, marrying, holding property and accepting public responsibilities. By the third quarter of that century there is evidence of a Roman legion, the *Legio Fulminata*, composed entirely or mainly of Christians, and at the end of the century the church father Tertullian reveals, by attacking them, that substantial numbers of Christians were serving in the Roman military in North Africa. This suggests that the picture was somewhat more complex.

Fundamentally, the problem is one of which evidence to count and how to read it. Those who argue that true Christianity is properly pacifist emphasize the examples of early Christians who were martyred for refusing military service, as well as authors such as Hippolytus and Origen who support the norm of rejecting military service. On the other side is the general pattern of Christians, from early in the second century, moving into closer acceptance of participation of life in the world, and the particular example of what seems to be a growing presence of Christians serving in the Roman military. Interpreting such contradictory evidence is analogous to determining the church's normative attitude towards priestly celibacy during the same period: on the one hand theological statements and canons enjoin celibacy; on the other there is evidence that large numbers of clergy were in fact married and had children.

Ecumenical movement

Whichever view one takes about what counts as normative within the church, the positions of the élite or the practice of larger numbers of ordinary Christians, the evidence is clear that acceptance of military service began more than a century before Constantine became emperor and two centuries before Augustine wrote on the just war. By the time of Augustine, Christian pacifism was no longer the normative position of the church; only monks and clergy were expected to refuse military service, though pacifism lived on among more radical, often heretical, groups.

Constantine's 'conversion'

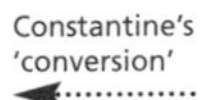

Augustine's comments on just war are relatively few and scattered among works on various other topics; he never produced a systematic treatise on just war comparable to the two he wrote on marriage. The creation of a coherent, systematic conception of just war began instead with the canonist Gratian in his *Decretum* in the mid-twelfth century. Gratian collected everything that

Canon law

Augustine and other authorities had said about just war and organized it by topics. Then in the mid-thirteenth century theologians such as Peter of Paris and Thomas Aquinas, working on the basis provided by canon law and Augustine's work before them, set the conception of just war into a broader theological frame. By the time of Thomas' *Summa Theologiae* the main line of the specifically Christian understanding of just war was established.

Anabaptists
Peace churches

Thomas' focus was on what later came to be called the *jus ad bellum*, how to determine if a given resort to force is just. He identified three requirements: that the use of force be on the authority of a sovereign working to ensure his responsibilities for the common good; that there be a just cause, defined as defending this common good, restoring that which has been wrongly taken, and punishing evil; and that there be a right intention, defined negatively as avoiding such intentions as bullying, self-aggrandizement, or implacable hatred of the other, and defined positively as the intention to secure a just, orderly peace. This peace, Augustine's tranquil order (*tranquillitas ordinis*), was understood to be a positive characteristic of good government, and the justified use of force was seen as a tool towards achieving and maintaining it. Canon law still set the terms of what came to be called the *jus in bello*, the requirements for moral conduct in war: lists of classes of non-combatants, who were not to be directly attacked, and efforts to ban or restrict certain weapons deemed disproportionately injurious (arrows, siege weapons). However, after Thomas Aquinas, up to the end of the Hundred Years War, the main contributions to just-war tradition came from secular spheres within Western Christian culture: the maturing code of chivalry, renewed attention to Roman law, and reflection on the right practice of government and the role of force in that practice.

Enlightenment

During this same period Christian pacifism exhibited the pattern already visible in Augustine's time: for the mainline church it was limited to the rejection of military service for monks and clergy, but it appeared in specific dissident groups, such as the Waldensians and the Cathars.

Waldensian Church

At the beginning of the modern era theorists such as Franciscus de Vitoria (1492–1547) and later Hugo Grotius (1583–1645) refashioned the inherited just-war tradition into an element of a new conception of the law of nations based on natural law and the law of nations (*jus gentium*). Among the Reformers, Martin Luther's position on just war was essentially that of Thomas Aquinas. John Calvin and the Reformed tradition modified this position only by giving a new critical look at the idea of sovereignty and who might justly use force to depose a tyrant. After the Peace of Westphalia, which brought the wars of religion to an end, focus on the moral issues treated in the *jus ad bellum* waned, as the question of just resort to force was reshaped into the concept of *compétence de guerre*. At the same time, in secular moral thought and theoretical writings on the law of nations, the *jus ad bellum* was given more emphasis. The limited wars of the eighteenth century reflected this emphasis, as has the development of positive international law on war beginning with the first Geneva Convention in 1864.

Wars of religion

The Reformation era, of course, also gave new life to the radical sectarian conception of Christian life in the form of the Anabaptist movement. Its descendants, the contemporary 'peace churches', maintain rejection of war and military service, though except for groups like the Amish they have moved into participation in other forms of public life.

Beginning with the era of the Enlightenment, Christians joined secular thinkers in defining a concept of 'perpetual peace', a peace to be achieved through international organization. So far as this position implied ending war as a part of political life, it is a form of pacifism, though a very different form from that of Christian sectarianism. In the twentieth century the distinction between these two approaches became blurred, and 'peace church' pacifism today often has elements of internationalism in it. Christian pacifism was diverse in the era of the two world wars and the coming of war itself led to splits among different sorts of Christian pacifists.

During the twentieth century much of main-line Christianity moved progressively in the direction of rejecting war, often arguing that its technology had become too destructive to be an instrument of justice. Nuclear pacifism, a product of the nuclear era, was a specific form of this larger modern-war pacifism. Beginning with the work of Paul Ramsey in the 1960s, however, there has been a vigorous effort to revive and develop just-war reasoning as a resource for Christian ethical reflection. An important landmark was the US Catholic bishops' 1983 pastoral, *The Challenge of Peace*, which tried to link Christian pacifism and just-war thinking in a common 'presumption against war'.

Whether these two positions are compatible is, however, another matter. The 'presumption against war' is nowhere found in Christian just-war tradition before the bishops adopted it. Christian pacifism and Christian just-war thought define distinct – and distinctive – positions not only on the question of the use of force but, more broadly, on how to conceive responsible Christian life.

JAMES TURNER JOHNSON

C. J. Cadoux, *The Early Christian Attitude to War* (1917), New York: Seabury Press 1982; Guy Franklin Hershberger, *War, Peace, and Nonresistance* (1944), Scottdale, PA and Kitchener, ON: Herald Press 1991; James Turner Johnson, *Just War Tradition and the Restraint of War*, Princeton, NJ: Princeton University

Press 1981; National Conference of Catholic Bishops, *The Challenge of Peace: God's Promise and Our Response*, Washington, DC: National Conference of Catholic Bishops 1983; Paul Ramsey, *Speak Up for Just War or Pacifism*, University Park, PA: Pennsylvania State University Press 1988

Wars of religion

In 1648 the Peace of Westphalia brought to an end a century of wars in which religion was a major cause of conflict. These affected every European country where the Roman Catholic ruler wanted to crush the newly-emerging Protestants, and where powerful forces within that country were willing to take up the Protestant cause. The only countries that escaped war were those in which the king himself was a Protestant convert (England and the Scandinavian monarchies), where the Protestants never gained powerful allies (Italy and Spain) or where a powerful but tolerant king ruled (Poland). Historians argue over the extent to which these wars should accurately be described as 'religious'; in every case many other factors were at work to cause conflict, but the struggle between Catholics and Protestants was present in all of them.

Conflict was almost inevitable in Germany once Martin Luther had declared his defiance of the Pope in 1517, attracted converts and started to create a new church. The country consisted of very many separate political units, nominally under the authority of the Holy Roman emperor. Lutheranism offered individual princes, counts and city-states the chance to escape from the emperor's control, and ordinary Germans a national cause. Add to this economic unrest and the great wealth of the Roman Catholic Church, as well as many intense personal rivalries among the leaders, and its rapid growth was inevitable.

Charles V as emperor was a deeply devout Catholic, desperate to maintain the authority of Rome throughout his dominions. He believed that the political unity of his empire could only be preserved through religious unity. Yet he remained reluctant to go to war against the Lutherans for many years, partly because continual crises in other parts of his wide lands absorbed his energies and resources, and partly because he hoped to bring about a reconciliation of the rival faiths based on reform of the Roman Catholic Church. He also hated the prospect of war against his own subjects, sharing the humanists' love of peace.

It was almost 30 years after Luther's original protest that war finally broke out. Earlier in that year (1546) Charles V had called yet another Diet (a meeting of all the rulers of the constituent states of the Holy Roman empire in Germany). It was a final attempt to find a peaceful solution to the Catholic-Protestant conflict, and it failed. Seeing war was inevitable, the Protestant princes had organized themselves into a defensive League. Disillusioned in his hopes, Charles accumulated troops and cash and launched an attack that brought him victory over the Protestant princes at Muhlberg in 1547. Several of their leaders were taken prisoner; mistakenly, Charles believed that Lutheranism would collapse with its leaders out of action. He always underestimated the strength of Protestant convictions. Where his troops occupied a town, the mass was reinstated; as soon as they had moved on, the Lutheran services began again. When he called a new Diet at Augsburg to draw up a compromise by which papal authority and Catholic doctrine were preserved (but the doctrine of justification by faith was accepted and clerical marriage allowed), almost no one supported it.

By now the Protestant princes still at large had realized that their cause needed outside help to succeed against the might of Charles, who had the resources of Spain and the Netherlands at his disposal. They approached Henry II of France, who agreed to help in return for control of Metz, Toul and Verdun (there was no religious motive here; Henry was a Catholic).

France declared war in 1552, seized the promised reward and defeated Charles, who had to flee in ignominy across the Brenner Pass. The emperor made a last attempt to reverse his defeat, but by now he was totally exhausted and ready to give up the struggle. He abdicated in 1555, dividing his burden by handing over the empire to his brother Ferdinand, and the throne of Spain and control of the Netherlands to his son Philip.

Martin Luther

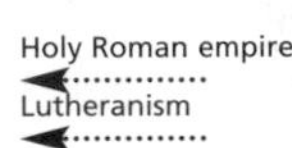

Holy Roman empire
Lutheranism

It was Ferdinand who presided over the Diet that brought the war to a formal end by drawing up the Peace of Augsburg later that year. Under its terms, each constituent part of the empire was to follow the religion of its ruler, Catholic or Lutheran (*cuius religio, eius regio*). In cities with equal numbers of followers of both religions, both were allowed. Those who did not agree with their ruler's religion were at liberty to move.

Roman Catholic Church

The wars of religion in France

Although Lutheranism had been the cause of the religious wars in Germany, it was Calvinism which provoked the Catholics to go to war to suppress it in France and the Netherlands. While Luther's church depended on the local ruler to provide its structure, Calvin's congregations were self-governing, enabling it to spread in lands where the government opposed it, and thus well-fitted to be the religion of the second phase of the Protestant Reformation.

Humanism

Reformation

Lutheranism had made a few converts in France in the 1520s; they escaped persecution until 1534, when a poster campaign alerted the king, Francis I, to the threat

John Calvin

they posed to Catholicism. John Calvin was among the Protestants who now fled France. He, like many other exiles, ended up in Geneva and began to create a new Protestant church that set out to win converts. In France it was particularly successful in the towns and among the nobility, with people who already had political and economic grievances. Both groups were seeing their standard of living fall through rapid inflation, and were aggrieved at their lack of any say in how the country was run.

As long as there was a strong king, the situation remained under control, but with the death of Henry II in 1559 France entered a long period of weak central authority. This unleashed the ambitions of three rival aristocratic families, and it was France's tragedy that these families were divided in religion. The most powerful, the Guises, were fanatical Catholics. The two others, the Chatillons and the Bourbons, were predominantly Protestant. As the new Calvinist congregations began to realize that persecution was a growing threat, they sought protection from local nobles who had converted to their faith. This meant they became part of the huge networks of clients with which the three rival families had already enmeshed the country.

The Guises were meanwhile consolidating their control over the young king, and over the royal army. They had great wealth and an immense power base in central and eastern France, while the Chatillons and Bourbons were strongest in the south west. By 1559 pressure was mounting to confront the Guises. Catherine de Medici, regent for her young sons, resented Guise control and favoured a policy of religious toleration. First she called the Colloquy of Poissy in 1561 to try to reconcile the two faiths. When that failed, she asked an assembly of leading nobles to give their assent to her Edict of January, relaxing the anti-heresy laws. This provoked the Guises into open preparation for war to re-assert their control over the court, and they deliberately risked starting war by attacking a congregation of Calvinists at Sunday worship near Vassy. (By this time Calvinists were more commonly called Huguenots; the origin of the name is unknown, but it could be a corruption of the Swiss-German *Eidgenossen* = confederates.)

In retaliation the Protestant leaders Condé and Coligny seized Orleans and rallied the Huguenot congregations to provide them with combatants as open war broke out. Both sides appealed for foreign support, the Guises to Spain and the Protestants to England and Germany. France descended into chaos, with local enmities adding to the spread of the fighting. Now a virtual prisoner of the Guises, Catherine de Medici made desperate appeals for peace. At first both sides rejected these, but the deaths in battle of several leading members of each side, in particular the Duke of Guise, led to greater willingness to negotiate.

The result was the Peace of Amboise in 1563, which gave freedom of worship to all nobles, and allowed one Huguenot place of worship in each of 90 districts. But these terms put such severe limitations on them that most Huguenots wanted to resume fighting to win more tolerance.

They felt increasingly threatened as the Cardinal of Lorraine took over as leader of the Guises, and Catherine de Medici misguidedly met the Duke of Alva, who was about to advance from Spain to the Netherlands to suppress Protestant rebellion there. The Huguenots feared that his army would invade France instead, and almost at once a second war broke out. A third war followed shortly.

By 1570 both sides were ready to agree to the Peace of St Germain. Now the Huguenots were allowed complete control of four fortress towns, but in reality central authority had become so weak during the wars that many Huguenot areas were virtually free to do as they wished. Several more leaders of the noble factions were now dead, and there was a general longing for a permanent peace.

Catherine de Medici believed tolerance of religious difference could be made permanent by the marriage of her daughter Margaret to a leading Protestant prince, Henry of Navarre. Coligny, another leading Protestant, had become a dominant figure at court, and tried to use his influence to persuade Catherine to agree to a French army being sent to aid the Netherlands Protestants against Spain. She opposed this, realizing it would provoke Philip of Spain to attack France to restore Guise and Catholic dominance.

During the wedding festivities in Paris, with many Huguenots thronging the capital, Coligny was shot and wounded. Although it was never proved, it seems probable that Catherine in a panic ordered the assassination of Coligny and leading Huguenots. But the killing got out of hand and spread far beyond Paris, gaining Catherine centuries-long notoriety as the instigator of the Massacre of St Bartholomew.

The fourth war broke out as a direct consequence. Many Huguenots now forsook all loyalty to the crown, having lost hope that it would ever succeed in imposing an effective policy of toleration. At the same time, moderate Catholics were realizing that the country could return to order and security only if the two religions lived in peace.

Catherine de Medici's reputation was in tatters, and the succession of her third son, Henry III, raised hopes that with an able adult on the throne, royal authority would be restored. Unfortunately these hopes were not realized; Henry could not control the noble factions, and war broke out yet again, from 1574 to 1580.

The death of the king's younger brother in 1584 left

the Protestant Henry of Navarre heir to the throne. The current Duke of Guise proclaimed his uncle Cardinal Bourbon as the true heir and forced the king to revoke all previous edicts of toleration, reviving his Catholic League of supporters to strengthen his hand. By 1588 Henry III was so humiliated by Guise attempts to dominate him that he had the Duke assassinated, only to be killed himself the following year.

Henry of Navarre now became king. At last a man of authority and integrity was on the throne of France, but it took a further ten years of intermittent fighting before royal authority was fully restored. The Catholic League had support from Spain, while English and German troops went to Henry IV's aid. By this time the League appeared more and more as the instrument of Spain, particularly after the death of Cardinal Bourbon, and the king was able to rally French national feeling to help expel the Spaniards.

Yet Henry IV came to realize that national unity and the defeat of the League would never be achieved while he remained a member of the minority religion. His religious convictions had never been strong; and for political expediency he abjured the Huguenot faith and was received as a Catholic in 1593. Quickly the last League strongholds were won over and the last Spaniards driven out.

The Huguenots remained loyal, but demanded major concessions in return for their support in the last stages of the war. Peace came in 1598 and with it the Edict of Nantes, giving the Huguenots complete liberty of conscience. But they were allowed public worship only in a limited number of places, mainly in southern and western France. They were also allowed certain garrisons, and an equal share in law courts which had jurisdiction over disputes concerning them.

As long as the crown supported the Edict, the Huguenots were safe. It remained in force until 1685, when Louis XIV revoked it and persecution resumed.

The Dutch revolt

When Protestantism first spread to the Netherlands, the area was under the authority of Charles V, his inheritance from his father as Duke of Burgundy. Charles V had given charge of it to his son Philip, king of Spain, when he abdicated in 1555. As in France, the first converts were Lutherans, who survived considerable persecution. Anabaptists followed, and suffered even harsher treatment. Calvinism was slower to penetrate here than in France, but received a boost when Huguenots sought refuge at the start of the French religious wars. It spread rapidly among all classes during the 1560s, particularly in the southern cities.

Philip II was determined to gain closer control of his territories in the Netherlands; he aimed to reduce the local aristocrats' share in running the country and to apply the anti-heresy laws far more strictly than his father had. This shocked the leading nobles into protest, and they were able to persuade Philip's regent, Margaret of Parma, to suspend the imposition of Philip's harsh edicts. Her hand was further forced when popular revolts broke out in Flanders, often encouraged by Calvinist ministers, and fuelled by food shortages and falling wages. Mobs got out of control and ransacked Catholic churches, and Margaret had to agree to the aristocrats' demand in return for their help in restoring order.

Philip was totally opposed to any measure of tolerance, and despatched the Duke of Alva to crush all opposition. Margaret resigned; William of Orange, known as William the Silent, a Dutch nobleman, and others fled the Netherlands to start organizing resistance from outside; and Alva set about punishing all rebels and heretics. The hatred this policy provoked was greatly increased when he also imposed a heavy tax on all sales, potentially crippling to a country so dependent on trade.

In exile, Orange now converted to Lutheranism and began to organize opposition to Alva. By 1572 he was ready to invade the Netherlands with help from English, French and German Protestants, and the group of semi-pirates who called themselves the Sea Beggars. Unplanned, these last precipitated armed conflict by seeking refuge in the port of Brill, and from there rapidly over-ran many towns in the provinces of Zealand and Holland. One month later Orange's forces invaded from the north-east, and Alva had to divide his troops. This early success did not last, and with the Massacre of St Bartholomew the French allies were withdrawn.

Orange now took a huge risk, dashing secretly across the country to link up with the Sea Beggars. Many more towns were won over to the rebels by the promise of freedom of worship and a more democratic form of town government. Orange had chosen well; this part of Holland and Zealand formed a natural fortress, with the sea and many rivers providing water on all sides. Here he was impregnable against Spanish might, and later his epic relief of the siege of Leyden, by water, awoke a spirit of national fervour in the northern Netherlands. Orange began to hope for the emergence of a new, free country where all religions were tolerated. He converted to Calvinism at this time, but tried to curb the iconoclasm of some of his extreme co-religionists. By now Alva was running out of money to pay for this war of attrition. Impatient for victory, Philip replaced Alva with Requesens, a realist who saw that straight victory over the rebels was unattainable. He was keen to negotiate with Orange, but Philip would not allow him to offer what the rebels demanded, religious toleration as well as the withdrawal of Spanish troops, and the war continued.

Anabaptists ←

François Dubois, *St Bartholomew's Day Massacre*, sixteenth century

By 1576 the Spanish troops were so behind in pay that they mutinied, and started to plunder the provinces of Flanders and Brabant. This 'Spanish Fury' provoked a huge outburst of anti-Spanish feeling throughout the Netherlands, uniting every part of the country against Spain for the first time. By the Pacification of Ghent, the leading great nobles in the States General (parliament) in Brussels agreed to combine forces with Orange as leader of Holland and Zealand to rid the Netherlands of the mutinous Spanish soldiers. The question of religious tolerance was deferred, since these grandees were all Catholics.

This united front was short-lived. Across Flanders, Brabant and Artois the Calvinists took the chance to seize control and ban Catholic worship, to Orange's despair. Few seemed to share his vision of a tolerant country. Many moderate Catholics were alarmed at the advance of militant Calvinism into the south of the Netherlands, while the grandees resented Orange's willingness to work with the representative States General and with people of all classes.

Eventually the three southern provinces, disgusted by Calvinist extremists, created their own Union of Arras and made peace with the latest Spanish governor, the Duke of Parma. The northern provinces replied by forming themselves into the Union of Utrecht, and promising religious toleration. Many Catholics feared that this would not be honoured, and made their way south, while Calvinists went north.

Parma now made it his goal to reconquer the north, and Orange tried to get help from France; when he was assassinated in 1584, the Union of Utrecht was dangerously weak. Although Parma was partially successful, he never won back the heartlands of Holland and Zealand, and his successors lacked his military skill. Orange's son, Maurice of Nassau, grew up to be an able soldier and some of the land was recovered.

Spain's resources were increasingly diverted to help the Catholic League in France and to prepare for the invasion of England. Spain simply could not afford to sustain further warfare. At the same time, the members of the Union of Utrecht (now calling themselves the United Provinces) were increasingly successful in welding themselves into a wealthy and politically cohesive nation. The southern provinces were beginning a slow economic decline under Spanish rule.

When England made peace with Spain in 1604, the United Provinces realized that they could not stand against Spain alone. By 1607 both sides were ready to negotiate an armistice. This was extended for a further twelve years by the Truce of Antwerp (1609). The war was renewed in 1621, and is known by the Dutch as the Eighty Years War, but the essential division of the Netherlands between the northern Calvinists and the southern Catholics had been effected long before.

The Thirty Years War

The wars described so far were mainly confined to one country, but after 1621 the struggles overlapped to involve many powers in the Thirty Years War. Religion became a diminishing motive among the combatants, with alliances being formed between Protestant and Catholic powers, and a major conflict emerging between two Catholic countries, France and Spain.

Spain had always intended to renew its struggle to win back the northern Netherlands when the twelve-year truce ran out, and it had renewed its strength. It was in desperate need of the revenue that they could provide, besides coveting their recovery for Catholicism. In preparation, Spain had secured a string of fixed points along the route that its troops would take from Genoa north across the Alps to the southern border of the United Provinces.

In Germany the Counter-Reformation had made headway, and Protestant princes feared that the emperor would try to win back property lost earlier by the Catholic Church. They created a defensive Evangelical Union, prompting the leading Catholic prince, Max of Bavaria, to form the Catholic League. Several confrontations between the two came to the brink of war, but it was the Bohemian revolt of 1618 which finally lit the flame.

Bohemia was mainly Protestant, but when Ferdinand, the heir to the imperial throne and an ultra-Catholic, was made king, the Protestant Deputies feared the loss of their religious freedom and chose the Protestant Elector of the Palatinate in his place. This amounted to rebellion, and was swiftly crushed by the imperial forces at the battle of the White Mountain in 1620. Ferdinand then enforced Catholicism throughout Bohemia, and drove the Elector Palatine out of his homeland on the Rhine in punishment.

These events alerted the rest of Europe to the Habsburg threat in the person of Ferdinand. France acted first, sending an army to block the route used by Spanish troops through the Alps. But it had been forced to make concessions, and by 1625 Spain was ready to launch a major attack to try to regain the United Provinces. Spain's initial success brought England, Denmark and parts of Germany as allies for their Dutch fellow-Protestants.

Spain knew how much the United Provinces' wealth depended on its overseas trade, and saw how it could weaken this by calling on the other Habsburg power, Austria, to win control of the north German coastal towns. The emperor authorized the brilliant military leader Wallenstein to raise an army on his behalf, and these troops quickly marched deep into Germany and defeated Denmark in 1629.

The Emperor Ferdinand believed that he was now strong enough to impose his Edict of Restitution, restoring to the Catholic Church much property lost to the Protestants in central and north Germany. Many Germans regarded this with horror, as evidence of Frederick's aim to make himself complete master of Germany in government as well as religion. It also brought a new force into the war, Gustavus Adolphus of Sweden. He saw himself as the saviour of the German Protestants, and made lightning progress from the Baltic southwards, defeating the imperial army at Breitenfeld in 1631. But Gustavus was killed the following year. A peaceful settlement now seemed possible, but fighting re-erupted again and again until the Swedes were finally defeated at Nordlingen and south Germany passed back under Habsburg control. Only in 1635 was peace signed at Prague. The Edict of Restitution was repealed for 40 years and Lutherans were allowed to keep all the church property they had held in 1627. Calvinists were still excluded from recognition, but the pattern of a Protestant north Germany and a Catholic south was confirmed.

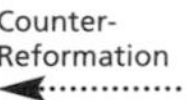
Counter-Reformation

War continued for another twelve years, but by now the motivation was almost entirely territorial gain. When France declared war on Spain in 1635, it was against a fellow Catholic power. During these years the United Provinces grew ever stronger, and the defeat of the Spanish navy in 1639 brought their enemy to the negotiating table. Spain at last recognized the United Provinces' independence by the Treaty of Münster in 1648. Though the Spanish-French struggle continued, all the other countries involved finally agreed to the Peace of Westphalia in 1648. The Holy Roman empire was the greatest loser, in terms both of territory and political authority. Within the empire, Protestant rights were acknowledged. The Treaty marks the secularization of politics, with religion left to individual conscience.

CATHERINE MULGAN

R. W. Scribner, *The German Reformation*, London: Macmillan 1986; M. P. Holt, *The French Wars of Religion*, Cambridge: CUP 1995; Geoffrey Parker, *The Dutch Revolt*, Harmondsworth: Penguin Books 1977 and *The Thirty Years War*, London: Routledge 1984

WOMEN IN CHRISTIANITY

Feminist theology, History, Interfaith dialogue, Jesus, Mary, Origins and background, Paul, Ministers and ministry, Monasticism, Religious orders, Sexuality, Theology

Christianity was shaped within two Mediterranean patriarchal cultures, Jewish and Graeco-Roman. These traditions mostly saw women as inferior and subordinate to men, and excluded women from public cultural and political leadership. But the early church was also shaped in Jewish prophetic and apocalyptic visions of hope for the liberation of oppressed people, as seen in the biblical narrative of the exodus and the writings of the prophets. Usually this liberation was understood as national emancipation and applied mostly to men, as leaders of the nation. However, in the first century a few Jewish thinkers applied this idea of liberation of the oppressed to those subjugated within the family, namely slaves and women. Christian history in relation to women is deeply shaped by this contradiction between a patriarchal view of women as subordinate and a prophetic view of women as sharing the same human nature as men and as liberated in Christ.

Prophecy

Apocalyptic

The New Testament

The conflict between these two world-views of patriarchy and liberation in early Christianity is reflected in the New Testament. On the liberationist side, one finds in the early strata of the New Testament a number of stories and teachings that suggest that redemption will transform traditional gender relations. The Gospel stories often set arrogant representatives of the leadership class – Pharisees and rulers – against women of despised groups – prostitutes, Samaritan and Canaanite women, poor widows and a woman with a flow of blood (making her unclean in Jewish law). These women are praised as having the true insight into Jesus' teachings, while the male religious leaders are rebuked as false teachers.

The coming of the messianic age heralded by Jesus is seen as turning the social system upside down. Mary, Jesus' mother, sings the praises of her coming child as the one who will 'put the mighty down from their thrones and lift up the lowly, fill the hungry with good things and send the rich empty away' (Luke 1.52–3). In his inaugural sermon in his home-town synagogue in Nazareth, Jesus announces that he has come to 'bring good news to the poor, the liberation of the captives, the setting at liberty of those who are oppressed' (Luke 4.18–19). In the outpouring of the Spirit at Pentecost slave women and men prophesy (Acts 2.18). Jesus declares that prostitutes and tax collectors will enter the kingdom of God ahead of the chief priests and elders of the people (Matthew 21.31).

Kingdom of God

The idea that redemption transforms gender, as well as class and race divisions, is expressed in an early baptismal creed cited by Paul: 'There is no longer Jew or Greek, slave or free, male and female, for you are all one in Christ Jesus' (Galatians 3.28). However, by Paul's time (some twenty years after the death of Jesus), the idea that women are made equal in Christ has taken on a particular meaning. It has become linked to celibacy. Women are seen as becoming spiritual equals with men by giving up their female functions as wives, renouncing sex and procreation and becoming 'spiritually male'.

Even this limited idea of gender equality became too threatening to Paul and his successors, particularly as women in their congregations claimed a new freedom to preach and travel as evangelists, while renouncing marriage and family. Later writers in the New Testament insist that equality in Christ is only spiritual. It does not change the actual power of masters, husbands and fathers over slaves, wives and children. Rather, they are commanded to obey. 'Wives obey your husbands, slaves obey your masters, children obey your parents' is an insistent theme in the later strata of the New Testament writings, such as Colossians 3, Ephesians 5–6 and 1 Peter 2–3. This demand for obedience itself testifies to the extent to which these power relations were seen as threatened by the liberationist tradition.

The letter to Timothy, written in the generation after Paul, seeks to give a definitive basis for women's continued subordination in the church and to refute any thought that this subordination has been changed by redemption in Christ. Woman was created second and was the originator of the fall of humanity into sin. This heritage locates woman as both secondary in God's original plan for creation, and also as subordinated as punishment for her primacy in sin. 'I permit no woman to teach or to have authority over a man; she is to keep silent … she will be saved by rearing children' (1 Timothy 2.11–15).

This text in 1 Timothy was to shape the dominant church teachings about women in Christianity until recent decades. It is still taken as authoritative by fundamentalist Christians. Yet the text also reveals that 1 Timothy was written in a context in which some women and men in the early church did not accept this teaching as the true meaning of Christianity. The author writes to try to silence Christian women in his own congregation who assume that they are liberated by Christ to depart from marriage in order to travel and preach the gospel.

Fundamentalism

The second to sixth centuries

This conflict between patriarchal and liberationist understandings of Christian faith continues in the second century after Christ. Writings of the time reveal that there were numerous currents in early Christianity which continued to assume some kind of transformation of gender relations. We read in these writings the story of Thecla, a young woman converted by Paul, who, against the wishes of her mother and her husband-to-be, renounces her coming marriage, cuts her hair and leaves home, to preach and baptize. Paul himself is portrayed as showing up at the end of the story to validate her ministry. We hear of church leaders, such as Priscilla and Maximilla, who abandon their husbands to engage in teaching as inspired prophets. Some groups of early Christians particularly revered the figure of Mary Magdalene, seen as the apostle to the apostles, whose special relation to Christ has given her an inside understanding of his teachings.

p. 850

The second to the fourth centuries saw a gradual suppression of these more radical understandings of Christianity in regard to women's roles. Christians with these views were declared heretical and expelled from churches increasingly dominated by male clergy who modelled themselves on the patriarchal rule of families and the governors of Roman cities and provinces. The Bishop of Rome would come to see himself as spiritual heir of the Roman emperor, who was supreme ruler of the church.

Heresy

Women continued to be given some minor ministries in the church into the sixth century. In some parts of the church deaconesses and orders of virgins and widows were regarded as ordained to these roles. But the major ordained roles of priest and bishop were reserved for men. Fourth-century church documents insist that women in these minor ministries must only pray and serve silently and not preach in the church, itself an indication that some women appointed to these ministries continued to assume that they were given a more active leadership.

The popularity of monastic life for both men and women also allowed many women to renounce marriage and childbearing to live in communities of women where they engaged in study, travelled to visit holy places in Egypt and Palestine, and founded their own institutions for service. Many of these female monastics became powerful leaders governing large communities of women and complexes of buildings. Bishops were often beholden to such women who came from the highest aristocratic families and owned great wealth.

In the Eastern Christian tradition Macrina, elder sister of Gregory of Nyssa and Basil the Great, is seen as the founder of the monastic life for her family. Gregory of Nyssa in his *Life of Macrina* credits her with converting their mother and his brothers Naucratius and Basil to the ascetic life and transforming their family estates into a monastic community. Gregory describes Macrina as his mentor in the path of spiritual ascent to union with God. For him women are as capable of the spiritual life as men and can be exemplary spiritual leaders for men as well as women. He does not see women taking public political roles in church or society, but for him these roles themselves are suspect and should be renounced by Christians seeking perfection.

Yet many bishops were suspicious of any real independence of such monastic women, insisting that they confine their leadership to a private world within the nunnery and not take public leadership roles. Abbesses should obey bishops in all things. But this struggle of male church leaders to control nuns and to confine them within the walls of cloisters was not to be completely successful. Nuns continued to see their women's communities as a base for independence from male control. This conflict has arisen again today in the Roman Catholic Church in the wake of the Second Vatican Council.

For the Western Christian tradition, the most influential bishop and theologian to try to resolve the conflict over women's place in Christianity was Augustine (354–430). Augustine was aware of the conflict between the teaching in Genesis 1.27, that women and men were created equally in the image of God, and that of Paul, that only men are made in the image of God. According to Paul, women have only a secondary reflection of the image of God under the male (1 Corinthians 11.2–10). There was also a contradiction between 1 Timothy's view that women in the church are to be defined as inferior because they have been made second in creation and were first in sin, and Paul's declaration in Galatians that women and men are now equal in Christ.

Augustine sought to resolve these contradictions in the tradition. His solution was to distinguish between a spiritual capacity in women's souls and their physical and psychological natures as female. The spiritual capacity of women's souls is made in the image of God. Women are as capable of being redeemed as males. But in their specific female bodily nature and reproductive roles they are inherently subordinate to the male, having been made so by God in the beginning. Moreover, by taking the lead in disobedience to God, Eve violated this subordination and became the cause of the fall. Women, as Eve's descendants, are then to be doubly subjugated, both as an expression of their original subordination and as punishment for their primacy in sin.

Sin

Augustine insisted that the choice of celibacy, while resulting in a higher life than marriage, does not liberate women from subordination to men. A celibate woman must submit her will to her bishop, rather than to a husband. The true Christian woman voluntarily accepts her place as one of silence and submission, and thereby shows that she is really in the path of redemption. At the end of the world, when the present worldly order is transformed into a heavenly one, women will be spiritually equal to men according to the spiritual merits of their lives. Sex and procreation will be no more, and so women will no longer be defined by these female roles. But here and now women's 'natural' subordination has not been changed, but rather reinforced in the church.

Augustine is also important for the understanding of sex and procreation in Latin Christianity.

Augustine believed that in the original creation, as intended by God, there would have been reproduction without sexual pleasure. One of the effects of the fall into sin is that sexual intercourse becomes accompanied by orgasmic pleasure. Augustine believed that this was inherently sinful, debasing to the 'manly mind'. The highest Christian life is to renounce sex and marriage for celibacy. For those who choose the lower path of marriage, sex is allowed, but only for procreation. Even then sex is sinful, but it is 'permitted' and so a sin that can be forgiven. Those who engage in sex, even in marriage, but deliberately avoid procreation, commit a mortal sin that severs their souls from God.

The medieval church

Augustine's teaching on women, sex and procreation would continue to shape Western Christianity to modern times. These teachings encapsulate the view of women as simultaneously equal in soul, capable of spiritual life and redemption in heaven, while being inherently inferior as female on earth. They are the foundation for the current negative Roman Catholic teaching on sexuality and birth control. One of the most important theologians to develop Augustine's views on women was the thirteenth-century Dominican Thomas Aquinas. Aquinas' teachings would become the basis for Roman Catholic orthodox theology in modern times, although in his own day he was regarded as radical.

Thomas Aquinas

Thomas incorporated an Aristotelian understanding of biological reproduction (which we now know to be false) into his understanding of gender. Aristotle taught that women were inherently inferior in mind, body and moral will. He defined women as 'defective': their very gestation was such as to produce a type of human that lacks the full and equal human capacities found in males. For Aristotle the relation of male and female is similar to the relation of mind and body, spirit and matter. The male alone possesses procreative power, while women contribute only the material substance that is formed by the male seed. In procreation the potency of the male seed shapes the female matter in the woman's womb, something like a sculptor shaping a piece of stone or wood.

According to Aristotle, if the seminal power of the male seed shapes the female matter fully, the result will be a male. If some defect occurs in the process, so that the matter is not fully formed, then a female will be produced. Females are characterized by a lack of full capacity for rationality, moral self-control and physical strength. Since women are inherently defective, they cannot govern themselves or govern others, but must be dependent and under the control of a male. Aquinas incorporated this Aristotelian understanding of biological reproduction into his theology.

Aquinas reasoned that, since women are inherently defective, they cannot represent the human species. Women are not normative exemplars of humanness. Therefore Christ had to be a male in order to be the representative of humanity in its full potential. Moreover, the priest who represents Christ must be a male as well. Because women are inherently dependent, they cannot hold any public offices or exercise leadership in the church or society. This dictate contradicted the actual existence of ruling queens and abbesses in Aquinas' own day and contributed to the illegitimatizing of such leadership by women. Roman Catholicism continues to insist even today that women cannot be ordained because Christ was and had to be a male, and therefore only a male can represent Christ. This view is rooted in Thomas' teachings.

Middle Ages

Medieval Catholic spirituality is characterized by extreme polarity in its view of the female. As wives and sexual beings women were seen as sources of the greatest temptation and sin, especially to a celibate clergy vowed to abstain from sex. As daughters of Eve women inherit her double subordination due to her insubordination to God's commands. In the later Middle Ages and the

Reformation era a widespread belief arose that Christian society was threatened by witchcraft. Hundreds of thousands of women and some men were burned at the stake or drowned as witches because it was believed that their willing submission to Satan opened the gates of hell upon the church and society.

Thomas' teachings that women are inherently defective shaped the views of Dominican inquisitors that witchcraft is an evil to which women were particularly prone. The fifteenth-century witch-hunter's manual, *Malleus Maleficarum* (The Hammer of Witches) states: 'It should be noted that there was a defect in the formation of the first woman, since she was formed from the bent rib, the rib of the breast which is bent in the contrary direction to a man … And since through the first defect in their intelligence they are always more prone to abjure the faith, so through their second defect of inordinate passions, they search for, brood over and inflict various vengeances, either by witchcraft or some other means. Wherefore it is no wonder that so great a number of witches exists in this sex.' The inquisitors offer thanks to God for the incarnation of God into the male sex, which has preserved males from so great an evil as witchcraft.

While the church excoriated the female as Eve, prone to witchcraft, it also exalted the feminine in the worship of the Virgin Mary. The theology of Mary and the veneration due to her expanded in medieval Christianity. She was ever-virgin. She was not only a virgin in the conception of Jesus, but she preserved her virginity in his birth and remained a virgin after his birth to the end of her life. This last teaching denied that Mary had any later children by Joseph after the birth of Jesus, even though brothers and sisters of Jesus are reported in several places in the New Testament. Her body did not decay at death, but she was physically assumed into heaven, there to be crowned Queen of Heaven, seated by the side of Christ. Catholic mariology taught that prayer to Mary will preserve even the worst sinner from ultimate perdition.

Some theologians in the later medieval church even speculated that Mary had been preserved from original sin in her own conception, although the Immaculate Conception would not be declared a doctrine of the Roman Catholic Church until 1954. This exaltation of Mary, however, had an ambivalent effect on actual women, who were still identified as daughters of Eve and prone to witchcraft. Male celibate devotion to Mary allowed them to cultivate love for an ideal virginal woman, while despising in-the-flesh females.

Nuns as virgins were more like Mary than married women. Some nuns cultivated a Marian piety that saw Mary as allowing them to share in nursing the baby Jesus, compensating for their own childlessness. In the earlier Middle Ages some abbesses held vast properties and exercised power as feudal lords. Many women mystics, such as Hildegard of Bingen, claimed their power to preach and teach as prophets inspired by God. In the earlier Middle Ages particularly the women's monastery could become a self-governing female world in which abbesses possessed many of the rights and titles of landed nobility: the right to rule over dependent villages, to coin money, raise armies and even be represented in parliament.

Hildegard of Bingen

Abbesses were also accorded some of the prerogatives of bishops, such as the mitre and crosier, and the right to license priests to function in their territories. Such great abbeys could be centres of independent learning, with schools and libraries. A stream of writing came forth from the pens of these learned women: treatises on mysticism, on science and medicine; literary compositions, such as plays and poetry; and treatises on humanistic learning. A great abbess like Hildegard of Bingen demonstrates many of these aspects of both independent rule and diverse forms of writing. As a recognized prophet she was also allowed to travel and to preach to mixed audiences.

However, the general trend of medieval Christianity was to curb the independence of nuns and to confine them behind cloister walls. In the later Middle Ages the educational level of nunneries declined as universities replaced monastic schools. Women under vows were forbidden entrance to university education. Yet these restrictions were also countered by the formation of new kinds of women's religious community. These women, known as Beguines, often belonged to the urban merchant or working classes. They took simple vows without restrictions of cloister and often made a living through manual labour. Their houses were under constant suspicion as hotbeds of dissent and heresy, and so they often ended by attaching themselves to male orders, such as the Dominicans, to win protection. Yet some of the most creative women mystics, such as Mechthild of Magdeburg, Hadewijch and Marguerite Porete, belonged to the Beguine tradition.

University

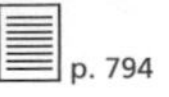

p. 794

The later Middle Ages saw the rise of many popular reform movements aimed at restoring a freer, more prophetic Christianity. Some, such as the twelfth-century Franciscans and Waldensians, took the form of popular preaching movements that sought to restore a lifestyle of poverty and simplicity. Following ancient Christian tradition that women as well as men were given the spirit of prophecy, Waldensians allowed women to preach. Among the Spiritual Franciscans the doctrine developed by the twelfth-century monk Joachim of Fiore that a Third Age of the Spirit would supersede the present clerical church became a language of dissent against the ecclesiastical hierarchy. Popes and bishops were seen as having departed from evangelical poverty and given themselves over to corruption. The true church was the church of monastic or evangelical reformers persecuted by the present corrupt church. A few female-led groups arose which even suggested that in the new dispensation the Holy Spirit would be disclosed in female form and women would be included among bishops and priests.

Waldensian Church

Holy Spirit

Thus medieval Christianity moved towards increasing sectarian strife and dissension between a hierarchical church grown ever more repressive, and popular reform movements which grew ever more alienated, each condemning the other as apostate. This sectarian strife of the later Middle Ages set the stage for full-blown schisms in the medieval Latin church, along both national and sectarian lines, in the era of the Protestant Reformation in the sixteenth century.

Reformation and Counter-Reformation

The Reformation as a whole did little to change the marginalization of women in Western Christianity. The major Reformers, Martin Luther and John Calvin, continued the traditional teaching that woman is second in creation and first in sin, and reiterated the ban on women's preaching or public teaching. Even the small space that was open to women as preachers and writers or as recognized prophets was closed by the magisterial Reformers, who declared that women as prophets were a special dispensation of the apostolic age that was no longer possible in the present church. Political and economic changes were removing the rights of women as landholders that they had enjoyed in the Middle Ages. Women were being excluded from independent guild membership and from professions they had previously followed through family ties and apprenticeship in popular folk-knowledge (such as medicine, midwifery and pharmacy).

Reformation

The Reformation also abolished celibacy and monasticism, which had been the mainstay of female vocations in the medieval church. But it did not include women in the new Protestant married clergy. Instead the Reformers continued the patriarchal reading of the Pauline tradition which enjoyed silence and submission on women both within the order of creation and as punishment for primacy in sin. Martin Luther argued that woman had been more equal in the original creation, but she had lost this through sin and is now subjugated to the rule of the husband.

John Calvin saw women as spiritually equal in soul, but subjugated to husbands, ministers and magistrates through that part of the image of God which women lack, namely the representation of God's dominion over lesser creatures. Rather, in the family and politics they themselves are under this dominion exercised by the ruling-class male. Husbands were enjoined to be kindly to their wives, but their right to rule was in no way dependent on these virtues. Thus women in the sixteenth and seventeenth centuries were being deprived of access to roles in which they had exercised some autonomous power, and confined to dependency as housewives in a male-controlled family economy as their sole 'vocation'.

Women's insubordination against this rightful male rule was seen as the source of the fall from paradise and the advent of the demonic in society. The Puritan divine William Perkins complemented his 1590 treatise on the *Domestical Oeconomie* with his 1596 treatise on *The Damned Art of Witchcraft*. In this treatise women are defined as more prone to witchcraft than men because of their 'weakness' and natural tendency to insubordination against constituted authority. This spirit of insubordination makes them easy targets for the Devil. Thus Puritanism continued the late medieval tradition of linking women's inferior nature with a proneness to witchcraft. This led to a renewal of witchcraft persecutions, particularly in Calvinist-ruled areas, such as Scotland and Puritan Massachusetts.

Puritans

Anabaptists

However, left-wing Puritans and Anabaptists championed the continuation of the lay conscience as the prophetic voice of the Holy Spirit. The oft-quoted New Testament text, 'your sons and your daughters shall prophesy', was used by many women in England in the Civil War era to insist that women were equally included in this exercise of the prophetic voice within both the church and society. Baptists allowed women to preach in this period, and John Rogers, the leader of an extreme Puritan group, the Fifth Monarchists (so called because its adherents believed that the fifth and final empire, after those of the Assyrians, Persians, Greeks and Romans, namely the Christian empire), was near, argued that women should be equal in all affairs of ministry and church governance. In the civil order there may be distinction of classes, but in the spiritual community all distinction of class and gender is abolished.

Baptist churches

Quakers

The Religious Society of Friends, commonly known as Quakers, became the most lasting representatives of this egalitarian trend of seventeenth-century radical Protestantism. The Quakers argued that women and men were equal in the original creation. But they changed the traditional woman-blaming view of the fall by claiming that the advent of sin took place through the 'usurpation of power of some over others'. This means that men in power, rather than insubordinate women, were the key source of sin, understood as a fall into illegitimate forms of domination, war and violence. Women were given the power of prophecy by God in biblical history. This culminated in the New Testament, where women were chosen to be the first witnesses of the resurrection and the source of the proclamation of the good news to the male disciples.

According to Margaret Fell's 1666 treatise *Women's Preaching justified according to the Scriptures*, this means that Christians accept the good news of Christ's resurrection only by at the same time accepting the legitimacy of women's preaching, since it is through women that this witness to the resurrection comes to the church. Paul's order to 'keep silence' applies only to those who have not yet received the good news and been transformed in the Spirit, in order that they may hear those who have received the Spirit. But women (and men) who have received the Spirit not only may but must speak and speak boldly to the church. The Quakers used this understanding of women's equal inclusion in prophecy to argue both for women's public preaching and also for their inclusion in local ministry through women's meetings.

Nineteenth- and twentieth-century Western Europe and the United States

The primary challenge to the traditional view of women's nature and role in church and society has sprung from the feminist movements of the nineteenth and twentieth centuries. An important impetus for the rise of feminism was liberalism, which developed the view that all 'men are created equal'. Liberalism challenged the traditional Christian view that class, race and gender hierarchies are the divinely founded 'order of creation'. It saw such hierarchies as false constructions by the ruling classes to secure their own power. The true and original 'order of nature' is one of equality. Societies are to be reformed, overthrowing old aristocracy and writing new constitutions that guarantee equal rights of all citizens before the law.

Roman Catholicism in the nineteenth century set itself as the foe of liberalism and the champion of the old feudal order, which it identified with Catholic society. In 1864 Pope Pius IX issued the Syllabus of Errors, condemning liberalism and socialism and decrying the ideas of democracy, freedom of thought, education, press and religion as modern errors. Pius IX consolidated both doctrinal and jurisdictional control over the church in the hands of the papacy by convening the First Vatican Council (1870), at which the Pope was declared to be infallible.

Papacy

Protestant and secular male liberals, too, were mostly not open to women's rights. They used liberal theory to reinforce male domination in political and economic affairs. The industrial revolution was shaping a new middle-class family based on the split between home and work. Paid work and politics was the sphere of men, while women were to be confined to non-paid housework and child-raising. Religion was being privatized. Spirituality became the sphere of women and the home, secular rationality the sphere of men in public life. Women's nature was redefined as intuitive, altruistic and maternal, but also non-sexual. Ideally women had no sexual feelings and endured sex for the sake of motherhood. This is a kind of secular mariology.

Industrial revolution

This new ideology of family and sentimental, non-sexual womanhood was congenial in somewhat different ways to Protestantism and to Roman Catholicism. The old medieval view of woman as Eve, the inferior, disobedient sexual temptress, was muted in favour of a view of woman's 'nature' as passive, ethereal, loving and maternal. The sexual temptress still lurked in the shadows of this definition, but she now became the 'bad' (among black people or the working class) or 'fallen' woman, who had lost her true nature. Woman's seclusion in the home was necessary to 'protect' her from the danger of becoming a fallen woman.

The American Protestant theologian Horace Bushnell argued in his 1869 treatise *Women's Suffrage. A Reform against Nature* that male and female 'natures' are comparable to the hierarchy of law and gospel. The law comes first and the gospel is dependent upon it. The law belongs to the rule of reason and force in the public sphere, while the gospel belongs in the private sphere as the realm where grace transforms hearts and turns them towards God. Thus women's feminine spiritual nature, while superior to the rough power of men, belongs strictly in the private realm of the home and is precluded from involvement in the public political realm of force and power.

From 1850 to 1920 the limitations of the old liberalism that confined the rights of 'man and the citizen' to white propertied males was being challenged. Slavery was gradually abolished. Women began to claim rights to property, higher education, professional employment and the vote. In 1848 the emergent women's rights leaders in the United States met in Seneca Falls, New York, where they laid claim not only to these public political rights, but also to ordained ministry. In the ringing conclusion to the Declaration of the Rights of Women issued by this conference, they called for 'the speedy overthrow of the male monopoly of the pulpit'.

In 1853 some Congregationalists responded to this call for equality for women in ministry with

Congregationalism

Women priests ordained in Bristol cathedral

the ordination of the first woman, Antoinette Brown. Brown was a graduate of Oberlin College, whose theological programme was the first to admit women. Luther Lee, the preacher at Brown's ordination, argued that the preaching ministry was identical with the prophetic ministry. Christ himself conferred the ministry on women by giving them the power of prophecy equally with men; thus it has always been wrong for the church to exclude women from ministry. Brown served briefly as pastor of a Congregational church, but soon dropped out because she found she could not preach a Calvinist theology of predestination. She returned to ministry in her later years as a Unitarian.

Predestination
Unitarians

Mainline denominations were slow to follow these beginnings of women's ordination in the United States. Some theological colleges were open to women in the 1880s, but the numbers remained small, about 5 per cent, until the 1960s. New non-ordained ministerial roles were opened to women, such as deaconesses, foreign missionaries and Christian educators. Women in theological colleges were mostly preparing for these non-ordained ministries. Besides Congregationalists, Unitarians, Universalists and Methodist Protestants began to ordain women in the late nineteenth century, but mainline Presbyterians, Methodists and Lutherans rejected women's ordination, seeking to direct women instead to non-ordained ministries.

In the United States the major advance toward women's ordination took place in 1956, when the Methodist Church and the Presbyterian Church, USA, changed their regulations to admit women to full clergy status. The impetus for this change came through new ecumenical ties of these American churches with the Reformed churches in Europe through the World Council of Churches. Women had served pastorates in many churches in Germany and Scandinavia during World War II. After the war these women insisted on continuing in ministry and called for full ordination. In the late 1950s and early 1960s women's ordination was accepted in these Lutheran and Reformed churches. In the US, liberal church leaders in charge of mainline denominations were convinced that they should follow suit, but they assumed that not many women would want to be ordained ministers.

Reformed churches

It was not until the late 1960s that the impact of this change really began to take effect in American theological colleges and churches. Women in the mainline Protestant churches began to attend theological seminaries in growing numbers. From 10 per cent in 1972, the numbers of women in theological colleges in the United States jumped to 27 per cent in 1987 (including seminaries of churches that did not ordain women). In 2003 in liberal seminaries it is common for women to be 50 per cent or more of the students of theological schools. The numbers of women with theological doctorates also began to climb. More and more seminaries began to include women as professors in all fields of study.

Feminist theological studies also began to expand rapidly in the 1970s and 1980s, with a growing literature in all fields of theology: Bible, theology, church history, ethics, pastoral psychology, liturgy and Christian education. From a few very general books on a feminist reading of Christian tradition, such as Mary Daly's 1968 book, *The Church and the Second Sex*, feminist theological studies have become more and more prolific and specialized. It is now possible to have major bibliographies of feminist studies in such fields as Hebrew scripture, New Testament, patristics, medieval Christianity and contemporary theology. Feminist sections became a major part of theological and scriptural conferences, such as the American Academy of Religion and the Society of Biblical Literature. However, the teaching of feminist theological studies in seminaries has not kept pace with its current development in research and writing. It is still typically treated as a special interest of a few women (and even less men), rather than a normal part of the curriculum as a whole.

The numbers of women in ordained ministry, as well as the number of churches that ordain women, have also continually expanded in the United States. After some struggle, the Episcopal Church granted women's ordination in 1976. Most mainline Christian Protestant churches now ordain women, and their numbers have grown to 20 per cent or more of the clergy. Women also began to move up the church hierarchy, with the United Methodist Church granting women's ordination to the episcopacy in 1984 and the Episcopal Church in 1989. Other churches in the Anglican Communion, such as New Zealand, have also elected a woman bishop. Lutheran churches in Germany and Scandinavia elected women to the episcopacy in 1992, as did the Evangelical Lutheran Church in America. After much struggle the Church of England accepted women priests, but has not yet accepted women bishops.

Lutheranism

Church of England

However, other churches have strongly rejected this trend. The Southern Baptist Church in the United States has not only rejected the possibility of women's ordination but has insisted that women's subordination under male headship is integral to biblical faith. Roman Catholicism also rejected women's ordination in a declaration issued in 1976 by the Congregation for the Doctrine of the Faith, *On the Question of the Admission of Women to the Ministerial Priesthood.* This asserts that women are not ordainable by their very nature as females, although it claims that the Catholic Church fully accepts women's civil rights in society. The papacy under Pope John Paul II has sought to cut off even the discussion of the issue of women's ordination in the Roman Catholic Church. Clergy and theologians who dissent on this issue are to be excluded from advancement to official leadership positions in the church. The Eastern Orthodox churches have also rejected women's ordination on the basis of tradition, although there remains some openness to the ordination of women to the deaconate, which was a part of Orthodox tradition into the twelfth century.

World Christianity

Christianity in Europe

Although American Christianity has been, in some ways, the pace-setter on women's ordination and feminist studies in religion, these developments are also taking place throughout world Christianity. In Germany, Scandinavia and the Netherlands women are now a substantial part of the pastoral ministry. For example, in Sweden in 2003 women were about a third of all ordained clergy and 15 per cent of vicars. Feminist studies are less well developed in universities in Germany, because of the hierarchical nature of these institutions. They are found more in networks of women theologians and theological students. The European Society for Women's Theological Research brings together women doing feminist theological studies every other year in a forum that includes Southern and Eastern Europe as well as Western Europe (although Western Europeans predominate in this network).

In England the organization Women in Theology (WIT) networked feminist theological studies. This group has recently disbanded as no longer needed because such work has grown in British universities. The journal *Feminist Theology* is a major outlet for feminist theological scholarship, and the Britain and Ireland School of Feminist Theology provides an important gathering place for such scholars. The School offers an MA in Feminist Theology through the University of Wales, Lampeter.

Christianity in Asia

In the so-called Third World (Africa, Asia and Latin America) the numbers of ordained women pastors is also growing. The Church of North India ordained the first woman in their church in 1924 and the Congregationalists in Japan ordained the first woman in 1932. Lutherans and other mainline churches in India now ordain women. In Korea, Methodists and the more liberal wing of Presbyterians ordain women. Mainline Protestants and Anglicans ordain women in Africa and Asia. As in Europe and the United States, their numbers as teachers and students in theological colleges and as pastors have grown steadily in the last two decades.

There are also growing networks for feminist theological reflection and journals that publish such work in all three regions. In Asia the journal *In God's Image* has maintained a network of writers from most Asian countries: India, Japan, the Philippines, Malaysia, Korea, Taiwan, Australia and Hong Kong, among others. It has published feminist writings from across Asia since the early 1980s. It is published by the Asian Women's Resource Center for Culture and Theology, currently located in Kuala Lumpur, Malaysia.

Christianity in Africa

In Africa the Circle of Concerned African Women Theologians networks Protestant and Catholic women across Anglophone Africa (to some extent also in Francophone and Portuguese-speaking Africa). These African feminist writers have published a number of book-length collections of articles, such as Mercy Amba Oduyoye and Musimbi Kanyora, *The Will to Arise: Women, Tradition and Church in Africa* (1992).

Christianity in Latin America

In Latin America the journal *Conspirando*, published in Chile with contributors from across Latin America, has maintained a stimulating series of monthly issues for over ten years. *Conspirando* works from an ecofeminist perspective. The *Conspirando* network has also published ecofeminist thought in book collections as well, such as the 2002 volume *Iluvia para Florecer* (Rain for Flourishing). This is a series of interviews of Latin American women on their life journey toward ecofeminism, edited by the *Conspirando* editor, Judy Ress.

Chung Hyun Kyung of Korea at celebrations before the World Council of Churches Assembly in Harare, 1990

In the 1970s the Ecumenical Association of Third World Theologians (EATWOT) was created to network liberation theologians across these three regions. In the mid-1980s EATWOT accepted the sponsorship of a parallel network of women theologians from Asia, Africa and Latin America. This Women's Commission of Third World women theologians meets on its own, as well as in general EATWOT meetings. It has been a major vehicle for the development of feminist theological reflection in Asia, Africa and Latin America.

The Women's Commission of EATWOT met first in national meetings, then in the three regions and then across all three regions from 1984 to 1986. It published a series of books from their conference papers. The collection *With Passion and Compassion: Third World Women Doing Theology* brought together the papers from the intercontinental meeting in Oaxtepec, Mexico, of December 1986. This network also met with First World women in Costa Rica in 1995 on the theme of violence against women, producing the book *Women Resisting Violence: Spirituality for Life* (edited by Mary John Mananzan et al., 1996).

While feminist journals, networks of communication, women in pastoral work and theological education and publication continue to grow, this hardly means that all issues of women's oppression have disappeared. On the contrary, fundamentalist movements across Protestant and Roman Catholic Christianity, as well as in other religions such as Islam, are also growing, and seek to return women to their traditional roles and definitions, by force if necessary. Among the major contested issues in this conflict are women's rights to control their reproductive functions, being

Fundamentalism

able to choose when and when not to have children; women's legal, educational and social equality in society; and the very definition of women as humans with similar natures to men who can aspire to all the roles in society, rather than being confined to domestic labour as wives and mothers.

Gay and lesbian theology

The question of women's options for other than heterosexual relations is also a vehemently contested issue. Conservative Catholicism and Protestantism are very active in seeking to deny women the option of legal abortion and even birth control and reject lesbianism as a valid form of sexual relationship and social bonding. Both forms of conservative Christianity seek to reinstate a view of male and female as having fundamentally different 'natures', according to divine design, that demands sharply distinct roles for men and women. Men alone should rule in public life, as well as 'head' the home, and women should remain subordinate and be confined to the home and domestic situations.

Sexual ethics
Bioethics

Both Roman Catholicism and Protestantism in the West inherit traditions from Augustine that rejected birth control and allowed sexuality only in the context of reproduction in heterosexual marriage. Most Protestants changed their views between 1930 and 1960, allowing artificial contraception within marriage. But Catholicism did not accept this development. In the period of the Second Vatican Council a strong movement developed to reconsider this ban on artificial contraception developed among Western Catholics. Pope Paul VI separated the issue from the Council by setting up a separate Birth Control Commission that met from 1964 to 1967. The outcome of this Commission was an overwhelming vote to change the teaching to allow any medically safe method of contraception within marriage.

p. 700

Vatican

But the vote was rejected by the Pope, on the advice of a few moral theologians who dissented from this majority. In the encyclical *Humanae vitae* (July 1968) the Pope reaffirmed the traditional teaching. Pope John Paul II has sought to give the anti-contraceptive position an unchangeable status in Catholic teaching, but the majority of Catholics reject this view in both theory and practice. Thus birth control has become a major area where an official teaching of the Vatican has not been 'received' by the vast majority of Catholics.

Recognizing major conflicts between the church and women, the US Catholic bishops set up a process of dialogue between the Bishop's Committee on Women and the Women's Ordination Conference in 1980. This dialogue resulted in a recommendation to study the issue of women in church and society and to write a bishops' pastoral letter on women. The first draft of the letter, *One in Christ: A Pastoral Response to the Concerns of Women for Church and Society* (1988), boldly asserted that 'sexism is sin'.

The pastoral letter sought to ground male/female relations in family, society and church in a model of 'partnership'. Men and women are created equally in the image of God and are to be partners in the family, partners in the world of work and partners in the ministry of the church. This approach revised the traditional anthropology of complementarity, the separation of masculine and feminine 'natures' and spheres of work and home. The bishops accepted that women are now a part of the world of work, although their 'vocation' was still seen as that of mother. (Men were never said to have a 'vocation' to be fathers.) There was also a recommendation to expand as much as possible the lay ministries available to women in the church. Ordained ministry was still off limits for discussion.

Pope John Paul II saw this pastoral letter as unacceptable. The Vatican intervened in its drafting to insist on more explicit condemnations of birth control, abortion and women's ordination. Moreover, the language of partnership was to be replaced by the Pope's preferred anthropology of complementarity. Women must be defined as having a 'different' feminine nature that fits them for the domestic world. Women are not forbidden work and public life, but this is seen as something forced upon them by inadequate social protection, not something due them as human beings. The US bishops' pastoral letter went through several drafts in an effort to satisfy these papal demands and was finally tabled by the bishops in recognition of its unacceptability to US Catholic women.

The Pope himself has issued a series of letters and declarations on women, in an effort to assert his own understanding of gender difference. In his 1988 letter, 'The Dignity and Vocation of Women', he expounds a mariological idealization of the 'feminine' as essential to the openness of the soul to God's redemptive work. Women's highest vocation is to represent and cultivate this feminine capacity of openness to divine grace and service to God. But this very nature of woman as feminine forbids her from taking those roles that represent divine power itself, most notably the priesthood as representative of Christ. For the Pope, this exclusion of women from the priesthood by no means makes women inferior. Rather it is based on valuing and protecting woman's true dignity and vocation.

This essentialist view of gender difference is increasingly unacceptable and even incomprehensible to many Catholic women and men. Catholic church teaching on women, the bans on birth control, abortion and women's ordination, represent a widening gap between church leaders and most Catholics. The refusal to open any dialogue on these issues has become an impasse that threatens the credibility of church authority and its ability to maintain its own pastoral ministry, which, with the current 'priest shortage', can hardly do without the services of women.

An impasse on the nature and role of women in church and society today divides liberal and conservative Catholics and Protestants. It is unlikely that this divide will be bridged any time soon. In many ways this impasse makes explicit the conflict between a patriarchal and a liberationist view of gender relations that has existed since the beginnings of Christianity. Although there has been a long history in Christian church teaching that has justified women's subordination in church and society, there have also been alternative views from the very beginning of Christianity that have affirmed women's full humanness and equality. These have been continually rediscovered and renewed through the centuries.

ROSEMARY RADFORD RUETHER

Anne Brotherton (ed), *Voices of the Turtledove: New Catholic Women in Europe*, New York and Mahwah, NJ: Paulist Press 1992; Elizabeth Clark, *Women in the Early Church*, Wilmington, DL: Michael Glazier Press 1983; Virginia Fabella and Mercy Amba Oduyoye, *With Passion and Compassion: Third World Women Doing Theology*, Maryknoll, NY: Orbis Books 1988; Mary T. Malone, *Women and Christianity* (3 vols), Maryknoll, NY: Orbis Books 2001–3; Barbara Newman, *From Virile Woman to WomanChrist: Studies in Medieval Religion and Literature*, Philadelphia: University of Pennsylvania Press 1995; Rosemary Radford Ruether and Rosemary Keller, *In Our Own Voices: Four Centuries of American Women's Religious Writing*, San Francisco: HarperSanFrancisco 1995; Rosemary Radford Ruether, *Women and Redemption: A Theological History*, Minneapolis: Fortress Press 1998 and London: SCM Press 1998; Merry E. Wiesner, *Women and Gender in Early Modern Europe*, Cambridge: CUP 1993

Work

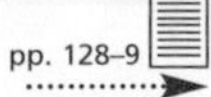

pp. 128–9

Any definition of work is likely to have a highly subjective character. How and what one thinks of it will depend on one's physical circumstances, one's social class, one's education, even one's politics. For the great majority of human beings, work is and always has been a necessity for survival, a laborious condition of human existence, the means of gaining the wherewithal to enjoy at least food and shelter; for a minority it is an opportunity for creativity and personal fulfilment; for a privileged few it is an optional activity, variously regarded as a virtuous service to others, a remedy for boredom or an obstacle both to pleasure and to the higher reaches of philosophical enquiry.

Monasticism

According to one strand of political thought, work is drudgery, and various forms of inducement are required (in the form of rewards or punishments) if it is to get done at all. According to another it is an activity that liberates and ennobles, appearing oppressive only because it is a means by which those with money and power exploit the labouring classes. The word itself is slippery, having come to mean anything from hard labour to artistic activity, and as a value it is ambivalent: an ambivalence which made possible the cruel irony of the slogan placed over the gate of a Nazi concentration camp, *Arbeit macht frei*, work is liberating.

Bible
Reformation
Martin Luther
John Calvin
Protestantism
p. 139
Puritans
Paul

Texts from the Bible can be found which support some, but by no means all, of these attitudes to work. There is no explicit discussion of work as such, but it is taken for granted that work is a universal condition that the human race has to endure in order to survive, and this is the clear implication of the words with which Adam and Eve were banished from the Garden of Eden: 'Cursed is the ground because of you: in toil shall you eat of it all the days of your life' (Genesis 3.17). The corollary that anyone who tries to avoid working is doing something both imprudent and anti-social and must be exhorted to industriousness is a theme which appears frequently in Proverbs and is invoked by the apostle Paul to prevent millenarian excitement from becoming a pretext for idleness (2 Thessalonians 3.11–12). However, Paul's own language is that of the more leisured classes: he had the option not to work but to live on the support provided by his churches; yet he deliberately chose not to be a 'burden' on them (2 Thessalonians 3. 8 and elsewhere) and prided himself on working in order to maintain his financial independence.

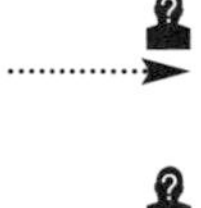

Further up the social scale still – and quite untypically of the Bible as a whole – the Jewish scholar Jesus ben Sirach reflected the pagan philosophical view that work is essentially *ascholia* (Greek), *negotium* (Latin), the denial of leisure, when he wrote, 'The wisdom of the scribe depends on the opportunity of leisure; only the one who has little business can be wise' (38.24) – a text conveniently ignored by Protestant theologians, since it occurs only in the Apocrypha. Yet even this variety of attitudes betrays a common perception. Work is an arduous necessity laid on all human beings: the notion of a 'leisured class' is altogether strange to the culture.

The tension between this general acceptance of the necessity of work and the pagan view (based on the acceptance of slave labour) that civilized activity and philosophical contemplation are impossible without leisure became apparent in the early monastic movement and resurfaced from time to time throughout the Middle Ages. The monastic rules of the fourth century stress the new social equality created between those who came from both the labouring and the leisured classes; and since all monks had to work for their living – Benedict of Nursia was to say that 'one is truly a monk when one lives by the work of one's hands' – it became necessary to establish that such work was not incompatible with prayer and contemplation. Hence a variety of arguments by which work may be seen to have a positive value: it is a means of 'taming the flesh', it is an antidote to idleness, it provides the resources for charitable giving, it can even be called a kind of 'prayer'. But this applied, of course, principally to those who had adopted the religious life. For the rest, work remained a laborious necessity, a punishment imposed on the human race for the sin of Adam; indeed extra work might even be undertaken as a form of penance.

The Reformation, as is well known, was impatient of any suggestion that true Christian discipleship was open only to priests and religious. As Martin Luther saw it, Christians must work out their salvation within their secular 'calling', which could be thought of as their own personal 'vocation'; while for John Calvin work was a duty, and any wealth resulting from it might be a sign of God's grace and of the worker's place among the elect. Hence (according to a widely accepted theory) the 'Protestant work ethic', which gave Christian endorsement to the entrepreneurial exploitation of the wealth arriving from the New World in the sixteenth and seventeenth centuries. In its Puritan form, this even gave a sense of guilt (inconceivable in antiquity or the Middle Ages) to those of the skilled or educated classes who failed to use all available hours of the day for productive work.

Subsequent economic theory found a measurable value in 'labour', which, added to the value of raw materials, could serve as a measure of industrial productivity. Meanwhile (mainly under the influence of G. W. F. Hegel) nineteenth-century philosophers came to see work as a means by which human beings achieve their true potential. By the time of Karl Marx's early writings, work had been transformed from a curse laid upon the human condition to an activity through which men and women might attain their true dignity and from which they had been 'alienated' only by the exploitation of the means of production by the wealthy.

But the same technological progress which, by placing new tools in the hands of human beings, had promised to reduce their hours of work, was now producing machines that had the opposite effect, vastly increasing the range and volume of the products of human labour, enriching the employers, but creating for the workers a regime of hard monotonous labour without even the remissions which the seasons had given to agricultural work or the relative security provided by employment on the land. Moreover the worker's opportunity to work had become totally dependent on the employer; and it was the new social evil of unemployment caused by circumstances outside the control of the workers which alerted the Christian conscience and stimulated Christian reflection on the importance of work for human dignity and well-being. The economic plight of the workless, and the social exclusion which tended to accompany it, was condemned by the church as an affront to human dignity.

To attack the scourge of unemployment and the exploitation of labour by wealthy entrepreneurs, an essentially bourgeois or middle-class conception of work was invoked. Work was redefined to include virtually any kind of creative activity: it became a form of co-operation with the work of the divine Creator, one of the blessings bestowed on human beings by God. Of course some work would always be drudgery; but in this case it could be likened to the 'work' of Christ in his passion and death and endured as a contribution to the continuing redemptive activity of Christ in the world.

So began a tradition of Roman Catholic teaching on work (first officially formulated in the papal encyclical *Rerum novarum*, in 1891, and given classical expression by John Paul II in *Laborem exercens*) which has continued to the present day and which is largely mirrored in such theological reflection as has issued from the other churches. In this, the 'curse' pronounced on Adam is quietly passed over; all the emphasis is on the dignity and creative potential of work. And so the idea was revived (which was first proposed, in quite another context, by the early church fathers) that the 'work' of human beings might be some kind of extension or continuation of the

p. 700

WORKER PRIESTS

In 1944, with the support of Cardinal Suhard, Archbishop of Paris, a group of volunteer French priests led by Fr Henri Perrin, who during the war had been deported to work in a factory in Germany, gave up clerical garb and life in clergy houses to work in factories and on building sites in Paris, then in Lyons and Marseilles, sharing the living and working conditions of those employed there. In so doing they were attempting to reach the working class, which had largely been alienated from the church. They were small in number, never exceeding 100.

The experiences of the priests changed their minds and they began to see their task as not simply bringing the poor back to the church but rethinking the whole mission of the church, as a witness to the kingdom of God and the bringer of good news to the poor. As a consequence of this they also began to join in workers' actions for better wages and living conditions. They saw membership of trade unions as essential for reform. In 1952 Perrin even headed the strike committee on a major dam-building site.

Kingdom of God

Roman Catholic industrialists and factory owners, who traditionally supported and were supported by the church, complained bitterly to the French bishops and to Rome. The priests were accused of being political and Marxist. In response the bishops issued a directive that they were to give up full-time work and return to their parishes. Some priests reluctantly complied, but around 50 chose to stay on.

By 1953 their position had become untenable. The Pope's representative, the papal nuncio in Paris, instructed the superiors of religious orders to recall their worker priests. Some struggled on nevertheless. In 1954 Pius XII ordered the movement to be discontinued.

In 1965, at the last session of the Second Vatican Council, after a unanimous vote by the French bishops, Paul VI again gave permission for worker priests, under strict conditions. The worker priests (*prêtres ouvriers*) were now officially called 'working priests' (*prêtres au travail*).The vocation appealed to younger priests, and in the early 1970s there were almost 1000 worker priests. Currently some 600 priests in France and 250 in neighbouring countries call themselves worker priests: they are not employed exclusively in manual work but are involved in other professions. They form a loose association, not a formal religious order. However, their number is declining steadily.

Inspired by the French worker priests, some Anglican priests, notably Bishop Leslie Hunter of Sheffield, focused their attention on involvement in the working-class world. The Sheffield Industrial Mission was formed, and elsewhere individual Anglican clergy became worker priests. However, they too came up against resistance from the established church and those who gave priority to its traditional approach, and the experiment was short-lived.

Oscar Arnal, *Priests in Working-Class Blue: The History of the Worker-Priests*, New York and Mahwah, NJ: Paulist Press 1986; John Mantle, *Britain's First Worker-Priests*, London: SCM Press 2000

Creation 'work' of God in creation. When human beings 'work', may they not be 'co-creators' with God? At this point a new text is invoked: 'Be fruitful and multiply, and fill the earth and subdue it' (Genesis 1.28). Admittedly there is no mention here of work. But it is 'beyond any doubt' (according to papal teaching) that it is by working that human beings fulfil the divine command to 'have dominion' over the earth. Creative work, by this reasoning, is a defining characteristic of human beings made in the image of God: through their work they share in God's own work of creation. And if New Testament validation is required for this line of argument, it is to be found in the statement of Mark 6.3 that Jesus was a *tekton* (though only the son of a *tekton* in Matthew 13.55), a carpenter, a practitioner (it is assumed) of essentially creative work who 'sanctified' such work by his example; and the circle is completed by the implication of John 5.17 that Jesus' 'work' (in this case the healing of a paralysed man) was of a piece with God's 'work'. Thus, by a radical extension of the meaning of the word 'work' to cover almost any purposeful activity, and clearly under the influence of nineteenth-century philosophy, the foundations were laid for a Christian doctrine of work as a vital component of human dignity, making all men (and in due course all women) 'co-creators' with God.

It is evident that this line of Christian thought, conditioned as it has been by social and economic circumstances and by the intellectual currents of the nineteenth and twentieth centuries, presents a partial and incomplete account of the matter. In affirming that work is co-operation with the divine creator it assumes that it is the work of the intellectual, the artist or the artisan which sets the standard: menial work is virtually ignored. Moreover, it sets aside a text that was formative for the Christian understanding of work for many centuries – the curse on Adam – and it appears to overlook that fact that the Old Testament sees as much evil potential in work as good.
Story From the story of Babel onwards, scripture makes it clear that human activity is as likely to lead to idolatry as to anything acceptable to God.

Moreover there are features of the modern 'world of work' which receive little attention. A tenth of all organized work in Britain is done by volunteers, who clearly perceive it not as 'co-creation' but as service to others (a theme that was very important to Augustine). Paid work no longer gives security and is unjustly distributed: many are highly paid for working excessively long hours, while others are excluded from the work-place. The disappearance of the language of virtues has made Christians apparently silent in the face of the evident vices of obsessive working or idleness disguised as delegation: the virtue of moderate industriousness forms no part of the modern Christian vocabulary.

But perhaps the most notable absence is any reference to the fact that the most explicit statements about work in the Old Testament (such as Exodus 20.8–11) are in relation to the sabbath: all work must be followed by a period of rest, and this 'rest' has the character of thankfulness, celebration and the strengthening of family ties. In the West today, increasing longevity and a social regime limiting the number of hours' work that can be demanded by employers have greatly increased the amount of time an individual can expect not to be working; consequently it is leisure rather than work that is looked to for providing satisfaction, fulfilment and human dignity. In such a world the distinctive Jewish undertanding of work, fully endorsed by Christianity, as taking its meaning and function from the divinely ordained 'rest' to which it leads, may yet become the most significant contribution which the Jewish and Christian traditions can make to the world of work in the twenty-first century.

ANTHONY HARVEY

R. H. Tawney, *Religion and the Rise of Capitalism* (1926), New Brunswick, NJ: Transaction Publications 1998; Alan Richardson, *The Biblical Doctrine of Work* (1952), London: SCM Press 1963; Josef Pieper, *Leisure: the Basis of Culture* (1963), South Bend, Indiana: St Augustine's Press 1998; Ronald Preston, *Religion and the Ambiguities of Capitalism*, London: SCM Press 1991; M. Volf, *Work in the Spirit*, New York and Oxford: OUP 1991; Anthony Harvey, *By What Authority? The Churches and Social Concern*, London: SCM Press 2001

WORLD

Animals, Church, Creation, Culture, Ecotheology, Environmental ethics, Evolution, History, Incarnation, Politics, Salvation, Science, Sin, Society

In its root meaning 'the world' (Greek *kosmos*) simply means 'that which is ordered', but it has come to be used by Christians in several different though related ways. It is sometimes synonymous with 'the heavens and the earth' of the Hebrew scriptures, and is closely bound up with the doctrine of creation and providence. The world is synonymous with what has been created by God and it comes under God's care: God is responsible for all that there is. He 'measured the waters in the hollow of his hand and marked the heavens with a span' (Isaiah 40.12), and it is through his spoken word that the world comes into existence (Psalm 33.6). This traditional doctrine provided the basis for the early Christians' understanding of creation, as in Acts 4.24, where God is invoked as sovereign Lord, maker of heaven and earth. This survived into the credal formularies of the next centuries, as in the opening of the Niceno-Constantinopolitan Creed of 381 CE, where God is described as maker of heaven and earth and of all things visible and invisible. Creed

In this understanding of the world the emphasis is on the contrast between the sovereignty of the creator and the subjugation or inferiority of what is created: the world belongs to God and it is in God that all things have their being: 'in him we live and move and have our being' (Acts 17.28). From the earliest times Christians have attributed a role in creation to Jesus himself – in Paul's writings, for instance, all things are seen as created through Christ (1 Corinthians 8.6), and in other writings the Word of God, the Logos, identified with Jesus, is seen as creating all things (Hebrews 11.3). Most influential in the New Testament is the Prologue to the Gospel of John, where all things are seen as being made through the Word (John 1.1–3), a doctrine that is maintained in the Niceno-Constantinopolitan Creed.

At other times the world is identified with the planet earth, or that place where human beings live and which provides them with the conditions for their sustenance, perhaps best described in modern terms as the natural world or the environment. A parallel meaning restricts this conception of the world to human society. Whereas in the first meaning of the term the world is fundamentally seen as good, and is seen as the counterpart to its creator (Genesis 1.12), the second meaning is more ambiguous. The natural and human world has a form of existence independent from God, and is capable of exerting its own often hostile power. Even though the world was created good, it has fallen into the hands of opposing forces. In John's Gospel the world is seen as rejecting the true light which had come into the world. Consequently, although the world was capable of reconciliation with God, and in the incarnation of the Son had become the place in which God's glory was to be glimpsed, that same world had rejected the light. The influential doctrines of the fall and of original sin, both emphasized by Augustine, which he saw as the result of rebellion by the primal human beings and by the angels, meant that the world displayed a tendency towards evil: what was good had been corrupted and needed to be restored.

There is a tendency in this view towards a dualism where the world is seen, not as morally neutral, but as in the grip of God's enemy, 'the prince of this world'. Although the world may not be beyond God's grasp, it is nevertheless held captive by opposing forces. Thus for many early Christians there was a belief in a Satanic power, the 'lawless one' (2 Thessalonians 2.8), who would bring disorder Satan and catastrophe: Christians were contending not against flesh and blood, 'but against the principalities, against the powers, against the world rulers of this present darkness, against the spiritual hosts of wickedness in the heavenly places' (Ephesians 6.12). The Christian life was consequently expressed in terms of a cosmic drama between God and his enemies, who temporarily ruled the world until the return of Christ and restoration of God's order.

Although in general the world was seen as being corrupted because of human disobedience, a theory which denied that God was directly responsible for evil, some Christians were more willing to accept alternative explanations of the origin of the world's evil. For many, the world of demons and hostile powers remained all-pervasive: some saw Christ as in a cosmic battle struggling to outwit the devil. Other theologians went still further and were labelled Gnostic heretics, accepting an alternative force of creation that set itself against what was good. Further dualistic movements with competing forces of good and evil like the Albigensians have recurred through Christian history, and have been subjected to harsh repression.

Evil

Gnosis

pp. 520–1

Given such a strong tendency towards dualism, Christians have from the very beginning sought escape from this hostile world where the 'sins of the flesh' held dominion. The domain of the spirit is thus contrasted with that of the flesh and world. The world thereby becomes synonymous with all those forces that the Christian should reject. In John's Gospel in particular the world is usually understood negatively, and Christians are given the capacity, through the 'conqueror of the world', to 'overcome' this world (John 16.33).

For many Christians this need to overcome the world stemmed from the belief that matter was inherently evil. Partly through the all-pervasive influence of Platonist philosophy in the early church, salvation required the transcending of the contingent sphere of the natural world, the world of becoming, in order to attain the world of pure being. Some Christians have maintained theories of the gradual ascent to union with the unchanging Godhead and escape from the transience of the world, as with the notion of deification that became a dominant model in the Eastern church. This often led to ascetic practices, some of which have produced almost pathological levels of self-abuse, even among the saints of the church, including Jerome, whose spiritual counsels led some of his followers to starvation: the attainment of holiness was a world-denying ordinance. In recent years there has been much criticism of this aspect of Christianity, which has been seen as devaluing the bodily and the material. Particularly among feminist theologians there has been a development of 'body' theologies that are usually rooted in the doctrine of the incarnation. This has sometimes led to more positive approaches to sexuality and marriage than those simply based on the need for procreation.

Feminist theology
Body
Incarnation
Sexuality

Apocalyptic

Other dualistic views of God and the world have derived from the strong sense of apocalyptic expectation that is such a dominant strand of the New Testament. Life in the present age is a life of waiting for the final catastrophe, when Christ will return to rule. Many passages in the New Testament are far more concerned with the future reign of God than with relationships with the present world. A consequence of the dualism of such apocalyptic theology has been to emphasize the spiritual at the expense of the material: this world just becomes a preparation for the true or 'higher' world, and is consequently of little ultimate significance. This can lead to political passivity, or even to the glorification of the suffering of the present age that was simply passing away (Romans 7.31). This transient world will be done away with to make way for the true world: as Paul suggested, this world, which was in bondage to decay, is groaning in childbirth as it awaits the new world (Romans 8.18). It comes as little surprise that some forms of Christianity, particularly those with a high doctrine of election or calling of Christians from out of the world, see true Christianity

Kingdom of God

Paul

as separation from the world of sin: the church or the sect exists as a parallel redeemed world in but not of the world. Indeed to see the church and the world as in any way related is an impossible compromise.

More recently, the rediscovery of apocalyptic in the twentieth century has been deeply influential on much New Testament interpretation and Christian theology and has had the effect of playing down Jesus' social teaching. The famous theologian Rudolf Bultmann could write that he did not believe that the Sermon on the Mount, the main digest of Jesus' social teaching, had any application in the real world, but was directed solely towards the higher world. In turn this form of theology has provoked a vigorous reaction from more socially-committed commentators, including the liberation theologians of Latin America.

p. 385

Liberation theology

In the twentieth century there has been a revival of more optimistic views of the world that emphasize the goodness of God's original blessing on the world rather than understanding the world solely in terms of human disobedience and the fall. Instead of simply being understood as sovereign over all creation, God is also seen as co-creator with humankind of a joint project. To some extent the Second Vatican Council's 'The Church in the Modern World' (*Gaudium et spes*) fell into this category as it tried to redirect the attention of the church towards the world in which it was set. Much of contemporary Christian concern for political and social issues stems from such teaching, which is reflected in far closer co-operation between ecclesiastical and secular agencies. Even such changes as the use of the vernacular in the church's liturgies have stressed the close relationship between church and world. The theology that underlies this form of social engagement is sometimes based on covenant theologies developed from the Old Testament with their strong sense of co-operation between God and his creation. Since human beings are created in the image of God, they are given the responsibility for helping to shape the created order, the world, in the direction intended by God. There is thus a sense of stewardship and responsibility for the world that comes from the human relationship with God.

p. 291

Covenant

Other recent thinkers, including the influential Roman Catholic theologian and scientist Pierre Teilhard de Chardin, have been more influenced by the rediscovery of the cosmic Christ (e.g. Colossians 1.15–20). Christ is understood as directing the universe to its final cosmic destiny as all things are gathered up into God. Sometimes, as with the writing of Matthew Fox, this has been developed in conscious opposition to the more pessimistic and dualistic theologies stemming from Paul and Augustine. Similarly, many process thinkers have understood the world less in terms of its origins than in terms of its goal. All things are moving towards that final age when God will be all in all, a doctrine sometimes called panentheism. Other theologians, particularly those influenced by the ecological movement, have been keen on stressing the mutual interaction between human beings and the rest of the world, both understood in relation to God. Hierarchical concepts of the past, which emphasize the dominion of human beings over nature, have made way for more symbiotic understandings, where human beings are simply one life force among others.

Ecotheology

All in all, Christian understandings of the world are ambiguous and point to a whole range of complex theological questions. Perhaps the most obvious direction for Christianity is to establish theologies of the world on the basis of the incarnation of Christ whereby God completely assumed the human flesh of Christ. This means that no aspect of the created order is beyond the reach of God, and however much it might have been corrupted, it is capable of being restored to its proper state. For some, it is the vocation of the church to remind the world that it has been restored and to point it in its proper direction. As the great English theologian, F. D. Maurice, wrote: 'The world contains the elements of which the church is composed. In the church, these elements are

penetrated by a uniting, reconciling power. The church is, therefore, human society in its normal state; the world, that same society irregular and abnormal. The world is the church without God; the church is the world restored to its relation with God, taken back by him into the state for which he created it.' While Christians are still divided on how to understand the world, it would seem that nearly all would agree that a world created by God can never be wholly bad despite human sin, but that nevertheless – at least after the entry of God into this world in the form of flesh – it can always get better.

MARK D. CHAPMAN

Peter Brown, *The Body and Society*, New York: Columbia University Press and London: Faber 1989; Matthew Fox, *Original Blessing*, Santa Fe: Bear & Co 1983; Jürgen Moltmann, *God in Creation*, London: SCM Press and Minneapolis: Fortress Press 1985; Richard Norris, *God and the World in Early Christian Thought*, London: A&C Black 1965; Pierre Teilhard de Chardin, *Hymn of the Universe*, London: Collins and New York: Harper & Row 1965

Worship

Going to church for worship is one of the most persistently identifiable features of Christianity. Despite changes in its shape, its intention and its component parts, despite incessant controversies over its proper mode and content, Christian worship has had the power to bind the faithful into community, to allow for the expression of religious feeling, to set the context for the encounter with God, and to shape individual Christian identity. More fully than ethics or doctrine, worship in all its myriad manifestations is the visible expression of Christianity.

Community
God
Ethics

This is not to say that there are not profound differences in the ways in which Christians have approached and interpreted what they are doing when they come together for common prayer. Most would agree that in worship both human action and divine action are at work, but the relationship between the two is a matter of varied interpretation. Most would also agree with the classic definition of worship as the church at prayer, but the form and content of that prayer varies widely. Going to church for worship provides many Christians with their primary experience of the scriptures, of praying, of praising God, and of the company of fellow believers. For others, gathering for worship on Sundays and holy days, and on occasions of family joy and sorrow, is just one thread in a richer tapestry of Christian living that could be described as worshipful.

Church
Prayer
Sacrifice
Covenant

The why of worship

There are six basic answers to the question, 'Why worship?' These different answers are given not only by large-scale traditions within the Christian family, past and present, but also by individual believers as they try to explain what worship is and why it claims them with such tenacity. Despite their individual differences, these six approaches are rooted in a common conviction that worship is an essential part of the shared world God graciously sets up with humankind, and each one takes worship seriously as an essential part of the Christian life and calling.

Many Christians have understood Christian worship as a *service* to God, a duty that God's human children perform in grateful obedience to the one who is the source of their life and their salvation. Indeed, the English word worship itself (from the Middle English *weorth-schippe*) carries with it this sense of ascribing to God the honour and worth which is due by right. And when Christians say they are attending a worship service, this same idea is being expressed; that they are undertaking worship as a way of serving Almighty God.

In many traditions, Christians pray that God will accept the *sacrifice* of their worship, and the language of sacrifice is another way of talking about worship as a service to God. The Old Testament bears witness to the belief that God established a system of sacrifices (the offering up of animals, birds and fruits of the harvest) which would be an effective sign of Israel's devotion and obedience, and a way of maintaining the covenant relationship. When Christians speak of their worship as a 'sacrifice of praise and thanksgiving' (from Leviticus 22.29 and Hebrews 13.15), they are suggesting that it functions in a similar way, as an effective sign that they offer to God all that they have and all that they are: heart and mind and possessions, body and soul. In hymns and prayers, in preaching and affirmations, Christians discharge the debt they owe to God for all blessings bestowed upon them. Most churches in the Reformed tradition (Presbyterians, for example) would find this a congenial view.

For other Christians, worship that takes place in church is an attempt to duplicate, to *recapitulate the worship of God* that takes place eternally in heaven. This model of Christian worship rests on the conviction that the ceaseless praise of God is the ultimate human destiny and calling, the activity for which human beings were created. In giving themselves over to worship here on earth, they are preparing themselves for their eternal vocation. For those who approach it this way, to enter into Christian worship is to enter into another dimension, where worshippers can gradually attune themselves with the ceaseless praises of the heavenly hosts. We can see this in the forms of worship of the Orthodox and Eastern-rite churches, where the chants, the prayers, the hymns take worshippers out of ordinary space and time and into a heavenly geography. Here it can be recognized that space and time are not to be used selfishly, but belong to God alone, and there will come a future when God will be all in all.

Still other Christians believe that the primary purpose of worship is to *affirm, inspire and support* believers in their Christian journey. They are convinced that to be a disciple of Jesus Christ is a difficult calling, if undertaken seriously and with dedication, setting Christians against the forces of evil. Like the Jesus they follow, they may be subject to misunderstanding, humiliation and betrayal, even death. But in Christian worship they are able to touch again and again the ground of their faith, and in so doing are enabled to renew the struggle against the forces of darkness that prevail around them. In prayers and testimonies, in the psalms and in songs of victory, believers are reinforced in the conviction that God is fighting on their side and are inspired to new heights of service and witness. Understandably, those Christians who stand on the frontlines of the struggle for justice and peacemaking, and those who are undergoing persecution for their faith are most likely to look at worship in this way, and we can see it clearly manifested, for example, among sectarian groups such as Mennonites and other Anabaptists.

Although all worship is understood in some measure to reinforce the God-human relationship, for some Christians the primary function of worship is to *make their relationship with God visible and tangible*, and in so doing to strengthen their relationships with fellow believers as well. Because worship is concerned with forming and maintaining essential bonds, the word communion is often used to describe what takes place in Christian worship. The English word communion translates the Greek word *koinonia*, which in the New Testament means fellowship, sharing or participation. It is used in descriptions of worship in the earliest Christian communities, which met to devote themselves to the apostles' teaching and fellowship (*koinonia*), to the breaking of bread and to the prayers (Acts 2. 42). This model of worship is marked by a spirit of mutuality, in which gifts are both given to God and received from God; it is assumed that gratitude and offering each demand to be given tangible form, and that both God and worshippers seek to make the divine-human relationship visible. This model is grounded in the paradigm of the incarnation: the same power by which God made love visible in Jesus now makes love visible in the rites and symbols of worship. So, too, do worshippers, made in God's image, incarnate their love of God in ritual form. Most clearly identified with Roman Catholic worship, it is also manifested among some Anglicans, Methodists and Lutherans.

Reformed churches

Incarnation

In many strands of Christian thought, the true, and perhaps only, Christian vocation is to *announce the good news of God in Christ*, to declare the redemptive workings of God in and for the world. Those who think of worship as the primary context for this proclamation wish to highlight the place of worship in the task of evangelization, and in the fostering of the church's participation in the mission of God. In worship, like-minded Christians gather together to say who and what they are, and in so doing to reinforce their own Christian identity. Indeed, the proclamation of Christ crucified and risen is the power that creates the worshipping community itself. As the first letter of Peter says of the church, 'You are a chosen race, a royal priesthood, a holy nation, God's own people, that you may proclaim the mighty acts of God who has called you out of darkness and into his marvellous light' (1 Peter 2.9). For Christians who view Christian worship through the lens of proclamation, including most evangelical Christians, it is only the dual action of remembering and declaring in worship that will allow the church to survive into the next generation.

Orthodox churches
Eastern-rite Catholic churches
Journeys

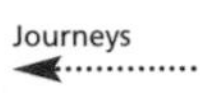

Evil

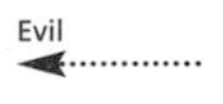

Evangelicals

For some Christians, however, all of the previous models suffer from a common defect: they turn Christian worship into something that is much too safe and predictable. They understand the goal of Christian worship as an immediate encounter with the living God, the holy, majestic and powerful God who transforms lives and sets hearts and souls on fire. They remember God's admonition to Moses in Exodus 3.5: 'Come no closer. Take your sandals from your feet, for the place where you are standing is holy ground.' And they are convinced that the same power by which God created the universe may at any moment be unleashed again. Just as Moses hid his face, for he was afraid to look at God, so too should Christian worshippers come into the presence of God with a sense of reverence, awe and expectation. Indeed, worship is constructed so that it established an arena conducive to this kind of holy

Peace churches
Anabaptists

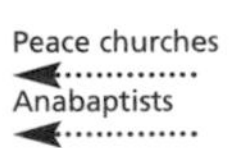

Holy Spirit
Resurrection

encounter, which is often understood to take place in the power of the Holy Spirit who acts as a mediator between the wholly otherness of God and the finite humanity. For different Christian communities, however, this arena will be constructed differently. In the Quaker meeting, for example, the most appropriate means of encouraging the divine presence is to wait in silence, clearing the mind and heart of worldly concerns, and listening carefully for the promptings of the Spirit. But in a Pentecostal or charismatic revival, patterned repetitions of sound and movement place worshippers into a receptive state, where the gifts of the Spirit can descend upon them.

Calendar

As we can see from this constellation of meanings that Christians have given to the act of coming together for worship in common, the theology of worship adopted in any given case depends on a number of factors. Since worship is integrated within a much larger complex of Christian values, assumptions and behaviours, it always implies an underlying attitude to the human person, and to human vocation and destiny. These models are never mutually exclusive, however; each affirms something basic and necessary to the understanding of the nature of Christian common prayer. Worship is at the same time proclamation and affirmation. It is a place to encounter divine transcendence and to renew and celebrate communion with God and fellow believers. Whenever the tension between and among these images of worship has collapsed, Christian worship has lost its vitality and strength. Both individuals and institutions can hold different views about the nature of worship at different times, and can fuse two or more understandings into a single theological model. But at the same time, the various Christian worship traditions also can be broadly identified by their emphasis on one of these theological approaches to worship over the others.

p. 465

It is also important to remember that for many people Christian worship is a primary source and context for the development of their own theology. The doctrine embedded in the hymns and prayers, the vision of God that is proclaimed and preached, gives worshippers food for thought as they form their Christian world-view. What is prayed and what is believed are mutually interdependent, and worship plays an essential role not only in expressing, but also in forming Christian belief.

The time for worship

Messiah
Festivals and fasts

Weekly worship on Sundays seems to have been a regular feature of Christian faith and life from a very early period, although Jewish Christians probably also participated, at least for a time, in temple, synagogue and domestic rites in addition to gatherings of those who believed the Messiah had come in Jesus of Nazareth. The symbolic associations that attached to Sunday were twofold. The first is a historical association: the synoptic Gospels describe the resurrection as taking place on the first day of the week, and it is most appropriate for the weekly celebration of the resurrection also to be held on a Sunday; the second is a more theological association, looking back to Genesis, where God finishes creation on the sixth day (Friday) and rests on the seventh (Saturday, or the sabbath). Now, in raising Jesus from the dead, God begins a new creation on the eighth day (which, of course in a seven-day week is, again, the first day, Sunday). A handful of contemporary Christian denominations such as Seventh-day Baptists and Seventh-day Adventists have refused to accept this symbolic logic, and follow the sabbath-keeping pattern demanded in the Old Testament, holding weekly services of worship on Saturday rather than Sunday.

Certainly by the middle of the second century, and perhaps much earlier, an annual celebration of the resurrection was held in association with the Jewish Passover, which fell on the fourteenth day of the lunar month of Nisan each year. Again the symbolic associations are clear. Not only did Jesus' death take place in the context of Passover, when the sacrifices in the temple and the eating of the ritual meal re-connected the Jewish community with the reality of God's saving action on their behalf, but Jesus himself appropriated the Passover motifs to interpret his own identity and destiny. Indeed, one of the earliest controversies over worship was over this question of the proper time for the annual celebration of the resurrection. Some Christians, called the Quartodecimans (the 'Fourteeners'), argued that these connections with Passover were so strong that the yearly celebration should coincide exactly with Passover and take place on 14 Nisan, whatever day of the week it fell upon. Others thought the symbolic associations between the resurrection and Sunday were stronger, and that the annual festival should be observed on the Sunday nearest to the Passover. The Quartodeciman Controversy lasted in some places until the sixth century, and although there are recurring suggestions that, for the sake of simplicity, the date of Easter ought to be fixed, Easter remains a so-called moveable feast, occurring each year on a Sunday somewhere between 21 March and 25 April.

The development of a more elaborate Christian calendar took place over the next several centuries. The first and historically pre-eminent of the dates celebrated were commemorations of events in the life and ministry of Jesus and the earliest Christian community. Forms of worship that marked the days leading up to Easter (Holy Week), which recalled the events of Pentecost, and which illuminated the meaning of the incarnation were in place in most Christian churches by the mid-fourth century. Thereafter there was a steady expansion of the calendar to include seasons of preparation for major festivals, and

POSTURES AND GESTURES

As in other religions, in Christianity the body is used in many ways in prayer and worship, extending even to forms of dance. The position of the body can be a powerful influence on prayer and worship

Dance

Postures

Standing, at times with hands uplifted, was the earliest posture used by Christians in praying, and today it is the posture for large parts of communal worship.

Kneeling to pray was originally associated with penitence, and in the early church it was actually forbidden in the Easter season. It became the general practice in the Middle Ages, and is associated with an increasing emphasis on penitence and sinfulness in public worship. It is a posture widely adopted in private prayer.

Forgiveness

Sitting is possible only when there are seats, and in worship originally a seat was provided only for the bishop or his representative. Later, with the development of long periods of prayer in monasteries, choir stalls were constructed and once sermons became part of worship, seats had to be provided for the congregation. Sitting is now accepted as a posture for prayer and meditation.

Prostration was the posture adopted in the early church by penitents and those being instructed in Christianity (catechumens), but now it is used only rarely, notably at the ordination of Roman Catholic priests.

Initiation

Gestures

The *hands* are used in many gestures. They are folded and sometimes raised in prayer, and are held out to receive communion. The laying on of hands is practised in ceremonies of healing, and by bishops at confirmation and ordination. The priest holds out his hand in blessing.

Sacraments

The right hand is used to make the *sign of the cross*, by individuals upon themselves, and by the clergy on persons and things in an act of blessing. It can be made with the thumb on the forehead, the whole hand, or just two fingers, touching forehead, breast, left and right (Western tradition) or right and left (Eastern tradition) shoulders, or with outstretched arm over a congregation. The right hand is also used in the gesture of *beating the breast* as an act of penitence.

The head and upper body are *bowed* as a gesture of humility and reverence; in *genuflection* the knee is bowed, as a sign of reverence, usually before the reserved sacrament.

In the worship of the early church, Christians greeted one another with a 'holy kiss', and this is mentioned by Paul (e.g. Romans 16.16). The practice was discontinued, but in modern times has been reintroduced as a sign of peace during the eucharist; however, it usually takes the form of a handshake or embrace rather than an actual kiss.

other biblical events such as the annunciation to Mary, the circumcision of Jesus, the transfiguration of Jesus, and the anniversaries of the deaths of the disciples. The lives of other, non-biblical, persons of great sanctity were gradually added, until by the late Middle Ages every day of the year was taken up with some form of commemoration. Major festivals, referred to as red letter days because they were originally printed in ecclesiastical calendars in red ink, generally took precedence over lesser, usually non-scriptural, festivals (Black Letter Days), but a complex set of calculations governed the relationships between and among holy days.

There is yet another pattern of worship which has nourished the Christian life and faith. Structures of daily prayer (also called the Daily Office, the Canonical Hours, and the Liturgy of the Hours) marking certain times of day with the prayer, hymn-singing, and the recitation of psalms has been a persistent feature of Christian practice, although it has been more significant for some Christian groups than for others. The history of daily prayer is the history of people trying to live out and manage the apostolic admonition to pray at all times (Ephesians 6.18). The ideal of perpetual prayerfulness has been a feature of many religious traditions, and in Christianity the expression of this ideal in forms of worship punctuating the day symbolizes a relationship with a God who is revealed in time.

The earliest forms of daily prayer were conceived as occasions for ordinary Christians to pray and praise God in the company of other Christians. As vehicles for popular devotion, these services were brief, colourful, simple, invariable, musical and thematically related to the time of day. Originally no readings from the Bible other than the psalms, no sermons, and no extended Christian teaching were included in these services, but only praise and thanksgiving to God (in the morning) and intercession and forms of confession of sin (in the evening). Gradually, however, those wishing to live a more intentional life in common with others took on the discipline of the Daily Office, and an increasingly complex pattern of

p. 966

Psalms

HIGH AND LOW

High and low have been used of various groups, objects and other things in Christianity. Here are some of them:

High church: Used since the end of the seventeenth century of those members of the Church of England who emphasize its continuity with the Catholic church and have 'high' views of the church, the priesthood, traditional ceremonial forms of worship and the sacraments. Anglo-Catholics share these concerns, and the Oxford Movement stood in the same tradition.

Low church: Those Anglicans who give a 'low' place to the priesthood and the sacraments and emphasize the connection of their church with the Protestantism of the Reformation. When the term was first used in the early eighteenth century in contrast to 'high church', confusingly it was applied to Anglicans like the Cambridge Platonists who attached little importance to any form of doctrine, church organization or worship, and who subsequently came to be called 'broad church'. It went out of use and then in the middle of the nineteenth century was revived to denote Evangelicals, whom it now tends to describe.

High mass: A mass celebrated at the high altar by three priests, termed celebrant, deacon and subdeacon, each with specific roles in the service, together with a choir to sing the musical setting and a number of servers or acolytes who assisted the priests in the sanctuary, and a thurifer to provide the incense. It could be very elaborate in form and presentation.

Low mass: Until modern times this was the most frequent form of the eucharist in the Western church, with only the priest celebrating, usually daily, and often in a side chapel rather than at the high altar. There was no music.
(Since the Second Vatican Council the terms 'high mass' and 'low mass' have disappeared from the Roman Catholic Church and the whole approach to celebrating the mass has been changed.)

High altar: The main altar in a church, traditionally at the centre of the east end. High mass would be celebrated there, the celebrant having his back to the congregation, and in old churches and cathedrals the altar would be separated from the people by the choir and often a screen. The Second Vatican Council decreed that the mass should be celebrated with the celebrant facing the people; this has led to the abandonment of the high altar and the erection of a new altar in the space between the choir and the people in the body of the church. There is no 'low' altar.

Low Sunday: A traditional name for the first Sunday after Easter, probably to contrast it with the 'high' feast of Easter, but nowadays equally plausibly taking its name from the usually small number of people in the congregation.

Higher criticism: An old-fashioned term, now obsolete, to describe the study of the literary methods and sources of the books of the Bible. This was to contrast it with textual criticism, which sought to establish the exact text that the biblical authors wrote.

daily prayer began to develop. Soon the popular forms of daily prayer died out as ordinary Christians relinquished the Daily Office to the religious professionals: monks, nuns and ordained ministers.

The corporate Daily Office is not the only form of worship during the day. Household worship in families has also had a long and unbroken history in the church. Parents generally supervised the prayer of their children, and devotional aids guided patterns of worship for use in the home. Usually the form and content of this prayer mirrored the worship that took place in church on Sundays, with prayers and hymns learned in the liturgy finding new meaning as they were used in domestic settings. Often in times of liturgical change and conflict the Christian home provided a safe place for the expression of alternative forms of worship, and often this was the place where women who were usually denied roles in the leadership of Christian public worship found their voice.

Buildings ➤

The space for worship

The space in which Christians have gathered for prayer in common has both shaped and been shaped by changes in the forms of worship. Until the mid-third century, meetings for Christian worship were held in the houses of influential leaders of the Jesus movement, and throughout the history of the church many Christian renewal groups throughout the centuries have returned to domestic settings in the hope of reduplicating the intimacy and spiritual power present in those most ancient Christian places of worship. There is some debate about the degree to which houses in this early period were adapted to the ritual demands of worship in the Christian mode: whether, for example, the reflecting pools that were a normal feature of Mediterranean atria were used to baptize new converts, and whether the family dining table was the setting for the ritual meal.

With the growing respectability of Christianity some

time before the turn of the third century, worship began to move into public buildings, first adapting existing buildings and then constructing purpose-built churches. As the church as a whole began to take on the trappings of the imperial court, including processions with singers and lighted candles, and badges of office such as the stole and the mitre, the appropriation of the Roman-style basilica for worship added to both the visibility and the prestige of Christianity. Changes in the setting for worship have reflected not only changes in the liturgy but also changes in theology and in the more general aesthetic sensitivities of the time. It is almost impossible to understand the trajectory of liturgical history without taking into account the trajectory of architectural history at the same time.

The shape of Christian worship

Several things have been historically understood to form the ritual core of Christian worship. Since the earliest gatherings of the post-resurrection Christian fellowship, the reading and exposition of the Bible has been at the centre of worship. Indeed, many would argue that the canon of scripture itself was formed in worship, as particular stories of Jesus, descriptions of the work of the first believers and pastoral letters that circulated around congregations were experienced as the Word of God. Gradually, lectionaries of Bible readings for each particular Sunday of the year began to be circulated. Eventually, and probably by the fifth century, three lessons (one from the Old Testament, one from the Epistles and one from the Gospels) and a psalm were appointed to be read on Sundays, and later as the Christian calendar became more complex, readings for special days of commemoration were added. Special prayers were devised to reflect the theme of the readings for a particular day, and together this combination of readings and accompanying prayers came to be known as the 'propers' of the service, that is, those elements that were specific to a particular day and season. (This is usually contrasted with those parts of worship that are invariable from week to week, which are referred to as the 'ordinary' parts of corporate worship.) Some of these elements of worship (such as the Lord's Prayer) are as old as Christianity itself; others may be being used for the first time at a particular gathering. But it is this creative combination of the ancient and the new that gives Christian worship its strength and vitality.

The second pole around which Christian worship has generally revolved is a ritual meal, enacted in remembrance of the last Passover *seder* that Jesus celebrated with his friends just before his crucifixion. In the earliest gatherings of Jesus' followers after his death, it is likely that this memorial meal was held once a year at Passover, but quite soon, and probably by the time of the earliest Christian writings, a commemorative meal was being held weekly on the first day of the week (Sunday). Originally, this would have been a full meal, with some of the bread and some of the wine set apart and used as a ritual link to the final meal of Jesus. It is possible that Jesus' words that identified the bread and wine with the sacrificial offering of his body and the shedding of his blood might have been recited (1 Corinthians 11.23–6), but much about this very earliest period of Christian worship history has yet to be discovered.

The earliest term for this meal is the Lord's Supper, a term we already find in the New Testament. Because the meal as a whole was understood to be, at least in part, a thanksgiving to God for the life, death and resurrection of Jesus, the word eucharist (from the Greek word for giving thanks) is also found in very early documents to describe the rite, and this term has become widely accepted in the contemporary ecumenical movement. The closing words of the medieval eucharistic rite were *Ite, missa est* (roughly translated 'Go, you are dismissed'), and it is from this that the term mass has its origins, and although almost universally abandoned by Protestants at the time of the Reformation, it is still common currency among Roman Catholics and some within the Anglican Communion. The communion is technically that portion of the rite during which the congregation receives the bread and wine, and many in the post-Reformation churches use the words holy communion to describe the rite as a whole. These various ways of talking about the Christian ritual meal have high sign-value, and different groups identify themselves by the term they most commonly use.

Architecture
Bible
Canon
Letters

Within the central prayer of the Christian eucharist, called variously the 'great thanksgiving', the 'canon of the mass', and the 'eucharistic prayer', one can find a fairly clear summary of Christian teaching. It begins with a recitation of the saving acts of God described in scripture, reaching a climax in the life, death and resurrection of Jesus. The power of the Holy Spirit is invoked, and the language of the community's self-offering is generally employed. In the communion, the bread and wine is shared among those present. Not all Christian communities feel it necessary to say such a complex prayer at the Lord's table; for many, including many in the Reformed churches, the recitation of the words of institution are sufficient to ensure that the rite is properly performed. At the same time, divergent interpretations of the meaning of this rite, of the necessary components and proper ministrants, and of its place in the Christian life and faith have fractured (and continue to fracture) the unity of the church.

Eucharist
p. 967
Sacraments

Of course other forms of Christian worship have been exceedingly important in its history. The water-rite with which new Christians are initiated, almost always called baptism, is, along with the Lord's Supper, a nearly-universal feature of Christian worship from earliest times.

LITURGICAL COLOURS

In the Roman Catholic, Anglican and Lutheran traditions the colours of the vestments worn by the clergy and some of the furnishings of the altar change with the season of the church's year. There was no system of colours to mark the seasons of the church's year in early Christianity, nor is there in the Orthodox churches today. Liturgical colours were first laid down in the twelfth century by Pope Innocent III. The developed system was:

White	*Red*	*Green*	*Purple*	*Black*
Trinity Sunday Feasts of Christ and Mary Corpus Christi Feasts of virgins and confessors Funerals (in some countries)	Pentecost Feasts of apostles and martyrs Palm Sunday Good Friday	Sundays and ordinary days from Epiphany to Lent and from Trinity Sunday to Advent	Lent and Advent Funerals	Funerals, masses and offices for the dead

pp. 288–9

However, with greater freedom in liturgical use, particularly after the Second Vatican Council, there is an increasing variety and combination of colours. Blue is often used, particularly in the United States, for the feasts of the Virgin Mary and increasingly throughout Advent instead of purple.

Unitarians

Controversies about baptism, like controversies about the eucharist, have divided and continue to divide the church. One fundamental debate centres on whether small children are appropriate candidates for baptism, or whether baptism should be reserved for adult believers upon mature profession of faith. Another rift divides those who believe that total submersion is the only proper mode of baptism from those who are not convinced that the quantity of water matters, but only the intention. Some Christians affirm that the act of baptism itself is a saving act of God, and others that it is a sign of a personal faith commitment made and affirmed by the candidate. Baptism has historically been one of a complex of initiatory practices, which have included the water bath itself, forms of catechesis, anointing with oil, and the laying-on-of-hands with prayer for the infusion of the Holy Spirit into the candidates' life. Once again, the appropriate relationship between and among these elements, their theological meaning, and the most proper and effective ritual to be employed has caused considerable dissention and fragmentation in the church.

Initiation

Marriage

Not all communities of faith that identify themselves as Christian insist on the centrality of the reading and preaching of the scriptures, the weekly celebration of the eucharist, and initiation into the community through baptism, although many would insist that these are the *sine qua non* of Christian belonging. The Religious Society of Friends (Quakers), founded in the seventeenth century on the spiritual insights of George Fox and others, is one notable example of a Christian tradition for which all visible rites and ceremonies are deemed to be contrary to the gospel. At the same time, Quakers would insist that baptism, the supper, and the proclamation of scripture are present in Quaker meetings for worship, but are received spiritually rather than materially. For most Unitarian Universalists, even those who would claim to be theistic and Christian, the right hand of fellowship has replaced baptism as the initiatory act.

Death

Quakers

Hope

Other acts of worship

To mark particular states and stages of human life with services of worship is common to many religious traditions. Puberty rites, marriage ceremonies, rituals around the sick bed, and words and actions by which the dead are buried and loss is lamented are hardly unique to Christianity. However, for Christians, these life-cycle rituals serve to place their own local and personal concerns into the context of the death and resurrection of Jesus, revealing the deeper meaning of their ordinary lives. In Christian marriage, for example, forms of worship have often proclaimed that the couple is forming a church in microcosm, a small-scale redemptive community in which the love of husband and wife embodies God's love for the world. Other traditions of worship carry the image of the marriage as a new Garden of Eden, where husband and wife are given a new chance at restoring the divine-human relationship as they honour in one another the image of God in which they were made.

The same process of reframing life events, placing them on a wider canvas, can be seen in the rites of death. Death has always been seen to be the most profound challenge to the Christian hope. But by linking the death of a particular Christian believer to the death and resurrection of Jesus, the worship that surrounds Christian burial proclaims that the Christian hope is not demolished, even when the future would seem to have been swallowed up

LITURGICAL OBJECTS

As with an ordinary meal, a number of vessels and cloths are used in the celebration of the eucharist or holy communion. These vary depending on the church concerned. Traditionally the altar, or table, has a cloth hanging down over the front, known as a *frontal*. A white cloth is placed along the top, hanging down at each end, and candles are placed upon it, which are lit for the service. Beside the altar is another table, called the *credence table*, also covered with a white cloth.

Eucharist

Another, smaller, rectangular cloth, the *corporal*, is laid at the centre of the altar and on it is placed the *chalice*, the cup which will contain the wine, usually of silver and sometimes of gold, with yet another a small linen cloth draped over it. This is known as a *purificator*, and is used to wipe the chalice after those taking communion have drunk from it. On top of these is placed the *paten*, a plate on which is placed the wafer of bread symbolically broken by the priest before communion. This is covered with a piece of white linen, stiffened by cardboard, known as the *pall*. All these are covered by a *veil*, a covering cloth in the liturgical colour of the season, often embroidered or decorated. On top of that is the *burse*, two stiffened squares of material again in the colour of the liturgical season, hinged together to form a pocket in which the corporal is put when not in use.

The consecrated bread for the eucharist (usually in the form of wafers) is put in a *ciborium*, and this, together with vessels

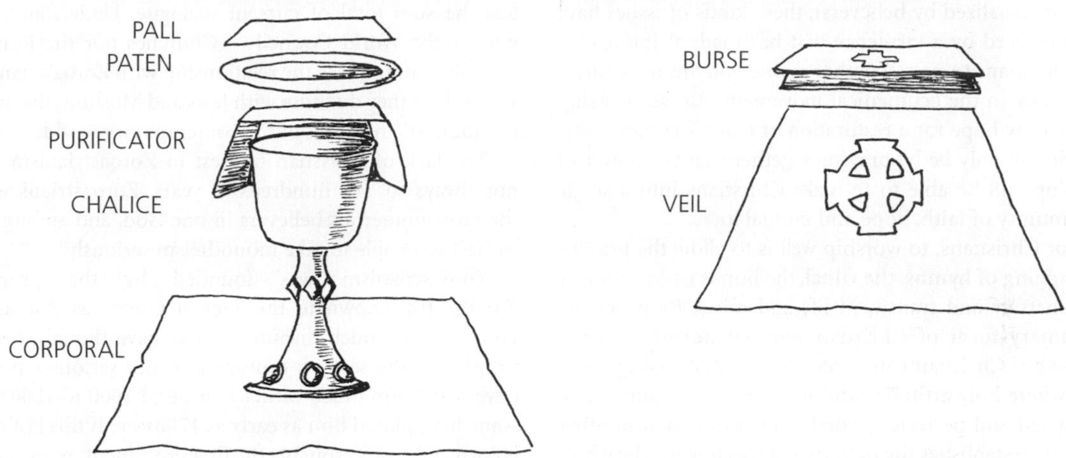

containing wine and water, traditionally known as *cruets*, are usually brought up to the altar at the offertory, before the prayer of thanksgiving. After the wine and water have been poured into the chalice, the cruets are put on the credence table, which also contains a further vessel containing water, a bowl and a small towel; these are used for the symbolic washing of the priest's hands after receiving the offerings of the people.

Incense is used at the eucharist in some traditions; this dates back to around the fifth century and was originally a mark of honour or of cleansing or exorcism. It is burned on hot charcoal in a *thurible*, a bowl suspended on three or more chains with a lid pierced with holes on another chain which can be lifted to insert the incense. The smoke then escapes through the holes. The person who carries it is known as a *thurifer*. A more generic term for an incense container is a *censer*: in the Eastern church incense is also burned in other devotions.

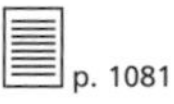
p. 1081

After the eucharist, consecrated bread (and wine) are kept for giving communion to sick people. The ciborium with the bread may be put in a *tabernacle*, a metal container covered with a cloth; alternatively it may be put in an *aumbry*, a niche in the wall secured by a door or grill. Another form of container used is the *pyx*, a name originally and widely used for the receptacles, suitable for carrying around, which are used in taking the sacrament to the sick.

In some churches, there is a service of devotion (Benediction of the Blessed Sacrament), which involves the display of a wafer consecrated at the eucharist. The wafer is put in an elaborately decorated container, known as a *monstrance*.

Devotions

by death. All Christian worship marking significant life events follows a similar pattern: to find meaning in the ordinary human situation by inserting it into the larger story of redemption.

Other forms of worship give voice to stages in individual spiritual growth. Confirmation rites allow those baptized as infants to make a first public profession of faith; rituals of penitence allow persons convicted of sin to express their repentance and to promise amendment of life; forms of thanksgiving for the birth or adoption of a child express gratitude to God for the gift of new beginnings. In all of these, the personal and communal, the private

Forgiveness

and the public, the interior disposition and the external action intertwine and inform each other. By setting these various human circumstances in a redemptive context, worship encourages the making of Christian meaning for individuals and communities.

Worship has not only been a persistent feature of Christianity but also a source of much division and dissent. Debates between groups of Christians over worship have fragmented the church almost since the beginning. Already in Paul's first letter to the Corinthians, division marks the community when the rich members bring lavish food to the Lord's Supper and eat it themselves, leaving the poor humiliated. Because of the understanding that it is in worship that Christian theology is most fully expressed (and internalized by believers), these kinds of issues have been marked by a virulence that has made it impossible for Christians to pray together as one body in the church. Ecumenical movement But many in the ecumenical movement also see worship as the only hope for a restoration of true Christian unity; that it will only be by praying together that the power of worship will be able to re-make Christians into a single community of faith, hope and mutual love.

For Christians, to worship well is to allow the prayers, Hymns the singing of hymns, the ritual, the bonds of community to penetrate and transform life and mind. By providing a primary form of Christian spiritual nurture, a place where the Christian can meet and be addressed by God, and where holy attitudes and forms of behaviour can be rehearsed and perfected, worship in common with other believers establishes the pattern and baseline for the whole of the Christian life.

SUSAN J. WHITE

Herbert Anderson and Edward Foley, *Mighty Stories, Dangerous Rituals*, San Francisco: Jossey-Bass 1997; Paul Bradshaw, *The Search for the Origins of Christian Worship*, Oxford: OUP [2]2002; Gail Ramshaw, *Worship: Searching for Language*, Washington DC: Pastoral Press 1988; Frank Senn, *Christian Liturgy: Catholic and Evangelical*, Minneapolis, MN: Fortress Press 1997; Dwight Vogel (ed), *Primary Sources of Liturgical Theology: A Reader*, Collegeville, MN: Liturgical Press 2000; Susan J. White, *The Spirit of Worship: The Liturgical Tradition*, London: SPCK and Maryknoll: Orbis 1999

Zoroastrianism and Christianity

Bible

It has been said that Zoroastrianism is the oldest of the revealed world religions, and has probably had more influence on humankind, directly and indirectly, than any other single faith. Yet there are no more than about 140,000 Zoroastrians in the world today. Only about 17,000 live in Iran, where the religion began. The vast majority (about 92,000) live in India, especially in Mumbai (Bombay) and surrounding areas in west India. Another 5000 or so live in North America, and the rest are scattered elsewhere.

Given that most Zoroastrians do not live in countries with numerous Christian populations, and given their tiny overall numbers anyway, it is not surprising that there is no strong tradition of Christian dialogue with Zoroastrianism. A few distinguished Zoroastrian scholars regularly attend international interfaith dialogue meetings, where they meet Christians and also members of other faiths. Christians occasionally meet Zoroastrians in interfaith groups in the UK, Canada, the USA or elsewhere. But that is more or less the sum total of current dialogue. Understandably, neither the World Council of Churches nor the Roman Catholic Church take the relationship with Zoroastrians as seriously as they do those with Jews and Muslims, the other monotheistic religions of the contemporary world.

The lack of Christian interest in Zoroastrianism was not always so. For hundreds of years, Zoroastrians were the most numerous believers in one God, and among the earliest of people to take monotheism seriously.

Zoroastrianism was founded by the prophet Zarathustra, known to the ancient Greeks as Zoroaster. His dates are much disputed. Many have thought him a prophet of the seventh century BCE, but serious scholars have dated him much earlier to around 1000 to 1200 BCE; some have placed him as early as 1700 BCE. If this last date is correct, he was probably the first prominent monotheist, earlier than the Egyptian 'heretic' pharaoh Akhenaten (officially Amenhotep IV) of the fourteenth century BCE, and Moses, who may have lived in the thirteenth and/or twelfth century BCE.

Zoroastrianism flourished in Persia (now Iran), and was the dominant religion in the Persian empire from about 550 BCE to the Muslim conquest of 651 CE. Thereafter, the numbers of Zoroastrians dwindled in their ancient heartland, and the few left in Iran now live chiefly in Yazd, Kernan and Tehran.

The Eastern Roman empire had occasionally sparred with Persia, the great power to its east. After the empire became Christian in 381 CE, Christians in Persia were intermittently persecuted by Zoroastrians on the grounds that they held the religion of a foreign and unfriendly culture. This persecution ceased after the coming of Islam.

Longer lasting and more important than any persecuting zeal was the impact of Zoroastrian beliefs upon Christianity, mostly through Judaism. The later documents of the Old Testament, and the inter-testamental literature, show both a confident monotheism (as opposed to henotheism, the belief that one's God is the most important of the deities) and a dualism, both of which no doubt derived in great part from influences from Persia. Specific Zoroastrian beliefs predate similar Jewish beliefs of that period.

Zoroastrians believe in a single God, Ahura Mazda, who is supreme. The Gathas, the original sacred text, declare that this God communicates with humans by a number of attributes, which are sometimes personified. Zoroastrians believe that the universe goes through a present period, where good and evil commingle, but that eventually they will be separated. One school of Zoroastrian thought describes this as a cosmic dualism between God and an evil spirit called Angra Mainyu, who opposes Ahura Mazda. This conflict compels humans and the rest of creation to choose which to follow. At the end of time, Angra Mainyu will be destroyed. After death, the soul is allowed three days to meditate upon its past life, then it is judged on the basis of its words and deeds and goes to either heaven or hell. A *saoshyant* (or saviour), born of a virgin and a descendant of Zoroaster, will judge everyone.

It is likely that, over the course of time, as Jews, Zoroastrians and Christians met and mingled, the influences described above went in every direction. Even so, it is clear how indebted Christianity has been to Zoroastrianism for its beliefs about God and Satan, heaven and hell, the soul, the saviour, final judgement and resurrection.

MARTIN FORWARD

Mary Boyce, *Zoroastrians. Their Religious Beliefs and Practices*, London and New York: Routledge 2001

Zwingli, Huldrych

Huldrych (originally Ulrich) Zwingli was born in 1484, in Toggenburg, an Alpine valley in the eastern part of modern-day Switzerland, to a poor peasant family, but as a bright young boy he was encouraged into education. He studied at the universities of Vienna and Basle (1498–1506), where he was exposed to the major currents that would shape his theology: late-medieval scholasticism and humanism. A talented linguist, Zwingli acquired an admirable grounding in Greek and Hebrew and was devoted to classical philosophy, so that his friends referred to him as 'Aristotle'. He was ordained to the priesthood and served in Glarus before going to the great Benedictine monastery of Einsiedeln (1516–19), whose rich library resources afforded the young priest the opportunity to deepen his knowledge of patristic and medieval writers. He would preach at the yearly official pilgrimages made by the citizens of Zurich to the Black Madonna of Einsiedeln, and as a result of his sermons there he became well known in the city. In 1519 he was called to the Grossmünster, the cathedral in Zurich, as stipendiary priest.

Zwingli's preaching made an enormous impact: he denounced ecclesiastical and political corruption, the receipt of foreign pensions by the leading families of the city and the mercenary service, and called on the people to purify themselves before God. Zurich was something of a backwater, without a university, but Zwingli created the mood for reform. It was never, however, a mass movement, but rather a small circle of like-minded priests, printers and magistrates who pushed forward the call for reform. Events developed around two disputations that took place in 1523 and for which Zwingli wrote his Sixty-Seven Theses, his first major work. As a result of them the city council made the cathedral independent of episcopal control. Steps were taken to abolish the mass, and Zwingli married. He sought to reform church and society, but he recognized that to do this he required the support of the magistrates, who needed to be reassured that reform was not social revolution.

Zwingli's position in Zurich was never wholly secure. The establishment of the new reformed order in Zurich at Easter 1525 was largely due to the influence of a couple of key magistrates who backed Zwingli. At the centre of his vision was the reform of worship, and the Reformation began with a celebration of the Lord's Supper in a new form. His reforms revealed a mixture of late-medieval and Erasmian impulses; institutional changes as well as moral legislation were drawn from the reform councils of the fifteenth century, and like Erasmus Zwingli believed that education was the key to the creation of a Christian society.

Reformation
Eucharist

Institutional reform under Zwingli was halting, largely because from 1525 until his death he was involved in a series of vicious polemical exchanges. Zwingli faced opposition from Catholics, his former mentor Erasmus, the so-called Anabaptists, and, most famously, Martin Luther. Virtually all of Zwingli's theological writings were hastily compiled responses to particular crises or attacks. Thus his work cannot be treated as systematic theology. The three major events in Zwingli's career after 1525 were the Baden Disputation (1526), which he refused to attend; the Berne Disputation (1528), which saw the Reformation adopted in major parts of the Swiss Confederation; and the Marburg Colloquy of 1529, where he and Luther came face to face. Zwingli's desire to bring the Reformation to the rest of the Swiss Confederation led to alliance-building, which made war with the Catholic states probable. This led to the disastrous First and Second Kappel Wars of 1529 and 1531. Zwingli was killed in a surprise attack in the night of 11 October 1531.

Martin Luther
Scholasticism
Humanism

On account of their acrimonious falling out over the Lord's Supper, the question of Luther's influence on Zwingli has remained highly contentious. Although Zwingli always maintained that he had arrived at his ideas of faith alone and scripture alone independently, it is clear that Luther's early works played a key role in his conversion to the Reformation. Certainly Zwingli keenly followed the 'Luther affair' and read all the German Reformer's works, which were being printed in Basle. On key theological points such as faith alone and scripture alone they were largely in agreement, but Zwingli had an entirely different agenda, which led to a theology of a different character. That background was shaped by two crucial aspects: Zwingli's own experience of serving in military campaigns (1513–15) and observing with horror the effects of the mercenary trade on the Swiss, and the form of Christian humanism prevalent in south-western Germany and the Swiss lands. The type of humanism that shaped Zwingli's thought concentrated on the practical Christian life and reform of the church, and it emphasized the role of the Old Testament. To this we can attribute most of the major themes in Zwingli's thought: the utter sovereignty of God, the covenantal nature of God's relationship with humanity, God's demand that his people be 'pure', and the centrality of ethics and the life of the regenerated Christian. Perhaps the most striking difference between the two Reformers came in their interpretation of the law; unlike Luther, Zwingli did not contrast law and gospel but rather interpreted God's law as a guide for Christian living.

Heinrich Bullinger ➤

Covenant

Zwingli saw the Reformation in terms of the renewal of the Christian community. He believed in the possibility of the Christian magistrate and he looked to the Old Testament model of the prophet and the king as his model form of governance. Civil authorities were to enforce the laws of the state, which were to be grounded in scripture. The prophets (clergy) were the interpreters of God's Word. Zwingli believed that the two authorities should stand side by side, but implicit in his teaching was the superiority of the prophet. Like Luther, Zwingli saw himself as God's prophet, but this approach was to go disastrously wrong when he was seen as responsible for leading Zurich into a disastrous war with Catholic cantons in 1531 that resulted in defeat and Zwingli's death. His influence endured, and in the hands of his successor Heinrich Bullinger, Zwingli's influence spread across Europe and to the New World.

BRUCE GORDON

📖 B. Gordon, *The Swiss Reformation*, Manchester; Manchester University Press 2002; G. W. Potter, *Zwingli*, Cambridge: CUP 1976; W. P. Stephens, *The Theology of Huldrych Zwingli*, Oxford: Clarendon Press 1986

WHO'S WHO

Abelard, Peter (1079–1142) French philosopher and theologian. Born in Brittany, he became a brilliant and popular teacher in Paris. There he fell in love with Heloise, the daughter of the canon of Notre Dame in whose house he lived; she had a child by him and he then married her, but to avoid further problems Heloise retired to a convent. Her father hired men who broke into Abelard's lodgings and castrated him, after which he became a monk, spending his last years at Cluny. He was primarily a philosopher, and his use of rational criticism and analysis, his stress on the importance of doubt, and his appeal to evidence left a great mark on theological method. In many respects he was a pioneer; moreover with his respect for the ancient pagan philosophers he might be said to have been a humanist before his time. With him theology moved so to speak from a monastic to a university context. His *Christian Theology* gave a new breadth to the term; his application of logic and dialectic to the doctrine of the Trinity proved highly controversial, as did his view of the atonement as primarily a moral influence. His *Know Yourself* focused on the role of conscience and the relevance of knowledge and intention to moral guilt. This new philosophical approach won him several condemnations by the church and the opposition of Bernard of Clairvaux. His autobiography, *The Story of My Misfortunes*, and his letters to Heloise illuminate his personal life.

📖 *The Letters of Abelard and Heloise*, Harmondsworth: Penguin Books 2003

Adam, Karl (1876–1966) German Catholic theologian. He was born in Bavaria, and after pastoral work taught at the University of Munich before becoming professor at Tübingen. He came to be known above all for his influential *The Spirit of Catholicism* (1924, English 1929). He was opposed to rationalism and liberal Protestantism, and although he believed God could not be known through unaided reason, his natural theology was based on a different approach from that of science. He believed that knowledge of Christ came through the church, which he regarded as virtually an extension of the incarnation; hierarchically structured by the papacy and the hierarchy, it swallowed up the individual in community.

📖 Karl Adam, *The Spirit of Catholicism*, New York: Crossroad 1997

Albertus Magnus (Albert the Great, 1193–1280) German theologian and scientist. Born near Ulm, he became a Dominican at Padua and taught in Hildesheim, Ratisbon, Cologne (where Thomas Aquinas was his pupil) and Paris before returning to Cologne. There he organized the university, becoming provincial of the German province and Bishop of Ratisbon. He is famous for establishing the study of nature as a respectable discipline for Christian thinkers. He wrote commentaries on all Aristotle's work and was concerned to reconcile Aristotle's philosophy with Christianity. Here he was an important predecessor of Thomas Aquinas, on whom his thinking made an impact.

📖 Simon Tugwell (ed), *Albert and Thomas. Selected Writings*, Classics of Western Spirituality, New York and Mahwah, NJ: Paulist Press 1989

Alcuin (*c.*740–804) English scholar. He was educated at the cathedral school of York, of which he became master. In 781 he met Charlemagne at Parma and became his adviser on religion

and education. He was made abbot of Tours in 796, and established a famous school and library there. He was an important figure in the revival of learning in Charlemagne's empire, particularly through setting up schools; he standardized the very varied scripts of different monasteries used for copying texts, insisting on a return to the earliest most authentic sources to be found in Rome and Monte Cassino; he was also involved in developing a new script which ultimately led to Roman type, and in revision of the Vulgate and the liturgy. He wrote educational books, poetry and letters.

📖 Donald A. Bullough: *Alcuin, Achievement and Reputation*, Leiden: Brill 2002

Alexander, Cecil Frances (1818–95) Hymn-writer. Mrs C. F. Alexander, to use the name by which she is almost always known, was born in Dublin Cecil Frances Humphreys, daughter of the land agent to the fourth Earl of Wicklow. She began writing at an early age and was influenced by the Oxford Movement, particularly John Keble, who edited her *Hymns for Little Children*. This collection includes three of the best-known of all children's hymns: 'All things bright and beautiful', 'There is a green hill far away' and 'Once in Royal David's City'. Tennyson said that her poem 'The Burial of Moses' was one of the few poems by a living author which he wished he had written. In 1850 she married the Revd William Alexander, who in 1867 became Bishop of Derry and Raphoe; he was six years younger, which was a matter of concern to her family. She was an indefatigable visitor of the poor and sick, and founded a nursing service.

📖 E. W. Lovell, *A Green Hill Far Away. A Life of Mrs C. F. Alexander*, Dublin: APCK 1970

Alfred the Great (849–99) King of Wessex. Born in Wantage, the youngest of five brothers and with a great interest in learning, he became king at the age of 22 and successfully repelled the Danes from his kingdom. Convinced that the Viking raids were a punishment for sins which arose out of a lack of learning, like Charlemagne he recruited a circle of scholars who translated many Latin Christian works, by Augustine, Bede, Boethius and Gregory the Great, among others, into Old English. This promotion of English was one of the foundations of the Anglo-Saxon Church. The Anglo-Saxon Chronicle dates from his reign. Alfred attempted, vainly, to revive monasticism.

📖 A. P. Smyth, *King Alfred the Great*, Oxford: OUP 1995

Alphonsus Liguori (1696–1787) Moral theologian. Born into an aristocratic family in Naples, he practised law for eight years until the loss of a major financial case led him to resign and become a mission preacher. In 1731 he reorganized a community of nuns in Scala, near Amalfi (later known as Redemptoristines), and the next year founded a religious congregation, the Redemptorists, which gained papal approval in 1749, devoted to pastoral work among the poor in country districts. He became its Superior-

General for life. The women's order was approved in 1750. Alphonsus was reluctantly consecrated bishop in 1762. He wrote many devotional and spiritual works; by the middle of the twentieth century they had gone through thousands of editions and had been translated into 60 languages. He had a simple approach to preaching, and rejected the rigoristic approach to the confessional and penance represented by the Jansenists; he felt that this was counter-productive. In his moral theology he developed a system known as 'equiprobabilism', which involved attempting to keep a balance between severity and laxity. His last years were overshadowed by controversies among the Redemptorists.

📖 F. M. Jones CSSR, *Alphonsus de Liguori: The Saint of Bourbon Naples*, Liguori, MO: Liguori Publications 1992

Ambrose (*c.* 339–97) Bishop of Milan. He was born in Trier, the son of a prefect of Gaul (now Germany). After practising law, in 374 he became governor of Aemilia-Liguria, with his seat in Milan. On the death of the bishop, the laity asked for Ambrose to succeed him, though Ambrose was not even baptized. He was then baptized, ordained and studied theology, becoming a famous preacher and defender of orthodoxy. A vigorous opponent of Arianism, both theologically and politically, he was one of the few Western churchmen to be able to read Greek. He was much concerned with the practical duties of being a bishop, including confrontation with the state (he disciplined the emperor Theodosius). He was also a major influence on Augustine because of the other-worldly, spiritual character of his faith and his defence of the Old Testament against the Manichaeans. His main work was a book on Christian ethics for the clergy, *On the Duties of Ministers*. He is said to have introduced antiphonal singing, and introduced a new form of hymn (of which 'O splendour of God's glory bright' is an example).

📖 F. Homes Dudden, *The Life and Times of St Ambrose*, Oxford: Clarendon Press 1935

Andrew of St Victor (died 1175) Biblical scholar. Of uncertain nationality, he studied at the famous abbey of St Victor in Paris under Hugh, and became a canon. He was then made abbot of a monastery in Hereford, England, but when it proved that he was more a scholar than an administrator he returned to France. However, about six years later he was recalled to Hereford, where he died. Inspired by Hugh and the example of Jerome, he approached scripture critically and literally and not only made use of Jewish sources but discussed biblical interpretation with Jews. His commentaries on the Bible thus differ strikingly from others of the time.

📖 B. Smalley, *The Study of the Bible in the Middle Ages*, Oxford: Blackwell [3]1983

Andrewes, Lancelot (1555–1626) English churchman. Born in what is now East London, he studied and taught at Cambridge, becoming Master of Pembroke Hall. In 1589 he was also made vicar of the London church of St Giles, Cripplegate, where he came to the attention of Elizabeth I. At first he declined bishoprics, and was made Dean of Westminster instead, but he went on to become Bishop of Chichester, Ely and then Winchester. Often involved in politics, he was a leading figure in forming a distinctive Anglican theology, reasonable and catholic, based on sound learning and with a high doctrine of the eucharist. He was most famous as a preacher; he also translated the first part of the Old Testament for the King James (Authorized) Version and wrote a classic set of daily devotions, *Private Prayers*, published posthumously (1648), full of quotations from the Greek fathers, scripture and liturgies.

📖 David Scott (ed), *Lancelot Andrewes*, London: SPCK 2002

Andrews, Charles Freer (1871–1940) Anglican missionary. Born in Newcastle, he studied and taught at Cambridge before joining the Cambridge Brotherhood in Delhi. In 1913 he joined Rabindranath Tagore's Institute in Bengal, of which he became vice-president. He was active in India and a champion of the oppressed. He spent that same year in South Africa helping in the Smuts-Gandhi Agreement, and soon afterwards paid two visits to Fiji with the aim of abolishing indentured Indian labour there. He was subsequently involved in much diplomatic work in this area. He wrote many books, on India and on Christianity; perhaps the best known are *The Renaissance in India* (1914), *Christ and Labour* (1923) and *Christ in the Silence* (1933).

📖 Nicol Macnicol, *C. F. Andrews: Friend of India*, London: James Clarke 1944

Anselm (*c.* 1033–1109) Philosopher and theologian. Son of a landowner in Aosta, Italy, he studied at the abbey of Bec in Normandy, where he became a monk and in due course prior. Later he became Archbishop of Canterbury. He was a pioneer in using linguistic analysis to solve philosophical problems, but his fame rests on his proofs of the existence of God. His arguments can be found in his *Monologion* (Soliloquy, 1078), which seeks to establish the existence of God on the basis of the ideas of truth and goodness, and *Proslogion* (Discourse, with the famous phrase 'faith seeking understanding', 1079), which contains his ontological argument, proof of God's existence from the concept of God (God is that than which nothing greater can be conceived; what exists in reality must be greater than what exists in the mind, therefore God exists). His other great book, *Cur Deus Homo?* (Why the God Man?, 1098), was on the atonement. In contrast to the view held since Origen that Christ died to pay a ransom to the devil, he argued that Christ offered himself willingly as the only one who could satisfy the outrage of sin to God's majesty. However, despite all Anselm's intellectual gifts, it was for his prayers and meditations that he was most known and revered during the Middle Ages. He also wrote many letters.

📖 R. W. Southern, *St Anselm and his Biographer*, Cambridge: CUP 1963

Anthony of Padua (1195–1231) Portuguese hermit. Born in Lisbon, he became a Franciscan and settled in Italy after illness cut short his missionary work in Morocco. He subsequently taught in Italy and France and was a fierce opponent of the Cathars and

Albigensians (he was known as 'Hammer of the Heretics'). He was a particularly famous preacher (later fable has him preaching to the fishes). He became the patron saint of the poor and was invoked for the return of lost property.

📖 E. Gilliat Smith, *Anthony of Padua according to his Contemporaries*, London: Dent and New York: E. P. Dutton 1926

Antony of Egypt (*c.* 251–356) Monk. The pioneer of solitary monasticism, around the age of 20 he gave away his possessions and about fifteen years later retired completely into the Egyptian desert. He was made famous in a *Life* by Athanasius which depicts him as austere, always at prayer, and constantly fighting with demons. He attracted disciples who followed his way of life. He influenced not only them but the supporters of orthodoxy against Arianism at the Council of Nicaea.

📖 Samuel Rubenson, *The Letters of St Antony: Monasticism and the Making of a Saint*, Minneapolis: Fortress Press 1995

Aphraates (Aphrahat, early fourth century) First of the Syrian church fathers. Little is known of his life except that he was an ascetic and held high office. He wrote a collection of *Homilies*, composed on the plan of an acrostic; they provide information about Persian Christianity.

📖 Works in *Nicene and Post-Nicene Fathers*, Peabody, Mass: Hendrickson 1994, Vol. XII

http:/www. ccel.org.fathers

Apollinarius of Laodicea (*c.* 310–90) Christian theologian. Son of a Beirut grammarian, and a friend of Athanasius, whose hostility to Arianism he shared, he became Bishop of Laodicea. He seceded from the church because he could not accept what was to become the orthodox view that Christ had a human spirit. He believed that the only active principle in Christ was the divine Logos, so that Christ had perfect Godhead but was not human as other human beings are. Little of his writings remain since he was condemned as a heretic.

📖 G. L. Prestige, *Fathers and Heretics*, London: SPCK 1940

Apollonius of Tyana (died *c.* 98) Neopythagorean philosopher. Founder of a school in Ephesus, he was said to have been so virtuous that his life was presented as a pagan counterpart to Christ – doing good, performing miracles and suffering trial for his actions. Unlike Christ he was said to have been delivered and to have gone to heaven.

📖 Philostratus, *Life of Apollonius of Tyana* ed G. W. Bowersock, Harmondsworth: Penguin Books 1971

Aristotle (384–322 BCE) Greek philosopher. He was born at Stagira on the Chalcidice peninsula, the son of a court physician. At the age of 17 he went to Athens and spent twenty years at Plato's academy as pupil and teacher. After twelve years away, for three of which he was tutor to Alexander the Great, he returned to Athens to found his own school, the Lyceum, where he taught for twelve years until forced out by hostile sentiment following Alexander's death. Most of his surviving works are lecture notes and memoranda. He created the discipline of logic and was a pioneer in ethics and physics. He differed from his teacher by his stress on empiricism and natural science; rather than beginning with 'ideas', he started from individual objects and reflected on the cause of their existence, which he analysed in some detail; among other things, this analysis led him to postulate a 'first cause', God, the unmoved prime mover. While his thought was by no means unknown during the first Christian millennium, its real impact on Christian theology came in the eleventh and twelfth centuries, when knowledge of his writings spread through Latin versions of Arabic translations of his works and commentaries on them. Initially, with their materialism and description of an eternal universe, these works came as a shock and were either banned or assigned to a separate area from Christianity; there was considerable controversy over this issue at the University of Paris in the thirteenth century. However, they were harmonized with Christian thinking by Albertus Magnus and Thomas Aquinas, leading to scholasticism. It is ultimately from Aristotle that many traditional theological concepts derive, particularly contrasting concepts like substance/accident, genus/species, potency/act, matter/form. The introduction of his thought into theology also underlies contrasts like those between philosophy and theology, faith and reason, and nature and supernature.

📖 J. L. Ackrill, *Aristotle the Philosopher*, Oxford: OUP 1981

Arius (*c.* 250–336) Christian theologian. Probably born in Libya, he was a popular preacher in charge of one of the main churches in Alexandria, Egypt, enjoying a reputation for asceticism. He came under criticism for his view that the Son had a beginning and was subordinate to the Father. There was a long and bitter controversy, in which he was not without his supporters, but as a result of the efforts particularly of Athanasius he was excommunicated. Arianism in its various forms was regarded as the main heresy of the fourth century, and the Council of Nicaea (325) was summoned in order to refute it; after the Council Arius was banished, and eventually died in Constantinople. Nowadays he is being reassessed and from his own perspective has more to be said for him than has been acknowledged in the past.

📖 Rowan Williams, *Arius: Heresy and Tradition*, London: SCM Press 2001 and Grand Rapids, MI: Eerdmans 2002

Arminius, Jacobus (1560–1609) Dutch theologian. Born Jakob Hermandszoon (Arminius is his Latin name) in Oudewater, son of a cutler, he studied at many European centres including Marburg, Geneva and Rome. He returned to Holland, first as a minister and then as professor at Leiden. He challenged Calvinistic views about predestination and later sought to revise the two main Calvinistic confessional documents of the Dutch church; at the same time he was drawn into political disputes. Since he gained many followers (Arminians or Remonstrants, after a Remonstrance, a statement of belief, issued in 1610), he caused a major split in the Reformed Church in Holland. He also had an influence abroad, e.g. on John Wesley.

📖 Carl Bangs, *Arminius: A Study in the Dutch Reformation*, Nashville TN: Abingdon Press 1971

Arndt, Johann (1555–1621) Lutheran mystical theologian. A follower of Melanchthon, after studies at Wittenberg, Strasbourg and Basle he held several pastorates, finally becoming general superintendent of Celle. His main work, *Four Books on True Christianity* (1606–9), which stressed the presence of Christ in the human heart, was a great influence on Pietism. Arndt claimed that orthodox belief was not enough, and that moral purification through righteous living and communion with God was also needed.

📖 *Johann Arndt: True Christianity*, Classics of Western Spirituality, New York and Mahwah, NJ: Paulist Press 1978

Arnold of Brescia (1100–55) Radical reformer. He studied in Paris, probably as a pupil of Abelard. On returning to Italy he attacked the church, arguing that clergy should not possess material goods or have secular authority, and that personal sinfulness in priests affected the validity of the sacraments. He also rejected the secular rule of the pope and took part in a revolutionary commune in Rome. Condemned, along with Abelard, on the instigation of Bernard of Clairvaux, he was excommunicated and eventually executed.

📖 G. W. Greenaway, *Arnold of Brescia*, Cambridge: CUP 1931

Arnold, Matthew (1822–88) English poet and critic. He was the oldest son of Thomas Arnold, the famous educational reformer and headmaster of Rugby School, who transformed the education of the sons of middle-class parents. After studying at Oxford he became a private secretary, government inspector of schools and Oxford Professor of Poetry. In addition to poetry he wrote a series of books which attacked many of the formal religious attitudes of his time and stressed the moral, personal and cultural aspects of Christianity. In addition to his famous *Culture and Anarchy* (1869) these include *St Paul and Protestantism* (1870) and *Literature and Dogma* (1873). He made the famous comment about religion that 'men cannot do without it; they cannot do with it as it is', and his view of Christianity reduced it to a non-dogmatic, non-supernatural faith. He was a major influence on Victorian England.

📖 Park Honan, *Matthew Arnold*, Cambridge, MA: Harvard University Press 1983

Asbury, Francis (1745–1816) Born in Birmingham, England, he went to America following an appeal by John Wesley, stayed through the Revolutionary War and identified himself with the new nation. In 1784 Wesley appointed him and Thomas Coke joint superintendents, and Asbury subsequently took the title of bishop. He was a key figure in shaping American Methodism.

📖 L. C. Rudolf, *Francis Asbury*, Nashville, TN: Abingdon Press 1966

Astruc, Jean (1684–1766) French Roman Catholic physician. The son of a Protestant pastor, converted to Catholicism, he became professor of anatomy at Toulouse, Montpellier and Paris. He is seen as one of the founders of modern biblical criticism, since in his *Conjectures on the Original Memoranda which Moses seems to have used to compose the Book of Genesis* (1753) he argued that Moses made use of earlier documents in writing Genesis, using the divine names Elohim and Jehovah as criteria.

📖 John Barton et al., *The Context and Legacy of Robert Lowth and Jean Astruc*, Oxford: OUP (forthcoming)

Athanasius (*c.*296–373) Theologian and bishop. Probably educated in Alexandria, he became secretary to the bishop there, Alexander, with whom he went to the Council of Nicaea; on Alexander's death he succeeded him as bishop. He was the main opponent of Arius, and because of the latter's popularity was attacked and much exiled. He wrote against paganism *(Contra Gentes)* and the Arians *(Contra Arianos)* and defended the incarnation *(De Incarnatione);* he also wrote a life of Antony. In his theology he stressed the role of the Logos and the *homoousion* (the Son 'of the same substance' as the Father).

📖 T. D. Barnes, *Athanasius and Constantius*, Cambridge, MA: Harvard University Press 1993

Athenagoras I (1886–1972) Ecumenical patriarch of Constantinople. Born Aristokles Spyrou, the son of a physician, he studied at the Theological School on the island of Halki near Constantinople. He rose rapidly in the church, becoming Metropolitan of Corfu in 1922 and Archbishop of the Greek Orthodox Church of North and South America in 1930, reorganizing and uniting the archdiocese and establishing new parishes, schools and a seminary. In 1948 he was appointed Ecumenical Patriarch: he aimed to achieve greater co-operation between the self-governing Orthodox Churches and greater unity in divided Christianity. In 1964, he met with Pope Paul VI in Jerusalem, the first meeting between Eastern and Western leaders since the schism of 1439; he and the Pope agreed to a withdrawal of the reciprocal decrees of excommunication issued at that time.

📖 Demetrios Tsakonas, *A Man Sent By God*, Brookline, MA: Holy Cross Orthodox Press 1977

Augustine of Canterbury (died *c.*604) Missionary. A Roman prior, he was sent by Pope Gregory the Great to refound the English church. In this work he clashed with other existing missions, notably that of the Celtic church, and was unable to reconcile the differences which arose between it and Rome. He became the first Archbishop of Canterbury.

📖 Margaret Deanesly, *Augustine of Canterbury*, London: Nelson 1964

Augustine of Hippo (354–430) Christian theologian. Born of a middle-class family at Tagaste, North Africa, with a pagan father and a Christian mother, Monica, he studied law at Carthage. Reading the Latin author Cicero aroused his interest in philosophy; he was then attracted by dualistic Manichaeanism, and moved to Rome. Here he became disillusioned and left to become professor of rhetoric in Milan. Influenced there by the preaching of Ambrose, he became a Christian: after his famous experience in a garden, where he heard a voice telling him to study the Bible ('Take and read'), he was baptized in 387. Returning to North Africa, he established a kind of monastery, but on a visit to Hippo by popular acclaim he was urged to become priest there; he subsequently became bishop, never to leave Africa again. He was a great controversialist, and it was in controversies that his influential views were expressed. Against the Manichaeans, he stressed that creation was good and that God is its sole creator; against the Donatists, with their stress on the character of the clergy, he argued that the church contains good and evil and that its sacraments cannot be affected by its ministers; against the Pelagians, with their view that human beings can take the first basic steps towards salvation, he stressed his view that original sin arises from the fall, with disastrous consequences which can be countered only by divine grace. His most famous works are his autobiographical *Confessions*, and *The City of God*, prompted by the sack of Rome in 410, which became an account of history in terms of two different 'cities'. In this vast work he contrasts the city of man as the rise and fall of empires with the city of God, made up of those who serve God. Refusing to see the hand of God at work in the history of his time, he argued that God's activity could not readily be identified. He was subsequently immensely influential in the Christian church through his views of the relationship between faith and reason, the love of God and renunciation, grace and free will, the corruption of human nature, the idea of the heart (which is restless until it finds rest in God) and his mediation of Platonism. He is sometimes said to have been the first modern man.

📖 Peter Brown, *Augustine of Hippo. A Biography*, Berkeley, CA: University of California Press and London: Faber 1967; Serge Lancel, *St Augustine*, Notre Dame, IN: University of Notre Dame Press and London: SCM Press 2002

Aulén, Gustaf (1879–1978) Swedish Lutheran theologian. After study at Uppsala, he taught there, and was then made professor at Lund, subsequently becoming Bishop of Strängnäs. His approach was to seek the essential truth behind the form in which a Christian doctrine is expressed. He wrote a much-used textbook, *The Faith of the Christian Church* (1923), but his best-known work is *Christus Victor* (1931), a restatement of the 'classic' view of the atonement as a victory. His theology generally proved to be critical of medieval scholasticism and Lutheran orthodoxy, contrasting them with the early church and Luther himself. He was also a musician and composer.

📖 Gustav Aulén, *Christus Victor*, London: SPCK 1965 and New York: Macmillan 1986

Averroes (Ibn Rushd, 1126–98) Islamic lawyer and philosopher. He was born in Cordova, Spain, and after ranging from medicine and mathematics to law and theology became *cadi* (magistrate) there and in Seville, subsequently being appointed physician to the caliph. He wrote commentaries on Aristotle, whom he understood in Neoplatonic terms, and through them Aristotle's thought entered the medieval Western world. Since these commentaries were not properly understood, even by Albertus Magnus and Roger Bacon (they in fact ruled out providence and personal immortality), they were even accepted as texts in the thirteenth-century University of Paris, where they were particularly championed by Siger of Brabant. Thomas Aquinas was one theologian who wrote against them, attacking what he saw as their view of a 'double truth' (religious and scientific), and eventually they were banned. In the Arab world, Averroes himself had been accused of heresy and exiled, though he was recalled just before his death.

📖 Oliver Leaman, *Averroes and His Philosophy*, Oxford: Clarendon Press 1986

Avicenna (Abu 'Ali al Hosain ibn 'Abdallah ibn Sina, 980–1037) Persian Muslim physician and philosopher. He wrote commentaries on Aristotle in a Neoplatonic vein, and a standard medical textbook (*Canon of Medicine*). Like Averroes after him, he was particularly important in mediating Aristotle to the Middle Ages.

📖 S. M. Afnan, *Avicenna: His Life and Works*, London: Greenwood Press 1980

Aylward, Gladys (1902–70) Missionary to China. A housemaid from North London, with little education, she wanted to go to China as a missionary but was turned down by the missionary societies. She saved her low wages for several years and in 1930 left for China on the Trans-Siberian railway. Despite being detained in Russia because of the Russo-Chinese war she arrived in Shanxi province, where she learned Mandarin and identified herself with the people. She became a Chinese citizen in 1936. She gained the support of the local mandarin, who gave her an official post supervising the welfare of young girls. She attracted children to an inn where she told Bible stories, and later opened an orphanage. On the Japanese invasion of China in 1940 she led 100 children to safety on an amazing journey, which was depicted in the 1959 film *The Inn of the Sixth Happiness* starring Ingrid Bergman. She returned to England during the Second World War and then returned, to Taiwan, where she founded an orphanage at which she worked until her death.

📖 Catherine Swift, *Gladys Aylward*, Minneapolis: Bethany House Publishing 1989 and London: Marshall, Morgan & Scott 1990

Azariah, Vednayakam Samuel (1874–1945) Ecumenical leader. The son of an Anglican minister, he was first involved in the YMCA and indigenous missionary societies. He was ordained priest in 1909 and went to Dornakal, near Madras; as the church there expanded he was consecrated bishop, the first native Indian to hold this office. He became a major Indian church leader and was host of the 1938 World Missionary Conference at Tambaram.

📖 Carol Graham, *Azariah of Dornakal*, London: SCM Press 1946

Bacon, Francis (1561–1626) English philosopher. Of a distinguished family, he studied at Cambridge and then became a lawyer and Member of Parliament, rising to the post of Lord Chancellor under James I, though in 1621 he was charged with corruption and banished from court. The first of the British empiricist philosophers, he believed that it was possible to discover basic principles by arguing from experience. His thinking was particularly forward-looking, as is evident from his frequent use of the word 'new', e.g. *Novum Organum* (1620) and *New Atlantis*, published posthumously in 1660. Seeing knowledge as power, he sought the separation of reason from revelation and was optimistic about the beneficial consequences science would have. He was also a pioneer in drawing attention to psychological motivations for philosophical positions.

📖 J. G. Crowther, *Francis Bacon: The First Statesman of Science*, London: Cresset Press 1960

Bacon, Roger (1214–94) British philosopher and scientist. He was born in Somerset, and studied in Oxford and Paris before returning to England. He then became a Franciscan and returned to Paris, where he was one of the first to lecture on Aristotle. A polymath, he was interested in science (he may well have invented a telescope and gunpowder), and also stressed the importance of knowing Greek and Hebrew in studying the scriptures. However, he did not leave behind any systematic body of thought.

📖 Brian Clegg, *The First Scientist: A Life of Roger Bacon*, London: Constable & Robinson 2003

Balthasar, Hans Urs von (1905–88) Swiss Roman Catholic theologian. Born in Lucerne, he studied in Vienna, Berlin and Zurich, and became a Jesuit; after post-doctoral studies he turned to freelance writing, becoming director of his own publishing house. He wrote an early, sympathetic study of Karl Barth; subsequently his work was influenced by his visionary colleague Adrienne von Speyr. His theology was ascetic, contemplative and eclectic, and deliberately élitist. His major, multi-volume work *The Glory of the Lord* (1961ff., English 1982ff.), which he called a theological aesthetics, brings together philosophy, literature and theology in a study of the beautiful, the good and true; it seeks to show how the biblical vision of divine glory revealed in the crucified and risen Christ fulfils and transcends the perception of Being in Western metaphysics.

📖 Bede McGregor and Thomas Norris (eds), *The Beauty of Christ: An Introduction to the Theology of Hans Urs von Balthasar*, Edinburgh: T&T Clark 1994

Barclay, Robert (1648–90) Scottish theologian and apologist. Born in Scotland, the son of a soldier, and part-educated in Paris as a Roman Catholic, he became a Quaker. He led a much-travelled life, with many ups and downs, ranging from friendship with royalty to imprisonment; in 1683 he was appointed governor of East New Jersey. One of the most substantial of apologists for Quaker principles, he wrote many books, the best-known being his *Apology for the True Christian Divinity. Being an Explanation and Vindication of the People Called Quakers* (1678). This is a classic account defending the doctrine of the 'inner light'.

📖 J. P. Wragge, *The Faith of Robert Barclay*, London: Friends Home Service Committee 1948

Barth, Karl (1886–1968) Swiss Reformed theologian. He was born in Basle and after studying at German universities became assistant pastor in Geneva and then pastor in the Swiss village of Safenwil. There, disillusioned with liberal theology at the outbreak of the First World War, he rediscovered the power of the Bible (commenting repeatedly on its 'strange, new world'; his views of this period are expressed in *The Word of God and the Word of Man*, English 1928), and in due course he wrote a revolutionary commentary on *The Epistle to the Romans* (1918; the second 1921 edition was completely rewritten, English 1933), which brought him widespread attention. His approach at the time was dominated by the idea of the Word of God breaking in vertically from above, making contact without any help from human beings, as a tangent touches a circle. His fame led to an invitation to a special theological chair at Göttingen, from where he moved to Münster, then to Bonn, being dismissed in 1935 for refusing to take an oath of allegiance to Hitler. His theology, termed 'dialectical' because of its characteristics, dominated the inter-war period in Germany, and he was also a leading light in the Confessing Church, playing a major part in the drafting of the famous Barmen Declaration of 1934. Having been forced to return to Switzerland, he became professor in Basle, devoting the rest of his life to writing a multi-volume *Church Dogmatics* (1936ff.), which he never finished. Massively centred on Christ, it represented a systematic account of Christian theology freed from the influence of philosophy and focused on the Bible and the theologians of the early church and the Reformation. Here as in all his later works Barth stressed the 'Godness' of God and the impossibility of human religion attaining to him, though as time went on his views about the role of humanity mellowed. However, 'Barthian' thought has long had a strong negative impact on inter-faith dialogue and on understanding the significance of culture for religious belief.

📖 Eberhard Busch, *Karl Barth*, London: SCM Press and Philadelphia: Fortress Press 1976

Basil of Caesarea ('The Great', *c.*330–79) Church father. He was trained in Athens, taught rhetoric and then became a hermit before being ordained and then consecrated bishop. One of the 'Cappadocian Fathers' (the others were Gregory of Nyssa and Gregory of Nazianzus), he stood up for the doctrine of the Council of Nicaea at a time when the emperor was an Arian. He was particularly important as a church leader, organizing monasteries, and establishing charitable institutions, hospitals and schools. He stressed the deity of the Spirit, which was not sufficiently emphasized at the time; his two main works are *Against Eunomius* and *On the Holy Spirit.*

📖 Philip Rousseau, *Basil of Caesarea*, Berkeley, CA: University of California Press 1994

Basilides (early second century) Gnostic theologian. All that is known of him is that he taught in Alexandria around 132–5 CE. He was very influential, but only fragments of his work survive in quotations from his orthodox critics. He is one of the earliest known authors of a biblical commentary. He adapted Christian ethics to Stoic categories and wrote poetry and songs; he also produced his own Gospel.

📖 Christoph Markschies, *Gnosis*, London: T&T Clark 2003

Baur, Ferdinand Christian (1792–1860) German church historian and dogmatician. Born in Württemberg, he studied at Tübingen, where he spent most of his teaching life. He is widely seen as one of the first to apply the historical method consistently to Christian theology. Thus in *Paul, The Apostle of Jesus Christ* (English 1873–5), he denied the authenticity of many Pauline letters and argued that in the early church there was opposition between Peter and Paul and that the Acts of the Apostles glosses over the split; he also stressed the historical value of the Synoptic Gospels as over against the then preferred Gospel of John. However, his views were dominated by the philosophy of Hegel, which led him to interpret his findings regularly in terms of a pattern of thesis-antithesis-synthesis. His major works include a five-volume *History of the Christian Church* (1852ff.) and a four-volume *Lectures on the History of Christian Dogma* (1865–7).

📖 Peter C. Hodgson, *The Formation of Historical Theology. A Study of Ferdinand Christian Baur*, New York: Harper & Row 1966

Baxter, Richard (1615–91) English Puritan divine. He was born in Shropshire and was self-educated. Acquaintance with Nonconformists aroused his sympathy for dissent, but he remained in the Church of England working as a curate in Kidderminster. He served as a Parliamentarian chaplain in the Civil War and worked for the return of King Charles II, but his objections to episcopacy led to his being debarred from holding church office and later suffering persecution. His many writings show his liberal and catholic sympathies, and his personal generosity and tolerance are evident in his two best-known books, *The Saints' Everlasting Rest* (1650) and *The Reformed Pastor* (1656).

📖 G. F. Nuttall, *Richard Baxter*, London: Nelson 1965

Beatrice of Nazareth (*c.*1200–68) Spiritual writer. Born into a wealthy family living near Brussels, at an early age she was sent to a Beguine community to be educated, following the death of her mother. From there she went on to a Cistercian convent at Bloemendaal, founded by her father. She joined the community and later became prioress of another house, at Notre-Dame-de-Nazareth near Antwerp, hence the name by which she is known. She remained there until her death. Around the age of 17 she had a mystical experience, and such experiences continued throughout her life. For twenty years she kept a journal, which is now lost; however, it was used by an anonymous priest who wrote her biography. She also wrote on 'Seven Manners of Love', developing the thought of Bernard of Clairvaux, and this has survived. These works provide important insights into the spirituality of the time.

📖 Roger de Ganck, *The Life of Beatrice of Nazareth*, Kalamazoo, MI: Cistercian Publications 1991

Bede, The Venerable (*c.*673–735) English monk, theologian and historian. He was born in Northumbria, sent to the monastery at Wearmouth and then to Jarrow, where he spent the rest of his life. His writings on chronology (related to the calculation of Easter) and history were instrumental in introducing the practice of dating events from the birth of Jesus. His *Ecclesiastical History of the English People* (731), the best-known of his works, is important for its identification of source material and its attempt to distinguish historical information from tradition and legend. He also wrote a scientific work *On the Nature of Things* (*c.*725) and a number of biblical commentaries.

📖 Benedicta Ward, *The Venerable Bede*, London: Continuum 1990

Bell, George Kennedy Allen (1881–1958) Anglican bishop and ecumenist. From a clergy family, he studied at Oxford and, after ordination and parish work, taught there. He became secretary to the Archbishop of Canterbury, and was involved in the 1920 Lambeth conference. In 1924 he became Dean of Canterbury and in 1929 Bishop of Chichester. Further international involvement in Life and Work, and later in the World Council of Churches, gave his life an ecumenical dimension. He was one of the first to recognize the threat of Nazism through his friendship with Dietrich Bonhoeffer and was hostile to Allied policies of unconditional surrender and saturation bombing during the Second World War.

📖 R. C. D. Jasper, *George Bell, Bishop of Chichester*, London: OUP 1967

Benedict of Nursia (*c.*480–547) Italian monk. Little is known of his life. After living as a hermit and establishing a number of monasteries, he eventually founded his best-known community on Monte Cassino, south of Rome, the beginning of the Benedictine order. Its basis was his famous Rule, which proved an important force by providing a disciplined focus for Christian life and thought throughout Europe. He is often called the father of Western monasticism, and became the patron saint of Europe.

📖 Patrick O'Donovan, *Benedict of Nursia*, London: Collins 1980

Berdyaev, Nicolai Aleksandrovich (1874–1948) Russian religious philosopher. Born in Kiev and educated in Moscow, he was originally a sceptic but joined the Orthodox Church after the 1905 Revolution. He later established a philosophical school in Berlin and then from 1922 lived in Paris. His theology is an ethical type of Christian existentialism which also affirms the primacy of a transcendental world of spirit, known by a near-mystical act of intuition, over the mere world of things. This does away with the need for formal worship, and doctrinal and moral definitions. Two important works are *The Destiny of Man* (1937) and his autobiography *Dream and Reality* (1951).

📖 Oliver Fielding Clarke, *Introduction to Berdyaev*, London: Geoffrey Bles 1950

Berkeley, George (1685–1753) Irish philosopher. He was educated at Trinity College, Dublin, where he then taught, becoming Dean of Derry and later Bishop of Cloyne; he also travelled abroad. He is particularly known for his 'immaterialism'. He argued that material objects do not exist unless someone perceives them, and since no one doubts that objects exist when we do not perceive them, there must be another mind aware of them – God. Only spirits have a primary existence. His best-known book is *Principles of Human Knowledge* (1710).

📖 K. P. Winkler, *Berkeley: An Interpretation*, Oxford: Clarendon Press 1989

Bernard of Clairvaux (1090–1153) Cistercian abbot. Born of noble parents near Dijon, he entered the monastery of Cîteaux, but three years later was asked by the abbot to establish a new monastery. His choice, Clairvaux, became one of the main Cistercian centres and Bernard as abbot was a very powerful man in church politics. He was bitterly hostile to the 'heretics' in Languedoc and supported the Second Crusade. However, he was above all an austere and saintly monk and is sometimes called the 'last of the fathers', since he stood at the end of a long tradition in seeing reason and faith as belonging closely together in the love of God. This made him an opponent of Abelard, whom he condemned. He wrote many books on spirituality, the best known of which is *On Loving God*.

📖 G. R. Evans, *Bernard of Clairvaux*, Oxford and New York: OUP 2000

Bérulle, Pierre de (1575–1629) French cardinal and reformer. Born in Champagne, after ordination he became a spiritual director. He was also a skilled diplomat. In 1611 he founded the French Oratory on the model of the Oratory of Philip Neri, and its members played a major role in reforming the French clergy. This trend became known as the French school of spirituality.

📖 W. M. Thompson (ed), *Bérulle and the French School. Selected Writings*, Classics of Western Spirituality, New York and Mahwah, NJ: Paulist Press 1989

Blake, William (1757–1827) English visionary poet. He lived in London, and when apprenticed to an engraver, spent much time in Westminster Abbey, falling under the influence of its Gothic style. Most of his poetry was engraved by hand and illustrated by coloured drawings. His best-known works are his collections of poems: *Songs of Innocence* (1789), *Songs of Experience* (1794) and *Jerusalem* (1818), and his set of engravings, *Illustrations of the Book* of *Job* (1825). Stressing the reality of the spiritual world, and using imagination to the full, his work made a deep impression precisely because of the religious depths of its art, which is not limited to any particular category.

📖 Peter Ackroyd, *Blake*, London: Minerva and New York: Knopf 1996

Blumhardt, Johann Christoph (1805–80) Protestant pietist. He was born in Stuttgart and studied in Tübingen, after which he worked with the Basle Mission, founded by his uncle. In 1838 he became pastor of Mottlingen, which experienced a revival accompanied by healings. This led him to resign and open up a healing centre at Bad Boll, which attracted much attention. His motto was 'Jesus is victor!'

📖 Vernard Eller (ed), *A Blumhardt Reader*, Grand Rapids, MI: Eerdmans 1980

Boehme, Jakob (1575–1624) German mystic. The son of a farmer, he became a shoemaker. He had mystical experiences on the basis of which he wrote obscure but significant works, much influenced by Paracelsus and drawing on Neoplatonism and the Jewish Kabbalah. He saw God as the primal abyss containing the possibilities of both good and evil. His works were banned in his lifetime, and became underground literature; he proved to be an influence on the Quakers, the Romantics and the Idealists.

📖 P. Erb (ed), *Jacob Boehme*, Classics of Western Spirituality, New York and Mahwah, NJ: Paulist Press 1978

Boethius, Anicius Manlius Severinus (*c.*480–*c.*524) Christian philosopher and statesman. He was brought up in a senatorial household in Rome, and then educated in Athens and became a consul and adviser to King Theodoric. He was imprisoned in Italy as a result of court intrigues, where he wrote his most famous book, *The Consolation of Philosophy*, to show how philosophy can lead the soul to a vision of God. Although not specifically Christian, it was extremely popular and was translated into English by, amongst others, King Alfred, Chaucer and Queen Elizabeth I. He himself translated two works of Aristotle, including his *Categories*, into Latin, and wrote commentaries on several others, thus preserving them through the Dark Ages. He was ultimately executed. He is a transitional figure between the ancient and modern worlds and laid the foundations for the later study of theology.

📖 Margaret Gibson (ed), *Boethius: His Life, Thought and Influence*, Oxford: Blackwell 1981

Boff, Leonardo (1938–) Brazilian Franciscan theologian. After studying under Karl Rahner in Germany, he became professor of theology in Petropolis, Brazil, and adviser to the Brazilian Conference of Bishops. His liberation theology gained prominence when as a result of his *Church: Charism and Power* (1981) he was summoned to Rome for censure, but accompanied by his bishops for support. Opposed to a hierarchical church, he stresses the church as the community of the people of God, especially for the dispossessed.

📖 Leonardo Boff, *The Path to Hope: Fragments from a Theologian's Journey*, Maryknoll, NY: Orbis Books 1993

Bonaventure (*c.*1217–74) Scholastic theologian and mystic. Born Giovanni di Fidanza, in Italy, he was educated in Paris and then became a Franciscan. He wrote a commentary on the *Sentences* of Peter Lombard. He later became minister-general of the order and played a major part in settling internal disputes. Subsequently he was made Cardinal Archbishop of Albano. Basically a conservative, in his theology he subordinated knowledge to faith; he believed that all human wisdom was folly compared to mystical illumination from God. His mystical account of the soul's journey to God *(Itineranum Mentis in Deum)* was particularly influential. He is known in the Roman Catholic church as the 'seraphic doctor'.

📖 Zachary Hastings (ed), *Bonaventure: Mystical Writings*, New York: Crossroad 1999

Bonhoeffer, Dietrich (1906–45) German Protestant theologian. Son of a Berlin professor of psychiatry, he studied in Tübingen and Berlin and then went to Barcelona and New York before returning to Berlin as lecturer and chaplain. Opposed to Nazism from the start, he became a leading member of the Confessing Church. When the preachers' seminary of which he was head was shut down, he joined the political resistance against Hitler, was imprisoned and ultimately executed. His main books reflect his life's work: *The Cost of Discipleship* (1937, English 1959) the demands on a Christian in an oppressive political situation; *Life Together* (1938, English 1954) life in the seminary; *Ethics* (1949, English 1955) the moral problems for Christians in the modern world. His posthumous *Letters and Papers from Prison* (English 1953, second edition 1971), smuggled out, are not only a moving human document but also contain pioneering radical thought, expressed in terms of the 'world come of age', 'religionless Christianity' and Jesus as 'the man for others'. It was widely discussed in the religious controversies of the 1960s.

📖 E. Bethge, *Dietrich Bonhoeffer: Theologian, Christian, Contemporary*, London: Collins and New York: Harper & Row 1970

Booth, William (1829–1912) English evangelist. Born in Nottingham, he was at first apprenticed to a pawnbroker. He was converted to Methodism but resigned because of its restrictions, becoming a free-lance evangelist in London's East End. He was fond of using military terminology, and the organization which was eventually founded in 1878 under his leadership, the Salvation Army, was run on military lines. It began to engage in social work from 1887, following a programme laid out in his *Darkest England – and the Way Out* (1890).

📖 Richard Collier, *The General Next to God: The Story of William Booth and the Salvation Army*, London: Collins Fontana 1968

Borromeo, Charles (1538–84) Catholic reformer. Of noble family, he was born by Lake Maggiore in Italy and given his first ecclesiastical appointment at the age of 12. After studying law at Pavia, at the age of 22 he was made cardinal and Archbishop of Milan. He was involved in the last stages of the Council of Trent and worked to implement its reforms, creating a model seminary, encouraging the religious orders, visiting widely, preaching and helping the poor.

📖 Margaret Yeo, *Reformer: Saint Charles Borromeo*, Milwaukeee: Bruce 1938

Bosco, John (1815–88) Educational pioneer. Born to a peasant family near Turin, following a vision he helped poor boys looking for work in the city. He provided education and encouragement, using minimum discipline and showing kindness and love. His activities led to the foundation of night schools and eventually technical schools and a church in Turin. In 1859 he founded the Society of St Francis of Sales (the Salesians) which spread round the world. He also had a deep concern for mission abroad.

📖 Lancelot C. Sheppard, *Don Bosco*, London: Burns & Oates 1957

Bossuet, Jacques-Bénigne (1627–1704) French Catholic preacher. Son of a judge in Dijon and an infant prodigy, he went to a Jesuit school and trained for the ministry in Paris, to which he returned after a period in Metz. He became Bishop, first of Condom and then of Meaux, and was also a tutor to the Dauphin. A precocious sermon preached when he was 16 revealed his most outstanding gift. He was also a skilled apologist, arguing for what was best in the religion of his time, and seeking to commend Catholicism to those who differed from it. His *Discourse on Universal History* (1681) was a classic account of the workings of providence and his *Meditations on the Gospel*, which appeared after his death, became a French devotional classic.

📖 W. J. Sparrow-Simpson, *A Study of Bossuet*, London: SPCK 1937

Bridget of Sweden (*c.* 1303–73) Religious, also known as Birgitta. Daughter of a wealthy provincial governor, she married and had eight children. She and her husband made a pilgrimage to Santiago de Compostela, but the next year he died and she embarked on a life of penance and prayer. Visions which she had had from early childhood became more frequent and as a result of them she urged the Pope to return from 'exile' in Avignon and condemned the moral decay in the church. As a result of these visions she also founded a religious order, the Brigittines, which lasted until the Reformation. In 1350 she went to live in Rome, where she spent the rest of her life, apart from a pilgrimage to the Holy Land, campaigning for reform.

📖 Helen Redpath, *God's Ambassadress – St Bridget of Sweden*, Milwaukeee: Bruce 1948

Brooks, Phillips (1835–93) Preacher and hymn-writer. Born in Boston, he went to Harvard and in 1859 was ordained into the Protestant Episcopal Church. After being rector of major churches in Philadelphia and Boston, he became Bishop of Massachusetts in 1869. He was influenced by the views of F. D. Maurice, and was known for his support in freeing slaves and allowing them the vote; he has been called the greatest American preacher of the nineteenth century. However, he is best known as the author of one of the most familiar Christmas carols, 'O little town of Bethlehem'.

📖 R. W. Albright, *Focus on Infinity: A Life of Phillips Brooks*, New York: Macmillan 1961

Browne, Robert (*c.* 1550–1633) English Puritan. He was born in Rutland and studied in Cambridge, where he came under Presbyterian influence. As a result he organized independent churches in East Anglia, was imprisoned, and then emigrated to Holland. After disputes there, he returned via Scotland to England and was formally reconciled with the Church of England, being ordained and given a parish in Northamptonshire. He died in prison after being arrested for attacking a policeman. He was an influence on the first Congregationalists (known as 'Brownists'). He believed that the civil powers had no spiritual jurisdiction over the church and that church membership was contractual rather than residential.

📖 C. Burrage, *The True Story of Robert Browne*, Oxford 1906.

Brunner, Heinrich Emil (1889–1966) Swiss Protestant theologian. Born in Winterthur, he was a pastor before becoming professor of theology in Zurich in 1922; on his retirement in 1953 he taught for three years at the International Christian University in Tokyo. Though often paired with Karl Barth because of his opposition to liberalism and his acceptance of dialectical theology and stress on the priority of revelation, Brunner's thought was independent; he was more influenced by Kierkegaard, by the Jewish philosopher Martin Buber, and by Christian Socialism. He parted company with Karl Barth in accepting the possibility of the revelation of God in history and the principle of analogy as a basis for knowledge of God. For him, there was a point of contact between the gospel and non-Christians. Of his many books, *The Mediator* (1927, English 1934) and *The Divine Imperative* (1932) are perhaps the best known.

📖 C. W. Kegley (ed), *The Theology of Emil Brunner*, New York: Macmillan 1962

Bruno, Giordano (1548–1600) Italian Renaissance philosopher. He became a Dominican in Naples in 1562, but was censured for unorthodoxy and had to flee, thenceforward leading an itinerant life until he was captured in Venice in 1592, imprisoned in Rome, and burnt as a heretic. He was a champion of Copernicus' new astronomy, but coupled this with a form of pantheism, an approach which led to his condemnation.

📖 D. W. Singer, *Giordano Bruno. His Life and Thought*, New York: Henry Schuman 1950

Bucer, Martin (1491–1551) German Reformer. Born in Alsace, he became a Dominican in 1506 but in 1518 came to know Martin Luther and three years later got a dispensation from his monastic vows, marrying the next year (one of the first German Reformers to do so). He was excommunicated for preaching reform and became leader of the Reformation in Strasbourg, where he had a formative influence on John Calvin. He remained there for more than twenty years, but problems in the city meant he was more effective outside it. Because of his skill in statesmanship he was involved in diplomacy all over Europe, and was also instrumental in providing constitutions for many Reformed churches. He tried to overcome the division between Luther and Huldrych Zwingli over eucharistic doctrine, but was less than successful. His opposition to the Augsburg interim settlement with the Catholics in Germany led to exile in 1548 and at Thomas Cranmer's invitation he went to England, where he became professor in Cambridge and influenced the production of the 1549 Book of Common Prayer. He was also the author of many biblical commentaries.

📖 D. F. Wright, *Martin Bucer: Reforming Church and Community*, Cambridge: CUP 1994

Bulgakov, Sergei (1871–1944) Russian religious philosopher. The son of a Russian priest; as a result of his acquaintance with Hegel's philosophy he became a sceptic. However, disillusioned with the 1905 Revolution he began to return to the church. He was expelled from Russia in 1922, after which he taught at the Orthodox Theological Seminary, which he helped to found and of which he became dean. His theology focused on divine wisdom or Sophia; this wisdom was the mediator between God and the world. His main works are *The Orthodox Church* (1935), *The Wisdom of God* (1937) and *The Bride of the Lamb* (1984).

📖 Sergei Bulgakov, *The Bride of the Lamb*, Grand Rapids, MI: Eerdmans 2001

Bullinger, Johann Heinrich (1504–75) Swiss Reformer. He was attracted to the Reformation after reading the works of Martin Luther and Philipp Melanchthon, and hearing Zwingli preach, and became chief pastor in Zurich after Zwingli. He played a part in the composition of the First and Second Helvetic Confessions and wrote much theology of a mediating kind. He had a particular interest in England and provided theological support for English monarchs.

📖 Bruce Gordon and Emidio Campi (eds), *Heinrich Bullinger and the Formation of the Reformed Faith*, Grand Rapids, MI: Baker Academic 2004

Bultmann, Rudolf (1884–1976) German New Testament scholar. Born in Oldenburg, after studying in Marburg, Tübingen and Berlin he spent most of his life as professor at Marburg. He was deeply involved in historical research along the lines of the

history-of-religions school and a pioneer of form criticism, analysing the pre-literary units of which the Synoptic Gospels are made up (*The History of the Synoptic Tradition*, 1921, English 1963), and wrote a classic *Theology of the New Testament* (1948–53, English 1952, 1955). He was associated with the dialectical theology of Karl Barth, but parted company with Barth when he saw Martin Heidegger's existentialist philosophy as crucial to interpreting the New Testament. In an attempt to help German army chaplains in their work he was led by this to propose the 'demythologization' of the New Testament, i.e. the reinterpretation of its mythology in terms of existentialist conceptuality (*Jesus Christ and Mythology*, 1958, English 1960).

📖 E. J. Tinsley, *Rudolf Bultmann*, London: Epworth Press 1973

Bunyan, John (1628–88) English Baptist minister. Brought up to be a tinker, after army service he joined a Baptist church in Bedford. He was imprisoned for twelve years after 1660 for belonging to what was then an illegal organization, and wrote a great deal in prison. Though his early spiritual autobiography *Grace abounding to the Chief of Sinners* (1666) aroused much attention, he is best known as author of *The Pilgrim's Progress* (1682).

📖 Gordon Wakefield, *John Bunyan the Christian*, London: Collins Fount 1992

Bushnell, Horace (1802–76) American Congregationalist theologian. Born in Connecticut, he graduated at Yale and after teaching and journalistic work returned there to study law. However, a revival renewed his faith and he became a pastor in Hartford, Connecticut, where he had a long ministry. His first book, *Christian Nurture* (1847), was opposed to the Puritan tradition and its new expression in revivalism, and with its stress on infant baptism and the family went back to an earlier tradition, looking to an audience on which revivalism made no mark. *God in Christ* (1849), on the social nature of language, atonement and the divinity of Christ, stands at the heart of his theology. The titles given him, the 'American Schleiermacher' and 'father of American religious liberalism', are not inappropriate. However, his thought always maintained a tension between the liberal and the conservative, which is particularly evident in his *Nature and the Supernatural* (1858).

📖 Barbara M. Cross, *Horace Bushnell: Minister to a Changing America*, Chicago: University of Chicago Press 1958

Butler, Joseph (1659–1752) Christian apologist. Born in Wantage, Berkshire, of Presbyterian parents, he abandoned his parents' beliefs and after study at Oxford became an Anglican priest. Having attracted attention for his brilliant preaching, he was marked out for preferment and eventually became Bishop of Bristol, then of Durham. He is particularly known for his *Analogy* of *Religion* (1736), a refutation of deism and a defence of natural theology. It was one of the most influential books of his time, arguing that probability must be the guide to understanding, and points to the existence of God.

📖 W. A. Spooner, *Bishop Butler*, London: Methuen 1901

Butler, Josephine Elizabeth (1828–1906) Social reformer. Born in Northumberland Josephine Grey, the extremely beautiful daughter of a wealthy landowner who was a strong advocate of social reform, she grew up to share her father's principles. In 1852 she married an Anglican clergyman, George Butler, who was a schools' examiner. In 1863 her only daughter was killed, and to cope with her grief, Josephine became involved in charity work. In 1867 the Butlers settled in Liverpool and she worked tirelessly to rescue women from violence and prostitution. In 1869 she formed the Ladies' National Association for the Repeal of the Contagious Diseases Acts and was instrumental in the founding of the International Federation for the Abolition of the State Regulation of Vice. She also fought against child prostitution and her campaign led parliament to raise the age of consent from 13 to 16. In 1896 she wrote her *Personal Reminiscences of a Great Crusade*. In her latter years she supported the suffragettes, though she was too old to join in their activities.

📖 Joseph Williamson, *Josephine Butler – the Forgotten Saint*, Leighton Buzzard: Faith Press 1977

Cajetan, Thomas de Vio (1469–1534) Born in Gaeta (hence his name, 'Gaetano'), he became a Dominican and taught in Padua, Pavia and Rome, becoming general of his order and later cardinal and Bishop of Gaeta. He came to be involved in controversy, opposing Luther and being against the planned divorce of Henry VIII of England. He wrote an important, if conservative, commentary on the *Summa Theologiae* of Thomas Aquinas and a number of works of scriptural exegesis.

Calvin, John (1509–64) French Reformer. He was born in Noyon, Picardy, second of five sons of a public notary in the service of the bishop. His father, who had secured two ecclesiastical positions for him, was prompted to send him to study theology in Paris, but on breaking with the bishop, ordered him to Orleans to study law. Calvin returned to Paris on his father's death, a young humanist scholar. Later he was converted to Protestantism, becoming active in the Reformation movement. In 1533, anti-Protestant feeling forced him to leave to avoid arrest, and he spent the next years travelling. However, this did not prevent him from writing in Latin a brief defence of Protestantism, entitled *Institution of the Christian Religion* (1536), which achieved considerable popularity. On his way to Strasbourg, where he could expect peace for study and writing, he stopped in Geneva and was invited to stay there to help to reform the church. So strict was his disciplinary approach, however, that he was exiled. Calvin was then invited to Strasbourg, where he became pastor to the French refugee congregation and married. He also wrote a commentary on Paul's letter to the Romans, drew up a form of worship and a metrical psalter, and laid the foundations for his later reputation. In 1541 he was urged back to Geneva, where he became the dominant figure. His aim to make it a holy city again caused conflict and indeed riots; Calvin even supervised the burning at the stake of Servetus, a physician who attacked the doctrine of the Trinity. Calvin's Reformation, and the strategic geographical position of Geneva, made the city a focal point for Reformed Christianity, and both Calvin and Geneva gained an international reputation. His 1536 Latin *Institution* was five times revised and rewritten in French as the *Institutes of the Christian Religion* (definitive edition 1559); as well as becoming a basic theological handbook for Protestants, it influenced the development of the French language. Calvin also wrote commentaries on most of the books of the Bible. His biblical theology, much influenced by Augustine, with its famous focus on predestination, left a lasting mark on Europe.

📖 T. H. L. Parker, *John Calvin*, Berkhamsted: Lion 1977

Camara, Helder (1909–99) Brazilian Roman Catholic archbishop. He was born in Fortaleza, Camara and in 1964 became Archbishop of Olinda and Reçife in North-East Brazil, the poorest region of the country. Though mention of his name was banned in the media, he became an international figure through his championship of the poor and of non-violent social change, inspired by Martin Luther King and Mahatma Gandhi. He became well known through his spiritual writings including *Church and Colonialism* (1969), *Spiral of Violence* (1971) and *The Desert is Fertile* (1976).

📖 José de Broucker, *The Conversions of a Bishop*, London: Collins 1979

Campbell, Alexander (1788–1866) Founder of the Disciples of Christ. Son of a Scottish Presbyterian, he emigrated to the United States. First becoming a Baptist, because of differences in belief he subsequently founded his own Disciples of Christ with a strong emphasis on the rejection of creeds and the expectation of an imminent second coming of Christ.

📖 D. R. Lindley, *Apostle of Freedom*, St Louis: Bethany Press 1957

Carey, William (1761–1834) Baptist missionary. Born in Northamptonshire and baptized an Anglican, he became a Baptist, preaching and teaching, while earning his living as a shoemaker, and learning foreign languages. He became a missionary and translated the New Testament into Bengali. In due course he was made professor in Calcutta and distinguished himself by producing many other translations, dictionaries and grammars. He also contributed, through his protests, to the abolition of suttee, the burning of widows alive on the deaths of their husbands.

📖 Mary Drewery, *William Carey: Shoemaker and Missionary*, London: Hodder & Stoughton and Grand Rapids, MI: Zondervan 1978:

Carroll, John (1735–1815) First Roman Catholic bishop in America. Born in Maryland, he was educated in Jesuit schools in

France, became a Jesuit, was ordained priest in 1769 and taught philosophy and theology in St Omer and Liège. When the Jesuits were dissolved he returned to America and became a leading Catholic there. In 1789 he was consecrated Bishop of Baltimore, a diocese which at that time covered the entire United States. In 1806 he laid the cornerstone of Baltimore cathedral and in 1808 he was made archbishop and the diocese was divided into four. During his time the Roman Catholic population of the US grew from 25,000 to 200,000.

📖 Annabelle M. Melville, *John Carroll of Baltimore*, New York: Scribner 1955

Cartwright, Thomas (1535–1603) English Puritan divine. After studying at Cambridge, he had to leave when Queen Mary came to the throne and did not return until after her death, eventually becoming professor there. His criticism of the Church of England led to his dismissal, and he left for Switzerland. From then on he was a vigorous supporter of Presbyterianism and Puritan values. He was one of the most gifted of the Puritans.

📖 William Haller, *The Rise of Puritanism*, New York: Columbia University Press 1957

Catherine of Genoa (1447–1510) Spiritual teacher. Born Caterinetta Fieschi of a noble Ligurian family, she was married at 16 for diplomatic reasons and after ten miserable years had a deep religious conversion; her husband, having fallen on hard times, was also converted and helped her in caring for the sick in a Genoa hospital until his death in 1497. Details of her teaching and spiritual life come from an anonymous compilation, *Life and Teaching*, published posthumously in 1551. Her teaching here focuses on purgatory as the continuation of a process of suffering which is necessary for souls seeking God, but this is a suffering which must inevitably end in perfect joy.

📖 *Catherine of Genoa*, Classics of Western Spirituality, New York and Mahwah, New Jersey: Paulist Press 1979

Catherine of Siena (*c.*1347–80) Italian mystic. Born Caterina Benincasa, one of the large family of a dyer, she became a Dominican lay sister, and after three years of seclusion began to work in public, forming a family of disciples around her. A long series of letters involved her in public affairs, notably contemporary conflicts surrounding the papacy, which was about to be involved in schism. This prompted a great concern for church reform.

📖 Guiliana Cavallini, *Catherine of Siena*, London: Geoffrey Chapman 1998

Caussade, Jean-Pierre de (1675–1751) Spiritual writer. He became a Jesuit in Toulouse at the age of 18, and was active throughout his life as a teacher and confessor in south-west France. He was important for rehabilitating mysticism at a time when it was under a shadow. He is known for a collection of notes from lectures not published until the nineteenth century, when along with some of his letters, they became a spiritual classic, *Self-Abandonment to Divine Providence*. His main emphasis was that every situation should be seen as God's purpose for the person concerned.

📖 Jean-Pierre de Caussade, *Self-Abandonment to Divine Providence*, London: Collins Fontana 1971

Celsus (second century) Pagan philosopher. He was author of the first known critique of Christianity, entitled *The True Doctrine*, criticizing miracles and absurdities; he was particularly offended at the incarnation and crucifixion. His work is known to us only through its refutation by Origen (*Contra Celsum*).

📖 Henry Chadwick (ed), *Origen Contra Celsum*, Cambridge: CUP ²1965

Charlemagne (*c.*742–814) Emperor. As King of the Franks he brought almost all the lands of Western Europe together in one state, and in 800 was crowned Holy Roman Emperor by Pope Leo III. In the Middle Ages he was regarded as the model Christian ruler. He is particularly important for Christianity because of his ambition also to make his court at Aachen, in what is now Germany, a centre of intellectual excellence. He summoned the best minds in the church, notably Alcuin of York and Einhard (*c.*770–840), who was to be his brilliant biographer and established the Palace School in Aachen. What is known as the Carolingian renaissance, which ensued, re-established Western culture. He was also interested and active in liturgy, canon law and theology.

📖 Matthias Becher, *Charlemagne*, New Haven: Yale University Press 2003

Claudel, Paul (1868–1955) French Catholic poet. Born into a French provincial family, he was converted to Christianity in Notre-Dame, Paris, in 1886. In 1893 he joined the diplomatic service, holding posts in the Far East, Europe and South America. He became ambassador in Tokyo in 1921, Washington in 1927 and finally Brussels (1933–6). He is known for his plays, the main theme of which is the rededication of the world to God in Christ. Most famous of them is *Le soulier de satin* (*The Silk Slipper*, 1929). He also wrote poems, prose and biblical commentaries.

📖 Richard Griffiths (ed), *Claudel: A Reappraisal*, London: Rapp & Whiting 1968

Clement of Alexandria (*c.*150–*c.*215) Christian scholar. Probably born in Athens, he became head of the famous catechetical school in Alexandria, but had to flee in the face of persecution. His trilogy, *Stromateis*, *Protrepticus* and *Paedagogus* ('Carpets', 'Exhortation' and 'The Tutor'), influenced by Gnosticism, attempted to bring Greek culture into a fruitful relationship with the truth of the faith of his time, in a concern to win over the educated classes.

📖 H. Chadwick, *Early Christian Thought and the Classical Tradition: Studies in Justin, Clement, and Origen*, Oxford: OUP 1966

Clovis (*c.*466–511) King of the Franks. Born a pagan, in 492 he married Clotilde, a Christian princess, and according to tradition was baptized in Reims on Christmas Day 496, following an unexpected victory in battle which he attributed to Christ. He expanded his kingdom by victories over the Arian Visigoths, and laid the foundations for modern France, making Paris his capital. His baptism is regarded as a major landmark in French history. His Merovingian dynasty lasted for 200 years until the rise of the Carolingian dynasty, of which Charlemagne is the most famous representative.

📖 J. M. Wallace-Hadrill, *Long-Haired Kings and Other Studies in Frankish History*, Toronto: University of Toronto Press 1982

Coke, Thomas (1747–1814) Methodist bishop. Originally an Anglican, born in Wales, he joined John Wesley, becoming his right-hand man. He was chosen by Wesley as superintendent for America and was made the first American Methodist bishop. He was vigorously opposed to slavery and was responsible for missionary work in the West Indies and Africa.

📖 John Vickers, *Thomas Coke: Apostle of Methodism*, London: Epworth Press 1969

Colenso, John William (1814–83) Missionary bishop. Born in Cornwall, he studied in Cambridge and after teaching mathematics at Harrow school, returned to Cambridge to teach and then became vicar of a Norfolk parish. In 1853 he was made missionary bishop of Natal, as a result of which he was forced to consider problems of biblical criticism. His *The Pentateuch and Book of Joshua Critically Examined* (1862–79), which brought out the absurdities of these books if taken literally, led to his excommunication. He also denied eternal punishment in hell.

📖 Peter Hinchliff, *John William Colenso*, London: Nelson 1964

Coleridge, Samuel Taylor (1772–1834) English romantic poet. Born in Devon, the son of a vicar, he studied in Cambridge and came into contact with the Wordsworths. A brilliant lecturer, he had to earn his living by public speaking; he had an unhappy life, complicated by painful rheumatism and an addiction to opium. As well as being a poet he had a philosophical interest, influenced by Immanuel Kant; he was the originator of the term 'existentialist'. Open-minded in religious matters, he helped to introduce German biblical criticism to England. He was profoundly original in his views, expressing a subjective religion based on moral experience. His best known book in this area is the posthumous *Confessions of an Inquiring Spirit* (1840).

📖 Richard Holmes, *Coleridge: Early Visions; Coleridge: Darker Reflections* (2 vols), London: Hodder & Stoughton 1989 and Flamingo 1998

John Colet (*c.* 1466–1519) Churchman and humanist. He was born in London, of which his father was twice Lord Mayor. After studying at Oxford, he travelled to Europe, where among other prominent figures he met Erasmus. After three years he returned to Oxford, was ordained priest and taught there, lecturing on the letters of St Paul. In 1505 he became Dean of St Paul's Cathedral, London, continuing to lecture on the Bible three times a week. He was also chaplain to Henry VIII and spiritual adviser to Sir Thomas More. He had a deep concern for reform in the church, attacking current abuses, and was tried for heresy, but acquitted. The fortune he inherited from his father enabled him to contribute to the cause of humanism; with it he gave financial support to Erasmus and founded St Paul's School.

📖 E. W. Hunt, *Dean Colet and his Theology*, London: SPCK 1956

Collins, Anthony (1676–1729) English deistic philosopher. Educated at Cambridge, he ultimately became deputy lieutenant of Essex. Influenced by John Locke, he wrote many works against the church and especially the clergy, which provoked retorts from churchmen. He argued against the accepted distinction between what is above and what is against human reason and for the efficacy of human reason and free enquiry. His main work is *A Discourse on Freethinking* (1713).

📖 J. O'Higgins, *Anthony Collins. The Man and His Works*, The Hague: Nijhoff 1970

Columba (*c.* 521–97) Celtic missionary. Born into a noble Irish family, he was trained in monasteries and went on to found several in Ireland himself. Around 553 he established a community on Iona which he used as a base for successful missionary work in the area.

📖 Adomnan of Iona, *Life of St Columba*, Harmondsworth: Penguin Books 1995

Comenius, John Amos (1592–1670) Bohemian Protestant educational reformer. Expelled from Bohemia as a non-Catholic during the Thirty Years' War, he settled in Leszno in Poland, where he became rector of the grammar school there. The great success of his book on teaching Latin, followed by his *magnum opus*, *Didacta Magna* (1657), on education, gave him an international reputation as an educational reformer. He travelled to England, Sweden and Hungary and ultimately settled in Amsterdam when Leszno was burnt by the Poles. His educational ideals were influenced by his own religious experience and he hoped that education and character development would lead to ecumenism.

📖 John Comenius, *The Labyrinth of the World and the Paradise of the Heart*, Classics of Western Spirituality, New York and Mahwah, NJ: Paulist Press 1998

Comte, Auguste (1798–1857) French mathematician and philosopher. Born in Montpellier, he studied science and mathematics in Paris, losing his faith in the process. He sought a philosophy which would command universal assent after the chaos of the French Revolution and replace lost religious faith, and produced positivism. His view was that the human race goes through three stages; theological, metaphysical and scientific. His fervour, which turned positivism into a substitute religion, with priests and sacraments and centred on humanity, cost him his job, leaving him dependent on followers, including the philosopher John Stuart Mill. His main work is his *Course of Positive Philosophy* (6 volumes, completed 1842, English 1903).

📖 Mary Pickering, *Auguste Comte: An Intellectual Biography*, Cambridge: CUP 1994

Congar, Yves (1904–95) French Catholic theologian. Born to a devout family in Sedan, he studied for the priesthood in Paris and became a Dominican, going to the study centre of Le Saulchoir, then basing himself in Belgium to escape church pressure. Work on the theologian Johann Adam Möhler took him to Germany, where he encountered Lutheranism. On his return to France he went to lectures given by Reformed church professors. He also visited England, encountering Anglicanism in Lincoln under Michael Ramsey. During the war he was a military chaplain and was imprisoned in Colditz; subsequently he developed a great interest in the Orthodox churches. However, after the war there was hostility to his ecumenical concerns; the open theology of Le Saulchoir was condemned by Rome and Congar's work was censured by his own order. For a while he was suspended from teaching, but the change of climate at Vatican II saved him; he played a major role in its preparation. Finally, he was made a cardinal. Prophetic yet traditional, a loyal critic, and a preacher and pastor rather than an original thinker, he wrote influential books, including *Lay People in the Church* (1953, English 1957), *Diversity and Communion* (1984), and *I Believe in the Holy Spirit* (1983).

📖 Aidan Nichols, *Yves Congar*, London and New York: Continuum 1989

Constantine the Great (Imperator Caesar Flavius Valerius Constantinus Augustus, 275–337) Roman emperor. Son of another emperor, he spent his childhood as a hostage in a divided and troubled empire. He was proclaimed emperor by his troops at York and established himself in power after the defeat of his rival Maxentius at the Milvian Bridge north of Rome, an event usually, but probably wrongly, associated with the conversion of Constantine to Christianity. Along with his co-ruler Licinius he decreed toleration for Christianity. He subsequently gave privileges to Christian clergy, and convened the Council of Nicaea in an attempt to establish church unity.

📖 A. H. M. Jones, *Constantine and the Conversion of Europe*, Harmondsworth: Penguin Books 1972

Copernicus, Nicolas (1473–1543) Polish clergyman, mathematician and astronomer. Born at Torun, he studied at Cracow and in Italy and then lived in Prussia all his life. Rejecting the established view of the universe dating from Ptolemaeus, with the earth as centre, in his book *On the Revolutions of the Heavenly Orbs* (1590) he argued that it was centred on the sun. His views were slow to spread, since their significance and truth were not at first appreciated, so he escaped the fate of Galileo, though his book was banned after his lifetime.

📖 Thomas S. Kuhn, *The Copernican Revolution: Planetary Astronomy in the Development of Western Thought*, Cambridge, MA: Harvard University Press 1990

Coverdale, Miles (1488–1568) Bible translator. He was born in Yorkshire and after ordination was an Augustinian friar in Cambridge. There, concern for church reform led him to leave his order and become a Lutheran. He had to flee the country because of his fervent preaching, and after helping William Tyndale in translation work he produced his own version, incorporating some of Tyndale's. This was the first English printed Bible, and Coverdale's translation of the Psalms was incorporated into the Anglican Book of Common Prayer. He eventually returned to England, becoming a Puritan leader.

📖 J. F. Mozley, *Coverdale and His Bibles*, London: Lutterworth Press 1953

Cranmer, Thomas (1489–1556) English Reformer. Born in Nottinghamshire, he studied and later taught at Cambridge. After his ordination, he was used by Henry VIII as a European ambassador in connection with his divorce of Catherine of Aragon and subsequently made Archbishop of Canterbury. He was later counsellor to Edward VI, and his ideas moved in an increasingly Protestant direction, in the hope of a union of all the European Reformation churches. His great contribution was to liturgical revision, and he was the architect of the Book of Common Prayer. He was burnt as a heretic under Queen Mary.

📖 Diarmaid MacCulloch, *Thomas Cranmer: A Life*, New Haven: Yale University Press 1996

Crowther, Samuel (*c.*1806–1891) Anglican bishop. Born Ajayi in Yorubaland (now part of Nigeria) he was sold into slavery at the age of 12 but rescued by the British Navy and taken to Sierra Leone, where he came under the care of the Church Missionary Society, and was baptized and educated. He went on a CMS Niger expedition in 1841 and his report was so impressive that he was sent to London for more training and in 1843 became the first African priest to be ordained. He worked in Yorubaland and then in the Niger mission which he founded, and in 1864 was consecrated Bishop of Western Africa outside colonial limits (i.e. not bishop of white clergy). Opposition from Europeans grew and his mission was eventually disbanded. He was succeeded by a white man.

📖 Jesse Page, *Samuel Crowther: The Slave Boy who became Bishop of the Niger*, London: S. W. Partridge 1908

Cyprian (Thascius Caecilius Cyprianus, died 258) The son of wealthy pagan parents in Carthage, he became a pagan rhetorician, but was converted to Christianity, and his skill and dedication to poverty and celibacy soon led him to be made bishop. His life was marked by persecution and controversy, and he suffered exile and ultimately martyrdom. He had a high view of the Catholic church ('outside the church there is no salvation') and was a rigorous disciplinarian. He wrote many fairly short works, chief among which is *On the Unity of the Catholic Church* (251).

📖 Peter Hinchliff, *Cyprian of Carthage and the Unity of the Christian Church*, London: Geoffrey Chapman 1974

Cyril (826–69) Until he became a monk his name was Constantine. With his brother Methodius, from a Greek senatorial family in Thessalonica, he worked as a librarian in Constantinople. Subsequently the brothers were sent to organize the Slav Church in Moravia. This led Cyril to invent a new alphabet based on Greek minuscules (equivalent to lower case characters), called Glagolitic (confusingly, not Cyrillic, as one would expect, though the Cyrillic alphabet is named after him). Cyrillic differs from Glagolitic in being based on Greek uncials (equivalent to capital letters). He died young, on a visit to Rome.

📖 A.-E. N. Tachiaos, *Cyril and Methodius of Thessalonica: The Acculturation of the Slavs*, Crestwood, NY: St Vladimir's Seminary Press 2000

Cyril of Alexandria (died 444) Christian theologian. He became Bishop of Alexandria in succession to his uncle. A ruthless controversialist, he vigorously attacked those whose views differed from his, especially Nestorius, whose condemnation he had secured, though in circumstances which also involved his own temporary deposition. He advocated above all a view of the person of Christ in which the divine was wholly dominant, a stress which favoured the rise of what later became the doctrine of Monophysitism (the view that Christ had only one, divine nature). He wrote many commentaries and letters.

📖 Frances M. Young, *From Nicaea to Chalcedon*, London: SCM Press and Philadelphia: Fortress Press 1983

Cyril of Jerusalem (*c.* 315–86) Bishop. Little is known of his early years; he became Bishop of Jerusalem at the age of 40. Jerusalem was a difficult place to be bishop of, and his inability to satisfy both his Arian superior and the orthodox Christians there, not to mention factions, led to much exile. Cyril is famous for his *Catechetical Lectures*, which give valuable information about the worship of the Palestinian church at the time; he also organized the church year into a series of historical anniversaries.

📖 Edward Yarnold, *Cyril of Jerusalem*, London and New York: Routledge 2000

Dante Alighieri (1265–1321) Italian poet and philosopher. He was born in Florence; little is known of his early life, except for his encounters with Beatrice, a woman he barely knew but who became for him the symbol of human perfection. After her death in 1290 he studied philosophy in Florence, but involvement in politics led to exile and a wandering life which took him as far as Paris. He died in Ravenna. A supporter of the emperor, in his *On Monarchy* (1310) he argued that for human happiness there was need of a universal monarchy independent of the church; this book was condemned. His *Divine Comedy* (1314) in three parts, 'Hell', 'Purgatory' and 'Paradise', belongs with the world's greatest literature. In his focus on the individual soul and its destiny he was a forerunner of the later Christian humanists and spiritual writers.

📖 George Holmes, *Dante*, Oxford: OUP 1979

Darwin, Charles (1809–82) English scientist. Born in Shrewsbury, after study in Cambridge in 1831 he sailed as a naturalist in a naval ship, *The Beagle*, on a five-year voyage to South America. During this time he collected evidence which he used in writing his pioneering book *The Origin of Species* (1859); this was followed by *The Descent of Man* (1871). His theory of evolution, that living beings evolve by natural selection from very few simple forms as a result of the survival of the fittest, led to vigorous controversy with Christian theologians during the nineteenth century. Darwin's views still continue to be opposed by many theologians because of their implications for an understanding of reality.

📖 Adrian Desmond and James Moore, *Darwin*, Harmondsworth: Penguin Books 1992

Day, Dorothy (1897–1980) American journalist. She was born in Brooklyn and grew up in Chicago where she went to the University of Illinois but did not graduate. Returning with her parents to New York in 1916, she became a left-wing journalist and worked for a period as a nurse. In 1927 she became a Roman Catholic. In 1933, with Peter Maurin, a French Catholic who pioneered a programme of social reconstruction, 'the green revolution', she founded the *Catholic Worker*, which was radical and pacifist. She also founded St Joseph's House of Hospitality in the New York slums. Left-wing Catholics such as Thomas Merton sought her out in the 1960s and she was a protestor against the Vietnam War, but to a younger generation she seemed reactionary on many moral issues. Her autobiography, *The Long Loneliness*, appeared in 1952.

📖 Robert Coles, *Dorothy Day: A Radical Devotion*, Boulder, CO: Perseus 1989

Derrida, Jacques (1930–2004) French philosopher. Born in El Biar, Algeria, he studied at the École Normale Supérieure in Paris, to which he returned as professor after a period teaching at the Sorbonne. Seeing philosophy as a critical reading of texts, he has made critical studies of thinkers from Greek philosophy via Hegel to phenomenology. A leading 'deconstructionist', taking up ideas from Heidegger and Nietzsche among others, he argued that it was wrong to seek an essential truth behind things, thus challenging the primacy of the word as the foundation of religion and metaphysics. The object of study should be language, which contains only differences. Hence the title of his best-known book, *Writing and Difference* (1967, English 1978).

📖 Nicholas Royle, *Jacques Derrida*, London and New York: Routledge 2003

Descartes, René (1596–1650) French philosopher. Born in La Haye, in the Loire valley, and educated by Jesuits, he studied law in Poitiers. In 1618 he began to travel in Holland and Germany and the next year conceived of a plan to reconstruct philosophy. Yet more travel took him also to Italy, but in 1628 he settled in Holland, where he lived quietly in the country and wrote his most important books. In 1649 Queen Christina of Sweden invited him to Stockholm to tutor her in philosophy. This proved fatal, since his habit had been to spend the morning in bed meditating; rising at 5 a.m. to teach the queen, he caught pneumonia and died the next year. The new philosophical method that he adopted was based on doubt. Making no prior assumptions, in a quest for certainty he began from the one thing of which he could be certain, 'I think, therefore I am,' and used the principle of radical doubt to achieve clarity. Coupled with this was a consequential distinction between, and total separation of, mind and matter, the relationship between which his philosophy never resolved ('Cartesian dualism'). His major works are the *Discourse on Method* (1637) and the *Meditations* (1641); their influence on subsequent thought has been prodigious.

📖 Tom Sorell, *Descartes: A Very Short Introduction*, Oxford: OUP 2000

Dibelius, Martin Franz (1883–1947) German New Testament scholar. Born in Dresden, after study at various German universities and a teaching post in Berlin he became professor at

Heidelberg. Initially interested in comparative languages, he came to concentrate on the New Testament, being one of the pioneers of form criticism; he argued from the assumed needs of the earliest Christian community to the forms of the material contained in the Gospels *(From Tradition to Gospel*, 1919). He made a major contribution to the understanding of Luke as an author in *Studies in the Acts of the Apostles* (1951). He also contributed towards the formation of the ecumenical movement as a leader of Faith and Order.

Martin Dibelius, *From Tradition to Gospel*, Cambridge: James Clarke 1982

Diderot, Dennis (1713–84) French encyclopaedist. Born at Langres and educated by the Jesuits, he became a Paris publisher's hack. His intellectual gifts brought him into a circle of advanced thinkers, and he was influenced by John Locke. Following a bookseller's suggestion, he embarked on what became his famous *Encyclopédie* (1751–72), which as well as collecting available knowledge sought to promote deism and enlightened ideas. His work had a considerable influence on Christian thinking.

Arthur M. Wilson, *Diderot*, New York: OUP 1972

Dionysius the (Pseudo-)Areopagite (*c.*500) Syrian mystic. Also known as Denys, he is named after Paul's convert in Athens (Acts 17), to whom his works were originally attributed. They combine Neoplatonic ideas with Christian thought and made a substantial impact on medieval theology, being an influence on, for example, Hugh of St Victor, Albertus Magnus, Thomas Aquinas, Dante and Milton. They comprise *The Celestial Hierarchy*, on the mediation of God by angels to men; *The Divine Names*, on the attributes of God; *The Ecclesiastical Hierarchy*, on the sacraments and the three ways of spiritual life, and the *Mystical Theology*, on the ascent of the soul to God.

Andrew Louth, *Denys the Areopagite*, London and New York: Continuum 2002

Domingo de Guzman (Dominic, 1170–1221) Founder of the Dominican order. Born of an ancient family from Castile, he studied at Palencia, where during a famine he is said even to have sold his books for food for the poor. After ordination, as canon of Osma he founded a community of which he became head until, as chaplain to his bishop, in 1203 he went to the south-west of France, where the spiritualist Albigensian movement was very active. Feeling challenged to combat it, Dominic and some volunteers stayed on and with papal permission went round preaching barefoot, adopting a life of ascetical poverty to further the conversion of the Albigensians. It was against this background that he founded religious communities, first a convent for women at Prouille and then one for men at Toulouse. Refusing a bishopric three times, Dominic consolidated and expanded his new order, but never forgot that its nature was to be a mendicant preaching order.

Simon Tugwell, *Early Dominicans: Selected Writings*, New York and Mahwah, NJ: Paulist Press and London: SPCK 1983

Donne, John (1571/2–1631) English poet. Originally a Roman Catholic, the son of a London ironmonger, he studied law and joined the Lord Chancellor's household. However, his elopement with the latter's niece led to his dismissal and unemployment. When all else failed he took Anglican orders and for his last decade was Dean of St Paul's. His poetry and sermons are among the great classics of English literature.

John Carey, *John Donne: Life, Mind and Art*, Oxford: OUP 1981

Dostoievsky, Fyodor Michaelovich (1821–81) Russian novelist. Son of a retired military surgeon, after private education he trained at the College of Military Engineering in St Petersburg, but resigned after three years. He was condemned to death for revolutionary activities, reprieved at the very last moment, and did four years forced labour in Siberia with only a Bible as reading matter before returning to the army. This led to a religious crisis and a conversion. From 1859 he was a journalist and devoted himself to writing. His experiences in Siberia are vividly reflected in *The House of the Dead* (1861). Impoverished and in debt through gambling, emotionally disturbed and a victim of epilepsy, he produced novels such as *Crime and Punishment* (1865) and *The Idiot* (1868). Along with Kierkegaard he proved immensely influential on existentialism and dialectical theology. He vividly brings home the problem of the individual torn between evil, the existence of which haunts him, and a quest for God through a faith which is quite detached from reason. Of all his famous novels, *The Brothers Karamazov* (1880), with its story of 'The Grand Inquisitor', representing the church as a falsifier of Christ, has been widely used in theology.

A. B. Gibson, *The Religion of Dostoevsky*, London: SCM Press 1973

Douglas, Mary (1921–96) English social anthropologist. After studying at Oxford she did fieldwork in the Belgian Congo, returning to teaching in London, Oxford and Northwestern University, Evanston. The focus of her study was symbols, and the lack of common symbols in our time, which she interpreted as indicating the lack of a sense of belonging in an ordered society. In arriving at this conclusion she used two factors, 'group' and 'grid', the former being the experience of a bounded social unit and the latter the rules relating one person to another on an ego-centred basis. In Western society, grid has come to eclipse group. Her views have had some influence on theology and biblical studies. Important books are *Purity and Danger* (1966) and *Natural Symbols* (1970).

Richard Fardon, *Mary Douglas: An Intellectual Biography*, www.ebooks4all.org

Duns Scotus, John (*c.*1265–1308) Scottish theologian. Little is known of his life: he was born at Duns, near Roxburgh, in Scotland and became a Franciscan, later studying and teaching in Oxford and Paris. At the end of his life he was moved to Cologne. Critical of the philosophy of Thomas Aquinas and its attempt to harmonize Aristotle and Christianity, he argued that faith cannot be established by any rational process, thus separating it from philosophy, a division which was to have far-reaching effects. In philosophy he made important contributions by restoring intelligibility to the individual (by his concept of *haeccitas*, 'thisness') in contrast to stress on the universal. His early death left his writings in disarray, and only recently have the genuine been distinguished from the inauthentic. As well as notes from his Paris and Oxford lectures there are a *Treatise on the First Principle* and discussions of Aristotle. He was also the first major theologian to defend Mary's immaculate conception. As a tribute to the complexity of his thought the church officially named him 'the subtle doctor'; Protestants found his ideas so obscure that they used his name as an insult: 'dunce'.

📖 Richard Cross, *Duns Scotus*, New York: OUP 1999

Durkheim, Emile (1858–1917) French sociologist. Born in Épinal, Lorraine, he studied in Paris and decided to devote his career to sociology with the aim of establishing an intellectually respectable science of society. He subsequently became professor in Bordeaux and Paris. He argued that social laws should not be inferred from biological laws. He is best known for his theory of 'collective consciousness', understanding human societies as *sui generis*, and his distinction between 'normal' and 'pathological' social types. In the sphere of religion he wrote a pioneering classic, *The Elementary Forms of the Religious Life* (1912), in which he saw religion, and particularly ritual, as a symbolic representation of a social bond.

📖 Anthony Giddens, *Durkheim*, London: Fontana 1985

Ebeling, Gerhard (1912–2001) German Lutheran theologian. Professor at Tübingen and Zurich, he was particularly concerned to relate the theology of the Reformers, especially Luther, to modern thought. He argued that both must be held together and that theologians must stand up to the tension between historical and dogmatic method, theology and proclamation. He wrote a major study of *Luther* (1970); his systematic thought is represented by *Word and Faith* (1963) and *The Study of Theology* (1979).

📖 Gerhard Ebeling, *The Study of Theology*, Philadelphia: Fortress Press 1979

Eckhart, Johannes ('Meister', *c.*1260–*c.*1328) German mystic. Born in Hochheim, he became a Dominican and studied in Paris, after which he was appointed provincial in Saxony and reformed the monastic houses in Bohemia. Returning to Paris, he taught there and made a name as a preacher and mystical teacher. In the last year of his life he was accused of heresy, but died before he was finally condemned. His spirituality centred on the creation and leads to creativity; he saw the soul as a divine spark: the divine Word is generated in the soul, producing a constant creative energy. His powerful imagery was influenced by Hildegard of Bingen and Mechthild of Magdeburg, and he in turn influenced such diverse figures as Luther, John of the Cross, Julian of Norwich and George Fox. As a result of his condemnation his thought went underground, but its effect has lasted over the centuries to modern times.

📖 Bernard McGinn, *The Mystical Thought of Meister Eckhart*, New York: Crossroad 2001

Eddy, Mary Baker (1821–1910) Founder of Christian Science. Born of a Congregationalist family in New Hampshire, she was subject to convulsions and had two ill-fated marriages. Cured by hypnosis, she worked out for herself a new understanding of Christianity as divine healing which she expressed in her *Science and Health with a Key to the Scriptures* (1875). She healed her invalid third husband and took his name when he died, thereafter founding her church. Her belief was that mind or God is the only reality and sin, evil, sickness and death are not real.

📖 Gillian Gill, *Mary Baker Eddy*, Cambridge, MA: Perseus Books 1998

Edwards, Jonathan (1703–58) American Calvinist theologian and philosopher. A precocious child, he had a deep interest in nature. He was educated at Yale, and then became a pastor in Northampton, Massachusetts, where there was a revival, but was dismissed after a controversy because he admitted to communion only those with a conversion experience. He then became a missionary pastor in Stockbridge, on the frontier; later he was appointed president of Princeton, but died soon afterwards. He was instrumental in two revivals, including the Great Awakening. Strict in his Calvinist views, he also rejected the idea of freedom (*The Freedom of the Will*, 1754). However, he kept his wonder at the divinity of nature, and also held that Calvinism fitted science better than other theological positions. His writing took on depth from the way in which he brought English empirical philosophy to bear on personal mystical knowledge of God; he was widely influential.

📖 George M. Marsden, *Jonathan Edwards: A Life*, New Haven: Yale University Press 2003

Eliot, George (Mary Ann Cross, née Evans, 1819–80) Novelist and translator. Daughter of the agent for a Warwickshire estate, she had her religious views broadened by Charles Bray, a Coventry manufacturer, and she translated David Friedrich Strauss's *Life of Jesus* and Ludwig Feuerbach's *Essence of Christianity*. In 1854 she went to live with George Henry Lewes, a prolific writer, and did so until his death. At this point her talent as a novelist emerged. Her novels, particularly *Middlemarch* (1871–2) and *Daniel Deronda* (1874–6), also brilliantly illustrate the religious sensibility of her time. She married John Walter Cross in the last year of her life.

📖 Peter C. Hodgson, *Theology in the Fiction of George Eliot*, London: SCM Press 2001

Eliot, Thomas Stearns (1888–1965) American/English poet and critic. Born in St Louis, he was educated at Harvard, the Sorbonne and Oxford. Originally a Unitarian, in 1927 he became an Anglican and took British citizenship. His poetry, with its indirect allusions to and influence from the mystics, especially *Four Quartets* (1944), has been particularly attractive to modern theologians. He specifically reflected on religion in *The Idea of a Christian Society* (1939).

📖 Peter Ackroyd, *T. S. Eliot*, London: Hamish Hamilton and New York: Simon & Schuster 1984

Emerson, Ralph Waldo (1803–82) American transcendentalist. Descended from a long line of ministers, he too became a Unitarian pastor in Boston after studying at Harvard, largely disliking his ministry. Resigning after the death of his wife and two brothers, he went to Europe, where he met Samuel Taylor Coleridge, William Wordsworth and the historian Thomas Carlyle, who had a great influence on him. He then remarried and settled in Concord, Massachusetts, staying there as a lecturer for the rest of his life. His books were largely based on his lectures, beginning with his influential *Nature* (1838). He stressed the 'beauty, dignity and infinite importance of the human soul' and combined a rational critique of traditional Christianity with mysticism. He believed in the divinity of human beings, but was stronger on the individual than on the collective. However, he was no democrat and only reluctantly supported the abolition of slavery.

📖 G. W. Allen, *Waldo Emerson. A Biography*, New York: Penguin Books 1981

Ephrem the Syrian (*c.*306–73) Syrian church father and poet. Perhaps the son of a pagan priest, after ordination he settled in Edessa where he spent the rest of his life, of which virtually nothing is known. His writings are ascetical and polemic and are mostly in verse. He is a valuable witness to the Syriac tradition and his poetry can be rich and vivid.

📖 Sebastian Brock, *The Luminous Eye: The Spiritual World of St Ephrem*, Rome: Cistercian Publications 1985

Epictetus (*c.*50–*c.*130) Stoic philosopher. Born a Phrygian slave in Hierapolis, he was given his freedom and taught in Rome until expelled by Domitian in 90, when he moved to southern France. He wrote nothing, and his teachings were collected by his pupil Arrian (*Discourses*). His views are closer to Christianity than those of most Stoics, including the Fatherhood of God and the brotherhood of man.

📖 C. Gill (ed), *The Discourses of Epictetus*, London: Phoenix 1995

Epicurus (342–270 BCE) Greek philosopher. He believed that the senses provide the sole criterion of truth, denying e.g. immortality. Although the term 'epicureanism' is often associated with a love of luxury, Epicurus himself argued that genuine pleasure is lived with prudence, honour and justice. Gods exist, but they have no relevance to human life. His philosophy became, with Stoicism, widely influential in the Roman world.

📖 J. M. Rist, *Epicurus: An Introduction*, Cambridge: CUP 1977

Epiphanius (*c.*315–403) Defender of orthodoxy. Born in Palestine, he founded a monastery in Judaea before being made Bishop of Salamis on Cyprus. Rigid in his orthodoxy and unable to understand other positions, he rejected learning, criticism and theological speculation. His *Panarion* (*Medicine Box: Refutations of all the Heresies*) is important for the information it contains, among all its polemic.

📖 Frances M. Young, *From Nicaea to Chalcedon*, London: SCM Press and Philadelphia: Fortress Press 1983

Erasmus, Desiderius (*c.*1469–1536) Dutch humanist. The illegitimate son of a Dutch priest, after his schooling he reluc-

tantly became a monk and was ordained. Encouraged by the Bishop of Cambrai he was able to travel, and studied in Paris, Oxford, Louvain and Turin. On the accession of Henry VIII (1509) he returned to England, and became professor at Cambridge, being the first to teach Greek there. He next went as royal councillor to the court at Brussels, and, after being relieved of all monastic obligations, settled in Basle until the Reformation arrived in 1529. He spent his last years in Freiburg im Breisgau. A great scholar, he produced an edition of the Greek New Testament which later became the basis of the standard text and editions of texts of many church fathers. His own works were read widely, the best known being *In Praise of Folly* (1509, against evils in the contemporary church and state) and *On the Freedom of the Will* (1524, against Luther). A complex person, he was his own man, remaining a Catholic and refusing many prestigious offers in order to keep his freedom.

📖 Leon E. Halkin, *Erasmus: A Critical Biography*, Oxford: Blackwell 1992

Eriugena, John Scotus (*c.*810–*c.*877) Irish theologian. Moving to France, under royal patronage he was head of the palace school at Leon. A philosopher in the Neoplatonist tradition, with a knowledge of Greek rare in the West of his time he was able to interpret Greek thought. In his *On the Divisions of Nature* (subsequently condemned for its suggestions of pantheism) he tried to reconcile Platonic emanation with the Christian view of creation, and in his *On Predestination* he asserted that God could not know evil and that evil was simply absence of good, bringing its own punishment.

📖 J. J. O'Meara, *Eriugena*, Oxford: Clarendon Press 1988

Eusebius (*c.*260–*c.*340) Church historian. Probably born in Palestine, he became Bishop of Caesarea. He attended the Council of Nicaea under suspicion of Arian sympathies and offered a compromise creed which was rejected for not containing the word *homoousios*, denoting that God the Father and God the Son are of the same substance. But his main claim to fame is as author of a uniquely valuable *Church History*, the main source for the history of Christianity before him apart from the Acts of the Apostles. It is more important for its source material than its judgements, which are influenced by his ideology. He was an apologist for the new development of Christianity under Constantine, whose life he wrote.

📖 Eusebius, *The History of the Church*, Harmondsworth: Penguin Books 1989

Faber, Frederick William (1814–63) English hymn writer. Born in Yorkshire and brought up as an Evangelical, at Oxford, where he studied and taught, he was influenced by the high church movement and after six years as an Anglican priest became a Roman Catholic. He joined John Henry Newman's Birmingham Oratory and then, on Newman's prompting, founded the London

Oratory. Concerned to bring spiritual life to the people of London, he was also open to science, natural beauty and secular culture. His many hymns include 'My God, how wonderful thou art'.

Ronald Chapman, *Father Faber*, London: Burns & Oates 1961

Fell, Margaret (1614–1702) 'Nursing mother' of Quakerism. She was born Margaret Askew into the landed gentry of Lancashire and in her late teens married an older man, Thomas Fell, who was a highly respected judge. Because he travelled a good deal, she was often left alone at their home, Swarthmoor Hall. In 1652 George Fox came to visit; she became convinced of the truth of his gospel and assisted him in his ministry. She inherited the estate on the death of her husband in 1658 and it became a centre for Quaker activities. The life of the early Quakers was by no means easy: George Fox was imprisoned twice, in 1659 and 1664, and Margaret was also imprisoned from 1664 to 1669. She married Fox in 1669, but because of his work and further imprisonments they rarely lived together. Her best-known pamphlet, *Women's Speaking Justified, Proved and Allowed by the Scriptures* (1666), has become a key feminist document.

Isabel Ross, *Margaret Fell. Mother of Quakerism*, London: Longmans 1949

Fénélon, François de Salignac de la Mothe (1651–1715) French Catholic mystic and quietist. Born in Perigord, he studied at Cahors and in Paris before ordination, and subsequently was involved in mission to the French Protestants in Saintogne. He then became tutor to the grandson of Louis XIV, and in 1695 was made Archbishop of Cambrai, by which time he had met Madame Guyon and become her defender. Two years later he was deposed, following attacks by Jacques-Bénigne Bossuet on his book defending mystical spirituality, and never returned to court favour. A distinguished preacher and spiritual director, he wrote letters of spiritual counsel which were published after his death and much read.

John McEwen, *Fénélon Letters*, London: Harvill Press 1964

Ferrar, Nicholas (1592–1637) A brilliant scholar at Cambridge, he had to leave for health reasons and travelled on the European continent for five years before being appointed to the Virginia Company, in which he held office, and becoming a Member of Parliament. However, in 1625 he turned his back on political life and settled on an estate at Little Gidding, in Huntingdonshire, where he formed a commune in accordance with the principles of the Church of England. Everyone learned a trade and the community specialized in bookbinding. There was also a school for local children. However, the Puritans were hostile and the community was destroyed by the parliamentary army in 1647, during the English Civil War.

A. L. Maycock, *Nicholas Ferrar of Little Gidding*, Grand Rapids, MI: Eerdmans 1980

Feuerbach, Ludwig Andreas (1804–72) German philosopher. He was born in Landshut and studied theology at Heidelberg, but in Berlin was persuaded by G. W. F. Hegel to change to philosophy. For most of his life he had no teaching post. His most celebrated work is *The Essence of Christianity* (1841), which was extremely influential, not least on Karl Marx. Denying transcendence, he saw religion as being the projection of human qualities and hopes on to a fictitious God. Theology is anthropology writ large.

Ludwig Feuerbach, *The Essence of Christianity*, Amherst, NY: Prometheus Books 1994

Ficino, Marsilio (1433–99) Italian humanist. Born near Florence, the son of the physician of Duke Cosimo de' Medici, under Cosimo's patronage he had leisure to translate many Platonic works into Latin, and founded the Platonic Academy. At the age of 40 he became a priest and later was a canon of Florence. Seeing a close link between Platonic philosophy and Christianity, he became widely influential well beyond the Renaissance and made a lasting mark on European thought.

P. O. Kristeller, *Marsilio Ficino and his Work after Five Hundred Years*, Florence: Olschki 1987

Forsyth, Peter Taylor (1848–1921) Scottish theologian. Son of a postman, he went to university in his home city of Aberdeen and studied under Albrecht Ritschl in Göttingen. After ordination into the Congregationalist church he held several church posts before becoming principal of Hackney College, London. At first interested in critical theology to the point of becoming suspect, he increasingly came to stress 'gospel truths' because he believed that liberal theology had no power, and wrote vigorously about sin and atonement. His greatest book, *The Person and Place of Christ* (1909), anticipated much that came a generation later, and he has been called a Barthian before Karl Barth.

W. L. Bradley, *P. T. Forsyth: The Man and His Work*, London: Independent Press 1952

Fosdick, Harry Emerson (1878–1960) American liberal preacher. Ordained a Baptist, after a pastorate in New Jersey he taught homiletics at Union Theological Seminary, New York. In 1918 he was called to a Presbyterian church but resigned over a sermon he preached against fundamentalism. Thereafter he was minister of Riverside Church, New York. He was an influential preacher and became a much-read author, through his works on personal religion, psychology and biblical criticism. Among his best known books are *The Manhood of the Master* (1913) and *The Meaning of Prayer* (1915).

H. E. Fosdick, *The Living of These Days*, New York: Harper & Bros 1956 and London: SCM Press 1957

Foucauld, Charles Eugène de (1858–1916) French hermit. Born an aristocrat, and very rich, he developed a passion for Africa through service as a cavalry officer. After a period of spiritual unrest, he was helped back to the Catholic faith. He made a pilgrimage to Palestine and then was ordained and became a Trappist monk, later going to Algeria to live as a hermit, first at Beni Abbes, then at Tamanrasset, among the Tuareg Muslims. For a decade until his assassination by one of them he devoted himself to their welfare, also producing dictionaries and translations. He composed rules for communities of 'Little Brothers' and 'Little Sisters', but had no companions during his lifetime; these communities were formed later.

📖 Robert Ellsberg, *Charles de Foucauld*, Maryknoll, NY: Orbis Books 1999

Foucault, Michel (1926–84) French philosopher. Born in Poitiers, he studied at the École Normale Supérieure and then taught in Clermond-Ferrand and Paris, being appointed professor at the Collège de France. He made his name in 1961 with the publication of *Madness and Civilization*, exploring the need of culture to define what lies outside it. Suspicious of any universals, instead he examined the role played by such concepts in history, exploring the ways in which they have been used in society. For him, knowledge is power and it is important to see how that power is used. Other major works are *The Archaeology of Knowledge* (1972) and *The History of Sexuality* (1976ff.).

📖 Paul Rabinow (ed), *The Foucault Reader*, Harmondsworth: Penguin Books 1991

Fox, George (1624–91) Founder of the Religious Society of Friends (Quakers). Son of a Leicestershire Puritan weaver, being disillusioned with the religion around him he became an itinerant preacher, suffering imprisonment and beatings. His mission proved successful in north-west England, where he gained the patronage of a local judge, Thomas Fell, whose widow Margaret Fell he later married. Thereafter he went on many missionary journeys abroad. He was led by personal experience to belief in guidance by the Inward Light, the Holy Spirit within. A charismatic figure, he also had considerable organizing ability and developed those who accepted his teaching into an identifiable society. He wrote a famous *Journal*, published posthumously (1694).

📖 H. L. Ingle, *First Among Friends: George Fox and the Creation of Quakerism*, New York: OUP 1994

Foxe, John (1516–87) Protestant historian. Born in Boston, Lincolnshire, he studied and taught at Oxford before becoming a tutor to the nobility, in which role he became interested in history. On the accession of Queen Mary he escaped to the continent and made many contacts there. When he returned, in collaboration with a London printer, with whom he worked for the rest of his life, he published his famous *Book of Martyrs* (1563), a great influence on the religious feeling of his time.

📖 V. N. Olsen, *John Foxe and the Elizabethan Church*, Berkeley, CA: University of California Press 1973

Francis of Assisi (1182–1226) Founder of the Franciscan order of friars. Son of a wealthy cloth merchant, he was converted after a wild youth and embraced a life of total poverty. As an itinerant preacher he attracted followers and in 1209 formed an order, the Friars Minor (so called because the Pope insisted they should take minor orders), centred on Assisi. (A women's order was founded three years later, called the Poor Clares, after a local heiress influenced by Francis.) In 1223 Francis handed over leadership of the order and spent the rest of his life as a hermit. His simple faith, humility and love of nature made him a popular saint, and his devotion was so deep that he is said to have received the stigmata, the wound marks of the crucified Jesus, on his body.

📖 Chiara Frugoni, *Francis of Assisi*, London: SCM Press 1998

Francis de Sales (1567–1622) Catholic bishop and devotional writer. Born in the Savoie of noble family, after studying at Annecy, Paris and Padua he gave up a brilliant career to become a priest. He had been haunted by the prospect of damnation, but a vision of Jesus dispelled his fear. At first he did missionary work near Geneva. but was then sent to Paris, where he proved to have deep spiritual gifts. Returning to Geneva as bishop he preached and acted as spiritual director, also writing his most important works, *An Introduction to the Devout Life* (1608) and *Treatise on the Love of God* (1616). His works were important in furthering the practice of spirituality outside the cloister.

📖 Michael de la Bedoyère, *Saintmaker: The Life of St Francis de Sales*, Manchester, NH: Sophia Institute Press 1999

Francis Xavier (1506–52) Catholic missionary. From an aristocratic Spanish family, he trained in Paris, where he met Ignatius Loyola, with whom he took vows of poverty and chastity and dedication to missionary work. Arriving in Goa, he first engaged in traditional mission, but came to realize the need to perceive the nature of the culture of the people among whom he was working. His work in Japan and India was highly successful and he made many converts.

📖 H. J. Coleridge, *The Life and Letters of Francis Xavier*, New Delhi: Asian Educational Services 1998

Freud, Sigmund (1856–1939) Founder of modern psychoanalysis. Born a Jew in Pribor, Czechoslovakia (then Freiburg, Moravia), he studied medicine in Vienna and specialized in neurology. He developed a method of dealing with hysterical disorders which eventually became what he himself termed psychoanalysis, and then went on to apply the method to himself. This led to two important books, *The Interpretation of Dreams* (1900, English 1913) and *Three Contributions to Sexual Theory* (1905, English 1910), which outlined his famous theories of infantile sexuality and libidinal development; from here he moved to the notion of repression and explanations of the nature of neurotic disorder. His books were burnt in Berlin when Hitler came to power, and after the Nazi occupation of Austria he moved to London, where he died. An atheist, and implacably hostile to religion in general and Christianity in particular (e.g. *The Future of an Illusion*, 1927), he seems to have accepted Enlightenment views of science and its powers of explanation. However, his analysis of himself may be seen as a quest for self-discovery in a godless world and thus not alien to theological enquiry. Precisely what he achieved by his psychotherapy is still a much-debated question within psychology and psychiatry, but his figure is an important focal point in modern culture.

📖 Peter Gay, *Freud: A Life for our Time*, New York: W. W. Norton 1998

Fry, Elizabeth (1780–1845) Quaker prison reformer. Born in Norwich the daughter of a banker, she married a London merchant and had a large family. In 1808 she founded a school in East London and in 1811 became a Quaker minister. In 1813 she became interested in prisons and began work among the

women prisoners in London's Newgate prison, teaching them to sew and reading the Bible to them. For the next 25 years she campaigned tirelessly for prison reform and on other social issues, including homelessness and begging, though her work was restricted when her husband went bankrupt in 1828. As well as reports on her activities she wrote *Texts for Every Day in the Christian Year* (1831).

📖 June Rose, *Elizabeth Fry*, London: Palgrave Macmillan 1981

Gabler, Johann Philipp (1753–1826) German biblical scholar, professor in Altdorf and Jena. He applied myth to Old Testament interpretation, but his main significance lies in being the first to distinguish between biblical and dogmatic theology. His major work is *On the Proper Distinction between Biblical and Dogmatic Theology and the Special Objectives of Each* (1787).

📖 His work on biblical and dogmatic theology is translated in *Scottish Journal of Theology* 33, 1980, pp. 133–58

Gadamer, Hans-Georg (1900–2002) German philosopher. Born in Marburg, he studied in his home city under Rudolf Bultmann and Martin Heidegger and went on to teach there before going to Leipzig. After the Second World War he became rector of the university and supervised its reconstruction under Russian occupation. He then became professor in Frankfurt and finally in Heidelberg. His *magnum opus Truth and Method* (1960) is a classic of hermeneutics, being influential not only in theology but in the social sciences and in literary criticism. It explores how truth emerges outside the natural sciences, examining the place of truth in the experience of art, its place in the humanities generally and its relation to language, and discusses the relation of tradition and prejudgement to language, arguing that the meaning of works emerges only through history.

📖 H.-G. Gadamer, *Truth and Method*, London and New York: Continuum 1993

Galileo Galilei (1564–1642) Italian astronomer. Born in Pisa, he was educated at a monastery near Florence and at the University of Pisa, where he then taught mathematics. He subsequently moved to Padua, where he became professor. He invented a telescope, and after observing Jupiter's moon came to support Nicolas Copernicus' theories of a universe centred on the sun. He had a long-drawn-out conflict with the Inquisition as a result, which led to his condemnation and recantation in 1616, and a second condemnation and house arrest in 1832. He is also important for theology because of his attempts to reconcile his findings with biblical statements ('Letter to Christina of Lorraine'), which mark one of the beginnings of biblical criticism.

📖 William R. Shea and Mariano Artigas, *Galileo in Rome: The Rise and Fall of a Troublesome Genius*, Oxford: OUP 2003

Gerhardt, Paul (1607–76) Lutheran poet and hymn writer. He was a tutor in Berlin before being ordained, and subsequently became pastor in Berlin and Archdeacon of Lübben. Though he was an uncompromising Lutheran, his devotional hymns show the influence of Catholic mysticism. They include 'O sacred head sore wounded' and 'The duteous day now closes'.

📖 T. B. Hewitt, *Paul Gerhardt as Hymnwriter and His Influence on English Hymnody*, New Haven: Yale University Press 1976

Gerson, Jean (1363–1429) French Catholic theologian. Born in the Ardennes, he studied at the University of Paris, taught there and eventually became chancellor. Living in a time of schism, he worked for reform in the church, through prayer and self-sacrifice, but the strain proved excessive and he left Paris to become dean of a church in Bruges. He later returned to Paris, and took part in the Council of Constance which condemned John Hus, at the same time incurring the hostility of the Duke of Burgundy by his views against tyrannicide, in which the Duke had been an accomplice. Barred from Paris, he lived in exile near Vienna before returning to France to spend his last days in spiritual and pastoral work. He was a vigorous exponent of the view that a general council was superior to the Pope, and in this way began the move towards a nationalist Catholicism in France (Gallicanism). Known in the Catholic Church as the 'most Christian doctor', he saw the church as the mystical body of Christ and held a mystical doctrine of identity between the soul and God in prayer.

📖 Jean Gerson, *Early Works*, Classics of Western Spirituality, New York and Mahwah, NJ: Paulist Press 1998

Gill, Eric (1882–1940) Letterer, sculptor and engraver. The son of an Anglican priest who had been a minister in the Countess of Huntingdon's Connexion, he became a Roman Catholic and Dominican tertiary. After studying lettering he turned to sculpture. He is known particularly for the Stations of the Cross in Westminster Cathedral (1914–18) and his sculptures on BBC Broadcasting House, London (1932), 'Nation shall speak peace unto nation'. He was also responsible for many war memorials. From 1915 he worked on engraving and lettering; his *Four Gospels* (1931) is his masterpiece. He also designed a number of typefaces, most notably Gill sans serif. He wrote controversially on the relationship of religion to work and art and uninhibitedly gloried in erotic love.

📖 Fiona MacCarthy, *Eric Gill*, London: Faber 1990

Gore, Charles (1853–1932) Anglo-Catholic bishop. A brilliant scholar, he rose through Oxford and Westminster to become Bishop of Worcester, the first Bishop of Birmingham and Bishop of Oxford before resigning to devote himself to writing. He was editor of *Lux Mundi* (1889), a collection of essays which made high churchmen take account of historical criticism, and provided his own provocative contribution. He also had a deep concern for social justice. He was founder of the Anglican Community of the Resurrection at Mirfield in Yorkshire. His trilogy, combined as *The Reconstruction of Belief* (1921–4), was widely influential.

📖 G. L. Prestige, *The Life of Charles Gore. A Great Englishman*, London: Heinemann 1935

Graham, William (Billy) Franklin (1918–) American revivalist. Born in North Carolina, he studied at Bob Jones University,

Florida Bible Institute and Wheaton College. After a brief pastorate he became an evangelist, but it was when he was President of Northwestern College, Minneapolis. that his fame began as a result of a crusade in Los Angeles. He founded the Billy Graham Evangelistic Association, and a successful crusade in 1954 made him a world-famous figure.

📖 John Pollock, *Billy Graham: The Authorized Biography*, London: Hodder & Stoughton 1966

Gratian (died *c.*1159) Little is known of his life other than that he was a Catholic monk who taught at Bologna. In his *Concordance of Differing Canons*, which came to be known as 'Gratian's Decree' (*Decretum Gratianum*), he collected a vast number of patristic texts, conciliar decrees and papal pronouncements, with the aim of resolving all their contradictions. It soon became a basic textbook, and Gratian is regarded as the father of church (canon) law.

📖 Anders Winroth, *The Making of Gratian's Decretum*, Cambridge: CUP 2000

Gregory of Nazianzus (329/30–389/90) Church theologian. Son of the Bishop of Cappadocia, he studied in Caesarea, where he met Basil. Together they went on to study in Athens. He became a monk and later his father had him ordained priest against his will, but he twice avoided being made bishop. He defended the Nicene faith against Arianism at the Council of Constantinople (381) and then returned home. His best known work is his *Theological Addresses,* which culminate in an argument that the Holy Spirit is of the same substance (*homoousios*) as the Father and the Son. With Basil he compiled a collection of Origen's works (the *Philokalia*). He, Basil and Gregory of Nyssa are known as the Cappadocian fathers.

📖 Anthony Meredith, *The Cappadocians*, London and New York: Continuum 1995

Gregory of Nyssa (*c.*330–*c.*395) Church theologian. Younger brother of Basil of Caesarea, he became a teacher of rhetoric, which displeased Basil. Penitent, Gregory became a monk and in 371 unwillingly accepted Basil's invitation to become Bishop of Nyssa. He played a leading role at the Council of Constantinople (381) and then disappears into obscurity. Superior to Basil in intellect, he made a more original contribution to theology. Under the influence of Origen, his thought was open and wide-ranging with a universalist hope; he was one of the first to link a theology of the sacraments with incarnational theology. He became known as the 'Father of fathers'. As well as writing polemic against Apollinarius and others in his *Catechetical Orations*, he expounded the doctrines of Trinity, incarnation and redemption, and the nature of baptism and the eucharist.

📖 Anthony Meredith, *The Cappadocians*, London and New York: Continuum 1995

Gregory Palamas (*c.*1296–1359) Greek theologian. Probably born in Constantinople to a noble family, he became a monk, and went with his two brothers to Mount Athos, where he became acquainted with the Hesychast tradition of silent, inner, mystical prayer. Political difficulties caused by the Turks disturbed his life at times, delaying his installation as Archbishop of Thessalonica. He was even imprisoned by them. He taught that human nature is a unity of body and soul and that the divine light ('uncreated light') could be seen physically, hence the inclusion of physical exercises in his spirituality. He is one of the most important theologians of the Greek church. His major work is *Triads in Defence of the Holy Hesychasts* (1336).

📖 John Meyendorff, *Gregory Palamas and Orthodox Spirituality*, Crestwood, NY: St Vladimir's University Press 1974

Gregory Thaumaturgus (*c.*213–70) Greek theologian. Born in Neocaesarea in Pontus of a noble family, he trained as a lawyer. On a visit to Palestine he was converted by Origen; returning to his native city, five years later he became its bishop. He owes his name, which means 'wonder-worker', to the miraculous answers to his prayers related in legends. A practical churchman, he was concerned to use all that was best in paganism.

📖 Robin Lane Fox, *Pagans and Christians*, Harmondsworth: Penguin Books 1988

Griffiths, Bede (1906–93) English mystic. After becoming a Benedictine, and later prior of Farnborough Abbey, in 1955 he went to India to found a contemplative community; from 1968 he was at Sacchidananda ashram in Tamil Nadu, a Christian community following the pattern of a Hindu ashram. Although still a Christian, he sought the mystery beyond all doctrinal formulations and revelations. Major books are *Return to the Centre* (1976) and *Marriage of East and West* (1982).

📖 Wayne Teasdale, *Bede Griffiths: An Introduction to his Interspiritual Thought*, Woodstock, VE: Skylight Paths Publishing 2003

Grosseteste, Robert (1175–1253) English bishop. He was born into a poor Suffolk family and his life is obscure until he became Chancellor of Oxford, where he had studied, and Bishop of Lincoln. He gained great fame as a teacher, and as well as being a vigorous reformer of his diocese had a wide range of scholarly interests, including astronomy and mathematics. His scientific experiments probably influenced Roger Bacon, and he played a part in regaining the legacy of antiquity from the Islamic world, which in many respects had been its custodian.

📖 James McEvoy, *Robert Grosseteste*, New York: OUP 2000

Grotius, Hugo (Huig de Groot, 1583–1645) Dutch lawyer and theologian. Born in Delft into an influential family, he was an infant prodigy. He was at the University of Leyden by the age of 11 and practising law at 16. Two years later he began to hold important state posts. However, his eirenic views involved him in conflict with the Calvinists, and he escaped life imprisonment only by being smuggled in a box of books to Paris. There, in poverty, he produced his famous *On the Law of War and Peace* (1625), which earned him the title 'father of international law'. It dissociated law from theology, and established the principle of justice in an unalterable law of nature. After a return to Holland, banishment, and further travels, he became Swedish ambassador in Paris, and never subsequently returned to his native land. His main religious work, *On the Truth of the Christian Religion* (1622), was written as a manual for sailors to refute pagans and Muslims, presenting a natural theology based on trust in providence and following the teaching of Christ; it was valued by Christians of all traditions. He was also a pioneer in biblical criticism. In modern times he has become known for his phrase *etsi deus non daretur*, ordering life 'as if there were no God'.

📖 Vreeland Hamilton, *Hugo Grotius: The Father of the Modern Science of International Law*, Buffalo, NY: William S. Hein 1986

Grundtvig, Nikolai Frederik Severin (1783–1872) Danish Lutheran. Two conversion experiences brought him first to Christian faith and later to an inability to accept orthodox views of the Bible. In his view the scriptures had now been destroyed by rationalism, so that faith had to be based, rather, on 'the living Word confessed down the ages'. His championship of freedom in church and society led him to be an educational reformer. For much of his life he was preacher at the Vartov Hospital in Copenhagen and was latterly given the title 'bishop'. He was also the author of many hymns. All this left a deep mark on the Danish church.

📖 A. M. Allchin, *N. F. S. Grundtvic*, London: Darton, Longman & Todd 1997

Gutiérrez, Gustavo (1928–) Founding father of liberation theology. A Peruvian priest of Indian descent, after studying in Louvain and Lyons he returned to Peru, where alongside being professor at the Catholic University in Lima he involved himself with the poor. He has been consultant to the Episcopal Conference of Latin America and lives and works in Rimac, a Lima slum. His theology is that salvation cannot be seen in any kind of dualistic approach as distinguishable from liberation. In his view Marxist philosophy is not incompatible with Christian theology, and the established violence of Latin American dictatorships may, if necessary, be responded to by violence. His major books are *Theology of Liberation* (1971, English 1973) and *We Drink from our Own* Wells (1984).

📖 James B. Nickoloff (ed), *Gustavo Gutiérrez – Essential Writings*, Maryknoll, NY: Orbis Books and London: SCM Press 1996

Guyon, Jeanne-Marie Bouvier de la Mothe (1648–1717) French mystic and champion of Quietism. Married to a much older rich husband and widowed, Madame Guyon (the name by which she is known) spent the rest of her life communicating her spiritual experience. For her, Christian life was one of contemplation of God in which the soul loses all concern for itself. Always controversial, and sure of being in the right, when she gained prominence in Paris she was imprisoned on suspicion of Quietism. Though soon released, she was twice condemned by the church and sent to the Bastille for a longer period, despite the support of Archbishop Fénélon, on whom she was a great influence. On submitting to discipline, she was released and spent her last years in Blois. Her teaching is recorded in *A Short and Very Easy Way of Praying* (1685).

📖 M. de la Bedoyère, *The Archbishop and the Lady: The Story of Fénélon and Madame Guyon*, London: Collins 1956

Hadewijch (thirteenth century) Flemish mystic. Little is known of her life; even her dates are uncertain. Though her letters were quoted in the fourteenth century by Jan van Ruysbroeck, manuscripts of her works were not discovered until the mid-nineteenth century. She seems to have been a Beguine, i.e. a devout woman who chose to lead a life of poverty and contemplation but without taking vows. Her writings indicate that her authority in the group was challenged and she may have been evicted. She was well read in the Bible, theology and French Romantic literature. She wrote visions, poems in stanzas and poems in couplets, and these are an important addition to our knowledge of medieval women mystics.

📖 Hadewijch, *The Complete Works*, Classics of Western Spirituality, New York and Mahwah, NJ: Paulist Press 1980

Hammarskjøld, Dag (1905–61) Swedish economist and statesman. The son of a Swedish Prime Minister, he studied law and economics at the universities of Uppsala and Stockholm and then taught political economy in Stockholm. In 1936 he joined the civil service, later becoming president of the board of the Bank of Sweden. In 1947 he moved to the ministry of foreign affairs, and in 1952 became head of the Swedish delegation to the United Nations. The next year he became the second Secretary-General of the United Nations, serving for five years and then being re-appointed. He was killed in a plane crash in the Congo to which he had sent a UN force at a time of civil war there. After his death a manuscript, *Markings*, was found among his papers, a spiritual diary which showed the depth of his religious life and proved to be a twentieth-century classic.

📖 Dag Hammarskjöld, *Markings*, London: Faber and New York: Alfred A. Knopf 1966

Harnack, Adolf von (1851–1930) German church historian. Son of a Lutheran scholar, after studying at Leipzig he became professor at Giessen, Marburg and Berlin (though because he had become suspect to it, the church denied him all recognition in this last post). A man of immense learning, he wrote major works on church history *(History of Dogma*, 1886–9; *The Mission and Expansion of Christianity*, 1902, enlarged 1924) as well as (in more conservative vein) *On the New Testament*. His theological views were popularized in his 1900 lectures *What is Christianity?*: for him, Christianity was about the Fatherhood of God, the infinite worth of the individual soul and the commandment to love. In his old age he clashed with Karl Barth, who was hostile to him for his liberal views and his support of the First World War. This was an encounter of total mutual incomprehension.

📖 G. Wayne Glick, *The Reality of Christianity. A Study of Adolf von Harnack as Historian and Theologian*, New York: Harper & Row 1967

Harris, William Wadé (*c.* 1860–1929) African prophet and evangelist. Born in Liberia of the Glebo people, at the age of 20 he had a conversion experience and became a Methodist lay preacher. After marrying the daughter of a teacher at a US Episcopal Church school he worked for the Episcopal mission from 1892–1908 as a teacher and evangelist, eventually coming to hold an apocalyptic view of the world. He also became official interpreter for the Glebo people. However, during this period his bishop, who opposed Harris' views, also became anti-Glebo and Harris was dismissed; in 1910 he was imprisoned for political activities, and while he was in prison he had a vision which convinced him that he was a prophet of the last times. He preached across the Ivory Coast to what is now Ghana, with such success that the French authorities imprisoned and then expelled him, so that his activities were confined to Liberia and Sierra Leone. He went around accompanied by women singers, with a turban, white robes and bare feet, carrying a staff in the form of a cross, a Bible, a rattle and a bowl to baptize people from. He taught the Lord's Prayer, the Ten Commandments and the strict observance of Sunday. He refused money for his ministry and sent those he baptized to Protestant or Catholic missionaries; where these were not available he nominated 'twelve apostles' from the locality. Prophet Harris became one of the best-known leaders of African mass movements in the early twentieth century.

📖 Sheila S. Walker, *Religious Revolution in the Ivory Coast: The Prophet Harris and the Harrisist Church*, Chapel Hill, NC: University of North Carolina Press 1983

Hartshorne, Charles (1897–2001) American philosopher. After study at Haverford and Harvard, Freiburg and Marburg he became professor in Chicago, at Emory and at the University of Texas. A 'process' philosopher, much indebted in his thought to Alfred North Whitehead but differing from him in approach, he was a leading advocate of a new view of God, characterized by the term 'panentheism', the doctrine that all is in God (this differs from pantheism by holding that God's reality is not exhausted by the fact that God includes the world). The most important difference between panentheism and the classical view of God is that it introduces change, temporality and relationality into the being of God. This view is claimed to have a close affinity to the biblical view of God. His major works include *Man's Vision of God* (1941), *The Divine Relativity* (1948), and *A Natural Theology for Our Time* (1967).

📖 Alan Gragg, *Charles Hartshorne*, Waco, TX: Word Books 1977

Hegel, Georg Wilhelm Friedrich (1770–1831) German philosopher. Born in Stuttgart, he studied theology in Tübingen and while tutor in Switzerland wrote a life of Christ, seeing him not as a moral teacher but as one in whom virtue and vice were transcended in an infinite life. After various teaching posts he became professor of philosophy first in Heidelberg and then in Berlin, succeeding the Kantian philosopher Johann Gottlieb Fichte. In the idealist tradition, he is well known for his view of historical development as a threefold process of thesis, antithesis, synthesis, representing a dialectical evolution of Spirit, i.e. God in process. Truth is a totality, rather than the property of individual disciplines. He also applied this approach to Christianity. His views were very influential, not least on Ferdinand Christian Baur, Ludwig Feuerbach, Karl Marx and David Friedrich Strauss. Many of his best-known books arose out of lecture courses in Berlin, including *Philosophy* of *History, Philosophy of Religion* and *Aesthetics.*

📖 Peter Singer, *Hegel. A Very Short Introduction*, Oxford: OUP 2001

Heidegger, Martin (1889–1976) German existentialist philosopher. Son of a Catholic sexton in Baden, after studying at a Jesuit seminary he went to Freiburg University. He lectured there, and then became professor of philosophy at Marburg, but returned to Freiburg in 1929. He remained in Freiburg until the end of the Second World War, when he came under justified suspicion for sympathies with the Nazi regime. Subsequently he lived in seclusion in the Black Forest. In his most important work, *Being and Time* (1927, English 1962), he analysed the distinctiveness of human existence as care, characterized by possibility, facticity and fallenness, seeing human beings as thrown into a world in which they have to cope with death and are faced with the alternatives of authentic and inauthentic existence. This existentialist philosophy was welcomed as a vehicle for the communication of Christianity in the modern world, especially by Rudolf Bultmann in his programme of demythologization. There is argument over how Heidegger's later philosophy relates to his early work, but it too has been influential on theology.

📖 Michael Inwood, *Heidegger. A Very Short Introduction*, Oxford: OUP 2000

Herbert of Cherbury, Edward (1583–1648) English philosopher. After an eventful youth he became ambassador to Paris, where he wrote (in Latin) a philosophical treatise attacking empiricism. He went on to write on religion. A forerunner of deism, he defended a rational religion based on innate ideas, namely that there is a God, who ought to be worshipped, principally through virtue; that repentance is a duty and that there is another life with rewards and punishments. He was the first Lord Herbert of Cherbury.

📖 J. M. Shuttleworth (ed), *Life of Lord Herbert of Cherbury, Written by Himself*, Oxford: OUP 1976

Herbert, George (1593–1633) English poet. Younger brother of Edward Herbert, he studied classics at Cambridge and was also a gifted musician. He became public orator at Cambridge, though he spent most of his time at court. The death of King James I and his patrons led him to be ordained five years later, and he spent the last years of his life as a parish priest near Salisbury. He wrote an account of the English clergyman, *A Priest to the Temple*, published posthumously. He is best known for his poems, full of Anglican spirituality.

📖 Christina Malcolmson, *George Herbert: A Literary Life*, London: Palgrave Macmillan 2003

Herrmann, Wilhelm (1846–1922) German theologian. After teaching at Halle, he became professor at Marburg. In the Idealist tradition, influenced by Kant and Ritschl, he saw God as the power of goodness and Jesus as an exemplary man; even if Jesus never existed, his portrait was still valid. His book *The Communion of the Christian with God* (1886) was regarded as almost a paradigm of the liberal theology against which Barth and dialectical theology reacted.

📖 W. Herrmann, *The Communion of the Christian with God*, Philadelphia: Fortress Press 1971 and London: SCM Press 1972

Hick, John Harwood (1922–) English philosopher of religion. He studied in Edinburgh, Oxford and Cambridge, becoming professor in Birmingham (where he was deeply involved in race relations) and Claremont. A United Reformed Church minister, he was twice indicted for heresy in the United States. He became well known through his *Evil and the God of Love* (1966), offering an alternative approach to the traditional interpretation of evil, predominantly based on Augustine, reviving the rather more optimistic views associated with Irenaeus. He remained in the public eye through his editorship of *The Myth of God Incarnate* (1977), which questioned the doctrine of the incarnation, and *The Myth of Christian Uniqueness* (1989), which argued for religious pluralism. In the latter book, with others he 'crossed the Rubicon' by claiming that Christians may believe that salvation need not necessarily be exclusively through Christ. In his philosophical work he introduced the idea of 'eschatological verification', namely that faith will be verified or not at the end of life, as a way of justifying Christian beliefs philosophically.

📖 John Hick, *John Hick. An Autobiography*, Oxford: Oneworld 2002

Hilary of Poitiers (*c.*315–67) French theologian. Born of a prominent family, after a classical education he was converted and made Bishop of Poitiers by popular acclaim. Banished to Phrygia for his defence of Athanasius in the anti-Arian disputes, he had an opportunity to get to know Eastern theology, which influenced him, to the degree that his christology is almost Monophysite (suggesting that Christ had only one, divine, nature). For his stance he became known as the 'Athanasius of the West'. Chief among his works, which are not easy to understand, is *On the Trinity*.

📖 C. F. A. Borchardt, *Hilary of Poitiers' Role in the Arian Struggle*, The Hague: Nijhoff 1966

Hildegard of Bingen (1098–1179) German mystic. Born of a noble family at Bockenheim on the river Nahe, and experiencing visions from childhood, she was brought up by a recluse called Jutta, who formed a Benedictine community. At the age of 18 she joined the community, and twenty years later became its abbess. She described her visions in her main work *Scivias*, which has an apocalyptic flavour. Her correspondence and travels in Germany and France made her influential and she also wrote on medicine and natural history, created an alphabet and language of her own, and composed music.

📖 Fiona Maddocks, *Hildegard of Bingen. The Woman of Her Age*, New York: Image Books 2003

Hippolytus of Rome (*c.*170–236) Roman churchman. Little is known of his life, probably because he was involved in disputes with the mainstream church (including one over the terms on which sinners could be readmitted to the church, in which he took a hard line) and because he wrote in Greek. This led to later confusion over his identity. He was the last major Eastern church writer working in Rome, and his *Apostolic Tradition* gives an important picture of church life there in the second century, particularly its liturgy; his *Refutation of all Heresies* is the longest of the anti-Gnostic treatises. His *Commentary on Daniel* is the oldest to come down to us in its entirety; he was the first to construct a scheme for calculating Easter independent of Judaism.

📖 Gregory Dix and Henry Chadwick (eds), *The Treatise on the Apostolic Tradition of Hippolytus of Rome*, London: Alban Books 1992

Hodge, Charles (1797–1878) American Calvinist theologian. He was born in Philadelphia, son of an army surgeon, and educated at Princeton, where he remained for the rest of his life. He was a great controversialist, upholding traditional Calvinism with rigorous arguments, in a system which he believed to be faithful to the Westminster Confession and the Reformation. He defended a supernaturally inspired Bible. This approach came to be known as Princeton theology and was a great influence on American Presbyterianism. He wrote a three-volume *Systematic Theology* (1871–3).

📖 H. T. Kerr, *Sons of the Prophets: Leaders in Protestantism from Princeton Seminary*, Princeton, NJ: Princeton University Press 1963

Hontheim, Johann Nikolaus von (1701–90) He was born in Trier, where, after study at Louvain, he spent most of his life, being ordained priest and later becoming assistant bishop. In 1742 he began to investigate the historical basis of the papacy and in the Latin work which resulted, *The State of the Church and the Legitimate Authority of the Roman Pontiff* (1763), while recognizing the Pope as head of the church, attacked the power the papacy had gained in the Middle Ages. He argued that church affairs should be basically under the control of bishops and civil authorities. The book was banned, but the pseudonym under which it was published, Justinus Febronius, gave its name to a movement, Febronianism. Hontheim later published a recantation, but with little change of view.

Hooker, Richard (*c.*1554–1600) Anglican churchman. Born near Exeter, he studied at Oxford, where he became a professor, though he spent most of his life in charge of parishes and as a chaplain to lawyers in London. He was a skilful champion of Anglicanism; his great work is the *Treatise on the Laws of Ecclesiastical Polity* (1594–7, some books appeared posthumously), which defended the Church of England against Puritan criticism with an appeal to natural law and common consent. However, he had a markedly low church view of the sacraments, reflected both in his eucharistic doctrine and his denial of the need for episcopal ordination.

📖 E. T. Davies, *The Political Ideas of Richard Hooker*, London: SPCK 1946

Hopkins, Gerard Manley (1844–89) English poet. Born in Stratford, Essex, and brought up as an Anglican, he was received into the Roman Catholic Church by Cardinal Newman when studying at Oxford. He then became a Jesuit. After ordination he held several teaching posts and in 1884 became professor of Greek in Dublin. His sensitive and often agonized poetry, the most noted of which is 'The Wreck of the Deutschland', was collected by Robert Bridges and published posthumously (1918).

📖 Paddy Kitchen, *Gerard Manley Hopkins*, London: Carcanet Press 1989

Hugh of St Victor (died 1142) Theologian. Little is known of his life, but he probably came from Lorraine or the Low Countries. He was the most distinguished of the Victorines, scholars living at the abbey of St Victor in Paris, a kind of chaplaincy to university students, and he was called a 'second Augustine'. He sought to integrate the new learning that was developing into the content of an introduction and guide to Bible study, in the process pioneering a new approach to scripture. He wrote on a wide range of topics, including biblical commentaries (on those books in which he was interested), history, grammar and geometry. He had a vivid imagination and a scientific curiosity; he learned Hebrew and talked with Jews. His interests were taken further by his pupil Andrew (see also Richard of St Victor).

📖 B. Smalley, *The Study of the Bible in the Middle Ages*, Oxford: Blackwell [3]1983

Hume, David (1711–76) Scottish philosopher and historian. He was born and educated in Edinburgh and held several administrative posts in England and abroad. His philosophy attacks reason by making it a product of experience: on the basis of experience the facts of reality can be established only with a degree of probability. This led, for example, to a challenge to belief in miracles. Since belief in God cannot be proved by reason, it must be a matter of faith. His major works in this area were *Philosophical Essays concerning Human Understanding* (1748) and the posthumous *Dialogues concerning Natural Religion*. His approach has been regarded as one of the most basic attacks on theology.

📖 David O'Connor, *Routledge Philosophy Guidebook to Hume on Religion*, London and New York: Routledge 2000

Huntingdon, Selina, Countess of (1707–91) English religious leader. She joined John and Charles Wesley's Methodist society, and at the age of 40, on her husband's death, devoted herself to its cause, opening her home, Trevecca House, in Breconshire, as a Methodist seminary. Legal objections to her appointing Methodist ministers as her chaplains led her to register her own chapels as dissenting. In disputes between John Wesley and George Whitefield she sided with the latter; this led to a split and the formation of the Calvinist Methodist 'Countess of Huntingdon's Connexion'.

📖 Faith Cook, *Selina Countess of Huntingdon. Her Pivotal Role in the Eighteenth-Century Evangelical Awakening*, Edinburgh: Banner of Truth 2001

Hus, John (1369–1415) Bohemian reformer. Born of a peasant family, he studied at Prague University, where he eventually became dean. He gained his influence as preacher of the Bethlehem chapel there. Attracted by Wyclif's doctrine, he attacked the morals of the clergy, a hierarchical and propertied church and the sale of indulgences. He was excommunicated in 1412 and went into exile, but was lured by promise of safe conduct to the Council of Constance, which condemned him and burnt him at the stake. He became a national hero.

📖 Matthew Spinka, *John Hus: A Biography*, London: Greenwood Press 1979

Hutter, Jacob (died 1536) Moravian Anabaptist leader. He became leader of disparate Anabaptist groups in 1529 and united and organized them with a view to communal production and consumption. This aroused fierce Roman Catholic opposition and he was burnt at the stake, but he succeeded in founding a tradition which has lasted to the present day.

📖 G. H. Williams, *The Radical Reformation*, Kirksville, MO: Truman State University Press [3]2001

Ignatius of Antioch (*c.*35–*c.*107) Martyr bishop. Little is known of his life; he was probably born in Syria and was one of the first bishops of Antioch. He was sent under escort to Rome, where he was executed. His letters, written from Smyrna while he was staying with Polycarp, and from Troas, are important evidence for the early church: in them he pleads for a unity of the church which is not only spiritual but bodily in the face of a threatened division through a heresy which seems to be some form of Gnosticism.

📖 Simon Tugwell, *The Apostolic Fathers*, London and New York: Continuum 1989

Ignatius Loyola (1491–1556) Founder of the Jesuit order. Son of a Spanish nobleman, he had a career in the court and the army, but at the age of 30 was wounded. During his convalescence he was converted to an ideal represented by Francis of Assisi and Dominic, and in a period of prayer and extreme austerity began writing his *Spiritual Exercises*. After an abortive attempt to settle in the Holy Land he studied theology and philosophy at Barcelona, Alcala and Salamanca. From there he went on to Paris and then, again prevented from going to Palestine, with the group of companions who had meanwhile gathered round him, put himself at the service of the Pope. The Jesuit order was given papal recognition by Paul III in 1540, with Ignatius as its reluctant superior general, and he spent the rest of his life organizing it.

📖 J. P. Donnelly, *Ignatius Loyola. Founder of the Jesuits*, London: Longman 2003

Illich, Ivan (1926–2002) Catholic educationalist. Born in Vienna, after studying in Rome and Salzburg he was ordained and went to the United States as assistant priest in a New York Irish-Puerto Rican parish. He later became vice-rector of the Catholic University of Puerto Rico. He was a co-founder of the Center for Intercultural Documentation in Cuernavaca, Mexico, and for many years directed research seminars on 'Institutional Alternatives in a Technological Society'. His *Deschooling Society* (1971) questioned much in current educational thinking, and his *Limits to Medicine* (1976) brought out the disadvantage of professional control over medicine. He argued that people need to be more involved in decision-making in matters which affect their lives, from education and health to transport and religion.

📖 Carl Mitcham and Lee Hoinacki, *The Challenges of Ivan Illich*, Albany, NY: State University Press of New York 2002

Irenaeus (*c.* 130–*c.* 200) Church father. Born in Asia Minor and acquainted with Polycarp, he studied in Rome before going to Lyons, of which he became bishop. His encounter with Gnosticism led him to write his *Against the Heresies* in five books, which now survive only in Latin. He is particularly known for his doctrine of recapitulation (Greek *anakephalaiosis*), that all those men and women who had lived before the saving work of Jesus were taken up into Christ in such a way that even Adam could be saved. His less dark view of sin and evil is often contrasted with that of Augustine and was espoused in modern times by John Hick.

📖 R. M. Grant, *Irenaeus of Lyons*, London and New York: Routledge 1997

Irving, Edward (1792–1834) Scottish minister. He was born in Dumfriesshire and studied in Edinburgh. After being assistant in Glasgow to Thomas Chalmers, the forceful evangelical minister who founded the Free Church of Scotland, he went to London, where he was so successful with a blend of Catholicism and Pentecostalism that a new church was built for him. But his popularity wore off and he became more extreme, turning to millenarian ideas among others, and these were a contributory factor to his downfall. He was excommunicated on the grounds of his belief that Christ's human nature was sinful, and removed from office. His followers constituted a new Catholic Apostolic Church (they are also known as 'Irvingites', though he did not found the church). Irving returned to Scotland until he was expelled from there, assuming a minor role in the sect which had grown from him.

📖 A. Dallimore, *The Life of Edward Irving: Fore-runner of the Charismatic Movement*, Edinburgh: Banner of Truth 1983

Isidore of Seville (560–636) Spanish scholar. Of a noble family, he had a monastic education and succeeded his brother as Archbishop of Seville. He was famous for his holiness and learning, and his works; some of them, meant as textbooks for cathedral schools, proved a storehouse of information for later ages, preserving the essentials of ancient learning until later medieval revivals.

📖 Ernest Brehaut, *An Encyclopedia of the Dark Ages. Isidore of Seville*, New York: Burt Franklin 1967

James, William (1842–1910) American psychologist and philosopher. He was born in New York, the son of a Swedenborgian theologian and brother of the novelist Henry James, and studied at Harvard and in Europe. He was originally a medical student, but his interests turned to psychology and philosophy, and after teaching at Harvard, in 1885 he became professor of philosophy there; he also lectured widely in America and Europe. He had a popular style; his psychological interests are expressed in his classic *The Varieties of Religious Experience* (1902), in which he analysed conversion and distinguished between once-born and twice-born believers. His philosophical interests are expressed in his *Pragmatism* (1901). He saw truth as something to be made and remade on the basis of experience; the truth of religion lay in the fact that it was virtually a universal experience.

📖 William James, *The Varieties of Religious Experience*, New York: Penguin Books 1983

Jansen, Cornelius Otto (1585–1638) Belgian theologian. Born in Utrecht, the son of the Bishop of Ghent, he studied at Louvain and in Paris, and then became director of a newly-founded college in Louvain. In 1636 he was made Bishop of Ypres. His *magnum opus* was *Augustinus* (1640), about grace and human freedom, based on Augustine and against scholasticism. It became the basis of the religious reform movement of Jansenism, to which Jansen gave his name. Jansenists had the pessimistic view that human beings cannot perform God's commands without his grace, and grace is irresistible.

📖 William Doyle, *Jansenism*, New York: St Martin's Press 2000

Jerome (Eusebius Hieronymus, *c.* 345–420) Hermit and biblical scholar. He was born on the Adriatic coast, educated in Rome, and after much travelling ultimately settled in Bethlehem, where he founded a monastery and devoted the rest of his life to biblical study. Mastering Greek and Hebrew, he translated the Bible into Latin, and this Vulgate, as it is called, influenced the church down to modern times; he also wrote commentaries on most biblical books. An ascetic and a great controversialist, he wrote, among others, against Augustine, Origen and Pelagius. His letters are particularly important.

📖 J. N. D. Kelly, *Jerome: His Life, Writings and Controversies*, London: Duckworth 1975

Joachim of Fiore (1132–1202) Italian mystic. Little is known of his life; after a pilgrimage to the Holy Land he became abbot of a Cistercian house in Calabria. However, a few years later he left to found his own congregation in Fiore. Allegedly on the basis of a vision in his youth, he interpreted history in terms of the Trinity: the Old Testament was the age of the Father; the New Testament was the age of the Son, which would end soon after his day; he identified the new age of the Spirit then to come with the millennium of the biblical book of Revelation. Some of his views were subsequently condemned, but his ideas of the new age caught the imagination of revolutionary groups. His main works were the *Book of Concord of the Old and New Testament, Psalter of Ten Strings*, and a commentary on Revelation.

📖 Marjorie Reeves, *Joachim of Fiore and the Prophetic Future*, Stroud: Sutton Publishing 1999

John Cassian (*c.* 360–435) Monk. Born in Scythia, he went to a monastery in Bethlehem, then to Egypt and Constantinople, before settling in Marseilles. He introduced Eastern monasticism to the West. His *Institutes* influenced the Rule of Benedict and was long regarded as a spiritual classic. His *Conferences* recount his conversations with the great leaders of Eastern monasticism.

📖 Owen Chadwick, *John Cassian. A Study in Mediaeval Monasticism*, Cambridge: CUP ²1968

John Chrysostom (*c.*347–407) Bishop and preacher. Born at Antioch of noble parents, he studied law and theology before becoming a monk. When the monastic rule damaged his health he returned to Antioch where he became a famous preacher (his name means 'golden mouth'). Somewhat against his will he became Patriarch of Constantinople, and proved a vigorous reformer. His measures caused hostility, leading him to be condemned for heresy and ultimately exiled. His works comprise hundreds of sermons and many letters.

📖 J. N. D. Kelly, *Golden Mouth*, Ithaca, NY: Cornell University Press 1995

John Climacus (*c.*570–649) Spiritual writer. A monk on Sinai, he became a hermit and later was abbot of Sinai. His writing *The Ladder* (Greek *climax*, hence his name) *of Paradise* presented the achievement of Christian perfection as climbing 30 steps of a ladder, to correspond to the years of Jesus' supposed age.

📖 Colm Luibheid (ed), *John Climacus: The Ladder of Divine Ascent*, New York and Mahwah, NJ: Paulist Press 1988

John of the Cross (Juan de Yepis y Alvarez, 1542–91) Spanish mystic. Son of a poor family of noble origin, he became a Carmelite, studied theology at Salamanca, and was ordained priest. With the help of Teresa of Avila he sought to reform his order, but this led to opposition, resulting in a split between calced and discalced Carmelites (those who did or did not wear sandals). Prior of several monasteries of the discalced, he eventually fell out with the vicar general and was banished to Andalusia, where he died. An unusually perceptive mystic, he is best known through *The Spiritual Canticle* (1578), *The Ascent of Mount Carmel* (1579), and *The Living Flame of Love* (1583). He is particularly noted for his account of 'the dark night of the soul'.

📖 R. A. Herrera, *Silent Music: The Life, Work and Thought of St John of the Cross*, Grand Rapids, MI: Eerdmans 2004

John of Damascus (*c.*655–*c.*750) Greek theologian. After serving as a Christian representative in the court of the caliph of Damascus, he moved to Jerusalem, where he became a priest. A traditionalist and systematician, in the controversy over icons he defended their use. His *Feast of Wisdom*, covering philosophy, heresies and orthodox belief, became a textbook in the Orthodox Church, but was long unknown in the West. He is regarded as the last of the great Eastern church fathers. He also wrote famous hymns, including 'The Day of Resurrection, earth tell it out abroad'.

📖 David Anderson, *John of Damascus: On the Divine Images*, Crestwood, NY: St Vladimir's Seminary Press 1980

Josephus, Flavius (37–100) Jewish historian. Son of a Palestinian priestly family, he lived in the desert with a hermit before becoming a Pharisee. He took part in the Jewish War and was captured by the Roman general Vespasian, whose favour he won by prophesying that Vespasian would become emperor. Freed when this happened, Josephus became a Roman citizen and had a pension which enabled him to devote his time to literary work. He is the most important primary source for Palestine in the New Testament period. His main works are *The Jewish War*, a personal account; *Jewish Antiquities*, a twenty-volume history of the Jews from creation; and his autobiography.

📖 Tessa Rajak, *Josephus*, London: Duckworth 2002

Julian of Norwich (*c.*1342–*c.*1420) English mystic. She lived in a cell beside St Julian's church in Norwich, from which she may have taken her name. Little is known of her life, but reflection on her visions is contained in her *Revelations of Divine Love*, one of the great spiritual classics, which emphasizes the love of God and contains the great assurance that 'all shall be well'.

📖 Julian of Norwich, *Revelations of Divine Love*, Harmondsworth: Penguin Books 1998

Jung, Carl Gustav (1875–1961) Swiss psychologist. Born in Thurgau canton, Switzerland, he studied in Basle and then worked in the Zurich psychiatric clinic. This led to collaboration with Freud, but in 1913 a break came with Freud's essentially sexually-orientated theories. Jung subsequently worked in Zurich, developing his own views under the name of analytical psychology. He postulated a collective unconscious common to all human beings through history, expressed through basic forms of archetypes. On this basis he saw the human psyche in terms of the shadow, the *animus* and the *anima*, which are projections from the archetypes. He regarded his analytical psychology as friendly to religion, seeing religion as a mythological description of how the psyche works and as a way of bringing healing to the psyche, but he was uninterested in the foundations of theology. His writings range widely and are collected in twenty volumes.

📖 C. G. Jung, *Memories, Dreams, Reflections*, London: Collins Fontana 1983 and New York: Vintage Books 1989

Justin Martyr (*c.*100–*c.*165) Roman apologist. Born of pagan parents in Shechem, Palestine, he studied the leading philosophies before being converted to Christianity. He taught in many great cities, and spent some time in Rome. He was denounced as a Christian and beheaded. He is important for his Christian interpretation of the Old Testament and the way in which he uses the Gospels as providing confirmation of the fulfilment of prophecy. He argued that Christianity was not immoral and was compatible with the best of Greek philosophy. His major works are his *Apology* and *A Dialogue with the Jew Trypho*.

📖 L. W. Barnard, *Justin Martyr: His Life and Thought*, Cambridge: CUP 1967

Justinian (483–565) Roman emperor. He did much to extend the empire and built many basilicas, notably in Ravenna and Constantinople (Santa Sophia). His lawyers drafted the basic code of Roman law. As a Christian he championed Chalcedonian orthodoxy and was concerned for collaboration between church and state in one body.

📖 A. H. M. Jones, *The Later Roman Empire 1*, Baltimore: Johns Hopkins University Press 1986

Kagawa, Toyohiko (1888–1960) Japanese social reformer. From a wealthy family, he was brought up a Buddhist. When he was converted to Christianity, his family disinherited him. He studied at the Presbyterian seminary in Kobe, and then, becoming aware of the social dimensions of Christianity, went to work in the slums. From 1914 he spent three years at Princeton Theological Seminary learning modern methods of social welfare and then returned to work among the poor. He helped to establish churches, schools and missions, and founded the first Japanese trade union and peasant union. Imprisoned during the Second World War, afterwards he became a democratic leader and member of the Japanese House of Peers. He wrote many books, including *The Religion of Jesus* (1931) and *Christ and Japan* (1934).

📖 C. J. Davey, *Kagawa of Japan*, London: Epworth Press and Nashville, TN: Abingdon Press 1960

Kähler, Martin (1835–1912) German systematic theologian. Born in Prussia the son of a Lutheran pastor, after university studies he spent his life as professor at Halle. Though he wrote a major book on Christian doctrine, he is best known for his collection of essays *The So-Called Historical Jesus and the Historic, Biblical Christ* (1892), in which he rejected the nineteenth-century quest for the historical Jesus; the real Christ is the Christ of preaching, as he is encountered in the church. Kähler's recognition that the Gospels are made up of units, each reflecting Christ in a variety of aspects, anticipated the form criticism of Rudolf Bultmann and Martin Dibelius.

📖 Martin Kahler, *The So-Called Historical Jesus and the Historic, Biblical Christ*, Philadelphia: Fortress Press 1964

Kant, Immanuel (1724–1804) German philosopher. He was born and died in Königsberg in Prussia and never went outside Prussia. Influenced by David Hume, he sought to demonstrate the role of reason in the gaining of knowledge. He undermined the metaphysical basis of orthodox and rational dogmatics by his argument that human beings do not know 'things in themselves' with the aim of 'removing knowledge to make room for faith'. The classical proofs for the existence of God were untenable. With these views, expressed in his *Critique of Pure Reason* (1781), he set the agenda for nineteenth-century theology, influencing such different figures as Friedrich Schleiermacher, Albrecht Ritschl, Ludwig Feuerbach and David Friedrich Strauss. His *Critique of Practical Reason* (1788) discussed the problem of morality and its implications for theism; his other major work was *Religion within the Limits of Reason Alone* (1793).

📖 Roger Scruton, *Kant: A Very Short Introduction*, Oxford: OUP 2001

Keble, John (1792–1866) English tractarian and poet. Son of a clergyman, after a distinguished career at Oxford, culminating in his appointment as professor of poetry, he spent most of his life in a country parish near Winchester. A leading figure in the Oxford Movement, which aimed at restoring high church ideals (John

Henry Newman regarded the 1833 Assize sermon which Keble preached as its start), he was a champion of apostolic succession in the church and of the centrality of the eucharist in worship. As well as writing many tracts, he joined Newman and Pusey in editing a library of the church fathers, which were then being rediscovered. But his best-known work is *The Christian Year* (1827), poems for Sundays and holy days, the source of many hymns.

📖 B. W. Martin, *John Keble: Priest, Professor and Poet*, London: Croom Helm 1976

Kempe, Margery (*c.*1373–*c.*1438) English mystic. Born in Norfolk, she married a local offical by whom she had fourteen children. Then after a pilgrimage to Canterbury, she and her husband took vows of chastity; she later went on pilgrimage to Europe and Palestine. She is known from *The Book of Margery Kempe*, an account of her travels and mystical experiences, which included visions and revelations; she was an acquaintance of Julian of Norwich.

📖 *The Book of Margery Kempe*, Harmondsworth: Penguin Books 1985

Ken, Thomas (1637–1711) Anglican bishop. He went to school at Winchester College, where he returned to teach after studying and teaching at Oxford, and looking after several parishes. He became a royal chaplain to Charles II, refusing to offer hospitality to Nell Gwynne; as a result of this principled stand the king made him Bishop of Bath and Wells. His principles also emerged in his refusal to sign either James II's Declaration of Indulgence which allowed freedom of worship to Non-conformists or the oath of allegiance to William of Orange. As a 'Non-juror' he was thereupon deposed and spent the rest of his life in retirement. He lived an ascetic life, and wrote an exposition of the catechism and many hymns, including 'Glory to thee, my God, this night'.

📖 H. A. L. Rice, *Thomas Ken: Bishop and Non-Juror*, London: SPCK 1964

Kierkegaard, Søren Aaby (1813–55) Danish philosopher. The son of a wealthy Lutheran hosier, he spent his life in Copenhagen. He was melancholy in disposition, with much unhappiness in his life, and his works are introspective and individualistic. But he was a great influence on subsequent philosophy and theology, particularly existentialism and dialectical theology, and a major figure of the nineteenth century. As indicated by his famous remark 'truth is subjectivity', he took as his focal point the individual in his existence, relegating reason to the lowest level of human activity. He saw the need to rise from being a mere spectator, through responsible decision and a sense of failure, to belief in Christ. Among his many works are: *Either/Or* (1843), *The Concept of Dread* (1844) and *Concluding Unscientific Postscript* (1846); these were succeeded by more 'Christian' works, including *Training in Christianity* (1850); he also wrote a *Journal*.

📖 Alastair Hannay, *Kierkegaard. An Intellectual Biography*, Cambridge: CUP 2002

Kimbangu, Simon (*c.*1889–1951) Church founder. Born in Lower Zaire, he was instructed in the Christian faith by the Baptist Missionary Society and baptized in 1915, but otherwise had no education. He experienced a visionary calling, and proved to have spiritual gifts of healing, but because of his lack of education, his application to become a missionary was rejected. In 1921 he embarked on a six-month period of public ministry, with many charismatic phenomena, proclaiming the direct intervention of God, the uselessness of African fetishes, and the coming end of colonial rule. Like Jesus he appointed twelve 'apostles'. This attracted police attention, as a result of which he surrendered to the Belgian authorities. He was sentenced to death, but this was commuted to life imprisonment, which he served, being regarded as a dangerous convict. On his death bed he was baptized into the Catholic Church. His apostles and thousands of his followers were banned, but Kimbanguism put down deep roots in what was then the Belgian Congo, offering Africans a new social vision, a new view of God's love in African terms, and an account of Black people's special place in the world.

📖 M. L. Martin, *Kimbangu: An African Prophet and his Church*, Oxford: Blackwell 1975 and Grand Rapids, MI: Eerdmans 1976

King, Martin Luther, Jr (1929–68) American civil rights leader. Born in Atlanta, after gaining a doctorate at Boston University he became a Baptist pastor in Alabama, then was co-pastor with his father in Atlanta. He became prominent in the movement to secure equal rights for blacks by non-violence, organized the Southern Christian Leadership Conference, led the 1963 March on Washington and was awarded the Nobel Peace Prize. He was assassinated by a white man in Memphis, Tennessee. A moving orator and preacher, he also wrote books, including *Stride toward Freedom* (1958) and *Why We Can't Wait* (1964).

📖 Stephen B. Oates, *Let The Trumpets Sound: The Life of Martin Luther King Jr*, New York: Harper & Row 1982

Kingsley, Charles (1819–75) English novelist and social reformer. He was born in Devon and educated at King's College, London and Cambridge. After being vicar of a country parish he was made professor of modern history at Cambridge before going on to canonries at Chester and Westminster. Influenced by F. D. Maurice, he became associated with Christian Socialism in a concern for reform in education and hygiene, as evidenced in his best-known novel *The Water Babies* (1863); he also wrote *Hereward the Wake* (1866) and many other novels. No great intellectual, he became associated with the phrase 'muscular Christianity'. He was a vigorous opponent of the high church Oxford Movement, and an ill-considered insult to John Henry Newman led the latter to write his *Apologia pro Vita Sua*.

📖 Brenda Colloms, *Charles Kingsley*, London: Constable 1975

Klopstock, Friedrich Gottlieb (1724–1823) German religious poet. Son of a lawyer, he studied theology at Jena and Leipzig. At school he conceived the plan of a religious epic, *The Messiah*, inspired by Milton's *Paradise Lost*, which he did not complete until 1773. Given a pension by the King of Denmark to enable him to finish the work, he lived first in Copenhagen, then in Hamburg. Its publication was a landmark in German literature. He also wrote other works and latterly devoted himself to philosophy.

📖 F. G. Klopstock, *The Messiah*, Bungay: C. Brightly 1808

Knox, John (*c.*1513–72) Scottish Reformer. Born in Haddington and educated at St Andrews, he was ordained and served as a tutor before being converted to Protestantism. Captured in a drive against heretics, he was sent as a galley slave to France. On his return to England, he continued his protests, and had to flee to the continent in the reign of Queen Mary, where at Calvin's prompting he became pastor to the English congregation in Frankfurt. Further disputes took him to Geneva, where he wrote *The First Blast of the Trumpet against the Monstrous Regiment of Women*, arguing against female sovereignty. In 1559 he returned to Scotland, where he was instrumental in shaping the Kirk of Scotland through the Scots Confession and the Book of Common Order. He also wrote a history of the Reformation in Scotland.

📖 J. Ridley, *John Knox*, Oxford: OUP 1968

Kraemer, Hendrik (1888–1966) Dutch missioner. After training in oriental languages, he was sent by the Netherlands Bible Society to serve in Indonesia, where he wrote his most famous book, The *Christian Message in a Non-Christian World* (1938), which argued that the Christian revelation is incomparable and *sui generis*, and that co-operation with non-Christian religions is a betrayal of truth. In 1937 he became professor of religion in the University of Leiden and in 1948 the first director of the World Council of Churches Ecumenical Institute at Bossey. His thought was very influential on the WCC.

📖 Hendrik Kraemer, The *Christian Message in a Non-Christian World*, London: Edinburgh House Press and New York: Harper & Bros 1938

Küng, Hans (1928–) Roman Catholic theologian. Born in Sursee, Switzerland, he studied at the German College in Rome and in Paris. His first major book, *Justification* (1957), which argued that Karl Barth's doctrine of justification and that of the medieval Council of Trent were virtually the same, caused a sensation and made him a marked man. After a brief period in a parish, in 1959 he became professor in the Catholic faculty of the University of Tübingen. Two further books, *The Council, Reform and Reunion* (1960) and *Structures of the Church* (1962), criticizing existing church structures and calling for reform, just antedated the Second Vatican Council, in which he played a major role as a theological expert. However, the situation deteriorated after publication of *The Church* (1967) and *Infallible? An Inquiry* (1970). His *On Being a Christian* (1974) and *Does God Exist?* (1978) became international bestsellers, reaching vast audiences, and were followed by the withdrawal of his licence to teach as a Catholic theologian. His attention turned to interfaith dialogue and a global ethic, and though still not recognized by the church he has become a statesman as well as a theologian.

📖 Hans Küng, *My Struggle for Freedom*, London: Continuum and Grand Rapids, MI: Eerdmans 2003

Kuyper, Abraham (1837–1920) Dutch Reformed theologian and politician. Son of a minister, at Leiden University he rebelled against the orthodoxy in which he had been brought up. However, he was unsatisfied emotionally by critical theology, and so turned to Calvinism in his first parish in Beesd. After moving to Utrecht and then Amsterdam, he was involved in politics and became leader of the Anti-Revolutionary Party. Elected to parliament, he mobilized the Calvinists for political support and drafted a programme of reform. He founded a Free University of Amsterdam and taught in its seminary and led an exodus from the Reformed Church to form a new branch of it. Ultimately in 1901 he became Prime Minister of the Netherlands. He remained an influential figure all his life.

📖 G. Vandenberg, *He Called My Name*, Grand Rapids, MI: Eerdmans 1944

Lacordaire, Jean-Baptiste Henri Dominique (1802–61) French Roman Catholic liberal. Originally a deist, after practising law he was persuaded of the truth of Christianity by reading the works of Lamennais, though he parted company with him later. He was ordained, and then became a revolutionary, arguing for separation of church and state and freedom of religion and the press, though theologically he supported the authority of Rome. He later became a Dominican and did much to revive the order in France.

📖 Lancelot C. Sheppard, *Lacordaire – A Biographical Essay*, London: Burns & Oates and New York: Macmillan 1964

Lactantius, Lucius Caecilius Firmianus (*c.*250–*c.*325) African Christian apologist. Appointed by the Emperor Diocletian teacher of rhetoric in Nicomedia, he was converted to Christianity, whereupon he lost his job. Later Constantine made him tutor to his son. His *Divine Institutions* (304–11) commend Christianity to educated people and are a first attempt in Latin to set out the main articles of Christian faith. His *The Deaths of the Persecutors* is an important source on the persecutions of the period.

📖 Arne S. Christensen, *Lactantius the Historian: An Analysis of the 'De Mortibus Persecutorum'*, Copenhagen: Museum Tusculanum Press 1980

Lamennais, Hugo Félicité Robert de (1782–1854) French political and social theorist. Born in St Malo, Brittany, to a well-to-do Roman Catholic family, he read widely, losing his faith under the influence of the works of Jean-Jacques Rousseau. He became a mathematics teacher at a local church college at the age of 22 and in the same year was converted to Roman Catholicism by his brother. Like his brother, he too became a priest; he retired to his grandfather's country house and founded a religious congregation and a journal, *L'Avenir* (The Future, 1830). After a first book demonstrating the futility of reason and calling for systematic organization of the clergy, which got him into trouble with Napoleon, he wrote his main work, 'Essay on Indifference in the Matter of Religion' (1817–23), arguing that the individual depends on the community for knowledge of the truth. His ideas developed and became more radical as time went on: first he called for a theocracy, with the Pope as supreme world ruler, then for the separation of the church and education from the state with freedom for the press. Pope Gregory XVI, initially favourable, later condemned these views, expressed in *L'Avenir*, and Lamennais left the church, turning to politics, seeing the future of society in liberal democracy and denying Catholicism and the supernatural. He was an important influence on later social and political ideas.

📖 A. R. Vidler, *Prophecy and Papacy. A Study of Lamennais, the Church and Revolution*, London: SCM Press 1954

Las Casas, Bartolomé de (1474–1566) Spanish Catholic missionary. Born in Seville, he studied law in Salamanca. He went to Haiti as legal adviser to the governor, and was ordained priest there. Disturbed at the treatment of the natives, from 1517–22 he travelled between Spain and America, seeking authority from the king to set up projects to improve their lot. His plans failed, and he became a Dominican; he continued his campaigning for the rest of his life, often in the face of bitter opposition from the colonists. He became Bishop of Chiapa in Mexico before retiring to Spain, where he wrote many books. The best known is *A Brief Relation of the Destruction of the Indies* (1552), published on his return to Spain.

📖 Gustavo Gutiérrez, *Las Casas: In Search of the Poor of Jesus Christ*, Maryknoll, NY: Orbis Books 1994

Law, William (1686–1761) English mystic. Born in Northampton, he studied and taught at Cambridge but lost his post on refusing to give the oath of allegiance to George I (i.e. he became a Non-juror). After a decade in London as a tutor he retired to Northampton, where he led a simple life and engaged in charitable work. His best-known book is *A Serious Call to a Devout and Holy Life* (1728), inspired by Ruysbroeck and Thomas à Kempis, which argues that all everyday virtues must be directed towards the glorification of God, in meditation and an ascetic life. Later in life he discovered Jakob Boehme, who influenced his last books. His writings were deeply influential on the thought of John Wesley during his early development.

📖 A. K. Walker, *William Law: His Life and Thought*, London: SPCK 1973

Lee, Ann (1736–84) 'Mother Ann', Shaker leader. She was the daughter of a Manchester blacksmith who was actually called Lees, and because she had to work in a textile mill from the age of 5 was illiterate. In 1758 she joined a group of 'Shaking Quakers'; in 1762 she married another blacksmith, Abraham Standerin. During 1770 she spent some time in a mental hospital, probably because of post-natal depression after the difficult birth of her fourth child; there she had a vision which convinced her that she was the 'woman clothed with the sun' in the book of Revelation,

Ann the Word, to whom God's light and power were revealed. On her release she became leader of the Shakers, the term by which the group came to be known, and after another vision, because of the persecution of the group, left with some of her followers for North America, where they founded a settlement near Albany, New York.

Ann's vision had convinced her that sexual desire hindered the work of God and preached celibacy. The Shaker movement spread widely and rapidly, and Ann was believed to be ushering in the Second Coming, embodying the feminine half of the deity as Jesus embodied the masculine half. A pacifist, in 1780 she refused to sign an oath of allegiance which would involve taking up arms against the British and was imprisoned. She spent the last two years of her life going round New England, where she was said to have performed miracles.

📖 Richard Francis, *Ann the Word*, New York: Arcade Publishing 2000

Lefebvre, Marcel (1905–91) Ultraconservative Roman Catholic archbishop. Born in Tourcoing, near Lille, he trained at the French seminary in Rome and then went to Africa as a missionary, becoming Archbishop of Dakar, Senegal, in 1948. He was involved in preparing conservative material for the Second Vatican Council which was vigorously rejected by the bishops at the Council, and subsequently denounced the decrees of the Council as heretical and satanic. From 1962 to 1968 he was superior general of the Holy Ghost Fathers and in 1969 founded the Priestly Confraternity of Saint Pius X in Switzerland, with a seminary in Ecône to train traditionalist priests. In 1976 he was suspended by Pope Paul VI, but defied the order, extending his movement further afield. In 1988 he was excommunicated after consecrating four traditionalist bishops at Ecône. By then his movement, declared schismatic, had 60,000 members.

📖 Marcel Lefebvre and François Laisney, *Archbishop Lefebvre and the Vatican, 1987–88*, Kansas City, MO: Angelus Press 1998

Leibniz, Gottfried Wilhelm von (1646–1716) German philosopher. A precocious child, born in Leipzig, he entered university at the age of 15 to study law, but became interested in philosophy and mathematics. He spent his life in service to local rulers, mostly the Duke of Brunswick in Hanover, whose historian/librarian he became, meeting many of the great intellectual figures of the day. Dissatisfied with the dualistic views of René Descartes, John Locke and Isaac Newton then current, in his *Monadology* (1714) he produced an optimistic account of the world as consisting of an infinite number of 'monads', each mirroring the universe in its own way. His conclusion that the world was 'the best of all possible worlds' was satirized by Voltaire in his *Candide*. He defended the proofs for the existence of God and was the first to use the word theodicy, the justification of God's ways to human beings. He also discovered calculus and was active in seeking to further international peace.

📖 Nicholas Rescher, *Leibniz. An Introduction to His Philosophy*, Oxford: Blackwell 1979

Lessing, Gotthold Ephraim (1729–81) German philosopher and dramatist. Born in Saxony the son of a Lutheran pastor, he studied at Leipzig and then made a name for himself as a playwright and critic (he has been called the father of German literature). He became interested in philosophy and theology and later was librarian to the Duke of Brunswick. His late play *Nathan the Wise* (1779) presents his view of religion as humanitarian morality through the figure of an ideal Jew. He was opposed to any historical revelation, as evidenced by his famous saying, 'Accidental truths of history can never become the proof of necessary truths of reason.' He was a key figure in the Enlightenment, and his *The Education of the Human Race* (1780) was an important work for later German Protestant liberalism. Albert Schweitzer saw Lessing's publication of Hermann Samuel Reimarus's posthumous writings ('the Wolfenbuttel fragments', 1774–8) as the beginning of the quest for the historical Jesus.

📖 G. Macdonald Ross, *Leibniz*, Oxford: OUP 1996

Lévi-Strauss, Claude (1908–) French social anthropologist. Born in Brussels, he studied in Paris and was soon appointed professor of sociology at Sao Paulo, Brazil; in 1938 he led an extended anthropological expedition to central Brazil. He spent the war years in the United States, returning to Paris in 1948, after which he held various academic posts in France, finally becoming professor at the Collège de France. A key figure in structuralism, his work focuses on the relationship of culture to nature, based on the human capacity to communicate through language; he gave a new methodology to ethnology, based on communication (*The Elementary Structures of Kinship*, 1969). His four-volume *Introduction to the Science of Mythology* (1964–72, English 1970–9) presents a structuralist account of myth, seeing myths as attempts to resolve problems of human existence and social organization rather than as explanations of natural phenomena.

📖 Boris Wiseman, *Introducing Lévi-Strauss and Structural Anthropology*, Cambridge, Icon Books 2000

Lewis, Clive Staples (1898–1963) Anglican writer. Born in Belfast, he studied and then taught for 30 years at Oxford University before becoming Professor of Medieval and Renaissance Literature at Cambridge. More than for his scholarly works he became famous for his vigorous, witty and clear defences of Christianity in radio broadcasts which resulted in books such as *The Problem of Pain* (1940), *The Screwtape Letters* (1942) and *Miracles* (1947). Two cycles of novels, the science-fiction trilogy beginning with *Out of the Silent Planet* (1938), and the Narnia novels for children beginning with *The Lion, the Witch and the Wardrobe* (1950), were deeply inspired by Christianity. He also wrote two intensely personal books, an account of his conversion, *Surprised by Joy* (1956), and of his bereavement by the death of his wife Joy Davidson, *A Grief Observed* (1961).

📖 A. N. Wilson, *C. S. Lewis: A Biography*, London: HarperCollins and New York: W. W. Norton 1990

Lightfoot, Joseph Barber (1828–89) New Testament scholar and bishop. At school in Birmingham he met Brooke Foss Westcott, who became a lifelong friend; Westcott was in fact his tutor in Cambridge, where Lightfoot had a brilliant career, holding two major professorial chairs in succession. In 1879 he was made Bishop of Durham, and as well as reorganizing the diocese, trained ordinands at his residence, Auckland Castle, and showed a particular concern for the poor and the working class. A brilliant scholar, he spoke seven languages fluently, had a highly retentive memory and was notable for the clarity of his thought and writing.

His most notable academic work was on the apostolic fathers, the authenticity of whose writings were then being questioned; he also contributed three commentaries on letters of Paul to a planned commentary on the whole of the New Testament to have been written by him, Lightfoot and F. J. A. Hort.

G. R. Eden and F. C. Macdonald (eds), *Lightfoot of Durham*, Cambridge: CUP 1932

Livingstone, David (1813–73) Scottish missionary and explorer. He left school at the age of 10 to work in a cotton mill, but studied while he worked and long into the night. He was converted to Christianity at the age of 17 and then went to college in Glasgow to read medicine and theology. In 1841 he went to Africa, where his famous travels took him from Cape Town to the Zambesi river, in the process of which he discovered what he named the Victoria Falls, and across the continent from east to west. He prompted the foundation of the Universities Mission to Central Africa in 1857and his reports on the Arab slave trade were a major contribution towards the abolishment of slavery.

Tim Jeal, *Livingstone*, New Haven and London: Yale University Press 2001

Locke, John (1632–1704) English philosopher. Born to a Somerset family of minor gentry, after studies at Oxford, where he was influenced by René Descartes and the scientist Robert Boyle, he became secretary to Lord Ashley, first Earl of Shaftesbury. Thereafter his career had its ups and downs, involving much forced travelling as he fell foul of the authorities; from 1691 he lived quietly in a manor house in Essex. He was the first major British empiricist philosopher and perhaps the most influential, and also helped to lay the foundation for liberal democracy. He combined his empiricism with a Christian rationalism. He argued that knowledge comes from experience alone, and that reality as such cannot be grasped by the human mind. However, the existence of God can be arrived at by reason, and Christianity has a secure rational base. In this area his major works are *An Essay Concerning Human Understanding* (1690) and *The Reasonableness of Christianity* (1695). A defender of free enquiry and toleration, he pleaded for religious freedom for all but Roman Catholics (because they owed allegiance elsewhere) and atheists (as a danger to the state). His *Two Treatises of Government*, published in 1690 but largely written earlier, defended constitutional rule and the freedom of the individual when both were threatened.

John Dunn, *Locke: A Very Short Introduction*, Oxford: OUP 2003

Loisy, Alfred Firmin (1857–1940) French Catholic Modernist. From a farming family in the Marne, he trained at the Catholic Institute in Paris, to which, after parish work, he returned to teach, later becoming professor. His critical work aroused suspicion and he was dismissed. After being chaplain to a Dominican convent and further teaching, he was forced to resign and was excommunicated for his critical views. He spent the rest of his working life as professor of the history of religions in the secular Collège de France. His *The Gospel and the Church* (1902), written in answer to Adolf von Harnack's *What is Christianity?*, which argued that the church did not develop according to a plan of Jesus ('Jesus preached the gospel and the church came'), and critical studies of John and the Synoptic Gospels paved the way for his excommunication. His subsequent works, culminating in *The Birth of Christianity* (1933), are widely regarded as erratic.

A. R. Vidler, *The Modernist Movement in the Roman Catholic Church*, Cambridge: CUP 1934

Lucian of Samosata (*c.* 115–200) Syrian pagan satirist. He was originally a lawyer in Antioch before turning to writing and becoming and itinerant lecturer. Author of satires on many subjects, he also wrote on Christianity particularly in *On the Death of Peregrinus*, in which he portrays Christians as being kind but credulous.

C. P. Jones, *Culture and Society in Lucian*, Cambridge, MA: Harvard University Press 1986

Lull, Ramon (1232–1316) Spanish missionary and philosopher. He was born in Majorca and educated as a knight. A vision of Christ when he was 30 made a deep impact, and he studied Arabic and Christian thought with a view towards converting Muslims. His *Book of Contemplation* was written in Arabic and translated into Catalan; he was the first medieval theologian not to write in Latin. In addition to teaching in Spain and France he travelled widely and wrote much. His thinking sought to arrive at a single system of language and belief to which all could adhere. His mystical theology anticipates that of Teresa of Avila and John of the Cross.

E. Allison Peers, *Fool of Love: The Life of Ramon Lull*, London: SCM Press 1946

Luther, Martin (1483–1546) German Reformer. Born in Eisleben, he studied at the University of Erfurt and then became a novice in the order of Augustinian Eremites. At the age of 25 he was transferred to the University of Wittenberg, where he later became professor, a post which he held until his death. Anxiety about his salvation led to a 'tower experience' in which he became convinced that the essence of the gospel was that justification is a gift of God through faith. This led him to deny the need for the priesthood and the church as mediator. Opposed to the indulgences (promises of remission of time in purgatory) from Pope Leo X, sold for renovating St Peter's, Rome, he nailed his famous Ninety-Five Theses attacking current Catholic abuses to the door of the castle church in Wittenberg. This inevitably led to conflict and his trial in Augsburg in 1518. In 1520 he appeared before the Emperor Charles V in Worms and was put under the ban. He was rescued by Elector Frederick III of Saxony, the ruler of Wittenberg, and concealed in Wartburg castle. After much agonizing, he then broke with the Roman Catholic Church, calling on the German princes to reform the church themselves: this appeal was contained in *To the Christian Nobility of the German Nation* (1520); also published the same year were *On the Babylonian Captivity of the Church*, rejecting the sacrifice of the mass and transubstantiation and putting forward a eucharistic theology including communion in both kinds; and *The Freedom of the Christian*, expounding justification by faith. As a result he was excommunicated. In personal danger, Luther continued to be protected by the Elector of Saxony. His teaching spread widely, favoured by the religious and political situation, extending to many countries. He left a permanent mark on the German language in his translation of the Bible, and wrote many fine hymns, including 'Ein feste Burg' ('A safe stronghold'). As the Reformation proceeded he came into conflict with other Reformers, calling for the suppression of the Peasants' Revolt and opposing Huldrych Zwingli's views on the eucharist. His contribution eventually led to the confessional documents included in the Lutheran Book of Concord. He criticized Erasmus' approach to church reform and wrote against his views in *The Bondage of the Will* (1525). That year he married Katharina von Bora, an ex-nun, and had a happy family life and home; his many volumes of biblical commentaries, sermons, etc. include his *Table Talk*. He died in Eisleben and was buried in Wittenberg.

📖 Roland H. Bainton, *Here I Stand: A Life of Martin Luther*, Harmondsworth: Penguin Books 2002

McPherson, Aimée Semple (1890–1944) Evangelist. Born in Canada, she was converted by the evangelist Robert J. Semple and went with him as a missionary to China. Widowed after three months, she returned home; her second marriage ended in divorce. Travelling widely with her mother through the United States, she developed her 'four-square' gospel: Christ as saviour and healer, the baptism of the Holy Spirit, speaking in tongues, and the second coming. She is supposed to have broadcast the first radio sermon. She organized the International Church of the Foursquare Gospel.

📖 Edith L. Blumhofer, *Aimée Semple McPherson: Everybody's Sister*, Grand Rapids, MI: Eerdmans 1993

Macrina (*c.* 327–80) Ascetic. The elder sister of the Cappadocian fathers Basil and Gregory of Nyssa. Widowed at a very early age, she devoted herself to an ascetic life of piety. She was a deep influence on her brothers and persuaded Basil away from a successful secular career to be ordained priest. She established one of the earliest communities of women ascetics on the family estate in Pontus. Gregory wrote a life of her.

📖 Gregory of Nyssa, *The Life of Macrina*, translated by W. K. L. Clarke, London: SPCK 1916

Maimonides (Moses ben Maimon, 1135–1204; known as Rambam) Spanish Jewish philosopher. Born in Cordova, and trained by his father as a Talmudist, he fled during a persecution and settled at Fez in Morocco, finally becoming head of the Jewish community in Cairo and physician to the sultan. His aim was to reconcile Jewish thought with Aristotelian philosophy as presented by contemporary Arab writers, doing for Judaism what Thomas Aquinas did for Christianity. He wrote a commentary on the Mishnah and produced a version of the Talmud classified by subject matter, but his most widely known work is his *Guide for the Perplexed*, written to reconcile reason with faith. His *Mishneh Torah* codified rabbinic law and ritual. His work influenced medieval thinkers like Albertus Magnus and Thomas Aquinas and later, differently, Benedict de Spinoza. He has been called 'the second Moses'.

📖 S. Pines (ed), *Moses Maimonides: The Guide of the Perplexed*, Chicago: University of Chicago Press 1974

Marcion of Pontus (died 160) Church founder. A wealthy ship owner from Sinope in Pontus (perhaps son of a bishop there), he joined the church in Rome but was excommunicated. He formed his followers into a separate community and his movement spread across the empire. He rejected the Old Testament and reduced the New Testament to an abbreviated Gospel of Luke and ten letters (which he edited) of Paul, whom he regarded as the only true apostle. He contrasted a gospel of love to the law, and believed that the God of the Old Testament, cruel, despotic and capricious, had nothing to do with the God of Jesus Christ. He was a major threat to the second-century church.

📖 E. C. Blackman, *Marcion and his Influence*, London: SPCK 1948

Marsilius of Padua (*c.* 1275–1342) Italian political philosopher. From the University of Padua he went to Paris to study medicine, became rector of the university, and after a spell in Avignon and northern Italy practised medicine there. His main work was *The Defender of Peace* (1324); this argued that civil order must be guaranteed by the state, which derives its authority from the people. The state must have a monopoly of coercion and the church has only the rights granted by the state. This approach undermined political arguments with a theological basis and paved the way for the Renaissance and subsequent developments. He was excommunicated, and spent the rest of his life in Munich at the court there.

📖 A. Gewirth, *Marsilius of Padua: The Defender of Peace*, New York: Columbia University Press 1956

Martyn, Henry (1781–1812) After being Charles Simeon's curate in Cambridge, he wanted to join the newly formed Church Missionary Society but was rejected; he then sailed to India as a chaplain to the East India Company in Calcutta. The style of his intense missionary work did not go down well with British congregations, and led to other postings, but the *Journals* published after his premature death are devotional classics. Ill-health took him on a voyage to Shiraz in Persia; he died in Armenia on the way home. A brilliant linguist, he translated the New Testament and Book of Common Prayer into Hindustani and later the Psalms and New Testament into Persian and the New Testament into Arabic.

📖 Constance E. Padwick, *Henry Martyn*, Leicester: Inter-Varsity Press 1953

Marx, Karl Heinrich (1818–83) German economist. Born in Trier to a family which stood in a long line of Jewish rabbis, he studied law, history and philosophy at Bonn, Berlin and Jena, discovering the thought of G. W. F. Hegel and Ludwig Feuerbach. He wrote his *Communist Manifesto* in 1847. He went to Paris during the 1848 revolution, and then returned to Cologne, from where he was expelled in 1849 after a trial for treason. He spent the rest of his life in England, where he wrote his *magnum* *opus, Das Kapital* (1867, English 1887). There is an important difference between what Marx himself wrote and what later came to be developed as Marxism. His early works are particularly important for theology, containing a more complex discussion of religion than is usually supposed in the light of his saying that it is the 'opium of the people'.

📖 Francis Wheen, *Karl Marx*, London: Fourth Estate 2000

Mather, Cotton (1663–1728) Puritan minister. Born in Boston, Massachusetts, he entered Harvard at the age of 12, gaining his MA at the age of 18 from his father, who was president of the college. He then served in his father's church in Boston, later becoming its senior pastor, and in 1690 was elected a fellow of Harvard. The most famous of all the New England Puritans, he devoted his life to prayer, preaching, writing (he wrote more than 400 works) and doing good. He had a wide range of interests about which he corresponded widely, especially science and medicine (he championed inoculation against smallpox). At the same time he believed in witchcraft. A great philanthropist, he supported a school for slaves. Though a firm supporter of the old order, in some respects he was ahead of his time.

📖 Barrett Wendell, *Cotton Mather. A Biography*, New York: Barnes & Noble 1992

Mathews, Shailer (1863–1941) American Baptist theologian. Born in Portland, Maine, he studied and taught at Colby College before moving to Chicago Divinity School. A champion of liberalism and the social gospel, he is regarded as the founder of the Chicago school of theology. His major work is *The Social Teaching of Jesus* (1897). He opposed a functionalist approach to current fundamentalism and was concerned that his theology should spread into the church.

📖 Shailer Mathews, *Jesus on Social Institutions*, Philadelphia: Fortress Press 1971

Maurice, John Frederick Denison (1805–72) English theologian. Born near Lowestoft, the son of a Unitarian, and brought up in Bristol, he studied at Cambridge. Religious objections to accepting the Anglican Thirty-Nine Articles, assent to which was then a necessary condition, prevented him from gaining a degree. Unable, therefore, to teach, he spent time writing in London. In 1830 he did become an Anglican and went to Oxford, and after a country parish held a hospital chaplaincy (during which he wrote his best-known book, *The Kingdom of Christ*, 1838, which contains a survey of religious and philosophical movements and churches with the famous conclusion that religious movements tend to be right in what they affirm and wrong in what they deny). He was then made professor at King's College, London. Following the 1848 revolutions he joined the Christian Socialists, where among others he met Charles Kingsley, and later he started a Working Men's College in London. However, his theological views, particularly his rejection of endless punishment in hell, forced him to resign his chair, and after a London parish post he became professor of moral philosophy at Cambridge. Individualistic and distinctive in his approach, and putting great stress on a loving God, he was one of the most important of English nineteenth-century theological figures.

📖 F. M. McClain, *Maurice: Man and Moralist*, London: SPCK 1972

Maximus the Confessor (*c.*580–662) Greek theologian and ascetic. As a young aristocrat he became chief secretary to the emperor, but then went to be a monk at Chrysopolis, where he was later abbot. When the Persians invaded, he fled to Africa. He was a determined opponent of monothelitism (the view that there was only one divine will in Christ), which was widespread in the East, and by his prolific writings became one of the main architects of Byzantine theology. The emphasis of his thought was that the purpose of history is the incarnation of God and the divinization of humanity by the restoration of the kingdom of God. His devotional writings include a mystical interpretation of the liturgy. His opposition to monothelitism and his sympathies with the Western church got him into trouble with the Byzantine emperor; his tongue and right hand were cut off and he was exiled to the Black Sea coast.

📖 A. Louth, *Maximus the Confessor*, London and New York: Routledge 1996

Mechthild of Magdeburg (*c.*1210–*c.*1282) German mystic. Descended from a noble family in Saxony, she left home to join an austere community of the Beguines in Magdeburg, later moving to a Cistercian convent at Helfta. A visionary, she wrote down her visions in *The Flowing Light of the Godhead*.

📖 Frank Tobin, *Mechthild of Magdeburg, Flowing Light of the Godhead*, New York and Mahwah, NJ: Paulist Press 1998

Melanchthon, Philipp (1497–1560) German Reformer. His family name was Schwarzerd (Black-earth), and Melanchthon, the Greek equivalent, came from an uncle as a tribute to his linguistic skill. He studied at the universities of Heidelberg, Tübingen (where he was noticed by Erasmus) and Wittenberg (where he became a professor and a supporter of Martin Luther). His *Loci communes* (1521) was the first systematic account of Lutheran theology. The leading humanist among the Lutheran Reformers, he was a moderate ready for compromise and openness, with a keen interest in education. He wrote textbooks and left his mark on schools and universities.

📖 Robert Stupperich, *Melanchthon*, Philadelphia: Westminster Press 1965

Men, Alexander (1935–90) Russian priest. He was born in Moscow, where his mother was a member of what was known as the 'catacomb' church, those priests and lay people who had managed to remain alive during the persecution of the Russian Orthodox Church by the Communist state. He studied biology but did not complete the course because he was expelled in 1958 when the authorities discovered his church connections. For the rest of his life he served in churches around Moscow and was able to win the trust of the intelligentsia; he was instrumental in bringing Alexander Solzhenitsyn into the church. With perestroika his position grew easier; he wrote a series of seven books, *In Search of the Way, the Truth and the Life*, on the world religions. He was very open and retained his love of science; he once remarked that 'God has given us two books, the Bible and nature'. He also gave many lectures and it was thought that he might broadcast on Russian television and become Dean of the Theological University. However, in 1990 he was murdered near his home; the murderer was never discovered.

📖 Elizabeth Roberts and Ann Shukman (eds), *Christianity for the Twenty-First Century: The Prophetic Writings of Alexander Men*, London: SCM Press 1996

Menno Simons (*c.* 1496–1561) Anabaptist leader. A parish priest in Friesland, he left the Roman Catholic Church because of doubts over infant baptism, and after reading Martin Luther joined the Anabaptists, then recovering from persecution. For 25 years he travelled round the Netherlands and Baltic Germany organizing congregations, spending his last years in Holstein. He gave his name to the Mennonites. He stressed Christianity as a closed community of believers who are 'new creatures', having entered on a spiritual resurrection with the church as a corporate new creation.

📖 Gerald R. Brunk, *Menno Simons: A Reappraisal*, Harrisonburg, CA: Eastern Mennonite College 1992

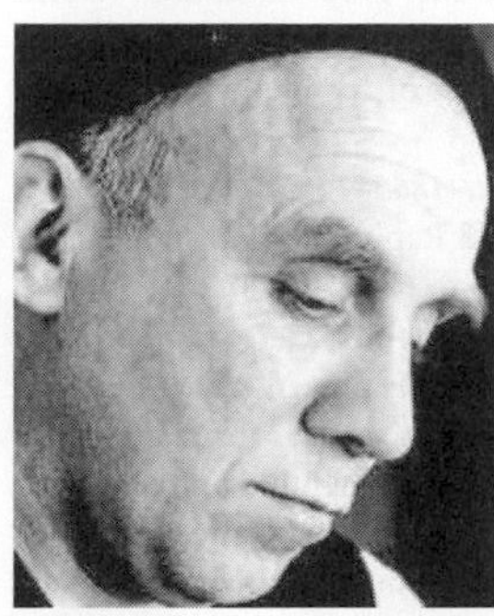

Merton, Thomas (1915–68) Catholic monk. Born in Prades, France, he had an unhappy and itinerant childhood; his parents, both artists, died when he was young. He was educated in Bermuda, France and England. After studying at Cambridge, he went to Columbia University, New York. There he joined the Catholic Church and became a Trappist monk in Gethsemani Abbey, Kentucky. He died at a monastic conference in Bangkok as the result of an accident. He became world-famous for his autobiography, *The Seven-Storey Mountain* (1948), and followed this by a wealth of other writing, displaying increasing openness. He was an articulate interpreter of the monastic experience, encountering tension between the solitary life and social involvement.

📖 Monica Furlong, *Merton. A Biography*, London: Collins 1980

Methodius (*c.* 815–85) Born to a Greek senatorial family in Thessalonica, with his brother Cyril he was sent to organize the Slav church in Moravia. On the premature death of his brother on a visit they paid to Rome, he was consecrated bishop and returned, only to be imprisoned through the action of hostile German bishops. His release was secured only at the price of using the Slavonic language in liturgy.

📖 A.-E. N. Tachiaos, *Cyril and Methodius of Thessalonica: The Acculturation of the Slavs*, Crestwood, NY: St Vladimir's Seminary Press 2000

Migne, Jacques-Paul (1800–75) French Catholic priest and publisher. Following disagreement with his bishop he went to Paris and after unsuccessful attempts at journalism decided to publish a universal library for the clergy. He ran a large publishing house which produced many works, but his memorial is the series of the Latin and Greek church fathers comprising the 221-volume *Patrologia Latina* (1844–1854) and the 162-volume *Patrologia Graeca* (1857–1866), the one edition which is anywhere near complete. His workshops and moulds were tragically destroyed in a disastrous fire in 1858.

📖 R. Howard Bloch, *God's Plagiarist: Being an Account of the Fabulous Industry and Irregular Commerce of the Abbé Migne*, Chicago: University of Chicago Press 1994

Milton, John (1608–74) English poet. Born in London, after studying at Cambridge he lived on his father's estate in Buckinghamshire and devoted himself to scholarship and literature. One of the greatest of English poets, he wrote his 'Ode on the Morning of Christ's Nativity' at the age of 21. Ten years later he moved to London, where he became involved in controversy; he joined the Presbyterians and in the Civil War supported the Commonwealth. He became blind in 1651. In danger of losing his life at the Restoration, he was pardoned. His poetry culminated in his epic *Paradise Lost* (1667), with its sequel *Paradise Regained* (1671), and also *Samson Agonistes*, which with its phrase 'eyeless in Gaza' reflects Milton himself. His theological work is *On Christian Doctrine*, published posthumously, which denies that all the persons of the Trinity are equal and eternal and that creation was from nothing.

📖 A. N. Wilson, *The Life of John Milton*, London: OUP 1983

Molina, Luis de (1535–1600) Spanish theologian. After becoming a Jesuit he taught in Coimbra and Evora and then spent several years writing in Lisbon; he retired to Cuenca and was appointed professor in Madrid the year he died. In *The Concord of Free Will with the Gift of Grace* (1588), a highly controversial work, he sought to defend, against Protestantism, the doctrine that human beings are free to resist or accept grace, a doctrine which became known as Molinism.

📖 Bernice Hamilton, *Political Thought in Sixteenth-Century Spain: A study of the political ideas of Vitoria, De Soto, Suarez, and Molina*, London: OUP 1963

Molinos, Miguel de (*c.* 1640–97) Spanish mystic. Born near Saragossa, after studying theology he was sent to Rome, where he became a distinguished confessor and spiritual director. His *Spiritual Guide* (1675), teaching that the soul achieves perfection when it abandons effort and desire and becomes lost in God, brought him fame, but because of the consequences drawn from this by the nuns he directed, he was condemned and sentenced to life imprisonment.

📖 Michael Molinos, *The Spiritual Guide*, Goleta, CA: Christian Books 1982

Moltmann, Jürgen (1926–) German Reformed theologian. Born in Hamburg, he was conscripted into the German army in the Second World War at 17, captured in Belgium, and held prisoner of war in England. After studying at Göttingen, where he was influenced by Karl Barth's theology, he served as a country pastor and became professor at Wuppertal and then at Bonn. He is now professor of theology in Tübingen. His first major book, *Theology of Hope* (1965), combined insights of the Marxist philosopher Ernst Bloch with a rediscovery of biblical eschatology and was widely influential; *The Crucified God* (1973) took up the issue of the nature of Christian belief after Auschwitz; *Church in the Power of the Spirit* (1975) sees the church as a messianic community. He followed this with a systematic theology.

📖 Geiko Müller Fahrenholz, *The Kingdom and the Power. The Theology of Jürgen Moltmann*, London: SCM Press and Minneapolis: Fortress Press 2000

Montanus (second century) Apocalyptic prophet. A convert to Christianity from Asia Minor, he claimed that the Holy Spirit spoke through him and that he was bringing the church into the final stage of revelation, the age of the Paraclete. He gathered a large following, the most notable among whom was Tertullian. Returning to the pattern of the earliest church, he included a large number of women in his movement. He has proved to be of renewed interest to modern Pentecostal movements.

📖 Christine Trevett, *Montanism; Gender, Authority and the New Prophecy*, Cambridge: CUP 2002

Moody, Dwight Lyman (1837–99) American evangelist. Born in Massachusetts, the son of a bricklayer, he had to work from the age of 13, and although he was converted to Christianity, his acceptance was delayed through lack of learning. He became a successful businessman in Chicago and organized a Sunday School, later deciding to devote himself to such work. With Ira Sankey, he had a triumphant mission to Britain, which formed the basis for equally eventful missions all over the United States. He also founded a Bible Institute in Chicago. His message was non-theological, non-denominational and conservative, prior to fundamentalist controversies.

📖 John Kent, *Holding the Fort. Studies in Victorian Revivalism*, London: Epworth Press 1978

More, Hannah (1745–1833) Evangelical writer and philanthropist. Initially a successful playwright whose plays were produced by David Garrick, she came under the influence of John Newton and William Wilberforce. Financed by members of the Clapham Sect she wrote religious tracts priced at a penny each which sold in the millions; she was also a pioneer in founding schools in and round Cheddar, near Bristol, where she had been born and where she spent her later life, providing training in spinning and domestic service. However, her views, like those of the Clapham Sect, were conservative, and she believed that the existing social order with all its poverty was divinely ordained.

📖 M. G. Jones, *Hannah More*, Cambridge: CUP 1952

More, Thomas (1478–1535) Lord Chancellor of England. Descended from a prominent London family, after studying at Oxford he became a lawyer, entered parliament and was appointed Lord Chancellor under Henry VIII. His famous *Utopia* (1516) was written early in his brilliant career: it describes an ideal community practising a natural religion and living by a natural law, and contains much satirical criticism of contemporary abuses. His career collapsed in 1532 when he opposed the King over his divorce; he later refused to forswear obedience to the Pope and accept royal supremacy in religious matters. This led to imprisonment in the Tower of London (during which he wrote *A Dialogue of Comfort against Tribulation)* and execution.

📖 Richard Marius, *Thomas More*, London: Weidenfeld & Nicolson 1999

Mott, John Raleigh (1865–1955) American churchman. A Methodist layman, he was born in New York; after studying in Iowa and Cornell he was converted and became involved in the YMCA. He helped to form the World Student Christian Federation and was president of the 1910 Edinburgh World Missionary Conference with its slogan 'the evangelization of the world in this generation'. For the rest of his life he was actively involved in ecumenical affairs.

📖 C. H. Hopkins, *John R. Mott, 1865–1955*, Geneva: World Council of Churches and Grand Rapids, MI: Eerdmans 1980

Mühlenberg, Henry Melchior (1711–87) German Lutheran clergyman. Son of a shoemaker in Hanover, after study in Göttingen and Jena he became inspector of an orphanage. He thought of going as a missionary to the East Indies but was called to Pennsylvania, where the Lutheran Church was in decline. In his revival work, he founded the first Lutheran synod in America there and did much to strengthen American Lutheranism generally.

📖 T. G. Tappert and J. W. Doberstein (trs and eds), *The Notebook of a Colonial Clergyman: Condensed from the Journals of Henry Melchior Muhlenberg*, Minneapolis, MN: Fortress Press [2]1998

Müntzer, Thomas (1489–1525) German Anabaptist and radical Reformer. After studying in Leipzig and Frankfurt, he became confessor to a convent in Thuringia. Under the influence of Hus, Luther and others he became a Protestant preacher, calling for radical social and religious reform. He believed that the church had fallen from purity after the apostles and that purity would be restored apocalyptically in his own times. His views constantly involved him in conflict and he eventually preached open revolt. He joined the Peasants' Revolt, and when they were defeated in battle he was captured and executed.

📖 Hans-Jürgen Goertz, *Thomas Müntzer. Apocalyptic Mystic and Revolutionary*, Edinburgh: T&T Clark 1993

Neale, John Mason (1818–66) Hymn writer. During his time as an undergraduate in Cambridge he became fascinated with high church views and church architecture, helping to found the Cambridge Camden Society, which championed Victorian Gothic. He was ordained in 1842 but because of ill health could not be appointed to a parish. Instead, he became warden of the Trollopian-style Sackville College, East Grinstead, where he founded the Sisterhood of St Margaret to educate girls and care for the sick. He wrote a commentary on the Psalms and a history of the Eastern church, but it is as a hymn writer that he became best known. Of the almost 100 hymns for which he was responsible, many are translations of ancient Greek and Latin hymns, like 'Jerusalem the Golden' and 'All Glory, Laud and Honour'.

He also wrote the carol 'Good King Wenceslas'. Not only was he immensely gifted as a hymn writer; he also seems to have had a sense of humour. It is said that on a visit to John Keble, while Keble was briefly out of the room, Neale translated one of his hymns into Latin. He then told Keble that Keble's hymn was not original, to the latter's perplexity.

M. Chandler, *The Life and Work of John Mason Neale 1818–1966*, Leominster: Gracewing 1995

Neri, Philip (1515–95) Founder of the Oratory. Born in Florence, he led an ascetic life in Rome, earning his living as a tutor, while studying and working among the poor. He had a mystical experience there, and was led to found a confraternity to care for pilgrims. After ordination he went to live with a community of priests at San Girolamo, which under his influence grew to become the Congregation of the Oratory (probably after the room where they met). His optimistic and attractive spirituality made him one of the most popular figures in Rome, much sought after for spiritual counsel, and the Oratory later gained papal approval.

Meriol Trevor, *Apostle of Rome: A Life of Philip Neri*, London: Macmillan 1966

Nestorius (died 451) Syrian theologian. He entered a monastery in Antioch and probably studied under Theodore of Mopsuestia. A famous preacher, he was made Bishop of Constantinople, where he was a vigorous defender of orthodoxy. However, he was opposed to the increasing use of the title *theotokos* (mother of God) for the Virgin Mary, which he thought unbalanced if left on its own. Here opinion consolidated against him, not least because of his forthright way of defending his views, and he was condemned as a heretic by the Council of Ephesus in 431. He was sent back to Antioch and later banished to Upper Egypt. Only fragments of his work survived until his *The Bazaar of Heracleides* was discovered in a Syriac translation in 1910. Whether his condemnation was a fair one in terms of the christology of the time is much disputed; at all events, bishops who found his views more satisfactory than the official line formed a church which has lasted to the present day.

F. Loofs, *Nestorius and his Place in Christian Doctrine* (1914), New York: Burt Franklin 1975

Newman, John Henry (1801–90) English theologian. Son of a London banker, and brought up an evangelical in the Church of England, he studied and taught at Oxford and became vicar of the university church. His sermons made him a nationally known figure. Along with others he wrote 'Tracts for the Times', in which he vigorously opposed the growing evangelical trends in the Church of England and sought to restore it to its Catholic past. His Tract 90 (1841), an attempt to reconcile the Thirty-Nine Articles of the Church of England with Roman Catholic doctrine, was highly controversial, and he was silenced by his bishop. He had already begun to have doubts about the Anglican Church, and four years later became a Roman Catholic, a move which he defended in his *Essay on the Development of Christian Doctrine* (1845). Although he later became a cardinal, his relations with the Roman Catholic Church were never easy. Other most famous works were a defence of his past, *Apologia pro Vita Sua* (1864), provoked by an attack from Charles Kingsley; *The Dream of Gerontius* (1865), a poem depicting a soul going to God at the hour of death and immortalized when set to music by Edward Elgar; and *A Grammar of Assent* (1870). His subsequent influence has been very great, not so much because of his theology as because of his views on doctrinal development and his psychological and moral insights.

Ian Ker, *John Henry Newman: A Biography*, Oxford: OUP 1990

Newton, Isaac (1642–1727) English mathematician and physicist. Born of a Lincolnshire farming family, he studied at Cambridge and became professor of mathematics there, later holding distinguished posts in London and serving as a Member of Parliament. He is well known for formulating the universal law of gravity, discovering differential calculus, and analysing light through a prism, but it is not always recognized that these discoveries are set in a religious context. He was converted at university and believed that his discoveries were communicated to him through the Holy Spirit, which was showing him the rationality of the universe. He kept his somewhat unorthodox religion in the private sphere: his interests extended to church history, chronology and prophecy.

James Gleick, *Isaac Newton*, London: Fourth Estate 2003

Newton, John (1725–1807) English evangelical. The son of a ship-master, he was press-ganged into the Navy, tried to escape, was arrested in West Africa, and spent two years as the slave of a slave trader. Converted in a storm on the voyage back home, he spent more time at sea and in the slave trade before becoming surveyor of the tides at Liverpool. Under the influence of George Whitefield he began to study and became curate of Olney, Buckinghamshire, where with the poet William Cowper he produced a famous set of *Olney Hymns* (1779). He later moved to London as a city rector and was an influence in the evangelical revival, not least on William Wilberforce. His hymns include 'Glorious Things of Thee are Spoken' and 'How Sweet the Name of Jesus Sounds'.

John Pollock, *Amazing Grace: John Newton's Story*, London: Collins 1981

Nicholas of Cusa (1401–64) German philosopher. From Cues on the Mosel, he studied at Heidelberg, Padua and Cologne. After ordination he became Dean of St Florin's, Koblenz. He did much work on behalf of Pope Nicholas V, as a result of which he was made a cardinal. Though appointed Bishop of Brixen in the Tyrol, he had trouble with the local ruler, as a result of which he eventually had to return to Rome, where he spent the rest of his life. His most important work was his treatise *On Learned Ignorance* (1440), in a Platonist vein: learned ignorance is the highest stage of knowledge possible to the human intellect, since absolute truth is unknowable and knowledge is complex, relative and approximate. In this approach he was a forerunner of the Renaissance.

📖 Christopher M. Bellitto and Thomas M. Izbicki (eds), *Introducing Nicholas of Cusa: A Guide to a Renaissance Man*, New York and Mahwah, NJ: Paulist Press 2004

Niebuhr, Reinhold (1892–1971) American theologian. Born in Missouri, he studied at Eden Theological College and Yale Divinity School and then for thirteen years was pastor of a Detroit church. Here he became involved in the Social Gospel movement, and his experience of industrial society shaped the rest of his life. His critical reaction to the liberal Protestantism in which he had been brought up was expressed in his first book *Does Civilization Need Religion?* (1928). His move to become professor at Union Theological Seminary, New York, virtually coincided with the beginning of the Great Depression. His classic *Moral Man and Immoral Society* (1932) argued that moral values when put into practice collectively produce behaviour which seems immoral from an individual perspective, and highlighted the weakness of liberal Protestant social ethics. He was much exercised in interpreting the political developments of the 1930s; at the same time in his writing he presented Christianity as a prophetic religion and offered his own *Interpretation of Christian Ethics* (1935). His greatest book, *The Nature and Destiny of Man* (1941, 1943), opposes a biblical view of human nature to Renaissance humanism, focusing on creation and fall, atonement and the second coming of Christ. In later years his interest moved to history and the theology of history; a stroke in 1952 hampered his activities thereafter. His prophetic approach and his political involvement made him a controversial figure whose full significance has perhaps yet to be appreciated.

📖 Richard Fox, *Reinhold Niebuhr, A Biography*, London and New York: HarperCollins 1987

Niebuhr, Helmut Richard (1894–1962) American theologian. Born in Missouri, he studied at Eden Theological Seminary, Washington University and Yale Divinity School; after serving as a pastor he returned to Eden to teach until 1931, with a brief period as president of Elmhurst College; he then moved to Yale Divinity School and in 1938 became professor at Yale University. His thought was particularly influenced by the work of Ernst Troeltsch. His first book, *The Social Sources of Denominationalism* (1929), advanced the church's acceptance of middle-class values; his interest in the relationship between culture and faith was continued in important books on *The Meaning of Revelation* (1941), *Christ and Culture* (1951) and *Radical Monotheism and Western Culture* (1960), all concerned with different forms of the relationship between Christianity and the modern world. The last of these books highlights the theocentric character of his theology. He was brother of Reinhold Niebuhr.

📖 Lonnie Kliever, *H. Richard Niebuhr*, Waco, TX: Word Books 1977

Nietzsche, Friedrich Wilhelm (1844–1900) German philosopher and philologist. Son of a Lutheran pastor in Saxony, he studied in Bonn and Leipzig, and was briefly professor in Basle before resigning through ill health. He became insane in 1889. He criticized Christianity and its ethics for otherworldliness and resented it for being a slave morality, which was condemning Europe to mediocrity. He was concerned with the will to power which can transform human values; claiming that God was dead, he saw this as the opening up of new horizons to those who accepted the challenge. In this context he envisaged the future superman, pursuing his goal without scruples, beyond good or evil, which were the values of a defunct Christianity. His ideas, prophetic and expressed in a disjointed and aphoristic way, were frequently misinterpreted, for example by the Fascists; nevertheless he has been a significant influence on twentieth-century thought. His major works include *The Gay Science* (1882), *Thus Spake Zarathustra* (1883), *Beyond Good and Evil* (1886) and *The Antichrist* (1888).

📖 Laurence Gane, *Introducing Nietzsche*, Cambridge: Icon Books 1999

Nil Sorsky (1433–1508) Russian monk and mystic. Born to an aristocratic Muscovite family, he became a monk in North Russia, but then visited Constantinople and Mount Athos, after which he was drawn to Hesychasm. Returning to Russia, he founded his own monastery by the river Sora (hence his name), introducing a new form of the monastic life, that of the small group (*skit*) guided by a spiritual father (*starets*). His writings and monastic rule proved influential for centuries to come.

📖 George A. Maloney, *Nil Sorsky, The Complete Writings*, Classics of Western Spirituality, New York and Mahwah, NJ: Paulist Press 2003

Nobili, Robert de (1577–1656) Italian missionary. From a wealthy family in Montepulciano, he became a Jesuit and went out to India, where he sought to understand the local culture, dressing as a *sannyasi* (a Hindu who renounces all he possibly can), and living in the Brahmin quarter. He was the first European to know Sanskrit and the Vedas. His methods led to opposition, but he was allowed to continue. His efforts to reconcile Christianity with local culture proved of permanent importance.

📖 Vincent Cronin, *A Pearl to India. The Life of Robert de Nobili*, New York: Dutton 1959

Nygrén, Anders (1890–1978) Swedish theologian. Born in Göteborg, he studied at Lund, where after a pastorate he became professor of systematic theology and then bishop. He was a leader in the World Council of Churches and in 1947 was elected first president of the Lutheran World Federation. His best-known book, *Agape and Eros* (1953), uses a method of motif research to trace the conflict between two forms of love, *agape* and eros, through Christianity.

📖 Anders Nygrén, *Agape and Eros*, New York: Harper Torchbooks 1969

Olier, Jean-Jacques (1608–57) Born in Paris, he studied with the Jesuits and at the Sorbonne. When in Rome for further studies he temporarily went blind; on recovering his sight he was converted to a religious life and after ordination met Vincent de Paul. He went on missions and in 1642 took charge of the Paris church of Saint-Sulpice, then in decline. He used it as the base for a seminary which became a model for other dioceses; its influence spread as far as Montreal. He wrote many books on spirituality.

Origen (*c.*185–*c.*254) Greek biblical scholar. He was born in Egypt and educated in Alexandria, where his mother had to prevent him forcibly from going out to seek martyrdom in the persecution in which his father was killed. He became head of the catechetical school, leading an extremely ascetical life; he even castrated himself. He was not ordained until 230, on a visit to Palestine; his own bishop deposed and exiled him because of the irregularity of his ordination and he settled in Caesarea, where he established what became a school. In a persecution in 250 he was imprisoned and tortured, and never really recovered. He wrote much, but because his teaching was later condemned, little survives in the original (there are some Latin translations). An imaginative biblical scholar, he produced a *Hexapla,* a work which set six versions of the Bible in parallel columns. His *De Principiis* is the first great systematic presentation of Christianity, in four books discussing God, the human and material world, free will and the Bible. He also wrote an apologetic work, *Against Celsus.* He interpreted the Bible as having three senses, literal, moral and allegorical, stressing the last, and divided Christians into two groups, the simple and the perfect. He believed that at a final restoration *(apokatastasis)* all creatures, even the devil, will be saved.

📖 Henri Crouzel, *Origen: The Life and Thought of the First Great Theologian,* Edinburgh: T&T Clark and San Francisco: Harper & Row 1989

Otto, Rudolf (1869–1937) German Protestant theologian. Born near Hanover, he studied at Erlangen and Göttingen, where he became professor, subsequently moving to Breslau and Marburg. Influenced by Friedrich Schleiermacher and Albrecht Ritschl, he was interested in the essence and truth of religion. However, he reacted against ethical and rational liberalism in favour of 'feelings' as valid experiences of the transcendental; the concept in which he expressed what was experienced was 'the holy, the numinous'. His most famous book is *The Idea of the Holy* (1917). He applied his approach via the numinous to eschatology in the Gospels in *The Kingdom of God and the Son of Man* (1934). He also wrote on Hinduism.

📖 P. C. Almond, *Rudolf Otto: An Introduction to His Philosophical Thought,* Chapel Hill, NC: University of North Carolina Press 1984

Pachomius (*c.*290–346) Egyptian monk. Brought up a pagan, he was converted as a conscript soldier by Christian kindness. He went on after training as a solitary to establish a community in a deserted village, modelled on the primitive community in Jerusalem, and by the time of his death he was leader of communal monasticism, based on a simple rule. This rule, which combined strict discipline with recognition of individual differences and emphasized productive work as well as prayer, influenced Basil of Caesarea, John Cassian and Benedict.

📖 Philip Rousseau, *Pachomius: The Making of a Community in Fourth-Century Egypt,* Berkeley, CA: University of California Press 1999

Paley, William (1743–1805) English scholar. Educated at Cambridge, he taught mathematics, looked after a Westmoreland parish and became Archdeacon of Carlisle. A popular communicator, he wrote a standard textbook on ethics, *The Principles of Moral and Political Philosophy* (1785), and in *Pauline Hours* (1790) made a historical comparison of Acts with the letters of Paul. His fame rests on *A View of the Evidences of Christianity* (1794) and *Natural Theology* (1802), in which he saw creation in mechanistic terms and argued for the existence of God in terms of design. He produced the famous illustration of finding a watch on the seashore and inferring that it is the creation of an intelligent mind.

📖 M. L. Clarke, *Paley: Evidences for the Man,* London: SPCK and Toronto: University of Toronto Press 1974

Parham, Charles Fox (1873–1929) Amerian Pentecostalist pioneer. Born in Iowa, he was converted at the age of 15 and went to the Methodist Southwestern Kansas College. He left in 1893 to serve in the Methodist Church, but a desire to return to New Testament Christianity led him after two years to practise an independent ministry. With a deep interest in holiness theology and faith healing, he opened a healing home and a Bible school in Topeka, Kansas. Believing that God would give his spirit to enable missionaries to preach in other known languages, in 1901 he and his students prayed to receive baptism in the Holy Spirit. This led to a revival, in which Parham and some of his students claimed to have experienced the Spirit, thus marking the beginning of the Pentecostal movement. In 1905 he opened a Bible school in Houston, Texas, where he influenced William J. Seymour, the key figure in the famous Azusa Street revival. Charges of sexual misconduct (later dropped) damaged Parham's leadership in the Pentecostal movement but his linking of speaking in tongues (later seen as 'unknown' tongues, i.e. glossolalia) became a powerful factor in its spread.

📖 James R. Goff, Jr, *Fields White unto Harvest: Charles F. Parham and the Missionary Origins of Pentecostalism,* Fayetteville, AR: University of Arkansas Press 1988

Pascal, Blaise (1623–62) French mathematician and theologian. Born in Clermont-Ferrand of a distinguished father, he was educated privately, moving with his father to Paris and then Rouen. A mathematical prodigy, he experimented from an early age, discovering the principles of the barometer and hydraulics, devising a calculator and working out the theory of probability. At the age of 23 he came into contact with the Jansenists, visiting Port Royal regularly on his return to Paris after his father's death. His *Letters to a Provincial* (1657), attacking Jesuit theories of grace and morality, were highly controversial and officially condemned by Rome. After a miraculous vision, in a 'night of fire' in 1654 which brought him deep assurance, he began a defence of the Christian religion, but never finished it, leaving only his notes, published as *Pensées.* He believed God could only be known by faith, not reason. His 'wager' is famous, as is his saying 'The heart has its reasons which reason does not know.'

📖 A. J. Krailsheimer, *Pascal,* Oxford: OUP 1980

Patrick (*c.*390–460) Irish bishop. His dates and the details of his life cannot be determined with certainty. Born in Britain, he was captured by Irish pirates, and spent six years in their custody in Ireland. Having prayed God to rescue him, when he did get home he was a changed man. He trained for the ministry in Britain and returned to Ireland where he spent the rest of his life as bishop, in the work of reconciliation, education and establishing religious institutions. He and his church were independent of Rome. Sadly, he does not seem to have composed the hymn ('St Patrick's Breastplate') attributed to him.

📖 R. P. C. Hanson, *Saint Patrick: His Origins and Career*, Oxford: OUP 1968

Péguy, Charles (1873–1914) French writer. Born of a poor and almost illiterate working-class family in Orleans, he went to the Sorbonne, but gave up his studies to run a bookshop. At first he was an ardent socialist and supporter of Dreyfus, the Jewish officer wrongly convicted of selling secrets to the Germans, defending Dreyfus in a journal of which he was co-founder. However, he later became a nationalist mystic with a love of medieval Catholicism and a deep eucharistic devotion, though he remained anti-clerical. He wrote a famous play, *The Mystery of the Charity of Joan of Arc* (1910, English 1950), and a vast religious poem, *Eve* (1914). An immense influence on later Catholic writers, he was killed in battle at the beginning of the First World War.

📖 M. H. Villiers, *Charles Péguy: A Study in Integrity*, London: Greenwood Press 1976

Pelagius (died *c.*410) British theologian. Trained in law, he was active in Rome at the end of the fourth century. Shocked by the moral laxity of his time, against dualistic views that human beings are intrinsically evil and therefore cannot be morally responsible he argued that they are free to choose good by nature. He subsequently moved to Africa and then Palestine, attracting followers. Though he does not seem to have denied the traditional Christian doctrine of original sin, a denial with which his name is associated, he was condemned for heresy. Initially he cleared himself, but was condemned again; Augustine was one of his vigorous opponents. Expelled from Palestine, he disappears from view; he may have died in Egypt. His influence continued and he has undergone a reassessment in modern times.

📖 John Ferguson, *Pelagius*, Cambridge: Heffer 1956

Penn, William (1644–1718) Quaker and founder of Pennsylvania. Son of an admiral and born in London, he was expelled from Oxford for non-conformist views. After travel (during which he became a Quaker, as a result of a sermon he heard in Cork) and service in the navy he studied law in London. His writings on Quakerism brought him imprisonment in the Tower of London. While there, undeterred, he wrote *No Cross, No Crown* (1669), which became a Quaker classic. On his release, becoming increasingly interested in founding a colony for Quakers in America, he established Pennsylvania, of which he became governor. He then returned to London, but was again persecuted and deprived of his governorship. In this period he also wrote *Primitive Christianity* (1696), comparing Quakerism with the early church. Returning to Pennsylvania only for a brief period, he spent the rest of his life in or near London.

📖 Catherine Owens Peare, *William Penn*, New York: Holt, Reinhart & Winston 1961

Peter Lombard (*c.*1095–1169) Born in Lombardy, after study in Bologna he went to Reims and Paris, where he taught at the cathedral school and became bishop. He is known for his *Sentences*, a four-volume compilation of quotations, principally from the Latin church fathers Augustine and Hilary but also from some Greek fathers like John of Damascus, previously unknown in the West. The resultant summary of doctrine covers the Trinity, creation and sin, the incarnation and virtue, the sacraments (first identified here as seven in number) and the 'last things'. After initial hostility it became the standard medieval textbook, and though it was eclipsed by the *Summa Theologiae* of Thomas Aquinas, it was still influential in the time of Luther and Calvin.

📖 Philip W. Rosemann, *Peter Lombard*, New York: OUP 2004

Philo (*c.*20 BCE–50 CE) Jewish philosopher and exegete. He came from a prosperous priestly family; nothing is known of his life except that he went with a delegation to Rome to plead with the Emperor Caligula for Jewish rights. A prolific author, he developed an allegorical interpretation of the Torah in terms of Platonic and Stoic philosophy, synthesizing Hebrew and Greek thought. His philosophy had a mystic dimension, moving towards the mystic vision of God in ecstasy. He was influential on Alexandrian Christian theologians like Clement and Origen, not least in his scriptural exegesis.

📖 Samuel Sandmel, *Philo of Alexandria: An Introduction*, New York: OUP 1979

Photius (*c.*820–91) Patriarch of Constantinople. From a noble family, he was a scholar and became a statesman. He taught at the university and became imperial secretary, then ambassador to Assyria. When palace intrigues led to the deposition of the current patriarch, though Photius was a layman, he was consecrated within a week and appointed. A controversy followed, at the end of which he was condemned by a Roman synod. This caused offence in Constantinople and the matter became political, complicated by the fact that there was a dispute as to whether newly-Christianized Bulgaria should depend on East or West. Photius in turn condemned the Roman addition of the *filioque* clause (the Holy Spirit proceeding from the Father *and the Son*) to the creed. A council in Constantinople excommunicated Pope Nicholas I. On a change of emperor, harmony was temporarily restored between East and West at the expense of deposing Photius, but he was later reinstated. On a further change of emperor he was deposed again and died in exile. The Photian schism, as it is called, was a forerunner of the final spilt between Eastern and Western churches. Photius' writings are important, not least for their bibliographical record of vanished works; he became a saint in the Eastern church.

📖 F. Dvornik, *The Photian Schism*, Cambridge: CUP 1948

Pio, Padre (1887–1968) Capuchin priest. He was born to a peasant family in Pietrelcina, southern Italy, and baptized Francesco Forgione. He became a Capuchin at the age of 15, when he took the name Pio, and was ordained priest in 1910; in 1918 he received the stigmata, the visible wounds of Christ. He spent his life in the monastery of S. Giovanni Rotondo in southern

Italy and became so famous for his powers of healing that the Vatican tried, unsuccessfully, for a time in the 1920s and 1930s to impose restrictions on access to him. In 1956 he built a House for the Relief of Suffering together with a large church to welcome all the pilgrims who came to him. He was canonized in 1999.

Renzo Allegri, *Padre Pio: Man of Hope*, Atlanta, GA: Charis Books 2000

www.padrepio.com

Plato (427–347 BCE) Greek philosopher. Born in Athens, he became a pupil of Socrates, after whose death he set up a school on the outskirts of Athens, the Academy, where he spent the rest of his life, apart from a brief visit to Sicily. In his philosophy he developed the notion of a world of 'forms' above and separate from our changing world and related to it as model to imperfect copy. From this world of forms (the Greek word is *idea*, hence idealism) eternal principles derive. True happiness comes from knowledge of these forms, and this knowledge is sought by the soul, pre-existent and surviving bodily death. Plato assumed that few if any people could actually achieve this level of knowledge. Through revivals of his doctrines from the first century BCE in a religious direction (Middle Platonism), he was influential on Christian thought, an influence which was further strengthened by the Neoplatonism developed by Plotinus, and then Porphyry and Boethius. Augustine helped to perpetuate his thinking. His *Republic*, setting out a model for an ideal state, was also widely influential in Western social thought and the formation of social institutions.

Richard Kraut (ed), *The Cambridge Companion to Plato*, Cambridge: CUP 1993

Plotinus (*c.*205–70) Greek Neoplatonist philosopher and mystic. Born in Lycopolis, Egypt, after travelling with the Emperor Gordian to Persia to acquaint himself with Eastern thought, he set up a school in Rome. His philosophy, reflecting dualism, sought to find a unifying principle behind the world and explain how the One, beyond the supreme mind and forms, gives rise to the Many. He attached great importance to contemplation as being the way by which the soul can gain knowledge and in so doing attain union with God by its own disciplined efforts, through asceticism and purity of heart. His works were edited in six groups of nine *(Enneads)* and published posthumously by Porphyry. They proved important because of their stress on the immaterial world.

D. J. O'Meara, *Plotinus: An Introduction to the Enneads*, Oxford: Clarendon Press 1995

Polycarp (*c.*69–155) Bishop of Smyrna and martyr. Little is known of his life; he is depicted as a champion of orthodoxy (against Marcion) and a faithful pastor. He was a leading Christian in Asia Minor; his great age linked him with much earlier days of the church. He paid a visit to Rome at the end of his life to discuss the date of Easter, a controversial issue; on his return he was arrested and burnt to death.

Simon Tugwell, *Apostolic Fathers*, London and New York: Continuum 2002

Porete, Marguerite (died 1310) Little is known of her life; she was burned at the stake for heresy in Paris in 1310. Her mystical work *The Mirror of Simple Souls* (*Le Miroir des simples âmes*) is regarded as the most important religious document in Old French.

Marguerite Porete, *The Mirror of Simple Souls*, Classics of Western Spirituality, New York and Mahwah, NJ: Paulist Press 1993

Porphyry (232–304) Neoplatonist philosopher. Born in Tyre, he travelled round Syria, Palestine and Egypt before studying philosophy in Athens. He met Plotinus in Rome, subsequently editing his works. He moved to Sicily, but returned to Rome at the end of his life. Sceptical of popular religion, he was especially hostile to Christianity, against which he wrote fifteen books: these are no longer extant because they were burned. He is important philosophically for the clarification he brings to Plotinus.

Porphyry's Life of Plotinus, Edmonds, WA: Holmes Publishing Group 1983

Priestley, Joseph (1733–1804) English Presbyterian minister and scientist. Born in Yorkshire in a strict Calvinist family, he was ordained and served as a minister in Suffolk before teaching at a dissenting academy in Warrington, distinguishing himself by his scholarship (he discovered oxygen). Moving to a ministry in Leeds, he became a Unitarian and as librarian to a nobleman found time to write. He then went to Birmingham, where his house was broken into and ransacked because of his support of the French Revolution. He moved to London, became one of the founders of the Unitarian Society, but subsequently emigrated to America and lived in Pennsylvania. His writings were controversial; they include *Institutes of Natural and Revealed Religion* (1772–4) and *History of Early Opinions Concerning Jesus Christ* (1786).

Robert E. Schofield, *The Enlightenment of Joseph Priestley*, Penn State University Press 1998

Priscillian (died 386) Spanish bishop. A nobleman with ascetic interests, he seems to have been influenced by Gnostic doctrines brought by an Egyptian called Marcus. He attracted many followers, particularly women, but including two bishops. Though condemned, he became Bishop of Avila; he and his followers were then exiled, going to France and then Rome to appeal to the Pope. Getting their exile annulled, Priscillian returned to Spain and his following grew. Not long after being tried for heresy by the emperor, he was executed for sorcery in Trier. His views seem to have been Manichaean: dualistic, anti-materialist, ascetic and astrological.

📖 Henry Chadwick, *Priscillian of Avila: The Occult and the Charismatic in the Early Church*, Oxford: OUP 1976

Prudentius (348–c.410) Poet and hymn writer. Aurelius Prudentius Clemens, to give him his full name, was a Spanish lawyer and civil servant. He was twice city prefect of Saragossa. Around the age of 50 he retired to live an ascetic life and to write poetry, of which Christians were still suspicious. Much influenced by the writers of classical antiquity he wrote didactic poems and hymns, the latter usually around 100 lines long. Some of his hymns, like 'Of the Father's Love Begotten' and 'Earth Has Many a Noble City', are still sung today.

📖 *The Poems of Prudentius* (2 vols), Fathers of the Church Vols 43, 52, Washington, DC: Catholic University of America Press 1962, 1965

Pusey, Edward Bouverie (1800–82) English theologian. He studied at Oxford and then at Göttingen and Berlin, where he met many leading German biblical critics, going on to become professor of Hebrew at Oxford, a post he held for the rest of his life. He later withdrew an early work which was thought to favour German theology, and from 1833 was associated with John Keble and John Henry Newman in the high church Oxford Movement, writing tracts and giving it intellectual backing. He was a gifted (and on occasion controversial) preacher; one of his sermons was instrumental in the reintroduction of private confession to a priest into the Anglican church. After his wife died in 1839 he became interested in the religious life. A conservative, he opposed university reform. In the latter part of his life he was involved in discussion with Rome in the hope of reunion. His views are expressed in his many tracts, letters and sermons.

📖 Leonard Prestige, *Pusey* (1933), Oxford: Mowbray 1982

Quiñones, Francisco de (1480–1540) Roman Catholic reformer. Born into a noble Spanish family, at the age of 18 he became a Franciscan, rising to become minister-general in 1523. In 1526 he was consecrated bishop. He was involved in the negotiations over Henry VIII's divorce, representing the interests of Catherine of Aragon. He was also involved in missionary work, sending twelve missionaries to Mexico, one of whom became the first bishop within the present territory of the United States. However, his main work was in the sphere of worship. He compiled a new breviary, reducing to a minimum the lives of the saints and providing for the recitation of the Psalter once a week and reading virtually all the Bible once a year. The Breviary proved too radical and was eventually banned, but it was a great influence on Thomas Cranmer in his preparation of the Anglican Book of Common Prayer.

Rahner, Karl (1904–84) German Catholic theologian. Born in Swabia, he became a Jesuit and studied in Freiburg, where he was influenced by Martin Heidegger, and Innsbruck, where he subsequently became professor; from 1964 he was professor in Munich. He was also involved in the Second Vatican Council. His main concern was to present thinking in the tradition of Thomas Aquinas (Thomistic theology) in such a way as to avoid the criticism of Immanuel Kant; he did this by means of the terminology of Heidegger. Under the influence of existentialism, he saw human experience as the key to all theological meaning; this is focused on transcendental experience, which becomes conscious when we reflect on the conditions for knowing. His reinterpretation of the traditional dogmas of the church in the light of the modern world was usually done in essay form. The results are summed up in *The Foundations of Christian Faith* (1978), and the essays themselves are collected in his *Theological Investigations*, which extend to more than twenty volumes.

📖 William V. Dych, *Karl Rahner*, London and New York: Continuum 2000

Raikes, Robert (1735–1811) Pioneer of the Sunday School movement. Son of the publisher of the *Gloucester Journal*, he was interested in social reform and hospital care. Seeing the neglect of local children and their bad behaviour on Sundays, in 1780 he engaged women to teach reading and the catechism on Sundays. The idea spread like wildfire and others took it up, so that in just over five years 200,000 children were being taught. The Sunday School Society was founded in 1783 and the Sunday School Union in 1803. He was also an influence on Hannah More.

📖 Frank Booth, *Robert Raikes*, Birmingham: National Christian Education Council 1980

Ramsey, Arthur Michael (1904–88) English theologian and archbishop. Son of the president of Magdalene College, Cambridge, where he studied, after pastoral work in Lincolnshire and a post at Lincoln Theological College he went on to become professor at Durham and Cambridge, Bishop of Durham, Archbishop of York and then of Canterbury. His patriarchal style earned him the reputation of being the last of the church fathers, and the quintessentially Anglican character of his theology gained him a wide readership. His major books were *The Gospel and the Catholic Church* (1936), studies on the resurrection and transfiguration, and a social history of Anglicanism, *From Gore to Temple* (1960).

📖 Owen Chadwick, *Michael Ramsey*, Oxford: Clarendon Press 1990

Rancé, Armand-Jean le Bouthillier de (1626–1700) Monastic reformer. As son of a secretary to the Queen of France and godson of Cardinal Richelieu, he had a good start in life, by the age of 10 having been made abbot of the Cistercian monastery of La Trappe and a canon of Notre-Dame, Paris, with the prospect of becoming Archbishop of Tours. He had a distinguished academic career and at the same time enjoyed attending the best Parisian salons. However, in 1657 he underwent a sudden conversion and resigned all his positions but that of abbot of La Trappe, to which he retired. He introduced stringent regulations, regarding penance and physical austerity as the basis of monastic life. He saw monks as criminals sentenced to a life of severity. Because La Trappe was the only Cistercian house in France to survive the Revolution, during the nineteenth century its rule became extremely influential.

📖 A. J. Krailsheimer, *Armand-Jean de Rancé, Abbot of La Trappe:*

His Influence on the Cloister and the World, Oxford: OUP 1974

Rauschenbusch, Walter (1861–1918) American theologian. Born in Rochester, New York, the son of a German Lutheran turned Baptist seminary teacher, he studied there and in Germany, and after twelve years as pastor in the Second German Baptist Church in New York City was called back to Rochester to teach in his turn. The social problems he had encountered in New York made a deep impression on him and he attempted to find a theology which went some way towards meeting them. He combined social analysis, theological liberalism and biblical piety, stressing that Jesus preached social salvation and reiterating the kingdom of God as a dominant principle and unifying concept. His major work was *Christianity and the Social Crisis* (1907); it was followed by *Christianity and the Social Order* (1912) and *A Theology for the Social Gospel* (1917). Despite opposition because of his German ancestry he became known as the father of the social gospel in America. He was highly suspect to his church for his liberal views.

📖 Christopher H. Evans, *The Kingdom is Always But Coming: A Life of Walter Rauschenbusch*, Grand Rapids, MI: Eerdmans 2004

Reimarus, Hermann Samuel (1694–1768) German deist and biblical critic. Born in Hamburg, after studying in Jena and teaching in Wittenberg he went to England, where he was influenced by the deists. From 1727 to his death he was professor in Hamburg. A thoroughgoing rationalist, he wrote a great deal, but it was only after his death, when Gotthold Lessing published fragments of his work, that his views became known and caused a sensation. He not only rejected miracles and the supernatural, but accused the biblical writers of fraud. Albert Schweitzer saw him as standing at the beginning of the quest for the historical Jesus.

📖 Reimarus, *Fragments* ed Charles H. Talbert, Philadelphia: Fortress Press 1970 and London: SCM Press 1971

Renan, Joseph Ernest (1823–92) French philosopher and theologian. Born in Brittany, he studied at a Paris seminary, but doubts caused him to leave. A work on Averroes established him as a scholar, and the emperor sent him to do archaeological work in the Near East. In Palestine he wrote his *Life of Jesus* (1863). This portrayed Jesus as a genial Galilean preacher and denied his divinity, causing a scandal. By now Renan was professor of Hebrew in the Collège de France, but because of the book he was dismissed. Later in life he turned to scientific rationalism.

📖 David C. J. Lee, *Ernest Renan: In the Shadow of Faith*, London: Duckworth 1996

Rhodes, Alexandre de (1591–1660) Jesuit missionary. Born in Avignon, he became a Jesuit in Rome in 1612 and in 1619 was sent as a missionary to Indochina (present-day Vietnam). He was expelled in 1630 because the authorities felt that his success was undermining the country's Confucianism, and then spent ten years as a professor of philosophy in Macao. He returned to south Vietnam in 1640, but in 1646 was condemned to death and saved only by his sentence being commuted to permanent exile. In Rome he argued for further missionary work in Vietnam and a native priesthood, but he was sent on mission to Persia, where he died. He produced a Vietnamese-Latin-Portuguese dictionary and developed a romanized form of script, known as Quoc Ngu, for Vietnamese.

📖 Peter C. Phan, *Apostle to Vietnam*, Maryknoll, NY: Orbis Books 1998

Ricci, Matteo (1552–1610) Italian Jesuit. After training in the sciences at the Roman College, he was sent to Goa and Macao, where he studied Chinese. His first visit to China in 1583 ended in expulsion after six years, but he immediately made a second attempt and lived there for the rest of his life, latterly in Nanking and Peking. He gained converts by his scientific knowledge and his adaptation of Christianity to Chinese ideas. His methods proved controversial and after his death were condemned by the Pope, but his *The True Doctrine of God* (1595), written in Chinese, became a standard missionary manual.

📖 Vincent Cronin, *The Wise Man from the West* (1984), London: Harvill Press 1999

Richard of St Victor (died 1173) Scholar and mystic. Born in Scotland, at an early age he entered the distinguished abbey of St Victor in Paris (he was less scholarly than Andrew and less intellectual than Hugh). There he spent his life, becoming prior. A mystic, he was attracted by the imagery of scripture; he also had a deep interest in architecture, which is reflected in his interpretaton of the visions of Ezekiel and the tabernacle and temple. He also stressed the importance of demonstration and argument in theology; his main work was *On the Trinity*, an attempt to understand the personal nature of God.

📖 B. Smalley, *The Study of the Bible in the Middle Ages*, Oxford: Blackwell [3]1983

Ricoeur, Paul (1913–) French philosopher. Born in Valence and orphaned at an early age, he was brought up by grandparents in Brittany. He studied in Rennes and the Sorbonne and became a schoolteacher until the outbreak of war. During military service he was awarded the Croix de Guerre. He was then put in a prisoner-of-war camp, in which he created a 'university'. After a period of research he was made professor at Strasbourg and Nanterre, subsequently holding chairs in both Paris and Chicago. He initially became interested in phenomenology, then because of the problem of evil he became interested in hermeneutics and symbolism. His first major work was his three-volume *Philosophy of the Will* (1950, English 1980). His *Essays on Biblical Interpretation* (1980) explore the different ways in which religious texts point to a hidden God. He is concerned to demonstrate how different positions can be both 'less than' and 'more than' one another.

📖 Karl Simms, *Paul Ricoeur*, London and New York: Routledge 2002

Ridley, Nicholas (*c.*1500–55) English Reformer. Born in Northumberland, he studied at Cambridge, the Sorbonne and Louvain. He then taught in Cambridge, and after being Cranmer's chaplain and a clergyman in Kent, he returned to Cambridge. Finally he became successively Bishop of Rochester and Bishop of London. His interest was aroused in eucharistic theology; he rejected the doctrine of a bodily eucharistic presence. Increasingly involved with the Reformers, in the reign of Queen Mary he was deposed, excommunicated and finally burned at the stake in Oxford.

📖 J. G. Ridley, *Nicholas Ridley: A Biography*, London: Longmans Green 1957

Ritschl, Albrecht Benjamin (1822–89) German Protestant theologian. Born in Berlin the son of a Lutheran bishop, after studying at Bonn, Halle, Heidelberg and Tübingen he became professor in Bonn and then Göttingen. Originally a disciple of Ferdinand Christian Baur, he moved to systematic theology, in which he became very influential. For him, faith was the main religious category, so philosophy was irrelevant. Christian revelation, he believed, is to a community, which makes the church important, but this has ethical consequences, so that religious doctrines are value judgements. His main work, *The Christian Doctrine of Justification and Reconciliation* (three volumes, 1870–84), covered what he believed to be the pivotal doctrine of Christianity. Adolf von Harnack, Ernst Troeltsch and Wilhelm Herrmann were among those whom he influenced.

📖 Philip Hefner, *Faith and the Vitalities of History*, New York: Harper & Row 1966

Robinson, John Arthur Thomas (1919–83) English New Testament scholar and theologian. Born in the cathedral close at Canterbury, he studied at Cambridge, where he taught before becoming Bishop of Woolwich; he then returned to Cambridge for the rest of his life. A conservative New Testament scholar, he nevertheless defied accepted opinions in his *Redating the New Testament* (1975), in which he argued that the bulk of the New Testament was composed before the fall of Jerusalem in 70 CE, and *The Priority of John* (1984), in which he argued that traditions in the Fourth Gospel antedate those of the Synoptics. He was interested in liturgical renewal long before that became the trend, and was much involved in the political and literary issues of the day. His *Honest to God* (1963), with its reflection of current radical thought in Germany and elsewhere, was an international sensation, but he never managed to develop its implications consistently.

📖 Eric James, *A Life of John A. T. Robinson: Scholar, Pastor, Prophet*, London: Collins and Grand Rapids, MI: Eerdmans 1987

Rolle of Hampole, Richard (*c.* 1300–49) English mystic. Born in Yorkshire, he studied at Oxford and then went to live as a hermit. He spent his last years near a convent of Cistercian nuns. He wrote prolifically in Latin and English, composing lyric poems as well as scholarly works. His spiritual writing expresses simple ideas and stresses grace. Orthodox in belief, he attacked corruption in the church.

📖 Rosamund S. Allen, *Richard Rolle: English Writings*, Classics of Western Spirituality, New York and Mahwah, NJ: Paulist Press and London: SPCK 1989

Rufinus, Tyrannius (*c.* 345–410) Italian monk, historian and translator. Born in Aquileia, he became friendly with Jerome in Rome and travelled first to Egypt, where he became interested in the works of Origen, and then to Jerusalem, where he founded a monastery on the Mount of Olives. He returned to Italy when Origen came under attack. Though he wrote works of his own, he is important for having translated the writings of the Greek fathers into Latin when knowledge of Greek was declining in the West. In many cases this ensured their survival.

📖 E. F. Morison, *Rufinus: Commentary on the Apostles' Creed*, London: Methuen 1916

Ruysbroeck, Jan van (1293–1381) Flemish mystic. Born near Brussels, he was educated there and spent three years as a priest before retiring to a local valley, Groenendaal, where he founded a monastery, and attracted visitors from far and wide. His major work is *The Spiritual Espousals*, emphasizing a loving union with God (he was accused of pantheism), humility, charity and light from the world. His prose helped to shape the Flemish language.

📖 Evelyn Underhill, *Ruysbroeck* (1914), Felinfach: Llanerch Press 2002

Saint-Cyran, Abbé de (Jean Duvergier de Hauranne, 1581–1643) French Jansenist leader. After studying at the Jesuit College at Louvain, and in Paris and Bayonne with Jansen, he was attracted to the works of Augustine, which he preferred to scholasticism. Being made abbot of Saint-Cyran, from then on he lived mostly in Paris. He was concerned to reform Roman Catholicism by reviving the teachings of Augustine, opposing the Jesuits and scholasticism and criticizing Roman Catholic abuses. Having incurred the enmity of Cardinal Richelieu, he spent the last five years of his life in prison.

📖 Dale van Kley, *The Jansenists and the Expulsion of the Jesuits from France*, New Haven: Yale University Press 1975

Savonarola, Girolamo (1452–98) Italian Reformer. After studies in Ferrara he became a Dominican and led an ascetic life, being made prior of San Marco in Florence. He passionately denounced the immorality of nobility and clergy; his popularity led to a revolution in Florence which forced out the ruling Medici family and created a theocracy. However, he made many enemies and was excommunicated by Alexander VI. He retorted by calling for the deposition of the Pope, but his support had dwindled and he was tortured and executed.

📖 Donald Weinstein, *Savonarola and Florence*, Princeton, NJ: Princeton University Press 1970

Schillebeeckx, Edward Cornelis Florentius Alfons (1914–) Belgian theologian. Born in Antwerp of a well-to-do family, he studied at the Jesuit College at Turnhout and then went on to the Dominican house in Ghent. After military service he studied theology at Louvain and taught there. Post-doctoral study in Paris broadened his horizons, and he met leading Dominicans. In 1958 he was called to be professor in Nijmegen, where he has been ever since. He was an expert adviser at the Second Vatican Council, but in subsequent years twice came under suspicion from the Vatican. His first major work was an existential interpretation of the sacraments,

Christ the Sacrament (1959, English 1963), but it was not until his *Jesus* (1974, English 1979) that he attracted international attention. In the book, influenced by modern biblical scholarship, he saw Jesus as an eschatological prophet; the sequel, *Christ* (1980) relates early Christian experience of salvation to contemporary Christian and non-Christian experience. A long interval separates these books from the last volume of his trilogy, *Church* (1990); two versions of a book he wrote on ministry during this period reflect his growing dissatisfaction with the move away from the ideas of Vatican II and the need for a revision of the Catholic theology of ministry. This dissatisfaction becomes even more evident in his latest work.

📖 John Bowden, *Edward Schillebeeckx*, London: SCM Press and New York: Crossroad 1983

Schlegel, Friedrich von (1772–1829) German Catholic apologist. A leader of the romantic movement, he lived in Berlin but lectured in Jena, Dresden and Paris. Most of his life was given to literary pursuits. He married a daughter of the Jewish philosopher Moses Mendelssohn and with her was converted to Catholicism. He then became opposed to the development of political and religious freedom in Germany and a vigorous defender of the Catholic medieval ideal against the rise of a German national state along Napoleonic lines.

📖 Hans Eichner, *Friedrich Schlegel*, New York: Twayne Publishers 1970

Schleiermacher, Friedrich Daniel Ernst (1768–1834) German theologian. Born in Breslau, the son of a Reformed army chaplain who was converted to the Herrnhuter Brethren, he had a Pietist education. Finding this too narrow, he went to the University of Halle, where he discovered Aristotle and Immanuel Kant. After being a tutor he was ordained, and served as a pastor in Berlin. He then became professor at Halle and, after a further Berlin pastorate, professor in Berlin. A gifted preacher, against the background of the Napoleonic wars he supported German national and church unity. His first major work, *On Religion: Speeches to its Cultured Despisers* (1799), was an apologia for religion as being a sense of the infinite without which human life was incomplete, locating religion in intuition and feeling, not dogma. His major work was *The Christian Faith* (1821–2), with its famous definition of religion as 'the feeling of absolute dependence', in which he sought a middle course between orthodoxy and natural theology. It was related to the corporate piety of the Christian community as an alternative basis to Christian knowledge constructed by Kant. He also wrote a life of Jesus. Of enormous influence, his theology seemed to point a way forward after Kant's criticism of theology and became the epitome of liberal theology.

📖 Keith W. Clements, *Friedrich Schleiermacher: Pioneer of Modern Theology*, London: Collins and Minneapolis: Fortress Press 1991

Schmidt, Karl-Ludwig (1891–1956) German New Testament scholar. He was professor at Giessen, Jena and then Bonn, from where he was dismissed by the Nazis in 1933, after which he taught in Basle. A pioneer in form criticism, he wrote an influential book on the framework of the Synoptic Gospels; further works were on church and state and Jewish-Christian relations.

📖 Karl-Ludwig Schmidt, *The Church*, London: A&C Black 1950

Schweitzer, Albert (1875–1965) Theologian, physician and musician. Born in Alsace, he studied in Strasbourg, Berlin and Paris. His first book was *The Mystery of the Kingdom of God* (1901), which saw Jesus' teaching as centred on the imminent coming of the kingdom. Its publication led to his being made a lecturer and head of a theological college, and he went on to write his classic *The Quest of the Historical Jesus* (1906), criticizing the orthodox and liberal nineteenth-century lives of Jesus as being projections of their authors and putting forward his own eschatological interpretation. Meanwhile he was studying for a medical degree, and in 1913 he gave up his academic career to devote himself to mission and the care of the sick in Lambarene, in French Equatorial Africa. He had to return to France because of the First World War, during which his hospital was destroyed, but he rebuilt it afterwards. While still writing as a biblical scholar he produced an influential book on Paul, *The Mysticism of Paul the Apostle* (1931), but his views changed to a philosophy of 'reverence for life': all life must be cherished, including insects and plants. He was also a fine organist, and wrote a study of Bach.

📖 James Brabazon, *Albert Schweitzer. A Biography*, London: Gollancz 1976

Seabury, Samuel (1729–96) American Episcopalian bishop. Born in Connecticut, he studied at Yale and Edinburgh, before serving in parishes in Jamaica, Long Island and Westchester. After being consecrated bishop in Aberdeen (because he could not take the oath of allegiance to the English crown), the first American to hold this office, he served as rector in New London, Connecticut, until his death.

📖 Bruce E. Steiner, *Samuel Seabury: A Study in High Church Tradition*, Athens, OH: Ohio University Press 1971

Sergei of Radonezh (*c.* 1314–92) Monastic reformer and mystic. Sergei, or Sergius, was originally called Bartholomew. He was born in Rostov, of a pious aristocratic family, who moved to Moscow when he was a boy. When he was 20, he and his brother went to live as hermits in the forest near Radonezh; in due course others joined them and they formed a community, building what became the Monastery of the Holy Trinity. Before he died Sergei had founded 40 monasteries in all and is celebrated as the father of Russian monasticism. He also influenced the politics of his time, mediating in disputes between Russian princes and inspiring resistance to Tartar invasions. Stories told about his love of animals recall Francis of Assisi, and his role for Russia resembles that of William Tell for Switzerland. Other religious buildings came to be built around the original monastery, which was destroyed in 1391, including two cathedrals and a seminary; under the Communists the settlement was known as Zagorsk, but it has now reverted to its original name of Sergiev Posad, north of Moscow.

📖 Nicolas Zernov, *St Sergius, Builder of Russia*, London: SPCK 1938

Seymour, William Joseph (1879–1922) African American Pentecostal leader. Born in Louisiana the son of former slaves and brought up as a Baptist, he later joined the Holiness movement. In 1905 he met Charles F. Parham, and accepted his teaching that God would bestow the gift of speaking other known languages in a baptism of the Spirit. In 1906 he moved to Los Angeles, where he met with his followers for prayer on Azusa Street. The revival there proved to be the most influential of the twentieth century in global impact, spreading all over the world. Seymour later dissociated himself from Parham's views but came to be especially loved by African American Pentecostalists for his emphasis on love and reconciliation.

📖 William J. Seymour, *The Doctrines and Discipline of the Azusa Street Apostolic Faith Mission* (1917), Pensacola, FL: Christian Life Books 2000

Shaftesbury, Anthony Ashley Cooper (1801–85) Social reformer. The seventh Earl of Shaftesbury, he was educated at Harrow School and Oxford and then became a Conservative Member of Parliament. He was concerned for the improvement of working conditions in factories and particularly those of women and children in the coal mines, and the use of young boys to sweep chimneys. A leading evangelical in the middle of the nineteenth century, he was president of the British and Foreign Bible Society, and was deeply interested in the work of the Church Missionary Society and YMCA. He had great influence over appointments to senior posts in the Church of England.

📖 John Pollock, *Shaftesbury, The Poor Man's Earl*, London: Hodder & Stoughton 1985

Siger of Brabant (1235–82) Radical Averroist philosopher. All that is known of him is that he taught at the University of Paris and was canon of St Paul's church in Liège. He was attacked by Bonaventure and Thomas Aquinas. When he arrived in Paris, Aristotle had recently been put on the curriculum and Siger wrote commentaries on his works. These brought out the conflict between Aristotle and orthodox Christianity, since Aristotle taught, for example, that the world was eternal and that there was no future life. Siger had to flee to escape charges of heresy because he was alleged to have taught a double truth, and is reported to have been killed in Orvieto by a mad cleric.

📖 N. Kretzmann et al., *The Cambridge History of Later Mediaeval Philosophy*, Cambridge: CUP 1982

Simeon the New Theologian (*c.* 949–*c.* 1022) Byzantine mystic and writer. He began his career in the imperial service, but in 977 became a monk at Studios, the famous monastery in Constantinople, and in 980 abbot of the monastery of St Mamas. Because of opposition to his teaching he was forced to resign in 1009 and was exiled to Asia Minor. Although the sentence was soon revoked, he preferred not to hold office again and spent the rest of his life at Chrysopolis near Constantinople. Regarded as the greatest of Byzantine mystical writers, he prepared the way for Hesychasm. His writings consist of catecheses (moral instructions), sermons, monastic rules and hymns. He attached great importance to the eucharist and the vision of divine light.

📖 G. A. Maloney, *The Mystic of Fire and Light: St Symeon the New Theologian*, Denville, NJ: Dimension Books 1975

Simeon, Charles (1759–1836) Evangelical Anglican. After school at Eton and studies at Cambridge he became an evangelical, and on ordination was appointed as Rector of Holy Trinity Church, Cambridge, where he spent the rest of his life. He was immensely influential in the evangelical revival, particularly in missionary work; he helped to found the Church Missionary Society and the British and Foreign Bible Society; his sermons were published in 21 volumes. The Simeon Trust, which bears his name and still exists, is patron of many Church of England parishes and appoints their ministers.

📖 H. E. Hopkins, *Charles Simeon of Cambridge*, Grand Rapids, MI: Eerdmans 1977

Simeon Stylites (*c.* 390–459) Born on the Cilician border, after time in a monastery he became a hermit and then spent his life on a pillar, the height of which was steadily increased. He produced no written works, but was a great influence on the religious and political life of his time, and an advocate of the orthodox Christian doctrine of the Council of Chalcedon.

📖 Robert Doran, *The Lives of Simeon Stylites*, Kalamazoo, MI: Cistercian Publications 1992

Simon, Richard (1638–1712) French biblical scholar. A member of the French Oratory, he was expelled for his *Critical History of the Old Testament* (1678), which denied that Moses wrote the Pentateuch, the first five books of the Bible traditionally attributed to him. However, his work was in fact written to defend orthodoxy against Benedict de Spinoza. He moved to Rouen and then Dieppe. where he wrote several books about the New Testament.

📖 William McKane, *Selected Christian Hebraists*, Cambridge: CUP 1989

Smith, Joseph (1805–44) Founder of the Church of Jesus Christ of Latter-day Saints (Mormons). Born into a frontier family in Vermont, he moved to Palmyra, New York, where he had a religious conversion. Claiming to have been shown by God golden plates covered with mysterious writing, he produced a translation of them as *The Book of Mormon*. This was followed by *Doctrine and Covenants* (1835), the basis of Mormon teaching. He formed a community and founded the city of Nauvoo, Illinois, but was killed by a mob angry at his financial failures and polygamy.

📖 Robert Vincent Remini, *Joseph Smith*, New York: Viking Books 2002

Smith, William Robertson (1848–94) Scottish Old Testament scholar. Son of a clergyman, he studied in Aberdeen, Edinburgh,

Bonn and Göttingen before becoming professor at the Free Church College in Aberdeen. Seven years later he was dismissed for writing articles in the *Encyclopedia Britannica* which were alleged to undermine belief in scriptural inspiration. He subsequently became editor-in-chief of the *Encyclopedia* and professor of Arabic at Cambridge. His most important book, *The Religion of the Semites* (1889), saw sacrifice as communion, not propitiation.

📖 J. S. Black and G. Chrystal, *The Life of William Robertson Smith*, London: A&C Black 1912

Söderblom, Nathan (1866–1931) Swedish Lutheran theologian. Born in Trönö, he studied in Uppsala, and wrote a book on *The Religion of Luther* (1893), whom he admired greatly, published in the year of his ordination. In Paris, where he was chaplain to the Swedish legation, he lectured on comparative religion, as he did subsequently in Leipzig, though by then he was professor at Uppsala. In 1914 he became archbishop, against some opposition from conservatives. He was prominent in the reunion movement and Life and Work, organizing a famous conference in Stockholm in 1927; he sought to bring about the practical co-operation of all Christian churches, especially in social problems, irrespective of doctrine. For this, he was posthumously awarded the Nobel Peace Prize. In his theological works, he defended biblical criticism, and argued that God's revelation is not limited to Bible or church. His major book, *The Living God*, appeared in English in 1933.

📖 Bengt Sundkler, *Nathan Söderblom: His Life and Work*, Lund: Gleerups 1968

Sölle, Dorothee (1929–2003) Radical German theologian. She studied in Cologne, Freiburg and Göttingen, and became professor of systematic theology at Union Theological Seminary, New York. She was also much involved as a freelance writer, journalist and in television work. Influenced by Marxism, she rejected traditional theism, believing that it put people in a position of dependence: God is loving solidarity. She also rejected existential and private forms of religion in favour of a political theology. Major books are *To Work and to Love* (1984) and *Thinking about God* (1990).

📖 Dorothee Sölle, *Choosing Life*, London: SCM Press and Philadelphia: Fortress Press 1981

Solovyov, Vladimir Sergyevich (1853–1900) Russian philosopher and theologian. The son of the rector of Moscow University, he studied and taught there. After extensive travel, and lecturing in philosophy in Moscow to an audience which included Fyodor Dostoievsky and Leo Tolstoy, he worked at the ministry of education in St Petersburg, but resigned after a controversial lecture against capital punishment. He then devoted himself to writing. Mystical experiences led him to construct a cosmic theology centred on the incarnation, death and resurrection of Christ and the need to realize unity by integration into the unity of the world. Though initially hostile to the Roman Catholic Church, he was increasingly drawn to church union. This approach led to a ban on his religious writings from the Holy Synod, so he turned to politics. In 1896 he seems to have become a Roman Catholic, a move also hinted at in his *Russia and the Universal Church* (1889).

📖 Jonathan Sutton, *The Religious Philosophy of Vladimir Solovyov*, New York: St Martin's Press 1988

Spener, Philipp Jakob (1635–1705) German Pietist. Born of devout parents in Alsace, he studied history and philosophy at Strasbourg. In subsequent travels he encountered Reformed Christianity, which made him want to change the Lutheranism he knew. A minister in Strasbourg and Frankfurt, he held devotional meetings in private homes, and in Frankfurt wrote his best-known work *Pia Desideria* (Pious Desires, 1675), which set out the essence of his pietism. He gained followers but, encountering opposition, moved to Dresden as court preacher. After more opposition there he went to Berlin, where the Elector of Brandenburg supported him. He was influential in founding the University of Halle, but more importantly his views left a permanent mark on German Lutheranism.

📖 Philipp Jakob Spener, *Pia Desideria*, Philadelphia: Fortress Press 1974

Spinoza, Benedict de (1632–77) Dutch Jewish philosopher. Born in Amsterdam of Portuguese parents, he read widely and developed unorthodox views, as a result of which he was expelled from the synagogue. He travelled around, earning his living by grinding lenses, and ended up in The Hague. His views were pantheistic: there is one reality which can be called God or nature and all other things are modifications of this. God only loves and hates in us. Religions like Judaism and Christianity do not express philosophical truth but convey moral truths to those incapable of seeing them by reason. However, he is perhaps most important in that his *Tractatus Theologico-politicus* (1670) shows him to be a forerunner of biblical criticism.

📖 Roger Scruton, *Spinoza*, London: Weidenfeld & Nicolson 1998

Spurgeon, Charles Haddon (1834–92) English Baptist preacher. Born in Essex into a family of Independent ministers, he became a Baptist minister; in South London his preaching drew such crowds that a new church had to be built for him. He also founded a college which still exists today under his name, and other evangelical organizations. A strict Calvinist, his views estranged him even from the Baptist Union. Books of his sermons spread round the world, and his devotional books are still used.

📖 Arnold Dallimore, *Spurgeon: A Biography*, Edinburgh: Banner of Truth 1985

Stanton, Elizabeth Cady (1815–1902) Born in Johnstown, New York, in addition to attending school and college she acquired an informal legal education from her father, who trained many of New York's leading lawyers. In 1840 she married Henry B. Stanton, a prominent figure in the anti-slavery and reform movements; they spent their honeymoon at the World's Anti-Slavery Convention in London. They had five children but this did not prevent her from writing assiduously on reform issues.

After the Civil War she travelled and spoke widely, and became one of the best-known women in American public life; she was tirelessly active in the cause of votes for women and was appointed president of the National Woman Suffrage Association. At the age of 65 she turned her attention to books and wrote a three-volume *History of Woman Suffrage* and a set of controversial Bible commentaries published as *The Woman's Bible*, among other things demonstrating how religious orthodoxy and male theology was a threat to women's independence.

📖 Elizabeth Griffith, *In Her Own Right: The Life of Elizabeth Cady Stanton*, New York: OUP 1984

Stein, Edith (1891–1942) Carmelite nun. Born of a Jewish family in Breslau, she studied at Göttingen and Freiburg and became a significant phenomenologist. She was converted to Roman Catholicism in 1922 and sought to interpret phenomenology in a Thomistic way. She became a Carmelite in Holland in 1934 and during the German occupation was deported by the Germans and killed in a concentration camp.

📖 Hilda Graef, *The Scholar and the Cross: The Life and Work of Edith Stein*, London: Longmans Green 1955

Strauss, David Friedrich (1808–74) German theologian. Born near Stuttgart, he studied under Ferdinand Christian Baur at Tübingen and in Berlin, but lost any prospect of an academic career by writing his controversial *The Life of Jesus Critically Examined* (1835–6). This argued consistently that the Gospels were myths developed from the Old Testament and elsewhere, with minimal historical foundation. The true significance of Christianity was to be seen in Hegelian philosophy. He later turned to biography before returning to theology and a second *Life* of Jesus, but never achieved the impact of his first work. That proved immensely influential in subsequent theology, and remains so to the present day.

📖 P. C. Hodgson (ed), *David Strauss, Life of Jesus translated by George Eliot*, Philadelphia: Fortress Press and London: SCM Press 1972

Sung, John (1901–44) Born the son of a Methodist minister in south-east China, he went to the United States to study science and philosophy at Ohio State University and Union Theological Seminary, New York. In 1927 he had a conversion experience and preached to his classmates so fervently that they feared he was unbalanced and he was put in a mental hospital for six months. On his return to China he became an evangelist, exerting such influence by his preaching and healing activities that he came to be known as the John Wesley or the Billy Graham of China. He suffered from intestinal tuberculosis and died at a relatively early age.

📖 Leslie Lyall, *John Sung: Flame for God in the Far East*, London: China Inland Mission 1956 and Chicago: Moody Press 1964

Suso, Heinrich (1295–1366) Swabian mystic. Of noble family, he entered a Dominican friary at Constance as a boy. Later he had a deep conversion and finished his studies at Cologne under Meister Eckhart. Back at Constance, a book in defence of Eckhardt was condemned and he was banned from teaching. He travelled as a director of women's convents and finally lived in Ulm, never far from criticism. *His Little Book of Eternal Wisdom* (1328), a practical book of meditation, is a spiritual classic, and was admired by Thomas à Kempis.

📖 Heinrich Suso, *The Life of the Servant*, Cambridge: James Clarke 1952

Swedenborg (Svedberg), Emanuel (1688–1772) Swedish philosopher. Son of a distinguished theologian, he studied at Uppsala and in England (where he was influenced by John Locke and Isaac Newton). A gifted scientist and inventor (he was the founder of crystallography), he was appointed to the Swedish Board of Mines. He already felt that the universe had a spiritual basis, and in 1734 wrote *On the Infinite and Final Cause of Creation* to demonstrate this. Ten years later he had a mystical conversion, in which he became conscious of direct contact with the supernatural and felt a call to be God's prophet and disseminate the doctrines of a 'new church', as a spiritual brotherhood. He resigned his government post and spent the rest of his life in Sweden, Holland and England. After his death, followers founded a Swedenborgian church based on his doctrines.

📖 Michael Stanley, *Emanuel Swedenborg*, Berkeley, CA: North Atlantic Books 2003

Tatian (active *c.* 160) Christian apologist. Born in Assyria, he was trained in Greek rhetoric and philosophy. He became a Christian in Rome and was a pupil of Justin Martyr. He is best known for his compilation, the *Diatessaron*, a harmony of the life of Christ based on the four Gospels. He wrote a defence of Christianity entitled *Oration to the Greeks*, a polemic against Greek culture, which he contrasted with the great age and purity of Christianity. He returned to Syria to found an ascetic sect, the Encratites.

📖 Molly Whittaker, *Tatian Oratio ad Graecos and Fragments*, Oxford: OUP 1982

Tauler, John (1300–61) German mystic. He became a Dominican at Strasbourg and seems to have been influenced by Meister Eckhart and Heinrich Suso. He gained a reputation as a preacher and spiritual director, and cared for the sick during the Black Death. He travelled widely and in his sermons was careful to commend a balance between active concern for everyday life and the inner quest. His only surviving works are transcripts of these sermons: they had a great influence on Martin Luther.

📖 Johannes Tauler, *Sermons*, Classics of Western Spirituality, New York and Mahwah, NJ: Paulist Press 1985

Taylor, James Hudson (1832–1905) Missionary. Born in Yorkshire, at the age of 17 he felt that God was calling him to China. He studied medicine and prepared himself by reading books on China, going out in 1853 under the auspices of the Chinese Evangelization Society. Ill health forced his return to England in 1860, but in 1865 he founded the interdenominational China Inland Mission, going out to China the next year with a group of 22 missionaries. The mission aimed to preach the gospel to all the provinces of China and at Taylor's death had 825 missionaries living in all the provinces of China. Taylor believed missionaries should be solely dependent on God with no guaranteed salary, should conform as far as possible to the Chinese way of life, should have an organization based in China, not abroad, and should preach an open evangelical faith.

Marshall Broomhall, *Hudson Taylor: The Man Who Believed God*, London and Philadelphia: China Inland Mission 1929

Taylor, Jeremy (1613–67) Anglican devotional writer. He lived, studied and taught in Cambridge, but after being noticed by Archbishop Laud, he was given a fellowship at All Souls', Oxford and was made chaplain to Charles I. After a parish in Uppingham, he served as chaplain to a member of the nobility before going to Ireland, where he became Bishop of Down and Connor and vice-chancellor of Dublin University. His best-known books are his *Holy Living* (1650) and *Holy Dying* (1651), which have become devotional classics, being clear, balanced and powerful. He was less balanced theologically, engaging in violent polemic against both Roman Catholics and Presbyterians. He influenced the thought of John Wesley during his early development.

P. G. Stanwood (ed), *Jeremy Taylor: Holy Living and Holy Dying*, Oxford: Clarendon Press 1989

Taylor, Nathaniel William (1786–1858) American theologian. Born in Connecticut, he studied at Yale, and after a pastorate in New Haven became the first professor of theology at Yale Divinity School. The last champion of New England theology, he sought to reconcile Calvinistic theology to revivalism, stressing that while sin was inevitable, each individual was responsible for his or her own moral choice. His *Practical Sermons, Lectures on the Moral Government of God* and *Essays and Lectures upon Select Topics in Revealed Religion* were published posthumously in 1859.

Douglas A. Sweeney, *Nathaniel Taylor, New Haven Theology, and the Legacy of Jonathan Edwards*, Oxford Scholarship Online, www.oxfordscholarship.com

Teilhard de Chardin, Pierre (1881–1955) French Catholic theologian and scientist. Born near Clermont-Ferrand, he trained as a Jesuit at Aix-en-Provence. He was particularly interested in geology and palaeontology, and after serving in the First World War worked in China, where he became a distinguished palaeontologist. Returning to France after the Second World War, he was forbidden to accept a professorship at the Collège de France because of his views, or to publish what became his best-known book, *The Phenomenon of Man* (1959). He then went to the United States. His books appeared only after his death and greatly increased his reputation. He saw the universe in evolutionary terms: God is part of the process, which has a Christic centre and moves towards the Omega Point; human beings form the noosphere, a spiritual area between the biosphere and the Omega point. His view, which saw the universe as Christ's body, was overly optimistic, but his concern to relate theology to science was important. His other major book is his devotional *Le milieu divin* (1960).

Claude Cuénot, *Teilhard de Chardin: A Biographical Study*, Baltimore: Helicon 1965

Temple, William (1881–1944) English theologian and philosopher. Son of an Archbishop of Canterbury, after studying and teaching at Oxford he became headmaster of Repton School, rector of St James', Piccadilly, canon of Westminster, Bishop of Manchester and successively Archbishop of York and Canterbury. Prominent in national life, he was concerned for social and economic justice; he was instrumental in founding the British Council of Churches and then developing the World Council of Churches. Remarkably, he found time to write significant books. Trained as a philosopher in the Idealist tradition, he produced *Mens Creatrix* (1917) and *Nature, Man and God* (1934); his devotional commentary, *Readings in St John's Gospel* (1939), became a classic. However, perhaps his most-read book was *Christianity and the Social Order* (1942).

F. A. Iremonger, *William Temple*, London: OUP 1963

Teresa of Avila (Teresa de Cepeda y Ahumada, 1515–82) Spanish mystic. Descended from an old Spanish family, she became a Carmelite nun in Avila. After a lax beginning, at 40 she began her mystic life, founding a house where the rule could be more strictly observed. There she wrote for her nuns *The Way of Perfection*; her other major work is *The Interior Castle*. She went on to found other houses and press for reform in the face of opposition, receiving support for her 'discalced' (without sandals, i.e. stricter) Carmelites from John of the Cross. Her religious life deepened to the point of what she called 'spiritual marriage'. She is important for her descriptions of the whole life of prayer.

The Life of Teresa of Avila by Herself, Harmondsworth: Penguin Books 1957

Teresa, Mother (1910–97) Missionary and nun. She was born Agnes Gonxha Bojaxhiu in Albania, the daughter of a grocer, and went to India in 1928, where she taught as a nun in the school of the Sisters of Loretto in Calcutta. She took the name Teresa after Thérèse of Lisieux. In 1946 she felt a call to work in the slums and founded her own Order of the Missionaries of Charity. She became an Indian citizen and she and her fellow religious wore blue saris as the habit of the order. The order opened a hospice, and centres for the disabled, lepers, the blind and the aged. By the time of her death it existed in more than 90 countries. She had outspoken conservative views on sexual ethics but through her tireless work among the poor proved to be a saint in her own lifetime.

Anne Sebba, *Mother Teresa: Beyond the Image*, New York: Bantam Doubleday Dell 2000

Tertullian (Quintus Septimius Florens Tertullianus, *c.* 160–*c.* 225) African theologian. Brought up in Carthage as a pagan, he was converted to Christianity and later joined the ascetic and apocalyptic sect of the Montanists. He wrote a large number of works and forms a bridge between the early Greek and Latin church fathers. Most of his writings are polemical: against the heretics, against Marcion, against a Praxeas who sees the Trinity simply as modes of God's being. A brilliant but difficult writer, he uses every rhetorical trick of the trade to demolish his opponents' views. His own views were rigorist, and his theology basically scriptural: he is well characterized by his two most famous sayings: 'I believe because it is absurd' and 'What has Athens to do with Jerusalem?'

📖 B. F. Osborn, *Tertullian, First Theologian of the West*, Cambridge: CUP 1997

Theodore of Mopsuestia (354–427) Theologian and biblical exegete. He studied rhetoric at Antioch, but then entered a monastery there with John Chrysostom. After ten years he became Bishop of Mopsuestia. In the Antiochene tradition, he rejected allegorical interpretation of the Bible. In his view of the person of Christ he explained the incarnation as a moral union brought about by the initiative of divine grace, talking of the 'assumed man': God dwells in Jesus as in the prophets and apostles, but Jesus is different in that God dwells in him as a Son. His views were later condemned – from a modem perspective, probably unjustly.

📖 R. A. Norris, *Manhood and Christ: A Study in the Christology of Theodore of Mopsuestia*, Oxford: OUP 1963

Theodoret of Cyrrhus (393–466) Theologian and bishop. Born and educated in Antioch, he gave up his possessions and entered a monastery. After becoming Bishop of Antioch he was a model pastor and administrator, but was caught up in the controversy between Cyril and Nestorius, whose friend he was. His support for the latter earned him deposition and exile, and he was only restored to his see after anathematizing Nestorius, after which he was left in peace. He is thought to have changed his views on christology during his life, the Council of Chalcedon being a watershed; he wrote on the Bible, and composed a church history and an apologia for Christianity.

📖 G. W. Ashby, *Theodoret of Cyrrhus as Exegete of the Old Testament*, Grahamstown 1972

Theodosius the Great (Imperator Caesar Flavius Theodosius Augustus, *c.* 346–95) Roman emperor. Taking Constantine's approval of Christianity one stage further, he made it the sole official religion of the Roman empire, forbidding assemblies of Christian heretics and ordering pagan temples to be closed. In 390, having ordered a massacre in Thessalonica after a riot, he publicly acknowledged his guilt to Ambrose.

📖 N. Q. King, *The Emperor Theodosius and the Rise of Christianity*, London: SCM Press and Philadelphia: Westminster Press 1961

Thérèse of Lisieux (Thérèse Martin, 1873–97) French Carmelite nun. Youngest daughter of a watchmaker in Alençon, and devout from a very early age, she entered the convent at Lisieux at the age of 15 and spent the rest of her life there. She wrote her autobiography (in English it appears under different titles, e.g. *Autobiography of a Saint, The Story of a Soul*) on the orders of her superiors; it was circulated to all Carmelite houses on her death and secured her fame. Her *Little Way*, which she described as 'spiritual childhood, confidence and abandonment in God', became a popular spiritual classic.

📖 Jean-François Six, *Light of the Night. The Last Eighteen Months in the Life of Thérèse of Lisieux*, London: SCM Press 1996

Thomas à Kempis (Thomas Hemerken, *c.* 1380–1471) German monk and devotional writer. Born at Kempen, near Cologne, of poor parents, he became a monk and spent his life in a monastery near Zwolle, writing, copying manuscripts and acting as a spiritual adviser. He is known solely through his *The Imitation of Christ* (1418), which with its clarity and perceptive insights is still one of the most popular of spiritual classics.

📖 Thomas à Kempis, *The Imitation of Christ*, Harmondsworth: Penguin Books 1952

Thomas Aquinas (1225–74) Dominican theologian. Born in Italy of a noble family, he was educated at the Benedictine abbey of Monte Cassino and then at the University of Naples. Against the wishes of his family, who imprisoned him at home for more than a year, he became a Dominican, going to Paris. He studied with Albertus Magnus, who introduced him to the works of Aristotle, newly rediscovered through the work of Arab philosophers, then went to Cologne. Much of his teaching life was subsequently spent in Paris, though he also taught for a decade in Italy and spent the last two years of his life setting up a Dominican school in Naples. He died on his way to the Council of Lyons. The greatest medieval theologian, his main achievement was to produce a system of Christian doctrine that reconciled it with the philosophy of Aristotle, which had seemed a great threat to Christian belief. Among other teachings he is well known for having established five 'ways to God', demonstrations of God's existence. His first great work was the *Summa contra Gentiles*, intended as a textbook for missionaries and a defence of natural theology. His *magnum opus* is the *Summa Theologiae*, the supreme medieval theological system.

📖 Aidan Nichols, *Discovering Aquinas: An Introduction to His Life, Work and Influence*, London: Darton, Longman & Todd 2003

Tillich, Paul Johannes (1886–1965) Philosopher and theologian. Son of a Lutheran pastor, he studied at Berlin, Tübingen, Halle and Breslau and served as an army chaplain in the First World War. He was then professor in Dresden, Marburg, Leipzig and Frankfurt, where he became a Religious Socialist. As a result he had to leave Germany when Hitler came to power in 1933, teaching at Union Theological Seminary, New York, Harvard and Chicago Divinity School. He wrote a great deal, but his most important work was his three-volume *Systematic Theology* (1951–64). In it he used a method of correlation between an analysis of the human situation and the symbols used in the Christian message: reason and revelation, being and God; human existence and Christ; life in ambiguities and the Spirit; the meaning of history and the kingdom of God. He understood God as the ground of Being, who is known through ultimate concern, and Jesus Christ as the New Being, points which he brought out in shorter books. In addition to *The Courage to Be* (1952) he produced two influential volumes of sermons: *The Shaking of the Foundations* (1948) and *The New Being* (1956).

Wilhelm and Marion Pauck, *Paul Tillich: His Life and Thought*, London: Collins 1977

Tillotson, John (1630–94) Anglican preacher. Born near Halifax, Yorkshire, of a Presbyterian family, he studied at Cambridge and became an Anglican. He was ordained, and in due course was appointed Dean of St Paul's and then Archbishop of Canterbury. Hostile to the Roman Catholic Church, he tried to bring all Protestant dissenters within the Church of England. He was a famous preacher, and his sermons, regarded as models, were read for well over a century.

Edward Hyams, *Tillotson*, New York: Simon & Schuster 1961

Tindal, Matthew (1655–1733) English deist. He studied and taught at Oxford; for a while he became a Roman Catholic but returned to the Church of England. He wrote two books making a rationalist criticism of the church, one of which was burned by order of Parliament. His best-known book, written towards the end of his life, was *Christianity as Old as the Creation* (1730), arguing that the gospel reinforces the immutable laws of nature and reason. It became a kind of deists' Bible.

Matthew Tindal, *Christianity as Old as the Creation*, New York: Garland Press 1978

Toland, John (1670–1722) Deist. An Irish Roman Catholic by birth, he became a Protestant at 16 and studied at Glasgow and Leiden universities. He then went to Oxford, where he finished his *Christianity not Mysterious* (1696), arguing that God and his revelation could be understood by human reason and that the so-called mysteries of Christianity were the tricks of priests. In Ireland, to which he had returned, his book was condemned and burned by parliament. He fled to England and over subsequent years travelled widely on the European continent, being welcomed at the Prussian court. He wrote other books and pamphlets, in his *Nazarenus* (1718) anticipating Ferdinand Christian Baur in distinguishing between Jewish and Gentile Christianity. He seems to have been the first to use the word pantheist, to describe the views of philosophers like Benedict de Spinoza.

Robert E. Sullivan, *John Toland and the Deist Controversy*, Cambridge, MA: Harvard University Press 1982

Tolstoy, Leo (1828–1910) Russian social critic and writer. He studied at the University of Kazan, but did not get a degree. The influence of Jean-Jacques Rousseau made him interested in social reform; he first joined the army and then travelled widely. In 1862 he married and wrote his famous novels *War and Peace* (1884–9) and *Anna Karenina* (1873–7), but later turned to books on moral and religious topics. He became critical of the Orthodox Church, by which he was eventually excommunicated. His was literally a gospel faith, but one shorn of the miraculous. He saw the key to religion in the Sermon on the Mount, which led to pacifism, chastity, rejection of oaths, refusal to serve as magistrate and love of enemies.

A. N. Wilson, *Tolstoy*, New York: W. W. Norton 2001

Torquemada, Tomás de (1420–98) Spanish Grand Inquisitor. Apparently from a family which was originally Jewish and son of a distinguished cardinal, he became a Dominican and proved eager to reform the order. In 1474 he was appointed prior of the monastery of Santa Cruz in Segovia where he stayed for many years. He was also confessor to Queen Isabella from her childhood. In 1482 he founded a new reformed priory in Avila, the first in the Dominican order to insist on purity of blood. The same year he was made an inquisitor in the Spanish Inquisition, and the next year became Grand Inquisitor with enormous powers. Convinced that the Moors and Jews in Spain posed a threat, he turned the Inquisition particularly against those who had been nominally converted. His attitude was instrumental in influencing Ferdinand and Isabella to expel the Jews from Spain in 1492.

Howard Fast, *Torquemada*, London: Methuen and New York: Doubleday 1966

Traherne, Thomas (1636–74) English poet. Born in Hereford, after studying at Oxford he returned there and after a decade moved to London, where he was chaplain to a government official as well as having a parish. Only one work appeared during his lifetime, *Roman Forgeries* (1673), a criticism of the Roman Catholic Church; his *Christian Ethics* appeared the year after he died. His poems, for which he is best known, were not published until the beginning of this century, as *Centuries of Meditation*. They are in the tradition of the metaphysical poets such as George Herbert.

Graham Dowell, *Enjoying the World: The Rediscovery of Thomas Traherne*, London and New York: Continuum 1990

Troeltsch, Ernst (1865–1923) German philosopher and theologian. Born in Augsburg, he was professor in Göttingen, Bonn, Heidelberg and Berlin. He was influenced by Albrecht Ritschl, and a friend of Max Weber, and may be regarded as the systematic theologian in the history-of-religions school. He is particularly important for having stressed the omnipresence of history and the consequent relativity of knowledge and institutions. A famous article 'On Historical and Dogmatic Method' crystallizes his views, which led him to write *The Absoluteness of Christianity* (1902), seeking to establish the status of Christianity from this perspective. His best-known work is *The Social Teaching of the Christian Churches* (1912), a sociological study in which he made a classic distinction between church and sect.

Hans Georg Drecher, *Ernst Troeltsch. His Life and Work*, London: SCM Press 1992

Truth, Sojourner (*c.* 1797–1883) African American evangelist and reformer. Isabella van Wagener was a slave who was the mother of five children by a fellow slave, freed in 1827 by one Isaac van Wagener, who gave her her name. She then took her youngest children to New York City, where she worked as a domestic servant. There she met a missionary, Elijah Pierson, and worked with him. She left New York in 1843 and became an itinerant missionary, singing and preaching in churches, at camp meetings and on street corners; from then on she called herself Sojourner Truth, supporting herself by her book *The Narrative of Sojourner Truth*. In the 1850s she settled at Battle Creek, Michigan, where she spent the rest of her life. She became involved in the abolitionist movement and the women's rights movements (making a famous speech 'Ain't I a woman?' at a convention in 1851), and during the Civil War worked for integration of black and white. After the proclamation of emancipation she moved to Washington, DC, where she was received by Abraham Lincoln in 1864 and worked with former slaves in a newly created 'Freedman's Village'. In her last years she returned to Battle Creek.

📖 Carleton Maybee and Susan Maybee Newhouse, *Sojourner Truth: Slave, Prophet, Legend*, New York: New York University Press 1997

Tyndale, William (*c.*1494–1536) English Bible translator and reformer. Born in Gloucester, he studied in Oxford and Cambridge. Around 1522 he planned to translate the Bible, and when the church would not support him, settled in Hamburg. His translation of the New Testament, after a chequered printing history, was published in Worms, Germany, and was attacked when it arrived in England. He then lived in Antwerp, beginning to translate the Old Testament and writing tracts against the church and defending the authority of scripture. Having been harried and pursued by secret agents all his life, he was eventually arrested and burned.

📖 Bryan Moynahan, *William Tyndale: If God Spare My Life – Martyrdom, Betrayal and the English Bible*, London: Abacus Books 2003

Tyrrell, George (1861–1909) Irish Modernist theologian. Born an Evangelical in Dublin, he became a Roman Catholic and entered the Jesuit college. After lecturing at Stonyhurst he was moved to the Jesuit church in Farm Street, London, where he became a sought-after confessor. He published meditations and lectures and became a friend of Baron Friedrich von Hügel. From 1899 he began to depart from traditional doctrine, particularly that of eternal punishment. He moved to Yorkshire and continued to write, but his works were now suspect and he was expelled from the Jesuits, was later excommunicated and refused Catholic burial. His later work was highly critical of the Roman Catholic Church, contrasting living faith with dead theology, and his last book, *Christianity at the Crossroads*, published posthumously, explored the possibility of a higher religion beyond Christianity.

📖 N. Sagovsky, '*On God's Side*': *A Life of George Tyrrell*, Oxford: Clarendon Press 1990

Ulfilas (*c.*311–83) Christian bishop and missionary. Born in Cappadocia, in his youth he spent much of his time in Constantinople and was consecrated bishop there around 341 by Eusebius of Nicomedia, who was an Arian. He then returned to Cappadocia and for the rest of his life was a missionary, especially among the Goths. He was the first to translate the Bible into Gothic and is said to have created the Gothic alphabet. Through his influence the Goths continued to be Arians for some centuries to come.

📖 E. A. Thompson, *The Visigoths in the Time of Ulfila*, Oxford: Clarendon Press 1966

Underhill, Evelyn (1875–1941) Anglo-Catholic writer on mysticism. The daughter of a barrister, she was educated at King's College, London, and travelled on the European continent. After a conversion experience in 1907, she became interested in mysticism and in relating personal spiritual experience to the formal theology of the church. Her *Mysticism* (1911) became a standard work. She met and was much influenced by Baron Friedrich von Hügel and became a much sought after spiritual director. She wrote many other books on mysticism, the most important of which is *Worship* (1936) which relates mysticism to Eastern Orthodox Christianity.

📖 C. J. R. Armstrong, *Evelyn Underhill*, Oxford: Mowbray 1975

Ussher, James (1581–1656) Irish archbishop and scholar. Born and educated in Dublin, he became professor there, and chancellor of St Patrick's Cathedral, and subsequently Bishop of Meath and Archbishop of Armagh. He was an ardent Calvinist, but is best known for producing a scheme of biblical chronology, published posthumously (*Sacred Chronology*, 1660), which concluded that the world was created in 4004 BCE. His dates were printed in many editions of the King James Version of the Bible.

📖 Robert Buick Knox, *James Ussher, Bishop of Armagh 1581–1656*, Cardiff: University of Wales Press 1968

Valentinus (second century) Gnostic theologian. Little is known of his life: he is said to have lived in Rome, hoped to have become a bishop, been passed over, and to have left the church, perhaps going to Cyprus. Only fragments of his work remain, unless he can be associated with some of the material discovered at Nag Hammadi. The most influential of the Gnostics, he had a large following and seems to have developed a systematic theology of a dualistic kind, based on a hierarchy of personifications of divine attributes, paired as male and female and making up the pleroma or spiritual world.

📖 Christoph Markschies, *Gnosis*, London: T&T Clark 2003

Vaughan, Henry (1622–95) English poet. From a Welsh family, he studied at Oxford, fought in the Civil War and spent the rest of his life as a country doctor. The author of religious poems, collected in *Silex Scintilians* (1650), he was influenced by George Herbert, but his work is more mystical. He also wrote a collection of meditations, *The Mount of Olives* (1652). His poems influenced William Wordsworth.

📖 Henry Vaughan, *The Complete Poems*, Harmondsworth: Penguin Books 1976

Venn, Henry (1725–1797) Anglican Evangelical. From a long line of clergymen, he was born in London and studied and taught in Cambridge. After various curacies he became vicar of

Huddersfield in Yorkshire for twelve years until health reasons compelled him to go to a country parish in Huntingdonshire. A gifted letter writer, he is best known for his book *The Complete Duty of Man* (1763). He was one of the founders of the evangelical Clapham Sect, of which his son John became a leading member.

📖 Wilbert R. Shenkl, *Henry Venn: Missionary Statesman*, Maryknoll, NY: Orbis Books 1983

Vianney, Jean-Baptiste-Marie (1786–1859) The Curé d'Ars. Born near Lyons, he had little formal education because of the Revolution and conscription. He wanted to become a priest, but was dismissed from two seminaries; he was finally ordained after private tuition. On ordination, he went to Ars-en-Dombes, a small country parish near Lyons, of which he was priest for 40 years. Thousands of penitents came each year to make their confessions to him and he was canonized as the patron saint of parish priests. He wrote no books, but led a deeply spiritual and ascetic life centred on the mass, and put great stress on the love of God.

📖 René Fourrey, *The Curé d'Ars*, London: Burns & Oates 1958

Vincent of Lérins (died before *c.*450) Presbyter. Little is known of his life, except that he lived in a monastery on the French island of Lérins (off Cannes). He was the author of two *Commonitoria*, the first of which contains what is known as the Vincentian canon: 'What has been believed everywhere, always, by all.' This he intended to be a yardstick for true doctrine.

📖 Vincent of Lérins, *Commonitory*, in *Nicene and Post-Nicene Fathers*, Peabody, Mass: Hendrickson 1994

http://www. ccel.org.fathers

Vincent de Paul (*c.*1580–1660) French Catholic pastor. Born of a peasant family in south-west France, he studied at Dax and Toulouse. He spent two years as a slave in Tunisia after being captured by pirates, and having come under the influence of Pierre de Bérulle in Paris, decided to devote his life to serving the poor. He worked among prisoners in the household of the general of the galleys, and founded charities for men and women. These culminated in the Lazarists, who trained clergy and carried on missions among country people; Louise de Marillac, under his direction, founded the Sisters of Charity, the first non-enclosed women's mission, devoted to the care of the sick and the poor. He was a firm opponent of Jansenism.

📖 Francis Ryan (ed), *Vincent de Paul and Louise de Marillac*, Classics of Western Spirituality, New York and Mahwah, NJ: Paulist Press 1995

Visser 't Hooft, Willem Adolf (1900–85) Dutch ecumenical leader. Born in Haarlem, he studied at the University of Leiden. A gifted multilinguist, in 1924 he became secretary of the world committee of the YMCA; in 1931 he moved on to become secretary of the World Student Christian Federation and in 1936 was ordained a minister of the Reformed church in Geneva. He was nominated General Secretary of the World Council of Churches as early as 1938, though because of World War II the Council was not formally constituted for another decade. A consummate statesman, he was a key figure in ecumenical circles in the postwar period, playing a major role in drawing into the WCC churches from communist countries and from the

emerging nations of Africa and Asia, along with the Orthodox churches. He was also a theologian in his own right and wrote numerous books on the ecumenical movement and the church.

📖 Robert C. Mackie and Charles C. West, *The Sufficiency of God. Essays in Honour of Visser 't Hooft*, London: SCM Press and Philadelphia: Westminster Press 1963

Vitoria, Francisco de (1483–1546) Spanish theologian. After becoming a Dominican he studied in Paris, where he encountered the ideas of Erasmus. He then became professor of theology in Salamanca, where he created a new school by replacing the *Sentences* of Peter Lombard with the *Summa Theologiae* of Thomas Aquinas as a textbook. At the same time he emphasized the Bible and the church fathers in his teaching. He is best known for his championing of the rights of the Indians in the New World, arguing that enlightened states like Spain could take over backward states only if it was in the latter's interests. Criticizing the Spanish methods of colonization in America, he laid down the conditions of a just war. His pioneering role in international law has led him to be set alongside Hugo Grotius.

📖 J. B. Scott, *Francisco de Vitoria and His Law of Nations*, London: OUP 1934

Voltaire (François Marie Arouet, 1694–1778) French philosopher and writer. Educated by the Jesuits in Paris, he was a lifelong enemy of the Catholic Church (he made a famous remark that it should be destroyed, *écrasez l'infame)*. He was exiled to England after a dispute; there he encountered deism and the philosophy of John Locke, and his *Letters on the English* (1734) idealized the country as a land of enlightenment. As a postscript he added an attack on Blaise Pascal. The book was burnt and he fled to Lorraine, where he lived on a country estate for sixteen years. In 1750 he went to the Court of Frederick II of Prussia; in 1758 he bought a country house at Ferney, on the Swiss border, and established a model village around it. Theologically he was concerned with the problem of theodicy, justifying the alleged actions of God, and though considering Gottfried Leibniz's solution, rejected it violently in his brilliant satire *Candide* (1759). He was in his element in this kind of work, and wrote more than twenty plays.

📖 John Gray, *Voltaire*, London: Weidenfeld & Nicolson 1998

Von Hügel, Friedrich (1852–1925) English Roman Catholic. Son of an Austrian diplomat, and inheriting the title Baron of the

Holy Roman Empire, he grew up in Tuscany and Belgium before settling in England and having a private education. Immensely learned, and having wide interests in science, philosophy and history, he became convinced of the validity of biblical criticism and was friendly with Modernists like Alfred Loisy and George Tyrrell. His major work was *The Mystical Element of Religion* (1908), focused on Catherine of Genoa. For all his liberal views he did not clash with the church; his openness and attractive personality comes out clearly in his published letters. He was more influential outside the Roman Catholic Church than within it.

📖 Michael de la Bedoyère, *The Life of Baron von Hügel*, London: Dent 1951

Ward, Mary (1585–1645) She was related to most of the great Catholic families of Yorkshire but in 1606 entered the convent of Poor Clares at St Omer in northern France as a lay sister (she could not take such a course in England). From there she founded a daughter house for Englishwomen at Gravelines, but left in 1609 to form a religious community modelled on the Society of Jesus. Members of this Institute, as it came to be called, did not live in a cloister, attend daily offices or wear a religious habit and were to be subject only to the Pope; it spread abroad to Flanders, Bavaria, Austria and Italy. However, it proved too radical; in 1630 it was suppressed and Mary Ward was confined in the Poor Clares Convent in Munich. On being freed, she gained support from Urban VIII and resumed her activities more informally. She returned to England in 1639, and died there. Today the order she inspired is worldwide and consists of two main groups, the Roman Branch and the Loreto Branch (formerly the Irish and North American Branches).

📖 Sister Margaret Mary, *Mary Ward*, London and New York: Continuum 2001

Warfield, Benjamin Breckinridge (1851–1921) American theologian. Born near Lexington, Kentucky, into an old American family, after private education he studied at Princeton and in Europe, becoming a minister in Baltimore and subsequently teaching New Testament at Westminster Theological Seminary, Philadelphia. He finally became professor at Princeton, succeeding Charles Hodge. A committed Calvinist, he held dogmatically to the inerrancy of scripture and sought to define the inspiration and total truthfulness of scripture in the face of biblical criticism, writing polemically against liberal scholars. He continues to be influential in evangelical circles. His books include *The Lord of Glory* (1907) and *Counterfeit Miracles* (1918).

📖 Mark A. Noll, David W. Bebbington and George A. Rawlyk (eds), *The Princeton Theology, 1812–1921: Scripture, Science, and Theological Method from Archibald Alexander to Benjamin Warfield*, Grand Rapids, MI: Baker Academic 2001

Watts, Isaac (1674–1748) Anglican hymn writer. Born in Southampton and educated in London, after a period as tutor he became pastor of a church near the Tower of London until he had to resign through ill health. He is known as the first great British hymn writer, composing among others, 'O God, our help in ages past', 'When I survey the wondrous cross' and 'Jesus shall reign where'er the sun'. He also wrote on prayer and had marked theological views, opposing the imposition of the doctrine of the Trinity on dissenters and leaning towards Unitarianism.

📖 A. P. Davis, *Isaac Watts*, London: Independent Press 1948

Weber, Karl Emil Maximilian (Max) (1864–1920) German sociologist. Born in Erfurt, he became professor of political economy at Freiburg and Heidelberg, suffering a breakdown between 1898 and 1903. A legacy enabled him to continue work privately. For a while he lived in the same house as Ernst Troeltsch, who influenced him. His main work, *The Protestant Ethic and the Spirit of Capitalism* (1904–5), argues that Calvinist asceticism arising out of the doctrine of predestination was an important factor in the formation of capitalist society. In his posthumously published writings on the sociology of religion he produced a system for classifying different types of religious leader, introducing the subsequently popular term 'charismatic'.

📖 Frank Parkin, *Max Weber*, London and New York: Routledge 2002

Weil, Simone (1909–43) French philosopher. Born in Paris to a secularized Jewish family, she studied philosophy. After graduation she taught for a while and then worked as a labourer in order to identify with the working class. She also served in the International Brigade against Franco in the Spanish Civil War. Profound religious experiences made her deeply interested in Roman Catholicism, though she was never baptized nor joined any church. In 1942 she escaped with her family to the United States, but returned to London to work for the Free French. She died of starvation and tuberculosis, refusing to eat to show solidarity with the French under German occupation. Her posthumously published books such as *Gravity and Grace* (English 1949) and *Waiting on God* (English 1950) revealed her serious and deeply personal religion, and she has been an influence on both religious thinkers and social activists.

📖 Richard Rees, *Simone Weil: Sketch for a Portrait*, Oxford: OUP 1966

Wellhausen, Julius (1844–1918) German biblical critic. Born in Hamelin the son of a Lutheran pastor, he studied in Göttingen and after teaching there became professor of Old Testament in Greifswald. He resigned his chair after ten years, claiming that his teaching was not helping his pupils to do what they were training for, namely to be church ministers. He then became professor of philosophy in Halle and later professor of Semitic studies at Marburg and Göttingen. He developed a classic theory about the sources of the Pentateuch; his dating of these sources transformed the history of Israel, putting the prophets before the law and not after it, as had commonly been supposed. In later years he turned to the New Testament, but his studies there did not have such influence and lasting effect. The classic expression of his views on the Old Testament is to be found in his *Prolegomena to the History of Ancient Israel* (1883).

📖 Julius Wellhausen, *Prolegomena to the History of Ancient Israel*, Eugen, OR: Wipf & Stock 2003

Wesley, Charles (1707–88) Anglican hymn writer and preacher. Eighteenth child of Samuel and Susanna Wesley and brother of

John Wesley, he was born at Epworth and studied at Oxford. After ordination, he went with John to Georgia, where he was secretary to the governor. On his return he had a conversion experience after an encounter with a group of Moravians. After an itinerant ministry he lived first in Bristol and then in London and was involved in preaching at City Road Chapel. However, he never left the Church of England. He was a gifted hymn writer, composing more than 7000, including 'Love divine, all loves excelling', 'Lo, he comes with clouds descending' and 'Jesus, lover of my soul'.

📖 M. R. Brailsford, *A Tale of Two Brothers, John and Charles Wesley*, Oxford: OUP 1954

Wesley, John (1703–91) Founder of Methodism. Brother of Charles Wesley, he studied at Oxford, was ordained, and taught there. He formed a 'Holy Club', whose members became known as Methodists (for reasons which have yet to be explained satisfactorily). He went with Charles on mission to Georgia, but fell foul of the colonists and returned home. An encounter with Moravians influenced him, and he went to their community at Herrnhut: in May 1738 he had a famous conversion experience. Taking up field preaching, he covered the whole of the British Isles in amazing journeys on horseback: he wrote countless letters and sermons (44 of which were selected as a kind of canon) and kept a journal. He started a conference of lay preachers which became annual, and the basis of the future Methodist constitution. From 1760 Methodism spread throughout America, and Wesley was persuaded to ordain ministers there. Though he wanted his movement to remain within the Church of England, it became increasingly independent.

📖 Henry Rack, *Reasonable Enthusiast. John Wesley and the Rise of Methodism*, London: Epworth Press [3]2002

Westcott, Brooke Foss (1825–1901) Anglican bishop. He went to school in Birmingham with J. B. Lightfoot, his lifelong friend, and then to Cambridge. He taught first at Harrow school and went on to become professor at Cambridge. Here, with F. J. A. Hort, he prepared a famous edition of the Greek text of the New Testament and wrote three commentaries for a planned series with Lightfoot and Hort. In 1889 he became president of Scott Holland's Christian Social Union and in 1890 Bishop of Durham, where he showed a deep concern for social issues, mediating in a coal miners' strike.

📖 David L. Edwards, *Leaders of the Church of England*, Oxford: OUP 1971

Whitefield, George (1714–70) English evangelist. Born in Gloucester, he met John and Charles Wesley at Oxford and joined the 'Holy Club', where he experienced an evangelical conversion. After ordination he proved a powerful preacher. He went with the Wesleys to Georgia and remained for some time after they left. When back in England he became a pioneer in open-air preaching, and covered vast distances, including fourteen visits to Scotland and seven to America, where he died. Since he was more Calvinistic than the Wesleys, differences arose, and he became associated with Selina, Countess of Huntingdon, working within her Connexion.

📖 John Pollock, *George Whitefield and the Great Awakening*, Garden City, NY: Doubleday 1972 and London: Hodder & Stoughton 1973

Whitehead, Alfred North (1861–1947) English philosopher and mathematician. He taught at Cambridge and London universities, and became professor at Harvard in 1924. Originally associated with Bertrand Russell, he broke away in search of a new comprehensive synthesis of knowledge, which among other things would integrate science and religion. He saw the world in dynamic terms as process; God is such that all the happenings in the world become part of his nature. His views led to the formation of schools of 'process philosophy' and 'process theology', which included figures like Charles Hartshorne. His major work is *Process and Reality* (1929).

📖 Lucien Price, *Dialogues of Alfred North Whitehead*, New York: Little, Brown 1954

William of Ockham (1285–1347) Scholastic theologian and philosopher. Born in Surrey, he studied at Oxford, where his views earned him a summons to Avignon to answer charges of heresy before Pope John XXII. After being excommunicated, he went from there to Bavaria, under the protection of its ruler, Louis. He is most famous for his principle of economy ('Ockham's razor': entities are not to be multiplied unnecessarily). Refusing to follow the current line of positing the existence of universals, he argued that these are mental constructs: only individuals exist, and awareness of them is the basis of knowledge (a view generally described as nominalism). Metaphysical analysis was replaced by logical analysis, destroying the foundation of earlier scholasticism. This was to be of importance in the future development of scientific exploration because of the way in which it destroyed the old idea of causality. Knowledge was limited to experience. He also differed from previous thought in arguing that the existence of God cannot be proved rationally: it is necessary to be content with faith and revelation, but this could be relied on, since it is God's world.

📖 Ernest A. Moody, *The Logic of William of Ockham*, New York: Russell & Russell 1965

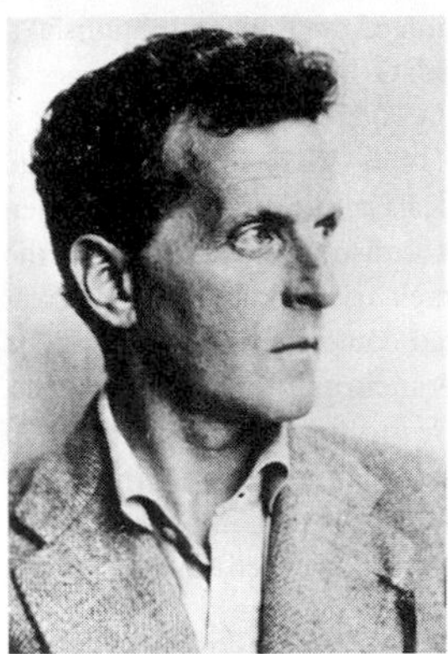

Wittgenstein, Ludwig Josef Johann (1889–1951) Austrian/English philosopher. Born in Vienna, he studied engineering in Berlin and Manchester and ultimately settled in England. He worked with Bertrand Russell in 1912–13 and served in the Austrian army during the First World War, during which he had a mystical experience. This led to his *Tractatus Logico-Philosophicus* (1921), the only one of his books to appear during his lifetime, on the limits of meaningful language (at this stage his philosophy was prescriptive, stating what must be true for language to work as it does); it contains his famous statement 'Whereof one cannot speak, thereon one must remain silent.' Also as a result of his experience he gave away a fortune he had inherited and worked as an elementary schoolteacher in Austria. However, in 1929 he returned to Cambridge, where in 1939 he became professor of philosophy. His posthumously published

Philosophical Investigations indicates a major move in his thought. By then he was talking in terms of 'language games', the different ways in which language is used. The important thing was now to discover the rules of the game. The latter approach, especially, has been of particular influence in religious discussion.

📖 Hans D. Sluga and David G. Stern, *The Cambridge Companion to Wittgenstein*, Cambridge: CUP 1996

Wrede, William (1859–1906) German New Testament scholar. He spent his career as professor at Breslau and was a founder-member of the history-of-religions school. His best-known work was *The Messianic Secret in the Gospels* (1901), in which he challenged the view that the Gospel of Mark was a historical account, and pointed to the role played by the messianic secret which, he argued, was read back into the Gospel record. Perhaps even more important, however, was his study of the nature of New Testament theology, raising questions which have still not been answered today.

📖 Robert Morgan, *The Nature of New Testament Theology. The Contribution of William Wrede and Adolf Schlatter*, London: SCM Press 1973

Wyclif, John (*c.* 1330–84) English reformer. Born in Yorkshire, he studied in Oxford, where he held many posts, also being in charge of parishes in *absentia*. In a sceptical age which separated natural knowledge from supernatural knowledge, he argued that human beings had their origin in God, and he resorted to the Bible and the church fathers rather than scholastic discussions. This led him to distinguish an ideal church from the actual church, so that, for example, he questioned the ownership of property by monasteries. He also saw the eucharistic doctrine of transubstantiation as popular superstition. This last view brought to breaking point tensions with the university: he was condemned and forced to retire to Lutterworth, one of his parishes. After his death he was condemned at the Council of Constance. He was a major influence on John Hus. Among many works, he wrote a *Summa Theologica* and initiated a translation of the Bible into English.

📖 Anthony Kenny, *Wyclif*, Oxford: OUP 1985

Ximenes de Cisneros, Francisco (1436–1517) Spanish cardinal. Born in Castile, he studied at Alcala and Salamanca and then in Rome. After the beginnings of a distinguished career in the Spanish church he suddenly became a friar, leading a life of great austerity. In 1492 he was appointed confessor to Queen Isabella and under her influence became Franciscan provincial in Castile, doing much to reform the order. He was finally made Archbishop of Toledo, the most influential post in Spain, but he continued his austere life and was concerned for the conversion of the Moors. On Isabella's death for a while he virtually ruled Castile; he was later made a cardinal. A patron of learning, he founded the University of Alcala (Latin name Complutum) and sponsored a multilingual Bible, the Complutensian Polyglot, with the Hebrew, Latin and Greek texts printed in parallel.

📖 Walter Starkie, *Grand Inquisitor. Being an Account of Ximenes de Cisneros and his Times*, London: Hodder & Stoughton 1940

Young, Brigham (1801–77) Second president of the Church of Jesus Christ of Latter-day Saints (Mormons). Born in Vermont, and with little education, he joined the Mormons in 1832 and in 1847 led them from Nauvoo, Illinois to Utah after the death of Joseph Smith. His gifts of leadership were instrumental in making Smith's system a successful social organization; he became governor of Utah territory, planned the Mormon Temple at Salt Lake City and founded the University of Utah.

📖 Newell G. Bringhurst, *Brigham Young*, London: Longmans 1987

Zinzendorf, Nicholas Ludwig, Count von (1700–60) Moravian pietist leader. Born in Dresden of noble family, and deeply religious, he hoped to be a missionary, but his family wanted him to go into government. He studied law in Wittenberg and entered the civil service, at the same time sponsoring religious gatherings at his home in Dresden. He then purchased an estate at Bethelsdorf where in 1722 he founded a Christian community with a group of Bohemian refugees which he called Herrnhut. Five years later he retired, to devote himself full time to the community. He stressed a religion of the heart and his piety was focused on Christ; he also had visions of ecumenical reunion. In 1737 he was ordained and his movement was eventually recognized, but circumstances forced it to become a separate organization, the Moravian church. He travelled around Europe founding communities, and also went abroad on mission to the West Indies and the United States.

📖 A. J. Lewis, *Zinzendorf. The Ecumenical Pioneer*, London: SCM Press and Philadelphia: Westminster Press 1962

Zwingli, Huldrych (1484–1531) Swiss Reformer. Son of a village magistrate, he studied in Berne, Vienna and Basle, and after a pastorate became chaplain to Swiss mercenaries in Italy. He then became priest at the Great Church in Zurich. His views of reformation were far more radical than those of Luther: he established a different style of discipline and organization, and his views differed on baptism, preaching and the eucharist. Much of his life was spent in political activity, though he never held political office; he was killed in battle. In his theology, baptism is a sign but cannot provide cleansing, and the eucharistic elements have no power without the believer's faith.

📖 G. W. Potter, *Zwingli*, Cambridge: CUP 1976

TIME CHART

Era	*Date*	*Events*	*Rulers and popes*	*Important figures*
BCE				Plato, Greek philosopher (427–347)
	333	Asia Minor invaded by Alexander; beginning of the 'Hellenization' of the Near East	Alexander the Great (356–323)	Aristotle, Greek philosopher (384–322)
	322–198	Palestine ruled by the Ptolemies from Alexandria		
	198–64	Palestine ruled by the Seleucids from Syria		
	167	Desecration of the Jerusalem temple by Antiochus	Antiochus IV Epiphanes (c. 215–164)	
	165	Maccabean revolt		
	164	Reconsecration of Jerusalem temple		
	142	Independent Jewish kingdom established (Hasmonean dynasty)		
	c. 125	Qumran community founded	Herod the Great (c. 73–4)	
	63	Pompey takes control of Palestine for Rome		
	37–4	Herod rules as client king for Rome		
	27	Roman empire begins with Augustus	Augustus, Roman emperor (27 BCE–14 CE)	
FIRST CENTURY	6	Judaea made a Roman province		
	c. 6	Jesus born		
	c. 30	Jesus crucified	Tiberius, Roman emperor 14–37	
	c. 35	Martyrdom of Stephen		Philo, Jewish philosopher (c. 20 BCE–50 CE)
	c. 36	Conversion of Paul		
APOSTOLIC AGE (period within the lifetime of the apostles)	45–58	Paul's missionary journeys	Claudius, Roman emperor 41–54	
	c. 49	'Apostolic' council in Jerusalem (Peter, Paul and James)		Flavius Josephus, Jewish historian (37–100)
	62	James the brother of Jesus stoned	Nero, Roman emperor 54–68	
	64	Great fire of Rome, persecution by Nero		
		Martyrdom of Peter (and Paul?)		Ignatius of Antioch, martyr bishop (c. 35–c. 107)
	66–70	First Jewish War against Rome		
	70	Destruction of Jerusalem	Vespasian, Roman emperor 69–79	
	c. 70–100	Composition of synoptic Gospels		
	84	Christians expelled from Jewish synagogues	Domitian, Roman emperor 81–96	
SECOND CENTURY AGE OF THE CHURCH FATHERS (c.100–c. 750)	Early	Christianity reaches Edessa, beyond the eastern frontier of the Roman empire	Trajan, Roman emperor 98–117	Polycarp, martyr bishop (c. 69–155)
				Basilides, Gnostic teacher (early 2nd century)
	c.125	Earliest extant papyrus fragment of a New Testament book (Gospel of John)	Hadrian, Roman emperor 117–38	
				Justin Martyr, Christian apologist (c. 100–c. 165)
	132–5	Second Jewish War		
	135	Jews defeated. Jerusalem rebuilt as Aelia Capitolina and Judaea renamed Palaestina. Jewish customs banned.		Marcion of Pontus, church founder (died 160)
				Irenaeus, church father (c. 130–c. 200)
Gnosticism (Gnosis) (2nd/3rd centuries)			Victor I, pope 189–98, attempts to settle controversy over date of Easter	Valentinus, Gnostic teacher (2nd century)
	End	Christian communities extend from Spain in the West to Afghanistan and possibly India in the East		Clement of Alexandria, Christian scholar (c. 150–c. 215)

Era	*Date*	*Events*	*Rulers and popes*	*Important figures*
THIRD CENTURY		Catacomb art begins	Fabian, pope 236–50, first martyr pope	Tertullian, African theologian (*c.* 160–225)
	c. 240	Earliest known baptistery in a house-church in Dura Europos, Syria	Decius, Roman emperor 249–51	Hippolytus of Rome, Roman churchman (*c.* 170–236)
	250	Persecution of Christians by Roman authorities	Cornelius, pope 251–3, tolerant to those who lapsed in persecution	Origen, Greek biblical scholar (*c.* 185–*c.* 254) Cyprian, martyr bishop, died 258)
	256	Council of Carthage attended by 88 bishops forbids women to baptize	Valerian, Roman emperor 253–60	Plotinus, Neoplatonist philosopher (*c.* 205–70)
	258	Christian clergy rounded up by Roman authorities and property confiscated	Stephen I, pope 254–7, first pope to appeal to Matthew 16.18 for his authority	Porphyry, Neoplatonist philosopher (232–304) Arius, Christian theologian (*c.* 250–336)
	c. 280	Conversion of Armenia by Gregory the Illuminator		
FOURTH CENTURY	Early	Christmas begins to be celebrated by Christians		Antony of Egypt, pioneer monk (*c.* 251 –356)
	c. 300	Armenia adopts Christianity as the state religion		Eusebius, church historian (*c.* 260–340)
Beginnings of monasticism	303	Persecution of Christians by Rome	Diocletian, Roman emperor 284–305	Pachomius, monk (*c.* 290–346)
	311	Donatist schism begins in North Africa	Constantine the Great, Roman emperor 306–37	Athanasius, theologian and bishop (*c.* 296–373)
	312	Constantine wins a decisive victory at the Milvian bridge which he attributes to the vision of a sign		Aphraates, first Syrian church father (Aphrahat, early 4th century)
	313	Edict of Milan tolerates all religious practices including Christianity	Miltiades, pope 310/11–14, first pope to enjoy government favour	Ephrem the Syrian, church father and poet (*c.* 306–73)
	319	Beginning of building of (the old) St Peter's, Rome		
	324	Constantine sole ruler		Apollinarius of Laodicea, Christian theologian (*c.* 310–90)
	325	Council of Nicaea: convened by Constantine to resolve Arian controversy		Ulfilas, bishop and missionary (*c.* 311–83)
	326	Helena, mother of Constantine, travels to the Holy Land		Cyril of Jerusalem, bishop and preacher (*c.* 315–86)
	330	Capital of the Roman empire moved to Byzantium, renamed Constantinople		Epiphanius, defender of orthodoxy (*c.* 315–403)
	335	Church of Holy Sepulchre in Jerusalem built	Julius I, pope 337–52, firm supporter of Nicene orthodoxy	Macrina, ascetic (*c.* 327–80)
	350	Frumentius ordained as head of church in Ethiopia	Liberius, pope 352–66, banished for his support of Nicene orthodoxy; he later recants	Basil of Caesarea ('The Great'), church father (*c.* 330–79)
		4 Codex Vaticanus Codex Sinaiticus		Gregory of Nazianzus, church theologian (329/30–389/90)
	381	Council of Constantinople: convened by Theodosius I finally to resolve Arian controversy	Damasus, pope 366–84, strengthens see of Rome	Gregory of Nyssa, church theologian (*c.* 330–*c.* 395)
	381–4	The devout Egeria goes on pilgrimage to the Holy Land and gives an account of what she finds there	Theodosius I ('The Great'), Roman emperor 379–95 Siricius, pope 384–99, author of first papal decretal	Ambrose, bishop and hymn writer (*c.* 339–97)
	395	Definitive division of Roman empire into East and West after the death of Theodosius I		John Chrysostom, bishop and preacher (*c.* 347–407)
FIFTH CENTURY	Early	Codex Alexandrinus	Innocent I, pope 402–17, sometimes called the first true pope	Theodore of Mopsuestia, theologian and biblical scholar (354–427)
	410	Rome sacked by Goths		Pelagius, British theologian (died *c.* 410)

Era	*Date*	*Events*	*Rulers and popes*	*Important figures*
FIFTH CENTURY (continued)	429–39	Vandals destroy Catholic Christianity in North Africa		Jerome, biblical scholar (*c.* 345–420)
	c. 431	Patrick engages in mission to Ireland		Augustine of Hippo, theologian (354–430)
	431	Council of Ephesus: excommunicates Nestorius and proclaims Mary *Theotokos*, 'Mother of God'		John Cassian, monk (*c.* 360–435) Cyril of Alexandria, theologian (died 444)
	451	Council of Chalcedon: produces the classic statement on the person of Christ, the Chalcedonian Definition	Leo I, pope 440–61, protects Rome when it is attacked by Huns and Vandals in 452 and 455	Nestorius, Syrian theologian (died 451) Simeon Stylites, pillar hermit (390–459)
	455	Capture of Rome by Vandals		Patrick, Irish bishop (*c.* 390–460)
	476	End of the Western Roman empire		
	496	Baptism of Clovis	Clovis, Frankish king (*c.* 466–511), converts to Catholicism	Dionysius the (Pseudo-) Areopagite, Syrian mystic (fifth century)
SIXTH CENTURY	523–37	Hagia Sophia built in Constantinople		Benedict of Nursia (*c.* 480–547), draws up a classic monastic rule
	525	System of dating by AD introduced by Dionysius Exiguus		
	527	Justinian reconquers north Africa from the Vandals and Italy from the Goths	Justinian, Roman emperor (527–65)	
	529	Benedict founds Monte Cassino monastery		Columba, Celtic missionary (*c.* 521–97), makes Iona his centre
	553	Second Council of Constantinople: convened by Justinian to condemn works favourable to Nestorius		
MIDDLE AGES (*c.* 500–1500)	589	Council of Toledo (inserts *filioque* into the Nicene Creed)		
	596	Gregory sends Augustine to convert the Anglo-Saxons	Gregory I (the Great), pope 590–604, one of the most important popes. His time sees the beginning of Gregorian chant	Augustine of Canterbury, missionary (died *c.* 604)
SEVENTH CENTURY	622	Hegirah, birth of Islam	Muhammad (570–632)	
	635	Christian monks first appear before Chinese emperor		Isidore of Seville, scholar (560–636)
	638	Arabs conquer Jerusalem		John Climacus, spiritual writer (*c.* 570–649)
	643–56	Final version of Qur'an		Maximus the Confessor, Greek theologian and ascetic (*c.* 580–662)
	664	Synod of Whitby: approves Roman rather than Celtic date for Easter		
	674	Glass first used in English church windows		
	681	Third Council of Constantinople: convened by Constantine IV to deal with Monothelitism		
	End	Lindisfarne Gospels		
EIGHTH CENTURY	*c.* 700	Conversion of Germany by Wilfred of York, Willibrord and Boniface		
	711	Rise of papal states		
	711–16	Arabs conquer Iberian peninsula		The Venerable Bede, historian (*c.* 673–735)
Iconoclastic controversy (726–87)	716	Boniface makes first missionary journey to Frisia		John of Damascus, Greek theologian (*c.* 655–*c.* 750)
	731	The first known church organ is installed		
	732	Charles Martel, leader of the Franks, stops the Arab advance at Poitiers in France		

Era	*Date*	*Events*	*Rulers and popes*	*Important figures*
EIGHTH CENTURY (continued)	786–7	Second Council of Nicaea: convened to end iconoclastic controversy	Stephen II (III), pope 752–67, the first to preside over a papal state	Alcuin, English scholar (*c.* 740–804), becomes adviser to Charlemagne
Carolingian renaissance (late 8th/early 9th century)	End	Book of Kells	Charlemagne, sole ruler from 771	
NINTH CENTURY	800	Charlemagne crowned emperor by Leo III; beginning of Holy Roman empire	Leo III, pope 795–816, crowns Charlemagne emperor	John Scotus Eriugena, Irish theologian (*c.* 810–*c.* 877)
Viking invasions of British Isles	829	Ansgar first known missionary to Denmark and Sweden		Methodius, missionary (*c.* 815–85)
Further iconoclastic controversy (815–42)	863–7	Photian schism, breach between Rome and Constantinople		Photius, Patriarch of Constantinople (*c.* 820–91)
	863	Cyril and Methodius set out for mission to the Slavs	Alfred the Great, king of Wessex (849–99), defeats the Danes and promotes Christian learning	
	869	Fourth Council of Constantinople, convened to condemn Photius; recognized only by the West		Cyril, missionary (826–69)
TENTH CENTURY	910	Foundation of Cluny, a great centre of monastic reform		Simeon the New Theologian, Byzantine mystic and writer (*c.* 949–*c.* 1022)
	928	End of Carolingian empire		
	962	Pope John XII crowns Otto King of Germany Holy Roman emperor		
	963	Foundation of Megisti Lavra on Mount Athos		Avicenna, Muslim philosopher (980–1037)
	988	Vladimir prince of Kiev baptized by Byzantine missionaries		
ELEVENTH CENTURY	1000	Christianity reaches Iceland		
Romanesque architecture	1054	Split between Eastern and Western churches	Leo IX, pope 1048–54, marks beginning of effective papal reform	
	1061	Virgin Mary appears to a widow in Walsingham		Anselm, philosopher and theologian (*c.* 1033–1109)
Investiture Controversy (1059–1122)	1077	Henry IV of Germany does penance at Canossa		
	1084	Foundation of Carthusian order	Gregory VII, pope 1073–85, makes the papacy a dominant force in Western Christianity	
	1085	Christian reconquest of Iberian peninsula begins		Abelard, Peter, philosopher and theologian (1079–1142)
	1095–9	First Crusade		
	1098	Foundation of abbey of Cîteaux and Cistercian order		
	1099	Crusaders take Jerusalem	Urban II, pope 1088–99, proclaims First Crusade	
TWELFTH CENTURY	1115	Foundation of abbey of Clairvaux		Hugh of St Victor, theologian (died 1142)
	1122	Suger elected abbot of St-Denis Concordat of Worms settles Investiture Controversy with a compromise		Bernard of Clairvaux, Cistercian abbot (1090–1153)
Gothic architecture (from c.1140)	1123	First Lateran Council: abolishes right of lay rulers to confer symbols of authority on bishops and abbots		Peter Lombard, theologian (*c.* 1095–1169) Hildegard of Bingen, German mystic (1098–1179)
	1139	Second Lateran Council: condemns teachings of the radical Arnold of Brescia		Gratian, church lawyer (died *c.* 1159)
	1147–9	Second Crusade	Eugenius III, pope 1145–53, commissions Bernard of Clairvaux to preach Second Crusade	Averroes, Muslim philosopher (1126–98)
	1150	Christianity reaches Finland		
	1150–70	Foundation of University of Paris		Richard of St Victor, scholar and mystic (died 1173)
	c. 1170	Waldo converted, beginning of Waldensian church		Andrew of St Victor, biblical scholar (died 1175)

Era	*Date*	*Events*	*Rulers and popes*	*Important figures*
TWELFTH CENTURY (continued)	1179	Third Lateran Council: restricts to a college of cardinals the right to elect the Pope		Joachim of Fiore, Italian mystic (1132–1202)
	1187	Jerusalem captured by Saladin		Maimonides, Spanish Jewish philosopher (1135–1204)
	1189–92	Third Crusade		
THIRTEENTH CENTURY	1200–4	Fourth Crusade	Innocent III, pope 1198–1216, preaches against Islam and the Albigensians, convenes Fourth Lateran Council	Domingo de Guzman (Dominic), founder of Dominican order (1170–1221)
	1204	Sack of Constantinople by Crusaders		
Scholasticism	1209	Albigensian Crusade launched		
	1212	Children's Crusade		Robert Grosseteste, English bishop (1175–1253)
	1215	Fourth Lateran Council: requires Christians to go to confession and communion twice a year; takes measures against Jews and heretics		Francis of Assisi, founder of the Franciscan order (1182–1226)
		Dominican order founded	Honorius III, pope 1216–27, produces a first book of canon law	Albertus Magnus, German theologian and scientist (1193–1280)
	1218–21	Fifth Crusade		
	1223	Approval of Franciscan rule		Anthony of Padua, Portuguese hermit (1195–1231)
	1226	Rule for Carmelites approved	Gregory IX, pope 1227–41, founds Inquisition (1232)	
	1237–40	Kievan Russia overrun by Tatars		
	1245	First Council of Lyons: excommunicates emperor and preaches a new crusade		Bonaventure, scholastic theologian (*c.* 1217–74)
	1248	Sainte-Chapelle in Paris built		Beatrice of Nazareth, spiritual writer (*c.* 1200–68)
	1261	Greek forces retake Constantinople		
	1274	Second Council of Lyons: forces Eastern church to capitulate over its differences with the West, including the *filioque* clause in the creed		Mechthild of Magdeburg, German mystic (*c.* 1210–*c.* 1282)
				Thomas Aquinas, theologian (1225–74)
	1291	Fall of Acre, the last crusader outpost		Ramon Lull, Spanish missionary and philosopher (1232–1316)
				Hadewijch (thirteenth century)
FOURTEENTH CENTURY	1309–77	Papacy at Avignon	Boniface VIII, pope 1294–1303, proclaims the universal jurisdiction of the Pope and the supremacy of spiritual power over secular power	Johannes Eckhart ('Meister'), mystic, (*c.* 1260–*c.* 1328)
	1311–12	Council of Vienne: convened to deal with the Templars and promote a new crusade		Dante Alighieri, Italian poet and philosopher (1265–1321)
	1324	In his *Defensor pacis* Marsilius of Padua argues that the church should be ruled by general councils and in turn be completely subordinate to the state	Clement V, a Frenchman, pope 1305–14, makes his residence in Avignon	John Duns Scotus, Scottish theologian (*c.* 1265–1308)
	1340	Sergei of Radonezh founds the Monastery of the Holy Trinity near Moscow		Gregory Palamas, Greek theologian (*c.* 1269–1359)
RENAISSANCE (*c.* 1350–1600)	1348–50	The Black Death		Marsilius of Padua, Italian political philosopher (*c.* 1275–1342)
	1374	Foundation of the Brethren of the Common Life by Geert de Groote in the Netherlands	Gregory XI, pope 1370–8, the last French pope	William of Ockham, scholastic theologian and philosopher (*c.* 1285–1347)
	1375–82	John Wyclif attacks the wealth of the church and the power of the Pope; his followers come to be known as Lollards		Sergei of Radonezh, monastic reformer and mystic (1319–92)
	1378–1415	Great Schism: popes in Avignon and Rome		John Wyclif, English reformer (*c.* 1330–84)
				Julian of Norwich, English mystic (*c.* 1342–*c.* 1420)

Era	*Date*	*Events*	*Rulers and popes*	*Important figures*
FOURTEENTH CENTURY (continued)				John Hus, Bohemian reformer (1369–1415)
FIFTEENTH CENTURY	1414–18	Council of Constance: convened to end the Great Schism; orders John Hus to be burnt		Thomas à Kempis, monk and devotional writer (*c.* 1380–1471)
	1431–49	Council of Basle: intended to continue the work of Constance; transferred to Ferrara and then to Florence		Nicholas of Cusa, German philosopher (1401–64) Tomas de Torquemada, Spanish Grand Inquisitor (1420–98)
	1436	Brunelleschi completes the dome of Florence Cathedral		Marsilio Ficino, Italian humanist (1433–99)
	1448	Russian churches independently elect Metropolitan of Moscow		Nil Sorsky, Russian monk and mystic (1433–1508)
	1453	Turks capture Constantinople; end of Eastern Roman empire		Catherine of Genoa, spiritual teacher (1447–1510)
	1455	Johannes Gutenberg prints his Bible with movable type		
	1478	Spanish Inquisition founded	Sixtus IV, pope 1471–84, approves the Spanish Inquisition and builds the Sistine Chapel	Girolamo Savonarola, Italian reformer (1452–98)
	1492	Muslims expelled from Spain with the conquest of Granada		
	1498	Leonardo da Vinci finishes his *Last Supper*		
SIXTEENTH CENTURY	1501	First diocese established in Hispaniola		John Colet, humanist (1467–1519)
	1506	Foundation stone of St Peter's laid in Rome		Desiderius Erasmus, humanist (c.1469–1536)
	1512	Michelangelo paints the Sistine Chapel (Last Judgement 1536)	Henry VIII, king of England 1509–47	Nicolas Copernicus, astronomer and mathematician (1473–1543)
REFORMATION (1517–1598)	1512–17	Fifth Lateran Council: concerned mainly with church discipline	Julius I, pope 1503–13, attacked by Luther over his indulgences for rebuilding St Peter's	
	1517	Luther's 95 theses		Bartolomé de Las Casas, Spanish Catholic missionary (1474–1566)
	1519	Luther's Catechisms		
	1524	Peasants' revolt in Germany Franciscan mission to Mexico	Leo X, pope 1513–21, excommunicates Luther	Jacob Hutter, Moravian Anabaptist leader (died 1536)
	1529	Diet of Speyer, 'protest' against Catholics, hence Protestantism		
	1530	Diet of Augsburg: Augsburg Confession		Martin Luther, German Reformer (1483–1546)
	1531	Virgin Mary appears to Juan Diego in Guadalupe		Huldrych Zwingli, Swiss Reformer (1484–1531)
	1533–5	Anabaptist 'new Jerusalem' in Münster		Miles Coverdale, Bible translator (1488–1568)
	1534	Act of Supremacy makes Henry VIII head of the Church of England Society of Jesus founded	Paul III, pope 1534–40, excommunicates Henry VIII, convenes Council of Trent	Thomas Müntzer, German Anabaptist and radical reformer (1489–1525)
	1536	First Helvetic Confession		Thomas Cranmer, English Reformer (1489–1556)
Wars of Religion (1546–1648)	1539–41	The Great Bible		
	1542	Geneva Catechism Francis Xavier arrives in India	Mary Tudor, queen of England 1553–8	Martin Bucer, German Reformer (1491–1551)
	1545–63	Council of Trent: major reforming council of the Roman Catholic Church		Ignatius Loyola, founder of Jesuit order (1491–1556)
	1546	Robert Estienne prints his Greek New Testament		William Tyndale, Bible translator and reformer (*c.* 1494–1536)
	1549	First English Book of Common Prayer		Menno Simons, Anabaptist leader (*c.* 1496–1561)
	1555	Peace of Augsburg, *cuius regio, eius religio*	Elizabeth I, queen of England, 1558–1603	
	1557	Index of Prohibited Books established by Rome		Philipp Melanchthon, German Reformer (1497–1550)
	1559	Act of Uniformity requires uniformity of worship in England		

Era	*Date*	*Events*	*Rulers and popes*	*Important figures*
SIXTEENTH CENTURY (continued) Puritans	1560	The Geneva Bible Reformed church established in Scotland: Scots Confession		Nicholas Ridley, English reformer (c. 1500–55) Johann Heinrich Bullinger, Swiss Reformer (1504–75)
	1563	Thirty-Nine Articles published	Pius IV, pope 1559–65, concludes Council of Trent	
	1566	Roman Catechism		
	1568	The Bishops' Bible		Francis Xavier, Catholic missionary (1506–52)
	1572	St Bartholomew's Day Massacre		
	1577	Formula of Concord		John Calvin, French Reformer (1509–64)
	1582	Douai New Testament	Gregory XIII, pope 1572–85, institutes the Gregorian calendar	
	1596	Council of Brest-Litovsk, at which the majority of Orthodox in the Ukraine join Rome	Sixtus V, pope 1585–90, known as the Iron Pope; reorganizes church administration	John Knox, Scottish Reformer (c. 1513–72) Teresa of Avila, Spanish mystic (1515–82)
	1598	Edict of Nantes proclaimed, giving guarantees to French Protestants		Philip Neri, founder of the Oratory (1515–95)
				John Foxe, Protestant historian (1516–87) John of the Cross, Spanish mystic (1542–91) Matteo Ricci, Jesuit missionary (1552–1610) Richard Hooker, Anglican churchman (c. 1554–1600)
SEVENTEENTH CENTURY	1601	Matteo Ricci evangelizes China	James I, king of Great Britain 1603–25	Lancelot Andrewes, English churchman (1555–1626)
Baroque (1600–1750)	1607	Settlement at Jamestown, Virginia		Galileo Galilei, Italian astronomer (1564–1642)
	1609	Douai Old Testament		
	1611	Authorized/King James Version		John Donne, English poet (1571–1631)
	1614	St Peter's in Rome completed		
		Prohibition of Christian worship in Japan		Jakob Boehme, German mystic (1575–1624)
Thirty Years War (1618–48)	1619	Canons of Dort condemn Arminianism	Charles I, king of Great Britain and Ireland 1625–49	Edward Herbert of Cherbury, English philosopher (1583–1648)
Caroline Divines (c. 1625–85)	1620	Mayflower sails for America		
	1642–9	English Civil War		Cornelius Otto Jansen, Belgian theologian (1585–1638)
	1643–9	Westminster Assembly meets to Reform Church of England		
Cambridge Platonists (c. 1650–80)	1646	Westminster Confession		Mary Ward, founder of a religious order (1585–1645)
	1647	Quakers founded		
ENLIGHTENMENT (c. 1650–1800)	1648	Peace of Westphalia ends Thirty Years War		Alexandre de Rhodes, Jesuit missionary (1591–1660)
		Westminster Catechisms	Oliver Cromwell, Lord Protector of England 1653–8	
Pietism (c. 1675–1760)	1662	Book of Common Prayer		
		Act of Uniformity		George Herbert, English poet (1593–1633)
	1666–7	Schism of Old Believers in Russia		
	1682	Quakers found Philadelphia	Charles II, King of Great Britain and Northern Ireland 1660–85	René Descartes, philosopher (1596–1650)
	1685	Edict of Nantes revoked		John Milton, English poet (1608–74)
				Margaret Fell, mother of Quakerism (1614–1702)
	1689	Oath of allegiance to William and Mary and Edict of Toleration grant freedom of religion to separatist Protestant groups	William (reigned 1689–1702) and Mary (reigned 1689-94), joint monarchs of Great Britain and Ireland	Richard Baxter, English Puritan divine (1615–91)
	1692	Imperial decree in China allows Christian worship		Blaise Pascal, French mathematician and theologian (1623–62)
	1698	Society for the Promotion of Christian Knowledge founded		George Fox, founder of the Society of Friends (1624–91)
				John Bunyan, English Baptist minister (1628–88)

Era	*Date*	*Events*	*Rulers and popes*	*Important figures*
SEVENTEENTH CENTURY (continued)				Benedict de Spinoza, Dutch Jewish philosopher (1632–77) John Locke, English philosopher (1632–1704) Philipp Jakob Spener, German Pietist (1635–1703) William Penn, Quaker and founder of Pennsylvania (1644–1718)
EIGHTEENTH CENTURY Rococo architecture (*c.* 1715–89) First Great Awakening (*c.* 1720–1750) American Revolution (1775–83) French Revolution (1789–99) Clapham Sect (1790–1830) Second Great Awakening (1798–1832)	1710 1721 1722 1738 1739 1742 1752 1773 1776 1780 1787 1792 1795 1799	The building of St Paul's Cathedral, London, is completed Peter the Great puts Russian church under government-controlled Holy Synod Count Zinzendorf founds Herrnhut colony Bach composes B minor Mass John Wesley begins to form Methodist societies within the Anglican Church First performance of Handel's *Messiah* Gregorian calendar adopted in Great Britain and Ireland First Methodist Conference in North America American Declaration of Independence Robert Raikes starts a Sunday school which is to shape a whole Sunday school movement US Constitution signed Baptist Missionary Society founded London Missionary Society founded Church Missionary Society founded	Anne, Queen of Great Britain and Ireland 1702–14 Clement XI, pope 1700–21, condemns practice of Chinese rites by Christians Benedict XIV, pope 1740–58, the highly respected pope of the century Clement XIV, pope 1769–74, suppresses Jesuit order (1773) George Washington (1732–99) becomes the first US President (1789)	Isaac Newton, English mathematician and physicist (1642–1727) Joseph Butler, Christian apologist (1659–1752) Cotton Mather, Puritan minister (1663–1728) Isaac Watts, Anglican hymn writer (1674–1728) Jean-Pierre de Caussade, spiritual writer (1675–1851) H. S. Reimarus, German deist and biblical critic (1694–1768) Voltaire, French philosopher and writer (1694–1778) Alphonsus Liguori, Catholic moral theologian (1696–1787) Nicholas Ludwig, Count von Zinzendorf, Moravian Pietist leader (1700–60) Jonathan Edwards, American Calvinist theologian and philosopher (1703–58) John Wesley, founder of Methodism (1703–91) Charles Wesley, Anglican hymn writer and preacher (1707–88) Selina, Countess of Huntingdon, English religious leader (1707–91) David Hume, Scottish philosopher and historian (1711–76) George Whitefield, English evangelist (1714–70) Immanuel Kant, German philosopher (1724–1804) Gotthold Ephraim Lessing, German philosopher and dramatist (1729–81)

Era	*Date*	*Events*	*Rulers and popes*	*Important figures*
EIGHTEENTH CENTURY (continued)				John Carroll, first Roman Catholic bishop in America (1735–1815) Ann Lee, Shaker leader (1736–84)
NINETEENTH CENTURY Romanticism Oxford Movement 1833–c. 1845 Christian Socialism	1804 1806 1807 1808 1811 1816 1829 1830 1840 1844 1847 1848 1849 1853 1864 1858 1859 1863 1865 1867 1869–70 1871 1875 1879 1888 1893	British and Foreign Bible Society founded Francis II, the last Holy Roman emperor, abdicates Slave trade abolished in British colonies Baltimore established as first Roman Catholic diocese American Board of Commissioners for Foreign Mission founded Disciples of Christ founded Methodist Episcopal Church founded Roman Catholic emancipation in Britain Virgin Mary appears in Paris to a nun Mormons (Church of Latter-day Saints) founded by Joseph Smith David Livingstone goes to Africa YMCA founded Mormons go to Salt Lake City under Brigham Young Birmingham Oratory founded by Newman Brompton Oratory founded by Newman Antoinette Brown ordained as first woman minister in the Congregational Church Publication of *Syllabus errorum* Virgin Mary appears in Lourdes to Bernadette Soubirous Publication of Charles Darwin, *The Origin of Species* Foundation of Seventh-day Adventist Church Salvation Army founded First Lambeth Conference Beginnings of the Holiness movement First Vatican Council: proclaims dogma of papal infallibility Formation of Old Catholic Churches Formation of World Alliance of Reformed and Presbyterian churches Virgin Mary appears to women in Knock Church of Christ, Scientist, founded by Mary Baker Eddy Lambeth Conference approves the Chicago-Lambeth Quadrilateral World's Parliament of Religions, Chicago	Victoria, Queen of Great Britain and Ireland 1836–1901 Pius IX, pope 1846–78, stresses the supreme authority of the Pope, condemns almost all modern intellectual movements in the *Syllabus errorum* and convenes the First Vatican Council Leo XIII, pope 1878–1903, sets out to reconcile the church with modernity but hardens later	Hannah More, evangelical writer and philanthropist (1745–1833) William Blake, English visionary poet (1757–1827) William Carey, Baptist missionary (1761–1834) Friedrich Schleiermacher, German theologian (1768–1834) Samuel Taylor Coleridge, English romantic poet (1772–1834) Elizabeth Fry, Quaker prison reformer (1780–1840) Henry Martyn, missionary in India (1781–1812) John Keble, English tractarian and poet (1792–1866) Sojourner Truth, African American evangelist and reformer (1797–1883) John Henry Newman, English theologian (1801–90) Horace Bushnell, American Congregationalist theologian (1802–76) Ludwig Feuerbach, German philosopher (1804–72) Joseph Smith, founder of the Mormons (1805–44) F. D. Maurice, English theologian (1805–72) Johann Christoph Blumhardt, Pietist (1805–80) David Friedrich Strauss, German theologian (1808–74) Charles Darwin, English scientist (1809–82) Søren Kierkegaard, Danish philosopher (1813–55) Elizabeth Cady Stanton, pioneer in women's suffrage (1815–1902) Karl Marx, German economist (1818–83) Fyodor Dostoievsky, Russian novelist (1821–81)

Era	*Date*	*Events*	*Rulers and popes*	*Important figures*
NINETEENTH CENTURY (continued)	1895	Beginnings of World Student Christian Federation (Student Christian Movement)		Matthew Arnold, English poet and critic (1822–88)
	1899	Gideons International founded		Josephine Butler, social reformer (1828–1906) Leo Tolstoy, Russian social critic and writer (1828–1910) William Booth, founder of the Salvation Army (1829–1912) William James, American psychologist and philosopher (1842–1910) Gerard Manley Hopkins, English poet (1844–89)
TWENTIETH CENTURY Social Gospel	1906	The Azusa Street revival marks the beginning of Pentecostalism	Pius X, pope 1903–14, condemns modernism and issues a revision of canon law	Adolf von Harnack, German church historian (1851–1930)
	1910	World Missionary Conference in Edinburgh		Friedrich von Hügel, liberal Roman Catholic (1852–1925)
First World War (1914–1918)	1910–15	Publication of *The Fundamentals*, the basis of fundamentalism	Benedict XV, pope 1914–22, works for reconciliation between nations	
	1917	Virgin Mary appears to children in Fatima		Sigmund Freud, founder of modern psychoanalysis (1856–1939)
	1925	Scopes 'monkey trial'		
	1927	Faith and Order Movement founded in Lausanne		William Wadé Harris, African prophet and evangelist (*c.* 1860–1929)
		Aimée Semple McPherson founds International Church of the Foursquare Gospel		Walter Rauschenbusch, American theologian (1861–1918)
Second World War (1939–45)	1928	Opus Dei founded	Joseph Stalin in power in Russia 1929–53	
	1929	Lateran Treaty between Vatican and Mussolini		Shailer Mathews, American Baptist theologian (1863–1941)
	1933	Eugenio Pacelli signs concordat with Hitler		
	1934	Creation of Confessing Church in Germany: Theological Declaration of Barmen	Pius XI, pope 1922–39, inaugurates Catholic Action	Ernst Troeltsch, German philosopher and theologian (1865–1923)
	1938	Frank Buchman launches Moral Rearmament		Nathan Söderblom, Swedish Lutheran theologian (1866–1931)
	1940	Taizé Community founded	Adolf Hitler in power in Germany 1933–1945	
	1944	Worker priest movement begins		Thérèse of Lisieux, Carmelite nun (1873–97)
	1945–6	Nag Hammadi Library discovered		
	1947	Church of South India formed	Pius XII, pope 1939–58, a controversial figure, particularly in connection with his silence over the Holocaust	
	1948	Dead Sea Scrolls discovered		Charles Fox Parham, American Pentecostal pioneer (1873–1929)
		Foundation of World Council of Churches, Amsterdam		
	1950	Dogma of the bodily assumption of Mary to heaven proclaimed		Carl Gustav Jung, Swiss psychologist (1875–1961)
	1951	Beginning of Three-self Patriotic Movement in China	Elizabeth II, Queen of Great Britain and Northern Ireland 1952–	Albert Schweitzer, theologian, physician and musician (1875–1965)
	1954	Worker priest movement dissolved		
		Methodist Church begins to ordain women		
	1962–5	Second Vatican Council: major reforming council of the Roman Catholic Church	John XXIII, pope 1958–63, a charismatic figure who convenes the Second Vatican Council	P. T. Forsyth, Scottish theologian (1878–1921) Harry Emerson Fosdick, American liberal preacher (1878–1960)
	1972	Formation of United Reformed Church	Paul VI, pope 1963–78, continues and concludes Vatican II, but with a conservative bent	Rudolf Bultmann, German New Testament scholar (1884–1976)

Era	*Date*	*Events*	*Rulers and popes*	*Important figures*
TWENTIETH CENTURY (continued)	1981	Virgin Mary appears to children in Medugorje	John Paul II, pope from 1978, the first Polish pope, much travelled but relentlessly conservative	Paul Tillich, philosopher and theologian (1886–1965)
	1982–6	Confession of Belhar		
Collapse of Communist regimes in Eastern European countries (1989–)	1988	Formation of Evangelical Lutheran Church in America		Athenagoras I, Ecumenical Patriarch of Constantinople (1886–1972)
		Election of a woman bishop in the US Episcopal Church		
	1992	*Catechism of the Catholic Church*		Karl Barth, Swiss Reformed theologian (1886–1968)
	1994	Church of England begins to ordain women to the priesthood		
				T. S. Eliot, American/English poet and critic (1888–1965)
				Simon Kimbangu, church founder (*c.* 1889–1951)
				Martin Heidegger, German existentialist philosopher (1889–1976)
				Edith Stein, Carmelite nun (1891–42)
				Reinhold Niebuhr, American theologian (1892–1971)
				C. S. Lewis, Anglican writer (1898–1963)
				Karl Rahner, German Catholic theologian (1904–84)
				Dietrich Bonhoeffer, German Protestant theologian (1906–45)
				Simone Weil, French philosopher (1909–43)
				Mother Teresa, missionary and nun (1910–97)
				Thomas Merton, Catholic monk (1915–68)
				Billy Graham, American revivalist (1918–)
				Gustavo Gutiérrez, founding father of liberation theology (1928–)
				Martin Luther King, Jr, American civil rights leader (1929–68)

GLOSSARY

This glossary contains words which appear regularly throughout *The Guide* and either are not part of everyday vocabulary or can bear a variety of different meanings. They are defined here in their usage in the context of Christianity

Allegory, allegorical From a Greek word meaning the description of one thing under the image of another. In an allegory, features of an account serve as symbols of something else lying outside the account.

Analogy An explanation that makes use of a relationship of similarity or proportionality, particularly in talking of God.

Anathema Complete exclusion from the church; a stronger term than excommunication.

Androcentric Male-centred.

Anglican Relating to a group of churches centred on the Church of England, their beliefs and practices.

Anglo-Catholicism A form of Anglicanism which has close affinities with Roman Catholicism.

Anthropocentric The view that human beings and their values are at the centre of the universe.

Anthropomorphic A view which gives God human features and qualities.

Antipope A rival claimant to the papacy.

Antitype The reality to which a 'type' points (sometimes called 'foretype').

Apocalyptic A form of literature which 'uncovers' (this is the meaning of the Greek word) what is to come in the future, especially at the end of the world, by means of symbolic dreams and visions.

Apocryphal Used of a variety of collections of books: the Apocrypha, those books included in the Greek version of the Hebrew Bible but not the Hebrew, which are accepted by Roman Catholics as scripture but not by Protestants; and early Christian books (New Testament Apocrypha), especially Gospels and Acts, which were not included in Christian scripture.

Apologetics, apologist, apology A reasoned account of the Christian faith and the one who gives it.

Apophatic Negative, used of the view that human categories are incapable of conceptualizing God.

Apostasy Renouncing the Christian faith.

Arian Relating to Arius, a fourth-century theologian who taught that Jesus was the highest created being but did not have the same status as God the Father. For some time Arianism was a powerful challenge to orthodox Christianity and it has come to be seen as the archetypal heresy.

Asceticism Discipline that involves renouncing desires or pleasures in order to do God's will.

Autocephalous Used of Eastern Orthodox churches that are in communion with one another but appoint their own heads.

Canon From a Greek word meaning 'rule'. The canon of scripture is the list of books accepted as the Bible. The central part of the eucharist is referred to as the canon. Canon law is church law based on canons, here decrees, from church bodies. A canon is a member of the staff of a cathedral or, in some cases, of a religious order.

Canonical hours The times of day when priests and religious orders say formal prayers.

Cataphatic Affirmative. The term is the opposite of apophatic and is used of the view that God can be conceptualized. Also spelt kataphatic.

Catechesis, catechism Instruction given to those preparing for membership of the Christian church and the form in which it is given

Catechumen Someone being instructed in the Christian faith.

Catholic From a Greek word meaning 'universal', originally applied to the one Christian church throughout the world. When this church was divided, the Eastern part came to be called Orthodox and the Western Catholic. When the Western church became fragmented after the Reformation, some churches which refused to accept the sovereignty of the Pope, such as the Anglican Church and later the Old Catholic churches, continued to call themselves Catholic. Here Roman Catholic denotes the church under the Pope and Catholic those Western churches claiming to belong to the Catholic tradition. The related noun is catholicity.

Celebrant Formerly used of the priest who leads the celebration of the mass. Because all worshippers are now seen to be actively involved, the term has widely been replaced by 'president'.

Chalcedon, Chalcedonian Shorthand term for the important Council of Chalcedon held in 451 which defined the relation of Jesus' divinity with his humanity.

Charism, charismatic From a Greek word meaning 'gift of grace'. The charismatic movement emphasizes the gifts of the Spirit, including speaking in tongues (Greek *glossolalia*) and healings.

Christ Christ is a title, the Greek translation of the Hebrew Messiah, and not a proper name, but it has come to be used as an alternative name for Jesus of

Nazareth, in the form Jesus Christ or Christ. Here Jesus denotes the historical figure and Christ the object of the church's faith.

Christocentric A view that gives Jesus Christ a central place.

Church fathers The name given to important theologians between the end of the first century and the end of the sixth century CE.

Clergy Ordained ministers of the church.

Communion Used to describe the receiving of the bread and wine at the eucharist, which is also called the communion service, or holy communion. It can also be used to denote those united in a common church fellowship.

Conciliar Relating to a council. Conciliarism was a movement beginning in the fifteenth century that held that supreme authority in the church lay with the council and not with the Pope. Conciliarity is understood to be a way of organizing the life of the church as a coherent whole.

Confession Can denote the act of acknowledging and speaking about one's sin. However, a confession of faith is a proclamation or statement of beliefs and by extension a religious group holding these beliefs can be called a confession.

Confessional As a noun the place where confessions are heard; as an adjective relating to a confession in the sense of a religious group.

Confessor Someone who hears confessions. In the early church, confessors were those who stood firm in their faith in time of persecution, but were not martyred.

Criticism Used to describe study of the Bible or other Christian sources, with no negative connotations: e.g. textual criticism, source criticism.

Cult, cultic Can denote the form and practice of worship; however, the noun is also used to denote a sect.

Daily Office Another name for canonical hours, the times of prayer for clergy and religious.

Decalogue From a Greek term meaning ten words. Another name for the Ten Commandments.

Deism The view that it is possible to know by reason of a God who created the world but then played no further part in it.

Denomination A religious group with distinctive beliefs and practices.

Dialectic A method of reasoning in which a conclusion emerges from the tension between two opposite positions.

Diaspora From the Greek word for dispersion. Originally those groups who lived outside Palestine, but now used of any religious group living outside its homeland.

Dispensation The way in which God relates to people, thought to be by a series of covenants.

Doctrine What is taught and believed to be true by a church.

Dogma A teaching or doctrine that has been officially endorsed by the church, used especially of the official teachings of the Roman Catholic Church.

Dogmatics An account of Christian doctrine presented in an organized and systematic way.

Dualism The view that there are two fundamental principles in the universe, such as good and evil or spirit and matter.

Dyophysitism The (orthodox) belief that Jesus Christ has two natures, human and divine.

Dyothelitism The belief that Jesus Christ had two wills, one human and one divine, but that these were never in conflict.

East, Eastern Used of the churches in the eastern Mediterranean which became the Eastern Orthodox churches to distinguish them from the Roman Church in the West.

Ecclesial Relating to the Christian church.

Ecclesiastical Relating to church organization or administration.

Ecclesiology The study of the church.

Ecumenical From a Greek word meaning the inhabited world. Thus the ecumenical councils were councils claiming to represent Christians from the whole world. The ecumenical patriarch is the primate of the Eastern Orthodox churches. However, the term is more widely used of the churches and their relationship with one another. The ecumenical movement strives for greater unity between them.

Election God's choosing of a people or an individual to carry out God's purposes in the world and to receive salvation.

Enlightenment A period in Europe between about 1650 and 1800 when groups of thinkers set out to base knowledge on the exercise of critical reason. It had far-ranging effects, but is also viewed negatively by many conservative and neo-orthodox Christians.

Episcopacy, episcopal Relating to bishops (for which the Greek is *episkopos*).

Epistemology The study of the way in which human knowledge is obtained.

Eschatology Study of the last things (Greek *eschata*). Particularly used of the second coming of Jesus and death, judgement, heaven and hell.

Established churches Official state churches.

Eucharist, eucharistic From the Greek word for thanksgiving. Relating to what is also called the Lord's supper, the mass or holy communion.

Evangelical In Europe the term is used of churches and their members standing in the Protestant tradition of the Reformation. In America and increasingly in the UK it is used of churches that emphasize evangelism and the need for a personal relationship with God through Jesus Christ.

Evangelism Communication of the 'good news' (Greek *euangelion*, English 'gospel') of Jesus Christ.

Excommunication Exclusion from receiving the sacraments of the church.

Exegesis, exegete From a Greek word meaning draw out. The explanation or interpretation of passages from the Bible and the person who engages in this.

Existential, existentialist Relating to human existence. Existentialist is used of a type of philosophy and theology that sees truth as being achieved by way of human subjectivity.

Fall, fallen Adam and Eve's act of disobedience towards God, according to the story in Genesis 3, through which sin is said to have entered the world, thus affecting all human beings, who are therefore fallen.

Fellowship Unity, sharing and community between Christians.

Filioque Latin 'and from the Son'. A term used by the West in describing the relations between the persons of the Trinity that was not accepted in the East and contributed to the schism between the churches.

Foundationalism, foundational A philosophical or theological approach that takes specific truths as the basis and criteria for all other truths.

Gentile Term originally used by Jews to denote non-Jews. Used in accounts of early Christianity to denote pagans.

Gnosis, Gnosticism From the Greek 'knowledge'. Movements contemporaneous with early Christianity that held that the human soul is imprisoned in evil matter and can free itself only by acquiring secret knowledge.

Gospel From the Anglo-Saxon *godspell*, good story or news. Used to describe the central message of Christianity. It is also the name for the first four books of the New Testament, accounts of the life of Jesus according to Matthew, Mark, Luke and John and other works modelled on them.

Grace God's gift to human beings to enable them to live good lives, a gift that is totally undeserved.

Great Awakenings Two revivals of Christianity in America during the eighteenth century.

Hebraic Relating to the Hebrew Bible (the Christian Old Testament) and its patterns of thought and culture; often contrasted with Hellenistic.

Hellenism, Hellenistic The Greek culture and thought which dominated the Mediterranean world from the time of Alexander the Great (356–323 BCE) onwards.

Hellenization The influence of Hellenistic thought and culture on Christianity.

Hermeneutics The methods used for searching for the meaning of writings, not least the Bible.

Hesychasm A form of Greek Orthodox mysticism in which silent contemplation plays a key role.

Heterodox Different from or counter to accepted, orthodox, belief.

Historical Jesus Jesus as he can be discovered by means of historical criticism, often opposed to 'the Christ of faith'.

Holy Communion A name for the eucharist or mass, used particularly by Protestants.

Homoousion Greek for 'of the same substance'. The name for the key statement affirming that Jesus Christ was identical in status to God the Father, and not inferior.

Host The bread, in the form of a wafer, consecrated at the eucharist or mass.

Humanism A viewpoint which emphasizes human worth and achievements. It need not necessarily be used in contrast to religious belief.

Idealism A type of philosophy or theology which sees the ideas of the human mind as the basis for understanding reality.

Ideology A set of ideas which determine thought and action, and which often hold together a particular group. These can be rigidly held and imposed on members.

Idolatry Worship of a false god or whatever is not God.

Image of God The condition in which human beings were created according to Genesis 1.26–8. There is much discussion as to what this might be.

Immanence, immanent The view that God is present in and with the created order; used as the opposite of transcendence.

Incarnation, incarnational The belief that God took human form and 'assumed flesh' (the meaning of the Latin word) in Jesus, and its consequences.

Index Shorthand for the *Index of Prohibited Books* maintained by the Roman Catholic Church from 1557 to 1966.

Indigenous Used of a church native to a particular area and controlled and shaped by those who live there.

Infallibility Free of all possible error. Used of the Bible and of official statements by the Pope on matters of faith and morals.

Inititation The means by which people enter the Christian church.

Intertestamental Relating to the period between the Old and New Testaments, and specifically the literature written during it.

Itinerant Used of preachers moving from place to place, initially of Jesus and then of preachers during the Great Awakenings and the revivals.

Justification, justify God's declaring individuals to be just or putting them right with God on the basis of the righteousness of Jesus Christ, thus bringing them salvation.

Kataphatic See Cataphatic.

Kenosis, kenotic From the Greek word meaning 'to empty'. A kenotic view of the incarnation holds that in becoming a human being in Jesus God emptied himself of all his divine attributes.

Kerygma, kerygmatic Greek 'proclamation'. The term is used for the content and form of the earliest Christian preaching, which kerygmatic theology regards as the starting point for interpreting the New Testament.

Koine From the Greek 'common'. The type of Greek used by first-century inhabitants of the Roman empire, in which the New Testament was written.

Labarum A military standard, particularly that of the Emperor Constantine which bore a symbol made up of the intersected Greek letters *chi* and *rho*, the beginning of the word Christ. See page 1164.

Laity, lay From the Greek *laos*, people. Pertaining to those members of the church who are not ordained.

Law Used most widely in theology of the Old Testament law, the Torah, which is contained in the first five books of the Bible, the Pentateuch, and includes the Ten Commandments. It is often contrasted with the gospel or with grace.

Lectionary A list of biblical readings for each day of the year, for use in public worship or by individuals.

Lesson A reading from the Bible.

Liturgy, liturgical Relating to worship. The form of service for the eucharist, mass or Lord's supper is called the liturgy.

Logos Greek for 'word' or 'reason'. A philosophical term for the rational force behind the universe that came to be identified with Jesus Christ.

Lord's Supper A name for the eucharist, mass or holy communion.

Magisterium The teaching authority of the Roman Catholic Church.

Marian, mariology Relating to the virgin Mary.

Mass The name given particularly in the Roman Catholic Church to the eucharist or Lord's Supper. From the last words of the Latin service, *Ite, missa est* (Go, this is the dismissal').

Metaphysics Greek 'beyond the physical'. A branch of philosophy concerned with questions of ultimate reality.

Millenarian Refers to the view that Jesus will return to earth imminently and establish a reign of peace on earth for a thousand years, and groups which hold it.

Mishnah A collection of tractates interpreting the Hebrew Bible made by rabbinic Jews in the second and third centuries CE.

Modernity, modernism Modernity denotes the period in Europe and North America after the Enlightenment dominated by the rise of science and technology. Modernism was a movement that sought to reinterpret Christianity in the light of modern thinking; the Roman Catholic version of it was condemned by the church.

Monophysitism The view that Jesus had only one, divine, nature rather than a human and a divine nature.

Monotheism Belief in one God.

Monothelitism The view that Jesus had only one, divine, will instead of two wills which were always in agreement.

Nativity A term used for the birth of Jesus.

Natural theology Knowledge of God believed to be attained by God's revelation in nature and the use of reason.

Nature A term used to describe the being of God or Jesus.

Nicaea, Nicene Shorthand term for the important Council of Nicaea held in 325 which defined Jesus' status in relation to that of God the Father.

Nominalism A medieval philosophical view that only individual things exist and universal ideas are names (Latin *nomina*). It was opposed to realism.

Non-conformist Not complying with an official church body.

Office Daily services prescribed to be said in churches of the Catholic tradition.

Ontology, ontological The philosophical study of being as being, i.e. the underlying principles of all things. The ontological argument for the existence of God is based on the necessity for God to exist.

Orders A term used for the church's organization (holy orders) and also for religious communities with a common rule of life (religious orders).

Orthodoxy Right belief. The term Orthodox churches is also used specifically of the Eastern churches under the Patriarch of Constantinople which were involved in a split with the Western churches in 1054.

Orthopraxy Right practice or conduct.

Parousia From the Greek, meaning the second coming of Christ.

Pasch, paschal Relating to Easter, from the Greek word for Passover.

Passion, passiontide From the Latin *passio*, 'suffering'. The spiritual and physical sufferings of Jesus up to and including his crucifixion commemorated during the two weeks before Easter.

Pastoral Relating to the care exercised by Christians towards people.

Pentateuch The first five books of the Hebrew Bible (from a Greek term), the Torah.

Person A term used of the three members of the Trinity, Father, Son and Holy Spirit: God in three persons.

Petrine Relating to the apostle Peter, also used in connection with the Pope.

Phenomenology A descriptive approach to experiences and practices.

Pluralism Diversity of views, values, cultures or religions.

Pneumatology The doctrine of the Holy Spirit.

Polity The form of government adopted by a church body.

Positivism, positivist The philosophical view that only facts are certain and that only what is experienced personally can be true.

Postmodernism A climate which is beyond the modernism introduced by the Enlightenment, characterized by a rejection of any claim to objective truth and universality. Truth is understood to be relative to particular communities.

Praxis A term used in liberation theology to denote a combination of action and reflection aimed at transforming the social order.

Pre-existence Used of Jesus, who is said to have existed from eternity prior to his incarnation.

Procession As well as denoting movement by people from place to place within a religious service the term is used to describe the order of relationships within the Trinity, e.g. the Son 'proceeds' from the Father.

Proper From the Latin *proprius*, 'own'. A text in the eucharist that changes according to the time of the church year.

Proselyte From the Greek meaning 'come to'. The word occurs only in the New Testament and denotes a former non-Jew who has become a Jew.

Protestant Someone who holds the views which emerged from the sixteenth-century Reformation.

Pseudepigrapha Writings that bear the name of those who cannot have been their actual authors, such as the Jewish Psalms of Solomon.

Qumran A place at the north-west end of the Dead Sea. The term is used as shorthand for the Essene community there which produced the Dead Sea Scrolls.

Rabbinic Judaism The Judaism which developed after the fall of Jerusalem in 70 CE.

Rapture An intense religious experience, but more commonly used of the belief that when Jesus returns, believers will be caught up into the air to be with him.

Realism In medieval philosophy the view that universals are independent of the mind that perceives them. It is the opposite of nominalism.

Reformation, Reformer Used especially of the movement beginning with Martin Luther in the sixteenth century that in its quest to reform the Roman Catholic Church broke away from it and formed the group of churches now called Protestant.

Religious Used specifically of a man or woman who joins a religious order.

Renaissance The cultural development which took place in the fourteenth to sixteenth centuries which saw a rediscovery of classical culture and the rise of humanism.

Righteousness A biblical term denoting the state of being right with God and God's action in bringing this about.

Satisfaction The re-establishment of a relationship with God through some means of making amends, used in an explanation of how Jesus' death does away with human sin.

Schism A formal division or break within a religious group. Two major schisms are confusingly both known as the 'Great Schism'. The first took place in 1054 when the Western and Eastern churches bitterly parted company, the one becoming what is now the Roman Catholic Church and the other the Orthodox Church. The other was within the Roman Catholic Church and lasted from 1378 to 1415: during this time there were popes in both Avignon and Rome.

Scholasticism An ordered theological approach adopted in the Middle Ages that made clear divisions and distinctions within its subject-matter.

Scripture An alternative term for the Bible.

Sect In sociology often contrasted with a church. It is a group with voluntary members and exclusive views, which separates itself from the world.

Secular As well as denoting the worldly, i.e. that which is not religious or spiritual, the term is used of Roman Catholic clergy who are not members of religious orders.

See From the Latin *sedes*, seat. The centre from which bishops, archbishops or a pope administer the area for which they are responsible.

Substance A term used to denote the eternal being of God.

Summa From the Latin meaning 'the main point'. A comprehensive system of theology in the Middle Ages, the most notable *summa* being that of Thomas Aquinas.

Syllabus (errorum) A list of erroneous modern beliefs condemned by Pope Pius IX in 1864.

Syncretism A mixing of views from different perspectives so that they lose their original points of reference. Thought to be a bad thing.

Talmud A commentary on the Mishnah, the main text of rabbinic Judaism, made in the fifth century CE. There are two Talmuds, the Babylonian (more important) and the Palestinian.

D

F

I

J

K

M

P

Q

R

S

T

X

Y

Z